SHORTER NINTH EDITION

We the People

AN INTRODUCTION TO AMERICAN POLITICS

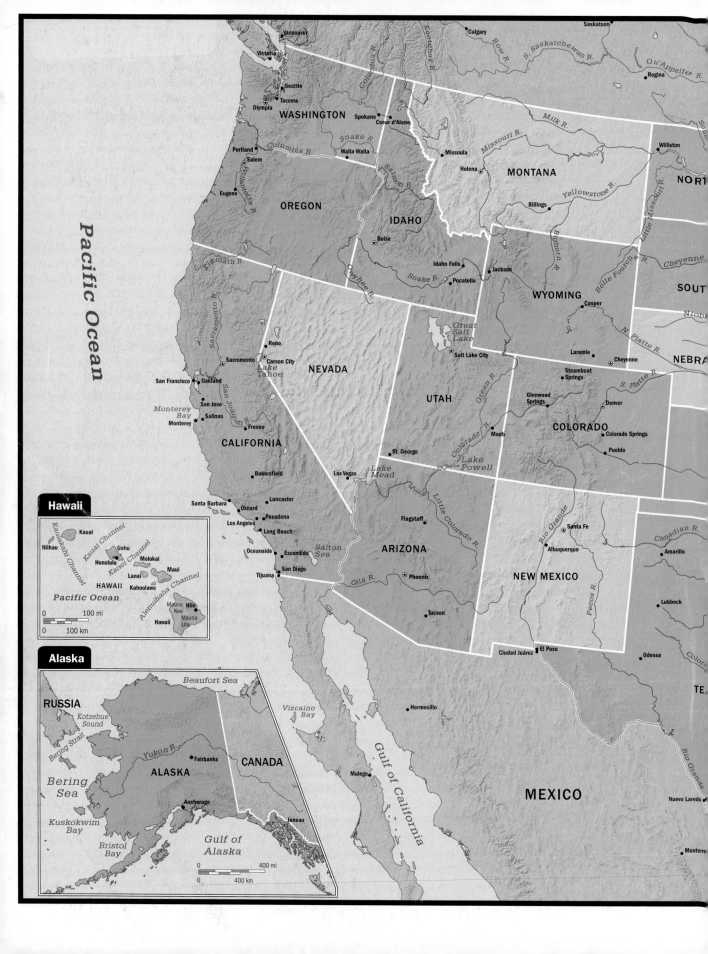

SHORTER NINTH EDITION

We the People

AN INTRODUCTION TO AMERICAN POLITICS

Benjamin Ginsberg
THE JOHNS HOPKINS UNIVERSITY

Theodore J. Lowi
CORNELL UNIVERSITY

Margaret Weir
UNIVERSITY OF CALIFORNIA AT BERKELEY

Caroline J. Tolbert
UNIVERSITY OF IOWA

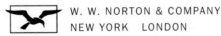
W. W. NORTON & COMPANY
NEW YORK   LONDON

W. W. Norton & Company has been independent since its founding in 1923, when William Warder Norton and Mary D. Herter Norton first published lectures delivered at the People's Institute, the adult education division of New York City's Cooper Union. The firm soon expanded its program beyond the Institute, publishing books by celebrated academics from America and abroad. By mid-century, the two major pillars of Norton's publishing program—trade books and college texts—were firmly established. In the 1950s, the Norton family transferred control of the company to its employees, and today—with a staff of four hundred and a comparable number of trade, college, and professional titles published each year—W. W. Norton & Company stands as the largest and oldest publishing house owned wholly by its employees.

Editor: Ann Shin
Associate Editor: Jake Schindel
Associate Editor, Ancillaries: Lorraine Klimowich
Manuscript Editor: Jenna Dolan
Project Editor: Christine D'Antonio
Electronic Media Editor: Pete Lesser
Editorial Assistant: Sarah Wolf
Editorial Assistant, Media: Jennifer Barnhardt
Marketing Manager, Political Science: Sasha Levitt
Senior Production Manager: Benjamin Reynolds
Photo Editor: Stephanie Romeo
Photo Researcher: Elyse Rieder
Permissions Manager: Megan Jackson
Text Design: Lissi Sigillo and Chris Welch
Information Graphics Design: Kiss Me I'm Polish LLC, New York
Art Director: Hope Miller Goodell
Composition: Jouve International—Brattleboro, VT
Manufacturing: R.R. Donnelley & Sons, Jefferson City, MO

Library of Congress Cataloguing-in-Publication Data has been applied for.

978-0-393-92109-0

W. W. Norton & Company, Inc., 500 Fifth Avenue, New York, N.Y. 10110
www.wwnorton.com

W. W. Norton & Company Ltd., Castle House, 75/76 Wells Street, London W1T 3QT

1 2 3 4 5 6 7 8 9 0

To Sandy, Cindy, and Alex Ginsberg

Angele, Anna, and Jason Lowi

Nicholas Ziegler

Dave, Jackie, Eveline, and Eddie Dowling

contents

4 ● Civil Liberties   112

PART II   Politics

7 ● The Media   250

8 ● Political Participation and Voting   292

9 ● Political Parties   338

PART III   Institutions

12 ● Congress   468

13 ● The Presidency   514

14 ● Bureaucracy in a Democracy   554

15 ● The Federal Courts   600

● Appendix   A1

preface

This book has been and continues to be dedicated to developing a satisfactory response to the question more and more Americans are asking: Why should we be engaged with government and politics? Through the first eight editions, we sought to answer this question by making the text directly relevant to the lives of the students who would be reading it. As a result, we tried to make politics interesting by demonstrating that students' interests are at stake and that they therefore need to take a personal, even selfish, interest in the outcomes of government. At the same time, we realized that students needed guidance in how to become politically engaged. Beyond providing students with a core of political knowledge, we needed to show them how they could apply that knowledge as participants in the political process. The "Get Involved/Go Online" sections in each chapter help achieve that goal.

As events from the last several years have reminded us, "what government does" can be a matter of life and death. Recent events have reinforced the centrality of government in citizens' lives. The U.S. government has fought two wars abroad, while claiming sweeping new powers at home that could compromise the liberties of its citizens. America's role in the world is discussed daily both inside and outside the classroom. Moreover, the Internet has opened up new avenues to participation and mobilization. Reflecting all of these trends, this new Ninth Edition shows more than any other book on the market (1) how students are connected to government; (2) how digital media are changing (or not changing) the way Americans experience politics; and (3) why students should think critically about government and politics. These themes are incorporated in the following ways:

- **New "Digital Citizens" boxes explore how new information technologies— especially the Internet—are changing the way we experience politics.** These boxes draw on recent scholarship to get students thinking critically about the rise of online politics. Examples include "The Digital Divide" (Chapter 5: Civil Rights), "Social Media, Crowdsourcing, and the 2012 Election" (Chapter 10: Campaigns and Elections), and "E-Government" (Chapter 14: Bureaucracy).

- **New "Get Involved/Go Online" units show students how to make a difference in politics.** These full-page boxes use contemporary examples to explain how young people (even those with busy lives!) can get involved in politics using the Internet, smart phones, and social media. Specific, step-by-step instructions guide students through a range of possible political activities related to each chapter's topic.

- **"Who Are Americans?" infographics ask students to think critically about how Americans from different backgrounds experience politics.** These sections use bold, engaging graphics to present a statistical snapshot of the nation related to each chapter's topic. Critical-thinking questions in each unit and related exercises on the StudySpace website give students a chance to compare their own views and experiences and consider the political implications. The "Who Are Americans?" PowerPoint slides include enhanced versions of the graphics for use in lectures.

- **Chapter introductions focus on "What Government Does and Why It Matters."** In recent decades, cynicism about "big government" has dominated the political zeitgeist. But critics of government often forget that governments do a great deal for citizens. Every year, Americans are the beneficiaries of billions of dollars of goods and services from government programs. Government "does" a lot, and what it does matters a great deal to everyone, including college students. At the start of each chapter, this theme is introduced and applied to the chapter's topic. The goal is to show students that government and politics mean something to their daily lives.

- **"America in the World" boxes show students how American government is connected to the world.** These one-page boxes in every chapter illustrate the important political role the United States plays abroad. Topics include "Should America Export Democracy?" "Human Rights and International Politics," "The American Health Care System in Comparison," and "What Is Congress's Role in Foreign Policy?" These boxes exemplify the critical-analytical approach that characterizes the text and include "For Critical Analysis" questions.

- **"For Critical Analysis" questions are incorporated throughout the text.** "For Critical Analysis" questions in the margins of every chapter prompt students' own critical thinking about the material in the chapter, encouraging them to engage with the topic. The two "For Critical Analysis" questions that conclude each "America in the World" box get students to think more deeply about America's role in the world. The questions at the end of each "Digital Citizens" box ask students to think critically about the intersection of politics and digital media. And the questions that accompany each "Who Are Americans?" unit ask students to consider how Americans from various backgrounds experience politics.

We continue to hope that our book will itself be accepted as a form of enlightened political action. This Ninth Edition is another chance. It is an advancement toward our goal. We promise to keep trying.

acknowledgments

We are pleased to acknowledge the many colleagues who had an active role in criticism and preparation of the manuscript. Our thanks go to:

First Edition Reviewers

Sarah Binder, Brookings Institution
Kathleen Gille, Office of Representative David Bonior
Rodney Hero, University of Colorado at Boulder
Robert Katzmann, Brookings Institution
Kathleen Knight, University of Houston
Robin Kolodny, Temple University
Nancy Kral, Tomball College
Robert C. Lieberman, Columbia University
David A. Marcum, University of Wyoming
Laura R. Winsky Mattei, State University of New York at Buffalo
Marilyn S. Mertens, Midwestern State University
Barbara Suhay, Henry Ford Community College
Carolyn Wong, Stanford University
Julian Zelizer, State University of New York at Albany

Second Edition Reviewers

Lydia Andrade, University of North Texas
John Coleman, University of Wisconsin at Madison
Daphne Eastman, Odessa College
Otto Feinstein, Wayne State University
Elizabeth Flores, Delmar College
James Gimpel, University of Maryland at College Park
Jill Glaathar, Southwest Missouri State University
Shaun Herness, University of Florida
William Lyons, University of Tennessee at Knoxville
Andrew Polsky, Hunter College, City University of New York
Grant Reeher, Syracuse University
Richard Rich, Virginia Polytechnic
Bartholomew Sparrow, University of Texas at Austin

Third Edition Reviewers

Bruce R. Drury, Lamar University
Andrew I. E. Ewoh, Prairie View A&M University
Amy Jasperson, University of Texas at San Antonio
Loch Johnson, University of Georgia

Mark Kann, University of Southern California
Robert L. Perry, University of Texas of the Permian Basin
Wayne Pryor, Brazosport College
Elizabeth A. Rexford, Wharton County Junior College
Andrea Simpson, University of Washington
Brian Smentkowski, Southeast Missouri State University
Nelson Wikstrom, Virginia Commonwealth University

Fourth Edition Reviewers

M. E. Banks, Virginia Commonwealth University
Lynn Brink, North Lake College
Mark Cichock, University of Texas at Arlington
Del Fields, St. Petersburg College
Nancy Kinney, Washtenaw Community College
William Klein, St. Petersburg College
Dana Morales, Montgomery College
Christopher Muste, Louisiana State University
Larry Norris, South Plains College
David Rankin, State University of New York at Fredonia
Paul Roesler, St. Charles Community College
J. Philip Rogers, San Antonio College
Greg Shaw, Illinois Wesleyan University
Tracy Skopek, Stephen F. Austin State University
Don Smith, University of North Texas
Terri Wright, Cal State, Fullerton

Fifth Edition Reviewers

Annie Benifield, Tomball College
Denise Dutton, Southwest Missouri State University
Rick Kurtz, Central Michigan University
Kelly McDaniel, Three Rivers Community College
Eric Plutzer, Pennsylvania State University
Daniel Smith, Northwest Missouri State University
Dara Strolovitch, University of Minnesota
Dennis Toombs, San Jacinto College–North
Stacy Ulbig, Southwest Missouri State University

Sixth Edition Reviewers

Janet Adamski, University of Mary Hardin–Baylor
Greg Andrews, St. Petersburg College
Louis Bolce, Baruch College
Darin Combs, Tulsa Community College
Sean Conroy, University of New Orleans
Paul Cooke, Cy Fair College
Vida Davoudi, Kingwood College
Robert DiClerico, West Virginia University
Corey Ditslear, University of North Texas
Kathy Dolan, University of Wisconsin, Milwaukee
Randy Glean, Midwestern State University
Nancy Kral, Tomball College
Mark Logas, Valencia Community College
Scott MacDougall, Diablo Valley College
David Mann, College of Charleston
Christopher Muste, University of Montana
Richard Pacelle, Georgia Southern University
Sarah Poggione, Florida International University
Richard Rich, Virginia Tech
Thomas Schmeling, Rhode Island College
Scott Spitzer, California State University–Fullerton
Dennis Toombs, San Jacinto College–North
John Vento, Antelope Valley College
Robert Wood, University of North Dakota

Seventh Edition Reviewers

Molly Andolina, DePaul University
Nancy Bednar, Antelope Valley College
Paul Blakelock, Kingwood College
Amy Brandon, San Jacinto College
Jim Cauthen, John Jay College
Kevin Davis, North Central Texas College
Louis DeSipio, University of California–Irvine
Brandon Franke, Blinn College
Steve Garrison, Midwestern State University
Joseph Howard, University of Central Arkansas
Aaron Knight, Houston Community College
Paul Labedz, Valencia Community College
Elise Langan, John Jay College
Mark Logas, Valencia Community College
Eric Miller, Blinn College
Anthony O'Regan, Los Angeles Valley College
David Putz, Kingwood College
Chis Soper, Pepperdine University
Kevin Wagner, Florida Atlantic University
Laura Wood, Tarrant County College

Eighth Edition Reviewers

Andrea Aleman, University of Texas at San Antonio
Stephen Amberg, University of Texas at San Antonio
Steve Anthony, Georgia State University
Brian Arbour, John Jay College, CUNY
Greg Arey, Cape Fear Community College
Ellen Baik, University of Texas–Pan American
David Birch, Lone Star College–Tomball
Bill Carroll, Sam Houston State University
Ed Chervenak, University of New Orleans
Gary Church, Mountain View College
Adrian Stefan Clark, Del Mar College
Casey Clofstad, University of Miami
Annie Cole, Los Angeles City College
Greg Combs, University of Texas at Dallas
Cassandra Cookson, Lee College
Brian Cravens, Blinn College
John Crosby, California State University–Chico
Scott Crosby, Valencia Community College
Courtenay Daum, Colorado State University, Fort Collins
Paul Davis, Truckee Meadows Community College
Peter Doas, University of Texas–Pan American
Vida Davoudi, Lone Star College–Kingwood
John Domino, Sam Houston State University
Doug Dow, University of Texas–Dallas
Jeremy Duff, Midwestern State University
Heather Evans, Sam Houston State University
Hyacinth Ezeamii, Albany State University
Bob Fitrakis, Columbus State Community College
Brian Fletcher, Truckee Meadows Community College
Paul Foote, Eastern Kentucky University
Frank Garrahan, Austin Community College
Jimmy Gleason, Purdue University
Steven Greene, North Carolina State University
Jeannie Grussendorf, Georgia State University
M. Ahad Hayaud-Din, Brookhaven College
Virginia Haysley, Lone Star College–Tomball
Alexander Hogan, Lone Star College–CyFair
Glen Hunt, Austin Community College
Mark Jendrysik, University of North Dakota
Krista Jenkins, Fairleigh Dickinson University
Carlos Juárez, Hawaii Pacific University
Melinda Kovas, Sam Houston State University
Paul Labedz, Valencia Community College
Boyd Lanier, Lamar University
Jeff Lazarus, Georgia State University
Jeffrey Lee, Blinn College
Alan Lehmann, Blinn College
Julie Lester, Macon State College
Steven Lichtman, Shippensburg University
Mark Logas, Valencia Community College
Fred Lokken, Truckee Meadows Community College
Shari MacLachlan, Palm Beach Community College
Guy Martin, Winston-Salem State University
Fred Monardi, College of Southern Nevada
Vincent Moscardelli, University of Connecticut
Jason Mycoff, University of Delaware
Sugmaran Narayanan, Midwestern State University
Adam Newmark, Appalachian State University
Larry Norris, South Plains College
Anthony Nownes, University of Tennessee, Knoxville

Elizabeth Oldmixon, University of North Texas
Anthony O'Regan, Los Angeles Valley College
John Osterman, San Jacinto College–Central
Mark Peplowski, College of Southern Nevada
Maria Victoria Perez-Rios, John Jay College, CUNY
Sara Rinfret, University of Wisconsin, Green Bay
Andre Robinson, Pulaski Technical College
Paul Roesler, St. Charles Community College
Susan Roomberg, University of Texas at San Antonio
Ryan Rynbrandt, Collin County Community College
Mario Salas, Northwest Vista College
Michael Sanchez, San Antonio College
Mary Schander, Pasadena City College
Laura Schneider, Grand Valley State University
Ronee Schreiber, San Diego State University
Subash Shah, Winston-Salem State University
Mark Shomaker, Blinn College
Roy Slater, St. Petersburg College
Scott Spitzer, California State University–Fullerton
Debra St. John, Collin College
John Vento, Antelope Valley College
Eric Whitaker, Western Washington University
Clay Wiegand, Cisco College
Walter Wilson, University of Texas at San Antonio
Kevan Yenerall, Clarion University
Rogerio Zapata, South Texas College

Ninth Edition Reviewers

Amy Acord, Lone Star College–CyFair
Milan Andrejevich, Ivy Tech Community College
Steve Anthony, Georgia State University
Phillip Ardoin, Appalachian State University
Gregory Arey, Cape Fear Community College
Joan Babcock, Northwest Vista College
Evelyn Ballard, Houston Community College
Robert Ballinger, South Texas College
Mary Barnes-Tilley, Blinn College
Robert Bartels, Evangel University
Nancy Bednar, Antelope Valley College
Annie Benifield, Lone Star College–Tomball
Donna Bennett, Trinity Valley Community College
Amy Brandon, El Paso Community College
Mark Brewer, The University of Maine
Gary Brown, Lone Star College–Montgomery
Joe Campbell, Johnson County Community College
Dewey Clayton, University of Louisville
Jeff Colbert, Elon University
Amanda Cook-Fesperman, Illinois Valley Community College
Kevin Corder, Western Michigan University
Kevin Davis, North Central Texas College
Paul Davis, Truckee Meadows Community College
Terri Davis, Lamar University
Jennifer De Maio, California State University, Northridge
Christopher Durso, Valencia College

Ryan Emenaker, College of the Redwoods
Leslie Feldman, Hofstra University
Glen Findley, Odessa College
Michael Gattis, Gulf Coast State College
Donna Godwin, Trinity Valley Community College
Precious Hall, Truckee Meadows Community College
Sally Hansen, Daytona State College
Tiffany Harper, Collin College
Todd Hartman, Appalachian State University
Virginia Haysley, Lone Star College–Tomball
David Head, John Tyler Community College
Rick Henderson, Texas State University–San Marcos
Richard Herrera, Arizona State University
Thaddaus Hill, Blinn College
Steven Holmes, Bakersfield College
Kevin Holton, South Texas College
Robin Jacobson, University of Puget Sound
Joseph Jozwiak, Texas A & M–Corpus Christi
Casey Klofstad, University of Miami
Samuel Lingrosso, Los Angeles Valley College
Mark Logas, Valencia College
Christopher Marshall, South Texas College
Larry McElvain, South Texas College
Elizabeth McLane, Wharton County Junior College
Eddie Meaders, University of North Texas
Rob Mellen, Mississippi State University
Jalal Nejad, Northwest Vista College
Adam Newmark, Appalachian State University
Stephen Nicholson, University of California, Merced
Cissie Owen, Lamar University
Suzanne Preston, St. Petersburg College
David Putz, Lone Star College–Kingwood
Auksuole Rubavichute, Mountain View College
Ronnee Schreiber, San Diego State University
Ronald Schurin, University of Connecticut
Jason Seitz, Georgia Perimeter College
Jennifer Seitz, Georgia Perimeter College
Shannon Sinegal, The University of New Orleans
John Sides, George Washington University
Thomas Sowers, Lamar University
Jim Startin, The University of Texas at San Antonio
Robert Sterken, University of Texas at Tyler
Bobby Summers, Harper College
John Theis, Lone Star College–Kingwood
John Todd, University of North Texas
Delaina Toothman, The University of Maine
David Trussell, Cisco College
Ronald Vardy, University of Houston
Linda Veazey, Midwestern State University
John Vento, Antelope Valley Community College
Clif Wilkinson, Georgia College
John Wood, Rose State College
Michael Young, Trinity Valley Community College
Tyler Young, Collin College

Students at several schools around the country participated in small focus groups that helped shape the Eighth Edition's pedagogical program. They included Brittany Boyle, Luan Do, Brent Harvey, Jorge Hernandez, Tiara Jackson, Josh Jacobs, Jimmy Johnson, Laura Konisek, Gabriela Maddox, Taylor Marcantel, Anna Mearidy, Lori Mendel, Jacob Minter, Mayela Montano, Diana Ortega, Natalie Pereira, Michael Rocca, Christine Sanders, Kirk Sharma, Andrea Soto-Innes, Mary Storey, Joe Street, Jamie Sula, and Mia Williams. We are grateful for their smart and candid feedback.

We are also grateful for the talents and hard work of several research assistants, whose contributions can never be adequately compensated. In particular, for his work on the Eighth Edition, we thank Peter Ryan.

Perhaps above all, we wish to thank those at W. W. Norton. For its first five editions, editor Steve Dunn helped us shape the book in countless ways. Our current editor, Ann Shin, has carried on the Norton tradition of splendid editorial work. We thank Elyse Rieder for devoting an enormous amount of time to finding new photos. For our student Web site and other media resources for the book, Peter Lesser has been an energetic and visionary editor, and Lorraine Klimowich has efficiently managed the test bank and instructor's manual. Michael Fleming was a thorough and thoughtful developmental editor. Jenna Dolan copyedited the manuscript, and project editor Christine D'Antonio devoted countless hours keeping on top of myriad details. Ben Reynolds has been dedicated in managing production. Finally, we wish to thank Roby Harrington, the head of Norton's college department.

Benjamin Ginsberg
Theodore J. Lowi
Margaret Weir
Caroline J. Tolbert

November 2012

SHORTER NINTH EDITION

We the People

AN INTRODUCTION TO AMERICAN POLITICS

Most Americans share the core political values of liberty, equality, and democracy and want their government and its policies to reflect these values. However, people often disagree on the meaning of these values and what government should do to protect them.

American Political Culture

WHAT GOVERNMENT DOES AND WHY IT MATTERS Americans sometimes appear to believe that the government is an institution that does things *to* them and from which they need protection. Business owners complain that federal health and safety regulations threaten their ability to make a profit. Farmers and ranchers complain that federal and state environmental rules intrude on their property rights. Motorists allege that municipal "red light" cameras, designed to photograph traffic violators, represent the intrusion of "Big Brother" into their lives. Civil libertarians express concern over what they view as sometimes overly aggressive police and prosecutorial practices. And almost everyone complains about federal, state, and local taxes.

Yet many of the same individuals who complain about what the government does *to* them also want the government to do a great deal *for* them. For example, most members of the Tea Party movement believe that the federal government has gotten too big and that government spending should be cut back. Even so, in poll after poll, the majority of those who identify with the Tea Party express support for two of the largest and fastest-growing federal programs, Social Security and Medicare.[1] Whatever they say about big government, most Americans expect to collect Social Security benefits when they retire and to obtain their health care from Medicare after they turn 65. In a similar vein, after the September 11, 2001, terrorist attacks on the World Trade Center and the Pentagon, Americans demanded government action. President George W. Bush responded by mobilizing powerful military forces and creating an Office of Homeland Security (later reorganized as a cabinet department). Congress authorized tens of billions of dollars in new federal expenditures to combat terrorism and to repair the damage already caused by terrorists. The states mobilized their own police and national guard forces, and local police and public safety departments were placed on high alert.

Americans also look to government for assistance with more routine matters. Farmers are the beneficiaries of billions in federal subsidies and research programs. Motorists would have no roads on which to be photographed by those hated cameras if not for the tens of billions of dollars spent each year on road construction and maintenance by federal, state, and municipal authorities. Individuals accused of crimes benefit from procedural safeguards and state-funded defense attorneys. Most Americans would not be here at all if it were not for federal immigration policies, which set the terms for entry into the United States and for obtaining citizenship. And, as for those detested taxes, without them there would be no government benefits at all.

government institutions and procedures through which a territory and its people are ruled

Government is the term generally used to describe the formal institutions through which a land and its people are ruled. As the government seeks to help and protect its citizens, it faces the challenge of doing so in ways that are true to the key American political values of liberty, equality, and democracy. Most Americans find it easy to affirm all three values in principle. In practice, however, matters are not always so clear; these values mean different things to different people, and they often seem to conflict. This is where politics comes in. **Politics** refers to conflicts and struggles over the leadership, structure, and policies of governments. As we will see in this chapter and throughout this book, much political conflict concerns policies and practices that seem to affirm one of the key American political values but appear to contradict another.

politics conflict over the leadership, structure, and policies of governments

chaptergoals

- Explore how Americans see their government (pages 5–8)
- Describe the role of the citizen in politics (pages 9–11)
- Define government and forms of government (pages 11–16)
- Show how the American people have changed over time (pages 16–23)
- Analyze whether the system of government upholds American political values (pages 23–30)

What Americans Think about Government

Explore how Americans see their government

Since the United States was established as a nation, Americans have been reluctant to grant government too much power, and they have often been suspicious of politicians. But over the course of the nation's history, Americans have also turned to government for assistance in times of need and have strongly supported the government in periods of war. In 1933 the power of the government began to expand to meet the crises created by the stock market crash of 1929, the Great Depression, and the run on banks of 1933. Congress passed legislation that brought the government into the businesses of home mortgages, farm mortgages, credit, and relief of personal distress. More recently, when the economy threatened to fall into a deep recession in 2008 and 2009, the federal government stepped in to shore up the financial system, oversee the restructuring of the ailing auto companies, and to inject hundreds of billions of dollars into the faltering economy. Today the national government is an enormous institution with programs and policies reaching into every corner of American life. It oversees the nation's economy; it is the nation's largest employer; it provides citizens with a host of services; it controls the world's most formidable military; and it regulates a wide range of social and commercial activities.

Much of what citizens have come to depend on and take for granted as somehow part of the natural environment is in fact created by government. Take the example of a typical college student's day, throughout which that student relies on a host of services and activities organized by national, state, and local government agencies. The extent of this dependence on government is illustrated by Table 1.1 on page 6.

Trust in Government

Ironically, even as popular dependence on the government has grown, the American public's view of government has turned more sour. Public trust in government has declined, and Americans are now more likely to feel that they can do little to influence the government's actions. The decline in public trust among Americans is striking. In the early 1960s, three-quarters of Americans said they trusted government most of the time. By 1994, only 21 percent of Americans expressed trust in government; three-quarters stated that they did not trust government most of the time.[2] Different groups vary somewhat in their levels of trust: African Americans and Latinos express more confidence in the federal government than do whites. But even among the most supportive groups, considerably more than half do not trust the government.[3] These developments are important because politically engaged citizens and public confidence in government are vital for the health of a democracy.

Public approval of government hit a record low in 2011 when Republicans and Democrats came into sharp conflict over the federal debt limit. While House Speaker John Boehner (a Republican) and President Barack Obama (a Democrat) struggled to find a compromise, many Americans worried that the delay in settling on a solution was harming the economy.

TABLE 1.1

The Presence of Government in the Daily Life of a Student at "State University"

TIME OF DAY	SCHEDULE
7:00 A.M.	Wake up. Standard time set by the national government.
7:10 A.M.	Shower. Water courtesy of local government, either a public entity or a regulated private company. Brush your teeth with toothpaste whose cavity-fighting claims have been verified by a federal agency. Dry your hair with an electric dryer manufactured according to federal government agency guidelines.
7:30 A.M.	Have a bowl of cereal with milk for breakfast. "Nutrition Facts" on food labels are a federal requirement, pasteurization of milk required by state law, freshness dating on milk based on state and federal standards, recycling the empty cereal box and milk carton enabled by state or local laws.
8:30 A.M.	Drive or take public transportation to campus. Air bags and seat belts required by federal and state laws. Roads and bridges paid for by state and local governments, speed and traffic laws set by state and local governments, public transportation subsidized by all levels of government.
8:45 A.M.	Arrive on campus of large public university. Buildings are 70 percent financed by state taxpayers.
9:00 A.M.	First class: Chemistry 101. Tuition partially paid by a federal loan (more than half the cost of university instruction is paid for by taxpayers), chemistry lab paid for with grants from the National Science Foundation (a federal agency) and smaller grants from business corporations made possible by federal income tax deductions for charitable contributions.
Noon	Eat lunch. College cafeteria financed by state dormitory authority on land grant from federal Department of Agriculture.
2:00 P.M.	Second class: American Government 101 (your favorite class!). You may be taking this class because it is required by the state legislature or because it fulfills a university requirement.
4:00 P.M.	Third class: Computer Lab. Free computers, software, and Internet access courtesy of state subsidies plus grants and discounts from IBM and Microsoft, the costs of which are deducted from their corporate income taxes; Internet built in part by federal government. Duplication of software prohibited by federal copyright laws.
6:00 P.M.	Eat dinner: hamburger and french fries. Meat inspected for bacteria by federal agencies.
7:00 P.M.	Work at part-time job at the campus library. Minimum wage set by federal government, books and journals in library paid for by state taxpayers.
10:00 P.M.	Go home. Street lighting paid for by county and city governments, police patrols by city government.
10:15 P.M.	Watch TV. Networks regulated by federal government, cable public-access channels required by city law. Weather forecast provided to broadcasters by a federal agency.
Midnight	Put out the garbage before going to bed. Garbage collected by city sanitation department, financed by "user charges."

In the aftermath of the September 11, 2001, terrorist attacks, a number of studies reported a substantial increase in popular trust in government. For example, in 2000, 44 percent of those surveyed said they trusted the government to "do the right thing" all or most of the time. After September 11, 2001, trust had jumped to 56 percent.[4] This view, expressed during a period of national crisis, may have been indicative less of a renewed *trust* in government to do the right thing than of a fervent *hope* that it would. And, indeed, by 2004, trust in government had neared its pre–September 11 level, with only 47 percent of Americans indicating that they trusted the government all or most of the time (see Figure 1.1).[5] Several fac-

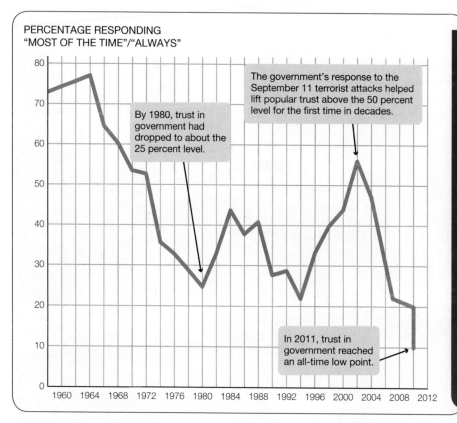

PERCENTAGE RESPONDING
"MOST OF THE TIME"/"ALWAYS"

By 1980, trust in government had dropped to about the 25 percent level.

The government's response to the September 11 terrorist attacks helped lift popular trust above the 50 percent level for the first time in decades.

In 2011, trust in government reached an all-time low point.

tors contributed to the decline in trust. Revelations about the faulty information that led up to the war in Iraq and ongoing concern about the war had increased Americans' distrust of government. In March 2007, 54 percent of those surveyed believed that the Bush administration had deliberately misled the American public about whether Iraq had weapons of mass destruction.

By 2012 the government's inability to get the economy moving had further undermined trust in government. Intense partisan conflict over the government's role in the economy fueled public discontent. The public watched with dismay as political differences over taxing and spending ended in repeated threats to shut down the federal government. By the fall of 2011, after a bitter congressional battle over raising the national debt limit—usually a routine matter—only 10 percent of Americans trusted government to do the right thing always or most of the time, the lowest level of trust ever recorded.[6]

Does it matter if Americans trust their government? For the most part, the answer is yes. As we have seen, most Americans rely on government for a wide range of services and laws that they simply take for granted. But long-term distrust in government can result in public refusal to pay taxes adequate to support such widely approved public activities. Low levels of confidence may also make it difficult for government to attract talented and effective workers to public service.[7] The weakening of government as a result of prolonged levels of distrust may ultimately harm the United States' capacity to defend its national interest in the world economy and may jeopardize its national security. Likewise, a weak government can do little to assist citizens who need help in weathering periods of sharp economic or technological change.

for critical analysis

What recent events have affected Americans' trust in government? Have the U.S. government's efforts to address the economic downturn since 2008 increased the public's trust in government?

In response to the terrorist attacks of September 11, 2001, Americans rallied around government officials and offered unprecedented support. Is support for the government during times of crisis at odds with Americans' distrust of government at other times?

Political Efficacy

political efficacy the ability to influence government and politics

Another important trend in American views about government has been a declining sense of **political efficacy**, the belief that ordinary citizens can affect what government does, that they can make government listen to them. In 2012, 62 percent of Americans said that elected officials don't care what people like them think; in 1960, only 25 percent felt so shut out of government. Accompanying this sense that ordinary people can't get heard is a growing belief that government is not run for the benefit of all the people. In 2012, 57 percent of the public disagreed with the idea that the "government is really run for the benefit of all the people."[8] These views are widely shared across the age spectrum.

This widely felt loss of political efficacy is bad news for American democracy. The feeling that you can't affect government decisions can lead to a self-perpetuating cycle of apathy, declining political participation, and withdrawal from political life. Why bother to participate if you believe it makes no difference? Yet the belief that you can be effective is the first step needed to influence government. Not every effort of ordinary citizens to influence government will succeed, but without any such efforts, government decisions will be made by a smaller and smaller circle of powerful people. Such loss of broad popular influence over government actions undermines the key feature of American democracy—government by the people.

Following the 2003 Iraq War and the ongoing fighting in Afghanistan, Americans' trust in government declined sharply. Why do you think so many Americans were critical of the government's handling of these conflicts?

Citizenship: Knowledge and Participation

Describe the role of the citizen in politics

The first prerequisite for achieving an increased sense of political efficacy is knowledge. Political indifference is often simply a habit that stems from a lack of knowledge about how your interests are affected by politics and from a sense that you can do nothing to affect politics. But political efficacy is a self-fulfilling prophecy: if you think you cannot be effective, chances are you will never try. Most research suggests that people active in politics have a high sense of their own efficacy. This means they believe they can make a difference— even if they do not win all the time. Most people do not want to be politically active every day of their lives, but it is essential to American political ideals that all citizens be informed and able to act.

Even though the Internet has made it easier than ever to learn about politics, the state of political knowledge in the United States today is spotty. Most Americans know little about current issues or debates. Numerous surveys indicate that the majority of Americans have significant gaps in their political knowledge. For example, in 2011 only 43 percent of those surveyed knew that Republicans held the majority in the House of Representatives, and only 47 percent knew that Chief Justice John Roberts Jr. is generally considered a conservative. On the other hand, the public is more knowledgeable about politicians and policy makers who have been prominent in the national media. For example, when shown pictures of public figures, 82 percent could identify Hillary Clinton as Secretary of State and 70 percent could identify Ben Bernanke as head of the Federal Reserve (see Table 1.2). But rather than dwell on the widespread political ignorance of many Americans, we

TABLE 1.2

What Americans Know about Government

RESPONDENTS WHO	PERCENTAGE
Knew that only citizens can vote in federal elections	48
Could identify two members of the president's cabinet and name their department	46
Knew how much of a majority is required for the U.S. Senate and House to override a presidential veto	38
Knew that Chief Justice John Roberts Jr. is generally considered a conservative	47*
Felt that the government spends more on Social Security than on foreign aid	18
Could identify Secretary of State Hillary Clinton (from a picture)	82*
Could identify House Speaker John Boehner	56*
Could identify Ben Bernanke's position as Federal Reserve chairman (when shown his picture)	70*

SOURCES: Center for Information and Research on Civic Learning and Engagement, www.civicyouth.org (accessed 2/4/08); and Pew Research Center for People and the Press, http://people-press.org (accessed 2/4/08).

*Pew Research Center for the People and the Press, "What the Public Knows—in Words and Pictures," November 7, 2011, www.people-press.org/files/legacy-pdf/11-7-11%20Knowledge%20Release.pdf (accessed 6/8/12)

prefer to view this as an opportunity for the readers of this book. Those of you who make the effort to become more knowledgeable will be much better prepared to influence the political system regarding the issues and concerns that you care most about.

After September 11, many commentators noted a revival in Americans' sense of citizenship, as manifested by ubiquitous flag displays and other demonstrations of patriotic sentiment. There seems to be little doubt that millions of Americans experienced a renewed sense of identification with their nation. Citizenship, however, has a broader meaning than just patriotism.

Beginning with the ancient Greeks, citizenship has meant membership in one's community. Citizenship entailed involvement in public discussion, debate, and activity designed to improve the welfare of the community. Our meaning for **citizenship** derives from the Greek ideal: enlightened political engagement.[9] To be politically engaged in a meaningful way, citizens require resources, especially political knowledge and information. Democracy functions best when citizens are informed. But citizenship in the full sense, as understood first by the ancient Greeks, goes beyond an occasional visit to a voting booth. A good citizen must be politically engaged and have the knowledge needed to participate in political debate.

citizenship informed and active membership in a political community

The Necessity of Political Knowledge

Political knowledge means more than having a few opinions to offer the pollster or to guide your decisions in a voting booth. It is important to know the rules and strategies that govern political institutions and the principles on which they are based, but it is more important to know them in ways that relate to your own interests. Citizens need knowledge in order to assess their interests and to know when to act on them. Knowledgeable citizens are more attentive to and engaged in politics because they understand how and why politics is relevant to their lives.

Without political knowledge, no citizen can be aware of her interests or her stake in a political dispute. In the year preceding the 2012 presidential election, for example, the prospective Republican candidates presented a diverse set of proposals on how to return the American economy to prosperity. These proposals could be easily accessed on the candidates' websites. How many voters paid enough attention to the discussion to be able to distinguish meaningfully among the various proposals and their implications? How many citizens attempted to ascertain whether they and their families would be better off under the tax proposals envisioned by Cain, Perry, or Romney, rather than the system favored by Obama? How could a voter participate intelligently without this knowledge? Various public and private interest groups devote enormous time and energy to understanding alternative policy proposals and their implications so they will know whom to support. Interest groups understand something that every citizen should also understand: effective participation requires knowledge.

Citizens need political knowledge also to identify the best ways to act on their interests. If your street is rendered impassable by snow, what can you do? Is snow removal the responsibility of the federal government? Is it a state or municipal responsibility? Knowing that you have a stake in a clear road does not help much if you do not know that snow removal is a city or a county responsibility and if you cannot identify the municipal agency that deals with the problem. Americans are fond of complaining that government is not responsive to their needs, but in some cases, it is possible that citizens simply lack the information they need to present their problems to the appropriate government officials.

Citizens need political knowledge also to ascertain what they cannot or should not ask of politicians and the government. We need to balance our need for protection and service with our equally pressing need for liberty. Particularly during periods when the nation's safety is threatened, Americans may be inclined to accept increased governmental intrusion into their lives in the name of national security. Since 2001, for example, Americans have accepted unprecedented levels of governmental surveillance and the erosion of some traditional restrictions on police powers in the name of preventing terrorism. It remains to be seen whether this exchange of liberty for the promise of security was a wise choice. Political knowledge, therefore, includes knowing the limits on (as well as the possibilities for) pursuing one's own individual interests through political action. This is, perhaps, the most difficult form of political knowledge to acquire.

for critical analysis

Many studies seem to show that most Americans know very little about government and politics. Can we have democratic government without knowledgeable and aware citizens?

● Government

Define government and forms of government

As we saw in the introduction to this chapter, government refers to the formal institutions through which a land and its people are ruled. To govern is to rule. A government may be as simple as a tribal council that meets occasionally to advise the chief, or as complex as the vast establishments, with their procedures, laws, and bureaucracies, found in many large countries today. In

Digital Citizens

As society and politics have migrated online, Americans have become "digital citizens." Digital citizens are daily Internet users. They go online for work, the news, communication with friends and family, entertainment, and information about politics, health, transportation, and more. Young people spend more time online than watching television, and many observers believed that the 2012 presidential election would be the first in which online politics trumps the television. In 2012, 80 percent of Americans used the Internet and 7 in 10 Americans went online daily. The Internet has become the backbone of a global digital infrastructure and an integral part of the information economy.

Digital citizenship is the ability to participate in society online, and it is increasingly important in politics. A 2012 Pew survey found that over 90 percent of Internet users in the United States use e-mail or have used a search engine, and 66 percent use a social networking site such as Facebook. Eight in 10 Internet users check the weather online, 75 percent read the news online (up from 61 percent in 2011), and more than six in 10 look up political information online. They also seek out government information; 67 percent visit a local, state, or federal government website (up from 56 percent in 2011). Economic activity online is widespread; 60 percent do banking online, 71 percent have purchased a product online, and 56 percent

look for information about a job. Online information even affects where you live; 4 in 10 Internet users look for a place to live online.

What does it take to become a digital citizen? Home access and high-speed access to the Internet are necessary for digital citizenship. Regular access and effective use enable full participation in society online. Research has shown that home access is important for activities connected with jobs, education, finances, politics, and community engagement.

Digital citizenship is beneficial to individuals, but it also has spillover benefits that provide advantages to society as a whole. Digital citizens are likely to be "good" citizens. They are more likely to be interested in politics and to discuss politics with friends, family, and coworkers than individuals who do not use online political information. They are also more likely to vote and participate in other ways in elections. When defined as those using the Internet at work, digital citizens earn higher wages (controlling for other factors), even among those with only a high school degree. Thus the Internet can encourage participation in politics and economic productivity.

However, individuals without Internet access or the skills to participate in politics and the economy online are being left further behind. Exclusion from

participation online is referred to as the digital divide (which we discuss further in Chapters 5 and 8).

Internet access and digital literacy are critical for full participation in American society in the twenty-first century. In much the same way that higher levels of education and literacy promoted democracy and economic growth in the nineteenth century, the Internet has the potential to benefit society as a whole and to facilitate political participation of individuals within society. At the same time, the rise of the Internet raises new questions about who is able to participate and whether digital politics is changing the traditional dynamics of American politics. Throughout this book, Digital Citizens boxes like this one will explore these questions.

SOURCES: Pew Internet and American Life, 2012, "What Internet Users Do Online," February 2012 Survey, http://pewinternet.org/Trend-Data-(Adults)/Online-Activites-Total.aspx (accessed 6/25/12). Karen Mossberger, Caroline Tolbert, and Ramona McNeal, *Digital Citizenship: The Internet, Society and Participation* (Cambridge, MA: MIT Press, 2008).

for critical analysis

1. Just as all Americans have the right to a public education and to be taught to read and write, should all Americans have access to the Internet and be taught skills to use information online?

2. Does the prevalence of economic and political activities online justify government intervention in providing broadband Internet access? Why or why not?

the history of civilization, governments have not been difficult to establish. There have been thousands of them. The hard part is establishing a government that lasts. Even more difficult is developing a stable government that is compatible with liberty, equality, and democracy.

Is Government Needed?

Americans have always harbored some suspicion of government and have wondered how extensive a role it should play in their lives. Thomas Jefferson famously observed that the best government was one that "governed least." Generally speaking, a government is needed to provide those services, sometimes called "public goods," that all citizens need but are not likely to be able to provide adequately for themselves. These might include defense against foreign aggression, maintenance of public order, enforcement of contractual obligations and property rights, and a guarantee of some measure of social justice. The precise extent to which government involvement in American society is needed has been debated throughout the nation's history and will continue to be a central focus of political contention.

Forms of Government

Governments vary in their structure, their size, and the way they operate. Two questions are of special importance in determining how governments differ: Who governs? And how much government control is permitted?

Some nations are governed by a single individual—a king or dictator, for example. This state of affairs is called **autocracy**. Where a small group—perhaps landowners, military officers, or wealthy merchants—controls most of the governing decisions, that government is said to be an **oligarchy**. If more people participate and have some influence over decision making, that government is a **democracy**.

Governments also vary considerably in terms of how they govern. In the United States and a small number of other nations, governments are limited as to what they are permitted to control (substantive limits) and how they go about it (procedural limits). Governments that are limited in this way are called **constitutional governments**, or liberal governments. In other nations, including many in Latin America, Asia, and Africa, though the law imposes few real limits, the government is nevertheless kept in check by other political and social institutions that it is unable to control and must come to terms with—such as autonomous territories, an organized religion, organized business groups, or organized labor unions. Such governments are generally called **authoritarian**. In a third group of nations, including the Soviet Union under Joseph Stalin, Nazi Germany, perhaps prewar Japan and Italy, and North Korea today, governments not only are free of legal limits but also seek to eliminate those organized social groups that might challenge or limit their authority. These governments typically attempt to dominate or control every sphere of political, economic, and social life and, as a result, are called **totalitarian**.

Americans have the good fortune to live in a nation in which limits are placed on what governments can do and how they can do it. Many of the world's people do not live in a constitutional democracy. By one measure, just 45 percent of the global population (those living in 87 countries) enjoy sufficient levels of political and personal freedom to be classified as living in a constitutional democracy.[10] And constitutional democracies were unheard of before the modern era. Prior to the eighteenth and nineteenth centuries, governments seldom sought—and rarely received—the support of their subjects. The available evidence strongly suggests

autocracy a form of government in which a single individual—a king, queen, or dictator—rules

oligarchy a form of government in which a small group—landowners, military officers, or wealthy merchants—controls most of the governing decisions

democracy a system of rule that permits citizens to play a significant part in the governmental process, usually through the election of key public officials

constitutional government a system of rule in which formal and effective limits are placed on the powers of the government

authoritarian government a system of rule in which the government recognizes no formal limits but may nevertheless be restrained by the power of other social institutions

totalitarian government a system of rule in which the government recognizes no formal limits on its power and seeks to absorb or eliminate other social institutions that might challenge it

that the ordinary people often had little love for the government or for the social order. After all, they had no stake in it. They equated government with the police officer, the bailiff, and the tax collector.[11]

Beginning in the seventeenth century, in a handful of Western nations, two important changes began to take place in the character and conduct of government. First, governments began to acknowledge formal limits on their power. Second, a small number of governments began to provide ordinary citizens with a formal voice in public affairs—through the vote. Obviously, the desirability of limits on government and the expansion of popular influence were at the heart of the American Revolution in 1776. "No taxation without representation," as we shall see in Chapter 2, was fiercely asserted from the beginning of the Revolution through the Founding in 1789. But even before the Revolution, a tradition of limiting government and expanding participation in the political process had developed throughout western Europe.

Limiting Government

America's Founders were influenced by the English thinker John Locke (1632–1704). Locke argued that governments need the consent of the people.

The key force behind the imposition of limits on government power was a new social class, the bourgeoisie, which became an important political force in the sixteenth and seventeenth centuries. *Bourgeois* is a French word for "freeman of the city," or *bourg*. Being part of the bourgeoisie later became associated with being "middle class" and with involvement in commerce or industry. In order to gain a share of control of government, joining or even displacing the kings, aristocrats, and gentry who had dominated government for centuries, the bourgeoisie sought to change existing institutions—especially parliaments—into instruments of real political participation. Parliaments had existed for centuries, but were generally aristocratic institutions. The bourgeoisie embraced parliaments as means by which they could exert the weight of their superior numbers and growing economic advantage on their aristocratic rivals. At the same time, the bourgeoisie sought to place restraints on the capacity of governments to threaten these economic and political interests by placing formal or constitutional limits on governmental power.

Although motivated primarily by the need to protect and defend their own interests, the bourgeoisie advanced many of the principles that would define the central underpinnings of individual liberty for all citizens—freedom of speech, freedom of assembly, freedom of conscience, and freedom from arbitrary search and seizure. The work of political theorists such as John Locke (1632–1704) and, later, John Stuart Mill (1806–73) helped shape these evolving ideas about liberty and political rights. However, it is important to note that the bourgeoisie generally did not favor democracy as we know it. They were advocates of electoral and representative institutions, but they favored property requirements and other restrictions so as to limit participation to the middle and upper classes. Yet once these institutions of politics and the protection of the right to engage in politics were established, it was difficult to limit them to the bourgeoisie.

John Stuart Mill (1806–73) presented a ringing defense of individual freedom in his famous treatise On Liberty. Mill's work influenced Americans' evolving ideas about the relationship between government and the individual.

Access to Government: The Expansion of Participation

The expansion of participation from the bourgeoisie to ever-larger segments of society took two paths. In some nations, popular participation was expanded by the Crown or the aristocracy, which ironically saw common people as potential political allies against the bourgeoisie. Thus in nineteenth-century Prussia, for example, it was the emperor and his great minister Otto von Bismarck who expanded popular participation in order to build political support among the lower orders.

In other nations, participation expanded because competing segments of the bourgeoisie sought to gain political advantage by reaching out and mobilizing the support of working- and lower-class groups that craved the opportunity to take part in politics—"lining up the unwashed," as one American historian put it.[12] To be sure, excluded groups often agitated for greater participation. But seldom was such agitation by itself enough to secure the right to participate. Usually, expansion of voting rights resulted from a combination of pressure from below and help from above.

The gradual expansion of voting rights by groups hoping to derive some political advantage has been typical of American history. After the Civil War, one of the chief reasons that Republicans moved to enfranchise newly freed slaves was to use the support of the former slaves to maintain Republican control over the defeated southern states. Similarly, in the early twentieth century, upper-middle-class Progressives advocated women's suffrage because they believed that women were likely to support the reforms espoused by the Progressive movement.

Influencing the Government through Participation: Politics

Expansion of participation means that more and more people have a legal right to take part in politics. *Politics* is an important term. In its broadest sense, it refers to conflicts over the character, membership, and policies of any organization to which people belong. As Harold Lasswell, a famous political scientist, once put it, politics is the struggle over "who gets what, when, how."[13] Although politics is a phenomenon that can be found in any organization, our concern in this book is narrower. Here, **politics** will be used to refer only to conflicts and struggles over the leadership, structure, and policies of governments. The goal of politics, as we define it, is to have a share or a say in the composition of the government's leadership, how the government is organized, or what its policies are going to be. Having a share is called having **power** or influence.

Politics can take many forms, including everything from blogging and posting opinion pieces online, sending e-mails to government officials, voting, lobbying legislators on behalf of particular programs, and participating in protest marches and even violent demonstrations. A system of government that gives citizens a regular opportunity to elect the top government officials is usually called a **representative democracy**, or **republic**. A system that permits citizens to vote directly on laws and policies is often called a **direct democracy**. At the national level, America is a representative democracy in which citizens select government officials but do not vote on legislation. Some states and cities, however, have provisions for direct legislation through popular initiative and ballot referendum. These procedures allow citizens to collect petitions requiring an issue to be brought directly to the voters for a decision. In 2012, more than 188 initiatives appeared on state ballots, dealing with matters that ranged from taxes and education to animal cruelty and affirmative action. Many hot-button issues are decided by initiatives. For example, in 2006, Michigan voters approved a measure that prohibits public institutions such as the University of Michigan from giving preferential treatment on the basis of race; in Colorado in 2010, voters passed a referendum that called on the state to sue the federal government to enforce immigration laws. Often, broad public campaigns promote controversial referenda, attempting to persuade voters to change existing laws. For example, in 2012 voters in Massachusetts approved the use of medical

politics conflict over the leadership, structure, and policies of governments

power influence over a government's leadership, organization, or policies

representative democracy/ republic a system of government in which the populace selects representatives, who play a significant role in governmental decision making

direct democracy a system of rule that permits citizens to vote directly on laws and policies

marijuana while voters in Arkansas defeated a similar measure. Voters in Colorado, Oregon, and Washington state enacted initiatives to legalize the recreational use of marijuana, a development that puts them at odds with federal law. Voters in Maryland, Maine, and Washington state approved same-sex marriage, the first victory for this issue at the ballot box.

Groups and organized interests do not vote (although their members do), but they certainly do participate in politics. Their political activities usually consist of such endeavors as providing funds for candidates, lobbying, and trying to influence public opinion. The pattern of struggles among interests is called group politics, or **pluralism**. Americans have always been ambivalent about pluralist politics. On the one hand, the right of groups to press their views and compete for influence in the government is the essence of liberty. On the other hand, Americans often fear that organized groups may sometimes exert too much influence, advancing special interests at the expense of larger public interests. (We will return to this problem in Chapter 11.)

Sometimes, of course, politics does not take place through formal channels at all but instead involves direct action. Direct-action politics can include either violent politics or civil disobedience, both of which attempt to shock rulers into behaving more responsibly. Direct action can also be a form of revolutionary politics, which rejects the system entirely and attempts to replace it with a new ruling group and a new set of rules. In recent years in the United States, groups ranging from animal-rights activists to right-to-life advocates to the Occupy Wall Street protesters have used direct action to underline their demands. Many forms of peaceful direct political action are protected by the U.S. Constitution. The country's Founders knew that the right to protest is essential to the maintenance of political freedom, even where the ballot box is available.

pluralism the theory that all interests are and should be free to compete for influence in the government; the outcome of this competition is compromise and moderation

Who Are Americans?

Show how the American people have changed over time

While American democracy aims to give the people a voice in government, the meaning of "we the people" has changed over time. Who are Americans? Through the course of American history, politicians, religious leaders, prominent scholars, and ordinary Americans have puzzled over and fought about the answer to this fundamental question. Since the Founding, the American population has grown from 3.9 million in 1790, the year of the first official census, to 314 million in 2012. As the American population has grown, it has become more diverse on nearly every dimension imaginable.[14]

At the time of the Founding, when the United States consisted of 13 states arrayed along the Eastern Seaboard, 81 percent of Americans counted by the census traced their roots to Europe, mostly England and northern Europe; nearly 20 percent were of African origin, the vast majority of whom were slaves.[15] Only 1.5 percent of the black population was free. There was also an unknown number of Native Americans, the original inhabitants of the land, not counted by the census because the government did not consider them Americans. The first estimates

An Increasingly Diverse Nation

Since the Founding, the American people have become increasingly diverse. This diversity and the changes in the population have frequently raised challenging questions in American politics.

Race

	1790*	1900*	2010

👤 = 1 million people

1790*		1900*		2010	
White	81%	White	88%	White	64%
Black	19%	Black	12%	Black	13%
		Other	0.5%	Hispanic	16%
				Asian	5%
				Native American	1%
				Other	1%
				2 or more races	2%

TOTAL POPULATION =	3,929,214	75,994,575	308,745,538

Geography

	1790	1900	2010

1790
50%
50%

Northeast 50%   South 50%

1900
28%
35%
6%
33%

Northeast 28%   Midwest 35%
South 33%   West 6%

2010
18%
22%
23%
37%

Northeast 18%   Midwest 22%
South 37%   West 23%

Age

	1900	2010

1900		2010	
0 - 19	44%	0 - 19	27%
20 - 44	38%	20 - 44	34%
45 - 64	14%	45 - 64	26%
65 +	4%	65 +	13%

for critical analysis

1. The 2010 census showed that the populations of the South and the West continued to grow more rapidly than the Northeast and Midwest. What are some of the political implications of this trend?

2. Today, Americans over age 37 outnumber Americans under 37—and older adults are more likely to participate in the political process. What do you think this means for the kinds of issues and policies taken up by the government?

* The 1790 census does not accurately reflect the population because it only counted blacks and whites. It did not include Native Americans or other groups. The 1900 census did not count Hispanic Americans.

SOURCE: U.S. Census Bureau, www.census.gov (accessed 8/16/12).

Native American societies, with their own forms of government, existed for thousands of years before the first European settlers arrived. By the time this photo of Red Cloud and other Sioux warriors was taken, around 1870, Native Americans made up about 1 percent of the American population.

of Native Americans and Hispanics in the mid-1800s showed that each group made up less than 1 percent of the total population.[16]

Flash forward to 1900. The country now stretched out across the continent, and waves of immigrants, mainly from Europe, boosted the population to 76 million. In 1900 the United States was predominantly composed of whites of European ancestry, but this number now included many from southern and eastern as well as northern Europe; the black population stood at 12 percent. Residents who traced their origin to Latin America or Asia each accounted for less than 1 percent of the entire population (see the infographic on page 17).[17] The large number of new immigrants was reflected in the high proportion of foreign-born people in the United States: the foreign-born population reached its height at 14.7 percent in 1910.[18]

Immigration and Ethnic Diversity

As the European-origin population grew more diverse, anxiety about Americans' ethnic identity mounted. In 1900 the author of a *New York Times* front-page article answered his own question—"Are the Americans an Anglo-Saxon People?"—in the affirmative.[19] But the growing numbers of immigrants from southern and eastern Europe who were crowding into American cities spurred heated debates about how long Anglo-Saxons could dominate. Much as today, politicians and scholars argued about whether the country could absorb such large numbers of immigrants. Concerns ranged from whether their political and social values were compatible with American democracy, to whether they would learn English, to alarm about the diseases they might bring into the United States.

The distinct ethnic backgrounds and language differences of the new immigrants were not the only characteristics that worried the Anglo-Saxon natives; immigrant religious affiliations also aroused concern. The first immigrants to the United States were overwhelmingly Protestant, many of them fleeing religious persecution. The arrival of Germans and Irish in the mid-1800s began to shift that balance with increasing numbers of Catholics. Even so, in 1900, four in five Americans were still Protestants. The large-scale immigration of the early twentieth century threatened

Millions of immigrants from Europe came to the United States in the early 1900s. Most passed through New York's Ellis Island, where they were checked for diseases before being admitted. Today many Americans trace their ancestry to immigrants who passed through Ellis Island.

to reduce the proportion of Protestants significantly. The eastern European immigrants pouring into the country, especially those from Russia, were heavily Jewish; the southern Europeans, especially Italians, were Catholic. A more religiously diverse country challenged the implicit Protestantism embedded in many aspects of American public life. For example, religious diversity introduced new conflicts into public schooling, as Catholics sought public funding for parochial schools and dissident Protestant sects lobbied to eliminate Bible reading and prayer in the schools.

Anxieties about immigration sparked intense debate. Should the numbers of immigrants entering the country be limited? Should restrictions be placed on the types of immigrants to be granted entry? After World War I, Congress responded to the fears swirling around immigration with new laws that sharply limited the number who could enter the country each year. It also established a new National Origins quota system, based on the nation's population in 1890, before the wave of immigrants from eastern and southern Europe arrived.[20] Supporters of ethnic quotas hoped to turn back the clock and revert to an earlier America in which northern Europeans dominated. The new system set up a hierarchy of admissions: northern European countries received generous quotas for new immigrants, whereas eastern and southern European countries were granted very small quotas. These restrictions ratcheted down the numbers of immigrants so that by 1970, the foreign-born population in the United States reached an all-time low of 5 percent.

Immigration and Race

Official efforts to use racial and ethnic criteria to restrict the American population were not new but had been used to draw boundaries around the American community from the start. The very first census, as just mentioned, did not count

Although the number of immigrants from Asia increased sharply in the 1970s, the number of Asian Americans who hold elected office is relatively small. When Nikki Haley (right) was elected governor of South Carolina in 2010, she became the second Indian American governor in the United States.

Native Americans; in fact, no Native Americans became citizens until 1924. Although the Constitution infamously declared that each slave would count as three-fifths of a person for purposes of apportioning representation among the states, most people of African descent were not officially citizens until 1868, when the Fourteenth Amendment to the Constitution conferred citizenship on the freed slaves.

Over half a century earlier, the federal government had sought to limit the nonwhite population with a 1790 law stipulating that only free whites could become naturalized citizens. Not until 1870 did Congress lift the ban on the naturalization of nonwhites. In addition to the restrictions on blacks and Native Americans, restrictions applied to Asians as well. The Chinese Exclusion Act of 1882 outlawed the entry of Chinese laborers to the United States. These provisions were not lifted until 1943, when China became America's ally during World War II. Additional barriers enacted after World War I meant that virtually no Asians entered the country as immigrants until the 1940s. People of Hispanic origin do not fit simply into the American system of racial classification. In 1930, for example, the census counted people of Mexican origin as nonwhite but reversed this decision a decade later—after protests by the Mexican-origin population and the Mexican government. Only in 1970 did the census officially begin counting persons of Hispanic origin, noting that they could be any race.[21]

Twenty-First-Century Americans

By 2000, immigration had profoundly transformed the nation's racial and ethnic profile once again. The primary cause was Congress's decision in 1965 to lift the tight restrictions of the 1920s, allowing for much-expanded immigration from Asia and Latin America (see Figure 1.2). One consequence of the shift has been the growth in the Hispanic, or Latino, population. Census figures for 2010 show that the total Hispanic proportion of the population is now 16 percent; the black, or African American, population is 12 percent of the total population. Asians made up 5 percent of the population. European Americans accounted for less than two-thirds of the population in 2010—their lowest share ever. Moreover, 2 percent of the population now identified itself as of "two or more races," a new category that the census added in 2000.[22] Although it is only a small percentage of the population, the multiracial category points toward a future in which the traditional labels of racial identification may be blurring, marking a major shift in the long-standing American tradition of strict racial categorization. The blurring of racial categories poses challenges to a host of policies—many of them put in place to remedy past discrimination—that rely on racial counts of the population.

Large-scale immigration means that many more residents are foreign born. In 2010, 12.36 percent of the population was born outside the United States, a figure comparable to foreign-born rates at the turn of the previous century.[23] Over half of the foreign born came from Latin America and the Caribbean—almost 1 in 10 from the Caribbean, nearly 4 in 10 from Central America (including Mexico), and 6.8 percent from South America. Those born in Asia constituted the next-largest group, making up over one-quarter of foreign-born residents. In sharp contrast to the immigration patterns of a century earlier, fewer immigrants came from

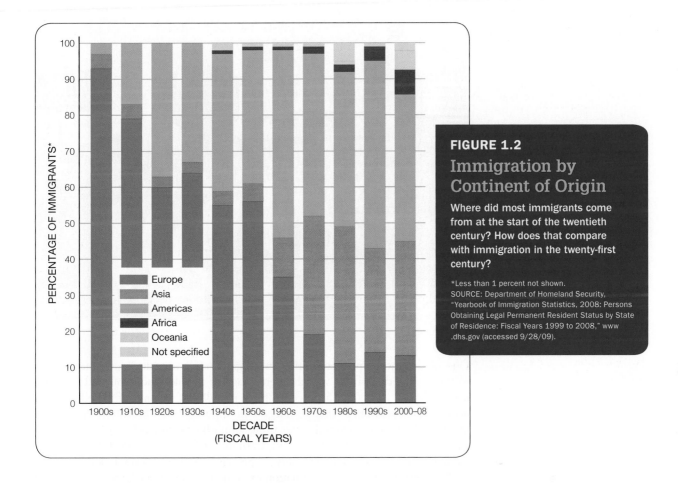

FIGURE 1.2

Immigration by Continent of Origin

Where did most immigrants come from at the start of the twentieth century? How does that compare with immigration in the twenty-first century?

*Less than 1 percent not shown.
SOURCE: Department of Homeland Security, "Yearbook of Immigration Statistics, 2008: Persons Obtaining Legal Permanent Resident Status by State of Residence: Fiscal Years 1999 to 2008," www .dhs.gov (accessed 9/28/09).

Europe. By 2010 only 12 percent of those born outside the United States came from Europe.[24]

These figures represent only legally authorized immigrants. One new feature of American society in recent years is the very large number of immigrants who live in the country without legal authorization. Estimates put the number of undocumented immigrants at 11 million, the majority of whom are from Mexico and Central America.[25] The large unauthorized population has become a flashpoint for controversy as states and cities have passed a variety of conflicting laws. Some states have offered driver's licenses to undocumented immigrants, while others have sought to bar them from public services, such as education and emergency health care, both of which are constitutionally guaranteed to unauthorized immigrants.[26] In 1982 the Supreme Court ensured access to education when it ruled in *Plyler v. Doe* that Texas could not deny funding for undocumented students.[27] In 1986, Congress guaranteed emergency medical care to all people regardless of immigration status when it passed the Emergency Medical Treatment and Active Labor Act (EMTALA).

The new patterns of immigration combined with differences in birth rates and underlying social changes to alter the religious affiliations of Americans. In 1900, 80 percent of the American adult population was Protestant; by 2008 only a little over half of Americans identified themselves as Protestants.[28] Catholics now made up a quarter of the population, and Jews accounted for 1.2 percent. A small Muslim population had also grown, with over one-half of 1 percent of the population.

In 1965, Congress loosened restrictions on immigration, allowing millions of people from Latin America and Asia to enter the country in the decades that followed. By 2002, Hispanics were the largest minority group in the United States. Here, Antonio Villaraigosa campaigns to become the first Latino mayor of Los Angeles in 130 years.

One of the most important shifts in religious affiliation during the latter half of the twentieth century was the percentage of people who professed no organized religion: in 2008, 15 percent of the population was not affiliated with an organized church. These changes suggest an important shift in American religious identity; although the United States thinks of itself as a "Judeo-Christian" nation—and indeed was 95 percent Protestant, Catholic, or Jewish from 1900 to 1968—by 2008, this number had fallen to only 77 percent of the adult population.[29]

As America grew and its population expanded and diversified, the country's age profile shifted with it. In 1900 only 4 percent of the population was over age 65. As life expectancy increased, the number of older Americans grew with it: by 2010, 13 percent of the population was over 65. The percentage of children under the age of 18 also changed; in 1900 this group comprised 43 percent of the American population; by 2010, children 18 and under had fallen to just over a quarter of the population.[30] Another way to think about the age of Americans is that in 1800, the median age of the population was 16 years; by 1900 it was 22.9 years, and by 2010 it was 37.2 years. Even though the median age of Americans has increased, Americans tend to be younger than citizens of many industrialized countries, mainly because of the large immigrant population in the United States. In most European countries, the median age was above 40 in 2000.[31] But an aging population poses challenges to the United States as well. As the elderly population grows and the working-age population shrinks, questions arise about how we will fund programs for the elderly, such as Social Security.

Over the nation's history, Americans have changed in other ways, moving from mostly rural settings and small towns to large urban areas. The idealization of country life in American culture traces its roots to the long period in which the majority of Americans lived in rural areas. Before 1920, less than half the population lived in urban areas; today 83.7 percent of Americans do.[32] Critics charge that the American political system—created when America was a largely rural society—underrepresents urban areas. The constitutional provision allocating each state two senators, for example, overrepresents sparsely populated rural states and underrepresents urban states, where the population is far more concentrated. In addition to becoming more urban over time, the American population has shifted regionally. During the past 50 years especially, many Americans left the Northeast and Midwest and moved to the South and Southwest. As congressional seats have been reapportioned to reflect the population shift, many problems that particularly plague the Midwest and Northeast, such as the decline in manufacturing jobs, receive less attention in national politics.

The shifting contours of the American people have regularly raised challenging questions about our politics and governing arrangements. Population growth has spurred politically charged debates about how the population should be apportioned among congressional districts. These conflicts have major implications for the representation of different regions of the country and for the balance of representation between urban and rural areas. Population growth has also transformed the close democratic relationship between congressional representatives and their constituents envisioned by the framers. For example, the framers stipulated that the number of representatives in the House of Representatives "shall not exceed one for every thirty Thousand" constituents; today the average member of Congress represents 710,767 constituents.[33] Immigration and the cultural and religious changes it entails provoked heated disputes 100 years ago and still spark passionate debate today. The different languages and customs that immigrants bring to the United States trigger fears that the country is changing in ways that may undermine American values and alter fundamental identities. The large number of unauthorized immigrants in the country today makes these anxieties even more acute. Yet a changing population has been one of the constants of American history. Indeed, each generation has confronted the myriad political challenges associated with answering anew "Who are Americans?"

● Thinking Critically about American Political Culture

Analyze whether the system of government upholds American political values

Underlying and framing political life in the United States are agreements on basic political values but disagreements over the ends or goals of government. Most Americans affirm the values of liberty, equality, and democracy. Values shape citizens' views of the world and define their sense of what is right and wrong, just and unjust, possible and impossible. If Americans shared no values, they would have difficulty communicating, much less agreeing on a common system of government and politics. However, sharing broad values does not guarantee political consensus. We can agree on principles but disagree over their application or how they are to be balanced. Much of the debate over the role of government has been over what government should do and how far it should go to reduce the inequalities within our society and political system while still preserving essential liberties.

Even though Americans have disagreed over the meaning of such political ideals as equality, they still agree on the importance of those ideals. The values, beliefs, and attitudes that form our **political culture** and hold together the United States and its people date back to the time of the founding of the Union.

political culture broadly shared values, beliefs, and attitudes about how the government should function. American political culture emphasizes the values of liberty, equality, and democracy

The essential documents of the American Founding—the Declaration of Independence and the Constitution—enunciated a set of political principles about the purposes of the new republic. In contrast with many other democracies, in the United States these political ideals did not just remain words on dusty documents. Americans actively embraced the principles of the Founders and made them central to the national identity. Let us look more closely at three of these ideals: liberty, equality, and democracy.

Liberty

liberty freedom from governmental control

limited government a principle of constitutional government; a government whose powers are defined and limited by a constitution

No ideal is more central to American values than liberty. The Declaration of Independence defined three inalienable rights: "Life, Liberty and the pursuit of Happiness." The preamble of the Constitution likewise identified the need to secure "the Blessings of Liberty" as one of the key reasons for drawing up the Constitution. For Americans, **liberty** means both personal freedom and economic freedom. Both are closely linked to the idea of **limited government**.

The Constitution's first 10 amendments, known collectively as the Bill of Rights, above all preserve individual personal liberties and rights. In fact, the word *liberty* has come to mean many of the freedoms guaranteed in the Bill of Rights: freedom of speech and writing, the right to assemble freely, and the right to practice religious beliefs without interference from the government. Over the course of American history, the scope of personal liberties has expanded, as laws have become more tolerant and as individuals have successfully used the courts to challenge restrictions on their individual freedoms. Far fewer restrictions exist today on the press, political speech, and individual moral behavior than in the early years of the nation. Even so, conflicts persist over how personal liberties should be extended and when personal liberties violate community norms. For example, a number of cities have recently passed "sit-lie" ordinances, which limit the freedom of individuals to sit or lie down on sidewalks. Designed to limit the presence of the homeless and make city streets more attractive to pedestrians, the ordinances have also been denounced as infringements on individual liberties.

Patrick Henry's famous "Give me liberty or give me death" speech demanded freedom at any cost and has resonated with Americans throughout the nation's history.

The central historical conflict regarding liberty in the United States was about the enslavement of blacks. The facts of slavery and the differential treatment of the races have cast a long shadow over all of American history. In fact, scholars today note that the American definition of freedom has been formed in relation to the concept of slavery. The right to control one's labor and the right to receive rewards for that labor have been central elements of our definition of freedom precisely because these freedoms were denied to slaves.[34]

laissez-faire capitalism an economic system in which the means of production and distribution are privately owned and operated for profit with minimal or no government interference

In addition to personal freedom, the American concept of liberty means economic freedom. Since the Founding, economic freedom has been linked to capitalism, free markets, and the protection of private property. Free competition, unfettered movement of goods, and the right to enjoy the fruits of one's labor are all essential aspects of economic freedom and American capitalism.[35] In the first century of the republic, support for capitalism often meant support for the doctrine of laissez-faire (literally, "leave alone" in French). **Laissez-faire capitalism** allowed very little room for the national government to regulate trade or restrict the use of private property, even in the public interest. Americans still strongly support capitalism and economic liberty, but they now also endorse some restrictions on economic freedoms to protect the public. Today, federal and state governments deploy a wide array of regulations in the name of public protection. These include health and safety laws, environmental rules, and workplace regulations.

Not surprisingly, fierce disagreements often erupt over what the proper scope of government regulation should be. What some people regard as protecting the public, others see as an infringement on their own freedom to run their businesses and use their property as they see fit. For example, in September 2009 the Food and Drug Administration banned the sale of flavored cigarettes under the terms of the Family Smoking Prevention and Tobacco Control Act passed by Congress three months earlier. The FDA and health care professionals argue that such cigarettes are manufactured primarily to lure children and teenagers into smoking. It is estimated that 3,600 children and teenagers start smoking each day; by banning flavored cigarettes, the agency hopes to reduce that number. Manufacturers of these products, however, are averse to such regulations, feeling that the government is limiting their freedom and their ability to make a profit.[36]

More recently, concerns about liberty have arisen in relation to the government's efforts to combat terrorism. In the months following September 11, hundreds of individuals, mainly of Middle Eastern origin, were arrested by federal authorities and held on immigration charges or by material witness warrants that allowed the government to incarcerate them without having to show any evidence they were linked to terrorist activities. Also in the immediate aftermath of September 11, President George W. Bush issued secret orders to the National Security Agency, authorizing the agency to monitor domestic phone traffic in search of possible communications among terrorist groups. This program meant that the calls of millions of Americans were secretly intercepted without a court warrant. Concerns about terrorism leave us with an extraordinary dilemma. On the one hand, we treasure liberty, but on the other hand, we recognize that the lives of thousands of Americans have already been lost and countless others are threatened by terrorism. Can we reconcile liberty and security? Liberty and order? In previous national emergencies, Americans accepted restrictions on liberty with the understanding that these would be temporary. But because the threat of terrorism has no clear end point, doubts have grown about whether special government powers that infringe on liberties should be continued.

Equality

The Declaration of Independence declares as its first "self-evident" truth that "all men are created equal." As central as it is to the American political creed, however, equality has been an even less well-defined ideal than liberty, because people interpret "equality" in different ways. Few Americans have wholeheartedly embraced the ideal of full equality of results, but most Americans share the ideal of **equality of opportunity**—that is, the notion that each person should be given a fair chance to go as far as his or her talents will allow. Yet it is hard for Americans to reach agreement on what constitutes equality of opportunity. Must *past* inequalities be remedied in order to ensure equal opportunity in the *present*? Should inequalities in the legal, political, and economic spheres be given the same weight? In contrast to liberty, which requires limits on the role of government, equality implies an *obligation* of the government to the people.[37]

Americans do make clear distinctions between political equality and social or economic equality. **Political equality** means that members of the American political community have the right to participate in politics on equal terms. Beginning from a very restricted definition of political community, which originally included only propertied white men, the United States has moved much closer to an ideal of political equality that can be summed up as "one person, one vote." Broad support

equality of opportunity a widely shared American ideal that all people should have the freedom to use whatever talents and wealth they have to reach their fullest potential

political equality the right to participate in politics equally, based on the principle of "one person, one vote"

for the ideal of political equality has helped expand the American political community and extend to all the right to participate. Although considerable conflict remains over whether the political system makes participation in it harder for some people and easier for others, and whether the role of money in politics has drowned out the public voice, Americans agree that all citizens should have an equal right to participate and that government should enforce that right.

In part because Americans believe that individuals are free to work as hard as they choose, they have always been less concerned about social or economic inequality. Many Americans regard economic differences as the consequence of individual choices, virtues, or failures. Because of this, Americans tend to be less supportive than most Europeans of government action to ensure economic equality. Yet when major economic forces, such as the Great Depression of the 1930s, affect many people, or when systematic barriers appear to block equality of opportunity, Americans support government action to promote equality. Even then, however, they have endorsed only a limited government role designed to help people get back on their feet or to open up opportunity.

Because equality is such an elusive concept, many conflicts have arisen over what it should mean in practice. Americans have engaged in three kinds of controversies about the public role in addressing inequality. The first is determining what constitutes equality of access to public institutions. In 1896 the Supreme Court ruled in *Plessy v. Ferguson* that "separate but equal" accommodation for blacks and whites was constitutional.[38] In 1954, in a major legal victory for the civil rights movement, the Supreme Court's decision in *Brown v. Board of Education* overturned the "separate but equal" doctrine (see Chapter 5).[39] Today, new questions have been raised about what constitutes equal access to public institutions. Some argue that the unequal financing of public schools in cities, suburbs, and rural districts is a violation of the right to equal education. To date, these claims have not been supported by the federal courts, which have rejected the notion that the unequal economic impacts of public policy outcomes are a constitutional matter.[40] Lawsuits arguing a right to "economic equal protection" stalled in 1973 when the Supreme Court ruled that a Texas school-financing law did not violate the Constitution even though the law affected rich and poor students differently.[41]

A second debate concerns the public role in ensuring equality of opportunity in private life. Although Americans generally agree that discrimination should not be tolerated, people disagree over what should be done to ensure equality of opportunity (see Table 1.3). Controversies about affirmative-action programs reflect these disputes. Supporters of affirmative action claim that such programs are necessary to compensate for past discrimination in order to establish true equality of opportunity today. Opponents maintain that affirmative action amounts to reverse discrimination and that a society that espouses true equality should not acknowledge gender or racial differences. The question of the public responsibility for private inequalities is central to gender issues. The traditional view, still held by many today, sees the special responsibilities

WE ALL DESERVE THE FREEDOM TO MARRY

Opponents of gay marriage have proposed amending the Constitution to define marriage as a union between one man and one woman. Supporters of gay rights argue that same-sex couples should have an equal right to marry.

TABLE 1.3

Equality and Public Opinion

Americans believe in some forms of equality more than others. How do these survey results reflect disagreement about what equality means in practice?

STATEMENT	PERCENTAGE WHO AGREE
Male and female citizens of the United States have equal rights.	97
Our society should do what is necessary to make sure that everyone has an equal opportunity to succeed.	86
Homosexuals should have equal rights in terms of job opportunities.	87
It should be legal for gay and lesbian couples to get married.	50
The fact that some are rich and some are poor is an acceptable part of the economic system.	52
We should make every possible effort to improve the position of blacks and other minorities even if it means preferential treatment (according to whites).	22
We should make every possible effort to improve the position of blacks and other minorities even if it means preferential treatment (according to blacks).	62

SOURCES: Pew Global Attitudes Project Poll, April 2010. Retrieved June 9, 2012 from the iPOLL Databank, The Roper Center for Public Opinion Research, University of Connecticut. www.ropercenter.uconn.edu/data_access/ipoll/ipoll.html. Pew Research Center for the People and the Press and for the Public, "Trends in American Values, 1987–2012, Partisan Polarization Surges in Bush, Obama Years," June 4, 2012, p. 104. Princeton Survey Research Associates International/Newsweek Poll, December 2008. Retrieved June 9, 2012 from the iPOLL Databank, The Roper Center for Public Opinion Research, University of Connecticut, www.ropercenter.uconn.edu/data_access/ipoll/ipoll.html. Polling Report.com, Gallup, May 3–June 12, 2012, pollingreport.com/civil.htm. Pew Research Center for the People and the Press and for the Public, "It's Not about Class Warfare, but Fairness Poll Analysis," March 2, 2012, www.peoplepress.org/2012/03/02/for-the-public-its-not-about-class-warfare-but-fairness/. (All accessed 6/9/12.)

of women in the family as falling outside the range of public concern. Indeed, from this perspective, the role of women within families is essential to the functioning of a democratic society. In the past 30 years especially, these traditional views have come under fire as advocates for women have argued that women occupy a subordinate place within the family and that such private inequalities *are* a topic of public concern.[42]

A third debate about equality concerns differences in income and wealth. Unlike in other countries, income inequality has not been an enduring topic of political controversy in the United States, which currently has the largest gap in income and wealth between rich and poor citizens of any developed nation. But Americans have generally tolerated great differences among rich and poor citizens, in part because of a pervasive belief that mobility is possible and that economic success is the product of individual effort.[43] This tolerance for inequality is reflected in America's tax code, which is more advantageous to wealthy taxpayers than that of almost any other Western nation. Indeed, tax changes enacted in recent years

Beginning in 2011, the Occupy movement drew attention to increasing inequality in the United States, arguing that the gap between the top 1 percent of earners and the other 99 percent was unfair.

for critical analysis

Economic inequality among Americans is now as high as it was 100 years ago. Many politicians and news commentators say that inequality is threatening the middle class. Is there any evidence that the American public is worried about the growth in inequality?

popular sovereignty a principle of democracy in which political authority rests ultimately in the hands of the people

majority rule, minority rights the democratic principle that a government follows the preferences of the majority of voters but protects the interests of the minority

have sharply reduced the tax burdens of upper-income Americans. Debate about taxes surfaced throughout the Obama presidency and during the 2012 election. President Obama defended the need to raise the tax rate of Americans earning more than $250,000 a year to support programs that benefit the middle class.[44] Even so, opposition among Republicans—and some Democrats—meant that tax rates remained untouched. The issue of inequality emerged in a new dramatic way in late 2011, when the Occupy Wall Street movement mounted protests across the country. Motivated by concerns about inequality, the movement did not develop a clear policy agenda, but concerns about inequality received new prominence. Polls showed that Americans are split in their views about whether government should aim to reduce economic inequality. In 2012, 52 percent viewed the gap between the rich and the poor as an acceptable part of the economic system while 45 percent considered it a problem that needs to be fixed. More Americans expressed concern about the power of the rich, with 77 percent agreeing that there was too much power in the hands of a few rich people and large corporations.[45]

Democracy

The essence of democracy is the participation of the people in choosing their rulers and the people's ability to influence what those rulers do. In a democracy, political power ultimately comes from the people. The idea of placing power in the hands of the people is known as **popular sovereignty**. In the United States, popular sovereignty and political equality make politicians accountable to the people. Ideally, democracy envisions an engaged citizenry prepared to exercise its power over rulers. As we noted earlier, the United States is a representative democracy, meaning that the people do not rule directly but instead exercise power through elected representatives. Forms of participation in a democracy vary greatly, but voting is a key element of the representative democracy that the American Founders established.

American democracy rests on the principle of **majority rule** with **minority rights**. Majority rule means that the wishes of the majority determine what government does. The House of Representatives—a large body elected directly by

Should America Export Democracy?

Americans are justifiably proud of their democratic political institutions and often believe that the people of all nations would benefit from living under American-style democratic rule. Indeed, on a number of occasions Americans have sought to transform other nations into democracies—a policy called "democratization." In the aftermath of World War II, American military forces occupied Japan and the western portion of Germany, imposing new democratic governments to replace the dictatorial regimes blamed for launching the war. More recently, after successful American military campaigns to overthrow the governments of Afghanistan and Iraq, the United States has undertaken an effort to build democratic governments in those nations.

Exporting democracy might be seen as a desirable goal for three reasons. The first of these is humanitarian. Generally speaking, individuals are better off when they possess civil liberties and political rights. Indeed, former president George W. Bush asserted that one of the main purposes of American policy in the Middle East was to bring democracy to the people of the region. "It is the calling of our country," Bush said.

A second reason sometimes given in support of American efforts to export democracy is the promotion of political stability. In a democracy, competing economic and social forces have a chance to work out their differences through lawful political struggle. Dictatorial regimes, by contrast, seldom provide opportunities for lawful political activity and usually seek to quash expressions of political dissent or opposition. Lacking lawful channels, political grievances in nations ruled by dictatorships usually manifest themselves in such forms as public protest, political violence, and terrorism. The uprisings of the "Arab Spring," including the prolonged struggle in Libya, overthrew dictators across the Arab world in 2011. Whether these major political shifts also build stable democratic regimes remains to be seen. A third reason Americans might wish to support policies of democratization is

that the spread of democracy may promote world peace. In his famous 1795 essay "Toward Perpetual Peace," the German philosopher Immanuel Kant observed that democratic regimes seldom made war on each other. Thus, he argued, the expansion of democracy would enhance the prospects for world peace. In recent years, a good deal of empirical research has supported Kant's hypothesis.

Although a more democratic world might, indeed, be more humane, stable, and peaceful, a policy of democratization faces daunting prospects. First, a huge percentage of the world's population lives in nations that are not democracies. It seems unlikely that America could actually democratize so much of the globe. Second, many nations might not be capable of sustaining democratic regimes even if they were established. Democracy is most likely to flourish where there are vigorous social institutions and a stable economy—conditions that do not exist in many regions of the world. Finally, the process of democratization can itself be dangerous for American interests because it may lead to political instability or the election of hostile governments. By 2009 some observers were questioning whether it would be possible to build democracies in Iraq and Afghanistan, where corruption and security challenges were undermining government stability. With the threat from the Taliban mounting in Afghanistan, the British ambassador there went so far as to suggest that it would take "an acceptable dictator" to unite the country.

for critical analysis

1. What are some of the factors that might help determine whether democratic politics can take root in a country that has not previously experienced democracy?

2. Is it appropriate for America to try to shape the governments and political arrangements of other countries?

the people—was designed in particular to ensure majority rule. But the Founders feared that popular majorities could turn government into a "tyranny of the majority" in which individual liberties would be violated. Concern for individual rights has thus been a part of American democracy from the beginning. The rights enumerated in the Bill of Rights and enforced through the courts provide an important check on the power of the majority.

Despite Americans' deep attachment to the *ideal* of democracy, many questions can be raised about our *practice* of democracy. The first is the restricted definition of the political community during much of American history. Property restrictions on the right to vote were eliminated by 1828; in 1870 the Fifteenth Amendment to the Constitution granted African Americans the vote, although later exclusionary practices denied them that right; in 1920 the Nineteenth Amendment guaranteed women the right to vote; and in 1965 the Voting Rights Act finally secured the right of African Americans to vote.

Just securing the right to vote does not end concerns about democracy, however. The organization of electoral institutions can have a significant impact on access to elections and on who can get elected. During the first two decades of the twentieth century, states and cities enacted many reforms, including strict registration requirements and scheduling of elections, that made it harder to vote. The aim was to rid politics of corruption, but the consequence was to reduce participation. Other institutional decisions affect which candidates stand the best chance of getting elected (see Chapter 10).

A further consideration about democracy concerns the relationship between economic power and political power. Money has always played an important role in elections and governing in the United States. Many argue that the pervasive influence of money in American electoral campaigns today undermines democracy. With the decline of locally based political parties that depend on party loyalists to turn out the vote, and the rise of political action committees, political consultants, and expensive media campaigns, money has become the central fact of life in American politics. Money often determines who runs for office; it can exert a heavy influence on who wins; and some argue that it affects what politicians do once they are in office.[46]

Low turnout for elections and a pervasive sense of apathy and cynicism characterized American politics for much of the past half-century. The widespread interest in the 2008 election and the near-record levels of voter turnout, which, at 61.7 percent, was the highest turnout since 1980, reversed this trend.[47] Nine million voters registered and voted for the first time in 2008, including near-record numbers of voters under the age of 24.[48] Volunteers found ways to become personally involved in politics. Although turnout in 2012 did not match 2008, these developments were a hopeful sign for those wishing to revitalize American democracy.

for critical analysis

Does the United States have the most democratic government possible? Do citizens make the decisions of government, or do they merely influence them?

Although most barriers to voting have been removed for Americans aged 18 and up, many people do not vote. In the 2012 election only only about 60 percent of eligible citizens turned out at the polls.

get involved/go online

Explore American Politics Online

Inform Yourself

 Keep up-to-date on political news. Political information websites are numerous and useful for checking on a daily or at least weekly basis to keep up-to-date on what is happing in terms of legislation, elections, and other political news. Websites for general political information include the Huffington Post (www.huffingtonpost .com) and Politico (www.politico.com). The Real Clear Politics website (www .realclearpolitics.com) focuses on elections and public opinion polling. Under the Polls tab there are opinion polls on hundreds of different upcoming races.

 Find out what's happening in Congress. To find out specifically what is happening in Washington, D.C., visit Roll Call (www.rollcall.com). The website features information on proposed legislation, the legislative process, and "who's who" on Capitol Hill. Visit the website and see what the headlines are in each of the drop-down categories.

 See what the public across the country is thinking. The Pew Research Center offers some of the highest-quality public opinion surveys available. At www.pewresearch .org you will find public opinion polls on a plethora of topics related to American politics. There is even a poll on the costs and benefits of a college education and student debt, with opinions of college students and their parents (http://pewresearch .org/pubs/2261/college-university-education-costs-student-debt). How should this information be used by politicians when making education policy? Do you think elected officials in Washington, D.C., will pay attention to this public opinion poll?

Express Yourself

 Visit the Rock the Vote website. Rock the Vote (www.rockthevote.org) was created to help young people express their political power. Its website offers opportunities to register to vote, find your polling place, volunteer for a campaign, contribute money, read blog posts and press releases, and more. Consider joining Rock the Vote for one of its "Road Trips" to mobilize and register young voters across the country. Summer 2012 music tours included the Vans Warped Tour, the Rock the Bells festival, and the band Blink-182. There are opportunities to volunteer for the shows and get free tickets.

Connect with Others

 Join the discussion on American Politics 411's Facebook page. This is a page linked to a bipartisan group of students "dedicated to redefining transparency in politics and the media." You can also find American Politics 411 on Twitter. Skim through the items on its Facebook time line or Twitter feed and determine what materials are "bipartisan" and what materials still have a clear political slant. Consider joining the discussion on one of its posts.

Find links to the sites listed above as well as related activities on wwnorton.com/studyspace.

study guide

 Practice online with: Chapter 1 Diagnostic Quiz ▪ Chapter 1 Key Term Flashcards

What Americans Think about Government

■ **Explore how Americans see their government (pp. 5–8)**

While Americans have always been hesitant about granting government too much power, they have frequently relied on it during times of national crisis and have become increasingly dependent on it to provide important services. Over the last few decades, the public's trust in government and their sense of political efficacy have declined significantly. Low levels of trust and efficacy may threaten American democracy by weakening the government and reducing the public's willingness to participate in political life.

Key Terms

government (p. 4)

politics (p. 4)

political efficacy (p. 8)

Practice Quiz

1. Political efficacy is the belief that (*p. 8*)
   a) government is wasteful and corrupt.
   b) government operates efficiently.
   c) government has grown too large.
   d) government cannot be trusted.
   e) one can influence what government does.

2. American's trust in their government (*pp. 5–7*)
   a) rose significantly between 1964 and 1980.
   b) increased immediately following September 11, 2001, but declined shortly thereafter.
   c) declined immediately after the September 11 attacks but has risen dramatically since 2004.
   d) has never been studied.
   e) has remained the same over the last 50 years.

 Practice Online
Video exercise: *Democracy Is . . .*

Citizenship: Knowledge and Participation

■ **Describe the role of the citizen in politics (pp. 9–11)**

Citizenship requires political knowledge. When citizens know about politics, they are better able to understand their interests and to identify the best way to act on those interests. Most Americans, however, do not know much about politics.

Key Term

citizenship (p. 10)

Practice Quiz

3. Generally speaking, Americans (*p. 9*)
   a) know very little about current political issues but are able to identify high-profile political leaders.
   b) know a great deal about current political issues but are not able to identify high-profile political leaders.
   c) know very little about current political issues and are not able to identify high-profile political leaders.
   d) know a great deal about current political issues and are able to identify high-profile political leaders.
   e) are extremely engaged with politics and trust the government to do what is right.

4. According to the authors, good citizenship requires (*p. 10*)
   a) political knowledge and political engagement.
   b) political knowledge but not political engagement.
   c) a good education.
   d) a significant amount of money.
   e) political engagement but not political knowledge.

 Practice Online
"Get Involved" exercise: *Political News in the Digital Age*

Government

 Define government and forms of government (pp. 11–16)

There are many different kinds of government. Prior to the modern era, governments accepted almost no limits on their behavior and provided citizens with few opportunities to participate in public affairs. Today, numerous countries, including the United States, are constitutional democracies. America's democracy provides citizens with the chance to elect top officials at all levels of government and even allows them to vote directly on laws in many states and localities.

Key Terms

autocracy (p. 13)

oligarchy (p. 13)

democracy (p. 13)

constitutional government (p. 13)

authoritarian government (p. 13)

totalitarian government (p. 13)

politics (p. 15)

power (p. 15)

representative democracy/republic (p. 15)

direct democracy (p. 15)

pluralism (p. 16)

Practice Quiz

5. What is the basic difference between autocracy and oligarchy? (*p. 13*)
   a) the extent to which the average citizen has a say in government affairs
   b) the means of collecting taxes and conscripting soldiers
   c) the number of people who control governing decisions
   d) the size and political influence of the military
   e) They are fundamentally the same thing.

6. The famous political scientist Harold Lasswell defined politics are the struggle over (*p. 15*)
   a) who gets elected.
   b) who is most popular.
   c) who gets what, when, how.
   d) who protests.
   e) who gets to vote.

7. Although not present at the national level, a number of states and cities permit citizens to vote directly on laws and policies. What is this form of rule called? (*p. 15*)
   a) a republic
   b) representative democracy
   c) direct democracy
   d) pluralism
   e) laissez-faire capitalism

8. *Pluralism* is a theory that says (*p. 16*)
   a) the means of economic production should be privately owned and operated without interference from the government.
   b) all interests in a society should be free to compete for influence over governmental decisions.
   c) government should always follow the preferences of the majority while also protecting the rights of those in the minority.
   d) american political culture should emphasize the values of liberty, equality, and democracy.
   e) one ruler should dominate all spheres of social, political, economic and cultural life.

Who Are Americans?

 Show how the American people have changed over time (pp. 16–23)

The United States is defined, in part, by its ever growing and changing population. During the last 200 years, America has become more racially, ethnically, geographically, and religiously diverse. Immigration has been an important reason for the country's shifting demographics, and it has frequently sparked intense debate about the nature of American identity and American democracy.

Practice Quiz

9. Since 1900, which of the following groups has increased as a percentage of the overall population in the United States? (*p. 20*)
   a) black, Hispanic, and Asian
   b) Hispanic only
   c) Asian only
   d) black only
   e) Hispanic and Asian only

10. The percentage of foreign-born individuals living in the United States (*pp. 19–20*)
    a) has increased significantly since reaching its low point in 1970.
    b) has decreased significantly since reaching its high point in 1970.
    c) has remained the same since 1970.
    d) has not been studied since 1970.
    e) has never been less than the percentage of native born individuals living in the United States.

 Practice Online
"Who Are Americans?" interactive exercise:
An Increasingly Diverse Nation

Thinking Critically About American Political Culture

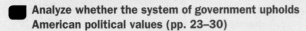 **Analyze whether the system of government upholds American political values (pp. 23–30)**

Most Americans espouse strong support for liberty, equality, and democracy. Agreement on these basic values does not mean, however, that political debate in the United States is without conflict. Questions about how to apply and balance the different elements of American political culture have motivated disagreements throughout the country's history.

Key Terms

political culture (p. 23)

liberty (p. 24)

limited government (p. 24)

laissez-faire capitalism (p. 24)

equality of opportunity (p. 25)

political equality (p. 25)

popular sovereignty (p. 28)

majority rule, minority rights (p. 28)

Practice Quiz

11. The principle of political equality can be best summed up as *(p. 25)*
    a) "equality of results."
    b) "equality of opportunity."
    c) "one person, one vote."
    d) "equality between the sexes."
    e) "leave everyone alone."

12. Which of the following is an important principle of American democracy? *(pp. 28–30)*
    a) popular sovereignty
    b) majority rule

    c) limited government
    d) minority rights
    e) All of the above are important principles of American democracy.

13. Which of the following is *not* related to the American conception of liberty? *(pp. 24–25)*
    a) freedom of speech
    b) free enterprise
    c) freedom of religion
    d) freedom of assembly
    e) All of the above are related to liberty.

14. Which of the following is *not* part of American political culture? *(p. 25)*
    a) belief in equality of results
    b) belief in democracy
    c) belief in individual liberty
    d) belief in free competition
    e) belief in equality of opportunity

15. Which of the following restrictions on voting have been repealed over the last 182 years of American history? *(p. 30)*
    a) property, gender, and race
    b) gender only
    c) race only
    d) property only
    e) race and gender only

 Practice Online
Interactive simulation: *Liberty vs. Security*

For Further Reading

Dahl, Robert. *Democracy and Its Critics*. New Haven, CT: Yale University Press, 1989.

Dalton, Russell. *The Good Citizen: How a Younger Generation Is Reshaping American Politics*. Rev. ed. Washington, DC: CQ Press, 2008.

Delli Carpini, Michael X., and Scott Keeter. *What Americans Know about Politics and Why It Matters*. New Haven, CT: Yale University Press, 1996.

Fischer, Claude S., and Michael Hout. *A Century of Difference: How America Changed in the Last One Hundred Years*. New York: Russell Sage Foundation, 2006.

Hibbing, John R., and Elizabeth Theiss-Morse. *Stealth Democracy: Americans' Belief about How Government Should Work*. New York: Cambridge University Press, 2002.

Huntington, Samuel. *Who Are We: The Challenges to America's National Identity*. New York: Simon & Schuster, 2004.

Lasswell, Harold. *Politics: Who Gets What, When, How*. New York: Meridian Books, 1958.

McCarty, Nolan, Keith T. Poole, and Howard Rosenthal, *Polarized America: The Dance of Ideology and Unequal Riches*. Cambridge, MA: MIT Press, 2008.

Page, Benjamin I., and Lawrence R. Jacobs. *Class War? What Americans Really Think about Economic Inequality*. Chicago: University of Chicago Press, 2009.

Tocqueville, Alexis de. *Democracy in America*. Translated by Phillips Bradley. New York: Knopf, Vintage Books, 1945; orig. published 1835.

Zakaria, Fareed. *The Future of Freedom*. New York: W.W.Norton, 2003.

Recommended Websites

American Democracy Project
www.aascu.org/programs/adp/
This is an effort by the Association of State Colleges and Universities to increase political engagement among college students. See what opportunities are available for you to become politically active.

Americans for Informed Democracy
www.aidemocracy.org
A nonpartisan organization that promotes democracy and seeks to build a new generation of globally conscious leaders. Find out how you can be politically active and coordinate a town hall meeting on campus, attend a leadership retreat, or publish your opinions on democracy.

DiversityInc
http://diversityinc.com
This site is dedicated to the promotion of American diversity and education. Here you can read about the issues that directly affect American minorities.

For Democracy
www.fordemocracy.com
Most Americans know little about our government. Log on to this independent site to find a plethora of information on the history of American democracy and related current events.

Future of Freedom Foundation
www.fff.org
This organization promotes individual liberty, free markets, private property, and limited government. Find out how some people are trying to protect freedom in the United States.

Institute for Learning Technologies
www.ilt.columbia.edu/publications/digitext.html#
Columbia University's Institute for Learning Technologies provides general information on early political thinkers such as Aristotle, Hobbes, Locke, and Rousseau. Take a moment to read some of the writings on topics such as popular sovereignty, democracy, and limited government.

Mobilize.org
http://mobilize.org
This all-partisan network is dedicated to educating, empowering, and energizing young people. Find out how politics affects America's youth and what they are doing about it by being engaged and active.

U.S. Census Bureau
www.census.gov
The website for the Bureau of the Census offers a statistical look at our country's population and economy. Check out some of the statistics to get a better idea of American diversity.

When the framers of the Constitution met in 1787, they set out to establish a political system that would protect liberty and place limits on government. They also believed a powerful government required a broad popular base. However, they debated how best to protect liberty and how to balance democracy with other concerns.

2

The Founding and the Constitution

WHAT GOVERNMENT DOES AND WHY IT MATTERS The framers of the U.S. Constitution knew why government mattered. In the Constitution's preamble, the framers tell us that the purposes of government are to promote justice, to maintain peace at home, to defend the nation from foreign foes, to provide for the welfare of the citizenry, and, above all, to secure the "blessings of liberty" for Americans. The remainder of the Constitution spells out a plan for achieving these objectives. This plan includes provisions for the exercise of legislative, executive, and judicial powers and a recipe for the division of powers among the federal government's branches and between the national and state governments. The framers' conception of why government matters and how it is to achieve its goals has been America's political blueprint for more than two centuries.

Today, some question the continuing value of the Constitution. Critics blame the constitutional division of powers for the gridlock that often seems to block legislation in the Congress. In 2011, when the United States very nearly defaulted on its debts because the president and Congress could not reach an agreement, the Constitution seemed more a hindrance to a solution than a recipe for effective governance. But, eventually, a decision was reached and the constitutional formula prevailed.

The story of America's Founding and the Constitution is generally presented as something both inevitable and glorious: it was inevitable that the American colonies would break away from Great Britain to establish their own country; and it was glorious in that the country established the best of all possible forms of government under a new constitution, which was easily adopted and quickly embraced, even by its critics. In reality, though, America's successful breakaway from Britain was by no means assured, and the Constitution was in fact highly controversial. Moreover, its ratification and durability were often in doubt. George Washington, the man chosen to preside over the Constitutional Convention of 1787, thought the document produced that hot summer in Philadelphia would probably last no more than 20 years, at which time leaders would have to convene again to come up with something new.

That Washington's expectation proved wrong is, indeed, a testament to the enduring strength of the Constitution. America's long-standing values of liberty, equality, and democracy were all major themes of the founding period and are all elements of the U.S. Constitution. However, the Constitution was a product of political bargaining and compromise, formed in very much the same way political decisions are made today. This fact is often overlooked because of what the historian Michael Kammen has called the "cult of the Constitution"—a tendency of Americans, going back more than a century, to venerate, sometimes to the point of near worship, the Founders and the document they created.[1] As this chapter will show, the Constitution reflects high principle as well as political self-interest, and also defines the relationship between American citizens and their government.

chaptergoals

- Describe the events that led to the Declaration of Independence and the Articles of Confederation (pages 39–43)

- Explain how the Constitution attempted to improve America's governance (pages 43–49)

- Outline the major institutions and rules established by the Constitution (pages 49–56)

- Present the controversies involved in the struggle for ratification (pages 56–62)

- Trace how the Constitution has changed over time through the amendment process (pages 62–66)

● The First Founding: Interests and Conflicts

Describe the events that led to the Declaration of Independence and the Articles of Confederation

Competing ideals and principles often reflect competing interests, and so it was in Revolutionary America. The American Revolution and the American Constitution were outgrowths and expressions of a struggle among economic and political forces within the colonies. Five sectors of society had interests that were important in colonial politics: (1) the New England merchants; (2) the southern planters; (3) the "royalists"—holders of royal lands, offices, and patents (licenses to engage in a profession or business activity); (4) shopkeepers, artisans, and laborers; and (5) small farmers. Throughout the eighteenth century, these groups were in conflict over issues of taxation, trade, and commerce. For the most part, however, the southern planters, the New England merchants, and the royal office and patent holders—groups that together made up the colonial elite—were able to maintain a political alliance that held in check the more radical forces representing shopkeepers, laborers, and small farmers. After 1760, however, by seriously threatening the interests of New England merchants and southern planters, British tax and trade policies split the colonial elite, permitting radical forces to expand their political influence, and set in motion a chain of events that culminated in the American Revolution.[2]

British Taxes and Colonial Interests

Beginning in the 1760s, the debts and other financial problems confronting the British government forced it to search for new revenue sources. This search rather quickly led to the Crown's North American colonies, which, on the whole, paid remarkably little in taxes to their parent country. The British government reasoned that a sizable fraction of its debt was, in fact, attributable to the expenses it had incurred in defense of the colonies during the French and Indian War, which ended in 1763, driving France from North America. The British also considered the cost of the continuing protection that British forces were giving the colonists from Indian attacks and that the British navy was providing for colonial shipping. Thus, during the 1760s, Britain sought to impose new, though relatively modest, taxes on the colonists.

Like most governments of the period, the British regime had limited ways in which to collect revenues. The income tax, which in the twentieth century became the single most important source of governmental revenues, had not yet been developed. In the mid-eighteenth century, governments relied mainly on tariffs, duties, and other taxes on commerce, and it was to such taxes, and to the Stamp Act, that the British turned during the 1760s.

The Stamp Act, and other taxes on commerce, such as the Sugar Act of 1764, which taxed sugar, molasses, and other commodities, most heavily affected the two groups in colonial society whose commercial interests and activities were most extensive—the New England merchants and the southern planters. United under

British colonists in America shipped many goods back to England, such as furs obtained by trading with Native Americans. The British government claimed that the colonists should pay more in taxes in light of the protection their shipments received from the British navy and the expenses Britain incurred defending the colonies.

the famous slogan "no taxation without representation," the merchants and planters sought to organize opposition to these new taxes. In the course of the struggle against British tax measures, the planters and merchants broke with their royalist allies and turned to their former adversaries—the shopkeepers, small farmers, laborers, and artisans—for help. With the assistance of these groups, the merchants and planters organized demonstrations and a boycott of British goods that ultimately forced the Crown to rescind most of its hated new taxes.

From the perspective of the merchants and planters, this was a victorious conclusion to their struggle with the mother country. They were anxious to end the unrest they had helped arouse, and they supported the British government's efforts to restore order. Indeed, most respectable Bostonians supported the actions of the British soldiers involved in the Boston Massacre—the 1770 killing of five colonists by British soldiers attempting to repel an angry mob gathered outside the Town House, the seat of the colonial government. In their subsequent trial, the soldiers were defended by John Adams, a pillar of Boston society and a future president of the United States. Adams asserted that the soldiers' actions were entirely justified, provoked by "a motley rabble of saucy boys, negroes and mulattoes, Irish teagues and outlandish Jack tars." All but two of the soldiers were acquitted.[3]

Despite the efforts of the British government and the better-to-do strata of colonial society, it proved difficult to bring an end to the political strife. The more radical forces representing shopkeepers, artisans, laborers, and small farmers, who had been mobilized and energized by the struggle over taxes, continued to agitate for political and social change. These radicals, whose leaders included Samuel Adams, a cousin of John Adams, asserted that British power supported an unjust political and social structure within the colonies, and began to advocate an end to British rule.[4]

Political Strife and the Radicalizing of the Colonists

The political strife within the colonies was the background for the events of 1773–74. In 1773 the British government granted the politically powerful East India Company a monopoly on the export of tea from Britain, eliminating a lucrative form of trade for colonial merchants. To add to the injury, the East India Com-

The British helped radicalize colonists through bad policy decisions in the years before the Revolution. For example, Britain gave the ailing East India Company a monopoly on the tea trade in the American colonies. Colonists feared that the monopoly would hurt colonial merchants' business and protested by throwing East India Company tea into Boston Harbor in 1773.

pany sought to sell the tea directly in the colonies instead of working through the colonial merchants. Tea was an extremely important commodity during the 1770s, and these British actions posed a serious threat to the New England merchants. Together with their southern allies, the merchants once again called on their radical adversaries for support. The most dramatic result was the Boston Tea Party. In three other colonies, anti-tax Americans succeeded in blocking the unloading of taxed tea, which then had to be returned to Britain. The royal governor of Massachusetts, however, refused to allow three shiploads of unsold tea to leave Boston Harbor. Anti-British radicals seized this opportunity: on the night of December 16, 1773, a group led by Samuel Adams, some of them hastily "disguised" as Mohawk Indians, boarded the three vessels and threw the entire cargo of 342 chests of tea into the harbor.

This event was of decisive importance in American history. The merchants had hoped to force the British government to rescind the Tea Act, but they did not support any further demands and did not seek independence from Britain. Samuel Adams and the other radicals, however, hoped to provoke the British government to take actions that would alienate its colonial supporters and pave the way for a rebellion. This was precisely the purpose of the Boston Tea Party, and it succeeded. By dumping the East India Company's tea into Boston Harbor, Adams and his followers goaded the British into enacting a number of harsh reprisals. Within five months after the incident in Boston, the House of Commons passed a series of acts that closed the port of Boston to commerce, changed the provincial government of Massachusetts, provided for the removal of accused persons to Britain for trial, and, most important, restricted movement to the West—further alienating the southern planters, who depended on access to new western lands. These acts of retaliation confirmed the worst criticisms of British rule and helped radicalize Americans. Radicals such as Samuel Adams and Christopher Gadsden (of South Carolina) had been agitating for more-violent measures against the British. But ultimately they needed Britain's political repression to create widespread support for independence.

Thus, the Boston Tea Party set in motion a cycle of provocation and retaliation that in 1774 resulted in the convening of the First Continental Congress—an assembly of delegates from all parts of the country— that called for a total boycott of British goods and, under the prodding of the radicals, began to consider the possibility of independence from British rule. The eventual result was the Declaration of Independence.

Britain eventually sent troops to subdue the American colonists. Grant Wood's Midnight Ride of Paul Revere *(1931) depicts Revere alerting colonists to the British army's arrival. The subsequent battle between colonial and British forces at Concord and Lexington began the Revolutionary War.*

The Declaration of Independence

In 1776, more than a year after open warfare had commenced in Massachusetts, the Second Continental Congress appointed a committee consisting of Thomas Jefferson of Virginia, Benjamin Franklin of Pennsylvania, Roger Sherman of Connecticut, John Adams of Massachusetts, and Robert Livingston of New York to draft a statement of American independence from British rule. The Declaration of Independence, written by Jefferson and adopted by the Second Continental Congress, was an extraordinary document both philosophically and politically. In philosophic terms,

THE DECLARATION OF INDEPENDENCE.
JULY 4TH 1776.

The year after fighting began between American colonists and the British army, the Continental Congress voted for independence on July 2, 1776, and approved the Declaration of Independence two days later, on July 4.

the Declaration was remarkable for its assertion that certain rights—the "unalienable rights" that include life, liberty, and the pursuit of happiness—could not be abridged by governments. In the world of 1776, a world in which some kings still claimed to rule by divine right, this was a dramatic statement. In political terms, the Declaration was remarkable because, despite the differences of interest that divided the colonists along economic, regional, and philosophical lines, it identified and focused on grievances, aspirations, and principles that might unify the various colonial groups. The Declaration was an attempt to identify and articulate a history and set of principles that might help forge national unity.[5]

The Articles of Confederation

Having declared their independence, the colonies needed to establish a governmental structure. In November 1777 the Continental Congress adopted the **Articles of Confederation**—the United States' first written constitution. Although it was not ratified by all the states until 1781, it was the country's operative constitution for almost 12 years, until March 1789.

The first goal of the Articles had been to limit the powers of the central government. The relationship between the national government and the states was called a **confederation**; as provided under Article II, "each state retains its sovereignty, freedom, and independence," much like the contemporary relationship between the United Nations and its member states. The central government was given no president or any other presiding officer. The entire national government was vested in a Congress, with execution of its few laws to be left to the individual states. And the Articles gave Congress very little power to exercise. Its members were not much more than delegates or messengers from the state legislatures: their salaries were paid out of the state treasuries; they were subject to immediate recall by state

Articles of Confederation America's first written constitution; served as the basis for America's national government until 1789

confederation a system of government in which states retain sovereign authority except for the powers expressly delegated to the national government authorities; and each state, regardless of its size, had only one vote. All 13 states had to agree to any amendments to the Articles.

Under the Articles of Confederation, Congress was given the power to declare war and make peace, to make treaties and alliances, to coin or borrow money, and to regulate trade with the Native Americans. It could also appoint the senior officers of the U.S. Army, but the national government had no army for those officers to command, because the nation's armed forces were composed of the state militias. Moreover, the central government could not prevent one state from discriminating against other states in the competition for foreign commerce. These extreme limits on the power of the national government made the Articles of Confederation hopelessly impractical.[6]

The Second Founding: From Compromise to Constitution

Explain how the Constitution attempted to improve America's governance

The Declaration of Independence and the Articles of Confederation were not sufficient to hold the new nation together as an independent and effective nation-state. A series of developments following the armistice with the British in 1783 highlighted the shortcomings of the Articles of Confederation.

International Standing and Balance of Power

There was a special concern for the country's international position. Competition among the states for foreign commerce allowed the European powers to play the states off one another, which created confusion on both sides of the Atlantic. At one point during the winter of 1786–87, John Adams of Massachusetts, a leader in the independence struggle, was sent to negotiate a new treaty with the British, one that would cover disputes left over from the war. The British government responded that since the United States under the Articles of Confederation was unable to enforce existing treaties, it would negotiate with each of the 13 states separately.

At the same time, the United States faced a threat from Spain, which still held vast territories in North and South America. Well-to-do Americans—in particular the New England merchants and southern planters—were especially troubled by the influence that "radical" forces exercised in the Continental Congress and in the governments of several of the states. The colonists' victory in the Revolutionary War had not only ended British rule but also significantly changed the balance of political power within the new states. As a result of the Revolution, one key segment of the colonial elite—the royal land, office, and patent holders—was stripped of its economic and political privileges. In fact, many of these individuals, along with tens of thousands of other colonists who considered themselves loyal British subjects, left for Canada after the British surrender. And although the prerevolutionary elite was weakened, the prerevolutionary radicals were better organized than ever and now controlled such states as Pennsylvania and Rhode Island, where they pursued economic and political policies that struck terror in the hearts of the prerevolutionary political establishment. In Rhode Island, for example, between 1783 and 1785, a legislature dominated by representatives of small farmers, artisans, and shopkeepers had instituted economic policies, including drastic currency inflation, that frightened business and property owners throughout the country. Of course, the central government under the Articles of Confederation was powerless to intervene. Similarly, the Pennsylvania government engaged in land redistribution, to the chagrin of property owners.

The Annapolis Convention

The continuation of international weakness and domestic economic turmoil led many Americans to consider whether their newly adopted form of government might not already require revision. In the fall of 1786, many state leaders accepted an invitation from the Virginia legislature for a conference of representatives of all the states, to be held in Annapolis, Maryland. Delegates from only five states actually attended, so nothing substantive could be accomplished. Still, this conference was the first step toward what is now known as the second founding. The one positive thing that came out of the Annapolis Convention was a carefully worded resolution calling on the Congress to send commissioners to Philadelphia at a later time "to devise such further provisions as shall appear to them necessary to render the Constitution of the Federal Government adequate to the exigencies of the Union."[7] But the resolution did not necessarily imply any desire to do more than improve and reform the Articles of Confederation.

Shays's Rebellion

It is quite possible that the Constitutional Convention of 1787 in Philadelphia would never have taken place at all except for a single event that occurred during the winter following the Annapolis Convention: Shays's Rebellion.

Daniel Shays, a former army captain, led a mob of farmers in a rebellion against the government of Massachusetts. The purpose of the rebellion was to prevent foreclosures on their debt-ridden land by keeping the county courts of western Massachusetts from sitting until after the next election. The state militia dispersed the mob, but for several days in February 1787, Shays and his followers terrified the state government by attempting to capture the federal arsenal at Springfield, provoking an appeal to the Congress to help restore order. Within a few days, the state government regained control and captured 14 of the rebels. Later that year, a newly elected Massachusetts legislature granted some of the farmers' demands.

The effects of the incident lingered and spread. Washington summed it up: "I am mortified beyond expression that in the moment of our acknowledged independence we should by our conduct verify the predictions of our transatlantic foe, and render ourselves ridiculous and contemptible in the eyes of all Europe."[8]

The Congress under the Confederation had been unable to act decisively in a time of crisis. This provided critics of the Articles of Confederation with precisely the evidence they needed to push the Annapolis resolution through the Congress. Thus, the states were asked to send representatives to Philadelphia to discuss constitutional revision. Seventy-four delegates were chosen. Of these, 55 would actually attend the convention, representing every state except Rhode Island, and 39 would eventually sign the newly drafted Constitution.

In the winter of 1787, Daniel Shays led a makeshift army against the federal arsenal at Springfield to protest heavy taxes levied by the Massachusetts legislature. The rebellion proved the Articles of Confederation too weak to protect the fledgling nation.

The Constitutional Convention

The delegates who convened in Philadelphia in May 1787 had political strife, international embarrassment, national weakness, and local rebellion fixed in their minds. Recognizing that these issues were symptoms of fundamental flaws in the Articles of Confederation, the delegates soon abandoned the plan to revise the Articles and committed themselves to a second founding—a second, and ultimately successful, attempt to create a legitimate and effective national system of government. This effort would occupy the convention for the next five months.

A Marriage of Interest and Principle For years, scholars have disagreed about the motives of the Founders in Philadelphia. Among the most controversial views of the framers' motives is the "economic interpretation" put forward by the historian Charles Beard and his disciples.[9] According to Beard's account, America's Founders were a collection of securities speculators and property owners whose only aim was personal enrichment. From this perspective, the Constitution's lofty principles were little more than sophisticated masks behind which the most venal interests sought to enrich themselves.

Contrary to Beard's approach is the view that the framers of the Constitution *were* concerned with philosophical and ethical principles. Indeed, they sought to devise a system of government consistent with the dominant philosophical and moral principles of the day. But in fact, these two views belong together; the Founders' interests were reinforced by their principles. The convention that drafted the American Constitution was chiefly organized by the New England merchants and southern planters. Although the delegates representing these groups did not all hope to profit personally from an increase in the value of their securities, as Beard would have it, they did hope to benefit in the broadest political and economic sense by breaking the power of their radical foes and establishing a system of government more compatible with their long-term economic and political interests. Thus, the framers sought to create a new government capable of promoting commerce and protecting property from radical state legislatures and populist forces hostile to the interests of the commercial and propertied classes.

The Great Compromise The proponents of a new government fired their opening shot on May 29, 1787, when Edmund Randolph of Virginia offered a resolution that proposed corrections and enlargements in the Articles of Confederation. The proposal was no simple motion but instead provided for virtually every aspect of a new government.

The portion of Randolph's motion that became most controversial was called the **Virginia Plan**. This plan provided for a system of representation in the national legislature based on the population of each state or the proportion of each state's revenue contribution to the national government, or both. (Randolph also proposed a second chamber of the legislature, to be elected by the members of the first chamber.) Since the states varied enormously in size and wealth, the Virginia Plan was thought to be heavily biased in favor of the large states.

While the convention was debating the Virginia Plan, opposition to it began to mount as more delegates arrived in Philadelphia. William Paterson of New Jersey introduced a resolution known as the **New Jersey Plan**. Its main proponents were delegates from the less-populous states, including Delaware, New Jersey, Connecticut, and New York, who asserted that the more populous states—Virginia, Pennsylvania, North Carolina, Massachusetts, and Georgia—would dominate the

Virginia Plan a framework for the Constitution, introduced by Edmund Randolph, that called for representation in the national legislature based on the population of each state

New Jersey Plan a framework for the Constitution, introduced by William Paterson, that called for equal state representation in the national legislature regardless of population

When the framers of the Constitution met in 1787, they set out to establish a political system that would protect liberty and place limits on government. They also believed that a powerful government required a broad popular base. However, they debated how best to protect liberty and how to balance democracy with other concerns.

Great Compromise the agreement reached at the Constitutional Convention of 1787 that gave each state an equal number of senators regardless of its population, but linked representation in the House of Representatives to population

new government if representation were to be determined by population. The smaller states argued that each state should be equally represented in the new regime regardless of that state's population.

The issue of representation threatened to wreck the entire constitutional enterprise. Delegates conferred, factions maneuvered, and tempers flared. James Wilson of Pennsylvania told the small-state delegates that if they wanted to disrupt the union, they should go ahead. The separation, he said, could "never happen on better grounds." Small-state delegates were equally blunt. Gunning Bedford of Delaware declared that the small states might, if forced, look elsewhere for friends. "The large states," he said, "dare not dissolve the confederation. If they do the small ones will find some foreign ally of more honor and good faith, who will take them by the hand and do them justice." These sentiments were widely shared. The union, as Oliver Ellsworth of Connecticut put it, was "on the verge of dissolution, scarcely held together by the strength of a hair."

The outcome of this debate was the Connecticut Compromise, also known as the **Great Compromise**. Under the terms of this compromise, in the first chamber of Congress—the House of Representatives—the representatives would be apportioned according to the population in each state. This, of course, was what delegates from the large states had sought. But in the second branch—the Senate—each state would have equal representation regardless of its size; this provision addressed the concerns of small states. This compromise was not immediately satisfactory to all the delegates. Indeed, two of the most vocal members of the small-state faction, John Lansing and Robert Yates of New York, were so incensed by the concession that their colleagues had made to the large-state forces that they stormed out of the convention. In the end, however, most of the delegates preferred compromise to the breakup of the Union, and the plan was accepted.

The Question of Slavery: The Three-Fifths Compromise Many of the conflicts that emerged during the Constitutional Convention were reflections of the fundamental differences between the slave and the nonslave states—differences that

Who Benefits from the Great Compromise?

The Great Compromise attempted to balance power between large and small states in the new Congress. The charts show the difference in representation for states in the House and Senate in the first Congress (1789–91). In the Senate each state has equal representation, which in the first Congress meant each had 1/13 of all seats. In the House the number of seats apportioned to each state is based on population; thus, the larger states have more representation.

Representation in the First Congress

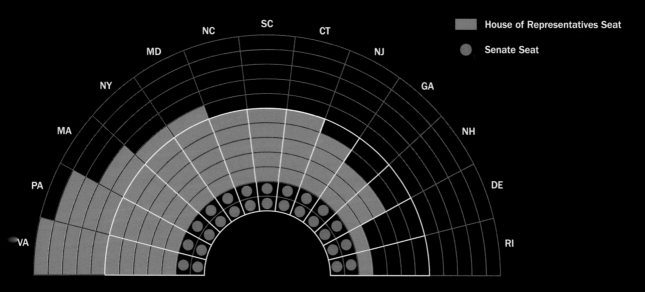

- ☐ House of Representatives Seat
- ⬤ Senate Seat

State Populations, 1790*

1.	Virginia	747,610
2.	Pennsylvania	433,373
3.	Massachusetts	378,787
4.	New York	340,120
5.	Maryland	319,728
6.	North Carolina	393,751
7.	South Carolina	249,073
8.	Connecticut	237,946
9.	New Jersey	184,139
10.	Georgia	82,548
11.	New Hampshire	141,885
12.	Delaware	59,096
13.	Rhode Island	68,825

The framers calculated the number of representatives per state in 1787 using population estimates. The first census was not taken until 1790. Total state population includes slave population. Slaves were counted as 3/5 of a person for purposes of apportioning seats in the House.

SOURCE: U.S. Census Bureau, www.census.gov (accessed 8/16/12).

for critical analysis

1. At the Constitutional Convention, large states supported the Virginia Plan, which would have made the whole Congress look like the House. Small states supported the New Jersey Plan, which would have made the whole Congress look like the Senate. How would each group have benefited from its favored plans?

2. What are the advantages of equal representation by states? What are the drawbacks? In your opinion, do the advantages outweigh the disadvantages?

pitted the southern planters and New England merchants against one another and would almost destroy the Republic in later years. In the midst of debate over large versus small states, James Madison observed,

> The great danger to our general government is the great southern and northern interests of the continent, being opposed to each other. Look to the votes in Congress, and most of them stand divided by the geography of the country, not according to the size of the states.[10]

More than 90 percent of the country's slaves resided in five states—Georgia, Maryland, North Carolina, South Carolina, and Virginia—where they accounted for 30 percent of the total population. In some places, slaves outnumbered nonslaves by as much as 10 to 1. If the Constitution were to embody any principle of national supremacy, some basic decisions would have to be made about the place of slavery in the general scheme. Madison hit on this point on several occasions as different aspects of the Constitution were being discussed. For example, he observed,

> It seemed now to be pretty well understood that the real difference of interests lay, not between the large and small but between the northern and southern states. The institution of slavery and its consequences formed the line of discrimination. There were five states on the South, eight on the northern side of this line. Should a proportional representation take place it was true, the northern side would still outnumber the other: but not in the same degree, at this time; and every day would tend towards an equilibrium.[11]

Northerners and southerners eventually reached agreement through the **Three-Fifths Compromise**. The seats in the House of Representatives would be apportioned according to a "population" in which five slaves would count as three

Three-Fifths Compromise
the agreement reached at the Constitutional Convention of 1787 that stipulated that for purposes of the apportionment of congressional seats, every slave would be counted as three-fifths of a person

Despite the Founders' emphasis on liberty, the new Constitution allowed slavery, counting each slave as three-fifths of a person in apportioning seats in the House of Representatives. In this 1792 painting, Liberty Displaying the Arts and Sciences, *the books, instruments, and classical columns at the left contrast with the kneeling slaves at the right—illustrating the divide between America's rhetoric of liberty and equality and the realities of slavery.*

free persons. The slaves would not be allowed to vote, of course, but the number of representatives would be apportioned accordingly.

The issue of slavery was the most difficult one faced by the framers, and it nearly destroyed the Union. Although some delegates believed slavery to be morally wrong, an evil and oppressive institution that made a mockery of the ideals and values espoused in the Constitution, morality was not the issue that caused the framers to support or oppose the Three-Fifths Compromise. Whatever they thought of the institution of slavery, most delegates from the northern states opposed counting slaves in the distribution of congressional seats. Wilson of Pennsylvania, for example, argued that if slaves were citizens, they should be treated and counted like other citizens. If, on the other hand, they were property, then why should not other forms of property be counted toward the apportionment of representatives? But southern delegates made it clear that they would never agree to the new government if the northerners refused to give in. William R. Davie of North Carolina heatedly said that it was time "to speak out." He asserted that the people of North Carolina would never enter the Union if slaves were not counted as part of the basis for representation. Without such agreement, he asserted ominously, "the business was at an end." Even southerners such as Edmund Randolph of Virginia, who conceded that slavery was immoral, insisted on including slaves in the allocation of congressional seats. Pierce Butler of South Carolina declared that the North and South were as different as Russia and Turkey. Eventually, the North and South compromised on the issue of slavery and representation. Indeed, northerners even agreed to permit a continuation of the odious slave trade in order to keep the South in the Union. But in due course, Butler proved to be correct, and a bloody war resulted when the disparate interests of the North and the South could no longer be reconciled.

● The Constitution

Outline the major institutions and rules established by the Constitution

The political significance of the Great Compromise and the Three-Fifths Compromise was to reinforce the unity of the mercantile and planter forces that sought to create a new government. The Great Compromise reassured those who feared that a new governmental framework would reduce the importance of their own local or regional influence. The Three-Fifths Compromise temporarily defused the rivalry between the merchants and planters. Their unity secured, members of the alliance supporting the establishment of a new government moved to fashion a constitutional framework consistent with their economic and political interests.

In particular, the framers sought a new government that, first, would be strong enough to promote commerce and protect property from radical state legislatures such as Rhode Island's. This became the constitutional basis for national control over commerce and finance, and for the establishment of national judicial supremacy and the effort to construct a strong presidency. Second, the framers sought to prevent what they saw as the threat posed by the "excessive democracy" of the state and national governments under the Articles of Confederation. This led to such constitutional principles as bicameralism (division of the Congress into two chambers), **checks and balances**, staggered terms in office, and indirect election

checks and balances
mechanisms through which each branch of government is able to participate in and influence the activities of the other branches; major examples include the presidential veto power over congressional legislation, the power of the Senate to approve presidential appointments, and judicial review of congressional enactments

TABLE 2.1

The Seven Articles of the Constitution

1. The Legislative Branch
   House: two-year terms, elected directly by the people.
   Senate: six-year terms (staggered so that only one-third of the Senate changes in any given election), appointed by state legislature (changed in 1913 to direct election).
   Expressed powers of the national government: collecting taxes, borrowing money, regulating commerce, declaring war, and maintaining an army and a navy; all other power belongs to the states, unless deemed otherwise by the elastic (necessary and proper) clause.
   Exclusive powers of the national government: states are expressly forbidden to issue their own paper money, tax imports and exports, regulate trade outside their own borders, and impair the obligation of contracts; these powers are the exclusive domain of the national government.

2. The Executive Branch
   Presidency: four-year terms (limited in 1951 to a maximum of two terms), elected indirectly by the electoral college.
   Powers: can recognize other countries, negotiate treaties, grant reprieves and pardons, convene Congress in special sessions, and veto congressional enactment.

3. The Judicial Branch
   Supreme Court: lifetime terms, appointed by the president with the approval of the Senate.
   Powers: include resolving conflicts between federal and state laws, determining whether power belongs to the national government or the states, and settling controversies between citizens of different states.

4. National Unity and Power
   Reciprocity among states: establishes that each state must give "full faith and credit" to official acts of other states and guarantees citizens of any state the "privileges and immunities" of every other state.

5. Amending the Constitution
   Procedure: requires approval by two-thirds of Congress and adoption by three-fourths of the states.

6. National Supremacy
   The Constitution and national law are the supreme law of the land and cannot be overruled by state law.

7. Ratification
   The Constitution became effective when approved by nine states.

electoral college the presidential electors from each state who meet after the popular election to cast ballots for president and vice president

Bill of Rights the first 10 amendments to the U.S. Constitution, ratified in 1791; they ensure certain rights and liberties to the people

separation of powers the division of governmental power among several institutions that must cooperate in decision making

federalism a system of government in which power is divided, by a constitution, between a central government and regional governments

(selection of the president by an **electoral college** rather than directly by voters and election of senators by state legislatures). Third, the framers, lacking the power to force the states or the public at large to accept the new form of government, sought to identify principles that would help secure support. This became the basis of the constitutional provision for direct popular election of representatives and, subsequently, for the addition of the **Bill of Rights** to the Constitution. Finally, the framers wanted to be certain that the government they created did not pose an even greater threat to its citizens' liberties and property rights than did the radical state legislatures they feared and despised. To prevent the new government from abusing its power, the framers incorporated principles such as the **separation of powers** and **federalism** into the Constitution. Let us assess the major provisions of the Constitution's seven articles (listed in Table 2.1) to see how each relates to these objectives.

The Legislative Branch

In Article I, Sections 1–7, the Constitution provided for a Congress consisting of two chambers: a House of Representatives and a Senate. Members of the House of Representatives were given two-year terms in office and were to be elected directly by the people. Members of the Senate were to be appointed by the state legislatures (this was changed in 1913 by the Seventeenth Amendment, which instituted direct election of senators) for six-year terms. These terms were staggered so that the appointments of one-third of the senators would expire every two years. The Constitution assigned somewhat different tasks to the House and Senate. Though the approval of each body was required for the enactment of a law, the Senate alone was given the power to ratify treaties and approve presidential appointments. The House, on the other hand, was given the sole power to originate revenue bills.

The character of the legislative branch was directly related to the framers' major goals. The House of Representatives was designed to be directly responsible to the people in order to encourage popular consent for the new Constitution and to help enhance the power of the new government. At the same time, to guard against "excessive democracy," the power of the House of Representatives was checked by the Senate, whose members were to be appointed by the states for long terms rather than elected directly by the people. The purpose of this provision, according to Alexander Hamilton, was to avoid "an unqualified complaisance to every sudden breeze of passion, or to every transient impulse which the people may receive."[12] Staggered terms of service in the Senate, moreover, were intended to make that body even more resistant to popular pressure. Since only one-third of the senators would be selected at any given time, the composition of the institution would be protected from changes in popular preferences transmitted by the state legislatures. This would prevent what James Madison called "mutability in the public councils arising from a rapid succession of new members."[13] Thus, the structure of the legislative branch was designed to contribute to governmental power, to promote popular consent for the new government, and at the same time to place limits on the popular political currents that many of the framers saw as a radical threat to the economic and social order.

The issues of power and consent were important throughout the Constitution. Section 8 of Article I specifically listed the powers of Congress, which include the authority to collect taxes, borrow money, regulate commerce, declare war, and maintain an army and navy. By granting Congress these powers, the framers indicated very clearly that they intended the new government to be far more influential than its predecessor. At the same time, by defining the new government's most important powers as belonging to Congress, the framers sought to promote popular acceptance of this critical change by reassuring citizens that their views would be fully represented whenever the government exercised its new powers.

As a further guarantee to the people that the new government would pose no threat to them, the Constitution implied that any powers not listed were not granted at all. This is the doctrine of **expressed powers**: the Constitution grants only those powers specifically expressed in its text. But the framers intended to create an active and powerful government, and so they included the necessary and proper clause, sometimes known as the **elastic clause**, which signified that the enumerated powers were meant to be a source of strength to the national government, not a limitation on it. In response to the charge that they intended to give the national government too much power, the framers included language in the Tenth Amendment stipulating that powers not specifically granted by the Constitution to the federal government were reserved to the states or to the people. As we will see in Chapter 3, the resulting tension between the elastic clause and the Tenth Amendment has been at the heart of constitutional struggles between federal and state powers.

Article I of the Constitution establishes the structure of Congress and lists certain specific powers of Congress. The language of the Constitution reflects the framers' desire to create a government that was powerful enough to be effective but not so powerful that it would threaten individual liberty.

expressed powers specific powers granted by the Constitution to Congress (Article I, Section 8) and to the president (Article II)

elastic clause Article I, Section 8, of the Constitution (also known as the necessary and proper clause), which enumerates the powers of Congress and provides Congress with the authority to make all laws "necessary and proper" to carry them out

THE CONSTITUTIONAL CONVENTION · 1787

According to Alexander Hamilton (left), the Constitution aimed toward "energy in the Executive." The framers wanted the president to be capable of timely and decisive action. This painting depicts Hamilton, James Wilson, James Madison, and Benjamin Franklin meeting in Franklin's garden.

bicameral having a legislative assembly composed of two chambers or houses; distinguished from *unicameral*

The Executive Branch

The Constitution provided for the establishment of the presidency in Article II. As Alexander Hamilton commented, the presidential article aimed toward "energy in the Executive." It did so in an effort to overcome the natural tendency toward stalemate that was built into the **bicameral** legislature and into the separation of powers among the three branches. The Constitution afforded the president a measure of independence from the people and from the other branches of government—particularly the Congress.

In line with the framers' goal of increased power to the national government, the president was granted the unconditional power to accept ambassadors from other countries; this amounted to the power to "recognize" other countries. The president was also given the power to negotiate treaties, although their acceptance required the approval of the Senate by a two-thirds vote. The president was given the unconditional right to grant reprieves and pardons, except in cases of impeachment. And the president was provided with the power to appoint major departmental personnel, convene Congress in special session, and veto congressional enactments. (The veto power is formidable, but it is not absolute, since Congress can override it by a two-thirds vote.)

The framers hoped to create a presidency that would make the federal government rather than the states the agency capable of timely and decisive action to deal with public issues and problems—hence the "energy" that Hamilton hoped to impart to the executive branch.[14] At the same time, however, the framers sought to help the presidency withstand excessively democratic pressures by creating a system of indirect rather than direct election through a separate electoral college.

for critical analysis

The framers sought to create an "energetic" presidency, but some observers believe that the presidency has become too powerful. Has the presidency become too powerful?

The Judicial Branch

In establishing the judicial branch in Article III, the Constitution reflected the framers' preoccupations with nationalizing governmental power and checking radical democratic impulses while preventing the new national government itself from interfering with liberty and property.

Under the provisions of Article III, the framers created a court that was literally a supreme court of the United States, and not merely the highest court of the national government alone. The most important expression of this intention was granting the Supreme Court the power to resolve any conflicts that might emerge between federal and state laws. In particular, the Supreme Court was given the right to determine whether a power was exclusive to the national government, concurrent with the states, or exclusive to the states. In addition, the Supreme Court was assigned jurisdiction over controversies between citizens of different states. The long-term significance of this provision was that as the country developed a national economy, it came to rely increasingly on the federal judiciary, rather than on the state courts, for the resolution of disputes.

Judges were given lifetime appointments to protect them from popular politics and from interference by the other branches. This, however, did not mean that the judiciary would remain totally impartial to political considerations or to the other branches, for the president was to appoint the judges, and the Senate to approve the appointments. Congress would also have the power to create inferior (lower) courts, change the jurisdiction of the federal courts, add or subtract federal judges, and even change the size of the Supreme Court.

No explicit mention is made in the Constitution of **judicial review**—the power of the courts to render the final decision when there is a conflict of interpretation of the Constitution or of laws between the courts and Congress, the courts and the executive branch, or the courts and the states. The Supreme Court eventually assumed the power of judicial review. Its assumption of this power, as we shall see in Chapter 15, was based not on the Constitution itself but on the politics of later decades and the membership of the Court.

judicial review the power of the courts to review and, if necessary, declare actions of the legislative and executive branches invalid or unconstitutional; the Supreme Court asserted this power in *Marbury v. Madison*

National Unity and Power

Various provisions in the Constitution addressed the framers' concern with national unity and power, including Article IV's provisions for comity (reciprocity) among states and among citizens of all states. Each state was prohibited from discriminating against the citizens of other states in favor of its own citizens. The Supreme Court was charged with deciding in each case whether a state had discriminated against goods or people from another state. The Constitution restricted the power of the states in favor of ensuring enough power to the national government to give the country a free-flowing national economy.

The framers' concern with national supremacy was also expressed in Article VI, in the **supremacy clause**, which provided that national laws and treaties "shall be the supreme Law of the Land." This meant that all laws made under the "Authority of the United States" would be superior to all laws adopted by any state or any other subdivision, and the states would be expected to respect all treaties made under that authority. The supremacy clause also bound the officials of all governments—state and local as well as federal—to take an oath of office to support the national Constitution. This meant that every action taken by the U.S. Congress would have to be applied within each state as though the action were in fact state law.

supremacy clause Article VI of the Constitution, which states that laws passed by the national government and all treaties are the supreme law of the land and superior to all laws adopted by any state or any subdivision

Amending the Constitution

The Constitution established procedures for its own revision in Article V. Its provisions are so difficult that Americans have successfully availed themselves of the amending process only 17 times since 1791, when the first 10 amendments were adopted. Many other amendments have been proposed in Congress, but fewer than 40 of them have even come close to fulfilling the Constitution's requirement of a two-thirds vote in Congress, and only a fraction have gotten anywhere near adoption by three-fourths of the states. Article V also provides that the Constitution can be amended by a constitutional convention. Occasionally, proponents of particular measures, such as a balanced-budget amendment, have called for a constitutional convention to consider their proposals. Whatever the purpose for which it were called, however, such a convention would presumably have the authority to revise America's entire system of government.

Ratifying the Constitution

The rules for the ratification of the Constitution were set forth in Article VII. Nine of the 13 states would have to ratify, or agree on, the terms in order for the Constitution to be formally adopted.

Constitutional Limits on the National Government's Power

Although the framers sought to create a powerful national government, they also wanted to guard against possible misuse of that power. To that end, the framers incorporated two key principles into the Constitution—federalism and the separation of powers. A third set of limitations, in the form of the Bill of Rights, was added to the Constitution to help secure its ratification when opponents of the document charged that it paid insufficient attention to citizens' rights.

The Separation of Powers No principle of politics was more widely shared at the time of the 1787 Founding than the principle that power must be used to balance power. The French political theorist Baron de la Brède et de Montesquieu (1689–1755) believed that this balance was an indispensable defense against tyranny. His writings, especially his major work, *The Spirit of the Laws*, "were taken as political gospel" at the Philadelphia Convention.[15] Although the principle of the separation of powers was not explicitly stated in the Constitution, the entire structure of the national government was built precisely on Article I, the legislature; Article II, the executive; and Article III, the judiciary (see Figure 2.1).

However, separation of powers is nothing but mere words on parchment without a method to maintain that separation. The method became known by the popular label "checks and balances" (see Figure 2.2). Each branch is given not only its own powers but also some power over the other two branches. Among the most familiar checks and balances are the president's veto as power over Congress and Congress's power over the president through its control of appointments to high executive posts and to the judiciary. Congress also has power over the president with its control of appropriations and (by the Senate) the right of approval of treaties. The judiciary was assumed to have the power of judicial review over the other two branches.

Another important feature of the separation of powers is the principle of giving each of the branches a distinctly different constituency. Theorists such as Montes-

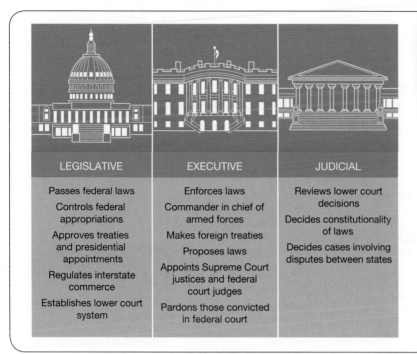

FIGURE 2.1
The Separation of Powers

LEGISLATIVE	EXECUTIVE	JUDICIAL
Passes federal laws	Enforces laws	Reviews lower court decisions
Controls federal appropriations	Commander in chief of armed forces	Decides constitutionality of laws
Approves treaties and presidential appointments	Makes foreign treaties	Decides cases involving disputes between states
Regulates interstate commerce	Proposes laws	
Establishes lower court system	Appoints Supreme Court justices and federal court judges	
	Pardons those convicted in federal court	

quieu called this a "mixed regime," with the president chosen, indirectly, by electors; the House, by popular vote; the Senate (originally), by state legislatures; and the judiciary, by presidential appointment. By these means, the occupants of each branch would tend to develop very different outlooks on how to govern, different definitions of the public interest, and different alliances with private interests.

Federalism Compared with the confederation principle of the Articles of Confederation, federalism was a step toward greater centralization of power. The delegates agreed that they needed to place more power at the national level, without completely undermining the power of the state governments. Thus, they devised a system of two sovereigns—the states and the nation—with the hope that competition between the two would be an effective limitation on the power of both.

The Bill of Rights Late in the Philadelphia Convention, a motion was made to include a list of citizens' rights in the Constitution. After a brief debate in which hardly a word was said in its favor and only one speech was made against it, the motion was almost unanimously turned down. Most delegates sincerely believed that since the federal government was already limited to its expressed powers, further protection of citizens was not needed. The delegates argued that the states should adopt bills of rights because their greater powers needed greater limitations. But almost immediately after the Constitution was ratified, a movement arose to adopt a national bill of rights. This is why the Bill of Rights, adopted in 1791, comprises the first 10 amendments to the Constitution rather than being part of the body of it. (We will have a good deal more to say about the Bill of Rights in Chapter 4.)

Executive over Legislative
Can veto acts of Congress
Can call Congress into a special session
Carries out, and thereby interprets, laws passed by Congress
Vice president casts tie-breaking vote in the Senate

Legislative over Judicial
Can change size of federal court system and the number of Supreme Court justices
Can propose constitutional amendments
Can reject Supreme Court nominees
Can impeach and remove federal judges

Legislative over Executive
Can override presidential veto
Can impeach and remove president
Can reject president's appointments and refuse to ratify treaties
Can conduct investigations into president's actions
Can refuse to pass laws or to provide funding that president requests

Judicial over Legislative
Can declare laws unconstitutional
Chief justice presides over Senate during hearing to impeach the president

JUDICIAL

Executive over Judicial
Nominates Supreme Court justices
Nominates federal judges
Can pardon those convicted in federal court
Can refuse to enforce Court decisions

Judicial over Executive
Can declare executive actions unconstitutional
Power to issue warrants
Chief justice presides over impeachment of president

EXECUTIVE

FIGURE 2.2
Checks and Balances

● The Fight for Ratification

Federalists those who favored a strong national government and supported the Constitution proposed at the American Constitutional Convention of 1787

Antifederalists those who favored strong state governments and a weak national government and who were opponents of the Constitution proposed at the American Constitutional Convention of 1787

Present the controversies involved in the struggle for ratification

The first hurdle faced by the Constitution was ratification by state conventions of delegates elected by the people of each state. This struggle for ratification was carried out in 13 separate campaigns. Each involved different people, moved at a different pace, and was influenced by local and national considerations. Two sides faced off throughout the states, however, calling themselves **Federalists** and **Antifederalists** (see Table 2.2). The Federalists (who more accurately should have called themselves "Nationalists," but who took their name to appear to follow in the revolutionary tradition) supported the Constitution and preferred a strong national government.

TABLE 2.2

Federalists versus Antifederalists

	FEDERALISTS	ANTIFEDERALISTS
Who were they?	Property owners, creditors, merchants	Small farmers, frontiersmen, debtors, shopkeepers, some state government officials
What did they believe?	Believed that elites were most fit to govern; feared "excessive democracy"	Believed that government should be closer to the people; feared concentration of power in hands of the elites
What system of government did they favor?	Favored strong national government; believed in "filtration" so that only elites would obtain governmental power	Favored retention of power by state governments and protection of individual rights
Who were their leaders?	Alexander Hamilton, James Madison, George Washington	Patrick Henry, George Mason, Elbridge Gerry, George Clinton

The Antifederalists opposed the Constitution and preferred a federal system of government that was decentralized; they took their name by default, in reaction to their better-organized opponents. The Federalists were united in their support of the Constitution, whereas the Antifederalists were divided over possible alternatives to the Constitution.

During the struggle over ratification of the Constitution, Americans argued about great political issues and principles. How much power should the national government be given? What safeguards would most likely prevent the abuse of power? What institutional arrangements could best ensure adequate representation for all Americans? Was tyranny of the many to be feared more than tyranny of the few?

Federalists versus Antifederalists

During the ratification struggle, thousands of essays, speeches, pamphlets, and letters were presented in support of and in opposition to the proposed Constitution. The best-known pieces supporting ratification were the 85 essays written between the fall of 1787 and the spring of 1788 under the name of "Publius," by Alexander Hamilton, James Madison, and John Jay. These **Federalist Papers**, as they are collectively known today, defended the principles of the Constitution and sought to dispel fears of a national authority. The Antifederalists published essays of their own, arguing that the new Constitution betrayed the Revolution and was a step toward monarchy. Among the best of the Antifederalist works were the essays, usually attributed to the New York State Supreme Court justice Robert Yates, that were written under the name of "Brutus" and published in the *New York Journal* at the same time the *Federalist Papers* appeared. The Antifederalist view was also ably presented in the pamphlets and letters written by a former delegate to the Continental Congress and future U.S. senator, Richard Henry Lee of Virginia, using the pen name "The Federal Farmer." These essays highlight the major differences of opinion between Federalists and Antifederalists. Federalists appealed to basic

Federalist Papers a series of essays written by Alexander Hamilton, James Madison, and John Jay supporting ratification of the Constitution

The American Constitution: A Model for the World?

The U.S. Constitution is often said to be both the world's oldest written constitution and a continuing model for the nations of the world. These assertions are *partly* accurate. Nearly two millennia before the delegates to America's Constitutional Convention met in Philadelphia, Greek city-states produced written constitutions.[a] And closer to home, all the first American states possessed written constitutions. Nevertheless, it might be said that the U.S. Constitution is the world's oldest written document that formally organizes the governmental processes of an entire nation.

As to the second assertion, the U.S. Constitution has indeed frequently been a model for others, but other nations' constitution writers often consciously sought to avoid rather than imitate American-style institutions and practices. One important American idea that has been widely copied is that of having a written constitution. After America wrote its constitution in 1789, both Poland and France adopted written constitutions in 1791. The French became so enamored of constitution writing that they put forth four different constitutions during the 1790s alone, as successive revolutionary

governments seized power.[b] As revolutions swept Europe during the nineteenth and early twentieth centuries, every new government viewed a written constitution both as an important legitimating instrument and as a declaration that the new regime categorically rejected the despotic and arbitrary practices of its predecessor. Today, virtually all the world's democracies have written constitutions. Britain, Israel, and New Zealand remain important exceptions.[c] Ironically, possession of a written constitution has become such an important attribute of political legitimacy and a symbol of freedom that even some despotic regimes have sham constitutions to provide the appearance, albeit not the substance, of popular government. For example, the former Soviet Union often boasted that it possessed the world's most democratic constitution.

Among the world's constitutional democracies, some have copied elements of the U.S. Constitution, but most have chosen patterns of government quite different from the American model. Judicial review of statutes, an American politi-

cal innovation, has been adopted by most democracies. In a number of instances, too, new constitutions have incorporated the principle of federalism to deal with the problem of ethnic or regional divisions. For example, with American encouragement, both Iraq and Afghanistan have made federalism an important principle in their new constitutional documents. However, it remains to be seen if these constitutions will survive after American troops leave those countries. Few democracies have copied the American system of checks and balances and separation of powers, with most opting, instead, for parliamentary government. Even the Japanese and German constitutions, written under the supervision of American occupation authorities following World War II, created parliamentary systems.

In addition to providing for parliamentary government, most of the world's constitutions have departed from the American model by specifying extensive lists of rights. For example, the constitution of the Czech Republic includes a lengthy "Charter of Fundamental Rights and Freedoms."

Thus, although the U.S. Constitution inspired many other nations to develop a written constitution, the precise form that national constitutions take can diverge considerably from the American model.

[a]Kim Lane Scheppele, "Constitutions around the World," www.constitutioncenter.org (accessed 2/9/08).
[b]Scheppele, "Constitutions."
[c]Scheppele, "Constitutions."

for critical analysis

1. Is America's Constitution appropriate for every nation? Which elements might have universal validity? Which features might be relevant mainly to the United States?

2. The U.S. Constitution is a brief document, whereas many new constitutions are lengthy documents. What are the advantages and disadvantages of America's constitutional model?

principles of government in support of their nationalist vision. Antifederalists cited equally fundamental precepts to support their vision of a looser confederacy of small republics.

Representation One major area of contention between the two sides was the question of representation. The Antifederalists asserted that representatives must be "a true picture of the people . . . [possessing] the knowledge of their circumstances and their wants."[16] This could be achieved, argued the Antifederalists, only in small, relatively homogeneous republics such as the existing states. In their view, the size and extent of the entire nation precluded the construction of a truly representative form of government. As Brutus put it, "Is it practicable for a country so large and so numerous . . . to elect a representation that will speak their sentiments? . . . It certainly is not."[17]

Federalists, for their part, saw no reason that representatives should be precisely like those they represented. In the Federalist view, one of the great advantages of representative government over direct democracy was precisely the possibility that the people would choose as their representatives individuals possessing ability, experience, and talent superior to their own. In Madison's words, rather than serving as a mirror or reflection of society, representatives must be "[those] who possess [the] most wisdom to discern, and [the] most virtue to pursue, the common good of the society."[18]

Tyranny of the Majority A second important issue dividing Federalists and Antifederalists was the threat of **tyranny**—unjust rule by the group in power. Both opponents and defenders of the Constitution frequently affirmed their fear of tyrannical rule. Each side, however, had a different view of the most likely source of tyranny and, hence, of the way in which to forestall the threat.

From the Antifederalist perspective, the great danger was the tendency of all governments—including republican governments—to become gradually more and more "aristocratic" in character, wherein the small number of individuals in positions of authority would use their stations to gain more and more power over the general citizenry. In essence, the few would use their power to tyrannize the many. For this reason, Antifederalists were sharply critical of those features of the Constitution that divorced governmental institutions from direct responsibility to the people—institutions such as the Senate, the executive, and the federal judiciary. The last, appointed for life, presented a particular threat: "I wonder if the world ever saw . . . a court of justice invested with such immense powers, and yet placed in a situation so little responsible," protested Brutus.[19]

The Federalists, too, recognized the threat of tyranny, but they believed that the danger particularly associated with republican governments was not aristocracy but majority tyranny. The Federalists were concerned that a popular majority, "united and actuated by some common impulse of passion, or of interest, adverse to the rights of other citizens," would endeavor to "trample on the rules of justice."[20] From the Federalist perspective, it was precisely those features of the Constitution that the Antifederalists attacked as potential sources of tyranny that actually offered the best hope of averting the threat of oppression. The size and extent of the nation, for instance, was for the Federalists a bulwark against tyranny, because a majority would have difficulty uniting in a large and populous nation.

Governmental Power A third major difference between Federalists and Antifederalists was the issue of governmental power. Both opponents and proponents of the Constitution agreed on the principle of **limited government**. They differed,

tyranny oppressive government that employs cruel and unjust use of power and authority

limited government a principle of constitutional government; a government whose powers are defined and limited by a constitution

The Constitution, the U.S. Postal System, and the Internet

Imagine living in a world where, in order to send a message to someone, you had to find a person willing to travel the distance to deliver the message personally, and you had to pay him for the time and effort it took to do this. Before the postal system was developed, this was the norm for people living in the British colonies that eventually became the United States.

The Founders knew the importance of the postal system, and thus wrote it into the Constitution, which gives Congress the power to "To establish post offices and post roads." Following the Founding, the postal service was the first major department created for the new United States of America, because it was one necessity all states could agree upon. The first postal system was founded in 1775, and the first postmaster was Benjamin Franklin. Until 1970 the U.S. Postal Service (USPS) was headed by a cabinet appointee and funded by tax dollars. After 1970 it became an independent agency, responsible for raising revenue through selling stamps and mailing packages to cover its expenses each year and (at least try to) to break even.

The U.S. post office was a cornerstone of many small rural towns over the past two centuries, a gathering place where citizens would meet to discuss local and national events. The invention of the Internet has changed this. In terms of volume of mail delivered, the peak year for the USPS was 2001; volume has declined almost 30 percent over the past decade. As e-mail, online bill paying, and competitors such as FedEx and UPS have reduced the volume of mail, operating costs (including salaries for employees, retirement benefits, health care, and gasoline) have risen. The USPS now spends more than it raises in rev-

enue. Since 2007 the USPS has been running a deficit, and in 2010 its shortfall reached $8.3 billion. The government has responded by closing 2,500 post offices in small towns since 2010. Plans include the closing of as many as 12,000 others, which would result in the layoff of more than 10,000 postal workers.

Even as more and more Americans turn to e-mail instead of letters and to online banking and online greeting cards, and as businesses rely on FedEx or UPS, the postal system remains one of the top five employers in America. It is the only publicly controlled method of delivering packages or mail. If the postal system collapsed, private companies such as FedEx and UPS could charge more, because they would not have to compete with the publicly controlled prices of the USPS. Moreover, e-mail and the other Internet services used for correspondence are generally controlled by private companies. The Founders could not have conceived of the ability to pay bills, talk to friends, or apply for jobs through the medium of the Internet. The decline of the postal system is in effect privatizing a service the Founders saw as important enough to write into the U.S. Constitution.

SOURCES: Josh Sanburn, "How the U.S. Postal Service Fell Apart," *Time*, May 11, 2011, www.time.com/time/nation/article/0,8599,2099187,00.html (accessed 6/11/12). United States Postal Service, "The United States Postal Service: An American History 1775–2006," http://about.usps.com/publications/pub100/welcome.htm (accessed 6/11/12).

for critical analysis

1. Does the closing of small-town post offices and the possible privatization of mail and package delivery violate the U.S. Constitution? Why or why not?

2. Should the federal government continue to deliver the mail to the homes of all Americans in an era of digital communication, or should it focus on operating post offices only?

however, on the fundamentally important question of how to place limits on governmental action. Antifederalists favored limiting and enumerating the powers granted to the national government in relation both to the states and to the people at large. To them, the powers given the national government ought to be "confined to certain defined national objects."[21] Otherwise, the national government would "swallow up all the power of the state governments."[22] Antifederalists bitterly attacked the supremacy clause and the elastic clause of the Constitution as unlimited and dangerous grants of power to the national government.[23] Antifederalists also demanded that a bill of rights be added to the Constitution to place limits on the government's exercise of power over the citizenry.

Federalists favored the construction of a government with broad powers to defend the nation against foreign foes, guard against domestic strife and insurrection, promote commerce, and expand the nation's economy. Antifederalists shared some of these goals but still feared governmental power. In reply, Federalists such as Hamilton acknowledged that every power could be abused but argued that the way to prevent misuse of power was not by depriving the government of the powers needed to achieve national goals but by adopting the Constitution's internal checks and controls. As Madison put it, "the power surrendered by the people is first divided between two distinct governments (state and national), and then the portion allotted to each subdivided among distinct and separate departments. Hence, a double security arises to the rights of the people. The different governments will control each other, at the same time that each will be controlled by itself."[24] The Federalists' concern with avoiding unwarranted limits on governmental power led them to oppose a bill of rights, which they saw as nothing more than a set of unnecessary restrictions on the government.

The Federalists acknowledged that abuse of power remained a possibility but felt that the risk had to be taken because of the goals to be achieved. "The very idea of power included a possibility of doing harm," said the Federalist John Rutledge during the South Carolina ratification debates. "If the gentleman would show the power that could do no harm," Rutledge continued, "he would at once discover it to be a power that could do no good."[25] This aspect of the debate between the Federalists and the Antifederalists, perhaps more than any other, continues to reverberate through American politics. Should the nation limit the federal government's power to tax and spend? Should Congress limit the capacity of federal agencies to issue new regulations? Should the government endeavor to create new rights for minorities, the disabled, and others? Though the details have changed, these are the same great questions that have been debated since the Founding.

Although there was much acrimonious debate and necessary compromise as the new Constitution was written, this print suggests that farmers, artisans, and "gentlemen" alike supported it after its ratification.

Reflections on the Founding

The final product of the Constitutional Convention would have to be considered an extraordinary victory for the groups that had most forcefully called for the creation of a new system of government to replace the Articles of Confederation. Antifederalist criticisms did force the Constitution's proponents to accept the addition of a bill of rights designed to limit the powers of the national government. In general, however, it was the Federalist vision of America that triumphed. The Constitution adopted in 1789 created the framework for a powerful national government that for more than 200 years has defended the nation's interests, promoted its commerce, and maintained national unity. In one notable instance, the national government fought and won a bloody war to prevent the nation from breaking apart. And despite this powerful government, the system of internal checks and balances has functioned reasonably well, as the Federalists predicted, to prevent the national government from tyrannizing its citizens.

Of course, the groups whose interests were served by the Constitution in 1789, mainly the merchants and planters, are not the same groups that benefit from the Constitution's provisions today. Once incorporated into law, political principles often take on lives of their own and have consequences that were never anticipated by their original champions. Indeed, many of the groups that benefit from constitutional provisions today did not even exist in 1789. Who would have thought that the principle of free speech would influence the transmission of data on the Internet? Who would have predicted that commercial interests that once sought a powerful government might come, two centuries later, to denounce governmental activism as "socialist"? Perhaps one secret of the Constitution's longevity is that it did not confer permanent advantage on any one set of economic or social forces.

Although they were defeated in 1789, the Antifederalists present us with an important picture of a road not taken and of an America that might have been. Would the Americans have been worse off if they had been governed by a confederacy of small republics linked by a national administration with severely limited powers? Were the Antifederalists correct in predicting that a government given great power in the hope that it might do good would, through "insensible progress," inevitably turn to evil purposes? Two hundred years of government under the federal Constitution are not necessarily enough to answer these questions definitively.

● The Citizen's Role and the Changing Constitution

> **Trace how the Constitution has changed over time through the amendment process**

The Constitution has endured for more than two centuries as the framework of government. But it has not gone unchanged. Without change, the Constitution might have become merely a sacred text, stored under glass.

Amendments: Many Are Called; Few Are Chosen

amendment a change added to a bill, law, or constitution

The inevitable need for change was recognized by the framers of the Constitution, and provisions for **amendment** were incorporated into Article V. Four methods of amendment are described:

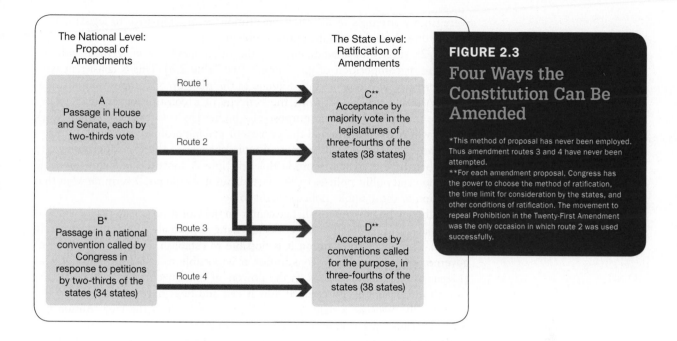

The National Level: Proposal of Amendments

The State Level: Ratification of Amendments

A
Passage in House and Senate, each by two-thirds vote

Route 1

Route 2

C**
Acceptance by majority vote in the legislatures of three-fourths of the states (38 states)

B*
Passage in a national convention called by Congress in response to petitions by two-thirds of the states (34 states)

Route 3

Route 4

D**
Acceptance by conventions called for the purpose, in three-fourths of the states (38 states)

FIGURE 2.3

Four Ways the Constitution Can Be Amended

*This method of proposal has never been employed. Thus amendment routes 3 and 4 have never been attempted.
**For each amendment proposal, Congress has the power to choose the method of ratification, the time limit for consideration by the states, and other conditions of ratification. The movement to repeal Prohibition in the Twenty-First Amendment was the only occasion in which route 2 was used successfully.

1. Passage in House and Senate by two-thirds vote; then ratification by majority vote of the legislatures of three-fourths (now 38) of the states.

2. Passage in House and Senate by two-thirds vote; then ratification by conventions called for the purpose in three-fourths of the states.

3. Passage in a national convention called for by Congress in response to petitions by two-thirds of the states; ratification by majority vote of the legislatures of three-fourths of the states.

4. Passage in a national convention (as in method 3); then ratification by conventions called for the purpose in three-fourths of the states.

Figure 2.3 illustrates each of these possible methods. Since no amendment has ever been proposed by national convention, however, methods 3 and 4 have never been employed. And method 2 has been employed only once (the Twenty-First Amendment, which repealed the Eighteenth Amendment, or Prohibition). Thus, method 1 has been used for all the others.

The Constitution has proved to be extremely difficult to amend. In the history of efforts to amend it, the most appropriate characterization is "many are called, few are chosen." Since 1789, more than 11,000 amendments have been formally offered in Congress. Of these, Congress officially proposed only 29, and 27 of these were eventually ratified by the states. Two of these—Prohibition and its repeal—cancel each other out, so that for all practical purposes, only 25 amendments have been added to the Constitution since 1791.

Which Were Chosen? An Analysis of the Twenty-Seven

There is more to the amending difficulties than the politics of campaigning and voting. It would appear that only a limited number of changes can actually be made to the Constitution. Most efforts to amend the Constitution have failed because they were simply attempts to use the Constitution as an alternative to legislation for dealing directly with a specific public problem.

The 25 successful amendments, on the other hand, are concerned with the structure or composition of government (see Table 2.3). This is consistent with the dictionary, which defines *constitution* as the makeup or composition of something. And it is consistent with the concept of a constitution as "higher law," because the whole point and purpose of a higher law is to establish a framework within which government and the process of making ordinary law can take place. Even those who would have preferred more changes to the Constitution have to agree that there is great wisdom in this principle. A constitution ought to enable legislation and public policies to be enacted, but it should not determine what that legislation or those public policies ought to be.

For those whose hopes for change center on the Constitution, it must be emphasized that the amendment route to social change is, and always will be, extremely limited. Through a constitution it is possible to establish a working structure of government, and through a constitution it is possible to establish basic rights of citizens by placing limitations on the powers of that government. Of course, the Constitution cannot enforce itself. But it can and does have a real influence on everyday life because a right or an obligation set forth in the Constitution can become a cause of action in the hands of an otherwise powerless person.

Private property is an excellent example. Property is one of the most fundamental and well-established rights in the United States; but it is well established not because it is recognized in so many words in the Constitution, but because legislatures and courts, working within an agreed-upon constitutional framework, have made it a crime for anyone, including the government, to trespass or to take away property without compensation. A constitution is good if it produces the cause of action that leads to good legislation, good case law, and appropriate police behavior. A constitution cannot eliminate power. But its principles can be a citizen's dependable defense against the abuse of power.

The Supreme Court and Constitutional Amendment

Although the process of constitutional amendment outlined in Article V has seldom been used successfully, another form of constitutional revision is constantly at work in the United States. This is, of course, judicial interpretation of the Constitution and its amendments by the Supreme Court as it reviews cases. In some instances, the Court may give concrete definition to abstract constitutional principles. For example, the Constitution's Fifth Amendment asserts in general terms that individuals accused of crimes are entitled to procedural rights. The Supreme Court, in a series of decisions, established principles giving effect to those rights. Every viewer of television crime programs knows that, upon being arrested, individuals must receive Miranda warnings informing them of their right to refuse to speak and their right to counsel. These required warnings are the result of a 1966 Supreme Court decision interpreting the meaning and implications of the Fifth Amendment.

In some instances, the Supreme Court does more than interpret or flesh out constitutional provisions: it seems to modify or augment the text itself. For example, in decisions in 1965 and 1973 on birth control and abortion, respectively, the Court said that Americans were constitutionally entitled to a right of privacy. No such right is mentioned anywhere in the Constitution. Similarly, the Court has held that the First Amendment prohibits many forms of government support for

TABLE 2.3

Amendments to the Constitution

AMENDMENT	PURPOSE	YEAR PROPOSED	YEAR ADOPTED
I	*Limits on Congress:* Congress is not to make any law establishing a religion or abridging speech, press, assembly, or petition freedoms.		
II, III, IV	*Limits on Executive:* The executive branch is not to infringe on the right of people to keep arms (II), is not arbitrarily to take houses for a militia (III), and is not to engage in the search or seizure of evidence without a court warrant swearing to belief in the probable existence of a crime (IV).		
V, VI, VII, VIII	*Limits on Courts:** The courts are not to hold trials for serious offenses without provision for a grand jury (V), a petit (trial) jury (VII), a speedy trial (VI), presentation of charges (VI), confrontation of hostile witnesses (VI), immunity from testimony against oneself (V), and immunity from more than one trial for the same offense (V). Neither bail nor punishment can be excessive (VIII), and no property can be taken without just compensation (V).		
IX, X	*Limits on National Government:* All rights not enumerated are reserved to the states or the people.		
XI	Limited jurisdiction of federal courts over suits involving the states.	1794	1798
XII	Provided separate ballot for vice president in the electoral college.	1803	1804
XIII	Eliminated slavery and eliminated the right of states to allow property in persons.	1865**	1865
XIV	(Part 1) Provided a national definition of citizenship.[†]	1866	1868
XIV	(Part 2) Applied due process of Bill of Rights to the states.	1866	1868
XV	Extended voting rights to all races.	1869	1870
XVI	Established national power to tax incomes.	1909	1913
XVII[††]	Provided direct election of senators.	1911	1913
XIX	Extended voting rights to women.	1919	1920
XX	Eliminated "lame duck" session of Congress.	1932	1933
XXII	Limited presidential term.	1947	1951
XXIII	Extended voting rights to residents of the District of Columbia.	1960	1961
XXIV	Extended voting rights to all classes by abolition of poll taxes.	1962	1964
XXV	Provided presidential succession in case of disability.	1965	1967
XXVI	Extended voting rights to citizens aged 18 and over.	1971	1971[†]
XXVII	Limited Congress's power to raise its own salary.	1789	1992

* These amendments also impose limits on the law-enforcement powers of federal (and especially) state and local executive branches.
** The Thirteenth Amendment was proposed on January 31, 1865, and adopted less than a year later, on December 18, 1865.
[†] In defining *citizenship*, the Fourteenth Amendment actually provided the constitutional basis for expanding the electorate to include all races, women, and residents of the District of Columbia. Only the "eighteen-year-olds' amendment" should have been necessary, since it changed the definition of citizenship. The fact that additional amendments were required following the Fourteenth suggests that voting is not considered an inherent right of U.S. citizenship. Instead, it is viewed as a privilege.
[††] The Eighteenth Amendment, ratified in 1919, outlawed the sale and transportation of liquor. It was repealed by the Twenty-First Amendment, ratified in 1933.
[†] The Twenty-Sixth Amendment holds the record for speed of adoption. It was proposed on March 23, 1971, and adopted on July 5, 1971.

religion and many forms of religious exercise in public institutions, such as schools. By doing this, the Court was saying that the framers of the First Amendment simply meant that the government was prohibited from declaring one religion to be the nation's official faith. They did not intend to prohibit nondenominational school prayer.

Of course, much of the Supreme Court's power is itself based on constitutional interpretation rather than on the text of the document. The Supreme Court claims the power of judicial review—the power to render the final decision when there is a conflict of interpretations of the Constitution or federal law among the courts, Congress, the executive branch, or the states. Nowhere does the Constitution mention this power. In a number of early cases, however, the Supreme Court asserted that the Constitution gave it the power of judicial review, and this interpretation has prevailed, enhancing the Court's power. Some commentators denounce constitutional amendment by the judiciary and demand that judges limit themselves to "strict construction" of the Constitution, adhering closely to the words of the document's text. Proponents of the idea of the *living Constitution*, on the other hand, assert that the Constitution is subject to change as conditions warrant, and they argue that the judiciary is the institution best qualified to adjust the Constitution's principles to new problems and times. Advocates of strict construction and champions of the living Constitution disagree about the desirability of constitutional amendment by the courts, but both acknowledge its reality.

The Equal Rights Amendment (ERA) is an example of an amendment that almost succeeded. The proposed amendment guaranteed equality under the law for women and made gender discrimination illegal. The ERA was ratified by 35 state legislatures but failed to get the 38 necessary to equaly three-fourths of the states.

Thinking Critically about Liberty, Equality, and Democracy in the Constitution

The Constitution's framers placed individual liberty ahead of all other political values, a concern that led many of the framers to distrust both democracy and equality. They feared that democracy could degenerate into a majority tyranny in which the populace, perhaps led by rabble-rousing demagogues, trampled on liberty. As for equality, the framers were products of their time and place; our contemporary ideas of racial and gender equality would have been foreign to them. The framers were concerned primarily with another manifestation of equality: they feared that those without property or position might be driven by what some called a "leveling spirit" to infringe on liberty in the name of greater economic or social equality. Indeed, the framers believed that this leveling spirit was most likely to produce demagoguery and majority tyranny. As a result, the basic structure of the Constitution—separated powers, internal checks and balances, and federalism—was designed to safeguard liberty, and the Bill of Rights created further safeguards for liberty. At the same time, however, many of the Constitution's other key provisions, such as indirect election of senators and the president, and the appointment of judges for life, were designed to limit democracy and, hence, the threat of majority tyranny.

By championing liberty, however, the framers virtually guaranteed that democracy and even a measure of equality would sooner or later evolve in the United States. For liberty promotes the growth of political activity and the expansion of political participation. In James Madison's famous phrase, "Liberty is to faction as air is to fire."[26] Where they have liberty, more and more people, groups, and interests will almost inevitably engage in politics and gradually overcome whatever restrictions might have been placed on participation. Indeed, this is precisely what happened in the early years of the American republic. During the Jeffersonian period, political parties formed. During the Jacksonian period, many state suffrage restrictions were removed and popular participation greatly expanded. Over time, liberty is conducive to democracy.

Liberty does not guarantee that everyone will be equal. It does, however, reduce the threat of inequality in one very important way. Historically, the greatest inequalities of wealth, power, and privilege have arisen where governments have used their power to allocate status and opportunity among individuals or groups. From the aristocracies of the early modern period to twentieth-century despotisms, the most extreme cases of inequality are associated with the most tyrannical regimes.

The other side of the coin, however, is that the absence of government intervention in economic affairs—in the name of liberty—may mean that there is no antidote to the inevitable inequalities of wealth produced by the marketplace. Economic inequalities, in turn, may lead to inequalities in political power as wealthy groups and individuals use their superior resources to elect politicians friendly to them and their aims and to influence the legislative process. Thus, liberty is a complex matter. In the absence of liberty, inequality is virtually certain. The existence of liberty, however, poses its own threat to political equality. Can we fully reconcile liberty and equality? Doing so remains a constant challenge in a democratic society.

Another limitation of liberty as a political principle is that limits on government action can also inhibit effective government. Consider, for example, one of the basic tasks of government, the protection of citizens' lives and property. A government limited by concerns over the rights of those accused of crimes may therefore

The Eighteenth Amendment was passed in 1919 and prohibited the manufacture, transportation, and sale of alcoholic beverages. Repealed in 1933 by the Twenty-First Amendment, the Prohibition Amendment can be seen as an attempt to legislate through the amendment process.

be limited in its ability to maintain public order. Recently, the U.S. government has asserted that protecting the nation against terrorists requires law-enforcement measures that seem at odds with legal and constitutional formalities.

Liberty is sometimes confused with the absence of government. The framers of the Constitution, though, saw liberty as a purpose or goal of government, not the result of governmental absence. The government they created was designed to "secure the Blessings of Liberty" by maintaining order, keeping the peace, and intervening where necessary to allow citizens to conduct their affairs in safety and freedom. Every generation of Americans ponders and reconsiders the work of the men who framed the Constitution.

Madison's Notes and the U.S. Constitution

Inform Yourself

 Read the Constitution. Visit the Library of Congress's "The Making of the U.S. Constitution" page (http://memory.loc.gov/ammem/amlaw/ac001/lawpres.html) to read a brief account of the Constitutional Convention followed by the text of the Constitution as originally adopted (that is, without the Bill of Rights and other amendments). The text of the Constitution also appears at the end of this book. Are you surprised by how short the document is? Does the text sound familiar? What did you not expect to find?

 Dip into James Madison's notes from the Constitutional Convention. To read what happened on those hot summer days in 1787 in Philadelphia, click on a day in the calendar on "The Debates in the Federal Convention of 1787" page to read that day's entry in Madison's journal (www.constitution.org/dfc/dfc_0000.htm). After reading the notes for any day, answer the following questions: What did the members of the Convention agree on? What issues did they disagree on? Can you find evidence of the debates between the small and large population states? Can you find evidence of the debates between slave-owning and non-slave-owning states? Can you find debate over the power of the presidency?

 Watch a slide show on the Bill of Rights. "Jump Back in Time" is also presented by the Library of Congress (www.americaslibrary.gov/jb/nation/jb_nation_bofright_1.html). Four short slides walk you through the adoption of the Bill of Rights.

Connect with Others

 Visit the United States Constitution page on Facebook. The U.S. Constitution has more than 200,000 Facebook fans. What type of posts appear on this page? Do the messages reflect different interpretations of the Constitution? What does this tell us about the Constitution? Is the Constitution a living document, or is it fixed in stone?

Find links to the sites listed above as well as related activities on wwnorton.com/studyspace.

⑤ Practice online with: Chapter 2 Diagnostic Quiz ▪ Chapter 2 Key Term Flashcards

The First Founding: Interests and Conflicts

■ **Describe the events that led to the Declaration of Independence and the Articles of Confederation (pp. 39–43)**

Dissatisfaction with British tax policies and discontent over retaliatory acts of political repression radicalized many colonists during the 1770s to push for independence from British rule. By identifying widely shared grievances, aspirations, and principles, the Declaration of Independence helped forge a sense of national unity among diverse elements in colonial society. The first written constitution of the United States, the Articles of Confederation, lefts most governmental responsibilities in the hands of states and placed serious limits on the powers of the national government.

Key Terms

Articles of Confederation (p. 42)

confederation (p. 42)

Practice Quiz

1. In their fight against British taxes such as the Stamp Act and the Sugar Act of 1764, New England merchants allied with which of the following groups? *(pp. 39–40)*
   a) artisans, southern planters, and laborers
   b) southern planters only
   c) laborers only
   d) artisans only
   e) southern planters and laborers only

2. How did the British attempt to raise revenue in the North American colonies? *(p. 39)*
   a) income tax
   b) taxes on commerce
   c) expropriation and government sale of land
   d) government asset sales
   e) requests for voluntary donations

3. The first governing document in the United States was *(p. 42)*
   a) the Declaration of Independence.
   b) the Articles of Confederation.
   c) the Constitution.
   d) the Bill of Rights.
   e) the Virginia Plan.

4. Where was the execution of laws conducted under the Articles of Confederation? *(p. 42)*
   a) the presidency
   b) the Congress
   c) the states
   d) the federal bureaucracy
   e) the federal judiciary

⑤ Practice Online
Video exercise: South Park, *"I'm a Little Bit Country"*

The Second Founding: From Compromise to Constitution

■ **Explain how the Constitution attempted to improve America's governance (pp. 43–49)**

International weakness, domestic economic problems and the national government's inability to act decisively in response to Shays's Rebellion led to a constitutional convention to replace the Articles of Confederation. The convention's delegates were deeply divided on the issues of slavery and representation in the national government. The Great Compromise and the Three-Fifths Compromise temporarily reconciled these divisions and allowed the Founders to move forward with creating a new constitutional framework for the United States.

Key Terms

Virginia Plan (p. 45)

New Jersey Plan (p. 45)

Great Compromise (p. 46)

Three-Fifths Compromise (p. 48)

Practice Quiz

5. Which of the following was *not* a reason that the Articles of Confederation seemed inadequate *(pp. 43–44)*
   a) the lack of a single voice in international affairs
   b) weakness of the national government

    c) persistent economic turmoil among states

    d) the power of radical forces in several states

    e) the power of radical forces in Congress

6. Which event led directly to the Constitutional Convention by providing evidence that the government created under the Articles of Confederation was unable to act decisively in times of national crisis? *(p. 44)*
   a) the Boston Tea Party
   b) the Boston Massacre
   c) Shays's Rebellion
   d) the Annapolis Convention
   e) the War of 1812

7. The draft constitution that was introduced at the start of the Constitutional Convention was authored by *(p. 45)*
   a) Edmund Randolph.
   b) Benjamin Franklin.
   c) James Madison.
   d) George Clinton.
   e) Thomas Jefferson.

8. Which state's proposal embodied a principle of representing states in the Congress according to their size and wealth? *(p. 45)*
   a) New Jersey
   b) Maryland
   c) Rhode Island
   d) Virginia
   e) Connecticut

9. The agreement reached at the Constitutional Convention that determined that every slave would be counted as a fraction of a person for the purposes of taxation and representation in the House of Representatives was called the *(pp. 48–49)*
   a) Connecticut Compromise.
   b) Three-Fifths Compromise.
   c) Great Compromise.
   d) Virginia Plan.
   e) New Jersey Plan.

 Practice Online

Interactive simulation: *The Role of a Delegate at the Constitutional Convention*

The Constitution

■ **Outline the major institutions and rules established by the Constitution (pp. 49–56)**

The Founders sought to create a stronger national government than existed under the Articles of Confederation. In particular, they hoped that the new constitution would promote commerce, protect private property, and avoid the perils of "excessive democracy." The Founders' concern with national power was expressed most clearly in the supremacy clause of Article VI. The national government, however, did not have unlimited power, and there were significant limits placed on it through the separation of powers, federalism, and the Bill of Rights.

Key Terms

checks and balances (p. 49)

electoral college (p. 50)

Bill of Rights (p. 50)

separation of powers (p. 50)

federalism (p. 50)

expressed powers (p. 51)

elastic clause (p. 51)

bicameral (p. 52)

judicial review (p. 53)

supremacy clause (p. 53)

Practice Quiz

10. What mechanism was instituted in the Congress to guard against "excessive democracy"? *(pp. 49–50)*
    a) bicameralism
    b) staggered terms in office
    c) checks and balances
    d) selection of senators by state legislatures
    e) all of the above

11. Which of the following best describes the Supreme Court as understood by the Founders? *(p. 53)*
    a) the highest court of the national government
    b) arbiter of disputes within the Congress
    c) the body that would choose the president
    d) a figurehead commission of elders
    e) a supreme court of the nation and its states

12. Theorists such as Montesquieu referred to the principle of giving each branch of government a distinctly different constituency as *(pp. 54–55)*
    a) laissez-faire.
    b) mixed regime.
    c) confederation.
    d) limited government.
    e) federalism.

 Practice Online

Video exercise: *Happy Constitution Day*

The Fight for Ratification

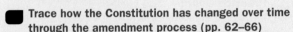

Present the controversies involved in the struggle for ratification (pp. 56–62)

Before the Constitution could go into effect, it had to be ratified by 9 of the 13 states. In the debate over ratification, the Federalists supported the Constitution and the Antifederalists opposed it. The three major areas of disagreement between Federalists and Antifederalists were the quality of representation, the threat of tyranny of the majority, and the extent of government power.

Key Terms

Federalists (p. 56)

Antifederalists (p. 56)

Federalist Papers (p. 57)

tyranny (p. 59)

limited government (p. 59)

Practice Quiz

13. Which of the following were the Antifederalists most concerned with? *(p. 59)*
    a) interstate commerce
    b) the protection of property
    c) the distinction between principles and interests
    d) abolishing slavery
    e) the potential for tyranny in the central government

The Citizen's Role and the Changing Constitution

Trace how the Constitution has changed over time through the amendment process (pp. 62–66)

The amendment process outlined in Article V of the Constitution creates significant hurdles to change that have rarely been cleared in American history. Attempts to solve specific social problems through the use of a constitutional amendment have been particularly unsuccessful at winning the support required to change the country's basic governing document. The Supreme Court, however, has provided new meaning and new substance to the Constitution on countless occasions during the last 200 years through their decisions on important cases.

Key Term

amendment (p. 62)

Practice Quiz

14. Which of the following best describes the process of amending the Constitution? *(pp. 62–63)*
    a) It is difficult and has rarely been used successfully to address specific public problems.
    b) It is difficult and has frequently been used successfully to address specific public problems.
    c) It is easy and has rarely been used successfully to address specific public problems.
    d) It is easy and has frequently been used successfully to address specific public problems.
    e) It is easy, but it has never been used for any purpose.

 Practice Online
"You Decide" exercise: *A Federal Marriage Amendment?*

For Further Reading

Amar, Akhil Reed. *America's Constitution: A Biography.* New York: Random House, 2006.

Beard, Charles. *An Economic Interpretation of the Constitution of the United States.* New York: Macmillan, 1913.

Beeman, Richard. *Plain, Honest Men: The Making of the American Constitution.* New York: Random House, 2010.

Breyer, Stephen G. *Active Liberty: Interpreting Our Democratic Constitution.* New York: Knopf, 2005.

Dahl, Robert A. *How Democratic Is the American Constitution?* 2nd ed. New Haven, CT: Yale University Press, 2002.

Ellis, Joseph. *American Creation: Triumphs and Tragedies at the Founding of the Republic.* New York: Knopf, 2007.

Hamilton, Alexander, James Madison, and John Jay. *The Federalist Papers.* Edited by Isaac Kramnick. New York: Viking, 1987.

Holton, Woody. *Unruly Americans and the Origins of the Constitution.* New York: Hill and Wang, 2007.

Jensen, Merrill. *The Articles of Confederation.* Madison: University of Wisconsin Press, 1963.

Keller, Morton. *America's Three Regimes.* New York: Oxford University Press, 2009.

Lewis, Anthony. *Freedom for the Thought That We Hate: A Biography of the First Amendment.* New York: Basic Books, 2008.

Main, Jackson Turner. *The Social Structure of Revolutionary America*. Princeton, NJ: Princeton University Press, 1965.

Rossiter, Clinton. *1787: Grand Convention*. New York: Macmillan, 1966.

Storing, Herbert, ed. *The Complete Anti-Federalist*. 7 vols. Chicago: University of Chicago Press, 1981.

Winik, Jay. *The Great Upheaval: America and the Birth of the Modern World, 1788–1800*. New York: HarperCollins, 2007.

Recommended Websites

The American Civil Liberties Union
www.aclu.org
The ACLU is committed to protecting, for all individuals, the freedoms found in the Bill of Rights. This sometimes controversial organization constantly monitors the government for violations of liberty and encourages its members to take political action.

Archiving Early America
www.earlyamerica.com
Revolutionary Americans were motivated by a variety of competing ideals, principles, and interests. Visit this website to learn more about the early colonists and the founding of our government.

Constitution Finder
http://confinder.richmond.edu
Is the American Constitution a model for the world? Explore the constitutions of many different nations and see what elements of the U.S. Constitution can be found in the governing documents of other countries.

Find Law
http://findlaw.com/casecode/state.html
The Find Law website provides all fifty states' constitutions. Click on your state and try to identify such constitutional principles as bicameralism, staggered terms of office, checks and balances, and separation of powers.

The National Archives
www.archives.gov
This government site provides information about and actual digital images of such founding documents as the Declaration of Independence, the U.S. Constitution, and the Bill of Rights.

The National Constitution Center
www.constitutioncenter.org
The National Constitution Center in Philadelphia maintains a website that provides in-depth instructional analysis of the U.S. Constitution. Check out the Interactive Constitution function and follow the document from its Preamble through the Twenty-Seventh Amendment.

Oyez
www.oyez.org
This website for U.S. Supreme Court Media has an excellent search engine for finding information on Supreme Court cases. See how the Court has interpreted the Constitution over time.

The PBS Liberty! Series
www.pbs.org/ktca/liberty
The PBS *Liberty!* series on the American Revolution offers an in-depth look at the Revolutionary War and includes information on historical events such as the Constitutional Convention.

The Supreme Court of the United States
www.supremecourtus.gov
The website for the U.S. Supreme Court provides information on recent decisions. Take a moment to read some oral arguments, briefs, or opinions

Federalism was at the center of the controversy concerning the Affordable Care Act, as 26 states sued the federal government over the health care reform law. When the Supreme Court heard arguments in the case in 2012, groups on both sides of the issue demonstrated outside the Court.

Federalism

WHAT GOVERNMENT DOES AND WHY IT MATTERS Few laws have attracted as much controversy as the Affordable Care Act, the Obama administration's signature legislation that aimed to make health care available to all Americans. From the time it was enacted in 2010, the law became the target of opponents in the states who charged that the federal government exceeded its constitutional powers in enacting the measure. The new law would require states to comply with federal rules on matters that had previously been decided by the states, such as who was eligible for Medicaid in the state. Twenty-six states sued the federal government, and the case made its way to the Supreme Court. In the Court's 2012 decision, Chief Justice John Roberts surprised many when he broke with the Court's conservative majority, penning an opinion that declared the main provisions of the Affordable Care Act constitutional.[1] Yet, the Court's ruling raised fundamental questions about federal power and about the relationship of the federal government to the states.

Although it upheld most of the Affordable Care Act and the federal government's power to force states to comply with the act, the decision also introduced the potential for significant new restrictions on federal power in two main ways. First, it limited the reach of the commerce clause, the main constitutional provision under which federal power has expanded for the past 80 years. Although the Court found the controversial "individual mandate"—the requirement that uninsured individuals buy health insurance—constitutional, it ruled that this provision could not be justified under the commerce clause. Instead, the decision stated, it was Congress's taxing power that justified the mandate.

Even more surprising was the Court's ruling that the federal government could not cut off all Medicaid funding to states that declined to expand the program as required in the Affordable Care Act.

Expanding Medicaid, the federal–state program that provides health care to low-income Americans, was one of the main ways the new law sought to reduce the number of uninsured. The Court's decision on Medicaid raises new questions far beyond the domain of health care. The federal government has long attached conditions to federal funding as a way to achieve national goals. For example, in 1984 the federal government pressured state governments to change the laws governing the age at which a person could legally drink alcohol to 21. It did so by threatening states with the loss of federal highway funds if they did not adopt the new drinking age. Eventually, all 50 states fell into line. The ruling on health care is likely to unleash challenges to the many federal laws that seek to influence what states do by attaching conditions to federal funds.

The debates about the Affordable Care Act engaged one of the oldest questions in American government: What is the responsibility of the federal government and what is the responsibility of the states? When should there be uniformity across the states and when is it better to let states adopt a diverse set of laws? Which approach serves the common good?

The United States is a federal system, in which the national government shares power with lower levels of government. Throughout American history, lawmakers, politicians, and citizens have wrestled with questions about how responsibilities should be allocated across the different levels of government. Some responsibilities, such as international relations, clearly lie with the federal government. Others, such as divorce laws, are controlled by state governments. In fact, most of the rules and regulations that Americans face in their daily lives are set by state and local governments. However, many government responsibilities are shared in American federalism and require cooperation among local, state, and federal governments. The debate about "who should do what" remains one of the most important discussions in American politics.

chaptergoals

- **Describe what the Constitution says about the powers of the national government and of the states (pages 77–81)**

- **Trace how the federal government became much stronger over time (pages 82–89)**

- **Analyze major developments in the federal framework since the 1930s (pages 89–105)**

Federalism in the Constitution

Describe what the Constitution says about the powers of the national government and of the states

The Constitution has had its most fundamental influence on American life through **federalism**. Federalism can be defined as the division of powers and functions between the national government and the state governments. Governments can organize power in a variety of ways. One of the most important distinctions is between unitary and federal governments. In a **unitary system**, the central government makes the important decisions, and lower levels of government have little independent power. In such systems, lower levels of government primarily implement decisions made by the central government. In France, for example, the central government was once so involved in the smallest details of local activity that the minister of education boasted that by looking at his watch he could tell what all French schoolchildren were learning at that moment because the central government set the school curriculum. In a **federal system**, by contrast, the central government shares power or functions with lower levels of government, such as regions or states. Nations with diverse ethnic or language groupings, such as Switzerland and Canada, are most likely to have federal arrangements. In federal systems, lower levels of government often have significant independent power to set policy in some areas, such as education and social programs, and to impose taxes. Yet the specific ways in which power is shared vary greatly: no two federal systems are exactly the same.

The United States was the first nation to adopt federalism as its governing framework. With federalism, the framers sought to limit the national government by creating a second layer of state governments. By granting a few "expressed powers" to the national government and reserving all the rest to the states, the original Constitution recognized two sovereigns, the principle of American federalism reinforced in the Bill of Rights.

The Powers of the National Government

As we saw in Chapter 2, the **expressed powers** granted to the national government are found in Article I, Section 8, of the Constitution. These 17 powers include the power to collect taxes, to coin money, to declare war, and to regulate commerce. Article I, Section 8, also contains another important source of power for the national government: the **implied powers** that enable Congress "to make all Laws which shall be necessary and proper for carrying into Execution the foregoing Powers." Not until several decades after the Founding did the Supreme Court allow Congress to exercise the power granted in this **necessary and proper clause**, but as we shall see later in this chapter, this doctrine allowed the national government to expand considerably the scope of its authority, although the process was a slow one. In addition to these expressed and implied powers, the Constitution affirmed the power of the national government in the supremacy clause (Article VI), which made all national laws and treaties "the supreme Law of the Land."

federalism a system of government in which power is divided, by a constitution, between a central government and regional governments

unitary system a centralized government system in which lower levels of government have little power independent of the national government

federal system a system of government in which the national government shares power with lower levels of government, such as states

expressed powers specific powers granted by the Constitution to Congress (Article I, Section 8) and to the president (Article II)

implied powers powers derived from the necessary and proper clause of Article I, Section 8, of the Constitution. Such powers are not specifically expressed, but are implied through the expansive interpretation of delegated powers

necessary and proper clause Article I, Section 8, of the Constitution, which provides Congress with the authority to make all laws "necessary and proper" to carry out its expressed powers

Especially since the mid-1990s, Republican Party leaders have contended that the national government has grown too powerful at the expense of the states and that the Tenth Amendment should restrict the growth of national power.

The Powers of State Government

One way in which the framers sought to preserve a strong role for the states was through the Tenth Amendment to the Constitution. The Tenth Amendment states that the powers that the Constitution does not delegate to the national government or prohibit to the states are "reserved to the States respectively, or to the people." The Antifederalists, who feared that a strong central government would encroach on individual liberty, repeatedly pressed for such an amendment as a way of limiting national power. Federalists agreed to the amendment because they did not think it would do much harm, given the powers of the Constitution already granted to the national government. The Tenth Amendment is also called the "**reserved powers** amendment," because it aims to reserve powers to the states.

The most fundamental power that the states retain is that of coercion—the power to develop and enforce criminal codes, to administer health and safety rules, to regulate the family via marriage and divorce laws. The states have the power to regulate individuals' livelihoods; if you're a doctor or a lawyer or a plumber or a barber, you must be licensed by the state. Even more fundamentally, the states have the power to define private property—private property exists because state laws against trespass define who is and is not entitled to use a piece of property. If you own a car, your ownership isn't worth much unless the state is willing to enforce your right to possession by making it a crime for anyone else to drive your car without your consent. These are fundamental matters, and the powers of the states regarding these domestic issues are much greater than the powers of the national government, even today.

A state's authority to regulate these fundamental matters is commonly referred to as the **police power** of the state and encompasses the state's power to regulate the health, safety, welfare, and morals of its citizens. Policing is what states do—they coerce you in the name of the community in order to maintain public order. And this was exactly the type of power that the Founders intended the states, not the federal government, to exercise.

In some areas, the states share **concurrent powers** with the national government, whereby they retain and share some power to regulate commerce and affect the currency—for example, by being able to charter banks, grant or deny corporate charters, grant or deny licenses to engage in a business or practice a trade, regulate the quality of products or the conditions of labor, and levy taxes (see the Digital Citizens box on page 81). Wherever there is a direct conflict of laws between the federal and the state levels, the issue will most likely be resolved in favor of national supremacy.

reserved powers powers, derived from the Tenth Amendment to the Constitution, that are not specifically delegated to the national government or denied to the states

police power power reserved to the state government to regulate the health, safety, and morals of its citizens

concurrent powers authority possessed by *both* state and national governments, such as the power to levy taxes

State Obligations to One Another

The Constitution also creates obligations among the states. These obligations, spelled out in Article IV, were intended to promote national unity. By requiring the states to recognize actions and decisions taken in other states as legal and proper, the framers aimed to make the states less like independent countries and more like components of a single nation.

Article IV, Section 1, calls for "Full Faith and Credit" among states, meaning that each state is normally expected to honor the "public Acts, Records, and judicial Proceedings" that take place in any other state. So, for example, if a couple is married in Texas—marriage being regulated by state law—in most cases, Missouri must also recognize that marriage, even though the couple was not married under Missouri state law.

This **full faith and credit clause** notwithstanding, if a practice is against their "strong public policy," states are not obligated to recognize it—even if it has been sanctioned by other states. A look at the history of interracial marriage, for example, offers some perspective on how much leeway states have to recognize marriages performed in other states. In 1952, 30 states prohibited interracial marriage. In 1967, when the Supreme Court struck down such laws as unconstitutional, 16 states still had these statutes on the books. Many of the states that prohibited interracial marriage also refused to recognize such marriages performed in other states. But many states that outlawed interracial marriage did recognize out-of-state marriages, depending on the circumstances.[2] In the case of same-sex marriage, the states that allow same-sex marriage (Connecticut, Iowa, Maine, Maryland, Massachussets, New Hampshire, New York, Vermont, and Washington) recognize same-sex marriages performed out of state, as does Rhode Island. In California, the governor signed a law in 2009 granting recognition of gay and lesbian marriages that were performed out of state during the five-month period in 2008 that these marriages were legal in California.[3]

Most states, however, do not recognize same-sex marriages performed in other states. And to underscore their opposition to same-sex marriage, a large majority of states have enacted provisions against gay marriage. By 2011, 38 states had passed "defense of marriage acts" or had adopted constitutional amendments that defined marriage as a union between one man and one woman only. Most of these states also outlaw recognition of gay marriages performed in other states. Anxious to show its disapproval of gay marriage, Congress passed the Defense of Marriage Act in 1996, which declared that states will *not* have to recognize a same-sex marriage, even if it is legal in one state. The act also said that the federal government will not recognize gay marriage—even if it is legal under state law—and that gay marriage partners will not be eligible for the federal benefits, such as Medicare and Social Security, normally available to spouses.[4]

Same-sex marriage is not the only issue in which the "full faith and credit" clause has come into play. It has played a role also in conflicts over gay adoption. In these cases, however, the courts have so far ruled that the full faith and credit clause requires states to accept the legal decisions of other states. Two states, Mississippi and Utah, explicitly ban gay adoption, and several other states sharply restrict it. An Oklahoma law banned state agencies from recognizing adoption orders to gay and lesbian couples approved in other states. Effectively, this meant that Oklahoma refused to issue birth certificates for children born in Oklahoma but legally adopted by same-sex couples in other states. In 2007 a federal appeals court struck down the Oklahoma law, ruling that the full faith and credit clause required Oklahoma to honor adoption orders approved by courts in other states.[5]

Article IV, Section 2, known as the "comity clause," also seeks to promote national unity. It provides that citizens enjoying the **privileges and immunities** of one state should be entitled to similar treatment in other states. What this has come to mean is that a state cannot discriminate against someone from another state or give special privileges to its own residents. For example, in the 1970s, when Alaska passed a law

Should same-sex marriages performed in one state be legally recognized in another state? State laws vary, and despite the Constitution's full faith and credit clause, these differences can lead to debate over controversial issues.

full faith and credit clause
provision, from Article IV, Section 1, of the Constitution, requiring that the states normally honor the public acts and judicial decisions that take place in another state

privileges and immunities clause
provision, from Article IV, Section 2, of the Constitution, that a state cannot discriminate against someone from another state or give its own residents special privileges

that gave residents preference over nonresidents in obtaining work on the state's oil and gas pipelines, the Supreme Court ruled the law illegal because it discriminated against citizens of other states.[6] The comity clause also regulates criminal justice among the states by requiring states to return fugitives to the states from which they have fled. Thus, in 1952, when an inmate escaped from an Alabama prison and sought to avoid being returned to Alabama on the grounds that he was being subjected to "cruel and unusual punishment" there, the Supreme Court ruled that he must be returned according to Article IV, Section 2.[7] This example highlights the difference between the obligations among states and those among different countries. In 2011, Portugal refused to return an American fugitive captured after more than 30 years on the run because he had become a Portuguese national and had a family in Portugal.[8] The Constitution clearly forbids states from doing something similar.

States' relationships with one another are also governed by the interstate compact clause (Article I, Section 10), which states that "No State shall, without the Consent of Congress . . . enter into any Agreement or Compact with another State." The Court has interpreted the clause to mean that states may enter into agreements with each other, subject to congressional approval. Compacts are a way for two or more states to reach a legally binding agreement about how to solve a problem that crosses state lines. In the early years of the republic, states turned to compacts primarily to settle border disputes. Today compacts are used for a wide range of issues but are especially important in regulating the distribution of river water, addressing environmental concerns, and operating transportation systems that cross state lines.[9] One unusual use of the interstate compact is the effort to enact the National Popular Vote compact. Initiated after George W. Bush won the presidency without winning the popular vote, the compact aims to make the popular vote, not the electoral college results, the criterion for victory. In signing onto the compact, a state agrees to award all its electoral college votes to the winner of the popular vote. By 2011, with eight states and the District of Columbia supporting the compact, the movement had obtained 49 percent of the 270 electoral votes needed for it to be effective.[10]

home rule power delegated by the state to a local unit of government to manage its own affairs

Local Government and the Constitution

Local government occupies a peculiar but very important place in the American system. In fact, the status of American local government is probably unique in world experience. First, it must be pointed out that local government has no status in the U.S. Constitution. *State* legislatures created local governments, and *state* constitutions and laws permit local governments to take on some of the responsibilities of the state governments. Local governments have always been subject to ultimate control by the states. This imbalance of power means that state governments could legally dissolve local governments or force multiple local governments to consolidate into one large locality. Most states amended their own constitutions to give their larger cities **home rule**—a guarantee of noninterference in various areas of local affairs. But local governments enjoy no such recognition and have no protected standing at all in the federal Constitution.[11]

Local governments became administratively important in the early years of the Republic because the states possessed little administrative capability. They relied on local governments—cities and counties—to implement state laws. Local government was an alternative to a statewide bureaucracy (see Table 3.1).

TABLE 3.1

89,527 Governments in the United States

TYPE	NUMBER
National	1
State	50
County	3,033
Municipal	19,492
Townships	16,519
School districts	13,051
Other special districts	37,381

SOURCE: U.S. Census Bureau, www.census.gov/govs/cog/GovOrgTab03ss.html (accessed 11/21/11).

E-Commerce and State Taxes

Where you buy a product can sig-nificantly affect how much it costs. Similar products in local stores often cost more than buying online, even after accounting for shipping costs. Have you ever wondered why? One reason is online stores don't have to pay rent for physical space, or hire sales clerks, or pay electrical bills. This allows them to share the cost savings with consumers. What began as an online bookstore, Amazon.com, for example, became the world's largest online retailer.

But a large part of the reason for the difference in cost is that we don't pay state sales tax on what we buy online unless the location the product is shipping from is in the same state as the shipping address (or the company has a warehouse in the state). We also do not pay local sales taxes on items bought online. This is one reason many people prefer to purchase expensive items, such as computers, online.

In our federal system, each state establishes its own state-level tax policies. Tax policies and rates vary from state to state, but most states collect a sales tax on items

that are not considered basic needs (such as food items). The rule that taxes are not charged for online purchases unless the business has a physical presence in the buyer's state dates back to a Supreme Court case in the 1990s that had nothing to do with online commerce. The decision concerned mail-order items and established the rules that now extend to Internet purchases.

This is not to say we do not technically owe the state taxes on items purchased online. Each year, when we file our state tax forms, we are supposed to report whether we bought items online, and if so, how much those items cost. But it is up to individuals to self-report purchases, and many people do not even know they are supposed to pay sales taxes on online purchases. In the majority of cases, the taxes are never paid.

The nonpayment of state sales taxes online has become a significant issue. Why? Traditional retailers have to collect state (and sometimes local) sales tax, which makes their items seem more expensive to consumers, which in turn hurts their business. More important, the sales tax is the leading source of revenue for state governments, so collectively, the states are missing out on billions of dollars in sales tax because of e-commerce. According to one estimate, over the last six years, the states lost more than $52 billion in sales taxes that went uncollected on online purchases. The year 2011 was the lowest collection year since 1967 because of the difficulty in collecting online sales taxes.

In response, more than 40 states have signed an agreement that simplifies and streamlines the various state taxes. Some major online sellers have agreed to start collecting state sales tax in a few years; others have not. For example, Amazon.com sued the state of Illinois in 2012 after the state government passed a law requiring all online vendors (regardless of where they were based) selling to residents of Illinois to collect Illinois sales taxes. Amazon has no physical presence in the state, and it fought the law, arguing that it violated the Internet Tax Freedom Act. The court ruled

that because Amazon does not have a presence in the state, the state government cannot force the company to collect taxes from the state's citizens for online purchases.

The Amazon case did not fully settle the question of whether the states can regulate e-commerce. Some observers argue that the patchwork of state and national laws threatens the growth of e-commerce, as many state laws place additional burdens on out-of-state commerce. The commerce clause in the U.S. Constitution gives the power to regulate commerce among the states to the federal government. However, while the states have been aggressive in collecting state taxes from online retailers, Congress is loath to be seen as raising taxes, and might not force retailers to collect the tax. Do the states have a right to force online retailers to collect sales taxes from consumers, or must Congress address this issue?

SOURCES: Dennis Cauchon, "Tax-Free Internet Sales, Exemptions Erode State Revenue." *USA Today*, February 28, 2012, www.usatoday.com/money/economy/story/2012-02-27/sales-tax-rate/53274224/1 (accessed 6/12/12). Jim Brunner, "States Fight Back against Amazon.com's Tax Deals." *Seattle Times*, April 2, 2012, http://seattletimes.nwsource.com/html/localnews/2017895493_amazonsalestax03.html (accessed 6/12/12). Rich Stim, "Sales Tax on the Internet: When Sales Tax Must Be Charged for Online Purchases," 2012, NOLO Law for ALL, www.nolo.com/legal-encyclopedia/sales-tax-internet-29919.html (accessed 6/12/12).

for critical analysis

1. What are the benefits of having the states (rather than the federal government) determine the rules for Internet sales to their residents? What are the possible disadvantages?

2. As commerce moves online and collecting sales taxes becomes more difficult, how can states replace lost revenue? What other taxes might state governments use to generate revenue?

The Changing Relationship between the Federal Government and the States

> **Trace how the federal government became much stronger over time**

At the time of the Founding, the states far outstripped the federal government in their power to influence the lives of ordinary Americans. In the system of shared powers between the states and the federal government, the states were most active in economic and social regulation, while Washington took a much more hands-off approach. Even so, the federal government gradually expanded its powers in the wake of important Supreme Court decisions. However, it was not until the New Deal in the 1930s that the federal government gained vast new powers.

Restraining National Power with Dual Federalism

dual federalism the system of government that prevailed in the United States from 1789 to 1937, in which most fundamental governmental powers were shared between the federal and state governments

As we have noted, the Constitution created two layers of government: the national government and the state governments. The consequences of this **dual federalism** are fundamental to the American system of government in theory and in practice; they have meant that states have done most of the fundamental governing. For evidence, look at Table 3.2, which lists the major types of public policies by which Americans were governed for the first century and a half under the Constitution. We call it the "traditional system" because it prevailed for much of American history and because it closely approximates the intentions of the framers of the Constitution.

Under the traditional system, the national government was quite small compared with both the state governments and the governments of other Western nations. Not only was it smaller than most governments of that time, but in fact it was also very narrowly specialized in the functions it performed. The national government built or sponsored the construction of roads, canals, and bridges (internal improvements). It provided cash subsidies to shippers and shipbuilders and distributed free or low-priced public land to encourage western settlement and business ventures. It placed relatively heavy taxes on imported goods (tariffs), not only to raise revenues but also to protect "infant industries" from competition from the more advanced European enterprises. It protected patents and provided for a common currency, which encouraged and facilitated enterprises and to expand markets.

What do these functions of the national government reveal? First, virtually all the functions were aimed at assisting commerce. It is quite appropriate to refer to the traditional American system as a "commercial republic." Second, virtually none of the national government's policies directly coerced citizens. The emphasis of governmental programs was on assistance, promotion, and encouragement—the allocation of land or capital to meet the needs of economic development.

Meanwhile, state legislatures were actively involved in economic regulation during the nineteenth century. In the United States, then and now, private property exists only in state laws and state court decisions regarding property, trespass, and real estate. American capitalism took its form from state property and trespass laws, and from state laws and court decisions regarding contracts, markets, credit, banking, incorporation, and insurance. Laws concerning slavery were a subdivision of property law in states where slavery existed. The practice of important

TABLE 3.2

The Federal System: Specialization of Governmental Functions in the Traditional System (1800–1933)

NATIONAL GOVERNMENT POLICIES (DOMESTIC)	STATE GOVERNMENT POLICIES	LOCAL GOVERNMENT POLICIES
Internal improvements	Property laws (including slavery)	Adaptation of state laws to local conditions
Subsidies	Estate and inheritance laws	Public works
Tariffs	Commerce laws	Contracts for public works
Public land disposal	Banking and credit laws	Licensing of public accommodation
Patents	Corporate laws	Assessible improvements
Currency	Insurance laws	Basic public services
	Family laws	
	Morality laws	
	Public health laws	
	Education laws	
	General penal laws	
	Eminent domain laws	
	Construction codes	
	Land-use laws	
	Water and mineral laws	
	Criminal procedure laws	
	Electoral and political party laws	
	Local government laws	
	Civil service laws	
	Occupations and professions laws	

professions, such as law and medicine, was (and is) illegal except as provided for by state law. To educate or not to educate a child has been a decision governed more by state laws than by parents. It is important to note also that virtually all criminal laws—regarding everything from trespass to murder—have been state laws. Most of the criminal laws adopted by Congress are concerned only with the District of Columbia and other federal territories.

All this (and more, as shown in the middle column of Table 3.2) demonstrates that most of the fundamental governing in the United States was done by the states. The contrast between national and state policies, as shown by Table 3.2, demonstrates the difference in the power vested in each. The list of items in the middle column could actually have been made longer. Moreover, each item on the list is a category of law that fills many volumes of statutes and court decisions.

This contrast between national and state governments is all the more impressive because it is basically what the framers of the Constitution intended. Since the 1930s the national government has expanded into local and intrastate matters far beyond what anyone could have foreseen in 1790, 1890, or even in the 1920s.

In 1815, President James Madison called for a federally funded program of "internal improvements," which was one of the few policy roles for the national government during the first half of the nineteenth century. By improving transportation through the construction of roads and canals, the government fostered the growth of the market economy and boosted federal power.

But this significant expansion of the national government did not alter the basic framework. The national government has become much larger, yet the states have continued to be central to the American system of government.

Herein lies probably the most important point of all: the fundamental impact of federalism on the way the United States is governed comes not from any particular provision of the Constitution but from the framework itself, which has determined which level of government does what and, through that, the political development of the country. By allowing state governments to do most of the fundamental governing, the Constitution saved the national government from many policy decisions that might have proven too divisive for a large and very young country. There is little doubt that if the Constitution had provided for a unitary rather than a federal system, the war over slavery would have come in 1789 or not long thereafter rather than in 1861; and if it had come that early, the South might very well have seceded and established a separate, slaveholding nation.

In helping the national government remain small and aloof from the most divisive issues of the day, federalism contributed significantly to the political stability of the nation, even as the social, economic, and political systems of many of the states and regions of the country were undergoing tremendous, profound, and sometimes violent, change.[12] As we shall see, some important aspects of federalism have changed, but the federal framework has survived two centuries and a devastating civil war.

Federalism and the Slow Growth of the National Government's Power

Having created the national government, and recognizing the potential for abuse of power, the states sought through federalism to constrain it. The "traditional system" of a weak national government prevailed for over a century, despite economic forces favoring its expansion and despite Supreme Court cases giving a pro-national interpretation to Article I, Section 8, of the Constitution.

That article delegates to Congress the power "to regulate commerce with foreign nations, and among the several States and with the Indian tribes." This **commerce clause** was consistently interpreted *in favor* of national power over the economy by the Supreme Court for most of the nineteenth century. The first and most important such case was *McCulloch v. Maryland* (1819), which involved the question of whether Congress had the power to charter a national bank—an explicit grant of power nowhere to be found in Article I, Section 8.[13] Chief Justice John Marshall answered that this power could be "implied" from other powers that were expressly delegated to Congress, such as the "powers to lay and collect taxes; to borrow money; to regulate commerce; and to declare and conduct a war."

By allowing Congress to use the necessary and proper clause to interpret its delegated powers expansively, the Supreme Court created the potential for an unprecedented increase in national government power. Marshall also concluded that whenever a state law conflicted with a federal law (as in the case of *McCulloch v. Maryland*), the state law would be deemed invalid since the Constitution states that "the Laws of the United States . . . shall be the supreme Law of the Land." Both parts of this great case are pro-national, yet Congress did not immediately seek to expand the policies of the national government.

Another major case, *Gibbons v. Ogden* (1824), reinforced this nationalistic interpretation of the Constitution. The important but relatively narrow issue was whether the state of New York could grant a monopoly to Robert Fulton's steamboat company to operate an exclusive service between New York and New Jersey. Chief Justice Marshall argued that New York state did not have the power to grant this particular monopoly, and so Marshall had to define what Article I, Section 8, meant by "commerce among the several states." He insisted that the definition was "comprehensive," extending to "every species of commercial intercourse." However, this comprehensiveness was limited "to that commerce which concerns more states than one." *Gibbons* is important because it established the supremacy of the national government in all matters affecting what later came to be called "interstate commerce."[14] But the precise meaning of interstate commerce would remain uncertain during several decades of constitutional discourse. Backed by the implied-powers decision in *McCulloch* and by the broad definition of "interstate commerce" in *Gibbons*, Article I, Section 8, was a source of power for the national government as long as Congress sought to facilitate commerce through subsidies, services, and land grants. Later in the nineteenth century, though, any effort of the national government to *regulate* commerce in such areas as fraud, the production of substandard goods, the use of child labor, or the existence of dangerous working conditions or long hours was declared unconstitutional by the Supreme Court as a violation of the concept of interstate commerce. Such legislation meant that the federal government was entering the factory and the workplace—local areas—and was attempting to regulate goods that had not yet passed into interstate commerce. To enter these local workplaces was to exercise police power—a power reserved to the states. No one questioned the power of the national government to regulate businesses that intrinsically involved interstate commerce, such as railroads, gas pipelines, and waterway transportation. But well into the twentieth century the Supreme Court used the concept of interstate commerce as a barrier against most efforts by Congress to regulate local conditions.

This aspect of federalism prevailed during an epoch of tremendous economic development, the period between the Civil War and the 1930s. It gave the American economy a freedom from federal government control that closely approximated the ideal of free enterprise. The economy was never entirely free, of course; in

commerce clause Article I, Section 8, of the Constitution, which delegates to Congress the power "to regulate commerce with foreign nations, and among the several States and with the Indian tribes." This clause was interpreted by the Supreme Court in favor of national power over the economy

fact, entrepreneurs themselves did not want complete freedom from government. They needed law and order. They needed a stable currency. They needed courts and police to enforce contracts and prevent trespass. They needed roads, canals, and railroads. But federalism, as interpreted by the Supreme Court for 70 years after the Civil War, made it possible for business to have its cake and eat it, too: entrepreneurs enjoyed the benefits of national policies facilitating commerce and were protected by the courts from policies regulating commerce by protecting the rights of consumers and workers.[15]

All this changed after 1937, when the Supreme Court issued a series of decisions that laid the groundwork for a much stronger federal government. Most significant was the Court's dramatic expansion of the commerce clause. By throwing out the old distinction between interstate and intrastate commerce, the Court converted the commerce clause from a source of limitations to a source of power for the national government. The Court upheld acts of Congress protecting the rights of employees to organize and engage in collective bargaining, regulating the amount of farmland in cultivation, extending low-interest credit to small businesses and farmers, and restricting the activities of corporations dealing in the stock market. The Court also upheld many other laws that contributed to the construction of

In 1916 the national government passed the Keating-Owen Child Labor Act, which excluded from interstate commerce all goods manufactured by children under age 14. The act was ruled unconstitutional by the Supreme Court, and the regulation of child labor remained in the hands of state governments until the 1930s.

the "welfare state."[16] With these rulings, the Court decisively signaled that the era of dual federalism was over. In the future, Congress would have very broad powers to regulate activity in the states.

The Changing Role of the States

As we have seen, the Constitution's commerce clause contained the seeds of a very expansive national government. For much of the nineteenth century, federal power remained limited. The Tenth Amendment was used to bolster arguments in favor of **states' rights**, which in their extreme version claimed that the states did not have to submit to national laws whenever they believed the national government had exceeded its authority. Prior to the Civil War, sharp differences between the North and the South over tariffs and slavery gave rise to arguments supporting nullification. Most fully articulated by John C. Calhoun, vice president under Andrew Jackson and later a senator from South Carolina, the doctrine of nullification proposed that states were not bound by federal laws that they considered unconstitutional. Such arguments were voiced less often after the Civil War, but the Supreme Court continued to use the Tenth Amendment to strike down laws that it thought exceeded national power, including the Civil Rights Act passed in 1875.

In the early twentieth century, however, reformers began to press for national regulations to limit the power of large corporations and to preserve the health and welfare of citizens. The Supreme Court approved some of these laws, but it struck down others, including a law combating child labor. The Court stated that the law violated the Tenth Amendment because only states should have the power to regulate conditions of employment. By the late 1930s, however, the Supreme Court had approved such an expansion of federal power that the Tenth Amendment appeared irrelevant. The desire to promote equal working conditions across the country had elevated the federal government over the states. In fact, in 1941, Justice Harlan Fiske Stone declared that the Tenth Amendment was simply a "truism," that it had no real meaning.[17]

states' rights the principle that the states should oppose the increasing authority of the national government. This principle was most popular in the period before the Civil War

States' rights have been embraced by many causes in the past 50 years. Governor George Wallace of Alabama, a vocal supporter of states' rights, defiantly turned away U.S. attorney general Nicholas Katzenbach, who tried to enroll two black students at the University of Alabama at Tuscaloosa in 1963.

International Trade Agreements and the States

The Constitution reserves for the federal government the power to make foreign policy and to enter into treaties. Yet the expansion of the global economy over the past three decades has increased the importance of the international arena for state and local governments. For states, the expansion of international trade offers new opportunities to promote economic development but also presents frustrations. This is because international trade agreements may tie the hands of states and because states have little formal voice in these agreements.

One of the most important such trade agreements is the North American Free Trade Agreement (NAFTA), a treaty signed by Canada, the United States, and Mexico in 1992 to open trade across the national borders of these three countries. It also created new trade rules that each national government is obligated to follow. Although U.S. state governments were not involved in creating these trade rules, the rules may significantly restrict their own policies. Other trade agreements, such as those negotiated through the World Trade Organization (WTO), also may limit what American states can do.

Trade agreements that have recently aroused concern in the states are proposed rulings that would label many common state procurement policies as barriers to trade and therefore unenforceable. Procurement policies determine who can sell goods and provide services to the state. States often impose conditions on the companies with which they do business. For example, some states have policies requiring them to buy local or American-made products in an effort to reduce the offshoring of jobs. Other states impose requirements aimed at improving the environment, including provisions for buying goods with recycled content or doing business with firms that use renewable energy sources. These conditions vary from state to state. As Maine's then-governor John Baldacci noted in a 2006 letter to the U.S. trade

representative, "The state of Maine's procurement laws have been developed to protect the interests of Maine's citizens and businesses and to reflect the state's commitment to spend its citizens' tax dollars in a socially and environmentally responsible way."[a]

The states have challenged the proposed national rules in international trade agreement as an infringement on state sovereignty. And some states have started to pass legislation to ensure that trade agreements are scrutinized by the state legislature. In 2007 the Hawaii state legislature passed legislation to ensure that only the state legislature could approve or reject the terms relating to procurement in international trade agreements. It became the third state to pass such legislation, joining Rhode Island and Maryland.

One of the major complaints that states have is that they have no voice in

the process of formulating trade agreement provisions even when such agreements significantly limit their sovereignty and regulatory authority. Five state legislatures (California, Maine, Minnesota, North Carolina, and Washington) have created formal committees on international trade and federalism. These committees assess the impact of trade agreements and gain expert and constituency views about the policies. They are also a point of contact for the state legislatures, the U.S. Trade Representative, and the members of Congress on issues related to trade and economic development. The potential for trade agreements to restrict the traditional decision-making powers of the states means that, in the future, states will have to consider the international repercussions of their actions as a normal part of state lawmaking.

[a]www.citizens.org (accessed 9/25/07).

for critical analysis

1. How do international treaties such as NAFTA and international organizations such as the World Trade Organization (WTO) affect the sovereign powers of the states?

2. What are states doing to ensure that their interests are considered when the federal government enters into international trade agreements?

Yet the idea that some powers should be reserved to the states did not go away. One reason is that groups with substantive policy interests often support states' rights as a means for achieving their policy goals. For example, in the 1950s, southern opponents of the civil rights movement revived the idea of states' rights to support racial segregation. In 1956, 96 southern members of Congress issued a "Southern Manifesto" in which they declared that southern states were not constitutionally bound by Supreme Court decisions outlawing racial segregation. They believed that states' rights should override individual rights to liberty and formal equality. With the eventual triumph of the civil rights movement, the slogan of "states' rights" became tarnished by its association with racial inequality.

The 1990s saw a revival of interest in the Tenth Amendment and important Supreme Court decisions limiting federal power. Much of the interest in the Tenth Amendment stemmed from conservatives who believed that a strong federal government encroached on individual liberties. They believed such freedoms were better protected by returning more power to the states through the process of devolution. In 1996, Bob Dole, the Republican presidential candidate, carried a copy of the Tenth Amendment in his pocket as he campaigned, pulling it out to read it aloud at rallies.[18] The Supreme Court's 1995 ruling in *United States v. Lopez* fueled further interest in the Tenth Amendment.[19] In that case, the Court, stating that Congress had exceeded its authority under the commerce clause, struck down a federal law that barred handguns near schools. This was the first time since the New Deal that the Court had limited congressional powers in this way. In 1997 the Court again relied on the Tenth Amendment to limit federal power in *Printz v. United States*.[20] The decision declared unconstitutional a provision of the Brady Handgun Violence Prevention Act that required state and local law-enforcement officials to conduct background checks on handgun purchasers. The Court declared that this provision violated state sovereignty guaranteed by the Tenth Amendment because it required state and local officials to administer a federal regulatory program.

The expansion of the power of the national government has not left the states powerless. State governments continue to make important laws. No better demonstration of the continuing influence of the federal framework can be offered than that the middle column of Table 3.2 is still a fairly accurate characterization of state government today. In each of these domains, however, states must now share power with the federal government.

for critical analysis

How have Supreme Court decisions affected the balance of power between the federal government and the states? Has the Supreme Court favored the federal government or the states?

Who Does What? Public Spending and the Federal Framework

Analyze major developments in the federal framework since the 1930s

Questions about how to divide responsibilities between the states and the national government first arose more than 200 years ago, when the framers wrote the Constitution to create a stronger union. But they did not solve the issue of who should do what. There is no "right" answer to that question; each generation of Americans has provided its own answer. In recent decades, many Americans have grown distrustful of the federal government and have supported giving more responsibility to the states.[21] Even so, they still want the federal government to set standards, promote equality, and provide security.

In political debates about the division of responsibility, some people argue for a strong federal role to set national standards, whereas others say the states should do more. These two goals are not necessarily at odds. The key is to find the right balance. In this section we will look at how the balance has shifted, and then we will consider current efforts to reshape the relationship between the national government and the states.

The New Deal

The door to increased federal action opened when states proved unable to cope with the demands brought on by the depression. Before the Great Depression of the 1930s, states and localities took responsibility for addressing the needs of the poor, usually through private charity. But the extent of the need created by the depression quickly exhausted local and state capacities. By 1932, 25 percent of the workforce was unemployed. The jobless lost their homes and settled into camps all over the country, called "Hoovervilles," after President Herbert Hoover. Elected in 1928, the year before the depression hit, Hoover steadfastly maintained that the federal government could do little to alleviate the misery caused by the depression. It was a matter for state and local governments, he said.

Yet demands mounted for the federal government to take action. In Congress, some Democrats proposed that the federal government finance public works to aid the economy and put people back to work. Other members of Congress introduced legislation to provide federal grants to the states to assist them in their relief efforts. Most of these measures failed to win congressional approval or were vetoed by President Hoover.

When Franklin Delano Roosevelt took office in 1933, he energetically threw the federal government into the business of fighting the depression through a number

The vast new programs created as part of the New Deal expanded the federal government's power. Programs like the Works Progress Administration (WPA), which provided jobs for the unemployed, were established to address the Great Depression, but the overall expansion of the national government lasted even after the depression ended.

of proposals known collectively as the New Deal. He proposed a variety of temporary measures to provide federal relief and work programs. Most of the programs he proposed were to be financed by the federal government but administered by the states. In addition to these temporary measures, Roosevelt presided over the creation of several important federal programs designed to provide future economic security for Americans. The New Deal signaled the rise of a more active national government.

Federal Grants

For the most part, the new national programs that the Roosevelt administration developed did not directly take power away from the states. Instead, Washington typically redirected states by offering them **grants-in-aid**, whereby Congress appropriates money to state and local governments on the condition that the money be spent for a particular purpose defined by Congress (see Figure 3.1). Franklin Roosevelt's New Deal expanded the range of grants-in-aid into social programs, providing grants to the states for financial assistance to poor children. Congress added more grants after World War II, creating new programs to help states fund activities such as providing school lunches and building highways. Sometimes the national government required state or local governments to match the national contribution dollar for dollar, but in some programs, such as the development of the interstate highway system, the congressional grants provided 90 percent of the cost of the program.

grants-in-aid programs through which Congress provides money to state and local governments on the condition that the funds be employed for purposes defined by the federal government

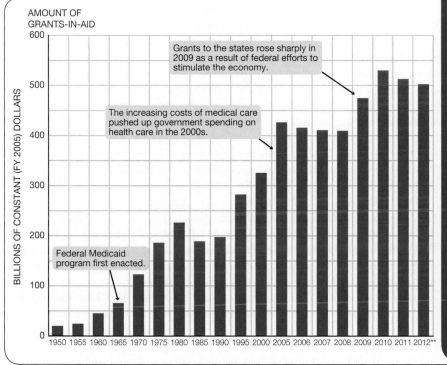

AMOUNT OF GRANTS-IN-AID

BILLIONS OF CONSTANT (FY 2005) DOLLARS

Grants to the states rose sharply in 2009 as a result of federal efforts to stimulate the economy.

The increasing costs of medical care pushed up government spending on health care in the 2000s.

Federal Medicaid program first enacted.

FIGURE 3.1

Historical Trend of Federal Grants-in-Aid,* 1950–2012

Spending on federal grants-in-aid to the states and local governments has grown dramatically since 1990. These increases reflect the growing public expectations about what government should do. What has been the most important cause of the steady increase in these grants?

*Excludes outlays for national defense, international affairs, and net interest.
**Estimate.

SOURCE: U.S. Budget for Fiscal Year 2013, *Historical Tables*, Table 12.2, www.gpo.gov/fdsys/pkg/BUDGET-2013-TAB/pdf/BUDGET-2013-TAB.pdf (accessed 6/10/12).

categorical grants congressional grants given to states and localities on the condition that expenditures be limited to a problem or group specified by law

These types of federal grants-in-aid are also called **categorical grants** because the national government determines the purposes, or categories, for which the money can be used. For the most part, the categorical grants created before the 1960s simply helped the states perform their traditional functions.[22] During the 1960s, however, the national role expanded and the number of categorical grants increased dramatically. For example, during the 89th Congress (1965–66) alone, the number of categorical grant-in-aid programs grew from 221 to 379.[23] The *value* of categorical grants also has risen dramatically, increasing from $2.3 billion in 1950 to an estimated $467 billion in 2008. The grants authorized during the 1960s announced national purposes much more strongly than did earlier grants. One of the most important—and expensive—was the federal Medicaid program, which provides states with grants to pay for medical care for the poor, the disabled, and many nursing home residents.

project grants grant programs in which state and local governments submit proposals to federal agencies and for which funding is provided on a competitive basis

formula grants grants-in-aid in which a formula is used to determine the amount of federal funds a state or local government will receive

Many of the categorical grants enacted during the 1960s were **project grants**, which require state and local governments to submit proposals to federal agencies. In contrast to the older, **formula grants**, which used a formula (composed of such elements as need and state and local capacities) to distribute funds, the project grants made funding available on a competitive basis. Federal agencies would give grants to the proposals they judged to be the best. In this way, the national government acquired substantial control over which state and local governments got money, how much they got, and how they spent it.

Cooperative Federalism

cooperative federalism a type of federalism existing since the New Deal era in which grants-in-aid have been used strategically to encourage states and localities (without commanding them) to pursue nationally defined goals. Also known as "intergovernmental cooperation"

The growth of categorical grants created a new kind of federalism. If the traditional system of two sovereigns performing highly different functions could be called dual federalism, historians of federalism suggest that the system since the New Deal could be called **cooperative federalism**. The political scientist Morton Grodzins characterized this as a move from "layer cake federalism" to "marble cake federalism,"[24] in which intergovernmental cooperation and sharing have blurred a once-clear distinguishing line, making it difficult to say where the national government ends and the state and local governments begin (see Figure 3.2). Figure 3.3 demonstrates the financial basis of the "marble cake" idea.

For a while in the 1960s, however, it appeared as if the state governments would become increasingly irrelevant to American federalism. Many of the new federal grants bypassed the states and instead sent money directly to local governments and even to local nonprofit organizations. The theme heard repeatedly in Washington was that the states simply could not be trusted to carry out national purposes.[25]

One of the reasons that Washington distrusted the states was the way African American citizens were treated in the South. The southern states' forthright defense of segregation, justified on the grounds of states' rights, helped tarnish the image of the states as the civil rights movement gained momentum. The national officials who planned the War on Poverty during the 1960s pointed to the racial exclusion practiced in the southern states as a reason for bypassing state governments. The political scientist James Sundquist described how this thinking affected the War on Poverty: "In the drafting of the Economic Opportunity Act, an 'Alabama syndrome' developed. Any suggestion within the poverty task force that the states be given a role in the administration of the act was met with the question, 'Do you want to give that kind of power to [then–Alabama governor] George Wallace?'"[26]

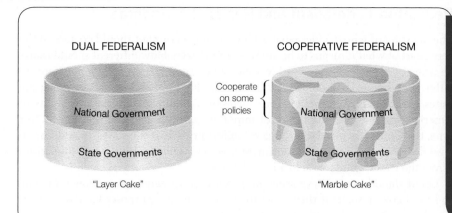

DUAL FEDERALISM

National Government

State Governments

"Layer Cake"

COOPERATIVE FEDERALISM

Cooperate on some policies

National Government

State Governments

"Marble Cake"

FIGURE 3.2

Dual versus Cooperative Federalism

In layer cake federalism, the responsibilities of the national government and state governments are clearly separated. In marble cake federalism, national policies, state policies, and local policies overlap in many areas.

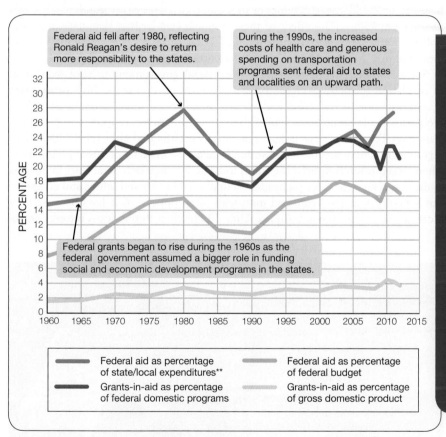

Federal aid fell after 1980, reflecting Ronald Reagan's desire to return more responsibility to the states.

During the 1990s, the increased costs of health care and generous spending on transportation programs sent federal aid to states and localities on an upward path.

Federal grants began to rise during the 1960s as the federal government assumed a bigger role in funding social and economic development programs in the states.

PERCENTAGE

1960 1965 1970 1975 1980 1985 1990 1995 2000 2005 2010 2015

Federal aid as percentage of state/local expenditures**

Federal aid as percentage of federal budget

Grants-in-aid as percentage of federal domestic programs

Grants-in-aid as percentage of gross domestic product

FIGURE 3.3

The Rise, Decline, and Recovery of Federal Aid, 1960–2012*

The level of federal aid has varied over the past several decades as program costs and politics have affected the role the national government plays in funding state and local services. The data in this figure show a rise, decline, and recovery of federal aid. What factors contributed to each of these trends?

*Data for 2012 estimated.
**Data for 2012 not available.

SOURCES: Office of Management and Budget, www.gpoaccess.gov (accessed 6/10/12), and U.S. Federal Budget for Fiscal Year 2013, *Analytical Perspectives*, Table 18.2, www.gpo.gov/fdsys/pkg/BUDGET-2013-PER/pdf/BUDGET-2013-PER.pdf (accessed 6/10/12).

Yet even though many national policies of the 1960s bypassed the states, other new programs, such as Medicaid—the health program for the poor—relied on state governments for their implementation. In addition, as the national government expanded existing programs run by the states, states had to take on more responsibility. These new responsibilities meant that the states were playing a very important role in the federal system.

Regulated Federalism and National Standards

The question of who decides what each level of government should do goes to the very heart of what it means to be an American citizen. How different should things be when one crosses a state line? In what policy areas is it acceptable for states to differ? In what areas should states be similar? How much inequality among the states is acceptable? Supreme Court decisions about the fundamental rights of American citizens provide the most important answers to these questions. Over time, the Court has pushed for greater uniformity across the states. In addition to legal decisions, the national government uses two other tools to create similarities across the states: grants-in-aid and regulations.

Grants-in-aid, as we have seen, are incentives: Congress gives money to state and local governments if they agree to spend it for the purposes Congress specifies. But as Congress began to enact legislation in new areas, such as environmental policy, it also imposed additional regulations on states and localities. Some political scientists call this a move toward **regulated federalism**.[27] The national government began to set standards of conduct or to require the states to set standards that met national guidelines. The effect of these national standards is that state and local policies in the areas of environmental protection, social services, and education are more uniform from coast to coast than are other nationally funded policies.

Some national standards require the federal government to take over areas of regulation formerly overseen by state or local governments. Such **preemption** occurs when state and local actions are found to be inconsistent with federal requirements. In some cases, federal laws and regulations are more stringent than state laws. For example, as federal regulations proliferated after the 1970s, Washington increasingly preempted state and local action in many different policy areas. These preemptions required the states to abide by tougher federal rules in policies as diverse as air and water pollution, occupational health and safety, and access for the handicapped. The regulated industries often oppose such laws because they increase the cost of doing business. After 1994, when Republicans retook control

regulated federalism a form of federalism in which Congress imposes legislation on states and localities, requiring them to meet national standards

preemption the principle that allows the national government to override state or local actions in certain policy areas; in foreign policy, the willingness to strike first in order to prevent an enemy attack

In 2005 the Supreme Court ruled that the federal government had the right to prosecute individuals for using medical marijuana, even in states that had made such use legal. Despite the Court's ruling, some states have continued to permit the dispensing and use of medical marijuana.

of Congress, the federal government used its preemption power in business's favor, limiting the ability of states to tax and regulate industry. For example, the Internet Tax Freedom Act (ITFA), first enacted by Congress in 1998 and subsequently renewed, prohibits states and localities from taxing Internet access services.

Congress is not the only federal body that can preempt the states; federal regulatory agencies can also issue rules that override state law. One controversial case involved a 2006 Food and Drug Administration drug-labeling rule preempting state laws that allow individuals to sue drug companies in state courts. Opponents—many of them trial lawyers—charged that such rules amounted to "stealth preemption" that "will deprive consumers of their right to hold negligent corporations accountable for injuries caused by defective products."[28] Supporters claimed that the rules were a proper use of federal authority. Although the Republicans came to power promising to grant more responsibility to the states, they ended up reducing state control in many areas by preemption.

State and local governments often contest federal preemptions. For example, in 2001, Attorney General John Ashcroft declared that Oregon's law permitting doctor-assisted suicide was illegal under federal drug regulations. In January 2006 the Supreme Court ruled in a 6–3 vote that the attorney general did not have the authority to outlaw the Oregon law.[29] Individuals have also challenged federal preemption. In 2009 the Supreme Court ruled against a drug manufacturer and in favor of a woman whose arm had to be amputated after she was improperly injected with a drug designed to counter nausea.[30] Although the drug company knew that such complications could arise, it argued that it was not responsible for the amputation because federal regulations did not require it to warn against this danger in labeling the drug. The Court, however, found the company liable for the damage. In its decision, the Court made it clear that federal regulations could not preempt state consumer protections and that states had the power to adopt stricter protections than those of the federal government.

In 2009, after only a few months in office, President Obama reversed the Bush administration's use of federal regulations to limit state laws. Under the new policy, federal regulations should preempt state laws only in extraordinary cases. The president directed agency leaders to review the regulations that had been put in place over the past ten years and consider amending them if they interfered with the "legitimate prerogatives of the states."[31] But as we will see below, the Obama administration did use its power of preemption to challenge state immigration laws, charging that states were making laws in a domain reserved for federal authority.

The growth of national standards has created some new problems and has raised questions about how far federal standardization should go. One problem that emerged in the 1980s was the increase in **unfunded mandates**—the product of a Democratic Congress that wanted to achieve liberal social objectives and Republican presidents who opposed increased social spending. Between 1983 and 1991, Congress mandated standards in many policy areas, including social services and environmental regulations, without providing additional funds to help the states meet those standards. Altogether, Congress enacted 27 laws that imposed new regulations or required states to expand existing programs.[32] For example, in the late 1980s, Congress ordered the states to extend the coverage provided by Medicaid, the medical insurance program for the poor. The aim was to make the program serve more people, particularly poor children, and to expand services. But Congress did not supply additional funding to help states meet these new requirements; the states had to shoulder the increased financial burden themselves.

for critical analysis

Is federal preemption of local laws desirable? Is preemption justified for some issues more than for others?

unfunded mandates regulations or conditions for receiving grants that impose costs on state and local governments for which they are not reimbursed by the federal government

States and localities quickly began to protest the cost of unfunded mandates. Although it is very hard to determine the exact cost of federal regulations, the Congressional Budget Office estimated that between 1983 and 1990, new federal regulations cost states and localities between $8.9 and $12.7 billion.[33] States complained that mandates took up so much of their budgets that they were not able to set their own priorities. These burdens became part of a rallying cry to reduce the power of the federal government—a cry that took center stage when a Republican Congress was elected in 1994. One of the first measures the new Congress passed was an act to limit the cost of unfunded mandates, the Unfunded Mandates Reform Act (UMRA). Under this law, Congress must estimate the cost of any proposal it believes will require more than $50 million.

New national problems inevitably raise the question of "who pays?" Recently, concern about unfunded mandates has arisen around health care reform. The major health care reform enacted during Obama's first two years as president, the Affordable Care Act of 2010 called for a major expansion of Medicaid. But because Medicaid is partly funded by the states, any major increase in the number of Medicaid recipients could impose a significant fiscal burden on the states. Although the law provided additional federal aid to support the new requirements, the Medicaid provisions became a target for state challenges to the health care law. One of the central claims in the 26 states' lawsuits charged that the federal government did not have the power to withhold Medicaid funds from states that did not implement the new expansions. Although a lower court rejected the states' arguments, the Supreme Court included the Medicaid challenge when it agreed to hear the case.[34] As we saw in the introduction to this chapter, the Court ultimately ruled that states could decline to expand Medicaid coverage without losing their existing Medicaid funds. After the Court's decision, a handful of Republican governors announced that they would not implement the expanded coverage. Whatever they decide to do, it is clear that the Court's decision has injected a whole new set of issues into the question of "who pays."

New Federalism and State Control

In 1970 the mayor of Oakland, California, told Congress that his city had 22 separate employment and training programs but that few poor residents were being trained for jobs that were available in the local labor market.[35] National programs had proliferated as Congress enacted many small grants, but little effort was made to coordinate or adapt programs to local needs. Today many governors argue for more control over such national grant programs. They complain that national grants do not allow for enough local flexibility and instead take a "one size fits all" approach.[36] These criticisms point to a fundamental challenge in American federalism: how to get the best results for the money spent. Do some divisions of responsibility between states and the federal government work better than others? Since the 1970s, as states have become more capable of administering large-scale programs, the idea of **devolution**—transferring responsibility for policy from the federal government to the states and localities—has become popular.

Proponents of more state authority have looked to **block grants** as a way of reducing federal control. Block grants are federal grants that allow the states considerable leeway in spending federal money. President Nixon led the first push for block grants in the early 1970s, as part of his **New Federalism**. Nixon's approach consolidated programs in the areas of job training, community development, and social services into three large block grants. These grants imposed some conditions on states and localities as to how the money should be spent, but not the narrow

devolution a policy to remove a program from one level of government by delegating it or passing it down to a lower level of government, such as from the national government to the state and local governments

block grants federal grants-in-aid that allow states considerable discretion in how the funds are spent

New Federalism attempts by Presidents Nixon and Reagan to return power to the states through block grants

regulations contained in the categorical grants. In addition, Congress provided an important new form of federal assistance to state and local governments, called **general revenue sharing**. Revenue sharing provided money to local governments and counties with no strings attached; localities could spend the money as they wished. In enacting revenue sharing, Washington acknowledged both the critical role that state and local governments play in implementing national priorities and their need for increased funding and enhanced flexibility in order to carry out that role (see Figure 3.4). Reagan's version of New Federalism also looked to block grants. Like Nixon, Reagan wanted to reduce the national government's control and return power to the states. But unlike Nixon, whose block grants increased federal spending, Reagan's block grants cut federal funding by 12 percent. His view was that the states could spend their own funds to make up the difference, if they chose to do so. Revenue sharing was also eliminated during the Reagan administration, leaving localities to fend for themselves. In all, Congress created 12 new block grants between 1981 and 1990.[37]

The Republican Congress elected in 1994 took this strategy even further, making substantial cuts in federal programs as well as supporting block grants. Their biggest success was the 1996 welfare reform law, which delegated to states important new responsibilities. Most of the other major proposed block grants or spending reductions, however, failed to pass Congress or were vetoed by President Clinton. The Republican congressional leadership had found that it was much easier to promise a "devolution revolution" than to deliver on that promise.[38]

Neither block grants nor reduced federal funding have proven to be magic solutions to the problems of federalism. For one thing, there is always a trade-off between accountability—that is, whether the states are using funds for the purposes intended—and flexibility. If the objective is to have accountable and efficient government, it is not clear that state bureaucracies are any more efficient or more capable than national agencies. In Mississippi, for example, the state Department of Human Services spent money from the child care block grant for office furniture

general revenue sharing the process by which one unit of government yields a portion of its tax income to another unit of government, according to an established formula. Revenue sharing typically involves the national government providing money to state governments

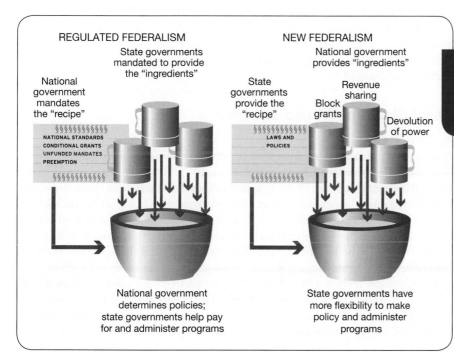

REGULATED FEDERALISM

State governments mandated to provide the "ingredients"

National government mandates the "recipe"

§§§§§§§§§§§§
NATIONAL STANDARDS
CONDITIONAL GRANTS
UNFUNDED MANDATES
PREEMPTION

§§§§§§§§§§§§

National government determines policies; state governments help pay for and administer programs

NEW FEDERALISM

National government provides "ingredients"

State governments provide the "recipe"

Block grants

Revenue sharing

Devolution of power

§§§§§§§§§§§§
LAWS AND
POLICIES

§§§§§§§§§§§§

State governments have more flexibility to make policy and administer programs

FIGURE 3.4

Regulated versus New Federalism

The debate over national-versus-state control of speed limits arose in 1973, when gas prices skyrocketed and supplies became scarce. Drivers nationwide were forced to wait in long lines at gas stations. The federal government responded to the gas crisis by instituting a national 55-mile-per-hour speed limit.

and designer salt and pepper shakers that cost $37.50 a pair. As one Mississippi state legislator said, "I've seen too many years of good ol' boy politics to know they shouldn't [transfer money to the states] without stricter controls and requirements."[39] Even after block grants were created, Congress reimposed regulations in order to increase the states' accountability.

At times the federal government has also moved to limit state discretion over spending in cases where it thinks states are too generous. For example, in 2007, President Bush issued regulations that prevented states from providing benefits under the State Children's Health Insurance Program (SCHIP) to children in families well above the poverty line. The Bush administration also barred states from providing chemotherapy to illegal immigrants, who are guaranteed emergency medical treatment under Medicaid.[40] These new rules embroiled states and the federal government in sharp conflicts over state discretion in spending decisions, once the hallmark of New Federalism.

Devolution: For Whose Benefit?

As Figure 3.5 indicates, federalism has changed dramatically over the course of American history. Finding the right balance among states and the federal government is an evolving challenge for American democracy, and since the expansion of the national government in the 1930s, questions about "who does what" have frequently provoked conflict. Why does such an apparently simple choice set off such highly charged political debate? One reason is that many decisions about federal-versus-state responsibility have implications for who benefits from government action.

Let's consider the benefits of federal control versus devolution in the realm of **redistributive programs**—programs designed primarily for the benefit of the poor. Many political scientists and economists maintain that states and localities should not be in charge of redistributive programs. They argue that since states and local governments have to compete with one another, they do not have the incentive to spend their money on the needy people in their areas. Instead, they want to keep

redistributive programs economic policies designed to control the economy through taxing and spending, with the goal of benefiting the poor

taxes low and spend money on things that promote economic development.[41] In this situation, states might engage in a "race to the bottom": if one state cuts assistance to the poor, neighboring states will institute similar or deeper cuts both to reduce expenditures and to discourage poorer people from moving to their states. As one New York legislator put it, "The concern we have is that unless we make our welfare system and our tax and regulatory system competitive with the states around us, we will have too many disincentives for business to move here. Welfare is a big part of that."[42]

In 1996, when Congress enacted major welfare reform, it followed a different logic. By changing welfare from a combined federal-state program into a block grant to the states, Congress gave the states more responsibility for programs that serve the poor. Supporters of the change hoped to reduce welfare spending and argued that states could act as "laboratories of democracy" by experimenting with many different approaches in order to find those that best met the needs of their citizens.[43] As states altered their welfare programs in the wake of the new law, they did indeed design diverse approaches. For example, Minnesota adopted an incentive-based approach that offers extra assistance to families that take low-wage jobs, while six other states imposed very strict time limits on receiving benefits, allowing welfare recipients less than the five-year limit in the federal legislation. After the passage of the law, welfare rolls declined dramatically. On average, they declined by more than half from their peak in 1994; in 12 states the decline was 70 percent or higher. Politicians have cited these statistics to claim that the poor have benefited from greater state control of welfare, yet most studies have found that the majority of those leaving welfare remain in poverty.

In some decisions about federalism, local concerns are overridden in the name of the national interest. The question of speed limits, traditionally a state and local responsibility, provides an example. In 1973, at the height of the oil shortage, Congress passed legislation to withhold federal highway funds from states that did not adopt a maximum speed limit of 55 miles per hour (mph) in order to reduce fuel consumption. Although Congress had not formally taken over the authority to set speed limits, the power of its purse was so important that every state adopted the new speed limit. As the crisis faded, concern about energy conservation diminished. The national speed limit lost much of its support, even though it was found to have reduced the number of traffic deaths. In 1995, Congress repealed the penalties for higher speed limits, and states once again became free to set their own speed limits. Many states with large rural areas raised their maximum to 75 mph; Montana initially set unlimited speeds in its rural areas during daylight hours. Research indicates that the number of highway deaths has indeed risen in the states that increased the limits.[44]

Because the division of responsibility in the federal system has important implications for who benefits, few conflicts over state-versus-national control will ever be settled once and for all. New evidence about the costs and benefits of different arrangements provides fuel for ongoing debates about what are properly the states' responsibilities and what the federal government should do. Likewise, changes in the political

In 1995, Congress removed its speed limit restrictions and allowed states to raise the limit above 55 miles per hour without losing federal highway funds. As a result, speed limits went up on many highways.

FIGURE 3.5
The Changing Federal Framework

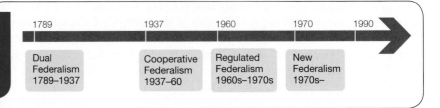

1789	1937	1960	1970	1990
Dual Federalism 1789–1937	Cooperative Federalism 1937–60	Regulated Federalism 1960s–1970s	New Federalism 1970s–	

control of the national government usually provoke a rethinking of responsibilities as new leaders seek to alter federal arrangements for the benefit of the groups they represent.

Federalism since 2000

During the past 13 years, many of the most controversial issues in American politics—including the appropriate size of public social spending, the rights and benefits of immigrants (legal as well as undocumented), government response to global climate change, and questions about whether and how government should regulate business and moral behavior—have been fought through the federal system. Politicians of all stripes regularly turn to the federal government to override decisions made by states. Likewise, when the federal government proves unable or unwilling to act, activists and politicians try to achieve their goals in states and localities. In many cases, it is up to the courts to decide which level of government should have the final say.

Although conservatives proclaim their preference for a small federal government and their support for more state autonomy, in fact they often expand the federal government and limit state autonomy. During the presidency of George W. Bush, the growth of government, the activist, free-spending Republican Congress, and a series of Supreme Court rulings supporting federal power over the states made it clear that conservatives do not always support small government; nor do they always favor returning power to the states. Once in power, many conservatives discovered not only that they needed a strong federal government to respond to public demands but also that they could use federal power to advance conservative policy goals.

For President Bush, the importance of a strong federal government dawned with force after the terrorist attacks in 2001. Aware that the American public was looking to Washington for protection, Bush worked with Congress to pass the Patriot Act, which greatly increased the surveillance powers of the federal government. A year later he created the enormous new federal Department of Homeland Security.

President Bush also expanded federal control and increased spending in policy areas far removed from concerns about security. The 2001 No Child Left Behind Act introduced unprecedented federal intervention in public education, traditionally a state and local responsibility. New, detailed federal testing requirements and provisions stipulating how states should treat failing schools were major expansions of federal authority in education. When a number of states threatened to defy some of the new federal requirements, Bush's Department of Education relaxed its tough stance and became more flexible in enforcing the act. The Obama administration increased flexibility even more by granting waivers to 19 states. The waivers released the states from the federal mandates around school accountability and performance, replacing them with state measures.

for critical analysis

The role of the national government has changed significantly from the Founding era to the present. Do you think the framers of the Constitution would be pleased with the current balance of power between the national government and the state governments?

In the Supreme Court, too, many decisions began to support a stronger federal role over the states. This was surprising to many observers, because in the 1990s it had appeared that the Rehnquist Court was embarked on a "federalism revolution" designed to return more power to the states. Instead, in several key decisions, the Court reaffirmed the power of the federal government. Decisions to uphold the federal Family and Medical Leave Act and the Americans with Disabilities Act asserted federal authority against state claims of immunity from the acts. In one important 2005 case, the Court upheld the right of Congress to ban medical marijuana, even though 11 states had legalized its use. Overturning a lower court ruling that said Congress did not have authority to regulate marijuana when it had been grown for noncommercial purposes in a single state, the Supreme Court ruled that the federal government did have the power to regulate use of all marijuana under the commerce clause. Even so, by 2011, 15 states had legalized medical marijuana. Amid this legal confusion, a medical marijuana industry began to flourish in states that allowed medical use of the drug. However, when the federal government unexpectedly began to crack down on marijuana dispensaries in 2011, some states began to reconsider their laws.[45]

One closely watched federalism case in 2006 was the challenge to Oregon's "right to die" law, which allows doctors to prescribe lethal doses of medicine for terminally ill patients who request it. Challengers claimed the law was illegal because Congress has the right to outlaw such use of drugs under the Controlled Substances Act, which regulates prescription drugs. In a 6–3 decision, the Court ruled in Oregon's favor.[46] Despite the ruling, only Washington state followed in Oregon's footsteps to make physician-assisted suicide legal. When challenged, other states, including Florida and Alaska, have upheld state prohibitions on physician-assisted suicide.

In other policy areas, states and localities have forged their own policies because the federal government has not acted. One of the most controversial of these issues is immigration legislation. In the first half of 2011, for example, state legislatures introduced more than 1,592 bills related to immigration.[47] Many state and local laws that govern immigration are not controversial, but some raise critical questions about what is the federal role and what are the responsibilities of state and local governments. In April 2010, Arizona enacted an extremely controversial immigration measure requiring immigrants to carry identity documents and requiring police to ask about immigration status when they stop drivers they suspect of being illegal immigrants. The federal Department of Justice joined several other groups in challenging the law, and the courts struck down the strongest provisions of the law. Even so, several states enacted similar laws. By 2012 the Department of Justice had sued three additional states—Alabama, South Carolina, and Utah—charging that their immigration laws were preempted by federal law. In the words of Attorney General Eric Holder, "It is clearly unconstitutional for a state to set its own immigration policy."[48] The Alabama law attracted national attention for its sweeping provisions, which made the failure to carry immigration papers a crime, gave police broad powers to stop suspected illegal immigrants, required employers and landlords to verify immigration status, and forced schools to check the legal status of students and their parents. In 2012 the Supreme Court ruled that Arizona's law did not preempt federal authority to make immigration law.[49] The decision allowed states to enact tough measures including immigration checks by local law enforcement officials. Even so, these laws will continued to be challenged on other grounds, such as racial profiling.

The presence of an estimated 11 million unauthorized immigrants in communities across the country is an especially volatile issue affecting many aspects of state lawmaking. In 2007 the federal Department of Homeland Security enlisted state and local officials in the effort to enforce federal immigration law. Under the program, state and local law-enforcement agencies can be deputized to arrest suspected unauthorized immigrants and to check the immigration status of those apprehended on unrelated offenses. Yet the aggressive use of these powers in some localities has led to calls for ending the program. In 2009 the Justice Department stripped Joe Arpaio, sheriff of Maricopa County (Phoenix), Arizona, of the authority to make immigration sweeps. Arpaio had gained national attention for his harsh treatment of those rounded up in immigration raids, which included housing the immigrants in tent cities in the Arizona desert and putting female inmates in chain gangs. The Justice Department launched a series of investigations into Arpaio's actions, including one charging that his department discriminated against Latinos. However, the federal government did not eliminate the program. Instead, it vowed to exercise greater oversight over local actions.[50]

In fact, the federal government launched an additional program, Secure Communities, which allows state and local authorities to check the fingerprints of people being booked into jail against a Homeland Security database. If the fingerprints find a match in the database, it is up to the federal Immigration and Customs Enforcement agents to take further action. The law led to a record number of deportations in 2009 and 2010. Some states have objected to the program, and Illinois pulled out of the agreement with the federal government on the grounds that the law was detaining too many undocumented immigrants who had never committed a crime. Despite these objections, the federal government has declared that participation of state and local law-enforcement authorities is mandatory.[51]

As the cases of immigration and medical marijuana show, the Obama administration signaled a much stronger role for the federal government on some dimensions. The stronger federal role was also evident in measures to jump-start the failing economy. In February 2009, Congress enacted the American Recovery and Reinvestment Act (ARRA), a $787 billion measure that, in addition to tax cuts, offered states substantial one-time funds for a variety of purposes, including education, road building, unemployment insurance, and health care. Many governors, strapped for cash, welcomed the new funds. Others, however, worried that the

In 2010, Arizona passed a controversial law that required police to check the immigration status of people stopped for even minor matters. Opponents of the law called on the federal government to intervene. In 2012 the Supreme Court upheld the main part of the law.

Who Opposed the Affordable Care Act?

Prior to the passage of the Affordable Care Act (ACA) in 2010, the states set the eligibility requirements for Medicaid, the government's health insurance program for lower-income Americans. States set various thresholds for Medicaid eligibility, which is shown below as a percentage of the federal poverty level (FPL); a lower number means it is harder to qualify for Medicaid benefits. The ACA would have required states to set Medicaid eligibility at 133% of the FPL. However, in June 2012, the U.S. Supreme Court struck the ACA's requirement of a national standard for Medicaid eligibility.

MEDICAID ELIGIBILITY

MN 215%

AR 17%

Percentage of FPL

- ● 15–39%
- ● 40–79%
- ● 80–119%
- ● 120–159%
- ● 160–215%

UNINSURED

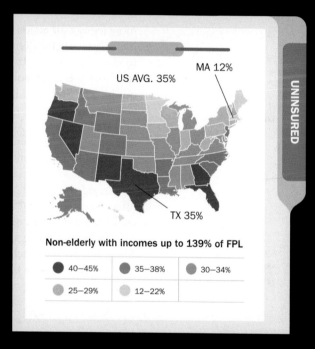

MA 12%

US AVG. 35%

TX 35%

Non-elderly with incomes up to 139% of FPL

- ● 40–45%
- ● 35–38%
- ● 30–34%
- ● 25–29%
- ● 12–22%

States That Challenged the ACA

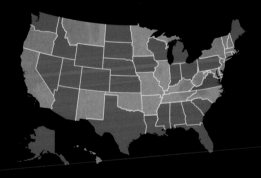

*Iowa is both a plaintiff and a supporter of the ACA. The attorney general filed a brief in support of the legislation while the governor, Terry Branstad, filed a motion to join the suit against it.

SOURCES: U.S. Census Bureau, www.census.gov; Kaiser Family Foundation, 50 State Comparisons, Health Coverage & Uninsured, www.statehealthfacts.org (both accessed 7/25/11); *National Federation of Independent Business v. Sebelius*, 567 U.S. ___ (2012).

AL	CA	DC	ID	KS	MD	MS	NV	NY	OK	SC	UT	WV
AK	CO	FL	IL	KY	MA	MO	NH	NC	OR	SD	VT	WI
AZ	CT	GA	IN	LA	MI	MT	NJ	ND	PA	TN	VA	WY
AR	DE	HI	IA*	ME	MN	NE	NM	OH	RI	TX	WA	

for critical analysis

1. Why do you think the states highlighted in green challenged the ACA? In general, were these states where the ACA made it easier or harder to get Medicaid?

2. In 2009, a family of four in Minnesota could earn up to $47,408 (215% of FPL) and still qualify for Medicaid benefits, while the same size family in Texas would be ineligible if they earned more than $5,733 (26% of FPL). Is it more important to provide equal access to health care or to preserve state choices?

federal government was using ARRA to dictate state spending priorities. Some of these governors sought to use the funds for purposes not allowed in the legislation or refused parts of the funds that they believed would tie their hands in the future. For example, former governor Mark Sanford of South Carolina, a Republican, asked the federal government for a waiver that would permit his state to use approximately $700 million of its estimated $2.8 billion ARRA allocation to pay down the state's debt. When the waiver was denied, Sanford vowed to reject the federal funds; however, the state legislature overrode his decision.[52] Several states objected to the unemployment funds, which required states to expand eligibility for unemployment insurance to many part-time and temporary workers. A handful of Republican southern governors refused to accept the funds on the grounds that expanded eligibility would place a future burden on employers. A majority of states, however, did change their laws in response to the federal requirements.[53]

In other ways, the Obama White House signaled that it would allow the states more leeway for action than they had under the Bush administration. This was particularly true in the domains of social policy and the environment when states sought to enact laws more stringent than those of the federal government. In the memo reversing the Bush policy of preemption, the White House noted, "Throughout our history, State and local governments have frequently protected health, safety, and the environment more aggressively than has the national Government."[54] Its new policy aimed to keep the federal government from infringing on these more aggressive state actions.

The most significant Obama law to affect the states was the 2010 health care overhaul. As we have seen, one controversial part of that legislation required states to expand their Medicaid programs to cover more low-income residents and to offer them additional services. The Court's ruling that the federal government could not impose all or nothing conditions on the states—implement the expansion or lose all Medicaid funding—represented a sharp departure from the past. The ruling has far-reaching potential to change the federal government's power to impose conditions on the states when it supplies the funds. The other controversial

The Affordable Care Act asserted federal power over the states by imposing new expansions of the Medicaid program in exchange for expanded funding. When the Supreme Court ruled that this "all or nothing" approach was too coercive, some states vowed to opt out of the law's Medicaid provisions.

provision of the Affordable Care Act was the "individual mandate," the requirement that individuals without health care insurance be required to purchase such insurance. The 26 states suing the federal government charged that Congress exceeded its power under the commerce clause when it enacted the mandate. They charged that Congress had no power to force individuals to purchase a product and argued that the act set up a "slippery slope" in which Congress could force individuals to make other purchases. As one judge (who upheld the law) asked, "Would it be unconstitutional to require people to buy broccoli?" In defending the law, the federal government argued that the complex interactions of the health care market made the individual mandate constitutional under Congress's power to regulate commerce among the states.[55] From the moment a person is born, he or she is part of the health care economy. Even if a person does not have health insurance, federal law requires that hospitals provide treatment in an emergency. Those costs are borne by all of the people who do pay for health insurance. Taking a more narrow view of the health care market, the Court rejected this argument on the grounds that the federal government cannot regulate economic inactivity, that is, the failure to purchase health insurance. Instead, it found that the Affordable Care Act could be justified by Congress's power to tax. The law requires individuals who do not receive insurance from their employers or their parents, and are not eligible for Medicaid, to purchase insurance or pay a penalty. The Court reasoned that the penalty could be considered a tax, and in that sense, passed constitutional muster. The complex and surprising decision marked a new era in American federalism. The Court placed limits on two of the key powers that have expanded the reach of the federal government since the New Deal—the power to regulate commerce and the power to spend for the general welfare. The decision will surely invite challenges to federal power in diverse areas, possibly including education programs, the drinking age, and environmental regulations.

for critical analysis

Why did the 2010 Affordable Care Act become controversial? How did the Supreme Court's decision about the law reflect the principles of federalism?

● Thinking Critically about the Federal System

It is often argued that liberals prefer a strong federal government because they value equality more than liberty. Conservatives are said to prefer granting more power to states and localities because they care most about liberty. Although this greatly oversimplifies liberal and conservative views, such arguments underscore the reality that ideas about federalism are linked to different views about the purposes of government. For what ends should government powers be used? What happens when widely shared national values conflict in practice? The connections between federalism and our fundamental national values have made federalism a focus of political contention throughout our nation's history.

The Constitution limited the power of the federal government in order to promote liberty. This decision reflected the framers' suspicions of centralized power, based on their experience with the British Crown. The American suspicion of centralized power lives on today in widespread dislike of "big government,"

Under the No Child Left Behind Act, schools can lose federal funding if students perform poorly on standardized tests. The Supreme Court's decision on the Affordable Care Act may open the door to new challenges from the states in areas such as education.

Will states attempt to change the drinking age in the future? The federal government required states to set the drinking age at 21 or risk losing federal highway funds, but some people feel this decision should be left to the states.

for critical analysis

What would be the advantages and disadvantages of a unitary system in which the federal government had all the power? What would be the advantages and disadvantages of a fully decentralized system in which the states had all the power?

which generally evokes a picture of a bloated federal government. But over the course of our history we have come to realize that the federal government is also an important guarantor of liberty. As we'll see in Chapter 4, it took enhanced federal power to ensure that local and state governments adhered to the fundamental constitutional freedoms in the Bill of Rights.

One of the most important continuing arguments for a strong federal government is its role in ensuring equality. A key puzzle of federalism is deciding when differences across states represent the proper democratic decisions of the states and when such differences represent inequalities that should not be tolerated. Sometimes a decision to eliminate differences is made on the grounds of equality and individual rights, as in the Civil Rights Act of 1964, which outlawed legally instituted racial segregation. At other times, a stronger federal role is justified on the grounds of national interest, as in the case of the oil shortage and the institution of a 55-mph speed limit in the 1970s. Yet advocates of a more limited federal role often point to the value of democracy. Public actions can more easily be tailored to fit distinctive local or state desires if states and localities have more power to make policy. Viewed this way, variation across states can be an expression of democratic will.

In recent decades, many Americans have grown disillusioned with the federal government and have supported efforts to give the states more responsibilities. After the terrorist attacks of 2001, however, support for the federal government soared. With issues of security topping the list of citizens' concerns, the federal government, which had seemed less important with the waning of the Cold War, suddenly reemerged as the central actor in American politics. As one observer put it, "Federalism was a luxury of peaceful times."[56] Yet polls show that trust in the federal government gradually dropped over the decade. In 2002, 64 percent of Americans expressed a positive view of the federal government; by 2008, only 37 percent did. Although approval of the federal government climbed to 42 percent after Obama's election in 2008, it fell as the economy stagnated. After the 2010 elections brought a Republican majority to the House of Representatives, political stalemate reduced approval of the federal government to new lows. By 2011, 89 percent of Americans did not trust the federal government to do the right thing.[57] Public views about state governments are generally more positive and more stable. However, the long recession took a toll: the proportion of those expressing a favorable view of states dropped from 62 percent in 2002 to 52 percent in 2012. Local governments remain most popular, with positive ratings of 67 percent in 2002 and 61 percent in 2012.[58]

American federalism remains a work in progress. As public problems shift and as local, state, and federal governments change, questions about the relationship between American values and federalism naturally emerge. The different views that people bring to this discussion suggest that federalism will remain a central issue in American democracy.

Mapping Federalism

Inform Yourself

Review the levels of government and their roles. The White House has a valuable website that discusses how states share power with the federal government and local governments (www.whitehouse.gov/our-government/state-and-local-government), in what is known as federalism.

Watch the cartoon "Federal Powers vs. State Powers" (www.youtube.com/watch?v=WQMZ2PT7kr0&feature=related). Consider what powers were reserved to the states. How has the federal government restricted these reserved powers over the last 50 years? When has the U.S. Supreme Court upheld laws that have taken power from the states? Do you believe this is constitutional?

Express Yourself

Go to the Patchwork Nation website (www.patchworknation.org/) to see hundreds of maps broken down by county, congressional district, and state government. Find the percentage of children who are on foods stamps by county. (Above the map of the United States, click on the "County Map" tab, and then on the "Latest Data" tab. Under "Select a Category," choose "Food Stamps." Click on a state to zoom in.) In South Dakota, for example, in some areas almost no children qualify for a free lunch, while in other counties over 80 percent of children qualify. How do state governments make one set of policies for areas as different as these?

The federal government faces similar issues when providing grant money to states. Consider the stimulus money provided for highway repairs. (Follow the directions just given by choosing the "County Map" and "Latest Data" tabs, but click on "Stimulus [via ProPublica].") If the money is broken down by number of people in the counties (per capita), the region receiving the most federal dollars for highway repairs is the Midwest. These maps offer many examples of how the federal government grants money to the states. What region of the country appears to benefit the most from federal tax dollars? Do populous states benefit more, or do the least-populated states? Looking at the data, do you think the current system is fair, or would you make changes in how money is allocated?

Consider texting or e-mailing your members of Congress your views about how federal government tax dollars should be spent and allocated. You can find your representatives and their contact information by using the tools "Find Your Senators" (www.senate.gov) and "Find Your Representative" (www.house.gov). Or send a letter (or e-mail) to the editor of your state/local newspaper expressing your views.

Find links to the sites listed above as well as related activities on wwnorton.com/studyspace.

Federalism in the Constitution

■ **Describe what the Constitution says about the powers of the national government and of the states (pp. 77–81)**

While the Founders wanted a national government that was stronger than it had been under the Articles of Confederation, they also wanted to preserve the autonomy of the states. The necessary and proper clause, supremacy clause, and the specific powers granted to Congress in Article I demonstrate the nation-centered focus of the Constitution. The Tenth Amendment, which grants all undelegated powers to the states, shows the state-centered focus of the Constitution. The Constitution also includes some concurrent powers that are shared by both the federal government and state governments.

Key Terms

federalism (p. 77)

unitary system (p. 77)

federal system (p. 77)

expressed powers (p. 77)

implied powers (p. 77)

necessary and proper clause (p. 77)

reserved powers (p. 78)

police power (p. 78)

concurrent powers (p. 78)

full faith and credit clause (p. 79)

privileges and immunities clause (p. 79)

home rule (p. 80)

Practice Quiz

1. Which term describes the sharing of powers between the national government and the state governments? *(p. 77)*
   a) home rule
   b) separation of powers
   c) federalism
   d) checks and balances
   e) unitary system

2. Which amendment to the Constitution stated that the powers not delegated to the national government or prohibited to the states were "reserved to the states"? *(p. 78)*
   a) First Amendment
   b) Fifth Amendment
   c) Tenth Amendment
   d) Fourteenth Amendment
   e) Twenty-Sixth Amendment

3. A state government's authority to regulate the health, safety, and morals of its citizens is frequently referred to as *(p. 78)*
   a) the reserved power.
   b) the police power.
   c) the expressed power.
   d) the concurrent power.
   e) the implied power.

4. Which constitutional clause has been central in debates over gay and lesbian marriage because it requires that states normally honor the public acts and judicial decisions of other states? *(p. 79)*
   a) privileges and immunities clause
   b) necessary and proper clause
   c) interstate commerce clause
   d) preemption clause
   e) full faith and credit clause

5. Many states have amended their constitutions to guarantee that large cities will have the authority to manage local affairs without interference from state government. This power is called *(p. 80)*
   a) home rule.
   b) devolution.
   c) preemption.
   d) states' rights.
   e) new federalism.

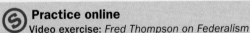

Ⓢ Practice online
Video exercise: *Fred Thompson on Federalism*

The Changing Relationship between the Federal Government and the States

■ **Trace how the federal government became much stronger over time (pp. 82–89)**

The relative importance of states and the federal government has changed significantly over time. During the first 100 years of American history, the national government was small and focused entirely on assisting commerce. Beginning in the 1930s, the Supreme Court dramatically expanded the power of the federal government through its expansive interpretation of the commerce clause. The growing power of the national government has not, however, left the states powerless and state governments continue to make important laws.

Key Terms

dual federalism (p. 82)

commerce clause (p. 85)

states' rights (p. 87)

Practice Quiz

6. The system of federalism that allowed states to do most of the fundamental governing from 1789 to 1937 was *(p. 82)*
   a) new federalism.
   b) home rule.
   c) regulated federalism.
   d) dual federalism.
   e) cooperative federalism.

7. In which case did the Supreme Court create the potential for increased national power by ruling that Congress could use the necessary and proper clause to interpret its delegated powers broadly? *(p. 85)*
   a) *United States v. Lopez*
   b) *Printz v. United States*
   c) *Marbury v. Madison*
   d) *McCulloch v. Maryland*
   d) *Gibbons v. Ogden*

8. In 1937 the Supreme Court laid the groundwork for a stronger federal government by *(p. 86)*
   a) issuing a number of decisions that dramatically narrowed the definition of the commerce clause.
   b) issuing a number of decisions that dramatically expanded the definition of the commerce clause.
   c) issuing a number of decisions that struck down the supremacy clause.
   d) issuing a number of decisions that struck down the privileges and immunities clause.
   e) issuing a number of decision that struck down the full faith and credit clause.

 Practice Online
Interactive simulation: *Power Distribution among Federal, State, and Local Governments*

Who Does What? Public Spending and the Federal Framework

■ **Analyze major developments in the federal framework since the 1930s (pp. 89–105)**

The Great Depression effectively ended the traditional system of dual federalism in which the states and the federal government performed very different functions. Today, American federalism includes elements of cooperative, coercive and "new" federalism. Most of the important public policy issues in recent years, including controversies about government spending, immigration, climate change and economic regulation, are debated and addressed through the United States' unique system of federalism.

Key Terms

grants-in-aid (p. 91)

categorical grants (p. 92)

project grants (p. 92)

formula grants (p. 92)

cooperative federalism (p. 92)

regulated federalism (p. 94)

preemption (p. 94)

unfunded mandates (p. 95)

devolution (p. 96)

block grants (p. 96)

New Federalism (p. 96)

general revenue sharing (p. 97)

redistributive programs (p. 98)

Practice Quiz

9. One of the most powerful tools by which the federal government has attempted to get the states to act in ways that are desired by the federal government is by *(p. 91)*
   a) defending states' rights.
   b) general revenue sharing.
   c) providing grants-in-aid.
   d) requiring licensing.
   e) granting home rule.

10. The form of regulated federalism that allows the federal government to take over areas of regulation formerly overseen by states or local governments is called *(p. 94)*
    a) project grants.
    b) preemption.
    c) devolution.
    d) categorical grants.
    e) formula grants.

11. When state and local governments must conform to costly regulations or conditions in order to receive grants but do not receive reimbursements for their expenditures from the federal government it is called *(p. 95)*
    a) a reciprocal grant.
    b) an unfunded mandate.
    c) general revenue sharing.
    d) a concurrent grant.
    e) a counterfunded mandate.

12. The process of returning more of the responsibilities of governing from the national level to the state level is known as *(p. 96)*
    a) devolution.
    b) dual federalism.
    c) incorporation.
    d) home rule.
    e) preemption.

13. To what does the term *New Federalism* refer? *(p. 96)*
    a) the era of federalism initiated by President Roosevelt during the late 1930s
    b) the national government's regulation of state action through grants-in-aid
    c) the type of federalism relying on categorical grants
    d) efforts to return more policy-making discretion to the states through the use of block grants
    e) the recent emergence of local governments as important political actors

14. A recent notable example of the process of giving the states more responsibility for administering government programs is *(p. 99)*
    a) campaign finance reform.
    b) prison reform.
    c) Social Security.
    d) welfare reform.
    e) trade reform.

 Practice Online
"Who Are Americans" interactive exercise: *Who Opposed the Affordable Health Care Act?*

For Further Reading

Bensel, Richard. *Sectionalism and American Political Development: 1880–1980.* Madison: University of Wisconsin Press, 1984.

Bowman, Ann O'M., and Richard C. Kearney. *The Resurgence of the States.* Englewood Cliffs, NJ: Prentice-Hall, 1986.

Derthick, Martha. *Keeping the Compound Republic: Essays on American Federalism.* Washington, DC: Brookings Institution Press, 2001.

Donahue, John D. *Disunited States.* New York: Basic Books, 1997.

Elazar, Daniel. *American Federalism: A View from the States.* 3rd ed. New York: Harper & Row, 1984.

Feiock, Richard C., and John T. Scholz, *Self-Organizing Federalism: Collaborative Mechanisms to Mitigate Institutional Collective Action Dilemmas.* New York: Cambridge University Press, 2009.

Gerston, Larry N. *American Federalism: A Concise Introduction.* Armonk, NY: M.E. Sharpe, 2007.

Grodzins, Morton. *The American System.* Chicago: Rand McNally, 1974.

Johnson, Kimberly S. *Governing the American State: Congress and the New Federalism, 1877–1929.* Princeton, NJ: Princeton University Press, 2007.

Kettl, Donald. *The Regulation of American Federalism.* Baltimore: Johns Hopkins University Press, 1987.

Robertson, David Brian. *Federalism and the Making of America.* New York: Routledge, 2011.

Van Horn, Carl E. *The State of the States.* 4th ed. Washington, DC: CQ Press, 2005.

Recommended Websites

Constitution Finder
http://confinder.richmond.edu

Governments can organize power in either unitary or federal systems. Examine the constitutions of different countries throughout the world and try to identify how those governments organize power.

Council of State Governments
www.csg.org

This organization provides information on a variety of state-federal policy areas. See what current issues concerning federalism are of prime importance to the state governments on this site.

Governing.com
www.governing.com

See what state-federal issues are important to your local government officials on the website for *Governing* magazine.

National Conference of State Legislatures
www.ncsl.org

National Governors Association
www.nga.org

These are two of the largest organizations dedicated to representing state and local government interests at the federal level.

Oyez: U.S. Supreme Court Media
www.oyez.org

Read here about one of the most important U.S. Supreme Court decisions regarding the division of federal and state power in the case of *McCulloch v. Maryland.*

Pew Center for the States
www.pewstates.org

The Pew Center on the States provides nonpartisan reporting and research, advocacy, and technical assistance to help states deliver better results and achieve long-term fiscal health by investing in programs that provide the strongest returns.

Urban Institute
www.newfederalism.urban.org

New Federalism gives state governments more flexibility to make public policy and administer programs. The Urban Institute's "Assessing the New Federalism" policy center takes a statistical look at the success and failure of recent government programs.

U.S. Census Bureau
www.census.gov

The Census Bureau maintains one of the largest collections of data about social and economic conditions of the nation's 50 states.

World Federalist Movement
www.wfm.org

This international organization is dedicated to the division of power and authority among all local, state, and international governmental agencies. Generally, it promotes federalism and constitutional democracy throughout the world.

Freedom of speech is one of the liberties protected by the First Amendment. Even speech that is hostile or offensive—such as the views expressed by these Ku Klux Klan members—cannot be prohibited so long as they do not incite illegal action.

Civil Liberties

WHAT GOVERNMENT DOES AND WHY IT MATTERS Today in the United States, we often take for granted the liberties contained in the Bill of Rights. In fact, few people in recorded history, including many American citizens before the 1960s, have enjoyed such protections. For more than 170 years after its ratification by the states in 1791, the Bill of Rights meant little to most Americans. As we shall see in this chapter, guaranteeing the liberties articulated in the Bill of Rights to all Americans required a long struggle. As recently as the early 1960s, criminal suspects in state cases did not have to be informed of their rights, some states required daily Bible readings and prayers in their public schools, and some communities regularly censored books that they deemed to be obscene.

Today, many Americans regard searches and, especially, full-body scans at airports as infringements upon their civil liberties, most notably their right to privacy. This right is mentioned nowhere in the Constitution but, instead, was invoked by the Supreme Court in its decisions striking down state restrictions on birth control and abortion. No court has yet been persuaded that airport searches violate the Constitution.

Thomas Jefferson said that a bill of rights "is what people are entitled to against every government on earth." Note the wording: *against government.* Civil liberties are *protections from* improper government action. Some of these restraints are substantive liberties, which put limits on *what* the government shall and shall not have power to do—such as establishing a religion, quartering troops in private homes without consent, or seizing private property without just compensation. Other restraints are procedural liberties, which deal with *how* the government is supposed to act. Civil liberties require a delicate balance between governmental power and governmental restraint. The government must be kept in check, with strict limits on its powers; yet, at the same time, the government must be given enough power to defend liberty and its benefits from those who seek to deprive others of them. This chapter will explore how this balance is struck. We will see how the Supreme Court, an inherently undemocratic institution, is especially important in establishing the balance. Civil liberties also reflect how well the democratic principle of majority rule with minority rights works. The rights enumerated in the Bill of Rights and enforced through the courts can provide an important check on the power of the majority.

chaptergoals

- Explain how the civil liberties included in the Bill of Rights were "nationalized" (pages 115–19)

- Describe how the First Amendment protects freedom of religion (pages 119–22)

- Describe how the First Amendment protects free speech (pages 122–32)

- Explore whether the Second Amendment means people have a right to own guns (pages 132–33)

- Explain the major rights that people have if they are accused of a crime (pages 133–43)

- Assess whether people have a right to privacy under the Constitution (pages 143–47)

A Brief History of the Bill of Rights

When the first Congress under the newly ratified Constitution met in late April of 1789, the most important item of business was the consideration of a proposal to add a bill of rights to the Constitution. Such a proposal had been turned down with little debate in the waning days of the Philadelphia Constitutional Convention in 1787, not because the delegates were against rights, but because, as the Federalists, led by Alexander Hamilton, later argued, it was "not only unnecessary in the proposed Constitution but would even be dangerous."[1] First, according to Hamilton, a bill of rights would be irrelevant to a national government that was given only delegated powers in the first place. To put restraints on "powers which are not granted" could provide a pretext for governments to claim more powers than were in fact granted: "For why declare that things shall not be done which there is no power to do?"[2] Second, the Constitution was to Hamilton and the Federalists a bill of rights in itself, containing provisions that amounted to a bill of rights without requiring additional amendments (see Table 4.1). For example, Article I, Section 9, included the right of **habeas corpus**, which prohibits the government from depriving a person of liberty without an open trial before a judge.

Despite the power of Hamilton's arguments, when the Constitution was submitted to the states for ratification, Antifederalists, most of whom had not been delegates in Philadelphia, picked up on the argument of Thomas Jefferson (who also had not been a delegate) that the omission of a bill of rights was a major imperfection of the new Constitution. The Federalists conceded that in order to gain ratification they would have to make an "unwritten but unequivocal pledge" to add a bill of rights that would include a confirmation (in what would become the Tenth Amendment) of the understanding that all powers not expressly delegated to the national government or explicitly prohibited to the states were reserved to the states.[3]

habeas corpus a court order demanding that an individual in custody be brought into court and shown the cause for detention

TABLE 4.1

Rights in the Original Constitution (Not in the Bill of Rights)

CLAUSE	RIGHT ESTABLISHED
Article I, Sec. 9	guarantee of habeas corpus
Article I, Sec. 9	prohibition of **bills of attainder**
Article I, Sec. 9	prohibition of **ex post facto laws**
Article I, Sec. 9	prohibition against acceptance of titles of nobility, etc., from any foreign state
Article III	guarantee of trial by jury in state where crime was committed
Article III	treason defined and limited to the life of the person convicted, not to the person's heirs

bill of attainder a law that declares a person guilty of a crime without a trial

ex post facto laws laws that declare an action to be illegal after it has been committed

"After much discussion and manipulation . . . at the delicate prompting of Washington and under the masterful prodding of Madison," the House of Representatives adopted 17 amendments; of these, the Senate adopted 12. Ten of the amendments were ratified by the necessary three-fourths of the states on December 15, 1791; from the start, these 10 were called the **Bill of Rights** (see Table 4.2).[4] The protections against improper government action contained in the Constitution and the Bill of Rights represent important **civil liberties**.

Nationalizing the Bill of Rights

The First Amendment provides that "Congress shall make no law . . ." But this is the only amendment in the Bill of Rights that addresses itself exclusively to the national government. For example, the Second Amendment provides that "the right of the people to keep and bear Arms, shall not be infringed." And the Fifth Amendment says, among other things, that "no person shall . . . be twice put in jeopardy of life or limb" for the same crime. Since the First Amendment is the only part of the Bill of Rights that is explicit in its intention to put limits on Congress and therefore on the national government, a fundamental question inevitably arises: Do the remaining provisions of the Bill of Rights put limits only on the national government, or do they limit the state governments as well?

The Supreme Court first answered this question in 1833 by ruling that the Bill of Rights limited only the national government and not the state governments.[5] But in 1868, when the Fourteenth Amendment was added to the Constitution, the question arose once again. The Fourteenth Amendment reads as if it were meant to impose the Bill of Rights on the states:

> No *State* shall make or enforce any law which shall abridge the privileges or immunities of citizens of the United States; nor shall any *State* deprive any person of life, liberty, or property, without due process of law; nor deny to any person within its jurisdiction the equal protection of the laws [emphasis added].

This language sounds like an effort to extend the Bill of Rights in its entirety to all citizens, wherever they might reside.[6] Yet this was not the Supreme Court's interpretation of the amendment for nearly 100 years. Within five years of ratification of the Fourteenth Amendment, the Court was making decisions as though the amendment had never been adopted.[7]

The only change in civil liberties during the first 50-odd years following the adoption of the Fourteenth Amendment came in 1897, when the Supreme Court held that the due process clause of the Fourteenth Amendment did in fact prohibit states from taking property for a public use without just compensation.[8] However, the Supreme Court had selectively "incorporated" into the Fourteenth Amendment only the property protection provision of the Fifth Amendment and no other clause of the Fifth or any other amendment of the Bill of Rights. In other words, although according to the Fifth Amendment, "due process" applied to the taking of life and liberty as well as property, only property was incorporated into the Fourteenth Amendment as a limitation on state power.

Although the Bill of Rights specifies certain rights and liberties, the interpretation and protection of those rights and liberties has evolved over time. The government's fight against terrorism has raised numerous civil liberties issues, such as whether suspected terrorists and "enemy combatants" are entitled to due process rights, such as a fair trial.

TABLE 4.2

The Bill of Rights

Amendment I: Limits on Congress	Congress cannot make any law establishing a religion or abridging freedoms of religious exercise, speech, assembly, or petition.
Amendments II, III, IV: Limits on the Executive	The executive branch cannot infringe on the right of the people to keep arms (II), cannot arbitrarily take houses for militia (III), and cannot search for or seize evidence without a court warrant swearing to the probable existence of a crime (IV).
Amendments V, VI, VII, VIII: Limits on the Judiciary	The courts cannot hold trials for serious offenses without provision for a grand jury (V), a trial jury (VII), a speedy trial (VI), presentation of charges and confrontation by the accused of hostile witnesses (VI), and immunity from testimony against oneself and immunity from trial more than once for the same offense (V). Furthermore, neither bail nor punishment can be excessive (VIII), and no property can be taken without "just compensation" (V).
Amendments IX, X: Limits on the National Government	Any rights not enumerated are reserved to the state or the people (X), and the enumeration of certain rights in the Constitution should not be interpreted to mean that those are the only rights the people have (IX).

No further expansion of civil liberties via the Fourteenth Amendment occurred until 1925, when the Supreme Court held that freedom of speech is "among the fundamental personal rights and 'liberties' protected by the due process clause of the Fourteenth Amendment from impairment by the states."[9] In 1931 the Court added freedom of the press to that short list of freedoms protected by the Bill of Rights from state action; in 1939 it added freedom of assembly.[10]

But that was as far as the Court was willing to go. As late as 1937 the Supreme Court was still unwilling to nationalize civil liberties beyond the First Amendment. The Constitution, as interpreted by the Supreme Court in *Palko v. Connecticut*, left standing the framework in which the states had the power to determine their own laws on a number of fundamental issues. The *Palko* case (described in more detail later in the chapter) established the principle of **selective incorporation**, by which the provisions of the Bill of Rights were to be considered one by one and selectively applied as limits on the states through the Fourteenth Amendment. In order to make clear that "selective incorporation" should be narrowly interpreted, Justice Benjamin Cardozo, writing for an 8–1 majority, asserted that although many rights have value and importance, some rights do not represent a "principle of justice so rooted in the traditions and conscience of our people as to be ranked as fundamental." He went on to remark that if the Fourteenth Amendment has absorbed such rights as freedom of thought and speech, "the process of absorption has had its source in the belief that neither liberty nor justice would exist if they were

selective incorporation the process by which different protections in the Bill of Rights were incorporated into the Fourteenth Amendment, thus guaranteeing citizens protection from state as well as national governments

TABLE 4.3

Incorporation of the Bill of Rights into the Fourteenth Amendment

SELECTED PROVISIONS AND AMENDMENTS	INCORPORATED	KEY CASE
Eminent domain (V)	1897	*Chicago, Burlington, and Quincy R.R. v. Chicago*
Freedom of speech (I)	1925	*Gitlow v. New York*
Freedom of press (I)	1931	*Near v. Minnesota*
Free exercise of religion (I)	1934	*Hamilton v. Regents of the University of California*
Freedom of assembly (I) and freedom to petition the government for redress of grievances (I)	1937	*DeJonge v. Oregon*
Freedom of assembly (I)	1939	*Hague v. CIO*
Nonestablishment of state religion (I)	1947	*Everson v. Board of Education*
Freedom from unnecessary search and seizure (IV)	1949	*Wolf v. Colorado*
Freedom from warrantless search and seizure (IV) ("exclusionary rule")	1961	*Mapp v. Ohio*
Freedom from cruel and unusual punishment (VIII)	1962	*Robinson v. California*
Right to counsel in any criminal trial (VI)	1963	*Gideon v. Wainwright*
Right against self-incrimination and forced confessions (V)	1964	*Mallory v. Hogan* *Escobedo v. Illinois*
Right to counsel and to remain silent (V)	1966	*Miranda v. Arizona*
Right against double jeopardy (V)	1969	*Benton v. Maryland*
Right to bear arms (II)	2010	*McDonald v. Chicago*

sacrificed."[11] *Palko* left states with most of the powers they had possessed even before the adoption of the Fourteenth Amendment, including the power to pass laws segregating the races—a power, in fact, that the 13 former Confederate states chose to continue to exercise on into the 1960s, despite *Brown v. Board of Education* in 1954. The constitutional framework also left states with the power to engage in searches and seizures without a warrant, to indict accused persons without a grand jury, to deprive accused persons of trial by jury, to deprive persons of their right not to have to testify against themselves, to deprive accused persons of their right to confront adverse witnesses, and to prosecute accused persons more than once for the same crime.[12] Few states chose to use these kinds of powers, but some states did, and the power to do so was available for any state whose legislative majority or courts so chose.

So, until 1961, only the First Amendment and one clause of the Fifth Amendment had been clearly incorporated into the Fourteenth Amendment as binding on the states as well as on the national government.[13] After that, one by one, most of the important provisions of the Bill of Rights were incorporated into the Fourteenth Amendment and applied to the states. Table 4.3 shows the progress of this revolution in the interpretation of the Constitution.

The final provision of the Bill of Rights to be incorporated by the Supreme Court was the Second Amendment, which protects the right to bear arms. In the 2010 case of *McDonald v. Chicago*, the Court held that the right of an individual "to keep and bear arms" is incorporated by the due process clause of the Fourteenth Amendment and applies to the states.[14]

The best way to examine the Bill of Rights today is the simplest way: to take the major provisions one at a time. Some of these provisions are settled areas of law; others are not. The Court can reinterpret any one of them at any time.

The First Amendment and Freedom of Religion

Describe how the First Amendment protects freedom of religion

Congress shall make no law respecting an establishment of religion, or prohibiting the free exercise thereof; or abridging the freedom of speech, or of the press; or the right of the people peaceably to assemble, and to petition the Government for a redress of grievances.

The Bill of Rights begins by guaranteeing freedom, and the First Amendment provides for that freedom in two distinct clauses: "Congress shall make no law [1] respecting an establishment of religion, or [2] prohibiting the free exercise thereof." The first clause is called the "establishment clause," and the second is called the "free exercise clause."

Separation between Church and State

The **establishment clause** and the idea of "no law" regarding the establishment of religion could be interpreted in several possible ways. One interpretation, which probably reflects the views of many of the First Amendment's authors, is that the government is prohibited from establishing an official church. Official state churches, such as the Church of England, were common in the eighteenth century and were viewed by many Americans as inconsistent with a republican form of government. Indeed, many American colonists had fled Europe to escape persecution for having rejected state-sponsored churches. A second possible interpretation is the view that the government may not take sides among competing religions but is not prohibited from providing assistance to religious institutions or ideas as long as it shows no favoritism. The United States accommodates religious beliefs in a variety of ways, from the reference to God on U.S. currency to the prayer that begins every session of Congress. These forms of religious establishment have never been struck down by the courts. The third view regarding religious

establishment clause the First Amendment clause that says that "Congress shall make no law respecting an establishment of religion." This law means that a "wall of separation" exists between church and state

The First Amendment affects everyday life in a multitude of ways. Because of the amendment's ban on state-sanctioned religion, the Supreme Court ruled in 2000 that student-initiated public prayer in school is illegal. Pregame prayer at public schools violates the establishment clause of the First Amendment.

Lemon test a rule articulated in *Lemon v. Kurtzman* that government action toward religion is permissible if it is secular in purpose, neither promotes nor inhibits the practice of religion, and does not lead to "excessive entanglement" with religion

establishment, which for many years dominated Supreme Court decision making in this realm, is the idea of a "wall of separation" between church and state—Jefferson's formulation—that cannot be breached by the government. For two centuries, Jefferson's words have had a powerful impact on our understanding of the proper relationship between church and state in America.

Despite the seeming absoluteness of the phrase "wall of separation," there is ample room to disagree on how high the wall is or of what materials it is composed. For example, the Court has been consistently strict in cases of school prayer, striking down such practices as Bible reading,[15] nondenominational prayer,[16] a moment of silence for meditation, and pre-game prayer at public sporting events.[17] In each of these cases, the Court reasoned that school-sponsored religious observations, even of an apparently non-denominational character, are highly suggestive of school sponsorship and therefore violate the prohibition against establishment of religion. On the other hand, the Court has been quite permissive (and, some would say, inconsistent) about the public display of religious symbols, such as city-sponsored nativity scenes in commercial or municipal areas.[18] And although the Court has consistently disapproved of government financial support for religious schools, even when the purpose has been purely educational and secular, it has permitted certain direct aid to students of such schools in the form of busing, for example. In 1971, after 30 years of cases involving religious schools, the Court attempted to specify some criteria to guide its decisions and those of lower courts, indicating, for example, in a decision invalidating state payments for the teaching of secular subjects in parochial schools, circumstances under which the Court might allow certain financial assistance. The case was *Lemon v. Kurtzman*; in its decision, the Supreme Court established three criteria to guide future cases—what came to be called the **Lemon** test. The Court held that government aid to religious schools would be accepted as constitutional if (1) it had a secular purpose, (2) its effect was neither to advance nor to inhibit religion, and (3) it did not entangle government and religious institutions in each other's affairs.[19]

Although these restrictions make the *Lemon* test hard to pass, imaginative authorities are finding ways to do so, and the Supreme Court has demonstrated a willingness to let them. For example, in 1995 the Court narrowly ruled that a student religious group at the University of Virginia could not be denied student activities funds merely because it was a religious group espousing a particular viewpoint about a deity. The Court called the denial "viewpoint discrimination" that violated the free speech rights of the group.[20]

In 2004 the question of whether the phrase "under God" in the Pledge of Allegiance violated the establishment clause was brought before the Court. Written without any religious references in 1892, the pledge had long been used in schools. But in 1954, in the midst of the Cold War, Congress voted to change the pledge in response to the "godless Communism" of the Soviet Union. The conversion was made by adding two key words, so that the revised version read, "I pledge allegiance to the flag of the United States of America and to the Republic for which it stands, one nation *under God*, indivisible, with liberty and justice for all."

Ever since the change was made, there has been a steady murmuring of discontent from those who object to an officially sanctioned profession of belief in a deity as a violation of the establishment clause of the First Amendment. When saying the pledge, those who object to the phrase have often simply stayed silent during the two key words and then resumed for the rest of the pledge. In 2003, Michael A. Newdow, the atheist father of a kindergarten student, forced the issue to the surface when he brought suit against the local California school district. Newdow argued that the reference to God turned the daily recitation of the pledge into a religious exercise. A federal court ruled that although students were not required to recite the pledge at all, having to stand and listen to "under God" still violated the First Amendment's establishment clause. The case was appealed to the Supreme Court, and on June 14, 2004—exactly 50 years to the day after the adoption of "under God" in the pledge—the Court ruled that Newdow lacked a sufficient personal stake in the case to bring the complaint. This inconclusive decision by the Supreme Court left "under God" in the pledge while keeping the issue alive for possible resolution in a future case.

Under what circumstances can religious freedom be abridged? Sultaana Freeman, a Muslim, sued the Florida state government for the right to wear a veil in her driver's license photo. Freeman argued that her religion required her to wear a veil in front of strangers.

In 2005 the Supreme Court ruled, again inconclusively, on government-sponsored displays of religious symbols. Two 2005 cases involved displays of the Ten Commandments. In *Van Orden v. Perry*, the Court decided by a 5–4 margin that a display of the Ten Commandments outside the Texas state capitol did not violate the Constitution.[21] However, in *McCreary County v. American Civil Liberties Union of Kentucky*, decided at the same time and also by a 5–4 margin, the Court determined that a display of the Ten Commandments inside two Kentucky courthouses was unconstitutional.[22] Justice Stephen Breyer, the deciding vote in the two cases, said that the display in *Van Orden* had a secular purpose, whereas the displays in *McCreary* had a purely religious purpose. The key difference between the two cases is that the Texas display had been exhibited in a large park for 40 years with other monuments related to the development of American law without any objections raised until this case, whereas the Kentucky display was erected much more recently and initially by itself, suggesting to some justices that its posting had a religious purpose. But most observers saw little difference between the two cases. Even Breyer was hard-pressed to explain his shifting votes, except to say that *Van Orden* was a "borderline" case. Obviously, the issue of government-sponsored displays of religious symbols has not been settled.

Free Exercise of Religion

The **free exercise clause** protects the right to believe and to practice whatever religion one chooses; it also protects the right to be a nonbeliever. The precedent-setting case involving free exercise is *West Virginia State Board of Education v. Barnette* (1943), which involved the children of a family of Jehovah's Witnesses who refused to salute and pledge allegiance to the American flag on the grounds that their religious faith did not permit it. Three years earlier, the Court had upheld such a requirement and had permitted schools to expel students for refusing to salute the flag. But the entry of the United States into a war to defend democracy,

free exercise clause the First Amendment clause that protects a citizen's right to believe and practice whatever religion he or she chooses

coupled with the ugly treatment to which the Jehovah's Witnesses' children had been subjected, induced the Court to reverse itself and to endorse the free exercise of religion even when it may be offensive to the beliefs of the majority.[23]

Although the Supreme Court has been fairly consistent and strict in protecting the free exercise of religious belief, it has taken pains to distinguish between religious beliefs and *actions* based on those beliefs. The 1940 case of *Cantwell v. Connecticut* established the "time, place and manner" rule. Americans are free to adhere to any religious beliefs, but the time, place, and manner of their exercise are subject to regulation in the public interest.[24]

In one case, for example, two Native Americans had been fired from their jobs for ingesting peyote, a cactus banned as an illegal drug. They claimed that they had been fired from their jobs unlawfully because the use of peyote was a religious sacrament protected by the free exercise clause. The Court disagreed with their claim in an important 1990 decision,[25] but Congress supported the claim and went on to engage in an unusual controversy with the Court, involving the separation of powers and the proper application of the separation of church and state. Congress literally reversed the Court's 1990 decision with the enactment of the Religious Freedom Restoration Act of 1993 (RFRA), forbidding any federal agency or state government from restricting a person's free exercise of religion unless the federal agency or state government demonstrates that its action "furthers a compelling government interest" and "is the least restrictive means of furthering that compelling governmental interest." One of the first applications of RFRA was to a case brought by St. Peter's Catholic Church against the city of Boerne, Texas, which had denied permission to the church to enlarge its building because the building had been declared a historic landmark. The case went to federal court on the argument that the city had violated the church's religious freedom as guaranteed by Congress in RFRA. The Supreme Court declared RFRA unconstitutional, but on grounds rarely utilized, if not unique to this case: Congress had violated the separation of powers principle, infringing on the powers of the judiciary by going so far beyond its lawmaking powers that it ended up actually expanding the scope of religious rights rather than just enforcing them. The Court thereby implied that questions requiring a balancing of religious claims against public policy claims were reserved strictly to the judiciary.[26]

● The First Amendment and Freedom of Speech and of the Press

Describe how the First Amendment protects free speech

Congress shall make no law . . . abridging the freedom of speech, or of the press.

Freedom of speech and of the press have a special place in American political thought. To begin with, democracy depends on the ability of individuals to talk to each other and to disseminate information and ideas. It would be difficult to conceive how democratic politics could function without free and open debate. Such debate, moreover, is seen as an essential mechanism for determining the quality or validity of competing ideas. As Justice Oliver Wendell Holmes said in 1919, "The best test of truth is the power of the thought to get itself accepted in the competition of the market. . . . That at any rate is the theory of our Constitution."[27] What is sometimes called the "marketplace of ideas" receives a good deal of protection from the courts. In 1938 the Supreme Court held that any legislation that attempts to restrict speech "is to be subjected to a more exacting judicial scrutiny . . . than are most other types of legislation."[28] This higher standard of judicial review came to be called "strict scrutiny."

The doctrine of strict scrutiny places a heavy burden of proof on the government if it seeks to regulate or restrict speech. Americans are assumed to have the right to speak and to broadcast their ideas unless some compelling reason can be identified to stop them. But strict scrutiny does not mean that speech can never be regulated. Over the past 200 years, the courts have scrutinized many different forms of speech and constructed different principles and guidelines for each. According to the courts, although virtually all speech is protected by the Constitution, some forms of speech are entitled to a greater degree of protection than others. Let us examine what the federal courts have said about some of the major forms of speech.

Political Speech

Political speech was the activity of greatest concern to the framers of the Constitution, even though some found it the most difficult form of speech to tolerate. Within seven years of the ratification of the Bill of Rights in 1791, Congress adopted the infamous Alien and Sedition Acts, which, among other things, made it a crime to say or publish anything that might tend to defame or bring into disrepute the government of the United States.

The first modern free speech case arose immediately after World War I. It involved persons who had been convicted under the federal Espionage Act of 1917 for opposing U.S. involvement in the war. The Supreme Court upheld the Espionage Act and refused to protect the speech rights of the defendants on the grounds that their activities—appeals to draftees to resist the draft—constituted a "**clear and present danger**" to national security.[29] This is the first and most famous "test" for when government intervention or censorship can be permitted.

It was only after the 1920s that real progress toward a genuinely effective First Amendment was made. Since then, political speech has been consistently protected by the courts even when it has been deemed "insulting" or "outrageous." Here is the way the Supreme Court put it in one of its most important statements on the subject:

> The constitutional guarantees of free speech and free press do not permit a State to forbid or proscribe advocacy of the use of force or of law violation *except where such advocacy is directed to inciting or producing imminent lawless action and is likely to incite or produce such action* [emphasis added].[30]

In other words, as long as speech falls short of actually inciting action, it cannot be prohibited, even if it is hostile to or subversive of the government and its policies. This statement was made in the case of a Ku Klux Klan leader, Charles Brandenburg, who had been arrested and convicted of advocating "revengent" action against the president, Congress, and the Supreme Court, among others, if they continued "to suppress the white, Caucasian race." Although Brandenburg was not carrying a weapon, some of the members of his audience were. Nevertheless, the Supreme Court reversed the state courts and freed Brandenburg while also

"clear and present danger" test test to determine whether speech is protected or unprotected, based on its capacity to present a "clear and present danger" to society

declaring Ohio's Criminal Syndicalism Act unconstitutional because it punished persons who "advocate, or teach the duty, necessity, or propriety [of violence] as a means of accomplishing industrial or political reform"; or who publish materials or "voluntarily assemble . . . to teach or advocate the doctrines of criminal syndicalism." The Supreme Court argued that the statute did not distinguish "mere advocacy" from "incitement to imminent lawless action." It would be difficult to go much further in protecting freedom of speech.

Another area of recent expansion of political speech, the participation of wealthy persons and corporations in political campaigns, was opened up in 1976 with the Supreme Court's decision in *Buckley v. Valeo*. Campaign finance reform laws of the early 1970s, arising out of the Watergate scandal, sought to put severe limits on campaign spending. In the *Buckley* case, a number of important provisions were declared unconstitutional on the basis of a new principle that spending money by or on behalf of candidates is a form of speech protected by the First Amendment. (For more details, see Chapter 10.)

The issue came up again in 2003, with passage of a new and still more severe campaign finance law, the Bipartisan Campaign Reform Act (BCRA). In *McConnell v. Federal Election Commission*, the 5–4 majority seriously reduced the area of speech protected by the *Buckley v. Valeo* decision by holding that Congress was well within its power to put limits on campaign spending. The Court argued that "the selling of access . . . has given rise to the appearance of undue influence [that justifies] regulations impinging on First Amendment rights . . . in order to curb corruption or the appearance of corruption."[31] In the *McConnell* case, the Court also upheld BCRA's limitations on "issue advertising." The act prohibited political advocacy groups from running ads that mentioned a candidate within 30 days of a primary election and 60 days of a general election. This ban was justified with the argument that wealthy special interests could affect election outcomes with last-minute ad campaigns. However, in its 2007 decision in the case of *Federal Election Commission v. Wisconsin Right to Life*, the Court reversed itself, declaring that such ads were protected speech and could not be prohibited so long as they focused mainly on issues and were not simply appeals to vote for or against a specific candidate.[32]

In the 2008 case of *Davis v. Federal Election Commission*, the Supreme Court struck down another element of BCRA, the so-called millionaire's amendment, which had increased contribution limits for opponents of wealthy, self-funded candidates.[33] Even more recently, in the 2010 case of *Citizens United v. Federal Election Commission*, the Supreme Court declared that the First Amendment prohibited BCRA's ban on corporate funding of independent political broadcasts aimed at electing or defeating particular candidates.[34] The case arose in 2008 when Citizens United, a conservative nonprofit organization, sought to show its film *Hillary: The Movie*, a documentary aimed at attacking Hillary Clinton's presidential bid during the 2008 Democratic primaries. In its 5–4 decision, the Supreme Court ruled that the Constitution prohibits the government from regulating political speech and that therefore the government could not ban this type of political spending by corporations. The Court's decision in this case has been controversial. Republicans, seeing themselves as the main beneficiaries of corporate ads, hailed the decision as a victory for free speech. Democrats denounced the decision, with President Obama calling it "a major victory for big oil, Wall Street banks, health insurance companies, and the other powerful interests that marshal their power every day in Washington to drown out the voices of everyday Americans."[35] Congressional Democrats vowed to rewrite the law to circumvent the Court's decision.

Symbolic Speech, Speech Plus, and the Rights of Assembly and Petition

The First Amendment treats the freedoms of religion and political speech as equal to the freedoms of assembly and petition—speech associated with action. Freedom of speech and freedom of assembly are closely related by the "public forum doctrine." In the 1939 case of *Hague v. Committee for Industrial Organization*, the Court declared that the government may not prohibit speech-related activities such as demonstrations or leafleting in public areas traditionally used for that purpose, though, of course, the government may impose rules designed to protect the public safety so long as these rules do not discriminate against particular viewpoints.[36]

Generally, the Supreme Court has sought to protect actions that are designed to send a political message. (Usually the purpose of a symbolic act is not only to send a direct message but also to draw a crowd—to do something spectacular in order to strengthen the message by attracting spectators. Therefore the Court held unconstitutional a California statute making it a felony to display a red Communist flag "as a sign, symbol or emblem of opposition to organized government."[37]Although today there are limits on how far one can go with actions that convey a message symbolically, the protection of such actions is very broad. Thus, although the Court upheld a federal statute making it a crime to burn draft cards to protest the Vietnam War, on the grounds that the government had a compelling interest in preserving draft cards as part of the conduct of the war itself, the Court also deemed the wearing of black armbands to school a protected form of assembly for symbolic action.

Another example is the burning of the American flag as a protest. In 1984, at a political rally held during the Republican National Convention in Dallas, Texas, a political protester burned an American flag, thereby violating a Texas statute that prohibited desecration of a venerated object. In a 5–4 decision, the Supreme Court declared the Texas law unconstitutional on the grounds that flag burning was expressive conduct protected by the First Amendment.[38] Congress reacted immediately with a proposal for a constitutional amendment reversing the Court's Texas decision, and when the amendment failed to receive the necessary two-thirds majority in the Senate, Congress passed the Flag Protection Act of 1989. Protesters promptly violated this act, and their prosecution moved quickly into the federal district court, which declared the new law unconstitutional. The Supreme Court, in another 5–4 decision, affirmed the lower court decision.[39] A renewed effort began in Congress to propose a constitutional amendment that would reverse the Supreme Court and place flag burning outside the realm of protected speech or assembly. Since 1995 the House of Representatives has four times passed a resolution for a constitutional amendment to ban this form of expressive conduct, but each time, the Senate has failed to go along.[40] In a 2003 decision, the Supreme Court struck down a Virginia cross-burning statute. In that case, the Court ruled that states could criminalize cross burning—typically an

The Supreme Court has interpreted the freedom of speech as extending to symbolic acts of political protest, such as flag burning. On several occasions—most recently in 2006—a resolution for a constitutional amendment to ban flag burning has passed in the House of Representatives but has never found enough support in the Senate.

expression of hatred of African Americans—as long as the statute required prosecutors to prove that the act of setting fire to the cross was intended to intimidate. Former justice Sandra Day O'Connor wrote for the majority that the First Amendment permits the government to forbid cross burning as a "particularly virulent form of intimidation," but not when the act was "a form of symbolic expression."[41] This decision will almost inevitably become a more generalized First Amendment protection of any conduct, including flag burning, that can be shown to be a form of symbolic expression.

In the 2011 case of *Snyder v. Phelps*, the Court sought to protect another form of symbolic speech. Members of the Westboro Baptist Church had frequently demonstrated at military funerals, claiming that the deaths of the soldiers were a sign that God disapproved of the acceptance of homosexuality in the United States. The father of a soldier killed in Iraq brought suit against the church and its pastor, claiming that the demonstrators had caused him and his family severe emotional distress. The Supreme Court ruled, however, that the First Amendment protected free speech in a public place against such suits.[42]

Closer to the original intent of the assembly and petition clause is the category of "**speech plus**"—following speech with physical activity such as picketing, distributing leaflets, and other forms of peaceful demonstration or assembly. Such assemblies are consistently protected by courts under the First Amendment; state and local laws regulating such activities are closely scrutinized and frequently overturned. But the same assembly on private property is quite another matter, and can in many circumstances be regulated. For example, the directors of a shopping center can lawfully prohibit an assembly protesting a war or supporting a ban on abortion. Assemblies in public areas can also be restricted under some circumstances, especially when the assembly or demonstration jeopardizes the health, safety, or rights of others. This condition was the basis of the Supreme Court's decision to uphold a lower court order that restricted the access that abortion protesters had to the entrances of abortion clinics.[43]

An unusual "speech plus" case, decided in 2006, was *Rumsfeld v. Forum for Academic and Institutional Rights*.[44] A number of law schools had banned military recruiters from their campuses to protest the military's antigay policies. The government responded by threatening to cut off federal funding to schools that joined the ban. The schools argued, in turn, that the government was violating their constitutional right to voice opposition to its policies. The Supreme Court ruled that the government could require schools to host recruiters as a condition for funding. Banning recruitment, said the Court, was not a form of expression protected by the Constitution; the schools remained completely free to voice their opposition to the military's policies even as they hosted the recruiters.

Freedom of the Press

For all practical purposes, freedom of speech implies and includes freedom of the press. With the exception of the broadcast media, which are subject to federal regulation, the press is protected under the doctrine against **prior restraint**. Beginning with the landmark 1931 case of *Near v. Minnesota*, the U.S. Supreme Court has held that, except under the most extraordinary circumstances, the First Amendment of the Constitution prohibits government agencies from seeking to prevent newspapers or magazines from publishing whatever they wish.[45] Indeed, in the case of *New York Times v. United States* (the so-called Pentagon Papers case), the Supreme Court ruled that the government could not block publication of secret

"speech plus" speech accompanied by conduct such as sit-ins, picketing, and demonstrations. Protection of this form of speech under the First Amendment is conditional, and restrictions imposed by state or local authorities are acceptable if properly balanced by considerations of public order

prior restraint an effort by a governmental agency to block the publication of material it deems libelous or harmful in some other way; censorship. In the United States, the courts forbid prior restraint except under the most extraordinary circumstances

Journalists often claim that the right to protect the names of their sources is essential to a free press. In 2005 a New York Times reporter, Judith Miller, went to jail rather than reveal the name of a confidential source in court.

Defense Department documents furnished to the *New York Times* by an opponent of the Vietnam War who had obtained the documents illegally.[46] In a 1990 case, however, the Supreme Court upheld a lower court order restraining Cable News Network (CNN) from broadcasting tapes of conversations between the former Panamanian dictator Manuel Noriega and his lawyer, supposedly recorded by the U.S. government. By a vote of 7 to 2, the Court held that CNN could be restrained from broadcasting the tapes until the trial court in the Noriega case had listened to the tapes and decided whether their broadcast would violate Noriega's right to a fair trial.[47]

Another press freedom issue that the courts have often been asked to decide is the question of whether journalists can be compelled to reveal their sources of information. Journalists assert that if they cannot ensure their sources' confidentiality, the flow of information will be reduced and press freedom effectively curtailed. Government agencies, however, aver that names of news sources may be relevant to criminal or even national security investigations. More than 30 states have "shield laws," which, to varying degrees, protect journalistic sources. There is, however, no federal shield law. The Supreme Court has held that the press has no constitutional right to withhold information in court.[48] In 2005 a *New York Times* reporter, Judith Miller, was jailed for contempt of court for refusing to tell a federal grand jury the name of a confidential source in a case involving the leaked identity of the CIA analyst Valerie Plame. Plame's husband, Joseph Wilson, had been critical of the Bush administration's Iraq policies.

Libel and Slander Some speech is not protected at all. If a written statement is made in "reckless disregard of the truth" and is considered damaging to the victim because it is "malicious, scandalous, and defamatory," it can be punished as **libel**. If such a statement is made orally, it can be punished as **slander**.

Most libel suits today involve freedom of the press, and the realm of free press is enormous. Historically, newspapers were subject to the law of libel, which provided that newspapers that printed false and malicious stories could be compelled to pay damages to those they defamed. In recent years, however, American courts

libel a written statement made in "reckless disregard of the truth" that is considered damaging to a victim because it is "malicious, scandalous, and defamatory"

slander an oral statement made in "reckless disregard of the truth" that is considered damaging to the victim because it is "malicious, scandalous, and defamatory" have greatly narrowed the meaning of libel and made it extremely difficult, particularly for politicians or other public figures, to win a libel case against a newspaper. In the important 1964 case of *New York Times v. Sullivan*, the Court held that to be deemed libelous, a story about a public official not only had to untrue, but also had to result from "actual malice" or "reckless disregard" for the truth.[49] In other words, the newspaper had to print false and malicious material deliberately. In practice, it is nearly impossible to prove that a paper *deliberately* printed maliciously false information, and it is especially difficult for a politician or other public figure to win a libel case. Essentially, the print media have been able to publish anything they want about a public figure.

However, the Court has opened up the possibility for public officials to file libel suits against the press. The Court has held that the press was immune to libel suits only when the printed material was "a matter of public concern."[50] In other words, a newspaper would have to show that the public official was engaged in activities that were indeed *public*. This principle has made the press more vulnerable to libel suits, but it still leaves an enormous realm of freedom for the press. For example, the Reverend Jerry Falwell, the leader of the Moral Majority, lost his libel suit against *Hustler* magazine even though the magazine had published a cartoon of Falwell showing him having drunken intercourse with his mother in an outhouse. A unanimous Supreme Court rejected a jury verdict in favor of damages for "emotional distress" on the grounds that parodies, no matter how outrageous, are protected because "outrageousness" is too subjective a test and thus would interfere with the free flow of ideas protected by the First Amendment.[51]

With the emergence of the Internet as an important communications medium, the courts have had to decide how traditional libel law applies to Internet content. In 1995 the New York courts held that an online bulletin board could be held responsible for the libelous content of material posted by a third party. To protect Internet service providers, Congress subsequently enacted legislation absolving them of responsibility for third-party posts. The federal courts have generally upheld this law and declared that service providers are immune from suits regarding the content of material posted by others.[52]

Obscenity and Pornography If libel and slander cases can be difficult because of the problem of determining the truth of statements and whether those statements are malicious and damaging, cases involving pornography and obscenity can be even stickier. It is easy to say that pornography and obscenity fall outside the realm of protected speech, but it is impossible to draw a clear line between protected and unprotected speech. Not until 1957 did the Supreme Court confront this problem, and it did so with a definition of obscenity that may have caused more confusion than it cleared up. In writing the Court's opinion, Justice William Brennan defined obscenity as speech or writing that appeals to the "prurient interest"—that is, books, magazines, films, and other material whose purpose is to excite lust, as this appears "to the average person, applying contemporary community standards." Even so, Brennan added, the work should be judged obscene only when it is "utterly without redeeming social importance."[53] Instead of clarifying the Court's view, Brennan's definition actually caused more confusion. In 1964, Justice Potter Stewart confessed that, although he found pornography impossible to define, "I know it when I see it."[54]

All attempts by the courts to define pornography and obscenity have proved impractical, because each instance required courts to screen thousands of pages of print material and feet of film alleged to be pornographic. The vague and impractical standards that had been developed meant ultimately that almost nothing could be banned on the grounds that it was pornographic and obscene. An effort was made to strengthen the restrictions in 1973, when the Supreme Court expressed its willingness to define pornography as a work that (1) as a whole, is deemed prurient by the "average person" according to "community standards"; (2) depicts sexual conduct "in a patently offensive way"; and (3) lacks "serious literary, artistic, political, or scientific value." This definition meant that pornography would be determined by local rather than national standards. Thus, a local bookseller might be prosecuted for selling a volume that was a best seller nationally but that was deemed pornographic locally.[55] This new definition of standards did not help much either, and not long after 1973, the Court began again to review all such community antipornography laws, reversing most of them.

In recent years, the battle against obscene speech has targeted "cyberporn"— pornography on the Internet. Opponents of this form of expression argue that it should be banned because of the easy access children have to the Internet. The first major effort to regulate the content of the Internet occurred in 1996, when the 104th Congress passed the Telecommunications Act. Attached to it was an amendment, called the Communications Decency Act (CDA), designed to regulate the online transmission of obscene material. The constitutionality of the CDA was immediately challenged in court by a coalition of interests led by the American Civil Liberties Union (ACLU). In the 1997 case of *Reno v. ACLU*, the Supreme Court struck down the CDA, ruling that it suppressed speech that "adults have a constitutional right to receive," and that governments may not limit the adult population to messages that are fit for children. Supreme Court justice John Paul Stevens described the Internet as the "town crier" of the modern age and said that the Internet was entitled to the greatest degree of First Amendment protection possible.[56] Congress again tried limiting children's access to Internet pornography with the 2001 Children's Internet Protection Act, which required public libraries to install antipornography filters on all library computers with Internet access. Though the act made cooperation a condition for receiving federal subsidies, it did permit librarians to unblock a site at the request of an adult patron. The law was challenged, but in 2003 the Court upheld it, asserting that its provisions did not violate library patrons' First Amendment rights.[57] In 2003, Congress enacted the PROTECT Act, which outlawed efforts to sell child pornography via the Internet. The Supreme Court upheld this act in the 2008 case of *United States v. Williams*, in which the majority said that criminalizing efforts to purvey child pornography did not violate free speech guarantees.[58]

In 2000 the Supreme Court extended the highest degree of First Amendment protection to cable (not broadcast) television. In *United States v. Playboy Entertainment Group*, the Court struck down a portion of the 1996 Telecommunications Act that required cable TV companies to limit the broadcast of sexually explicit programming to late-night hours. In its decision, the Court noted that the law already provided parents with the means to restrict access to sexually explicit cable channels through various blocking devices. Moreover, such programming could come into the home only if parents decided to purchase such channels in the first place.[59]

Closely related to the issue of obscenity is the matter of violent broadcast content. Can a state or the federal government prohibit broadcasts or publications deemed to be excessively violent? Here, too, the Court has generally upheld freedom of speech. For example, in the 2011 case of *Brown v. Entertainment Merchants Association*, the Court struck down a California law banning the sale of violent video games to children, saying that the law violated the First Amendment.[60]

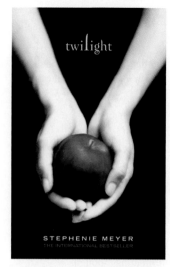

One of the more visible issues of free speech has been the banning of certain books in public schools. For example, in recent years, one of the most frequently banned books has been Twilight, *a vampire saga by Stephenie Meyer.*

Fighting Words and Hate Speech Speech can also lose its protected position when it moves toward the sphere of action. "Expressive speech," for example, is protected until it moves from the symbolic realm to the realm of actual conduct—to direct incitement of damaging conduct with the use of so-called **fighting words**. In 1942 a man called a police officer a "goddamned racketeer" and "a damn Fascist," and was arrested and convicted of violating a state law forbidding the use of offensive language in public. When his case reached the Supreme Court, the arrest was upheld on the grounds that the First Amendment provides no protection for such offensive language because such words "are no essential part of any exposition of ideas."[61] This decision was reaffirmed in the important 1951 case of *Dennis v. United States* when the Supreme Court held that

> there is no substantial public interest in permitting certain kinds of utterances: the lewd and obscene, the profane, the libelous, and the insulting or "fighting" words—those which by their very utterance inflict injury or tend to incite an immediate breach of the peace.[62]

Since that time, however, the Supreme Court has reversed almost every conviction based on arguments that the speaker had used "fighting words." But again, it does not mean this is an absolutely settled area. In recent years, the increased activism of minority and women's groups has prompted a movement against words that might be construed as offensive to members of a particular group. But how should we determine what words are "fighting words" and therefore fall outside the protections of the freedom of speech?

Scores of universities have attempted to develop speech codes to suppress utterances deemed to be racial or ethnic slurs. Similar developments have taken place in large corporations, both public and private, with many successful complaints and lawsuits alleging that the words of employers or their supervisors created a "hostile or abusive working environment." The Supreme Court has held that a "hostile working environment" results from "sexual harassment," including "unwelcome sexual advances, requests for sexual favors, and other *verbal* or physical conduct of a sexual nature [emphasis added]."[63] A fundamental free speech issue is involved in these regulations of hostile speech.

Many jurisdictions have drafted ordinances banning hate speech—forms of expression designed to assert hatred toward one or another group, be they African Americans, Jews, Muslims, or others. Such ordinances seldom pass constitutional muster. The leading Supreme Court case in this realm is the 1992 decision in *R.A.V. v. City of St. Paul*.[64] Here, a white teenager was arrested for burning a cross on the lawn of a black family in violation of a municipal ordinance that banned cross burning. The Court ruled that such an ordinance must be *content neutral*—that is, it must not prohibit actions directed at some groups but not others. The statute in question prohibited only cross burning—which is typically directed at African Americans. Since a statute banning all forms of hateful expression would be deemed overly broad, the *R.A.V.* standard suggests that virtually all hate speech is constitutionally protected.

One category of conditionally protected speech is the speech of high school students in public schools. In 1986 the Supreme Court backed away from a broad protection of student free speech rights by upholding the punishment of a high school student for making a sexually suggestive speech. The Court opinion held that such speech interfered with the school's goal of teaching students the limits of socially acceptable behavior.[65] Two years later the Supreme Court took another conser-

fighting words speech that directly incites damaging conduct

for critical analysis

Should hate speech be protected? Is it contradictory that many who strongly support free thought and expression draw the line at protecting "thought we hate"?

The Supreme Court has ruled that high school students' speech can be restricted. In a 2007 case involving a student who displayed the banner at left, the Court found that the school principal had not violated the student's right to free speech by suspending him.

vative step by restricting students' speech and press rights even further, defining them as part of the educational process and not to be treated with the same standard as adult speech in a regular public forum.[66] A later case involving high school students is the 2007 case of *Morse v. Frederick*.[67] This case dealt with the policies of Juneau-Douglas High School in Juneau, Alaska. In 2002 the Olympic torch relay had passed through Juneau on its way to Salt Lake City for the opening of the Winter Olympics. As the torch passed Juneau-Douglas High, a senior, Joseph Frederick, unfurled a banner reading "Bong Hits 4 Jesus." The school's principal promptly suspended Frederick, who then brought suit for reinstatement, alleging that his free speech rights had been violated. Like most of America's public schools, Juneau High prohibits assemblies or expressions on school grounds that advocate illegal drug use, saying that some federal aid is contingent on this policy. Civil libertarians, of course, see such policies as restricting students' right to free speech. Speaking for the Court's majority, Chief Justice Roberts said that the First Amendment did not require schools to permit students to advocate illegal drug use.

Commercial Speech Commercial speech, such as newspaper or television advertisements, does not have full First Amendment protection because it cannot be considered political speech. Initially considered to be entirely outside the protection of the First Amendment, commercial speech is still subject to some regulation. For example, the prohibition of false and misleading advertising by the Federal Trade Commission is an old and well-established power of the federal government. The Supreme Court long ago approved the constitutionality of laws prohibiting the electronic media from carrying cigarette advertising.[68] It has upheld city ordinances prohibiting the posting of all commercial signs on public property (as long as the ban is total, so that there is no hint of selective censorship).[69] And the Supreme Court, in a contentious 5–4 decision written by Chief Justice William

Rehnquist, upheld Puerto Rico's statute restricting gambling advertising aimed at residents of Puerto Rico.[70]

However, the gains far outweigh the losses in the effort to expand the protection of commercial speech under the First Amendment. "In part, this reflects the growing appreciation that commercial speech is part of the free flow of information necessary for informed choice and democratic participation."[71] For example, in 1975 the Supreme Court struck down a state statute making it a misdemeanor to sell or circulate newspapers encouraging abortions; the Court ruled that the statute infringed on constitutionally protected speech and on the right of the reader to make informed choices.[72] On a similar basis, the Court reversed its own earlier decisions upholding laws that prohibited dentists and other professionals from advertising their services. For the Court, medical service advertising was a matter of health that could be advanced by the free flow of information.[73] In 1996 the Court struck down Rhode Island laws and regulations banning the advertisement of liquor prices as a violation of the First Amendment.[74] And in a 2001 case, the Court ruled that a Massachusetts ban on all cigarette advertising violated the First Amendment right of the tobacco industry to advertise its products to adult consumers.[75] These instances of commercial speech, significant in themselves, are all the more significant because they indicate the breadth and depth of the freedom existing today to direct appeals to a large public, not only to sell goods and services but also to mobilize people for political purposes.

● The Second Amendment and the Right to Bear Arms

A loophole in gun purchase laws allowed a student at Virginia Tech with a history of mental illness to purchase the handguns he used to kill 32 people, including instructors and fellow students, and wound many others. Following the tragedy, both the state of Virginia and the national government strengthened the requirements for background checks on gun buyers.

> **Explore whether the Second Amendment means people have a right to own guns**

A well regulated Militia, being necessary to the security of a free State, the right of the people to keep and bear Arms, shall not be infringed.

The point and purpose of the Second Amendment is the provision for militias; they were to be the backing of the government for the maintenance of local public order. "Militia" was understood at the time of the Founding to be a military or police resource for state governments, and militias were specifically distinguished from armies and troops, which came within the sole constitutional jurisdiction of Congress.

Thus, the right of the people "to keep and bear Arms" is based on and associated with participation in state militias. The reference to citizens keeping arms underscored the fact that in the 1700s, state governments could not be relied on to provide firearms to militia members, so citizens eligible to serve in militias (white males between the ages of 18 and 45) were expected to keep their own firearms at the ready. In the late nineteenth century, some citizens sought to form their own *private* militias, but

The Second Amendment arouses as much controversy as the First. The right to bear arms is constitutionally guaranteed, although an estimated 80 percent of Americans support some form of gun control.

the Supreme Court cut that short with a ruling that militias are a military or police resource of state governments.[76] In 2008 the U.S. Supreme Court declared that the Second Amendment also protected an individual's right to possess a firearm for private use.[77] In the case of *District of Columbia v. Heller*, the Court struck down a Washington, D.C., law that was designed to make it nearly impossible for private individuals to purchase firearms legally. The District of Columbia is an entity of the federal government, and the Court did not indicate that its ruling applied to state firearms laws. However, in the 2010 case of *McDonald v. Chicago*, the Court struck down a Chicago firearms ordinance and applied the Second Amendment to the states as well,[78] making this the first new incorporation decision by the Court in 40 years.

● Rights of the Criminally Accused

Explain the major rights that people have if they are accused of a crime

Except for the First Amendment, most of the battle to apply the Bill of Rights to the states has been fought over the various protections granted to individuals who are accused of a crime, who are suspects in the commission of a crime, or who are brought before the court as a witness to a crime (Table 4.4). The Fourth, Fifth, Sixth, and Eighth amendments, taken together, are the essence of the **due process of law**, even though these precise words for this fundamental concept do not appear until the end of the Fifth Amendment. In the next sections, we will look at specific cases that illuminate the dynamics of this important constitutional issue. The procedural safeguards that we will discuss may seem remote to most law-abiding citizens, but they help define the limits of government action against the personal liberty of every citizen. Many Americans believe that "legal

due process of law the right of every citizen against arbitrary action by national or state governments

technicalities" are responsible for setting many actual criminals free. In many cases, this is absolutely true. In fact, setting defendants free is the very purpose of the requirements that constitute due process. One of America's traditional and most strongly held juridical values is that "it is far worse to convict an innocent man than to let a guilty man go free."[79] In civil suits, verdicts rest on "the preponderance of the evidence," but in criminal cases, guilt has to be proven "beyond a reasonable doubt"—a far higher standard. The provisions for due process in the Bill of Rights were added in order to improve the probability that the standard of "reasonable doubt" would be respected.

The Fourth Amendment and Searches and Seizures

> The right of the people to be secure in their persons, houses, papers, and effects, against unreasonable searches and seizures, shall not be violated, and no Warrants shall issue, but upon probable cause, supported by Oath or affirmation, and particularly describing the place to be searched, and the persons or things to be seized.

The purpose of the Fourth Amendment is to guarantee the security of citizens against unreasonable (i.e., improper) searches and seizures. In 1990 the Supreme Court summarized its understanding of the Fourth Amendment brilliantly and succinctly: "A search compromises the individual interest in privacy; a seizure deprives the individual of dominion over his or her person or property."[80] But how are we to define what is reasonable and what is unreasonable?

The 1961 case of *Mapp v. Ohio* illustrates one of the most important of the principles that have grown out of the Fourth Amendment—the **exclusionary rule**, which prohibits evidence obtained during an illegal search from being introduced in a trial. Acting on a tip that Dollree (Dolly) Mapp was harboring a suspect in a bombing incident, several policemen forcibly entered Mapp's house, claiming they had a warrant to look for the bombing suspect. The police did not find the bombing suspect but did find some materials connected to a local numbers racket (an illegal gambling operation) and a quantity of "obscene materials," in violation of

exclusionary rule the ability of courts to exclude evidence obtained in violation of the Fourth Amendment

Under what circumstances can the police search an individual's car? The Fourth Amendment protects against "unreasonable searches and seizures," but the Supreme Court has had to interpret what is unreasonable.

TABLE 4.4

The Rights of the Accused from Arrest to Trial

No improper searches and seizures (Fourth Amendment)

No arrest without probable cause (Fourth Amendment)

Right to remain silent (Fifth Amendment)

No self-incrimination during arrest or trial (Fifth Amendment)

Right to be informed of charges (Sixth Amendment)

Right to counsel (Sixth Amendment)

No excessive bail (Eighth Amendment)

Right to grand jury (Fifth Amendment)

Right to open trial before a judge (Article I, Section 9)

Right to speedy and public trial before an impartial jury (Sixth Amendment)

Evidence obtained by illegal search not admissible during trial (Fourth Amendment)

Right to confront witnesses (Sixth Amendment)

No double jeopardy (Fifth Amendment)

No cruel and unusual punishment (Eighth Amendment)

an Ohio law banning possession of such materials. Although no warrant was ever produced, the evidence that had been seized was admitted by a court, and Mapp was charged and convicted of illegal possession of obscene materials.

By the time Mapp's appeal reached the Supreme Court, the issue of obscene materials had faded into obscurity, and the question before the Court was whether any evidence produced under the circumstances of the search of her home was admissible. The Court's opinion affirmed the exclusionary rule: under the Fourth Amendment (applied to the states through the Fourteenth Amendment), "all evidence obtained by searches and seizures in violation of the Constitution . . . is inadmissible."[81] This means that even people who are clearly guilty of the crime of which they are accused must not be convicted if the only evidence for their conviction was obtained illegally. This idea was expressed by Supreme Court justice Benjamin Cardozo nearly a century ago, when he wrote that "the criminal is to go free because the constable has blundered."

The exclusionary rule is the most dramatic restraint imposed by the courts on police behavior because it rules out precisely the evidence that produces a conviction; it frees those people who are *known* to have committed the crime of which they have been accused. Thus, in recent years the Court has softened the application of the exclusionary rule, and federal courts have relied on its discretionary use, whereby they make a judgment as to the "nature and quality of the intrusion." It is thus difficult to know ahead of time whether a defendant will or will not be protected from an illegal search under the Fourth Amendment.[82] In 2006, in the case of *United States v. Grubbs*, the Supreme Court ruled that the police could conduct searches using such "anticipatory warrants"—warrants issued when the police know that incriminating material is not yet present but have reason to believe that it will eventually arrive at a particular premises.[83] The warrants are held until the police are ready to conduct their search. In some instances, such as during an arrest, the authorities can conduct searches without obtaining any warrants at all.

The Fourth Amendment is also at issue in the controversy over mandatory drug testing. Such tests are most widely applied to public employees, and in 1989 the Supreme Court upheld the U.S. Customs Service's drug-testing program for its employees.[84] That same year, the Court approved drug and alcohol tests for railroad workers if they were involved in serious accidents.[85] Since then, more than 40 federal agencies have initiated mandatory employee drug tests, giving rise to public appeals against the general practice of "suspicionless testing" of employees, in violation of the Fourth Amendment. A 1995 case, in which the Court upheld a public school district's policy requiring all students participating in interscholastic sports to submit to random drug tests, surely contributed to the efforts of federal, state, and local agencies to initiate random and suspicionless drug and alcohol testing.[86]

The most recent cases suggest, however, that the Court is beginning to consider limits on the war against drugs. In 2001 the Court found it unconstitutional for police to use trained dogs in roadblocks set up to look for drugs in cars. Unlike drunk-driving roadblocks, where public safety is directly involved, narcotics roadblocks "cannot escape the Fourth Amendment's requirement that searches be based on suspicion of individual wrongdoing."[87] In a decisive 8–1 decision in 1997, the Court applied the Fourth Amendment as a shield against "state action that diminishes personal privacy" in cases that do not involve high-risk or safety-sensitive tasks.[88] That same year, the Court extended protection against unlawful searches to passengers in cars that have been stopped by the police, giving passengers the same right as drivers to challenge the validity of a search.[89] The Court also ruled that a public hospital cannot constitutionally test maternity patients for illegal drug use without their consent,[90] and that the police may not use thermal imaging devices to detect suspicious patterns of heat emerging from private homes without obtaining the usual search warrant.[91] In 2009 the Court ruled against an Arizona school district that conducted a strip search of a thirteen-year-old student suspected of hiding ibuprofen in her underwear.[92]

The Fifth Amendment

No person shall be held to answer for a capital, or otherwise infamous crime, unless on a presentment or indictment of a Grand Jury, except in cases arising in the land or naval forces, or in the Militia, when in actual service in time of War or public danger; nor shall any person be subject for the same offence to be twice put in jeopardy of life or limb; nor shall be compelled in any criminal case to be a witness against himself, nor be deprived of life, liberty, or property, without due process of law; nor shall private property be taken for public use, without just compensation.

grand jury jury that determines whether sufficient evidence is available to justify a trial; grand juries do not rule on the accused's guilt or innocence

Grand Juries The first clause of the Fifth Amendment, the right to a **grand jury** to determine whether a trial is warranted, is considered "the oldest institution known to the Constitution."[93] Grand juries play an important role in federal criminal cases. However, the provision for a grand jury is the one important civil liberties provision of the Bill of Rights that was not incorporated into the Fourteenth Amendment to apply to state criminal prosecutions. Thus, some states operate without grand juries. In such states, the prosecuting attorney simply files a "bill of information" affirming that there is sufficient evidence available to justify a trial. If the accused person is to be held in custody, the prosecutor must take the available information before a judge to determine that the evidence shows probable cause.

Who Is in Prison?

Despite the many freedoms protected by the Bill of Rights, the United States imprisons more of its people than any other country. Although African Americans make up only about 13 percent of the total U.S. population, they make up 38 percent of the prison population. People convicted of violent crimes make up the majority of prison inmates, with drug offenders as the second largest group.

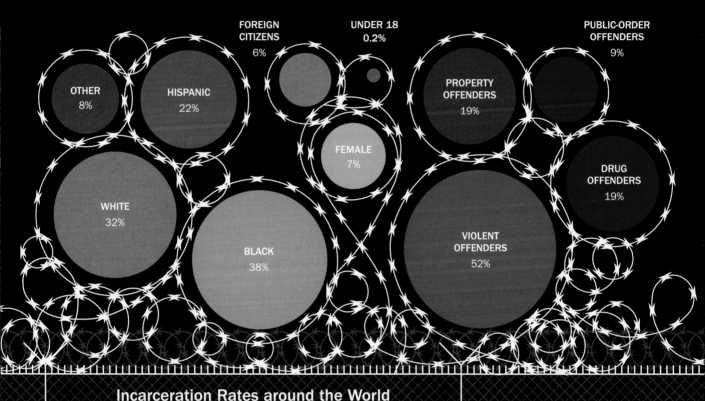

OTHER
8%

HISPANIC
22%

FOREIGN CITIZENS
6%

UNDER 18
0.2%

PROPERTY OFFENDERS
19%

PUBLIC-ORDER OFFENDERS
9%

FEMALE
7%

DRUG OFFENDERS
19%

WHITE
32%

BLACK
38%

VIOLENT OFFENDERS
52%

Incarceration Rates around the World
per 100,000 of the national population

RWANDA
595

UNITED STATES
743

RUSSIAN FEDERATION
568

SOUTH AFRICA
316

IRAN
291

ISRAEL
319

BRAZIL
253

MEXICO
200

MYANMAR
120

CHINA
122

FRANCE
96

SWITZERLAND
79

JAPAN
58

INDIA
32

NIGERIA
31

SOURCES: Bureau of Justice Statistics, "Prisoners in 2010" (2011); Roy Walmsley, "World Prison Population List," Ninth Edition (2011), International Centre for Prison Studies, School of Law, King's College, London.

for critical analysis

1. Due process guarantees the same legal protections to anyone accused of a crime. However, studies have shown that African Americans and Hispanics are more likely to be jailed—and jailed for longer—than whites convicted of similar crimes. Is this a violation of civil liberties?

2. Some people have argued that prison terms for relatively minor drug offenses violate the Eighth Amendment's ban on cruel and unusual punishment. What do you think?

double jeopardy the Fifth
Amendment right providing that a
person cannot be tried twice for
the same crime

Double Jeopardy "Nor shall any person be subject for the same offence to be twice put in jeopardy of life or limb" is the constitutional protection from **double jeopardy**, or being tried more than once for the same crime. The protection from double jeopardy was at the heart of the *Palko* case in 1937, which, as we saw earlier in this chapter, also established the principle of selective incorporation of the Bill of Rights. In that case, a Connecticut court had found Frank Palko guilty of second-degree murder and sentenced him to life in prison. Unhappy with the verdict, the state of Connecticut appealed the conviction to its highest court, won the appeal, got a new trial, and then succeeded in getting Palko convicted of first-degree murder. Palko appealed to the Supreme Court on what seemed an open-and-shut case of double jeopardy. Yet, although the majority of the Court agreed that this could indeed be considered a case of double jeopardy, they decided that double jeopardy was *not* one of the provisions of the Bill of Rights incorporated into the Fourteenth Amendment as a restriction on the powers of the states. It took more than 30 years for the Court to nationalize the constitutional protection against double jeopardy. Because Frank Palko lived in the state of Connecticut rather than in a state whose constitution included a guarantee against double jeopardy, he was eventually executed for the crime.

Self-Incrimination Perhaps the most significant liberty found in the Fifth Amendment, and the one most familiar to the many Americans who watch television crime shows, is the guarantee that no citizen "shall be compelled in any criminal case to be a witness against himself." The most famous case concerning self-incrimination is one of such importance that Chief Justice Earl Warren assessed its results as going "to the very root of our concepts of American criminal jurisprudence."[94] Twenty-three-year-old Ernesto Miranda was sentenced to between 20 and 30 years in prison for the kidnapping and rape of an eighteen-year-old woman. The woman had identified him in a police lineup, and after two hours of questioning, Miranda confessed, subsequently signing a statement that his confession had been made voluntarily, without threats or promises of immunity. These confessions were admitted into evidence, served as the basis for Miranda's conviction, and also served as the basis for the appeal of his conviction all the way to the Supreme Court. Following

The case of Ernesto Miranda resulted in the creation of Miranda rights, which must be read to those arrested to make them aware of their constitutional rights.

DEFENDANT		LOCATION	
SPECIFIC WARNING REGARDING INTERROGATIONS			
1. YOU HAVE THE RIGHT TO REMAIN SILENT.			
2. ANYTHING YOU SAY CAN AND WILL BE USED AGAINST YOU IN A COURT OF LAW.			
3. YOU HAVE THE RIGHT TO TALK TO A LAWYER AND HAVE HIM PRESENT WITH YOU WHILE YOU ARE BEING QUESTIONED.			
4. IF YOU CANNOT AFFORD TO HIRE A LAWYER ONE WILL BE APPOINTED TO REPRESENT YOU BEFORE ANY QUESTIONING, IF YOU WISH ONE.			
SIGNATURE OF DEFENDANT		DATE	
WITNESS		TIME	
☐ REFUSED SIGNATURE SAN FRANCISCO POLICE DEPARTMENT			PR.9.1.4

one of the most intensely and widely criticized decisions ever handed down by the Supreme Court, Ernesto Miranda's case produced the rules the police must follow before questioning an arrested criminal suspect. The reading of a person's "Miranda rights" became a standard scene in every police station and on virtually every dramatization of police action on television and in the movies. *Miranda* advanced the civil liberties of accused persons not only by expanding the scope of the Fifth Amendment clause covering coerced confessions and self-incrimination but also by confirming the right to counsel (discussed later). The Supreme Court under Burger and Rehnquist considerably softened the *Miranda* restrictions, but the **Miranda rule** still stands as a protection against egregious police abuses of arrested persons. The Supreme Court reaffirmed *Miranda* in *Dickerson v. United States* (2000). However, in the 2010 case of *Berghuis v. Thompkins*, the Supreme Court introduced an important qualification to the Miranda rule.[95] In a 5–4 decision, the Court said that statements made by suspects who did not expressly waive their rights (usually by signing a form) could be used against them. The dissenting justices feared that this decision might open the way for police abuses and misleading claims.

Miranda rule the requirement, articulated by the Supreme Court in *Miranda v. Arizona*, that persons under arrest must be informed prior to police interrogation of their rights to remain silent and to have the benefit of legal counsel

Eminent Domain The other fundamental clause of the Fifth Amendment is the "takings clause," which extends to each citizen a protection against the "taking" of private property "without just compensation." Although this part of the Fifth Amendment is not specifically concerned with protecting persons accused of crimes, it is nevertheless a fundamentally important instance where the government and the citizen are adversaries. The power of any government to take private property for public use—a power essential to the very concept of sovereignty—is called **eminent domain**. The Fifth Amendment neither invents eminent domain nor takes it away; its purpose is to put limits on that inherent power through procedures that require a showing of a public purpose and the provision of fair payment for the taking of someone's property. This provision is now universally observed in all U.S. principalities, but it has not always been meticulously observed.

eminent domain the right of government to take private property for public use

The first modern case confronting the issue of public use involved a mom-and-pop grocery store in a run-down neighborhood on the southwest side of the District of Columbia. In carrying out a vast urban redevelopment program, the city government of Washington, D.C., took the property as one of a large number of privately owned lots to be cleared for new housing and business construction. The owner of the grocery store, and his successors after his death, took the government to court on the grounds that it was an unconstitutional use of eminent domain to take property from one private owner and eventually to turn that property back, in altered form, to another private owner. In 1945 the store owners lost their case. The Supreme Court's argument was a curious but very important one: the "public interest" can mean virtually anything a legislature says it means. In other words, since the overall slum clearance and redevelopment project was in the public interest, according to the legislature, the eventual transfers of property were justified.[96] This principle was reaffirmed in the 2005 case of *Kelo v. City of New London*, where the Court held that the city could seize land from one private owner and transfer it to another as part of a redevelopment plan.[97]

The Sixth Amendment and the Right to Counsel

In all criminal prosecutions, the accused shall enjoy the right to a speedy and public trial, by an impartial jury of the State and district wherein the crime shall have been committed, which district shall have been previously ascertained by law, and to be informed of the nature and cause of the accusation; to be confronted with the witnesses against him; to have compulsory process for obtaining witnesses in his favor, and to have the Assistance of Counsel for his defence.

Like the exclusionary rule of the Fourth Amendment and the self-incrimination clause of the Fifth Amendment, the "right to counsel" provision of the Sixth Amendment is notable for sometimes freeing defendants who seem to be guilty as charged. Other provisions of the Sixth Amendment, such as the right to a speedy trial and the right to confront witnesses before an impartial jury, are less controversial in nature.

Gideon v. Wainwright (1963) is the perfect case study because it involved a disreputable person who seemed patently guilty of the crime of which he was convicted. In and out of jails for most of his 51 years, Clarence Earl Gideon received a five-year sentence for breaking and entering a poolroom in Panama City, Florida. While serving time in jail, Gideon became a fairly well-qualified "jailhouse lawyer," made his own appeal on a handwritten petition, and eventually won the landmark ruling on the right to counsel in all felony cases.[98]

The right to counsel has been expanded during the past few decades, even as the courts have become more conservative. For example, although at first the right to counsel was met by judges assigning lawyers from the community as a formal public obligation, now most states and cities have created an office of public defender; these state-employed professional defense lawyers typically provide poor defendants with much better legal representation. And although these defendants cannot afford to hire their own defense attorney, they do have the right to appeal a conviction on the grounds that the counsel provided by the state was deficient. For example, in 2003 the Supreme Court overturned the death sentence of a Maryland death row inmate, holding that the defense lawyer had failed to inform the jury fully of the defendant's history of "horrendous childhood abuse."[99] Moreover, the right to counsel extends beyond serious crimes to any trial, with or without a jury, that holds the possibility of imprisonment.[100] In the 2006 case of *United States v. Gonzalez-Lopez*, the Court held that a defendant had been deprived of his Sixth Amendment rights because the trial court had refused to allow him to make use of the particular counsel of his own choosing.[101]

The Eighth Amendment and Cruel and Unusual Punishment

Excessive bail shall not be required, nor excessive fines imposed, nor cruel and unusual punishment inflicted.

Virtually all the debate over Eighth Amendment issues focuses on the last clause of the amendment: one of the greatest challenges in interpreting this provision consistently is that what is considered "cruel and unusual" varies from culture to culture and from generation to generation.

In 1972 the Supreme Court overturned several state death-penalty laws, not because they were cruel and unusual but because they were being applied unevenly—that is, blacks were much more likely than whites to be sentenced to death, and the poor more likely than the rich, and men more likely than women.[102] Very soon after that decision, a majority of states revised their capital punishment provisions to meet the Court's standards, and the Court reaffirmed that the death penalty could be used if certain standards were met.[103] Since 1976, the Court

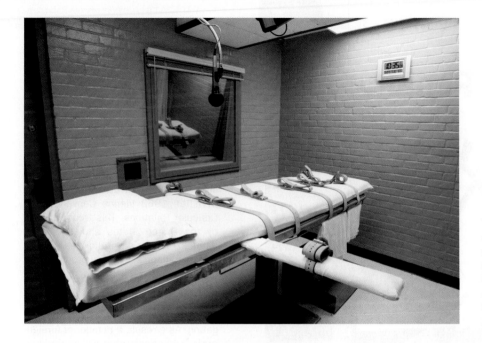

Thirty-seven states currently have the death penalty for the most serious crimes. Although a majority of Americans support the death penalty, it has always been controversial and is sometimes seen as a violation of the Eighth Amendment.

has consistently upheld state laws providing for capital punishment, although the Court also continues to review numerous death-penalty appeals each year.

Between 1976 and 2012, states executed 1,307 people. Most of those executions occurred in southern states, with Texas leading the way at 489. As of 2012, 33 states had statutes providing for capital punishment for specified offenses, a move approved of by about three-quarters of all Americans. And criminal conduct is traditionally defined by the states. In recent years, though, Congress has expanded federal criminal law, even imposing capital punishment for more than 50 federal crimes.

Despite the seeming popularity of the death penalty, the debate has become, if anything, more intense. Many death-penalty supporters assert its deterrent effects on other would-be criminals. Although studies of capital crimes usually fail to demonstrate any direct deterrent effect, this failure may be due to the lengthy delays—typically years and even decades—between convictions and executions. A system that eliminates undue delays might enhance deterrence. And deterring even one murder or other heinous crime, proponents argue, is ample justification for such laws. Beyond that, the death penalty is seen by proponents as a proper expression of retribution, embodying the biblical phrase "an eye for an eye": people who commit vicious crimes deserve to forfeit their lives in exchange for the suffering they have inflicted.

Death-penalty opponents are quick to counter that the death penalty has not been proved to deter crime, either in the United States or abroad. In fact, America is the only Western nation that still executes criminals. If the government is to serve as an example of proper behavior, say foes of capital punishment, it has no business sanctioning killing when incarceration will similarly protect society. Furthermore, execution is time-consuming and expensive—more expensive than life imprisonment—precisely because the government must make every effort to ensure that it is not executing an innocent person. Curtailing legal appeals would make the possibility of a mistake too great. And although most Americans do support the death penalty, people also support life imprisonment without the possibility of parole as an alternative. Race also intrudes in death-penalty cases: people of

The Death Penalty

The United States is the only Western democracy that continues to make use of capital punishment as a form of criminal sanction. Thirty-seven of the 50 states provide for the death penalty, as do the federal government and the military. Since 1976 the states have executed more than 1,000 convicted criminals. In 2011 alone, 43 individuals were put to death by state authorities. Though this is a small number compared with, say, China, which executed several thousand persons for a variety of crimes in 2011, it was enough executions to rank the United States fifth, just behind Yemen, in its use of execution as a form of punishment.

Though a majority of Americans support capital punishment, America's continuing use of the death penalty has put the United States at odds with its European allies and with Canada and Mexico, which have all abolished capital punishment. One area of conflict concerns the extradition of criminals. If an individual charged with or convicted of a crime flees to another country, the fugitive's home country may ask that he or she be returned home to face trial or punishment. The United States has extradition treaties with many nations. In recent years, however, a number of European nations have resisted extraditing fugitives to the United States if there has been a possibility that

those fugitives might face a death sentence upon their return.

One of the most important of these cases involved Jens Soering. Soering was arrested in the United Kingdom in 1986 on a U.S. extradition warrant charging that he and his girlfriend had murdered her parents in Virginia. The European Court of Human Rights ruled that Soering's extradition to the United States would violate the European Convention on Human Rights, which prohibited torture or other degrading forms of punishment, because, if convicted in Virginia, he could be sentenced to death. To obtain Soering's extradition, the United States had to assure Britain that he would not be prosecuted for capital murder. Subsequently, Soering was returned, tried, and sentenced to 99 years in prison. Since the Soering case, European authorities have generally made extradition to the United States conditional on American assurances that the individual sought by American

authorities not face capital charges if he or she is returned.

A second realm in which America's continuing use of capital punishment has created conflict with other nations stems from the 1963 Vienna Convention on Consular Relations. This treaty, signed by the United States and 162 other nations, requires the authorities to notify foreign nationals in their custody of their right to contact their own consulates for assistance before they are brought to trial. Police and courts in the United States often fail to comply with this obligation. As a result, a number of foreigners have been convicted of capital crimes and sentenced to death without having been allowed to contact their consulates for help. In 2001 the International Court of Justice ruled that the United States had violated its treaty obligations with Germany by executing a German citizen, Walter LaGrand, without notifying him of his treaty rights. In recent years, the Mexican government has challenged the convictions and death sentences of several Mexican nationals in the United States on the grounds that the individuals in question were not allowed to contact the Mexican consulate in a timely manner. In 2003, Mexico won a judgment against the United States in the International Court of Justice, but the U.S. Supreme Court ruled that Texas courts were not bound by this decision. Generally, U.S. courts have not been particularly hospitable to Vienna Convention claims.

SOURCE: William A. Schabas, "Indirect Abolition: Capital Punishment's Role in Extradition Law and Practice," *Loyola Los Angeles International and Comparative Law Review* 25 (2003): 581–604.

for critical analysis

1. America's continued use of capital punishment has complicated its relations with its neighbors and allies. Should the United States adjust its laws to accommodate the wishes of other nations?

2. What might explain why the United States continues to use capital punishment, whereas other Western nations have abandoned the practice?

color are disproportionately more likely than whites charged with identical crimes to be given the ultimate punishment.

The Supreme Court has long struggled to establish principles to govern executions. In recent years, the Court has issued a number of death-penalty opinions, declaring that death was too harsh a penalty for a child rapist[104] and invalidating a death sentence for a black defendant after the prosecutor improperly excluded African Americans from the jury.[105] On the other hand, in a decision that received worldwide attention, the Court ruled that the International Court of Justice had no authority to order a Texas court to reopen a death-penalty case involving a foreign national.[106] The Court also upheld Kentucky's policy of execution by lethal injection despite arguments that this form of execution was likely to cause considerable pain.[107]

● The Right to Privacy

> **Assess whether people have a right to privacy under the Constitution**

A **right to privacy** was not granted in the Bill of Rights, but a clause in the Fourth Amendment provides for "the right of the people to be secure in their persons, houses, papers, and effects, against unreasonable searches and seizures." In a 1928 case, Justice Louis Brandeis argued in a dissent that the Fourth Amendment should be extended to a more general principle of "privacy in the home."[108] Another step in this direction was taken when several Jehovah's Witnesses directed their children not to salute the flag or say the Pledge of Allegiance in school because the first of the Ten Commandments prohibits the worship of "graven images." They lost their case in 1940, but the Supreme Court, reversing itself in 1943, held that the 1940 case had been "wrongly decided" and recognized "a right to be left alone" as part of the free speech clause of the First Amendment.[109] Another small step was taken in 1958, when the Supreme Court recognized "privacy in one's association" in its decision that the state of Alabama could not use the membership list of the National Association for the Advancement of Colored People (NAACP) in state investigations.[110]

right to privacy the right to be left alone, which has been interpreted by the Supreme Court to entail individual access to birth control and abortions

> **for critical analysis**
> Read the Third, Fourth, Fifth, and Ninth amendments in the appendix at the end of this book. In your opinion, do American citizens have a right to privacy?

Birth Control

The sphere of privacy was formally recognized in 1965, when the Court ruled that a Connecticut statute forbidding the use of contraceptives violated the right of marital privacy. Estelle Griswold, the executive director of the Planned Parenthood League of Connecticut, was arrested by the state of Connecticut for providing information, instruction, and medical advice about contraception to married couples. She and her associates were found guilty as accessories to the crime and fined $100 each. The Supreme Court reversed the lower court decisions and declared the Connecticut law unconstitutional because it violated "a right of privacy older than the Bill of Rights—older than our political parties, older than our school system."[111] Justice William O. Douglas, author of the majority decision in the *Griswold* case, argued that this right of privacy is also grounded in the Constitution, because it fits into a "zone of privacy" created by a combination of the Third, Fourth, and Fifth amendments. A concurring opinion, written by Justice Arthur Goldberg, attempted to strengthen Douglas's argument by adding that "the concept of liberty . . . embraces the right of marital privacy though that right is not mentioned explicitly in the Constitution [and] is supported by numerous decisions of this Court . . . and *by the language and history of the Ninth Amendment* [emphasis added]."[112]

Abortion

The right to privacy was confirmed and extended in 1973 in one of the most important Supreme Court decisions in American history: *Roe v. Wade.* This decision established a woman's right to seek an abortion and prohibited states from making abortion a criminal act.[113] The Burger Court's decision in *Roe* took a revolutionary step toward establishing the right to privacy. It is important to emphasize that the preference for privacy rights and for their extension to include the rights of women to control their own bodies was not something the Supreme Court invented in a vacuum. Most states did not regulate abortions in any fashion until the 1840s, at which time only 6 of the 26 existing states had any regulations governing abortion. In addition, many states had begun to ease their abortion restrictions well before the 1973 *Roe* decision, although in recent years a number of states have reinstated some restrictions on abortion.

By extending the umbrella of privacy, this sweeping ruling dramatically changed abortion practices in America. In addition, it galvanized and nationalized

One of the most important cases related to the right to privacy was Roe v. Wade, *which established a woman's right to seek an abortion. However, the decision has remained highly controversial, with opponents arguing that the Constitution does not guarantee this right.*

the abortion debate. Groups opposed to abortion, such as the National Right to Life Committee, organized to fight the liberal new standard, while abortion rights groups have sought to maintain that protection. In recent years, the legal standard shifted against abortion rights supporters in two key Supreme Court cases. In *Webster v. Reproductive Health Services* (1989), the Court narrowly upheld (by a 5–4 majority) the constitutionality of restrictions on the use of public medical facilities for abortion.[114] And in the 1992 case of *Planned Parenthood of Southeastern Pennsylvania v. Casey*, another 5–4 majority of the Court upheld *Roe* but narrowed its scope, refusing to invalidate a Pennsylvania law that significantly limits freedom of choice. The Court's decision defined the right to an abortion as a "limited or qualified" right subject to regulation by the states as long as the regulation does not constitute an "undue burden."[115] In the 2000 case of *Stenberg v. Carhart*, the Court, by a vote of 5 to 4, struck down Nebraska's ban on partial-birth abortions because the law had the "effect of placing a substantial obstacle in the path of a woman seeking an abortion."[116] However, in the 2006 case of *Ayotte v. Planned Parenthood of Northern New England*, the Court held that a law requiring parental notification before a minor could obtain an abortion was not an undue burden.[117] And in *Gonzales v. Carhart*, the Court effectively reversed its earlier *Carhart* decision by upholding the federal partial-birth abortion ban, which was virtually identical to the Nebraska law it had struck down in 2000.[118]

Homosexuality

In the last two decades, the right to be left alone began to include the privacy rights of homosexuals. One morning in Atlanta, Georgia, in the mid-1980s, a police officer came to the home of Michael Hardwick to serve a warrant for Hardwick's arrest for failure to appear in court to answer charges of drinking in public. One of Hardwick's unknowing housemates invited the officer to look in Hardwick's room, where he found Hardwick and another man engaging in "consensual sexual behavior" and then proceeded to arrest him under Georgia's laws against heterosexual and homosexual sodomy. Hardwick filed a lawsuit against

The right to privacy has also included the rights of gay men and lesbians. Here, supporters of gay rights celebrate the repeal in 2011 of the military's "don't ask don't tell" policy, which was seen as discriminatory in part because a service member could be dismissed based on his or her private sexual conduct.

A Right to Privacy Online?

While the right to privacy is not explicitly written into the Constitution, the common understanding is that Americans do enjoy a right to privacy. The Courts have wavered in terms of how far to extend this right. Many observers predict that in the coming years the major cases in this area will involve individuals seeking protection of their privacy online.

Currently it is not illegal for a potential employer to ask for an individual's password and Facebook login to see what that person has been doing. Companies will often Google an individual they are considering hiring to see if his or her behavior online can inform hiring decisions. A 2012 survey found that 46 percent of company executives said their company does and will continue to consider an individual's "online profiles" (including Facebook, Twitter, blogs, and the like) in hiring decisions. Almost half of those surveyed consider inappropriate content on social networking sites also as a legitimate reason for termination of a current employee.

What we post online affects more than our economic opportunities. If, for example, you share a picture in which you are keying an ex-boyfriend's car or committing another crime, the police can use that as evidence against you. No warrant is needed, and the image is not protected by a right to privacy. Government agencies ranging from local police to the FBI routinely check Facebook, Twitter, and other online social media sites for evidence of illegal activities, as individuals who commit crimes often post pictures of their crimes or other evidence online. Even street gangs now have Facebook pages where fans can "like" their photos and comments. Headline news was made when the Justice Department sought Twitter account information from individuals working with WikiLeaks, the website that spills government secrets. Twitter went to court to fight for permission to notify its subscribers that the government had requested their account information.

Other concerns about online privacy involve the tracking of Internet users. Google and other large technology companies have admitted to tracking user habits, data, and personal information and selling this information to outside marketing companies without the users' permission. This practice, and other instances of companies using individuals' information without permission, led to the Consumer Privacy Bill of Rights promoted by the Obama administration in 2012. The Consumer Privacy Bill of Rights is a blueprint for giving citizens more control over  how their personal information is used on the Internet. The Commerce Department will begin convening companies' representatives, privacy advocates, and other stakeholders to develop and implement enforceable privacy policies based on the Consumer Privacy Bill of Rights. However, these guidelines are not yet law.

While the White House, Congress, and many state legislatures are considering how to protect people's personal information online, there is still no formal right to privacy online. What you post can and likely will be used to determine whether you've committed any crimes and your suitability for hiring by a potential employer. Even if the Consumer Privacy Bill of Rights or some comparable law is eventually passed, the police, the FBI, and others involved in law enforcement will still be able to use what you post as evidence if you are charged with a crime. The proposed "privacy bills" are aimed at stopping companies from tracking your usage and selling your information, not at protecting you from the consequences of sharing information online.

SOURCES: Stan Finger, "Police: Street Gangs Embrace Social Media, Too," *Wichita Eagle*, June 10, 2012, www.kansas.com/2012/06/10/2366765/police-street-gangs-embrace-social.html (accessed 6/14/12). David Goldman, David, "White House Pushes Online Privacy Bill of Rights." CNN Money, February 23, 2012, http://money.cnn.com/2012/02/23/technology/privacy_bill_of_rights/index.htm (accessed 6/14/12). Daniel Hong, "Your Facebook Profile Could Affect Your Hiring Potential," PRWeb, May 31, 2012, www.prweb.com/releases/prweb2012/5/prweb9556895.htm (accessed 6/14/12).

for critical analysis

1. With the migration of more personal information online via social networking sites, should Congress pass a law to protect citizens' privacy online? Why or why not?

2. How does a right to privacy differ from our other constitutionally protected rights?

the state, challenging the constitutionality of the Georgia law, and won his case in the federal court of appeals. The state of Georgia, in an unusual move, appealed the court's decision to the Supreme Court. The majority of the Court reversed the lower court decision, holding against Hardwick on the grounds that "the federal Constitution confers [no] fundamental right upon homosexuals to engage in sodomy," and that therefore there was no basis to invalidate "the laws of the many states that still make such conduct illegal and have done so for a very long time."[119]

Seventeen years later, and to almost everyone's surprise, in *Lawrence v. Texas* (2003) the Court overturned *Bowers v. Hardwick* with a dramatic pronouncement that gays are "entitled to respect for their private lives"[120] as a matter of constitutional due process. Drawing from the tradition of negative liberty, the Court maintained, "In our tradition the State is not omnipresent in the home. And there are other spheres of our lives and existence outside the home, where the State should not be a dominant presence." Explicitly encompassing lesbians and gay men within the umbrella of privacy, the Court concluded that the "petitioners are entitled to respect for their private lives. The State cannot demean their existence or control their destiny by making their private sexual conduct a crime."[121] This decision added substance to the "right of privacy."[122]

The Right to Die

Another area ripe for litigation and public discourse is the so-called right to die. A number of highly publicized physician-assisted suicides in the 1990s focused attention on whether people have a right to choose their own death and to receive assistance in carrying it out. Can this become part of the privacy right? Or is it a new substantive right? The Supreme Court has not definitively answered this question. However, the Court refused to intervene in the well-publicized case of Terri Schiavo, a woman who suffered irreversible brain damage and was kept alive in a vegetative state via a feeding tube for 15 years. During this period, Schiavo's husband wanted to withdraw life support, citing his wife's wishes, while her parents wanted support continued indefinitely. The case was heard multiple times in the Florida state courts and the federal courts. In 2005, Schiavo's husband finally prevailed, and she was removed from life support and subsequently died. In the 2006 case of *Gonzales v. Oregon*, however, the Supreme Court did intervene to uphold a law allowing doctors to use drugs to facilitate the deaths of terminally ill patients who requested such assistance.[123] Thus, although the Court has not ruled definitively on the right-to-die question, it does not seem hostile to the idea.

● Thinking Critically about the Future of Civil Liberties

In the months after the September 11 terrorists attacks against the United States, President George W. Bush issued a series of executive orders to combat the threat of terrorism. He authorized the indefinite detention at the Guantánamo Bay military prison in Cuba of individuals whom he designated enemy combatants, the creation of special military tribunals to try enemy combatants, and the initiation of a massive warrantless surveillance program by the National Security Agency (NSA) to monitor communications into and out of the United States. The president averred that these policies were necessary to protect the nation, but each

The dilemma of balancing liberty and security has continued during the Obama administration. The introduction of full-body scanners at some airports was criticized as an intrusion on individual rights but also has been defended as a necessary step to prevent terrorist attacks.

of his orders was denounced by civil libertarians as an intrusion on constitutional rights and was challenged in the courts.

In the 2004 case of *Hamdi v. Rumsfeld*, the Supreme Court ruled that those declared enemy combatants could challenge their detention before a judge, but the Court affirmed the president's power to declare even U.S. citizens to be enemy combatants.[124] In 2006, in the case of *Hamdan v. Rumsfeld*, the Court invalidated the military tribunals established by presidential order, because their procedures did not accord with current law. The Court, however, accepted the principle that the president could order the creation of such tribunals as long as their procedures had some statutory basis. Congress provided that basis in the 2006 Military Commissions Act, which mainly reaffirmed the procedures that had been devised by the president.[125] The act also seemed partially to reverse the *Hamdi* decision by declaring that prisoners at Guantánamo could not present habeas corpus petitions to the federal courts to challenge their detention. The legality of that portion of the act is currently being debated in the federal courts.

As for the NSA surveillance program, in 2007 the Sixth Circuit Court of Appeals upheld the program's validity, but the ACLU has appealed the decision to the Supreme Court. Under new rules established by President Bush, the NSA requests warrants from the Foreign Intelligence Surveillance (FISA) Court, a secretive panel established to hear top-secret cases. The president, however, reserved the right to order warrantless searches if he deemed them to be necessary. The Obama administration took the same position and sent government lawyers to defend the program. As these "war on terrorism" cases illustrate, battles over civil liberties are not abstract, historical matters. They are part of our lives today.

When President Obama took office in 2009, civil libertarians were confident that the new administration would move quickly to curb what many saw as the civil liberties abuses of the Bush years, primarily those associated with the war on terrorism. After Obama's first year in office, however, civil libertarians gave the president a mixed review. Anthony Romero, director of the ACLU, declared that the Obama administration had "made some significant strides toward restoring civil liberties and the rule of law."[126] Nevertheless, the ACLU took the Obama administration to task for continuing a number of Bush's policies. Thus, while Obama issued executive orders closing the Guantánamo Bay prison, which housed a number of terrorism suspects, the prison actually remained open, holding detainees without charge or trial while the administration considered what to do with them. Similarly, although Obama ordered an end to the harsh interrogation of terrorist suspects countenanced by the Bush administration, he showed little interest in investigating charges of prisoner abuse by the military and intelligence agencies. The ACLU criticized Obama for not bringing an end to government spying on Americans, the monitoring of political activists, and the continued use of secret detentions and removals of terrorist suspects to overseas facilities.

Many Americans believe that America's reputation in the world has been hurt by the image of prisoners being held without proper legal process, and they are eager to find ways to restore America's reputation as a bastion of liberty. At the same time, of course, no president wishes to see dangerous foes of the United States do harm to Americans. The dilemma of liberty versus security is rarely easy to resolve.

Freedom of Speech, the Right to Privacy, and Digital Media

Inform Yourself

Know your rights and protect your information online. Visit the Electronic Frontier Foundation's (EFF) website (www.eff.org), which is dedicated to protecting freedom on the Internet. Since there is no established right to privacy online, the EFF works to defend digital rights, including privacy, free speech, innovation, and consumer rights. Click on the "Our Work" tab to see the EFF's "Whitepapers" (reports). Your computer, phone, and other digital devices hold vast amounts of personal information about you and your family. Read the "Know Your Rights" (June 2011) white paper to learn how to protect your personal documents.

Understand current issues in digital rights. The EFF's Deeplink Blog provides up-to-the-minute reporting on current political issues and issues of civil liberties that may affect you and others you know. There are posts on online video privacy, drones, bloggers' rights, coders' rights, free speech, surveillance self-defense, worldwide Internet censorship, cell phone tracking data from wireless carriers, personal data and social media, patent problems, and much more.

Think critically about civil liberties issues. The American Civil Liberties Union (www.aclu.org) is one of the country's oldest and most active groups working to protect civil liberties. Visit its website and select a "Key Issue," such as Internet privacy, rights of individuals accused of a crime, immigration, religion, reproductive freedom, or flag burning. Read the arguments for protecting these rights. Do you agree or disagree with the ACLU's position on the issue? Why?

Express Yourself

Read and consider signing the petitions available at the EFF's website to defend digital rights online, by clicking the "Take Action" tab. Do you believe in a free and open Internet? What about the rights of bloggers who are the victims of frivolous lawsuits for legitimate online content? How do you feel about criminal penalties for online streaming of copyrighted videos? (Congress is considering such a law.)

Would you burn a virtual flag? The Flag Burning Page (www.esquilax.com/flag/index2.shtml) gives visitors the opportunity to burn a virtual flag, and points out that if the Constitution were amended to ban flag desecration (as has been proposed), the page would be illegal. The Supreme Court considers burning the American flag an act protected by the First Amendment right to free speech. Do you agree or disagree?

Find links to the sites listed above as well as related activities on wwnorton.com/studyspace.

Ⓢ **Practice online with:** Chapter 4 Diagnostic Quiz ▪ Chapter 4 Key Term Flashcards

A Brief History of the Bill of Rights

■ **Explain how the civil liberties included in the Bill of Rights were "nationalized" (pp. 115–19)**

Although some believed that a bill of rights was unnecessary and potentially dangerous, the Federalists made a pledge to add one in order to secure support for the Constitution during the ratification process. During the first hundred years of American history, the Bill of Rights was interpreted to limit only the actions of the federal government. One by one, most of the important provisions of the first 10 amendments have eventually been incorporated into the Fourteenth Amendment and applied to the states.

Key Terms

habeas corpus (p. 115)

bill of attainder (p. 115)

ex post facto laws (p. 115)

Bill of Rights (p. 116)

civil liberties (p. 116)

selective incorporation (p. 117)

Practice Quiz

1. From 1789 until the end of the nineteenth century, the Bill of Rights put limits on *(pp. 116–19)*
   a) the national government only.
   b) the state government only.
   c) both the national and state governments.
   d) neither the national nor the state government.
   e) political parties and interest groups.

2. Which of the following rights were *not* included in the original Constitution? *(p. 115)*
   a) prohibition of bills of attainder
   b) prohibition of ex post facto laws

c) guarantee of habeas corpus
   d) guarantee of trial by jury in the state where the crime was committed
   e) None—they were all included in the original Constitution.

3. Which of the following provided that all of the protections contained in the Bill of Rights applied to the states as well as national government? *(pp. 116–19)*
   a) the First Amendment
   b) the Fourteenth Amendment
   c) *Palko v. Connecticut*
   d) *Gitlow v. New York*
   e) none of the above

4. The process by which some of the liberties in the Bill of Rights were applied to the states (or nationalized) is known as *(p. 117)*
   a) preemption.
   b) selective incorporation.
   c) judicial activism.
   d) civil liberties.
   e) establishment.

5. Which of the following provisions of the Bill of Rights was incorporated in 2010? *(p. 119)*
   a) the right to counsel in any criminal trial
   b) the right against self-incrimination
   c) freedom from unnecessary searches and seizures
   d) freedom to petition the government for redress of grievance
   e) the right to bear arms

 Practice Online
Video exercise: *Where Do Civil Liberties Come From?*

The First Amendment and Freedom of Religion

■ **Describe how the First Amendment protects freedom of religion (pp. 119–22)**

Two parts of the First Amendment touch on religious freedom: the establishment clause and the free exercise clause. The courts have been somewhat inconsistent in determining how porous the establishment clause's "wall of separation" between church and state actually is in practice. While the courts have been more consistent in protecting the free exercise of religious beliefs, they have

taken pains to distinguish between religious beliefs and actions based on those beliefs.

Key Terms

establishment clause (p. 119)

Lemon **test** (p. 120)

free exercise clause (p. 121)

Practice Quiz

6. Which of the following protections are *not* contained in the First Amendment? *(pp. 119–32)*
   a) the establishment clause
   b) the free exercise clause
   c) freedom of the press
   d) the right to peaceably assemble
   e) All of the above are First Amendment protections.

7. The so-called *Lemon* test, derived from the Supreme Court's ruling in *Lemon v. Kurtzman*, concerns the issue of *(p. 120)*
   a) school desegregation.
   b) aid to religious schools.
   c) cruel and unusual punishment.
   d) obscenity.
   e) prayer in school.

 Practice Online
Video exercise *Religious Freedom and Contraception*

The First Amendment and Freedom of Speech and of the Press

■ **Describe how the First Amendment protects free speech (pp. 122–32)**

Given the importance of freedom of speech and of the press to the functioning of democratic government, Americans are assumed to have the right to speak and broadcast their ideas unless there is some compelling reason to stop them. According to the courts, although virtually all speech is protected by the Constitution, some forms of speech are entitled to a greater degree of protection than others, Libel, slander, and speech that incites lawless action are examples of speech that can be limited by the government.

Key Terms

"clear and present danger" test (p. 123)

"speech plus" (p. 126)

prior restraint (p. 126)

libel (p. 127)

slander (p. 127)

fighting words (p. 130)

Practice Quiz

8. The judicial doctrine that places a heavy burden of proof on the government when it seeks to regulate or restrict speech is called *(p. 123)*
   a) judicial restraint.
   b) judicial activism.
   c) habeas corpus.
   d) prior restraint.
   e) strict scrutiny.

9. Which of the following describes a written statement made in "reckless disregard of the truth" that is considered damaging to a victim because it is "malicious, scandalous, and defamatory"? *(p. 137)*
   a) slander
   b) libel
   c) speech plus
   d) fighting words
   e) expressive speech

 Practice Online
Video exercise: The Daily Show with Jon Stewart, *Headlines—Flame Retarded*

The Second Amendment and the Right to Bear Arms

■ **Explore whether the Second Amendment means people have a right to own guns (pp. 132–33)**

The Second Amendment granted Americans the right "to keep and bear Arms" in order to provide for state militias. Prior to 2010, the Second Amendment was not incorporated. In *McDonald v. Chicago*, the Supreme Court asserted that the right to bear arms applies to both state governments and the federal government.

Practice Quiz

10. In *McDonald v. Chicago*, the Supreme Court ruled that *(p. 133)*
    a) states can require citizens to own firearms.

    b) federal grants can be used to support the formation of state militias.
    c) felons can be prevented from purchasing assault rifles.
    d) the Second Amendment applies to states as well as the federal government.
    e) the Second Amendment applies only to the federal government and not to states.

Rights of the Criminally Accused

 Explain the major rights that people have if they are accused of a crime (pp. 133–43)

The essence of the Constitution's due process of the law is found in the Fourth, Fifth, Sixth, and Eighth amendments. The Fourth Amendment protects individuals from unreasonable searches and seizures. The Fifth Amendment provides individuals with the right to a grand jury, protection from double jeopardy, and a guarantee against self-incrimination. The Sixth Amendment provides the right to legal counsel, the right to a speedy trial, and the right to confront witnesses before an impartial jury. The Eighth Amendment protects individuals against "cruel and unusual" punishment.

Key Terms

due process of law (p. 133)

exclusionary law (p. 134)

grand jury (p. 136)

double jeopardy (p. 138)

Miranda rule (p. 139)

eminent domain (p. 139)

Practice Quiz

11. The Fourth, Fifth, Sixth, and Eighth amendments, taken together, define *(p. 133)*
    a) freedom of religion.
    b) due process of law.
    c) free speech.
    d) the right to bear arms.
    e) civil rights of minorities.

12. In *Mapp v. Ohio,* the Supreme Court ruled that *(p. 134)*
    a) evidence obtained from an illegal search could not be introduced in a trial.
    b) the government must provide legal counsel for defendants who are too poor to provide it for themselves.
    c) persons under arrest must be informed prior to police interrogation of their rights to remain silent and to have the benefits of legal counsel.
    d) the government has the right to take private property for public use if just compensation is provided.
    e) a person cannot be tried twice for the same crime.

13. Which famous case deals with Sixth Amendment issues? *(p. 140)*
    a) *Roe v. Wade*
    b) *Mapp v. Ohio*
    c) *Gideon v. Wainwright*
    d) *Terry v. Ohio*
    e) *Miranda v. Arizona*

 Practice Online
"You Decide" exercise: *The USA PATRIOT Act*

The Rights to Privacy

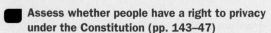 **Assess whether people have a right to privacy under the Constitution (pp. 143–47)**

A right to privacy is never explicitly mentioned in the Constitution. In fact, it was not until 1965 that the Supreme Court interpreted the Third, Fourth, Fifth, and Ninth amendments to create a constitutional "zone of privacy." The right to privacy has since been used to strike down laws limiting access to birth control, outlawing abortion, and criminalizing gay and lesbian sexual activity.

Key Term

right to privacy (p. 143)

Practice Quiz

14. In what case was a right to privacy first found in the Constitution? *(p. 152)*
    a) *Griswold v. Connecticut*
    b) *Roe v. Wade*
    c) *Lemon v. Kurtzman*
    d) *Planned Parenthood v. Casey*
    e) *Baker v. Carr*

15. In which case did the Supreme Court rule that state governments no longer had the authority to make private sexual behavior a crime? *(p. 147)*
    a) *Texas v. Johnson*
    b) *Webster v. Reproductive Health Services*
    c) *Gonzales v. Oregon*
    d) *Lawrence v. Texas*
    e) *Bowers v. Hardwick*

Practice Online
Video exercise: *Stop the Spying! People for the American Way and the Electronic Frontier Foundation*

For Further Reading

Barendt, Eric. *Freedom of Speech.* 2nd ed. New York: Oxford University Press, 2007.

Brandon, Mark. *The Constitution in Wartime.* Durham, NC: Duke University Press, 2005.

Cash, Arthur. *John Wilkes: The Scandalous Father of Civil Liberties.* New Haven, CT: Yale University Press, 2007.

Cook, Byrne. *Reporting the War: Freedom of the Press from the American Revolution to the War on Terror.* New York: Palgrave Macmillan, 2007.

Domino, John. *Civil Rights and Liberties in the 21st Century.* 3rd ed. New York: Longman, 2009.

Dworkin, Ronald. *Justice in Robes.* Cambridge, MA: Belknap Press, 2006.

Fisher, Louis. *Military Tribunals and Presidential Power.* Lawrence: University Press of Kansas, 2005.

Friendly, Fred W. *Minnesota Rag: The Dramatic Story of the Landmark Supreme Court Case that Gave New Meaning to Freedom of the Press.* New York: Vintage, 1982.

Glendon, Mary Ann. *Rights Talk: The Impoverishment of Political Discourse.* New York: Free Press, 1991.

Hentoff, Nat. *The First Freedom: The Tumultuous History of Free Speech in America.* New York: Basic Books, 1994.

Lewis, Anthony. *Gideon's Trumpet.* New York: Random House, 1964.

David M O'Brien, *Constitutional Law and Politics: Civil Rights and Civil Liberties.* 8th ed. Vol. 2. New York: W. W. Norton, 2011.

Sundby, Scott. A Life and Death Decision: A Jury Weighs the Death Penalty. New York: Palgrave Macmillan, 2007.

Recommended Websites

The American Civil Liberties Union (ACLU)
www.aclu.org

The ACLU is committed in protecting for all individuals the freedoms found in the Bill of Rights. This sometimes controversial organization constantly monitors the government for violations of liberty and encourages its members to take political action.

Electronic Privacy Information Center
http://epic.org/privacy

For an extensive list of privacy issues, go to the Web page for the Electronic Privacy Information Center. Here you will find civil liberties concerns as they relate to all forms of information technology, including the Internet.

The Free Expression Network
www.freeexpression.org

The Free Expression Network is an organization "dedicated to preserving the right to free expression." On its website you can find links to important First Amendment issues and organizations.

Freedom Forum
www.freedomforum.org

Freedom of speech and freedom of the press are considered critical in any democracy; however, only some kinds of speech are fully protected against restrictions. Freedom Forum is a nonpartisan agency that investigates and analyzes such First Amendment restrictions.

National Abortion and Reproductive Rights Action League
www.naral.org

National Right to Life Committee
www.HRIC.org

The National Abortion and Reproductive Rights Action League and the National Right to Life Committee are two of the nation's largest interest groups weighing in on the abortion issue. See what these opposing groups have to say about privacy rights.

Religious Freedom Page
http://religiousfreedom.lib.virginia.edu

The establishment clause of the U.S. Constitution has been interpreted to mean a "wall of separation" between government and religion. On the Religious Freedom Page you can find information on a variety of issues pertaining to religious freedom in the United States and around the world.

U.S. Supreme Court Media
www.oyez.org

This website for U.S. Supreme Court media has a great search engine for finding information on cases affecting civil liberties, such as *Lemon v. Kurtzman*, *Miranda v. Arizona*, *Mapp v. Ohio*, and *New York Times v. Sullivan*, to name a few.

Today, many conflicts about civil rights relate to immigration law and Latinos. In 2011 the debate over the rights of immigrants erupted into mass protests after Arizona and Georgia passed controversial laws targeting Latino immigrants.

Civil Rights

WHAT GOVERNMENT DOES AND WHY IT MATTERS In 2011 the federal Department of Justice accused the Maricopa County Sheriff's Office in Phoenix, Arizona, of violating the civil rights of Latinos. The results of a three-year investigation showed that the Sheriff's Department had routinely used racial profiling to detain and arrest Latinos and that county jails discriminated against people who spoke limited English. Both practices, Justice officials declared, were unconstitutional. At the same time, however, advocates charged that the federal government itself violated the Constitution in implementing the Secure Communities program. A centerpiece of the Obama administration's immigration policy, Secure Communities connects local police with the Department of Homeland Security to identify and deport undocumented residents who break the law. However, studies show that the program also has detained American citizens, who have been held illegally for days at a time.[1] The presence of an estimated 11 million undocumented immigrants in the United States presents the government with a thorny set of questions about civil rights. How aggressively should the government seek out and deport undocumented immigrants? How can the civil rights of Americans and legal residents be protected as the government enforces immigration laws?

Today, many conflicts about civil rights relate to immigration laws and Latinos. Fifty years ago, the African American struggle for equal rights took center stage. Many goals of the civil rights movement that once aroused bitter controversy are now widely accepted as part of the American commitment to equal rights. But even today the question of what is meant by "equal rights" is hardly settled. Although most Americans reject the idea that government should create equal outcomes for its citizens, they do widely endorse government action to prohibit public and private discrimination, and they do support the idea of equality of opportunity. However, even these concepts are elusive. When immigration law leads to civil rights violations and discrimination against Latinos, should the enforcement efforts be abandoned? When past denial of rights creates unequal starting points for some groups, should government take additional steps to ensure equal opportunity? What kinds of groups should be specially protected against discrimination? Should the disabled receive special protection? Should lesbians and gay men? What about individuals who identify as bisexual and transgender? Finally, what kinds of steps are acceptable to remedy discrimination, and who should bear the costs? These questions are at the heart of contemporary debates over civil rights.

The answers that Americans give to these questions have shifted dramatically over the course of our nation's history. But ideas about civil rights did not change easily; advocates who challenged barriers to civil rights often struggled against strong resistance. The election of Barack Obama as the nation's first black president is a testament to the successes of those struggles but does not by itself alter persistent social and economic differences across racial lines. The black civil rights movement inspired a new wave of movements for equality, as groups including women, gay men and lesbians, Native Americans, Latinos, and the disabled launched campaigns for equal rights.

This chapter will show how inequalities between races and genders were tolerated and even enforced by law during much of our country's history. Although the United States was founded on the ideals of liberty, equality, and democracy, its history of civil rights reveals a gap between these principles and actual practice. This history also demonstrates how the struggle to attain those ideals has helped narrow this gap. More recently, the ongoing struggle for political and social equality also shows how liberty and equality are not mutually supportive. In fact, these principles are often in conflict with each other. This chapter's concluding discussion of affirmative action illustrates this conflict.

chaptergoals

- **Trace the legal developments and social movements that expanded civil rights (pages 157–76)**

- **Describe how different groups have won protection of their rights (pages 176–90)**

- **Contrast arguments for and against affirmative action (pages 190–95)**

● The Struggle for Civil Rights

Trace the legal developments and social movements that expanded civil rights

In the United States the history of slavery and legalized racial **discrimination** against African Americans coexists uneasily with a strong tradition of individual liberty. Indeed, for much of our history Americans have struggled to reconcile such exclusionary racial practices with our notions of individual rights. With the adoption of the Fourteenth Amendment in 1868, **civil rights** became part of the Constitution, guaranteed to each citizen through "equal protection of the laws." This **equal protection clause** launched a century of political movements and legal efforts to press for racial equality.

For African Americans, the central fact of political life for most of American history has been a denial of full citizenship rights. By accepting the institution of slavery, the Founders embraced a system fundamentally at odds with the "Blessings of Liberty" promised in the Constitution. Their decision set the stage for two centuries of African American struggles to achieve full citizenship. For women as well, electoral politics was a decidedly masculine world. Until 1920, not only were women barred from voting in national politics, but electoral politics was closely tied to such male social institutions as lodges, bars, and clubs. Yet the exclusion of women from this political world did not prevent them from engaging in public life. Instead, women carved out a "separate sphere" for their public activities. Emphasizing female stewardship of the moral realm, women became important voices in social reform well before they won the right to vote.[2] Prior to the Civil War, women played leading roles in the abolitionist movement.

discrimination the use of any unreasonable and unjust criterion of exclusion

civil rights obligation imposed on government to take positive action to protect citizens from any illegal action of government agencies and of other private citizens

equal protection clause provision of the Fourteenth Amendment guaranteeing citizens "the equal protection of the laws." This clause has been the basis for the civil rights of African Americans, women, and other groups

African American men won the right to vote after the Civil War, and many former slaves began registering and voting in state elections as early as 1867. This political influence soon evaporated in the face of Jim Crow laws and the end of Reconstruction.

Slavery and the Abolitionist Movement

No issue in the nation's history so deeply divided Americans as that of slavery. The importation and subjugation of Africans kidnapped from their native lands was a practice virtually as old as the country itself: the first slaves brought to what became the United States arrived in 1619, a year before the Plymouth colony was established in Massachusetts. White southerners built their agricultural economy (especially cotton production) on a large slave labor force. By 1840 nearly half of the populations of Alabama and Louisiana consisted of black slaves. Even so, only about a quarter of southern white families owned slaves.

Slavery was so much a part of southern culture that efforts to restrict or abolish the institution were met with fierce resistance. Despite the manifest cruelties of the slave system, southerners referred to it merely as the "peculiar institution." This quaint label meant little to slavery's opponents, however, and an abolitionist movement grew and spread among northerners in the 1830s (although abolitionist sentiment could be traced back to the prerevolutionary era). Slavery had been all but eliminated in the North by this time, but few northerners favored outright abolition. In fact, most whites held attitudes toward blacks that would be considered racist today.

The abolitionist movement spread primarily through local organizations in the North. Antislavery groups coalesced in New York, Ohio, New Hampshire, Pennsylvania, New Jersey, and Michigan. In addition, the movement spawned two political parties: the staunchly antislavery Liberty Party and the larger but more moderate Free Soil Party, which sought primarily to restrict slavery from spreading into new western territories. In 1857 the infamous case of *Dred Scott v. Sandford* "roused passions as never before"[3] by splitting the country deeply, with the U.S. Supreme Court holding that Scott had no due process rights because, as a slave, he was his master's permanent property, regardless of his master's having taken him to a free state or territory.[4]

Some opponents of slavery took matters into their own hands, aiding in the escape of runaway slaves along the Underground Railroad. Even today, private homes and churches scattered throughout the Northeast, once used to hide blacks on their trips to Canada, still attest to the involvement of local citizenry. In the South, a similar, if contrary, fervor prompted mobs to break into post offices in order to seize and destroy antislavery literature.

The emotional power of the slavery issue was such that it precipitated the nation's bloodiest conflict, the Civil War. From the ashes of the Civil War came the Thirteenth, Fourteenth, and Fifteenth amendments, which would redefine civil rights from that time on.

The Link to the Women's Rights Movement

The quiet upstate New York town of Seneca Falls played host to what would later come to be known as the starting point of the modern women's movement. Convened in July 1848 and organized by the activists Elizabeth Cady Stanton and Lucretia Mott, the Seneca Falls Convention drew 300 delegates to formulate plans for advancing the political and social rights of women.

The centerpiece of the convention was its Declaration of Sentiments and Resolutions. Patterned after the Declaration of Independence, the Seneca Falls document declared, "We hold these truths to be self-evident: that all men and women are created equal" and "The history of mankind is a history of repeated injuries and usurpations on the part of man toward woman, having in direct object the establishment of an absolute tyranny over her." The most controversial provision of the declaration, nearly rejected as too radical, was the call for the right to vote for

Although a few women could vote in the early American republic, such as these New Jersey women who satisfied state property qualifications, laws were soon enacted to block women from the ballot box. At the beginning of the nineteenth century, no American woman could legally vote.

women. Although most of the delegates were women, about 40 men participated, including the renowned abolitionist Frederick Douglass.

The link to the antislavery movement was not new. Stanton and Mott had attended the World Anti-Slavery Convention in London in 1840 but had been denied delegate seats because of their sex. This rebuke helped precipitate the 1848 convention in Seneca Falls. The movements for women's rights and the abolition of slavery were also closely linked with the temperance movement (because alcohol abuse was closely linked to male abuses of women). The convergence of the antislavery, temperance, and suffrage movements was reflected in the views and actions of some women's movement leaders, such as Susan B. Anthony.

The convention and its participants were subjected to widespread ridicule, but similar conventions were organized in other states, and in the same year as the Seneca Falls Convention, New York State passed the Married Women's Property Act in order to restore the right of married women to own property.

The Civil War Amendments to the Constitution

The hopes of African Americans for achieving full citizenship rights initially seemed fulfilled when three constitutional amendments were adopted after the Civil War: the **Thirteenth Amendment** abolished slavery, the **Fourteenth Amendment** guaranteed equal protection under the law, and the **Fifteenth Amendment** guaranteed voting rights for blacks. Protected by the presence of federal troops, African American men were able to exercise their political rights immediately after the war. Between 1869 and 1877, blacks were elected to many political offices: two black senators were elected from Mississippi and a total of 14 African Americans were elected to the House of Representatives. African Americans also held many state-level political offices. As voters and public officials, black citizens found a home in the Republican Party, which had secured the ratification of the three constitutional amendments guaranteeing black rights. After the war, the Republican Party continued to reach out to black voters as a means to build party strength in the South.[5]

This political equality was short-lived, however. The national government withdrew its troops from the South and turned its back on African Americans in 1877,

Thirteenth Amendment one of three Civil War amendments; it abolished slavery

Fourteenth Amendment one of three Civil War amendments; it guaranteed equal protection and due process

Fifteenth Amendment one of three Civil War amendments; it guaranteed voting rights for African American men when Reconstruction ended. In the Compromise of 1877, southern Democrats agreed to allow the Republican candidate, Rutherford B. Hayes, to become president after a disputed election. In exchange, northern Republicans dropped their support for the civil liberties and political participation of African Americans. After that, southern states erected a "Jim Crow" system of social, political, and economic inequality that made a mockery of the promises in the Constitution. The first **Jim Crow laws** were adopted in the 1870s, in each southern state, to criminalize intermarriage of the races and to segregate trains and depots. These were promptly followed by laws segregating all public accommodations, and within 10 years all southern states had adopted laws segregating the schools.

Immediately after the Civil War, when male ex-slaves won the franchise, some women pressed for the right to vote at the national level, but politicians in both parties rejected women's suffrage as disruptive and unrealistic. Women also started to press for the vote at the state level in 1867, when a referendum to give women the vote in Kansas failed. Frustration with the general failure to win reforms in other states accelerated suffrage activism. In 1872, Susan B. Anthony and several other women were arrested in Rochester, New York, for illegally registering and voting in that year's national election. (The men who allowed the women to register and vote were also indicted; Anthony paid their expenses and eventually won presidential pardons for them.) At Anthony's trial, Judge Ward Hunt ordered the jury to find her guilty without deliberation. Yet Anthony was allowed to address the court, saying, "Your denial of my citizen's right to vote is the denial of my right of consent as one of the governed, the denial of my right of representation as one of the taxed, the denial of my right to a trial of my peers as an offender against the law."[6] Hunt assessed Anthony a fine of $100 but did not sentence her to jail. She refused to pay the fine.

Civil Rights and the Supreme Court: "Separate but Equal"

Resistance to equality for African Americans in the South led Congress to adopt the Civil Rights Act of 1875, which attempted to protect blacks from discrimination by proprietors of hotels, theaters, and other public accommodations. But

Jim Crow laws laws enacted by southern states following Reconstruction that discriminated against African Americans

The 1896 Supreme Court case of Plessy v. Ferguson *upheld legal segregation and created the "separate but equal" rule, which fostered national segregation. Overt discrimination in public accommodations was common.*

the Court declared the legislation unconstitutional on the grounds that the act sought to protect blacks against discrimination by *private* businesses, whereas the Fourteenth Amendment, according to the Court's interpretation, was intended to protect individuals from discrimination only against actions by *public* officials of state and local governments.

In the infamous case of *Plessy v. Ferguson* (1896), the Court went still further by upholding a Louisiana statute that *required* segregation of the races on trolleys and other public carriers (and, by implication, in all public facilities, including schools). Homer Plessy, a man defined as "one-eighth black," had violated a Louisiana law that provided for "equal but separate accommodations" on trains and levied a $25 fine on any white passenger who sat in a car reserved for blacks or on any black passenger who sat in a car reserved for whites. The Supreme Court held that the Fourteenth Amendment's equal protection clause was not violated by racial distinction as long as the facilities were equal, thus establishing the **"separate but equal" rule** that prevailed through the mid-twentieth century. People generally pretended that segregated accommodations were equal as long as some accommodation for blacks existed. The Court said that although "the object of the [Fourteenth] Amendment was undoubtedly to enforce the absolute equality of the two races before the law, . . . it could not have intended to abolish distinctions based on color, or to enforce social, as distinguished from political, equality, or a commingling of the two races upon terms unsatisfactory to either."[7] What the Court was saying in effect was that the use of race as a criterion of exclusion in public matters was not unreasonable.

"separate but equal" rule doctrine that public accommodations could be segregated by race but still be considered equal

Organizing for Equality

The National Association for the Advancement of Colored People The creation of a Jim Crow system in the southern states and the lack of a legal basis for "equal protection of the laws" prompted the beginning of a long process in which African Americans built organizations and devised strategies for asserting their constitutional rights.

One such strategy sought to win political rights through political pressure and litigation. This approach was championed by the National Association for the Advancement of Colored People (NAACP), established in 1909 by a group of black and white reformers that included W. E. B. Du Bois, one of the twentieth century's most influential and creative thinkers on racial issues. Because the northern black vote was so small in the early 1900s, the NAACP relied primarily on the courts to press for black political rights. After the 1920s it built a strong membership base, with some strength in the South, which would be critical when the civil rights movement gained momentum in the 1950s.

The great migration of blacks to the North beginning around World War I enlivened a protest strategy. Although protest organizations had existed in the nineteenth century, the continuing migration of blacks made protest an increasingly useful tool. The black labor leader A. Philip Randolph forced the federal government to address racial discrimination in hiring practices during World War II by threatening a massive march on Washington. The federal government also grew more attentive to blacks as their voting strength increased as a result of the northward migration. By the 1940s the black vote had swung away from Republicans, but the Democratic hold on black votes was by no means absolute.

Women's Organizations and the Right to Suffrage The 1886 unveiling in New York Harbor of the Statue of Liberty, depicting liberty as a woman, prompted

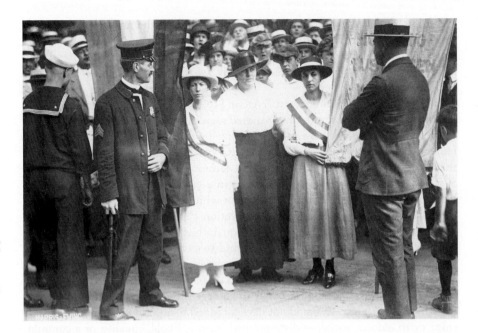

People had been agitating for women's right to vote since the 1830s, especially during the Civil War era. Here, early twentieth-century suffragists protest in front of the White House. Women gained the constitutional right to vote in 1920.

women's rights advocates to call it "the greatest hypocrisy of the nineteenth century," in that "not one single woman throughout the length and breadth of the Land is as yet in possession of political Liberty."[8] Suffragists used the occasion of the Constitution's centennial in 1887 to protest the continued denial of their rights. For these women, the centennial represented "a century of injustice."

The climactic movement toward suffrage had been formally launched in 1878 with the introduction of a proposed constitutional amendment in Congress. Parallel efforts were made in the states. Many states granted women the right to vote before the national government did; western states with less entrenched political systems opened politics to women earliest. When Wyoming became a state in 1890, it was the first state to grant full suffrage to women. Colorado, Utah, and Idaho all followed suit in the next several years. Suffrage organizations grew—the National American Woman Suffrage Association (NAWSA), formed in 1890, claimed 2 million members by 1917—and staged mass meetings, parades, petitions, and protests. NAWSA organized state-by-state efforts to win the right for women to vote. Members of a more militant group, the National Woman's Party, staged pickets and got arrested in front of the White House to protest President Wilson's opposition to a constitutional amendment granting women this right. When the Nineteenth Amendment was ratified in 1920, women were finally guaranteed the right to vote.

Litigating for Equality after World War II

The shame of discrimination against black military personnel during World War II, plus revelations of Nazi racial atrocities, moved President Harry S. Truman finally to bring the problem of racial discrimination to the White House and national attention, with the appointment in 1946 of the President's Commission on Civil Rights. In 1948 the commission submitted its report, *To Secure These Rights*, which laid bare the extent of the problem and its consequences. The report also revealed the success of experiments with racial integration in the armed forces during

World War II, to demonstrate to southern society that it had nothing to fear. But the commission recognized that the national government had no clear constitutional authority to pass and implement civil rights legislation. It proposed tying such legislation to the commerce power described in Article I of the Constitution, which allows Congress to regulate interstate commerce, although it was clear that discrimination was not itself related to the flow of interstate commerce.[9] The committee even suggested using the treaty power as a source of constitutional authority for civil rights legislation.[10]

The Supreme Court had begun to change its position on racial discrimination before World War II by being stricter about the criterion of equal facilities in the "separate but equal" rule. In 1938, for example, the Court rejected Missouri's policy of paying the tuition of qualified blacks to out-of-state law schools rather than admitting them to the University of Missouri Law School.[11]

After the war, modest progress resumed. In 1950 the Court rejected Texas's claim that its new "law school for Negroes" afforded education equal to that of the all-white University of Texas Law School, anticipating its future civil rights rulings by opening the question of whether *any* segregated facilities could be truly equal.[12] But in ordering the admission of blacks to all-white state law schools, the Supreme Court did not directly confront the "separate but equal" rule, because the Court needed only to recognize the absence of *any* equal law school for blacks. The same had been true in 1944, when the Supreme Court struck down the southern practice of "white primaries," which legally excluded blacks from participation in the nominating process. Here the Court simply recognized that primaries could no longer be regarded as the private affairs of the parties but were an integral aspect of the electoral process, making parties "an agency of the State." Therefore any practice of discrimination against blacks was "state action within the meaning of the Fifteenth Amendment."[13] The most important pre-1954 decision was probably *Shelley v. Kraemer*, in which the Court ruled against the widespread practice of "restrictive covenants" whereby the seller of a home added a clause to the sales contract requiring the buyer to agree never to sell the home to any non-Caucasian, non-Christian, and so on. The Court ruled that such covenants could not be judicially enforced, since the Fourteenth Amendment prohibits any organ of the state, including the courts, from denying equal protection of its laws.[14]

Although none of those pre-1954 cases confronted "separate but equal" and the principle of racial discrimination as such, they were extremely significant to black leaders in the 1940s and gave them encouragement to believe that at last they had an opportunity and enough legal precedent to change the constitutional framework itself. Much of this legal work was done by the Legal Defense and Educational Fund of the NAACP. Until the late 1940s, lawyers working for the Legal Defense Fund had concentrated on winning small victories within the existing framework. Then, in 1948, the Legal Defense Fund upgraded its approach by simultaneously filing suits in different federal districts and through each level of schooling, with complaints ranging from unequal provision of kindergarten for blacks to unequal sports and science facilities in all-black high schools. After nearly two years of these mostly successful equalization suits, the lawyers decided the time was ripe to confront the "separate but equal" rule head-on, but they felt they needed some heavier artillery to lead the attack. Their choice was the African American lawyer Thurgood Marshall, who had been fighting, and often winning, equalization suits since the early 1930s. Marshall was pessimistic about the readiness of the Supreme Court for a full confrontation with segregation itself and the constitutional principle sustaining it. But the unwillingness of Congress after the 1948 election to consider fair-employment legislation seems to have convinced Marshall that the courts were the only hope.

The NAACP was formed in 1909 to promote the political rights of blacks. In the decades following the 1920s, the NAACP expanded its membership significantly and played an important role in the civil rights movement of the 1950s and '60s.

Brown v. Board of Education
the 1954 Supreme Court decision that struck down the "separate but equal" doctrine as fundamentally unequal. This case eliminated state power to use race as a criterion of discrimination in law and provided the national government with the power to intervene by exercising strict regulatory policies against discriminatory actions

During the next four years there emerged a clear indication that the Supreme Court itself was willing to take more civil rights cases on appeal. Yet this was no guarantee that the Court would reverse *on principle* the separate-but-equal precedent of *Plessy v. Ferguson*. All through 1951 and 1952, as cases were winding slowly through the lower-court litigation maze, intense discussions and disagreements arose among NAACP lawyers as to whether a full-scale assault on *Plessy* was good strategy, or whether it might not be better to continue with specific cases alleging unequal treatment and demanding relief with a Court-imposed policy of equalization.[15] For some lawyers, including Marshall, such victories could amount to a defeat. For example, under the leadership of Governor James F. Byrnes, a former Supreme Court justice, South Carolina had undertaken a strategy of large-scale equalization of school services, both to satisfy the *Plessy* rule and to head off or render moot any litigation against the principle of separate but equal.

In the fall of 1952, the Court had on its docket cases from Delaware, Kansas, South Carolina, Virginia, and the District of Columbia challenging the constitutionality of school segregation. Of these, the case filed in Kansas became the one chosen by the NAACP. It seemed to be ahead of the pack in its district court, and it had the advantage of being located in a state outside the Deep South.[16]

Oliver Brown, the father of three girls, lived "across the tracks" in a low-income, racially mixed Topeka neighborhood. Every school day, Linda Brown took the school bus to the Monroe Elementary School, for black children, about a mile away. In September 1950, Oliver Brown took Linda to the all-white Sumner School, which was closer to home, to enter her into the third grade, in defiance of state law and local segregation rules. When they were refused, Brown took his case to the NAACP, and soon thereafter, the case **Brown v. Board of Education** was born. In mid-1953 the Court announced that the several cases on their way up would be re-argued within a set of questions having to do with the intent of the Fourteenth Amendment. Almost exactly a year later, the Court responded to those questions in one of the most important decisions in its history.

In deciding the *Brown* case, the Court, to the surprise of many, basically rejected as inconclusive all the learned arguments about the intent and the history of the Fourteenth Amendment and committed itself instead to considering only the consequences of segregation:

> Does segregation of children in public schools solely on the basis of race, even though the physical facilities and other "tangible" factors may be equal, deprive the children of the minority group of equal educational opportunities? We believe that it does. . . . We conclude that in the field of public education the doctrine of "separate but equal" has no place. Separate educational facilities are inherently unequal.[17]

The *Brown* decision altered the constitutional framework in two fundamental respects. First, after *Brown*, the states no longer had the power to use race as a criterion of discrimination in law. Second, the national government from then on had the power (and eventually the obligation) to intervene with strict regulatory policies against the discriminatory actions of state or local governments, school boards, employers, and many others in the private sector.

Civil Rights after *Brown v. Board of Education*

Brown v. Board of Education withdrew all constitutional authority to use race as a criterion of exclusion, and it signaled more clearly the Court's determination to use the **strict scrutiny** test in cases related to racial discrimination. This meant that the burden of proof would fall on the government to show that the law in question *was* constitutional—not on the challengers to show the law's *uncon*stitutionality.[18] Although the use of strict scrutiny would give an advantage to those attacking racial discrimination, the historic decision in *Brown v. Board of Education* was merely a small opening move. First, most states refused to cooperate until sued, and many ingenious schemes were employed to delay obedience (such as paying the tuition for white students to attend newly created "private" academies). Second, even as southern school boards began to cooperate by eliminating their legally enforced (**de jure**) school segregation, extensive actual (**de facto**) school segregation remained, in the North as well as in the South, as a consequence of racially segregated housing that could not be addressed by the 1954–55 *Brown* principles. Third, discrimination in employment, public accommodations, juries, voting, and other areas of social and economic activity were not directly touched by *Brown*.

School Desegregation, Phase One Although the District of Columbia and some of the school districts in the border states began to respond almost immediately to court-ordered desegregation, the states of the Deep South responded with a

strict scrutiny a test used by the Supreme Court in racial discrimination cases and other cases involving civil liberties and civil rights that places the burden of proof on the government rather than on the challengers to show that the law in question is constitutional

de jure literally, "by law"; refers to legally enforced practices, such as school segregation in the South before the 1960s

de facto literally, "by fact"; refers to practices that occur even when there is no legal enforcement, such as school segregation in much of the United States today

"Massive resistance" among white southerners attempted to block the desegregation efforts of the national government. For example, at Little Rock Central High School in 1957, an angry mob of white students prevented black students from entering the school.

for critical analysis

Describe the changes in American society between the *Plessy v. Ferguson* and the *Brown v. Board of Education* decisions. How might changes in society have interacted with the changes in civil rights policy in America since the *Brown* case?

carefully planned delaying tactic commonly called "massive resistance" by the more demagogic southern leaders and "nullification" and "interposition" by the centrists. Either way, southern politicians stood shoulder to shoulder to declare that the Supreme Court's decisions and orders were without effect. The legislatures in these states enacted statutes ordering school districts to maintain segregated schools and state superintendents to terminate state funding wherever there was racial mixing in the classroom. Some southern states violated their own long traditions of local school autonomy by centralizing public school authority under the governor or the state board of education, and they gave themselves the power to close the schools and to provide alternative private schooling wherever local school boards might be inclined to obey the Supreme Court.

Most of these plans of "massive resistance" were tested in the federal courts and were struck down as unconstitutional.[19] But southern resistance was not confined to legislation. For example, in Arkansas in 1957, Governor Orval Faubus mobilized the Arkansas National Guard to intercede against enforcement of a federal court order to integrate Little Rock Central High School, and President Eisenhower was compelled to deploy U.S. troops and place the city under martial law. The Supreme Court considered the Little Rock confrontation so historically important that the opinion it rendered in that case was not only agreed to unanimously but was, unprecedentedly, signed personally by every one of the justices.[20] The end of massive resistance, however, became simply the beginning of still another southern strategy. "Pupil placement" laws authorized school districts to place each pupil in a school according to a variety of academic, personal, and psychological considerations, never mentioning race at all. This put the burden of transferring to an all-white school on the nonwhite children and their parents, making it almost impossible for a single court order to cover a whole district, let alone a whole state. This delayed desegregation awhile longer.[21]

Social Protest after Brown Ten years after *Brown*, fewer than 1 percent of black school-age children in the Deep South were attending schools with whites.[22] A decade of frustration made it fairly obvious to all observers that adjudication alone would not succeed. The goal of "equal protection" required positive, or affirmative, action by Congress and by administrative agencies. And given massive southern resistance and a generally negative national public opinion toward racial integration, progress would not be made through courts, Congress, or federal agencies without intense, well-organized support. Figure 5.1 shows the increase in the number of civil rights demonstrations for voting rights and public accommodations during the years following *Brown*. The number of organized demonstrations began to mount slowly but surely after *Brown v. Board of Education*. Only a year after *Brown*, black citizens in Montgomery, Alabama, challenged the city's segregated bus system with a yearlong boycott. The boycott began with the arrest of Rosa Parks, who refused to give up her seat for a white man. A seamstress who worked with civil rights groups, Parks eventually became a civil rights icon, as did one of the ministers leading the boycott, Martin Luther King Jr. But the boycott was a group effort, a carefully planned

The 1955–56 Montgomery bus boycott began with the arrest of Rosa Parks, who refused to give up her seat for a white man. The boycott lasted a year and drew national attention to the cause of civil rights.

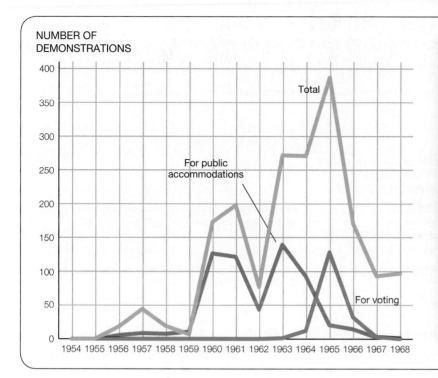

NUMBER OF
DEMONSTRATIONS

Total

For public
accommodations

For voting

1954 1955 1956 1957 1958 1959 1960 1961 1962 1963 1964 1965 1966 1967 1968

FIGURE 5.1

Peaceful Civil Rights Demonstrations, 1954–68

Peaceful demonstrations were an important part of the civil rights movement. Why did the number of demonstrations grow after 1955? Why do you think the focus shifted from public accommodations to voting rights after 1964?

NOTE: The data are drawn from a search of the *New York Times* index for all references to civil rights demonstrations.

SOURCE: Jonathan D. Casper, *The Politics of Civil Liberties* (New York: Harper and Row, 1972), p. 90.

campaign in which nearly all the black citizens of Montgomery took part. After a year of private carpools and walking, Montgomery's bus system desegregated, but only after the Supreme Court ruled the system unconstitutional. The lengthy boycott and the white violence that accompanied it riveted national attention on the emerging civil rights movement. By the 1960s the many organizations that made up the civil rights movement had accumulated experience and built networks capable of launching large-scale direct-action campaigns against southern segregationists. The Southern Christian Leadership Conference, the Student Nonviolent Coordinating Committee, and many other organizations had built a movement that stretched across the South, using the media to attract nationwide attention and support. The image of protesters being beaten, attacked by police dogs, and set upon with fire hoses did much to win broad sympathy for the cause of black civil rights and to discredit state and local governments in the South. In the massive March on Washington in 1963, the Reverend Martin Luther King Jr. staked out the movement's moral claims in his famous "I Have a Dream" speech. Steadily, the movement created intense pressure for a reluctant federal government to take more assertive steps to defend black civil rights.

The Civil Rights Acts

It is important to observe here the mutual dependence of the courts and legislatures: the legislatures need constitutional authority to act, and the courts need legislative assistance to implement court orders and focus political support. Consequently, even as the U.S. Congress finally moved into the field of school desegregation (and other areas of "equal protection"), the courts continued to exercise their powers, not only by placing court orders against recalcitrant school districts but also by extending

TABLE 5.1

Cause and Effect in the Civil Rights Movement

Political action and government action worked in tandem to produce dramatic changes in American civil rights policies.

JUDICIAL AND LEGAL ACTION	POLITICAL ACTION
1954 *Brown v. Board of Education*	**1955** Montgomery, Alabama, bus boycott
1956 Federal courts order school integration; of special note is one ordering Autherine Lucy admitted to the University of Alabama, with Governor Wallace officially protesting	
1957 Civil Rights Act creating Civil Rights Commission; President Eisenhower sends 101st Airborne Division paratroops to Little Rock, Arkansas, to enforce integration of Central High School	**1957** Southern Christian Leadership Conference (SCLC) formed, with Martin Luther King Jr. as president
1960 First substantive Civil Rights Act, primarily voting rights	**1960** Student Nonviolent Coordinating Committee formed to organize protests, sit-ins, freedom rides
1961 Interstate Commerce Commission orders desegregation on all buses and trains, and in terminals	
1961 JFK favors executive action over civil rights legislation	
1963 JFK shifts, supports strong civil rights law; JFK's assassination; LBJ asserts strong support for civil rights	**1963** Nonviolent demonstrations in Birmingham, Alabama, lead to King's arrest and his "Letter from Birmingham Jail"
	1963 March on Washington
1964 Congress passes historic Civil Rights Act covering voting, employment, public accommodations, education	
1965 Voting Rights Act	**1965** King announces drive to register 3 million blacks in the South
1966 War on Poverty in full swing	**Late 1960s** Movement diverges: part toward litigation, part toward community action programs, part toward war protest, part toward more militant "Black Power" actions

and reinterpreting aspects of the equal protection clause to support legislative and administrative actions (see Table 5.1). But after a decade of very frustrating efforts, the courts and Congress ultimately came to the conclusion that the federal courts alone were not adequate to the task of changing the social rules, and that legislation and administrative action would be needed.

Three civil rights acts were passed during the first decade after the 1954 Supreme Court decision in *Brown v. Board of Education*. But these acts were of only marginal importance. The first one, in 1957, created the U.S. Commission on Civil Rights, to study abuses. The second, in 1960, established that the Fourteenth Amendment to the Constitution, adopted almost a century earlier, could no longer be disregarded, particularly with regard to voting. The third, the Equal Pay Act of 1963, was more important, but it was concerned with women, did not touch the question of racial discrimination, and, like the 1960 legislation, had no enforcement mechanisms.

By far the most important piece of legislation passed by Congress concerning equal opportunity was the Civil Rights Act of 1964. It not only put some teeth in the voting rights provisions of the 1957 and 1960 acts but also went far beyond voting to attack discrimination in public accommodations, segregation in the schools, and, at long last, the discriminatory conduct of employers in hiring, promoting, and laying off their employees. Discrimination against women was also included, extending the important 1963 provisions. The 1964 act seemed bold at the time, but it was enacted 10 years after the Supreme Court had declared racial discrimination "inherently unequal" under the Fifth and Fourteenth amendments. And it was enacted long after blacks had demonstrated that discrimination was no longer acceptable. The choice in 1964 was not between congressional action or inaction but between legal action and expanded violence.

Public Accommodations After the passage of the 1964 Civil Rights Act, public accommodations quickly removed some of the most blatant forms of racial discrimination. Signs defining "colored" and "white" restrooms, water fountains, waiting rooms, and seating arrangements were removed, and a host of other practices that relegated black people to separate and inferior arrangements was ended. In addition, the federal government filed more than 400 antidiscrimination suits in federal courts against hotels, restaurants, taverns, gas stations, and other "public accommodations."

Many aspects of legalized racial segregation—such as separate Bibles in the courtroom—seem like ancient history today. But the issue of racial discrimination in public settings is by no means over. In 1993, six African American Secret Service agents filed charges after a Denny's restaurant in Annapolis, Maryland, failed to serve them; white Secret Service agents at a nearby table had received prompt service. Similar charges citing discriminatory service at Denny's restaurants surfaced across the country. Faced with evidence of a pattern of systematic discrimination and numerous lawsuits, Denny's paid $45 million in damages to plaintiffs in Maryland and California in what is said to be the largest settlement ever in a public accommodations case.[23] In addition to the settlement, the chain vowed to expand employment and management opportunities for minorities in its restaurants. Other forms of racial discrimination in public accommodations are harder to challenge, however. For example, there is considerable evidence that taxicabs often refuse to pick up black passengers.[24] Such practices may be common, but they are difficult to prove and remedy through the law.

School Desegregation, Phase Two The 1964 Civil Rights Act also declared discrimination by private employers and state governments (school boards, etc.) illegal, and then went further to provide for administrative agencies to help the courts implement these laws. Title IV of the act, for example, authorized the executive branch, through the Justice Department, to implement federal court orders to desegregate schools, and to do so without having to wait for individual parents to bring complaints. Title VI of the act vastly strengthened the role of the executive branch and the credibility of court orders by providing that federal grants-in-aid to state and local governments for education must be withheld from any school system practicing racial segregation. Title VI became the most effective weapon for desegregating schools outside the South because the situation in northern communities was subtler and more difficult to address. In the South, the problem was segregation by law coupled with overt resistance to the national government's efforts to change the situation. In contrast, outside the South, segregated facilities were the outcome of hundreds of thousands of housing choices made by individuals and families. Once racial residential patterns emerged, racial homogeneity, property values, and neighborhood schools and churches were defended by real estate agents, neighborhood organizations, and the like. Thus, in order to eliminate discrimination nationwide, the 1964 Civil Rights Act gave (1) the president, through the Justice Department's Office for Civil Rights, the power to withhold federal education grants,[25] and (2) the attorney general of the United States the power to initiate suits (rather than having to await complaints) wherever there was a "pattern or practice" of discrimination.[26]

In the decade following the 1964 Civil Rights Act, the Justice Department brought legal action against more than 500 school districts. During the same period, administrative agencies filed lawsuits against 600 school districts, threatening to suspend federal aid to education unless real desegregation steps were taken.

Busing One step taken toward desegregation was busing children from poor urban school districts to wealthier suburban ones. In 1971 the Supreme Court held that state-imposed desegregation could be brought about by busing children across school districts:

> If school authorities fail in their affirmative obligations, judicial authority may be invoked. Once a right and a violation have been shown, the scope of a district court's equitable powers to remedy past wrongs is broad. . . . Bus transportation [is] a normal and accepted tool of educational policy.[27]

But the decision went beyond that, adding that under certain limited circumstances even racial quotas could be used as the "starting point in shaping a remedy to correct past constitutional violations," and that pairing or grouping schools and reorganizing school attendance zones would also be acceptable.

Three years later, however, this principle was severely restricted when the Supreme Court determined that only cities found guilty of deliberate and de jure racial segregation would have to desegregate their schools,[28] effectively exempting most northern states and cities from busing because school segregation in northern

The 1964 Civil Rights Act made desegregation a legal requirement. The policy of busing from black neighborhoods to white schools bitterly divided the black and white communities in Boston. In 1976 a protester waved an American Flag threateningly at an innocent black bystander— a lawyer on his way to his office—as another white man sought to help him get out of the way.

cities is generally the de facto result of segregated housing and thousands of acts of private discrimination against blacks and other minorities.

Boston provides a good illustration of the agonizing problem of making further progress in civil rights in the schools under the constitutional framework established by these decisions. Boston school authorities were found guilty of deliberately building school facilities and drawing school districts "to increase racial segregation." After vain efforts by Boston school authorities to draw up an acceptable plan to remedy the segregation, federal judge W. Arthur Garrity ordered an elaborate desegregation plan of his own, involving busing between the all-black neighborhood of Roxbury and the nearby white, working-class community of South Boston. The city's schools were so segregated and uncooperative that even the conservative administration of President Richard Nixon had already initiated a punitive cutoff of funds. But even many liberals criticized Judge Garrity's plan as being badly conceived for involving two neighboring communities with a history of tension and mutual resentment. The plan did work well at the elementary school level but proved explosive at the high school level, generating a continuing crisis for the city of Boston and for the whole nation.[29]

The prospects for further school integration diminished with a 1991 Supreme Court decision holding that lower federal courts could end supervision of local school boards if they could show "good faith" compliance with court orders to desegregate and could show that "vestiges of past discrimination" had been eliminated "to the extent practicable."[30] It is not necessarily easy for a school board to prove that the new standard has been met, but this was the first time since *Brown* and the 1964 Civil Rights Act that the Court had opened the door at all to retreat.

That door was opened further by a 1995 Court ruling that the remedies being applied in Kansas City, Missouri, were improper.[31] In accordance with a lower-court order, the state was pouring additional funding into salaries and remedial programs for Kansas City schools, which had a history of segregation. The aim of the spending was to improve student performance and to attract white students from the suburbs into the city schools. The Supreme Court declared the interdistrict goal improper, and reiterated its earlier ruling that states can free themselves of court orders by showing a good-faith effort. This decision indicated the Court's new willingness to end desegregation plans even when predominantly minority schools continued to lag significantly behind white suburban schools. In 2007 the Court's ruling in *Parents Involved in Community Schools v. Seattle School District No. 1* limited school integration measures still further. By making race one factor in assigning students to schools, the cities of Seattle and Louisville had hoped to achieve greater racial balance across the public schools. The Court ruled that these plans (even though the cities had voluntarily adopted them) were unconstitutional because they discriminated against white students on the basis of race. Many observers described the decision as the end of the *Brown* era because it eliminated one of the few public strategies left to promote racial integration. Others argued that Justice Anthony Kennedy's concurring opinion, which recognized the harm of racial isolation, may provide the basis for new efforts to promote integration in the future.[32]

Outlawing Discrimination in Employment

Despite the agonizingly slow progress of school desegregation, some progress was made in other areas of civil rights during the 1960s and '70s. Voting rights were established and fairly quickly began to revolutionize southern politics. Service on juries was no longer denied to minorities.

for critical analysis

Many people believe that despite the significance of the *Brown v. Board of Education* decision, it has failed to fulfill its promise. What did *Brown* really accomplish? Can courts bring about social change?

But progress in the right to participate in politics and government dramatized the relative lack of progress in the economic domain, where battles over civil rights were increasingly being fought.

The federal courts and the Justice Department entered this area through Title VII of the Civil Rights Act of 1964, which outlawed job discrimination by all private and public employers, including governmental agencies (such as fire and police departments) that employed more than 15 workers. We have already seen (in Chapter 3) that the Supreme Court gave "interstate commerce" such a broad definition that Congress had the constitutional authority to cover discrimination by virtually any local employers.[33] Title VII makes it unlawful to discriminate in employment on the basis of color, religion, sex, or national origin, as well as race.

Title VII delegated some of the powers to enforce fair-employment practices to the Justice Department's Civil Rights Division and others to a new agency created in the 1964 act, the Equal Employment Opportunity Commission (EEOC). By executive order, these agencies had the power of the national government to revoke public contracts for goods and services and to refuse to engage in contracts with any private company that could not guarantee that its rules for hiring, promotion, and firing were nondiscriminatory. Executive orders in 1965, 1967, and 1969, by Presidents Johnson and Nixon, extended and reaffirmed nondiscrimination practices in employment and promotion in the federal government service. And in 1972, President Nixon and a Democratic Congress cooperated to strengthen the EEOC by giving it authority to initiate suits rather than wait for grievances.

But one problem with Title VII was that the complaining party had to show that deliberate discrimination was the cause of the failure to get a job or a training opportunity. Rarely, of course, does an employer explicitly admit discrimination on the basis of race, sex, or any other illegal reason. Recognizing this, the courts have allowed aggrieved parties (the plaintiffs) to make their case if they can show that an employer's hiring practices had the *effect* of exclusion. A leading case in 1971 involved a "class action" by several black employees in North Carolina attempting to show with statistical evidence that blacks had been relegated to only one department in the Duke Power Company, which involved the least desirable manual-labor jobs, and that they had been kept out of contention for better jobs because the employer had added attainment of a high school education and the passing of specially prepared aptitude tests as qualifications for higher jobs. The Supreme Court held that although the statistical evidence did not prove intentional discrimination, and although the requirements were race-neutral in appearance, their effects were sufficient to shift the burden of justification to the employer to show that the requirements were a "business necessity" that bore "a demonstrable relationship to successful performance."[34] The ruling in this case was subsequently applied to other hiring, promotion, and training programs.[35]

Voting Rights Although 1964 was the *most* important year for civil rights legislation, it was not the only important year. In 1965, Congress significantly strengthened legislation protecting voting rights by barring literacy and other tests as a condition for voting in six southern states[36] by setting criminal penalties for interference with efforts to vote and by providing for the replacement of local registrars with federally appointed registrars in counties designated by the attorney general as significantly resistant to registering eligible blacks to vote. The right to vote was further strengthened with ratification in 1964 of the Twenty-Fourth Amendment, which abolished the poll tax, and in 1975 with legislation permanently outlawing literacy tests in all 50 states and mandating bilingual ballots or oral assistance for Spanish speakers; Chinese, Japanese, Korean, and Native Americans; and Alaska natives.

In the long run, the laws extending and protecting voting rights could prove to be the most effective of all the great civil rights legislation because the progress in black political participation produced by these acts has altered the shape of American politics. In 1965, in the seven states of the Old Confederacy covered by the Voting Rights Act (VRA), 29.3 percent of the eligible black residents were registered to vote, compared with 73.4 percent of the white residents (see Table 5.2). Mississippi was the extreme case, with 6.7 percent black and 69.9 percent white registration. By 1971–72, 56.6 percent of the eligible blacks in the seven states were registered, compared with 67.8 percent of the eligible whites, a gap of 11.2 points. By 1972 the gap between black and white registration in the seven states was only 11.2 points, and in Mississippi the gap had been reduced to 9.4 points. At one time, white leaders in Mississippi had attempted to dilute the influence of this growing black vote by **gerrymandering** districts to ensure that no blacks would be elected to Congress. But the black voters changed Mississippi before Mississippi could change them. In 1988, 11 percent of all elected officials in Mississippi were black, a figure closely approximating the size of the national black electorate, which at the time was just over 11 percent of the American voting-age population. Mississippi's blacks had made significant gains (as they had in other Deep South states) as elected state and local representatives, and Mississippi was one of only

gerrymandering the apportionment of voters in districts in such a way as to give unfair advantage to one racial or ethnic group or political party

TABLE 5.2

Registration by Race and State in Southern States Covered by the Voting Rights Act (VRA)

The VRA had a direct impact on the rate of black voter registration in the southern states, as measured by the gap between white and black voters in each state. Further insights can be gained by examining changes in white registration rates before and after passage of the Voting Rights Act and by comparing the gaps between white and black registration. Why do you think registration rates for whites increased significantly in some states and dropped in others? What impact could the increase in black registration have had on public policy?

	BEFORE THE ACT*			AFTER THE ACT* 1971–72		
	WHITE %	BLACK %	GAP** %	WHITE %	BLACK %	GAP %
Alabama	69.2	19.3	49.9	80.7	57.1	23.6
Georgia	62.6	27.4	35.2	70.6	67.8	2.8
Louisiana	80.5	31.6	48.9	80.0	59.1	20.9
Mississippi	69.9	6.7	63.2	71.6	62.2	9.4
North Carolina	96.8	46.8	50.0	62.2	46.3	15.9
South Carolina	75.7	37.3	38.4	51.2	48.0	3.2
Virginia	61.1	38.3	22.8	61.2	54.0	7.2
TOTAL	73.4	29.3	44.1	67.8	56.6	11.2

*Available registration data as of March 1965 and 1971–72.
**The gap is the percentage-point difference between white and black registration rates.

SOURCE: U.S. Commission on Civil Rights, *Political Participation* (1968), Appendix VII: Voter Education Project, attachment to press release, October 3, 1972.

eight states in the country in which a black judge presided over the highest state court. (Four of the eight were Deep South states.)[37]

Several provisions of the 1965 act were scheduled to expire in 2007. However, in 2006, responding to charges that black voters still faced discrimination at the polls, Congress renewed the act for another 25 years. Pressure for renewal of the act had been intense since the disputed 2000 presidential election. The U.S. Commission on Civil Rights conducted hearings on the election in Florida, at which black voters testified about being turned away from the polls and wrongly purged from the voting rolls, and about the unreliable voting technology in their neighborhoods. On the basis of this testimony and after an analysis of the vote, the commission charged that there had been extensive racial discrimination.[38] Most recently, Texas has come under fire for gerrymandering congressional districts that discriminate against Latino voters. Due to population growth, most of it among Latinos, Texas gained four new congressional seats after the 2010 census. The heavily Republican state legislature drew a map designed to ensure that three of the new seats would go to Republican candidates. However, a coalition of minority groups and the Justice Department contested the map in court, charging that it failed to create a sufficient number of majority-minority districts. After extensive legal wrangling, the new redistricting plan included three majority-minority districts.[39]

Housing The Civil Rights Act of 1964 did not address housing, but in 1968, Congress passed another civil rights act specifically to outlaw housing discrimination. Called the Fair Housing Act, the law prohibited discrimination in the sale or rental of most housing—eventually covering nearly all the nation's housing. Housing was among the most controversial of discrimination issues because of deeply entrenched patterns of residential segregation across the United States. Such segregation was not simply a product of individual choice. Local housing authorities deliberately segregated public housing, and federal guidelines had sanctioned discrimination in Federal Housing Administration mortgage lending, effectively preventing blacks from joining the exodus to the suburbs in the 1950s and '60s. Nonetheless, Congress had been reluctant to tackle housing discrimination, fearing the tremendous controversy it could arouse. But just as the housing legislation was being considered in April 1968, the civil rights leader Martin Luther King Jr. was assassinated; this tragedy brought the measure unexpected support in Congress.

Although it pronounced sweeping goals, the Fair Housing Act had little effect on housing segregation, because its enforcement mechanisms were so weak. Individuals who believed they had been discriminated against had to file suit themselves. The burden was on the individual to prove that housing discrimination had occurred, even though such discrimination is often subtle and difficult to document. Although local fair-housing groups emerged to assist individuals in their court claims, the procedures for proving discrimination constituted a formidable barrier to effective change. These procedures were not altered until 1988, when Congress passed the Fair Housing Amendments Act. This new law put more teeth in the enforcement procedures and allowed the Department of Housing and Urban Development (HUD) to initiate legal action in cases of discrimination.[40]

Other attempts to challenge residential segregation had similarly mixed success. HUD tried briefly in the early 1970s to create racially "open communities" by withholding federal funds to suburbs that refused to accept subsidized housing. Confronted with charges of "forced integration" and bitter local protests, however, the administration quickly backed down. Efforts to prohibit discrimination in lending have been somewhat more promising. Several laws passed in the 1970s

The mortgage crisis that led to foreclosures on many homes in 2008 and 2009 hit minority communities especially hard. Civil rights organizations argued that some lenders discriminated against African American and Latino home buyers, making it harder for them to get a fair deal on a mortgage.

required banks to report information about their mortgage lending patterns, making it more difficult for them to engage in **redlining**, the practice of refusing to lend to entire neighborhoods. The 1977 Community Reinvestment Act required banks to lend in neighborhoods in which they do business. Through vigorous use of this act, many neighborhood organizations have reached agreements with banks that, as a result, have significantly increased investment in some poor neighborhoods.

Even so, racial discrimination in home mortgage lending remains a significant issue. In 2007 the issue of predatory lending—offering loans well above market rates, often with complex provisions that borrowers do not understand—attracted nationwide attention as the number of home foreclosures skyrocketed. Several lawsuits charged that these loans were particularly targeted at minority borrowers. In 2009, civil rights organizations; several states, including California, Illinois, Massachusetts, and New York; and some cities, including Baltimore, filed charges against banks and other lenders claiming they had illegally discriminated against African American and Latino home buyers. Minority home buyers, the suits charged, had been offered subprime mortgage products, with higher interest rates, in contrast to whites with similar income levels, who were offered loans at lower interest rates. By 2012 some of these lawsuits had resulted in the largest financial settlements ever issued for lending discrimination. In announcing one settlement, the Justice Department vowed to "vigorously pursue those who would take advantage of certain Americans because of their race, national origin, gender or disability," noting that such discrimination "betrays the promise of equal opportunity that is enshrined in our Constitution and our legal framework."[41]

Marriage The Civil Rights Act of 1964 was also silent on the question of interracial marriage, which 16 states continued to outlaw in 1967. In that year, the Supreme Court ruled in *Loving v. Virginia* that such state laws were unconstitutional. The case concerned a Virginia couple, a white man and a black woman, who married in Washington, D.C., where such unions were legal. When they moved back to Virginia, which outlawed interracial marriage, authorities charged

redlining a practice in which banks refuse to make loans to people living in certain geographic locations

the couple with violating Virginia law. The Lovings moved back to Washington, D.C., and challenged the Virginia law. Nine years later the Supreme Court struck down state laws banning marriage on the basis of racial classifications. In so doing, the Court declared marriage "one of the 'basic civil rights of man,' fundamental to our very existence and survival."[42]

● Extending Civil Rights

> **Describe how different groups have won protection of their rights**

Even before equal-employment laws began to have a positive effect on the economic situation of blacks, something far more dramatic began happening: the extension of civil rights to other groups. The right not to be discriminated against was being successfully claimed by the other groups listed in Title VII of the 1964 Civil Rights Act, those defined by sex, religion, or national origin, and eventually by still other groups defined by age or sexual preference. This extension of civil rights has become the new frontier of the civil rights struggle.

Once gender discrimination began to be seen as an important civil rights issue, other groups rose to demand recognition and active protection of their civil rights. Under Title VII, any group or individual can try, and in fact is encouraged to try, to convert goals and grievances into questions of rights and of the deprivation of those rights. A plaintiff must establish only that his or her membership in a group is an unreasonable basis for discrimination—that is, that the unequal treatment cannot be proven to be a "job-related" or otherwise clearly reasonable and relevant decision. In the United States today, the list of individuals and groups claiming illegal discrimination is lengthy.

Women and Gender Discrimination

Title VII provided a valuable tool for the growing women's movement in the 1960s and '70s. In fact, in many ways the law fostered the growth of the women's movement. The first major campaign of the National Organization for Women (NOW)

Political equality did not end discrimination against women in the workplace or in society at large. African Americans' struggle for civil rights in the 1950s and '60s spurred a parallel equal rights movement for women in the 1960s and '70s.

Have Women Achieved Equal Rights?

Title VII of the 1964 Civil Rights Act prohibits gender discrimination, and the Supreme Court has consistently upheld the principle that women should have the same rights as men. Since 1960, the United States has made great strides toward gender equality in some areas but, as the data show, still has a long way to go in other areas.

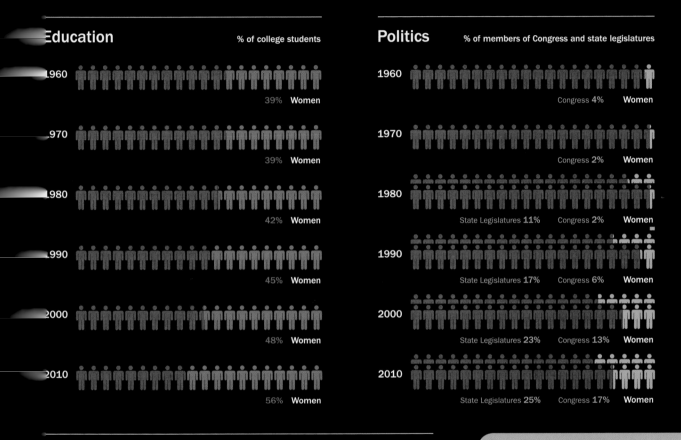

Education
% of college students

1960 — 39% **Women**
1970 — 39% **Women**
1980 — 42% **Women**
1990 — 45% **Women**
2000 — 48% **Women**
2010 — 56% **Women**

Politics
% of members of Congress and state legislatures

1960 — Congress 4% **Women**
1970 — Congress 2% **Women**
1980 — State Legislatures 11% Congress 2% **Women**
1990 — State Legislatures 17% Congress 6% **Women**
2000 — State Legislatures 23% Congress 13% **Women**
2010 — State Legislatures 25% Congress 17% **Women**

Women's Income as a Percentage of Men's
Weekly earnings, by occupation, 2010

81%

74%
Professional
Men: $1,256
Women: $923

81%
Office/Sales
Men: $736
Women: $597

Educators
Men: $1,065
Women: $862

78%
Service
Men: $543
Women: $423

74%
Production
Men: $640
Women: $473

SOURCES: U.S. Census Bureau, census.gov; Center for American Women and Politics, cawp.rutgers.edu accessed 7/18/12).

for critical analysis

1. How much do each of these factors—education, political office holders, and income—say about gender equality in the United States?

2. While most Americans support the principle of equal opportunity for all groups, there is disagreement over how much the government should do to ensure equal outcomes. Discuss the difference between equal opportunity and equal outcomes in the context of women's rights.

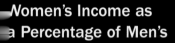

involved picketing the EEOC for its refusal to ban sex-segregated employment advertisements. NOW also sued the *New York Times* for continuing to publish such ads after the passage of Title VII. Another organization, the Women's Equity Action League (WEAL), pursued legal action on a wide range of sex-discrimination issues, filing lawsuits against law schools and medical schools for discriminatory admission policies, for example.

Building on these victories and the growth of the women's movement, feminist activists sought an "Equal Rights Amendment" (ERA) to the Constitution. The proposed amendment was short: its substantive passage stated that "equality of rights under the law shall not be denied or abridged by the United States or by any State on account of sex." The amendment's supporters believed that such a sweeping guarantee of equal rights was a necessary tool for ending all discrimination against women and for making gender roles more equal. Opponents charged that the amendment would be socially disruptive and would introduce changes (such as unisex restrooms) that most Americans did not want. The amendment easily passed Congress in 1972 and won quick approval in many state legislatures, but it fell three states short of the 38 needed to ratify it by the 1982 deadline.[43]

Despite the failure of the ERA, efforts to stop gender discrimination expanded dramatically as an area of civil rights law. In the 1970s the conservative Burger Court (under Chief Justice Warren Burger) helped establish gender discrimination as a major and highly visible civil rights issue. Although the Supreme Court refused to treat gender discrimination as the equivalent of racial discrimination,[44] it did make it easier for plaintiffs to file and win suits on the basis of gender discrimination by applying an "intermediate" level of review to these cases.[45] This **intermediate scrutiny** is midway between traditional rules of evidence, which put the burden of proof on the plaintiff, and the doctrine of strict scrutiny, which requires the defendant to show that unequal treatment is both reasonable and necessary. Intermediate scrutiny shifts the burden of proof partially onto the defendant.

One major step was taken in 1992, when the Court decided in *Franklin v. Gwinnett County Public Schools* that violations of Title IX of the 1972 Education Act could be remedied with monetary damages.[46] Title IX forbade gender discrimination in education, but it initially sparked little litigation because of its weak enforcement provisions. The Court's 1992 ruling that monetary damages could be awarded for gender discrimination opened the door for more legal action in the area of education. The greatest impact has been in the areas of sexual harassment (the subject of the *Franklin* case) and in equal treatment of women's athletic programs. The potential for monetary damages has made universities and public schools take the problem of sexual harassment more seriously. And in the two years after the *Franklin* case, complaints to the Education Department's Office for Civil Rights about unequal treatment of women's athletic programs nearly tripled. In several high-profile legal cases, some prominent universities were ordered to create more women's sports programs, prompting many other colleges and universities to follow suit in order to avoid potential litigation.[47] In 1997 the Supreme Court refused to hear a petition by Brown University challenging a lower-court order that the university establish strict sex equity in its athletic programs. The Court's decision meant that in colleges and universities across the country, varsity athletic positions for men and women must reflect the schools' overall enrollment numbers.[48] By 2012, 40 years after Title IX was first enacted, it was clear that the had a major impact on college athletic programs. But advocates for gender equality noted that many differences between men and women students continued to exist. They pointed to gender barriers in important fields such as science, technology, engineering, and math, which women students are much less likely to enter.[49]

intermediate scrutiny a test used by the Supreme Court in gender discrimination cases that places the burden of proof partially on the government and partially on the challengers to show that the law in question is unconstitutional

Kim Messer, pictured here with a group of male cadets, was one of the first women admitted to the Citadel, a military college in South Carolina. The Supreme Court ruled in 1996 that state-sponsored schools must be open to both men and women.

In 1996 the Supreme Court made another important decision about gender and education by putting an end to all-male schools supported by public funds. It ruled that the Virginia Military Institute's (VMI) policy of not admitting women was unconstitutional.[50] Along with the Citadel, an all-male military college in South Carolina, VMI had never admitted women in its 157-year history. VMI argued that the unique educational experience it offered (including intense physical training and the harsh treatment of freshmen) would be destroyed if women students were admitted. The Court, however, ruled that the male-only policy denied "substantial equality" to women. Two days after the ruling, the Citadel announced that it would accept women. VMI considered becoming a private institution in order to remain all-male, but in September 1996, the school's board finally voted to admit women. Even without formal barriers to entry, the experience of the new female cadets at these schools was not easy. The first female cadet at the Citadel, Shannon Faulkner, won admission in 1995 under a federal court order but quit after four days. Of the four women admitted to the Citadel after the Supreme Court decision, two quit within months. They charged harassment from male students, including attempts to set the female cadets on fire.[51]

Courts began to find sexual harassment to be a form of sex discrimination during the late 1970s. Although sexual harassment law applies to education, most such law has been developed by courts through interpretation of Title VII of the 1964 Civil Rights Act. In 1986 the Supreme Court recognized two forms of sexual harassment. One type is "quid pro quo" harassment, which involves an explicit or strongly implied threat that submission is a condition of continued employment. The second is harassment that creates offensive or intimidating employment conditions amounting to a "hostile environment."[52]

Employers and many employees have complained that "hostile environment" sexual harassment is too ambiguous. When can an employee bring charges? When is the employer liable? In 1986 the Court said that sexual harassment may be legally actionable even if the employee did not suffer tangible economic or job-related losses in relation to it. In 1993 the Court said that sexual harassment may be legally actionable even if the employee did not suffer tangible psychological costs as a result of it.[53] In two 1998 cases, the Court further strengthened the law when it said that whether or not sexual harassment results in economic harm to the employee, an employer is liable for the harassment if it was committed by someone with authority over the employee—by a supervisor, for example. But the Court also said that an employer may defend itself by showing that it had a sexual harassment prevention and grievance policy in effect.[54]

The fight against gender discrimination as an important part of the civil rights struggle has coincided with the rise of women's politics as a discrete movement in American politics. As with the struggle for racial equality, the relationship between changes in government policies and political action suggests that, to a great degree, changes in government policies produce political action. Today, the existence of a powerful women's movement derives in large measure from the enactment of Title VII of the Civil Rights Act of 1964 and from the Burger Court's vital steps in applying that law to protect women. The recognition of women's civil rights has become an issue that in many ways transcends the usual distinctions of American political discourse. In the heavily partisan debate over the federal crime bill enacted in 1994, for instance, the section of the bill that enjoyed the widest support was the Violence Against Women Act, whose most important feature was that it defined gender-biased violent crimes as a matter of civil rights, with a civil rights remedy for women, the crimes' victims. The Supreme Court's 2000 decision ruling the act unconstitutional signaled a defeat for women's rights.[55] Another setback occurred in 2007, when the Court ruled against a claim of pay discrimination at work. The case, *Ledbetter v. Goodyear Tire and Rubber Co.*, involved a woman supervisor named Lily Ledbetter, who learned late in her career that she was being paid up to 40 percent less than male supervisors, including those with less seniority. Ledbetter filed a grievance with the EEOC, charging sex discrimination.[56] The Supreme Court denied her claim, ruling that according to the law, workers must file their grievance 180 days after the discrimination occurs. Many observers found the ruling unfair because workers often do not know about pay differentials until well after the initial decision to discriminate has been made. Justice Ruth Bader Ginsburg, the only female member of the Court, marked her disagreement by reading her dissent aloud, a rare occurrence. In January 2009 the Lily Ledbetter Fair Pay Act became the first bill that President Obama signed into law. The new law gave workers expanded rights to sue in cases, such as Ledbetter's, when an employee learns of discriminatory treatment well after it has started.

Latinos

The labels *Latino* and *Hispanic* encompass a wide range of groups with diverse national origins, distinctive cultural identities, and particular experiences. As a result, civil rights issues for them have varied considerably by group and by place. For example, the early political experiences of Mexican Americans were shaped by race and by region. For the earliest Mexican Americans in the Southwest, the United States came to them, rather than the other way around. In 1848, under the Treaty of Guadalupe Hidalgo, Mexico ceded to the United States territory that now comprises Arizona, California, New Mexico, and parts of Colorado, Nevada, and Utah, as well as extending the Texas border to the Rio Grande. Although the treaty guaranteed full civil rights to the residents of these territories, Mexican Americans in fact experienced ongoing discrimination, which they sought to remedy through the courts. In 1898 the courts reconfirmed Mexican Americans' formal political rights, including the right to vote. In many places, however, and especially in Texas, Mexican Americans were segregated and prevented from voting through such means as the white primary and the poll tax.[57]

There were regional differences, too. In contrast to the northeastern and midwestern cities to which most European ethnics immigrated, the Southwest did not have a tradition of ethnic mobilization associated with machine politics. Particularly after the political reforms enacted in the first decade of the twentieth century, city politics in the Southwest was dominated by small groups of Anglo elites. In the countryside, when Mexican Americans participated in politics, it was often as part of a political organization dominated by a white landowner, or *patrón*. Texas established separate schools for Mexicans, a practice also common in Southern California. In the housing markets, Mexicans were often banned by restrictive covenants from buying or renting houses in many neighborhoods.

The 1947 Mendez v. Westminster *case challenged segregation of Mexican American students in California and was an important precursor to later school segregation cases. In 2007 a U.S. postal stamp was issued to commemorate the* Mendez *case.*

The earliest Mexican American independent political organizations included the League of United Latin American Citizens (LULAC), founded in 1929, and the GI Forum, created in 1948. Both groups worked to stem discrimination against Mexican Americans. LULAC pursued a legal strategy like the NAACP's to eliminate the segregation of Mexican American students. One of its earliest victories came in 1931, when it successfully challenged a Texas school district's decision to establish separate schools for Anglos and Mexicans.[58] LULAC also litigated the 1947 *Mendez v. Westminster* case, which overturned school segregation in Orange County, California. This case was an important precursor to *Brown v. Board of Education*, and many of the same actors were involved. For example, Thurgood Marshall of the NAACP, the lead attorney on *Brown* (and later a Supreme Court justice), filed a brief supporting desegregation in the *Mendez* case. Moreover, Earl Warren, the California governor who signed the legislation outlawing school segregation there after the *Mendez* decision, served as chief justice when the Supreme Court ruled on *Brown* seven years later. By the late 1950s the first Mexican American was elected to Congress, and four others followed in the 1960s.

In the 1960s a new kind of Mexican American political movement was born. A central inspiration for political mobilization emerged from the United Farm Workers union and its charismatic leader, César Chávez. In an era of unprecedented economic prosperity, California's farmworkers, mainly Mexican migrants, remained poorly paid and lacked basic rights for fair treatment on the job. Employing novel tactics such as the national grape boycott, the union drew Americans' attention to the plight of farmworkers and the injustices that confronted Mexican migrants and Mexican Americans in the fields. Chávez, whose hunger strikes and inspirational speeches kept the movement in the public eye, came to symbolize the quest for Mexican American civil rights more broadly.[59] The fields were not the only focus of conflict. In the late 1960s, Mexican American students, inspired by the black civil rights movement, launched boycotts of high school classes in East Los Angeles, Denver, and San Antonio. Students in colleges and universities across California joined in as well. Among their demands were bilingual education, an end to discrimination, and more cultural recognition. In Crystal City, Texas, which had been dominated by Anglo politicians despite a population that was overwhelmingly Mexican American, the newly formed La Raza Unida Party took over the city government.[60]

Cesar Chavez, a leader of the United Farm Workers, advocated for the rights of Mexican Americans. During the 1960s, Chavez and his supporters used hunger strikes and other protests to draw attention to the discriminatory treatment of Mexican Americans.

Since that time, Latino political strategy has developed along two tracks. One is a traditional ethnic group path of voter registration and voting along ethnic lines. The second is a legal strategy using the various civil rights laws designed to ensure fair access to the political system. The Mexican American Legal Defense and Education Fund (MALDEF), founded in 1968, has played a key role in designing and pursuing the latter strategy.

Immigrants and Civil Rights Since the 1960s, rights for Latinos have been intertwined with immigrant rights. Latino organizations opposed the Immigration Reform and Control Act of 1986 because it imposed sanctions on employers who hire undocumented workers. Such sanctions, they feared, would lead employers to discriminate against Latinos. These suspicions were confirmed in a 1990 report by the General Accounting Office that found employer sanctions had created a "widespread pattern of discrimination" against Latinos and others who appear foreign.[61] Organizations such as MALDEF monitor and challenge such discrimination. These groups have turned their attention to the rights of legal and illegal immigrants, as anti-immigrant sentiment has grown in recent years.

For much of American history, legal immigrants were treated much the same as citizens. But growing immigration—including an estimated 300,000 unauthorized immigrants per year—and mounting economic insecurity have undermined this sense of equality. Groups of voters across the country now strongly support drawing a sharper line between immigrants and citizens. The Supreme Court has ruled that unauthorized immigrants are eligible for education and emergency medical care but can be denied other social benefits. The movement to deny benefits to noncitizens gathered steam in California, which experienced sharp economic distress in the early 1990s and has the highest levels of immigration of any state. In 1994, California voters approved Proposition 187, denying unauthorized immigrants all services except emergency medical care. Supporters of the measure hoped to discourage unauthorized immigration and to pressure those already in the country to leave. Opponents contended that denying basic services to unauthorized immigrants risked creating a subclass of residents in the United States whose poor health and lack of education would threaten all Americans. In 1994 and 1997 a federal court declared most of Proposition 187 unconstitutional, affirming previous rulings that unauthorized immigrants should be granted public education. A booming economy helped reduce public concern about unauthorized immigration, but these worries soon emerged again.

Questions about the rights of unauthorized immigrants became especially contentious in 2007. That year, Congress considered a complex compromise bill—running some 761 pages long—that attempted to accomplish three goals: increase border security to reduce illegal immigration; provide unauthorized immigrants who had been in the country for at least five years with a pathway to legal citizenship; and ensure employers an adequate supply of temporary immigrant workers through a guest worker program. The compromise failed in the face of opposition from the Right, which disliked the provision for creating a path to legal citizenship, and from the Left, which opposed the proposed guest worker program.

Some states and cities have tried to address illegal immigration by enacting stricter laws than those under consideration by Congress. This worker protested one such law with a sign reading, "I am a day laborer, not a criminal."

In the aftermath of the failed legislation, unauthorized immigration has continued to be a hot-button political issue with important repercussions for civil rights. Antagonism against undocumented immigrants has spilled over into violence against Latinos. One priority for civil rights groups is to ensure that such violence is classified as a hate crime by the federal Justice Department, thus carrying significantly heavier penalties than would otherwise be the case. In 2009 a Shenandoah, Pennsylvania, jury imposed a very light sentence on three teenage defendants who had beaten a Mexican man to death while shouting ethnic slurs. The National Council of La Raza (a Latino civil rights advocacy organization) and MALDEF collected 50,000 signatures on a petition urging the Justice Department to declare the murder a hate crime.[62]

Another ongoing issue is federal cooperation with local and state law enforcement agencies to enforce federal immigration laws. Programs first initiated by the Department of Homeland Security in the final years of the George W. Bush administration led to immigrant "sweeps," which rounded up Latinos, many of whom were legal immigrants or even American citizens. A broad coalition of civil rights organizations opposed the program for engaging in racial profiling and violating civil rights, and the congressional Hispanic Caucus called on the new president to end it. Yet, as we saw in the introduction to this chapter, the Obama administration's Secure Communities program, which initially sought to focus on major drug offenders, violent criminals, and those already in prison, has come under fire for illegally detaining citizens and legal immigrants. In the case of Maricopa County (Phoenix) sheriff Joe Arpaio, the federal government took strong measures to limit local discriminatory behavior. Charging that the Sheriff's Office had "a pervasive culture of discriminatory bias against Latinos," the Justice Department threatened to withdraw all federal money from the county if it did not agree to change its practices.[63]

Finally, as we saw in Chapter 3, a number of states, including Arizona, Utah, South Carolina, Indiana, Georgia, and Alabama passed very strict immigration laws. Civil rights groups have contested the laws in court, and the federal Justice Department has instituted its own legal challenges. Arizona's 2010 law provided the inspiration for these far-reaching state measures. Arizona's law required immigrants to carry identity documents with them at all times, made it a crime for an undocumented immigrant to apply for a job, gave the police greater powers to stop anyone they suspected of being an unauthorized immigrant, and required them to check the immigration status of a person they detain if they suspect that person is an unauthorized immigrant. The Justice Department challenged the law on the grounds that the federal government was responsible for making immigration law, not the states. The Supreme Court's 2012 decision was a partial victory for the federal government. The court struck down three parts of the Arizona law on the grounds that they preempted federal responsibility. These included the provision that immigrants carry identity papers, that undocumented immigrants cannot apply for jobs, and that police can stop persons they suspect of being undocumented immigrants. The Court let stand the provision that required local police to check the immigration status of an individual detained for other reasons, if they had grounds to suspect that the person was in the country illegally. Opponents of the police checks vowed to challenge that part of the law on the grounds that it led to illegal racial profiling.[64]

Asian Americans

Like the term *Latino*, the label *Asian American* encompasses a wide range of people from very different national backgrounds who came to the United States at different moments in history. As a consequence, Asian Americans have had very diverse experiences.

The early Asian experience in the United States was shaped by a series of naturalization laws dating back to 1790, the first of which declared that only white aliens were eligible for citizenship. Chinese immigrants began arriving in California in the 1850s, drawn by the boom of the gold rush, but they were immediately met with virulent antagonism. In 1870, Congress declared Chinese immigrants ineligible for citizenship; in 1882 the first Chinese Exclusion Act suspended the entry of Chinese laborers.

At the time of the Exclusion Act, the Chinese community was composed predominantly of single male laborers, with few women and children. The few Chinese children in San Francisco were initially denied entry to the public schools; only after parents of American-born Chinese children pressed legal action were the children allowed to attend public school. Even then, however, they were segregated into a separate Chinese school. American-born Chinese children could not be denied citizenship, however; this right was confirmed by the Supreme Court in 1898, when it ruled in *United States v. Wong Kim Ark* that anyone born in the United States was entitled to full citizenship.[65] Still, new Chinese immigrants were barred from the United States until 1943, after China had become a key wartime ally and Congress repealed the Chinese Exclusion Act and permitted Chinese residents to become citizens.

The earliest Japanese immigrants, who came to California in the 1880s, at the height of the anti-Chinese movement, faced similar discrimination. Like Chinese immigrants, Japanese immigrants were ineligible to become citizens because of their race. During the first part of the twentieth century, California and several other western states enacted laws that denied Japanese immigrants the right to own property. The denial of basic civil rights to Japanese Americans culminated in the decision to

Asian immigrants faced discrimination throughout much of American history. During World War II, Americans of Japanese descent were forced from their homes and confined in internment camps. At the time, the Supreme Court supported this denial of civil rights as a necessary security measure.

forcibly remove Americans of Japanese descent as well as Japanese noncitizen residents from their homes and confine them in internment camps during World War II. Despite a vigorous legal challenge, the Supreme Court ruled that the internment was constitutional on the grounds of military necessity.[66] Not until the Civil Liberties Act of 1988 did the federal government formally acknowledge this denial of civil rights as a "grave injustice" that had been "motivated largely by racial prejudice, wartime hysteria, and a failure of political leadership."[67] Along with a formal apology from the president, Congress issued each surviving internee a $20,000 check.

Asian immigration increased rapidly after the 1965 Immigration Act, which lifted discriminatory quotas. In spite of this and other developments, limited English proficiency barred many new Asian American and Latino immigrants from full participation in American life. Two developments in the 1970s, however, established rights for language minorities. In 1974 the Supreme Court ruled in *Lau v. Nichols*, a suit filed on behalf of Chinese students in San Francisco, that school districts have to provide education for students whose English is limited.[68] It did not mandate bilingual education, but it established a duty to provide instruction that the students could understand. As we saw earlier, the 1970 amendments to the Voting Rights Act permanently outlawed literacy tests in all 50 states and mandated bilingual ballots or oral assistance for those who speak Chinese, Japanese, Korean, Spanish, or Native American or Alaskan languages.

The Digital Divide

Digital inequality, or the digital divide, refers to the gap between Internet users and individuals or groups who do not have access to the Internet. Those least likely to be online and use the Internet daily are the poor, racial and ethnic minorities, non-English speakers, the less educated, and the elderly. The same groups are also less likely to have digital literacy skills. Thus, addressing the divide requires both access and skills, the two components necessary for digital citizenship, or full participation in today's increasingly digital politics and society.

It is hard to image that less than 20 years ago (1995) only one in 10 adults in the United States was online. In contrast, in 2012 almost 8 out of 10 adults were online. When the Pew Research Center first began tracking the role of the Internet in American life (in 1995) there were stark demographic differences between who was on- and offline. Today, these differences still exist, especially when it comes to broadband access at home.

While the overall number of Internet users has increased dramatically, almost 4 in 10 don't have high-speed access at home. As we discussed in Chapter 1, home access and high-speed access are necessary for digital citizenship and full participation in society online. A 2011 Pew survey found that two-thirds (66 percent) of whites have high-speed Internet at home, but only half of African Americans (49 percent) and Hispanics (51 percent) have such access. The 2011 survey also found gaps based on age, income, and educational attainment. Among those who earn less than $30,000 per year, only 41 percent have such access. This compares with 89 percent of those making at least $75,000 per year. Thus

Internet access follows a similar socio-economic pattern as voter turnout (see Chapter 8), potentially reinforcing political inequalities as some groups participate more than others in politics.

The ways in which people connect to the Internet are more varied today than they were a decade ago. Some people argue that mobile access will solve the digital divide. Mobile access on smartphones is a primary way the poor and racial and ethnic minorities go online. Among smartphone users, the groups that are more likely than other groups to say that their phone is their main source of Internet access are young adults, minorities, those with no college experience, and those with lower household income levels. In 2012 over 40 percent of Americans used a smartphone that could connect to the Internet, while over 60 percent went online wirelessly using a laptop, tablet, or cell phone.

However, in a 2011 New York Times editorial, Yeshiva University law school Professor Susan Crawford argued that although smartphones have many benefits, they provide "second-class access" compared with high-speed broadband. There are significant gaps in the activities online for broadband users versus for individuals with mobile access only. A 2009 Federal Communications Commission (FCC) survey found that only 52 percent of the less connected read national or international news online, compared to 77 percent of those with broadband at home. Of the less connected, only 57 percent used state, local, or federal government websites compared with

79 percent with broadband a home. The growth in mobile phone use has not erased inequalities in participation online and seems unlikely to do so.

What are the reasons people give for remaining offline? For rural residents, broadband is often not available. But the number one reason people report for not having home broadband is price. Despite President Obama's promise to build a digital highway across America and despite the adoption of the National Broadband Plan, the United States lags behind numerous other countries in broadband investment, ranking 15th in the percentage of broadband subscribers in 2010. Government spending has focused on subsidizing rural broadband wiring rather than addressing the high cost of access. In 2012 the FCC began experimenting with subsidizing broadband access for the poor. At this point it is a pilot project, but future government policy may help provide Internet access for those who are unable to afford it.

SOURCES: Karen Mossberger, Caroline Tolbert, and Mary Stansbury, *Virtual Inequality: Beyond the Digital Divide* (Washington, DC: Georgetown University Press, 2003). Karen Mossberger, Caroline Tolbert, and William Franko, *Digital Cities: The Internet and the Geography of Opportunity* (New York: Oxford University Press, 2012). Pew Internet and American Life, *Digital Differences*, April 2012.

for critical analysis

1. In 2011 the United Nations declared that access to the Internet is a human right Do you think the government has an obligation to provide Internet access to all Americans?

2. The Internet has the potential to increase participation in politics, but does this matter if the same groups that have historically been underrepresented in politics also have less access to digital politics?

Native Americans

The political status of Native Americans was left unclear in the Constitution. But by the early 1800s the courts had defined each of the Indian tribes as a nation. As members of Indian nations, Native Americans were thus declared noncitizens of the United States. The political status of Native Americans changed in 1924, when congressional legislation granted citizenship to all persons born in the United States. A variety of changes in federal policy toward Native Americans during the 1930s paved the way for a later resurgence of their political power. Most important was the federal decision to encourage Native Americans on reservations to establish local self-government.[69] Since the 1920s and '30s, Native American tribes have sued the federal government for illegal land seizures; both monetary reparations and land have been awarded as damages, but only in small amounts. Native American tribes have been more successful in winning federal recognition of their sovereignty. Sovereign status has, in turn, allowed them to exercise greater self-determination.

The Native American political movement gathered force in the 1960s as Native Americans began to use protest, litigation, and assertion of tribal rights to improve their situation. In 1968, Dennis Banks, Herb Powless, and Clyde Bellecourt cofounded the American Indian Movement (AIM), the most prominent Native American rights organization. AIM won national attention in 1969 when 200 of its members, representing 20 different tribes, took over the famous prison island of Alcatraz in San Francisco Bay, claiming it for Native Americans. The federal government responded to the rise in Native American activism with the Indian Self-Determination and Education Assistance Act, which began to give Native Americans more control over their own land.[70]

As a language minority, Native Americans also benefited from the 1975 amendments to the Voting Rights Act and the *Lau* decision, which established the right of Native Americans to be taught in their own languages. This marked quite a change from the boarding schools by the Bureau of Indian Affairs, where members of Native American tribes were forbidden to speak their own languages until reforms began in the 1930s. In addition to these language-related issues, Native Americans have sought to expand their rights on the basis of their sovereign status. Most significant in economic terms was a 1987 Supreme Court decision that freed Native American tribes from most state regulations prohibiting gambling. The establishment of casino gambling on Native American lands has brought a substantial flow of new income onto desperately poor reservations.

Disabled Americans

The concept of rights for the disabled began to emerge in the 1970s as the civil rights model spread to other groups. The seed was planted in a little-noticed provision of the 1973 Rehabilitation Act, which outlawed discrimination against individuals on the basis of disabilities. As in many other cases, the law itself helped give rise to the movement demanding rights for the handicapped.[71] Inspired by the NAACP's use of a Legal Defense Fund, the disability movement founded a Disability Rights Education and Defense Fund to press its legal claims. The movement achieved its greatest success with the passage of the Americans with Disabilities Act (ADA) of 1990, which guarantees equal employment rights and access to public businesses for the disabled and prohibits discrimination in employment, housing, and health care. Claims of discrimination in violation of this act are considered by the EEOC. The impact of the law has been far-reaching, as businesses and public facilities have installed ramps, elevators, and other devices to meet the act's requirements.[72] In 1998 the Supreme Court interpreted the ADA to apply not only to people with AIDS but to those with HIV as well. The case arose when a dentist refused to fill a cavity for a woman with HIV unless the procedure were done in a hospital setting. The woman sued on the grounds that HIV had already disabled her because it was discouraging her from having children. Despite widespread concerns that the ADA was being applied too broadly and that costs were becoming too burdensome, corporate America did not seem to be disturbed by the Court's ruling. Stephen Bokat, general counsel of the U.S. Chamber of Commerce, said businesses in general had already been accommodating people with HIV as well as those with AIDS and that the case presented no serious problem.[73]

Older Americans

The 1967 federal Age Discrimination in Employment Act (ADEA) makes age discrimination illegal when practiced by employers with at least 20 employees. Many states have added to the federal provisions with their own age discrimination laws, and some such state laws are stronger than the federal provisions. The major lobbyist for seniors, AARP, formerly the American Association of Retired Persons (see Chapter 11), with its claim to more than 30 million members, has been active in pushing for these laws and making sure that they are vigorously implemented. Rights for older workers received a setback, however, in a 2009 Supreme Court decision in the case of *Gross v. FBL Financial Services*.[74] The Court ruled that a 54-year-old employee who had challenged his demotion on the grounds of age discrimination would have to show that this action was a direct result of discrimination. This was a major change in the law: in the past, the burden of proof had been on employers to demonstrate that they had valid reasons other than age for demoting or terminating one of their employees.

Gay Men and Lesbians

In less than 30 years, the lesbian, gay, bisexual, and transgender (LGBT) movement has become one of the largest civil rights movements in contemporary America. From its beginnings with the Stonewall Riots in New York City's Greenwich Village in 1969, the movement has grown into a sophisticated and well-financed lobby. The Human Rights Campaign is the primary national political action committee (PAC) focused on gay rights; it provides campaign financing and volunteers to work for political candidates endorsed by the group. The movement has also formed legal-rights organizations, including the Lambda Legal Defense and Education Fund.

Gay rights drew national attention in 1993, when President Bill Clinton confronted the question of whether gays should be allowed to serve in the military. As a candidate, Clinton had said he favored lifting the ban on homosexuals in the military. The issue set off a huge controversy in the first months of Clinton's presidency. After nearly a year of deliberation, the administration enunciated a compromise: its "Don't Ask, Don't Tell" policy allowed gay men and lesbians to serve in the military as long as they did not openly proclaim their sexual orientation or engage in homosexual activity. The administration maintained that the ruling would protect gay men and lesbians against witch hunt investigations, but many advocates of gay men and lesbians expressed disappointment, charging the president with reneging on his campaign promise. After nearly 20 years of challenges, President Obama signed an executive order repealing "Don't Ask, Don't Tell," and beginning in September 2011, gay men and lesbians could serve openly in the military.

But until 1996, there was no Supreme Court ruling or national legislation explicitly protecting gay men and lesbians from discrimination. In the first gay rights case it decided, *Bowers v. Hardwick*, the Court ruled against a right to privacy that would protect consensual homosexual activity.[75] After the *Bowers* decision, the gay rights movement sought suitable legal cases to test the constitutionality of discrimination against gay men and lesbians, much as the black civil rights movement had done in the late 1940s and '50s. As one advocate put it, "lesbians and gay men are looking for

In 2008, California voters passed Proposition 8, which restricted marriage to couples consisting of a man and woman. Opponents of the proposition argued that same-sex couples should be treated equally under the law and allowed the right to marry.

their *Brown v. Board of Education*."[76] Test cases stemmed from local ordinances restricting gay rights (including the right to marry), allowing job discrimination, and affecting family law issues such as adoption and parental rights. In 1996 the Supreme Court, in *Romer v. Evans*, explicitly extended fundamental civil rights protections to gay men and lesbians by declaring unconstitutional a 1992 amendment to the Colorado state constitution that prohibited local governments from passing ordinances to protect gay rights.[77] In its decision, the Court highlighted the connection between gay rights and civil rights.

In *Lawrence v. Texas* (2003), the Court overturned *Bowers* and struck down a Texas statute criminalizing certain intimate sexual conduct between consenting partners of the same sex.[78] A victory for gay men and lesbians every bit as significant as *Roe v. Wade* was for women, *Lawrence v. Texas* extends the right to privacy to sexual minorities. However, this decision does not undo the various exclusions that deprive gay men and lesbians of full civil rights, including the right to marry, which became a hot-button issue in the 1990s and remains one today. In 1993, Hawaii's supreme court declared the state's ban on same-sex marriage discriminatory, raising the possibility that such marriages could become legal. In Washington, D.C., the Republican congressional majority responded with the Defense of Marriage Act, which defined marriage as the union of a man and a woman for purposes of federal law and benefits, such as Social Security.

Although Hawaii's voters and its legislature eventually outlawed same-sex marriage, other states took up the issue. A significant victory came in 2004, when the Supreme Judicial Court of Massachusetts ruled that under that state's constitution, same-sex couples were entitled to marry. After that, 10 other states and the District of Columbia passed laws that allowed such couples to marry, including Maryland and Washington state, which passed laws approving same-sex marriage in 2012. Some of these laws, however, have faced challenges. In California, voters repealed the law five months after its passage, although lower courts subsequently declared the California vote as unconstitutional discrimination. In 2012 voters for the first time approved same-sex marriage at the ballot box, with measures winning a majority in Maine, Maryland, and Washington state. Voters in Minnesota blocked an effort to place a ban on same-sex marriage in the state constitution. Gay rights advocates won a significant victory of a different kind in national politics. New legislation extended the definition of hate crimes to include crimes against gay and transgender people. Such legislation had been sought since the 1998 murder of Matthew Shepard, a Wyoming college student who was brutally slain because of his sexual orientation. The new law allows for tougher penalties when a crime is designated a hate crime.

● Affirmative Action

> **Contrast arguments for and against affirmative action**

The politics of rights has spread to increasing numbers of groups in American society since the 1960s. The relatively narrow goal of equalizing opportunity by eliminating discriminatory barriers evolved into the far broader goal of **affirmative action**, compensatory action to overcome the consequences of past discrimination. Affirmative action policies take race or some other status into account in order to provide greater opportunities to groups that have previously been at a disadvantage due to discrimination.

affirmative action government policies or programs that seek to redress past injustices against specified groups by making special efforts to provide members of those groups with access to educational and employment opportunities

President Lyndon Johnson put the case emotionally in 1965: "You do not take a person who, for years, has been hobbled by chains . . . and then say you are free to compete with all the others, and still just believe that you have been completely fair."[79] Johnson issued executive orders directing agency heads and personnel officers vigorously to pursue a policy of minority employment in the federal civil service and in companies doing business with the national government. But affirmative action did not become a prominent goal of the national government until the 1970s.

Affirmative action also took the form of efforts by the agencies in the Department of Health, Education, and Welfare to shift their focus from "desegregation" to "integration."[80] Federal agencies, sometimes with court orders and sometimes without them, required school districts to present plans for busing children across district lines, for pairing schools, for closing certain schools, and for redistributing faculties as well as students, or face the loss of grants-in-aid from the federal government. The guidelines constituted preferential treatment to compensate for past discrimination, and without this legislatively assisted approach to integration, there would certainly not have been the dramatic increase in the number of black children attending integrated classes. The yellow school bus became a symbol of hope for many and defeat for others.

Affirmative action was also initiated in the area of employment opportunity. The EEOC has often required plans whereby employers must attempt to increase the number of their minority employees, and the Department of Labor's Office of Federal Contract Compliance Programs has used the threat of contract revocation for the same purpose. These programs did not require the use of formal quotas.

The Supreme Court and the Burden of Proof

Efforts by the executive, legislative, and judicial branches to shape the meaning of affirmative action today tend to center on one key issue: What is the appropriate level of review in affirmative action cases—that is, on whom should the burden of proof be placed, the plaintiff or the defendant? Affirmative action was first addressed

TABLE 5.3

Supreme Court Rulings on Affirmative Action

CASE	COURT RULING
Regents of the University of California v. Bakke, 438 U.S. 265 (1978)	Affirmative action upheld, but quotas and separate admission for minorities rejected; burden of proof on defendant
Wards Cove v. Atonio, 490 U.S. 642 (1989)	All affirmative action programs put in doubt: burden of proof shifted from defendant to plaintiff (victim), then burden of proof shifted back to employers (defendants)
St. Mary's Honor Center v. Hicks, 113 S. Ct. 2742 (1993)	Required victim to prove discrimination was intentional
Adarand Constructors v. Peña, 515 U.S. 200 (1995)	All race-conscious policies must survive "strict scrutiny," with burden of proof on government to show the program serves "compelling interest" to redress past discrimination
Hopwood v. Texas, 78 F3d 932 (5th Cir., 1996)	Race can *never* be used as a factor in admission, even to promote diversity (Supreme Court refusal to review limited application to the Fifth Circuit—Texas, Louisiana, Mississippi)
Gratz v. Bollinger, 123 S. Ct. 2411 (2003)	Rejection of a "mechanical" point system favoring minority applicants to University of Michigan as tantamount to a quota; *Bakke* reaffirmed
Grutter v. Bollinger, 123 S. Ct. 2325 (2003)	Upheld race-conscious admission to Michigan Law School, passing strict scrutiny with diversity as a "compelling" state interest, as long as admission was "highly individualized" and not "mechanical," as in *Gratz*

formally by the Supreme Court in the case of Allan Bakke (see Table 5.3). Bakke, a white male, brought suit against the University of California at Davis Medical School on the grounds that, in denying him admission, the school had discriminated against him on the basis of his race. (That year, the school had reserved 16 of 100 available slots for minority applicants.) Bakke argued that his grades and test scores had ranked him well above many students who had been accepted at the school and that the only possible explanation for his rejection was that he was white, whereas those others accepted were black or Latino. In 1978, Bakke won his case before the Supreme Court and was admitted to the medical school, but the Court stopped short of declaring affirmative action unconstitutional. The Court rejected the procedures at the University of California because its medical school had used both a quota *and* a separate admissions system for minorities. The Court accepted the argument that achieving "a diverse student body" was a "compelling public purpose," but found that the method of a rigid quota of student slots assigned on the basis of race was incompatible with the Fourteenth Amendment's equal protection clause. Thus,

Allan Bakke sued the University of California at Davis Medical School after he was denied admission. The school had reserved 16 of 100 available slots for minority students. The Supreme Court ordered the school to admit Bakke, who is shown here on his first day of classes in 1978.

the Court permitted universities (and presumably other schools, training programs, and hiring authorities) to continue to take minority status into consideration, but severely limited the use of quotas to situations (1) in which previous discrimination had been shown, and (2) where quotas were used more as a guideline for social diversity than as a mathematically defined ratio.[81]

For nearly a decade after *Bakke*, the Supreme Court was tentative and permissive about efforts by universities, corporations, and governments to experiment with affirmative action programs.[82] But in 1989, with the case of *Wards Cove Packing Co. v. Atonio*, the Court backed away further from affirmative action by easing the way for employers to prefer white males, holding that the burden of proof of unlawful discrimination should be shifted from the defendant (the employer) to the plaintiff (the person claiming to be the victim of discrimination).[83] Congress responded with the Civil Rights Act of 1991, which shifted the burden of proof in employment discrimination cases back to employers.

In 1995 the Supreme Court's ruling in *Adarand Constructors v. Peña* further weakened affirmative action. This decision stated that race-based policies, such as preferences given by the government to minority contractors, must survive strict scrutiny, placing the burden on the government to show that such affirmative action programs serve a compelling government interest and are narrowly tailored to address identifiable past discrimination.[84] President Clinton responded to the *Adarand* decision by ordering a review of all government affirmative action policies and practices, and adopted an informal policy of trying to "mend, not end" affirmative action.

This betwixt-and-between status of affirmative action was how things stood in 2003, when the Supreme Court took two cases against the University of Michigan that were virtually certain to clarify, if not put closure on, affirmative action. The first suit, *Gratz v. Bollinger* (Lee Bollinger, the university president), challenged the University of Michigan's undergraduate admissions policy and practices, alleging that by using a point-based ranking system that automatically awarded 20 points (out of 150) to African American, Latino, and Native American applicants, the university discriminated unconstitutionally against white students of otherwise equal or superior academic qualifications. The Supreme Court agreed, 6–3, arguing that something tantamount to a quota was involved because undergraduate admissions lacked the necessary "individualized consideration" and had employed instead a "mechanical one," based too much on the favorable minority points.[85] The Court's ruling in *Gratz v. Bollinger* was not surprising, given *Bakke*'s (1978) holding against quotas and given recent decisions calling for strict scrutiny of all racial classifications, even those that are intended to remedy past discrimination or promote future equality.

The second case, *Grutter v. Bollinger*, broke new ground. Barbara Grutter sued the law school on the grounds that it had discriminated in a race-conscious way against white applicants with equal or superior grades and law boards. A precarious 5–4 decision for the first time aligned the majority of the Supreme Court with Justice Powell's lone plurality opinion in *Bakke*. Powell had argued that (1) diversity in education is a compelling state interest, and (2) race could be constitutionally considered as a plus factor in admissions decisions. In *Grutter*, the Court reiterated Powell's holding and, applying strict scrutiny to the law school's policy, found that the law school's admissions process was narrowly tailored to the school's compelling state interest in diversity because it gave a "highly individualized, holistic review of each applicant's file" in which race counted but was not used in a "mechanical" way.[86] The Court's ruling that racial categories can be deployed to serve a compelling state interest put affirmative action on stronger ground. But in 2012 the Court agreed to hear a case that might spell the end of affirmative action in higher education. In *Fisher v. University of Texas*, a white student challenged the use of race as one factor among many in the admissions decision.[87] Many observers believed that the Court's decision to hear the case suggested it was ready to revisit the Grutter decision.

Referenda on Affirmative Action

The courts have not been the only center of action: during the 1990s, challenges to affirmative action also emerged in state and local politics. One of the most significant state actions was the passage by referendum in 1996 of the California Civil Rights Initiative, also known as Proposition 209. Proposition 209 outlawed affirmative action programs in the state and local governments of California, thus prohibiting those governments from using race or gender preferences in their decisions about hiring, contracting, or university admissions. Following a heated political battle, the measure passed with 54 percent of the vote, including 27 percent of the black vote, 30 percent of the Latino vote, and 45 percent of the Asian American vote.[88] In 1997 the Supreme Court refused to hear a challenge to the new law. Proposition 209 was framed as a civil rights initiative: "the state shall not discriminate against, or grant preferential treatment to, any individual or group on the basis of race, sex, color, ethnicity, or national origin."

Different wording can produce quite different outcomes. A 1997 ballot initiative asked Houston voters whether they wanted to ban affirmative action in city contracting and hiring, not whether they wanted to end preferential treatment. Fifty-five percent of Houston voters decided in favor of affirmative action.[89] In 2006, 58 percent of Michigan voters supported a measure, modeled after California's Proposition 209, to amend the state constitution by outlawing affirmative action in public education, contracting, and employment. Although University of Michigan officials initially declared that they would continue to use affirmative action criteria in the admissions process until all legal appeals were exhausted, in early 2007 the university announced

The election of Barack Obama as the country's first black president raised questions about whether America's racial problems had been solved and whether policies such as affirmative action were still needed. Does the election of an African American as president mean we are closer to achieving racial equality?

Human Rights and International Politics

When Barack Obama entered office, many observers expected the United States to place a stronger emphasis on human rights in its international engagement. In some respects, the new administration has fulfilled those expectations, but in other ways, it has pursued international policies that some view as hostile to the goal of promoting human rights around the world.

In March 2009 the new administration signaled that it would engage international concerns about human rights when it sought and won a seat on the UN Human Rights Council. The Bush administration had refused to join the council on the grounds that the United Nations was biased and that the United States could better protect international human rights by remaining outside the council.

However, when it comes to foreign policy, the Obama administration has made it clear that advancing human rights is not its sole goal. Instead, the administration has balanced support for human rights with the recognition that the United States often has to work with countries that may violate those rights. For example, concerned with offending the Chinese president before their November 2009 meeting, Obama delayed a meeting with the Dalai Lama, who has long led resistance to Chinese rule in Tibet. This was in sharp contrast to the

approach taken by President George W. Bush, who presented the Dalai Lama with the Congressional Gold Medal. Both decisions were mainly symbolic. Bush wanted to send a message that the United States opposed violations of human rights in Tibet and elsewhere. Obama's decision was seen as part of a broader effort by the administration to cultivate Chinese support, an approach that has been called "strategic reassurance." On her visit to China soon after becoming secretary of state, Hillary Clinton suggested that concern for human rights should not "interfere with the global economic crisis, the global climate-change crisis, and the security crisis"—a reference to the U.S. desire for North Korean nuclear disarmament—all of which required the Chinese to work with the United States.[a]

The Obama administration's stance toward Myanmar (also known as Burma)

provides another example of its effort to balance human rights advocacy with foreign policy realism. Myanmar is ruled by a military junta that seized power almost five decades ago and has blocked democratic elections ever since. The United States long imposed sanctions on Myanmar for its failure to hold elections and for its continued imprisonment of opposition leaders, most notably Nobel Peace Prize–winner Aung San Suu Kyi. However, the Obama administration concluded that sanctions alone haven't worked. Therefore, in late September 2009, the administration announced that it would start talks with the country's military junta for the first time. At the same time, it declared that it would increase humanitarian assistance to the country. In response to Myanmar's return to civilian rule in 2010 and its implementation of some reforms, Hillary Clinton became the first American leader to visit Myanmar in more than 55 years. In 2012 after Myanmar had released hundreds of political prisoners, Washington restored diplomatic ties. Soon after the country held its first elections in two decades.

Striking the right balance between human rights and achieving America's other international interests is not simple. As the Obama administration seeks to advance America's interests in the world, it will have to determine how best to reconcile those interests with its support for international human rights.

[a]John Pomfret, "Obama's Meeting with the Dalai Lama Is Delayed," *Washington Post*, October 5, 2009, www.washingtonpost.com (accessed 10/24/09).

for critical analysis

1. How has the Obama administration sought to balance support for human rights and the United States' international interests?

2. Are symbolic meetings, such as that with the Dalai Lama, important for advancing international human rights? Will better relations with Chinese leaders lead to stronger human rights in the long run or will they compromise the United States' ability to serve as a leader in this field?

that it would stop using affirmative action procedures in admissions. Buoyed by their success in Michigan, affirmative action opponents planned to place similar initiatives on the ballot in other states. However, in 2008 they succeeded in gaining sufficient signatures to bring the measure before voters only in Colorado, where the initiative failed to obtain voter approval, and Nebraska, where voters approved the measure.

● Thinking Critically about Civil Rights and Affirmative Action

The election of Barack Obama as the nation's first black president fueled discussions about whether America's racial problems had been solved. Polls taken just before Obama's inauguration revealed a sharp upturn in positive views about progress toward racial equality, but the euphoria about racial equality did not last for long. A Gallup poll in October 2009 revealed that broad attitudes about America's racial divisions remained remarkably stable. When asked whether they were hopeful that a solution to problems between blacks and whites would be worked out, 56 percent responded positively. This response was nearly identical to that in 1963, when 55 percent indicated that they were hopeful. After Obama's election, the proportion of those believing that racism against blacks was widespread dropped somewhat. Even so, in October 2009, nearly three-quarters of blacks and close to half of all whites continued to view racism against blacks as a widespread problem.[90]

Such beliefs indicate that the election of a black president will not make the debate about civil rights and affirmative action disappear, because Americans hold fundamentally different views about whether and how the government should recognize racial distinctions. At the risk of gross oversimplification, we can divide those with differing views into two groups, and label them liberals and conservatives.[91] Conservatives argue, first, that rights in the American tradition are *individual* rights, and affirmative action violates this concept by concerning itself with "group rights," an idea said to be alien to the American tradition. Second, conservatives argue that the Constitution is "color blind" and that any discrimination, even if it is called positive or benign, must inevitably rely on quotas and thus ultimately violate the equal protection clause.

Liberals agree that rights ultimately come down to individuals but argue that since the essence of discrimination is the unreasonable and unjust exclusion of *an entire group* from something valuable the society has to offer, discrimination itself has to be attacked on a group basis. Despite progress toward racial equality (see Table 5.4), liberals argue that race still matters. They can also cite Supreme Court history, because the first definitive interpretation of the Fourteenth Amendment by the Court, in 1873, stated that

> the existence of laws in the state where the newly emancipated Negroes resided, which discriminated with gross injustice and hardship against them *as a class*, was the evil to be remedied by this clause [emphasis added].[92]

As to the conservative argument concerning quotas, the liberal response is that the Supreme Court has already accepted ratios (a form of quota) that are admitted as evidence to prove a "pattern or practice of discrimination" sufficient to reverse the burden of proof—to obligate the employer to show that there was *not* an intent to discriminate. Further, benign quotas have often been used by Americans

TABLE 5.4

Americans' Opinions on Racial Equality

"How much of a role, if any, do you think the government should have in trying to improve the social and economic position of blacks and other minority groups in this country: a major role, a minor role, or no role at all?"

	MAJOR ROLE %	MINOR ROLE %	NO ROLE %	UNSURE %
All	27	46	26	1
Blacks	59	32	8	1
Whites	19	50	30	1

SOURCE: USA Today/Gallup Poll, August 4–7, 2011, www.pollingreport.com/race.htm (accessed 6/23/12).

both to compensate for some bad action in the past or to provide some desired distribution of social characteristics—that is, diversity. For example, a long-respected policy in the United States is the "veterans' preference" by which the government automatically gives extra consideration in hiring to persons who have served in the country's armed forces. And the goal of social diversity has long justified "positive discrimination," especially in higher education—the very institution where conservatives have most adamantly argued against positive quotas for blacks and women. For example, all the Ivy League schools and many other private colleges and universities regularly and consistently reserve admissions places not only for students from minority groups but also for the children of loyal alumni and of their own faculty, even when, in a pure competition based solely on test scores and high school records, many of those same students would not have been admitted. These practices certainly underscore the liberal argument that affirmative or compensatory action for minorities is not alien to American experience.

If we think of the debate about affirmative action in terms of American political values, it is clear that conservatives emphasize liberty, whereas liberals stress equality. Conservatives believe that actively using government to promote equality for minorities and women infringes on the rights of white men. Lawsuits challenging affirmative action often cite this "reverse discrimination" as a justification. Liberals, on the other hand, traditionally have defended affirmative action as the best way to achieve equality. In recent years, however, the debate over affirmative action has become more complex and has divided liberals. One study of public opinion found that many self-identified liberals were angry about affirmative action, feeling that in the name of equality, affirmative action actually violates norms of fairness and equality of opportunity by giving special advantages to some.[93] Moreover, it is argued, affirmative action is broadly unpopular, making it questionable in terms of democratic values. Because our nation has a history of slavery and legalized racial discrimination, and because discrimination continues to exist (although it has declined), the question of racial justice, more than any other issue, highlights the difficulty of reconciling our values to our practice.

Explore Civil Rights Online

Inform Yourself

 Watch video of key moments in the struggle to end racial discrimination. The Gettysburg Address in 1863, during the height of the Civil War, is considered a turning point in Americans' understanding of equality and freedom. Read the text of the speech at www.gettysburg.com/bog/address.htm. Next, watch a video of Martin Luther King Jr.'s famous "I Have a Dream" speech during the March on Washington at www.youtube.com/watch?v=1UV1fs8IAbg&feature=related, and consider how far the country had come since the Gettysburg address a century earlier. Finally, watch a video of Barack Obama's speech as he accepted the Democratic Party's nomination for president in 2008 (www.youtube.com/watch?v=tQGsP8mnHsg) and consider that, just 45 years after Martin Luther King Jr., an African American is president of the United States. Will African Americans achieve full equality with whites in the years to come?

 Learn about the women's suffrage movement. The fight for equality in the political sphere was also a long one for women seeking the right to vote in elections, and continues today in the fight for policy representation and political influence in government. Visit the Library of Congress's photo collection of the women's suffrage movement (http://memory.loc.gov/ammem/vfwhtml/vfwhome.html).

 Hear an argument for LGBT rights. Secretary of State Hillary Clinton released a video in 2011 stating that LGBT (lesbian, gay, bisexual, and transgender) individuals deserve equal rights, and that LGBT rights are human rights. Learn more about her argument by clicking the video link at www.state.gov/secretary/rm/2011/12/178368.htm.

Connect with Others

 Connect with rights organizations. The objective of the Leadership Conference, an organization with more than 200 subsidiary organizations, is "to promote and protect the civil and human rights of all persons in the United States." Go to its "Action Center" page (www.civilrights.org/action_center/action-center.html) and read through the current issues. Consider signing one of its online petitions to show your support for the issues relating to you.

Find links to the sites listed above as well as related activities on wwnorton.com/studyspace.

study guide

The Struggle for Civil Rights

■ **Trace the legal developments and social movements that expanded civil rights (pp. 157–76)**

Discrimination against individuals on the basis of their race and gender was tolerated and even enforced by government policy throughout much of American history. With the adoption of the Fourteenth Amendment in 1868, civil rights became a part of the Constitution. The political struggles of African Americans and women have narrowed the gap between Americans' belief in equality and the reality of life in the United States, but they have not eliminated it.

Key Terms

discrimination (p. 157)

civil rights (p. 157)

equal protection clause (p. 157)

Thirteenth Amendment (p. 159)

Fourteenth Amendment (p. 159)

Fifteenth Amendment (p. 159)

Jim Crow laws (p. 160)

"separate but equal" rule (p. 161)

Brown v. Board of Education (p. 164)

strict scrutiny (p. 165)

de jure (p. 165)

de facto (p. 165)

gerrymandering (p. 173)

redlining (p. 175)

Practice Quiz

1. When did civil rights become part of the Constitution? *(p. 157)*
   a) in 1789 at the Founding
   b) with the adoption of the Fourteenth Amendment in 1868
   c) in 2008 when Barack Obama was elected president
   d) with the adoption of the Nineteenth Amendment in 1920
   e) in the 1954 *Brown v. Board of Education* case

2. Which of the following could be described as a Jim Crow law? *(p. 160)*
   a) a law forcing blacks and whites to ride on separate trains
   b) a law criminalizing interracial marriage

   c) a law requiring blacks and whites to attend different schools
   d) a law segregating all public accommodations, such as hotels, restaurants, and theaters
   e) all of the above

3. Which civil rights case established the "separate but equal" rule? *(p. 161)*
   a) *Plessy v. Ferguson*
   b) *Grotter v. Bollinger*
   c) *Brown v. Board of Education*
   d) *Regents of the University of California v. Bakke*
   e) *Adarand Constructors v. Peña*

4. Which of the following organizations established a Legal Defense Fund to challenge segregation? *(p. 163)*
   a) the Association of American Trial Lawyers
   b) the National Association of Evangelicals
   c) the National Association for the Advancement of Colored People
   d) the Student Nonviolent Coordinating Committee
   e) the Southern Christian Leadership Council

5. The judicial test that places the burden of proof on government to show that a race-based policy serves a compelling government interest and is narrowly tailored to address identifiable past discrimination is called *(p. 165)*
   a) strict scrutiny.
   b) intermediate scrutiny.
   c) limited scrutiny.
   d) de facto segregation.
   e) de jure segregation.

6. "Massive resistance" refers to efforts by southern states during the late 1950s and early 1960s to *(p. 165)*
   a) build public housing for poor blacks.
   b) defy federal mandates to desegregate public schools.
   c) give women the right to have an abortion.
   d) bus black students to white schools.
   e) stage large-scale protests against Jim Crow laws.

7. Which of the following made discrimination by private employers and state governments illegal? *(pp. 168–69)*
   a) the Fourteenth Amendment
   b) the Fifteenth Amendment
   c) *Brown v. Board of Education*
   d) the 1964 Civil Rights Act
   e) *Regents of the University of California v. Bakke*

8. The Voting Rights Act of 1965 significantly extended and protected voting rights by doing which of the following? *(p. 172)*
   a) barring literacy tests as a condition for voting in six southern states
   b) requiring all voters to register two weeks before any federal election
   c) eliminating all federal-level registration requirements
   d) allowing voters to sue election officials for monetary damages in civil court
   e) all of the above

 Practice Online
Video exercise: *John F. Kennedy—Address on Civil Rights*

Extending Civil Rights

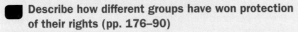 **Describe how different groups have won protection of their rights (pp. 176–90)**

In the 1970s the civil rights model created by African Americans began to spread beyond racial and ethnic groups to include groups defined by sex, religion, national origin, age, and sexual preference. For many of these groups, government polices played an important role in giving rise to movements that demanded equal treatment.

Key Term

intermediate scrutiny (p. 178)

Practice Quiz

9. In what way does the struggle for gender equality most resemble the struggle for racial equality? *(p. 180)*
   a) There has been very little political action in realizing the goal.
   b) Changes in government policies to a great degree produced political action.
   c) The Supreme Court has not ruled on the issue.
   d) The Constitution has not been invoked by proponents of the movement.
   e) No legislation has passed adopting the aims of the movement.

10. Which of the following is *not* an example of an area in which women have made progress since the 1970s in guaranteeing certain civil rights? *(pp. 176–80)*
    a) sexual harassment
    b) integration into all-male publicly supported universities
    c) more equal funding for college women's varsity athletic programs
    d) the passage of the Equal Rights Amendment
    e) None—these are all examples of areas in which women have made progress.

11. The Supreme Court's decision in *Mendez v. Westminster* was significant because it *(p. 181)*
    a) served as a precursor for *Brown v. Board of Education* by ruling that the segregation of Anglos and Mexican Americans into separate schools was unconstitutional.
    b) determined that anyone born in the United States was entitled to full citizenship.
    c) allowed school districts to achieve racial integration through busing.
    d) held that public accommodations could be segregated by race but still be equal.
    e) eliminated state power to use race as a criterion for discrimination in law.

12. Which of the following civil rights measures dealt with access to public businesses and accommodations? *(p. 187)*
    a) the 1990 Americans with Disabilities Act and the 1964 Civil Rights Act
    b) the 1964 Civil Rights Act only
    c) the 1990 Americans with Disabilities Act only
    d) the Equal Rights Amendment only
    e) the Equal Rights Amendment and the 1964 Civil Rights Act

13. Which of the following cases represents the *Brown v. Board of Education* case for lesbians and gay men? *(p. 189)*
    a) *Bowers v. Hardwick*
    b) *Lau v. Nichols*
    c) *Romer v. Evans*
    d) *Regents of the University of California v. Bakke*
    e) There has not been a Supreme Court ruling explicitly protecting gay men and lesbians from discrimination.

 Practice Online
"Get Involved" exercise: *Online Activism and Contemporary Civil Rights*

Affirmative Action

■ **Contrast arguments for and against affirmative action (pp. 190–95)**

Affirmative action policies take race or some other status into account in order to provide greater educational and employment opportunities to groups that have been discriminated against. The Supreme Court has ruled that the government must show evidence that affirmative action programs serve a compelling government interest and are narrowly tailored to address identifiable past discrimination in order to be ruled constitutional. In recent years, challenges to affirmative action have also emerged at the state and local levels.

Key Term

affirmative action (p. 190)

Practice Quiz

14. In what case did the Supreme Court find that rigid quotas are incompatible with the equal protection clause of the Fourteenth Amendment? *(p. 191)*
    a) *Regents of the University of California v. Bakke*
    b) *Korematsu v. United States*
    c) *Brown v. Board of Education*
    d) *United States v. Nixon*
    e) *Immigration and Naturalization Service v. Chadha*

15. The Supreme Court's decision in *Grutter v. Bollinger* was significant because *(p. 193)*
    a) it stated that race can never be used as a factor in university admissions.
    b) it stated that diversity is a compelling state interest and that university admissions that take racial categorized into account are constitutional as long as they are highly individualized.
    c) it outlawed quotas and separate university admission standards for members of minority groups.
    d) it rejected mechanical point systems that favor minority applicants in university admissions.
    e) it declared that affirmative action policies would no longer be subject to strict scrutiny from the courts.

 Practice Online
"You Decide" exercise: *Affirmative Action*

For Further Reading

Chen, Anthony S. *The Fifth Freedom: Jobs, Politics, and Civil Rights in the United States, 1941–1972.* Princeton, NJ: Princeton University Press, 2009.

Garrow, David J. *Bearing the Cross: Martin Luther King and the Southern Christian Leadership Conference: A Personal Portrait.* New York: Morrow, 1986.

Greenberg, Jack. *Crusaders in the Courts: How a Dedicated Band of Lawyers Fought for the Civil Rights Revolution.* New York: Basic Books, 1994.

Katznelson, Ira. *When Affirmative Action Was White: The Untold Story of Racial Inequality in Twentieth-Century America.* New York: W.W. Norton, 2006.

Klinkner, Philip A., with Rogers M. Smith. *The Unsteady March: The Rise and Decline of Racial Equality in America.* Chicago: University of Chicago Press, 1999.

McClain, Paula D., and Joseph Stewart Jr. *"Can We All Get Along?" Racial Minorities in American Politics.* 4th ed. Boulder, CO: Westview Press, 2005.

Mink, Gwendolyn. *Hostile Environment: The Political Betrayal of Sexually Harassed Women.* Ithaca, NY: Cornell University Press, 2000.

Nava, Michael. *Created Equal: Why Gay Rights Matter to America.* New York: St. Martin's, 1994.

Rosales, Francisco. *Chicano! The History of the Mexican American Civil Rights Movement.* Houston: Arte Público Press, 1997.

Rosenberg, Gerald N. *The Hollow Hope: Can Courts Bring About Social Change?* Chicago: University of Chicago Press, 1991.

Russell, Nancy. *Freedom Is Not Enough: The Opening of the American Workplace.* Cambridge, MA: Harvard University Press, 2006.

Valelly, Richard. *The Voting Rights Act.* Washington, DC: CQ Press, 2005.

Recommended Websites

ADA Home Page
www.ada.gov

The Americans with Disabilities Act (ADA), enacted in 1990, guarantees equal employment rights and access to public businesses for the physically disabled. The U.S. Department of Justice maintains this website, which offers general information on ADA standards, changes in regulation, and policy enforcement.

The Martin Luther King, Jr., Research and Education Institute
http://mlk-kpp01.stanford.edu

Dr. Martin Luther King Jr. was a key leader in the fight for civil rights and desegregation. At this website you can find Dr. King's important speeches and papers, as well as other information about social injustice.

Equal Employment Opportunity Commission (EEOC)
www.eeoc.gov

This website provides information on the federal agency and current employment laws. At this site you can even find out how someone might file a harassment or discrimination charge against an employer.

Equality Now
www.equalitynow.org

This is an organization dedicated to ending gender discrimination around the world. Read about how this group is fighting for the rights of women in Africa or campaigning against female genital mutilation and sex trafficking.

Federal Bureau of Investigation
www.fbi.gov/hq/cid/civilrights/hate.htm

Civil rights violations fall under the jurisdiction of the Federal Bureau of Investigation. Find out what steps the FBI is taking to combat the problem of hate crimes and view some comprehensive statistical data.

Human Rights Campaign (HRC)
www.hrc.org

Gay and Lesbian Alliance against Defamation (GLAAD)
www.glaad.org

These two prominent interest groups are dedicated to equal rights for lesbians and gay men and ending gender discrimination.

League of United Latin American Citizens (LULAC)
www.lulac.org

LULAC has worked to stem discrimination against Mexican Americans since World War II and is now the largest and oldest Hispanic organization in the United States. See what this group is doing to guarantee racial equality based on the Fourteenth Amendment's equal protection clause.

Mexican American Legal Defense and Education Fund (MALDEF)
www.maldef.org

MALDEF is the leading nonprofit Latino litigation, advocacy, and educational outreach institution in the United States. At this site, you will learn about litigation and other activities that MALDEF has initiated related to the rights of Latinos and of immigrants more generally.

NAACP
www.naacp.org

The NAACP is one of the oldest and largest civil rights organizations that is dedicated to equal rights and putting an end to racial discrimination. This group was particularly influential in the landmark case *Brown v. Board of Education,* which led to the desegregation of public schools.

National Organization for Women
www.now.org

Feminist Majority Foundation
www.feminist.org

These leading women's rights groups continue to fight for gender equality and equal rights.

U.S. Commission on Civil Rights
www.usccr.gov

The U.S. Commission on Civil Rights was created by Congress in the late 1950s and continues to investigate complaints of discrimination in American society.

U.S. Supreme Court Media
www.oyez.org

This website has a good search engine for finding information on such landmark civil rights cases as *Plessy v. Ferguson*, *Brown v. Board of Education*, *Lawrence v. Texas*, and *United States v. Wong Kim Ark*, to name only a few.

How closely should the government follow public opinion? Public opinion is sometimes sharply divided over policies or even over the role of government. In other cases, citizens seem to lack the political knowledge necessary for informed opinions. These circumstances can make it difficult for lawmakers to follow the will of the people.

Public Opinion

6

WHAT GOVERNMENT DOES AND WHY IT MATTERS The "consent of the governed"—demanded in the Declaration of Independence—is critical for the functioning of a democracy. We expect the government to pay attention to public opinion, and research has shown that public opinion does indeed have a significant impact on public policy, especially foreign policy.[1] However, many Americans have very little knowledge about government, and their opinions about what government should do are often shifting and inconsistent.

More than halfway through Barack Obama's first presidential term, nearly one in five Americans believed he was a Muslim or had been born outside the United States and thus, as a noncitizen, was ineligible for the presidency. Among Republicans, those doubting the president's citizenship numbered more than two in five.[2] This belief persisted even as the verified details of Obama's personal life were widely available and included ample evidence of his American citizenship. To counter the widespread misperception, the White House eventually posted to the Internet a photograph of President Obama's "long-form" birth certificate, showing that he was born in a hospital in Honolulu, Hawaii, on August 4, 1961, at 7:24 P.M.[3] In over two centuries since the Founding, a sitting president had never before been forced to prove his citizenship publicly. Why did this happen? If public opinion did not matter, why would President Obama have released his birth certificate?

In 2008, as many as 40 percent of voters said they were unsure when asked about Obama's religion. Before Obama was elected president, about 12 percent of Americans believed he was a Muslim, when in fact he and his family are practicing Christians.[4] To be sure, Hussein, Obama's middle name, is a common name in Muslim countries. Obama's unusual background (Kenyan black father; American white mother; raised in Indonesia, Kansas, and Hawaii) was highlighted by both his supporters and opponents. But why did the misperception that he was a Muslim or noncitizen *increase* among some groups after he became president? We would expect that as Americans learned more about Obama over time, these misperceptions would decrease.

In the decade following the September 11, 2001, terrorist attacks and the beginning of the Iraq War in 2003, anti-Muslim sentiment in the United States grew substantially.[5] During the 2008 election some of Obama's opponents waged a media attack insinuating that he had ties to the Muslim community. For example, photographs of Obama with his extended family in Indonesia, some wearing turbans, were widely circulated online. Political scientist Tali Mendelberg has found that nonverbal campaign messages (such as the photos in this case) can be used to exploit discriminatory attitudes among the public.[6] From a base of uncertainty laid by this media campaign, misperceptions of Obama's religion grew.

Are people who believe that Obama was not born in the United States or is a Muslim simply ill-informed, despite the substantial media coverage of the facts? Research shows that facts do not mean much to those who believe that Obama is not American.[7] This disregard of evidence is not unique to those who dislike Obama. Individuals often ignore or discount new information that goes against their feelings about an individual or issue.[8] Emotions in part color how we process information about politics. Moreover, studies have shown that Americans have little interest in politics and political information. Can we have government by the people if the people are not well informed?

chaptergoals

- Define public opinion and identify broad types of values and beliefs Americans have about politics (pages 205–19)

- Explain the major factors that shape specific individual opinions (pages 219–28)

- Describe basic survey methods and other techniques researchers use to measure public opinion (pages 228–41)

- Analyze the relationship between public opinion and government policies (pages 241–43)

● Defining Public Opinion

Define public opinion and identify broad types of values and beliefs Americans have about politics

The term **public opinion** is used to denote the attitudes that people have about issues, events, elected officials, and, of course, politics and policy. It is useful to distinguish between values and beliefs on the one hand and attitudes and opinions on the other. **Values (or beliefs)** constitute a person's basic orientation to politics. Values underlie deep-rooted goals, aspirations, and ideals that shape an individual's perceptions of political issues and events. Liberty, democracy, and equality of opportunity, for example, are basic political values held by most Americans. Another useful term for understanding public opinion is *ideology*. **Political ideology** refers to a complex set of beliefs and values that, as a whole, form a general philosophy about government.

For example, many Americans believe that governmental solutions to problems are inherently inferior to solutions offered by the private sector. The Tea Party movement, for example, advocates private-sector solutions to the problems that face society. Such a general belief may, in turn, lead individuals to form negative views of specific government programs even before they know much about them. An **attitude (or opinion)** is a specific view about a particular issue, person, or event. An individual may have an attitude toward American policy in Iraq or an opinion about Barack Obama's citizenship. The attitude or opinion may have emerged from a broad belief about military intervention or about Democrats, but the opinion itself is very specific. Some attitudes may be short-lived and can change based on changing circumstances or new information.

When we think of public opinion, we often think in terms of differences of opinion. The media are fond of reporting political differences between Democrats and Republicans, blacks and whites, men and women, the young and the old, and so on. Certainly Americans differ on many issues, and often these differences do seem to be associated with race, religion, gender, age, or other social characteristics. For example, opinion polls show that roughly half of Americans sympathize with

public opinion citizens' attitudes about political issues, leaders, institutions, and events

values (or beliefs) basic principles that shape a person's opinions about political issues and events

political ideology a cohesive set of beliefs that forms a general philosophy about the role of government

attitude (or opinion) a specific preference on a particular issue

Attitudes may change over time based on new information, but many Americans who doubted President Obama's U.S. citizenship did not change their views even as ample evidence of his citizenship became available. Finally, the White House published the president's "long-form" birth certificate.

the Tea Party movement and half with the Occupy Wall Street movement. Those who support the Wall Street protestors have very different beliefs regarding the cause of the poor economy (the banks and elected officials are held captive by corporate interests) from those of people supporting the Tea Party (government regulation is strangling the private sector, preventing an economic rebound). While both Occupy Wall Street and the Tea Party are populist economic movements, they have very different underlying opinions, attitudes, and ideologies about the economy and government.

Differences of political opinion are often associated with income, education, and occupation. Similarly, factors such as race, gender, ethnicity, age, religion, and region—which not only influence individuals' interests but also shape their experiences and upbringing—have enormous influence on their beliefs and opinions. For example, individuals whose incomes differ substantially have correspondingly different views on the desirability of any number of important economic and social programs. In general, the poor, who are the chief beneficiaries of these programs, support them more strongly than do those who are wealthier and pay more of the taxes that fund the programs. Religious individuals are much more likely to oppose allowing gays and lesbians to wed than citizens who do not regularly attend church. Blacks and whites have different views on issues that touch upon civil rights and race relations (such as affirmative action)—presumably reflecting differences of interest and historical experience. In recent years, many observers have begun to take note of various differences between the views expressed by men and those expressed by women, especially on foreign policy questions, where women appear to be much more concerned with the dangers of war. Political attitudes are also strongly influenced by partisanship (Republican versus Democrat; see Chapter 9) and ideology (conservative versus liberal).

Today there is a renewed understanding that opinions about issues and politics have emotional underpinnings as well.[9] Emotional responses to candidates or policies run the gamut from strongly positive to strongly negative, and these emotions are traditionally measured by survey questions asking if a candidate (or individual, event, or issue) makes the respondent feel fearful, anxious, hopeful, or enthusiastic. Contrary to the idea that public opinion is purely rational, feelings are complicated and often irrational; once individuals become emotionally attached to particular beliefs, they tend to hold on to them even in the face of contradictory information. Using emotions as a guide, individuals will form opinions quickly in response to current events.[10]

Political Values

liberty freedom from governmental control

Most Americans share a common set of values, including a belief in the principles, if not always the actual practice, of liberty, equality, and democracy. The United States was founded on the principle of individual **liberty**. Americans have always voiced strong support for the idea of liberty, and typically support the notion that governmental interference with individuals' lives and property should be kept to a minimum. (Although, in recent years, Americans have grown accustomed to greater levels of governmental intervention than would have been deemed acceptable by the founders of liberal theory.) Liberty was highlighted in Republican Ron Paul's campaign for president in 2012.

Concerns about liberty have increased since the September 11 terrorist attacks, with the Patriot Act and policies adopted under President George W. Bush. In 2012, President Obama signed into law the National Defense Authorization Act

Most Americans share certain basic political values, including a belief in equality of opportunity. For example, most people believe that all individuals should be allowed to pursue success based on their own efforts and abilities—and not on their social background.

(NDAA), which was overwhelmingly approved by Congress. Under the law, even an American citizen on U.S. soil can be held in military prison indefinitely without charge or a trial. Proponents contend that the law is necessary to prevent another terrorist attack on the United States. Critics, such as the American Civil Liberties Union (ACLU), argue the law is unconstitutional, in that it violates the rights of the accused to a trial and can be used to militarily detain people captured far from a battlefield.[11] Concerns about due process are rooted in the value of liberty.

Similarly, **equality of opportunity** has always been an important theme in American society. Most Americans believe that all individuals should be allowed to seek personal and material success. Moreover, Americans generally believe that such success should be the result of individual effort and ability, rather than family connections or other forms of special privilege. Quality public education is one of the most important mechanisms for obtaining equality of opportunity in that it allows individuals, regardless of personal or family wealth, a chance to get ahead. Today, Internet access is emerging as an important form of equality of opportunity by providing online access to news, politics, jobs, the economy, health care, and other benefits of digital citizenship.[12] Economic opportunity, defined as a good job and a decent standard of living, is a core value in American politics.

Most Americans also believe in **democracy**. They presume that every person should have the opportunity to take part in the nation's governmental and policy-making processes and to have some say in determining how they are governed, including the right to vote in elections.[13] (See Chapter 8 for a discussion of rules affecting voting in elections.) Figure 6.1 shows there is consensus among Americans on fundamental values: for instance, 88 percent believe the government should support equality of opportunity with public policy, and 71 percent believe government censorship is a bigger threat than illegal downloading.

Obviously, the principles that Americans espouse have not always been put into practice. For 200 years, Americans embraced the principles of equality of opportunity and individual liberty while denying them in practice to generations of African Americans. Yet the strength of the principles ultimately helped overcome practices that deviated from those principles. This is echoed in speeches by President Lincoln leading up to the Civil War. Proponents of slavery and, later, of segregation

equality of opportunity a widely shared American ideal that all people should have the freedom to use whatever talents and wealth they have to reach their fullest potential

democracy a system of rule that permits citizens to play a significant part in the governmental process, usually through the election of key public officials

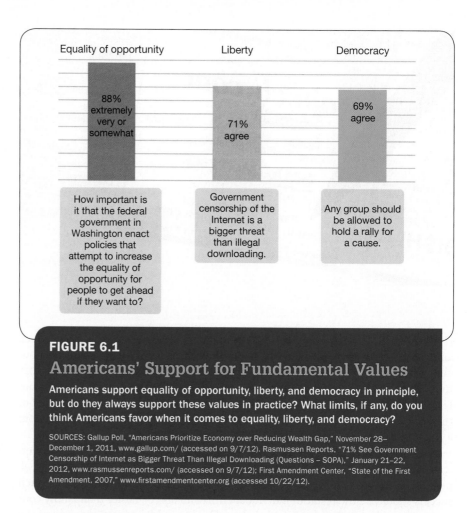

FIGURE 6.1

Americans' Support for Fundamental Values

Americans support equality of opportunity, liberty, and democracy in principle, but do they always support these values in practice? What limits, if any, do you think Americans favor when it comes to equality, liberty, and democracy?

SOURCES: Gallup Poll, "Americans Prioritize Economy over Reducing Wealth Gap," November 28–December 1, 2011, www.gallup.com/ (accessed on 9/7/12). Rasmussen Reports, "71% See Government Censorship of Internet as Bigger Threat Than Illegal Downloading (Questions – SOPA)," January 21–22, 2012, www.rasmussenreports.com/ (accessed on 9/7/12); First Amendment Center, "State of the First Amendment, 2007," www.firstamendmentcenter.org (accessed 10/22/12).

were defeated in the arena of public opinion because their practices differed so sharply from the fundamental principles accepted by most Americans.

Yet even when there is broad agreement over principles, practical *interpretations* of principles can differ. For example, in contemporary politics Americans' fundamental commitment to equality of opportunity has led to divisions over racial policy, with both proponents and opponents of affirmative action programs citing their belief in equality of opportunity as the justification for their position. Proponents of these programs see them as necessary to ensure equality of opportunity, whereas opponents believe that affirmative action is a form of preferential treatment that violates basic American values.[14]

Political Socialization and Public Opinion

People's attitudes about political issues and elected officials tend to be shaped by their underlying political beliefs and values. For example, an individual who has negative feelings about government intervention into America's economy and society would probably be predisposed to oppose the development of new social and health care programs. Similarly, someone who distrusts the military would likely be suspicious of any call for the use of U.S. troops. The processes through which these underlying political beliefs and values are formed are collectively called **political socialization**.

political socialization the induction of individuals into the political culture; learning the underlying beliefs and values on which the political system is based

Probably no nation, and certainly no democracy, could survive if its citizens did not share some fundamental beliefs. If Americans had few common values or perspectives, it would be very difficult for them to reach agreement on particular issues. In contemporary America, some elements of the socialization process tend to produce differences in outlook, whereas others promote similarities. Four of the most important **agents of socialization** that foster differences in political perspectives are the family and social networks, membership in social groups, education, and political environment.

Of course, no brief list of the agents of socialization can fully explain the development of a given individual's basic political beliefs. In addition to the factors that are important for everyone, experiences and influences that are unique to each individual also play a role in shaping political orientation. An early encounter with a single member of another racial group, for example, can have a lasting impact on an individual's view of the entire group. A highly salient political event, such as the Vietnam War or September 11, can leave an indelible mark on a person's political consciousness. And some deep-seated personality characteristic, such as paranoia, may strongly influence the formation of someone's political beliefs. One recent experiment revealed that individuals displaying measurably higher physiological reactions to sudden noises and threatening visual images were more likely to favor defense spending, capital punishment, patriotism, and the Iraq War. That is, people who are more fearful appear to support policies that protect the existing social structure from both external and internal threats.[15] Nevertheless, even if we cannot fully explain the development of any given individual's political outlook, let us look at some of the most important agencies of socialization that do affect one's beliefs.

The Family and Social Networks Most people acquire their initial orientation to politics from their families. As might be expected, differences in family background tend to produce divergent political perspectives. Although relatively few parents spend much time directly teaching their children about politics, political conversations occur in many households, and children tend to absorb the political views of parents and other caregivers, often without realizing it. Studies find, for example, that party preferences are initially acquired at home. Children raised in households in which the primary caregivers are Democrats tend to become Democrats, whereas children raised in homes where their caregivers are Republicans tend to favor the Republican Party.[16] Similarly, children reared in politically liberal households are more likely than not to develop a liberal outlook, whereas children raised in politically conservative settings are likely to see the world through conservative lenses. (Obviously not all children absorb their parents' political views. Two of the late conservative Republican president Ronald Reagan's three children, for instance, rejected their parents' conservative values and became active on behalf of Democratic candidates.) Moreover, even those children whose views are initially shaped by parental values may change their minds as they mature and experience political life for themselves.

Nevertheless, family, friends, coworkers, and neighbors are an important source of political orientation for nearly everyone. Political scientist Betsy Sinclair argues that people are "social citizens" whose political opinion and behavior are significantly shaped by peer influence.[17] Sinclair shows that social networks can and do have the power to change public opinion, including the decision to declare oneself a Democrat or

agents of socialization social institutions, including families and schools, that help to shape individuals' basic political beliefs and values

The terrorist attacks of September 11, 2001, certainly influenced public opinion in the months immediately following the attacks and likely also had a long-term effect on many Americans' basic political beliefs.

a Republican. When members of a social network express a particular political opinion or belief, Sinclair finds, others notice and conform, particularly if their conformity is likely to be highly visible. The conclusion is that basic political acts are surprisingly subject to social pressures. Online social networks such as Facebook and Twitter likely increase the role of peers in shaping public opinion.

Social Groups Another important source of political values are the social groups to which individuals belong. Social groups include those to which individuals belong involuntarily (national, religious, gender, and racial groups, for example) as well as those they join willingly (political parties, labor unions, the military, and environmental, educational, and occupational groups).

Membership in a particular group can give individuals experiences and perspectives that shape their view of political and social life. In American society, for example, the experiences of blacks and whites can differ significantly. Blacks are a minority and have been victims of persecution and discrimination throughout American history. Blacks and whites also have different educational and occupational opportunities, often live in separate communities, and may attend separate schools. Such differences tend to produce distinctive political outlooks. For example, blacks and whites differ considerably in their perceptions of the extent of racism in America (see Figure 6.2). Indeed, according to a CNN poll, 47 percent of white respondents thought racism fairly or very common, while almost half (49 percent) thought it was rare in the United States, according to a survey. Among African Americans, on the other hand, fully 86 percent thought racism was common and only 12 percent said it was rare, almost a 40 point difference between blacks and whites.[18] Interestingly, Hispanic Americans, who have also been victims of racism in the United States, are less likely than African Americans to see America as a racist society; in a 2008 survey, 52 percent of Hispanic Americans and 55 percent of white Americans said that race relations in the United States were generally good. Only 29 percent of black Americans agreed.[19]

Men and women have important differences of opinion as well. Reflecting differences in social roles and occupational patterns, women tend to oppose military intervention more than men, are more likely than men to favor policies to protect the environment, and are more likely to support government social and health care programs (see Table 6.1). Perhaps because of these differences on issues, women are more likely than men to vote for Democratic candidates. This tendency of men's and women's opinions to differ is known as the **gender gap**.

Party Affiliation Political party membership—that is, voluntary membership of a social group—is one of the most important factors affecting political orientation.[20] We can think of partisanship as red-tinted or blue-tinted glasses that color public opinion on a vast array of issues. Partisans tend to rely on party leaders and the media for cues on the appropriate positions to take on major political issues.[21] Walter Lippmann, an influential political commentator of the mid-twentieth century, argued that public opinion is but an echo of elite positions on policy issues, and many others studying public opinion agree.

In recent years, partisan realignment in the South and congressional redistricting have reduced the number of conservative Democrats and all but eliminated liberal Republicans from the Congress and from positions of prominence in the party. As a result, the leadership of the Republican Party has become increasingly conservative, whereas that of the Democratic Party has become somewhat more liberal. Polarization among party leaders has been reflected in the views of party adherents

gender gap a distinctive pattern of voting behavior reflecting the differences in views between women and men

RACE RELATIONS IN THE UNITED STATES

Racism is a very serious problem.

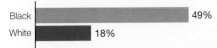

Black 49%
White 18%

Percentages who think only a few white people dislike blacks, many white people dislike blacks, or just about all white people dislike blacks.

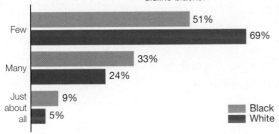

Few 51%
69%

Many 33%
24%

Just about all 9%
5%

■ Black
■ White

EDUCATIONAL OPPORTUNITY

Do black children have as good a chance as white children to get a good education?

Black responses 31% Yes
69% No

White responses 63% Yes
37% No

TREATMENT BLACKS RECEIVE

Discrimination against blacks is rare today.

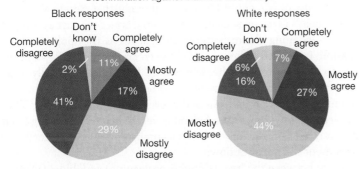

Black responses

Completely disagree
Don't know
Completely agree
2%
11%
Mostly agree
17%
41%
29%
Mostly disagree

White responses

Don't know
Completely disagree
Completely agree
6%
7%
16%
Mostly agree
27%
44%
Mostly disagree

Percent who favor affirmative action programs.

Blacks 93%
Whites 65%

FIGURE 6.2

Disagreement among Blacks and Whites

In the United States, racial and ethnic groups may not perceive race relations in precisely the same way. How, according to the data in this figure, do blacks and whites differ in their views on race relations? Which group is more likely to think that race relations are good? What factors help to account for these differences in perception?

SOURCES: CNN, www.cnn.com; Gallup, Inc., www.gallup.com; and Pew Research Center Publications, http://pewresearch.org (accessed 4/1/08).

TABLE 6.1

Disagreements among Men and Women on National Security Issues

For the most part, fewer women than men favor the use of military force as an instrument of foreign policy. Is this pattern reflected consistently in the data? What might explain gender differences in this realm?

GOVERNMENT ACTION	PERCENTAGE APPROVING OF ACTION	
	MEN	WOMEN
Agree that torture of terrorism suspects is acceptable	50	31
Favor withdrawing troops from Iraq within a year	43	55
Agree that NSA surveillance program is needed	60	50
Oppose sending more troops to Iraq	52	69
Favor cutting off funding for Iraq War	48	57
Believe United States should send more troops to Afghanistan (2009)	49	36

SOURCES: ABC, 2009; *Ms.*, 2006; UPI/Zogby, 2007; *USA Today*, 2007; *Washington* Post/ABC, 2007; CBS, 2009.

and the general public. According to recent studies, differences between Democratic and Republican partisans on a variety of political and policy questions are greater today than during any other period for which data are available. On issues of national security, for example, Republicans have become very "hawkish," whereas Democrats have become quite "dovish." In an October 2003 survey, 85 percent of Republicans but only 39 percent of Democrats thought that America's war against Iraq was a good idea.[22] Gaps on social and economic issues are just as broad. Some refer to the ever-widening chasm between the parties as the "politics of extremism." An example is the 2011 showdown between congressional Republicans and Democrats as to whether to raise the debt ceiling. Republicans initially refused to raise the amount the federal government could borrow, which would have caused the government to default on its loans and prevent it from operating.[23] The "debt ceiling fiasco" led to a lowering of the federal government's credit rating (so it pays a higher interest rate to borrow money), but a compromise was eventually reached and the government did not shut down.

Despite the rift between the "red" (Republican-leaning) and "blue" (Democratic-leaning) states that seems deeper than ever, political scientist Morris Fiorina and colleagues refute the common belief that Americans are deeply divided in their fundamental political views, showing that on a broad range of issues, ranging from homosexuality to abortion, most Americans hold moderate opinions.[24] While political elites and members of Congress may be highly polarized, there is general agreement among most Americans—even on those issues thought to be most divisive. Fiorina and colleagues argue that relatively small differences are often magnified by the rhetoric used to present policy issues. For example, survey data showed that the average opinions of self-identified liberals and conservatives regarding abortion differ only regarding the specific conditions under which they think abortion should be legal, not the legality of abortion in general (which is generally accepted). Overall, in fact, the so-called culture war appears to be between polarized political parties and their activists, with the mass public in the middle being forced to choose between them. Fiorina and colleagues' study suggests that America divides itself because we have little choice when presented with highly divided political parties and elected officials. (See Chapter 9 on why we have a two-party system.) However, contemporary debates over abortion and birth control that emerged in the 2012 Republican presidential primaries may further widen the gap between liberals and conservatives over social issues. As of 2012, 53 percent of Americans believe abortion should be legal in all or most cases, and 41 percent say that abortion should be illegal in all or most cases.[25]

Other Social Groups Other kinds of social affiliations affect individuals' political attitudes. Different religions, for example, provide unique historical experiences and philosophical perspectives that lead their members to see the world in different ways. And social groups can affect individuals' political orientations through the direct efforts of the groups themselves to influence their members. Environmental groups may shape the opinions of their members on issues ranging from public open space and recycling to the wisdom of producing energy from wind power. Labor unions often use meetings, rallies, and literature to shape their members' understanding of politics and to make them more amenable to supporting the political positions favored by union leaders. Women's groups, minority groups, religious groups, and the like often endeavor to structure their members' political views through intensive educational programs. Women who belong to women's organizations, for example, are likely to differ from men in their political views to a greater extent than women without such affiliations.[26] Some analysts have found that African Americans who belong to black organizations are likely to differ more from whites in their political orientations than are blacks who don't belong to such organizations.[27]

Self-Interest and Public Opinion Another way that membership in social groups can affect political beliefs is through what might be called objective political interests. On many economic issues, for example, the interests of the rich and the poor differ significantly. Inevitably, these differences in interests will produce differences in political outlook. The framers of the Constitution thought that the inherent gulf between the rich and the poor would always be the most important source of conflict in political life. More recently, the Occupy Wall Street protesters have decried the chasm between the 99 percent of income earners and the top 1 percent. Struggles over welfare, minimum wage, job creation, health care policy, Social Security, the bailout of the banks, and so forth are fueled by differences in interest between wealthier and poorer Americans. Latinos consider the issue of immigration to be significantly more important than non-Latinos, while African Americans are more supportive of affirmative action programs than non-blacks. Difference in public opinion on these issues is influenced by group self-interest.

However, some researchers find little evidence that economic self-interest has much effect on public opinion, and most people don't translate broad concerns about inequality or their own economic self-interest into specific policy preferences.[28] The public, both rich and poor, is far from demanding redistribution, for example, and has actually become more conservative even as economic inequality in the United States has increased over the past two decades.[29] Political scientist Larry Bartels found that when asked if the income difference between the rich and poor had changed

Is there a culture war between the "red" states of "middle America" and the liberal "blue" states? The television program King of the Hill *took a more nuanced perspective on middle American values, showing that most individuals are less rigid and extreme in their opinions than party leaders. Recent political science research supports this view.*

During the Vietnam War era, public opinion was sharply divided over the war and numerous other issues. Anti–Vietnam War protestors staged passionate demonstrations.

in recent decades, nearly 75 percent of the Americans asked believed that the difference had increased.[30] Of those who stated that the gap between the rich and the poor had grown, over half said that this was a "bad thing." Only 5 percent of the respondents thought it was a "good thing"; the rest said they had not thought about whether rising inequality was good or bad. Despite this concern about inequality, two-thirds of Americans favored the 2000 federal tax cuts supported by President George W. Bush, even though the tax disproportionately benefited the very wealthy, and would therefore likely increase economic inequality. The poor, middle class, and affluent alike favored the tax cuts. Bartels concludes that the public does not seem able to translate a concern for economic self-interest into policy preferences that would benefit average citizens.

Differences in interest also exist among the generations, not just among economic classes. Senior citizens and younger Americans have very different views on such diverse issues as the war on drugs, Social Security, and criminal justice. The young, for example, are much more accepting of allowing same-sex couples to marry legally than are those who are older. And in recent decades major differences in opinion and political orientation have developed between American civilians and members of the armed services. Military officers, in particular, are far more conservative in their domestic and foreign policy views than the public at large and are heavily Republican in their political leanings.[31] Support for the Republican Party among military officers climbed sharply during the 1980s and '90s, decades in which the GOP championed large military budgets.

Nevertheless, group membership can never fully explain a given individual's political views. One's unique personality and life experiences may produce political views very different from those of the group to which one might nominally belong. Some African Americans are conservative Republicans, and the occasional wealthy businessperson is also very liberal. Group membership is conducive to particular outlooks, but it is not determinative.

Education After family and social groups, education can be a third important source of differences in political perspectives. Indeed, education may be the great equalizer. Governments use public education to try to teach all children a common set of civic values; it is mainly in school that Americans acquire their basic belief in liberty, equality, and democracy. In history classes, students are taught that the Founders fought for the principle of liberty. In the course of studying such topics as the Constitution, the Civil War, and the civil rights movement, students are taught the importance of equality. Research finds education to be a strong predictor of tolerance for racial minorities.[32] Through participation in class elections and student government, students are taught the virtues of democracy. These lessons are repeated in every grade, and in a variety of contexts. It is no wonder they constitute such an important element in Americans' beliefs.

At the same time, differences in formal education are strongly associated with differences in political outlook. In particular, those who attend college are often exposed to modes of thought that will distinguish them from their friends and neighbors who do not pursue college diplomas. One of the major differences between college graduates and other Americans can be seen in levels of political participation. Table 6.2 outlines some general differences of opinion found between college graduates and other Americans. College graduates vote, join campaigns, take part in protests, and generally make their voices heard.[33]

TABLE 6.2

Education and Public Opinion

The figures show the percentage of respondents in each category who agree with the statement. Are college graduates generally more or less liberal than other Americans? Which data support your claim? Can you think of economic or political explanations for these findings?

	PERCENTAGE WHO AGREE, BY EDUCATION LEVEL			
ISSUE	GRADE SCHOOL	HIGH SCHOOL	SOME COLLEGE	COLLEGE GRADUATE
Women and men should have equal roles.	38	75	83	86
Abortion should never be allowed.	21	10	7	4
The government should adopt national health insurance.	35	47	42	49
The United States should not concern itself with other nations' problems.	45	26	20	8
Government should see to fair treatment in jobs for African Americans.	49	28	30	45
Government should provide fewer services to reduce government spending.	8	17	19	27

SOURCE: The American National Election Studies, 2004 data, provided by the Inter-University Consortium for Political and Social Research, University of Michigan.

Political Environment A fourth set of factors that shape political attitudes and values are the conditions under which individuals and groups are recruited into and become involved in political life. Although political beliefs are influenced by family background and group membership, the content and character of these views is, to a large extent, determined by political circumstances. For example, the baby-boom generation that came of age in the 1960s was exposed to both the Vietnam War itself and also widespread antiwar protests on college campuses and in urban areas throughout the nation. This experience fundamentally shaped the opinions of this age cohort, just as September 11 and the war on terrorism helped shape the political lives of those who came of age in the 1990s and 2000s.

Similarly, the views held by members of a particular group can shift drastically over time, as political circumstances change. For example, American white southerners were staunch members of the Democratic Party from the Civil War through the 1960s. As Democrats, they became key supporters of liberal New Deal and post–New Deal social programs that greatly expanded the size and power of the American national government. The 1960s mark the beginning of the South's move from the Democratic to the Republican camp—mainly because of white southern opposition to the Democratic Party's integrationist racial policies and because of determined Republican efforts to win white southern support. Since the 1960s a majority of southern whites has shifted to the Republican Party. Now southern whites provide a solid base of support for efforts to scale back social programs and sharply reduce the size and power of the national government—hence the popularity of the Tea Party movement in the South.[34] It was not a change in the character of white southerners but a change in the political environment in which they found themselves that induced this major shift in partisanship in the South.

Another example of partisan realignment due to an evolving political environment can be seen in the West. California's Republican governor in the 1970s, Ronald Reagan, went on in the 1980s to become one of the most admired Republican presidents, ushering in the tax revolt and regulating many government policies. But since the 1990s, California, once a Republican stronghold, has become solidly Democratic. Some argue that the realignment began with a series of ballot measures targeting racial and ethnic minorities endorsed by the Republican Party in the 1990s, including immigration, affirmative action, and bilingual education. These ballot measures triggered a backlash, especially among Latinos, who had previously voted in very low numbers. In the 1990s, registration and voting by Latinos increased dramatically, and favored Democratic political candidates. With Latinos and blacks combined making up more than 50 percent of California's population, this demographic environmental change moved California to a solid Democratic state.[35]

In sum, public opinion cannot be inferred simply from the character of groups or the political climate of an era. Any group's political outlooks and orientations are shaped by the political circumstances in which that group finds itself, and those outlooks can change as circumstances change. The generation of American students now coming of political age after the September 11 terrorist attacks will have a very different view of the use of American military power from that of their parents—members of a generation that reached political consciousness during the 1960s, when opposition to the Vietnam War and military conscription was, for many, a defining political stance.

Political Ideology

libertarianism a political ideology that emphasizes freedom and voluntary association with small government

socialism a political ideology that emphasizes social ownership or collective government ownership and strong government

As we have seen, people's beliefs about government can vary widely. But for some individuals, a set of beliefs can fit together into a coherent philosophy about government. The set of underlying orientations, ideas, and beliefs through which we come to understand and interpret politics is called a *political ideology*. Ideologies take many different forms. Some people may view politics primarily in religious terms. During the course of European political history, for example, Protestantism and Catholicism were often political ideologies as much as they were religious creeds. Each set of beliefs included not only elements of religious practice but also distinct ideas about secular authority and political action. Other people may see politics through a racial lens. In mid-twentieth-century Germany, Nazi ideology placed race at the center of political life and sought to interpret politics in terms of racial categories.

In America today, a variety of ideologies compete for attention and support. **Libertarianism**, for example, argues that government is wasteful and interferes with free markets and society, and so it should be limited to as few spheres of activity as possible. In 2012, Republican presidential candidate Ron Paul, a staunch libertarian, gained support among many young voters for his opposition to foreign wars and his support of civil liberties and smaller government. While Libertarians believe in less government intervention in economic and social realms, **socialists**, on the other hand, argue that more government is necessary to promote justice and to reduce economic and social inequality. Although many Americans subscribe to libertarianism, socialism, and other ideologies in part, most Americans describe themselves as either liberals or conservatives, or some shade of the two. Like the political ideologies already described, liberalism and conservatism comprise beliefs about the role of the government, preferences regarding specific public policies, and ideas about which groups in society should exercise power and how they should do so (see Boxes 6.1 and 6.2).

The definitions of both *liberal* and *conservative* have changed over time. To some extent, contemporary liberalism and conser-

Although liberalism and conservatism are the most common political ideologies in the United States today, other ideologies, such as libertarianism, offer different perspectives on the role of government, policy issues, and society. For example, libertarians advocate a smaller role for government, less involvement overseas, and more freedom for businesses.

vatism can be seen as differences in emphasis with regard to the fundamental American political values of liberty and equality. For liberals, equality is the most important of the core values. Liberals encourage government action in such areas as college admissions and business practices to enhance race, class, and gender equality, or in terms of social programs and redistributive taxation that promote equality. For conservatives, on the other hand, liberty is the core value. Conservatives oppose many efforts of the government, however well intentioned, to interfere in private life and the marketplace.

Liberalism In classical political theory, a **liberal** was someone who favored individual initiative and was suspicious of the motives of government and of its ability to manage economic and social affairs—a definition akin to that of today's libertarian. Liberals saw government as a foe of freedom. The proponents of a larger and more active government, on the other hand, called themselves progressives. In the early twentieth century, though, many liberals and progressives coalesced around the doctrine of "social liberalism," which represented recognition that government action might be needed to preserve individual liberty. Today's liberals are social liberals rather than classical liberals.

In contemporary politics being a liberal has come to imply supporting political and social reform, government intervention in the economy, the expansion of federal social services and health care, more vigorous efforts on behalf of the poor and minorities, and greater concern for consumers and the environment. Liberals generally support abortion rights and rights for gay men and lesbians, and are concerned with protecting the rights of people accused of crimes. Liberals oppose state involvement in religious institutions and state sanction of religious expression. In international affairs, liberals often support arms control, aid to poor nations, and international organizations such as the United Nations and the European Union; liberals generally oppose the development and testing of nuclear weapons, and the use of American troops to influence the affairs of developing nations. Many liberals are opposed to military wars. Under the broad umbrella of liberalism, some liberals have a specific focus: Occupy Wall Street groups, for instance, demonstrate for greater economic equality, and environmentalists view global warming and other ecological threats as the most important issues facing humanity today.

liberal today this term refers to those who generally support social and political reform; extensive governmental intervention in the economy; the expansion of federal social services; more vigorous efforts on behalf of the poor, minorities, and women; and greater concern for consumers and the environment

BOX 6.1

Profile of a Liberal: Representative Nancy Pelosi

- Supports abortion rights and birth control.

- Opposes prayer in the public schools.

- Supports affirmative action.

- Supports same-sex marriage.

- Favors expanded health coverage for all Americans.

- Advocates increased funding for education.

- Supports further increases in the minimum wage.

BOX 6.2

Profile of a Conservative: House Speaker John Boehner

- Wants to trim the size of the federal government.

- Wants to diminish government regulation of business.

- Favors prayer in the public schools.

- Opposes gay rights legislation.

- Favors making most abortions illegal.

- Supports harsher treatment of criminals.

- Opposes many affirmative action programs.

- Favors tax cuts.

conservative today this term refers to those who generally support the social and economic status quo and are suspicious of efforts to introduce new political formulae and economic arrangements. Conservatives believe that a large and powerful government poses a threat to citizens' freedom

Conservatism By contrast, **conservatives** believe strongly that a large and powerful government poses a threat to the freedom of individual citizens. Ironically, today's conservatives espouse the views of classical liberalism. Premodern conservatives were the defenders of monarchy and aristocracy—doctrines that seem completely antiquated today. Today, in the domestic arena, conservatives generally oppose the expansion of governmental activity, asserting that solutions to social and economic problems can and should be developed in the private sector. Conservatives particularly oppose efforts to impose government regulation on business, maintaining that regulation frequently leads to economic inefficiency, is costly, and can ultimately lower the entire nation's standard of living. In terms of social policy, many conservatives support school prayer and traditional family arrangements, and are concerned about law and order; conservatives generally oppose abortion, same-sex marriage, and the use of mandatory school busing to achieve the racial integration of schools. In international affairs, conservatism has come to mean support for military intervention and the maintenance of American military power.

Mixing Ideologies Both liberalism and conservatism are far from monolithic ideologies, and most Americans consider themselves moderates, with shades of liberal or conservative values. Figure 6.3 shows that the percentage of Americans who consider themselves moderates has declined slightly since 2008, but overall Americans' ideology has been fairly stable. Many conservatives support at least some government social programs. Republican president George W. Bush called himself a "compassionate conservative," to indicate that he favored programs that assist the poor and needy. Other conservatives dismissed Bush as a "big government" Republican, and therefore not a true conservative. Many staunch conservatives joined the rising Tea Party movement in 2009 to protest President Obama's efforts to expand the role of the federal government, especially in health care. And while President Obama is liberal in supporting health care reform and other social programs, he has been criticized by those on the left for extending the tax policies of his Republican predecessor, Bush, which benefited the affluent, and for expanding U.S. military involvement in Afghanistan and other countries. In short, some

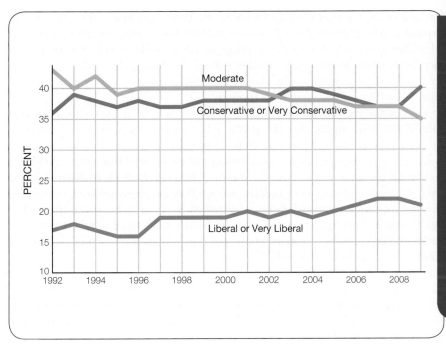

FIGURE 6.3

Americans' Ideology, 1972–2012

Over the past two decades, more Americans have identified themselves as "conservatives" than "liberals." During this same period, however, Americans have elected two Democratic presidents and have, several times, elected Democratic majorities in Congress. What might account for this apparent discrepancy between ideology and partisanship?

SOURCE: Gallup Poll, "Conservatives Remain the Largest Ideological Group in U.S." January 12, 2012, www.gallup.com/poll/152021/conservatives-remain-largest-ideological-group.aspx (accessed 9/7/12).

of Obama's economic and foreign policies are associated with conservatives, and some with liberals. The real political world is far too complex to be seen simply in terms of a struggle between liberals and conservatives.

Sometimes political ideologies provide little guidance in a crisis. At the root of the financial collapse in 2008 was a sudden collapse in real estate values and an accompanying breakdown in the home mortgage system, one that has been blamed for wiping out much of the wealth of American families. The ensuing bailout of the home mortgage industry, including the federally backed mortgage institutions Freddie Mac and Fannie Mae, is estimated to have cost taxpayers hundreds of billions of dollars.[36] In October 2008 many conservatives in Congress, and some liberals, voted against the Bush administration's emergency plan to address the nation's financial crisis because they opposed the partial government takeover of banks and other financial institutions as a massive government intervention in the nation's economy; they believed that even the risk of a catastrophic financial meltdown did not justify the expansion of government power in the marketplace, or the high cost to taxpayers. Some conservatives, though, strongly favored actions designed to rescue American capitalism in a time of crisis. Reducing the national debt, creating jobs, improving the economy, and keeping American safe are "valence principles"—that is, unifying because they are deemed important by conservatives and liberals alike.

How We Form Political Opinions

Explain the major factors that shape specific individual opinions

Few individuals possess ideologies so cohesive that they will automatically shape all their opinions. Most people have at least some conflicting underlying attitudes. Most conservatives support some federal programs—defense, national security, or tax deductions for businesses, for example—and wish to see them, and hence the government, expanded. Many liberals favor American military intervention in other nations for what they deem to be humanitarian purposes but generally oppose American military intervention in the affairs of other nations. For most individuals, attitudes on specific issues are not shaped by ideological predispositions. Let's explore what we know about how public opinion is formed.

One of the most important studies of public opinion is by political scientist John Zaller, who argues that the public relies on elite cues, or bits of information from the media and political leaders, when forming opinions about complex policies.[37] Opinions on survey questions are often derived from the individual's feeling on the issue at the time the question is asked. Individuals form opinions from the most recent news or media coverage they have remembered, responding to survey questions with whatever information happens to be at the "top of the head," which is mentally sampled when an individual is asked to take a stance on an issue. Responses to questions about policy positions are based largely on the way survey questions are asked. The answer to a question about a specific policy is usually determined by the framing of the question, or by relevant events being discussed by political elites and mass media at that time. Opinions are often unreliable, primarily because these elite sources provide competing information, causing public opinion polls to measure whatever recent elite message (or media story) an individual has stored in his or her short-term memory. One should thus expect a fair amount of variability in people's responses to survey questions.

Zaller's work tells us that most people don't hold consistent opinions for every policy issue. Individuals are often ambivalent or have many different opinions about most issues. Zaller suggests that more general aspects of political awareness—best proxied with political knowledge—are critical for shaping public opinion. Political knowledge is what allows individuals to connect underlying attitudes with opinions on politics and policy. But other research has shown that individuals are quite stable and rational in their policy attitude formation. Individuals do not just guess about their policy preferences on foreign policy issues, for example, but tend to have fairly constrained and structured attitudes.[38]

Political Knowledge and Public Opinion

What best explains whether citizens are generally consistent in their political views or inconsistent and open to the influence of others? In general, knowledgeable citizens are better able to evaluate new information and determine if it is relevant to and consistent with their beliefs and opinions.[39] As a result, better-informed individuals can recognize their political interests and act consistently to further those interests. But political knowledge is generally low in America.[40]

Using public opinion surveys, political scientist Adam Berinsky has found that certain segments of the population may lack sufficient knowledge of public policy to give informed opinions. When asked about preferences toward social welfare policy, disadvantaged groups are more likely than any other group to abstain from giving answers—mainly due to the lack of politically relevant information available to those with few resources. This not only leads to a potential underreporting of support for welfare policy among the poor, but also limits the political voice of those who are most likely to support social welfare policies.[41]

This raises the question of how much political knowledge is necessary for one to act as an effective citizen. In an important study of political knowledge in the United States, the political scientists Michael X. Delli Carpini and Scott Keeter found that

How Americans View the World and Vice Versa

When they are not being accused of seeking to conquer the world, Americans are often charged with failing to pay enough attention to international affairs. It is true that many Americans lack a basic knowledge of world history and geography and have considerable difficulty naming the leaders of other nations. Several surveys have indicated that some Americans think Canada is one of the 50 states.

Nevertheless, Americans do have strong opinions about which foreign nations are America's friends in the world and which are its foes. Topping the list of friends is Great Britain, seen by 74 percent of recent poll respondents as a "close ally." Curiously, 2 percent of those surveyed viewed Britain as an enemy. Perhaps they have not forgotten King George's mistreatment of the colonists in 1775. When it comes to China, now one of America's most important trading partners, only 9 percent of Americans believe China is a close ally, whereas 54 percent think China is not friendly or even is America's enemy. It is interesting to note also that France, traditionally an American ally, came to be viewed less favorably than Russia, America's Cold War adversary, in the wake of vocal French opposition to America's Middle East policy.

Just as Americans have opinions about the world, citizens of other nations have their own opinions about America. Americans sometimes complain that their efforts on behalf of other nations are not properly appreciated and feel envied and disliked by the rest of the world. Only Kenyan, Nigerian, and Filipino respondents to a recent survey had an overwhelmingly positive view of America. Even normally friendly Europeans seem to have developed a negative view of the United States.

During the American occupation of Iraq, antagonism toward American foreign policy has hardened even more in most Muslim countries. An overwhelming majority of those polled in the Middle East expressed strongly anti-American senti-

ment. The enduring popularity of Osama bin Laden in these countries also reinforces Muslim attitudes generally toward the United States. Worldwide, a majority of people believed that the United States'

war on terror is actually an attempt to control the Middle East's oil or to dominate the world. The Bush administration's foreign policies earned few converts abroad and lost support at home as well.

the average American exhibits little knowledge of political institutions, processes, leaders, or policy debates.[42] Many Americans cannot even name their own congressional representatives. Does this ignorance of key political facts matter? Delli Carpini and Keeter also found that political knowledge is not evenly distributed throughout the population. Those with higher education, income, and occupational status, and who are members of social or political organizations, are more likely to know about and be active in politics. As a result, individuals with a disproportionate share of income and education also have a disproportionate share of knowledge and influence and thus are better able to get what they want from government.

Presidential elections provide ample illustration of the relationship between political knowledge and public opinion. Despite the obvious fact that most Republicans prefer Republican candidates and most Democrats prefer Democratic candidates (see Chapter 9 for a discussion of party identification), some voters are swayed by the information they receive during a campaign. During the 2008 presidential campaign, for instance, voters weighed the arguments of Barack Obama against those of John McCain to determine who was more qualified to oversee the U.S. economy. Many independents and Republican voters turned to Obama because they held the GOP responsible for the nation's financial crisis and found Obama's economic proposals more credible than McCain's. In the 2012 presidential campaign, both candidates campaigned aggressively on their ability to improve the nation's economy. In exit polls, voters said the economy was the most important issue in the election. The polls found that voters were evenly divided as to whether they blamed Obama or his predecessor, George W. Bush, for the poor economic conditions. In this close presidential race, Obama was re-elected with the highest unemployment rate since Franklin Delano Roosevelt.[43]

Latino voters provide another example. Republican president George W. Bush made a concerted effort to attract Latino voters, and was rewarded with about 40 percent of the Latino vote in the 2004 elections. Latino support helped Bush win battleground

Members of various social groups may see political issues in different ways. After a racially-charged incident in 2009 involving Harvard professor Henry Louis Gates Jr. (second from left) and police officer James Crowley (second from right), President Obama tried to address the tensions surrounding the incident by bringing the two men together for a "beer summit" at the White House.

states such as Colorado, Florida, Nevada, and New Mexico, which all have large Latino electorates. In the 2012 election, Republican presidential candidate Romney had the support of only 3 in 10 Latinos, in part due to his opposition to immigration and his promise to repeal the Patient Protection and Affordable Care Act.[44] Romney's harsh rhetoric on these subjects did not resonate with this large and growing minority population. In a June 2011 Latinos Decisions tracking poll, three-quarters of Latinos want the president to "stop deporting immigrants who are married to U.S. citizens and have families here in the U.S. and two-thirds of Latino voters support executive orders to stop the deportation of youth who would be eligible for the Dream Act" (Development, Relief, and Education for Alien Minors).[45] Obama took a step in this direction with an Executive Order implementing parts of the Dream Act in 2012. Clearly, Latinos have a high level of political knowledge about the issue of immigration, and the president's policies may shape their voting behavior in the 2012 elections.

Shortcuts and Cues Because being informed politically requires a substantial investment of time and energy, most Americans seek to acquire political information and to make political decisions "on the cheap" by making use of shortcuts for political evaluation and decision making rather than engaging in a lengthy process of information gathering. Researchers have found that the public relies on cues and heuristics (problem-solving strategies) from party elites and the media to aid in attitude formation.[46] Other "inexpensive" ways to become informed involve taking cues from trusted friends, relatives, colleagues, and perhaps religious leaders. Political scientists Richard Lau and David Redlawsk argue that most public opinion is formed by taking cues from trusted political elites: elected officials, the media, and interest groups.[47] By means of these informational shortcuts, average citizens can form political opinions that are, in most instances, consistent with their underlying preferences. They call this "voting correctly." Results find that even individuals with low levels of political knowledge are able to make relatively informed political choices by relying on these voter cues. It is generally accepted by scholars in political science that people are cognitive misers and rely on shortcuts in forming public opinion on politics and public policy.[48]

Even the best-informed citizens often assess new issues and events through the lens of their more general beliefs and orientations, and sometimes the outcome is less than optimal. Partisanship and general ideological orientations can often be poor guides to decision making. For example, few Americans read the details of the health care reform proposals debated in the House and Senate in 2009, and instead took their cues from politicians whose views, they assumed, were similar to their own. Yet many liberals who took their cues from President Obama might have preferred no bill at all to a bill without the "public option"—a comprehensive, nationalized system of financing health care coverage—which the president agreed to drop. And many conservatives who took their cues from House and Senate Republican leaders might have found much to like in the legislation these same politicians castigated. Surveys have consistently shown strong public approval of ideas such as maintaining health care coverage for young adults on their parents' insurance, and prohibiting insurance companies from denying coverage due to "preexisting conditions"—ideas contained in the bill that eventually became law.

Costs to Democracy? If political scientists are correct in their findings that so many citizens base their opinions (and votes) on inadequate knowledge and an overreliance on cues from political elites, this raises a critical question: If political

In 2012 the billionaire Warren Buffett argued that is was not right that he—one of the richest people in the world—paid a lower tax rate than his secretary, Debbie Bosanek (pictured here). However, many Americans may not understand how changes in the tax code will affect them.

knowledge is necessary for effective citizenship, how does a general lack of such knowledge affect the way we govern ourselves?

Although understandable and, perhaps, inevitable, low levels of political knowledge and engagement weaken American democracy in two ways. First, those who lack political information cannot effectively defend their own political interests and can easily become losers in political struggles. The presence of large numbers of politically inattentive or ignorant individuals means that political power can more easily be manipulated by political elites, the media, and wealthy special interests that seek to shape public opinion.

Second, if knowledge is power, then a lack of knowledge can contribute to growing political and economic inequality. When individuals are unaware of their interests or how to pursue them, it is virtually certain that political outcomes will not favor them. One of the most important areas of government policy is taxation. America has the largest gap between the super rich and the poor than any other nation in the world. But rather than raise taxes, over the past several decades, the United States has substantially reduced the rate of taxation levied on its wealthiest citizens. Most recently, tax cuts signed into law by George W. Bush in 2001, and extended by President Obama in 2010, provided a substantial tax break mainly for the top 1 percent of the nation's wage earners. Political scientist Larry Bartels shows that, surprisingly, most Americans favored the tax cuts, including millions of middle- and lower-middle-class citizens who did not stand to benefit from the tax policy. Additionally, 40 percent of Americans had no opinion at all regarding the Bush tax cuts. The explanation for this odd state of affairs appears to be a lack of political knowledge. Millions of individuals who were unlikely to derive benefit from President Bush's tax policy thought they would. Since most Americans think they pay too much in taxes, they favored the policy, even if the wealthy benefited much more than the middle class.

Bartels has employed the cartoon character Homer Simpson to explain how people don't realize what is in their economic interest: Homer wants a tax cut, and even if he gets only $1 and Mr. Burns, his boss, takes $1,000, Homer still wants his dollar in savings.[49] Homer is a fool to want his dollar in tax savings: the overall lost tax revenues, collected mainly from the wealthy, would have funded programs that benefit middle-class taxpayers like Homer. Upper-bracket taxpayers, who are more informed and knowledgeable, are more likely to see to it that their economic self-interest aligns with government policy—and vice versa. This example illustrates that basic political knowledge matters in American politics.

The Media, Government, and Public Opinion

marketplace of ideas the public forum in which beliefs and ideas are exchanged and compete

When individuals attempt to form opinions about particular political issues, events, and personalities, they seldom do so in isolation. Typically, they are confronted with—sometimes bombarded by—the efforts of a host of individuals and groups seeking to persuade them to adopt a particular point of view. In the approach to the 2012 presidential election, someone trying to decide what to think about Barack Obama or Mitt Romney could hardly avoid an avalanche of opinions expressed through the media, in meetings, or in conversations with friends. The **marketplace of ideas** is the interplay of opinions and views that takes place as competing forces attempt to persuade as many people as possible to accept a particular position on a particular issue. Given this constant exposure to the ideas of others, it is virtually impossible for most individuals to resist some modification of their own beliefs. Three forces that play important roles in shaping opinions in the marketplace are the government, private groups, and the news media.[50]

Government and the Shaping of Public Opinion All governments try to influence, manipulate, or manage their citizens' beliefs. But the extent to which public opinion is actually affected by governmental public relations can be limited. Often, governmental claims are disputed by the media, by interest groups, and at times even by opposing forces within the government itself.

This hasn't stopped modern presidents from focusing a great deal of attention on shaping public opinion to boost support for their policy agendas. Franklin Delano Roosevelt promoted his policy agenda directly to the American people through his famous "fireside chats" radio broadcasts. A hallmark of the Clinton administration was the employment of techniques such as those used in election campaigns to bolster popular enthusiasm for White House initiatives. The president established a political "war room" similar to the one that operated in his campaign headquarters, where representatives from all departments met daily to discuss and coordinate the president's public-relations efforts. Many of the same consultants and pollsters who had directed the successful Clinton election campaign then became employed in the selling of the president's programs.[51]

The George W. Bush administration developed an extensive public-relations program to bolster popular support for the president's policies. Working with the conservative TV personality Mary Matalin, the White House worked to maintain popular support for the administration's war against terrorism. These efforts included presidential speeches, media appearances by administration officials, numerous press conferences, and thousands of press releases presenting the administration's views.[52] Using the runway of an aircraft carrier as his stage, a confident Commander in Chief Bush, dressed in military fatigues, proclaimed the end of the Iraq War. His statement was premature by nearly half a decade, but it effectively maintained public support for the Iraq War effort. His speech proved hollow compared to President Reagan's command that Mikhail Gorbachev "tear down this wall!" (referring to the Berlin Wall)—a tearing down that actually occurred—dramatically calling an end to the Cold War.

Like its predecessors, the Obama administration has sought to shape public opinion in the United States and abroad, relying upon the power of the president's oratorical skills to build support for his administration's initiatives in domestic and foreign policy. But Obama's White House is unique in using social media to promote the president's policy agenda. President Obama has been as theatrical as Bush and Reagan, but largely through the digital media. In spring 2012, Barack Obama's Facebook page had 26 million "likes" and counting, compared to 1.7 million fans for his 2012 challenger, Romney.[53] Hourly posts on Facebook promote his policies, campaign, and serve to personalize the president. In one of the most humanizing publicly available photographs in the history of the American presidency, a young boy touches the hair of Obama, who has bowed down to accommodate the child's request to see what his hair feels like. The photograph hangs in the White House and was widely shared online and via social media. Obama's adept use of e-mail, Twitter, Facebook, online videos, and other methods helped to solidify his re-election in 2012.

Private Groups and the Shaping of Public Opinion The ideas that become prominent in political life are developed and spread not only by government officials but also by important economic and political groups searching for issues that will advance their causes. One especially notable example is the abortion issue, which has inflamed American politics over the past 30 years. The notion of a fetal "right to life," whose proponents seek to outlaw abortion and overturn the Supreme Court's 1973 *Roe v. Wade* decision, was developed by conservative politicians who saw the issue of abortion as a means of uniting Catholic and Protestant conservatives and linking both groups to the Republican Party.[54] To advance their cause, leaders of the right-to-life movement sponsored well-publicized Senate hearings at which testimony, photographs, and other exhibits were presented to illustrate the violent results of abortion procedures. At the same time, publicists for the movement produced leaflets, articles, books, and films such as *The Silent Scream* to highlight the agony and pain ostensibly felt by the "unborn" when they were being aborted. All this underscored the movement's claim that abortion was nothing more or less than the murder of more than a million innocent human beings annually in the United States. Finally, Catholic and evangelical Protestant religious leaders were organized to denounce abortion from their church pulpits and, increasingly, from their electronic pulpits on the Christian Broadcasting Network (CBN) and the various other television forums available for religious programming. Religious leaders have also organized demonstrations, pickets, and disruptions at abortion clinics throughout the nation.[55] The abortion rights issue remains a potent one.

In recent years, the issue of same-sex marriage has played out in much the same way as the abortion debate, and with many of the same opposing constituencies. In 2009, Iowa's seven-member supreme court ruled unanimously that the state's constitution guarantees gay men and lesbians the right to wed, as in a handful of other states with similar laws. At the time, polls showed about a third of Iowans supporting gay marriage, a third opposing gay marriage but supporting legalized civil unions, and a third opposing both gay marriage and civil unions. In the 2010 midterm elections, Iowa's incumbent Democratic governor Chet Culver was attacked by his Republican opponents not only for the state's poor economy but also the court's decision to legalize same-sex marriage. Hundreds of thousands of dollars poured in from out-of-state religious and "527" organizations (see Chapter 10) such as the National Organization for Marriage to fund negative campaign ads denouncing same-sex marriage and the Iowa Supreme Court, and encouraging voters to vote against retaining the justices who had ruled that same-sex marriage is constitutional. Polls conducted after the election revealed that many people turned out to vote because of the judicial retention elections, not the midterm elections for public office.[56] That is, the judicial elections became a referendum, akin to the politics of direct democracy, on the court's ruling to legalize gay marriage. And the 527 groups were key to shaping public opinion about the issue.[57] The headline story of the Iowa 2010 elections was not Culver's loss to his Republican challenger, but the fact that Iowans had

Opponents and proponents of a woman's right to choose often clash with one another. Large well-financed groups on both sides of the debate try to influence public opinion and government policy.

overwhelmingly voted not to retain three state supreme court judges who had ruled to legalize same-sex marriage a year earlier. Never in the 60 years since retention elections were instituted in the state had supreme court judges not been retained.

Ideas are marketed most effectively by groups with access to financial resources, public or private institutional support, and sufficient skill or education to select, develop, and draft ideas that will attract interest and support. The development and promotion of conservative themes and ideas in recent years have been greatly facilitated by the millions of dollars that conservative corporations and business organizations such as "super PACs" (see Chapter 10), the U.S. Chamber of Commerce, and the Public Affairs Council spend each year on public information. In addition, conservative business leaders have contributed millions of dollars to such conservative institutions as the Heritage Foundation, the Hoover Institution, and the American Enterprise Institute.[58] Many of the ideas that helped those on the right influence political debate were first developed and articulated by scholars associated with institutions such as these.

In much the same way, liberal organizations vie for public attention armed with ample financial assets, access to the media, and well-honed skills in creating, communicating, and using ideas. In recent decades, various left-leaning public-interest groups, relying heavily on voluntary contributions of time, effort, and money from their members, have organized in parallel with the rise of such institutions on the right. Through groups such as Common Cause, the National Organization for Women, the Sierra Club, the World Wildlife Federation, and Friends of the Earth, liberal intellectuals and professionals have been able to apply their organizational skills and educational resources to developing and promoting their ideas.[59] Often, research conducted in universities and in liberal "think tanks" such as the Brookings Institution provides the ideas that ultimately become law through the efforts of liberal politicians.

The News Media and the Shaping of Public Opinion The media are among the most powerful forces operating in the marketplace of ideas. As we shall see in Chapter 7, the mass media are not simply neutral messengers for ideas developed by others. Instead, the media are very much opinion makers in their own right and have an enormous impact on popular attitudes. For example, for the past 40 years since the publication of the Pentagon Papers by the *New York Times* and the exposure of the Watergate scandal led by the *Washington Post*, the national news media have relentlessly investigated personal and official wrongdoing on the part of politicians and public officials. The continual media presentation of corruption in government and venality in politics has undoubtedly contributed to the cynicism toward and distrust of government that prevails in much of the general public. Approval of Congress reached a new record low in 2011, with just 11 percent of Americans approving of the job Congress is doing. It is the lowest single rating in Gallup's history of asking this question since 1974.[60] In 1964, on the eve of the Vietnam War, 77 percent of Americans expected their government to "do the right thing" always or most of the time, according to opinion polls. Ten years later, after Vietnam and Watergate, 77 percent had become 36. Today, just one in five Americans has that confidence in the federal government.[61] Very low trust in government is a defining feature of contemporary American politics.

At the same time, the ways in which media coverage interprets or "frames" specific events can have a major impact on popular responses and opinions about these events.[62] Given the critical importance of media framing to the way the public perceives the news, the Bush administration went to great lengths to persuade broadcasters to follow its lead in their coverage of both terrorism and America's response to terrorism in the months following the September 11, 2001, attacks. For the most part, the media acquiesced, presenting the administration's military campaigns in Afghanistan and Iraq, as well as its domestic antiterrorist efforts, in a positive light. Even supposedly liberal newspapers such as the *New York Times*, which had strongly opposed Bush in the 2000 election, praised his leadership and published articles supportive of the president's bellicose rhetoric against the Iraqi regime prior to March 2003, when President Bush ordered the invasion of Iraq.

● Measuring Public Opinion

> **Describe basic survey methods and other techniques researchers use to measure public opinion**

As recently as 50 years ago, American political leaders gauged public opinion by the presence of crowds at meetings and their applause. This direct exposure to the people's views did not necessarily produce accurate knowledge of public opinion. It did, however, give political leaders confidence in their public support—and therefore confidence in their ability to govern by consent.

Abraham Lincoln and Stephen Douglas debated each other seven times during the summer and autumn of 1858, two years before they became presidential nominees. Their debates took place before audiences in parched cornfields and courthouse squares. A century later, the presidential debates, although seen by millions, take place in television studios, before a few reporters, technicians, and audiences instructed not to applaud or make noise. Only rarely, such as in the grassroots or "retail" politics of the Iowa caucuses or New Hampshire presidential primary, can politicians gauge the public's response directly.[63] Retail politics is where candidates meet citizens face-to-face to discuss politics.[64]

As Chapter 7 on the media illustrates, the media convey information to millions of people, but the media are not yet as efficient at getting information back to leaders, although the rise of social media, such as Facebook and Twitter, has created improved feedback for elected officials. Today public officials make extensive use of **public-opinion polls** to help them decide whether to run for office, what policies to support, how to vote on important legislation, and what types of appeals to make in their campaigns. All recent presidents and other major political figures have worked closely with polls and pollsters.

public-opinion polls scientific instruments for measuring public opinion

Measuring Public Opinion from Surveys

It is not feasible to interview the 311 million-plus Americans residing in the United States on their opinions of who should be the next president or what should be done about important policy issues such as how to improve the economy and create jobs. Instead, pollsters take a **sample** of the population and use it to make inferences (i.e., extrapolations and educated guesses) about the preferences of the population as a whole. For a political survey to be an accurate representation of the population, it must meet certain requirements, including an appropriate sampling method, a sufficient sample size, and the avoidance of selection bias.[65]

sample a small group selected by researchers to represent the most important characteristics of an entire population

Political Knowledge and Opinion in a "Scan-and-Skim" Culture

The transformation of political information in the digital era has had a profound effect on the way the news is reported and how citizens obtain information about politics. A 2012 survey conducted by the Pew Internet and American Life Project found that 36 percent of social networking site users say those sites are important for their political information, and more than three in four Americans read the news online or seek political information online. Recent research also indicates a trend in journalism toward shorter articles and flashier headlines, as the number of articles published by reputable newspapers such as *The Wall Street Journal* have doubled within the last decade. Americans today are likely to read the news by scanning and skimming multiple headlines online, in bits and bytes, rather than by reading long news articles. They also learn about politics in online discussion with family and friends.

Has the rise of digital politics and online news affected mass public opinion? *Newsweek's* July 2012 cover story

by Tony Dokoupil asked the question "Is the Web Driving Us Mad?" And Nicholas Carr's best-selling book, *The Shallows: What the Internet Is Doing to Our Brains,* asks, "Is Google making us stupid?" The answer from a review of scientific data conducted by both authors is, in part, yes.

Nicholas Carr's carefully researched study details the decline in the deep processing that underpins "mindful knowledge acquisition, inductive analysis, critical thinking, imagination, and reflection." He argues that although the Internet may seem to be making us smarter by virtue of giving us access to more data faster than ever, it also seriously threatens the type of intelligence that is measured by depth of thought rather than sheer speed. The Internet has encouraged "cursory reading, hurried and distracted thinking, and superficial learning"; a scan-and-skim culture rather than one practicing deep and reflectful thought. The habits of browsing, scanning, and reading in a nonlinear fashion have undermined the capacity to immerse oneself in longer works of writing, such as books. A study conducted by University College London found that people tend to go online to avoid reading in the traditional sense, and instead rely on new forms of reading to "power browse" horizontally through titles, contents pages, and abstracts. In order to maintain their profits, magazine and newspaper editors have yielded to this tendency by offering brief capsules of news instead of longer stories.

Carr argues that throughout the history of human evolution the ways in which we obtain information have actually changed our brain processes. He explains how human thought has been shaped over time by "tools of the mind"—from the alphabet to maps, to the printing press, the clock, and the computer. Our brains change in response to our experiences. The technologies we employ to find, store, and share information can literally

reroute our neural pathways. The rise of digital media is actually changing the way we think.

Extending this logic to politics, the implications are that public opinion will be less rational and more erratic, as individuals will lack a carefully developed understanding on which to base their opinions, despite the overwhelming volume of information about politics online. This trend might explain the significant percentage of Americans who believe political stories that are untrue or based on misinformation, such as the claim that President Obama is not a U.S. citizen (as discussed in the introduction to this chapter). However, as we've seen in this chapter, some research indicates that most individuals use simple cues and shortcuts to process political information. If this is correct, scanning and skimming headlines might provide a reasonable way to be informed about politics without extensive time or effort.

SOURCE: Nicholas Carr, *The Shallows: What the Internet Is Doing to Our Brains* (New York: W.W. Norton, 2011).

for critical analysis

1. Will the Internet have a positive or negative impact on how we process political information and form opinions about politics? Why?

2. While the Internet provides less depth of information, it also offers a more interactive environment for discussing politics. Will the use of social media and other online forums to share political information and opinions help increase political knowledge as well as interest in politics in general?

Representative Sample The most representative sample is what statisticians call a **simple random sample** (or **probability sample**). To draw such a sample, one would need a complete list of all the people in the United States, and individuals would be randomly selected from that list. Imagine that everyone's name were entered into a lottery, with names then drawn blindly from an enormous box. If everyone had an equal chance of selection, we would have a truly random sample. Since we don't have a complete list of all Americans, pollsters use census data, lists of households (for in-person or telephone surveys), and telephone numbers (telephone surveys) to create lists, drawing samples from regions and then neighborhoods within regions. Just as in a simple random sample, everyone has an equal chance of being selected for the survey. Rolls of registered voters are often used in political surveys designed to predict the outcome of an election.

Another method of drawing samples of the national population is a technique called **random digit dialing** of landline and cell phone numbers, but not business phones or inoperative home telephones. A computer random number generator is used to produce a list of 10-digit telephone numbers. Given that 95 percent of Americans have telephones (cell phones or landlines), this technique usually results in a random national sample. Until recently, opinion polls did not include cell phone numbers, but because so many young people, urban residents, and other demographic groups (the poor) don't have landlines, cell phone numbers are included in many opinion polls. It allows almost every citizen a chance of being included in the survey. Telephone surveys are fairly accurate, cost-effective, and flexible in the type of questions that can be asked. Websites such as RealClearPolitics.com list the results of every political survey released each day; during elections, this can be as many as 20 different surveys daily. Every week, the opinions of Americans regarding candidates and public policies are measured, but also opinions on a vast array of products (toothpaste), entertainment (movie star romances), and even college political science textbooks!

Sample Size A sample must be large enough to provide an accurate representation of the population. Surprisingly, though, the size of the population being measured doesn't matter, only the size of the *sample*. A survey of 1,000 people is just as effective for measuring the opinions of all Texans (25 million residents) as the opinions of all Americans (over 300 million residents).

Flipping a coin shows how this works. After tossing a coin ten times, the number of heads and tails may not be close to five and five. After 100 tosses of the coin, though, the percentage of heads should be close to 50 percent, and after 1,000 tosses, very close to 50 percent (assuming it is a fair coin). In fact, after 1,000 tosses there is a 95 percent chance that the number of heads will be somewhere between 46.9 percent and 53.1 percent. This 3.1 percent variation from 50 percent is called the sampling error or margin of error. The chance that the sample used does not accurately represent the population from which it is drawn is called the **sampling error** (or **margin of error**). It is the amount of error we can expect with a typical 1,000-person survey. Normally, samples of 1,000 people are considered sufficient for accurately measuring public opinion through the use of surveys.

Larger sample sizes can yield more accurate predictions of the opinions of a population, but there is a trade-off in terms of cost, since it is also more expensive to poll more people. Why is a sample size of only 1,000 generally accepted as adequately representative of much larger populations? Consider the "diminishing returns" of sampling more and more people. The sample error from a sample of 500 people is 4.4 percent. With 1,000 respondents, it drops to 3.1 percent, and

probability sampling a method used by pollsters to select a representative sample in which every individual in the population has an equal probability of being selected as a respondent

random digit dialing a polling method in which respondents are selected at random from a list of ten-digit telephone numbers, with every effort made to avoid bias in the construction of the sample

sampling error (or margin of error) polling error that arises based on the small size of the sample

Who Thinks Economic Inequality Is a Problem?

Percentage who said there are "strong" or "very strong" conflicts between rich and poor

An individual's ideology and party identification may influence his or her opinions on specific issues. As this study showed, the percentage of Americans concerned about economic inequality was rougly similar for all income groups. However, the differences between liberals and conservatives, and between Democrats and Republicans, were more significant.

By income

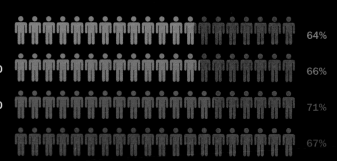

< $20,000	64%
$20,000–40,000	66%
$40,000–75,000	71%
> $75,000	67%

By ideology

Conservative	55%
Moderate	68%
Liberal	79%

By party

Republican	55%
Independent	68%
Democrat	73%

for critical analysis

1. Do the findings in this study show that opinions are shaped by economic self-interest? Why or why not?

2. Which ideological group and which party are most likely to support government action to address inequality? Are the other groups not concerned about inequality? Use the data to explain your answers.

SOURCE: Pew Research Center, "Rising Share of Americans See Conflict between Rich and Poor," January 11, 2012, www.pewsocialtrends.org/2012/01/11/rising-share-of-americans-see-conflict-between-rich-and-poor/ accessed 5/10/12)

with 1,500 to 2.5 percent. That is, the smaller and smaller gains in accuracy have to be weighed against the steadily increasing costs of polling more and more people. The consensus among statisticians and pollsters is that the optimal trade-off point is 1,000—hence 1,000 is the "gold standard."

When an election poll of 1,000 people indicates that 51 percent of voters surveyed favor the Republican candidate, say, Mitt Romney, and 49 percent support the Democratic candidate, Barack Obama, the outcome is considered too close to call because the difference, 2 percent, is within the margin of error. That is, a figure of 51 percent really means that between 48 and 54 percent of voters in the population *probably* favor the Republican, while a figure of 49 percent indicates that between 46 and 52 percent of all voters *probably* support the Democrat. Thus, in this example, a 52-to-48 percent Democratic victory would still be consistent with polls predicting a 51-to-49 percent Republican triumph. Table 6.3 shows how accurate two of the major national polling organizations, Gallup and Harris, have been in predicting the outcomes of presidential elections. As you can see, the two firms have mostly been correct in their predictions. When the media refer to a "scientific poll" conducted by a highly respected polling firm such as Gallup or Harris, they actually mean a poll that has followed the steps just outlined: a poll based on a random (representative) sample of the population that is sufficiently large and avoids selection bias.

Survey Design and Question Wording Even with reliable sample procedures and a large sample, surveys may fail to reflect the true distribution of opinion within a target population. One frequent source of measurement error is the wording of survey questions. The precise words used in a question can have an enormous impact on the answers it elicits. The reliability of survey results can also be adversely affected by poor question format, faulty ordering of questions, poor vocabulary, ambiguity of questions, or questions with built-in biases.

Often, seemingly minor differences in the wording of a question can convey vastly different meanings to respondents and thus produce quite different response

TABLE 6.3

Two Pollsters and Their Records, 1948–2012

Since their poor showing in 1948, the major pollsters have been close to the mark in every national presidential election. In 2000, though, neither Gallup nor Harris accurately predicted the outcome. From what you have learned about polling, what were some of the possible sources of error in these two national polls?

	HARRIS (%)	GALLUP (%)	ACTUAL OUTCOME (%)
2012			
Obama	NA	49	50
Romney		50	48
2008			
Obama	50	51	53
McCain	44	43	46
2004			
Bush	49	49	51
Kerry	48	49	48
Nader	1	1	0

	HARRIS (%)	GALLUP (%)	ACTUAL OUTCOME (%)
2000			
Bush	47	48	48
Gore	47	46	49
Nader	5	4	3
1996			
Clinton	51	52	49
Dole	39	41	41
Perot	9	7	8
1992			
Clinton	44	44	43
Bush	38	37	38
Perot	17	14	19
1988			
Bush	51	53	54
Dukakis	47	42	46
1984			
Reagan	56	59	59
Mondale	44	41	41
1980			
Reagan	48	47	51
Carter	43	44	41
Anderson		8	
1976			
Carter	48	48	51
Ford	45	49	48
1972			
Nixon	59	62	61
McGovern	35	38	38
1968			
Nixon	40	43	43
Humphrey	43	42	43
Wallace	13	15	14
1964			
Johnson	62	64	61
Goldwater	33	36	39
1960			
Kennedy	49	51	50
Nixon	41	49	49
1956			
Eisenhower	NA	60	58
Stevenson		41	42
1952			
Eisenhower	47	51	55
Stevenson	42	49	44
1948			
Truman	NA	44.5	49.6
Dewey		49.5	45.1

NOTE: All figures except those for 1948 are rounded. NA = Not asked.

SOURCES: Data from the Gallup Poll and the Harris Survey, *Chicago Tribune*–New York News Syndicate, various press releases 1964–2012. Courtesy of the Gallup Organization and Louis Harris Associates.

patterns (see Box 6.3). For example, for many years the University of Chicago's National Opinion Research Center has asked respondents whether they think the federal government is spending too much, too little, or about the right amount of money on "assistance for the poor." Answering the question posed this way, about two-thirds of all respondents seem to believe that the government is spending too little. However, the same survey also asks whether the government spends too much, too little, or about the right amount for welfare. When the word *welfare* is substituted for "assistance for the poor," about half of all respondents indicate that too much is being spent.[66]

BOX 6.3

It Depends on How You Ask

THE SITUATION
The public's desire for tax cuts can be hard to measure. In 2000, pollsters asked what should be done with the nation's budget surplus and got different results depending on the specifics of the question.

THE QUESTION
President Clinton has proposed setting aside approximately two-thirds of an expected budget surplus to fix the Social Security system. What do you think the leaders in Washington should do with the remainder of the surplus?

VARIATION 1
Should the money be used for a tax cut, or should it be used to fund new government programs?

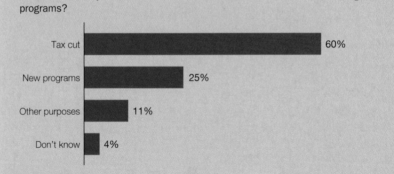

VARIATION 2
Should the money be used for a tax cut, or should it be spent on programs for education, the environment, health care, crime fighting, and military defense?

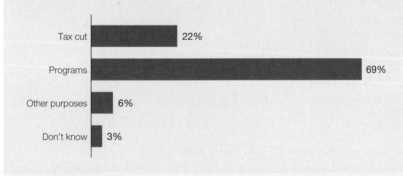

SOURCE: Pew Research Center, reported in the *New York Times*, January 30, 2000, p. WK 3.

Internet Surveys Today, pollsters are increasingly turning to the use of online surveys, often using similar techniques to those of telephone surveys. But Internet surveys can be more efficient, less costly, and more accurate than standard phone surveys, and they include larger samples of young people and yield more accurate results within age cohorts. Many surveys you will find online do not use probability sampling (random sampling), and thus are not representative of the American population. Instead, they reflect those willing to take a quiz online, or on Facebook.

Knowledge Networks (KN) and YouGov are leaders in Internet polling using random sampling methods in which respondents complete surveys online instead of being interviewed on the phone. KN has a large population of respondents (hundreds of thousands of individuals) identified using probability sampling, so the sample is representative of the American population in terms of age, education, income, gender, race, political interest, region, partisanship, and other attributes. Individuals without Internet access are given free subscriptions and, if necessary, a computer or WebTV; those with Internet access are given free subscriptions to complete the surveys. If a client commissions a survey, KN randomly draws a sample of, say, 1,000 respondents from its population of online respondents. Because respondents have agreed to complete a number of surveys in exchange for free Internet access, they are more likely to complete the surveys.

Other polling companies, such as YouGov, use other methods for conducting Internet surveys, often by using statistical weights to make the surveys generally representative of the American population.[67] Internet surveys such as the Cooperative Congressional Election Study (CCES) can have very large samples, up to 50,000 people. In the future, Internet surveys may be more representative of the American population than traditional telephone surveys, and may replace telephone surveys entirely, especially given falling response rates and the growing number of households without landline phones but using cell phones exclusively.

Critics of Internet surveys contend that the samples may still be biased by not including enough respondents from groups that are more likely to be offline, especially non–English speakers, Latinos, African Americans, the elderly, and the poor.

Because not everyone has Internet access at home, obtaining a representative sample for an online survey can be difficult. However, polling companies such as YouGov are developing methods to improve accuracy, and online surveys may eventually offer a more efficient and affordable alternative to telephone surveys.

Online surveys may include more "politicos," or respondents who are interested in politics, than the normal population. Proponents contend that minorities and the poor are increasingly online, but via mobile access, and that the samples are representative of the American population. Because Internet surveys have proved to be accurate in forecasting elections, and some argue they are more accurate than random digital telephone surveys, Internet surveys are likely here to stay.

Face-to-Face Surveys With more than 60 years' experience studying American politics, the American National Election Studies (ANES) is the premier omnibus survey. The ANES traditionally has conducted surveys using face-to-face interviews, but because interviewing respondents in person is very costly, the ANES uses a multi-stage, stratified probability sample of 2,000-plus respondents from regions of the country (what they call primary sampling units). While this method approximates a simple random sample of the entire population, it does not guarantee random samples within states; all respondents from Iowa may be from Des Moines, for example. This can cause problems for generalizing the results for individual states. Even the ANES has begun experimenting with adding Internet surveys to its traditional face-to-face surveys. However, in-person surveys remain one of the most valuable and accurate ways to conduct interviews, and thus the ANES is an important source of survey data in political science.

Framing Experiments within Surveys

Surveys are increasingly drawing on experimental techniques in which one group of respondents is given a treatment, or unique question wording, and responses are compared to a control group of respondents that does not receive the treatment. For example, the widespread tendency to base survey responses on the way questions are worded or "framed" provides a way to measure public opinion—through what are called framing experiments. Because of the media's power to shape public opinion, framing experiments are an important tool for measuring how the media and government shape political attitudes. Let us return to the opening example of this chapter. For more people to have become convinced that Obama is Muslim during his presidency than when he was running for office, there must have been some underlying misperception in the first place; that is, citizens were unsure enough about Obama to consider and ultimately embrace the idea.

Researchers often use framing experiments (in surveys or laboratory experiments) to understand how subtle changes in the structure of political information can result in the expression of different political opinions. In one experiment, individuals in one group were exposed to a frame arguing that affirmative action is necessary to correct past discrimination, while those in a second group received a competing frame arguing that affirmative action gives African Americans special treatment. Not surprisingly, those in the first group showed greater support for affirmative action than did those in the second group for the same policies. By using a treatment and control group design, framing experiments provide more leverage in assessing cause and effect in measuring changes in public opinion.

Dennis Chong and Jamie Druckman have extended how we measure framing effects on public opinion by testing the effect of multiple countervailing frames to create more realistic models of real-world political debate, where citizens are exposed to multiple perspectives on candidates and political issues.[68] Such competing frames can be expected to have different effects in shaping public opinion on a policy. In the marketplace of ideas, it matters crucially whether, say, the wealthiest

Americans are characterized as "the super-rich" and "1-percenters," or "business leaders" and "job creators." Framing experiments help researchers understand how public opinion changes in the face of new information. John Zaller's work shows that framing by the media, political groups, or candidates is important because individuals form opinions based on the latest information and arguments they are exposed to—what is "on the top of their heads"—and as a result, public opinion polls often merely measure whatever recent elite cues (or media stories) individual respondents happen to have stored in their short-term memory.[69] Thus framing experiments are an important way to understand how public opinion moves in response to political elites and the mass media.

When Polls Are Wrong

The history of polling over the past century contains many instances of getting it wrong and learning valuable lessons in the process. As a result, polling techniques have grown more and more sophisticated, and pollsters have a more and more nuanced understanding of how public opinion is formed and how it is revealed.

Social Desirability Effects and List Experiments Political scientists have found that survey results can be inaccurate when the surveys include questions about sensitive issues for which individuals do not wish to share their true preferences. For example, respondents tend to overreport voting in elections and the frequency of their church attendance. Why? These activities are deemed socially appropriate, so even if the respondents did not vote or do not attend church regularly, they may feel social pressure to do so, and thus they may respond inaccurately on a survey. Political scientist Adam Berinsky calls this the **social desirability effect**, whereby respondents report what they expect the interviewer wishes to hear or whatever they think is socially acceptable, rather than what they actually believe or know to be true.[70] Additionally, surveys tend to report a high degree of nonresponse to questions about income; researchers have found that those most likely not to report their income in surveys are the poor.

social desirability effect
the effect that results when respondents in a survey report what they expect the interviewer wishes to hear rather than what they believe

Questions that ask directly about race or gender are particularly problematic. New research finds that social desirability makes it difficult to learn voters' true opinions about touchy subjects such as racial attitudes, because respondents hide their preferences from the interviewer for fear of social retribution (against what might be deemed "politically incorrect"). However, surveys using experiments can be designed to tap respondents' latent or hidden feelings about sensitive issues without directly asking them to express overt opinions. For example, one such survey examined support for a generic black presidential candidate; the study was conducted in mid-2007, well before Barack Obama became president. The survey was designed to tap underlying attitudes toward a black candidate, allowing researchers to compare openly expressed support for such a candidate with unvoiced hidden attitudes toward the same candidate. Results show that 30 percent of Americans exhibited reluctance about voting for a generic black presidential candidate, even though, when asked directly, nearly 85 percent had claimed they would support such a candidate.[71] However, there may be a significant difference between expressing support for a generic candidate and supporting a real candidate in the heat of an actual campaign. Yet, in 2008, another study found that 30 percent of white Americans were "troubled" by the prospect of "Obama as the first black president," almost the identical percentage as the previous study.[72] The fact that both studies found that roughly one-third of Americans had misgivings about a black president suggests that racism may be a factor.

Both of the studies just described made use of so-called list experiments, which rely on comparisons between subsamples (a treatment and a control group) that receive slightly different survey questions (see Box 6.4). List experiments work like this: One randomly assigned control group receives a list of items to which they are asked to respond by indicating how many of those items "trouble" them. The treatment group receives the same list, with one different "target item," and is similarly asked to report how many items are troubling. The respondents are not asked to share which statements bother them, only how many. The simple difference in the average number of statements between the treatment and control groups provides a measure of the percentage of the treatment group that is troubled by the target item, since otherwise all items are the same for both groups. And because the treatment group is a random subset of the full sample, results can be generalized to the larger population from which the random sample is drawn.

In examining the emotional underpinnings of attitudes about Obama as the first black president, David Redlawsk and his colleagues found that anxiety and enthusiasm were driving hidden racial opinions. Their study's results suggest that Obama's victory in the 2008 presidential election, despite a high level of concern about his race, was at least partly a result of the intense enthusiasm his campaign generated. This makes sense, given that Obama's campaign message focused on hope. Their

BOX 6.4

Measuring Opinion about Obama's Race

In this experiment, half the participants were given Version A, which included the target item ("he is the first black president") and the other half were given Version B, which didn't include that statement. By comparing the average responses from the two groups, researchers were able to measure opinion on Obama's race.

VERSION A (TREATMENT GROUP)

Some people approve of the job Barack Obama is doing as president, and some people do not. Regardless of your overall feelings toward him, please indicate how many of the following facts about President Obama trouble you. We are not interested in WHICH ONES, only HOW MANY. Just enter a number from 0 to 5.

1. As a child, he spent several years in Indonesia.
2. He is the first black president.
3. He sometimes smokes cigarettes.
4. He is a former law professor.
5. He was a community organizer.

VERSION B (CONTROL GROUP)

Some people approve of the job Barack Obama is doing as president, and some people do not. Regardless of your overall feelings toward him, please indicate how many of the following five facts about President Obama trouble you. We are not interested in WHICH ONES, only HOW MANY. Just enter a number from 0 to 5.

1. As a child, he spent several years in Indonesia.
2. He has two children.
3. He sometimes smokes cigarettes.
4. He is a former law professor.
5. He was a community organizer.

enthusiasm for Obama may have allowed some white voters to overcome latent concerns about his race. The lesson here, once again, is that public opinion cannot be understood without understanding the public's underlying emotions.

Other racial attitude surveys conducted during the 2008 election—many of which do reveal substantial prejudice even when obscured by social desirability effects—tend to estimate that closer to 5 percent of Americans hold such attitudes.[73] List experiments were also employed to reveal that a quarter of Americans would not vote for a female president, and that it is common to hide true opinions about race and racial policies, such as affirmative action.[74] The list experiment provides a way to measure public opinion on sensitive issues and does so without respondents knowing what information is being sought.

Selection Bias The importance of accurate sampling was brought home early in the history of political polling. A 1936 *Literary Digest* poll predicted that the Republican candidate, Alf Landon, would defeat the Democratic incumbent, Roosevelt, in that year's presidential election. The actual election, of course, ended in a Roosevelt landslide. The main problem with the survey was what is called **selection bias** in drawing the sample. The pollsters had relied on telephone directories and automobile registration rosters to produce the survey sample. During the Great Depression, though, only wealthier Americans owned telephones and automobiles. Thus, the millions of working-class Americans who constituted Roosevelt's principal base of support were excluded from the sample.

A more recent instance of polling error caused by selection bias was the 1998 Minnesota gubernatorial election. A poll conducted by the *Minneapolis Star Tribune* just six weeks before the election showed independent candidate and former professional wrestler Jesse Ventura running a distant third behind the Democratic candidate, Hubert Humphrey III, who seemed to have the support of 49 percent of the electorate, and the Republican candidate, Norm Coleman, whose support stood at 29 percent. Only 10 percent of those polled said they were planning to vote for Ventura. Yet on Election Day, Ventura garnered more votes than either Humphrey or Coleman. Analysis of exit poll data showed why the polls had been so wrong. In an effort to be more accurate, preelection pollsters often take into account the likelihood that respondents will actually vote, and so the *Star Tribune* poll was conducted only among individuals who had voted in the previous election. Ventura, however, attracted to the polls not only individuals who had not voted in the last election but also many people who had never voted before in their lives; in fact, a full 12 percent of Minnesota's voters in 1998 said they came to the polls only because Ventura was on the ballot. This surge in turnout was facilitated by the fact that Minnesota permits same-day voter registration. (See Chapter 8 for a discussion of the effects of registration rules.) Thus, the pollsters were wrong because Ventura changed the composition of the electorate.[75]

In recent years, the issue of selection bias has been complicated by the fact that growing numbers of individuals refuse to answer pollsters' questions, or they use such devices as answering machines and caller ID to screen unwanted callers. As noted previously, the increasing number of Americans who use cell phones (including many who do not have a landline at all) may be a problem in surveys that only include landline phone numbers. Individuals most likely to rely on cell phones alone include the young, urban residents, the poor, and minorities. These individuals would be less likely to be contacted if a telephone survey did not include cell phone numbers.

Additionally, response rates for surveys—the percentage of calls attempted that are completed—have been falling steeply. Response rates for the Pew Research

selection bias (surveys) polling error that arises when the sample is not representative of the population being studied, which creates errors in overrepresenting or underrepresenting some opinions

Though public opinion is important, it is not always easy to interpret, and polls often fail to predict accurately how Americans will vote. In 1948, election-night polls showed Thomas Dewey defeating Harry S. Truman for the presidency.

Center's highly respected surveys, for example, are less than one in five individuals called, or 20 percent. If pollsters could be certain that those who responded to their surveys simply reflected the views of those who refused to respond, there would be no problem. Some studies, however, suggest that the views of respondents and non-respondents can differ, especially along social class lines. Upper-class individuals are often less willing to respond to surveys or less likely to be at home than their working-class counterparts, which can bias telephone surveys. And women are significantly more likely to answer telephone surveys than men. Additionally, as discussed, most young people (ages 18–25) and a majority of minorities do not have landline phones, only cell phones, and are often excluded from telephone surveys. This can lead to incorrect inferences of public opinion.

push polling a polling technique in which the questions are designed to shape the respondent's opinion

Push Polling Push polling introduces a different type of bias into public opinion polling. Push polls are not scientific polls, as just discussed, and are not intended to yield accurate information about a population. Instead, they involve asking a respondent a loaded question about a political candidate designed to elicit the response sought by the pollster and, simultaneously, to shape the respondent's perception of the candidate in question. One of the most notorious uses of push polling occurred in the 2000 South Carolina Republican presidential primary, in which George W. Bush defeated John McCain and went on to win the presidency. Callers working for Bush supporters asked conservative white voters if they would be more or less likely to vote for McCain if they knew he had fathered an illegitimate black child. Because McCain often campaigned with a daughter whom he and his wife had adopted from Mother Teresa's orphanage in Bangladesh, many voters accepted the premise of the "poll." This push poll was often cited by McCain as one of the political smear tactics that made him reluctant to expose his family to the stresses of the 2008 presidential race. More than 100 consulting firms across the nation now specialize in push polling.[76] Calling push polling the "political equivalent of a drive-by shooting," Representative Joe Barton (R-Tex.)

launched a congressional investigation into the practice.[77] Push polls may be one reason Americans are becoming increasingly skeptical about the practice of polling and increasingly unwilling to answer pollsters' questions.[78]

The Bandwagon Effect By influencing perceptions, public opinion polls can even influence political realities. In fact, sometimes polling can even create its own reality. The so-called **bandwagon effect** occurs when polling results influence people to support the candidate marked as the probable victor. This is especially true in the presidential nomination process, where there may be multiple candidates within one party vying to be the party's nominee. Todd Donovan and his coauthors found that the change in national media coverage received by a candidate before and after the Iowa caucuses, the first nominating event, was a major predictor of how well the candidate would do in the New Hampshire primary (the second nominating event) and in presidential primaries nationwide, controlling for other factors, including money and standing in the polls.[79] A candidate who has "momentum"—that is, one who demonstrates a lead in the polls—usually finds it considerably easier to raise campaign funds than a candidate whose poll standing is poor. And with these additional funds, poll leaders can often afford to pay for television time and other campaign activities that will generate positive media attention and thus cement their advantage.

bandwagon effect a shift in electoral support to the candidate whom public opinion polls report as the front-runner

Public Opinion and Government Policy

> Analyze the relationship between public opinion and government policies

In 1960, Angus Campbell and the other authors of the *American Voter* argued that few Americans think about politics ideologically or consistently, so one would naturally expect public opinion to vary, as discussed earlier.[80] In fact, one of the reasons elected officials sometimes do not follow public opinion is that it tends to be unpredictable. Given the general lack of political knowledge among voters, the sometimes volatile nature of public opinion, and the difficulty of measuring the public will accurately, it's little wonder that politicians are sometimes unable, or unwilling, to act solely on the basis of public opinion. In fact, John Zaller's work on how Americans form specific opinions calls into question whether government leaders should consult public opinion at all when they make policy decisions—but consulting public opinion is their democratic duty. So how responsive is government policy to public opinion?

Government Responsiveness to Public Opinion

Even though there is no one-to-one correlation between public opinion and the policy decisions made on the public's behalf, studies generally do suggest that elected officials are constrained by the preferences of the public. For example, political scientists Benjamin Page and Robert Shapiro have studied the relationship between macro-level changes in opinion toward various political issues and the policy outcomes that most closely correspond to the issues.[81] The results show that shifts in public opinion on particular issues do in fact tend to lead to changes in public policy. This is especially true when there are wide swings in opinion regarding particularly high-profile issues that are relatively simple. Other researchers have

Professional polling companies gather extensive information about public opinion, but do politicians do what the public wants? In general, policies appear to follow the broad preferences of the public, but specific policies may not always align with what the majority of constituents want.

median voter theorem
a proposition predicting that when policy options can be arrayed along a single dimension, majority rule will pick the policy most preferred by the voter whose ideal policy is to the left of half of the voters and to the right of exactly half of the voters

found similar evidence that government policy generally does track public opinion. By measuring public opinion over time, political scientists Gerald Wright, Robert Erikson, and John McIver have found, unsurprisingly, that states where conservative opinions predominate tend to adopt more conservative laws, and states with more liberal public opinion adopt more liberal policies.[82]

In order to maintain their positions in public office—that is, in order to be re-elected or reappointed—politicians will naturally attempt to create policies that align with the preferences of their constituents. One of the most important theories of how legislators make policy is the **median voter theorem**, proposed by Anthony Downs in 1957. This view suggests that, in order for a politician to get re-elected, the most reliable strategy for him or her to take is to adopt the preferences of the median voter. Representing centrist opinion will allow politicians to garner the largest number of votes, even though this approach also has the potential to alienate supporters holding more extreme opinions.

However, not only do public officials know how unreliable public opinion can be, it's also true that voters may not know exactly what positions the officials actually support. So the fact that voters and government leaders will not always be certain about each other's preferences provides elected officials some latitude in which to pursue their own goals—so long as they do not stray so far from centrist opinion as to jeopardize their position of power.[83] Sometimes officials act on their own preferences if they believe it will benefit government or society, and studies have indeed shown that lawmakers typically do use their own judgment when making policy choices.[84] The bailout of the banks in 2008, for example, was carried out despite polls showing that a majority of Americans opposed this policy. When elected officials pursue policies not aligned with centrist opinion, it is often because they view particular groups of the electorate as more important than others. Inevitably, loyal voting blocs or interest groups that regularly contribute to a candidate may have their interests more closely represented than the general public.[85]

Does Everyone's Opinion Count Equally?

In a democracy, it is assumed that elected representatives should implement the policies favored by the people, and in a general sense this happens in the United States. But when policy issues are more complicated, the public is likely to have less of a voice. Further, citizens who are more affluent and more educated may have a disproportionate influence over politics and public-policy decisions. This has been shown when comparing the responsiveness of elected officials to low- and high-income individuals, voters and nonvoters, and whites and minorities. The view that some groups in a society have more influence over the political process is not new, but it is quite different from the traditional pluralist view of all citizens having equal access to the political sphere—the democratic ideal outlined by Robert Dahl. By contrast, E. E. Schattschneider's famous critique argues that "the flaw in the pluralist heaven is that the heavenly chorus sings with a strong upper-class accent."

How do more affluent and educated citizens manage to wield outsize influence over policy makers? One way is obvious: they vote and they are more likely to contribute money to political campaigns. As we will discuss in Chapter 8, voters and individuals making political contributions tend to be more affluent and educated than nonvoters. Indeed, there is some evidence supporting the common, but generally untested, assumption that voters are better represented than nonvoters. In a comparative study of the roll call votes of U.S. senators, political scientists John Griffin and Brian Newman demonstrate that elected officials are indeed responsive to the policy preferences (and public opinion) of voters, but not to those of nonvoters.[86] Political scientist Larry Bartels finds that U.S. senators from both the Republican and Democratic parties are less likely to respond to the opinions of low-income constituents than to those of constituents with higher incomes.[87] Senate roll call votes on such varied issues as the minimum wage, civil rights, and abortion are more likely to reflect the opinions of the upper-income constituency. Additionally, Bartels's study shows that, when weighing the opinions of those who vote and have high levels of political knowledge, senators are still more responsive to the rich. Bartels argues that government policies such as tax cuts for the ultra-wealthy, failure to increase the minimum wage, and the elimination of the inheritance tax have created greater inequality between the ultra-rich and average Americans than at any other time in American history.[88]

Because of the importance of public opinion, most presidents have made major efforts both to ascertain the public's views and to promote opinions favorable to themselves and their policies. Bill Clinton was often criticized for retaining a number of pollsters to chart shifts in public opinion on a daily basis.

As an alternative to analyzing legislative roll call votes, political scientist Martin Gilens uses survey results to confirm that those with higher incomes are more likely to have their policy preferences represented by actual policies.[89] He considers public opinion surveys on a wide variety of policy issues conducted over 20 years and compares the responses of upper- and lower-income groups to related federal policy outcomes. Gilens finds a moderately strong relationship between what the public wants and what the government actually does, albeit with a strong bias toward the status quo. But when Americans with different income levels differ in their policy preferences, actual policies strongly reflect the preferences of the most affluent and show little or no relationship to the preferences of poor or middle-income Americans. Robert Dahl may be right when he argues that every American citizen has an equal right to voice opinions in the political arena, but his critics are also right to point out that some voices receive a very attentive listening while others are hardly heard at all.

● Thinking Critically about Public Opinion and Democracy

This chapter has focused on the role of public opinion in American politics. A major purpose of democratic government, with its participatory procedures and representative institutions, is to ensure that political leaders will heed the public will. And, indeed, a good deal of evidence suggests that they do. There are many instances in which public policy and public opinion do not coincide, but often the government's actions are consistent with citizens' preferences, at least in the most general sense.[90]

Some political scientists argue, however, that government policy is much less responsive to public opinion on the issues that really count, and that when the interests of elites are at stake, government officials are much more likely to represent the opinions of the affluent than the poor.[91] There is often a disconnect between public opinion and policy. For example, most Americans oppose U.S. military intervention in

Wealthy people, groups, and corporations have more access to policy makers and may have greater influence on government. Here, Vice President Joe Biden (who was a senator at the time) poses for a photo with two lobbyists at a gala dinner.

other nations' affairs in the principle, yet such interventions continue to take place in the Middle East and Africa, often winning public approval—at least at first. The overwhelming majority of Americans supported the Bush administration's decision to attack Afghanistan after September 11, and a year and a half later, most Americans were persuaded that invading Iraq and toppling the regime of Saddam Hussein was necessary for U.S. national security and to prevent a repeat of September 11.

The migration of politics online has greatly expanded the amount of information available and the ease of becoming informed. And as we will see in Chapter 7, online media are more diverse than traditional media. Given this new media environment, we might expect public opinion to be more accurate, even about the nuances of public policy. Digital citizenship offers the promise of a more informed electorate, with citizens having multiple venues in which to translate their opinions into political action and demand improved representation from political leaders.

At the same time, the Internet raises the same concerns about the accuracy and consistency of public opinion that were a central focus of the pre-Internet-era work on public opinion by John Zaller. As Chapter 7 will show, Americans may become trapped in a "filter bubble" in which they are exposed only to news consistent with their political preferences. There are Internet vandals, or "bomb-throwers," who defame other people and their opinions in ways that may negatively color public opinion. Misinformation—rumor masked as legitimate news—may be more common, especially in blogs, as the confusion regarding Barack Obama's religion illustrates. Some research finds that the gap between the haves and the have-nots in terms of political knowledge actually increases with more information. The implications are significant, given the explosion of political coverage online. The research suggests that with more information, public opinion may actually be less consistent.[92]

In a recent book, *The Shallows*, author Nicholas Carr poses another concern: "Is Google making us stupid?"[93] That is, as we enjoy the endless information available online, are we sacrificing our ability to read closely and think deeply, to evaluate competing claims and draw reasoned conclusions? Carr argues that human thought has been shaped through the centuries by "tools of the mind"—from the earliest alphabets and maps to the printing press, the clock, and the computer. Our brain structure changes in response to our experiences. Using the Internet to find, store, and share information can literally reroute our neural pathways. While the printed book served to focus our attention, promoting in-depth thought, the Internet, in contrast, encourages the rapid, distracted sampling of small bits of information from multiple sources, such as updates in Facebook, Twitter, or Google News. While we are becoming ever more adept at scanning and skimming, Carr wonders if we are losing our capacity for concentration, contemplation, and reflection.

The Internet may be reshaping what is public opinion. The effects of new media—vast and still unfolding—include the wide dissemination of public opinion polls and the rise of Internet polling. Do new media make public opinion more or less important? Do they make elected officials more or less responsive to the citizens? Time will tell.

Measuring Public Opinion— Including Your Own

Inform Yourself

Consider opinion on current issues. Visit the Polling Report (www.pollingreport .com) and click on a topic. For example, what percentage of Americans approve of the president's job performance? How has that figure changed over the last year? Next look for polls on same-sex marriage. What percentage of Americans approves of allowing gay men/lesbians to marry and what percentage opposes?

Compare multiple surveys on the same topic. An important clearinghouse for election polls is Real Clear Politics (www.realclearpolitics.com). Click "Polls" and then "Latest Polls." Each day, you can find the results of opinion polls that have been conducted, often including several on the same topic. This website has become increasingly important because it aggregates the results of so many surveys. How much do the results of different polls on the same topic vary? Does aggregating the results from many surveys make the findings more reliable?

Watch a video about opinion on the economy. Watch the Pew Research Center's video on "The Lost Decade of the Middle Class" (www.pewsocialtrends .org/2012/08/22/video-lost-decade-of-the-middle-class/). Then click on the report with the same name on the top right of the page. Who do Americans blame for the economic losses of the middle class? Which groups are most optimistic about their future economic prospects? Which are least optimistic?

Connect with Others

What is your political ideology? First take the very short political quiz at www .theadvocates.org/quiz. What was your result? Next take the Pew Research Center's political typology quiz (www.people-press.org/typology/quiz). How are your results for the two quizzes similar or different? Were you surprised by the findings? How would you redesign the questions to better measure political ideology? Share the political quizzes on your Facebook page or on Twitter.

Find links to the sites listed above as well as related activities on wwnorton.com/studyspace.

Defining Public Opinion

Define public opinion and identify broad types of values and beliefs Americans have about politics (pp. 205–19)

Public opinion refers to the attitudes that people have about issues, events, elected officials, and public policy. Individuals' attitudes are shaped by their underlying political beliefs and values. A number of factors, including the family, membership in social groups, education, and political conditions, help form people's underlying political beliefs and values in a process called *political socialization*. Despite differences in opinion on many issues, most Americans share a common set of values, including a belief in the principles of liberty, equality, and democracy.

Key Terms

public opinion (p. 205)

values (or beliefs) (p. 205)

political ideology (p. 205)

attitude (or opinion) (p. 205)

liberty (p. 206)

equality of opportunity (p. 207)

democracy (p. 207)

political socialization (p. 208)

agents of socialization (p. 209)

gender gap (p. 210)

libertarianism (p. 216)

socialist (p. 216)

liberal (p. 217)

conservative (p. 218)

Practice Quiz

1. The term *public opinion* is used to describe *(p. 205)*
   a) the collected speeches and writings made by a president during his or her term in office.
   b) the analysis of events broadcast by news reporters during the evening news.
   c) the beliefs and attitudes that people have about issues.
   d) decisions of the Supreme Court.
   e) any political statement that is made by a citizen outside of their private residencies or places of employment.

2. Variables such as income, education, race, gender, and ethnicity *(p. 206)*
   a) often create differences of political opinion in America.
   b) have consistently been a challenge to America's core political values.
   c) have little impact on political opinions.
   d) help explain why public opinion polls are so unreliable.
   e) matter only for people's opinions on moral issues but not for their opinions on economic issues.

3. The process by which Americans learn political beliefs and values is called *(p. 208)*
   a) brainwashing.
   b) propaganda.
   c) indoctrination.
   d) political socialization.
   e) political development.

4. Which of the following is an agency of socialization? *(p. 209)*
   a) the family
   b) social groups
   c) education
   d) political conditions
   e) all of the above

5. When men and women respond differently to issues of public policy, they are demonstrating an example of *(p. 210)*
   a) liberalism.
   b) educational differences.
   c) the gender gap.
   d) party politics.
   e) feminism.

6. A politician who opposes abortion, government regulation of business, and gay rights legislation would be best described as a *(p. 218)*
   a) liberal.
   b) conservative.
   c) libertarian.
   d) socialist.
   e) communist.

 Practice Online
"Get Involved" exercise: *Public-Opinion Polls*

How We Form Political Opinions

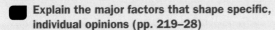

■ **Explain the major factors that shape specific, individual opinions (pp. 219–28)**

As a result of the fact that being politically informed requires a substantial investment of time and energy, most Americans know relatively little about the political world. In fact, most people acquire political information and make political decisions by relying on cues and heuristics from party elites, trusted acquaintances, and the mass media. These informational shortcuts can allow average citizens to from political opinions that are, in most instances, consistent with their underlying preferences and interests.

Key Term

marketplace of ideas (p. 224)

Practice Quiz

7. The fact that the public is inattentive to politics and must frequently rely on informational shortcuts has which of the following effects on American democracy? *(p. 224)*
   a) It strengthens it by providing politicians with more freedom to act on a wider variety of issues.
   b) It strengthens it by increasing the number of people who participate in politics.
   c) It weakens it by making it easier for various institutions and political actors to manipulate the political process.
   d) It weakens it by making every citizen equally empowered to produce outcomes that are consistent with their interests on every issue.
   e) It has no effect on it.

8. Which of the following are the most important external influences on how political opinions are formed in the marketplace of ideas? *(p. 224)*
   a) the government, private groups, and the news media
   b) the unemployment rate, the Dow Jones industrial average, and the NASDAQ composite
   c) random digit dialing surveys, push polls, and framing experiments
   d) the Constitution, the Declaration of Independence, and the Federalist Papers
   e) the legislative branch, the executive branch, and the judicial branch

 Practice Online
Video exercise: *Constructing Public Opinion—Media Education Foundation*

Measuring Public Opinion

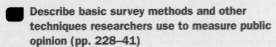

■ **Describe basic survey methods and other techniques researchers use to measure public opinion (pp. 228–41)**

Politicians frequently use public-opinion surveys to decide whether to run for office, what policies to support, how to vote on important pieces of legislation, and what types of appeals to make in their campaigns. Surveys can provide a very accurate description of the true distribution of opinion on an issue if they employ an appropriate sampling method and include a sufficient sample size. In addition to the characteristics of the sample, the reliability of surveys is also determined by the ordering and wording of the questions pollsters choose to ask.

Key Terms

public-opinion polls (p. 228)

sample (p. 228)

simple random sample (or probability sample) (p. 230)

random digit dialing (p. 230)

sampling error (or margin of error) (p. 230)

social desirability effect (p. 237)

selection bias (surveys) (p. 239)

push polling (p. 240)

bandwagon effect (p. 241)

Practice Quiz

9. Which of the following is the term used in public-opinion polling to denote the small group representing the opinions of the whole population? *(p. 228)*
   a) control group
   b) sample
   c) micropopulation
   d) respondents
   e) median voters

10. A poll that includes many poorly worded or ambiguous questions has a high degree of *(p. 232)*
    a) sampling error.
    b) measurement error.
    c) selection bias.
    d) validity error.
    e) attribution error.

11. A push poll is a poll in which *(p. 240)*
    a) the questions are designed to shape the respondent's opinion rather than measure the respondent's opinion.
    b) the questions are designed to measure the respondent's opinion rather than shape the respondent's opinion.
    c) the questions are designed to reduce measurement error.

d) the sample is chosen to include only undecided or independent voters.
e) the sample is not representative of the population it is drawn from.

12. A familiar polling problem is the "bandwagon effect," which occurs when *(p. 241)*
   a) the same results are used over and over again.
   b) polling results influence people to support the candidate marked as the probable victor in a campaign.

c) polling results influence people to support the candidate who is trailing in a campaign.
d) background noise makes it difficult for a pollster and a respondent to communicate with each other.
e) a large number of people refuse to answer a pollster's questions.

 Practice Online
Video exercise: *What Do You Do for a Living? with Andrew Kohut*

Public Opinion and Government Policy

 Analyze the relationship between public opinion and government policies (pp. 241–43)

In a democracy, elected officials should pursue policies that are favored by the public. Although there are many instances where government policy differs from the desires of the public, academic research has shown that there is generally a strong connection between what government does and what people want. Academic research has also shown, however, that the government is less responsive to the public on complex issues and that more affluent and more educated citizens have a disproportionate influence over policy decisions.

Key Term

median voter theorem (p. 242)

Practice Quiz

13. The median voter theorem suggests that *(p. 242)*
   a) the most reliable strategy for a politician to take in winning reelection is to adopt policies that are consistent with the preferences of ideologically extreme voters.

b) the most reliable strategy for a politician to take in winning re-election is to adopt policies that are consistent with the preferences of centrist voters.
c) the average American voter is uninformed about the details of most government policies.
d) the average American voter is well informed about the details of most government policies.
e) government policy should always reflect what a majority of Americans want.

 Practice Online
"You Decide" exercise: *School Prayer*

For Further Reading

Althaus, Scott. *Collective Preferences in Democratic Politics.* New York: Cambridge University Press, 2003.

Bartels, Larry. *Unequal Democracy.* Princeton, NJ: Princeton University Press, 2008.

Berinsky, Adam. *Silent Voices: Public Opinion and Political Participation in America.* Princeton, NJ: Princeton University Press, 2005.

Bishop, George. *The Illusion of Public Opinion.* New York: Rowman and Littlefield, 2004.

Clawson, Rosalee, and Zoe Oxley. *Public Opinion: Democratic Ideals and Democratic Practice.* Washington, DC: CQ Press, 2008.

Erikson, Robert, and Kent Tedin. *American Public Opinion.* 7th ed. New York: Longman, 2004.

Fiorina, Morris. *Culture War: The Myth of a Polarized America.* New York: Longman, 2005.

Gallup, George. *The Pulse of Democracy.* New York: Simon and Schuster, 1940.

Ginsberg, Benjamin. *The Captive Public: How Mass Opinion Promotes State Power.* New York: Basic Books, 1986.

Glynn, Carol et al., ed. *Public Opinion.* Boulder, CO: Westview, 2004.

Jacobs, Lawrence R., and Robert Y. Shapiro. *Politicians Don't Pander: Political Manipulation and the Loss of Democratic Responsiveness.* Chicago: University of Chicago Press, 2000.

Lee, Taeku. *Mobilizing Public Opinion.* Chicago: University of Chicago Press, 2002.

Lippman, Walter. *Public Opinion.* New York: Harcourt, Brace, 1922.

Norrander, Barbara, and Clyde Wilcox. *Understanding Public Opinion.* Washington, DC: CQ Press, 2009.

Zaller, John. *The Nature and Origins of Mass Opinion.* New York: Cambridge University Press, 1992.

Recommended Websites

American Association for Public Opinion Research
www.aapor.org

This website is one of the premier academic sites for public opinion data on a host of political and social topics.

eTalkinghead
http://directory.etalkinghead.com

Political blogs have become an increasingly popular way for Americans to express and discuss political opinions. This Web page provides a directory of political blogs by ideology and issue.

Gallup
www.gallup.com

The Gallup Organization has been involved in the scientific study of public opinion for more than 70 years and is very highly regarded. This website contains public-opinion data archives, video archives, and international polls.

The Political Compass
www.politicalcompass.org

A political ideology is a cohesive set of beliefs that form a general philosophy about government; however, people are often unsure if they are liberal, moderate, or conservative. Go to the website for the Political Compass and take the test to see if it helps you identify your ideology.

Polling Report
http://pollingreport.com

This independent, nonpartisan resource tracks trends in American public opinion. On this site you will find countless political opinion polls by all the major media outlets, all in one place.

Public Agenda
www.publicagenda.org

Measuring public opinion from surveys can be problematic. Often samples contain selection bias, or surveys have measurement error. Public Agenda is an organization that studies public opinion on major policy issues. Its website contains critiques of public opinion.

ThisNation.com
www.thisnation.com/socialization.html

The process through which underlying political beliefs and values are formed is called political socialization. This civic-minded Web page offers a brief discussion of political socialization with some related Web links.

Political candidates who receive positive news coverage gain momentum, which helps them attract campaign contributions and endorsements and eventually win votes. The influence of the media on political campaigns is just one example of its important role in American democracy.

The Media

WHAT GOVERNMENT DOES AND WHY IT MATTERS One area in which our government's role is intended to be minimal is the realm of the news media. The Constitution's First Amendment guarantees freedom of the press, and most Americans believe that a free press is an essential condition for both liberty and democratic politics. Today the media (new and old) play a central role in American politics, not only in setting the agenda of topics that Americans think about and discuss, but often in swaying opinions on political issues and candidates.

Political candidates who receive positive news coverage gain momentum, pick up political endorsements, attract campaign contributions, and win support from voters.[1] In the 2008 campaign for the Democratic Party's presidential nomination, Barack Obama exceeded the media's expectations with his early win in the Iowa caucuses, in which he upset the front-runner, Hillary Clinton. Obama's unexpected victory earned him greatly increased press attention and eventually led him to the White House.[2] But candidates who disappoint media expectations see their political endorsements, campaign contributions, and polling numbers dwindle.

The influence of the media on political campaigns is just one example of the media's vitally important role in American democracy. Without the media's investigations, citizens would be forced to rely entirely on the information provided by politicians and the government, and would be deprived of an indispensable opportunity to evaluate issues carefully and form reasoned opinions.

The rise of the Internet has brought important changes to the media industry and its influence in politics. In fact, the Internet is fundamentally altering the media's role in politics and American democracy. Just 20 years ago the majority of Americans got their political news from a daily newspaper, from radio, or by watching the local evening news and the national evening news from one of the three major networks (ABC, CBS, NBC). In the twenty-first century, America is becoming a nation of "digital citizens"—daily Internet users who turn to the Internet for politics and news.[3] Overall 80 percent of Americans have used the Internet, although just under 7 in 10 have high-speed home access.[4] Among Internet users in 2012, 3 in 4 read the news online and 6 in 10 go online for information about politics.[5] In fact, more Americans now read the news online than read a print newspaper, and those reading online news are more likely to vote and participate in politics in other ways.[6] Today mainstream media must compete with niche media outlets that tailor news to their readers and viewers, and Americans increasingly find political content via blogs and social media such as Facebook and Twitter.

The sharing of information and opinions is critical to democracy. Discussing the right of press freedom, Thomas Jefferson wrote, "The basis of our government being the opinion of the people, the very first object should be to keep that right; and were it left to me to decide whether we should have a government without newspapers or newspapers without a government, I should not hesitate a moment to prefer the latter." In the twenty-first century, newspapers and other traditional media have been joined by today's electronic and digital media as an essential component of American democracy.

chaptergoals

- Describe the role of print and broadcast media in providing political information (pages 253–56)

- Explain how the Internet has transformed the news media (pages 256–68)

- Describe trends in who owns mass media companies (pages 268–70)

- Analyze the ways the media can influence public opinion and politics (pages 270–77)

- Explain how politicians and others try to shape the news (pages 278–83)

- Trace the evolution of rules that govern broadcast media (pages 283–85)

Traditional Media

Describe the role of print and broadcast media in providing political information

The American news media are among the world's freest and most diverse. Americans have literally thousands of available options in political reporting. The wide variety of newspapers, newsmagazines, broadcast media, and online sources regularly present information that is at odds with the government's claims, and editorial opinions sharply critical of high-ranking officials. The freedom to speak one's mind is one of the most cherished of American political values.

Americans get their news from three main sources: **broadcast media** (radio and television), print media (newspapers and magazines), and, increasingly, the Internet. Each of these sources has distinctive characteristics. We discuss the first two in this section, and in the next section, we will take a close look at the emergence of the Internet and how it is changing the media industry and the way Americans get political news.

broadcast media television, radio, or other media that transmit audio and/or video content to the public

Broadcast Media

Television news reaches more Americans than any other single news source. It is estimated that over 95 percent of Americans have a television, although the percentage of Americans with cable television may be dropping among the young, as the Internet becomes the preferred vehicle for news, communication, and entertainment. The 2012 presidential elections may be the first time digital media trumped television media. Yet tens of millions of people watch national and local news programs every day. Television news, however, covers relatively few topics and provides little depth of coverage. It serves the extremely important function of alerting viewers to issues and events, but generally doesn't provide much more than a series of sound bites—brief quotes

When Rick Perry made a major gaffe in a 2012 Republican primary debate, the scene was broadcast on national television—and then viewed millions of times on YouTube.

and short characterizations of the day's events, often little more than a few seconds in length. Because they are aware of the character of television news coverage, politicians and others often seek to manipulate the news by providing the media with sound bites that will dominate news coverage for at least a few days. Twenty-four-hour news stations such as Cable News Network (CNN) offer more detail and commentary than the networks' half-hour evening news shows. Even CNN and the others, however, offer more headlines and sound bites than analysis, especially during their prime-time broadcasts. Politicians generally consider local broadcast news a friendlier venue than the national news. National reporters are often inclined to criticize and question, whereas local reporters are more likely to accept the pronouncements of national leaders at face value.

Radio news is also essentially a headline service. In the short time they devote to news (usually five minutes per hour), radio stations announce the day's major events without providing much detail. All-news stations such as WTOP in Washington, D.C., and New York's WCBS assume that most listeners are in their cars and that, as a result, the people in the audience change throughout the day as listeners reach their destinations. Thus, rather than use their time to flesh out a given set of stories, they repeat the same stories each hour to present them to new listeners. In the 1990s, radio talk shows became important sources of commentary and opinion. A number of conservative radio hosts such as Rush Limbaugh and Sean Hannity have huge audiences and have helped to mobilize support for conservative political causes and candidates. In the political center or left center, National Public Radio is a coveted source for moderate talk radio and provides in-depth political reporting, while the now-defunct Air America hoped to achieve on the left what Limbaugh had achieved on the right.

Comedy talk shows with political content, like The Colbert Report, *have become a significant source of political information for some Americans.*

Comedy talk shows with political content, such as *The Daily Show* or *The Colbert Report*, have become increasingly important, attracting millions of television viewers. Comedian Stephen Colbert went so far as to establish a political action committee during the 2012 presidential primaries and to enter the Republican primary in his home state of South Carolina in an effort to draw attention to problems with current campaign finance laws. *Colbert, The Daily Show,* and other late-night talk shows use cutting-edge humor, sarcasm, and social criticism to cover almost every major political event. Yet talk shows that cover political topics are not just for fun. They have become increasingly important sources of political news, especially for younger viewers. Pew surveys show that many Americans get political news from these shows and that followers of comedic talk shows are well informed about politics.[7]

The broadcast media are also diversifying as they adapt to changes in the American population, especially the growing number of Latinos. California and Texas are both projected to become majority Hispanic by the middle of the twenty-first century. In both states, as well as others, the Latino-oriented television channels Telemundo, Univision, and MSN Latino attract large audiences. These channels have Spanish-language programming, including political reporting and other news. They also may focus on topics or perspectives of particular interest to their audience. Coverage of the Arizona and Alabama illegal immigration laws, for example, in Hispanic media outlets was significantly different from that of mainstream media. News outlets aimed at other ethnic groups have also become common in many areas. As America has become more multicultural, multiethnic television—a form of niche media—has broadened news media.

Print Media

Newspapers, though no longer the primary news source for most Americans, remain important nevertheless, because they are influential among the political elite. The broadcast media also rely on leading newspapers such as the *New York Times* and the *Washington Post* to set their news agenda. In fact, the broadcast media engage in very little actual reporting; they primarily cover stories that have been "broken," or initially reported, by the print media or online media. For example, sensational charges that President Bill Clinton had had an affair with a White House intern were reported first by the Drudge Report, a popular news aggregation website, and then picked up by the *Washington Post* and *Newsweek* before being trumpeted around the world by the broadcast media. Print and online media, as written text, also provide more detailed and complete information than radio or television media, offering a better context for analysis. The nation's economic, social, and political elite tend to rely on the detailed coverage provided by the print media to inform and influence their views about important public matters. The print media may have a smaller audience than their cousins in broadcasting, but they have an especially influential audience.

For most traditional newspapers, though, recent decades have been ruinous. Competition from broadcast media and, more recently, free content online, combined with simultaneous declines in advertising revenue and circulation levels, have undermined the traditional business model of newspapers, bringing financial disaster to traditional print media.[8] Daily newspaper print circulation has declined from 62 million to 49 million nationwide over the past 20 years. Circulation for the *New York Times*, for example, dropped more than 10 percent from 2010 to 2011, and in 2011 alone the paper lost 25 percent of its revenue.[9] For the first time, advertisers prefer online media; advertising revenue at print newspapers has dropped by 25 percent since 2006.[10] Major newspapers such as the *Chicago Tribune*, the *Minneapolis Star Tribune*, and the *Philadelphia Inquirer* have all sought bankruptcy protection. Many newspapers, such as the *Rocky Mountain News*, have gone out of business altogether. The *Los Angeles Times* has reduced its news staff by half over the past decade. Newspapers have cut costs by closing their foreign bureaus and their offices in Washington, D.C.

To counter these trends, traditional media organizations have been forced to adapt, and most now have a significant online presence, blurring the distinction between old media and new. Faced with shrinking revenues from their print versions, a few news organizations, such as the *Washington Post*, the *New York Times*, and the *Economist*, have begun to charge customers for reading the news online, while others, such as the *Seattle Post-Intelligencer* and the *Christian Science Monitor*, have become online only. If this approach succeeds, we may see more online subscription newspapers in the future, and a more viable business model for the digital press.

● New Media and Online News

Explain how the Internet has transformed the news media

The twenty-first century has already experienced a profound transformation of the media. The impact of the Internet in communications technology parallels that of the printing press in nineteenth-century America, which saw the rise of the **penny press** and widespread literacy.[11] Today, even as the newspaper business struggles for its life, readership of online news has soared. Nielsen estimates that 75 million Americans read the news online, a number higher than that for print newspapers.[12] Beside online-only newspapers, other forums include news websites, blogs, Facebook, YouTube, and Twitter. **News aggregators**, such as Google News and Real Clear Politics, provide links to thousands of stories covered in the news each day, as well as the latest public opinion polls and their own synthesis of the headline news. Younger Americans are more likely to rely on the Internet than any other news source, which suggests that this trend will continue in the future.[13] One great advantage of online news is that it is frequently updated. After the September 11, 2001, terrorist attacks, many Americans relied on the Internet for news about terrorism, bioterrorism, and the wars in Iraq and Afghanistan, as well as for viewing video of the Twin Towers falling. In general, news watchers have quickly grown accustomed to following world events unfolding in real time. Online media are more diverse and have created a more democratic and participatory press, one in which citizens and nonprofit organizations now play a prominent role. No longer relegated to the letters-to-the-editor section found in most print publications, readers can now post comments online and participate in a community providing feedback on almost all online news articles. Online media, by representing a wider range of political views than traditional media, have created a more democratic press.

The term *digital citizenship* refers to the ability to participate in society and politics online. In much the same way that education and literacy promoted democracy and economic growth in the nineteenth century, today's Internet has the potential to benefit society as a whole and to facilitate political participation by individuals within society. Like education, the Internet helps provide the information and skills needed for democratic engagement and economic opportunity.[14] It facilitates social inclusion through greater access to political information and news.[15]

However, regular and effective use of the Internet requires high-speed access, technical skills, and literacy to evaluate and use information online.[16] Individuals

penny press cheap, tabloid-style newspaper produced in the nineteenth century, when mass production of inexpensive newspapers first became possible due to the steam-powered printing press; a penny press cost one cent compared to other papers, which cost more than five cents

news aggregator an application or feed that collects Web content such as news headlines, blogs, podcasts, online videos, and more in one location for easy viewing

The rise of new media has made it easier for Americans with Internet access to get political news, but 1 in 5 Americans is still completely offline. For example, there are neighborhoods in large cities like Chicago where over 80 percent of households lack broadband access.

Who Gets Political Information Online?

Percentage of Internet Users Who Go Online to Find...

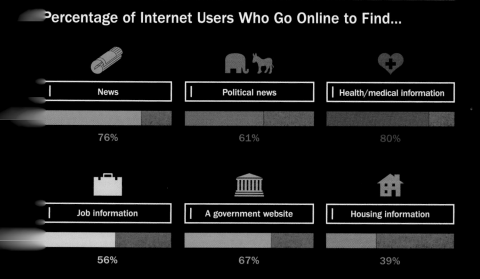

News	Political news	Health/medical information
76%	61%	80%

Job information	A government website	Housing information
56%	67%	39%

In a democracy like the United States, people need political information to understand current issues and their government's actions. With the rise of the Internet as a news source, Americans are increasingly likely to get political and other important information online. However, not everyone has the same level of access to the Internet and thus to information.

Who Has High-Speed Internet at Home?

SOURCES: Pew Internet and American Life Project, "Trend Data: Adults" 2011, http://pewinternet.org/Trend-Data-(Adults)/Online-Activites-Total.aspx; National Telecommunications & Information Administration, "Digital Nation: Understanding Internet Usage," February 2011, www.ntia.doc.gov/files/ntia/publications/ntia_internet_use_report_february_2011.pdf (both accessed 5/23/12).

Income

< $15,000	32.1%
$15,000–24,999	42.6%
$25,000–34,999	50.6%
$35,000–49,999	63.4%
$50,000–74,999	73.6%
$75,000–99,999	80.8%
00,000–149,999	85.5%
> $150,000	89.6%

Race/Ethnicity

Hispanic	45.2%
Black	49.9%
White	68.3%
Asian	68.8%

Age

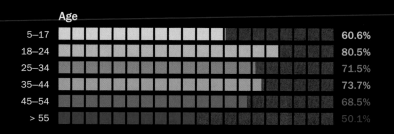

5–17	60.6%
18–24	80.5%
25–34	71.5%
35–44	73.7%
45–54	68.5%
> 55	50.1%

for critical analysis

1. Which groups are less likely to have access to high-speed Internet? Why might this be a concern in American politics?

2. In the past, young people have been less likely than older Americans to use news sources, like newspapers or television news programs. Will digital politics change this pattern?

without the access or skills to use the Internet may be increasingly uninformed and excluded from the world of politics online. As of 2011, almost 7 in 10 Americans were **digital citizens**, individuals with high-speed access at home (beyond mobile access), and nearly 8 in 10 Americans used the Internet in some location (e.g., home, school, library). However, 1 in 5 Americans are completely offline. Moreover, just half of African Americans, Latinos, and the poor are digital citizens by this definition (home access), as well as the poor, which suggests that there are significant inequalities in access to digital media.[17] Additionally, up to 20 percent of adult Americans fall into the lowest literacy category. Although most people in this category were not illiterate (completely unable to read or write), they lacked the basic skills necessary to read a simple newspaper article.[18] Digital citizenship requires literacy skills for reading and understanding printed information, as well as regular Internet access.

In this section we look at the major types of online news available to citizens today. While many traditional news sources, such as newspapers, now publish online, other Web news outlets tend to be smaller and more specialized, and have lower personnel and overhead costs than mainstream publishers. Sharing videos online through sites such as YouTube is fundamentally altering broadcast news, as dedicated channels provide analysis, commentary, and comedy, just as podcasts are restructuring radio news. Beyond news aggregation websites, online news sources include niche journalism, citizen journalism and blogs, nonprofit journalism, and social media.

Niche Journalism

In the gap opened by the decline of traditional print media, the last decade has seen the rise of **niche journalism** and specialty publications. Bloomberg News, one of the most successful specialty online sources, has hundreds of thousands of readers paying a large annual fee for detailed business-related news. In politics, Roll Call, The Hill, the National Journal, Congressional Quarterly, Salon, the Huffington Post, Real Clear Politics, and Politico, the niche leader, have detailed political reporting inside the Beltway (that is, in Washington, D.C., which is encircled by freeways). *The Onion*, a satiric publication also available in print, has an avid following among the young and liberals. Niche journalism feeds citizens' interest in politics from the full range of the political spectrum. These niche outlets are supplemented by a rich array of international and foreign online news sources.

News consumers have shifted from a few general-purpose sources, such as the evening television news and a local newspaper, to a large number of niche publications and specialized new sources: business news from one source; weather from another; sport, politics and commentary from others. Just 10 years ago Americans tuned to local evening news for weather; today many Americans use Weather.com or Weather Channel applications on smartphones. Two-thirds of Americans go online wirelessly using a laptop, tablet computer, or smartphone, while 46 percent of Americans have a smartphone that connects to the Internet as of 2012.[19] The radio has long been a primary medium for information about local traffic, but today Google Maps on smartphones provides up-to-the-minute traffic information and routing with the touch of a screen. Sports fans once depended on local evening news for information about their favorite teams but now find it online through a variety of niche media outlets, including EPSN online. The rise of niche journalism has fundamentally changed how Americans consume news and what they read.

Citizen Journalism and Blogs

The old media system was dominated by professional journalists, trained in journalism schools, who served as gatekeepers in determining what was front-page news and how political events were to be interpreted. This system had benefits and costs: the quality was high, but the diversity of opinions was relatively low. The media's gatekeeper role continues, but the diversity of online media is changing traditional journalism and the very nature of "news coverage." Even five years ago, most establishment journalists took their cues exclusively from a small handful of outlets (such as the Drudge Report), but now many of them use a much more extensive and diversified roster of sources, including blogs, Twitter, and independent political commentators, such as Nate Silver's FiveThirtyEight blog on elections (now published on the *New York Times* website). Online news is creating a new generation of whistle-blowers, enhancing the media's traditional role as a watchdog for the people against government corruption, and it is creating new venues for the political activism of ideological conservatives, liberals, and moderates.

A distinguishing feature of the digital media is **citizen journalism**, which is interactive and participatory. Citizen journalism includes news reporting and political commentary by ordinary citizens, and even crisis coverage from eyewitnesses on the scene. If the September 11 attacks had occurred in 2011 instead of 2001, the Web would be populated by citizen videos of the devastating terrorist attack on U.S. soil. In just 10 years, news reporting has dramatically changed. Because it involves a wider range of voices in gathering news and interpreting political events, contemporary news reporting and commentary are more democratic. Magnifying the power of the Internet is the near-universal availability of digital cameras and camera-equipped cell phones, which gives millions of Americans the capacity to photograph or film events. At the same time, Internet sites such as YouTube permit users to upload photos and video clips that are then viewed by hundreds of thousands of subscribers or relayed by the mainstream media for even wider dissemination. When a citizen using a mobile phone captured video of police pepper-spraying peaceful Occupy Wall Street demonstrators at the University of California–Davis in November 2011, it became headline news; the video was viewed by millions and fueled mounting concerns about police brutality toward the Occupy protesters.

A growing number of readers turn to online blogs (short for "Web logs"). There are thousands of blogs, covering virtually every topic imaginable, and a large share of these include political news and commentary on local, national, and world events. Many blogs are citizen-run and are more interactive and representative of the diversity of American views than traditional news, which generally reflects the priorities of political elites. A number of blogs, such as the Daily Kos, Nate Silver's FiveThirtyEight, and Salon's Glen Greenwald, have thousands of loyal readers who regularly critique stories presented by the print and broadcast media. These online discussion and comment forums create a community for readers, further interpreting the news.

Citizen journalism supplements the work of professional journalists in many important ways. The diversity of online media has created new opinion leaders, new voices, and even, at times, improved information. In recent years, for example, bloggers have uncovered major factual errors in media reports and forced the networks and newspapers to issue corrections. Sharp-eyed bloggers have proven adept at recognizing faked or Photoshopped photographs in news stories—for example, pointing out that major news outlets, including the *New York Times*, the *Los Angeles*

citizen journalism news reported and distributed by citizens, rather than professional journalists and for-profit news organizations

In 2011 an ordinary citizen recorded video of police pepper-spraying peaceful Occupy protesters at the University of California–Davis. This video was widely shared on the Internet and the story became headline news.

Times, Reuters, and the Associated Press, had presented doctored photos in their reports from Iraq, Afghanistan, and the Israeli-Palestinian conflict.[20] Because bloggers do not have strict editorial boards, they can post a story within minutes. This ability to scoop the mainstream media often means that bloggers are now the ones framing stories about political candidates, and candidates have only minutes to respond to accusations before the story breaks in the mainstream media.[21] By sharply lowering the technological and financial barriers that previously prevented all but a few individuals and interests from reaching mass audiences, blogs (at least potentially) increase the ability of ordinary people to engage in effective political action. (In Chapter 8, we will take a closer look at the Internet's effects on political participation.)

To be sure, the open, freewheeling nature of blogging often means that there's little of the traditional quality control employed by "respectable," institutional old media. Many of the claims found in blogs are unsupported or simply untrue. And because they do not face the burden of fact-checking required for the mainstream media, even well-meaning bloggers can post false information. This could be one reason why misinformation about political issues is higher among blog readers than those reading online news from the mainstream press.[22] Moreover, niche bloggers may not be subject to the moderating influences felt by mainstream publications, which try to appeal to the widest possible readership. In 2008, for example, bloggers were responsible for some of the harshest attacks of the presidential campaign, often focusing on negative stories and even scurrilous rumors. Republican bloggers circulated the unfounded claim that Barack Obama was a Muslim intent on subverting the U.S. government, or that Obama was a noncitizen. (This false rumor is covered in detail in Chapter 6.) Democratic bloggers, for their part, circulated unflattering stories about John McCain's personal history and made much of an allegation that Sarah Palin's infant son was actually her daughter's baby. These blog-driven rumors became widespread enough to receive attention in the mainstream media.

Nonprofit Journalism

As traditional news organizations have cut budgets and especially investigative journalism, political information is increasingly emanating from universities, think tanks, nonprofit organizations, and private foundations. Think tanks such as the Brookings Institution, the Cato Institute, the Hoover Institution, the Heritage Foundation, the Center for American Progress, and the American Enterprise Institute provide information and analysis on current events in order to influence public debate. Universities have expended their public outreach, encouraging faculty to explain their findings for a general audience; as a result, university faculty are increasingly cited in the mainstream media. Universities have even constructed television studios and entire networks, such as the Big Ten Network, which includes athletic and academic programming, and polling during presidential elections. Community-based nonprofit newspapers are supported by local foundations seeking to fill the void in local news as local papers close their doors. Corporations are players, too. The Bill and Melinda Gates Foundation, established by Microsoft founder Bill Gates, provides extensive funding to National Public Radio. The Pew Research Center's 2010 report entitled the "State of the Media 2010" estimates that, in the past four years, $14 million in nonprofit funding has been spent in new media. But this represents only one-tenth of the $1.6 billion in print newspaper revenue lost during this same period.[23]

Social Media

Social media, such as Twitter and Facebook, are the most recent players in news and political communication. Nearly half of the U.S. population of 311 million is registered as users on Facebook. Pew surveys show that 15 percent of Americans who use the Internet use Twitter, and this figure has been rising over the past few years; 8 percent use Twitter on a typical day.[24] Young adults, African Americans, and mobile users have the highest rates of using Twitter. Both Facebook and Twitter are online networking forums that allow users to share content, news stories, photos, and videos with others, from a handful of close friends to thousands of people. Because they are more personalized and interactive than anonymous news organizations, social media are becoming increasing popular means for Americans to receive political information from the candidates and interest groups they support. In turn, candidates for political office, elected officials, political organizations, and interest groups have been quick to adopt Facebook and Twitter as means of communicating with their supporters and providing them a continual feed of new information. For example, in 2007, Chris Hughes, one of the founders of Facebook, helped the Obama presidential campaign establish a Facebook site that allowed Obama supporters to "like" the senator's page. At the site's resource center, visitors could download flyers, videos, and other campaign materials, and could create or join online groups to

social media Web-based and mobile-based technologies that are used to turn communication into interactive dialogue between organizations, communities, and individuals; social media technologies take on many different forms including blogs, Wikis, podcasts, pictures, video, Facebook, Twitter, and more

Barack Obama's Facebook page was an important tool in his 2008 and 2012 campaigns, offering a way to inform and organize supporters. As of summer 2012, Obama had 26 million friends on Facebook.

share ideas and organize events. The site's fund-raising section allowed visitors to set personal fund-raising goals and to invite other registered friends to help them reach those goals. The Obama site attracted more than a million visitors during the campaign for the 2008 Democratic presidential nomination,[25] and as of 2012, Obama's Facebook page has 26 million friends.

Both Facebook and Twitter have contributed to political mobilization and information sharing by creating virtual social networks where groups of like-minded individuals, or individuals with shared interests, can quickly and easily share information. Twitter was the communication tool of choice for organizing the Occupy Wall Street demonstrations in 2011, as thousands of Americans camped out in cities across the United States to protest growing income inequality between the top 1 percent of American income earners and the bottom 99 percent. In another example, from outside the United States, bloggers and Twitter users helped organize protests around the Middle East during the 2010 "Arab Spring," bringing down the Egyptian dictator Hosni Mubarak and other governments.

Benefits of Online News

So why have new media become so popular? We have just touched on many of the reasons: Americans may prefer online news because of (1) the convenience of getting the news online; (2) the up-to-the-moment currency of the information available online; (3) the depth of the information available online; and (4) the diversity of online viewpoints.[26] At the same time, changes to the media arising from the rapid proliferation of the Internet have raised a multitude of concerns, as we will see in the section "Concerns about Online News."

Convenience Information online is convenient and always available for those who have regular access to the Internet at home or, increasingly, through mobile devices such as smartphones. Pew surveys show that nearly half of those who use online news and political information cite its convenience.[27] Finding specific information is simplified by search engines, links, and search functions within Web pages. Google News, for example, reports the headline news (domestic and international) from thousands of sources updated by the minute, with 24-hour-a-day convenience, providing access to information with much more depth than that found when tuning into the national evening news on television. Twitter, Facebook, Google News, and Weather Channel applications provide news updates on smartphones. Because political knowledge is central to the formation of political attitudes, the convenience of online political news may lead to a more informed and engaged citizenry. Use of online political information is associated with more interest in politics, greater knowledge of politics, and a greater likelihood of discussing politics with friends and family.[28]

Currency One of the fundamental changes ushered in by an era of online news is the speed with which local, national, and international events are covered, as well as the scope of coverage. Major news stories regularly break first online, and are later reported through print newspapers and television. Social media have accelerated even further the speed with which news travels around the globe. News of Osama bin Laden's death in May 2011 spread rapidly through text-messaging, smartphones, and social media outlets such as Facebook and Twitter even before it could be verified by traditional media. When the Twin Towers fell on September 11, online videos spread rapidly, with the most updated information about the terrorist attack found online. Likewise, many Americans watched online videos of millions of gallons of crude oil gushing into the Gulf of Mexico in 2010. Viewership peaked with "top kill" efforts by British Petroleum (BP) to stop the leak on the *Deepwater Horizon* rig.

Depth Online news provides more information than the 60-second sound bites found in television and radio news. By blending more-detailed treatment of topics with the visual and emotive appeal of streaming videos, the Internet shares qualities both of print media (promoting knowledge) and of the visual aspects of television (promoting interest and engagement).[29] Online news covers events and issues with the same immediacy as television, but with the in-depth treatment that is typical of newspapers. The multimedia capacity of the Internet notwithstanding, most websites still rely heavily upon written text, and most political "Web surfing" consists mainly of reading, which facilitates greater recall of information and, in turn, encourages the acquisition of political knowledge.[30]

Diversity Like the myriad products sold in a modern grocery store or available for purchase on Amazon.com, the American media industry is now highly fragmented, with hundreds of thousands of sources presenting political information. Online sources are much more diverse than those found in the traditional media, and this diversity may lead to an increase in political knowledge and interest.[31] While major players online certainly do include mainstream outlets (such as websites sponsored by television networks and major newspapers in the United States),[32] the Internet remains populated by a wide range of information sources. By making foreign media such as the British Broadcasting Company (BBC) and Al Jazeera television easily available, the Internet has reduced the importance of physical proximity and created a truly global shared culture. Millions went online to watch live broadcasts of Egyptian citizens protesting for democratic freedoms in 2011. News aggregators provide links to a broad international array of sources; Google News, for example, draws from more than 25,000 publishers around the world and offers its services in two dozen languages. Sites such as RealClearPolitics .com focus on politics, presenting links to commentary, the latest polling results, and

Traditional Media vs. Social Media

The Internet, especially Twitter, has transformed how political campaigns interact with the media, and how Americans get campaign news. Before the rise of the Internet, news reached the public through television, radio, or newspapers. Each of these sources required journalists (to find stories), editors, and researchers (to ensure the information was accurate), as well as time to distribute the story. Stories used to take hours if not days to reach the public, and controversial or scandalous stories sometimes did not appear at all because journalists had trouble verifying the information. To publish a story based on hearsay opens the publisher to a libel charge if the information turns out to be false. Today, blogs, Twitter, and other sites repeat rumors (as well as breaking news) at lightning speed, while political campaigns and journalists are forced to play catchup.

The changing standards of the news have become evident in presidential elections. Campaigns used to hire strategists who were friendly with reporters, in the hope that tips about forthcoming stories would give the campaign team time to prepare a response to a negative story. Since the 2000 presidential election, however, the 24-hour news cycle has meant that campaign staffers have had to scour the Internet for any possible negative information about their candidate and respond immediately. Campaigns cannot afford to take an entire day to respond to negative information.

Another trend is that traditional media tend to focus on campaign strategy among the candidates, while social media focus more on the likability of the candidates, their positions on issues, and the candidates' personal lives. One study analyzed more than 20 million tweets in the run-up to the 2012 primary election, and researchers found that the discourse on Twitter was much more opinionated and candidate-biased than mainstream media coverage. There is also more of it on Twitter. Discussions

of the 2012 presidential candidates on Twitter outnumbered those found in blogs by nine to one.

The content of traditional and social media also differs. In 2012, coverage of Republican presidential candidate Ron Paul was virtually nonexistent in the mainstream news, but Paul had a loyal following of supporters online who posted their "news" daily. Paul enjoyed the most favorable tone on Twitter of all candidates; 55 percent of the statements made about him were positive. However, the study found that overall political discussion on Twitter is slightly more negative than that in the mainstream news.

In recent years, there is evidence that individuals have become more skeptical of major news outlets and have increasingly turned to Twitter, blogs, social media, and other online sources for information. A National Journal/Heartland Monitor poll conducted in the summer of 2012 found that input from personal relationships was more important than information from major newspapers in voting decisions in the 2012 presidential election. Three in four Americans relied on conversations and information shared

by friends, family, and acquaintances. Only 6 in 10 relied on editors' opinions in news magazines and major newspapers. Social media allows information from individuals' social networks to loom large in political decisions.

As news consumers increasingly turn to social networks, they need to be mindful of where the information has come from and whether it is a reputable news source or an unregulated rumor. While there are still some restraints on major outlets, bloggers and tweeters have free rein to write whatever they want. Bloggers have been known to fabricate entire stories about candidates they do not like. Candidates and parties, in turn, must be ready at a second's notice to refute claims made on these unregulated "news" sites.

SOURCES: Jeff Howe, "The Next Economy: The Dialogue Economy, Social Media and the Marketplace," *A Special Supplement to the Atlantic Monthly* (a joint project with the National Journal) (Summer 2012). Tom Rosenstiel, Mark Jurkowitz, and Tricia Sartor. "How the Media Covered the 2012 Primary Campaign," Pew Research Center, April 23, 2012, www.journalism.org/analysis _report/romney_report?src=prc-headline (accessed 6/23/12). Tom Rosenstiel, Mark Jurkowitz, et al. "Twitter and the Campaign: How the Discussion on Twitter Varies from Blogs and News Coverage and Ron Paul's Twitter Triumph." Pew Research Center, December 8, 2011, www .journalism.org/analysis_report/twitter_and_campaign" (accessed 6/23/12).

for critical analysis

1. Do you think today's 24-hour news cycle and multitude of news sources create a more informed citizenry? Why or why not?

2. What are some of the benefits of getting political information from trusted friends or family members? What are some of the possible drawbacks?

The Egyptian Revolution in 2011 showed how new media—from citizen journalism to social media—can empower citizens. The Egyptian government shut down Internet access and cell phone service in an effort to keep the protesters from organizing and publicizing their cause.

news analysis from newspapers nationwide. By including links to columns by ideological liberals, moderates, conservatives, and libertarians, such sites highlight the diversity of political news online. Such a vast array of voices, of course, means that online sources also can provide questionable information, misinformation, or outright lies—just as can happen in mainstream media and even presidential debates. To verify media reports found in both traditional and online media, there are new websites, such as FactCheck.org and PolitiFact.com, devoted exclusively to checking the veracity of political claims.

Decentralization and Local News A long-standing concern of scholars of traditional media has been the "nationalization of the news" that results when most political news emanates from inside the Washington, D.C., Beltway, to the detriment of local news coverage. Ten years ago the dominance of national wire services, such as the Associated Press, and budget constraints by local newspapers resulted in a dearth of relevant local news reporting. As the seat of national government, Washington has been the focus for traditional print and television media. New media have decentered the political news. In 2010 the Pew Research Center's Project for Excellence in Journalism found that many traditional national news outlets were in irreversible decline, and when unavoidable belt-tightening meant cuts in overall staff numbers and news-gathering bureaus, the first to go were often the D.C. offices. NBC and CBS cut their Washington bureaus by 50 percent over the past five years, while the number of newspaper reporters based in Washington bureaus declined by 50 percent.[33] And many newspapers, including the *Chicago Tribune* and the *Los Angeles Times*, closed their Washington bureaus altogether. While the cost to traditional journalism is apparent, the decentralization of online news may have a silver lining resulting in a revival of local news coverage. Online local newspapers; blogs; city and local government websites and Facebook pages; community newsletters; email listservs; social media; and other new sources have made local news and local political news more available than in previous decades. Almost every city government has a Facebook page and website, which publish news and events, as well as offer services. A 2011 survey from the Pew Internet and American Life found 67 percent of American adult Internet users had visited a local, state, or federal government website; over 50 percent of Americans use the Internet to get community or neighborhoods news.[34] Readily available local news coverage may engage citizens in politics in their communities.

Concerns about Online News

While online news holds significant promise for improving access to the political information citizens need, the shift toward online media has also given rise to several major concerns. These potential disadvantages include a decline in investigative journalism, uneven quality in news content, and negative effects on knowledge and tolerance.

Loss of Investigative Power In a democracy, the press is expected to be a watchdog for the people and to inform citizens about government abuses of power. Stated another way, democracies depend upon news organizations to inform the people about current events and to help citizens hold their leaders accountable for their actions. The greatest challenge for contemporary news organizations is to generate enough revenue to finance traditional investigative journalism.[35] This activity requires more time and resources than other aspects of the news, and it may be the most important. When readers paid subscription fees to read the news, circulation was high and advertising provided sufficient revenue to allow newspapers and, later, broadcasters to cover both basic news (weather, sports, business) and political events. Revenue from publishing basic news would subsidize political analysis and investigative journalism. By breaking apart mainstream news organizations, online news may actually reduce the media's ability to engage in the kind of sustained, in-depth reporting that is critical to the media's watchdog role and thus to the health of American democracy.

More Variation in the Quality of News As already noted, the growing diversity of online news has led to substantial variation in the quality of available information. Multiple perspectives certainly do provide citizens with a well-stocked marketplace of ideas, but the freewheeling nature of the Internet also means that hate speech, unsubstantiated rumors, and outdated information can overwhelm thoughtful, original, and civic-oriented voices. And while viral media may elevate the watchdog function of the media, the misinformation and unsubstantiated rumors that are part of viral media can substitute for objective truth as claims are widely repeated. This is especially so in anonymous online forums, where sexism and racism can be freely communicated in unedited form. Political scientist Dianne Bystrom has noted that "the online universe of political commentary operates outside traditional media editorial boundaries and is sometimes incisive but often offensive and unsubstantiated."[36]

Political candidates and political leaders are particularly susceptible to attack when negative stories go viral and spread quickly without the traditional media filters of fact-checking and respect for the privacy of public figures. This can have real consequences; for example, scholars have found that Hillary Clinton's 2008 presidential campaign was hurt by negative and arguably sexist discussion on the blogs.[37] False rumors that President Obama was not a natural-born citizen and therefore not eligible to be president under Article II of the U.S. Constitution spread rapidly on the Internet and spilled over into mainstream news. These "birther movement" conspiracy theories, promoted by real estate tycoon Donald Trump and his allies, alleged that Obama was born in Kenya, not Hawaii, or that his birth certificate was a forgery. Extensive media coverage of the birther movement allowed what many viewed as an attack against a sitting president to become the nation's headline news, something that may not have occurred in a pre-Internet era. Belief in these theories has persisted, despite Obama's pre-election release of his official long-form birth certificate from Hawaii in 2008, the posting of a copy of his birth certificate online, and confirmation by the Hawaii Department of Health based on the original documents. The birther movement is an example of a story that went viral based on claims that were proven to be untrue. (See Chapter 6 for a related discussion.)

Another case of viral media occurred when Penn State assistant football coach Jerry Sandusky was charged by a grand jury of 67 counts of child sexual abuse involving up to a dozen victims. More than 10,000 stories appeared in Google News each day for weeks as a member of America's iconic Big Ten football program was charged with an egregious crime against a number of youths and university officials were accused of not protecting children from violence. The fury caused the ouster of Hall of Fame football coach Joe Paterno and the school's longtime president. While a court would eventually determine Sandusky's innocence or guilt, viral media created a tsunami of media coverage, increasing the importance of the media in politics and society. As Sandusky's lawyer complained, "my client has been tried in the court of public opinion."[38] The implication is that Sandusky's reputation was ruined by the viral mass media even before he was convicted in a court of law.

Potential Effects on Knowledge and Tolerance Perhaps the greatest concern about politics in the digital age goes to the heart of modern democracy: Do online media ultimately help or hinder progress toward the ideal of a well-informed citizenry that can govern itself effectively? One study has found that while readers of online news from major websites (largely offshoots of the traditional print and broadcast media) are more knowledgeable than average citizens, those who get their political news mainly from blogs are actually worse off.[39] And the very diversity of online news, in fact, may actually *lower* tolerance for social and political diversity. Most new media do not abide by traditional media's principle of objective

Some online news sources like Politico.com have developed a reputation for accuracy and professionalism. Here, a Politico reporter talks with Treasury Secretary Timothy Geithner. However, the quality of information from many online news sources varies and isn't always reliable.

journalism, in which both sides of an argument are reported. Instead, the specialization of information online and on cable television means that liberals and conservatives alike can turn to specialized websites and television channels that cater to their underlying assumptions and that avoid exposing readers/viewers to information that might challenge their preconceived beliefs. Online news outlets, for their part, serve certain self-selected groups and are unlikely to cover stories that do not conform to what that group wants to hear.[40] Even the active nature of the online experience can contribute to the "balkanization," or compartmentalization, of the electorate. On the Internet, an individual must seek out information, compared with the passive process of simply watching or listening to television.[41] The natural tendency to select online news that conforms with our own beliefs is exacerbated by the way search engines cater to our individual preferences—what one scholar has called the "filter bubble," which screens out exposure to information that might challenge or broaden our worldview.[42]

The undeniable benefits and possibilities created by digital media for the American political process may well outweigh these concerns about accuracy, reliability, ethical practices, and depth of reporting. If the new media are to realize their potential as a boon to informed democratic participation, citizens must have "information literacy," or the ability to find, evaluate, and apply information.[43] Greater access to information online makes education and critical thinking among citizens more important than ever before.

● Mass Media Ownership

Describe trends in who owns mass media companies

Ironically, and in sharp contrast to the immense diversity in online news sources, the second most significant trend in America's largely unregulated media system is the growing concentration in ownership of traditional media. The popularity of online news may in part be a response to the growing homogenization of traditional corporate media that has been occurring over the last three decades.

The United States boasts approximately 1,400 daily newspapers, 2,000 television stations, and more than 13,000 radio stations (20 percent of which are devoted to news, talk, or public affairs). Despite these substantial numbers overall, the number of traditional news-gathering sources operating nationally is actually quite small—several wire services, four broadcast networks, public radio and television, two elite newspapers, three newsmagazines, and a smattering of other sources, such as the national correspondents of a few large local papers and several small, independent radio networks. More than three-fourths of the daily newspapers in the United States are owned by large media conglomerates such as the Hearst, McClatchy, and Gannett corporations. Much of the national news that is published by local newspapers is provided by one wire service, the Associated Press, while additional coverage is provided by services run by several major newspapers, including the *New York Times* and the *Chicago Tribune*. More than 500 of the nation's television stations are affiliated with one of the four networks and carry that network's evening news programs. Dozens of others carry PBS (Public Broadcasting System) news. Several hundred local radio stations also carry network news or National Public Radio news broadcasts.

At the same time, though, there are only three truly national newspapers: the *Wall Street Journal*, the *Christian Science Monitor*, and *USA Today*; two other papers, the *New York Times* and the *Washington Post*, are read by political leaders and other influential Americans throughout the nation. National news is also carried to millions of Americans by the newsmagazine *Time*, though it is declining in readership. Beginning in the late 1980s, CNN became another major news source for Americans, especially after its coverage of the Persian Gulf War. However, the number of news sources—those doing actual news-gathering, not simply relying on news reporting by others—has remained essentially the same, or has declined. Some of the most popular online news outlets are electronic versions of the conventional print or broadcast media.

The trend toward less variety in traditional media has been accelerated by changes in media ownership, which became possible in large part due to the relaxation of government regulations in the 1980s and '90s. The enactment of the 1996 Telecommunications Act opened the way for additional consolidation in the media industry, and a wave of mergers and consolidations has further reduced the field of independent media across the country. For example, the Australian press baron Rupert Murdoch owns the Fox network plus a host of radio, television, and newspaper properties around the world, known collectively as News Corporation, the world's second-largest media conglomerate. In 2007, Murdoch won control of the *Wall Street Journal*, consolidating his position as one of the world's most powerful publishers. News Corporation owns 800 media companies in more than 50 countries and has a net worth of $5 billion. A small number of giant corporations now control a wide swath of media holdings, including television networks, movie studios, record companies, cable channels and local cable providers, book publishers, magazines, and newspapers. Clear Channel Communications, for example, a Texas-based media conglomerate, owns 850 radio stations—by far the largest number controlled by a single company. These developments have prompted questions about whether enough competition exists among the media to produce a truly diverse set of views on political and corporate matters, or even whether the United States has become a prisoner of media monopolies.[44]

As major newspapers, television stations, and radio networks fall into fewer and fewer hands, the risk increases that politicians and citizens who express less-popular or minority viewpoints will have difficulty finding a public forum. Examples include 2012 Republican presidential candidate Ron Paul, who despite favorable showing in early nominating events, such as the Iowa caucuses and the New Hampshire primary, received little national media coverage because his libertarian ideas were outside the mainstream of his political party. **Media monopolies** may also be a reason for the relatively scant mainstream media coverage of the Occupy Wall Street protests, which have sought to bring attention to the issue of income inequality. (See Chapter 8 for more discussion of the Occupy movement.) The mainstream media are often committed to the status quo, which is why they were less enthusiastic about the Occupy protests or, at the other end of the political spectrum, the Tea Party. Increasingly, these groups turn to the Internet to express their views. The Internet is an important mechanism for linking communities of adherents, but can it mitigate traditional media's homogeneous point of view in terms of what constitutes news coverage, or its treatment of opinions that challenge the status quo? Can the diversity of media sources available online, including blogs and social media, help balance the corporate concentration of media ownership?

for critical analysis

In recent years, a number of major media corporations have acquired numerous newspapers, television stations, and radio properties. Is media concentration a serious problem? Why or why not?

media monopoly the ownership and control of the media by a few large corporations

One negative consequence of media concentration may be a steadily growing distrust of the press. Jonathan Ladd argues that from the 1950s through the 1970s, competition in American party politics and the media industry reached historic lows.[45] When competition later intensified in both of these realms, the public's distrust of the institutional media grew, leading the public to resist the mainstream press's reporting about policy outcomes and to turn toward alternative partisan media outlets—those expressly favored by Republicans or Democrats. As a result, public opinion and voting behavior are now increasingly shaped by partisan media, such as Fox News on the right and MSNBC on the left. While it is impossible to suppress party and media competition in the twenty-first century, and certainly not in a new media environment, Ladd argues that we need new ways to augment the public's political knowledge. In an age of digital media having uneven and unpredictable quality, it is more important than ever for citizens to find, evaluate, and apply information.

● Media Influence

Analyze the ways the media can influence public opinion and politics

The content and character of news and public affairs programming—what the media choose to present and how they present it—can have far-reaching political consequences. The media can shape and modify, if not fully form, the public's perception of events, issues, and institutions. Media coverage can rally support for, or intensify opposition to, national policies on matters as weighty as health care, the economy, or international wars. Media disclosures can greatly enhance, or fatally damage, the careers of public figures, as discussed earlier. At the same time, the media are influenced by the individuals or groups who are subjects of the news. The president, in particular, has the power to set the news agenda through speeches and actions. All politicians, for that matter, seek to shape or manipulate their media images by cultivating good relations with reporters and through news leaks and staged news events.

In recent American political history, the media have played a central role in many major events. For example, the media were a critically important factor in the civil rights movement of the 1950s and '60s. Television images showing peaceful civil rights marchers attacked by club-swinging police helped to generate sympathy among northern whites for the civil rights struggle and greatly increased the pressure on Congress to bring an end to segregation.[46] To take a second example, the media were instrumental in compelling the Nixon administration to negotiate an end to American involvement in the Vietnam War. Beginning in 1967 the national media, reacting in part to a shift in elite opinion, portrayed the war as misguided and unwinnable, and as a result helped turn popular sentiment against continued American involvement.[47]

The media were also central actors in the Watergate affair, the cluster of scandals that ultimately forced President Richard Nixon, the landslide victor in the 1972 presidential election, to resign from office in disgrace just two years later. A relentless series of investigations launched by the *Washington Post*, the *New York Times*, and the television networks led to disclosures of the various abuses of which Nixon was guilty, ultimately forcing him to choose between resignation and almost certain impeachment.

During the 1960s, civil rights protesters learned a variety of techniques designed to elicit sympathetic media coverage. Television images of police brutality in Alabama led directly to the enactment of the 1965 Civil Rights Act.

More recently, the media were crucial actors in the U.S. decision to invade Iraq in March 2003, despite the fact that Iraq had not invaded a neighboring country or attacked the United States. In the wake of the September 11 terrorist attacks, harsh media coverage of Iraqi leader Saddam Hussein, combined with White House claims that Iraq was harboring weapons of mass destruction (WMDs), led 70 percent of Americans to approve of the invasion of Iraq. (It was later determined that, in fact, Iraq did not have any WMDs. The news media, including the *New York Times*, issued a public apology to readers for some of its coverage of claims of Iraqi WMDs.) The Pew Research Center reported in a 2003 survey that individuals getting the news from mainstream American media were more supportive of the Iraq invasion, while those relying on foreign news coverage, political comedy shows, or online news were more likely to oppose the invasion.

Conservatives have long charged that the liberal biases of reporters and journalists result in distorted news coverage.[48] A 2004 survey conducted by the Pew Research Center found that 34 percent of national news reporters identified themselves as liberal, whereas only 7 percent said they were conservative.[49] While journalists may lean in a Democratic direction, journalists generally defend their professionalism, insisting that their personal political leanings do not affect the way they perform their jobs. Moreover, those who decry "the liberal media" seldom acknowledge the partisan or ideological leanings of media

for critical **analysis**

To what extent, do you think, are the media biased? As more news sources have become available, has this led to more or less bias in the media?

owners. Rupert Murdoch, the CEO of News Corporation (the parent company of Fox News and the *Wall Street Journal*), is a politically active conservative. Philip Anschutz, owner of the *Examiner* newspapers in San Francisco, Washington, and other cities, has been a major financial contributor to the Republican Party and to GOP candidates, including George W. Bush. As discussed in detail in the previous section, the diversity of online news sources, however, may mean that debates about liberal or conservative bias in the mainstream media are becoming less important.

How the Media Influence Politics

Traditional and new media influence American politics in a number of important ways.[50] The power of all media collectively, both traditional and online, lies in their ability to shape what issues Americans think about (agenda setting) and what opinions Americans hold about those issues (framing and priming).

agenda setting the power of the media to bring public attention to particular issues and problems

Agenda Setting and Selection Bias The first source of media power is **agenda setting**; that is, the media help to set the agenda for political discussion. Agenda setting involves identifying the issues that will receive attention by the media, which means that some things are deemed important while others are not. Groups and forces that wish to bring their ideas before the public in order to generate support for policy proposals or political candidacies must secure media coverage. If the media are persuaded that an idea is newsworthy, then they may declare it an "issue" that must be confronted or a "problem" to be solved, thus clearing the first hurdle in the policy-making process. If, on the other hand, an idea lacks or loses media appeal, its chance of resulting in new programs or policies is diminished.

After September 11, President George W. Bush had little difficulty convincing the media that terrorism and his administration's efforts to forestall further terrorist attacks merited a dominant place on the national agenda. Not surprisingly, the American-led military campaigns in Afghanistan and Iraq dominated the news throughout 2002 and 2003. Some stories have such overwhelming significance that

In April 2004, 60 Minutes II's broadcast of the story of American soldiers' abuse of Iraqi inmates at Abu Ghraib prison was seen around the world. Initial efforts by the Bush administration to contain the Abu Ghraib scandal and limit the blame to a handful of soldiers failed.

the main concern of political leaders is not whether a story will receive attention—wars and natural disasters always receive attention—but whether the leaders themselves will figure prominently and positively in media accounts. This was certainly true in 2005, when Hurricane Katrina struck the Gulf Coast. There was no question that this storm and the damage it caused would be on the national agenda; the question was how the press and the public would apportion blame and credit. As the story took shape, the media found little to praise in the belated, haphazard emergency and relief efforts. Local, state, and national leaders were all faulted for the region's lack of preparedness and a botched relief plan, with the Bush administration and the Federal Emergency Management Agency (FEMA) receiving the largest share of blame for these failures In 2008 and 2009 the news agenda was dominated by the global financial crisis and the severe economic recession that ensued. Continuing media attention created enormous pressure for the government to "do something" even as the crisis began to ease, and the new Obama administration's "honeymoon period" was cut short by public frustration over the government's inability to solve economic problems quickly. In 2010 the media's focus on a massive oil spill in the Gulf of Mexico contributed to widespread anger at the Obama administration's seeming helplessness to contain the environmental disaster.

In many instances, the media serve as conduits for agenda-setting efforts by competing groups and forces. Occasionally, however, journalists themselves are instrumental in setting the agenda of political discussion. The Watergate scandal that destroyed Nixon's presidency was in some measure initiated and driven by the *Washington Post* and the national television networks.

Because the media are businesses, and because the media seek to attract the largest possible audiences, they naturally tend to cover stories with dramatic or entertainment value, giving less attention to important stories that are less compelling. News coverage often focuses on crimes and scandals, especially those involving prominent individuals. This **selection bias** means that the media may provide less information about important political issues that the public depends upon. For example, the Democratic partisan predisposition of many journalists did not prevent a media frenzy in January 1998 when reports surfaced that President Clinton (a Democrat) might have had an affair with a White House intern. It was the Republicans' turn in 2012 when the extramarital affairs of presidential candidates Herman Cain and Newt Gingrich made headlines. Partisanship and ideology notwithstanding, the age-old journalistic instinct for sensational stories to tell often trumps both the media's responsibility to inform the public about what really matters and the public's responsibility to demand that from the media.

What the mainstream media decide to report on and what they ignore has important implications. For example, the mainstream media published few stories critical of the U.S. invasion of Iraq leading up to the war in March 2003. As of 2012, the Iraq and Afghanistan wars have cost an estimated $3 trillion, with more than 6,000 American troops killed and 46,000 wounded in Iraq and Afghanistan, not to mention the hundreds of thousands of citizens of these two nations who have been killed or wounded. Both wars lasted far longer than predicted. Similarly, the press shied away from other controversial topics, including the government's failure to close the Guantánamo Bay prison camp, where suspected terrorist and alleged Al Qaeda personnel have been held without a trial since 2002. In 2009, President Obama gave orders for the detention camp to be closed by 2010, but as of 2012 the camp remains open. The media provided little coverage of the Bush tax cuts in 2001, although they dramatically increased the federal budget deficit and widened the gap between the

selection bias (news) the tendency to focus news coverage on only on aspect of an event or issue, avoiding coverage of over aspects

AMERICA IN THE WORLD

What the Media Tell Americans about the World and the World about America

It is often said that we live in an age of "globalization," when events anywhere in the world affect everyone in the world. Nevertheless, the American news media are surprisingly parochial in their orientation. Few news organizations have foreign bureaus or foreign correspondents. Indeed, in the face of globalization, the number of foreign bureaus operated by major news organizations has actually decreased. One veteran CBS reporter, Tom Fenton, said that when he joined the network in 1970, "I was one of three correspondents in the Rome bureau. We had bureaus in Paris, Bonn, Warsaw, Cairo, and Nairobi. Now you can count the number of foreign correspondents on two hands and have three fingers left over."[a] Despite vital American interests in the Middle East, most reporters know very little about the history, culture, and languages of the region. U.S. correspondents sent to cover the Iraq war could not speak directly with Iraqis or understand Arabic news media.[b]

On a typical Sunday, most major American newspapers devote roughly 20 percent of their news coverage to international events. It is interesting to note that the bulk of the international news featured in these papers involved war, terrorism, and political violence. To the extent that Americans derive their understanding of the world from the newspapers, they might reasonably see much of it as a very dangerous place.

However, before we dismiss the American news media as parochial, we should compare U.S. coverage of international events with that presented on the same day by one of the world's oldest and most famous newspapers, *The Times* of London. *The Times* did, indeed, devote a considerably greater portion of its news coverage to international events than did the American newspapers. Slightly more than 44 percent of the stories in *The Times* focused on world affairs—twice the percentage found in the typical American paper.

The Times and other international newspapers devote enormous attention to the United States because America's economic and military power mean that American actions are likely to have important consequences throughout the world. In their news pages and editorial commentary, newspapers in Europe, Asia, Africa, Latin America, and the Middle East seek to dissect American policy to understand its intentions and significance for their own nations. Often, this coverage is less than flattering, even when American policy appears to be successful. Most European newspapers were sharply critical of the Bush administration's decision to go to war against Iraq without UN approval, and, in 2009 the president of the Czech Republic, which held the six-month rotating presidency of the European Union, called the Obama administration's economic policies "a road to Hell" that would cause global inflation. However, not all foreign news coverage of U.S. politics is critical.

[a]Michael Massing, "The Unseen War," *New York Review of Books,* May 29, 2003, p. 17.
[b]Massing, "Unseen War," p. 17.

for critical analysis

1. In 2004, American news coverage of the abuse of Iraqi prisoners by U.S. soldiers shocked the world. Should the American media present a more positive image of the United States to foreigners?

2. American newspapers offer more coverage of local events than of world affairs. What factors might explain the local focus of the American press?

super rich and most other Americans in terms of wealth.[51] Access to the print and broadcast media is such an important political resource that political forces that lack media access, such as the Occupy Wall Street protestors, have only a very limited opportunity to influence the political process. The selection bias of traditional media run by a handful of powerful corporations, however, may be balanced out by the diversity of media sources available online, especially the growing influence of social media sites such as Twitter and Facebook.

Election campaigns are important because the officials we elect set public policy, but successful campaigners know that politics in a democracy is about not only policy issues but also spectacle and entertainment. Media coverage of election campaigns typically focuses on the "horse race" (that is, who is ahead and by how much), which sometimes deflects attention from issues and candidate records. In the year preceding the 2008 national elections, for example, it appeared that Senator Hillary Clinton was nearly certain to become the Democratic nominee. Looking for a horse race, however, the national media gave enormous publicity to Senator Barack Obama. Months of positive coverage helped transform Obama into a serious presidential contender.

Framing The language and context in which the media presents the news, known as **framing**, can determine how the American people interpret political events. Knowing this, politicians take care to choose language that presents their ideas in the most favorable light possible. Public opinion on politics naturally changes with facts, but few citizens read legislation, so when forming opinions about policy and politics, the public relies on media coverage. This means that arguments made by elected officials and other political actors, or frames, are critical to the process of forming opinions. Political elites have some (but certainly not complete) freedom to determine the dimensions along which policies will be debated, and the frames and arguments elites use can have a powerful influence on how the public evaluates not only candidates for elected office but also public policy.

For example, the Obama administration labeled its health care initiative the Patient Protection and Affordable Care Act, thus framing the proposal as a matter of compassionate responsibility and good economic sense. As the bill was debated in Congress, early press coverage framed it as "health care reform." Sensing that Americans generally approve of the idea of "reform," Republican opponents of the legislation chose language that framed it quite differently. The law's provisions for limiting excessive medical testing were labeled as "health care rationing," for example, and proposals to create committees to advise patients about end-of-life care were called "death panels." Public support for the legislation waned as media coverage gravitated to the Republicans' framing of the issues involved; the bill that barely passed in 2010 was a much-watered-down version of the original proposal.

One of the most important aspects of the 2008 election was that for the first time in American history an African American was a major party contender for the presidency of the United States. Political scientists Michael Tesler and David O. Sears found that the 2008 election was more polarized by racial attitudes than any other presidential election on record. There were two sides: racial opposition *to* Obama and racially liberal support *for* Obama. Obama's campaign was given a boost in the primaries from racial liberals that extended well beyond that usually offered to ideologically similar white candidates, such as Hillary Clinton.[52] The media coverage of the campaign reflected this, and regarded race as more significant than Hillary Clinton's bid to become the first woman to serve as president. Partly because they regarded the fact that Obama was America's first serious black

framing the power of the media to influence how events and issues are interpreted

presidential candidate as newsworthy, the media gave Obama much more attention and scrutiny than they afforded other candidates. This extra attention frequently allowed Obama to dominate the news and led his opponents constantly to charge that the media were biased in his favor. Obama was able to take advantage of the extra media attention he was given to generate popular enthusiasm for his campaign and raise tens of millions of dollars in small contributions via the Internet. By devoting enormous quantities of ink and airtime to Obama, the media were not so much exhibiting bias as reflecting what they saw as the historic importance of the story. Nevertheless, they may have contributed to Obama's presidential victory in 2008.

In the 2012 Republican presidential primaries, the media frequently framed front-runner Mitt Romney as not a "real conservative," a notion stemming either from his position as governor of Massachusetts, a northern and liberal-leaning state, or from his Mormon religion. (Evangelical Christians dominate the ranks of the strongest conservatives in the Republican Party.) This created opportunities for many Republican challengers to do better than expected in primary elections, especially Newt Gingrich and Rick Santorum. A counter media frame was that only Mitt Romney, a moderate Republican, could beat President Obama in the general election among those seeking the Republican presidential nomination, and opinion polls cited widely in the media showed the closest margin in head-to-head races between Obama and Romney in the 2012 general election. Framing Romney as able to beat President Obama may have increased support for him. The mass media framed the general election as a toss-up. Political pundits claimed that either candidate might win, predicting a 1 percent margin in the popular vote. But this widely touted media frame may have misled voters, as many pollsters predicted a decisive Obama victory. Election forecaster Nate Silver predicted an Obama win months before the election.

Priming A third important way the media can shape political events is known as **priming**, which is closely related to framing. This occurs when media coverage affects the way the public evaluates political leaders, issues, and events. Priming involves "calling attention to some matters while ignoring others."[53] Often candidate research is described as "priming" while research on political issues is called "framing." Both may examine subliminal priming of subjects using varying forms media frames. For example, media praise for President George W. Bush's speeches in the wake of the September 11, 2001, terrorist attacks prepared, or *primed*, the public to view Bush's subsequent response to terrorism in an extremely positive light, at least initially, even though some aspects of the administration's efforts, most notably the invasion of Iraq, eventually lost public support.

In the case of political candidates, the media have considerable influence over whether a particular individual will receive public attention and be taken seriously as a viable contender. Thus, if the media find a candidate interesting, they may treat him or her as a serious contender despite possible weaknesses and shortcomings. For example, in the 2012 Republican presidential primaries there were positive stories covering New Jersey governor Chris Christie as a possible candidate (though Christie ultimately did not run). Similarly, the media may report that a candidate has "momentum," a property that the media confer on candidates when they exceed the media's own expectations. After winning the 2008 Iowa caucuses in the Democratic primaries, the media declared that Barack Obama had momentum, as his fund-raising and poll numbers had exceeded early projections.[54] Nothing Hillary Clinton was able to do seemed to deprive Obama of

priming process of preparing the public to take a particular view of an event or political actor the coveted momentum the media had granted him—momentum soon becomes a feedback loop by which media attention generates public enthusiasm, which in turn garners further media attention. Republican presidential candidate Mitt Romney was anointed with "momentum" by the media in the 2012 primaries.

In 2004, controversial measures banning same-sex marriage were placed on 13 statewide ballots as referenda by Republican state lawmakers or as initiatives by conservative interest groups sympathetic to the Republican Party. All 13 ballot measures were approved by voters. The well-coordinated, high-profile campaigns urging passage of the measures garnered extensive media coverage in these states and may have primed citizens to vote for the Republican presidential incumbent, George W. Bush. One study found that citizens residing in one of the states with such ballot measures were more likely to rank the issue of gay marriage as very important in the presidential election, tracking a higher volume of media coverage, compared with voters in the 37 states that didn't vote on this issue. When evaluating the 2004 presidential candidates, voters in these 13 states who believed that the issue of same-sex marriage was very important were more likely to vote for the Republican candidate. The research suggests that the ballot measures on a same-sex-marriage ban may have helped re-elect President Bush in the 2004 election.[55]

Media coverage of ballot measures can benefit Democratic candidates in much the same way. In 2006 coordinated ballot-measure campaigns in six states to raise the minimum wage were successful in modifying support for the policy among partisan subsamples (with Democrats becoming more likely and Republicans less likely to support the measure), thus increasing the saliency of the economy as an issue in general among these targeted populations, and priming support for Democratic candidates for Congress and governor.[56]

In the 2012 primaries, positive media attention gave Mitt Romney momentum, helping him secure the Republican presidential nomination.

● News Coverage

News coverage, or the content of the news, includes information and leaks to the press. Such media leaks are key for investigative journalism, as are press releases and the tradition of adversarial journalism.

Media Leaks

leak a disclosure of confidential information to the news media

The media may also report information that is leaked by government officials. A **leak** is the disclosure of confidential information to the news media. Leaks may emanate from a variety of sources, including "whistle-blowers," lower-level officials who hope to publicize what they view as their bosses' or the government's improper activities. In 1971, for example, a minor Defense Department staffer named Daniel Ellsberg sought to discredit official justifications for America's involvement in Vietnam by leaking top-secret documents to the press. The "Pentagon Papers"—the Defense Department's own secret history of the war, differing widely from the Pentagon's public pronouncements—were published by the *New York Times* and the *Washington Post* after the U.S. Supreme Court ruled that the government could not block their release.[57] Pentagon credibility was severely damaged, hastening the erosion of public support for the war. In 2005, President George W. Bush was infuriated when he learned that a still-unidentified source, presumed to be a whistle-blower, had leaked information concerning the president's secret orders authorizing the National Security Agency to conduct clandestine, warrantless surveillance of suspected terrorists. Bush ordered the Justice Department to launch a probe of the leak. In 2006 another unidentified source leaked part of a secret intelligence summary that seemed to contradict the administration's claims of progress in the war in Iraq. In 2009 a leak to journalist Bob Woodward embarrassed the Pentagon by revealing General Stanley McChrystal's secret report to the president on the failures of American military efforts in Afghanistan.

Most leaks, though, originate not with low-level whistle-blowers but rather with senior government officials, prominent politicians, and political activists. These individuals cultivate long-term relationships with journalists to whom they regularly leak confidential information, knowing that it is likely to be published on a priority basis in a form acceptable to them. In turn, of course, journalists are likely to regard high-level sources of confidential information as valuable assets whose favor must be retained. For example, during the George W. Bush administration, Lewis "Scooter" Libby, Vice President Dick Cheney's chief of staff, was apparently such a valuable source of leaks to so many journalists that his name was seldom even mentioned in the newspapers, despite his prominence in Washington and his importance as a decision maker.[58] Further, the more that recipients of leaked information strive to keep their sources secret, the more difficulty other journalists will have in checking that information's validity.

Through such tacit alliances with journalists, prominent figures can manipulate news coverage and secure the publication of stories that serve their purposes. One recent case that revealed the complexities of this culture of leaks was the 2005 Valerie Plame affair. Plame was an undercover CIA analyst who happened to be married to Joseph Wilson, a prominent career diplomat. Wilson had angered the

In 2010 and 2011, WikiLeaks published thousands of classified documents after they were leaked by Bradley Manning (center). As a member of the military, Manning was tried for breaking the laws related to how classified information is handled. However, many observers debated whether WikiLeaks broke the law by publishing the documents.

Bush White House by publicly questioning the president's stated rationales for threatening the invasion of Iraq. In an apparent effort to discredit Wilson, one or more administration officials informed prominent journalists that Plame had improperly used her position to help Wilson. In so doing, these officials may have violated a federal statute prohibiting disclosure of the identities of covert intelligence operatives. The subsequent investigation revealed that the story had been leaked to several journalists, including the *Washington Post*'s Bob Woodward, who did not use it, and the *New York Times*'s Judith Miller, who did. Miller initially refused to name her source and spent several weeks in jail for contempt of court. When Miller was finally compelled to testify before a federal grand jury looking into the leak, Scooter Libby was charged with having been the source of the leak, though it later emerged that the leak had actually come from a former State Department official, Richard Armitage. The leak in the Plame case came to light only because it was illegal. Thousands of other leaks each year are quietly and seamlessly incorporated into the news.

New technology and online media have taken the cat-and-mouse game of leaks to a new level. WikiLeaks, an independent nonprofit organization dedicated to publishing classified information, posts leaked documents to its website and uses an anonymous drop-box system so leakers cannot be identified. In recent years, WikiLeaks has released thousands of secret government documents involving instances of government corruption, war crimes in Afghanistan and Iraq, torture at the Guantánamo Bay detention camp, and numerous embarrassing private communiqués sent by U.S. diplomats abroad. WikiLeaks also shares its treasure trove of leaked government documents with major international papers, including the *New York Times*. In July 2007, gunners aboard two U.S. Army helicopters killed over a dozen people, including two Reuters news staffers, in the Iraqi suburb of New Baghdad. When Reuters subsequently learned that the U.S. military had video footage of the attack, it tried to obtain the video through the Freedom of Information Act, but without success. The video was leaked to WikiLeaks, however, which released it in April 2010. Shot through an Apache helicopter gunsight, the video clearly shows the slaying of a wounded Reuters employee and his would-be rescuers; it led to a worldwide storm of condemnation of U.S. military action in the Iraq War.

Critics of WikiLeaks argue that posting government documents online is not journalism, that governments must have some secrets, and that the release of some government documents may jeopardize American soldiers and their local allies by revealing their identities. The whistle-blower behind the Pentagon Papers, Daniel Ellsberg, and many others, including Congressman Ron Paul and Salon's Glenn Greenwald, defend WikiLeaks, arguing that it has played a vital role in informing the public of government wrongdoings.

Press Releases

Also seamlessly incorporated into daily news reports each year are thousands of press releases—stories written by advocates or publicists and distributed to the media in the hope that journalists will publish them, under their own bylines, with little or no revision. The originator of the press release, or news release, was a well-known New York public-relations consultant named Ivy Lee. In 1906 a train operated by one of Lee's clients, the Pennsylvania Railroad, was involved in a serious wreck. Lee quickly wrote a story about the accident that presented the railroad in a favorable light, and he distributed the account to reporters. Many papers published Lee's slanted story as their own objective account of events, and the railroad's reputation for quality and safety remained untarnished.

Consistent with Lee's example, today's press release presents facts and perspectives that serve an advocate's interests but is written in a way that mimics the factual news style of the paper, periodical, or television news program to which the press release has been sent. A well-designed press release can be nearly impossible to distinguish from an actual news story. Newspapers, of course, understand that, in publishing press releases, they are allowing themselves to be used, but they have a strong financial incentive to publish material that, in effect, allows them to fill their pages at little cost. The White House regularly issues press releases—for example, in preparation for a State of the Union address or major legislation supported by the president. Polling companies, such as Gallup, use press releases to share the results of election surveys.

The capacity of news subjects to influence the news is hardly unlimited. Media consultants and issues managers may shape the news for a time, but it is generally not difficult for the media to penetrate the smoke screens thrown up by news sources if they have a reason to do so. Thus, for example, despite the Obama administration's media management, press accounts of continuing U.S. casualties in Afghanistan, coupled with stories about the corruption and incompetence of the Afghan government, forced the White House to declare in 2009 that America's commitment to Afghanistan was not open-ended and to indicate that there would be a timetable for the withdrawal of American forces from that country.

for critical analysis

Before he left office in June 2007, the long-time British prime minister Tony Blair called the news media a "feral beast." Why are many politicians hostile to media? Do you share their views?

Adversarial Journalism

The political power of the news media vis-à-vis the government has greatly increased in recent years through the growing prominence of "adversarial journalism," a form of reporting in which the media adopt a skeptical or even hostile posture toward the government and public officials.

During the nineteenth century, American newspapers were subordinate to the political parties. Newspapers depended on official patronage (legal notices and party subsidies) for their financial survival and were controlled by party leaders.

(A vestige of that era survived into the twentieth century in such newspaper names as the *Springfield Republican* and the *St. Louis Globe-Democrat*.) At the turn of the twentieth century, with the development of commercial advertising, newspapers became financially independent, making possible the emergence of a formally non-partisan press.

Presidents were the first national officials to make use of the opportunities presented by this development. By communicating directly to the electorate through newspapers and magazines, Theodore Roosevelt and Woodrow Wilson established political constituencies for themselves, independent of party organizations, and thereby strengthened their own power relative to that of Congress. President Franklin Delano Roosevelt used the radio, most notably in his famous fireside chats, to reach out to voters throughout the nation and to make himself the center of American political life. Roosevelt was also adept at developing close personal relationships with reporters, which enabled him to obtain favorable news coverage despite the fact that, in his day, a majority of newspaper owners and publishers were staunch conservatives. Following Roosevelt's example, subsequent presidents have all sought to use the media to enhance their popularity and power. John F. Kennedy, for example, used televised news conferences to mobilize public support for his domestic and foreign policy initiatives.

During the 1950s and early 1960s a few members of Congress also made successful use of the media, especially television, to mobilize national support for their causes. Senator Joseph McCarthy of Wisconsin made himself a powerful national figure through his well-publicized investigations of alleged Communist infiltration of key American institutions. However, through the mid-1960s, the executive branch continued to generate the bulk of news coverage, and the media became a cornerstone of presidential power.

The Vietnam War shattered this amicable relationship between the press and the presidency. During the early stages of U.S. involvement, American

This famous photograph of the aftermath of a napalm attack was one of many media images that shaped the American public's views on the Vietnam War. Media accounts critical of the war helped to turn public opinion against it and hastened the withdrawal of American troops.

officials in Vietnam who disapproved of the way the war was being conducted leaked to reporters information critical of administrative policy. Publication of this material infuriated the White House, which pressured publishers to block its release—on one occasion, President Kennedy went so far as to ask the *New York Times* to reassign its Saigon correspondent. However, the national broadcast media and especially the two leading national newspapers, the *Washington Post* and the *New York Times*, discovered an audience for critical coverage and investigative reporting among segments of the public skeptical of administration policy. As the Vietnam War dragged on, adverse media coverage fanned antiwar sentiment. Moreover, growing opposition to the war among liberals encouraged some members of Congress to break with the White House, by then occupied by Lyndon Johnson. In turn, these shifts in popular and congressional sentiment emboldened journalists and publishers to continue to present news reports critical of the war. Gradually a generation of journalists developed a commitment to adversarial journalism, and a constituency emerged that would rally to the defense of the media whenever it came under attack from the White House.

This pattern persisted through the 1970s and into the 1980s. Political forces opposed to presidential policies, along with many members of Congress and the national news media, began to find that their interests often overlapped. Opponents of the Nixon, Carter, Reagan, and Bush administrations welcomed news accounts detailing the failures of executive agencies and officials involved with U.S. conduct abroad and domestic matters such as race relations, the environment, and regulatory policy. In addition, many senators and representatives found it politically advantageous to champion causes favored by the antiwar, consumer, or environmental movements because, by conducting televised hearings on such issues, they were able to mobilize national constituencies, become national figures, and, in a number of instances, become serious contenders for their party's presidential nomination.

As for the national media, aggressive use of the techniques of investigation, publicity, and exposure allowed them to enhance their autonomy and carve out a prominent place for themselves in American government and politics. Without aggressive media coverage, would we have known of Bill Clinton's extramarital affair or of the illegal break-in to the Democratic Party headquarters in the Watergate Building by Nixon's "Committee to Re-elect the President" and the White House's subsequent cover-up of the scandal? Without aggressive media coverage, would important questions be raised about the conduct of American foreign and domestic policy, including drone attacks, torture, and civil liberty violations? It is easy to criticize the media for their aggressive tactics, but would our democracy function effectively without the critical role of the press? Independent media are needed as the watchdogs of American politics.

Of course, in October 2001 the adversarial relationship between the government and the media was at least temporarily transformed into a much more supportive association as the media helped rally the American people for the fight against terrorism. The *Washington Post* and the *New York Times* were complicit with the government in the buildup to the Iraq War in 2003, publishing few stories critical of the invasion. Since the September 11 terrorist attacks, the mainstream media and the government have at times prevented the release of information that may have been damaging to U.S. foreign policy. Adversarial journalism waned in the surge of "patriotism" following the September 11 terrorist attacks when it was considered unpatriotic to oppose President Bush's response to the attacks, including the war on terrorism. The adversarial relationship between the government and segments of the press partially resumed in the wake of the 2003 Iraq War. The

LIVE

DAVID BLOOM
WITH THE THIRD INFANTRY DIVISION
IN IRAQ
LITY ▲ NOW ON MSNBC.COM: U.S. STEPS UP NBC.

Prior to the Iraq War, the Bush administration invited more than one hundred news correspondents and photographers to accompany American forces into battle. These "embedded" journalists developed considerable rapport with the soldiers and provided generally sympathetic war coverage.

same newspapers that had been largely uncritical of the U.S. invasion (for example, the *Washington Post* and the *New York Times*) castigated President Bush for going to war without the support of some of America's major allies. When American forces failed to uncover evidence that Iraq possessed WMDs—a major reason cited by the administration for launching the war—these newspapers intimated that the war had been based on intelligence failures, if not outright presidential deceptions.

New media has ushered in a new watchdog of government wrongdoing. The release of confidential government documents by WikiLeaks showed the world that the American government and press (including the *New York Times*) sometimes concealed news, including war crimes against civilians and the use of torture by American forces. One advantage of new media is that they are less likely to be co-opted by the government, as WikiLeaks is not dependent on the U.S. government in terms of regulation or taxation. A website controlled by an Australian citizen, with Web servers in many nations worldwide, including Iceland, WikiLeaks is indicative of the lawless environment that now characterizes the new media, and of how the new media are challenging even traditional media, taking the adversarial role of the press to new heights.

● Regulation of the Media

Trace the evolution of rules that govern broadcast media

In many countries, such as China, the government exercises strict control over traditional media content. In others, the government owns the broadcast media (for example, the BBC in Britain) but does not tell the media what to say.

In the United States, the print and online media are essentially free from government interference. The broadcast media, on the other hand, are subject to federal regulation. American radio and television are regulated by the Federal Communications Commission (FCC), an independent agency established in 1934. Radio and TV stations must have FCC licenses, which must be renewed every five years. Licensing provides a mechanism for allocating radio and TV frequencies in order to prevent broadcasts from interfering with and garbling one another. License renewals are almost always granted automatically by the FCC. Indeed, renewal requests are now filed by postcard.

Through regulations prohibiting obscenity, indecency, and profanity, the FCC has also sought to prohibit radio and television stations from airing explicit sexual and excretory references between 6 A.M. and 10 P.M., the hours when the audience is most likely to include children. Generally speaking, FCC regulation applies only to the over-the-air broadcast media. It does not apply to cable television, the Internet, or satellite radio. As a result, explicit sexual content and graphic language that would run afoul of the rules on broadcast television are regularly available on cable channels. This explains why "shock jock" Howard Stern moved his program to satellite radio after years of incurring fines and penalties while he was on broadcast radio. A number of bills have been introduced in recent congresses to extend the rules to apply to cable TV and satellite radio, but none has succeeded so far.

For more than 60 years, the FCC sought not only to regulate but also to promote competition in the broadcast industry, but in 1996, Congress passed the Telecommunications Act, a broad effort to end most regulations in effect since 1934. The legislation loosened restrictions on media ownership and allowed telephone companies, cable television providers, and broadcasters to compete with one another to provide telecommunication services. Following the passage of the Telecommunications Act, several mergers between telephone and cable companies and among different segments of the entertainment media produced an even greater concentration of media ownership than had been possible since regulation of the industry began in 1934.

The Telecommunications Act of 1996 included an attempt to regulate the content of material transmitted over the Internet. This law, known as the Communications Decency Act, made it illegal to make "indecent" sexual material on the Internet accessible to those under age 18. The act was immediately denounced by civil libertarians and became the subject of lawsuits. In 1997 the Supreme Court ruled that the Communications Decency Act was an unconstitutional infringement of the right to freedom of speech guaranteed by the First Amendment (see Chapter 4).

Although the government's ability to regulate the content of the Internet has been curtailed, the FCC has used its licensing power to impose several regulations that can affect the political content of radio and TV broadcasts. The first of these is the **equal time rule**, under which broadcasters must provide to candidates for the same political office equal opportunities to communicate their messages to the public. If, for example, a television station sells commercial time to a state's Republican gubernatorial candidate, it may not refuse to sell time to the Democratic candidate for the same office. Under the terms of the Telecommunications Act, during the 45 days before an election, broadcasters are required to make time available to candidates at the lowest rate charged for that time slot.

The second regulation affecting the content of broadcasts is the **right of rebuttal**, which requires that individuals be given the opportunity to respond to personal attacks. In the 1969 case of *Red Lion Broadcasting Company v. FCC*, for example, the U.S. Supreme Court upheld the FCC's determination that a radio station was required to provide a liberal author with an opportunity to respond to a conservative commentator's attack that the station had aired.[59]

equal time rule the requirement that broadcasters provide candidates for the same political office equal opportunities to communicate their messages to the public

right of rebuttal a Federal Communications Commission regulation giving individuals the right to have the opportunity to respond to personal attacks made on a radio or television broadcast

For many years, a third important federal regulation was the **fairness doctrine**. Under this rule, broadcasters who aired programs on controversial issues were required to provide time for opposing views. In 1985, however, the FCC stopped enforcing the fairness doctrine on the grounds that there were so many radio and television stations—to say nothing of newspapers and newsmagazines—that in all likelihood many different viewpoints were already being presented without each station being required to try to present all sides of every argument. Critics of this FCC decision charged, and continue to charge, that in many media markets the number of competing viewpoints is actually quite small. During the past several years, Democratic members of Congress, including Nancy Pelosi, John Kerry, and Richard Durbin, have sought to revive the fairness doctrine in response to what they see as the "unfairness" of conservative talk radio.

The rise of online media requires revising our thinking about regulation of the media, as it is more difficult—some say impossible—to regulate political content online. The United Nations recently declared that access to the Internet is a human right.[60] While this declaration came in response to threats by authoritarian governments against Internet access—the Egyptian government, for example, disabled Internet access for the entire nation during protests in 2011—the UN's position demonstrates the significance of information technology in modern life. Many authoritarian countries continue to censor the Internet, sometimes blocking the transmission of stories that contain specific terms or information from specific websites.[61] In the United States, controversy erupted in 2012 over proposed congressional legislation that would have regulated content on the Internet, commonly referred to as SOPA and PIPA. In the face of mass online protests organized by Google, Wikipedia, and thousands of technology companies and websites, congressional leaders from both parties withdrew their support for the legislation. (See Chapter 8 for further discussion.) The government does have the power to regulate the Internet if a website infringes U.S. copyright law. In January 2012 the U.S. Department of Justice shut down a website, Megaupload, that ran services for file storing and viewing. The owners of the Hong Kong–based company, in operation since 2005, were arrested on charges of copyright infringement. The U.S. government claimed it had the right to shut down the website because the company used an Internet server located in Virginia.

Federal Communications Commission (FCC) regulations prohibit obscenity, indecency, and profanity in American television and radio broadcasts. The radio personality Howard Stern incurred millions of dollars in FCC fines before moving to satellite radio, which is not regulated by the FCC.

fairness doctrine a Federal Communications Commission requirement for broadcasters who air programs on controversial issues to provide time for opposing views; the FCC ceased enforcing this doctrine in 1985

● Thinking Critically about Digital Citizens, the Media, and Democracy

The free media comprise an institution essential to democratic government. Ordinary citizens depend on the media to investigate wrongdoing, to publicize and explain governmental actions, to evaluate programs and politicians, and to bring to light matters that might otherwise be known to only a handful of governmental insiders. In short, without free and active media, democratic government would be virtually impossible. Citizens would have few means through which to know or assess the government's actions—other than the claims or pronouncements of the government itself. Moreover, without active (indeed, aggressive) media, citizens would be hard-pressed to make informed choices among competing candidates at the polls.

Today's media are not only adversarial but also increasingly partisan. Debates about the liberalism and conservatism of the mass media make it clear that many readers and viewers perceive more and more bias in newspapers, radio, and television. Blogs, niche media, social media, and other Internet outlets, of course, are often unabashedly partisan. To some extent, increasing ideological and partisan stridency is an inevitable result of the expansion and proliferation of news sources. When the news was dominated by three networks and a handful of national papers, each sought to appeal to the entire national audience. This required a moderate and balanced tone so that consumers would not be offended and transfer their attention to a rival network or newspaper. Today, there are so many news sources that few can aim for a broad-based national audience. Instead, each targets a partisan or ideological niche and aims to develop a strong relationship with consumers in that audience segment by catering to their biases and predispositions. The end result may be to encourage greater division and disharmony among Americans.

The media can make or break reputations, help to launch or destroy political careers, and build support for or rally opposition to programs and institutions.[62] Wherever there is so much power, at least the potential exists for its abuse or overly zealous use. All things considered, free media are so critically important to the maintenance of a democratic society that Americans must be prepared to take the risk that the media will occasionally abuse their power. Governmental controls that would prevent the media from misusing their power would also certainly destroy freedom. The ultimate beneficiaries of free and active media are the American people.

Has the rise of citizen journalism and the Internet fundamentally changed how political information is gathered and distributed? As more and more Americans go online to read the news and learn about politics, even the definition of "journalist" is being challenged. Is WikiLeaks a media organization protected by First Amendment guarantees of press freedom, or is it a website engaged in illegal activity? Are Twitter feeds from protestors on the ground in Egypt or in an Occupy Wall Street camp examples of citizen journalism? In an era of online news, regular citizens create content and distribute the news through personal pages and blogs. Is this real news or just local gossip on a global scale? Wikipedia, the free online encyclopedia founded by Jimmy Wales, has millions of pages providing relatively unbiased content on virtually every political topic imaginable. The information is compiled by legions of volunteers working in teams in almost every country in the world, including China. Wikipedia is the only nonprofit among the 10 most popular websites worldwide. Social media (Facebook, Twitter, and countless others), Wikipedia, and all Wiki-type sites involve people working collaboratively to write and create information and to transmit knowledge. Is Wikimedia the future of the media?

In the twenty-first century, political campaigns are covered wall to wall by the Internet; on newspapers' sites updated throughout the day; and on blogs, tweets, social media, and cable television. There is no doubt that the new digital media are more diverse, more representative of multiple viewpoints, more interactive and participatory, and, to many, more interesting than traditional news media. Time will tell whether the shift to online news strengthens or harms American democracy.

Become a Critical Consumer of Political News

Inform Yourself

 Visit news sources outside the traditional mainstream media. Many blogs and websites serve as media watchdogs and alternative voices. Have you read or heard of the Drudge Report (www.drudgereport.com"), the Huffington Post (www .huffingtonpost.com), Salon's blog (www.salon.com), the National Review (www .nationalreview.com), the Weekly Standard (www.weeklystandard.com), Truth Out (www.truthout.org), Moveon.org, or www.rightmarch.org? What about TheMonkeyCage.org? Can you tell which news sites represent the ideological left versus the right, and which are created by scholars on neither the right nor the left?

 Check the facts. Candidates and political groups use the Internet and social media to deliver their messages directly to the public, unfiltered by editors. One downside to this process is that lies and misinformation are more common online. Visit the popular Factcheck website (www.factcheck.org) and its Viral Spiral page (from the site's top menu). What are the current Internet rumors? Who are the subjects of these rumors? Do you see a pattern?

Express Yourself

 Share your view of the media. HBO's *The Newsroom* is a show about how the mainstream media care more about ratings than reporting the news. Consider the clip at www.youtube.com/watch?v=og3D5UwxjU0. What does the character say that you agree with? What does he say that you disagree with? Share your thoughts on the *Newsroom* clip and the media with others and see what your friends think.

Connect with Others

 What is news? Go to the Drudge Report website (www.drudgereport.com) and find two articles that never became headline news. Why do you think these stories never made mainstream news? What does this tell us about what is thought of as news? Consider sharing the stories and your opinion on your Facebook page, Twitter, or in class with other students.

Find links to the sites listed above as well as related activities on wwnorton.com/studyspace.

study guide

Traditional Media

■ **Describe the role of print and broadcast media in providing political information (pp. 253–56)**

Americans have traditionally gotten their political information from broadcast media (radio and television) and print media (newspapers and magazines). Television reaches the largest audience but provides little depth of coverage. Radio news is essentially a headline service that alerts listeners to important events without providing much detail. Newspapers, by contrast, are read by political elites for their in-depth coverage and are important in setting the agenda of the broadcast media.

Key Term

broadcast media (p. 253)

Practice Quiz

1. Which of the following statements is *not* true about old-fashioned newspapers? *(p. 255)*
   a) They typically offer readers a better context for analysis by providing more detailed and complete information than other forms of media.
   b) They are the read on a daily basis by almost all Americans.
   c) They serve as the primary source of news for the nation's social and political elite.
   d) Broadcast media organizations rely heavily on newspapers to set their news agenda.
   e) Daily newspaper circulation in the United States has declined over the last 20 years.

> **Practice Online**
> Interactive simulation: *Editor-in-chief of a Daily Newspaper*

News Media and Online News

■ **Explain how the Internet has transformed the news media (pp. 256–68)**

Online political information includes news aggregation websites, niche journalism, citizen journalism, nonprofit journalism, blogs, and social media. The convenience, currency, and diversity of online news have led many Americans to prefer it to more traditional sources. Changes arising from the emergence of the Internet have also raised of concerns that online news may produce a decline in investigative journalism, a decrease in the quality of news content, and a reduction in political knowledge and tolerance.

Key Terms

penny press (p. 256)

news aggregator (p. 256)

digital citizen (p. 258)

niche journalism (p. 258)

citizen journalism (p. 259)

social media (p. 261)

Practice Quiz

2. *Penny press* refers to *(p. 256)*
   a) the very low wages paid to reporters.
   b) the single-page newspapers released on a weekly basis during the colonial era.
   c) the emergence of low-cost online news sources.
   d) the fact that most Americans see very little value in the information provided to them by the media.
   e) the cheap, tabloid style newspapers produced in the nineteenth century.

3. News reporting that is targeted in its content toward a narrow segment of the population is called *(p. 258)*
   a) nonprofit journalism.
   b) for-profit journalism.
   c) niche journalism.
   d) citizen journalism.
   e) adversarial journalism.

4. Which of the following is *not* a reason that Americans may prefer online news? *(pp. 262–65)*
   a) the convenience of getting news online.
   b) the up-to-the-moment currency of the information available online.
   c) the depth of the information available online.

d) the diversity of online viewpoints.

e) the accuracy and objectivity compared to traditional media outlets.

 Practice Online
"Get Involved" interactive exercise: *Become a Critical Consumer of Political News*

Mass Media Ownership

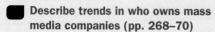 **Describe trends in who owns mass media companies (pp. 268–70)**

One of the most important trends for the American media system over the last few decades has been the growing concentration in ownership of print and broadcast media outlets. Although there are thousands of newspapers, magazines, and television and radio stations across the country, the number of traditional news-gathering sources operating nationally is quite small and may be declining. As major newspapers, television stations, and radio networks fall into fewer and fewer hands, there is a growing risk that the diversity of viewpoints heard by the public will decline.

Key Term

media monopoly (p. 269)

Practice Quiz

5. Consolidation of the media was accelerated by *(p. 269)*
   a) the Supreme Court's decision in *Red Lion Broadcasting Company v. FCC.*
   b) the declining number of reporters working for the major media outlets.
   c) the enactment of the 1996 Telecommunications Act.
   d) the purchase of influential newspapers and magazines by foreign corporations.
   e) the purchase of major networks and newspapers by the federal government.

 Practice Online
"You Decide" exercise: *Regulation of Media Ownership*

Media Influence

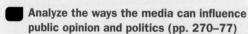 **Analyze the ways the media can influence public opinion and politics (pp. 270–77)**

The content and character of news programming can have far-reaching political consequences. In recent American political history, the media have played a central role in numerous major events, such as the civil rights movement of the 1950s and '60s, the Vietnam War, and the Watergate affair. The power of the media lies in their ability to shape what issues Americans think about (agenda setting) and what opinions Americans hold about those issues (framing and priming).

Key Terms

agenda setting (p. 272)

selection bias (news) (p. 273)

framing (p. 275)

priming (p. 276)

Practice Quiz

6. The media's powers to determine what becomes a part of political discussion and to shape how political events are interpreted are known as *(p. 272)*
   a) media consolidation and selection bias.
   b) issue definition and protest power.
   c) agenda setting and framing.
   d) the illusion of saliency and the bandwagon effect.
   e) the equal time rule and the right of rebuttal.

7. Which of the following best describes the media's role in the Watergate affair? *(p. 273)*
   a) They played a central role in reporting on President Nixon's resignation but did little to reveal his abuses of power while he was president.
   b) They played a central role in President Nixon's decision to resign from the presidency by revealing his abuses of power to the public.
   c) They played a central role in disproving claims that President Nixon had abused his power while in office.
   d) They played almost no role in the Watergate affair because they were legally prohibited from discussing ongoing police investigations.
   e) They played almost no role in the Watergate affair because they refused to investigate claims that President Nixon had abused his power.

8. Media coverage of election campaigns typically focuses on which of the following? *(p. 275)*
   a) the details of each candidate's domestic policy proposals
   b) the details of each candidate's foreign policy proposals
   c) the biography of each of the candidates
   d) the records of each of the candidates
   e) the "horse race" (that is, who is ahead and by how much)

 Practice Online
Video exercise: *The Word—Media Culpa*

News Coverage

■ **Explain how politicians and others try to shape the news (pp. 278–83)**

Leaks, press releases, and the tradition of adversarial journalism are important in determining the content of news coverage. Leaks, which are confidential pieces of information disclosed to members of the media, have driven press coverage on issues ranging from foreign policy to government corruption. Also incorporated into daily news coverage are thousands of press releases authored by advocates of influential political interests. "Adversarial journalism," a form of reporting in which the media adopt a skeptical or even hostile posture toward public officials, has increased the political power of the press in recent years.

Key Term

leak (p. 278)

Practice Quiz

9. Most leaks originate with *(p. 278)*
   a) low-level, government whistle-blowers.
   b) senior government officials, prominent politicians, and political activists.
   c) members of the public who witness misbehavior.
   d) ambassadors from foreign countries.
   e) members of the media.

10. Which of the following best describes the media's use of press releases? *(p. 280)*
   a) Press releases are never incorporated into daily news reports because it is illegal under federal law.
   b) Press releases are never incorporated into daily news reports because reporters view the information they contain as biased and politically motivated.
   c) Thousands of press releases are incorporated into daily news reports every year because press releases allow news organizations to fill their pages at little cost.
   d) Press releases are rarely incorporated into daily news reports because reporters view the information as biased and politically motivated.
   e) Every press release written by a political party, interest group, candidate, or government official is incorporated into daily news reports because reporters view the information as newsworthy.

11. *Adversarial journalism* refers to *(p. 280)*
   a) the recent shift in American society away from general purpose sources of information and toward narrowly focused niche sources.
   b) an era in American history when political parties provided all of the financing for newspapers.
   c) a form of reporting in which the media adopt a skeptical or even hostile posture toward the opinions and behaviors of their audience.
   d) a form of reporting in which the media adopt an accepting and friendly posture toward the government and public officials.
   e) a form of reporting in which the media adopt a skeptical or even hostile posture toward the government and public officials.

12. Which event shattered the amicable relationship between the press and the presidency? *(p. 281)*
   a) September 11, 2001
   b) the Vietnam War
   c) Watergate
   d) World War II
   e) the Monica Lewinsky affair

 Practice Online
Video Exercises: *Press Secretary's "Zumtrel Flooby" Answer May Be Attempt to Evade Question—Onion News Network*

Regulation of the Media

■ **Trace the evolution of rules that govern broadcast media (pp. 283–85)**

Although American print and online media are free from government interference, broadcast media are subject to significant federal regulation. Radio and television stations in the United States are licensed by the Federal Communications Commission. The FCC has used its licensing power to impose several regulations, such as the equal time rule, the right of rebuttal, and the fairness doctrine, that affect the political content of radio and television broadcasts.

Key Terms

equal time rule (p. 284)

right of rebuttal (p. 284)

fairness doctrine (p. 285)

Practice Quiz

13. In general, FCC regulations apply only to *(p. 284)*
   a) cable television.
   b) Internet websites.
   c) over-the-air broadcast media.
   d) satellite radio.
   e) newspapers and magazines.

14. The now defunct requirement that broadcasters provide time for opposing views when they air programs on controversial issues was called *(p. 285)*
   a) the equal time rule.
   b) the free speech doctrine.
   c) the fairness doctrine.
   d) the right of rebuttal.
   e) the response rule.

For Further Reading

Ansolabehere, Stephen, and Shanto Iyengar. *Going Negative*. New York: Simon & Schuster, 1997.

Carr, Nicholas. *The Shallows: What the Internet Is Doing to Our Brains*. New York: W.W. Norton & Company, 2011.

De Zengotita, Thomas. *Mediated: How the Media Shapes Our World and the Way We Live in It*. New York: Bloomsbury, 2006.

Fenton, Tom. *Bad News: The Decline of Reporting, the Business of News, and the Danger to Us All*. New York: Harper-Collins, 2005.

Fox, Richard, and Jennifer Ramos. *iPolitics: Citizens, Elections and Governing in the New Media Era*. New York: Cambridge University Press, 2011.

Hamilton, James T. *All the News That's Fit to Sell*. Princeton, NJ: Princeton University Press, 2004.

Iyengar, Shanto, and Donald Kinder. *News That Matters: Television and American Public Opinion*. Chicago: University of Chicago Press, 2010.

Jamieson, Kathleen, and Paul Waldman. *The Press Effect*. New York: Oxford University Press, 2004.

Mossberger, Karen, Caroline Tolbert, and Ramona McNeal. *Digital Citizenship: The Internet, Society and Participation*. Cambridge, MA: MIT Press, 2008.

Pariser, Eli. *The Filter Bubble: What the Internet Is Hiding from You*. New York: Penguin, 2011.

Weaver, David, et al. *The American Journalist in the 21st Century: U.S. News People at the Dawn of a New Millennium*. New York: Erlbaum, 2006.

West, Darrell. *The Next Wave: Using Digital Technology to Further Social and Political Innovation*. Washington, DC: Brookings Institution Press, 2011.

Recommended Websites

Accuracy in Media
www.aim.org
This nonprofit, watchdog group attempts to ensure accuracy in media reporting by identifying botched or slanted stories and then "setting the record straight."

Federal Communications Commission
www.fcc.gov
The FCC is an independent regulatory agency established by the U.S. government in 1934 to regulate the broadcast media. On the official FCC website you can read about the rules and regulations that affect the media, along with other current topics of interest.

Journalism.org
www.journalism.org
This nonprofit, nonpolitical site, sponsored by the Project for Excellence in Journalism, examines the overall performance of the press as providers of information. Their aim is to help both consumers and producers of the news.

National Newspaper Association
www.nnawes.org
The NNA is one of the oldest and largest professional associations in the print media today. As ownership of major newspapers falls into fewer and fewer hands, the NNA is trying to protect, promote, and enhance America's community newspapers.

Newseum
www.newseum.org
Newseum is the Web page for an interactive museum of news journalism. On this site you can browse the front pages of over 500 daily national and international newspapers and explore the galleries and theaters of the news museum in Washington, D.C.

The Pew Research Center for the People and the Press
http://people-press.org
This independent survey research organization studies attitudes toward the press and numerous political issues.

For much of the country's history, large groups of Americans were denied the right to vote. Most restrictions on voting have been eliminated for Americans age 18 and older, but voter turnout remains relatively low, especially among young voters. Will the rise of online politics increase participation?

Political Participation and Voting

WHAT GOVERNMENT DOES AND WHY IT MATTERS In many ways, Barack Obama's 2008 presidential campaign rewrote the rules for engaging supporters in electoral campaigns. Seeking to replace cynicism and apathy with idealism and hope, the Obama campaign focused on mobilizing new voters—the young in particular—and on making effective use of the Internet. The campaign linked online point-to-point communication to traditional offline opportunities to volunteer, thus engaging many who were not previously interested in politics. By opening 700 field offices across the country and developing a state-of-the-art website, the campaign made it easier for potential supporters to connect with campaign activities. Obama's team frequently communicated with supporters through e-mail, texting, and social networking sites such as Facebook and Twitter to make personal pleas for contributions, raising over $600 million in small contributions (a record) from 3 million donors.

Obama's 2008 campaign also took advantage of early-voting laws, newly adopted by many states, which allowed citizens to vote up to 40 days prior to the actual election. The campaign employed a sophisticated voter registration database to get out the vote, calling, messaging, and e-mailing supporters until it was confirmed that a ballot had been cast. The combination of excitement and mobilization (online and offline) spurred 62 percent of eligible citizens to vote, a modern record and the highest turnout since the 1960s. Participation increased among many categories of voters. African Americans turned out at historically high levels, inspired by the first major-party black presidential nominee in American history. Young voters (ages 18–29), traditionally the most apathetic segment of the electorate, increased their turnout to 51 percent, but their participation was still lower than expected.[1]

Despite the success of their 2008 campaign, however, Democrats had trouble mobilizing African Americans and young voters just two years later, for the 2010 midterm elections. Young voters, who made up 18 percent of the electorate in 2008, comprised only 10 percent in 2010. Use of the Internet for information about politics and mobilization continued to grow by leaps and bounds in 2012, but young voters still turned out at low rates.

It is not just the young who vote at low rates: nearly 40 percent of eligible American adults do not vote. Along with young adults, nonvoters are also disproportionately poor, uneducated, and nonwhite.[2] Their reasons for not voting are many: some find the process of voting and registering to vote onerous; some are not interested in politics because of uncompetitive elections without active campaigns. And for some people the decision to stay away from politics has been reinforced by a perception that politics is corrupt.[3]

So who does vote? Wealth, education, and strong partisanship are all associated with a greater likelihood of voting and other forms of political participation, such as contributing money to candidates or contacting elected officials. Political interest and knowledge are important predictors of whether an individual will vote. Some people vote because they view voting as a patriotic duty of citizenship. In fact, many people consider higher voter turnout to be an important goal in itself.[4] But many citizens, of course, vote because they want their preferred candidates, parties, and policies to win. As we will see in this chapter, who participates in politics matters because it affects the issues that candidates and elected officials put at the top of their agenda.

chaptergoals

- Describe the major types of traditional and online participation in politics (pages 295–304)

- Examine voter turnout in American elections (pages 305–6)

- Explain the factors that influence whether individuals vote or not (pages 306–20)

- Describe the patterns of participation among major social groups (pages 320–31)

Forms of Political Participation

Describe the major types of traditional and online participation in politics

We can think of political participation as falling into two major categories. Traditional participation in politics includes voting, of course, as well as attending campaign events, party business meetings, and fund-raisers. It also includes volunteering, canvassing, displaying campaign signs, and contributing to candidates and parties, or even challenging a law in court. Even protests and demonstrations can be considered age-old forms of participatory politics. Many, but not all, are face-to-face forms of participation in politics.

In addition to traditional participation there is a growing online world of digital politics—not just the exchange of information, but also fund-raising and voter mobilization. Some observers contend that digital politics is just a new way of engaging in traditional politics, while others argue that it is fundamentally different. There may be some truth to both arguments, but it is clear that digital politics is increasingly intertwined with traditional participation and is changing participation in important ways that may increase engagement in politics overall. We will see in this chapter that digital and traditional participation are combining to broaden the ways Americans participate in politics.

Traditional Political Participation

Traditional political participation refers to a wide range of activities designed to influence government, politics, and policy. For most citizens today, voting is the most common form of political participation. (Voting will be discussed at length later in this chapter.) Yet ordinary people took part in politics long before the advent of the election or any other formal mechanism of popular involvement in political life. If there is any natural or spontaneous form of popular political participation, it is not the election but the riot. In fact, for much of American history, fewer Americans exercised their right to vote than participated in urban riots and rural uprisings, as voting was for a long time limited to white, male, landowning citizens. Civil unrest played an important role in American politics in the 1960s and '70s. As recently as 1999, protests helped labor unions and other opponents of trade liberalization slow the pace of change in the rules governing world trade.

traditional political participation activities designed to influence government including voting and face-to-face activities such as protesting or volunteering for a campaign

Protests and rallies are forms of political participation. At this rally, demonstrators gathered in support of immigrants' rights. They hoped to draw attention to their cause and to influence the government to adopt policies that would result in better conditions for immigrant workers.

Volunteering for a campaign—for example, making calls on behalf of a candidate—is one traditional form of political participation.

protest participation that involves assembling crowds to confront a government or other official organization

The vast majority of Americans, of course, reject rioting or violence for political ends, but peaceful **protest** is protected by the First Amendment and is generally recognized as a legitimate and important form of political activity. During the height of the civil rights movement in the 1960s, hundreds of thousands of Americans took part in peaceful protests to demand social and political rights for African Americans. More recently, peaceful marches and demonstrations have been employed by a host of groups, ranging from opponents of the war in Iraq to antiabortion activists and conservative Tea Party activists. The Occupy Wall Street movement began in September 2011 in New York City's Financial District, using peaceful demonstrations to protest high unemployment, undue corporate influence on government, and growing inequality between the super rich and the middle class—or, in the lingo of the Occupy Wall Street movement, the 1 percent versus the 99 percent of Americans. The protests in New York sparked similar Occupy movements, and their tent cities, across America. Opinion polls suggest that the movement has been especially successful in raising awareness of income inequality. For example, a Pew Research Center survey found that in 2012, two-thirds of Americans (66 percent) believed there were "very strong" or "strong" conflicts between the rich and the poor—an increase of 19 percentage points since 2009.[5]

Elections are the hallmark of political participation in a democracy, of course. In addition to voting, citizens can give money to politicians or political organizations, volunteer in campaigns, contact political officials, sign petitions, attend public meetings, join organizations, display campaign signs and pins, write letters to the editor, publish articles, attend rallies, or lobby their representatives in Congress; they can even sue the government or run for elected office. They can also join interest groups, which will be discussed in Chapter 11. These other forms of political action generally require more time, effort, or money than voting. In a 2008 survey of participation, just 22 percent of respondents said they had attended a local community meeting in the previous year; 16 percent said they had contacted a public official. Only 10 percent of those surveyed reported giving money to a candidate's campaign during the election, while 9 percent said they had attended a rally or political meeting. Fewer than 5 percent of those questioned said they had actually spent time volunteering for a political campaign.[6] (See Figure 8.1.)

Such activities differ from voting because they can communicate much more detailed information to public officials than voting can. Voters may support a can-

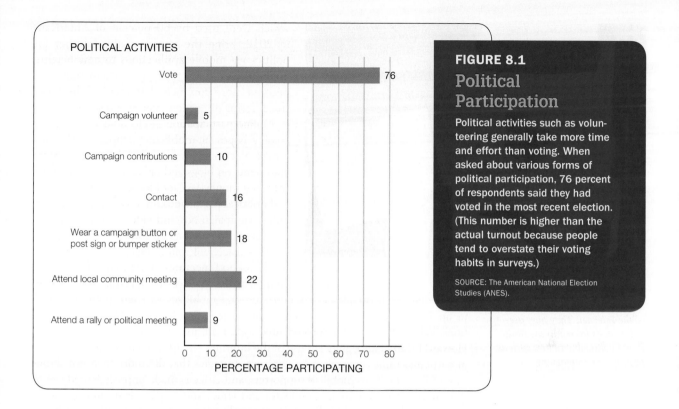

POLITICAL ACTIVITIES

Activity	Percentage
Vote	76
Campaign volunteer	5
Campaign contributions	10
Contact	16
Wear a campaign button or post sign or bumper sticker	18
Attend local community meeting	22
Attend a rally or political meeting	9

PERCENTAGE PARTICIPATING

FIGURE 8.1

Political Participation

Political activities such as volunteering generally take more time and effort than voting. When asked about various forms of political participation, 76 percent of respondents said they had voted in the most recent election. (This number is higher than the actual turnout because people tend to overstate their voting habits in surveys.)

SOURCE: The American National Election Studies (ANES).

didate for many reasons, but their actual votes do not indicate specifically what they like and don't like, nor do they tell officials how intensely voters feel about issues. By volunteering for a political campaign or writing to their member of Congress or attending a protest, people can convey much more specific information. For that reason, people often find these other political activities more satisfying than voting.[7]

Online Political Participation

Online political participation is rapidly changing the way Americans experience politics. While traditional forms of participation remain important, the Internet gives citizens greater access to political information and, at least potentially, a greater role in politics than ever before. Many forms of online participation build on traditional forms of participation, but the Internet makes many of these activities easier and gives them greater potential as community-building tools. The Internet offers an active, two-way form of communication with feedback, rather than the more passive, one-way communication involved in reading printed newspapers, watching television, or listening to the radio. The Internet allows person-to-person communication as well as broadcast capability through online text, video, and visual images where information can be widely shared. For these reasons the Internet has been called a telephone, library, soapbox, storehouse of information, and channel for communication—all in one.

As of 2012, nearly 7 in 10 Americans read the news online, and nearly as many use online political information. Smartphones, or Internet-enabled mobile devices,

online political participation
activities designed to influence government using the Internet, including visiting a candidate's website, organizing events online, or signing an online petition

Americans are increasingly likely to participate in politics through digital means, such as cell phones or the Internet. They may use online tools to coordinate traditional political activities such as protests or campaigning.

which were used by 60 percent of Americans in 2012, bring the power of the Internet for politics via mobile applications to new heights. Today these online forms of participation have become more common than most of the traditional forms of participation just discussed.[8]

Online participation in elections includes discussing issues or mobilizing supporters through e-mail, electronic messaging, and Twitter; posting comments on blogs and online news stories; contributing money to candidates; visiting candidate and political party websites; creating and viewing online campaign ads and videos on sites such as YouTube; campaigning on social networking sites such as Facebook; and organizing face-to-face neighborhood meetings on sites such as Meetup.com. With each successive election, the Internet creates new platforms for communication and mobilization about politics. Digital technology brought fresh vigor to citizen participation in the 2008 and 2012 elections. While this wasn't unprecedented—after all, in 2004, presidential candidate Howard Dean made significant use of the Internet—in 2008, Democratic candidates in particular built comprehensive Internet strategies that did more than just duplicate offline efforts to mobilize supporters, and citizens made unprecedented use of the Internet to learn about candidates and issues and to participate in campaigns. While only 4 percent of likely voters went online for election information in 1996, a full 61 percent of American voters reported looking at information online or discussing politics online in 2012 according to Pew's Internet and American Life Project.[9] During the 2008 general election, over half of American adults used the Internet to learn about the candidates or to express their views.[10]

The 2012 presidential elections saw increasing sophistication of online campaigning and improved integration of online and offline participation opportunities. Facebook and Twitter, independent journalism (blogs), and political videos became critical means of organizing and communicating during the 2012 presidential elections. Many analysts believe that television, which had dominated presidential campaigns for the past half century, may have played second fiddle. Every serious presidential candidate had a Facebook page, with millions of fans who received weekly if not daily updates from the campaigns and candidates. These fans, in turn, signaled to their "friends" which candidates they supported for elected office, making politics part of everyday discussion.

The young (ages 18–29) were significantly more likely than middle-aged and older respondents to be engaged in presidential electoral activities online. Among young Americans who were registered to vote, 22 percent were highly engaged in the 2008 presidential primaries online, while another 43 percent were moderately active online (two to three activities). Thus, 65 percent of those young people registered to vote were moderately or highly active in the presidential nomination by way of online activities. In comparison, of those in the oldest age group (age 60 and older), only 5 percent were very active online, another 19 percent were moderately active online, and most (76 percent) reported little (one activity) or no political involvement online.[11] If these trends are sustained, they may result in greater overall levels of political interest and activity. Those who benefit most from online politics are likely to be those who are most active online: the young.[12]

Why is digital politics so effective with young people? Young Americans tend to move from place to place more often than citizens aged 40 years and older, so traditional "snail mail" campaigns are less likely to mobilize them. Young people are especially likely to be online, increasingly via mobile phones or smartphones rather than landlines. A 2011 survey found that the young (ages 18–29) made up 55 percent of citizens with only mobile Internet access (no Internet connection at home). In contrast, the young accounted for just 14 percent of individuals with an Internet connection at home. Similar patterns are found for blacks and Latinos and the less affluent, who disproportionately rely on mobile phones for Internet access.[13] Thus candidates and political campaigns are turning more and more to digital politics to reach young Americans, especially using mobile applications.

Does Online Participation Lead to Offline Participation? An important question is whether online political participation influences offline participation, especially voting. Political participation requires that people be motivated and have an interest in the outcome of the election. They must have the knowledge or capacity to understand how to participate, and they must be mobilized.[14] Digital technology encourages information-gathering and interaction between users by combining features of traditional media in content and interpersonal communication for discussion and mobilization. Because of this combination of information and interactivity, the Internet has the potential to promote interest in politics and to transform the nature of political participation. The Digital Citizens section on page 301 describes the case of the Occupy movement, in which the use of the Internet and cell phones was crucial in mobilizing participants.

A growing body of research indicates that activities such as reading online news, commenting on blogs, or sending or receiving political e-mails increase the likelihood that someone will not only vote but also contribute to political campaigns and candidates, attend campaign meetings, volunteer for campaigns, engage in community activities, and even contact elected officials.[15]

For example, one study found that participating in politics online—reading online news, commenting on blogs, or sending or receiving political e-mails—increases the likelihood of voting and participating in others ways offline. Online participation is also linked with discussing politics with friends or family, having an interest in politics, and being politically knowledgeable.

Researchers who study this subject have suggested at least six possible reasons online politics may increase participation. First, information, which is necessary for effective political participation, is easier to obtain online and is available 24 hours a day for those who have regular access to the Internet. The Internet is increasingly compared to the invention of the printing press, which stimulated the demand for greater literacy in society.[16] The Internet, like printed material, conveys information to the masses, and indeed, more Americans now read the news online than read print newspapers. Surveys show that nearly half of those who use online news and political information cite the Internet's convenience.[17]

Second, online news may "accidentally" engage individuals who otherwise would not be involved in politics at all. The political scientist Doris Graber has referred to the "accidental" mobilization of the electorate through the election news coverage that many Americans were exposed to by default when there were only a few television networks.[18] The Internet has created a new version of the "accidental mobilization" of those who are greeted by political information when they open their e-mail, check their Facebook accounts, or conduct online searches—sometimes politics finds the individual, rather than the other way around.[19] Candidates regularly place political ads on social media sites and in Google searches. Individuals may be "accidently" exposed to these ads and learn about politics, even if their motives for being online do not involve politics. Some research shows that individuals with low to moderate interest in politics, who are frequently online, are more likely to participate than individuals with low interest who are are not online.[20]

The flexibility of the Internet allows candidates to micro-target campaign ads to voters:[21] sophisticated techniques enable political campaigns to target information that will be of interest to potential supporters while those potential supporters are doing Google searches. This micro-targeting by candidates and campaigns may drive accidental political mobilization.[22]

Third, digital media have unique characteristics that enhance participation and even democratic accountability. The Internet effectively combines the qualities of print media that promote knowledge with the visual aspects of television that generate interest, engagement, and emotion.[23] Online news covers events and issues with the same immediacy as television, but with the in-depth treatment that is typical of newspapers. Emotional responses to political candidates or issues learned in online media, positive or negative, have been shown to trigger interest in politics and engagement.[24] In 2012, for example, Senate candidate Elizabeth Warren became a national sensation overnight with a video in which she passionately rebutted the idea that taxing the wealthy is "class warfare." Her campaign video was viewed more than 100,000 times on YouTube in one week.

Online readers can also post comments and participate in a community by providing feedback on news articles. A parallel experience for the print media does not exist outside of letters to the editor, a forum that can never have the potential scope of online feedback.

Fourth, online sources are more diverse than those found in the traditional media, and this diversity, too, may influence participation through its effects on political knowledge and interest. While online news is dominated by mainstream outlets available in other modes,[25] such as the websites of major newspapers or television networks, the Web is populated also by a wide range of information sources that reduce the impact of distance, making foreign media or media that appeal mainly to a narrow segment of the population easily available to anyone. This diversity matters, as surveys show that one-third of those who get their political information online believe that other information media are inadequate in comparison.[26] Many argue that the diversity of news sources online is good for democracy and that it makes debates about the purported liberal or conservative bias of the mainstream media irrelevant.

Fifth, online politics lowers the barriers for entry, making it easier for people to participate in ways that require less effort. By its very nature online political participation occurs in ways that are less location dependent than traditional politics: *community* takes on a very different meaning in an online context compared to a voter's actual neighborhood precinct or a local political party office. The Internet facilitates participation that is potentially broad, but with looser connections between participants than in more traditional networks of coworkers or neighbors.[27] The breadth of networks—for example, on Facebook or Twitter—is encouraged by the ease of sending information or appeals through hyperlinked websites, videos, and blogs as well as e-mail. While this may promote more extensive organizing efforts, it also encourages forms of participation that are low-intensity and sporadic, possibly attracting individuals with only moderate political interest.

Occupy Wall Street

The movement that became known as Occupy Wall Street started with one simple e-mail sent to 90,000 individuals in July 2011. The idea was vague, but the goal was to get 20,000 people to protest economic inequality on September 17, 2011, in New York. Only 2,000 showed up. Many of those involved feared the event would fail to have an impact.

However, viral media fueled the flames of the populist economic protest, as

people around the country shared videos of young protesters being arrested by the police. After two weeks, the protesters coordinated occupations in hundreds of other cities via the Internet. The mainstream media and the rest of the country began to pay attention. When a citizen using a mobile phone captured video of police pepper-spraying peaceful Occupy demonstrators at the University of California–Davis in November 2011, it became headline news; the video was viewed by millions.

Twitter was the communication tool of choice, offering a way to connect with the thousands of Americans camped out in cities across the United States as part of the protest. One month after the movement's humble beginnings, Occupy Wall Street's Twitter account had over 85,000 followers, and in the first week of October 2011 approximately 400,000 people visited their website *per day*, making Occupy Wall Street the first mass protest in the United States built on new media.

One debate about digital politics is whether it mainly affects the people most likely to participate anyway or whether it can mobilize new groups and individuals. The Occupy movement represents a high-water mark in the use of online communications to mobilize offline political protest. But did it mobilize people who were otherwise unlikely to get involved? An in-person random sample of 200 New York protesters found that almost half were under age 30, and about half reported this event as the first time they were involved in a protest, rally, or march. Just over half had voted in the 2008 presidential election.[a] Additionally Occupy protes-

tors were economically hard pressed; a third reported they were "struggling" in the labor market. These findings suggest that the Occupy movement and the use of digital media may indeed have helped mobilize groups—such as the young, the poor, and nonvoters—who tend to have lower rates of political participation.

On Facebook, the main Occupy site had over 167,000 "likes" as of June 2012. There are four other general pages and dozens of other Occupy pages dedicated to specific cities. The Occupy protests indicate that digital politics can lead to offline participation.

[a]Douglas E. Schoen, "Occupy Wall Street Survey Topline," http://www.douglasschoen.com/pdf/Occupy_Wall_Street_Poll_Douglas_Schoen.pdf (data collected October 10 and 11, 2011).

for critical analysis

1. Will online politics benefit those most likely to participate in politics already, such as the affluent and educated, or will digital politics help level the playing field, giving greater voice to the young, minorities, less affluent, and lower educated?

2. Does social media provide a new way to mobilize young people, a group with traditionally low voter turnout, to participate in politics? Or will the same barriers that have prevented young people from participating still apply, despite the Internet?

Thus participation online may be broader, but also less intense, possibly leading more people to participate in ways that require less effort. Forwarding an e-mail to a friend, posting a link on Facebook, or uploading a brief comment to a local newspaper website is an individual act that doesn't require commitment to organizational membership. However, it may improve political knowledge, interest, and participation. The political scientist Bruce Bimber has shown that some interest groups are responding to this new political climate of sporadic participation by focusing more outreach on the Web and by making it possible for individuals to support a specific issue or campaign without making a commitment to membership in the organization as a whole.[28] If citizens with low to moderate interest can become engaged in politics online, this will widen the pool of people participating in politics.

Finally, the Internet enables new forms of political expression through the creation of content on blogs, videos, social media, and websites.[29] This expressive capacity of the technology can lead to increased citizen involvement in politics, much of it through citizen journalism. Online news is creating a new generation of whistle blowers and citizen journalists, enhancing the media's traditional role as a watchdog for the people against government corruption. Although writing a blog is an obviously creative activity, 67 percent of those who follow blogs say that they also consider reading them an expression of their political beliefs.[30] The scholar Russell Dalton argues that, in fact, participation isn't declining at all but rather is changing by including norms of citizenship that are more expressive than voting.[31] For many citizens, becoming a "fan" of a candidate page on Facebook is a first step toward active participation in politics.

For all these reasons, digital media may foster a new kind of community-building that has the potential to reverse the trends in voter turnout and political participation, which have been declining over the past four decades. Explanations for these trends vary, but many analysts cite reduced trust in government, failures of the party system, and a diminishing stock of what Robert Putnam, author of *Bowling Alone*, calls social capital—community networks that motivate political participation.[32] By making political information, discussion, communication, and online mobilization easier, the Internet may help Americans grow a new kind of social capital, one based on shared political experiences in cyberspace.[33]

Online Protest against SOPA and PIPA Online protests to preserve Internet freedom provide a striking example of how new media can be used to mobilize offline participation in politics. Media "content producers" have long complained of severe economic losses due to online piracy—the illegal downloading of music, movies, TV shows, and other copyrighted material posted by foreign piracy websites. Early in 2012, at the urging of media companies and industry associations, legislation designed to clamp down on U.S.-based websites that facilitated international piracy was brought before Congress. These proposed laws, known as SOPA and PIPA,[34] represented an attempt to extend U.S. copyright laws beyond U.S. borders.

In what became characterized as a duel pitting Hollywood against Silicon Valley, proponents of the anti-piracy legislation, including the U.S. Chamber of Commerce and the motion picture industry, said that SOPA and PIPA were necessary to prevent digital thievery. While acknowledging that online piracy was a problem, the technology industry objected to provisions that would have held them liable for policing any website they linked to that might contain pirated content, such as a video or song. Google, for example, links to millions and millions

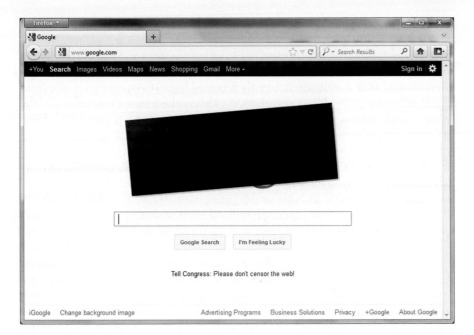

In 2012 an online protest prompted Congress to reconsider legislation designed to regulate the Internet and protect intellectual property rights. Numerous major websites "went dark" to draw attention to the issue, and Google displayed a black censorship bar along with a link to an online petition against the proposed law.

of websites. More generally, opponents of SOPA and PIPA said that the proposals would allow government censorship of the Internet and would damage free and open online communication. They argued further that the legislation could stifle innovation and job creation in the twenty-first-century economy, especially among small businesses reliant on the Internet.

At least initially, the bills had broad bipartisan support and appeared destined to be enacted into law. Then, on January 18, 2012, more than a hundred websites launched a coordinated protest—the largest online protest in history. It included a 24-hour shutdown of the online encyclopedia Wikipedia, a nonprofit organization and one of the top 10 most-visited websites worldwide. Users were redirected to a black screen providing information on the bills and links for users to click on to contact their member of Congress. According to Wikipedia, in one day there were 160 million visits to the site, and more than 4 million people accessed the information about contacting their member of Congress. (To put this figure in perspective, remember that there are 311 million citizens in the United States.). Google users, meanwhile, faced a black censorship bar blocking the Google logo and a link reading "Tell Congress: Please don't censor the web!" The search engine directed users to a petition opposing the bills; 10 million people signed the petition in 24 hours. Craigslist, Facebook, Twitter, and hundreds of other tech giants participated as well, either blacking out their content or posting information about the issue in order to raise awareness.[35] Yahoo, Microsoft, and many other major Internet companies opposed the legislation with public statements.

To be sure, this was a different form of protest: quiet compared to a traditional street rally, but loud in its impact on the media industry and government. Overnight, protest as a tool was transformed as people turned from traditional constituent lobbying techniques (scripted calls and form letters) and toward the use of new media. Mark Zuckerberg, founder and CEO of Facebook, tweeted, "Tell your congressmen you want them to be pro-Internet." Members of Congress faced a barrage of phone calls, e-mails, and tweets from concerned citizens voicing opposition to the anti-piracy laws. In response, at least eight members of Congress publicly changed their position on the legislation within the day, many more withdrew their support in the following days, and the bills' momentum was stalled. As former senator Chris Dodd said, "No Washington player can safely assume that a well-wired, heavily financed legislative program is safe from a sudden burst of Web-driven populism. . . . This is altogether a new effect."[36] The websites and citizens participating in the blackout created a grassroots backlash against Congress.

Are There Drawbacks to Online Participation? Traditional political participation and online participation are not mutually exclusive, of course. Many people are equally comfortable in both worlds, using websites such as Meetup.com to facilitate organizing face-to-face neighborhood meetings, using the Internet to seek out information about where to vote, or using social media for information about a local campaign event.

As we described in Chapter 1, digital citizens are daily Internet users, requiring regular and effective access to the technology, and the skills to use the technology, including language skills.[37] A barrier to participation in politics online is the digital divide—defined as the line separating citizens with Internet access from those without. Those on the wrong side of the divide tend to be poorer, lower educated, African American and Latino, and older. This creates new inequalities as the world of politics moves online.[38] Nearly one-third of Americans lack high-speed Internet access at home, although a growing number of Americans connect to the Internet through mobile devices such as cell phones, even if they lack home access, especially racial minorities and the young.[39] However, one in five Americans remains completely offline as of 2012. For some, Internet access is prohibitively costly or difficult to use, precluding online activities such as participation in politics altogether. Racial minorities and the poor are more likely to cite affordability and cost as reasons for their lacking Internet access at home compared to other groups. A lack of skills is a primary reason for being offline for Latinos, while a lack of interest is the primary reason among the elderly.[40] Inequality in access to political information online is an important public policy issue, separating the digital "haves" from the "have-nots." (See Chapter 7 for more discussion.)

The Future of Online Participation? Inequality in technology access notwithstanding, a growing number of voters finds the advantages of online participation to be overwhelming—and in any case, the Internet isn't going away. So what does this mean for American politics? The breakthrough success of the 2008 Obama campaign's use of the Internet to attract donations and the tidal wave of digital protest against SOPA and PIPA strongly suggest that online participation will play an increasingly important role in real-world offline politics.

Perhaps the most transformative aspect of digital media is how they affect not the participation of ordinary citizens, but rather that of candidates and officeholders. Running for office can be enormously expensive, but new media may level the playing field by reducing candidate reliance on money from corporations, special interests, and wealthy donors. Dark-horse and third-party candidates can now reach voters because of the relatively low cost and the 24-hour availability of the Internet. Despite recent Supreme Court rulings against legislative attempts to limit the influence of money in politics (*Citizens United*), new media offer the promise of reinvigorating a more grassroots and participatory American democracy.[41] But it also costs money to advertise online, which may benefit wealthy candidates.

● Voter Participation

Examine voter turnout in American elections

Whether voting is as effective or satisfying as protest (online or offline) and other forms of political action is an open question. It is clear, however, that for most Americans, voting remains one of the most important forms of political activity. The right to vote gives ordinary Americans a more equal chance to participate in politics than almost any other form of political activity. Voting is especially important because this act selects the officials who make the laws that the American people must follow, including laws compelling them to pay taxes. Voting is the single most important political act for most Americans, and it is the most common way that individuals involve themselves in politics. In the remainder of this chapter, therefore, we will turn to voting in America.

Voting Rights

The right to vote, or **suffrage**, is a legal right. During the colonial and early national periods of American history, suffrage was generally restricted to white males over the age of 21. Many states further limited voting to those who owned property or paid more than a specified amount of annual tax. The Founders gave to the state legislatures the authority to regulate congressional elections, a decision that would have profound consequences for voting rights throughout American history. Until the early 1900s, state legislatures elected U.S. senators, and there were no direct elections for members of the Electoral College (who in turn elect the president), so elections for the U.S. House as well as state and local offices were the primary venue for citizen participation in government.

During the nineteenth and early twentieth centuries, the right to vote was not distributed equally across the American population. The states often acted to restrict expanding suffrage, initially through poll taxes (fees to vote) and literacy tests designed to curtail immigrant voting in northern cities controlled by political machines, and later imported to the southern states to disenfranchise African Americans and uneducated whites during the Jim Crow era. Voter eligibility requirements often varied greatly from state to state. Some states openly prevented the right to vote on the basis of race; others did not. Some states required property ownership for voting; others had no such restrictions. Most states mandated lengthy residency requirements, which meant that persons moving from one state to another sometimes lost their right to vote for as much as a year.[42]

Over the past two centuries of American history, a dominant trend has been federal statutes, court decisions, and constitutional amendments designed to override state voting laws and expand suffrage to non-landowners, African Americans, Asian Americans, women, young adults, and others.[43] In the South, black voting rights were established by the Fifteenth Amendment (1870), which prohibited denying the right to vote on the basis of race. Despite the Fifteenth Amendment, the voting rights of African Americans were effectively rescinded during the 1880s by the states of the former Confederacy. During the 1950s and '60s, through the civil rights movement led by Martin Luther King Jr. and others, African Americans demanded their voting rights. This goal was achieved with the enactment of the 1965 Voting Rights Act, which authorized the federal government to register voters in states that discriminated against minority citizens. The result was the reenfranchisement of southern blacks for the first time since the 1860s.

suffrage the right to vote; also called franchise

for critical analysis

Describe the expansion of suffrage in the United States since the Founding. Why might the government have denied participation to so many for so long? What forces influenced the expansion of voting rights?

Women won the right to vote in 1920, through the adoption of the Nineteenth Amendment. This amendment resulted primarily from the activism of the women's suffrage movement, led by Elizabeth Cady Stanton, Susan B. Anthony, and Carrie Chapman Catt, among others, during the late nineteenth and early twentieth centuries. The "suffragists" held rallies, demonstrations, and protest marches for more than half a century before achieving their goal. The cause of women's suffrage was ultimately advanced by World War I, when President Woodrow Wilson and members of Congress became convinced that women would be more likely to support the war effort if they were granted the right to vote.

The most recent expansion of the right to vote in the United States, the Twenty-Sixth Amendment, lowering the voting age from 21 to 18, was ratified during the Vietnam War, in 1971. Unlike black suffrage and women's suffrage, which came about in part because of the demands of groups that had been deprived of the right to vote, the Twenty-Sixth Amendment was not a response to the demands of young people to be given the right to vote. Instead, the right to vote was intended to channel the disruptive protest activities of students involved in the anti–Vietnam War movement into peaceful participation at the ballot box.

Current Trends in Voter Turnout Today voting rights are granted to all American citizens age 18 and older, although some states revoke this right from those who have committed a felony or are mentally incompetent. (This will be discussed in detail below.) Despite granting suffrage to women, racial minorities, and young adults, however, America's rate of voting participation, or **turnout**, is low. Only 6 in 10 eligible Americans vote in presidential elections, and turnout for midterm elections (elections that fall between presidential elections) is typically much lower, around 33 percent of eligible voters; for local elections, turnout is even lower.[44] Turnout in state and local races that do not coincide with national contests is typically much lower. (In most European countries and other Western democracies, by contrast, national voter turnout is usually between 70 and 90 percent;[45] see America in the World.)

Participation in U.S. presidential elections dropped significantly after 1960, when 64 percent of eligible voters cast ballots. In 1996, participation reached a modern low when only 52 percent of eligible voters went to the polls. Since then, though, overall trends have improved somewhat. In 2004, major efforts to get out the vote brought turnout to over 60 percent—the first significant increase in voting in 40 years. The trend continued in 2008, when nearly 62 percent of the population eligible to vote did so, a modern-day record, and in the 2006 and 2010 midterm elections, turnout rose to more than 40 percent although turnout dropped slightly in 2012 (see Figure 8.2).

turnout the percentage of eligible individuals who actually vote

● Explaining Political Participation: The Individual in Context

Explain the factors that influence whether individuals vote or not

A common starting point for understanding who votes and who does not is to consider that individuals face a number of costs and benefits related to their decision to become involved in politics, just as in any other activity in life. According to such an analysis, an individual is likely to participate only if the benefits of voting in an election outweigh the costs.[46] One benefit associated with voting, for instance, may be the

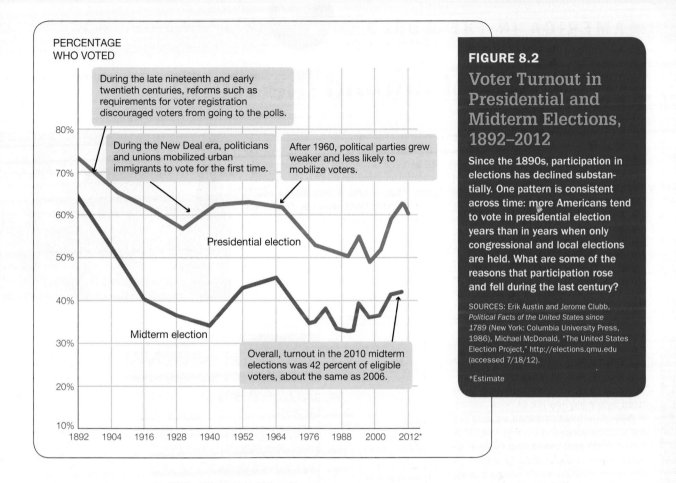

PERCENTAGE
WHO VOTED

During the late nineteenth and early twentieth centuries, reforms such as requirements for voter registration discouraged voters from going to the polls.

During the New Deal era, politicians and unions mobilized urban immigrants to vote for the first time.

After 1960, political parties grew weaker and less likely to mobilize voters.

Presidential election

Midterm election

Overall, turnout in the 2010 midterm elections was 42 percent of eligible voters, about the same as 2006.

FIGURE 8.2

Voter Turnout in Presidential and Midterm Elections, 1892–2012

Since the 1890s, participation in elections has declined substantially. One pattern is consistent across time: more Americans tend to vote in presidential election years than in years when only congressional and local elections are held. What are some of the reasons that participation rose and fell during the last century?

SOURCES: Erik Austin and Jerome Clubb, *Political Facts of the United States since 1789* (New York: Columbia University Press, 1986), Michael McDonald, "The United States Election Project," http://elections.qmu.edu (accessed 7/18/12).

*Estimate

favorable policies that might result from having one's preferred candidate or party in office, which the potential voter weighs against the slim likelihood of his or her vote actually influencing the outcome of the election. Another benefit of voting is the sense of pride gained from fulfilling one's civic duty. The costs related to voting can include the time and resources needed to cast a ballot and the citizen's ability to gather political information and become informed. This may in part explain why the poor and the less educated are less likely to vote.

Beyond the costs and benefits of voting, political scientists have focused on understanding the individual in his or her political environment and how contextual factors affect whether or not that person decides to cast a ballot on Election Day. A simple example is headline news stories declaring an early winner in the exit polls in presidential elections. If a candidate is proclaimed the winner, there is little incentive for individuals to vote; in fact nonvoting is rational. This occurs every four years when voters on the West Coast, located in a time zone three hours later than that of the East Coast, learn that the presidential race is effectively over. Turnout in California and other western states naturally plummets.

The factors that organize our understanding of voting in elections can be grouped into three general categories: (1) a person's socioeconomic status and attitudes about politics, (2) the political environment in which elections take place, such as campaigns that seek to mobilize voters and whether an election is contested among two political candidates, and finally, (3) the state electoral laws that shape the political process.

Voter Turnout around the World

In the United States voter turnout was 38 percent in the 2010 midterm election and about 60 percent in the 2008 presidential election; which is an average of 48 percent. Over the decades since 1945, the average in the United States was a bit higher but still lower than many other nations. The average among the other advanced democracies of the OECD is around 70 percent of the adult population, though there are considerable differences among countries. As the graph below shows, we also find a range of voting rates in developing countries like Thailand and Brazil.

Why is there so much variation in electoral participation around the world? One simple explanation is different electoral rules and electoral systems. These rules determine how the game of politics is played. In most countries citizens are automatically registered to vote when they turn a given age, based on a national ID number (like a social security number in the United States). In the United States, citizens have to register to vote. If they move residences, citizens must reregister to vote in the new district. Not being registered to vote is a primary reason people do not vote. Another reason is that many countries, including Australia, have compulsory voting laws. Citizens can be fined or ticketed for nonvoting. In the United States, there is no penalty for nonvoting. These two simple rules go a long way towards explaining why participation in elections is so low in the United States compared to other nations.

Additionally, many adults in the United States are either noncitizens (and thus denied voting rights) or are ex-felons who have been denied voting rights. The graph measures turnout as a percentage of the voting-age population. If voting rates are calculated as the percent of the population that is *eligible* to vote instead of the adult population, participation in U.S. elections is somewhat higher. Political scientist Michael McDonald's Voter Election Project calculates turnout as the number of votes for the highest office divided by the voting-eligible population (VEP), which excludes noncitizens

and the disenfranchised. Calculated this way, turnout in the 2010 elections was 42 percent, and in the 2008 presidential election was almost 62 percent of Americans. That is only 8 percentage points lower than the OECD average. The lesson is that how we count matters.

[a]www.citizens.org (accessed 9/25/07).

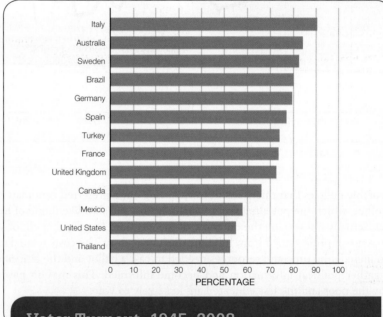

Voter Turnout, 1945–2008

NOTE: Average between 1945 and 2008.

SOURCE: International Institute for Democracy and Electoral Assistance. www.idea.int/vt/ (accessed 12/5/09); note that for some of the countries, the most recent election data are from 2007; for Brazil the average is calculated for the period after 1989, when democracy was restored. Turnout is based on percentage of voting-age population.

for critical analysis

1. Would compulsory voting laws and automatic voter registration laws be useful to adopt in the United States? Or should participation in elections be purely by choice?

2. Does it matter if everyone votes? Do you think ex-felons should be allowed to vote? What about permanent residents who are not citizens? Why or why not?

Socioeconomic Status

One of the most important and consistent findings from surveys about participation is that Americans with higher levels of education, more income, and higher-level occupations—collectively, what social scientists call higher **socioeconomic status**—participate much more in politics than do those with less education and less income.[47] Education level is the single most important factor in predicting not only whether an individual will vote, but also most kinds of participation, but income is an important factor (not surprisingly) when it comes to making contributions. People who are more affluent have the money, time, education, and capacity to participate effectively in the political system. These characteristics are also related to attitudes toward politics. Higher levels of political interest and psychological involvement in politics, such as political efficacy, are associated with individuals higher on the socioeconomic scale.[48]

Figure 8.3 on next page shows the differences in voter turnout linked to ethnic group, income and education level, and age. In 2008, for example, just 54 percent of those earning under $25,000 a year voted in the presidential election, compared with 79 percent of those earning more than $100,000 a year.[49] In addition to education and income, other individual characteristics affect participation. For example, African Americans and Latinos are less likely to participate than are whites, although when differences in education and income are taken into account, African Americans participate at similar levels as do whites.[50] Finally, young people are far less likely to participate in politics than are older people. (We will take a closer look at these groups later in this chapter.) Individuals with strong partisan ties—mainly those who affiliate with the Republican or Democratic parties—are more likely to vote than nonpartisans or independents.

But individual-level factors are not the only explanations for voter turnout. Our incomplete understanding of participation is evident when we compare voting across countries. For example, if more political resources lead to a greater likelihood of voting, why does the United States, one of the most prosperous countries in the world, have such a dismal history of participation? And Americans have become more educated over the past century, with more people finishing high school and attending college; so, given the well-documented links between educational attainment and voting, why has participation declined during this period?[51] These puzzles mean we need to look beyond the socioeconomic characteristics of individuals and to the larger political environment in which participation occurs.

Political Environment

However important such individual factors as age and socioeconomic class may be in determining political participation, political environments and state election laws have increasingly proven to be even more significant. Whether or not people have resources, feel engaged, or are recruited to participate in politics depends very much on their social setting—what their parents are like, whom they know, what associations they belong to. In the United States, churches are one important social institution for helping foster political participation. Through their church activities people learn the civic skills that prepare them to participate in the political world more broadly. However, Robert Putnam argues that, over the past five decades, America has experienced a collapse of community organizations (or social capital), which may explain low participation. Younger generations are less likely to be engaged in community organizations that are involved in politics than, say, generations that came of age during World War II.

socioeconomic status status in society based on level of education, income, and occupational prestige

for critical analysis

As voter turnout has declined since its peak in the late 1800s, inequality in political participation has become more severe. Why are upper-income Americans more likely to be voters than lower-income Americans?

FIGURE 8.3

The Percentage of Americans Who Voted, 1976–2008

Voting rates vary substantially by race and ethnicity, education, employment status, and age. Which groups have the highest rates of voter turnout? Among which groups has participation increased the most since 1992?

SOURCES: U.S. Census Bureau, "Reported Voting and Registration by Race, Hispanic Origin, Sex, and Age Groups: November 1964 to 2008"; "Reported Voting and Registration by Region, Educational Attainment, and Labor Force: November 1964 to 2008," www .census.gov (accessed 11/24/09).

PERCENTAGE OF POPULATION
REPORTING THEY VOTED

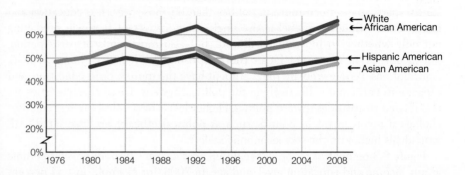

← White
← African American
← Hispanic American
← Asian American

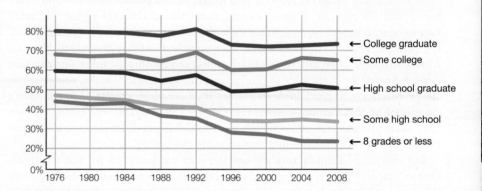

← College graduate
← Some college
← High school graduate
← Some high school
← 8 grades or less

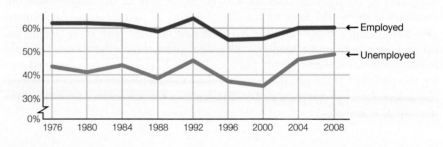

← Employed
← Unemployed

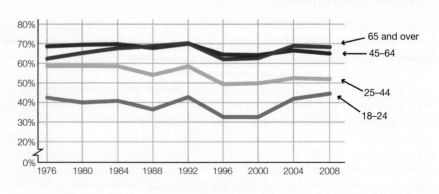

← 65 and over
← 45–64
← 25–44
← 18–24

Still, arguments about long-term declines in community involvement may not give enough attention to the actual political environments where participation takes place. Participation depends not only on what people think politics has to offer them and their communities, but also on whether citizens are motivated and mobilized to participate and on whether there are formal obstacles in the political system.

Mobilization A critical aspect of political environments is whether people are mobilized—by parties, candidates, campaigns, interest groups, and social movements. A recent comprehensive study of the decline in political participation in the United States found that half of the drop-off could be accounted for by reduced **mobilization** efforts.[56] People become much more likely to participate when someone—preferably someone they know—asks them to get involved.

A series of experiments conducted by the political scientists Donald Green and Alan Gerber demonstrates the importance of personal contact for mobilizing voters. Evaluating the results of several get-out-the-vote drives, Gerber and Green showed that face-to-face interaction with a canvasser greatly increased the chances that the person contacted would go to the polls. They estimated that personal contact boosted voter turnout by 9.8 percent. The impact of direct mail was much smaller, causing only a 0.6 percent increase in voting.[53] Impersonal calls from a phone bank had no measurable effect on voter turnout. Green and Gerber also evaluated the impact of mobilization on young voters by studying a series of get-out-the-vote campaigns conducted near college campuses during the 2000 election. In these campaigns, phone contacts that were chattier and more informal than standard phone-bank messages increased turnout by an estimated 5 percent. Face-to-face contact again proved even more powerful, increasing turnout by 8.5 percent.[54] Recent research has shown that text messaging has a positive impact on youth turnout. In 2008 one study showed that sending text messages to young voters on the day before a presidential primary election increased turnout by 2.1 percent; sending messages on the day of the election increased turnout by 4.6 percent.[55]

In previous decades, political parties and social movements relied on personal contact to mobilize voters. As we will see in Chapter 9, during the nineteenth century, American political party machines employed hundreds of thousands of workers to organize and mobilize voters as well as bring them to the polls. The result was an extremely high turnout rate, typically more than 90 percent of eligible voters.[56] But political party machines began to decline in strength at the beginning of the twentieth century, and by now have, for the most part, disappeared. By the late twentieth century, political parties had become essentially fund-raising and advertising organizations rather than mobilizers of people. Without party workers to encourage eligible voters to go to the polls, and even bring them there if necessary, many of them will not participate. Nevertheless, competitive presidential elections since 2000 have once again motivated both parties to build strong grassroots organizations to reach voters and turn them out on Election Day. In the 2004 elections, Republicans were more successful in their organizational efforts than Democrats. Republicans

mobilization the process by which large numbers of people are organized for a political activity

People are more likely to turn out to vote if someone asks them face-to-face. Direct mail and impersonal phonecalls are less likely to have an effect on turnout.

for critical analysis

Why do efforts toward direct
mobilization seem to be more
successful than television
advertising in promoting voter
turnout? How is the Internet
becoming an important
tool for increasing political
participation?

built an organization with more than 1.4 million volunteers who were trained to
make calls, go door to door to register voters, write letters to the editor in support
of President Bush, post blogs online, and phone local radio call-in shows.

During the 2008 campaign, though, the Democrats built a more extensive organization to contact and turn out voters than did Republicans. Barack Obama's campaign made mobilization a centerpiece of its strategy from the start. Inspired by
Obama's own experience as a community organizer, the campaign sought to organize a base of volunteers to go door to door seeking support for their candidate.
Many of Obama's crucial primary victories, including his initial win in Iowa and his
later success in states that, like Iowa, used the caucus system to select presidential
candidates, relied on direct voter mobilization. These victories in the primaries led
the Obama campaign to create a nationwide organization of paid staff and volunteers for the general election, rather than focusing on battleground states as his predecessors had done. The expansion of the electorate through mobilization became
a central pillar of the Obama strategy. The campaign opened more than 700 offices
in the battleground states, where paid staff coordinated the work of tens of thousands of volunteers. The Internet, as discussed earlier, played a significant role in
this mobilization strategy. In contrast, the McCain campaign put less emphasis on
building an organization of paid staff and volunteers, relying instead on traditional
voter mobilization tactics and the battleground-state strategy that had worked four
years earlier for George W. Bush.

Analyses of the 2008 election have suggested that the Democrats' organization
and mobilization helped Barack Obama win the White House. By mobilizing support in places where Democrats had not seriously contended in the past, including largely Republican states such as Indiana, the Obama campaign expanded the
electoral map. In 2012, Obama swept most almost all of the battleground states
besides North Carolina. The marriage of technology, money, early voting, and field
organization that the Obama campaign assembled for the 2008 campaign was
repeated in 2012, and will surely be imitated in future elections.

In the past, social movements, such as the labor movement in the 1930s and the
civil rights movement of the 1960s, played an important role in mobilizing people
into politics. Since then, social movements, interest groups, and political parties
have generally reduced their efforts at direct mobilization, although some—such
as the labor movement, the Christian right, and the Tea Party movement—have
revived direct mobilization in recent years. The number of interest groups has
grown dramatically, but the connection that most members have to such groups
often extends no further than their checkbooks. Rather than promoting political
activity through personal contact, membership in an organization is likely to bring
solicitation letters through the mail, requesting donations. And rather than providing a venue for meeting new people and widening a citizen's circle of engagement,
organizational membership is more likely to land one's name on yet another mailing list, generating still more requests for funds.

Electoral Competition To be motivated to vote, individuals must be interested in
the election and knowledgeable about the candidates. An important factor, often
overlooked in analyzing political participation, is whether elections are competitive; that is, whether there are at least two parties (and their candidates) actively
contesting a position in government.[57] Competitive elections, and the campaign
spending and mobilization efforts that go along with them, have been identified as
playing an important role in turnout rates in the United States and cross-nationally.[58]
Conversely, limited exposure to competitive elections may be one reason for the

lower levels of turnout recorded since the 1960s. In many congressional, statewide, and local races, a candidate (often the incumbent) runs unopposed or is expected to win by such a large margin that the challenger's chances are virtually nil. When congressional districts are drawn to favor one political party over another—what is termed *gerrymandering*—election outcomes can be highly lopsided in favor of one candidate over another. This is a primary reason why most members of Congress win elections by landslides—that is, by overwhelming margins.

One political scientist, Todd O. Donovan, uses a baseball analogy to explain the importance of competitive elections in mobilizing people to participate in politics: "People watch a game to see their team win, or because of interest in an important game. Perfect scoring is meaningless if only one team takes the field, and attendance will suffer if two teams are playing that no one can cheer for."[59] When candidates and political parties spend more effort and money to compete for an elected office, more information becomes available to voters in the form of media ads, newspaper coverage, door-to-door campaigns, online campaigns, and more. Electoral competition may reduce the cost to individuals of becoming informed, leading to higher turnout. Conversely, if elections are uncompetitive or uncontested, they generate little political information. Without active campaigns, individuals have fewer opportunities to be interested in an election, and may have less motivation to vote.[60] Under these conditions, the cost of being informed and actually voting is high.

The American states vary dramatically in the competitiveness of presidential elections, congressional elections, gubernatorial elections, and substantive ballot measures. Some U.S. House districts are so uncompetitive that a single candidate often runs in an uncontested election; in some states, up to one-third of congressional races are uncontested in some election years.[61] With only one name appearing on the election ballot, there is little incentive for a rational citizen to vote, as voting will not affect the outcome. On average over the past 40 years, only two dozen U.S. House races have been very competitive every two years, producing a

A baseball game in which only one team competed or where neither team had many fans would not attract much interest. Similarly, an uncontested (or noncompetitive) election is unlikely to motivate citizens to participate.

victory margin of 5 percentage points or less by the winning candidate over the losing candidate—for example, the winning candidate gets 52 percent of the vote and the losing candidate 48 percent. Many studies have shown that more electoral competition and increased campaign spending on the part of candidates lead to higher voter turnout.[62]

Beyond candidate races, ballot measures (initiatives and referenda) have been found to increase voter turnout, especially among less educated citizens.[63] Elections that include controversial initiatives on the state ballot—in which citizens vote directly on policy questions such as affirmative action, increasing the minimum wage, or bans on same-sex marriage—have also been found to increase political interest, political knowledge, and contributions to interest groups.[64] In many states, ballot measure campaigns are increasingly important for mobilizing voter turnout and can have spillover effects on candidate races.[65] In the 2004 presidential election, for example, laws prohibiting same-sex marriage appeared on the ballot in 13 states. Scholars have found that the ballot measure campaigns and media attention increased the importance of marriage as an issue when voters evaluated the 2004 presidential candidates in these states. The issue was also a more important factor in voting for the president in the 13 states where marriage was on the ballot than in the states without such ballot measures. That is, the same-sex-marriage ballot measures may have helped re-elect George W. Bush in the 2004 presidential elections by priming voters to make the issue of same-sex marriage more salient, which had the effect of benefiting the Republican candidate over the Democratic candidate.[66] These studies point to ballot measure campaigns providing the motivation to engage citizens to participate in politics.

An important source of variation in electoral competition is America's unique structure for presidential elections. No other country uses an electoral college to mediate between a national or direct vote for presidential candidates and the actual winner. To win, a U.S. presidential candidate must receive a majority of the votes in the electoral college (270), which are awarded to states based on the size of their congressional delegation. (The electoral college is covered in more detail in Chapter 10.) Some citizens reside in highly competitive battleground states, such as Ohio, Florida, and Pennsylvania. These states are defined by high levels of competition between the Democratic and Republican parties, with half the voters affiliating with the Republicans and half with the Democrats. Most Americans, however, live in non-battleground states such as California, New York, and Texas, where one or the other of the major parties, Democratic or Republican, is generally assured of victory in presidential elections. Every four years, residents of battleground states get smothered with attention from candidates and media, while citizens in states with few electoral votes or where one political party has a solid majority barely get noticed. Hence, presidential elections are often decided by a relatively small number of voters in America's dozen or so battleground states.[67] One study found that voter turnout in battleground states is higher than in non-battleground states and less skewed in terms of participation by the poor and young. Furthermore, the poor in battleground states are more interested in politics than the poor in non-battleground states.[68] Since the number of battleground states has been decreasing, fewer and fewer Americans are exposed to high-intensity presidential campaigns, which may be another reason for lower levels of turnout since the 1960s.

Even the structure for nominating presidential candidates has implications for participation in government. Selecting presidential candidates involves a sequence of statewide primary elections and caucuses; the early phase of this process is dominated by a handful of small-population states. The resulting privileged position of Iowa and New Hampshire, sites of the nation's first caucus and first primary election, respectively, can boost political participation. Similarly, studies have shown that citizens residing in early-voting states, such as Iowa, New Hampshire, or the "Super Tuesday" states (the two dozen states that hold primaries or caucuses on a single day about six weeks after the New Hampshire primary), are more likely to vote in presidential primaries and be interested in the election.[69] For residents of late-voting states, by contrast, turnout in primaries is often very low. Frequently the nomination contest is over almost before it starts, as one candidate secures a significant lead in early primaries, leaving many citizens (sometimes the majority of Americans) with no role in selecting their party's nominee. Turnout in these later states naturally plummets. For example, California's 2012 primary election was in June, well after the Republican nominee, Mitt Romney, had already been chosen; turnout in the primary was thus very low.

State Electoral Laws

As stipulated by the Constitution, the states retain control of voter registration and voting itself. This decentralized system continues to create wide variation in the laws governing elections and voting, as well as participation in politics.[70] Voter turnout in presidential elections in the last decade ranges from a high of over 70 percent of eligible voters in Minnesota to 45 percent in Mississippi, a 25-point difference. State electoral laws can create formal barriers to voting—costs to be weighed against the potential benefits of voting—that can reduce participation.

Registration Requirements An important factor reducing voter turnout in the United States is our nation's unique state-by-state patchwork of registration rules. In most other democracies in the world, citizens are automatically registered to vote, but the United States requires a two-step process: registering to vote and then voting. In every American state but North Dakota, individuals who are eligible to vote must register with the state election board before they are actually allowed to vote, although a handful of states now allow this to occur on Election Day itself. Registration requirements (another voting cost) were introduced at the end of the nineteenth century in response to the demands of the Progressive movement. Historical Progressive reformers hoped to make voting more difficult, both to reduce multiple voting and other forms of corruption and to discourage immigrant and working-class voters from going to the polls so political parties would be more responsive to middle-class voters and professionals. In some states, registration requirements reduced voter turnout by as much as 50 percent. Once voters are registered, they participate at very high levels—80 to 90 percent of those registered have voted in recent elections.

Registration requirements particularly reduce voting by the young, those with low education, and those with low incomes because registration requires a greater degree of political involvement (a cost) than does the act of voting itself. Those with relatively little education may become interested in politics once the issues of a particular campaign become salient, but by then it may be too late for them to register, especially if they live in states that require registration up to a month before the election. And because young people tend to change residences more often than older people, registration requirements place a greater burden on them. As a result, registration requirements not only diminish the size of the electorate but also tend to create an electorate that is, on average, better educated, more affluent, and composed of fewer young people and minorities than the citizenry as a whole (see Figure 8.4). In Europe, there is typically no registration burden on the individual voter; voter registration is handled automatically by the government. This is one reason that voter turnout rates in Europe are higher than those in the United States.

Other Formal Barriers A barrier to voting that has grown more important in recent years is the restriction on the voting rights of people who have committed a felony. Forty-eight states and the District of Columbia prohibit prison inmates who are serving a felony sentence from voting.[71] In 36 states, felons on probation or parole are not permitted to vote. There are also numerous restrictions on the voting rights of felons who have served their sentences. In 11 states, a felony record can result in a lifetime ban on voting.

With the sharp rise in incarceration rates in the 1980s and '90s, these restrictions have had a significant impact on voting rights. By one estimate, 5.3 million people (2.4 percent of the voting-age population) have lost their voting rights as a result of these restrictions. Further, such restrictions disproportionately affect minorities because 60 percent of the prison population is African American or Latino, though these groups make up only roughly 25 percent of the population. One in eight black men cannot vote because of a criminal record. In the states that deny the vote to all ex-felons, nearly one in three black men has lost the right to vote.[72] The impact of felon disenfranchisement has been especially strong in the South, where Republican candidates have benefited from the reduction in the numbers of minority voters. Concern over the impact of these voting restrictions has led to campaigns to restore voting rights to people who have committed a felony. Since 1997, 19 states have reduced voting restrictions for people with a felony record.[73] Such reforms may have an important impact on politics: one study showed that if all people with felony records had been allowed to vote, Al Gore would have won the 2000 election.[74]

A relatively recent barrier is a requirement that voters provide proof of identity. Thirty-one states require all voters to show ID before voting at the polls: in 15 states a voter must provide photo identification to vote; in the remaining 16, non-photo forms of ID are acceptable. Georgia and Indiana have what the National Conference of State Legislatures (NCSL) calls strict photo identification laws, requiring government photo ID. In 2011 and 2012, six additional states (Kansas, Mississippi, South Carolina, Tennessee, Texas, and Wisconsin) passed similar laws. Voter identification laws in the states disproportionately affect minority citizens and the less affluent, reducing voter turnout of certain groups.[75]

Another barrier to voting has received less attention. In the United States, elections are held on Tuesdays—regular working days. In most European countries, by contrast, elections are held on Sundays or holidays. In some countries, such as India, polls remain open for several days. Holding elections on working days may make it difficult for some people to vote due to the demands of work and family. The United States has addressed this problem somewhat by expanding the use of absentee ballots, early voting, and voting by mail. Some reformers have called for an Election Day holiday, as is commonly used in Europe. This would underscore the importance of voting in America, making democratic participation a priority.

Voting and Registration Reforms Election reform efforts over the past quarter-century have focused mainly on making voter registration and voting easier and more convenient. These reforms are based on the premise that reducing the cost of voting (in the sense of cost-benefit analysis) should increase voter turnout.[76] Lever-

for critical **analysis**

Why is voter turnout so low in the United States? What are the consequences of low voter turnout?

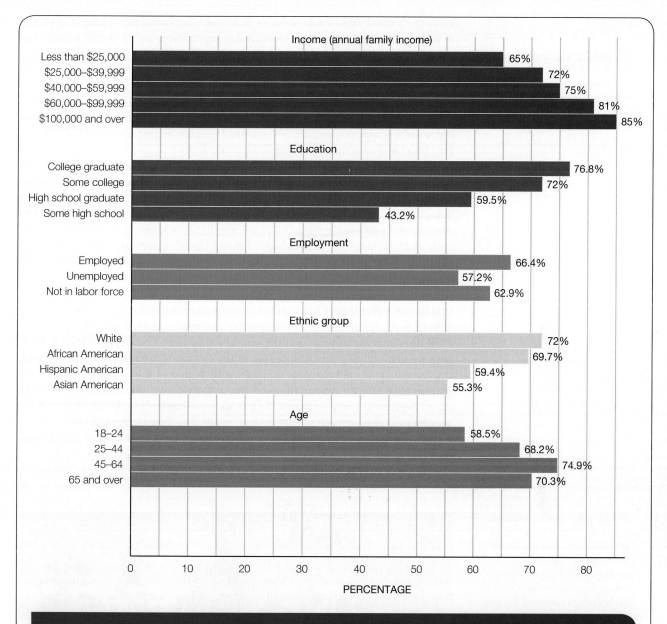

FIGURE 8.4

Voter Registration Rates by Social Group, 2008

Some political analysts argue that registration requirements depress turnout. The percentage of the population that is registered to vote varies according to education level, employment status, race and ethnicity, and age. Are people with a lower income more or less likely to register to vote? Are less educated people more or less likely to register? Would the rates of participation among these groups change if registration requirements were altered?

Sources: U.S. Census Bureau, "Reported Voting and Registration by Race, Hispanic Origin, Sex, and Age Groups: November 1964 to 2008"; "Reported Voting and Registration by Region, Educational Attainment, and Labor Force: November 1964 to 2008," www.census.gov (accessed 11/24/09); U.S. Census Bureau, "Reported Voting and Registration by Region, Educational Attainment, and Labor Force: November 1964 to 2008," www.census.gov (accessed 11/24/09); Douglass R. Hess and Jody Herman, "Representational Bias in the 2008 Electorate," November 2009, www.projectvote.org (accessed 11/21/09).

aging the natural variation in the American states, scholars have studied the effects of early voting, voting by mail, election-day registration, and absentee voting laws, among other such reforms.[77] **Election-Day registration** (EDR) combines the two-step process of voting—registering to vote and casting a ballot on Election Day—into one. On the same day, citizens can both register to vote and actually cast a ballot. A dozen states have EDR laws, with North Carolina and Iowa the two most recent adopters, in 2008. Proposals to adopt EDR have been considered in other states, but are often opposed because of concerns (whether legitimate or not) of Election Day fraud and noncitizens voting.

As might be expected, in states that do not require registration (North Dakota) or that allow registration on the day of the election (Idaho, Iowa, Minnesota, Maine, Montana, New Hampshire, North Carolina, Wisconsin, and Wyoming), not only is voter turnout higher than the national average, but younger and less affluent voters turn out in larger percentages.[78] On average, EDR increases turnout by 5 percent, with all other factors held constant.[79] One of the most sophisticated studies, conducted by political scientist Michael Hamner, measured change in voter turnout after the statewide adoption of EDR, comparing turnout rates with those of similar states without EDR. The study controlled for the possibility that states adopting registration reforms may have higher turnout rates in the first place and a political culture that supports citizen participation. The results of Hamner's study indicate EDR does increase turnout, but the effects are modest. The largest effects of EDR laws are in modifying the composition of the electorate; turnout among the young, the less educated, and the poor is significantly higher in the dozen states allowing citizens to register to vote on the same day as the election, compared to states with longer registration requirements.[80] Thus the real effect of state election reforms may be in altering *who* turns out to vote, rather than *how many* turn out.

New portable voter registration requirements in some states, for example, eliminate the need to reregister after changing residences and may reduce the bias of the electorate by removing one barrier to participation by young people and others

Why is voter turnout relatively low in the United States? One reason may be that the United States requires a two-step process to vote—registering and then voting. Some states have tried to make voting easier and less time-consuming by offering Election-Day registration, early voting, or voting, by mail, and by providing ballots and other information in multiple languages.

who tend to move frequently.[81] In 1988, Oregon voters adopted a ballot measure to create a system for voting exclusively by mail, thus eliminating polling places altogether. Individual voters fill out their ballot at home and place it in the mail or in drop-boxes throughout the state. Washington State followed suit a few years later, and the majority of Californians and citizens of other Western states now cast votes using **permanent absentee ballots**, which are mailed.[82] In Colorado, a state that promotes absentee voting, 78.6 percent of the vote was cast via absentee ballot in 2008.[83] The western states tend to have higher voter turnout than other parts of the country besides the Midwest, making it difficult to disentangle whether mail voting or regional political culture drives higher turnout.

Another reform that has been adopted by many states is **early voting**, which allows registered voters to cast a ballot at their regular polling place up to 40 days before the election. In contrast to EDR or mail voting, early voting may not significantly increase turnout or alter the demographic composition of the electorate.[84] One study from Oregon found that voting by mail increased voter turnout, but only among those groups already predisposed to vote; early voting reinforces higher turnout among the upper class and older citizens, and nonvoting among the lower class.[85]

Removing formal obstacles to voting, or reducing voting costs, may not be enough to ensure that people participate, as the example of the National Voter Registration Act passed in 1993 shows. Popularly known as the Motor Voter Act, the law aimed to increase participation by making it easier to register to vote. The law allowed people to register at the Department of Motor Vehicles when they applied for a driver's license and at other public facilities. An estimated 3.4 million people registered to vote as a result of the Motor Voter Act, but turnout in the 1996 election—the first presidential election held after the law went into effect—actually declined by 6 percent from that in 1992.[86] The limited success of the Motor Voter Act suggests that people need motivation to vote, such as active candidate campaigns and competitive elections, not simply the removal of registration barriers.

The political scientist Adam Berinksy provides an explanation for these seemingly contradictory findings that overall voter turnout has not increased despite efforts to make voting easier and more convenient. He suggests that making voting more convenient (e.g., voting by mail, early voting, and absentee voting) simply reinforces the behavior of those most likely to vote. These reforms do not lower the costs of voting enough to engage those with few political resources, but instead lower the costs enough for the upper classes to vote more consistently. One study shows that different election reforms may produce different outcomes. Reducing barriers to registration can increase the likelihood of voting among those not already a part of the electoral system, and voting that is more convenient mainly helps those most likely to vote anyway, while EDR has a relatively strong influence on turning out lower-income voters.[87]

Of all the reforms, EDR has shown the most promise for increasing turnout in general and in increasing voting among the young and those with few resources. But voter turnout isn't the only outcome that matters. One estimate put the number of early votes at one-third of the national total in 2008, with Obama outperforming his Republican opponent, John McCain, in early-voting ballots.[88] Thus state election laws allowing early voting may have helped Obama win office in 2008.[89] Obama wisely made early voting a key part of his campaign in 2008 and again in 2012, encouraging his supporters to vote early and thus avoid problems that occur on Election Day, such as long lines, poor weather, or malfunctioning voting machines.

Recent Restrictions on Voting Rights: A Backlash? Not everyone agrees that increasing voter turnout is a worthy goal. In recent years, despite the general trend

permanent absentee ballots the option in some states to have a ballot sent automatically to your home for each election, rather than having to request an absentee ballot each time

early voting the option in some states to cast a vote at a polling place or by mail before the election

throughout American history toward encouraging wider political participation, there have been efforts in many states to reimpose restrictions on voting rights.

As just noted, more than half of the states—31 as of 2012—have introduced requirements that would-be voters must produce proof of identity at their polling places. The issue of whether to require voters' proof of identity has become bitterly partisan. Proponents of such measures, mainly Republicans, insist that the possibility of voter fraud threatens "the sanctity of the vote"; opponents, mainly Democrats, counter that there have been almost no significant instances of voter fraud in the modern era and that the new photo ID laws are actually designed to suppress the vote of segments of the population most likely to vote for Democrats but also least likely to have photo ID—racial minorities, the elderly, and the poor.

● Diversity and Participation

> **Describe the patterns of participation among major social groups**

America's racial and ethnic diversity distinguishes it from many other democracies; participation by varying groups is important, as government must balance the demands of varying segments of the population. We've seen that individual characteristics, especially socioeconomic status, are associated with different levels and types of political participation.

Why does minority participation matter? One study of black political participation, for example, found that African Americans in cities run by a black mayor were more likely to vote, participate in campaigns, and contact public officials.[90] African Americans and Latinos are also more likely to vote when residing in states with increased representation in the state legislature, as measured by the percentage of black or Latino lawmakers.[91] One study found that African Americans represented by a black member of Congress are more likely to vote in elections and to have a sense of efficacy—the belief that the government is responsive to them—and have higher levels of political knowledge.[92] The same pattern is found for Latinos, with Latino representation in Congress and in state legislatures increasing Latino voting participation.[93] This phenomenon is commonly referred to as descriptive representation—when individuals are represented in government by officials of their same race, ethnicity, or gender.

When meaningful descriptive representation occurs, minority groups may have a greater ability to affect policy outcomes, thus incorporating minority populations and their concerns and interests into the political system. Descriptive representation may also confer symbolic benefits, such as reducing levels of political alienation among racial and ethnic minorities.[94] Since racial and ethnic groups generally hold different political opinions and support different political parties, elected officials disproportionately represent those who participate, which potentially leads to policies that pay little heed to nonvoters.[95] We discuss descriptive representation again in Chapter 12.

African Americans

As we saw earlier in Chapter 5, in the South during much of the twentieth century, the widespread use of the poll tax, literacy tests, and other measures such as the white primary deprived African Americans (and many poor whites) of the right to vote. This system of legal segregation meant that black Americans in the South had few avenues for participating in politics.

Political and legal pressure, as well as protest, all played a part in the modern civil rights movement, which became a major force for change in the 1950s (see Chapter 5). The movement drew on an organizational base and network of communication rooted in black churches, the NAACP, and black colleges.

The nonviolent protest tactics adopted by local clergy members, including Reverend Martin Luther King Jr., eventually spread across the South and brought national attention to the movement. The clergy organized themselves into a group called the Southern Christian Leadership Conference (SCLC). Students also played a key role. The most important student organization was the Student Nonviolent Coordinating Committee (SNCC). In 1960, four black students in Greensboro, North Carolina, sat down at the lunch counter of a Woolworth's department store, which, like most southern establishments, did not serve African Americans. Their sit-in was the first of many. Through a combination of protest, legal action, and political pressure, the civil rights movement compelled a reluctant federal government to enforce black civil and political rights.

The victories of the civil rights movement made blacks full citizens and stimulated a tremendous growth in the number of black public officials at all levels of government as blacks exercised their newfound political rights. By voting as a cohesive bloc, African American voters began to wield considerable political power. When such legal barriers as the poll tax and the white primary were removed in the 1960s, black political participation shot up, with rates of turnout approaching those of southern whites as early as 1968.[96] Yet despite these successes, racial segregation remains a fact of life in the United States, and new problems have emerged. Most troubling is the persistence of black urban poverty, now coupled with deep social and economic isolation.[97] These conditions, often called concentrated poverty, raise new questions about African American political participation. One such question concerns black political cohesion: Will blacks continue to vote as a bloc, given the sharp economic differences that now divide a large black middle class from an equally large group of deeply impoverished African Americans? Public opinion and voting evidence indicate that African Americans have indeed continued to vote cohesively despite their economic differences.[98] Surveys of black voters show that blacks across the income spectrum believe that their fates are linked because of their race. This sense of shared experience and a common fate has united blacks at the polls and in politics.[99]

In the decades after the Civil War, newly enfranchised African American voters overwhelmingly supported Republicans, the "Party of Lincoln." When Franklin Delano Roosevelt ran for the presidency in 1932, however, most black voters joined the coalition that, through the many social programs that composed the New Deal, redefined not only the Democratic Party but also government itself. Especially since the 1960s when the Democratic Party favored the civil rights movement and white southerners began to desert the Democratic Party of Lyndon Johnson's Great Society, blacks have largely chosen Democratic candidates (roughly 90 percent of blacks vote Democratic), and black candidates have sought election under the Democratic banner. African Americans are one of the most cohesive groups in voting Democratic. Republican hostility to affirmative action and other programs of racial preference is likely to prevent any large-scale black migration to the Republican Party. At the same time, however, the black community has been considerably frustrated that their loyalty to the Democratic Party, even under African American president Barack Obama, has not been rewarded with economic opportunity. Because Republicans have not sought to win the black vote and Democrats take it for granted, neither party is willing to support bold measures to address the problems of poor African Americans.

With Barack Obama running in 2008 as the first black major-party candidate for president, African American interest in the election surged. Exit polls indicated that 95 percent of African Americans who voted cast ballots for Obama. The 2008 election also witnessed a significant increase in minority participation and marked an end to the long-standing gap in the level of black and white voter turnout. Black turnout rose 5 percent from 2004 to 2008, while there was only a 3 percent increase for Latinos. White non-Hispanic turnout was 67 percent in 2004 and 66 percent in 2008. The black-white gap went from 7 percent in 2004 to 1 percent in 2008.[100] Was this surge in minority voting merely an anomaly sparked by the Obama campaign, or was it indicative of a more general relationship between the election of minorities to public office and voter turnout?

Latinos

For many years, analysts called the Latino vote "the sleeping giant" because Latinos as a group had relatively low levels of political mobilization. One important reason for this was the low rate of naturalization, which meant that many Latinos, as noncitizens, were not eligible to vote. Among those who were eligible to vote, registration and turnout rates were relatively low.

Today politicians and political parties view Latinos as a political group of critical importance, as they have become the largest minority group in the United States. Rapid population growth, increased political participation, and uncertain party attachment all magnify the importance of the Latino vote.[101] The Latino population stands at 50.5 million people as of 2010, or 16.3 percent of Americans, making Hispanics significantly more numerous than African Americans.[102] In large states such as California, Latinos approach 50 percent of the population. Although Latino registration and turnout are still significantly lower than those of whites and African Americans, these numbers have been steadily increasing. In 2008 a record 9.75 million Hispanics voted, accounting for 7.4 percent of the total national vote. In 2012, these numbers increased, with Latinos accounting for 10 percent of voters.[103]

Latinos have tended to favor the Democrats in national elections, though not as strongly or consistently as African Americans. Indeed, many Republicans believe that the tendency of Hispanic voters to be more socially conservative on issues of marriage, abortion, and religion than other groups within the Democratic Party provides the GOP with an opportunity to attract support from this growing constituency. President George W. Bush was especially committed to cultivating support in the Latino community, winning upwards of 44 percent of Latino votes in the 2004 presidential election, more than any other Republican presidential candidate in modern history. However, Republican opposition to immigration reform prompted Latinos to return to their more typical Democratic voting patterns in 2006 and 2008.

President Obama, much like his predecessor, has actively courted Latino voters. Nowhere was this more evident than in his nomination in May 2009 of Sonia Sotomayor to be the nation's first Latina Supreme Court justice. Obama also appointed two Latino lawmakers, Ken Salazar and Hilda Solis, to his cabinet and named a record number of Hispanics to positions within the administration. Obama's expansion of health insurance coverage was far more popular within the Latino community than the nation at large, mainly because of the high percentage of Latinos without insurance coverage.[104] The Obama administration has also aggressively reached out to Spanish-speaking media in an effort to connect to Latino voters: it held the first bilingual White House press briefing and partnered with Spanish-language networks Univision and Telemundo to broadcast White House events. Latino voters retained their strong allegiance to Democratic candidates in the 2010 midterm elections.[105]

However, Obama's failure to adopt immigration reform, combined with increased deportations of illegal immigrants during his first term, led to disaffection among some in the Latino community. Latinos were disappointed that, during the first four years of the Obama administration, more illegal immigrants were deported than during the eight years of the George W. Bush administration. However, Latinos leaned back toward the Democratic Party after the decision from the Obama administration in 2012 not to deport young people who came to the United States as children of illegal immigrants. In 2012, Obama and his challenger Mitt Romney both tried to appeal to Latino voters, but according to exit polls, Obama won 70 percent of the Latino vote.

Asian Americans

Asian Americans are a smaller group than whites, Latinos, or African Americans, comprising 4.8 percent of the U.S. population in 2010. Yet, individuals who were Asian combined with at least one other race made up 5.6 percent of the nation's population. However, in particular states, such as California, home to 33 percent of the nation's Asian population, the group has become an important political presence. While the Asian population is just over 5 percent nationally, in California it is 13.4 percent of the population, according to the 2010 census. In terms of socioeconomic status, Asian Americans are more similar to non-Hispanic whites as

Although Asian Americans come from diverse national backgrounds and hold diverse political opinions, efforts have been made recently to increase overall turnout among Asian American voters and increase their influence as a group. In 2008, the Center for Asian Americans United for Self-Empowerment (CAUSE) undertook a major effort to register Asian Pacific voters.

a group, with education and income levels closer to those of whites than of Latinos or African Americans. Asians often vote similarly to whites.

No one national group dominates among the Asian American population, and their diversity has impeded the development of group-based political power. This diversity means that Asian Americans often have different political concerns, stemming from their different national backgrounds and experiences in the United States. Historically, these groups have united most effectively around common issues of ethnic discrimination or anti-Asian violence, federal immigration policies, and discriminatory mortgage loan practices.

Turnout rates among Asian Americans have been generally lower than those of other groups, though they have been gradually increasing; in 2008, 47.6 percent of Asian Americans turned out to vote, their second-highest percentage turnout since the census began tracking their participation in 1990.[106] In terms of political orientation, Asian Americans are a diverse group, but they have been moving, along with other minority groups, toward the Democratic Party in recent elections. Although a majority of Asian Americans voted Republican in the early 1990s, in the 2000s they have been voting increasingly Democratic,[107] and 73 percent of Asian Americans voted to re-elect Barack Obama in 2012.

Gender and Participation

Today women register and vote at rates similar to or higher than those of men. The ongoing significance of gender issues in American politics is best exemplified by the **gender gap**—a distinctive pattern of male and female voting decisions—in electoral politics. Women tend to vote in higher numbers for Democratic candidates, whereas Republicans win more male votes. In 1980, men voted heavily for the Republican candidate, Ronald Reagan; women divided their votes between Reagan and the incumbent Democratic president, Jimmy Carter. Since that election, gender differences have emerged in congressional and state elections as well. In the 2004 election, George W. Bush narrowed the gender gap substantially, winning 48 percent of the female vote.[108] By 2006 the gender gap had reappeared, with 55 percent of women voting Democratic and only 43 percent Republican.[109] In the 2008 presidential election, observers expressed doubt about how women would vote, especially disappointed supporters of Democratic candidate Hillary Clinton. In fact, women voted strongly Democratic in 2008, with exit polls showing that 58 percent of women cast their ballots for the Obama-Biden ticket and 43 percent for the McCain-Palin ticket. In 2012, both parties considered women's votes as potentially decisive in the close race. However, Obama won the majority of women's votes again; according to exit polls, 55 percent of women voters cast their vote for compared to 44 percent favoring Romney.

Behind these voting patterns are differing assessments of key policy issues. Women are more likely than men to oppose military activities, especially war, and are more likely to support social spending. In 2003, 79 percent of men supported the Iraq War, for example, compared with 65 percent of women—a 14-point difference. This split continued during the debate about when to withdraw from Iraq. In 2007, 51 percent of men stated that they were in favor of keeping troops in Iraq until civil order was restored, whereas only 35 percent of women supported keeping troops there with such an indefinite time horizon.[110] On social programs, women tend to want stronger action from government: 37 percent of men express satisfaction with the Social Security and Medicare systems, whereas only 33 percent of women do; 45 percent of men were content with the quality of public education, whereas only 39 percent of women

gender gap a distinctive pattern of voting behavior reflecting the differences in views between women and men

Women won the right to vote with the adoption of the Nineteenth Amendment in 1920, in part because many officials were convinced that women's suffrage would increase female support for American involvement in World War I. However, women have generally been less likely than men to support military activities.

were.[111] These differences do not mean that all women vote more liberally than all men. In fact, the voting differences between women who are homemakers and women who are in the workforce are almost as large as the differences between men and women.[112]

One key development in gender politics in recent years is the growing number of women in elective office (see Figure 8.5), an increasingly significant form of descriptive representation. Journalists dubbed 1992 the "Year of the Woman" because so many women were elected to Congress: women doubled their numbers in the House and tripled them in the Senate. By 2009, women held 17.2 percent of the seats in the House of Representatives, including that held by the first female Speaker of the House, Nancy Pelosi. A total of 17 women served in the 100-member Senate in 2009–11, which represented an all-time high for an institution that had had only 38 female senators in its entire history.[113] Following the 2012 elections, 20 women served in the Senate, including 4 freshmen, notably Elizabeth Warren (D-Mass.) and Tammy Baldwin (D-Wisc.). Baldwin is also the first openly gay person elected to the senate. A record 28 women of color were elected to House, including 13 African American women, 9 Latinas, and 6 Asian/Pacific Islander Americans.

Recent research has shown that one key to increasing the number of women in political office is to encourage more women to run for election and by asking women to run for political office. Although women are just as likely to win an election as men, women are less likely to run for office, even if they are equally qualified as men. They are also disadvantaged as candidates not because they are women, but because male candidates are more likely to have the advantage of incumbency.[114] Organizations supporting female candidates have worked to encourage more women to run for office and have supported them financially. In addition to the bipartisan National Women's Political Caucus (NWPC), the Women's Campaign

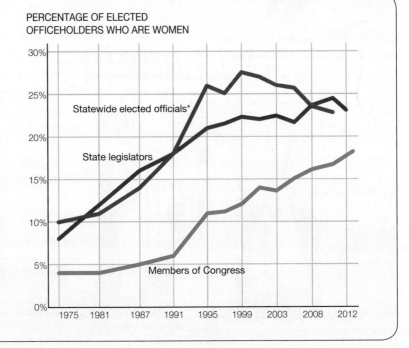

FIGURE 8.5

Increase in Number of Women in Elective Office, 1975–2013

The number of women holding elected office has always been larger in state offices than in Congress. When did the percentage of women elected to office begin to rise more rapidly?

*Governors, attorneys general, etc.

SOURCES: Cynthia Costello, Shari Miles, and Anne J. Stone, eds., *The American Woman, 2001–2002* (New York: W.W. Norton, 2002), p. 328; and Center for American Women and Politics, www.cawp.rutgers.edu (accessed 11/8/12).

PERCENTAGE OF ELECTED OFFICEHOLDERS WHO ARE WOMEN

Statewide elected officials*

State legislators

Members of Congress

Fund (WCF), and EMILY's List ("Early Money Is Like Yeast—it helps raise the dough") provide prochoice Democratic women with early campaign financing, which is critical to establishing electoral momentum.

Women candidates gained special prominence in the 2008 elections, with Senator Hillary Clinton's strong campaign for the Democratic presidential nomination and the selection of Alaska's governor Sarah Palin to run as vice president on the Republican ticket. Although neither succeeded in winning office, their campaigns marked important milestones in the road to power for women politicians. Clinton's nearmiss for the Democratic presidential nomination, in particular, is likely to make it easier for women to be considered credible presidential candidates in the future. Some research suggests that women were more likely to vote for Hillary Clinton in the 2008 presidential primaries than for the male candidates.

Why does the gender gap matter? Although women in public office by no means take uniform positions on policy issues, surveys show that, on the whole, female legislators are more supportive of women's rights and education and health care spending, and are more attentive to children's and family issues.[115] Recent surveys have shown that voters judge public officials differently on the basis of gender. While women are evaluated more positively on issues such as education and health care and are viewed as more skilled at striking compromises, the public views male officials as far more capable of dealing with national security and defense, and with crime and public safety.[116]

Age and Participation

Older people have much higher rates of participation than young people. In the 2008 presidential elections, youth turnout was at its highest level in decades, with

51 percent of those aged 18 to 29 voting. However, this figure is still far lower than the number of older (65 and over) voters who turned out: an estimated 70 percent of those voters cast ballots in 2008.[117] Moreover, in midterm elections, youth turnout has historically been extremely low. In 2012, for example, young voters made up 19 percent of the electorate (up from 18 percent in 2008) but only slightly more than 10 percent in the midterm elections of 2010.

One reason younger people vote less is that political campaigns have rarely targeted young voters. A study of political advertising in the 2000 elections found that 64 percent of campaign television advertising was directed at people over 50. Only 14.2 percent of advertising was aimed at eighteen- to thirty-four-year-olds.[118] Another reason that political campaigns target older voters is that the elderly are better organized to participate than young people. The most important organization representing the elderly is AARP (formerly the American Association of Retired People), which has a membership of 40 million. AARP's ability to mobilize many thousands of individuals to weigh in on policy proposals has made the organization one of the most powerful in Washington. Young people have no comparable organization.

Since the early 1990s, several campaigns have been designed to increase the participation of young voters. Rock the Vote, which began in 1990, uses musicians and actors to urge young people to vote. It has spawned other initiatives aimed at young voters, including Rap the Vote and Rock the Vote a lo Latino.

The Obama campaign made young voters central to its electoral strategy in 2008 and 2012. The campaign posted videos on YouTube and used social media to reach out to young people. It sought to increase participation of young voters through a major voter registration campaign. In 2008, 22.3 million eighteen- to twenty-nine-year-olds (51 percent) turned out to vote, which represented a slight increase from 2004 and a big increase from the 2000 election, in which just

for critical analysis

When the Twenty-Sixth Amendment changed the voting age from 21 to 18 in 1971, observers expected that the youth vote would add a significant new voice to American politics. Why has the youth vote turned out to be less important than was hoped? What changes would engage more young people in the political system?

Registration requirements make it harder to vote because voters have to plan ahead and register, rather than just showing up at the polls on election day. Some groups try to increase voting rates by getting more people registered in advance of elections.

At this 2008 Rock the Vote concert, musicians such as Pharrell Williams, from the band N*E*R*D, performed to support efforts to get young people to vote. Particularly since 2000, campaigns like Rock the Vote have contributed to increases in the youth vote.

40 percent of young voters cast ballots.[119] Exit polls showed that 66 percent of younger voters choose Barack Obama in 2008, with 60 percent supporting Obama in 2012.[120]

Relatively low voter turnout by the young has implications for the policies addressed by government at the local, state, and federal levels. Young people share older Americans' concerns about the economy and national security, but they tend to have more positive views about the role of government and express support for stronger environmental laws, funding for public education and colleges, and more tolerance for personal freedoms than older people do. They also are more likely to oppose military intervention overseas.[121] And although young people are less likely to engage in politics than older generations, they do have a strong interest in community service. One recent survey found that 19 percent of young people are involved in community service projects, with numbers higher among those with college experience.[122] Another survey found that 57 percent of young people felt that they could have a role in solving the problems in their community. Yet that same survey revealed cynicism about politics, with 61 percent of young people responding that "politics is a way for the powerful to keep themselves powerful."[123]

Who Made Up the Electorate in 2012?

The electorate—those citizens who vote in elections—does not necessarily resemble the American population. For example, in 2012, Latinos made up at least 16 percent of the population but only 10 percent of the electorate in the 2012 presidential election (though this percentage has been steadily increasing over recent elections). Americans older than 65 made up about 13 percent of the population but 16 percent of the electorate.

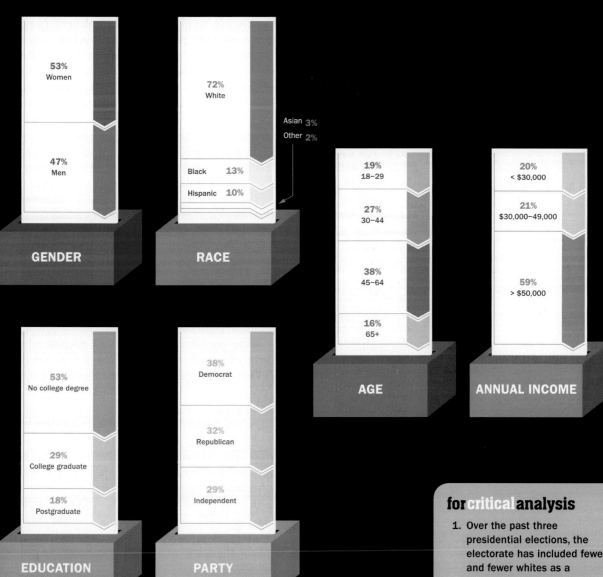

GENDER
- 53% Women
- 47% Men

RACE
- 72% White
- Black 13%
- Hispanic 10%
- Asian 3%
- Other 2%

AGE
- 19% 18–29
- 27% 30–44
- 38% 45–64
- 16% 65+

ANNUAL INCOME
- 20% < $30,000
- 21% $30,000–49,000
- 59% > $50,000

EDUCATION
- 53% No college degree
- 29% College graduate
- 18% Postgraduate

PARTY
- 38% Democrat
- 32% Republican
- 29% Independent

for critical analysis

1. Over the past three presidential elections, the electorate has included fewer and fewer whites as a percentage of total voters. What does this mean for candidates and parties?

2. Does it matter if the electorate reflects the overall population? Why or why not?

SOURCE: Data are based on exit polls available at
http://elections.nytimes.com/2012/results/president/exit-polls (accessed 11/12/12).

Religious Identity

Religious identity plays an important role in American life and has come to the forefront with 2008 and 2012 Republican presidential candidate Mitt Romney, a Mormon, as a front-runner. For many citizens, religious groups provide an organizational infrastructure for political participation, especially around issues of special group concern. Black churches, for example, were instrumental in the civil rights movement, and black religious leaders continue to play important roles in national and local politics. Jews have also been active as a group in politics, but less through religious bodies than through a variety of social action agencies, including the American Jewish Congress, the American Jewish Committee, and the Anti-Defamation League.

For most of American history, religious language, symbols, and values have been woven deeply into the fabric of public life. Until the mid-twentieth century, public school students generally began the day with prayers or Bible readings; city halls displayed crèches during the Christmas season. But over the past 35 years, a variety of court decisions has greatly reduced this kind of overt religious influence on public life. In 1962 the Supreme Court ruled in *Engel v. Vitale* that prayer in public schools was unconstitutional—that government should not be in the business of sponsoring official prayers.[124]

These decisions helped to spawn a countermovement of religious activists seeking to roll back these decisions and restore the prominent role of religion in civic life. The mobilization of religious organizations and other groups that aim to reintroduce their moral views into the public sphere has been one of the most significant political developments of the past two and a half decades. Some of the most divisive conflicts in politics today, such as those over abortion and same-sex marriage, hinge on differences over religious and moral beliefs. These divisions have become so salient that they now constitute a major clash of cultures, with repercussions throughout the political system and across many different areas of policy.

One of the most significant drivers of this new politics has been the mobilization of white evangelical Protestants into a cohesive political force. The Moral Majority, the first broad-based political organization of evangelical Christians, was founded in 1979 and quickly rose to prominence in the 1980 election when it aligned with the Republican Party, eventually backing Ronald Reagan for president. Over the next few years, evangelicals strengthened their movement by registering voters and mobilizing them with sophisticated, state-of-the-art political techniques such as direct-mail campaigns and telephone hotlines. Their success was evident in the 1984 election, when 80 percent of evangelical Christian voters cast their ballots for Reagan. The 1988 election was a turning point in the political development of the Christian right. The televangelist Pat Robertson ran for president, and, although his candidacy was unsuccessful, his effort laid the groundwork for future political strength. Robertson's supporters gained control of some state Republican parties and won positions of power in others. With this new organizational base and sharply honed political skills, Robertson formed a new organization, the Christian Coalition, which capitalized on its ability to mobilize a large grassroots base to become one of the most important groups in American politics during the 1990s.

President George W. Bush was closely aligned with religious conservatives, and the religious right played an important role in mobilizing voters to support him in the 2000 and 2004 elections. Many analysts viewed Bush's Office of Faith-Based and Community Initiatives (whose programs were generally known as faith-based initiatives), which sought to funnel government assistance to religious groups engaged in charitable work, as a way to reward conservative Christian groups for supporting his candidacy. In fact, conservative religious groups spoke out against the initiative at first because they feared that government control would accompany federal dollars.[125]

● Thinking Critically about the Future of Political Participation

The American political community has expanded over the course of history, with new groups winning and asserting political rights. This expansion has brought American politics more closely into line with the fundamental values of liberty, equality, and democracy. But for much of the twentieth century, the electoral system in the United States failed to mobilize an active citizenry, giving rise to an uneven pattern of political participation that gives some people more of a voice in politics than others and thus goes against the American values of equality and democracy. Since 2000 a series of highly competitive presidential elections has spurred political campaigns to pay more attention to drawing greater numbers of voters into the political process, but many Americans still do not participate in politics.

Naturally enough, one of the most important factors in sustaining participation is a sense of political efficacy, the feeling that average citizens can help shape what government actually does. One important study found that elected officials respond more to the preferences of voters than nonvoters, confirming long-held assumptions that the affluent, more educated, and older citizens have more voice in politics and public policy.[126] A study by the political scientist Larry Bartels showed that senators (both Republicans and Democrats) are much less responsive to the policy preferences of low-income citizens—who are also less likely to be active voters.[127] If the voices of only the more affluent are heard during election time, the issues that concern lower-income Americans may not find a place at the top of the political agenda.

What would it take to increase political engagement among citizens of all backgrounds? For decades the conventional wisdom of reformers was to limit the role of money in politics so that the voices of ordinary Americans couldn't be easily drowned out by wealthy individuals and well-financed special interests. In 1976, however, the Supreme Court ruled that individual contributions to candidates were a form of free speech and that it would be a curtailment of liberty to forbid such spending so long as it was not formally connected with political campaigns.[128] And the Supreme Court's 2010 ruling in *Citizens United v. Federal Election Commission* increases the role of money in campaigns. Again defending campaign spending as free speech, the Court ruled that corporations and labor unions could directly spend unlimited amounts of money in favor of candidates as long as the corporations and unions did not coordinate directly with the candidates' campaign organizations. (See Chapter 10 for a discussion of this decision.) The *Citizens United* decision may increase the

For much of American history, formal barriers restricted the right to vote and created a pattern of unequal participation in politics. Today, most of those barriers have been eliminated, but voter turnout remains relatively low, especially among young voters. In 2008, these voters cast their ballots at a polling station in a fraternity house near the UCLA campus.

political influence of the affluent and special interests, such as corporations, potentially weakening the voice of the middle class and poor in politics.[129]

Nonetheless, other recent developments promise to give more people more of a voice in American government. Over the past few decades innovative states have led the way by reforming and modernizing America's patchwork election system, with innovations ranging from EDR to early and mail voting, and even portable registration that eliminates altogether the need to reregister after moving to a new residence. Hawaii registers all high school students to vote, while permanent voter registration, akin to voting systems used in European countries, is increasingly a popular reform at the state level. Some states, such as Iowa, use nonpartisan boards to draw legislative districts, which tend to boost competition in congressional and state legislative races. Increased competition, in turn, often results in a more informed and energized electorate, thus increasing turnout.

Drawing on the American states as laboratories of democracy allows policy makers to test what works and what does not. Reforms found to be successful at the state level may be adopted at the national level: Congress debated legislation to create early voting nationally in 2008. Eighteen states granted women's suffrage before adoption of the Nineteenth Amendment in 1920 gave women the right to vote nationally, and many states allowed the direct election of U.S. senators before the Seventeenth Amendment to the Constitution established direct election of senators by popular vote in each state. If more Americans voted, the policies adopted by their governments would be more representative of the majority preferences in this country.

The explosive growth in online communication as a means of organizing political participation has been especially apparent during recent elections. New technologies have supplied political leaders and candidates with new avenues for reaching out to citizens and have given citizens novel (and even enjoyable) ways to learn about and engage with politics. As we have learned, individuals who learn about politics online are more likely to vote and participate in politics in myriad other ways. Astonishingly diverse online news sources have given rise to new opinion leaders and new voices.

Nevertheless, the new media revolution has some drawbacks for American politics. Misinformation spreads as quickly through the Internet as good information, and false rumors and gender or racial sterotypes can proliferate. Inequality in access to the Internet remains a barrier to full participation in a digital democracy. Those most likely to be offline include the poor, the less educated, the elderly, and racial and ethnic minorities, such as Latinos and African Americans—all the same demographic groups who, along with young Americans, have been least likely to vote. It's possible, then, that these overlapping disadvantages may make the electorate even more unrepresentative. However, mobile access on cell phones is most common among racial minorities and the young, partially bridging the digital divide. Digital politics offers hope for reinvigorating American democracy and participation in politics.

Whatever promise digital politics holds for increasing political participation, it also raises the same fundamental questions that have arisen with every major new development in America's political history: How can citizens turn participation in politics into meaningful representation in government? And how, in turn, can representation result in public policies that reflect the needs of the greatest number of American citizens?

Become a Voter

Inform Yourself

Find out *when* the next election is, and *what* is on the ballot. Go to vote411 .org (a website from the League of Women Voters), and locate "On Your Ballot." Select your state from th e drop-down menu. Either click on the link to all of your state's elections or use the form for "Personalized Ballot" to get information about what is on the ballot in the next election. *Where* do you vote? Enter your street address in the "Polling Place Finder" (on the main vote411.org page) to receive your voting location.

Express Yourself

Register to vote. Voting is one of the most important forms of expression in politics. In most states, you must be registered in order to vote. One way to do so is by visiting vote411.org and selecting "Register to Vote." Your state's page on the site also includes information on what type of ID is necessary to vote.

Ask about voting. If you have questions about how to register to vote or wish to request an absentee ballot, call or e-mail the your state's secretary of state or board of elections. Contact information is provided on the state pages at vote411.org. Most states allow voting via an absentee ballot, which is mailed to your home.

Connect with Others

Get involved in the next election. If there is an election coming up, your local newspaper's website will likely have a guide to the candidates and issues. Many candidates have Facebook pages or personal websites where you can learn about upcoming campaign events and how to get involved (donating money? displaying a sign? attending a meeting?).

Know your current representatives. Even if there's not an election coming up soon, it's a safe bet that some of your current representatives in government will be running for re-election in the next election. Will you support them? Find out who represents you by entering your zip code at the Project Vote Smart website (www .votesmart.org). Choose two of your representatives, and visit their personal websites or Facebook pages to see what types of messages they are posting and whether you agree with the policies they support.

Find links to the sites listed above as well as related activities on wwnorton.com/studyspace.

Forms of Political Participation

■ **Describe the major types of traditional and online participation in politics (pp. 295–304)**

Political participation refers to a wide range of activities designed to influence government, politics, and policy. These activities fall into two major categories: traditional political participation, which refers to long-standing activities, such as voting, volunteering, and contributing to a candidate; and online political participation, which refers to a newer set of activities carried out through the Internet, such as posting comments on a blog or Twitter, or visiting a political party's website. There are many reasons to believe that the opportunities created by Internet in turn increase traditional political participation among large segments of the population.

Key Terms

traditional political participation (p. 295)

protest (p. 296)

online political participation (p. 297)

Practice Quiz

1. Which of the following is not a form of traditional political participation? *(pp. 295–97)*
   a) volunteering in a campaign
   b) attending an abortion-rights rally
   c) contributing to the Democratic Party
   d) voting in an election
   e) uploading a political video to YouTube

2. Online sources of information *(pp. 299–302)*
   a) are less diverse than those found in the traditional media.
   b) are more diverse than those found in the traditional media.
   c) are exactly the same as those found in the traditional media.
   d) do not influence political knowledge, political interest, or political participation.
   e) never "accidentally" engage individuals who otherwise would not be involved in politics at all.

3. The *digital divide* refers to *(p. 304)*
   a) the line separating citizens who watch television news from those who do not.
   b) the fact that newspapers rarely publish the same stories on their websites that they do in their print editions.
   c) the fact that few politicians maintain websites once they are elected to office.
   d) the line separating citizens with Internet access from those without.
   e) the fact that people who learn about politics online are less informed than those who learn about it through traditional media.

> **⑤ Practice Online**
> "Get Involved" exercise: *Become a Voter*

Voter Participation

■ **Examine voter turnout in American elections (pp. 305–6)**

Voting is the most important and most common form of political participation in the United States. Although suffrage was once limited to white males over age 21, numerous federal statutes, court decisions, and constitutional amendments over the last 200 years have extended voting rights to minority groups, women, and young adults. The dramatic expansion of voting rights has not, however, increased voting participation in the United States. Only 60 percent of Americans vote in presidential elections, and turnout in congressional, state, and local elections is much lower.

Key Terms

suffrage (p. 305)

turnout (p. 306)

Practice Quiz

4. What is the most common form of political participation? *(p. 305)*
   a) lobbying
   b) contributing money to a campaign
   c) protesting
   d) voting
   e) creating a political website

5. Which of the following best describes the composition of the electorate during the colonial and early national periods of American history? *(p. 305)*
   a) landowning white males over age 21
   b) all white males
   c) all literate males
   d) "universal suffrage"
   e) no suffrage for any citizen

6. Women won the right to vote in _____ with the adoption of the _____ Amendment. *(p. 306)*
   a) 1791; Fifth
   b) 1868; Fourteenth
   c) 1920; Nineteenth
   d) 1971; Twenty-Sixth
   e) 1965; Twenty-First

7. Voter turnout in presidential election years has *(p. 306)*
   a) been consistently higher than in years when only congressional and local elections are held.
   b) been consistently lower than in years when only congressional and local elections are held.
   c) been the same as in years when only congressional and local elections are held.
   d) consistently increased since 1892.
   e) consistently decreased since 1892.

 Practice Online
Interactive simulation: *Getting People to the Polls*

Explaining Political Participation: The Individual in Context

■ **Explain the factors that influence whether individuals vote or not (pp. 306–20)**

Three general sets of factors help explain why some Americans vote and others do not: (1) a person's socioeconomic status and attitudes about politics, (2) features of the political environment in which elections take place, and (3) state-level electoral laws. Research has consistently shown, for example, that people with higher levels of education, more income, and higher-level occupations participate in elections much more frequently than those with less education, less income, and lower-level occupations. Similarly, people mobilized by political parties, candidates, campaigns, interest groups, and social movements are more likely to participate than those who are not. Electoral laws passed by state governments, such as registration requirements, can create formal barriers to voting that also influence who participates and who does not.

Key Terms

socioeconomic status (p. 309)

mobilization (p. 311)

Election-Day registration (p. 318)

permanent absentee ballots (p. 319)

early voting (p. 319)

Practice Quiz

8. Americans who vote are more likely to be _____ than the population as a whole. *(p. 309)*
   a) poorer
   b) employed in lower-level occupations
   c) less educated
   d) better educated
   e) residents of states with strict registration requirements

9. On average over the last 40 years, how many U.S. House races have been very competitive in each election? *(pp. 312–15)*
   a) 0
   b) 24
   c) 100
   d) 217
   e) 435

10. Which of the following factors is not currently an obstacle to voting in the United States? *(pp. 315–16)*
    a) registration requirements
    b) that elections occur on Tuesdays
    c) the restriction of voting rights for people who have committed a felony
    d) literacy tests
    e) that many states provide for absentee voting

11. After passage of the Motor Voter Act in 1993, participation in the 1996 elections *(p. 319)*
    a) increased dramatically.
    b) increased somewhat.
    c) declined somewhat.
    d) declined dramatically.
    e) was not affected, since few people registered to vote as a result of the act.

Diversity and Participation

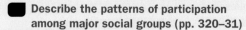 **Describe the patterns of participation among major social groups** (pp. 320–31)

Race, gender, age, and religious affiliation are associated with different levels and types of political participation. Generally speaking, whites, older people, and women vote most frequently. In recent elections, African Americans, Latinos, women and young people have been more likely to support Democratic candidates than whites, males, and older people.

Key Term

gender gap (p. 324)

Practice Quiz

12. In the decades immediately following the Civil War, African Americans voted *(p. 321)*
    a) overwhelmingly in support of the Democratic Party.
    b) overwhelmingly in support of the Republican Party.
    c) for mostly independent or third-party candidates.
    d) in nearly equal numbers for the Democratic and Republican parties.
    e) with slightly larger numbers supporting the Democratic Party.

13. Currently, African Americans *(pp. 320–22)*
    a) almost never participate in politics.
    b) consistently support the Republican Party in elections.
    c) vote at much lower rates than they did 15 years ago.
    d) vote differently from one another based on income.
    e) vote cohesively despite economic differences.

14. One reason that there are fewer women than men in elected office is that *(pp. 324–26)*
    a) there is a limit set by the Constitution on the number of women who can serve in the House of Representatives.
    b) fewer women are eligible to run for office under the rules created by state and local governments.
    c) women are less attentive to politics than men.
    d) women are less likely to run for office than men.
    e) women are less likely to win elections than men.

15. Which of the following statements most accurately characterizes the rates of political participation among different age groups? *(pp. 326–28)*
    a) Older people have much lower rates of participation than young people.
    b) Older people have much higher rates of participation than young people.
    c) Both older people and younger people participate in politics at extremely low rates.
    d) Both older people and younger people participate in politics at extremely high rates.
    e) There is no consistent pattern because sometimes younger people participate more than older people and sometimes older people participate more than younger people.

 Practice Online
Video exercise: *Rock the Vote*

For Further Reading

Bimber, Bruce, and Richard Davis. *Campaigning Online: The Internet in U.S. Elections.* Oxford, UK: Oxford University Press, 2003.

Cain, Bruce E., Todd Donovan, and Caroline J. Tolbert, eds. *Democracy in the States: Experiments in Election Reform.* Washington, DC: Brookings Institution Press, 2008.

Crenson, Matthew A., and Benjamin Ginsberg. *Downsizing Democracy: How America Sidelined Its Citizens and Privatized Its Public.* Baltimore: Johns Hopkins University Press, 2004.

Dalton, Russell J. *The Good Citizen: How a Younger Generation Is Reshaping American Politics.* Washington, DC: CQ Press, 2008.

Donovan, Todd, and Shawn Bowler. *Reforming the Republic: Democratic Institutions for the New America.* Upper Saddle River, NJ: Pearson/Prentice Hall, 2004.

Green, Donald P., and Alan S. Gerber. *Get Out the Vote! How to Increase Voter Turnout.* Washington, DC: Brookings Institution Press, 2004.

Griffin, John D., and Brian Newman. *Minority Report: Evaluating Political Equality in America.* Chicago: University of Chicago Press, 2008.

Hahn, Hahrie. *Moved to Action: Motivation, Participation, and Inequality in American Politics.* Stanford, CA: Stanford University Press, 2009.

Hanmer, Michael J. *Discount Voting: Voter Registration Reforms and Their Effects.* New York: Cambridge University Press, 2009.

Lewis-Beck, Michael S., William G. Jacoby, Helmut Norpoth, and Herbert F. Weisberg. *The American Voter Revisited.* Ann Arbor: University of Michigan Press, 2008.

McDonald, Michael P., and John Samples, eds. *The Market-place of Democracy: Electoral Competition and American Politics*. Washington, DC: Brookings Institution Press, 2006.

Manza, Jeff, and Christopher Uggen. *Locked Out: Felon Disenfranchisement and American Democracy*. New York: Oxford University Press, 2006.

Mossberger, Karen, Caroline Tolbert, and Ramona McNeal. *Digital Citizenship: The Internet, Society and Participation*. Cambridge, MA: MIT Press, 2008.

Nicholson, Steven P. *Voting the Agenda: Candidates Elections and Ballot Propositions*. Princeton, NJ: Princeton University Press, 2005.

Patterson, Thomas E. *The Vanishing Voter: Public Involvement in an Age of Uncertainty*. New York: Vintage, 2003.

Piven, Frances Fox, and Richard Cloward. *Why Americans Don't Vote*. New York: Pantheon, 1988.

Putnam, Robert D. *Bowling Alone: The Collapse and Revival of American Community*. New York: Simon and Schuster, 2000.

Rosenstone, Steven J., and John Mark Hansen. *Mobilization, Participation and Democracy in America*. New York: Macmillan, 1993.

Smith, Daniel, and Caroline Tolbert. *Educated by Initiative: The Effects of Direct Democracy on Citizens and Political Organizations in the American States*. Ann Arbor: University of Michigan Press, 2004.

Verba, Sidney, Kay Lehman Schlozman, and Henry Brady. *Voice and Equality: Civic Voluntarism in American Politics*. Cambridge, MA: Harvard University Press, 1995.

Recommended Websites

CQ MoneyLine
http://moneyline.cq.com/pml/home.do

Campaign contributions are a form of political participation that is both necessary and controversial. This website uses data from the Federal Election Commission (FEC) to publish the names of those who give elected officials campaign money and those who may be receiving preferential treatment.

Declare Yourself
http://declareyourself.com

Statistics on political participation show that older people are much more likely to vote than are young people. Declare Yourself is a national nonpartisan, nonprofit campaign dedicated to closing the intergenerational divide by energizing and empowering a new movement of young voters.

League of Women Voters
www.lwv.org

Established in 1920 as part of the women's suffrage movement, the League of Women Voters encourages informed and active participation in government.

Project Vote
www.projectvote.org

Since 1982, Project Vote has worked to increase the participation of low-income, minority, youth and other marginalized and under-represented voters. The organization sponsors voter registration drivers, get-out-the-vote programs, and monitors election laws across the states. As a community organizer, Barack Obama worked for Project Vote, registering voters in Chicago.

Project Vote Smart
www.votesmart.org

This nonpartisan site is dedicated to providing citizens with information on political candidates and elected officials. Here you can easily view candidates' biographical information, positions on issues, and voting records, so that you can make an informed choice on Election Day.

U.S. Census Bureau: Voting and Registration
www.census.gov/population/www/socdemo/voting.html

The U.S. Census Bureau collects statistics on voting and registration by various demographic and socioeconomic characteristics. See if you can find differences in voter turnout by race, age, sex, or socioeconomic status.

At their 2012 national convention, Republicans formally nominated Mitt Romney as their presidential candidate. While many Americans express frustration over partisan conflict, political parties play an important role in organizing American politics and government.

Political Parties

9

WHAT GOVERNMENT DOES AND WHY IT MATTERS In the United States, political parties force the government to concern itself with the needs of its citizens. Strong parties and energetic party competition make it more likely that the political system will support basic American values.

Liberty requires coherent and well-organized opposition to those in power. Political parties organize the collective interests of those who, as individuals, might lack the resources and knowledge to compete with elites and interest groups. Democracy is promoted when parties mobilize large numbers of individuals to participate in the political arena, and to vote.

Political parties are a core feature of the American political system. They provide guideposts for citizens and politicians alike by helping to organize the political world and simplify complex policy debates. Individual partisanship is the most important factor in predicting whom Americans vote for. In Congress, parties are key in setting the terms of policy conflict; they exercise significant influence over the votes of individual members of Congress on many important issues. Parties also play central roles in mobilizing citizens to vote and ensuring that the public voice is heard in policy making.

The importance of parties in organizing congressional debate and mobilizing citizens was evident in the 2009 debate over national health care, one of President Obama's central achievements in office. Democratic Party leaders in the House of Representatives and in the Senate worked to build support among their members for a health care reform bill. Although the bill passed the House with 84 percent support from Democrats and won all 60 Democratic votes in the Senate, crafting a compromise between the two houses of Congress presented a major challenge, and led to significant changes that diluted the final legislation. Democratic leaders had to work hard to win the support of enough Democrats in the House and Senate to send a final bill to President Obama. The role of parties was also evident in the nearly unanimous opposition of the Republican Party to the health care legislation. Republican opposition stemmed from both policy and political concerns. Most Republicans prefer policy approaches that require less government regulation of the market and less public spending. As the opposition party, however, Republicans were also aware that a major policy win would likely strengthen Democrats. Republican Party leaders mobilized staunch opposition to the Democratic health care reform proposals in both the House and the Senate. In the end, only one Republican in the House voted for the health care reform bill. Unified Republican opposition led Senate Democratic leaders to use the reconciliation process, a procedure that requires only a majority vote to pass legislation, in order to enact their health care reform.

Today, the political parties in Congress are more polarized than at any time in recent history, with over 90 percent of the votes in Congress passed with unanimous party-line voting.[1] Partisanship was also important in the 2012 elections, with most Democrats voting for the Democratic candidates and most Republicans voting for the Republican candidates, but many Americans expressed concern that "partisan politics" was distracting the candidates and the government from the real issues facing the nation. Are the major political parties fulfilling their role in American democracy?

chaptergoals

- Define political parties and their general role in politics (pages 341–42)

- Describe how the party system in the United States has changed over time and its main features today (pages 342–55)

- Describe how the major American parties are structured at the national, state, and local levels (pages 355–60)

- Identify the social groups that tend to support the Republicans and the Democrats (pages 360–66)

- Explain the roles parties play in elections (pages 366–67)

- Explain how parties organize legislative business and influence policy (pages 367–70)

● What Are Political Parties?

Define political parties and their general role in politics

Political parties, like interest groups, are organizations that seek influence over government. Ordinarily, they can be distinguished from interest groups on the basis of their orientation. A party seeks to control the government by electing its members to office, thereby controlling the government. As we will see in Chapter 11, interest groups don't control the operation of government and its personnel, but rather try to influence government policies.

In the United States today, the relationship between parties and government is more complex than this basic definition suggests. Political parties have been the chief points of contact between government, on the one side, and individual citizens and interest groups, on the other. Through organized political parties, citizens and groups can gain some control over governmental policies. Simultaneously, the government often seeks to organize and influence important groups in society through political parties. All political parties have this dual character: they are instruments through which citizens and government attempt to influence each other.

political parties organized groups that attempt to influence the government by electing their members to important government offices

The Democratic Party of the United States is the world's oldest political party. It can trace its history back to Thomas Jefferson's Jeffersonian Republicans and, later, to Andrew Jackson's Jacksonian Democrats. The Jacksonians expanded voter participation and ushered in the political era of the common person, as shown in this image of Jackson's inauguration celebration.

As long as political parties have existed, they have been criticized for introducing selfish, "partisan" concerns into public debates and national policy. Yet political parties are extremely important to the proper functioning of a democracy. As we will see, parties increase participation in politics, provide a central cue for citizens to cast informed votes, and organize the business of Congress and governing. Some argue that the problem in America today is that political elites in Congress and the parties are too polarized (liberal versus conservative), whereas the majority of Americans hold moderate opinions and values, and thus Congress and the parties do a poor job representing the citizens.[2] Others argue that the problem is not that politics is too partisan but that our parties are not strong enough to function effectively—one reason that America has such low levels of political involvement and voter turnout.[3] Still others argue that the rules governing our election system need to be updated—what is called "election reform"—so that there are more than two major political parties and so representation of the citizens can be improved.[4]

● The Two-Party System in America

Describe how the party system in the United States has changed over time and its main features today

Over the past 200 years, Americans' conception of political parties has changed considerably. In the early years of the Republic, parties were seen as threats to the social order, and were referred to as factions. In *The Federalist Papers*, both Alexander Hamilton and James Madison condemned "factions" that pursued narrow self-interest over the broader well-being of the nation as a whole.[5] In his 1796 Farewell Address, President George Washington warned his countrymen to shun partisan politics. Nonetheless, a **two-party system** emerged early in the history of the new Republic. Beginning with the Federalists and the Jeffersonian Republicans in the late 1780s, two major parties have dominated national politics, although *which* particular two parties has changed with the times and issues. This two-party system today includes Democrats and Republicans (see Figure 9.1).

two-party system a political system in which only two parties have a realistic opportunity to compete effectively for control

Unlike many other countries in the world that use a proportional representation system, in which seats are allocated to political parties based on their share (percentage) of the total vote cast in the election, the United States uses geographic single-member districts combined with a winner-take-all system. It doesn't matter, for example, if the contest for a U.S. House seat is won by 1 percent or 20 percent of the total votes, the candidate (and his/her party) with the largest number of votes (plurality) in that district wins the seat in Congress. Unlike in proportional systems, runners-up do not gain representation in first-past-the-post system. In the United States, proportional representation systems are uncommon, especially above the local level, and are absent at the national level. Voters thus have an incentive not to vote for small or third parties for fear of wasting their vote, as only one party (usually one of the two largest parties) can win the election. This winner-take-all system has helped create our two-party-dominant system, and third parties have historically not won seats in Congress, or won the presidency. Third parties are discussed in more detail later in this chapter.

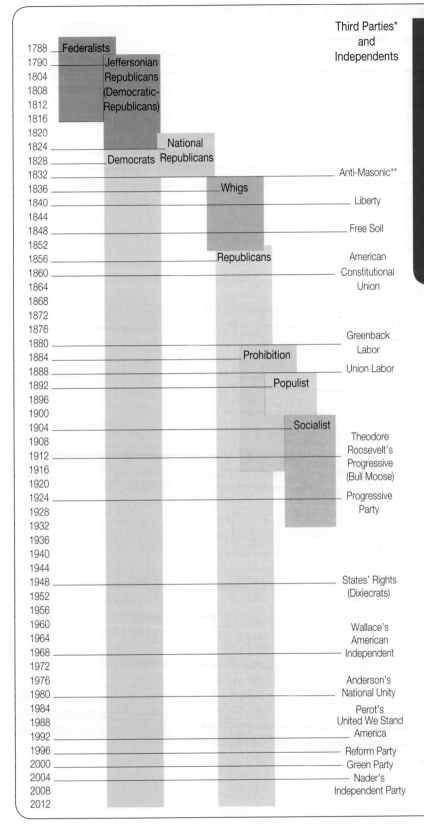

FIGURE 9.1

How the Party System Evolved

During the nineteenth century, the Democrats and the Republicans emerged as the two dominant parties in American politics. As the American party system evolved, many third parties emerged, but few of them remained in existence for very long.

*Or in some cases, fourth parties; most of these parties lasted through only one term.

**The Anti-Masonics had the distinction of being not only the first third party but also the first party to hold a national nominating convention and the first to announce a party platform.

How Do Political Parties Form?

Historically, parties form in one of two ways. The first, which could be called "internal mobilization," occurs when political conflicts prompt officials and competing factions within government to mobilize popular support. This is precisely what happened during the early years of the American Republic. Competition in the Congress between northeastern merchants and southern agricultural factions led first the southerners and then the northeasterners to attempt to organize their supporters. The result was the foundation of America's first national parties: the Jeffersonians, whose primary base was in the South, and the Federalists, whose strength was greatest in the New England states.

The second way that parties may form, which could be called "external mobilization," takes place when a group of politicians outside government organizes popular support to win governmental power. For example, during the 1850s, a group of state politicians who opposed slavery, especially the expansion of slavery in America's territorial possessions, built what became the Republican Party by constructing party organizations and mobilizing popular support in the Northeast and West.

America's two major parties now, of course, are the Democrats and the Republicans. Both trace their roots back over 150 years to the nineteenth century, and both have evolved over time. Since they were formed, the two major parties have undergone significant shifts in their positions, their goals, and their membership. These changes have been prompted both by issues and events and by demographic and social developments and population growth in the United States. Parties also change as they compete with one another to win support among voters and interest groups for political office, different policies, and enduring power. Because of this, it is important to understand parties in relation to one another.

Party Systems

Historians often refer to the set of parties that are important at any given time as a nation's "party system." The most obvious feature of a party system is the number of major parties competing for power. The United States has usually had a two-party system, meaning that only two parties have a serious chance to win national elections. Of course, we have not always had the same two parties, and as we shall see, minor parties often put forward candidates.

The term *party system*, however, refers to more than just the number of parties competing for power. It also includes the organization of the parties, the balance of power between and within party coalitions, the parties' social and institutional bases, and the issues and policies around which party competition is organized. Seen from this broader perspective, the character of a nation's party system can change even if the number of parties remains the same and even when the same two parties seem to be competing for power. Today's American party system is very different from the country's party system of 50 years ago, but the Democrats and Republicans continue to be the major competing forces.

The character of a nation's party system can have profound consequences for the types of issues and policies that reach the nation's political agenda, and for critically important issues such as the distribution of wealth and economic inequality. For example, the contemporary American political parties mainly compete for the support of different groups of middle-class Americans. As a result, issues that concern the middle and upper-middle classes, such as the environment, health care, retirement benefits, and taxation, are very much on the political agenda, whereas issues that concern working-class and poorer Americans, such as welfare and housing, receive short shrift from both parties.[6] Some argue that the government and the political parties have become more responsive to the wealthy over the past few decades, rather than to the middle or working class.[7] Political scientist Larry Bartels shows in an important study that neither the Democrats nor the Republicans in Congress are responsive to the poor, Americans in the bottom one-third of the income distribution. Both political parties respond some of the time to the middle class (those in the middle third of the income distribution), and the Republican Party is the most responsive to the wealthy, those in the top third of incomes.[8] Bartels shows that over the past half century, income of the poor and working class grew more under Democratic Party presidents than Republican administrations.

Over the course of American history, changes in political forces and alignments have produced six distinctive party systems.

The First Party System: Federalists and Jeffersonian Republicans The first party system emerged in the 1790s and pitted the Federalists against the Jeffersonian Republicans. The Federalists spoke mainly for New England merchants and supported a program of protective tariffs to encourage manufacturing, assumption of the states' Revolutionary War debts, the creation of a national bank, and resumption of commercial ties with Britain. The Jeffersonians, led by southern agricultural interests, opposed these policies and instead favored free trade, the promotion of agricultural over commercial interests, and friendship with France. The Federalists sought, unsuccessfully, to use the force of law against the Jeffersonians by enacting the Alien and Sedition Acts to outlaw criticism of the government. These acts, however, proved virtually impossible to enforce, and the Jeffersonians gradually expanded their base from the South into the Middle Atlantic states. In the election of 1800, Jefferson defeated the incumbent Federalist president, John Adams, and led his party to power. Over the following years, the Federalists gradually weakened. The party disappeared altogether after the pro-British sympathies of some Federalist leaders during the War of 1812 led to charges of treason against the party.

From the collapse of the Federalists until the 1830s, America had only one political party, the Jeffersonian Republicans, who gradually came to be known as the Democrats. This period of one-party politics is sometimes known as the Era of Good Feelings, to indicate the absence of party competition. Throughout this period, however, there was intense factional conflict within the Democratic Party, particularly between the supporters and opponents of General Andrew Jackson, America's great military hero of the War of 1812. Jackson's opponents united to deny him the presidency in 1824, but Jackson won elections in 1828 and 1832. Jackson's support was in the South and West, and he generally espoused a program of free trade and policies that appealed to those regions.

The Second Party System: Democrats and Whigs During the 1830s, groups opposing Jackson united to form a new political force, the Whig Party—thus giving rise to the second American party system. Both the Democrats and the Whigs built party organizations throughout the nation, and both sought to enlarge their bases of support by expanding the right to vote. They increased the number of eligible voters through the elimination of property restrictions and other barriers to voting—at least voting by white males. Support for the new Whig Party

In the 1930s the Whig Party emerged as the Democrats' main rival. This drawing depicts a Whig rally and parade during the 1840 election, which became known as the "hard cider" campaign.

was stronger in the Northeast than in the South and West and stronger among merchants than among small farmers. Hence, in some measure, the Whigs were the successors of the Federalists. Yet conflict between the two parties revolved more around personalities than policies. The Whigs were a diverse group united more by opposition to the Democrats than by agreement on programs. In 1840 the Whigs won their first presidential election under the leadership of General William Henry Harrison, a military hero known as "Old Tippecanoe." The Whig campaign carefully avoided issues—since the party could agree on almost none—and emphasized the personal qualities and heroism of the candidate. The Whigs also invested heavily in campaign rallies and entertainment to win the hearts, if not exactly the minds, of the voters. The 1840 campaign came to be called the "hard cider" campaign because of the practice of using food and especially drink to win votes.

During the late 1840s and early 1850s, conflicts over slavery produced sharp divisions within both the Whig and the Democratic parties, despite the efforts of party leaders to develop compromises. By 1856 the Whig Party had all but disintegrated under the strain, and many Whig politicians and voters, along with antislavery Democrats, joined the new Republican Party, which pledged to ban slavery from the western territories. In 1860 the Republicans nominated Abraham Lincoln for the presidency. Lincoln's victory strengthened southern calls for secession from the Union and, soon thereafter, for all-out civil war.

The Civil War and Post–Civil War Party System: Republicans and Democrats During the course of the war, President Lincoln depended heavily on Republican governors and state legislatures to raise troops, provide funding, and maintain popular support for a long and bloody military conflict. The secession of the South had stripped the Democratic Party of many of its leaders and supporters, but the Democrats remained politically competitive throughout the war and nearly won the 1864 presidential election because of war weariness on the part of the northern public. With the defeat of the Confederacy in 1865, some congressional Republicans sought to convert the South into a Republican bastion through a program of Reconstruction that enfranchised newly freed slaves. This Reconstruction program collapsed in the 1870s as a result of disagreement within the Republican Party in Congress and violent resistance by southern whites. With the end of Reconstruction, the former Confederate states regained full membership in the Union and full control of their internal affairs. Throughout the South, African Americans were deprived of political rights, including the right to vote, despite post–Civil War constitutional guarantees to the contrary. The post–Civil War South was solidly Democratic in its political affiliation, and with a firm southern base, the national Democratic Party was able to confront the Republicans on a more or less equal basis. From the end of the Civil War to the 1890s, the Republican Party remained the party of the North, with strong business and middle-class support, while the Democrats were the party of the South, with support also from working-class and immigrant groups.

The System of 1896: Republicans and Democrats During the 1890s, profound and rapid social and economic changes led to the emergence of a variety of protest parties, including the Populist Party, which won the support of hundreds of thousands of voters in the South and West. The Populists appealed mainly to small farmers but also attracted western mining interests and urban workers. In the 1892 presidential election, the Populist Party carried four states and elected governors in eight. In 1896 the Populist Party effectively merged with the Democrats, who nominated William Jennings Bryan, a Democratic senator with pronounced

Populist sympathies, for the presidency. The Republicans nominated the conservative senator William McKinley. In the ensuing campaign, northern and midwestern businesses made an all-out effort to defeat what they saw as a radical threat from the Populist-Democratic alliance. When the dust settled, the Republicans had won a resounding victory. The GOP ("Grand Old Party"), or Republican Party, had carried the more heavily populated northern and midwestern states and confined the Democrats to their smaller bases of support in the South and far West. For the next 36 years, the Republicans were the nation's majority party, carrying 7 of 9 presidential elections and controlling both houses of Congress in 15 of 18 contests. The Republican Party of this era was very much the party of American business, advocating low taxes, high tariffs on imports, and a minimum of government regulation. The Democrats were far too weak to offer much opposition. Southern Democrats, moreover, were too concerned with maintaining the region's autonomy on issues of race to challenge the Republicans on other fronts.

The New Deal Party System: Reversal of Fortune Soon after the Republican presidential candidate Herbert Hoover won the 1928 presidential election, the nation's economy collapsed. The Great Depression, which produced unprecedented economic hardship, stemmed from a variety of causes, but from the perspective of millions of Americans, the Republican Party did not do enough to promote economic recovery. In 1932, Americans elected Franklin Delano Roosevelt and a solidly Democratic Congress. Roosevelt developed a program for economic recovery that he dubbed the "New Deal." Under the auspices of the New Deal, the size and reach of America's national government increased substantially. The federal government took responsibility for economic management and social welfare to an extent that was unprecedented in American history. Roosevelt designed many of his programs specifically to expand the political base of the Democratic Party. He rebuilt and revitalized the party around a nucleus of unionized workers, upper-middle-class intellectuals and professionals, southern farmers, Jews, Catholics, and African Americans—the so-called New Deal coalition that made the Democrats the nation's majority party for the next 36 years. Groping for a response to the New Deal, Republicans often wound up supporting popular New Deal programs such as Social Security in what was sometimes derided as "me too" Republicanism. Even the relatively conservative administration of Dwight D. Eisenhower in the 1950s left the principal New Deal programs intact.

The New Deal coalition was severely strained during the 1960s by conflicts over civil rights and the Vietnam War. The struggle over civil rights initially divided northern Democrats who supported the civil rights cause from white southern Democrats who defended the system of racial segregation. Subsequently, as the civil rights movement launched a northern campaign aimed at securing access to jobs and education and an end to racial discrimination in

Following the Civil War, the Republican Party remained dominant in the North. This poster supporting Republican Benjamin Harrison in the 1888 election promises protective tariffs, and other policies that appealed to the industrial states in the North.

such realms as housing, northern Democrats also split, often along income lines. The struggle over the Vietnam War further divided the Democrats, with upper-income liberal Democrats strongly opposing the Johnson administration's decision to greatly expand the numbers of U.S. troops fighting in Southeast Asia. These schisms within the Democratic Party provided an opportunity for the GOP, which returned to power in 1968 under the leadership of Richard Nixon.

The Contemporary American Party System The Republican Party widened its appeal in the second half of the twentieth century. In 1964, for example, the Republican presidential candidate Barry Goldwater argued in favor of substantially reduced levels of taxation and spending, less government regulation of the economy, and the elimination of many federal social programs. Though Goldwater was defeated by Lyndon Johnson, the ideas he espoused continued to be major themes for the Republican Party. It took Richard Nixon's "southern strategy" to give the GOP the votes it needed to end Democratic dominance of national politics. Nixon appealed to disaffected white southerners, and with the help of the independent candidate and former Alabama governor George Wallace, he sparked the shift of voters that gave the party a strong position in all the states of the former Confederacy. The movement of white southerners to the Republican Party was in part because of opposition to desegregation of the South and to the civil rights movement supported by Democratic leaders, including President Kennedy. During the 1980s, under the leadership of President Ronald Reagan, Republicans added two additional important groups to their coalition. The first were religious conservatives who were offended by Democratic support for abortion and gay rights and by alleged Democratic disdain for traditional cultural and religious values. The second were working-class whites who were drawn to Reagan's tough approach to foreign policy and his positions against affirmative action.

While Republicans built a political base around economic and social conservatives and white southerners, the Democratic Party maintained its support among a majority of unionized workers and upper-middle-class intellectuals and professionals. Democrats also appealed strongly to racial minorities. The 1965 Voting

Richard Nixon's "southern strategy" helped broaden the Republican Party's base in the late 1960s and the 1970s by appealing the white southerners. Here, Nixon meets supporters in Georgia in 1973.

Rights Act had greatly increased black voter participation in the South and helped the Democratic Party retain some House and Senate seats in southern states. And whereas the Republicans appealed to social conservatives, the Democrats appealed strongly to Americans concerned with abortion rights, gay rights, feminism, environmentalism, and other progressive social causes.

Despite the success of Republican presidential candidates in attracting votes from groups previously associated with the Democratic Party, Republicans generally did not do as well at the state and local levels until the 1990s, when conservative religious groups made a concerted effort to expand their influence within the Republican Party. This effort led to conflict between these members of the "religious right" and more traditional "country club" Republicans, whose major concerns were economic matters such as taxes and federal regulation of business. The two factions of the party came together when the Republicans won both houses of Congress in 1994 (the first time in almost half a century). The Republicans retained control of Congress in 1996, despite President Clinton's re-election in that year. In 2000, George W. Bush united the party's centrist and right wings behind a program of tax cuts, education reform, military strength, and family values.

However, by 2006, the public's disapproval of the Bush administration and the war in Iraq led to major losses for Republicans in both houses of Congress. Campaigning during the worst financial crisis since the 1930s and burdened with a president whose approval ratings had sunk to historic lows, Republicans again fared poorly in the 2008 elections. With the party in disarray, contending factions sought to redefine a strategy that would allow Republicans to regain the influence they had enjoyed in the early days of George W. Bush's presidency.

In 2008, Democrats reached beyond their base by appealing to moderate voters in states that had once been Republican strongholds, and they won control of Congress as well as the presidency for the first time since 1995. However, the continuation of sharp partisan differences in Congress signaled that intense party conflict would continue to characterize American politics. Republicans won control of the House of Representatives in 2010, and although Obama was re-elected to the presidency in 2012, control of Congress remained divided.

Electoral Alignments and Realignments

The points of transition between party systems in American history are sometimes called **electoral realignments**. During these periods, the coalitions that support the parties and the balance of power between the parties are redefined. In historical terms, realignments occur when new issues, combined with economic or political crises, mobilize new voters and persuade large numbers of them to reexamine their traditional partisan loyalties and permanently shift their support from one party to another. Figure 9.2 charts the sequence of party systems and realignments in American history.

electoral realignment the point in history when a new party supplants the ruling party, becoming in turn the dominant political force; in the United States, this has tended to occur roughly every 30 years

Although scholars dispute the timing of realignments, there is some agreement that five have occurred since the Founding. The first took place around 1800, when the Jeffersonian Republicans defeated the Federalists and became the dominant force in American politics. The second realignment took place in about 1828, when the Jacksonian Democrats seized control of the White House and the Congress. In the third period of realignment, centered on 1860, the newly founded Republican Party, led by Abraham Lincoln, won power, in the process destroying the Whig Party, which had been one of the nation's two major parties since the 1830s. Many northern voters who had supported the Whigs or the Democrats on the basis of their economic stands shifted their support to the Republicans as slavery replaced

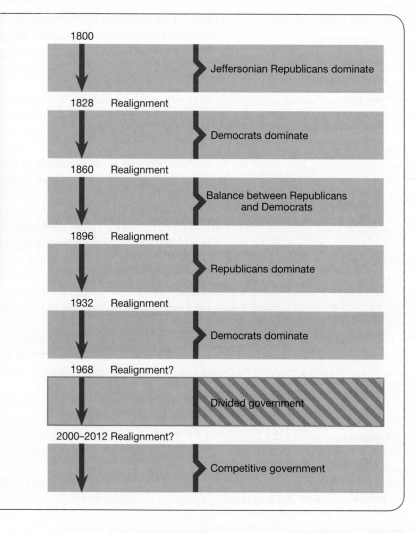

1800

Jeffersonian Republicans dominate

1828   Realignment

Democrats dominate

1860   Realignment

Balance between Republicans and Democrats

1896   Realignment

Republicans dominate

1932   Realignment

Democrats dominate

1968   Realignment?

Divided government

2000–2012 Realignment?

Competitive government

tariffs and economic concerns as the central item on the nation's political agenda. Many southern Whigs shifted their support to the Democrats. The new sectional alignment of forces that emerged was solidified by the trauma of the Civil War and persisted almost to the turn of the century.

In the 1890s, this alignment was at least partially supplanted by an alignment of political forces based on economic and cultural factors, bringing about the fourth electoral realignment. In the election of 1896, the Republican candidate, William McKinley, emphasizing business, industry, and urban interests, defeated the Democrat, William Jennings Bryan, who spoke for sectional interests, farmers, and fundamentalism.

Republican dominance lasted until the fifth realignment, during the period 1932–36, when the Democrats, led by Franklin Delano Roosevelt, took control of the White House and Congress and, despite sporadic interruptions, maintained control of both through the 1960s. Since that time, American party politics has been characterized primarily by **divided government**, wherein the presidency is controlled by one party while the other party controls one or both houses of Congress.

Such periods of electoral realignment in American politics have had extremely important policy consequences. Realignments occur when new issue concerns, coupled with economic or political crises, weaken the established political elite

divided government the condition in American government wherein the presidency is controlled by one party while the opposing party controls one or both houses of Congress and permit new groups of politicians to create coalitions of forces capable of capturing and holding the reins of governmental power. The construction of new governing coalitions during these realigning periods has effected major changes in American governmental institutions and policies. Each period of realignment was a turning point in American politics. The choices made by the national electorate during these periods helped shape the course of American political history for the following generation.[9]

Party Polarization

A distinguishing feature of the contemporary party system is **party polarization**. Polarization in Congress is measured by party unity in roll call votes. In 2010, for example, Republicans in both the House and Senate voted with their fellow Republican colleagues on 91 percent of roll call votes.[10] Similarly, Democrats in Congress voted in unity with their party over 90 percent of the time. Both parties are more unified than at any time since 1956. And frequently, the Democrats and Republicans in Congress vote in exactly the opposite ways. Legislation is often enacted by the slimmest of vote margins in Congress. While the majority of Americans hold moderate views, representatives in Congress tend to be strong conservatives among Republicans and strong liberals among Democrats; many of these members are elected from "safe" districts, where a majority of voters identify with their party, which means they have little chance of losing in the next election. Both Republicans and Democrats in Congress are usually re-elected in landslide elections. (The average winning margin of victory in the House is over 40 percentage points. That means incumbents, on average, win 70 percent of the popular vote compared with challengers' 30 percent.)[11] Of the 435 House races, only a dozen are highly contested, measured by a vote margin of 5 percent or less. Uncompetitive elections in Congress and safe seats are associated with growing party polarization.

This polarization among the parties in Congress does not match the ideology of the American public. Imagine if we could line up all 311 million Americans on a continuum from the most liberal on the left to the most conservative on the right. There would be far fewer very strong liberals and very strong conservatives than moderates. The majority of Americans would fall somewhere in between, somewhat left of center or just right of center. Opinion polls show that the distribution of ideology in the United States represents a single hump (like a one-humped camel), with the majority of Americans holding a moderate ideology. Now imagine lining up the members of Congress on the same continuum from most liberal to most conservative. Few lawmakers would fall in the middle, with the majority either to the far left (strong Democrat) or the far right (strong Republican)—essentially a two-humped camel. This suggests that party polarization in Congress has created a Congress that does not match the aggregate ideology of the American public. Approval of Congress in 2012 stood at just under 10 percent of the American public, the lowest level on record.[12] This extreme polarization has led not only to low approval of government, but also an inability of Congress to compromise and adopt policies that would benefit the majority of Americans.

Should we believe the media pundits who tell us that Americans are deeply divided between the red states and the blue states? Is the American population really polarized on hot-button moral, religious, and cultural issues? Political scientist Morris Fiorina and his colleagues debunk the commonly held myth that Americans are deeply divided in their fundamental political views, showing that on a broad range of topics from homosexuality to abortion, most Americans hold moderate opinions.[13] While political elites and members of Congress may be

party polarization the division between the two major parties on most policy issues, with members of each party unified around their party's positions with little crossover

for critical analysis

What are the principal issues dividing the two major parties today? What are the chief areas of agreement between the two parties? Doe the parties agree or disagree on questions of liberty and democracy?

highly polarized, with sharp divisions between Republicans and Democrats, most Americans are moderates in terms of public opinion. Both the Democratic and Republican parties are essentially centrist parties.

Third Parties

Although the United States has a two-party-dominant system, the country has always had more than two parties. Typically, **third parties** in the United States have represented social and economic interests that for one or another reason were not given voice by the two major parties.[14] Such parties have had a good deal of influence on ideas and elections in the United States. The Populists, a party centered in the rural areas of the West and Midwest, and the Progressives, spokesmen for the urban middle classes in the late nineteenth and early twentieth centuries, are the most important examples in the past 100 years. More recently, Ross Perot, who ran in 1992 as an independent and in 1996 as the Reform Party's nominee, won the votes of almost one in five Americans.

Because third parties almost always lose at the national level, such parties exist as a protest movement against the two parties or to promote specific issues. Third parties profoundly affect American elections, as they steal votes from the two major parties, often swinging the election in favor of the Democrats or the Republicans. In the extremely close 2000 presidential election, for example, third-party candidate Ralph Nader won just 3 percent of the popular vote, but that was enough to swing the election to Republican George W. Bush. While the majority of Americans favored the Democratic Party in 2000, having a third party in the race split the Democratic vote, so the party lost the White House. Most Nader voters would have preferred Al Gore over George Bush, but by voting for Nader they inadvertently enabled Bush to win. The same thing happened in 1992 and 1996, but this time it was the conservative vote that was split between two parties. At times third parties have become a major force in presidential politics. H. Ross Perot's Reform Party won roughly 18.9 percent of the popular vote in 1992 (the highest third-party vote share since Roosevelt), which allowed Democrat Bill Clinton to win the presidency with just 43.0 percent of the popular vote (to Republican George H. W. Bush's 37.4 percent). In 1996, Perot won just over 8.0 percent of the popular vote, and Democrat Bill Clinton again won the White House, with less than 50 percent of the popular vote (49.2 to Republican Bob Dole's 40.7). Because of these dramatic losses, leaders in both major political parties fear third-party challenges in presidential elections. In 1912, Theodore Roosevelt made a run for the presidency on the Progressive Party, and Abraham Lincoln, our most revered president, won the presidency in a four-way race with less than 40 percent of the popular vote.

Table 9.1 lists the top candidates in the presidential election of 2012, including the top third-party and independent candidates who ran. In addition to the candidates listed in Table 9.1, the Socialist Party, the Prohibition Party, and several other parties nominated candidates for the presidency in 2012.

In 2000, Ralph Nader ran as the candidate of the Green Party and won 3 percent of the vote, mainly at the expense of the Democratic candidate, Al Gore. Many observers believed that Gore would have won the 2000 election had Nader dropped out. In 2004 and 2008, Nader ran again as an independent candidate, receiving less than 1 percent of the vote.

Third Parties at the State and Local Levels Third parties are active not only in presidential races. Third-party and independent candidacies also arise at the state and local levels. In New York, the Liberal and Conservative parties have been on the ballot for decades. In 1998, Minnesota elected a third-party governor, the former professional wrestler Jesse Ventura. During the 2002 midterm elections, third-party candidates ran for state office and for congressional seats in

TABLE 9.1

Parties and Candidates in 2012

CANDIDATE	PARTY	VOTE TOTAL*	PERCENTAGE OF VOTE*
Barack Obama	Democratic	62,088,847	50.5%
Mitt Romney	Republican	58,783,137	48
Gary Johnson	Libertarian	1,198,942	1
Jill Stein	Green	424,676	0.4
Virgil Goode	Constitution	117,877	0.1

*With 99 percent of votes tallied.

SOURCE: http://elections.huffingtonpost.com/2012/results# (accessed 11/12/12).

many states. Libertarian Party gubernatorial candidates received at least 2 percent of the vote in 15 states, including a whopping 11 percent of the vote in Wisconsin. The Green Party was also active throughout the nation. The Green Party candidate for governor in Massachusetts, Jill Stein, may have affected the race between Republican Mitt Romney and his Democratic rival by drawing votes away from the Democrats in a close race. In races with razor-thin margins between the Republican and Democratic candidates, any fraction of the vote going to a third-party candidate can make a difference. In Florida in 2012, Barack Obama was .05 percent ahead of Mitt Romney, but Libertarian Party candidate Gary Johnson won .05 percent of the popular vote, likely from voters who otherwise would have supported Romney. In 2012, third party or independent candidates won Senate races in Maine and Vermont.

Obstacles Facing Third Parties Americans usually assume that only candidates nominated by one of the two major parties have any chance of winning an election. Thus, a vote cast for a third-party or independent candidate is often seen as a vote wasted. Voters who would prefer a third-party candidate may feel compelled to vote for the major-party candidate whom they regard as the "lesser of two evils," to avoid wasting their votes in a futile gesture.

Under federal election law, any minor party receiving more than 5 percent of the national presidential vote is entitled to federal funds. The Reform Party qualified by winning 8.2 percent in 1996. Ralph Nader, the Green Party candidate in 2000, hoped to win the 5.0 percent of the vote that would entitle the Green Party to federal funds, but failed to achieve that threshold.

As discussed earlier, third-party prospects are also hampered by America's single-member district system for allocating seats. In many other nations, several individuals can be elected to represent each legislative district—a system of multiple-member districts, which are more favorable to minor-party candidates. Add to that the plurality, or winner-take-all, system of voting discussed earlier in this chapter, where candidates need to win more votes (usually over 50 percent) than in countries using the proportional representation system. (In a proportional system, parties can earn seats in government with 15–20 percent of the popular vote.) This higher American threshold discourages minor parties.[15]

Green Party candidate Jill Stein ran for president in 2012 and received less than 1 percent of the vote. Although minor party candidates do not have much chance of winning the presidency, their campaigns can affect the issues that the major parties put on their agendas.

The Influence of Third Parties

Although the Republican Party was the only American third party to make itself permanent (by replacing the Whigs), other third parties have enjoyed an influence far beyond their electoral size. This is because large parts of their programs were adopted by one or both of the major parties, which sought to appeal to the voters mobilized by the new party, and so expand their own electoral strength. The Democratic Party, for example, became a great deal more liberal when it adopted most of the Progressive program early in the twentieth century. Many socialists felt that President Roosevelt's New Deal had adopted most of their party's program, including old-age pensions, unemployment compensation, an agricultural marketing program, and laws guaranteeing workers the right to organize into unions. This kind of influence explains the short lives of third parties. Their causes are usually eliminated when the major parties absorb their programs and draw their supporters into the mainstream.

Although it is not technically a political party, the Tea Party movement had a considerable impact on the Republican Party primaries in 2010, when Tea Party candidates defeated several incumbents and candidates endorsed by Republican Party leaders. Some high-profile Tea Party candidates, including Rand Paul (R-Ky.), then went on to win office in the 2010 midterm elections, but on the whole, the Tea Party succeeded in electing only about 32 percent of their candidates. Although it took the name Tea Party and sponsored a national convention, the Tea Party movement is not a formal party. It is an organized challenge to incumbents by the most conservative wing of the Republican Party.[16]

Election Reform and Third Parties In part because third parties have become increasingly common in American politics, despite election rules favoring a two-party system, one-third of all winning presidential candidates since the Civil War have been elected with a plurality (simply more votes than any other candidate) but not a majority (more than 50 percent of all votes) of the national popular vote.[17] When one considers those voting for the losing major-party presidential candidate and a losing third-party candidate (e.g., Perot, Nader), a majority of Americans who cast a vote for president in recent elections are on the "losing side" about a third of the time. If the party that wins the presidency in one out of three elections is not favored by a majority of voters, that calls into question the legitimacy of our election system. Some scholars suggest that the failure to secure majorities may continue in the future with the rise of independent candidates and dissatisfaction with the two major political parties.[18]

Some proponents of election reform argue that two major parties are not sufficient to represent the varied interests of America's 311 million people, and that more political parties would improve representation. Forms of proportional representation, multiple-member districts, or instant run-off voting would increase the probability of third-party representation in American politics. State ballot access laws are another major impediment for third parties. Third parties often fail to meet criteria to get on the ballot, such as registration fees or petition requirements in which a certain number of voters must sign a petition in order for the third party or independent candidate to gain ballot access. States with lower access hurdles, such as Minnesota, have more third-party candidates. Those who favor a stronger role for third parties argue that states should make it easier to get on the ballot. Supporters of the current system, on the other hand, contend that America's two-party system creates stability in governing and prevents the need for a coalition government, where multiple small parties work together to form a majority to govern.

● Party Organization

> **Describe how the major American parties are structured at the national, state, and local levels**

In the United States, **party organizations** exist at virtually every level of government (see Figure 9.3). These organizations are usually committees made up of a number of active party members. State law and party rules prescribe how such committees are constituted. Usually committee members are elected at local party meetings, called **caucuses**, or as part of the regular primary election. The best-known examples of these committees are at the national level: the Democratic National Committee and the Republican National Committee.

party organization the formal structure of a political party, including its leadership, election committees, active members, and paid staff

caucus (political) a normally closed meeting of a political or legislative group to select candidates, plan strategy, or make decisions regarding legislative matters

National Convention

At the national level, the party's most important institution is the **national convention**. The convention, held every four years, is attended by delegates from each of the states; as a group, they nominate the party's presidential and vice-presidential candidates, draft the party's campaign platform for the presidential race, and approve changes in the rules and regulations governing party procedures. Before World War II, presidential nominations occupied most of the time, energy, and

national convention a national party political institution that nominates the party's presidential and vice presidential candidates, establishes party rules, and writes and ratifies the party's platform

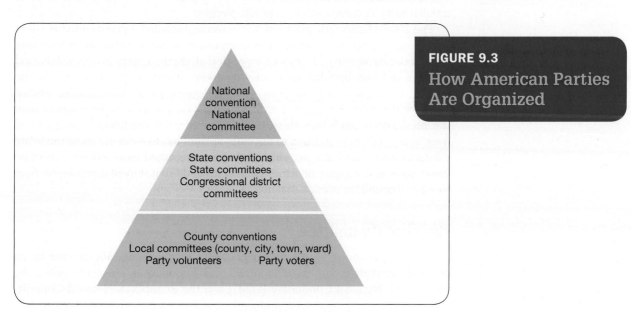

FIGURE 9.3
How American Parties Are Organized

National convention
National committee

State conventions
State committees
Congressional district committees

County conventions
Local committees (county, city, town, ward)
Party volunteers   Party voters

effort expended at the national convention. The nomination process required days of negotiation and compromise among state party leaders and often required many ballots before a nominee was selected. In recent years, however, presidential candidates have been chosen by winning enough delegate support in primary elections to win the official nomination on the first ballot. The actual convention has become symbolic.

The convention's other two tasks, determining the party's rules and its platform, remain important. Party rules can determine the relative influence of competing factions within the party and can also increase or decrease the party's chances for electoral success. In 1972, for example, the Democratic National Convention adopted a new set of rules favored by the party's liberal wing. Under these rules, state delegations to the Democratic Convention were required to include women and members of minority groups in rough proportion to those groups' representation among the party's membership in that state. Liberals correctly calculated that women and African Americans would generally support liberal ideas and candidates. The rules also called for the use of the proportional representation voting system, which liberals thought would give them an advantage by allowing the election of more women and minority delegates. The Republican Party used proportional representation voting for the first time in the 2012 presidential nomination.

platform a party document, written at a national convention, that contains party philosophy, principles, and positions on issues

The convention also approves the party **platform**. Platforms are often dismissed as documents filled with platitudes that voters seldom read. To some extent this criticism is well founded. Not one voter in a thousand so much as glances at the party platform, and even the news media pay little attention to the documents. Furthermore, the parties' presidential candidates make little use of the platforms in their campaigns; usually they prefer to develop and promote their own themes. Nonetheless, the platform can be an important document. The platform should be understood as a contract in which the various party groups attending the convention state their terms for supporting the ticket. For one, welfare reform may be a key issue. For another, tax reduction may be more important. For a third, the critical issue might be deficit reduction. When one of these "planks" is included in the platform, its promoters are asserting that this is what they want in exchange for their support for the ticket, while other party factions might be agreeing that the plank seems reasonable and appropriate. Thus, party platforms should be seen more as internal party documents than as public pledges.

The 2008 Democratic platform, for example, included a plank aimed at cities, promising to "strengthen the federal commitment to cities." Urban areas have long formed the backbone of Democratic political strength; a party plank pledging aid to cities and metropolitan areas rewards a key constituency whose enthusiastic support is crucial to a Democratic victory. Because party platforms are written more for the delegates than for ordinary voters, they tend to be less centrist than the presidential candidates themselves. A presidential candidate hoping to win over "swing" voters in addition to the party faithful has to stake out more moderate positions. Thus, the 2008 Republican platform presented more extreme views on issues such as the rights of same-sex couples and environmental regulation than those of Republican presidential nominee John McCain.

National Committee

Between conventions, each national political party is technically headed by its national committee. For the Democrats and Republicans, these are called the Democratic National Committee (DNC) and the Republican National Commit-

tee (RNC), respectively. These national committees raise campaign funds, head off factional disputes within the party, and endeavor to enhance the party's media image. The actual work of each national committee is overseen by its chairperson. During every election cycle prior to the enactment of the campaign finance reforms of 2002, the DNC and RNC each raised tens of millions of dollars of so-called **soft money**, which could be used to support party candidates throughout the nation. The 2002 Bipartisan Campaign Reform Act (BCRA), sometimes known as the McCain-Feingold Act, outlawed this practice. To circumvent BCRA, however, each party has established a set of "shadow parties." These are **527 committees**, groups organized to promote and publicize political issues. As such, they can claim tax-exempt status under Section 527 of the Internal Revenue Code, which defines and provides tax-exempt status for nonprofit political advocacy groups.

Under the law, 527 committees can raise and spend unlimited amounts of money as long as their activities are not coordinated with those of the formal party organizations. Although some 527 committees are actually independent, many are directed by former Republican and Democratic party officials and run shadow campaigns on behalf of the parties.[19] In the 2008 election cycle, nonprofit organizations formed specifically to support particular candidates became an additional source of soft money. This change was the result of a 2007 Supreme Court decision that overturned parts of the BCRA, allowing corporations, including nonprofits, to run issue advertisements in the days leading up to the primaries and general elections.[20] Soft money played a less prominent role in the 2008 presidential election, in part because the presidential candidates and their parties created such successful fund-raising operations. But a diverse array of outside groups, including the U.S. Chamber of Commerce, the National Rifle Association, and Defenders of Wildlife Action Fund, continued to raise and spend large sums of money on competitive congressional races. In 2010, the Supreme Court's decision in *Citizens United v. Federal Election Committee* again changed the terms for campaigning. As we will see in Chapter 10, the amount of money spent in the 2012 presidential primaries broke new records because the 2010 Court decision allowed unlimited corporate contributions to political campaigns.[21]

soft money money contributed directly to political parties and other organizations for political activities that is not regulated by federal campaign spending laws; in 2002 federal law prohibited unregulated donations to national party committees

527 committees nonprofit independent groups that receive and disburse funds to influence the nomination, election, or defeat of candidates. Named after Section 527 of the Internal Revenue Code, which defines and grants tax-exempt status to nonprofit advocacy groups

When a party controls the White House, that party's national committee chair is appointed by the president. Typically, this means that the party's national committee becomes little more than an adjunct to the White House staff. For a first-term president, the committee devotes the bulk of its energy to the re-election campaign. The national committee chair of the party not in control of the White House is selected by the committee itself and usually takes a broader view of the party's needs, raising money and performing other activities on behalf of the party members in Congress and in the state legislatures.

Congressional Campaign Committees

Each party also forms House and Senate campaign committees to raise funds for House and Senate election campaigns. Their efforts may or may not be coordinated with the activities of the national committees. Within the party that controls the White House, the national committee and the congressional campaign committees are often rivals, since both groups are seeking donations from the same people but for different candidates: the national committee seeks funds for the presidential race, while the congressional campaign committees approach the same contributors for support for the congressional contests. In recent years, the Republican Party has attempted to coordinate the fund-raising activities of all its committees. Republicans have also sought to give the GOP's national institutions the capacity to invest funds in those close congressional, state, and local races where they can do the most good. The Democrats soon followed suit. Their aggressive stance and party unity allowed them to win back Congress in 2006.

State and Local Party Organizations

Each of the two major parties has a central committee in each state. The parties traditionally also have county committees and, in some instances, state senate district committees, judicial district committees, and, in the case of larger cities, citywide party committees and local assembly district "ward" committees. Congressional districts also may have party committees. Some cities also have precinct committees. Precincts are not districts from which any representative is elected but instead are legally defined subdivisions of wards that are used to register voters and set up ballot boxes or voting machines. A precinct is typically composed of 300 to 600 voters.

During the nineteenth and early twentieth centuries, many cities, counties, and occasionally even a few states had such well-organized parties that they were called **machines**, whose leaders were called "bosses." The famous old machines of New York, Chicago, and Boston relied on "precinct captains" and a fairly tight group of party members around them. Precinct captains were usually members of long standing in neighborhood party clubhouses, which were important social centers and places for distributing favors to constituents.[22] Traditional party machines depended heavily on **patronage**, their power to control government jobs. With thousands of jobs to dispense, party bosses were able to recruit armies of political workers, who in turn mobilized millions of voters.

Some of the major reform movements in American history were motivated by the excessive powers and abuses of these machines and their bosses. Few, if any, machines are left today. With civil-service reform, party leaders no longer control many positions. Nevertheless, state and local party organizations are very active in recruiting candidates and conducting voter registration drives. In addition,

machines strong party organizations in late-nineteenth- and early-twentieth-century American cities. These machines were led by "bosses" who controlled party nominations and patronage

patronage the resources available to higher officials, usually opportunities to make partisan appointments to offices and to confer grants, licenses, or special favors to supporters

Party Power in a Digital Age

Parties in the United States are considered to be ground-up organizations, meaning that they get their power from the members of the mass public who support them at the local level. However, until fairly recently, political party bosses controlled the party platform, the party message, and often, through early money to candidates, who held elected office and who won the nomination for president. Even with the decline of party machines and the increased use of primaries in the nominations process in the twentieth century, party elites retained a great deal of control over these decisions. Local party leaders would then spread the message from the elites by word of mouth and at local events to gain new supporters and keep existing supporters in line.

While this elite-driven process still occurs today, the process of party formation and many aspects of party politics have been turned upside down with the digital revolution in communication. Four resources that political parties use to contest and win elections (time, money, expertise, and organization) have all been altered by the Internet. New

media are decentralizing party power, as citizens can volunteer and give money to the party of their choice without ever being contacted by a party official. Online fund-raising allows millions of donors to give small contributions to parties, and new media allow the party to spread its message far and wide online. This is beneficial for parties because more people are involved, but at the same time, there are more divergent opinions that must be recognized and appeased. No longer can party leaders craft their own message and relay it to the field; they must also listen to what their supporters want. If the party does not appeal to the mass public, members of the mass public will form their own groups, or even competing parties.

This is exactly what happened in the case of the Tea Party movement in 2010. A large number of Republican supporters felt the party was not listening to their concerns and decided to create their own groups. Without the Internet, the Tea Party groups may not have been able to form, let alone influence the Republican Party as they did in the 2010 elections. Fearing a major split in the party and a mass exodus of party supporters, the Republican Party was forced to change its platform to reincorporate these supporters.

The Republican Party had to move farther away from the center and become more conservative to appease a core group of supporters. As online news becomes more important, the Internet is increasingly cited as a cause for the growing polarization of the political parties, where they agree on fewer and fewer political issues. In a 2010 Pew survey, over half of those interviewed agreed that "the Internet increases the influence of those with extreme political views" while only 30 percent believed that

the Internet is decreasing the power of party extremists.

Whether the Internet increases polarization or not, it seems clear that, the days of political elites deciding the party agenda behind closed doors are gone. The term *party leader* still invokes images of powerful governors, senators, and presidents; however, with the changes to party makeup in a world of digital politics, the term more appropriately applies to the average citizen watching what the party does from his computer or smartphone, with party leaders sending out texts, tweets, e-mails, or Facebook posts.

SOURCES: Bruce Bimber, *Information and American Democracy: Technology in the Evolution of Political Power* (Cambridge, UK: Cambridge University Press, 2003). Marty Cohen, David Karol, Hans Noel, and John Zaller, *The Party Decides: Presidential Nominations before and after Reform* (Chicago: University of Chicago Press, 2008). Thomas Mann, and Norman Ornstein, *It's Even Worse Than It Looks: How the American Constitutional System Collided with the New Politics of Extremism* (Washington, DC: Brookings Institution Press, 2012). Trygve Olson, and Terry Nelson, "The Internet's Impact on Political Parties and Campaigns," International Reports, 2010, www.kas.de/wf/en/33.19706/ (accessed 6/23/12). Adam Smith, "Attitudes towards the Internet's Impact on Politics," Pew Internet and American Life Project, 2011, http://pewinternet.org/Reports/2011/The-Internet-and-Campaign-2010/Section-4.aspx (accessed 6/24/12).

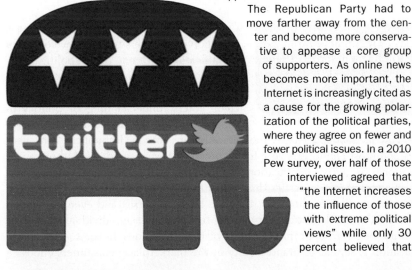

for critical analysis

1. Can you image a new political party that makes online communication its primary mode of operation? Why or why not? Why did the experiment in an online political party, Americans Elect, fail?

2. Do political elites and party bosses still control party politics in the United States, or have new media fostered a more democratic and participatory process for average Americans? Explain your answer.

Local party offices may work in tandem with the national and state party organizations, but they also have a good deal of independence to decide which local candidates and issues to support.

under current federal law, state and local party organizations can spend unlimited amounts of money on "party-building" activities such as voter registration and get-out-the-vote drives (though in some states such practices are limited by state law). As a result, for many years the national party organizations, which had enormous fund-raising abilities but were restricted by law in how much they could spend on candidates, transferred millions of dollars to the state and local organizations. The state and local parties, in turn, spent this soft money to promote national, state, and local political activities. In this process, local organizations became linked financially to the national parties and American political parties became somewhat more integrated and nationalized than ever before. At the same time, the state and local party organizations came to control large financial resources and play important roles in elections despite the collapse of the old patronage machines.[23]

● Parties and the Electorate

> **Identify the social groups that tend to support the Republicans and the Democrats**

party identification an individual voter's psychological ties to one party or another

One reason why parties are so important is that individual voters tend to develop **party identification** with one of the political parties. Party identification has been compared to wearing blue- or red-tinted glasses: they color voters' understanding of politics in general, and are the most important cue in how to vote in elections. That is, most Republicans vote for Republican Party candidates, and most Democrats vote for Democratic Party candidates. Although it is an emotional tie, party identification also has a rational component. Voters generally form attachments to parties that reflect their views and interests. Once those attachments are formed, however, they are likely to persist and even be handed down to children, unless some very strong factors convince individuals that their party is no longer an appropriate object of their affections. In some sense, party identification is similar to brand loyalty in the marketplace: consumers choose a

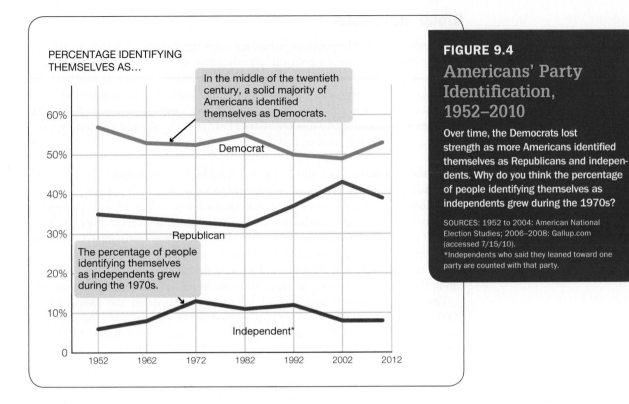

PERCENTAGE IDENTIFYING THEMSELVES AS...

In the middle of the twentieth century, a solid majority of Americans identified themselves as Democrats.

Democrat

Republican

The percentage of people identifying themselves as independents grew during the 1970s.

Independent*

1952   1962   1972   1982   1992   2002   2012

FIGURE 9.4

Americans' Party Identification, 1952–2010

Over time, the Democrats lost strength as more Americans identified themselves as Republicans and independents. Why do you think the percentage of people identifying themselves as independents grew during the 1970s?

SOURCES: 1952 to 2004: American National Election Studies; 2006–2008: Gallup.com (accessed 7/15/10).
*Independents who said they leaned toward one party are counted with that party.

brand of automobile for its appearance or mechanical characteristics and stick with it out of loyalty, habit, and unwillingness to reexamine their choices, but they may eventually change if the old brand no longer serves their interests.

On any general-election ballot, there are likely to be only two or three candidacies where the nature of the office and the characteristics and positions of the candidates are well known to voters. But what about the choices for judges, the state comptroller, the state attorney general, and many other elected positions? Parties and campaigns help by providing information when voters must choose among obscure candidates. Without knowledge of local races or judges, most voters fall back on their partisanship, voting for Republican candidates or Democratic candidates for these positions.

Although roughly one in three Americans is independent, roughly a third are Republican and a third Democrat, and most independents "lean" toward one major party (see Figure 9.4). Party identification gives citizens a stake in election outcomes that goes beyond the particular race at hand. This is why strong party identifiers are more likely to go to the polls and, of course, are more likely than others to support the party with which they identify. **Party activists** are drawn from the ranks of the strong identifiers. Activists are those who not only vote but also contribute their time and effort to party affairs. No party could succeed without the thousands of volunteers who undertake the tasks needed to keep the organization going. Many party activists devote their time to politics because they have strong beliefs on particular policy issues. Across a range of issues, the views of Democratic activists are more liberal than those of Democratic voters, whereas the views of Republican activists are more conservative than those of Republican voters. One study that compared the views of party activists and rank-and-file voters across a range of issues found that since the 1990s, the views of Republican Party activists have diverged most sharply from those of the average voter.[24]

party activists partisans who contribute time, energy, and effort to support their party and its candidates

Group Affiliations

The Democratic and Republican parties are currently America's only truly national parties. They are the only political organizations that draw support from most regions of the country and from Americans of every racial, economic, religious, and ethnic group. The two parties do not draw equal support from members of every social stratum, however. In the United States today, a variety of group characteristics is associated with party identification. These include race and ethnicity, gender, religion, class, ideology, region, and age.

Race and Ethnicity Since the 1930s and Franklin Delano Roosevelt's New Deal, African Americans have been overwhelmingly Democratic in their party identification. More than 90 percent of African Americans describe themselves as Democrats and support Democratic candidates in national, state, and local elections. In 2012, over 90 percent of African Americans supported the Democrat Barack Obama for president. Latino voters are less monolithic, by contrast, but tend to support the Democratic Party. Cuban Americans, for example, have generally leaned Republican in their party affiliations, whereas Mexican Americans favored the Democrats.

This mix of partisan preferences shifted strongly toward the Democrats in 2008, when the exit polls showed that 67 percent of Latinos supported Obama. The trend continued in 2012, with over 70 percent voting for Obama. The Latino vote is particularly important because it can help alter the electoral map. In 2012 the Latino vote in swing states such as Florida and Colorado helped bring the Democrats to victory. Asian Americans have been divided in past elections, but in 2012, 73 percent of Asian Americans voted for Barack Obama, and 26 percent voted for Mitt Romney, according to exit polls.

gender gap a distinctive pattern of voting behavior reflecting the differences in views between women and men

Gender Women are somewhat more likely to support Democrats, and men are somewhat more likely to support Republicans, in surveys of party affiliation. This difference is known as the **gender gap**. The gender gap has varied between 6 and 11 percent since 1992. For example, George W. Bush's first election, in 2000, had

In 2012 both major parties tried to appeal to Latino and Hispanic voters. Mitt Romney called on members of his family who speak Spanish to appear at campaign events with Latino groups.

a sizable gender gap of 53 percent support among men and 43 percent among women. In 2004 the gender gap decreased slightly, with 55 percent of men voting for Bush compared with 48 percent of women. In 2008 the gap remained on the small side, with 56 percent of women and 49 percent of men supporting Barack Obama for president but it widened again in 2012, with 55 percent of women supporting Obama as compared with just 45 percent of men.[25]

Religion Jews are among the Democratic Party's most loyal constituent groups and have been since the New Deal. Nearly 90 percent of all Jewish Americans describe themselves as Democrats. Catholics were also once a strongly pro-Democratic group but have been shifting toward the Republican Party since the 1970s, when the party focused on abortion and other social issues deemed to be important to Catholics. Protestants are more likely to identify with the Republicans than with the Democrats. Evangelical Protestants, in particular, have been drawn to the Republicans' conservative stands on social issues, such as marriage and abortion. The importance of religious conservatives to the Republican Party became more evident after 2000, when George W. Bush awarded federal grants and contracts to religious groups. By using so-called faith-based groups as federal contractors, Bush sought to ensure that these groups would have a continuing stake in Republican success. Religious conservatives, particularly white born-again Christians, overwhelmingly supported President Bush in 2004, accounting for one-third of his votes. Almost 80 percent of white born-again Christians voted for President Bush; only 21 percent supported the Democratic candidate, Senator John Kerry. Yet the 2004 election results also revealed that religiosity, as measured by frequency of attendance at religious services, had a larger impact on voting than denominational affiliation. Voters who attended religious services weekly were more likely to vote for Bush, regardless of their religion, than were voters who were less observant. In 2008 and 2012, white evangelicals continued to vote overwhelmingly Republican.[26]

Class The patterns of class voting that emerged from the New Deal of the 1930s were simple: upper-income Americans were considerably more likely to affiliate with the Republicans, whereas lower-income Americans were far more likely to identify with the Democrats. This divide is reflected in the differences between the two parties on economic issues. In general, the Republicans support cutting taxes and social spending—positions that reflect the interests of the wealthy. The Democrats, however, favor increasing social spending—a position consistent with the interests of less-affluent Americans. But beginning in the 1970s, many white working-class voters, concerned about "law and order," moral issues, and racial liberalism, started voting Republican, and have remained in the Republican Party. Analysts disagree about the trend of class voting, because there is no widely accepted definition of class. When the electorate is divided into thirds on the basis of income, the relationship between lower-income voters and Democratic allegiance remains strong. When class is measured by education, however, white workers without a college degree have voted heavily for Republicans in recent elections.[27]

Ideology Ideology and party identification are very closely linked. Most individuals who describe themselves as conservatives identify with the Republican Party, whereas most who call themselves liberals support the Democrats. This division has increased in recent years as the two parties have taken very different positions on social and economic issues. Before the 1970s, when party differences were more blurred, it was not uncommon to find Democratic conservatives and Republican liberals. Both of these species are rare today. Yet important differences remain among conservatives and liberals. Economic conservatives care most about reducing government regulation and taxes. Social conservatives are concerned about social issues such as abortion and same-sex marriage. The Republican Party includes both groups, but at times the interests of these two kinds of conservatives conflict. Likewise, many Democrats who are economic liberals, in favor of generous social spending, are conservative when it comes to matters such as gun control.

Region After the 2000 election, red and blue maps appeared showing the regional distribution of the vote. Democrats, represented as "Blue America," were clustered on the coasts and the upper Midwest and across the northern states. Republicans, represented as "Red America," were concentrated in the Mountain West, the Southwest, and the South.

The explanations for these regional variations are complex. Between the Civil War and the 1960s, the "Solid South" was a Democratic bastion. Today the South is solidly Republican. Southern Republicanism has come about because conservative white southerners identify the Democratic Party with the civil rights movement, racial liberalism, and with liberal positions on abortion, school prayer, and other social issues. Republican strength in the South is also related to the weakness of organized labor in these regions, and to the dependence of the two regions on military programs supported by the Republicans. Democratic strength in the Northeast and Midwest is a function of the continuing influence of organized labor in the large cities of these regions, and of the regions' large populations of minority and elderly voters, who benefit from Democratic social programs. The coastal West, especially California, shifted toward the Democrats in the 1990s, in part because of the growing importance of the Latino vote.[28]

Age Age is another factor associated with partisanship. In 2008 the shift toward the Democratic Party affected all age groups, but it was particularly strong among young voters. Polls showed that, while older voters preferred Democrats by 11–12 percent, those born after 1977 favored Democrats by 24 percent. There is nothing about a particular numerical age that leads to a particular party loyalty. Rather, individuals from the same age cohort are likely to have experienced a similar set of events during the period when their party loyalties were formed. Thus, Americans between the ages of 50 and 64 came of political age during the Cold War, Vietnam, and civil rights eras. Apparently, among voters whose initial perceptions of politics were shaped during this period, more responded favorably to the role played by the Democrats than to the actions of the Republicans. Young people who came of age during the Bush presidency had the strongest Democratic Party identification of any age group.

Recent Trends in Party Affiliation

After the 1960s, many analysts began to express concern that American parties had become too weak to play their vital role in converting popular political participation into effective government. These scholars noted such trends as a decline in partisan attachment within the electorate, the growth in the numbers of voters identifying as independents, and a rise in so-called split-ticket voting. This overall trend, sometimes termed dealignment, was seen as a product of growing social diversity and educational attainment, which made voters less reliant on parties to guide their political decision making. The growth of the mass media, particularly television, also seemed to reduce the role of parties in elections, as television tends to focus on the personality of indi-

for critical analysis

What are the major components of each party's political coalition? What factors tie these groups to their respective parties?

Who Identifies with Which Party?

Party identification varies by income, race, and gender. For example, as these statistics from 2008 show, Americans with higher incomes are significantly more likely to support the Republican Party. Women and African Americans are more likely than white men to identify with the Democratic Party.

Gender		Republican	Independent	Democratic
	Men	42%	11%	47%
	Women	34%	11%	55%

Age				
	18-29	33%	10%	58%
	30-49	39%	10%	50%
	50-64	38%	11%	51%
	65 and over	40%	11%	49%

Race				
	White	44%	10%	46%
	Black	7%	8%	86%
	Hispanic	27%	11%	62%
	All others	15%	12%	73%

Income				
	Under $20K	24%	12%	63%
	$20K–$29,999	32%	10%	58%
	$30K–$49,999	36%	9%	54%
	$50K–$74,999	51%	8%	41%
	$75K and over	48%	8%	45%

Region				
	East	34%	11%	55%
	Midwest	38%	12%	50%
	South	41%	10%	49%
	West	37%	10%	53%

Education				
	< High school	27%	13%	60%
	High school grad.	38%	11%	52%
	College grad.	43%	10%	47%
	Postgraduate	38%	9%	53%

Republican Party

Democratic Party

Independent

for critical analysis

1. How do younger Americans differ from older Americans in their party identification? How—and how much—do regions of the country differ?

2. Do you think of yourself as a Democrat, Republican, or independent? Are other Americans of your gender, age, race, region, and income level likely to share your party preference?

SOURCE: Harold W. Stanley and Richard G. Niemi, *Vital Statistics on American Politics, 2011-2012* (Washington, DC: Congressional Quarterly Press, 2011), p. 110.

vidual candidates rather than the "institution" of the party. Today, party loyalties in America continue to be in a state of flux. On the one hand, the percentage of voters who declare no party loyalty remains at an all-time high.[29] On the other hand, party identification among a large number of the most active voters has grown stronger.[30]

The Who Are Americans? feature indicates the relationship between party identification and a number of social criteria. Race and income seem to have the greatest influence on Americans' party affiliations. Neither of these social characteristics is inevitably linked to partisan identification, however. The general party identifications just discussed are broad tendencies that both reflect and reinforce the issue and policy positions the two parties take in the national and local political arenas.

● Parties and Elections

> **Explain the roles parties play in elections**

Parties have always been central to the electoral process, and in recent years they have taken on a renewed role in recruiting candidates, coordinating campaigns, mobilizing voters, and raising money.[31] One of the most important but least noticed party activities is the recruitment of candidates for local, state, and national office. Each election year, candidates must be found for thousands of state and local offices as well as congressional seats. Where they do not have an incumbent running for re-election, party leaders attempt to identify strong candidates and to interest them in entering the campaign.

An ideal candidate will have an unblemished record and the capacity to raise enough money to mount a serious campaign. Party leaders are usually not willing to provide financial backing to candidates who are unable to raise substantial funds on their own. For a House seat, this can mean several hundred thousand dollars; for a Senate seat, a serious candidate must be able to raise several million dollars. Often party leaders have difficulty finding attractive candidates and persuading them to run. Candidate recruitment is problematic in an era when political candidates must assume that their personal lives will be intensely scrutinized in the press and even subjected to mudslinging campaigns by their opponents.[32]

Nominations

Article I, Section 4, of the Constitution makes only a few provisions for elections. It delegates to the states the power to set the "times, places, and manner" of holding elections, even for U.S. senators and representatives. The Constitution has been amended from time to time to expand the right to participate in elections. Congress has also occasionally passed laws regulating elections, congressional districting, and campaign practices. But the Constitution and the laws are almost completely silent on nominations, setting only age and citizenship requirements for candidates. The president must be at least 35 years of age, a native-born citizen, and a resident of the United States for 14 years. A senator must be at least 30, a U.S. citizen for at least nine years, and a resident of the state he or she represents. A member of the House must be at least 25, a U.S. citizen for 7 years, and a resident of the state he or she represents.

Nomination is the process by which a party selects a single candidate to run for each elective office. The nominating process can precede the election by many months, as it does when the many candidates for the presidency are eliminated

nomination the process by which political parties select their candidates for election to public office

from consideration through a grueling series of debates and state primaries until there is only one survivor in each party: the party's nominee.

Mobilizing Voters

The actual election period begins immediately after the nominations. Throughout American history, this has been a time of glory for the political parties, whose popular base of support is fully displayed. All the paraphernalia of party committees (signs, bumper stickers, buttons) are on display, and all the committee members are activated into local party workforces. The first step involves voter registration. There was a time when party workers were responsible for virtually all this kind of electoral activity, but they have been supplemented by civic groups such as the League of Women Voters, unions, and Chambers of Commerce, although the parties frequently mail notices and call voters to ensure that they are registered. Those who have registered have to decide on Election Day if they will actually go to the polling place, stand in line, and vote for the various candidates and referenda on the ballot. If they are voting by mail in one of the states that allow this, they have to request the ballot, fill it out, and return it (see Chapter 8).

Political parties, candidates, and campaigning can make a big difference in persuading voters to vote. Voter mobilization, once an art, has now become a science. In recent years, each of the two major parties has developed an extensive database on hundreds of millions of potential voters, which allows the parties to bring their search for votes, contributions, and campaign help down to named individuals. The Republican Party calls its archive Voter Vault. To compete with the technologically sophisticated Republicans, in the mid-2000s the Democratic National Committee began to use a state-of-the-art Web-based system, originally called Demzilla and later renamed VoteBuilder, for collecting and sharing voter information. In the 2008 and 2012 elections, the DNC made the voter file available to state parties, and this technology became one of the keys to their successful mobilization and get-out-the-vote activities those years.

Since the 1980s, the Republicans have appealed to "values voters" concerned about social issues like school prayer, abortion, and gay marriage with promises to enact new policies in these areas. In 2011, Mitt Romney spoke at the Values Voter Summit in Washington, D.C.

● Parties and Government

> **Explain how parties organize legislative business and influence policy**

When the dust of the campaign has settled, does it matter which party has won? It does. Especially when the parties are sharply divided ideologically, as they have been in recent years, the party that controls government can make significant changes by moving policy in new directions.

Parties and Policy

One of the most familiar complaints about American politics is that the two major parties try to be all things to all people, and are therefore indistinguishable from each other. But since the 1980s, important differences have emerged between the positions of Democratic and Republican party leaders on a number of key issues, and these differences are still apparent today.

FRC*Action*.org

★ ★ ★

★ Values ★

Voter

For example, the national leadership of the Republican Party supports maintaining high levels of military spending, cuts in social programs, tax relief for upper-income voters, tax incentives for businesses, and the "social agenda" backed by members of conservative religious denominations. The national Democratic leadership, on the other hand, supports expanded social welfare spending, cuts in military spending, increased regulation of business, and a variety of consumer and environmental programs.

These differences reflect differences in philosophy and differences in the core constituencies to which the parties seek to appeal. The Democratic Party at the national level seeks to unite organized labor, the poor and working class, members of racial minorities, and liberal upper-middle-class professionals. The Republicans, by contrast, appeal to business, upper-middle- and upper-class groups in the private sector, white working-class voters, and social conservatives. Often party leaders will seek to develop issues they hope will add new groups to their party's constituent base. During the 1980s, for example, under the leadership of Ronald Reagan, the Republicans devised a series of "social issues," including support for school prayer, opposition to abortion, and opposition to affirmative action, designed to cultivate the support of white southerners. This effort was extremely successful in increasing Republican strength in the once solidly Democratic South. In the 1990s, under the leadership of Bill Clinton, who called himself a "new Democrat," the Democratic Party sought to develop new social programs designed to solidify the party's base among working-class and poor voters, and new, somewhat more conservative economic programs aimed at attracting the votes of middle- and upper-middle-class voters. In 2000, George W. Bush labeled himself a "compassionate conservative" to signal to the Republican base that he was a conservative while seeking to reassure moderate and independent voters that he was not an opponent of federal social programs.

As these examples suggest, parties do not always support policies just because their constituents already favor those policies. Instead, party leaders can play the

policy entrepreneur an individual who identifies a problem as a political issue and brings a policy proposal into the political agenda

role of **policy entrepreneurs**, seeking ideas and programs that will expand their party's base of support while eroding that of the opposition. It is one of the essential characteristics of party politics in America that a party's programs and policies often lead, rather than follow, public opinion. Like their counterparts in the business world, party leaders seek to identify and develop "products" (programs and policies) that will appeal to the public. The public, of course, has the ultimate voice. With its votes it decides whether or not to "buy" new policy offerings.

Thus, for example, in 2010 many Republican congressional candidates vowed to repeal the major health care reform act signed by President Obama earlier in the year. Republican presidential candidates in 2012 also vowed to repeal what they referred to as Obamacare, but it was not clear whether they would be able to obtain the necessary votes in Congress. There are, however, a number of legal cases that have challenged the individual mandate requiring individuals to purchase health care insurance if they are not covered by their employer. In 2012 the Supreme Court ruled arguments concerning the individual mandate was constitutional.

Parties in Congress

Congress depends more on the party system than is generally recognized. For one thing, the speakership of the House is essentially a party office. All the members of the House take part in the election of the Speaker. But the actual selection is made

Within the government, parties help like-minded politicians achieve their policy goals. In Congress party members work together to try to pass legislation, and they also work with the president. Here, President Barack Obama meet with the Democrats' congressional leaders in the Oval Office.

by the **majority party**—the party that holds a majority of seats in the House. (The other party is known as the **minority party**.) When the majority party caucus presents a nominee to the entire House, its choice is then invariably ratified in a straight vote along party lines. The committee system of both houses of Congress is also a product of the two-party system. For example, each party is assigned a quota of members for each committee, depending on the percentage of total seats held by the party. As we shall see in Chapter 12, the assignment of individual members to committees is a party decision. Each party has a "committee on committees" to make such decisions. Granting permission to transfer to another committee is also a party decision, as is advancement up the committee ladder toward the chair. Since the late nineteenth century, most advancements have been automatic—based on the length of continual service on the committee. This seniority system has existed only because of the support of the two parties, however, and either party can depart from it by a simple vote.

The importance of parties in Congress became especially evident in the months after the Republicans won control of Congress in 1994. The Republican leadership was able to maintain nearly unanimous support among party members on vote after vote as it sought to implement the GOP's legislative agenda, and Democrats were rarely able to match the Republicans' strong party discipline. After 2006, however, when Democrats won back the Congress, they showed considerably more party discipline than they had in past decades. After Obama's election, Republican members of Congress also showed remarkable party discipline in their united party-line opposition to the president's major initiatives ranging from economic stimulus to major health care reform, which led Democrats to decry the GOP as "the party of No."

President and Party

Strong presidents with broad popular support can depend on party ties to get their legislation enacted in Congress. Yet there has been a trade-off in using the

majority party the party that holds the majority of legislative seats in either the House or the Senate

minority party the party that holds a minority of legislative seats in either the House or the Senate

party machinery to support the president's legislative agenda and building it to support the party in congressional elections. The political scientist Daniel Galvin argues that since the Eisenhower presidency, Republicans have paid much more attention to party building than have Democrats.[33] Given their minority status in the electorate for much of the past 50 years, Republican presidents have sought to enhance the party's capabilities to mobilize voters and win elections. George W. Bush's adviser Karl Rove hoped to build a strong party apparatus that would ensure a permanent Republican majority. Democratic presidents have put much less energy into building the party apparatus, focusing instead on their legislative agenda and their own re-election. It was only after their 2004 election defeat that Democrats began to pour their energies into building a stronger party. Under the chairmanship of Howard Dean, a previous presidential candidate and a former Vermont governor, the Democratic National Committee invested heavily in new technology and in creating party-mobilizing capabilities in states across the country, not just the traditionally "blue" states that have reliably voted Democratic.

The Obama campaign was able to use this party machinery as a springboard for its own mobilizing organization, Obama for America. With detailed information about Democratic Party activists, Obama for America's database became, in turn, an important political resource for the mobilizing capacities of the Democratic Party. After Obama took office, the organization was renamed Organizing for America (OFA) and became an independent project of the Democratic National Committee. During Obama's first year in office, the president used Organizing for America to mobilize grassroots support for his legislative agenda. For example, OFA took a very active part in lobbying members of Congress to support health care reform. Organizing for America provides training for volunteers to learn how to become organizers and it has established offices in nearly every state.

● Thinking Critically about Why Political Parties Matter

Political parties are bulwarks of liberty. The Constitution certainly provides for freedom of speech, freedom of assembly, and freedom of the press. Maintaining these liberties, though, requires more than parchment guarantees. Of course, as long as freedom is not seriously threatened, abstract guarantees suffice to protect it. If, however, those in power actually do threaten citizens' liberties, the preservation of freedom may come to depend on the presence of a coherent and well-organized opposition. As noted earlier, in the first years of the Republic, it was not the Constitution or the courts that preserved free speech in the face of Federalist efforts to silence the government's critics; it was the vigorous opposition of the Jeffersonian Republicans. To this day, the presence of an opposition party is a fundamentally important check on attempts by those in power to skirt the law and infringe on citizens' liberties.

Competition among the political parties is a key factor in stimulating voter turnout. Competition gives citizens an incentive to vote and politicians an incentive to get them to vote.[34] The origins of the American national electorate can be traced to the earliest days of the Republic. According to the historian David Fischer, "the Jeffersonians revolutionized electioneering" during the 1790s, and the Federalists, although initially reluctant, soon adopted the same techniques for mobilizing voters: "mass meetings, barbecues, stump-speaking, festivals of many kinds, processions

Political Parties and the World

Few Americans are aware of the international involvements of our two major political parties. Since the mid-1980s each political party has been associated with a formal foreign policy institute. The International Republican Institute (IRI) was founded in 1983, and the National Democratic Institute for International Affairs (NDI) was established in 1985. Each party's institute is led by a cadre of the party's former officials and elected officeholders.

Both the IRI and the NDI work to encourage citizen participation and democracy throughout the world, particularly in regions that lack a historical and institutional base for democratic politics. Both party institutes work with local politicians, civic leaders, and community activists to encourage understanding of democratic political techniques and respect for democratic values.

Although the programs of the party institutes have many similarities, they diverge in ways that reflect the differences between the two American political parties. NDI programs pay special attention to women and young people—groups cultivated by the Democratic Party in the United States—and to trade unions, another bulwark of the U.S. Democratic Party. Thus, for example, an NDI program in Senegal was designed to increase the involvement of women in local government and in the leadership of the nation's political parties.

The IRI, for its part, has emphasized cultivating relationships with government officials and business leaders, and whereas the NDI's approach is decidedly grassroots in character, the IRI, like the Republican Party, emphasizes political technology. For example, in Macedonia, the IRI has taught public officials the elements of media relations, public-opinion polling, and "message development." Differences are also evident in which countries each institute emphasizes. For example, the IRI pays special attention to the issue of democracy in Cuba, reflecting the significance of the Cuban American vote to the Republican Party.

Although promoting democracy sounds uncontroversial, intervention into the affairs of other countries can lead to results that are anything but democratic. The case of the IRI's activities in Haiti provide an example. A 2006 investigative article in the *New York Times* charged that the IRI deliberately worked to destabilize democracy in Haiti in 2003–04.[a] At the time, Haiti was in a political crisis, with two opposing sides seeking to reach a political reconciliation. According to interviews and public records, the IRI's representative in Haiti provided one-sided support to the opponents of the elected president, Bertrand Aristide. Aristide was a controversial leader who was seen as a voice for Haiti's poor. Although the U.S. ambassador to Haiti at the time protested the involvement of the IRI, the group continued to operate with little accountability. Aristide's opponents launched a coup in 2004, sending the country into chaos for years to come.

Despite criticism, the IRI has grown and in 2008 employed 400 people working on democracy projects in seventy countries.[b]

[a]Walt Bogdanich and Jenny Nordberg, "Mixed U.S. Signals Helped Tilt Haiti toward Chaos," *New York Times,* January 29, 2006, p. 1.
[b]Mike McIntire, "Democracy Group Gives Donors Access to McCain," *New York Times,* July 28, 2008, p. A1.

for critical analysis

1. What are the similarities and differences between the NDI and the IRI? Do these parallel the similarities and differences between the Democratic and Republican parties?

2. How can Americans ensure that the activities of groups such as the IRI and NDI are accountable to the taxpayers who fund them?

for critical analysis

Describe the factors that have contributed to the overall strength and weakness of political parties in America. What are the advantages of a political system in which political parties organize conflict?

and parades, runners and riders, door-to-door canvassing, the distribution of tickets and ballots, . . . free transportation to the polls, outright bribery and corruption of other kinds."[35] The result of this competition for votes was described by the historian Henry Jones Ford in his classic *Rise and Growth of American Politics.*[36] Ford examined the popular clamor against John Adams and Federalist policies in the 1790s that made government a "weak, shakey affair" and appeared to contemporary observers to mark the beginnings of popular insurrection.[37] Attempts by the Federalists to suppress mass discontent, Ford observed, might have "caused an explosion of force which would have blown up the government."[38] What intervened to prevent rebellion was Jefferson's creation of an opposition party that served to "open constitutional channels of political agitation" that diverted opposition to the administration into electoral channels.[39] Party competition gave citizens a sense that their votes were valuable and that it was thus not necessary to take to the streets to have a political impact.

Finally, political parties make democratic government possible. We often fail to appreciate that *democratic government* is a contradiction in terms: *government* implies policies, programs, and decisive action, while *democracy* implies an opportunity for all citizens to participate fully in the governmental process. But full participation by everyone is often inconsistent with getting anything done. At what point should participation stop and governance begin? The problem of democratic government is especially acute in the United States because of the Constitution's system of separated powers, making it very difficult to link popular participation with effective decision making. Often, after the citizens have spoken and the dust has settled, no single set of political forces has been able to win control of enough of the scattered levers of power actually to do anything. Instead of governance, we have continual political struggle. Strong political parties, then, are a partial antidote to the inherent contradiction between participation and government: they can both encourage popular involvement and convert participation into effective government.

There is an old saying that politics is the art of compromise, but politics is more than that—it is also the challenge of making choices. Parties help to crystallize a world of possible government actions into a set of distinct choices. In so doing, they make it easier for ordinary citizens to understand politics, evaluate candidates, and make their own choices.

Connect with Political Parties

Inform Yourself

Learn about third (and fourth and fifth) parties. Most people in the United States are aware of the two major political parties. Many do not know of the dozens of smaller parties that operate on a national scale. Visit the webpage: http://www .politics1.com/parties.htm and read the platforms of each of the major and minor parties. Does any of the information about these parties surprise you?

Compare videos from a range of parties. The Procon website (2012election .procon.org) lists the candidates who ran for office in 2012 from the major two parties and third parties, including their mission statements and platforms. Using the menu on the left side of the screen, you can watch videos of the candidates and hear their speeches. The summary chart shows the candidates' positions on 61 issues (http://2012election.procon.org/view.source-summary -chart.php?topic=64).

Express Yourself

Are concerns about today's major parties valid? When parties began to form in the early 1790s, President Washington was concerned about their potential power. Read his Farewell Address at http://thehistoryprofessor.us/bin/ history/politics.html, and consider what Washington might have said about political parties today. Were his concerns valid? What would the Founders have said about the platforms and roles of the modern parties? Consider posting your opinion on the Facebook page of one of parties listed under "Connect."

Connect

Both the Republican and Democratic national committees have Facebook pages. Dozens of third-party committees do as well. Visit their Facebook pages at www .facebook.com/#!/electdemocrats, www.facebook.com/#!/GOP, www.facebook .com/#!/GreenPartyUS, or www.facebook.com/#!/libertarians. (There are many others.) Read a few of the posts on each page and consider whether you agree with any of the comments. If one in particular stands out to you, consider commenting on the post.

Find links to the sites listed above as well as related activities on wwnorton.com/studyspace.

study guide

 Practice online with: Chapter 9 Diagnostic Quiz ▪ Chapter 9 Key Term Flashcards

What Are Political Parties

■ **Define political parties and their general role in politics (pp. 341–42)**

A political party is an organization that seeks influence over government by electing its members to office. Although some people are critical of political parties, they are extremely important to the functioning of a democracy because they increase participation in politics, provide a central cue for citizens to cast informed votes, and organize the business of Congress and governing.

Key Term

political parties (p. 341)

Practice Quiz

1. A political party is different from an interest group in that a political party *(p. 341)*
   a) seeks to control the entire government by electing its members to office and thereby controlling the government's personnel.
   b) seeks to control only limited, very specific functions of government.
   c) is entirely nonprofit.
   d) has a much larger membership.
   e) has a much smaller membership.

The Two-Party System in America

■ **Describe how the party system in the United States has changed over time and its main features today (pp. 342–55)**

Historically, political parties in the United States have formed through either "internal mobilization" or "external mobilization." A nation's party system refers to the organization of the parties within the country, the balance of power between and within party coalitions, the parties' social and institutional bases, and the issues and policies around which party competition is organized. Over the course of American history, changes in political forces and alignments have produced six distinctive party systems. Although third parties have occasionally influenced election outcomes and placed new ideas on the political agenda, numerous factors limit their long-term success and they have rarely been able to win elections at the national level.

Key Terms

two-party system (p. 342)

electoral realignment (p. 349)

divided government (p. 350)

party polarization (p. 351)

third parties (p. 352)

Practice Quiz

2. External mobilization occurs when *(p. 344)*
   a) political activists from a foreign country seek to influence American politics by financing the formation of a new political party in the United States.
   b) a politician seeks to pursue a moderate course that places him or her midway between the positions of conservative Republicans and liberal Democrats.
   c) the presidency is controlled by one party while the opposing party controls one or both houses of Congress.
   d) a group of politicians outside government organizes popular support to win governmental power.
   e) political conflicts within government break out and competing factions seek to mobilize popular support.

3. A proportional-representation electoral system is *(p. 342)*
   a) a system that gives each political party representation in proportion to its percentage of the total vote.
   b) a system where a candidate needs to win at least three-fourths of the vote to win the election.
   c) a system where the candidate with the most votes wins the election.
   d) a system where every candidate that wins at least 5 percent of the overall vote is given a seat in the legislature.

e) a system that gives each political party an equal number of seats in the legislature regardless of how many votes they receive in the election.

4. Which party was founded as a political expression of the antislavery movement? *(p. 346)*
   a) American Independent
   b) Prohibition
   c) Republican
   d) Democratic
   e) Whig

5. The periodic episodes in American history in which an "old" dominant political party is replaced by a "new" dominant political party are called *(p. 349)*
   a) constitutional revolutions.
   b) party turnovers.

c) governmental realignments.
d) presidential elections.
e) electoral realignments.

6. Historically, when do realignments occur? *(p. 349)*
   a) typically, every 20 years
   b) whenever a minority party takes over Congress
   c) when large numbers of voters permanently shift their support from one party to another
   d) in even-numbered years
   e) in odd-numbered years

 Practice Online
Video exercise: *Time Ripe for a Third Party?*

Party Organization

■ **Describe how the major American parties are structured at the national, state, and local levels (pp. 355–60)**

Party organizations exist at virtually every level of government in the United States, and they play an important role in structuring electoral competition. At the national level, for example, party organizations assemble conventions every four years that nominate the party's presidential and vice-presidential candidates, draft the party's campaign platform for the presidential race and approve changes in the rules governing party procedures. Similarly, at the state and local level, party organizations are active in recruiting candidates to run for office and in conducting voter registration and get-out-the-vote drives.

Key Terms

party organization (p. 355)

caucus (political) (p. 355)

national convention (p. 355)

platform (p. 356)

soft money (p. 357)

527 committees (p. 357)

machines (p. 358)

patronage (p. 358)

Practice Quiz

7. Which of the following is *not* determined at a party's national convention? *(p. 355)*
   a) the party's candidate for president
   b) the party's candidate for vice president

c) the party's campaign platform for the presidential race
d) the congressional committees party representatives will be assigned to
e) the rules and regulations governing party procedures.

8. The Bipartisan Campaign Reform Act *(p. 357)*
   a) outlawed patronage.
   b) outlawed caucuses.
   c) outlawed hard money.
   d) outlawed soft money.
   e) outlawed party machines.

9. An independent, nonprofit group that receives and disburses funds to influence election campaigns is called *(p. 357)*
   a) a party election committee.
   b) a 527 committee.
   c) a political machine.
   d) a party organization.
   e) a third party.

10. Through which mechanism did party leaders in the late nineteenth and early twentieth centuries maintain their control? *(p. 358)*
    a) civil service reform
    b) soft money contributions
    c) machine politics
    d) electoral reform
    e) political action committees.

 Practice Online
Interactive simulation: *Running for Local Office*

Parties and the Electorate

■ **Identify the social groups that tend to support the Republicans and the Democrats (pp. 360–66)**

Party identification refers to the psychological and emotional attachments people have to one of the political parties. In contemporary American politics, a wide variety of group characteristics, including race, ethnicity, gender, religion, class, ideology, region, and age, are associated with an individual's party identification. Party loyalties in the United States are currently in a state of flux, and roughly one-third of Americans identify themselves as independents rather than as Democrats or Republicans.

Key Terms

party identification (p. 360)

party activists (p. 361)

gender gap (p. 362)

Practice Quiz

11. Which of the following best describes in the current state of Americans' party identification? (*p. 361*)
    a) Roughly one-third identify as Democrats, roughly one-third identify as Republicans and roughly one-third identify as independents.
    b) Roughly half identify as Republicans and half identify as Democrats.
    c) Roughly half identify as Democrats, roughly 25 percent identify as Republicans, and roughly 25 percent identify as independents.
    d) Roughly half identify as Republicans, roughly 25 percent identify as Democrats, and roughly 25 percent identify as independents.
    e) A majority of Americans do not identify with any party.

12. The decline in partisan attachment in the electorate is referred to as (*p. 364*)
    a) polarization.
    b) independentification.
    c) unalignment.
    d) realignment.
    e) dealignment.

Practice Online
Video exercise: *Party Identification and Voting Behavior*

Parties and Elections

■ **Explain the roles parties play in elections (pp. 366–67)**

While political parties have always been important to the electoral process, they have recently taken on a renewed role in recruiting candidates and mobilizing voters. The Constitution sets age and citizenship requirements for candidates but says nothing about who can be recruited for office or who can be nominated by the political parties. As a result, party leaders attempt to identify strong candidates and to interest them in entering the campaign. Once the party's nominee has been selected, parties devote a great deal of energy registering people to vote and convincing them to show up on election day.

Key Term

nomination (p. 366)

Practice Quiz

13. Parties today are most important in the electoral process in (*p. 366*)
    a) recruiting and nominating candidates for office.
    b) financing all of the campaign's spending.
    c) providing millions of volunteers to mobilize voters.
    d) creating a responsible party government.
    e) changing the electoral laws to make voting easier.

Practice Online
Video exercise: *Pinellas County Republican Executive Committee (PCREC)*

Parties and Government

■ **Explain how parties organize legislative business and influence policy (pp. 367–70)**

Political parties exert a great deal of influence over the content of public policy, the structure of Congress and the behavior of presidents. The sharp ideological divisions between Democrats and Republicans in recent years mean that election outcomes matter greatly for the kinds of laws that government enacts. Many of the most important organizational features of Congress, such as Speaker, the committee system, and seniority, also depend on the party system. In order to overcome their minority status in the electorate, Republican presidents have spent significantly more time mobilizing voters than Democratic presidents.

Key Terms

policy entrepreneur (p. 368)

majority party (p. 369)

minority party (p. 369)

Practice Quiz

14. Which of the following feature of the House of Representatives is determined by a vote of the whole membership rather than by decisions within each party? *(p. 368)*
    a) the assignments of individual members to particular committees.
    b) advancement up the committee ladder.
    c) the ability of individual members to transfer from one committee to another.
    d) the use of the seniority system for determining committee chairs.
    e) selection of the Speaker of the House.

15. Which of the following statements best describes party-building activities from the 1960s to 2004 *(pp. 369–70)*
    a) Party-building activities were legally allowed but both political parties chose to ignore them.
    b) Democrats and Republicans paid equally high levels of attention to party-building.
    c) Democrats paid more attention to party-building than Republicans.
    d) Republicans paid more attention to party-building than Democrats.
    e) Party-building activities were outlawed under federal law.

For Further Reading

Aldrich, John H. *Why Parties? The Origin and Transformation of Political Parties in America.* Chicago: University of Chicago Press, 1995.

Bartels Larry. *Presidential Primaries and the Dynamics of Public Choice.* Princeton, NJ: Princeton University Press, 1988.

Burnham, Walter Dean. *Critical Elections and the Mainsprings of American Politics.* New York: W.W. Norton, 1970.

Cohen, Marty, David Karol, Hans Noel, and John Zaller. *The Party Decides: Presidential Nominations Before and After Reform.* Chicago: University of Chicago Press, 2008.

Donovan, Todd, and Shaun Bowler. *Reforming the Republic: Democratic Institutions for the New America.* Englewood Cliffs, NJ: Prentice Hall, 2003.

Green, Donald, Bradley Palmquist, and Eric Schickler. *Partisan Hearts and Minds: Political Parties and the Social Identities of Voters.* New Haven, CT: Yale University Press, 2002.

Maisel, L. Sandy. *Political Parties and Elections: A Very Short Introduction.* New York: Oxford University Press, 2007.

McCarty, Nolan, Keith Poole, and Howard Rosenthal. *Polarized America: The Dance of Ideology and Unequal Riches.* Cambridge, MA: MIT Press, 2006.

Polsby, Nelson W. *The Consequences of Party Reform.* New York: Oxford University Press, 1983.

Redlawsk, David, Caroline Tolbert, and Todd Donovan. *Why Iowa? How Caucuses and Sequential Elections Improve the Presidential Nominating Process.* Chicago: University of Chicago Press, 2011.

Schattschneider, E. E. *The Semi-sovereign People.* New York: Harcourt Brace, 1960.

Shefter, Martin. *Political Parties and the State: The American Historical Experience.* Princeton, NJ: Princeton University Press, 1994.

Recommended Websites

D.C.'s Political Report
www.dcpoliticalreport.com/Disclaimer.htm
  Here you can find almost every organization that identifies itself as a political party, including such obscure groups as the American Beer Drinker's Party or the Scorched Earth Party.

Democratic Party
www.dnc.org

Republican Party
www.GOP.com, www.rnc.org
  These are the official websites for the Democrats and Republicans. Compare the platforms of the two main U.S. parties and see if there's "not a dime's worth of difference" between the two of them.

Green Party
www.gp.org

Libertarian Party
www.lp.org
  The Green Party and Libertarian Party are two of the largest and most successful third parties in recent years. Find out what these parties are trying to accomplish.

National Annenberg Election Survey
http://annenbergpublicpolicycenter.org
  Individual voters tend to develop psychological ties to one party or another. The National Annenberg Election Survey (NAES) uses survey data to track party identification by state every two years. Find out if your state has more Democratic or Republican identifiers.

In the 2012 elections, Barack Obama and Mitt Romney competed for the presidency, offering Americans a choice between two approaches to government and the major issues facing the nation. Elections determine who is in government and thus influence what issues and policies will be taken up by the government.

10

Campaigns and Elections

WHAT GOVERNMENT DOES AND WHY IT MATTERS In many ways, the 2012 presidential election seemed like a repeat of 2008 but sung in a slightly lower key and with a few new notes. Barack Obama was elected to a second term as president in a close race against Republican challenger Mitt Romney. Sixty percent of eligible voters turned out to vote in the general election, down slightly from 62 percent in 2008. Obama's campaign message that he would keep the nation moving "forward" replaced his 2008 theme of "hope," but the technical aspects of Obama's ground game in swing states remained the same. Notably, Obama's efforts to mobilize Democratic voters were more important than efforts to persuade Republicans or independents to vote for him. Obama won nearly every battleground state, including Colorado, Iowa, Ohio, New Hampshire, Virginia, Wisconsin, and Florida. Republicans retained control of the House, and Democrats retained control of the Senate.

The biggest issue for voters in 2012 was the economy, with three-quarters saying that economic conditions were poor. Historically, a weak economy and high unemployment makes re-election difficult for an incumbent president. However, the electorate was evenly divided as to whether responsibility for the country's economic woes rested with Obama or his predecessor, George W. Bush. Obama was re-elected with the highest unemployment rate of any incumbent since Franklin Delano Roosevelt.

Who supported Obama in 2012? While Obama's support among young and black voters did decline slightly from 2008, he still received large majorities of the vote from both groups. Obama's biggest gains came from Asian and Latino voters. Over 70 percent of Latinos voted for Obama, up from 61 percent in 2008. Minority voters accounted for 45 percent of Obama's support, reflecting the expanded power of black, Latino, and Asian voters. While whites made up 77 percent of the electorate in 2004 and 74 percent in 2008, they accounted for just 72 percent in 2012, according to exit polls released immediately after the election. Romney won among whites, men, older people, affluent voters, evangelical Christians, and those from suburban and rural counties.

As expected, the 2012 presidential election shattered previous records for campaign spending. In the aftermath of the Supreme Court's 2010 *Citizens United* decision, which allowed unlimited political spending by unaffiliated groups, both majority party candidates opted out of the campaign financing system that imposes spending limits in return for government financing. Spending in the presidential race, including expenditures by "super PACs," was $2.6 billion, and the combined cost of congressional and presidential races, including money spent by candidates' campaigns, their parties, and super PACs, was a staggering $6 billion, up from $5.3 billion in 2008 and $4.2 billion in 2004.

Finally, the influence of digital media and political pollsters reached new heights in 2012. While many in the mass media painted the election as a too-close-to-predict nail-biter, the growing sophistication of opinion polling suggested otherwise, predicting a solid victory for Obama. By aggregating thousands of polling results, experts like Nate Silver of the FiveThirtyEight blog accurately forecast the electoral outcomes well in advance of November. Not only did the Internet continue to grow as a forum for political news, but the art of predicting election outcomes became a science.

chaptergoals

- Describe the major rules and procedures of elections in the United States (pages 381–94)

- Explain how campaigns are typically conducted (pages 394–403)

- Identify the major factors that influence voters' decisions (pages 403–8)

- Analyze the strategies, issues, and outcomes of the 2012 elections (pages 408–18)

- Describe how candidates raise the money they need to run (pages 419–25)

Elections in America

Describe the major rules and procedures of elections in the United States

Voting in elections is the most important form of participation in American politics, and the most common. Elections allow average citizens to hold their elected representatives in government accountable. Elections are at the heart of democracy. In the United States, elections are held at regular intervals. National presidential elections take place every four years, on the first Tuesday in November; congressional elections are held every two years, also on the first Tuesday in November. Congressional elections that do not coincide with a presidential election are sometimes called **midterm elections**. Elections for state and local office also often coincide with national elections. Some state and local governments, however, prefer to schedule their local elections in years that do not coincide with national elections, to avoid having national considerations distract from or unduly influence local contests.

In the American federal system, the responsibility for running elections is highly decentralized, and rests largely with state and county governments. State laws specify how elections are to be administered, determine the boundaries of

midterm elections congressional elections that do not coincide with a presidential election; also called off-year elections

Elections are the most important way that Americans participate in politics. Some of the rules for American elections have been in place since the Founding, while others have evolved over time. This painting shows election day in Philadelphia in 1815.

electoral districts, and specify candidate and voter qualifications. Elections are administered by state, county, and city election boards that are responsible for establishing and staffing polling places and verifying the eligibility of individuals who come to vote.

Types of Elections

Four types of elections are held in the United States: primary elections, general elections, runoff elections, and initiative and referendum elections, (in which proposed laws are placed on the ballot for a popular vote). We discuss the first three types here; we will take a closer look at ballot initiatives and referenda later in the section "Direct-Democracy Elections."

Primary elections are held to select each party's candidates for the general election. In the case of local and statewide offices, the winners of primary elections face one another as their parties' nominees in the general election. At the presidential level, however, primary elections are indirect; they are used to select state delegates to the national conventions, at which the major party presidential candidates are chosen. America is one of few nations in the world to hold primary elections. In most countries, nominations are controlled by party officials, as they once were in the United States. The primary system was introduced at the turn of the twentieth century by Progressive reformers who hoped to weaken the power of party leaders by taking candidate nominations out of their hands.

Under the laws of some states, only registered members of a political party may vote in a primary election to select that party's candidates. This is called a **closed primary**. Other states allow all registered voters to choose on the day of the primary in which party's primary they will participate. This is called an **open primary**. A primary election is like a prelim in a sporting event. It is used to select the best candidate to represent the political party in the general election. Thus primary elections are races where Democrats compete against Democrats and Republicans against

primary elections elections held to select a party's candidate for the general election

closed primary a primary election in which voters can participate in the nomination of candidates, but only of the party in which they are enrolled for a period of time prior to primary day

open primary a primary election in which the voter can wait until the day of the primary to choose which party to enroll in to select candidates for the general election

Iowa caucus-goers were the first to vote in the 2012 presidential primaries. The United States is one of few nations in the world to hold primary elections and caucuses.

Republicans. Today, party conventions are largely symbolic, and the delegates won by each candidate in the primary elections largely determine who the party nominee is.

The primary is followed by the **general election**, the decisive electoral contest. The winner of the general election is elected to office for a specified term. In some states, however, mainly in the Southeast, if no candidate wins an absolute majority in the primary, a **runoff election** is held before the general election. This situation is most likely to arise if there are more than two candidates, none of whom has received a majority of the votes cast. A runoff election is held between the two candidates who received the largest number of votes.

Plurality and Winner-Take-All Electoral Rules

In some countries, to win a seat in the parliament or other governing body, a candidate must receive an absolute majority (50 percent plus 1) of all the votes cast in the relevant district. This type of electoral system is called a **majority system**. In the United States, it is used in primary elections by some southern states. Majority systems usually include a provision for a runoff election between the two top candidates, because if the initial race draws several candidates, there is little chance that any one will receive a majority.

In other nations, as in the United States, candidates for office need not win an absolute majority of the votes cast to win an election. Instead, victory is awarded to the candidate who receives the most votes, regardless of the actual percentage this represents. A candidate receiving 50 percent, or 30 percent, or even 20 percent, of the popular vote can win if no other candidate receives more votes. This type of electoral system is called a **plurality system** and is used in virtually all general elections in the United States. In part because of plurality election rules, the United States has usually had only two significant political parties, whereas with proportional representation, many European countries have developed multiparty systems. (See Chapter 9 for more on the two-party system in the United States.)

Most European nations employ a third type of electoral system, called **proportional representation**. Under proportional rules, competing political parties are awarded legislative seats in rough proportion to the percentage of popular votes that each party won. A party that wins 30 percent of the vote will receive roughly 30 percent of the seats in the parliament or other representative body. In the United States, proportional representation is used by many states in presidential primary elections, but not in general election for president or Congress. Proportional representation benefits smaller groups because it usually allows a party to win legislative seats with fewer votes than would be required under a majority or plurality system. A party that wins 10 percent of the national vote might win 10 percent of the parliamentary seats. In the United States, by contrast, a party that wins 10 percent of the vote would probably win no seats in Congress. Because they give small parties little chance of success, plurality and majority systems tend to reduce the number of competitive political parties.

The Ballot

Before the 1890s, voters cast ballots according to political parties. Each party printed its own ballots, listed only its own candidates for each office, and employed party workers to distribute the ballots at the polls. Because voters had to choose which party's ballot to use, it was very difficult for a voter to cast anything other than a **straight-ticket vote**. The advent of a new, neutral ballot during the Progressive era

general election a regularly scheduled election involving most districts in the nation or state, in which voters select officeholders; in the United States, general elections for national office and most state and local offices are held on the first Tuesday following the first Monday in November in even-numbered years (every four years for presidential elections)

runoff election a "second round" election in which voters choose between the top two candidates from the first round

majority system a type of electoral system in which, to win a seat in the parliament or other representative body, a candidate must receive a majority of all the votes cast in the relevant district

plurality system a type of electoral system in which, to win a seat in the parliament or other representative body, a candidate need only receive the most votes in the election, not necessarily a majority of votes cast

proportional representation a multiple-member district system that allows each political party representation in proportion to its percentage of the total vote

straight-ticket voting selecting candidates from the same political party for all offices on the ballot

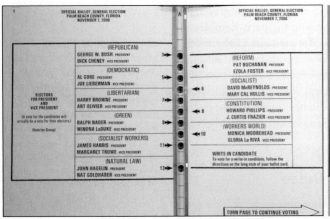

Some of the devices that have been used to record votes in the United States are notably prone to errors that can affect election results. For example, in 2000 in Florida's Palm Beach County, some voters were confused by the "butterfly ballot" (left), which made it difficult to match candidates and votes. In the 2012 elections, many of the nation's voters cast their ballots on electronic touch-screen machines. Critics of touch-screen voting systems, however, question the machines for their accuracy and security against fraud.

(at the turn of the twentieth century) brought a significant change to electoral procedure. The new ballot (call the Australian ballot) was prepared and administered by the government rather than the political parties. Each ballot was identical and included the names of all candidates for office. This ballot reform made it possible for voters to make their choices on the basis of the individual rather than the collective merits of a party's candidates.

Because all candidates for the same office now appeared on the same ballot, voters were no longer forced to choose straight-ticket voting. This gave rise to the phenomenon of split-ticket voting in American elections, where voters may vote for a Democrat for Congress and a Republican for governor. If a voter supports candidates from more than one party in the same election, he or she is said to be casting a split-ticket vote. Voters who support only one party's candidates are casting a straight-ticket vote. Straight-ticket voting occurs most often when a voter casts a ballot for a party's presidential candidate and then "automatically" votes for the rest of that party's candidates. The result of this voting pattern is known as the **coattail effect**.

Prior to the reform of the ballot, it was not uncommon for an entire incumbent administration to be swept from office and replaced by an entirely new set of officials. In the absence of a real possibility of split-ticket voting, the electorate could express any desire for change only as a vote against all candidates of the party in power. Because of this, the possibility always existed, particularly at the state and local levels, that an insurgent slate committed to policy change could be swept into power. The party ballot thus increased the potential impact of elections on the government's composition. Although this potential may not always have been realized, the party ballot at least increased the chance that electoral decisions could lead to policy changes. By contrast, because it permitted choice on the basis of candidates' individual appeal, ticket splitting led to increasingly divided partisan control of government.

The actual ballots used by voters vary from county to county across the United States. Some counties employ paper ballots, while most use mechanical voting machines or computerized systems. Not surprisingly, the controversy surrounding Florida's presidential vote in 2000 led to a closer look at the different balloting systems, and it became apparent that some of them produced unreliable results. When many counties moved to introduce computerized voting systems, critics

coattail effect the result of voters casting their ballot for president or governor and "automatically" voting for the remainder of the party's ticket warned that they might be vulnerable to unauthorized use or "hacking." During the 2008 Ohio primaries a software error was discovered that potentially affected electronic voting machines used in 34 states. The machine's manufacturer moved to correct the error before the November national elections, and the 2008, 2010, and 2012 elections produced few complaints about electronic voting.

Legislative Elections and Electoral Districts

The boundaries for congressional and state legislative districts in the United States are usually redrawn by the states every 10 years in response to population changes determined by the U.S. Census. This redrawing of district boundaries is called **redistricting**. The geographic shape of district boundaries is influenced by several factors. Some of the most important influences have been federal court decisions. In the 1963 case of *Gray v. Sanders*, and in the 1964 cases of *Wesberry v. Sanders* and *Reynolds v. Sims*, the Supreme Court held that legislative districts within a state must include roughly equal populations, so as to accord with the principle of "one person, one vote."[1] During the 1980s the Supreme Court also declared that legislative districts should, insofar as possible, be contiguous, compact, and consistent with existing political subdivisions.[2]

Despite these legal cases, state lawmakers routinely seek to influence electoral outcomes to favor one political party over another (or incumbents over challengers) in drawing electoral districts for Congress and state legislatures. This strategy is called **gerrymandering**, named for a nineteenth-century Massachusetts governor, Elbridge Gerry, who was alleged to have designed a district in the shape of a salamander to promote his party's interests. The principle behind gerrymandering is simple: different populations of voters in districts can produce different electoral results. For example, by dispersing the members of a particular group across two or more districts, state legislators can dilute that group's voting power and prevent it from electing a representative in any district. (In the lingo of gerrymandering, this is called "cracking.") Alternatively, by concentrating the members of a party in as few districts as possible, state lawmakers can try to ensure that their opponents will elect as few representatives as possible. (This is referred to as "packing.") The widespread practice of gerrymandering has created many safe districts in Congress, where incumbents rarely face a serious challenger, even if there are elections every two years in the House. This is one reason most members of Congress are elected in landslide elections, and why 98 percent of incumbents are re-elected.

The federal government has supported congressional districts made up primarily of minority group members, a practice intended to increase the number of African Americans and Latinos elected to public office. The Supreme Court has viewed this effort as constitutionally dubious, however. Beginning with the 1993 case of *Shaw v. Reno*, the Court has generally rejected efforts to create such **majority-minority districts**.[3] The Court has asserted that districting based exclusively on racial criteria is unlawful.

Presidential Elections

While many of the rules related to presidential elections and congressional elections are the same, presidential elections have certain special features. First, the president is technically elected by the electoral college, not by popular vote. Second, presidential candidates from the

redistricting the process of redrawing election districts and redistributing legislative representatives. This happens every ten years to reflect shifts in population or in response to legal challenges in existing districts

gerrymandering apportionment of voters in districts in such a way as to give unfair advantage to one racial or ethnic group or political party

majority-minority district a gerrymandered voting district that improves the chances of minority candidates by making selected minority groups the majority within the district

The drawing of electoral districts is always a matter of controversy, with opponents accusing one another of "gerrymandering"— drawing district boundaries in such a way as to serve a particular group's interests. The original gerrymander was a districting plan attributed to the Massachusetts governor Elbridge Gerry (1744–1814) that had the shape of a salamander.

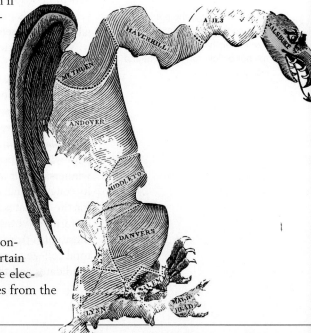

In a number of recent cases, black, white, and Hispanic voters have claimed to be the victims of racial gerrymanders. For instance, in 1995 the Supreme Court held that one Georgia district, which was 64 percent African American, was unfairly based on race. Meanwhile, no challenge was made to Texas's 6th District, which was predominantly white. In 2006, the Supreme Court rejected part of a Texas redistricting plan on the grounds that it suppressed minority votes, though the Court upheld most of the plan.

two major parties are officially nominated at the parties' national conventions, following primary elections and caucuses to select delegates to the conventions. While primary elections are also used to select candidates in congressional and other types of elections, the national convention delegate system for nominating candidates is unique to presidential elections.

The Electoral College In the early history of popular voting, nations often made use of indirect elections. In these elections, voters would choose the members of an intermediate body. These members would, in turn, select public officials. The assumption underlying such a process was that ordinary citizens were not qualified to choose their leaders and could not be trusted to do so directly. The last vestige of this procedure in America is the **electoral college**, the group of electors who formally select the president and vice president of the United States.

When Americans go to the polls on Election Day, they are technically not voting directly for presidential candidates. Instead, voters within each state are choosing among slates of electors selected by each state's party and pledged, if elected, to support that party's presidential candidate. These are indirect elections. To win, a U.S. presidential candidate must receive a majority of the votes in the electoral college, which are awarded to states based on the size of their congressional delegation.[4] In each state (except Maine and Nebraska), the party candidate who wins the popular vote wins all the electoral college votes for that state, in a winner-take-all fashion.[5] Each state has electoral college votes equal to the size of its congressional delegation (House plus Senate), for a total of 538 electoral votes for the 50 states and the District of Columbia. The presidential candidate with a majority of votes in the electoral college—not necessarily the candidate with the most votes from the people—becomes president. No other country uses an electoral college to mediate between a national or direct/popular vote for presidential candidates and the winner.

electoral college the presidential electors from each state who meet after the popular election to cast ballots for president and vice president

Support for changing the election rules in the United States has been gaining momentum since the contested 2000 presidential election, which was followed by a lengthy legal battle in Florida that ultimately ended with the U.S. Supreme Court's decision in *Bush v. Gore*.[6] The decision resolved the dispute in Florida, which handed George W. Bush the presidency. Even though the Democratic candidate, Vice President Al Gore, had won 500,000 more votes nationwide, Republican George W. Bush won a majority of the electoral college and was elected president. Only on rare occasions in American history has the winner of the popular vote been defeated, but this controversial election created ripple effects in motivating efforts to reform American elections.

Another rare occurrence is if an elector breaks his or her pledge and votes for the other party's candidate. For example, in 1976, when the Republicans carried the state of Washington, one Republican elector from that state refused to vote for Gerald Ford, the Republican presidential nominee. Many states have now enacted statutes formally binding electors to their pledges, but some constitutional authorities doubt whether such statutes are enforceable.

Throughout history there have been a few cases where the electoral college failed to produce a majority for any candidate. In the election of 1800, Thomas Jefferson, the Jeffersonian Republican Party's presidential candidate, and Aaron Burr, that party's vice-presidential candidate, received an equal number of votes in the electoral college, throwing the election to the House of Representatives. (The electoral rules at that time made no distinction between presidential and vice-presidential candidates, specifying only that the individual receiving a majority of electoral votes would be named president, and that the individual receiving the second most votes would be the vice president.) Some members of the Federalist Party in Congress suggested that they should seize the opportunity to damage the Republican cause by supporting Burr and denying Jefferson the presidency. The Federalist leader Alexander Hamilton put a stop to this mischievous notion, however, and made certain that his party supported Jefferson. Hamilton's actions enraged Burr and helped lead to the infamous duel between the two men, in which Burr killed Hamilton. The Twelfth Amendment, ratified in 1804, was designed to prevent a repetition of such an inconclusive election by providing for separate electoral college votes for president and vice president.

In the 1824 election, four candidates—John Quincy Adams, Andrew Jackson, Henry Clay, and William H. Crawford—divided the electoral vote; no one of them received a majority. The House of Representatives eventually chose Adams over the others, even though Jackson had won more electoral and popular votes. After 1824 the two major political parties began to dominate presidential politics to such an extent that by December of each election year, only two candidates remained for the electors to choose between, thus ensuring that one would receive a majority.

On all but three occasions since 1824, the electoral vote has simply ratified the nationwide popular vote. Since electoral votes are won on a state-by-state basis, it is mathematically possible for a candidate who receives a nationwide popular plurality to fail to carry states whose electoral votes would add up to a majority. Thus, in 1876, Rutherford B. Hayes was the winner in the electoral college despite receiving fewer popular votes than his rival, Samuel Tilden. In 1888, Grover Cleveland received more popular votes than Benjamin Harrison, but received fewer electoral votes. And in 2000, Al Gore outpolled his opponent, George W. Bush, by more than 500,000 votes, but narrowly lost the electoral college by a mere four electoral votes.

Calls for eliminating the electoral college and using a national popular vote for president are widespread, as surveys show that more than three in four Americans would prefer such a direct election for the president.[7] Replacing the electoral college with another system would require a constitutional amendment that most agree would be extremely difficult to pass. However, reform is still possible, since the constitution allows states to choose the method of selecting presidential electors. One example of a recent attempt to reform the electoral college is the National Popular Vote plan, which has been introduced as a bill in a number of state legislatures.[8] Under the proposed rule change, a state's Electoral College votes would go to the candidate who won the national popular vote, not the candidate with a plurality of votes in that specific state. States would enter a compact with other states making the same change, which would go into effect when a number of states representing a majority in the electoral college (270 electoral votes) approved it. The reform would effectively bypass the electoral college without the need for an amendment to the U.S. Constitution. To date, 10 states have enacted the bill into law. Replacing the electoral college with a national popular vote would dramatically alter the influence of states and change the nature of presidential campaigns. Competition would no longer be confined to a few large battleground states, such as Florida, Ohio, and Pennsylvania, but would likely focus more on urban areas where the most votes are found.[9]

Nominating Presidential Candidates: Primaries and Caucuses Before the general election, the two major parties must select candidates to represent the parties in the general election. The major-party presidential nominations are quite different from the nominating process employed for other political offices. In years when an incumbent president is running for re-election, as in 2012, one party's nomination may not be contested. When the Democratic or Republican presidential nomination is contested, however, candidates typically compete to win national convention delegates in all 50 states. Most states hold primary elections to choose their delegates, but about a third of the states hold **caucuses**, essentially a party business meeting rather than an election, to choose candidates for president. Caucuses begin with precinct-level meetings throughout the state.

The most famous caucuses are those in Iowa, the first state to select presidential candidates in the calendar year. Citizens attending the caucuses typically elect delegates to statewide conventions, at which delegates to the national party conventions are then chosen.

The primaries and caucuses traditionally begin in January of a presidential election year and end in June (see Table 10.1). Early voting states, such as Iowa and New Hampshire, are important because they can help candidates secure media attention, campaign contributions, and increased standing in the polls, or what is called "momentum." Candidates spend months courting voter support in these two states. A candidate who performs better than expected in Iowa and New Hampshire will usually be able to secure public support and media coverage for subsequent races. A candidate who fares poorly in these two states may be written off as a loser, and drop out of the race. Gradually, the presidential nomination has become "front-loaded," with states vying with one another to increase their political influence by holding their nominating processes earlier. But is it fair that two relatively small states (in terms of population) such as Iowa and New Hampshire should have such outsize influence in picking presidents?

caucus (political) a normally closed political party business meeting of citizens or law makers to select candidates elect officers, plan strategy, or make decisions regarding legislative matters

In the election of 1800, the electoral college didn't produce a majority for any candidate; it was split between Thomas Jefferson, Aaron Burr, and John Adams, with Jefferson and Burr tied at 73 electoral votes each. The decision was put to the House of Representatives, which chose Jefferson.

TABLE 10.1

The 2012 Primaries and Caucuses Calendar

DATE	STATE	ELECTION TYPE
January 3	Iowa	Caucus
January 10	New Hampshire	Primary
January 21	South Carolina	Primary (R)
	Nevada	Caucus (D)
January 31	Florida	Primary
February 4	Nevada	Caucus (R)
February 4–11	Maine	Caucus (R)
February 7	Colorado, Minnesota	Caucus (R)
	Missouri	Primary
February 28	Arizona, Michigan	Primary
March 3	Washington	Caucus (R)
March 6	Alaska, Idaho	Caucus (R)
	Minnesota	Caucus (D)
	North Dakota	Caucus
	Georgia, Massachusetts, Ohio, Oklahoma, Tennessee, Vermont	Primary
	Virginia	Primary (R)
March 6–10	Wyoming	Caucus (R)
March 7	Hawaii	Caucus (D)
March 10	Kansas	Caucus (R)
March 11	Maine	Caucus (D)
March 13	Alabama, Mississippi	Primary
	Hawaii	Caucus (R)
	Utah	Caucus (D)
March 17	Missouri	Caucus (R)
March 20	Illinois	Primary
March 24	Louisiana	Primary
April 3	District of Columbia, Maryland, Wisconsin	Primary
April 9	Alaska	Caucus (D)
April 14	Idaho, Kansas, Nebraska, Wyoming	Caucus (D)
April 15	Washington	Caucus (D)
April 24	Connecticut, Delaware, New York, Pennsylvania, Rhode Island	Primary
May 8	Indiana, North Carolina, West Virginia	Primary
May 19–June 1	Colorado	Caucus (D)
May 15	Nebraska, Oregon	Primary
May 22	Arkansas, Kentucky	Primary
May 29	Texas	Primary
June 5	California, Montana, New Jersey, New Mexico, South Dakota	Primary
	North Dakota	Caucus (D)
June 26	Utah	Primary (R)

NOTES: Many states will not hold a Democratic nominating contest if only one candidate qualified for the ballot. The Missouri primary is non-binding. The Missouri Republican Party chose convention delegates in a March 17 caucus.

SOURCE: The United States Elections Project, http://elections.gmu.edu (accessed 8/16/12).

As we saw in Chapter 7, if Barack Obama had not won in Iowa, most commentators believe he would not have been able to go on to capture the Democratic nomination for president in 2008. One study found that the change in mass media coverage that candidates receive before and after the Iowa caucuses predicts how well they will do in the New Hampshire primary, and in presidential primaries nationwide measured by vote share.[10] It is not winning the Iowa caucuses that matters, but doing better than expected by the media. President Carter came in second (after "undecided") in the 1976 Iowa caucuses, for example, but beat media expectations and used this success to propel his nomination to the White House. With the rise of the Internet, media coverage of early nominating events is even greater, and may further increase the importance of states holding early primaries and caucuses.[11]

As noted in Chapter 9, the Democratic Party requires that state presidential primaries allocate delegates on the basis of proportional representation; Democratic candidates win delegates in rough proportion to their percentage of the primary vote. The Republican Party does not require proportional representation, but most states have now written proportional representation requirements into their election laws. A few states use the winner-take-all system, by which the candidate with the most votes wins all the party's delegates in that state. When the primaries and caucuses are concluded, it is usually clear which candidates have won their parties' nominations.

Nominating Presidential Candidates: Party Conventions For more than 50 years after America's founding, presidential nominations were controlled by each party's congressional caucus—all the party's members in the House and the Senate. Critics referred to this process as the "King Caucus" and charged that it did not fairly represent the views of party members throughout the nation. In 1824 the King Caucus method came under severe attack when the Democratic Party caucus failed to nominate Andrew Jackson, the candidate with the greatest support among both party members and supporters outside the capital. In the 1830s the party convention was devised as a way of allowing party leaders throughout the nation to participate in selecting presidential candidates, although the U.S. Constitution is silent on procedures for picking presidents. The first such convention was held by the Anti-Masonic Party in 1831. The Democratic Party held its first convention in 1832, when Andrew Jackson was nominated for a second term.

As it developed during the course of the next century, the convention became the decisive institution in the presidential nominating processes of the two major parties. The convention was a deliberative body in which party groups argued, negotiated, and eventually reached a decision. The convention was composed of delegations from each state. The size of a state's delegation depended on the state's population, and each delegate was allowed one vote for the purpose of nominating the party's presidential and vice-presidential candidates. Before 1936, victory required the support of two-thirds of the delegates. Until 1968, state delegations voted according to the "unit rule," by which all the members of the state delegation would vote for the candidate favored by the majority of the state's delegates. This practice was designed to maximize a state's influence in the nominating process. In 1968 both major parties abolished the unit rule.

Between the 1830s and World War II, national convention delegates were generally selected by a state's party leaders. Usually the delegates were public officials, political activists, and party notables from all regions of the state, representing most major party factions. Some delegates would arrive at the convention having pledged in advance to give their support to a particular presidential candidate. Most delegates were uncommitted, however. This fact, coupled with the unit rule, allowed state party leaders (i.e., the delegates) to negotiate with one another and with presidential candidates for their support. Typically, many votes were needed before the nomination could be decided. Often deadlocks developed among the most powerful party factions, and state leaders would be forced to compromise, sometimes choosing a little-known candidate. Among the more famous "dark horse" nominees were James Polk in 1844 and Warren Harding in 1920. Although he was virtually unknown, Polk won the Democratic nomination when it became clear that none of the more established candidates could win. Similarly, Harding, another political unknown, won the Republican nomination after the major candidates had fought one another to a standstill.

Over time, reformers came to view the convention as a symbol of rule by party leaders. During the Progressive era, at the turn of the twentieth century, many states adopted primary elections to choose presidential candidates, at which average citizens would have a voice in picking presidents. Today, as we saw earlier in this chapter, the nomination is determined in a series of primary elections and local party caucuses held in virtually all 50 states during the months prior to the party's national convention. These primaries and caucuses determine how each state's convention delegates will vote. Candidates now arrive at the convention knowing who has enough delegate support in hand to assure a victory in the first round of balloting. State party leaders no longer serve as power brokers, and the party's presidential and vice-presidential choices are made relatively quickly.

Even though the party convention no longer controls presidential nominations, it still has a number of important tasks. The first of these is the adoption of party rules concerning such matters as convention delegate selection and future presidential primary elections. In 1972, for example, the Democratic convention accepted rules requiring convention delegates to be broadly representative of the party's membership in terms of race and gender. After those rules were passed, the convention refused to seat several state delegations that were deemed not to meet this standard. Another important task for the convention is the drafting of a party **platform**, a statement of principles and pledges around which the delegates can unite. Although the two major parties' platforms tend to contain many similar principles and platitudes, differences between their platforms can be significant. In recent years, for example, the Republican platform has advocated tax cuts and taken strong positions opposing affirmative action and abortion. The Democratic platform, on the other hand, has focused on the importance of maintaining welfare and regulatory programs. A close reading of the party platforms can reveal many of the ideological differences between the parties.

Today, convention **delegates** are generally political activists with strong positions on social and political issues. In states such as Michigan and Iowa, local party caucuses choose many of the delegates who will actually attend the national convention. In most of the remaining states, primary elections determine how a state's delegation will vote, but the actual delegates are selected by state party officials. Delegate votes won in primary elections are apportioned to candidates on the basis of proportional representation. Thus, a candidate who received 30 percent of the vote in the California Democratic primary would receive roughly 30 percent of the state's delegate votes at the party's national convention.

Although the party's nominees for the president and the vice president are "officially" announced at the party conventions, they are actually selected much earlier through caucuses and primary elections. In 2012, Mitt Romney and Paul Ryan formally accepted the Republican nomination at the national convention.

platform a party document, written at a national convention, that contains party philosophy, principles, and positions on issues

delegate political activist selected to vote at a party's national convention

As was mentioned earlier, the Democratic Party requires that a state's convention delegation be representative of that state's Democratic electorate in terms of race, gender, and age. Republican delegates, by contrast, are more likely to be male and white. The Democrats also reserve slots for elected Democratic Party officials, called **superdelegates**. All the Democratic governors and about 80 percent of the party's members of Congress now attend the national convention as delegates.

superdelegate a convention delegate position, in Democratic conventions, reserved for party officials

Once the nominations have been settled and most other party business has been resolved, the presidential and vice-presidential nominees deliver acceptance speeches. These speeches are opportunities for the nominees to begin their formal campaigns on a positive note, and they are usually meticulously crafted to make as positive an impression on the electorate as possible.

Direct-Democracy Elections

ballot initiative a proposed law or policy change that is placed on the ballot by citizens or interest groups for a popular vote

Beyond presidential and congressional elections, 24 states also provide for the initiative process, as we saw in Chapter 1. **Ballot initiatives** allow citizens to circulate petitions to place policy change or proposed laws directly on the ballot for a popular vote. If a ballot measure receives majority support, it becomes law. Controversial issues frequently appear on the ballot of states with the initiative process—for example, proposals to ban same-sex marriage, raise the minimum wage, adopt legislative term limits, and reform the election process. In recent years, voters in several states have voted to cut taxes, to prohibit social services for illegal immigrants, to end affirmative action, to protect open space and the environment, and to prevent offshore drilling. At the turn of the twentieth century, ballot initiatives were used to grant women suffrage (the right to vote), to prevent child labor, to limit the work day to eight hours, and to allow voters to elect U.S. senators directly (rather than having them chosen by state legislatures). Ballot initiative campaigns often involve high spending by proponents and opponents, and mass media campaigns than can rival that of congressional and presidential candidates within a state. All 50 states have the legislative **referendum**, in which the state legislature refers laws to the voters for a popular vote. Referendum votes are required for changes to state constitutions.

referendum the practice of referring a proposed law passed by a legislature to the vote of the electorate for approval or rejection

The initiative and the referendum, both adopted by Progressive reformers at the turn of the twentieth century, are examples of what is called direct democracy. They allow voters to govern directly without intervention by government officials or the political parties. The validity of ballot measure results, however, is subject to judicial action. If a court finds that an initiative violates the state or national constitution, it can overturn the result. This happened in the case of a 1994 California initiative curtailing social services to illegal aliens and again in 2012 when the federal courts overturned California's Proposition 8 banning same-sex marriage.[12]

Ballot initiatives not only change policy but also appear to affect political engagement. One study found that states with initiatives on the ballot have higher voter turnout over time. Citizens living in direct-democracy states report more interest in politics, and are more likely to discuss politics. Why is this so? If electoral rules offer people more opportunities to participate in decisions, those institutions may have an "educative" effect on those people.[13] Representative democracy allows citizens to vote on who gets to make political decisions; ballot propositions go further, offering voters the possibility of directly making public policy. By having more opportunities to act politically, citizens may learn to participate more, and come to believe their participation has meaning.

Issue elections provide information to voters in the form of political campaigns and attention in the mass media. Ballot measures concerning controversial policy issues such as same-sex marriage, taxes for the wealthy, nonpartisan redistricting, and immigration rights generate their own campaigns, with television, newspaper, and Internet ads; professional campaign consultants; and organized interests that contact potential voters.[14] Like candidate races, issue elections generate free media coverage, paid media campaigns, and grassroots mobilization efforts. Legislative hearings, court disputes, and signature-gathering petition drives to qualify ballot measures may generate additional media attention. Initiative campaigns and the mass media provide information and appeals to the electorate that can stimulate political participation.[15]

Hundreds of initiatives and referenda appear on state election ballots every two years, often with millions of dollars in campaign expenditures. Initiative campaigns can pump millions of dollars into the American states each election. In the 2002 elections, almost $9.00 per capita was spent on initiative campaigns in Arizona, more than the amount spent on any single candidate race, congressional or statewide. In the 2004 presidential elections, Oregon topped the list, with $8.98 on ballot initiative expenditure per capita, followed by Nevada ($6.65) and California ($5.95).[16] More money was spent per capita on initiatives in California in 2004 than on any of the other major candidate races in the state. Spending on ballot initiatives continues to rise with each election. Although not well recognized, ballot measures and their associated campaigns often draw more media attention and spending than prominent candidate races. For example, in 2012, Colorado and Washington voters approved measures to legalize marijuana sale and consumption. More initiatives and referenda have appeared on state ballots in the last 30 years than at any other time in American history, outside of the Progressive era.

Controversial ballot propositions can have spillover effects, shaping both the national agenda and evaluations of and voting for gubernatorial and congressional candidates.[17] The tax revolt in the late 1970s, with initiatives and referenda on many state ballots lowering taxes, may have contributed to Republican Ronald Reagan's successful bid for the White House in 1980. Ballot measures banning same-sex marriage placed on the ballot of 13 states may have primed voting for the Republican presidential candidate in the 2004 election, George W. Bush. In 2006, coordinated ballot measures in multiple state raising the minimum wage may have influenced voters to focus on the economy, and increased voting for Democrats in Congress and for Democratic governors. Placing issues on the ballot as part of an effort to influence candidate elections is a relatively new, but important strategy, for political campaigns. Such effects on candidate races highlight just how important issue elections are in American politics.

Eighteen states also have legal provisions for **recall** elections, which allow voters to remove governors and other state officials from office prior to the expiration of their terms. Generally, a recall effort begins with a petition campaign. In California, for example, if 12 percent of those who voted in the last general election

In 2010, voters in Missouri decided several referenda, including a proposition to block government-mandated health insurance.

recall a procedure to allow voters to remove state officials from office before their terms expire by circulating petitions to call a vote

sign petitions demanding a special recall election, one must be scheduled by the state board of elections. In 2003 many California voters blamed Governor Gray Davis for the state's $38 billion budget deficit, allowing his opponents to secure enough signatures to force a vote. In October 2003, Davis became only the second governor in American history to be recalled by his state's electorate. Under California law, voters are also asked to choose a replacement for the official whom they've dismissed, and in 2003 they elected Arnold Schwarzenegger to be their governor. Federal officials, such as the president and members of Congress, are not subject to recall.

● Election Campaigns

Explain how campaigns are typically conducted

campaign an effort by political candidates and their supporters to win the backing of donors, political activists, and voters in their quest for political office

A **campaign** is an effort by political candidates (and their supporters) to win the backing of donors, political activists, and voters in their quest for political office. Campaigns precede every primary and general election. Because of the complexity of the campaign process, and because of the amount of money that candidates must raise, presidential campaigns usually begin almost two years before the November presidential elections. The campaign for any office consists of a number of steps. Candidates must first organize an exploratory committee consisting of supporters who will help them raise funds and bring their names to the attention of the media and potential donors. This step is relatively easy for a candidate currently in office, known as an **incumbent**. Incumbents usually are already well known and have little difficulty attracting supporters and contributors—unless of course they have been subject to damaging publicity while in office.

incumbent a candidate running for reelection to a position that he or she already holds

Advisers

The next step in a typical campaign involves recruiting advisers and creating a formal campaign organization (see Figure 10.1). Most candidates, especially for national or statewide office, will need a campaign manager, a media consultant, a pollster, a financial adviser, and a press spokesperson, as well as a staff director to coordinate the activities of volunteer and paid workers. For a local campaign, candidates generally need hundreds of workers, both professionals and volunteers. State-level campaigns call for thousands of workers, and presidential campaigns require tens of thousands of workers nationwide.

Virtually all serious contenders for national and statewide office retain the services of professional campaign consultants. Increasingly, candidates for local office, too, have come to rely on professional campaign managers. Consultants offer candidates the expertise necessary to conduct accurate opinion polls, produce television commercials, organize direct-mail campaigns, and make use of sophisticated computer analyses. Professional political consultants have taken the place of the old-time party bosses who once controlled political campaigns, and naturally they prefer to work for candidates who seem to have a reasonable chance of winning. Most consultants who direct campaigns specialize in politics, although some are drawn from the ranks of corporate advertising or public relations, and they may

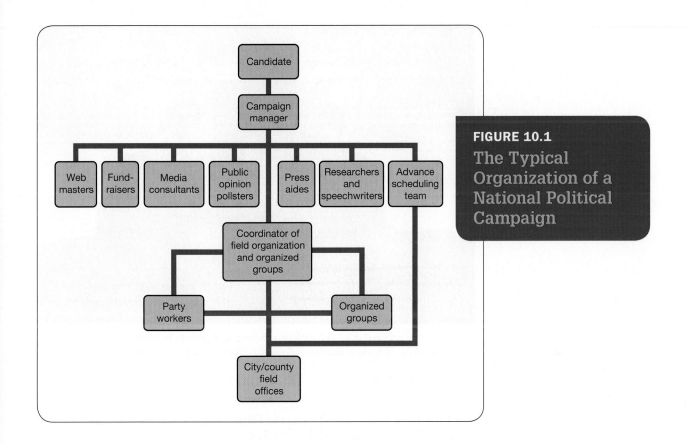

FIGURE 10.1

The Typical Organization of a National Political Campaign

work with commercial clients in addition to politicians. Campaign consultants conduct public opinion polls, produce television commercials, organize direct-mail campaigns, and develop the issues and advertising messages the candidate will use to mobilize support. George W. Bush's former chief political strategist, Karl Rove, not only played a key role in two presidential campaigns but is also widely credited with crafting the strategy that brought about a Republican victory in the 2002 national congressional races.

Fund-Raising

Modern national political campaigns are fueled by enormous amounts of money. Together with their advisers, candidates must begin serious fund-raising efforts at an early stage in the campaign, usually by appealing both to the altruism of small donors and to the self-interest of large donors. To have a reasonable chance of winning a seat in the House of Representatives, a candidate may need to raise more than $500,000; in 2008, incumbent candidates in competitive House races typically spent close to $2 million to hold on to their seats. In 2008 Senate races, the average winner spent more than $4 million. In recent years, some Senate contests have cost $25 million or more, as have some races for governorships. In fact, 2010 California Republican gubernatorial candidate Meg Whitman spent more than $160 million, including $140 million of her own money, in an ultimately unsuccessful bid for office. Presidential candidates in particular must raise huge amounts of money. In 2012 fund-raising by presidential campaign shattered previous records.

Candidates for national office hire professional campaign advisers to guide their campaigns and direct volunteers. Here, Mitt Romney talks with advisers Stuart Stevens and Eric Fehrnstrom in 2012.

The Obama campaign, the Democratic Party, and the Priorities USA Action super PAC raised $934 million, while Mitt Romney's campaign, the Republican Party, and the Restore Our Future super PAC raised $881 million. These figures are unprecedented.

Candidates generally begin raising funds long before they face an election, and many politicians spend more time soliciting donations than engaging in any other campaign activity. Once in office, members of Congress find it much easier to raise campaign funds and are thus able to outspend their challengers (see Figure 10.2).[18] Members of the majority party in the House and Senate are particularly attractive to donors who want access to those in power.[19] In the "Money and Politics" section later in this chapter, we will discuss further the critical role that money plays in the electoral process.

Polling

Virtually all contemporary campaigns for national and statewide office, and many local campaigns, make extensive use of opinion polling. To be competitive, a candidate must collect voting and poll data to assess the electorate's needs, hopes, fears, and past behavior. Polls, conducted throughout most political campaigns, provide the basic information that candidates and their staff use to craft campaign strategies—that is, to select issues, to assess the candidates' strengths and weaknesses and those of the opposition, to check voter response to the campaign, and to measure the degree to which various constituent groups may respond to campaign appeals. The themes, issues, and messages that candidates present during a campaign are generally based on polls and small face-to-face sessions with voters, called "focus groups." In recent years, pollsters have become central figures in most national campaigns, and some have continued as advisers to their clients after they've won the election.

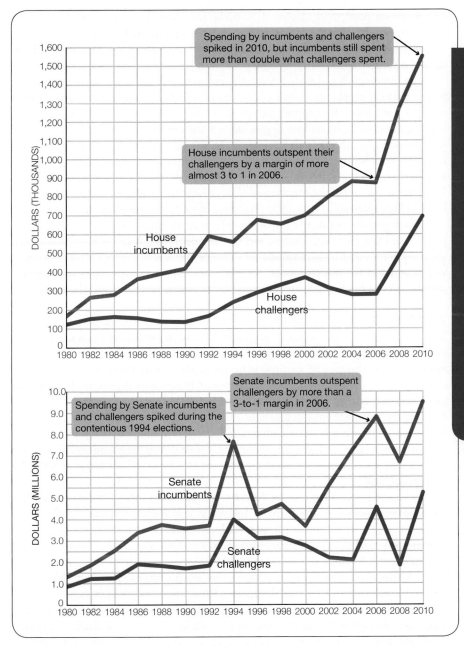

FIGURE 10.2

Average House and Senate Campaign Expenditures, 1980–2010 (Net Dollars)

The average amount spent by House and Senate incumbents to secure reelection has risen sharply in recent years, whereas spending by challengers has remained more stable. What would you expect to see as a consequence of this trend? Is legislation needed to level the playing field?

SOURCES: Norman J. Ornstein, Thomas E. Mann, and Michael J. Malbin. eds., *Vital Statistics on Congress, 2001–2002* (Washington, DC: American Enterprise Institute, 2002), 87, 93; and Campaign Finance Institute, www.cfinst.org (accessed 8/16/12).

Within the figure (top chart):

> Spending by incumbents and challengers spiked in 2010, but incumbents still spent more than double what challengers spent.

> House incumbents outspent their challengers by a margin of more almost 3 to 1 in 2006.

House incumbents

House challengers

Within the figure (bottom chart):

> Senate incumbents outspent challengers by more than a 3-to-1 margin in 2006.

> Spending by Senate incumbents and challengers spiked during the contentious 1994 elections.

Senate incumbents

Senate challengers

Media Coverage and the Internet

For those candidates lucky enough to survive the nominating process, the last hurdle is the general election. There are essentially two types of general election in the United States today. The first type is the organizationally driven, labor-intensive election. Candidates campaign in local elections and many congressional elections by recruiting large numbers of volunteer workers to hand out leaflets and organize rallies. The candidates make appearances at receptions, community group meetings, local rallies, and even in shopping malls and on busy street corners. Generally, local and congressional campaigns depend less on issues and policy proposals

The Internet is an increasingly important tool in fundraising. Building on Obama's success in raising money online in 2008, his 2012 campaign introduced a new iPhone app and other new tools for soliciting donations.

spot (advertisement) a 15-, 30-, or 60-second television campaign commercial that permits a candidate's message to be delivered to a target audience

and more on hard work designed to make the candidate more visible than his or her opponent. Statewide campaigns, some congressional races, and of course the national presidential election fall into the second category: the media-driven, capital-intensive electoral campaign.

In the nineteenth and early twentieth centuries, political campaigns were waged by the parties' enormous armies of patronage workers. Throughout the year, party workers cultivated the support of voters by assisting them with legal problems, helping them find jobs, and serving as liaisons with local, state, and federal agencies. On Election Day, throughout the nation, hundreds of thousands of party workers marched from house to house reminding their supporters to vote, helping the aged and infirm reach the polls, and calling in the favors they had accrued during the year. Campaigns resembled the maneuvers of huge infantries vying for victory. Historians have, in fact, referred to this traditional style of party campaigning as "militarist."

Contemporary political campaigns rely less on infantries and more on "air power" and the Internet. That is, rather than deploying huge armies of workers, contemporary campaigns make use of a number of communications tools to reach voters and bid for their support. Six tools are especially important: the media, debates, phone banks, direct mail, professional public relations, and the Internet.

The Media Extensive use of the broadcast media, television in particular, is the hallmark of the modern political campaign. Candidates endeavor to secure as much positive news and feature coverage as possible. This type of coverage is called *free media* because the cost of air time is borne by the media themselves. Candidates can secure free media coverage by participating in newsworthy events. Incumbents introduce legislation, sponsor hearings, undertake inspection tours of the sites of fires and floods, meet with delegations of foreign dignitaries, and so on, to capture the attention of the television cameras. Challengers announce new policy proposals, visit orphanages and senior centers, and demand that their opponents agree to a series of debates. Generally speaking, incumbents have the advantage in securing free media time.

In addition to pursuing free media coverage, candidates spend millions of dollars for *paid media* time, in the form of television and radio ads. Many of these ads consist of 15-, 30-, or 60-second **spots (advertisements)** that permit a candidate's message to be delivered to a target audience before uninterested or hostile viewers can tune it out. Examples of extremely effective spots include George H. W. Bush's 1988 "Willie Horton" ad, which implied that Bush's opponent, Michael Dukakis, coddled criminals, and Lyndon Johnson's 1964 "daisy" ad, which suggested that Johnson's opponent, Barry Goldwater, would lead the United States into nuclear war. Television spots are used to establish candidate name recognition, to create a favorable image of the candidate and a negative image of the opponent, to link the candidate with desirable groups in the community, and to communicate the candidate's stands on selected issues.

Often in the late stages of a campaign, candidates will "go negative," putting out ads attacking their opponents' character by exposing sordid incidents or unsavory associations. Though voters consistently say they reject so-called negative campaigning, attacks such as the 1988 "Willie Horton" ad can be devastatingly effective in the heat of a closely contested race, even when the ads are misleading or patently false. The targets of these attacks are forced to issue denials and use valuable campaign time defending themselves rather than promoting their ideas.

Journalists, voters, and scholars frequently complain that such ads undermine elections and even democratic government itself. The argument is that voters are

Formation of an Exploratory Committee
Formed 18 to 24 months before the election, this committee begins fund-raising and bringing the candidate's name to the attention of the media and influential groups.

Fund-Raising
Presidential candidated must develop fundraising strategies, hire expert fundraisers, and quickly build a subtantial "war chest" early on to show they are serious contenders.

Campaigning
Months before the primaries, candidates begin meetings with local leaders, public appearances, ad campaigns, and other strategies.

Primaries and Caucuses
Candidates need to do well in early contests such as Iowa and New Hampshire in order to build momentum and win their party's nomination. Party debates give candidates an opportunity to impress large television audiences.

The Convention
The Democratic and Republican parties hold national conventions in September prior to the November general election. The party's nominees for president and vice president are "officially" announced.

The General Election Campaign
In the months leading up to the November election, candidates focus on battleground or swing states as they aim to win at leat 270 votes in the electoral college. They run television ads and use new media to reach voters. They must continue to raise money throughout this process.

The Debates
In October, the major party candidates engage in several televised debates along with one vice presidential debate.

The General Election
On the Tuesday following the first Monday in November, voters in each state cast ballots. In most states, the candidate who wins the most votes in the state wins all of the state's votes in the electoral college.

The Electoral College
The electors meet in their state capitals in December, and their votes are officially counted in January.

The Inauguration
The president is officially inaugurated on January 20.

FIGURE 10.3
Electing the President: Steps in the Process

turned off by the negativity of politics and the media, and in turn are uninformed about politics and less likely to vote. Americans tend to see negative campaign ads as just that: negative. But political scientist John Geer has found that negative campaigns are more effective than positive campaigns in shaping voter decisions. He argues that when political candidates attack each other, raising doubts about each other's views and qualifications, voters benefit.[20] Negative ads are more likely to address important policy differences between candidates and provide supporting evidence. Positive ads tend to focus on candidates' personal characteristics rather than issues, and do not provide any supporting evidence regarding the candidates' claims. Thus voters may learn more from negative ads than positive ads.

In addition to ads sponsored by the candidates, numerous campaign ads are sponsored by the political parties and by political advocacy groups seeking to influence the outcome of the election. As discussed in Chapter 4, the 2003 Bipartisan Campaign Reform Act (BCRA) prohibited advocacy groups from running ads that mentioned a candidate's name within 30 days of a primary election and 60 days of a general election. The purpose of the ban was to prevent well-heeled groups from conducting ad blitzes just before an election, thus possibly distorting the results. In its 2007 decision in *Federal Election Commission v. Wisconsin Right to Life*, the Supreme Court struck down the ad ban as an unconstitutional restriction on speech.[21] Following the 2010 *Citizens United* decision, advocacy groups can form super PACs and run unlimited campaign ads for or against candidates, as long as the organizations are "independent" of the candidate's campaign. This decision prevented the spending limits in BCRA from playing a significant role in election campaigns.

The 1992 presidential campaign introduced two new media techniques that are still important today: the talk show interview and the "electronic town hall meeting." Candidates used interviews on television and radio talk shows to reach the large audiences drawn to this popular entertainment program format. The **town hall meeting** format allows candidates the opportunity to interact with ordinary citizens, thus showing the candidates' concern with the views and needs of the voters. Both talk show appearances and town hall meetings allow candidates to deliver their messages to millions of Americans without the input of journalists or commentators who might criticize or question the candidates' assertions.

town hall meeting an informal public meeting in which candidates meet with ordinary citizens. Allows candidates to deliver messages without the presence of journalists or commentators

Debates Public debates were a critical part of the democratic process of ancient Greece, where they were both a vital form of public entertainment and the principal means of what today would be called "voter education." Many successful American politicians, such as Abraham Lincoln, came to prominence largely because of their skill as debaters. Today, both presidential and vice-presidential candidates hold debates, as do candidates for statewide and even local offices. Debates give voters the opportunity to see how the candidates fare in direct, face-to-face exchanges outside the "campaign bubble" of stage-managed public appearances and carefully scripted speeches. Candidates who can "think on their feet" may be seen as demonstrating the kind of on-the-spot decision making that is more like actual governing than anything else they do in a campaign.

Televised presidential debates began with the famous 1960 Kennedy-Nixon clash. Kennedy's strong performance in the debate and the perception of many voters that the youthfully vigorous Kennedy "looked presidential" were major factors in bringing about his victory over the much better-known Richard Nixon. In 1980, Ronald Reagan was able to dispel misgivings that some voters had about his age with a well-timed joke about the "youth and inexperience" of his Democratic

American Campaign Techniques Conquer the World

Since the 1950s, American elec-tion campaigns have been characterized by a reliance on technology in place of organization and personnel and by the rise of a new type of campaigner, the professional political consultant, in place of the old-time party boss. More and more, these campaign methods and even the consultants who wield them have spread to other parts of the world. American campaign consultants with their polls and phone banks and spot ads have directed campaigns in Europe, Latin America, and Asia. One American consultant recently said, "[We have] worked a lot in South America, Israel, [and the] Philippines and one of the things that I've discovered through that work is that the tools and techniques and strategies that we have developed here are applicable everywhere."[a]

This phenomenon, which is sometimes called the Americanization of politics, has important political implications. For the most part, the substitution of technology for organization in political campaigns works to the advantage of politicians and political forces repre-

senting the upper ends of the social spectrum versus those representing the lower classes. Strong party organization was generally introduced by working-class parties as a way of maximizing their major political resource—the power of numbers. When politics is based mainly on organization and numbers, working-class parties can compete quite successfully. The growing use of technology in place of organization shifts the advantage to middle- and upper-class parties, which generally have better access to the financial resources needed to fuel the polls and television ads on which new-style campaigns depend.

In Britain and France, new techniques were introduced first by conservative parties and then copied by their opponents.

The development of the new technology in Europe and other parts of the world followed the American pattern.

This phenomenon is now becoming apparent in Africa. For example, in Kenya's 2008 presidential contest, President Mwai Kibaki made use of consultants, opinion polls, and media technology in his nation's presidential race. The linchpin of Kibaki's effort was the cell-phone campaign. Many Kenyan voters, especially in rural areas, lack Internet access or television service. Most, however, own cell phones. The president's ads, plastered on billboards throughout the nation, provided a cell-phone number and urged voters to call in their views. Voters were also likely to receive cell-phone calls and text messages from Kibaki supporters asking them to vote for the president. Not to be outdone, Kibaki's main rival, the populist Raila Odinga, hired Dick Morris, a former consultant to Bill Clinton, to offer advice to his campaign. Odinga used television ads designed by a media consultant and organized his own cell-phone campaign.[b]

Unfortunately, when Kibaki lost the election, he refused to cede power and a period of fighting ensued before a power-sharing agreement was reached. American consultants scurried for cover when the bullets flew.

[a]Paul Baines, Fritz Plasser, and Christian Scheucher, "Operationalising Political Marketing: A Comparison of US and Western European Consultants and Managers," Middlesex University Discussion Paper Series, No. 7, July 1999.
[b]Stephanie McCrummen, "Kenya Tests New Style of Politicking," *Washington Post,* December 22, 2007, p. A10.

for critical analysis

1. Which foreign political parties were first to adopt American-style campaign techniques? Why?

2. What are the political implications and consequences of the shift from old-fashioned campaign styles to American-style, technology-intensive politics?

rival, Senator Walter Mondale. Indeed, candidates can make or break their campaigns with the strength of their debate performances, including even unconscious gestures and the nuances of their facial expressions. President George H. W. Bush was thought to have "lost" a 1992 debate when he was seen nervously glancing at his watch while his opponent, Bill Clinton, was speaking. In the 2012 presidential primaries, the Republicans held a dozen nationally televised debates, more than ever before, and the debates were spread out over the course of many months. In contrast with a process focusing on the state holding a primary or caucus that week, this series of debates before a nationwide audience had the effect of nationalizing the selection of the Republican presidential candidate. It also made or broke the presidential chances of a number of candidates. Before the debates, Texas governor Rick Perry was considered the ideal candidate to take the White House, given his policy positions and standing within the party. But a number of high-profile gaffes during the debates—including one in which he could not remember the name of one of the U.S. government departments he wished to eliminate if he were elected president—turned voters off. On the other hand, for former Speaker of the U.S. House Newt Gingrich, who has always been a natural orator, the televised debates allowed him to gain confidence. Throughout the series of debates, Gingrich was considered a front-runner at times, although he eventually lost to Mitt Romney. Candidates spend a great deal of time preparing for debate appearances, rehearsing their responses to likely questions and devising gambits to catch their opponents off guard. But because debates force candidates to react spontaneously, many voters believe that they provide the most important and revealing moments of a campaign.

Phone Banks Through the broadcast media, candidates communicate with voters en masse and impersonally. Phone banks, on the other hand, allow campaign workers to make personal contact with hundreds of thousands of voters. Personal contact of this sort is thought to be extremely effective. Again, polling data identify the groups that will be targeted for phone calls. Computers select phone numbers from areas in which members of these groups are concentrated. Staffs of paid or volunteer callers, using computer-assisted dialing systems and prepared scripts, then place calls to deliver their candidate's message. The targeted groups are generally those identified by polls as either uncommitted or weakly committed, and even strong supporters of the candidate who are contacted simply to be encouraged to vote. In 2008 and 2012 the presidential campaigns of both parties also placed hundreds of thousands of automated "robo calls" urging voters to support their candidates. In surveys of likely Iowa caucus attendees, as many respondents said they had been contacted by a robo call as by a live person. These types of campaign contacts are extremely effective and widespread.[22]

Direct Mail Direct mail is both a vehicle for communicating with voters and a mechanism for raising funds. The first step in a direct-mail campaign is the purchase or rental of a computerized mailing list of voters deemed to have some particular perspective or social characteristic. Often magazine subscription lists or lists of donors to various causes are employed. For example, a candidate interested in reaching conservative voters might rent subscription lists from the *National Review, Human Events,* or *Conservative Digest*; a candidate interested in appealing to liberals might rent subscription lists from the *New York Review of Books* or *The Nation.* Considerable fine-tuning is possible. After obtaining the appropriate mailing lists, candidates usually send pamphlets, letters, and brochures describing themselves and their views to voters believed to be sympathetic. Different types of mail appeals are made to different electoral subgroups. Often the letters sent to voters are personalized. The recipient is addressed by name in the text, and the letter appears actually to have been signed by the candidate. Of course, these "personal" letters and even the signatures are generated by a computer.

In addition to its use as a political advertising medium, direct mail has also become an important source of campaign funds. Computerized mailing lists permit campaign strategists to pinpoint individuals whose interests, background, and activities suggest that they may be potential donors to the campaign. Letters of solicitation are sent to these potential donors. Some of the money raised is then used to purchase additional mailing lists. Direct-mail solicitation can be enormously effective.

Professional Public Relations Modern campaigns are typically directed by professional public-relations consultants, who have expertise in contemporary communications strategies. Virtually all serious contenders for national and statewide office retain the services of professional campaign consultants. Increasingly, candidates for local office, too, have come to rely on professional campaign managers. Consultants offer candidates the expertise necessary to conduct accurate opinion polls, produce television commercials, organize direct-mail campaigns, and make use of sophisticated computer analyses.

The Internet The Internet has become a major weapon in modern political campaigns. The 2008 and 2012 campaigns made the Internet more central to their political strategies than ever before. Beginning with the primaries, every campaign developed an Internet strategy for fund-raising, generating interest in the candidate, mobilizing supporters, and getting out the vote. The Clinton primary campaign made extensive use of the Internet to mobilize potential supporters and to raise money. The innovative Obama campaign used the Internet to create events such as walkathons, community meet-ups, and fund-raisers all around the country. Both Obama and John McCain created social networking sites that allowed supporters to post information about themselves and chat with one another. (See Chapters 7 and 8 for more on this.) These sites help build enthusiasm and are potent fund-raising tools. Obama's website played a major role in the Illinois senator's ability to raise money and build strong ties to supporters.[23] The Digital Citizens box on the following page discusses the use of social media, such as Facebook, in recent campaigns.

● How Voters Decide

Identify the major factors that influence voters' decisions

Whatever the capacity of those with the money and power to influence the electoral process, it is the millions of individual decisions on Election Day that ultimately determine electoral outcomes. Sooner or later the choices of voters weigh more heavily than the schemes of campaign advisers or the leverage of interest groups.

Three factors influence voters' decisions at the polls: partisan loyalty, issues and policy preferences and candidate characteristics.

Social Media, Crowdsourcing, and the 2012 Election

While the Internet has created new challenges for political parties and candidates in the realm of campaigns and elections, it has also provided many new opportunities for campaign outreach and organization. Social media are remaking the face of political campaigning—and that face might be yours!

Social media sites give candidates a free way to organize supporters across a district, a state, or the country. The ability to reach millions of people instantly with a message, a call for volunteers, money, or whatever else the campaign needs is revolutionary. By fall 2012, Barack Obama had 30 million "friends" on Facebook, and Mitt Romney had less than half as many.

Social media sites allow not only candidates to communicate directly with their supporters, but also supporters to *retransmit* that information instantly to all their friends. What used to take weeks can take a candidate less than a day. This is critical, as only a small percentage of social media users (an estimated 7 percent of Facebook users, for example) actually "friend" political campaigns,

but the messages they retransmit reach all their friends, and often friends of their friends—eventually reaching thousands of people the campaign would not otherwise have reached. Research shows that we trust information more when we hear it from a trusted friend or someone who is like us. Thus, social media and the retransmission of information by supporters expose candidates to a wide audience that trusts the source of the information.

The ability of candidates to promote their campaign by extending their network through friends of friends on Facebook or other social media sites leverages the power of crowdsourcing. *Wired* magazine writer Jeff Howe coined the term *crowdsourcing* to describe how the Internet has enabled large, widely distributed teams of citizens to do work that was previously the domain of isolated experts or corporations. Linux and Wikipedia are only two of hundreds of examples of this phenomenon. While originally applied to business, crowdsourcing may increasingly be a driving force in political campaigns.

The 2008 elections showed how social media's unique ability to transfer

information quickly was indispensable to campaigns, and social media played an even larger role in the 2012 election. More than 3 in 4 Americans went online for election news in 2012. In the run-up to the election, Facebook abounded with memes about the candidates and debates, which were shared by millions. Citizens' social media habits, browser histories, and mobile applications became new goldmines for the campaigns. New in 2012 was a flurry of online advertising, as Obama and Romney campaign ads popped up everywhere, from YouTube to Google. The 2012 election was dominated by data, election forecasts, live-streaming debates, Facebook memes, and tweets of horserace results, all side by side with traditional political journalism and political pundits. As the election unfolded, the story was shared by millions online via social media.

SOURCES: Jeffry Howe, *Crowdsourcing: Why the Power of the Crowd Is Driving the Future of Business.* New York: Crown Business, 2009. Lee Rainie, "Social Media and the 2012 U.S. Presidential Elections." Washington, DC: U.S. Department of State, 2012, http://fpc.state.gov/193458.htm (accessed 6/25/12).

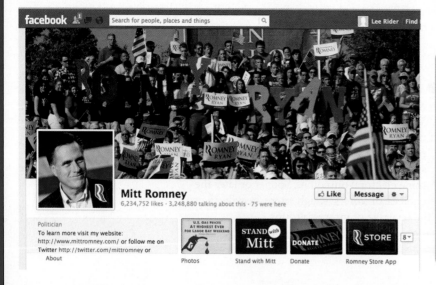

for critical analysis

1. What are some of the advantages and disadvantages of using social media for election campaigns?

2. *Crowdsourcing* is a term applied to communities of citizens doing work previously dominated by experts. Are citizens playing a larger role in political campaigns via social media? Why or why not?

Partisan Loyalty

Partisan loyalty was considerably stronger during the 1940s and '50s than it is today, but even now most voters feel a certain sense of identification or kinship with the Democratic or Republican party. This sense of identification is often handed down from parents to children and is reinforced by social and cultural ties. Partisan identification predisposes voters in favor of their party's candidates and against those of the opposing party (see Figure 10.4). At the level of the presidential contest, issues and candidate personalities may become very important, although even here many Americans supported Mitt Romney or Barack Obama in the 2012 race only because of partisan loyalty. But partisanship is more likely to assert itself in the less visible races, where issues and the candidates are not as well known. State legislative races, for example, are often decided by voters' party ties. Once formed, voters' partisan loyalties seldom change. Voters tend to keep their party affiliations unless some crisis causes them to reexamine the bases of their loyalties and to conclude that they have not given their support to the appropriate party. During these relatively infrequent periods of electoral change, millions of voters can change their party ties. For example, at the beginning of the New Deal era, between 1932 and 1936, millions of former Republicans transferred their allegiance to Franklin Roosevelt and the Democrats.

Issues and Policy Preferences

Policy preferences are a second factor influencing voters' choices at the polls. Voters may cast their ballots for the candidate whose position on economic issues they believe to be closest to their own, or the candidate who has what they believe to be the best record on foreign policy. Issues are more important in some races than others. If candidates articulate and publicize very different positions on important policy issues, voters are more likely to be able to identify and act on whatever policy preferences they may have.

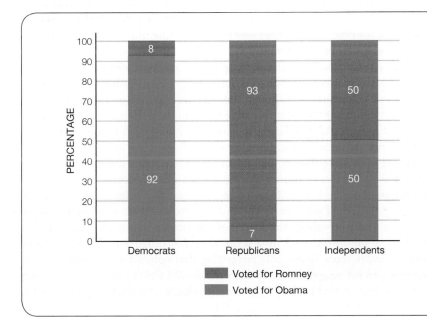

FIGURE 10.4

The Effect of Party Identification on the Vote, 2012

In 2012, more than 90 percent of Democrats and Republicans supported their party's presidential candidate. Should candidates devote their resources to converting voters who identify with the opposition or to winning more support among independents? What factors might make it difficult for candidates to simultaneously pursue both courses of action?

The ability of voters to make choices on the basis of policy preferences is diminished, however, if competing candidates do not differ substantially or do not focus their campaigns on policy matters. Very often, candidates deliberately take the safe course and emphasize positions that will not offend any voters. Thus, they often trumpet their opposition to corruption, crime, and inflation—things favored, presumably, by few voters. Such a strategy, though perfectly reasonable, makes it extremely difficult for voters to make their issue or policy preferences the basis for their choices at the polls.

Voters' issue choices usually involve a mix of their judgments about the past behavior of competing parties and candidates and their hopes and fears about candidates' future behavior. Political scientists call choices that focus on future behavior **prospective voting**, whereas those based on past performance are called **retrospective voting**. To some extent, whether prospective or retrospective evaluation is more important in a particular election depends on the strategies of competing candidates. Candidates always endeavor to define the issues of an election in terms that will serve their interests. Incumbents running during a period of prosperity will seek to take credit for the economy's happy state and will define the election as revolving around their record of success. This strategy encourages voters to make retrospective judgments. By contrast, an insurgent running during a period of economic uncertainty will tell voters it is time for a change and ask them to make prospective judgments. Thus, Bill Clinton focused on change in 1992 and prosperity in 1996, and through well-crafted media campaigns was able to define voters' agenda of choices.

The most important issue for voters in the 2012 election was the economy. Mitt Romney campaigned aggressively on his ability to turn around the deepest economic downturn since the Great Depression, and in exit polls was seen as the candidate better equipped to handle the economy. The Obama campaign touted the rebound of the auto industry after the president's bailout package in 2009, especially in Ohio, and his health care policy.

The Economy As we identify the strategies and tactics employed by opposing political candidates and parties, we should keep in mind that the best-laid plans of politicians often go awry. Election outcomes are affected by a variety of forces that candidates for office cannot fully control. Among the most important of these forces is the condition of the economy. If voters are satisfied with their economic prospects, they tend to support the party in power, while voter unease about the economy tends to favor the opposition. Thus, George H. W. Bush lost in 1992 during an economic downturn even though the American-led victory in the Gulf War had briefly given him a 90 percent favorable rating in the polls just one year earlier. And Bill Clinton won in 1996 during an economic boom even though voters had serious concerns about his moral fiber. As we shall see later in this chapter, the 2008 financial crisis gave Barack Obama and the Democrats a significant advantage. Over the past quarter-century, the Consumer Confidence Index, calculated by the Conference Board, a business research group, has been a fairly accurate predictor of presidential outcomes. The index is based on surveys asking voters how optimistic they are about the future of the economy. It would appear that a generally rosy view, indicated by a score over 100, augurs well for the party in power. An index score under 100, suggesting that voters are pessimistic about the economy's trend, suggests that incumbents should worry about their own job prospects (see Figure 10.5). The 2012 elections deviated from this pattern, with

prospective voting voting based on the imagined future performance of a candidate or political party

retrospective voting voting based on the past performance of a candidate or political party

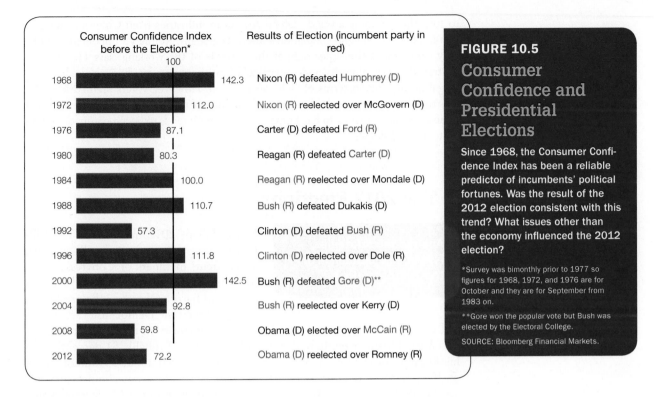

FIGURE 10.5

Consumer Confidence and Presidential Elections

Since 1968, the Consumer Confidence Index has been a reliable predictor of incumbents' political fortunes. Was the result of the 2012 election consistent with this trend? What issues other than the economy influenced the 2012 election?

*Survey was bimonthly prior to 1977 so figures for 1968, 1972, and 1976 are for October and they are for September from 1983 on.

**Gore won the popular vote but Bush was elected by the Electoral College.

SOURCE: Bloomberg Financial Markets.

Obama re-elected despite a Consumer Confidence Index score of 72.2 before the election.

Candidate Characteristics

Candidates' personal attributes always influence voters' decisions. Some analysts claim that voters prefer tall candidates to short ones, candidates with shorter names to candidates with longer names, and candidates with lighter hair to candidates with darker hair. Perhaps these rather frivolous criteria do play some role. But the more important candidate characteristics that affect voters' choices are race, ethnicity, religion, gender, geography, and social background. In general, voters may be proud to see someone of their ethnic, religious, or geographic background in a position of leadership, and they may presume that such candidates are likely to have views and perspectives close to their own. This is why, for many years, politicians sought to "balance the ticket," making certain that their party's ticket included members of as many important groups as possible.

Just as candidates' personal characteristics may attract some voters, they may repel others. Many voters are prejudiced against candidates from certain ethnic, racial, or religious groups. And for many years, voters were reluctant to support the candidacies of women, although this appears to be changing. Indeed, the fact that in 2008 the Democratic candidate was a black man and the Republican vice-presidential candidate a woman indicates the ongoing collapse of previously rigid political barriers.

Voters also pay attention to candidates' personality characteristics, such as "decisiveness," "honesty," and "vigor." In recent years, integrity has become a key election issue. In the 2012 election, Obama's opponents painted him as a weak leader, unable to turn the economy around, defend American industries from China's rising economic power, or defend the nation's interests globally. Romney's opponents said he only cared about the super rich, at the expense of the working class. He was also portrayed as anti-minority and, in particular, anti-Latino, as his rhetoric was harsh on illegal immigrants in terms of "self" deportation. However, voters seemed less concerned with these matters than with the ability of the candidates to deal with the nation's economic woes. In hard times, the electorate tends to become impatient with partisan mudslinging.

● The 2012 Elections

Analyze the strategies, issues, and outcomes of the 2012 elections

In the fall of 2012, more than 123 million Americans went to the polls to select a president, members of Congress, governors, and numerous other officials. Voters re-elected Barack Obama to the presidency and confirmed the Democratic Party's control of the Senate and the Republican Party's majority in the House of Representatives. Obama won more than 62 million votes, or roughly 51 percent, while his Republican challenger, Mitt Romney, had received about 59 million votes, or 48 percent. Though the president's margin of victory was about 5 percentage points less than in 2008, it was enough to give him 332 electoral votes, 62 more than the 270 needed to win the constitutionally mandated electoral college majority. The president's margin of victory was built on a coalition of women, working-class voters, and minority voters in several key battleground states. Despite the billions of dollars spent by candidates and the hoopla of the campaign, the 2012 election was decided more by demographic realities than political rhetoric.

Generally speaking, incumbent presidents have a substantial advantage when they seek re-election to a second term. During the course of American history, incumbent presidents standing for re-election have won about 70 percent of the time. Despite this advantage of incumbency, the re-election of President Barack Obama in 2012 was never a foregone conclusion. Obama had won handily in 2008 over his Republican rival, Senator John McCain. Obama had promised "Change we can believe in," and energized legions of young supporters who saw in the senator from Illinois a charismatic and energetic politician who would pursue a progressive social agenda and bring an end to America's wars in the Middle East. Many liberal voters had also been eager to elect America's first black president and thus make a break with the nation's long and unhappy history of racial oppression and discrimination.

Once in office, Obama was eager to make good on his promise of change. He worked to bring an end to the war in Iraq and to wind down the war in Afghanistan, partly in order to shift the nation's spending priorities from military to domestic social needs. In the realm of domestic policy, between 2008 and 2010, with the cooperation of a Congress controlled by the Democrats, the president succeeded in bringing about a massive overhaul of America's health care system. Under the terms of what came to be known as "Obamacare," tens of millions of previously uninsured Americans would be required to purchase federally subsidized health insurance policies through state insurance exchanges. Despite some

Many winning candidates of the 2010 elections were supported by Tea Party groups. Here, Senator Rand Paul campaigns at a Tea Party event. The question was whether these trends would continue in 2012.

initial doubt, the Supreme Court upheld the main provisions of Obamacare in 2012. The president also signed into law a major new program, the Dodd-Frank Wall Street Reform and Consumer Protection Act, aimed at protecting the nation's financial system from a future crisis like the one that nearly brought about a global financial catastrophe in 2008–09. The Dodd-Frank Act provided for tighter regulation of banks, prohibitions on some risky investment activities, and protections for consumers and borrowers. The president also signed a $700 billion economic stimulus bill to create jobs and spur investment and growth.

Despite the successes claimed by President Obama and his allies, Democrats lost control of the House of Representatives in the 2010 midterm elections. It is often the case that the president's party loses some seats in the midterm elections, but in 2010 the Democrats received a much larger drubbing than usual, losing 60 seats and ceding control of the House to the Republicans. In Senate races, the GOP failed to win enough seats to take control of the upper chamber but, with 46 seats, had enough votes to sustain filibusters if necessary. It seemed that what Obama and the Democrats had viewed as major accomplishments were seen by conservative Republican voters as a series of disasters. These voters saw Obamacare as a costly government takeover of a major industry and an unwarranted intrusion into the lives of all Americans. These same voters saw financial reform as a policy that would strangle America's financial services industry. With encouragement and momentum from the Tea Party movement, conservatives defeated numerous members of Congress who had supported Obama and left the president with a Republican House of Representatives that vowed to block any new presidential initiatives. Over the next two years, the president and Congress engaged in acrimonious battles over the federal budget and the federal government's borrowing power (the debt limit) that twice brought the U.S. government to the brink of financial ruin before last-minute compromises temporarily averted disaster.

All the while, the nation's economy, which had been battered by the 2007–08 recession, was showing only tepid signs of recovery. For much of the president's first term, unemployment remained in the uncomfortably high 8–9 percent range;

The Romney campaign and other Republican groups attacked Obama's handling of the economy. As a sitting president presiding over a somewhat shaky economy, with unemployment uncomfortably high, Obama's re-election was not at all certain.

the housing market was weak; a number of major financial institutions seemed tottering on the edge of failure; and job seekers, including hundreds of thousands of recent college graduates, found themselves unemployed or underemployed. Against this backdrop, President Obama's re-election hardly seemed assured. However, the Republicans needed to find a candidate who could defeat the president and appeal to the various factions of their party.

Political Parties in 2012: Unity and Division

As recently as the 1950s, each of America's major political parties had been a coalition that included both liberal and conservative elements. The Democrats included the liberal forces of organized labor and the big cities and the more conservative groups in the states of the South. The Republicans, for their part, mobilized midwestern conservatives and the liberals of the northeastern Protestant establishment. Each party was said to be a "big tent."

As we saw in Chapter 9, the political upheavals of the 1960s and '70s, especially the civil rights revolution, triggered a national realignment of political forces. Angered by the national Democratic leadership's stances on civil rights issues, white Southerners largely shifted their allegiance to the GOP. At the same time, liberal Republicans on the East and West coasts shifted their support to the Democrats. Over time, the Democrats became a much more liberal party and the Republicans a much more conservative political force. This ideological realignment of the two parties is one reason that partisan struggles in Congress—and between Congress and the White House when party control of the two branches is divided—have become especially intense in recent years.

The growing ideological split between the two parties has not meant that each party is ideologically uniform. In fact, disputes among the various liberal groups within the Democratic Party and among the disparate conservative groups in the GOP have also been quite heated. Some liberal Democrats, for example, castigated President Obama as too moderate because he did not move quickly enough to end the wars in Iraq and Afghanistan and did not seek to create a fully nationalized health care system on the European or Canadian model. The GOP, for its part, is divided among fiscal conservatives, social conservatives, and other factions. For the fiscal conservatives, the major issues facing the nation today are excessive taxation and regulation. The social conservatives are more concerned with ending abortion, preventing same-sex marriage, and restoring the place of religion in American public life. The neoconservatives, a small group in the electorate but an influential element in the party's leadership, favor a robust military policy and an internationalist foreign policy. The paleoconservatives are suspicious of America's foreign involvements, favor restrictions on immigration, and generally have an isolationist bent. In 2012 divisions among the Democrats were relatively inconsequential for the simple reason that the party's presidential nominee was a given. Like it or not, all the party's factions had to accommodate themselves to President Obama. The Republican nomination, on the other hand, was sharply contested by several candidates representing different factions in the party. Former Massachusetts governor and successful financier Mitt Romney spoke for fiscal conservatives. Former Pennsylvania senator Rick Santorum and Minnesota congresswoman Michele Bachmann were the champions of the social conservatives. Libertarian Texas congressman Ron Paul spoke for the paleoconservatives, and former House Speaker Newt Gingrich represented neoconservatives. Several other candidates, who lacked significant bases of support, including business executive Herman Cain, Texas governor Rick Perry, former Utah governor and ambassador Jon Huntsman, former New Mexico governor Gary Johnson, and former Minnesota governor Tim Pawlenty, sought to stake out positions that might attract supporters if the front runners faltered.

Between May 2011 and February 2012, Republican hopefuls engaged in a series of televised debates where each argued that he or she would be best able to defeat the Democrats. The candidates were generally polite to one another and saved their criticisms for Obama and the Democrats. Gradually, candidates who found themselves unable to attract much support dropped out of the race, and by February 2012, only four remained: Gingrich, Paul, Romney, and Santorum. Over the next several months, these four candidates faced one another in a series of Republican primaries and caucuses, competing for the votes of 2,286 Republican convention delegates, with 1,144 needed to win the nomination.

From the beginning, Romney's superior organization and financial base made him the front-runner. The GOP's social and religious conservatives, though, were unenthusiastic about the former Massachusetts governor. Some saw him as a liberal in Republican clothing while others, particularly evangelical Protestants, were unhappy about the idea of a member of the Mormon faith leading the party. These groups gave their support to Rick Santorum, who eventually carried 11 states and more than 20 percent of the primary vote. By April 2012, though, Romney had clearly won the delegate votes needed for the nomination, and Santorum suspended his campaign. In the end, Romney carried 42 states and territories, and Santorum 11. Gingrich and Paul turned out to be nearly irrelevant, with the former Speaker carrying two states and the Texas congressman only one.

Having won the Republican nomination, Romney moved to reassure the party's social conservatives that he was worthy of their enthusiastic support in the general election. Conservatives would not jump to the Obama camp, but anything less than enthusiastic participation in the campaign on the part of social conservatives would doom the GOP's ticket to defeat. Accordingly, Romney endorsed a party platform that would appeal to this group. Its provisions included a constitutional amendment to ban abortion; elimination of government-funded family planning programs, with the exception of abstinence training; and a program of detention for "dangerous" aliens. Other provisions included partial privatization of the Medicare program, elimination of the federal income tax, and an end to various forms of federal regulation. As icing on the conservative cake, Romney chose as his vice-presidential running mate Congressman Paul Ryan of Wisconsin. Ryan had vigorously opposed Democratic fiscal and social policies and was enthusiastically supported by the GOP's social and fiscal conservatives. Yet, many conservatives remained unconvinced about Romney. Radio talk show hosts such as Glenn Beck and Michael Savage continued to attack the Massachusetts governor. But, particularly with Ryan on the ticket, most fell into line, and as the party became more united behind his candidacy, Romney was ready to face Obama and the Democrats.

The General Election

In recent years, the bedrock base of GOP support has consisted of reasonably affluent, educated, middle-aged, middle-class white men living in suburban and rural areas. The Democrats, on the other hand, have been able to rely upon the votes of a majority of women, less affluent Americans, urban residents, younger voters, African Americans, and, increasingly, Hispanic voters. While there are certainly poor Republicans and affluent Democrats, this split approaches a classic division between the "have mores" and "have lesses." Romney alluded to this division when he said, in what he thought to be a closed-door meeting with Republican donors, that 47 percent of Americans paid few taxes, depended on government handouts, and would never vote for him. When news of Romney's comments leaked, Republicans sought to contain the damage but did not necessarily dispute the accuracy of Romney's analysis.

The division of the electorate into "have mores" and "have lesses" also dictated a major struggle in the campaign. In a number of states, Republican governors and legislatures enacted voter ID laws requiring prospective voters to present valid, government-issued photo identification cards at the polls. Republicans said such laws were needed to prevent fraudulent voting. The GOP's calculus, though, was that less-educated and minority voters (who tend to vote Democratic) were less likely to be able to produce valid ID at the polls and would thus be barred from voting. Two dozen states enacted voter ID laws, and though Democrats mounted court challenges, many of these laws were in effect on Election Day.

While America, of course, consists of 50 states, presidential elections are usually fought in only 9 or 10 states. This is so because some states are solidly Republican (sometimes called the red states) while others are solidly Democratic (known as the blue states). The states of the Deep South and mountain West, for example, are so securely in the Republican camp that Democratic presidential candidates hardly bother to campaign there. Most of the states of the Northeast and West Coast, on the other hand, are heavily committed to the Democrats and receive little attention from the GOP. In 2012 opinion polls indicated that only 8 of the 50 states were actually toss-ups. These were Colorado, Florida, Iowa, Nevada, New Hampshire, Ohio, Virginia, and Wisconsin. A handful of other states, including Michigan, Minnesota, New Mexico, and Pennsylvania were seen as leaning toward Obama, while Arizona, Indiana, and North Carolina were viewed as leaning toward Romney. The remaining 35 states seemed to be solidly in either the Democratic or Republican camp.

Romney's remark—made at a private fundraiser—that 47 percent of Americans were dependent on government and not worth his campaign's time offended many Americans. The issue highlighted the division of the electorate into "have mores" and "have lesses."

Thus, the 2012 presidential race was waged in 8 to 10 battleground states. Here the Obama and Romney campaigns and their various supporters spent hundreds of millions of dollars on television and online advertising, phone banks, voter registration drives, and rallies as well as numerous candidate visits. While voters in many states would hardly have reason to notice the presidential contest, voters in the battleground states could hardly turn on their television sets or answer their phones without being urged to support Obama or Romney.

The Debates

Of course, while most campaigning was undertaken on a state-by-state basis, the candidates did face each other in one major set of national forums. These were the three nationally televised presidential debates along with the one vice-presidential debate. The first presidential debate, focusing on domestic policy, was held at the University of Colorado on October 3, 2012. The debate, which was watched by 67 million people, was more remarkable for style than substance. In terms of substance, the candidates discussed the economy, the federal deficit, Social Security, and the Affordable Care Act, with Romney criticizing Obama's record and the president defending his accomplishments. Though both candidates made mistakes and factual errors, both seemed to possess a thorough knowledge of the details of major American domestic policies. In terms of style, however, Obama and Romney differed sharply. Governor Romney seemed alert and aggressive, making points assertively and methodically as he accused the president of increasing the nation's debt, failing to bolster the economy, and undermining the private sector in favor of government-run programs. The president, for his part, appeared disengaged and listless. In the wake of the first debate, the national polls, which had constantly shown Obama with a slim lead over his Republican opponent, now suggested that the race was neck and neck. Republicans were elated and Democrats dismayed by the debate and its results.

The president improved his performance in the next two debates and was generally judged to have been the winner, as was Vice President Biden in his confrontation with Republican vice-presidential candidate Paul Ryan. As one commentator noted, however, Obama and Biden had won their victories on points while Romney had scored a knockout in the first debate. To add to the president's problem, in the 34 states that allowed early voting in 2012, hundreds of thousands of voters had cast their ballots after the first debate but before the other debates, introducing a wild card that would be discussed long after the election. At any rate, with the damage done, Obama had two weeks after the debates to slow his opponent's growing momentum.

Obama responded by redoubling his efforts in battleground states, with speeches and campaign commercials labeling Romney a multimillionaire who was out of touch with ordinary Americans and who sent American jobs overseas. The Obama campaign argued that Romney had favored allowing Detroit to go bankrupt, despite the potential loss of hundreds of thousands of jobs. Obama also coined the term *Romnesia*, to suggest that Romney continually changed positions for reasons of expedience and expected voters to forget what his previous positions had been. These efforts succeeded in shoring up Obama's

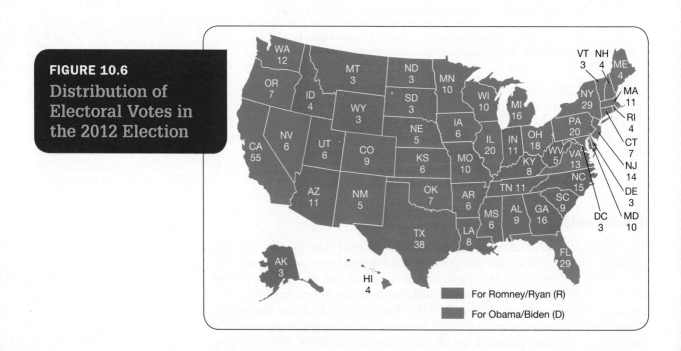

FIGURE 10.6
Distribution of Electoral Votes in the 2012 Election

For Romney/Ryan (R)

For Obama/Biden (D)

Who Supported Obama in 2012?

Barack Obama defeated Mitt Romney in the 2012 presidential election, winning 50 percent of the popular vote to Romney's 48 percent. The map in Figure 10.6, to the left, shows who won each state; there, red seems to dominate. However, if we adjust the map to show each state in proportion to its population, blue states—those won by Obama—clearly dominate.

Election Results by State's Population

Mitt Romney (R)

Barack Obama (D)

Votes in Electoral College

55	California	10	Maryland	06	Utah
38	Texas	10	Minnesota	05	New Mexico
29	Florida	10	Wisconsin	05	Nebraska
29	New York	10	Missouri	05	West Virginia
20	Illinois	09	Colorado	04	Hawaii
20	Pennsylvania	09	Alabama	04	Maine
18	Ohio	09	South Carolina	04	New Hampshire
16	Michigan	08	Louisiana	04	Rhode Island
16	Georgia	08	Kentucky	04	Idaho
15	North Carolina	07	Connecticut	04	Delaware
14	New Jersey	07	Oregon	03	District Of Columbia
13	Virginia	07	Oklahoma	03	Vermont
12	Washington	06	Iowa	03	Alaska
11	Massachusetts	06	Nevada	03	Montana
11	Indiana	06	Arkansas	03	North Dakota
11	Arizona	06	Kansas	03	South Dakota
11	Tennessee	06	Mississippi	03	Wyoming

for critical analysis

1. With the exception of Texas, Obama won the states with the largest populations—California, New York, Florida, and Illinois. How are these states different from those that Romney won? What do these differences tell us about the political differences between more densely populated areas (urban areas) and those with lower populations (rural areas)?

2. What do you think causes the differences between urban and rural America? Do you think these differences will continue long into the future?

In 2012, as in past elections, both campaigns focused on a few battleground states. Romney and Obama campaigned extensively in Ohio, Florida, Virginia, Wisconsin, Colorado, Nevada, Iowa, and New Hampshire, and voters in these states saw thousands of campaign ads.

support among working-class Americans. According to exit polls, the president won 63 percent of the votes of those whose family incomes were less than $30,000 per year and 57 percent of those who earned between $30,000 and $49,000 per year. Among more affluent voters, by contrast, Romney was the winner, taking 52 percent of the votes of those who earned between $50,000 and $100,000 per year and about 54 percent of the votes of those whose annual family incomes exceeded $100,000.

The Obama campaign also redoubled its efforts among women voters. In recent years, women have tended to give a majority of their votes to the Democrats, producing a so-called gender gap in the electoral arena. Democratic ads reminded women that it was the Democratic Party that supported such issues as equal pay. Foolish remarks on rape and abortion by GOP senatorial candidates in Indiana and Missouri were highlighted by the Democrats to underscore Republican insensitivity to women's concerns. On Election Day, 55 percent of women voters supported Obama, while Romney received the votes of 52 percent of America's men.

Finally, Obama campaign workers were determined to ensure high levels of turnout among minority voters, who potentially could be decisive in several battleground states. African American voters were a loyal Democratic constituency and could be counted upon to turn out for the president. But the Democrats had been making enormous efforts to bring Asian and, especially, Latino voters into their camp, too. Latinos are the most rapidly growing group in the American population and were responsible for about 10 percent of the votes cast in 2012. The Democratic Party had made a major effort to court Latinos on such issues as immigration and, in 2012, Democrats had pushed for ballot initiatives in a number of states that offered undocumented young Latinos who had been raised in the United States the opportunity to attend public colleges at the in-state tuition rate. These so-called "American Dream" referenda not only cemented the relationship between the Democratic Party and the Latino community, but also helped bring Latinos to the polls in large numbers. This strategy proved extremely successful. Not only did Obama capture 93 percent of the African American vote, but he also won approximately 70 percent of the Latino vote across the country. Among whites, by contrast, Romney received 58 percent of the vote.

Taken together, working-class voters, women, and minority constituents gave Obama the votes he needed for victory. This "one-two-three punch" was particularly important in the battleground states. Astonishingly, President Obama carried all the battleground states, and in each one, exit polls suggested that the critical margin was provided by low-income groups, minorities, and women.

Digital Media in the 2012 Elections

The 2012 elections also reflected an ongoing change in how campaigns and elections are conducted since the rise of the Internet. Even more so than in 2008, both parties and candidates at all levels had to take account of the growing importance of online videos, mobile applications, social media, and digital fundraising.

According to reports released by the Pew Research Center soon after the election, in 2012 fully 55 percent of registered voters watched political videos online, including news reports about the election, debates, humorous and parody videos, and political ads. One in two registered voters had received recommendations for political videos to watch. Mobile phone politics also hit new highs in the 2012 election. Twenty-seven percent of registered voters who own a cell phone used their phone in this election campaign to keep up with news related to the election or politics. One in five cell phone owners sent text messages related to the campaign to friends, family members, or others.

Political discussions frequently took place via social media, where people tried to convince their friends how to vote. In the last 30 days of the campaigns, 30 percent of registered voters heard from family and friends via Facebook or Twitter that they should vote for Obama or Romney. This compares to 48 percent who had similar face-to-face conversations. Perhaps most important, one in five registered voters was the mobilizer, encouraging friends and family to get out and vote by posting on these forums.

Campaign donations continued to go digital in 2012, following Obama's successful campaign in 2008. Thirteen percent of American adults donated to one of the presidential candidates in 2012, a higher than average percentage roughly matching 2008. While 67 percent of these contributors donated in person, over the telephone, or by mail, roughly half donated online or via e-mail in 2012. There are partisan differences: 57 percent of Democratic campaign donors gave online or via e-mail in 2012, compared with just 34 percent of Republican donors. In 2012 the Federal Election Commission allowed political campaigns to accept campaign contributions via text message, and again, Democrats were more likely to contribute using the new technology.

While many factors—especially demographic trends—contributed to Obama's victory in 2012, it is also notable that the Obama campaign pioneered online fundraising and organizing techniques in 2008 and built on these successful strategies in 2012. The Republicans made up some ground and introduced a few online strategies of their own in 2012, but the Democrats appeared to hold an advantage in the effective use of digital politics.

Looking toward the Future

As they surveyed the results, Republicans consoled themselves that 2012 had not been a complete disaster. To be sure, in Senate races, Democrats increased their majority by a net gain of two, from 51 to 53 seats. Democrats won formerly Republican seats in Massachusetts and Indiana as well as the Connecticut seat previously held by Independent Joe Lieberman. Republicans, for their part, captured a formerly Democratic seat in Nebraska. A formerly Republican seat long held by retiring senator Olympia Snowe was won by Independent former governor Angus King, who refused to say whether he planned to caucus with the Democrats or Republicans. Nevertheless, the GOP had successfully defended its bastion in the House of Representatives. In House races, the Democrats added only seven seats to their total, falling fall short of the number needed to take control of the lower chamber. And it appeared that Republicans might add one gubernatorial slot, North Carolina, to their tally of state chief executives.

But while 2012 was not an unmitigated disaster for the GOP; many Republicans reviewing the results of the election believed that their party must change, that it must reach out to women, Latinos, and others. If the GOP remained merely the party of affluent white men, particularly as the U.S. population became less white, demographics would doom it to the status of a permanent minority. Thus, ironically, if it hoped to become a party capable of winning majorities, the GOP would have to become a party able to woo minorities.

Senator Claire McCaskill was one of several Democratic incumbents who were considered vulnerable in the 2012 elections. However, McCaskill won re-election, in part because her opponent Todd Akin lost support after making remarks on rape that were widely criticized.

Money and Politics

During the nineteenth century, national political campaigns in the United States employed millions of people. Indeed, as many as 2.5 million individuals did political work during the 1880s.[24] Most of these workers, however, were volunteers, so the direct cost of campaigns was relatively low. For example, in 1860, Abraham Lincoln spent only $100,000—which was approximately twice the amount spent by his chief opponent, Stephen A. Douglas.

Campaign tasks that were once performed by masses of party workers with some cash now require fewer personnel but a great deal more money, for the new political style depends on surveys, computers, and other electronic communication methods. The modern political campaign is enormously expensive. A 60-second spot on prime-time network television costs hundreds of thousands of dollars each time it is aired. Polling expenses in a statewide race can easily reach or exceed the six-figure mark. Campaign consultants can charge substantial fees. A serious national direct-mail campaign requires at least $1 million in "front-end cash" to pay for mailing lists, printing, envelopes, and postage.[25]

Certainly "people power" is not irrelevant to modern political campaigns. Candidates continue to use the political services of tens of thousands of volunteer workers, especially for grassroots get-out-the-vote drives. Still, even the recruitment of campaign workers has become a job for electronic technology. Employing a technique called "instant organization," paid staff use phone banks to contact potential campaign workers in areas targeted by a computer (which they also do when contacting potential voters, as discussed earlier). Volunteer workers are recruited from among those called.

In the nineteenth century, labor-intensive campaigns allowed parties whose chief support came from groups nearer the bottom of the social scale to use their

One way candidates raise money is through fundraisers, like this Republican Party event in Pennsylvania where Mitt Romney spoke. Supporters typically donate a certain amount in order to attend.

numerical superiority as a partial counterweight to the institutional and economic resources more readily available to the opposition. The capital-intensive campaign of the modern era, by contrast, has given a major boost to the political fortunes of candidates whose supporters are able to furnish the large sums now needed to compete effectively.[26] Candidates with the most campaign dollars usually win, and that was certainly the case with President Obama, who in 2008 out-fund-raised his Republican opponent, John McCain. It was also the case with Republican Mitt Romney, who out-fund-raised his Republican challengers in 2012, including Newt Gingrich and Rick Santorum. Dominated by expensive technology, therefore, electoral politics has become a contest in which the wealthy and powerful have a decided advantage. The use of the Internet for campaigns offers hope for more equality, with millions of dollars in small donations increasingly raised in online fund-raising, as was the case with Obama in the 2008 presidential elections (see Chapter 8). The 2012 presidential election shattered previous records for campaign spending. In the aftermath of the 2010 Supreme Court decision allowing unlimited political spending by unaffiliated groups, both majority party candidates opted out of the campaign financing system. Spending by candidates, political parties and interest groups on the congressional and presidential races was $6 billion combined in 2012, as compared with $5.3 billion in 2008 and $4.2 billion in 2004.

Sources of Campaign Funds

According to the Center for Responsive Politics, about 10 percent of the $3 billion spent by candidates for federal offices in 2008 came from **political action committees (PACs)**, mainly in support of congressional races; the remainder came from individual donors. Several million individuals donated money to political campaigns in that year, some in contributions of as little as five or ten dollars. One of the sources of Barack Obama's fund-raising advantage in the 2008 campaign was his ability to generate more than 2 million small- and medium-size contributions to his campaign.[27] Another $500 million in 2008 was raised and spent by individuals and advocacy groups—the so-called 527 and 501c(4) groups operating outside the structure of the Democratic and Republican campaigns. According to early estimates, as much as $4 billion was spent by candidates and their supporters during the 2010 midterm elections in the wake of the Supreme Court's ruling in the *Citizens United* case and other federal court decisions which eliminated many of the previous limits on campaign spending.[28]

political action committee (PAC) a private group that raises and distributes funds for use in election campaigns

Individual Donors Politicians spend a great deal of time asking people for money. Money is solicited via direct mail, through the Internet, over the phone, and in numerous face-to-face meetings. Under federal law, individuals may donate as much as $2,300 per candidate per election, $5,000 per PAC per calendar year (to a maximum of $65,500), $28,500 per national party committee per calendar year, and $10,000 to state and local committees per calendar year. Federal rules also impose an overall limit on individual contributors of $108,200 per election cycle. Individuals may contribute freely—without limits—to 527 committees and to 501c(4) groups. Additionally, they may attempt to enhance their influence by "bundling" their contributions with those of friends and associates.

Political Action Committees PACs are organizations established by corporations, labor unions, or interest groups to channel the contributions of their members into political campaigns. Under the terms of the 1971 Federal Election Campaign Act, which governs campaign finance in the United States, PACs are permitted to make larger contributions to any given candidate than individuals are allowed to make (see Table 10.2). Moreover, allied or related PACs often coordinate their campaign contributions, greatly increasing the amount of money a candidate actually receives from the same interest group. More than 4,500 PACs are registered with the Federal Election Commission (FEC), which oversees campaign finance practices in the United States. Nearly two-thirds of all PACs represent corporations, trade associations, and other business and professional groups. Alliances of bankers, lawyers, doctors, and merchants all sponsor PACs. The National Beer Wholesalers Association PAC was known for many years as "SixPAC." Labor unions also sponsor PACs, as do ideological, public interest, and nonprofit groups. The National Rifle Association sponsors a PAC, as does the Sierra Club. Many congressional and party leaders have established PACs, known as leadership PACs, to provide funding for their political allies.

Independent Spending: 527, 501c(4), and Super PAC Committees Committees known as **527s** and **501c(4)s** are independent groups that are currently not covered by the campaign-spending restrictions imposed in 2002 by the BCRA. These groups, named for the sections of the tax code under which they are organized, can raise and spend unlimited amounts on political advocacy as long as their efforts are not coordinated with those of any candidate's campaign. A 527 is a group established specifically for the purpose of political advocacy, whereas a

527 committees nonprofit independent groups that receive and disburse funds to influence the nomination, election, or defeat of candidates. Named after Section 527 of the Internal Revenue Code, which defines and provides tax-exempt status for nonprofit advocacy groups

501c(4) committees nonprofit groups that also engage in issue advocacy. Under Section 501c(4) of the federal tax code such a group may spend up to half its revenue for political purposes

TABLE 10.2

The Rules for Campaign Contributions

WHO	MAY CONTRIBUTE . . .	TO . . .	IF . . .
Individuals	up to $2,300	a candidate	they are contributing to a single candidate in a single election.
Individuals	up to $28,500	a national party committee.	
Individuals	up to $5,000	a PAC.	
PACs	up to $5,000	a candidate	they contribute to the campaigns of at least five candidates.
Individuals and PACs	unlimited funds	a 527 committee	the funds are used for Issue advocacy and the 527 committee's efforts are not coordinated with any political campaign.
Individuals and	up to $10,000	a state party committee	the money is used for Voter registration and get-out-the-vote efforts.

During the 2004 presidential campaign, dozens of independent 527 committees spent hundreds of millions of dollars on television advertising. One of the most notorious of these ads was the "Swift Boat Veterans for Truth," which challenged John Kerry's military record and activism against the Vietnam War.

501c(4) is a nonprofit group, such as an environmental or other public interest group, that also engages in advocacy. A 501c(4) may not spend more than half its revenue for political purposes. Yet, unlike a 527, a 501c(4) is not required to disclose where it gets its funds or exactly what it does with them. As a result, it has become a common practice for wealthy and corporate donors to route campaign contributions far in excess of the legal limits through 501c(4)s. A new form of independent group, the independent expenditure committee, or "super PAC," came about as a result of an FEC ruling that the Supreme Court's 2010 decision in *Citizens United v. FEC* permitted individuals and organizations to form committees that could raise unlimited amounts of money to run advertising for and against candidates so long as their efforts were not coordinated with those of the candidates.[29] Outside spending via 527s and 501c(4)s played an unprecedented role in the 2012 presidential race, as groups ran extensive television ads. Priorities USA Action super PAC raised $64 million to support Democrats, while the Restore Our Future super PAC raised $132 million to help Republicans. The top spending super PACs were primarily those advocating against Obama, including American Crossroads ($85 million), the Republican National Committee ($41 million), Americans for Prosperity ($34 million), and the National Rifle Association of America Political Victory Fund ($7.4 million). Super PACs on both sides relied on very large contributions. Table 10.3 lists the top super PAC donors in 2012.

Political Parties Before 2002, most campaign dollars took the form of "soft money," unregulated contributions to the national parties nominally to assist in party building or voter registration efforts rather than for particular campaigns. Federal campaign finance legislation crafted by Senators John McCain and Russell Feingold and enacted in 2002 sought to ban soft money by prohibiting the national parties from soliciting and receiving contributions from corporations, unions, or individuals and preventing them from directing such funds to their affiliated state parties. However, it did not reduce the overall importance of money in politics, and political parties continue to play a major role in financing political campaigns. Under federal rules, a national political party committee may make unlimited "independent expenditures" advocating support for its own presidential candidate or advocating the defeat of the opposing party's candidate as long as these expenditures are not coordinated with the candidate's own campaign. A national party committee may

TABLE 10.3

Top Donors to Super PACs, 2012

DEMOCRATIC SUPER PAC DONORS

AMOUNT DONATED (IN MILLIONS)	DONOR
3.5	Fred Eychaner An Obama bundler and Chicago media mogul.
3.5	James H. Simons President of Euclidean Capital and Board Chair of Renaissance Technologies Corp., a hedge fund company.
3.0	Jeffrey Katzenberg Chief executive of Dreamworks Animation.
2.0	United Association of Journeymen & Apprentices of the Pipe Fitting Industry Trade union.
2.0	Irwin Jacobs Founder of chipmaker Qualcomm and former M.I.T. professor.
2.0	Jon Stryker Gay rights activist and founder of the Arcus Foundation.
2.0	Steve Mostyn Texas trial lawyer.
2.0	Anne Cox Chambers Part owner of Cox Enterprises, the media conglomerate.
1.5	Ann Wyckoff Seattle philanthropist.
1.2	National Air Traffic Controllers Association PAC PAC of the air traffic controllers union.

REPUBLICAN SUPER PAC DONORS

AMOUNT DONATED (IN MILLIONS)	DONOR
10.0	Sheldon Adelson Billionaire casino owner and Newt Gingrich's longtime friend and patron.
10.0	Miriam Adelson Physician; wife of Sheldon Adelson.
10.0	Bob J. Perry Houston homebuilder who was a major financier of Swift Boat Veterans for Truth in 2004.
2.8	Oxbow Carbon LLC An oil and gas company based in West Palm Beach, Florida. It was founded by William Koch, the brother of David H. and Charles Koch, wealthy conservative businessmen and founders of Americans for Prosperity.
2.3	Harold Simmons Dallas billionaire who was among the top donors to Governor Rick Perry of Texas.
2.2	Julian Robertson Founder of Tiger Management, a hedge fund.
1.6	Robert Reynolds Chief executive of Putman Investments.
1.6	Kenneth C. Griffin Founder and chief executive of Citadel LLC.
1.5	A. Jerrold Perenchio Billionaire and former chairman of Univision.
1.2	Stanley Herzog Chairman and chief executive of Herzog Contracting Corp., a highway and railroad construction firm.

SOURCE: http://elections.nytimes.com/2012/campaign-finance (accessed 11/11/12).

also spend up to $19 million in coordination with its Presidential candidate's campaign even if its candidate has accepted public funding. Thus, for example, even though John McCain accepted full public funding for his 2008 presidential bid, the national Republican Party helped fund McCain's advertising up to the federal limit. Neither major party candidate accepted public financing in 2012. As a result, many observers believe that the 2008 race may be the last time that a major-party candidate will forgo his or her own fund-raising in favor of public funding. Candidates who accept public funding may not engage in fund-raising for their own campaigns.

Rules governing campaign finance have been the object of intense debate in recent years. Many Americans worry that government policies favor groups—such as Wall Street financiers—who make large donations to campaigns.

Public Funding The Federal Election Campaign Act also provides for public funding of presidential campaigns. As they seek a major-party presidential nomination, candidates become eligible for public funds by raising at least $5,000 in individual contributions of $250 or less in each of 20 states. Candidates who reach this threshold may apply for federal funds to match, on a dollar-for-dollar basis, all individual contributions of $250 or less they receive. Currently, candidates who accept matching funds may spend no more than $42 million, including the matching funds, in their presidential primary campaigns. The funds are drawn from the Presidential Election Campaign Fund. Taxpayers may contribute $3 to this fund, at no additional cost to themselves, by checking a box on the first page of their federal income tax returns. Major-party presidential candidates receive a lump sum (about $91 million in 2012) during the summer prior to the general election. They must meet all their general expenses from this money. Third-party candidates are eligible for public funding only if they received at least 5 percent of the vote in the previous presidential race. This stipulation effectively blocks pre-election funding for third-party or independent candidates, although a third party that wins more than 5 percent of the vote can receive public funding after the election. In 1980, John Anderson persuaded banks to lend him money for an independent candidacy on the strength of poll data showing that he would receive more than 5 percent of the vote and thus would obtain public funds with which to repay the loans.

Under current law, no candidate is required to accept public funding for either the nominating races or general presidential election. Candidates who do not accept public funding are not affected by any expenditure limits. In 2008, John McCain accepted public funding for the general election campaign, receiving $84 million, but Barack Obama declined, choosing to rely on his own fund-raising prowess. Obama was ultimately able to outspend McCain by a wide margin. Candidates who accept public funding may not engage in fund-raising for their own campaigns. In 2010 the U.S. Supreme Court ruled in *Citizens United v. Federal Election Commission* that the government could not restrict independent expenditures by corporations or unions to political campaigns.[30] The Court said such restrictions violated the First Amendment. The United States has entered a new era of campaign finance in which corporations and unions can spend unlimited sums. These independent expenditures, meaning there is no coordination with the official candidate campaign, run through super PACs, or super political action committees.

The Candidates Themselves On the basis of the Supreme Court's 1976 decision in *Buckley v. Valeo*, the right of individuals to spend their *own* money to campaign for office is a constitutionally protected matter of free speech and is not subject to limitation.[31] Thus, extremely wealthy candidates often contribute millions of dollars to their own campaigns. The New Jersey Democrat Jon Corzine, for example, spent approximately $60 million of his own funds in a successful U.S. Senate bid in 2000 and another $40 million when he ran for governor of New Jersey in 2005. The only exception to the *Buckley* rule concerns presidential candidates who accept federal funding for their general election campaigns. Such individuals are limited to $50,000 in personal spending.

● Thinking Critically about Elections and Democracy

The important role played by private funds in American elections affects the balance of power among contending economic groups. Politicians need large amounts of money to campaign successfully for major offices. This fact inevitably ties their interests to the interests of the groups and forces that can provide this money: the affluent. In a nation as large and diverse as the United States, to be sure, campaign contributors represent many different groups and, often, clashing interests. Business groups, labor groups, environmental groups, and pro-choice and right-to-life forces all contribute millions of dollars to political campaigns. One set of trade associations may contribute millions to win politicians' support for telecommunications reform, whereas another set may contribute just as much to block the same reform efforts. Insurance companies may contribute millions of dollars to Democrats to win their support for changes in the health care system, whereas physicians may contribute equal amounts to prevent the same changes from becoming law.

Interests that donate large amounts of money to campaigns expect and often receive favorable treatment from elected officials in return for their contributions. For example, in 2000 a number of major interest groups with specific policy goals made substantial donations to the Bush presidential campaign. These included airlines, energy producers, banks, tobacco companies, and a number of others. After Bush's election, these interests pressed the new president to promote their legislative and regulatory agendas. For instance, MBNA America Bank was a major donor to the 2000 Bush campaign. The bank and its executives gave Bush $1.3 million. The bank's president helped raise millions more for Bush and personally gave an additional $100,000 to the president's inaugural committee after the election. All told, MBNA and other banking companies donated $26 million to the GOP in 2000. Within weeks of his election, President Bush signed legislation providing

MBNA and the others with something they had sought for years: bankruptcy laws making it more difficult for consumers to escape credit card debt.

Similarly, a coalition of manufacturers led by the U.S. Chamber of Commerce and the National Association of Manufacturers also provided considerable support for Bush's 2000 campaign. This coalition sought, among other things, the repeal of federal rules promulgated in 2000 by the federal Occupational Safety and Health Administration (OSHA) that were designed to protect workers from repetitive-motion injuries. Again, within weeks of his election, the president approved a resolution rejecting the rules. In the 2010 and 2012 elections a number of corporate interests and labor unions took advantage of the Supreme Court's lifting of restrictions on campaign spending to pour tens of millions of dollars into congressional races. Corporate America, for the most part, supported the GOP. Labor, particularly public-sector unions fearing job cuts under the Republicans, gave tens of millions of dollars to support Democrats.

Despite the diversity of contributors, not all interests play a role in financing political campaigns. Only those groups that have a good deal of money to spend can make their interests known in this way. The poor and the downtrodden also live in America and have a stake in the outcome of political campaigns. Who speaks for them? Who benefits from the American system of private funding of campaigns? The Internet and online campaigns offer promise for levelling the playing field in elections.

Explore Issues in Campaigning

Inform Yourself

 Consider how the electoral college system influences presidential campaign strategy. Presidential campaigns don't try to win over every voter in every state; rather, they focus on winning enough states to get to 270 votes in the electoral college. Check out www.270towin.org to see the battleground states in the 2012 election, compared to the 2008 and 2004 elections. Which states have changed? Which have stayed the same?

 Consider alternatives to the electoral college. One proposed electoral reform is called the National Popular Vote. View the video *Make Every State Purple* (www .youtube.com/watch?v=JhOZCKac6os). What are the advantages of a system based on the popular vote? What are the advantages of the electoral college system?

 Find out who pays for campaigns. Visit the *New York Times* 2012 Money Race (http://elections.nytimes.com/2012/campaign-finance) to see how much was money was raised and spent during the election. How much was raised by the candidates, the parties, and Super PACs? Visit Open Secrets via its Facebook page to see who the big spenders were in 2012. Are you surprised?

Express Yourself

 Share your thoughts on where presidential candidates should campaign. View a map of state populations using the 2010 census (http://2010.census .gov/2010census/popmap/). About a third of the population lives in one of five states (Texas, California, Florida, New York, or Illinois), yet only one of these has recently been a battleground state. The average voter in a battleground state will view nearly 300 television ads during the campaign, compared to just a half dozen in a non-swing state. Campaign ads and other campaign events help educate voters about the candidates and their policy positions. Where do you think candidates should campaign?

 Follow the money in your area. Go to Follow the Money (www.followthemoney .org) and look up how much money was spent on elections in your state in the last few years. Enter your address to find out about money spent in your legislative district, or click on the "Who represents me?" boxes to find out. Which groups or industries provide the most money to your lawmakers? With this information, consider e-mailing or calling your lawmaker to express your opinion about money in politics.

Find links to the sites listed above as well as related activities on wwnorton.com/studyspace.

study guide

Ⓢ Practice online with: Chapter 10 Diagnostic Quiz ▪ Chapter 10 Key Term Flashcards

Elections in America

⬛ **Describe the major rules and procedures of elections in the United States (pp. 381–94)**

There are four types of American elections: primary elections, general elections, runoff elections, and initiative and referendum elections. While each election operates under its own set of rules, most elections in the United States today use the Australian ballot and operate under plurality, rather than the majority or the proportional representation, system. Unlike members of the House of Representatives, who are elected through a direct vote from districts whose boundaries are usually redrawn every 10 years, presidents are elected indirectly by the electoral college.

Key Terms

midterm elections (p. 381)

primary elections (p. 382)

closed primary (p. 382)

open primary (p. 382)

general election (p. 383)

runoff election (p. 383)

majority system (p. 383)

plurality system (p. 383)

proportional representation (p. 383)

straight-ticket vote (p. 383)

coattail effect (p. 384)

redistricting (p. 385)

gerrymandering (p. 385)

majority-minority district (p. 385)

electoral college (p. 386)

caucus (political) (p. 388)

platform (p. 391)

delegate (p. 391)

superdelegate (p. 392)

ballot initiative (p. 392)

referendum (p. 392)

recall (p. 393)

Practice Quiz

1. A closed primary is a primary election in which *(p. 382)*
   a) one's vote is kept private.
   b) only registered members of the party may vote.
   c) only registered members of the party may run.
   d) only two candidates are allowed to run.
   e) voting is conducted by mail.

2. Beginning with the 1993 case *Shaw v. Reno*, the Supreme Court has *(p. 385)*
   a) generally rejected efforts to create majority-minority districts and asserted that districting based exclusively on race is unlawful.
   b) generally supported efforts to create majority-minority districts and asserted that districting based exclusively on race is lawful.
   c) generally rejected efforts to create majority-minority districts but asserted that districting based exclusively on race is lawful.
   d) generally supported efforts to reduce the amount of soft money in election campaigns.
   e) generally rejected efforts to reduce the amount of soft money in election campaigns.

3. When a voter casts a ballot for a party's presidential candidate and then "automatically" votes for the rest of that party's candidates, it is referred to as *(p. 383)*
   a) primary voting.
   b) one-way voting.
   c) proportional representation.
   d) straight-ticket voting.
   e) split-ticket voting.

4. If a state has 10 members in the U.S. House of Representatives, how many electoral votes does that state have? *(p. 386)*
   a) 2
   b) 10
   c) 12
   d) 20
   e) It cannot be determined from this information.

Election Campaigns

 Explain how campaigns are typically conducted (pp. 394–403)

In order to successfully run for political office, candidates must organize exploratory committees and create formal campaign organizations that employ a campaign manager, a media consultant, a pollster, a financial advisor, a press spokesperson, and a staff director. Although local and congressional candidates campaign by recruiting large numbers of volunteer workers, most contemporary political campaigns rely less on labor-intensive mobilizations and more on "air power" and the Internet. These activities require enormous amounts of money, and many politicians spend more time soliciting donations than engaging in anything else.

Key Terms

campaign (p. 394)

incumbernt (p. 394)

spot (advertisement) (p. 398)

town hall meeting (p. 400)

Practice Quiz

5. The average amount of money spent by House incumbents to secure re-election has *(pp. 395–97)*
   a) been surpassed by the average amount of money spent by challengers since 1980.
   b) declined to zero after the passage of the Bipartisan Campaign Reform Act in 2003.
   c) remained the same as the average amount spent by challengers since 1980.
   d) increased at a greater rate than the average amount spent by challengers since 1980.
   e) decreased at a greater rate than the average amount spent by challengers since 1980.

 Practice Online
Interactive simulation: *Running a Successful Campaign*

How Voters Decide

 Identify the major factors that influence voters' decisions (pp. 403–8)

Three factors influence the decisions that voters make at the polls: partisan loyalty, issues and policy preferences, and candidate characteristics. Partisan attachments are usually handed down from parents to children and, once formed, tend to remain an important influence on which candidates a voter chooses to support. In addition, voters consider the past and future behavior of competing parties and candidates when casting a ballot. A candidate's race, ethnicity, religion, gender, and social background are also weighed by voters on election day.

Key Terms

prospective voting (p. 406)

retrospective voting (p. 406)

Practice Quiz

6. Partisan loyalty *(p. 405)*
   a) is often handed down from parents to children.
   b) changes frequently.
   c) is currently much stronger than it was in the 1940s and 1950s.
   d) is mandated in states with closed primaries.
   e) has little impact on voting in congressional and state-level elections.

7. When a voter decides which candidate to vote for based on past performance, the voter is engaged in *(p. 406)*
   a) prospective voting.
   b) retrospective voting.
   c) the coattail effect.
   d) candidate-centered voting.
   e) ticket splitting.

8. The Consumer Confidence Index *(p. 406)*
   a) measures how business leaders rate the federal government's regulation of the economy during election years.
   b) was a federal government program designed to increase economic growth during the Reagan administration.
   c) has been an inaccurate predictor of presidential outcomes.
   d) has been a fairly accurate predictor of presidential outcomes.
   e) is based on government reports of objective economic indicators.

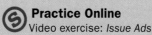 **Practice Online**
Video exercise: *Issue Ads*

The 2012 Elections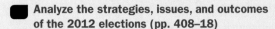

■ **Analyze the strategies, issues, and outcomes of the 2012 elections (pp. 408–18)**

In the 2012, voters re-elected Barack Obama to the presidency, and Democrats retained control of the Senate while Republicans retained control of the House of Representatives. In the primaries, Mitt Romney competed with several other candidates to win the Republican nomination for the presidency. Throughout the campaigns both parties argued that they had a better plan for addressing the economic challenges facing the nation and other issues.

Practice Quiz

9. The biggest issue in the 2012 national elections was (pp. 408–10)
   a) same-sex marriage.
   b) energy policy.
   c) abortion.
   d) the economy.
   e) Medicare.

10. During the Republican primaries, which faction within the party did Romney represent? (p. 411)
   a) social conservatives
   b) fiscal conservatives
   c) neoconservatives
   d) paleoconservatives
   e) extreme conservatives

11. In 2012, Romney and the Republicans received a majority of votes from (pp. 416–17)
   a) whites, Asian Americans, and young voters.
   b) whites, Latinos, and women.
   c) whites, men, and more affluent voters.
   d) African Americans, women, and more affluent voters.
   e) African Americans, Latinos, and young voters.

12. Which statement best characterizes the role of the Internet in the 2012 elections? (pp. 417–18)
   a) The Internet was less important than in previous elections.
   b) The Internet played a larger role than ever.
   c) The Internet was important mainly for the Democrats.
   d) The Internet was important mainly for the Republicans.
   e) Presidential candidates used the Internet as a campaign tool for the first time.

Money and Politics

■ **Describe how candidates raise the money they need to run (pp. 419–25)**

Modern political campaigns in the United States are enormously expensive and candidates with the most money usually win. Candidates finance their campaigns with money from their own bank accounts, individual donors, political action committees, political parties, and independent 527 and 501c(4) groups. The Federal Elections Campaign Act also provides for public funding of presidential campaigns.

Key Terms

political action committee (p. 420)

527 committees (p. 421)

501c(4) committees (p. 421)

Practice Quiz

14. In 2002, federal campaign finance legislation crafted by John McCain and Russell Feingold sought to (p. 422)
   a) ban soft money by prohibiting national parties from soliciting and receiving contributions from corporations, unions, or individuals.
   b) increase the amount of soft money in elections by encouraging national parties to solicit and receive contributions from corporations, unions, and individuals.
   c) ban candidates from using their own personal resources in election campaigns.
   d) give corporations the power to contribute unlimited amounts of money to influence the outcome of election campaigns.
   e) create a system of publicly financed election campaigns.

15. In *Buckley v. Valeo*, the Supreme Court ruled that (p. 425)
   a) PAC donations to campaigns are constitutionally protected.
   b) candidates cannot spend any of their own money to run for office.
   c) the right of individuals to spend their own money to campaign is constitutionally protected.
   d) the political system is corrupt.
   e) the Federal Elections Campaign Act is unconstitutional.

 Practice Online
Video exercise: *Campaign Ads and PACs*

For Further Reading

Abramson, Paul, John Aldrich, and David Rohde. *Change and Continuity in the 2008 Elections.* Washington, DC: Congressional Quarterly Press, 2009.

Ackerman, Bruce, and Ian Avres. *Voting with Dollars.* New Haven, CT: Yale University Press, 2004.

Browning, Graeme. *Electronic Democracy.* New York: Cyberage, 2002.

Ginsberg, Benjamin, and Martin Shefter. *Politics by Other Means: Institutional Conflict and the Declining Significance of Elections in America.* New York: Norton, 1999.

Heilemann, John, and Mark Halperin. *Game Change: Obama and the Clintons, McCain and Palin, and the Race of a Lifetime.* New York: Harper, 2010.

Maass, Matthias. *The World Views of the 2008 U.S. Presidential Election.* New York: Palgrave, 2009.

Nelson, Michael, ed. *The Elections of 2008.* Washington, DC: CQ Press, 2009.

Polsby, Nelson, Aaron Wildavsky, and David Hopkins. *Presidential Elections.* 12th ed. New York: Rowman and Littlefield, 2007.

Raymond, Allen, and Ian Spiegelman. *How to Rig an Election.* New York: Simon & Schuster, 2008.

Schier, Steven. *You Call This an Election?* Washington, DC: Georgetown University Press, 2003.

Wayne, Stephen. *Is This Any Way to Run a Democratic Election?* 3rd ed. Washington, DC: CQ Press, 2007.

Recommended Websites

Center for Voting and Democracy
www.fairvote.org

The Center for Voting and Democracy is dedicated to open access to voting, equal representation, and a voice for all Americans. Read about some of their electoral reform proposals such as runoff elections, proportional representation, and alternatives to the electoral college.

The Color of Money
www.colorofmoney.org

Campaign funding affects the balance of power among contending social groups in America. Politicians are tied to groups that provide them with the large amounts of money needed to campaign for major office. This website examines federal campaign contributions with a focus on race and ethnicity to show how campaign money has the potential to skew government policy decisions.

ElectionMail.com
www.electionmail.com

Are you thinking about running for office? Whether you aspire to be student government president or president of the United States, here you can find links to affordable political printing, including political brochures, campaign literature, and campaign signs.

Federal Election Commission
www.fec.gov

The Federal Election Commission (FEC) is an independent government agency that was created in 1975 to administer and enforce the Federal Election Campaign Act (FECA). At the official FEC website you can read about the rules and regulations that govern the financing of federal elections and other topics of interest.

JibJab.com
www.jibjab.com

This website became famous for its political video clips during the 2004 presidential campaign. For a good laugh check out some of the political jokes or rummage through the video archives to find one of the original Bush or Kerry clips.

MultiEducator.com
www.multied.com/elections/

MultiEducator's History Central website features a major section on elections. Here you can find the history of every U.S. national election, including popular and electoral votes, turnout, and a map of the states carried by each competing candidate.

National Archives and Records Administration
www.archives.gov/federal-register/electoral-college/index.html

The U.S. National Archives and Records Administration's Electoral College page is a great resource on presidential elections. Find answers to frequently asked questions about our electoral system, read about how electors vote, or try predicting who will win the next presidential election with the electoral college calculator.

OpenSecrets.org
www.opensecrets.org

Campaign funds come from a variety of sources, including individual donors, political action committees (PACs), self-contributions, independent spending, parties, and public funding. At this site you can research funding for all federal officials, including your own members of Congress.

Project Vote Smart
www.votesmart.org

Project Vote Smart is a nonpartisan site dedicated to providing citizens with information on political candidates and elected officials. Here you can easily view a candidate's biographical information, position on issues, and voting record, so that you can make an informed choice on Election Day.

Voter Information Services
www.vis.org

Voter Information Services (VIS) is a nonpartisan, nonprofit organization dedicated to helping interested citizens learn about their elected members of Congress. Here you can obtain a Congressional Report Card for your members of Congress and find out where they stand on the issues.

The use of "fracking" to recover gas has brought environmental groups into conflict with the energy industry. Both sides have tried to influence government regulations related to fracking.

Groups and Interests

WHAT GOVERNMENT DOES AND WHY IT MATTERS For the past several years, environmental groups and the nation's energy industry have been locked in a struggle over the issue of "hydraulic fracking." This is a method for recovering natural gas trapped in shale formations deep beneath the earth's surface. The energy industry, which stands to make enormous profits from extracting this gas, asserts that fracking is the key to achieving American energy independence. Environmental groups, on the other hand, argue that fracking produces greenhouse gas emissions, undermines air quality, and contaminates drinking water while discouraging investment in cleaner, renewable forms of energy.

Despite these environmental concerns, large sections of the United States, including tracts in New York, Pennsylvania, and Ohio, are being fracked for their natural gas. Environmental groups appear to be losing the battle. Why? The energy industry, organized in groups such as the Natural Gas Alliance, the Independent Petroleum Association of America, and the American Gas Association, has deployed an army of nearly 800 lobbyists, including former members of Congress and other former high-ranking government officials, to promote their cause on Capitol Hill and in the state capitals. The industry has also spent tens of millions of dollars on advertising and campaign contributions—filling the coffers of Democrats and Republicans alike. Even President Obama, a self-proclaimed environmentalist, was moved to declare in his 2011 State of the Union address that natural gas produced in America was an important part of America's energy future.

The case of fracking exemplifies the power of interest groups in action. Tens of thousands of organized groups have formed in the United States, ranging from civic associations to huge nationwide groups such as the National Rifle Association (NRA), whose chief cause is opposition to restrictions on gun ownership, and Common Cause, a public interest group that advocates a variety of liberal political reforms. Despite the array of interest groups in American politics, however, not all interests are represented equally, and the results of competition among various interests are not always consistent with the common good. In this chapter we will examine the nature and consequences of interest-group politics in the United States.

chaptergoals

- Describe the major types of interest groups and whom they represent (pages 435–43)

- Analyze why the number of interest groups has grown in recent decades (pages 443–45)

- Explain how interest groups try to influence government (pages 445–60)

● The Character of Interest Groups

Describe the major types of interest groups and whom they represent

The framers of the U.S. Constitution feared the power that could be wielded by organized interests. Yet they believed that interest groups thrived because of liberty— the freedom that all Americans enjoy to organize and to express their views. If the government were given the power to regulate or in any way to forbid efforts by organized interests to interpose themselves in the political process, it would in effect have the power to suppress liberty. The solution to this dilemma was presented by James Madison:

> Take in a greater variety of parties and interests [and] you make it less probable that a majority of the whole will have a common motive to invade the rights of other citizens. . . . [Hence the advantage] enjoyed by a large over a small republic.[1]

According to Madison, a good constitution encourages multitudes of interests so that no single interest, which he called a "faction," can ever tyrannize the others. The basic assumption is that all the competing interests will regulate one another, producing balance.[2] Today, this Madisonian principle is called **pluralism**. According to pluralist theory, all interests are and should be free to compete for influence in the United States. Moreover, according to pluralist doctrine, the outcome of this competition is compromise and moderation, since no group is likely to be able to achieve any of its goals without accommodating itself to some of the views of its many competitors.[3]

An **interest group** is an organized group of people that makes policy-related appeals to government. This definition of interest groups includes membership organizations as well as businesses, corporations, universities, and other institutions that restrict membership to particular occupational groups or other categories of persons. Individuals form groups in order to increase the chance that their views

pluralism the theory that all interests are and should be free to compete for influence in the government. The outcome of this competition is compromise and moderation

interest group individuals who organize to influence the government's programs and policies

As long as there is government, there will be interests trying to influence it. During the 1890s, for instance, business interests fought for protective tariffs from Congress and President McKinley. This 1897 cartoon satirizes their success in capturing Congress.

Public interest groups often advocate for interests that are not addressed by traditional lobbies. For example, in addition to many other activities, the Public Interest Research Group (PIRG) publishes an annual toy safety report to help protect consumers and to encourage policymakers to address problems in this area.

will be heard and their interests treated favorably by the government. Interest groups are sometimes referred to as "lobbies." They are also sometimes confused with political action committees, which are actually groups that focus on influencing elections rather than trying to influence the elected (see Chapter 10). One final distinction is that interest groups are also different from political parties: interest groups tend to concern themselves with the *policies* of government; parties tend to concern themselves with the *personnel* of government.

The number of interest groups in the United States is enormous, and millions of Americans are members of one or more groups, at least to the extent of paying dues or attending an occasional meeting. By representing the interests of such large numbers of people and encouraging political participation, organized groups can and do enhance American democracy. Organized groups educate and mobilize their members for elections and grassroots lobbying efforts, thus encouraging participation. Groups lobby members of Congress and the executive, engage in litigation, and generally represent their members' interests in the political arena. Interest groups also monitor government programs to make certain that their members are not adversely affected by these programs. In all these ways, organized interests can be said to promote democratic politics. But because not all interests are represented equally, interest-group politics works to the advantage of some and the disadvantage of others.

It is also important to remember that not all organized interests are successful. Struggles among interest groups have winners and losers, and even large groups well represented in Washington are sometimes defeated in political struggle. In recent years, for example, despite relentless lobbying, physicians' groups such as the American Medical Association (AMA) have been unable to persuade Congress to increase Medicare funding for physicians' services. One reason for this failure is that physicians are forced to compete for funding with insurers, drug companies, and hospitals. The doctors have simply been overmatched.

Common Types of Interest Groups

Business and Agricultural Groups Interest groups come in as many shapes and sizes as the interests they represent. The most obvious are groups with a direct economic interest in governmental actions. These groups are generally supported by groups of producers or manufacturers in a particular economic sector, such as the American Fuel and Petrochemical Manufacturers and the American Farm Bureau Federation. In addition to these broadly representative groups, specific companies, such as Exxon, IBM, and General Motors, may be active in Washington on certain issues that are of particular concern to them.

Labor Groups Labor organizations are equally active lobbyists. The AFL-CIO, the United Mine Workers, and the Teamsters all lobby on behalf of organized labor. In recent years, groups have arisen to further the interests of public employees, the most significant among these being the American Federation of State, County, and Municipal Employees (AFSCME).

Professional Associations Professional lobbies such as the American Bar Association and the AMA have been particularly successful at furthering their members' interests in state and federal legislatures. Financial institutions, represented by organizations such as the American Bankers Association and the National Savings and Loan League, although often less visible than other lobbies, also play an important role in shaping legislative policy.

Public Interest Groups Recent years have witnessed the growth of a powerful "public interest" lobby, purporting to represent the general good rather than its own selfish interests. **Public interest groups** have been most visible in the consumer protection and environmental policy areas, although public interest groups cover a broad range of issues. The Natural Resources Defense Council, the Sierra Club, the Union of Concerned Scientists, and Common Cause are all examples of public interest groups. Claims to represent *only* the public interest should be viewed with caution, however: it is not uncommon to find decidedly private interests seeking to hide behind the term *public interest*. For example, the benign-sounding Partnership to Protect Consumer Credit is a coalition of credit card companies fighting for less federal regulation of credit abuses, and Project Protect is a coalition of logging interests promoting increased timber cutting.[4]

Ideological Groups Closely related to and overlapping public interest groups are ideological groups, organized in support of a particular political or philosophical perspective. People for the American Way, for example, promotes liberal values, whereas the Christian Coalition focuses on conservative social goals, and the National Taxpayers Union campaigns to reduce the size of the federal government.

Public-Sector Groups The perceived need for representation on Capitol Hill has generated a public-sector lobby in the past several years, including the National League of Cities and the "research" lobby. The latter group comprises think tanks and universities that have an interest in obtaining government funds for research and support, and it includes such diverse institutions as Harvard University, the Brookings Institution, and the American Enterprise Institute. Indeed, universities have expanded their lobbying efforts even as they have reduced faculty positions and course offerings.[5]

What Interests Are Not Represented?

It is difficult to categorize unrepresented interests precisely because they are not organized and are not able to present to us (or governments) their identity and their demands. The political scientist David Truman referred to these interests as "potential interest groups."[6] And he is undoubtedly correct that at any time, as long as there is freedom, any interest shared by a lot of people can develop through "voluntary association" into a genuine interest group that can demand, usually successfully, to get some representation. But the fact remains that many interests—including some very widely shared interests—do not get organized and recognized. Such "potential interests" might include everything from the homeless through tall people.

Organizational Components

Although interest groups are many and varied, most share certain key organizational components. These include leadership, money, an agency or office, and members.

public interest groups groups that claim they serve the general good rather than only their own particular interest

Do Foreign Interests Exert Influence in the United States?

Discussions of interest groups often focus on the efforts of competing domestic forces—business, labor, public interest groups, and so on—to influence the government. Often, however, foreign interests and foreign governments also lobby vigorously to influence U.S. policy. Much of this lobbying is undertaken by foreign firms hoping to do business in the United States or directly with the U.S. government on favorable terms. For example, every year, Americans purchase billions of dollars of goods manufactured in China. In some instances, these Chinese products fail to comply with American health and safety standards, leading to demands that the United States restrict Chinese imports. To protect their access to the U.S. market, Chinese firms, like those in many other countries, retain the services of international trade lobbyists. These lobbyists guide foreign firms through the intricacies of U.S. laws and customs and introduce foreign executives to American power brokers, movers, and shakers. Some see American citizens who work as international trade lobbyists as corporate traitors, but American lobbyists and their counterparts in other countries play an important role in promoting world trade and diminishing international rivalries.

Questions of loyalty are also often raised by the activities of another form of foreign lobby in the United States: the ethnic lobby. Many Americans retain a sense of identification with their family's country of origin or with those who share their religion in another country. Individuals with such ethnic or religious ties to another country are often willing to lobby vigorously on that country's behalf. The best-known case is that of the pro-Israel lobby. Through such organizations as AIPAC, the American Israel Public Affairs Committee, some Jewish Americans have worked to secure American

military, financial, and economic support for Israel since that nation's founding. Largely because of the pro-Israel lobby's activities, Israel is the largest recipient of American foreign aid and is usually supported by the United States in its conflicts with the Arab nations of the Middle East. Interestingly, Jewish Americans are not the only pro-Israel lobbyists. Israel is also strongly supported by so-called Christian Zionists, evangelical Protestants who see Israel's existence as the fulfillment of biblical prophecy.

In addition to the pro-Israel lobby, a number of other ethnic lobbies are active in Washington. Americans from the Indian subcontinent have lobbied effectively for the improvement of U.S.-Indian relations. Some Irish Americans have lobbied against British rule in Northern Ireland. Recently, despite a good deal of lobbying by Armenian Americans, Congress failed to pass a resolution condemning the murder of hundreds of thousands of Armenians by Turkish forces between 1914 and 1917. Turkey, an important U.S. military ally, was able to defeat the resolution with a lobbying campaign of its own.

Often, lobbying by foreign firms and governments is accompanied by extensive public-relations campaigns. One foreign government that lobbies vigorously in the United States and also spends tens of millions of dollars each year on public relations is the Kingdom of Saudi Arabia. For example, in a recent issue of *The New Republic*—a magazine read mainly by upper-middle-class professionals and intellectuals in New York, Washington,

and Boston—the Kingdom of Saudi Arabia sponsored a full-page ad promoting its efforts to combat terrorism.[a]

In point of fact, however, the Saudi government's long-standing practice has been to subsidize and support Islamic radicals as long as they do not make trouble within Saudi Arabia.[b] The Saudi ad campaign is designed to gloss over this rather embarrassing and politically inconvenient fact.

[a]*New Republic*, December 5, 2005, back cover.
[b]Craig Unger, *House of Bush, House of Saud* (New York: Scribner's, 2004).

forcriticalanalysis

1. Should foreign firms be allowed to lobby in the United States?
2. Is it un-American or disloyal for ethnic and religious groups to lobby on behalf of a foreign country with which they identify?

First, every group must have a leadership and decision-making structure. For some groups, this structure is very simple. For others, it can be quite elaborate and involve hundreds of local chapters that are melded into a national apparatus. Interest-group leadership is, in some respects, analogous to business leadership. Many interest groups are initially organized by political entrepreneurs with a strong commitment to a particular set of goals. Such entrepreneurs see the formation of a group as a means both for achieving those goals and for enhancing their own influence in the political process. And just as is true in the business world, successful groups often become bureaucratized; the initial entrepreneurial leadership is replaced by a paid professional staff. In the 1960s, for example, Ralph Nader led a ragtag band of consumer advocates (Nader's Raiders) in a crusade for product safety that resulted in the enactment of numerous laws and regulations, such as the requirement that all new cars be equipped with seat belts. Today, Nader remains active in the consumer movement, and his loosely organized band of raiders has been transformed into a well-organized and well-financed phalanx of interlocking groups led by professional staff.

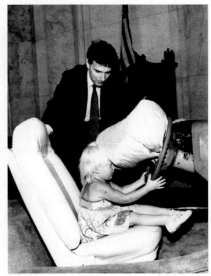

Although there have always been groups trying to influence the government, since the 1960s the number of organized interests in Washington, D.C., has increased substantially. For instance, the consumer activist Ralph Nader, shown here at a demonstration in support of mandatory airbags in cars, founded a network of consumer advocacy groups.

Second, every interest group must build a financial structure capable of sustaining an organization and funding the group's activities. Most interest groups rely on membership dues and voluntary contributions from sympathizers. Many also sell some ancillary services to members, such as insurance and vacation tours. Third, most groups establish an agency that actually carries out the group's tasks. This may be a research organization, a public relations office, or a lobbying office in Washington or a state capital.

Finally, almost all interest groups must attract and keep members. Somehow, groups must persuade individuals to invest the money, time, energy, or effort required to take part in the group's activities. Members play a larger role in some groups than in others. In **membership associations**, group members actually serve on committees and engage in projects. In the case of labor unions, members may march on picket lines; in the case of political or ideological groups, members may participate in demonstrations and protests. In another set of groups, **staff organizations**, a professional staff conducts most of the group's activities; members are called on only to pay dues and make other contributions. Among the well-known public interest groups, some, such as the National Organization for Women (NOW), are membership groups; others, such as Defenders of Wildlife and the Children's Defense Fund, are staff organizations.

membership association
an organized group in which members actually play a substantial role, sitting on committees and engaging in group projects

staff organization a type of membership group in which a professional staff conducts most of the group's activities

The Characteristics of Members Membership in interest groups is not randomly distributed in the population. People with higher incomes, higher levels of education, and management or professional occupations are much more likely to become members of groups than are those who occupy the lower rungs on the socioeconomic ladder.[7] Well-educated, upper-income business and professional people are more likely to have the time, money, concerns, and skills needed to play a role in a group or association. Moreover, for business and professional people, group membership may provide personal contacts and access to information that can help advance their careers. At the same time, of course, corporate entities—businesses and the like—usually have ample resources to form or participate in groups that seek to advance their interests.

The result is that interest-group politics in the United States tends to have a very pronounced upper-class bias. Certainly, many interest groups and political associations have a working-class or lower-class membership—labor organizations

The NRA is a group that promotes the interests of gun owners. In addition to lobbying the government, the NRA offers members a wide range of services, from providing information about gun laws to organizing gun shows.

or welfare-rights organizations, for example—but the great majority of interest groups and their members is drawn from the middle and upper-middle classes. In general, the "interests" served by interest groups are the interests of society's "haves." Even when interest groups take opposing positions on issues and policies, the conflicting positions they espouse usually reflect divisions among upper-income strata rather than conflicts between the upper and lower classes.

In general, to obtain adequate political representation, forces from the bottom rungs of the socioeconomic ladder must be organized on the massive scale associated with political parties. Parties can organize and mobilize the collective energies of large numbers of people who, as individuals, may have very limited resources. Interest groups, on the other hand, generally organize smaller numbers of the better-to-do. Thus, the relative importance of political parties and interest groups in American politics has far-ranging implications for the distribution of political power in the United States. In recent years, interest groups, as we shall see in the section "The Proliferation of Groups," have become much more numerous, more active, and more influential in American politics, with lobby groups and super PACs playing major roles in Congress and in electoral politics.

The "Free Rider" Problem Whether they need individuals to volunteer or merely to write checks, both types of groups need to recruit and retain members. Yet many groups find this task difficult, even when it comes to recruiting members who agree strongly with the group's goals. Why? As the economist Mancur Olson explains, the benefits of a group's success are often broadly available and cannot be denied to nonmembers.[8] Such benefits can be called **collective goods**. This term is usually associated with certain government benefits, but it can also be applied to beneficial outcomes of interest-group activity.

Olson offers this example: suppose a number of private property owners live near a mosquito-infested swamp. Each owner wants this swamp cleared. But if one or a few of the owners were to clear the swamp alone, their actions would benefit all the other owners as well, without any effort on the part of those other owners. Each of the inactive owners would be a **free rider** on the efforts of the ones who

collective goods benefits, sought by groups, that are broadly available and cannot be denied to nonmembers

free riders those who enjoy the benefits of collective goods but did not participate in acquiring them

cleared the swamp. Thus, there is a disincentive for any of the owners to undertake the job alone. Since the number of concerned owners is small in this particular case, they might eventually be able to organize themselves to share the costs as well as to enjoy the benefits of clearing the swamp.

But suppose the number of interested people is increased. Suppose the common concern is not the neighborhood swamp but polluted air or groundwater involving thousands of residents in a region, or in fact millions of residents in a whole nation. National defense is the most obvious collective good whose benefits are shared by all residents, regardless of the taxes they pay or the support they provide. As the number of involved persons increases, or as the size of the group increases, the free rider phenomenon becomes more of a problem. The group would no doubt be more influential if all concerned individuals were active members—if there were no free riders.

Why Join? Individuals do not have much incentive to become active members and supporters of a group that is already working more or less on their behalf. But groups do not reduce their efforts just because free riders get the same benefits as dues-paying activists. In fact, groups may try even harder precisely because there are free riders, with the hope that the free riders will be encouraged to join in, often by the lure of various "selective benefits" available only to group members. These benefits can be informational, material, solidary, or purposive. Of course, groups sometimes offer combinations of benefits. A community association, for example, can offer its members a sense of belonging (solidary benefit), involvement in community decision making (purposive benefit), and reduced rates on home-owners' insurance (material benefit). Table 11.1 gives some examples of the range of benefits in each of these categories.

forcriticalanalysis

Could college students be organized as an interest group? What would such a group advocate? What might be some impediments to the creation of a National Organization of College Students?

TABLE 11.1

Selective Benefits of Interest-Group Membership

CATEGORY	BENEFITS
Informational benefits	Conferences Professional contacts Training programs Publications Coordination among organizations Research Legal help Professional codes Collective bargaining
Material benefits	Travel packages Insurance Discounts on consumer goods
Solidary benefits	Friendship Networking opportunities
Purposive benefits	Advocacy Representation before government Participation in public affairs

SOURCE: Adapted from Jack Walker Jr., *Mobilizing Interest Groups in America: Patrons, Professions, and Social Movements* (Ann Arbor: University of Michigan Press, 1991), p. 86.

informational benefits special newsletters, periodicals, training programs, conferences, and other information provided to members of groups to entice others to join

material benefits special goods, services, or money provided to members of groups to entice others to join

solidary benefits selective benefits of group membership that emphasize friendship, networking, and consciousness raising

purposive benefits selective benefits of group membership that emphasize the purpose and accomplishments of the group

Informational benefits are the most widespread and important category of selective benefits offered to group members. Information is provided through conferences, training programs, and newsletters and other periodicals sent automatically to those who have paid membership dues. **Material benefits** include anything that can be measured monetarily, such as discount purchasing, shared advertising, and, perhaps most valuable of all, health and retirement insurance. **Solidary benefits** include the friendship and networking opportunities that membership provides. Extremely important to many of the newer nonprofit and citizen groups is "consciousness raising." One example of this can be seen in the claims of many women's organizations that active participation conveys to each member an enhanced sense of her own value and a stronger ability to advance individual as well as collective rights. Members of associations based on ethnicity, race, or religion also derive solidary benefits from interacting with individuals they perceive as sharing their own backgrounds, values, and perspectives.

A fourth type of benefit involves the appeal of the purpose of an interest group. An example of these **purposive benefits** is businesses' joining trade associations to further their economic interests. Similarly, individuals join consumer, environmental, or other civic groups to pursue goals important to them. Many of the most successful interest groups of the past 20 years have been citizen groups or public interest groups organized largely around shared ideological goals, including government reform, election and campaign reform, civil rights, economic equality, "family values," and even opposition to government itself.

AARP and the Benefits of Membership One group that has been extremely successful in recruiting members and mobilizing them for political action is AARP. The organization was founded as the American Association of Retired Persons in 1958 as a result of the efforts of a retired California high school principal, Ethel Percy Andrus, to find affordable health insurance for herself and the thousands of members of the National Retired Teachers Association (NRTA). In 1955 she found an insurer who was willing to give NRTA members a low group rate. In 1958, partly at the urging of the insurer (who found that insuring the elderly was quite profitable), Andrus founded AARP. For the insurer, it provided an expanded market; for Andrus, it was a way to serve the ever-growing elderly population, whose problems and needs were expanding along with their numbers and their life expectancy.

Today, AARP is a large and powerful organization with 38 million members and an annual income of $900 million. In addition, the organization receives $90 million in federal grants. Its national headquarters in Washington, D.C., staffed by nearly 3,000 full-time employees, is so large that it has its own zip code. Its monthly periodical, *AARP: The Magazine*, has a circulation larger than that of America's leading newsmagazines.[9]

How did this large organization overcome the free rider problem and recruit 38 million older people as members? First, no other organization on earth has ever more successfully provided the selective benefits necessary to overcome the free rider problem. It helps that AARP began as an organization to provide affordable health insurance for aging members rather than as an organization to influence public policy. But that fact only strengthens the argument that members need short-term individual benefits if they are to invest effort in a longer-term and less concrete set of benefits. As AARP evolved into a political interest group, its leadership added more selective benefits for individual members. It provided guidance against consumer fraud, offered low-interest credit cards, evaluated and endorsed products that were deemed valuable to members, and provided auto insurance and a discounted mail-order pharmacy.

In a group as large as AARP, members are bound to disagree on particular subjects, often creating serious factional disputes. But the resources of AARP are so extensive that its leadership has been able to mobilize itself for each issue of importance to the group. One of its most successful methods of mobilization for political action is the "telephone tree," with which AARP leaders can quickly mobilize thousands of members for and against proposals that affect Social Security, Medicare, and other questions of security for the aging. A "telephone tree" in each state enables the state AARP chair to phone all of the AARP district directors, who then can phone the presidents of the dozens of local chapters, who can call their local officers and individual members. Within 24 hours, thousands of individual AARP members can be contacting local, state, and national officials to express their opposition to proposed legislation. It is no wonder that AARP is respected and feared throughout Washington. In 2009, AARP's endorsement of the health care bill proposed by the House leadership convinced many wavering members of Congress to support the bill rather than risk offending such a powerful lobby group.

● The Proliferation of Groups

> **Analyze why the number of interest groups has grown in recent decades**

Interest groups and concerns about them are not new phenomena. As long as there is government, as long as government makes policies that add value or impose costs, and as long as there is liberty to organize, interest groups will abound; and if government expands, so will interest groups. There was, for example, a spurt of growth in the national government during the 1880s and '90s, arising largely from the first government efforts at economic intervention to fight large monopolies and to regulate some aspects of interstate commerce. In the latter decade, a parallel spurt of growth occurred in national interest groups, including the imposing National Association of Manufacturers (NAM) and numerous other trade associations. Many groups organized around specific agricultural commodities as well. This period also marked the beginning of the expansion of trade unions as interest groups. Later, in the 1930s, interest groups with headquarters and representation in Washington began to grow significantly, concurrent with that decade's historic and sustained expansion within the national government (see Chapter 3).

Over the past decades, there has been an even greater increase both in the number of interest groups seeking to play a role in the American political process and in the extent of their opportunity to influence that process. This explosion of interest-group activity has two basic origins: first, the expansion of the role of government during this period, and second, the coming-of-age of a new and dynamic set of political forces in the United States—forces that have relied heavily on "public interest" groups to advance their causes.

The Expansion of Government

Modern governments' extensive economic and social programs have powerful politicizing effects, often sparking the organization of new groups and interests. The activities of organized groups are usually viewed in terms of their effects on governmental action. But interest-group activity is often as much a consequence as an antecedent of governmental programs. Even when national policies begin as responses to the appeals of pressure groups, government involvement in any area can be a powerful stimulus for political organization and action by those whose interests are affected. For example, during the 1970s, expanded federal regulation of the automobile, oil, gas, education, and health care industries impelled each of these interests to increase substantially its efforts to influence the government's behavior. These efforts, in turn, spurred the organization of other groups to augment or counter the activities of the first.[10] Similarly, federal social programs have occasionally sparked political organization and action on the part of clientele groups seeking to influence the distribution of benefits and, in turn, the organization of groups opposed to the programs or their cost. For example, federal programs and court decisions in such areas as abortion and school prayer sparked political organization and action by fundamentalist religious groups. Thus, the expansion of government in recent decades has also stimulated increased group activity and organization.

The New Politics Movement and Public Interest Groups

The second factor accounting for the explosion of interest-group activity in recent years has been the emergence of a new set of forces in American politics that can collectively be called the New Politics movement.

The **New Politics movement** is made up of upper-middle-class professionals and intellectuals for whom the civil rights and antiwar movements were formative experiences, just as the Great Depression and World War II had been for their parents. The crusade against racial discrimination and the Vietnam War led these young men and women to see themselves as a political force, and in more recent years they have focused attention on issues such as environmental protection, women's rights, and nuclear disarmament.

New Politics movement a political movement that began in the 1960s and '70s, made up of professionals and intellectuals for whom the civil rights and antiwar movements were formative experiences. The New Politics movement strengthened public interest groups

NOW (the National Organization for Women) emerged from the New Politics movement. Founded in 1966, the group continues to lobby government on issues such as abortion, gender discrimination, and economic rights. In 2012, NOW members held a vigil to mark the 39th anniversary of the Roe v. Wade *decision.*

Members of the New Politics movement founded or strengthened public interest groups such as Common Cause, the Sierra Club, the Environmental Defense Fund, Physicians for Social Responsibility, and NOW. New Politics forces were able to influence the media, Congress, and even the judiciary, and enjoyed a remarkable degree of success during the late 1960s and early 1970s in securing the enactment of policies they favored. New Politics activists played a major role in securing the enactment of environmental, consumer, and occupational health and safety legislation.

Among the factors contributing to the rise and success of New Politics forces was technology. In the 1970s and '80s, computerized direct-mail campaigns allowed public interest groups to reach hundreds of thousands of potential sympathizers and contributors. Today, the Internet and e-mail serve the same function even more efficiently. Electronic communication allows relatively small groups to identify their adherents and mobilize them throughout the nation.

● Strategies: The Quest for Political Power

Explain how interest groups try to influence government

Interest groups work to improve the likelihood that they and their policy interests will be heard and treated favorably by all branches and levels of the government. The quest for political influence or power takes many forms. Insider strategies include access to key decision makers and use of the courts. Outsider strategies include going public and using electoral politics. These strategies do not exhaust all the possibilities, but they paint a broad picture of ways that groups use their resources in the fierce competition for power (see Figure 11.1).

Many groups employ a mix of insider and outsider strategies. For example, environmental groups such as the Sierra Club lobby members of Congress and key congressional staff members; participate in bureaucratic rule making by offering comments and suggestions to agencies on new environmental rules; and bring lawsuits under various environmental acts such as the Endangered Species Act, which authorizes groups and citizens to come to court if they believe the act is being violated. At the same time, the Sierra Club attempts to influence public opinion through media campaigns and to influence electoral politics by supporting candidates who it believes share its environmental views and by opposing candidates it views as foes of environmentalism.

Direct Lobbying

Lobbying is an attempt by a group to influence the policy process through persuasion of government officials. Most Americans tend to believe that interest groups exert their influence through direct contact with members of Congress, but lobbying encompasses a broad range of activities that groups engage in with all sorts of government officials and the public as a whole.

The 1946 Federal Regulation of Lobbying Act defines a lobbyist as "any person who shall engage himself for pay or any consideration for the purpose of attempting to influence the passage or defeat of any legislation of the Congress of the United States." The 1995 Lobbying Disclosure Act requires all organizations employing

lobbying a strategy by which organized interests seek to influence the passage of legislation by exerting direct pressure on members of the legislature

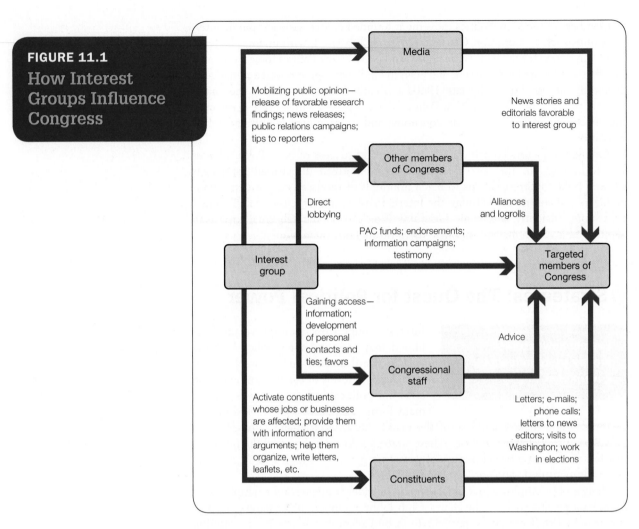

FIGURE 11.1
How Interest Groups Influence Congress

Media

Mobilizing public opinion—release of favorable research findings; news releases; public relations campaigns; tips to reporters

News stories and editorials favorable to interest group

Other members of Congress

Direct lobbying

Alliances and logrolls

PAC funds; endorsements; information campaigns; testimony

Interest group

Targeted members of Congress

Gaining access—information; development of personal contacts and ties; favors

Advice

Congressional staff

Activate constituents whose jobs or businesses are affected; provide them with information and arguments; help them organize, write letters, leaflets, etc.

Letters; e-mails; phone calls; letters to news editors; visits to Washington; work in elections

Constituents

lobbyists to register with Congress and to disclose whom they represent, whom they lobby, what they are looking for, and how much they are paid. More than 12,000 lobbyists are currently registered.[11]

Lobbying involves a great deal of activity on the part of someone speaking for an interest, and lobbyists attempt to influence the policy process in a variety of ways.[12] Lobbyists badger and buttonhole legislators, administrators, and committee staff members with facts about pertinent issues and facts or claims about public support of certain issues or facts.[13] They often testify on behalf of their clients at congressional committee and agency hearings. Lobbyists talk to reporters, place ads in newspapers, and organize letter-writing and e-mail campaigns. They also play an important role in fund-raising, helping to direct clients' contributions to members of Congress and presidential candidates.

Further, sophisticated lobbyists win influence by providing information about policies to busy members of Congress. As one lobbyist noted, "You can't get access without knowledge. . . . I can go in to see [the former Energy and Commerce Committee chair] John Dingell, but if I have nothing to offer or nothing to say, he's not going to want to see me."[14] In 1978, during debate on a bill to expand the requirement for lobbying disclosures, the Democratic senators Edward Kennedy of Massachusetts and Dick Clark of Iowa joined with the Republican senator Robert Stafford of Vermont to issue the following statement: "Government without lobbying could not function. The flow of information to Congress and to every federal agency is a vital part of our democratic system."[15]

Lobbying Congress Traditionally, the term *lobbyist* referred mainly to individuals who sought to influence the passage of legislation in the Congress. The First Amendment to the Constitution provides for the right to "petition the Government for a redress of grievances." But as early as the 1870s, *lobbying* became the common term for petitioning. And since petitioning cannot take place on the floor of the House or Senate, petitioners must therefore confront members of Congress in the lobbies of the legislative chamber—hence the term *lobbying.*

The influence of lobbyists, in many instances, is based on personal relationships and the behind-the-scenes services they are able to perform for lawmakers. Many of Washington's top lobbyists have close ties to important members of Congress or were themselves important political figures, thus virtually guaranteeing that their clients will have direct access to congressional leaders. According to the Capitol Hill newspaper, *The Hill*, examples include Jim Blanchard of DLA Piper, who was a governor of Michigan; Chuck Brain of Capitol Hill Strategies, who worked in the White House Legislative Affairs office under President Clinton; Alfonse D'Amato of Park Strategies, who was a senator from New York; Mitchell Feuer of the Rich Feuer Group, who was counsel to the Senate Banking Committee; and Broderick Johnson of Bryan Cave, who was a senior aide in the Clinton White House. The list goes on.[16] Some important lobbyists have more than a business relationship to lawmakers: quite a few, in fact, are married to prominent political figures. For example, Linda Daschle of LHD and Associates is the wife of former Senate majority leader Tom Daschle, and Hadassah Lieberman, wife of Senator Joseph Lieberman, was for many years a lobbyist for the pharmaceutical industry.

Corporate interests endeavor to be strategic in their choice of lobbyists, often hiring lobbyists whom they know to be key fund-raisers for the politicians they hope to influence. In so doing, they are not making a campaign contribution that would have to be reported to the Federal Election Commission but are nevertheless seeking to ensure that the lobbyist promoting their interests will be seen by the targeted politician as an important source of campaign money. For example, a coalition of television networks seeking to loosen rules governing their ownership of local TV stations hired Gregg Hartley as their lobbyist. Hartley, formerly a top aide to former House Majority Whip Roy Blunt, whose support the coalition sought, was one of Blunt's top fund-raisers. Companies hiring Hartley to lobby for them were almost certain of receiving a positive reception from Blunt. Many members of Congress list lobbyists as treasurers of their re-election committees,[17] and, in turn, many of Washington's lobbyists also serve as campaign treasurers and major fund-raisers for political candidates.[18] Lobbyists such as Peter Hart, Tommy Boggs, Peter Knight, Ken Duberstein, and Vin Weber are influential, in part, because of their ability to raise money for politicians. Several members of the powerful House Appropriations Committee sponsor political action committees headed by lobbyists with business before the committee.[19]

POLITICAL MARKET.

Concern about business having too much influence in Washington dates back to the early days of the country. Here, a mid-nineteenth-century cartoon lampoons the ease with which corporate executives could bribe politicians.

In 2008, the Senate Commerce and Labor Committee heard from lobbyists for the "payday loan" industry, which offers small loans at very high interest rates. Public advocacy groups complained that the payday lenders were taking advantage of consumers and should be regulated more closely by government. Lobbyists for the lenders argued that the industry provides a beneficial service to consumers and does not need stricter regulation.

Through their lobbyists, interest groups also have substantial influence in setting the legislative agenda. They help to craft specific language in legislation and build broader coalitions and comprehensive campaigns around particular policy issues.[20] These coalitions do not rise from the grass roots but instead are put together by Washington lobbyists who launch comprehensive lobbying campaigns that combine simulated grassroots activity with information and campaign funding for members of Congress. In recent years, the Republican leadership worked so closely with lobbyists that critics charged that the boundaries between lobbyists and legislators had been erased and that lobbyists had become "adjunct staff to the Republican leadership."[21]

What happens to interests that do not engage in extensive lobbying? They often find themselves "Microsofted," that is, marginalized in the political process. In 1998 the software giant was facing antitrust action from the Justice Department and had few friends in Congress. One member of the House, Representative Billy Tauzin (R-La.), told Microsoft's chairman, Bill Gates, that without an extensive investment in lobbying, the corporation would continue to be "demonized." Gates responded by quadrupling Microsoft's lobbying expenditures and hiring a group of lobbyists with strong ties to Congress. The result was congressional pressure on the Justice Department resulting in a settlement of the Microsoft suit on terms favorable to the company.

Similarly, in 1999, members of Congress advised Wal-Mart that its efforts to win approval to operate savings and loans in its stores were doomed to failure if the retailer did not greatly increase its lobbying efforts. "They don't give money. They don't have congressional representation—so nobody here cares about them," said one influential member. Like Microsoft, Wal-Mart learned its lesson, hired more lobbyists, and got what it wanted.[22] By 2005, Wal-Mart had become a seasoned political player, creating a "war room" in its Arkansas headquarters. Staffed by a phalanx of veteran political operatives from both parties, the war room is the nerve center of the giant retailer's lobbying and public relations efforts.[23] Today, Wal-Mart spends about $5 million a year on its lobbying efforts.

Lobbying the President So many individuals and groups clamor for the president's time and attention that only the most skilled and best-connected members of the lobbying community can hope to influence presidential decisions. Typically, a president's key political advisers and fund-raisers will include individuals with ties to the lobbying industry who can help their friends gain access to the White House. For example, one of President George W. Bush's top fund-raisers was Tom Kuhn, a Washington lobbyist representing the electric power industry. Kuhn, also the president's personal friend and college classmate, was able to prevent the Environmental Protection Agency (EPA) from imposing new controls on electric power plant emissions of mercury, representing a savings of hundreds of millions of dollars for the industry.

During the 2008 presidential campaign, Barack Obama said, "Lobbyists won't find a job in my White House." Soon after his election, however, Obama appointed David Axelrod as his senior adviser. Before joining the Obama campaign and administration, Axelrod was a partner in ASK Public Strategies, a consulting group that had helped the giant Illinois utility Commonwealth Edison obtain a major

Interest groups may also try to influence the president's decisions. In 2009, President Obama met with business leaders to discuss how a new health care policy would affect their employees' health insurance plans.

rate hike. At least 30 other senior Obama administration officials have a lobbying background.[24] The lobbying industry is so much a part of Washington that it probably would have been impossible for the president to keep his campaign pledge.

Lobbying the Executive Branch Even when an interest group is very successful at getting its bill passed by Congress and signed by the president, the prospect of full and faithful implementation of that law is not guaranteed. Often a group and its allies do not pack up and go home as soon as the president turns their lobbied-for new law over to the appropriate agency. In some respects, interest-group access to the executive branch is promoted by federal law. The Administrative Procedure Act, first enacted in 1946 and frequently amended in subsequent years, requires most federal agencies to provide notice and an opportunity for comment before implementing proposed new rules and regulations. This "notice and comment rulemaking" is designed to allow interests an opportunity to make their views known and to participate in the implementation of federal legislation that affects them. In 1990, Congress enacted the Negotiated Rulemaking Act to encourage administrative agencies to engage in direct and open negotiations with affected interests when developing new regulations. These two pieces of legislation—which have been strongly enforced by the federal courts—have played an important role in opening the bureaucratic process to interest-group influence. Today, few federal agencies would consider attempting to implement a new rule without consulting affected interests, known in Washington as "stakeholders."[25]

Cultivating Access

In 2005 a prominent Washington lobbyist, Jack Abramoff, was indicted on numerous charges of fraud and violations of federal lobbying laws. During the investigation of his activities, it was revealed that Abramoff, along with his associate Michael Scanlon, had collected tens of millions of dollars from several American Indian tribes that operated lucrative gambling casinos. (Indian gambling is currently a $16 billion industry in the United States.) What Abramoff provided in exchange was access to key Republican members of Congress, who helped his clients shut down rival casino operators. Abramoff was closely associated with several House members, including the former House majority leader Tom DeLay as well as senators John Cornyn, Conrad Burns, and David Vitter. Millions of tribal dollars apparently found their way into the campaign war chests of Abramoff's friends in Congress. Thus, through a well-connected lobbyist, money had effectively purchased access and influence. Abramoff and several of his associates subsequently pleaded guilty to federal bribery and fraud charges, and Abramoff was sentenced to more than five years in prison.

This photo from 2002 was introduced as evidence in the 2006 Abramoff case. It shows the lobbyist Jack Abramoff (left) with Senator Bob Ney (right) and the GSA chief of staff David Safavian (second from right) on a luxurious golf trip to Scotland that was arranged by Abramoff.

In a similar vein, GOP representative Randy "Duke" Cunningham of California was found guilty of accepting $2.4 million in bribes from a defense contractor. Cunningham allegedly used his position on a defense appropriations subcommittee to funnel millions of dollars in contracts to the firm. In 2009, Democratic representative William Jefferson of Louisiana acquired considerable notoriety when FBI agents found $90,000 hidden in the congressman's freezer. He was later found guilty of accepting bribes.

For the most part, though, access to decision makers does not require bribes or other forms of illegal activity. In many areas, interest groups, government agencies, and congressional committees routinely work together for mutual benefit. The interest group provides campaign contributions for members of Congress, and it lobbies for larger budgets for the agency. The agency, in turn, provides government contracts for the interest group and constituency services for friendly members of Congress. The congressional committee or subcommittee, meanwhile, supports the agency's budgetary requests and the programs the interest group favors. This so-called **iron triangle** has one angle in an executive branch program, another angle in a Senate or House legislative committee or subcommittee, and a third angle in some highly stable and well-organized interest group. The angles in the triangular relationship are mutually supporting; they count as access only if they last over a long period of time. For example, access to a legislative committee or subcommittee requires that at least one committee member support the interest group in question. This member also must have built up considerable seniority in Congress. An interest cannot feel comfortable about its access to Congress until it has one or more of its "own" people with 10 or more years of continuous service on the relevant committee or subcommittee. Figure 11.2 illustrates one of the most important iron triangles in recent American political history: that of the defense industry.

A number of important policy domains, such as the environmental and welfare arenas, are controlled not by highly structured and unified iron triangles but by broader **issue networks**. These networks consist of like-minded politicians,

iron triangle the stable, cooperative relationship that often develops among a congressional committee, an administrative agency, and one or more supportive interest groups. Not all of these relationships are triangular, but the iron triangle is the most typical

issue network a loose network of elected leaders, public officials, activists, and interest groups drawn together by a specific policy issue

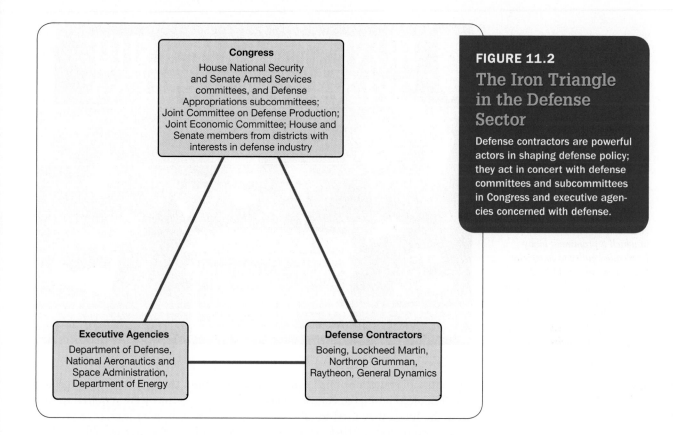

Congress
House National Security and Senate Armed Services committees, and Defense Appropriations subcommittees; Joint Committee on Defense Production; Joint Economic Committee; House and Senate members from districts with interests in defense industry

Executive Agencies
Department of Defense, National Aeronautics and Space Administration, Department of Energy

Defense Contractors
Boeing, Lockheed Martin, Northrop Grumman, Raytheon, General Dynamics

FIGURE 11.2

The Iron Triangle in the Defense Sector

Defense contractors are powerful actors in shaping defense policy; they act in concert with defense committees and subcommittees in Congress and executive agencies concerned with defense.

consultants, public officials, political activists, and interest groups having some concern with the issue in question. Activists and interest groups recognized as being involved in the area (the stakeholders) are customarily invited to testify before congressional committees or give their views to government agencies considering action in their domain.

Attempts to Regulate Lobbying To counter the growing influence of the lobbying industry, stricter guidelines regulating the actions of lobbyists have been adopted in the last decade. For example, as of 1993, businesses may no longer deduct lobbying costs as a business expense. Trade associations must report to members the proportion of their dues that goes toward lobbying, and that proportion of the dues may not be reported as a business expense. The most important attempt to limit the influence of lobbyists was the 1995 Lobbying Disclosure Act, which significantly broadened the definition of people and organizations that must register as lobbyists. This has led, as we saw earlier, to more than 12,000 registrations today.

In 1996, Congress passed legislation limiting the size of gifts to its own members: no gift could be worth more than $50, and no member could receive more than $100 from a single source. It also banned the practice of honoraria for giving speeches, which special interests had used to supplement congressional salaries. In 2007, congressional Democrats secured the enactment of a new package of ethics rules designed to fulfill their 2006 campaign promise to bring an end to lobbying abuses. The new rules prohibited lobbyists from paying for most meals, trips, parties, and gifts for members of Congress. Lobbyists were also required to disclose the

After the Abramoff scandal, in which a prominent lobbyist pleaded guilty to conspiring to bribe members of Congress, both parties called for reform of the lobbying process. In 2007, Democrats in the House of Representatives passed new ethics rules designed to end lobbying abuses.

amounts and sources of small campaign contributions they collected from clients and "bundled" into large contributions. And interest groups were required to disclose the funds they used to rally voters to support or oppose legislative proposals. According to the *Washington Post*, however, within a few weeks, lobbyists had learned how to circumvent many of the new rules, and lobbying firms were as busy as ever.[26]

Using the Courts (Litigation)

Interest groups sometimes turn to litigation when they lack access or when they are dissatisfied with government in general or with a specific government program and feel they have insufficient influence to change the situation. Interest groups can use the courts to affect public policy in at least three ways: (1) by bringing suit directly on behalf of the group itself, (2) by financing suits brought by individuals, or (3) by filing a companion brief as an *amicus curiae* (literally "friend of the court") to an existing court case (see Chapter 15 for a discussion of *amicus curiae* briefs).

Among the best-known illustrations of using the courts for political influence is found in the history of the NAACP. The most important of these court cases was, of course, *Brown v. Board of Education of Topeka, Kansas*, in which the U.S. Supreme Court held that legal segregation of the schools was unconstitutional.[27] Later, extensive litigation accompanied the "sexual revolution" of the 1960s and the emergence of the movement for women's rights.

The 1973 Supreme Court case of *Roe v. Wade*, which took away a state's power to ban abortions, sparked a controversy that brought conservatives to the fore on a national level.[28] Since 1973, conservative groups have made extensive use of the courts to whittle away at the scope of the privacy doctrine initially defined by the Supreme Court in *Roe v. Wade*. They obtained rulings, for example, that prohibit the use of federal funds to pay for voluntary abortions. And in 1989, right-to-life groups were able to use the case of *Webster v. Reproductive Health Services* to restore the right of states to place restrictions on abortion, thus undermining the *Roe v.*

Wade decision (see Chapter 4).[29] The *Webster* case brought more than 300 interest groups on both sides of the abortion issue to the Supreme Court's door.

Litigation involving large businesses is especially mountainous in such areas as taxation, antitrust, interstate transportation, patents, and product quality and standardization. Often a business is brought to litigation against its will by virtue of initiatives taken against it by other businesses or by government agencies. But many individual businesses bring suit themselves to influence government policy, and business groups also frequently use the courts because of the number of government programs applied to them. Major corporations and their trade associations pay tremendous amounts of money each year in fees to the most prestigious Washington law firms. Some of this money is expended in gaining access. A great proportion of it, however, is used to keep the best and most experienced lawyers prepared to represent the corporations in court or before administrative agencies when necessary.

New Politics forces made significant use of the courts during the 1970s and '80s, and judicial decisions were instrumental in advancing their goals. Facilitated by changes in the rules governing access to the courts ("standing" is discussed in Chapter 15), the New Politics agenda was clearly visible in court decisions handed down in several key policy areas. In the environmental policy area, New Politics groups were able to force federal agencies to pay attention to environmental issues, even when an agency was not directly involved in activities related to environmental quality. For example, the Federal Trade Commission (FTC) became very responsive to the demands of New Politics activists during the 1970s and '80s. The FTC stepped up its activities considerably, litigating a series of claims arising under regulations prohibiting deceptive advertising in cases ranging from false claims for over-the-counter drugs to inflated claims about the nutritional value of children's cereal.

Mobilizing Public Opinion

Going public is a strategy that attempts to mobilize the widest and most favorable climate of opinion. Many groups consider it imperative to maintain this climate at all times, even when they have no issue to fight about. An increased use of this kind of strategy is usually associated with modern advertising. As early as the 1930s, political analysts were distinguishing between the "old lobby" of direct group representation before Congress and the "new lobby" of public-relations professionals addressing the public at large to reach Congress.[30]

Institutional Advertising One of the best-known ways of going public is the use of **institutional advertising**. A casual scanning of important mass-circulation magazines and newspapers will provide numerous examples of expensive and well-designed ads by the major oil companies, automobile and steel companies, other large corporations, and trade associations. The ads show how much these organizations are doing for the country, for the protection of the environment, or for the defense of the American way of life. The purpose of the ads is to create and maintain a strongly positive association between an organization and the community at large in the hope of drawing on these favorable feelings as needed for specific political campaigns later on.

institutional advertising
advertising designed to create a positive image of an organization

Protests and Demonstrations Many groups resort to going public because they lack the resources, the contacts, or the experience to use other political strategies. The sponsorship of boycotts, sit-ins, mass rallies, and marches by Martin Luther King Jr.'s Southern Christian Leadership Conference (SCLC) and related organizations during the 1950s and '60s is one of the most significant and successful cases of going public to create a more favorable climate of opinion by calling attention to abuses. The success of these events inspired similar efforts by women's groups. Organizations such as NOW used public strategies in their drive for legislation and in their efforts to gain ratification of the Equal Rights Amendment. In 2004 and 2005, antiwar groups demonstrated near President Bush's ranch in Crawford, Texas, to demand an end to the American military presence in Iraq. The 2010 GOP takeover of the House of Representatives began with the spontaneous self-organization of the Tea Party movement in 2009 as an angry response to the Obama administration's health care initiatives. In 2011 the Occupy Wall Street movement sparked demonstrations across America and around the world, giving voice to those who are outraged by economic inequality.

grassroots mobilization

a lobbying campaign in which a group mobilizes its membership to contact government officials in support of the group's position

Grassroots Mobilization Another form of going public is **grassroots mobilization**, in which a lobby group mobilizes its members and their families throughout the country to write to their elected representatives in support of the group's position. Among the most effective users of the grassroots effort in contemporary American politics is the religious right. Networks of evangelical churches have the capacity to generate hundreds of thousands of letters and phone calls to Congress and the White House. For example, the religious right was outraged when President Clinton announced soon after taking office that he planned to end the military's ban on gay and lesbian soldiers. The Reverend Jerry Falwell, an evangelical leader, called on viewers of his television program to dial a telephone number that would add their names to a petition urging Clinton to retain the ban on gays in the military. Within a few hours, 24,000 people had called to support the petition.[31]

Grassroots campaigns have been so effective in recent years that a number of Washington consulting firms have begun to specialize in this area. In 2007, for

Many interest groups stage protests and demonstrations to draw attention to their cause and mobilize public opinion. This Sierra Club demonstration was intended to call attention to the problem of toxic pollution in Oregon's Willamette River.

Online Petitions and Group Mobilization

You may have received e-mail or social media notices about how you can take action by participating in an online petition. Websites like Change.org provide groups—from upstart community groups to national organizations—a way to mobilize and educate supporters by circulating and signing online petitions. Groups are increasingly turning to online petitions as a way to pressure elected officials. A petition with hundreds or thousands of signatures can become headline news in local and national newspapers, enhancing the legitimacy of the group's cause. Such petitions are also an important way for interest groups to overcome the challenge of getting individuals to contribute to a common cause even though they may not benefit personally. The ability to petition elected officials online—from local school boards to members of Congress—is a powerful new avenue that requires little effort on the part of citizens.

Online petitions are especially effective for communicating with members of Congress. A high-water mark for online petitions was January 11, 2011, when many major websites held an Internet blackout to protest proposed congressional legislation regulating the Internet (see Chapter 8 for more information on the SOPA/PIPA protests). Users of the online encyclopedia Wikipedia, for example, were redirected to a page providing information on the bills and links for users to click on to contact their members of Congress. In one day 4 million people accessed the information about contacting their member of Congress. In response to the online protests, Congress shelved the controversial legislation.

Groups can also organize grassroots e-mail campaigns using online petition forms. Groups provide pre-written messages that can be personalized simply by the user entering his or her name and address (or sometimes only the zip code). (The user's location is used to determine the appropriate representative.) From there the signed e-mail is routed automatically to the user's elected official. Before the advent of these easy petitions, individuals had to either call their elected representative or take the time to mail a letter. Often these mailed letters were simply form letters created by interest groups trying to mobilize their supporters, but the individual had to invest more time and effort than simply clicking a button.

A 2009 Pew survey showed that 20 percent of Internet users had signed an online petition in the previous year. Another survey found that among all adults 32 percent had signed a petition at some point (either online or offline). Among individuals who were active online, 61 percent had signed a petition; while among those who were not online, only 13 percent had signed a petition.

Interest groups wishing to bombard elected officials with requests from supporters are much more likely to use online petitions and e-mail campaigns than the old-fashioned paper petitions. It saves them money, time, and effort, and the response is higher than with paper petitions. Since interest groups form to lobby for or against government legislation, the ability to send elected officials hundreds or thousands of e-mails in one day is an important form of grassroots mobilization.

Research has found that petitions matter beyond their immediate effect on elected officials. Individuals who sign petitions are more likely to vote and participate in other ways. And individuals who use political information (including the information often included with online petitions) are more likely to initiate contact with government or elected officials.

Interest groups want the volume available through form petitions, but research has found that a well-written, personalized letter (or e-mail) holds vastly more weight with elected officials than 100 form letters (or form e-mails), as it shows the time and thought a person took in formulating his or her opinion. This is why on almost every petition there is a space for a personal message—the hope being that if enough people personalize the form e-mail, the elected official will take the petition more seriously.

SOURCES: J. Thomas and G. Streib, "The New Face of Government: Citizen-Initiated Contacts in the Era of E-Government," *Journal of Public Administration Theory and Research* 13, no. 1 (2003): 83–102.
Caroline Tolbert and Ramona McNeal, "Unraveling the Effects of the Internet on Political Participation." *Political Research Quarterly* 56, no. 2 (2003): 175–85.
Aaron Smith, Kay Lehman Schlozman, Sydney Verba, and Henry Brady, "The Internet and Civic Engagement," September 1, 2009, http://pewinternet.org/Reports/2009/15–The-Internet-and-Civic-Engagement.aspx (accessed 7/1/12).

for critical analysis

1. Do you think online petitions are more or less effective than paper petitions for interest groups lobbying members of Congress? Why?

2. Do you think petitions are likely to be effective in shaping government policy, or do elected officials still respond primarily to well-established business interests, rather than citizen groups? Are online petitions more for show than for substance?

example, a grassroots firm called Grassfire.org led the drive to kill the immigration reform bill supported by President Bush and a number of congressional Democrats that would have legalized the status of many illegal immigrants. Grassfire.org used the Internet and talk radio programs to generate a campaign that yielded 700,000 signatures on petitions opposing the bill. The petitions, along with tens of thousands of phone calls, letters, and e-mails generated by Grassfire and several other groups, led to the bill's defeat in the U.S. Senate.[32]

Sometimes, unfortunately, such efforts are not genuine grassroots campaigns but instead represent "Astroturf lobbying" (a play on the name of the artificial grass used on many sports fields). Such campaigns, often using e-mail, have increased in frequency in recent years as members of Congress have grown more and more skeptical of Washington lobbyists and far more attentive to demonstrations of support for a particular issue by their actual constituents. Often Astroturf campaigns are carefully scripted efforts on behalf of corporate interests using names designed to disguise their true goals to help them gather public support for their efforts. For example, the Save Our Species Alliance is an industry group seeking to weaken the Endangered Species Act, and Citizens for Asbestos Reform seeks to limit the ability of individuals harmed by asbestos to seek redress in the courts. The Coalition to Protect America's Health Care is a group of for-profit hospitals that runs ads calling for increased federal funding for those entities. Citizens for Better Medicare actually represents the pharmaceutical industry. Voices for Choices was the alias used by a coalition of telecommunications companies that unsuccessfully advertised on behalf of continued regulation of local phone services. Both Americans for Balanced Energy Choices and the Coalition for Clean, Affordable, Reliable Energy sponsor ads promoting the virtues of coal as an energy source. "Some of us invest lots of time and money into making the world cleaner," announces the pitchman for Americans for Balanced Energy Choices. "And one thing that's helping is electricity from coal."

By the logic of these aliases, a coalition of strip-mining interests might call itself Citizens for a Cleaner Earth, while perhaps a coalition of health insurers—companies notorious for raising premiums but refusing to pay subscribers' claims—might operate under the alias Citizens against Costly Medical Services. A Senate bill proposed in 2006 would have required lobby groups using such aliases to disclose their true identities. Many groups treated this proposal as a vicious attack on their freedom of speech. Wayne LaPierre, president of the NRA, suggested that this sort of disclosure requirement would have thwarted the activities of the Revolutionary-era pamphleteer Tom Paine and perhaps undermined the American Revolution. The proposal ultimately failed.

Using Electoral Politics

In addition to attempting to influence members of Congress and other government officials, interest groups also seek to use the electoral process to elect the right legislators in the first place and to ensure that those who are elected will owe them a debt of gratitude for their support. If we view matters in perspective, groups invest far more resources in lobbying than in electoral politics. Nevertheless, financial support and campaign activism can be important tools for organized interests.

Political Action Committees By far the most common electoral strategy employed by interest groups is that of giving financial support to the parties or to particular candidates. But such support can easily cross the threshold into outright bribery. Therefore, Congress has occasionally attempted to regulate this strategy. For example, the Federal Election Campaign Act of 1971 (amended in 1974) limits campaign contributions and requires that each candidate or campaign committee itemize the full name and address, occupation, and principal business of each person who contributes more than $100. These provisions have been effective up to a point, resulting in numerous embarrassments, indictments, resignations, and criminal convictions in the aftermath of the 1972 Watergate scandal.

The Watergate scandal was triggered by the illegal entry of a group of clandestine agents employed by the president's re-election committee into the office of the Democratic National Committee in the Watergate apartment and hotel complex. An investigation quickly revealed numerous violations of campaign finance laws, involving millions of dollars in unregistered cash from corporate executives to President Nixon's re-election committee. Reaction to Watergate produced further legislation on campaign finance in 1974 and 1976, but the effect was to restrict individual rather than interest-group campaign activity. Today, individuals may contribute no more than $2,300 to any candidate for federal office in any primary or general election. A **political action committee (PAC)**, however, can contribute $5,000, provided it contributes to at least five different federal candidates each year. (Campaign finance regulations are discussed in more detail in Chapter 10.) Beyond this, the laws permit corporations, unions, and other interest groups to form PACs and to pay the costs of soliciting funds from private citizens for the PACs. In other words, PACs are interest groups that operate in the electoral arena in addition to whatever they do within the interest-group system. The option to form a PAC was made available by law only in the early 1970s. Until then, it was difficult, if not downright illegal, for corporations, including unions, to get directly involved in elections by supporting parties and candidates.

The flurry of reform legislation of the 1970s attempted to reduce the influence that special interests have over elections, but the effect has been almost the exact opposite. Electoral spending by interest groups has been increasing steadily. The number of PACs has also increased significantly—from 480 in 1972 to more than 5,500 in 2012 (see Figure 11.3). Opportunities for legally influencing campaigns

political action committee (PAC)
a private group that raises and distributes funds for use in election campaigns

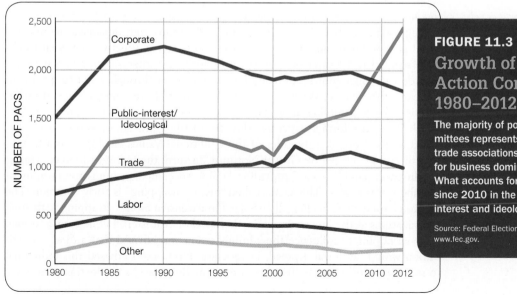

FIGURE 11.3

Growth of Political Action Committees, 1980–2012

The majority of political action committees represents corporations or trade associations. What accounts for business dominance of PACs? What accounts for the huge increase since 2010 in the number of public interest and ideological PACs?

Source: Federal Election Commission, www.fec.gov.

are now widespread. PACs contributed roughly 15 percent of the more than $5 billion spent on national, state, and local elections in 2012. As much as 50 percent was contributed or spent by 527s, 501c(4) groups, and super PACs, which can spend far more than is allowed under federal law for PACs.

Given the enormous costs of television commercials, polls, computers, and other elements of contemporary political technology, most politicians are eager to receive PAC contributions and are at least willing to give a friendly hearing to the needs and interests of contributors. Most politicians probably will not simply sell their services to the interests that fund their campaigns, but there is some evidence that interest groups' campaign contributions do influence the overall pattern of political behavior in Congress and in the state legislatures.

Concern about PACs grew through the 1980s and '90s, creating a constant drumbeat for reform of federal election laws. Proposals to abolish PACs were introduced in Congress on many occasions, with perhaps the most celebrated being the McCain-Feingold bill, which became the Bipartisan Campaign Reform Act (BCRA) of 2002. When originally proposed in 1996, McCain-Feingold was aimed at reducing or eliminating PACs. But in a stunning about-face, when campaign finance reform was adopted in 2002, it did not restrict PACs in any significant way. Rather, it eliminated unrestricted "soft money" donations to the national political parties. One consequence of this reform, as we saw in Chapters 9 and 10, was the creation of a host of new organizations, which include 527 committees, organizations created to promote particular ideas or candidates, and super PACs, formally called "independent expenditure-only committees," which were created for the purpose of promoting whatever candidacies their organizers wish. 527 committees and super PACs are nominally unaffiliated with the two parties but often directed by former party officials. This change has had the effect of strengthening interest groups and weakening parties.

Activist groups carefully keep their campaign spending separate from party and candidate organizations to avoid the restrictions of federal campaign finance laws. As long as a group's campaign expenditures are not coordinated with those of a candidate's campaign, the group is free to spend as much money as it wishes. Such expenditures are viewed as "issue advocacy" and are protected by the First Amendment. The Supreme Court's 2010 *Citizens United* decision increased the flow of money into 527s and super PACs by removing restrictions on corporate political spending, freeing business to back whatever politicians it chose.[33]

One powerful but little-known campaign finance tactic is the formation of strategic alliances between corporate interest groups and ideological or not-for-profit groups. Politicians are reluctant to accept money directly from what might have seemed to be unsavory sources, and corporate interests may find it useful to hide campaign contributions by laundering them through a not-for-profit. In the case of the former Washington super-lobbyist Jack Abramoff, discussed earlier in this chapter, gambling interests made contributions to religious groups led by Ralph Reed, the former executive director of the Christian Coalition, and Reverend Louis P. Sheldon, founder of the Traditional Values Coalition, and to tax-reform groups headed by Grover Norquist. In turn, these groups lobbied against the Internet gambling ban, providing laundered campaign funds for prominent members of Congress. This tactic, called "money swapping," is fairly common. The Clinton administration allegedly engaged in extensive money swapping with such organizations as the International Brotherhood of Teamsters. In one case, a foreign national hoping to influence the administration was advised that a direct contribution would be illegal. Instead, Democratic fund-raisers advised this individual to make a contribution to Teamster president Ron Carey's re-election campaign.

Who Is Represented by PACs?

Following recent Supreme Court decisions that ended many restrictions on campaign spending and issue advocacy, the number of "nonconnected," or ideological, PACs has increased dramatically, making this the largest PAC category in terms of the number of groups. These groups are not connected to a specific corporation, labor organization, or membership association, and they work to elect candidates who support their ideals or agenda. However, in terms of contributions to candidates, spending by ideological groups is dwarfed by the combined contributions of PACs from various business sectors.

PAC Contributions to Federal Candidates in 2010

By sector

Corporate

Nonconnected/ideological

Labor

Other

Labor
$63,665,882

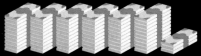

Finance, insurance & real estate
$62,909,712

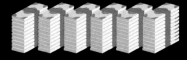

Ideological
$60,279,974

Health
$54,641,685

Misc. business
$37,791,850

Energy & natural resources
$28,858,057

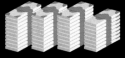

Communications/electronics
$24,972,482

Agribusiness
$22,950,208

Transportation
$21,118,906

Lawyers & lobbyists
$15,916,526

Construction
$15,534,354

Defense
$14,263,964

Other
$1,344,461

Registered PACs in 2011–12

By category

Nonconnected/
Ideological
2,442

Other
153

Labor
297

Trade/
Membership/
Health
989

Corporate
1,786

for critical analysis

1. Business PACs are the biggest spenders. What effect might this have on which candidates get elected and what policies they pass?

2. If ideological PACs are now the most numerous type, what effects might this have on American politics and government?

SOURCES: www.fec.gov; www.opensecrets.org (accessed 9/26/12).

The Teamsters, in turn, made a legal contribution to the Clinton campaign. Such money swapping is illegal but almost impossible to prove.

Campaign Activism Financial support is not the only way that organized groups seek influence through electoral politics. Sometimes activism can be even more important than campaign contributions. Campaign activism on the part of conservative groups played a very important role in bringing about the Republican capture of both houses of Congress in 1994. For example, Christian Coalition activists played a role in many races, including those in which Republican candidates were not strongly identified with the religious right. One postelection study suggested that more than 60 percent of the more than 600 candidates supported by the Christian right were successful in state, local, and congressional races in 1994, especially in the South.[34] In many congressional districts, Christian Coalition efforts were augmented by grassroots campaigns launched by the NRA, which had been outraged by Democratic support for gun-control legislation, and the National Federation of Independent Business (NFIB), which had been energized by its campaign against employer mandates in the failed Clinton health care reform initiative. Both groups are well-organized at the local level and were able to mobilize their members across the country to participate in congressional races.

Initiatives Another political tactic that interest groups sometimes use is sponsorship of ballot initiatives at the state level. The initiative, a device adopted by a number of states around 1900, allows proposed laws to be placed on the general election ballot and submitted directly to the state's voters, bypassing the state legislature and the governor. The initiative was originally promoted by late-nineteenth-century Populists as a mechanism that would allow the people to govern directly—an antidote to interest-group influence in the legislative process.

Many studies have suggested that, ironically, most initiative campaigns today are actually sponsored by interest groups seeking to circumvent legislative opposition to their goals. In recent years, for example, initiative campaigns have been sponsored by the insurance industry, trial lawyers' associations, and tobacco companies.[35] The success of business groups promoting antitax initiatives and conservative activists seeking to ban same-sex marriage has led liberal activists to develop their own initiative campaigns to promote issues such as same-sex marriage, clean energy, and abortion rights. In 1998, liberal activists established the Ballot Initiative Strategy Center (BISC) to provide national coordination for these efforts, which led to successes such as the 2010 Oregon campaign for Propositions 66 and 67, which increased taxes for corporations and high-income wage earners. The role of interest groups in initiative campaigns should come as no surprise, since such campaigns can cost millions of dollars.

● Thinking Critically about Groups and Interests: The Dilemmas of Reform

We would like to think that policies are products of legislators representing the public interest. The truth of the matter is that few programs and policies ever reach the public agenda without the vigorous efforts of important national interest groups. In the realm of economic policy, social policy, international trade policy, and even such seemingly interest-free areas as criminal justice policy—where, in fact, private prison corporations lobby for longer sentences for lawbreakers—the activity of interest groups is a central feature.

for critical analysis

Describe the different techniques of influence that organized interests employ. When is one technique preferable to another?

for critical analysis

How has the U.S. government sought to regulate interest-group activity in order to balance the competing values of liberty and equality? What else might government do to make group politics less biased?

Some citizens worry that well-funded narrow interests, such as business groups, are better able to organize and lobby the government, while ordinary citizens have less influence in politics.

James Madison wrote that "liberty is to faction as air is to fire."[36] By this he meant that the organization and proliferation of interests were inevitable in a free society. To seek to place limits on the organization of interests, in Madison's view, would be to limit liberty itself. Madison believed that interests should be permitted to regulate themselves by competing with one another. As long as competition among different interests were free, open, and vigorous—that is, as long as pluralism thrived—there would be some balance of power among them, and no one interest would be able to dominate the political or governmental process.

Indeed, there is considerable competition among organized groups in the United States. Pro-choice and antiabortion forces, for example, continue to be locked in a bitter struggle. Nevertheless, interest-group politics is not as balanced as Madisonian theory might suggest. Although the weak and poor do occasionally become organized to assert their rights, interest-group politics is generally a form of political competition best suited to the wealthy and powerful. In the realm of group politics, liberty seems inconsistent with equality.

Moreover, although groups sometimes organize to promote broad public concerns, they more often represent relatively narrow, selfish interests. Small, self-interested groups can be organized much more easily than large and more diffuse collectives. For one thing, the members of a relatively small group—say, bankers or hunting enthusiasts—are usually able to recognize their shared interests and the need to pursue them in the political arena. Members of large and more diffuse groups—say, consumers or potential victims of firearms—often find it difficult to recognize their shared interests or the need to engage in collective action to achieve them.[37]

To make matters still more complicated, group politics seems to go hand in hand with government. As we saw earlier, government programs often lead to a proliferation of interest groups as competing forces mobilize to support, oppose, or take advantage of the government's actions. Often the government explicitly encourages the formation of interest groups. Agencies such as the Department of Veterans' Affairs, the Social Security Administration, and the Department of Agriculture devote a great deal of energy to the organization and mobilization of groups of "stakeholders" to support the agencies and their efforts. One reason the Social Security program has endured despite its fiscal shortcomings is that it is so strongly supported by a powerful group: AARP. Significantly, the Social Security Administration played an important early role in the formation of AARP, precisely because agency executives realized that this group could become a useful ally.

The responsiveness of government agencies to interest groups is a challenge to democracy. Groups sometimes seem to have a greater impact than voters on the government's policies and programs. Yet, before we decide that we should do away with interest groups, we should think carefully: If there were no organized interests, would the government pay more attention to ordinary voters? Or would the government simply pay less attention to everyone? In his work *Democracy in America*, Alexis de Tocqueville argued that the proliferation of groups promoted democracy by encouraging governmental responsiveness. Does group politics foster democracy or impede democracy? It does both.

Learn about Lobbying

Inform Yourself

What counts as an interest group? The number of interest groups and lobbyists has grown dramatically over the last 50 years. There is no central database of all these groups, but a relatively complete list is available at http://pag.vancouver.wsu.edu/. Click on a few of the categories and see what groups are listed there. Does any of them surprise you as being classified as an interest group?

Consider the example of professional sports interest groups. The groups that lobby government are diverse. In professional sports, there are unions representing players, staff, and referees; there are corporations that run the teams; there are leagues themselves—each of these entities also lobbies the government for favorable policies. Check out the report at http://firststreetresearch.cqpress.com/2012/05/16/sports-lobby-is-a-multi-million-dollar-enterprise/.

Express Yourself

Watch a video on the pros and cons of lobbying. The American League of Lobbyists has created a video arguing that lobbying is beneficial to American politics. Watch it at: www.alldc.org/video.cfm. Compare what the first video argues with the factual information from the video available at www.youtube.com/watch?v=R2DUM6jVasw. Consider sharing your opinion on what you learn.

Are current regulations on lobbying strong enough? Explore how heavily regulated lobbyists are in Washington, D.C., today at www.voanews.com/content/lobbying-regulated-to-prevent-abuse-in-us-101407789/174277.html. Do you think lobbyists are regulated enough, or should we take further action against their influence? Contact your members of Congress to let them know your views.

Connect with Others

Connect with interest groups. A small sample of the groups on Facebook include AARP, MADD, the NRA, NOW, and the National Chamber of Commerce. Visit the Facebook pages of these groups (they all have Twitter pages as well) or find others that interest you. Find a post by one of the groups and join in the discussion. You can also join a membership group if you find one whose goals you share.

Find links to the sites listed above as well as related activities on wwnorton.com/studyspace.

The Character of Interest Groups

■ **Describe the major types of interest groups and whom they represent (pp. 435–43)**

An interest group is an organized group of people that makes policy-related appeals to government. Although organized groups form around many different political interests, almost all interest groups share a similar set of organizational components, including leadership, money, an office and members. In order to overcome the free rider problem, interest groups attempt to provide their potential members with informational, material, solidary and purposive benefits.

Key Terms

pluralism (p. 435)

interest group (p. 435)

public interest groups (p. 437)

membership association (p. 439)

staff organization (p. 439)

collective goods (p. 440)

free riders (p. 440)

informational benefits (p. 442)

material benefits (p. 442)

solidary benefits (p. 442)

purposive benefits (p. 442)

Practice Quiz

1. The theory that competition among organized interests will produce balance, with all the interests regulating one another is *(p. 435)*
   a) pluralism.
   b) elite power politics.
   c) democracy.
   d) socialism.
   e) libertarianism.

2. Groups that have an interest in obtaining government funds for research, such as Harvard University, the Brookings Institution, and the American Enterprise Institute, are referred to as *(p. 437)*
   a) membership associations.
   b) public interest groups.
   c) professional associations.
   d) ideological groups.
   e) public-sector groups.

3. To overcome the free rider problem, groups *(p. 441)*
   a) provide general benefits.
   b) litigate.
   c) provide selective benefits.
   d) provide collective goods.
   e) go public.

4. Friendship and networking are examples of _____, while discount purchasing and health insurance are examples of _____. *(p. 442)*
   a) purposive benefits; material benefits
   b) purposive benefits; solidary benefits
   c) solidary benefits; purposive benefits
   d) material benefits; solidary benefits
   e) solidary benefits; material benefits

5. Which of the following best describes the reputation of AARP in the Washington, D.C., community? *(p. 443)*
   a) It is respected and feared.
   b) It is believed to be ineffective.
   c) It always wins the political battles it fights.
   d) It is corrupt and unrepresentative of most Americans.
   e) It is supported and well liked by all political forces.

 Practice Online
"Who Are Americans?" exercise: *Who Is Represented by PACs?*

The Proliferation of Groups

■ **Analyze why the number of interest groups has grown in recent decades (pp. 443–45)**

In recent decades there has been a significant growth in the number of interest groups seeking to influence the American political process. One reason for this change has been the dramatic expansion of the role of American government over the last four decades. Another reason for this change has been the emergence of a new set of political forces in the United States called the "New Politics" movement.

Key Term

New Politics movement (p. 444)

Practice Quiz

6. Which of the following is an important reason for the enormous increase in the number of groups seeking to influence the American political system? *(p. 443)*

   a) the decrease in the size and activity of government during the last few decades
   b) the increase in the size and activity of government during the last few decades
   c) the increase in the amount of soft money in election campaigns in recent decades
   d) the increase in legal protection provided to interest groups as a result of the Supreme Court's evolving interpretation of the First Amendment
   e) the increase in the number of people identifying themselves as an independent in recent decades

7. Which types of interest groups are most often associated with the New Politics movement? *(p. 445)*

   a) political action committees
   b) professional associations
   c) government groups
   d) labor groups
   e) public interest groups

Strategies: The Quest for Political Power

■ **Explain how interest groups try to influence government (pp. 445–60)**

Interest groups take action to improve the probability that their policy interests will be treated favorably by all branches and all levels of government. These actions often take many different forms. Insider strategies include direct lobbying, cultivating access to decision makers and using the court system. Outsider strategies include mobilizing public opinion and using electoral politics.

Key Terms

lobbying (p. 445)

iron triangle (p. 450)

issue network (p. 450)

institutional advertising (p. 453)

grassroots mobilization (p. 454)

political action committee (PAC) (p. 457)

Practice Quiz

8. Which of the following best describes the federal government's laws regarding lobbying? *(pp. 445–46)*

   a) Federal law allows lobbying but only on issues related to taxation.
   b) Federal law allows lobbying but only if the lobbyists receive no monetary compensation for their lobbying.
   c) Federal law strictly prohibits any form of lobbying.
   d) Federal law requires all organizations employing lobbyists to register with Congress and to disclose whom they represent, whom they lobby, what they are looking for, and how much they are paid.
   e) There are no laws regulating lobbying because the federal government has never passed any legislation on the legality of the activity.

9. A loose network of elected leaders, public officials, activists, and interest groups drawn together by a public policy issue is referred to as *(p. 450)*

   a) an issue network.
   b) a public interest group.
   c) a political action committee.
   d) pluralism.
   e) an iron triangle.

10. Which of the following is a way that interest groups use the courts to influence public policy? *(p. 452)*

    a) supplying judges with solidary benefits
    b) joining an issue network
    c) creating an iron triangle
    d) forming a political action committee
    e) filing *amicus* briefs

11. Which of the following are examples of the "going public" strategy? *(pp. 453–56)*

    a) free riding, pluralism, and issue networking
    b) donating money to political parties, endorsing candidates, and sponsoring ballot initiatives

c) institutional advertising, grassroots advertising, and protests and demonstrations

d) providing informational benefits, providing solidary benefits, and providing material benefits

e) filing an amicus brief, bringing a lawsuit, and financing those who are filing a lawsuit

12. According to this text, what is the limit a PAC can contribute to a candidate in a primary or general election campaign? *(p. 457)*
   a) $1,000
   b) $5,000
   c) $10,000
   d) $50,000
   e) $100,000

13. Which of the following is *not* an activity in which interest groups frequently engage? *(pp. 456–60)*
   a) starting their own political party
   b) litigation
   c) sponsoring ballot initiatives at the state level
   d) lobbying
   e) contributing to campaigns

14. "Money swapping" occurs when *(p. 458)*
   a) a member of a congressional committee trades his or her vote for a cash payment from an interest group.
   b) a candidate who is running in a competitive race convinces interest groups to contribute to a candidate who is running in a competitive race.
   c) an interest group combines its campaign spending with that of a political party or candidate organization.
   d) a lobbyist is paid to testify before a congressional committee.
   e) a corporate interest group attempts to hide its campaign contributions by laundering them through a not-for-profit group.

 Practice Online
Interactive simulation: *Legislative Affairs Director*

For Further Reading

Abramoff, Jack. *Capitol Punishment: The Hard Truth about Washington Corruption from America's Most Notorious Lobbyist.* New York: WIND Books, 2011.

Ainsworth, Scott. *Analyzing Interest Groups.* New York: W.W. Norton, 2002.

Alexander, Robert, ed. *The Classics of Interest Group Behavior.* New York: Wadsworth, 2005.

Baumgartner, Frank, Jeffrey M. Berry, Beth L. Leech, David C. Kimball, and Marie Hojnacki. *Lobbying and Policy Change: Who Wins, Who Loses and Why.* Chicago: University of Chicago Press, 2009.

Berry, Jeffrey. *Interest Group Society.* 5th ed. New York: Longman, 2008.

Cigler, Allan J., and Burdett A. Loomis, eds. *Interest Group Politics.* 7th ed. Washington, DC: CQ Press, 2006.

Esterling, Kevin. *The Political Economy of Expertise.* Ann Arbor: University of Michigan Press, 2004.

Goldstein, Kenneth. *Interest Groups, Lobbying, and Participation in America.* New York: Cambridge University Press, 2008.

Kaiser, Robert. *So Damn Much Money: The Triumph of Lobbying and the Corrosion of American Government.* New York: Vintage, 2010.

Lessig, Lawrence. *Republic, Lost: How Money Corrupts Congress—and a Plan to Stop It.* New York: Twelve/Hachette Book Group, 2011.

Lowi, Theodore J. *The End of Liberalism: The Second Republic of the United States.* 2nd ed. New York: W.W. Norton, 1979.

Moe, Terry M. *The Organization of Interests: Incentives and the Internal Dynamics of Political Interest Groups.* Chicago: University of Chicago Press, 1980.

Nownes, Anthony. *Total Lobbying: What Lobbyists Want and How They Try to Get It.* New York: Cambridge University Press, 2006.

Olson, Mancur, Jr. *The Logic of Collective Action: Public Goods and the Theory of Groups.* Cambridge, MA: Harvard University Press, 1965.

Rozell, Mark, Clyde Wilcox, and David Madland. *Interest Groups in American Campaigns.* Washington, DC: CQ Press, 2005.

Sheingate, Adam. *The Rise of the Agricultural Welfare State: Institutions and Interest Group Power in the United States, France, and Japan.* Princeton, NJ: Princeton University Press, 2003.

Strolovitch, Dara. *Affirmative Advocacy: Race, Class, and Gender in Interest Group Politics.* Chicago: University of Chicago Press, 2007.

Truman, David B. *The Governmental Process: Political Interests and Public Opinion.* New York: Knopf, 1951.

Recommended Websites

AARP
www.aarp.org

AARP (formerly the American Association of Retired Persons) is one of the largest and most significant interest groups in the United States. Read about the history of this organization, its group benefits, and how it is affecting political issues and elections.

AFL-CIO Legislative Alert Center
www.aflcio.org/issues/legislativealert/

Created in 1955, the AFL-CIO represents more than 10 million working men and women. See how this influential labor group is active and involved in political issues.

American Civil Liberties Union
www.aclu.org
American Conservative Union
www.conservative.org

The American Civil Liberties Union and the American Conservative Union are two of the nation's largest and most influential ideological interest groups. See what these opposing groups have to say about our government and current political issues.

American Israel Public Affairs Committee (AIPAC)
www.aipac.org

Due to globalization, interest groups cannot limit their activities to one country. Decisions made in Washington, D.C., can affect countries around the world. The American Israel Public Affairs Committee (AIPAC) works with Republicans and Democrats to maintain a strong relationship between the United States and Israel.

MoveOn
www.moveon.org

This progressive interest group is dedicated to bringing ordinary citizens back into the political process and electing liberal members of government. See how this group uses electoral politics, via political action committees and campaign activism, to achieve its agenda.

National Rifle Association (NRA)
www.nra.org
Coalition to Stop Gun Violence
www.csgv.org
Brady Campaign to Prevent Gun Violence
www.bradycampaign.org

Lobbying is an attempt by a group to influence the policy process by persuading government officials. These three groups employ a variety of lobbying techniques on the issue of gun control.

U.S. PIRG (United States Public Interest Research Group)
www.uspirg.org

This public interest group stands up for ordinary citizens. Its special emphasis is on consumer rights and the environment. U.S. PIRG mobilizes public opinion via institutional advertising, social movements, and grassroots efforts. PIRG chapters can be found in most states and at many colleges and universities.

World Wildlife Fund
www.wwf.org

The World Wildlife Fund is dedicated to protecting nature. They provide information to policy makers about conservation and advocate policies to help preserve the natural environment.

In addition to its lawmaking powers, Congress plays a critical role in American democracy as a representative institution. The members of Congress—100 senators and 435 representatives—represent the voices of the people across America. Yet some observers worry that Congress does not represent all voices equally.

IN GOD WE TRUST

12

Congress

WHAT GOVERNMENT DOES AND WHY IT MATTERS Early in 2012, Wikipedia went dark for a day. Visitors to the popular free online encyclopedia saw a black screen and an ominous warning: "Imagine a World without Free Knowledge." The day before, Wikipedia's cofounder Jimmy Wales sent out a tweet advising students, "Do your homework early."[1] Professors, of course, normally recommend that students not rely on Wikipedia's public-sourced format for their homework assignments. Still, the website made a point that day, with the help of other big names on the Internet, including Google. By organizing online petitions and e-mails, the sites succeeded in preventing Congress from enacting the Stop Online Piracy Act (SOPA) and the Protect Intellectual Property Act (PIPA). These regulatory measures would have given the Justice Department power to order websites to remove links suspected of copyright violation. To supporters in the film and recording industries, the proposed laws offered vital protection to writers, filmmakers, and recording artists, ensuring that they would receive appropriate compensation for their intellectual property. To opponents of SOPA and PIPA, the measures amounted to censorship, the heavy hand of the government stifling the free flow of information and the creativity that the Internet makes possible.

The conflict over the proposed laws highlighted how power works in Congress. For years, leaders in the entertainment industry, the key supporters of the restrictive legislation, had showered funds on members of Congress through campaign contributions. They also lobbied intensely, relying on expensive Washington-based lobbying firms to represent them. By contrast, Internet companies had paid much less attention to Congress, and most had only recently begun to build a presence in Washington.[2] Congress's initial support for SOPA and PIPA reflected the workings of power behind closed doors "inside the Beltway," as politics in Washington is sometimes called. But the success of the online mobilization in leading Congress to postpone its decision reflected the impact that broad-based mobilization of millions of citizens can have on Congress. It also revealed the power of the Internet as a way to mobilize people whose voices are often not heard in Washington.

Congress has vast authority over most aspects of American life. Laws related to federal spending, taxing, and regulation all pass through Congress. While the debates over these laws may seem hard to follow because they are complex and technical or because heated, partisan struggles distract from the substance of the issue, it is important for the American people to learn about what Congress is doing. As the example of SOPA and PIPA indicates, actions taken—or not taken—in Congress affect the everyday experiences we take for granted. With its power to spend and tax, Congress also affects the choices that people face and the opportunities they can expect in life. With so much information about Congress available on the Internet, it is not hard to get beyond the heated rhetoric and simplistic headlines and ask your own questions about a proposed law. How will it affect my life and the lives of people I care about? What is the impact on my country? Making laws is often compared to making sausage, because it is such a complex and often messy process. Even so, it is vital for citizens to monitor what Congress does because the laws it passes are so central to their lives.

chaptergoals

- Describe who serves in Congress and how they represent their constituents (pages 471–84)

- Explain how party leadership, the committee system, the staff system, and caucuses help structure congressional business (pages 484–91)

- Outline the steps in the process of passing a law (pages 491–96)

- Analyze the factors that influence which laws Congress decides to pass (pages 496–504)

- Describe the oversight, "advice and consent," and impeachment powers of Congress (pages 504–7)

Congress: Representing the American People

Describe who serves in Congress and how they represent their constituents

Congress is the most important representative institution in American government. Each member's primary responsibility is to the district, to his or her **constituency**, not to the congressional leadership, a party, or even Congress itself. Yet the task of representation is not a simple one. Views about what constitutes fair and effective representation differ, and constituents may have very different expectations of their representatives. Members of Congress must consider these diverse views and expectations as they represent their districts.

constituency the residents in the area from which an official is elected

House and Senate: Differences in Representation

The framers of the Constitution provided for a **bicameral** legislature—that is, a legislative body consisting of two chambers. As we saw in Chapter 2, the framers intended each of these chambers, the House of Representatives and the Senate, to serve a different constituency. Members of the Senate, appointed by state legislatures for six-year terms, were to represent society's elite. Today, members of both House and Senate are elected directly by the people. The 435 members of the House are elected from districts apportioned according to population; the 100 members of the Senate are elected by their states, with two senators from each. Senators continue to have much longer terms in office and usually represent much larger and more diverse constituencies than do their counterparts in the House (see Table 12.1).

bicameral characterized as having a legislative assembly composed of two chambers or houses' distinguished from *unicameral*

The House and Senate play different roles in the legislative process. In essence, the Senate is the more deliberative of the two bodies—the forum in which any and all ideas that senators raise can receive a thorough public airing. The House is the more centralized and organized of the two bodies—better equipped to play a routine role in the governmental process. In part, this difference stems from the different rules governing the two bodies. These rules give House leaders more control over the legislative process and allow House members to specialize in certain

TABLE 12.1

Differences between the House and the Senate

	HOUSE	SENATE
Minimum age of member	25 years	30 years
U.S. citizenship	At least 7 years	At least 9 years
Length of term	2 years	6 years
Number representing each state	1–53 per state (depends on population)	2 per state
Constituency	Local	Local and state-wide

For its first 128 years, Congress was a decidedly masculine world. In 1917, three years before the ratification of the Nineteenth Amendment, Jeanette Rankin (R-Mont.) (pictured back row, far right) became the first woman to serve in Congress.

sociological representation a type of representation in which representatives have the same racial, gender, ethnic, religious, or educational backgrounds as their constituents. It is based on the principle that if two individuals are similar in background, character, interests, and perspectives, then one could correctly represent the other's views

agency representation the type of representation in which a representative is held accountable to a constituency if he or she fails to represent that constituency properly. This is incentive for good representation when the personal backgrounds, views, and interests of the representative differ from those of his or her constituency

legislative areas. The rules of the much smaller Senate give its leadership relatively little power and discourage specialization.

Both formal and informal factors contribute to differences between the two chambers of Congress. Differences in the length of terms and requirements for holding office, specified by the Constitution, generate differences in how members of each body develop their constituencies and exercise their powers of office. The result is that members of the House most effectively and frequently serve as the agents of well-organized local interests with specific legislative agendas—for instance, used-car dealers seeking relief from regulation, labor unions seeking more favorable legislation, or farmers looking for higher subsidies. The small size and relative homogeneity of their constituencies and the frequency with which they must seek re-election make House members more attuned to the legislative needs of local interest groups.

Senators, on the other hand, serve larger and more heterogeneous constituencies. As a result, they are somewhat better able than members of the House to act as the agents for groups and interests organized on a statewide or national basis. Moreover, with longer terms in office, senators have more time to consider "new ideas" or to bring together new coalitions of interests rather than simply serving existing ones.

Sociological versus Agency Representation

We have become so accustomed to the idea of representative government that we tend to forget what a peculiar concept representation really is. A representative claims to act or speak for some other person or group. But how can one person be trusted to speak for another? How do we know that those who call themselves our representatives are actually speaking on our behalf, rather than simply pursuing their own interests?

There are two circumstances under which one person reasonably might be trusted to speak for another. The first occurs if the two individuals are so similar in background, character, interests, and perspectives that anything said by one would very likely reflect the views of the other as well. This principle is at the heart of what is sometimes called **sociological representation**—the sort of representation that takes place when representatives have the same racial, gender, ethnic, religious, or educational backgrounds as their constituents. The assumption is that sociological similarity helps to promote good representation; thus the composition of a properly constituted representative assembly should mirror the composition of society.

The second circumstance under which one person might be trusted to speak for another occurs if the two are formally bound together so that the representative is in some way accountable to those he or she is supposed to represent. If representatives can somehow be punished for failing to speak properly for their constituents, then we know they have an incentive to provide good representation even if their own personal backgrounds, views, and interests differ from the backgrounds of those they represent. This principle is called **agency representation**—the sort of representation that takes place when constituents have the power to hire and fire their representatives.

Both sociological and agency representation play a role in the relationship between members of Congress and their constituencies.

The Social Composition of the U.S. Congress The extent to which the U.S. Congress is representative of the American people in a sociological sense can be seen by examining social characteristics of the House and Senate today. For example, the religious affiliations of members of both the House and Senate are overwhelmingly Protestant—the distribution is very close to the proportion in the population at large—although the Protestant category comprises more than 15 denominations. Catholics are the second-largest category of religious affiliation, and Jews a much smaller, third category.[3] Religious affiliations directly affect congressional debate on a limited range of issues where different moral views are at stake, such as abortion.

African Americans, women, Latinos, and Asian Americans have increased their congressional representation in the past two decades (see Figure 12.1), but the representation of minorities in Congress is still not comparable to their proportions in the general population. After the Democrats won a majority in the House in November 2006, Nancy Pelosi (D-Calif.) became the first female Speaker of the House and held that position through 2010. Following the 2012 elections, the 113th Congress (2013–14) included at least 77 women in the House of Representatives and 20 women in the Senate, an all-time high. Since many important contemporary national issues cut along racial and gender lines, pressure for reform in the representative process is likely to continue until all groups are fully represented.

The occupational backgrounds of members of Congress have always been a matter of interest because so many issues split along economic lines that are

for critical analysis

Why is sociological representation important? If congressional representatives have racial, religious, or educational backgrounds similar to those of their constituents, are they better representatives? Why or why not?

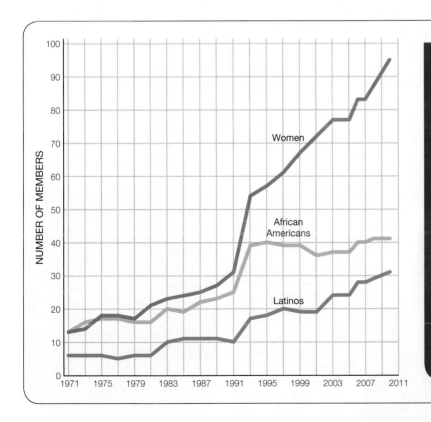

FIGURE 12.1

Women, African Americans, and Latinos in the U.S. Congress, 1971–2010

Congress has become much more socially diverse since the 1970s. After a gradual increase from 1971 to 1990, the number of women and African American members grew quickly during the first half of the 1990s. How does the pattern of growth for Latino representatives compare with that of women and African Americans?

SOURCES: Harold W. Stanley and Richard G. Niemi, eds., *Vital Statistics on American Politics 2003–2004* (Washington, DC: CQ Press, 2003), 207, Table 5–2; and Mildred Amer and Jennifer E. Manning, *Membership of the 11th Congress: A Profile*, Congressional Research Service 7-5700, December 31, 2008, assets.opencrs.com (accessed 1/31/10).

New Media and Women Candidates for Congress

Congress has entered the digital age. As of 2009, 186 members of the House used Twitter, and 291 had Facebook pages. Every member of Congress had a website. Additionally, almost half of House members had a dedicated blog. However, there are differences in who is using these online avenues for constituent communication.

The 113th Congress (2013–14) includes 20 women serving in the 100-person Senate and at least 77 women serving in the House of Representatives (out of 435 members). These figures represent an all-time high. Yet women account for over 50 percent of the U.S. population but just 18 percent of the members of Congress. Are new media and digital communication helping or hurting women political candidates?

Members of Congress use blogs to claim credit and to raise awareness of issues. It is not uncommon for lawmakers to "leak" information to other bloggers to mobilize support for policy positions they favor. Members also use their own blogs because it allows unfiltered messages to reach constituents and the news media. Traditional media may report a 20-second clip of an interview, but a blog or website allows the member to get the full message to the public. Winning Senate candidate

Elizabeth Warren (D-Mass.) became an overnight sensation when her campaign speech went viral on YouTube; in the video Warren talks about the need to raise taxes so all Americans, including large corporations, pay their fair share.

Members of the House are more likely to be on Twitter than Senators; however, use of Facebook is about the same in the two chambers. Republican officeholders are more likely than Democratic officeholders to be on either of these sites; in 2009, 69 percent of Republican lawmakers used Facebook, compared to only 45 percent of Democrats.

When broken down by gender, the posts reveal differences in format and content. Congresswomen are more likely than Congressmen to be on Facebook and are more likely to stress advertising and position taking. Women politicians try to downplay personal and procedural issues online, compared to men. Surveys show that women constituents also prefer Facebook to other forms of new media.

If women lawmakers are taking advantage of online media more often than men, does this translate into more support for women in elections? The answer is unclear. While new media such as Facebook, Twitter, blogs, and YouTube can offer female legislators an easier way to reach supporters and raise campaign funds, the Internet can also have a negative impact on women candidates.

Women running for Congress are often faced with a barrage of negative advertising, and online messages can be especially harsh and inaccurate. Bloggers can invert stories about a candidate, and by the time the message is corrected the damage to her legitimacy has been done. Of course male candidates face the same danger,

but because women candidates face more criticism based on gender, negative press can be more damaging, reinforcing existing gender stereotypes.

Another reason the new media world can be problematic for women politicians is because individuals self-select information, thus only seeing "facts" that support their pre-existing opinions. People who believe in gender stereotypes and think women candidates are inferior to men may only be exposed to information online that supports their view. In contrast, mainstream media outlets tend to offer more balanced news coverage and avoid gender stereotypes. Research by political scientist Jennifer Lawless on the effects of new media on support for women candidates shows that individuals who rely primarily on blogs for political information are less likely to believe women candidates are competent, and are less likely to vote for women candidates, holding all else even.

SOURCES: Richard Davis, *Typing Politics: The Role of Blogs in American Politics* (New York: Oxford University Press, 2009). Jennifer L. Lawless, "Twitter and Facebook: New Ways for Members of Congress to Send the Same Old Messages?" in *iPolitics: Citizens, Elections, and Governing in the New Media Era*, ed. Richard L. Fox and Jennifer M. Ramos (Cambridge, UK: Cambridge University Press, 2012), pp. 206–32.

for critical analysis

1. From a constituent's perspective, is it more helpful to receive information directly from your members of Congress via the Internet or through the news media? Why?

2. Do you think the use of online media will ultimately help or hurt women running for Congress and other political offices? Why?

The increasing racial and ethnic diversity Congress is shown in the membership of the Congressional Hispanic Caucus, Black Caucus, and Asian Pacific American Caucus. Here, members of those three groups hold a press conference on the federal budget and debt.

relevant to occupations and industries. The legal profession is the dominant career of most members of Congress prior to their election. Public service or politics is also a significant background, with many members coming from positions in state and local government. In addition, many members of Congress have important ties to business and industry.[4] Moreover, members of Congress are much more highly educated than most Americans. More than 9 in 10 members hold university degrees, and close to half of them have law degrees.[5] This is not a portrait of the U.S. population. Congress is not a sociological microcosm of American society.

Can Congress still legislate fairly or take account of a diversity of views and interests if it is not a sociologically representative assembly? The task is certainly much more difficult. Yet there is reason to believe it can. Representatives, as we shall see shortly, can serve as the agents of their constituents even if they do not precisely mirror their sociological attributes. Yet sociological representation is a matter of some importance, even if it is not an absolute prerequisite for fair legislation by members of the House and Senate. At the least, the social composition of a representative assembly is important for symbolic purposes: to demonstrate to groups in the population that the government takes them seriously. If Congress is not representative symbolically, then its own authority, and indeed that of the entire government, is reduced.[6]

Representatives as Agents A good deal of evidence indicates that whether or not members of Congress share their constituents' sociological characteristics, they *do* work very hard to speak for their constituents' views and to serve their constituents' interests. The idea of representative as agent is similar to the relationship of lawyer and client. True, the relationship between the member of Congress and an average of 710,767 "clients" in the district, or the senator and millions of "clients" in the state, is very different from that of the lawyer and client. But the criteria of performance are comparable. One expects at the very least that each representative will constantly seek to discover the interests of the constituency and take those interests into account as he or she governs. Whether members of Congress always represent the interests of their constituents is another matter, as we will see later in this chapter.[7]

There is constant communication between constituents and congressional offices, and the volume of e-mail from constituents and advocacy groups has grown so large so quickly that congressional offices have struggled to find effective ways to respond in a timely manner.[8] At the same time, members of Congress have found new ways to communicate with constituents. They have created websites describing their achievements, established a presence on social networking sites, and issued e-newsletters that alert constituents to current issues. Many also have set up blogs and used Twitter accounts to establish a more informal style of communication with constituents.

The seriousness with which members of the House attempt to behave as representatives can be seen in the amount of time they spend on behalf of their constituents. One way to measure the amount of time members of Congress devote to constituency service (called "casework") is to look at the percentage of personal House and Senate staff (personal staff being non-committee member staff) assigned to district and state offices. In 1972, 22.5 percent of House members' personal staff were located in district offices; by 2005 the number had grown to 50.7 percent.[9] For the Senate, the staff in state offices grew from 12.5 percent in 1972 to 39 percent in 2005. The service that these offices provide is not merely a matter of handling correspondence. It includes talking to constituents, providing them with minor services, presenting special bills for them, and attempting to influence decisions by regulatory commissions on their behalf.

Although no members of Congress are above constituency pressures (and they would not want to be), on many issues, constituents do not have very strong views, and representatives are free to act as they think best. Foreign policy issues often fall into this category. But in many districts, there are two or three issues on which constituents have such pronounced opinions that representatives feel they have little freedom of choice. For example, representatives from districts that grow wheat, cotton, or tobacco probably will not want to exercise a great deal of independence on relevant agricultural legislation. In oil-rich states such as Oklahoma and Texas, senators and members of the House are likely to be leading advocates of oil interests. For one thing, representatives are probably fearful of voting against their district interests; for another, the districts are unlikely to have elected representatives who would *want* to vote against them.

The influence of constituencies is so pervasive that both parties have strongly embraced the informal rule that nothing should be done to endanger the re-election chances of any member. Party leaders obey this rule fairly consistently by not asking any member to vote in a way that might conflict with a district interest.

The Electoral Connection

The sociological composition of Congress and the activities of representatives once they are in office are very much influenced by electoral considerations. Three factors related to the U.S. electoral system affect who gets elected and what they do once in office. The first factor concerns who decides to run for office and which candidates have an edge over others. The second issue is that of incumbency advantage. Finally, the way congressional district lines are drawn can greatly affect

Who Are the Members of Congress?

Gender

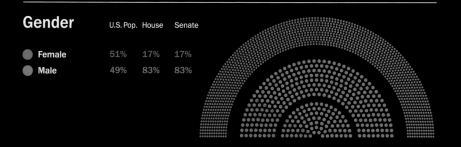

	U.S. Pop.	House	Senate
Female	51%	17%	17%
Male	49%	83%	83%

Key

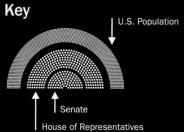

U.S. Population

Senate

House of Representatives

Race

	U.S. Pop.	House	Senate
White	64%	82%	96%
Black	13%	10%	0%
Hispanic	16%	7%	2%
Asian	5%	3%	2%
Native American	1%	.002%	0%

Although the number of women, African Americans, and Latinos in Congress has increased in recent decades, Congress is still much less diverse than the American population. Members of Congress are predominantly male, white, Protestant Christian, and most commonly come from a professional and educational background as lawyers. These data compare the 112th Congress, which took office in 2011, with the U.S. population as a whole.

Religion

	U.S. Pop.	House	Senate
Protestant	51%	57%	56%
Catholic	24%	30%	24%
Mormon	2%	2%	5%
Jewish	2%	6%	12%
All Others	21%	4%	4%

for critical analysis

1. Does it matter if the backgrounds of members of Congress reflect the population as a whole? Can members still represent their constituents effectively if they do not come from similar backgrounds?

2. Visit www.house.gov and www.senate.gov to identify your representatives in Congress and visit their Web pages. How similar are their backgrounds to yours? How closely do their policy positions, as expressed on their web pages, match your own?

Education

Highest level attained:

	U.S. Pop.	House	Senate
< High school	15%	0	0
High school grad.	58%	8%	1%
Bachelor's degree	18%	26%	24%
Professional/ law degree	2%	38%	55%
Other advanced degree	8%	28%	20%

Average Age

U.S. Pop. 37   House 57   Senate 62

SOURCE: Jennifer E. Manning, "Membership of the 112th Congress: A Profile," CRS Report R41647, March 1, 2011, www.senate.gov (accessed 8/15/12).

the outcome of an election. Let us examine more closely the impact that these considerations have on representation.

Who Runs for Congress Voters' choices are restricted from the start by who decides to run for office. In the past, decisions about who would run for a particular elected office were made by local party officials. A person who had a record of service to the party, or who was owed a favor, or whose "turn" had come up, might be nominated by party leaders. Today, few party organizations have the power to slate candidates in this way. Instead, parties try to ensure that well-qualified candidates run for Congress. During the 1990s, the Republican Party developed "farm teams" of local officials who were groomed to run for Congress. Their success led Democrats to attempt a similar strategy. Even so, the decision to run for Congress is a personal choice, and one of the most important factors determining who runs for office is an individual candidate's ambition.[10] A potential candidate may also assess whether he or she can attract enough money to mount a credible campaign. The ability to raise money depends on connections with other politicians, interest groups, and national party organizations. In the past, the difficulty of raising campaign funds posed a disadvantage to female candidates. Since the 1980s, however, a number of powerful political action committees (PACs) have emerged to recruit women and fund their campaigns. The largest of them, EMILY's List (an acronym for "Early Money Is Like Yeast," which raises dough), has become a powerful fundraiser. Research shows that money is no longer the barrier it once was to women running for office.[11] Even so, women candidates tend to face more competition in their primary elections.

Features distinctive to each congressional district also affect the field of candidates. For example, the way the congressional district overlaps with state legislative boundaries may affect a candidate's decision to run. A state-level legislator who is considering running for the U.S. Congress is more likely to assess her prospects favorably if her state district coincides with the congressional district (because the voters will already know her). And for any candidate, decisions about running must be made early, because once money has been committed to already declared candidates, it is harder for new candidates to break into a race. Thus, the outcome of a November election is partially determined many months earlier, when decisions to run are finalized.

Incumbency Incumbency plays a very important role in the American electoral system and in the kind of representation citizens get in Washington. Once in office, members of Congress gain access to an array of tools they can use to stack the deck in favor of their re-election. The most important of these is constituency service: taking care of the problems and requests of individual voters. Through such services and through regular newsletter mailings, incumbents seek to establish a "personal" relationship with their constituents. The success of this strategy is evident in the high rates of re-election for congressional incumbents: as high as 98 percent for House members and

incumbency holding a political office for which one is running

One reason women have not increased their numbers more quickly in Congress is the incumbency advantage. Incumbents are more likely to win elections and most incumbents are men. In 2012, Senator Orrin Hatch (R-Utah) won re-election to his seventh term.

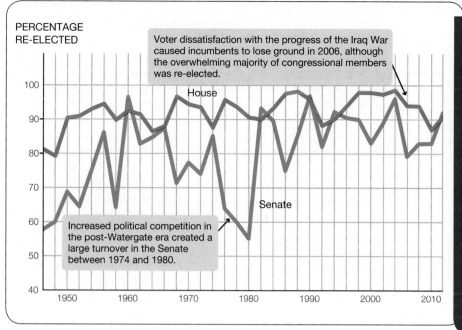

PERCENTAGE
RE-ELECTED

Voter dissatisfaction with the progress of the Iraq War caused incumbents to lose ground in 2006, although the overwhelming majority of congressional members was re-elected.

House

Senate

Increased political competition in the post-Watergate era created a large turnover in the Senate between 1974 and 1980.

100
90
80
70
60
50
40

1950   1960   1970   1980   1990   2000   2010

FIGURE 12.2

The Power of Incumbency

Members of Congress who run for re-election have a very good chance of winning. Senators have at times found it difficult to use the power of incumbency to protect their seats, as the sharp decline in Senate incumbency rates between 1974 and 1980 indicates. Has the incumbency advantage generally been greater in the House or in the Senate?

SOURCES: Norman J. Ornstein et al., eds., *Vital Statistics on Congress, 1999–2000* (Washington, DC: AEI Press, 2000), pp. 57–58; and authors' update.

90 percent for members of the Senate in recent years (see Figure 12.2). It is also evident in what is called "sophomore surge"—the tendency for candidates to win a higher percentage of the vote when seeking subsequent terms in office. Based on early estimates of the 2012 elections, approximately 92 percent of incumbents were re-elected in the House and roughly 93 percent in the Senate.

Incumbency can help a candidate by scaring off potential challengers. In many races, potential candidates may decide not to run because they fear that the incumbent simply has too much money or is too well liked or too well known, or that a district's partisan leanings are too unfavorable. The efforts of incumbents to raise funds to ward off potential challengers start early. A Connecticut Democrat, Joe Courtney, who earned the nickname "Landslide Joe" with his 91-vote margin of victory in 2006, began fund-raising for the 2008 election even before he was sworn in for his first term. In addition, the Democratic Congressional Campaign Committee placed him on its "Frontline team," a group of the 29 most vulnerable Democrats. The Democratic leadership took special efforts to raise the profile of these members of Congress. For example, Courtney and others in the Frontline team received high-profile speaking assignments on the floor of Congress and were appointed to key congressional committees. In 2008, Courtney won his seat by a comfortable margin, and he was easily re-elected in 2010 and again in 2012.[12]

The advantage of incumbency thus tends to preserve the status quo in Congress. This fact has implications for the social composition of Congress. For example, incumbency advantage makes it harder for women to increase their numbers in Congress because most incumbents are men. Women who run for open seats—that is, seats for which there are no incumbents—are just as likely to win as male candidates.[13] Supporters of **term limits** argue that such limits are the only way to get new faces into Congress. They believe that incumbency advantage and the tendency

term limits legally prescribed limits on the number of terms an elected official can serve

of many legislators to view politics as a career mean that very little turnover will occur in Congress unless limits are imposed on the number of terms a legislator may serve.

Yet the percentage of incumbents who are returned to Congress after each election also depends on how many members decide to run again. Because, each year, some members decide to retire, turnover in Congress is greater than the re-election rates of incumbents suggest. On average, 10 percent of the House and Senate decide to retire each election. In some years, the number of retirements is higher, as in 1992, when 20 percent of House members decided to retire; thus the 90 percent of incumbents who were re-elected that year was a subset of all the eligible incumbents (80 percent). The precarious economy and the backlash against the party in power made 2008 and 2010 difficult election years for some incumbents. Democrats felt particularly vulnerable in 2010, given that their party controlled the presidency and both houses of Congress in a year when economic woes contributed to strong anti-incumbent sentiment.[14] Even with these retirements during primaries, 54 incumbent Democratic members of the House and two incumbent Democratic senators lost their seats in 2010, including two who lost in the primaries. Incumbents fared better in the 2012 elections. In the House, 13 incumbents lost primary races and preliminary results showed that 22 incumbents lost their seats in the general election; while one incumbent Senator lost in the primaries and one lost the general election.

Apportionment and Redistricting The final factor affecting who wins a seat in Congress is the way congressional districts are drawn. Every ten years, state legislatures must redraw congressional districts to reflect population changes. Because the number of congressional seats has been fixed at 435 since 1929, redistricting is a zero-sum process; in order for one state to gain a seat, another must lose one. The process of allocating congressional seats among the 50 states is called **apportionment**. States with population growth gain additional seats; states with a population decline or with less population growth lose seats. Over the past several decades, the shift of the American population to the South and the West has greatly increased the size of the congressional delegations from those regions (see Figures 12.3 and 12.4). This trend continued after the 2010 census. Texas emerged as the biggest winner, with a gain of four additional seats, while Florida added two seats and Arizona, Georgia, Nevada, South Carolina, Utah, and Washington all added one extra seat.[15]

Not surprisingly, **redistricting** is a highly political process: districts are shaped to create an advantage for the party with a majority in the state legislature, which controls the redistricting process. In this complex process, those charged with drawing districts use sophisticated computer technologies to come up with the most favorable district boundaries. Redistricting can create open seats and may pit incumbents of the same party against one another, ensuring that one of them will lose. Redistricting can also give an advantage to one party by clustering voters with some ideological or sociological characteristics in a single district, or by separating those voters into two or more districts. The manipulation of electoral districts to serve the interests of a particular group is known as **gerrymandering** (see Chapter 10).

Redistricting attracts close political attention because the way districts are drawn always benefits one party over the other. In the redistricting following the 2000 census, the close balance of power in the House—with party control hinging on only six seats—made the process especially charged. Both Republicans and Democrats went to court to challenge remaps they viewed as unfair. In 2003, Texas Republicans took the unprecedented step of redrawing the lines set in 2001 rather than waiting for the next census. Even after Texas Democrats fled to Oklahoma

apportionment the process, occurring after every decennial census, that allocates congressional seats among the 50 states

redistricting the process of redrawing election districts and redistributing legislative representatives. This happens every 10 years to reflect shifts in population or in response to legal challenges to existing districts

gerrymandering the apportionment of voters in districts in such a way as to give unfair advantage to one racial or ethnic group or political party

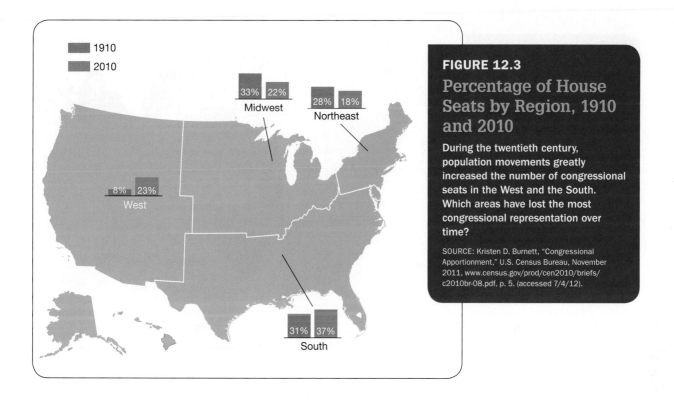

FIGURE 12.3

Percentage of House Seats by Region, 1910 and 2010

During the twentieth century, population movements greatly increased the number of congressional seats in the West and the South. Which areas have lost the most congressional representation over time?

SOURCE: Kristen D. Burnett, "Congressional Apportionment," U.S. Census Bureau, November 2011, www.census.gov/prod/cen2010/briefs/c2010br-08.pdf, p. 5. (accessed 7/4/12).

1910
2010

33% 22%
Midwest

28% 18%
Northeast

8% 23%
West

31% 37%
South

and New Mexico to prevent passage of the plan, the state legislature eventually approved the new map. Republicans benefited from the post-2010 redistricting, in part as a result of the population gains in states that have tended to vote Republican in the past. But they also benefited because Republicans control the state legislatures in the majority of the states in line to gain additional seats, which allowed them to redraw the districts in ways that consolidated Republican gains in 2010 and maximized the Republicans' future advantage.[16] As we saw in Chapter 10, since the passage of the 1982 amendments to the Voting Rights Act of 1965, race has become a major, and controversial, consideration in drawing voting districts. These amendments, which encouraged the creation of districts in which members of racial minorities have decisive majorities, have greatly increased the number of minority representatives in Congress. After the 1991–92 redistricting, the number of predominantly minority districts doubled, rising from 26 to 52. Among the most fervent supporters of the new minority districts were white Republicans, who used the opportunity to create more districts dominated by white Republican voters. These developments raise thorny questions about representation. Some analysts argue that the system may grant minorities greater sociological representation but has made it more difficult for minorities to win substantive policy goals. Others dispute this argument, noting that the strong surge of Republican voters was a more significant factor in Republican congressional victories than any Democratic losses due to racial redistricting.[17]

In the case of *Miller v. Johnson* (1995), the Supreme Court limited racial redistricting by ruling that race could not be the predominant factor in creating electoral districts.[18] The distinction between race being the "predominant" factor and its being one factor among many is very hazy. As a result, concerns about

for critical analysis

How does redistricting alter the balance of power in Congress? Why do political parties care so much about the redistricting process?

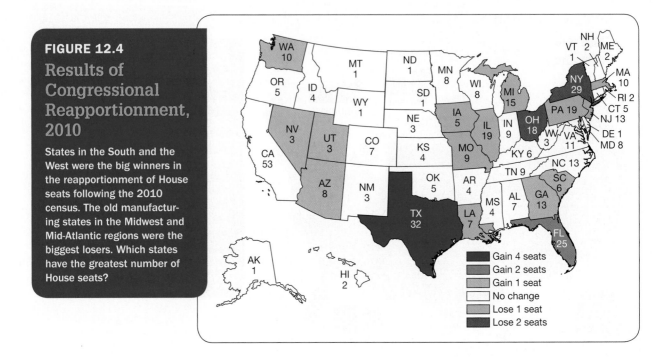

FIGURE 12.4

Results of Congressional Reapportionment, 2010

States in the South and the West were the big winners in the reapportionment of House seats following the 2010 census. The old manufacturing states in the Midwest and Mid-Atlantic regions were the biggest losers. Which states have the greatest number of House seats?

Legend:
- Gain 4 seats
- Gain 2 seats
- Gain 1 seat
- No change
- Lose 1 seat
- Lose 2 seats

redistricting and representation have not disappeared.[19] Questions about minority representation emerged in 2011 in Texas, which gained four new seats as a result of reapportionment. The Republican legislature drew a map that advantaged Republicans in three of those districts. But the plan drew a legal challenge on the grounds that it underrepresented Hispanic voters, who accounted for most of the state's population growth. Although federal judges drew a map more favorable to minorities (and Democrats), the Supreme Court ruled that the state did not have to use the map drawn by judges. The state ultimately agreed to a map that added two Latino-dominated districts. However, federal courts ruled that this map also weakened Latino and African American political power. Because the drawing of district boundaries affects incumbents as well as the field of candidates who decide to run for office, it continues to be a key battleground on which political parties fight about the meaning of representation.

Direct Patronage

As agents of their constituents, members of Congress have numerous opportunities to provide direct benefits, or **patronage**, for their districts. The most important such opportunity for direct patronage is in so-called **pork-barrel** legislation, which specifies a project to be funded within a particular district. Many observers of Congress argue that pork-barrel bills are the only ones that some members are serious about moving toward actual passage, because they are seen as so important to members' re-election bids.

A common form of pork-barreling is the "earmark," by which members of Congress insert into bills language that provides special benefits for their own constituents. When the Democrats took over Congress in 2007, they vowed to limit the use of earmarks, which had grown from 1,439 per year in 1995 to 15,268 in 2006. More troubling, earmarks were connected to congressional scandals. For example, the Republican House member Randy "Duke" Cunningham (R-Calif.)

patronage the resources available to higher officials, usually opportunities to make partisan appointments to offices and to confer grants, licenses, or special favors to supporters

pork barrel (or pork) appropriations made by legislative bodies for local projects that are often not needed but that are created so that local representatives can win re-election in their home districts

was sent to jail in 2005 for accepting bribes by companies hoping to receive earmarks in return.[20] The House passed a new rule requiring that those representatives supporting each earmark identify themselves and guarantee that they have no personal financial stake in the requested project. A new ethics law applied similar provisions to the Senate. The new requirements appear to have had some impact: the 2007 military bill, for example, cut in half the value of earmarks contained in the military bill passed in 2006. But in the midst of the sharp economic downturn in 2009, Congress passed an economic stimulus bill that contained more than 8,000 earmarks. In many cases, Republicans and some Democrats who voted against the bill were later happy to take credit from their constituents for the earmarks they had placed in it. In his 2010 State of the Union address, President Obama called for Congress to publish a list of all earmark requests on a single website. Congress not only failed to enact such legislation, but in 2010 it set a new record by passing 11,320 earmarks worth $32 billion. Still, in 2011 the House and the Senate agreed to a two-year moratorium on earmarks in spending bills. Despite the moratorium, some members of Congress charged that special provisions were creeping back into legislation, and few members of Congress supported making the moratorium permanent.[21]

Highway bills are a favorite vehicle for congressional pork-barrel spending. A 2005 highway bill was full of such items, containing more than 6,000 projects earmarked for specific congressional districts. These measures often have little to do with transportation needs, instead serving as evidence for constituents that congressional members can bring federal dollars back home. Perhaps the most extravagant item in the 2005 bill—and the one least needed for transportation—was a bridge in Alaska designed to connect a barely populated island to the town of Ketchikan, population just under 8,000. At a cost that could soar to $2 billion, the bridge would have replaced an existing five-minute ferry ride. Alaska's representative, Don Young (R), proudly claimed credit. After Hurricane Katrina, "the bridge to nowhere" became a symbol of wasteful congressional spending. Sensitive to this criticism, Congress removed the earmarks for the bridge from the final legislation. Even so, it allowed Alaska to keep the funds for other unspecified transportation projects. In 2007 the state quietly dropped the project.

There are a few other types of direct patronage (see Figure 12.5). One important form of constituency service is intervention with federal administrative agencies on behalf of constituents. Members of the House and Senate and their staff spend a great deal of time on the telephone and in administrative offices seeking to secure favorable treatment for constituents and supporters. For example, members of Congress can assist senior citizens who are having Social Security or Medicare benefit eligibility problems. Most members of Congress have a "constituent services" section on their websites, providing information about what they can and cannot do to assist their constituents. For example, Representative Tom Petri's (R-Wisc.) website puts it this way: "If you can't get an answer from a federal agency in a timely fashion, or if you feel you have been treated unfairly, my office may be able to help resolve a problem or get you the information you need. While we cannot guarantee you a favorable outcome, we will do our best to help you receive a fair and timely response to your problem."[22] A small but related form of patronage is securing an appointment to one of the military academies for the child of a constituent. Traditionally, these appointments are allocated one to a district.

A different form of patronage is the **private bill**. Unlike a public bill, which is supposed to deal with general rules and categories of behavior, people, and institutions, a private bill proposes to grant some kind of relief, special privilege, or exemption to the person named in the bill. As many as 75 percent of all private

for critical **analysis**
Why are earmarks so difficult to eliminate?

private bill a proposal in Congress to provide a specific person with some kind of relief, such as a special exemption from immigration quotas

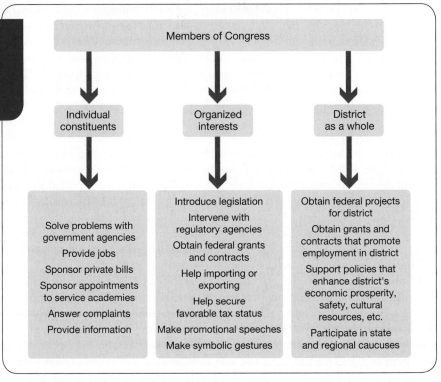

FIGURE 12.5
How Members of
Congress Represent
Their Districts

Members of Congress

Individual constituents

Organized interests

District as a whole

Solve problems with government agencies
Provide jobs
Sponsor private bills
Sponsor appointments to service academies
Answer complaints
Provide information

Introduce legislation
Intervene with regulatory agencies
Obtain federal grants and contracts
Help importing or exporting
Help secure favorable tax status
Make promotional speeches
Make symbolic gestures

Obtain federal projects for district
Obtain grants and contracts that promote employment in district
Support policies that enhance district's economic prosperity, safety, cultural resources, etc.
Participate in state and regional caucuses

bills introduced (and one-third of those that pass) are concerned with obtaining citizenship for foreign nationals who do not have resident status in the United States. For example, in 2010 a private bill granted legal immigrant status to the widow of a U.S. Marine from Tennessee who gave birth to their son after the marine was killed in Iraq in 2008.[23] Private legislation is a congressional privilege that could be abused, but it is impossible to imagine members of Congress completely giving up one of the easiest, cheapest, and most effective forms of patronage available to them. It can be defended as an indispensable part of the process by which members of Congress seek to fulfill their role as representatives. And obviously they like the privilege because it helps them win re-election.

● The Organization of Congress

Explain how party leadership, the committee system, the staff system, and caucuses help structure congressional business

The U.S. Congress is not only a representative assembly; it is also a legislative body. For Americans, representation and legislation go hand in hand, but many parliamentary bodies in other countries are representative without the power to make laws. It is no small achievement that the U.S. Congress both represents and governs.

To exercise its power to make laws, Congress must first bring about something close to an organizational miracle. The building blocks of congressional organization include the political parties, the committee system, congressional staff, the caucuses, and the parliamentary

conference a gathering of House Republicans every two years to elect their House leaders. Democrats call their gathering the caucus

caucus (political) a normally closed meeting of a political or legislative group to select candidates, plan strategy, or make decisions regarding legislative matters

rules of the House and Senate. Each of these factors plays a key role in the organization of Congress and in the process through which Congress formulates and enacts laws.

Party Leadership in the House

Every two years, at the beginning of a new Congress, the members of each party gather to elect their House leaders. House Republicans call their gathering the **conference**. House Democrats call theirs the **caucus**. The elected leader of the majority party is later proposed to the whole House and is automatically elected to the position of **Speaker of the House**, with voting along straight party lines. The House majority conference or caucus then also elects a **majority leader**. The minority party goes through the same process and selects a **minority leader**. Each party also elects a **whip** to line up party members on important votes and to relay voting information to the leaders.

Next in order of importance for each party after the Speaker and majority or minority leader is what Democrats call the Steering and Policy Committee—Republicans have a separate steering committee and a separate policy committee—whose tasks are to assign new legislators to committees and to deal with the requests of incumbent members for transfers from one committee to another. At one time, party leaders strictly controlled committee assignments, using them to enforce party discipline. Today, in principle, representatives receive the assignments they want. But often several individuals seek assignments to the most important committees, which gives the leadership an opportunity to cement alliances when it resolves conflicting requests.

Generally, representatives seek assignments that will allow them to influence decisions of special importance to their districts. Representatives from farm districts, for example, may request seats on the Agriculture Committee.[24] Seats on powerful committees such as Ways and Means, which is responsible for tax legislation, and Appropriations are especially popular.

Party Leadership in the Senate

Within the Senate, the majority party usually designates a member with the greatest seniority to serve as president pro tempore, a position of primarily ceremonial leadership. Real power is in the hands of the majority leader and minority leader, each elected by party conference. Together they control the Senate's calendar, or agenda for legislation.

Each party also elects a policy committee, which advises the leadership on legislative priorities. The structure of majority party leadership in the House and the Senate is shown in Figures 12.6 and 12.7.

The Committee System

The committee system is central to the operation of Congress. At each stage of the legislative process, Congress relies on committees and subcommittees to do the hard work of sorting through alternatives and writing legislation. There are several different kinds of congressional committees: standing committees, select committees, joint committees, and conference committees.

Standing Committees The most important arenas of congressional policy making are **standing committees**. These committees remain in existence from

Speaker of the House the chief presiding officer of the House of Representatives. The Speaker is the most important party and House leader, and can influence the legislative agenda, the fate of individual pieces of legislation, and members' positions within the House

majority leader the elected leader of the majority party in the House of Representatives or in the Senate. In the House, the majority leader is subordinate in the party hierarchy to the Speaker of the House

minority leader the elected leader of the minority party in the House or Senate

whip a party member in the House or Senate responsible for coordinating the party's legislative strategy, building support for key issues, and counting votes

standing committee a permanent committee with the power to propose and write legislation that covers a particular subject, such as finance or agriculture

As Speaker of the House, John Boehner attempted to keep his party unified, despite disagreements between the Tea Party members and other Republicans. Especially during the 2011 debate over the national debt, Boehner worked hard to persuade House Republicans to fall into line.

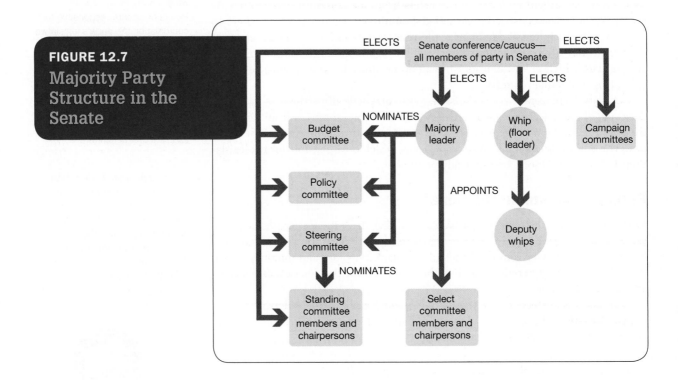

FIGURE 12.6

Majority Party Structure in the House of Representatives

*Includes Speaker, majority leader, chief and deputy whips, caucus chair, chairs of five major committees, members elected by regional caucuses, members elected by recently elected representatives, and at-large members appointed by the Speaker.

FIGURE 12.7

Majority Party Structure in the Senate

one session of Congress to the next; they have the power to propose and write legislation. The jurisdiction of each standing committee covers a particular subject matter, which in most cases parallels a major department or agency in the executive branch (see Table 12.2). Among the most important standing committees are those in charge of finances. The House Ways and Means Committee and the Senate Finance Committee are powerful because of their jurisdiction over taxes, trade, and expensive entitlement programs such as Social Security and

TABLE 12.2

Permanent Committees of Congress

HOUSE COMMITTEES

Agriculture	Judiciary
Appropriations	Natural Resources
Armed Services	Oversight and Government Reform
Budget	Rules
Education and Labor	Science and Technology
Energy and Commerce	Small Business
Financial Services	Standards of Official Conduct
Foreign Affairs	Transportation and Infrastructure
Homeland Security	Veterans' Affairs
House Administration	Ways and Means

SENATE COMMITTEES

Agriculture, Nutrition, and Forestry	Foreign Relations
Appropriations	Health, Education, Labor, and Pensions
Armed Services	Homeland Security and Governmental Affairs
Banking, Housing, and Urban Affairs	Judiciary
Budget	Rules and Administration
Commerce, Science, and Transportation	Select Intelligence
Energy and Natural Resources	Small Business and Entrepreneurship
Environment and Public Works	Veterans' Affairs
Finance	

Medicare. The Senate and House Appropriations committees also play important ongoing roles because they decide how much funding various programs will actually receive; they also determine exactly how the money will be spent. A seat on an appropriations committee allows a member the opportunity to direct funds to a favored program—perhaps one in his or her home district.

Except for the House Rules Committee, all standing committees receive proposals for legislation and process them into official bills. The House Rules Committee decides the order in which bills come up for a vote on the House floor and determines the specific rules that govern the length of debate and opportunity for amendments. The Senate, which has less formal organization and fewer rules, does not have a rules committee.

Select Committees Select committees are usually not permanent and usually do not have the power to present legislation to the full Congress. (The House and Senate Select Intelligence committees are permanent, however, and do have the power to report legislation, which means they can send legislation to the full House or

select committees (usually) temporary legislative committees set up to highlight or investigate a particular issue or address an issue not within the jurisdiction of existing committees

Senate for consideration. These committees hold hearings and serve as focal points for the issues they are charged with considering. Congressional leaders form select committees when they want to take up issues that fall outside the jurisdictions of existing committees, to highlight an issue, or to investigate a particular problem. Examples of select committees investigating political scandals include the Senate Watergate Committee of 1973, the committees set up in 1987 to investigate the Iran-Contra affair, and the Whitewater Committee of 1995–96. Select committees set up to highlight ongoing issues have included the House Select Committee on Hunger, established in 1984, and the House Select Committee on Energy Independence and Global Warming, created in 2007 but abolished in 2011, when Republicans assumed control of the House. A few select committees have remained in existence for many years, such as the select committees on aging; hunger; children, youth, and families; and narcotics abuse and control. In 1995, however, congressional Republicans abolished most of these select committees, both to streamline operations and to remove a forum used primarily by Democratic representatives and their allies. In 2003 an important select committee, the House Select Committee on Homeland Security, was created to oversee the new Department of Homeland Security. Unlike most select committees, this one had the ability to present legislation. Initially the committee had only temporary status. It was made a regular permanent committee in 2005.

Joint Committees **Joint committees** involve members from both the Senate and the House. There are four such committees: economic, taxation, library, and printing. These joint committees are permanent, but they do not have the power to present legislation. The Joint Economic Committee and the Joint Taxation Committee have often played important roles in collecting information and holding hearings on economic and financial issues. In 2011, Congress created the Joint Select Committee on Deficit Reduction and, in an unusual move, gave the committee the power to write and report legislation. Informally known as "the supercommittee," the committee was charged with coming up with $1.2 trillion in debt reduction. Formed after a contentious debate about raising the debt limit (usually a routine matter), the supercommittee proved unable to come to an agreement and disbanded less than four months after it was created.

joint committees legislative committees formed of members of both the House and Senate

Conference Committees Finally, **conference committees** are temporary committees whose members are appointed by the Speaker of the House and the presiding officer of the Senate. These committees are charged with reaching a compromise on legislation once it has been passed by the House and the Senate. Conference committees play an extremely important role in determining the laws that are actually passed, because they must reconcile any differences in the legislation passed by the House and Senate.

When control of Congress is divided between two parties, each is guaranteed significant representation in conference committees. When a single party controls both houses, the majority party is not obligated to offer such representation to the minority party. In 2003, Democrats complained that Republicans took this power to the extreme by excluding them and adding new provisions to legislation at the conference committee stage. Democrats even prevented several conference committees from convening in order to protest their near exclusion from conference committees on major energy, health care, and transportation laws. After they returned to power in 2007, the Democrats also largely bypassed the conference committees; when their early efforts to reach compromises in committee were

conference committees joint committees created to work out a compromise on House and Senate versions of a piece of legislation

derailed by partisan differences, the Democrats began making closed-door agreements between top leaders in the House and the Senate. Although the process facilitated compromises across the two chambers, it meant that important changes to bills were made in private, without the transparency that would have been part of the conference committee process. After 2010, Congress continued to avoid conference committees. Instead, the Republican House and Democratic Senate exchanged amendments as they sought to reach agreement on the final version of a bill, a practice known informally as "ping pong."[25]

Politics and the Organization of Committees Within each committee, hierarchy has usually been based on **seniority** determined by years of continuous service on that particular committee. In general, each committee is chaired by the most senior member of the majority party. But the principle of seniority is not absolute. When the Republicans took over the House in 1995, they violated the principle of seniority in the selection of key committee chairs. House Speaker Newt Gingrich defended the new practice, saying, "You've got to carry the moral responsibility of fielding the team that can win or you cheat the whole conference."[26] Since then, Republicans have continued to depart from the seniority principle, often choosing committee chairs on the basis of loyalty or fund-raising abilities rather than seniority. In 2007, Democrats returned to the seniority principle for choosing committee chairs but altered traditional practices in other ways by offering freshman Democrats choice committee assignments in order to increase their chances of re-election.[27]

> **seniority** the ranking given to an individual on the basis of length of continuous service on a committee in Congress

Over the years, Congress has reformed its organizational structure and operating procedures. Most changes have been made to improve efficiency, but some reforms have also been a response to political considerations. In the 1970s, for example, Congress increased the number of subcommittees and gave greater autonomy to subcommittee chairs. (Subcommittees are responsible for considering a specific subset of issues under a committee's jurisdiction.) In the past, committee chairs had exercised considerable power; they determined hearing schedules, selected subcommittee members, appointed committee staff, and sometimes used their power to block consideration of bills they opposed. By enhancing subcommittee power and allowing more members to chair subcommittees and appoint subcommittee staff, the reforms undercut the power of committee chairs. Yet the reforms of the 1970s created new problems for Congress: power became more fragmented, making it harder to reach agreement on legislation. The Republican leadership of the 104th Congress (1995–97), seeking to reverse this fragmentation of congressional power and concentrate more authority in the party leadership, reduced the number of subcommittees and limited the time committee chairs could serve to three terms. They made good on this in 2001, when they replaced 13 committee chairs.

As a consequence of these changes, committees no longer have the central role they once held in policy making. When the Democrats took control of Congress in 2007, they repealed the term limits on committee chairs, but Republicans reinstated the practice when they reassumed control of the House in 2010. Still, sharp partisan divisions have made it difficult for committees to deliberate and bring bipartisan expertise to bear on policy making as in the past. With committees less able to engage in effective decision making, they typically do not deliberate for very long or call witnesses, and it has become more common in recent years for party-driven legislation to go directly to the floor, bypassing committees altogether.[28] Nonetheless, committees continue to play an important role in the legislative process, especially on issues that are not sharply partisan.[29]

The Staff System: Staffers and Agencies

The congressional institution second in importance only to the committee system is the staff system. Every member of Congress employs many staff members whose tasks include handling constituent requests and, to a large extent, dealing with legislative details and the activities of administrative agencies. Staffers often bear the primary responsibility for formulating and drafting proposals, organizing hearings, dealing with administrative agencies, and negotiating with lobbyists. Indeed, legislators typically deal with one another through staff, rather than through direct personal contact. Staffers even develop policy ideas, draft legislation, and, in some instances, have a good deal of influence over the legislative process. Representatives and senators together employ 11,500 staffers in their Washington and home offices. In addition, Congress also employs roughly 2,000 committee staffers. These individuals make up the permanent staff that stays attached to every House and Senate committee regardless of turnover in Congress and that is responsible for organizing and administering the committee's work, including doing research, scheduling, organizing hearings, and drafting legislation. Committee staffers can play key roles in the legislative process.

One example of the importance that members of Congress attach to committee staffers was the conflict over hiring a new staff director for the House Ethics Committee in 2005. The Ethics Committee (officially known as the Committee on Standards of Official Conduct) has the power to investigate members for unethical practices and can issue reprimands or censures when it finds that members have violated House rules. The staff director is critical in determining how energetically and effectively the committee pursues its investigations. With allegations of ethics violations swirling around the congressional leadership, and criminal investigations of congressional lobbyist Jack Abramoff under way, the Ethics Committee was in a pivotal position. But for the first half of 2005, the committee was at a standstill as Republicans and Democrats fought over who would have the job of staff director. Despite House rules calling for the committee staff director to be nonpartisan, the committee chair, Doc Hastings (R-Wash.), initially sought to appoint a partisan Republican to the job. After nearly half a year of wrangling, Hastings agreed to appoint a staff director acceptable to both parties.

Not only does Congress employ personal and committee staff, but it has also established **staff agencies** designed to provide the legislative branch with resources and expertise independent of the executive branch. These agencies enhance Congress's capacity to oversee administrative agencies and to evaluate presidential programs and proposals. They include the Congressional Research Service, which performs research for legislators who wish to know the facts and competing arguments relevant to policy proposals or other legislative business; the Government Accountability Office, through which Congress can investigate the financial and administrative affairs of any government agency or program; and the Congressional Budget Office, which assesses the economic implications and likely costs of proposed federal programs. A fourth agency, the Office of Technology Assessment, which provided Congress with analyses of scientific or technical issues, was abolished by the Republican-dominated Congress in 1995.

staff agencies legislative support agencies responsible for policy analysis

Members of Congress rely heavily on their personal staffs and on committee staffs, who often play an important role in the legislative process.

Informal Organization: The Caucuses

In addition to the official organization of Congress, an unofficial organizational structure also exists: the caucuses. **Caucuses** are groups of senators or representatives who share certain opinions, interests, or social characteristics. A large number of caucuses are composed of legislators representing particular economic or policy interests, such as the Travel and Tourism Caucus, the Steel Caucus, the Mushroom Caucus, and Concerned Senators for the Arts. Legislators who share common backgrounds have organized caucuses such as the Congressional Black Caucus, the Congressional Caucus for Women's Issues, and the Hispanic Caucus. All these caucuses seek to advance the interests of the groups they represent by promoting legislation, encouraging Congress to hold hearings, and pressing administrative agencies for favorable treatment. In recent years, some caucuses have evolved into powerful lobbying organizations, well funded by interest groups. For example, the Sportsmen's Caucus receives funds from a nonprofit foundation that itself benefits from donations from the National Rifle Association, sports equipment manufacturers, and firearms manufacturers. In 2010 conservative Republicans in the House and Senate formed the Tea Party Caucus to advance anti-spending policies.

caucuses (congressional) associations of members of Congress based on party, interest, or social group, such as gender or race

Rules of Lawmaking: How a Bill Becomes a Law

> **Outline the steps in the process of passing a law**

The institutional structure of Congress is a key factor in shaping the legislative process. A second and equally important set of factors is the rules of congressional procedure. These rules govern everything from the introduction of a **bill** through its submission to the president for signing (see Figure 12.8). Not only do these regulations influence the fate of every bill, but they also help determine the distribution of power in the Congress.

bill a proposed law that has been sponsored by a member of Congress and submitted to the clerk of the House or Senate

Committee Deliberation

The first step in getting a law passed is drafting legislation. Members of Congress, the White House, and federal agencies all take roles in developing and drafting initial legislation. The bill is then officially submitted by a senator or representative to the clerk of the House or Senate and referred to the appropriate committee for deliberation. During the course of its deliberations, the committee typically refers the bill to one of its subcommittees, which may hold hearings, listen to expert testimony, and amend the proposed legislation before referring it to the full committee for consideration. The full committee may then accept the recommendation of the subcommittee or hold its own hearings and prepare its own amendments.

The next steps in the process are the **committee markup** sessions, in which committees rewrite bills to reflect changes discussed during the hearings. In the partisan fighting that has characterized Congress in recent years, the minority party has charged that its members are often not given enough time to study proposed legislation before markup. In 2003 conflict over this issue drew the Capitol police to

committee markup the session in which a congressional committee rewrites legislation to incorporate changes discussed during hearings on the bill

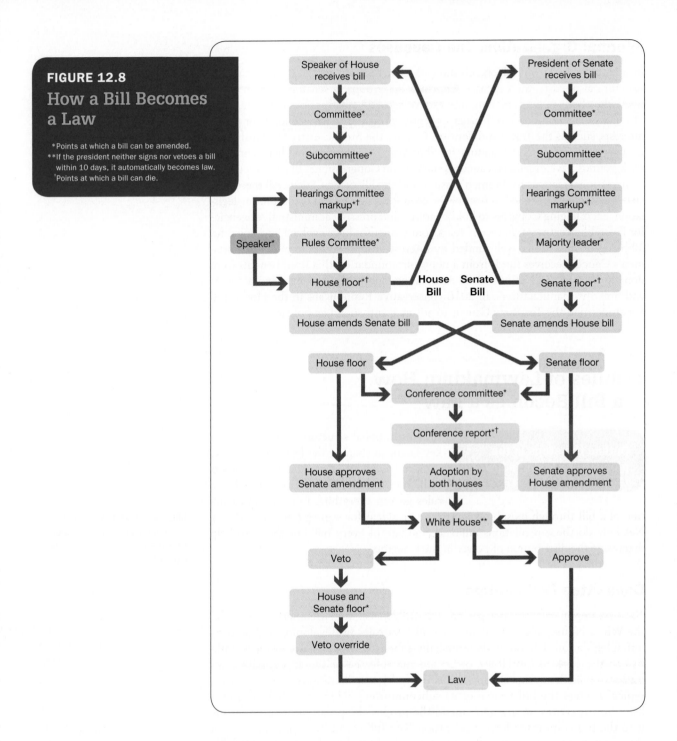

FIGURE 12.8

How a Bill Becomes a Law

*Points at which a bill can be amended.
**If the president neither signs nor vetoes a bill within 10 days, it automatically becomes law.
†Points at which a bill can die.

Speaker of House receives bill → Committee* → Subcommittee* → Hearings Committee markup*† → Rules Committee* → House floor*†

President of Senate receives bill → Committee* → Subcommittee* → Hearings Committee markup*† → Majority leader* → Senate floor*†

Speaker*

House Bill   Senate Bill

House amends Senate bill   Senate amends House bill

House floor   Senate floor

Conference committee*

Conference report*†

House approves Senate amendment   Adoption by both houses   Senate approves House amendment

White House**

Veto   Approve

House and Senate floor*

Veto override

Law

the House and almost resulted in a fistfight among representatives when Democrats protested their treatment by the House Ways and Means Committee. Charging that they had been given a complex pension bill only 10 hours before markup, House Democrats walked out. The ensuing commotion, with Republicans calling the police and a Democratic congressman threatening a Republican, presented a sorry spectacle for the evening news. Although Democrats lost a resolution to censure the committee for its actions, the committee chair, Bill Thomas (R-Calif.), later broke down in tears as he apologized on the House floor.

Frequently, the committee and subcommittee do little or nothing with a bill that has been submitted to them. Many bills are simply allowed to "die in committee" without serious consideration. Often, members of Congress introduce legislation that they neither expect nor even desire to see enacted into law but present merely to please a constituency group. These bills die a quick and painless death. Other pieces of legislation have ardent supporters and die in committee only after a long battle. But in either case, most bills are never reported out of the committees to which they are assigned. In a typical congressional session, 95 percent of the roughly 8,000 bills introduced die in committee.

In the House, the relative handful of bills that are presented out of committee must pass one last hurdle within the committee system—the Rules Committee, which determines the rules that will govern action on the bill on the House floor. In particular, the Rules Committee allots the time for debate and decides to what extent amendments to the bill can be proposed from the floor. A bill's supporters generally prefer a **closed rule**, which puts severe limits on floor debate and amendments. Opponents of a bill usually prefer an **open rule**, which permits potentially damaging floor debate and makes it easier to add amendments that may cripple the bill or weaken its chances for passage. Thus, the outcome of the Rules Committee's deliberations can be extremely important, and the committee's hearings can be an occasion for sharp conflict. In recent years, the Rules Committee has become less powerful because the House leadership exercises so much influence over its decisions.

closed rule a provision by the House Rules Committee limiting or prohibiting the introduction of amendments during debate

open rule a provision by the House Rules Committee that permits floor debate and the addition of new amendments to a bill

Debate

The next step in getting a law passed is debate on the floor of the House and Senate. Party control of the agenda is reinforced by the rule giving the Speaker of the House and the president of the Senate the power of recognition during debate on a bill. Usually the chair knows the purpose for which a member intends to speak well in advance of the occasion. Spontaneous efforts to gain recognition are often foiled. For example, the Speaker may ask, "For what purpose does the member rise?" before deciding whether to grant recognition.

In the House, virtually all the time allotted by the Rules Committee for debate on a given bill is controlled by the bill's sponsor and by its leading opponent. In almost every case, these two people are the committee chair and the ranking minority member of the committee that processed the bill—or those they designate. These two participants are, by rule and tradition, granted the power to allocate most of the debate time in small amounts to members who are seeking to speak for or against the measure. Preference in the allocation of time goes to the members of the committee whose jurisdiction covers the bill.

In the Senate, the leadership has much less control over floor debate. Indeed, the Senate is unique among the world's legislative bodies for its commitment to unlimited debate. Once given the floor, a senator may speak as long as he or she wishes. On a number of memorable occasions, senators have used this opportunity to prevent action on legislation that they opposed. Through this tactic, called the **filibuster**, small minorities or even one individual in the Senate can force the majority to give in. Filibusters can be ended by a Senate vote to cut off debate, called **cloture**. From 1917 to 1975, it took two-thirds of the Senate or 67 votes to end a filibuster. In 1975 the Senate changed the rules to three-fifths of the Senate or 60 votes

filibuster a tactic used by members of the Senate to prevent action on legislation they oppose by continuously holding the floor and speaking until the majority backs down. Once given the floor, senators have unlimited time to speak, and it requires a vote of three-fifths of the Senate to end a filibuster

cloture a rule allowing a majority of two-thirds or three-fifths of the members of a legislative body to set a time limit on debate over a given bill. In the U.S. Senate, 60 senators (three-fifths) must agree in order to impose such a limit

needed for cloture. The threat of a filibuster ensures that, in crafting legislation and proposing judicial appointments, the majority takes into account the viewpoint of the political minority. For much of American history, senators only rarely used the filibuster, though during the 1950s and '60s, opponents of civil rights legislation often used filibusters to block its passage. In the last 20 years, the filibuster has become so common that observers routinely note that it takes 60 votes to get anything passed in the Senate. The 111th Congress (2009–10) holds the record, with 137 cloture votes; with 109 cloture votes, the 112th Congress (2011–12) had the third highest in history. Frustrated at the difficulty of moving his agenda through the Senate, President Obama noted in his 2010 State of the Union Address, "You had to cast more votes to break filibusters last year than in the entire 1950s and '60s combined."[30] Yet the filibuster is a tool that both parties have used, and with a 67-vote majority required to eliminate it, the filibuster is likely to remain a feature of American politics for the foreseeable future.

The filibuster is not the only technique used to block Senate debate. Under Senate rules, members have virtually unlimited ability to propose amendments to a pending bill. Each amendment must be voted on before the bill can come to a final vote. The introduction of new amendments can be stopped only by unanimous consent. This, in effect, can permit a determined minority to filibuster by amendment, indefinitely delaying the passage of a bill. Senators can also place "holds," or stalling devices, on bills to delay debate. Senators place holds on bills when they fear that openly opposing them will be unpopular. Because holds are kept secret, the senators placing the holds do not have to take public responsibility for their actions. There have been several efforts to eliminate holds. In 1997, opponents of this practice introduced an amendment that would have required publicizing the identity of the senator putting a bill on hold. But when the Senate voted on the measure, the proposal to end the practice of anonymous holds had "mysteriously disappeared."[31] Although no one took credit for killing the measure, it was evident that the majority of senators wanted to maintain the practice. In 2007, reformers succeeded in passing the Honest Leadership and Open Government Act. Although the new law did not eliminate holds, it contained provisions requiring senators who imposed a hold to identify themselves in the *Congressional Record* after six days and state the reasons for the hold.[32] Even with this provision,

In 2010, Senator Bernard Sanders of Vermont held the Senate floor for over eight hours, to draw attention to concerns about a tax plan. Sanders's long speech wasn't technically a filibuster (because it did not stop any Senate business), but it provides an example of the rule that a senator can speak as long he or she wants once given the floor.

senators have continued to impose holds on legislation and especially on presidential appointees. Senator Richard Shelby (R-Ala.) aroused the ire of the White House in 2010 for placing a "blanket hold" on more than 70 presidential nominees. Unusual in its sweeping nature, Shelby's hold aimed to force the White House to support several defense-related contracts that would benefit the state of Alabama.[33]

Once a bill is debated on the floor of the House and the Senate, the leaders schedule it for a vote on the floor of each chamber. By this time, congressional leaders know what the vote will be; leaders do not bring legislation to the floor unless they are fairly certain it is going to pass. As a consequence, it is unusual for the leadership to lose a bill on the floor. On rare occasions, the last moments of the floor vote can be very dramatic, as each party's leadership puts its whip organization into action to make sure that wavering members vote with the party. In September 2008 the House of Representatives surprisingly rejected a $700 billion bank rescue plan, which led the Dow Jones Industrial Index to decline nearly 7 percent in a single day—one of the biggest drops in recent history. As the *New York Times* reported, lawmakers were "almost speechless" on hearing that the bill had not passed; not only did the White House and the congressional leadership of both parties expect the bill to prevail, albeit narrowly, but so did even its most ardent opponents. As the end of the voting period drew close, it was clear that the bill was going down to defeat, with 205 votes for the bill and 228 against. Since members of the House can change their votes during the voting period, the Speaker decided to extend the period to forty minutes in order to corral votes. Despite the efforts of both Democratic and Republican leaders, they could not persuade enough members to switch their votes. A few days later, the House passed a revised version of the bill by 263 to 171 votes.[34]

Conference Committee: Reconciling House and Senate Versions of Legislation

Getting a bill out of committee and through both houses of Congress is no guarantee that the bill will be enacted into law; it must be considered by a conference committee. Frequently, bills that begin with similar provisions in both chambers emerge with little resemblance to each other. Alternatively, a bill may be passed by one chamber but undergo substantial revision in the other chamber. In such cases, a conference committee composed of the senior members of the committees or subcommittees that initiated the bill may be required to iron out differences between the two now-dissimilar pieces of legislation. Sometimes members or leaders will let objectionable provisions pass on the floor, knowing that they will get the chance to make changes in conference. Usually, conference committees meet behind closed doors. Agreement requires a majority of each of the two delegations. Legislation that emerges successfully from a conference committee is more often a compromise than a clear victory of one set of forces over another. In recent years, as we have seen, polarization in Congress has led to much less reliance on conference committees. Instead, leaders exchange amendments in the hope of reaching agreement.

When a bill comes out of conference, it faces one more hurdle. Before it can be sent to the president for signing, the House-Senate conference committee's version of the bill must be approved on the floor of each chamber. Usually such approval is given quickly. Occasionally, however, a bill's opponents use this round of approval as one last opportunity to defeat a piece of legislation.

Presidential Action

The final step in passing a law is presidential approval. Once adopted by the House and Senate, a bill goes to the president, who may choose to sign the bill into law or veto it. If the president does not sign the bill or veto it within 10 days, and Congress is in session, the bill automatically becomes law. The **veto** is the president's constitutional power to reject a piece of legislation. To veto a bill, the president returns it unsigned within 10 days to the house of Congress in which it originated. If Congress adjourns during the 10-day period, and the president has taken no action, the bill is also considered to be vetoed. This latter method is known as the **pocket veto**. The possibility of a presidential veto affects how willing members of Congress are to push for different pieces of legislation at different times. If they think a proposal is likely to be vetoed they might shelve it until a later time.

A presidential veto may be overridden by a two-thirds vote in both the House and Senate. A veto override says much about the support that a president can expect from Congress, and it can deliver a stinging blow to the executive branch. Presidents will often back down from a veto threat if they believe that Congress will override the veto.

veto the president's constitutional power to turn down acts of Congress. A presidential veto may be overridden by a two-thirds vote of each house of Congress

pocket veto a presidential veto that is automatically triggered if the president does not act on a given piece of legislation passed during the final 10 days of a legislative session

● How Congress Decides

> **Analyze the factors that influence which laws Congress decides to pass**

What determines the kinds of legislation that Congress ultimately produces? According to the simplest theories of representation, members of Congress respond to the views of their constituents. In fact, the process of creating a legislative agenda, drawing up a list of possible measures, and deciding among them is a very complex one, in which a variety of influences from inside and outside government play important roles. External influences include a legislator's constituency and various interest groups. Influences from inside government include party leadership, congressional colleagues, and the president. Let us examine each of these influences individually and then consider how they interact to produce congressional policy decisions.

Constituency

Because members of Congress, for the most part, want to be re-elected, we would expect the views of their constituents to be a primary influence on the decisions that legislators make. Yet constituency influence is not so straightforward. In fact, most constituents pay little attention to politics and often do not even know what policies their representatives support. Nonetheless, members of Congress spend a lot of time worrying about what their constituents think, because they realize that the choices they make may be scrutinized in a future election and used as ammunition by an opposing candidate. Because of this possibility, members of Congress do try to anticipate their constituents' policy views, especially if they think that voters will take them into account during elections.[35] In this way, constituents may affect congressional policy choices even when there is little direct evidence of their influence. In October 1998, for example, 31 House Democrats broke party ranks and voted in favor of an impeachment inquiry against President Clinton because they believed a "no" vote could cost them re-election that November. In 2002 the White House successfully pressed to schedule the vote authorizing the use of force in Iraq right before the midterm elections in order to pressure members to vote for it.

Interest Groups

Interest groups are another important external influence on congressional policies. When members of Congress are making voting decisions, those interest groups that have some connection to constituents in particular members' districts are most likely to be influential, and those groups with the ability to mobilize followers in many congressional districts may be especially influential. In recent years, Washington-based interest groups with little grassroots strength have recognized the importance of locally generated activity. Accordingly, they have sought to simulate grassroots pressure with so-called Astroturf lobbying (see Chapter 11). Such campaigns encourage constituents to sign form letters, postcards, or e-mails, which are then sent to congressional representatives. Campaigns set up toll-free telephone numbers for a system in which simply reporting your name and address to the listening computer will generate a letter to your congressional representative. One Senate office estimated that such organized campaigns to demonstrate "grassroots" support account for two-thirds of the mail the office received. As such campaigns increase, however, they become less influential, because members of Congress are aware of how rare real constituent interest actually is.[36]

Many interest groups now also use legislative "scorecards" that rate how members of Congress vote on issues of importance to that group. A high or low rating by an important interest group may provide a potent weapon in the next election. Interest groups can increase their influence over a particular piece of legislation by signaling their intention to include it in their scoring. Among the most influential groups that use scorecards, often posting them on their websites for members and the public to see, are the National Federation of Independent Business, the AFL-CIO, National Right to Life, the League of Conservation Voters, and the National Rifle Association.

Interest groups also have substantial influence in setting the legislative agenda and in helping to craft specific language in legislation. Today, sophisticated lobbyists win influence by providing information about policies to busy members of Congress. In the 2009–10 health reform effort, the biotechnology firm Genentech ghostwrote statements that more than a dozen members of Congress placed into the *Congressional Record.* Genentech's role came to light when it became evident that some members had used the exact same language in their entries.[37] In recent years, interest groups have also begun to build broader coalitions and comprehensive campaigns around particular policy issues. These coalitions do not rise from the grass roots but instead are put together by Washington lobbyists, who launch comprehensive lobbying campaigns that combine simulated grassroots activity with information and campaign funding for members of Congress.

Close financial ties between members of Congress and interest-group lobbyists often raise eyebrows because they

Members of Congress often spend a great deal of time in their electoral districts meeting with constituents. Representative Elijah E. Cummings of Maryland is shown here greeting constituents at an event in Baltimore.

suggest that interest groups get special treatment in exchange for political donations. Concerns about the influence of lobbyists in Congress mounted in the early 2000s when Republicans launched the K Street Project, named after the street in Washington where many high-powered lobbyists have offices. The K Street Project placed former Republican staffers in key lobbying positions and ensured a large and steady flow of corporate cash into Republican coffers. Congressional relationships to lobbyists came under close scrutiny when the lobbyist Jack Abramoff, a self-proclaimed big supporter of the K Street Project, pled guilty in early 2006 to charges of conspiracy, mail fraud, and tax evasion.

Concern over such corruption led Congress to enact new ethics legislation in 2007. The new law sets new restrictions on the gifts lobbyists can bestow on lawmakers and limits privately funded travel. The law also prohibits members of Congress from lobbying for two years after they retire and requires lawmakers to identify the earmarks they insert in legislation. Further, it aims to shine light on the practice of "bundling," whereby lobbyists assemble money from a number of clients to make a single political donation. Now lobbyists are required to disclose the names of the individual contributors to these political donations. Although the new law provides additional transparency, revealing more about the relationship between lobbyists and members of Congress, it is widely viewed as lacking sufficient authority to go after those who are suspected of ethics violations.[38] Moreover, the large sums of cash raised by "super PACs"—discussed in Chapter 10—have introduced a whole new set of questions about the role of special interests in politics, especially because donors to super PACs can remain anonymous. Although they cannot openly coordinate with candidates, super PACs can endorse candidates by name and are often run by people close to the candidates they support. In 2012 super PACs poured unprecedented sums of money into the race for president, but they also targeted key congressional contests in an effort to affect the balance of power between the parties in Congress.[39]

Party

In both the House and Senate, party leaders have a good deal of influence over the behavior of their party members. This influence, sometimes called "party discipline," was once so powerful that it dominated the lawmaking process. In the late 1800s, party leaders could often command the allegiance of more than 90 percent of their members. A vote in which half or more of the members of one party take one position while at least half of the members of the other party take the opposing position is called a **party unity vote**. At the beginning of the twentieth century, nearly half of all **roll-call votes** in the House of Representatives were party votes. For much of the twentieth century, the number of party votes declined as bipartisan legislation became more common. The 1990s witnessed a return to strong party discipline as partisan polarization drew sharper lines between Democrats and Republicans, and congressional party leaders aggressively used their powers to promote party discipline. In 2005 party discipline was close to its all-time high.

Typically, party unity is greater in the House than in the Senate. House rules grant greater procedural control of business to the majority party leaders, which gives them more influence over House members. In the Senate, however, the leadership has few sanctions over its members. The former Senate minority leader Tom Daschle once observed that a Senate leader seeking to influence other senators has as incentives "a bushel full of carrots and a few twigs."[40]

party unity vote a roll-call vote in the House or Senate in which at least 50 percent of the members of one party take a particular position and are opposed by at least 50 percent of the members of the other party

roll-call vote a vote in which each legislator's yes or no vote is recorded as the clerk calls the names of the members alphabetically

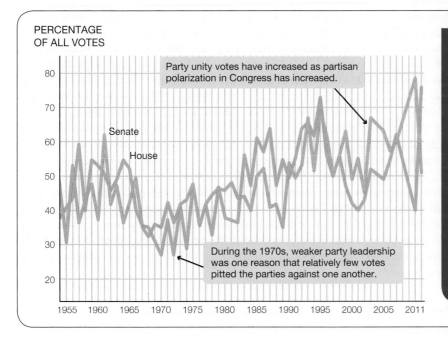

PERCENTAGE OF ALL VOTES

Party unity votes have increased as partisan polarization in Congress has increased.

Senate

House

During the 1970s, weaker party leadership was one reason that relatively few votes pitted the parties against one another.

1955 1960 1965 1970 1975 1980 1985 1990 1995 2000 2005 2011

FIGURE 12.9

Party Unity Votes by Chamber

Party unity votes are roll-call votes in which a majority of one party lines up against a majority of the other party. Party unity votes increase when the parties are polarized and when the party leadership can enforce discipline. Why did the percentage of party unity votes decline in the 1970s? Why has it risen in recent years?

SOURCES: Shawn Zeller, "2010 Vote Studies: Party Unity," *CQ Weekly*, January 3, 2012, p. 37; Emily Ethridge, "2011 Vote Studies: Party Unity," *CQ Weekly*, January 16, 2012, p. 111.

Though it has not reached nineteenth-century levels, party unity has been on the rise in recent years because the divisions between the parties have deepened on many high-profile issues such as abortion, health care, and financial reform (see Figure 12.9). Party unity scores rise when congressional leaders try to put a partisan stamp on legislation. For example, in 1995, then-Speaker Newt Gingrich sought to enact a Republican "Contract with America" that few Democrats supported. The result was more party unity in the House than in any year since 1954. Since then, the polarization of political parties has resulted in very high party unity scores. In 2011, House Democrats voted with the majority 87 percent of the time, slightly short of their all-time high of 92 percent in 2007 and 2008. In 2011, Senate Democrats set a record for party unity by voting with their caucus 92 percent of the time. In 2011, House Republicans voted with their party 91 percent of the time, matching their all-time high; Senate Republicans voted with their party 86 percent of the time.[41]

To some extent, party unity is based on ideology and background. Republican members of the House are more likely than Democrats to have been elected by rural or suburban districts. Democrats are likely to be more liberal on economic and social questions than their Republican colleagues in both houses. These differences certainly help to explain roll-call divisions between the two parties. Ideology and background, however, are only part of the explanation for party unity. The other part has to do with party organization and leadership. Among the resources that party leaders have at their disposal are (1) leadership PACs, (2) committee assignments, (3) access to the floor, (4) the whip system, (5) logrolling, and (6) the presidency.

Leadership PACs Leaders have increased their influence over members in recent years with aggressive use of leadership political action committees. Leadership PACs are organizations that members of Congress use to raise funds that they then distribute to other members of their party running for election. Republican congressional leaders pioneered the aggressive use of leadership PACs to win their congressional majority in 1995, and the practice has spread widely since that time. The former House majority leader Tom DeLay was especially aggressive in raising funds, creating several important PACs, including Americans for a Republican Majority (ARMPAC), Retain Our Majority Program (ROMP), and the Republican Majority Issues Committee. In recent years, Democrats have also formed well-funded leadership PACs. Money from leadership PACs can be directed to the most vulnerable candidates or to candidates who are having trouble raising money. It can also be used to influence primary elections. In 2010 and 2012, conservatives in the House and Senate used leadership PACs to support conservative candidates in Republican primaries. For example, Senator Jim DeMint's (R-S.C.) Senate Conservatives Fund was an early supporter of three conservative candidates who won in 2010: Marco Rubio (R-Fla.), Rand Paul (R-Ky.), and Pat Toomey (R-Pa.). Although leadership PACs have traditionally enhanced the power of the party and created a bond between the leaders and the members who receive their help, the aggressive use of PACs by Republican conservatives highlights their use for wings of the party who want to increase their power.[42]

Committee Assignments Leaders can create debts among members by helping them get favorable committee assignments. These assignments are made early in the congressional careers of most members and cannot be taken from them if they later balk at party discipline. Nevertheless, if the leadership goes out of its way to get the right assignment for a member, this effort is likely to create a bond of obligation that can be called on without any other payments or favors. This is one reason the Republican leadership gave freshmen favorable assignments when the Republicans took over Congress in 1995. When Nancy Pelosi assumed the position of Speaker in 2007, she sought to spread power more widely by limiting the number of committees that any one member could chair. She also gave freshmen representatives access to key committees that would raise their political stature.[43] By offering attractive committee assignments to members in competitive races, especially to new members, she sought to boost her party's chances in the next elections.

Floor time—the opportunity to speak on the floor of Congress—gives members to argue their point of view and to show their constituents that they are actively working on their behalf. In 2011, Senator Roy Blunt (R-Mo.), spoke on the floor about the need for disaster relief funding for Missourians.

Access to the Floor The most important everyday resource available to the parties is control over access to the floor. With thousands of bills awaiting passage and most members clamoring for access in order to influence a bill or publicize themselves, floor time is precious. In the Senate, the leadership allows ranking committee members to influence the allocation of floor time—who will speak for how long; in the House, the Speaker, as head of the majority party (in consultation with the minority leader), allocates large blocks of floor time. Thus, floor time is allocated in both houses of Congress by the majority and minority leaders. More important, the Speaker of the House and the majority leader in the Senate possess the power of recognition. This seemingly insubstantial authority is, in fact, quite formidable and can be used to stymie a piece of legislation completely or frustrate a member's attempts to speak on a particular issue. Because the power is significant, members of Congress usually attempt to stay on good terms with the Speaker and the majority leader to ensure they will continue to be recognized.

As House Speaker, Nancy Pelosi was particularly generous in offering freshmen Democrats and other especially vulnerable Democrats an opportunity to speak on the floor. When Republicans assumed control of the House in 2010, they likewise ensured that the voices of freshmen Republicans were heard on the House floor.[44]

The Whip System Some influence accrues to party leaders through the whip system, which is primarily a communications network for conveying the leaders' wishes and plans to the members. Between 12 and 20 assistant and regional whips are selected to operate at the direction of the majority or minority leader and the whip. They poll all the members in order to learn their intentions on specific bills, enabling the leaders to know if they have enough support to allow a vote as well as whether the vote is so close that they will need to put pressure on undecided members. In those instances, the Speaker or a lieutenant will go to a few party members who have indicated they will switch if their vote is essential—an expedient that the leaders try to limit to a few times per session.

The whip system helps maintain party unity in both houses of Congress, but it is particularly critical in the House of Representatives because of the large number of legislators whose positions and votes must be accounted for. The majority and minority whips and their assistants must be adept at inducing compromise among legislators who hold widely differing viewpoints. The whips' personal styles and their perception of their function significantly affect the development of legislative coalitions and the compromises that emerge. As Republican House whip from 1995 to 2002, Tom DeLay established a reputation as an effective vote counter and a tough leader, earning the nickname the Hammer. DeLay also expanded the reach of the whip, building alliances with Republicans outside Congress, particularly those in ideological and business-oriented groups. Since Republicans retook control of the House following the 2010 elections, the whip operation has been faced with significant challenges from the large number of freshmen members of Congress. An unusually high number of members (87) were freshmen, 40 percent of whom had never held elected office before, calling themselves "citizen politicians." More important, many of these new members identified themselves as members of the Tea Party movement. Given the divisions between more experienced and moderate members in leadership and the new influx of conservative freshmen, Speaker John Boehner adopted an unusually loose approach to party discipline, as typified by his statement "Let the House work its will."[45] This approach created problems for the leadership, forcing the Speaker to end his "grand bargain" negotiations with President Obama surrounding deficit reduction and a raise in the debt ceiling in summer 2011. It also led to the rejection by the Republican conference of a payroll tax cut extension that had previously been passed by a large bipartisan majority in the Senate in late 2011, although a two-month extension did eventually pass.

Logrolling An agreement between two or more members of Congress who have nothing in common except the need for support is called **logrolling**. The agreement states, in effect, "You support me on bill X, and I'll support you on another bill of your choice." Since party leaders are the center of the communications networks

logrolling a legislative practice whereby agreements are made between legislators in voting for or against a bill; vote trading

in the two chambers, they can help members create large logrolling coalitions. Hundreds of logrolling deals are made each year, and although there are no official record-keeping books, it would be a poor party leader whose whips did not know who owed what to whom. In some instances, logrolling produces strange alliances. A most unlikely alliance emerged in Congress in October 1991, an alliance that one commentator dubbed "the corn for porn plot."[46] The alliance joined Senate supporters of the National Endowment for the Arts (NEA) with senators seeking limits on the cost of grazing rights on federal lands. The NEA, which provides federal funding to the arts, had been under fire from the conservative senator Jesse Helms (R-N.C.) for funding some controversial artists whose work Helms believed to be indecent. In an effort to block federal support for such works, Helms attached a provision to the NEA's funding that would have prohibited the agency from awarding grants to any work that in a "patently offensive way" depicted "sexual or excretory activities or organs." Supporters of the NEA condemned such restrictions as a violation of free speech and pointed out that many famous works of art could not have been funded under such restrictions. When it appeared that the amendment would pass, NEA supporters offered western senators a deal. In exchange for voting down the Helms amendment, they would eliminate a planned hike in grazing fees. Republican senators from 16 western states switched their votes and defeated the Helms amendment. Although Helms called his defeat the product of "back-room deals and parliamentary flimflam," his amendment was simply the victim of the time-honored congressional practice of logrolling.[47] This type of logrolling has become much less common in recent years, as sharp partisan differences have limited the possibilities for compromise.

The Presidency Of all the influences that maintain the clarity of party lines in Congress, the influence of the presidency is probably the most important. Indeed, the office is a touchstone of party discipline in Congress. Since the late 1940s, under President Harry Truman, presidents each year have identified a number of bills that they want to be considered part of their administration's program. By the mid-1950s, both parties in Congress began to look to the president for these proposals, which became the most significant part of Congress's agenda. The president's support is a criterion for party loyalty, and party leaders are able to use it to rally some members. Since 2011, with the presidency in Democratic hands and the House of Representatives controlled by Republicans, party polarization has limited the president's agenda-setting powers. Instead, his proposals have become targets for congressional opponents.

When Congress Can't Decide

We've considered the major factors that influence congressional decisions, but what happens if Congress as a whole can't decide and fails to act? In February 2012, Congress received the lowest levels of approval ever recorded in public opinion polls. Just 10 percent of those questioned approved of the job Congress was doing, while 86 percent expressed disapproval.[48] Two concerns lay behind the public's dissatisfaction with Congress. The first was the inability of the Republican House and the Democratic Senate to make decisions on numerous issues. The second was the pervasive belief that members of Congress listen more to special interests than to the American public.

By the end of 2011, 50 percent of Americans, a record high, said that the current Congress "had accomplished less than recent congresses."[49] Indeed partisan divisions

Congress has been polarized in recent years. For example, Democrats and Republicans were sharply divided over the Affordable Care Act passed in 2010 to reform the health care system. Representative Michele Bachmann joined Tea Party supporters and other Republicans in calling for the repeal of the act.

mired the 112th Congress in contentious arguments and prevented it from making many decisions. As we have seen, many of the usual procedures through which Congress enacted laws in the past—congressional committees to consider legislation, conference committees to reconcile House and Senate versions of legislation, a whip system to support leaders in the House of Representatives, logrolling, and presidential agenda setting—no longer functioned in the divided Congress. Even extraordinary efforts, such as the joint "supercommittee" appointed to reduce the deficit in 2011, failed to prompt Congress to reach agreement. Unable to decide the big issues, Congress resorted to passing short-term extensions of existing legislation.

The partisan divisions that prevented Congress from making decisions were especially acute because the unusually large class of freshman Republicans, many associated with the Tea Party movement, believed they had been sent to Congress to put an end to business as usual. Dedicated to reducing government spending, they used their power to hold up routine decisions, such as extension of the debt limit, as a way to extract concessions on government spending. Even when Republican leader John Boehner attempted to make a "grand bargain" with President Obama over taxes and spending—one very favorable to Republicans—conservative Republicans in the House rejected it as not going far enough. The political standoffs, which included regular threats of a government shutdown and resulted in the decision by rating agency Moody's to downgrade the U.S. credit rating, tarnished Congress's reputation with the public.

The public's disapproval of Congress was intensified by the belief that members of Congress pay attention to special interests. Much of the dissatisfaction with Congress appeared to be directed at members of Congress, not at the institution itself. In fact, a 2011 poll found that nearly half of those responding believed that most members of Congress are corrupt.[50] Both Occupy Wall Street on the left and the Tea Party movement on the right charged that Congress has been captured by special interests. This sense was intensified by the rise of super PACS after 2010, when several court decisions, including *Citizens United v. Federal Election Commission*, allowed outside groups and individuals to spend unlimited amounts of money on elections.[51]

Congressional gridlock is here to stay so long as voters elect representatives with sharply different views about what government should and shouldn't do. Until there is more agreement about the role of government and the best way to manage the budgetary challenges that face the country, congressional stand-offs on major legislation will remain a regular feature of American politics.

● Beyond Legislation: Other Congressional Powers

> **Describe the oversight, "advice and consent," and impeachment powers of Congress**

In addition to the power to make the law, Congress has at its disposal an array of other instruments through which to influence the process of government. The Constitution gives the Senate the power to approve treaties and appointments. And Congress has a number of other powers through which it can share with the other branches the capacity to administer the laws.

oversight the effort by Congress, through hearings, investigations, and other techniques, to exercise control over the activities of executive agencies

appropriations the amounts of money approved by Congress in statutes (bills) that each unit or agency of government can spend

Congress may call on members of the executive branch and others to testify at hearings. Here, Sandra Thompson of the FDIC testifies at a hearing on bank stability and the TARP program in 2011.

Oversight

Oversight, as applied to Congress, refers to the effort to oversee or to supervise how the executive branch carries out legislation. Oversight is carried out by committees or subcommittees of the Senate or the House, which conduct hearings and investigations in order to analyze and evaluate bureaucratic agencies and the effectiveness of their programs. Their purpose may be to locate inefficiencies or abuses of power, to explore the relationship between what an agency does and what a law intends, or to change or abolish a program. Most programs and agencies are subject to some oversight every year during the course of hearings on **appropriations**, the funding of agencies and government programs.

Committees or subcommittees have the power to subpoena witnesses, administer oaths, cross-examine, compel testimony, and bring criminal charges for contempt (refusing to cooperate) and perjury (lying under oath). Hearings and investigations are similar in many ways, but they differ on one fundamental point. A hearing is usually held on a specific bill, and the questions asked are usually intended to build a record with regard to that bill. In an investigation, the committee or subcommittee does not begin with a particular bill, but examines a broad area or problem and then concludes its investigation with one or more proposed bills.

In recent years, congressional oversight power has increasingly been used as a tool of partisan politics. The Republican Congress aggressively investigated President Clinton, racking up 140 hours of sworn testimony on whether the president had used the White House Christmas card list for partisan purposes. By contrast, the Republican-controlled Congress failed to scrutinize seriously the actions of the Bush administration during Bush's first six years in office. The investigation into the abuse of prisoners in Iraq's Abu Ghraib prison, for example, entailed only 12 hours of sworn testimony. Moreover, the few oversight hearings that the Republican Congress held sought mainly to support the leadership's policy goals—during a hearing on Arctic oil drilling, for example, much testimony was devoted to the benefits of such drilling. Congress also convened oversight hearings on issues that had nothing to do with the executive branch, such as the high-profile hearings on steroid use in Major League Baseball in 2005 and 2008.[52]

When the Democrats took control of Congress in 2007, congressional oversight increased dramatically. To highlight the importance of oversight, Democrats renamed the House Government Reform Committee, calling it the Committee on Oversight and Government Reform, and added four new subcommittees dedicated to oversight. They also hired more than 200 new investigative staffers.[53] Armed with these resources, Congress stepped up the number of oversight hearings: during its first six months in power, the Democratic Congress held 942 oversight hearings, compared with 579 for the same period when Republicans controlled Congress in 2005.[54] Congressional leaders are quite aware of oversight hearings as political tools. In 2012, with the presidential race looming, Republican House Speaker John Boehner urged Republicans to use their oversight powers aggressively, telling them, "Our obligation is to use our majority to shine a spotlight on the places where the president's failed policies are getting in the way of American job creation. And that means stepped-up oversight of the Obama administration's policies."[55]

Advice and Consent: Special Senate Powers

The Constitution has given the Senate another special power, one that is not based on lawmaking. The president has the power to make treaties and to appoint top executive officers, ambassadors, and federal judges—but only "with the Advice and Consent of the Senate" (Article II, Section 2). For treaties, two-thirds of those present must concur; for appointments, a simple majority is required.

The power to approve or reject presidential requests includes the power to set conditions: In fact, the Senate only occasionally exercises its power to reject treaties and appointments, and despite recent debate surrounding judicial nominees, only a handful of judicial nominees have been rejected by the Senate during the past century, whereas hundreds have been approved.

Most presidents make every effort to take potential Senate opposition into account in treaty negotiations with foreign powers. Instead of treaties, presidents frequently resort to **executive agreements** that do not need Senate approval. The Supreme Court has held that such agreements are equivalent to treaties.[56] In the past, presidents sometimes concluded secret agreements without informing Congress of the agreements' contents, or even their existence. For example, American involvement in the Vietnam War grew in part out of a series of secret arrangements made between American presidents and the South Vietnamese during the 1950s and '60s. Congress did not even learn of the existence of these agreements until 1969. In 1972, Congress passed the Case Act, which requires that the president inform Congress of any executive agreement within 60 days of its having been reached. This provides Congress with the opportunity to cancel agreements it opposes. In addition, Congress can limit the president's ability to conduct foreign policy through executive agreement by refusing to appropriate the funds needed to implement an agreement. In this way, for example, Congress can modify or even cancel executive agreements to provide American economic or military assistance to foreign governments.

executive agreement an agreement, made between the president and another country, that has the force of a treaty but does not require the Senate's "advice and consent"

Impeachment

The Constitution also grants Congress the power of **impeachment** over the president, vice president, and other executive officials. Impeachment means to charge a government official (president or otherwise) with "Treason, Bribery, or

impeachment the formal charge by the House of Representatives that a government official has committed "Treason, Bribery, or other high Crimes and Misdemeanors"

What Is Congress's Role in Foreign Policy?

During World War II, national security dominated the congressional agenda. With the massive mobilization of American troops and economic production geared to support the war effort, domestic policy commanded only modest attention in Congress. Congress focused on supporting the president as the nation faced total mobilization for war. During other periods, Congress has been much less supportive of the president's foreign policy. For example, in the late 1960s, as widespread doubts about the wisdom of the Vietnam War began to grow, Congress convened hearings that questioned administration assumptions and priorities.

Americans disagree about Congress's proper role in foreign policy. Such disagreements become especially salient in times of war. Should Congress primarily support the president as commander in chief of the armed forces? Or should Congress play the role of watchdog, delving into the details of foreign policy to ensure that the president's policies best serve the public interest?

Intensive congressional scrutiny of the president's foreign policy is counterproductive, say those who believe Congress should unite behind the president. Some believe that congressional objec-

tions to the president's priorities only strengthen the nation's enemies by weakening our American resolve to take the measures needed to ensure the country's defense. Congress is more likely than the president to adopt a short-term, politicized perspective. Congress is also more likely to put domestic concerns ahead of foreign-policy priorities. These tensions grew more pronounced after public disenchantment with the war in Iraq gave control of Congress to the Democrats in the 2006 midterm election. House and Senate leaders pressed the president to announce a new strategy for reducing American forces in Iraq. The president insisted, however, that U.S. troops needed to stay in Iraq to end sectarian violence. In the end, some feel presidents are better equipped than Congress to know what needs to be done to

conduct a successful foreign policy. They have a large national security apparatus with extensive expertise, and they are able to keep the big picture in mind.

Critics disagree, arguing that Congress has a vital role to play in foreign policy. The absence of ongoing congressional scrutiny can lead to poor policy, detached from democratic accountability. The continuing violence in Iraq and the lack of progress toward political stability provided only one example where congressional leaders claimed the Bush administration had lost touch with the electorate. From this viewpoint, democratic checks and balances must extend to foreign policy. If the executive branch refuses to adjust its foreign policies in response to public opinion, then Congress may have to exercise its power of the purse by cutting off funds. Ultimately, Congress must closely monitor the executive to ensure that the arguments and evidence for U.S. foreign policy are sound.

Former president Bush's handling of the war in Iraq and the threat of terrorism brought tensions between Congress and the White House to a level not seen since the Vietnam War. President Obama, however, found he was not immune to these tensions. Although Obama succeeded in winning congressional approval for additional troops in Afghanistan, many members of Congress did not support his request. The president's reputation rests far more heavily on success or failure in foreign policy than do the reputations of members of Congress. Meanwhile, Congress is more responsive to popular pressures that also have a place in foreign policy.

for critical analysis

1. Why is the president better equipped than Congress to conduct foreign policy, especially in matters such as terrorism?

2. Why is congressional oversight essential to good foreign policy? How does the experience of the war in Iraq point to the importance of strong congressional involvement in foreign policy?

other high Crimes and Misdemeanors" and bring him or her before Congress to determine guilt. Impeachment is thus like a criminal indictment in which the House of Representatives acts like a grand jury, voting (by simple majority) on whether the accused ought to be impeached. If a majority of the House votes to impeach, the impeachment trial moves to the Senate, which acts like a trial jury by voting whether to convict and forcibly remove the person from office (which requires a two-thirds majority of the Senate). The impeachment power is a considerable one; its very existence in the hands of Congress is a highly effective safeguard against the executive tyranny so greatly feared by the framers of the Constitution.

Controversy over Congress's impeachment power has arisen over the grounds for impeachment, especially the meaning of "high Crimes and Misdemeanors." A strict reading of the Constitution suggests that the only impeachable offense is an actual crime. But a more common working definition is that "an impeachable offense is whatever the majority of the House of Representatives considers it to be at a given moment in history."[57] In other words, impeachment, especially impeachment of a president, is a political decision.

The Senate possesses the power to impeach federal officials. In American history, 16 federal officials have been impeached, including two presidents. In 1998 the House impeached President Bill Clinton for lying under oath about his affair with the intern Monica Lewinsky.

The political nature of impeachment was very clear in the two instances of impeachment that have occurred in American history. In the first, in 1867, President Andrew Johnson, a southern Democrat who had battled a congressional Republican majority over Reconstruction, was impeached by the House but saved from conviction by one vote in the Senate. In 1998 the House impeached President Bill Clinton on two counts, for lying under oath and obstructing justice during the investigation into his sexual affair with the White House intern Monica Lewinsky. The vote was highly partisan, with only five Democrats voting for impeachment on each charge. In the Senate, where a two-thirds majority was needed to convict the president, only 45 senators voted to convict on the first count of lying and 50 voted to convict on the second charge of obstructing justice. As in the House, the vote for impeachment was highly partisan, with all Democrats and only five Republicans supporting the president's ultimate acquittal.

● Thinking Critically about Congress and Democracy

Much of this chapter has described the major institutional components of Congress and has shown how they work as Congress makes policy. But what do these institutional features mean for how Congress represents the American public? Does the organization of Congress promote the equal representation of all Americans? Or are there institutional features of Congress that allow some interests more access and influence than others?

As we noted at the beginning of this chapter, Congress instituted a number of reforms in the 1970s to make itself more accessible and to distribute power more

for critical **analysis**

Two of Congress's chief responsibilities are representation and lawmaking. How do these responsibilities support and reinforce each other? How might they also conflict with each other?

widely within the institution. These reforms sought to respond to public views that Congress had become a stodgy institution ruled by a powerful elite that made decisions in private. We have seen that these reforms increased the number of subcommittees, prohibited most secret hearings, and increased the staff support for Congress. These reforms spread power more evenly throughout the institution and opened new avenues for the public to contact and influence Congress.

But the opening of Congress ultimately did not benefit the broad American public, as reformers had envisioned. In fact the congressional reforms enacted during the 1970s actually made Congress less effective and, ironically, more permeable to special interests. Open committee meetings made it possible for sophisticated interest groups to monitor and influence every aspect of developing legislation. The unanticipated, negative consequences of these reforms highlighted the trade-off between representation and effectiveness in Congress.[58] Efforts to improve representation by opening Congress up made it difficult for Congress to be effective.

For the Founders, Congress was the national institution that best embodied the ideals of representative democracy. Throughout U.S. history, Congress has symbolized the American commitment to democratic values. Members of Congress, working to represent their constituents, bring these democratic values to life. A member of Congress can interpret his or her job as representative in two different ways: as a **delegate**, acting on the express preferences of his constituents; or as a **trustee**, more loosely tied to constituents and empowered to make the decisions he or she thinks best. The delegate role appears to be the more democratic because it forces representatives to heed the desires of their constituents. But this requires the representative to be in constant touch with constituents; it also requires constituents to follow each policy issue very closely. The problem with this form of representation is that most people do not follow every issue so carefully; instead they focus only on the issue or issues of particular interest to them. Many people are too busy to get the information necessary to make informed judgments even on issues they care about. Thus, adhering to the delegate form of representation runs the risk that the voices of only a few active and informed constituents get heard. Although it seems more democratic at first glance, the delegate form of representation may actually open Congress up to even more influence by special interests.

When congressional members act as trustees, on the other hand, they may not pay sufficient attention to the wishes of their constituents. In this scenario, the only way the public can exercise influence is by voting every two years for representatives or every six years for senators. In fact, most members of Congress take this electoral check very seriously. They try to anticipate the wishes of their constituents even when they don't know exactly what those wishes are, because they know that unpopular decisions can be used against them in the coming election. What the public dislikes most about Congress stems from suspicions that Congress acts as neither a trustee nor a delegate of the broad public interest, but instead is swayed by narrow special interests with lots of money.[59] Ideally, representative democracy grants all citizens equal opportunity to select their leaders and to communicate their preferences to these elected representatives. Yet, in reality, some citizens have more wealth, are more politically savvy, or belong to more effective organizations. Despite past efforts to reform Congress, these advantages provide special access for some interests even as they mute the voices of much of the American public. The dilemma that congressional reformers confront is how to devise safeguards that reduce the influence of special interests while allowing Congress to remain open to the wishes of the voting public.

delegate a representative who votes according to the preferences of his or her constituency

trustee a representative who votes based on what he or she thinks is best for his or her constituency

for critical **analysis**

Why is it so hard to make the voice of the public heard in Congress over that of the special interests? What reforms can enhance the public's influence in congressional deliberations?

Know Your Members of Congress

Inform Yourself

Know your members of Congress. Find out who represents your college or hometown in the House of Representatives and the Senate by using the "Find your senators/representative" tool at www.house.gov and www.senate.gov.

Check your representatives' records. After you've identified your senators and representative, go to www.rollcall.com and complete the Legislator Profiles report. Who gives them money and how long have they been in office? What was the last bill they sponsored and does it benefit you or a friend or family member? How well do their policy positions align with your own?

Express Yourself

Let your members of Congress know how you feel about issues that are important to you by sending them an e-mail. Members' e-mail addresses are given on their Web pages. Your message may be especially effective if Congress is expected to consider and vote on the issue in the near future.

Connect with Others

Connect with Congress and other constituents. Most members of Congress have Facebook pages (often linked through their websites) where you can learn about campaign events and policies and connect with other constituents the House district or state. What has your member of Congress posted in the past month? Which posts were the most popular in terms of "likes" or shares? Does visiting the Facebook page of your member of Congress change your evaluation of your representative?

Consider how congressional districting affects who represents you and other Americans. Play the "Redistricting Game" at www.redistrictinggame.org (all five steps, including creating a partisan gerrymander and ending with a nonpartisan redistricting). After drawing the districts yourself, do you think legislative districts should be drawn using the partisan composition of the district or other criteria? Why are legislative districts so important to members of Congress?

Find links to the sites listed above as well as related activities on wwnorton.com/studyspace.

Congress: Representing the American People

■ **Describe who serves in Congress and how they represent their constituents (pp. 471-84)**

A member of Congress's primary responsibility is to his or her district and to his or her constituency. The House and Senate operate according to a very different set of rules and play very different roles in the legislative process. Although members of Congress do not share their constituents' sociological characteristics, they do work hard to speak for their constituents' views and to serve their constituents' interests. Generally speaking, there are three factors related to the U.S. electoral system that affect who gets elected and what they do once in office: who decides to run for Congress, the incumbency advantage, and the way congressional districts are drawn.

Key Terms

constituency (p. 471)

bicameral (p. 471)

sociological representation (p. 472)

agency representation (p. 472)

incumbency (p. 478)

term limits (p. 479)

apportionment (p. 480)

redistricting (p. 480)

gerrymandering (p. 480)

patronage (p. 482)

pork-barrel (or pork) (p. 482)

private bill (p. 483)

Practice Quiz

1. Because they have larger and more heterogeneous constituencies, senators *(pp. 471–72)*
   a) have less freedom to consider "new ideas" or to bring together new coalitions of interests.
   b) are more attuned to the needs of localized interest groups.
   c) care more about re-election than House members.
   d) can better represent the national interest.
   e) face less competition in elections than House members.

2. What type of representation is described when constituents have the power to hire and fire their representative? *(p. 472)*
   a) agency representation
   b) sociological representation
   c) democratic representation
   d) trustee representation
   e) economic representation

3. Sociological representation is important in understanding the U.S. Congress because *(p. 475)*
   a) members often vote on the basis of their religion.
   b) Congress is a microcosm of American society.
   c) most people vote for people who are just like them.
   d) the symbolic composition of Congress is important for the authority of the government.
   e) there is a distinct "congressional sociology."

4. Some have argued that the creation of minority congressional districts has *(p. 481)*
   a) made it easier to draw districts.
   b) lessened the sociological representation of minorities in Congress.
   c) made it more difficult for minorities to win substantive policy goals.
   d) been a result of the media's impact on state legislative politics.
   e) lessened the problem of "pork-barrel" politics.

5. One way members of Congress can work as agents of their constituents is by *(p. 482)*
   a) providing direct patronage.
   b) taking part in a party vote.
   c) joining a caucus.
   d) supporting term limits.
   e) spending time on fund-raising for their re-election campaign.

 Practice Online
"Get Involved" exercise: *Know Your Members of Congress*

The Organization of Congress

■ **Explain how party leadership, the committee system, the staff system, and caucuses help structure congressional business (pp. 484–91)**

Congress is a representative body and lawmaking institution. The political parties, the committee system, congressional staff, the caucuses, and the parliamentary rules of the House and Senate play key roles in the process through which Congress formulates and enacts law. the committee system is particularly important to the legislative process because Congress relies on committees and subcommittees to do the difficult work of sorting through alternatives and writing bills.

Key Terms

conference (p. 485)

caucus (political) (p. 485)

Speaker of the House (p. 485)

majority leader (p. 485)

minority leader (p. 485)

whip (p. 485)

standing committee (p. 485)

select committees (p. 487)

joint committees (p. 488)

conference committees (p. 488)

seniority (p. 489)

staff agencies (p. 490)

caucus (congressional) (p. 491)

Practice Quiz

6. Which of the following types of committees does not include members of both the House and the Senate? *(pp. 485–89)*
   a) conference committee
   b) joint committee
   c) 527 committees
   d) No committees include both House members and senators.

7. A series of reforms instituted by Congress in the 1970s, including an increase in the number of subcommittees and greater autonomy for subcommittee chairs, was intended to *(p. 489)*
   a) reduce the power of committee chairs.
   b) increase the power of committee chairs.
   c) secure re-election for all committee chairs.
   d) ending the filibuster.
   e) guarantee the electoral defeat of all committee chairs.

 Practice Online
Video exercise: *What will It Take to Close the Partisan Rift in Congress?*

Rules of Lawmaking: How a Bill Becomes a Law

■ **Outline the steps in the process of passing a law (pp. 491–96)**

The rules of congressional procedure influence the fate of every bill and determine the distribution of power in Congress. Debate over bills is much less restricted in the Senate than in the House, and the filibuster gives tremendous power to individual senators. The president's veto power also exerts an important influence on Congress's lawmaking because the possibility of a presidential veto affects how willing members of Congress are to push for different pieces of legislation.

Key Terms

bill (p. 491)

committee markup (p. 491)

closed rule (p. 493)

open rule (p. 493)

filibuster (p. 493)

cloture (p. 493)

veto (p. 496)

pocket veto (p. 496)

Practice Quiz

8. The difference between a closed rule and an open rule in the House is *(p. 493)*
   a) a closed rule puts severe limits on floor debate and amendments, whereas an open rule permits floor debate and makes amendments easier.
   b) an open rule puts severe limits on floor debate and amendments, whereas a closed rule permits floor debate and makes amendments easier.
   c) a closed rule allows journalists and members of the public to listen to debates about a bill, whereas an open rule prevents journalists and members of the public from listening to debates about the bill.
   d) an open rule allows journalists and members of the public to listen to debates about a bill, whereas a closed rule prevents journalists and members of the public from listening to debates about the bill.
   e) a closed rule prevents the federal judiciary from declaring a bill unconstitutional once passed, whereas an open rule allows the federal judiciary to declare a bill unconstitutional.

9. Which of the following is *not* a technique that can be used to block debate about a bill in the Senate? *(pp. 493–94)*
   a) filibuster
   b) caucus
   c) the introduction of new amendments
   d) cloture
   e) placing holds on bills

How Congress Decides

■ **Analyze the factors that influence which laws Congress decides to pass (pp. 496–504)**

A variety of influences from inside and outside government play a role in congressional decision making. External influences include the policy preferences of the legislator's constituency and the lobbying of various interest groups. Party leaders within Congress use committee assignments, access to the floor, the whip system, logrolling and the president's support to influence how representatives behave.

Key Terms

party unity vote (p. 498)

roll-call vote (p. 498)

logrolling (p. 501)

Practice Quiz

10. Which of the following is *not* an important influence on how members of Congress vote on legislation? *(p. 496)*
    a) the media
    b) constituency
    c) the president
    d) interest groups
    e) party leaders

11. Which of the following is *not* a resource that party leaders in Congress use to create party discipline? *(pp. 498–502)*
    a) leadership PACs
    b) committee assignments
    c) access to the floor
    d) the whip system
    e) roll-call votes

12. An agreement between members of Congress to trade support for each other's bills is known as *(p. 501)*
    a) oversight.
    b) filibuster.
    c) logrolling.
    d) patronage.
    e) cloture.

 Practice Online
Video exercise: *Clay Shirky on the Influence of Interest Groups and the People*

Beyond Legislation: Other Congressional Powers

■ **Describe the oversight, "advice and consent," and impeachment powers of Congress (pp. 504-7)**

Congress has many other powers than simply lawmaking. Using hearings, investigations and other techniques, Congress exercises control over the agencies of the executive branch. Under the Constitution, the president can only make treaties and appoint top executive officers, ambassadors, and federal judges "with the Advice and Consent of the Senate." The Constitution also grants Congress the power of impeachment over the president, vice president, and other executive officials.

Key Terms

oversight (p. 504)

appropriations (p. 504)

executive agreement (p. 505)

impeachment (p. 505)

delegate (p. 508)

trustee (p. 508)

Practice Quiz

13. When Congress conducts an investigation to explore the relationship between what a law intended and what an executive agency has done, it is engaged in *(p. 504)*
    a) oversight.
    b) advice and consent.
    c) appropriations.
    d) executive agreement.
    e) direct patronage.

14. Which of the following statements about impeachment is *not* true? *(pp. 505–7)*
    a) The president is the only official who can be impeached by Congress.

b) Impeachment means to charge a government official with "Treason, Bribery, or other high Crimes and Misdemeanors."

c) The House of Representatives decides by simple majority vote whether the accused ought to be impeached.

d) The Senate decides whether to convict and remove the person from office.

e) There have only been two instances of impeachment in American history.

For Further Reading

Adler, E. Scott. *Why Congressional Reforms Fail.* Chicago: University of Chicago Press, 2002.

Dodd, Lawrence C., and Bruce I. Oppenheimer, eds. *Congress Reconsidered.* 9th ed. Washington, DC: CQ Press, 2008.

Dodson, Debra L. *The Impact of Women in Congress.* New York: Oxford University Press, 2006.

Fenno, Richard F. *Homestyle: House Members in Their Districts.* Boston: Little, Brown, 1978.

Fiorina, Morris. *Congress: Keystone of the Washington Establishment.* 2nd ed. New Haven, CT: Yale University Press, 1989.

Fowler, Linda, and Robert McClure. *Political Ambition: Who Decides to Run for Congress?* New Haven, CT: Yale University Press, 1989.

Hamilton, Lee. *How Congress Works.* Bloomington: Indiana University Press, 2004.

Koger, Gregory. *Filibustering: A Political History of Obstruction in the House and Senate.* Chicago: University of Chicago Press, 2010.

Mann, Thomas E., and Norman J. Ornstein. *The Broken Branch: How Congress Is Failing America and How to Get It Back on Track.* New York: Oxford University Press, 2006.

Mayhew, David R. *Congress: The Electoral Connection.* New Haven, CT: Yale University Press, 1974.

Palmer, Barbara, and Denise Simon. *Breaking the Political Glass Ceiling: Women and Congressional Elections.* 2nd ed. New York: Routledge, 2008.

Redman, Eric. *The Dance of Legislation.* Seattle: University of Washington Press, 2001.

Recommended Websites

Cook Political Report
www.cookpolitical.com

The Cook Political Report, by Charlie Cook, is a nonpartisan analysis of electoral politics. Check out current House and Senate races for an in-depth analysis of past elections and previews of future congressional elections.

Library of Congress: Thomas
http://thomas.loc.gov

The Library of Congress's "Thomas" website is a superb place to find information about the U.S. Congress. Roll-call votes, current legislation, the full text of the *Congressional Record*, and committee reports are just a few of the archives you will find.

National Committee for an Effective Congress
www.ourcampaigns.com

Congressional redistricting is the process of redrawing House districts every 10 years to account for shifts in population. For information about redistricting in your state, log on to the Redistricting Resource Center, provided by the National Committee for an Effective Congress.

Roll Call
www.rollcall.com

Roll Call, the newspaper of Capitol Hill, provides daily coverage on the members, legislation, and events taking place in and around the U.S. legislature.

The Sunlight Foundation and Taxpayers for Common Sense
http://earmarkwatch.org

Earmarks are language that members of Congress insert in legislation that dedicates funds for specific uses, many whose broad benefits can be questioned. The Sunlight Foundation and Taxpayers for Common Sense are two watchdog groups that have joined forces to publish a database of congressional earmarks. Earmarks can be searched by state, congressional sponsor, recipient, and description of the project.

U.S. House of Representatives
www.house.gov

U.S. Senate
www.senate.gov

These are the official websites for the U.S. House of Representatives and the U.S. Senate. Here you can find information on your members of Congress, key congressional leaders, bills currently under consideration, and legislative committees.

In 2012, Americans re-elected Barack Obama to the presidency. During the campaign, Obama made promises about how he would use the powers of the office to address the challenges facing the nation.

The Presidency

WHAT GOVERNMENT DOES AND WHY IT MATTERS As President Barack Obama began his second term, his administration confronted a number of problems. While the U.S. economy—which had been in recession since 2007—had gradually begun to recover, the unemployment rate was still high and new job creation lagged. Obama had accused his Republican challenger, Mitt Romney, of sending American jobs overseas when Romney was a business manager. Bringing those jobs back, though, might not be so easy for the president. The economy was also threatened by budget deficits, as government spending outpaced income from taxes, and no consensus existed on how to solve that problem. On the international front, Obama had brought an end to the long and costly wars in Iraq and Afghanistan. However, the nation was still threatened by shadowy terrorist groups, while Iran seemed to be working to build a nuclear weapon, despite American pressures and economic sanctions. The president also faced an economic crisis in Europe, unrest in the Arab world, challenges from China, and a host of other problems, large and small. Obama's campaign slogan in 2012 had been "Forward!" but just how to go forward was not entirely obvious.

The president also inherited a presidency considerably more powerful than the institution imagined by the framers of the U.S. Constitution. Ironically, the same wars that presented such an enormous challenge to the new administration also had the potential to enhance its power.

Presidential power generally increases during times of war. For example, President Abraham Lincoln's 1862 declaration of martial law and Congress's 1863 legislation giving the president the power to make arrests and use military tribunals to try suspects amounted to a "constitutional dictatorship" that lasted through the Civil War and Lincoln's re-election in 1864. During World War II, Franklin Delano Roosevelt, like Lincoln, did not bother to wait for Congress but took executive action first and expected Congress to follow. One dissenter on the Supreme Court called the president's assumption of emergency powers "a loaded weapon ready for the hand of any authority that can bring forward a plausible claim of an urgent need."

On the domestic side, however, presidents often wish they had more power. During the budget and deficit crises of 2011, President Obama seemed unable to persuade House Republicans to follow his lead and was forced to accept compromises not at all to his liking. With their control of the House of Representatives, Republicans threatened to bring about a default on federal debt unless the president accepted their proposals, and there was little Obama could do besides agree.

In this chapter, we examine the foundations of the American presidency and assess the origins and character of presidential power in the twenty-first century. National emergencies are one source of presidential power, but presidents are also empowered by democratic political processes and, increasingly, by their ability to control and expand the institutional resources of the office.

chaptergoals

- Explain the role of the president in the American political system (pages 517–19)

- Outline the powers the Constitution gives the president (pages 519–32)

- Identify the institutional resources presidents have to help them exercise their powers (pages 532–37)

- Explain how modern presidents have become even more powerful (pages 538–47)

Establishing the Presidency

Explain the role of the president in the American political system

The presidency was established by Article II of the Constitution, which begins by asserting, "The executive power shall be vested in a President of the United States of America." Article II describes the manner in which the president is to be chosen and defines the basic powers of the presidency. By vesting the executive power in a single president, the framers were emphatically rejecting proposals for various forms of collective leadership. Some delegates to the Constitutional Convention had argued in favor of a multiheaded executive or an "executive council" in order to avoid undue concentration of power in the hands of one individual. Most of the framers, however, wanted to provide for "energy" in the executive, and they thought that a unitary executive would be more energetic than some form of collective leadership. They believed that a powerful executive would help protect the nation's interests vis-à-vis other nations and promote the federal government's interests relative to the states.

The presidential selection process defined by Article II resulted from a struggle between those delegates who wanted the president to be selected by, and thus be responsible to, Congress and those delegates who preferred that the president be elected directly by the people. Direct popular election would create a more independent and more powerful presidency. With the adoption of a scheme of indirect election through an electoral college, with electors to be selected by the state legislatures (and close elections to be resolved in the House of Representatives), the framers hoped to achieve a "republican" solution: a strong president responsible to state and national legislators rather than directly to the electorate. This indirect method of electing the president probably did dampen the power of most presidents in the nineteenth century.

The framers of the Constitution wanted an "energetic" presidency, capable of quick, decisive action. However, when George Washington was sworn in as the first president, in 1789, the presidency was a less powerful office than it is today.

As the method of selecting presidents became more democratic, the president came to be seen as the direct representative of the American people, increasing the power of the office. Here, President Ronald Reagan attends a memorial service for American soldiers killed in the 1983 bombing of the American embassy in Beirut, Lebanon.

caucus (political) a normally closed political party business meeting of citizens or law makers to select candidates, elect officers, plan strategy, or make decisions regarding legislative matters

The presidency was strengthened somewhat in the 1830s with the introduction of the national convention system of nominating presidential candidates. Until then, presidential candidates had been nominated by their party's congressional delegates through a **caucus** system, derisively called "King Caucus" because any candidate for president was beholden to the party's leaders in Congress both for the party's nomination and for their support in the presidential election. The national nominating convention arose outside Congress in order to provide some representation for a party's voters who lived in districts where they were in the minority. The political party in each state made its own provisions for selecting delegates to attend the presidential nominating convention, and in virtually all states, the selection was dominated by the party leaders. (Only in recent decades have state laws intervened to regularize the selection process and to provide, in all but a few instances, for open election of delegates.) The convention system quickly became the most popular method of nominating candidates for all elective offices and remained so until well into the twentieth century, when it succumbed to the criticism that it was undemocratic and dominated by a few leaders in a "smoke-filled room." But during the nineteenth century, the convention system was seen as a victory for democracy against the congressional elite. Furthermore, the national convention gave the presidency a base of power independent of Congress.

This additional independence did not immediately transform the presidency into the office familiar to us today, but the national convention did begin to open the presidency to larger social forces and newly organized interests in society. In other words, it gave the presidency a broad popular base that would eventually demand and support increased presidential power. Improvements in the telegraph, the telephone, and other forms of mass communication enabled individuals to share their complaints and allowed national leaders (especially presidents and presidential candidates) to reach out directly to the people. Eventually, though more slowly, the presidential selection process began to be further democratized with the adoption of primary elections through which millions of ordinary citizens were given an opportunity to take part in the presidential nominating process by popular selection of convention delegates.

But despite political and social conditions favoring the enhancement of the presidency, the development of presidential government as we know it today did not mature until the middle of the twentieth century. For a long period, even as the national government began to grow, Congress was careful to keep a tight rein on the president's power. The real turning point in the history of American national government came during the administration of Franklin Delano Roosevelt. Since FDR and his "New Deal" of the 1930s, every president has been strong whether or not he was committed to the goal of a strong presidency.

● The Constitutional Powers of the Presidency

Outline the powers the Constitution gives the president

Whereas Section 1 of Article II of the Constitution explains how the president is to be chosen, Sections 2 and 3 outline the powers and duties of the president. These two sections identify two sources of presidential authority. Some presidential powers, called the **expressed powers** of the office, are specifically established by the language of the Constitution. For example, the president is authorized to make treaties, grant pardons, and nominate judges and other public officials. These specifically defined powers cannot be revoked by Congress or any other agency without an amendment to the Constitution. Other expressed powers include the authority to receive ambassadors and the command of the military forces of the United States.

expressed powers specific powers granted by the Constitution to Congress (Article I, Section 8) and to the president (Article II)

In addition to the president's expressed powers, Article II declares that the president "shall take Care that the Laws be faithfully executed." Since the laws are enacted by Congress, this language implies that Congress is to delegate to the president the power to implement or execute its will. Powers given to the president by Congress are called **delegated powers**. In principle, Congress delegates to the president only the power to identify or develop the means through which to carry out its decisions. So, for example, if Congress determines that air quality should be improved, it might delegate to a bureaucratic agency in the executive branch the power to identify the best means of bringing about such an improvement as well as the power to implement the actual cleanup process. In practice, of course, decisions about how to clean the air are likely to have an enormous impact on businesses, organizations, and individuals throughout the nation. By delegating power to the executive branch, Congress substantially enhances the importance of the presidency. In most cases, Congress delegates power to bureaucratic agencies in the executive branch rather than to the president, but as we shall see, contemporary presidents have found ways to capture a good deal of this delegated power for themselves.

delegated powers constitutional powers that are assigned to one governmental agency but that are exercised by another agency with the express permission of the first

Presidents have claimed a third source of power beyond expressed and delegated powers. These are powers not specified in the Constitution or the law but said to stem from "the rights, duties and obligations of the presidency."[1] Referred to as the **inherent powers** of the presidency, they are most often asserted by presidents in times of war or national emergency. For example, after the fall of Fort Sumter and the outbreak of the Civil War, President Abraham Lincoln issued a series of executive orders for which he had no clear legal authority. Without even calling Congress into session, Lincoln combined the state militias into a 90-day national volunteer force, called for 40,000 new volunteers, enlarged the regular

inherent powers powers claimed by a president that are not expressed in the Constitution but are inferred from it

army and navy, diverted $2 million in unspent appropriations to military needs, instituted censorship of the U.S. mail, ordered a blockade of southern ports, suspended the writ of habeas corpus in the border states, and ordered the arrest by military police of individuals whom he deemed to be guilty of engaging in or even merely contemplating treasonous actions.[2] Lincoln asserted that these extraordinary measures were justified by the president's inherent power to protect the nation.[3] Subsequent presidents, including Franklin Delano Roosevelt and George W. Bush, have made similar claims.

Expressed Powers

The president's expressed powers, as defined by Sections 2 and 3 of Article II, fall into several categories:

1. *Military.* Article II, Section 2, provides for the power as "Commander in Chief of the Army and Navy of the United States, and of the Militia of the several States, when called in to the actual Service of the United States."

2. *Judicial.* Article II, Section 2, also provides the power to "grant Reprieves and Pardons for Offences against the United States, except in Cases of Impeachment."

3. *Diplomatic.* Article II, Section 2, further provides the power "by and with the Advice and Consent of the Senate to make Treaties." Article II, Section 3, provides the power to "receive Ambassadors and other public Ministers."

4. *Executive.* Article II, Section 3, also authorizes the president to see to it that all the laws are faithfully executed; Section 2 gives the chief executive power to appoint, remove, and supervise all executive officers and to appoint all federal judges.

5. *Legislative.* Article I, Section 7, and Article II, Section 3, give the president the power to participate authoritatively in the legislative process.

commander in chief the role of the president as commander of the national military and the state National Guard units (when called into service)

Military Power The president's military powers are among the most important exercised by the chief executive. The position of **commander in chief** makes the president the highest military authority in the United States, with control of the entire defense establishment. The president is also head of the nation's intelligence network, which includes not only the Central Intelligence Agency (CIA) but also the National Security Council (NSC), the National Security Agency (NSA), the Federal Bureau of Investigation (FBI), and a host of less well known but very powerful international and domestic security agencies.

War and Inherent Presidential Power The Constitution gives Congress the power to declare war. Presidents, however, have gone a long way toward capturing this power for themselves. Congress has not declared war since December 1941, but since then, American military forces have engaged in numerous campaigns throughout the world under the orders of the president. When North Korean forces invaded South Korea in June 1950, Congress was actually prepared to declare war, but President Harry S. Truman asserted that the president and not Congress could decide when and where to deploy America's military might. Truman dispatched American forces to Korea without a congressional declaration, and in the face of the emergency, Congress felt it had to acquiesce, and so passed a resolution approving the president's actions. This became the pattern for future

In 2010, President Obama visited American troops in Afghanistan. A few months earlier, Obama ordered a "surge" of 30,000 reinforcements to be sent to Afghanistan. Although the strategy was controversial, even among Obama's own party, Congress approved funding for the increase in troops.

congressional-executive relations in the military realm: the wars in Vietnam, Bosnia, Afghanistan, and Iraq, and a host of lesser conflicts, were all fought without declarations of war.

In 1973, Congress responded to presidential unilateralism by passing the **War Powers Resolution** over President Richard M. Nixon's veto. This resolution reasserted the principle of congressional war power, required the president to inform Congress of any planned military campaign, and stipulated that forces must be withdrawn within 60 days if there is no specific congressional authorization for their continued deployment. Presidents, however, have generally ignored the War Powers Resolution, claiming inherent executive power to defend the nation. Thus, President George W. Bush responded to the September 2001 attacks by Islamic terrorists by organizing a major military campaign to overthrow the Taliban regime in Afghanistan, which had sheltered the terrorists. In 2003, Bush ordered the invasion of Iraq, which he accused of posing a threat to the United States. U.S. forces overthrew the government of the Iraqi dictator, Saddam Hussein, and occupied the country. In both instances, Congress passed resolutions approving the president's actions, but the president was careful to assert that he did not need congressional authorization. The War Powers Resolution was barely mentioned on Capitol Hill and was ignored by the White House.

War Powers Resolution a resolution of Congress that the president can send troops into action abroad only by authorization of Congress, or if American troops are already under attack or serious threat

Military Sources of Domestic Power   The president's military powers extend into the domestic sphere. Article IV, Section 4, provides that the "United States shall [protect] every State . . . against Invasion . . . and . . . domestic Violence." Congress has made this an explicit presidential power through statutes directing the president as commander in chief to discharge these obligations.[4] The Constitution restrains the president's use of domestic force by providing that a state legislature (or governor when the legislature is not in session) must request federal troops before the president can send them into the state to provide public order. Yet this proviso is not absolute. First, presidents are not obligated to deploy national troops merely because the state legislature or governor makes such a request. More

The President versus the World: How Presidents Seized Control of the War Power

The 1973 War Powers Resolution provided that presidents could not deploy military forces for more than 60 days without securing congressional authorization. Many in Congress saw this time limit as a restraint on presidential action, though it gave the president more discretion than the framers of the Constitution had provided. President Gerald Ford had carefully followed the letter of the law when organizing a military effort to rescue American sailors held by North Korea. But this was the first and last time that the War Powers Act was fully observed. Between 1982 and 1986, President Reagan presented Congress with a set of military faits accomplis that undermined the War Powers Act and, in effect, asserted a doctrine of sole presidential authority in the security realm.

In October 1983, while American forces were still in Lebanon, President Reagan ordered an invasion of the Caribbean island of Grenada after a coup had led to the installation of a pro-Cuban government on the island. Congress threatened to invoke the War Powers Act, but Reagan withdrew American troops before the Senate acted. In 1986, Reagan ordered the

bombing of Libya in response to a terrorist attack in Berlin that the administration blamed on Libyan agents. In both cases, Reagan acted without consulting Congress and claimed that his authority had come directly from the Constitution.

Reagan's successor, George H. W. Bush, ordered an invasion of Panama designed to oust the Panamanian strongman General Manuel Noriega. Congress made no official response to the invasion. In 1990–91, the Bush administration sent a huge American military force into the Persian Gulf in response to Iraq's invasion and occupation of Kuwait. Both houses of Congress voted to authorize military action against Iraq, but Bush made it clear that he did not feel bound by any congres-

sional declaration. Indeed, the president later pointed out that he had specifically avoided asking Capitol Hill for "authorization" since such a request might improperly imply that Congress "had the final say in . . . an executive decision."[a]

In 1994, President Clinton planned an invasion of Haiti under the cover of a UN Security Council resolution. Congress expressed strong opposition to Clinton's plans, but he pressed forward nonetheless, claiming that he did not need congressional approval. In a similar vein, between 1994 and 1998, the administration undertook a variety of military actions in the former Yugoslavia without formal congressional authorization.

In 2001, President George W. Bush ordered an attack that soon toppled Afghanistan's Taliban regime. In 2003, he sent American forces to oust Saddam Hussein's government in Iraq. Bush had congressional support for his actions but, like his predecessors, asserted that he did not need Congress's permission to undertake military action. In 2011, President Obama ordered American forces to assist in the ultimately successful NATO campaign to oust Libya's leader, Mu'ammar Qaddafi. Like his predecessors, Obama claimed Congress had no authority in this matter. It is no longer clear what war powers, if any, remain in the hands of Congress.

[a]George H. W. Bush and Brent Scowcroft, *A World Transformed* (New York: Knopf, 1998), p. 441.

for critical analysis

1. Article I of the Constitution gives Congress the power to declare war. Why have modern presidents consistently refrained from asking Congress for such a declaration?

2. The scholar Edward Corwin said that the Constitution invited the president and Congress to struggle over war powers. What advantages have allowed presidents gradually to prevail in this struggle over the past century?

important, the president may deploy troops in a state or city without a specific request from the state legislature or governor if the president considers it necessary to maintain an essential national service during an emergency, to enforce a federal judicial order, or to protect federally guaranteed civil rights.[5]

One historic example of the unilateral use of presidential emergency power, even when the states don't request it, is the decision by President Dwight D. Eisenhower in 1957 to send troops into Little Rock, Arkansas, against the wishes of the state of Arkansas, to enforce court orders to integrate Little Rock's Central High School. The governor of Arkansas, Orval Faubus, had posted the Arkansas National Guard at the entrance to Central High School to prevent the court-ordered admission of nine black students. After an effort to negotiate with Governor Faubus failed, President Eisenhower reluctantly sent 1,000 paratroopers to Little Rock; they stood watch while the black students took their places in the all-white classrooms.

In most instances of domestic disorder, whether from human or from natural causes, presidents tend to exercise unilateral power by declaring a "state of emergency," thereby making available federal grants, insurance, and direct assistance. In 1992, in the aftermath of devastating riots in Los Angeles and hurricanes in Florida, American troops, sent in by the president, were very much in evidence, more in the role of Good Samaritans than of military police. In 2005, President Bush declared a state of emergency to allow the Federal Emergency Management Agency (FEMA) to coordinate the government's response to Hurricane Katrina, an immense storm that devastated the city of New Orleans. Bush sent federal troops to bolster local efforts.

Military emergencies have typically also led to expansion of the domestic powers of the executive branch. This was true during the First and Second World Wars and has been true in the wake of the "war on terror" as well. Within a month of the September 11, 2001, attacks, the White House had drafted and Congress had enacted the USA PATRIOT Act, expanding the power of government agencies to engage in domestic surveillance activities, including electronic surveillance, and restricting judicial review of such efforts. The act also gave the attorney general greater authority to detain and deport aliens suspected of having terrorist affiliations. The following year, Congress created the Department of Homeland Security, combining offices from 22 federal agencies into one huge new cabinet department that would be responsible for protecting the nation from attack and responding to natural disasters. The new agency includes the U.S. Coast Guard, Transportation

TABLE 13.1

The Roles of the President

Chief of State (acting on behalf of all Americans)

Commander in Chief (in charge of the military)

Chief Jurist (judicial responsibilities)

Chief Diplomat (managing U.S. relations with other nations)

Chief Executive (as "boss" of the executive branch)

Chief Legislator (legislative powers)

Chief Politician (party leadership)

Security Administration, FEMA, Immigration and Customs Enforcement (ICE), and offices from the departments of Agriculture, Energy, Transportation, Justice, Health and Human Services, Commerce, and the General Services Administration, as well as other agencies. The actual reorganization plan was drafted by the White House, but Congress weighed in to make certain that the new agency's workers had civil service and union protections.

Judicial Power   The presidential power to grant reprieves, pardons, and amnesty involves power over all individuals who may be a threat to the security of the United States. Presidents may use this power on behalf of a particular individual, as did Gerald Ford when he pardoned Richard Nixon in 1974 "for all offenses against the United States which he . . . has committed or may have committed." Or they may use it on a large scale, as did President Andrew Johnson in 1868, when he gave full amnesty to all southerners who had participated in the "Late Rebellion," and President Carter in 1977, when he declared an amnesty for all the draft evaders of the Vietnam War. This power of life and death over others helped elevate American presidents to the level of earlier conquerors and kings, before whom supplicants might come to make their pleas for mercy.

Diplomatic Power   The president is America's "head of state," its chief representative in dealings with other nations, having the power to make treaties for the United States (with the advice and consent of the Senate). When President George Washington received Edmond Genêt ("Citizen Genêt") as the formal emissary of the revolutionary government of France in 1793 and had his cabinet officers and Congress back his decision, he established a greatly expanded interpretation of the power to "receive Ambassadors and other public Ministers," extending it to the power to "recognize" other countries. That power gives the president the almost unconditional authority to review the claims of any new ruling groups in order to determine whether they indeed control the territory and population of their country, so that they can commit it to treaties and other agreements.

As head of state, the president is America's chief representative in dealings with other countries. At an official state dinner in 2011, President Obama and Michelle Obama welcomed Chinese president Hu Jintao to the White House.

In recent years, presidents have expanded the practice of using executive agreements instead of treaties to establish relations with other countries.[6] An **executive agreement** is exactly like a treaty because it is a contract between two countries, but it does not require Senate approval. There are actually two types of executive agreements. One is the executive-congressional agreement. For this type of agreement, the president will submit the proposed arrangement to Congress for a simple majority vote in both houses, usually easier for presidents to win than the two-thirds approval of the Senate that is required for a treaty. The other type of executive agreement is the sole executive agreement, which is simply an understanding between the president and a foreign state and is not submitted to Congress for approval. In the past, sole executive agreements were used to flesh out commitments already made in treaties or to arrange for matters well below the level of policy. Since the 1930s, however, presidents have entered into sole executive agreements on important issues when they were uncertain about their prospects for securing congressional approval. For example, the General Agreement on Tariffs and Trade (GATT), one of the cornerstones of U.S. international economic policy in the post–World War II era, was based on an executive agreement. The courts have held that executive agreements have the force of law, as though they were formal treaties.

During the 1960s, Congress discovered that several presidents had entered into agreements with foreign governments and not informed Congress. This discovery led to the enactment of the 1972 Case-Zablocki Act, requiring the president to provide Congress each year with a complete list of all executive agreements signed during the course of that year. Presidents have not fully complied with this law. If they wish to keep an agreement secret, they call it by another name, such as "national security memorandum," and claim that it is not covered by the Case-Zablocki Act.

Executive Power   The Constitution focuses executive power and legal responsibility on the president. The famous sign on President Truman's desk, "The Buck Stops Here," was not merely an assertion of Truman's personal sense of responsibility but also his recognition of the legal and constitutional responsibility of the president. The most important basis of the president's power as chief executive is to be found in Article II, Section 3, of the Constitution, which stipulates that the president must see that all the laws are faithfully executed, and Section 2, which provides that the president will appoint, remove, and supervise all executive officers, and appoint all federal judges (with Senate approval). The power to appoint the principal executive officers and to require each of them to report to the president on subjects relating to the duties of their departments makes the president the true chief executive officer (CEO) of the nation. The president is subject to some limitations, because the appointment of all such officers, including ambassadors, ministers, and federal judges, is subject to a majority approval by the Senate. But these appointments are at the discretion of the president, and the loyalty and the responsibility of each appointee are presumed to be directed toward the president.

Another component of the president's power as chief executive is **executive privilege**, the claim that confidential communications between a president and close advisers should not be revealed without presidential consent. Presidents have made this claim ever since George Washington refused a request from the House of Representatives to deliver documents concerning negotiations of an important treaty. Washington refused (successfully) on the grounds that, first, the House was not constitutionally part of the treaty-making process, and second, diplomatic negotiations required secrecy.

executive agreement an agreement, made between the president and another country, that has the force of a treaty but does not require the Senate's "advice and consent"

executive privilege the claim that confidential communications between a president and close advisers should not be revealed without the consent of the president

The Supreme Court's decision in United States v. Nixon *is often seen as a blow to presidential power because Nixon was required to turn over secret tapes related to the Watergate scandal, despite his claim of executive privilege.*

Although many presidents have claimed executive privilege, the concept was not tested in the courts until the 1971 "Watergate" affair. President Richard Nixon refused congressional demands that he turn over secret White House tapes that congressional investigators suspected would establish his complicity in illegal activities. In *United States v. Nixon* (1974), the Supreme Court ordered Nixon to turn over the tapes.[7] The president complied with the order and was forced to resign from office. The *United States v. Nixon* case is often seen as a blow to presidential power, but in actuality, the Court's ruling recognized for the first time the legal validity of executive privilege, though holding that it did not apply in this particular instance. Subsequent presidents have cited *United States v. Nixon* in support of their claims of executive privilege. For example, the George W. Bush administration successfully invoked executive privilege when it refused congressional demands for records of Vice President Dick Cheney's 2001 energy task force meetings.

Legislative Power   The president plays a role not only in the administration of government but also in the legislative process. Two constitutional provisions are the primary sources of the president's power in the legislative arena. The first of these is the portion of Article II, Section 3, providing that the president "shall from time to time give to the Congress Information of the State of the Union, and recommend to their Consideration such Measures as he shall judge necessary and expedient." Delivering a "State of the Union" address may at first appear to be little more than the president's obligation to make recommendations for Congress's consideration. But as political and social conditions began to favor an increasingly prominent presidential role, each president, especially since Franklin Delano Roosevelt, began to rely on this provision in order to become the primary initiator of proposals for legislative action in Congress and the most important single participant in legislative decision making, as well as the principal source for public awareness of national issues.[8]

The second of the president's legislative powers is the veto power assigned by Article I, Section 7.[9] The **veto** is the president's constitutional power to reject acts of Congress (see Figure 13.1), making the president the most important single legislative leader.[10] No bill vetoed by the president can become law unless both the House and Senate override the veto by a two-thirds vote. In the case of a **pocket veto**, Congress does not have the option of overriding the veto, but must reintroduce the bill in the next session. Usually, if a president is presented with a bill and does not sign it within 10 days, it automatically becomes law. But this is true only while Congress is in session. If a president chooses not to sign a bill presented within the last 10 days of a legislative session, and Congress is out of session when the 10-day limit expires, instead of becoming law, the bill is vetoed.

Use of the veto varies according to the political situation each president confronts. George W. Bush did not find it necessary to use his veto power until 2007, when the Democrats took control of both houses of Congress. During his last two years in office, Bush vetoed 10 bills, including legislation designed to prohibit the use of harsh interrogation tactics, saying it "would take away one of the most valuable tools in the war on terror."[11] President Obama, who during his first two years in office initially enjoyed solid Democratic majorities in both houses of Congress, used his veto power only once during his

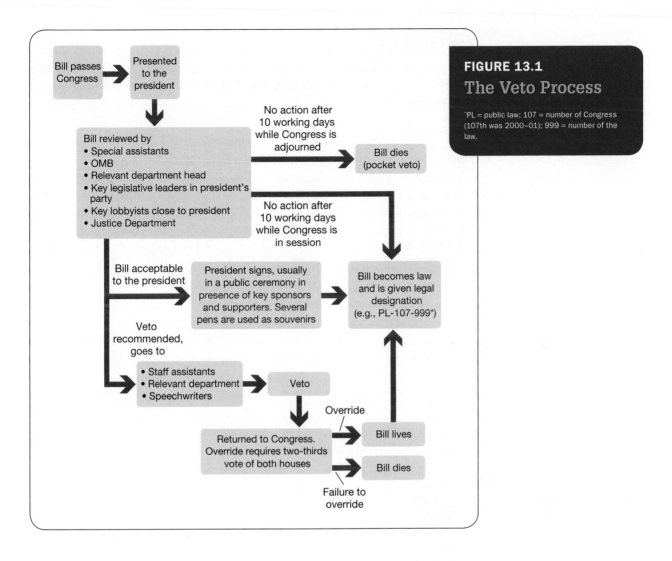

FIGURE 13.1

The Veto Process

*PL = public law; 107 = number of Congress (107th was 2000–01); 999 = number of the law.

Bill passes Congress → Presented to the president

Bill reviewed by
• Special assistants
• OMB
• Relevant department head
• Key legislative leaders in president's party
• Key lobbyists close to president
• Justice Department

No action after 10 working days while Congress is adjourned → Bill dies (pocket veto)

No action after 10 working days while Congress is in session

Bill acceptable to the president → President signs, usually in a public ceremony in presence of key sponsors and supporters. Several pens are used as souvenirs

Bill becomes law and is given legal designation (e.g., PL-107-999*)

Veto recommended, goes to → • Staff assistants • Relevant department • Speechwriters → Veto

Returned to Congress. Override requires two-thirds vote of both houses

Override → Bill lives

Failure to override → Bill dies

first year. As shown by Table 13.2, presidential vetoes are seldom overridden. Since the time of George Washington, presidents have used their veto power 2,560 times, and on only 109 occasions has Congress overridden them.

Though not explicitly, the Constitution also provides the president with the power of **legislative initiative**. The framers of the Constitution clearly saw legislative initiative as one of the keys to executive power. "Initiative" implies the ability to formulate proposals for important policies, and the president, as an individual with a great deal of staff assistance, is able to initiate decisive action more frequently than Congress, with its large assemblies that have to deliberate and debate before taking action. With some important exceptions, Congress depends on the president to set the agenda of public policy. And quite clearly, initiative confers the power of being able to set the terms of discourse in the making of public policy.

For example, during the weeks immediately following September 11, George W. Bush took many presidential initiatives to Congress, and each was given almost unanimous support—from commitments to pursue Al Qaeda, remove the Taliban, and reconstitute the Afghanistan regime, all the way to almost unlimited approval

legislative initiative the president's inherent power to bring a legislative agenda before Congress

TABLE 13.2

Presidential Vetoes, 1789–2012

PRESIDENT	CONGRESSES	TOTAL VETOES	VETOES OVERRIDDEN
Washington	1st–4th	2	.....
Adams	5th–6th	.....	.....
Jefferson	7th–10th	.....	.....
Madison	11th–14th	7	.....
Monroe	15th–18th	1	.....
John Quincy Adams	19th–20th	.....	.....
Jackson	21st–24th	12	.....
Van Buren	25th–26th	1	.....
Harrison	27th	.....	.....
Tyler	27th–28th	10	1
Polk	29th–30th	3	.....
Taylor	31st	.....	.....
Fillmore	31st–32nd	.....	.....
Pierce	33rd–34th	9	5
Buchanan	35th–36th	7	.....
Lincoln	37th–39th	7	.....
Johnson	39th–40th	29	15
Grant	41st–44th	93	4
Hayes	45th–46th	13	1
Garfield	47th	.....	.....
Arthur	47th–48th	12	1
Cleveland	49th–50th	414	2
Harrison	51st–52nd	44	1
Cleveland	53rd–54th	170	5
McKinley	55th–57th	42	.....
Theodore Roosevelt	57th–60th	82	1
Taft	61st–62nd	39	1
Wilson	63rd–66th	44	6
Harding	67th	6	.....
Coolidge	68th–70th	50	4
Hoover	71st–72nd	37	3
Franklin Delano Roosevelt	73rd–79th	635	9
Truman	79th–82nd	250	12
Eisenhower	83rd–86th	181	2
Kennedy	87th–88th	21	.....
Johnson	88th–90th	30	.....
Nixon	91st–93rd	43	7
Ford	93rd–94th	66	12
Carter	95th–96th	31	2
Reagan	97th–100th	78	9
George H. W. Bush	101st–102nd	44	1
Clinton	103rd–106th	37	2
George W. Bush	107th–110th	10	3
Barack Obama	111th–112th	2	....
Total	....	**2562**	**109**

for mobilization of both military force and the power to regulate American civil liberties.

The president's initiative does not end with congressional policy making and the making of laws in the ordinary sense of the term. The president has still another legislative role (in all but name) within the executive branch. This is designated as the power to issue **executive orders**. The executive order is first and foremost simply a normal tool of management, a power that virtually any CEO has to make "company policy"—rules-setting procedures, etiquette, chains of command, functional responsibilities, and so on. But evolving out of this normal management practice is a recognized presidential power to promulgate rules that have the effect and the formal status of legislation. Most presidential executive orders provide for the reorganization of structures and procedures or otherwise direct the affairs of the executive branch—to be applied either across the board to all agencies or to a single agency or department. One of the most important examples is Executive Order No. 8248, September 8, 1939, establishing the divisions of the Executive Office of the President. Another one of equal importance is President Nixon's executive order in 1970–71 establishing the Environmental Protection Agency (EPA), which included establishment of the Environmental Impact Statement.

This legislative or policy leadership role of the presidency is an institutionalized feature of the office that exists independent of the occupant of the office. That is to say, anyone duly elected president would possess these powers regardless of his or her individual energy or leadership characteristics.[12]

executive order a rule or regulation issued by the president that has the effect and formal status of legislation

Delegated Powers

Many of the powers exercised by the president and the executive branch are not found in the Constitution but are the products of congressional statutes and resolutions. Over the past century, Congress has voluntarily delegated a great deal of its own legislative authority to the executive branch. To some extent, this delegation of power has been an almost inescapable consequence of the expansion of government activity in the United States since the New Deal. Given the vast range of the federal government's responsibilities, Congress cannot execute and administer all the programs it creates and the laws it enacts. Inevitably, Congress must turn to the hundreds of departments and agencies in the executive branch or, when necessary, create new agencies to implement its goals. Thus, for example, in 2002, when Congress sought to protect America from terrorist attacks, it established a Department of Homeland Security with broad powers in the realms of law enforcement, public health, and immigration. Similarly, in 1970, when Congress enacted legislation designed to improve the nation's air and water quality, it assigned the task of implementing its goals to the new EPA, created by President Nixon's executive order and empowered by Congress to set and enforce air- and water-quality standards.

As they implement congressional legislation, federal agencies collectively develop thousands of rules and regulations and issue thousands of orders and findings every year. Agencies interpret Congress's intent, promulgate rules aimed at implementing that intent, and issue orders to individuals, firms, and organizations to impel them to conform to the law. When it establishes an agency, Congress sometimes grants it only limited discretionary authority, providing very specific guidelines and standards that must be followed by the administrators charged with the program's implementation. Take the Internal Revenue Service (IRS), for

for critical **analysis**
Presidents have expressed, delegated, and inherent sources of power. Which of the three do you think most accounts for the powers of the presidency?

In 2011 the Obama administration instructed the Justice Department to stop enforcing the Defense of Marriage Act, a federal law that defines marriage as the union of one man and one woman. Although Congress makes the laws, the president (as head of the executive branch) oversees the agencies that implement the laws.

example. Most Americans view the IRS as a powerful agency whose dictates can have an immediate and sometimes unpleasant impact on their lives. In fact, congressional tax legislation is very specific and detailed, leaving little to the discretion of IRS administrators.[13] The agency certainly develops numerous rules and procedures to enhance tax collection. It is Congress, however, that establishes the structure of the tax liabilities, tax exemptions, and tax deductions that determine each taxpayer's burdens and responsibilities.

In most instances, though, congressional legislation is not very detailed. Often, Congress defines a broad goal or objective and delegates enormous discretionary power to administrators to determine how that goal is to be achieved. For example, the 1970 act creating the Occupational Safety and Health Administration (OSHA) states as Congress's purpose "to assure so far as is possible every working man and woman in the nation safe and healthful working conditions." The act, however, neither defines such conditions nor suggests how they might be achieved.[14] The result is that agency administrators have enormous discretionary power to draft rules and regulations that have the effect of law. Indeed, the courts treat these administrative rules like congressional statutes. For all intents and purposes, when Congress creates an agency such as OSHA or the Department of Homeland Security, giving it a broad mandate to achieve some desirable outcome, it transfers its own legislative power to the executive branch.

During the nineteenth and early twentieth centuries, Congress typically wrote laws that provided fairly clear principles and standards to guide executive implementation. For example, the 1923 tariff act empowered the president to increase or decrease duties on certain manufactured goods in order to reduce the difference in costs between domestically produced products and those manufactured abroad. The act authorized the president to make the final determination, but his discretionary authority was quite constrained. The statute listed the criteria the president was to consider, fixed the permissible range of tariff changes, and outlined the procedures to be used to calculate the cost differences between foreign and domestic goods. When an importer challenged a particular executive decision as an abuse of

Who Are America's Presidents?

American presidents have all been men and have all been Christians. Until the election of Barack Obama in 2008, they had all been white. As the data show, a majority of presidents have come from the southeastern United States, with Virginia producing the most American presidents, especially in the nation's first decades.

U.S. Presidents, 1789–2013

PRESIDENT	PARTY	RACE	RELIGION	STATE
Washington	■	●	✚	VA
Adams	■	●	✚	MA
Jefferson	■	●	✚	VA
Madison	■	●	✚	VA
Monroe	■	●	✚	VA
Quincy Adams	■■■	●	✚	MA
Jackson	■	●	✚	*
Van Buren	■	●	✚	NY
W. Harrison	■	●	✚	VA
Tyler	■■	●	✚	VA
Polk	■	●	✚	NC
Taylor	■	●	✚	VA
Fillmore	■	●	✚	NY
Pierce	■	●	✚	NH
Buchanan	■	●	✚	PA
Lincoln	■■	●	✚	KY
A. Johnson	■■	●	✚	NC
Grant	■	●	✚	OH
Hayes	■	●	✚	OH
Garfield	■	●	✚	OH
Arthur	■	●	✚	VT
Cleveland	■	●	✚	NJ

PRESIDENT	PARTY	RACE	RELIGION	STATE
B. Harrison	■	●	✚	OH
McKinley	■	●	✚	OH
T. Roosevelt	■	●	✚	NY
Taft	■	●	✚	OH
Wilson	■	●	✚	VA
Harding	■	●	✚	OH
Coolidge	■	●	✚	VT
Hoover	■	●	✚	IA
F. Roosevelt	■	●	✚	NY
Truman	■	●	✚	MO
Eisenhower	■	●	✚	TX
Kennedy	■	●	✚	MA
L. Johnson	■	●	✚	TX
Nixon	■	●	✚	CA
Ford	■	●	✚	NE
Carter	■	●	✚	GA
Reagan	■	●	✚	IL
G.H.W. Bush	■	●	✚	MA
Clinton	■	●	✚	AR
G.W. Bush	■	●	✚	CT
Obama	■	●	✚	HI

Key

PARTY
- ■ Federalist
- ■ Democratic-Republican
- ■ Whig
- □ Unionist
- ■ Democrat
- ■ Republican

RACE
- ● White
- ● African American

RELIGION
- ✚ Christian: Protestant
- ✚ Christian: Catholic

*Waxhaw area, on North Carolina–South Carolina border

U.S. Presidents, by Region

Presidents
- ○ 0
- ● 1
- ● 2
- ● 4
- ● 7
- ● 8

SOURCE: The Miller Center, "American President: A Reference Resource," millercenter.org (accessed 10/15/12).

for critical analysis

1. Why do you think all presidents have been Christian men and all but one have been white? Do you think this is likely to change in coming years?

2. Why do you think so many presidents have come from the South and the East? What electoral or historical factors may have produced this trend?

delegated power, the Supreme Court had no difficulty finding that the president was merely acting in accordance with Congress's directives.[15]

At least since the New Deal, however, Congress has tended to give executive agencies broad mandates and to draft legislation that offers few clear standards or guidelines for implementation by the executive. For example, the 1933 National Industrial Recovery Act gave the president the authority to set rules to bring about fair competition in key sectors of the economy without ever defining what the term meant or how it was to be achieved.[16] Similarly, the 1938 Agricultural Adjustment Act, which led to a system of commodity price supports and agricultural production restrictions, authorized the secretary of agriculture to make agricultural marketing "orderly" but offered no guidance regarding the commodities to be affected, how markets were to be organized, or how prices should be determined. All these decisions were left to the discretion of the secretary and his agents.[17] This pattern of broad delegation became typical in the ensuing decades. The 1972 Consumer Product Safety Act, for example, authorizes the Consumer Product Safety Commission to reduce unreasonable risk of injury from household products but offers no suggestions to guide the commission's determination of what constitutes reasonable and unreasonable risks or how these are to be reduced.[18]

This shift from the nineteenth-century pattern of relatively well-defined congressional guidelines for administrators to the more contemporary pattern of broad delegations of congressional power to the executive branch is, to be sure, partially a consequence of the great scope and complexity of the tasks that America's contemporary government has undertaken. During much of the nineteenth century, the federal government had relatively few domestic responsibilities, and Congress could pay close attention to details. Today, the operation of an enormous executive establishment and literally thousands of programs under varied and changing circumstances requires that administrators be allowed some considerable measure of discretion to carry out their jobs. Nevertheless, the end result is to shift power from Congress to the executive branch.

● The Presidency as an Institution

> **Identify the institutional resources presidents have to help them exercise their powers**

The framers of the Constitution, as we saw, created a unitary executive because they thought this would make the presidency a more energetic institution. Nevertheless, since the ratification of the Constitution, the president has been joined by thousands of officials and staffers who work for, assist, or advise the chief executive (see Figure 13.2). Collectively, these individuals could be said to make up the institutional presidency and to give the president a capacity for action that no single individual, however energetic, could duplicate. The first component of the institutional presidency is the president's Cabinet.

Cabinet the secretaries, or chief administrators, of the major departments of the federal government. Cabinet secretaries are appointed by the president with the consent of the Senate

The Cabinet

In the American system of government, the **Cabinet** is the traditional but informal designation for the heads of all the major federal government departments. The

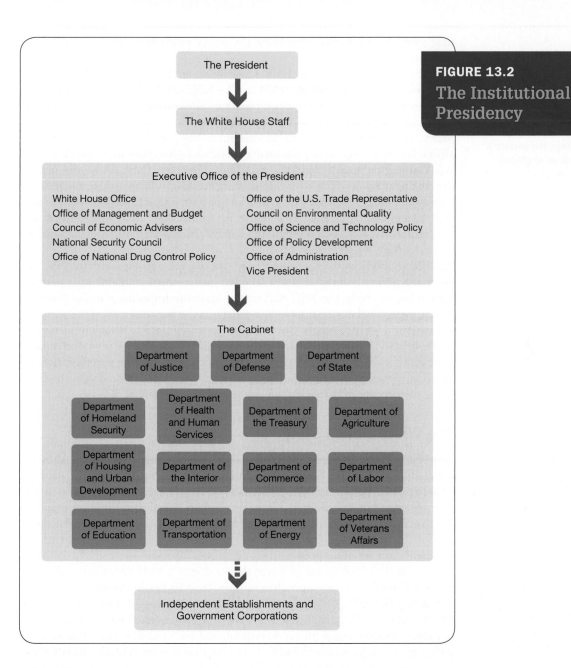

FIGURE 13.2
The Institutional
Presidency

The President

The White House Staff

Executive Office of the President

White House Office
Office of Management and Budget
Council of Economic Advisers
National Security Council
Office of National Drug Control Policy

Office of the U.S. Trade Representative
Council on Environmental Quality
Office of Science and Technology Policy
Office of Policy Development
Office of Administration
Vice President

The Cabinet

Department of Justice

Department of Defense

Department of State

Department of Homeland Security

Department of Health and Human Services

Department of the Treasury

Department of Agriculture

Department of Housing and Urban Development

Department of the Interior

Department of Commerce

Department of Labor

Department of Education

Department of Transportation

Department of Energy

Department of Veterans Affairs

Independent Establishments and Government Corporations

Cabinet has no constitutional status. Unlike in Great Britain and many other parliamentary countries, where the cabinet is the government, the American Cabinet is not a collective body. It meets but makes no decisions as a group. Each appointment must be approved by the Senate, but cabinet members are not responsible to the Senate or to Congress at large.

Since cabinet appointees generally have not shared political careers with the president or with one another, and since they may meet literally for the first time only after their selection, this motley collection of appointees is unlikely to form an effective governing group. Although President Clinton's insistence on a cabinet diverse enough "to look like America" could be considered an act of political wisdom, it virtually guaranteed that few of his appointees had ever spent much time working together or even knew the policy positions or beliefs of the other appointees.[19]

Some presidents have relied more heavily on an "inner cabinet." This includes the **National Security Council (NSC)**. The NSC, established by law in 1947, is composed of the president, the vice president, the secretary of state, the secretary of defense, and other officials invited by the president. It has its own staff of foreign policy specialists run by the special assistant to the president for national security affairs. For these highest appointments, presidents often turn to people from outside Washington, usually longtime associates. The inner Cabinet also can include the ranking officials of the White House staff. President Obama (at least in his early months in office) relied heavily on his chief of staff, Rahm Emanuel, who resigned in 2010 and was replaced by Pete Rouse; his former chief campaign strategist and now senior adviser, David Axelrod; the deputy chief of staff, Jim Messina; and the press secretary, Robert Gibbs.

Different presidents have had different working relationships with the NSC and other subcabinet bodies, because executive management is inherently a personal matter. For example, the NSC staff was of immense importance under President Nixon, especially because it served essentially as the personal staff of the presidential assistant Henry Kissinger. But it was of less importance to President George H. W. Bush, who turned much more to the Joint Chiefs of Staff for advice on military policy matters. Despite all the personal variations, however, one generalization can be made: presidents have increasingly preferred the White House staff to the Cabinet as their means of managing the gigantic executive branch.

The White House Staff

The **White House staff** is composed mainly of analysts and advisers.[20] Although many of the top White House staff members are given the title "special assistant" for a particular task or sector, the judgments and advice they are supposed to provide are a good deal broader and more generally political than those coming from the Executive Office of the President or from the cabinet departments. The members of the White House staff also tend to be more closely associated with the president than are other presidentially appointed officials.

From an informal group of fewer than a dozen people (popularly called the **Kitchen Cabinet**) and no more than four dozen at its height during the Roosevelt presidency in 1937, the White House staff has grown substantially.[21] Richard Nixon employed 550 people in 1972. President Carter, who found so many of the trappings of presidential power distasteful, and who publicly vowed to keep his staff small and decentralized, built an even larger and more centralized staff. President Clinton reduced the White House staff by 20 percent, but a large White House staff is still essential.

The Executive Office of the President

Created in 1939, the **Executive Office of the President (EOP)** is a major part of what is often called the "institutional presidency"—the permanent agencies that perform defined management tasks for the president. Somewhere between 1,500 and 2,000 highly specialized people work for EOP agencies.[22] The importance of each agency in the EOP varies according to the personal orientation of each president. The most important and the largest EOP agency is the Office of Management and Budget (OMB). Its roles in preparing the national budget, designing the president's program,

National Security Council (NSC) a presidential foreign policy advisory council composed of the president, the vice president, the secretary of state, the secretary of defense, and other officials invited by the president

White House staff analysts and advisers to the president, each of whom is often given the title "special assistant"

Kitchen Cabinet an informal group of advisers to whom the president turns for counsel and guidance. Members of the official Cabinet may or may not also be members of the Kitchen Cabinet

Executive Office of the President (EOP) the permanent agencies that perform defined management tasks for the president. Created in 1939, the EOP includes the OMB, the CEA, the NSC, and other agencies

reporting on agency activities, and overseeing regulatory proposals connect the OMB to every conceivable presidential responsibility. The status and power of the OMB have grown in importance with each successive president, and the director of the OMB is now one of the most powerful officials in Washington. At one time the process of budgeting was a "bottom-up" procedure, with expenditure and program requests passing from the lowest bureaus through the departments to "clearance" in the OMB and thence to Congress, where each agency could be called in to explain what its "original request" was before the OMB revised it. Now the budgeting process is "top-down": the OMB sets the terms of discourse for agencies as well as for Congress.

The staff of the Council of Economic Advisers (CEA) constantly analyzes the economy and economic trends in order to help the president anticipate events, rather than waiting and reacting to them. The Council on Environmental Quality was designed to do for environmental issues what the CEA does for economic issues. The NSC—the "inner Cabinet" mentioned earlier—is composed of designated cabinet officials who meet regularly with the president to give advice on the large national security picture. The staff of the NSC assimilates and analyzes data from all intelligence-gathering agencies (CIA, etc.). Other EOP agencies perform more specialized tasks.

The Vice Presidency

The vice presidency is a constitutional anomaly even though the office was created along with the presidency by the Constitution. The vice president exists for two purposes only: to succeed the president in case of death, resignation, or incapacity and to preside over the Senate, casting a tie-breaking vote when necessary.[23]

The main value of the vice president as a political resource for the president is electoral. Traditionally, presidential candidates choose running mates who can win the support of at least one state (preferably a large one) that may not otherwise support the ticket. It is very doubtful that John Kennedy would have won in 1960 without his vice-presidential candidate, Lyndon Johnson, and the contribution Johnson made to winning in Texas. Another traditional guideline holds that the vice-presidential nominee should provide some regional balance and, wherever possible, ideological or ethnic balance as well. In 2008, Barack Obama chose Senator Joseph Biden of Delaware to be his running mate for a number of reasons. To begin with, Biden is Catholic and has blue-collar origins. Obama believed correctly

Vice President Joseph Biden had 35 years' experience in the Senate before Barack Obama picked him as his running mate. In particular, Biden's foreign policy experience was seen as an important strength in the campaign and the Obama administration. Here, Biden meets with Jordan's King Abdullah II.

that Biden would appeal to these important groups in such must-win states as Pennsylvania and Ohio. Perhaps even more important, Biden possesses enormous foreign policy experience and chaired the Senate Foreign Relations Committee. The Republicans had often pointed to Obama's lack of experience in the international realm as indicating that he was not ready to be president; Democrats hoped that Biden's presence on the ticket would put the "experience" issue to rest.

As the institutional presidency has grown in size and complexity, most presidents of the past 25 years have sought to use their vice presidents as a management resource after the election. President Clinton, for example, relied greatly on his vice president, Al Gore, to oversee the National Performance Review (NPR), an ambitious program to "reinvent" the way the federal government conducts its affairs. President George W. Bush granted unprecedented power and responsibility to his vice president, Dick Cheney, who helped shape the "war on terror." In the Obama White House, Vice President Biden is said to be regarded as the "skeptic-in-chief."[24] Biden's role is to question and criticize policy recommendations made to the president—until, of course, the president makes a decision, at which point the vice president falls loyally into step.

The vice president is also important because, in the event of the death or incapacity of the president, he or she will succeed to the nation's highest office. During the course of American history, six vice presidents have had to replace presidents who died in office. One vice president, Gerald Ford, found himself at the head of the nation when President Richard Nixon was forced to resign as a result of the Watergate scandal. During the 2004 vice-presidential debates, Dick Cheney sought to distinguish himself from the Democratic vice-presidential nominee, John Edwards, by averring that he, unlike the less-experienced Edwards, had been chosen for his ability to serve as president if that became necessary.

Until the ratification of the Twenty-Fifth Amendment in 1965, the succession of the vice president to the presidency was a tradition, launched by John Tyler when he assumed the presidency after William Henry Harrison's death, rather than a constitutional or statutory requirement. The Twenty-Fifth Amendment codified this tradition by providing that the vice president would assume the presidency in the event of the chief executive's death or incapacity and setting forth the procedures that would be followed. In the event that both the president and vice president are killed, the Presidential Succession Act of 1947 establishes an order of succession, beginning with the Speaker of the House and continuing with the president of the Senate and the Cabinet secretaries. This piece of legislation, adopted during the Cold War and prompted by fear of a nuclear attack, has taken on new importance in an age of global terrorism.

During the 2008 and 2012 presidential campaigns, Michelle Obama campaigned for her husband, speaking at rallies and appearing on talk shows. As first lady, she has worked on numerous issues, including childhood obesity.

The First Spouse

The president serves as both chief executive and chief of state—the equivalent of Great Britain's prime minister and monarch rolled into one, simultaneously leading the government and representing the nation at official ceremonies and functions.

Because they are generally associated exclusively with the head-of-state aspect of America's presidency, presidential spouses are usually not subject to the same sort of media scrutiny or partisan attack as that aimed at the president. Traditionally, most first ladies have limited their activities to the ceremonial portion of the presidency: greeting foreign dignitaries, visiting other countries, and attending important national ceremonies.

Some first spouses, however, have had considerable influence over policy. Franklin Roosevelt's wife, Eleanor, was widely popular, but also widely criticized, for her active role in many elements of her husband's presidency. During the 1992 campaign, Bill Clinton often implied that his wife would be active in the administration; he joked that voters would get "two for the price of one." And indeed, after the election, Hillary Clinton took a leading role in many policy areas, most notably heading the administration's health care reform effort. She also became the first first lady to seek public office on her own, winning a seat in the U.S. Senate in 2000 and then running for president in 2008. Later, President Obama named Clinton secretary of state. Barack Obama's wife, Michelle, is a lawyer and served for a number of years as a senior administrator at the University of Chicago's Pritzker School of Medicine. Given her legal and policy background, Michelle Obama seemed likely to become a visible and activist first lady on the Hillary Clinton model, but generally she has played a mainly behind-the-scenes role.

The President and Policy

The president's powers and institutional resources, taken together, give the chief executive a substantial voice in the nation's policy-making processes. Strictly speaking, presidents cannot introduce legislation—only members of Congress can formally propose new programs and policies. Nevertheless, a great many of the major bills acted on by the Congress are crafted by the president and his aides and then introduced by friendly legislators. Congress has come to expect the president to propose the government's budget, and the nation has come to expect presidential initiatives to deal with major problems. Some of these initiatives have come in the form of huge packages of programs—Franklin Delano Roosevelt's "New Deal" and Lyndon Johnson's "Great Society." Sometimes presidents craft a single program they hope will have a significant impact on the nation and on their political fortunes. For example, Bill Clinton developed a major health care reform initiative whose political defeat marked a significant setback for his presidency. George W. Bush made the "war on terror" the centerpiece of his administration and brought about the creation of a new cabinet department, the Department of Homeland Security, and the enactment of legislation such as the USA PATRIOT Act to give the executive branch more power to confront the terrorist threat. Bush also presided over a huge expansion of the Medicare program to provide prescription drug benefits for senior citizens. Bush may have lacked a strong claim of popular support in the wake of the controversial 2000 election, but the expressed and delegated powers of the office gave him the resources through which to achieve significant goals. President Barack Obama emphasized health care for all Americans by making the Affordable Care Act the centerpiece of his presidency.

At one time, historians and journalists liked to debate the question of strong versus weak presidents. Some presidents, such as Abraham Lincoln and FDR, were called "strong" for their leadership and their ability to guide the nation's political agenda. Others, such as James Buchanan and Calvin Coolidge, were seen as "weak" for failing to develop significant legislative programs and seeming to observe rather than shape political events. Today, the strong-versus-weak categorization has become moot. Every president is strong, not so much as a function of personal charisma or political savvy but as a reflection of the increasing power of the presidency. Let us see how this came about.

The Contemporary Bases of Presidential Power

Explain how modern presidents have become even more powerful

During the nineteenth century, Congress was America's dominant institution of government, and members of Congress sometimes treated the president with disdain. Today, however, no one would assert that the presidency is unimportant. Presidents seek to dominate the policy-making process and claim the power to lead the nation in time of war. The expansion of presidential power over the course of the past century has come about not by accident but as the result of an ongoing effort by successive presidents to enlarge the powers of the office.

Generally, presidents can expand their power in three ways: through the party, through popular mobilization, and through the administration. In the first instance, presidents may create or strengthen partisan institutions that can exert influence in the legislative process and can help implement their programs. In addition, presidents may use popular appeals to create a mass base of support that will allow them to dominate their political foes, a tactic called "going public."[25] Third, presidents may seek to bolster their control of established executive agencies or to create new administrative institutions and procedures that will reduce their dependence on Congress and give them a more independent governing and policy-making capability. Perhaps the most obvious example of this is the use of executive orders to achieve policy goals in lieu of seeking to persuade Congress to enact legislation.

Party as a Source of Power

Each president has relied on his own party to implement his legislative agendas. President George W. Bush, for example, worked closely with congressional GOP leaders on such matters as energy policy and Medicare reform. But the president does not control his party; party members have considerable autonomy. Moreover, in America's system of separated powers, the president's party may be in the minority in Congress and unable to do much for the chief executive's programs (see Figure 13.3). Consequently, although their party is valuable to chief executives, it has not been a fully reliable presidential tool. As a result, contemporary presidents are more likely to use the two other methods, popular mobilization and executive administration, to achieve their political goals.

Going Public

In the nineteenth century, it was considered inappropriate for presidents to engage in personal campaigning on their own behalf or in support of programs and policies. When Andrew Johnson broke this unwritten rule and made a series of speeches vehemently seeking public support for his Reconstruction program, even some of his supporters were shocked at what they saw as his lack of decorum and dignity. The president's opponents cited his "inflammatory" speeches in one of the articles of impeachment drafted by the Congress.[26]

In the twentieth century, though, popular mobilization became a favored weapon in the political arsenals of most presidents. The first to make systematic

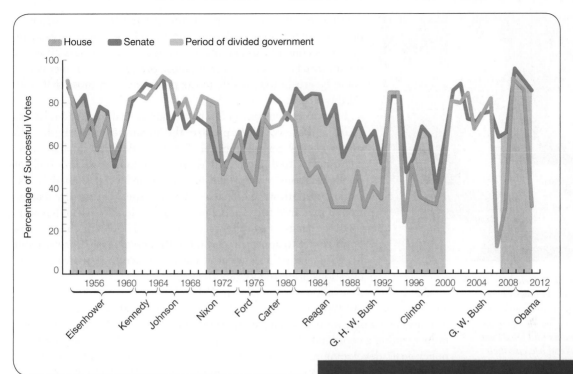

FIGURE 13.3

Presidential Success on Congressional Votes, 1953–2011*

Presidents have more success in Congress when their party is in the majority. Can you identify the periods when presidents had majority support in Congress and when they did not?

*Percentages based on votes on which presidents took a position.
SOURCE: *Congressional Quarterly*
CREDIT: *Nelson HSU/NPR*

use of appeals to the public were Theodore Roosevelt and Woodrow Wilson, but the president who used public appeals most effectively was Franklin Delano Roosevelt. FDR was "firmly persuaded of the need to form a direct link between the executive office and the public."[27] Roosevelt developed a number of tactics for forging such a link. He often embarked on speaking trips around the nation to promote his programs. On one such tour, he told a crowd, "I regain strength just by meeting the American people."[28] In addition, FDR made effective use of a new electronic medium, the radio, to reach millions of Americans. In his famous "fireside chats," the president's voice could be heard in every living room in the country, discussing programs and policies and generally assuring Americans that Franklin Delano Roosevelt was aware of their difficulties and working diligently toward solutions.

Roosevelt was also an innovator in the realm of what now might be called press relations. When he entered the White House, FDR faced a mainly hostile press, typically controlled by conservative members of the business establishment. As the president wrote, "All the fat-cat newspapers—85 percent of the whole—have been utterly opposed to everything the Administration is seeking."[29] Roosevelt hoped to be able to use the press to mold public opinion, but to do so he needed to circumvent the editors and publishers who were generally unsympathetic to his goals. To this end, the president worked to cultivate the reporters who covered the White House. Roosevelt made himself available for biweekly press conferences where he offered candid answers to reporters' questions and made certain to make important policy announcements that would provide the reporters with significant stories

President Franklin Delano Roosevelt's direct appeals to the American people allowed him to "reach over the heads" of congressional opponents and force them to follow his lead because their constituents demanded it.

for their papers.[30] Roosevelt was the first president to designate a press secretary, Stephen Early, who was charged with organizing the press conferences and making certain that reporters observed the informal rules distinguishing those presidential comments that could be attributed directly to the president from those that were off the record.

Every president since FDR has sought to craft a public-relations strategy that would emphasize the incumbent's strengths and maximize his popular appeal. For John F. Kennedy, handsome and quick-witted, the televised press conference was an excellent public-relations vehicle. Johnson and Nixon lacked Kennedy's charisma, but both were effective television speakers, usually reading from a prepared text. Bill Clinton made extensive use of televised town meetings—carefully staged events that gave the president an opportunity to appear to consult with rank-and-file citizens about his goals and policies without having to face the sorts of pointed questions preferred by reporters.

One Clinton innovation was to make the White House Communications Office an important institution within the EOP. The Communications Office became responsible not only for responding to reporters' queries but also for developing and implementing a coordinated communications strategy—promoting the president's policy goals, developing responses to adverse news stories, and making certain that a favorable image of the president would, insofar as possible, dominate the news. George W. Bush relied heavily on material crafted by the Communications Office, whereas Barack Obama often relies on his own formidable speaking abilities.

The Limits of Going Public Some presidents have been able to make effective use of popular appeals to overcome congressional opposition. Popular support, though, has not been a firm foundation for presidential power: the public is notoriously fickle. During his first two years in office, Ronald Reagan's approval rating ranged from a high of 59 percent in 1981 to a low of 37 percent in early 1983.[31] As Reagan's poll standing fell, his ability to overawe Democratic opponents and retain the support of wavering Republicans diminished sharply. After America's triumph in the 1990 Persian Gulf War, President George H. W. Bush scored a remarkable 90 percent approval rating in the polls. Two years later, however, after the 1991 budget crisis, Bush's support plummeted, and the president was defeated in his bid for re-election. His son, President George W. Bush, maintained an approval rating of over 70 percent for more than a year following the September 11 terrorist attacks. By the end of 2005, however, President Bush's approval rating had dropped to 39 percent as a result of the growing unpopularity of the Iraq War, the administration's inept handling of hurricane relief, and a number of White House scandals, including the conviction of Vice President Cheney's chief of staff on charges of lying to a federal grand jury. Such declines in popular approval during a president's term in office are nearly inevitable and follow a predictable pattern.[32] Both before and after they are elected, presidents generate popular support by promising to undertake important programs that will contribute directly to the well-being of large numbers of Americans. Almost without exception, presidential performance falls short of promises and popular expectations, leading to a decline in public support and the ensuing weakening of presidential influence.[33] It is a rare American president, such as Bill Clinton, who exits the White House more popular than when he went in.

The Digital President

As the only elected official accountable to all Americans, the president has to make communication between him or herself and the people a priority. Communication with the people is also a key tool presidents can use to pressure Congress to enact their policy agendas. FDR's fireside chats were broadcast on the radio and brought the words of the president into citizens' homes during the crises of the Great Depression and World War II. In the early 1960s, President John F. Kennedy was the first to use television to communicate with the mass public.

President Barack Obama has also been the first to make full use of a new communication medium—in this case, the Internet. Some political commentators argue that without the Internet, Barack Obama would not have been elected president in 2008. Drawing on the interactive tools of the Web, Obama's campaign changed the way politicians organize supporters, advertise to voters, defend against attacks, and communicate with their constituents. His website, www.barackobama.com, was also the centerpiece of his 2012 campaign.

One reason the Internet is such an effective means of organizing presidential campaigns is because of cost. Obama's campaign organized supporters online, a feat that in the past would have required an army of volunteers and paid organizers on the ground. The Internet allows the organization of volunteers at a fraction of the cost of traditional campaigns. Obama's campaigns took advantage of free advertising on YouTube rather than relying exclusive on television ads. Online political videos may be more effective than television ads because viewers make a conscious choice to watch them, instead of having their television program interrupted by an unwanted ad. Obama's YouTube video ads in the 2008 election were watched for 14.5 million hours. By comparison, purchasing 14.5 million hours on broadcast TV would have cost an estimated $47 million. President Obama's 37-minute speech on race ("A More Perfect Union") was watched online by 7 million people. The efficient use of the Internet allowed the Obama campaign to spend the vast funds raised from supporters more efficiently.

The Internet has not only changed the way modern presidents campaign but also how they govern. The Whitehouse .gov website keeps the president's constituents abreast of his policy agenda with a weekly streaming video address by the president, press briefings, speeches and remarks, a daily blog, photos of the president, the White House schedule, and other information. Virtually everything the president does is recorded online. YouTube airs Obama's press conferences and public appearances on a daily basis. Every presidential address is now streamed live online. Circumventing television and other traditional media, the Internet allows the president to broadcast his policy ideas directly to the citizens. In March 2012, Obama broke new media ground again, appearing on Bill Simmons's "B.S. Report" (a regular series of podcasts on ESPN's website) in the first-ever podcast with a sitting U.S. president.

Obama's Facebook page personalizes the president's connection with his constituents and the causes they care about. As of July 2012, Barack Obama's Facebook page had more than 27 million "likes." In June 2012, Obama had 16.5 million Twitter followers.

A social media analysis firm found that social media users appear to be less influenced by negative advertising, which dominates campaign communications on television. Facebook users were more interested in positive posts focusing on successes, accomplishments, and the candidates' private lives than in standard campaign rhetoric. This suggests that new media hold promise for creating a positive forum for political discussion and increasing confidence in presidential leadership.

Websites, podcasts, Facebook, and other new media forums facilitate direct communication between the president and the people, creating a virtual network of constituents. Like FDR in the 1930s and '40s, and Kennedy in the 1960s, Obama may have changed how presidents govern for some time to come.

SOURCES: Juliana Gruenwald, "New Data Show Obama ahead in Social-Media Race." *National Journal*, June 14, 2012. Claire Cain Miller, "How Obama's Internet Campaign Changed Politics." *New York Times*, November 7, 2008. David Plouffe, *The Audacity to Win: The Inside Story and Lessons of Barack Obama's Historic Victory* (New York: Penguin Group Publishers, 2009).

for critical analysis

1. Will the Internet and social media become more important to modern presidents than television, just as television replaced FDR's radio addresses?

2. What are the advantages and disadvantages of presidents governing via digital media?

President Obama has held town hall meetings on issues such as health care reform and the economy, as a way to consult (or appear to consult) ordinary Americans about goals and policies.

The Administrative State

Contemporary presidents have increased the administrative capabilities of their office in three ways. First, they have enhanced the reach and power of the EOP. Second, they have sought to increase White House control over the federal bureaucracy. Third, they have expanded the role of executive orders and other instruments of direct presidential governance. Taken together, these three components of what might be called the White House "administrative strategy" have given presidents a capacity to achieve their programmatic and policy goals even when they are unable to secure congressional approval. Indeed, some recent presidents have been able to accomplish a great deal with remarkably little congressional, partisan, or even public support.

The Growth of the EOP The EOP has grown from six administrative assistants in 1939 to today's 400 employees working directly for the president in the White House office, along with some 1,400 individuals staffing the several (currently eight) divisions of the Executive Office.[34] The creation and growth of the White House staff gives the president an enormously enhanced capacity to gather information, plan programs and strategies, communicate with constituencies, and exercise supervision over the executive branch. The staff multiplies the president's eyes, ears, and arms, becoming a critical instrument of presidential power.[35]

In particular, the OMB serves as a potential instrument of presidential control over federal spending and hence a mechanism through which the White House has greatly expanded its power. The OMB has the capacity to analyze and approve all legislative proposals, not only budgetary requests, emanating from all federal agencies before being submitted to Congress. This procedure, now a matter of routine, greatly enhances the president's control over the entire executive branch. All legislation originating in the White House as well as all executive orders also go through the OMB.[36]

Thus, through one White House agency, the president has the means to exert major influence over the flow of money and the shape and content of national legislation.

Regulatory Review   A second tactic that presidents have used to increase their power and reach is the process of regulatory review, through which presidents have sought to seize control of rule making by the agencies of the executive branch (see also Chapter 14). Whenever Congress enacts a statute, its actual implementation requires the promulgation of hundreds of rules by the agency charged with administering the law and effecting the will of Congress. Some congressional statutes are quite detailed and leave agencies with relatively little discretion. Typically, however, Congress enacts a relatively broad statement of legislative intent and then delegates to the appropriate administrative agency the power to fill in many important details.[37] In other words, Congress typically says to an administrative agency, "Here is the problem: deal with it."[38]

The discretion that Congress delegates to administrative agencies has provided recent presidents with an important avenue for expanding their own power. For example, President Clinton believed the president had full authority to order agencies of the executive branch to adopt such rules as the president thought appropriate.

During the course of his presidency, Clinton issued 107 directives to administrators ordering them to propose specific rules and regulations. In some instances, the language of the rule to be proposed was drafted by the White House staff; in other cases, the president asserted a priority but left it to the agency to draft the precise language of the proposal. Republicans, of course, denounced Clinton's actions as a usurpation of power.[39] However, after President George W. Bush took office, he made no move to surrender the powers Clinton had claimed—quite the contrary. Bush vigorously continued the Clinton-era practice of issuing presidential directives to agencies, spurring them to issue new rules and regulations. Obama's first regulatory director, Cass Sunstein, not only issued a number of major regulatory directives to federal agencies but also launched a "look back" program. Under this program, the administration sought to eliminate several hundred existing federal rules it deemed obsolete.[40]

Governing by Decree: Executive Orders   A fourth mechanism through which contemporary presidents have sought to enhance their power to govern unilaterally is through the use of executive orders and other forms of presidential decrees, including executive agreements, national security findings and directives, proclamations, reorganization plans, signing statements, and a host of others.[41] Executive orders have a long history in the United States and have been the vehicles for a number of important government policies, including the purchase of Louisiana, the annexation of Texas, the emancipation of the slaves, the internment of Japanese Americans, the desegregation of the military, the initiation of affirmative action, and the creation of important federal agencies, among them the EPA, the FDA, and the Peace Corps.[42]

Although wars and national emergencies produce the highest volume of executive orders, such presidential actions also occur frequently in peacetime (see Figure 13.4). In the realm of foreign policy, unilateral presidential actions in the form of executive agreements have virtually replaced treaties as the nation's chief foreign policy instruments.[43] Presidential decrees, however, are often used for purely domestic purposes.

Presidents may not use executive orders to issue whatever commands they please. The use of such decrees is bound by law. If a president issues an executive order, proclamation, directive, or the like, in principle he does so pursuant to the powers granted to him by the Constitution or delegated to him by Congress, usually through

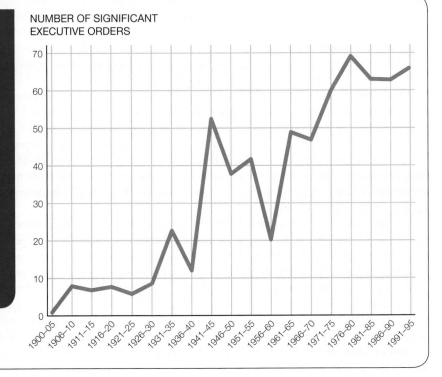

FIGURE 13.4

Significant Executive Orders, 1900–95

Over the twentieth century, presidents made increasingly frequent use of executive orders to accomplish their policy goals. What factors explain this development? How has Congress responded to increased presidential assertiveness? What might explain the large number of executive orders issued during the 1940s?

SOURCE: William Howell, "The President's Powers of Unilateral Action: The Strategic Advantages of Acting Alone" (Ph.D. diss., Stanford University, 1999).

NUMBER OF SIGNIFICANT EXECUTIVE ORDERS

a statute. When presidents issue such orders, they generally state the constitutional or statutory basis for their actions. For example, when President Truman ordered the desegregation of the armed services, he did so pursuant to his constitutional powers as commander in chief. In a similar vein, when President Lyndon Johnson issued Executive Order No. 11246, he asserted that the order was designed to implement the 1964 Civil Rights Act, which prohibited employment discrimination. Where an executive order has no statutory or constitutional basis, the courts have held it to be void. The most important such is *Youngstown Co. v. Sawyer* (1952).[44] Here, the Supreme Court ruled that President Truman's seizure of the nation's steel mills during the Korean War had no statutory or constitutional basis and was thus invalid.

A number of court decisions, though, have established broad boundaries that leave considerable room for presidential action. For example, the courts have held that Congress might approve presidential action after the fact or, in effect, ratify presidential action through "acquiescence" by not objecting for long periods of time or by continuing to provide funding for programs established by executive orders. Further, the courts have indicated that some areas, most notably the realm of military policy, are presidential in character, allowing presidents wide latitude to make policy by executive decree. Thus, within the very broad limits established by the courts, presidential orders can be important policy tools.

President Clinton issued numerous orders designed to promote a coherent set of policy goals: protecting the environment, strengthening federal regulatory power, shifting America's foreign policy from a unilateral to a multilateral focus, expanding affirmative action programs, and helping organized labor.[45] President George W. Bush also did not hesitate to use executive orders, issuing more than 300 between his inauguration and the end of 2008. During his first months in office, Bush issued

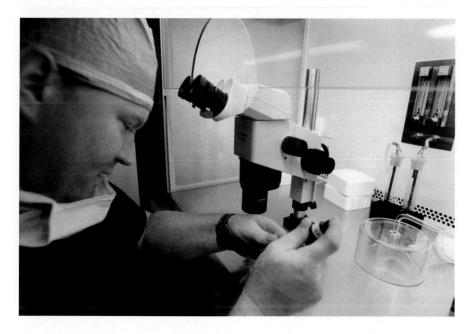

In 2001, President Bush issued an executive order limiting the use of stem cells in federally funded research. In 2009, President Obama issued an executive order overturning Bush's order and allowing federal science programs more freedom.

orders prohibiting the use of federal funds to support international family-planning groups that provided abortion counseling services, and limiting the use of embryonic stem cells in federally funded research projects. Throughout his administration, Bush made very aggressive use of executive orders in response to the threat of terrorism. In November 2001, for example, he issued a directive authorizing the creation of military tribunals to try noncitizens accused of involvement in acts of terrorism against the United States. In May 2007 he issued controversial national security directives that gave the president sole responsibility for determining when and how constitutional government could be reestablished in the event of a catastrophic attack on the United States.

During his first year in office, President Obama also issued a number of executive orders, many of which rescinded Bush-era orders. Thus, Obama ordered the closing of the Guantánamo prison and ordered an end to what were deemed unlawful methods of interrogation of terror suspects. In February 2010, with many elements of his legislative agenda stalled in Congress, Obama indicated that he might make increased use of executive orders to advance energy, environmental, fiscal, and other domestic priorities.[46] In June 2012, Obama issued an order designed to halt the deportation of undocumented immigrants who had come to the United States as children. These individuals would become eligible for work permits. Immigrant rights groups hailed the order while Republicans criticized the president for circumventing Congress.

Signing Statements   To negate congressional actions to which they objected, recent presidents have made frequent and calculated use of presidential **signing statements** when signing bills into law.[47] The signing statement is an announcement made by the president, at the time of signing a congressional enactment into law, that offers the president's interpretation of the law and usually innocuous remarks predicting the many benefits the new law will bring to the nation. Occasionally, presidents have used signing statements to point to sections of the law they have deemed improper or even unconstitutional, and to instruct executive branch

signing statements
announcements made by the president when signing bills into law, often presenting the president's interpretation of the law

agencies how to execute the law.[48] President Harry Truman, for example, accompanied his approval of the 1946 Hobbs Anti-Racketeering Act with a message offering his interpretation of ambiguous sections of the statute and indicating how the federal government would implement the new law.[49]

Presidents have made signing statements throughout American history, though many were not recorded and did not become part of the official legislative record. Ronald Reagan's attorney general, Edwin Meese, is generally credited with transforming the signing statement into a routine tool of presidential direct action.[50] Meese believed that carefully crafted signing statements would provide a basis for action by executive agencies and, perhaps even more important, would become part of the history and context of a piece of legislation if and when judicial interpretation became necessary. Indeed, to make certain of this, Meese reached an agreement with the West Publishing Company to include them in its authoritative texts of federal legislation.[51]

With the way thus paved, Reagan, followed by George H. W. Bush, Clinton, and George W. Bush, proceeded to use detailed and artfully designed signing statements—prepared by the Department of Justice—to reinterpret congressional enactments. For example, when signing the 1986 amendments to the Safe Drinking Water Act, President Reagan issued a statement that interpreted sections of the act to allow discretionary enforcement even though Congress seemed to call for mandatory enforcement.[52] Reagan hoped the courts would accept his version of the statute when examining subsequent enforcement decisions. In other cases, Reagan used his signing statements to attempt to nullify portions of statutes. George W. Bush issued more than 161 signing statements and used them to rewrite the law on numerous occasions. As a candidate, President Obama criticized Bush for excessive use of signing statements. As president, Obama has issued signing statements, but in far smaller numbers.[53]

The Advantages of the Administrative Strategy   Through the course of American history, party leadership and popular appeals have played important roles in presidential efforts to overcome political opposition, and both continue to be instruments of presidential power. Reagan's tax cuts and Clinton's budget victories were achieved with strong partisan support. George W. Bush, lacking the oratorical skills of Reagan or Roosevelt, nevertheless made effective use of sophisticated communications strategies to promote his agenda. Yet, as we have seen, in the modern era parties have waned in institutional strength, and the effects of popular appeals have often proven evanescent. The limitations of the alternatives have increasingly impelled presidents to try to expand the administrative capabilities of the office and their own capacity for unilateral action as means of achieving their policy goals. And in recent decades, the expansion of the Executive Office, the development of regulatory review, and the use of executive orders and signing statements have given presidents a substantial capacity to achieve significant policy results despite congressional opposition to their legislative agendas.

In principle, perhaps, Congress could respond more vigorously to unilateral policy making by the president than it has. Certainly, a Congress willing to impeach a president should have the mettle to overturn his or her administrative directives. But the president has significant advantages in such struggles with Congress. In battles over presidential directives and orders, Congress is on the defensive, reacting to presidential initiatives. The framers of the Constitution saw "energy," or the ability to take the initiative, as a key feature of executive power.[54] When the president takes action by issuing an order or an administrative directive, Congress must respond through the cumbersome and time-consuming lawmaking process, overcome internal divisions, and enact legislation that the president may ultimately veto. Moreover, as the political scientist Terry Moe has argued, in such battles Congress faces a significant collective action problem: members are likely to be more sensitive to the substance of a president's actions and its short-term effects on their constituents than to the more general long-term implications of presidential power for the vitality of their institution.[55]

● Thinking Critically about Presidential Power and Democracy

The framers of the Constitution created a system of government in which the Congress and the executive branch were to share power. At least since the New Deal, however, the powers of Congress have waned, whereas those of the presidency have expanded dramatically. An instance of congressional retreat in the face of presidential assertiveness occurred in October 2002, when both houses of Congress, pressed by President George W. Bush, voted overwhelmingly to authorize the White House to use military force against Iraq. The resolution adopted by Congress expressly allowed the president complete discretion to determine whether, when, and how to attack Iraq. The president had rejected language that might have implied even the slightest limitations on his prerogatives. Indeed, Bush's legal advisers had pointedly declared that the president did not actually need specific congressional authorization to attack Iraq if he deemed such action to be in America's interest. "We don't want to be in the legal position of asking Congress to authorize the use of force when the president already has that full authority," said one senior administration official. Few members of Congress even bothered to object to this apparent rewriting of the U.S. Constitution.

There is no doubt that Congress continues to be able to confront presidents and even, on occasion, hand the White House a sharp rebuff. During the 2011 debt crisis, President Obama was unable to force House Republicans to accept his plan for dealing with the nation's deficits and was compelled to accede to many of the GOP's demands in order to prevent a potentially disastrous default on government debt.

In the larger view, however, presidents' occasional defeats, however dramatic, have to be seen as temporary setbacks in a gradual but decisive shift toward increased presidential power. Louis Fisher, a leading authority on the separation of powers, recently observed that in what are arguably the two most important policy arenas, national defense and the federal budget, the powers of Congress have been in decline for at least the past 50 years. The last time Congress exercised its constitutional power to declare war was December 8, 1941, and yet, since that time, American forces have been committed to numerous conflicts around the world by order of the president. The much-hailed 1973 War Powers Resolution, far from limiting presidential power, actually allowed the president considerably more discretionary authority than what was granted by the Constitution, which seems to require congressional authorization before troops can be deployed for even one day. The War Powers Resolution gave the president the authority to deploy forces abroad for 60 days without congressional authority. And presidents have ignored even this stipulation.

Presidents are not all-powerful. President Obama succeeded in getting health care legislation passed in his first term, but not without making major concessions to Congress regarding the type and scope of the reforms. Here, Obama signs the Affordable Care Act into law in 2010.

As to spending powers, the framers of the Constitution conceived the "power of the purse" to be Congress's most fundamental prerogative. For more than a century this power was jealously guarded by powerful congressional leaders such as Taft-era House speaker "Uncle" Joe Cannon, who saw congressional control of the budget as a fundamental safeguard against "Prussian-style" militarism and autocracy. Since the New Deal, however, successive Congresses have yielded to steadily increasing presidential influence over the budget process. In 1939, Congress allowed Franklin Delano Roosevelt to take a giant step toward presidential control of the nation's purse strings when it permitted him to bring the Bureau of the Budget (BoB) into the newly created EOP. Roosevelt and his successors used the BoB (now called the OMB) effectively to seize the nation's legislative and budgetary agenda. In 1974, Congress attempted to respond to Richard Nixon's efforts to further enhance presidential control of spending when it enacted the Budget and Impoundment Control Act, legislation centralizing Congress's own budgetary process and apparently reinforcing congressional power. Yet, less than 10 years later, Congress watched as President Ronald Reagan essentially seized control of the congressional budget process. Subsequently, Congress has surrendered more and more power to the president.

Representative assemblies such as the U.S. Congress derive their influence from the support of groups and forces in civil society that believe these institutions serve their interests. A chief executive, such as the president of the United States, on the other hand, fundamentally derives power from the command of bureaucracies, armies, and the general machinery of the state. Presidents can certainly benefit from popular support. If we imagine, however, a fully demobilized polity in which neither institution could count on much support from forces in civil society, the president would still command the institutions of the state, whereas Congress would be without significant resources. In a fully mobilized polity, on the other hand, Congress might have a chance to counterbalance the president's institutional powers with the support of significant social forces.

A powerful presidency, a weak Congress, and a partially demobilized electorate make for a dangerous mix. Presidents have increasingly asserted the right to govern unilaterally and now appear able to overcome most institutional and political constraints. Presidential power, to be sure, can be a force for good. To cite one example from the not-so-distant past, it was President Lyndon Johnson, more than Congress or the judiciary, who faced up to the task of smashing America's racial apartheid system. Yet, as the framers knew, unchecked power is always dangerous. Americans of the founding generation feared that unchecked presidential power would lead to *monocracy*, a republican form of monarchy without a king. Inevitably, we will pay a price for our undemocratic politics.

<aside>
for critical analysis

The presidency and Congress are both democratic institutions. Which is the more democratic? Why?
</aside>

Connect with the Presidency

Inform Yourself

Who are America's presidents? To learn about American presidents past and present, visit the University of Virginia's Miller Center (http://millercenter.org/president), which provides a one-stop reference for American presidents. See photos of each president, learn how long he served, his religion, home state, and much more. You can also visit the White House website www.whitehouse.gov/about/presidents,which counts down the presidencies from the first to the most recent.

Understand the president's role as head of the executive branch. Freedom Project has created a 10-minute video that focuses on the powers and limitations of the executive branch (www.youtube.com/watch?v=mQGp4acvBs0&feature=related). The White House also has a section on how the modern executive branch is organized. Visit www.whitehouse.gov/our-government/executive-branch to understand the power of the modern executive branch.

Evaluate America's presidents. Presidents in the United States are ranked by a multitude of factors. However, there is always disagreement about what should be considered in the rankings. After considering the many different types of rankings available at http://en.wikipedia.org/wiki/Historical_rankings_of_Presidents_of_the_United_States, consider the conservative blog's argument at www.theamericanconservative.com/articles/ranking-the-presidents/. What do you think should be considered when ranking the "best" and "worst" presidents? Whom would you list as the five best and five worst presidents?

Express Yourself

Respond to the White House blog. The White House website has a constantly updated blog on key issues and events involving the executive branch. Go to www.whitehouse.gov/blog and see the current events of the day. After reading a blog post, consider making a comment online.

Send an e-mail to the president. Use the Whitehouse website to send a letter to the President (and his staffers) about what you would like to see changed in how the executive branch operates. This form will allow you send "questions, comments, concerns, or well-wishes to the President or his staff": www.whitehouse.gov/contact/submit-questions-and-comments.

Find links to the sites listed above as well as related activities on wwnorton.com/studyspace.

study guide

(S) **Practice online with:** Chapter 13 Diagnostic Quiz ▪ Chapter 13 Key Term Flashcards

Establishing the Presidency

■ **Explain the role of the president in the American political system (pp. 517–19)**

During the writing of the Constitution, the framers debated whether executive authority should be concentrated in the hands of one individual and whether this individual should be directly by the people. Once the idea of an "executive council" was rejected in favor of a creating "energy" in the executive branch, the framers chose to design an indirect system of selecting the president that would make the president responsible to state and national legislators rather than to the public. It was not until the emergence of the national convention system in the 1830s that the presidency obtained the broad popular base needed to increase presidential power.

Key Term

caucus (political) (p. 518)

Practice Quiz

1. Which article of the Constitution establishes the presidency? *(p. 517)*
   a) Article I
   b) Article II
   c) Article III
   d) Article IV
   e) Article V

2. The Founders chose to select the president through an indirect election in order to *(p. 517)*
   a) increase the strength and influence of political parties.
   b) build an imperial presidency that would overwhelm the power of Congress.
   c) force the president to be responsive to the will of the people.
   d) make the president responsible to the state and national legislatures.
   e) create a more independent chief executive.

> (S) **Practice Online**
> Video exercises: "*My Job*" on The Daily Show with Jon Stewart

The Constitutional Powers of the Presidency

■ **Outline the powers the Constitution gives the president (pages 519–32)**

Presidents have three kinds of powers: expressed, delegated and inherent. The president's expressed powers, as defined by Article II of the Constitution, fall into several broad categories: military, judicial, diplomatic, executive, and legislative. The president's delegated powers are not found in the Constitution but are, instead, the product of congressional statutes and resolutions that voluntarily transfer authority from the legislative to the executive branch. The president's inherent powers grow from "the rights, duties and obligations of the presidency" that presidents often assert during times of war and national crisis.

Key Terms

expressed powers (p. 519)
delegated powers (p. 519)
inherent powers (p. 519)
commander in chief (p. 520)
War Powers Resolution (p. 521)
executive agreement (p. 525)

executive privilege (p. 525)
veto (p. 526)
pocket veto (p. 526)
legislative initiative (p. 527)
executive order (p. 529)

Practice Quiz

3. Which of the following war powers does the Constitution *not* assign to the president? *(p. 520)*
   a) command of the army and navy of the United States
   b) the power to declare war
   c) command of the state militias
   d) the power to make treaties
   e) The Constitution assigns all of the powers above to the president.

4. The War Powers Resolution of 1973 was an act passed by Congress that *(p. 521)*
   a) required the CIA to collect inteligence on all Americans born in a foreign country.
   b) outlawed presidential use of executive agreements.
   c) created the National Security Council.

d) granted the president the authority to declare war.

e) stipulated military forces must be withdrawn within 60 days in the absence of a specific congressional authorization for their continued deployment.

5. Which of the following does *not* require the advice and consent of the Senate? *(p. 525)*
   a) an executive agreement
   b) a treaty
   c) appointment of ambassadors
   d) Supreme Court nominations
   e) All of the above require the advice and consent of the Senate.

6. What did the Supreme Court rule in *United States v. Nixon*? *(p. 526)*
   a) Nixon had to turn his secret White House tapes over to congressional investigators because presidents do not have the power of executive privilege.
   b) Nixon did not have to turn his secret White House tapes over to congressional investigators because, in general, presidents have the power of executive privilege.
   c) Nixon had to turn his secret White House tapes over to congressional investigators but, in general, presidents have the power of executive privilege.
   d) Nixon did not have to turn his secret White House tapes over to congressional investigators but, in

general, presidents do not have the power of executive privilege.

   e) All presidents are immune from criminal investigations and cannot, therefore, be tried in any court of law.

7. What are the requirements for overriding a presidential veto? *(p. 526)*
   a) 50 percent plus one vote in both houses of Congress
   b) two-thirds vote in both houses of Congress
   c) two-thirds vote in the Senate only
   d) three-fourths vote in both houses of Congress.
   e) A presidential veto cannot be overridden by Congress.

8. When the president issues a rule or regulation that reorganizes or otherwise directs the affairs of the executive branch, such as the directives that established the Executive Office of the President and the Environmental Protection Agency, it is called *(p. 529)*
   a) an executive agreement.
   b) an executive order.
   c) an executive mandate.
   d) administrative oversight.
   e) legislative initiative.

 Practice Online
Video exercise: *The Word—The Defining Moment*

The Presidency as an Institution

▌ **Identify the institutional resources presidents have to help them exercise their powers (pp. 532–37)**

The institutionalized presidency is made up of the Cabinet, White House staff, Executive Office of the President, the Vice Presidency, and the First Spouse. Through their advice and assistance. these thousands of individuals give the president a capacity for action that he could never have by himself. When coupled with the president's formal powers, the institutionalized presidency makes the chief executive an important player in the country's policy-making process.

Key Terms

Cabinet (p. 532)

National Security Council (NSC) (p. 534)

White House staff (p. 534)

Kitchen Cabinet (p. 534)

Executive Office of the President (EOP) (p. 534)

Practice Quiz

9. Which of the following statements about vice presidents is *not* true? *(pp. 535–36)*
   a) The vice president succeeds the president in case of death, resignation, or incapacitation.
   b) The vice president casts the tie-breaking vote in the Senate when necessary.

   c) The vice president also serves as an honorary member of the Supreme Court.
   d) Six vice presidents have had to replace presidents who died in office during American history.
   e) Presidential candidates typically select a vice presidential candidate who is likely to bring the support of a state that would not otherwise support the ticket.

10. The Office of Management and Budget is part of *(p. 533)*
    a) the Executive Office of the President.
    b) the White House staff.
    c) the Kitchen Cabinet.
    d) the Congressional Budget Office.
    e) the Bureau of Economic Analysis.

11. How many people work for agencies within the Executive Office of the President? *(p. 534)*
    a) 25 to 50
    b) 700 to 1,000
    c) 1,500 to 2,000
    d) 4,500 to 5,000
    e) 25,000 to 30,000

 Practice Online
Interactive simulation exercise: *Special Assistant to the President*

The Contemporary Bases of Presidential Power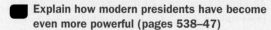

 Explain how modern presidents have become even more powerful (pages 538–47)

Although Congress was the dominant institution in the American political system throughout the nineteenth century, recent presidents have expanded the policy-making power of their office in number of ways. While some presidents have relied primarily on the support of party members to advance their legislative goals, contemporary, presidents more commonly turn to popular mobilization and executive administration in pursuing policy change.

Key Term

signing statements (p. 545)

Practice Quiz

12. What are the three ways that presidents can expand their power? *(p. 538)*
    a) weakening national partisan institutions, avoiding popular appeals, and loosening their control of executive agencies
    b) strengthening national partisan institutions, using popular appeals, and bolstering their control of executive agencies
    c) weakening national partisan institutions, using popular appeals, and loosening their control of executive agencies

    d) strengthening national partisan institutions, avoiding popular appeals, and bolstering their control of executive agencies
    e) weakening national partisan institutions, avoiding popular appeals, and bolstering their control of executive agencies

13. The Supreme Court case *Youngstown Co. v. Sawyer* was significant because *(pp. 543–544)*
    a) it showed that the courts would never invalidate an executive order.
    b) it showed that the courts would invalidate executive orders that have no statutory or constitutional basis.
    c) it asserted that pocket vetoes were unconstitutional.
    d) it upheld the notion of executive privilege.
    e) it struck down the Budget and Impoundment Control Act.

14. When the president makes an announcement about his interpretation of a congressional enactment that he is signing into law, it is called *(p. 545)*
    a) a signing statement.
    b) a line item veto.
    c) an executive order.
    d) legislative initiative.
    e) executive privilege.

Ⓢ Practice Online
"You Decide" exercise: *Presidential Power and Warrantless Wiretapping*

For Further Reading

Barber, James David. *The Presidential Character*. Englewood Cliffs, NJ: Prentice-Hall, 1992.

Crenson, Matthew, and Benjamin Ginsberg. *Presidential Power: Unchecked and Unbalanced*. New York: W.W. Norton, 2007.

Draper, Robert. *Dead Certain: The Presidency of George Bush*. New York: Free Press, 2007.

Edwards, George. *Why the Electoral College Is Bad for America*. New Haven, CT: Yale University Press, 2004.

Edwards, George, and Stephen Wayne. *Presidential Leadership: Politics and Policy Making*. New York: Wadsworth, 2009.

Goldsmith, Jack. *The American Presidency: Power and Constraint*. New York: W.W. Norton, 2012.

Hayes, Stephen F. *Cheney: The Untold Story of America's Most Powerful and Controversial Vice President*. New York: HarperCollins, 2007.

Lowi, Theodore J. *The Personal President: Power Invested, Promise Unfulfilled*. Ithaca, NY: Cornell University Press, 1985.

Milkis, Sidney. *The American Presidency: Origins and Development*. Washington, DC: CQ Press, 2011.

Neustadt, Richard E. *Presidential Power: The Politics of Leadership from Roosevelt to Reagan*. Rev. ed. New York: Free Press, 1990.

Pfiffner, James. *Understanding the Presidency*. 6th ed. New York: Longman, 2010.

Pika, Joseph, and John A. Maltese. *Politics of the Presidency*. Washington, DC: Congressional Quarterly Press, 2009.

Skowronek, Stephen. *The Politics Presidents Make: Leadership from John Adams to Bill Clinton*. Cambridge, MA: The Belknap Press of Harvard University Press, 1997.

Yoo, John. *The Powers of War and Peace*. Chicago: University of Chicago Press, 2005.

Recommended Websites

Almanac of Policy Issues: War Powers Resolution
www.policyalmanac.org/world/archive/war_powers
_resolution.shtml

The War Powers Resolution was passed in 1973 to define and limit the president's power during times of war. Read the full text of the resolution on this website.

Dave Leip's Atlas of U.S. Presidential Elections
www.uselectionatlas.org

For information on upcoming and past presidential elections, refer to this website. Experiment with the electoral college calculator to see how your state could affect the electoral outcome.

The American Presidency Project
www.americanpresidency.org

Directed by Gerhard Peters and John T. Woolley at UC Santa Barbara, this site contains over 88,000 documents related to the study of the presidency, including party platforms, candidates' remarks, statements of administration policy, documents released by the Office of the Press Secretary, and election debates. This site is also an excellent resource for data related to the study of the presidency.

The National Archives: Executive Branch
www.archives.gov/executive/

Research official executive branch documents at the Executive Branch website, provided by the U.S. National Archives and Records Administration.

Vicepresidents.com
www.vicepresidents.com

This website is dedicated to providing lots of interesting facts and archives about vice presidents, along with some lively humor.

The White House
www.whitehouse.gov

This is the official website of the White House. Here you can read about current presidential news, the president's Cabinet, executive orders, and presidential appointments.

White House Historical Association
www.whitehousehistory.org

The White House Historical Association is dedicated to the understanding, appreciation, and preservation of the White House. At its website you can find historical facts and take a detailed online tour of the numerous rooms and the property.

The White House: Past First Ladies
www.whitehouse.gov/history/firstladies/

The first lady is an important resource for the president in his role as head of state. Read about the current and past first ladies on this website.

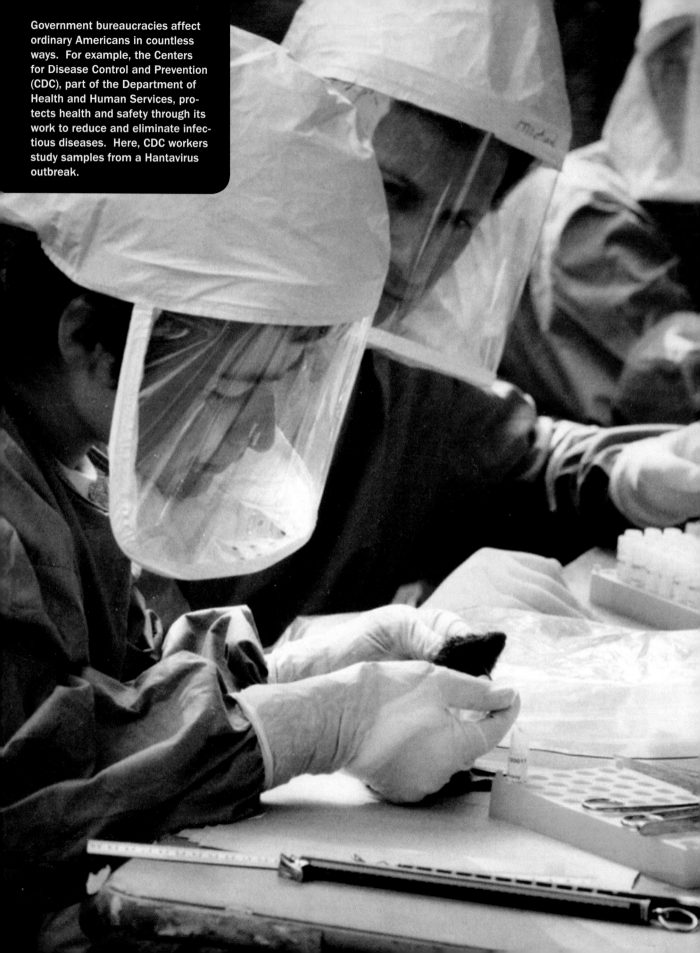

Government bureaucracies affect ordinary Americans in countless ways. For example, the Centers for Disease Control and Prevention (CDC), part of the Department of Health and Human Services, protects health and safety through its work to reduce and eliminate infectious diseases. Here, CDC workers study samples from a Hantavirus outbreak.

Bureaucracy in a Democracy

14

WHAT GOVERNMENT DOES AND WHY IT MATTERS Americans depend on government bureaucracies to accomplish the most spectacular achievements as well as the most mundane. Yet they often do not realize that public bureaucracies are essential for providing the services they use every day and rely on in emergencies. On a typical day, a college student might check the weather forecast, drive on an interstate highway, mail the rent check, drink from a public water fountain, check the calories on the side of a yogurt container, attend a class, log on to the Internet, and meet a relative at the airport. Each of these activities is possible because of the work of a government bureaucracy: the U.S. Weather Service, the U.S. Department of Transportation, the U.S. Postal Service, the Environmental Protection Agency, the Food and Drug Administration, the student loan programs of the U.S. Department of Education, the Advanced Research Projects Agency (which developed the Internet in the 1960s), and the Federal Aviation Administration. Without the ongoing work of these agencies, many of these common activities would be impossible, unreliable, or more expensive. Even though bureaucracies provide essential services that all Americans rely on, they are often disparaged by politicians and the general public alike as "big government," and come into public view only when they are charged with fraud, waste, and abuse.

In emergencies, the national perspective on bureaucracy and, indeed, on "big government" shifts. After the September 11 terrorist attacks, all eyes turned to Washington. The federal government responded by strengthening and reorganizing the bureaucracy to undertake a whole new set of responsibilities designed to keep America safe. In the biggest government reorganization in over half a century, Congress created the Department of Homeland Security in 2002. The massive new department merged 22 existing agencies into a single department employing nearly 170,000 workers.

As we shall see in this chapter, Americans have a love-hate relationship with the federal bureaucracy. This ambivalence sometimes prompts politicians to promise that they will slash the federal bureaucracy or move government responsibilities to the private sector. Yet they rarely follow through on such promises. Because Americans rely on government in so many aspects of their lives, significant reductions in the federal bureaucracy would create disruptions that no one wishes to experience.

chaptergoals

- **Define bureaucracy and describe the basic features of the executive branch** (pages 557–66)

- **Describe the major goals we expect federal agencies to promote** (pages 566–80)

- **Evaluate some of the ways politicians have tried to make the bureaucracy more efficient** (pages 580–88)

- **Explain why it is often difficult to control the bureaucracy** (pages 588–93)

● Bureaucracy and Bureaucrats

Define bureaucracy and describe the basic features of the executive branch

Bureaucracy is nothing more nor less than a form of organization, a complex structure of offices, tasks, and rules. *Bureau*, a French word, can mean either "office" or "desk." *Cracy* is from the Greek word for "rule" or "form of rule." Taken together, *bureau* and *cracy* produce an interesting definition: bureaucracy is rule by offices and desks. Each member of an organization has an office, meaning both a place and a set of responsibilities. That is, each "office" comprises a set of tasks that are specialized to the needs of the organization, and the person holding that office (or position) performs those specialized tasks. Specialization and repetition are essential to the efficiency of any organization. Therefore, when an organization is inefficient, it is often because it is not "bureaucratized" enough! But bureaucracies do not only perform specialized tasks that require routine action. As we shall see, they also undertake politically controversial tasks that require them to exercise a great deal of discretion and professional judgment. In many areas of policy, Congress writes laws that are very broad, and it is up to the bureaucracy to define what the policy will mean in practice. The decisions that bureaucrats make, often based on professional judgments, can themselves become politically contentious.

Both routine and exceptional tasks require the organization, specialization, and expertise found in bureaucracies. To provide services, government bureaucracies employ specialists such as meteorologists, doctors, and scientists. To do their jobs effectively, these specialists require resources and tools (ranging from paper to blood samples); they have to coordinate their work with others (for example, the traffic engineers must communicate with construction engineers); and there must be effective outreach to the public (for example, private doctors must be made aware of health warnings). Bureaucracy is a means of coordinating the many different parts that must work together for the government to provide useful services.

bureaucracy the complex structure of offices, tasks, rules, and principles of organization that are employed by all large-scale institutions to coordinate the work of their personnel

After September 11, the federal government assumed a new role in airport security. With the passage of the Secure Aviation and Transportation Act, the federal government became involved with screening passengers and baggage.

The Size of the Federal Service

For decades, politicians from both parties have asserted that the federal government is too big. Ronald Reagan led the way in 1981 with his assertion that government was the problem, not the solution. Fifteen years later President Bill Clinton abandoned the traditional Democratic defense of government, declaring that "the era of big government is over." President George W. Bush voiced similar sentiments when he accepted his party's nomination for president in 2000, proclaiming, "Big government is not the answer!" President Obama struck a different tone. Addressing Congress on the topic of health care reform, he noted that while Americans had a "healthy skepticism about government," they also believed that "hard work and responsibility should be rewarded by some measure of security and fair

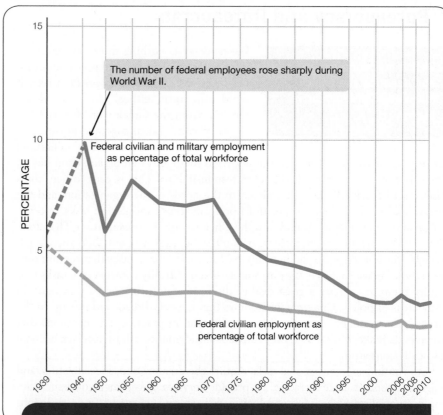

FIGURE 14.1

Employees in the Federal Service and in the National Workforce, 1939–2010

Since 1950 the ratio of federal employment to the total workforce has gradually declined. The lower line in this figure shows that the federal service has tended to grow at a rate that keeps pace with the economy and society. The upper line shows that variations in federal employment since 1946 have been in the military and are directly related to war and the Cold War. When did military employment begin its sharp decline?

SOURCES: "Federal Civilian Employment and Annual Payroll by Branch: 1970–2010," Table 496, and "Department of Defense Personnel: 1960–2010," Table 510. Both tables are from the U.S. Census Bureau's *Statistical Abstract of the United States, 2012.*

play" and recognized "that sometimes government has to step in to help deliver that promise."[1] Despite fears of bureaucratic growth getting out of hand, however, the federal service has hardly grown at all during the past 35 years; it reached its peak postwar level in 1968, with 3.0 million civilian employees plus an additional 3.6 million military personnel (a figure swollen by the war in Vietnam). The number of civilian federal employees has since fallen to approximately 2.8 million in 2010; the number of military personnel totals only 1.4 million.[2]

The growth of the federal service over the past 50 years is even less imposing when placed in the context of the total workforce and when compared with the size of state and local public employment. Figure 14.1 indicates that since 1950,

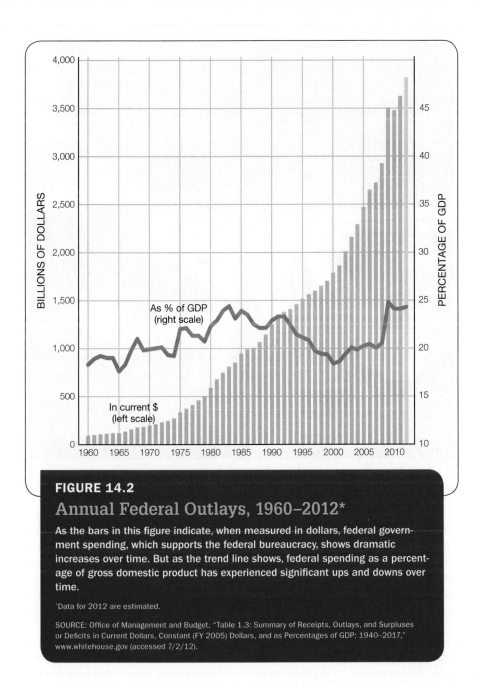

FIGURE 14.2

Annual Federal Outlays, 1960–2012*

As the bars in this figure indicate, when measured in dollars, federal government spending, which supports the federal bureaucracy, shows dramatic increases over time. But as the trend line shows, federal spending as a percentage of gross domestic product has experienced significant ups and downs over time.

*Data for 2012 are estimated.

SOURCE: Office of Management and Budget, "Table 1.3: Summary of Receipts, Outlays, and Surpluses or Deficits in Current Dollars, Constant (FY 2005) Dollars, and as Percentages of GDP: 1940–2017," www.whitehouse.gov (accessed 7/2/12).

the ratio of federal employment to the total workforce has been steady, and in fact has *declined* slightly in the past 30 years. In 1950 there were 4.3 million state and local civil service employees (about 6.5 percent of the country's workforce). In 2009 there were close to 20 million state and local employees (more than 14 percent of the nation's workforce).[3] Federal employment, in contrast, exceeded 5 percent of the workforce only during World War II, and almost all of that temporary growth was military.

Another useful comparison is to be found in Figure 14.2. Although the dollar increase in federal spending shown by the bars looks impressive, the trend line

The Coast Guard, an agency within the federal bureaucracy, led the efforts to contain and clean up the Deepwater Horizon *oil spill in 2010. These efforts included relocating endangered wildlife threatened by the spill. Here, pelicans rescued from the oil slick are loaded onto Coast Guard planes for release in a safer wildlife reserve.*

indicating the relation of federal spending to the gross domestic product (GDP) remained close to what it had been in 1960. This changed in 2009, when the recession pushed spending up dramatically, as the federal government sought to stimulate the economy, and spending rose on other recession-related programs, such as unemployment insurance. After 2009 the budget also reflected the costs of the wars in Iraq and Afghanistan, which had not been included in the Bush administration's budgets.

In sum, the national government is indeed "very large," but it has not been growing any faster than the economy or society. The same is roughly true of the growth pattern of state and local public personnel. Bureaucracy keeps pace with society, despite people's seeming dislike of it, because the control towers, the prisons, the Social Security system, and other essential elements of modern-day society cannot be operated without bureaucracy. Indeed, the recent growth of government spending does not reflect a growth in the federal bureaucracy but rather an increase in payments to individuals for valued social programs such as Social Security, and Medicare (which provides health care for people over 65), and a temporary boost in federal grants to the states to help them weather the recession.

Although the federal executive branch is large and complex, everything about it is commonplace because its many bureaucracies touch so many aspects of daily life. Government bureaucracies implement the decisions made through the political process. Bureaucracies are full of routine because that ensures the regular delivery of services and also the fulfillment of each agency's mandate. Public bureaucracies are powerful because legislatures and chief executives, and indeed the people, delegate vast power to them to make sure that society's collective needs are addressed, providing most citizens with the freedom to pursue their private ends.

Bureaucrats

"Government by offices and desks" conveys to most people a picture of hundreds of office workers shuffling millions of pieces of paper. There is a lot of truth in that image, but we have to look more closely at what papers are being shuffled and why. More than 70 years ago, an astute observer defined bureaucracy as "continuous routine business."[4] As we saw at the beginning of this chapter, almost any organization succeeds by reducing its work to routine tasks performed by different specialists. But with specialization, one worker's output becomes another worker's input, making the timing of such relationships essential and therefore requiring these workers to stay in communication with each other. In fact, bureaucracy was the first information network.

What Do Bureaucrats Do? Congress is responsible for making the laws, but in most cases legislation only sets the broad parameters for government action. Bureaucracies are responsible for filling in the blanks by determining how the laws should be implemented. This requires bureaucracies to draw up detailed rules that guide the process of **implementation** and also to play a key role in enforcing the laws. Congress needs the bureaucracy to engage in rule making and implementation for several reasons. One is that bureaucracies employ people who have much more specialized expertise in specific policy areas than do members of Congress. Decisions about how to achieve many policy goals—from managing the national parks to regulating air quality to ensuring a sound economy—rest on the judgment of specialized experts. A second reason that Congress needs bureaucracy is that because updating legislation can take many years, bureaucratic flexibility can ensure that laws are administered in ways that take new conditions into account. Finally, members of Congress often prefer to delegate politically difficult decision making to bureaucrats.

    One of the most important things that government agencies do is issue rules that provide more detailed and specific indications of what a given congressional policy will actually mean. For example, the Clean Air Act empowers the Environmental Protection Agency (EPA) to assess whether current or projected levels of air pollutants pose a threat to public health, to determine whether motor vehicle emissions are contributing to such pollution, and to create rules designed to regulate these emissions. Under the George W. Bush administration, the EPA claimed it did not have the authority to regulate a specific group of pollutants commonly referred to as "greenhouse gases" (for example, carbon dioxide). In 2007 the Supreme Court ruled that the EPA did have that authority and had to provide a justification for not regulating such emissions.[5] In the first year of the Obama administration, the agency ruled that greenhouse gases posed a threat to public health and that the emissions from new motor vehicles contributed to greenhouse gas pollution.[6] The agency then imposed new emission standards for automobiles, which would raise the average per-vehicle fuel economy for new vehicles to 35.5 miles per gallon starting in 2016, a standard later boosted to 54.4 miles per gallon by 2025.[7] Not only will this finding by the EPA have a significant effect on the automobile industry, but it could also lead to far-reaching regulations in the

implementation the efforts of departments and agencies to translate laws into specific bureaucratic rules and actions

future governing all industries that generate greenhouse gases. Not surprisingly, the agency's findings soon faced legal challenges by industries affected by the ruling.[8]

The rule-making process is thus a highly political one. Once a new law is passed, the relevant agency studies the legislation and proposes a set of rules to guide implementation. These proposed rules are then open to comment by anyone who wishes to weigh in. Representatives for the regulated industries and advocates of all sorts commonly submit comments. But anyone who wishes to can go to the website www.regulations.gov to read proposed rules, enter comments, and view the comments of others. Once rules are approved, they are published in the *Federal Register* and have the force of law.

In addition to rule making, bureaucracies play an essential role in enforcing the laws, thus exercising considerable power over private actors. For example, in 2011, Facebook reached a settlement with the Federal Trade Commission, which charged that the company had deceived consumers with unkept promises about privacy. Facebook agreed to change a number of its privacy practices and comply with the requirement that the company "obtain consumers' affirmative express consent before enacting changes that override their privacy preferences."[9] In 2010, to comply with federal regulations, the auto manufacturer Toyota was forced to recall several car models after identifying problems with their gas pedals and accelerators. The National Highway Traffic Safety Commission launched an investigation of Toyota and found that it had known of the defect but had installed the accelerators in cars anyway. The National Highway Traffic Safety Commission charged the company a fine of $16.4 million for failing to notify regulators of these problems. It also began to consider new rules designed to prevent such accidents in the future, such as new technical requirements for brake systems.[10]

Government bureaucrats do essentially the same things that bureaucrats in large private organizations do, and neither type deserves the disrespect often implied in the term *bureaucrat*. But because of the authoritative, coercive nature of government, far more constraints are imposed on public bureaucrats than on private bureaucrats, even when their jobs are the same. During the 1970s and '80s, the length of time required to develop an administrative rule from a proposal to actual publication in the *Federal Register* (when it takes on full legal status) grew from an average of 15 months to an average of 35 to 40 months. Inefficiency? No. Most of the increased time is attributable to new procedures requiring more public notice, more public hearings, more hearings held out in the field rather than in Washington, more cost-benefit analysis, and stronger legal obligations to prepare "environmental impact statements" demonstrating that the proposed rule or agency action will not have an unacceptably large negative impact on the human or physical environment.[11] Thus, a great deal of what is popularly decried as the lower efficiency of public agencies can be attributed to the political, judicial, legal, and public-opinion restraints and extraordinarily high expectations imposed on public bureaucrats. If a private company such as Microsoft were required to open up all its decision processes and management practices to full view by the media, its competitors, and all interested citizens, Microsoft—despite its profit motive and the pressure of competition—would likely appear far less efficient, perhaps no more efficient than public bureaucracies.

A good case study of the important role agencies can play is the story of how ordinary federal bureaucrats created the Internet. Yes, it's true: what became the Internet

The rules established by regulatory agencies have the force of law. In 2010 the car company Toyota was forced by federal regulators to recall six million vehicles in the United States owing to safety defects with the gas pedal in some models.

Who Are "Bureaucrats"?

Executive Branch Employees, 2010 (in thousands)

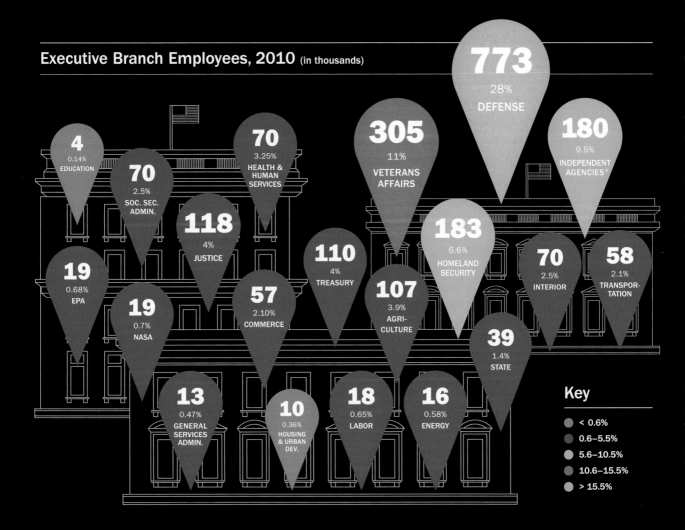

4
0.14%
EDUCATION

70
2.5%
SOC. SEC. ADMIN.

70
3.25%
HEALTH & HUMAN SERVICES

305
11%
VETERANS AFFAIRS

773
28%
DEFENSE

180
9.5%
INDEPENDENT AGENCIES*

118
4%
JUSTICE

19
0.68%
EPA

19
0.7%
NASA

57
2.10%
COMMERCE

110
4%
TREASURY

183
6.6%
HOMELAND SECURITY

107
3.9%
AGRI-CULTURE

70
2.5%
INTERIOR

58
2.1%
TRANSPOR-TATION

39
1.4%
STATE

13
0.47%
GENERAL SERVICES ADMIN.

10
0.36%
HOUSING & URBAN DEV.

18
0.65%
LABOR

16
0.58%
ENERGY

Key

- ● < 0.6%
- ● 0.6–5.5%
- ● 5.6–10.5%
- ● 10.6–15.5%
- ● > 15.5%

Location, 2008

320
17%
WASHINGTON, D.C., AREA

1,589
83% — OTHER

* Independent agencies include NASA, the EPA, and the Social Security Administration (shown here), as well as other agencies.

SOURCES: U.S. Census Bureau 2012 Statistical Abstract; Bureau of Labor Statistics.

Contrary to popular notions of "paper pushers," the people who work in the federal bureaucracy perform a range of tasks essential to the functioning of American society. Nearly 2 million executive branch employees are involved in protecting the nation's security, managing the economy, and promoting public welfare through various means including environmental protection and health and safety regulations. Most federal employees work outside the Washington, D.C., area.

for critical analysis

1. Which category of departments and agencies—security, economic, or public welfare—employs the most people? Why?

2. With 2 million people working for the executive branch, mostly outside of the Washington, D.C., area, how can Congress and the president be sure that they are serving the public's interests?

was developed largely by the U.S. Department of Defense, and defense considerations still shape the basic structure of the Internet. In 1957, immediately following the profound American embarrassment over the Soviet Union's launching of *Sputnik*, Congress authorized the establishment of the Advanced Research Projects Agency (ARPA) to develop, among other things, a means of maintaining communications in the event of a strategic attack on the existing telecommunications network (the telephone system). Since the telephone network was highly centralized and therefore could have been completely disabled by a single attack, ARPA developed a decentralized, highly redundant network with an improved probability of functioning after an attack. The full design, called by the acronym ARPANET, took almost a decade to create. By 1971 around 20 universities were connected to the ARPANET. The forerunner to the Internet was born.[12]

The Merit System: How to Become a Bureaucrat Although they face more inconveniences than their counterparts in the private sector, public bureaucrats are rewarded in part with greater job security than employees of most private organizations. More than a century ago the federal government attempted to imitate business by passing the Civil Service Act of 1883, which was followed by almost universal adoption of equivalent laws in state and local governments. These laws required that appointees to public office be qualified for the job to which they were appointed. This policy came to be called the **merit system**; its goal was not merely to put an end to political appointments under the "spoils system" but also to create a system of competitive examinations through which the very best candidates were to be hired for every job. At the higher levels of government agencies, including such posts as cabinet secretaries and assistant secretaries, many jobs are filled with political appointees and are not part of the merit system.

As a further safeguard against political interference (and to compensate for the lower-than-average pay given to public employees), merit-system employees (genuine civil servants) were given legal protection against being fired without a show of cause. Reasonable people may disagree about the value of such job security and how far it should extend in the civil service, but the justifiable objective of this job protection, cleansing bureaucracy of political interference while upgrading performance, cannot be disputed.

merit system a product of civil service reform, in which appointees to positions in public bureaucracies must objectively be deemed qualified for those positions

The Organization of the Executive Branch

Cabinet departments, agencies, and bureaus are the operating parts of the bureaucratic whole. Figure 14.3 is an organizational chart of one of the largest and most important of the 15 **departments**, the Department of Agriculture. At the top is the head of the department, who in the United States is called the "secretary" of the department.[13] Below the secretary and the deputy secretary is a second tier of "undersecretaries," who have management responsibilities for one or more operating agencies, shown in the smaller print directly below each undersecretary's title. Those operating agencies are the third tier of the department, yet they are the highest level of responsibility for the actual programs around which the entire department is organized. This third tier is generally called the "bureau level." Each bureau-level agency usually operates under a statute, enacted by Congress, that set up the agency and gave it its authority and jurisdiction. The names of these bureau-level agencies are often quite well known to the public—the Forest

department the largest subunit of the executive branch. The secretaries of the 15 departments form the Cabinet.

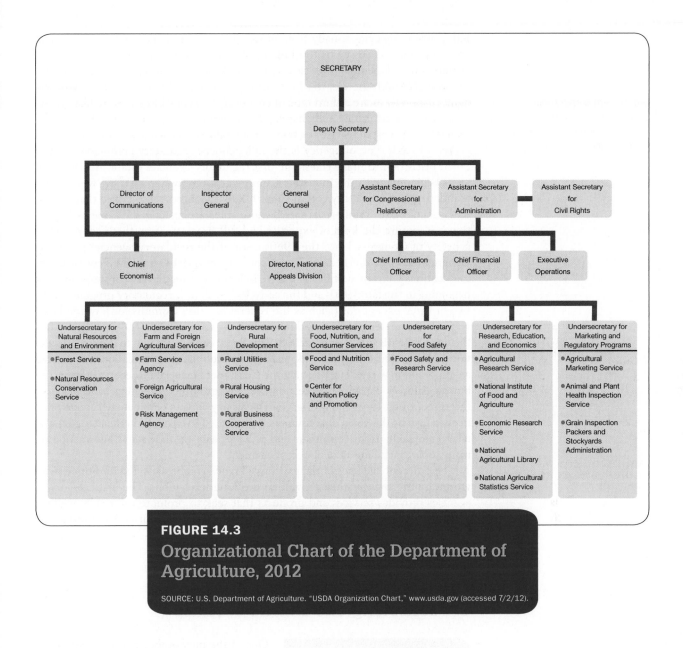

FIGURE 14.3

Organizational Chart of the Department of Agriculture, 2012

SOURCE: U.S. Department of Agriculture. "USDA Organization Chart," www.usda.gov (accessed 7/2/12).

Service and the Food Safety and Inspection Service, for example. These are the so-called line agencies, those that deal directly with the public. Sometimes these agencies are officially called "bureaus," such as the Federal Bureau of Investigation (FBI), which is part of the third tier of the Department of Justice. But "bureau" is also the conventional term for this level of administrative agency, even though many agencies or their supporters have preferred over the years to adopt a more politically palatable designation, such as "service" or "administration." Each bureau is, of course, even further subdivided into divisions, offices, or units—all are parts of the bureaucratic hierarchy.

Not all government agencies are part of cabinet departments. Some **independent agencies** are set up by Congress outside the departmental structure altogether, even though the president appoints and directs the heads of these agencies.

independent agency agency that is not part of a cabinet department

Independent agencies usually have broad powers to provide public services that are either too expensive or too important to be left to private initiatives. Some examples of independent agencies are the National Aeronautics and Space Administration (NASA), the Central Intelligence Agency (CIA), and the EPA. **Government corporations** are a third type of government agency but are more like private businesses in performing and charging for a market service, such as delivering the mail (the U.S. Postal Service) or transporting railroad passengers (Amtrak).

government corporation
government agency that performs a service normally provided by the private sector

Yet a fourth type of agency is the independent regulatory commission, given broad discretion to make rules. The first regulatory agencies established by Congress, beginning with the Interstate Commerce Commission in 1887, were set up as independent regulatory commissions because Congress recognized that regulatory agencies are "minilegislatures," whose rules are exactly the same as legislation but require the kind of expertise and full-time attention that is beyond the capacity of Congress. Until the 1960s most of the regulatory agencies set up by Congress, such as the Federal Trade Commission (1914) and the Federal Communications Commission (1934), were independent regulatory commissions. But beginning in the late 1960s and the early 1970s, all new regulatory programs, with two or three exceptions (such as the Federal Election Commission), were placed within existing departments and made directly responsible to the president. After the financial crisis that began in 2008, Congress passed legislation to improve regulation of banks and other nonbank financial institutions. The legislation also created an important new regulatory agency, the Consumer Financial Protection Bureau. The bureau enforces consumer protection laws; for example, regulating bank practices that affect credit cards and mortgages. The agency aims to eliminate deceptive practices and act as the voice of consumers. Its website (www.consumerfinance.gov) also takes complaints from consumers and provides easy to understand information on many topics, including student debt repayment.

The different agencies of the executive branch can be classified into three main groups by the services they provide to the American public. The first category of agencies provides services and products that seek to promote the public welfare. The second group of agencies works to promote national security. The third group provides services that help maintain a strong economy. Let us look more closely at what each set of agencies offers to the American public.

● Promoting the Public Welfare

Describe the major goals we expect federal agencies to promote

One of the most important activities of the federal bureaucracy is to promote the public welfare. Americans often think of government welfare as a single program that goes only to the very poor; but a number of federal agencies provide services, build infrastructure, and enforce regulations designed to enhance the well-being of the vast majority of citizens. Departments that have important responsibilities for promoting the public welfare in this sense include the Department of Housing and Urban Development, the Department of Health and Human Services, the Department of Veterans Affairs, the Department of the Interior, the Department of Education, and the Department of Labor. Ensuring the public welfare is also the main activity of agencies in other departments, such as the Department of Agriculture's Food and Nutrition Service, which administers the federal school lunch program and the

Supplemental Nutrition Assistance Program (formerly known as food stamps). In addition, multiple independent regulatory agencies enforce regulations that aim to safeguard the public health and welfare.

How Do Federal Bureaucracies Promote the Public Welfare? Federal bureaucracies promote the public welfare with a diverse set of services, products, and regulations. The Department of Health and Human Services (HHS), for example, administers the program that comes closest to the popular understanding of welfare: Temporary Assistance for Needy Families (TANF). Yet this program is one of the smallest activities of the department. HHS also oversees the National Institutes of Health (NIH), which is responsible for cutting-edge biomedical research and for two major health programs of the federal government: Medicaid, which provides health care for low-income families and for many elderly and disabled people; and Medicare, which is the health insurance available to all elderly people in the United States.

A different notion of the public welfare but one highly valued by most Americans is provided by the National Park Service, under the Department of the Interior. First created in 1916, the National Park Service is responsible for the care and upkeep of national parks. Since the nineteenth century, Americans have seen protection of the natural environment as an important public goal and have looked to federal agencies to implement laws and administer programs that preserve natural areas and keep them open to the public.

The United States has no "Department of Regulation" but has many **regulatory agencies**. Some of these are bureaus within departments, such as the Food and Drug Administration (FDA), within the Department of Health and Human Services, and the Occupational Safety and Health Administration (OSHA), in the Department of Labor. As we saw earlier, other regulatory agencies are independent regulatory commissions, such as the Consumer Product Safety Commission, the FCC, and the EPA. But whether departmental or independent, an agency or commission is regulatory if Congress delegates to it relatively broad powers over a sector of the economy or a type of commercial activity and authorizes it to make rules within that jurisdiction. Rules made by regulatory agencies have the force and effect of law.

Often working behind the scenes, these agencies seek to promote the welfare of all Americans. The FDA, for example, works to protect public health by setting standards for food quality and inspecting plants to ensure that those standards are met. The EPA sets standards to limit polluting emissions from automobiles,

regulatory agency a department, bureau, or independent agency whose primary mission is to impose limits, restrictions, or other obligations on the conduct of individuals or companies in the private sector

The agencies of the federal bueaucracy provide a range of services. The EPA creates and enforces regulations related to the environment, for example by testing for pollution (left). Amtrak, a government corporation, offers rail service throughout much of the United States.

among other functions. On numerous occasions, EPA regulations have required automobile manufacturers to change the way they designed cars. The result has been cleaner air in many metropolitan areas.

Bureaucracies, Clienteles, and the Public Some of the public agencies that provide services are tied to a specific group or segment of American society that is often thought of as the main clientele of that agency. For example, the Department of Agriculture was established in 1862 to promote the interests of farmers. Likewise, the Department of Veterans Affairs has strong links to veterans' organizations such as the American Legion and the Veterans of Foreign Wars. The Department of Education relies on teachers' organizations for support. Figure 14.4 is a representation of this type of politics. This configuration is known as an **iron triangle**, a pattern of stable relationships among an agency in the executive branch, a congressional committee or subcommittee, and one or more organized groups of agency clientele. (Iron triangles were discussed in detail in Chapter 11.)

These relationships with particular clienteles are often important in preserving agencies from political attack. During his 1980 campaign, Ronald Reagan promised to dismantle the Department of Education as part of his commitment to get government "off people's backs." After his election, Reagan even appointed a secretary of the department who was publicly committed to eliminating it. Yet by the end

iron triangle the stable, cooperative relationship that often develops among a congressional committee, an administrative agency, and one or more supportive interest groups. Not all of these relationships are triangular, but the iron triangle is the most typical.

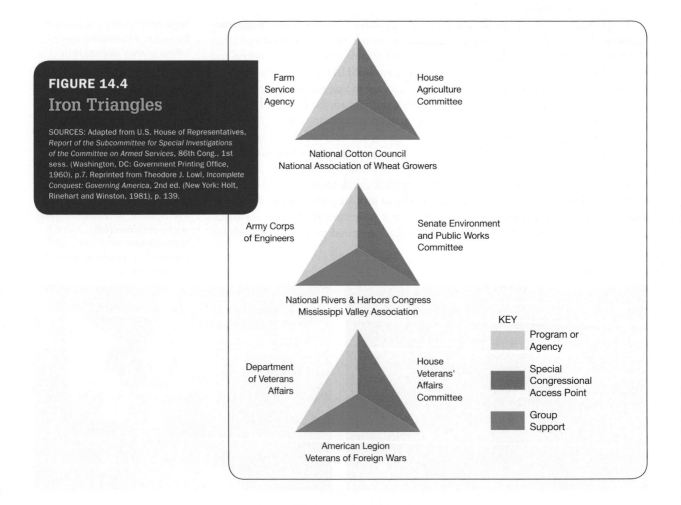

FIGURE 14.4
Iron Triangles

SOURCES: Adapted from U.S. House of Representatives, *Report of the Subcommittee for Special Investigations of the Committee on Armed Services*, 86th Cong., 1st sess. (Washington, DC: Government Printing Office, 1960). p.7. Reprinted from Theodore J. Lowi, *Incomplete Conquest: Governing America*, 2nd ed. (New York: Holt, Rinehart and Winston, 1981), p. 139.

Farm Service Agency

House Agriculture Committee

National Cotton Council
National Association of Wheat Growers

Army Corps of Engineers

Senate Environment and Public Works Committee

National Rivers & Harbors Congress
Mississippi Valley Association

Department of Veterans Affairs

House Veterans' Affairs Committee

American Legion
Veterans of Foreign Wars

KEY

Program or Agency

Special Congressional Access Point

Group Support

of his administration, the Department of Education was still standing and barely touched. In 1995 the Republican Congress vowed to eliminate the Department of Education, along with two other departments, but it, too, failed. The educational constituency of the department (its clientele) mobilized to save it each time.

Nevertheless, the ability of clientele groups to get their way is not automatic, as agencies have to balance limited resources, competing interests, and political pressures. For example, the Department of Veterans Affairs long resisted the efforts of Vietnam veterans to be compensated for exposure to Agent Orange, a chemical defoliant used extensively during the Vietnam War. Veterans charged that exposure to Agent Orange had left them with a variety of diseases ranging from cancer to severe birth defects in their children. Only after decades of lobbying, lawsuits, and federally sponsored studies did the Department of Veterans Affairs provide assistance to affected veterans.

Moreover, federal agencies increasingly seek public support outside their direct clients for their activities. In some cases, key clientele groups will work to build more widespread support for agency activities. For example, the American Federation of Labor and Congress of Industrial Organizations (AFL-CIO), which represents organized labor, built a broad coalition of student organizations, church groups, consumer groups, and civil rights activists opposed to sweatshops in the United States. These groups helped support the Department of Labor's campaign to uncover and eliminate such manufacturing practices in the United States. Agency failure to consider public opinion can result in embarrassment, which bureaucrats prefer to avoid. The Department of Homeland Security's color-coded system for warning about terrorism failed to command public respect and came in for ridicule by late-night television comedians. The public gradually began to ignore the alerts, especially as suspicions mounted that the system was being politically manipulated. Eventually, the federal government stopped issuing new alerts.

Attentiveness to the public often means making them aware of services and improving the way services are delivered. The Social Security Administration is an independent agency that administers old-age and disability insurance, the federal government's most important and expensive welfare program. Old-age insurance, or Social Security, is supported by AARP, an interest group representing people over 50, generally considered to be the most powerful interest group operating in the United States today. But worried that younger workers are losing confidence in Social Security, the agency began to issue annual statements to each worker, outlining the benefits that they can count on from Social Security when they retire and indicating what benefits are available if they become disabled before retirement.

for critical analysis

What is the impact of iron triangles on inequality in the United States? Do the ties among agencies, congressional committees, and organized groups promote inequality?

Providing National Security

One of the remarkable features of American federalism is that the most vital agencies for providing security for the American people (namely, the police) are located in state and local governments. But some agencies vital to maintaining national security are located in the national government, and they can be grouped into two categories: (1) agencies to confront threats to internal national security and (2) agencies to defend American security from external threats. The departments of greatest influence in these two areas are Homeland Security, Justice, Defense, and State.

Agencies for Internal Security The task of maintaining domestic security changed dramatically after the terrorist attacks of September 11, 2001. The creation of the Department of Homeland Security in late 2002 signaled the high priority that domestic security would now have. The orientation of domestic agencies shifted as well, as agencies geared up to prevent terrorism, a very different task from their former charge of investigating crime. With this shift in responsibility came broad new powers, many of them controversial, including the power to detain terrorist suspects and to engage in extensive domestic intelligence-gathering about possible terrorists.

Before September 11, most of the effort put into maintaining internal national security took the form of legal work related to prosecuting federal crimes. The largest and most important unit of the Justice Department is the Criminal Division. Lawyers in the Criminal Division represent the U.S. government when it is the plaintiff enforcing federal criminal laws, except for those cases (about 25 percent) specifically assigned to other divisions or agencies. Criminal litigation is handled by U.S. attorneys, who are appointed by the president. There is one U.S. attorney in each of the 94 federal judicial districts; he or she supervises the work of a number of assistant U.S. attorneys.

The Civil Division of the Justice Department deals with litigation in which the United States is the defendant being sued for injury and damages allegedly inflicted by a government official or agency. The missions of the other divisions of the Justice Department—Antitrust, Civil Rights, Environment and Natural Resources, and Tax—are described by their names.

When the prevention of terrorism took center stage, the Justice Department reoriented its activities accordingly. The Patriot Act, enacted by Congress soon after September 11, gave the Justice Department broad new powers, allowing the attorney general to detain any foreigner suspected of posing a threat to internal security. The Patriot Act also expanded the government's ability to use wiretaps and to issue search warrants without notifying suspects immediately. It required public libraries to keep lists of the public's book and Internet use for federal inspection. Although initially popular with most Americans, these measures created concern about civil liberties. In 2007, high-profile congressional hearings revealed extensive conflicts between the Justice Department and the White House over the use of warrantless wiretapping in the United States. Both publicly and behind the scenes, since 2001 the Justice Department has played a central role in setting the balance between national security and civil liberties.

In 2002 the new Department of Homeland Security joined the Justice Department as the major bureaucracy charged with domestic security. The department took over some of the security-oriented agencies previously controlled by other departments (see Table 14.1). For example, the Immigration and Naturalization Service (INS) was moved from Justice to Homeland Security. Once inside the new department, the INS was abolished; immigration services were consolidated into the newly created U.S. Citizenship and Immigration Services, and the enforcement functions of the old INS were combined with the U.S. Customs Services (formerly part of the Treasury Department) to create a new Bureau of Immigration and Customs Enforcement, known as ICE. ICE has extensive investigative capacities, with field offices around the United States and bureaus in more than 30 countries. Other agencies that were transferred to the Department of Homeland Security include the Coast Guard, the Secret Service, and the Federal Emergency Management Agency (FEMA).

Growing pains were evident in Homeland Security's first years. Different bureaucratic cultures, now part of a single operation, quickly became embroiled in turf battles with one another and with the FBI (which remained in the Justice

for critical analysis

Why was the Department of Homeland Security created? What problems has the new department faced?

TABLE 14.1

The Shape of a Domestic Security Department

DEPARTMENT OF HOMELAND SECURITY	AGENCIES AND DEPARTMENTS THAT WERE MOVED TO THE DEPARTMENT OF HOMELAND SECURITY	DEPARTMENT OR AGENCY THEY WERE PREVIOUSLY UNDER	FROM THE 2012 BUDGET REQUEST	
			BUDGET REQUEST, IN MILLION $	ESTIMATED NUMBER OF EMPLOYEES
Border and Transportation Security	U.S. Customs and Border Protection	Treasury Department	11,845	61,354
	Immigration and Customs Enforcement	Justice Department	5,823	20,546
	U.S. Citizenship and Immigration Services	Justice Department	2,907	11,633
	National Protection and Program Directorate (includes domestic preparedness)	General Services Administration	2,555	3,167
	Transportation Security Administration	Transportation Department	8,115	58,401
	Federal Law Enforcement Training Center	Treasury Department	276	1,103
Emergency Preparedness and Response	Federal Emergency Management Agency	Independent agency	10,063	10,255
Domestic Nuclear Detection Office	(new)	(new)	332	142
Science and Technology	(multiple programs)	Department of Energy	1,176	505
Secret Service	Secret Service (includes presidential protection units)	Treasury Department	1,943	7,054
Coast Guard	Coast Guard	Transportation Department	10,339	50,682
Office of Health Affairs	(new)	(new)	160.9	118
Total DHS			56,983	220,601

SOURCE: U.S. Department of Homeland Security, "Budget-in-Brief, Fiscal Year 2012," www.dhs.gov (accessed 7/4/12).

Department) as the two departments attempted to sort out their respective responsibilities. The department's most public failure was its terrible performance during Hurricane Katrina in 2005. Not only did Homeland Security, through FEMA, fail to move quickly to assist stranded residents of New Orleans, it mismanaged contracts and grants associated with the recovery efforts, which led to massive cost overruns and poor performance. Alarm bells went off again in 2007 when the Coast Guard, the largest agency under Homeland Security, renewed a $24 billion

The Federal Bueau of Investigation (FBI) investigates crime and gathers intelligence within the United States. In 2010, FBI agents searched the apartment of Faisal Shazad, who had attempted to detonate a bomb in Times Square, New York City.

contract for fleet modernization only 11 days after department officials testified about major flaws in the program.[14] Since 2009 the Department of Homeland Security has become embroiled in conflicts over immigration. In its Secure Communities program, the department, through ICE, works with the FBI and local police to detain suspected criminals who may be undocumented immigrants. In addition to provoking claims of civil rights violations, the program has attracted opposition from state and local politicians and some local police departments. These critics charge that the program undermines effective policing by reducing Latinos' and immigrants' trust in the government.[15]

Agencies for External National Security Two departments occupy center stage in maintaining external national security: the departments of State and Defense.

The State Department's primary mission is diplomacy. As the most visible public representative of American diplomacy, the Secretary of State works to promote American perspectives and interests in the world. For example, in 2011 Secretary of State Hillary Clinton made a widely publicized trip to Myanmar (also known as Burma) to underscore American support for democracy in that country and to pressure Myanmar's leaders to adopt more far-reaching democratic reforms. Although diplomacy is the primary task of the State Department, diplomatic missions are only one of its organizational dimensions. As of 2012 the State Department comprised 35 bureau-level units, each under the direction of an assistant secretary.[16]

These bureaus support the responsibilities of the elite foreign-service officers (FSOs), who staff U.S. embassies around the world and who hold almost all the most powerful positions in the department below the rank of ambassador.[17] The ambassadorial positions, especially the plum positions in the major capitals of the world, are filled by presidential appointees, many of whom get their posts by having been important donors to victorious political campaigns.

Despite the importance of the State Department in foreign affairs, fewer than 20 percent of all U.S. government employees working abroad are directly under its authority. By far the largest number of career government professionals working abroad are under the authority of the Defense Department.

The creation of the Department of Defense by legislation between 1947 and 1949 was an effort to unify the two historic military departments, the War Department and the Navy Department, and to integrate them with a new branch of the military, the U.S. Air Force. Real unification, however, did not occur. The Defense Department simply added another layer to an already pluralistic national security establishment. That establishment became more complex in 1952, with the creation of the National Security Agency, charged with electronic surveillance and intelligence gathering.

The American military, following worldwide military tradition, is organized according to a "chain of command," a tight hierarchy of clear responsibility and rank, made clearer by uniforms, special insignia, and detailed organizational charts and rules of order and etiquette. At the top of the chain of command of each branch of the military are, respectively, the chief of staff of the army, the chief of naval operations, the commandant of the marines, and the chief of staff of the air force. These officers also constitute the membership of the Joint Chiefs of Staff, the center of military policy and management.

In 2002 the Defense Department created the U.S. Northern Command, a regional command charged with ensuring homeland defense, directing military operations inside the nation's borders and providing emergency backup to state and local governments, which are the first responders to any security disaster. The creation of a regional command within the United States was an unprecedented move, breaching a long-standing line between domestic law enforcement and foreign military operations.

As the creation of a military capacity within the United States suggests, addressing the threat of terrorism calls for greater coordination of internal and external security. In 2004 the National Commission on Terrorist Attacks upon the United States (the 9/11 Commission) issued a widely read report that called for a major reorganization of bureaucratic responsibilities for internal and external security.[18] The report revealed that different departments of the American government had information that, if handled properly, might have prevented the attacks of September 11, 2001. To correct this, the commission made major recommendations designed to promote unity of effort across the bureaucracy.

The 9/11 Commission's work prompted a major reorganization of the fragmented intelligence community. In 2005 a new office, the Office of the Director of National Intelligence, took over responsibility for coordinating the efforts of the 16 different agencies that gather intelligence. The DNI reports directly to the president each morning.

National Security and Democracy Of all the agencies in the federal bureaucracy, those charged with providing national security most often come into conflict with the norms and expectations of American democracy. Two issues in particular arise as these agencies work to ensure the national security: (1) the trade-offs between respecting the personal rights of individuals versus protecting the general public, and (2) the need for secrecy in matters of national security versus the public's right to know what the government is doing. Standards for acceptable trade-offs vary depending on the nature of the threats facing national security and whether the country is at war or peace. Needless to say, Americans often disagree about what activities the government should be able to pursue to defend U.S. national security.

Leading through Civilian Power

During the opening years of the twenty-first century, the military dominated America's presence in the world. The wars in Iraq and Afghanistan mobilized hundreds of thousands of troops and military contractors to engage in conflicts where decisive victories proved hard to win. Aiming to provide an alternative vision for America's international engagement, in 2010 the Department of State and the U.S. Agency for International Development (USAID) issued a blueprint for "leading through civilian power."[a]

The new plan called for the Department of State and USAID to play a more prominent role in preventing and resolving international conflicts. It highlighted the unique capacities of both organizations to offer distinct perspectives on conflict and alternative approaches to addressing international problems. For example, housed in missions across the world, State Department employees possess deep knowledge of the types of ethnic conflicts that bedeviled the military efforts in Iraq and Afghanistan. USAID, an independent agency of the U.S. government, has long experience in supporting successful economic development, which may help prevent conflict. By making use of civilian power, the State

Department aimed not only to pursue America's global interests more effectively but also to reflect more fully American values of democracy and human rights. In announcing its new approach, State Department officials emphasized that "civilian power has to be the first face of American power."[b]

As part of this new vision, the Department of State developed a reorganization plan that proposed several new bureaus. One of these, the Bureau of Conflict and Stabilization Operations, was established in late 2011. Responsible for promoting effective civilian engagement in states that are vulnerable to instability and conflict, the bureau is designed to coordinate the activities of different federal departments and nongovernmental agencies (NGOs). The new bureau builds on the work of the Office of the Coordinator for Reconstruction and

Stabilization (S/CRS), which was created in 2004 to promote civilian engagement in the reconstruction of Iraq and Afghanistan. One major lesson from these wars was that stabilizing insecure nations requires much more than military expertise. It involves mobilizing experts in areas including municipal administration; reconstruction of water supply, electricity, and telecommunications; humanitarian relief; housing; education; banking; and agriculture, to name just a few. Long-range stability entails strengthening political institutions and, where necessary, planting the seeds of entirely new institutions such as political parties, legislative assemblies, courts, and local governments. By coordinating the activities of diverse civilian experts, the Bureau of Conflict and Stabilization Operations will aim to address the root causes of instability and conflict.

The State Department's ambitious plan charts a new direction for advancing American interests in the world, one that relies much less on military capabilities than in the past. But building "civilian power" is a complex bureaucratic task. Whether the State Department can mobilize the resources and build the interdepartmental cooperation needed to carry out this new mission remains to be seen.

[a]U.S. Department of State and U.S. Agency for International Development, *Leading Through Civilian Power: The First Quadrennial Diplomacy and Development Review* (Washington, DC: 2010), www.state.gov/documents/organization/153142.pdf (accessed 1/4/12).
[b]Charles S. Clark, "State Department Review Promises Transparency, Civilian 'Face,'" *Government Executive*, December 20, 2010, www.govexec.com/dailyfed/1210/122010cc1.htm.

for critical analysis

1. Why does the United States need so many different kinds of expertise to prevent and resolve conflicts abroad?
2. What are the pros and cons of assigning more responsibility for conflict prevention and resolution to the State Department instead of the Department of Defense?

When national security is at stake, federal agencies have taken actions that are normally considered incompatible with individual rights. For example, during World War II thousands of American citizens of Japanese descent were interned in camps due to national security concerns. Although the Supreme Court approved this action, the federal government has since acknowledged that it constituted unjustified discrimination and has offered reparations to those who were interned. In the 1960s, FBI director J. Edgar Hoover authorized extensive wiretaps to eavesdrop on telephone calls of the civil rights leader Martin Luther King Jr.; most people today would regard this as an illegal invasion of his personal privacy.

With the advent of the war on terrorism, the government gained unprecedented powers to detain foreign suspects, carry out wiretaps and searches, conduct secret military tribunals, and build an integrated law enforcement and intelligence system. Congress hastily enacted many of these sweeping provisions of the Patriot Act several weeks after the terrorist attacks, with little debate. Since then, extensive doubts about the broad powers of the Patriot Act have spread from civil libertarians on the left to libertarians on the right and even to librarians and city governments, who objected to its surveillance provisions. When Congress debated renewing the Patriot Act in 2005–06, these concerns about individual liberties threatened to block renewal. The act that was finally approved in 2006 did include modest revisions, such as exempting most libraries from having to turn over users' records to the government. Nonetheless, many in Congress felt the safeguards to individual liberties did not go far enough.

Protecting national security often requires the government to conduct its activities in secret. Yet, as Americans have come to expect a more open government in the past three decades, many believe that federal agencies charged with national security keep too many secrets from the American public. As one critic put it, "the United States government must rest, in the words of the Declaration of Independence, on 'the consent of the governed.' And there can be no meaningful consent where those who are governed do not know to what they are consenting."[19] The effort to make information related to national security more available to the public began in 1966 with the passage of the Freedom of Information Act (FOIA). Strengthened in 1974 after Watergate, the act allows any person to request classified information from any federal agency. The information obtained through the Freedom of Information Act often reveals unflattering or unsuccessful aspects of national security activities. One private organization, the National Security Archive, makes extensive use of FOIA to obtain information about the activities of national security agencies. The National Security Archive has published many of these documents on its website and maintains an archive in Washington, D.C., that is open to the public. For example, the organization's website contains "The Torture Archive," a searchable database of documents related to the detention of individuals in the Global War on Terror and the authorized use of torture by the American government.

The tension between secrecy and democracy sharpened dramatically with the threat of terrorism. FOIA was curtailed, and the range of information deemed sensitive has greatly expanded. President George W. Bush defended the new secrecy, declaring, "We're an open society, but we're at war. Foreign terrorists and agents must never again be allowed to use our freedoms against us." Although most Americans agreed that enhanced secrecy was needed to ensure domestic security, concerns about excessive secrecy mounted. Some analysts worried that secrecy would prevent Congress from carrying out its basic oversight responsibilities. They also claimed that much of the secrecy had nothing to do with

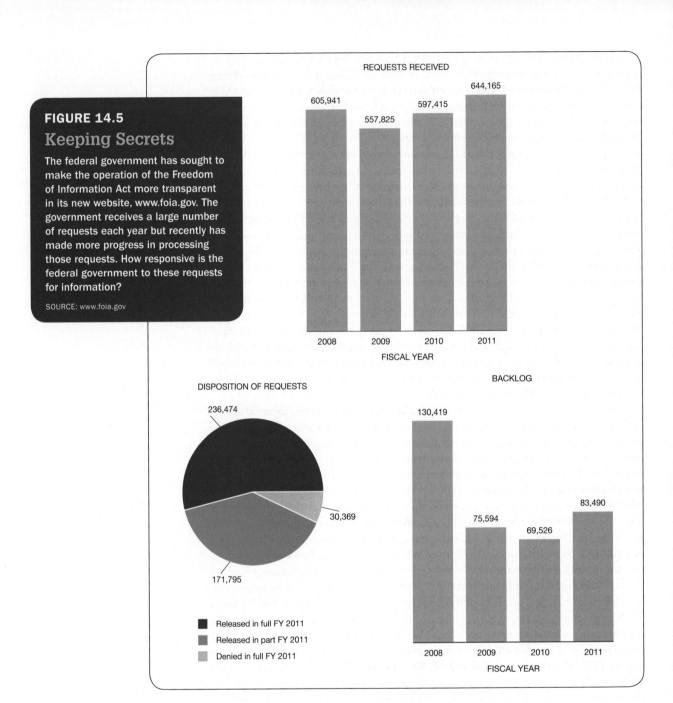

FIGURE 14.5

Keeping Secrets

The federal government has sought to make the operation of the Freedom of Information Act more transparent in its new website, www.foia.gov. The government receives a large number of requests each year but recently has made more progress in processing those requests. How responsive is the federal government to these requests for information?

SOURCE: www.foia.gov

REQUESTS RECEIVED

605,941
557,825
597,415
644,165

2008 2009 2010 2011

FISCAL YEAR

DISPOSITION OF REQUESTS

236,474
30,369
171,795

Released in full FY 2011
Released in part FY 2011
Denied in full FY 2011

BACKLOG

130,419
75,594
69,526
83,490

2008 2009 2010 2011

FISCAL YEAR

national security. As a candidate, President Obama promised to reduce government secrecy. The day after his election, he launched a process that would culminate in an Open Government Directive. He also instructed federal agencies that they should administer the FOIA law liberally: when in doubt, err on the side of openness. In 2011 the Department of Justice created the website www.foia.gov so that the public could learn more about the FOIA process. The site presents data about the number of FOIA requests by agency and the size of the backlog in processing those requests (see Figure 14.5). And in the most substantive change, at the end of his first year in office, Obama issued an executive order designed to promote more rapid declassification of secret documents. However, the Obama administration also continued some of the secrecy practices initiated in the Bush years. Most notably, it invoked the state secrets privilege to prevent lawsuits related to warrantless wiretapping and torture from going to trial.[20] The cost of government secrecy has risen dramatically since 2001. In 2011 the federal government spent an estimated $13 billion protecting its secrets, up from $4.7 billion in 2000, as much as the entire budget of the Environmental Protection Agency.[21] Even so, secrecy is increasingly difficult to preserve. In 2010–11 the Australian anti-secrecy activist Julian Assange shocked the world by releasing hundreds of thousands of U.S. government classified documents online through WikiLeaks. The incident, which made secret State Department cables and other documents available online, underscored the vulnerability of government secrets in the Internet age. In an era when national security is foremost in the public's mind, conflicts between democracy and secrecy are sure to increase.

Maintaining a Strong Economy

In our capitalist economic system, the government does not directly run the economy. Yet many federal government activities are critical to maintaining a strong economy. Foremost among these are the agencies responsible for fiscal and monetary policy. Other agencies, such as the Internal Revenue Service (IRS), transform private resources into use for public purposes. Tax policy may also strengthen the economy through decisions about whom to tax, how much, and when. Finally, the federal government, through such agencies as the Department of Transportation, the Commerce Department, and the Energy Department, may directly provide services or goods that bolster the economy.

Fiscal and Monetary Agencies **Fiscal policy** can refer to any government policy having to do with public finance. However, Americans often reserve *fiscal* for taxing and spending policies and use *monetary* for policies having to do with banks, credit, and currency.

While the responsibility for making fiscal policy lies with Congress, the administration of fiscal policy occurs primarily in the Treasury Department. In addition to collecting income, corporate, and other taxes, the Treasury also manages the enormous national debt: $16 trillion in 2012.[22] The Treasury Department is also responsible for printing U.S. currency, but currency is only a tiny proportion of the entire money economy. Most of the trillions of dollars used in the transactions of the private and public sectors of the U.S. economy exist virtually—in computerized accounts rather than actual currency.

A key monetary agency is the **Federal Reserve System**, which is headed by the Federal Reserve Board. The Federal Reserve System (called simply the Fed) has authority over the interest rates and lending activities of the nation's most important banks. Congress established the Fed in 1913 as a clearinghouse responsible for adjusting the supply of money and credit to the needs of commerce and industry in different regions of the country. The Fed is also responsible for ensuring that banks do not overextend themselves, a policy that guards against a chain of bank failures during a sudden economic scare, such as occurred in 1929 and again in 2008. The Federal Reserve Board directs the operations of the 12 district Federal Reserve Banks, which are essentially "bankers' banks," serving the monetary needs of the hundreds of member banks in the national banking system.[23] The Treasury and the Federal Reserve took center stage when a string of bank failures threatened

fiscal policy the government's use of taxing, monetary, and spending powers to manipulate the economy

Federal Reserve System a system of 12 Federal Reserve Banks that facilitates exchanges of cash, checks, and credit; regulates member banks; and uses monetary policies to fight inflation and deflation

The Treasury Department helps maintain the economy in various ways. Here, Treasury Secretary Timothy Geithner meets with economic experts and business leaders to discuss oversight of the Troubled Asset Relief Program, which was designed to address the financial crisis that began in 2008.

economic catastrophe in 2008. These agencies designed a $700 billion bailout package and convinced Congress that a rapid response was needed to avert a worldwide depression. Although the Treasury and the Federal Reserve sprang into action when economic calamity loomed, critics charged that the crisis could have been prevented if these agencies had exercised more regulatory oversight over the financial sector during the previous decade. In 2010 the Congress and the president created the Financial Stability Oversight Council, headed by the treasury secretary, with the Federal Reserve chairman also playing a key role. This body is responsible for identifying systemwide risks to the financial sector. The council initiated rule-writing processes designed to set up its operations and to implement new regulations related to financial stability. Most significant among the issues it has considered is whether to make nonbank financial institutions, such as hedge funds, subject to greater regulatory oversight, comparable to that which banks now receive.[24] The financial industry kept a close eye on these developments, aiming to limit the regulatory reach of the new council.[25]

Revenue Agencies One of the first actions Congress took under President George Washington was to create the Department of the Treasury, and probably its oldest function is the collection of taxes on imports, called tariffs. Now part of the Department of Homeland Security, federal customs agents are located at every U.S. seaport and international airport to oversee the collection of tariffs. But far and away the most important of the **revenue agencies** is the IRS. The U.S. Customs and Border Protection is one bureau of seven within the Department of Homeland Security, while the IRS is a bureau within the Treasury Department.

The IRS is the government agency that Americans love to hate. As one expert put it, "probably no organization in the country, public or private, creates as much clientele *dis*favor as the Internal Revenue Service. The very nature of its work brings it into an adversarial relationship with vast numbers of Americans every year [emphasis added]."[26] Taxpayers complain about the IRS's needless complexity, its lack of sensitivity and responsiveness to individual taxpayers, and its overall lack of

revenue agency an agency responsible for collecting taxes. Examples include the Internal Revenue Service for income taxes, the U.S. Customs Service for tariffs and other taxes on imported goods, and the Bureau of Alcohol, Tobacco, Firearms and Explosives for collection of taxes on the sale of those particular products.

efficiency. Such complaints led Congress to pass the IRS Restructuring and Reform Act of 1998, which instituted a number of new protections for taxpayers. By 2005, however, concern was shifting toward the problem of tax dodgers. When a 2005 report indicated that the gap between true income and income reported to the IRS was at an all-time high, the IRS vowed to step up enforcement activities, focusing especially on foreign tax shelters favored by the wealthy. The Obama administration has put an emphasis on shutting down overseas tax "havens." Aided by a 13 percent increase in funding for enforcement, the IRS has become more aggressive about pursuing wealthy individuals suspected of avoiding U.S. tax by illegally sheltering their income abroad. After the U.S. government reached deals with the Swiss and Maltese governments to turn over details of U.S. citizens with holdings in banks in those countries, more than 14,000 U.S. taxpayers came forward as part of an amnesty program, with some accounts amounting to as much as $100 million.[27] The Department of Justice continued to pursue the matter and, in 2012, charged employees of a Swiss bank with helping to shield $1.2 billion in American taxpayer assets from the IRS. The results of these efforts are limited, however, because many overseas tax shelters are legal. Despite several efforts, Congress has failed to enact legislation limiting such shelters.[28]

The politics of the IRS is most interesting because, although thousands upon thousands of corporations and wealthy individuals have a strong and active interest in American tax policy, key taxation decisions are set by agreements among the president, the Treasury Department, and the leading members of the two tax committees in Congress, the House Ways and Means Committee and the Senate Finance Committee. External influence is not spread throughout the 50 states but is much more centralized in the majority political party, a few key figures in Congress, and a handful of professional lobbyists. Suspicions of unfair exemptions and favoritism are widespread, and they do exist, but these exemptions come largely from Congress, *not* from the IRS itself.

Economic Development Agencies Federal agencies also conduct programs designed to strengthen particular segments of the economy or to provide specific services aimed at strengthening the entire economy. Created in 1889, the Department of Agriculture is the fourth-oldest cabinet department. Its initial mission, to strengthen American agriculture by providing information about effective farming practices, reflected the enormous importance of farming in the American economy. Through its Agricultural Extension Service, the Department of Agriculture established an important presence in rural areas throughout the country. It also built strong support for its activities among the nation's farmers and at the many land-grant colleges, where agricultural research has been conducted for over 100 years.

At first glance, the Department of Transportation, which oversees the nation's highway and air traffic systems, may seem to have little to do with economic development. But effective transportation is the backbone of a strong economy. The interstate highway system, for example, is widely acknowledged as a key factor in promoting economic growth in the decades after World War II. The departments of Commerce and Energy also oversee programs designed to ensure a strong economy. The Small Business Administration, in the Department of Commerce, provides loans and technical assistance to small businesses across the country.

In recent decades, dissatisfaction with government has led to calls to keep government out of the economy. Yet if the federal government were to disappear, the economy would almost certainly fall into chaos. There is widespread agreement that the federal government should set the basic rules for economic activity and should intervene—through such measures as setting interest rates—to keep the economy strong. Some analysts argue that the government's role should go beyond rule setting to include more active measures such as investment in infrastructure. Advocates of government action point to the economic benefits of government investments in the interstate highway system and of the government research in the 1960s that led to the creation of the Internet.

Can the Bureaucracy Be Reformed?

Evaluate some of the ways politicians have tried to make the bureaucracy more efficient

When citizens complain that government is too bureaucratic, what they often mean is that government bureaucracies seem inefficient and waste money. The epitome of such bureaucratic inefficiency in the late 1980s was the Department of Defense, which was revealed to have spent $640 apiece for toilet seats and $435 apiece for hammers—although erroneous reports of $16 muffins bought by the Justice Department captured headlines in 2011.[29] Many citizens also had negative personal experience with the federal government: mountains of forms to fill out, lengthy waits, and unsympathetic service. Why can't government do better? many citizens asked. The application of new technologies and innovative management strategies in the private sector during the 1980s made government agencies look even more lumbering and inefficient by comparison. People were coming to expect faster service and more customer-friendly interactions in the private sector. But how can public-sector bureaucracies become more effective?

The government has sought to find various ways to make the federal bureaucracy more efficient. The key strategies used to promote reform include reinventing bureaucratic procedures, termination, devolution, and privatization. In general,

In recent years there have been several attempts to "reinvent" government. In 1993, President Bill Clinton and Vice President Al Gore established the National Performance Review to reinvent government. Gore promoted this on David Letterman's show, where he railed against the government's procurement requirements, which even specified the number of pieces into which a government ashtray may shatter.

NASA's space shuttle program was terminated in 2011. In July of that year Atlantis *flew its last mission.*

Democratic administrations have aimed to make the existing bureaucracy work more effectively, whereas Republican administrations have sought to sideline the bureaucracy, especially by contracting out government work to private companies.

Reinventing the Bureaucracy

In 1993, President Clinton launched the National Performance Review (NPR)—part of his promise to "reinvent government"—to make the federal bureaucracy more efficient, accountable, and effective. The NPR sought to prod federal agencies into adopting flexible, goal-driven practices. Clinton promised that the result would be a government that would "work better and cost less." Virtually all observers agreed that the NPR made substantial progress. Its original goal was to save more than $100 billion over five years, in large part by cutting the federal workforce by 12 percent (more than 270,000 jobs) by the end of 1999. In fact, by 2000, $136 billion in savings were already assured through legislative or administrative action, and the federal workforce had been cut by 426,200.[30] The streamlining of government business procedures did help make government work more effectively, but it did not institute the more sweeping approach to reform demanded by some political leaders. These leaders have instead pursued efforts to terminate, devolve, or contract out government functions.

Termination

The only *certain* way to reduce the size of the bureaucracy is to eliminate programs. Variations in the levels of federal personnel and expenditures (as were shown in Figures 14.1 and 14.2) demonstrate the futility of trying to make permanent cuts in existing agencies. Furthermore, most agencies have a supportive constituency that will fight to reinstate any cuts that are made. Termination (a rare occurrence) is the only way to ensure an agency's reduction. Even in the 12 years of the Reagan and George H. W. Bush administrations, both of which proclaimed a strong commitment to the reduction of the national government, not a single national government agency or program was terminated. In the 1990s, Republicans did succeed in eliminating two small agencies.

The overall difficulty in terminating bureaucracy is a reflection of Americans' love-hate relationship with the national government. As antagonistic as Americans may be toward bureaucracy in general, they benefit from the services being rendered and the protections being offered by particular bureaucratic agencies. They fiercely defend their favorite agencies while perceiving no inconsistency in their hostility toward the bureaucracy in general. A good case in point is the agonizing problem of closing military bases in the wake of the end of the Cold War with the former Soviet Union, when the United States no longer needed so many bases. Since every base was in some congressional member's district, it proved impossible for Congress to decide to close any of them. Consequently, beginning in 1988, Congress established the Defense Base Closure and Realignment Commission (BRAC) to decide on base closings, allowing Congress only an up or down vote on the commission's proposals.[31] Five different BRAC reports, the most recent in 2005, have formed the basis for closing bases and modifying the operations in the remaining bases.

Elected leaders have come to rely on a more incremental approach to downsizing the bureaucracy. Much has been done by budgetary means, reducing the budgets of all agencies across the board by small percentages and cutting some less-supported agencies by larger amounts. Yet these changes are still incremental, leaving the existence of agencies unaddressed.

Devolution

The next most effective approach to genuinely reducing the size of the federal bureaucracy is **devolution**, downsizing the federal bureaucracy by delegating the implementation of programs to state and local governments. Devolution often alters the pattern of who benefits most from government programs. Opponents of devolution in social policy, for example, charge that it reduces the ability of the government to remedy inequality. They argue that state governments, which cannot run deficits, as the federal government does, and which have more limited taxing capabilities, will inevitably cut spending on programs that serve low-income residents. They point to the State Children's Health Insurance Program (SCHIP), which was created in 1997 to extend health insurance to low-income children. When the economy was booming, states added children to the rolls and some states even extended benefits to the children's parents. But by 2002, as states faced significant budget crises, many cut back on SCHIP. Although the federal government was initially able to compensate for state funding problems, states have found it difficult to keep pace with the rising number of children without health insurance. Moreover, because state revenues can fluctuate widely from year to year, states are often forced to cut back on expensive health coverage programs. By 2010, many states faced their worst budget crises since the Great Depression. Even though the federal government provided substantial assistance to states through a massive stimulus program, as those funds dried up in 2011, a number of states began to cut health benefits for children. Many of these children will now receive insurance through state health exchanges and

devolution a policy to remove a program from one level of government by delegating it or passing it down to a lower level of government, such as from the national government to the state and local governments

insurance subsidies, both established by the Affordable Care Act. Others will be covered through the expansions of Medicaid mandated in the act. However, if states take advantage of the Supreme Court ruling on the act that allows them to opt out of expanded coverage, many low-income people may remain without health insurance.[32] Immediately after the court decision, the governors of Florida and South Carolina announced their intention to opt out, citing the burden of Medicaid on state budgets. Other states expressed doubts about whether they would accept the expansion. While some saw this as the beginning of a trend that would leave millions uninsured, others predicted that in the end, the favorable terms of the Medicaid expansion—the federal government pays for all the expanded coverage until 2016 and 90 percent thereafter—would lead states to participate in the program.[33]

Often the central aim of devolution is to provide more efficient and flexible government services. Yet by its very nature, devolution entails variation across the states. In some states, government services may improve as a consequence of devolution. In other states, services may deteriorate as the states use devolution as an opportunity to cut spending and reduce services. This has been the pattern in the implementation of the welfare reform passed in 1996, the most significant devolution of federal government social programs in many decades. Some states, such as Wisconsin, have used the flexibility of the reform to design innovative programs that respond to clients' needs; other states, such as Idaho, have virtually dismantled their welfare programs. The recession that began in 2008 provided the first real evidence about what increased state flexibility meant for low-income Americans. Studies showed that the number of people on public assistance rose by 14 percent even as the unemployment rate increased by 88 percent between 2007 and 2010.[34] Moreover, states varied widely in how they responded: for example, although unemployment rose by 146 percent in Arizona, public assistance rolls actually fell by 48 percent. In Oregon, by contrast, public assistance cases rose by 70 percent although unemployment grew by only 41 percent. The overall lack of growth and state variation in welfare contrasts sharply with the rise in the rise of food stamp recipients during 2008–09. Food stamp recipients grew by 45 percent between 2009 and 2010 and pulled an estimated 9 percent of Americans out of poverty in 2009.[35] Critics argued that devolution gave the states too much flexibility to design their own welfare programs and that the result has been a program unable to assist the poor when they need it most.

This is the dilemma that devolution poses. Up to a point, variation can be considered one of the virtues of federalism. But in a democracy, it is inherently dangerous to have large variations in the provisions of services and benefits.

Privatization

Most of what is called privatization is the provision of government goods and services by private contractors under direct government supervision. Except for top-secret strategic materials, virtually all military hardware, from boats to bullets, is produced on a privatized basis by private contractors. Research services worth billions of dollars are bought under contract by governments from universities and from ordinary industrial corporations and private "think tanks." **Privatization** simply means that a formerly public activity is picked up under contract by a private company or companies. But such programs are still very much government programs—paid for by government and supervised by government. Privatization

privatization the transfer of all or part of a program from the public sector to the private sector

downsizes the government only in that the workers providing the service are no longer counted as part of the government bureaucracy.

President George W. Bush made privatization a central component of his effort to reform the federal bureaucracy. He introduced new procedures that would subject more than 800,000 federal jobs, nearly half the federal civilian workforce, to competitive outsourcing. If it were determined that a company could do the job more efficiently, the work would be contracted out. Under Bush, government outsourcing grew dramatically as the government sought to staff the new Department of Homeland Security and pursue wars in Afghanistan and Iraq without increasing the numbers of federal employees. One estimate of the growth of contracting showed that at the end of the Cold War in 1990, there were three and a half contractors and grantees for every civil servant; by 2005 the buildup connected with national security had altered the ratio to five and a half contractors and grantees for every civil servant.[36] Payments for federal contracts grew from $209 billion in 2000 to $528 billion in 2008.[37] Although military contracts account for much of the growth, contracting is common throughout the federal bureaucracy. In fact, contracting is now so widespread that it has been called a "virtual fourth branch of government."[38]

The central aim of privatization is to reduce the cost of government. Depending on how it is conducted, competitive outsourcing may not lead to extensive privatization; instead, competition may improve government performance by forcing federal agencies to reexamine how they can do their work more efficiently. When private contractors can perform a task as well as government can, but for less money, taxpayers win. But private firms are not necessarily more efficient or less costly than government, especially when there is little competition among private firms and when public bureaucracies are not granted a fair chance to bid in the contracting competition. In 2005 only 34 percent of existing contracts were subject to competition, whereas 45 percent were open to competition in 2000 (Figure 14.6).[39] When private firms have a monopoly on service provision, they may

One strategy to carry out the tasks of government is privatization. The United States' military operations have increasingly been privatized, with private contractors providing security services in Iraq and Afghanistan.

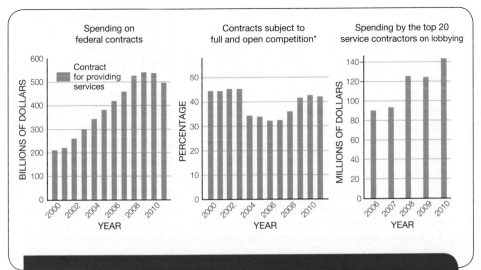

FIGURE 14.6

Outsourcing the Government

As spending on federal contracts has grown, the number of contracts subject to open competition has declined substantially. At the same time, the rise in spending by private contractors on lobbying and campaign contributions raises questions about improper political influence on government contracting decisions.

'Includes both new contracts and payments against existing contracts.

SOURCES: Fedspending.org, "Summary of Federal Spending: Financial Assistance and Procurement," www .fedspending.org (accessed 7/4/12); Fedspending.org, "Federal Contract Awards by Extent of Competition," www .fedspending.org (accessed 7/4/12); Government Executive, "Top 200 Federal Contractors," August 15, 2010, www.govexec.com (accessed 7/4/12); Center for Responsive Politics, "Lobbying Database," www.opensecrets.org (accessed 7/4/12).

be less efficient than government and more expensive. In fact, there is no good evidence that privatization saves the government money.

Concerns about adequate government oversight and accountability escalated as the scale of contracting has dramatically increased. Consider the use of private contractors in Iraq and Afghanistan. Congressional hearings revealed massive cost overruns by KBR (formerly a subsidiary of Halliburton, the firm that former vice president Dick Cheney headed), which held $9 billion in no-bid contracts to provide services ranging from supplying fuel for the military to preparing cafeteria meals in Iraq. Army auditors have challenged $1.9 billion of KBR's bills as improper, citing violations ranging from unserved meals to inflated gas prices.[40]

Private security firms pose even more serious oversight issues. The Department of Defense has made heavy use of such firms to provide services in Iraq and Afghanistan that were previously provided by the military directly. In 2011 a congressional commission reported that more than 260,000 private workers operated in Iraq and Afghanistan in 2010. Private workers outnumbered the federal military and federal civilian workforce in these countries.[41] High-profile congressional hearings into the role of Blackwater, a private security firm, in civilian killings in Iraq illustrated the difficulties of relying on private contractors to conduct a war. With a billion dollars of government contracts, Blackwater played an essential role in providing security in Iraq. But because they are not bound by the same rules of conduct as the military, private security forces were accused of being more likely than the regular military to kill civilians who posed little threat. And because the private security forces are not subject to the military code of justice, illegal behavior is difficult to sanction.

The private military is also costlier. Noting that "sergeants in the military generally cost the Government between $50,000 to $70,000 per year" and that "a comparable position at Blackwater costs the Federal Government over $400,000, six times as much," congressional critics have questioned whether the private military is cost effective.[42] Disparities in pay not only are demoralizing to the troops, but they also lure trained troops away from the military to the private contractors. Even more troubling is the possibility that private contractors undermined the mission in Iraq by creating hostility among the Iraqi people as reports of unprovoked civilian killings came to light.[43]

In most aspects of government activity, contract employees work side by side with government employees in what has been called a "blended workforce."[44] Many agencies that rely on technical expertise, such as the National Oceanographic and Atmospheric Administration, routinely rely on contractors. But although federal regulations forbid the outsourcing of "inherently governmental work," no clear line separates governmental and nongovernmental work. For example, in 2006 the General Services Administration hired a private firm, CACI International, to help it examine cases of fraud by other private contractors. Not only did the private contract workers hired by the GSA in this case cost double their public counterparts, but they were engaged in oversight of other private contractors, a clear conflict of interest.[45]

As alarm over the activities of contractors has grown, there have been several efforts to increase accountability. In 2002 the federal government created a centralized database to record how well contractors have performed. The aim of the database is to provide a resource for agencies as they offer new contracts. However, research by the Government Accountability Office (GAO) showed that after seven years, the database was poorly documented and was seldom used in agency decision making.[46] As part of the 2009 National Defense Authorization Act, Congress called for the creation of an additional database that will keep track of contractors who commit legal or contractual violations.[47] In 2008, Congress also responded to the concerns about contractors by creating a "Commission on Wartime Contracting." The commission, modeled on the 1941 Truman Commission set up to investigate wartime profiteering in World War II, had a two-year charge to investigate contracting abuse and waste in Afghanistan and Iraq. Its final report sharply criticized the use of private contractors, estimating that the practice had wasted between $31 billion and $60 billion during the two wars. It made numerous recommendations for reform but noted that successful reforms would require congressional action and funding for new oversight capabilities.[48]

Some members of Congress have sought far-reaching regulations on contractors. For example, Senator Chuck Schumer (D-N.Y.) and Representative Chris Van Hollen (D-Md.) proposed legislation in 2010 that would prohibit government contractors from making political contributions.[49] Members of Congress have also proposed forbidding contractors from performing sensitive functions in war settings, including interrogations, security, and intelligence functions. In 2011 the Obama administration considered issuing an executive order requiring federal contractors to disclose their contributions to groups that engage in politics. Proposals for such

E-Government

E-government refers to the delivery of government information and services online via the Internet or other digital means. E-government holds promise for improved delivery of many types of public services, including online transactions such as filing taxes, applying for financial aid or licenses, reserving a campsite in a national or state park, or paying parking tickets. It also makes it easier to get information about the operation of government (for example, snow plow routes, evacuation routes, traffic delays, real-time rail and bus routes, and community events). E-government can improve communication between citizens and government. Perhaps most importantly, it can save money.

Before digital government, interacting with government was often slow and time-consuming. A typical transaction required travel to a government office, waiting in line, requesting a form, calling the office if there were questions about how to fill out the form, mailing it in, and so on. The Department of Motor Vehicles (DMV) is an example of a government office that still requires in-person visits, and usually waiting in long lines, to obtain a driver's license.

E-government is one of the fastest-growing online activities, and 2012 survey data show that more than three in four Internet users report using a federal, state, or local government website. The federal government has a central portal for all federal services (www.usa.gov), all 50 states have sophisticated websites, and most local governments maintain websites.

Trust in government has been declining for more than half a century, as the federal bureaucracy in particular has been seen as slow, inefficient, and unresponsive. E-government has been proposed as a way to improve citizen evaluations of government. Why might this occur?

By making available the information and services that citizens want, and by improving the speed and ease of interactions, e-government may enhance government responsiveness. Government websites, e-mail, and social media create convenient new opportunities for interaction with officials. Single, integrated portals and links to other sites have the potential to make information and services from a number of agencies available through a single website. Searchable databases can improve the accessibility of information, as does access to information seven days a week, 24 hours a day. E-government may improve participation in government by providing for citizen input via online town meetings, online forums, and deliberative processes for e-rulemaking. It may also improve government transparency through the posting of data, policies, laws, meeting schedules and minutes, and contact information.

A recent study drawing on Pew survey data found that people who use e-government tend to have more positive attitudes about government. Specifically, use of a local government website appears to be related to trust in local governments, and to other positive assessments of federal, state, and local governments in terms of responsiveness, accessibility, communication, and transparency.

Perhaps most important, e-government improves efficiency through use of the latest technology to automate processes, improve service delivery, produce budget savings, and save time. Online transactions and downloadable forms are examples of more efficient processes through e-government. More generally, however, automation emulates the convenience and efficiency of e-commerce, and suggests that government is adopting state-of-the-art private-sector practices. The political scientist Darrell West found that receiving information about e-government was associated with positive attitudes about government efficiency.

Darrell West argues that new technology requires organizational change, and this type of change is necessary for government innovation. The private sector has quickly adapted to a world of commerce online, using technology for organizational change, including "flattening" organizations so that there is less hierarchy. Government bureaucracies are typically hierarchical; to take full advantage of the new technology, they may need to decentralize. But can they?

SOURCES: Darrell West, *The Next Wave: Using Digital Technology to Further Social and Political Innovation* (Washington, DC: Brookings Institution Press, 2011). Darrell West, *Digital Government: Technology and Public-Sector Performance* (Princeton, NJ: Princeton University Press, 2005). Caroline Tolbert, Karen Mossberger, and Ramona McNeal, "Institutions, Policy Innovation and E-Government in the American States, *Public Administration Review* 68, no. 3 (2008): 549–63.

for critical analysis

1. Beyond cost savings, what are the benefits of digital government or e-government? What are the disadvantages?

2. Can government bureaucracies update their organizational structure to take advantage of advances in information technology as private-sector organizations have done? Or is there a limit to the efficiency gains from new technology?

major reforms, however, are difficult to enact given the political connections of many federal contractors.

The Obama administration has sought to address the concerns about contracting in several ways. In July 2009 the White House Office of Management and Budget (OMB) took steps to reduce the government's reliance on outside contractors. Departments and agencies were told to cut contract spending by 7 percent over the next two years.[50] By 2011 the administration announced that for the first time in 13 years, spending on outside contractors had declined.[51]

Managing the Bureaucracy

Explain why it is often difficult to control the bureaucracy

By their very nature, bureaucracies pose challenges to democratic governance. Although bureaucracies provide the expertise needed to implement the public will, they can also become entrenched organizations that serve their own interests. The public's task is neither to retreat from bureaucracy nor to attack it, but to take advantage of its strengths while making it more accountable to the demands of democratic politics and representative government.

We must return to James Madison's observation "You must first enable the government to control the governed; and in the next place oblige it to control itself."[52] Today, after more than 200 years, millions of employees, and trillions of dollars since the Founding, the problem is the same. Now, though, the process has a name, administrative accountability, which implies that some higher authority will guide and judge the actions of the bureaucracy. The highest authority in a democracy is *demos* ("the people"), and the guidance for bureaucratic action is the popular will. But that ideal of accountability must be translated into practical terms by the president and Congress.

The President as Chief Executive

In 1937, President Franklin Roosevelt's Committee on Administrative Management officially addressed a plea that had been growing increasingly urgent: "The president needs help." The national government had grown rapidly during the preceding 25 years, but the structures and procedures necessary to manage the burgeoning executive branch had not yet been established. The response to the call for "help" for the president initially took the form of three management policies: (1) All communications and decisions that related to executive policy decisions must pass through the White House. (2) In order to cope with such a flow, the White House must have adequate staff of specialists in research, analysis, legislative and legal writing, and public affairs. (3) The White House must have additional staff to ensure that presidential decisions are made, communicated to Congress, and carried out by the appropriate agency.

Making the Managerial Presidency The story of the modern presidency can be told largely as a series of responses to the plea for managerial help. Indeed, each expansion of the national government into new policies and programs in the twentieth century was accompanied by a parallel expansion of the president's management authority. This pattern began even before FDR's presidency, with the policy innovations of President Woodrow Wilson between 1913 and 1920. Congress responded to Wilson's policies with the 1921 Budget and Accounting Act, which turned over the prime legislative power of budgeting to the White House. Each successive president has continued this pattern, creating what we now know as the "managerial presidency."[53]

President Jimmy Carter, in particular, was probably more preoccupied with administrative reform and reorganization than any other twentieth-century president. His reorganization of the civil service will long be recognized as one of the most significant contributions of his presidency. The Civil Service Reform Act of 1978 was the first major revamping of the federal civil service since its creation in 1883. The 1978 act abolished the century-old Civil Service Commission (CSC) and replaced it with three agencies, each designed to handle one of the CSC's functions on the theory that the competing demands of these functions had given the CSC an "identity crisis." The Merit Systems Protection Board (MSPB) was created to defend competitive merit recruitment and promotion from political encroachment. A separate Federal Labor Relations Authority (FLRA) was set up to administer collective bargaining and to address individual personnel grievances. The third new agency, the Office of Personnel Management (OPM), was created to manage recruiting, testing, training, and the retirement system. The Senior Executive Service—a top management rank for civil servants—was also created to recognize and foster "public management" as a profession and to facilitate the movement of "supergrade" career officials across agencies and departments.[54]

Carter also tried to impose a stringent budgetary process on all executive agencies. Called "zero-based budgeting," it was a method of budgeting from the bottom up whereby each agency was required to rejustify its entire mission rather than merely its next year's increase. Zero-based budgeting did not succeed, but the effort was not lost on President Reagan. Although Reagan gave the impression of being a hands-off president, he actually centralized management to an unprecedented degree. From Carter's "bottom-up" approach, Reagan went to a "top-down" approach, whereby the initial budgetary decisions would be made in the White

Following the government's slow and inadequate response to Hurricane Katrina in 2005, some questioned President Bush's management of executive agencies. When Hurricane Rita threatened the Gulf states a month later, Bush worked closely with FEMA to make sure the error was not repeated.

House and the agencies would be required to abide by those decisions. This process converted the OMB into an agency of policy determination and presidential management.[55] President George H. W. Bush took Reagan's centralization strategy even further in using the White House staff instead of cabinet secretaries for managing the executive branch.[56]

President Clinton was often criticized for the way he managed his administration. His loose approach to administration even included all-night "bull sessions," complete with pizza. Yet, as we have seen, Clinton also inaugurated one of the most systematic efforts "to change the way government does business" in his NPR. Heavily influenced by the theories of management consultants who prized decentralization, customer responsiveness, and employee initiative, Clinton sought to infuse these new practices into government.[57]

George W. Bush was the first president with a degree in business. His management strategy followed a standard business school dictum: select skilled subordinates and delegate responsibility to them. Bush followed this model closely in his appointment of highly experienced officials to cabinet positions and in his selection of Dick Cheney for vice president. But critics contended that the Bush administration's distrust of the bureaucracy led the administration to exercise inappropriate political control. Political appointees occupied high agency positions that allowed them to suppress the work of agency experts when they threatened to undercut the administration's political goals.

The Obama administration has sought to reinvigorate federal agencies, which reflects the Democrats' greater support for strong government institutions. Obama's approach to the managerial presidency features a deep belief in the importance of scientific expertise in government service. The president's appointments to head key regulatory agencies, including the EPA, OSHA, and the FDA, reflected this conviction. Some of the new agency leaders were well-known academic experts; others had won recognition for their achievements in state or local administrative settings.

Congress holds hearings to determine whether federal agencies are successfully performing their jobs. In 2009, Attorney General Eric Holder testified at a congressional hearing on oversight of the Justice Department. Members of Congress were concerned about a recent Justice Department decision to try the suspects in the September 11 terrorist attacks in New York.

Decades of reform have increased the managerial capacity of the presidency, but such reforms themselves do not ensure democratic accountability—presidents must put their managerial powers to use. Although Ronald Reagan was an enormously popular president, he was faulted for his disengaged management style. During his administration, the National Security Council staff was not prevented from running its own policies toward Iran and Nicaragua for at least two years (1985–86) after Congress had explicitly restricted activities toward Nicaragua and the president had forbidden negotiations with Iran. The Tower Commission, appointed to investigate the Iran-Contra affair, concluded that although there was nothing fundamentally wrong with the institutions involved in foreign-policy making, there had been a "flawed process," "a failure of responsibility," and a thinness of the president's personal engagement in the issues. The Tower Commission found that "at no time did [President Reagan] insist upon accountability and performance review."[58] In 2008, Congress held hearings to investigate the financial crisis. Members grilled banking and insurance executives and the former chairman of the Federal Reserve, Alan Greenspan. Greenspan, once hailed as a financial wizard, memorably admitted that inadequate regulation of lending practices had played a role in causing the crisis.

Presidents may also use their managerial capacities to limit democratic accountability if they believe it is a hindrance to effective government. Even in the unusual circumstances of the war on terrorism, critics question whether the Bush administration was too quick to assert **executive privilege** and shield its actions from public scrutiny. In such circumstances, the separation of powers among the branches of government may be the best way to ensure democratic accountability.

Congressional Oversight

Congress is constitutionally essential to responsible bureaucracy because ultimately the key to bureaucratic responsibility is legislation. When a law is passed and its intent is clear, the accountability for implementation of that law is also clear. Then the president knows what to "faithfully execute," and the responsible agency understands what is expected of it. But when Congress enacts vague legislation, agencies must resort to their own interpretations. The president and the federal courts often step in to tell agencies what the legislation intended. And so do the most intensely interested groups. Yet when everybody, from president to courts to interest groups, gets involved in the actual interpretation of legislative intent, to whom and to what is the agency accountable?

Congress's answer is **oversight**. The more power Congress has delegated to the executive, the more it has sought to re-involve itself in directing the interpretation of laws through committee and subcommittee oversight of each agency. The standing committee system in Congress is well suited to oversight, inasmuch as most of the congressional committees and subcommittees have jurisdictions roughly parallel to one or more departments and agencies, and members of Congress who sit on these committees can develop expertise equal to that of the bureaucrats. The exception is the Department of Homeland Security, whose activities are now overseen by more than 20 committees. One of the central recommendations of the 9/11 Commission—as yet unimplemented—was to create a single committee with oversight of the Department of Homeland Security. Appropriations committees, as well as authorization committees, have oversight powers—as do their

executive privilege the claim that confidential communications between a president and close advisers should not be revealed without the consent of the president

oversight the effort by Congress, through hearings, investigations, and other techniques, to exercise control over the activities of executive agencies

respective subcommittees. In addition to these, the Committee on Oversight and Government Reform (in the House) and the Homeland Security and Governmental Affairs Committee (in the Senate) have oversight powers not limited by departmental jurisdiction.

The most visible indication of Congress's oversight efforts is the use of public hearings, before which bureaucrats and other witnesses are summoned to discuss and defend agency budgets and past decisions. In 2011 and 2012, for example, Congress held high-profile hearings on topics as diverse as programs of the Bureau of Alcohol, Tobacco, Firearms and Explosives that inadvertently put guns into the hands of Mexican drug cartels; and VIP loans provided to prominent politicians by the defunct mortgage company Countrywide Financial Corporation.

The data drawn from systematic studies of congressional committee and subcommittee hearings and meetings show quite dramatically that Congress has tried through oversight to keep pace with the expansion of the executive branch. The annual number of oversight hearings has grown over time as the bureaucracy has expanded. Oversight hearings in both the Senate and the House increased dramatically in the 1970s in the aftermath of the Watergate scandal. In recent years, oversight has become a topic of substantial political concern. After the Republicans took over Congress in 1995, they concentrated their oversight power on investigating scandal. When George W. Bush became president in 2001, congressional oversight virtually disappeared. In the words of the congressional scholars Thomas Mann and Norman Ornstein, Republican members of Congress saw "themselves as field lieutenants in the president's army far more than they [did] as members of a separate and independent branch of government."[59] In Mann and Ornstein's view, Congress's failure to exercise its oversight role led to poor government performance and bureaucracies that were not accountable to the American people. After winning back Congress in 2006, the Democrats revived the oversight role, holding hearings on such issues as the use of government contractors in the Iraq and Afghanistan wars and the Troubled Asset Relief Program (TARP), which was instituted to help bail out the banks in 2008. When Republicans took control of the House in 2010, oversight hearings focused on the Democratic administration's programs, such as the Consumer Financial Protection Bureau.

Individual members of Congress can also carry out oversight inquiries. Such standard congressional "casework" can address significant questions of public responsibility even when they are motivated only by the demands of an individual constituent. Oversight also encompasses the communications between congressional staff and agency staff. In addition, Congress has created for itself three large agencies whose obligations are to engage in constant research on matters related to the executive branch. These are the GAO, the Congressional Research Service (CRS), and the Congressional Budget Office (CBO), each designed to give Congress information independent of the information it can get directly from the executive branch through hearings and other communications.[60] Another source of information for oversight is directly from citizens through the FOIA, which, as we have seen, gives ordinary citizens the right to gain access to agency files and agency data. Nevertheless, the information citizens gain through FOIA can be made effective only through the institutionalized channels of congressional committees and, though rarely, through public interest litigation in the federal courts.

Most Americans dislike the idea of "big government," but they want the bueaucracy to be responsive when they need government services. Americans are increasingly likely to use the Internet to get information and help from bureaucratic agencies—a trend that may improve perceptions of government efficiency.

The increasing use of federal contractors raises new questions about democratic accountability. When government work is outsourced, federal monitoring is essential to ensure that funds are spent in accordance with the public will and to confirm that the costs are fair. Yet government contracting is now so extensive that such monitoring has become extremely difficult. Even with monitoring, accountability may be hard to achieve; many of the mechanisms of democratic accountability do not apply to private firms that contract to perform public work. For example, private corporations can resist FOIA requests, and they are not constrained by the same ethics rules as public employees. Moreover, because private firms do not have to disclose information about their operations in the same way that public bureaucracies do, Congress has much more limited oversight. The move to privatization clearly presents major challenges to democratic accountability.

One of the most troubling aspects of outsourcing is that private contractors donate millions of dollars each year to political campaigns and lobbying. As Figure 14.6 shows, the top 20 federal contractors have substantially increased their spending on lobbying since 2000. These expenditures raise troubling questions about how assertive members of Congress are likely to be in scrutinizing the business practices of important political donors or in moving activities from the private to the public sector.

for critical analysis

Through elected officials (that is, the president and the Congress) the public can achieve some control over the bureaucracy. What are the relative advantages and disadvantages of presidential and congressional control of the bureaucracy?

● Thinking Critically about Responsible Bureaucracy in a Democracy

Americans' views about the federal government bureaucracy present something of a paradox. On the one hand, the public expresses dislike for "big government," exemplified by bureaucracy. From this perspective, the federal government is too large, inherently wasteful, and at odds with individual freedom. On the other hand, Americans support many government programs and have high expectations for government. Indeed, high expectations lead many Americans to blame bureaucrats when the country faces problems, such as the prolonged economic downturn of recent years. One consequence of these divergent views is that public discussion about bureaucracy is often high on emotion and short on facts.

Arguments contending that the federal government is too large ignore the fact that the number of government employees has not grown disproportionately large when compared with the size of the American workforce. Charges that government wastes the taxpayers' money must also be put into perspective. As we have seen in this chapter, outsourcing government activities to private contractors does not offer a remedy for wasteful spending. In fact, private firms may be more wasteful than the public sector unless there is strong government oversight of private activities. Finally, it is true that bureaucratic rules often limit the freedom of individuals and corporations. But the laws that bureaucracies implement were enacted by our elected representatives in Congress. They are, in fact, the product of our democratic political system. As these considerations suggest, building a bureaucracy that reflects American values is not a simple task. Adequate congressional oversight is one important part of the solution because a bureaucracy that is shielded from the public eye may wind up pursuing its own interests rather than those of the public. Even so, an administration whose every move is subject to intense public scrutiny may be hamstrung in its efforts to carry out the public interest. Finding the right balance between bureaucratic autonomy and public scrutiny is a central task of creating an effective government; it requires both presidential and congressional vigilance to build an effective and responsive bureaucracy.

Untangling Bureaucratic Red Tape?

Inform Yourself

 Explore federal agencies. Go to the FirstGov A–Z Department and Agency Index (www.usa.gov/directory/federal/index.shtml) and select one of the federal agencies listed. What does it do? Under whose jurisdiction does it fall? Are you surprised by how many government agencies there are? Are you surprised that, in addition to well-known agencies such as the Postal Service and NASA, the list includes more obscure agencies such as Radio Free Asia and the Committee for the Implementation of Textile Agreements?

 See how the bureaucracy has grown. The federal bureaucracy did not always exist in the large form it does today. The specialization and growth of the bureaucracy of the federal government occurred over the course of the country's 200-year history. Read about the development of the bureaucracy at www.ushistory.org/gov/8a.asp.

 Watch a *Futurama* clip portraying bureaucrats. The modern-day perception of the bureaucracy has been portrayed in thousands of television episodes and movies. Watch the clip from Futurama at www.comedycentral.com/video-clips/fqqyi0/futurama-bureaucrat-s-song. Consider whether this is a fair description of federal bureaucrats.

Connect with Others

 Find government agencies on Facebook. Search for and visit at least one federal department's Facebook page and see what information members of the bureaucracy are posting. What are the responses to these posts? Consider whether you are affected by the regulations/rules discussed in the postings and what your response to them would be. Post a response if you feel strongly enough about the issue. Federal departments on Facebook include (but are not limited to) the Department of the Treasury, the Department of State, the Department of the Interior, and the U.S. Department of Commerce.

Find links to the sites listed above as well as related activities on wwnorton.com/studyspace.

Bureaucracy and Bureaucrats

■ **Define bureaucracy and describe the basic features of the executive branch (pp. 557–66)**

Bureaucracy is defined as the complex structure of offices, tasks, and rules that private and public organizations use to coordinate the work of their personnel. The federal executive branch is composed of cabinet departments, independent agencies, government corporations, and independent regulatory commissions. Although many people express concerns that the national government is too large, the federal service has actually grown very little over the last 35 years. Through their rule making and enforcement decisions, the federal service touches on many important aspects of daily life.

Key Terms

bureaucracy (p. 557)

implementation (p. 561)

merit system (p. 564)

department (p. 564)

independent agency (p. 565)

government corporation (p. 566)

Practice Quiz

1. Which of the following best describes the growth of the federal service in the past 35 years? *(p. 558)*
   a) rampant, exponential growth
   b) little growth at all
   c) decrease in the total number of federal employees
   d) vast, compared to the growth of the economy and the society
   e) the federal service has been eliminated in favor of more state government employees

2. What task must bureaucrats perform if Congress charges them with enforcing a law through explicit directions? *(p. 561)*
   a) constitutional revisions
   b) implementation
   c) interpretation
   d) lawmaking
   e) quasi-judicial decision making

3. State and local laws similar to the Civil Service Act of 1883 require that appointees to public office *(p. 564)*
   a) pledge an oath of loyalty to the United States.
   b) be qualified for the job to which they are appointed.
   c) not belong to any political party.
   d) cannot be fired for any reason.
   e) cannot serve more than four years.

4. Which of the following are *not* part of the executive branch? *(pp. 564–66)*
   a) Cabinet departments
   b) government corporations
   c) independent regulatory commissions
   d) agencies
   e) All of the above are parts of the executive branch.

5. Which of the following is an example of a government corporation? *(p. 566)*
   a) National Aeronautics and Space Administration
   b) United States Postal Service
   c) Social Security Administration
   d) National Science Foundation
   e) Federal Express

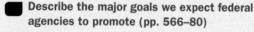
S **Practice Online**
"Who Are Americans?" exercise: *Who Are Bureaucrats?*

Promoting the Public Welfare

■ **Describe the major goals we expect federal agencies to promote (pp. 566–80)**

The federal bureaucracy promotes the public's welfare through a diverse set of services, products, and regulations. Some federal agencies, such as the Federal Reserve System and the Internal Revenue Service, promote the public's welfare by helping maintain a strong economy. Other federal agencies, such as the Department of Defense, the Department of Justice, and the Department of Homeland Security, promote the public's welfare by protecting the country against internal and external security threats.

Key Terms

regulatory agency (p. 567)

iron triangle (p. 568)

fiscal policy (p. 577)

Federal Reserve System (p. 577)

revenue agency (p. 578)

Practice Quiz

6. A stable relationship between a bureaucratic agency, a clientele group, and a legislative committee is called *(p. 568)*
   a) a standing committee.
   b) a conference committee.
   c) a cabinet.
   d) an issue network.
   e) an iron triangle.

7. Americans refer to government policy about banks, credit and currency as *(p. 577)*
   a) interstate commerce policy.
   b) deficit policy.
   c) fiscal policy.
   d) monetary policy.
   e) regulatory policy.

 Practice Online
Interactive simulation: *Director of an Executive Agency*

Can Bureaucracy Be Reformed?

Evaluate some of the ways politicians have tried to make the bureaucracy more efficient (pp. 580–88)

Many Americans express frustration with the performance of the federal bureaucracy. As a result, politicians have frequently explored various methods of making the federal bureaucracy more efficient. In general, politicians have attempted four strategies to promote bureaucratic reform: "reinventing" government, termination of programs, devolution, and privatization.

Key Terms

devolution (p. 582)

privatization (p. 583)

Practice Quiz

8. Which president instituted the bureaucratic reform of the National Performance Review? *(p. 581)*
   a) Richard Nixon
   b) Lyndon Johnson
   c) Jimmy Carter
   d) Bill Clinton
   e) George W. Bush

9. Devolution refers to *(p. 582)*
   a) the gradual decline in efficiency that always comes when government begins to implement a new program.
   b) removing all or part of a program from the public sector to the private sector.
   c) a policy of reducing or eliminating regulatory restraints on the conduct of individuals or private institutions.
   d) a policy to remove a program from one level of government by passing it down to a lower level of government.
   e) reducing the overall number of regulatory agencies in the federal bureaucracy.

10. Which of the following is *not* a way in which the bureaucracy might be reduced? *(pp. 581–88)*
    a) devolution
    b) termination
    c) privatization
    d) eminent domain
    e) all of the above

11. Which of the following best describes the changes in government contracting since 2000? *(p. 584)*
    a) Spending on government contracts has decreased while the number of government contracts subject to open competition has increased.
    b) Spending on government contracts has decreased while the number of government contracts subject to competition has decreased.
    c) Government contracting ended in 2000 as a result of the Supreme Court's decision in *Immigration and Naturalization Service v. Chadha*.
    d) Spending on government contracts has increased while the number of government contracts subject to open competition has decreased.
    e) Spending on government contracts has increased while the number of government contracts subject to open competition has increased.

 Practice Online
Video exercise: *World News Tonight—Wasteful Government Spending*

Managing the Bureaucracy

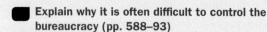 **Explain why it is often difficult to control the bureaucracy (pp. 588–93)**

The federal bureaucracy provides the expertise that is needed to implement the law but they can also become entrenched organizations that serve their own interests rather than the public will. While the emergence of the "managerial presidency" during the twentieth century has given the president more authority over the bureaucracy, presidents have sometimes used their managerial capacities to limit rather than promote democratic accountability. Congress can exert control over the federal bureaucracy by enacting specific legislation and engaging in vigorous oversight.

Key Terms

executive privilege (p. 591)

oversight (p. 591)

Practice Quiz

12. Which of the following is a power sometimes invoked by presidents to shield their administration's actions from public scrutiny? *(p. 591)*
    a) executive oversight
    b) executive privilege
    c) executive protection
    d) congressional oversight
    e) administrative adjudication

13. The concept of *oversight* refers to the effort made by *(p. 591)*
    a) Congress to make executive agencies accountable for their actions.
    b) the president to make executive agencies accountable for their actions.
    c) the president to make Congress accountable for its actions.
    d) the courts to make executive agencies responsible for their actions.
    e) the states to make the executive branch accountable for its actions.

14. Which of the following agencies were created by Congress to engage in research on problems taking place in or confronted by the executive branch? *(p. 592)*
    a) Government Accountability Office, Congressional Research Service, Congressional Budget Office
    b) Department of Justice, Department of the Interior, Department of the Treasury
    c) Congressional Oversight Organization, Bureau of Government Performance, National Performance Review Association
    d) Office of Management and Budget, Council of Economic Advisors, Oversight and Government Reform Agency
    e) Congressional Oversight Organization, Council of Economic Advisors, Department of Justice

For Further Reading

Aberbach, Joel D., and Mark A. Peterson, eds. *Institutions of American Democracy: The Executive Branch* (Institutions of American Democracy Series). New York: Oxford University Press, 2006.

Arnold, Peri E. *Making the Managerial Presidency: Comprehensive Organization Planning.* Princeton, NJ: Princeton University Press, 1986.

Gormley, William, and Stephen Balla. *Bureaucracy and Democracy: Accountability and Performance.* 3rd ed. Washington, DC: CQ Press, 2012.

Kettl, Donald F., and James W. Fesler. *The Politics of the Administrative Process.* 4th ed. Washington, DC: CQ Press, 2008.

Light, Paul C. *A Government Ill Executed: The Decline of the Federal Service and How to Reverse It.* Cambridge, MA: Harvard University Press, 2008.

Verkuil, Paul. *Outsourcing Sovereignty: Why Privatization of Government Functions Threatens Democracy and What We Can Do about It.* New York: Cambridge University Press, 2007.

Weiner, Tom. *Legacy of Ashes: The History of the CIA.* New York: Doubleday, 2007.

Wildavsky, Aaron. *The New Politics of the Budget Process.* 2nd ed. New York: HarperCollins, 1992.

Wilson, James Q. *Bureaucracy: What Government Agencies Do and Why They Do It.* New York: Basic Books, 1989.

Recommended Websites

Central Intelligence Agency
www.cia.gov

The Central Intelligence Agency (CIA) is one of several bureaucracies responsible for providing national security. A major problem facing this clandestine agency is how to provide security and meet the public's right to know what the government is doing. At the official website for the CIA, see what questions are often asked.

Department of Homeland Security
www.dhs.gov

The Department of Homeland Security was created after 9/11 to promote bureaucratic communication and domestic security. See what the department is doing to protect America from foreign threats.

Federal Emergency Management Agency
www.fema.org

In the aftermath of Hurricane Katrina, the Federal Emergency Management Agency (FEMA) became infamous for its role in the disaster relief efforts. View the disaster history of your state and see what FEMA is currently doing to prevent disasters and assist Americans in need.

Official U.S. Executive Branch Websites
www.loc.gov

This resource page at the Library of Congress website provides links to every federal department, independent agency, and regulatory commission in the federal bureaucracy.

Reason Foundation
reason.org/areas/topic/privatization

The Reason Foundation is dedicated to promoting libertarian principles and limited government. Their website includes studies and opinion pieces on a range of policy issues, including many related to the size and effectiveness of the federal bureaucracy.

Project on Government Oversight
www.pogo.org

The Project on Government Oversight is an independent, nonprofit organization that seeks to make government more accountable by investigating corruption and misconduct. Originally set up to focus on the military, this organization now examines all types of government bureaucracies.

U.S. Agency for International Development
www.usaid.gov

In 1961 Congress created the U.S. Agency for International Development (USAID) to provide economic and social development assistance to foreign countries. Often criticized for promoting American values and foreign policy objectives, USAID is currently involved in numerous global issues.

...me Court may seem like
...nd mysterious institution
...isions affect ordinary
... in countless ways. From
... to immigration to free
... campus, the Court's
... a direct impact on
...fe.

The Federal Courts

15

WHAT GOVERNMENT DOES AND WHY IT MATTERS Many Americans may think of the Supreme Court as a distant and mysterious institution whose decisions affect only giant corporations, wealthy individuals, and powerful politicians. They may see no direct relationship between the black-robed justices and the everyday lives of ordinary people. Occasionally, however, the Supreme Court is asked to hear questions that touch students' lives in a very direct way. One recent example, from 2007, is the case of *Morse v. Frederick*.[1] This case dealt with the policies of Juneau-Douglas High School in Juneau, Alaska. In 2002 the Olympic torch relay passed through Juneau on its way to Salt Lake City for the opening of the Winter Olympics. As the torch passed Juneau-Douglas High, a senior, Joseph Frederick, unfurled a banner that read, "Bong Hits 4 Jesus." The school's principal promptly suspended Frederick, who then brought suit for reinstatement, alleging that his right to freedom of speech had been violated.[2]

Like most of America's public schools, Juneau-Douglas High prohibits on school grounds any assemblies or expressions that advocate illegal drug use. Schools say that some federal aid is contingent on this policy. Civil libertarians see such policies as restricting students' right to free speech—a right that has been recognized by the Supreme Court since a 1969 case in which it ruled that an Iowa public school could not prohibit students from wearing antiwar armbands. Unfortunately for Joseph Frederick, today's Supreme Court has a more conservative cast than it did in 1969. Speaking for the Court's majority, Chief Justice John G. Roberts said that the First Amendment did not require schools to permit students to advocate illegal drug use. This decision affected not only Joseph Frederick, but

601

also millions of other students whose views might be seen as inappropriate by school administrators. Far from being a remote institution, the Supreme Court turns out to have reached into every public school in America. The same could be said for a 2012 decision involving a religious school in Michigan that fired a teacher for actions that, in the school's view, violated church doctrine. The teacher brought a federal employment discrimination suit against the school, claiming that she had been fired in retaliation for filing an employment discrimination claim against the school. In a unanimous decision, the Supreme Court asserted what it called a "ministerial exception," allowing religious institutions wide latitude in their personnel decisions.[3]

Every year, nearly 25 million cases are tried in American courts, and one American in every nine is directly involved in litigation. Cases can arise from disputes between citizens, from efforts by government agencies to punish wrongdoing, or from citizens' efforts to prove that their rights have been infringed on as a result of government action—or inaction. Many critics of the U.S. legal system assert that Americans have become too litigious (ready to use the courts for all purposes). But the heavy use that Americans make of the courts is also an indication of the extent of conflict in American society. And given the existence of social conflict, it is far better that Americans seek to settle their differences through the courts than resort to violence or otherwise take matters into their own hands. The framers of the American Constitution called the Supreme Court the "least dangerous branch" of American government. Today, though, it is not unusual to hear the Court described as an all-powerful "imperial judiciary." Before we can understand this transformation and its consequences, we must look in some detail at America's judicial process.

chaptergoals

- Identify the general types of cases and types of courts in our legal system (pages 603–8)

- Describe the different levels of federal courts and their functions (pages 608–14)

- Explain how the Supreme Court exercises the power of judicial review (pages 614–31)

- Consider the political influences on the courts (pages 632–34)

The Legal System

Identify the general types of cases and types of courts in our legal system

Originally, a "court" was the place where a sovereign ruled—where the king or queen governed. Settling disputes between citizens was part of governing. In modern democracies, courts and judges have taken over the power to settle conflicts by hearing the facts on both sides and deciding which side possesses the greater merit. But since judges are not kings, they must have a basis for their authority. That basis in the United States is the Constitution and the law. Courts decide cases by hearing the facts on both sides of a quarrel and applying the relevant law or principle to the facts. This can be a sensitive matter because courts have been given the authority to settle disputes between not only citizens but also citizens and the government itself, where the courts are obliged to maintain the same neutrality and impartiality as they do in disputes involving two citizens. This is the essence of the "rule of law": that "the state" and its officials must be judged by the same laws as the citizenry.

Cases and the Law

Court cases in the United States proceed under two broad categories of law: criminal law and civil law, each with myriad subdivisions.

Cases of **criminal law** are those in which the government charges an individual with violating a statute that has been enacted to protect public health, safety, morals, or welfare. In criminal cases, the government is always the **plaintiff** (the party that brings charges) and alleges that a criminal violation has been committed by a named **defendant**. Most criminal cases arise in state and municipal courts and involve matters ranging from traffic offenses to robbery and murder. Although the great bulk of criminal law is still a state matter, a large and growing body of federal criminal law deals with matters ranging from tax evasion and mail fraud to acts of

criminal law the branch of law that regulates the conduct of individuals, defines crimes, and specifies punishment for criminal acts

plaintiff the individual or organization that brings a complaint in court

defendant the one against whom a complaint is brought in a criminal or civil case

In criminal cases, the government charges an individual with violating a statute protecting health, safety, morals, or welfare. Most such cases arise in state and municipal courts. Here, an Illinois county court hears testimony in a murder case.

terrorism and the sale of narcotics. Defendants found guilty of criminal violations may be fined or sent to prison.

Cases of **civil law** involve disputes among individuals, groups, corporations, and other private entities, or between such litigants and the government in which no criminal violation is charged. Unlike in criminal cases, the losers in civil cases cannot be fined or sent to prison, although they may be required to pay monetary damages for their actions. In a civil case, the one who brings a complaint is the plaintiff and the one against whom the complaint is brought is the defendant. The two most common types of civil cases involve contracts and torts. In a typical contract case, an individual or corporation charges that it has suffered because of another's violation of a specific agreement between the two. For example, the Smith Manufacturing Corporation may charge that Jones Distributors failed to honor an agreement to deliver raw materials at a specified time, causing Smith to lose business. Smith asks the court to order Jones to compensate it for the damage it allegedly suffered. In a typical tort case, one individual charges that he or she has been injured by another's negligence or malfeasance. Medical malpractice suits are one example of tort cases. Another important area of civil law is administrative law, which involves disputes over the jurisdiction, procedures, or authority of administrative agencies. A plaintiff may assert, for example, that an agency did not follow proper procedures when issuing new rules and regulations. A court will then examine the agency's conduct in light of the Administrative Procedure Act, the legislation that governs agency rule making.

In deciding cases, courts apply statutes (laws) and legal **precedents** (prior decisions). State and federal statutes, for example, often govern the conditions under which contracts are and are not legally binding. Jones Distributors might argue that it was not obliged to fulfill its contract with the Smith Manufacturing Corporation because actions by Smith, such as the failure to make promised payments, constituted fraud under state law. Precedents established in previous cases also guide courts' decisions in new cases. Attorneys for a physician being sued for malpractice might search for prior instances in which courts ruled that actions similar to those of their client did not constitute negligence. Such precedents are applied under the doctrine of **stare decisis**, a Latin phrase meaning "let the decision stand."

If a case involves the actions of the federal government or a state government, a court may also be asked to examine whether the government's conduct was consistent with the Constitution. In a criminal case, for example, defendants might assert that their constitutional rights were violated when the police searched their property. Similarly, in a civil case involving federal or state restrictions on land development, plaintiffs might assert that government actions violated the Fifth Amendment's prohibition against taking private property without just compensation. Thus, both civil and criminal cases may raise questions of constitutional law.

Types of Courts

In the United States, systems of courts have been established both by the federal government and by the governments of the individual states. Both systems have several levels, as shown in Figure 15.1. More than 99 percent of all court cases in the United States are heard in state courts. The overwhelming majority of criminal cases, for example, involve violations of state laws prohibiting such actions as murder, robbery, fraud, theft, and assault. If such a case is brought to trial, it will be heard in a state **trial court**, in front of a judge and sometimes a jury, who will determine whether the defendant violated state law. If the defendant is convicted, he or

civil law the branch of law that deals with disputes that do not involve criminal penalties

precedent prior case whose principles are used by judges as the basis for their decision in a present case

stare decisis literally, "let the decision stand." The doctrine that a previous decision by a court applies as a precedent in similar cases until that decision is overruled

trial court the first court to hear a criminal or civil case

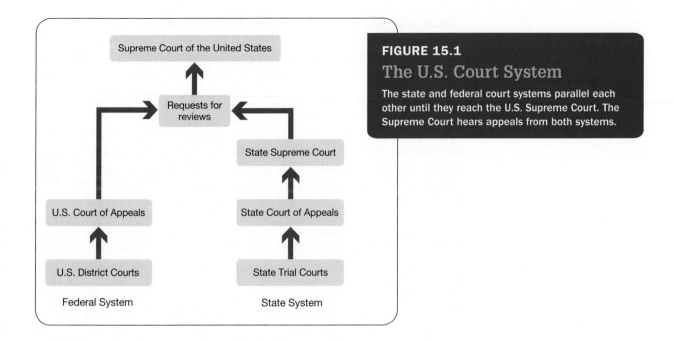

FIGURE 15.1

The U.S. Court System

The state and federal court systems parallel each other until they reach the U.S. Supreme Court. The Supreme Court hears appeals from both systems.

she may appeal the conviction to a higher court, such as a state **court of appeals**, and from there to a court of last resort, usually called the state's **supreme court**.

Similarly, in civil cases, most litigation is brought in the courts established by the state in which the activity in question took place. For example, a patient bringing suit against a physician for malpractice would file the suit in the appropriate court in the state where the alleged malpractice occurred. The judge hearing the case would apply state law and state precedent to the matter at hand. There is some variation in court structure among the 50 states. Several states lack an intermediate appellate level, and the court of last resort is the only appellate court. Two states, Oklahoma and Texas, have established two state courts of last resort, one for civil appeals and the other for criminal appeals. It should be noted that in both criminal and civil matters, most cases are settled before trial through negotiated agreements between the parties. In criminal cases these agreements are called **plea bargains**.

Although each state has its own set of laws, these laws have much in common from state to state. Murder and robbery, of course, are illegal in all states, although the range of possible punishments varies from state to state. Some states, for example, provide for capital punishment (the death penalty) for murder and other serious offenses; other states do not. However, some acts that are criminal offenses in one state may be legal in another state. Prostitution, for example, is legal in some Nevada counties, although it is outlawed in all other states. Considerable similarity among the states is also found in the realm of civil law. In the case of contract law, most states have adopted the Uniform Commercial Code in order to reduce interstate differences. In areas such as family law, however, which covers such matters as divorce and child custody arrangements, state laws vary greatly.

Cases are heard in the federal courts if they involve federal laws, treaties with other nations, or the U.S. Constitution; these areas are the official **jurisdiction** of the federal courts. In addition, any case in which the U.S. government is a party is heard in the federal courts. If, for example, an individual is charged with violating

court of appeals a court that hears appeals of trial court decisions

supreme court the highest court in a particular state or in the United States. This court primarily serves an appellate function

plea bargain a negotiated agreement in a criminal case in which a defendant agrees to plead guilty in return for the state's agreement to reduce the severity of the criminal charge or prison sentence the defendant is facing

jurisdiction the sphere of a court's power and authority

a federal criminal statute, such as evading the payment of income taxes, charges are brought before a federal judge by a federal prosecutor. Civil cases involving the citizens of more than one state and in which more than $75,000 is at stake may be heard in either the federal or the state courts, usually depending on the preference of the plaintiff.

But even if a matter belongs in federal court, how do we know which federal court should exercise jurisdiction over the case? The answer to this seemingly simple question is somewhat complex. The jurisdiction of each federal court is derived from the U.S. Constitution and federal statutes. Article III of the Constitution gives the Supreme Court appellate jurisdiction in all federal cases and original jurisdiction in cases involving foreign ambassadors and issues in which a state is a party. Article III assigns original jurisdiction in all other federal cases to the lower courts that Congress was authorized to establish. Over the years, as Congress enacted statutes creating the federal judicial system, it specified the jurisdiction of each type of court it established. For the most part, Congress has assigned jurisdictions on the basis of geography. The nation is currently, by statute, divided into 94 judicial districts, including one court for each of three U.S. territories. Each of the 94 U.S. district courts exercises jurisdiction over federal cases arising within its territorial domain. The judicial districts are, in turn, organized into 11 regional circuits and the D.C. circuit (see Figure 15.2). Each circuit court exercises appellate jurisdiction over cases heard by the district courts within its region.

Geography, however, is not the only basis for federal court jurisdiction. Congress has also established several specialized courts that have nationwide original jurisdiction in certain types of cases. These include the U.S. Court of International Trade, created to deal with trade and customs issues, and the U.S. Court of Federal Claims, which handles damage suits against the United States. Congress has also established a court with nationwide appellate jurisdiction, the U.S. Court of Appeals for the Federal Circuit, which hears appeals involving patent law and those arising from the decisions of the trade and claims courts. Other federal courts assigned specialized jurisdictions by Congress include the U.S. Court of Appeals for Veterans Claims, which exercises exclusive jurisdiction over cases involving veterans' claims, and the U.S. Court of Military Appeals, which deals with questions of law arising from trials by court-martial.

With the exception of the claims court and the Court of Appeals for the Federal Circuit, these specialized courts were created by Congress on the basis of the powers the legislature exercises under Article I, rather than Article III, of the Constitution. Article III is designed to protect judges from political pressure by granting them life tenure and prohibiting reduction of their salaries while they serve. The judges of Article I courts, by contrast, are appointed by the president for fixed terms of 15 years and are not protected by the Constitution from salary reduction. As a result, these "legislative courts" are generally viewed as less independent than the courts established under Article III of the Constitution. The three territorial courts (for Guam, the U.S. Virgin Islands, and Northern Mariana Islands) were also established under the provisions in Article I, and their judges are appointed for 10-year terms.

The appellate jurisdiction of the federal courts also extends to cases originating in the state courts. In both civil and criminal cases, a decision of the highest state court can be appealed to the U.S. Supreme Court by raising a federal issue. A defendant who appeals a lower-court decision in federal court might assert, for example, that they were denied the right to counsel or were otherwise deprived of

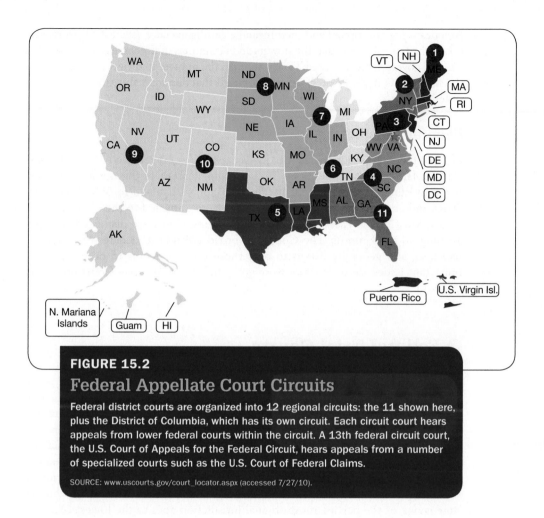

FIGURE 15.2

Federal Appellate Court Circuits

Federal district courts are organized into 12 regional circuits: the 11 shown here, plus the District of Columbia, which has its own circuit. Each circuit court hears appeals from lower federal courts within the circuit. A 13th federal circuit court, the U.S. Court of Appeals for the Federal Circuit, hears appeals from a number of specialized courts such as the U.S. Court of Federal Claims.

SOURCE: www.uscourts.gov/court_locator.aspx (accessed 7/27/10).

the **due process of law** guaranteed by the federal Constitution, or they might assert that important issues of federal law were at stake in the case. The U.S. Supreme Court is not obligated to accept such appeals, and will do so only if it believes that the matter has considerable national significance. In addition, in criminal cases, defendants who have been convicted in a state court may request a **writ of *habeas corpus*** from a federal district court. Sometimes known as the "Great Writ," *habeas corpus* is a court order to the authorities to release a prisoner deemed to be held in violation of his or her legal rights. In 1867 its distrust of southern courts led Congress to authorize federal district judges to issue such writs to prisoners who they believed had been deprived of constitutional rights in state court. Generally speaking, state defendants seeking a federal writ of *habeas corpus* must show that they have exhausted all available state remedies and must raise issues not previously raised in their state appeals. Federal courts of appeals and, ultimately, the U.S. Supreme Court have appellate jurisdiction for federal district court *habeas* decisions.

Although the federal courts hear only a small fraction of all the civil and criminal cases decided each year in the United States, their decisions are extremely important. It is in the federal courts that the Constitution and federal laws that govern all

due process of law the right of every citizen against arbitrary action by national or state governments

writ of *habeas corpus* a court order that the individual in custody be brought into court and shown the cause for detention. *Habeas corpus* is guaranteed by the Constitution and can be suspended only in cases of rebellion or invasion

Americans are interpreted and their meaning and significance established. Moreover, it is in the federal courts that the powers and limitations of the increasingly powerful national government are tested. Finally, through their power to review the decisions of the state courts, it is ultimately the federal courts that dominate the American judicial system.

Federal Jurisdiction

In 2010 federal district courts (the lowest federal level) received 363,428 cases. Though large, this number is approximately 1 percent of the number of cases heard by state courts. The federal courts of appeal listened to 56,097 cases in 2010, and about 15 percent of the verdicts were appealed to the U.S. Supreme Court. Most of the cases filed with the Supreme Court are dismissed without a ruling on their merits. The Court has broad latitude to decide what cases it will hear, and generally listens to only those cases it deems to raise the most important issues. Only 76 cases were given full-dress Supreme Court review in 2010–11.[4]

● Federal Trial Courts

Describe the different levels of federal courts and their functions

Most of the cases of original federal jurisdiction are handled by the federal district courts. Courts of **original jurisdiction** are the courts that are responsible for discovering the facts in a controversy and creating the record on which a judgment is based. Although the Constitution gives the Supreme Court original jurisdiction in several types of cases, such as those affecting ambassadors and those in which a state is one of the parties, most original jurisdiction goes to the lowest courts— the trial courts. (In courts that have appellate jurisdiction, judges receive cases after the factual record is established by the trial court. Ordinarily, new facts cannot be presented before appellate courts.)

There are 89 district courts in the 50 states, plus one in the District of Columbia and one in Puerto Rico, and three territorial courts. These courts are staffed by 679 federal district judges. District judges are assigned to district courts according to the workload; the busiest of these courts may have as many as 28 judges. Only one judge is assigned to each case, except where statutes provide for three-judge courts to deal with special issues. The routines and procedures of the federal district courts are essentially the same as those of the lower state courts, except that federal procedural requirements tend to be stricter. States, for example, do not have to provide a grand jury, a 12-member trial jury, or a unanimous jury verdict. Federal courts must provide all these things.

original jurisdiction the authority to initially consider a case. Distinguished from appellate jurisdiction, which is the authority to hear appeals from a lower court's decision.

Federal Appellate Courts

Roughly 20 percent of all lower-court cases, along with appeals from some federal agency decisions, are subsequently reviewed by federal appeals courts. As

President George W. Bush nominated John Roberts (left photo, center) first as a Supreme Court justice and then as chief justice after the death of former chief justice William Rehnquist. Although Roberts's nomination was approved fairly easily in the Senate, President Bush's next nominee, Samuel Alito (right), was subjected to harsher questioning before being confirmed. Democratic senators were worried that Alito, who was replacing a more moderate justice, would shift the overall balance of the Court toward the right.

noted, the country is divided geographically into 11 regional circuits and the D.C. circuit, each of which has a U.S. Court of Appeals. Every state, the District of Columbia, and each of the territories is assigned to the circuit in the continental United States that is closest to it. A 13th appellate court, the U.S. Court of Appeals for the Federal Circuit, has a subject matter, rather than a geographical, jurisdiction.

Except for cases selected for review by the Supreme Court, decisions made by the appeals courts are final. Because of this finality, certain safeguards have been built into the system. The most important is the provision of more than one judge for every appeals case. Each court of appeals has from 6 to 28 permanent judgeships, depending on the workload of the circuit. Although normally three judges hear appealed cases, in some instances a larger number of judges sits together en banc.

Another safeguard is provided by the assignment of a Supreme Court justice as the circuit justice for each of the 12 circuits. The circuit justice deals with requests for special action by the Supreme Court. The most frequent and best-known action of circuit justices is that of reviewing requests for stays of execution when the full Court is unable to do so—primarily during the summer, when the Court is in recess.

The Supreme Court

The Supreme Court is America's highest court. Article III of the Constitution vests "the judicial power of the United States" in the Supreme Court, and this court is supreme in fact as well as form. The Supreme Court is the only federal court established by the Constitution. The lower federal courts are created by statute and can be restructured or, presumably, even abolished by the Congress. The Supreme Court is made up of the chief justice of the United States and eight associate justices. The **chief justice** presides over the Court's public sessions and

chief justice justice on the Supreme Court who presides over the Court's public sessions and whose official title is chief justice of the United States

conferences. In the Court's actual deliberations and decisions, however, the chief justice has no more authority than his or her colleagues. Each justice casts one vote. The chief justice, though, is always the first to speak and the last to vote when the justices deliberate. In addition, if the chief justice has voted with the majority, he or she decides which of the justices will write the formal opinion for the court. The character of the opinion can be an important means of influencing the evolution of the law beyond the mere affirmation or denial of the appeal on hand. To some extent, the influence of the chief justice is a function of his or her own leadership ability. Some chief justices, such as the late Earl Warren, have been able to lead the court in a new direction. In other instances, forceful associate justices, such as the late Felix Frankfurter, are the dominant figures on the Court.

The Constitution does not specify the number of justices who should sit on the Supreme Court; Congress has the authority to change the Court's size. In the early nineteenth century, there were six Supreme Court justices; later there were seven. Congress set the number of justices at nine in 1869, and the Court has remained that size ever since. In 1937, President Franklin Delano Roosevelt, infuriated by several Supreme Court decisions that struck down New Deal programs, asked Congress to enlarge the Court so that he could add a few sympathetic justices to the bench. Although Congress balked at Roosevelt's "court packing" plan, the Court gave in to FDR's pressure and began to take a more favorable view of his policy initiatives. The president, in turn, dropped his efforts to enlarge the Court.

How Judges Are Appointed

Federal judges are appointed by the president and confirmed by the Senate. They are generally selected from among the more prominent or politically active members of the legal profession. Many federal judges previously served as state court judges or state or local prosecutors. Before the president makes a formal nomination, however, the senators from the candidate's own state must indicate that they

In 2010, Barack Obama nominated former solicitor general Elena Kagan to the Supreme Court, bringing the number of women justices to three. Kagan's nomination was approved by the Senate, and she was sworn in by Chief Justice John Roberts (right) in August 2010.

Who Are Federal Judges?

factor among many that presidents may take into account when selecting judicial nominees is diversity. The number upreme Court justices is relatively small, so it is easy to count the number of African Americans who have served as reme Court justices (2), female justices (4), and Hispanic justices (1). How diverse is the rest of the federal judiciary? first section below shows the racial, ethnic, and gender composition of the lower federal courts.

deral Judges in 2009, by Race and Gender

 = 10 federal judges

e men 860

African American men 84

Hispanic men 58

e women 225

African American **women** 40

Hispanic women 26

pointments to Federal Courts, by Administration

- White men
- White women
- African American men
- African American women
- Hispanic men
- Hispanic women
- Asian American men
- Asian American women

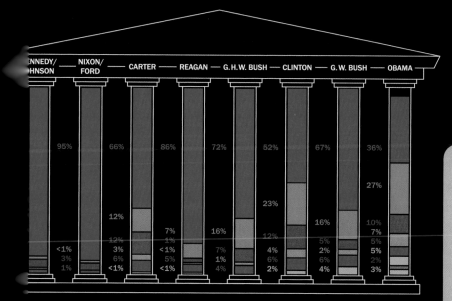

	NNEDY/ OHNSON	NIXON/ FORD	CARTER	REAGAN	G. H. W. BUSH	CLINTON	G. W. BUSH	OBAMA
	95%	66%	86%	72%	52%	67%	36%	
							27%	
		12%			23%			
			7%	16%		16%	10%	
		12%	1%		12%		7%	
	<1%	3%	<1%	7%	4%	5%	5%	
	3%	6%	5%	1%	6%	2%	2%	
	1%		<1%	<1%	4%	2%	6%	4%	3%

for critical analysis

1. Would you describe the federal judiciary as diverse? Does racial, ethnic, and gender diversity of federal judges matter? Why or why not?

2. What similarities and differences do you notice among the judicial appointments of the presidents shown? What might account for the differences in terms of the diversity of their appointees?

CE: Russell Wheeler, "The Changing Face of the Federal Judiciary" (Washington, DC: Brookings Institution, 2009). n first section above are from August 2009.

support the nominee. This is an informal but seldom violated practice called **senatorial courtesy**. If one or both senators from a prospective nominee's home state belong to the president's political party, the president will almost invariably consult them and secure their blessing for the nomination. Because the president's party in the Senate will rarely support a nominee opposed by a home-state senator from its ranks, this arrangement gives these senators virtual veto power over appointments to the federal bench in their own states. Senators also see nominations to the judiciary as a way to reward important allies and contributors in their states. If the state has no senator from the president's party, the governor or members of the state's House delegation may make suggestions. The practice of "courtesy" generally does not apply to Supreme Court appointments, only to district and circuit court nominations.

Federal appeals court nominations follow much the same pattern. Since appeals court judges preside over jurisdictions that include several states, however, senators do not have so strong a role in proposing potential candidates. Instead, potential appeals court candidates are generally suggested to the president by the Justice Department or by important members of the administration. The senators from the nominee's own state are still consulted before the president will formally act.

There are no formal qualifications for service as a federal judge. In general, presidents endeavor to appoint judges who possess legal experience and good character and whose partisan and ideological views are similar to their own. Once the president has formally nominated an individual, the nominee must be considered by the Senate Judiciary Committee and confirmed by a majority vote in the full Senate. In recent years, a good deal of partisan conflict has surrounded judicial appointments. Senate Democrats have sought to prevent Republican presidents from appointing conservative judges while Senate Republicans have worked to prevent Democratic presidents from appointing liberal judges. During the early months of the Obama administration, Republicans were able to slow the judicial appointment process through various procedural maneuvers so that only three of the president's 23 nominations for federal judgeships were confirmed by the Senate.[5] Some of Obama's allies urged the president to take a more aggressive stance, or risk allowing Republicans to block what had been considered a key Democratic priority, and by the beginning of his fourth year in office, the president had secured the appointment of 97 new district court judges and 25 new appeals court judges.[6]

If political factors play an important role in the selection of district and appellate court judges, they are decisive when it comes to Supreme Court appointments.

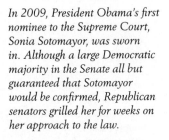

In 2009, President Obama's first nominee to the Supreme Court, Sonia Sotomayor, was sworn in. Although a large Democratic majority in the Senate all but guaranteed that Sotomayor would be confirmed, Republican senators grilled her for weeks on her approach to the law.

TABLE 15.1

Supreme Court Justices, 2012 (in Order of Seniority)

NAME	YEAR OF BIRTH	PRIOR EXPERIENCE	APPOINTED BY	YEAR OF APPOINTMENT
Antonin Scalia	1936	Law professor, federal judge	Reagan	1986
Anthony Kennedy	1936	Federal judge	Reagan	1988
Clarence Thomas	1948	Federal judge	G. H. W. Bush	1991
Ruth Bader Ginsburg	1933	Federal judge	Clinton	1993
Stephen Breyer	1938	Federal judge	Clinton	1994
John Roberts Jr. (*Chief Justice*)	1955	Federal judge	G. W. Bush	2005
Samuel Alito	1950	Federal judge	G. W. Bush	2006
Sonia Sotomayor	1954	Federal judge	Obama	2009
Elena Kagan	1960	Solicitor general	Obama	2010

Because the high court has so much influence over American law and politics, virtually all presidents have made an effort to select justices who share their political philosophies.

It is important to note that five of the nine current justices as of 2012 were appointed by Republican presidents (Table 15.1). This conservative majority, consisting of Chief Justice Roberts and Justices Alito, Kennedy, Scalia, and Thomas, has propelled the Court in a more conservative direction in a variety of areas. In 2009 and 2010, for example, in a series of 5–4 decisions, the Court overturned limits on corporate campaign spending, ruled that the Federal Communications Commission was justified in penalizing the use of expletives on the airwaves, and blocked a suit against former attorney general John Ashcroft by a terrorist suspect alleging that the suspect had been mistreated in prison. In 2011 and 2012, however, Chief Justice Roberts responded to charges that the Court's decisions were political rather than judicial by joining the liberal bloc in two important cases. The first was the Court's decision to invalidate portions of an Arizona law designed to identify and apprehend illegal aliens.[7] The second was the Court's 5–4 decision to uphold the Affordable Care Act, President Obama's major legislative achievement. Critics had charged that the Act's requirement that all Americans purchase health insurance was unconstitutional. Roberts wrote that this requirement was just another federal tax.[8]

In recent decades, Supreme Court nominations have come to involve intense partisan struggle. Typically, after the president has named a nominee, interest groups opposed to the nomination mobilize opposition in the media, among the public, and in the Senate. When President George H. W. Bush proposed the conservative judge Clarence Thomas for the Court, for example, liberal groups launched a campaign to discredit Thomas. After extensive research into his background, opponents of the nomination were able to produce evidence suggesting that Thomas had sexually harassed a former subordinate, Anita Hill. Thomas denied the charge.

After contentious Senate Judiciary Committee hearings, highlighted by testimony from both Thomas and Hill, Thomas narrowly won confirmation.

Likewise, conservative interest groups carefully scrutinized Bill Clinton's somewhat more liberal nominees, hoping to find information about them that would sabotage their appointments. During his two opportunities to name Supreme Court justices, Clinton was compelled to drop several potential appointees because of information unearthed by political opponents.

In 2009, when President Obama nominated federal Judge Sonia Sotomayor to replace retiring justice David Souter, conservatives denounced Sotomayor as a "reverse racist" because of her support for affirmative action. Many Republican senators, however, were reluctant to oppose a Hispanic nominee. For several years the GOP has made efforts to attract America's rapidly growing Hispanic population. Republicans feared that opposing Sotomayor would undermine these efforts.[9] In 2010, Republicans severely criticized Obama's nomination of Elena Kagan, solicitor general and former Harvard law dean, to replace retiring justice John Paul Stevens. Kagan was, nevertheless, confirmed by the Senate.

● The Power of the Supreme Court: Judicial Review

judicial review the power of the courts to review and, if necessary, declare actions of the legislative and executive branches invalid or unconstitutional. The Supreme Court asserted this power in *Marbury v. Madison*.

> **Explain how the Supreme Court exercises the power of judicial review**

The term **judicial review** refers to the power of the judiciary to examine and, if necessary, invalidate actions undertaken by the legislative and executive branches if it finds them unconstitutional. The term is sometimes used also to describe the scrutiny that appellate courts give to the actions of trial courts, but, strictly speaking, this is an improper use. A higher court's examination of a lower court's decisions might be called "appellate review," but it is not judicial review.

Judicial Review of Acts of Congress

Because the Constitution does not give the Supreme Court the power of judicial review over congressional enactments, the Court's exercise of it is something of a usurpation. It is not known whether the framers of the Constitution opposed judicial review, but "if they intended to provide for it in the Constitution, they did so in a most obscure fashion."[10] Disputes over the intentions of the framers were settled in 1803 in the case of *Marbury v. Madison*.[11] This case arose after Thomas Jefferson replaced John Adams in the White House. Jefferson's secretary of state, James Madison, refused to deliver an official commission to William Marbury, who had been appointed to a minor office by Adams just before he left the presidency. Marbury petitioned the Supreme Court to order Madison to deliver the commission. Jefferson and his followers did not believe that the Court had the power to undertake such an action and might have resisted the order. Chief Justice John Marshall was determined to assert the power of the judiciary but knew he must avoid a direct confrontation with the president. Accordingly, Marshall turned down Marbury's petition but gave as his reason the unconstitutionality of the legislation upon which Marbury had based his claim. Thus, Marshall asserted the power of judicial review but did so in a way that would not provoke a battle with Jefferson.

In Marbury v. Madison (1803), Chief Justice John Marshall established the Supreme Court's power to rule on the constitutionality of federal and state laws. This power makes the Court a lawmaking body.

The Supreme Court's decision in this case established the power of judicial review. The Court said:

> It is emphatically the province and duty of the Judicial Department [the judicial branch] to say what the law is. Those who apply the rule to particular cases must, of necessity, expound and interpret that rule. If two laws conflict with each other, the Courts must decide on the operation of each. . . . So, if a law [e.g., a statute or treaty] be in opposition to the Constitution, if both the law and the Constitution apply to a particular case, so that the Court must either decide that case conformably to the law, disregarding the Constitution, or conformably to the Constitution, disregarding the law, the Court must determine which of these conflicting rules governs the case. This is of the very essence of judicial duty.

Although Congress and the president have often been at odds with the Court, the Court's legal power to review acts of Congress has not been seriously questioned since 1803. One reason for this is that the Supreme Court makes a self-conscious effort to give acts of Congress an interpretation that will make them constitutional. In more than two centuries, the Court has concluded that only some 160 acts of Congress directly violate the Constitution. For example, in 2007 and 2010 the high court struck down key portions of the Bipartisan Campaign Reform Act, through which Congress had sought to regulate spending in political campaigns.[12] The Court found that provisions of the act limiting political advertising violated the First Amendment.

supremacy clause Article VI of the Constitution, which states that laws passed by the national government and all treaties are the supreme law of the land and superior to all laws adopted by any state or any subdivision

Judicial Review of State Actions

The power of the Supreme Court to review state legislation or other state action and to determine its constitutionality is neither granted by the Constitution nor inherent in the federal system. But the logic of the **supremacy clause** of Article VI of the Constitution, which declares the Constitution itself and laws made under its

In 2011 the Supreme Court struck down a California law that regulated the sale of violent video games to children, saying it violated the First Amendment. California state senator Leland Yee, who proposed the ban, held up some of the games the law would have regulated.

authority to be the supreme law of the land, is very strong. Furthermore, in the Judiciary Act of 1789, Congress conferred on the Supreme Court the power to reverse state constitutions and laws whenever they are clearly in conflict with the U.S. Constitution, federal laws, or treaties.[13] This power gives the Supreme Court appellate jurisdiction over all the millions of cases that American courts handle each year.

The supremacy clause of the Constitution not only established the federal Constitution, statutes, and treaties as the "supreme Law of the Land," but also provided that "the Judges in every State shall be bound thereby, any Thing in the Constitution or Laws of the State to the Contrary notwithstanding." Under this authority, the Supreme Court has frequently overturned state constitutional provisions or statutes and state court decisions it deems to contravene rights or privileges guaranteed under the federal Constitution or federal statutes.

The civil rights arena abounds with examples of state laws that the Supreme Court has overturned because the statutes violated guarantees of due process and equal protection contained in the Fourteenth Amendment to the Constitution. For example, in the 1954 case of *Brown v. Board of Education*, the Court overturned statutes from Kansas, South Carolina, Virginia, and Delaware that either required or permitted segregated public schools, ruling that such statutes denied black school-children equal protection under the law.[14] In 1967 the Court's ruling in *Loving v. Virginia* invalidated a Virginia statute prohibiting interracial marriages.[15]

State statutes in other areas of law are equally subject to challenge. In *Griswold v. Connecticut*, the Court invalidated a Connecticut statute prohibiting the general distribution of contraceptives to married couples on the basis that the statute violated the couples' rights to marital privacy.[16] In *Brandenburg v. Ohio*, the Court overturned an Ohio statute forbidding any person to urge criminal acts as a means of inducing political reform or to join any association that advocated such activities. The Court found that the statute punished "mere advocacy" and therefore violated the free speech provisions of the Constitution.[17]

One realm in which the Court constantly monitors state conduct is the area of law enforcement. As we saw in Chapter 4, over the years, the Supreme Court has developed a number of principles regulating police conduct to ensure that the police do not violate constitutional liberties. These principles, however, must often be updated to keep pace with changes in technology. In a 2012 decision, the Supreme Court found that police use of a GPS tracker—a device invented more than two centuries after the adoption of the Bill of Rights—constituted a "search" as defined by the Fourth Amendment. In the case of *United States v. Jones*, the Court ruled that the police were prohibited from attaching a global-positioning device to a car belonging to a suspected drug dealer without first obtaining a valid warrant.[18]

for critical analysis

During his 2005 confirmation hearings, senators asked Chief Justice Roberts why the Supreme Court was more willing to declare acts of Congress unconstitutional than it was to confront the president on the constitutionality of his actions. What reasons might you identify?

Judicial Review of Federal Agency Actions

Although Congress makes the law, as we saw in Chapters 12 and 14, it can hardly administer the thousands of programs it has enacted and must therefore delegate power to the president and to a huge bureaucracy to achieve its purposes. For example, if Congress wishes to improve air quality, it cannot possibly anticipate all the conditions and circumstances that may arise with respect to that general goal. Inevitably, Congress must delegate to the executive substantial discretionary power to make judgments about the best ways to bring about improved air quality in the face of changing circumstances. Thus, over the years, almost any congressional program will result in thousands upon thousands of pages of administrative regulations developed by executive agencies nominally seeking to implement the will of the Congress.

Delegation of power to the executive poses a number of problems for Congress and the federal courts. If Congress delegates broad authority to the president, it risks seeing its goals subordinated to and subverted by those of the executive branch.[19] If Congress attempts to limit executive discretion by enacting precise rules and standards to govern the conduct of the president and the executive branch, it risks writing laws that do not conform to real-world conditions and that are too rigid to be adapted to changing circumstances.[20]

Over the past two centuries, the issue of delegation of power has led to a number of court decisions regarding the scope of the delegation. Courts have also been called on to decide whether the regulations adopted by federal agencies are consistent with Congress's express or implied intent.

As presidential power expanded during the New Deal era, one indication of increased congressional subordination to the executive was the enactment of laws that contained few, if any, principles limiting executive discretion. Congress enacted legislation, often at the president's behest, that gave the executive virtually unfettered authority to address a particular concern. For example, the Emergency Price Control Act of 1942 authorized the executive to set "fair and equitable" prices without spelling out what those terms might mean.[21] Although the Court initially challenged these delegations of power to the president during the New Deal, it retreated from its position when faced with a confrontation with President Franklin Delano Roosevelt. Perhaps as a result, no congressional delegation of power to the president since then has been struck down as impermissibly broad. Particularly in recent years, the Supreme Court has found that so long as federal agencies developed rules and regulations "based upon a permissible construction" or "reasonable interpretation" of Congress's statute, the judiciary would accept the views of the executive branch. Generally, the courts give considerable deference to administrative agencies as long as those agencies engage in a formal rule-making process as prescribed by the various statutes governing agency rule making.

Judicial Review and Presidential Power

The federal courts are also called on to review the actions of the president. On many occasions, members of Congress as well as individuals and groups have challenged presidential orders and actions in the federal courts. In recent years, the federal bench

The courts have the authority to settle disputes between not only individuals and other private entities but also individuals and the government. In recent "enemy combatant" cases, the Supreme Court has ruled on the rights of prisoners being held in the U.S. base in Guantánamo, Cuba. In 2008, demonstrators dressed as Guantánamo detainees protested outside the Court.

has, more often than not, upheld assertions of presidential power in such realms as foreign policy, war and emergency powers, legislative power, and administrative authority. In June 2004, however, the Supreme Court ruled on three cases involving President George W. Bush's antiterrorism initiatives and claims of executive power, and in two of the three cases appeared to place some limits on presidential authority.

One important case was *Hamdi v. Rumsfeld*.[22] Yaser Esam Hamdi, apparently a Taliban soldier, was captured by American forces in Afghanistan and brought to the United States, where he was incarcerated at the Norfolk Naval Station. Hamdi was classified as an enemy combatant and denied civil rights, including the right to counsel, despite the fact that he had been born in Louisiana and held American citizenship. In June 2004 the Supreme Court ruled that Hamdi was entitled to a lawyer and "a fair opportunity to rebut the government's factual assertions." Thus the Supreme Court did assert that presidential actions were subject to judicial scrutiny and that the Court could place some constraints on the president's power. But at the same time, the Court affirmed the president's single most important claim: the unilateral power to declare individuals, including U.S. citizens, "enemy combatants," who could be detained by federal authorities under adverse legal circumstances. Several of the justices intimated that once designated an enemy combatant, a U.S. citizen might be tried before a military tribunal, without the normal presumption of innocence.

In the 2006 case of *Hamdan v. Rumsfeld*, Salim Hamdan, a Taliban fighter, was captured in Afghanistan and held at the Guantánamo Bay naval base. The Bush administration planned to try Hamdan before a military commission authorized by a 2002 presidential order. The Supreme Court ruled that the commissions created by the president planned to use procedures that would violate federal law and U.S. treaty obligations.[23] President Bush responded by demanding that Congress rewrite the law. Congress quickly obliged and enacted the Military Commissions Act, which gave the president statutory authority for his actions. In Section 7 of the act, Congress declared that Guantánamo prisoners could not bring *habeas corpus* petitions to federal courts to seek their release. In the 2008 case of *Boumediene v. Bush*, however, the Supreme Court struck down Section 7 and declared *habeas corpus* to be a fundamental right.[24]

Judicial Review and Lawmaking

Much of the work of the courts involves the application of statutes to the particular case at hand. Over the centuries, judges have also developed a body of rules and principles of interpretation that are not grounded in specific statutes. This body of judge-made law is called **common law**.

common law law made through court precedent rather than legislative enactments

The appellate courts, however, are in another realm. Their rulings can be considered laws, but they govern the behavior only of the judiciary. The written opinion of an appellate court is about halfway between common law and statutory law. As in common law, the opinion is judge-made and draws heavily on the precedents of previous cases. But, as in statutory law, it tries to articulate the rule of law controlling the case in question and future cases like it. It differs from a statute in that a statute addresses itself to the future conduct of citizens, whereas a written opinion addresses itself mainly to the future willingness or ability of courts to take cases and render favorable opinions. Decisions by appellate courts affect citizens by opening or closing access to the courts.

A specific case illustrates the distinction. Before the Second World War, one of the most insidious forms of racial discrimination was the "restrictive covenant," a clause in a contract whereby the purchasers of a house agreed that if they later decided to sell the home, they would sell only to a Caucasian. When a test case finally reached the Supreme Court in 1948, the Court ruled unanimously that citizens had a right to discriminate with restrictive covenants in their sales contracts but that the courts could not enforce those contracts. Its argument was that enforcement would constitute violation of the Fourteenth Amendment provision that no state shall "deny to any person within its jurisdiction equal protection under the law."[25] The Court was thereby predicting what it would and would not do in future cases of this sort. Most states have now enacted statutes that forbid homeowners from placing such covenants in sales contracts.

Many areas of civil law have been constructed in the same way: by judicial messages to other judges, some of which are eventually codified into legislative enactments. An example of great concern to employees and employers is that of liability for injuries sustained at work. Courts have sided with employees so often that it has become virtually useless for employers to fight injury cases. It has become "the law" that employers are liable for such injuries, without regard to claims of negligence. But the law in this instance is simply a series of messages to lawyers that they should advise their corporate clients not to appeal injury decisions. In recent years, the Supreme Court has also been developing law in the realm of sexual harassment in the workplace. In a 2006 case, for example, the Court said that a victim of sexual harassment who was transferred from her job could sue her employer even though the company disciplined the perpetrator when the harassment was reported.[26]

The appellate courts cannot decide what types of behavior will henceforth be a crime. They cannot directly prevent the police from forcing confessions from suspects or intimidating witnesses. In other words, they cannot directly change the behavior of citizens or eliminate abuses of government power. What they can do, however, is make it easier for mistreated persons to gain redress.

In redressing wrongs, the appellate courts—and even the Supreme Court itself—often call for a radical change in legal principle. Changes in race relations, for example, would probably have taken a great deal longer if the Supreme Court had not rendered the 1954 decision *Brown v. Board of Education*, which redefined the rights of African Americans.

Similarly, the Supreme Court interpreted the doctrine of the separation of church and state so as to alter significantly the practice of religion in public institutions. For example, in a 1962 case, *Engel v. Vitale*, the Court declared that a once widely observed ritual—the recitation of a prayer by students in a public school—was unconstitutional under the establishment clause of the First Amendment.[27] Almost all the dramatic changes in the treatment of criminals and of persons accused of crimes have been made by the appellate courts, especially the Supreme Court. The Supreme Court brought about a veritable revolution in the criminal process with three cases over less than five years: *Gideon v. Wainwright*, in 1963, established the obligation of state courts to provide legal counsel to defendants who could not afford their own attorneys.[28] *Escobedo v. Illinois*, in 1964, gave suspects the right to remain silent and the right to have counsel present during questioning. But the *Escobedo* decision left confusions that allowed differing decisions to be made by lower courts.[29] In *Miranda v. Arizona*, in 1966, the Supreme

Due process of law is an area in which federal courts have been critical in "making law" since the 1960s. In 2009 the Court heard the case of Savana Redding, who was strip-searched by school officials who suspected she was hiding prescription pills. The Court ruled that the search was illegal.

Court cleared up these confusions by setting forth what is known as the Miranda rule: arrested people have the right to remain silent, the right to be informed that anything they say can be held against them, and the right to counsel before and during police interrogation (see Chapter 4).[30] In 2000 the Supreme Court considered overruling *Miranda* in *Dickerson v. United States*, but it decided that the wide acceptance of Miranda rights in the legal culture was "adequate reason not to overrule" it.[31]

One of the most significant changes brought about by the Supreme Court was the revolution in legislative representation unleashed by the 1962 case of *Baker v. Carr*.[32] In this landmark case, the Supreme Court held that it could no longer avoid reviewing complaints about the apportionment of seats in state legislatures. Following that decision, the federal courts went on to force reapportionment of all state, county, and local legislatures in the country.

The Supreme Court in Action

Given the millions of disputes that arise every year, the job of the Supreme Court would be impossible if it were not able to control the flow of cases and its own caseload. The Supreme Court has original jurisdiction in a limited variety of cases defined by the Constitution. The original jurisdiction includes (1) cases between the United States and one of the 50 states, (2) cases between two or more states, (3) cases involving foreign ambassadors or other ministers, and (4) cases brought by one state against citizens of another state or against a foreign country. The most important of these cases are disputes between states over land, water, or old debts. Generally, the Supreme Court deals with these cases by appointing a "special master," usually a retired judge, to hear the case and present a report. The Supreme Court then allows the states involved in the dispute to present arguments for or against the master's opinion.[33] The fact that a matter falls within the Supreme Court's jurisdiction does not mean that the Court will necessarily hear the case.

Rules of Access Over the years, the courts have developed specific rules that govern which cases within their jurisdiction they will and will not hear. In order to be heard by the courts, cases must meet certain criteria that are initially applied by the trial court but may be reconsidered by appellate courts. These rules of access can be broken down into three major categories: case or controversy, standing, and mootness.

Article III of the Constitution and Supreme Court decisions define judicial power as extending only to "cases and controversies." This means that the case before a court must be an actual controversy, not a hypothetical one, with two truly adversarial parties. The courts have interpreted this language to mean that they do not have the power to render advisory opinions to legislatures or agencies about the constitutionality of proposed laws or regulations. Furthermore, even after a law is enacted, the courts will generally refuse to consider its constitutionality until it is actually applied.

standing the right of an individual or organization to initiate a court case, on the basis of their having a substantial stake in the outcome

Parties to a case must also have **standing**—that is, they must show that they have a substantial stake in the outcome of the case. The traditional requirement for standing has been to show injury to oneself; that injury can be personal, economic, or even aesthetic, such as a neighbor's building a high fence that blocks one's view of the ocean. In order for a group or class of people to have standing (as in class-action suits), each member must show specific injury. This means that a general interest in the environment, for instance, does not provide a group with sufficient basis for standing.

The Supreme Court also uses a third criterion in determining whether it will hear a case: that of **mootness**. In theory, this requirement disqualifies cases that are brought too late—after the relevant facts have changed or the problem has been resolved by other means. The criterion of mootness, however, is subject to the discretion of the courts, which have begun to relax the rules of mootness, particularly in cases where a situation that has been resolved is likely to come up again. In the abortion case *Roe v. Wade*, for example, the Supreme Court rejected the lower court's argument that because the pregnancy in question had already come to term, the case was moot. The Court agreed to hear the case because no pregnancy was likely to outlast the lengthy appeals process.[34]

mootness a criterion used by courts to screen cases that no longer require resolution

Putting aside the formal criteria, the Supreme Court is most likely to accept cases that involve conflicting decisions by the federal circuit courts, cases that present important questions of civil rights or civil liberties, and cases in which the federal government is the appellant. Ultimately, however, the question of which cases to accept can come down to the preferences and priorities of the justices. If a group of justices believes that the Court should intervene in a particular area of policy or politics, they are likely to look for a case or cases that will serve as vehicles for judicial intervention. For many years, the Court was not interested in considering challenges to affirmative action or other programs designed to provide particular benefits to minorities. In recent years, however, several of the Court's more conservative justices have been eager to push back the limits of affirmative action and racial preference, and have therefore accepted a number of cases that would allow them to do so. In the 2009 case of *Ricci v. DeStefano*, for example, the Court ruled that officials in New Haven, Connecticut, had discriminated against white firefighters when they threw out the results of a test in which whites had outscored minority candidates for promotion. The Court said employers must have a "strong basis in evidence" that a test is defective, rather than simply relying on disparate outcomes.[35] The case is also notable because it was an appeal following a decision by Judge Sonia Sotomayor, who, a few months later, joined the Supreme Court. In 2012 the Court was poised to rule on the constitutionality of "race-conscious" college admissions.

The justices' preferences and priorities influence which cases are heard by the Supreme Court. Recently, the Court's conservative justices have been interested in cases involving challenges to affirmative action. In 2009 the Court found that officials in New Haven, Connecticut, including Mayor John DeStefano (pictured here), had discriminated against white firefighters in an effort to protect the rights of minority firefighters.

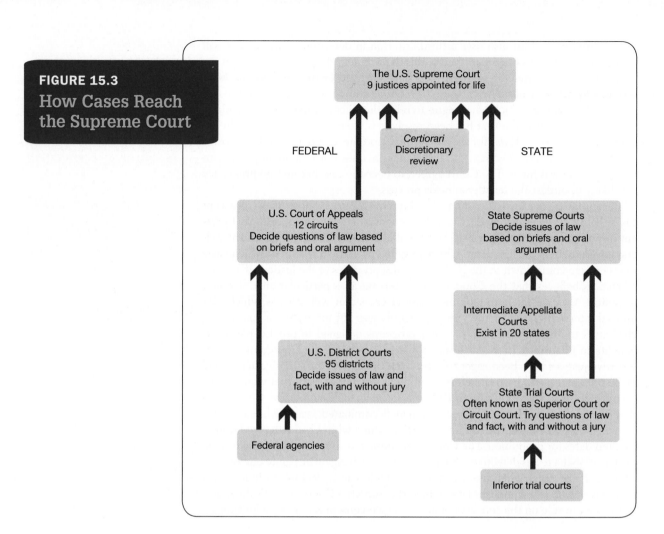

FIGURE 15.3
How Cases Reach the Supreme Court

The U.S. Supreme Court
9 justices appointed for life

FEDERAL

Certiorari
Discretionary review

STATE

U.S. Court of Appeals
12 circuits
Decide questions of law based on briefs and oral argument

State Supreme Courts
Decide issues of law based on briefs and oral argument

U.S. District Courts
95 districts
Decide issues of law and fact, with and without jury

Intermediate Appellate Courts
Exist in 20 states

Federal agencies

State Trial Courts
Often known as Superior Court or Circuit Court. Try questions of law and fact, with and without a jury

Inferior trial courts

writ of *certiorari* a decision of at least four of the nine Supreme Court justices to review a decision of a lower court; *certiorari* is Latin, meaning "to make more certain"

Writs Most cases reach the Supreme Court through a **writ of *certiorari*** (see Figure 15.3). *Certiorari* is an order to a lower court to deliver the records of a particular case to be reviewed for legal errors. The term *certiorari* is sometimes shortened to *cert*, and cases deemed to merit *certiorari* are referred to as "certworthy." An individual who loses in a lower federal court or state court and wants the Supreme Court to review the decision has 90 days to file a petition for a writ of *certiorari* with the clerk of the U.S. Supreme Court. There are two types of petitions: paid petitions and petitions *in forma pauperis* ("in the form of a pauper"). The former requires payment of filing fees, submission of a certain number of copies, and compliance with a variety of other rules. For *in forma pauperis* petitions, usually filed by prison inmates, the Court waives the fees and most other requirements. Petitions for thousands of cases are filed with the Court every year (see Figure 15.4).

Since 1972, most of the justices have participated in a "*certiorari* pool" in which their law clerks work together to evaluate the petitions. Each petition is reviewed by one clerk, who writes a memo for all the justices participating in the pool, summarizing the facts and issues and making a recommendation. Clerks for the other justices add their comments to the memo. After the justices have reviewed the memos, any one of them may place any case on the "discuss list," which is circulated by the chief justice. If a case is not placed on the discuss list, it

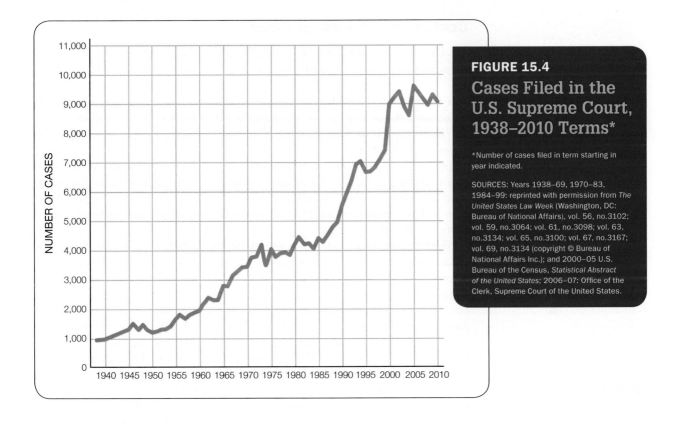

FIGURE 15.4

Cases Filed in the U.S. Supreme Court, 1938–2010 Terms*

*Number of cases filed in term starting in year indicated.

SOURCES: Years 1938–69, 1970–83, 1984–99: reprinted with permission from *The United States Law Week* (Washington, DC: Bureau of National Affairs), vol. 56, no.3102; vol. 59, no.3064; vol. 61, no.3098; vol. 63, no.3134; vol. 65, no.3100; vol. 67, no.3167; vol. 69, no.3134 (copyright © Bureau of National Affairs Inc.); and 2000–05 U.S. Bureau of the Census, *Statistical Abstract of the United States*; 2006–07: Office of the Clerk, Supreme Court of the United States.

is automatically denied *certiorari*. Cases placed on the discuss list are considered and voted on during the justices' closed-door conference.

For *certiorari* to be granted, four justices must be convinced that the case satisfies Rule 10 of the Rules of the U.S. Supreme Court. Rule 10 states that *certiorari* is not a matter of right but is to be granted only when there are special and compelling reasons. These include conflicting decisions by two or more circuit courts, conflicts between circuit courts and state courts of last resort, conflicting decisions by two or more state courts of last resort, decisions by circuit courts on matters of federal law that should be settled by the Supreme Court, and a circuit court decision on an important question that conflicts with Supreme Court decisions. It should be clear from this list that the Court will usually take action under only the most compelling circumstances—when there are conflicts among the lower courts about what the law should be, when an important legal question has been raised in the lower courts but not definitively answered, or when a lower court deviates from the principles and precedents established by the high court. Few cases are able to gain the support of four justices needed for *certiorari*. In recent sessions, although thousands of petitions were filed, the Court has granted *certiorari* to barely more than 80 petitioners each year—about 1 percent of those seeking a Supreme Court review.

A handful of cases reach the Supreme Court through avenues other than *certiorari*. One of these is the writ of certification, which can be used when a U.S. court of appeals asks the Supreme Court for instructions on a point of law that has never been decided. A second alternative avenue is the writ of appeal, which is used to appeal the decision of a three-judge district court.

Controlling the Flow of Cases

In addition to the judges, other actors play important roles in shaping the flow of cases through the federal courts: the solicitor general and federal law clerks.

The Solicitor General If any single person has greater influence than individual judges over the federal courts, it is the **solicitor general** of the United States. The solicitor general is the third-ranking official in the Justice Department (below the attorney general and the deputy attorney general) but the top government lawyer in virtually all cases before the Supreme Court in which the government is a party. The solicitor general has the greatest control over the flow of cases; his or her actions are not reviewed by any higher authority in the executive branch. More than half the Supreme Court's total workload consists of cases under the direct charge of the solicitor general.

The solicitor general exercises especially strong influence by screening cases before any agency of the federal government can appeal them to the Supreme Court; indeed, the justices rely on the solicitor general to "screen out undeserving litigation and furnish them with an agenda to government cases that deserve serious consideration."[36] Typically, more requests for appeals are rejected than are accepted by the solicitor general. Agency heads may lobby the president or otherwise try to circumvent the solicitor general, and a few of the independent agencies have a statutory right to make direct appeals, but without the solicitor general's support, these requests are seldom reviewed by the Court. At best, they are doomed to **per curiam** ("by the court") rejection—rejection through a brief, unsigned opinion by the whole Court. Congress has given only a few agencies, including the Federal Communications Commission, the Federal Maritime Commission, and in some cases the Department of Agriculture (even though it is not an independent agency), the right to appeal directly to the Supreme Court without going through the solicitor general.

The solicitor general can enter a case even when the federal government is not a direct litigant by writing an **amicus curiae** ("friend of the court") brief. A friend of the court is not a direct party to a case but has a vital interest in its outcome. Thus, when the government has such an interest, the solicitor general can file an *amicus* brief or a federal court can invite such a brief because it wants an opinion in writing. Other interested parties may file briefs as well.

In addition to exercising substantial control over the flow of cases, the solicitor general can shape the arguments used before the federal courts. Indeed, the Supreme Court tends to give special attention to the way the solicitor general characterizes the issues. The solicitor general is the person who appears most frequently before the Court and, theoretically at least, is the most disinterested. The credibility of the solicitor general is not hurt when several times each year he or she comes to the Court to withdraw a case with the admission that the government has made an error.

The solicitor general's sway over the flow of cases does not, however, entirely overshadow the influence of the other agencies and divisions in the Department of Justice. The solicitor general is counsel for the major divisions in the department, including the Antitrust, Tax, Civil Rights, and Criminal divisions. Their activities generate a great part of the solicitor general's agenda. This is particularly true of the Criminal Division, whose cases are appealed every day. These cases are generated by initiatives taken by the U.S. attorneys and the district judges before whom they practice.

solicitor general the top government lawyer in all cases before the Supreme Court where the government is a party

per curiam a brief, unsigned decision by an appellate court, usually rejecting a petition to review the decision of a lower court

amicus curiae literally, "friend of the court"; individuals or groups who are not parties to a lawsuit but who seek to assist the Supreme Court in reaching a decision by presenting additional briefs

Law Clerks Every federal judge employs law clerks to research legal issues and assist with the preparation of opinions. Each Supreme Court justice is assigned four clerks, almost always honors graduates of the nation's most prestigious law schools. A clerkship with a Supreme Court justice is a great honor and generally indicates that the fortunate individual is likely to reach the very top of the legal profession. The work of the Supreme Court clerks is a closely guarded secret, but it is likely that some justices rely heavily on their clerks for advice in writing opinions and in deciding whether the Court should hear specific cases. In a recent book, a former law clerk to the late justice Harry Blackmun charged that Supreme Court justices yielded "excessive power to immature, ideologically driven clerks, who in turn use that power to manipulate their bosses."[37]

Lobbying for Access: Interests and the Court

At the same time that the Court exercises discretion over which cases it will review, groups and forces in society often seek to persuade the justices to listen to their problems. Lawyers representing interest groups try to choose the proper client and the proper case, so that the issues in question are most dramatically and appropriately portrayed. They also have to pick the right district or jurisdiction in which to bring the case. Sometimes they even have to wait for an appropriate political climate. Group litigants have to plan carefully when to make use of and when to avoid publicity. They must also attempt to develop a proper record at the trial court level, one that includes some constitutional arguments and even, when possible, errors on the part of the trial court. One of the most effective strategies that litigants use in getting cases accepted for review by the appellate courts is to bring the same type of suit in more than one circuit (that is, to develop a "pattern of cases"), in the hope that inconsistent treatment by two different courts will improve the chance of a Supreme Court review.

The two most notable users of the pattern-of-cases strategy in recent years have been the National Association for the Advancement of Colored People (NAACP) and the American Civil Liberties Union (ACLU). For many years, the NAACP (and its Defense Fund—now a separate group) has worked through local chapters and with many individuals to encourage litigation on issues of racial discrimination and segregation. Sometimes it distributes petitions to be signed by parents and filed with local school boards and courts, deliberately sowing the seeds of future litigation. The NAACP and the ACLU often encourage private parties to bring suit and then join the suit as *amici curiae*.

In many states, it is considered unethical and illegal for attorneys to engage in "fomenting and soliciting legal business in which they are not parties and have no pecuniary right or liability." The NAACP was sued by the state of Virginia in the late 1950s in an attempt to restrict or eliminate its efforts to influence the pattern of cases. The Supreme Court reviewed the case in 1963, recognized that the strategy was being used, and held that the NAACP strategy was protected by the First and Fourteenth amendments, just as other forms of speech and petition are protected.[38]

Thus, many pathbreaking cases are eventually granted *certiorari* because repeated refusal to review one or more of them would amount to a rule of law just as much as if the courts had handed down a written opinion. In this sense, the flow of cases, especially the pattern of significant cases, influences the behavior of the appellate judiciary.

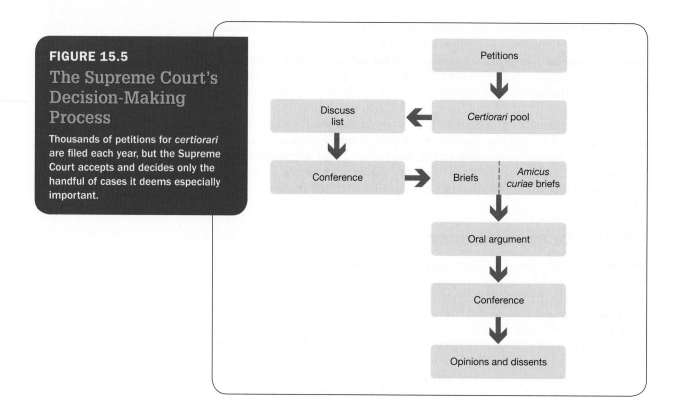

FIGURE 15.5

The Supreme Court's Decision-Making Process

Thousands of petitions for *certiorari* are filed each year, but the Supreme Court accepts and decides only the handful of cases it deems especially important.

Petitions → *Certiorari* pool → Discuss list → Conference → Briefs / *Amicus curiae* briefs → Oral argument → Conference → Opinions and dissents

The Supreme Court's Procedures

The Supreme Court's decision to accept a case is the beginning of what can be a lengthy and complex process (see Figure 15.5). After a petition is filed and *certiorari* is granted, the Court considers the reasoning on both sides as presented in briefs and oral argument, the justices discuss the case in conference, and opinions are carefully drafted.

The Preparation First, the attorneys on both sides must prepare **briefs**, written documents in which the attorneys explain why the Court should rule in favor of their client. Briefs are filled with referrals to precedents specifically chosen to show that other courts have frequently ruled in the same way the attorneys are requesting that the Supreme Court rule. The attorneys for both sides muster the most compelling precedents they can in support of their arguments.

As the attorneys prepare their briefs, they often ask sympathetic interest groups for their help. These groups are asked to file *amicus curiae* briefs that support the claims of one or the other litigant. In a case involving separation of church and state, for example, liberal groups such as the ACLU and People for the American Way are likely to be asked to file *amicus* briefs in support of strict separation, whereas conservative religious groups are likely to file *amicus* briefs advocating increased public accommodation of religious ideas. Often dozens of briefs will be filed on each side of a major case. *Amicus* filings are one of the primary methods used by interest groups to lobby the Court. By filing these briefs, groups indicate to the Court where they stand and signal to the justices that they believe the case to be an important one.

briefs written documents in which attorneys explain, using case precedents, why the court should find in favor of their client

Oral Argument The next stage of a case is **oral argument**, in which attorneys for both sides appear before the Court to present their positions and answer the justices' questions. Each attorney has only a half hour to present his or her case, and this time includes interruptions for questions. Certain members of the Court, such as Justice Antonin Scalia, are known to interrupt attorneys dozens of times. Others, such as Justice Clarence Thomas, seldom ask questions. For an attorney, the opportunity to argue a case before the Supreme Court is a singular honor and a mark of professional distinction. It can also be a harrowing experience, as when justices interrupt a carefully prepared presentation. Nevertheless, oral argument can be very important to the outcome of a case. It allows justices to understand better the heart of the case and to raise questions that might not have been addressed in the opposing sides' briefs. It is not uncommon for justices to go beyond the strictly legal issues and ask opposing counsel to discuss the implications of the case for the Court and the nation at large.

oral argument the stage in Supreme Court procedure in which attorneys for both sides appear before the Court to present their positions and answer questions posed by justices

The Conference Following oral argument, the Court discusses the case in its Wednesday or Friday conference, a strictly private meeting that no outsiders are permitted to attend. The chief justice presides over the conference and speaks first; the other justices follow in order of seniority. The justices discuss the case and eventually reach a decision on the basis of a majority vote. If the Court is divided, a number of votes may be taken before a final decision is reached. As the case is discussed, justices may try to influence or change one another's opinions. At times, this may result in compromise decisions.

Opinion Writing After a decision has been reached, one of the members of the majority is assigned to write the **opinion**. This assignment is made by the chief justice or by the most senior justice in the majority if the chief justice is on the losing side. The assignment of the opinion can make a significant difference to the interpretation of a decision. Every opinion of the Supreme Court sets a major precedent for future cases throughout the judicial system. Lawyers and judges in the lower courts will examine the opinion carefully to ascertain the Supreme Court's intent. Differences in wording and emphasis can have important implications for future litigation. Thus, in assigning an opinion, the justices must give serious thought to the impression the case will make on lawyers and on the public, and to the probability that one justice's opinion will be more widely accepted than another's.

opinion the written explanation of the Supreme Court's decision in a particular case

One of the more dramatic instances of this tactical consideration occurred in 1944, when Chief Justice Harlan F. Stone chose Justice Felix Frankfurter to write the opinion in the "white primary" case *Smith v. Allwright*. The chief justice believed that this sensitive case, which overturned the southern practice of prohibiting black participation in nominating primaries, required the efforts of the most brilliant and scholarly jurist on the Court. But the day after Stone made the assignment, Justice Robert H. Jackson wrote a letter to Stone urging a change of assignment and arguing that Frankfurter, a foreign-born Jew from New England, would not win the South with his opinion, regardless of its brilliance. Stone accepted the advice and substituted Justice Stanley Reed, an American-born Protestant from Kentucky and a southern Democrat in good standing.[39]

Once the majority opinion is drafted, it is circulated to the other justices. Some members of the majority may agree with both the outcome and the rationale but wish to emphasize or highlight a particular point. For that purpose, they draft a concurring opinion, called a *regular concurrence*. In other instances, one or more justices may agree with the majority but disagree with the rationale presented in

Is Everyone on Facebook Now a "Constitutional Scholar"?

The Supreme Court is used to working in relative anonymity until a major case is decided, at which point the Court's decision attracts substantial public attention. This trend existed since before the 1954 *Brown v. Board of Education* decision to integrate the public schools, and was in full view immediately after the 1973 *Roe v. Wade* ruling allowing women the right to an abortion. But the aftermath of the Court's 2012 decision on the Patient Protection and Affordable Care Act, public interest reached a new level, as political discussion online exploded. In one day, Chief Justice John Roberts became a household name.

Googling "Supreme Court Affordable Care Act" in June 2012 immediately following the announcement of the decision resulted in more than 214 million stories. In Google News alone, the same search term found more than 150,000 results. The 2010 Affordable Care Act included an individual mandate that virtually all Americans buy health insurance. Five of the nine justices agreed that the penalty someone must pay if he or she refuses to buy health insurance is a kind of tax that Congress can impose using its taxing power. The

Court's decision meant that the controversial mandate was constitutional, and President's Obama universal health care bill would become law.

With the decision, the Supreme Court was shoved to the forefront of a political divide in the United States. The individual justices were simultaneously heroes and villains, depending on whether one supported or opposed the act. A Gallup poll taken immediately after the ruling found Americans evenly divided over the Supreme Court decision, with 46 percent agreeing and 46 percent disagreeing with the Court's ruling that the law is constitutional. Opinion largely followed party lines, with Republicans opposing and Democrats favoring. While there were millions of posts, blogs, articles, and tweets about the decision, only a small percentage reflected a deep understanding and analysis of the decision's significance.

While the justices were all in the spotlight in the aftermath of this decision, Chief Justice Roberts took the brunt of the blame from those opposed to the health care act, and he became a champion to supporters. Roberts is usually a member of the conservative bloc of justices, so his vote to uphold the individual mandate shocked the nation. Hundreds of people gathered around the Supreme Court building in Washington, D.C., the day the decision was released, including many Tea Party supporters who had organized online to have a protest rally if the act was upheld.

A clever picture caption (or "meme") with more than 30,000 "shares" on the social networking site Facebook became popular in blogs and other online media surrounding the Court's decision. It read, "Brace Yourselves: Everyone on Facebook Is About to Become a Constitutional Scholar." While making fun of the hoopla surrounding the decision and the strident arguments being made on both sides following the Court's ruling, the underlying mes-

sage referred to the educative effects of social media on citizens' political knowledge about the Court. Research has found that individuals who get political information online have higher levels of general political knowledge and are more likely to discuss politics with friends and family. While supporters of the Patient Protection and Affordable Care Act celebrated the Court's decision, and opponents ranted and railed against the Court and promised to overturn the act, the average American became one notch more informed about constitutional law.

SOURCES: "The Health Care Decision, Explained in 1 Paragraph on SCOTUSblog." *The Atlantic*, June 28, 2012. Karen Mossberger, Caroline Tolbert, and Ramona McNeal. *Digital Citizenship: The Internet, Society and Participation* (Cambridge, MA: MIT Press, 2008). Lydia Saad, "Americans Issue Split Decision on Healthcare Ruling," Gallup Organization, June 29, 2012.

for critical analysis

1. Will the Internet and social media make the Supreme Court more responsive to public opinion, or will the Court continue to operate as it has for the past two centuries?

2. Does discussing politics on social networking sites make the public more informed about the court system and legal issues? Or do citizens merely gain a surface understanding of the issues, without substantive political knowledge?

the majority opinion. These justices may draft *special concurrences*, explaining their disagreements with the majority.

Dissent Justices who disagree with the majority decision of the Court may choose to publicize the character of their disagreement in the form of a **dissenting opinion**. The dissenting opinion is generally assigned by the senior justice among the dissenters. Dissents can be used to express irritation with an outcome or to signal to defeated political forces in the nation that their position is supported by at least some members of the Court. Ironically, the most dependable way an individual justice can exercise a direct and clear influence on the Court is to write a dissent. Because there is no need to please a majority, dissenting opinions can be more eloquent and less guarded than majority opinions. The current Supreme Court often produces 5–4 decisions, with dissenters writing long and detailed opinions that, they hope, will help them persuade a swing justice to join their side on the next round of cases dealing with a similar topic. During the Court's 2006–07 term, Justice Ruth Bader Ginsburg was so unhappy about the majority's decisions in a number of cases that she twice violated her own long-standing practice and read forceful dissents from the bench, thus underscoring her disagreement with current legal trends and pointing the way toward other possibilities.

Dissent plays a special role in the work and impact of the Court because it amounts to an appeal to lawyers all over the country to keep bringing similar cases. Therefore, an effective dissent influences the flow of cases through the Court and the arguments that lawyers will use in later cases. Even more important, dissent points out that although the Court speaks with a single opinion, it is the opinion only of the majority—and one day the majority might go the other way.

Explaining Supreme Court Decisions

The Supreme Court explains its decisions in terms of law and precedent. But it is the Court itself that decides what the laws actually mean and what importance the precedent will actually have. Throughout its history, the Court has shaped and reshaped the law. In the late nineteenth and early twentieth centuries, for example, the Supreme Court held that the Constitution, law, and precedent permitted racial segregation in the United States. Beginning in the late 1950s, however, the Court found that the Constitution prohibited segregation on the basis of race and indicated that the use of racial categories in legislation was always suspect. By the 1970s and '80s, the Court once again held that the Constitution permitted the use of racial categories—when such categories were needed to help members of minority groups achieve full participation in American society. Since the 1990s, the Court has retreated from this position, too, indicating that governmental efforts to provide extra help to racial minorities could represent an unconstitutional infringement on the rights of the majority.

Activism and Restraint One element of judicial philosophy is the issue of activism versus restraint. Over the years, some justices have believed that courts should interpret the Constitution according to the stated intentions of its framers and defer to the views of Congress when interpreting federal statutes. Justice Felix Frankfurter, for example, advocated judicial deference to legislative bodies and avoidance of the "political thicket" in which the Court would entangle itself by deciding questions that were essentially political rather than legal in character. Advocates of

On several occasions, Justice Ruth Bader Ginsburg has read her dissenting opinions aloud from the bench, to emphasize her strong disagreement with the majority. Dissenting opinions can encourage lawyers to bring similar cases in the future by letting the public know that not all the justices support the majority decision.

dissenting opinion a decision written by a justice in the minority in a particular case in which the justice wishes to express his or her reasoning in the case

judicial restraint judicial philosophy whose adherents refuse to go beyond the clear words of the Constitution in interpreting the document's meaning

judicial activism judicial philosophy that posits that the Court should go beyond the words of the Constitution or a statute to consider the broader societal implications of its decisions

for critical analysis

In its 2008 decision in the case of *District of Columbia v. Heller*, the Supreme Court struck down a District of Columbia law that prohibited most private citizens from keeping handguns in their homes. How does the *Heller* decision affect gun laws outside the District of Columbia?

judicial restraint are sometimes called "strict constructionists," because they look strictly to the words of the Constitution in interpreting its meaning.

The alternative to restraint is **judicial activism**. Activist judges such as Chief Justice Earl Warren believed that the Court should go beyond the words of the Constitution or a statute to consider the broader societal implications of its decisions. Activist judges sometimes strike out in new directions, promulgating new interpretations or inventing new legal and constitutional concepts when they believe these to be socially desirable. For example, Justice Harry Blackmun's opinion in *Roe v. Wade* was based on a constitutional right to privacy that is not found in the words of the Constitution but was, rather, from the Court's prior decision in *Griswold v. Connecticut*.[40] Blackmun and the other members of the majority in the *Roe* case argued that the right to privacy was implied by other constitutional provisions. In this instance of judicial activism, the Court knew the result it wanted to achieve and was not afraid to make the law conform to the desired outcome.

Activism and restraint are sometimes confused with liberalism and conservatism. For example, conservative politicians often castigate "liberal activist" judges and call for the appointment of conservative jurists who will refrain from reinterpreting the law. To be sure, some liberal jurists are activists and some conservatives have been advocates of restraint, but the relationships are by no means synonymous. Indeed, the Rehnquist court, dominated by conservatives, was among the most activist courts in American history, particularly in such areas as federalism and election law. The Roberts court is continuing along the same route. As the examples of these conservative courts illustrate, a judge may be philosophically conservative and believe in strict construction of the Constitution but also be jurisprudentially activist and believe that the courts must play an active and energetic role in policy making, if necessary striking down acts of Congress to ensure that the intent of the framers is fulfilled.

Political Ideology The philosophy of activism versus restraint is sometimes a smokescreen for political ideology, and indeed, the liberal or conservative attitudes of justices play an important role in their decisions.[41] In the past, liberal judges have often been activists, willing to use the law to achieve social and political change, whereas conservatives have been associated with judicial restraint. Interestingly, however, in recent years some conservative justices who have long called for restraint have actually become activists in seeking to undo some of the work of liberal jurists.

From the 1950s to the 1980s, the Supreme Court took an activist role in such areas as civil rights, civil liberties, abortion, voting rights, and police procedures. For example, the Supreme Court was more responsible than any other governmental institution for breaking down America's system of racial segregation. Since that time, however, the conservative justices appointed by presidents Ronald Reagan, George H. W. Bush, and George W. Bush have become the dominant bloc on the Court and, as we saw earlier, have moved the Court to the right on a number of issues, including affirmative action and abortion.

The political struggles of recent years amply illustrate the importance of judicial ideology. Is abortion a fundamental right or a criminal activity? How much separation must there be between church and state? Does application of the Voting Rights Act to increase minority representation constitute a violation of the rights of whites? The answers to these and many other questions cannot be found in the words of the Constitution. They must be located, instead, in the hearts and minds of the judges who interpret that text.

The Supreme Court and International Law

For most of its history the American judiciary has been a particularly domestic institution. But in this epoch of globalization, the Court has had to give up what Justice Ruth Bader Ginsburg in 2003 called "our 'island' or 'lone ranger' mentality." Ginsburg went on to note that increasingly the justices were considering the perspectives of comparative and international law. Despite Ginsburg's comment, one of the most important Supreme Court decisions in this realm, *Medellin v. Texas*, decided in March 2008, seemed to uphold our "island" mentality.[a] In that case the Court said that an international treaty is not binding domestic law unless Congress enacts statutes implementing it. Lacking such statutory authority, the president has no power to enforce a treaty or decision of an international tribunal. In the Medellin case, the defendant, a Mexican national, had been convicted of rape and murder in Texas and sentenced to death. Medellin said, however, that when he was arrested he had not been notified of his right to contact the Mexican consulate as required by international treaty. Medellin received a favorable ruling from the International Court of Justice, a UN entity recognized by the United States, which declared that Medellin was entitled to a review and reconsideration of his conviction. The U.S. Supreme Court, however, declared that U.S. courts were not bound by the rulings of an international tribunal unless Congress had enacted legislation to that effect. Medellin was executed.

Despite the Medellin case, America's relationship to international law is changing. Along One numerous cases involves such things as interpreting the terms of an international treaty that regular "cross-border transactions" in which international law not only is relevant but could be the governing law. U.S. courts had a difficult time with these because they required research on international law and decisions by foreign courts. And our various courts continually disagree over the weight to put on the rulings of foreign tribunals: Are these foreign decisions to be taken as precedents in our courts? Or do U.S. courts apply U.S. law to such transnational cases?

A second path of change is the extent to which our courts should be influenced by international opinion and by the decisions by foreign legislators and courts in their domestic disputes. One of the most striking was the 2003 decision that a Texas statute making it a crime for two persons of the same sex to engage in consensual sexual conduct violated the due process clause.[b] More controversial than the ruling itself was part of its argument: that other nations, including Great Britain, had repealed such laws 10 years earlier. Another decision of equal import was the 2002 decision in which the majority opinion noted that "within the world community the imposition of the death penalty for crimes committed by mentally retarded offenders is overwhelmingly disapproved." Chief Justice Rehnquist and Justice Scalia vigorously dissented on this point.

Another international influence is the UN treaty to establish an International Criminal Court (ICC), to be given jurisdiction over the conduct of military personnel in any international campaign. Since the ICC's creation in 1998, 130 countries have signed the treaty. Although President Clinton signed for the United States, he continued to bargain over terms, and the U.S. Senate has never had to confront a vote on ratification. However, Clinton's signature committed the United States to avoid acting in any way that would undermine the treaty. Consequently, fears persist that U.S. military personnel could be subject to prosecution if one of the ratifying UN member states comes forward with an allegation that a "war crime" has been committed. The Bush administration was generally hostile to the ICC, asserting that its actions infringed on American sovereignty. The Obama administration, on the other hand, indicated a desire to cooperate with the ICC and suggested that it might be time to renegotiate and revise the treaty establishing the court to deal with American concerns and potentially secure U.S. ratification.

[a]*Medellin v. Texas*, 552 U.S. 491 (2008).
[b]*Lawrence v. Texas*, 539 U.S. 558 (2003).
[c]*Atkins v. Virginia*, 536 U.S. 304 (2002).

for critical analysis

1. Who should have jurisdiction if American soldiers are charged by the Iraqi government with war crimes for having mistreated Iraqi prisoners and civilians during the conflict there? Iraqi courts? American courts? The ICC?

2. Who should have jurisdiction if an American soldier is arrested by Afghan police and charged with molesting an Afghan woman?

Judicial Power and Politics

One of the most important institutional changes to occur in the United States during the past half-century has been the striking transformation of the role and power of the federal courts, and of the Supreme Court in particular. Understanding how this transformation came about is the key to understanding the contemporary role of the courts in America.

Traditional Limitations on the Federal Courts

For much of American history, the power of the federal courts was subject to a number of limitations.[42] To begin with, unlike other governmental institutions, courts cannot exercise power on their own initiative. Judges must wait until a case is brought to them before they can make authoritative decisions. Traditionally, moreover, courts were constrained by judicial rules of standing that limited access to the bench. Claimants who simply disagreed with governmental action or inaction could not obtain access to the courts, which was limited to individuals who could show that they were particularly affected by the government's behavior in some area. This limitation on access diminished the judiciary's capacity to forge links with important political and social forces.

Second, courts were traditionally limited in the character of the relief they could provide. In general, courts acted only to offer relief or assistance to individuals and not to broad social classes, again inhibiting the formation of alliances between the courts and important social forces.

Third, courts lacked enforcement powers of their own and were compelled to rely on executive or state agencies to ensure compliance with their edicts. If the executive or state agencies were unwilling to assist the courts, judicial enactments could go unheeded, as when President Andrew Jackson declined to enforce Chief Justice John Marshall's 1832 order to the state of Georgia to release two missionaries it had arrested on Cherokee lands. Marshall asserted that the state had no right to enter the lands without the Cherokees' assent.[43] Jackson is reputed to have said, "John Marshall has made his decision, now let him enforce it."

Fourth, federal judges are, of course, appointed by the president (with the consent of the Senate). As a result, the president and Congress can shape the composition of the federal courts and ultimately, perhaps, the character of judicial decisions. Finally, Congress has the power to change both the size and jurisdiction of the Supreme Court and other federal courts. In many areas, federal courts obtain their jurisdiction not from the Constitution but from congressional statutes. On a number of occasions, Congress has threatened to take matters out of the Court's hands when it was unhappy with the Court's policies.[44] For example, in 1996, Congress enacted several pieces of legislation designed to curb the jurisdiction of the federal courts. One of these laws was the Prison Litigation Reform Act, which limits the ability of federal judges to issue "consent decrees," under which the judges could take control of state prison systems. As to the size of the Court, on one memorable occasion that we mentioned earlier, presidential and congressional threats to expand the size of the Supreme Court—Franklin Delano Roosevelt's "court packing" plan—encouraged the justices to drop their opposition to New Deal programs.

for critical analysis

Are the federal courts "imperial," or are they subordinate to the elected branches of government? In what respect does the federal judiciary still play a "checks and balances" role?

As a result of these limitations on judicial power, through much of their history the chief function of the federal courts was to provide judicial support for executive agencies and to legitimize acts of Congress by declaring them to be consistent with constitutional principles. Only on rare occasions have the federal courts dared to challenge Congress or the executive branch.[45]

Two Judicial Revolutions

Since the Second World War, however, the role of the federal judiciary has been strengthened and expanded. There have been two judicial revolutions in the United States since then. The first and more visible of these was the substantive revolution in judicial policy. As we saw earlier in this chapter and in Chapters 4 and 5, in many policy areas, including school desegregation, legislative apportionment, and criminal procedure, and in obscenity, abortion, and voting rights, the Supreme Court was at the forefront of a series of sweeping changes in the role of the U.S. government and, ultimately, the character of American society.[46] But at the same time that the courts were introducing important policy innovations, they were also bringing about a second, less visible revolution. During the 1960s and '70s, the Supreme Court and other federal courts instituted a series of changes in judicial procedures that fundamentally expanded the power of the courts in the United States.

First, the federal courts liberalized the concept of standing to permit almost any group that seeks to challenge the actions of an administrative agency to bring its case before the federal bench. In 1971, for example, the Supreme Court ruled that public interest groups could use the National Environmental Policy Act to challenge the actions of federal agencies by claiming that the agencies' activities might have adverse environmental consequences.[47]

Congress helped to make it even easier for groups dissatisfied with government policies to bring their cases to the courts by adopting Section 1983 of the U.S. Code, which permits the practice of "fee shifting"—that is, allowing citizens who successfully bring a suit against a public official for violating their constitutional rights to collect their attorneys' fees and costs from the government. Thus, Section 1983 encourages individuals and groups to bring their problems to the courts rather than to Congress or the executive branch. These changes have given the courts a far greater role in the administrative process than ever before. Many federal judges are concerned that federal legislation in areas such as health care reform will create new rights and entitlements that give rise to a deluge of court cases. "Any time you create a new right, you create a host of disputes and claims," warned Barbara Rothstein, chief judge of the federal district court in Seattle, Washington.[48]

Second, the federal courts broadened the scope of relief to permit themselves to act on behalf of broad categories or classes of persons in "class action" cases, rather than just on behalf of individuals.[49] A **class-action suit** is a procedural device that permits large numbers of persons with common interests to join together under a representative party to bring or defend a lawsuit. One example of a class-action suit is the case of *In re Agent Orange Product Liability Litigation*, in which a federal judge in New York certified Vietnam War veterans as a class with standing to sue a manufacturer of herbicides for damages allegedly incurred from exposure

class-action suit a legal action by which a group or class of individuals with common interests can file a suit on behalf of everyone who shares that interest

Today, the Supreme Court is frequently at the center of major political issues. In 2012 it decided a case related to the state versus federal power in immigration policy. In the past, the power of the courts was generally more limited than it is today.

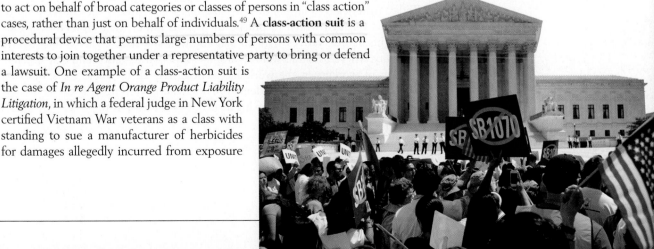

to the defendant's product while in Vietnam.[50] The class potentially numbered in the tens of thousands.

Third, the federal courts began to employ so-called structural remedies, in effect retaining jurisdiction of cases until the court's mandate had actually been implemented to its satisfaction.[51] The best known of these instances was federal judge W. Arthur Garrity Jr.'s effort to operate the Boston school system from his bench in order to ensure its desegregation. Between 1974 and 1985, Judge Garrity issued 14 decisions relating to different aspects of the Boston school desegregation plan that had been developed under his authority and put into effect under his supervision.[52] In 1985, as a result of a suit brought by the NAACP five years earlier, federal judge Leonard B. Sand imposed fines that would have forced the city of Yonkers, New York, into bankruptcy if it had refused to accept his plan to build public housing in white neighborhoods. Twenty-two years and $1.6 million in fines later, in 2007, the city finally gave in to the judge's ruling.

Through these three judicial mechanisms, the federal courts paved the way for an unprecedented expansion of national judicial power. In essence, liberalization of the rules of standing and expansion of the scope of judicial relief drew the federal courts into linkages with important social interests and classes, while the introduction of structural remedies enhanced the courts' ability to serve these constituencies. Thus, during the 1960s and '70s, the power of the federal courts expanded in the same way the power of the executive expanded during the 1930s: through links with constituencies, such as civil rights, consumer, environmental, and feminist groups, that staunchly defended the Supreme Court in its battles with Congress, the executive, and other interest groups.

● Thinking Critically about the Judiciary, Liberty, and Democracy

In the original conception of the framers, the judiciary was to be the institution that would protect individual liberty from the government. As we saw in Chapter 2, the framers believed that in a democracy the great danger was what they termed "tyranny of the majority"—the possibility that a popular majority, "united or actuated by some common impulse or passion," would "trample on the rules of justice."[53] The framers hoped that the courts would protect liberty from the potential excesses of democracy. And for most of American history, the federal courts' most important decisions were those that protected the freedoms—to speak, worship, publish, vote, and attend school—of groups and individuals whose political views, religious beliefs, or racial or ethnic backgrounds made them unpopular.

Today, Americans of all political persuasions seem to view the courts as useful instruments through which to pursue their goals rather than protectors of individual rights. Conservatives want to ban abortion and help business maintain its profitability, whereas liberals want to promote school integration and help enhance the power of workers in the workplace. These may all be noble goals, but they present a basic dilemma for students of American government. If the courts are simply one more set of policy-making institutions, who is left to protect the liberty of individuals?

Explore the Court System

Inform Yourself

Watch a video on the power of the courts. The perception and power of the federal court system have changed over the course of the nation's history. Even at the Constitutional Convention, held in 1787, there were disagreements over what exactly the court system should look like. Watch the Standard Deviants' introduction to the judicial branch at www.youtube.com/watch?v=YdCkCRLyfpk and consider what was included in the Constitution versus the Judiciary Act.

Compare the jurisdictions of federal and state courts. The federal courts are not the only courts in the United States. Which cases are heard by state courts? The cases that are deemed federal or state fall into specific categories, listed at www .uscourts.gov/EducationalResources/FederalCourtBasics/CourtStructure/ JurisdictionOfStateAndFederalCourts.aspx. Do any of these classifications surprise you?

Express Yourself

Take a stand on free speech and technology. The American Civil Liberties Union (ACLU) often files *amicus curiae* briefs on cases that involve civil rights or civil liberties infringements. A recent case originating in Virginia argues that "liking" something on Facebook is equivalent to protected speech and that employers should not be able to fire employees for this action. Read the ACLU post at www .aclu.org/blog/free-speech-technology-and-liberty/aclu-facebook-tell-appeals-court-free-speech. Consider whether you would rule for the plaintiff or the defendant in this case. Share your opinion by posting a comment to the ACLU blog or Facebook page.

Weigh in on judicial elections. Are judicial elections held in your state? View the map of the United States and see whether members of your home state's supreme court are elected or appointed (www.justiceatstake.org/state//index .cfm). If they are elected, are they elected in partisan or non-partisan elections? If they are appointed, is it using the merit plan or another system?

After viewing this information on the appointment versus the election of judges, what is your opinion? What is the fairest method of selecting judges? Follow the "Justice at Stake" Twitter feed (http://twitter.com/justicestake) and consider sharing your opinion online. If your state holds judicial elections, how will you choose between judicial candidates in the next race?

Find links to the sites listed above as well as related activities on wwnorton.com/studyspace.

study guide

The Legal System

■ **Identify the general types of cases and types of courts in our legal system (pp. 603–8)**

American court cases proceed under two broad categories of law: criminal law and civil law. There are court systems at both the federal and state level in the United States. While state courts hear only cases involving questions of state law, the federal courts decide cases addressing federal laws, treaties with other nations and the Constitution.

Key Terms

criminal law (p. 603)

plaintiff (p. 603)

defendant (p. 603)

civil law (p. 604)

precedent (p. 604)

stare decisis (p. 604)

trial courts (p. 604)

court of appeals (p. 605)

supreme court (p. 605)

plea bargain (p. 605)

jurisdiction (p. 605)

due process of law (p. 607)

writ of *habeas corpus* (p. 607)

Practice Quiz

1. What is the name for the body of law that involves disputes between private parties? *(p. 604)*
   a) civil law
   b) privacy law
   c) plea bargains
   d) household law
   e) common law

2. By what term is the practice of the courts to uphold precedent known? *(p. 604)*
   a) *habeas corpus*
   b) *certiorari*
   c) *stare decisis*
   d) rule of four
   e) senatorial courtesy

3. Where do most trials in America take place? *(p. 604)*
   a) state and local courts
   b) appellate courts
   c) federal courts
   d) federal circuit courts
   e) the Supreme Court

4. The term "writ of *habeas corpus*" refers to *(p. 607)*
   a) a court order that an individual in custody be brought into court and shown the cause for his or her detention.
   b) a criterion used by courts to screen cases that no longer require resolution.
   c) a decision of at least four of the nine Supreme Court justices to review a decision of a lower court.
   d) a short, unsigned decision by an appellate court, usually rejecting a petition to review the decision of a lower court.
   e) a brief filed by the solicitor general when the federal government is not a direct litigant in a Supreme Court case.

Federal Trial Courts

■ **Describe the different levels of federal courts and their functions (pp. 608–14)**

The federal courts hear a very small percentage of the cases decided in the United States each year. Presidents typically nominate judges for the federal judiciary who are prominent members of the legal profession and who share their partisan and ideological views. The importance of appointments to the federal judiciary has made the confirmation process in the Senate increasingly contentious in recent years.

Key Terms

original jurisdiction (p. 608)

chief justice (p. 609)

senatorial courtesy (p. 612)

Practice Quiz

5. Under what authority is the number of Supreme Court justices decided? *(p. 610)*
   a) the president
   b) the chief justice
   c) the Department of Justice
   d) Congress
   e) the Constitution

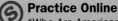
Practice Online
"Who Are Americans?" exercise: *Who Are Federal Judges?*

The Power of the Supreme Court: Judicial Review

■ **Explain how the Supreme Court exercises the power of judicial review (pp. 614–31)**

Although the Supreme Court reviews a small number of cases each year under its original jurisdiction, most cases arrive at the Supreme Court by a writ of *certiorari*. The Supreme Court is most likely to grant a writ of *certiorari* to cases that involve conflicting decisions by the federal circuit courts, cases that present important questions of civil rights or civil liberties, and cases in which the federal government is the appellant. Much of the Supreme Court's power in the American political system comes from its power to invalidate actions taken by the legislative and executive branches of government if they violate Constitution.

Key Terms

judicial review (p. 614)

supremacy clause (p. 615)

common law (p. 618)

standing (p. 620)

mootness (p. 621)

writ of *certiorari* (p. 622)

solicitor general (p. 624)

per curiam (p. 624)

amicus curiae (p. 624)

briefs (p. 626)

oral argument (p. 627)

opinion (p. 627)

dissenting opinion (p. 629)

judicial restraint (p. 630)

judicial activism (p. 630)

Practice Quiz

6. The Supreme Court's decision in *Marbury v. Madison* was important because *(pp. 614–15)*
   a) it invalidated state laws prohibiting interracial marriage.
   b) it ruled that the recitation of prayers in public schools are unconstitutional under the establishment clause of the First Amendment.
   c) it established that arrested people have the right to remain silent, the right to be informed that anything they say can be held against them, and the right to counsel before and during police interrogation.
   d) if provided an expansive definition of "commerce" under the interstate commerce clause.
   e) it established the power of judicial review.

7. Which of the following cases involved the "right to privacy"? *(p. 616)*
   a) *Griswold v. Connecticut*
   b) *Brown v. Board of Education*
   c) *Schneckloth v. Bustamante*
   d) *Marbury v. Madison*
   e) *Texas v. Johnson*

8. Which of the following Supreme Court cases did not involve the rights of criminal suspects? *(p. 620)*
   a) *Gideon v. Wainwright*
   b) *Miranda v. Arizona*
   c) *Escobedo v. Illinois*
   d) *Baker v. Carr*
   e) *Dickerson v. United States*

9. Which of the following is *not* included in the original jurisdiction of the Supreme Court? *(p. 620)*
   a) cases between the United States and one of the 50 states
   b) cases brought by one state against citizens of another state or against a foreign country
   c) cases involving challenges to the constitutionality of state laws
   d) cases between two or more states
   e) cases involving foreign ambassadors or other ministers

10. Which of the following influences the flow of cases heard by the Supreme Court? *(p. 624)*
    a) the attorney general and the Secretary of State
    b) the solicitor general and law clerks
    c) the president and Congress
    d) state legislatures
    e) the federal district and circuit courts

11. Which government official is responsible for arguing the federal government's position in cases before the Supreme Court? *(p. 624)*
    a) the vice president
    b) the attorney general
    c) the chief justice
    d) the U.S. district attorney
    e) the solicitor general

12. Which of the following is a brief submitted to the Supreme Court by someone other than one of the parties in the case? *(p. 624)*
    a) *amicus curiae*
    b) *habeas corpus*
    c) solicitor general
    d) *ex post* brief
    e) *de jure* brief

13. Justices who favored going beyond the words of the Constitution to consider the broader societal implications of the Supreme Court's decisions would be considered advocates of which judicial philosophy? *(p. 630)*
    a) original intent
    b) judicial restraint
    c) judicial activism
    d) judicial constitutionalism
    e) *stare decisis*

 Practice Online
Video exercise: *Interviews with Supreme Court Justices*

Judicial Power and Politics

■ **Consider the political influences on the courts (pp. 632–34)**

Throughout most of American history, the federal courts avoided confrontations with the other branches of government and worked primarily to provide support for executive actions and congressional laws by declaring them to be consistent with constitutional principles. During the 1960s and '70s, the federal courts liberalized the concept of standing, broadened the scope of relief courts could provide, and began to employ structural remedies. As a result of these changes, the power of the federal court system expanded dramatically.

Key Term

class-action suit (p. 633)

Practice Quiz

14. Which of the following would *not* be accurately characterized as a traditional limitation on the power of the federal courts? *(p. 632)*
    a) The president can dissolve the Supreme Court if it oversteps its powers.
    b) Courts lack enforcement powers of their own and are compelled to rely on executive or state agencies to ensure compliance with their rulings.
    c) Congress has the power to change both the size and jurisdiction of the federal courts.
    d) Courts can act to offer relief or assistance to broad social classes but not to specific individuals.
    e) Courts cannot exercise power on their own initiative and must wait for cases to be brought to them.

15. How have changes in judicial policy areas and judicial procedure affected the power of the federal judiciary since World War II? *(p. 633)*
    a) Strong involvement in sweeping policy change has expanded the courts' power, but changes in procedure have sought to limit judicial power.
    b) Changes in procedure have expanded the courts' power, but the courts have played only minor roles in policy change.
    c) Both policy and procedure changes have expanded judicial power.
    d) Both policy and procedure changes have lessened judicial power.
    e) Judicial policy and judicial procedure have remained largely unchanged since World War II.

 Practice Online
"Video exercise: *The End of Choice?*

For Further Reading

Baum, Lawrence. *The Supreme Court.* Washington, DC: CQ Press, 2009.

Cross, Frank. *Decision Making in the U.S. Courts of Appeals.* Stanford, CA: Stanford University Press, 2007.

Dorsen, David. *Henry Friendly, Greatest Judge of His Era.* Cambridge, MA: Harvard University Press, 2012.

Epstein, Lee. *Constitutional Law for a Changing America.* Washington, DC: CQ Press, 2007.

Greenberg, Jan Crawford. *Supreme Conflict: The Inside Story of the United States Supreme Court.* New York: Penguin, 2008.

Hall, Kermit L., James W. Ely Jr., and Joel B. Grossman. *The Oxford Companion to the Supreme Court of the United States.* 2nd ed. New York: Oxford University Press, 2005.

Irons, Peter. *A People's History of the Supreme Court.* New York: Penguin, 2006.

McClosky, Robert, and Sanford Levinson. *The American Supreme Court.* Chicago: University of Chicago Press, 2004.

O'Brien, David M. *Storm Center: The Supreme Court in American Politics.* 8th ed. New York: W.W. Norton, 2008.

Peppers, Todd, and Artemus Ward. *In Chambers: Stories of Supreme Court Law Clerks and Their Justices,* Charlottesville, VA: University of Virginia Press, 2012.

Raskin, Jamin B. *We the Students: Supreme Court Decisions for and about Students.* Washington, DC: Congressional Quarterly Press, 2003.

Rehnquist, William H. *The Supreme Court.* New York: Vintage, 2002.

Rosen, Jeffrey. *The Supreme Court: The Personalities and Rivalries That Defined America.* New York: Henry Holt, 2007.

Rosenberg, Gerald. *The Hollow Hope: Can Courts Bring about Social Change?* Chicago: University of Chicago Press, 1991.

Rossum, Ralph. *Antonin Scalia's Jurisprudence.* Lawrence: University Press of Kansas, 2006.

Stevens, John Paul. *Five Chiefs: A Supreme Court Memoir.* Boston: Little, Brown, 2011.

Sunstein, Cass. *Are Judges Political?* Washington, DC: Brookings Institution Press, 2006.

Toobin, Jeffrey. *The Nine: Inside the Secret World of the Supreme Court.* New York. Anchor Books 2008.

Whittington, Keith. *Political Foundations of Judicial Supremacy: The President, the Supreme Court, and Constitutional Leadership in U.S. History.* Princeton, NJ: Princeton University Press, 2008.

Recommended Websites

Concourts

www.concourts.net

The U.S. Supreme Court has the responsibility for examining and interpreting the Constitution. The Concourts website assumes a comparative perspective and looks at systems of constitutional review in over 150 countries.

FindLaw

www.findlaw.com

FindLaw's website provides answers to most legal questions and helps individuals find legal counsel.

Justice Talking

www.justicetalking.org

Justice Talking is a public radio program that examines current legal issues and important court cases.

Legal Information Institute

www.law.cornell.edu

The Legal Information Institute at Cornell University is a wonderful website for conducting legal research.

Office of the Solicitor General

www.usdoj.gov/osg

The solicitor general conducts litigation on behalf of the U.S. Supreme Court and has a tremendous amount of control over the cases that it hears. See what cases are currently being considered by this powerful official of the Justice Department.

U.S. Courts

www.uscourts.gov

The U.S. court system consists of trial, appellate, and supreme courts. The U.S. Courts website provides a look at the different types of courts in the federal judiciary.

U.S. Supreme Court

www.supremecourtus.gov

The website for the U.S. Supreme Court provides information on recent decisions. Take a moment to read some oral arguments, briefs, or court opinions.

U.S. Supreme Court Media

www.oyez.com

The website for U.S. Supreme Court Media has a great search engine for finding information on such landmark cases as *Marbury v. Madison, Miranda v. Arizona,* and *Roe v. Wade.*

The Declaration of Independence

In Congress, July 4, 1776

The unanimous Declaration of the thirteen united States of America,

When in the Course of human events, it becomes necessary for one people to dissolve the political bands which have connected them with another, and to assume among the powers of the earth, the separate and equal station to which the Laws of Nature and of Nature's God entitle them, a decent respect to the opinions of mankind requires that they should declare the causes which impel them to the separation.

We hold these truths to be self-evident, that all men are created equal, that they are endowed by their Creator with certain unalienable Rights, that among these are Life, Liberty and the pursuit of Happiness.—That to secure these rights, Governments are instituted among Men, deriving their just powers from the consent of the governed.—That whenever any Form of Government becomes destructive of these ends, it is the Right of the People to alter or to abolish it, and to institute new Government, laying its foundation on such principles and organizing its powers in such form, as to them shall seem most likely to effect their Safety and Happiness. Prudence, indeed, will dictate that Governments long established should not be changed for light and transient causes; and accordingly all experience hath shewn, that mankind are more disposed to suffer, while evils are sufferable, than to right themselves by abolishing the forms to which they are accustomed. But when a long train of abuses and usurpations, pursuing invariably the same Object evinces a design to reduce them under absolute Despotism, it is their right, it is their duty, to throw off such Government, and to provide new Guards for their future security.—Such has been the patient sufferance of these Colonies; and such is now the necessity which constrains them to alter their former Systems of Government. The history of the present King of Great Britain is a history of repeated injuries and usurpations, all having in direct object the establishment of an absolute Tyranny over these States. To prove this, let Facts be submitted to a candid world.

He has refused his Assent to Laws, the most wholesome and necessary for the public good.

He has forbidden his Governors to pass Laws of immediate and pressing importance, unless suspended in their operation till his Assent should be obtained; and when so suspended, he has utterly neglected to attend to them.

He has refused to pass other Laws for the accommodation of large districts of people, unless those people would relinquish the right of Representation in the Legislature, a right inestimable to them and formidable to tyrants only.

He has called together legislative bodies at places unusual, uncomfortable, and distant from the depository of their public Records, for the sole purpose of fatiguing them into compliance with his measures.

He has dissolved Representative Houses repeatedly, for opposing with manly firmness his invasions on the rights of the people.

He has refused for a long time, after such dissolutions, to cause others to be elected; whereby the Legislative powers, incapable of Annihilation, have returned to the People at large for their exercise; the State remaining in the mean time exposed to all the dangers of invasion from without, and convulsions within.

He has endeavoured to prevent the population of these States; for that purpose obstructing the Laws for Naturalization of Foreigners; refusing to pass others to encourage their migrations hither, and raising the conditions of new Appropriations of Lands.

He has obstructed the Administration of Justice, by refusing his Assent to Laws for establishing Judiciary powers.

He has made Judges dependent on his Will alone, for the tenure of their offices, and the amount and payment of their salaries.

He has erected a multitude of New Offices, and sent hither swarms of Officers to harrass our people, and eat out their substance.

He has kept among us, in times of peace, Standing Armies without the Consent of our legislatures.

He has affected to render the Military independent of and superior to the Civil power.

He has combined with others to subject us to a jurisdiction foreign to our constitution, and unacknowledged by our laws; giving his Assent to their Acts of pretended Legislation:

For Quartering large bodies of armed troops among us:

For protecting them, by a mock Trial, from punishment for any Murders which they should commit on the Inhabitants of these States:

For cutting off our Trade with all parts of the world:

For imposing Taxes on us without our Consent:

For depriving us in many cases, of the benefits of Trial by Jury:

For transporting us beyond Seas to be tried for pretended offences:

For abolishing the free System of English Laws in a neighboring Province, establishing therein an Arbitrary government, and enlarging its Boundaries so as to render it at once an example and fit instrument for introducing the same absolute rule into these Colonies:

For taking away our Charters, abolishing our most valuable Laws, and altering fundamentally the Forms of our Governments:

For suspending our own Legislatures, and declaring themselves invested with power to legislate for us in all cases whatsoever.

He has abdicated Government here, by declaring us out of his Protection and waging War against us.

He has plundered our seas, ravaged our Coasts, burnt our towns, and destroyed the lives of our people.

He is at this time transporting large Armies of foreign Mercenaries to compleat the works of death, desolation and tyranny, already begun with circumstances of Cruelty & perfidy scarcely paralleled in the most barbarous ages, and totally unworthy the Head of a civilized nation.

He has constrained our fellow Citizens taken Captive on the high Seas to bear Arms against their Country, to become the executioners of their friends and Brethren, or to fall themselves by their Hands.

He has excited domestic insurrections amongst us, and has endeavoured to bring on the inhabitants of our frontiers, the merciless Indian Savages, whose known rule of warfare, is an undistinguished destruction of all ages, sexes and conditions.

In every stage of these Oppressions We have Petitioned for Redress in the most humble terms: Our repeated Petitions have been answered only by repeated injury. A Prince whose character is thus marked by every act which may define a Tyrant, is unfit to be the ruler of a free people.

Nor have We been wanting in attentions to our Brittish brethren. We have warned them from time to time of attempts by their legislature to extend an unwarrantable jurisdiction over us. We have reminded them of the circumstances of our emigration and settlement here. We have appealed to their native justice and magnanimity, and we have conjured them by the ties of our common kindred to disavow these usurpations, which, would inevitably interrupt our connections and correspondence. They too have been deaf to the voice of justice and of consanguinity. We must, therefore, acquiesce in the necessity, which denounces our Separation, and hold them, as we hold the rest of mankind, Enemies in War, in Peace Friends.

We, Therefore, the Representatives of the United States of America, in General Congress, Assembled, appealing to the Supreme Judge of the world for the rectitude of our intentions, do, in the Name, and by Authority of the good People of these Colonies, solemnly publish and declare, That these United Colonies are, and of Right ought to be Free and Independent States; that they are Absolved from all Allegiance to the British Crown, and that all political connection between them and the State of Great Britain, is and ought to be totally dissolved; and that as Free and Independent States, they have full Power to levy War, conclude Peace, contract Alliances, establish Commerce, and to do all other Acts and Things which Independent States may of right do. And for the support of this Declaration, with a firm reliance on the protection of divine Providence, we mutually pledge to each other our Lives, our Fortunes and our sacred Honor.

The foregoing Declaration was, by order of Congress, engrossed, and signed by the following members:

John Hancock

NEW HAMPSHIRE
Josiah Bartlett
William Whipple
Matthew Thornton

MASSACHUSETTS BAY
Samuel Adams
John Adams
Robert Treat Paine
Elbridge Gerry

RHODE ISLAND
Stephen Hopkins
William Ellery

CONNECTICUT
Roger Sherman
Samuel Huntington
William Williams
Oliver Wolcott

NEW YORK
William Floyd
Philip Livingston
Francis Lewis
Lewis Morris

NEW JERSEY
Richard Stockton
John Witherspoon
Francis Hopkinson
John Hart
Abraham Clark

PENNSYLVANIA
Robert Morris
Benjamin Rush
Benjamin Franklin
John Morton
George Clymer
James Smith
George Taylor
James Wilson
George Ross

DELAWARE
Caesar Rodney
George Read
Thomas M'Kean

MARYLAND
Samuel Chase
William Paca
Thomas Stone
Charles Carroll,
of Carrollton

VIRGINIA
George Wythe
Richard Henry Lee
Thomas Jefferson
Benjamin Harrison
Thomas Nelson, Jr.
Francis Lightfoot Lee
Carter Braxton

NORTH CAROLINA
William Hooper
Joseph Hewes
John Penn

SOUTH CAROLINA
Edward Rutledge
Thomas Heyward, Jr.
Thomas Lynch, Jr.
Arthur Middleton

GEORGIA
Button Gwinnett
Lyman Hall
George Walton

Resolved, That copies of the Declaration be sent to the several assemblies, conventions, and committees, or councils of safety, and to the several commanding officers of the continental troops; that it be proclaimed in each of the United States, at the head of the army.

The Articles of Confederation

Agreed to by Congress November 15, 1777;
ratified and in force March 1, 1781

To all whom these Presents shall come, we the undersigned Delegates of the States affixed to our Names, send greeting. Whereas the Delegates of the United States of America, in Congress assembled, did, on the fifteenth day of November, in the Year of Our Lord One thousand Seven Hundred and Seventy seven, and in the Second Year of the Independence of America, agree to certain articles of Confederation and perpetual Union between the States of Newhampshire, Massachusetts-bay, Rhodeisland and Providence Plantations, Connecticut, New-York, New-Jersey, Pennsylvania, Delaware, Maryland, Virginia, North-Carolina, South-Carolina and Georgia in the words following, viz. "Articles of Confederation and perpetual Union between the states of Newhampshire, Massachusettsbay, Rhodeisland and Providence Plantations, Connecticut, New-York, New-Jersey, Pennsylvania, Delaware, Maryland, Virginia, North-Carolina, South-Carolina and Georgia.

Art. I. The Stile of this confederacy shall be "The United States of America."

Art. II. Each state retains its sovereignty, freedom and independence, and every Power, Jurisdiction and right, which is not by this confederation expressly delegated to the United States, in Congress assembled.

Art. III. The said states hereby severally enter into a firm league of friendship with each other, for their common defence, the security of their Liberties, and their mutual and general welfare, binding themselves to assist each other, against all force offered to, or attacks made upon them, or any of them, on account of religion, sovereignty, trade, or any other pretence whatever.

Art. IV. The better to secure and perpetuate mutual friendship and intercourse among the people of the different states in this union, the free inhabitants of each of these states, paupers, vagabonds and fugitives from Justice excepted, shall be entitled to all privileges and immunities of free citizens in the several states; and the people of each state shall have free ingress and regress to and from any other state, and shall enjoy therein all the privileges of trade and commerce, subject to the same duties, impositions and restrictions as the inhabitants thereof respectively, provided that such restriction shall not extend so far as to prevent the removal of property imported into any state, to any other state, of which the Owner is an inhabitant; provided also that no imposition, duties or restriction shall be laid by any state, on the property of the united states, or either of them.

If any Person guilty of, or charged with treason, felony, or other high misdemeanor in any state, shall flee from Justice, and be found in any of the united states, he shall, upon demand of the Governor or executive power, of the state from which he fled, be delivered up and removed to the state having jurisdiction of his offence.

Full faith and credit shall be given in each of these states to the records, acts and judicial proceedings of the courts and magistrates of every other state.

Art. V. For the more convenient management of the general interests of the united states, delegates shall be annually appointed in such manner as the legislature of each state shall direct, to meet in Congress on the first Monday in November, in every year, with a power reserved to each state, to recall its delegates, or any of them, at any time within the year, and to send others in their stead, for the remainder of the Year.

No state shall be represented in Congress by less than two, nor by more than seven Members; and no person shall be capable of being a delegate for more than three years in any term of six years; nor shall any person, being a delegate, be capable of holding any office under the united states, for which he, or another for his benefit receives any salary, fees or emolument of any kind.

Each state shall maintain its own delegates in a meeting of the states, and while they act as members of the committee of the states.

In determining questions in the united states, in Congress assembled, each state shall have one vote.

Freedom of speech and debate in Congress shall not be impeached or questioned in any Court, or place out of Congress, and the members of congress shall be protected in their persons from arrests and imprisonments, during the time of their going to and from, and attendance on congress, except for treason, felony, or breach of the peace.

Art. VI. No state without the Consent of the united states in congress assembled, shall send any embassy to, or receive any embassy from, or enter into any conference, agreement, or alliance or treaty with any King, prince or state; nor shall any person holding any office or profit or trust under the united states, or any of them, accept of any present, emolument, office or title of any kind whatever from any king, prince or foreign state; nor shall the united states in congress assembled, or any of them, grant any title of nobility.

No two or more states shall enter into any treaty, confederation or alliance whatever between them, without the consent of the united states in congress assembled, specifying accurately the purposes for which the same is to be entered into, and how long it shall continue.

No state shall lay any imposts or duties, which may interfere with any stipulations in treaties, entered into by the united states in congress assembled, with any king, prince or state, in pursuance of any treaties already proposed by congress, to the courts of France and Spain.

No vessels of war shall be kept up in time of peace by any state, except such number only, as shall be deemed necessary by the united states in congress assembled, for the defence of such state, or its trade; nor shall any body of forces be kept up by any state, in time of peace, except such number only, as in the judgment of the united states, in congress assembled, shall be deemed requisite to garrison the forts necessary for the defence of such state; but every state shall always keep up a well regulated and disciplined militia, sufficiently armed and accoutred, and shall provide and constantly have ready for use, in public stores, a due number of field pieces and tents, and a proper quantity of arms, ammunition and camp equipage.

No state shall engage in any war without the consent of the united states in congress assembled, unless such state be actually invaded by enemies, or shall have received certain advice of a resolution being formed by some nation of Indians to invade such state, and the danger is so imminent as not to admit of a delay, till the united states in congress asssembled can be consulted; nor shall any state grant commissions to any ships or vessels of war, nor letters of marque or reprisal, except it be after a declaration of war by the united states in congress assembled, and then only against the kingdom or state and the subjects thereof, against which war has been so declared, and under such regulations as shall be established by the united states in congress assembled, unless such state be infested by pirates; in which case vessels of war may be fitted out for that occasion, and kept so long as the danger shall continue, or until the united states in congress assembled shall determine otherwise.

Art. VII. When land-forces are raised by any state for the common defence, all officers of or under the rank of colonel, shall be appointed by the legislature of each state respectively, by whom such forces shall be raised, or in such manner as such state shall direct, and all vacancies shall be filled up by the state which first made the appointment.

Art. VIII. All charges of war, and all other expences that shall be incurred for the common defence or general welfare, and allowed by the united states in congress assembled, shall be defrayed out of a common treasury, which shall be supplied by the several states in proportion to the value of all land within each state, granted to or surveyed for any Person, as such land and the buildings and improvements thereon shall be estimated according to such mode as the united states in congress assembled, shall from time to time direct and appoint.

The taxes for paying that proportion shall be laid and levied by the authority and direction of the legislatures of the several states within the time agreed upon by the united states in congress assembled.

Art. IX. The united states in congress assembled, shall have the sole and exclusive right and power of determining on peace and war, except in the cases mentioned in the sixth article—of sending and receiving ambassadors—entering into treaties and alliances, provided that no treaty of commerce shall be made whereby the legislative power of the respective states shall be restrained from imposing such imposts and duties on foreigners, as their own people are subjected to, or from prohibiting the exportation of any species of goods or commodities whatsoever—of establishing rules for deciding in all cases, what captures on land or water shall be legal, and in what manner prizes taken by land or naval forces in the service of the united states shall be divided or appropriated—of granting letters of marque and reprisal in times of peace—appointing courts for the trial of piracies and felonies committed on the high seas and establishing courts for receiving and determining finally appeals in all cases of captures, provided that no member of congress shall be appointed a judge of any of the said courts.

The united states in congress assembled shall also be the last resort on appeal in all disputes and differences now subsisting or that hereafter may arise between two or more states concerning boundary, jurisdiction or any other cause whatever; which authority shall always be exercised in the manner following. Whenever the legislative or executive authority or lawful agent of any state in controversy with another shall present a petition to congress stating the matter in question and praying for a hearing, notice thereof shall be given by order of congress to the legislative or executive authority of the other state in controversy, and a day assigned for the appearance of the parties by their lawful agents, who shall then be directed to appoint by joint consent, commissioners or judges to constitute a court for hearing and determining the matter in question: but if they cannot agree, congress shall name three persons out of each of the united states, and from the list of such persons each party shall alternately strike out one, the petitioners beginning, until the number shall be reduced to thirteen; and from that number not less than seven, nor more than nine names as congress shall direct, shall in the presence of congress be drawn out by lot, and the persons whose names shall be so drawn or any five of them, shall be commissioners or judges, to hear and finally determine the controversy, so always as a major part of the judges who shall hear the cause shall agree in the determination: and if either party shall neglect to attend at the day appointed, without shewing reasons, which congress shall judge sufficient, or being present shall refuse to strike, the congress shall proceed to nominate three persons out of each state, and the secretary of congress shall strike in behalf of such party absent or refusing; and the judgment and sentence of the court to be appointed, in the manner before prescribed, shall be final and conclusive; and if any of the parties shall refuse to submit to the authority of such court, or to appear to defend their claim or cause, the court shall nevertheless proceed to pronounce sentence, or judgment, which shall in like manner be final and decisive, the judgment or sentence and other proceedings being in either case transmitted to congress, and lodged among the acts of congress for the security of the parties concerned: provided that every commissioner, before he sits in judgment, shall take an oath to be administered by one of the judges of the supreme or superior court of the state, where the cause shall be tried, "well and truly to hear and determine the matter in question, according to the best of his judgment, without favour, affection or hope of reward:" provided also, that no state shall be deprived of territory for the benefit of the united states.

All controversies concerning the private right of soil claimed under different grants of two or more states, whose jurisdictions as they may respect such lands, and the states which passed such grants are adjusted, the said grants or either of them being at the same time claimed to have originated antecedent to such settlement of jurisdiction, shall on the petition of either party to the congress of the united states, be finally determined as near as may be in the same manner as is before prescribed for deciding disputes respecting territorial jurisdiction between different states.

The united states in congress assembled shall also have the sole and exclusive right and power of regulating the alloy and value of coin struck by their own authority, or by that of the respective states—fixing the standard of weights and measures throughout the united states—regulating the trade and managing all affairs with the Indians, not members of any of the states, provided that the legislative right of any state within its own limits be not infringed or violated—establishing and regulating post-offices from one state to another, throughout all the united states, and exacting such postage on the papers passing thro' the same as may be requisite to defray the expences of the said office—appointing all officers of the land forces, in the service of the united states, excepting regimental officers—appointing all the officers of the naval forces, and commissioning all officers whatever in the service of the united states—making rules for the government and regulation of the said land and naval forces, and directing their operations.

The united states in congress assembled shall have authority to appoint a committee, to sit in the recess of congress, to be denominated "A Committee of the States," and to consist of one delegate from each state; and to appoint such other committees and civil officers as may be necessary for managing the general affairs of the united states under their direction—to appoint one of their number to preside, provided that no person be allowed to serve in the office of president more than one year in any term of three years; to ascertain the necessary sums of Money to be raised for the service of the united states, and to appropriate and apply the same for defraying the public expenses—to borrow money, or emit bills on the credit of the united states, transmitting every half year to the respective states an account of the sums of money so borrowed or emitted,—to build and equip a navy—to agree upon the number of land forces, and to make requisitions from each state for its quota, in proportion to the number of white inhabitants in such state; which requisition shall be binding, and thereupon the legislature of each state shall appoint the regimental officers, raise the men and cloath, arm and equip them in a soldier like manner, at the expense of the united states; and the officers and men so cloathed, armed and equipped shall march to the place appointed, and within the time agreed on by the united states in congress assembled: But if the united states in congress assembled shall, on consideration of circumstances judge proper that any state should not raise men, or should raise a smaller number than its quota, and that any other state should raise a greater number of men than the quota thereof, such extra number shall be raised, officered, cloathed, armed and equipped in the same manner as the quota of such state, unless the legislature of such state shall judge that such extra number cannot be safely spared out of the same, in which case they shall raise officer, cloath, arm and equip as many of such extra number as they judge can be safely spared. And the officers and men so cloathed, armed and equipped, shall march to the place appointed, and within the time agreed on by the united states in congress assembled.

The united states in congress assembled shall never engage in a war, nor grant letters of marque and reprisal in time of peace, nor enter into any treaties or alliances, nor coin money, nor regulate the value thereof, nor ascertain the sums and expenses necessary for the defence and welfare of the united states, or any of them, nor emit bills, nor borrow money on the credit of the united states, nor appropriate money, nor agree upon the number of vessels of war, to be built or purchased, or the number of land or sea forces to be raised, nor appoint a commander in chief of the army or navy, unless nine states assent to the same: nor shall a question on any other point, except for adjourning from day to day be determined, unless by the votes of a majority of the united states in congress assembled.

The congress of the united states shall have power to adjourn to any time within the year, and to any place within the united states, so that no period of adjournment be for a longer duration than the space of six Months, and shall publish the Journal of their proceedings monthly, except such parts thereof relating to treaties, alliances or military operations, as in their judgment require secrecy; and the yeas and nays of the delegates of each state on any question shall be entered on the Journal, when it is desired by any delegate; and the delegates of a state, or any of them, at his or their request shall be furnished with a transcript of the said Journal, except such parts as are above excepted, to lay before the legislatures of the several states.

Art. X. The committee of the states, or any nine of them, shall be authorised to execute, in the recess of congress, such of the powers of congress as the united states in congress assembled, by the consent of nine states, shall from time to time think expedient to vest them with; provided that no power be delegated to the said committee, for the exercise of which, by the articles of confederation, the voice of nine states in the congress of the united states assembled is requisite.

Art. XI. Canada acceding to this confederation, and joining in the measures of the united states, shall be admitted into, and entitled to all the advantages of this union: but no other colony shall be admitted into the same, unless such admission be agreed to by nine states.

Art. XII. All bills of credit emitted, monies borrowed and debts contracted by, or under the authority of congress, before the assembling of the united states, in pursuance of the present confederation, shall be deemed and considered as a charge against the united states, for payment and satisfaction whereof the said united states and the public faith are hereby solemnly pledged.

Art. XIII. Every state shall abide by the determinations of the united states in congress assembled, on all questions which by this confederation are submitted to them. And the Articles of this confederation shall be inviolably observed by every state, and the union shall be perpetual; nor shall any alteration at any time hereafter be made in any of them; unless such alteration be agreed to in a congress of the united states, and be afterwards confirmed by the legislatures of every state.

And Whereas it hath pleased the Great Governor of the World to incline the hearts of the legislatures we respectively represent in congress, to approve of, and to authorize us to ratify the said articles of confederation and perpetual union. Know Ye that we the undersigned delegates, by virtue of the power and authority to us given for that purpose, do by these presents, in the name and in behalf of our respective constituents, fully and entirely ratify and confirm each and every of the said articles of confederation and perpetual union, and all and singular the matters and things therein contained: And we do further solemnly plight and engage the faith of our respective constituents, that they shall abide by the determinations of the united states in congress assembled, on all questions, which by the said confederation are submitted to them. And that the articles thereof shall be inviolably observed by the states we respectively represent, and that the union shall be perpetual. In Witness whereof we have hereunto set our hands in Congress. Done at Philadelphia in the state of Pennsylvania the ninth day of July, in the Year of our Lord one Thousand seven Hundred and Seventy-eight, and in the third year of the independence of America.

The Constitution of the United States of America

[PREAMBLE]

We the People of the United States, in Order to form a more perfect Union, establish Justice, insure domestic Tranquility, provide for the common defence, promote the general Welfare, and secure the Blessings of Liberty to ourselves and our Posterity, do ordain and establish this Constitution for the United States of America.

Article I

SECTION 1

[LEGISLATIVE POWERS]

All legislative Powers herein granted shall be vested in a Congress of the United States, which shall consist of a Senate and House of Representatives.

SECTION 2

[HOUSE OF REPRESENTATIVES, HOW CONSTITUTED, POWER OF IMPEACHMENT]

The House of Representatives shall be composed of Members chosen every second Year by the People of the several States, and the Electors in each State shall have the Qualifications requisite for Electors of the most numerous Branch of the State Legislature.

No Person shall be a Representative who shall not have attained to the Age of twenty five Years, and been seven Years a Citizen of the United States, and who shall not, when elected, be an Inhabitant of that State in which he shall be chosen.

Representatives and *direct Taxes*[1] shall be apportioned among the several States which may be included within this Union, according to their respective Numbers, *which shall be determined by adding to the whole Number of free Persons, including those bound to Service for a Term of Years, and excluding Indians not taxed, three fifths of all other Persons.*[2] The actual Enumeration shall be made within three Years after the first Meeting of the Congress of the United States, and within every subsequent Term of ten Years, in such Manner as they shall by Law direct. The Number of Representatives shall not exceed one for every thirty Thousand, but each State shall have at Least one Representative; *and until such enumeration shall be made, the State of New Hampshire shall be entitled to chuse three, Massachusetts eight, Rhode-Island and Providence Plantations one, Connecticut five, New-York six, New Jersey four, Pennsylvania eight, Delaware one, Maryland six, Virginia ten, North Carolina five, South Carolina five, and Georgia three.*[3]

When vacancies happen in the Representation from any State, the Executive Authority thereof shall issue Writs of Election to fill such Vacancies.

The House of Representatives shall chuse their Speaker and other Officers; and shall have the sole Power of Impeachment.

SECTION 3

[THE SENATE, HOW CONSTITUTED, IMPEACHMENT TRIALS]

The Senate of the United States shall be composed of two Senators from each State, *chosen by the Legislature thereof,*[4] for six Years; and each Senator shall have one Vote.

Immediately after they shall be assembled in Consequence of the first Election, they shall be divided as equally as may be into three Classes. The Seats of the Senators of the first Class shall be vacated at the Expiration of the second Year, of the second Class at the Expiration of the fourth Year, and of the third Class at the Expiration of the sixth Year, so that one third may be chosen every second Year; *and if Vacancies happen by Resignation, or otherwise, during the Recess of the Legislature of any State, the Executive thereof may make temporary Appointments until the next Meeting of the Legislature, which shall then fill such Vacancies.*[5]

No Person shall be a Senator who shall not have attained to the Age of thirty Years, and been nine Years a Citizen of the United States, and who shall not, when elected, be an Inhabitant of that State for which he shall be chosen.

The Vice President of the United States shall be President of the Senate, but shall have no Vote, unless they be equally divided.

The Senate shall chuse their other Officers, and also a President pro tempore, in the Absence of the Vice President, or when he shall exercise the Office of President of the United States.

---

[1] Modified by Sixteenth Amendment.

[2] Modified by Fourteenth Amendment.

[3] Temporary provision.

[4] Modified by Seventeenth Amendment.

[5] Modified by Seventeenth Amendment.

The Senate shall have the sole Power to try all Impeachments. When sitting for that Purpose, they shall be on Oath or Affirmation. When the President of the United States is tried, the Chief Justice shall preside: And no Person shall be convicted without the Concurrence of two thirds of the Members present.

Judgment in Cases of Impeachment shall not extend further than to removal from Office, and disqualification to hold and enjoy any Office of honor, Trust or Profit under the United States: but the Party convicted shall nevertheless be liable and subject to Indictment, Trial, Judgment and Punishment, according to Law.

SECTION 4
[ELECTION OF SENATORS AND REPRESENTATIVES]
The Times, Places and Manner of holding Elections for Senators and Representatives, shall be prescribed in each State by the Legislature thereof; but the Congress may at any time by Law make or alter such Regulations, except as to the Places of chusing Senators.

The Congress shall assemble at least once in every Year, and such Meeting shall be on the first Monday in December, unless they shall by Law appoint a different Day.[6]

SECTION 5
[QUORUM, JOURNALS, MEETINGS, ADJOURNMENTS]
Each House shall be the Judge of the Elections, Returns and Qualifications of its own Members, and a Majority of each shall constitute a Quorum to do Business; but a smaller Number may adjourn from day to day, and may be authorized to compel the Attendance of absent Members, in such Manner, and under such Penalties as each House may provide.

Each House may determine the Rules of its Proceedings, punish its Members for disorderly Behaviour, and, with the Concurrence of two thirds, expel a Member.

Each House shall keep a Journal of its Proceedings, and from time to time publish the same, excepting such Parts as may in their Judgment require Secrecy; and the Yeas and Nays of the Members of either House on any questions shall, at the Desire of one fifth of those Present, be entered on the Journal.

Neither House, during the Session of Congress, shall, without the Consent of the other, adjourn for more than three days, nor to any other Place than that in which the two Houses shall be sitting.

SECTION 6
[COMPENSATION, PRIVILEGES, DISABILITIES]
The Senators and Representatives shall receive a Compensation for their Services, to be ascertained by Law, and paid out of the Treasury of the United States. They shall in all Cases, except Treason, Felony and Breach of the Peace, be privileged from Arrest during their Attendance at the Session of their respective Houses, and in going to and returning from the same; and for any Speech or Debate in either House, they shall not be questioned in any other Place.

No Senator or Representative shall, during the Time for which he was elected, be appointed to any civil Office under the Authority of the United States, which shall have been created, or the Emoluments whereof shall have been encreased during such time; and no Person holding any Office under the United States, shall be a Member of either House during his Continuance in Office.

SECTION 7
[PROCEDURE IN PASSING BILLS AND RESOLUTIONS]
All Bills for raising Revenue shall originate in the House of Representatives; but the Senate may propose or concur with Amendments as on other Bills.

Every Bill which shall have passed the House of Representatives and the Senate, shall, before it become a Law, be presented to the President of the United States: If he approve he shall sign it, but if not he shall return it, with his Objections to that House in which it shall have originated, who shall enter the Objections at large on their Journal, and proceed to reconsider it. If after such Reconsideration two thirds of that House shall agree to pass the Bill, it shall be sent, together with the Objections, to the other House, by which it shall likewise be reconsidered, and if approved by two thirds of that House, it shall become a Law. But in all such Cases the Votes of both Houses shall be determined by yeas and Nays, and the Names of the Persons voting for and against the Bill shall be entered on the Journal of each House respectively. If any Bill shall not be returned by the President within ten Days (Sundays excepted) after it shall have been presented to him, the Same shall be a Law, in like Manner as if he had signed it, unless the Congress by their Adjournment prevent its Return, in which Case it shall not be a Law.

Every Order, Resolution, or Vote to which the Concurrence of the Senate and House of Representatives may be necessary (except on a question of Adjournment) shall be presented to the President of the United States; and before the Same shall take Effect, shall be approved by him, or being disapproved by him, shall be repassed by two thirds of the Senate and House of Representatives, according to the Rules and Limitations prescribed in the Case of a Bill.

SECTION 8
[POWERS OF CONGRESS]
The Congress shall have Power

To lay and collect Taxes, Duties, Imposts and Excises, to pay the Debts and provide for the common Defence and general Welfare of the United States; but all Duties, Imposts and Excises shall be uniform throughout the United States;

To borrow Money on the credit of the United States;

---

[6]Modified by Twentieth Amendment.

To regulate Commerce with foreign Nations, and among the several States, and with the Indian Tribes;

To establish an uniform Rule of Naturalization, and uniform Laws on the subject of Bankruptcies throughout the United States;

To coin Money, regulate the Value thereof, and of foreign Coin, and fix the Standard of Weights and Measures;

To provide for the Punishment of counterfeiting the Securities and current Coin of the United States;

To establish Post Offices and post Roads;

To promote the Progress of Science and useful Arts, by securing for limited Times to Authors and Inventors the exclusive Right to their respective Writings and Discoveries;

To constitute Tribunals inferior to the supreme Court;

To define and punish Piracies and Felonies committed on the high Seas, and Offences against the Law of Nations;

To declare War, grant Letters of Marque and Reprisal, and make Rules concerning Captures on Land and Water;

To raise and support Armies, but no Appropriation of Money to that Use shall be for a longer Term than two Years;

To provide and maintain a Navy;

To make Rules for the Government and Regulation of the land and naval Forces;

To provide for calling forth the Militia to execute the Laws of the Union, suppress Insurrections and repel Invasions;

To provide for organizing, arming, and disciplining, the Militia, and for governing such Part of them as may be employed in the Service of the United States, reserving to the States respectively, the Appointment of the Officers, and the Authority of training the Militia according to the discipline prescribed by Congress;

To exercise exclusive Legislation in all Cases whatsoever, over such District (not exceeding ten Miles square) as may, by Cession of particular States, and the Acceptance of Congress, become the Seat of the Government of the United States, and to exercise like Authority over all Places purchased by the Consent of the Legislature of the State in which the Same shall be, for the Erection of Forts, Magazines, Arsenals, dock-Yards, and other needful Buildings;—And

To make all Laws which shall be necessary and proper for carrying into Execution the foregoing Powers, and all other Powers vested by this Constitution in the Government of the United States, or in any Department or Officer thereof.

SECTION 9

[SOME RESTRICTIONS ON FEDERAL POWER]
The Migration or Importation of such Persons as any of the States now existing shall think proper to admit, shall not be prohibited by the Congress prior to the Year one thousand eight hundred and eight, but a Tax or duty may be imposed on such Importation, not exceeding ten dollars for each Person.[7]

The Privilege of the Writ of Habeas Corpus shall not be suspended, unless when in Cases of Rebellion or Invasion the public Safety may require it.

No Bill of Attainder or ex post facto Law shall be passed.

No Capitation, or other direct, Tax shall be laid, unless in Proportion to the Census or Enumeration herein before directed to be taken.[8]

No Tax or Duty shall be laid on Articles exported from any State.

No Preference shall be given by any Regulation of Commerce or Revenue to the Ports of one State over those of another; nor shall Vessels bound to, or from, one State, be obliged to enter, clear, or pay Duties in another.

No Money shall be drawn from the Treasury, but in Consequence of Appropriations made by Law; and a regular Statement and Account of the Receipts and Expenditures of all public Money shall be published from time to time.

No Title of Nobility shall be granted by the United States: And no Person holding any Office of Profit or Trust under them, shall, without the Consent of the Congress, accept of any present, Emolument, Office, or Title, of any kind whatever, from any King, Prince, or foreign State.

SECTION 10

[RESTRICTIONS UPON POWERS OF STATES]
No State shall enter into any Treaty, Alliance, or Confederation; grant Letters of Marque and Reprisal; coin Money; emit Bills of Credit; make any Thing but gold and silver Coin a Tender in Payment of Debts; pass any Bill of Attainder, ex post facto Law, or Law impairing the Obligation of Contracts, or grant any Title of Nobility.

No State shall, without the Consent of the Congress, lay any Imposts or Duties on Imports or Exports, except what may be absolutely necessary for executing its inspection Laws: and the net Produce of all Duties and Imposts, laid by any State on Imports or Exports, shall be for the Use of the Treasury of the United States; and all such Laws shall be subject to the Revision and Control of the Congress.

No State shall, without the Consent of Congress, lay any Duty of Tonnage, keep Troops, or Ships of War in time of Peace, enter into any Agreement or Compact with another State, or with a foreign Power, or engage in War, unless actually invaded, or in such imminent Danger as will not admit of delay.

Article II

SECTION 1

[EXECUTIVE POWER, ELECTION,
QUALIFICATIONS OF THE PRESIDENT]
The executive Power shall be vested in a President of the United States of America. *He shall hold his Office during the*

---

[7]Temporary provision.

[8]Modified by Sixteenth Amendment.

Term of four Years, and, together with the Vice President, chosen for the same Term, be elected, as follows[9]

Each State shall appoint, in such Manner as the Legislature thereof may direct, a Number of Electors, equal to the whole Number of Senators and Representatives to which the State may be entitled in the Congress: but no Senator or Representative, or Person holding an Office of Trust or Profit under the United States, shall be appointed an Elector.

The electors shall meet in their respective States, and vote by ballot for two Persons, of whom one at least shall not be an Inhabitant of the same State with themselves. And they shall make a List of all the Persons voted for, and of the Number of Votes for each; which List they shall sign and certify, and transmit sealed to the Seat of the Government of the United States, directed to the President of the Senate. The President of the Senate shall, in the Presence of the Senate and House of Representatives, open all the Certificates, and the Votes shall then be counted. The Person having the greatest Number of Votes shall be the President, if such Number be a Majority of the whole Number of Electors appointed; and if there be more than one who have such Majority, and have an equal Number of Votes, then the House of Representatives shall immediately chuse by Ballot one of them for President; and if no Person have a Majority, then from the five highest on the List the said House shall in like Manner chuse the President. But in chusing the President, the Votes shall be taken by States, the Representation from each State having one Vote; A quorum for this Purpose shall consist of a Member or Members from two thirds of the States, and a Majority of all the States shall be necessary to a Choice. In every Case, after the Choice of the President, the person having the greatest Number of Votes of the Electors shall be the Vice President. But if there should remain two or more who have equal Votes, the Senate shall chuse from them by Ballot the Vice President.[10]

The Congress may determine the Time of chusing the Electors, and the Day on which they shall give their Votes; which Day shall be the same throughout the United States.

No Person except a natural born Citizen, or a Citizen of the United States, at the time of the Adoption of this Constitution, shall be eligible to the Office of President; neither shall any Person be eligible to that Office who shall not have attained to the Age of thirty five Years, and been fourteen Years a Resident within the United States.

In Case of the Removal of the President from Office, or his Death, Resignation, or Inability to discharge the Powers and Duties of the said Office, the Same shall devolve on the Vice President, and the Congress may by Law provide for the Case of Removal, Death, Resignation or Inability, both of the President and Vice President, declaring what Officer shall then act as President, and such Officer shall act accordingly, until the Disability be removed, or a President shall be elected.

The President shall, at stated Times, receive for his Services, a Compensation, which shall neither be increased nor diminished during the Period for which he shall have been elected, and he shall not receive within that Period any other Emolument from the United States, or any of them.

Before he enter on the Execution of his Office, he shall take the following Oath or Affirmation:—"I do solemnly swear (or affirm) that I will faithfully execute the Office of President of the United States, and will to the best of my Ability, preserve, protect and defend the Constitution of the United States."

SECTION 2

[POWERS OF THE PRESIDENT]

The President shall be Commander in Chief of the Army and Navy of the United States, and of the Militia of the several States, when called into the actual Service of the United States; he may require the Opinion, in writing, of the principal Officer in each of the executive Departments, upon any Subject relating to the Duties of their respective Offices, and he shall have Power to grant Reprieves and Pardons for Offences against the United States, except in Cases of Impeachment.

He shall have Power, by and with the Advice and Consent of the Senate, to make Treaties, provided two thirds of the Senators present concur; and he shall nominate, and by and with the Advice and Consent of the Senate, shall appoint Ambassadors, other public Ministers and Consuls, Judges of the supreme Court, and all other Officers of the United States, whose Appointments are not herein otherwise provided for, and which shall be established by Law: but the Congress may by Law vest the Appointment of such inferior Officers, as they think proper, in the President alone, in the Courts of Law, or in the Heads of Departments.

The President shall have Power to fill up all Vacancies that may happen during the Recess of the Senate, by granting Commissions which shall expire at the End of their next Session.

SECTION 3

[POWERS AND DUTIES OF THE PRESIDENT]

He shall from time to time give to the Congress Information of the State of the Union, and recommend to their Consideration such Measures as he shall judge necessary and expedient; he may, on extraordinary Occasions, convene both Houses, or either of them, and in Case of Disagreement between them, with Respect to the Time of Adjournment, he may adjourn them to such Time as he shall think proper; he shall receive Ambassadors and other public Ministers; he shall take Care that the Laws be faithfully executed, and shall Commission all the Officers of the United States.

SECTION 4

[IMPEACHMENT]

The President, Vice President and all civil Officers of the United States, shall be removed from Office on Impeachment

---

[9]Number of terms limited to two by Twenty-Second Amendment.

[10]Modified by Twelfth and Twentieth Amendments.

for, and Conviction of, Treason, Bribery, or other high Crimes and Misdemeanors.

Article III

SECTION 1

[JUDICIAL POWER, TENURE OF OFFICE]
The judicial Power of the United States, shall be vested in one supreme Court, and in such inferior Courts as the Congress may from time to time ordain and establish. The Judges, both of the supreme and inferior Courts, shall hold their Offices during good Behaviour, and shall, at stated Times, receive for their Services, a Compensation, which shall not be diminished during their Continuance in Office.

SECTION 2

[JURISDICTION]
The judicial Power shall extend to all Cases, in Law and Equity, arising under this Constitution, the Laws of the United States, and Treaties made, or which shall be made, under their Authority;—to all Cases affecting Ambassadors, other public Ministers and Consuls;—to all Cases of admiralty and maritime Jurisdiction;—to Controversies to which the United States shall be a Party;—to Controversies between two or more States;— *between a State and Citizens of another State;*—between Citizens of different States,—between Citizens of the same State claiming Lands under Grants of different States, *and between a State,* or the Citizens thereof, *and foreign States, Citizens or Subjects.* [11]

In all Cases affecting Ambassadors, other public Ministers and Consuls, and those in which a State shall be Party, the supreme Court shall have original Jurisdiction. In all the other Cases before mentioned, the supreme Court shall have appellate Jurisdiction, both as to Law and Fact, with such Exceptions, and under such Regulations as the Congress shall make.

The Trial of all Crimes, except in Cases of Impeachment, shall be by Jury; and such Trial shall be held in the State where the said Crimes shall have been committed; but when not committed within any State, the Trial shall be at such Place or Places as the Congress may by Law have directed.

SECTION 3

[TREASON, PROOF, AND PUNISHMENT]
Treason against the United States, shall consist only in levying War against them, or in adhering to their Enemies, giving them Aid and Comfort. No Person shall be convicted of Treason unless on the Testimony of two Witnesses to the same overt Act, or on Confession in open Court.

The Congress shall have Power to declare the Punishment of Treason, but no Attainder of Treason shall work Corruption of Blood, or Forfeiture except during the Life of the Person attainted.

Article IV

SECTION 1

[FAITH AND CREDIT AMONG STATES]
Full Faith and Credit shall be given in each State to the public Acts, Records, and judicial Proceedings of every other State. And the Congress may by general Laws prescribe the Manner in which such Acts, Records and Proceedings shall be proved, and the Effect thereof.

SECTION 2

[PRIVILEGES AND IMMUNITIES, FUGITIVES]
The Citizens of each State shall be entitled to all Privileges and Immunities of Citizens in the several States.

A Person charged in any State with Treason, Felony or other Crime, who shall flee from Justice, and be found in another State, shall on Demand of the executive Authority of the State from which he fled, be delivered up, to be removed to the State having Jurisdiction of the Crime.

No person held to Service or Labour in one State, under the Laws thereof, escaping into another, shall, in Consequence of any Law or Regulation therein, be discharged from such Service or Labour, but shall be delivered up on Claim of the Party to whom such Service or Labour may be due. [12]

SECTION 3

[ADMISSION OF NEW STATES]
New States may be admitted by the Congress into this Union; but no new State shall be formed or erected within the Jurisdiction of any other State; nor any State be formed by the Junction of two or more States, or Parts of States, without the Consent of the Legislatures of the States concerned as well as of the Congress.

The Congress shall have Power to dispose of and make all needful Rules and Regulations respecting the Territory or other Property belonging to the United States; and nothing in this Constitution shall be so construed as to Prejudice any Claims of the United States, or of any particular State.

SECTION 4

[GUARANTEE OF REPUBLICAN GOVERNMENT]
The United States shall guarantee to every State in this Union a Republican Form of Government, and shall protect each of them against Invasion; and on Application of the Legislature, or of the Executive (when the Legislature cannot be convened), against domestic Violence.

Article V

[AMENDMENT OF THE CONSTITUTION]
The Congress, whenever two thirds of both Houses shall deem it necessary, shall propose Amendments to this Constitution, or, on the Application of the Legislatures of two thirds of the

---

[11]Modified by Eleventh Amendment.

[12]Repealed by the Thirteenth Amendment.

several States, shall call a Convention for proposing Amendments, which, in either Case, shall be valid to all Intents and Purposes, as Part of this Constitution, when ratified by the Legislatures of three fourths of the several States, or by Conventions in three fourths thereof, as the one or the other Mode of Ratification may be proposed by the Congress; *Provided that no Amendment which may be made prior to the Year One thousand eight hundred and eight shall in any Manner affect the first and fourth Clauses in the Ninth Section of the first Article;*[13] and that no State, without its Consent, shall be deprived of its equal Suffrage in the Senate.

Article VI

[DEBTS, SUPREMACY, OATH]
All Debts contracted and Engagements entered into, before the Adoption of this Constitution, shall be as valid against the United States under this Constitution, as under the Confederation.

This Constitution, and the Laws of the United States which shall be made in Pursuance thereof; and all Treaties made, or which shall be made, under the Authority of the United States, shall be the supreme Law of the Land; and the Judges in every State shall be bound thereby, any Thing in the Constitution or Laws of any State to the Contrary notwithstanding.

The Senators and Representatives before mentioned, and the Members of the several State Legislatures, and all executive and judicial Officers, both of the United States and of the several States, shall be bound by Oath or Affirmation, to support this Constitution; but no religious Test shall be required as a Qualification to any Office or public Trust under the United States.

Article VII

[RATIFICATION AND ESTABLISHMENT]
The Ratification of the Conventions of nine States, shall be sufficient for the Establishment of this Constitution between the States so ratifying the Same.[14]

Done in Convention by the Unanimous Consent of the States present the Seventeenth Day of September in the Year of our Lord one thousand seven hundred and Eighty seven and of the Independence of the United States of America the Twelfth. *In Witness* whereof We have hereunto subscribed our Names,

---

[14]The Constitution was submitted on September 17, 1787, by the Constitutional Convention, was ratified by the conventions of several states at various dates up to May 29, 1790, and became effective on March 4, 1789.

---

[13]Temporary provision.

G:⁰ WASHINGTON—
Presidt. and deputy from Virginia

NEW HAMPSHIRE
John Langdon
Nicholas Gilman

MASSACHUSETTS
Nathaniel Gorham
Rufus King

CONNECTICUT
Wm. Saml. Johnson
Roger Sherman

NEW YORK
Alexander Hamilton

NEW JERSEY
Wil: Livingston
David Brearley
Wm. Paterson
Jona: Dayton

PENNSYLVANIA
B Franklin
Thomas Mifflin
Robt. Morris
Geo. Clymer
Thos. FitzSimons
Jared Ingersoll
James Wilson
Gouv Morris

DELAWARE
Geo: Read
Gunning Bedford jun
John Dickinson
Richard Bassett
Jaco: Broom

MARYLAND
James McHenry
Dan of St Thos. Jenifer
Danl. Carroll

VIRGINIA
John Blair—
James Madison Jr.

NORTH CAROLINA
Wm. Blount
Richd. Dobbs Spaight
Hu Williamson

SOUTH CAROLINA
J. Rutledge
Charles Cotesworth Pinckney
Charles Pinckney
Pierce Butler

GEORGIA
William Few
Abr Baldwin

Amendments to the Constitution

Proposed by Congress and Ratified by the Legislatures of the Several States, Pursuant to Article V of the Original Constitution.

Amendments I–X, known as the Bill of Rights, were proposed by Congress on September 25, 1789, and ratified on December 15, 1791.

Amendment I
[FREEDOM OF RELIGION, OF SPEECH, AND OF THE PRESS]
Congress shall make no law respecting an establishment of religion, or prohibiting the free exercise thereof; or abridging the freedom of speech, or of the press; or the right of the people peaceably to assemble, and to petition the Government for a redress of grievances.

Amendment II
[RIGHT TO KEEP AND BEAR ARMS]
A well regulated Militia, being necessary to the security of a free State, the right of the people to keep and bear Arms, shall not be infringed.

Amendment III
[QUARTERING OF SOLDIERS]
No Soldier shall, in time of peace be quartered in any house, without the consent of the Owner, nor in time of war, but in a manner to be prescribed by law.

Amendment IV
[SECURITY FROM UNWARRANTABLE SEARCH AND SEIZURE]
The right of the people to be secure in their persons, houses, papers, and effects, against unreasonable searches and seizures, shall not be violated, and no Warrants shall issue, but upon probable cause, supported by Oath or affirmation, and particularly describing the place to be searched, and the persons or things to be seized.

Amendment V
[RIGHTS OF ACCUSED PERSONS IN CRIMINAL PROCEEDINGS]
No person shall be held to answer for a capital, or otherwise infamous crime, unless on a presentment or indictment of a Grand Jury, except in cases arising in the land or naval forces, or in the Militia, when in actual service in time of War or in public danger; nor shall any person be subject for the same offence to be twice put in jeopardy of life or limb; nor shall be compelled in any criminal case to be a witness against himself, nor be deprived of life, liberty, or property, without due process of law; nor shall private property be taken for public use, without just compensation.

Amendment VI
[RIGHT TO SPEEDY TRIAL, WITNESSES, ETC.]
In all criminal prosecutions, the accused shall enjoy the right to a speedy and public trial, by an impartial jury of the State and district wherein the crime shall have been committed, which district shall have been previously ascertained by law, and to be informed of the nature and cause of the accusation; to be confronted with the witnesses against him; to have compulsory process for obtaining witnesses in his favor, and to have the Assistance of Counsel for his defence.

Amendment VII
[TRIAL BY JURY IN CIVIL CASES]
In suits at common law, where the value in controversy shall exceed twenty dollars, the right of trial by jury shall be preserved, and no fact tried by a jury, shall be otherwise reexamined in any Court of the United States, than according to the rules of the common law.

Amendment VIII
[BAILS, FINES, PUNISHMENTS]
Excessive bail shall not be required, nor excessive fines imposed, nor cruel and unusual punishments inflicted.

Amendment IX
[RESERVATION OF RIGHTS OF PEOPLE]
The enumeration in the Constitution, of certain rights, shall not be construed to deny or disparage others retained by the people.

Amendment X
[POWERS RESERVED TO STATES OR PEOPLE]
The powers not delegated to the United States by the Constitution, nor prohibited by it to the States, are reserved to the States respectively, or to the people.

Amendment XI

[Proposed by Congress on March 4, 1794; declared ratified on January 8, 1798.]

[RESTRICTION OF JUDICIAL POWER]

The Judicial power of the United States shall not be construed to extend to any suit in law or equity, commenced or prosecuted against one of the United States by Citizens of another State, or by Citizens or Subjects of any Foreign State.

Amendment XII

[Proposed by Congress on December 9, 1803; declared ratified on September 25, 1804.]

[ELECTION OF PRESIDENT AND VICE PRESIDENT]

The Electors shall meet in their respective states and vote by ballot for President and Vice-President, one of whom, at least, shall not be an inhabitant of the same state with themselves; they shall name in their ballots the person voted for as President, and in distinct ballots the person voted for as Vice-President, and they shall make distinct lists of all persons voted for as President, and of all persons voted for as Vice-President, and of the number of votes for each, which lists they shall sign and certify, and transmit sealed to the seat of the government of the United States, directed to the President of the Senate;—the President of the Senate shall, in presence of the Senate and House of Representatives, open all the certificates and the votes shall then be counted;—The person having the greatest number of votes for President, shall be the President, if such number be a majority of the whole number of Electors appointed; and if no person have such majority, then from the persons having the highest numbers not exceeding three on the list of those voted for as President, the House of Representatives shall choose immediately, by ballot, the President. But in choosing the President, the votes shall be taken by states, the representation from each state having one vote; a quorum for this purpose shall consist of a member or members from two-thirds of the states, and a majority of all the states shall be necessary to a choice. And if the House of Representatives shall not choose a President whenever the right of choice shall devolve upon them, before the fourth day of March next following, then the Vice-President shall act as President, as in the case of the death or other constitutional disability of the President.—The person having the greatest number of votes as Vice-President, shall be the Vice-President, if such number be a majority of the whole number of Electors appointed, and if no person have a majority, then from the two highest numbers on the list, the Senate shall choose the Vice-President; a quorum for the purpose shall consist of two-thirds of the whole number of Senators, and a majority of the whole number shall be necessary to a choice. But no person constitutionally ineligible to the office of President shall be eligible to that of Vice-President of the United States.

Amendment XIII

[Proposed by Congress on January 31, 1865; declared ratified on December 18, 1865.]

SECTION 1

[ABOLITION OF SLAVERY]

Neither slavery nor involuntary servitude, except as a punishment for crime whereof the party shall have been duly convicted, shall exist within the United States, or any place subject to their jurisdiction.

SECTION 2

[POWER TO ENFORCE THIS ARTICLE]

Congress shall have power to enforce this article by appropriate legislation.

Amendment XIV

[Proposed by Congress on June 13, 1866; declared ratified on July 28, 1868.]

SECTION 1

[CITIZENSHIP RIGHTS NOT TO BE ABRIDGED BY STATES]

All persons born or naturalized in the United States, and subject to the jurisdiction thereof, are citizens of the United States and of the State wherein they reside. No State shall make or enforce any law which shall abridge the privileges or immunities of citizens of the United States; nor shall any State deprive any person of life, liberty, or property, without due process of law; nor deny to any person within its jurisdiction the equal protection of the laws.

SECTION 2

[APPORTIONMENT OF REPRESENTATIVES IN CONGRESS]

Representatives shall be apportioned among the several States according to their respective numbers, counting the whole number of persons in each State, excluding Indians not taxed. But when the right to vote at any election for the choice of electors for President and Vice-President of the United States, Representatives in Congress, the Executive and Judicial officers of a State, or the members of the Legislature thereof, is denied to any of the male inhabitants of such State, being twenty-one years of age, and citizens of the United States, or in any way abridged, except for participation in rebellion, or other crime, the basis of representation therein shall be reduced in the proportion which the number of such male citizens shall bear to the whole number of male citizens twenty-one years of age in such State.

SECTION 3

[PERSONS DISQUALIFIED FROM HOLDING OFFICE]

No person shall be a Senator or Representative in Congress, or elector of President and Vice-President, or hold any office, civil or military, under the United States, or under any State, who, having previously taken an oath, as a member of Congress, or as an officer of the United States, or as a member of any State legislature, or as an executive or judicial officer of any State, to support the Constitution of the United States, shall have engaged in insurrection or rebellion against the same, or given aid or comfort to the enemies thereof. But Congress may by a vote of two-thirds of each House, remove such disability.

SECTION 4
[WHAT PUBLIC DEBTS ARE VALID]
The validity of the public debt of the United States, authorized by law, including debts incurred for payment of pensions and bounties for services in suppressing insurrection or rebellion, shall not be questioned. But neither the United States nor any State shall assume or pay any debt or obligation incurred in aid of insurrection or rebellion against the United States, or any claim for the loss or emancipation of any slave; but all such debts, obligations and claims shall be held illegal and void.

SECTION 5
[POWER TO ENFORCE THIS ARTICLE]
The Congress shall have power to enforce, by appropriate legislation, the provisions of this article.

Amendment XV
[*Proposed by Congress on February 26, 1869;*
declared ratified on March 30, 1870.]

SECTION 1
[NEGRO SUFFRAGE]
The right of citizens of the United States to vote shall not be denied or abridged by the United States or by any State on account of race, color, or previous condition of servitude.

SECTION 2
[POWER TO ENFORCE THIS ARTICLE]
The Congress shall have power to enforce this article by appropriate legislation.

Amendment XVI
[*Proposed by Congress on July 2, 1909;*
declared ratified on February 25, 1913.]
[AUTHORIZING INCOME TAXES]
The Congress shall have power to lay and collect taxes on incomes, from whatever source derived, without apportionment among the several States, and without regard to any census or enumeration.

Amendment XVII
[*Proposed by Congress on May 13, 1912;*
declared ratified on May 31, 1913.]
[POPULAR ELECTION OF SENATORS]
The Senate of the United States shall be composed of two Senators from each State, elected by the people thereof, for six years; and each Senator shall have one vote. The electors in each State shall have the qualifications requisite for electors of the most numerous branch of the State legislatures.

When vacancies happen in the representation of any State in the Senate, the executive authority of such State shall issue writs of election to fill such vacancies: *Provided,* That the legislature of any State may empower the executive thereof to make temporary appointments until the people fill the vacancies by election as the legislature may direct.

This amendment shall not be so construed as to affect the election or term of any Senator chosen before it becomes valid as part of the Constitution.

Amendment XVIII
[*Proposed by Congress December 18, 1917;*
declared ratified on January 29, 1919.]

SECTION 1
[NATIONAL LIQUOR PROHIBITION]
After one year from the ratification of this article the manufacture, sale, or transportation of intoxicating liquors within, the importation thereof into, or the exportation thereof from the United States and all territory subject to the jurisdiction thereof for beverage purposes is hereby prohibited.

SECTION 2
[POWER TO ENFORCE THIS ARTICLE]
The Congress and the several States shall have concurrent power to enforce this article by appropriate legislation.

SECTION 3
[RATIFICATION WITHIN SEVEN YEARS]
This article shall be inoperative unless it shall have been ratified as an amendment to the Constitution by the legislatures of the several States, as provided in the Constitution, within seven years from the date of the submission hereof to the States by the Congress.[1]

Amendment XIX
[*Proposed by Congress on June 4, 1919;*
declared ratified on August 26, 1920.]
[WOMAN SUFFRAGE]
The right of citizens of the United States to vote shall not be denied or abridged by the United States or by any State on account of sex.

Congress shall have power to enforce this article by appropriate legislation.

---

[1]Repealed by the Twenty-First Amendment.

Amendment XX

[*Proposed by Congress on March 2, 1932;
declared ratified on February 6, 1933.*]

SECTION 1
[TERMS OF OFFICE]
The terms of the President and Vice President shall end at noon on the 20th day of January, and the terms of Senators and Representatives at noon on the 3d day of January, of the years in which such terms would have ended if this article had not been ratified; and the terms of their successors shall then begin.

SECTION 2
[TIME OF CONVENING CONGRESS]
The Congress shall assemble at least once in every year, and such meeting shall begin at noon on the 3d day of January, unless they shall by law appoint a different day.

SECTION 3
[DEATH OF PRESIDENT-ELECT]
If, at the time fixed for the beginning of the term of the President, the President elect shall have died, the Vice President elect shall become President. If a President shall not have been chosen before the time fixed for the beginning of his term, or if the President elect shall have failed to qualify, then the Vice President elect shall act as President until a President shall have qualified; and the Congress may by law provide for the case wherein neither a President elect nor a Vice President elect shall have qualified, declaring who shall then act as President, or the manner in which one who is to act shall be selected, and such person shall act accordingly until a President or Vice President shall have qualified.

SECTION 4
[ELECTION OF THE PRESIDENT]
The Congress may by law provide for the case of the death of any of the persons from whom the House of Representatives may choose a President whenever the right of choice shall have devolved upon them, and for the case of the death of any of the persons from whom the Senate may choose a Vice President whenever the right of choice shall have devolved upon them.

SECTION 5
[AMENDMENT TAKES EFFECT]
Sections 1 and 2 shall take effect on the 15th day of October following the ratification of this article.

SECTION 6
[RATIFICATION WITHIN SEVEN YEARS]
This article shall be inoperative unless it shall have been ratified as an amendment to the Constitution by the legislatures of three-fourths of the several States within seven years from the date of its submission.

Amendment XXI

[*Proposed by Congress on February 20, 1933;
declared ratified on December 5, 1933.*]

SECTION 1
[NATIONAL LIQUOR PROHIBITION REPEALED]
The eighteenth article of amendment to the Constitution of the United States is hereby repealed.

SECTION 2
[TRANSPORTATION OF LIQUOR INTO "DRY" STATES]
The transportation or importation into any State, Territory, or Possession of the United States for delivery or use therein of intoxicating liquors, in violation of the laws thereof, is hereby prohibited.

SECTION 3
[RATIFICATION WITHIN SEVEN YEARS]
This article shall be inoperative unless it shall have been ratified as an amendment to the Constitution by conventions in the several States, as provided in the Constitution, within seven years from the date of the submission hereof to the States by the Congress.

Amendment XXII

[*Proposed by Congress on March 21, 1947;
declared ratified on February 27, 1951.*]

SECTION 1
[TENURE OF PRESIDENT LIMITED]
No person shall be elected to the office of President more than twice, and no person who has held the office of President or acted as President, for more than two years of a term to which some other person was elected President shall be elected to the office of the President more than once. But this Article shall not apply to any person holding the office of President when this Article was proposed by the Congress, and shall not prevent any person who may be holding the office of President, or acting as President, during the term within which this Article becomes operative from holding the office of President or acting as President during the remainder of such term.

SECTION 2
[RATIFICATION WITHIN SEVEN YEARS]
This article shall be inoperative unless it shall have been ratified as an amendment to the Constitution by the legislatures of three-fourths of the several States within seven years from the date of its submission to the States by the Congress.

Amendment XXIII

[*Proposed by Congress on June 16, 1960;
declared ratified on March 29, 1961.*]

SECTION 1

[ELECTORAL COLLEGE VOTES FOR THE DISTRICT OF COLUMBIA]

The District constituting the seat of Government of the United States shall appoint in such manner as the Congress may direct:

A number of electors of President and Vice President equal to the whole number of Senators and Representatives in Congress to which the District would be entitled if it were a State, but in no event more than the least populous State; they shall be in addition to those appointed by the States, but they shall be considered, for the purposes of the election of President and Vice President, to be electors appointed by a State; and they shall meet in the District and perform such duties as provided by the twelfth article of amendment.

SECTION 2

[POWER TO ENFORCE THIS ARTICLE]

The Congress shall have power to enforce this article by appropriate legislation.

Amendment XXIV

[*Proposed by Congress on August 27, 1962;
declared ratified on January 23, 1964.*]

SECTION 1

[ANTI-POLL TAX]

The right of citizens of the United States to vote in any primary or other election for President or Vice President, for electors for President or Vice President, or for Senator or Representative of Congress, shall not be denied or abridged by the United States or any State by reason of failure to pay any poll tax or other tax.

SECTION 2

[POWER TO ENFORCE THIS ARTICLE]

The Congress shall have power to enforce this article by appropriate legislation.

Amendment XXV

[*Proposed by Congress on July 6, 1965;
declared ratified on February 10, 1967.*]

SECTION 1

[VICE PRESIDENT TO BECOME PRESIDENT]

In case of the removal of the President from office or his death or resignation, the Vice President shall become President.

SECTION 2

[CHOICE OF A NEW VICE PRESIDENT]

Whenever there is a vacancy in the office of the Vice President, the President shall nominate a Vice President who shall take the office upon confirmation by a majority vote of both houses of Congress.

SECTION 3

[PRESIDENT MAY DECLARE OWN DISABILITY]

Whenever the President transmits to the President pro tempore of the Senate and the Speaker of the House of Representatives his written declaration that he is unable to discharge the powers and duties of his office, and until he transmits to them a written declaration to the contrary, such powers and duties shall be discharged by the Vice President as Acting President.

SECTION 4

[ALTERNATE PROCEDURES TO DECLARE AND
TO END PRESIDENTIAL DISABILITY]

Whenever the Vice President and a majority of either the principal officers of the executive departments, or of such other body as Congress may by law provide, transmit to the President pro tempore of the Senate and the Speaker of the House of Representatives their written declaration that the President is unable to discharge the powers and duties of his office, the Vice President shall immediately assume the powers and duties of the office as Acting President.

Thereafter, when the President transmits to the President pro tempore of the Senate and the Speaker of the House of Representatives his written declaration that no inability exists, he shall resume the powers and duties of his office unless the Vice President and a majority of either the principal officers of the executive department, or of such other body as Congress may by law provide, transmit within four days to the President pro tempore of the Senate and the Speaker of the House of Representatives their written declaration that the President is unable to discharge the powers and duties of his office. Thereupon Congress shall decide the issue, assembling within forty eight hours for that purpose if not in session. If the Congress, within twenty one days after receipt of the latter written declaration, or, if Congress is not in session, within twenty one days after Congress is required to assemble, determines by two-thirds vote of both Houses that the President is unable to discharge the powers and duties of his office, the Vice President shall continue to discharge the same as Acting President; otherwise, the President shall resume the powers and duties of his office.

Amendment XXVI

[*Proposed by Congress on March 23, 1971;*
declared ratified on July 1, 1971.]

SECTION 1

[EIGHTEEN-YEAR-OLD VOTE]
The right of citizens of the United States, who are eighteen years of age or older, to vote shall not be denied or abridged by the United States or by any State on account of age.

SECTION 2

[POWER TO ENFORCE THIS ARTICLE]
The Congress shall have power to enforce this article by appropriate legislation.

Amendment XXVII

[*Proposed by Congress on September 25, 1789;*
declared ratified on May 8, 1992.]

[CONGRESS CANNOT RAISE ITS OWN PAY]
No law varying the compensation for the services of the Senators and Representatives, shall take effect, until an election of representatives shall have intervened.

The Federalist Papers

No. 10: Madison

Among the numerous advantages promised by a well constructed Union, none deserves to be more accurately developed than its tendency to break and control the violence of faction. The friend of popular governments never finds himself so much alarmed for their character and fate, as when he contemplates their propensity to this dangerous vice. He will not fail therefore to set a due value on any plan which, without violating the principles to which he is attached, provides a proper cure for it. The instability, injustice, and confusion introduced into the public councils have, in truth, been the mortal diseases under which popular governments have everywhere perished, as they continue to be the favorite and fruitful topics from which the adversaries to liberty derive their most specious declamations. The valuable improvements made by the American constitutions on the popular models, both ancient and modern, cannot certainly be too much admired; but it would be an unwarrantable partiality to contend that they have as effectually obviated the danger on this side, as was wished and expected. Complaints are everywhere heard from our most considerate and virtuous citizens, equally the friends of public and private faith and of public and personal liberty, that our governments are too unstable, that the public good is disregarded in the conflicts of rival parties, and that measures are too often decided, not according to the rules of justice and the rights of the minor party, but by the superior force of an interested and overbearing majority. However anxiously we may wish that these complaints had no foundation, the evidence of known facts will not permit us to deny that they are in some degree true. It will be found, indeed, on a candid review of our situation, that some of the distresses under which we labor have been erroneously charged on the operation of our governments; but it will be found, at the same time, that other causes will not alone account for many of our heaviest misfortunes; and, particularly, for that prevailing and increasing distrust of public engagements and alarm for private rights which are echoed from one end of the continent to the other. These must be chiefly, if not wholly, effects of the unsteadiness and injustice with which a factious spirit has tainted our public administration.

By a faction I understand a number of citizens, whether amounting to a majority or minority of the whole, who are united and actuated by some common impulse of passion, or of interest, adverse to the rights of other citizens, or to the permanent and aggregate interests of the community.

There are two methods of curing the mischiefs of faction: the one, by removing its causes; the other, by controlling its effects.

There are again two methods of removing the causes of faction: the one, by destroying the liberty which is essential to its existence; the other, by giving to every citizen the same opinions, the same passions, and the same interests.

It could never be more truly said than of the first remedy, that it is worse than the disease. Liberty is to faction what air is to fire, an aliment without which it instantly expires. But it could not be a less folly to abolish liberty, which is essential to political life, because it nourishes faction, than it would be to wish the annihilation of air, which is essential to animal life, because it imparts to fire its destructive agency.

The second expedient is as impracticable, as the first would be unwise. As long as the reason of man continues fallible, and he is at liberty to exercise it, different opinions will be formed. As long as the connection subsists between his reason and his self-love, his opinions and his passions will have a reciprocal influence on each other; and the former will be objects to which the latter will attach themselves. The diversity in the faculties of men, from which the rights of property originate, is not less an insuperable obstacle to a uniformity of interests. The protection of these faculties is the first object of Government. From the protection of different and unequal faculties of acquiring property, the possession of different degrees and kinds of property immediately results; and from the influence of these on the sentiments and views of the respective proprietors, ensues a division of the society into different interests and parties.

The latent causes of faction are thus sown in the nature of man; and we see them everywhere brought into different degrees of activity, according to the different circumstances of civil society. A zeal for different opinions concerning religion, concerning Government, and many other points, as well of speculation as of practice; an attachment to different leaders ambitiously contending for pre-eminence and power; or to persons of other descriptions whose fortunes have been interesting to the human passions, have in turn divided mankind into parties, inflamed them with mutual animosity, and rendered them much more disposed to vex and oppress each other, than to co-operate for their common good. So strong is this propensity of mankind to fall into mutual animosities, that where no substantial occasion presents itself, the most frivolous and fanciful distinctions have been sufficient to kindle their unfriendly passions, and excite their most violent conflicts. But the most common and durable source of factions has been the various and unequal distribution of property. Those who hold and those who are without property have ever formed distinct interests in society. Those who are creditors, and those who are debtors, fall under a like discrimination. A landed interest, a manufacturing interest, a mercantile interest, a moneyed interest, with many lesser interests, grow up of necessity in civilized nations, and divide them into different classes, actuated by different sentiments and views. The regulation of these various and interfering interests forms the principal task of modern Legislation, and involves the spirit of party and faction in the necessary and ordinary operations of Government.

No man is allowed to be judge in his own cause, because his interest would certainly bias his judgment and, not improbably, corrupt his integrity. With equal, nay with greater reason, a body of men are unfit to be both judges and parties at the same time; yet what are many of the most important acts of legislation but so many judicial determinations, not indeed concerning the rights of single persons, but concerning the rights of large bodies of citizens; and what are the different classes of legislators but advocates and parties to the causes which they determine? Is a law proposed concerning private debts? It is a question to which the creditors are parties on one side and the debtors on the other. Justice ought to hold the balance between them. Yet the parties are, and must be, themselves the judges; and the most numerous party, or in other words, the most powerful faction must be expected to prevail. Shall domestic manufacturers be encouraged, and in what degree, by restrictions on foreign manufacturers? are questions which would be differently decided by the landed and the manufacturing classes, and probably by neither with a sole regard to justice and the public good. The apportionment of taxes on the various descriptions of property is an act which seems to require the most exact impartiality; yet there is, perhaps, no legislative act in which greater opportunity and temptation are given to a predominant party to trample on the rules of justice. Every shilling with which they overburden the inferior number is a shilling saved to their own pockets.

It is in vain to say that enlightened statesmen will be able to adjust these clashing interests and render them all subservient to the public good. Enlightened statesmen will not always be at the helm. Nor, in many cases, can such an adjustment be made at all without taking into view indirect and remote considerations, which will rarely prevail over the immediate interest which one party may find in disregarding the rights of another or the good of the whole.

The inference to which we are brought is that the *causes* of faction cannot be removed and that relief is only to be sought in the means of controlling its *effects*.

If a faction consists of less than a majority, relief is supplied by the republican principle, which enables the majority to defeat its sinister views by regular vote. It may clog the administration, it may convulse the society; but it will be unable to execute and mask its violence under the forms of the Constitution. When a majority is included in a faction,

the form of popular government, on the other hand, enables it to sacrifice to its ruling passion or interest both the public good and the rights of other citizens. To secure the public good and private rights against the danger of such a faction, and at the same time to preserve the spirit and the form of popular government, is then the great object to which our enquiries are directed. Let me add that it is the great desideratum by which alone this form of government can be rescued from the opprobrium under which it has so long labored and be recommended to the esteem and adoption of mankind.

By what means is this object attainable? Evidently by one of two only. Either the existence of the same passion or interest in a majority at the same time must be prevented, or the majority, having such co-existent passion or interest, must be rendered, by their number and local situation, unable to concert and carry into effect schemes of oppression. If the impulse and the opportunity be suffered to coincide, we well know that neither moral nor religious motives can be relied on as an adequate control. They are not found to be such on the injustice and violence of individuals, and lose their efficacy in proportion to the number combined together, that is, in proportion as their efficacy becomes needful.

From this view of the subject it may be concluded that a pure Democracy, by which I mean a Society consisting of a small number of citizens, who assemble and administer the Government in person, can admit of no cure for the mischiefs of faction. A common passion or interest will, in almost every case, be felt by a majority of the whole; a communication and concert results from the form of Government itself; and there is nothing to check the inducements to sacrifice the weaker party or an obnoxious individual. Hence it is that such Democracies have ever been spectacles of turbulence and contention; have ever been found incompatible with personal security or the rights of property; and have in general been as short in their lives as they have been violent in their deaths. Theoretic politicians, who have patronized this species of Government, have erroneously supposed that by reducing mankind to a perfect equality in their political rights, they would at the same time be perfectly equalized and assimilated in their possessions, their opinions, and their passions.

A Republic, by which I mean a Government in which the scheme of representation takes place, opens a different prospect and promises the cure for which we are seeking. Let us examine the points in which it varies from pure Democracy, and we shall comprehend both the nature of the cure and the efficacy which it must derive from the Union.

The two great points of difference between a Democracy and a Republic are: first, the delegation of the Government, in the latter, to a small number of citizens elected by the rest; secondly, the greater number of citizens and greater sphere of country over which the latter may be extended.

The effect of the first difference is, on the one hand, to refine and enlarge the public views by passing them through the medium of a chosen body of citizens, whose wisdom may best discern the true interest of their country and whose patriotism and love of justice will be least likely to sacrifice it to temporary or partial considerations. Under such a regulation it may well happen that the public voice, pronounced by the representatives of the people, will be more consonant to the public good than if pronounced by the people themselves, convened for the purpose. On the other hand, the effect may be inverted. Men of factious tempers, of local prejudices, or of sinister designs, may, by intrigue, by corruption, or by other means, first obtain the suffrages, and then betray the interests of the people. The question resulting is, whether small or extensive Republics are most favorable to the election of proper guardians of the public weal; and it is clearly decided in favor of the latter by two obvious considerations.

In the first place it is to be remarked that however small the Republic may be, the Representatives must be raised to a certain number in order to guard against the cabals of a few; and that however large it may be they must be limited to a certain number in order to guard against the confusion of a multitude. Hence, the number of Representatives in the two cases not being in proportion to that of the Constituents, and being proportionally greatest in the small Republic, it follows that if the proportion of fit characters be not less in the large than in the small Republic, the former will present a greater option, and consequently a greater probability of a fit choice.

In the next place, as each Representative will be chosen by a greater number of citizens in the large than in the small Republic, it will be more difficult for unworthy candidates to practise with success the vicious arts by which elections are too often carried; and the suffrages of the people being more free, will be more likely to centre on men who possess the most attractive merit and the most diffusive and established characters.

It must be confessed that in this, as in most other cases, there is a mean, on both sides of which inconveniencies will be found to lie. By enlarging too much the number of electors, you render the representative too little acquainted with all their local circumstances and lesser interests; as by reducing it too much, you render him unduly attached to these, and too little fit to comprehend and pursue great and national objects. The Federal Constitution forms a happy combination in this respect; the great and aggregate interests being referred to the national, the local and particular to the State legislatures.

The other point of difference is the greater number of citizens and extent of territory which may be brought within the compass of Republican than of Democratic Government; and it is this circumstance principally which renders factious combinations less to be dreaded in the former than in the latter. The smaller the society, the fewer probably will be the distinct parties and interests composing it; the fewer the distinct parties and interests, the more frequently will a majority be found of the same party; and the smaller the number of individuals composing a majority, and the smaller the compass within which they are placed, the more easily will they concert and execute their plans of oppression. Extend the sphere and you take in a greater variety of parties and interests; you make it

less probable that a majority of the whole will have a common motive to invade the rights of other citizens; or if such a common motive exists, it will be more difficult for all who feel it to discover their own strength and to act in unison with each other. Besides other impediments, it may be remarked, that where there is a consciousness of unjust or dishonorable purposes, communication is always checked by distrust in proportion to the number whose concurrence is necessary.

Hence, it clearly appears that the same advantage which a Republic has over a Democracy in controlling the effects of faction is enjoyed by a large over a small republic—is enjoyed by the Union over the States composing it. Does this advantage consist in the substitution of representatives whose enlightened views and virtuous sentiments render them superior to local prejudices and to schemes of injustice? It will not be denied that the representation of the Union will be most likely to possess these requisite endowments. Does it consist in the greater security afforded by a greater variety of parties, against the event of any one party being able to outnumber and oppress the rest? In an equal degree does the increased variety of parties comprised within the Union increase this security? Does it, in fine, consist in the greater obstacles opposed to the concert and accomplishment of the secret wishes of an unjust and interested majority? Here again the extent of the Union gives it the most palpable advantage.

The influence of factious leaders may kindle a flame within their particular States but will be unable to spread a general conflagration through the other States: a religious sect may degenerate into a political faction in a part of the Confederacy; but the variety of sects dispersed over the entire face of it must secure the national Councils against any danger from that source: a rage for paper money, for an abolition of debts, for an equal division of property, or for any other improper or wicked project, will be less apt to pervade the whole body of the Union than a particular member of it; in the same proportion as such a malady is more likely to taint a particular county or district than an entire State.

In the extent and proper structure of the Union, therefore, we behold a republican remedy for the diseases most incident to Republican Government. And according to the degree of pleasure and pride we feel in being republicans ought to be our zeal in cherishing the spirit and supporting the character of federalist.

PUBLIUS

No. 51: Madison

To what expedient, then, shall we finally resort, for maintaining in practice the necessary partition of power among the several departments as laid down in the constitution? The only answer that can be given is that as all these exterior provisions are found to be inadequate the defect must be supplied, by so contriving the interior structure of the government as that its several constituent parts may, by their mutual relations, be the means of keeping each other in their proper places. Without presuming to undertake a full development of this important idea I will hazard a few general observations which may perhaps place it in a clearer light, and enable us to form a more correct judgment of the principles and structure of the government planned by the convention.

In order to lay a due foundation for that separate and distinct exercise of the different powers of government, which to a certain extent is admitted on all hands to be essential to the preservation of liberty, it is evident that each department should have a will of its own; and consequently should be so constituted that the members of each should have as little agency as possible in the appointment of the members of the others. Were this principle rigorously adhered to, it would require that all the appointments for the supreme executive, legislative, and judiciary magistracies should be drawn from the same fountain of authority, the people, through channels having no communication whatever with one another. Perhaps such a plan of constructing the several departments would be less difficult in practice than it may in contemplation appear. Some difficulties, however, and some additional expense would attend the execution of it. Some deviations, therefore, from the principle must be admitted. In the constitution of the judiciary department in particular, it might be inexpedient to insist rigorously on the principle: first, because peculiar qualifications being essential in the members, the primary consideration ought to be to select that mode of choice which best secures these qualifications; second, because the permanent tenure by which the appointments are held in that department must soon destroy all sense of dependence on the authority conferring them.

It is equally evident that the members of each department should be as little dependent as possible on those of the others for the emoluments annexed to their offices. Were the executive magistrate, or the judges, not independent of the legislature in this particular, their independence in every other would be merely nominal.

But the great security against a gradual concentration of the several powers in the same department consists in giving to those who administer each department the necessary constitutional means and personal motives to resist encroachments of the others. The provision for defence must in this, as in all other cases, be made commensurate to the danger of attack. Ambition must be made to counteract ambition. The interest of the man must be connected with the constitutional rights of the place. It may be a reflection on human nature that such devices should be necessary to control the abuses of government. But what is government itself but the greatest of all reflections on human nature? If men were angels, no government would be necessary. If angels were to govern men, neither external nor internal controls on government would be necessary. In framing a government which is to be administered by men over men, the great difficulty lies in this: You must first enable the government to control the governed; and in the next place oblige it to control itself. A dependence on the people is, no doubt, the primary control on the government; but experience has taught mankind the necessity of auxiliary precautions.

This policy of supplying, by opposite and rival interests, the defect of better motives, might be traced through the whole system of human affairs, private as well as public. We see it particularly displayed in all the subordinate distributions of power, where the constant aim is to divide and arrange the several offices in such a manner as that each may be a check on the other; that the private interest of every individual may be a sentinel over the public rights. These inventions of prudence cannot be less requisite in the distribution of the supreme powers of the State.

But it is not possible to give to each department an equal power of self-defense. In republican government, the legislative authority necessarily predominates. The remedy for this inconveniency is to divide the legislature into different branches; and to render them, by different modes of election and different principles of action, as little connected with each other as the nature of their common functions and their common dependence on the society will admit. It may even be necessary to guard against dangerous encroachments by still further precautions. As the weight of the legislative authority requires that it should be thus divided, the weakness of the executive may require, on the other hand, that it should be fortified. An absolute negative on the legislature appears, at first view, to be the natural defense with which the executive magistrate should be armed. But perhaps it would be neither altogether safe nor alone sufficient. On ordinary occasions it might not be exerted with the requisite firmness, and on extraordinary occasions it might be perfidiously abused. May not this defect of an absolute negative be supplied by some qualified connection between this weaker branch of the stronger department, by which the latter may be led to support the constitutional rights of the former, without being too much detached from the rights of its own department?

If the principles on which these observations are founded be just, as I persuade myself they are, and they be applied as a criterion to the several State constitutions, and to the federal Constitution, it will be found that if the latter does not perfectly correspond with them, the former are infinitely less able to bear such a test.

There are, moreover, two considerations particularly applicable to the federal system of America, which place that system in a very interesting point of view.

First. In a single republic, all the power surrendered by the people is submitted to the administration of a single government; and usurpations are guarded against by a division of the government into distinct and separate departments. In the compound republic of America, the power surrendered by the people is first divided between two distinct governments, and then the portion allotted to each subdivided among distinct and separate departments. Hence a double security arises to the rights of the people. The different governments will control each other, at the same time that each will be controlled by itself.

Second. It is of great importance in a republic not only to guard the society against the oppression of its rulers, but to guard one part of the society against the injustice of the other part. Different interests necessarily exist in different classes of citizens. If a majority be united by a common interest, the rights of the minority will be insecure. There are but two methods of providing against this evil: The one by creating a will in the community independent of the majority—that is, of the society itself; the other, by comprehending in the society so many separate descriptions of citizens as will render an unjust combination of a majority of the whole very improbable, if not impracticable. The first method prevails in all governments possessing an hereditary or self-appointed authority. This, at best, is but a precarious security; because a power independent of the society may as well espouse the unjust views of the major as the rightful interests of the minor party, and may possibly be turned against both parties. The second method will be exemplified in the federal republic of the United States. Whilst all authority in it will be derived from and dependent on the society, the society itself will be broken into so many parts, interests and classes of citizens, that the rights of individuals, or of the minority, will be in little danger from interested combinations of the majority. In a free government the security for civil rights must be the same as that for religious rights. It consists in the one case in the multiplicity of interests, and in the other in the multiplicity of sects. The degree of security in both cases will depend on the number of interests and sects; and this may be presumed to depend on the extent of country and number of people comprehended under the same government. This view of the subject must particularly recommend a proper federal system to all the sincere and considerate friends of republican government: Since it shows that in exact proportion as the territory of the Union may be formed into more circumscribed Confederacies, or States, oppressive combinations of a majority will be facilitated; the best security, under the republican form, for the rights of every class of citizens, will be diminished; and consequently the stability and independence of some member of the government, the only other security, must be proportionally increased. Justice is the end of government. It is the end of civil society. It ever has been and ever will be pursued until it be obtained, or until liberty be lost in the pursuit. In a society under the forms of which the stronger faction can readily unite and oppress the weaker, anarchy may as truly be said to reign as in a state of nature, where the weaker individual is not secured against the violence of the stronger: And as, in the latter state, even the stronger individuals are prompted, by the uncertainty of their condition, to submit to a government which may protect the weak as well as themselves: So, in the former state, will the more powerful factions or parties be gradually induced, by a like motive, to wish for a government which will protect all parties, the weaker as well as the more powerful. It can be little doubted that if the State of Rhode Island was separated from the Confederacy and left to itself, the insecurity of rights under the popular form of government within such narrow limits would be displayed by such reiterated oppressions of factious majorities that some power altogether independent of the people would soon be called for by the voice of the very factions whose misrule had proved the necessity of it. In the extended republic of the United States, and among the great variety of interests, parties, and sects which it embraces, a coalition of a majority of the whole society could seldom take place on any other principles than those of justice and the general good; and there being thus less danger to a minor from the will of the major party, there must be less pretext, also, to provide for the security of the former, by introducing into the government a will not dependent on the latter, or, in other words, a will independent of the society itself. It is no less certain than it is important, notwithstanding the contrary opinions which have been entertained, that the larger the society, provided it lie within a practicable sphere, the more duly capable it will be of self-government. And happily for the *republican cause*, practicable sphere may be carried to a very great extent by a judicious modification and mixture of the *federal principle*.

PUBLIUS

Presidents and Vice Presidents

	PRESIDENT	VICE PRESIDENT		PRESIDENT	VICE PRESIDENT
1	George Washington *(Federalist 1789)*	John Adams *(Federalist 1789)*	12	Zachary Taylor *(Whig 1849)*	Millard Fillmore *(Whig 1849)*
2	John Adams *(Federalist 1797)*	Thomas Jefferson *(Dem.-Rep. 1797)*	13	Millard Fillmore *(Whig 1850)*	
3	Thomas Jefferson *(Dem.-Rep. 1801)*	Aaron Burr *(Dem.-Rep. 1801)*	14	Franklin Pierce *(Democratic 1853)*	William R. D. King *(Democratic 1853)*
		George Clinton *(Dem.-Rep. 1805)*	15	James Buchanan *(Democratic 1857)*	John C. Breckinridge *(Democratic 1857)*
4	James Madison *(Dem.-Rep. 1809)*	George Clinton *(Dem.-Rep. 1809)*	16	Abraham Lincoln *(Republican 1861)*	Hannibal Hamlin *(Republican 1861)*
		Elbridge Gerry *(Dem.-Rep. 1813)*			Andrew Johnson *(Unionist 1865)*
5	James Monroe *(Dem.-Rep. 1817)*	Daniel D. Tompkins *(Dem.-Rep. 1817)*	17	Andrew Johnson *(Unionist 1865)*	
6	John Quincy Adams *(Dem.-Rep. 1825)*	John C. Calhoun *(Dem.-Rep. 1825)*	18	Ulysses S. Grant *(Republican 1869)*	Schuyler Colfax *(Republican 1869)*
7	Andrew Jackson *(Democratic 1829)*	John C. Calhoun *(Democratic 1829)*			Henry Wilson *(Republican 1873)*
		Martin Van Buren *(Democratic 1833)*	19	Rutherford B. Hayes *(Republican 1877)*	William A. Wheeler *(Republican 1877)*
8	Martin Van Buren *(Democratic 1837)*	Richard M. Johnson *(Democratic 1837)*	20	James A. Garfield *(Republican 1881)*	Chester A. Arthur *(Republican 1881)*
9	William H. Harrison *(Whig 1841)*	John Tyler *(Whig 1841)*	21	Chester A. Arthur *(Republican 1881)*	
10	John Tyler *(Whig and Democratic 1841)*		22	Grover Cleveland *(Democratic 1885)*	Thomas A. Hendricks *(Democratic 1885)*
11	James K. Polk *(Democratic 1845)*	George M. Dallas *(Democratic 1845)*	23	Benjamin Harrison *(Republican 1889)*	Levi P. Morton *(Republican 1889)*

	PRESIDENT	VICE PRESIDENT		PRESIDENT	VICE PRESIDENT
24	Grover Cleveland *(Democratic 1893)*	Adlai E. Stevenson *(Democratic 1893)*	34	Dwight D. Eisenhower *(Republican 1953)*	Richard M. Nixon *(Republican 1953)*
25	William McKinley *(Republican 1897)*	Garret A. Hobart *(Republican 1897)*	35	John F. Kennedy *(Democratic 1961)*	Lyndon B. Johnson *(Democratic 1961)*
		Theodore Roosevelt *(Republican 1901)*	36	Lyndon B. Johnson *(Democratic 1963)*	Hubert H. Humphrey *(Democratic 1965)*
26	Theodore Roosevelt *(Republican 1901)*	Charles W. Fairbanks *(Republican 1905)*	37	Richard M. Nixon *(Republican 1969)*	Spiro T. Agnew *(Republican 1969)*
27	William H. Taft *(Republican 1909)*	James S. Sherman *(Republican 1909)*			Gerald R. Ford *(Republican 1973)*
28	Woodrow Wilson *(Democratic 1913)*	Thomas R. Marshall *(Democratic 1913)*	38	Gerald R. Ford *(Republican 1974)*	Nelson Rockefeller *(Republican 1974)*
29	Warren G. Harding *(Republican 1921)*	Calvin Coolidge *(Republican 1921)*	39	James E. Carter *(Democratic 1977)*	Walter Mondale *(Democratic 1977)*
30	Calvin Coolidge *(Republican 1923)*	Charles G. Dawes *(Republican 1925)*	40	Ronald Reagan *(Republican 1981)*	George H. W. Bush *(Republican 1981)*
31	Herbert Hoover *(Republican 1929)*	Charles Curtis *(Republican 1929)*	41	George H. W. Bush *(Republican 1989)*	J. Danforth Quayle *(Republican 1989)*
32	Franklin D. Roosevelt *(Democratic 1933)*	John Nance Garner *(Democratic 1933)*	42	William J. Clinton *(Democratic 1993)*	Albert Gore, Jr. *(Democratic 1993)*
		Henry A. Wallace *(Democratic 1941)*	43	George W. Bush *(Republican 2001)*	Richard Cheney *(Republican 2001)*
		Harry S. Truman *(Democratic 1945)*	44	Barack H. Obama *(Democratic 2009)*	Joseph R. Biden, Jr. *(Democratic 2009)*
33	Harry S. Truman *(Democratic 1945)*	Alben W. Barkley *(Democratic 1949)*			

glossary

affirmative action   government policies or programs that seek to redress past injustices against specified groups by making special efforts to provide members of those groups with access to educational and employment opportunities

agency representation   the type of representation in which a representative is held accountable to a constituency if he or she fails to represent that constituency properly. This is incentive for good representation when the personal back grounds, views, and interests of the representative differ from those of his or her constituency

agenda setting   the power of the media to bring public attention to particular issues and problems

agents of socialization   social institutions, including families and schools, that help to shape individuals' basic political beliefs and values

amendment   a change added to a bill, law, or constitution

amicus curiae   literally, "friend of the court"; individuals or groups who are not parties to a lawsuit but who seek to assist the Supreme Court in reaching a decision by presenting additional briefs

Antifederalists   those who favored strong state governments and a weak national government and who were opponents of the Constitution proposed at the American Constitutional Convention of 1787

apportionment   the process, occurring after every decennial census, that allocates congressional seats among the 50 states

appropriations   the amounts of money approved by Congress in statutes (bills) that each unit or agency of government can spend

Articles of Confederation   America's first written constitution; served as the basis for America's national government until 1789

attitude (or opinion)   a specific preference on a particular issue

authoritarian government   a system of rule in which the government recognizes no formal limits but may nevertheless be restrained by the power of other social institutions

autocracy   a form of government in which a single individual—a king, queen, or dictator—rules

ballot initiative   a proposed law or policy change that is placed on the ballot by citizens or interest groups for a popular vote

bandwagon   effect a shift in electoral support to the candidate whom public opinion polls report as the front-runner

bicameral   having a legislative assembly composed of two chambers or houses; distinguished from *unicameral*

bill   a proposed law that has been sponsored by a member of Congress and submitted to the clerk of the House or Senate

bill of attainder   a law that declares a person guilty of a crime without a trial

Bill of Rights   the first 10 amendments to the U.S. Constitution, ratified in 1791; they ensure certain rights and liberties to the people

block grants   federal grants-in-aid that allow states considerable discretion in how the funds are spent

briefs   written documents in which attorneys explain, using case precedents, why the court should find in favor of their client

broadcast media   television, radio, or other media that transmit audio and/or video content to the public

Brown v. Board of Education   the 1954 Supreme Court decision that struck down the "separate but equal" doctrine as fundamentally unequal. This case eliminated state power to use race as a criterion of discrimination in law and provided the national government with the power to intervene by exercising strict regulatory policies against discriminatory actions

bureaucracy   the complex structure of offices, tasks, rules, and principles of organization that are employed by all large-scale institutions to coordinate the work of their personnel

Cabinet   the secretaries, or chief administrators, of the major departments of the federal government. Cabinet secretaries are appointed by the president with the consent of the Senate

campaign   an effort by political candidates and their supporters to win the backing of donors, political activists, and voters in their quest for political office

categorical grants   congressional grants given to states and localities on the condition that expenditures be limited to a problem or group specified by law

caucus (political) a normally closed political party business meeting of citizens or law makers to select candidates, elect officers, plan strategy, or make decisions regarding legislative matters

caucuses (congressional) associations of members of Congress based on party, interest, or social group, such as gender or race

checks and balances mechanisms through which each branch of government is able to participate in and influence the activities of the other branches; major examples include the presidential veto power over congressional legislation, the power of the Senate to approve presidential appointments, and judicial review of congressional enactments

chief justice justice on the Supreme Court who presides over the Court's public sessions and whose official title is chief justice of the United States

citizen journalism news reported and distributed by citizens, rather than professional journalists and for-profit news organizations

citizenship informed and active membership in a political community

civil law the branch of law that deals with disputes that do not involve criminal penalties

civil liberties areas of personal freedom with which governments are constrained from interfering

civil rights obligation imposed on government to take positive action to protect citizens from any illegal action of government agencies and of other private citizens

class-action suit a legal action by which a group or class of individuals with common interests can file a suit on behalf of everyone who shares that interest

"clear and present danger" test test to determine whether speech is protected or unprotected, based on its capacity to present a "clear and present danger" to society

closed primary a primary election in which voters can participate in the nomination of candidates, but only of the party in which they are enrolled for a period of time prior to primary day

closed rule a provision by the House Rules Committee limiting or prohibiting the introduction of amendments during debate

cloture a rule allowing a majority of two-thirds or three-fifths of the members of a legislative body to set a time limit on debate over a given bill. In the U.S. Senate, 60 senators (three-fifths) must agree in order to impose such a limit.

coattail effect the result of voters casting their ballot for president or governor and "automatically" voting for the remainder of the party's ticket

collective goods benefits, sought by groups, that are broadly available and cannot be denied to nonmembers

commander in chief the role of the president as commander of the national military and the state National Guard units (when called into service)

commerce clause Article I, Section 8, of the Constitution, which delegates to Congress the power "to regulate commerce with foreign nations, and among the several States and with the Indian tribes." This clause was interpreted by the Supreme Court in favor of national power over the economy

committee markup the session in which a congressional committee rewrites legislation to incorporate changes discussed during hearings on the bill

common law law made through court precedent rather than legislative enactments

concurrent powers authority possessed by *both* state and national governments, such as the power to levy taxes

confederation a system of government in which states retain sovereign authority except for the powers expressly delegated to the national government

conference a gathering of House Republicans every two years to elect their House leaders. Democrats call their gathering the caucus

conference committees joint committees created to work out a compromise on House and Senate versions of a piece of legislation

conservative today this term refers to those who generally support the social and economic status quo and are suspicious of efforts to introduce new political formulae and economic arrangements. Conservatives believe that a large and powerful government poses a threat to citizens' freedom

constituency the residents in the area from which an official is elected

constitutional government a system of rule in which formal and effective limits are placed on the powers of the government

cooperative federalism a type of federalism existing since the New Deal era in which grants-in-aid have been used strategically to encourage states and localities (without commanding them) to pursue nationally defined goals. Also known as "intergovernmental cooperation"

court of appeals a court that hears appeals of trial court decisions

criminal law the branch of law that regulates the conduct of individuals, defines crimes, and specifies punishment for criminal acts

de facto literally, "by fact"; refers to practices that occur even when there is no legal enforcement, such as school segregation in much of the United States today

de jure literally, "by law"; refers to legally enforced practices, such as school segregation in the South before the 1960s

defendant the one against whom a complaint is brought in a criminal or civil case

deficit the total amount the government owes its creditors

delegate a representative who votes according to the preferences of his or her constituency

delegated powers constitutional powers that are assigned to one governmental agency but that are exercised by another agency with the express permission of the first

democracy a system of rule that permits citizens to play a significant part in the governmental process, usually through the election of key public officials

department   the largest subunit of the executive branch. The secretaries of the 15 departments form the Cabinet.

devolution   a policy to remove a program from one level of government by delegating it or passing it down to a lower level of government, such as from the national government to the state and local governments

digital citizen   a daily Internet user with high-speed home Internet access and the technology and literacy skills to go online for employment, news, politics, entertainment, commerce, and other activities

direct democracy   a system of rule that permits citizens to vote directly on laws and policies

discrimination   the use of any unreasonable and unjust criterion of exclusion

dissenting opinion   a decision written by a justice in the minority in a particular case in which the justice wishes to express his or her reasoning in the case

divided government   the condition in American government wherein the presidency is controlled by one party while the opposing party controls one or both houses of Congress

double jeopardy   the Fifth Amendment right providing that a person cannot be tried twice for the same crime

dual federalism   the system of government that prevailed in the United States from 1789 to 1937, in which most fundamental governmental powers were shared between the federal and state governments

due process of law   the right of every citizen against arbitrary action by national or state governments

early voting   the option in some states to cast a vote at a polling place or by mail before the election

elastic clause   Article I, Section 8, of the Constitution (also known as the necessary and proper clause), which enumerates the powers of Congress and provides Congress with the authority to make all laws "necessary and proper" to carry them out

Election-Day registration   the option in some states to register on the day of the election, at the polling place, rather than in advance of the election

electoral college   the presidential electors from each state who meet after the popular election to cast ballots for president and vice president

electoral realignment   the point in history when a new party supplants the ruling party, becoming in turn the dominant political force; in the United States, this has tended to occur roughly every 30 years

eminent domain   the right of government to take private property for public use

equal protection clause   provision of the Fourteenth Amendment guaranteeing citizens "the equal protection of the laws." This clause has been the basis for the civil rights of African Americans, women, and other groups

equal time rule   the requirement that broadcasters provide candidates for the same political office equal opportunities to communicate their messages to the public

equality of opportunity   a widely shared American ideal that all people should have the freedom to use whatever talents and wealth they have to reach their fullest potential

establishment clause   the First Amendment clause that says that "Congress shall make no law respecting an establishment of religion." This law means that a "wall of separation" exists between church and state

ex post facto laws   laws that declare an action to be illegal after it has been committed

exclusionary rule   the ability of courts to exclude evidence obtained in violation of the Fourth Amendment

executive agreement   an agreement, made between the president and another country, that has the force of a treaty but does not require the Senate's "advice and consent"

Executive Office of the President (EOP)   the permanent agencies that perform defined management tasks for the president. Created in 1939, the EOP includes the OMB, the CEA, the NSC, and other agencies

executive order   a rule or regulation issued by the president that has the effect and formal status of legislation

executive privilege   the claim that confidential communications between a president and close advisers should not be revealed without the consent of the president

expressed powers   specific powers granted by the Constitution to Congress (Article I, Section 8) and to the president (Article II)

fairness doctrine   a Federal Communications Commission requirement for broadcasters who air programs on controversial issues to provide time for opposing views; the FCC ceased enforcing this doctrine in 1985

Federal Reserve System   a system of 12 Federal Reserve Banks that facilitates exchanges of cash, checks, and credit; regulates member banks; and uses monetary policies to fight inflation and deflation

federal system   a system of government in which the national government shares power with lower levels of government, such as states

federalism   a system of government in which power is divided, by a constitution, between a central government and regional governments

Federalist Papers   a series of essays written by Alexander Hamilton, James Madison, and John Jay supporting ratification of the Constitution

Federalists   those who favored a strong national government and supported the Constitution proposed at the American Constitutional Convention of 1787

Fifteenth Amendment   one of three Civil War amendments; it guaranteed voting rights for African American men

fighting words   speech that directly incites damaging conduct

filibuster   a tactic used by members of the Senate to prevent action on legislation they oppose by continuously holding the floor and speaking until the majority backs down. Once given the floor, senators have unlimited time to speak, and it requires a vote of three-fifths of the Senate to end a filibuster

fiscal policy the government's use of taxing, monetary, and spending powers to manipulate the economy

501c(4) committees nonprofit groups that also engage in issue advocacy. Under Section 501c(4) of the federal tax code such a group may spend up to half its revenue for political purposes

527 committees nonprofit independent groups that receive and disburse funds to influence the nomination, election, or defeat of candidates. Named after Section 527 of the Internal Revenue Code, which defines and grants tax-exempt status to nonprofit advocacy groups

formula grants grants-in-aid in which a formula is used to determine the amount of federal funds a state or local government will receive

Fourteenth Amendment one of three Civil War amendments; it guaranteed equal protection and due process

framing the power of the media to influence how events and issues are interpreted

free exercise clause the First Amendment clause that protects a citizen's right to believe and practice whatever religion he or she chooses

free riders those who enjoy the benefits of collective goods but did not participate in acquiring them

full faith and credit clause provision, from Article IV, Section 1, of the Constitution, requiring that the states normally honor the public acts and judicial decisions that take place in another state

gender gap a distinctive pattern of voting behavior reflecting the differences in views between women and men

general election a regularly scheduled election involving most districts in the nation or state, in which voters select officeholders; in the United States, general elections for national office and most state and local offices are held on the first Tuesday following the first Monday in November in even-numbered years (every four years for presidential elections)

general revenue sharing the process by which one unit of government yields a portion of its tax income to another unit of government, according to an established formula. Revenue sharing typically involves the national government providing money to state governments

gerrymandering the apportionment of voters in districts in such a way as to give unfair advantage to one racial or ethnic group or political party

government institutions and procedures through which a territory and its people are ruled

government corporation government agency that performs a service normally provided by the private sector

grand jury jury that determines whether sufficient evidence is available to justify a trial; grand juries do not rule on the accused's guilt or innocence

grants-in-aid programs through which Congress provides money to state and local governments on the condition that the funds be employed for purposes defined by the federal government

grassroots mobilization a lobbying campaign in which a group mobilizes its membership to contact government officials in support of the group's position

Great Compromise the agreement reached at the Constitutional Convention of 1787 that gave each state an equal number of senators regardless of its population, but linked representation in the House of Representatives to population

habeas corpus a court order demanding that an individual in custody be brought into court and shown the cause for detention

home rule power delegated by the state to a local unit of government to manage its own affairs

impeachment the formal charge by the House of Representatives that a government official has committed "Treason, Bribery, or other high Crimes and Misdemeanors"

implementation the efforts of departments and agencies to translate laws into specific bureaucratic rules and actions

implied powers powers derived from the necessary and proper clause of Article I, Section 8, of the Constitution. Such powers are not specifically expressed, but are implied through the expansive interpretation of delegated powers

incumbency holding a political office for which one is running

incumbent a candidate running for reelection to a position that he or she already holds

independent agency agency that is not part of a cabinet department

informational benefits special newsletters, periodicals, training programs, conferences, and other information provided to members of groups to entice others to join

inherent powers powers claimed by a president that are not expressed in the Constitution but are inferred from it

institutional advertising advertising designed to create a positive image of an organization

interest group individuals who organize to influence the government's programs and policies

intermediate scrutiny a test used by the Supreme Court in gender discrimination cases that places the burden of proof partially on the government and partially on the challengers to show that the law in question is unconstitutional

iron triangle the stable, cooperative relationship that often develops among a congressional committee, an administrative agency, and one or more supportive interest groups. Not all of these relationships are triangular, but the iron triangle is the most typical

issue network a loose network of elected leaders, public officials, activists, and interest groups drawn together by a specific policy issue

Jim Crow laws laws enacted by southern states following Reconstruction that discriminated against African Americans

joint committees legislative committees formed of members of both the House and Senate

judicial activism judicial philosophy that posits that the Court should go beyond the words of the Constitution or a statute to consider the broader societal implications of its decisions

judicial restraint judicial philosophy whose adherents refuse to go beyond the clear words of the Constitution in interpreting the document's meaning

judicial review the power of the courts to review and, if necessary, declare actions of the legislative and executive branches invalid or unconstitutional; the Supreme Court asserted this power in *Marbury v. Madison*

jurisdiction the sphere of a court's power and authority

Kitchen Cabinet an informal group of advisers to whom the president turns for counsel and guidance. Members of the official Cabinet may or may not also be members of the Kitchen Cabinet

laissez-faire capitalism an economic system in which the means of production and distribution are privately owned and operated for profit with minimal or no government interference

leak a disclosure of confidential information to the news media

legislative initiative the president's inherent power to bring a legislative agenda before Congress

***Lemon* test** a rule articulated in *Lemon v. Kurtzman* that government action toward religion is permissible if it is secular in purpose, neither promotes nor inhibits the practice of religion, and does not lead to "excessive entanglement" with religion

libel a written statement made in "reckless disregard of the truth" that is considered damaging to a victim because it is "malicious, scandalous, and defamatory"

liberal today this term refers to those who generally support social and political reform; extensive governmental intervention in the economy; the expansion of federal social services; more vigorous efforts on behalf of the poor, minorities, and women; and greater concern for consumers and the environment

libertarianism a political ideology that emphasizes freedom and voluntary association with small government

liberty freedom from governmental control

limited government a principle of constitutional government; a government whose powers are defined and limited by a constitution

lobbying a strategy by which organized interests seek to influence the passage of legislation by exerting direct pressure on members of the legislature

logrolling a legislative practice whereby agreements are made between legislators in voting for or against a bill; vote trading

machines strong party organizations in late-nineteenth- and early-twentieth-century American cities. These machines were led by "bosses" who controlled party nominations and patronage

majority leader the elected leader of the majority party in the House of Representatives or in the Senate. In the House, the majority leader is subordinate in the party hierarchy to the Speaker of the House

majority party the party that holds the majority of legislative seats in either the House or the Senate

majority rule, minority rights the democratic principle that a government follows the preferences of the majority of voters but protects the interests of the minority

majority system a type of electoral system in which, to win a seat in the parliament or other representative body, a candidate must receive a majority of all the votes cast in the relevant district

majority-minority district a gerrymandered voting district that improves the chances of minority candidates by making selected minority groups the majority within the district

marketplace of ideas the public forum in which beliefs and ideas are exchanged and compete

material benefits special goods, services, or money provided to members of groups to entice others to join

media monopoly the ownership and control of the media by a few large corporations

median voter theorem a proposition predicting that when policy options can be arrayed along a single dimension, majority rule will pick the policy most preferred by the voter whose ideal policy is to the left of half of the voters and to the right of exactly half of the voters

membership association an organized group in which members actually play a substantial role, sitting on committees and engaging in group projects

merit system a product of civil service reform, in which appointees to positions in public bureaucracies must objectively be deemed qualified for those positions

midterm elections congressional elections that do not coincide with a presidential election; also called off-year elections

minority leader the elected leader of the minority party in the House or Senate

minority party the party that holds a minority of legislative seats in either the House or the Senate

Miranda rule the requirement, articulated by the Supreme Court in *Miranda v. Arizona*, that persons under arrest must be informed prior to police interrogation of their rights to remain silent and to have the benefit of legal counsel

mobilization the process by which large numbers of people are organized for a political activity

mootness a criterion used by courts to screen cases that no longer require resolution

national convention a national party political institution that nominates the party's presidential and vice presidential candidates, establishes party rules, and writes and ratifies the party's platform

National Security Council (NSC) a presidential foreign policy advisory council composed of the president, the vice president, the secretary of state, the secretary of defense, and other officials invited by the president

necessary and proper clause Article I, Section 8, of the Constitution, which provides Congress with the authority to make all laws "necessary and proper" to carry out its expressed powers

New Federalism   attempts by Presidents Nixon and Reagan to return power to the states through block grants

New Jersey Plan   A framework for the Constitution, introduced by William Paterson, that called for equal state representation in the national legislature regardless of population

New Politics movement   a political movement that began in the 1960s and '70s, made up of professionals and intellectuals for whom the civil rights and antiwar movements were formative experiences. The New Politics movement strengthened public interest groups

news aggregator   an application or feed that collects Web content such as news headlines, blogs, podcasts, online videos, and more in one location for easy viewing

niche journalism   news reporting devoted to a targeted portion (subset) of a journalism market sector or for a portion of readers/viewers based on content or ideological presentation

nomination   the process by which political parties select their candidates for election to public office

oligarchy   a form of government in which a small group—landowners, military officers, or wealthy merchants—controls most of the governing decisions

online political participation   acti-vities designed to influence government using the Internet, including visiting a candidate's website, organizing events online, or signing an online petition

open primary   a primary election in which the voter can wait until the day of the primary to choose which party to enroll in to select candidates for the general election

open rule   a provision by the House Rules Committee that permits floor debate and the addition of new amendments to a bill

opinion   the written explanation of the Supreme Court's decision in a particular case

oral argument   the stage in Supreme Court procedure in which attorneys for both sides appear before the Court to present their positions and answer questions posed by justices

original jurisdiction   the authority to initially consider a case. Distinguished from appellate jurisdiction, which is the authority to hear appeals from a lower court's decision.

oversight   the effort by Congress, through hearings, investigations, and other techniques, to exercise control over the activities of executive agencies

party activists   partisans who contribute time, energy, and effort to support their party and its candidates

party identification   an individual voter's psychological ties to one party or another

party organization   the formal structure of a political party, including its leadership, election committees, active members, and paid staff

party polarization   the division between the two major parties on most policy issues, with members of each party unified around their party's positions with little crossover

party unity vote   a roll-call vote in the House or Senate in which at least 50 percent of the members of one party take a particular position and are opposed by at least 50 percent of the members of the other party

patronage   the resources available to higher officials, usually opportunities to make partisan appointments to offices and to confer grants, licenses, or special favors to supporters

penny press   cheap, tabloid-style newspaper produced in the nineteenth century, when mass production of inexpensive newspapers first became possible due to the steam-powered printing press; a penny press cost one cent compared to other papers, which cost more than five cents

per curiam   a brief, unsigned decision by an appellate court, usually rejecting a petition to review the decision of a lower court

permanent absentee ballots   the option in some states to have a ballot sent automatically to your home for each election, rather than having to request an absentee ballot each time

plaintiff   the individual or organization that brings a complaint in court

platform   a party document, written at a national convention, that contains party philosophy, principles, and positions on issues

plea bargain   a negotiated agreement in a criminal case in which a defendant agrees to plead guilty in return for the state's agreement to reduce the severity of the criminal charge or prison sentence the defendant is facing

pluralism   the theory that all interests are and should be free to compete for influence in the government; the outcome of this competition is compromise and moderation

plurality system   a type of electoral system in which, to win a seat in the parliament or other representative body, a candidate need only receive the most votes in the election, not necessarily a majority of votes cast

pocket veto   a presidential veto that is automatically triggered if the president does not act on a given piece of legislation passed during the final 10 days of a legislative session

police power   power reserved to the state government to regulate the health, safety, and morals of its citizens

policy entrepreneur   an individual who identifies a problem as a political issue and brings a policy proposal into the political agenda

political action committee (PAC)   a private group that raises and distributes funds for use in election campaigns

political culture   broadly shared values, beliefs, and attitudes about how the government should function. American political culture emphasizes the values of liberty, equality, and democracy

political efficacy   the ability to influence government and politics

political equality   the right to participate in politics equally, based on the principle of "one person, one vote"

political ideology   a cohesive set of beliefs that forms a general philosophy about the role of government

political parties organized groups that attempt to influence the government by electing their members to important government offices

political socialization the induction of individuals into the political culture; learning the underlying beliefs and values on which the political system is based

politics conflict over the leadership, structure, and policies of governments

popular sovereignty a principle of democracy in which political authority rests ultimately in the hands of the people

pork barrel (or pork) appropriations made by legislative bodies for local projects that are often not needed but that are created so that local representatives can win re-election in their home districts

power influence over a government's leadership, organization, or policies

precedent prior case whose principles are used by judges as the basis for their decision in a present case

preemption the principle that allows the national government to override state or local actions in certain policy areas; in foreign policy, the willingness to strike first in order to prevent an enemy attack

primary elections elections held to select a party's candidate for the general election

prior restraint an effort by a governmental agency to block the publication of material it deems libelous or harmful in some other way; censorship. In the United States, the courts forbid prior restraint except under the most extraordinary circumstances

priming process of preparing the public to take a particular view of an event or political actor

private bill a proposal in Congress to provide a specific person with some kind of relief, such as a special exemption from immigration quotas

privatization the transfer of all or part of a program from the public sector to the private sector

privileges and immunities clause provision, from Article IV, Section 2, of the Constitution, that a state cannot discriminate against someone from another state or give its own residents special privileges

probability sampling a method used by pollsters to select a representative sample in which every individual in the population has an equal probability of being selected as a respondent

project grants grant programs in which state and local governments submit proposals to federal agencies and for which funding is provided on a competitive basis

proportional representation a multiple-member district system that allows each political party representation in proportion to its percentage of the total vote

prospective voting voting based on the imagined future performance of a candidate or political party

protest participation that involves assembling crowds to confront a government or other official organization

public interest groups groups that claim they serve the general good rather than only their own particular interest

public opinion citizens' attitudes about political issues, leaders, institutions, and events

public-opinion polls scientific instruments for measuring public opinion

purposive benefits selective benefits of group membership that emphasize the purpose and accomplishments of the group

push polling a polling technique in which the questions are designed to shape the respondent's opinion

random digit dialing a polling method in which respondents are selected at random from a list of ten-digit telephone numbers, with every effort made to avoid bias in the construction of the sample

recall a procedure to allow voters to remove state officials from office before their terms expire by circulating petitions to call a vote

redistributive programs economic policies designed to control the economy through taxing and spending, with the goal of benefiting the poor

redistricting the process of redrawing election districts and redistributing legislative representatives. This happen every 10 years to reflect shifts in population or in response to legal challenges to existing districts

redlining a practice in which banks refuse to make loans to people living in certain geographic locations

referendum the practice of referring a proposed law passed by a legislature to the vote of the electorate for approval or rejection

regulated federalism a form of federalism in which Congress imposes legislation on states and localities, requiring them to meet national standards

regulatory agency a department, bureau, or independent agency whose primary mission is to impose limits, restrictions, or other obligations on the conduct of individuals or companies in the private sector

representative democracy/republic a system of government in which the populace selects representatives, who play a significant role in governmental decision making

reserved powers powers, derived from the Tenth Amendment to the Constitution, that are not specifically delegated to the national government or denied to the states

retrospective voting voting based on the past performance of a candidate or political party

revenue agency an agency responsible for collecting taxes. Examples include the Internal Revenue Service for income taxes, the U.S. Customs Service for tariffs and other taxes on imported goods, and the Bureau of Alcohol, Tobacco, Firearms and Explosives for collection of taxes on the sale of those particular products

right of rebuttal a Federal Communications Commission regulation giving individuals the right to have the opportunity to respond to personal attacks made on a radio or television broadcast

right to privacy right to be left alone, which has been interpreted by the Supreme Court to entail individual access to birth control and abortions

roll-call vote a vote in which each legislator's yes or no vote is recorded as the clerk calls the names of the members alphabetically

runoff election a "second round" election in which voters choose between the top two candidates from the first round

sample a small group selected by researchers to represent the most important characteristics of an entire population

sampling error polling error that arises based on the small size of the sample

select committees (usually) temporary legislative committees set up to highlight or investigate a particular issue or address an issue not within the jurisdiction of existing committees

selection bias (news) the tendency to focus news coverage on only on aspect of an event or issue, avoiding coverage of over aspects

selection bias (surveys) polling error that arises when the sample is not representative of the population being studied, which creates errors in overrepresenting or underrepresenting some opinions

selective incorporation the process by which different protections in the Bill of Rights were incorporated into the Fourteenth Amendment, thus guaranteeing citizens protection from state as well as national governments

senatorial courtesy the practice whereby the president, before formally nominating a person for a federal judgeship, seeks the indication that senators from the candidate's own state support the nomination

seniority the ranking given to an individual on the basis of length of continuous service on a committee in Congress

"separate but equal" rule doctrine that public accommodations could be segregated by race but still be considered equal

separation of powers the division of governmental power among several institutions that must cooperate in decision making

signing statements announcements made by the president when signing bills into law, often presenting the president's interpretation of the law

slander an oral statement made in "reckless disregard of the truth" that is considered damaging to the victim because it is "malicious, scandalous, and defamatory"

social desirability effect the effect that results when respondents in a survey report what they expect the interviewer wishes to hear rather than what they believe

social media Web-based and mobile-based technologies that are used to turn communication into interactive dialogue between organizations, communities, and individuals; social media technologies take on many different forms including blogs, Wikis, podcasts, pictures, video, Facebook, Twitter, and more

socialism a political ideology that emphasizes social ownership or collective government ownership and strong government

socioeconomic status status in society based on level of education, income, and occupational prestige

sociological representation a type of representation in which representatives have the same racial, gender, ethnic, religious, or educational backgrounds as their constituents. It is based on the principle that if two individuals are similar in background, character, interests, and perspectives, then one could correctly represent the other's views

soft money money contributed directly to political parties and other organizations for political activities that is not regulated by federal campaign spending laws; in 2002 federal law prohibited unregulated donations to national party committees

solicitor general the top government lawyer in all cases before the Supreme Court where the government is a party

solidary benefits selective benefits of group membership that emphasize friendship, networking, and consciousness raising

Speaker of the House the chief presiding officer of the House of Representatives. The Speaker is the most important party and House leader, and can influence the legislative agenda, the fate of individual pieces of legislation, and members' positions within the House

"speech plus" speech accompanied by conduct such as sit-ins, picketing, and demonstrations. Protection of this form of speech under the First Amendment is conditional, and restrictions imposed by state or local authorities are acceptable if properly balanced by considerations of public order

spot (advertisement) a 15-, 30-, or 60-second television campaign commercial that permits a candidate's message to be delivered to a target audience

staff agencies legislative support agencies responsible for policy analysis

staff organization a type of membership group in which a professional staff conducts most of the group's activities

standing committee a permanent committee with the power to propose and write legislation that covers a particular subject, such as finance or agriculture

standing the right of an individual or organization to initiate a court case, on the basis of their having a substantial stake in the outcome

stare decisis literally, "let the decision stand." The doctrine that a previous decision by a court applies as a precedent in similar cases until that decision is overruled

states' rights the principle that the states should oppose the increasing authority of the national government. This principle was most popular in the period before the Civil War

straight-ticket voting selecting candidates from the same political party for all offices on the ballot

strict scrutiny a test used by the Supreme Court in racial discrimination cases and other cases involving civil liberties and civil rights that places the burden of proof on the government rather than on the challengers to show that the law in question is constitutional

suffrage the right to vote; also called franchise

superdelegate a convention delegate position, in Democratic conventions, reserved for party officials

supremacy clause Article VI of the Constitution, which states that laws passed by the national government and all treaties are the supreme law of the land and superior to all laws adopted by any state or any subdivision

supreme court the highest court in a particular state or in the United States. This court primarily serves an appellate function

term limits legally prescribed limits on the number of terms an elected official can serve

third parties parties that organize to compete against the two major American political parties

Thirteenth Amendment one of three Civil War amendments; it abolished slavery

Three-Fifths Compromise the agreement reached at the Constitutional Convention of 1787 that stipulated that for purposes of the apportionment of congressional seats, every slave would be counted as three-fifths of a person

totalitarian government a system of rule in which the government recognizes no formal limits on its power and seeks to absorb or eliminate other social institutions that might challenge it

town hall meeting an informal public meeting in which candidates meet with ordinary citizens. Allows candidates to deliver messages without the presence of journalists or commentators

traditional political participation activities designed to influence government including voting and face-to-face activities such as protesting or volunteering for a campaign

trial court the first court to hear a criminal or civil case

trustee a representative who votes based on what he or she thinks is best for his or her constituency

turnout the percentage of eligible individuals who actually vote

two-party system a political system in which only two parties have a realistic opportunity to compete effectively for control

tyranny oppressive government that employs cruel and unjust use of power and authority

unfunded mandates regulations or conditions for receiving grants that impose costs on state and local governments for which they are not reimbursed by the federal government

unitary system a centralized government system in which lower levels of government have little power independent of the national government

values (or beliefs) basic principles that shape a person's opinions about political issues and events

veto the president's constitutional power to turn down acts of Congress. A presidential veto may be overridden by a two-thirds vote of each house of Congress

Virginia Plan A framework for the Constitution, introduced by Edmund Randolph, that called for representation in the national legislature based on the population of each state

War Powers Resolution a resolution of Congress that the president can send troops into action abroad only by authorization of Congress, or if American troops are already under attack or serious threat

whip a party member in the House or Senate responsible for coordinating the party's legislative strategy, building support for key issues, and counting votes

White House staff analysts and advisers to the president, each of whom is often given the title "special assistant"

writ of *certiorari* a decision of at least four of the nine Supreme Court justices to review a decision of a lower court; *certiorari* is Latin, meaning "to make more certain"

writ of *habeas corpus* a court order that the individual in custody be brought into court and shown the cause for detention. *Habeas corpus* is guaranteed by the Constitution and can be suspended only in cases of rebellion or invasion

endnotes

Chapter 1

1. Theda Skocpol and Vanessa Williamson, *The Tea Party and the Making of Republican Conservatism* (New York: Oxford University Press, 2012), pp. 59–64.
2. The ANES Guide to Public Opinion and Electoral Behavior, "Trust the Federal Government, 1958–2008," www.electionstudies.org/nesguide/toptable/tab5a_1 .htm (accessed 6/8/12).
3. Pew Research Center for the People and the Press, "Distrust, Discontent, Anger, and Partisan Rancor," April 18, 2010, www.people-press.org/2010/04/18/section-1-trust -in-government-1958-2010/ (accessed 10/14/2011).
4. ANES Guide to Public Opinion and Electoral Behavior, "Trust the Federal Government."
5. ANES Guide to Public Opinion and Electoral Behavior, "Trust the Federal Government."
6. The New York Times/CBS News Poll, "Americans' Approval of Congress Drops to Single Digits," October 25, 2011, www.nytimes.com/interactive/2011/10/25/ us/politics/approval-of-congress-drops-to-single-digits .html?ref=politics (accessed 6/8/12).
7. Joseph S. Nye Jr., "Introduction: The Decline of Confidence in Government," in *Why People Don't Trust Government*, ed. Joseph S. Nye Jr., Philip D. Zelikow, and David C. King (Cambridge, MA: Harvard University Press, 1997), p. 4.
8. The Pew Research Center for the People and the Press, "Partisan Polarization Surges in Bush, Obama Years; Trends in American Values: 1987–2012, Section 4: Values about Government and the Social Safety Net," www .people-press.org/2012/06/04/section-4-values-about -government-and-the-social-safety-net/ (accessed 6/8/12).
9. This definition is taken from Norman H. Nie, Jane Junn, and Kenneth Stehlik-Barry, *Education and Democratic Citizenship in America* (Chicago: University of Chicago Press, 1996).
10. Freedom House, "Freedom in the World Report, 2011, Tables and Charts," www.freedomhouse.org/images/File/fiw/ Tables%2C%20Graphs%2C%20etc%2C%20FIW%20 2011_Revised%201_11_11.pdf (accessed 10/10/11).
11. See Eugen Weber, *Peasants into Frenchmen: The Modernization of Rural France, 1870–1914* (Stanford, CA: Stanford University Press, 1976), chap. 5.
12. See V. O. Key, *Politics, Parties, and Pressure Groups* (New York: Crowell, 1964), p. 201.
13. Harold Lasswell, *Politics: Who Gets What, When, How* (New York: Meridian Books, 1958).
14. Susan B. Carter, Scott Sigmund Gartner, Michael R. Haines, Alan L. Olmstead, Richard Sutch, and Gavin Wright, eds., *Historical Statistics of the United States: Millennial Edition Online*, Table Aa145-184, Population, by Sex and Race: 1790–1990 (New York: Cambridge University Press, 2006). Data from 2012 available at U.S. Census Bureau, www.census.gov (accessed 2/25/12).
15. Carter et al., *Historical Statistics of the United States*, Table Aa145-184, Population, by Sex and Race: 1790–1990.
16. Carter et al., *Historical Statistics of the United States*, Table Aa145-184, Population, by Sex and Race: 1790–1990; Table Aa2189-2215, Hispanic Population Estimates.
17. U.S. Census Bureau, www.census.gov; Claude S. Fischer and Michael Hout, *A Century of Difference: How America Changed in the Last One Hundred Years* (New York: Russell Sage Foundation, 2006), p. 36.
18. Carter et al., *Historical Statistics of the United States*, Table Aa22-35, Selected Population Characteristics.
19. Fischer and Hout, *A Century of Difference*, p. 24.
20. Michael B. Katz and Mark J. Stern, *One Nation Divisible: What America Was and What It Is Becoming* (New York: Russell Sage Foundation, 2006), p. 16.
21. Carter et al., *Historical Statistics of the United States*, Table Aa145-184, Population, by Sex and Race: 1790–1990, p. 23. Karen R. Humes, Nicholas A. Jones, and Roberto R. Ramirez, "Overview of Race and Hispanic Origin: 2010," *2010 Census Briefs*, Number C210BR-02 (Washington, DC: U.S. Census Bureau, March 2011), p. 4, www.census.gov/prod/cen2010/briefs/c2010br-02.pdf (accessed 10/14/2011).
22. Karen R. Humes, Nicholas A. Jones, and Roberto R. Ramirez, "Overview of Race and Hispanic Origin: 2010," U.S. Census Bureau, March 2010, Table 2 (accessed 6/9/12).

23. U.S. Census, "Table 1.1. Population by Sex, Age, Nativity, and U.S. Citizenship Status: 2010," www.census.gov/population/foreign/data/cps2010.html (accessed 10/14/11).

24. Yesenia D. Acosta and D. Patricia de la Cruz, "The Foreign Born from Latin America and the Caribbean: 2010," *American Community Survey Briefs*, Number ACSBR/10-15 (Washington DC: U.S. Census Bureau, September 2011), p. 2, www.census.gov/prod/2011pubs/acsbr10-15.pdf (accessed 10/14/11).

25. Michael Hoefer, Nancy Rytina, and Bryan C. Baker, "Estimates of the Unauthorized Immigrant Population Residing in the United States: January 2010, *Population Estimates*, Office of Immigration Statistics, Department of Homeland Security, February 2011, www.dhs.gov/xlibrary/assets/statistics/publications/ois_ill_pe_2010.pdf (accessed 10/14/11).

26. Anthony Faiola, "States' Immigrant Policies Diverge," *Washington Post*, October 15, 2007, p. A1.

27. *Plyer v. Doe*, 457 U.S. 202 (1982).

28. Fischer and Hout, *A Century of Difference*, p. 187. "U.S. Census Bureau, *The 2012 Statistical Abstract: Population*, Table 75: Self-Described Religious Identification of Adult Population, 1990, 2001, and 2008," www.census.gov/compendia/statab/cats/population.html (accessed 10/14/11).

29. U.S. Census Bureau, *The 2012 Statistical Abstract: Population*, Table 75: Self-Described Religious Identification of Adult Population, 1990, 2001, and 2008, www.census.gov/compendia/statab/cats/population.html (accessed 10/14/2011).

30. Lindsay M. Howden and Julie A. Meyer, "Age and Sex Composition: 2010 Census Briefs, Number C2010BR-03" (Washington, DC: U.S. Census Bureau, May 2011), pp. 4, 2, www.census.gov/prod/cen2010/briefs/c2010br-03.pdf (accessed 10/14/11).

31. Eurostat, "Population Structure and Ageing," October 2010, http://epp.eurostat.ec.europa.eu/statistics_explained/index.php/Population_structure_and_ageing (accessed 10/14/11).

32. U.S. Census, "Apportionment Population and Number of Representatives, by State: 2010 Census," http://2010.census.gov/news/pdf/apport2010_table1.pdf (accessed 6/22/12).

33. Constitution of the United States of America, Article I, Section 2; U.S. Census, "Congressional Apportionment: 2010 Apportionment Results," www.census.gov/population/apportionment/data/2010_apportionment_results.html (accessed 6/9/12).

34. See Judith N. Shklar, *American Citizenship: The Quest for Inclusion* (Cambridge, MA: Harvard University Press, 1991).

35. Herbert McClosky and John Zaller, *The American Ethos: Public Attitudes toward Capitalism and Democracy* (Cambridge, MA: Harvard University Press, 1984), p. 19.

36. Gardiner Harris, "Flavors Banned from Cigarettes to Deter Youths," *New York Times*, September 22, 2009, www.nytimes.com/2009/09/23/health/policy/23fda.html (accessed 9/24/09).

37. J. R. Pole, *The Pursuit of Equality in American History* (Berkeley: University of California Press, 1978), p. 3.

38. *Plessy v. Ferguson*, 163 U.S. 537 (1896).

39. *Brown v. Board of Education*, 347 U.S. 483 (1954).

40. See Rogers M. Smith, *Liberalism and American Constitutional Law* (Cambridge, MA: Harvard University Press, 1985), chap. 6.

41. The case was *San Antonio Independent School District v. Rodriguez*, 411 U.S. 1 (1973). See the discussion in Smith, *Liberalism and American Constitutional Law*, pp. 163–64.

42. See the discussion in Eileen McDonagh, "Gender Political Change," in *New Perspectives on American Politics*, ed. Lawrence C. Dodd and Calvin C. Jillson (Washington, DC: CQ Press, 1994), pp. 58–73. The argument for moving women's issues into the public sphere is made by Jean Bethke Elshtain, *Public Man, Private Woman* (Princeton, NJ: Princeton University Press, 1981).

43. Roger Lowenstein, "The Way We Live Now: The Inequality Conundrum," *New York Times Magazine*, June 10, 2007, p. 11.

44. Associated Press, "Obama: Tax Cuts Will Be Felt by April 1," February 21, 2009, www.msnbc.msn.com/id/29314485/ (accessed 9/28/09).

45. Reuters, "Obama to Allow Bush Tax Cuts to Expire on Schedule," February 21, 2009, www.reuters.com/article/topNews/idUSTRE51K1ZF20090221 (accessed 9/28/09); Pew Research Center for the People and the Press and for the Public, "Trends in American Values, 1987–2012, Partisan Polarization Surges in Bush, Obama Years," June 4, 2012, www.people-press.org/2012/06/04/partisan-polarization-surges-in-bush-obama-years p. 89 (accessed 6/9/12).

46. Kevin Phillips, *Arrogant Capital: Washington, Wall Street, and the Frustration of American Politics* (Boston: Little, Brown, 1994).

47. United States Election Project, "Voter Turnout: Turnout 1980–2008," http://elections.gmu.edu/voter_turnout.htm (accessed 9/29/09).

48. Center for the Study of the American Electorate, "2008 Turnout Report: African-Americans, Anger, Fear and Youth Propel Turnout to Highest Level since 1960," news release, December 17, 2008, www.american.edu/ia/cdem/csae/pdfs/2008pdfoffinaledited.pdf (accessed 9/29/09).

Chapter 2

1. Michael Kammen, *A Machine That Would Go of Itself* (New York: Vintage, 1986), p. 22.

2. The social makeup of colonial America and some of the social conflicts that divided colonial society are discussed in Jackson Turner Main, *The Social Structure of Revolu-*

tionary America (Princeton, NJ: Princeton University Press, 1965).

3. George B. Tindall and David E. Shi, *America: A Narrative History*, 8th ed. (New York: Norton, 2010), p. 202.

4. For a discussion of events leading up to the Revolution, see Charles M. Andrews, *The Colonial Background of the American Revolution* (New Haven, CT: Yale University Press, 1924).

5. See Carl Becker, *The Declaration of Independence* (New York: Knopf, 1942).

6. An excellent and readable account of the development from the Articles of Confederation to the Constitution will be found in Alfred H. Kelly, Winfred A. Harbison, and Herman Belz, *The American Constitution: Its Origins and Development*, 7th ed. (New York: Norton, 1991), vol. 1, chap. 5.

7. Reported in Samuel E. Morrison, Henry Steele Commager, and William Leuchtenberg, *The Growth of the American Republic* (New York: Oxford University Press, 1969), vol. 1, p. 244.

8. Quoted in Morrison et al., *The Growth of the American Republic*, vol. 1, p. 242.

9. Charles A. Beard, *An Economic Interpretation of the Constitution of the United States* (New York: Macmillan, 1913).

10. Madison's notes, along with the somewhat less complete records kept by several other participants in the convention, are available in a four-volume set. See Max Farrand, ed., *The Records of the Federal Convention of 1787*, 4 vols., rev. ed. (New Haven, CT: Yale University Press, 1966).

11. Farrand, ed., *The Records of the Federal Convention of 1787*, vol. 1, p. 476.

12. Alexander Hamilton, James Madison, and John Jay, *The Federalist Papers*, ed. Clinton L. Rossiter (New York: New American Library, 1961), no. 71.

13. *The Federalist Papers*, no. 62.

14. *The Federalist Papers*, no. 70.

15. Max Farrand, *The Framing of the Constitution of the United States* (New Haven, CT: Yale University Press, 1962), p. 49.

16. Melancthon Smith, quoted in Herbert J. Storing, *What the Anti-Federalists Were For* (Chicago: University of Chicago Press, 1981), p. 17.

17. "Essays of Brutus," no. 1, in *The Complete Anti-Federalist*, ed. Herbert Storing (Chicago: University of Chicago Press, 1981).

18. *The Federalist Papers*, no. 57.

19. "Essays of Brutus," no. 15, in Storing, ed., *The Complete Anti-Federalist*.

20. *The Federalist Papers*, no. 10.

21. "Essays of Brutus," no. 7, in Storing, ed., *The Complete Anti-Federalist*.

22. "Essays of Brutus," no. 6, in Storing, ed., *The Complete Anti-Federalist*.

23. Storing, *What the Anti-Federalists Were For*, p. 28.

24. *The Federalist Papers*, no. 51.

25. Quoted in Storing, *What the Anti-Federalists Were For*, p. 30.

26. *The Federalist Papers*, no. 10.

Chapter 3

1. *National Federation of Independent Business v. Sebeilus*, 11–393 (2012).

2. Adam Liptak, "Bans on Interracial Unions Offer Perspective on Gay Ones," *New York Times*, March 17, 2004, p. A22.

3. National Conference of State Legislators, Same Sex Marriage, Civil Unions and Domestic Partnerships, Last Update: August, 2009, www.ncsl.org/IssuesResearch/Human-Services/SameSexMarriage/tabid/16430/Default.aspx (accessed 10/16/09); "California Bill to Recognize Some Same-Sex Marriages," www.cnn.com/2009/US/10/12/california.samesex.marriage (accessed 10/16/09).

4. Ken I. Kersch, "Full Faith and Credit for Same-Sex Marriages?" Political Science Quarterly 112 (Spring 1997): 117–36; Joan Biskupic, "Once Unthinkable, Now under Debate," *Washington Post*, September 3, 1996, p. A1.

5. Barbara Hoberock, "State Won't Fight Same-Sex Adoption Ruling," *Tulsa World*, August 17, 2007, p. A9.

6. *Hicklin v. Orbeck*, 437 U.S. 518 (1978).

7. *Sweeny v. Woodall*, 344 U.S. 86 (1953).

8. Raphael Minder, "Court Refuses to Extradite Killer Wanted in Hijacking," *New York Times*, November 18, 2011, p. A29.

9. Patricia S. Florestano, "Past and Present Utilization of Interstate Compacts in the United States," *Publius* 24 (Fall 1994): 13–26.

10. See the discussion in www.nationalpopularvote.com (accessed 11/21/11); for a critique of the effort, see David Gringer, "Note: Why the National Popular Vote Is the Wrong Way to Abolish the Electoral College," *Columbia Law Review* 108 (January 2008): 182–230.

11. A good discussion of the constitutional position of local governments is in Richard Briffault, "Our Localism: Part I, The Structure of Local Government Law," *Columbia Law Review* 90, no. 1 (January 1990): 1–115. For more on the structure and theory of federalism, see Larry N. Gerston, *American Federalism: A Concise Introduction* (Armonk, NY: M.E. Sharpe, 2007), and Martha Derthick, "Up-to-Date in Kansas City: Reflections on American Federalism" (1992 John Gaus Lecture), *PS: Political Science & Politics* 25 (December 1992): 671–5.

12. For a good treatment of the contrast between national political stability and social instability, see Samuel P. Huntington, *Political Order in Changing Societies* (New Haven, CT: Yale University Press, 1968), chap. 2.

13. *McCulloch v. Maryland*, 4 Wheaton 316 (1819).

14. *Gibbons v. Ogden*, 9 Wheaton 1 (1824).

15. The Sherman Antitrust Act, adopted in 1890, for example, was enacted not to restrict commerce, but rather to protect it from monopolies, or trusts, in order to prevent unfair trade practices and to enable the market again to become self-regulating. Moreover, the Supreme Court sought to uphold liberty of contract to protect businesses.

For example, in *Lochner v. New York*, 198 U.S. 45 (1905), the Court invalidated a New York law regulating the sanitary conditions and hours of labor of bakers on the grounds that the law interfered with liberty of contract.

16. The key case in this process of expanding the power of the national government is generally considered to be *NLRB v. Jones & Laughlin Steel Corporation*, 301 U.S. 1 (1937), in which the Supreme Court approved federal regulation of the workplace and thereby virtually eliminated interstate commerce as a limit on the national government's power.

17. *United States v. Darby Lumber Co.*, 312 U.S. 100 (1941).

18. W. John Moore, "Pleading the 10th," *National Journal*, July 29, 1995, p. 1940.

19. *United States v. Lopez*, 14 U.S. 549 (1995).

20. *Printz v. United States*, 521 U.S. 98 (1997).

21. See the poll reported in Guy Gugliotta, "Scaling Down the American Dream," *Washington Post*, April 19, 1995, p. A21. See also John Kincaid and Richard L. Cole, "Citizens' Attitudes toward Issues of Federalism in Canada, Mexico and the United States," *Publius: The Journal of Federalism* 41, no. 1 (2011): 53–75.

22. Kenneth T. Palmer, "The Evolution of Grant Policies," in *The Changing Politics of Federal Grants*, ed. Lawrence D. Brown, James W. Fossett, and Kenneth T. Palmer (Washington, DC: Brookings Institution Press, 1984), p. 15.

23. Palmer, "The Evolution of Grant Policies," p. 6.

24. Morton Grodzins, *The American System*, ed. Daniel J. Elazar (Chicago: Rand McNally, 1966).

25. See Terry Sanford, *Storm over the States* (New York: McGraw-Hill, 1967).

26. James L. Sundquist, with David W. Davis, *Making Federalism Work* (Washington, DC: Brookings Institution Press, 1969), p. 271. George Wallace was mistrusted by the architects of the War on Poverty because he was a strong proponent of racial segregation and "states' rights."

27. See Donald F. Kettl, *The Regulation of American Federalism* (Baton Rouge: Louisiana State University Press, 1983).

28. Cindy Skrzycki, "Trial Lawyers on the Offensive in Fight against Preemptive Rules," *Washington Post*, September 11, 2007, p. D2.

29. *Gonazales v. Oregon*, 546 U.S. 243 (2006).

30. *Wyeth v. Levine*, 555 U.S. 555 (2009).

31. Philip Rucker, "Obama Curtails Bush's Policy of 'Preemption,'" *Washington Post*, May 22, 2009, p. A3.

32. See U.S. Advisory Commission on Intergovernmental Relations, *Federal Regulation of State and Local Governments: The Mixed Record of the 1980s* (Washington, DC: Advisory Commission on Intergovernmental Relations, July 1993).

33. U.S. Advisory Commission on Intergovernmental Relations, *Federal Regulation of State and Local Governments*, p. iii.

34. Adam Liptak, "Justices to Hear Health Care Case as Race Heats Up," *New York Times*, November 15, 2011, p. A1.

35. Quoted in Timothy Conlon, *New Federalism: Intergovernmental Reform from Nixon to Reagan* (Washington, DC: Brookings Institution Press, 1988), p. 25.

36. For the emergence of complaints about federal categorical grants, see Palmer, "The Evolution of Grant Policies," pp. 17–18. On the governors' efforts to gain more control over federal grants after the 1994 congressional elections, see Dan Balz, "GOP Governors Eager to Do Things Their Way," *Washington Post*, November 22, 1994, p. A4.

37. U.S. Advisory Commission on Intergovernmental Relations, *Federal Regulation of State and Local Governments*.

38. For an assessment of the achievements of the 104th and 105th Congresses, see Timothy Conlan, *From New Federalism to Devolution: Twenty-Five Years of Intergovernmental Reform* (Washington, DC: Brookings Institution Press, 1998).

39. Robert Frank, "Proposed Block Grants Seen Unlikely to Cure Management Problems," *Wall Street Journal*, May 1, 1995, p. 1.

40. Sarah Kershaw, "U.S. Rule Limits Emergency Care for Immigrants," *New York Times*, September 22, 2007, p. A1.

41. U.S. Committee on Federalism and National Purpose, *To Form a More Perfect Union* (Washington, DC: National Conference on Social Welfare, 1985). See also the discussion in Paul E. Peterson, *The Price of Federalism* (Washington, DC: Brooking Institution Press, 1995), esp. chap. 8.

42. Malcolm Gladwell, "Remaking Welfare: In States' Experiments, a Cutting Contest," *Washington Post*, March 10, 1995, p. 6.

43. The phrase "laboratories of democracy" was coined by Supreme Court Justice Louis Brandeis in his dissenting opinion in *New State Ice Co. v. Liebman*, 285 U.S. 262 (1932).

44. "Motor Vehicle Fatalities in 1996 Were 12 Percent Higher on Interstates, Freeways in 12 States That Raised Speed Limits," Insurance Institute for Highway Safety, press release, October 10, 1997.

45. William Yardley, "New Federal Crackdown Confounds States That Allow Medical Marijuana," *New York Times*, May 8, 2011, p. A13.

46. *Gonzales v. Oregon* (2006).

47. National Conference of State Legislatures, "2011 State Immigration-Related Bills," www.ncsl.org/default.aspx?TabID=756&tabs=951,102#951 (accessed 11/27/11).

48. Associated Press, "Justice Department Sues Utah over State's Illegal Immigration Enforcement Law," *Washington Post*, November 22, 2011, www.washingtonpost.com/national/us-department-of-justice-sues-utah-over-immigration-enforcement-law/2011/11/22/gIQAJeJEmN_story.html (accessed 11/27/11).

49. *Arizona v. United States*, 11–182 (2012).

50. David Nasaw, "Toughest US Sheriff Loses Power to Arrest Illegal Immigrants: Stripping of Federal Duties Political Move, Says Officer: Female Chain Gangs among Criti-

cized Tactics," *The Guardian*, October 10, 2009, p. 27; Anna Gorman, "ICE-Local Alliance to Stay; but the Immigration Enforcement Will Be Subject to More Federal Oversight, Officials Say," *Los Angeles Times*, October 17, 2009, p. A16.

51. Julia Preston, "States Resisting Program Central to Obama's Immigration Strategy," *New York Times*, May 6, 2011, p. A18; Gretchen Gavett, "Why Three Governors Challenged Secure Communities," PBS *Frontline*, October 18, 2011, www.pbs.org/wgbh/pages/frontline/race-multicultural/lost-in-detention/why-three-governors-challenged-secure-communities/ (accessed 11/27/11).

52. Kate Phillips, "South Carolina Governor Rejects Stimulus Money," *New York Times*, March 20, 2009, http://thecaucus.blogs.nytimes.com/2009/03/20/round-2-omb-rejects-sc-governors-stimulus-plan/ (accessed 10/6/09).

53. Robert Pear and J. David Goodman, "Governors' Fight over Stimulus May Define G.O.P.," *New York Times*, February 22, 2009, www.nytimes.com/2009/02/23/us/politics/23governors.html (accessed 10/7/09).

54. The White House, Office of the Press Secretary, Memorandum for the Heads of Executive Departments and Agencies, Subject: Preemption, May 20, 2009, http://theusconstituion.org/blog.history/wp-content/uploads/2009/05/obama-preemption-memo-5202009.pdf (accessed 10/17/09).

55. Adam Liptak, "In Health Law, Asking Where U.S. Power Stops," *New York Times*, November 14, 2011, p. A1.

56. This was a comment from Walter E. Dellinger, President Clinton's acting solicitor general. Linda Greenhouse, "Will the Court Reassert National Authority?" *New York Times*, September 30, 2001, Week in Review, p. 14.

57. Jeff Zeleny and Megan Thee-Brenan, "New Poll Finds a Deep Distrust of Government," *New York Times*, October 26, 2011, p. A1.

58. The Pew Research Center for People and the Press, "Growing Gap in Favorable Views of Federal, State Governments," April 26, 2012, www.people-press.org/2012/04/26/growing-gap-in-favorable-views-of-federal-state-governments/ (accessed 6/10/12).

Chapter 4

1. Alexander Hamilton, James Madison, and John Jay, *The Federalist Papers*, ed. Clinton Rossiter (New York: New American Library, 1961), no. 84, p. 513.

2. *The Federalist Papers*, no. 84, p. 513.

3. Clinton Rossiter, *1787: The Grand Convention* (New York: W.W. Norton, 1987), 302.

4. Rossiter, *1787*, p. 303. Rossiter also reports that "in 1941 the States of Connecticut, Massachusetts, and Georgia celebrated the sesquicentennial of the Bill of Rights by giving their hitherto withheld and unneeded assent."

5. *Barron v. Baltimore*, 7 Peters 243, 246 (1833).

6. The Fourteenth Amendment also seems designed to introduce civil rights. The final clause of the all-important Section 1 provides that no state can "deny to any person within its jurisdiction the equal protection of the laws." It is not unreasonable to conclude that the purpose of this provision was to obligate the state governments as well as the national government to take positive actions to protect citizens from arbitrary and discriminatory actions, at least those based on race. This will be explored in Chapter 5.

7. For example, *The Slaughterhouse Cases*, 16 Wallace 36 (1883).

8. *Chicago, Burlington and Quincy Railroad Company v. Chicago*, 166 U.S. 226 (1897).

9. *Gitlow v. New York*, 268 U.S. 652 (1925).

10. *Near v. Minnesota*, 283 U.S. 697 (1931); *Hague v. C.I.O.*, 307 U.S. 496 (1939).

11. *Palko v. Connecticut*, 302 U.S. 319 (1937).

12. All of these were implicitly included in the *Palko* case as "not incorporated" into the Fourteenth Amendment as limitations on the powers of the states.

13. There is one interesting exception, which involves the Sixth Amendment right to public trial. In the 1948 case *In re Oliver*, 33 U.S. 257, the right to the public trial was, in effect, incorporated as part of the Fourteenth Amendment. However, the issue in that case was put more generally as "due process," and public trial itself was not actually mentioned in so many words. Later opinions, such as *Duncan v. Louisiana*, 391 U.S. 145 (1968), cited the *Oliver* case as the precedent for more explicit incorporation of public trials as part of the Fourteenth Amendment.

14. *McDonald v. Chicago*, 561 U.S. 3025 (2010).

15. *Abington School District v. Schempp*, 374 U.S. 203 (1963).

16. *Engel v. Vitale*, 370 U.S. 421 (1962).

17. *Wallace v. Jaffree*, 472 U.S. 38 (1985).

18. *Lynch v. Donnelly*, 465 U.S. 668 (1984).

19. *Lemon v. Kurtzman*, 403 U.S. 602 (1971). The *Lemon* test is still good law, but as recently as the 1994 Court term, four justices have urged that the test be abandoned. Here is a settled area of law that may soon become unsettled.

20. *Rosenberger v. Rector and Visitors of the University of Virginia*, 515 U.S. 819 (1995).

21. *Van Orden v. Perry*, 545 U.S. 677 (2005).

22. *McCreary v. ACLU*, 545 U.S. 844 (2005).

23. *West Virginia State Board of Education v. Barnette*, 319 U.S. 624 (1943). The case it reversed was *Minersville School District v. Gobitus*, 310 U.S. 586 (1940).

24. *Cantwell v. Connecticut*, 310 U.S. 296 (1940).

25. *Employment Division, Department of Human Resources of Oregon v. Smith*, 494 U.S. 872 (1990).

26. *City of Boerne v. Flores*, 521 U.S. 507 (1997).

27. *Abrams v. U.S.*, 250 U.S. 616 (1919).

28. *U.S. v. Carolene Products Company*, 304 U.S. 144 (1938), note 4. This footnote is one of the Court's most important doctrines. See Alfred H. Kelly, Winfred A. Harbison, and Herman Belz, *The American Constitution: Its Origins and Development*, 7th ed. (New York: Norton, 1991), vol. 2, 519–23.

29. *Schenk v. United States*, 249 U.S. 47 (1919).

30. *Brandenburg v. Ohio*, 395 U.S. 444 (1969).

31. *McConnell v. Federal Election Committee*, 540 U.S. 93 (2003).

32. *Federal Election Commission v. Wisconsin Right to Life*, 551 U.S. 449 (2007).

33. *Davis v. Federal Election Commission*, 554 U.S. 724 (2008).

34. *Citizens United v. Federal Election Commission*, 558 U.S. 50 (2010).

35. Arthur Delaney, "Supreme Court Rolls Back Campaign Finance Restrictions," *Huffington Post*, updated May 25, 2011, www.huffingtonpost.com/2010/01/21/supreme-court-rolls-back_n_431227.html (accessed 7/9/12).

36. *Hague v. Committee for Industrial Organization*, 307 U.S. 496 (1939).

37. *Stromberg v. California*, 283 U.S. 359 (1931).

38. *Texas v. Johnson*, 488 U.S. 884 (1989).

39. *United States v. Eichman*, 496 U.S. 310 (1990).

40. Lizette Alvarez, "Measure to Ban Flag Burning Falls 4 Votes Short in the Senate," *New York Times*, March 30, 2000, p. A24; Adam Clymer, "House, in Ritual Vote, Opposes Flag Burning," *New York Times*, July 18, 2001, p. A20.

41. *Virginia v. Black*, 528 U.S. 343 (2003).

42. *Snyder v. Phelps*, 09–751 (2011).

43. For a good general discussion of speech plus, see Louis Fisher, *American Constitutional Law* (New York: McGraw-Hill, 1990), 544–6. The case upholding the buffer zone against the abortion protesters is *Madsen v. Women's Health Center*, 512 U.S. 753 (1994).

44. *Rumsfeld v. Forum for Academic and Institutional Rights*, 547 U.S. 47 (2006).

45. *Near v. Minnesota*, 283 U.S. 697 (1931).

46. *New York Times v. United States*, 403 U.S. 731 (1971).

47. *Cable News Network, Inc., v. Noriega*, 498 U.S. 976 (1990).

48. *Branzburg v. Hayes*, 408 U.S. 656 (1972).

49. *New York Times v. Sullivan*, 376 U.S. 254 (1964).

50. Shannon Hutzler, "Protecting Informed Public Participation," *Valparaiso University Law Review* 41, no. 3 (Spring 2007): 1235–84.

51. *Hustler Magazine v. Falwell*, 485 U.S. 46 (1988).

52. See *Zeran v. America Online*, 129 F3d 327 (4th Cir. 1977).

53. *Roth v. United States*, 354 U.S. 476 (1957).

54. Concurring opinion in *Jacobellis v. Ohio*, 378 U.S. 184 (1964).

55. *Miller v. California*, 413 U.S. 15 (1973).

56. *Reno v. American Civil Liberties Union*, 521 U.S. 844 (1997).

57. *United States v. American Library Association*, 539 U.S. 194 (2003).

58. *United States v. Williams*, 553 U.S. 285 (2008).

59. *United States v. Playboy Entertainment Group*, 529 U.S. 803 (2000).

60. *Brown v. Entertainment Merchants Association*, 08-1448 (2011).

61. *Chaplinsky v. State of New Hampshire*, 315 U.S. 568 (1942).

62. *Dennis v. United States*, 341 U.S. 494 (1951), which upheld the infamous Smith Act of 1940, which provided criminal penalties for those who "willfully and knowingly conspire to teach and advocate the forceful and violent overthrow and destruction of the government."

63. *Capital Broadcasting Company v. Acting Attorney General*, 405 U.S. 1000 (1972).

64. *R.A.V. v. City of St. Paul*, 506 U.S. 377 (1992)

65. *Bethel School District No. 403 v. Fraser*, 478 U.S. 675 (1986).

66. *Hazelwood School District v. Kuhlmeier*, 484 U.S. 260 (1988).

67. *Morse v. Frederick*, 551 U.S. 393 (2007).

68. *Meritor Savings Bank v. Vinson*, 477 U.S. 57 (1986).

69. *City Council v. Taxpayers for Vincent*, 466 U.S. 789 (1984).

70. *Posadas de Puerto Rico Associates v. Tourism Company of Puerto Rico*, 479 U.S. 328 (1986).

71. Fisher, *American Constitutional Law*, p. 546.

72. *Bigelow v. Virginia*, 421 U.S. 809 (1975).

73. *Virginia State Board of Pharmacy v. Virginia Citizens Consumer Council*, 425 U.S. 748 (1976). Later cases restored the rights of lawyers to advertise their services.

74. *44 Liquormart, Inc. and Peoples Super Liquor Stores Inc., Petitioners v. Rhode Island and Rhode Island Liquor Stores Association*, 517 U.S. 484 (1996).

75. *Lorillard Tobacco v. Reilly*, 533 U.S. 525 (2001).

76. *Presser v. Illinois*, 116 U.S. 252 (1886).

77. *District of Columbia v. Heller*, 554 U.S. 570 (2008).

78. *McDonald v. Chicago*, 561 U.S. 3025 (2010).

79. *In re Winship*, 397 U.S. 361 (1970). An outstanding treatment of due process in issues involving the Fourth through Seventh amendments will be found in Fisher, *American Constitutional Law*, chap. 13.

80. *Horton v. California*, 496 U.S. 128 (1990).

81. *Mapp v. Ohio*, 367 U.S. 643 (1961). Although Mapp went free in this case, she was later convicted in New York on narcotics trafficking charges and served 9 years of a 20-year sentence.

82. For a good discussion of the issue, see Fisher, *American Constitutional Law*, pp. 884–9.

83. *United States v. Grubbs*, 547 U.S. 90 (2006).

84. *National Treasury Employees Union v. Von Raab*, 39 U.S. 656 (1989).

85. *Skinner v. Railroad Labor Executives' Association*, 489 U.S. 602 (1989).

86. *Vernonia School District 47J v. Acton*, 515 U.S. 646 (1995).

87. *Indianapolis v. Edmund*, 531 U.S. 32 (2000), 531 U.S. 32 (2000).

88. *Chandler v. Miller*, 520 U.S. 305 (1997).

89. *Brendlin v. California*, 551 U.S. 249 (2007).

90. *Ferguson v. Charleston*, 532 U.S. 67 (2001).

91. *Kyllo v. United States*, 533 U.S. 27 (2001).

92. *Safford Unified School District No. 1 v. No. Redding*, 08–477 (2009).

93. Edwin S. Corwin and J. W. Peltason, *Understanding the Constitution* (New York: Holt, 1967), p. 286.

94. *Miranda v. Arizona*, 348 U.S. 436 (1966).

95. *Berghuis v. Thompkins*, 08–1470 (2010).

96. *Berman v. Parker*, 348 U.S. 26 (1954). For a thorough analysis of the case, see Benjamin Ginsberg, "*Berman v. Parker*: Congress, the Court, and the Public Purpose," *Polity* 4 (1971): 48–75. For a later application of the case that suggests that "just compensation"—defined as something approximating market value—is about all a property owner can hope for protection against a public taking of property, see Theodore Lowi et al., *Poliscide: Big Government, Big Science, Lilliputian Politics*, 2nd ed. (Lanham, MD: University Press of America, 1990), pp. 267–70.

97. *Kelo v. City of New London*, 545 U.S. 469 (2005).

98. *Gideon v. Wainwright*, 372 U.S. 335 (1963).

99. *Wiggins v. Smith*, 539 U.S. 510 (2003).

100. For further discussion of these issues, see Corwin and Peltason, *Understanding the Constitution*, pp. 319–23.

101. *United States v. Gonzalez-Lopez*, 548 U.S. 140 (2006).

102. *Furman v. Georgia*, 408 U.S. 238 (1972).

103. *Gregg v. Georgia*, 428 U.S. 153 (1976).

104. *Kennedy v. Louisiana*,, 554 U.S. 407 (2008).

105. *Snyder v. Louisiana*, 552 U.S. 472 (2008).

106. *Medellin v. Texas*, 552 U.S. 491 (2008).

107. *Baze v. Rees*, 553 U.S. 35 (2008).

108. *Olmstead v. United States*, 227 U.S. 438 (1928). See also David M. O'Brien, *Constitutional Law and Politics*, 6th ed. (New York: W.W. Norton, 2005), vol. 1, pp. 76–84.

109. *West Virginia State Board of Education v. Barnette* (1943).

110. *NAACP v. Alabama ex rel. Patterson*, 357 U.S. 447 (1958).

111. *Griswold v. Connecticut*, 381 U.S. 479 (1965).

112. *Griswold v. Connecticut*, concurring opinion. In 1972 the Court extended the privacy right to unmarried women: *Eisenstadt v. Baird*, 405 U.S. 438 (1972).

113. *Roe v. Wade*, 410 U.S. 113 (1973).

114. *Webster v. Reproductive Health Services*, 492 U.S. 490 (1989), which upheld a Missouri law that restricted the use of public medical facilities for abortion. The decision opened the way for other states to limit the availability of abortion.

115. *Planned Parenthood of Southeastern Pennsylvania v. Casey*, 505 U.S. 833 (1992).

116. *Stenberg v. Carhart*, 530 U.S. 914 (2000).

117. *Ayotte v. Planned Parenthood*, 546 U.S. 320 (2006).

118. *Gonzales v. Carhart*, 550 U.S. 124 (2007).

119. *Bowers v. Hardwick*, 478 U.S. 186 (1986).

120. *Lawrence v. Texas*, 539 U.S. 558 (2003).

121. *Lawrence v. Texas* (2003).

122. It is worth recalling here the provision of the Ninth Amendment: "The enumeration in the Constitution, of certain rights, shall not be construed to deny or disparage others retained by the people."

123. *Gonzales v. Oregon*, 546 U.S. 243 (2006).

124. *Hamdi v. Rumsfeld*, 542 U.S. 507 (2004).

125. *Hamdan v. Rumsfeld*, 548 U.S. 557 (2006).

126. *ACLU v. NSA*, 06-2095 (6th Cir. 2007).

Chapter 5

1. See Julia Preston, "Immigration Crackdown Also Snares Americans," *New York Times*, December 14, 2011, p. A20; on the charges against the Maricopa County Sheriff's Office, see "Assistant Attorney General Thomas E. Perez Speaks at the Maricopa County Sheriff's Office Investigative Findings Announcement," December 15, 2011, www.justice.gov/crt/opa/pr/speeches/2011/crt-speech -111215.html (accessed 12/15/11).

2. Paula Baker, "The Domestication of Politics: Women and American Political Society, 1780–1920," *American Historical Review* 89 (June 1984): 620–47.

3. Oscar Handlin, *America—A History* (New York: Holt, Rinehart and Winston, 1968), p. 474.

4. *Dred Scott v. Sandford*, 19 Howard 393 (1857).

5. August Meier and Elliot Rudwick, *From Plantation to Ghetto* (New York: Hill and Wang, 1976), pp. 184–8.

6. Jill Dupont, "Susan B. Anthony," New York Notes (Albany: New York State Commission on the Bicentennial of the U.S. Constitution, 1988), p. 3.

7. *Plessy v. Ferguson*, 163 U.S. 537 (1896).

8. Dupont, "Susan B. Anthony," p. 4.

9. The prospect of a "fair employment practices" law tied to the commerce power produced the Dixiecrat break with the Democratic Party in 1948. The Democratic Party organization of the States of the Old Confederacy seceded from the national party and nominated its own candidate, the then-Democratic governor of South Carolina, Strom Thurmond, who later became a Republican senator. This almost cost President Truman the election.

10. This was based on the provision in Article VI of the Constitution that "all treaties made, . . . under the Authority of the United States" shall be the "supreme Law of the Land." The commission recognized that if the U.S. Senate ratified what became the Universal Declaration of Human Rights (a treaty), then that power could be used as the constitutional umbrella for effective civil rights legislation. The Supreme Court had recognized in *Missouri v. Holland*, 252 U.S. 416 (1920), that a treaty could enlarge federal power at the expense of the states.

11. *Missouri ex rel. Gaines v. Canada*, 305 U.S. 337 (1938).

12. *Sweatt v. Painter*, 339 U.S. 629 (1950).

13. *Smith v. Allwright*, 321 U.S. 649 (1944).

14. *Shelley v. Kraemer*, 334 U.S. 1 (1948).

15. Kermit L. Hall, *The Magic Mirror: Law in American History* (New York: Oxford University Press, 1989), pp. 322–4. See also Richard Kluger, *Simple Justice* (New York: Random House, Vintage Edition, 1977), pp. 530–7.

16. The District of Columbia case came up, too, but since the District of Columbia is not a state, this case did not directly involve the Fourteenth Amendment and its

equal protection clause. The plaintiffs confronted the Court on the same grounds, however—that segregation is inherently unequal. Their victory in effect was "incorporation in reverse," with equal protection moving from the Fourteenth Amendment to become part of the Bill of Rights. See *Bolling v. Sharpe*, 347 U.S. 497 (1954).

17. *Brown v. Board of Education of Topeka, Kansas*, 347 U.S. 483 (1954).

18. The Supreme Court first declared that race was a suspect classification requiring strict scrutiny in the decision *Korematsu v. United States*, 323 U.S. 214 (1944). In this case, the Court upheld President Roosevelt's executive order of 1941 allowing the military to exclude persons of Japanese ancestry from the West Coast and to place them in internment camps. It is one of the few cases in which classification based on race survived strict scrutiny.

19. The two most important cases were *Cooper v. Aaron*, 358 U.S. 1 (1958), which required Little Rock, Arkansas, to desegregate, and *Griffin v. Prince Edward County School Board*, 377 U.S. 218 (1964), which forced all the schools of that Virginia county to reopen after five years of closing to avoid desegregation.

20. In *Cooper v. Aaron*, the Supreme Court ordered immediate compliance with the lower court's desegregation order and went beyond that with a stern warning that it is "emphatically the province and duty of the judicial department to say what the law is."

21. *Shuttlesworth v. Birmingham Board of Education*, 358 U.S. 101 (1958), upheld a "pupil placement" plan purporting to assign pupils on various bases, with no mention of race. This case interpreted *Brown* to mean that school districts had to stop explicit racial discrimination but were under no obligation to take positive steps to desegregate. For a while black parents were doomed to case-by-case approaches.

22. For good treatments of this long stretch of the struggle of the federal courts to integrate the schools, see Paul Brest and Sanford Levinson, *Processes of Constitutional Decision-Making: Cases and Materials*, 2nd ed. (Boston: Little, Brown, 1983), pp. 471–80; and Alfred Kelly et al., *The American Constitution: Its Origins and Development*, 6th ed. (New York: W.W. Norton, 1983), pp. 610–16.

23. Pierre Thomas, "Denny's to Settle Bias Cases," *Washington Post*, May 24, 1994, p. A1.

24. See Hamil Harris, "For Blacks, Cabs Can Be Hard to Get," *Washington Post*, July 21, 1994, p. J1.

25. For a thorough analysis of the Office for Civil Rights, see Jeremy Rabkin, "Office for Civil Rights," in James Q. Wilson, ed., *The Politics of Regulation* (New York: Basic Books, 1980).

26. This was an accepted way of using quotas or ratios to determine statistically that blacks or other minorities were being excluded from schools or jobs, and then, on the basis of that statistical evidence, to authorize the Justice Department to bring suits in individual cases and class-action suits. In most segregated situations outside the South, it is virtually impossible to identify and document an intent to discriminate.

27. *Swann v. Charlotte-Mecklenberg Board of Education*, 402 U.S. 1 (1971).

28. *Milliken v. Bradley*, 418 U.S. 717 (1974).

29. For a good evaluation of the Boston effort, see Gary Orfield, *Must We Bus? Segregated Schools and National Policy* (Washington, DC: Brookings Institution, 1978), pp. 144–6. See also Bob Woodward and Scott Armstrong, *The Brethren: Inside the Supreme Court* (New York: Simon and Schuster, 1979), pp. 426–7; and J. Anthony Lukas, *Common Ground* (New York: Random House, 1986).

30. *Board of Education v. Dowell*, 498 U.S. 237 (1991).

31. *Missouri v. Jenkins*, 515 U.S. 70 (1995).

32. John A. Powell, "Segregated Schools Ruling Not All Bad: In Rejecting Seattle's Integration Bid, Top Court Majority Also Held that Avoiding Racial Isolation Is a Legitimate Public Goal," *Newsday*, July 16, 2007, p. A33.

33. See especially *Katzenbach v. McClung*, 379 U.S. 294 (1964). Almost immediately after passage of the Civil Rights Act of 1964, a case was brought challenging the validity of Title II, which covered discrimination in public accommodations. Ollie's Barbecue was a neighborhood restaurant in Birmingham, Alabama. It was located 11 blocks away from an interstate highway and even farther from railroad and bus stations. Its table service was for whites only; there was only a take-out service for blacks. The Supreme Court agreed that Ollie's was strictly an intrastate restaurant, but since a substantial proportion of its food and other supplies was bought from companies outside the state of Alabama, there was a sufficient connection to interstate commerce; therefore, racial discrimination at such restaurants would "impose commercial burdens of national magnitude upon interstate commerce." Although this case involved Title II, it had direct bearing on the constitutionality of Title VII.

34. *Griggs v. Duke Power Company*, 401 U.S. 24 (1971). See also Allan Sindler, *Bakke, DeFunis, and Minority Admissions* (New York: Longman, 1978), pp. 180–9.

35. For a good treatment of these issues, see Charles O. Gregory and Harold A. Katz, *Labor and the Law* (New York: W.W. Norton, 1979), chap. 17.

36. In 1970 this act was amended to outlaw for five years literacy tests as a condition for voting in all states.

37. Joint Center for Political Studies, *Black Elected Officials: A National Roster—1988* (Washington, DC: Joint Center for Political Studies Press, 1988), pp. 9–10. For a comprehensive analysis and evaluation of the Voting Rights Act, see Bernard Grofman and Chandler Davidson, eds., *Controversies in Minority Voting: The Voting Rights Act in Perspective* (Washington, DC: Brookings Institution Press, 1992).

38. Ford Fessenden, "Ballots Cast by Blacks and Older Voters Were Tossed in Far Greater Numbers," *New York Times*, November 12, 2001, p. A17.

39. Aaron Blake, "Texas Redistricting Case: Five Things You Need to Know," *Washington Post*, December 13, 2011, www

.washingtonpost.com/blogs/the-fix/post/texas
-redistricting-case-five-things-you-need-to-know/2011/
12/13/gIQAdowHsO_blog.html (accessed 6/22/12);
Manny Fernandez, "Federal Judges Approve Final
Texas Redistricting Maps," *New York Times*, February 28,
2012, www.nytimes.com/2012/02/29/US/final-texas
-redistricting-maps-approved.html (accessed 6/22/12).

40. See Douglas S. Massey and Nancy A. Denton, *American Apartheid: Segregation and the Making of the Underclass* (Cambridge, MA: Harvard University Press, 1993), chap. 7.

41. Michael Powell, "Bank Accused of Pushing Mortgage Deals on Blacks," *New York Times*, June 6, 2009; Charlie Savage, "Countrywide Will Settle a Bias Suit," *New York Times*, December 22, 2011, p. B1.

42. *Loving v. Virginia*, 388 U.S. 1. (1967).

43. See Jane J. Mansbridge, *Why We Lost the ERA* (Chicago: University of Chicago Press, 1986), and Gilbert Steiner, *Constitutional Inequality* (Washington, DC: Brookings Institution Press, 1985).

44. See *Frontiero v. Richardson*, 411 U.S. 677 (1973).

45. See *Craig v. Boren*, 423 U.S. 1047 (1976).

46. *Franklin v. Gwinnett County Public Schools*, 503 U.S. 60 (1992).

47. Jennifer Halperin, "Women Step Up to Bat," *Illinois Issues* 21 (September 1995): 11–14.

48. Joan Biskupic and David Nakamura, "Court Won't Review Sports Equity Ruling," *Washington Post*, April 22, 1997, p. A1.

49. Debra DeMeis and Rosanna Hertz, "Sex, Sports, and Title IX on Campus: The Triumphs and Travails," *Daily Beast*, June 22, 2012, www.dailybeast.com/articles/2012/06/22/sex-sports-and-title-ix-on-campus-the-triumphs-and-travails.html (accessed 6/22/12).

50. *United States v. Virginia*, 518 U.S. 515 (1996).

51. Judith Havemann, "Two Women Quit Citadel over Alleged Harassment," *Washington Post*, January 13, 1997, p. A1.

52. *Meritor Savings Bank v. Vinson*, 477 U.S. 57 (1986). See also Gwendolyn Mink, *Hostile Environment—The Political Betrayal of Sexually Harassed Women* (Ithaca, NY: Cornell University Press, 2000), pp. 28–32.

53. *Harris v. Forklift Systems, Inc.*, 510 U.S. 17 (1993).

54. *Burlington Industries v. Ellerth*, 524 U.S. 742 (1998); *Faragher v. City of Boca Raton*, 524 U.S. 775 (1998).

55. *United States v. Morrison*, 529 U.S. 598 (2000).

56. *Ledbetter v. Goodyear Tire and Rubber Co.*, 550 U.S. 618 (2007).

57. New Mexico had a different history because not many Anglos settled there initially. (*Anglo* is the term for a non-Hispanic white, generally of European background.) Mexican Americans had considerable power in territorial legislatures between 1865 and 1912. See Lawrence H. Fuchs, *The American Kaleidoscope* (Hanover, NH: University Press of New England, 1990), pp. 239–40.

58. *Salvatierra v. Del Rio Independent School District*, 1931 (Texas).

59. On the United Farm Workers and César Chávez, see Marshall Ganz, *Why David Sometimes Wins: Leadership, Organization, and Strategy in the California Farm Worker Movement* (New York: Oxford University Press, 2009); Miriam Pawel, *The Union of Their Dreams: Power, Hope and Struggle in Cesar Chavez's Farm Worker Movement* (New York: Bloomsbury Press, 2010); and Jacques E. Levy, *Cesar Chavez: Autobiography of La Causa* (Minneapolis: University of Minnesota Press, 2007).

60. On La Raza Unida Party, see "La Raza Unida Party and the Chicano Student Movement in California," in *Latinos in the American Political System* ed. F. Chris Garcia (Notre Dame, IN: University of Notre Dame Press, 1988), pp. 213–35.

61. Dick Kirschten, "Not Black and White," *National Journal*, March 2, 1991, p. 497.

62. Krissah Thompson, "Justice Department to Address Backlog of Civil Rights Complaints," September 25, 2009, www.washingtonpost.com/wp-dyn/content/article/2009/09/25/AR2009092502151.html?nav=emailpage (accessed 10/27/09).

63. Anna Gorman, "ICE-Local Alliance to Stay; but Immigration Enforcement Will Be Subject to More Federal Oversight, Officials Say," *Los Angeles Times*, October 17, 2009, p. 16. For recent criticism, see Preston, "Immigration Crackdown Also Snares Americans," and the PBS *Frontline* documentary "Lost in Detention," available at www.pbs.org/wgbh/pages/frontline/lost-in-detention (accessed 12/15/11). On the charges against the Maricopa County Sheriff's Office, see Marc Lacey, "U.S. Says Arizona Sheriff Shows Pervasive Bias against Latinos," *New York Times*, December 16, 2011, p. A1.

64. *Arizona v. United States*, 567 U.S.___ (2012); Robert Barnes and N. C. Aizenmann, "Supreme Court Rejects Much of Arizona Immigration Law," *Washington Post*, June 25, 2012, www.washingtonpost.com/politics/supreme-court-rules-on-arizona-immigration-law/2012/06/25/gJQA0Nrm1V_story.html?hpid=zl (accessed 6/25/12).

65. *United States v. Wong Kim Ark*, 169 U.S. 649 (1898).

66. *Korematsu v. United States*, 323 U.S. 214 (1944).

67. Children of the Camps, "Historical Documents: The Civil Liberties Act of 1988," http://pbs.org/childofcamp/history/civilact.html (accessed 2/17/08).

68. *Lau v. Nichols*, 414 U.S. 563 (1974).

69. Not all Native American tribes agreed with this, including the Navajos. See Ronald Takaki, *A Different Mirror: A History of Multicultural America* (Boston: Little, Brown: 1993), pp. 238–45.

70. On the resurgence of Native American political activity, see Stephen Cornell, *The Return of the Native: American Indian Political Resurgence* (New York: Oxford University Press, 1990); and Dee Brown, *Bury My Heart at Wounded Knee* (New York: Holt, Rinehart, 1971).

71. See the discussion in Robert A. Katzmann, *Institutional Disability: The Saga of Transportation Policy for the Disabled* (Washington, DC: Brookings Institution Press, 1986).

72. For example, after pressure from the Justice Department, one of the nation's largest rental-car companies agreed to make special hand controls available to any customer requesting them. See "Avis Agrees to Equip Cars for Disabled," *Los Angeles Times*, September 2, 1994, p. D1.

73. The case and the interview with Stephen Bokat were reported in Margaret Warner, "Expanding Coverage," *The NewsHour with Jim Lehrer*, July 1, 1998, www.pbs.org/newshour/bb/law/jan-june98/hiv_6-30.html (accessed 2/18/08).

74. *Gross v. FBL Financial Services, Inc.*, 557 U.S.___(2009).

75. *Bowers v. Hardwick*, 478 U.S. 186 (1986).

76. Quoted in Joan Biskupic, "Gay Rights Activists Seek a Supreme Court Test Case," *Washington Post*, December 19, 1993, p. A1.

77. *Romer v. Evans*, 517 U.S. 620 (1996).

78. *Lawrence v. Texas*, 539 U.S. 558 (2003).

79. From Lyndon B. Johnson, *The Vantage Point* (New York: Holt, Rinehart, and Winston, 1971), p. 166.

80. The Department of Health, Education, and Welfare (HEW) was the cabinet department charged with administering most federal social programs. In 1980, when education programs were transferred to the newly created Department of Education, HEW was renamed the Department of Health and Human Services.

81. *Regents of the University of California v. Bakke*, 438 U.S. 265 (1978).

82. See, for example, *United Steelworkers v. Weber*, 443 U.S. 193 (1979), and *Fullilove v. Klutznick*, 448 U.S. 448 (1980).

83. *Wards Cove v. Atonio*, 490 U.S. 642 (1989).

84. *Adarand Constructors v. Peña*, 515 U.S. 200 (1995).

85. *Gratz v. Bollinger*, 539 U.S. 244 (2003).

86. *Grutter v. Bollinger*, 539 U.S. 306 (2003).

87. *Fisher v. University of Texas*, 11–345 (2012).

88. Michael A. Fletcher, "Opponents of Affirmative Action Heartened by Court Decision," *Washington Post*, April 13, 1997, p. A21.

89. See Sam Howe Verhovek, "Houston Vote Underlined Complexity of Rights Issue," *New York Times*, November 6, 1997, p. A1.

90. Frank Newport, "Little 'Obama Effect' on Views about Race Relations; Attitudes toward Race Not Significantly Improved from Previous Years," October 29, 2009, www.gallup.com/poll/123944/Little-Obama-Effect-Views-Race-Relations.aspx (accessed 10/30/09).

91. There are still many genuine racists in America, but with the exception of a lunatic fringe, made up of neo-Nazis and members of the Ku Klux Klan, most racists are too ashamed or embarrassed to take part in normal political discourse. They are not included in either category here.

92. *Slaughterhouse Cases*, 16 Wallace 36 (1873).

93. See Paul M. Sniderman and Edward G. Carmines, *Reaching beyond Race* (Cambridge, MA: Harvard University Press, 1997).

Chapter 6

1. See, for example, John H. Aldrich, Christopher Gelpi, Peter Feaver, Jason Reifler, and Kristin Thompson Sharp, "Foreign Policy and the Electoral Connection" *Annual Review of Political Science* 9: 477–502 (2006). John H. Aldrich, John L. Sullivan, and Eugene Borgida "Foreign Affairs and Issue Voting: Do Presidential Candidates 'Waltz before a Blind Audience'?" *American Political Science Review 81:* 123–41 (1989).

2. Pew Research Center, "No Decline in Belief That Obama Is a Muslim: Nearly One-in-Five White Evangelicals Think So" April 1, 2009, http://pewresearch.org/pubs/1176/obama-muslim-opinion-not-changed (accessed 9/7/12). The same survey also found that 28 percent of Americans think Muslims should not be eligible to sit on the Supreme Court, while fully one-third believe that Muslims should be barred from running for president. See also David Redlawsk, "A Matter of Motivated Reasoning," *New York Times*, April 22, 2011, www.nytimes.com/roomfordebate/2011/04/21/barack-obama-and-the-psychology-of-the-birther-myth/a-matter-of-motivated-reasoning (accessed 9/7/12).

3. www.whitehouse.gov/sites/default/files/rss_viewer/birth-certificate-long-form.pdf (accessed 9/7/12).

4. A July 15, 2008, Pew Research Center survey found that about 12 percent of voters nationwide thought Obama was Muslim (http://pewresearch.org/pubs/898/belief-that-obama-is-muslim-is-bipartisan-but-most-likely-to-sway-democrats, accessed 9/7/12). A November 2008 Pew survey reports that even after the election, about 12 percent of American still believed Obama to be Muslim (http://pewresearch.org/pubs/1176/obama-muslim-opinion-not-changed, accessed 9/7/12). An October 2008 University of Iowa Hawkeye Poll, using an open-ended question, asked a national sample of respondents to name both McCain and Obama's religions. For Obama's religion, 37.9 percent of likely voters said they did not know, somewhat higher than Pew's 25 percent. The difference likely stems from Pew's use of a closed-ended question, where options were given to the respondent, compared to an open-ended one, for which the respondent must come up with an answer.

5. Matt Barreto and Dino Bozonelos, "Democrat, Republican, or None of the Above? The Role of Religiosity in Muslim American Party Identification" *Politics and Religion* 2 (2009): 200–29. Jaihyun Park, Karla Felix, and Grace Lee, "Implicit Attitudes toward Arab-Muslims and the Moderating Effects of Social Information" *Basic and Applied Social Psychology* 29, no. 1 (2007): 35–45.

6. Tali Mendelberg, *The Race Card: Campaign Strategy, Implicit Messages, and the Norm of Equality* (Princeton, NJ: Princeton University Press, 2001).

7. Redlawsk, "A Matter of Motivated Reasoning."

8. David Redlawsk, "Hot Cognition or Cool Consideration? Testing the Effects of Motivated Reasoning on

Political Decision Making," *Journal of Politics* 64 (2002): 1021–44. See also David Redlawsk, Andrew Civettini, and Karen Emmerson, "The Affective Tipping Point: Do Motivated Reasoners Ever 'Get It'?" *Political Psychology* 31, no. 4 (2010).

9. M. Lodge and C. S. Taber, "Three Steps toward a Theory of Motivated Political Reasoning," in A. Lupia, M. McCubbins, and S. Popkin, eds., *Elements of Reason: Cognition, Choice, and the Bounds of Rationality* (London: Cambridge University Press, 2000). George E. Marcus, W. Russell Neuman, and Michael MacKuen, *Affective Intelligence and Political Judgment* (Chicago: University of Chicago Press, 2000); Redlawsk, "Hot Cognition or Cool Consideration?"; Redlawsk, Civettini, and Emmerson, "The Affective Tipping Point."

10. Marcus, Neuman, and MacKuen, *Affective Intelligence and Political Judgment.*

11. ACLU Statement on Obama's Signing of NDAA, "President Obama Signs Indefinite Detention Bill into Law," GG Drafts, December 31, 2011, http://ggdrafts.blogspot.com/2011/12/aclu-statement-on-obamas-signing-of.html?spref=fb (accessed 9/7/12).

12. See Karen Mossberger, Caroline Tolbert, and Ramona McNeal, *Digital Citizenship: The Internet, Society and Participation* (Cambridge: MIT Press, 2008).

13. See Harry Holloway and John George, *Public Opinion* (New York: St. Martin's, 1986). See also Paul R. Abramson, *Political Attitudes in America* (San Francisco: Freeman, 1983).

14. See Paul M. Sniderman and Edward G. Carmines, *Reaching beyond Race* (Cambridge, MA: Harvard University Press, 1997).

15. Douglas R. Oxley, Kevin B. Smith, John R. Alford, Matthew V. Hibbing, Jennifer L. Miller, Mario Scalora, Peter K. Hatemi, and John R. Hibbing, "Political Attitudes Vary with Physiological Traits," *Science* 321, no. 5896 (September 19, 2008): 1667–70. See also Jeffrey Mondak, *Personality and the Foundation of Political Behavior* (Cambridge, UK: Cambridge University Press, 2010).

16. See Angus Campbell et al., *The American Voter* (New York: Wiley, 1960), p. 147.

17. Betsy Sinclair, *The Social Citizen: Peer Networks and Political Behavior* (Chicago: University of Chicago Press, 2012).

18. CNN Poll, 2009.

19. CBS News/New York Times Poll, 2008.

20. Donald Green, Bradley Palmquist, and Eric Schickler, *Partisan Hearts and Minds: Political Parties and the Social Identities of Voters* (New Haven, CT: Yale University Press, 2002).

21. See Richard Lau and David Redlawsk, *How Voters Decide: Information Processing during an Election Campaign* (New York: Cambridge University Press, 2006).

22. David S. Broder, "Partisan Gap Is at a High, Poll Finds," *Washington Post*, November 9, 2003, p. A6.

23. Broder, "Partisan Gap Is at a High, Poll Finds." See also Thomas E. Mann and Norman J. Ornstein, *It's Even Worse Than It Looks: How the American Constitutional System Collided with the New Politics of Extremism* (New York: Basic Books, 2012).

24. Morris Fiorina, Samuel Abrams, and Jeremy Pope, *Culture War? The Myth of a Polarized America* (New York: Longman Publishers, 2004).

25. Pew Research Center, The Complicated Politics of Abortion, August 22, 2012, http://www.people-press.org/2012/08/22/the-complicated-politics-of-abortion/ (accessed 9/7/12)

26. Pamela Johnston Conover, "The Role of Social Groups in Political Thinking," *British Journal of Political Science* 18 (1988): 51–78.

27. See also Michael C. Dawson, *Behind the Mule: Race, Class, and African American Politics* (Princeton, NJ: Princeton University Press, 1994).

28. Jack Citrin, Donald Green, Christopher Muste, and Cara Wong, "Public Opinion toward Immigration Reform: The Role of Economic Motivations," *Journal of Politics* 59 (1997): 858–81. David Sears and Jack Citrin, *Something for Nothing in California* (Berkeley, CA: University of California Press, 1982).

29. Nathan J. Kelly and Peter K. Enns, "Inequality and the Dynamics of Public Opinion: The Self-Reinforcing Link between Economic Inequality and Mass Preferences," *The American Journal of Political Science* 54, no. 4 (2010): 855–70. Jacob S. Hacker and Paul Pierson, *Winner-Take-All Politics: How Washington Made the Rich Richer—and Turned Its Back on the Middle Class* (New York: Simon and Schuster, 2010).

30. Larry M. Bartels, "Homer Gets a Tax Cut: Inequality and Public Policy in the American Mind," *Perspectives on Politics* 3, no. 1 (2005): 15–31. Larry Bartels, *Unequal Democracy* (Princeton, NJ: Princeton University Press, 2008).

31. O. R. Holsti, "A Widening Gap between the Military and Society? Some Evidence, 1976–1996," *International Security* 23 (Winter 1998/1999): 5–42

32. Jennifer A. Heerwig and Brian J. McCabe, "Education and Social Desirability Bias: The Case of a Black Presidential Candidate," *Social Science Quarterly* 90, no. 3 (2009): 674–86.

33. Raymond E. Wolfinger and Steven J. Rosenstone, *Who Votes?* (New Haven, CT: Yale University Press, 1980). See also Steven J. Rosenstone and John Mark Hansen, *Mobilization, Participation, and Democracy in America* (New York: Macmillan, 1993).

34. Mann and Ornstein, *It's Even Worse Than It Looks.*

35. Shaun Bowler, Gary Segura, and Stephen Nicholson, "Earthquakes and Aftershocks: Race, Direct Democracy, and Partisan Change," *American Journal of Political Science* 50 (2006): 146–59. For a more general discussion of the spillover effects of ballot measures on public opinion, see Stephen Nicholson, *Voting the Agenda: Candidates*

Elections and Ballot Propositions (Princeton, NJ: Princeton University Press, 2005).

36. Paul Davidson, "Fannie, Freddie Bailout to Cost Taxpayers $154 Billion," *USA Today*, October, 22, 2010.

37. John R. Zaller, *The Nature and Origins of Mass Opinion* (New York: Cambridge University Press, 1992).

38. Benjamin I. Page and Robert Y. Shapiro, *The Rational Public: Fifty Years of Trends in Americans' Policy Preferences* (Chicago: University of Chicago Press, 1995); Eugene Wittkopf, *Faces of Internationalism: Public Opinion and Foreign Policy* (Durham, NC: Duke University Press, 1990).

39. Zaller, *Nature and Origins of Mass Opinion*.

40. Carol Glynn et al., *Public Opinion*, 2nd ed. (Boulder, CO: Westview, 2004), p. 293. See also Michael X. Delli Carpini and Scott Keeter, *What Americans Know about Politics and Why It Matters* (New Haven, CT: Yale University Press, 1996).

41. Adam J. Berinsky, "The Two Faces of Public Opinion,"*American Journal of Political Science* 43, no. 4 (1999): 1209–30.

42. Delli Carpini and Keeter, *What Americans Know about Politics and Why It Matters.*

43. Michael Lewis Beck, *Economics and Elections: The Major Western Democracies* (Ann Arbor: University of Michigan Press, 1990).

44. Matt Barreto, "Watch for 'Sí Se Puede' Signs at Obama Rallies," *New York Times*, May 23, 2012, www.nytimes .com/roomfordebate/2012/05/23/securing-the-hispanic -vote/watch-for-si-se-puede-signs-at-obama-rallies (accessed 6/6/12).

45. Pilar Marrero, "June Tracking Poll: Immigration Is a Critical Issue for Voters," *Latino Decisions*, June 10, 2011, www.latinodecisions.com/blog/2011/06/10/june -tracking-poll-immigration-is-a-critical-issue-for-voters/ (accessed 6/6/12).

46. Adam J. Berinsky, "Assuming the Costs of War: Events, Elites and American Support for Military Conflict," *The Journal of Politics* 69, no. 4 (2007): 975–97; Zaller, *Nature and Origins of Mass Opinion*.

47. Richard R. Lau and David P. Redlawsk, "Advantages and Disadvantages of Cognitive Heuristics in Political Decision Making," *American Journal of Political Science* 45 (October 2001): 951–71. Lau and Redlawsk, *How Voters Decide.*

48. For a discussion of the role of information politics, see Arthur Lupia and Matthew D. McCubbins, *The Democratic Dilemma: Can Citizens Learn What They Need to Know?* (New York: Cambridge University Press, 1998). See also Shaun Bowler and Todd Donovan, *Demanding Choices: Opinion and Voting in Direct Democracy* (Ann Arbor: University of Michigan Press, 1998). See also Samuel Popkin, *The Reasoning Voter: Communication and Persuasion in Presidential Campaigns* (Chicago: University of Chicago Press, 1991); Arthur Lupia, "Shortcuts Versus Encyclopedias: Information and Voting Behavior in California Insurance Reform Elections," *American Political Science Review* 88 (1994): 63–76; and Wendy

Rahn, "The Role of Partisan Stereotypes in Information Processing about Political Candidates," *American Journal of Political Science* 37 (1993): 472–96.

49. Bartels, *Unequal Democracy.*

50. Benjamin Ginsberg, *The American Lie: Government by the People and Other Political Fables* (Boulder, CO: Paradigm, 2007).

51. Gerald F. Seib and Michael K. Frisby, "Selling Sacrifice," *Wall Street Journal*, February 5, 1993, p. 1.

52. Peter Marks, "Adept in Politics and Advertising, 4 Women Shape a Campaign," *New York Times*, November 11, 2001, p. B6.

53. Facebook pages accessed May 2012.

54. *Roe v. Wade*, 410 U.S. 113 (1973).

55. See Gillian Peele, *Revival and Reaction* (Oxford, UK: Clarendon, 1985). Also see Connie Paige, *The Right-to-Lifers* (New York: Summit, 1983).

56. For example, see the poll conducted for the Des Register by Selzer and Co. Inc. of Des Moines, October 26–29. The sample includes 1,093 Iowans 18 and older, with a margin of error of 3.5 percent.

57. Caroline Tolbert and Amanda Keller, "Iowa's 2010 Gubernatorial Race: Money, the Economy and Same-Sex Marriage," in *Pendulum Swing*, ed. Larry J. Sabato (New York: Longman Publishers, 2011). See also Daniel A. Smith and Caroline Tolbert, *Educated by Initiative: The Effects of Direct Democracy on Citizens and Political Organizations in the American States* (Ann Arbor: University of Michigan Press, 2004).

58. See David Vogel, "The Power of Business in America: A Reappraisal," *British Journal of Political Science* 13 (January 1983): 19–44.

59. See David Vogel, "The Public Interest Movement and the American Reform Tradition," *Political Science Quarterly* 96 (Winter 1980): 607–27.

60. Frank Newport, "Congress Ends 2011 with Record-Low 11% Approval," Gallup Politics, December 19, 2011, www .gallup.com/poll/151628/Congress-Ends-2011-Record -Low-Approval.aspx (accessed 6/6/12).

61. Mann and Ornstein, *It's Even Worse Than It Looks.*

62. See Shanto Iyengar, *Is Anyone Responsible? How Television Frames Political Issues* (Chicago: University of Chicago Press, 1991); and Shanto Iyengar, *Do the Media Govern?* (Thousand Oaks, CA: Sage, 1997).

63. David Redlawsk, Caroline Tolbert, and Todd Donovan. *Why Iowa? How Caucuses and Sequential Elections Improve the Presidential Nominating Process* (Chicago: University of Chicago Press, 2011).

64. Redlawsk, Tolbert, and Donovan, *Why Iowa?*

65. Herbert Asher, *Polling and the Public* (Washington, DC: CQ Press, 2001), 64.

66. Michael Kagay and Janet Elder, "Numbers Are No Problem for Pollsters, Words Are," *New York Times*, August 9, 1992, p. E6.

67. Lynn Vavreck and Douglas Rivers, "The 2006 Cooperative Congressional Election Study," *Journal of Elections*,

Public Opinion and Parties 18, no. 4 (2008): 355–66. See also Simon Jackman and Lynn Vavreck, "Primary Politics: Race, Gender, and Age in the 2008 Democratic Primary," *Journal of Elections, Public Opinion and Parties* 20, no. 2 (2010): 153–86.

68. Dennis Chong and James N. Druckman, "A Theory of Framing and Opinion Formation in Competitive Elite Environments," *Journal of Communication* 57 (2007): 99–118. See also Stephen P. Nicholson and Robert M. Howard, "Framing Support for the Supreme Court in the Aftermath of Bush v. Gore," *Journal of Politics* 65, no. 3 (2003): 676–95; and Dennis Chong and James N. Druckman, "Framing Public Opinion in Competitive Democracies" *American Political Science Review* 101, no. 4 (2007): 637–55.

69. John R. Zaller, *The Nature and Origins of Mass Opinion* (New York: Cambridge University Press, 1992).

70. See Adam Berinsky, "The Two Faces of Public Opinion," *American Journal of Political Science* 43, no. 4 (1999): 1209–30. See also Adam Berinsky, "Political Context and the Survey Response: The Dynamics of Racial Policy Opinion," *Journal of Politics* 64, no. 2 (2002): 567–84.

71. Jennifer A. Heerwig and Brian J. McCabe, "Education and Social Desirability Bias: The Case of a Black Presidential Candidate," *Social Science Quarterly* 90, no. 3 (2009): 674–86.

72. David Redlawsk, Caroline Tolbert, and William Franko, "Voters, Emotions, and Race in 2008: Obama as the First Black President," *Political Research Quarterly* 63, no. 3 (2010): 875–89.

73. Michael Tesler and David O. Sears, *Obama's Race: The 2008 Election and the Dream of a Post-Racial America* (Chicago: University of Chicago Press, 2010).

74. See James H. Kuklinski, Michael D. Cobb, and Martin Gilens, "Racial Attitudes and the 'New South,'" *Journal of Politics* 59, no. 2 (1997): 323–49; and James H. Kuklinski, Paul M. Sniderman, Kathleen Knight, Thomas Piazza, Philip E. Tetlock, Gordon R. Lawrence, and Barbara Mellers, "Racial Prejudice and Attitudes Toward Affirmative Action," *American Journal of Political Science* 41, no. 2 (1997): 402–19. See also Jeffrey A. Karp and David Brockington, "Social Desirability and Response Validity: A Comparative Analysis of Overreporting Voter Turnout in Five Countries," *Journal of Politics* 67, no. 3 (2005): 825–40; and Matthew J. Streb, Barbara Burrell, Brian Frederick, and Michael A. Genovese, "Social Desirability Effects and Support for a Female American President," *Public Opinion Quarterly* 72, no. 1 (2008): 76–89.

75. Carl Cannon, "A Pox on Both Our Parties," in *The Enduring Debate*, ed. David C. Canon et al. (New York: W.W .Norton, 2000), p. 389.

76. "Dial S for Smear," *Memphis Commercial Appeal*, September 22, 1996.

77. Amy Keller, "Subcommittee Launches Investigation of Push Polls," *Roll Call*, October 3, 1996.

78. For a discussion of the growing difficulty of persuading people to respond to surveys, see John Brehm, *Phantom Respondents* (Ann Arbor: University of Michigan Press, 1993).

79. Redlawsk, Tolbert and Donovan, *Why Iowa?*

80. Angus Campbell et al. *The American Voter* (New York: Wiley, 1960).

81. Benjamin I. Page and Robert Y. Shapiro, "Effects of Public Opinion on Policy," *American Political Science Review* 77, no. 1 (1983): 175–90.

82. Gerald C. Wright, Rober S. Erikson, and John P. McIver, "Public Opinion and Policy Liberalism in the American States," *American Journal of Political Science* 31, no. 4 (November 1987): 980–1001.

83. Richard F. Fenno, *Home Style: House Members in Their Districts* (Boston: Little, Brown and Co., 1978); and Lawrence R. Jacobs and Robert Y Shapiro, *Politicians Don't Pander: Political Manipulation and the Loss of Democratic Responsiveness* (Chicago: University of Chicago Press, 2000).

84. Malcolm E. Jewell, *Representation in State Legislatures* (Lexington: University Press of Kentucky, 1982).

85. Jacobs and Shapiro, *Politicians Don't Pander.*

86. John Griffin and Brian Newman, "Are Voters Better Represented?" *Journal of Politics* 67 (2005): 1206–27.

87. Bartels, *Unequal Democracy.*

88. Other authors have endorsed Bartels's view that government policy exacerbates income inequality. See, for example, Jacob S. Hacker and Paul Pierson, *Winner-Take-All Politics: How Washington Made the Rich Richer—And Turned Its Back on the Middle Class* (New York: Simon and Schuster, 2010).

89. Martin Gilens, "Inequality and Democratic Responsiveness," *Public Opinion Quarterly* 69, no. 5 (2005): 778–96; and Martin Gilens, "Preference Gaps and Inequality in Representation," *PS: Political Science and Politics* 42, no. 2 (2009): 335–41.

90. Christopher Wlezien and Stuart Soroka, "The Relationship between Public Opinion and Policy," in Russell Dalton and Hans-Dieter Klingemann, eds., *Oxford Handbook of Political Behavior* (New York: Oxford University Press, 2009), pp. 799–817.

91. Gilens, "Inequality and Democratic Responsiveness"; Bartels, *Unequal Democracy.*

92. Ryan Claassen and Benjamin Highton, "Does Policy Debate Reduce Information Effects in Public Opinion? Analyzing the Evolution of Public Opinion on Health Care," *Journal of Politics* 68, no. 2 (2006): 410–20.

93. Nicholas Carr, *The Shallows: What the Internet Is Doing to Our Brains* (New York: W.W. Norton, 2011).

Chapter 7

1. Larry M. Bartels, *Presidential Primaries and the Dynamics of Public Choice* (Princeton, NJ: Princeton University Press, 1988).

2. David Redlawsk, Caroline Tolbert and Todd Donovan, *Why Iowa? How Caucuses and Sequential Elections Improve the Presidential Nominating Process* (Chicago: University of Chicago Press, 2011).

3. Karen Mossberger, Caroline Tolbert, and Ramona McNeal, *Digital Citizenship: The Internet, Society and Participation* (Cambridge, MA: MIT Press, 2008). See also J. E. Katz and R. E. Rice, *Social Consequences of Internet Use: Access, Involvement, and Interaction* (Cambridge, MA: MIT Press, 2002).

4. Karen Mossberger, Caroline Tolbert and William Franko, *Digital Cities: The Internet and the Geography of Opportunity* (New York: Oxford University Press, 2012). See also the National Telecommunications and Information Administration, *Digital Nation: 21st Century America's Progress toward Universal Broadband Access* (Washington, DC: U.S. Department of Commerce, 2011).

5. Pew Internet and American Life, "Trend Data (Adults): What Internet Users Do Online," February 2012, http://pewinternet.org/Static-Pages/Trend-Data-(Adults)/Online-Activites-Total.aspx (accessed 6/12/12).

6. Caroline Tolbert and Ramona McNeal, "Unraveling the Effects of the Internet on Political Participation," *Political Research Quarterly* 56, no. 2 (2003): 175–85. See also Bruce Bimber, "Information and Political Engagement in America: The Search for Effects of Information Technology at the Individual Level," *Political Research Quarterly* 54 (2001): 53–67; Bruce Bimber, *Information and American Democracy: Technology in the Evolution of Political Power* (Cambridge, UK: Cambridge University Press, 2003); and Brian S. Krueger, "Assessing the Potential of Internet Political Participation in the United States," *American Politics Research* 30 (2002): 476–98.

7. Pew Research Center Publications, "The Internet's Broader Role in Campaign 2008," January 11, 2008, http://pewresearch.org/pubs/689/the-internets-broader-role-in-campaign-2008, and *"The Daily Show*: Journalism, Satire or Just Laughs?" May 8, 2008, http://pewresearch.org/pubs/829/the-daily-show-journalism-satire-or-just-laughs (accessed 9/7/12).

8. Robert McChesney and John Nichols, *The Death and Life of American Journalism: The Media Revolution that Will Begin the World Again* (New York: Nation Books, 2010).

9. Pew Research Center Publications, "State of the News Media 2010," March 15, 2010, http://pewresearch.org/pubs/1523/state-of-the-news-media-2010 (accessed 9/11/12).

10. Darrell West, *The Next Wave: Using Digital Technology to Further Social and Political Innovation* (Washington, DC: Brookings Institution Press, 2011).

11. West, *The Next Wave*; Edward Glaeser, *Triumph of the City: How Our Greatest Invention Makes Us Richer, Smarter, Greener, Healthier, and Happier* (New York: Penguin Press, 2011).

12. West, *The Next Wave*.

13. Mossberger, Tolbert and McNeal, *Digital Citizenship*.

14. Mossberger, Tolbert and McNeal, *Digital Citizenship*; Brian A. Krueger, "A Comparison of Conventional and Internet Political Mobilization, *American Politics Research* 34, no. 6 (2006): 759–76.

15. Antony Wilhelm, *Digital Nation: Toward an Inclusive Information Society* (Cambridge, MA: MIT Press, 2006). P. DiMaggio, E. Hargittai, et al., "Social Implications of the Internet," *Annual Review of Sociology* 27, no. 1 (2001): 307–36.

16. Karen Mossberger, Caroline Tolbert, and Mary Stansbury, *Virtual Inequality: Beyond the Digital Divide* (Washington, DC: Georgetown University Press, 2003); Pippa Norris, *Digital Divide: Civic Engagement, Information Poverty, and the Internet Worldwide* (New York: Cambridge University Press, 2001).

17. National Telecommunications and Information Administration, *Digital Nation: 21st Century America's Progress Toward Universal Broadband Access* (Washington, DC: U.S. Department of Commerce, 2011).

18. Eric R. A. N. Smith, *The Unchanging American Voter* (Berkeley: University of California Press, 1989), chap. 4.

19. See Pew Internet and American Life, "Trend Data (Adults): Online Activities, 2000-2009," February 2012, http://pewinternet.org/Static-Pages/Trend-Data-(Adults)/Online-Activites-Total.aspx (accessed 6/28/12). See also Kathryn Zickuhr and Aaron Smith, "Digital Differences," Pew Internet and American Life, April 13, 2012, http://www.pewinternet.org/Reports/2012/Digital-differences.aspx (accessed 6/28/12).

20. June Kronholz and Amy Schatz, "How Conservatives Enhanced Online Voice," *Wall Street Journal*, July 3, 2007, p. A5.

21. Richard Davis, "Interplay: Political Blogging and Journalism," in *iPolitics: Citizens, Elections, and Governing in the New Media Era*, ed. Richard L. Fox and Jennifer M. Ramos (Cambridge, UK: Cambridge University Press, 2012), pp. 76–99.

22. Zoe M. Oxley, "More Sources, Better Informed Public? New Media and Political Knowledge," in *iPolitics*, Fox and Ramos, ed. pp. 25–47. James Fallows, "Bit by Bit It Takes Shape: Media Evolution from the 'Post-Truth' Age." *The Atlantic*, August 29, 2012, http://www.theatlantic.com/politics/archive/2012/08/bit-by-bit-it-takes-shape-media-evolution-for-the-post-truth-age/261741/ (accessed 9/10/12).

23. Pew Research Center, "State of the Media, 2010"; West, *The Next Wave*.

24. Aaron Smith and Joanna Brenner, "Social Networking: Twitter Use 2012." Pew Internet and American Life Project, May 31, 2012, http://pewinternet.org/topics/Social-Networking.aspx?typeFilter=5 (accessed 6/28/12).

25. Amy Schatz, "BO, UR So Gr8: How a Young Tech Entrepreneur Translated Barack Obama into the Idiom of Facebook," *Wall Street Journal*, May 26, 2007, p. 1.

26. Karen Mossberger and Caroline Tolbert, "Digital Democracy," in *Oxford Handbook of American Elections*

and Political Behavior, ed. Jan Leighley (New York: Oxford University Press, 2010).

27. Tolbert and McNeal, "Unraveling the Effects of the Internet."

28. Mossberger, Tolbert, and McNeal, *Digital Citizenship*. See Richard L. Fox and Jennifer M. Ramos, eds., *iPolitics: Citizens, Elections, and Governing in the New Media Era* (Cambridge, UK: Cambridge University Press, 2011).

29. W. R. Neuman, M. R. Just, A. N. Crigler, *Common Knowledge: News and the Construction of Political Meaning* (Chicago: University of Chicago Press, 1992).

30. A. Healy and D. McNamara, "Verbal Learning and Memory: Does the Modal Model Still Work?" in *Annual Review of Psychology*, Vol. 47, ed. J. Spense, J. Darley, and D. Foss (Palo Alto, CA: Annual Reviews, 1996), pp. 143–72.

31. Cass Sunstein, *Republic.com* (Princeton, NJ: Princeton University Press, 2001). See also Mossberger and Tolbert "Digital Democracy."

32. Michael Margolis and David Resnick*Politics as Usual: The Cyberspace "Revolution"* (Thousand Oaks, CA: Sage, 2000).

33. West, *The Next Wave*.

34. See Pew Internet and American Life, "Trend Data (Adults): What Internet Users Do Online." See also Karen Mossberger, Caroline Tolbert and Allison Hamilton, "Measuring Digital Citizenship: Mobile Access and Broadband." *International Journal of Communication* 6 (2012): 2492–528.

35. West, *The Next Wave*; McChesney and Nichols, *The Death and Life of American Journalism*.

36. Dianne Bystrom, "Advertising, Web Sites, and Media Coverage: Gender and Communication along the Campaign Trail," in *Gender and Elections: Shaping the Future of American Politics*, 2nd ed., ed. Susan J. Carroll and Richard L. Fox (Cambridge, UK: Cambridge University Press, 2010), pp. 239–62.

37. Regina G. Lawrence and Melody Rose, *Hillary Clinton's Race for the White House: Gender Politics and Media on the Campaign Trail* (Boulder, CO: Lynne Reinner Publishers, 2010).

38. Joe Sterling and Phil Gast, "Assistant Coach Who Reported Penn State Incident Threatened, Won't Be at Game," *CNN*, November 10, 2011, www.cnn.com (accessed 10/22/12).

39. Oxley, "More Sources, Better Informed Public?"

40. Matthew A. Baum, "Preaching to the Choir or Converting the Flock: Presidential Communication Strategies in the Age of Three Medias," in *iPolitics*, ed. Fox and Ramos, pp. 183–205.

41. Ann Crigler, Marion Just, Lauren Hume, Jesse Mills, and Parker Hevron, "YouTube and TV Advertising Campaigns: Obama versus McCain in 2008," in *iPolitics*, ed. Fox and Ramos, pp. 103–24.

42. Eli Pariser, *The Filter Bubble: What the Internet Is Hiding from You* (New York: Penguin Press, 2011).

43. Karen Mossberger, Caroline Tolbert, and Mary Stansbury, *Virtual Inequality: Beyond the Digital Divide* (Washington, DC: Georgetown University Press, 2003).

44. For a criticism of the increasing consolidation of the media, see the essays in Patricia Aufderheide et al., *Conglomerates and the Media* (New York: New Press, 1997).

45. Jonathan M. Ladd, *Why Americans Hate the Media and How It Matters* (Princeton, NJ: Princeton University Press, 2012).

46. David J. Garrow, *Protest at Selma: Martin Luther King, Jr., and the Voting Rights Act of 1965* (New Haven, CT: Yale University Press, 2001).

47. See Todd Gitlin, *The Whole World Is Watching* (Berkeley: University of California Press, 1980).

48. Tim Groseclose, *Left Turn: How Liberal Media Bias Distorts the American Mind* (New York: St. Martin's Press, 2011).

49. Pew Research Center Publications, "How Journalists See Journalists in 2004: Views on Profits, Performance and Politics," May 2004, http://people-press.org/http://people-press.org/files/legacy-pdf/214.pdf (accessed on 9/7/2012)

50. Doris Graber, ed., *Media Power in American Politics*, 5th ed. (Washington, DC: Congressional Quarterly Press, 2006).

51. Larry Bartels, *Unequal Democracy* (Princeton, NJ: Princeton University Press, 2008).

52. Michael Tesler and David O. Sears, *Obama's Race: The 2008 Election and the Dream of a Post-Racial America.* (Chicago: University of Chicago Press, 2010). See also Redlawsk, Tolbert, and Donovan, *Why Iowa?*

53. Iyengar Shanto and Donald R. Kinder, *News That Matters: Television and American Opinion* (Chicago: University of Chicago Press, 1987), p. 63.

54. Redlawsk, Donovan, and Tolbert, *Why Iowa?*

55. Todd Donovan, Caroline Tolbert, and Daniel Smith, "Priming Presidential Votes with Direct Democracy," *Journal of Politics* 70, no. 4 (2008): 1217–31.

56. Daniel Smith and Caroline Tolbert, "Direct Democracy, Public Opinion, and Candidate Choice," *Public Opinion Quarterly* 74 (1 (2010): 85–108.

57. *New York Times v. United States*, 403 U.S. 713 (1971).

58. Michael Massing, "The Press: The Enemy Within," *New York Review of Books*, December 15, 2005, p. 6.

59. *Red Lion Broadcasting Company v. FCC*, 395 U.S. 367 (1969).

60. United Nations General Assembly, "Report of the Special Rapporteur on the Promotion and Protection of the Right to Freedom of Opinion and Expression," 2011.

61. Andrew Chadwick, *Internet Politics: States, Citizens, and New Communication Technologies* (Oxford, UK: Oxford University Press, 2006).

62. See Martin Linsky, *Impact: How the Press Affects Federal Policymaking* (New York: W.W. Norton, 1986).

Chapter 8

1. Douglas R. Hess and Jody Herman, "Representational Bias in the 2008 Electorate, November 2009," www.projectvote.org/reports-on-the-electorate-/440.html (accessed 11/21/09).

2. Angus Campbell, Philip E. Converse, Warren E. Miller, and Donald E. Stokes, *The American Voter* (New York: Wiley, 1960); Raymond E. Wolfinger and Steven J. Rosenstone, *Who Votes?* (New Haven, CT: Yale University Press, 1980); Frances Fox Piven and Richard A. Cloward, *Why Americans Don't Vote* (New York: Pantheon, 1988).

3. Joanne Laucius, "Vote or Die?" *Ottawa Citizen*, November 4, 2004, p. A8.

4. Bruce E. Cain, Todd Donovan, and Caroline J. Tolbert, *Democracy in the States: Experiments in Election Reform* (Washington, DC: Brookings Institution Press, 2008).

5. Pew Research Center for the People and the Press, "No Consensus about Whether Nation Is Divided Into 'Haves' and 'Have-Nots,'" September 29, 2011, http://pewresearch.org/pubs/2109/haves-have-nots-economic-divisions (accessed 9/14/12).

6. The American National Election Studies (ANES), "American National Election Study, 2008: Pre- and Post-Election Survey" [computer file], ICPSR25383-v1, Ann Arbor, MI: Inter-university Consortium for Political and Social Research [distributor], 2009-06-10. doi:10.3886/ICPSR25383 (accessed 12/4/09).

7. Sidney Verba, Kay Lehman Schlozman, and Henry E. Brady, *Voice and Equality: Civic Voluntarism in American Politics* (Cambridge, MA: Harvard University Press, 2005), chap. 3, for kinds of participation, and pp. 66–7 for prevalence of local activity.

8. Karen Mossberger, Caroline Tolbert, and Ramona McNeal, *Digital Citizenship: The Internet, Society, and Participation* (Cambridge, MA: MIT Press, 2008).

9. Pew Internet and American Life Project, "Trend Data (Adults): What Internet Users Do Online," April 2012, http://pewinternet.org/Trend-Data-%28Adults%29/Online-Activites-Total.aspx (accessed 7/26/12).

10. Aaron Smith, "The Internet's Role in Campaign 2008," Pew Research Center for the People and the Press, November 2008.

11. David Redlawsk, Caroline Tolbert, and Todd Donovan, *Why Iowa? How Caucuses and Sequential Elections Improve the Presidential Nominating Process* (Chicago: University of Chicago Press, 2011). See also Karen Mossberger and Caroline Tolbert, "Digital Democracy," in *The Oxford Handbook of American Elections and Political Behavior*, ed. Jan Leighley (New York: Oxford University Press, 2010).

12. Mossberger, Tolbert, and McNeal, *Digital Citizenship*; B. S. Krueger, "Assessing the Potential of Internet Political Participation in the United States," *American Politics Research* 30 (2002): 476–98; B. S. Krueger, "A Comparison of Conventional and Internet Political Mobilization," *American Politics Research* 34, no. 6 (2006): 759–76; Andrew Chadwick, *Internet Politics: States, Citizens, and New Communication Technologies* (Oxford, UK: Oxford University Press, 2006); Bruce Bimber, *Information and American Democracy: Technology in the Evolution of Political Power* (Cambridge, UK: Cambridge University Press, 2003); and

Rachel Gibson, Wainer Lusoli, and Steven Ward, "Online Participation in the UK: Testing a 'Contextualized' Model of Internet Effects,"*British Journal of Politics and International Relations* 7, no. 4 (2006): 561–83.

13. Karen Mossberger, Allison Hamilton, and Caroline Tolbert, "Measuring Digital Citizenship: Mobile Access and the Less Connected," *International Journal of Communication*, forthcoming.

14. Verba, Schlozman, and Brady, *Voice and Equality*.

15. Caroline Tolbert and Ramona McNeal, "Unraveling the Effects of the Internet on Political Participation." *Political Research Quarterly* 56, no. 2 (2003): 175–85; see also Bruce Bimber, "Information and Political Engagement in America: The Search for Effects of Information Technology at the Individual Level," *Political Research Quarterly* 54 (2001): 53–67; Bruce Bimber, *Information and American Democracy: Technology in the Evolution of Political Power* (Cambridge, UK: Cambridge University Press, 2003); and Brian Krueger, "Assessing the Potential of Internet Political Participation in the United States," *American Politics Research* 30 (2002): 476–98. Thomas, J. and G. Streib, "The New Face of Government: Citizen-Initiated Contacts in the Era of E-Government," *Journal of Public Administration Theory and Research* 13, no. 1(2003): 83–102; D. V. Shah, J. Cho, William P. Eveland, and N. Kwak, "Information and Expression in a Digital Age: Modeling Internet Effects on Civic Participation," *Communication Research* 32, no. 5 (2005): 531–65; K. Kenski and N. J. Stroud, "Connections Between Internet Use and Political Efficacy, Knowledge, and Participation," *Journal of Broadcasting and Electronic Media* 50, no. 2 (2006): 173–92; Arthur Lupia and G. Sin, "Which Public Goods Are Endangered? How Evolving Communication Technologies Affect the Logic of Collective Action," *Public Choice* 117 (2003): 315–31.

16. Smith, "Internet's Role in Campaign 2008." See also Darrell West, *The New Wave* (Washington DC: Brookings Institution Press, 2011).

17. Pew Internet and American Life Project, "Post-Election 2004 Tracking Survey," November 22, 2004, http://www.pewinternet.org/Shared-Content/Data-Sets/2004/Post Election-2004-Tracking-Survey.aspx (accessed 12/29/08).

18. Doris Graber, *Processing the News: How People Tame the Information Tide*, 2nd ed. (New York: Longman, 1988).

19. Mossberger and Tolbert, "Digital Democracy."

20. Caroline Tolbert and Allison Hamilton, "Political Engagement and the Internet in the 2008 U.S. Presidential Election: A Panel Survey," in Eva Anduiza, Mike Jensen, and Laia Jorba, eds., *Digital Media and Political Engagement Worldwide: A Comparative Study* (Cambridge, UK: Cambridge University Press, 2012).

21. Sunshine Hillygus and Todd Shields, *The Persuadable Voter: Wedge Issues in Presidential Campaigns* (Princeton, NJ: Princeton University Press, 2008).

22. Karen Mossberger and Caroline Tolbert, "Digital Democracy," in *Oxford Handbook of American Elections*

and Political Behavior, ed. Jan Leighley (New York: Oxford University Press, 2010).

23. W. R. Neuman, M. R. Just, and A. N. Crigler, *Common Knowledge: News and the Construction of Political Meaning* (Chicago: University of Chicago Press, 1992).

24. David P. Redlawsk, "Hot Cognition or Cool Consideration: Testing the Effects of Motivated Reasoning," *Journal of Politics* 64 (2002): 1021–44.

25. Michael Margolis and D. Resnick, *Politics as Usual: The Cyberspace "Revolution"* (Thousand Oaks, CA: Sage, 2000).

26. Pew Internet and American Life Project, "Post-Election 2004 Tracking Survey."

27. Manuel Castells, *The Rise of the Network Society: The Information Age: Economy, Society, and Culture* (Oxford, UK: Blackwell, 1997).

28. Bimber, *Information and American Democracy*; Bruce Bimber and Richard Davis, *Campaigning Online: The Internet in U.S. Elections* (Cambridge, UK: Cambridge University Press, 2003).

29. D. Stolle and M. Micheletti, "The Expansion of Political Action Repertoires: Theoretical Reflections on Results from the Nike Email Exchange Internet Campaign," American Political Science Association, Washington, D.C., 2005.

30. Joseph Graf, "The Audience for Political Blogs: New Research on Blog Readership," Institute for Politics, Democracy & the Internet, October 2006.

31. Russell Dalton, *The Good Citizen: How a Younger Generation Is Reshaping American Politics* (Washington, DC: CQ Press, 2008).

32. Robert Putnam. *Bowling Alone: The Collapse and Revival of American Community* (New York: Simon and Schuster, 2000).

33. Mossberger, Tolbert, and McNeal, *Digital Citizenship*; Pippa Norris, *Digital Divide: Civic Engagement, Information Poverty, and the Internet Worldwide* (New York: Cambridge University Press, 2001); Benjamin Barber, "The New Telecommunications Technology: Endless Frontier or the End of Democracy?" *Constellations* 4, no. 2 (2011): 208–28; Tolbert and McNeal, "Unraveling the Effects of the Internet"; H. Rheingold, *The Virtual Community: Homesteading on the Electronic Frontier* (Reading, MA: Addison-Wesley, 1993).

34. Acronyms for the Stop Online Piracy Act (SOPA) and the PROTECT IP Act (Preventing Real Online Threats to Economic Creativity and Theft of Intellectual Property Act, or PIPA).

35. "A Political Coming of Age for the Tech Industry" *New York Times*, January 18, 2012.

36. "Public Outcry over Antipiracy Bills Began as Grass-Roots Grumbling: Suddenly, Hollywood Wants to Sit Down and Talk," *New York Times*, January 20, 2012, p. B1.

37. Mossberger, Tolbert, and McNeal, *Digital Citizenship*.

38. Pippa Norris, *Digital Divide: Civic Engagement, Information Poverty, and the Internet Worldwide* (New York: Cambridge University Press, 2001). See also Karen Mossberger, Caroline Tolbert, and May Stansbury. *Virtual Inequality: Beyond the Digital Divide* (Washington, DC: Georgetown University Press, 2003).

39. U.S. Department of Commerce. "Digital Nation," National Telecommunications and Information Administration, Washington, DC, 2011.

40. Karen Mossberger, Caroline Tolbert, and William Franko, *Digital Cities: The Internet and the Geography of Opportunity* (New York: Oxford University Press, 2012).

41. *Citizens United v. Federal Election Commission*, 558 U.S. 50 (2010).

42. Michael P. McDonald, "American Voter Turnout in Historical Perspective," in *The Oxford Handbook of American Elections and Political Behavior*, pp. 125–43.

43. Todd Donovan and Shaun Bowler, *Reforming the Republic: Democratic Institutions for the New America* (Upper Saddle River, NJ: Pearson Education, 2004).

44. For a discussion of the decline in voter turnout over time, see Ruy A. Teixeira, *The Disappearing American Voter* (Washington, DC: Brookings Institution Press, 1992). See also Michael McDonald and Samuel Popkin, "The Myth of the Vanishing Voter" *American Political Science Review*, 95 (2001): 963–74, and Michael McDonald, "Voter Turnout," *United States Election Project*, http://elections.gmu.edu/voter_turnout.htm (accessed 9/14/12).

45. Robert Jackman, "Political Institutions and Voter Turnout in the Democracies," *American Political Science Review* 81 (June 1987): 420.

46. Anthony Downs, *An Economic Theory of Democracy* (New York: Harper and Row, 1957); William H. Riker and Peter C. Ordeshook, "A Theory of the Calculus of Voting," *American Political Science Review* 62, no. 1 (1968): 25–42.

47. Angus Campbell, Philip E. Converse, Warren E. Miller, and Donald E. Stokes, *The American Voter* (New York: Wiley, 1960); Steven Rosenstone and John Mark Hansen, *Mobilization, Participation, and Democracy in America* (New York: Macmillan, 1993).

48. Sidney Verba and Norman H. Nie, *Participation in America: Political Democracy and Social Equality* (New York: Harper and Row, 1972).

49. Douglas R. Hess and Jody Herman, "Representational Bias in the 2008 Electorate," November 2009, www.projectvote.org/reports-on-the-electorate-/440.html (accessed 11/21/09).

50. Jan E. Leighley and Jonathan Nagler, "Socioeconomic Class Bias in Turnout, 1964–1988: The Voters Remain the Same," *American Political Science Review* 86, no. 3 (1992): 725–36.

51. See Richard A. Brody, "The Puzzle of Political Participation in America," in *The New American Political System*, ed. Anthony King (Washington, DC: American Enterprise Institute, 1978), chap. 8.

52. Rosenstone and Hansen, *Mobilization, Participation, and Democracy*, p. 59.

53. Alan S. Gerber and Donald P. Green, "The Effects of Canvassing, Telephone Calls, and Direct Mail on Voter

Turnout: A Field Experiment," *The American Political Science Review* 94, no. 3 (September 2000): 660.

54. Donald P. Green and Alan S. Gerber, "Getting Out the Youth Vote: Results from Randomized Field Experiments," December 29, 2001, pp. 26–7, www.youngvoterstrategies.org (accessed 3/8/08).

55. Student PIRGs New Voter Project, "Text Reminders Increase Primary Youth Turnout," October 2008, www.newvotersproject.org/research/text-messaging (accessed 11/30/09).

56. Erik Austin and Jerome Chubb, *Political Facts of the United States since 1789* (New York: Columbia University Press, 1986), pp. 378–9.

57. Michael P. McDonald and John Samples, eds., *The Marketplace of Democracy: Electoral Competition and American Politics* (Washington, DC: Brookings Institution Press, 2006).

58. Mark N. Franklin, "Electoral Participation," in *Comparing Democracies: Elections and Voting in Global Perspective*, ed. Lawrence LeDuc, Richard G. Niemi, and Pippa Norris (Thousand Oaks, CA: Sage, 1996), pp. 216–35; G. Bingham Powell, "American Voter Turnout in Comparative Perspective," *American Political Science Review* 80, no. 1 (1986): 17–43.

59. Todd Donovan, "A Goal for Reform: Make Elections Worth Stealing," *PS: Political Science and Politics* 40, no. 4 (2007): 681–6.

60. Donovan, "A Goal for Reform"; Gary W. Cox and Michael C. Munger, "Closeness, Expenditures, and Turnout in the 1982 U.S. House Elections," *American Political Science Review* 83, no. 1 (1989): 217–31; James G. Gimpel, Karen M. Kaufmann, and Shanna Pearson-Merkowitz, "Battleground States versus Blackout States: The Behavioral Implications of Modern Presidential Campaigns," *Journal of Politics* 69, no. 3 (2007): 786–97.

61. Donovan and Bowler, *Reforming the Republic*; McDonald and Samples, *Marketplace of Democracy*; Gary Jacobson, *The Politics of Congressional Elections*, 7th ed. (New York: Longman, 2008).

62. Samuel C. Patterson and Gregory A. Caldeira, "Getting Out the Vote: Participation in Gubernatorial Elections," *American Political Science Review* 77, no. 3 (1983): 675–89; Gregory A. Caldeira and Samuel C. Patterson, "Contextual Influences on Participation in U.S. State Legislative Elections," *Legislative Studies Quarterly* 7, no. 3 (1982): 359–81; Cox and Munger, "Closeness, Expenditures, and Turnout"; Gary W. Copeland, "Activating Voters in Congressional Elections," *Political Behavior* 5, no. 4 (1983): 391–401; Robert A. Jackson, "The Mobilization of U.S. State Electorates in the 1988 and 1990 Elections," *Journal of Politics* 59, no. 2 (1997): 520–37; Thomas M. Holbrook and Scott D. McClurg, "The Mobilization of Core Supporters: Campaigns, Turnout, and Electoral Composition in United States Presidential Elections," *American Journal of Political Science* 49, no. 4 (2005):

689–703; Andre Blais, "What Affects Voter Turnout?" *Annual Review of Political Science* 9 (2006): 111–25; Andre Blais and Agnieszka Dobrzynska, "Turnout in Electoral Democracies," *European Journal of Political Research* 33, no. 2 (2003): 239–61.

63. Caroline Tolbert, Daniel C. Bowen, and Todd Donovan, "Initiative Campaigns: Direct Democracy and Voter Mobilization," *American Politics Research* 37, no. 1 (2009): 155–92.

64. Caroline Tolbert, John A. Grummel, and Daniel A. Smith, "The Effects of Ballot Initiatives on Voter Turnout in the American States," *American Politics Research* 29, no. 6 (2001): 625–48; Mark A. Smith, "The Contingent Effects of Ballot Initiatives and Candidate Races on Turnout," *American Journal of Political Science* 45, no. 3 (2001): 700–706; Caroline J. Tolbert and Daniel A. Smith, "The Educative Effects of Ballot Initiatives on Voter Turnout," *American Politics Research* 33, no. 2 (2005): 283–309; Daniel A. Smith and Caroline J. Tolbert, *Educated by Initiative: The Effects of Direct Democracy on Citizens and Political Organizations in the American States* (Ann Arbor: University of Michigan Press, 2004).

65. Stephen Nicholson, *Voting the Agenda: Candidates, Elections, and Ballot Propositions* (Princeton, NJ: Princeton University Press, 2005).

66. Todd Donovan, Caroline Tolbert, and Daniel Smith, "Priming Presidential Votes with Direct Democracy, *Journal of Politics* 70, no. 4 (2008): 1217–31.

67. Jeffrey Karp and Caroline Tolbert, "Support for Nationalizing Presidential Elections," *Presidential Studies Quarterly* 40, no. 4 (2010): 771–93; Daron Shaw, *The Race to 270: The Electoral College and the Campaign Strategies of 2000 and 2004* (Chicago: University of Chicago Press, 2006).

68. Gimpel, Kaufmann, Pearson-Merkowitz, "Battleground States versus Blackout States"; Julianna Sandell Pacheco, "Political Socialization in Context: The Effect of Political Competition on Youth Voter Turnout," *Political Behavior* 30, no. 4 (2008): 415–36; Keena Lipsitz, "The Consequences of Battleground and 'Spectator' State Residency for Political Participation," *Political Behavior* 31, no. 2 (2009): 187–209.

69. Redlawsk, Tolbert, and Donovan, *Why Iowa?*

70. Cain, Donovan, and Tolbert, *Democracy in the States.*

71. The data in this paragraph are drawn from the Sentencing Project and Human Rights Watch, "Losing the Vote: The Impact of Felony Disenfranchisement Laws in the United States" (October 1998), www.sentencingproject.org/tmp/File/FVR/fd_losingthevote.pdf (accessed 2/22/08).

72. Sentencing Project, "Expanding the Vote: State Felony Disenfranchisement Reform, 1997–2008," September 25, 2008, www.sentencingproject.org/detail/news/cfm?news_id=492 (accessed 11/30/09).

73. Ryan S. King, "Expanding the Vote: State Felony Disenfranchisement Reform, 1997–2008" (Sentencing Project, Septem-

ber 2008), www.sentencingproject.org/doc/publications/fd_statedisenfranchisement.pdf (accessed 12/5/09).

74. Chris Uggen and Jeffrey Manza, "Democratic Contraction: Political Consequences of Felon Disenfranchisement in the United States," *American Sociological Review 2002* 67, no. 6 (2002): 777–803.

75. Matt Barreto, Stephen Nuño, and Gabriel Sanchez, "The Disproportionate Impact of Voter-ID Requirements on the Electorate—New Evidence from Indiana," *PS: Political Science & Politics* 42 (2009): 111–16.

76. Benjamin Highton, "Easy Registration and Voter Turnout," *Journal of Politics* 59 (1997): 565–75; Benjamin Highton, "Voter Registration and Turnout in the United States," *Perspectives on Politics* 2, no. 3 (2004): 507–15; Michael J. Hanmer, *Discount Voting: Voter Registration Reforms and Their Effects* (New York: Cambridge University Press, 2009); Cain, Donovan, and Tolbert, *Democracy in the States.*

77. Cain, Donovan, and Tolbert, *Democracy in the States.*

78. Robert A. Jackson, Robert D. Brown, and Gerald C. Wright, "Registration, Turnout and the Electoral Representativeness of U.S. State Electorates," *American Politics Quarterly* 26, no. 3 (July 1998): 259–87. See also Benjamin Highton, "Easy Registration and Voter Turnout," *Journal of Politics* 59, no. 2 (April 1997): 565–87.

79. Highton "Easy Registration and Voter Turnout"; Stephen Knack and James White, "Election-Day Registration and Turnout Inequality," *Political Behavior* 22, no. 1 (2000): 29–44; Craig Leonard Brians and Bernard Grofman, "When Registration Barriers Fall, Who Votes? An Empirical Test of a Rational Choice Model," *Public Choice* 99 (1999): 161–76; Michael J. Hanmer, *Discount Voting: Voter Registration Reforms and Their Effects* (New York: Cambridge University Press, 2009); Mary Fitzgerald, "Greater Convenience But Not Greater Turnout: The Impact of Alternative Voting Methods on Electoral Participation in the United States," *American Politics Research* 33, no. 6 (2005): 842–67; Caroline J. Tolbert, Todd Donovan, Bridgett King, and Shaun Bowler, "Election Day Registration, Competition, and Voter Turnout," in *Democracy in the States: Experiments in Election Reform*, ed. Bruce E. Cain, Todd Donovan, and Caroline J. Tolbert (Washington, DC: Brookings Institution Press, 2008), pp. 83–98.

80. Hanmer, *Discount Voting;* Robert A. Jackson, Robert D. Brown, and Gerald C. Wright, "Registration, Turnout, and the Electoral Representativeness of U.S. State Electorates," *American Politics Quarterly* 26, no. 3 (1998): 259–87; Robert D. Brown, Robert A. Jackson, and Gerald C. Wright, "Registration, Turnout, and State Party Systems," *Political Research Quarterly* 52, no. 3 (1999): 463–79.

81. Michael P. McDonald, 2008. "Portable Voter Registration," *Political Behavior* 30, no. 4 (2008): 491–501.

82. Cain, Donovan, and Tolbert, *Democracy in the States.*

83. Michael McDonald, "2008 Early Voting Statistics," *United States Election Project*, http://elections.gmu.edu/early vote 2008.html (accessed 11/20/09).

84. Paul Gronke, Eva Galanes-Rosenbaum, and Peter Miller, "Early Voting and Turnout," *PS: Political Science and Politics* 40, no. 4 (October 2007): 639–45; Fitzgerald "Greater Convenience but Not Greater Turnout"; Adam J. Berinsky, "The Perverse Consequences of Electoral Reform in the United States," *American Politics Research* 33, no. 4 (2005): 471–91.

85. Jeffrey Karp and Susan Banducci, "Going Postal: How All-Mail Elections Influence Turnout," *Political Behavior* 22, no. 3 (2000): 223–39.

86. Connie Cass, "'Motor Voter' Impact Slight," *Chattanooga News-Free Press*, June 20, 1997, p. A5. On the need to motivate voters, see Marshall Ganz, "Motor Voter or Motivated Voter?" *American Prospect* 28 (September–October 1996): 41–9. On the hopes for Motor Voter, see Frances Fox Piven and Richard A. Cloward, "Northern Bourbons: A Preliminary Report on the National Voter Registration Act," *PS: Political Science and Politics* 29, no. 1 (March 1996): 39–42. On turnout in the 1996 election, see Barbara Vobejda, "Just under Half of Possible Voters Went to the Polls," *Washington Post*, November 7, 1996, p. A3.

87. Elizabeth Rigby and Melanie J. Springer, "Does Electoral Reform Increase (or Decrease) Political Equality?" *Political Research Quarterly* (2010): 1–15.

88. Democracy Corps, "The 2008 Early Voting Statistics," *United States Election Project*, http://elections.gmu.edu/early vote 2008.html (accessed 11/20/09).

89. "Voting by Mail and Turnout: A Replication and Extension," Early Voting Information Center, www.earlyvoting.net/blog/node/155 (accessed 12/5/09); Paul Gronke, Eva Galanes-Rosenbaum, and Peter Miller, "Early Voting and Turnout," *PS: Political Science and Politics* 40, no. 4 (October 2007): 639–45.

90. Lawrence Bobo and Franklin D. Gilliam, "Race, Sociopolitical Participation, and Black Empowerment," *American Political Science Review* 24, no. 2 (June 1990): 377–93.

91. Rene Rocha, Caroline Tolbert, Daniel Bowen, and Chris Clark, "Race and Turnout: Does Descriptive Representation in State Legislatures Increase Minority Voting?" *Political Research Quarterly* 63, no. 3 (2010): 890–907.

92. Susan Banducci, Todd Donovan, and Jeffrey Karp, "Minority Representation, Empowerment and Participation," *Journal of Politics* 66, no. 2 (2004): 34–556.

93. Matt Barreto, Gary Segura, and Nathan Woods, "The Mobilizing Effect of Majority—Minority Districts on Latino Turnout," *American Political Science Review* 98 (2004): 65–75.

94. Adrian Pantoja and Gary Segura, "Does Ethnicity Matter? Descriptive Representation in the Statehouse and Political Alienation Among Latinos," *Social Science Quarterly* 84 (2003): 441–60.

95. Ryan Claassen, "Political Opinion and Distinctiveness: The Case of Hispanic Ethnicity," *Political Research Quarterly* 57 (2004): 609–20.

96. Connie Cass, "'Motor Voter' Impact Slight," *Chattanooga News-Free Press*, June 20, 1997, p. A5. On the need to motivate voters see Marshall Ganz, "Motor Voter or Motivated Voter?" *American Prospect*, no. 28 (September–October 1996): 41–49. On the hopes for Motor Voter, see Fox Piven and Cloward, "Northern Bourbons." On turnout in the 1996 election, see Barbara Vobejda, "Just under Half of Possible Voters Went to the Polls," *Washington Post*, November 7, 1996, p. A3.

97. See William Julius Wilson, *The Truly Disadvantaged: The Inner City, the Underclass, and Public Policy* (Chicago: University of Chicago Press, 1987); and Douglas Massey and Nancy Denton, *American Apartheid: Segregation and the Making of the American Underclass* (Cambridge, MA: Harvard University Press, 1993).

98. See Michael C. Dawson, *Behind the Mule: Race and Class in African-American Politics* (Princeton, NJ: Princeton University Press, 1994), chaps. 5 and 6.

99. Dawson, *Behind the Mule*.

100. Mark Hugo Lopez and Paul Taylor, "Dissecting the 2008 Electorate: Most Diverse in U.S. History," Pew Research Center, April 30, 2009, www.pewhispanic.org/2009/04/30/dissecting-the-2008-electorate-most-diverse-in-us-history/ (accessed 9/14/12).

101. Barreto, Nuño, and Sanchez, "The Disproportionate Impact of Voter ID Requirements."

102. U.S. Census Bureau, "Resident Population by Race, Hispanic Origin Status, and Age—Projections," www.census.gov/compendia/statab/cats/population/estimates_and_projections_by_age_sex_raceethnicity.html (accessed 11/25/09).

103. Douglas R. Hess and Jody Herman, "Representational Bias in the 2008 Electorate, November 2009," www.projectvote.org/reports-on-the-electorate-/440.html (accessed 11/21/09). The 2012 data are from exit polls available at http://elections.nytimes.com (accessed 11/11/12).

104. Center for Health Policy, University of New Mexico, "New Survey Shows Overwhelming Support among Latinos for Health Care Reform That Includes Public Option," November 30, 2009, http://healthpolicy.unm.edu/resources/new-survey-shows-overwhelming-support-among-latinos-health-care-reform-includes-public-opt (accessed 12/1/09).

105. Liz Sidoti, "Keeping Latino Support a Big Challenge for Obama," *Associated Press*, November 29, 2009, www.chron.com/disp/story.mpl/nation/6743401.html (accessed 11/29/09).

106. U.S. Census Bureau, "Resident Population by Race, Hispanic Origin Status, and Age—Projections," www.census.gov/compendia/statab/cats/population/estimates_and_projections_by_age_sex_raceethnicity.html (accessed 11/24/09).

107. U.S. Census Bureau, "Reported Voting and Registration by Race, Hispanic Origin, Sex, and Age Groups: November 1964 to 2008"; "Reported Voting and Registration by Region, Educational Attainment, and Labor Force: November 1964 to 2008," CNN National Exit Poll 2008, www.cnn.com/ELECTION/2008/results/polls/#USP00p1 (accessed 11/22/09).

108. Anne E. Kornblut, "Bush Plan to Win Over Democratic Voters Lags," *Boston Globe*, April 27, 2003, p. A1.

109. CNN.com, "America Votes, 2006."

110. Dan Balz and Jon Cohen, "Majority in Poll Favor Deadline for Iraq Pullout," *Washington Post*, February 27, 2007, p. A1.

111. Gallup Poll, January 2003.

112. Center for American Women and Politics, "Gender Gap in 2004 Presidential Race Is Widespread" (November 10, 2004), www.cawp.rutgers.edu/Facts/Elections/GG2004widespread.pdf (accessed 2/22/08).

113. National Conference of State Legislatures, "Women in State Legislatures: 2009 Legislative Session," www.ncsl.org/default.aspx?tabid=15398 (accessed 11/25/09).

114. Kira Sanbonmatsu, "Political Parties and the Recruitment of Women to State Legislatures," *Journal of Politics* 64, no. 3 (August 2002): 791–809; Jennifer L. Lawless and Richard L. Fox, *Why Are Women Still Not Running for Public Office?* (Washington, DC: Brookings Institution Press, 2008).

115. Center for American Women and Politics, "The Impact of Women in Public Office: Findings at a Glance" (New Brunswick, NJ: Rutgers University Press, n.d.).

116. Paul Taylor, Rich Morin, D'Vera Cohn, April Clark, and Wendy Wang, "A Paradox in Public Attitudes: Men or Women: Who's the Better Leader?" Pew Research Center, Washington, DC, August 25, 2008, p. 25, http://pewsocialtrends.org/assets/pdf/gender-leadership.pdf (accessed 12/6/09).

117. Emily Hoban Kirby and Kei Kawashima-Ginsberg, "The Youth Vote in 2008," Center for Information and Research on Civic Learning and Engagement, August 17, 2009, www.civicyouth.org/?page_id=241 (accessed 11/25/09).

118. Michael DeCourcy Hinds, "Youth Vote 2000: They'd Rather Volunteer," *Carnegie Reporter* 1, no. 2 (Spring 2001): 2.

119. Kirby and Kei Kawashima-Ginsberg, "The Youth Vote in 2008," *The Center for Information & Research on Civic Learning & Engagement*, August 17, 2009, www.civicyouth.org/?page_id=241 (accessed 11/25/09).

120. CNN National Exit Poll 2008, www.cnn.com/ELECTION/2008/results/polls/#UPS00p1 (accessed 11/22/09).

121. The OnLine NewsHour, Generation Next: Speak Up Be Heard, "Iraq, Economy Weigh on Minds of Young Voters," August 31, 2007, www.pbs.org/newshour/generation-next/demographic/youthvote_08-31.html (accessed 2/21/08).

122. Emily Hoban Kirby, Karlo Barrios Marcelo, and Kei Kawashima-Ginsberg, "Volunteering and the College

Experience," Center for Information and Research on Civic Learning and Engagement, August 2009, www.civicyouth.org/?page_id=237 (accessed 11/25/09).

123. The Center of Information and Research on Civic Learning and Engagement, "Millennials Talk Politics: A Study of College Student Political Engagement," 2007, www.civicyouth.org/?page_id=250 (accessed 11/29/09).

124. *Engel v. Vitale*, 370 U.S. 421 (1962); *Abington School District v. Schempp*, 374 U.S. 203 (1963).

125. Laurie Goodstein, "Bush's Charity Plan Is Raising Concerns for Religious Right," *New York Times*, March 3, 2001, p. A1.

126. John Griffin, and Michael Keane, "Are Voters Better Represented?" *Journal of Politics* 67, no. 4 (2005): 1206–27.

127. Larry Bartels, *Unequal Democracy: The Political Economy of the New Gilded Age* (Princeton, NJ: Princeton University Press, 2008).

128. *Buckley v. Valeo*, 424 U.S. 1 (1976).

129. *Citizens United v. Federal Election Commission*.

Chapter 9

1. Todd Donovan and Shaun Bowler, *Reforming the Republic: Democratic Institutions for the New America* (Upper Saddle River, NJ: Prentice Hall, 2003).

2. Morris Fiorina, Samuel Abrams, and Jeremy Pope. *Culture War? The Myth of a Polarized America* (New York: Pearson Longman, 2004).

3. E. E. Schattschneider, *The Semi-Sovereign People: A Realist's View of Democracy in America* (New York: Holt, Rinehart, Winston, 1960).

4. Donovan and Bowler, *Reforming the Republic*.

5. James Madison, *The Federalist Papers*, no. 10: "The Same Subject Continued: The Union as a Safeguard against Domestic Faction and Insurrection. The New York Packet. Friday, November 23, 1787," http://thomas.loc.gov/home/histdox/fed_10.html (accessed 11/11/12).

6. See Matthew Crenson and Benjamin Ginsberg, *Downsizing Democracy* (Baltimore: Johns Hopkins University Press, 2002).

7. Jacob S. Hacker and Paul Pierson, *Winner-Take-All Politics: How Washington Made the Rich Richer—and Turned Its Back on the Middle Class* (New York: Simon & Schuster, 2010).

8. Larry Bartels, *Unequal Democracy: The Political Economy of the New Guilded Age* (Princeton, NJ: Princeton University Press, 2008).

9. Benjamin Ginsberg, *The Consequences of Consent* (New York: Random House, 1982), chap. 4.

10. Nolan McCarty, Keith T. Poole, and Howard Rosenthal. *Polarized America: The Dance of Ideology and Unequal Riches*. Cambridge, MA: MIT Press, 2006. For 2010

data, see Voteview.com, http://voteview.com/polarized_america.htm#POLITICALPOLARIZATION.

11. Donovan and Bowler, *Reforming the Republic*.

12. Frank Newport, "Congress Ends 2011 with Record-Low 11% Approval," Gallup Politics, December 19, 2011, www.gallup.com/poll/151628/Congress-Ends-2011-Record-Low-Approval.aspx (accessed 9/16/12)

13. Fiorina, Abrams, and Pope. *The Myth of a Polarized America*.

14. For a discussion of third parties in the United States, see Daniel Mazmanian, *Third Parties in Presidential Elections* (Washington, DC: Brookings Institution Press, 1974).

15. See Maurice Duverger, *Political Parties* (New York: Wiley, 1954).

16. Alex Isenstadt, "Tea Party Candidates Falling Short," *Politico*, March 7, 2010, www.politico.com/news/stories/0310/34041.html (accessed 3/11/10).

17. Donovan and Bowler, *Reforming the Republic*.

18. Andri Blais. *To Keep or To Change First Past the Post? The Politics of Election Reform* (New York: Oxford University Press, 2008).

19. Glen Justice, "F.E.C. Declines to Curb Independent Fund Raisers," *New York Times*, May 14, 2004, p. A16.

20. Jim Rutenberg and David D. Kirkpatrick, "A New Channel for Soft Money Appears in Race," *New York Times*, November 12, 2007, p. A1.

21. *Citizens United v. Federal Election Commission*, 558 U.S. 50 (2010).

22. See Harold Gosnell, *Machine Politics Chicago Model*, rev. ed. (Chicago: University of Chicago Press, 1968).

23. For a useful discussion, see John Bibby and Thomas Holbrook, "Parties and Elections," in *Politics in the American States*, ed. Virginia Gray and Herbert Jacob (Washington, DC: CQ Press, 1996), pp. 78–121.

24. Kyle L. Saunders and Alan I. Abramowitz, "Ideological Realignment and Active Partisans in the American Electorate," *American Politics Research* 32 (May 2004): 285–309.

25. Based on exit polls available at http://elections.nytimes.com/2012/results/president/exit-polls (accessed 11/12/12).

26. The Pew Forum on Religion and Public Life, "How the Faithful Voted: 2012 Preliminary Analysis," www.pewforum.org/Politics-and-Elections/How-the-Faithful-Voted-2012-Preliminary-Exit-Poll-Analysis.aspx#rr (accessed 11/12/12).

27. Christopher Shea, "Who Are You Calling Working Class?" *Boston Globe*, February 12, 2006, www.boston.com/news/globe/ideas/articles/2006/02/12/who_are_you_calling_working_class/ (accessed 2/24/08).

28. Shaun Bowler, Gary Segura, and Stephen Nicholson. "Earthquakes and Aftershocks: Race, Direct Democracy, and Partisan Change," *American Journal of Political Science* 50 (January 2006): 146–59.

29. See Morris Fiorina, "Parties and Partisanship: A Forty Year Retrospective," *Political Behavior* 24, no. 2 (June 2002): 93–115.

30. On the limited polarization among ordinary voters, see Fiorina, Abrams, and Pope, *Culture War?*; on growing partisan attachment among a subset of voters, see Alan Abramowitz and Kyle Saunders, "Why Can't We Just Get Along? The Reality of a Polarized America," *The Forum* 3, no. 2 (2005): 1–22.

31. Raymond J. La Raja, "Political Parties in the Era of Soft Money," in *The Parties Respond: Changes in American Parties and Campaigns*, 4th ed., ed. Sandy L. Maisel (Boulder, CO: Westview Press, 2002), pp. 163–88.

32. For an excellent analysis of the parties' role in recruitment, see Paul Herrnson, *Congressional Elections: Campaigning at Home and in Washington* (Washington, DC: CQ Press, 1995).

33. Daniel Galvin, *Presidential Party Building: Dwight D. Eisenhower to George W. Bush* (Princeton, NJ: Princeton, University Press, 2009).

34. Stanley Kelley Jr., Richard E. Ayres, and William Bowen, "Registration and Voting: Putting First Things First," *American Political Science Review* 61 (June 1967): 359–70.

35. David H. Fischer, *The Revolution of American Conservatism* (New York: Harper & Row, 1965), p. 93.

36. Henry Jones Ford, *The Rise and Growth of American Politics: A Sketch of Constitutional Development* (1898 reprint; New York: Da Capo Press, 1967 edition), chap. 9.

37. Ford, *The Rise and Growth of American Politics*, p. 125.

38. Ford, *The Rise and Growth of American Politics*, p. 125.

39. Ford, *The Rise and Growth of American Politics*, p. 126.

Chapter 10

1. *Gray v. Sanders*, 372 U.S. 368 (1963); *Wesberry v. Sanders*, 376 U.S. 1 (1964); *Reynolds v. Sims*, 377 U.S. 533 (1964).

2. *Thornburg v. Gingles*, 478 U.S. 613 (1986).

3. *Shaw v. Reno*, 509 U.S. 113 (1993).

4. Daron Shaw, *The Race to 270: The Electoral College and the Campaign Strategies of 2000 and 2004* (Chicago: University of Chicago Press, 2006).

5. State legislatures determine the system by which electors are selected. Almost all states use this "winner-take-all" system. Maine and Nebraska, however, provide that one electoral vote goes to the winner in each congressional district and two electoral votes go to the winner statewide.

6. *Bush v. Gore*, 531 U.S. 98 (2000).

7. Jeffrey Karp and Caroline J. Tolbert, "Explaining Support for Nationalizing Presidential Elections," Midwest Political Science Association (2009)

8. See www.nationalpopularvote.com for details (accessed 9/26/12).

9. Karp and Tolbert, *Explaining Support*; Shaw, *Race to 270*.

10. David Redlawsk, Caroline J. Tolbert, and Todd Donovan, *Why Iowa? How Caucuses and Sequential Elections Improve the Presidential Nomination Process* (Chicago: University of Chicago Press, 2011).

11. Redlawsk, Tolbert, and Donovan, *Why Iowa?*

12. Adam Nagourney, "Court Strikes Down Ban on Gay Marriage in California," *New York Times*, February 7, 2012, www.nytimes.com/2012/02/08/us/marriage-ban-violates -constitution-court-rules.html (accessed 8/21/12).

13. Daniel Smith and Caroline J. Tolbert, *Educated by Initiative: The Effects of Direct Democracy on Citizens and Political Organizations in the American States* (Ann Arbor: University of Michigan Press, 2004).

14. Shaun Bowler, Todd Donovan, and Caroline J. Tolbert. *Citizens as Legislators: Direct Democracy in the United States* (Columbus: Ohio State University Press, 1998).

15. Caroline Tolbert, Daniel Bowen, and Todd Donovan, "Initiative Campaigns; Direct Democracy and Voter Mobilization," *American Politics Research* 37, no.1 (2009): 155–192.

16. Caroline Tolbert, Daniel Bowen and Todd Donovan, "Initiative Campaigns: Direct Democracy and Voter Mobilization," *American Politics Research* 37, no. 1 (2009): 155–92.

17. Stephen Nicholson, *Voting the Agenda: Candidates, Elections, and Ballot Propositions* (Princeton, NJ: Princeton University Press, 2005).

18. Stephen Ansolabehere and James Snyder, "Campaign War Chests and Congressional Elections," *Business and Politics* 2 (2000): 9–34.

19. Gary W. Cox and Eric Magar, "How Much Is Majority Status in the U.S. Congress Worth?" *American Political Science Review* 93 (1999): 299–309.

20. John Greer, *In Defense of Negativity: Attack Ads in Presidential Campaigns* (Chicago: University of Chicago Press, 2006).

21. *Federal Election Commission v. Wisconsin Right to Life, Inc.*, 551 U.S. 449 (2007).

22. Redlawsk, Tolbert, and Donovan, *Why Iowa?*

23. Amy Schatz, "BO, UR So Gr8," *Wall Street Journal*, May 26, 2007.

24. M. Ostrogorski, *Democracy and the Organization of Political Parties* (New York: Macmillan, 1902).

25. Timothy Clark, "The RNC Prospers, the DNC Struggles as They Face the 1980 Election," *National Journal*, October 27, 1980, p. 1619.

26. For discussions of the consequences of this, see Thomas Edsall, *The New Politics of Inequality* (New York: W.W .Norton, 1984). Also see Thomas Edsall, "Both Parties Get the Company's Money—but the Boss Backs the GOP," *Washington Post*, National Weekly Edition, September 16, 1986, p. 14; and Benjamin Ginsberg, "Money and Power: The New Political Economy of American Elections," in *The Political Economy*, ed. Thomas Ferguson and Joel Rogers (Armonk, NY: M.E. Sharpe, 1984).

27. Michael Luo and Jeff Zeleny, "Straining to Reach Money Goal, Obama Presses Donors" *New York Times*, September 9, 2008, p. 1.

28. *Citizens United v. Federal Election Commission*, 558 U.S. 50 (2010).

29. *Citizens United v. Federal Election Commission*.

30. *Citizens United v. Federal Election Commission*.

31. *Buckley v. Valeo*, 424 U.S. 1 (1976).

Chapter 11

1. Alexander Hamilton, James Madison, and John Jay, *The Federalist Papers*, ed. Clinton L. Rossiter (New York: New American Library, 1961), no. 10, p. 83.
2. *The Federalist Papers*, no. 10.
3. The best statement of the pluralist view is in David Truman, *The Governmental Process* (New York: Knopf, 1951), chap. 2.
4. Erika Falk, Erin Grizard, and Gordon McDonald, "Legislative Issue Advertising in the 108th Congress: Pluralism or Peril?" *Harvard International Journal of Press/Politics* 11, no. 4 (Fall 2006): 148–64, http://hij.sagepub.com/cgi/reprint/11/4/148 (accessed 3/2/08).
5. Betsy Wagner and David Bowermaster, "B.S. Economics," *Washington Monthly*, November 1992, pp. 19–21.
6. Truman, *The Governmental Process*.
7. Kay Lehman Schlozman and John T. Tierney, *Organized Interests and American Democracy* (New York: Harper and Row, 1986), p. 60.
8. Mancur Olson, *The Logic of Collective Action* (Cambridge, MA: Harvard University Press, 1965).
9. Timothy Penny and Steven Schier, *Payment Due: A Nation in Debt, a Generation in Trouble* (Boulder, CO: Westview, 1996), pp. 64–65.
10. John Herbers, "Special Interests Gaining Power as Voter Disillusionment Grows," *New York Times*, November 14, 1978.
11. Center for Responsive Politics, "Lobbying Database," www.opensecrets.org/lobby/index.php (accessed 11/6/12).
12. See Frank Baumgartner and Beth Leech, *Basic Interests* (Princeton, NJ: Princeton University Press, 1998).
13. For discussions of lobbying, see Allan J. Cigler and Burdett A. Loomis, eds., *Interest Group Politics* (Washington, DC: CQ Press, 1983). See also Jeffrey M. Berry, *Lobbying for the People* (Princeton, NJ: Princeton University Press, 1977).
14. Daniel Franklin, "Tommy Boggs and the Death of Health Care Reform," *Washington Monthly*, April 1995, p. 36.
15. "The Swarming Lobbyists," *Time*, August 7, 1978, p. 15
16. "Top Lobbyists: Hired Guns," *The Hill*, May 14, 2009, p. 1.
17. Brody Mullins, "Growing Role for Lobbyists: Raising Funds for Lawmakers," *Wall Street Journal*, January 27, 2006, p. 1.
18. Eliza Carney, "Cleaning House," *National Journal*, January 28, 2006, p. 36.
19. Jonathan Weisman and Charles H. Babcock, "K Street's New Ways Spawn More Pork," *Washington Post*, January 27, 2006, p. 1.
20. Marie Jojnacki, "Interest Groups' Decisions to Join Alliances or Work Alone," *American Journal of Political Science* 41 (1997): 61–87; Kevin W. Hula, *Lobbying Together: Interest Groups Coalitions in Legislative Politics* (Washington, DC: Georgetown University Press, 1999).
21. Peter H. Stone, "Follow the Leaders," *National Journal*, June 24, 1995, p. 1641.
22. Common Cause, "The Microsoft Playbook: A Report from Common Cause," September 25, 2000.
23. Michael Barbaro, "A New Weapon for Wal-Mart: A War Room," *New York Times*, November 1, 2005, p. 1.
24. *The Washington Times*, "Editorial: Obama's Lobbyists," May 7, 2009, www.washingtontimes.com/news/2009/may/07/obamas-lobbyists (accessed 9/6/12).
25. For an excellent discussion of the political origins of the Administrative Procedure Act, see Martin Shapiro, "APA: Past, Present, Future," 72 *Virginia Law Review* 72, no. 477 (March 1986): 447–92.
26. David Kirkpatrick, "Congress Finds Ways of Avoiding Lobbyist Limits," *Washington Post*, February 11, 2007, p. 1.
27. *Brown v. Board of Education of Topeka, Kansas*, 347 U.S. 483 (1954).
28. *Roe v. Wade*, 410 U.S. 113 (1973).
29. *Webster v. Reproductive Health Services*, 492 U.S. 490 (1989).
30. E. Pendleton Herring, *Group Representation before Congress* (New York: McGraw-Hill, 1936).
31. Michael Weisskopf, "Energized by Pulpit or Passion, the Public Is Calling," *Washington Post*, February 1, 1993, p. 1.
32. Julia Preston, "Grass Roots Roared and Immigration Bill Collapsed," *New York Times*, June 10, 2007, p. 1.
33. *Citizens United v. Federal Election Commission*, 558 U. S. 50 (2010).
34. Richard L. Burke, "Religious-Right Candidates Gain as GOP Turnout Rises," *New York Times*, November 12, 1994, p. 10.
35. Elisabeth R. Gerber, *The Populist Paradox* (Princeton, NJ: Princeton University Press, 1999).
36. *The Federalist Papers*, no. 10.
37. Olson, *The Logic of Collective Action*.

Chapter 12

1. Tim Walker, "WWW: World without Wikipedia," *The Independent*, January 19, 2012, www.independent.co.uk/life-style/gadgets-and-tech/news/www-world-without-wikipedia-6291597.html (accessed 1/23/12).
2. Rebecca MacKinnon, "Why Doesn't Washington Understand the Internet?" *Washington Post*, January 20, 2012, www.washingtonpost.com/opinions/why-doesnt-washington-understand-the-internet/2012/01/17/gIQAGPzWEQ_story.html (accessed 1/23/12).
3. Mildred Amer and Jennifer E. Manning, *Membership of the 112th Congress: A Profile*, Congressional Research Service 7-5700, September 20, 2011, pp. 5–6, fpc.state.gov/documents/organization/174246.pdf (accessed 1/23/12).
4. Amer and Manning, *Membership of the 112th Congress*, p. 2.
5. Amer and Manning, *Membership of the 112th Congress*, p. 3.
6. For a discussion, see Benjamin Ginsberg, *The Consequences of Consent* (New York: Random House, 1982), chap. 1.
7. See Kristen D. Burnett, "Congressional Apportionment" (Washington, DC: U.S. Census Bureau, November 2011),

www.census.gov/prod/cen2010/briefs/c2010br-08 .pdf (accessed 1/23/12). For some interesting empirical evidence, see Angus Campbell, Philip Converse, Warren Miller, and Donald Stokes, *Elections and the Political Order* (New York: Wiley, 1966), chap. 11; for more recent considerations about the relationship between members of Congress and their constituents, see Lawrence Jacobs and Robert Y. Shapiro, *Politicians Don't Pander: Political Manipulation and the Loss of Democratic Responsiveness* (Chicago: University of Chicago Press, 2000), and Larry M. Bartels, *Unequal Democracy: The Political Economy of the New Gilded Age* (Princeton, NJ: Princeton University Press, 2008).

8. Congressional Management Foundation, *Communicating with Congress: How Citizen Advocacy Is Changing Mail Operations on Capitol Hill* (Washington, DC: Partnership for a More Perfect Union at the Congressional Management Foundation, 2011), http://congressfoundation.org/ storage/documents/CMF_Pubs/cwc-mail-operations .pdf (accessed 1/23/12).

9. Norman J. Ornstein, Thomas E. Mann, and Michael J. Malbin, *Vital Statistics on Congress 2008* (Washington, DC: Brookings Institution, 2009), pp. 111–2.

10. See Linda Fowler and Robert McClure, *Political Ambition: Who Decides to Run for Congress* (New Haven, CT: Yale University Press, 1989); and Alan Ehrenhalt, *The United States of Ambition: Politicians, Power, and the Pursuit of Office* (New York: Three Rivers Press, 1992).

11. Barbara Palmer and Denise Simon, *Breaking the Political Glass Ceiling: Women and Congressional Elections*, 2nd ed. (New York: Routledge, 2008); Jennifer L. Lawless and Kathryn Pearson, "The Primary Reason for Women's Underrepresentation? Reevaluating the Conventional Wisdom," *Journal of Politics* 70 (2008): 67–82.

12. Michael Leahy, "House Rules," *Washington Post*, June 10, 2007, p. W12.

13. See Barbara C. Burrell, *A Woman's Place Is in the House: Campaigning for Congress in the Feminist Era* (Ann Arbor: University of Michigan Press, 1994), and David Broder, "Key to Women's Political Parity: Running," *Washington Post*, September 8, 1994, p. A17.

14. Dan Balz, "Dodd, Dorgan, and Ritter to Retire as Democrats Face a Difficult Mid-Term Year," *Washington Post*, January 7, 2010.

15. U.S. Census Bureau, "Map: Apportionment of the U.S. House of Representatives Based on the 2010 Census," *U.S. Census Bureau Congressional Apportionment*, www .census.gov/population/apportionment/data/2010 _apportionment_results.html (accessed 02/6/12).

16. Aaron Blake, "GOP's Redistricting Advantage, Muted but Real," *Washington Post*, June 15, 2011, www.washingtonpost .com/blogs/the-fix/post/gops-redistricting-advantage -is-real-but-muted/2011/06/14/AGwaQDWH_blog .html (accessed 1/23/12).

17. "Did Redistricting Sink the Democrats?" *National Journal*, December 17, 1994, p. 2984.

18. *Miller v. Johnson*, 515 U.S. 900 (1995).

19. Bernie Becker, "Reapportionment Roundup," *New York Times*, December 24, 2009, http://thecaucus.blogs .nytimes.com/2009/12/24/reapoortionment-roundup/ (accessed 1/31/10).

20. Tom Hamburger and Richard Simon, "Everybody Will Know if It's Pork," *Los Angeles Times*, January 6, 2007, p. A1.

21. Jared Allen, "Lawmakers Pushing for Earmark Reform Think Obama Boosted Their Chances," *The Hill*, January 30, 2010, http://thehill.com/homenews/house/78869 -lawmakers-think-obama-boosted-earmark-reform- (accessed 1/31/10); David S. Fallis, Scott Higham and Kimberly Kindy, "Congressional Earmarks Sometimes Used to Fund Projects Near Lawmakers' Properties," *Washington Post*, February 6, 2012, p. 1.

22. Congressman Tom Petri, "Constituent Services," http:// petrihouse.gov/serving-you/help-federal-agency (accessed 7/4/12).

23. Associated Press, "Congress Passes Rare Private Immigration Bills," Associated Press, December 15, 2010, www .aolnews.com/2010/12/15/congress-passes-rare-private -immigration-bills/ (accessed 2/1/12).

24. Richard Fenno Jr., *Home Style: House Members in Their Districts* (Boston: Little, Brown, 1978).

25. Edward Epstein, "Dusting Off Deliberation," CQ *Weekly*, June 14, 2010, pp. 1436–42. Sarah Binder, "Where Have All the Conference Committees Gone?" *The Monkey Cage* (blog), December 21, 2011, themonkeycage.org/ blog/2011/12/21/where-have-all-the-conference -committees-gone/ (accessed 2/7/12).

26. Derek Willis, "Republicans Mix It Up When Assigning House Chairmen for the 108th," *Congressional Quarterly Weekly*, January 11, 2003, p. 89.

27. Rebecca Kimitch, "CQ Guide to the Committees: Democrats Opt to Spread the Power," *Congressional Quarterly Weekly*, April 16, 2007, p. 1080.

28. Richard E. Cohen, "Crackup of the Committees," *National Journal*, July 31, 1999, pp. 2210–16.

29. David W. Rohde, "Committees and Policy Formulation," in *Institutions of American Democracy: The Legislative Branch*, ed. Paul J. Quirk and Sarah A. Binder (New York: Oxford University Press, 2005), pp. 201–23.

30. U.S. Senate, "Cloture Motions—111th Congress," www .senate.gov/pagelayout/reference/cloture_motions/ 111.htm (accessed 2/1/12); U.S. Senate, "Cloture Motions— 112th Congress," www.senate.gov/pagelayout/reference/ cloture_motions/112.shtml (accessed 2/1/12). For Obama's 2010 speech, see Matt Negrin, "Comparing the 1950s with 2009," *Politico*, February 4, 2010, www .politico.com/politico44/perm/0210/about_those_ filibusters_ac215c69-38c3-4ad8-ad44-183d81490ce2 .html (accessed 2/9/12).

31. See Robert Pear, "Senator X Kills Measure on Anonymity," *New York Times*, November 11, 1997, p. 12.

32. Jonathan Weisman, "House Votes 411–18 to Pass Ethics Overhaul," *Washington Post*, August 1, 2007, p. A1.

33. Kate Phillips and Jeff Zeleny, "White House Blasts Shelby Hold on Nominees," *New York Times*, February 5, 2010, http://thecaucus.blogs.nytimes.com/2010/02/05/white-house-blasts-shelby-hold-on-nominees/ (accessed 2/5/10).

34. Carl Hulse and David M. Herszenhorn, "Defiant House Rejects Huge Bailout; Next Step Is Uncertain," *New York Times*, September 29, 2008, www.nytimes.com/2008/09/30/business/30cong.html?pagewanted=1&_r=1 (accessed 2/4/10); Reuters. "House Passes Bailout, Focus Shifts to Fallout," October 3, 2008, www.reuters.com/article/idUSTRE49267J20081003 (accessed 2/4/10).

35. See John W. Kingdon, *Congressmen's Voting Decisions* (New York: Harper and Row, 1973), chap. 3; and R. Douglas Arnold, *The Logic of Congressional Action* (New Haven, CT: Yale University Press, 1990).

36. Jane Fritsch, "The Grass Roots, Just a Free Phone Call Away," *New York Times*, June 23, 1995, p. A1.

37. Robert Pear, "In House, Many Spoke with One Voice: Lobbyists," *New York Times*, November 14, 2009, p. A1.

38. Eliza Newlin Carney, "For Ethics Hawks, Congress Could Be Next," *National Journal Online*, February 17, 2009, www.nationaljournal.com/njonline/rg_20090217_2426.php (accessed 2/5/10).

39. Dan Eggen, "SuperPACs Target Congressional Races," *Washington Post*, January 29, 2012, www.washingtonpost.com/politics/super-pacs-target-congressional-races/2012/01/26/gIQAyRfnaQ_story.html (accessed 2/9/12).

40. Holly Idelson, "Signs Point to Greater Loyalty on Both Sides of the Aisle," *Congressional Quarterly Weekly Report*, December 19, 1992, p. 3849.

41. "Vote Studies 2011," in Graphics, CQ.com, http://media.cq.com/media/2011/votestudy_2011/graphics/(accessed 2/1/12).

42. Alexander Bolton, "DeMint's Leadership PAC Battles Leaders in Fight for the Future of Senate GOP Caucus," *The Hill*, August 4, 2011, http://thehill.com/homenews/senate/175397-demints-leadership-pac-battles-leaders-in-fight-for-future-of-senate (accessed 1/23/12); for a list of leadership PACs, see the Open Secrets website, www.opensecrets.org/industries/indus.php?Ind=Q03 (accessed 1/23/12).

43. Kimitch, "CQ Guide to the Committees," p. 1080.

44. Leahy, "House Rules," p. W12; Marin Cogan, "Freshmen Jump Line for Floor Speeches," *Politico*, January 18, 2011, www.politico.com/news/stories/0111/47791.html (accessed 2/9/12).

45. Robert Draper, "How Kevin McCarthy Wrangles the Tea Party in Washington," *New York Times*, July 13, 2011, www.nytimes.com/2011/07/17/magazine/how-kevin-mccarthy-wrangles-the-tea-party.html?pagewanted=all (accessed 2/1/12).

46. James J. Kilpatrick, "Don't Overlook Corn for Porn Plot," *Chicago Sun-Times*, January 3, 1992, p. 23.

47. Dennis McDougal, "Cattle Are Bargaining Chip of the NEA," *Los Angeles Times*, November 2, 1991, p. F1.

48. Frank Newport, "Congress' Job Approval at New Low of 10%," Gallup Politics, www.gallup.com/poll/152528/ Congress-Job-Approval-New-Low.aspx (accessed 2/10/12).

49. Pew Research Center for the People and the Press, "Frustration with Congress Could Hurt Republican Incumbents, GOP Base Critical of Party's Washington Leadership," December 15, 2011, www.people-press.org/2011/12/15/section-1-congress-the-parties-and-the-anti-incumbent-mood/ (accessed 2/10/11).

50. Rasmussen Reports, "New High: 48% Say Most Members of Congress Are Corrupt," December 31, 2011, www.rasmussenreports.com/public_content/politics/general_politics/december_2011/new_high_48_say_most_members_of_congress_are_corrupt (accessed 2/10/12).

51. *Citizens United v. Federal Election Commission*, 558 U.S. 50 (2010).

52. Susan Milligan, "Congress Reduces Its Oversight Role; Since Clinton, a Change in Focus," *Boston Globe*, November 20, 2005, p. A1; Bill Shaikin, "Clemens Is Star Attraction at Hearing," *Los Angeles Times*, February 12, 2008, p. D1.

53. Elizabeth Williamson, "Revival of Oversight Role Sought; Congress Hires More Investigators, Plans Subpoenas," *Washington Post*, April 25, 2007, p. A1.

54. Thomas E. Mann, Molly Reynolds, and Peter Hoey, "A New, Improved Congress?" *New York Times*, August 26, 2007, p. 11.

55. John Stanton and Daniel Newhowser, "House GOP Uses Retreat to Lay 2012 Plans," *The Hill*, January 23, 2012, www.rollcall.com/issues/57_82/house_gop_uses_retreat_lay_2012_plans-211670-1.html (accessed 2/9/12).

56. *United States v. Pink*, 315 U.S. 203 (1942). For a good discussion of the problem, see James W. Davis, *The American Presidency* (New York: Harper and Row, 1987), chap. 8.

57. Carroll J. Doherty, "Impeachment: How It Would Work," *Congressional Quarterly Weekly Report*, January 31, 1998, p. 222.

58. See Kenneth A. Shepsle, "Representation and Governance: The Great Legislative Trade-off," *Political Science Quarterly* 103, no. 3 (1988): 461–84.

59. John R. Hibbing and Elizabeth Theiss-Morse, *Congress as Public Enemy: Public Attitudes toward American Political Institutions* (New York: Cambridge University Press, 1996), p. 105.

Chapter 13

1. *In re Neagle*, 135 U.S. 1 (1890).

2. James G. Randall, *Constitutional Problems under Lincoln* (New York: Appleton, 1926), chap. 1.

3. Edward S. Corwin, *The President: Office and Powers*, 4th rev. ed. (New York: New York University Press, 1957), p. 229.

4. These statutes are contained mainly in Title 10 of the United States Code, Sections 331, 332, and 333.

5. The best study covering all aspects of the domestic use of the military is that of Adam Yarmolinsky, *The Military Establishment* (New York: Harper and Row, 1971). Probably the most famous instance of a president's unilateral use of the power to protect a state "against domestic violence" was President Grover Cleveland's dealing with the Pullman Strike of 1894. The famous Supreme Court case that ensued was *In re Debs*, 158 U.S. 564 (1895).

6. In *United States v. Pink*, 315 U.S. 203 (1942), the Supreme Court confirmed that an executive agreement is the legal equivalent of a treaty, despite the absence of Senate approval. This case approved the executive agreement that was used to establish diplomatic relations with the Soviet Union in 1933. An executive agreement, not a treaty, was used in 1940 to exchange "fifty over-age destroyers" for 99-year leases on some important military bases.

7. *United States v. Nixon*, 418 U.S. 683 (1974).

8. For a different perspective, see William F. Grover, *The President as Prisoner: A Structural Critique of the Carter and Reagan Years* (Albany: State University of New York Press, 1988).

9. A third source of presidential power is implied from the provision for "faithful execution of the laws." This is the president's power to impound funds—that is, to refuse to spend money Congress has appropriated for certain purposes. One author referred to this as a "retroactive veto power" (Robert E. Goosetree, "The Power of the President to Impound Appropriated Funds," *American University Law Review* [January 1962]). This impoundment power has been used freely and to considerable effect by many modern presidents, and Congress has occasionally delegated such power to the president by statute. But in reaction to the Watergate scandal, Congress adopted the Congressional Budget and Impoundment Control Act of 1974, which was designed to circumscribe the president's ability to impound funds by requiring that the president must spend all appropriated funds unless both houses of Congress consented to an impoundment within 45 days of a presidential request. Therefore, since 1974, the use of impoundment has declined significantly. Presidents have had either to bite their tongues and accept unwanted appropriations or to revert to the older and more dependable but politically limited method of vetoing the entire bill.

10. For more on the veto, see Robert J. Spitzer, *The Presidential Veto: Touchstone of the American Presidency* (Albany: State University of New York Press, 1989).

11. Dan Eggen, "Bush Announces Veto of Waterboarding Ban," WashingtonPost.com, March 8, 2008, www.washingtonpost.com/wp-dyn/content/article/2008/03/08AR2008030800304.html (accessed 6/10/10).

12. For a good review of President Clinton's legislative leadership in the first session of his last Congress, see *Congressional Quarterly Weekly*, November 13, 1999, especially the cover story by Andrew Taylor, "Clinton Gives Republicans a Gentler Year-End Beating," pp. 2698–700.

13. Kenneth F. Warren, *Administrative Law*, 3rd ed. (Upper Saddle River, NJ: Prentice-Hall, 1996), p. 250.

14. Theodore J. Lowi, *The End of Liberalism*, 2nd ed. (New York: W.W. Norton, 1979), pp. 117–18.

15. *J. W. Hampton & Co. v. United States*, 276 U.S. 394 (1928).

16. 48 Stat. 200.

17. David Schoenbrod, *Power without Responsibility: How Congress Abuses the People through Delegation* (New Haven, CT: Yale University Press, 1993), pp. 49–50.

18. Lowi, *The End of Liberalism*, p. 117.

19. Adam Clymer, "The Transition: Push for Diversity May Cause Reversal on Interior Secretary," *New York Times*, December 23, 1992, p. 1.

20. A substantial portion of this section is taken from Theodore J. Lowi, *The Personal President* (Ithaca, NY: Cornell University Press, 1985), pp. 141–50.

21. All the figures since 1967, and probably 1957, are understated, because additional White House staff members were on "detail" service from the military and other departments (some secretly assigned) and are not counted here because they were not on the White House payroll.

22. The actual number is difficult to estimate because, as with White House staff, some EOP personnel, especially in national security work, are detailed to the EOP from outside agencies.

23. Article I, Section 3, provides that "The Vice-President . . . shall be President of the Senate, but shall have no Vote, unless they be equally divided." This is the only vote the vice president is allowed.

24. David Ignatius, "A Skeptical Biden's Role," RealClearPolitics.com, November 26, 2009, www.realclearpolitics.com/articles/2009/11/26/a_skeptical_bidens_role_99320.html (accessed 5/12/09).

25. Samuel Kernell, *Going Public: New Strategies of Presidential Leadership*, 3rd ed. (Washington, DC: CQ Press, 1997); also Jeffrey K. Tulis, *The Rhetorical Presidency* (Princeton, NJ: Princeton University Press, 1987).

26. Tulis, *The Rhetorical Presidency*, p. 91.

27. Sidney M. Milkis, *The President and the Parties* (New York: Oxford University Press, 1993), p. 97.

28. James MacGregor Burns, *Roosevelt: The Lion and the Fox* (New York: Harcourt, Brace, 1956), p. 317.

29. Burns, *Roosevelt*, p. 317.

30. Kernell, *Going Public*, p. 79.

31. Tulis, *The Rhetorical Presidency*, p. 161.

32. Lowi, *The Personal President*.

33. Lowi, *The Personal President*, p. 11.

34. Harold W. Stanley and Richard G. Niemi, *Vital Statistics on American Politics, 2001–2002* (Washington, DC: Congressional Quarterly Press, 2001), pp. 250–51.

35. Milkis, *The President and the Parties*, p. 128.

36. Milkis, *The President and the Parties*, p. 160.

37. The classic critique of this process is Lowi, *The End of Liberalism*.

38. Kenneth Culp Davis, *Administrative Law Treatise* (St. Paul, MN: West Publishing, 1958), p. 9.

39. For example, Douglas W. Kmiec, "Expanding Power," in *The Rule of Law in the Wake of Clinton*, ed. Roger Pilon (Washington, DC: Cato Institute Press, 2000), pp. 47–68.

40. John M. Broder, "Powerful Shaper of U.S. Rules Quits, Leaving Critics in Wake," *New York Times*, August 4, 2012, p. A1.

41. A complete inventory is provided in Harold C. Relyea, "Presidential Directives: Background and Review," Congressional Research Service Report 98–611 (Washington, DC: Library of Congress, November 9, 2001).

42. Terry M. Moe and William G. Howell, "The Presidential Power of Unilateral Action," *Journal of Law, Economics and Organization* 15, no. 1 (January 1999): 133–4.

43. Moe and Howell, "The Presidential Power of Unilateral Action," p. 164.

44. *Youngstown Sheet & Tube Co. v. Sawyer*, 346 U.S. 579 (1952).

45. Todd Gaziano, "The New 'Massive Resistance,'" *Policy Review* (May–June 1998): 283.

46. Mark Killenbeck, "A Matter of Mere Approval: The Role of the President in the Creation of Legislative History," *University of Arkansas Law Review* 48, no. 239 (1995).

47. Philip Cooper, *By Order of the President* (Lawrence: University Press of Kansas, 2002), p. 201.

48. Corwin, *The President*, p. 283.

49. Cooper, *By Order of the President*, p. 201.

50. Cooper, *By Order of the President*, p. 203.

51. Cooper, *By Order of the President*, p. 216.

52. Peter Baker, "Obama Is Making Plans to Use Executive Power for Action on Several Fronts," *New York Times*, February 13, 2010, p. A12.

53. Baker, "Obama Is Making Plans," p. A12.

54. Alexander Hamilton, James Madison, and John Jay, *The Federalist Papers*, ed. Clinton Rossiter (New York: New American Library, 1961), no. 70, pp. 423–30.

55. Terry Moe, "The Presidency and the Bureaucracy: The Presidential Advantage," in *The Presidency and the Political System*, ed. Michael Nelson (Washington, DC: Congressional Quarterly Press, 2002), pp. 416–20.

Chapter 14

1. "Obama's Health Care Speech to Congress," *New York Times*, September 9, 2009, www.nytimes.com/2009/09/10/us/politics/10obama.text.html (accessed 2/10/10).

2. U.S. Census Bureau, "Federal Civilian Employment and Annual Payroll by Branch: 1970 to 2010," *Statistical Abstract of the United States 2012*, Table 496, www.census.gov/compendia/statab/2012/tables/12s0496.pdf (accessed 1/2/12); U.S. Census Bureau, "Department of Defense Personnel: 1960–2010," *Statistical Abstract of the United States 2010*, Table 510, www.census.gov/compendia/statab/2012/tables/12s0510.pdf (accessed 1/2/12).

3. U.S. Census Bureau, Table 461, "Government Employment and Payrolls, 1982–2009," *Statistical Abstract of the United States 2012*, www.census.gov/compendia/statab/2012/tables/12s0462.pdf (accessed 1/2/12), and Table 602, "Employed Civilians and Weekly Hours 1980 to 2010, www.census.gov/compendia/statab/2012/tables/12s0602.pdf (accessed 1/2/12).

4. Arnold Brecht and Comstock Glaser, *The Art and Techniques of Administration in German Ministries* (Cambridge, MA: Harvard University Press, 1940), p. 6.

5. Linda Greenhouse, "Justices Say E.P.A. Has Power to Act on Harmful Gases," *New York Times*, April 3, 2007, www.nytimes.com/2007/04/03/washington/03scotus.html?ex=1333339200&en=e0d0a1497263d879&ei=5124&partner=permalink&exprod=permalink (accessed 2/15/10).

6. Environmental Protection Agency, "Endangerment and Cause or Contribute Findings for Greenhouse Cases under Section 202(a) of the Clean Air Act," epa.gov/climatechange/endangerment.html (accessed 2/16/10).

7. Environmental Protection Agency, "Regulations and Standards: Vehicles/Engines," www.epa.gov/oms/climate/regulations.htm (accessed 2/16/10).

8. Juliet Eilperin, "EPA Needed More Data before Ruling on Greenhouse Gas Emissions, Report Says," *Washington Post* September 28, 2011, www.washingtonpost.com/national/health-science/epa-needed-more-data-before-ruling-on-greenhouse-gas-emissions-report-says/2011/09/28/gIQABs2X5K_story.html (accessed 1/2/12).

9. Federal Trade Commission, "Facebook Settles FTC Charges That It Deceived Consumers by Failing to Keep Privacy Promises," November 29, 2011, http://ftc.gov/opa/2011/11/privacysettlement.shtm (accessed 7/4/12)

10. Greg Gardner, "U.S. Probes Toyota Recall, Could Levy $16.4M Fine If Carmaker Acted Too Slowly," *Detroit Free Press*, www.freep.com/article/20100216/BUSINESS01/100216030/1318/U.S.-probes-Toyota-recall-could-levy-16.4M-fine-if-carmaker-acted-too-slowly (accessed 2/16/10); Ralph Vartabedian, "Sudden Acceleration in Toyota Vehicles Not an Electronic Issue, U.S. Study Finds," *Los Angeles Times* February 9, 2011, articles.latimes.com/2011/feb/09/business/la-fi-toyota-nasa-20110209 (accessed 1/3/12).

11. Gary Bryner, *Bureaucratic Discretion* (New York: Pergamon Press, 1987).

12. This account is drawn from Alan Stone, *How America Got On-Line: Politics, Markets, and the Revolution in Telecommunications* (Armonk, NY: M.E. Sharpe, 1997), pp. 184–7.

13. There are historical reasons that American cabinet-level administrators are called "secretaries." During the Second Continental Congress and the subsequent confederal government, standing committees were formed to deal with executive functions related to foreign affairs, military and maritime issues, and public financing. The heads of those committees were called "secretaries" because their primary task was to handle all correspondence and documentation related to their areas of responsibility.

14. Rob Margetta, "Homeland Security for Hire," *Congressional Quarterly Weekly*, November 12, 2007, pp. 3392–9, http://library.cqpress.com/cqweekly/weeklyreport 110 -000002625610 (accessed 11/14/07).

15. Julia Preston, "States Resisting Program Central to Obama's Immigration Strategy," *New York Times*, May 5, 2011, p. A18.

16. U.S. Department of State, "Department Organization Chart," www.state.gov/r/pa/ei/rls/dos/99494.htm (accessed 2/16/10).

17. For more details, consult John E. Harr, *The Professional Diplomat* (Princeton, NJ: Princeton University Press, 1972), p. 11; and Nicholas Horrock, "The CIA Has Neighbors in the 'Intelligence Community,'" *New York Times*, June 29, 1975, sec. 4, p. 2. See also Morton H. Halperin and Priscilla Clapp, with Arnold Kanter, *Bureaucratic Politics and Foreign Policy*, 2nd ed. (Washington, DC: Brookings Institution Press, 2007).

18. *The 9/11 Commission Report: Final Report of the National Commission on Terrorist Attacks upon the United States* (New York: W.W. Norton, 2004).

19. Daniel Patrick Moynihan, "The Culture of Secrecy," *Public Interest* (Summer 1997): 55–71.

20. Charlie Savage, "Obama Curbs Secrecy of Classified Documents," *New York Times*, December 30, 2009, p. A19. See the comprehensive evaluation in Citizens for Responsibility and Ethics in Washington, OpenTheGovernment.org, "Measuring Transparency under the FOIA: The Real Story behind the Numbers, December 2011, crew.3cdn.net/591 1487fbaaa8cb0f8_9xm6bgari.pdf (accessed 1/3/12).

21. Scott Shane, "Cost to Protect U.S. Secrets Doubles to Over $11 Billion," *New York Times*, July 3, 2012, p. A11. The official figure was $11 billion, but that did not include the expenses of the Central Intelligence Agency and the National Security Agency, which were estimated at $2 billion.

22. U.S. Department of the Treasury, "The Debt to the Penny and Who Holds It," www.treasurydirect.gov/NP/BPDLogin?application=np (accessed 2/18/10).

23. For an excellent political analysis of the Fed, see Donald Kettl, *Leadership at the Fed* (New Haven, CT: Yale University Press, 1986).

24. Annie Lowrey, "Regulators Move Closer to Oversight of Nonbanks," *New York Times*, April 4, 2012, p. B3, www.nytimes.com/2012/04/04/business/economy/regulators-move-closer-to-scrutinizing-nonbanks.html (accessed 7/3/12)

25. For an account of the Financial Stability Oversight Council and passage of the Dodd-Frank financial regulatory legislation, see John T. Woolley and J. Nicholas Ziegler, "The Two-Tiered Politics of Financial Reform in the United States," in *Crisis and Control. Institutional Change in Financial Market Regulation*, ed. Renate Mayntz (Frankfurt: Campus/MPIfG, 2012); the council's early activities are described in Financial Stability Oversight Council, Annual Report 2011, www.treasury.gov/initiatives/fsoc/Documents/FSOCAR2011.pdf (accessed 1/3/12), and in Edward V. Murphy and

Michael B. Bernier, "Financial Stability Oversight Council: A Framework to Mitigate Systemic Risk," (Washington DC: Congressional Research Service, Novem-ber 15, 2011), www.llsdc.org/attachments/wysiwyg/544/CRS-R42083.pdf (accessed 1/3/2012).

26. George E. Berkley, *The Craft of Public Administration* (Boston: Allyn and Bacon, 1975), p. 417.

27. OMB Watch, "IRS Gets Serious about Tax Enforcement," November 24, 2009. www.ombwatch.org/node/10583 (accessed 2/18/10).

28. On the Swiss banks, see "U.S. Charges 3 Swiss Bank Employees with Aiding Tax Evasion," *New York Times*, January 4, 2012, http://dealbook.nytimes.com/2012/01/04/u-s-charges-swiss-bank-employees-with-tax-evasion/ (accessed 1/4/12); David Kocieniewski, "Senate Bill Seeks to Raise Revenue by Closing Tax Havens," *New York Times*, July 13, 2011, p. B12.

29. Eric Schmitt, "Washington Talk: No $435 Hammers, but Questions," *New York Times*, October 23, 1990, p. A16; Jerry Markon, "A $16 Muffin? Justice Dept. Audit Finds 'Wasteful' and Extravagant Spending, *Washington Post*, September 20, 2011, www.washingtonpost.com/politics/a-16-muffin-justice-dept-audit-finds-wasteful-and-extravagant-spending/2011/09/20/gIQAXKyhiK_story.html (accessed 1/3/12); and Charlie Savage, "The $16 Muffin That Wasn't," *New York Times*, October 29, 2011, p. A14.

30. Vice President Gore's National Partnership for Reinventing Government, "Appendix F, History of the National Partnership for Reinventing Government Accomplishments, 1993–2000, A Summary," http://govinfo.library.unt.edu/npr/whoweare/appendixf.html (accessed 3/28/08).

31. Public Law 101–510, Title XXIX, Sections 2,901 and 2,902 of Part A (Defense Base Closure and Realignment Commission); see the 2005 commission's Web site, Defense Base Closure and Realignment Commission, www.brac.gov (accessed 1/3/12).

32. *National Federation of Independent Business v. Sebelius*, 567 U.S.__(2012).

33. Robert Pear, "Republican Governor of Florida Says State Won't Expand Medicaid," *New York Times*, July 3, 2012, p. A10.

34. Sheila Zedlewski and Pamela Loprest with Erika Huber, "What Role Is Welfare Playing in This Period of High Unemployment?" Urban Institute, Fact Sheet 3, August 2011, www.urban.org/UploadedPDF/412378-Role-of-Welfare-in-this-Period-of-High-Unemployment.pdf (accessed 7/4/12)

35. Sabrina Tavernise, "Food Stamps Helped Reduced Poverty Rate, Study Says," *New York Times*, April 10, 2012, A16.

36. Paul C. Light, "The New True Size of Government," Organizational Performance Initiative, Research Brief no. 2, p. 8, Wagner School of Public Service, New York University, http://wagner.nyu.edu/performance/files/True_Size.pdf (accessed 3/11/08).

37. OMB Watch, "Total Spending by Year," FedSpending.org, www.fedspending.org/fpds/chart_total.php (accessed 1/2/12).

38. Scott Shane and Ron Nixon, "In Washington, Contractors Take on Biggest Role Ever," *New York Times*, February 4, 2007, p. A1.

39. Shane and Nixon, "In Washington, Contractors Take on Biggest Role Ever."

40. Matt Kelley, "GAO Challenges $150B Contract Awarded by Army," *USA Today*, October 31, 2007, p. 5A.

41. Commission on Wartime Contracting in Iraq and Afghanistan, *Transforming Wartime Contracting: Controlling Costs, Reducing Risks: Final Report to Congress*, p.18, August 2011, www.wartimecontracting.gov (accessed 1/4/12); Congressional Research Service, "The Department of Defense's Use of Private Contractors in Iraq and Afghanistan: Background, Analysis, and Options for Congress," September 29, 2009, fpc.state.gov/documents/organization/130803.pdf (accessed 2/18/10).

42. Committee on Oversight and Government Reform, Hearings on Blackwater USA, preliminary transcript, October 2, 2007, http://oversight.house.gov/documents/20071127131151.pdf (accessed 3/10/08).

43. Committee on Oversight and Government Reform, Hearings on Blackwater USA.

44. Shane and Nixon, "In Washington, Contractors Take on Biggest Role Ever."

45. Shane and Nixon, "In Washington, Contractors Take on Biggest Role Ever."

46. General Accountability Office, *Federal Contractors: Better Performance Information Needed to Support Agency Contract Award Decisions*, April 2009, GAO-09-374; www.gao.gov/new.items/d09374.pdf (accessed 2/26/10).

47. Neil Gordon, "Move Over FCMD, Make Way for FAPIIS," Project on Government Oversight, http://pogoblog.typepad.com/pogo/2009/09/move-over-fcmd-make-way-for-fapiis.html (accessed 2/26/10).

48. For the estimates on waste, see Commission on Wartime Contracting in Iraq and Afghanistan, *Transforming Wartime Contracting*.

49. Dan Egan, "Democrats Proposing New Limits on Corporate Campaign Donations," *Boston Globe*, February 12, 2010, www.boston.com/news/nation/washington/articles/2010/02/12/democrats proposing new limits on corporate campaign donations/ (accessed 2/27/10).

50. Joe Davidson, "OMB Moves to Cut Outside Contractors," *Washington Post*, July 29, 2009, www.washingtonpost.com/wp-dyn/content/article/2009/07/28/AR2009072802812.html (accessed 2/18/10)

51. Joe Davidson, "Deficit-Cutters Must Also Weigh the Cost of Contractors," *Washington Post*, February 4, 2011, www.washingtonpost.com/wp-dyn/content/article/2011/02/03/AR2011020306809.html?nav=emailpage (accessed 1/2/12).

52. Alexander Hamilton, James Madison, and John Jay, *The Federalist Papers*, ed. Clinton Rossiter (New York: New American Library, 1961), no. 51, p. 322.

53. The title of this section was inspired by Peri Arnold, *Making the Managerial Presidency* (Princeton, NJ: Princeton University Press, 1986).

54. For more details and evaluations, see David Rosenbloom, *Public Administration* (New York: Random House, 1986), pp. 186–221; Charles H. Levine, with the assistance of Rosslyn S. Kleeman, *The Quiet Crisis of the Civil Service: The Federal Personnel System at the Crossroads* (Washington, DC: National Academy of Public Administration, 1986).

55. Lester Salamon and Alan Abramson, "Governance: The Politics of Retrenchment," in *The Reagan Record*, ed. John Palmer and Isabel Sawhill (Cambridge, MA: Ballinger, 1984), p. 40.

56. Colin Campbell, "The White House and the Presidency under the 'Let's Deal' President," in *The Bush Presidency. First Appraisals*, ed. Colin Campbell and Bert A. Rockman (Chatham, NJ: Chatham House, 1991), pp. 185–222.

57. See John Micklethwait, "Managing to Look Attractive," *New Statesman* 125, November 8, 1996, p. 24.

58. Quoted in I. M. Destler, "Reagan and the World: An 'Awesome Stubborness,'" in *The Reagan Legacy: Promise and Performance*, ed. Charles O. Jones, (Chatham, NJ: Chatham House, 1988), pp. 244–57. The source of the quote is *Report of the President's Special Review Board* (Washington, DC: Government Printing Office, 1987).

59. Thomas E. Mann and Norman J. Ornstein. *The Broken Branch: How Congress Is Failing America and How to Get It Back on Track* (New York: Oxford University Press, 2006), p. 155.

60. The Office of Technology Assessment (OTA) was a fourth research agency serving Congress until 1995. It was one of the first agencies scheduled for elimination by the 104th Congress. Until 1983, Congress had still another tool of legislative oversight: the legislative veto. Each agency operating under such provisions was obliged to submit to Congress every proposed decision or rule, which would then lie before both chambers for 30 to 60 days. If Congress took no action by one-house or two-house resolution explicitly to veto the proposed measure during the prescribed period, the measure became law. The legislative veto was declared unconstitutional by the Supreme Court in 1983 on the grounds that it violated the separation of powers—the resolutions Congress passed to exercise its veto were not subject to presidential veto, as required by the Constitution. See *Immigration and Naturalization Service v. Chadha*, 462 U.S. 919 (1983).

Chapter 15

1. *Morse v. Frederick*, 551 U.S. 393 (2007).

2. Charles Lane, "Court Backs School on Speech Curbs," *Washington Post*, June 26, 2007, p. A6.

3. *Hosanna-Tabor Evangelical Lutheran Church and School v. Equal Employment Opportunity Commission*, 565 U.S. ___ (2012).

4. U.S. Bureau of the Census, *Statistical Abstract of the United States* (Washington, DC: Government Printing Office, 2012).

5. Michael A. Fletcher, "Obama Criticized as Too Cautious on Judicial Posts," *Washington Post*, October 15, 2009, www.washingtonpost.com/wp-dyn/content/article/2009/10/15/AR2009101504083.html (accessed 3/1/10).

6. Russell Wheeler, "Judicial Nominations and Confirmations after Three Years—Where Do Things Stand?" Governance Studies at Brookings, January 13, 2012. [give URL and date accessed]

7. *Arizona v. United States*, 11–182 (2012).

8. *National Federation of Independent Business v. Sebelius*, 11–393 (2012).

9. Peter Wallsten and Richard Simon, "Sotomayor Nomination Splits GOP," *Los Angeles Times*, May 27, 2009, http://articles.latimes.com/2009/may/27/nation/na-court-access27 (accessed 3/1/10).

10. C. Herman Pritchett, *The American Constitution* (New York: McGraw-Hill, 1959), p. 138.

11. *Marbury v. Madison*, 1 Cr. 137 (1803).

12. *Federal Election Commission v. Wisconsin Right to Life*, 551 U.S. 449 (2007).

13. This review power was affirmed by the Supreme Court in *Martin v. Hunter's Lessee*, 1 Wheat. 304 (1816).

14. *Brown v. Board of Education*, 347 U.S. 483 (1954).

15. *Loving v. Virginia*, 388 U.S. 1 (1967).

16. *Griswold v. Connecticut*, 381 U.S. 479 (1965).

17. *Brandenburg v. Ohio*, 395 U.S. 444 (1969).

18. *United States v. Jones*, 10-1259 (2012).

19. Theodore J. Lowi, *The End of Liberalism*, 2nd ed. (New York: W.W. Norton, 1979); also David Schoenbrod, *Power without Responsibility: How Congress Abuses the People through Delegation* (New Haven, CT: Yale University Press, 1993).

20. Kenneth Culp Davis, *Discretionary Justice* (Baton Rouge: Louisiana State University Press, 1969), pp. 15–21.

21. Emergency Price Control Act, 56 Stat. 23 (January 30, 1942).

22. *Hamdi v. Rumsfeld*, 542 U.S. 507 (2004).

23. *Hamdan v. Rumsfeld*, 548 U.S. 557 (2006).

24. *Boumediene v. Bush*, 553 U.S. 723 (2008).

25. *Shelley v. Kraemer*, 334 U.S. 1 (1948).

26. *Burlington Northern v. White*, 548 U.S. 53 (2006).

27. *Engel v. Vitale*, 370 U.S. 421 (1962).

28. *Gideon v. Wainwright*, 372 U.S. 335 (1963).

29. *Escobedo v. Illinois*, 378 U.S. 478 (1964).

30. *Miranda v. Arizona*, 384 U.S. 436 (1966).

31. *Dickerson v. United States*, 530 U.S. 428 (2000).

32. *Baker v. Carr*, 369 U.S. 186 (1962).

33. Walter F. Murphy, "The Supreme Court of the United States," in *Encyclopedia of the American Judicial System*, ed. Robert J. Janosik (New York: Scribner's, 1987).

34. *Roe v. Wade*, 410 U.S. 113 (1973).

35. *Ricci v. DeStefano*, 200 U.S. 321 (2009).

36. Robert Scigliano, *The Supreme Court and the Presidency* (New York: Free Press, 1971), p. 162. For an interesting critique of the solicitor general's role during the Reagan administration, see Lincoln Caplan, "Annals of the Law," *New Yorker*, August 17, 1987, pp. 30–62.

37. Edward Lazarus, *Closed Chambers* (New York: Times Books, 1998), p. 6.

38. *NAACP v. Button*, 371 U.S. 415 (1963). The quotation is from the opinion in this case.

39. *Smith v. Allwright*, 321 U.S. 649 (1994).

40. *Griswold v. Connecticut*, 381 U.S. 479 (1965).

41. R. W. Apple Jr., "A Divided Government Remains, and with It the Prospect of Further Combat," *New York Times*, November 7, 1996, p. B6.

42. For limits on judicial power, see Alexander Bickel, *The Least Dangerous Branch* (Indianapolis: Bobbs-Merrill, 1962).

43. *Worcester v. Georgia*, 6 Pet. 515 (1832).

44. See Walter Murphy, *Congress and the Court* (Chicago: University of Chicago Press, 1962).

45. Robert Dahl, "The Supreme Court and National Policy Making," *Journal of Public Law* 6 (1958): 279.

46. Martin Shapiro, "The Supreme Court: From Warren to Burger," in *The New American Political System*, ed. Anthony King (Washington, DC: American Enterprise Institute, 1978).

47. *Citizens to Preserve Overton Park v. Volpe*, 401 U.S. 402 (1971).

48. Toni Locy, "Bracing for Health Care's Caseload," *Washington Post*, August 22, 1994, p. A15.

49. See "Developments in the Law—Class Actions," *Harvard Law Review* 89 (1976): 1318.

50. *In re Agent Orange Product Liability Litigation*, 100 F.R.D. 718 (D.C.N.Y. 1983).

51. See Donald Horowitz, *The Courts and Social Policy* (Washington, DC: Brookings Institution Press, 1977).

52. *Moran v. McDonough*, 540 F2d 527 (1 Cir., 1976; *cert. denied*, 429 U.S. 1042 [1977]).

53. Alexander Hamilton, James Madison, and John Jay, *The Federalist Papers*, ed. Clinton Rossiter (New York: New American Library, 1961), no. 10, p. 78.

answer key

Chapter 1
1. e
2. b
3. c
4. a
5. c
6. c
7. c
8. b
9. e
10. a
11. c
12. e
13. e
14. a
15. a

Chapter 2
1. a
2. b
3. b
4. c
5. e
6. c
7. a
8. d
9. b
10. e
11. e
12. b
13. e
14. a

Chapter 3
1. c
2. c
3. b
4. e
5. a
6. d

7. d
8. b
9. a
10. c
11. b
12. b
13. d
14. d

Chapter 4
1. a
2. e
3. b
4. b
5. e
6. e
7. b
8. e
9. b
10. d
11. b
12. a
13. c
14. a
15. d

Chapter 5
1. b
2. e
3. a
4. c
5. a
6. b
7. d
8. a
9. b
10. d
11. a
12. a
13. c

14. a
15. b

Chapter 6
1. c
2. a
3. e
4. d
5. c
6. b
7. c
8. a
9. b
10. b
11. a
12. b
13. b

Chapter 7
1. b
2. e
3. c
4. e
5. c
6. c
7. e
8. b
9. b
10. c
11. b
12. e
13. c
14. c

Chapter 8
1. e
2. b
3. d
4. d
5. a

6. c
7. a
8. d
9. b
10. d
11. c
12. b
13. e
14. d
15. b

Chapter 9
1. a
2. d
3. a
4. c
5. e
6. c
7. d
8. d
9. b
10. c
11. a
12. e
13. a
14. e
15. d

Chapter 10
1. b
2. a
3. d
4. c
5. d
6. a
7. b
8. d
9. d
10. b
11. c

12. b
13. a
14. c

Chapter 11
1. a
2. e
3. c
4. e
5. a
6. b
7. e
8. d
9. a
10. e
11. c
12. b
13. a
14. e

Chapter 12
1. d
2. a
3. d
4. c
5. a
6. c
7. a
8. a
9. b
10. a
11. e
12. c
13. a
14. a

Chapter 13
1. b
2. d
3. b

4. e

5. a

6. c

7. b

8. b

9. c

10. a

11. c

12. b

13. b

14. a

Chapter 14

1. b

2. b

3. b

4. e

5. b

6. e

7. d

8. d

9. d

10. d

11. d

12. b

13. a

14. a

Chapter 15

1. a

2. c

3. a

4. a

5. d

6. e

7. a

8. d

9. c

10. b

11. e

12. a

13. c

14. a

15. c

photo credits

West/Alamy; p. 313: Paul Spinelli/MLB Photos via Getty Images; p. 318: AP Photo; p. 323: CAUSE (www.causeusa.org); p. 325: Library of Congress; p. 327: William Thomas Cain/Getty Images; p. 328: AP Photo; p. 331: AP Photo. **Chapter 9:** Page 338: Mladen Antonov/AFP/Getty Images; p. 341: Granger Collection; p. 345: Granger Collection; p. 347: Granger Collection; p. 348: Nixon Presidential Library & Museum; p. 352: AP Photo; p. 354: AP Photo; p. 357: Ken Cedeno/Corbis; p. 360: Douglas Graham/Roll Call via Getty Images; p. 362: AP Photo; p. 367: Jeff Malet Photography/Newscom; p. 369: Pete Souza/White House-Photolink.net/Newscom; p. 371: AFP/Getty Images. **Chapter 10:** Page 378: Bruce Bennett/Getty Images; p. 381: Courtesy The Historical Society of Pennsylvania; p. 382: Bob Daemmrich/Alamy; p. 384 (left): Reuters/Corbis; (right): AP Photo; p. 385: Granger Collection; p. 386 (both): AP Photo; p. 388: Stock Montage/Getty Images; p. 391: Reuters/Mike Segar/Landov; p. 393: AP Photo; p. 396: Chip Somodevilla/Getty Images; p. 398: Joel Kowsky/Bloomberg/Getty Images; p. 401: AP Photo; p. 404: Mitt Romney Campaign; p. 409: Photo by Gage Skidmore. http://www.creativecommons.org/licenses/by-sa/2.0/deed.en; p. 410: Alliance Images/Alamy; p. 413: Patrick Farrell/MCT/Newscom; p. 416: Ty Wright/Getty Images; p. 418: AP Photo; p. 419: T.J. Kirkpatrick; p. 422: Courtesy of Roy Hoffmann; p. 424: Jason Reed/Reuter/Landov. **Chapter 11:** Page 432: Courtesy Stefanie Penn Spear/ecowatch.org; p. 435: Granger Collection; p. 436: Zunique/Newscom; p. 438: Chip Somodevilla/Getty Images; p. 439: Bettmann/Corbis; p. 440: Daniel Acker/The New York Times/Redux Pictures; p. 444: Brendan Hoffman/Getty Images; p. 447: Corbis; p. 448: AP Photo; p. 449: Ron Sachs/Pool/CNP/Corbis; p. 450: AP Photo; p. 452: AP Photo; p. 454: AP Photo; p. 455: Tim Roberts/Digital Vision/Getty Images; p. 461: AFP/Getty Images. **Chapter 12:** Page 468: Mladen Antonov/AFP/Getty Images; p. 472: Bettmann/Corbis; p. 474: Bill Clark/Roll Call Photos/Newscom; p. 475: Alex Wong/Getty Images; p. 478: AP Photo;

p. 485: Alex Wong/Getty Images; p. 490: Scott J. Ferrell/Congressional Quarterly/Getty Images; p. 494: Courtesy Bernie Sanders/C-Span; p. 497: Photo by Jay Tinker/Courtesy of Maryland Society for Sight, founded in 1909 with the mission of saving sight; p. 500: YouTube/Senator Blunt; p. 503: Alex Wong/Getty Images; p. 504: Andrew Harrer/Bloomberg via Getty Images; p. 506: Ernesto Hernandez Fonte/NATO Training Mission-Afghanistan via Getty Images; p. 507: William Philpott/AFP/Getty Images. **Chapter 13:** Page 514: Zhan Jun/Xinhua Press/Corbis; p. 517: Granger Collection; p. 518: The Reagan Library, National Archives; p. 521: Pete Souza/Corbis; p. 522: Larry Downing/Reuters/Corbis; p. 524: Alex Wong/Getty Images; p. 526: NBCU Photo Bank/Getty Images; p. 530: Terry Schmitt/UPI/Newscom; p. 535: Salah Malkawi/Getty Images; p. 536: Jason Reed/Reuters/Corbis; p. 540: Bettmann/Corbis; p. 541: Official White House Photo by Pete Souza; p. 542: Benjamin J. Myers/Corbis; p. 545: Sandy Huffaker/Corbis; p. 547: AP Photo. **Chapter 14:** Page 554: CDC/PHIL/Corbis; p. 557: Stephen Crowley/The New York Times/Redux; p. 560: AP Photo; p. 562: AP Photo; p. 567 (left): AP Photo; (right): Michael Doolittle/Alamy; p. 572: AP Photo; p. 574: Gray Tappan, USGS/EROS, Courtesy USAID; p. 578: Chip Somodevilla/Getty Images; p. 580: CBS/courtesy Everett Collection; p. 581: Gene Blevins/LA Daily News/Corbis; p. 584: Scott Peterson/Getty Images; p. 587: Ashrafov/Dreamstime.com; p. 589: Ron Sachs/CNP/Corbis; p. 590: Michael Reynolds/epa/Corbis; p. 593: Jeff Greenberg/Alamy. **Chapter 15:** Page 600: Blakeley/Dreamstime; p. 603: AP Photo; p. 609 (both): AP Photo; p. 610: J. Scott Applewhite/Pool/CNP/Corbis; p. 612: Steve Petteway, Collection of the Supreme Court of the United States; p. 614: Bettmann/Corbis; p. 615: AP Photo; p. 617: AP Photo; p. 619: AP Photo; p. 621: AP Photo; p. 628: AP Photo; p. 629: Collection of the Supreme Court of the United States, photo by: Steve Petteway; p. 631: AP Photo; p. 633: Mandel Ngan/AFP/Getty Images.

index

Consumer Privacy Bill of Rights, 146
Consumer Product Safety Act of 1972, 532
controlled Substances Act, 101
Coolidge, Calvin, 537
cooperative federalism, 91–93, *93*
Cornyn, John, 450
Corzine, Jon, 425
Council of Economic Advisers (CEA), 535
Council on Environmental Quality, 535
counsel, right to, 139–40
court cases, 603–4
Courtney, Joe, 479
court of appeals, 605
courts, 603; *see also* federal courts
Craigslist, 303
Crawford, Susan, 186
Crawford, William H., 387
criminal cases, 603–5
criminal justice
    and judicial review, 619–20
    rights of the criminally accused, 133–43, *136*
    states' return of fugitives, 80
criminal law, 603
cross burning, 125–26
crowdsourcing, 404
Crowley, James, *222*
cruel and unusual punishment, 140–43
Cuba, 371
Culver, Chet, 226, 227
Cummings, Elijah E., *497*
Cunningham, Randy "Duke," 450, 482–83
Czech Republic, 58, 274

D

Dahl, Robert, 242, 243
Dalai Lama, 194
Dalton, Russell, 302
D'Amato, Alfonse, 447
Daschle, Linda, 447
Daschle, Tom, 498
Davie, William R., 49
Davis, Gray, 394
Davis v. Federal Election Commission, 124
Dean, Howard, 298, 370

death penalty, 140–43, *141*
debates
    campaign, 400, 402
    congressional, 493–95
decision making
    by Congress, 496–504
    by the Supreme Court, *626*
    by voters in elections, 403–8
Declaration of Independence, 24, 25, 41–42
Declaration of Sentiments and Resolutions, 158
de facto, 165
defendant, 603
Defense, Department of, 573, 580, 585
Defense Base Closure and Realignment Commission (BRAC), 582
Defense of Marriage Act of 1996, 79, 189, *530*
defense of marriage acts, 79
de jure, 165
Delaware, 164
DeLay, Tom, 450, 500, 501
delegated powers, 519, 529–32, 617
delegates
    congressional, 508
    to political conventions, 391
Delli Carpini, Michael X., 220, 222
DeMint, Jim, 500
democracy, 28–30
    as basic political value, 23
    and Congress, 507–8
    in the Constitution, 67–68
    constitutional, 13
    in Constitutional Amendments, 67–68
    defined, 13, 207
    and elections, 381, 425–26
    exporting, 29
    function of political parties in, 339, 342
    function of the press in, 266
    ideal of vs. practice of, 30
    interest groups as challenge to, 460–62
    and the judiciary, 634
    and the media, 285–86
    and national security, 573, 575–77
    and opinions based on inadequate knowledge, 223–24

and political culture, 28–30
    and presidential power, 547–48
    and public opinion, 243–44
    responsible bureaucracy in, 593–94
Democracy in America (Tocqueville), 462
democratic government (term), 372
Democratic National Committee (DNC), 356–57, 367, 370, 457
Democratic Party, *341*, 344–49, 362; *see also* political parties
    African Americans' support for, 321
    Asian Americans' support for, 324
    characteristics of, 210, 211
    and civil rights of African Americans, 160
    congressional party unity, 498–99, *499*
    fund-raising activities of, 358
    and health care reform bill, 339–40
    key policy positions of, 367–68
    liberalism of, 354
    mobilization efforts of, 312
    organizational efforts of, 311
    party-building by, 370
    party identification, 360–61
    and primary delegates, 390
    and public works financing, 89
    recruitment of candidates by, 478
    and redistricting, 480–82
    responsiveness of, 345
    tax and social spending views of, 363
    and tax debate, 28
    white southerners in, 215
democratization policy, 29
demonstrations, 453–54
Dennis v. United States, 130
department, defined, 564
descriptive representation, 320
DeStefano, John, *621*
devolution, 96, 98–100, 582–83
DHS. *See* Homeland Security, Department of
Dickerson v. United States, 139, 620
dictatorships, 29
digital citizens, 12, 252, 258; *see also* Internet

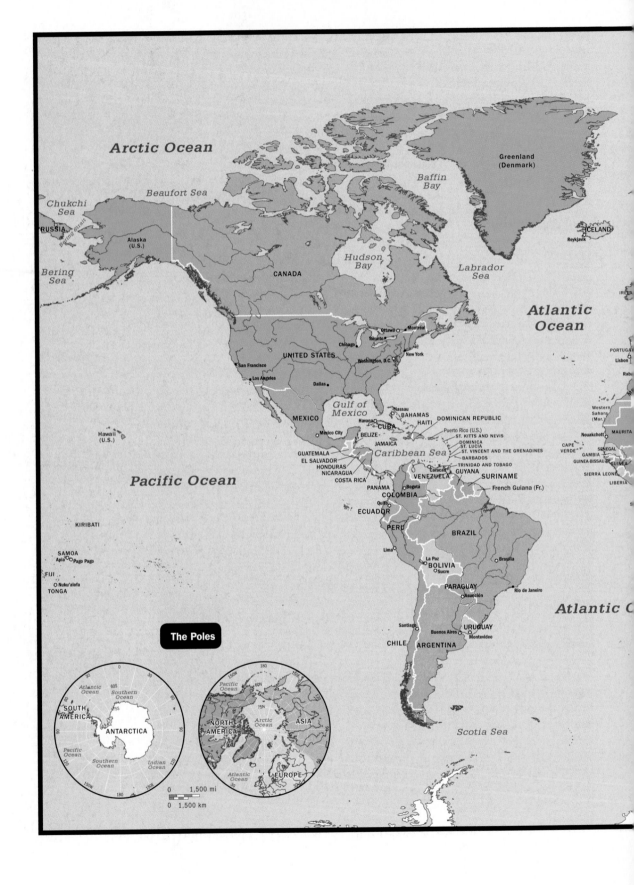

Arctic Ocean

Chukchi
Sea

Beaufort Sea

RUSSIA

Bering Strait

Bering
Sea

Alaska
(U.S.)

CANADA

Hudson
Bay

Baffin
Bay

Greenland
(Denmark)

Labrador
Sea

ICELAND

Reykjavik

Atlantic
Ocean

IRELA

Ottawa Montreal

Chicago Toronto

UNITED STATES

New York

Washington, D.C.

San Francisco

Los Angeles

Dallas

Hawaii
(U.S.)

MEXICO

Gulf of
Mexico

Nassau BAHAMAS

Havana CUBA HAITI DOMINICAN REPUBLIC

Mexico City BELIZE

JAMAICA

Puerto Rico (U.S.)
ST. KITTS AND NEVIS
DOMINICA
ST. LUCIA
ST. VINCENT AND THE GRENADINES
BARBADOS

PORTUGA

Lisbon

Raba

Western
Sahara
(Mor.)

Nouakchott

CAPE
VERDE

MAURITA

SENEGAL

GAMBIA

GUINEA-BISSAU

GUINEA

SIERRA LEONE

LIBERIA

Pacific Ocean

KIRIBATI

SAMOA
Apia Pago Pago

FIJI
Nuku'alofa
TONGA

GUATEMALA
EL SALVADOR
HONDURAS
NICARAGUA
COSTA RICA
PANAMA

Caribbean Sea

TRINIDAD AND TOBAGO

Caracas GUYANA SURINAME

VENEZUELA

French Guiana (Fr.)

Bogotá

COLOMBIA

Quito
ECUADOR

PERU

Lima

BRAZIL

La Paz
BOLIVIA
Sucre

Brasília

PARAGUAY

Asunción

Rio de Janeiro

Santiago

Buenos Aires

CHILE ARGENTINA

URUGUAY

Montevideo

Atlantic O

Scotia Sea

The Poles

Atlantic
Ocean

60S

Southern
Ocean

SOUTH
AMERICA

75S

ANTARCTICA

Pacific
Ocean

Southern
Ocean

Indian
Ocean

150W

180

150E

Pacific
Ocean

60N

180

150E

75N

NORTH
AMERICA

Arctic
Ocean

ASIA

Atlantic
Ocean

EUROPE

0 1,500 mi

0 1,500 km

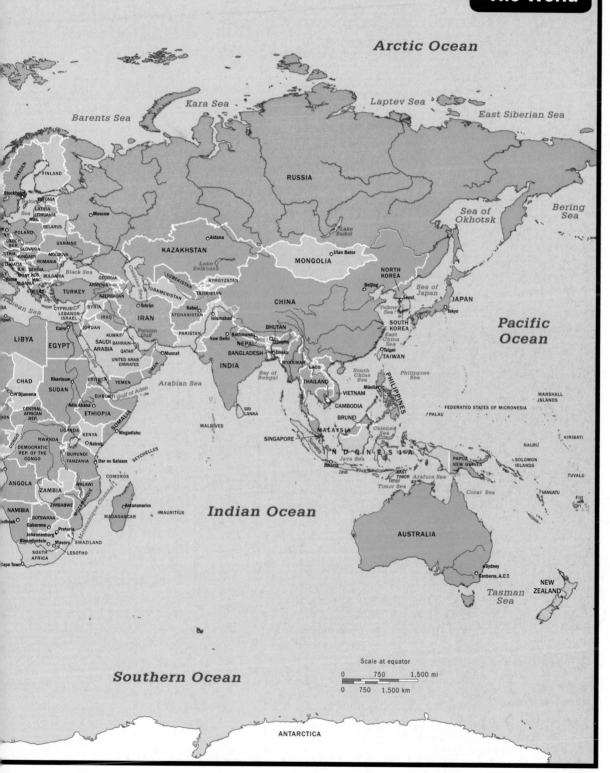

The World

Arctic Ocean

Barents Sea

Kara Sea

Laptev Sea

East Siberian Sea

SWEDEN

FINLAND

Stockholm

Baltic
Sea

ESTONIA

LATVIA

LITHUANIA

RUS.

BELARUS

POLAND

N.Y.

CZECH
REP.

SLOVAKIA

AUSTRIA

HUNGARY

MOLDOVA

SL.

CROATIA

ROMANIA

B.H.

SERBIA

Rome

MONT. KOS.

MAC.

ALBANIA

BULGARIA

Black Sea

GREECE

TURKEY

GEORGIA

ARMENIA

AZERBAIJAN

CYPRUS

LEBANON

ISRAEL

SYRIA

Tehrān

IRAQ

IRAN

Kabul

AFGHANISTAN

Islamabad

Tripoli

JORDAN

KUWAIT

LIBYA

EGYPT

SAUDI
ARABIA

BAHRAIN

QATAR

Cairo

Persian
Gulf

UNITED ARAB
EMIRATES

OMAN

Muscat

CHAD

Khartoum

ERITREA

YEMEN

Gulf of Aden

Arabian Sea

N'Djamena

SUDAN

DJIBOUTI

CENTRAL
AFRICAN
REP.

Adis Ababa

ETHIOPIA

SOMALIA

UGANDA

KENYA

Mogadishu

CONGO

RWANDA

Nairobi

DEMOCRATIC
REP. OF THE
CONGO

BURUNDI

TANZANIA

Dar es Salaam

SEYCHELLES

ANGOLA

ZAMBIA

MALAWI

COMOROS

NAMIBIA

ZIMBABWE

Antananarivo

MAURITIUS

BOTSWANA

MOZAMBIQUE CHANNEL

MADAGASCAR

Windhoek

Gaborone

Pretoria

Johannesburg

Bloemfontein

Maseru

SWAZILAND

SOUTH
AFRICA

LESOTHO

Cape Town

Moscow

KAZAKHSTAN

Astana

Lake
Balkhash

UZBEKISTAN

KYRGYZSTAN

TURKMENISTAN

TAJIKISTAN

Caspian Sea

New Delhi

PAKISTAN

INDIA

Kathmandu

NEPAL

BHUTAN

Thimphu

BANGLADESH

Dhaka

MYANMAR

Bay of
Bengal

SRI
LANKA

MALDIVES

RUSSIA

Lake
Baikal

MONGOLIA

Ulan Bator

Ulian Bator

CHINA

Beijing

NORTH
KOREA

Seoul

SOUTH
KOREA

Yellow
Sea

Sea of
Japan

JAPAN

Tokyo

East
China
Sea

Taipei

TAIWAN

LAOS

THAILAND

VIETNAM

CAMBODIA

South
China
Sea

Manila

PHILIPPINES

Philippine
Sea

Sea of
Okhotsk

Bering
Sea

Pacific
Ocean

MARSHALL
ISLANDS

FEDERATED STATES OF MICRONESIA

PALAU

NAURU

KIRIBATI

SOLOMON
ISLANDS

TUVALU

VANUATU

FIJI

BRUNEI

SINGAPORE

MALAYSIA

Sumatra

I N D O N E S I A

Jakarta

Java

Java Sea

Celebes
Sea

EAST
TIMOR

Timor

Arafura Sea

Timor Sea

PAPUA
NEW GUINEA

Coral Sea

AUSTRALIA

Sydney

Canberra, A.C.T.

Tasman
Sea

NEW
ZEALAND

Indian Ocean

Southern Ocean

ANTARCTICA

Scale at equator

| 0 | 750 | 1,500 mi |

| 0 | 750 | 1,500 km |

Mind
on
Statistics

Second Edition

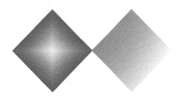

DUXBURY

Mind on Statistics

Second Edition

JESSICA M. UTTS
University of California, Davis

ROBERT F. HECKARD
Pennsylvania State University

THOMSON

™

BROOKS/COLE

Australia • Canada • Mexico • Singapore • Spain • United Kingdom • United States

THOMSON

BROOKS/COLE

Senior Acquisitions Editor: Carolyn Crockett
Development Editor: Cheryll Linthicum
Assistant Editor: Ann Day
Editorial Assistant: Julie Bliss
Technology Project Manager: Burke Taft
Marketing Manager: Joseph Rogove
Marketing Assistant: Jessica Perry
Advertising Project Manager: Tami Strang
Project Manager, Editorial Production: Karen Haga
Print/Media Buyer: Judy Inouye

Permissions Editor: Kiely Sexton
Production Service: Martha Emry Production Services
Text Designer: Terri Wright, John Edeen
Photo Researcher: Pat Quest
Copy Editor: Pamela Rockwell
Illustrator: Lisa Torri, G&S Typesetters
Cover Designer: Rob Hugel
Cover Printer: Lehigh Press
Compositor: G&S Typesetters
Text printer: Transcontinental Printing

Text printed in Canada
2 3 4 5 6 7 07 06 05 04 03

For more information about our products, contact us at:
Thomson Learning Academic Resource Center
1-800-423-0563

For permission to use material from this text, contact us by:
Phone: 1-800-730-2214   **Fax:** 1-800-730-2215
Web: http://www.thomsonrights.com

MINITAB is a trademark of Minitab, Inc., and is used herein with the owner's permission. Portions of MINITAB Statistical Software input and output contained in this book are printed with permission of Minitab, Inc.

All products mentioned herein are used for identification purposes only and may be trademarks or registered trademarks of their respective owners.

Library of Congress Control Number: 2002116149

Student Edition: ISBN 0-534-39305-5

Instructor's Edition: ISBN 0-534-39306-3

Brooks/Cole—Thomson Learning
10 Davis Drive
Belmont, CA 94002
USA

Asia
Thomson Learning
5 Shenton Way #01-01
UIC Building
Singapore 068808

Australia/New Zealand
Thomson Learning
102 Dodds Street
Southbank, Victoria 3006
Australia

Canada
Nelson
1120 Birchmount Road
Toronto, Ontario M1K 5G4
Canada

Europe/Middle East/Africa
Thomson Learning
High Holborn House
50/51 Bedford Row
London WC1R 4LR
United Kingdom

Latin America
Thomson Learning
Seneca, 53
Colonia Polanco
11560 Mexico D.F.
Mexico

Spain/Portugal
Paraninfo
Calle/Magallanes, 25
28015 Madrid, Spain

*To Bill Harkness—energetic, generous, and innovative
educator, guide, and friend—who launched our careers in statistics
and continues to share his vision.*

Brief Contents

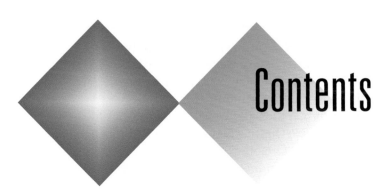

Contents

CHAPTER 3   Gathering Useful Data   58

CHAPTER 4   Sampling: Surveys and How to Ask Questions   88

CHAPTER 5   Relationships Between Quantitative Variables   130

CHAPTER 12 **More About Confidence Intervals   390**

CHAPTER 13 **More About Significance Tests   436**

CHAPTER **14**   More About Regression   **492**

CHAPTER **15**   More About Categorical Variables   **526**

CHAPTER **16**   Analysis of Variance   **560**

CHAPTER **17** Turning Information into Wisdom   **592**

SUPPLEMENTAL TOPIC **1** Additional Discrete Random Variables   **S1-1**

SUPPLEMENTAL TOPIC **2** Nonparametric Tests of Hypotheses   **S2-1**

SUPPLEMENTAL TOPIC **3** Multiple Regression   **S3-1**

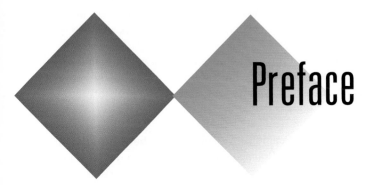

Preface

A CHALLENGE

Before you continue, think about how you would answer the question in the first bullet, and read the statement in the second bullet. We will return to them a little later in this Preface.

- What do you *really know* is true, and how do you know it?
- The diameter of the moon is about 2160 miles.

WHAT IS STATISTICS AND WHO SHOULD CARE?

Because people are curious about many things, chances are that your interests include topics to which statistics has made a useful contribution. As written in Chapter 17, "information developed through the use of statistics has enhanced our understanding of how life works, helped us learn about each other, allowed control over some societal issues, and helped individuals make informed decisions. There is almost no area of knowledge that has not been advanced by statistical studies."

Statistical methods have contributed to our understanding of health, psychology, ecology, politics, music, lifestyle choices, and dozens of other topics. A quick look through this book, especially Chapters 1 and 17, should convince you of this. Watch for the influences of statistics in your daily life as you learn this material.

Although statistics courses are often offered through a mathematics department, statistics is not a branch of mathematics. Mathematics is to statistics as wood, hammer, and nails are to building a house: a partial set of materials and tools. Statistics also draws materials and tools from philosophy, graphics, computing, psychology, and language.

HOW IS THIS BOOK DIFFERENT?
TWO BASIC PREMISES OF LEARNING

We wrote this book because we were tired of being told that what statisticians do is boring and difficult. We think statistics is useful and not difficult to learn, and yet the majority of college graduates we've met seemed to have had a negative experience taking a statistics class in college. We hope this book will help to overcome these misguided stereotypes.

Let's return to the two bullets at the beginning of this Preface. Without looking, do you remember the diameter of the moon? Unless you already had a pretty good idea, or have an excellent memory for numbers, you probably don't remember. One premise of this book is that new material is much easier to learn and remember if it is related to something interesting or previously known. The diameter of the moon is about the same as the air distance between Atlanta and Los Angeles, San Francisco and Chicago, London and Cairo, or Moscow and Madrid. Picture the moon sitting between any of those pairs of cities, and you are not likely to forget the size of the moon again. Throughout this book, new material is presented in the context of interesting and useful examples. The first and last chapters (1 and 17) are exclusively devoted to examples and case studies, which illustrate the wisdom that can be generated through statistical studies.

Now answer the question asked in the first bullet: What do you really know is true and how do you know it? If you are like most people, you know because it's something you have experienced or verified for yourself. It is not likely to be something you were told or heard in a lecture. The second premise of this book is that new material is easier to learn if you actively ask questions and answer them for yourself. *Mind on Statistics* is designed to help you learn statistical ideas by actively thinking about them. Throughout most of the chapters there are boxes entitled *Turn On Your Mind*. Thinking about the questions in those boxes will help you to discover and verify important ideas for yourself. We encourage you to think and question, rather than simply read and listen.

TOOLS FOR EXPANDED LEARNING

There are a number of tools provided in this book and beyond to enhance your learning of statistics.

Turn On Your Mind boxes appear throughout each chapter to help you develop your statistical reasoning and intuition. *Hints* are now provided to help you develop these skills.

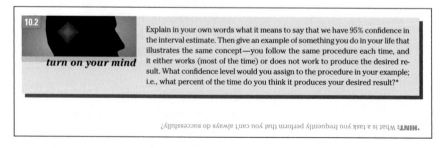

10.2

turn on your mind

Explain in your own words what it means to say that we have 95% confidence in the interval estimate. Then give an example of something you do in your life that illustrates the same concept—you follow the same procedure each time, and it either works (most of the time) or does not work to produce the desired result. What confidence level would you assign to the procedure in your example; i.e., what percent of the time do you think it produces your desired result?*

HINT: What is a task you frequently perform that you can't always do successfully?

New to this edition: *Turn On Your Computer* features provide additional opportunities for independent, hands-on exploration of key statistical concepts.

 **Random Sampling in Action**

It should be obvious to you by now that each time you take a random sample from a population you are likely to get a different group of individuals, even though the population remains fixed. The **Sampling** applet on the CD for this text allows us to watch what happens when we repeatedly take random samples from the same population. Figure 4.1 illustrates how the applet appears when it starts. Each stick figure represents one member of a population of 100 college students: 55 females (blue) and 45 males (red). Their heights have been recorded as well, and if you look carefully you will see that the little stick figures are all of slightly different heights. The mean height for the population is 68 inches.

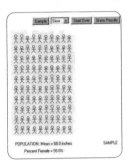

FIGURE 4.1 **The sampling applet starting point**

Examples throughout the chapters tie statistical concepts to everyday life occurrences.

EXAMPLE 10.2
If I Won the Lottery I'd Consider Quitting

What would you do for the rest of your life if you won a lot of money in a lottery? In a 1997 poll conducted by the Gallup Organization, one of the questions was "If you won 10 million dollars in the lottery would you continue to work, or would you stop working?" The results were reported at the Gallup Organization's website (www.gallup.com).

Surprisingly, 59% of the 616 employed respondents answered that they would continue working, 40% said they would stop working, and 1% had no opinion. The website article also gave this information about the poll:

The current results are based on telephone interviews with a randomly selected sample of 1,014 adults, conducted August 22–25, 1997. Among this group, 616 are employed full-time or part-time. For results based on this sample of "workers," one can say with 95% confidence that the error attributable to sampling could be plus or minus 4 percentage points.

Gallup describes the margin of error with the phrase "could be plus or minus 4 percentage points," but the phrase "could be *as large as* plus or minus 4 percentage points" would have been more informative. The margin of error is a likely upper limit on the sampling error. Here, there is a 95% chance that the sampling error is actually smaller than 4 percentage points. ◆

Key Terms at the end of each chapter, organized by section, can be used as a "quick-finder" and as a review tool.

KEY TERMS

Section 9.1
statistic, 294, 296
parameter, 294, 296
sampling distribution, 294–295, 296

Section 9.2
sample proportion, 296
normal curve approximation rule for sample proportions, 297, 298
sampling distribution of $\hat{p}$, 298
standard deviation of $\hat{p}$, 300
standard error of $\hat{p}$, 300

Section 9.3
normal curve approximation rule for sample means, 302–303, 304

sampling distribution of $\bar{x}$, 304
sampling distribution of the mean, 304
standard deviation of the sample mean, 304
standard error of the mean, 305
law of large numbers, 306

Section 9.4
central limit theorem, 309

Section 9.6
standardized statistic, 313–314
standardized z-statistic, 313–314, 315

Section 9.7
Student's t-distribution, 314
t-distribution, 314
degrees of freedom, (df), 315
standardized t-statistic, 315

Section 9.8
statistical inference, 316
confidence interval, 317
hypothesis testing, 317
significance testing, 317
statistical significance, 317

Special *Tech Note* boxes provide additional technical discussion as well as details about using MINITAB® statistical software* and Microsoft® Excel®.

Additional Notes on Creating Histograms

tech note ◆ Consider using intervals that make the range and width of each interval convenient. For instance, to create a histogram of ages at death for First Ladies, it would be convenient to use ten-year periods—died in her 30s, died in her 40s, and so on, up to 90s. This would create seven intervals.

◆ To show relative frequency, you can use either the proportion or the percent that are in an interval.

New to this edition: *Mind on the Basics* Exercises focus on practice and review; these exercises, color-coded in blue and appearing at the beginning of each exercise section, complement the conceptual and data-analysis exercises.

EXERCISES

1.1 A five-number summary for the heights in inches of the women who participated in the survey in Case Study 1.1 is

	Female Heights (Inches)	
Median	65	
Quartiles	63.5	67.5
Extremes	59	71

a. What is the median height for these women?
b. What is the range of heights, that is, the difference in heights between the shortest and the tallest women?
c. What is the interval of heights containing the shortest 1/4 of the women?
d. What is the interval of heights containing the middle 1/2 of the women?

1.2 In the year 2000, Vietnamese American women had the highest rate of cervical cancer in the country. Suppose that among 200,000 Vietnamese American women, 86 developed cervical cancer.

1.8 Suppose that an observational study showed that students who get at least 7 hours of sleep performed better on exams than students who didn't. Which of the following are possible confounding variables, and which are not? Explain why in each case.
a. Number of courses the student took that term.
b. Weight of the student.
c. Number of hours the student spent partying in a typical week.

1.9 Explain the distinction between statistical significance and practical significance. Can the result of a study be statistically significant but not practically significant?

1.10 A headline in a major newspaper read, "Breast-Fed Youth Found to Do Better in School."
a. Do you think this statement was based on an observational study or a randomized experiment? Explain.
b. Given your answer in part (a), which of these two alternative headlines do you think would be preferable: "Breast-feeding Leads to Better School Performance" or "Link Found Between Breast-feeding and School Performance"? Explain.

A Student's Suite CD provided with the book includes the *Turn On Your Computer* applets, tutorial quizzes, InfoTrac® College Edition and Internet exercises, Microsoft PowerPoint® presentation slides, links to both the Book Companion Web Site and *Internet Companion for Statistics* by Michael Larsen, Supplemental Topics identified in the Table of Contents, datasets formatted for MINITAB, Microsoft Excel, SPSS®, SAS®, JMP®, and ASCII, and technology manuals designed for use with MINITAB, SPSS, Excel, and the TI-83.

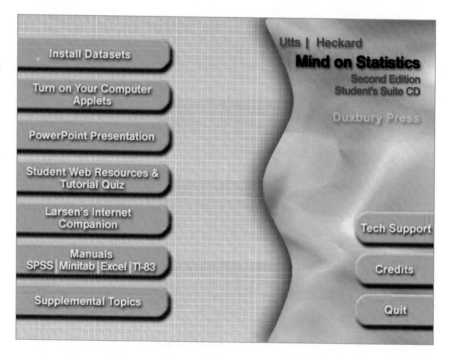

* MINITAB is a trademark of Minitab, Inc. and is used herein with the owner's permission (www.minitab.com).

Case Studies apply statistical ideas to intriguing news stories. As the *Case Studies* are developed, they model the statistical reasoning process.

CASE STUDY 6.1
Drinking, Driving, and the Supreme Court

In the early 1970s a young man challenged an Oklahoma State law that prohibited the sale of 3.2% beer to males under 21 but allowed its sale to females in the same age group. The case (*Craig* v. *Boren*, 429 U.S. 190, 1976) was ultimately heard by the U.S. Supreme Court.

Laws are allowed to use gender-based differences as long as they "serve important governmental objectives" and "are substantially related to the achievement of these objectives" (Gastwirth, 1988, p. 524). The defense argued that traffic safety was an important governmental objective and that data clearly show that young males are more likely to have alcohol-related accidents than young females.

The Supreme Court examined evidence from a "random roadside survey" that measured information on age, gender, and whether or not the driver had been drinking alcohol in the previous two hours. Although the survey was called a "random" survey of drivers, it probably was not. In roadside surveys, police tend to stop all drivers at certain locations at the time of the survey. This procedure does not really provide a random sampling of drivers in an area, but we'll treat it as though it does. Table 6.8 gives the results of the roadside survey for the drivers under 20 years of age.

TABLE 6.8 ■ **Results of Roadside Survey for Young Drivers**

| | Drank Alcohol in Last Two Hours? | | | |
	Yes	No	Total	Percent Who Drank
Males	77	404	481	16.0%
Females	16	122	138	11.6%
Total	93	526	619	15.0%

Source: Gastwirth, 1988, p. 526.

Notice that the percentage of young men who had been drinking alcohol is slightly higher than the percentage of young women. The difference is 16% − 11.6% = 4.4%. However, we cannot rule out chance as a reasonable explanation for this difference. In other words, if there really is no difference between the percents of young male and female drivers in the population who drink and drive, we could possibly see a difference as large as the one observed in a sample of this size.

In Figure 6.6, we present the results of asking the Minitab program to compute the chi-square statistic for this example. The chi-square summary statistic is 1.637, and the *p*-value for this statistic is 0.201. This *p*-value tells us that if there's really no association in the population (the null hypothesis), there's about a 20% chance that the sample would have a chi-square statistic as large as 1.637, or larger. In other words, the observed relationship could easily have occurred even if there is no relationship in the population represented by the sample.

The Supreme Court overturned the law, concluding that "the showing offered by the appellees does not satisfy us that sex represents a legitimate, accurate proxy for the regulation of drinking and driving" (Gastwirth, 1988, p. 527). Based on the chi-square analysis, you can see why the Supreme Court was reluctant to conclude that the difference in the sample represented sufficient evidence for a real difference in the population.

Expected counts are printed below observed counts

| | | Drank in Last 2 Hours? | | |
	Yes	No	Total	
Males	77	404	481	
	72.27	408.73		
Females	16	122	138	
	20.73	117.27		
Total	93	526	619	

Chi-Sq = 0.310 + 0.055 +
         1.081 + 0.191 = 1.637
DF = 1, P-Value = 0.201

FIGURE 6.6 **Minitab output for Case Study 6.1**

In Summary boxes appear at appropriate points to enhance key concepts and calculations; many are new in this edition.

in summary **Possible Reasons for Outliers and Reasonable Actions**

♦ *A mistake was made while taking a measurement or entering it into the computer.* If this can be verified, the values should be discarded or corrected.

♦ *The individual in question belongs to a different group than the bulk of individuals measured.* Values may be discarded if a summary is desired and reported for the majority group only.

♦ *The outlier is a legitimate data value and represents natural variability for the group and variable(s) measured.* Values may not be discarded in this case—they provide important information about location and spread.

Many *Exercises* (indicated by bold numbers) have complete or partial solutions, found in the *Answers to Selected Exercises* at the back of the book, to check your answers on those exercises and guide your thinking on similar exercises.

 # Answers to Selected Exercises

Chapter 1

1.2   a. .00043
1.5   a. 400
1.7   c. Randomized experiment.
       d. Observational study.
1.11 189/11,034, or about 17/1000, based on placebo group.
1.15 a. 150 mph.
       b. 55 mph.
       c. 80 mph.
       d. 1/2
       e. 51
1.19 No.
1.22 The base rate for that type of cancer.
1.26 a. $212/1525 = .139$.
       b. $1/\sqrt{1525} = .026$.
       c. .113 to .165.
1.28 a. Self-selected or volunteer.
       b. No. Readers with strong opinions will respond.

Chapter 2

2.1   a. Categorical.
       b. Quantitative.
       c. Quantitative.
       d. Categorical.
2.2   a. Categorical.
       b. Ordinal.
2.4   a. Not continuous.
2.5   a. Explanatory is amount of walking or running; response is lung function.
2.6   a. Population.
       b. Sample.
2.8   a. Support ban or not; categorical.
       b. Gain on verbal and math SATs after program; quantitative.

       c. Smoker or not and Alzheimer sufferer or not; both categorical.
2.9   a. Question 1a.
2.11 Example: Letter grades (A, B, etc.) converted to GPA.
2.14 a. $1427/2530 = .564$, or 56.4%.
       b. $100\% - 56.4\% = 43.6\%$.
2.15 a. $1700/2470 = .688$, or 67.8%.
       b. $1056/1700 = .621$, or 62.1%.
2.16 c. Overweight = 26.57%; about right = 69.23%; underweight = 4.20%.
2.18 a. Explanatory is smoked or not; response is developed Alzheimer's disease or not.
2.21 Either could be justified as being more informative.
2.23 a. Skewed to the right.
       b. 13 ear pierces may be an outlier.
       c. 2 ear pierces; about 45 women had this number.
       d. About 32 or so.
2.25 a. Roughly symmetric.
       b. Highest = 92.
       c. Lowest = 64.
       d. 5/20 = .25, or 25%
2.29 Example: The age of a person who is 80 years old would be an outlier at a traditional college, but not at a retirement home.
2.31 Whether it's the male author (then not an outlier) or the female author (then an outlier).
2.34 Yes. Values inconsistent with the bulk of the data will be obvious.
2.36 a. This is personal preference; some may prefer a very large family.
       b. An outlier (in the high direction).
2.37 a. Median = $(72 + 76)/2 = 74$; mean = 74.33.
       b. Median = 7; mean = 25.
2.39 a. Range = $225 - 123 = 102$.
       b. IQR = 35.
       c. 50%

A Note to Instructors

The Instructor's Suite CD includes everything featured on the Student's Suite CD, plus a Test Bank in Microsoft Word® format, sample course outlines and syllabi, Web resources for examples and case studies, complete solutions to the exercises found in the text, suggested answers for the *Turn On Your Mind* questions, recommended in-class noncomputer-oriented projects, and information on how to correlate text material with the AP Statistics curriculum. Additional Instructor's Resources are available through your Duxbury/Thomson representative.

ACKNOWLEDGMENTS

We thank William Harkness, Professor of Statistics at Penn State University, for continued support and feedback throughout our careers and during the writing of this book, and for his remarkable dedication to undergraduate statistics education. Preliminary editions of *Mind on Statistics* were used at Penn State, the University of California at Davis, and Texas A & M University, and we thank the many students who provided comments and suggestions on those and on the first edition. Thanks to Dr. Melvin Morse (Valley Children's Clinic and University of Washington) for suggesting the title for Chapter 17 and to Deb Niemeier, University of California, Davis, for suggesting that we add a supplemental chapter on Ethics (on the CD). At Penn State, Dave Hunter, Steve Arnold, and Tom Hettmansperger have provided many helpful insights. At the University of California at Davis, Rodney Wong has provided insights as well as material for some exercises and the Test Bank. The following reviewers offered valuable suggestions: Patti B. Collings, Brigham Young University; James Curl, Modesto Junior College; Donald Harden, Georgia State University; Rosemary Hirschfelder, University Sound; Sue Holt, Cabrillo Community College; Tom Johnson, North Carolina University; Andre Mack, Austin Community College; D'Arcy Mays, Virginia Commonwealth; Mary Murphy, Texas A & M University; N. Thomas Rogness, Grand Valley State University; Heather Sasinouska, Clemson University; Robert Alan Wolf, University of San Francisco; Elizabeth Clarkson, Wichita State University; Megan Meece, University of Florida; Thomas Nygren, Ohio State University; Wade Ellis, West Valley College; David Robinson, St. Cloud University; Jay Gregg, Colorado State University; Mark Johnson, University of Central Florida; and Nancy Pfenning, University of Pittsburgh.

Our sincere appreciation and gratitude goes to Carolyn Crockett and the staff of Duxbury, without whom this book could not have been written, and to Martha Emry who kept us on track throughout the editing and production of both editions of the book. Finally, for their support, patience, and numerous prepared dinners, we thank our families and friends, especially Candace Heckard, Molly Heckard, Wes Johnson, Claudia Utts-Smith, and Dennis Smith.

Jessica Utts
Robert Heckard

CHAPTER 1

Statistics Success Stories and Cautionary Tales

If they could drive faster, would they? See Case Study 1.1.

The seven stories in this chapter are meant to bring life to the term *statistics*. When you are finished reading these stories, if you still think the subject of statistics is lifeless or gruesome, check your pulse!

L et's face it. You're a busy person. Why should you spend your time learning about a subject that sounds as dull as statistics? In this chapter we give seven examples of situations in which statistics either provided enlightenment or misinformation. With these examples, we hope to convince you that learning about this subject will be interesting and useful.

Each of the stories in this chapter illustrates one or more concepts that will be developed throughout the book. These concepts are given as "the moral of the story" after a case is presented. Definitions of some terms used in the story also are provided following each case. By the time you read all of these stories, you already will have an overview of what statistics is all about. ◆

1.1 | WHAT IS STATISTICS?

When you hear the word *statistics* you probably think of lifeless or gruesome numbers, like the population of your state or the number of violent crimes committed in your city last year. The word *statistics,* however, actually is used to mean two different things. The better-known definition is that statistics are numbers measured for some purpose. A more complete definition, and the one that forms the substance of this book, is the following:

definition **Statistics** is a collection of procedures and principles for gathering data and analyzing information in order to help people make decisions when faced with uncertainty.

The stories in this chapter are meant to bring life to this definition. When you are finished reading them, if you still think the subject of statistics is lifeless or gruesome, check your pulse!

1.2 | SEVEN STATISTICAL STORIES WITH MORALS

The best way to gain an understanding of some of the ideas and methods used in statistical studies is to see them in action. Each of the seven stories presented in this chapter includes interesting lessons about how to gain information from data. The methods and ideas will be expanded throughout the book, but these seven stories will give you an excellent overview of why it is useful to study statistics. To help you understand some basic statistical principles, each case study is accompanied by a "moral of the story" and by some definitions. All of the ideas and definitions will be discussed in greater detail in subsequent chapters.

CASE STUDY 1.1
Who Are Those Speedy Drivers?

A survey taken in a large statistics class at Penn State University contained the question "What's the fastest you have ever driven a car? _____mph." The *data* provided by the 87 males and 102 females who responded are listed here.

Males: 110 109 90 140 105 150 120 110 110 90 115 95 145 140 110 105 85 95 100 115 124 95 100 125 140 85 120 115 105 125 102 85 120 110 120 115 94 125 80 85 140 120 92 130 125 110 90 110 110 95 95 110 105 80 100 110 130 105 105 120 90 100 105 100 120 100 100 80 100 120 105 60 125 120 100 115 95 110 101 80 112 120 110 115 125 55 90

Females: 80 75 83 80 100 100 90 75 95 85 90 85 90 90 120 85 100 120 75 85 80 70 85 110 85 75 105 95 75 70 90 70 82 85 100 90 75 90 110 80 80 110 110 95 75 130 95 110 110 80 90 105 90 110 75 100 90 110 85 90 80 80 85 50 80 100 80 80 80 95 100 90 100 95 80 80 50 88 90 90 85 70 90 30 85 85 87 85 90 85 75 90 102 80 100 95 110 80 95 90 80 90

From these numbers, can you tell which sex tends to have driven faster, and by how much? Notice how difficult it is to make sense of the *data* when you are simply presented with a list. Even if the numbers had been presented in numerical order, it would be difficult to compare the two sexes.

Your first lesson in statistics is how to formulate a simple summary of a long list of numbers. The *dotplot* shown in Figure 1.1 helps us see the pattern in the data. In the plot, each dot represents the response of an individual student. We can see that the men tend to claim a higher "fastest ever driven" speed than do the women.

The graph shows us a lot, and calculating some statistics that summarize the data will provide additional insight. There are a variety of ways to do so, but for this example we examine a *five-number summary* of the data for males and females. The five numbers are the lowest value, the cutoff points for 1/4, 1/2, and 3/4 of the data, and the highest value. The three middle values of the summary (the cutoff points for 1/4, 1/2, and 3/4 of the data)

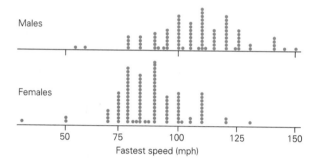

FIGURE 1.1   Responses to "What's the fastest you've ever driven?"

are called the *lower quartile, median,* and *upper quartile.* Five-number summaries can be represented like this:

	Males **(87 Students)**		**Females** **(102 Students)**	
Median		110		89
Quartiles	95	120	80	95
Extremes	55	150	30	130

Some interesting facts become immediately obvious from these summaries. By looking at the medians, you see that half of the men have driven 110 miles per hour or more, whereas the halfway point for the women is only 89 miles per hour. In fact, 3/4 of the men have driven 95 miles per hour or more, but only 1/4 of the women have done so. These facts were not at all obvious from the original lists of numbers.

Moral of the Story: *Simple summaries of data can tell an interesting story and are easier to digest than long lists.*

Definitions: Data is a plural word referring to numbers or non-numerical labels (such as male/female) collected from a set of entities (people, cities, and so on). The **median** of a numerical list of data is the value in the middle when the numbers are put in order. For an even number of entities, the median is the average of the middle two values. The **lower quartile** and **upper quartile** are (roughly) the medians of the lower and upper halves of the data.

CASE STUDY 1.2
Safety in the Skies?

Air travelers already have enough concerns, with the potential for delays, lost baggage, and so on. So if you do a lot of air travel, or know anyone who does, you may have been disturbed by the headline in *USA Today* that read, "Planes get closer in midair as traffic control errors rise" (Levin, 1999). You may have been even more disturbed by the details: "Errors by air traffic controllers climbed from 746 in fiscal 1997 to 878 in fiscal 1998, an 18% increase." Don't cancel your next vacation yet. A look at the statistics indicates that the news is actually pretty good! And, there is some reassurance when we are told that "most [errors] involve planes passing so far apart that there is no danger of collision."

The headline and details do sound ominous—all those errors and an increase of almost 20%! If things continue at that rate, won't your next flight be quite likely to suffer from air traffic controller error? The answer is a resounding "no," which becomes obvious when we are told the *base rate* or *baseline risk* for errors. "The errors per million flights handled by controllers climbed from 4.8 to 5.5." So, the original *rate* of errors in 1997, from which the 18% increase was calculated, was less than 5 errors per million flights.

Fortunately, the rates for the two years were provided in the story. This is not always the case in news reports of increases in rates. For instance, an article may say that the rate of a certain type of cancer is doubled if you eat a certain unhealthful food. But what good is that information unless you know the actual risk? Doubling your chance of getting cancer from 1 in a million to 2 in a million is trivial, but doubling your chance from 1 in 50 to 2 in 50 is not.

Moral of the Story: *When discussing the change in the rate or risk of occurrence of something, make sure you also include the base rate or baseline risk.*

Definitions: The **rate** at which something occurs is simply the number of times it occurs per number of opportunities for it to occur. In fiscal year 1998, the rate of errors was 5.5 per million flights. The **risk** of a bad outcome in the future can be estimated using the past rate for that outcome, if it is assumed the future is like the past. Based on 1998 data, the estimated risk of an error for any given flight in 1999 would be 5.5/1,000,000, or .0000055. The **base rate** or **baseline risk** is the rate or risk at a beginning time period or under specific conditions. For instance, the base rate of air traffic controller errors was 4.8 per million flights in fiscal year 1997.

CASE STUDY 1.3
Did Anyone Ask Whom You've Been Dating?

"According to a new *USA Today*/Gallup Poll of teenagers across the country, 57 percent of teens who go out on dates say they've been out with someone of another race or ethnic group" (Peterson, 1997). That's over half of the dating teenagers, so of course it was natural for the headline in the *Sacramento Bee* to read, "Interracial dates common among today's teenagers." The article contained other information as well, such as: "In most cases, parents aren't a major obstacle. Sixty-four percent of teens say their parents don't mind that they date interracially, or wouldn't mind if they did."

There are millions of teenagers in the United States whose experiences are being reflected in this story. How could the poll-takers manage to ask so many teenagers these questions? The answer is that they didn't. The article states that "the results of the new poll of 602 teens, conducted Oct. 13–20, reflect the ubiquity of interracial dating today. . . ." They asked only 602 teens? Could such a small sample possibly tell us anything about the millions of teenagers in the United States? The answer is "yes" if those teens constituted a *random sample* from the *population* of interest.

The featured statistic of the article is that "57 percent of teens who go out on dates say they've been out with someone of another race or ethnic group." Only 496 of the 602 teens in the poll said they date, so the 57% value is actually a percent based on 496 responses. In other words, the pollsters were using information from only 496 teenagers to estimate something about all teenagers. Figure 1.2 illustrates this situation.

How accurate could this sample possibly be? The answer may surprise you. The results of this poll are accurate to within a *margin of error* of about 4.5%. As surprising as it may seem, the true percentage of all teens in the United States who date interracially is reasonably likely to be within 4.5% of the reported percentage that's based only on the 496 teens asked! We'll be conservative and round the 4.5% margin of error up to 5%. The percent of all teenagers in the United States who date that would say they have dated interracially is likely to be in the range 57% $\pm$ 5%, or between 52% and 62%. (The symbol $\pm$ is read "plus and minus" and means that the value on the right should be added to and subtracted from the value on the left, to create an interval.)

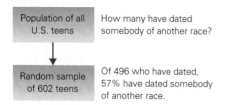

FIGURE 1.2   Population and sample for the survey

Polls and *sample surveys* are frequently used to assess public opinion and to estimate population characteristics like the percent of teens who have dated interracially. Many sophisticated methods have been developed that allow pollsters to gain the information they need from a very small number of individuals. The trick is to know how to select those individuals. In Chapter 4 we examine a number of other strategies used to ensure that sample surveys provide reliable information about populations.

Moral of the Story: *A representative sample of only a few thousand, or perhaps even a few hundred, can give reasonably accurate information about a population of many millions.*

Definitions: A **population** is a collection of all individuals about which information is desired. The "individuals" are usually people, but could also be schools, cities, pet dogs, agricultural fields, and so on. A **random sample** is a subset of the population selected so that every individual has a specified probability of being part of the sample. In a **sample survey,** the investigators gather opinions or other information from each individual included in the sample. The **margin of error,** for a properly conducted survey, is a number that is added to and subtracted from the sample information to produce an interval that is 95% certain to contain the truth about the population. In the most common types of sample surveys, the margin of error is approximately equal to 1 divided by the square root of the number of individuals in the sample. Hence, a sample of 496 teenagers who have dated produces a margin of error of about $1/\sqrt{496} = .045$, or about 4.5%.

CASE STUDY 1.4
Who Are Those Angry Women?

A well-conducted survey can be very informative, but a poorly conducted one can be a complete disaster. As an extreme example, Moore (1997, p. 11) reports that for her highly publicized book *Women and Love,* Shere Hite sent questionnaires to 100,000 women asking about love, sex, and relationships. Only 4.5% of the women responded, and Hite used those responses to write her book. As Moore notes, "The women who responded were fed up with men and eager to fight them. For example, 91% of those who were divorced said that they had initiated the divorce. The anger of women toward men became the theme of the book." Do you think that women who were angry with men would be likely to answer questions about love relationships in the same way as the general population of women?

The Hite sample exemplifies one of the most common problems with surveys—the sample data may not represent the pop-

ulation. Extensive *nonresponse* from a random sample, or the use of a *self-selected* (i.e., *all-volunteer*) *sample,* will probably produce biased results. Those who voluntarily respond to surveys tend to care about the issue and thus have stronger and different opinions than those who do not respond.

Moral of the Story: *An unrepresentative sample, even a large one, tells you almost nothing about the population.*

Definitions: Nonresponse bias can occur when many people who are selected for the sample either do not respond at all or do not respond to some of the key survey questions. This may occur even when an appropriate random sample is selected and contacted. The survey is then based on a nonrepresentative sample, usually those who feel strongly about the issues. Some surveys don't even attempt to contact a random sample, but instead ask anyone who wishes to respond to do so. Magazines, television stations, and Internet websites routinely conduct this kind of poll, and those who respond are called a **self-selected** sample or a **volunteer sample.** This kind of sample tells you nothing about the larger population at all; it only tells you about those who responded.

CASE STUDY 1.5
Does Prayer Lower Blood Pressure?

Newspaper headlines are notorious for making one of the most common mistakes in the interpretation of statistical studies—jumping to unwarranted conclusions. A headline in *USA Today* read, "Prayer can lower blood pressure" (Davis, 1998). The story that followed continued the possible fallacy it began by stating, "Attending religious services lowers blood pressure more than tuning into religious TV or radio, a new study says." The words "attending religious services lowers blood pressure" imply a direct cause-and-effect relationship. This is a strong statement, but it's not a statement that is justified by the research project described in the article.

The article was based on an *observational study* conducted by the U.S. National Institutes of Health, which followed 2391 people aged 65 or older for six years. The article described one of the study's principal findings: "People who attended a religious service once a week and prayed or studied the Bible once a day were 40% less likely to have high blood pressure than those who don't go to church every week and prayed and studied the Bible less" (Davis, 1998). So, the researchers did observe a relationship, but it's a mistake to think that this justifies the conclusion that prayer actually *causes* lower blood pressure.

When groups are compared in an observational study, the groups usually differ in many important ways that may contribute to the observed relationship. In this example, people who attended church and prayed regularly may have been less likely than the others to smoke or to drink alcohol. These could affect the results because smoking and alcohol use are both believed to affect blood pressure. The regular church attendees may have had a better social network, a factor that could lead to reduced stress, which in turn could reduce blood pressure. People who were generally somewhat ill may not have been as willing or able to go out to church. We're sure you can think of other possibilities for *confounding variables* that may have contributed to the observed relationship between prayer and lower blood pressure.

Moral of the Story: *Cause-and-effect conclusions cannot generally be made based on an observational study.*

Definitions: An **observational study** is one in which participants are merely observed and measured. Comparisons based on observational studies are comparisons of naturally occurring groups. A **variable** is a characteristic that differs from one individual to the next. It may be numerical, like blood pressure, or it may be categorical, like whether or not someone attends church regularly. A **confounding variable** is a variable that is not the main concern of the study, but may be partially responsible for the observed results.

CASE STUDY 1.6
Does Aspirin Reduce Heart Attack Rates?

In 1988, the Steering Committee of the Physicians' Health Study Research Group released the results of a five-year *randomized experiment* conducted using 22,071 male physicians between the ages of 40 and 84. The purpose of the experiment was to determine if taking aspirin reduces the risk of a heart attack. The physicians had been *randomly assigned* to one of the two *treatment* groups. One group took an ordinary aspirin tablet every other day, while the other group took a *placebo*. None of the physicians knew whether he was taking the actual aspirin or the placebo.

TABLE 1.1 ■ The Effect of Aspirin on Heart Attacks

Treatment	Heart Attacks	Doctors in Group	Attacks Per 1000 Doctors
Aspirin	104	11,037	9.42
Placebo	189	11,034	17.13

The results, shown in Table 1.1, support the conclusion that taking aspirin does indeed help reduce the risk of having a heart attack. The rate of heart attacks in the group taking aspirin was only about half the rate of heart attacks in the placebo group. In the aspirin group, there were 9.42 heart attacks per 1000 participating doctors, while in the placebo group, there were 17.13 heart attacks per 1000 participants.

Because the men in this experiment were randomly assigned to the two conditions, other important risk factors like age, amount of exercise, and dietary habits should have been similar for both groups. The only important difference between the two groups should have been whether they took aspirin or placebo. This makes it possible to conclude that taking aspirin actually *caused* the lower rate of heart attacks for that group. In a later chapter, you will learn how to determine that the difference seen in this sample is *statistically significant*. In other words, the observed sample difference probably reflects a true difference within the population.

To what population does the conclusion of this study apply? The participants were all male physicians, so the conclusion that aspirin reduces the risk of a heart attack may not hold for the general population of men. No women were included, so the conclusion may not apply to women at all. More recent evidence, however, has provided additional support for the benefit of aspirin in broader populations.

Moral of the Story: *Unlike with observational studies, cause-and-effect conclusions can generally be made on the basis of randomized experiments.*

Definitions: A **randomized experiment** is a study in which treatments are randomly assigned to participants. A **treatment** is a specific regimen or procedure assigned to participants by the experimenter. A **random assignment** is one in which each participant has a specified probability of being assigned to each treatment. A **placebo** is a pill or treatment designed to look just like the active treatment but with no active ingredients. A **statistically significant** relationship or difference is one that is large enough to be unlikely to have occurred in the sample if there was no relationship or difference in the population.

CASE STUDY 1.7
Does the Internet Increase Loneliness and Depression?

It was big news. Researchers at Carnegie Mellon University had found that "greater use of the Internet was associated with declines in participants' communication with family members in the household, declines in size of their social circle, and increases in their depression and loneliness" (Kraut et al., 1998, p. 1017). An article in the *New York Times* reporting on this study was entitled "Sad, lonely world discovered in cyberspace" (Harmon, 1998). The study included 169 individuals in 73 households in Pittsburgh, Pennsylvania who were given free computers and Internet service in 1995. The participants answered a series of questions at the beginning of the study and either one or two years later, measuring social contacts, stress, loneliness, and depression. The *New York Times* reported:

> In the first concentrated study of the social and psychological effects of Internet use at home, researchers at Carnegie Mellon University have found that people who spend even a few hours a week online have higher levels of depression and loneliness than they would if they used the computer network less frequently . . . it raises troubling questions about the nature of "virtual" communication and the disembodied relationships that are often formed in cyberspace. (Harmon, 1998)

Given these dire reports, one would think that using the Internet for a few hours a week is devastating to your mental health. But a closer look at the findings reveals that the changes were actually quite small, although statistically significant. Internet use averaged 2.43 hours per week for participants. The number of people in the participants' "local social network" decreased from an average of 23.94 people to an average of 22.90 people, hardly a noticeable loss. On a scale from 1 to 5, self-reported loneliness decreased from an average of 1.99 to 1.89 (lower scores indicate greater loneliness). And on a scale from 0 to 3, self-reported depression dropped from an average of 0.73 to an average of 0.62 (lower scores indicate higher depression).

The *New York Times* did report the magnitude of some of the changes, noting for instance, that "one hour a week on the Internet was associated, on average, with an increase of 0.03, or 1 percent on the depression scale." But the attention the research received masked the fact that the impact of Internet use on depression, loneliness, and social contact was actually quite small.

As a follow-up to this study, in July 2001 *USA Today* (Elias, 2001) reported that in continued research, the bad effects had mostly disappeared. The article, titled "Web use not always a downer: Study disputes link to depression," began with the statement "Using the Internet at home doesn't make people more depressed and lonely after all." However, the article noted that the lead researcher, Robert Kraut of Carnegie Mellon University, believes that the earlier findings were correct, but that "the Net has become a more social place since the study began in 1995." His explanation for the change in findings is that "either the Internet has changed, or people have learned to use it more constructively, or both." Whether the link ever existed will never be known, but it is not surprising, given the small magnitude of the original finding, that it subsequently disappeared.

Moral of the Story: *A "statistically significant" finding does not necessarily have practical importance. When a study reports a statistically significant finding, find out the magnitude of the relationship or difference. A secondary moral to this story is that the implied direction of cause and effect may be wrong. In this case, it could be that people who were more lonely and depressed were more prone to use the Internet. And, as the follow-up research makes clear, remember that "truth" doesn't necessarily remain fixed across time. Any study should be viewed in the context of society at the time it was done.*

1.3 | THE COMMON ELEMENTS IN THE SEVEN STORIES

The seven stories were meant to bring life to our definition of statistics. Let's consider that definition again:

> **Statistics** is a collection of procedures and principles for gathering data and analyzing information in order to help people make decisions when faced with uncertainty.

Think back over the seven stories. In every story, *data are used to make a judgment about a situation.* This common theme is what statistics is all about.

The Discovery of Knowledge

Each story illustrates part of the process of discovery of new knowledge, for which statistical methods can be very useful. The basic steps in this process are

1. *Asking the right question(s).*
2. *Collecting useful data*, which includes deciding how much is needed.
3. *Summarizing and analyzing data*, with the goal of answering the questions.
4. *Making decisions and generalizations* based on the observed data.
5. *Turning the data and subsequent decisions into new knowledge.*

We'll explore these five steps throughout the book, concluding with a chapter on "Turning Information into Wisdom." We're confident that your active participation in this exploration will benefit you in your everyday life and in your future professional career.

In a practical sense, almost all decisions in life are based on knowledge obtained by gathering and assimilating data. Sometimes the data are quantitative, as when an instructor must decide what grades to give based on a collection of homework and exam scores. Sometimes the information is more qualitative and the process of assimilating it is informal, such as when you decide what you are going to wear to a party. In either case, the principles in this book will help you understand how to be a better decision maker.

1.1

turn on your mind

Think about a decision that you recently had to make. What "data" did you use to help you make the decision? Did you have as much information as you would have liked? If you could freely use them, how would you use the principles in this chapter to help you gain more useful information?*

in summary   **Some Important Statistical Principles**

The "moral of the story" items for the case studies presented in this chapter give a good overview of many of the important ideas covered in this book. Here is a summary:

- Simple summaries of data can tell an interesting story and are easier to digest than long lists.

- When discussing the change in the rate or risk of occurrence of something, make sure you also include the base rate or baseline risk.

- A representative sample of only a few thousand, or perhaps even a few hundred, can give reasonably accurate information about a population of many millions.

- An unrepresentative sample, even a large one, tells you almost nothing about the population.

- Cause-and-effect conclusions cannot generally be made based on an observational study.

- Cause-and-effect conclusions can generally be made on the basis of randomized experiments.

- A statistically significant finding does not necessarily have practical importance. When a study reports a statistically significant finding, find out the magnitude of the relationship or difference.

KEY TERMS

Every term in this chapter is discussed more extensively in later chapters, so don't worry if you don't understand all of the terminology that's been introduced here. The following list indicates the page number(s) where the important terms in this chapter are introduced and defined.

EXERCISES Blue = Basics   Bold, **Bold** = Answer in back

1.1 A five-number summary for the heights in inches of the women who participated in the survey in Case Study 1.1 is

Female Heights (Inches)		
Median		65
Quartiles	63.5	67.5
Extremes	59	71

  a. What is the median height for these women?
  b. What is the range of heights, that is, the difference in heights between the shortest and the tallest women?
  c. What is the interval of heights containing the shortest 1/4 of the women?
  d. What is the interval of heights containing the middle 1/2 of the women?

1.2 In the year 2000, Vietnamese American women had the highest rate of cervical cancer in the country. Suppose that among 200,000 Vietnamese American women, 86 developed cervical cancer.
  a. Calculate the rate of cervical cancer for these women.
  b. What is the estimated risk of developing cervical cancer for Vietnamese American women in the next year?
  c. Explain the conceptual difference between the rate and the risk, in the context of this example.

1.3 Explain the difference between a population and a sample.

1.4 For a survey based on a random sample of 2000 adults, what is the approximate margin of error?

1.5 What sample size produces each of the following values as the approximate margin of error?
  a. Margin of error = .05 or 5%.
  b. Margin of error = .30 or 30%.

1.6 A proposed study design is to leave 100 questionnaires by the checkout line in a student cafeteria. The questionnaire could be picked up by any student and returned to the cashier. Explain why this volunteer sample is a poor study design.

1.7 For each of the examples given here, decide whether the study was an observational study or a randomized experiment.
  a. A group of 100 students was randomly divided, with 50 assigned to receive vitamin C and the remaining 50 to receive a placebo, to see if vitamin C helps prevent colds.
  b. All patients who received a hip transplant operation at Stanford University Hospital during 1990 to 2000 will be followed for 10 years after their operation to determine the success (or failure) of the transplant.
  c. A group of students who were enrolled in an introductory statistics course were randomly assigned to take a Web-based course or to take a traditional lecture course. The two methods were compared by giving the same final examination in both courses.
  d. A group of smokers and another group of nonsmokers who visited a particular clinic were asked to come in for a physical exam every 5 years for the rest of their lives in order to monitor and compare their health status.

1.8 Suppose that an observational study showed that students who get at least 7 hours of sleep performed better on exams than students who didn't. Which of the following are possible confounding variables, and which are not? Explain why in each case.
  a. Number of courses the student took that term.
  b. Weight of the student.
  c. Number of hours the student spent partying in a typical week.

1.9 Explain the distinction between statistical significance and practical significance. Can the result of a study be statistically significant but not practically significant?

1.10 A headline in a major newspaper read, "Breast-Fed Youth Found to Do Better in School."
  a. Do you think this statement was based on an observational study or a randomized experiment? Explain.
  b. Given your answer in part (a), which of these two alternative headlines do you think would be preferable: "Breast-feeding Leads to Better School Performance" or "Link Found Between Breast-feeding and School Performance"? Explain.

1.11 Refer to Case Study 1.6, in which the relationship between aspirin and heart attack rates was examined. Using the results of this experiment, what do you think is the base rate of heart attacks for men like the ones in this study? Explain.

1.12 A random sample of 1001 University of California faculty members taken in December 1995 was asked, "Do you favor or oppose using race, religion, sex, color, ethnicity, or national origin as a criterion for admission to the University of California?" (Roper Center, 1996). Fifty-two percent responded "favor."
  a. What is the population for this survey?
  b. What is the approximate margin of error for the survey?
  c. Based on the results of the survey, could it be concluded that a majority (over 50%) of *all* University of California faculty members favor using these criteria? Explain.

1.13 In this chapter you learned that cause and effect can be concluded from randomized experiments but generally not from observational studies. Why don't researchers simply conduct all studies as randomized experiments rather than observational studies?

1.14 Give an example of a question you would like to have answered, such as whether eating chocolate helps prevent depression. Then explain how a randomized experiment or an observational study could be done to study this question.

1.15 Refer to the data and five-number summaries given in Case Study 1.1. Give a numerical value for each of the following:
  a. The fastest speed driven by anyone in the class.
  b. The slowest speed driven by a male.
  c. The speed for which 1/4 of the women had driven at that speed or faster.
  d. The proportion of females who had driven 89 mph or faster.
  e. The number of females who had driven 89 mph or more.

1.16 Why was the study described in Case Study 1.5 conducted as an observational study instead of an experiment?

1.17 Students in a statistics class at Penn State were asked, "About how many minutes do you typically exercise in a week?" Responses from the *women* in the class were

60, 240, 0, 360, 450, 200, 100, 70, 240, 0, 60, 360, 180, 300, 0, 270

Responses from the *men* in the class were

180, 300, 60, 480, 0, 90, 300, 14, 600, 360, 120, 0, 240

a. Compare the women to the men using a dotplot. What does your plot show you about the difference between the men and the women?
b. For each gender, determine the median response.
c. Do you think there's a "significant" difference between the weekly amount that men and women exercise? Explain.

1.18 Refer to the previous exercise.
a. Create a five-number summary for the men's responses. Show how you found your answer.
b. Use your five-number summary to describe in words the exercise behavior of this group of students.

1.19 Case Study 1.6 reported that the use of aspirin reduces the risk of heart attack and that the relationship was found to be "statistically significant." Does either of the cautions in the "moral of the story" for Case Study 1.7 apply to this result? Explain.

1.20 An article in the magazine *Science* (Service, 1994) discussed a study comparing the health of 6000 vegetarians and a similar number of their friends and relatives who were not vegetarians. The vegetarians had a 28% lower death rate from heart attacks and a 39% lower death rate from cancer, even after the researchers accounted for differences in smoking, weight, and social class. In other words, the reported percentages were the remaining differences after adjusting for differences in death rates due to those factors.
a. Is this an observational study or a randomized experiment? Explain.
b. On the basis of this information, can we conclude that a vegetarian diet causes lower death rates from heart attacks and cancer? Explain.
c. Give an example of a potential confounding variable and explain what it means to say that this is a confounding variable.

1.21 Refer to the previous exercise, comparing vegetarians and nonvegetarians for two causes of death. Were base rates given for the two causes of death? If so, what were they? If not, explain what a base rate would be for this study.

1.22 An article in the *Sacramento Bee* (March 8, 1984, p. A1) reported on a study finding that "men who drank 500 ounces or more of beer a month (about 16 ounces a day) were three times more likely to develop cancer of the rectum than nondrinkers." In other words, the rate of cancer was triple in the beer-drinking group when compared with the nonbeer drinkers in this study. What important numerical information is missing from this report?

1.23 Dr. Richard Hurt and his colleagues (Hurt et. al., 1994) randomly assigned volunteers wanting to quit smoking to wear either a nicotine patch or a placebo patch to determine whether wearing a nicotine patch improves the chance of quitting. After 8 weeks of use, 46% of those wearing the nicotine patch but only 20% of those wearing the placebo patch had quit smoking.
a. Was this a randomized experiment or an observational study?
b. The difference in the percent of participants who quit (20% versus 46%) was statistically significant. What conclusion can be made on the basis of this study?
c. Why was it advisable to assign some of the participants to wear a placebo patch?

1.24 Refer to the study in the previous exercise, in which there was a statistically significant difference in the percent of smokers who quit using a nicotine patch and a placebo patch. Now read the two cautions in the "moral of the story" for Case Study 1.7. Discuss each of them in the context of this study.

1.25 Refer to the study in the previous two exercises, comparing the percent of smokers who quit using a nicotine patch and a placebo patch. Refer to the definition of statistics given on page 1, and explain how it applies to this study.

1.26 The Roper Organization conducted a poll in 1992 (Roper, 1992) in which one of the questions asked was whether or not the respondent had ever seen a ghost. Of the 1525 people in the 18 to 29-year-old age group, 212 said "yes."
a. What is the risk of someone in this age group seeing a ghost?
b. What is the approximate margin of error that accompanies the proportion in (a)?
c. What is the interval that is 95% certain to contain the actual proportion of people in this age group who have seen a ghost?

1.27 Refer to the previous exercise. The Roper Organization selected a random sample of adults in the United States for this poll. Suppose listeners to a late-night radio talk show were asked to call and report whether or not they had ever seen a ghost.
a. What is this type of sample called?
b. Do you think the proportion reporting that they had seen a ghost for the radio poll would be higher or lower than the proportion for the Roper poll? Explain.

1.28 A popular Sunday newspaper magazine often includes a yes or no survey question such as "Do you think there is too much violence on television?" or "Do you think parents should use physical discipline?" Readers are asked to mail their answers to the magazine and the results are reported in a subsequent issue.
a. What is this type of sample called?
b. Do you think the results of these polls represent the opinions of all readers of the magazine? Explain.

1.29 Refer to Case Study 1.6. Go through the five steps listed for "The Discovery of Knowledge" in Section 1.3, and show how each step was addressed in this study.

1.30 Refer to Case Study 1.5. Explain what mistakes were made in the implementation of steps 4 and 5 of "The Discovery of Knowledge" when *USA Today* reported the results of this study.

REFERENCES

Davis, Robert (1998). "Prayer can lower blood pressure," *USA Today,* August 11, 1998, p. 1D.

Elias, Marilyn (2001). "Web use not always a downer. Study disputes link to depression," *USA Today,* July 23, 2001, p. 1D.

Harmon, Amy (1998). "Sad, lonely world discovered in cyberspace," *New York Times,* August 30, 1998, p. A3.

Hite, Shere (1987). *Women and Love,* New York: Knopf.

Hurt, R., L. Dale, P. Fredrickson, C. Caldwell, G. Lee, K. Offord, G. Lauger, Z. Maruisic, L. Neese, and T. Lundberg (1994). "Nicotine patch therapy for smoking cessation combined with physician advice and nurse follow-up," *Journal of the American Medical Association,* Feb. 23, 1994, Vol. 271, No. 8, pp. 595–600.

Kraut, R., V. Lundmark, M. Patterson, S. Kiesler, T. Mukopadhyay, and W. Scherlis (1998). "Internet paradox: A social technology that reduces social involvement and psychological well-being?" *American Psychologist,* Vol. 53, No. 9, pp. 1017–1031.

Levin, Alan (1999). "Planes get closer in midair as traffic control errors rise," *USA Today,* February 24, 1999, p. 1A.

Moore, David S. (1997). *Statistics: Concepts and Controversies,* 4th ed., New York: W. H. Freeman.

Peterson, Karen S. (1997). "Interracial dates common among today's teenagers," *Sacramento Bee,* November 3, 1997, p. A6.

Roper Center (1996). "University of California Faculty Opinion Survey on Affirmative Action Policies," Roper Center for Public Opinion Research, Press Release, January 15, 1996.

The Roper Organization (1992). *Unusual personal experiences: An analysis of the data from three national surveys,* Las Vegas: Bigelow Holding Corp.

Service, R. F. (1994). "Dropping cholesterol—safely," *Science,* Nov 25, 1994, Vol. 266, No. 5189, p. 1323.

The Steering Committee of the Physicians' Health Study Research Group (1988). "Preliminary report: Findings from the aspirin component of the ongoing Physicians' Health Study," *New England Journal of Medicine,* Vol. 318, No. 4, Jan. 28,1988, pp. 262–264.

CHAPTER 2

Turning Data Into Information

The average weight of the men in this boat might be lower than you think. See Example 2.7.

Bob Daemmrich /Stock Boston /PictureQuest

Looking at a long list of numbers is about the same as looking at a scrambled set of letters. To get information from numerical data, you have to organize it in ways that allow you to answer questions of concern to you.

I n Case Study 1.1, we analyzed the responses that 189 college students gave to the question "What's the fastest you've ever driven a car?" The "moral of the story" for that case study was that *simple summaries of data can tell an interesting story and are easier to digest than long lists.* In this chapter, you will learn how to create simple summaries and pictures from various kinds of raw data. ◆

2.1 | RAW DATA

Raw data is a term used for numbers and category labels that have been collected but have not yet been processed in any way. For example, here is a list of questions that were asked in a large statistics class and the "raw data" given by one of the students:

1. What is your sex (m = male, f = female)?   Raw data: m
2. How many hours did you sleep last night?   Raw data: 5 hours
3. Randomly pick a letter—*S* or *Q*.   Raw data: *S*
4. What is your height in inches?   Raw data: 67 inches
5. Randomly pick a number between 1 and 10.   Raw data: 3
6. What's the fastest you've ever driven a car (mph)?   Raw data: 110 mph
7. What is your right handspan in centimeters?   Raw data: 21.5 cm
8. What is your left handspan in centimeters?   Raw data: 21.5 cm

For questions 7 and 8, a centimeter ruler was provided on the survey form and handspan was defined as the distance covered on the ruler by a stretched hand, from the tip of the thumb to the tip of the small finger. You may be wondering why questions 3 and 5 were asked. Your curiosity will be satisfied as you keep reading this chapter!

2.1
turn on your mind

There were almost 200 students who answered these survey questions. Formulate four interesting questions you would like to answer using the data from these students. What kind of summary information would help you answer your questions?*

Data from Populations and Samples

tech note   In Chapter 1, Case Study 1.3, we learned that data from a representative sample can provide information about the larger population represented by the data. When measurements are taken from a subset of a population, they represent **sample data.** When all individuals in a population are measured, the measurements represent **population data.** Sometimes the reason for collecting the data is important in making this distinction. For instance, data measured in a statistics class is population data if just that class is of interest but is sample data if it is to be used to represent a larger collection of students.

The use of sample data to make inferences about populations is a major theme of this book, and it is important to determine whether raw data were obtained from a sample or from the complete population. However, the material in this chapter explains how to summarize data, and these descriptive methods are the same for both sample and population data. Therefore, in this chapter we will distinguish between sample and population data only when the notation differs for the two situations.

The generic names used for summary measures from sample and population data also differ. A summary measure computed from sample data is called a **statistic,** while a summary measure for an entire population is called a **parameter.** However, this distinction is often overlooked when numerical summaries are the only information of interest from either a population or a sample. In that case, the summary numbers for either a population or a sample are simply called **descriptive statistics.** We will begin to emphasize the distinction between populations and samples in Chapter 9.

2.2 | TYPES OF DATA

Different types of summaries are appropriate for different types of data. It makes sense, for example, to calculate the average number of hours of sleep last night for the members of a group, but it doesn't make sense to calculate the average sex (male, female) for the group. For gender data, it makes more sense to determine the proportion of the group that's male and the proportion that's female.

A **variable** is a characteristic that differs from one individual to the next. A variable may be a *categorical* characteristic, like a person's sex, or a *numerical* characteristic, like hours of sleep last night. To determine what type of summary

*HINT: An example is, "What was the average amount of sleep for these students?" Case Study 1.1 could be utilized to generate another example.

might provide meaningful information, you first have to recognize which type of variable you want to summarize.

The raw data from a **categorical variable** consists of group or category names that don't necessarily have any logical ordering. Each individual falls into one and only one category. For a categorical variable, the most fundamental summaries are how many individuals and what percent of the group fall into each category. Here are a few examples of categorical variables and their possible categories:

Variable	Possible Categories
Dominant hand	Left-handed, Right-handed
Regular church attendance	Yes, No
Opinion about marijuana legalization	Yes, No, Not sure
Eye color	Brown, Blue, Green, Hazel

Raw data from **quantitative variables** are recorded as numerical values, and the data are either measurements or counts taken on each individual. All individuals can be meaningfully ordered according to these values, and averaging and other arithmetic operations make sense for these data. Some examples of quantitative variables are height, weight, hours of sleep last night, years of education, and number of classes missed this week.

Quantitative variable, **measurement variable,** and **numerical variable** are all similar terms for quantitative data. The term **continuous variable** can also be used for quantitative data when every value within some interval is a possible result. For example, height is a continuous quantitative variable because any height within some range is possible. The limitations of measuring tapes, however, don't allow us to measure heights accurately enough to find that a person's actual height is 66.5382617 inches. Even if we could measure that accurately, we would usually prefer to round such a height to 66.5 inches.

Not all numbers fit the definition of a quantitative variable. For instance, Social Security numbers or student identification numbers may carry some information (like region of the country where the Social Security number was obtained), but it is not generally meaningful to put them into numerical order or to determine the average Social Security number.

A data type can be a function of how something is measured. For instance, household income is a numerical value with two digits after the decimal place, and if it's recorded this way, it is a quantitative variable. Researchers, however, often collect household income data using ordered categories like 1 = less than $25,000; 2 = $25,000 to $50,000; 3 = $50,000 to $75,000; and so on. When household income is recorded using categories like these, it becomes a categorical variable. In some situations, household income could be categorized very broadly, as when it is used to determine whether or not someone qualifies for a loan. In that case, income may either be "high enough" to qualify for the loan or "not high enough."

Sometimes the distinction between categorical and quantitative data is ambiguous or depends on the purpose. For example, "shoe size" could be used as a categorical variable if the Army needed to know how many of each size to manufacture for new soldiers, but used as a quantitative variable as a measure of foot size. As another example, suppose that you are asked to rate your driving skills compared to the skills of other drivers, using the codes 1 = better than average,

2 = average, and 3 = worse than average. The response is a categorical variable with arbitrary numbers attached to the category labels. It could, however, still be informative to find the average of the responses to see if it is close to 2, which it should be if everyone gives an honest appraisal. On the other hand, it would not make sense to talk about "average household income" using the numerical codes attached to the income categories described in the previous paragraph (1 = less than $25,000; 2 = $25,000 to $50,000; and so on).

When a categorical variable has ordered categories, the term **ordinal variable** is sometimes used to describe the data. Both the rating of driver skill variable and the categorized household income variable just described could be called ordinal variables. Another example of an ordinal variable is the response to the instruction "On a scale of 1 to 7 where 1 = poor and 7 = excellent, rate your teacher."

---

in summary **Types of Variables**

♦ Raw data from *categorical variables* consist of group or category names that don't necessarily have a logical ordering. Examples: eye color, country of residence.

♦ Categorical variables for which the categories have a logical ordering are called *ordinal variables*. Examples: highest educational degree earned, tee shirt size (S, M, L, XL).

♦ Raw data from *quantitative variables* consist of numerical values taken on each individual. Examples: height, number of siblings.

turn on your mind

Review the data collected in the statistics class, listed in Section 2.1, and identify a type for each variable. The only one that is ambiguous is question 5. That question asks for a numerical response, but as we will see later in this chapter, it is more interesting to summarize the responses as if they are categorical.*

Asking the Right Questions

As with most situations in life, the information you get when you summarize a data set depends on how careful you are about asking for what you want. Here is a brief summary of the questions that are most commonly of interest for various kinds of variables and combinations, with an example given in each case.

One Categorical Variable

Question 1a: How many and what percentage of individuals fall into each category?

---

*HINT: For each variable, consider whether the raw data are meaningful quantities or category names.

Example: What percentage of college students favor the legalization of marijuana, and what percentage of college students oppose legalization of marijuana?

Question 1b: Are individuals equally divided across categories, or do the percentages across categories follow some other interesting pattern?

Example: When individuals are asked to choose a number from 1 to 10, are all numbers equally likely to be chosen?

Two Categorical Variables

Question 2a: Is there a relationship between the two variables, so that the category into which individuals fall for one variable seems to depend on which category they are in for the other variable?

Example: In Case Study 1.6, we asked if the risk of having a heart attack was different for the physicians who took aspirin than for those who took a placebo.

Question 2b: Do some combinations of categories stand out because they provide information that is not found by examining the categories separately?

Example: The relationship between smoking and lung cancer was detected, in part, because someone noticed that the *combination* of being a nonsmoker and having lung cancer is unusual.

One Quantitative Variable

Question 3a: What are the interesting summary measures, like the average or the range of values, that help us understand the collection of individuals who were measured?

Example: What is the average handspan measurement, and how much variability is there in handspan measurements?

Question 3b: Are there individual data values that provide interesting information because they are unique or stand out in some way?

Example: What is the oldest recorded age of death for a human? Are there many people who have lived nearly that long, or is the oldest recorded age a unique case?

One Categorical and One Quantitative Variable

Question 4a: Are the measurements similar across categories?

Example: Do men and women drive at the same "fastest speeds" on average?

Question 4b: When the categories have a natural ordering (an ordinal variable), does the measurement variable increase or decrease, on average, in that same order?

Example: Do high school dropouts, high school graduates, college dropouts, and college graduates have increasingly higher average incomes?

Two Quantitative Variables

Question 5a: If the measurement on one variable is high (or low), does the other one also tend to be high (or low)?

Example: Do taller people also tend to have larger handspans?

Question 5b: Are there individuals whose combination of data values provides interesting information because that combination is unusual?

Example: An individual who has a very low IQ score but can perform complicated arithmetic operations very quickly may shed light on how the brain works. Neither the IQ nor the arithmetic ability may stand out as uniquely low or high, but it is the combination that is interesting.

Sometimes it's the summary or aggregate information that is most interesting, and sometimes it is the uniqueness of certain individuals. Part of the fun and creativity of analyzing data comes from deciding which questions to ask in each context. When you encounter a dataset, return to these questions and others we will add as we encounter new situations to guide your exploration.

Explanatory and Response Variables

Many of the questions just listed were questions about the relationship between two variables (questions 2a, 2b, 4a, 4b, 5a, and 5b). In these instances, it is useful to identify one variable as the **explanatory variable** and the other variable as the **response variable.** In general, the value of the explanatory variable for an individual is thought to partially explain the value of the response variable for that individual. For example, in examining the relationship between smoking and lung cancer, whether or not an individual smokes is the explanatory variable, and whether or not he or she develops lung cancer is the response variable. If we note that people with higher education levels generally have higher incomes, education level is the explanatory variable and income is the response variable. The identification of one variable as "explanatory" and the other as "response" does not imply that there is a *causal* relationship. It simply implies that knowledge of the value of the explanatory variable may help provide knowledge of the value of the response variable for an individual.

2.3 | SUMMARIZING ONE OR TWO CATEGORICAL VARIABLES

Numerical Summaries

The first step in summarizing a categorical variable is to simply count how many individuals fall into each category. Because percents are usually more informative than counts, the second step is to calculate the percent in each category. This simple method can also be used to summarize a combination of two categorical variables.

EXAMPLE 2.1
The Importance of Order

In the sample survey described in Section 2.1, there were 92 students who responded to question 3, "Randomly pick a letter—*S* or *Q*." The results are displayed in Table 2.1.

Notice that about 66% picked the first choice they were given, *S,* and only 34% picked the second choice, *Q*. This result raises an interesting question that might be relevant when you read the results of a survey or look at the results of an election. When people are given a set of options, are they more likely to pick the first choice?

A second possible explanation of the result is that the students liked the letter *S* better than the letter *Q*. For the 92 students described above, the letter *S* was always the first letter presented, so we can't tell if there was a general preference for the first possible choice or for the letter *S*. To clarify this confusion, the teacher actually used two different forms of the question, randomly distributed among the class. The second form asked students to "Randomly pick a letter—*Q* or *S*." The order of presenting the two letters has been reversed.

TABLE 2.1 ■ Letter Picked When Asked to Pick Either *S* or *Q*

Letter Picked	Frequency	Percent
S	61	66%
Q	31	34%
Total	92	100%

TABLE 2.2 ■ Order of Letters on Form and Choice of Letter

	S Picked	*Q* Picked	Total
S Listed First	61 (66%)	31 (34%)	92
Q Listed First	45 (46%)	53 (54%)	98
Total	106 (56%)	84 (44%)	190

The results are displayed in Table 2.2. There was a clear propensity for picking the letter that was presented first. This tendency was stronger when *S* was listed first. In that case, 66% of the students picked the first choice (*S*). With *Q* listed first, 54% picked the first choice (*Q*). In all, $(61 + 53)/190 = 60\%$ of the 190 respondents picked the first letter.

One more explanation for the results should be considered. Perhaps everyone really did pick randomly, and the results were this unbalanced just by chance. In Chapter 6, we will learn how to determine that the chance such unbalanced results would occur if everyone picked randomly is less than 1 in 200. This isn't much of a chance, so a "chance luck" explanation seems unreasonable. ◆

EXAMPLE 2.2
Lighting the Way to Nearsightedness

A survey of 479 children found that those who had slept with a nightlight or in a fully lit room before the age of 2 had a higher incidence of nearsightedness (myopia) later in childhood (*Sacramento Bee,* May 13, 1999, pp. A1, A18). The raw data for each child consisted of two categorical variables, each with three categories. Table 2.3 gives the categories and the number of children falling into each combination of them. The pattern in Table 2.3 is striking. As the amount of sleeptime light increases, the incidence of myopia also increases. However, this study does not prove that sleeping with light actually *caused* myopia in more children. There are other possible explanations. For example, myopia has a genetic component, so those children whose parents have myopia are more likely to suffer from it themselves. Maybe nearsighted parents are more likely to provide light while their children are sleeping. ◆

TABLE 2.3 ■ Nighttime Lighting in Infancy and Eyesight

Slept with:	No Myopia	Myopia	High Myopia	Total
Darkness	155 (90%)	15 (9%)	2 (1%)	172
Nightlight	153 (66%)	72 (31%)	7 (3%)	232
Full Light	34 (45%)	36 (48%)	5 (7%)	75
Total	342 (71%)	123 (26%)	14 (3%)	479

2.3

turn on your mind

Can you think of possible explanations for the observed relationship between use of nightlights and myopia, other than direct cause and effect? What additional information might help provide an explanation?*

*HINT: Reread Example 2.2 where one possible explanation is mentioned. What data would we need to investigate the possible explanation mentioned there?

Explanatory and Response Variables for Categorical Variables

In both Example 2.1 and Example 2.2, percentages were given across rows. For instance, Table 2.3 in Example 2.2 shows that 90% (100% × 155/172) of those who slept in darkness were free of myopia, but only 45% of those who slept in full light were free of myopia. The table does not provide "column percentages" such as the fact that 34/342 or about 10% of those who were free of myopia had slept in full light.

When summarizing two categorical variables, it may be possible to identify one variable as a response variable (or **outcome variable**), and the other as an explanatory variable. In Example 2.1, the outcome variable is the letter chosen and the explanatory variable is the question form the student received. In Example 2.2, the outcome variable is degree of myopia and the explanatory variable is the amount of sleeptime lighting.

Notice that in both examples, the categories of the explanatory variable defined the rows of the table and the categories of the response variable defined the columns. Tables often are formed this way, and when they are, the row percentages are of more interest than the column percentages. No matter how the table is constructed, you should determine if one variable is a response variable and the other is an explanatory variable. Within each explanatory group, we are interested in knowing what percent fell into each response or outcome.

Minitab Tip

 tech note   **Numerically Describing One or Two Categorical Variables**

◆ To determine how many and what percent fall into the categories of a categorical variable, use **Stat>Tables>Tally**. In the dialog box, specify a column containing the raw data for a categorical variable, and click on any desired options for counts and percents.

◆ To create a two-way table for two categorical variables, use **Stat>Tables>Cross Tabulation.** In the dialog box, specify the two columns containing the raw data for the variables, and then choose any desired percents (row and/or column and/or total).

Visual Summaries for Categorical Variables

There are two simple visual summaries used for categorical data:

◆ **Pie charts** are useful for summarizing a single categorical variable if there are not too many categories.

◆ **Bar graphs** are useful for summarizing one or two categorical variables and are particularly useful for making comparisons when there are two categorical variables.

Both of these simple graphical displays are easy to construct and interpret, as the following examples demonstrate.

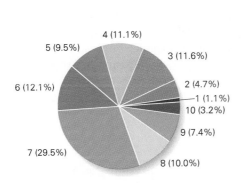

FIGURE 2.1   **Pie chart of numbers picked**

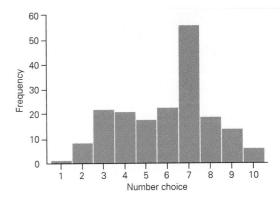

FIGURE 2.2   **Bar graph of numbers picked**

EXAMPLE 2.3
Humans Are Not Good Randomizers

Question 5 in the class survey described in Section 2.1 asked students to "Randomly pick a number between 1 and 10." The pie chart shown in Figure 2.1 illustrates that the results are not even close to being evenly distributed across the numbers. Notice that almost 30% of the students chose 7 while only just over 1% chose the number 1.

Figure 2.2 illustrates the same results with a bar graph. This bar graph shows the actual frequencies of responses on the vertical axis. The display makes it even more obvious that the number of students who chose 7 was more than double that of the next most popular choice. We also see that very few students chose either 1 or 10. ◆

EXAMPLE 2.4
Revisiting Nightlights and Nearsightedness

Figure 2.3 illustrates the data presented in Example 2.2 with a bar chart showing, for each lighting group, the percent that ultimately had each level of myopia. This bar chart differs from the one in Figure 2.2 in two respects. First, it is used to present data for two categorical variables instead of just one. Second, the vertical axis represents percents instead of counts, with the percents for myopia status computed separately within each lighting category. ◆

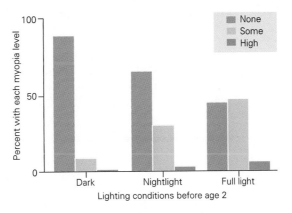

FIGURE 2.3   **Bar chart for myopia and nighttime lighting in infancy**

2.4

turn on your mind

Redo the bar graph in Figure 2.3 using counts instead of percents. The necessary data are given in Table 2.3. Would the comparison of frequency of myopia across the categories of lighting be as easy to make using the bar graph with counts? Generalize your conclusion to provide guidance about what should be done in similar situations.*

---

in summary   Bar Graphs for Categorical Variables

In a bar graph for *one categorical variable,* you can choose one of the following to display as the height of a bar for each category, indicated by labeling the vertical axis:

◆ Frequency or count

◆ Relative frequency = number in category/overall number

◆ Percent = relative frequency × 100%

In a bar graph for *two categorical variables,* if an explanatory and response variable can be identified it is most common to:

◆ Draw a separate group of bars for each category of the explanatory variable.

◆ Within each group of bars, draw one bar for each category of the response variable.

◆ Label the vertical axis with percents and make the heights of the bars for the response categories sum to 100% within each explanatory category group. It can sometimes be useful to make the heights of the bars equal the counts in the category groups instead of percents.

Minitab Tip

tech note   **Graphically Describing a Categorical Variable**

◆ To draw a *bar graph* of a categorical variable, use **Graph> Chart.** In the dialog box, specify a column containing the raw data for a categorical variable as the X variable. Do not make any other specifications.

◆ To draw a *pie chart* of a categorical variable, use **Graph>Pie Chart.**

---

graph of percents?

graphs? What could be learned from the graph of counts that isn't apparent from the

***HINT:** Which graph makes it easier to compare the percent with myopia for the three*

2.4 | FINDING INFORMATION IN QUANTITATIVE DATA

Looking at a long list of numbers is about the same as looking at a scrambled set of letters. To get information from numerical data, you have to organize it in ways that allow you to answer questions of concern to you. For instance, do you know if, compared to others of your sex, your hands are large, small, or average? Table 2.4 displays the raw data for the right handspan measurements (in centimeters) made by the students in the survey described in Section 2.1.

Find a ruler with a centimeter scale and use the ruler to measure your own handspan. Stretch out your hand and measure from the tip of your thumb to the tip of your small finger. Can you see how your measurement compares to the students of your sex in Table 2.4? That's probably hard to see because the list of data values is disorganized.

Five-Number Summaries

In the "fastest ever driven" example of Case Study 1.1, you learned how to display a **five-number summary** of a list of data values by finding the extremes (high, low), the median, and the quartiles (roughly, the medians of the lower and upper halves of the values). A five-number summary provides a quick overview of the data values and information about the center, spread, and shape of the data as well. Specific instructions for finding the median and quartiles are given in Section 2.6. In this section, the focus is on interpreting these summary values.

EXAMPLE 2.5
Right Handspans

Here are five-number summaries for male and female responses to the survey question asking students to measure the span of their right hands:

	Males (87 Students)		Females (103 Students)	
Median		22.5		20.0
Quartiles	21.5	23.5	19.0	21.0
Extremes	18.0	26.0	12.5	23.25

Remember that the five-number summary divides the dataset into approximate quarters. For example, about 25% of the handspans of females are between

TABLE 2.4 ■ **Stretched Right Handspans (cm) of 190 College Students**

Males (87 students):
21.5, 22.5, 23.5, 23, 24.5, 23, 26, 23, 21.5, 21.5, 24.5, 23.5, 22, 23.5, 22, 24.5, 23, 22.5, 19.5, 22.5, 22, 23, 22.5, 20.5, 21.5, 23, 22.5, 21.5, 25, 24, 21.5, 21.5, 18, 20, 22, 24, 22, 23, 22, 22, 23, 22.5, 25.5, 24, 23.5, 21, 25.5, 23, 22.5, 24, 21.5, 22, 22.5, 23, 18.5, 21, 24, 23.5, 24.5, 23, 22, 23, 23, 24, 24.5, 20.5, 24, 22, 23, 21, 22.5, 21.5, 24.5, 22, 22, 21, 23, 22.5, 24, 22.5, 23, 23, 23, 21.5, 19, 21.5

Females (103 Students):
20, 19, 20.5, 20.5, 20.25, 20, 18, 20.5, 22, 20, 21.5, 17, 16, 22, 22, 20, 20, 20, 20, 21.7, 22, 20, 21, 21, 19, 21, 20.25, 21, 22, 18, 20, 21, 19, 22.5, 21, 20, 19, 21, 20.5, 21, 22, 20, 20, 18, 21, 22.5, 22.5, 19, 19, 19, 22.5, 20, 13, 20, 22.5, 19.5, 18.5, 19, 17.5, 18, 21, 19.5, 20, 19, 21.5, 18, 19, 19.5, 20, 22.5, 21, 18, 22, 18.5, 19, 22, 17, 12.5, 18, 20.5, 19, 20, 21, 19, 19, 21, 18.5, 19, 21.5, 21.5, 23, 23.25, 20, 18.8, 21, 21, 20, 20.5, 20, 19.5, 21, 21, 20

12.5 and 19.0 centimeters, about 25% are between 19 and 20 cm, about 25% are between 20 and 21 cm, and about 25% are between 21 and 23.25 cm. The five-number summary should give you a sense of where your own handspan measurement fits into the distribution of handspans for your gender. ◆

Interesting Summary Features of Quantitative Variables

For most quantitative variables, there are three summary characteristics of the overall distribution of the data that tend to be of the most interest. These are the **location** (center, average), the **spread** (variability), and the **shape** of the data. From a five-number summary, you can learn about location and spread. The median is an estimate of the *location* or *center* of the data. The difference between the two extremes and the difference between the two quartiles tell us about the *spread* of the data. Later in this section, you'll learn how to characterize the *shape* of a distribution.

Outliers

Another interesting feature to consider is whether any individual values are **outliers.** There is no precise definition for an outlier, but in general, an outlier is a data point that is not consistent with the bulk of the data. For a single variable, an outlier is a value that is unusually high or low. When two variables are considered, an outlier is an unusual combination of values. For instance, if you look back at Example 2.5, you will see that a female with a handspan of 24.5 cm would be an outlier because this handspan is well past the largest of the measurements made by the 103 females. On the other hand, a male with a handspan of 24.5 cm is not an outlier because this measurement is clearly within the normal range for males.

The next example illustrates that sometimes the extreme points are the most interesting features of a dataset.

EXAMPLE 2.6
Ages of Death
of U.S. First Ladies

Much has been written about ages of U.S. Presidents when elected and at death, but what about their wives? Do these women tend to live short lives or long lives? Table 2.5 lists the First Ladies of the United States and their approximate ages at death (to within one year) as listed in late 2002 at the White House website.[1] It is not completely accurate to label all of these women "First Ladies" if the strict definition is "the wife of a President while in office." For example, Harriet Lane served socially as "First Lady" to President James Buchanan, but he was unmarried and she was his niece. A few of the women listed died before their husband's term in office. Nonetheless, we will use the data as provided by the White House and summarize the ages at death for these women. Here is a five-number summary for these ages:

	First Ladies' Ages at Death	
Median		70
Quartiles	60	81.5
Extremes	34	97

---

[1]http://www.whitehouse.gov/WH/glimpse/firstladies/html/firstladies.html

TABLE 2.5 ■ The First Ladies of the United States of America

Name	Born–Died	Age at Death
Martha Dandridge Custis Washington	1731–1802	71
Abigail Smith Adams	1744–1818	74
Martha Wayles Skelton Jefferson	1748–1782	34
Dolley Payne Todd Madison	1768–1849	81
Elizabeth Kortright Monroe	1768–1830	62
Louisa Catherine Johnson Adams	1775–1852	77
Rachel Donelson Jackson	1767–1828	61
Hannah Hoes Van Buren	1783–1819	36
Anna Tuthill Symmes Harrison	1775–1864	89
Letitia Christian Tyler	1790–1842	52
Julia Gardiner Tyler	1820–1889	69
Sarah Childress Polk	1803–1891	88
Margaret Mackall Smith Taylor	1788–1852	64
Abigail Powers Fillmore	1798–1853	55
Jane Means Appleton Pierce	1806–1863	57
Harriet Lane	1830–1903	73
Mary Todd Lincoln	1818–1882	64
Eliza McCardle Johnson	1810–1876	66
Julia Dent Grant	1826–1902	76
Lucy Ware Webb Hayes	1831–1889	58
Lucretia Rudolph Garfield	1832–1918	86
Ellen Lewis Herndon Arthur	1837–1880	43
Frances Folsom Cleveland	1864–1947	83
Caroline Lavinia Scott Harrison	1832–1892	60
Ida Saxton McKinley	1847–1907	60
Edith Kermit Carow Roosevelt	1861–1948	87
Helen Herron Taft	1861–1943	82
Ellen Louise Axson Wilson	1860–1914	54
Edith Bolling Galt Wilson	1872–1961	89
Florence Kling Harding	1860–1924	64
Grace Anna Goodhue Coolidge	1879–1957	78
Lou Henry Hoover	1874–1944	70
Anna Eleanor Roosevelt Roosevelt	1884–1962	78
Elizabeth Virginia Wallace Truman	1885–1982	97
Mamie Geneva Doud Eisenhower	1896–1979	83
Jacqueline Lee Bouvier Kennedy Onassis	1929–1994	65
Claudia Taylor Johnson	1912–	
Patricia Ryan Nixon	1912–1993	81
Elizabeth Bloomer Ford	1918–	
Rosalynn Smith Carter	1927–	
Nancy Davis Reagan	1923–	
Barbara Pierce Bush	1925–	
Hillary Rodham Clinton	1947–	
Laura Welch Bush	1946–	

If you are at all interested in history, this summary will make you curious about the extreme points. Who died at 34? Who lived to be 97? The extremes are more interesting features of this dataset than the summary of ages in the middle, which tend to match what we would expect for ages at death. From Table 2.5 you can see that Thomas Jefferson's wife Martha died in 1782 at age 34, almost 20 years before he entered office. He reportedly was devastated and he never remarried, although historians believe that he may have had other children in his relationship with Sally Hemmings. At the other extreme, Bess Truman died in 1982 at age 97; her husband Harry preceded her in death by ten years, but he too lived a long life—he died at age 88. ◆

How to Handle Outliers

Should we attach the label "outlier" to either of the most extreme points in the list of ages at death for the First Ladies? To study this issue, we have to examine all of the data to see if the two extremes clearly stand apart from the other values. If you look over Table 2.5, you may be able to form an opinion about whether Martha Jefferson and Bess Truman should be called outliers. Making sense of a list of numbers, however, is difficult. The most effective way to look for outliers is to graph the data, which we will learn to do later in this chapter.

Outliers need special attention because they can have a big influence on conclusions drawn from a dataset, and because they can lead to erroneous conclusions if they are not treated appropriately. Remember that outliers are data values that are not consistent with the bulk of the data, for either a single variable or a combination of variables.

Outliers can also cause complications in some statistical analysis procedures, as you will learn throughout this book. As a result, some researchers wrongly discard them rather than treat them as legitimate data. Outliers should never be discarded without justification. The first step in deciding what to do with outliers is determining why they exist, so that appropriate action can be taken.

in summary **Possible Reasons for Outliers and Reasonable Actions**

- *A mistake was made while taking a measurement or entering it into the computer.* If this can be verified, the values should be discarded or corrected.

- *The individual in question belongs to a different group than the bulk of individuals measured.* Values may be discarded if a summary is desired and reported for the majority group only.

- *The outlier is a legitimate data value and represents natural variability for the group and variable(s) measured.* Values may not be discarded in this case—they provide important information about location and spread.

Let's consider each of these possible reasons for outliers, and what to do about them.

A Mistake Was Made While Taking a Measurement or Entering It into the Computer

Sometimes faulty equipment or unclear instructions can cause an outlier. For example, a data value of 8 would be recorded for a woman's right handspan measurement if she had a span of 20 cm but misunderstood and reported the measurement in inches instead of centimeters. A faulty thermometer or a clock with a dying battery can result in erroneous measurements of temperature and time. Misuse of equipment or inexperienced technicians can distort measurements. More blatant mistakes can occur when data values are recorded or typed incorrectly, such as when a height of 68 inches is recorded as 86 inches. Fortunately, outliers caused by these kinds of problems are often easy to identify and should be removed from the dataset or, if possible, corrected and retained.

*The Individual in Question Belongs to a
Different Group Than the Bulk of Individuals Measured*

Sometimes a collection of measurements is taken on a group that contains a few individuals who are not like everyone else. For instance, a college class may include mostly traditional-age students (perhaps 18 to 22) but a few retirees. Measurements taken on variables related to age, such as total dollar value of assets owned, may result in outliers for the retirees. Or consider the relationship in real estate sales between the size of a house (square feet) and sales price for the house and property. If the home sales in an area are mostly suburban dwellings but a few farms are included, the sales prices for the farms will be much higher than comparable houses of the same size.

When outliers result from the inclusion of a few individuals who are different from the others for an obvious reason, the decision about whether to retain the outliers must be made based on the question of interest. For example, in measuring assets owned by college students, if interest is in the value of assets owned by traditional-age students, then the measurements taken on students who are not in that age range should be discarded before the dataset is analyzed. If the question of interest concerns all college students, then all measurements should be retained. In that case, the relationship between age and assets may be of primary interest.

**EXAMPLE 2.7
Tiny Boatsmen**

Here are the weights (in pounds) of 18 men who were on the crew teams at Oxford and Cambridge universities (*The Independent,* March 31, 1992, also Hand, D. J. et al., 1994, p. 337.):

> *Cambridge:* 188.5, 183.0, 194.5, 185.0, 214.0, 203.5, 186.0, 178.5, 109.0
> *Oxford:* 186.0, 184.5, 204.0, 184.5, 195.5, 202.5, 174.0, 183.0, 109.5

Read over the list. Do you notice anything unusual? The last weight given in each list is very different from the others. In fact, those two men were the coxswains for their teams, while the other men were the rowers. What is the mean weight for the crew team members? If all members are included, it is 181 pounds. If only the rowers are included, it is 190 pounds. Different questions, different answers. ◆

*The Outlier Is a Legitimate Data Value and Represents
Natural Variability for the Group and Variable(s) Measured*

Characterizing the natural variability in a collection of measurements is one of the most important themes in statistics and data analysis. Outliers that are inherent in measurements of a particular type should never be discarded unless the goal is to study only a partial range of the possible values. As we will see in the next section, the two smallest female handspan measurements, 12.5 cm and 13.0 cm, were well below the remainder of the measurements. But they provide important information about the spectrum of possibilities. Discarding them for no reason would result in an erroneous depiction of these measurements, with a mean that was too high and measure of spread that was too low.

2.5 | PICTURES FOR QUANTITATIVE DATA

There are three similar types of pictures that are used to represent quantitative variables, all of which are valuable for assessing center, spread, shape, and outliers. **Histograms** are similar to bar graphs and can be used for any number of

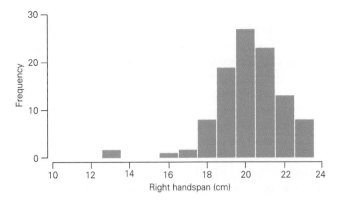

```
12 | 5
13 | 0
14 |
15 |
16 | 0
17 | 005
18 | 00000005558
19 | 0000000000000005555
20 | 000000000000000000000022555555
21 | 0000000000000000055557
22 | 00000000555555
23 | 02
```

Example: | 12 | 5 = 12.5

FIGURE 2.5   Stem-and-leaf plot of women's right handspans

FIGURE 2.4   Histogram of women's right handspans

data values. **Stem-and-leaf plots** and **dotplots** present all individual values, so for very large datasets, they are not as useful as histograms. Another kind of picture, called a **boxplot** or **box-and-whisker plot,** is useful for summarizing quantitative data and for comparing summary measures for two or more groups. Boxplots visually display the type of information given in a five-number summary and will be discussed in the next section along with some other methods for summarizing quantitative variables.

Figures 2.4 to 2.6 illustrate a histogram, stem-and-leaf plot, and dotplot, respectively, for the females' right handspans displayed in Table 2.4. Examine the three figures. Notice that if the stem-and-leaf plot were turned on its side, all three pictures would look similar.

Interpreting Histograms, Stem-and-Leaf Plots, and Dotplots

Each of these pictures is useful for assessing the location, spread, and shape of a distribution, and each is also useful for detecting outliers. For the data presented in Figures 2.4 to 2.6, notice that the values are "*centered*" around 20 cm, which we learned in Example 2.5 is indeed the median value. There are two possible *outlier* values that are low compared to the bulk of the data. These are identifiable in the stem-and-leaf plot as 12.5 and 13.0 cm, but are evident in the other two pictures as well. Except for those values, the handspans *range* from about 16 to 23 cm, and tend to be "clumped" around 20 and taper off toward 16 and 23.

Describing Shape

The *shape* of a dataset is usually described as either **symmetric** or **skewed.** A skewed dataset is either *skewed to the left* or *skewed to the right.* The shape in

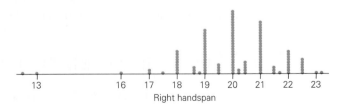

FIGURE 2.6   Dotplot of women's right handspans

Figures 2.4 to 2.6 is called "skewed to the left" because the values trail off to the left. Were it not for the two low values, the shape would be relatively "symmetric," meaning that it is similar on both sides of the center. A symmetric dataset can either be **bell-shaped** or not. Without the two low values, the data set in Figures 2.4 to 2.6 would be considered bell-shaped because the pictures would look somewhat like the shape of a bell. We will learn much more about bell-shaped curves in Section 2.7.

There are many computer programs that you can use to create these pictures. Figures 2.4, 2.5, and 2.6, for instance, are slight modifications of pictures created using Minitab. We'll go through the steps for creating each type of picture by hand, but keep in mind that statistical software like Minitab automates most of the process.

Creating a Histogram

A histogram is a bar chart of a quantitative variable that shows how many values are in various intervals of the data. The steps in creating a histogram are

Step 1: Decide how many *equally spaced* intervals to use for the horizontal axis. The experience of many researchers is that somewhere between 6 and 15 intervals is a good number. The data in Figure 2.4 ranged from 12.5 to 23.25, and Minitab chose to use 11 intervals, with each interval *centered* on an integer (12.5 to 13.5 is centered on 13, 13.5 to 14.5 is centered on 14, and so on). The intervals *must* all be the same width, so there will often be gaps like we see in Figure 2.4.

Step 2: Decide whether to use *frequencies* or *relative frequencies* on the vertical axis. Frequencies simply represent the actual number of individuals who fall into each interval. Relative frequencies represent the proportion. For instance, 2 of the 36 First Ladies died in their 30s. A relative frequency histogram would show a bar with a height of 2/36 or about .056 (or 5.6%) for the interval 30–40. It is useful to use relative frequencies when you want to compare histograms for groups with different numbers of individuals.

Step 3: Draw the appropriate number of equally spaced intervals on the horizontal axis, making sure you cover the entire range of the data. Determine the frequency or relative frequency of data values in each interval and draw a bar with corresponding height. You have to decide what rule to use for values that fall on the border between two intervals. For Figure 2.4, Minitab assigned individuals with handspans of exactly 13.5 to the interval 13.5 to 14.5, those with exactly 14.5 to the interval 14.5 to 15.5, and so on.

Additional Notes on Creating Histograms

 tech note ♦ Consider using intervals that make the range and width of each interval convenient. For instance, to create a histogram of ages at death for First Ladies, it would be convenient to use ten-year periods—died in her 30s, died in her 40s, and so on, up to 90s. This would create seven intervals.

♦ To show relative frequency, you can use either the proportion or the percent that are in an interval.

Creating a Dotplot

The dotplot in Figure 2.6 was created using the Minitab Statistical Package, and the online help feature in Minitab gives a good description of how it's done: "A dotplot displays a dot for each observation along a number line. If there are multiple occurrences of an observation, or if observations are too close together, then dots will be stacked vertically. If there are too many points to fit vertically in the graph, then each dot may represent more than one point" (Minitab, Release 12.1, 1998).

Creating a Stem-and-Leaf Plot

A stem-and-leaf plot is created much like a histogram, except every individual data value is shown. This type of plot is a quick way to summarize small datasets and is also a useful tool for ordering from lowest to highest. The basic structure of the plot is that the "stem" contains all but the last digit of a number, and the "leaf" is the last digit of the number, regardless of whether it falls before or after a decimal point.

To simplify the work, data values sometimes are truncated or rounded off. To truncate a value, digits are simply dropped. The number 23.58 is truncated to 23.5, but it is rounded off to 23.6. In Figure 2.5 the handspan values are truncated to one digit after the decimal point. The largest handspan is 23.25 cm, which is truncated to 23.2. This number is shown on the "23" stem along with the value of 23.0 cm. These two handspans are displayed as |23| 02. In other words, this stem has two leaves, each representing a different individual.

Here are the steps required to create a stem-and-leaf plot:

Step 1: Determine the stem values. Remember that the "stem" contains all but the last of the displayed digits of a number. As with histograms, it is reasonable to have between 6 and 15 stems (each stem defines an interval of values). The stems should define equally spaced intervals.

Step 2: For each individual, attach a "leaf" to the appropriate stem. A "leaf" is the last of the displayed digits of a number. It is standard, but not mandatory, to put the leaves in increasing order at each stem value.

Note: There will be more than one way to define equally spaced stems. For example, the ages at death of First Ladies range from 34 to 97. We could have stem values representing the decades (3, 4, . . . , 9) for a total of seven stems, *or* we could allow two stem values for each decade, for a total of 14 stem values. With two stems for each decade, the first instance of each stem value would receive leaves of 0 to 4 and the second would receive leaves of 5 to 9. So, the two deaths in the 30s, at ages 34 and 36, could be represented in two different ways:

$$|3| \; 46 \quad \text{or} \quad \begin{array}{c|c} 3 & 4 \\ 3 & 6 \end{array}$$

The first method, with fewer stem values, is generally preferable for small datasets, while the second, with more stem values, is preferable for larger datasets.

For the First Ladies data, could you use three stems for each decade? Why or why not? Could you use five stems for each decade? Why or why not?*

EXAMPLE 2.8
Big Music Collections

About how many music CDs do you own? Responses to this question for 24 students in a senior-level statistics course in 1999 at Penn State University were

220, 20, 50, 450, 300, 30, 20, 50, 200, 35, 25, 50,
250, 100, 0, 100, 20, 13, 200, 2, 125, 150, 90, 60

Here is a stem-and-leaf plot of these data:

Reported music CDs owned for *n* = 24 Penn State students (stem unit = 100s, leaf unit = 10s)

```
0 | 001222233
0 | 55569
1 | 002
1 | 5
2 | 002
2 | 5
3 | 0
3 |
4 |
4 | 5
```

(Source: Class data collected by Robert Heckard.)

Notice that the numbers range from 0 to about 450. The stem unit is "100s" and the leaf unit within a row is "10s." The final digit of the response is truncated. For instance, the row |1| 002 represents the data values 100, 100, and 125. There is a clear outlier, with someone reporting that they own 450 CDs. Even without the outlier of 450, the data are skewed to the right (turn the picture on its side to see this), with the bulk of the values in the 0 to 90 range. The median number of CDs owned is 55. The arithmetic average or mean is about 105. The outlier of 450 is a legitimate part of the data, but (along with the skewness) causes a big difference between the mean and the median. ◆

Minitab Tip

 tech note **Visually Describing a Quantitative Variable**

- ◆ To draw a *histogram* of a quantitative variable, use **Graph>Histogram.** In the dialog box, specify under X a column containing the raw data for a quantitative variable. Use the ***Options*** button if you want to display percents rather than counts or if you want to control how many intervals are created.
- ◆ To draw a *dotplot* of a quantitative variable, use **Graph>Dotplot.**
- ◆ To draw a *stemplot* of a quantitative variable, use **Graph>Stem-and-Leaf.**

2.6 | NUMERICAL SUMMARIES OF QUANTITATIVE VARIABLES

We have discussed the interesting features of a quantitative dataset and learned how to look for them with pictures. The final stage of the process is to compute numerical summaries of these features.

Notation for Raw Data

formula n = the number of individuals in a dataset

$x_1, x_2, x_3, \ldots, x_n$ represent the individual raw data values

Example: A dataset consists of handspan values in centimeters for six females; the values are 21, 19, 20, 20, 22, and 19. Then,

$n = 6$

$x_1 = 21, x_2 = 19, x_3 = 20, x_4 = 20, x_5 = 22,$ and $x_6 = 19$

Describing the Location of a Dataset

The words *location* and *center* often are used as synonyms for the middle of a dataset. There are two common ways to describe this feature. The **mean** is simply the numerical average, calculated as the sum of the data values divided by the number of values. The **median** is either the middle value (for an odd number of individuals) or the average of the middle two values (for an even number of individuals).

In a perfectly symmetric dataset, the mean and the median are equal, but in a skewed data set they differ. When the data are skewed to the left, the mean will tend to be smaller than the median. When the data are skewed to the right, the mean will tend to be larger than the median. Example 2.8 illustrates an extreme case with data skewed to the right, and the mean of about 105 CDs is much larger than the median of 55.

Determining the Mean and Median

formula   **The Mean**

The symbol $\bar{x}$ is nearly always used to represent the mean of a sample. Notation for calculating the sample mean of a list of values is

$$\bar{x} = \frac{\Sigma x_i}{n}$$

The capital Greek letter sigma, written as Σ, is the universal symbol meaning "add up whatever follows." Therefore, for a dataset with individual values $x_1, x_2, x_3, \ldots, x_n$, the notation Σx_i is the same as saying "add together all the values."

The Median
It would require more notation than is convenient to write a formula for the median, so we simply write the rule:

- If n is odd, the median M is the middle of the ordered values. Find M by counting $(n + 1)/2$ up from the bottom or down from the top of the ordered list.

- If n is even, the median M is the average of the middle two of the ordered values. Find M by averaging the values that are $(n/2)$ and $(n/2) + 1$ from the top or the bottom of the ordered list.

Note: If you're determining a median "by hand," your first step should be to put the data in order from lowest to highest!

EXAMPLE 2.8—CONTINUED
Median Number of CDs Owned

In Example 2.8, we gave data for the number of music CDs owned by $n = 24$ college students in a statistics class, and also reported that the median number owned was 55 CDs. To find the median of a data set, first write the values in order from lowest to highest. For the music CDs owned data, the ordered list is

$$0 \;\; 2 \;\; 13 \;\; 20 \;\; 20 \;\; 20 \;\; 25 \;\; 30 \;\; 35 \;\; 50 \;\; 50 \;\; 50$$
$$60 \;\; 90 \;\; 100 \;\; 100 \;\; 125 \;\; 150 \;\; 200 \;\; 200 \;\; 220 \;\; 250 \;\; 300 \;\; 450$$

From the display of the ordered data, it's easy to see that the median is located between 50 and 60, the 12th- and 13th-highest values in the dataset, which are the two middle values among the 24 observations. The median is found by averaging these two middle values, which gives $M = (50 + 60)/2 = 55$. ◆

EXAMPLE 2.9
Will "Normal" Rainfall Get Rid of Those Odors?

A company (that will remain unnamed) located near Davis, California, was having an odor problem in its wastewater facility. Blame it on the weather:

> [According to a company official] "Last year's severe odor problems were due in part to the 'extreme weather conditions' created in the Woodland area by El Niño." She said Woodland saw 170 to 180 percent of its normal rainfall. "Excessive rain means the water in the holding ponds takes longer to exit for irrigation, giving it more time to develop an odor." (Amy Goldwitz, *The Davis Enterprise,* March 4, 1998, p. A1)

This wording is typical of weather-related stories in which it is often remarked that rainfall is vastly "above normal" or "below normal." In fact, these stories occur so frequently that one wonders if there is *ever* a normal year. The rainfall (in inches) for Davis, California, for 47 years is shown in Table 2.6. A histogram is shown in Figure 2.7.

What is the "normal" annual rainfall in Davis? The mean in this case is 18.69 inches and the median is 16.72 inches. For the year under discussion in the article (1997–98), rainfall was 29.69 inches, hence the comment that it was "170 to 180

TABLE 2.6 ■ **Annual Rainfall for Davis, California (July 1–June 30), in Inches**

Year	Rainfall	Year	Rainfall	Year	Rainfall	Year	Rainfall
1951	20.66	1964	18.56	1977	27.69	1990	13.84
1952	16.72	1965	11.41	1978	17.25	1991	17.46
1953	13.51	1966	27.64	1979	25.06	1992	29.84
1954	14.1	1967	11.49	1980	12.03	1993	11.86
1955	25.37	1968	24.67	1981	31.29	1994	31.22
1956	12.05	1969	17.04	1982	37.42	1995	24.5
1957	28.74	1970	16.34	1983	16.67	1996	19.52
1958	10.98	1971	8.6	1984	15.74	1997	29.69
1959	12.55	1972	27.69	1985	27.47		
1960	12.75	1973	20.87	1986	10.81		
1961	14.99	1974	16.88	1987	16.3		
1962	27.1	1975	6.14	1988	11.38		
1963	11.2	1976	7.69	1989	15.79		

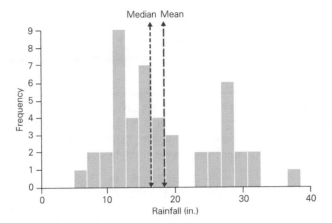

FIGURE 2.7   **Annual rainfall in Davis, California**

percent of normal." But, 29.69 inches of rain is within the range of rainfall values over this 47-year period, and more rain occurred in 4 of the other 46 years. The next time you hear about weather conditions that are not "normal," pay attention to whether they are truly outliers or just different from the *average* value. In this case, the company's excuse for the problem just doesn't hold water. ◆

The Influence of Outliers on the Mean and Median

Outliers have a larger influence on the mean than the median. Outliers at the high end will increase the mean, while outliers at the low end will decrease it. For instance, suppose there had been only five First Ladies, with ages at death of 70, 72, 74, 76, and 78. Then the median and the mean age of death would both be 74. But now suppose the youngest age had been 35 instead of 70. The median would *still* be 74 years old. But the mean would be

$$\bar{x} = \frac{35 + 72 + 74 + 76 + 78}{5} = 67 \text{ years}$$

You should remember this when you hear statistics about "average life expectancy." Those values are calculated based on averaging the anticipated age at death for all babies born in a given time period. The majority of individuals will live to be older than this "average," but those who die in infancy are the outliers that pull down the average. Datasets that are skewed to the right or that have large outliers at the high end generally have higher means than medians. Examples include annual incomes of executives and sales prices of homes for a large area.

Describing Spread: Range and Interquartile Range

Three summary measures that describe the *spread* or *variability* of a dataset are

- ◆ **Range** = high value − low value
- ◆ **Interquartile range** = upper quartile − lower quartile. The notation **IQR** is often used to represent the interquartile range.
- ◆ **Standard deviation**

The standard deviation is easiest to interpret in the context of bell-shaped data, so we postpone a description of it until Section 2.7, where bell-shaped distributions are discussed. In this section, we describe how to calculate the range and the interquartile range.

EXAMPLE 2.10
Range and Interquartile Range for Fastest Speeds Ever Driven

In Case Study 1.1 we summarized responses to the question "What's the fastest you've ever driven a car?" The five-number summary for the 87 males surveyed is

	Males (87 Students)	
Median		110
Quartiles	95	120
Extremes	55	150

This summary provides substantial information about the location, spread, and possible outliers. Remember that the median, 110 mph in this case, measures the *center* or *location* of the data. The other four numbers in the five-number summary can be used to describe how *spread out* or *variable* the responses are.

- The two *extremes* describe the spread over 100% of the data. Here, the responses are spread from 55 mph to 150 mph.
- The two *quartiles* describe the spread over approximately the middle 50% of the data. About 50% of the men gave responses between 95 and 120 mph.

Given the values of the extremes and the quartiles, it's simple to calculate the range and the interquartile range (IQR). For the fastest speed reportedly driven by males, values for these two measures of variability are

- Range = high − low = 150 − 55 = 95 mph
- IQR = upper quartile − lower quartile = 120 − 95 = 25 mph

While the range from the smallest to the largest data point is 95 mph, the middle 50% of the data fall in a relatively narrow range of only 25 mph. In other words, the responses are more densely clumped near the center of the data and are more spread out toward the extremes. ◆

Finding Quartiles

tech note Q_1 = **lower quartile** = median of lower half of the ordered values
Q_3 = **upper quartile** = median of upper half of the ordered values

A simple way to find the quartiles is to split the ordered values into the half that is below the median and the half that is above the median.

- The lower quartile (Q_1) is the median of the data values that are below the median.
- The upper quartile (Q_3) is the median of the data values that are above the median.

These values are called **quartiles** because, along with the median, they divide the ordered data into quarters.

Note: The Minitab program uses a different procedure, so its quartile estimates could occasionally differ slightly from the estimates determined by the procedure described here.

EXAMPLE 2.10—CONTINUED
Fastest Driving Speeds for Men

Here are the 87 males' responses to the question about how fast they have driven a car, as given in Case Study 1.1, except now the data are in numerical order. To make it easier to count, the data are arranged in rows of ten numbers:

```
55 60 80 80 80 80 85 85 85 85
90 90 90 90 90 92 94 95 95 95
95 95 95 100 100 100 100 100 100 100
100 100 101 102 105 105 105 105 105 105
105 105 109 110 110 110 110 110 110 110
110 110 110 110 110 112 115 115 115 115
115 115 120 120 120 120 120 120 120 120
120 120 124 125 125 125 125 125 125 130
130 140 140 140 140 145 150
```

The median is the middle value in an ordered list, so for 87 values, the median is the $(87 + 1)/2 = 88/2 = 44$th value in the list. The 44th value is 110, and this value is shown in bold in the data list. Aside from the middle value of 110, there were 43 values at or below 110, and another 43 values at or above 110. Notice that there are many responses of 110, which is why we are careful to say that 43 of the values are *at or above* the median.

There are 43 values on either side of the median. To find the *quartiles,* simply find the median of each of those sets of 43 values. The lower quartile is the $(43 + 1)/2 = 22$nd value from the bottom of the data, and the upper quartile is the 22nd value from the top. These values are in bold and italics in the data list; $Q_1 = 95$ and $Q_3 = 120$. Notice that the 87 values have been partitioned as follows:

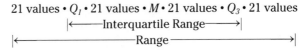

21 values • Q_1 • 21 values • M • 21 values • Q_3 • 21 values

|←——Interquartile Range——→|

|←————————Range————————→|

The median and quartiles divide the data into equal numbers of values but do not necessarily divide the data into equally wide intervals. For example, the lowest 1/4 of the males had responses ranging over the 40-mph interval from 55 mph to 95 mph, while the next 1/4 had responses ranging over only a 15-mph interval, from 95 to 110. Similarly, the third quarter had responses in only a 10-mph interval (110 to 120), while the top 1/4 had responses in a 30-mph interval (120 to 150). It is common to see the majority of values clumped in the middle and the remainder tapering off into a wider range. ◆

2.6

turn on your mind

A **resistant statistic** is a numerical summary of the data that is "resistant" to the influence of outliers. In other words, an outlier is not likely to have a major influence on its numerical value. Two of the summary measures from the list *mean, median, range,* and *interquartile range* are *resistant,* while the other two are not. Explain which two are resistant and which two are not.*

Percentiles

The quartiles and the median are special cases of **percentiles** for a dataset. In general, the kth *percentile* is a number that has k% of the data values at or below it and $(100 - k)\%$ of the data values at or above it. The lower quartile, median, and upper quartile are also the 25th percentile, 50th percentile, and 75th percentile, respectively. If you are told that you scored at the 90th percentile on a standardized test (like the SAT), it indicates that 90% of the scores were at or below your score, while 10% were at or above your score.

Using Excel to Find Summary Measures

 tech note   Suppose the dataset has been stored in a range of cells, which we represent by the word "list" in what follows. For instance, if the dataset is in column A, rows 1 to 30, then "list" is A1:A30. You can also "list" the actual numerical values themselves, rather than the range of cells containing them. All of these commands are part of the "statistical functions" provided by Excel. You can insert them directly into a cell by preceding the command with the symbol @. Some values have multiple options. For instance, there are many commands that give the minimum value.

Average(list) = mean

Quartile(list, 0) = *Min(list)* = minimum value

Quartile(list, 1) = lower quartile

Quartile(list, 2) = *Median(list)* = median

Quartile(list, 3) = upper quartile

Quartile(list, 4) = *Max(list)* = maximum value

Small(list,k) gives the kth-smallest value, for example, *small(list,1)* = minimum

Large(list,k) gives the kth-largest value, for example, *large(list,n)* = minimum

Percentile(list,p) gives the kth percentile where $p = k/100$. In other words, you must express the desired percentile as a proportion rather than a percent. For instance, to find the 90th percentile, use *percentile(list,.9)*.

Count(list) = n, the number of values in the dataset.

Note: As with most computer programs, Excel uses a more precise algorithm to find the upper and lower quartiles than the one we recommend using if you are finding them "by hand," so your values may differ slightly.

Minitab Tip

tech note   **Numerical Summaries of a Quantitative Variable**

♦ To determine summary statistics for a quantitative variable, use **Stat**>**Basic Statistics**>**Display Descriptive Statistics.** In the dialog box, specify a column(s) containing the raw data for a quantitative variable(s). The ***Graphs*** button, of the dialog box provides options for several different graphs.

♦ If you wish to compare numerical summaries of a quantitative variable across categories (for example, compare the handspans of men and women), check "By Variable" and specify the variable that defines the categories.

Note: The output from **Stat**>**Basic Statistics**>**Display Descriptive Statistics** includes the mean, the median, the elements of the five-number summary, and the standard deviation, a statistic that we'll discuss in the next section.

Picturing Location and Spread with Boxplots

We have already seen how to create a simple and informative five-number summary using the extremes, the quartiles, and the median. A simple way to picture that information is to use a **boxplot.** This type of graph is particularly useful for comparing two or more groups and also is an effective tool for identifying outliers.

Figure 2.8 uses boxplots to compare the spans of the right hands of males and females. For each group, the box covers the middle 50% of the data, and the line within a box marks the median value. With the exception of possible outliers, the lines extending from a box reach to the minimum and maximum data values. Possible outliers are marked with an asterisk. In Figure 2.8, the vertical axis is used for the quantitative variable (handspan), but the graph could also be drawn so that the horizontal axis is used for the quantitative variable.

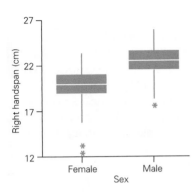

FIGURE 2.8   Boxplots for right handspans of men and women

How to Draw a Boxplot and Identify Outliers

Step 1: Label either a vertical axis or a horizontal axis with numbers from the minimum to the maximum of the data.

Step 2: Draw a box with the lower end of the box at Q_1 and the upper end at Q_3.

Step 3: Draw a line through the box at the median M.

Step 4: Draw a line that extends from the Q_1 end of the box to the smallest data value that is not further than $1.5 \times$ IQR from Q_1. Also draw a line that extends from the Q_3 end of the box to the largest data value that is not further than $1.5 \times$ IQR from Q_3.

Step 5: Mark data points further than $1.5 \times$ IQR from either edge of the box with an asterisk. *Points represented with asterisks are considered to be outliers.*

In Figure 2.8, we see that several features of each group are immediately obvious. The comparison between the two groups is simplified as well. The only feature of a dataset that is not obvious from a boxplot is the shape, although there is information about whether the values tend to be clumped in the middle or tend to stretch more toward one extreme than the other.

EXAMPLE 2.7—*CONTINUED*
Five-number Summary
and Outlier Detection for
the Cambridge Boatsmen

In Example 2.7, the weights (in pounds) given for nine men on the Cambridge crew team were

188.5, 183.0, 194.5, 185.0, 214.0, 203.5, 186.0, 178.5, 109.0

The first step in finding a five-number summary is to write the data in order from smallest to largest. Here, the ordered values are

109.0   178.5   183.0   185.0   **186.0**   188.5   194.5   203.5   214.0

The median, 186.0, is underlined and in bold typeface in the ordered list. Because the number of data values is odd ($n = 9$), the median value is the middle of the ordered values. The lower quartile is the median of the four values below the median (186.0), which are 109.0, 178.5, 183.0, and 185.0. Thus, the lower quartile is $Q_1 = (178.5 + 183)/2 = 180.75$. The upper quartile is the median of the four values above the median. These are 188.5, 194.5, 203.5, and 214.0, so the value of the upper quartile is $Q_3 = (194.5 + 203.5)/2 = 199.0$.

The value 109.0, the weight of the coxswain, is an obvious outlier. We'll use this value to illustrate the criterion for identifying outliers on a boxplot. A value below the lower quartile is marked as an outlier if it is more than $1.5 \times$ IQR below Q_1. The interquartile range for these data is IQR $= Q_3 - Q_1 = 199.0 - 180.75 = 18.25$, and $1.5 \times$ IQR $= 1.5 \times 18.25 = 27.375$. Any value smaller than $Q_1 - 1.5 \times$ IQR $= 180.75 - 27.375 = 153.375$ would be marked as an outlier on a boxplot, the case for the weight 109.0. No other values would be identified as outliers in this example. For instance, a value above the upper quartile would have to be larger than $Q_3 + 1.5 \times$ IQR $= 199.0 + 27.375 = 226.375$ to be identified as an outlier. None of the crew team members was that heavy. ◆

2.7

turn on your mind

Using the boxplots in Figure 2.8, what can you say about the respective handspans for males and females? Are there any surprises, or do you see what you would expect?*

Minitab Tip

tech note   **Drawing a Boxplot**

♦ To draw a *boxplot* of a quantitative variable, use **Graph>Boxplot.** In the dialog box, specify a column containing the raw data for a quantitative variable under Y. It is not necessary to enter anything under X.

♦ To use **Graph>Boxplot** to create a boxplot that compares a quantitative response variable across categories of an explanatory variable, specify the response variable under Y and specify the categorical explanatory variable under X. Figure 2.8 is an example of this type of plot.

2.7 | BELL-SHAPED DISTRIBUTIONS OF NUMBERS

Nature seems to follow a predictable pattern for many kinds of measurements. Most individuals are clumped around the center, and the greater the distance a value is from the center, the fewer individuals have that value. Except for the two outliers at the lower end, that pattern is evident in the females' right handspan measurements in Figures 2.4 to 2.6. If we were to draw a smooth curve connecting the tops of the bars on a histogram with this shape, the smooth curve would resemble the shape of a bell.

Numerical variables that follow this pattern are said to follow a **bell-shaped curve,** or to be "bell-shaped." A special case of this distribution of measurements is so common it is also called a **normal distribution** or **normal curve.** There is a precise mathematical formula for this smooth curve, which we will study in more depth in Chapter 8, but in this chapter we will limit ourselves to a few convenient descriptive features for data of this type. Most variables with a bell shape do not fit the mathematical formula for a normal distribution exactly, but they come close enough that the results in this section can be applied to them to provide useful information.

*HINT: Is there a difference in the location of the data for the two graphs? Is either group more spread out than the other?

EXAMPLE 2.11
The Shape of
British Women's Heights

A representative sample of 199 married British couples, taken in 1980, provided information on five variables: height of each spouse (in millimeters), age of each spouse, and husband's age at the time they were married (Hand et al., 1994). Figure 2.9 displays a histogram of the wives' heights, with a normal curve superimposed. The particular normal curve shown in Figure 2.9 was generated using Minitab statistical software, and of all the possible curves of this type, it was chosen because it is the best match for the histogram. The mean height for these women is 1602 millimeters, and the median at 1600 millimeters is very close. Although it is difficult to tell precisely in Figure 2.9, the normal curve is centered at the mean of 1602. For bell-shaped curves, there is a useful measure of spread called the *standard deviation,* which we describe next. ◆

Minitab Tip

 tech note **Superimposing a Normal Curve onto a Histogram**

◆ To draw a normal curve onto the histogram of a quantitative variable, use **Stat**>**Basic Statistics**>**Display Statistics.** Specify the column of interest, click the ***Graphs*** button, and choose the *Histogram of data, with Normal Curve* option.

Describing Spread with Standard Deviation

Because normal curves are so common in nature, a whole set of descriptive features has been developed that apply mostly to variables with that shape. In fact, two summary features uniquely determine a normal curve, so that if you know those two summary numbers, you can draw the curve precisely. The first summary number is the mean, and the bell shape is centered on that number. The second summary number is called the **standard deviation,** and it is a measure of the spread of the values.

The Concept of Standard Deviation

You can think of the **standard deviation** as *roughly the average distance values fall from the mean.* Put another way, it measures variability by summarizing how

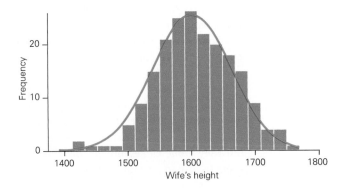

FIGURE 2.9 **Histogram of wife's height and normal curve**

far individual data values are from the mean. Consider, for instance, the standard deviations for the following two sets of numbers, both with a mean of 100:

Set	Numbers	Mean	Standard Deviation
1	100, 100, 100, 100, 100	100	0
2	90, 90, 100, 110, 110	100	10

In the first set of numbers, all values equal the mean value so there is no variability or spread at all. For this set, the standard deviation is 0, as will *always* be the case for such a set of numbers. In the second set of numbers, one number equals the mean, while the other four numbers are each 10 points away from the mean, so the average distance away from the mean is about 10, the standard deviation for this set of data.

Calculating the Standard Deviation

The formula for calculating the standard deviation is a bit more involved than the conceptual interpretation just discussed. This is the first instance of a summary measure that differs based on whether the data represent a sample or an entire population. The version given here is appropriate when the dataset is considered to represent a sample from a larger population. This distinction will become clear later in the book.

The Formula for the Standard Deviation

formula   The formula for the (sample) standard deviation is

$$s = \sqrt{\frac{\Sigma(x_i - \bar{x})^2}{n - 1}}$$

The value of s^2 is called the (sample) **variance.**

An equivalent formula for the (sample) standard deviation that is easier to compute on a calculator is

$$s = \sqrt{\frac{\Sigma x_i^2 - n\bar{x}^2}{n - 1}}$$

In practice, statistical software like Minitab or a spreadsheet program like Excel typically is used to find the standard deviation for a dataset. For situations where you have to calculate the standard deviation by hand, here is a step-by-step guide to the steps involved:

Step 1: Calculate $\bar{x}$, the sample mean.

Step 2: For each observation, calculate the difference between the data value and the mean.

Step 3: Square each difference calculated in step 2.

Step 4: Sum the squared differences calculated in step 3, and then divide this sum by $n - 1$. The answer for this step is called the **variance.**

Step 5: Take the square root of the variance calculated in step 4.

EXAMPLE 2.12
Calculating a
Standard Deviation

Calculate the standard deviation of the four pulse rates 62, 68, 74, 76.

Step 1: The sample mean is

$$\bar{x} = \frac{62 + 68 + 74 + 76}{4} = \frac{280}{4} = 70$$

Steps 2 and 3: For each observation, calculate the difference between the data value and the mean. Then, square this difference. The results of these two steps are shown here:

Data Value	Step 2 Value − Mean	Step 3 (Value − Mean)^2
62	62 − 70 = −8	$(-8)^2 = 64$
68	68 − 70 = −2	$(-2)^2 = 4$
74	74 − 70 = 4	$4^2 = 16$
76	76 − 70 = 6	$6^2 = 36$

Step 4: The sum of step 3 quantities is $64 + 4 + 16 + 36 = 120$. Divide this sum by $n - 1 = 4 - 1$ to get the variance:

$$s^2 = \frac{120}{4 - 1} = \frac{120}{3} = 40$$

Step 5: Take the square root of the variance computed in step 4:

$$s = \sqrt{40} = 6.3 \; \blacklozenge$$

Population Mean and Standard Deviation

tech note   For reasons that will become clear later in this book, datasets are commonly treated as if they represent a sample from a larger population. However, in situations where the dataset includes measurements for an entire population, the notations for the mean and standard deviation are different, and the formula for the standard deviation is also slightly different. A **population mean** is represented by the symbol μ ("mu"), and

$$\textbf{population standard deviation} = \sigma = \sqrt{\frac{\Sigma(x_i - \mu)^2}{n}}$$

Notice that the difference between this formula and the sample version is that the denominator is now n instead of $n - 1$. Also, the appropriate notation for the mean (population) is used.

Excel Tip

tech note   The **Excel** commands for the standard deviation and variance are

Stdev(list) = sample standard deviation

Stdevp(list) = population standard deviation

Var(list) = sample variance

Varp(list) = population variance

Interpreting the Standard Deviation for Bell-Shaped Curves: The Empirical Rule

Once you know the mean and standard deviation for a bell-shaped curve, you can also determine the approximate proportion of the data that will fall into any specified interval. We will learn much more about how to do this in Chapter 8, but for now, here are some useful benchmarks.

> **definition** The **Empirical Rule** states that for any bell-shaped curve, approximately
>
> ◆ 68% of the values fall within 1 standard deviation of the mean in either direction
>
> ◆ 95% of the values fall within 2 standard deviations of the mean in either direction
>
> ◆ 99.7% of the values fall within 3 standard deviations of the mean in either direction

Combining the Empirical Rule with knowledge that bell-shaped variables are symmetric allows the "tail" ranges to be specified as well. The first statement of the Empirical Rule implies that about 16% of the values fall more than 1 standard deviation *below* the mean, and 16% fall more than 1 standard deviation *above* the mean. Similarly, about 2.5% fall more than 2 standard deviations below the mean, and so on.

The Empirical Rule, the Standard Deviation, and the Range

The Empirical Rule implies that the range from the minimum to maximum data values equals about 4 to 6 standard deviations for data with an approximate bell shape. *You can get a rough idea of the value of the standard deviation by dividing the range of the data values by 6.* In other words, the standard deviation of bell-shaped data can be approximated as

$$s \approx \frac{\text{Range}}{6}$$

Generally, if the rough estimate of standard deviation based on dividing the range by 6 is decidedly different from the actual standard deviation, the dataset might contain outliers or could have a skewed shape. In this case, the Empirical Rule won't work well.

EXAMPLE 2.11—*CONTINUED*
Women's Heights and the Empirical Rule

The mean for the 199 British women's heights is 1602 millimeters, and the standard deviation is 62.4 millimeters. Figure 2.10 illustrates how the Empirical Rule would apply if the distribution exactly followed a normal curve.

For instance, about 68% of the 199 heights would fall into the range 1602 ± 62.4, or 1539.6 to 1664.4 mm. (The symbol "±" is read "plus or minus" and indicates that you form an interval by first subtracting and then adding the value that follows the symbol from the value that precedes it.) About 95% of the heights would fall into the interval 1602 ± (2 × 62.4), or 1477.2 to 1726.8 mm. And about 99.7% of the heights would be in the interval 1602 ± (3 × 62.4), or 1414.8

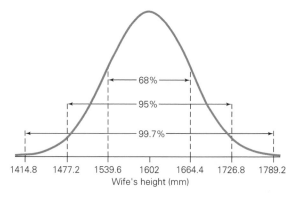

FIGURE 2.10   **The Empirical Rule applied to British women's heights**

to 1789.2 mm. In fact, these intervals work well for the actual data. Here is a summary of how well the Empirical Rule compares with the actual numbers and percents of heights falling within 1, 2, and 3 standard deviations (s.d.) of the mean:

Interval	Numerical Interval	Empirical Rule % and Number	Actual Number	Actual Percent
Mean ± 1 s.d.	1539.6 to 1664.4	68% of 199 = 135	140	140/199 or 70%
Mean ± 2 s.d.	1477.2 to 1726.8	95% of 199 = 189	189	189/199 or 95%
Mean ± 3 s.d.	1414.8 to 1789.2	99.7% of 199 = 198	198	198/199 or 99.5%

Notice that the women's heights, although not perfectly "bell-shaped," follow the Empirical Rule quite well. The minimum height was 1410 mm, while the maximum was 1760, for a range of $1760 - 1410 = 350$ mm. Therefore, a reasonable guess for the standard deviation is Range/6 = 350/6 = 58.3 mm. This is indeed close to the actual standard deviation of 62.4 mm. ◆

Standardized z-Scores

The standard deviation is also useful as a "yardstick" for measuring how far an individual value falls from the mean. Suppose you were told that scores on your last statistics exam were bell-shaped (they often are) and that your test score was 2 standard deviations above the mean for the class. Without even knowing your score or the mean score, you would know that only about 2.5% of the students had scores exceeding yours. From the Empirical Rule, we know that the scores for about 95% of the class are within 2 standard deviations of the mean. Of the remaining 5% of the scores, about half, or 2.5%, will be more than 2 standard deviations above the mean.

The **standardized score** or **z-score** is a useful measure of the relative value of any observation in a dataset. The formula for this score is simple:

$$z = \frac{\text{Observed value} - \text{Mean}}{\text{Standard deviation}}$$

Notice that a z-score is simply the distance between the observed value and the mean, measured in terms of number of standard deviations. Data values below the mean have negative z-scores, and values above the mean have positive z-scores.

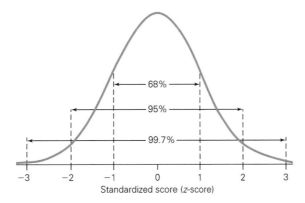

FIGURE 2.11   **The Empirical Rule applied to standardized scores (z-scores)**

As an example, suppose that the mean resting pulse rate for adult men is 70 beats per minute, the standard deviation is 8 beats per minute, and we calculate the standardized score for a resting pulse rate of 80 beats per minute. The calculation is

$$z = \frac{80 - 70}{8} = 1.25$$

The value $z = 1.25$ indicates that a pulse rate of 80 is 1.25 standard deviations above the mean pulse rate for adult men.

> ***definition*** The **Empirical Rule** for bell-shaped data can be restated as follows:
>
> ◆ About 68% of values have z-scores between -1 and $+1$
> ◆ About 95% of values have z-scores between -2 and $+2$
> ◆ About 99.7% of values have z-scores between -3 and $+3$
>
> Figure 2.11 illustrates this version of the Empirical Rule.

Many computer programs and calculators will find the approximate proportion of a bell-shaped variable falling below any z-score you specify. For instance, the function NORMSDIST(z) in Excel does this. Remember that a common special case of a bell-shaped distribution is called the "normal distribution," and it is this special case that is used by Excel. As an example, NORMSDIST(-1) = 0.158655, or 15.8655%, corresponding to the information from the Empirical Rule that about 16% of values fall more than 1 standard deviation below the mean. In Chapter 8 you will learn a more precise interpretation for z-scores.

2.8

turn on your mind

Why do you think measurements with a bell-shaped distribution are so common in nature? For example, why do you think women's heights are distributed in this way, rather than, for instance, being equally spread out from about 5 feet tall to 6 feet tall?*

HINT: What factors contribute to persons' adult height? Considering these factors, why would it be more likely that heights are close to the mean than far from the mean?

The Empirical Rule in Action

The **Empirical** applet on the CD accompanying this book can be used to explore how well the Empirical Rule works for each of eight variables, some with bell-shaped distributions and some with skewed distributions. The data are from the **UCDavis1** and **pennstate1** datasets on the CD for this book. A general description of the eight variables is given at the top of the Web page that includes the applet. For each variable, the applet will display a histogram along with information about the intervals **mean±s** and **mean±2s**. The percent of the sample contained in each interval is reported. When the Empirical Rule applies, these two percents should be about 68% and 95%, respectively.

What to Do

Open the **Empirical** applet. Figure 2.12 shows the initial applet display, a summary of the hours of sleep the previous night for $n = 173$ students in a UC Davis statistics class. A histogram of the hours of sleep data is displayed with superimposed vertical lines indicating the intervals **mean±s** and **mean±2s**. Notice that the histogram has approximately a bell shape. Below the histogram, we see that the sample mean = 6.935 hours and the standard deviation is $s = 1.705$. Notice also that the interval **mean±s** = (5.23, 8.64) contains 114 of the 173 data values, which is 65.9%. The interval **mean±2s** = (3.525, 10.35) contains 166/173 = 95.95% of the data values. These percents are consistent with the Empirical Rule—not surprising since the distribution is approximately bell-shaped.

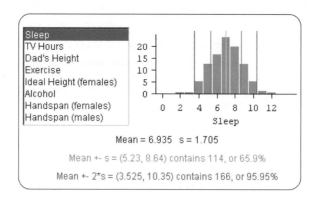

FIGURE 2.12   **The Empirical applet summary of hours of sleep reported by $n = 173$ students**

After examining the results for the hours of sleep variable, click on **TV Hours,** the second variable in the menu at the left of the applet display. Figure 2.13 displays the result, a summary of self-reported weekly hours of watching television for the same 173 students in the hours of sleep example. Notice that the distribution is skewed to the right, and there's an extreme outlier at 100 hours, so the Empirical Rule won't work well. Here, the interval **mean±s**, given as -1.484 to 19.26 hours, contains about 89% of the dataset, much more than the (approximate) 68% that would be in this interval if the Empirical Rule applied. Another difficulty is that the lower value of the interval is negative, an impossible value for weekly hours of watching television. This also is the case for the interval $mean \pm 2s = (-11.86, 29.63)$.

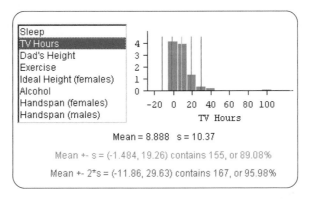

FIGURE 2.13   **The Empirical applet display of weekly hours watching television reported by** $n = 173$ **students**

Click on each of the other six variables, to further explore the connection between the shape of the histogram and the applicability of the Empirical Rule. For each variable, judge the shape of the distribution and take note of the percents in the two intervals given. Which of the variables are well described by the Empirical Rule? Typically, what is the approximate shape of the distributions of these variables? Which variables are not well described by the Empirical Rule? What shape do the distributions of these variables typically have?

Lessons Learned

You'll see that the Empirical Rule works well when the distribution is more or less bell-shaped. But, when the distribution is skewed or an extreme outlier is present, you'll see that the interval $mean \pm s$ tends to include noticeably more than 68% of the dataset, and the values in the interval $mean \pm 2s$ generally don't match the characteristics of the actual data.

KEY TERMS

Section 2.1
raw data, 13
sample data, 14
population data, 14
statistic, 14
parameter, 14
descriptive statistics, 14

Section 2.2
variable, 14
categorical variable, 15
quantitative variable, 15, 16

measurement variable, 15
numerical variable, 15
continuous variable, 15
ordinal variable, 16
questions for variable types, 16–18
explanatory variable, 18, 20
response variable, 18, 20

Section 2.3
outcome variable, 20
pie chart, 20–21
bar graph, 20–22

Section 2.4
five-number summary, 23
location, 24
spread, 24, 34
shape, 24, 28
outlier, 24, 26–27, 34, 38–39

Section 2.5
histogram, 27, 29
stem-and-leaf plot, 28, 30
dotplot, 28, 30
boxplot, 28, 38

EXERCISES   Blue = Basics   Bold, **Bold** = Answer in back

Sections 2.1 and 2.2

2.1   For each of the following variables, indicate whether the variable is categorical or quantitative:
   a. Importance of religion to respondent (very, somewhat, or not very important).
   b. Hours of sleep last night.
   c. Weights of adult women, measured in pounds.
   d. Favorite color for an automobile.

2.2   For each of the following, indicate whether the variable is ordinal or not. If the variable is not ordinal, indicate its variable type.
   a. Opinion about a new tax law (favor or oppose).
   b. Letter grade in a statistics course (A, B, and so on).
   c. Whether the person believes in love at first sight.
   d. Student rating of teacher effectiveness on a 7-point scale where 1 = not at all effective and 7 = extremely effective.

2.3   For each of the following characteristics of an individual, indicate whether the variable is categorical or quantitative:
   a. Length of forearm from elbow to wrist (in cm).
   b. Whether the person has ever been the victim of a crime.
   c. Number of music CDs owned.
   d. Feeling about own weight (overweight, about right, underweight).

2.4   For each of the following quantitative variables, explain whether the variable is continuous or not:
   a. Number of classes a student misses in a week.
   b. Head circumference (cm).
   c. Time it takes students to walk from their dorm to a classroom.
   d. Number of coins presently in someone's pockets and/or purse.

2.5   For each pair of variables, specify which variable is the explanatory variable and which is the response variable in the relationship between them.
   a. Amount person walks or runs per day, and performance on a test of lung function.
   b. Feeling about importance of religion, and age of respondent.
   c. Score on the final exam, and the final course grade in a psychology course.
   d. Opinion about the death penalty (favor or oppose), and gender (male or female).

2.6   In each situation, explain whether it would be more appropriate to treat the observed data as a sample from a larger population or as data from the whole population.
   a. An instructor surveys all students in her class to determine whether students would prefer a take-home exam or an in-class exam.
   b. The Gallup organization polls 1000 individuals to estimate the percent of American adults who approve of the President's job performance.
   c. A historian summarizes the ages at death for all past Presidents of the United States.
   d. A nutritionist wants to determine which of two weight-loss programs is more effective. He assigns 25 volunteers to each program, and records the weight loss after two months for each participant.

2.7   Refer to the previous exercise. In each part, identify the variable of interest, and specify whether that variable is a categorical variable or a quantitative variable.

2.8   For each of the following situations reported in the news, specify what variable(s) were measured on each individual and whether they are best described as categorical, ordinal, or quantitative.
   a. A *Los Angeles Times* survey found that 60% of the 1515 adult Californians polled supported a recent state law banning smoking in bars (*Sacramento Bee*, May 28, 1998, p. A3).
   b. According to the *College Board News* (Dec. 1998, p. 1), "Students using either one of two major coaching programs [for the SAT] were likely to experience an average gain of 5 to 19 points on verbal and 5 to 38 points on math."
   c. According to the *Associated Press* (June 19, 1998), "Smokers are twice as likely as lifetime nonsmokers to develop Alzheimer's disease and other forms of dementia . . . [according to a study that] followed 6,870 men and women ages 55 and older."

2.9   Review the questions listed in Section 2.2 labeled "Asking the Right Questions." For each of the situations in exercise 2.8, determine which of those questions is being answered.

2.10   Give an example of an ordinal variable that is likely to be treated as a categorical variable because numerical summaries like the average would not make much sense.

2.11   Give an example of an ordinal variable for which a numerical summary like the average would make sense.

2.12 To answer the following questions, researchers would need to measure two variables for each individual unit measured or observed in the study. In each case, specify the two variables, and whether each one would most likely be categorical, ordinal, or quantitative. Then, specify which of the two variables you would call the explanatory variable and which you would designate as the response variable.

a. Is the average IQ of left-handed people higher than the average IQ of right-handed people?

b. For married couples, is there a relationship between owning a pet and whether or not they get divorced?

c. For college students, is there a relationship between grade point average (GPA) and number of hours spent studying each week?

d. Individuals in the United States fall into one of a small number of tax brackets based on level of income. Is there a relationship between a person's tax bracket and the percent of income donated to charities?

2.13 Find an example of a study in a magazine, newspaper, or website. Determine what variables were measured, and, for each variable, determine its type. Which of the questions listed under "Asking the Right Questions" were addressed in this study? Describe the question(s) in the context of the study, then explain what answer was found.

Section 2.3

2.14 The Youth Risk Behavior Surveillance System (YRBSS) is a biennial survey of American high school students that is sponsored by the U.S. Centers for Disease Control. In the 2001 survey, students were asked how often they wear a seatbelt when they drive. A summary of the responses given by 2530 students in the 12th grade who said they drive is as follows:

Response	Frequency
Never	105
Rarely	248
Sometimes	286
Most times	464
Always	1427
http://www.cdc.gov/nccdphp/dash/yrbs/	

a. What percent of the 12th-grade students who drive said they always wear a seatbelt when driving?

b. What percent of the 12th-grade students who drive do not always wear a seatbelt when they drive?

c. Find the percent in each of the five response categories.

d. Draw a bar graph of the percents found in part (c).

2.15 Refer to the previous exercise. Students also were asked what grades they usually get in school. For 12th-grade students who responded to this question and the question about how often they wear seatbelts when driving, a summary of frequency counts for combinations of responses to the two questions is as follows:

	Usual School Grades			
Wears Seatbelt	**A and B**	**C**	**D and F**	**Total**
Never	52	32	18	102
Rarely	128	93	22	243
Sometimes	166	104	8	278
Most times	298	128	24	450
Always	1056	300	41	1397
Total	1700	657	113	2470

a. The total number of students in the table is 2470. What percent of these 2470 students said they usually get A's and B's in school?

b. What percent of the 1700 students who said they usually get A's and B's said they always wear a seatbelt when driving?

c. What percent of the 657 students who said they usually get C's said they always wear a seatbelt when driving?

d. What percent of the 113 students who said they usually get D's and F's said they always wear a seatbelt when driving?

2.16 A sample of college students is asked how they feel about their weight. Of the 143 women in the sample who responded, 38 women said they felt overweight, 99 felt their weight was about right, and 6 felt they were underweight. Of the 78 men in the sample, 18 men felt they were overweight, 35 felt their weight was about right, and 25 felt they were underweight. (*Data source:* **pennstate3** dataset on the CD for this book.)

a. In the relationship between feelings about weight and gender, which variable is the explanatory variable and which is the response variable?

b. Summarize the observed counts by creating a table similar to Table 2.3.

c. For the 149 women, find the percent responding in each category for how they feel about their weight.

d. For the 78 men, find the percent responding in each category for how they feel about their weight.

e. Using the percents found in parts (c) and (d), summarize how the women and men differed in how they felt about their weight.

2.17 Refer to the previous exercise about gender and feelings about weight. To compare the men and women, draw a bar graph of the percents found in parts (c) and (d). Use Figure 2.3 for guidance.

2.18 For each of the following situations, which is the explanatory variable and which is the response variable?

a. The two variables are whether or not someone smoked and whether or not they developed Alzheimer's disease.

b. The two variables are whether or not somebody voted in the last election and their political party (Democrat, Republican, Independent, or Other).

c. The two variables are income level and whether or not the person has ever been subjected to a tax audit.

2.19 Refer to the data in Example 2.1 and Table 2.2.

a. Reconstruct the table using the two categorical variables "letter listed first (S or Q)" and "ordering of letter chosen (listed first or second)."

b. Draw an appropriate picture to accompany your numerical summary.

c. Explain whether you think the variables used in Example 2.1 or the variables used in this exercise were more appropriate for illustrating the point of this dataset.

2.20 Each of the following quotes is taken from an article entitled "Education seems to help in selecting husbands" (*Sacramento Bee,* Dec. 4, 1998, p. A21), which reported on new data in the *Statistical Abstract of the United States.* Draw an appropriate graph to represent each situation.

a. "The data show that 3.8 percent of women who didn't complete high school had four or more husbands. For high school graduates, the share with four or more partners drops to 3 percent. Among those who attended college 2 percent had four or more husbands, and that fell to 1 percent for those with college degrees."

b. "From 1997 on, 5.5 percent of children lived with their grandparents, a share that has been rising steadily. It was only 3.6 percent in 1980, and by 1990 it was 4.9 percent."

c. "The center said 20.1 percent of Americans took part in some regular activity—21.5 percent of men and 18.9 percent of women."

2.21 According to Krantz (1992, p. 190) the percentage of women having their first child at various ages is as follows (for all women who have children):

Under 20	20–24	25–29	30–34	35 and Over
25%	33%	25%	12.5%	4%

(The numbers do not sum to 100% due to rounding them off.) Draw a pie chart and a bar graph to represent the data. Explain which picture you think is more informative.

Sections 2.4 and 2.5

2.22 Hand et al. (1994, p. 148) provide data on the number of words in each of 600 randomly selected sentences from the book *Shorter History of England* by G. K. Chesterton. They summarized the data as follows:

Number of Words	Frequency
1–5	3
6–10	27
11–15	71
16–20	113
21–25	107
26–30	109
31–35	68
36–40	41
41–45	28
46–50	18
51–55	12
56–60	3

a. Create a histogram for the number of words in sentences in the *Shorter History of England.*

b. Provide a summary of the dataset based on your histogram.

c. Explain why you could not create a stem-and-leaf plot for this dataset.

d. Count the number of words in the first 20 sentences in Chapter 1 of this book (not including headings), and create a histogram of sentence lengths. Compare the sentence lengths to those in the *Shorter History of England.*

2.23 The figure for this exercise is a histogram summarizing the responses given by 137 college women to a question asking how many ear pierces they have. (*Data source:* **pennstate2** dataset on the CD for this book.)

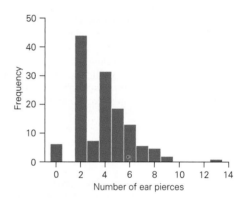

EXERCISE 2.23

a. Describe the shape of the dataset. Explain whether it is symmetric or skewed.

b. Are there any outliers? For any outlier, give a value for the number of ear pierces, and explain why you think the value is an outlier.

c. What number of ear pierces was the most frequently reported value? Roughly, how many women said they have this number of ear pierces?

d. Roughly, how many women said they have four ear pierces?

2.24 The figure for this exercise (see next page) is a histogram summarizing the responses given by 116 college students to a question asking how much they had slept the previous night. (*Data source:* **sleepstudy** dataset on the CD for this book.)

a. Describe the shape of the dataset. Explain whether it is symmetric or skewed.

b. Are there any outliers? For any outlier, give an approximate value for the amount of sleep, and explain why you think the value is an outlier.

c. What was the most frequently reported value (approximately) for the amount of sleep the previous night?

d. Roughly, how many students said they slept eight hours the previous night?

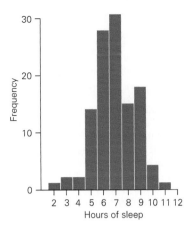

EXERCISE 2.24

2.25 The following stem-and-leaf plot is for the mean August temperatures (Fahrenheit) in 20 U.S. cities. The "stem" (row label) gives the first digit of a temperature, while the "leaf" gives the second digit. (*Data source:* **temperature** dataset on the CD for the book.)

```
6 | 44
6 | 89
7 | 01124
7 | 56667
8 | 1223
8 | 5
9 | 2
```

   a. Describe the shape of the dataset. Is it skewed or is it symmetric?
   b. What is the highest temperature in the dataset?
   c. What is the lowest temperature in the dataset?
   d. What percent of the 20 cities have a mean August temperature in the 80s?

2.26 A set of fifteen exam scores is

   75, 84, 68, 95, 87, 93, 56, 87, 83, 82, 80, 62, 91, 84, 75

   a. Draw a stem-and-leaf plot of the scores.
   b. Draw a dotplot of the scores.

2.27 Case Study 1.1 presented data on the fastest speed men and women had driven a car, and dotplots were shown for each sex. Data for the men are also on the **pennstate1M** dataset on the CD for the text.[1]
   a. Create a stem-and-leaf plot for the male speeds.
   b. Create a histogram for the male speeds.
   c. Compare the pictures created in (a) and (b) and the dotplot in Case Study 1.1. Comment on which is more informative, if any of them are, and comment on any other differences you think are important.
   d. How would you describe the shape of this dataset?

2.28 In the data discussed in Section 2.1, one student reported having slept 16 hours the previous night.

a. What additional information do you need in order to determine whether or not this value is an outlier?
b. If you do determine that the data value of 16 hours of sleep is an outlier, what additional information do you need to decide whether or not to discard it before summarizing the data?

2.29 A male whose height is 78 inches might be considered to be an outlier among males in a statistics class but not among males who are professional basketball players. Give another example in which the same measurement taken on the same individual would be considered to be an outlier in one dataset but not in another dataset.

2.30 Annual rainfall for Davis, California, for 1951 to 1997 is given in Table 2.6 in Section 2.6 and in the **rainfall** dataset on the CD for the text. A histogram is shown in Figure 2.7.
   a. Create a stem-and-leaf plot for the rainfall data, rounded (not truncated) to the nearest inch.
   b. Create a dotplot for the rainfall data, rounded to the nearest inch.
   c. Describe the shape of the rainfall data.
   d. Discuss whether there are any outliers, and if so, whether to discard them or not.

2.31 One of the authors of this book (one male, one female) has a right handspan measurement of 23.5 cm. Would you consider this value to be an outlier? What additional information do you need to make your decision?

2.32 Here are the ages, arranged in order, for the CEOs of the 60 top-ranked small companies in America in 1993 (*Forbes,* "America's Best Small Companies," Nov. 8, 1993; also at http://lib.stat.cmu.edu/DASL/Datafiles/ceodat.html). These data are part of the **ceodata** dataset on the CD for the text.

   32, 33, 36, 37, 38, 40, 41, 43, 43, 44, 44, 45, 45, 45, 45, 46, 46, 47, 47, 47, 48, 48, 48, 48, 49, 50, 50, 50, 50, 50, 50, 51, 51, 52, 53, 53, 53, 55, 55, 55, 56, 56, 56, 56, 57, 57, 58, 58, 59, 60, 61, 61, 61, 62, 62, 63, 69, 69, 70, 74

   a. Create a histogram for these ages.
   b. Create a stem-and-leaf plot for these ages.
   c. Create a dotplot for these ages.
   d. Describe the shape of this dataset.
   e. Are there any outliers in this dataset?
   f. In general, would outliers be more likely to occur in the salaries of heads of companies or in the ages of heads of companies? Explain.

2.33 Does a five-number summary provide sufficient information to determine whether a dataset contains an outlier? Explain.

2.34 Does a stem-and-leaf plot provide sufficient information to determine whether a dataset contains an outlier? Explain.

2.35 For the following situations, would you be most interested in knowing the average value, the spread, or the maximum value for each dataset? Explain. If you think it would be equally useful to know more than one of these summaries, explain that as well. (Answers may differ for different individuals. It is your reasoning that is important.)
   a. A dataset with the annual salaries for all employees in a large company that has offered you a job.

[1] A small CD next to an exercise indicates that the data used in the exercise are on the CD and that it may be useful to use statistical software to answer the question.

b. You need to decide from which of two statistics instructors you will take a class. You have two datasets, with previous final exam scores given by each of the two instructors.

c. A dataset with ages at death for 20 of your relatives who died of natural causes.

2.36 For each of the following situations, would you prefer your value to be average, a low outlier, or a high outlier? Explain.
   a. Number of children you have.
   b. Your annual salary.
   c. Gas mileage for your car.
   d. Crime rate in the city or town where you live.

Section 2.6

2.37 Find the mean and the median for each list of values:
   a. 64, 68, 72, 76, 80, 86
   b. 10, 6, 2, 7, 100
   c. 30, 10, 40, 30

2.38 Refer to part (b) of the previous exercise. Explain why there is such a large difference between the mean and median values.

2.39 Sixty-three college men were asked what they thought was their ideal weight. A five-number summary of the responses (in pounds) is

Median	175	
Quartiles	155	190
Extremes	123	225

(*Data source:* **idealwtmen** dataset on the CD for the text)
   a. Find the value of the range for these data.
   b. Find the value of the interquartile range (IQR).
   c. About what percent of the men gave a response that falls in the interval 155 to 190 pounds?

2.40 Students in a statistics class wrote as many letters of the alphabet as they could in 15 seconds using their nondominant hand. The figure for this exercise is a boxplot that compares the number of letters written by males and females in the sample. (*Data source:* **letters** dataset on the CD for this book.)
   a. What is the median number of letters written by females?
   b. What is the median for males?

c. Explain whether the interquartile range is larger for males or for females.
   d. Find the value of the range for males.
   e. Find the value of the range for females.

2.41 A set of eight systolic blood pressures is

110, 123, 132, 150, 127, 118, 102, 122

   a. Find the median value for the dataset.
   b. Find the values of the lower and upper quartiles.
   c. Find the value of the interquartile range (IQR).
   d. Identify any outliers in the dataset. Use the criterion that a value is an outlier if it is either more than $1.5 \times$ IQR above Q_3 or more than $1.5 \times$ IQR below Q_1.
   e. Draw a boxplot of the dataset.

2.42 Create side-by-side boxplots for the "fastest ever driven a car" data from Case Study 1.1, one for males and one for females. Compare the two sexes using the information displayed in the boxplots. The data are in the **pennstate1** dataset on the CD for the text.

2.43 Refer to "Asking the Right Questions" in Section 2.2, and notice the two questions that are asked for one quantitative variable (questions 3a and 3b). Use those questions as a basis for describing the age of First Ladies' death data in Table 2.5. Compute whatever numerical summaries you think are appropriate, then write a narrative summary based on the computed information. Include pictures if appropriate.

2.44 Refer to the previous exercise. Repeat that exercise to describe the rainfall data in Table 2.6.

2.45 Refer to Example 2.9, Table 2.6, and Figure 2.7 for the rainfall data. Specify whether the shape is skewed to the left or to the right, and explain whether the relationship between the mean and the median (which one is higher) is what you typically expect for data with that shape.

2.46 Create a five-number summary for the rainfall data in Example 2.9, Table 2.6. Write a few sentences describing the dataset. The data are in the **rainfall** dataset on the CD.

2.47 Refer to the sentence-length dataset in exercise 2.22. Notice that you cannot compute exact summary values. Provide as much information as you can about the median, interquartile range, and range for sentence lengths in the *Shorter History of England.*

For Exercises 2.48 to 2.50 use the data for the number of CDs owned by students, listed in Example 2.8, and in the **Music-CDs** *dataset on the CD for this book.*

2.48 Create a five-number summary for the number of music CDs owned by the students listed in Example 2.8. Write a few sentences describing the dataset.

2.49 Create a boxplot for the number of music CDs owned by the students listed in Example 2.8.

2.50 a. Find the mean and median for the number of music CDs owned by the students listed in Example 2.8.
   b. Compare the two measures and discuss which one is a more representative "average" for these values.
   c. Is the relationship between the mean and median what you typically expect for data with the shape of this dataset? Explain.

For Exercises 2.51 to 2.53 use the data for the ages of CEOs, listed in Exercise 2.32 and in the **ceodata** *dataset on the CD for this book.*

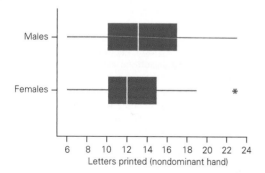

Males

Females

| | 6 | 8 | 10 | 12 | 14 | 16 | 18 | 20 | 22 | 24 |

Letters printed (nondominant hand)

EXERCISE 2.40

2.51 Create a five-number summary for the ages of CEOs of small companies listed in exercise 2.32. Write a few sentences describing the dataset.

2.52 Create a boxplot for the ages of CEOs of small companies listed in exercise 2.32.

2.53 Find the mean and median for the ages of CEOs of small companies listed in exercise 2.32. Is the relationship between them what you would typically expect for data with the shape of this dataset? Explain.

Section 2.7

2.54 The typical amount of sleep per night for college students has a bell-shaped distribution with a mean of 7 hours and a standard deviation equal to 1.7 hours. Use the Empirical Rule to complete each sentence:
a. About 68% of college students typically sleep between ____ and ____ hours per night.
b. About 95% of college students typically sleep between ____ and ____ hours per night.
c. About 99.7% of college students typically sleep between ____ and ____ hours per night.

2.55 Refer to the previous exercise about hours of sleep per night for college students. Draw a picture of the distribution. Indicate the locations of the three intervals found in the previous exercise. Use Figure 2.10 for guidance.

2.56 Suppose that the mean weight for men 18 to 24 years old is 170 pounds, and the standard deviation is 20 pounds. In each part, find the value of the standardized score (z-score) for the given weight:
a. 200 pounds
b. 140 pounds
c. 170 pounds
d. 230 pounds

2.57 Find the mean and standard deviation for each sample of values:
a. 18, 19, 20, 21, 22
b. 20, 20, 20, 20, 20
c. 1, 5, 7, 8, 79

2.58 The scores on the final exam in a course have approximately a bell-shaped distribution. The mean score was 70, the highest score was 98, and the lowest score was 41.
a. Find the value of the range for the exam scores.
b. Refer to the previous part. Use the value of the range to estimate the value of the standard deviation for the exam scores.

2.59 A sample of $n = 500$ individuals is asked how many hours they typically spend using a computer in a week. The mean response is $\bar{x} = 8.3$ hours and the standard deviation is $s = 7.2$ hours. Find values for the interval $\bar{x} \pm 2s$, and explain why the result is evidence that the distribution of weekly hours spent using the computer is not bell-shaped.

2.60 The mean for the women's right handspans is about 20 cm, with a standard deviation of about 1.8 cm. Using the stem-and-leaf plot in Figure 2.5, determine how well this set of measurements fits with the Empirical Rule.

2.61 Do you think the "ages at death" in Table 2.5 are likely to fit a bell-shaped curve? Explain why or why not.

2.62 a. Would the "ages at death" in Table 2.5 be considered a population of measurements or a sample from some larger population? Explain.
b. Find the appropriate standard deviation (sample or population) for the "ages at death" data in Table 2.5.

2.63 The interquartile range and the standard deviation are two different measures of spread. Which measure do you think is more affected by outliers? Explain.

2.64 Explain why women's heights are likely to have a bell shape but their ages at marriage do not.

2.65 Can a categorical variable have a bell-shaped distribution? Explain.

2.66 The data for 103 women's right handspans are shown in Figures 2.4 to 2.6, and a five-number summary is given in Example 2.5.
a. Examine Figures 2.4 to 2.6 and comment on whether or not the Empirical Rule should hold.
b. The mean and standard deviation for these measurements are 20.0 cm and 1.8 cm, respectively. Determine whether the range of the data (found from the five-number summary) is about what would be expected using the Empirical Rule.

2.67 Refer to the women's right handspan data. As you can see in Figures 2.4 to 2.6, there are two apparent outliers, at 12.5 cm and 13.0 cm.
a. If these values are removed, do you think the mean will increase, decrease, or remain the same? What about the standard deviation? Explain.
b. With the outliers removed, the mean and standard deviation for the remaining 101 values are 20.2 cm and 1.45 cm, respectively. The range is 7.25, from 16.0 to 23.25. Determine whether the Empirical Rule for mean $\pm$ 3 standard deviations appears to hold for these values.
c. Refer to Figures 2.4 to 2.6. Based on those figures, do you think the Empirical Rule should hold when the outliers are removed? How about when the outliers have not been removed? Explain.
d. Is there any justification for removing the two outliers? Explain.

2.68 Heights for traditional college-age students in the United States have means and standard deviations of approximately 70 inches and 3 inches for males and 65 inches and 2.5 inches for females. Specify your own height and find the z-score for a college-age student of your sex and height.

2.69 a. If a data value has a z-score of 0, the value equals one of the summary measures discussed in this chapter. Which summary is that?
b. Verify that a data value having a z-score of 1.0 is equal to the mean plus 1 standard deviation.

2.70 Using a computer or calculator that provides proportions falling below a specified z-score, determine the approximate proportion for each of the following situations. In each case, assume the values are approximately bell-shaped.
a. The proportion of SAT scores falling below 450 for a group with a mean of 500 and a standard deviation of 100.
b. The proportion of boys with heights below 36.5 inches for a group with mean height of 34 inches and standard deviation of 1 inch.
c. The proportion of a large class that scored below you

on a test for which the mean was 75, the standard deviation was 8, and your score was 79.

d. The proportion of a large class that scored below you on a test for which the mean was 75, the standard deviation was 4, and your score was 79.

2.71 If you learn that your score on an exam was 80 and the mean was 70, would you be more satisfied if the standard deviation was 5 or if it was 15? Explain.

2.72 Write a set of seven numbers with a mean of 50 and a standard deviation of 0. Is there more than one possible set of numbers? Explain.

2.73 Remember that a resistant statistic is a numerical summary whose value is not unduly influenced by an outlier of any magnitude. Is the standard deviation a resistant statistic? Justify your answer by giving an example of a small dataset, then adding a very large outlier and noting how the standard deviation is affected.

2.74 For a bell-shaped dataset with a large number of values, approximately what z-score would correspond to a data value equaling each of the following?
a. The median.
b. The lowest value.
c. The highest value.
d. The mean.

2.75 Refer to exercise 2.32, in which the ages for the 60 CEOs of America's best small companies of 1993 were given. These data are in the **ceodata** dataset.
a. Find the mean and standard deviation for these ages.
b. Recall that the range should be equivalent to 4 to 6 standard deviations for bell-shaped data. Determine whether that relationship holds for these ages.
c. Find the z-scores for the youngest and oldest CEO. Are they about what you would expect? Explain.

Chapter Exercises

2.76 In an experiment conducted by one of this book's authors, 26 students were asked to estimate (in millions) the population of Canada, which was about 30 million at that time. Before they made their estimates, ten of the students (group 1) were told that the population of the United States was about 290 million at that time. Nine of the students (group 2) were told that the population of Australia was roughly 20 million at that time. The other seven students (group 3) were not given any information. The estimates (millions) made by the students in these three groups were

Group 1: 2, 30, 35, 70, 100, 120, 135, 150, 190, 200
Group 2: 8, 12, 16, 29, 35, 40, 45, 46, 95
Group 3: 5, 23, 50, 55, 150, 150, 300

a. Find the median estimate in group 1.
b. Find the median estimate in group 2.
c. Find the median estimate in group 3.
d. Compare the values of the range for the three groups. Which group had the largest range? Which group had the smallest range?

2.77 Refer to the previous exercise.
a. Find values of the lower and upper quartiles for the data in group 1.

b. Find values of the lower and upper quartiles for the data in group 2.
c. Find values of the lower and upper quartiles for the data in group 3.
d. Draw a boxplot that compares the three groups. Refer to Figure 2.8 for guidance.

2.78 Specify the type (categorical, ordinal, quantitative) for each of the following variables recorded in a survey of telephone usage in student households:
a. Telephone exchange (first three numbers after area code).
b. Number of telephones in the household.
c. Dollar amount of last month's phone bill.
d. Long-distance phone company used.

2.79 In the same survey for which wives' heights are given in Example 2.11, husbands' heights were also recorded. A five-number summary of husbands' heights (mm) is

	Husbands' Heights ($n = 199$)	
Median	1725	
Quartiles	1691	1774
Extremes	1559	1949

a. Construct a boxplot for the husbands' heights.
b. Use the range to approximate the standard deviation for these heights.
c. What assumption did you need to make in part (b) to make the approximation appropriate?
d. The mean and standard deviation for these heights are 1732.5 mm and 68.8 mm. Use the Empirical Rule to construct an interval that should cover 99.7% of the data, and compare your interval to the extremes. Does the interval cover both extremes?

2.80 Can a variable be *both* of the following types? If so, give an example.
a. An explanatory variable and a categorical variable.
b. A continuous variable and an ordinal variable.
c. A quantitative variable and a response variable.
d. A bell-shaped variable and a categorical variable.
e. A bell-shaped variable and a response variable.

2.81 Reach into your wallet, pocket, or wherever you can find at least ten coins, and sort all of the coins you have by type.
a. Count how many of each kind of coin you have (pennies, nickels, and so on, or the equivalent for your country). Draw a pie chart illustrating the distribution of your coins.
b. In part (a), "kind of coin" was the variable of interest for each coin. Is that a categorical, ordinal, or quantitative variable?
c. Now consider the total monetary value of all of your coins as a single data value. What type of variable is it?
d. Suppose you had similar data for all of the students in your statistics class. Write a question for which the variable "kind of coin" is the data of interest for answering the question. Then write a question for which the variable "total monetary value of the coins" is the data of interest for answering the question.

2.82 Look around your living space or current surroundings

and find a categorical variable for which there are at least three categories and for which you can collect at least 20 observations (example: color of the shirts in your closet). Collect the data.

a. Draw a pie chart for your data.

b. Draw a bar graph for your data.

c. Is one of the pictures more informative than the other? Explain. (Your answer may depend on the variable you chose.)

2.83 Look around your living space or current surroundings and find a quantitative variable for which you can collect at least 20 observations (example: monetary amounts of the last 25 checks you wrote). List the data with your response.

a. Create a five-number summary.

b. Draw a boxplot.

c. Draw your choice of a histogram, stem-and-leaf plot, or dotplot.

d. Refer to your picture in part (c) and comment on the shape and presence or absence of outliers.

e. Compute the mean and compare it to the median. Explain whether the relationship between them is what you would expect based on the information you discussed in part (d).

2.84 For each of the following two sets of data, explain which one is likely to have a larger standard deviation:

a. Set 1: Heights of the children in a kindergarten class.
Set 2: Heights of all of the children in an elementary school.

b. Set 1: Systolic blood pressure for a single individual taken daily for 30 days.
Set 2: Systolic blood pressure for 30 people who visit a health clinic in 1 day.

c. Set 1: SAT scores (which range from 200 to 800) for the students in an honors class.
Set 2: Final examination scores (which range from 0 to 100) for all of the students in the English classes at a high school.

2.85 For each of the following datasets, explain whether you would expect the mean or the median of the observations to be higher:

a. In a rural farming community, for each household the number of children is measured.

b. For all households in a large city, yearly household income is measured.

c. For all students in a high school (not just those who were employed), income earned in a job outside the home in the past month is measured.

d. For the coins in someone's pocket that has 1/3 pennies, 1/3 nickels, and 1/3 quarters, the monetary value of each coin is recorded.

2.86 For each of the following research questions, explain what two variables would have to be measured for each individual in the study.

a. Is there a relationship between the amount of beer people drink and their systolic blood pressure?

b. Is there a relationship between calories of protein consumed per day and incidence of colon cancer?

c. Is there a relationship between eye color and whether or not corrective lenses are needed by age 18?

d. For women who are HIV positive when they get pregnant, is there a relationship between whether or not the HIV is transmitted to the infant and the length of time the woman had been infected prior to getting pregnant?

2.87 Refer to the previous exercise. In each case, specify which of the two variables is the explanatory variable and which is the response variable. If it is ambiguous, explain why.

Exercises 2.88 to 2.91 each describe one or two variables and the individuals for whom they were measured. Determine which question listed under "Asking the Right Questions" in Section 2.2 is of interest, and state the question in the context of the situation, as is done for the examples listed in the text with the questions.

2.88 Individuals are all of the kindergarten children in a school district.
One variable: Adult(s) with whom the child lives (both parents, mother only, father only, one or both grandparents, other).

2.89 Individuals are all mathematics majors at a college.
Two variables: Grade point average and hours spent studying last week.

2.90 Individuals are a representative sample of adults in a large city.
Two variables: Ounces of coffee consumed per day and marital status (currently married or not).

2.91 Individuals are a representative sample of college students.
Two variables: Male or female and whether the person dreams in color (yes or no).

Dataset Exercises

2.92 The data for this exercise are in the **GSS-93** dataset. The variable ***gunlaw*** is whether a respondent favors or opposes stronger gun control laws.

a. Determine the percent of respondents who favor stronger gun control laws and the percent of respondents who oppose stronger gun control laws. (*Note:* Not all survey participants were asked the question about gun laws so the sample size for ***gunlaw*** is smaller than the overall sample size.)

b. Draw a graphical summary of the ***gunlaw*** variable.

c. Create a two-way table of counts that shows the relationship between gender (variable name ***sex***) and opinion about stronger gun control laws. From looking at this table of counts, are you able to judge whether the two variables are related? Briefly explain.

d. What percent of females favors stronger gun control laws? What percent of males favors stronger gun control laws?

e. Based on the percents found in part (d), do you think that gender and opinion about gun control are related? Briefly explain.

2.93 Use the **pennstate1** dataset for this exercise. The data for the variable ***HrsSleep*** are responses by $n = 190$ students to the question "How many hours did you sleep last night?"

a. Draw a histogram of the data for the ***HrsSleep*** variable. Describe the shape of this histogram, and comment on any other interesting features of the data.

b. Determine the five-number summary for these data.

c. What is the range of the data? What is the interquartile range?

2.94 Use the **pennstate2** dataset for this exercise. The variable **CDs** is the approximate number of music CDs owned by a student.
   a. Draw a stem-and-leaf plot for the **CDs** variable.
   b. Draw a histogram for the **CDs** variable.
   c. Draw a dotplot for the **CDs** variable.
   d. Describe the shape of the data for the **CDs** variable, and comment on any other interesting features of the data.
   e. Calculate the mean number and the median number of CDs. Compare these two values.
   f. For these data, do you think the mean or the median is a better description of the location of the data? Briefly explain.

2.95 For this exercise, use the **GSS-93** dataset. The variable **cappun** is the respondent's opinion about the death penalty for persons convicted of murder, and the variable **polparty** is the respondent's political party preference (Democrat, Republican, Independent, Other).
   a. In this dataset, what percent favors the death penalty? What percent opposes the death penalty?
   b. Create a table that displays the relationship between political party and opinion about the death penalty. Calculate an appropriate set of conditional percentages for describing the relationship.
   c. Are the variables **polparty** and **cappun** related? Explain.

2.96 Use the **cholest** dataset for this exercise. The dataset contains cholesterol levels for 30 "control" patients and 28 heart attack patients at a medical facility. For the heart attack patients, cholesterol levels were measured 2 days, 4 days, and 14 days after the heart attack.
   a. Calculate the mean, the standard deviation, and the five-number summary for the control patients.
   b. Calculate the mean, the standard deviation, and the five-number summary for the heart attack patients' cholesterol levels 2 days after their attacks.
   c. Generally, which group has the higher cholesterol levels? How much difference is there in the *location* of the cholesterol levels of the two groups?
   d. Which group of measurements has a larger *spread*? Compare the groups with regard to all three measures of spread introduced in Sections 2.6 and 2.7.
   e. Compare the controls and the heart attack patients using a comparative dotplot (as in Case Study 1.1). Briefly explain what this plot indicates about the difference between the two groups.

2.97 Use the **pennstate1** dataset.
   a. Draw a histogram of the **height** variable.
   b. What is the shape of this histogram? Why do you think it is not a bell shape?
   c. Draw a boxplot of the height variable.
   d. Which graph, the histogram or the boxplot, is more informative about this dataset? Briefly explain.

2.98 Use the **GSS-93** dataset. The variable **degree** indicates the highest educational degree achieved by a respondent.
   a. Is the **degree** variable quantitative, categorical, or ordinal? Explain.
   b. Determine the number and percent falling into each degree category.

c. What percent of the sample has a degree that is beyond a high school degree?
   d. The variable **tvhours** is the self-reported number of hours of watching television in a typical day. Find the mean number of television-watching hours for each of the five degree groups.
   e. Is there a relationship between self-reported hours of watching television and educational degree? Explain.
   f. Draw any visual summary of the variable **tvhours** (for the whole sample). What are the interesting features of your graph?

Turn On Your Computer

*For Exercises 2.99 to 2.103, use the **Empirical** applet described in Section 2.7. It is on the CD for this text.*

2.99 Examine the results given by the applet for each of the eight variables.
   a. Among the eight variables, which variables are best described by the Empirical Rule, and which are not well described by the Empirical Rule?
   b. Generally, what is the shape of the histogram for the variables that are well described by the Empirical Rule? What is the shape of the histogram for the variables that are not well described by the Empirical Rule?

2.100 The parts of this exercise concern the variable **Dad's Height**, which is data for father's height as reported by $n = 167$ college students.
   a. What is the shape of the histogram given for the variable **Dad's Height**? Are there any outliers?
   b. Refer to part (a). Based on the shape of the histogram, explain whether the Empirical Rule will apply or not.
   c. What numerical values are given by the applet for the interval $Mean \pm s$? What percent of the data values are in this interval? Compare this percent to the percent that would be expected if the Empirical Rule applies.
   d. What numerical values are given by the applet for the interval $Mean \pm 2s$? What percent of the data values are in this interval? Compare this percent to the percent that would be expected if the Empirical Rule applies.

2.101 The parts of this exercise concern the variable **Alcohol**, which is data for number of alcoholic beverages consumed in a typical week as reported by $n = 167$ college students.
   a. What is the shape of the histogram given for **Alcohol**? Are there any outliers?
   b. Refer to part (a). Based on the shape of the histogram, explain whether the Empirical Rule will apply or not.
   c. What numerical values are given by the applet for the interval $Mean \pm s$? What percent of the data values are in this interval? Compare this percent to the percent that would be expected if the Empirical Rule applies.
   d. What numerical values are given by the applet for the interval $Mean \pm 2s$? Explain why this interval is not a good description of possible values for the variable **Alcohol**.

2.102 The parts of this exercise concern the variable **Ideal Height**, which is the respondent's desired height as reported by $n = 149$ college women.
   a. Use information given by the applet to explain whether the Empirical Rule applies for **Ideal Height**.

b. Assuming the Empirical Rule applies, give numerical values for the interval that will contain about 99.7% of the data values.

c. Compare the interval found in part (b) to the histogram of the data. Explain whether or not the interval is a reasonable description of the data.

2.103 The data for each of the following variables includes one or more outliers. In each case, identify the outlier(s).

Then explain whether the Empirical Rule would apply to the remaining data if the outlier(s) were removed from the dataset.

a. *TV Hours.*

b. *Handspan (females).*

c. *Dad's Height.*

REFERENCES

Hand, D. J., F. Daly, A. D. Lunn, K. J. McConway, and E. Ostrowski (1994). *A Handbook of Small Data Sets,* London: Chapman and Hall.

Krantz, Les (1992). *What the Odds Are,* New York: Harper-Perennial.

CHAPTER 3

Gathering Useful Data

Tom Stewart/The Stock Market

What can you tell about a book by its cover? See Example 3.4.

Probably the biggest misinterpretation made when reporting studies is to imply that a *cause-and-effect* relationship can be concluded on the basis of an observational study. Groups that naturally differ for the explanatory variable of interest are almost certain to differ in other ways, any of which may contribute to differences in the responses.

An old saying that we should retire immediately is that "the data speaks for itself." In fact, data should never be allowed to speak without a good translator. Part of the intent of this book is to develop your translation skills. The knowledge of how the data were generated is one of the key ingredients for translating data intelligently. In this chapter, and the next, we focus on how to collect useful data. ◆

3.1 | DESCRIPTION OR DECISION? USING DATA WISELY

There are two major categories of statistical techniques that can be applied to data. The first category is **descriptive statistics,** in which we use numerical and graphical summaries to characterize a dataset. We partially covered descriptive statistics in Chapter 2, and we will introduce additional descriptive techniques in Chapters 5 and 6. Descriptive statistics such as the mean, interquartile range, and so on, as well as graphical displays, can be applied to any set of data. They are generally not difficult to interpret.

The second important category of statistical techniques is **inferential statistics,** in which we use sample information to make conclusions about a broader range of individuals than just those who are observed. For example, based on the 22,071 physicians who participated in the study described in Case Study 1.6, we can *infer* that taking aspirin helps prevent heart attacks for all men similar to the participants.

Inference methods can only be applied when it is reasonable to assume that the data in hand are *representative* for the question being considered about a larger group. In Chapters 3 and 4 you will learn how to collect representative data and the extent to which it can be used to generalize to a larger group. The key concept requires you to think about *both* the source of the data *and* the question(s) of interest. A dataset may contain representative information for certain questions but not for others.

> *definition* The **Fundamental Rule for Using Data for Inference** is that available data can be used to make inferences about a much larger group *if the data can be considered to be representative with regard to the question(s) of interest.*

EXAMPLE 3.1
Do First Ladies Represent Other Women?

If we were interested in how old American women live to be, it would not make sense to use the ages of death given in Chapter 2 for the First Ladies. Even if you ignore the fact that most of the First Ladies did not live in modern times with modern health care, you can probably think of many reasons why those women do not represent the full population of American women. In fact, there is probably no larger group for which these women are representative. Past First Ladies are not even likely to be representative of future First Ladies on the question of age at death, since medical, social, and political conditions keep changing in ways that may affect their health. ◆

EXAMPLE 3.2
Do Penn State Students Represent Other College Students?

One dataset in Chapter 2 was collected at Penn State University. Do Penn State students represent all college students? This probably depends on the question. If we wanted to know the average handspan of female college students in the United States, we could convincingly argue that the data collected in statistics classes at Penn State University are indeed representative. We could even argue that the Penn State women are representative of all females in the same age group, not just college students. On the other hand, Penn State students may not be representative of all college students when questioned about how fast they have ever driven a car. Penn State is in rural Pennsylvania, where there are many country roads and little traffic. Students in larger cities, even nearby ones like New York or Philadelphia, may not have access to the same open spaces and may not have had the opportunity to drive a car as fast as students in rural areas. Many students in larger cities may not even drive cars at all. ◆

As you can see from these examples, it may require knowledge of the subject matter to determine whether a sample is representative of the larger group for the question of interest. There are, however, a small number of common strategies that researchers use to improve the likelihood that the data they collect can be used to make inferences about a larger population. We will examine some of those strategies in the remainder of this chapter and the next. Also, we will discuss the strengths of those strategies and some problems that may arise when they are used.

Populations, Samples, and Simple Random Samples

In most statistical studies, the objective is to use a small group of units to make an inference about a larger group. The larger group of units about which inferences are to be made is called the **population.** The smaller group of units actually measured is called the **sample.** Sometimes measurements *are* taken on the whole group of interest, in which case *these measurements comprise the whole population.* Occasionally you will see someone make the mistake of trying to make inferences to some hypothetical "larger group" when there isn't one.

Remember the fundamental rule for making valid inferences about the group represented by the sample for which the data were measured: *The data must be representative of the larger group with respect to the question of interest.* The principal way to guarantee that sample data will be representative of the population is to use a **simple random sample** from the population.

> *definition* With a **simple random sample,** every conceivable group of units of the required size from the population has the same chance to be the selected sample.

Although obtaining a simple random sample of the population of interest is ideal, for most research studies it is not possible for both practical and ethical reasons. For instance, suppose researchers wanted to study the effect of using marijuana for the reduction of pain in cancer patients. It would not be practical or ethical to select a random sample of all cancer patients to use in the study. Instead, researchers would use volunteers who wanted to participate and would hope that they were representative of the larger population of all cancer patients.

Simple random samples and related sampling methods *are* typically used for one type of statistical study: sample surveys or polls. Remember from Chapter 1 that in a *sample survey* the investigators gather opinions or other information from each individual included in the sample. Because this gathering of information is usually not time-consuming or invasive, it is often both practical and ethical to contact a large random sample from the population of interest. In Chapter 4 we will learn more about how to select simple random samples and how to conduct sample surveys.

Most research studies must rely on volunteers or on samples that are readily available rather than on random samples. Therefore, when you read the results of a study it is important to pay attention to how the participants were chosen. You can then decide for yourself to what extent you think the results can be extended to a larger group. You will learn much more about how to critically assess statistical studies and surveys in the remainder of this chapter and in Chapter 4.

3.2 | SPEAKING THE LANGUAGE OF RESEARCH STUDIES

Although there are a number of different strategies for collecting meaningful data, there is common terminology used in most of them. Statisticians tend to borrow words from common usage and apply a slightly different meaning, so be sure you are familiar with the special usage of a word in a statistical context.

Types of Research Studies

There are two basic types of statistical research studies:

- *observational studies*
- *experiments*

In an **observational study,** the researchers simply observe or question the participants about opinions, behaviors, or outcomes. Participants are not asked to do anything differently. For example, Case Study 1.5 described an observational study in which blood pressure and frequency of certain types of religious activity (like prayer and church attendance) were measured. The goal was to see if people with higher frequency of religious activity had lower blood pressure. Two special cases of observational studies are *sample surveys* and *case-control* *studies.* We will examine case-control studies later in this chapter and take an in-depth look at sample surveys in Chapter 4.

In an **experiment,** researchers manipulate something and measure the effect of the manipulation on some outcome of interest. **Randomized experiments** are experiments in which the participants are *randomly assigned* to participate in one condition or another. The different "conditions" are called **treatments.**

Case Study 1.6 described a randomized experiment in which physicians were randomly assigned to take an aspirin or a placebo every other day. The goal was to see if regular intake of aspirin resulted in lower risk of heart attacks than that experienced by the group taking only a placebo. The two possible treatments were taking aspirin or taking a placebo. The random assignment should have ensured that the groups were similar in all other respects, so any difference in heart attack rates could actually be attributed to the difference in the pill they took (aspirin or placebo).

In many cases, there are practical and ethical issues that prevent researchers from conducting an experiment. For instance, it would not be reasonable to randomly assign some people to attend church and pray and others not to do so. Or, in an investigation of the effect of oral contraceptive usage on blood pressure, it would certainly not be reasonable to randomly assign some women to use oral contraceptives and others to use a placebo.

Researchers often recruit volunteers to participate in randomized experiments. These volunteers agree to receive whichever treatment is assigned to them, and they often don't know which treatment it is until the experiment is concluded. For example, volunteers in a study of the effectiveness of a new vaccine may be randomly assigned to receive either the vaccine or a placebo. Because the volunteers sign an "informed consent" to participate, it is deemed ethically acceptable to ask them to accept whichever treatment is assigned to them.

Observational Study or Randomized Experiment?

In some cases, researchers can choose between the strategies for collecting data and must weigh the advantages and disadvantages of each strategy. For instance, suppose researchers want to study whether people lose more weight by exercising or by limiting their fat intake. They could conduct an *observational study,* in which they question people about their exercise and eating habits, as well as their history of weight loss, and compare people who exercise with those who eat limited fat. Or, they could conduct a *randomized experiment* in which they randomly assign people to either exercise or eat a specific diet, and then measure and compare weight loss. As we will see later in this chapter, there are advantages and disadvantages to each type of study.

3.1

turn on your mind

Many randomized experiments recruit volunteers who agree to accept whichever treatment is randomly assigned to them. Why do you think this strategy cannot always be used, thus requiring observational studies to be used instead?*

Who Is Measured: Units, Subjects, Participants

Researchers use a variety of terms to describe who is measured. The generic term **unit** is used to indicate a single individual or object being measured. In experiments, the most basic entity (person, plant, and so on) to which different treatments can be assigned is called an **experimental unit.** For instance, in Case Study 1.6 each physician was an experimental unit, since each one was randomly assigned to take aspirin or a placebo. When the experimental units are people, they often are called **subjects.** In both experiments and observational studies, the subjects may also be called **participants.**

Roles Played by Variables — Measured or Not

Most experiments and observational studies are conducted because researchers want to learn about the relationship between two or more variables. For instance, in the observational study in Case Study 1.5, the researchers wanted to know if religious activity and blood pressure were related. In the randomized experiment in Case Study 1.6, they wanted to know if aspirin consumption and risk of heart attack were related.

It is useful to assign generic names to the different roles played by the variables of interest. An **explanatory variable** is one that may explain or may cause differences in a **response variable** (sometimes called an **outcome variable**). For example, in Case Study 1.5, frequency of religious activity is the explanatory variable and blood pressure is the response variable. We distinguished between explanatory variables and response variables in Chapter 2 when creating summaries for categorical variables. The data for a response variable or an explanatory variable may be either categorical or quantitative.

Another term used for a response variable is **dependent variable** because the values are sometimes thought to *depend* on the values of the explanatory variable(s). In contrast, and completely separate from the common usage of the word *independent,* explanatory variables are sometimes called **independent variables.**

Most relationships are complex, and it is unlikely that any explanatory variable is the direct and sole explanation for the values of the response variable. In many studies, particularly in observational studies, *confounding* variables may be present. For example, suppose that an observational study finds that people who take at least 500 mg of vitamin C every day get fewer colds than other people do. But, perhaps people who take vitamins also eat more healthful foods and the better diet reduces the risk of a cold. Or, perhaps the extra glass of water used to take the vitamin pill helped to prevent colds.

definition A **confounding variable** is a variable that both *affects the response variable* and also *is related to the explanatory variable.* The effect of a confounding variable on the response variable cannot be separated from the effect of the explanatory variable.

Confounding might cause the appearance of a nonexistent meaningful relationship between the explanatory and response variables, or it can even mask an actual relationship. The term **lurking variable** is sometimes used to describe a potential confounding variable that is not measured and is not considered in the interpretation of a study. Notice that whether or not the researchers measure confounding variables, such variables are an inherent property of the nature of the relationship between explanatory and response variables. When interpreting the results of an observational study, always consider the possibility that confounding variables may exist.

EXAMPLE 3.3
What Confounding Variables Lurk Behind Lower Blood Pressure?

In Case Study 1.5, the people who attended church regularly had lower blood pressure than people who stayed home and watched religious services on television. But it may be that those who attended church had lower blood pressure as a result of a strong social support network rather than from attending church regularly. If this is the case, the "amount of social support" is a *confounding* variable. Notice that two conditions must be met for "amount of social support" to qualify as a confounding variable:

◆ Amount of social support (confounding variable) *affects* blood pressure (the response variable).

◆ Amount of social support (confounding variable) *is related to* attending church regularly (the explanatory variable) because the same people who attend church regularly are likely to have a strong social support network.

Health status is another possible confounding variable, since those who are not well may not be able to attend church regularly. There are numerous other possibilities, like age, attitude toward life, and so on, that could affect the observed relationship between religious activity and blood pressure. ◆

3.2

turn on your mind

Choose a possible confounding variable for this situation (Case Study 1.5), and explain how it meets the two conditions necessary to qualify as a confounding variable.*

EXAMPLE 3.4
The Fewer the Pages, the More Valuable the Book?

If you peruse the bookshelves of a typical college professor, you will find a variety of books, ranging from textbooks to esoteric technical publications to paperback novels. In order to determine whether or not there is a relationship between the price of a book and the number of pages it contains, a college professor recorded the number of pages and price for 15 books on one shelf.

The numbers are shown in Table 3.1. The books are ordered from fewest to most number of pages. Do prices increase accordingly, with the books with the fewest number of pages costing the least? No, the trend appears to be the reverse—many of the books with fewer pages seem to be more expensive than many of the books with a larger number of pages!

*HINT: Think of something that would probably be different for people who attend church compared to those who don't and that might affect blood pressure.

TABLE 3.1 ■ **Pages Versus Price for the Books on a Professor's Shelf**

Book #	Pages	Price	Book #	Pages	Price
1	104	32.95	9	417	4.95
2	188	24.95	10	417	39.75
3	220	49.95	11	436	5.95
4	264	79.95	12	458	60.00
5	336	4.50	13	466	49.95
6	342	49.95	14	469	5.99
7	378	4.95	15	585	5.95
8	385	5.99			

Why does the relationship seem to be the opposite of what we might expect? The answer is that there is a confounding variable, the type of book. The books on the professor's shelf consisted of paperback novels, which tend to be long but inexpensive, and hardcover technical books, which tend to be shorter but expensive. As illustrated in Figure 3.1, when we look at the relationship between price (the response variable) and pages (the explanatory variable) for each type of book separately, we see that the price does tend to increase with number of pages, especially for the technical books. Notice that type of book (confounding variable) *affects* price (response variable) and type of book (confounding variable) *is related to* number of pages (explanatory variable), because hardcover technical books tend to have fewer pages than paperback novels. ◆

As these examples illustrate, it is unlikely that any explanatory variable is the direct and sole explanation for the values of the response variable. There are almost always confounding variables. These confounding variables might be measured and accounted for in the analysis of the data, or they could be unmeasured lurking variables. In either case, always think about the possible effect of confounding variables when you consider the results of statistical studies. Confounding variables can be especially problematic when interpreting the results of observational studies. Randomized experiments are designed to help control the influence of confounding variables.

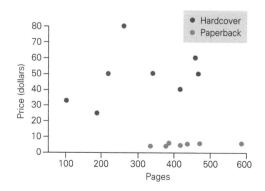

FIGURE 3.1   **Price versus pages for two types of books**

CASE STUDY 3.1
Lead Exposure and Bad Teeth

The following article appeared on the *USA Today* website (www.usatoday.com/life/health/). As you read the article, identify the explanatory and response variables and any possible lurking or confounding variables mentioned.

Lead exposure linked to bad teeth in children

Children exposed to lead are more likely to suffer tooth decay, and vitamin C might help lower blood lead levels, say two studies out Thursday. In the first of the reports in the *Journal of the American Medical Association,* researchers calculate that lead exposure could account for tooth decay in 2.7 million children. "Other people may debate that, but that's our position," says head researcher Mark Moss of the University of Rochester (N.Y.) School of Medicine and Dentistry. Prior studies showed that lead exposure can depress a child's IQ. "There are a lot worse things that lead can do to you than hurt your teeth," Moss says. He notes, however, that one of the key questions in dentistry is why low-income people experience more tooth decay than higher-income people. "This study suggests lead might be one of the reasons," he says.

The study involved 24,901 children ages 2 and older. It showed that the greater the child's exposure to lead, the more decayed or missing teeth. "The risk of getting tooth decay increased as the amount of lead went up," Moss says.

Thomas Matte of the Centers for Disease Control and Prevention says that nearly 1 million U.S. children younger than age 6 still have too much lead in their blood, particularly poor children living in older housing. An estimated 57 million residences still have lead paint on the walls, Matte says. He cautions in an editorial, however, that the problems with tooth decay might be associated with something other than lead, perhaps a sugar-rich diet or poor access to fluoridated water. "Those are good points," Moss says. "But I doubt it. We controlled for income level, the proportion of diet due to carbohydrates, calcium in the diet and the number of days since the last dental visit. We still saw this consistent pattern between dental decay and blood lead level—whether they were baby teeth or adult teeth."

In the second study, Joel Simon and his colleagues at the University of California at San Francisco studied 19,578 people who had no history of excess lead exposure. They found that the higher a person's intake of vitamin C, the lower his blood lead level. (Steve Sternberg, *USA Today*, June 23, 1999, Internet.)

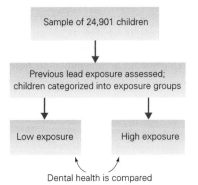

FIGURE 3.2   An observational study in Case Study 3.1: Researchers assess prior lead exposure and compare dental health of low and high exposure groups

Discussion of Case Study 3.1

The *USA Today* article is based on two *observational studies,* the first of which is described in the most detail.

Figure 3.2 illustrates the process the researchers used in the first study. Because it is an observational study, there is no randomization step in the process. The steps for this study include identifying the participants, measuring the explanatory and response variables on each participant, and making appropriate comparisons.

The researchers are interested in studying the relationship between exposure to lead and tooth decay and loss. The *explanatory variable* is level of exposure to lead, and the *response variable* is the extent to which the child has missing or decayed teeth. The article mentions a number of possible *confounding variables.* Remember that confounding variables are variables whose effect on the response variable cannot be separated from the effect of the explanatory variable. In this example, these are factors that may differ for children exposed to high and low amounts of lead and that may also affect tooth decay. The researchers measured some of these and tried to account for their impact, including "income level, the proportion of diet due to carbohydrates, calcium in the diet and the number of days since the last dental visit." They did not measure or account for other possible *lurking variables* that could also be confounding variables, such as amount of fluoride in the water and amount of general health care available to these children, which may differ for those exposed to high and low amounts of lead.

3.3

turn on your mind

For most randomized experiments, such as medical studies comparing a new treatment with a placebo, it is unrealistic to recruit a simple random sample of people to participate. Why is this the case? What can be done instead to make sure the Fundamental Rule for Using Data for Inference is not violated?*

3.3 | DESIGNING A GOOD EXPERIMENT

An *experiment* measures the effect of manipulating the environment of the participants in some way. With human participants, the manipulation may include receiving a drug or medical treatment, going through a training program, agreeing to a special diet, and so on. Most experiments on humans use volunteers because you can't very well force someone to accept a manipulation. Experiments are also done on other kinds of experimental units, such as when different growing conditions are compared for their effect on plant yield, or different paints are applied on highways to see which ones last longer. The idea is to measure the effect of the feature being manipulated, the explanatory variable, on the response variable.

Randomized experiments are particularly important because, unlike most other studies, they often allow us to determine **cause and effect.** The participants in randomized experiments are usually randomly assigned to either receive a specific treatment or to take part in a control group. The purpose of the random assignment is to make the groups approximately equal in all respects except for the explanatory variable, which is purposely manipulated. Differences in the response variable between the groups, if large enough to rule out natural chance variability, can then be attributed to the manipulation of the explanatory variable.

CASE STUDY 3.2
Kids and Weight Lifting

Is weight training good for children? If so, is it better for them to lift heavy weights for a few repetitions or moderate weights a larger number of times? Researchers at the University of Massachusetts set out to answer this question with a randomized experiment using 43 young volunteers between the ages of 5.2 and 11.8 years old. The children, recruited from a YMCA after-school program, were randomly assigned to one of three groups. Group 1 performed 6 to 8 repetitions with a heavy load, group 2 performed 13 to 15 repetitions with a moderate load, and group 3 was a control group.

Figure 3.3 illustrates the process used in this study. The steps for this randomized experiment include recruiting volunteers to participate, randomly assigning participants to the three groups, carrying out the weight-lifting treatments (the explanatory variable), and comparing muscular strength and endurance (the response variable) for the three groups.

*HINT: As an example, in a study to test a new medication to treat people with athlete's foot, would it be possible to identify the population of those afflicted, get a random sample, and get their cooperation? How might a "representative" sample be found instead?

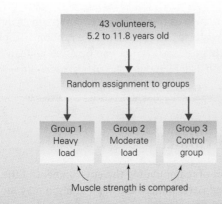

43 volunteers,
5.2 to 11.8 years old

↓

Random assignment to groups

↓   ↓   ↓

Group 1   Group 2   Group 3
Heavy   Moderate   Control
load   load   group

↖   ↑   ↗

Muscle strength is compared

FIGURE 3.3   **The randomized experiment in Case Study 3.2:
Children were randomly assigned to one of three different groups**

The exercises were performed twice a week for eight weeks. According to the research report, the higher-repetition, moderate-load group (group 2) showed the best results. Here is a sample of the results:

> Leg extension strength significantly increased in both exercise groups compared with that in the control subjects. Increases of 31.0% and 40.9%, respectively, for the low repetition–heavy load and high repetition–moderate load groups were observed. (Faigenbaum et al., 1999, p. e5)

Because the children were randomly assigned to the exercise groups, they should have been similar, on average, before the weight-training intervention. Therefore, it is reasonable to conclude that the different training programs actually *caused* the difference in results.

Who Participates in Randomized Experiments?

In most cases, the participants in randomized experiments are **volunteers.** Sometimes they are passive volunteers, such as when all patients treated at a particular medical facility are asked to sign a consent form agreeing to participate in a study. Often, researchers recruit volunteers through the newspaper. For instance, a "Well-Being" feature page in *The Sacramento Bee* had an article titled "Volunteers for Study." It said:

> People who suffer from anxiety disorders are needed for a study being conducted by the University of California, Davis, Department of Psychiatry. Researchers are examining the effectiveness of a new medication on moderate-to-severe symptoms of anxiety. The study requires volunteers who are at least 18 and in generally good health and who are not taking oral medications for their anxiety. The study lasts 14 weeks and requires routine visits to the Department of Psychiatry. All study procedures, visits and medications are free. To enroll, call . . . (*Sacramento Bee,* July 7, 1999, p. G5)

When researchers recruit volunteers for studies, they may be able to extend the results to a larger population, but this is not always the case. For instance, investigators often recruit volunteers by offering a small payment or free medical care as compensation for participation. Those who respond are more likely to be from lower socioeconomic backgrounds, and the results may not apply to the general population.

Remember the Fundamental Rule for Using Data for Inference: Available data can be used to make inferences about a much larger group *if the data can be considered to be representative with regard to the question(s) of interest.* In many randomized experiments, the question of interest is whether the treatment and control groups differ on the outcome variable(s). Common sense should enable you to figure out if the volunteers in the study are representative of a larger population for that question.

Randomization: The Crucial Element

Researchers do experiments to reduce the likelihood that the results will be affected by confounding variables and other sources of bias that often are present in observational studies. The simple principle of **randomization** is the key to doing this.

In experimentation, we want to make sure that the experimenters do not have the flexibility to choose which of the units (people, animals, etc.) receive each of the potential treatments, or in some cases, the order in which each unit receives multiple treatments. For instance, in Case Study 3.2 it was important for the researchers to randomly assign the kids to different weight-lifting routines. If they handpicked which kids received which routine, they could have chosen the strongest kids to receive the treatment they wanted to show was superior.

In many experiments, each experimental unit receives or participates in only a single treatment, such as in Case Study 1.6, when the physicians were given either aspirin or a placebo. In these experiments, the treatments are randomly assigned to the experimental units, or equivalently, the experimental units are assigned to the treatment groups. In other experiments, each experimental unit receives or participates in all of the treatments, such as when people are asked to taste and compare three brands of soda. In this case, the order in which the treatments are presented must be randomized. In Chapter 4 we will learn how both of these types of randomization are actually accomplished. For now, we discuss why randomization is necessary.

Randomizing the Type of Treatment

Randomly assigning the treatments to the experimental units keeps the researchers from making assignments favorable to their hypotheses and also helps protect against hidden or unknown biases. For example, suppose that in the experiment in Case Study 1.6, approximately the first 11,000 physicians who enrolled were given aspirin and the remaining physicians were given placebos. It could be that the healthier, more energetic physicians enrolled first, thus giving aspirin an unfair advantage.

In statistics, "random" is not synonymous with "haphazard," despite what your thesaurus might say. As we have seen, random assignments may not be possible or ethical under some circumstances. But in situations where randomization is feasible, it is usually not difficult to accomplish. It can be done with a table of random digits, a computer, or even, if done carefully, by physical means like flipping a coin or drawing numbers from a hat. The important feature, ensured by proper randomization, is that the chances of being assigned to each condition are the same for each participant.

Randomizing the Order of Treatments

In some experiments, all treatments are applied to each unit. In that case, randomization should be used to determine the *order* in which they are applied. For example, suppose an experiment is conducted to determine the extent to which drinking alcohol or smoking marijuana impairs driving ability. Because drivers are all different, it makes sense to test the same drivers under all three conditions (alcohol, marijuana, and sober) rather than using different drivers for each condition. But if everyone were tested under alcohol first, then marijuana, then sober, the performances could improve on the second and third times just from having learned something about the test.

A better method would be to randomly assign some drivers to each of the possible orderings, so the learning effect would average out over the three treatments. Notice that it is important that the assignments be made *randomly*. If we let the experimenter decide which drivers to assign to which ordering, assignments could be made to give an unfair advantage to one of the treatments.

Control Groups, Placebos, and Blinding

Control Groups

In order to determine whether or not a drug, weight-lifting routine, meditation technique, and so on has an effect, we need to know what would have happened to the response variable if the treatment had not been applied. To find that out, experimenters create **control groups,** which are treated identically in all respects except that they don't receive the active treatment. Occasionally, a control group will receive a standard or existing treatment against which a new treatment is to be compared.

Placebos

A special kind of control group is often used in studies of the effectiveness of drugs. A substantial body of research shows that people respond not only to active drugs but also to **placebos.** A placebo looks like the real drug but has no active ingredients. Placebos can be amazingly effective; studies have shown that they can help up to 62% of headache sufferers, 58% of those suffering from seasickness, and 39% of those with postoperative wound pain.

Because the **placebo effect** is so strong, drug research is generally conducted by randomly assigning half of the volunteers to receive the drug and the other half to receive a placebo, without telling them which they are receiving. The placebo looks just like the real thing, so the participants will not be able to distinguish between it and the actual drug and thus will not be influenced by belief biases.

Blinding

It isn't only the patient who can be affected by knowing whether or not he or she has received an active drug. If the researcher who is measuring the reaction of the patients were to know which group they were in, the measurements could be taken in a biased fashion.

To avoid these biases, good experiments use **double-blind** procedures. A double-blind experiment is one in which neither the participant nor the researcher taking the measurements knows who had which treatment. A **single-blind** experiment is one in which the participants do not know which treatment they have been assigned. An experiment would also be called *single-blind* if the participants knew the treatments but the researcher was kept blind.

Although double-blind experiments are preferable, they are not always possible. For example, to test the effect of meditation on blood pressure, the subjects would obviously know if they were in the meditation group or the control group. Only a single-blind study is possible, in which the person taking the blood pressure measurement would not know who was in which group.

Double Dummy

Sometimes in an experiment to compare two treatments it is impossible to mask which treatment is which, so each group receives one active treatment and one placebo treatment. For instance, suppose researchers wanted to compare the effects of nicotine patches to nicotine gum for helping people quit smoking. Obviously, participants would know if they were wearing a patch or chewing gum. So participants are asked to both wear a patch and to chew gum. One of the two will have the active ingredient (nicotine), but the other will be a placebo. In other words, the treatments would be

Group One: Nicotine patch, placebo gum
Group Two: Placebo patch, nicotine gum

This method of giving each participant two "treatments" to ensure that the experiment is blind is called **double dummy.** Sometimes a third group is used and given placebos of both methods to compare the results from each treatment method to what would happen with no active treatment at all. In our example, a third group would receive a placebo patch and placebo gum.

Pairing and Blocking

It is sometimes easier and more efficient to have each person in a study serve as his or her own control. That way, differences that inherently exist among individuals don't obscure the treatment effects. We encountered this idea when we discussed how to compare driving ability under the influence of alcohol and marijuana and when sober.

Sometimes instead of using the same individual for the treatments, researchers will match people on traits that are likely to be related to the outcome, such as age, IQ, or weight. They will then randomly assign each of the treatments to one member of each matched pair or grouping. For example, in a study comparing chemotherapy to surgery to treat cancer, patients might be matched by sex, age, and level of severity of the illness. One from each pair would then be randomly chosen to receive the chemotherapy and the other to receive surgery. (Of course, such a study would only be ethically feasible if there were no prior knowledge that one treatment was superior to the other. Patients in such cases are always required to sign an informed consent.)

Matched-Pair Designs

Experimental designs that use either two matched individuals or the same individual to receive each of two treatments are called **matched-pair designs.** The important feature of these designs is that randomization is used to assign the order of the two treatments. Of course, it is still important to try to conduct the experiment in a double-blind fashion, so that neither the participant nor the researcher knows which *order* was used.

Block Designs

The matched-pair design is a special case of a **block design.** Experimental units are divided into homogeneous groups called **blocks,** and each treatment is randomly assigned to one or more units in each block. Sometimes the "blocks" are individuals, and the "experimental units" are the repeated time periods in which they receive the varying treatments. The method discussed for comparing drivers under three conditions was a block design. Each driver is a block, and the experimental units are the three time periods during which they drove sober, with alcohol, and with marijuana. This somewhat peculiar terminology results from the fact that these ideas were first used in agricultural experiments, where the experimental units were plots of land that had been subdivided into homogeneous blocks. In the social sciences, designs such as these, in which the same participants are measured repeatedly under differing conditions, are referred to as **repeated-measures designs.**

Block designs are sometimes used when the experimental units are different enough on an important variable that experimenters group them on that variable, then assign all treatments within each group. For instance, an experiment to compare two methods for increasing memorization skills might first block participants into age groups (young, middle-aged, elderly) and then randomly assign the two methods to half of the individuals in each age group. Comparison of the two

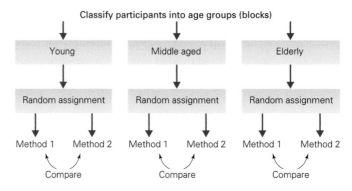

Classify participants into age groups (blocks)

| Young | Middle aged | Elderly |

| Random assignment | Random assignment | Random assignment |

| Method 1   Method 2 | Method 1   Method 2 | Method 1   Method 2 |

Compare   Compare   Compare

FIGURE 3.4   **A blocked experiment to compare two memorization methods. Within each of three age groups (blocks), individuals are randomly allocated to the two methods.**

treatments would be done separately in each age group so that differences in memorization capacity with age would not mask the differences in the two methods. Figure 3.4 illustrates the steps that would be taken in such an experiment.

3.4

turn on your mind

Students are sometimes confused by the reasons for blocking and for randomization. One method is used to control *known* sources of variability among the experimental units, and the other is used to control *unknown* sources of variability. Explain which is which, and provide examples illustrating these ideas.*

Design Terminology and Examples

If the treatments in an experiment are randomly assigned to experimental units without using matched pairs or blocks, the experiment has what is called a **completely randomized design.** When matched-pairs are used, the experiment has a **matched-pairs design,** and when blocks are used, the experiment has a **randomized block design.** When researchers design an experiment, they must decide whether to use matched-pairs, blocks, or neither. Blocks or matched-pairs are used to reduce known sources of variability in the response variable across experimental units and should be used when such sources are known and can be determined for each experimental unit. For example, if you wanted to study the relationship between exercise and weight loss, it would make sense to separate people based on whether they were initially underweight, overweight, or about right. Initial weight would be used to create matched-pairs or blocks.

Notice that there is some overlap in the terminology used for these designs because a matched-pairs design could also be considered to be a randomized block design, with each pair representing one block. Therefore, matched-pairs designs are a subset of randomized block designs, in which there are only two treatments, each assigned only once within each block.

To help you distinguish the types of experimental design, here are two examples of experiments that might be done using those designs and how each design would be accomplished.

Experiment 1: The Effect of Caffeine on Swimming Speed

Suppose a researcher wants to know if taking caffeine an hour before swimming affects the time that it takes swimmers to complete a one-mile swim and that 50 volunteers are available for the study.

◆ *Completely randomized design.* Randomly assign 25 volunteers to take a caffeine pill and the remaining 25 to take a placebo, have them all swim a mile, and compare the times for the two groups as the analysis.

◆ *Matched-pairs design.* There are two ways this could be done.

Method 1: Have each of the 50 swimmers take both treatments, with adequate time, perhaps a week, between them. In week one, randomly assign swimmers to take either a caffeine pill or a placebo. Have them swim a mile and record the time. The next week, give each swimmer the treatment he or she did not have the previous week, have them swim a mile, and record the time. For each swimmer, take the difference in the two times and use those measurements for the analysis.

Method 2: Create 25 pairs of swimmers based on speed. Before assigning treatments, measure how long it takes each one to swim a mile. Match the two fastest swimmers as one pair, the next two as the second pair, and so on. A week later, randomly assign one swimmer in each pair to take a caffeine pill and the other to take a placebo. Measure their times to swim a mile. For each pair, take the difference in the two times and use those measurements for the analysis.

◆ *Randomized block design.* This would be most appropriate if there were different types of swimmers. For instance, suppose that 10 of the volunteers were males who swim competitively, 20 were males who don't swim competitively, 8 were females who swim competitively, and the remaining 12 were females who don't swim competitively. Then each of these four groups would constitute a block, and half of each block would be randomly assigned to take a caffeine pill while the other half would take a placebo. Each person would swim a mile. The times for caffeine versus placebo would be compared within each block as well as across the four blocks combined.

Experiment 2: Advertising Strategies for Selling Coffee Near Colleges

Suppose that a national chain of coffee cafes wants to compare three methods for increasing sales at their cafes near college campuses. Each method involves placing a weekly advertisement in the campus newspaper. With method one, a coupon for a free cup of coffee is included in the ad. With method two, a coupon for a free cookie with any coffee drink is included in the ad. The third method is to place the ad without any coupons. They place the ads for one full semester and measure how much sales change from the same semester the previous year.

◆ *Completely randomized design.* For this design, they would randomly choose one-third of the campuses in the study to receive each of the treatments, and the analysis would compare the change in sales for the three treatment groups.

◆ *Matched-pairs design.* This design would not be possible if they want to compare all three treatments.

◆ *Randomized block design.* Decide what known factors contribute to differing sales across campuses. Group or "block" the campuses based on those factors. For instance, they might categorize the campuses based on size of the student body (small or large) and population of the town or city (small, medium, large) for a total of six blocks. Once the campuses have been blocked, randomly assign one-third of the campuses within each block to receive each treatment. Compare change in sales within each block, then across blocks. Other blocking variables might include initial sales, distance from the campus, and whether or not there is a competing cafe in the neighborhood.

Debate About How Many Blocks To Use

tech note Some statisticians argue that the number of experimental units in a block should only equal the number of treatments, so that each treatment is assigned only once in each block. That allows as many sources of known variability as possible to be controlled. For the example of the effect of caffeine on swimming speed there are two treatments, so blocks of size two (matched pairs) would be created. This could be accomplished by matching people on known variables such as sex, initial swim speed, usual caffeine consumption, age, and so on.

CASE STUDY 3.3
Quitting Smoking with Nicotine Patches

There is no longer any doubt that smoking cigarettes is hazardous to your health and to those around you. Yet, for someone addicted to smoking, quitting is no simple matter. One promising technique is to apply a patch to the skin that dispenses nicotine into the blood. In fact, these nicotine patches have become one of the most frequently prescribed medications in the United States.

In order to test the effectiveness of these patches on the cessation of smoking, Dr. Richard Hurt (1994) and his colleagues recruited 240 smokers at Mayo Clinics in Rochester, Minnesota, Jacksonville, Florida, and Scottsdale, Arizona. Volunteers were required to be between the ages of 20 and 65, have an expired carbon monoxide level of 10 ppm or greater (showing that they were indeed smokers), be in good health, have a history of smoking at least 20 cigarettes per day for the past year, and be motivated to quit.

Volunteers were randomly assigned to receive either 22-mg nicotine patches or placebo patches for eight weeks. They were also provided with an intervention program recommended by the National Cancer Institute, in which they received counseling before, during, and for many months after the eight-week period of wearing the patches.

After the eight-week period of patch use, almost half (46%) of the nicotine group had quit smoking, while only one-fifth (20%) of the placebo group had. Having quit was defined as "self-reported abstinence (not even a puff) since the last visit and an expired air carbon monoxide level of 8 ppm or less" (p. 596). After a year, rates in both groups had declined, but the group that had received the nicotine patch still had a higher percentage who successfully quit than did the placebo group, 27.5% versus 14.2%.

The study was double-blind, so neither the participants nor the nurses taking the measurements knew who had received the active nicotine patches. The study was funded by a grant from Lederle Laboratories and was published in the *Journal of the American Medical Association*. Because this was a well-designed randomized experiment, it is likely that the nicotine patches actually *caused* the additional percentage who had quit in the nicotine patch group compared with the control group.

3.4 | DESIGNING A GOOD OBSERVATIONAL STUDY

Observational studies start with a distinct *disadvantage* compared to experiments when trying to establish causal links. The researchers observe, but cannot control, the explanatory variables. However, they have the *advantage* that they are more likely to measure participants in their natural setting. Before looking at some complications that can arise, let's look at an example of a well-designed observational study.

CASE STUDY 3.4
Baldness and Heart Attacks

On March 8, 1993, *Newsweek* announced, "A really bad hair day: Researchers link baldness and heart attacks" (p. 62). The article reported that "men with typical male pattern baldness ... are anywhere from 30 to 300 percent more likely to suffer a heart attack than men with little or no hair loss at all." (Pattern baldness is the type affecting the crown or vertex and not the same thing as a receding hairline; it affects approximately one-third of middle-aged men.)

The report was based on an observational study conducted by researchers at Boston University School of Medicine. They compared 665 men who had been admitted to the hospital with their first heart attack to 772 men in the same age group (21 to 54 years old) who had been admitted to the same hospitals for other reasons. There were 35 hospitals involved, all in eastern Massachusetts and Rhode Island. Lesko, Rosenberg, and Shapiro reported the full results in the *Journal of the American Medical Association* (1993).

The study found that the percentage of men who showed some degree of pattern baldness was substantially higher for those who had had a heart attack (42%) than for those who had not (34%). Further, when they used sophisticated statistical tests to ask the question in the reverse direction, they found that there was an increased risk of heart attack for men with any degree of pattern baldness. The analysis methods included adjustments for age and other heart attack risk factors. The increase in risk was more severe with increasing severity of baldness, after adjusting for age and other risk factors.

The authors of the study speculated that a third variable, perhaps a male hormone, might simultaneously increase the risk of heart attacks and the propensity for baldness. With an observational study such as this one, scientists can establish a connection, and they can then look for causal mechanisms in future investigations.

Special Types of Observational Studies

Retrospective or Prospective Studies

Observational studies can be classified according to whether they are **retrospective,** in which participants are asked to recall past events, or **prospective,** in which participants are followed into the future and events are recorded. The prospective approach is a better procedure, because people often do not remember past events accurately.

Case-Control Studies

In a **case-control study,** "cases" who have a particular attribute or condition are compared to "controls" who do not. The idea is to compare the cases and controls to see how they differ on an explanatory variable of interest. In medical settings, the cases usually are individuals who have been diagnosed with a particular disease. Researchers then identify a group of controls who are as similar as possible to the cases, except that they don't have the disease. In order to achieve this similarity, researchers often use patients hospitalized for other causes as the controls.

Case Study 3.4 is an example of a case-control study. In this example, men who had been admitted to the hospital with a heart attack were the cases, and men who had been admitted for other reasons were the controls. The cases and controls were compared on a variable of interest, which in Case Study 3.4 was the degree of baldness. In essence, the explanatory variable is whether a participant is a case or a control (heart attack or not), and the response variable is

FIGURE 3.5   The case-control design in Case Study 3.4: Samples of male heart attack patients (cases) and other male hospital patients (controls) were compared for the extent of baldness

the measurement of interest (degree of baldness). Figure 3.5 illustrates the steps taken in this study.

Sometimes cases are matched with controls on an individual basis. That type of design is similar to a matched-pair experimental design. The analysis proceeds by first comparing the pair, then summarizing over all pairs. Unlike a matched-pair experiment, the researcher does not randomly assign treatments within pairs, but is restricted to how they occur naturally. For example, to identify whether or not left-handed people die at a younger age, researchers might match each left-handed case with a right-handed sibling as a control and compare their ages at death. Handedness could obviously not be randomly assigned to the two individuals, so confounding factors (like the fact that most tools are made for right-handed people) might be responsible for any observed differences.

Advantages of Case-Control Studies

Case-control studies have become increasingly popular in medical research, with good reason. They do not suffer from the ethical considerations inherent in the random assignment of potentially harmful or beneficial treatments. In addition, case-control studies can be efficient in terms of time, money, and the inclusion of enough people with the disease.

Efficiency

In an exercise given later in this book, researchers were interested in whether or not owning a pet bird is related to the incidence of lung cancer. Imagine trying to design an experiment to study this problem. You would randomly assign people to either own a bird or not and then wait to see how many in each group contracted lung cancer. The problem is that you would have to wait a long time, and even then, you would observe very few cases of lung cancer in either group. In the end, you may not have enough cases for a valid comparison.

A case-control study, in contrast, would identify a large group of people who had just been diagnosed with lung cancer, then ask them whether or not they had owned a pet bird. A similar control group would be identified and asked the same question. A comparison would then be made between the proportion of cases (lung-cancer patients) who had birds and the proportion of controls who had birds.

Reducing Potential Confounding Variables

Another advantage of case-control studies over other observational studies is that the controls are chosen to try to reduce potential confounding variables. For example, in Case Study 3.4, suppose it was simply the case that balding men were less healthy than other men and were therefore more likely to get sick in some way. An observational study that recorded only whether or not someone had baldness and whether or not he had experienced a heart attack would not be able to control for that fact. By using other hospitalized patients as the controls, the researchers were able to partially account for general health as a potential confounding factor.

You can see that careful thought is needed to choose controls that reduce potential confounding factors and do not introduce new ones. For example, suppose we want to know if heavy exercise induces heart attacks, and as cases we use people recently admitted to the hospital with a heart attack. We would certainly not want to use other newly admitted patients as controls. People who are sick enough to enter the hospital (for anything other than sudden emergencies) would probably not have been recently engaging in heavy exercise. When you read the results of a case-control study, you should pay attention to how the controls were selected.

3.5 | DIFFICULTIES AND DISASTERS IN EXPERIMENTS AND OBSERVATIONAL STUDIES

There are a number of complications that can arise if researchers are not careful in conducting and reporting experiments and observational studies. Some apply only to observational studies, some only to experiments, and some to both settings. The first step in reading the results of a study is to determine if it's an experiment or an observational study. The conclusions you can make differ for the two types. We first list the possible problems, then describe each one in detail.

Difficulties and Disasters in Experiments and Observational Studies

- Confounding variables and the implication of causation in observational studies
- Extending results inappropriately
- Interacting variables
- Placebo, Hawthorne, and experimenter effects
- Ecological validity and generalizability
- Relying on memory or secondhand sources

Confounding Variables and the Implication of Causation in Observational Studies

Probably the biggest single misinterpretation made when reporting studies is to imply that a *cause-and-effect* relationship can be concluded on the basis of an observational study. There is simply no way to separate the role of confounding variables from the role of explanatory variables in producing the outcome variable if randomization has not been used.

A partial solution is for researchers to measure possible confounding variables and include them in the analysis to see if they are related to the outcome variable. Another partial solution can be achieved in case-control studies by choosing the controls to be as similar as possible to the cases. In Chapter 17 we discuss some nonstatistical considerations that can help you determine whether a causal link is plausible based on observational studies. The other part of the solution is up to you as a consumer of information: Don't be misled into thinking a causal relationship exists when it doesn't.

EXAMPLE 3.5
Will Preventing Artery
Clog Prevent Memory Loss?

An observational study based on a random sample of over 6000 older people (average age 70 when the study began) found that 70% of the participants did not lose cognitive functioning over time. One important finding, however, was that "those who have diabetes or high levels of atherosclerosis in combination with a gene for Alzheimer's disease are eight times more likely to show a decline in cognitive function." This finding led one of the researchers to comment that "that has implications for prevention, which is good news. If we can prevent atherosclerosis, we can prevent memory loss over time, and we know how to do that with behavior changes—low-fat diets, weight control, exercise, not smoking, and drug treatments." (*Source:* "Study: Age doesn't sap memory," *Sacramento Bee,* Kathryn Doré Perkins, July 7, 1999. pp. A1 and A10.)

But notice that this conclusion assumes that the memory loss is *caused* by atherosclerosis. This conclusion is not justified on the basis of an observational study. Perhaps certain people have a genetic predisposition to artherosclerosis and to memory loss, in which case preventing the former condition with lifestyle changes will not reduce the memory loss. Or perhaps people who suffer from depression tend to eat poorly, not exercise well, and also suffer from memory loss. There are simply too many possible confounding factors that could be related to both artherosclerosis and memory loss to conclude that preventing artherosclerosis would prevent memory loss. ◆

Extending Results Inappropriately

In interpreting both randomized experiments and observational studies, keep in mind the Fundamental Rule for Using Data for Inference: Available data can be used to make inferences about a much larger group *if the data can be considered to be representative with regard to the question(s) of interest.* Some observational studies are based on random samples, in which case the results can readily be extended to the population from which the sample was drawn. Example 3.5 is one such example; the study on aging and memory loss was part of the large Cardiovascular Health Study, sponsored by the National Heart, Lung and Blood Institute, part of the National Institutes of Health.

Many observational studies and almost all randomized experiments use convenience samples or volunteers. It is up to you to determine whether or not the results can be extended to any larger group for the question of interest. For example, the weight-lifting experiment in Case Study 3.2 used 11 girls and 32 boys who volunteered to participate in the study. There is no reason to suspect that these volunteers would differ from other children in terms of the differential effects of no training, moderate lifting, and heavy lifting measured in the study. Thus, although the sample consisted solely of volunteers, the results can probably be extended to other children in this age group.

Interacting Variables

Sometimes a second variable *interacts* with the explanatory variable in its relationship with the outcome variable. This can be a problem if the results of a study are reported without taking the interaction into account. Although the reported results may be true on average, they may not hold for specific subgroups.

For example, in Case Study 3.3, there was an interaction between the treatment (nicotine or placebo patch) and whether there were other smokers at

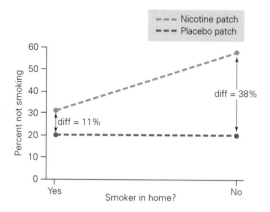

FIGURE 3.6   Interaction in Case Study 3.3: The difference between the nicotine and placebo patches is greater when there are no smokers in the home than when there are smokers in the home

home. The researchers measured and reported this interaction, which is illustrated in Figure 3.6. When there were no other smokers in the participant's home, the eight-week success rate was actually 58% for the nicotine patch users compared to 20% for the placebo patch group. When there were other smokers in the home, the eight-week success rate for the nicotine patch was only 31%, but the success rate for the placebo users remained at about 20%. In other words, the amount by which the nicotine and placebo groups differed was affected by whether other smokers were present in the home. Therefore, it would be misleading to merely report that 46% of the nicotine recipients had quit without also providing the information about the interaction.

Hawthorne and Experimenter Effects

We have already discussed the fact that a placebo can have a very strong effect on experimental outcomes, since the power of suggestion is somehow able to affect the result. A similar difficulty is that participants in an experiment respond differently than they otherwise would, just because they are in the experiment. This is called the **Hawthorne effect** because it was first detected in 1924 when studying factory workers at the Hawthorne, Illinois plant of the Western Electric Company. (The phrase was not actually coined until much later; see French, 1953.)

The Hawthorne effect is a common problem in medical research. Many treatments have been observed to have a higher success rate in clinical trials than they do in actual practice. This may occur because patients and researchers are highly motivated to correctly carry out a treatment protocol in a clinical trial.

Related to these effects are numerous ways in which the experimenter can bias the results. These **experimenter effects** include recording the data erroneously to match the desired outcome, treating subjects differently based on which condition they are receiving, or subtly making the subjects aware of the desired outcome. Most of these problems can be overcome by using double-blind designs and by including a placebo group or a control group that gets identical handling except for the active part of the treatment. Other problems, such as incorrect data recording, should be addressed by allowing data to be automatically entered into a computer when it is collected, if possible. Depending on the experiment, there may still be subtle ways in which experimenter effects can sneak into the results. You should be aware of these possibilities when you read the results of a study.

EXAMPLE 3.6
Dull Rats

In a classic experiment designed to test whether or not the expectations of the experimenter could really influence the results, Rosenthal and Fode (1963) deliberately conned 12 experimenters. They gave each one 5 rats that had been taught to run a maze. They told 6 of the experimenters that the rats had been bred to do well (i.e., they were "maze bright") and told the other 6 that their rats were "maze dull" and should not be expected to do well. Sure enough, the experimenters who had been told they had bright rats found learning rates far superior to those found by the experimenters who had been told they had dull rats. Hundreds of other studies have since confirmed the experimenter effect. ◆

Ecological Validity and Generalizability

Suppose you want to compare three assertiveness-training methods to see which is more effective in teaching people how to say "no" to unwanted requests for their time. Would it be realistic to give participants the training, then measure the results by asking them to role-play in situations in which they should say "no"? Probably not, since everyone involved would know that they were only role-playing. The usual social pressures to say "yes" would not be as present.

This is an example of an experiment with little **ecological validity.** The variables have been removed from their natural setting and are measured in the laboratory or in some other artificial setting. Thus, the results do not accurately reflect the impact of the variables in the real world or in everyday life. Whenever you read the results of a study you should question its ecological validity and its generalizability.

EXAMPLE 3.7
***Real Smokers
with a Desire to Quit***

The researchers in Case Study 3.3, the nicotine patch study, did many things to help ensure ecological validity and generalizability. First, they used a standard intervention program available from and recommended by the National Cancer Institute, instead of inventing their own, so that other physicians could follow the same program. Next, they used participants at three different locations around the country rather than in one community only, and they involved a wide range of ages (20 to 65). They included individuals who lived in households with other smokers as well as those who did not. Finally, they recorded numerous other variables (sex, race, education, marital status, psychological health, etc.) and checked to make sure these were not related to the response variable or the patch assignment. ◆

Relying on Memory or Secondhand Sources

Retrospective observational studies can be particularly unreliable because they ask people to recall past behavior. Some studies, in which the response variable is whether or not someone has died, can be even worse because they rely on the memories of relatives and friends rather than the actual participants to measure explanatory and other variables. Retrospective studies also suffer from the fact that variables that confounded things in the past may no longer be similar to those that would currently be confounding variables, and researchers may not think to measure them.

If at all possible, prospective studies should be used. That's not always possible. For example, researchers who first considered the potential causes of AIDS or toxic-shock syndrome had to start with those who were ill and try to find common factors from their pasts. If possible, retrospective studies should use authoritative sources such as medical records rather than rely on memory.

EXAMPLE 3.8
Do Left-Handers Die Young?

A few years ago, a highly publicized study pronounced that left-handed people did not live as long as right-handed people (Coren and Halpern, 1991). In one part of the study, the researchers had sent letters to next of kin for a random sample of recently deceased individuals, asking which hand the deceased had used for writing, drawing, and throwing a ball. They found that the average age of death for those who had been left-handed was 66, while for those who had been right-handed it was 75.

What the researchers failed to take into account was that in the early part of the 20th century many children were forced to write with their right hands, even if their natural inclination was to be left-handed. Therefore, people who died in their 70s and 80s during the time of this study were more likely to be right-handed than those who died in their 50s and 60s. The confounding factor of how long ago one learned to write was not taken into account. A better study would be a prospective one, following current left- and right-handers to see which group survived longer, but you can imagine the practical difficulties of conducting such a study. The participants could well outlive the researchers. ◆

KEY TERMS

EXERCISES   Blue = Basics   **Bold, Bold** = Answer in back

Sections 3.1 and 3.2

3.1 The median income for a random sample of households in a school district was found to be $36,300. From this information, the school board decided that the median income for all households in the district was probably between about $32,000 and $40,000. Describe the difference between descriptive statistics and inferential statistics in the context of this example.

3.2 According to the Fundamental Rule for Using Data for Inference, when can available data be used to make inferences about a much larger group?

3.3 In a class of 20 students (John, Maria, Inez, Bill, etc.), a simple random sample of two people will be selected from the class. Use the definition of a simple random sample to compare the chance that John and Maria will be the group selected with the chance that Maria and Bill will be the group selected.

3.4 Suppose a statistics teacher wants to know whether the number of hours students spend studying in a group affects the final course grade. In each part, explain whether the research method described is a randomized experiment or an observational study.
  a. Each student keeps a log of the hours he or she spends studying in a group, and reports the total after the course is completed.
  b. Students are randomly assigned to study groups. The teacher tells each group how often to meet. This varies from one hour the day before each exam to two hours per week.
  c. Students voluntarily join groups based on how often the groups will meet. The groups are designated as meeting weekly, meeting only before exams, or meeting whenever enough members feel it is necessary.

3.5 To estimate the percent of households in the United States that use a DVD player, a researcher surveys a randomly selected sample of 500 households and asks about DVD player usage.
  a. What is the unit being measured in this survey?
  b. What is the population of interest in this survey?
  c. What is the sample in this survey?

3.6 In each part, identify the response variable and the explanatory variable in the relationship between the two given variables.
  a. Daughter's height and mother's height.
  b. Age and weight for children between the ages of 3 and 10 years old.
  c. Opinion about the death penalty for persons convicted of murder and political party membership (Democrat, Republican, etc.)
  d. Smoking habits and performance on a test of lung function.

3.7 Remember that a confounding variable affects the response variable and is related to the explanatory variable. For each of the following situations, explain how the given confounding variable meets these criteria.
  a. *Response variable* = Math skills of children aged 6 to 12 years old; *explanatory variable* = shoe size; *confounding variable* = age.

  b. *Response variable* = Whether or not a student gets a cold during a school term; *explanatory variable* = whether or not the student procrastinates in doing assignments; *confounding variable* = number of hours per week the student spends socializing.
  c. *Response variable* = Child's IQ at age 10; *explanatory variable* = whether mother smokes or not; *confounding variable* = mother's educational level.
  d. *Response variable* = Number of missing or decayed teeth a child has; *explanatory variable* = amount of past exposure to lead; *confounding variable* = number of visits to a dentist child has made in the past three years.

3.8 For each of the following situations explain whether or not the Fundamental Rule for Using Data for Inference holds.
  a. *Available Data:* Salaries for a random sample of male and female professional basketball players.
    Research Question: Are women paid less than men who are in equivalent jobs?
  b. *Available Data:* Pulse rates for smokers and nonsmokers in a large statistics class at a major university.
    Research Question: Do college-age smokers have higher pulse rates than college-age nonsmokers?
  c. *Available Data:* Opinions on whether or not the legal drinking age should be lowered to 19 years old, collected from a random sample of 1000 adults in the state.
    Research Question: Does a majority of adults in the state support lowering the drinking age to 19?
  d. *Available Data:* Opinions on whether or not the legal drinking age should be lowered to 19 years old, collected from a random sample of parents of high school students in the state.
    Research Question: Does a majority of adults in the state support lowering the drinking age to 19?

3.9 For each of the following research scenarios, explain whether a randomized experiment could be used.
  a. To study the relationship between long-term practice of meditation and blood pressure.
  b. To determine whether a special training program improves scores on a standard college admissions test.
  c. To compare two programs to reduce the number of commuters who drive to work: providing discount coupons for the bus, or providing shuttle service for people who need to run errands during the workday.
  d. To study the relationship between age and opinion about whether marijuana should be legal.

3.10 Refer to exercise 3.9. In each case, state the explanatory variable and the response variable.

3.11 Refer to exercise 3.9. In each case, give an explanation of a possible confounding variable that could be present if an observational study were done.

3.12 Give an example of an observational study, and explain the difference between a confounding variable and a lurking variable in the context of your example.

3.13 Explain whether a variable can be both
  a. A confounding variable and a lurking variable.
  b. A response variable and a confounding variable.
  c. An explanatory variable and a dependent variable.

3.14 Refer to the first observational study described in Case Study 3.1. Give an example of a possible confounding variable in addition to those described in the text. Explain why it could be a confounding variable.

3.15 A friend has recommended the work of a musician who has recorded five CDs, each containing ten selections. You decide to visit a music store and listen to a simple random sample of four songs. Explain how you could select the four songs.

3.16 Refer to the previous exercise. Suppose you randomly chose four of the CDs, then randomly chose one song from each one. Would this be considered a simple random sample of the musician's songs? Explain.

3.17 A news article on the *Reuters Health* website, Dec. 18, 1998 reported that

> A study of over 1200 people over age 65 showed that the "owls"—those who go to sleep after 11 p.m. and rise after 8 a.m.—tend to be as healthy and intelligent as "larks"—those who go to bed before 11 p.m. and rise before 8 a.m.—according to a report in the December 19/26 issue of the *British Medical Journal* [Vol. 317, pp. 1675–1677]. The researchers also found that owls tend to have higher average income than the early birds.

a. Do you think this is based on an observational study or a randomized experiment? Explain.

b. It is mentioned that the "owls" have higher average income than the "larks." Explain whether or not income is a possible confounding variable in this study.

c. Give an example of a possible confounding variable that is not mentioned.

d. Draw a figure similar to Figure 3.2, illustrating the steps in this study.

3.18 A news article by *Reuters* on October 6, 1998 reported:

> In a new study, Dr. Matti Uhari and colleagues at the University of Oulu in Finland, randomly gave 857 healthy children in daycare centers xylitol in syrup, gum or a lozenge form, or a placebo gum or syrup in five doses per day for 3 months. According to a report in the October issue of the journal *Pediatrics* [Vol. 102, pp. 879–884, 971–972, 974–975], the incidence of ear infections were reduced by 40% in children given xylitol chewing gum, 30% in those given syrup and 20% in those given lozenges when compared to children given a placebo.

a. Is this an observational study or a randomized experiment? Explain.

b. What are the explanatory and response variables?

c. Are confounding variables likely to be a problem in this study? Explain.

Sections 3.3 and 3.4

3.19 Twenty students agreed to participate in a study on colds. Ten were randomly assigned to receive vitamin C, and the remaining 10 received a tablet that looked and tasted like vitamin C but in fact contained only sugar and flavoring. The students did not know whether they were taking vitamin C or not, but the investigators did. The students were followed for two months to see who came down with a cold and who didn't. Explain whether each of the following terms applies to this study.

a. Observational study.

b. Randomized experiment.

c. Placebo.

d. Single-blind.

e. Double-blind.

f Matched pairs.

g. Repeated measures.

3.20 A school district has 20 elementary schools and each school has 12 classes that can be used for a study.

a. Describe a randomized block design to compare three teaching methods, using schools as blocks.

b. Explain why schools should be used as blocks.

3.21 Twenty volunteers aged 40 to 65 years old will participate in an experiment done to compare two methods of memorizing information. The age variation in the participants concerns the researchers because memorization skills decrease with age.

a. Describe how the study could be done using a matched-pair design.

b. Explain why a matched-pair design is a good idea in this situation.

3.22 Refer to Case Study 3.2, "Kids and Weight Lifting." Did the experiment described use a completely randomized design, a matched-pair design, or a randomized block design? Explain.

3.23 Students who had meningitis were matched with other students without meningitis on gender, undergraduate (or graduate) status, and college. The purpose of the study was to discover risk factors for meningitis. Explain whether each of the following terms applies to this observational study.

a. Prospective study.

b. Retrospective study.

c. Case-control study.

3.24 Students whose undergraduate major was economics were followed for 10 years after graduation to study the number of different jobs they took. Explain whether each of the following terms applies to this observational study.

a. Prospective study.

b. Retrospective study.

c. Case-control study.

3.25 What type of variable is being described by, "a variable that affects the response variable and is also related to the explanatory variable?"

3.26 Refer to Case Study 3.3, "Quitting Smoking with Nicotine Patches," which used a completely randomized design. Explain how the experiment could have been done using a randomized block design instead.

3.27 Explain whether each of the following experiments was single-blind, double-blind, or neither.

a. An electric company wanted to know if residential customers would use less electricity during peak hours if they were charged more during those hours. One hundred customers were randomly selected to receive the special time-of-day rates, and they were matched with 100 customers who were similar in terms of past electrical use and household size. Special meters were installed for all 200 customers, and at the end of three months the usage during peak hours was compared for each pair. The technician who read the meters did not know who had which rate plan.

b. To test an herbal treatment for depression, 100 volunteers who suffered from mild depression were randomly divided into two groups. Each person was given a month's supply of tea bags. For one group, the tea contained the herb mixed with a spice tea, whereas for the other group, the bags contained only the spice tea. Participants were not told which type of tea they had and were asked to drink one cup of the tea per day for a month. At the end of the month, a psychologist evaluated them to determine if their mood had improved. The psychologist did not know who had the tea with the herbal ingredient added.

c. To compare three packaging designs for a new food, a manufacturer randomly selected three grocery stores in each of 50 cities. The three designs were randomly assigned to the three stores in each city, and sales were compared for a two-month period.

3.28 Refer to exercise 3.27. In each case, explain whether the experiment was a matched-pair design, a block design, or neither.

3.29 Refer to exercise 3.27. In each case, designate the explanatory variable and the response variable.

3.30 Refer to exercise 3.27. In each case, explain whether a control group was used and whether a placebo treatment was used.

3.31 Refer to exercise 3.27. In each case, explain the extent to which you think the results from the sample in the experiment could be extended to a larger population.

3.32 Explain why confounding variables are more of a problem in observational studies than in randomized experiments. Give an example.

3.33 Echinacea is an herb that may help prevent colds and flu. Explain how researchers could conduct a double-blind, double-dummy experiment to compare echinacea tea with chewable vitamin C pills for effectiveness in preventing colds.

3.34 Suppose researchers were interested in determining the relationship, if any, between the use of cellular telephones and the incidence of brain cancer. Would it be better to use a randomized experiment, a case-control study, or an observational study that did not use cases and controls? Explain.

3.35 Find an example of an observational study in the news. Determine whether or not it was a case-control study and if it was prospective or retrospective. Specify the explanatory and response variables, and explain whether confounding variables were likely to be a major problem in interpreting the results. Be sure to include the news article with your response.

3.36 Reuters (June 24, 1997) reported on a study published in the *Journal of the American Medical Association* (1997, Vol. 277, pp. 1940–1944) in which researchers recruited 276 volunteers (aged 18 to 55) and used nose drops to infect them with a cold virus. The volunteers were then quarantined and observed to see if they came down with a cold or infection. They also answered questions about their social lives, including the number of different types of contacts they had (family, work, community, religious groups, and so on). *Reuters* reported that "those with one to three types of social contacts were 4.2 times as likely to come down with cold symptoms and signs of infection compared to those with six or more contacts."

a. Was this an observational study or a randomized experiment? Explain.

b. What were the explanatory and response variables of interest to the researchers?

c. The researchers in this study took an unusual step to help reduce the impact of confounding variables. Explain what they did and why it might have helped to reduce the impact of confounding variables.

3.37 A story at ABCNEWS.com ("Pet Contact" by Rita Rubin, March 17, 1998) reported: Karen Allen, a researcher at the University of Buffalo, found that couples who own cats or dogs have more satisfying marriages and are less stressed-out than those who don't own pets. Pet owners also have more contact with each other and with other people. Allen compared 50 couples who owned either cats or dogs with 50 pet-free couples. The volunteers completed a standard questionnaire assessing their relationship and how attached they were to their pets. They also kept track of their social contacts over a two-week period. To see how the couples responded to stress, Allen monitored their heart rates and blood pressure while they discussed sore subjects. Pet-owning couples started out with lower blood pressure readings than the others, and their numbers didn't rise as much when they argued.

a. Was this a case-control study, a randomized experiment, or an observational study that was not case-controlled?

b. What are the explanatory and response variables in this study?

c. Give an example of a possible confounding variable.

d. Draw a figure illustrating the steps in this study, similar to Figures 3.2 through 3.5.

Section 3.5

3.38 For each of the following, explain whether the study summary describes an interacting variable or a confounding variable.

a. A comparison of the mean grade point averages of male and female students finds more difference for fraternity and sorority members than for students living in dorms and off-campus.

b. A study finds that wine drinkers tend to have better health than beer drinkers, but also finds that wine drinkers tend to smoke less than beer drinkers.

c. It is found that drawing a happy face on a restaurant bill increases mean tip percent for female servers but does not increase mean tip percent for male servers.

3.39 Researchers have found that women who take oral contraceptives (birth control pills) are at higher risk of having a heart attack or stroke and that the risk is substantially higher if a woman smokes. In investigating the relationship between taking oral contraceptives (the explanatory variable) and having a heart attack or stroke (the response variable), would smoking be called a confounding variable or an interacting variable? Explain.

3.40 In a study on worker productivity done in 1927 in Cicero, Illinois, it was observed that productivity improved when the lighting was increased. However, it was observed that productivity also improved when the lighting was decreased. What term is used to describe the fact that productivity increased simply because the subjects knew they were in an experiment?

3.41 A new medication is observed to cause a weight loss in women but a weight gain in men. Identify what the response variable, explanatory variable, and interacting variable are in this situation.

3.42 An investigator believes that a new medication will help reduce anxiety and that a placebo will not. In a single-blind study (patients are blind), she finds that the group taking the new medication had reduced anxiety while the placebo group did not. Explain how the experimenter effect may have played a role in the results.

3.43 In a sample of 500 college students aged 18 to 21, it was found that offering discount coupons for restaurant meals substantially increased the likelihood that they would eat at those restaurants. Explain how "extending results inappropriately" may be a problem in the interpretation of this study.

3.44 An experiment on elephants in captivity was done to see if breeding would occur more often when the elephants were kept together in a herd or when a male was isolated with a female. Explain how ecological validity affects the ability to generalize these results to wild elephants.

3.45 A retrospective study of 517 veterans who never smoked was done to see if there was an association between lung disease and exposure to workplace gases, dust, and fumes (Clawson, *Stanford Report*, November 1, 2000). In this study, subjects were asked whether or not they remembered being exposed to gases, dust, or fumes in the workplace. A concern expressed by the investigator was that "patients who have histories of lung diseases may be more likely to recall a history of exposure—whether accurate or not—than subjects reporting good health." Discuss whether each of the following is likely to be a problem in this study.
    a. Relying on memory.
    b. Confounding variable.
    c. Hawthorne effect.

3.46 Refer to exercise 3.37, describing a study about pet ownership and marriage. Explain whether each of the following is likely to be a problem for that study:
    a. Confounding variables and the implication of causation in observational studies.
    b. Placebo, Hawthorne, and experimenter effects.
    c. Ecological validity and generalizability.

3.47 Refer to exercise 3.27. For each of the experiments described, pick one of the "Difficulties and Disasters" described in Section 3.5, and explain how it might be a problem in that experiment.

3.48 Is the experimenter effect more likely to be a problem in a study that is double-blind, single-blind, or not blind at all? Explain.

3.49 Pick the two "Difficulties and Disasters" most likely to be a problem in each of the following studies, and explain why they would be a problem:
    a. To compare marketing methods, a marketing professor randomly divides a large class into three groups and randomly assigns each group to watch one of three television commercials. The students are then asked to rate how likely they would be to buy the advertised product.
    b. Volunteers are recruited through a newspaper article to participate in a study of a new vaccine for hepatitis C, which is transmitted by contact with infected blood and is a particular problem for intravenous drug users. The article specifically requests both in-

travenous drug users and medical workers to volunteer, assuring them confidentiality and offering them free medical care for the life of the study. Volunteers are then randomly assigned to receive either a placebo or the vaccine, and a year later they are tested to see if they have the disease.
    c. A researcher at a large medical clinic wants to determine if a high-fat diet in childhood is more likely to result in heart disease in later life. As a case-control study, she gives a questionnaire to 500 patients with heart disease and 500 other clinic patients matched by age and sex. The questionnaire asks about childhood diet.

3.50 Refer to part (c) of the previous exercise, describing a case-control study relating childhood diet and heart disease. Comment on the extent to which each of the following is likely to be a problem.
    a. Confounding variables and the implication of causation in observational studies.
    b. Extending results inappropriately.
    c. Interacting variables.
    d. Placebo, Hawthorne, and experimenter effects.
    e. Ecological validity and generalizability.
    f. Relying on memory or secondhand sources.

3.51 A categorical interacting variable defines subgroups for which the effect of the explanatory variable on the outcome variable differs. For instance, as explained in the text, for the nicotine patch experiment described in Case Study 3.3, one interacting variable was whether or not there were other smokers at home. When the difference in subgroups is thought to hold for the population, the subgroup variable is sometimes called an **effect modifier.** Explain why this term makes sense, using the context of the smokers at home in the nicotine experiment. For instance, what "effect" is being modified?

Chapter Exercises

Exercises 3.52 to 3.60 refer to a study published in the Journal of the American Medical Association *and reported in the* Sacramento Bee *on Jan. 26, 2000 ("Study ties hormone replacement, cancer" by Shari Roan, p. A1). A sample of 46,355 postmenopausal women were studied for 15 years and asked about their use of hormone therapy and whether or not they had breast cancer; 2082 developed the disease. The article reported that "for each year of combined [estrogen and progestin] therapy, a woman's risk of breast cancer was found to increase by 8 percent compared to a 1 percent increase in women taking estrogen alone.*

3.52 Do you think this research was an observational study or a randomized experiment? Explain.

3.53 Discuss whether this research is the following:
    a. A case-control study.
    b. A retrospective study or a prospective study.

3.54 What are the explanatory and response variables for this study? Are they quantitative or categorical? If they are categorical, what are the categories?

3.55 Refer to the questions listed under "Asking the Right Questions" in Section 2.2 of Chapter 2. Which of those questions is being answered in this research? Give the general question, and the specific question in the context of this study.

3.56 To whom are the women taking combined therapy and estrogen alone being compared when the increased risks of 8% and 1% are computed?

3.57 Assuming the women and their physicians made the decision about which treatment to pursue (combined hormones, estrogen alone, or no hormones), discuss the possibility of confounding variables in this study.

3.58 Near the end of the *Sacramento Bee* article, it was noted that "the NCI researchers analyzed their results by the woman's weight.... There was no increased breast cancer risk in heavier women." Which of the "Difficulties and Disasters" in Section 3.5 is represented by this statement? Explain.

3.59 One drawback of the study quoted in the *Sacramento Bee* was that "people who develop breast cancer are much more likely to remember whether they took hormones compared to women who don't develop the disease." Which of the "Difficulties and Disasters" in Section 3.5 is represented by this statement? Explain.

3.60 Another drawback of the study quoted in the *Sacramento Bee* was that "the women in the study may not resemble women today, because many women now take lower doses of progestin than was used during the follow-up years of the study (1979–95)." Which of the "Difficulties and Disasters" in Section 3.5 is represented by this statement? Explain.

Exercises 3.61 to 3.66 refer to a study described in a Sacramento Bee *article titled "Much ado over those bad hairdos" (Jan. 26, 2000, p. A21). Here is part of the article:*

> Researchers surveyed 60 men and 60 women from 17 to 30, most of them Yale students. They were separated into three groups. One group was questioned about times in their lives when they had bad hair. The second group was told to think about bad product packaging, like leaky containers, to get them in a negative mind-set. The third group was not asked to think about anything negative. The groups were tested for self-esteem and self-judgment, and the bad hair group scored lower than the others.

3.61 Was this an observational study or a randomized experiment? Explain.

3.62 What were the explanatory and response variables for this study? Were they categorical variables or quantitative variables?

3.63 Refer to the questions listed under "Asking the Right Questions" in Chapter 2, Section 2.2. Which of those questions is being answered in this research? Give the general question, and the specific question in the context of this study.

3.64 Discuss whether this study could have been blind or double-blind, and whether you think it was blind or double-blind.

3.65 Discuss each of the following "Difficulties and Disasters" in the context of this research.
   a. Ecological validity.
   b. Extending results inappropriately.
   c. Experimenter effect.

3.66 The article also reported that "contrary to popular belief men's self-esteem may take a greater licking than women's when their hair just won't behave. Men were likely to feel less smart and less capable when their hair stuck out, was badly cut or otherwise mussed." In the context of this quote, is male/female a confounding variable, an interacting variable, or neither?

3.67 For each of the following examples from the text, explain whether there would be more interest in descriptive statistics (for the acquired data set only) or in inferential statistics (extending results to a larger population).
   a. Ages at death of First Ladies.
   b. The relationship between nicotine patch use and cessation of smoking.
   c. Annual rainfall data for Davis, California.
   d. The relationship between nightlights and myopia.

3.68 Refer to the study reported in Example 2.2, relating the use of nightlights in childhood and the incidence of subsequent myopia.
   a. Was the research based on an observational study or a randomized experiment? Explain.
   b. Which one of the "Difficulties and Disasters" in Section 3.5 do you think is most likely to be a problem in this research? Explain.

3.69 Find an example of an observational study in the news. Answer the following questions about it. Be sure to include the news article with your response.
   a. What are the explanatory and response variables, or is this distinction not possible?
   b. Briefly describe how the study was done. For instance, was it a case-control study, a prospective or retrospective study?
   c. Discuss possible confounding variables. For instance, were any possible confounding variables included in the study and news report? Were other lurking confounding variables mentioned in the report? Can you think of possible confounding variables that were not mentioned?
   d. Pick one of the "Difficulties and Disasters" in Section 3.5 and discuss how it applies to the study.

3.70 Find an example of a randomized experiment in the news. Answer the following questions about it. Be sure to include the news article with your response.
   a. What are the explanatory and response variables? What relationship was found, if any?
   b. What treatments were assigned? Was a control group or placebo used?
   c. Was the study a matched-pair design, a block design, or neither? Explain.
   d. Was the study single-blind, double-blind, or neither? Explain.

3.71 Researchers want to design a study to compare topical cream (applied to the skin) and a drug taken in capsule form for the treatment of a certain type of skin rash. Sixty volunteers who have the rash agree to participate in the study.
   a. If each volunteer is given only one treatment can the study be double-blind? Explain.
   b. If each volunteer is given only one treatment can the study be single-blind? Explain.
   c. Could a double-blind, double-dummy study be done? If not, explain why not. If so, explain how it would be done.

3.72 Specify what an individual "unit" is in each of the following studies. Then specify what two variables were measured on each unit.
   a. A study found that tomato plants raised in full sunlight produced more tomatoes than tomato plants raised in partial shade.
   b. A study found that gas mileage was higher for automo-

biles when the tires were inflated to their maximum possible pressure than when the tires were underinflated.

   c. Ten randomly selected classrooms in a school district were assigned to have a morning fruit snack break, and another ten classrooms of the same grade level in similar schools were measured as a control group. The number of children who performed better than average on standardized tests was measured for each classroom.

3.73 Refer to the previous exercise and answer these questions.

   a. For each study, based on the information given, is it clearly a randomized experiment? If not, explain what additional information would make it clear that the study was a randomized experiment rather than an observational study.

   b. For each study, discuss whether or not matched pairs were used. If it is not clear, explain what additional information would make it clear.

   c. Discuss whether any of the studies would suffer from each of the following: the Hawthorne effect, interacting variables, ecological validity.

3.74 Is it possible for each of the following to be used in the same study (on the same units)? Explain or give an example of such a study.

   a. A placebo and a double-blind procedure.

   b. A matched-pair design and a retrospective study.

   c. A case-control study and random assignment of treatments.

3.75 Refer to the nicotine patch study described in Case Study 3.3. Draw a figure similar to those in Figures 3.2 through 3.5, illustrating the steps for that study.

3.76 Refer to the study in Example 3.8, comparing ages at death for left-handed and right-handed people. Draw a figure similar to those in Figures 3.2 through 3.5, illustrating the steps for that study.

3.77 Refer to Case Study 1.6 in which physicians were randomly assigned to take aspirin or a placebo and heart attack rates were compared. Draw a figure similar to Figures 3.2 through 3.5, illustrating the steps for that study.

3.78 A study was done (fictional) to compare the proportion of children who developed myopia after sleeping with and without a nightlight. The study found that the results differed based on whether at least one parent suffered from myopia by age 20. The percents of children suffering from myopia were as follows:

	Parent(s) Had Myopia	Parent(s) Did Not Have Myopia
Slept with:	% with Myopia	% with Myopia
No Light	10%	10%
Some Light	50%	30%

   a. Identify the explanatory variable, the response variable, and an interacting variable.

   b. Draw a figure similar to Figure 3.6, illustrating the interaction in this study.

   c. Write a few sentences that would be understood by someone with no training in statistics explaining the concept of interaction in this study.

3.79 A fast-food chain sells its burgers alone or as part of a "value meal," which includes fries and a drink. They know some customers are health-conscious. They want to do an experiment to see if the proportion of customers choosing the meal would increase if they offered baby carrots with the meal as an alternative to fries. They will compare three treatments: (1) status quo, (2) offering carrots as an alternative but with no advertising, and (3) offering carrots as an alternative and advertising this option in the local area. They have restaurants in three types of areas—cities, suburban areas, and along major highways.

   a. Explain how they would do this experiment using a completely randomized design.

   b. Explain how they would do this experiment using a randomized block design.

   c. Explain why it makes sense to use the type of area in which a restaurant is located as a block determinant in this experiment.

   d. Explain why a matched-pair design could not be used for this experiment.

3.80 Refer to Example 3.6, "Dull Rats," which was done using a completely randomized design.

   a. What were the treatments in this experiment?

   b. Were the experimental units the 60 individual rats or the 12 individual experimenters? Explain.

   c. Explain how the experiment could have been done using a matched-pair design instead.

REFERENCES

Coren, S., and D. Halpern (1991). "Left-handedness: A marker for decreased survival fitness," *Psychological Bulletin,* Vol. 109, No. 1, pp. 90–106.

Faigenbaum, A. D., W. L. Westcott, R. LaRosa Loud, and C. Long (1999). "The effects of different resistance training protocols on muscular strength and endurance development in children," *Pediatrics Electronic Article,* Vol. 104, No. 1 (July), p. e5.

French, J. R. P (1953). "Experiments in field settings," in L. Festinger and D. Katz (eds.), *Research Method in the Behavioral Sciences,* New York: Holt, pp. 98–135.

Hurt, R., L. Dale, P. Fredrickson, C. Caldwell, G. Lee, K. Offord, G. Lauger, Z. Maruisic, L. Neese, and T. Lundberg (1994).

"Nicotine patch therapy for smoking cessation combined with physician advice and nurse follow-up," *Journal of the American Medical Association,* Vol. 271, No. 8, (Feb. 23), pp. 595–600.

Lesko, S. M., L. Rosenberg, and S. Shapiro (1993). "A case-control study of baldness in relation to myocardial infarction in men," *Journal of the American Medical Association,* Vol. 269, No. 8, (Feb. 24), pp. 998–1003.

Rosenthal, R., and K. L. Fode (1963). "The effect of experimenter bias on the performance of the albino rat," *Behavioral Science,* Vol. 8, pp. 183–189.

CHAPTER 4

Sampling: Surveys and How to Ask Questions

Do they have your number? See Example 4.7.

Here is a fact that may astound you. If you use proper methods to sample 1500 people from a population of millions and millions, you can almost certainly gauge the percent of the entire population who have a certain trait or opinion to within 3%. The tricky part is that you have to use a proper sampling method.

P eople are curious about each other. When a newsworthy event occurs, people want to know what others think. In the midst of election campaigning, people want to know which candidates are in the lead. We devour news stories about the behavior and opinions of others. For this reason, news organizations like *USA Today* and CNN often conduct sample surveys. Many recent surveys can be found on the Web. In this chapter we learn how to conduct surveys, how to make sure they are representative, and what can go wrong. ◆

4.1 | THE BEAUTY OF SAMPLING

In a **sample survey,** a subgroup of a large population is questioned on a set of topics. The investigator simply asks the participants to answer some questions. There is no manipulation of a respondent's behavior in this type of research. In other words, sample surveys are a special type of observational study.

The results from a sample survey are used as if they are representative of the larger population, which they will be if the sample is chosen correctly and if those selected cooperate in responding. National polling organizations like the Gallup organization often question only slightly over 1000 individuals. How can a survey of such a small number of individuals possibly obtain accurate information about the opinions of millions?

Here is some information that may astound you. If you use commonly accepted methods to sample 1500 people from an entire population of millions and millions, you can almost certainly gauge the percent of the entire population who have a certain trait or opinion to within 3%. Even more amazing is the fact that this result doesn't depend on how big the population is. It only depends on how many are in the sample! A sample of 1500 would do about equally well for a population of 4 billion as it would for a population of 10 million. Of course, the tricky part is that you have to use a proper sampling method, a topic that we examine in this chapter.

You can see why researchers are content to rely on public opinion polls rather than trying to ask everyone for their opinions. It is much cheaper to ask 1500 people than several million, especially when you can get an answer that is almost as accurate. It also takes less time to conduct a sample survey than it does to conduct a **census,** in which everyone in the population is measured. And because fewer interviewers are needed for a survey than for a census, there may be better quality control of interviewing procedures when only a small sample of individuals is measured.

The Margin of Error: The Accuracy of Sample Surveys

Sample surveys often are used to estimate the *proportion* or *percent* of people who have a certain trait or opinion. For example, the Nielsen ratings, used to determine the percent of American television sets tuned to a particular show, are based on a sample of a few thousand households. Newspapers and magazines routinely survey only one or two thousand people to determine public opinion on current topics of interest. As we have said, if properly conducted, these surveys are amazingly accurate.

When a survey is used to find a proportion based on a sample of only a few thousand individuals, the obvious question is how close that proportion comes to the truth for the entire population. This measure of accuracy in sample surveys is a number called the **margin of error.** The *sample proportion* and the *population proportion* with a certain opinion or trait differ by *less than* the margin of error *more than* 95% of the time, or in at least 19 in 20 surveys. In other words, the margin of error provides an upper limit on the amount by which the sample proportion differs from the true population proportion, and this upper limit holds for at least 95% of all samples. To express results in terms of percents instead of proportions, simply multiply everything by 100.

> **definition** The amount by which the sample proportion differs from the true population proportion is less than the quantity $1/\sqrt{n}$ in at least 95% of all random samples. The letter n represents the number of people in the sample. Survey results reported in the media are usually expressed as percents and are accompanied by a margin of error, nearly always calculated as
>
> $$\frac{1}{\sqrt{n}} \times 100\%.$$
>
> We call this a **conservative margin of error.**

In Chapter 10 we will learn a more complicated and precise formula for the margin of error that depends on the actual sample proportion. It will never give an answer larger than the formula given here, so we call this formula a *conservative* margin of error. For simplicity, many media reports use the conservative formula. For example, with a sample of 1600 people, we will usually get an estimate that is accurate to within $1/\sqrt{1600} = 1/40 = 0.025 = 2.5\%$ of the truth. You might see results such as, "Fifty-five percent of respondents support the President's economic plan. The margin of error for this survey is plus or minus 2.5 percentage points." This means that it is almost certain that between 52.5% and 57.5% of the entire population supports the plan. In other words, add and subtract the margin of error to the sample value (55% in this example), to create an interval. If you were to follow this method every time you read the results of a properly conducted survey, the interval would miss covering the truth only about 1 in 20 times (5%) and would cover the truth the remaining 95% of the time.

---

in summary Margin of Error and Confidence Interval

(Conservative) margin of error $= 1/\sqrt{n}$ (or $100\% \times 1/\sqrt{n}$ for a percent), where $n =$ number of individuals in the sample. For about 95% of all sample proportions found in properly conducted sample surveys,

$$|\text{population proportion} - \text{sample proportion}| \le \frac{1}{\sqrt{n}}$$

Simply stated, for about 95% of properly conducted sample surveys, the interval

$$\textit{sample proportion} - \frac{1}{\sqrt{n}} \text{ to } \textit{sample proportion} + \frac{1}{\sqrt{n}}$$

will contain the actual population proportion. This interval is called an approximate "95% **confidence interval**" for the population proportion. In Chapter 10, a more precise formula will be given.

Another way of writing the approximate 95% confidence interval is

$$\textit{sample proportion} \pm \frac{1}{\sqrt{n}}$$

To report the results in percents instead of proportions, multiply everything by 100%.

Here are three examples of polls, with the margin of error and an approximate 95% confidence interval for each one. In each case the poll is based on a nationwide random sample of Americans aged 18 and older.

EXAMPLE 4.1
The Importance of Religion for Adult Americans

For a CNN/*USA Today*/Gallup Poll conducted on September 2 to 4, 2002, a random sample of $n = 1003$ adult Americans was asked, "How important would you say religion is in your own life: very important, fairly important, or not very important?" (http://www.pollingreport.com/religion.htm, September 17, 2002). The percents that selected each response were

Very important	65%
Fairly important	23%
Not very important	12%
No opinion	0%

Conservative margin of error: $\dfrac{1}{\sqrt{1003}} = .03$ or $.03 \times 100\% = 3\%$

Approximate 95% confidence interval for the proportion and percent of *all* adult Americans who would say religion is very important:

Proportion: $.65 \pm .03$ or $[.65 - .03 \text{ to } .65 + .03]$ or .62 to .68
Percent: $65\% \pm 3\%$ or $[65\% - 3\% \text{ to } 65\% + 3\%]$, or 62% to 68% ◆

EXAMPLE 4.2
Would You Eat Those Modified Tomatoes?

An ABC News.com poll conducted by TNS Intersearch on June 13 to 17, 2001 posed the following question to a random sample of $n = 1024$ adult Americans: "Scientists can change the genes in some food crops and farm animals to make them grow faster or bigger and be more resistant to bugs, weeds and disease. Do you think this genetically modified food, also known as bio-engineered food, is or is not safe to eat?" (http://www.pollingreport.com/science.htm, September 17, 2002). The percents that selected each response were

Is safe	35%
Is not safe	52%
No opinion	13%

Conservative margin of error: $\dfrac{1}{\sqrt{1024}} = .03$ or $.03 \times 100\% = 3\%$

Approximate 95% confidence interval for the proportion and percent of *all* adult Americans who would say genetically modified food is *not* safe to eat:

Proportion: $.52 \pm .03$ or $[.52 - .03$ to $.52 + .03]$ or .49 to .55
Percent: $52\% \pm 3\%$ or $[52\% - 3\%$ to $52\% + 3\%]$, or 49% to 55% ◆

EXAMPLE 4.3
Cloning Human Beings

A Pew Research Center for the People & the Press and Pew Forum on Religion & Public Life survey conducted by Princeton Survey Research Associates between February 25 and March 10, 2002 asked a random sample of $n = 2002$ adult Americans, "Do you favor or oppose scientific experimentation on the cloning of human beings?" (http://www.pollingreport.com/science.htm, September 17, 2002). The percents that selected each response were

Favor	17%
Oppose	77%
Don't know/Refused	6%

Conservative margin of error: $\dfrac{1}{\sqrt{2002}} = .022$ or $.022 \times 100\% = 2.2\%$

Approximate 95% confidence interval for the proportion and percent of *all* adult Americans who would say they *favor* this experimentation:

Proportion: $.17 \pm .022$ or $[.17 - .022$ to $.17 + .022]$ or .148 to .192
Percent: $17\% \pm 2.2\%$ or $[17\% - 2.2\%$ to $17\% + 2.2\%]$, or 14.8% to 19.2% ◆

Interpreting the Confidence Intervals in Examples 4.1 to 4.3

In each of the three examples of surveys, an approximate 95% confidence interval was found. There is no way to know whether all, some, or none of these intervals actually covers the population value of interest. For instance, the interval from 62% to 68% may or may not capture the percent of adult Americans who considered religion to be very important in their lives in September of 2002. But, in the long run, this procedure will produce intervals that capture the unknown population values about 95% of the time, as long as it is used with properly conducted surveys. This long-run performance is usually expressed after an interval is computed by saying that we are 95% confident that the population value is covered by the interval.

tech note   Because the margin of error used in this chapter is "conservative," the procedure actually works slightly more than 95% of the time. Details will be covered in Chapters 10 and 12.

Advantages of a Sample Survey over a Census

When a Census Isn't Possible

Suppose you need a laboratory test to see whether or not your blood has too high a concentration of a certain substance. Would you prefer that the lab measure the entire population of your blood, or would you prefer to give them a sample? Similarly, suppose a manufacturer of firecrackers wants to know what percent of its products are duds. It would not make much of a profit if it tested them all, but it could get a reasonable estimate of the desired percentage by testing a properly selected sample. As these examples illustrate, there are situations where measurements destroy the units being tested and thus a census is not feasible.

Speed

Another advantage of a sample survey over a census is speed. For instance, it takes several years to successfully plan and execute a census of the entire population of the United States, something done every ten years. Getting figures like monthly unemployment rates would be impossible with a census; they would be quite out-of-date by the time they were released. It is much faster to collect a sample than a census if the population is large.

Accuracy

A final advantage to a sample survey is that you can devote your resources to getting the most accurate information possible from the sample you have selected. It is easier to train a small group of interviewers than a large one, and it is easier to track down a small group of nonrespondents than the larger one that would inevitably result from trying to conduct a census.

Bias: How Surveys Can Go Wrong

Not all surveys produce trustworthy results. The purpose of most surveys is to use a characteristic of the sample (such as the proportion with a certain opinion) as an estimate of the corresponding characteristic of the population from which the sample was selected. While it is unlikely that the sample value will equal the population value precisely, the goal of a good survey is to get an **unbiased** sample value. Results based on a survey are **biased** if the method used to obtain those results would consistently produce values that are either too high or too low.

There are three common types of bias that might occur in surveys:

- **Selection bias** occurs if the method for selecting the participants produces a sample that does not represent the population of interest. For instance, if shoppers at a mall are surveyed to determine attitudes about raising the sales tax, the results are not likely to represent all area residents.

- **Nonresponse bias** occurs when a representative sample is chosen for a survey, but a subset cannot be contacted or does not respond. For instance, a survey conducted by phoning people at home in the evening would omit people who work during that time. Their opinions would not be represented, so if they were much different, the sample results would be biased.

- ◆ **Response bias** occurs when participants respond differently from how they truly feel. The way questions are worded, the way the interviewer behaves, as well as many other factors might lead an individual to provide false information. For instance, surveys about socially unacceptable behavior such as heavy smoking or drinking, abusive behavior, and so on must be worded and conducted carefully to minimize the possibility of response bias.

4.1

The terms *nonresponse bias* and *response bias* sound very similar. Do they refer to two aspects of the same kind of problem? Explain.*

turn on your mind

4.2 | SIMPLE RANDOM SAMPLING AND RANDOMIZATION

The ability of a relatively small sample to accurately reflect a huge population does not happen haphazardly. It only happens if proper sampling methods are used. The basic idea is that everyone in the population must have a specified chance of making it into the sample, and methods with this characteristic are called **probability sampling plans.** Let's look at how to implement the most basic method of accomplishing this goal, which is to use a **simple random sample.** Remember (from Chapter 3) that with a simple random sample, every conceivable group of units of the required size has the same chance of being the selected sample.

Choosing a Simple Random Sample

Choosing a simple random sample is somewhat like choosing the winning numbers in many state lotteries. For instance, in the former California Super Lotto, six numbers were randomly selected from the choices 1, 2, . . . , 51. Every possible set of six numbers was equally likely to be the winning set. There are actually 18,009,460 different possible sets, which is why the odds of any specific individual guessing the winning set are so small! Similarly, the chances of any *particular* group of units getting selected to be the random sample from a large population is quite small, but whatever group is selected is likely to be *representative.* For instance, in a simple random sample of 1000 people in your state or country, it is extremely unlikely that you and your next-door neighbor would be selected. But it is extremely likely that someone in the sample will be representative of each of you, having similar opinions to yours.

To actually produce a simple random sample, you need only two things. First, you need a list of the units in the population. For instance, in drawing the winning lottery numbers, the list of units is the numbers 1, 2, . . . , 51. In selecting a simple random sample of students from your school, the list of units is all students in the school (which the registrar can usually produce).

Second, you need a source of **random numbers.** Random numbers can be found in tables called **tables of random digits,** or they can also be generated using either a computer or the right calculator. If the population isn't too large, physical methods can be used, such as in the lottery, where the numbers were written on small hollow plastic balls and six of them physically selected.

Table 4.1 illustrates a portion of a table of random digits. It is organized into numbered rows to make it easier to find specific sections of the Table. There are only 10 rows in Table 4.1, so they are labeled using the single digits 0 to 9. A larger table would have to use longer identifying numbers for the rows. The digits are grouped into columns of 5 for easier reading. These tables are generated by the equivalent of writing the digits from 0 to 9 on slips of paper, mixing them well, choosing one, and then repeating this process over and over again. No single digit, pair of consecutive digits, triplet of digits, and so on are any more or less likely to occur than any others.

Using Table 4.1 to Choose a Simple Random Sample

Here are the steps for selecting a simple random sample using Table 4.1.

1. Number the units in the population using the same number of digits for each one.
   Example: Suppose there are 270 students in a class and the teacher wants to choose a simple random sample of 10 of them to call on in class. Number the students from 001 to 270.
2. Choose a starting point in Table 4.1. You can close your eyes and point, or use any other method as long as you haven't studied the table and then chosen numbers that give a favorable sample for your purpose.
   Example: Start in row 3, column 2 (10484 . . .)
3. From the starting point, read across the row to get numbers with the correct number of digits to identify a unit. Continue with consecutive rows. For instance, if the units are numbered 001 to 270, read three-digit numbers.
   Example: Reading three-digit numbers starting with row 3, column 2 results in 104, 842, 461, 613, 466, 416, 180, 855, 118, 314, 577, 002, 896, and so on.
4. If a number is in the range of the unit numbers, select that unit number. Otherwise, continue along the row, choosing more potential unit numbers

TABLE 4.1 ■ A Table of Random Digits

Row								
0	00157	37071	79553	31062	42411	79371	25506	69135
1	38354	03533	95514	03091	75324	40182	17302	64224
2	59785	46030	63753	53067	79710	52555	72307	10223
3	27475	10484	24616	13466	41618	08551	18314	57700
4	28966	35427	09495	11567	56534	60365	02736	32700
5	98879	34072	04189	31672	33357	53191	09807	85796
6	50735	87442	16057	02883	22656	44133	90599	91793
7	16332	40139	64701	46355	62340	22011	47257	74877
8	83845	41159	67120	56273	67519	93389	83590	12944
9	12522	20743	28607	63013	60346	71005	90348	86615

until you have a sample of the desired size. (But see step 5 for a more efficient method.) Because each unit can only be used once, if a unit number occurs that has already been selected, simply ignore that number and continue.

Example: Unit numbers can only be 001 to 270, so most of the numbers chosen are simply ignored. Select units 104, 180, 118, 002, then keep going until the required 10 students have been selected.

5. Step 4 is very inefficient. To make it more efficient, reassign some of the higher numbers onto the range of unit numbers in a way that still ensures that each unit number has an equal chance of selection. For instance, suppose the units are numbered 001 to 270. If a number between 301 and 570 is chosen, subtract 300 and use it. If a number between 601 and 870 is chosen, subtract 600 and use it. As in step 4, if a unit number occurs more than once, simply ignore subsequent occurrences after the first one. For instance, in the scenario just given, if unit 017 has already been selected, then any subsequent occurrence of 017, 317, or 617 would be discarded.

Example: Now the string generated earlier is more useful. Let's see what decision follows each three-digit entry:

Three-digit Number	Using Step 4, Choose Unit	Using Step 5, Choose Unit
104	104	104
842	Discard	242 (subtracted 600)
461	Discard	161 (subtracted 300)
613	Discard	013 (subtracted 600)
466	Discard	166 (subtracted 300)
416	Discard	116 (subtracted 300)
180	180	180
855	Discard	255 (subtracted 600)
118	118	118
314	Discard	014 (subtracted 300)
577	Discard	Not needed, 10 already selected
002	002	Not needed

Using the method in step 4, the first 4 students selected would be those numbered 104, 180, 118, and 002, and the process would continue until six more were selected. Using the method in step 5, the sample of 10 units would include 104, 242, 161, 013, 166, 116, 180, 255, 118, and 014, and unit 002 would not be needed.

Minitab Tip

 tech note   **Picking a Random Sample**

- ◆ To create a column of ID numbers, use **Calc>Make Patterned Data>Simple Set of Numbers.** In the dialog box, specify a column for storing the ID numbers, and specify the first and last possible ID number for the population.

- ◆ To sample values from a column, use **Calc>Random Data> Sample from Columns.** In the dialog box, specify how many items (rows) will be selected from a particular column, and specify a column where the sample will be stored.

Note: Items can be randomly selected from a column of names or data values, so it may not be necessary to assign ID numbers to the units in the population in order to select a sample.

EXAMPLE 4.4
Representing the
Heights of British Women

In Example 2.11 of Chapter 2, we examined data on the heights of 199 British women. Suppose you had a list of these 199 women and wanted to choose 10 of them to test drive a sporty, but small, automobile model and give their opinions about its comfort. The heights of the women in the sample should be representative of the range of heights in the larger group. You would not want your sample of 10 to include only short women or only tall women. Here's how you could choose a simple random sample:

1. Assign an ID number from 001 to 199 to each woman.
2. Use a table of random digits, a computer, or a calculator to randomly select ten numbers between 001 and 199, and sample the heights of the women with those ID numbers.

We used the statistical package Minitab to choose a simple random sample of heights, then used Table 4.1 to choose another one. The samples are listed next along with their sample means and the list of ten random numbers between 001 and 199 that generated them (with leading zeros dropped). In Chapter 2 the heights were given in millimeters, but here they have been converted to inches.

Sample 1 (Minitab)

ID numbers of the women selected: 176, 10, 1, 40, 85, 162, 46, 69, 77, 154
Heights: 60.6, 63.4, 62.6, 65.7, 69.3, 68.7, 61.8, 64.6, 60.8, 59.9; mean = 63.7 inches

Sample 2 (Table 4.1)

ID numbers of the women selected: 41, 93, 167, 33, 157, 131, 110, 180, 185, 196
Heights: 59.4, 66.5, 63.8, 62.6, 65.0, 60.2, 67.3, 59.8, 67.7, 61.8; mean = 63.4 inches

Sample 2 was selected by starting with the third set of five digits in the row labeled 5 (04189). Numbers from 001 to 199 can be used directly; for numbers between 201 and 399, subtract 200; for numbers between 401 and 599, subtract 400; and so on. The only numbers that would need to be discarded using this method are 000, 200, 400, 600, and 800. You can test your understanding of the use of Table 4.1 by starting at 04189 (third set in row 5), selecting 10 consecutive sets of three digits, and determining if you correctly identify the 10 women in sample 2.

As you can see, each sample is different but each should be representative of the whole collection of 199 women. Within each sample, the range of heights is from about 60 inches to about 69 inches. The sample means are both close to the mean height for the larger group, which was given in Chapter 2 as 1602 mm, or about 63 inches. ◆

Using a Table of Random Digits in a Randomized Experiment

In Chapter 3 we learned that randomization plays a key role in designing experiments to compare treatments. Remember that for a *completely randomized design*, experimental units are randomly assigned to the treatment conditions. For a *matched-pair design* or a *randomized block design*, the order in which treatments are assigned within a pair or block is randomized. In all of these designs, the randomization can be viewed as a special case of simple random sampling. As with choosing a simple random sample, a table of random digits, a computer program, or a physical method of randomization can be used. In the next example, Table 4.1 is used to randomize the treatments in a completely randomized design.

EXAMPLE 4.5
Assigning Children to Lift Weights

Case Study 3.2 involves a randomized experiment in which 43 children were assigned to one of three treatment groups. Children in group 1 were asked to perform weight-lifting repetitions with a heavy load, group 2 performed more repetitions but with a moderate load, and group 3 served as a control group and did not lift weights. According to the study report (Faigenbaum et al., 1999, p. e5), there were 15 children assigned to group 1, 16 to group 2, and the remaining 12 to group 3. Assuming no blocks or pairs were used, how would you use Table 4.1 to assign the children to the treatment groups?

First, choose the 15 children to participate in group 1. Do this by labeling the 43 children from 01 to 43, then choosing a simple random sample of 15. This can be done using Table 4.1 by choosing two-digit numbers. If the table entry is 01 to 43, choose the child with that number. For 51 to 93, subtract 50 then choose the child with that number. Discard numbers 00, 44 to 50, and 94 to 99. Let's start at the beginning of the row labeled 7. The resulting sample of 15 children for group 1 is

> 16, 33, 24, 01, 39, 14 (64 − 50), 20 (70 − 50), (14 has already been used so skip), 13 (63 − 50), 05 (55 − 50), 12 (62 − 50), 34, 02, (20 has already been used, so skip), 11, (discard 47), 25, 27 (77 − 50)

In numerical order, the children assigned to group 1 are those numbered 1, 2, 5, 11, 12, 13, 14, 16, 20, 24, 25, 27, 33, 34, and 39.

There are now 43 − 15 = 28 remaining children, of whom 16 are to be assigned to group 2 and 12 to the control group. Because 12 is the smaller number, it will be faster to choose a random sample of 12 from the 28 remaining children to assign to the control group. The 16 remaining children will constitute group 2.

There are other methods of making the random assignments that would also work. For instance, you could write the names of the children on identical slips of paper, put them in a bag, and mix well. Reach in and select 15 of them for group 1, another 16 for group 2, and the remaining 12 would constitute the control group. ◆

EXAMPLE 4.6
Redesigning Case Study 3.2

In the original research report about Case Study 3.2 (Faigenbaum et al., 1999), it was noted that the 43 children were not all available at the start of the study. The 31 children in the two weight-lifting groups were available and were randomly assigned to the two groups in a method similar to that described in Example 4.5. According to the article, "twelve children who enrolled in this study after the recruitment of the experimental groups acted as nontraining control subjects." In other words, the control group enrolled after the children in the two treatment groups.

The late enrollment may help explain another characteristic described in the research report, which may confound the results. The average weights of the children in the three groups were 35.4 kg for group 1, 39.8 kg for group 2, and only 27.7 kg for the control group. Because change in muscle strength was the response variable of interest, it would be better if the three groups were matched more closely on initial average weight.

One way to make sure that happened would be to use a randomized block design instead of a completely randomized design. Recall from Chapter 3 that a block is a collection of similar experimental units. In this situation, measure the initial weight of each child and create one block consisting of the heaviest three children, one consisting of the next three heaviest, and so on. Within each block, the children would be of similar weight. Number the children in each block 1, 2, and 3. Randomly assign the three children in each block to the three treatment groups. The assignment can be done in a variety of ways using Table 4.1. The important feature is that each child in the block has an equal chance of receiving each treatment. For instance, choose a starting point and get three unique digits. Label the three children in a block with those digits. The child with the lowest digit gets treatment 1, the one with the middle digit gets treatment 2, and the one with the highest digit goes in the control group. For instance, if the three digits are 843, then treatment assignments for children 1, 2, and 3 are control group, treatment 2, and treatment 1, respectively. ◆

Random Sampling in Action

It should be obvious to you by now that each time you take a random sample from a population you are likely to get a different group of individuals, even though the population remains fixed. The **Sampling** applet on the CD for this text allows us to watch what happens when we repeatedly take random samples from the same population. Figure 4.1 illustrates how the applet appears when it starts. Each stick figure represents one member of a population of 100 college students: 55 females (blue) and 45 males (red). Their heights have been recorded as well, and if you look carefully you will see that the little stick figures are all of slightly different heights. The mean height for the population is 68 inches.

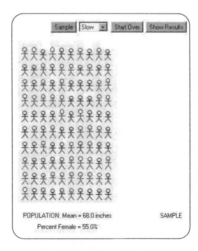

FIGURE 4.1 **The sampling applet starting point**

If we repeatedly take simple random samples of 10 people from this population, how much do you think the proportion of females in the samples will vary? Will it almost always be 50% or 60%, given that it must be a multiple of 10 and the population is 55% female? Will the sample ever consist of all males or all females? Pick one of the stick figures to represent yourself. How often do you think you would end up in the sample? Will the mean height of the sample always be close to the mean height of all 100 students, at 68 inches? If the mean height were to be 70 inches, would that indicate a possible problem in the selection of the sample, or is such a large value to be expected in some samples? In Chapters 7 to 9 you will learn the mathematical answers to these questions, but playing with the applet can give you a good intuitive idea of what happens.

What Happens

The applet always chooses a simple random sample of 10 individuals when you press the button labeled **Sample.** You can control the speed of the sampling to be slow, fast, or batch. With slow and fast sampling, you get to watch each individual move from the population into the sample, which is illustrated to the right of the population. With batch sampling, the whole sample appears as soon as you press the **Sample** button. Figures 4.2 and 4.3 illustrate two examples of the results after pressing the **Sample** button. Notice that in Figure 4.2 only 3 females were selected, so 30% of the sample is female. Not surprisingly, given that the sample has a higher percentage of men than the population, the mean height for the sample (69.6 inches) is higher than the 68-inch mean height for the population. The reverse happens in Figure 4.3, in which females make up 60% of the sample and the mean height is 67.2 inches.

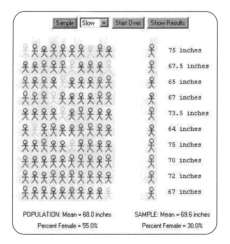

FIGURE 4.2   Sampling applet results

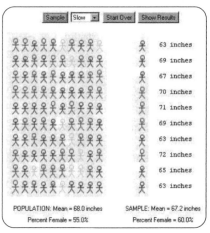

FIGURE 4.3   Additional sampling applet results

What to Do

Open the **Sampling** applet on the CD, and then repeatedly press the **Sample** button to choose many samples. You can decide if you want to select a sample slowly, so you can carefully watch each person being taken from the population and placed in the sample; fast (you can still watch); or in a batch. This decision won't change the results. Do *not* press the **Start Over** button.

Notice how the percent of females changes for each sample and how the mean height changes. Pick one of the stick figures to represent yourself, and notice how often you make it into the sample. At any time, you can see a summary of the samples you have selected so far by pushing the button labeled **Show Results.** When you press the **Start Over** button, all past results are cleared.

Take dozens of samples, then press **Show Results.** Are the percent female values and the mean height values for the samples more, or less, spread out than you would have anticipated? The number of females must be 0 or 1 or 2, etc., up to 10, so the "percent female" can only be one of 11 possibilities: 0%, 10%, 20%, 30%, etc., up to 100%. Count how often each of the 11 possibilities occurred in your repeated sampling. Does the result surprise you or is it what you expected? Draw a histogram of the means from the samples you chose. What do you notice? Do mean values far away from the "truth" of 68 inches occur as often as mean values close to 68 inches? Would you suspect a problem with the sample if a sample had a mean of 70 inches? How about 72 inches?

Note for Minitab Users: The results in the "Show Results" window can be copied and then pasted into a Minitab worksheet. Minitab can then be used to analyze the results. For instance, **Graph**>**Histogram** could be used to draw a histogram of the means of the chosen samples.

Lessons Learned

This applet lets you see simple random sampling in action. Much of the remaining material in this book follows from the idea that although samples vary, the amount by which they vary over the long run can be quantified. Remember that a simple random sample is supposed to be representative of the population. However, it should be obvious to you that with only 10 individuals per sample, both the percent of females and the mean height vary considerably from sample to sample. In fact, the conservative margin of error for a sample of $n = 10$ is over 30%! Therefore, you should expect to see a wide range in the percent of females across samples.

4.3 | OTHER SAMPLING METHODS

For large populations it may not be practical to take a simple random sample because it may be difficult to get a numbered list of the units. For instance, if a polling organization wanted to take a simple random sample of all voters or all adults in a country or region, they would need to get a numbered list of them, which is simply an impossible task in most cases. Instead, they rely on more complicated sampling methods, all of which are good substitutes for simple random sampling in most situations. In fact, they often have advantages over simple random sampling. For instance, one of these other methods, stratified random sampling, can be used to increase the chance that the sample represents important subgroups within the population.

To visually illustrate the various sampling plans discussed in this chapter, let's suppose a college administration would like to survey a sample of students living in dormitories. The college has undergraduate and graduate dormitories. The undergraduate dormitories have three floors each with 12 rooms per floor. The graduate dormitories have five floors each with 8 rooms per floor.

Figure 4.4 illustrates a simple random sample of 30 rooms in the dormitories. Any collection of 30 rooms has an equal chance of being the selected sample. Notice that for the sample illustrated there are 12 undergraduate rooms and 18 graduate rooms in the sample.

Stratified Random Sampling

Sometimes the population of units falls into natural groups, called **strata.** For example, public opinion pollsters often take separate samples from each region of the country so that they can spot regional differences as well as measure

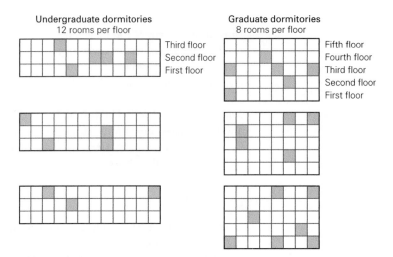

FIGURE 4.4   A simple random sample of 30 dorm rooms

national trends. Political pollsters may sample separately from each political party in order to compare opinions by party.

A **stratified random sample** is collected by first dividing the population of units into groups (strata) and then taking a simple random sample from each one. For example, the strata might be regions of the country or political parties. You can often recognize this type of sampling when you read the results of a survey because the results will be listed separately for each of the strata.

Figure 4.5 illustrates a stratified sample for the college survey. There are two strata, the undergraduate and graduate dorms. A random sample of 15 rooms is taken from each of the two strata. Each collection of 15 undergraduate rooms has an equal chance of being the selected sample for the undergraduate dorms, and each collection of 15 graduate rooms has an equal chance of being the selected sample for the graduate dorms. But, the total of 15 rooms within each strata is fixed before the sample is selected.

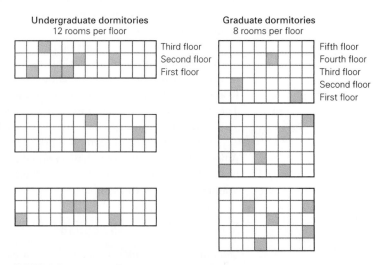

FIGURE 4.5   A stratified sample of 15 undergraduate and 15 graduate dorm rooms

Stratified sampling has other advantages in addition to the fact that results are available separately by strata. One is that different interviewers may work best with different people. For example, people from separate regions of the country (South, Northeast, etc.) may feel more comfortable with interviewers from the same region. It may also be more convenient to stratify before sampling. If we were interested in opinions of college students across the country, it would probably be easier to train interviewers at each college rather than to send the same interviewer to all campuses.

So far we have been focusing on measuring categorical variables, such as opinions or traits people might have. Surveys are also used to measure quantitative variables, such as age at first intercourse or number of cigarettes smoked per day. We are often interested in the population average for such measurements.

The accuracy with which we can estimate the average depends on the natural variability among the measurements. The less variable they are, the more precisely we can assess the population average on the basis of the sample values. For instance, if everyone in a relatively large sample reports that the age at first intercourse was between 16 years 3 months and 16 years 4 months, then we can be relatively sure that the average age in the population is close to that. On the other hand, if the reported ages range from 13 years to 25 years, then we cannot pinpoint the average age for the population nearly as accurately.

Stratified sampling can help to solve this problem. Suppose we could figure out how to stratify in a way that there is little natural variability in the answers within each strata. We could then get an accurate estimate for each stratum and combine them to get a much more precise answer for the group than if we measured everyone together. For example, if we wanted to estimate the average weight loss for participants in a new exercise program, we could do so more accurately by dividing the participants into groups based on their initial weight. Heavy people are more likely to lose weight during the first few days, but light individuals might even gain weight as they build muscles.

Cluster Sampling

Cluster sampling is often confused with stratified sampling, but actually it is a radically different concept and can be much easier to accomplish. The population units are again divided into groups, called **clusters,** but rather than sampling within each group, *we select a random sample of clusters and measure only those clusters.* In most applications of stratified sampling, the population is divided into a few *large* strata, such as regions of the country, and a small subset within each one is randomly sampled. In most applications of cluster sampling, the population is divided into *small* clusters, such as city blocks, a large number of clusters are randomly sampled, and everyone in those clusters is measured.

Figure 4.6 illustrates a cluster sampling plan for the college survey. Each floor of each dormitory is a cluster. A random sample of five floors is selected, and all students on those floors are surveyed. Any collection of five floors has an equal chance of being the selected sample, but once those floors are selected, all rooms on them are surveyed.

One obvious advantage of cluster sampling is that you need only a list of clusters instead of a list of all individual units. City blocks are commonly used as clusters in surveys that require door-to-door interviews. To measure customer satisfaction, airlines sometimes randomly sample a set of flights, then distribute a survey to everyone on those flights. Each flight is a cluster. It is clearly much

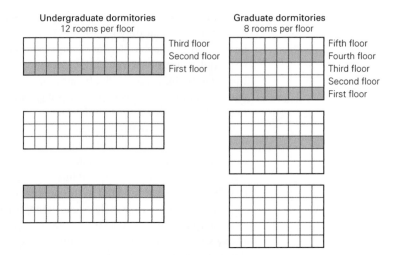

FIGURE 4.6   **A cluster sample in which five floors (clusters) are randomly selected**

easier for the airline to choose a random sample of flights than it would be to identify and locate a random sample of individual passengers to whom to distribute surveys.

If cluster sampling is used, the analysis must proceed differently because there may be similarities among the members of the clusters that must be taken into account. Numerous books are available that describe proper analysis methods based on which sampling plan was employed. (See, for example, *Sampling: Design and Analysis* by Sharon Lohr, Duxbury Press, 1999.)

Systematic Sampling

Suppose you have a list of 5000 names and telephone numbers from which you want to select a sample of 100 individuals. That means you would want to select 1 out of every 50 people on the list. You would not want to simply choose the first 100 names because, depending on how the list was ordered, they might not constitute a representative sample.

An idea that would work in most cases is to choose every 50th name on the list. If you did so, you would be using a **systematic sampling plan.** With this plan, you divide the list into as many consecutive segments as you need, randomly choose a starting point in the first segment, then sample at that same point in each segment. In our example, you would randomly choose a starting point in the first 50 names, then sample every 50th name after that. When you were finished, you would have selected one person from each of 100 segments, equally spaced throughout the list. As another example, suppose a company wanted to assess the quality of items produced on an assembly line. They might use a systematic sampling plan by selecting every 200th unit that was produced and testing its quality. This would be a much simpler plan than trying to make a list of all units produced and selecting a simple random sample of them.

Systematic sampling is often a good alternative to random sampling. In a few instances it can lead to a biased sample, and common sense must be used to avoid those. As an example, suppose you were doing a survey of potential noise problems in a high-rise college dormitory. Further, suppose a list of residents was provided, arranged by room number, with 20 rooms per floor and two people

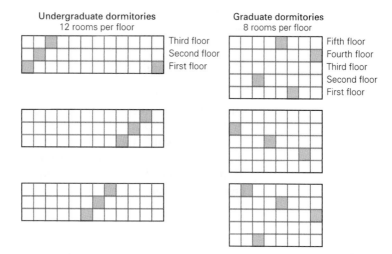

FIGURE 4.7   **A systematic sample of every eleventh room, randomly starting with the third room**

per room. If you were to take a systematic sample of, say, every 40th person on the list, you would get people who lived in the same location on every floor and thus a biased sampling of opinions about noise problems.

Figure 4.7 illustrates a systematic sample of the college dormitory rooms that were shown in Figures 4.4 through 4.6. Consider an ordered list of rooms starting with the top floor of the first undergraduate dorm, numbering those rooms 1 to 12. The second-floor rooms are numbered 13 to 24 and so on, continuing with the undergraduate dorms, then moving to the fifth floor of the first graduate dorm. In the figure, room 3 was randomly selected as a starting point chosen from the first 11 rooms. After that, every eleventh room is sampled. Notice that there is some pattern to the rooms selected, which may or may not lead to biased results, depending on the questions asked in the survey.

Random-Digit Dialing

Most of the national polling organizations and many of the government surveys in the United States now use a method of sampling called **random-digit dialing.** This method results in a sample that approximates a simple random sample of all households in the United States that have telephones.

The method proceeds as follows. First, the polling organization makes a list of all possible telephone *exchanges,* where the exchange consists of the area code and the next three digits. Then, a computer is used to generate a sample of exchanges. Using numbers listed in the white pages, the pollsters can approximate the proportion of all households in the country that have a specific exchange, and this proportion governs the chance that the exchange is sampled. Next, the same method is used to randomly sample *banks* within each exchange, where a bank consists of the next two numbers. Phone companies assign numbers using banks, so that certain banks are mainly assigned to businesses, certain ones are held for future neighborhoods, and so on. Finally, to complete the number, the computer randomly generates the last two digits from 00 to 99.

Once a phone number has been determined, the pollsters should make multiple attempts to reach someone at that household. Sometimes they will ask to speak to a male because females are more likely to answer the phone and would thus be overrepresented if the researchers always survey the first individual who answers the phone.

Multistage Sampling

Many large surveys use a combination of the methods we have discussed. The survey designers might stratify the population by region of the country, then stratify by urban, suburban, and rural, and then choose a random sample of communities within those strata. They would then divide those communities into city blocks or fixed areas, as clusters, and sample some of those. Everyone on the block or within the fixed area may then be sampled. This is called a **multi-stage sampling plan.**

---

in summary   **Getting a Representative Sample**

All of the sampling plans described in this section will provide samples that are representative of the population from which they are drawn, except for special problems where noted (such as improper use of a systematic sample). It might be possible to get a representative sample without using one of these plans, but caution must be used. As we will learn in Section 4.4, there are sampling methods that are complete disasters. For instance, relying on volunteers to respond to a survey in a magazine will not provide a sample that represents any population. Results of such a survey cannot be extended beyond those people who actually respond. When you read the results of a survey, make sure you learn how the sample was obtained.

EXAMPLE 4.7
The Nationwide Personal Transportation Survey

Every five years, the U.S. Department of Transportation conducts The Nationwide Personal Transportation Survey to learn about the amount and type of personal travel by people in the United States. The 1995 survey included 21,000 households nationally. Interviews were conducted by telephone, using a **computer-assisted telephone interviewing (CATI)** system. This system helps interviewers keep track of which additional questions to ask based on specific answers, when to skip entire sections, and so on. Here is a description of who was interviewed:

> Interviews are conducted for all persons age 5 and older in the household. Persons 14 and older are interviewed directly and a household adult is asked to report for children age 5–13. A list-assisted Random Digit Dialing sample framework is used. The sample is stratified by region of the country, size of metropolitan area and presence or absence of a subway system. (Liss, 1997, p. 15)

Notice that this is a multistage sample. U.S. households are *stratified* by region of the country, size of metropolitan area, and whether there is a subway system. Households are then selected by *random-digit dialing*. Finally, everyone in a selected household is included, so each household is a *cluster*. ◆

EXAMPLE 4.8
A Los Angeles Times
National Poll
on the Millennium

Most polling agencies now include information on recent polls on their websites, including a brief description of how the poll was conducted. For example, a poll reported by the *Los Angeles Times,* taken in early 1999, reported these results:

> A full quarter of Americans surveyed in a recent Los Angeles Times poll said they believe the onset of a new millennium heralds the second coming of Jesus Christ. While half of Americans polled said they view Jan. 1, 2000, as "just another New Year's Day," considerable numbers say they expect an increase in natural disasters (26%) or civil unrest (30%). About one in 10 report that they are stockpiling goods. (Teresa Watanabe, Mar. 31, 1999)

A description of how the poll was conducted was also given, as follows:

> The Times Poll contacted 1,249 adults nationwide by telephone February 27–28. Telephone numbers were chosen from a list of all exchanges in the nation. Random-digit dialing techniques were used so that listed and non-listed numbers could be contacted.

In other words, the poll was taken over a two-day period in February 1999, by telephone, using a simple random-digit dialing sample. ◆

4.2

turn on your mind

In Chapter 3, the Fundamental Rule for Using Data for Inference stated that "available data can be used to make inferences about a much larger group *if the data can be considered to be representative with regard to the question(s) of interest.*" Read the description of how the *Los Angeles Times* poll in Example 4.8 was conducted. Do you think the results of the poll can be extended to a larger group than the 1249 people in the sample? If so, to what group can the results be extended and why?*

4.4 | DIFFICULTIES AND DISASTERS IN SAMPLING

In theory, designing a good sampling plan is easy and straightforward. However, the real world rarely cooperates with well-designed plans, and trying to collect a proper sample is no exception. Difficulties that can occur in practice need to be considered when you evaluate a study. If a proper sampling plan is never implemented, this can lead to very misleading and inaccurate conclusions. Some problems can occur even when a sampling plan has been well designed. Here is a list of possible problems:

- ◆ Using the wrong sampling frame
- ◆ Not reaching the individuals selected
- ◆ Nonresponse or volunteer response
- ◆ Self-selected sample
- ◆ Convenience or haphazard sample

*HINT: Read the section on random-digit dialing in this chapter.

Using the Wrong Sampling Frame

> *definition*   The **sampling frame** is the list of units from which the sample is
> selected. This list may or may not be the same as the list of all
> units in the desired "target" population.

Sometimes a sampling frame either will include unwanted units or exclude desired units. For example, if we sample from a list of registered voters in order to predict election outcomes, we will include individuals who are not likely to vote as well as those who are likely to do so. Using a telephone directory to survey the general population excludes those who move often, those with unlisted home numbers (like many physicians and teachers), and those who cannot afford a telephone. Using the wrong sampling frame is one way to create selection bias. Figure 4.8 illustrates this situation.

Common sense can often lead to a solution for this problem. In the example of registered voters, interviewers may try to first ascertain the voting history of the people contacted by asking them where they vote and then continuing the interview only if the person knows the answer. Instead of using a telephone directory, surveys use random-digit dialing. This still excludes those without phones, but not those who didn't happen to be in the last printed directory.

Not Reaching the Individuals Selected

Even if a proper sample of units is selected, the desired units may not be reached. For example, *Consumer Reports* magazine mails a lengthy survey to its subscribers in order to obtain information on the reliability of various products. If you were to receive such a survey and you had a close friend who had been having trouble with a highly rated automobile, you may very well decide to pass the questionnaire on to your friend to answer. That way, he would get to register his complaints about the car, but *Consumer Reports* would not have reached the intended recipient.

Telephone surveys tend to reach a disproportionate number of women since they are more likely to answer the phone. Researchers sometimes ask to speak to the oldest adult male at home to try to counter that problem. Surveys are also likely to have trouble contacting people who work long hours and are rarely

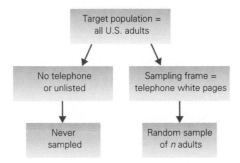

FIGURE 4.8   **The sampling frame doesn't cover the target population, leading to selection bias**

home or those who tend to travel extensively. Some people screen their calls or simply refuse to cooperate even when they do answer the phone.

In recent years, there has been pressure on news organizations to produce surveys of public opinions quickly. When a controversial story breaks, people want to know how others feel about it. This pressure results in what *Wall Street Journal* reporter Cynthia Crossen calls "**quickie polls.**" As she notes, these are "most likely to be wrong because questions are hastily drawn and poorly pre-tested, and it is almost impossible to get a random sample in one night" (Crossen, 1994, p. 102). Even if the computer can randomly generate phone numbers for the sample, there will be groups of people who are not likely to be home that night, and they may have different opinions from those who are likely to be home. Most responsible reports about polls include information about the dates during which the poll was conducted. For instance, the millennium poll in Example 4.8 was conducted on a Saturday and Sunday, so people who frequently travel on weekends may be underrepresented.

It is very important once a sample has been selected that those individuals are the ones who are actually measured. It is better to put resources into getting a smaller sample than to get one that has been biased by moving on to the next person on the list when someone is initially unavailable. Failing to contact or measure the individuals who were selected in the sampling plan leads to nonre-sponse bias.

Nonresponse or Volunteer Response

Even the best surveys are not able to contact everyone on the list, and not every-one contacted will respond. The General Social Survey (GSS), run by the presti-gious National Opinion Research Center (NORC) at the University of Chicago, noted in its September 1993 *GSS News:*

> In 1993 the GSS achieved its highest response rate ever, 82.4%. This is five percentage points higher than our average over the last four years. Given the long length of the GSS (90 minutes), the high response rates of the GSS are testimony to the extraordinary skill and dedication of the NORC field staff.

The GSS is now conducted biennially, and the response rates for 1994, 1996, and 1998 have been 78%, 76%, and 76%, respectively, according to the NORC web-site (http://www.norc.uchicago.edu/gss/homepage.htm). Beyond having a ded-icated staff, not much can be done about getting everyone in the sample to re-spond. Response rates should be reported in research summaries.

As a reader, remember that the lower the response rate, the less the re-sults can be generalized to the population as a whole. Responding to a survey (or not) is voluntary, and those who respond are likely to have stronger opin-ions than those who do not respond. As mentioned earlier, this type of **nonre-sponse bias** can lead to systematically over- or underestimating the truth about a population.

With mail surveys, it may be possible to compare those who respond imme-diately with those who need a second prodding, and in telephone surveys you could compare those who are home on the first try with those who require nu-merous call-backs. If those groups differ on the measurement of interest, then those who were never reached are probably different as well.

In a mail survey, it is best not to rely solely on **volunteer response.** In other words, researchers should not just accept that those who did not respond the first time can't be cajoled into responding. Often, sending a reminder with a brightly colored stamp or following up with a personal phone call will produce the desired effect. Surveys that simply use those who respond voluntarily are sure to be biased in favor of those with strong opinions or with time on their hands.

4.3

turn on your mind

Suppose you want to know how students at your school feel about the computer services that are offered. You are able to obtain the list of e-mail addresses for all students taking statistics classes, so you send a survey to a simple random sample of 100 of those students and 65 respond. Using the difficulties discussed so far in this section, explain to whom you could extend the results of your survey and why.*

EXAMPLE 4.9
***Which Scientists
Trashed the Public?***

According to a poll taken among scientists and reported in the prestigious journal *Science* (Mervis, 1998), scientists don't have much faith in either the public or the media. The article reported that based on the results of a "recent survey of 1400 professionals" in science and in journalism, 82% of scientists "strongly or somewhat agree" with the statement, "The U.S. public is gullible and believes in miracle cures or easy solutions." Eighty percent agreed that "the public doesn't understand the importance of federal funding for research." Eighty-two percent also trashed the media, agreeing with the statement, "The media do not understand statistics well enough to explain new findings." It isn't until the end of the article that we learn who responded: "The study reported a 34% response rate among scientists, and the typical respondent was a white, male physical scientist over the age of 50 doing basic research." Remember that those who feel strongly about the issues in a survey are the most likely to respond. With only about a third of those contacted responding, it is inappropriate to generalize these findings and conclude that most scientists have so little faith in the public and the media. This is especially true since we were told that the respondents represented only a narrow subset of scientists. ◆

Disasters in Sampling

Basing a sample survey on a **self-selected sample** (also called a **volunteer sample**) or a **convenience sample** is usually so problematic that the results cannot be extended to anyone beyond the sample. This warning applies only to sample surveys and to some observational studies. As we learned in Chapter 3, randomized experiments often make use of volunteers and convenience samples.

Self-Selected Sample
While relying on volunteer responses from a random sample presents somewhat of a difficulty in determining the extent to which surveys can be generalized, relying on a self-selected sample consisting of only those who volunteer to partic-

ipate is usually a complete waste of time. If a television or radio station, magazine, or Internet site presents a survey and asks any readers or viewers who are interested to respond, the results reflect the opinions of only those listeners or readers who decide to take the trouble to respond. And people who weren't watching or listening, or reading the magazine or Internet site, would not even know the poll existed.

As noted earlier, those who have a strong opinion about the question are more likely to respond than those who do not have a strong opinion. Thus, the self-selected responding group is simply not representative of any larger group. Most media outlets now acknowledge that such polls are "unscientific" when they report the results, but most readers are not likely to understand how misleading the results can be. The next example illustrates the contradiction that can result between a scientific poll and one relying solely on a self-selected sample.

EXAMPLE 4.10
A Meaningless Poll

On the 18th of February, 1993, shortly after Bill Clinton became President of the United States, a television station in Sacramento, California asked viewers to respond to the question, "Do you support the President's economic plan?" The next day the results of a properly conducted study that asked the same question were published in the newspaper. Here are the results from these two different surveys:

	Television Poll	Survey
Yes (support plan)	42%	75%
No (don't support plan)	58%	18%
Not sure	0%	7%

As you can see, those who were dissatisfied with the President's plan were much more likely to respond to the television poll than those who supported it, and no one who was "Not sure" called the television station, since they were not invited to do so. Trying to extend those results to the general population is misleading. It is irresponsible to publicize such studies, especially without a warning that they result from an unscientific survey and are not representative of general public opinion. You should never interpret such polls as anything other than a count of who bothered to respond. ◆

Convenience or Haphazard Sample

Another worthless sampling technique for surveys is to use the most convenient group available or to decide haphazardly on the spot who to sample. It is almost always the case that these types of samples break the Fundamental Rule of Using Data for Inference given in Section 3.1. Rarely do the responses from a **convenience sample** or **haphazard sample** represent any larger population for the question of interest.

EXAMPLE 4.11
Haphazard Sampling

A few years ago, the student newspaper at a California university announced as a front-page headline "Students ignorant, survey says." The article explained that a "random survey" indicated that American students were less aware of current events than international students were.

The article quoted the undergraduate researchers, who were international students themselves, as saying "the students were randomly sampled on the quad." The quad is a wide expanse of lawn where students relax, eat lunch, and so on. There is simply no proper way to collect a random sample of students by selecting them in an area like that. In such situations, the researchers are likely to approach people whom they think will support the results they intended for their survey. Or, they are likely to approach friendly looking people who look like they will easily cooperate. This is called a haphazard sample, and it cannot be expected to be representative at all. ◆

You have seen the proper way to collect a sample and have been warned about the many difficulties and dangers inherent in the process. Here is a famous example that helped researchers learn some of these pitfalls.

CASE STUDY 4.1
The Infamous Literary Digest *Poll of 1936*

Before the election of 1936, a contest between Democratic incumbent Franklin Delano Roosevelt and Republican Alf Landon, the magazine *Literary Digest* had been extremely successful in predicting the results in U.S. presidential elections. But 1936 turned out to be the year of its downfall, when it predicted a 3-to-2 victory for Landon. To add insult to injury, young pollster George Gallup, who had just founded the American Institute of Public Opinion in 1935, not only correctly predicted Roosevelt as the winner of the election, he also predicted that the *Literary Digest* would get it wrong. He did this before they even conducted their poll! And Gallup surveyed only 50,000 people, while the *Literary Digest* sent questionnaires to 10 million people (Freedman, Pisani, Purves, and Adhikari, 1991, p. 307).

The *Literary Digest* made two classic mistakes. First, the lists of people to whom they mailed the 10 million questionnaires were taken from magazine subscribers, car owners, telephone directories, and, in a few instances, lists of registered voters. In 1936, those who owned telephones or cars, or

subscribed to magazines, were more likely to be wealthy individuals who were not happy with the Democratic incumbent.

Despite what many accounts of this famous story conclude, the bias produced by the more affluent list was not likely to have been as severe as the second problem (Bryson, 1976). *The main problem was volunteer response.* They received 2.3 million responses, a response rate of only 23%. Those who felt strongly about the outcome of the election were most likely to respond. And that included a majority of those who wanted a change, the Landon supporters. Those who were happy with the incumbent were less likely to bother to respond.

Gallup, on the other hand, knew the value of random sampling. He was not only able to predict the election but he also predicted what the results of the *Literary Digest* poll would be to within 1%. How did he do this? According to Freedman et al. (1991, p. 308), "he just chose 3,000 people at random from the same lists the *Digest* was going to use, and mailed them all a postcard asking them how they planned to vote."

This example illustrates the beauty of random sampling and the idiocy of trying to base conclusions on nonrandom and biased samples. The *Literary Digest* went bankrupt the following year, so it never had a chance to revise its methods. The organization founded by George Gallup has flourished, although it has made a few sampling blunders as well. (See exercise 4.46.)

4.5 | HOW TO ASK SURVEY QUESTIONS

You may be surprised at how much the answers to questions can change based on simple changes in wording. Here is one example. Loftus and Palmer (1974, quoted in Plous, 1993, p. 32) showed college students films of an automobile accident, after which they asked them a series of questions. One group was asked the question, "About how fast were the cars going when they contacted each other?" The average response was 31.8 miles per hour. Another group was asked, "About how fast were the cars going when they collided with each other?" In that group, the average response was 40.8 miles per hour. Simply changing from the word *contacted* to the word *collided* increased the estimates of speed by 9 miles per hour, or 28%, even though the respondents had witnessed the same film.

The wording and presentation of questions can significantly influence the results of a survey. The seven pitfalls discussed in this section are all possible sources of response bias in surveys.

Possible Sources of Response Bias in Surveys

Many pitfalls can be encountered when asking questions in a survey or experiment. Here are some of them, each of which will be discussed in turn:

- Deliberate bias
- Unintentional bias
- Desire to please
- Asking the uninformed
- Unnecessary complexity
- Ordering of questions
- Confidentiality and anonymity

Deliberate Bias

Sometimes, if a survey is being conducted to support a certain cause, questions are deliberately worded in a biased manner. Be careful about survey questions that begin with phrases like "Do you agree that . . . ?" Most people want to be agreeable and will be inclined to answer "yes" unless they have strong feelings the other way.

For example, suppose an antiabortion group and a prochoice group each wanted to conduct a survey in which it would find the best possible agreement with its position. Here are two questions that would each produce an estimate of the proportion of people who think abortion should be completely illegal. The questions are almost certain to produce different estimates:

1. Do you agree that abortion, the murder of innocent beings, should be outlawed?
2. Do you agree that there are circumstances under which abortion should be legal, to protect the rights of the mother?

The wording of a question should not indicate a desired answer. For instance, a Gallup Poll conducted in June 1998 contained the question, "Do you think it was a good thing or a bad thing that the atomic bomb was developed?" Notice that the question does not indicate which answer is preferable (61% of the respondents said "bad," while 36% said "good" and 3% were undecided).

Unintentional Bias

Sometimes questions are worded in such a way that the meaning is misinterpreted by a large percentage of the respondents. For example, if you were to ask people whether or not they use drugs, you would need to specify if you mean prescription drugs, illegal drugs, over-the-counter drugs, or common substances like caffeine. If you were to ask people to recall the most important date in their life, you would need to clarify if you meant the most important calendar date or the most important social engagement with a potential partner. (It is unlikely that anyone would mistake the question as being about the shriveled fruit, but you can see that the same word can have multiple meanings.)

EXAMPLE 4.12
Laid Off or Fired?

Plewes (1994) described a number of changes implemented at the beginning of 1994 to the Current Population Survey (CPS), which is a monthly survey used to determine government unemployment figures and other government statistics in the United States. One change involved clarification and expansion of questions about being laid off. Plewes explained that people were answering that they had been laid off, when in reality they had been fired: "The CPS concept of 'on layoff' differs from the everyday usage by respondents. CPS defines 'on layoff' as embodying an expectation of recall to the job; common usage considers it a euphemism for 'fired'" (p. 38). ◆

Desire to Please

Most survey respondents have a desire to please the person who is asking the question. They tend to understate their responses about undesirable social habits and opinions, and vice versa. For example, in recent years estimates of the prevalence of cigarette smoking based on surveys do not match those based on cigarette sales. Either people are not being completely truthful, or lots of cigarettes are ending up in the garbage.

EXAMPLE 4.13
Most Voters Don't Lie but Some Liars Don't Vote

Abelson, Loftus, and Greenwald (1992) discuss how the National Election Surveys always find that more people claim to vote than actually did. They explain that researchers have tried to make it more socially acceptable to admit to not voting by adding a preamble to questions about voting. The preamble reads, "In talking to people about elections, we often find that a lot of people were not able to vote because they weren't registered, they were sick, or they just didn't have time. How about you—did you vote in the elections this November?" (p. 139). In a survey six to seven months after the November 1986 election, the authors of the report surveyed people for whom they knew whether or not they had actually voted. The question started with the preamble and finished with "did you vote in the 1986 elections for United States Congress?" (p. 141). They found that of the 211 respondents who had actually voted, 203 (96%) accurately reported that they did. But of the 98 respondents who had *not* voted, 39 (40%) claimed that they *did* vote. ◆

Asking the Uninformed

People do not like to admit that they don't know what you are talking about when you ask them a question. Crossen (1994, p. 24) gives an example: "When the American Jewish Committee studied Americans' attitudes toward various ethnic groups, almost 30% of the respondents had an opinion about the fictional Wisians, rating them in social standing above a half-dozen other real groups, including Mexicans, Vietnamese and African blacks."

Political pollsters, who are interested in surveying only those who will actually vote, learned long ago that it is useless to simply ask people if they plan to vote. Most of them will say "yes." Instead, they ask questions to establish a history of voting, such as "Where did you go to vote in the last election?"

Unnecessary Complexity

If questions are to be understood, they must be kept simple. A question like "Shouldn't former drug dealers not be allowed to work in hospitals after they are released from prison?" is sure to lead to confusion. Does a "yes" answer mean they should or should not be allowed to work in hospitals? It would take a few readings to figure that out.

Another way in which a question can be unnecessarily complex is by actually asking more than one question at once. An example would be a question like "Do you support the president's health care plan, since it would ensure that all Americans receive health coverage?" If you agree with the idea that all Americans should receive health coverage but disagree with the remainder of the plan, do you answer "yes" or "no"? Or what if you support the president's plan, but not for that reason?

EXAMPLE 4.14
Why Weren't You at Work Last Week?

In the work leading to the revision of the Current Population Survey discussed in Example 4.13, researchers discovered that some questions were too complex to be understood by many respondents. For instance, as Plewes (1994, p. 38) described, one such question on the old version was "Did you have a job from which you were temporarily absent or on layoff LAST WEEK?" In the revised version of the questionnaire, people are first asked if they were absent in the last week, and if they were, further questions about temporary absence are asked. A new and separate series of questions asks about layoffs. ◆

Ordering of Questions

If one question requires respondents to think about something that they may not have otherwise considered, then the order in which questions are presented can change the results. For example, suppose a survey were to ask, "To what extent do you think teenagers today worry about peer pressure related to drinking alcohol?" and then ask, "Name the top five pressures you think face teenagers today." It is quite likely that respondents would use the idea they had just been given and name peer pressure related to drinking alcohol as one of the five choices.

EXAMPLE 4.15
Is Happiness Related to Dating?

Clark and Schober (1992, p. 41) report on a survey that asked the following two questions:

1. How happy are you with life in general?
2. How often do you normally go out on a date? about ＿＿ times a month

When the questions were asked in this order, there was almost no relationship between the two answers. But when question 2 was asked first, the answers were highly related. Clark and Schober speculate that in that case, respondents interpreted question 1 to mean "Now, considering what you just told me about dating, how happy are you with life in general?" ◆

Confidentiality and Anonymity

People will often answer questions differently based on the degree to which they believe they are anonymous. Because researchers often need to perform follow-up surveys, it is easier to try to ensure confidentiality than anonymity. In ensuring **confidentiality,** the researcher promises not to release identifying information about respondents. In an **anonymous** survey, the researcher does not know the identity of the respondents.

Questions on issues like sexual behavior and income are particularly difficult because people consider those to be private matters. A variety of techniques have been developed to help ensure confidentiality, but surveys on such issues are hard to conduct accurately.

The problems discussed in this section are well known to professional pollsters, and most reputable polling agencies go to great lengths to overcome them to the extent possible. The survey questions in Examples 4.1 to 4.3 in Section 4.1 are excellent illustrations of how questions should be worded. For instance, the question in Example 4.3, "Do you favor or oppose scientific experimentation on the cloning of human beings?" is worded so as not to suggest which answer the interviewer would prefer. Here are two examples that illustrate attempts to overcome bias but also illustrate how difficult that can be.

EXAMPLE 4.16
When Will Adolescent Males Report Risky Behavior?

It is particularly difficult to measure information on behavior that is sensitive, risky, or illegal. In an article in *Science*, Turner et al. (1998) describe the use of audio, computer-assisted self-interviews as part of the 1995 National Survey of Adolescent Males (aged 15 to 19). The respondents were randomly assigned to answer the survey using the traditional paper form ($n = 368$) or using a laptop computer ($n = 1361$). The paper questionnaire was filled out and sealed in an envelope to return to the surveyor but was accompanied by identifying code numbers. The computer method included listening to questions through headphones, then recording the answers on a laptop computer. The authors believed this method would allow respondents to feel that their responses were more private. In particular, respondents who could not read would need to have the paper version read to them, whereas the audio-computer method allowed complete self-administration of the survey.

Results indicated that the additional perception of privacy increased the reported incidence of certain behaviors, while decreasing others. The behaviors with increased reported incidence for the audio-computer version tended to be less socially acceptable, while those with higher incidence for the paper version tended to be more socially acceptable (for the adolescent males in this survey). Here are some examples reported in the article:

Question:	Estimated Prevalence per 100 Males in Population	
Have you ever . . .	Paper Version	Audio-Computer Version
Had sex with a prostitute	0.7	2.5
Had intercourse with a female	68.1	63.9
Made a girl pregnant	7.9	6.5
Had sex with another male	1.5	5.5
Taken street drugs using a needle	1.4	5.2

◆

EXAMPLE 4.17
Politics Is All in the Wording

Crossen (1994, p. 112) described three very different sets of responses to a question about whether the president of the United States should be able to veto specific items in the federal budget. The first set came from a questionnaire published in *TV Guide* in which founder of the Reform Party and presidential candidate Ross Perot asked, "Should the president have the line item veto to eliminate waste?" Respondents were volunteers who mailed in the survey. Of those who responded, 97% said "yes." The second set of responses came from asking a properly selected random sample the same question, and 71% said "yes." But clearly the question is written to elicit a "yes" answer. When the question was reworded to read, "Should the president have the line item veto, or not?" and a proper random sample was queried, only 57% answered yes.

Cohn and Cope (2001, pp. 145–146) report that Perot also asked the question "Should laws be passed to eliminate all possibilities of special interests giving huge sums of money to candidates?" Again the "yes" responses were an overwhelming 99%. When a properly selected random sample was asked the same, biased version of the question, 80% said "yes." But when a properly selected random sample was asked, "Should laws be passed to prohibit interested groups from contributing to campaigns, or do groups have a right to contribute to the candidate they support?" only 40% said that such laws should be passed. ◆

4.4

turn on your mind

You have now learned that survey results have to be interpreted in the context of *who* responded and *to what questions* they responded. When you read the results of a survey, for which of these two areas do you think it would be easier for you to recognize and assess possible biases? Why?*

Be Sure You Understand What Was Measured

Sometimes words mean different things to different people. When you read about survey results, you should get a precise definition of what was actually asked or measured. Here are two examples that illustrate that even common terminology may mean different things to different people.

EXAMPLE 4.18
Teenage Sex

A letter to advice columnist Ann Landers stated, "According to a report from the University of California at San Francisco . . . sexual activity among adolescents is on the rise. There is no indication that this trend is slowing down or reversing itself." The letter went on to explain that these results were based on a national survey (*Davis Enterprise,* Feb. 19, 1990, p. B-4). On the same day, in the same newspaper, an article entitled "Survey: Americans Conservative with Sex" reported that "teenage boys are not living up to their reputations. [A study by the Urban Institute in Washington] found that adolescents seem to be having sex less often, with fewer girls and at a later age than teenagers did a decade ago" (*Ibid.,* p. A-9).

Here we have two apparently conflicting reports on adolescent sexuality, both reported on the same day in the same newspaper. One indicated that teenage sex was on the rise, while the other indicated that it was on the decline. Although neither report specified exactly what was measured, the letter to Ann Landers proceeded to note that "national statistics show the average age of first intercourse is 17.2 for females and 16.5 for males." The article stating that adolescent sex was on the decline measured it in terms of *frequency.* It was based on interviews with 1880 boys between the ages of 15 and 19, in which "the boys said they had had six sex partners, compared with seven a decade earlier. They reported having had sex an average of three times during the previous month, compared with almost five times in the earlier survey."

Thus it is not enough to know that both surveys were measuring adolescent or teenage sexual behavior. In one case the author was, at least partially, discussing the *age* of first intercourse, whereas in the other case the author was discussing the *frequency*. ◆

EXAMPLE 4.19
The Unemployed

Ask people whether or not they know anyone who is unemployed and invariably they will say that they do. Most people, however, don't realize that to be officially unemployed and included in the unemployment statistics given by the U.S. government, you must meet very stringent criteria. The government excludes "discouraged workers" who are "identified as persons who, though not working or seeking work, have a current desire for a job, have looked for one within the past year [but not within the past four weeks], and are currently available for work" (U.S. Dept. of Labor, 1992, p. 10). If you knew someone who fit that definition, you would undoubtedly think of him or her as unemployed. But they are not included in the official statistics. You can see that the true number of people who are not working is higher than the government statistics would lead you to believe. ◆

Some Concepts Are Hard to Precisely Define

Sometimes it is not the language but the concept itself that is ill-defined. For example, there is still not universal agreement on what should be measured with intelligence, or IQ, tests. The tests were originated at the beginning of the 20th century in order to determine the mental level of schoolchildren. The intelligence quotient (IQ) of a child was found by dividing the child's "mental level" by his or her chronological age. The "mental level" was determined by comparing the child's performance on the test with that of a large group of "normal" children to find the age group the individual's performance matched. Thus, if an 8-year-old child performed as well on the test as a "normal" group of 10-year-old children, he or she would have an IQ of $100 \times (10/8) = 125$.

IQ tests have been expanded and refined since the early days, but they continue to be surrounded by controversy. One reason is that it is very difficult to define what is meant by intelligence. It is hard to measure something if you can't even agree on what it is you are trying to measure. If you are interested in knowing more about these tests and the surrounding controversies, you can find numerous books on the subject. Anastasi (1988) provides a detailed discussion of a large variety of psychological tests, including IQ tests.

Measuring Attitudes and Emotions

Similar problems exist with trying to measure attitudes and emotions like self-esteem and happiness. The most common method for trying to measure such things is to have respondents read statements and determine the extent to which they agree with the statement. For example, a test for measuring happiness might ask respondents to indicate their level of agreement, from "strongly disagree" to "strongly agree," with statements such as "I generally feel optimistic when I get up in the morning." In order to produce agreement on what is meant by characteristics such as "introversion," psychologists have developed standardized tests that claim to measure those attributes.

Open or Closed Questions: Should Choices Be Given?

An **open question** is one in which respondents are allowed to answer in their own words, while a **closed question** is one in which they are given a list of alternatives from which to choose their answer. Usually the latter form offers a choice of "other" in which the respondent is allowed to fill in the blank.

Problems with Closed Questions

To show the limitation of closed questions, Schuman and Scott (1987) asked about "the most important problem facing this country today." Half of the sample, 171 people, were given this as an open question. The most common responses were

> Unemployment (17%)
> General economic problems (17%)
> Threat of nuclear war (12%)
> Foreign affairs (10%)

In other words, one of these four choices was volunteered by over half of the respondents.

The other half of the sample was given the question as a closed question, with the list of choices and the percent who chose them being

> The energy shortage (5.6%)
> The quality of public schools (32.0%)
> Legalized abortion (8.4%)
> Pollution (14.0%)

These choices combined were mentioned by only 2.4% of respondents in the open question survey, yet they were selected by 60% when they were the only specific choices given. Don't think respondents had no choice; in addition to the list of four, they were told, "If you prefer, you may name a different problem as most important." On the basis of the closed-form questionnaire, policymakers would have been seriously misled about what is important to the public. It is possible to avoid this kind of astounding discrepancy. If closed questions are preferred, they first should be presented as open questions to a test sample before the real survey, and the most common responses should then be included in the list of choices for the closed question. This kind of exercise is usually done as part of what's called a "pilot survey" in which various aspects of a study design can be tried before it's too late to change them.

Problems with Open Questions

The biggest problem with open questions is that the results can be difficult to summarize. If a survey includes thousands of respondents, it can be a major chore to categorize their responses. Another problem, found by Schuman and Scott (1987), is that the wording of the question might unintentionally exclude answers that would have been appealing had they been included in a list of choices (such as in a closed question). To test this, they asked 347 people to "name one or two of the most important national or world event(s) or change(s) during the past 50 years." The most common choices and the percent who mentioned them were

> World War II (14.1%)
> Exploration of space (6.9%)
> Assassination of John F. Kennedy (4.6%)
> The Vietnam war (10.1%)
> Don't know (10.6%)
> All other responses (53.7%)

The same question was then repeated in closed form to a new group of 354 people. Five choices were given, the preceding ones and "invention of the computer." Of the 354 respondents, the percent who selected each choice were

World War II (22.9%)
Exploration of space (15.8%)
Assassination of John F Kennedy (11.6%)
The Vietnam war (14.1%)
Invention of the computer (29.9%)
Don't know (0.3%)
All other responses (5.4%)

The most frequent response was "invention of the computer," which had been mentioned by only 1.4% of respondents in the open question. Clearly, the wording of the question led respondents to focus on "events" rather than "changes" and the invention of the computer did not readily come to mind. When it was presented as an option, however, people realized that it was indeed one of the most important events or changes during the past 50 years.

In summary, there are advantages and disadvantages to both approaches. One compromise is to ask a small test sample to list the first several answers that come to mind, then use the most common of those. These could be supplemented with additional answers, like "invention of the computer," that may not readily come to mind.

Remember that, as the reader, you have an important role in interpreting the results. You should always be informed as to whether questions were asked in open or closed form, and if the latter, you should be told what the choices were. You should also be told whether or not "don't know" or "no opinion" was offered as a choice in either case.

CASE STUDY 4.2
No Opinion of Your Own? Let Politics Decide

This is an excellent example of how people will respond to survey questions when they do not know about the issues, and how the wording of questions can influence responses. In 1995, the *Washington Post* decided to expand on a 1978 poll taken in Cincinnati, Ohio in which people were asked whether they "favored or opposed repealing the 1975 Public Affairs Act" (Morin, 1995, p. 36). There was no such act, but about one-third of the respondents expressed an opinion about it.

In February 1995, the *Washington Post* added this fictitious question to its weekly poll of 1000 randomly selected respondents: "Some people say the 1975 Public Affairs Act should be repealed. Do you agree or disagree that it should be repealed?" Almost half (43%) of the sample expressed an opinion, with 24% agreeing that it should be repealed and 19% disagreeing!

The *Post* then tried another trick that produced even more disturbing results. This time, they polled two separate groups of 500 randomly selected adults. The first group was asked: "President Clinton [a Democrat] said that the 1975 Public Affairs Act should be repealed. Do you agree or disagree?" The second group was asked: "The Republicans in Congress said that the 1975 Public Affairs Act should be repealed. Do you agree or disagree?" Respondents were also asked about their party affiliation.

Overall, 53% of the respondents expressed an opinion about repealing this fictional act! The results by party affiliation were striking: For the Clinton version, 36% of the Democrats but only 16% of the Republicans agreed that the act should be repealed. For the "Republicans in Congress" version, 36% of the Republicans but only 19% of the Democrats agreed that the act should be repealed.

KEY TERMS

EXERCISES   Blue = Basics   **Bold, Bold** = Answer in back

Section 4.1

4.1 Briefly explain the difference between a sample survey and a census.

4.2 A survey is planned to estimate the proportion of voters in a community who plan to vote for candidate Y. Calculate the conservative margin of error, as a proportion and as a percent, for each of the following possible sample sizes:
a. $n = 100$.
b. $n = 400$.
c. $n = 900$.

4.3 The Nielsen survey produces the rankings of television shows. The survey is based on a random sample of about 5000 households with TV sets. Calculate a conservative margin of error for this survey as a proportion and as a percent.

4.4 In a random sample of 90 students at a university, 72 students (80% or .80 of the sample) say they use a laptop computer.
a. Calculate the conservative margin of error for the survey.
b. Compute an approximate 95% confidence interval for the population *proportion* that uses a laptop computer.

4.5 Briefly explain what it means to say that a survey method is biased.

4.6 For each definition, identify the correct term for the type of bias being defined. Possible answers are selection bias, nonresponse bias, response bias.
a. Participants respond differently from how they truly feel.
b. The method for selecting the participants produces a sample that does not represent the population of interest.

c. A representative sample is chosen, but a subset of the sample cannot be contacted or does not respond.

4.7 In each of the following situations, indicate whether the potential bias is a selection bias, a nonresponse bias, or a response bias.
a. A survey question asked of unmarried men was, "What is the most important feature you consider when deciding whether to date somebody?" The results were found to depend upon whether the interviewer was male or female.
b. In a study of women's opinions about community issues, investigators randomly selected a sample of households and interviewed a woman from each selected household. When no woman was present in a selected household, a next-door neighbor was interviewed instead. The survey was done during daytime hours, so working women might have been disproportionately missed.
c. A telephone survey of 500 residences is conducted. People refused to talk to the interviewer in 200 of the residences.

4.8 In a CNN/*Time* poll conducted December 17–18, 1998, a sample of $n = 1031$ adults in the United States was asked, "Do you think the police should or should not be allowed to collect DNA information from suspected criminals, similar to how they take fingerprints?" Of those sampled, 66% answered "should" (http://www.pollingreport.com/crime.htm).
a. Calculate the conservative margin of error for the survey, as a percent.
b. Compute an approximate 95% confidence interval for the percent of all American adults who think police should be allowed to collect DNA information from suspected criminals.

4.9 In an ABC News Poll conducted between January 21st and 26th, 2000 a random sample of $n = 1006$ adult Americans was asked, "Compared to buying things by mail order or in a store, do you think that buying things over the Internet poses more of a threat to your personal privacy, less of a threat, or about the same?" (http://www.pollingreport.com/computer.htm, September 17, 2002). The percents that selected each response were

More of a threat	40%
Less of a threat	7%
About the same	47%
No opinion	6%

a. What is the margin of error for this poll? Give your answer as both a proportion and a percent.

b. What is a conservative 95% confidence interval for the population proportion that would have responded "More of a threat?" Give your answer for the population percent as well.

c. Write a sentence or two interpreting the interval you found in part (b).

d. Based on the interval you found in part (b), could you conclude that in January 2000 fewer than half of all adult Americans perceived Internet shopping as posing more of a threat than buying things by mail order or in a store? Explain.

4.10 Suppose a national polling agency conducted 100 polls in a year, using proper random sampling, and reported a 95% confidence interval for each poll. About how many of those confidence intervals would be wrong, i.e., would not cover the true population value?

4.11 The question about the importance of religion in Example 4.1 was asked in a survey of elementary statistics students at Penn State University in the fall of 2001 and spring of 2002. The results were as follows:

Very important	460 =	27%
Fairly important	703 =	41%
Not very important	543 =	32%
Total	1706 =	100%

Because these students were not a random sample from a larger population, and because statistics students may not represent other students on questions of religion, treat these 1706 students as a population. Therefore, we know that for the population of elementary statistics students at Penn State in the 2001–2002 academic year, 27% felt that religion was very important in their lives.

a. Based on the results in Example 4.1, can we conclude that this percent differs from the percent of the population of all adult Americans who felt religion was very important in their lives in September 2002? Explain.

b. Based on the preceding results and those in Example 4.1, answer the question in part (a) for the percent who felt religion was fairly important and for the percent who felt it was not very important.

c. Write a short news article comparing the two surveys as if you were writing it for the student newspaper.

d. Suppose we believe the Penn State sample is representative of all students in the academic programs that require the elementary statistics course. Calculate an approximate 95% confidence interval for the population proportion that would say religion is very important in their lives.

4.12 Give an example of a situation where a sample must be used because a census is not possible.

4.13 The U.S. government gathers numerous statistics based on random samples, but every ten years it conducts a census of the U.S. population. What can it learn from a census that cannot be learned from a sample?

4.14 An Internet report on a 1999 Gallup Poll (August 2, 1999, http://www.gallup.com/poll/index.asp) included the statement: "The results below are based on telephone interviews with a randomly selected national sample of 1,021 adults, 18 years and older, conducted July 22–25, 1999. For results based on this sample, one can say with 95 percent confidence that the maximum error attributable to sampling and other random effects is plus or minus 3 percentage points." What is the margin of error for this survey? Give two separate ways in which you know this is the answer.

4.15 Refer to the previous exercise. One of the questions asked was "Do you think there will or will not come a time when Israel and the Arab nations will be able to settle their differences and live in peace?" The choices and percent choosing them were "Yes, will be a time" (49%), "No, will not" (47%), "No opinion" (4%).

a. Give the interval of values that is likely to cover the true proportion of the population who would answer, "Yes, will be a time."

b. Give the interval of values that is likely to cover the true proportion of the population who would answer, "No, will not."

c. Compare your answers in parts (a) and (b). Is there a clear majority of the population for either opinion? Explain.

4.16 A poll commissioned by the Student Aid Alliance sampled 1022 American adults in May 1999 and was reported to have a margin of error of 3.1%. Respondents were asked, "How important do you think it is to increase the current level of federal funding for each of the following things?" The programs and the percent of the sample who answered "Very important" or "Somewhat important" were "Health care" (90%), "Social Security" (89%), "Financial aid for college students" (87%), "Defense" (77%), "Welfare" (56%), and "Foreign aid" (47%). (*Source:* NASULGC[1] *Newsline,* July–August 1999, p. 7.) Write a short news article explaining these results. Address the question of which program(s) the highest percentage of *all* adult Americans think it is at least somewhat important to fund at increased levels.

4.17 Refer to the three types of bias given in Section 4.1. Which type of bias do you think would be introduced in each of the following situations?

a. A list of registered automobile owners is used to select a random sample for a survey about whether people think homeowners should pay a surtax to support public parks.

b. A survey is mailed to a random sample of residents in a city asking if they think the current mayor is doing an acceptable job.

[1]NASULGC is the National Association of State Universities and Land Grant Colleges.

c. In a college town, college students are hired to conduct door-to-door interviews, based on a multistage cluster sample, to determine if city residents think there should be a law forbidding loud music at parties.

d. A magazine sends a survey to a random sample of its subscribers asking them if they would like the frequency of publication reduced from biweekly to monthly or would prefer that it remain the same.

e. A random sample of registered voters is contacted by phone and asked whether or not they are going to vote in the upcoming presidential election.

Section 4.2

4.18 Define each of the following terms:
a. Probability sampling plan.
b. Simple random sample.

4.19 There are 8000 items in a population, and these items are labeled using four-digit numbers ranging from 0000 to 7999. Use the following stream of random digits to select four items from the population. Explain how you determined your answer.

Random Digits: 76429 69730 23395 12694 43387

4.20 Ten grocery stores, numbered from 0 to 9, will participate in an experiment to compare the effectiveness of two methods for displaying a product. Five of these stores will be randomly selected to use the first method, while the other five stores will use the second method. Use the following stream of random digits to select the five stores that will use the first display method.

Random Digits: 68538 70621 32205 23593 61396

4.21 Refer to Example 4.5, in which 43 children were randomly assigned to three treatment groups. The example demonstrated how the children for group 1 were selected. Use Table 4.1 to select the 12 children (from the remaining 28) to go into the control group. Number the children from 1 to 28. Start at the beginning of the row labeled 4, explain your process, and list the unit numbers of the children selected.

4.22 A lottery game is played by choosing six whole numbers between 1 and 49. The grand prize is won if all six numbers chosen match the winning numbers drawn.
a. Use Table 4.1 to draw six numbers. Start at the beginning of the table, explain your process, and write down the six numbers chosen.
b. George plays this game weekly. Assume the winning numbers are drawn fairly, so that any number has the same chance of occurrence. Would George have a better chance of winning if he chose the same numbers every week or chose different numbers every week, or doesn't it matter?

4.23 One hundred volunteers agree to participate in an experiment. There are four treatments, each of which will be assigned to 25 participants. Explain how you could use Table 4.1 to assign the treatments.

4.24 Refer to the previous exercise. Suppose the participants were grouped into 25 blocks of 4 each, with each treatment assigned once per block. Explain how you could use Table 4.1 to assign the treatments.

4.25 A radio station has a daily contest in which they randomly select one birthday (month and day, not year) and announce it on the air. The first person with that birthday who calls the station wins a prize. Each day the station selects a new birthday, and it doesn't mind if the same birthday is selected multiple times over the course of the contest. Explain how it could use Table 4.1 to select the birthdays. Start at the beginning of the row labeled 9 and write down the first five birthdays the station would use.

4.26 Refer to Figure 4.2, showing the results of taking a simple random sample of 10 stick figures from Figure 4.1. Label the stick figures in Figure 4.1 from 00 to 99, going across rows. Suppose a table of random digits had been used to select the sample in Figure 4.2. Write down a stream of random digits that would have led to the selection of the sample shown.

4.27 Refer to the previous exercise and write down a stream of random digits that would have led to the selection of the sample shown in Figure 4.3.

4.28 An exercise in Chapter 3 described the following scenario: To compare three packaging designs for a new food, a manufacturer randomly selected three grocery stores in each of 50 cities. The three designs were randomly assigned to the three stores in each city, and sales were compared for a two-month period.
a. Explain how you would use Table 4.1 to choose the three grocery stores in each city.
b. Explain how you would use Table 4.1 to randomly assign the three packaging designs to the three stores in each city.

4.29 The right handspan measurements for 103 female college students in Table 2.4 in Chapter 2 are given again here and in the **pennstate1F** dataset on the CD.

Females (103 Students): 20, 19, 20.5, 20.5, 20.25, 20, 18, 20.5, 22, 20, 21.5, 17, 16, 22, 22, 20, 20, 20, 21.7, 22, 20, 21, 21, 19, 21, 20.25, 21, 22, 18, 20, 21, 19, 22.5, 21, 20, 19, 21, 20.5, 21, 22, 20, 20, 18, 21, 22.5, 22.5, 19, 19, 19, 22.5, 20, 13, 20, 22.5, 19.5, 18.5, 19, 17.5, 18, 21, 19.5, 20, 19, 21.5, 18, 19, 19.5, 20, 22.5, 21, 18, 22, 18.5, 19, 22, 17, 12.5, 18, 20.5, 19, 20, 21, 19, 19, 21, 18.5, 19, 21.5, 21.5, 23, 23.25, 20, 18.8, 21, 21, 20, 20.5, 20, 19.5, 21, 21, 20

a. Draw three simple random samples of ten measurements each from this data set (an individual can be in more than one of your samples). Explain how you chose the samples and list the ten handspan measurements in each sample.

b. Find the median for each of your three samples. Compare them to the median for the full data set (20.0 cm).

c. Find the mean for each of your three samples. Compare them to the mean for the full data set (also 20.0 cm).

d. There were 21 women whose recorded handspan measurements were 20.0 cm. Would it be possible to have a random sample of ten measurements with a mean of 20.0 and a standard deviation of 0? Explain.

Section 4.3

4.30 A class of 200 students is numbered from 1 to 200, and a table of random digits is used to choose 60 students from the class. Is the group of students selected a simple ran-

dom sample, a stratified random sample, a cluster sample, or a systematic sample?

4.31 In each part, identify whether the sample is a stratified random sample or a cluster sample.
   a. A class of 200 students is seated in 20 rows of 10 students per row. Three students are randomly selected from every row.
   b. An airline company randomly chooses one flight from a list of all flights taking place that day. All passengers on that selected flight are asked to fill out a survey on meal satisfaction.

4.32 In a factory producing television sets, every 100th set produced is inspected. Is the collection of sets inspected a simple random sample, a stratified random sample, a cluster sample, or a systematic sample?

4.33 The **Sampling** applet described in Section 4.2 drew a simple random sample of 10 individuals from a population of 45 men and 55 women and measured their heights. The average height for the sample could be used as an estimate of the average height in the population. Another possibility for estimating the average height would be to use stratified sampling, where men and women are the two strata, then estimate the heights of men and women separately and use the knowledge that 45% of the population is male to combine the two estimates. Do you think stratified sampling would be a more accurate or a less accurate method than simple random sampling for estimating the mean height in the population? Explain.

4.34 Suppose a state has 10 universities, 25 four-year colleges, and 50 community colleges, each of which offer multiple sections of an introductory statistics class each year. Researchers want to conduct a survey of students taking introductory statistics in the state. Explain a method for collecting each of the following types of samples:
   a. A stratified sample.
   b. A cluster sample.
   c. A simple random sample.

4.35 Refer to the previous question. Give one advantage of each sampling method in the context of the problem.

4.36 Find an example of a survey routinely conducted by the U.S. government. (The Internet is a good source, for instance, try http://www.fedstats.gov.) Explain how the survey is conducted and identify the type(s) of sampling used.

4.37 Is a sample found using random-digit dialing more like a stratified sample or a cluster sample? Explain.

Sections 4.4 and 4.5

4.38 A group of biologists wants to estimate the abundance of barrel cactus in a desert. They divide the desert into a grid of 100 rectangular areas, but exclude 10 of those areas because they are difficult to access. The biologists then measure the density of cactus in a randomly selected sample of 40 of the 90 accessible areas.
   a. What was the sampling frame in this study, and how did it differ from the population of interest?
   b. Explain why "using the wrong sampling frame" might lead to a biased estimate of the abundance of cactus in the desert.

4.39 A local government wants to determine whether taxpayers support increasing local taxes in order to provide more public funding to schools. They randomly select 500 schoolchildren from a list of all children enrolled in local schools and then survey the parents of these children about possible tax increases.
   a. What is the population of interest for the local government?
   b. What sampling frame did the government use for the survey?
   c. Explain why "using the wrong sampling frame" might lead to a biased estimate of taxpayer support for increasing taxes.

4.40 In each part, indicate whether the sample should be called a self-selected sample or a convenience sample.
   a. To assess passenger satisfaction, an airline distributed questionnaires to 100 passengers in the airline's frequent flyer lounge. All 100 individuals responded, and 95 respondents said they had a high degree of satisfaction with the airline.
   b. A magazine contains a survey about sexual behavior. Readers are asked to mail in their answers, and $n = 2000$ readers do so.
   c. A political scientist surveys the 80 people in a class he teaches in order to evaluate student political views.

4.41 A survey question will be asked to determine whether people think smoking should be banned on all airline flights.
   a. Write a version of the question that is as neutral and unbiased as possible.
   b. Write a version of the question likely to get people to respond that smoking should be forbidden on all flights.
   c. Write a version of the question likely to get people to respond that smoking should be allowed on airline flights.

4.42 An example of an unnecessarily complex survey question is "Shouldn't former drug dealers not be allowed to work in hospitals after they are released from prison?" Restate this question so that it is clearer.

4.43 In a planned survey about moviegoing, two questions that will be asked are:
   ♦ How many times per month do you go to the movies?
   ♦ Do you consider yourself to be well-informed about recent movies, or not?
   The questions could be asked in either order. Briefly explain how you think the question order for asking them might affect how people answer them.

4.44 In presidential election years in the United States, a Gallup Poll is conducted in which the first survey question asks which presidential candidate the voter prefers. Subsequent questions concern other political, social, and election issues. Explain why this question order might be the best order for estimating how people may vote in the presidential election.

4.45 Medical tests, such as those for detecting HIV, sometimes concern such sensitive information that people do not want to give their names when they take the test. In some instances, a person taking such a medical test is given a number or code that they can use later to learn the test result by phone. Explain whether this procedure is an example of anonymous testing or confidential testing.

4.46 Despite his success in 1936, George Gallup failed miserably in trying to predict the winner of the 1948 U.S. presi-

dential election. His organization, as well as two others, predicted that Thomas Dewey would beat incumbent Harry Truman. All three used what is called **quota sampling.** The interviewers were told to find a certain number, or quota, of each of several types of people. For example, they might have been told to interview six women under age 40, one of whom was black and the other five of whom were white. Imagine that you are one of their interviewers, trying to follow these instructions. Who would you ask? Now explain why you think these polls failed to predict the true winner and why quota sampling is not a good method.

4.47 Explain why the main problem with the *Literary Digest* poll is described as "volunteer response" and not "volunteer sample."

4.48 Gastwirth (1988, p. 507) describes a court case in which Bristol Myers was ordered by the Federal Trade Commission to stop advertising that "twice as many dentists use Ipana as any other dentifrice" and that more dentists recommended it than any other dentifrice. Bristol Myers had based its claim on a survey of 10,000 randomly selected dentists from a list of 66,000 subscribers to two dental magazines. They received 1983 responses, with 621 saying they used Ipana and only 258 reporting that they used the second most popular brand. As for the recommendations, 461 respondents recommended Ipana, compared with 195 for the second most popular choice.

a. Specify the sampling frame for this survey, and explain whether or not you think "using the wrong sampling frame" was a difficulty here, based on what Bristol Myers was trying to conclude.

b. Of the remaining four "Difficulties and Disasters in Sampling" listed in Section 4.4 (other than "using the wrong sampling frame"), which do you think was the most serious in this case? Explain.

c. What could Bristol Myers have done to improve the validity of the results after it had mailed the 10,000 surveys and received 1983 of them back? Assume it kept track of who had responded and who had not.

4.49 An Internet poll sponsored by a site called About.com asked Internet users to pick one of two choices in response to the question, "Should jurors opposed to gun control laws refuse to convict defendants even if they have clearly broken gun laws?" The two choices and the number and percent choosing them were

◆ Yes, that's an effective way to defeat unjust laws (16,864, 23%).

◆ No, that undermines the legal system (55,519, 77%). Discuss this poll, including whether or not you think the results are representative of all adults and whether you think the wording is appropriate.

4.50 A Gallup Poll released on July 9, 1999 included a series of questions about possible religious activities in public schools. The poll was based on telephone interviews with a randomly selected sample of 1016 U.S. adults conducted June 25–27, 1999. The questions, asked in random order, included the following:

◆ Do you favor or oppose teaching creationism ALONG WITH evolution in public schools? Favor—68%, Oppose—29%, No opinion—3%.

◆ Do you favor or oppose teaching creationism INSTEAD OF evolution in public schools? Favor—40%, Oppose—55%, No opinion—5%.

a. What is the margin of error for this poll?

b. Write a few sentences describing the results of the survey, being truthful but biasing the story in favor of teaching creationism.

c. Repeat part (b), but bias the story in favor of not teaching creationism.

d. Repeat part (b), but write an unbiased story.

e. Explain which of the pitfalls in Section 4.5 is illustrated by this example.

4.51 Suppose a community group wants to convince city officials to put more trash containers on the city streets. They decide to conduct a survey, but rather than a scientifically valid result, they want their results to show that as many citizens as possible want additional trash containers. Give an example of how they could use each of the following to their advantage:

a. Self-selected sample.

b. Deliberate bias.

c. Ordering of questions.

d. Desire to please.

4.52 Find an example of a poll based on a self-selected sample. Report the wording of the questions and the number who chose each response. Comment on whether or not you think the results can be extended to any population.

4.53 Give an example of two survey questions for which you think the results would be substantially different depending on which order they were asked.

4.54 Explain which of three methods—a door-to-door interview, a telephone interview, or a mail survey—would be *most* likely and which would be *least* likely to suffer from each of the following problems:

a. Bias due to desire to please the interviewer.

b. Volunteer response.

c. Bias due to perceived lack of confidentiality.

4.55 Find an example of a poll conducted by a reputable scientific polling organization. Write a few paragraphs describing how the poll was conducted, what was asked, and the results. Explain whether or not any of the problems discussed in Sections 4.4 and 4.5 were likely to have biased the results of the poll.

4.56 Refer to Example 4.16, "When Will Adolescent Males Report Risky Behavior?" Explain which two of the seven "Possible Sources of Response Bias in Surveys" are illustrated by this example.

4.57 An advertiser of a certain brand of aspirin (let's call it Brand B) claims that it is the preferred painkiller for headaches, based on the results of a survey of headache sufferers. But further investigation reveals that the choices given to respondents were: Tylenol, Extra-Strength Tylenol, Brand B aspirin, Advil.

a. Is this an open- or closed-form question? Explain.

b. Comment on the choices given to respondents.

c. Comment on the advertiser's claim.

d. What choices do you think should have been given? Explain.

4.58 An NBC News/*Wall Street Journal* poll conducted at the end of the 20th century (September 9–12, 1999) asked a random sample of $n = 1010$ adult Americans, "Which one of the following do you consider to be the best American

movie of the 20th century?" The choices given and the percent who chose them were: *Gone With the Wind* 28%, *Schindler's List* 18%, *Titanic* 11%, *Star Wars* 11%, *Casablanca* 8%, *The Godfather* 7%, *Citizen Kane* 6%, *The Graduate* 1%, Not sure 4%. In addition, 2% volunteered the answer "all of them," and 4% volunteered an answer not listed (http://www.pollingreport.com/hollywoo.htm, September 29, 2002).

   a. Was this asked as an open-form or closed-form question?

   b. Do you think the form used was appropriate for trying to ascertain what movies adult Americans thought were the best of the 20th century? Explain.

   c. Give one advantage and one disadvantage each for open-form and closed-form questions in this situation.

4.59 Rock singer Elvis Presley died on August 16, 1977 and his life received substantial publicity as the 25th anniversary of his death approached on August 16, 2002. On August 7–11, 2002 an ABC News poll asked a random sample of $n = 1023$ adult Americans, "Who do you think is the greatest rock 'n' roll star of all time?" There were 128 different stars volunteered by respondents. The top responses and the percent they received were: Elvis Presley 38%, Jimi Hendrix 4%, John Lennon 2%, Mick Jagger 2%, Bruce Springsteen 2%, Paul McCartney 2%, Eric Clapton 2%, Michael Jackson 2%, Other 25%, None 7%, No opinion 15% (http://abcnews.go.com/sections/us/DailyNews/elvis_poll.html, Sept 29, 2002).

   a. Was this an open- or closed-form question?

   b. Do you think the percent who responded "Elvis Presley" was influenced by the timing of the poll? Explain.

   c. Do you think the percent who responded "Elvis Presley" would have been higher, lower, or about the same if the question had given specific choices?

4.60 Refer to the previous exercise. Another question asked in the poll was "Do you consider yourself a fan of Elvis Presley, or not?" The responses were almost equally split, with 49% saying "yes" and 51% saying "no." Do you think the order in which this question and the one in the previous exercise were asked would influence the results to either question? Explain (http://www.pollingreport.com/music.htm, September 29, 2002).

Chapter Exercises

4.61 Refer to Example 4.17, "Politics Is All in the Wording."

   a. Explain which one of the "Difficulties and Disasters" listed in Section 4.4 is illustrated by this example.

   b. Explain which one of the seven "Possible Sources of Response Bias in Surveys" is illustrated by this example.

4.62 Refer to Example 4.3 in which a survey question was "Do you favor or oppose scientific experimentation on the cloning of human beings?" Suppose an agency that advocated cloning of human beings wanted to conduct a survey that would show support for their cause. Explain how they might use each of the following to do so:

   a. Selection bias.

   b. Deliberate bias.

   c. Desire to please.

   d. Ordering of questions.

4.63 Suppose you wanted to estimate the proportion of adults who write with their left hands and decide to watch a sample of n people signing credit card receipts at a mall.

   a. Do you think this sample would be representative for the question of interest? Explain.

   b. Assuming the sample was representative, how many people would you have to include to estimate the proportion with a margin of error of 5%?

   c. Suppose you observed 500 people and 60 of them signed with their left hand. What interval of values would you give as being likely to contain the true proportion of people in the larger population who would sign with their left hand?

   d. Is the sampling plan used a probability sampling plan? Explain.

4.64 The faculty senate at a large university wanted to know what proportion of the students thought a foreign language should be required for everyone. The statistics department offered to cooperate in conducting a survey, and a simple random sample of 500 students was selected from all students enrolled in statistics classes. A survey form was sent by e-mail to these 500 students. Discuss the extent to which each of the three types of bias would be likely to occur in this survey:

   a. Selection bias.

   b. Nonresponse bias.

   c. Response bias.

   d. Which of these three types of bias do you think would be the most serious? Explain.

4.65 Refer to the previous exercise.

   a. What is the population of interest to the faculty senate?

   b. What is the sampling frame?

   c. What is the sample?

   d. Is the sample representative of the population of interest? Explain.

4.66 A large medical professional organization with membership consisting of doctors, nurses, and other medical employees wanted to know how its members felt about HMOs (health maintenance organizations). Name the type of sampling plan they used in each of the following scenarios:

   a. They randomly selected 500 members from each of the lists of all doctors, all nurses, and all other employees and surveyed those 1500 members.

   b. They randomly selected ten cities from all cities in which its members lived, then surveyed all members in those cities.

   c. They randomly choose a starting point from the first 50 names in an alphabetical list of members, then chose every 50th member in the list starting at that point.

4.67 An article in the *Sacramento Bee* was headlined "Drop found in risky behavior among teens over last decade" (June 7, 2000, p. A6; reprinted from the *Los Angeles Times*). The article reported that "the findings show that for the general population [not a specific ethnic group], the share of teens abstaining from all 10 risky behaviors jumped from 20 percent to 25 percent [from the beginning to the end of the 1990s]." The article did not say who was measured, but was obviously based on *samples* taken at each end of the decade. What additional information would you need to know to determine whether or not this drop rep-

resents a real drop in the percent of the *population* of teens abstaining? Explain.

4.68 Case Study 3.3 discussed an experiment in which smokers wore a nicotine patch or a placebo patch. Of the 120 participants wearing a nicotine patch, 46% had quit smoking after eight weeks. Assume this group is equivalent to a random sample of smokers desiring to quit.
   a. What is the margin of error accompanying this percent?
   b. What is the approximate 95% confidence interval accompanying this percent?
   c. Suppose the manufacturer of the nicotine patches was to claim that "evidence shows that a majority of smokers with a desire to quit may be helped by nicotine patches." Comment on this statement, referring to your answer in part (b).

4.69 One evening around 6 P.M. authorities in a major metropolitan area received hundreds of phone calls from people reporting that they had just seen an unidentified flying object (UFO). A local television station would like to report the story on their 10 P.M. news and wants to include an estimate of the proportion of area residents who witnessed the UFO. Explain how each of the following methods of obtaining this information would be biased, if at all:
   a. A "quickie poll" taken between 7 P.M. and 9 P.M. that evening, using random-digit dialing for residents of the area.
   b. During commercial breaks between 7 P.M. and 9 P.M. that evening, providing two numbers for viewers to phone—one if they had seen the UFO, and one if they had not.
   c. A door-to-door survey taken between 7 P.M. and 9 P.M., based on a multistage sampling plan, in which ten city blocks (or equivalent area) were randomly selected and interviewers knocked on the doors of all homes in those areas and surveyed those who answered the door.
   d. An e-mail survey sent at 7 P.M. to all e-mail addresses for local residents served by a local Internet Service Provider in the area, using responses received by 9 P.M.

4.70 Refer to the previous exercise. Acknowledging that some bias is inevitable when information is required on such short notice, which of the four methods would you recommend that the television station use to get the information it desires? Explain.

4.71 Refer to the previous two exercises. Suppose that a local newspaper conducted a survey during the next week, based on random-digit dialing of 1400 residents of the area, and found that 20% of them reported having seen a UFO on the evening in question.
   a. What is the margin of error for the survey?
   b. Give an interval of values that probably covers the true percentage of the population that saw the UFO.

4.72 Refer to the survey described in Example 4.9, "Which Scientists Trashed the Public?" Explain which type of bias (selection, nonresponse, or response) was the most problematic in that survey.

4.73 Suppose an (unscrupulous!) organization wanted to conduct a survey in which the results supported its position that drinking coffee in public should be illegal except in designated coffee bars. Explain how they could use each of the following sources of bias to help produce the results they wanted:

   a. Selection bias.
   b. Nonresponse bias.
   c. Response bias.

4.74 Suppose a survey reported that 55% of respondents favored gun control, with a margin of error of ±3 percentage points.
   a. What was the approximate size of the sample?
   b. What is an approximate 95% confidence interval for the percent of the corresponding population who favor gun control?
   c. Based on the material in this chapter, write a statement interpreting the interval you found in part (b) that could be understood by someone with no training in statistics. (In Chapter 10 you will learn a more precise way to interpret this type of interval.)

4.75 Refer to the *Literary Digest* poll in Case Study 4.1. Discuss the extent to which each type of bias (selection, nonresponse, and response) played a role in producing the disastrous results, if at all.

4.76 Use the data in Case Study 1.1 (p. 2) or in the file **pennstate1** on the CD accompanying this book for this exercise.
   a. Select a random sample of ten males and a random sample of ten females and write down their answers to the question "What's the fastest you've ever driven a car?"
   b. Compare the males' and females' responses using appropriate numerical and/or graphical summary information.
   c. Recall from Chapters 1 and 2 that there was an obvious difference between male and female responses for the set of all students. Is this difference obvious in your samples? Explain.
   d. It is true in statistics that the larger the actual difference between two groups is in the population, the smaller the sample sizes needed to detect the difference. Discuss your answer to part (c) in the context of this statement.

Exercises 4.77–4.80 are based on a report of a Field Poll printed in the Sacramento Bee *on July 7, 2000 (Dan Smith, p. A4) with the headline "Ratings up for Boxer, Feinstein in new poll." The results were reported with a graphical display containing the information that "results are based on a statewide survey of 750 adults conducted June 9–18. The sample includes 642 voters considered likely to vote in the Nov. 7 general election. The margin of error is 3.8 percentage points."*

4.77 The text of the article said that the 750 adults surveyed were actually 750 *registered voters.* Based on the information about who was surveyed, if the poll results are to be used to predict the proportion of voters likely to vote for Senator Feinstein in November, should the results of all 750 voters be used? Explain, using the Fundamental Rule for Using Data for Inference in your explanation.

4.78 The report stated that the margin of error was 3.8 percentage points. This value is based on the 642 voters considered likely to vote and uses the precise formula you will learn in Chapter 10.
   a. Compute the conservative margin of error for this poll based on those likely to vote, and compare it to the precise margin of error presented.

b. For this sample, 57% reported that they approve of Dianne Feinstein's job performance. What is an approximate 95% confidence interval for the percent of all likely voters who approve of her performance?

4.79 Read the headline that accompanied the article, which stated that ratings were "up" for both senators. For the June 2000 poll, 57% approved of Feinstein's performance, compared with 56% and 53%, respectively, for similar polls taken in February 2000 and October 1999. Presumably, the headline refers to all registered voters in the state, and not just those in the samples. Considering the margin of error accompanying each poll, do you agree with the headline? Explain.

4.80 The article also reported that "among GOP voters, 39 percent give Feinstein high marks." Would the margin of error accompanying this result be larger, smaller, or the same as the margin of error for the entire sample? Explain.

Exercises 4.81–4.83 refer to a survey of University of California faculty members on affirmative action policies for the university (Roper Center, 1996). The survey was based on telephone interviews with a random sample of 1001 faculty members conducted in December 1995.

4.81 One of the questions asked was "Do you favor or oppose using race, religion, sex, color, ethnicity, or national origin as a criterion for admission to the University of California?" Of the 804 male respondents, 47% said "Favor," and of the 197 female respondents, 73% said "Favor."
a. Find the conservative margin of error for the males, and use it to compute an approximate 95% confidence interval for the percent of males in the population who favor this policy.
b. Repeat the analysis in part (a) for females.
c. Compare the approximate 95% confidence intervals you found in parts (a) and (b), and comment on whether you think male and female faculty members in the population differed on this question.

4.82 Refer to the previous exercise. Of the 166 arts and humanities faculty members, 66% favored the policy, while of the 229 engineering, mathematical, and physical sciences faculty, 38% favored it.
a. Find the conservative margin of error for the arts and humanities faculty, and use it to compute an approximate 95% confidence interval for the percent of them in the population who favor this policy.
b. Repeat the analysis in part (a) for the engineering and sciences faculty.
c. Compare the approximate 95% confidence intervals you found in parts (a) and (b), and comment on whether you think faculty members in these disciplines in the population differed on this question.

4.83 One question asked was as follows: "The term affirmative action has different meanings to different people. Please tell me which statement best describes what you mean by the term: First, affirmative action means granting preferences to women and certain racial and ethnic groups. Second, affirmative action means promoting equal opportunities for all individuals without regard to their race, sex, or ethnicity." The options "Neither" or "Both" were not given and were recorded only if the respondent offered them. The first statement was chosen by 37%, the second one by 43%, "Neither" by 13%, and "Both" by 2%. The remainder said, "Don't know." The organization that commissioned the poll, the California Association of Scholars, issued a press release that said in reference to this question, "These findings demolish the claim that the faculty at UC wants preferential policies." Refer to the "Possible Sources of Response Bias" in Section 4.5, and discuss them in the context of this question and resulting press release.

Turn On Your Computer

*For Exercises 4.84–4.88, use the **Sampling** applet described in Section 4.2. The applet is on the CD accompanying this text.*

4.84 Choose one stick figure to represent yourself and identify which one it was in your answers to this exercise by giving the row number (1 to 10) and column number (1 to 10) where you reside.
a. Suppose you are in a class of 100 individuals, represented by these stick figures. Your teacher randomly selects 10 people each class period and asks them to answer a question about the reading assignment. What are your chances of being in the sample each day?
b. Repeat the sample selection process 20 times, each time noting whether you made it into the sample. How many times did you make it into the sample? Does that surprise you or is it about what you expected?

4.85 Repeat the sampling process 50 times without pressing the **Start Over** button. Use **Show Results** to display the results of the 50 samples. Cut and paste the results into Minitab or another program.
a. Display a histogram of the 50 means of the chosen samples.
b. Describe the histogram in part (a), including shape, center, and spread.
c. Display a histogram of the 50 values of "percent female."
d. Describe the histogram in part (c).

4.86 Repeat the sampling process 20 times without pressing the **Start Over** button. Use **Show Results** to display the results of the 20 samples. Write down the results, or cut and paste them into a computer program.
a. What is the median of the 20 sample means?
b. What is the range of the 20 sample means?
c. Display a boxplot of the 20 sample means.
d. We know that the population has a mean height of 68 inches. Based on your results in parts (a), (b), and (c), discuss how useful the mean of a sample of size 10 is for estimating the population mean in this situation.

4.87 Repeat the sampling process 20 times without pressing the **Start Over** button. Use **Show Results** to display the results of the 20 samples. Write down the results, or cut and paste the results into a computer program. Find the mean of the 20 sample means. This value represents the mean of all 200 sample values. Is this combined mean a better estimate of the population mean of 68 than most of the individual sample means? Is that what you would expect, or not? Explain.

4.88 Generate one random sample and print the display showing the applet and your result. Show what stream of numbers from a table of random digits would have produced your sample, numbering the stick figures from 00 to 99, starting at the top and going across rows.

REFERENCES

Abelson, R. P., E. F. Loftus, and A. G. Greenwald (1992). "Attempts to improve the accuracy of self-reports of voting," in *Questions about Questions*, J. M. Tanur (ed.), New York: Russell Sage Foundation, pp. 138–153.

Anastasi, Anne (1988). *Psychological Testing*, 6th ed., New York: Macmillan.

Bryson, M. C. (1976). "The *Literary Digest* poll: Making of a statistical myth," *American Statistician*, Vol. 30, pp. 184–185.

Clark, H. H., and M. F. Schober (1992). "Asking questions and influencing answers," in *Questions about Questions*, J. M. Tanur (ed.), New York: Russell Sage Foundation, pp. 15–48.

Cohn, Victor, and Lewis Cope (2001). *News and Numbers: A Guide to Reporting Statistical Claims and Controversies in Health and Other Fields*, 2nd ed., Ames, IA: Iowa State University Press.

Crossen, Cynthia (1994). *Tainted Truth*, New York: Simon and Schuster.

Freedman, D., R. Pisani, R. Purves, and A. Adhikari (1991). *Statistics*, 2nd ed., New York: W. W. Norton.

Gastwirth, Joseph L. (1988). *Statistical Reasoning in Law and Public Policy*, Vol. 2: *Tort Law, Evidence and Health*, Boston: Academic Press.

Liss, Susan (1997). "The Effects of Survey Methodology Changes in the NPTS," Technical Report, Office of Highway Policy Information, Federal Highway Administration.

Loftus, E. F., and J. C. Palmer (1974). "Reconstruction of automobile destruction: An example of the interaction between language and memory," *Journal of Verbal Learning and Verbal Behavior*, Vol. 13, pp. 585–589.

Mervis, Jeffrey (1998). "Report deplores science-media gap," *Science*, Vol. 279, p. 2036.

Morin, Richard (1995). "What informed public opinion?" *The Washington Post National Weekly Edition*, April 10–16, 1995, p. 36.

Plewes, Thomas J. (1994). "Federal agencies introduce redesigned Current Population Survey," *Chance*, Vol. 7, No. 1, pp. 35–41.

Plous, Scott (1993). *The Psychology of Judgment and Decision Making*, New York: McGraw-Hill.

Roper Center (1996). "University of California Faculty Opinion Survey on Affirmative Action Policies," Roper Center for Public Opinion Research, Press Release, January 15, 1996.

Schuman, H. and J. Scott (1987). "Problems in the use of survey questions to measure public opinion," *Science*, Vol. 236, May 22, 1987, pp. 957–959.

Turner, C. F., L. Ku, S. M. Rogers, L. D. Lindberg, J. H. Pleck, F. L. Sonenstein (1998). "Adolescent sexual behavior, drug use, and violence: Increased reporting with computer survey technology," *Science*, Vol. 280, pp. 867–873.

U.S. Department of Labor, Bureau of Labor Statistics (1992). *BLS Handbook of Methods*, Sept. 1992, Bulletin 2414.

Relationships Between Quantitative Variables

David Hurrell, Rex Interstock/Stock Connection/PictureQuest

Do college students give up study time to sleep, or vice versa? See Example 5.9.

A *statistical relationship* is different from a *deterministic relationship,* for which the value of one variable can be determined exactly from the value of the other variable. In a statistical relationship, there is variation from the average pattern. Our ability to predict what happens for an individual depends on the amount of natural variability from that pattern.

The description and confirmation of relationships between variables is so important in research that entire courses are devoted to the topic. You have already seen several examples that involved a potential relationship. For instance, in the observational study in Case Study 3.4, the investigators wanted to know if male pattern baldness and the risk of a heart attack were related. In the randomized experiment in Case Study 1.6, the researchers wanted to know if aspirin consumption and risk of heart attack were related.

In this chapter, we will learn how to describe the relationship between two *quantitative variables.* Remember (from Chapter 2) that the terms *quantitative variable* and *measurement variable* are synonyms for data that can be recorded as numerical values and then ordered according to those values. The relationship between weight and height is an example of a relationship between two quantitative variables.

The questions we ask about the relationship between two variables often concern specific numerical features of the association. For example, we may want to know how much weight will increase on average for each 1-inch increase in height. Or, we may want to estimate what the college grade point average will be for a student whose high school grade point average was 3.5.

We will use three tools to describe, picture, and quantify the relationship between two quantitative variables:

- ◆ **Scatterplot,** a two-dimensional graph of data values.
- ◆ **Correlation,** a statistic that measures the *strength and direction* of a linear relationship between two quantitative variables.
- ◆ **Regression equation,** an equation that describes the average relationship between a quantitative response variable and an explanatory variable. ◆

5.1

turn on your mind

For adults, there is a *positive association* between weight and height. For used cars, there is a *negative association* between the age of the car and the selling price. Explain what it means for two variables to have a positive association. Explain what it means when two variables have a negative association. What is an example of two variables that would have *no association*?*

5.1 | LOOKING FOR PATTERNS WITH SCATTERPLOTS

A **scatterplot** is a two-dimensional graph of the measurements for two numerical variables. A point on the graph represents the combination of measurements for an individual observation. The vertical axis, which is called the *y axis,* is used to locate the value of one of the variables. The horizontal axis, called the *x axis,* is used to locate the value of the other variable.

As we learned in Chapter 2, when looking at relationships we can often identify one of the variables as an **explanatory variable** that may explain or cause differences in the **response variable.** The term **dependent variable** is used as a synonym for *response variable.* In a scatterplot, the response variable is plotted on the vertical axis (the *y* axis), so it may also be called the **y variable.** The explanatory variable is plotted along the horizontal axis (the *x* axis) and may be called the **x variable.**

Questions to Ask About a Scatterplot

◆ What is the *average* pattern? Does it look like a straight line or is it curved?

◆ What is the direction of the pattern?

◆ How much do individual points vary from the average pattern?

◆ Are there any unusual data points?

EXAMPLE 5.1
Height and Handspan

TABLE 5.1 ■ Handspans and Height

Height (in.)	Span (cm)
71	23.5
69	22.0
66	18.5
64	20.5
71	21.0
72	24.0
67	19.5
65	20.5
76	24.5
67	20.0
70	23.0
62	17.0

and so on, for *n* = 167 observations.

Table 5.1 displays the first 12 observations of a dataset that includes the heights (in inches) and fully stretched handspans (in centimeters) of 167 college students. The data values for all 167 students are the raw data for studying the connection between height and handspan. Imagine how difficult it would be to see the pattern in the data if all 167 observations were shown in Table 5.1. Even when we just look at the data for 12 students, it takes a while to confirm that there does seem to be a tendency for taller people to have larger handspans.

Figure 5.1 is a scatterplot that displays the handspan and height measurements for all 167 students. The handspan measurements are plotted along the vertical axis (*y*), and the height measurements are plotted along the horizontal axis (*x*). Each point represents the two measurements for an individual.

We see that taller people tend to have greater handspan measurements than shorter people do. When two variables tend to increase together, as they do in Figure 5.1, we say that they have a **positive association.** Another noteworthy characteristic of the graph is that we can describe the general pattern of this re-

*HINT: Average weight increases as height increases. The selling price decreases as a car's age increases. Use these patterns to define positive and negative association more generally.

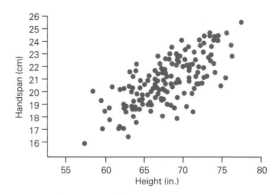

FIGURE 5.1   **Handspans and height**

lationship with a straight line. In other words, the handspan and height measurements may have a **linear relationship.** ◆

> *definition* ◆ Two variables have a **positive association** when the values of one variable tend to increase as the values of the other variable increase.
>
> ◆ Two variables have a **negative association** when the values of one variable tend to decrease as the values of the other variable increase.

EXAMPLE 5.2
Driver Age and the Maximum Legibility Distance of Highway Signs

In a study of the legibility and visibility of highway signs, a Pennsylvania research firm determined the maximum distance at which each of 30 drivers could read a newly designed sign. The 30 participants in the study ranged in age from 18 to 82 years old. The government agency that funded the research hoped to improve highway safety for older drivers and wanted to examine the relationship between age and the sign legibility distance.

Table 5.2 lists the data and Figure 5.2 shows a scatterplot of the ages and distances. The sign legibility distance is the response variable, so that variable is plotted on the *y* axis (the vertical axis). The maximum reading distance tends to

TABLE 5.2 ■ **Data Values for Example 5.2**

Age	Distance	Age	Distance	Age	Distance
18	510	37	420	68	300
20	590	41	460	70	390
22	560	46	450	71	320
23	510	49	380	72	370
23	460	53	460	73	280
25	490	55	420	74	420
27	560	63	350	75	460
28	510	65	420	77	360
29	460	66	300	79	310
32	410	67	410	82	360

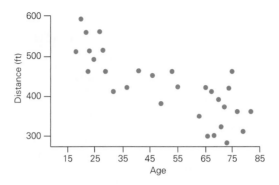

FIGURE 5.2   **Driver age and the maximum distance at which highway sign is read**
(Source: Adapted from data collected by Last Resource, Inc., Bellefonte, PA.)

decrease as age increases, so there is a negative association between distance and age. This is not a surprising result. As a person gets older, his or her eyesight tends to get worse, so we would expect the distances to decrease with age.

The researchers collected the data to determine numerical estimates for two questions about the relationship:

- ◆ How much does the distance decrease when age is increased?
- ◆ For drivers of any specific age, what is the average distance at which the sign can be read?

We'll examine these questions in the next section. For now, we simply point out that the pattern in the graph looks *linear,* so a straight-line equation that links distance to age will help us answer these questions. ◆

Curvilinear Patterns

A linear pattern is common, but it is not the only type of relationship. Sometimes, a curve describes the pattern of a scatterplot better than a line does, and when that's the case the relationship is called **nonlinear,** or **curvilinear.**

EXAMPLE 5.3
The Development
of Musical Preferences

Will the music that you like now always be your favorite music? If you are about 20 years old, the answer is likely to be "yes" according to research reported in a 1989 issue of the *Journal of Consumer Research* (Holbrook and Schindler, 1989). The research finding was that popular music preferences are acquired in late adolescence and early adulthood.

The researchers asked 108 participants from 16 to 86 years old to listen to 28 top hits from the years 1932 to 1986. Each song had been on *Billboard*'s Top 10 list for popular music. Respondents rated the 28 songs using a 10-point scale on which the value "1" corresponded to the statement "I dislike it a lot" and the value "10" corresponded to "I like it a lot." After collecting the data, the researchers adjusted the music-preference scores so that the mean score for each individual was 0. On this scale, a positive score indicates that a song rating was above average for the respondent, and a negative score indicates a below-average rating for the respondent. This was done to adjust for person-to-person

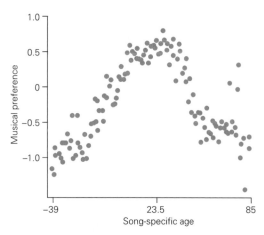

FIGURE 5.3   Scatterplot of music-preference score versus song-specific age
(Source: Figure adapted from Holbrook and Schindler, 1989, p. 122.)

variation in the rating levels because some respondents gave all songs high ratings while others assigned low ratings to all songs.

The researchers also created an adjusted age variable that they called the song-specific age of the respondent. This was the respondent's "age" in the year the song was popular. If the song was popular before the respondent was born, the song-specific age is negative. For example, if a song was on the *Billboard* Top 10 list in 1934 and the respondent was born in 1954, the song-specific age is −20, because the song was popular 20 years before the respondent was born.

Figure 5.3 shows the relationship between the preference rating and song-specific age. The overall pattern looks somewhat like an inverted U, and the maximum preference ratings occur when the song-specific age is in the late teens and early twenties. With this pattern, we can't characterize the relationship as being either generally positive or negative. Also, a straight line does not describe the overall pattern, so the association is nonlinear (or curvilinear). ◆

Indicating Groups Within the Data on Scatterplots

When we examined the connection between height and handspan in Example 5.1, you may have wondered whether we should be concerned about student gender. Both height and handspan tend to be greater for men than for women, so we should consider the possibility that gender differences might be completely responsible for the observed relationship.

It's easy to indicate subgroups on a scatterplot. We just use different symbols or different colors to represent the different groups. Figure 5.4 is the same as Figure 5.1, but now different symbols are used for males and females. Notice that the positive association between handspan and height appears to hold within each sex. For both men and women, handspan tends to increase as height increases. It's not always the case that the pattern in each subgroup is consistent with the pattern in the whole group. Later in this chapter, we will see that when we combine subgroups inappropriately, the relationship for the combined group can misrepresent the relationship that we see in each subgroup.

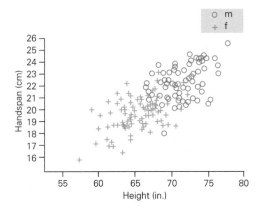

FIGURE 5.4   **Handspan and height by gender**

Look for Outliers

Outliers can have a big impact when we quantify a relationship, as we will see in more detail later in this chapter. When we consider two variables, an **outlier** is a point that has an unusual combination of data values. For instance, a man 6′7″ tall who weighs 145 pounds would probably be an outlier in a scatterplot of weights and heights because this is an unusual *combination* of weight and height measurements. Outliers can occur because there are interesting and unusual data points, or they may occur because mistakes were made when the data were recorded or entered into the computer.

EXAMPLE 5.4
Heights and Foot
Lengths of College Women

Figure 5.5 shows the relationship between foot length (in centimeters) and height (in inches) for a sample of 41 college women. The two shortest women have much greater foot lengths than we would predict based on the rest of the data. On the other side of the height scale, the tallest woman (74 inches) has a much shorter foot length than we might expect. Fortunately, the students submitted their measurements on a paper form, and a look at those forms revealed that the heights of the three "unusual" women were incorrectly entered into the computer. The woman who appears to be 74 inches tall is actually 64 inches tall.

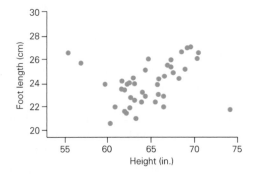

FIGURE 5.5   **Outliers in the relationship between the heights and foot lengths of women**
(Data Source: Collected in class by one of the authors.)

The women with heights of 55 inches and 57 inches on the plot were actually 65 and 67 inches tall. ◆

Minitab Tip

 tech note   **Graphing the Relationship Between Two Quantitative Variables**

◆ To draw a scatterplot, use **Graph**>**Plot**. In the dialog box, specify the columns containing the raw data for Y and X.

◆ To mark different subgroups with different symbols, use the "Data display:" area of the Plot dialog box, put the word Group under "For each," and specify the column that defines the groups under "Group Variables."

5.2

turn on your mind

Suppose you were to make a scatterplot of (adult) daughters' heights versus mothers' heights by collecting data on both variables from several of your female friends. You would now like to predict how tall your infant niece will be when she grows up. How would you use your scatterplot to help you make this prediction? What other variables, aside from her mother's height, might be useful for improving your prediction? How could you use these variables in conjunction with the mother's height?*

5.2 | DESCRIBING LINEAR PATTERNS WITH A REGRESSION LINE

Scatterplots show us a lot about a relationship, but we often want more specific numerical descriptions of how the response and explanatory variables are related. Imagine, for example, that we are examining the weights and heights of a sample of college women. We might want to know what the increase in average weight is for each 1-inch increase in height. Or, we might want to estimate the average weight for women with a specific height, like 5′10″.

Regression analysis is the area of statistics used to examine the relationship between a quantitative response variable and one or more explanatory variables. A key element of regression analysis is the *estimation of an equation* that describes how, on average, the response variable is related to the explanatory variables. This **regression equation** can be used to answer the types of questions that we just asked about the weights and heights of college women.

A regression equation can also be used to make **predictions.** For instance, it might be useful for colleges to have an equation for the connection between verbal SAT score and college grade point average (GPA). They could use that equation to predict the potential GPAs of future students, based on their verbal SAT scores. Some colleges actually do this kind of prediction to decide whom to admit, but they use a collection of variables to predict GPA. The prediction equation for GPA usually includes high school GPA, high school rank, verbal and math SAT scores, and possibly other factors such as a rating of the student's high school or the quality of an application essay.

There are many types of relationships and many types of regression equations. *The simplest kind of relationship between two variables is a straight line,* and that's the only type we will discuss here. Straight-line relationships occur frequently in practice, so this is a useful and important type of regression equation. Before we use a straight-line regression model, however, we should always examine a scatterplot to verify that the pattern actually is linear. We remind you of the music preference and age example where a straight line definitely does not describe the pattern of the data.

> *definition* When the best equation for describing the relationship between *x* and *y* is a straight line, the resulting equation is called the **regression line.** This line is used for two purposes:
>
> ♦ to *estimate the average value* of *y* at any specified value of *x*
> ♦ to *predict the value* of *y* for an individual, given that individual's *x* value

EXAMPLE 5.1—*CONTINUED*
Describing Height and Handspan with a Regression Line

In Figure 5.1, we saw that the relationship between handspan and height has a straight-line pattern. Figure 5.6 displays the same scatterplot as Figure 5.1, but now a line is shown that describes the average relationship between the two variables. To determine this line, we used statistical software (Minitab) to find the "best" line for this set of measurements. We'll discuss the criterion for "best" later. Presently, let's focus on what the line tells us about the data.

The line drawn through the scatterplot is the regression line, and it describes how average handspan is linked to height. For example, when the height is 60 inches, the vertical position of the line is at about 18 centimeters. To see this, locate 60 inches along the horizontal axis (*x* axis), look up to the line, and then read the vertical axis to determine the handspan value. The result is that we can estimate that people 60 inches tall have an *average* handspan of about 18 centimeters (roughly 7 inches). We can also use the line to *predict* the handspan for an individual whose height is known. For instance, someone 60 inches tall is *predicted* to have a handspan of about 18 centimeters. ♦

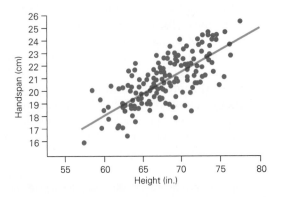

FIGURE 5.6   **Regression line describing handspan and height**

If we estimate the average handspan at a different height, we can determine how much handspan changes, on average, when height is varied. Let's use the line to estimate the average handspan for people who are 70 inches tall. We see that the vertical location of the regression line is somewhere between 21 and 22 centimeters, perhaps about 21.5 centimeters (roughly 8.5 inches). So, when height is increased from 60 inches to 70 inches, average handspan increases from about 18 centimeters to about 21.5 centimeters.

The average handspan increased by 3.5 centimeters (about 1.5 inches) when the height was increased by 10 inches. This is a rate of 3.5/10 = 0.35 centimeter per one inch increase in height, which is the **slope** of the line. For each 1-inch difference in height, there is about a 0.35-centimeter average difference in handspan.

Algebra Reminder

formula   The equation for a straight line relating y and x is

$$y = b_0 + b_1 x$$

where b_0 is the "y **intercept**" and b_1 is the slope. When $x = 0$, y is equal to y intercept.

The **slope** of a line can be determined by picking any two points on the line, and then calculating

$$\text{Slope} = \frac{\text{Difference between } y \text{ values}}{\text{Difference between } x \text{ values}} = \frac{y_2 - y_1}{x_2 - x_1}$$

The letter y represents the vertical direction, and x represents the horizontal direction. The *slope* tells us how much the y variable changes for each increase of one unit in the x variable.

We ordinarily don't have to "read" the regression line as we just did. Statistical software will tell us the *regression equation,* the specific equation used to draw the line. For the handspan and height relationship, the regression equation determined by statistical software is

Handspan = −3 + 0.35 Height

When emphasis is on using the equation to estimate the average handspans for specific heights, we may write

Average handspan = −3 + 0.35 Height

When emphasis is on using the equation to predict an individual handspan, we might instead write

Predicted handspan = −3 + 0.35 Height

In most situations, the correct statistical interpretation of a regression equation is that it estimates the average value of a response variable (y) for individuals with a specific value of the explanatory variable (x). The equation Handspan = −3 + 0.35 (Height) tells us how to draw the line, but not all individuals follow this pattern exactly. Look again at Figure 5.6, in which we see that the line describes the overall pattern, but we also see substantial individual deviation from this line.

Let's use the regression equation to estimate the average handspans for some specific heights.

For height = 60, average handspan = −3 + 0.35(60) = −3 + 21 = 18 cm.
For height = 70, average handspan = −3 + 0.35(70) = −3 + 24.5 = 21.5 cm.

In the equation, the value 0.35 multiplies the height. This value is the *slope* of the straight line that links handspan and height. Consistent with our previous estimates, the slope in this example tells us that handspan increases by 0.35 centimeter, on average, for each increase of 1 inch in height. We can use the slope to estimate the average difference in handspan for any difference in height. If we consider two heights that differ by 7 inches, our estimate of the difference in handspans would be 7 × 0.35 = 2.45 centimeters, or approximately 1 inch.

Statistical Relationships Versus Deterministic Relationships

A **statistical relationship** is different from a **deterministic relationship.** In a *deterministic relationship,* if we know the value of one variable we can exactly determine the value of the other variable. For example, the relationship between the volume and weight of water is deterministic. Every pint of water weighs 1.04 pounds, so we can determine exactly the weight of any number of pints of water.

You can see from Figure 5.6 that the regression line does not predict exactly what will happen for each individual. Most individuals do not have a handspan exactly equal to −3 + 0.35 (Height), the handspan that would be predicted from the regression equation. In a *statistical relationship,* there is variation from the average pattern.

A regression equation is most useful for describing the pattern of the *average* relationship for a group. Our ability to predict what happens for an individual depends on the amount of natural variability from the overall pattern. If most measurements are close to the regression line, we may be able to accurately predict what will happen for an individual. When there is substantial variation from the line, we will not be able to accurately predict what will happen for an individual.

The Equation for the Regression Line

All straight lines can be expressed by the same formula in which y is the variable on the vertical axis and x is the variable on the horizontal axis. The equation for a regression line is

$$\hat{y} = b_0 + b_1 x$$

In any given situation, the sample is used to determine numbers that replace b_0 and b_1.

- $\hat{y}$ is spoken as "y-hat," and it is also referred to either as **predicted y** or **estimated y**.
- b_0 is the *intercept* of the straight line. The intercept is the value of y when $x = 0$.
- b_1 is the *slope* of the straight line. The slope tells us how much of an increase (or decrease) there is for the y variable when the x variable increases by one unit. The sign of the slope tells us whether y increases or decreases when x increases.

> ### *in summary* Interpreting a Regression Line
>
> - $\hat{y}$ estimates the average y for a specific value of x. It also can be used as a prediction of the value of y for an individual with a specific value of x.
> - The slope of the line estimates the average increase in y for each one unit increase in x.
> - The intercept of the line is the value of y when $x = 0$. Note that interpreting the intercept in the context of statistical data only makes sense if $x = 0$ is included in the range of observed x values.

EXAMPLE 5.2—CONTINUED
Driver Age and the Maximum Legibility Distance of Highway Signs

The regression line $\hat{y} = 577 - 3x$ describes how the maximum sign legibility distance (the y variable) is related to driver age (the x variable). Statistical software was used to calculate this equation and to create the graph shown in Figure 5.7. Earlier, we asked these two questions about distance and age:

- How much does the distance decrease when age is increased?
- For drivers of any specific age, what is the average distance at which the sign can be read?

The slope of the equation can be used to answer the first question. Remember that the slope is the number that multiplies the x variable and the sign of the slope indicates the direction of the association. Here, the slope tells us that, on average, the legibility distance decreases 3 feet when age increases by one year. This information can be used to estimate the average change in distance for any difference in ages. For an age *increase* of 30 years, the estimated *decrease* in legibility distance is 90 feet because the slope is -3 feet per year.

The question about estimating the average legibility distances for a specific age is answered by using the specific age as the x value in the regression equation. To emphasize this use of the regression line, we write it as

$$\text{Average distance} = 577 - 3 \text{ Age}$$

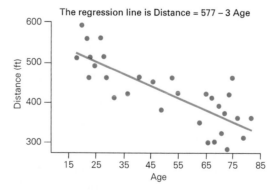

The regression line is Distance = 577 – 3 Age

FIGURE 5.7 **Regression line for driver age and sign legibility distance**

Here are the results for three different ages:

Age	Average Distance
20	$577 - 3(20) = 517$ feet
50	$577 - 3(50) = 427$ feet
80	$577 - 3(80) = 337$ feet

The equation can also be used to predict the distance measurement for an *individual* driver with a specific age. To emphasize this use of the regression line, we write the equation as

$$\text{Predicted distance} = 577 - 3 \, \text{Age}$$

For example, we can predict that the legibility distance for a 20-year-old will be 517 feet, and for an 80-year-old it will be 337 feet. ◆

Extrapolation

It is risky to use a regression equation to predict values outside the range of the observed data, a process called **extrapolation.** There is no guarantee that the relationship will continue beyond the range for which we have observed data. Suppose that a sample of adult men is used to estimate a regression equation that relates weight to height, and the equation of the line is Weight $= -180 + 5$ (Height). This equation should work well in the range of heights that we see in adult men, but it won't describe the weights of children. If we use the equation to estimate the weight of a boy 36 inches tall, the answer is $-180 + 5(36) = 0$ pounds. The straight-line equation developed for adult men doesn't accurately describe the connection between the weights and heights of children.

Extrapolation also is an issue when regression methods are used to predict future values of a variable. For instance, a straight line describes the relationship between $y =$ winning time in Olympic women's 100-meter backstroke swim and $x =$ Olympic year. This straight line could be used to predict the winning time in the near future, but it should not be used to predict the time in the year 3000.

Prediction Errors and Residuals

For any given line, we can calculate the predicted value $\hat{y}$ for each point in the observed data. To do this for any particular point, we use the observed x value in the regression equation. The **prediction error** for an observation is the difference between the observed y value and the predicted value $\hat{y}$; the formula is $error = (y - \hat{y})$. The terminology "error" is somewhat misleading, since the amount by which an individual differs from the line is usually due to natural variation rather than "errors" in the measurements. A more neutral term for the difference $(y - \hat{y})$ is that it is the **residual** for that individual.

EXAMPLE 5.2—*CONTINUED*
Prediction Errors for
the Highway Sign Data

Example 5.2 described a study in which $y =$ maximum distance at which a person can read a highway sign was related to $x =$ age. The regression equation for these data is $\hat{y} = 577 - 3x$. To calculate $\hat{y}$ for an individual, substitute his or her age for x in the equation. For individuals in the sample, an observed value of y is available and the residual $(y - \hat{y})$ can then be found. For the first three individuals shown in Table 5.2, the *residuals*, or *prediction errors*, are calculated as follows:

x = Age	y = Distance	$\hat{y} = 577 - 3x$	Residual = $y - \hat{y}$
18	510	$577 - 3(18) = 523$	$510 - 523 = -13$
20	590	$577 - 3(20) = 517$	$590 - 517 = 73$
22	516	$577 - 3(22) = 511$	$516 - 511 = 5$

This process could be carried out for any of the 30 observations in the dataset. The seventh individual in Table 5.2, for instance, has age = 27 years and distance = 560 feet. The predicted distance for this person is $\hat{y} = 577 - 3(27) = 496$ feet, so the residual is $(y - \hat{y}) = 560 - 496 = 64$ feet. A positive residual indicates that the individual had an observed value that was higher than what would be predicted for someone of that age. In this case, the 27-year-old in the study could see the sign at a distance 64 feet longer than would be predicted for someone of that age. Figure 5.8 illustrates this residual by showing that the residual is the vertical distance from a data point to the regression line. ◆

The Least Squares Criterion

We can use statistical software to estimate the regression line, but how does the computer find the best-fitting equation for a set of data? A mathematical criterion called **least squares** is nearly always the basis for estimating the equation of a regression line. The term *least squares* is a shortened version of "least sum of squared errors." This criterion focuses on the prediction errors $(y - \hat{y})$, the differences between the values of the response variable (y) and the predicted values. The response variable is emphasized because we often use the equation to predict that variable for specific values of the explanatory variable x. Therefore, we should minimize how far predictions will be off in that direction.

A **least squares line** has the property that the sum of squared differences between the observed values of y and the predicted values is smaller for that line than it is for any other line. Put more simply, the least squares line minimizes the sum of squared prediction errors for the observed data set. The notation **SSE,** which stands for sum of squared errors, is used to represent the sum of squared prediction errors. Thus, we can also say that that the least squares line (the regression line) has a smaller SSE than any other regression line that might be used to predict the response variable.

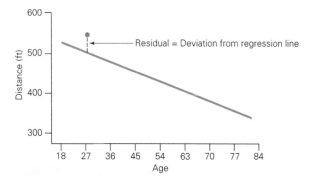

FIGURE 5.8   **Residual from regression line for 27-year-old who saw sign at a distance of 560 feet. The residual, also called the prediction error, is the difference between observed y = 560 feet and $\hat{y}$ = 496 feet.**

There is a mathematical solution that produces general formulas for computing the slope and intercept of the least squares line. These formulas are used by all statistical software, spreadsheet programs, and statistical calculators. To be complete, we include the formulas. In practice, however, regression analysis is done using a computer so we don't include an example showing how to calculate the slope and intercept for the least squares line "by hand."

Formulas for the Slope and Intercept of the Least Squares Line

formula b_1 is the slope and b_0 is the y intercept.

$$b_1 = \frac{\sum_i (x_i - \bar{x})(y_i - \bar{y})}{\sum_i (x_i - \bar{x})^2}$$

$$b_0 = \bar{y} - b_1 \bar{x}$$

x_i represents the x measurement for the ith observation.

y_i represents the y measurement for the ith observation.

$\bar{x}$ represents the mean of the x measurements.

$\bar{y}$ represents the mean of the y measurements.

EXAMPLE 5.5
Calculating the Sum of Squared Errors

Suppose that $x =$ score on exam 1 in a course and $y =$ score on exam 2, and that the first two rows in Table 5.3 (shown below) give x values and y values for $n = 6$ students. For these data, the least squares regression line is $\hat{y} = 20 + 0.8x$ (found using Minitab). Values of $\hat{y}$ for all observations are given in the third row of Table 5.3, and the fourth row gives the corresponding values of the prediction errors $(y - \hat{y})$. For instance, $x = 70$ and $y = 75$ for the first observation shown in Table 5.3, so $\hat{y} = 20 + 0.8(70) = 76$ and $(y - \hat{y}) = 75 - 76 = -1$. The sum of the squared prediction errors for the regression line is

$$\text{SSE} = (-1)^2 + (2)^2 + (-4)^2 + (2)^2 + (2)^2 + (-1)^2$$
$$= 1 + 4 + 16 + 4 + 4 + 1 = 30$$

The line $\hat{y} = 20 + 0.8x$ is the least squares line, so any other line will have a sum of squared errors greater than 30. As an example, if the line $\hat{y} = 4 + x$ were used to predict the values of y, the sum of squared values of $(y - \hat{y})$ would be

$$(75 - 74)^2 + (82 - 79)^2 + (80 - 84)^2 + (86 - 84)^2 + (90 - 89)^2$$
$$+ (91 - 94)^2 = 40 \quad \blacklozenge$$

Why Regression Is Called Regression

You may wonder why the word *regression* is used to describe the study of statistical relationships. Most of the vocabulary used by statisticians has at least

TABLE 5.3 ▪ **Values of x, y, $\hat{y}$, and $(y - \hat{y})$ for Example 5.5**

$x =$ Exam 1 score	70	75	80	80	85	90
$y =$ Exam 2 score	75	82	80	86	90	91
$\hat{y} = 20 + 0.8\,x$	76	80	84	84	88	92
$(y - \hat{y})$	-1	2	-4	2	2	-1

some connection to the common usage of the words, but this doesn't seem to be true for *regression*. The statistical use of the word *regression* dates back to Francis Galton, who studied heredity in the late 1800s. (See Stigler, 1986 or 1989, for a detailed historical account.) One of Galton's interests was whether or not a man's height as an adult could be predicted by his parents' heights. He discovered that it could, but the relationship was such that very tall parents tended to have children who were shorter than they were, and very short parents tended to have children taller than themselves. He initially described this phenomenon by saying that there was "reversion to mediocrity" but later changed to the terminology "regression to mediocrity." Thereafter the technique of determining such relationships was called *regression*.

5.3

turn on your mind

Suppose the statistics community is having a contest to rename "regression" to something more descriptive of what it actually does. What would you suggest as a name for the whole procedure? As a name for the regression line?*

5.3 | MEASURING STRENGTH AND DIRECTION WITH CORRELATION

The linear pattern is so common that a statistic was created to characterize this type of relationship. The statistical **correlation** between two quantitative variables is a number that *indicates the strength and the direction of a straight-line relationship*.

♦ The *strength* of the relationship is determined by the *closeness of the points to a straight line*.

♦ The *direction* is determined by whether one variable generally increases or generally decreases when the other variable increases.

As used in statistics, the meaning of the word *correlation* is much more specific than it is in everyday life. A statistical correlation only describes *linear relationships*. Whenever a correlation is calculated, a straight line is used as the frame of reference for evaluating the relationship. When the pattern is nonlinear, as it was for the music preference data shown in Figure 5.3, a correlation is not an appropriate way to measure the strength of the relationship.

Correlation is represented by the letter *r*. Sometimes this measure is called the "Pearson product moment correlation" or the "correlation coefficient." It doesn't matter which of the two variables is called the *x* variable and which is called the *y* variable. The value of the correlation is the same either way. For instance, the correlation between height and foot length is the same regardless of whether you use height as the *y* variable or use foot length as the *y* variable. Another useful feature of the correlation coefficient is that its value doesn't change when the measurement units are changed for either or both of the variables. For instance, the correlation between weight and height is the same whether the measurements are in pounds and inches, or in kilograms and centimeters.

The formula for calculating the correlation coefficient looks complicated, although it can be described rather simply in terms of standardized scores (introduced in Section 2.7). Approximately, the correlation value is the average product of standardized scores for variables x and y. Calculating a correlation value by hand, however, generally involves much labor, so all statistical software programs and many calculators provide a way to easily calculate this statistic. In this section, we focus on how to interpret the correlation coefficient rather than how to calculate it.

A Formula for Correlation

formula $$r = \frac{1}{n-1}\sum_i \left(\frac{x_i - \bar{x}}{s_x}\right)\left(\frac{y_i - \bar{y}}{s_y}\right)$$

n is the sample size.

x_i is the x measurement for the ith observation.

$\bar{x}$ is the mean of the x measurements.

s_x is the standard deviation of the x measurements.

y_i is the y measurement for the ith observation.

$\bar{y}$ is the mean of the y measurements.

s_y is the standard deviation of the y measurements.

Interpreting the Correlation Coefficient

Some specific features of the correlation coefficient are

- Correlation coefficients are always between -1 and $+1$.
- The magnitude of the correlation indicates the strength of the relationship, which is the overall closeness of the points to a straight line. The sign of the correlation does not tell us about the strength of the linear relationship.
- A correlation of either $+1$ or -1 indicates that there is a perfect linear relationship and all data points fall on the same straight line.
- The sign of the correlation indicates the direction of the relationship. A *positive* correlation indicates that the two variables tend to increase together (a positive association). A *negative* correlation indicates that when one variable increases the other is likely to decrease (a negative association).
- A correlation of 0 indicates that the best straight line through the data is exactly horizontal, so that knowing the value of x does not change the predicted value of y.

EXAMPLE 5.1—*CONTINUED*
The Correlation Between Handspan and Height

The relationship between handspan and height appears to be linear, so a correlation is useful for characterizing the strength of the relationship. For these data, the correlation is $r = +0.74$, a value that indicates a somewhat strong positive relationship. A look back at Figure 5.1 shows us that average handspan definitely increases when height increases, but within any specific height there is some natural variation among individual handspans. ◆

EXAMPLE 5.2—*CONTINUED*
The Correlation Between Age and Sign Legibility Distance

The correlation for the data shown in Figure 5.2, relating driver age and sign legibility distance, is $r = -0.8$. This value indicates a somewhat strong negative association between the variables. ◆

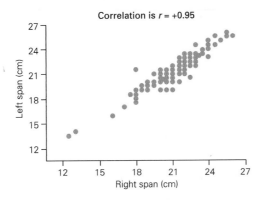

FIGURE 5.9 **Left handspan versus right handspan**

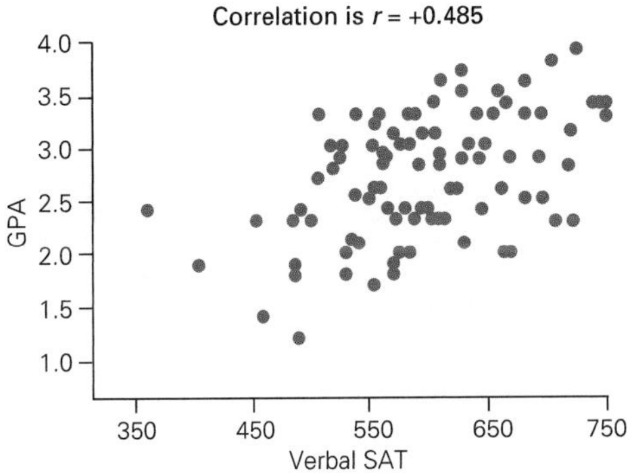

FIGURE 5.10 **Verbal SATs and grade point average**

EXAMPLE 5.6
Left and Right Handspans

If you know the span of a person's right hand, do you think you could accurately estimate his or her left handspan? Figure 5.9 displays the relationship between the right and left handspans (in centimeters) of the 190 college students in the dataset of Chapter 2. In the plot, the points nearly fall into a straight line. The correlation coefficient for this strong positive association is +0.95. ◆

EXAMPLE 5.7
Verbal SAT and GPA

The scatterplot in Figure 5.10 shows the grade point averages (GPAs) and verbal SAT scores for a sample of 100 students at a university in the northeastern United States. The correlation for the data in the scatterplot is $r = 0.485$, a value that indicates only a moderately strong relationship. ◆

EXAMPLE 5.8
Age and Hours of Television Viewing per Day

On a typical day, how many hours do you spend watching television? The National Opinion Research Center asks this question in its General Social Survey. In Figure 5.11, we see the relationship between respondent age and hours of daily television viewing for 1913 respondents in the 1996 survey. There does not seem to be much of a relationship between age and television hours, and the correlation of only +0.12 confirms this weak connection between the variables. We also see some odd responses. A few respondents claim to watch television more than 20 hours per day! ◆

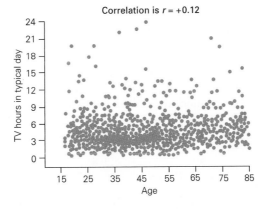

FIGURE 5.11 **Age and hours of television per day**

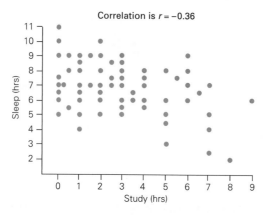

FIGURE 5.12   **Hours of sleep versus hours of study**
(Source: Class data collected by one of the authors.)

EXAMPLE 5.9
Hours of Sleep
and Hours of Study

Figure 5.12 displays, for a sample of 116 college students, the relationship between the reported hours of sleep during the previous 24 hours and the reported hours of study during the same period. The correlation value for this scatterplot is $r = -0.36$, indicating a negative association that is not particularly strong. On average, the hours of sleep decrease as hours of study increase, but there is substantial variation in the hours of sleep for any specific hours of study. ◆

turn on your computer

Exploring Correlation

The **Correlation** applet on the CD accompanying this book can be used to explore how the correlation coefficient, r, is sensitive to the strength and direction of the relationship between two quantitative variables. Remember that the strength of a linear relationship is measured by the absolute value of the correlation coefficient. The sign of the correlation value indicates whether the two variables have a positive association or a negative association.

What Happens

Your goal is to create a scatterplot so that the correlation value for the points on the graph is close to a "goal" value. You place points onto a graph by using the mouse to click on locations in a graph. The applet recalculates and displays the correlation value after each point is added. The applet will declare "Goal Reached!" when the correlation is within ± 0.05 of the goal value after 15 or more points have been added to the plot.

What to Do

Open the **Correlation** applet. You'll see three different scatterplot regions, each with a different goal value for the correlation. Figure 5.13 shows the first of these regions before any points have been added. For that region, the goal is $r = 0.5$,

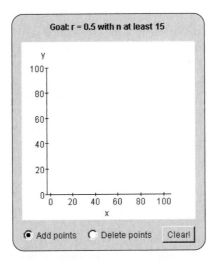

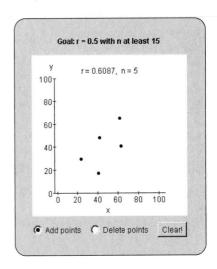

FIGURE 5.13   Starting point for the Correlation applet. The goal is *r* = 0.5 and at least 15 points should be placed on the graph.

FIGURE 5.14   Appearance of Correlation applet after 5 points have been added. For these 5 points, the correlation is *r* = 0.6087, a value shown at the top of the scatter plot.

so your task is to create a graph with at least 15 data points for which the correlation is anywhere between 0.45 and 0.55.

Begin adding points to the graph by using the mouse to click on desired locations. An example of how the applet might look after 5 data points have been added is displayed in Figure 5.14. Notice that for the 5 points shown in the figure, the correlation is *r* = 0.6087. Continue adding points until the goal is reached. You can delete points by clicking on the ***Delete*** radio button and then clicking on the point you wish to delete. The ***Clear*** button can be used to remove all points.

The correlation goals for the second and third scatterplots on the applet page are *r* = −0.8 and *r* = 0, respectively. Create scatterplots that achieve those targets. In each instance, first try achieving the correlation by making your *x* values range from about 10 to 90, and not including any outliers. Remember that at least 15 points should be placed on a graph. Figures 5.2, 5.10, and 5.11 in this chapter provide models for the three target correlations in the applet.

After reaching your goals, clear the plots and then explore how an outlier affects a correlation value. For instance, try reaching the *r* = 0.5 goal for the first scatterplot by adding 14 points for which the correlation is above 0.8, then adding an outlier that brings the correlation down to about 0.5. Or, where the goal is *r* = −0.8, put 14 points in the upper left portion of the graph so the correlation for those points is between −0.2 and +0.2, then add an outlier that makes the correlation become about −0.8.

Lessons Learned

The three target correlations exemplify how correlation is related to the strength and direction of a relationship. The algebraic sign of the correlation value gives the direction of the relationship. For linear relationships with no outliers present in the data, the absolute value of the correlation measures the strength of a relationship, which has to do with the overall closeness of points to a line. By using the applet to put outliers on the plots, you will see that an outlier can either increase or decrease a correlation.

The Interpretation of r^2, the Squared Correlation

The squared value of the correlation is frequently used to describe the strength of a relationship. A **squared correlation, r^2,** always has a value between 0 and 1, although some computer programs will express its value as a percent between 0 and 100%. By squaring the correlation, we retain information about the strength of the relationship, but we lose information about the direction.

Researchers typically use the phrase "**proportion of variation explained by x**" in conjunction with the squared correlation, r^2. For example, if $r^2 = 0.60$ (or 60%), the researcher may write that the explanatory variable explains 60% of the variation in the response variable. If $r^2 = 0.10$ (or 10%), the explanatory variable only explains 10% of the variation in the response variable. This interpretation stems from the use of the least squares line as a prediction tool.

In Example 5.6, the correlation between left and right handspans is 0.95, so r^2 is 0.90, or about 90%. This indicates that the span of one hand is very predictable if we know the span of the other hand (see Figure 5.9). In Example 5.8, the correlation between television viewing hours and age is only $r = 0.12$. The squared correlation is about $r^2 = 0.014$, only about 1.4%. As we can see from the scatterplot in Figure 5.11, knowing a person's age doesn't help us much in predicting how much television he or she watches per day.

Let's consider Example 5.1 again. For that example, the regression equation is Handspan $= -3.5 + 0.35$ (Height). The correlation is 0.74 and $r^2 = (0.74)^2 = 0.55$ (or 55%). We can say that height explains 55% of the variation in handspan, but what does it mean to say this?

Suppose that we ignore the height information when we make predictions of handspan. In other words, suppose we don't use the least squares line to predict handspan. For the 167 students in the dataset, $\bar{y}$, the average handspan, is about 20.8 centimeters. If we ignore the least squares line, we could use this value to predict the handspan for any individual, regardless of his or her height. Our prediction "equation" is simply Handspan $= 20.8$. For both this equation and the least squares equation involving height, we can compute the sum of squared differences between the actual handspan values and the predicted values.

- The sum of squared differences between observed y values and the sample mean $\bar{y}$ is called the *total variation in y* or **sum of squares total** and is denoted by **SSTO.**

- The sum of squared differences between observed y values and the predicted values based on the least squares line is called the **sum of squared errors** and is denoted by **SSE.** Remember that errors are sometimes called residuals, and a synonym for sum of squared errors is **residual sum of squares.**

Whenever the correlation is not 0, the least squares line will produce generally better predictions than the sample mean, so SSE will be smaller than SSTO. The squared correlation expresses the reduction in squared prediction error as a fraction of the total variation. This leads to the formula

$$r^2 = \frac{\text{SSTO} - \text{SSE}}{\text{SSTO}}$$

It can be shown (using algebra) that this quantity is exactly equal to the square of the correlation.

EXAMPLE 5.5—CONTINUED
Calculation of r^2

Example 5.5 involved the following six observations for x = score on exam 1 and y = score on exam 2:

x = Exam 1 score	70	75	80	80	85	90
y = Exam 2 score	75	82	80	86	90	91

The regression equation is $\hat{y} = 20 + 0.8x$, and we found in Example 5.5 that the sum of squared errors is SSE = 30. For the y values, the mean is $\bar{y} = 84$. Values of SSTO and r^2 are

$$\text{SSTO} = (75 - 84)^2 + (82 - 84)^2 + (80 - 84)^2 + (86 - 84)^2 + (90 - 84)^2 + (91 - 84)^2 = 190$$

$$r^2 = \frac{\text{SSTO} - \text{SSE}}{\text{SSTO}} = \frac{190 - 30}{190} = 0.842$$

We also can find that the correlation between x and y in this example is $r = \sqrt{0.842} = 0.918$. ◆

EXAMPLE 5.6—CONTINUED
Getting to Know the Left Hand Based on the Right Hand

Many statistical computer packages are available that will do all of the regression calculations for you. The box below illustrates the basic results of using the statistical package Minitab for the data in Figure 5.9. The explanatory variable is right handspan, and the response variable is left handspan.

```
The regression equation is
LftSpan = 1.46 + 0.938 RtSpan

Predictor      Coef       StDev        T        P
Constant     1.4635      0.4792      3.05    0.003
RtSpan       0.93830     0.02252    41.67    0.000

S = 0.6386     R-Sq = 90.2%      R-Sq(adj) = 90.2%

Analysis of Variance

Source          DF       SS        MS        F        P
Regression       1     708.15    708.15   1736.38   0.000
Residual Error  188      76.67      0.41
  Total         189     784.82
```

In Chapter 14, we will revisit regression and the meaning of all of the computer results will become clear. For now, you should be able to recognize the following features:

◆ Regression equation: $\hat{y} = b_0 + b_1x = 1.46 + 0.938\ x$, where x = right handspan.

◆ Slope: $b_1 = 0.938$, expanded in another part of the display to 0.93830.

◆ Intercept: $b_0 = 1.46$, expanded in another part of the display to 1.4635.

◆ $r^2 = 0.902$, or 90.2%.

◆ SSTO = 784.82.

◆ SSE = 76.67. ◆

Minitab Tip

 tech note **Determining the Regression Line and Calculating a Correlation**

♦ To find a simple regression equation, use **Stat>Regression>Regression.** In the dialog box, specify the column containing the raw data for the response variable (Y) as the "Response," and specify the column containing the data for the explanatory variable (X) as a "Predictor."

♦ To find a regression line and also have Minitab draw this line onto a scatterplot of the data, use **Stat>Regression>Fitted Line Plot.** Specify the response variable (Y) and the predictor (X) in the dialog box.

♦ To calculate a correlation coefficient, use **Stat>Basic Statistics>Correlation.** Specify two (or more) columns as the Variables.

Excel Tip

tech note **Finding the Correlation and Regression Equation**

First, enter the y values and x values into separate columns. We refer to the range of cells as *y-range* and *x-range* in what follows:

CORREL(y-range,x-range) = the correlation.

RSQ(y-range,x-range) = squared correlation or proportion of variation explained by x.

INTERCEPT(y-range,x-range) = intercept of the regression equation.

SLOPE(y-range,x-range) = slope of the regression equation.

For the correlation and squared correlation, the ranges can be entered in either order, but for the intercept and slope, the y-range must be listed first.

5.4

turn on your mind

Sometimes the main purpose of a regression analysis is to determine the nature of the relationship between two variables, and sometimes the main purpose is to use the equation in the future to predict a y value when the x value is known. Explain which purpose is likely to be the main reason for a regression analysis between

x = percent fat consumed in diet, y = blood pressure
x = SAT score, y = college grade point average
x = height at age 4, y = height at age 21
x = hours of sleep per night, y = score on IQ test*

5.4 | WHY THE ANSWERS MAY NOT MAKE SENSE

As with all numerical summaries, a number of situations can cause misleading correlation and regression results. Each of the following actions will produce an illegitimate description of a relationship:

*HINT: Colleges use SAT scores to predict GPAs of applicants, so predicting a future y value is more likely in that instance.

- ◆ Allowing outliers to overly influence the results
- ◆ Combining groups inappropriately
- ◆ Using correlation and a straight-line equation to describe curvilinear data

The Influence of Outliers

Outliers can have an impact on correlation and regression results. This is particularly true for small samples. In Example 5.4, we learned that sometimes outliers occur because mistakes are made when the data are recorded or are entered into the computer. In these cases, we may be able to make the necessary corrections. When outliers are legitimate data, we have to carefully consider their effect on the analysis. We may exclude outliers from some analyses, but we shouldn't forget about them. As in everyday life, the unusual data is often the most interesting data.

Outliers with extreme x values have the most *influence* on correlation and regression and are called **influential observations.** Depending on whether these points "line up" with the rest of the data, they can either deflate or inflate a correlation. An outlier at an extreme x value can also have a big effect on the slope of the regression line.

EXAMPLE 5.4—*CONTINUED*
Height and Foot Length
of College Women

Figure 5.5 displayed a scatterplot of the foot lengths and heights of 41 college women. We saw three outliers in that plot, all of which occurred because heights were incorrectly entered into the computer. If we don't correct these mistakes, the correlation between the foot lengths and heights in Figure 5.5 is only $r = 0.28$. For the corrected data set, the correlation is $r = 0.69$, a markedly higher value. The outliers also have a big effect on the equation of the *least squares* line.

- ◆ For the uncorrected data set, foot length = 15.4 + 0.13 height
- ◆ For the corrected data set, foot length = −3.2 + 0.42 height

The slope of the correct line is more than three times the size of the slope of the incorrect data. This is a big difference. For instance, let's consider a 12-inch difference in heights. The correct estimate of the associated difference in average foot lengths is $12 \times 0.42 \approx 5$ centimeters (about 2 inches). If we use the incorrect data, the estimated difference in average foot lengths is only $12 \times 0.13 \approx 1.6$ centimeters (about 5/8 of an inch). ◆

EXAMPLE 5.10
Earthquakes in the
Continental United States

Table 5.4 lists the major earthquakes that occurred in the continental United States between 1850 and 1992. The correlation between deaths and magnitude for these six earthquakes is 0.73, showing a relatively strong association. It implies that, on average, higher death tolls accompany stronger earthquakes.

TABLE 5.4 ■ **Major Earthquakes in the Continental United States, 1850–1992**

Date	Location	Deaths	Magnitude
August 31, 1886	Charleston, SC	60	6.6
April 18–19,1906	San Francisco	503	8.3
March 10, 1933	Long Beach, CA	115	6.2
February 9, 1971	San Fernando Valley, CA	65	6.6
October 17, 1989	San Francisco area	62	6.9
June 28, 1992	Yuca Valley, CA	1	7.4

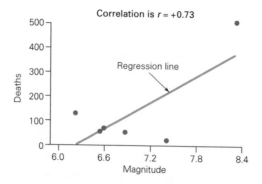

FIGURE 5.15   **Deaths and earthquake magnitude**

However, if you examine the scatterplot of the data shown in Figure 5.15, you will notice that the correlation is entirely due to the famous San Francisco earthquake of 1906. In fact, for the remaining earthquakes, the trend is actually *reversed*. Without the 1906 quake, the correlation for these five earthquakes is strongly *negative*, at −0.96, indicating that fewer deaths are associated with greater magnitudes.

Clearly, trying to interpret the correlation between magnitude and death toll for this small group of earthquakes is a misuse of statistics. The largest earthquake, in 1906, occurred before earthquake building codes were enforced. The next largest quake, with magnitude 7.4, killed only one person but occurred in a very sparsely populated area. ◆

The next example demonstrates another situation that leads to illegitimate results. We'll give you a hint—outliers don't cause the difficulty.

EXAMPLE 5.11
Does It Make Sense?
Height and Lead Feet

For a sample of college students, a scatterplot of their heights and their responses to the question "What is the fastest you have ever driven a car?" is displayed in Figure 5.16. Height is the *x* variable and the fastest-speed response is the *y* variable. We see that the fastest-speed response tends to increase as height increases. The correlation is +0.39, and the *least squares* line that describes the

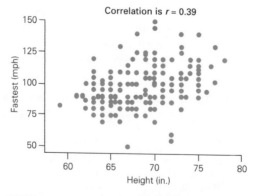

FIGURE 5.16   **Height and the fastest that college students have ever driven**
(Data Source: Class data collected in 1998 by one of the authors.)

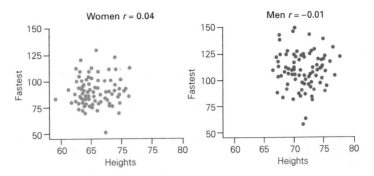

FIGURE 5.17 **Fastest speed and height separately for men and women**

average pattern is $\hat{y} = -20 + 1.7x$. The slope of the equation tells us that for every 1-inch increase in height, there is an average increase of 1.7 mph for the fastest-speed response. This means that for a 12-inch difference in heights, we would estimate the difference in the fastest-speed response to be $12 \times 1.7 \approx 20$ mph. The newspaper headline might read "Height and Lead Foot Go Together." Is this a sensible conclusion? Why might these results be misleading?

We know that men tend to be taller than women. Those of you with good memories may recall Case Study 1.1, which indicated that men tend to claim a higher fastest speed than women do. These gender differences could be causing the positive association that we see in Figure 5.16. One way to examine this possibility is to look separately at men and women. Figure 5.17 shows two scatterplots, one for each gender. For men, the correlation between height and fastest speed is -0.01, basically 0. For women, the correlation is 0.04, also basically 0. In other words, there is no relationship between height and fastest speed within either sex. The observed association in the combined data occurs only because men tend to have higher values than women do for both variables. ◆

Inappropriately Combining Groups

The height and fastest-speed example demonstrates a common mistake that can lead to an illegitimate correlation, which is combining two or more groups when the groups should be considered separately. Example 3.4 of Chapter 3 described a relationship between the cost of a book and the number of pages in the book. Surprisingly, there seemed to be a negative relationship. As the number of pages increased, the cost tended to decrease. The data included hardcover and softcover books, and this explains the unexpected negative association. The hardcover books generally had fewer pages than the softcover books, but their cost was higher. When the book types are considered separately, the association between pages and cost is positive for each type.

Once again, we should think about the association between handspan and height described in Example 5.1. In Figure 5.4, we saw that the positive association holds for each gender. The correlation for the combined group is 0.74, but within each gender the correlation is about 0.6. Combining males and females does inflate the correlation somewhat, but gender differences are not the sole reason for the observed association.

The next example shows us that it's important to look at a scatterplot before we calculate a regression line.

EXAMPLE 5.12
Does It Make Sense?
Don't Predict without a Plot

Table 5.5 lists the population of the United States (in millions) for each census year between 1790 and 1990. There is, of course, a positive association between y = population size and x = year, because the population size has been steadily increasing through the years. The correlation between population size and year is $r = +0.96$, indicating a very strong relationship. The *least squares* line for these data has the equation $\hat{y} = -2218 + 1.218$ (Year). If we use this equation to predict the population in 2030, our estimate is about 255 million. Does this estimate make sense? What's wrong with this analysis?

Your first thought may be that we shouldn't extrapolate a prediction to 2030 because that's too far past the end of the data. That's a good thought, but the extrapolation issue is not the biggest problem here. You'll realize that something is wrong if you compare the estimate for 2030 to the 1990 population. The year 2030 estimate of 255 million is only 6 million higher than the 1990 population size. The population increased by about 20 million between 1980 and 1990, so it doesn't make sense that the increase will only be 8 million between 1990 and 2030. Also, on September 16, 1999, the United States population was already estimated to be about 273 million (*source:* http://www.census.gov).

Why does the regression line produce such a poor estimate for 2030? The reason is that the pattern of population growth is actually *curved,* so a straight-line equation isn't the right type of equation to use. Figure 5.18 shows the situation. The *least squares* line is shown as well as a curve that traces the actual data pattern. The curve is extended to the year 2030 to provide a projection of the population in that year. It looks like the population might be around 350 million at that point in time. By the way, the United States Census Bureau projects a population size of 347 million in the year 2030 (http://www.census.gov). ◆

TABLE 5.5 ■ United States Population (millions) in Census Years Since 1790

Year	Pop.	Year	Pop.
1790	3.9	1900	76.2
1800	5.3	1910	92.2
1810	7.2	1920	106.0
1820	9.6	1930	123.2
1830	12.9	1940	132.2
1840	17.1	1950	151.3
1850	23.2	1960	179.3
1860	31.4	1970	203.3
1870	35.6	1980	228.5
1880	50.2	1990	248.8
1890	63.0		

Source: United States Census Bureau, http://www.census.gov.

Curvilinear Data

The United States population example illustrates that we can make big mistakes if we use a straight line to describe curved data. We should describe a curvilinear pattern with an equation for a curve. This is simpler said than done. There are many different types of equations that describe curves, and it's hard to judge which type we should use just by looking at the scatterplot.

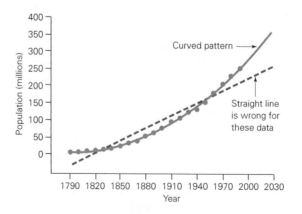

FIGURE 5.18   **Estimating the United States population in 2030**

The music-preference and age relationship in Example 5.3 illustrates another way that correlation can be misleading when the pattern is curvilinear. For the data shown in Figure 5.3, the correlation will be around 0. This value could make us believe that there is no relationship, but in fact there is. Remember that the frame of reference for calculating a correlation is a straight line. For the inverted U pattern in Figure 5.3, the best straight line will be nearly horizontal, so the correlation will be around 0. Clearly, a straight line shouldn't be used to describe these data, so the correlation value is meaningless.

5.5

turn on your mind

Sketch a scatterplot with an outlier that would inflate the correlation between the two variables. Sketch a scatterplot with an outlier that would deflate the correlation between the two variables.*

5.5 | CORRELATION DOES NOT PROVE CAUSATION

Many spirited disagreements about the interpretation of research results revolve around whether a change in one variable actually *causes* a change in another variable. The saying "correlation does not imply causation" is used so frequently in these arguments that you may already have encountered it in everyday life or in another academic course. It is easy to construct silly, obvious examples of observed associations that don't have a causal connection. For example, weekly flu medication sales and weekly sweater sales for an area with extreme seasons would exhibit a positive association because both tend to go up in the winter and down in the summer.

The problem is that the explanation for an observed relationship usually isn't so obvious as it is in the flu medication and sweater sales example. Suppose the finding in an observational study is that people who use vitamin supplements get fewer colds than people who don't use vitamin supplements. It may be that the use of vitamin supplements causes a reduced risk of a cold, but it is also easy to think of other explanations for the observed association. Perhaps those who use supplements also sleep more and it's actually the sleep difference that causes the difference in the frequency of colds. Or, the users of vitamin supplements may be worried about good health and will take several different actions designed to reduce the risk of getting a cold.

Interpretations of an Observed Association

There are at least four possible interpretations of an observed relationship between an explanatory variable and a response variable.

1. There is causation. The explanatory variable is indeed causing a change in the response variable.
2. There may be causation, but confounding factors contribute as well and make this causation difficult to prove.

*HINT: Examples 5.4 and 5.10 might be helpful.

3. There is no causation. The association is explained by how the explanatory and response variables are both affected by other variables.
4. The response variable is causing a change in the explanatory variable.

Interpretation 1—Causation

It isn't easy to prove that a cause-and-effect relationship exists. Ideally, we would be able to keep everything in the environment constant except the explanatory variable. If we change only one variable, we can learn whether these changes cause changes in the outcome variable.

The use of a designed experiment is the most legitimate way to establish a causal connection statistically. As we learned in Chapter 3, in designed experiments we try to rule out confounding variables through random assignment of the experimental units to specific values of the explanatory variable. If we have a large sample, and if we use proper randomization, we can assume that the levels of confounding variables will be about equal in the different treatment groups. This reduces the chances that an observed association is due to confounding variables, even those that we have neglected to measure.

Interpretation 2—There May Be Causation, but Confounding Factors Contribute as Well and Make This Causation Difficult to Prove

The data from an observational study, in the absence of any other evidence, simply cannot be used to establish causation. It is nearly impossible to separate the effect of *confounding variables* from the effect of the explanatory variable. For example, even if we observe that smokers tend to have higher blood pressure than nonsmokers, we can't definitively say that smoking causes high blood pressure because there may be alternative explanations. Perhaps smokers are more stressed than nonsmokers and this causes the higher blood pressure.

A partial solution is to measure possible confounding variables and include them in the analysis to see how they are related to the outcome variable. Some other considerations can be taken into account as well. Each of the following items provides evidence for causation:

◆ There is a reasonable explanation of cause and effect.
◆ The connection occurs under varying circumstances.
◆ Potential confounding variables are ruled out.

The second item was instrumental in establishing that smoking causes the risk of lung cancer to increase. Numerous observational studies have related cigarette smoking and lung cancer. Further, the studies have shown that the higher the number of cigarettes smoked, the greater the chances of developing lung cancer; similarly, a connection has been established with the age at which smoking began. These facts make it more plausible that smoking actually causes lung cancer.

Interpretation 3—The Association Is Explained by How Other Variables Affect the Explanatory and Response Variables

The association between height and fastest speed in Example 5.11 had this interpretation. As another example of an observed association that doesn't imply causation, recall the association between verbal SAT scores and college GPAs exhibited in Example 5.7. We would certainly not conclude that higher SAT scores caused higher grades in college, except perhaps for a slight benefit of boosted self-esteem. However, we could probably agree that the causes responsible for one variable being high (or low) are the same as those responsible for the other being high (or low). Those causes would include things like intelligence, motivation, and ability to perform well on tests.

Interpretation 4—The Response Variable Is Causing a Change in the Explanatory Variable

Sometimes the causal connection is the opposite of what might be expected or claimed. If an observational study finds, for men and women over 60 years old, that regular church attendance is associated with better health, should we believe that church attendance causes good health? An alternative explanation is that the causation may be in the opposite way. Healthy people are more able to attend church, so good health could increase the likelihood of church attendance.

5.6

turn on your mind

An article in the *Centre Daily Times* (April 19, 1997, p. 8A) included data from the United States and several European countries that indicated a negative correlation between the cost of cigarettes and annual per capita cigarette consumption. Does this result mean that if the United States increased its cigarette tax in order to increase the price of cigarettes, the result would be that people would smoke less? What are some other explanations for the negative correlation between cigarette price and annual cigarette consumption?*

CASE STUDY 5.1
A Weighty Issue

In a large statistics class, students (119 females and 63 males) were asked to report their actual and their ideal weights. It's well known that males and females differ with regard to actual weights and their views of their weight, so the two genders should be separated for the analysis. Table 5.6 displays the mean actual and ideal weights for men and women. For women, the mean ideal is 10.7 pounds less than the mean actual, while for men, the mean ideal is only about 2.5 pounds less than mean actual.

We can use a scatterplot and regression to learn more about the connection between actual and ideal weight. Figure 5.19 shows a scatterplot of the two variables for the females, and Figure 5.20 is the same plot for the males. Each point represents one student (or multiple students with the same values), whose ideal weight can be read on the vertical axis and actual weight can be read on the horizontal axis.

If everyone had responded that his or her ideal weight was the same as his or her actual weight, all points would fall on a line with the equation

Ideal = Actual

TABLE 5.6 ■ Mean Actual and Ideal Weights by Gender (in pounds)

	Actual	Ideal	Difference
Females (*n* = 119)	132.8	122.1	10.7
Males (*n* = 63)	176.1	173.6	2.5

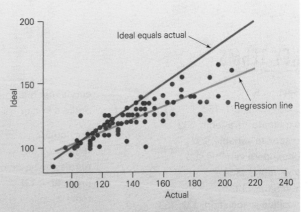

FIGURE 5.19   **Ideal and actual weight: females**

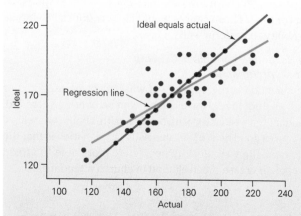

FIGURE 5.20   Ideal and actual weight: males

That line is drawn in each figure. Most of the women fall below that line, indicating that their ideal weight is *below* their actual weight. The situation is not as clear for the men, but a pattern is still evident. The majority of men weighing less than 175 pounds would prefer to weigh the same or more than they do, and they fall on or above the line. The majority of men weighing over 175 pounds fall on or below the line and would prefer to weigh the same or less than they do.

The *least squares regression line* is also shown on each scatterplot. The approximate regression equations are

Women: Average ideal = 44 + 0.6 Actual

Men: Average ideal = 53 + 0.7 Actual

The regression equations tell us the "average pattern" of the connection between actual and ideal weight. By substituting some different actual weights into the equations, we can explore how the ideal weight is associated with the actual weight for each gender. Table 5.7 shows regression calculations for students 15 pounds below the mean of the actual weights for their sex and for students 15 pounds above the mean of the actual weights for their sex.

TABLE 5.7 ■ Regression Estimates of Ideal Weight

Students with Actual Weight 15 Pounds Below the Mean for Their Sex:			
Gender	Actual	Ideal Based on Regression	Average Preference
Female	118	44 + 0.6(118) ≈ 115	Lose 3 pounds
Male	161	53 + 0.7(161) ≈ 166	Gain 5 pounds

Students with Actual Weight 15 Pounds Above the Mean for Their Sex:			
Gender	Actual	Ideal Based on Regression	Average Preference
Female	148	44 + 0.6(148) ≈ 133	Lose 15 pounds
Male	191	53 + 0.7(191) ≈ 187	Lose 4 pounds

The results in Table 5.7 reveal interesting gender differences. For instance, consider women who weigh 118 pounds, which is about 15 pounds less than the mean weight for women. On average, their ideal weight is about 115 pounds, which is 3 pounds less than their actual weight. On the other hand, men who weigh 15 pounds less than the mean for men would, on average, like to gain about 5 pounds. Women who weigh 15 pounds more than the mean for women would like to lose about 15 pounds. Men who weigh 15 pounds more than the mean for men would like to lose only about 4 pounds.

KEY TERMS

Section 5.1

scatterplot, 131, 132
explanatory variable, 132
response variable, 132
dependent variable, 132
y variable, 132
x variable, 132
positive association, 132, 133
linear relationship, 133
negative association, 133
nonlinear relationship, 134

curvilinear relationship, 134
outliers in regression, 136

Section 5.2

regression analysis, 137
regression equation, 137
prediction, 137
regression line, 138
slope of a straight line, 139, 140
intercept of a straight line, 139, 140
statistical relationship, 140

deterministic relationship, 140
predicted *y*, 140
estimated *y*, 140
extrapolation, 142
prediction error, 142
residual, 142
least squares, 143
least squares line, 143
SSE, 143
sum of squared errors (SSE), 143

EXERCISES   Blue = Basics   **Bold, Bold** = Answer in back

Section 5.1

5.1 For each of the following pairs of variables, is there likely to be a positive association, a negative association, or no association? Briefly explain your reasoning.
  a. Amount of alcohol consumed and performance on a test of coordination.
  b. Height and grade point average for college students.
  c. Miles of running per week and time for a 5-kilometer run.
  d. Forearm length and foot length.

5.2 The figure for this exercise is a scatterplot of y = average math SAT score in 1998 versus x = percent of graduating seniors who took the test that year for the 50 states and the District of Columbia The data are from the **sats98** dataset on the CD for this text.
  a. Does the plot show a positive association, a negative association, or no association between the two variables? Explain.
  b. Explain whether you think the pattern of the plot is linear or curvilinear.
  c. About what was the highest average math SAT for the 50 states and District of Columbia? Approximately, what percent of graduates took the test in that state?
  d. About what was the lowest average math SAT for the 50 states and District of Columbia? Approximately, what percent of graduates took the test in that state?

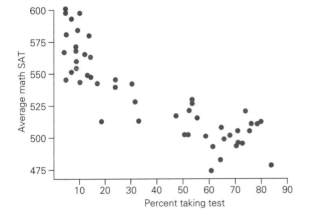

EXERCISE 5.2

5.3 Identify whether a scatterplot would or would not be an appropriate visual summary of the relationship between the following variables. In each case, explain your reasoning.
  a. Blood pressure and age.
  b. Region of country and opinion about stronger gun control laws.
  c. Verbal SAT score and math SAT score.
  d. Handspan and gender (male or female).

5.4 The figure for this exercise is a scatterplot of y = head circumference (centimeters) versus x = height (inches) for the thirty females in the **physical** dataset on the CD for this text.

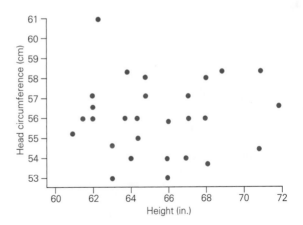

EXERCISE 5.4

  a. Does the plot show a positive association, a negative association, or no association between the two variables? Explain.
  b. One data point appears to be an outlier. What are the approximate values of height and head circumference for that point?

5.5 The figure for this exercise is a scatterplot of y = pulse rate after marching in place for one minute versus x = resting pulse rate measure before marching in place. (The data are in the **pulsemarch** dataset on the CD for this text.)

a. Does the plot show a positive association, a negative association, or no association between the two variables? Explain.

b. Explain whether you think the pattern of the plot is linear or curvilinear.

c. Explain whether there are any obvious outliers. If there are outliers, describe where they are located on the plot.

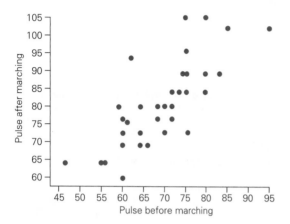

EXERCISE 5.5

5.6   The data in the following tables are the geographic latitudes and the average August temperatures (Fahrenheit) for 20 cities in the United States. The cities are listed in south to north geographic order. (These data are part of the **temperature** dataset on the CD for the text.)

a. Draw a scatterplot of y = August temperature versus x = latitude.

b. Is the pattern linear or curvilinear? What is the direction of the association?

c. Are there any outliers? If so, which cities are outliers?

Geographic Latitude and Mean August Temperature

City	Latitude	Aug Temp
Miami FL	26	83
Houston TX	30	82
Mobile AL	31	82
Phoenix AZ	33	92
Dallas TX	33	85
Los Angeles CA	34	75
Memphis TN	35	81
Norfolk VA	37	77
San Francisco CA	38	64
Baltimore MD	39	76
Kansas City MO	39	76
Washington DC	39	74
Pittsburgh PA	40	71
Cleveland OH	41	70
New York NY	41	76
Boston MA	42	72

Geographic Latitude and Mean August Temperature *(continued)*

City	Latitude	Aug Temp
Syracuse NY	43	68
Minneapolis MN	45	71
Portland OR	46	69
Duluth MN	47	64

Data Source: *The World Almanac and Book of Facts,* 1999, p. 220 and p. 456. Reprinted by permission.

5.7   The following data show the relationship between the speed of a car (mph) and the average stopping distance (feet) after the brakes are applied:

Speed (mph)	0	10	20	30	40	50	60	70
Distance (ft)	0	20	50	95	150	220	300	400

Source: *Defensive Driving: Managing Time and Space,* American Automobile Association, Pamphlet #3389, 1991.

a. In the relationship between these two variables, which is the response variable (y) and which is the explanatory variable (x)?

b. Draw a scatterplot of the data. Characterize the relationship between stopping distance and speed.

5.8   The following table shows sex, height (inches), and mid-parent height (inches) for a sample of 18 college students. The variable mid-parent height is the average of mother's height and father's height. (These data are in the dataset **UCDchap5**; they are sampled from the larger dataset **UCDavis2.**)

Sex, Height, and Mid-Parent Height for 18 College Students

Sex	Height	Mid-Parent Height
M	71	64.0
F	60	63.5
F	66	67.0
M	70	64.5
F	65	65.5
F	66	69.5
M	74	72.5
F	67	67.5
F	63	65.5
M	67	64.0
F	69	70.0
M	65	63.0
M	72	69.0
M	68	67.0
F	63	63.0
F	61	63.0
M	74	69.5
F	65	67.5

a. In the relationship between height and mid-parent height, which variable is the response variable (y) and which is the explanatory variable (x)?

b. Draw a scatterplot of the data for the y and x variables defined in part (a). Use different symbols for males and females.

c. Briefly interpret the scatterplot. Does the association appear to be linear? What are the differences between the males and females? Which points, if any, are outliers?

d. Calculate the difference between height and mid-parent height for each student, and draw a scatterplot of y = difference versus x = mid-parent height. Use different symbols for males and females. What does this graph reveal about the connection between height and mid-parent height?

Section 5.2

5.9   Suppose that a regression equation for the relationship between y = weight (pounds) and x = height (inches) for men aged 18 to 29 years old is

$$\text{Average weight} = -250 + 6\,\text{Height}$$

a. Estimate the average weight for men in this age group who are 70 inches tall.

b. What is the slope of the regression line for average weight and height? Write a sentence that interprets this slope in terms of how much average weight changes when height is increased by one inch.

5.10   Refer to the previous exercise in which a regression equation is given that relates average weight and height for men in the 18-to-29-year-old age group.

a. Suppose a man in this age group is 72 inches tall. Use the regression equation given in the previous exercise to predict the weight of this man.

b. Suppose this man, who is 72 inches tall, weighs 190 pounds. Calculate the residual (prediction error) for this individual.

5.11   Refer to the scatterplot for exercise 5.2 showing the relationship between the average math SAT score and the percent of high school graduates taking the test for the 50 states and District of Columbia. The regression line for these data is

$$\text{Average Math} = 575 - 1.11\,\text{Percent Took}$$

a. The slope of the equation is -1.11. Interpret this value in the context of how average math SAT changes when the percent of graduates taking the test changes.

b. In Missouri, only 8% of graduates take the SAT test. What is the predicted average math SAT score for Missouri?

c. In 1998, the average math SAT score for Missouri was 573. What is the residual (prediction error) for Missouri?

5.12   The equation for converting a temperature from x = degrees Celsius to y = degrees Fahrenheit is $y = 32 + 1.8x$. Does this equation describe a statistical relationship or a deterministic relationship? Briefly explain your answer.

5.13   The average August temperatures (y) and geographic lat-

itudes (x) of 20 cities in the United States were given in the table for exercise 5.6. The regression equation for these data is

$$\hat{y} = 113.6 - 1.01x$$

a. What is the slope of the line? Interpret the slope in terms of how mean August temperature is affected by a change in latitude.

b. Estimate the mean August temperature for a city with latitude of 32.

c. San Francisco has a mean August temperature of 64 and its latitude is 38. Use the regression equation to estimate the mean August temperature in San Francisco, and then calculate the prediction error (residual) for San Francisco.

d. Why should we not use this regression equation to estimate the mean August temperature at the equator (latitude = 0)? If we did use the equation for this purpose, what would be the estimated August temperature at the equator?

5.14   A regression equation for y = handspan (cm) and x = height (in.) was discussed in Section 5.2. If the roles of the variables are reversed and only women are considered, the regression equation is Average height = $51.1 + 0.7$ Handspan.

a. Interpret the slope of 0.7 in terms of how height changes as handspan increases.

b. What is the estimated average height of women with a handspan of 20 centimeters?

c. Molly has a handspan of 20 centimeters and is 66.5 inches tall. What is the prediction error (residual) for Molly?

5.15   Imagine a regression line that relates y = average systolic blood pressure to x = age. The average blood pressure for people 30 years old is 120, while for those 50 years old the average is 130.

a. What is the slope of the regression line?

b. What is the estimated average systolic blood pressure for people who are 34 years old?

5.16   Iman (1994) reports that for professional golfers, a regression equation relating x = putting distance (in feet) and y = success rate (percent) based on observations of distances ranging from 5 feet to 15 feet is

$$\text{Success rate} = 76.5 - 3.95\,\text{Distance}$$

a. What percent success would you expect for these professional golfers if the putting distance was 10 feet?

b. Explain what the slope of -3.95 means in terms of how success changes with distance.

5.17   Refer to the previous exercise. The original data for the putting success of professional golfers included values beyond those used for that exercise (5 feet to 15 feet), in both directions. At a distance of 2 feet, 93.3% of the putts were successful, while at a distance of 20 feet, 15.8% of the putts were successful.

a. Use the equation in exercise 5.16 to predict success rates for those two distances (2 feet and 20 feet). Compare the predictions to the actual success rates.

b. Utilize your results from part (a) to explain why it is not a good idea to use a regression equation to predict information beyond the range of values from which the equation was determined.

c. Draw a picture of what you think the relationship between putting distance and success rate would look like for the entire range from 2 feet to 20 feet.

5.18 The *least squares* regression equation for the data immediately below is $\hat{y} = 5 + 2x$.

x	4	4	7	10	10
y	15	11	19	21	29

a. Calculate the value of $\hat{y}$ for each data point.
b. Calculate the sum of squared errors for this equation.

Section 5.3

5.19 Which of the numbers $0, 0.25, -1.7, -0.5, 2.5$ could not be values of a correlation coefficient? In each case, explain why.

5.20 For $n = 188$ students, the correlation between $y =$ fastest speed ever driven and $x =$ number "randomly" picked between 1 and 10 is about $r = 0$. Describe what this correlation indicates about the association between the maximum speed driven and picking a number between 1 and 10.

5.21 For 19 female bears, the correlation between $x =$ length of the bear (inches) and $y =$ chest girth (inches) is $r = +0.82$ (*Data source:* **bears-female** dataset on the CD for this text).
  a. Describe how chest girth will change when length is increased.
  b. Assuming there are no outliers and the relationship is linear, explain what the correlation indicates about the strength of the relationship.
  c. If the measurements were made in centimeters rather than inches, what would be the value of the correlation coefficient?

5.22 Suppose a value of r^2 is 100% for the relationship between two variables.
  a. What is indicated about the strength of the relationship?
  b. What are the two possible values for the correlation coefficient for the two variables?

5.23 Which implies a stronger linear relationship, a correlation of $+0.4$ or a correlation of -0.6? Briefly explain.

5.24 In Figure 5.9, we observed that the correlation between the left and right handspans of college students was 0.95. The handspans were measured in centimeters. What would be the correlation if the handspans were converted to inches? Explain.

5.25 Explain how two variables can have a perfect curved relationship and yet have zero correlation. Draw a picture of a set of data meeting those criteria.

5.26 For Example 5.7 in this chapter, the correlation between verbal SAT and grade point average is $r = +0.485$. Calculate r^2 and write a sentence that interprets this value.

5.27 The following figure shows four graphs. Assume that all four graphs have the same numerical scales for the two axes.

a. Which graph shows the strongest relationship between the two variables? Which graph shows the weakest?
b. In scrambled order, correlation values for these four graphs are $-0.9, 0, +0.3, +0.6$. Match these correlation values to the graphs.

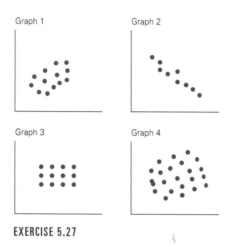

EXERCISE 5.27

5.28 Refer to exercise 5.8 and the table for exercise 5.8 in which heights and mid-parent heights are given for 18 college students (*Data source:* **UCDchap5** dataset on the CD for this text). Draw a scatterplot for the data, using different symbols for males and females as instructed in part (b) of that exercise. Based on the scatterplot, would you say that the correlation between height and mid-parent is higher for the females in the sample, or for the males? Or, are the correlation values about the same for males and females? Explain your reasoning.

5.29 In a regression analysis the total sum of squares (SSTO) is 800 and the error sum of squares (SSE) is 200. What is the value for r^2?

5.30 Suppose you know that the slope of a regression line is $b_1 = +3.5$. Based on this value, explain what you know and do not know about the strength and direction of the relationship between the two variables.

Sections 5.4 and 5.5

5.31 Explain why a strong correlation would be found between weekly sales of firewood and weekly sales of cough drops over a 1-year period.

5.32 An article in the *Sacramento Bee* (29 May, 1998, p. A17) noted "Americans are just too fat, researchers say, with 54 percent of all adults heavier than is healthy. If the trend continues, experts say that within a few generations virtually every U.S. adult will be overweight." This prediction is based on extrapolation, which assumes the current rate of increase will continue indefinitely. Is that a reasonable assumption? Do you agree with the prediction? Explain.

5.33 The **physical** dataset on the CD for this book gives heights (inches) and head circumferences (cm) for a sample of college students. For females only, the correlation between the two variables is 0.05, while for males only, the correlation is 0.19. For the combined sample of males and females, however, the correlation is 0.42. Explain why the correlation in the combined sample is higher than in the separate samples of males and females. Refer to Example 5.11 for guidance.

5.34 The **pennstate2** dataset on the book's CD includes heights and the total number of ear pierces for each person in a sample of college students. The correlation between the two variables is -0.495. What third variable may explain this observed correlation? Explain how that third variable could create the negative correlation.

5.35 Based on the data for the past 50 years in the United States, there is a strong correlation between yearly beer sales and yearly per capita income. Would you interpret this to mean that increasing a person's income will cause him or her to drink more beer? Explain.

5.36 Refer back to exercise 5.7 about stopping distance and vehicle speed. The least squares line for these data is

$$\text{Average distance} = -45 + 5.7 \text{ Speed}$$

a. Use this equation to estimate the average stopping distance when the speed is 80 miles per hour. Do you think this is an accurate estimate? Explain.

b. Draw a scatterplot of the data, as instructed in exercise 5.7(b). Use the scatterplot to estimate the average stopping distance for a speed of 80 mph.

c. Do you think the data on stopping distance and vehicle speed shown in exercise 5.7 describe the relationship between these two variables for all situations? What are some other variables that should be considered when the relationship between stopping distance and vehicle speed is analyzed?

5.37 When a correlation value is reported in research journals there often is not an accompanying scatterplot. Explain why reported correlation values should be supported with either a scatterplot or a description of the scatterplot.

5.38 A memorization test is given to ten women and ten men. The researchers find a negative correlation between scores on the test and height. Explain which of the reasons listed at the beginning of Section 5.4 for misleading correlations might explain this finding. Sketch a scatterplot for the relationship between the variables that is consistent with your explanation.

5.39 Sketch a scatterplot in which the presence of an outlier decreases the observed correlation between the response and explanatory variables.

5.40 Suppose a positive relationship had been found between each of the following sets of variables. For each set, discuss possible reasons why the connection may not be causal. Refer to the list of possible reasons for an observed association in Section 5.5.

a. Number of deaths from automobiles and soft drink sales for each year from 1950 to 2000.

b. Amount of daily walking and quality of health for men over 65 years old.

c. Number of ski accidents and average wait time for the ski lift for each day during one winter at a ski resort.

5.41 Suppose that in an observational study, it is observed

that the risk of heart disease increases as the amount of dietary fat consumed increases. Write a paragraph discussing why this result does not imply that diets high in fat cause heart disease.

Chapter Exercises

5.42 For each pair of variables, identify whether the pair is likely to have a positive correlation, a negative correlation, or no correlation. Briefly indicate your reasoning.

a. Hours of television watched per day and grade point average for college students.

b. Number of liquor stores and number of ministers in Pennsylvania cities.

c. Performance on a strength test and age for people between 40 and 80 years old.

d. Verbal skills and age for children under 12 years old.

e. Height of husband and height of wife.

5.43 The regression line relating verbal SAT scores and GPA for the data exhibited in Figure 5.10 is

$$\text{Average GPA} = 0.539 + 0.00362 \text{ Verbal SAT}$$

a. Estimate the average GPA for those with verbal SAT scores of 600.

b. Explain what the slope of 0.00362 represents in terms of the relationship between GPA and SAT.

c. For two students whose verbal SAT scores differ by 100 points, what is the estimated difference in college GPAs?

d. The lowest possible SAT score is 200. Does the intercept have any useful meaning for this example? Explain.

5.44 For Example 5.2 in this chapter, the correlation between sign legibility distance and age is $r = -0.8$. Calculate r^2 and write a sentence that interprets this value.

5.45 The heights (inches) and foot lengths (centimeters) of 33 college men are shown in the following table. (These data are in the dataset **heightfoot** on the CD for the text.)

Height (inches) and Foot Length (cm)
for 33 College Students

Student	Height	Foot Length	Student	Height	Foot Length
1	66.5	27.0	18	68.0	25.0
2	73.5	29.0	19	72.5	28.0
3	70.0	25.5	20	78.0	31.5
4	71.0	27.9	21	79.0	30.0
5	73.0	27.0	22	71.0	28.0
6	71.0	26.0	23	74.0	29.0
7	71.0	29.0	24	66.0	25.5
8	69.5	27.0	25	71.0	26.7
9	73.0	29.0	26	71.0	29.0
10	71.0	27.0	27	71.0	28.0
11	69.0	29.0	28	84.0	27.0
12	69.0	27.2	29	77.0	29.0
13	73.0	29.0	30	72.0	28.0
14	75.0	29.0	31	70.0	26.0
15	73.0	27.2	32	76.0	30.0
16	72.0	27.5	33	68.0	27.0
17	69.0	25.0			

Data Source: William Harkness.

a. Draw a scatterplot with y = foot length (cm) and x = height (inches). Does the relationship appear to be linear? Are there any outliers? If so, do you think the outliers are legitimate data values?

b. Use statistical software or a calculator to calculate the correlation between height and foot length. If heights were converted to centimeters, what would be the correlation between height and foot length?

c. If there are any outliers, remove them and recalculate the correlation. Describe how the correlation changed from part (b).

5.46 Refer to the previous exercise about y = foot length and x = height (*Data source:* **heightfoot** dataset). If the person who reportedly is 84 inches tall is excluded, the regression equation for the remaining 32 men is $\hat{y}$ = 0.25 + 0.384x.

a. How much does average foot length increase for each 1-inch increase in height?

b. Predict the difference in the foot lengths of men whose heights differ by 10 inches.

c. Suppose Max is 70 inches tall and has a foot length of 28.5 centimeters. Based on the regression equation, what is the predicted foot length for Max? What is the value of the prediction error (residual) for Max?

5.47 Refer to Case Study 5.1, in which regression equations are given for males and females relating ideal weight to actual weight. The equations are

Women: Ideal = 44 + 0.6 Actual
Men: Ideal = 53 + 0.7 Actual

a. Predict the ideal weight for a man who weighs 140 pounds and for a woman who weighs 140 pounds. Compare the results.

b. Do the intercepts have logical physical interpretations in the context of this example? Explain.

c. Do the slopes have logical interpretations in the context of this example? Explain.

5.48 Calculate r^2 for Example 5.9 in this chapter (about hours of sleep and hours of study) in which the correlation is −0.36. Write a sentence that interprets this value.

5.49 The winning time in the Olympic men's 500-meter speed skating race over the years 1924 to 1992 can be described by the regression equation

Winning time = 255 − 0.1094 Year

a. Is the correlation between winning time and year positive or negative? Explain.

b. In 1994, the actual winning time for the gold medal was 36.33 seconds. Use the regression equation to predict the winning time for 1994, and compare the prediction to what actually happened.

c. Explain what the slope of −0.1094 indicates in terms of how winning times change from year to year.

d. Why should we not use this regression equation to predict the winning time in the 2050 Winter Olympics?

5.50 The following lists the number of pages and the price for 15 books. Eight of the books are hardcover and 7 are softcover. (These data are in the dataset **ProfBooks** on the data CD.)

Pages versus Price for Books,
Type H = hardcover, S = softcover

Pages	Price	Type	Pages	Price	Type
104	32.95	H	417	4.95	S
188	24.95	H	417	39.75	H
220	49.95	H	436	5.95	S
264	79.95	H	458	60.00	H
336	4.50	S	466	49.95	H
342	49.95	H	469	5.99	S
378	4.95	S	585	5.95	S
385	5.99	S			

a. Draw a scatterplot of y = price versus x = pages. Use different symbols for hardcover and softcover books.

b. For all 15 books, determine the correlation between price and pages.

c. Separate the books by type. Determine the correlation between price and pages for hardcover books only. Determine the correlation between price and pages for softcover books only.

d. Which of the reasons listed in Section 5.4 for misleading correlations is illustrated in this exercise?

5.51 Give an example of a prediction that is an extrapolation. Do not give an example that is already in this chapter.

5.52 Researchers have shown that there is a positive correlation between the average fat intake and the breast cancer rate across countries. In other words, countries with higher fat intake tend to have higher breast cancer rates. Does this correlation prove that dietary fat is a contributing cause of breast cancer? Explain.

5.53 United States Census Bureau estimates of the average number of persons per household in the United States for census years between 1850 and 2000 are shown in the following table. (On the data CD, these data are in the file **perhouse**.)

Persons per Household
in the United States

Year	Per House	Year	Per House
1850	5.55	1930	4.11
1860	5.28	1940	3.67
1870	5.09	1950	3.37
1880	5.04	1960	3.35
1890	4.93	1970	3.14
1900	4.76	1980	2.76
1910	4.54	1990	2.63
1920	4.34	2000	2.59

Data Source: *The World Almanac and Book of Facts*, 1999, p. 383, and Bureau of the Census.

a. Draw a scatterplot for the relationship between persons per household and year. Is the relationship linear or curvilinear? Is the association between persons per household and year positive or negative?

b. On your scatterplot, add a line that you believe fits the data pattern. Extend this line to the year 2010. Based on this line, estimate the persons per household in the United States in the year 2010.

5.54 Refer to the previous exercise about the trend in persons per household.

a. Using statistical software, determine the least squares line for these data. Use the equation of this line to estimate the persons per household in the year 2010 (*Data source:* **perhouse** dataset).

b. What is the slope of the line? Interpret the slope in the context of these variables.

c. Based on the regression line, what would be the predicted persons per household in the year 2200? What is the lowest possible value of the persons per household number? How does the estimate for 2200 compare to this value?

d. Part (c) illustrates that the observed pattern can't possibly continue in the same manner forever. Sketch the pattern for the trend in persons per household that you think might occur between now and the year 2200.

5.55 For a statistics class project at a large northeastern university, a student examined the relationship between

x = body weight (in pounds)
y = time to chug a 12-ounce beverage (in seconds)

We'll leave it to you to imagine the beverage. The student collected data from 13 individuals, and those data are in the following table. (On the data CD, this dataset is named **chugtime.**)

Body Weight (pounds) and Chug Time (seconds) for 13 College Students

Person	Weight	Chug Time
1	153	5.6
2	169	6.1
3	178	3.3
4	198	3.4
5	128	8.2
6	183	3.5
7	177	6.1
8	210	3.1
9	243	4.0
10	208	3.2
11	157	6.3
12	163	6.9
13	158	6.7

Data Source: William Harkness.

a. Draw a scatterplot of the measurements. Characterize the relationship between chug time and body weight.

b. The heaviest person appears to be an outlier. Do you think that observation is a legitimate observation or do you think an error was made in recording or entering the data?

c. Outliers should not be thrown out unless there's a good reason, but there are several reasons why it may be legitimate to conduct an analysis without them (for instance, see part (e)). Delete the data point for the heaviest person, and determine a regression line for the remainder of the data.

d. Use the regression line from part (c) to estimate the chug time for an individual who weighs 250 pounds. Do you think this time could be achieved by anybody?

e. Sometimes the relationship between two variables is linear for a limited range of x values, then changes to a different line or curve. Using this idea, draw a sketch that illustrates what you think the actual relationship between weight and chug time might be for the range of weights from 100 to 300 pounds.

f. Discuss plausible reasons why the heaviest person appears to be an outlier with regard to his combination of weight and chug-time measurements.

5.56 The data for this exercise are

x	1	2	3	4
y	4	10	14	16

a. Determine the sum of squared errors (SSE) for each of the following two lines:

$$\text{Line 1: } \hat{y} = 3 + 3x$$
$$\text{Line 2: } \hat{y} = 1 + 4x$$

b. By the least squares criterion, which of the two lines is better for these data? Why is it better?

5.57 Measure the heights and weights of ten friends of the same sex.

a. Draw a scatterplot of the data, with weight on the vertical axis and height on the horizontal axis. Draw a line onto the scatterplot that you believe describes the average pattern. Based on two points on this line, estimate the slope of the relationship between weight and height.

b. Using statistical software, compute the least squares line, and compare the slope to your estimated slope from part (a).

5.58 The data in the following table come from the time when the United States still had a maximum speed limit of 55 miles per hour. An issue of some concern at that time was whether lower speed limits reduce the highway death rate. (On the CD, these data are called **speedlimit.**)

a. In the relationship between death rate and speed limit, which variable is the response variable and which is the explanatory variable?

b. Plot the data in the table, and discuss the result. Does there appear to be an association? Are there any outliers? If so, what is their influence on the correlation?

Highway Death Rates and Speed Limits

Country	Death Rate (per 100 million veh. miles)	Speed Limit (in miles per hour)
Norway	3.0	55
United States	3.3	55
Finland	3.4	55
Britain	3.5	70
Denmark	4.1	55
Canada	4.3	60
Japan	4.7	55
Australia	4.9	60
Netherlands	5.1	60
Italy	6.1	75

Source: "Fifty-five mph speed limit is no safety guarantee," D. J. Rivkin, *New York Times* (letters to the editor), Nov. 25, 1986, p. 26.

Dataset Exercises

5.59 Use the dataset **sats98** for this exercise. The variable **Verbal** contains the average scores on the verbal SAT in 1998 for the 50 states and the District of Columbia. **PctTook** is the percent of high school graduates, in each state, who took the SAT that year.

a. Make a scatterplot showing the connection between average *verbal* SAT and the percent of graduates who took the SAT in a state. Describe the relationship between these two variables.

b. Compute the least squares regression line for the relationship between these two variables. Write a sentence that interprets the slope of this equation in a way that could be understood by people who don't know very much about statistics.

c. Based on the appearance of the scatterplot, do you think that a straight line is an appropriate mathematical model for the connection between **Verbal** and **PctTook**? Why or why not?

d. Explain why the intercept of the equation computed in part (b) would not have a sensible interpretation for these two variables.

5.60 Use the **sats98** dataset.

a. Plot the relationship between average verbal (**Verbal**) and average math (**Math**) SAT scores in the 50 states. Describe the characteristics of the relationship.

b. What states are outliers? In what specific way are they outliers?

5.61 Use the dataset **idealwtmen**. It contains data for the men used for Case Study 5.1. The variable **diff** is the difference between actual and ideal weights and was computed as **diff = actual − ideal.**

a. Plot **diff** versus **actual** (actual weight). Does the relationship appear to be linear or is it curvilinear?

b. Compute the equation of the regression line for the relationship between **diff** and **actual**. Estimate the average difference for men who weigh 150 pounds. On average, do 150-pound men want to weigh more or less than they actually do?

c. Repeat part (b) for men who weigh 200 pounds.

d. What is the value of r^2 for the relationship between **diff** and **actual**?

5.62 Use the dataset **ceodata**. The ages of 60 CEOs for America's best small companies were given in exercise 2.32 of Chapter 2. The annual salaries (in thousands of dollars) for 59 of these CEOs are in the dataset along with the ages.

a. Plot **Salary** versus **Age.**

b. Compute the correlation coefficient and r^2.

c. Characterize the relationship between annual salary and age. What is the pattern of the relationship? How strong is the association?

5.63 Use the dataset **UCDwomht**. For a sample of college women, the variable **height** is student's height (in inches) and the variable **midparent** is the average height of the student's parents, in inches as reported by the student.

a. Compute the regression equation for predicting a student's height from the average of her parents' heights.

b. Use the regression equation to predict the height for a college woman with parents who have an average height of 68 inches.

c. Use the regression equation to predict the height of a college woman whose mother is 62 inches tall and whose father is 70 inches tall.

d. What other summaries of the data should be done in order to determine the strength of the relationship between **height** and **midparent** height?

5.64 Use the dataset **temperature**. A portion of this dataset was presented in exercise 5.6 in which the relationship between mean August temperature and geographic latitude was analyzed. For predicting mean April temperature (**AprTemp**), which of these two variables in the dataset is a stronger predictor: geographic latitude (**latitude**) or mean January temperature (**JanTemp**)? Support your answer with relevant statistics and plots.

Turn On Your Computer

*For these exercises, use the **Correlation** applet described in Section 5.3. It is on the CD for this text. In each exercise, you are asked to sketch a facsimile of a graph you create with the applet. Alternatively, you might use "Print Screen" on your keyboard to copy the screen image; then paste it to a word processing document.*

5.65 Using the applet, create a plot for the target correlation $r = +0.5$. Don't include any outliers. Sketch an approximate facsimile of your resulting graph.

5.66 Using the applet, create a plot for the target correlation $r = −0.8$. Don't include any outliers. Sketch an approximate facsimile of your resulting graph.

5.67 Using the applet, create a plot for the target correlation $r = 0$. Don't include any outliers. Sketch an approximate facsimile of your resulting graph.

5.68 Using the applet, create a plot for the target correlation $r = +0.5$ in which one point is an outlier that decreases the correlation. Make the plot such that if the outlier were removed, the correlation for the remaining points would be greater than $r = 0.7$. Sketch an approximate facsimile of your resulting graph.

5.69 Using the applet, create a plot for the target correlation $r = −0.8$ in which one point is an outlier that inflates the correlation. Make the plot such that if the outlier were removed, the correlation for the remaining points would be between $−0.2$ and $+0.2$. Sketch an approximate facsimile of your resulting graph. *Hint:* Start by putting points in the upper left corner of the plot.

5.70 Using the applet, with the target correlation $r = 0$, make a plot that has a curvilinear pattern for which the correlation is 0. Sketch an approximate facsimile of your resulting graph.

REFERENCES

Holbrook, M. B., and R. M. Schindler (1989). "Some exploratory findings on the development of musical tastes," *Journal of Consumer Research,* Vol. 16, pp. 119–124.

Iman, R. L. (1994). *A Data-Based Approach to Statistics,* Belmont, CA: Wadsworth.

CHAPTER 6

Relationships Between Categorical Variables

What else do they have on their bodies? See Example 6.2 and Exercise 6.45.

Whenever risk statistics are reported, there is a risk that they are misreported. Journalists often present risk data in a way that produces the best story rather than in a way that provides the best information. Very commonly, news reports either don't contain or don't emphasize the information you need to understand risk.

This chapter is about the analysis of the relationship between two categorical variables, so let's begin by recalling the meaning of the term *categorical variable.* The raw data from categorical variables consist of group or category names that don't necessarily have any ordering. Eye color and hair color, for instance, are categorical variables.

We can also use the methods of this chapter to examine *ordinal* variables. Ordinal variables can be thought of as categorical variables for which the categories have a natural ordering. For example, a researcher might define categories for quantitative variables, like age, income, or years of education.

Although there are many questions that we can and will ask about two categorical variables, in most cases the principal question that we ask is: Is there a relationship between the two variables, so that the category into which individuals fall for one variable seems to depend on the category they are in for the other variable? ◆

6.1

turn on your mind

Hair color and eye color are related characteristics. What exactly does it mean to say that these two variables are related? Suppose that you know the hair colors and the eye colors of 200 individuals. How would you assess whether the two variables are related for those individuals?*

6.1 | DISPLAYING RELATIONSHIPS BETWEEN CATEGORICAL VARIABLES

We have already encountered several examples of the type of problem we will study in this chapter. In Chapter 2, for instance, we described a study of 479 children that found that children who slept either with a nightlight or in a fully lit

*HINT: Read the sentence just before the Turn on Your Mind box.

171

room before the age of two had a higher incidence of myopia (nearsightedness) later in childhood. The following table was used to examine this relationship:

Slept with:	No Myopia	Myopia	High Myopia	Total
Darkness	155 (90%)	15 (9%)	2 (1%)	172
Nightlight	153 (66%)	72 (31%)	7 (3%)	232
Full Light	34 (45%)	36 (48%)	5 (7%)	75
Total	342 (71%)	123 (26%)	14 (3%)	479

The table displays the number of children in each combination of the categories of two categorical variables: the sleep-time lighting condition and the child's eyesight classification at the time of the study. The table also gives row percents, the percents of children within each row who fall into the different eyesight categories. For example, 90% (155/172) of those who slept in darkness had no myopia, but only 45% (34/75) of those who slept in full light had no myopia.

Notice that the row percents show us that the two variables are related. From these percents we learn that the incidence of myopia increases when the amount of sleep-time light increases. This result doesn't prove that sleeping with light *causes* myopia, but we can say that, for some reason, the characteristics of eyesight and sleep-time lighting are *associated* characteristics.

Displays like the table above are often called **contingency tables** because they cover all contingencies for the combinations of the two variables. Because the categories of two variables are used to create the table, a contingency table is also referred to as a **two-way table.** Each row and column combination of the table is called a **cell.**

The first step in analyzing the relationship between two categorical variables is to count how many observations fall into each cell of the contingency table. It's difficult, however, to look at a table of counts and make useful judgments about a relationship. Usually, we need to consider the **conditional percents** within either the rows or the columns of the table.

There are two types of conditional percents that we can compute for a contingency table. **Row percents,** like the percents in the myopia table, are the percents across a row of a contingency table. These percents are based on the total number of observations in the row. **Column percents** are the percents down a column of a contingency table. These percents are based on the total number of observations in the column.

In some cases, one variable can be designated as the *explanatory variable* and the other variable as the *response variable.* As we learned in Chapter 2, in these situations it is customary to define the rows using the categories of the explanatory variable and the columns using the categories of the response variable. When this is done, the row percents can be used to examine the relationship because they tell us what percent *responded* in each possible way. We can then see if individuals responded equivalently for each category of the explanatory variable. For instance, we can see if the myopia response was the same for different lighting conditions.

EXAMPLE 6.1
Smoking and the Risk of Divorce

Table 6.1 displays data on smoking habits and divorce history for the 1669 respondents who had ever been married in the 1991 and 1993 General Social Surveys done by the National Opinion Research Center at the University of Chicago.

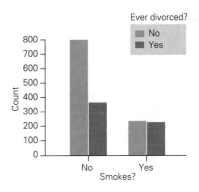

FIGURE 6.1   **Frequency counts for smoking habits and divorce**

TABLE 6.1 ■ **Smoking and Divorce, GSS Surveys 1991–1993**

	Ever Divorced?		
Smoke?	*Yes*	*No*	*Total*
Yes	238	247	485
No	374	810	1184
Total	612	1057	1669

Data Source: SDA archive at UC Berkeley website (www.csa.berkeley.edu:7502/).

The frequency counts in the cells of this table are visually summarized in Figure 6.1, using a bar graph as described in Chapter 2. In the bar graph, we see evidence of an association between smoking habits and the likelihood of divorce because the set of bars for smokers has a different pattern than the set of bars for nonsmokers. Among those who smoke, the number who have ever been divorced is about equal to the number who have not been divorced. Among those who do not smoke, the proportion ever divorced is clearly a minority. We also see that the majority of the sample does not smoke.

To describe the relationship, we should calculate row percents because we are interested in comparing divorce rates between smokers and nonsmokers. We are not interested in comparing smoking rates between those who have been divorced and those who have not. Among the respondents who smoke, 49% (238/485) have been divorced and 51% have not been divorced. Among those who don't smoke, only 32% (374/1184) have been divorced, while 68% have not been divorced. The difference between the two sets of row percents indicates a relationship. ◆

EXAMPLE 6.2
Tattoos and Ear Pierces

From 1996 through 1998, students in several statistics classes at Penn State provided responses to these two questions:

1. Do you have a tattoo?
2. How many total ear pierces do you have?

The responses from 565 men are displayed in Table 6.2. In the table, the very few men who had more than two ear pierces are lumped with the men who had two ear pierces.

For this table, we could ask questions about the conditional percents in either direction because there is no clear explanatory and response variable distinction. For instance, does the likelihood that a man has a tattoo differ based on whether or not he has an ear pierce? Or, we could ask if men with tattoos are more likely to have an ear pierce? Let's consider the row percents.

TABLE 6.2 ■ **Ear Pierces and Tattoos for Men ($n = 565$)**

Ear Pierces	No Tattoo	Tattoo	Total
0	381	43	424
1	54	16	70
2 or more	45	26	71
Total	480	85	565

◆ Among men with no ear pierces, 43/424 = 10% have a tattoo.

◆ Among men with one ear pierce, 16/70 = 23% have a tattoo.

◆ Among men with two or more ear pierces, 26/71 = 37% have a tattoo.

Clearly, the percent with a tattoo increases as the number of ear pierces increases, so the two characteristics are related. We also see the relationship when we consider the column percents. Those percents are shown in the bar chart of Figure 6.2. Men with tattoos are more likely to have an ear pierce.

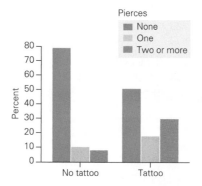

FIGURE 6.2   **Column percents for the ear pierce and tattoo data**

Percents based on the total sample can also be of interest. These percents don't provide information about the relationship, but they do provide useful descriptions of the overall group. For example, 381/565 = 67% of the men in the overall sample have neither a tattoo nor an ear pierce, while (16 + 26)/565 = 42/565 = 7.4% have both. The overall percent with an ear pierce is (70 + 71)/565 = 25%, and the overall percent with a tattoo is 85/565 = 15%. ◆

EXAMPLE 6.3
Gender and Reasons for Taking Care of Your Body

In a 1997 poll conducted by the *Los Angeles Times,* 1218 southern California residents were surveyed about their health and fitness habits. The respondents were selected using random-digit dialing methods. One of the questions was: "What is the most important reason why you try to take care of your body: Is it mostly because you want to be attractive to others, or mostly because you want to keep healthy, or mostly because it helps your self-confidence, or what?"

The percent distribution of the responses is shown for men and for women in Table 6.3. Notice that the pattern of responses is more or less the same for men and women. It seems reasonable to conclude that the response to the question was not related to the gender of the respondent. ◆

TABLE 6.3 ■ **Reasons for Taking Care of Body and Gender**

	Healthy	Self-Confidence	Attractive	Don't Know
Men	76%	16%	7%	1%
Women	74%	20%	4%	2%

Source: www.latimes.com, poll archives, study #401.

6.2

turn on your mind

In Example 6.1, the risk of divorce was associated with smoking habits. Were the data collected in an observational study or in an experiment? Do you think cigarette smoking may cause an increase in the divorce rate? Do you think getting divorced may cause a person to start smoking? How would you explain the association between smoking habits and the likelihood of divorce?*

*HINT: Do you think participants were randomly assigned to smoke or not? Think about possible confounding variables.

6.2 | RISK, RELATIVE RISK, ODDS RATIO, AND INCREASED RISK

When a particular outcome is undesirable, researchers and journalists may describe the *risk* of that outcome. The **risk** that a randomly selected individual within a group falls into the undesirable category is simply the proportion in that category.

$$\text{Risk} = \frac{\text{Number in category}}{\text{Total number in group}}$$

It is commonplace to express risk as a percent rather than as a proportion. Suppose, for instance, that within a group of 200 individuals, asthma affects 24 people. In this group the *risk* of asthma is 24/200 = 0.12, or 12%.

Relative Risk

We often want to know how the risk of an outcome relates to an explanatory variable. One statistic used for this purpose is **relative risk,** which is the ratio of the risks in two different categories of an explanatory variable.

$$\text{Relative risk} = \frac{\text{Risk in category 1}}{\text{Risk in category 2}}$$

Relative risk describes the risk in one group as a multiple of the risk in another group. For example, suppose that a researcher states that, for those who drive while under the influence of alcohol, the relative risk of an automobile accident is 15. This means that the risk of an accident for those who drive under the influence is 15 times the risk for those who don't drive under the influence.

Some features of relative risk are

- When two risks are the same, the relative risk is 1.
- When two risks are different, the relative risk is different from 1; and when the category in the numerator has higher risk, the relative risk is greater than 1.
- The risk in the denominator (the bottom) of the ratio is often the **baseline risk,** which is the risk for the category in which no additional treatment or behavior is present.

6.3

turn on your mind

Based on the study in Section 6.1, the relative risk of developing any myopia later in childhood is 5.5 for babies sleeping in full light compared with babies sleeping in darkness. Restate this information in a sentence that the public would understand.*

EXAMPLE 6.1—*CONTINUED*
Smoking and the Relative Risk of Divorce

Refer to Table 6.1 on page 173. To compute the relative risk of divorce for smokers, we first find the risk of divorce in each smoking category:

- For those who smoke, the risk of divorce is 238/485 = 0.491, or about 49%.
- For nonsmokers, the risk of divorce is 374/1184 = 0.316, or about 32%. This can be considered to be the *baseline risk* of divorce.

HINT: See the interpretation of relative risk in Example 6.1—continued.

The relative risk of divorce is the ratio of these two risks.

$$\text{Relative risk} = \frac{49\%}{32\%} = 1.53$$

In this sample, the risk of divorce for smokers is 1.53 times the risk of divorce for nonsmokers. ◆

Percent Increase or Decrease in Risk

Sometimes an increase or decrease in risk is presented as a percent change instead of a multiple. The **percent increase** (or decrease) **in risk** can be calculated as follows:

$$\text{Percent increase in risk} = \frac{\text{Difference in risks}}{\text{Baseline risk}} \times 100\%$$

Equivalently, when the relative risk has already been determined, the percent increase in risk can be calculated using the relationship

$$\text{Percent increase in risk} = (\text{relative risk} - 1) \times 100\%$$

When a risk is smaller than the baseline risk, the relative risk is less than 1 and the percent "increase" will actually be negative. In this situation, the term *percent decrease* should be used to describe the percent change in the risks.

EXAMPLE 6.1—*CONTINUED*
Percent Increase in the Risk
of Divorce for Smokers

Because we've already calculated the relative risk, the easiest way to determine the percent increase in the risk of divorce for smokers is

$$\text{Percent increase in risk} = (1.53 - 1) \times 100\% = 53\%$$

We can get the same answer for the percent increase in risk by calculating

$$\text{Percent increase in risk} = \frac{\text{Difference in risks}}{\text{Baseline risk}} \times 100\%$$

$$= \frac{49 - 32}{32} \times 100\% = 53\%$$

So, the risk of divorce is 53% higher for smokers than it is for nonsmokers. ◆

Odds Ratio

Sometimes counts for the outcomes of a categorical variable are summarized by comparing the **odds** of one outcome to another, rather than by comparing one outcome to the total. For instance, the *odds* of getting a divorce to *not* getting a divorce for nonsmokers are 374 divorced to 810 not divorced, or equivalently about 0.46 divorced to 1 not divorced (divide both counts by 810 to get this). For smokers, on the other hand, the odds are 238 divorced to 247 not divorced, or 0.96 to 1, approximately even odds. Notice that odds are expressed using a phrase with the structure "a to b," so a ratio is implied but not actually computed.

The **odds ratio** is used to compare the odds of a certain behavior or event within two different groups. For example, we may want to compare the odds of success versus failure for two different treatments of clinical depression. The formula for the odds ratio will be given in a moment, but a numerical example should make it easy for you to see how it is computed. In Example 6.1, the odds ratio comparing the odds of divorce for smokers and nonsmokers is

$$\frac{\text{Odds of divorce for smokers}}{\text{Odds of divorce for nonsmokers}} = \frac{238/247}{374/810} = \frac{0.96}{0.46} = 2.1$$

This odds ratio tells us that the odds of ending up divorced instead of still married for smokers are about double the odds of ending up divorced for nonsmokers.

A useful characteristic of the odds ratio is that its value stays the same if the roles of the response and explanatory variables are reversed. In the previous paragraph, we compared the odds of divorce for smokers and nonsmokers. If we had, instead, compared the odds of being a smoker for those who have been divorced and those who have never divorced, the answer would still be 2.1. The calculation is

$$\frac{\text{Odds of smoking for divorced}}{\text{Odds of smoking for never divorced}} = \frac{238/374}{247/810} = \frac{0.636}{0.305} = 2.1$$

The interpretation here is that the odds of being a smoker for those who have been divorced are about double the odds of being a smoker for those who have never been divorced.

---

in summary   Statistics on Risk, Relative Risk, Odds, and Odds Ratios

Let's summarize the various ways in which risk, relative risk, odds, and odds ratios are constructed from a two-way contingency table. These measures are usually employed when there is a definable explanatory and response variable and when there is a baseline condition, so we present them using those distinctions. In situations where those distinctions cannot be made, simply be clear about which condition is in the numerator and which is in the denominator.

	Response Variable		
Explanatory Variable	*Category 1*	*Category 2*	*Total*
Category of Interest	A_1	A_2	T_A
Baseline Category	B_1	B_2	T_B

- Risk (of response 1) for category of interest $= A_1/T_A$
- Odds (of response 1 to response 2) for category of interest $= A_1$ to A_2
- Relative risk $= \dfrac{A_1/T_A}{B_1/T_B}$
- Odds ratio $= \dfrac{A_1/A_2}{B_1/B_2}$

6.3 | MISLEADING STATISTICS ABOUT RISK

6.4

turn on your mind

Suppose a newspaper article claims that drinking coffee doubles your risk of developing a certain disease. Assume the statistic was based on legitimate, well-conducted research. What additional information would you want about the risk before deciding whether or not to quit drinking coffee?*

Whenever risk statistics are reported, there is a risk that they are misreported. Unfortunately, journalists often present risk data in a way that produces the best story rather than in a way that provides the best information. Very commonly, news reports either don't contain or don't emphasize the information you need to understand risk. You should always ask the following questions when you encounter statistics about risk:

1. What are the actual risks? What is the baseline risk?
2. What is the population for which the reported risk or relative risk applies?
3. What is the time period for this risk?

EXAMPLE 6.4
Disaster in the Skies?
Case Study 1.2 Revisited

Case Study 1.2 described a *USA Today* article that told us: "Errors by air traffic controllers climbed from 746 in fiscal 1997 to 878 in fiscal 1998, an 18% increase." To airplane travelers this may sound frightening, but a look at the risk of controller error per flight should ease their fear. In 1998, there were only 5.5 errors per million flights compared to 4.8 errors per million flights in 1997. The risk of controller error did increase, but the actual risk is extremely small. ◆

EXAMPLE 6.5
Dietary Fat and
Breast Cancer

"Italian scientists report that a diet rich in animal protein and fat—cheeseburgers, french fries, and ice cream, for example—increases a woman's risk of breast cancer threefold," according to *Prevention Magazine's Giant Book of Health Facts* (1991, p. 122). The statement attributed to the Italian scientists is nearly useless information for at least two reasons:

1. We don't how the data were collected, so we don't know what population these women represent.
2. We don't know the ages of the women studied, so we don't know the baseline rate of breast cancer for these women.

Age is a critical factor. A frequently stated statistic about breast cancer is that one in nine women will develop breast cancer, but this is actually an accumulated lifetime risk to the age of 85, so a woman who dies before she reaches age 85 does not have a one in nine risk. According to the *University of California at Berkeley Wellness Letter* (July 1992, p. 1) the accumulated lifetime risk of a woman developing breast cancer by certain ages is as follows:

by age 50: 1 in 50
by age 60: 1 in 23
by age 85: 1 in 9

Also, the annual risk of developing breast cancer is only about 1 in 3700 for women in their early 30s (Fletcher, Black, Harris, Rimer, and Shapiro, 1993, p. 1644). If the Italian study had been done on very young women, the threefold increase in risk represents a small increase. Unfortunately, *Prevention Magazine's Giant Book of Health Facts* did not even give enough information to lead us to the original research report, so it is impossible to intelligently evaluate the claim. ◆

EXAMPLE 6.6
Is Smoking More Dangerous for Women?

"Higher heart risk in women smokers" was the headline of an April 3, 1998, article at the YAHOO® Health news website. The article, due to the Reuters news agency, described Danish research that was interpreted as evidence that smoking affects the risk of a heart attack more for women than for men. Here is part of the article:

> Women who smoke have a greater than 50% higher risk of a heart attack than male smokers according to a study from Denmark. The researchers suggest that this difference may be related to the interaction of tobacco smoke and the female hormone, estrogen.
>
> "Women may be more sensitive than men to some of the harmful effects of smoking," the team writes in the April 4th edition of the *British Medical Journal.*
>
> Analyzing data from nearly 25,000 Danish men and women, Dr. Eva Prescott of the University of Copenhagen and colleagues report that women who smoke have a 2.24 relative risk of myocardial infarction, or heart attack, compared with nonsmokers. This is significantly higher than the relative risk of male smokers compared with nonsmokers.

Unfortunately, the only information we're given, for each sex, is the *relative risk* of a heart attack for smokers. What's missing from the article is any mention of the estimated risk of a heart attack for any group of interest. A look at those risks makes the research interpretation debatable.

The *British Medical Journal* article (Prescott, Hippe, Schnor, and Vestbo, 1998) provided more complete information about the risks. That information is displayed in Table 6.4. Based on the data in the table, do you agree with the conclusion stated in the Web article?

TABLE 6.4 ■ Smoking, Gender, and the Risk of a Heart Attack

	Sample Size	Heart Attacks	Risk of Heart Attack
Men			
Smokers	8490	902	10.62% (902/8490)
Nonsmokers	4701	349	7.42% (349/4701)
Women			
Smokers	6461	380	5.88% (380/6461)
Nonsmokers	5011	132	2.63% (132/5011)

We see from the table that the risk of a heart attack is generally greater for men than it is for women. In particular, for men who smoke the risk of a heart attack is 10.62%, which is clearly higher than the risk of 5.88% for women who smoke. These numbers contradict the Web article's headline and first sentence, which both imply that the risk of a heart attack is greater for women smokers than for men smokers.

The researchers focused on relative risk, which is the ratio of two risks. We can easily verify that the relative risks provided in the Web article are correct.

◆ For women who smoke, the relative risk of a heart attack is 5.88%/2.63% = 2.24.

◆ For men who smoke, the relative risk of a heart attack is 10.62%/7.42% = 1.43.

The first sentence of the article actually refers to a comparison of these two *relative* risks, which are not the *actual* risks for women and men smokers. In other words, the *relative risk* value for women, 2.24, is 50% higher than the *relative risk* for men, 1.43.

In a subsequent issue of the *British Medical Journal,* several letter writers argued that the correct interpretation of these data is

◆ For both smokers and nonsmokers, men have a higher risk of heart attack than women do.

◆ For both men and women, smoking *adds* about 3.2% to the risk experienced by nonsmokers. In other words, the effect of smoking is the same for the two sexes.

The researchers' response to these letters was that they believed that it was valid to consider the multiplicative effect of smoking on risk. Dr. Prescott and her colleagues believe it is important that, for women, smoking multiplies the risk of a heart attack by 2.24, but for men, smoking multiplies the risk by only 1.43. ◆

The moral of the story in Example 6.6 is that a *relative risk* is affected by the *baseline risk,* so it's important to know the baseline risk. If a risk increases to 3% from a baseline risk of 1%, the relative risk is 3. If a risk increases to 22% from a baseline risk of 20%, the relative risk is only 22/20 = 1.1, although the difference in risks is still 2%. Is an increase in risk from 1% to 3% more serious than an increase from 20% to 22%? That may depend on the situation.

6.5

turn on your mind

If you were a frequent beer drinker and were worried about getting colon cancer, would it be more informative to you to know the *risk* of colon cancer for frequent beer drinkers or the *relative risk* of colon cancer for frequent beer drinkers compared to nondrinkers? Which of those statistics would likely be of more interest to the media? Explain your responses.*

*HINT: Suppose the relative risk is 3.0. Does that mean the same to you as an individual if the disease is rare as it does if it is common?

6.4 | THE EFFECT OF A THIRD VARIABLE AND SIMPSON'S PARADOX

In previous chapters, you have seen several examples in which a confounding or lurking variable may have affected the relationship between an explanatory variable and a response variable. In observational studies, a confounding variable might explain an apparent relationship between two variables or, in some instances, it can mask a relationship. Whenever the data are the product of an observational study, you should carefully consider the possibility that a third variable may affect the observed relationship.

EXAMPLE 6.7
Educational Status and Driving after Substance Use

In December of 1998, the U.S. government's Substance Abuse and Mental Health Services Administration released a report with information about drug use, alcohol use, and driving that was gathered in a 1996 nationwide survey of 11,847 individuals aged 16 and over (SAMSHA, 1998). A principal response variable throughout the report was a categorical variable that described whether a respondent had on any occasion in the previous year driven within two hours of using either alcohol or drugs. This response variable had three categories:

- ◆ never drove while impaired
- ◆ drove within two hours of alcohol use, but never after drug use
- ◆ drove within two hours of drug use and possibly after alcohol use

Figure 6.3 displays the association between this variable and educational status. The vertical axis of the bar chart is the proportion within an educational category that falls into a particular category of the response variable. The bar chart clearly shows that as the amount of education increases, the proportion who drove within two hours of alcohol use also increases. The data suggest a possible way to reduce the problem of drinking and driving: Let's not give out

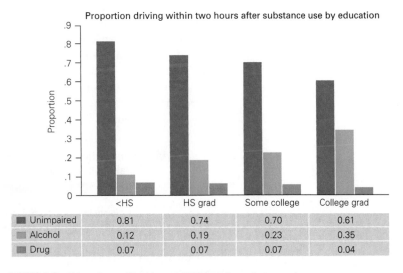

Proportion driving within two hours after substance use by education

	<HS	HS grad	Some college	College grad
Unimpaired	0.81	0.74	0.70	0.61
Alcohol	0.12	0.19	0.23	0.35
Drug	0.07	0.07	0.07	0.04

FIGURE 6.3 **Education and incidence of driving after substance abuse**

any more college degrees. We hope, for many reasons, that you disagree with this solution.

What's going on here? This is an observational study, so we should consider the possibility of confounding. We should ask if the various educational groups differ in ways that may affect the response variable. One likely difference between the educational groups has to do with age. In the survey, about 13% of the respondents were under 21 years old. It is probable that almost none of these younger respondents were in the college degree group. It is also possible that many members of the "less than high school group" were under 21.

Age differences could at least partially explain the results. Another table in the report showed that about 80% of those under 21 fell into the "never while impaired category," but only 70% of the 21 or over age group fell into this category. Unfortunately, the report didn't contain the information necessary to sort out the relative effects of age and educational status, so we'll have to classify age as a lurking variable.

The amount of alcohol consumed within two hours of driving should also be considered. The report indicates that compared to younger drivers, older drivers were more likely to say that they had never had more than one drink before driving. ◆

Simpson's Paradox

Occasionally, the effect of a confounding factor is strong enough to produce a paradox known as **Simpson's Paradox.** The paradox is that the relationship appears to be in a different direction when the confounding variable is not considered than when the data are separated into the categories of the confounding variable.

EXAMPLE 6.8
Blood Pressure and Oral Contraceptive Use

We will illustrate Simpson's Paradox with a hypothetical example of an observational study done to examine the association between oral contraceptive use and blood pressure. Although the data are hypothetical, they are similar to data from several actual studies of the same problem. Suppose that 2400 women are categorized according to whether or not they use oral contraceptives and whether or not they have high blood pressure. The results shown in Table 6.5 indicate that the percent with high blood pressure is about the same among oral contraceptive users as it is for nonusers. In fact, a slightly higher percentage of the nonusers have high blood pressure.

We're certain that you can think of many factors that affect blood pressure. If the users and nonusers of oral contraceptives differ with respect to one of

TABLE 6.5 ■ **Percent with High Blood Pressure for Users and Nonusers of Oral Contraceptives**

	Sample Size	Number with High B.P.	% with High B.P.
Use Oral Contraceptives	800	64	64 of 800 = 8.0%
Don't Use Oral Contraceptives	1600	136	136 of 1600 = 8.5%

TABLE 6.6 ■ Controlling for the Effect of Age

	Age 18–34		Age 35–49	
	Sample Size	n and % with High B.P.	Sample Size	n and % with High B.P.
Use Oral Contraceptives	600	36 (6%)	200	28 (14%)
Don't Use Oral Contraceptives	400	16 (4%)	1200	120 (10%)

these factors, that factor confounds the results in Table 6.5. As in the previous example, age is a critical factor. The users of oral contraceptives tend to be younger than the nonusers are. This is important because blood pressure increases with age.

One way to control for the effect of age is to create separate contingency tables for women in different age groups. Table 6.6 divides the data from our hypothetical study into two age groups. In each age group, the percentage with high blood pressure is higher for the users than for the nonusers. This contradicts the direction of the relationship that we see when the age factor is not considered. In Table 6.5, not controlling for age differences masked the true nature of the relationship. Notice that the older women were less likely to be oral contraceptive users but more likely to have high blood pressure. ◆

6.5 | ASSESSING THE STATISTICAL SIGNIFICANCE OF A 2 × 2 TABLE

Most of the material you have seen thus far involves *descriptive statistics*, which are methods for describing the data in hand. This section introduces a special case of *hypothesis testing*, one of the two most common statistical procedures making up *inferential statistics*. The other common inference procedure is the use of a *confidence interval* to estimate a population value. Confidence intervals were introduced in Chapter 4. Hypothesis testing and confidence intervals will be covered in detail in Chapters 10 to 16, but this brief introduction will help you become familiar with some basic concepts and will help prepare you for those chapters.

Remember that observed data often represent a sample from a larger population. When this is the case, the purpose of collecting the data is usually to use the sample information to make generalizations about the population. Because this involves *inferring* something rather than being sure, the statistical methods used are called *inferential statistics*. When the data represent two categorical variables, the question of interest is whether a relationship observed in the sample data can also be inferred to hold in the population represented by the data.

When we see differences in the conditional distributions within the rows (or columns) of the contingency table, we say that the variables are related in the sample. A large difference between conditional distributions may convince us that the relationship is real. Small differences in conditional distributions, however, might not convince us. It is unlikely that any set of observed conditional distributions would ever be exactly the same for all categories of an explanatory variable. Small differences in observed conditional distributions could simply be the result of chance and may not represent a real relationship in the population.

6.6

turn on your mind

A random sample includes 110 women and 90 men. Of the women, approximately 9% are left-handed, while approximately 11% of the men are left-handed. Based on this observed data, do you think there is a relationship between gender and handedness in the population represented by this sample? Why or why not?*

Case Study 1.6 described the Physician's Health Study in which about 22,000 physicians were randomized to take either aspirin or a placebo daily. Over a five-year period, the percentage of physicians experiencing heart attacks was lower in the aspirin group than in the placebo group. The difference was found to be **statistically significant,** and it was inferred that the observed difference reflected an actual difference in the population.

In the definitions following Case Study 1.6, the term *statistically significant* was defined as follows:

> A **statistically significant relationship** or difference is one that is large enough to be unlikely to have occurred in the observed sample if there is no relationship or difference in the population.

The practical upshot of calling an observed relationship statistically significant is that we are inferring that the relationship exists in the population. We make this inference by establishing that if there were really no relationship, it would be unlikely that we would have observed such a strong relationship in the sample.

The Five Steps to Determining Statistical Significance

There are five steps required in any hypothesis-testing situation. These steps lead to a decision about whether a statistically significant effect can be inferred about the population. The steps are

Step 1: Determine the null and alternative hypotheses.
Step 2: Verify necessary data conditions, and if met, summarize the data into an appropriate test statistic.
Step 3: Assuming the null hypothesis is true, find the *p*-value.
Step 4: Decide whether or not the result is statistically significant based on the *p*-value.
Step 5: Report the conclusion in the context of the situation.

In this section we describe how these steps are implemented for a 2×2 contingency table. In Chapter 15 you will learn how to implement them for any contingency table.

Step 1: Null and Alternative Hypotheses
The question we are considering is whether or not the sample data permit us to conclude that two variables are related. Another way to describe our objective is that we are deciding between two possible hypotheses about the population.

***HINT:** Consider *how many* men and women in the samples are left-handed. Now consider how the percents would change if one more or one fewer had been left-handed.

In statistical language, the possibilities are called the **null hypothesis** and the **alternative hypothesis,** and they can be stated as follows:

null hypothesis: The two variables are not related.
alternative hypothesis: The two variables are related.

The two hypotheses just given are specific to the context of two-way tables. In Chapters 11 and 13, you will learn how to write null and alternative hypotheses for a broad range of research questions.

Step 2: The Chi-square Statistic

The statistical significance of the association between two categorical variables can be examined using a value known as the **chi-square statistic.** This statistic measures the difference between the **observed counts** in the contingency table and the counts that would be **expected** if there were no relationship (the null hypothesis). A large difference between the observed and expected counts occurs when a relationship is present in the observed table. To simplify our discussion of the chi-square statistic, we will consider only 2×2 contingency tables so each variable will have just two categories. The same principles apply to larger tables, and we'll learn the details for larger tables in Chapter 15.

What follows is a brief discussion of the computation of the chi-square value. Don't worry too much about technical detail. Statistical software can be used to compute the chi-square statistic. You should, at this point, principally worry about the general ideas and how to use the computer output to decide whether you can declare statistical significance.

The first step in the calculation of a chi-square statistic is to determine a table of **expected counts.** These are the counts that would be expected to fall into the cells of the contingency table if there were no relationship between the two variables. They are found by making the row percents across columns equal for each row. To accomplish this, simply determine what percent of the total sample falls into each column, then split the total for each row into columns according to those same percents.

A table of expected counts has these two properties:

1. There is no association between the two variables. For instance, there are no differences between the conditional distributions in the rows (or columns) of a table of expected counts.
2. The expected counts in each row and column sum to the same totals as the observed numbers.

EXAMPLE 6.9
A Table of Expected Counts

Suppose that 90 men and 110 women are each asked about his or her handedness. Of the 200 total individuals, 20 are left-handed and 180 are right-handed. If gender and handedness are not related, what counts would we see in the cells of a contingency table? A strategy for determining these "expected counts" is to first calculate that $20/200 = 10\%$ of the overall sample is left-handed (falls into the first column), and to then make 10% of each gender be left-handed. The result is

	Left-handed	Right-handed	Total
Men	9 (10%)	81 (90%)	90
Women	11 (10%)	99 (90%)	110
Total	20 (10%)	180 (90%)	200

Keep in mind that these counts are what we would see if there were no relationship between gender and handedness. The row percents are the same for the two genders, and the total counts for each row and each column match the characteristics of the observed data. ◆

Calculating Expected Counts

 formula   The expected count for each cell can be calculated as

$$\frac{\text{Row total} \times \text{Column total}}{\text{Total } n \text{ for table}}$$

For example, in Example 6.9, the expected count for the number of women who are left-handed could be calculated as

$$\frac{110 \times 20}{200} = 11$$

Verifying Conditions for the Test

tech note   The method described in this section won't work if the sample is too small. Proceed as long as at least three of the four expected counts are 5 or more and all of them are 1 or more.

Calculating the Chi-square Statistic

The specific way in which the chi-square statistic (χ^2) measures the difference between the observed and expected counts is relatively simple:

◆ First, for each cell in the table, we compute

$$\frac{(\text{Observed count} - \text{Expected count})^2}{\text{Expected count}}$$

◆ Then, we total these quantities over all cells of the table:

$$\chi^2 = \text{Sum of } \frac{(\text{Observed count} - \text{Expected count})^2}{\text{Expected count}}$$

Step 3: The p-value of the Chi-square Test

Now we're faced with a bit of a mystery. A large chi-square value indicates a relationship, but how large should the value be in order for us to declare statistical significance? In practice, this question is transformed into a different but equivalent question, which is: If there is actually no relationship in the population, what is the likelihood that the chi-square statistic could be as large as it is or larger?

definition   The **p-value** for a chi-square test is computed by assuming the null hypothesis is true and then determining the likelihood of observing data that would produce a chi-square statistic as large as the one observed, or larger. It answers the question, "How likely is it that a relationship of the magnitude observed, or one even stronger, would occur in the sample if there is no relationship in the population?"

The p-value is used to decide if the relationship observed in the sample is statistically significant and can be inferred to hold in the population. The p-value will be part of the computer output provided by almost any statistical software. If you are computing the chi-square statistic "by hand" instead of using statistical software, you can use Excel to find the *p*-value; see the Excel Tip on page 188. If that isn't possible, you can still determine whether the result is statistically significant using a standard rule, but the reason it works will remain a mystery until you encounter it again in Chapter 15. The decision process is as follows.

Steps 4 and 5: Making and Reporting a Decision

Generally, a large chi-square statistic and subsequently small *p*-value provide evidence that a real relationship exists in the population. To determine whether to decide in favor of the alternative hypothesis, that a real relationship exists, we'll use the rule that most researchers commonly use:

◆ When the *p*-value is less than or equal to 0.05 (5%) we will assume that the observed relationship did not occur by chance. In that case, we *can* say that the relationship is statistically significant, and we reject the null hypothesis in favor of the alternative hypothesis. For a chi-square statistic based on a 2 × 2 contingency table, this is equivalent to finding a chi-square statistic of at least 3.84.

◆ When the *p*-value is greater than 0.05 (5%), we will say that the observed relationship could have occurred just by chance. In that case, we *cannot* say that the relationship is statistically significant, and we cannot reject the null hypothesis. For a chi-square statistic based on a 2 × 2 contingency table, this is equivalent to finding a chi-square statistic of less than 3.84.

EXAMPLE 6.10
Randomly Pick S or Q

Example 2.2 of Chapter 2 described an experiment in which 92 college students were given a form that read, "Randomly choose one of the letters *S* or *Q*." Of these 92 students, 66% (61/92) picked *S*. Another 98 students were given a form that read, "Randomly choose one of the letters *Q* or *S*." Of these students only 46% (45/98) picked *S*. Is this sufficient evidence to generalize that the order of the letters on the form and the response are related?

Figure 6.4 displays computer output for testing the significance of the relationship for this experiment. The output was produced using the Minitab com-

```
Expected counts are printed below observed counts

                  Letter Picked
Form          S            Q         Total
S first       61           31          92
            51.33        40.67

Q first       45           53          98
            54.67        43.33

  Total      106           84         190

Chi-Sq = 1.823 +  2.301 +
          1.712 +  2.160 = 7.995
DF = 1, P-Value = 0.005
```

FIGURE 6.4   **Minitab output for the *S* or *Q* experiment (Example 6.10)**

puter program. From the output, we learn that the *p*-value is 0.005. Because the *p*-value is less than 0.05, we can say that the relationship is statistically significant, and we reject the null hypothesis that there is no relationship. In other words, we infer that the observed result also holds in the population represented by these students.

Notice that the value of the chi-square statistic is 7.995. The *p*-value tells us that the chance is only 0.005 (which is 5 in 1000) that we would get a chi-square as large as 7.995 (or larger) if there really is no relationship between the order of the letters on the form and the letter that would be picked by people in this population. ◆

Minitab Tip

tech note   **Computing a Chi-square Test for a Two-Way Table**

◆ If the raw data are stored in columns of the worksheet, use **Stat>Tables>Cross Tabulation.** In the dialog box, specify the two columns of interest and also click on "Chi-square analysis."

◆ If the data are already summarized into counts, enter the table of counts into columns of the worksheet and then use **Stat>Tables>Chi-Square Test.** In the dialog box, specify the columns containing the counts.

Excel Tip

tech note   The *p*-value can also be computed using Microsoft Excel. The function CHIDIST(x,df) provides the *p*-value, where x is the value of the chi-square statistic and df is a number called "degrees of freedom," which will be explained later in this book. The formula for df is (#rows − 1)(#columns − 1). For instance, corresponding to the information in Figure 6.4, $x = 7.995$, df = $(2 − 1)(2 − 1) = 1$ and the *p*-value is CHIDIST(7.995,1) = 0.00469, or about 0.005 as given by Minitab. Excel will also calculate the *p*-value directly from the data using the function CHITEST, but unlike Minitab, the user must provide the expected counts as well as the observed counts. Use the command *CHITEST(array1,array2),* where the observed counts are in table format covered by the cells in *array1* and the expected counts are in *array2.* For example, if the observed counts are in a 2×2 table in the first four cells of a worksheet, *array1* would be given as A1:B2. Unlike Minitab and other statistical software, Excel gives only the *p*-value, and not the value of the chi-square statistic.

EXAMPLE 6.11
Breast Cancer Risk Stops Hormone Replacement Therapy Study

On July 17, 2002, the *Journal of the American Medical Association* published the results of a study that affected the lives of millions of women. The study was the first large randomized experiment to test the effects of combined estrogen and progestin, the most commonly prescribed hormone replacement therapy for postmenopausal women. The big news was that "On May 31, 2002, after a mean of 5.2 years of follow-up, the data and safety monitoring board recommended stopping the trial of estrogen plus progestin vs placebo because the test statistic for invasive breast cancer exceeded the stopping boundary for this adverse effect and the global index statistic supported risks exceeding benefits" (Writing Group for the Women's Health Initiative Investigators, 2002, p. 321).

TABLE 6.7 ■ **Results of a Randomized Experiment Comparing Hormone Therapy and Placebo**

	Invasive Breast Cancer?			Risk of Breast Cancer
	Yes	No	Total	
Hormones	166	8,340	8,506	.0195
Placebo	124	7,978	8,102	.0153
Total	290	16,318	16,608	.0175

The study measured several medical outcomes, but the two that received the most attention were breast cancer and coronary heart disease. Table 6.7 shows the results for breast cancer; results for coronary heart disease are given in the exercises. Is there a statistically significant effect of the hormone treatment on breast cancer?

Step 1: The Hypotheses

Null hypothesis: Occurrence of breast cancer is unrelated to hormone therapy.

Alternative hypothesis: Occurrence of breast cancer is related to hormone therapy.

Steps 2 and 3: The Conditions and Test Statistic

The expected count for the "Hormones, Yes" cell is $[(8,506)(290)]/16,608 = 148.53$. The other expected counts can be found similarly, or they can be found by subtraction because the row and column totals are the same as they are for the observed counts. For instance, the expected count for the "Hormones, No" cell is $290 - 148.53 = 141.47$. The sample size condition is met, since all expected counts exceed 5. The chi-square statistic is

$$\frac{(166-148.53)^2}{148.53} + \frac{(8340-8357.47)^2}{8357.47} + \frac{(124-141.47)^2}{141.47} + \frac{(7978-7960.53)^2}{7960.53} = 4.288$$

Steps 4 and 5: The p-value and Decision in Context

Using Excel, the *p*-value is found as CHIDIST(4.288,1) = 0.038382, or about 0.04. Using the standard convention, the result is statistically significant because 0.04 < 0.05. In the context of the problem, this means that there is a statistically significant relationship between hormone therapy and occurrence of breast cancer *in the population similar to the women in this experiment.* Because the data are from a randomized experiment, it can be concluded that hormone therapy *causes* a change in the incidence of breast cancer. It was for this reason that the study was terminated early. ◆

Factors That Affect Statistical Significance

In general, whether or not we can infer that an observed relationship represents a "real" relationship depends on two factors:

- ◆ the strength of the observed relationship
- ◆ how many people were studied

For 2×2 tables, the strength of the relationship can be measured by the difference between the two categories of the explanatory variable with respect to the percent falling into a particular category of the response variable. For instance, in Example 6.10, we saw that 66% of those with the "*S* or *Q*" order picked *S*, while only 46% of those with the "*Q* or *S*" form picked *S*. The difference between these two percents reflects the strength of the observed relationship between the order of the letters on the form and letter choice.

The sample size of a study also affects the significance of the results. Imagine, for example, that a psychiatric researcher compares the effectiveness of two treatments for depression by conducting a randomized experiment in which only ten patients receive each treatment. The results are that after three months, eight of the ten patients using treatment A show improvement, but among those who used treatment B, only five of ten patients show improvement. Although the difference between the percentages showing improvement is large (80% − 50%), the study is too small to safely infer that treatment A is the better treatment for the larger population of patients. The chi-square statistic and *p*-value would be 1.978 and 0.16. On the other hand, if 100 patients were in each treatment group and the same percents were observed (80% and 50%), the chi-square statistic would be 19.78 and the *p*-value would be 8.7×10^{-8}. We would almost certainly believe that treatment A was really better than treatment B in that case.

Practical Versus Statistical Significance

Statistical significance does not mean the two variables have a relationship that you would necessarily consider to be of *practical* importance. A table based on a very large number of observations will have little trouble achieving the status of statistical significance even if the relationship between the two variables in the population is only minor.

On the other hand, an interesting relationship in a population may fail to achieve statistical significance if there are only a few observations in the sample. Whenever a study "fails to find a relationship" between two variables, it does not necessarily mean that a relationship was not observed or does not exist in the population. It means that whatever relationship was observed in the sample did not achieve statistical significance. It is hard to rule out chance unless you have either a very strong relationship or a sufficiently large sample.

In the following example, you will see that with a large sample size, a relatively small arithmetic difference can be statistically significant. Remember that "statistical significance" means that we are convinced that a real relationship exists in the larger population represented by the sample. It makes sense that if we have a very large sample and it is exhibiting a relationship, we would be more convinced that it is real than we would be if a very small sample exhibited that same relationship.

EXAMPLE 6.12
Aspirin and Heart Attacks

In Case Study 1.6, the possible categories for the explanatory and response variables were

Explanatory variable = took placebo or took aspirin
Response variable = heart attack or no heart attack

```
Expected counts are printed below observed counts

              Heart Attack?
            Yes        No      Total
Aspirin     104      10933     11037
          146.52   10890.48

Placebo     189      10845     11034
          146.48   10887.52

Total       293      21778     22071

Chi-Sq = 12.339 + 0.166 +
         12.343 + 0.166 = 25.014
DF = 1, P-Value = 0.000
```

FIGURE 6.5   **Minitab output for aspirin study (Example 6.12)**

Figure 6.5 shows the results of asking the Minitab program to compute the chi-square statistic. We see that the p-value is 0.000, so we can declare statistical significance. This p-value tells us that there is almost no chance that we could observe such a strong relationship if there is really no difference between the effects of aspirin and placebo.

Because the p-value is less than 0.05, we can reject the null hypothesis of no relationship. Among those in the placebo group, 189/11,034 = 1.71% had a heart attack during the study period, while among those in the aspirin group, 104/11,037 = 0.94% had a heart attack. The difference has practical importance because the percent decrease in risk for those taking aspirin is (1.71 − 0.94)/1.71 = 45%. However, the arithmetic difference in the percent experiencing a heart attack is 1.71% − 0.94% = 0.77%, or less than 1%. If a smaller study had been done, the researchers may not have been able to declare statistical significance, but since they used a sample with over 22,000 participants they were able to detect this important relationship. ◆

Interpreting a Nonsignificant Result

When we cannot claim statistical significance, we have to be careful about how we state the conclusion. The correct interpretation of a **nonsignificant result** is that the sample results are not strong enough to safely conclude that there is a relationship in the population. A p-value that's too large for us to declare significance simply means that the observed relationship could have resulted by chance, even if there is no relationship in the population. This is not the same as saying that we believe there is no relationship.

In the following case study, the difference between the relevant conditional percentages is larger than the difference we saw in the aspirin example. The result of the chi-square test, however, will be that we cannot declare statistical significance. You will see that the sample size for the case study is much smaller than the sample size for the aspirin study. Remember that the sample size affects our ability to declare significance.

CASE STUDY 6.1
Drinking, Driving, and the Supreme Court

In the early 1970s a young man challenged an Oklahoma State law that prohibited the sale of 3.2% beer to males under 21 but allowed its sale to females in the same age group. The case (*Craig* v. *Boren*, 429 U.S. 190, 1976) was ultimately heard by the U.S. Supreme Court.

Laws are allowed to use gender-based differences as long as they "serve important governmental objectives" and "are substantially related to the achievement of these objectives" (Gastwirth, 1988, p. 524). The defense argued that traffic safety was an important governmental objective and that data clearly show that young males are more likely to have alcohol-related accidents than young females.

The Supreme Court examined evidence from a "random roadside survey" that measured information on age, gender, and whether or not the driver had been drinking alcohol in the previous two hours. Although the survey was called a "random" survey of drivers, it probably was not. In roadside surveys, police tend to stop all drivers at certain locations at the time of the survey. This procedure does not really provide a random sampling of drivers in an area, but we'll treat it as though it does. Table 6.8 gives the results of the roadside survey for the drivers under 20 years of age.

TABLE 6.8 ■ **Results of Roadside Survey for Young Drivers**

	Drank Alcohol in Last Two Hours?			
	Yes	*No*	*Total*	*Percent Who Drank*
Males	77	404	481	16.0%
Females	16	122	138	11.6%
Total	93	526	619	15.0%

Source: Gastwirth, 1988, p. 526.

Notice that the percentage of young men who had been drinking alcohol is slightly higher than the percentage of young women. The difference is 16% − 11.6% = 4.4%. However, we cannot rule out chance as a reasonable explanation for this difference. In other words, if there really is no difference between the percents of young male and female drivers in the population who drink and drive, we could possibly see a difference as large as the one observed in a sample of this size.

In Figure 6.6, we present the results of asking the Minitab program to compute the chi-square statistic for this example. The chi-square summary statistic is 1.637, and the *p*-value for this statistic is 0.201. This *p*-value tells us that if there's really no association in the population (the null hypothesis), there's about a 20% chance that the sample would have a chi-square statistic as large as 1.637, or larger. In other words, the observed relationship could easily have occurred even if there is no relationship in the population represented by the sample.

The Supreme Court overturned the law, concluding that "the showing offered by the appellees does not satisfy us that sex represents a legitimate, accurate proxy for the regulation of drinking and driving" (Gastwirth, 1988, p. 527). Based on the chi-square analysis, you can see why the Supreme Court was reluctant to conclude that the difference in the sample represented sufficient evidence for a real difference in the population.

Expected counts are printed below observed counts

		Drank in Last 2 Hours?		
	Yes	No	Total	
Males	77	404	481	
	72.27	408.73		
Females	16	122	138	
	20.73	117.27		
Total	93	526	619	

Chi-Sq = 0.310 + 0.055 +
         1.081 + 0.191 = 1.637
DF = 1, P-Value = 0.201

FIGURE 6.6   Minitab output for Case Study 6.1

KEY TERMS

Section 6.1
contingency table, 172
two-way table, 172
cell, 172
conditional percents, 172
row percents, 172
column percents, 172

Section 6.2
risk, 175
relative risk, 175

baseline risk, 175
percent increase in risk, 176
odds, 176
odds ratio, 176

Section 6.4
Simpson's Paradox, 182

Section 6.5
statistically significant relationship, 184

statistical significance, 184
null hypothesis, 185
alternative hypothesis, 185
chi-square statistic, 185
observed counts, 185
expected counts, 185, 186
p-value, 186
practical significance, 190
nonsignificant result, 191

EXERCISES   Blue = Basics   **Bold, Bold** = Answer in back

Section 6.1

6.1 Each fall, auditions for the band and orchestra are held at a large university. Last fall, the numbers of males and females in each class who auditioned were

Class	Female	Male	Total
Freshman	170	100	270
Sophomore	50	50	100
Junior	60	20	80
Senior	20	30	50
Total	300	200	500

a. Calculate the row percent for freshman females and explain what it means.

b. Calculate the column percent for freshman females and explain what it means.

c. Which class had the highest percentage of female applicants? Support your answer with numbers.

d. Which gender had a higher percentage of sophomore applicants? Support your answer with numbers.

6.2 Anton and Edward often play a game together, so they decide to see if who goes first affects who wins. They keep track of 50 games, with each going first 25 times. Of the 25 times Anton went first, he won 15 times. Of the 25 times Edward went first, he won 12 times. In constructing a contingency table for these results, the two variables are "Who went first" and "Did the person who went first win?"

a. What are the categories for each of the two variables?

b. If the explanatory variable is used to define the rows of the contingency table, which variable would be the row variable?

c. Construct a contingency table for the results.

d. Overall, what percent of the games were won by the person who went first?

e. Is there an advantage to going first? Explain.

6.3 For each pair of variables, indicate whether or not a two-way table would be appropriate for summarizing the relationship. In each case, briefly explain why or why not.

a. Political party (Republican, Democrat, etc.) and opinion about new gun control law.

b. Age group (under 20, 21–29, etc.) and rating of a song on 1 to 5 scale (1 = hate it, 5 = love it).

c. Weight (pounds) and height (inches).

d. Gender and opinion about capital punishment.

e. Head circumference (centimeters) and gender.

6.4 Suppose a study on the relationship between gender and political party included 200 men and 200 women and found 180 Democrats and 220 Republicans. Is that information sufficient for you to construct a contingency table for the study? If so, construct the table. If not, explain why not.

6.5 Students in a class were asked whether they preferred an in-class or a take-home final exam and were then categorized as to whether or not they had received an A on the in-class midterm. Of the 25 A students, 10 preferred a take-home exam, while of the 50 non-A students, 30 preferred a take-home exam.

a. Display the data in a contingency table.

b. In the relationship between grade on the midterm and opinion about type of final, which variable is the response variable and which is the explanatory variable?

c. Determine an appropriate set of conditional percents for determining if there is a relationship between grade on the midterm and opinion about the type of final. Based on these percents, does it appear that there is a relationship? Why or why not?

6.6 Do grumpy old men have a greater risk of having coronary heart disease than men who aren't so grumpy? Harvard Medical School researchers examined this question in a prospective observational study reported in the November 1996 issue of *Circulation* (Kawachi et al., 1994). For seven years, the researchers studied men between the ages of 46 and 90 years old. All study participants completed a survey of anger symptoms at the beginning of the study period. Among 199 men who had no anger symptoms, there were 8 cases of coronary heart disease. Among 559 men who had the most anger symptoms, there were 59 cases of coronary heart disease.

a. Construct a contingency table for the relationship

between degree of anger and the incidence of heart disease.

b. Among those with no anger symptoms, what percent had coronary heart disease?

c. Among those with the most anger symptoms, what percent had coronary heart disease?

d. Draw a bar graph of these data. Based on this graph, does there appear to be an association between anger and the risk of coronary heart disease? Explain.

6.7 In a class survey, Penn State statistics students were asked, "Regarding your weight, do you think you are: About right? Overweight? Underweight?" The following table displays the results by sex:

Gender and Perception of Weight

	Perception of Weight			
Sex	*About Right*	*Overweight*	*Underweight*	*Total*
Female	87	39	3	129
Male	64	3	16	83
Total	151	42	19	212

Source: The authors.

a. Write a sentence that explains what would be measured by the row percents for this table. Make your answer specific to this situation.

b. Determine the row percents.

c. Draw a bar graph of the row percents.

d. Briefly describe how males and females differ in their perceptions of weight.

e. An important objective of statistics is the use of sample information to make generalizations about a larger population. What population do you think is represented by this sample?

6.8 Refer back to Example 6.1 about smoking and divorce.

a. Figure 6.1 is a bar graph of the observed counts. Draw a bar graph of the row percents. Does this graph confirm the relationship? Explain.

b. Among those who were ever divorced, what percent smoke?

c. Among those who were never divorced, what percent smoke?

d. What percent of all respondents in the table have ever been divorced?

6.9 In a case-control study done in England, Voss and Mulligan (2000) collected data on height (short or not) and whether or not the student had ever been bullied in school for 209 secondary school students. The following table displays a contingency table of the data. A student was categorized as short if he or she was below the third percentile for height upon school entry, but because this was a case-control study, short people (cases) constitute almost half of the sample.

Height and Bullying in School

	Ever Bullied		
Height	*Yes*	*No*	*Total*
Short	42	50	92
Not Short	30	87	117
Total	72	137	209

a. Among students in the "short" category, what percent have ever been bullied?

b. Among students in the "not short" category, what percent have ever been bullied?

c. Is there a relationship between height and the likelihood of having been bullied? Briefly justify your answer.

Sections 6.2 and 6.3

6.10 For each of the following measures, give the value that implies no difference between the two groups being compared.

a. Relative risk.

b. Odds ratio.

c. Percent increase in risk.

For Exercises 6.11 to 6.14: A study is done to compare side effects for those taking a drug versus those taking a placebo. One hundred people are given the drug and 100 are given the placebo. Results are as shown in the following table.

	Headache?		**Nausea?**		**Insomnia?**	
	Yes	*No*	*Yes*	*No*	*Yes*	*No*
Drug	10	90	15	85	6	94
Placebo	5	95	5	95	4	96

6.11 For each of the following side effects, compute the risk of the side effect when taking the drug.

a. Headache.

b. Nausea.

c. Insomnia.

6.12 For each of the following side effects, compute the relative risk of the side effect when taking the drug compared to when taking the placebo.

a. Headache.

b. Nausea.

c. Insomnia.

6.13 For each of the following side effects, compute the odds ratio for the side effect for those taking the drug compared to those taking the placebo.

a. Headache.

b. Nausea.

c. Insomnia.

6.14 For each of the following side effects, compute the percent increase (or decrease) in risk of side effect for those taking the drug compared to those taking the placebo.

a. Headache.

b. Nausea.

c. Insomnia.

6.15 If the baseline risk of a certain disease for nonsmokers is 1% and the relative risk of the disease is 5 for smokers compared to nonsmokers, what is the risk of the disease for smokers?

6.16 For a relative risk of 2.1, what is the percent increase in risk?

6.17 For an increase in risk of 40%, what is the relative risk?

6.18 The relative risk of contracting a certain coronary disease is 2.0 for male smokers compared to male nonsmokers and 3.0 for female smokers compared to female nonsmokers. Is this enough information to determine whether male smokers or female smokers are more likely to contract the disease? If so, make that determination. If not, explain what additional information would be needed to make that determination.

6.19 *Science News* (Feb. 25, 1995, p. 124) reported a study of 232 people, aged 55 or over, who had heart surgery. The patients were asked whether their religious beliefs give them feelings of strength and comfort and whether they regularly participate in social activities. Of those who said yes to both, about 1 in 50 died within six months after their operation. Of those who said no to both, about 1 in 5 died within six months after their operation. What is the relative risk of death (within six months) for the two groups? Write your answer in a sentence or two that would be understood by someone with no training in statistics.

6.20 Refer back to exercise 6.6 about anger symptoms and the incidence of heart disease.
  a. For those with the most anger symptoms, what is the relative risk of heart disease (compared to those with no anger symptoms)?
  b. For those with the most anger symptoms, what is the percent increase in the risk of heart disease?

6.21 Refer back to exercise 6.9 about height and the risk of being bullied.
  a. For each height category, calculate the risk of having been bullied.
  b. What is the relative risk for short students of having been bullied? Write a sentence that interprets this relative risk.
  c. What is the increased risk of having been bullied for short students? Write a sentence that interprets this increased risk.
  d. Calculate the odds ratio that compares the odds of having been bullied for the short students to the odds for students who are not short. Write a sentence that interprets this ratio.

6.22 Using the terminology of this chapter, what name applies to each of the boldface numbers in the following quotes (e.g., odds, risk, relative risk)?
  a. "Fontham found increased risks of lung cancer with increasing exposure to secondhand smoke, whether it took place at home, at work, or in a social setting. A spouse's smoking alone produced an overall **30** percent increase in lung-cancer risk" (*Consumer Reports,* Jan. 1995, p. 28).
  b. "What they found was that women who smoked had a risk [of getting lung cancer] **27.9** times as great as nonsmoking women; in contrast, the risk for men who smoked regularly was only **9.6** times greater than that for male nonsmokers" (Taubes, 1993, p. 1375).
  c. "**One student in five** reports abandoning safe-sex practices when drunk" (*Newsweek,* Dec. 19, 1994, p. 73).

6.23 The Roper Organization (1992) conducted a study as part of a larger survey to ascertain the number of American adults who had experienced phenomena such as seeing a ghost, "feeling as if you left your body," and seeing a UFO. A representative sample of adults (18 and over) in the continental United States were interviewed in their homes during July, August, and September 1991. The results when respondents were asked about seeing a ghost are shown in the following table.

	Reportedly Has Seen a Ghost		
	Yes	*No*	*Total*
Aged 18 to 29	212	1313	1525
Aged 30 or over	465	3912	4377
Total	677	5225	5902

Data Source: The Roper Organization (1992), *Unusual Personal Experiences,* Las Vegas: Bigelow Holding Corp., p. 35.

  a. In each age group, find the percent who reported seeing a ghost.
  b. What is the *relative risk* of reportedly seeing a ghost for one group compared to the other? Write your answer in the form of a sentence that could be understood by someone who knows nothing about statistics.
  c. Repeat part (b) using *increased risk* instead of relative risk.
  d. What are the odds of reportedly seeing a ghost to not seeing one in the older group?

6.24 Suppose a newspaper article states that drinking three or more cups of coffee per day doubles the risk of gall bladder cancer. Before giving up coffee, what questions should be asked by a person who drinks this much coffee?

Section 6.4

6.25 Refer to Case Study 1.5, "Does Prayer Lower Blood Pressure?" One of the results quoted in that study was, "People who attended a religious service once a week and prayed or studied the Bible once a day were 40% less likely to have high blood pressure than those who don't go to church every week and prayed and studied the Bible less."
  a. What is the explanatory variable in this study?
  b. What is the response variable in this study?
  c. Give an example of a third variable that might at least partially account for the observed relationship.

6.26 Refer to the previous exercise, in which one or more third variables are at least partially likely to account for the observed relationship between religious activities and reduced incidence of high blood pressure. Is this an example of Simpson's Paradox? Explain.

6.27 This exercise presents a real example of Simpson's paradox (Wagner, 1982). The total income and total taxes paid in each of five income categories are given for two years, 1974 and 1978, in the following table.
  a. The "tax rate" for any income category is calculated as Tax divided by Income. Calculate the tax rates for each income bracket in each year.

	1974		**1978**	
Adjusted Gross Income	*Income*	*Tax*	*Income*	*Tax*
Under $5,000	41,651,643	2,244,467	19,879,622	689,318
$5,000 to $9,999	146,400,740	13,646,348	122,853,315	8,819,461
$10,000 to $14,999	192,688,922	21,449,597	171,858,024	17,155,758
$15,000 to $99,999	470,010,790	75,038,230	865,037,814	137,860,951
$100,000 or more	29,427,152	11,311,672	62,806,159	24,051,698
Total	880,179,247	123,690,314	1,242,434,934	188,577,186

b. Calculate the overall tax rate for each of the two years.

c. Did the tax rates within each income bracket increase or decrease from 1974 to 1978?

d. Did the overall tax rate increase or decrease from 1974 to 1978?

e. Compare your results in parts (c) and (d). Explain them in terms of Simpson's Paradox.

6.28 In a 1997 Marist College Institute for Public Opinion survey of 995 randomly selected Americans, 31% of the men and 12% of the women surveyed said they have dozed off while driving (*Source:* www.mipo.marist.edu). Think of a third variable that might at least partially explain the observed relationship between gender and dozing when driving. Briefly explain your answer.

6.29 Suppose two hospitals are willing to participate in an experiment to test a new treatment, and both hospitals agree to include 1100 patients in the study. Because the researchers conducting the experiment are on the staff of hospital A, they decide to perform the majority of cases with the new procedure. They randomly assign 1000 patients to the new treatment, with the remaining 100 receiving the standard treatment. Hospital B, which is a bit reluctant to try something new on too many patients, agrees to randomly assign 100 patients to the new treatment, leaving 1000 to receive the standard treatment. The following table displays the results.

Survival Rates for Standard and New Treatments at Two Hospitals

	Hospital A			Hospital B		
Treatment	*Survive*	*Die*	*Total*	*Survive*	*Die*	*Total*
Standard	5	95	100	500	500	1000
New	100	900	1000	95	5	100
Total	105	995	1100	595	505	1100

a. Which treatment was more successful in hospital A? Justify your answer with relevant percents.

b. Which treatment was more successful in hospital B? Justify your answer with relevant percents.

c. Combine the data from the two hospitals into a single contingency table that shows the relationship between treatment and outcome. Which treatment has the higher survival rate in this combined table? Justify your answer.

6.30 A researcher observes that, compared to students who do not procrastinate, students who admit to frequent procrastination are more likely to miss class due to illness. Does this mean that procrastinating increases illness? What is another explanation?

6.31 The success rates of two treatments (A and B) for clinical depression are being compared. The research team included five doctors, and the participants were 200 patients with depression. The doctors were supposed to randomly assign treatments to patients, but two doctors didn't do this. Instead, they often assigned more severely depressed patients to use treatment A and less severely depressed patients to use treatment B.

a. Three variables measured by the investigators were the outcome of treatment (successful or not), method

of treatment (A or B), and a rating of the initial severity of the depression (mild or severe). Which of these variables is the response variable in this investigation?

b. The doctors were surprised by the final result, which was that treatment B had a higher success rate than treatment A. Based on results attained by other investigators, they had expected the opposite to occur. Explain how the actions of the two doctors who did not always randomly assign treatments may have caused an unfair comparison of the two treatments.

c. Taking Example 6.8 into consideration, describe how the researchers might control for the effect of the initial severity of patient depression when they analyze the relationship between treatment method and outcome.

Section 6.5

6.32 The following 2 × 2 contingency table shows data for gender and opinion on the death penalty for respondents in the 1993 General Social Survey (**GSS-93** dataset on the CD for this text).

Opinion on Death Penalty

	Oppose	Favor	All
Male	113	535	648
Female	224	616	840
All	337	1151	1488

a. State null and alternative hypotheses about the relationship between the two variables.

b. Calculate the expected counts for a chi-square test.

6.33 The following 2 × 2 contingency table shows data for gender and opinion about the legalization of marijuana for respondents in the 1993 General Social Survey (**GSS-93** dataset on the CD for this text).

Opinion on Marijuana

	Don't Legalize	Legalize	All
Male	295	118	413
Female	475	116	591
All	770	234	1004

a. Verify that the value of the chi-square statistic is approximately 10.9.

b. The p-value is 0.001. Are the results statistically significant? Explain.

c. Write a conclusion in the context of the situation.

6.34 For each of the following results, explain what conclusion can be made about the null hypothesis that there is no relationship between two variables that form a 2 × 2 contingency table.

a. p-value = 0.001.

b. p-value = 0.101.

c. p-value = 0.900.

d. p-value = 0.049.

e. p-value = 0.755.

f. Chi-square statistic = 4.01.

g. Chi-square statistic = 2.98.

6.35 If a relationship is statistically significant, does that guarantee it also has practical significance? Explain.

6.36 If a relationship has practical significance, does it guarantee that statistical significance will be achieved in every study that examines it? Explain.

6.37 Explain whether each of the following is possible.

a. A relationship exists in the observed sample but not in the population from which the sample was drawn.

b. A relationship does not exist in the observed sample but does exist in the population from which the sample was drawn.

c. A relationship does not exist in the observed sample but an analysis of the sample shows that there is a statistically significant relationship, so it is inferred that there is a relationship in the population.

6.38 Refer back to exercise 6.23 in which data were presented for the relationship between age group and whether a person reports having ever seen a ghost (see table).

a. Write null and alternative hypotheses about the possible relationship between the two variables.

b. The Minitab output for a chi-square test of the relationship follows. Based on this output, what can be concluded about the relationship? What is the basis for this conclusion?

c. Notice in the Minitab output that the *p*-value is 0.001. Write a sentence that interprets this number.

```
Expected counts are printed below observed counts

              Yes        No       Total
18-29         212       1313       1525
            174.93    1350.07

30+           465       3912       4377
            502.07    3874.93

Total         677       5225       5902

Chi-Sq = 7.857 + 1.018 +
         2.737 + 0.355 = 11.967
DF = 1, P-Value = 0.001
```

6.39 Refer to the Minitab output for the previous exercise.

a. Demonstrate how the *expected count* was computed for the "age 18–29 yes" cell of the table.

b. Verify that the expected count for the "age 30+ yes" cell can be determined by subtracting the answer for part (a) from the total count for the "yes" column of the table.

c. In each row of the table, express the *expected count* for yes as a percent of the total count for that row. How do these two percents compare to each other?

6.40 Imagine that 50 men and 50 women are asked, "Do you favor or oppose capital punishment for those convicted of murder?" In the observed data, $38/50 = 76\%$ of the men favor capital punishment compared to $32/50 = 64\%$ of the women.

a. Write null and alternative hypotheses about the possible relationship between gender and opinion about capital punishment.

b. A chi-square test of the statistical significance of the relationship has a *p*-value of 0.19. Is this evidence that there is or is not a relationship? What is the justification for this conclusion?

6.41 Refer to the previous exercise about the relationship between gender and opinion about capital punishment.

a. Calculate the value of the chi-square statistic.

b. In the previous exercise, the *p*-value was given as 0.19. Write a sentence that interprets this number.

c. Suppose that 500 men and 500 women had been surveyed, rather than 50 of each sex. Further suppose that the proportions in favor of capital punishment remained the same, at 380/500 or 76% of the men and 320/500 or 64% of the women. Calculate the chi-square statistic in this case.

d. The *p*-value for the chi-square statistic in part (c) is 0.000035. Is this evidence that there is a relationship between gender and opinion about capital punishment?

e. Explain the reason for the discrepancy between the result in exercise 6.40b and the result in part (d) of this exercise .

6.42 Considering the effect of sample size on the chi-square test, explain why a finding that a relationship is "not statistically significant" should not be interpreted as absolute proof that there is no relationship in the population.

6.43 Refer to Example 6.11, in which a statistically significant relationship was found between hormone therapy and invasive breast cancer. In the same study, the following observed counts were found for death from coronary heart disease (CHD). Carry out the five steps leading to a conclusion about whether there is a statistically significant relationship between hormone therapy and death from CHD.

	Death from CHD?		
	Yes	*No*	*Total*
Hormones	33	8473	8506
Placebo	26	8076	8102
Total	59	16,549	16,608

Chapter Exercises

6.44 Wechsler and Kuo (2000) used data from the 1999 College Alcohol Study to examine the relationship between student alcohol use and student definitions of binge drinking. In the study, approximately 14,000 college students from 119 schools answered questions about drinking habits. Using the definition that binge drinking is five consecutive drinks for men and four consecutive drinks for women, the researchers categorized students into four "type of drinker" categories based on their answers to questions about personal alcohol use. Students in the survey were also asked how many drinks in a row they thought constituted binge drinking for men and for women. The following is a contingency table showing the relationship between the student definitions of binge drinking for a man and student alcohol use:

Type of Drinker and Personal Definition of Binge Drinking

Type of Drinker	Definition of Binge Drinking for Men (Drinks in a Row)				
	≤4	5	6	≥7	Total
Abstainer	814	659	484	702	2659
Nonbinge	714	1129	997	2223	5063
Occasional Binge	231	471	480	1780	2962
Frequent Binge	179	442	367	2147	3135
Total	1938	2701	2328	6852	13,819

a. Among all students, what percent defined binge drinking for men as being seven or more drinks in a row?

b. Write a sentence describing what would be measured by row percents in the table. Make your answer specific to these variables.

c. Write a sentence describing what would be measured by column percents in this table. Make your answer specific to these variables.

d. Calculate the row percents in the table. In a few sentences, describe the relationship between type of drinker and the personal definition of drinking.

6.45 Example 6.2 presented data on how many college men have ear pierces and tattoos. The following table contains data on ear pierces and tattoos for a sample of 678 college women. The ear pierce response is the total number of ear pierces for a woman, and this has been categorized.

**Ear Pierces and Tattoos,
678 College Women**

Pierces	No Tattoo	Have Tattoo
2 or less	245	19
3 or 4	210	26
5 or 6	91	32
7 or more	25	30

Data Source: One of the authors.

a. For each ear-pierce category, determine the percent with a tattoo. Based on these percents, would you say there is a relationship between these two variables? Explain.

b. Draw a bar graph of the column percents. What does the graph show us about the relationship between having a tattoo and the number of ear pierces?

c. Calculate the percent with at least five ear pierces for women who have a tattoo, and separately for women who don't have a tattoo.

d. What percent of the total sample has a tattoo?

e. What percent of the total has two or fewer ear pierces and also does not have a tattoo?

6.46 Refer back to Example 6.2.

a. Redraw the bar chart in Figure 6.2 using counts rather than percents. What features of the data does this plot reveal that are not revealed by Figure 6.2?

b. Briefly explain what would be measured by the row percents for the data in Table 6.2.

6.47 In a retrospective observational study, researchers asked women who were pregnant with planned pregnancies how long it took them to get pregnant (Baird and Wilcox,

1985; see also Weiden and Gladen, 1986). Length of time to pregnancy was measured according to the number of cycles between stopping birth control and getting pregnant. Women were also categorized on whether or not they smoked, with smoking defined as having at least one cigarette per day for at least the first cycle during which they were trying to get pregnant. The following table summarizes the observed counts.

**Time to Pregnancy for Smokers
and Nonsmokers**

	Pregnancy Occurred After	
	First Cycle	Two or More Cycles
Smoker	29	71
Nonsmoker	198	288

a. Among smokers, what percent was pregnant after the first cycle?

b. Among nonsmokers, what percent was pregnant after the first cycle?

c. Draw a bar graph that can be used to examine the relationship between smoking and how long it took to get pregnant.

d. Among those who were pregnant after the first cycle, what percent smoked?

e. Among those who took two or more cycles to become pregnant, what percent smoked?

f. Do you think there is a relationship between smoking and how long it takes to get pregnant? Explain.

6.48 In the 1996 General Social Survey, religious preference and opinion about when premarital sex might be wrong were among the measured variables. The contingency table of counts for these variables is shown in the following table.

Religious Preference and Opinion about Premarital Sex

Religion	When Is Premarital Sex Wrong?				
	Always	Almost Always	Sometimes	Never	Total
Protestant	355	117	227	384	1083
Catholic	62	37	120	226	445
Jewish	0	3	14	34	51
None	20	13	45	147	225
Other	15	13	23	40	91
Total	452	183	429	831	1895

Source: SDA archive at csa.berkely.edu:7502.

a. For each religious preference category, determine the percent of respondents who think premarital sex is always wrong.

b. Do the percents computed in part (a) indicate that there is a relationship between the two variables? Briefly explain why or why not.

6.49 A case-control study in Berlin, reported by Kohlmeier, Arminger, Bartolomeycik, Bellach, Rehm, and Thamm (1992) and by Hand et al. (1994), asked 239 lung-cancer patients and 429 controls (matched to the cases by age and sex) whether or not they had kept a pet bird during adulthood. Of the 239 lung-cancer cases, 98 said yes. Of the 429 controls, 101 said yes.

  a. Construct a contingency table for the data.

  b. Compute the risk of lung cancer for bird owners and for those who had never kept a bird.

  c. Can the risks computed in part (b) be used as baseline risks for the populations of those who have and have not owned birds? Explain.

  d. What is the relative risk of lung cancer for bird owners?

  e. What additional information about the risk of lung cancer would you want before you made a decision about whether or not to own a pet bird?

  f. Can these data be used to establish a causal connection between owning a bird and the risk of lung cancer? Explain.

  g. For any study of lung cancer, the effect of smoking should be considered. How would you determine if smoking might be a confounding variable in this study?

6.50 Compute the chi-square statistic and assess the statistical significance for the relationship between bird ownership and lung cancer, based on the data in the previous exercise. State a conclusion about the relationship.

6.51 Pagano and Gauvreau (1993, p. 133) reported data for women participating in the first National Health and Nutrition Examination Survey (Carter, Jones, Schatzkin, and Brinton, 1989). The explanatory variable was whether or not the woman gave birth to her first child at the age of 25 or older, and the outcome variable was whether or not she developed breast cancer. Observed counts are in the following table.

Age at Birth of First Child and Breast Cancer

Age at First Child	Breast Cancer	No Breast Cancer	Total
25 or Older	31	1597	1628
Under 25	65	4475	4540
Total	96	6072	6168

Source: Pagano and Gauvreau (1993).

  a. Calculate the risk of breast cancer for women who were under 25 years old when they had their first child.

  b. Calculate the risk of breast cancer for women who were 25 or older when they had their first child.

  c. Calculate the relative risk of breast cancer for women who were 25 or older when they had their first child compared with women who were under 25. Write a sentence that interprets this relative risk in the context of this problem.

  d. What is the percent increase in the risk of breast cancer for women who were 25 or older when they had their first child?

  e. Can these data be used as evidence of a causal connection between age at first child and the risk of breast cancer? Explain.

6.52 Refer to Example 6.11, in which a statistically significant relationship was found between hormone therapy and invasive breast cancer. There were 166 cases of invasive breast cancer out of 8506 women taking hormones and 124 cases of invasive breast cancer out of 8102 women taking placebo.

  a. What is the relative risk of invasive breast cancer when taking hormones compared with taking placebo?

  b. What is the baseline risk of invasive breast cancer, assuming that the placebo group is representative of the relevant population of women?

  c. Explain why it is important to report the baseline risk found in part (b) when reporting the relative risk found in part (a).

6.53 A well-known example of Simpson's Paradox, published by Bickel, Hammel, and O'Connell (1975), examined admission rates for men and women who had applied to graduate programs at the University of California at Berkeley. The actual breakdown of data for specific programs is confidential, but the point can be made with similar, hypothetical numbers. For simplicity, we will assume there are only two graduate programs. The figures for acceptance to each program are shown in the following table.

Data for Exercise 6.31

	Program A		Program B	
	Admit	Deny	Admit	Deny
Men	400	250	50	300
Women	50	25	125	300

  a. Combine the data for the two programs into one table. What percent of all men who applied was admitted? What percent of all women who applied was admitted? Which sex was more successful in the admissions process?

  b. What percent of the men who applied did program A admit? What percent of the women who applied did program A admit? Repeat the question for program B. Which sex was more successful in getting admitted to program A? program B?

  c. Explain how this problem is an example of Simpson's Paradox. Provide a potential explanation for the observed figures by guessing what type of programs A and B might have been.

6.54 Compute the chi-square statistic and assess the statistical significance for the relationship between smoking and time to pregnancy in exercise 6.47. State a conclusion about the relationship.

6.55 Refer to Example 6.11, in which a statistically significant relationship was found between hormone therapy and invasive breast cancer. One of the results reported in the paper was "Absolute excess risks per 10,000 person-years attributable to estrogen plus progestin were . . . 8 more invasive breast cancers" (Writing Group for the Women's Health Initiative Investigators, p. 321). In other words, for every 10,000 "person-years" of women taking the hormones instead of a placebo, there would be 8 additional cases of invasive breast cancer. Discuss practical versus statistical significance in this situation.

6.56 Exercise 6.6 concerned the relationship between anger and the risk of heart disease. Some computer output for a chi-square test is shown below. What do the results indicate about the relationship? Explain.

```
Expected counts are printed below observed counts

                      Heart Disease
                   Yes          No
   No Anger          8          191        199
                   17.59       181.41

   Most Anger       59          500        559
                   49.41       509.57

   Total            67          691        758

Chi-Sq = 5.228 +  0.507 +
           1.861 + 0.180 = 7.777
DF = 1, P-Value = 0.0005
```

6.57 Refer to the data in the previous exercise, showing the frequency of heart disease for men with no anger and men with the most anger. Show how the numbers in the following statement were calculated: The odds of remaining free of heart disease versus getting heart disease are about 24 to 1 for men with no anger, whereas those odds are only about 8.5 to 1 for men with the most anger.

6.58 Refer to the previous two exercises. Find the odds ratio for remaining free of heart disease for men with no anger compared with men with the most anger. Give the result in a sentence that someone with no training in statistics would understand.

6.59 "Saliva test predicts labor onset" was the headline of a Reuters Health story that appeared May 23, 2000 at the Yahoo Health News website, and the story described a medical test called SalEst. A positive SalEst test indicates an elevated estrogen level, and this knowledge may help predict how soon a pregnant woman will give birth because estrogen level increases in the 2 to 3 weeks before delivery. Researchers employed by the manufacturers of SalEst tested 642 women who had been pregnant for 39 weeks. Among the 615 women who delivered before the 42nd week of the pregnancy, about 59% had a positive SalEst test. Among the 27 women who delivered in the 42nd week or later, 33% had a positive SalEst test.
  a. Construct a contingency table of counts for the relationship between the SalEst test result and the time of delivery.
  b. Which of the two variables used to make the contingency table is the explanatory variable and which is the response variable?
  c. Among all 642 women, what percent delivered before 42 weeks?
  d. The article states that if a test result is positive, there is a 98% chance the woman will deliver before 42 weeks. Based on the contingency table, justify this claim.
  e. Among those who had a negative test, what percent delivered before 42 weeks?
  f. Would you advise a pregnant woman to spend $90 for the test? Explain why or why not.

6.60 According to a study on partner abuse reported by the *Sacramento Bee* (July 14, 2000, p. A6, Associated Press), 25% of women with male partners had been assaulted by their current or a former partner, whereas 11% of women with female partners had been assaulted. What is the rel-

ative risk of assault for women with male partners compared to women with female partners? Write your answer in a sentence that would be understood by someone with no training in statistics.

6.61 In exercise 6.53 data were given for admissions to two graduate programs for men and women. The data are given again here for use in this exercise, with the combined data presented as well.

	Program A		Program B		Combined	
	Admit	Deny	Admit	Deny	Admit	Deny
Men	400	250	50	300	450	550
Women	50	25	125	300	175	325

  a. Give the odds of being admitted versus being denied to program A separately for men and women. Then give the odds ratio for women compared to men. Write a sentence explaining the odds ratio in words.
  b. Give the odds of being admitted versus being denied for the combined programs separately for men and women. Then give the odds ratio for women compared to men. Write a sentence explaining the odds ratio in words.
  c. Using the results from parts (a) and (b), write one sentence that sounds as if the university favors women applicants and another sentence that sounds as if the university favors male applicants.

Dataset Exercises

6.62 Use the dataset **UCDavis2** for this exercise. The variable *WtFeel* contains UC Davis student responses to the question, "Do you think you are: Underweight? About Right? Overweight?"
  a. Create a contingency table for the relationship between *sex* (female or male) and perception of weight (*WtFeel*).
  b. For each sex category, calculate the conditional percents for the perception of weight variable. Of the men, what percent thinks they are underweight? Of the women, what percent thinks they are underweight?
  c. In Section 6.5, the chi-square test was only used for 2 × 2 tables, but it can be used for larger tables as well. Use software to do a chi-square test of statistical significance for the relationship between sex and perception of weight. What is the *p*-value of the test? Based on this *p*-value, what conclusion can be made about the relationship?
  d. Penn State student responses to essentially the same question are summarized in exercise 6.7 (see table). Do the Penn State and UC Davis students differ in how they respond to the question about weight? If so, describe the differences.

6.63 Use the **UCDavis2** dataset for this exercise. The variable *Cheat* contains answers to a question about whether the respondent would tell the instructor if he or she saw another student cheating on an examination.
  a. Create a two-way table for the relationship between *sex* (male or female) and the variable *Cheat.* Of all stu-

dents, what percent said they would tell the instructor about witnessing cheating?

b. Of the females, what percent said they would tell the instructor about witnessing cheating? What percent of the males said they would do this?

c. Is the observed relationship between sex and response to the cheating question statistically significant? Justify your answer by reporting the results of a chi-square test.

d. For this question about cheating, what population do you think is represented by the students in the data set?

6.64 Use the **GSS-93** dataset for this exercise. The variable *gunlaw* has responses to a question about whether the respondent would favor a law requiring a police permit to be obtained before the purchase of any gun. The variable *owngun* indicates whether or not there are any guns in the respondent's home (including garages and sheds).

a. Write null and alternative hypotheses about the possible relationship between *owngun* and *gunlaw*.

b. Create a two-way table that summarizes the relationship between *owngun* and *gunlaw*. What percent of all respondents had a gun in their home?

c. Among those with a gun in their home, what percent favors a gun permit law? Among those with no gun in their home, what percent favors a gun permit law? Based on the difference between these two percents, would you say there is a relationship between the two variables? Why or why not?

d. What is the *p*-value of a chi-square test of statistical significance for the relationship between *owngun* and *gunlaw*? Is the observed relationship statistically significant?

e. Explain what it means to say that an observed relationship is statistically significant.

6.65 Use the dataset **GSS-93** for this exercise. Write a paragraph that describes the relationship between *race* (respondent's race) and *cappun* (opinion about capital punishment). Include a two-way table of counts and a relevant set of conditional percents.

| REFERENCES

Baird, D. D., and A. J. Wilcox (1985). "Cigarette smoking associated with delayed conception," *Journal of the American Medical Association,* Vol. 253, pp. 2979–2983.

Bickel, P. J., E. A. Hammel, and J. W. O'Connell (1975). "Sex bias in graduate admissions: Data from Berkeley," *Science,* Vol. 187, pp. 298–304.

Carter, C. L., D. Y Jones, A. Schatzkin, and L. A. Brinton (1989). "A prospective study of reproductive, familial, and socioeconomic risk factors for breast cancer using NHANES I data," *Public Health Reports,* Vol. 104, January–February 1989, pp. 45–49.

Fletcher, S. W., B. Black, R. Harris, B. K. Rimer, and S. Shapiro (1993). "Report of the international workshop on screening for breast cancer," *Journal of the National Cancer Institute,* Vol. 85, No. 20, Oct. 20, 1993, pp. 1644–1656.

Gastwirth, J. L. (1988). *Statistical Reasoning in Law and Public Policy,* Academic Press: New York.

Hand, D. J., E. Daly, A. D. Lunn, K, J. McConway, and E. Ostrowski (1994). *A Handbook of Small Data Sets,* Chapman and Hall: London.

Kawachi, I., D. Sparrow, A. Spiro III, P. Vokonas, and S. T. Weiss (1994). "A prospective study of anger and coronary heart disease: The normative aging study," *Circulation,* Vol. 94, pp. 2090–2095.

Kohlmeier, L., G. Arminger, S. Bartolomeycik, B. Bellach, J. Rehm, and M. Thamm (1992). "Pet birds as an independent risk factor for lung cancer: Case-control study," *British Medical Journal,* Vol. 305, pp. 986–989.

Pagano, M., and K Gauvreau (1993). *Principles of Biostatistics,* Duxbury Press: Belmont, CA.

Prescott, E., M. Hippe, H. O. H. Schnor, and J. Vestbo (1998). "Smoking and risk of myocardial infarction in women and men: Longitudinal population study," *British Medical Journal,* Vol. 316, pp. 1043–1047.

Prevention Magazine's Giant Book of Health Facts (1991). John Feltman (ed.), New York: Wings Books.

SAMSHA (1998). "Driving After Drug and Alcohol Use: Findings from the 1996 National Household Survey on Drug Abuse." United States Department of Health and Human Services.

Taubes, G. (1993). "Claim of higher risk for women smokers attacked," *Science,* Vol. 262, Nov. 26, 1993, p. 1375.

The Roper Organization (1992). *Unusual Personal Experiences: An Analysis of the Data from Three National Surveys,* Las Vegas: Bigelow Holding Corp.

Voss, L. D., and J. Mulligan (2000). "Bullying in school: Are short pupils at risk? Questionnaire study in a cohort," *British Medical Journal,* Vol. 320, pp. 612–613.

Wagner, C. H. (1982). "Simpson's Paradox in real life," *The American Statistician,* Vol. 36, No. 1, pp. 46–48.

Wechsler, H., and M. Kuo (2000). "College students define binge drinking and estimate its prevalence: Results of a national survey," *Journal of American College Health,* Vol. 49, pp. 57–64.

Weiden, C. R., and B. C. Gladen (1986). "The beta-geometric distribution applied to comparative fecundability studies," *Biometrics,* Vol. 42, pp. 547–560.

Writing Group for the Women's Health Initiative Investigators (2002). "Risks and benefits of estrogen plus progestin in healthy postmenopausal women: Principal results from the Women's Health Initiative randomized controlled trial," *Journal of the American Medical Association*, Vol. 288, No. 3, pp. 321–333.

Probability

CHAPTER 7

Will Hart /PhotoEdit /PictureQuest

How is a teacher to choose? See Case Study 7.1.

We rarely stop to think about the precise meaning of the word *probability.* When we speak of the probability that we will win a lottery based on buying a single ticket, are we using the word in the same way that we do when we speak about the probability that we will buy a new house in the next five years?

Statistical methods are used to evaluate information in uncertain situations and probability plays a key role in that process. Remember our definition of statistics from Chapter 1: *Statistics is a collection of procedures and principles for gathering data and analyzing information in order to help people make decisions when faced with uncertainty.* Decisions like whether to buy a lottery ticket, whether to buy an extended warranty on a computer, or which of two courses to take are examples of decisions that you may have to make that involve uncertainty and the evaluation of probabilities.

Probability calculations also are a key element of *statistical inference.* In Chapter 6 we introduced *p*-values, which are probabilities used to determine if the results of a study are statistically significant. As a reminder of how *p*-values are used, consider Case Study 1.6 in which 22,071 physicians were randomly assigned to take either aspirin or a placebo. There were 189 heart attacks in the placebo group but only 104 in the aspirin group. Could this have happened just by the luck of how the physicians were randomized to the treatment groups?

Suppose that regardless of which group they were in, $104 + 189 = 293$ of the men would have had heart attacks anyway. What is the probability that, just by the luck of random assignment, the numbers of heart attacks in the two groups would have been so different? In other words, if aspirin and placebo are equally effective (or ineffective), what is the probability that we would see such a large discrepancy in the proportion of heart attacks in the two groups? The answer is the *p*-value, which is less than .00001. This is strong evidence that these results did not just occur by chance. From this, we conclude that aspirin really did reduce the number of heart attacks in the group that took it. ◆

7.1 | RANDOM CIRCUMSTANCES

The next case study is hypothetical but contains the kinds of situations that people encounter every day involving probability. We will use the elements of this story throughout the chapter to illustrate the concepts and calculations necessary to understand the role probability plays in our lives.

CASE STUDY 7.1
A Hypothetical Story—Alicia Has a Bad Day

Last week, Alicia went to her physician for a routine medical exam. This morning her physician phoned to tell her that one of her tests came back positive, indicating that she may have a disease we will simply call D. Thinking there must be some mistake, Alicia inquired about the accuracy of the test. The physician told her that the test is 95% accurate whether someone has disease D or not. In other words, when someone has D, the test detects it 95% of the time. When someone does not have D, the test is rightly negative 95% of the time.

Therefore, according to the physician, even though only 1 out of 1000 women of Alicia's age actually has D, the test is a pretty good indicator that Alicia may have the disease. Alicia doesn't know it yet, but her physician is wrong to imply that it's likely that Alicia has the disease. Actually, her chance of hav-ing the disease is small, even given the positive test result. Later in this chapter you will discover why this is true.

Understandably, the physician's call upsets Alicia. She had planned to spend the morning studying for her statistics class, but instead she uses the time to search the Web for information about disease D. Her statistics professor randomly selects 3 separate students at the beginning of each class to answer questions about the material. Alicia reasons that with 50 students in the class she is unlikely to be one of the 3 selected. The students' names are placed on slips of paper in a bag, and one name is drawn (without replacement) for each question. Probability didn't go in Alicia's favor this day. After twice breathing a sigh of relief, she is picked to answer the third question.

Random Circumstances in Alicia's Day

A **random circumstance** is one in which the outcome is unpredictable. In many cases, *the outcome is not determined until we observe it.* It was not predetermined that Alicia would be selected to answer one of the questions in class. This happened when the professor drew her name out of the bag. In other cases, *the outcome is already determined, but our knowledge of it is uncertain.* Alicia either has disease D or not, but she and her physician don't know which possibility is true.

One lesson of this chapter is that the probabilities associated with random circumstances sometimes depend on other random circumstances. Alicia's test results were positive. The probability that Alicia would have a positive test depends on another random circumstance, which is whether or not she actually has disease D. In her statistics class, Alicia was not selected to answer questions 1 or 2. So, at the time of the drawing of a name for the third question, the probability that she would be selected was 1/48 because there were only 48 names left in the bag instead of the original 50. If she had been selected to answer either question 1 or question 2, her probability of being selected to answer question 3 would have been 0.

Here is a list of the random circumstances in Alicia's story and the possible outcomes for each of them:

Random Circumstance 1: Disease status

- ◆ Alicia has D.
- ◆ Alicia does not have D.

Random Circumstance 2: Test result

◆ Test is positive.

◆ Test is negative.

Random Circumstance 3: First student's name is drawn

◆ Alicia is selected.

◆ Alicia is not selected.

Random Circumstance 4: Second student's name is drawn

◆ Alicia is selected.

◆ Alicia is not selected.

Random Circumstance 5: Third student's name is drawn

◆ Alicia is selected.

◆ Alicia is not selected.

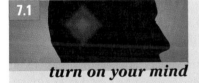

7.1

turn on your mind

At the beginning of Alicia's day, the outcomes of the five random circumstances listed were uncertain to her. Which of them were uncertain because *the outcome was not yet determined* and which were uncertain because of Alicia's *knowledge of the outcome*?*

Assigning Probabilities to the Outcomes of a Random Circumstance

We said the probability was 1/48 that Alicia would be picked for the third question given that she had not been picked for either of the first two. Note that this probability is expressed as a fraction. A probability is a value between 0 and 1 and is written either as a fraction or as a decimal fraction. From a purely mathematical point of view, a **probability** simply is a number between 0 and 1 that is assigned to a possible outcome of a random circumstance. Additionally, for the complete set of distinct possible outcomes of a random circumstance, the total of the assigned probabilities must equal 1.

In practice, of course, we should assign probabilities to outcomes in a meaningful way. A probability should provide information about how likely it is that a particular outcome will be the result of a random circumstance. In the next section, we discuss two different ways to assign and interpret probabilities. One of these ways, the relative frequency definition of probability, forms the foundation for the statistical inference methods that we will examine in later chapters.

7.2

turn on your mind

Based on your understanding of probability and random events, assign probabilities to the two possible outcomes for Random Circumstance 3.**

7.2 | INTERPRETATIONS OF PROBABILITY

The word *probability* is so common that in all probability you may encounter it today in everyday language. But, we rarely stop to think about the precise meaning of the word. When we speak of the probability that we will win a lottery based on buying a single ticket, are we using the word in the same way that we do when we speak about the probability that we will buy a new house in the next five years? We can quantify the chance of winning the lottery exactly, but our assessment of the chance that we will buy a new house is based on our personal and subjective belief about how life will evolve for us.

The conceptual difference illustrated by these two different situations creates two different interpretations of what is meant by the word *probability*. In most situations in statistics, a probability is assigned to a possible outcome based on what will or has happened over the long run of repeatedly observing a random circumstance. There are situations, however, where a probability may be assigned based on the expert assessment of an individual.

The Relative Frequency Interpretation of Probability

The relative frequency interpretation of probability applies to situations in which we can envision repeatedly observing the results of a random circumstance. For example, it is easy to imagine flipping a coin over and over again and counting the number of heads and tails. It makes sense to interpret the probability that the coin lands with heads up to be the relative frequency, over the long run, with which it lands with heads up. When we say that the probability of flipping heads is 1/2, we can interpret this to mean that about half of a large number of flips will result in heads.

Here are some other situations to which the relative frequency interpretation of probability can be applied:

- Buying lottery tickets regularly and observing how often you win.
- Drawing a student's name out of a hat and seeing how often a particular student is selected.
- Commuting to work daily and observing whether or not a certain traffic signal is red when we encounter it.
- Surveying many adults and determining what proportion smokes.
- Observing births and noting how often the baby is a female.

definition In situations that we can imagine repeating many times, we define the **probability** of a specific outcome as *the proportion of times it would occur over the long run.* This also is called the **relative frequency** of that particular outcome.

Notice the emphasis on what happens *in the long run*. We cannot accurately assess the probability of a particular outcome by observing it only a few times. For example, consider a family with five children in which only one child is a boy. We should not take this as evidence that the probability of having a boy is only 1/5. To more accurately assess the probability that a baby is a boy, we have to observe many births.

TABLE 7.1 ■ Relative Frequency of Male Births over Time

Weeks of Watching	Total Births	Total Boys	Proportion of Boys
1	30	19	.633
4	116	68	.586
13	317	172	.543
26	623	383	.615
39	919	483	.526
52	1237	639	.517

EXAMPLE 7.1
Probability of Male Versus Female Births

According to the *Information Please Almanac* (1991, p. 815), the long-run relative frequency of males born in the United States is about .512. In other words, over the long run, there are 512 male babies and 488 female babies born per 1000 births.

Suppose we were to tally births and the relative frequency of male births in a certain city for the next year. Table 7.1, which was generated with a computer simulation, shows what we might observe. In the simulation, the chance was .512 that any individual birth was a boy, and the average number of births per week was 24. Notice how the *proportion* or *relative frequency* of male births is relatively far from .512 over the first few weeks, but then settles down to around .512 in the long run. After 52 weeks, the *relative frequency* of boys was 639/1237 = .517. If we used only the data from the first week to estimate the probability of a male birth, our estimate would have been far from the actual value. We need to look at a large number of observations to accurately estimate a probability. ◆

Determining the Relative Frequency Probability of an Outcome

There are two ways to determine a relative frequency probability. The first method involves *making an assumption about the physical world*. The second method involves *making a direct observation of how often something happens*.

Method 1: Make an Assumption about the Physical World Sometimes, it's reasonable to assign probabilities to possible outcomes based on what we think about physical realities. We generally assume, for example, that coins are manufactured in such a way that they are equally likely to land with heads or tails up when flipped. Therefore, we conclude that the probability of a flipped coin showing heads up is 1/2.

EXAMPLE 7.2
A Simple Lottery

A lottery game run by many states in the United States is one in which players choose a three-digit number between 000 and 999. A player wins if his or her three-digit number is chosen. If we assume that the physical mechanism used to draw the winning number gives each possibility an equal chance, we can determine the probability of winning. There are 1000 possible three-digit numbers (000, 001, 002, . . . , 999), so the probability that the state picks the player's number is 1/1000. In the long run, a player should win about 1 out of 1000 times. Note that this does not mean that a player will win *exactly* once in every thousand plays. ◆

EXAMPLE 7.3
The Probability That Alicia Has to Answer a Question

In Case Study 7.1, there were 50 student names in the bag when a student was selected to answer the first question. If we assume the names have been well mixed in the bag, then each student is equally likely to be selected. Therefore, the probability that Alicia would be selected to answer the first question was 1/50. ◆

Method 2: Observe the Relative Frequency   Another way to determine the probability of a particular outcome is by *observing the relative frequency of the outcome over many, many repetitions of the situation.* We illustrated this method with Example 7.1 when we observed the relative frequency of male births in a given city over a year. If we consider many births, we can get a very accurate figure for the probability that a birth will be a male. As mentioned, the relative frequency of male births in the United States has been consistently close to .512 (*Information Please Almanac,* 1991, p. 815). In 1987, for example, there were a total of 3,809,394 live births in the United States, of which 1,951,153 were males. Assuming that the probability does not change in the future, the probability that a live birth will result in a male is about 1,951,153/3,809,394 = .5122.

EXAMPLE 7.4
***The Probability
of Lost Luggage***

According to Krantz (1992, p. 33; original source U.S. Department of Transportation), 1 in 176 passengers on U.S. airline carriers will temporarily lose their luggage. This number is based on data collected over the long run and is found by dividing the number of passengers who temporarily lost their luggage by the total number of passengers. Another way to state this fact is to say that the probability is 1/176, or about .006, that a randomly selected passenger on a U.S. carrier will temporarily lose luggage. ◆

Proportions and Percentages as Probabilities

Relative frequency probabilities are often derived from the proportion of individuals who have a certain characteristic, or a certain outcome in a random circumstance. The relative frequency probabilities are therefore numbers between 0 and 1. It is commonplace, however, to be somewhat loose in how relative frequencies are expressed. For instance, here are four ways to express the relative frequency of lost luggage:

- The proportion of passengers who lose their luggage is 1/176 or about .006.
- About 0.6% of passengers lose their luggage.
- The probability that a randomly selected passenger will lose his or her luggage is about .006.
- The probability that you will lose your luggage is about .006.

This last statement is not exactly correct, because *your* probability of lost luggage depends on a number of factors, including whether or not you check any luggage and how late you arrive at the airport for your flight. The probability of .006 really only applies to the long-run relative frequency across all passengers, or the probability that a *randomly selected* passenger is one of the unlucky ones.

Estimating Probabilities from Observed Categorical Data

When appropriate data are available, the long-run relative frequency interpretation of probability can be used to estimate probabilities of outcomes and combinations of outcomes for categorical variables. Assuming the data are representative, the probability of a particular outcome is estimated to be the relative frequency (proportion) with which that outcome was observed. As we learned in Case Study 1.3 and also in Chapter 4, such estimates are not precise, and an approximate margin of error for the estimated probability is calculated as $1/\sqrt{n}$. We'll learn a more precise way to calculate the margin of error in Chapter 10.

TABLE 7.2 ■ Nighttime Lighting in Infancy and Eyesight

Slept with:	No Myopia	Myopia	High Myopia	Total
Darkness	155 (90%)	15 (9%)	2 (1%)	172
Nightlight	153 (66%)	72 (31%)	7 (3%)	232
Full Light	34 (45%)	36 (48%)	5 (7%)	75
Total	342 (71%)	123 (26%)	14 (3%)	479

EXAMPLE 7.5
Nightlights and
Myopia Revisited

In an example discussed in Chapters 2 and 6, we investigated the relationship between nighttime lighting in early childhood and the incidence of myopia later in childhood. The results are shown again in Table 7.2.

Assuming these data are representative of a larger population, what is the approximate probability that someone from that population who sleeps with a nightlight in early childhood will develop some degree of myopia? There were 232 infants who slept with a nightlight. Of those, 72 developed myopia and 7 developed high myopia, for a total of 79 who developed some degree of myopia. Therefore, the relative frequency of some myopia among nightlight users is $(72 + 7)/232 = 79/232 = .34$. From this we can conclude that the approximate probability of developing some myopia, given that an infant slept with a nightlight, is .34. This estimate is based on a sample of 232 people, so there is a margin of error of about $1/\sqrt{232} = .066$. ◆

The Personal Probability Interpretation

The relative frequency interpretation of probability clearly is limited to repeatable conditions. Yet, uncertainty is a characteristic of most events, whether or not they are repeatable under similar conditions. We need an interpretation of probability that can be applied to situations even if they will never happen again.

If you decide to drive downtown this Saturday afternoon, will you be able to find a good parking space? Should a movie studio release its potential new hit movie before Christmas, when many others are released, or wait until January when it might have a better chance to be the top box-office attraction? If the United States enters into a trade alliance with a particular country, will that cause problems in relations with another country? Will you have a better time if you go to Cancun or to Florida for your next spring break?

These are unique situations, not likely to be repeated. They require people to make decisions based on an assessment of how the future will evolve. We could each assign a personal probability to these events, based on our own knowledge and experiences, and we could use that probability to help us with our decision. Different people may not agree on what the probability of an event happening is, but nobody would be considered to be wrong.

definition We define the **personal probability** of an event to be the degree to which a given individual believes the event will happen. Sometimes the term **subjective probability** is used because the degree of belief may be different for each individual.

There are very few restrictions on personal probabilities. They must fall between 0 and 1 (or, if expressed as a percent, between 0 and 100%). They must also fit together in certain ways if they are to be **coherent.** By being coherent, we mean that your personal probability of one event doesn't contradict your personal probability of another. For example, if you thought that the probability of finding a parking space downtown Saturday afternoon was .20, then to be coherent you must also believe that the probability of not finding one is .80. We will explore some of these logical rules later in this chapter.

How We Use Personal Probabilities

People routinely base decisions on personal probabilities. This is why committee decisions are often so difficult. For example, suppose a committee is trying to decide which candidate to hire for a job. Each member of the committee has a different assessment of the candidates, and they may disagree on the probability that a particular candidate would best fit the job. We are all familiar with the problem juries sometimes have when trying to agree on someone's guilt or innocence. Each member of the jury has his or her own personal probability of guilt and innocence. One of the benefits of committee or jury deliberations is that they may help members reach some consensus in their personal probabilities.

Personal probabilities often take relative frequencies of similar events into account. For example, the late astronomer Carl Sagan believed that the probability of a major asteroid hitting the Earth soon is high enough to be of concern. "The probability that the Earth will be hit by a civilization-threatening small world in the next century is a little less than one in a thousand" (Jane Arraf, "Leave Earth or perish: Sagan," *China Post,* Taiwan, Dec. 14, 1994, p. 4). To arrive at that probability, Sagan obviously could not use the long-run frequency definition of probability. He would have to use his own knowledge of astronomy, combined with past asteroid behavior.

Notice that unlike relative frequency probabilities, personal probabilities assigned to unique events are not equivalent to proportions or percentages. For instance, it does not make sense to say that major asteroids will hit approximately 1 out of 1000 Earths in the next century.

Mysteries of the Past

There is some debate about how to represent probability when an outcome has been determined but is still unknown, such as if you have flipped a coin but not yet looked at it. Technically, any particular outcome has either happened or not. If it has happened, its probability of happening is 1, and if it hasn't, its probability of happening is 0.

For instance, in Case Study 7.1, Alicia either has the disease or not, but no one knows which is true. Because 1 out of 1000 women of her age have the disease, without any additional information, we might say that the probability that Alicia has it is 1/1000. But one could argue that this probability statement is meaningless, because she either has the disease or not.

As another example, suppose a woman is pregnant but no one knows the sex of the fetus. Is the probability that she will have a boy either 0 or 1, or is it .512? Suppose you flip a coin but cover it with your hand before anyone sees it. Is the probability of a head still 1/2, until it is revealed?

The answer to the dilemma in these kinds of situations is that technically, once an outcome has been determined, a relative frequency probability statement no longer makes sense. However, a personal probability statement about what outcome has occurred or may ultimately be revealed does make sense. This interpretation is often what is meant when we discuss such occurrences in everyday life, even in situations where relative frequency information is used to determine the probability value, such as in the three examples just discussed.

Another example of this type of situation is the construction of a 95% confidence interval, introduced in Chapter 4, which we will study in detail in Chapters 10 and 12. Before the sample is chosen, a probability statement makes sense. The probability is .95 that a sample will be selected for which the computed 95% confidence interval covers the truth. After the sample has been chosen, "the die is cast." Either the computed confidence interval will cover the truth, or it won't. That's why we say that we have *95% confidence* that the interval is correct, rather than saying that *the probability* that it is correct is .95.

7.3

turn on your mind

You are about to enroll in a course for which you know that 20% of the students will receive a grade of A. Do you think that the probability that *you* will receive an A in the class is .20? Do you think the probability that a randomly selected student in the class will receive an A is .20? Explain the difference in these two probabilities, using the distinction between relative frequency probability and personal probability in your explanation.*

in summary Interpretations of Probability

The *relative frequency probability* of an outcome is the proportion of times the outcome would occur over the long run. Relative frequency probabilities can be determined by any of these methods:

◆ Making an assumption about the physical world and using it to find relative frequencies

◆ Observing outcomes over the long run

◆ Measuring a representative sample and observing relative frequencies of the sample that fall into various categories

The *personal probability* of an outcome is the degree to which a given individual believes it will happen. Sometimes data from similar events in the past and other knowledge are incorporated when determining personal probabilities.

7.3 | PROBABILITY DEFINITIONS AND RELATIONSHIPS

One of the key factors for being able to calculate and interpret probabilities is to be able to define specific outcomes or events of interest and how these events are related to each other. There are just a few definitions of these relationships. The first set of definitions has to do with the possible outcomes of a random circumstance. A specific possible outcome is called a **simple event,** and the

***HINT:** Look at the "In Summary" box immediately following. Which of the four methods described apply in each case?

collection of all possible outcomes is called the **sample space** for the random circumstance. The term **event** is used to describe any collection of one or more possible outcomes.

> *definition* ◆ The **sample space** is the collection of unique, nonoverlapping possible outcomes of a random circumstance.
>
> ◆ A **simple event** is one outcome in the sample space. In other words, a simple event is a possible outcome of a random circumstance.
>
> ◆ An **event** is a collection of one or more simple events in the sample space. Events are often written using capital letters A, B, C, and so on.

EXAMPLE 7.6
Days per Week of Drinking Alcohol

Suppose that we randomly sample college students and ask each student how many days he or she drinks alcohol in a typical week. The *simple events* in the *sample space* of possible outcomes are 0 days, 1 day, 2 days, and so on, up to 7 days. These simple events certainly are not equally likely. We might be interested to learn the probability of the *event* that a randomly selected student drinks alcohol on 4 or more days in a typical week. The *event* "4 or more" is comprised of the *simple events* {4 days, 5 days, 6 days, and 7 days}. ◆

Assigning Probabilities to Simple Events

A probability is assigned to each *simple event* (unique outcome) using relative frequency or personal probabilities. The relative frequency method is used most often. The notation $P(A)$ is used for the probability of an event A.

Conditions for Valid Probabilities
The assigned probabilities for the possible outcomes of a random circumstance must meet the following two conditions:

1. Each probability is between 0 and 1.
2. The sum of the probabilities over all possible simple events is 1. In other words, the total probability for all possible outcomes of a random circumstance is equal to 1.

Equally Likely Simple Events
If there are k simple events in the sample space and they are all equally likely, then the probability of the occurrence of each one is $1/k$. For instance, suppose a fair 6-sided die is rolled and the number that lands face up is observed. Then the sample space is {1,2,3,4,5,6} and each outcome has probability 1/6. Suppose two fair coins are tossed and the outcome of interest is the combination of results on the first toss then the second toss. There are four equally likely events, {HH, HT, TH, TT}, where H = heads and T = tails, so each outcome has probability 1/4.

EXAMPLE 7.2—CONTINUED
Probabilities for Some Lottery Events

Random Circumstance: A three-digit winning lottery number is selected.
Sample Space: {000,001,002,003, . . . ,997,998,999}. There are 1000 simple events.
Probabilities for Simple Event: The probability that any specific three-digit number is a winner is 1/1000. We assume that all three-digit numbers are equally likely.

Probabilites for Some Events:

- Let event A = the last digit is a 9. Notice that event A contains the subset of all simple events that end with a 9. We can write this as A = {009,019, . . . ,999}. Notice that since one out of ten numbers will be included in this set, $P(A) = 1/10$.

- Let event B = the three digits are all the same. This event includes ten simple events, which are {000,111,222,333,444,555,666,777,888,999}. Because event B contains 10 of the 1000 equally likely simple events, $P(B) = 10/1000$, or 1/100. ◆

Complementary Events

> *definition* One event is the **complement** of another event if the two events do not contain any of the same simple events *and* together they cover the entire sample space. For an event A, the notation A^C represents the complement of A.

An event either happens or it doesn't. A randomly selected person either has blue eyes or does not have blue eyes. Alicia either has a disease or does not. "Opposite" events are called **complementary events.** Because the total probability for a sample space must be equal to 1, the probabilities of complementary events must sum to 1. In symbols, $P(A) + P(A^C) = 1$.

EXAMPLE 7.2—CONTINUED
The Probability of
Not Winning the Lottery

If A is the event that a player buying a single lottery ticket wins, then A^C is the event that he or she does not win. As we have seen, $P(A) = 1/1000$, so it makes sense that $P(A^C) = 999/1000$. ◆

Mutually Exclusive Events

> *definition* Two events are **mutually exclusive** if they do not contain any of the same simple events (outcomes). Equivalent terminology is that the two events are **disjoint.**

We sometimes are interested in two events that involve distinctly separate simple events, but the two events may not cover all possible outcomes in the sample space. For example, we may want to know the probability that a randomly selected man is unusually short or tall. We might want to know the probability that he is either at least 4 inches taller than the mean height, or at least 4 inches shorter than the mean height. The events "at least 4 inches taller than the mean" and "at least 4 inches shorter than the mean" are separate events that cannot occur simultaneously, and they are called *mutually exclusive* or *disjoint events*.

EXAMPLE 7.2—CONTINUED
Mutually Exclusive Events
for Lottery Numbers

Here are two mutually exclusive (disjoint) events when a winning lottery number is drawn from the set 000 to 999. Notice that they do not cover all possibilities, so they are not complements:

A = All three digits are the same.

B = The first and last digits are different. ◆

Independent and Dependent Events

> *definition* ◆ Two events are **independent** of each other if knowing that one will occur (or has occurred) does not change the probability that the other occurs.
>
> ◆ Two events are **dependent** if knowing that one will occur (or has occurred) changes the probability that the other occurs.

The definitions of independent and dependent events have to do with whether the fact that one event has taken place affects the probability that a second event could happen. The definitions can apply *either* to events *within the same random circumstance* or to events *from two separate random circumstances.* As an example of two dependent events within the same random circumstance, suppose a random digit from 0 to 9 is selected. If we know that the randomly selected digit is an *even number,* our assignment of a probability to the event that *the number is 4* changes from 1/10 to 1/5. Often, we examine questions about the dependence of the outcomes of two separate random circumstances. For instance, does the knowledge of whether a randomly selected person is male or female (random circumstance 1) affect the probability that he or she is opposed to abortion (random circumstance 2)? If the answer is yes, the outcomes of the two random circumstances are dependent events.

EXAMPLE 7.7
Winning a Free Lunch

Some restaurants display a glass bowl in which customers deposit their business cards, and a drawing is held once a week for a free lunch. Suppose you and your friend Vanessa each deposit a card in two consecutive weeks. Define:

Event A = You win in week 1.
Event B = Vanessa wins in week 1.
Event C = Vanessa wins in week 2.

Notice that events A and B refer to the same random circumstance, the drawing in week 1. They are *not* independent. If you win (event A), then Vanessa cannot win (event B). So if A occurs, then $P(B) = 0$. Knowing that A has or will occur changes $P(B)$.

Notice that events A and C refer to *different* random circumstances, the drawings in separate weeks. Those events *are* independent. Knowing that A occurred does not give any information about the probability that C will occur. ◆

EXAMPLE 7.3—CONTINUED
The Probability That Alicia Has to Answer a Question

It is not always the case that events related to two separate random circumstances are independent. Define:

Event A = Alicia is selected to answer question 1.
Event B = Alicia is selected to answer question 2.

In Example 7.3 we determined that $P(A) = 1/50$. Are A and B independent? Notice that they refer to different random circumstances, but $P(B)$ is affected by knowing whether or not A occurred. If Alicia answered question 1, her name is already out of the bag, so $P(B) = 0$. If event A does not occur, there are 49 names left in the bag including Alicia's, so $P(B) = 1/49$. Therefore, knowing whether or not A occurred changes $P(B)$. ◆

Conditional Probabilities

Suppose that two events are dependent. From the definition of dependent events, it follows that knowing that one event will occur (or has occurred) *does* change the probability that the other occurs. Therefore, we need to distinguish between two probabilities:

- ◆ $P(B)$, the unconditional probability that the event B occurs
- ◆ $P(B|A)$, read "probability of B given A," the conditional probability that the event B occurs *given that we know A has occurred or will occur*

> *definition* The **conditional probability of the event B, given that the event A occurs,** is the long-run relative frequency with which event B occurs when circumstances are such that A also occurs. This probability is written as **$P(B|A)$.**

EXAMPLE 7.8
Probability That a Teenager Gambles Depends upon Gender

Based on a survey of nearly all of the 9th and 12th graders in Minnesota public schools in 1998, a total of 78,564 students, Stinchfield (2001) reported proportions admitting that they gambled at least once a week during the previous year. He found that these proportions differed considerably for males and females, as well as for 9th and 12th graders. One result he found was that 22.9% of the 9th-grade boys but only 4.5% of the 9th-grade girls admitted gambling at least weekly. Assuming these figures are representative of all Minnesota 9th graders, we can write these as conditional probabilities for 9th-grade Minnesota students:

$P(\text{student is weekly gambler}|\text{student is boy}) = .229$
$P(\text{student is weekly gambler}|\text{student is girl}) = .045$

Notice the dependence between the outcomes for the random circumstance "weekly gambling habit" and the outcomes for the random circumstance "gender." Knowledge of a student's gender changes the probability that he or she is a weekly gambler. ◆

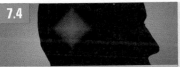

7.4

turn on your mind

Remember that there were 50 students in Alicia's statistics class and that student names were not put back in the bag after being selected. Define the events A = Alicia is selected to answer question 1 and B = Alicia is selected to answer question 2. Describe each of these four conditional probabilities in words and determine a value for each.

$P(B|A), \qquad P(B^C|A), \qquad P(B|A^C), \qquad P(B^C|A^C)$

Now, based on your answers, can you formulate a rule about the value of $P(B|A) + P(B^C|A)$?*

*HINT: For $P(B|A)$ and $P(B|A^C)$, see Example 7.3—CONTINUED.

---

in summary   **Key Probability Definitions**

- The **sample space** is the collection of unique, nonoverlapping possible outcomes of a random circumstance.
- A **simple event** is one outcome in the sample space. In other words, a simple event is a possible outcome of a random circumstance.
- An **event** is a collection of one or more simple events in the sample space. Events are often written using capital letters A, B, C, and so on.
- One event is the **complement** of another event if the two events do not contain any of the same simple events *and* together they cover the entire sample space. For an event A, the notation A^C represents the complement of A.
- Two events are **mutually exclusive** if they do not contain any of the same simple events (outcomes). Equivalent terminology is that the two events are **disjoint.**
- Two events are **independent** of each other if knowing that one will occur (or has occurred) does not change the probability that the other occurs.
- Two events are **dependent** if knowing that one will occur (or has occurred) changes the probability that the other occurs.
- The **conditional probability of the event B, given that the event A occurs,** is the long-run relative frequency with which event B occurs when circumstances are such that A also occurs. This probability is written as $P(B|A)$.

7.4 | BASIC RULES FOR FINDING PROBABILITIES

We already have been able to determine some probabilities based on our knowledge of physical situations and long-run relative frequencies. We also have stated two conditions that must apply to probabilities. Namely, that they are always between 0 and 1, and that the sum of the probabilities for all simple events must be 1.

In this section, we introduce four more rules that can be used to find probabilities for complicated events. When stating these rules, we use the letters A and B to represent events, and $P(A)$ and $P(B)$ for their respective probabilities. Each rule is followed by examples that translate the formulas into words. Common words that signal the use of the rule are shown in *italic* in the examples.

Probability an Event Does Not Occur

definition   **Rule 1 (for "not the event"):** To find the probability of A^C, the complement of A, use $P(A^C) = 1 - P(A)$.

Rule 1 follows directly from the observation that $P(A) + P(A^C) = 1$, which was stated as an immediate consequence after the definition of A^C. Therefore, if $P(A)$ is known, it's easy to find the probability that A does not occur. Simply subtract $P(A)$ from 1. For instance, in Example 7.2—*CONTINUED*, it was easy to determine that the probability of *not* winning the lottery was .999, once we knew that the probability of winning was .001.

Rule 1 is simple but surprisingly useful. When you are confronted with finding the probability of an event, always ask yourself if it would be easier to find the probability of its complement, and then subtract that from 1.

EXAMPLE 7.9
Probability a Stranger Does Not Share Your Birth Date

Assuming all 365 birth dates are equally likely, the probability that the next stranger you meet will share your birthday is 1/365. Therefore, the probability that they will *not* share your birthday is $1 - (1/365) = (364/365) = .9973$. This does not hold if you were born on Feb. 29, but if that's you, you are used to ingenuity when it comes to birthdays! ◆

Probability That Either of Two Events Happens

definition **Rule 2 (addition rule for "either/or"):** To find the probability that either A *or* B happens:

Rule 2a (general): $P(A \text{ or } B) = P(A) + P(B) - P(A \text{ and } B)$
Rule 2b (for mutually exclusive events): *If* A and B are *mutually exclusive* events, $P(A \text{ or } B) = P(A) + P(B)$

Rule 2b is a special case of Rule 2a because when A and B are mutually exclusive events, $P(A \text{ and } B) = 0$.

To find the probability that either of two *mutually exclusive* events will be the outcome of a random circumstance, we add the probabilities for the two events. For instance, the probability that a randomly selected integer between 1 and 10 is either 3 or 7 is $.1 + .1 = .2$. When the two events are not mutually exclusive, we modify the sum of the probabilities in the manner described in Rule 2a and illustrated in Example 7.10.

EXAMPLE 7.10
Roommate Compatibility

Brett is off to college. There are 1000 additional new male students, and one of them will be randomly assigned to share Brett's dorm room. He is hoping it won't be someone who likes to party or who snores. The 2×2 table for the 1000 students is

	Snores	Doesn't Snore	Total
Likes to Party	150	100	250
Doesn't Like to Party	200	550	750
Total	350	650	1000

What is the probability that Brett will be disappointed and get a roommate who *either* likes to party or snores? Relevant events and their probabilities are

A = likes to party $\qquad\qquad P(A) = \dfrac{250}{1000} = .25.$

B = snores $\qquad\qquad\qquad\quad P(B) = \dfrac{350}{1000} = .35$

A and B = likes to party *and* snores $\quad P(A \text{ and } B) = \dfrac{150}{1000} = .15$

Using Rule 2a, $P(A \text{ or } B) = P(A) + P(B) - P(A \text{ and } B) = .25 + .35 - .15 = .45$. The probability is .45 that Brett will be assigned a roommate who either likes to party, or snores, or both. Notice that the probability is therefore $1 - .45 = .55$ that he will get a roommate who is acceptable, using Rule 1. We could also determine this probability from the table of counts because there are 550 suitable roommates out of 1000 possibilities. ◆

We can use Example 7.10 to illustrate why Rule 2a makes sense. In order to find $P(A \text{ or } B)$ we need to include all possible outcomes involved in either event. In Brett's case, 250 (.25) of the potential roommates like to party and 350 (.35) snore, for a total of 600 (.6). But notice that the 150 guys who like to party *and* who snore have been counted twice. So, we need to subtract them once, resulting in $250 + 350 - 150 = 450$ people out of the 1000 total who have one or both traits. So, Rule 2a tells you to add the probabilities for all of the outcomes that are part of event A, plus the probabilities for all of the outcomes that are part of event B, then to subtract the probabilities for all of the outcomes that have been counted twice, $P(A \text{ and } B)$.

EXAMPLE 7.11
Probability of **Either** *Two Boys or Two Girls in Two Births**

What is the probability that a woman who has two children has *either* two girls *or* two boys? The question asks about two *mutually exclusive* events because with only two children she can't have two girls and two boys. Rule 2b applies to this situation. We'll use the information in Example 7.1 that the probability of a boy is .512 and the probability of a girl is .488, and we'll also take a sneak peek at Rule 3 introduced next.

Event A = two girls. From Rule 3b (next), $P(A) = (.488)(.488) = .2381$.
Event B = two boys. From Rule 3b (next), $P(B) = (.512)(.512) = .2621$.

Therefore, the probability that the woman has *either* two girls *or* two boys is

$$P(A \text{ or } B) = P(A) + P(B) = .2381 + .2621 = .5002 \quad ◆$$

Probability That Two or More Events Occur Together

Rule 2 allowed us to answer "either or both" questions about events. But what if we want to restrict consideration to the combination of both events only? In that case, we want to find $P(A \text{ and } B)$. For instance, if you flip a nickel and a dime, what is the probability that they *both* land heads up? You probably know intuitively that the answer is 1/4, or could be convinced of that by noting that the four possibilities, HH, HT, TH and TT, are equally likely. A more general way of arriving at the answer is to notice that 1/4 is the result of multiplying $1/2 \times 1/2$, the two individual probabilities of heads. This general method works for finding $P(A \text{ and } B)$ as long as A and B are independent events.

If A and B are dependent events, then finding the probability that they both occur requires that we know more than their individual probabilities. Sometimes we can find P(A and B) directly as a relative frequency. In Example 7.10, the probability that Brett's roommate will be someone who likes to party *and* who snores can be found directly as $150/1000 = .15$. If we can't find P(A and B) directly, then we need to know either P(A|B) and P(B), or P(B|A) and P(A).

> **definition** **Rule 3 (multiplication rule for "and"):** To find the probability that two events both occur simultaneously or in a sequence:
>
> **Rule 3a (general):** $P(A \text{ and } B) = P(A)P(B|A)$
> **Rule 3b (for independent events):** *If* A and B are *independent* events, $P(A \text{ and } B) = P(A)P(B)$
> **Extension of Rule 3b to more than two independent events:** For several independent events, $P(A_1 \text{ and } A_2 \ldots \text{ and } A_n) = P(A_1)P(A_2) \cdots P(A_n)$

Rule 3b is a special case of Rule 3a because when A and B are independent, P(B|A) is equal to P(B).

To find the probability that two or more independent events occur together, multiply the probabilities of the events. For instance, the probability is $(.5)(.5)(.5) = .125$ that the next three people of your sex you see all are taller than the median height for your sex. (Remember that the median is the value for which half of a group has a greater value and half has a smaller value, so the probability is .5 that a randomly selected person is taller than the median. We are assuming the probability of being exactly at the median is essentially 0.)

EXAMPLE 7.8—*CONTINUED*
Probability a Randomly Selected 9th Grader Is a Male and a Weekly Gambler

In a 1998 survey of most of the 9th-grade students in Minnesota, 22.9% of the boys and 4.5% of the girls admitted that they gambled at least once a week during the previous year (Stinchfield, 2001). The population consisted of 50.9% girls and 49.1% boys. Assuming these students represent all 9th-grade Minnesota teens, what is the probability that a randomly selected student will be a male *who also* gambles at least weekly?

Event A = A male is selected.
Event B = A weekly gambler is selected.

Events A and B are dependent, so we use Rule 3a (general multiplication rule) to determine the probability that A and B occur together. We know that $P(A) = .491$. We also know that the *conditional* probability that the selected teen is a weekly gambler, given that a male is selected, is $P(B|A) = .229$. The answer to our question is therefore:

$$P(\text{male } and \text{ weekly gambler}) = P(A \text{ } and \text{ } B) = P(A)P(B|A) = (.491)(.229)$$
$$= .1124$$

About 11% of all 9th-grade teenagers are males *and* weekly gamblers. ◆

EXAMPLE 7.12
Probability Two Strangers Both Share Your Birth Month

Assuming birth months are equally likely, what is the probability that the next two unrelated strangers you meet *both* share your birth month? Because the strangers are unrelated, we assume independence between the two events that have to do with them sharing your birth month. Define:

Event A = first stranger shares your birth month; $P(A) = 1/12$.
Event B = second stranger shares your birth month; $P(B) = 1/12$.

The events are independent, so Rule 3b applies. The probability that *both* individuals share your birth month is the probability that A occurs *and* B occurs:

$$P(A \text{ and } B) = P(A)P(B) = \frac{1}{12} \times \frac{1}{12} = \frac{1}{144} = .007$$

The Extension of Rule 3b allows this result to be generalized. For instance, the probability that four unrelated strangers *all* share your birth month is $(1/12)^4$. ◆

Determining a Conditional Probability

definition **Rule 4 (conditional probability):** This rule is simply an algebraic restatement of Rule 3a, but it is sometimes useful to use the following form of that rule:

$$P(B|A) = \frac{P(A \text{ and } B)}{P(A)}$$

The assignment of letters to events A and B is arbitrary, so it is also true that

$$P(A|B) = \frac{P(A \text{ and } B)}{P(B)}$$

Often, a conditional probability is given to us directly. In Example 7.8, for instance, it was reported that the estimated conditional probability is .045 that a 9th grader is a weekly gambler if the student is a female. In other cases, the physical situation can make it easy to determine a conditional probability. For instance, in drawing 2 cards from an ordinary deck of 52 cards, the probability that the second card drawn is red, *given* that the first card drawn was red, is 25/51 because 25 of the remaining 51 cards are red. Occasionally, it is useful to use Rule 4, an algebraic restatement of the multiplication rule (Rule 3a), to calculate a conditional probability.

EXAMPLE 7.13
Probability Alicia Is Picked for the First Question Given That She's Picked to Answer a Question

Here is an example for which it is easy to see the logical answer. If *we know* that Alicia is picked to answer one of the questions, what is the probability that it was the first question? Once we know she had to answer one of the three questions, the conditional probability that it was the first one should be 1/3. All three questions would be equally likely to be the question for which Alicia was picked.

Let's use Rule 4 to verify this logic. Define:

A = Alicia is called on to answer the first question; $P(A) = 1/50$.
B = Alicia is called on to answer any one of the questions; $P(B) = 3/50$, since there are 50 students and 3 students are chosen to answer questions.

Notice that the event that A and B *both* occur is synonymous with the event A occurring, since A is a subset of B. If A has occurred, then B also has occurred. Therefore, $P(A \text{ and } B) = 1/50$. Applying Rule 4:

$$P(A|B) = \frac{P(A \text{ and } B)}{P(B)} = \frac{1/50}{3/50} = \frac{1}{3} \quad ◆$$

EXAMPLE 7.14
The Probability of Guilt and Innocence Given a DNA Match

This example is modified from one given by Paulos (1995, p. 72). Suppose there has been a crime and it is known that the criminal is a person within a population of 6,000,000. Further, suppose it is known that in this population only about one person in a million has a DNA type that matches the DNA found at the crime scene, so let's assume there are six people in the population with this DNA type. Someone in custody has this DNA type. *We know* the person's DNA matches, but what is the probability that he is actually innocent? In the absence of any other evidence beyond the DNA match, the probability of guilt is 1/6 because the criminal is one of the six individuals who have this DNA type in the population. Therefore, the probability of innocence is 5/6.

We now know the answer, but to illustrate Rule 4 we'll look at how it can be used to determine this probability. Imagine randomly selecting someone from the population. Define:

Event A = DNA of randomly chosen person matches DNA at the crime scene
Event B = person selected is innocent of the crime

We want to determine

$$P(B|A) = \frac{P(A \text{ and } B)}{P(A)}$$

The event "A and B" is the event that the selected person is innocent *and* the DNA matches. There are five such people in the population so $P(A \text{ and } B) = 5/6,000,000$. The probability of a DNA match is $P(A) = 6/6,000,000$, and

$$P(B|A) = \frac{P(A \text{ and } B)}{P(A)} = \frac{5/6,000,000}{6/6,000,000} = \frac{5}{6}$$

If you were on the jury, it would be important to realize that without additional evidence, the probability that this person is *innocent* is 5/6, even though the DNA matches. The prosecutor surely would emphasize a different conditional probability, specifically, the very small probability that an innocent person's DNA type would match the crime scene DNA (remember, there are 5,999,999 innocent people). Do not confuse these two different conditional probabilities. ◆

7.5

turn on your mind

Continuing the DNA example, verify that the conditional probability

$$P(\text{DNA match} \mid \text{innocent person}) = \frac{5}{5,999,999} = .00000083$$

Then provide an explanation that would be understood by a jury for the distinction between the two statements:

◆ The probability that a person who has a DNA match is innocent is 5/6.

◆ The probability that a person who is innocent has a DNA match is .00000083.*

> ***in summary***   **Independent and Mutually Exclusive Events and Probability Rules**
>
> Students sometimes confuse the definitions of independent and mutually exclusive events. Remember these two concepts:
>
> - When two events are *mutually exclusive* and one happens, it turns the probability of the other one to 0.
> - When two events are *independent* and one happens, it leaves the probability of the other one alone.
>
> Probabilities under these two situations follow these rules:
>
> | When Events Are: | $P(A\ or\ B)$ is: | $P(A\ and\ B)$ Is: | $P(A|B)$ Is: |
> |---|---|---|---|
> | Mutually Exclusive | $P(A) + P(B)$ | 0 | 0 |
> | Independent | $P(A) + P(B) - P(A)P(B)$ | $P(A)P(B)$ | $P(A)$ |
> | Any | $P(A) + P(B) - P(A\ and\ B)$ | $P(A)P(B|A)$ | $\dfrac{P(A\ and\ B)}{P(B)}$ |

Sampling with and without Replacement

Suppose a classroom has 30 students in it and 3 of the students are left-handed. If the teacher randomly picks one student, the probability a left-handed student is selected is 3/30 or 1/10. The probability that a right-handed student is selected is 27/30 or 9/10. Now suppose the teacher randomly picks a student again. What is the probability that another left-handed student is chosen? The answer is that it depends on whether the first student selected is eligible to be selected again.

> *definition* ◆ A **sample** is drawn **with replacement** if individuals are returned to the eligible pool for each selection.
>
> ◆ A **sample** is drawn **without replacement** if sampled individuals are not eligible for subsequent selection.

To determine the probability of a sequence of events, we use the multiplication rule. If sampling is done *with replacement,* the Extension of Rule 3b holds. If sampling is done *without replacement,* probability calculations are more complicated because the probabilities of the possible outcomes at any specific time in the sequence are *conditional* on previous outcomes.

Consider randomly drawing two left-handed students from a class of 30 where 3 students are left-handed. Here is how you would find the probability that a left-handed student is drawn both times if sampling is with replacement and if sampling is without replacement:

$$\textit{Sampled with replacement: } P(\text{Left and Left}) = \left(\frac{3}{30}\right)\left(\frac{3}{30}\right) = \frac{9}{900} = \frac{1}{100}$$

$$\textit{Sampled without replacement: } P(\text{Left and Left}) = \left(\frac{3}{30}\right)\left(\frac{2}{29}\right) = \frac{6}{870} = \frac{1}{145}$$

The probability that the second student is left-handed, given that the first student was left-handed, is a conditional probability. It is found by noticing that there are 29 students remaining, of whom 2 are left-handed.

If a sample is drawn from a very large population, the distinction between sampling with and without replacement becomes unimportant. For example, suppose a city has 300,000 people of whom 30,000 are left-handed. If two people are sampled, the probability that they are both left-handed is $1/100 = .01$ if drawn with replacement, and .0099997 if drawn without replacement. In most polls, individuals are drawn without replacement, but the analysis of the results is done as if they were drawn with replacement. The consequences of making this simplifying assumption are negligible.

7.5 | STRATEGIES FOR FINDING COMPLICATED PROBABILITIES

Much like we build complicated sentences using basic words and simple rules, we can compute complicated probabilities using the basic rules for probability relationships. Finding probabilities of complicated events is somewhat like trying to drive from one city to another. There often are many different routes that get you there. Some routes are faster than others, but all will get you to your destination. When you attempt to solve a probability problem, remember that you may take a different approach than this book or your professor or friend. The important thing is that you all get to the same answer eventually.

---

in summary **Probability Rules 1 Through 4**

Rule 1 (for "not the event"): To find the probability of A^C, the complement of A, use $P(A^C) = 1 - P(A)$

Rule 2 (addition rule for "either or"): To find the probability that either A *or* B happens:

> **Rule 2a (general):** $P(A \text{ or } B) = P(A) + P(B) - P(A \text{ and } B)$

> **Rule 2b (for mutually exclusive events):** *If* A and B are *mutually exclusive* events: $P(A \text{ or } B) = P(A) + P(B)$

Rule 3 (multiplication rule for "and"): To find the probability that two events both occur simultaneously or in a sequence:

> **Rule 3a (general):** $P(A \text{ and } B) = P(A)P(B|A)$

> **Rule 3b (for independent events):** *If* A and B are *independent* events, $P(A \text{ and } B) = P(A)P(B)$

> **Extension of Rule 3b to more than two independent events:** For several independent events, $P(A_1 \text{ and } A_2 \ldots \text{ and } A_n) = P(A_1)P(A_2) \cdots P(A_n)$

Rule 4 (conditional probability): To find the probability that B occurs given that A has occurred:

$$P(B|A) = \frac{P(A \text{ and } B)}{P(A)}$$

The assignment of letters to events A and B is arbitrary, so it is also true that

$$P(A|B) = \frac{P(A \text{ and } B)}{P(B)}$$

EXAMPLE 7.2—CONTINUED
Winning the Lottery

Suppose you have purchased a lottery ticket with the number 956. What is the probability that you will win? Let the event A = winning number is 956. Here are two methods for finding $P(A)$:

Method 1: With the physical assumption that all 1000 possibilities are equally likely, it is clear that $P(A) = 1/1000$.

Method 2: Define three events,

B_1 = first digit drawn is 9
B_2 = second digit drawn is 5
B_3 = third digit drawn is 6

Event A occurs if and only if all three of these events occur. With the physical assumption that each of the ten digits $(0, 1, \ldots, 9)$ is equally likely on each draw, $P(B_1) = P(B_2) = P(B_3) = 1/10$. Since these events are all independent, we can apply the Extension of Rule 3b to find $P(A) = (1/10)^3 = 1/1000$.

Both of these methods are effective in determining the correct answer, but the first method is faster. ◆

Hints and Advice for Finding Probabilities

- To find $P(A \text{ and } B)$, define the combined event in physical terms and see if you know its probability. If this fails, try the multiplication rule (Rule 3).

- To find the probability that a series of independent events all happen, simply multiply all individual probabilities (Extension of Rule 3b).

- To find the probability that one of a collection of mutually exclusive events happens, simply add all of the individual probabilities (Rule 2b extended).

- It is sometimes easier to find the probability of the *complement* of the event of interest and then subtract it from 1 (applying Rule 1).

- To find the probability that *none* of a collection of mutually exclusive events happens, find the probability that one of them happens, and then subtract that from 1.

- To find a conditional probability, define the event in physical terms and see if you know its probability. If this fails, try Rule 4. See the next bullet as well.

- If you know $P(B|A)$ but are trying to find $P(A|B)$, you can use Rule 3a to find the two pieces in $P(B) = P(A \text{ and } B) + P(A^C \text{ and } B)$, then use Rule 4 to find $P(A|B)$.

Bayes Rule

formula The last tip is an informal statement of **Bayes Rule**, which states:

$$P(A|B) = \frac{P(A \text{ and } B)}{P(B|A)P(A) + P(B|A^c)P(A^c)}$$

This rule looks complicated, but note that the denominator is simply $P(B)$ broken into two parts, $P(A \text{ and } B) + P(A^C \text{ and } B)$, each written using Rule 3a.

A Specific Set of Steps for Finding Probabilities

Here are a series of steps that usually work for solving probability problems. You may prefer to take a different route to solve problems, which is fine as long as you reach the same final destination.

Step 1: List each separate random circumstance involved in the problem.

Step 2: List the possible outcomes for each random circumstance.

List mutually exclusive events covering all possibilities. Determine the simplest events for which you want to specify probabilities. For instance, when we determined whether or not Alicia was called upon to answer question 1, we did not need to list each of the possible outcomes, the 50 students, separately. We simply listed whether or not Alicia was selected.

Step 3: Assign whatever probabilities you can with the knowledge you have.

Sometimes this will require making physical assumptions, sometimes it will be based on long-run frequencies, and sometimes it will be based on personal probabilities. Sometimes the probabilities you know how to assign are conditional probabilities.

Step 4: Specify the event for which you want to determine the probability.

Do this in terms of the possible outcomes listed in step 2.

Step 5: Determine which of the probabilities from step 3 and which probability rules can be combined to find the probability of interest.

Remember that there may be several ways to do this.

EXAMPLE 7.15
Family Composition

Assume the probability that each birth in a family is a boy is .512 and that the outcomes of successive births are independent. If the family has three children, what is the probability that they have two boys and one girl (in any order)? Here are two equally correct solutions to this problem:

Example 7.15, Solution 1
Define each birth as a separate "random circumstance."

Step 1: List all of the separate random circumstances involved in the problem.

Step 2: List the possible outcomes for each random circumstance.

Step 3: Assign whatever probabilities you can with the knowledge you have.

For these three steps, define three random circumstances to be birth of first child, birth of second child, and birth of third child. For each of these circumstances, there are two possible outcomes, boy and girl. Let B_1, B_2, and B_3 be the event that birth 1, birth 2, and birth 3, respectively, result in a boy. Then $P(B_1) = P(B_2) = P(B_3) = .512$. Similarly, let G_1 be the event that the first birth results in a girl. (Notice that we could write this as B_1^C, but the notation is awkward.) Similarly define G_2 and G_3 as girls for births 2 and 3. Then $P(G_1) = P(G_2) = P(G_3) = 1 - .512 = .488$.

Step 4: Specify the event for which you want to determine the probability.

The event "two boys and one girl" can happen in any of the following three ways:

(B_1 and B_2 and G_3) *or* (B_1 and G_2 and B_3) *or* (G_1 and B_2 and B_3).

Step 5: Determine which of the probabilities from step 3 and which probability rules can be combined to find the probability of interest.

Since birth outcomes are independent, and since the events in step 4 involve "and" statements, use the Extension of Rule 3b to find:

$$P(B_1 \text{ and } B_2 \text{ and } G_3) = (.512)(.512)(.488) = .1279$$
$$P(B_1 \text{ and } G_2 \text{ and } B_3) = (.512)(.488)(.512) = .1279$$
$$P(G_1 \text{ and } B_2 \text{ and } B_3) = (.488)(.512)(.512) = .1279$$

Finally, because these are disjoint, $P[(B_1 \text{ and } B_2 \text{ and } G_3)$ *or* $(B_1 \text{ and } G_2 \text{ and } B_3)$ *or* $(G_1 \text{ and } B_2 \text{ and } B_3)] = .1279 + .1279 + .1279 = .3837$. There is about a 38% chance that the family will have two boys and one girl.

Example 7.15, Solution 2

Define the collection of births in the family as one "random circumstance." This requires listing all possible sets of three births. We use the notation BGB to indicate that the first birth is a boy, the second is a girl, and the third is a boy, and similarly for all of the possible outcomes.

Step 1: List all of the separate random circumstances involved in the problem.

Step 2: List the possible outcomes for each random circumstance.

For steps 1 and 2, the random circumstance is the three births, and the possible outcomes are {GGG,GGB,GBG,BGG,BBG,BGB,GBB,BBB}.

Step 3: Assign whatever probabilities you can with the knowledge you have.

Since the births are independent, the probability of each outcome is found by multiplying .512 for each B and .488 for each G. For instance, $P(BGG) = (.512)(.488)(.488) = .1219$.

Step 4: Specify the event for which you want to determine the probability.

The event "two boys and one girl" consists of the following subset of the sample space: {BBG,BGB,GBB}.

Step 5: Determine which of the probabilities from step 3 and which probability rules can be combined to find the probability of interest.

Using Rule 2b, add the probabilities of the three disjoint outcomes listed in step 4. Each one has probability $(.512)(.512)(.488) = .1279$, so the combined probability of two boys and one girl is $.1279 + .1279 + .1279 = .3837$. ◆

EXAMPLE 7.16
Prizes in Cereal Boxes

A particular brand of cereal contains a prize in each box. There are four possible prizes, and any box is equally likely to contain each of the four prizes. What is the probability that you will receive two different prizes if you purchase two boxes? Here are the known facts:

◆ The probability of receiving each prize is 1/4 for each box.

◆ The prizes you receive in two boxes are independent of each other.

There are a number of equally correct ways to solve this problem. The simplest method is to recognize that no matter what you receive in the first box, the probability of receiving a different prize in the second box is 3/4. Therefore, the probability of receiving two different prizes is 3/4. Here is a more detailed method.

Label the four prizes as a,b,c,d and define an "outcome" as the pair of prizes from the first and second box. Since outcomes are independent, the probability of any pair is found from Rule 3b to be $(1/4)(1/4) = 1/16$. The sample space is

{aa,ab,ac,ad,ba,bb,bc,bd,ca,cb,cc,cd,da,db,dc,dd}

There are 12 disjoint ways to get two different prizes, so reapplying Rule 2b, the probability of getting two different prizes is $12(1/16) = 12/16 = 3/4$. ◆

EXAMPLE 7.17
Optimism for Alicia —
She Is Probably Healthy

If you were in Alicia's position, you would be most interested in finding the probability of having the disease, *given* that the test was positive. Let's use these steps to find that probability.

Steps 1 to 3: Random circumstances, possible outcomes and known probabilities.

Random circumstance 1:   Alicia's disease status

    Possible Outcomes: A = disease

                        A^C = no disease

       Probabilities: $P(A) = 1/1000 = .001$ (from her physician's knowledge)

                        $P(A^C) = 999/1000 = .999$

Random circumstance 2:   Alicia's test results

    Possible Outcomes: B = test is positive

                        B^C = test is negative

Probabilities: We only know conditional probabilities, from her physician:

$P(B|A) = .95$ (positive test given disease)

$P(B^C|A) = .05$ (negative test given disease)

$P(B|A^C) = .05$ (positive test given no disease)

$P(B^C|A^C) = .95$ (negative test given no disease)

Step 4: Specify the event for which you want to determine the probability.

We would like to know $P(\text{disease}|\text{positive test}) = P(A|B)$.

Step 5: Determine which of the probabilities from step 3 and which probability rules can be combined to find the probability of interest.

The first thing to notice is that this is a conditional probability, so we first try to use either the definition of conditional probability or Rule 4. Neither of these works immediately, but notice that we have conditional probabilities in one direction and want them in the other direction. Using the last of the above tips, we follow these steps:

$P(B) = P(A \text{ and } B) + P(A^C \text{ and } B)$, since these are the disjoint and complete ways B can happen.

From Rule 3a, find $P(A \text{ and } B) = P(B|A)P(A)$, similarly find $P(A^C \text{ and } B)$. Add them to get $P(B)$.

$$P(A \text{ and } B) = P(B|A)P(A) = (.95)(.001) = .00095$$
$$P(A^C \text{ and } B) = P(B|A^C)P(A^C) = (.05)(.999) = .04995$$
$$P(B) = .0509$$

From Rule 4 and the pieces you just found, you can now find $P(A|B)$:

$$P(A|B) = \frac{P(A \text{ and } B)}{P(B)} = \frac{.00095}{.0509} = .019$$

Notice what this tells Alicia! Even though her test was positive, the probability that she *actually has disease D is only .019.* There is less than a 2% chance that Alicia has the disease, even though her test was positive. The fact that so many more people are disease-free than diseased means that the 5% of disease-free people who falsely test positive far outweigh the 95% of those with the disease who legitimately test positive. ◆

Two-Way Tables and Tree Diagrams — Two Useful Tools

There are two useful tools for illustrating combinations of events and answering questions about them. The two tools, constructing a hypothetical two-way table and constructing a tree diagram, are particularly useful when conditional probabilities are already known in one direction, such as $P(A|B)$. The tools can then be used to find $P(A$ and $B)$, $P(B|A)$, and other probabilities of interest.

Constructing a Two-Way Table:
The "Hypothetical Hundred Thousand"

When conditional or joint probabilities are known for two events, it is sometimes useful to construct a hypothetical two-way table of outcomes for a round number of individuals, and 100,000 is a good number because usually it results in whole numbers of people in each cell. Therefore, we will call this method the *hypothetical hundred thousand.* Let's illustrate the idea with an example.

EXAMPLE 7.8—*CONTINUED*
Teens and Gambling

In Example 7.8, a study was reported in which 9th-grade Minnesota teens were asked whether they had gambled at least once a week during the past year. The sample consisted of 49.1% boys and 50.9% girls. The proportion of boys who had gambled weekly was .229, while the proportion of girls who had done so was only .045. If we were to construct a table for a hypothetical group of 100,000 teens reflecting these proportions, there would be $(.491)(100,000) = 49,100$ boys, and 50,900 girls. Of the 49,100 boys, $(.229 \times 49,100)$ or 11,244 would be weekly gamblers, and of the 50,900 girls, .045, or 2,291 girls would be weekly gamblers. The "hypothetical hundred thousand" table can be constructed by starting with these numbers and filling in the rest by subtraction and addition. Here is the resulting table:

	Weekly Gambler	Not Weekly Gambler	Total
Boy	11,244	37,856	49,100
Girl	2,291	48,609	50,900
Total	13,535	86,465	100,000

It's easy to find various probabilities from this table. Here are some examples:

- ◆ P(boy and weekly gambler) $= 11,244/100,000 = .11244$, so about 11% of 9th graders are boys who gamble weekly.
- ◆ P(boy|weekly gambler) $= 11,244/13,535 = .8307$, so about 83% of weekly gamblers are boys.
- ◆ P(weekly gambler) $= 13,535/100,000 = .13535$, so about 13.5% of 9th graders are weekly gamblers. ◆

Tree Diagrams

Another useful tool for combinations of events is a tree diagram. A **tree diagram** is a schematic representation of the sequence of events and their probabilities, including conditional probabilities based on previous events for events that happen sequentially. It is easiest to illustrate by example.

EXAMPLE 7.18
Alicia's Possible Fates

Let's consider what could have happened with Alicia's medical test, and the probabilities associated with those options. There are two random circumstances involved. The first circumstance is whether or not she has the disease (*D* or *not D*), and the second circumstance is whether the test result is positive or negative (*positive test* or *negative test*). We have already specified the probabilities of each of the pieces, and using Rule 3a we can find the probabilities of the various combinations, like the probability that Alicia has the disease but the test result is negative.

Figure 7.1 illustrates these probabilities in a tree diagram. The initial set of branches shows the two possibilities and associated probabilities for her disease status. The next set of branches shows the two possibilities for the outcome of the test and associated *conditional probabilities* depending on whether or not she has the disease. The "final probability" shown for each combination of branches is found by multiplying the probabilities on the branches, applying Rule 3a. Thus, for instance, the probability that Alicia has D *and* has a positive test is .00095. ◆

Here are the general steps for creating a tree diagram:

Step 1: Determine the first random circumstance in the sequence, and create the first set of branches to illustrate possible outcomes for it. Create one branch for each outcome, and write the associated probability on the branch.

Step 2: Determine the next random circumstance, and append branches for the possible outcomes to each of the branches in step 1. Write the associated *conditional probabilities* on the branches, where the outcome for step 2 is *conditional* on the branch taken in step 1.

Step 3: Continue this process for as many steps (and sets of branches) as necessary.

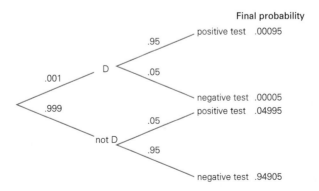

FIGURE 7.1 **Tree diagram for Alicia's medical test**

Step 4: To determine the probability of following any particular sequence of branches, multiply the probabilities on those branches. This is an application of Rule 3a.

Step 5: To determine the probability of any collection of sequences of branches, add the individual probabilities for those sequences, as found in step 4. This is an application of Rule 2b.

EXAMPLE 7.18 — *CONTINUED*
The Probability That
Alicia Has a Positive Test

Notice that Alicia's test is positive if she follows branch D and then branch "positive test" *or* if she follows branch "not D" and then branch "positive test." The overall probability that the test is positive can be found by adding the probabilities from these two sets of branches. Hence,

$$P(\text{positive test}) = (.001)(.95) + (.999)(.05) = .00095 + .04995 = .0509$$

In other words, for all women like Alicia who are tested, including the .001 of them with the disease and the .999 of them without the disease, a positive test will occur with probability .0509. This is equivalent to saying that .0509 or 5.09% of these women will have a positive test. ◆

It is always the case that the first set of branches in a tree diagram displays probabilities for the outcomes of one random circumstance, then the second set of branches displays *conditional* probabilities for the outcomes of another random circumstance, *given* what happened on the first one. In general, the first set of branches corresponds to the circumstance that occurs first chronologically, if the events have a time order. If they don't have a time order, then think about what probabilities are known. You must know the unconditional probabilities of outcomes for the events on the first set of branches.

EXAMPLE 7.8 — *CONTINUED*
Teens and Gambling

Let's construct a tree diagram using the information provided in Example 7.8 about the gambling behavior of 9th-grade Minnesota teenagers. For a randomly selected 9th grader, the two random circumstances are gender (boy or girl) and weekly gambler (yes or no). We know the unconditional probabilities for gender: $P(\text{boy}) = .491$ and $P(\text{girl}) = .509$. We know the *conditional* probabilities of weekly gambling, *given* gender: $P(\text{weekly gambler}|\text{boy}) = .229$ and $P(\text{weekly gambler}|\text{girl}) = .045$. Therefore, the first set of branches represents gender and the second set represents weekly gambler or not. Figure 7.2 illustrates the completed tree diagram.

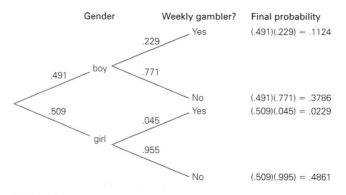

FIGURE 7.2 **Tree diagram for 9th-grade teens and weekly gambling**

Once the tree diagram is completed, we can easily find probabilities for any combination of gender *and* weekly gambling by multiplying the probabilities across branches. For instance,

$$P(\text{boy and weekly gambler}) = (.491)(.229) = .1124$$

$$P(\text{girl and not weekly gambler}) = (.509)(.955) = .4861$$

We can find other probabilities by adding outcomes from two sets of branches. For instance,

$$P(\text{weekly gambler}) = P(\text{boy and weekly gambler}) + P(\text{girl and weekly gambler}) = (.1124) + (.0229) = .1353$$

Finally, we can find conditional probabilities in the opposite direction to those known by finding probabilities such as those we just found and then applying Rule 4. For instance,

$$P(\text{boy}|\text{weekly gambler}) = \frac{P(\text{boy and weekly gambler})}{P(\text{weekly gambler})} = \frac{.1124}{.1353} = .8307. \; \blacklozenge$$

Probabilities, Proportions, and Percents

tech note In many of the examples in this chapter we have discussed probabilities associated with a "randomly selected individual" from a population. These are equivalent to percents in the population with specific characteristics, but multiplying percents doesn't work. For instance, in Example 7.8, 49.1% or .491, of the teens were boys and of those, 22.9%, or .229, were weekly gamblers. To find what *percent* of the teens were boys *and* weekly gamblers, it would not work to multiply (49.1%)(22.9%) = 1124.39%. Instead, convert everything to proportions, multiply, then convert back to a percent by multiplying by 100%: (.491)(.229) = .1124, or .1124 × 100% = 11.24% of the teens are boys who gamble weekly. Proportions can always be interpreted as percents in this manner. For instance, in Example 7.18— *CONTINUED,* we found that for all women like Alicia who are tested for this disease, .0509 × 100% = 5.09% will have a positive test, including 4.995% who do not have the disease and test positive and only .095% who have the disease and test positive.

7.6

turn on your mind

Explain why the tree diagram in Figure 7.1 displayed disease status first and test results second rather than the other way around.*

7.6 | USING SIMULATION TO ESTIMATE PROBABILITIES

Some probabilities are so difficult or time-consuming to calculate that it is easier to simulate the situation repeatedly using a computer or calculator and observe the relative frequency of the event of interest. If you simulate the random circumstance n times and the outcome of interest occurs in x out of those n

*HINT: See the paragraph just before the previous Example, 7.8—*CONTINUED.*

times, then the estimated probability for the outcome of interest is x/n. This is an estimate of the long-run relative frequency with which the outcome would occur in real life.

EXAMPLE 7.19
Getting All the Prizes

Refer to the situation in Example 7.16. Suppose cereal boxes each contain one of four prizes, and any box is equally likely to contain any of the four prizes. You would like to collect all four prizes. If you buy six boxes of cereal, how likely is it that you will get all four prizes?

It would be quite time-consuming to solve this problem using the rules presented in the previous sections. It is much simpler to simulate the situation using a computer or calculator. Table 7.3 shows 50 simulations using the Minitab computer software. In each case, six digits were drawn, each equally likely to be 1, 2, 3 or 4. The outcomes that contain all four digits are highlighted in bold.

Counting the outcomes in bold reveals that 19 out of 50, or .38, of these simulations satisfy the condition that all four prizes are collected. In fact, this simulation had particularly good results. There are $4^6 = 4096$ equally likely possible outcomes for listing six digits randomly chosen from 1, 2, 3, 4, and 1560 of those outcomes include all four digits. So the actual probability of getting all four prizes is $1560/4096 = .3809$. ◆

In general, determining the accuracy of simulation for estimating a probability is similar to determining the margin of error when estimating a proportion from a sample survey. The probability estimated by simulation will be no farther off than $1/\sqrt{n}$ most of the time, where n is the number of simulated repetitions of the situation.

This information about the accuracy of the simulation approach for estimating probabilities should make it clear that you need to repeat the simulated situation a large number of times to obtain accurate results. Therefore, it is most useful if you can use a computer to generate the simulated outcomes and also to count how many of them satisfy the event of interest.

EXAMPLE 7.20
Finding Gifted ESP Participants

An ESP test is conducted by randomly selecting one of five video clips and playing it in one building, while a participant in another building tries to describe what is playing. Later, the participant is shown the five video clips and is asked to determine which one best matches the description he or she had given. By chance, the participant would get this correct with probability 1/5. Individual participants are each tested eight times, with five new video clips each time. They are identified as "gifted" if they guess correctly at least five times out of the

TABLE 7.3 ■ 50 Simulations of Prizes from Cereal Boxes

112142	443222	323324	321223	**332314**
224123	342324	**232413**	121123	422244
244412	**342431**	121333	**244132**	434224
234323	**144332**	121142	**432121**	144313
443313	211141	**421342**	441211	111134
113432	433424	**312314**	241114	313411
214443	222422	144441	**213141**	312232
312341	411124	111422	312213	**323314**
143124	111131	**441233**	121223	424433
213341	114333	**243311**	442244	**214133**

eight tries. Suppose people actually do have some ESP and can guess correctly with probability .30 (instead of the .20 expected by chance). What is the probability that a participant will be identified as "gifted"?

In Chapter 8 you will learn how to solve this kind of problem, but we can simulate the answer using a random number table or generator that produces the digits 0, 1, 2, . . . , 9 with equal likelihood. Table 4.1 (page 95) is an example of a random number table. Many calculators and computers will simulate these digits. Here are the steps needed for one "repetition":

- Each "guess" is simulated with a digit, equally likely to be 0 to 9.
- For each participant, we simulate eight "guesses" resulting in a string of eight digits.
- If a digit is 7, 8, or 9, we count that guess as "correct" so $P(\text{correct}) = 3/10 = .3$, as required in the problem. If the digit is 0 to 6, the guess is "incorrect." (There is nothing special about 7, 8, 9; we could have used any three digits.)
- If there are five or more "correct" guesses (digits 7, 8, 9), we count that as "gifted."

The entire process is repeated many times, and the proportion of times the result is a "gifted" participant is an estimate of the desired probability.

Process and Results Using Minitab

1. Generate 1000 rows of 8 columns, using random integers from 0 to 9. Each row represents the 8 guesses for one participant.
2. Use the "code" feature to recode all of the values, $(7,8,9) \rightarrow 1$, $(0,1,2,3,4,5,6) \rightarrow 0$.
3. Sum the 8 columns; for each row (each participant) the sum is the number of "correct" guesses. This is equivalent to the number of 1s in the row after recoding.
4. The sums are now in a column with 1000 rows. Tally this column to find out how many of the participants had five or more "correct guesses."
5. The results of doing this were as follows:

Number Correct	0	1	2	3	4	5	6	7	8
Frequency	64	187	299	271	119	44	14	2	0

Notice that there were $44 + 14 + 2 + 0 = 60$ individuals who got five or more correct, so the probability of finding a "gifted" participant each time is about $60/1000 = .06$. In other words, if everyone is equally talented, and each guess is correct with probability .3, then there will be five or more correct guesses out of eight tries with probability .06, or about 6% of the time. ◆

7.7

turn on your mind

Does using simulation to estimate probabilities rely on the relative frequency or the personal probability interpretation of probability? Explain. Whichever one you chose, could simulation be used to find probabilities for the other interpretation? Explain.*

*HINT: Could you tell a computer what proportions to use if you and your friend do not agree on what to use?

7.7 | COINCIDENCES AND INTUITIVE JUDGMENTS ABOUT PROBABILITY

People do not have good intuition about probability assessments. In Case Study 7.1, Alicia's physician made a common mistake by informing her that the medical test was a good indicator of her disease status since it was 95% accurate whether or not she had the disease. As we learned in Example 7.17, the probability that she actually has the disease is small, about 2%. In this section, we explore this phenomenon, called "Confusion of the Inverse," and some other ways in which intuitive probability assessments can be seriously flawed.

Confusion of the Inverse

Eddy (1982) posed the following scenario to 100 physicians:

> One of your patients has a lump in her breast. You are almost certain that it is benign, in fact you would say there is only a 1% chance that it is malignant. But just to be sure, you have the patient undergo a mammogram, a breast X-ray designed to detect cancer.
>
> You know from the medical literature that mammograms are 80% accurate for malignant lumps and 90% accurate for benign lumps. In other words, if the lump is truly malignant, the test results will say that it is malignant 80% of the time and will falsely say it is benign 20% of the time. If the lump is truly benign, the test results will say so 90% of the time and will falsely declare that it is malignant only 10% of the time.
>
> Sadly, the mammogram for your patient is returned with the news that the lump is malignant. What are the chances that it is truly malignant?

Most of the physicians to whom Eddy posed this question thought the probability that the lump was truly malignant was about 75% or .75. In truth, given the probabilities described in the scenario, *the probability is only .075.* The physicians' estimates were ten times too high! When Eddy asked the physicians how they arrived at their answers, he realized they were confusing the answer to the actual question with the answer to a different question. "When asked about this, the erring physicians usually report that they assumed that the probability of cancer given that the patient has a positive X-ray was approximately equal to the probability of a positive X-ray in a patient with cancer" (1982, p. 254).

Robyn Dawes has called this phenomenon **confusion of the inverse** (Plous, 1993, p. 132). The physicians were confusing the conditional probability of cancer *given a positive X-ray* with the inverse, the conditional probability of a positive X-ray *given that the patient has cancer!*

It is not difficult to see that the correct answer is indeed .075. Let's construct a hypothetical table of 100,000 women who fit this scenario. In other words, these are women who would present themselves to the physician with a lump for which the probability that it was malignant seemed to be about 1%. Thus, of the 100,000 women, about 1%, or 1000 of them, would have a malignant lump. The remaining 99%, or 99,000, would have a benign lump.

Further, given that the test was 80% accurate for malignant lumps, it would show a malignancy for 800 of the 1000 women who actually had one. Given that it was 90% accurate for the 99,000 women with benign lumps, it would show benign

TABLE 7.4 ■ Breakdown of Actual Status Versus Test Status for a Rare Disease

	Test is Malignant	Test is Benign	Total
Actually Malignant	800	200	1000
Actually Benign	9900	89,100	99,000
Total	10,700	89,300	100,000

for 90%, or 89,100 of them, and malignant for the remaining 10%, or 9900 of them. Table 7.4 shows how the 100,000 women would fall into these possible categories.

Let's return to the question of interest. Our patient has just received a positive test for malignancy. Given that her test showed malignancy, what is the actual probability that her lump is malignant? Of the 100,000 women, 10,700 of them would have an X-ray show malignancy. But of those 10,700 women, only 800 of them actually have a malignant lump! Thus, given that the test showed a malignancy, the probability of malignancy is just 800/10,700 = 8/107 = .075.

Sadly, many physicians are guilty of confusion of the inverse. Remember, in a situation where the *base rate* for a disease is very low and the test for the disease is less than perfect, there will be a relatively high probability that a positive test result is a false positive. If you ever find yourself in a situation similar to the one just described, you may wish to construct a table like the one above.

To determine the probability of a positive test result being accurate, you only need three pieces of information.

1. What the base rate or probability that you are likely to have the disease is, without any knowledge of your test results.
2. What the **sensitivity** of the test is, which is the proportion of people who correctly test positive when they actually have the disease.
3. What the **specificity** of the test is, which is the proportion of people who correctly test negative when they don't have the disease.

Notice that items 2 and 3 are measures of the accuracy of the test. They do not measure the probability that people have the disease when they test positive or the probability that they do not have the disease when they test negative. Those probabilities, which are obviously the ones of interest to the patient, can be computed by constructing a table similar to Table 7.4 or by the other methods shown earlier in this chapter.

Specific People Versus Random Individuals

According to the Federal Aviation Administration, between 1987 and 1996 there were 39 fatal airline accidents for regularly scheduled flights on U.S. carriers. During that same time period, there were 76,557,000 flight departures. That means that the relative frequency of fatal accidents was about one accident per 2 million departures. Based on these kinds of statistics you will sometimes hear statements like "The probability that you will be in a fatal plane crash is 1 in 2 million" or "The chance that your marriage will end in divorce is 50%."

Do these probability statements really apply to you personally? In an attempt to personalize the information, reporters express probability statements in terms of individuals when they actually apply to the aggregate. Obviously, if you never fly, the probability that you will be in a fatal plane crash is 0. Here are two equivalent, correct ways to restate the aggregate statistics about fatal plane crashes:

◆ In the long run, about 1 out of every 2 million flight departures end in a fatal crash.

◆ The probability that a randomly selected flight departure ends in a fatal crash is about 1/2,000,000.

If you have had a terrific marriage for 30 years, it is not likely to end in divorce now. Your probability of a divorce surely is less than the 50% figure often reported in the media. Here are two correct ways to express aggregate statistics about divorce:

◆ In the long run, about 50% of marriages end in divorce.

◆ At the beginning of a randomly selected marriage, the probability that it will end in divorce is about .50.

Notice the emphasis on "random selection" in the second version of each statement. Sometimes the phrase "randomly selected" is omitted, but it should always be understood that randomness is part of the communication.

Coincidences

When one of the authors of this book was in college in upstate New York, she visited Disney World in Florida during summer break. While there, she ran into three people she knew from her college, none of whom were there together. A few years later, she visited the top of the Empire State Building in New York City and ran into two friends (who were there together) and two additional unrelated acquaintances. Years later, when traveling from London to Stockholm she ran into a friend at the airport in London while waiting for the flight. Not only did the friend turn out to be taking the same flight but had been assigned an adjacent seat.

These events are all examples of what would commonly be called coincidences. They are certainly surprising, but are they improbable? Most people think that coincidences have low probabilities of occurring, but we shall see that our intuition can be quite misleading regarding such phenomena. We will adopt the definition of **coincidence** proposed by Persi Diaconis and Fred Mosteller:

> *definition* A **coincidence** is a surprising concurrence of events, perceived as meaningfully related, with no apparent causal connection. (1989, p. 853)

The mathematically sophisticated reader may wish to consult the article by Diaconis and Mosteller, in which they provide some instructions on how to compute probabilities for coincidences. For our purposes, we will need nothing more sophisticated than the simple probability rules we encountered earlier in this chapter.

Following are some examples of coincidences that at first glance seem highly improbable.

EXAMPLE 7.21
Two George D. Brysons

"My next-door neighbor, Mr. George D. Bryson, was making a business trip some years ago from St. Louis to New York. Since this involved weekend travel and he was in no hurry, . . . and since his train went through Louisville, he asked the conductor, after he had boarded the train, whether he might have a stopover in Louisville.

"This was possible, and on arrival at Louisville he inquired at the station for the leading hotel. He accordingly went to the Brown Hotel and registered. And then, just as a lark, he stepped up to the mail desk and asked if there was any mail for him. The girl calmly handed him a letter addressed to Mr. George D. Bryson, Room 307, that being the number of the room to which he had just been assigned. It turned out that the preceding resident of Room 307 was another George D. Bryson" (Weaver, 1963, pp. 282–283). ◆

EXAMPLE 7.22
Identical Cars and Matching Keys

Plous (1993, p. 154) reprinted an Associated Press news story describing a coincidence in which a man named Richard Baker and his wife were shopping on April Fool's Day at a Wisconsin shopping center. Mr. Baker went out to get their car, a 1978 maroon Concord, and drove it around to pick up his wife. After driving for a short while, they noticed items in the car that did not look familiar. They checked the license plate, and sure enough, they had someone else's car. When they drove back to the shopping center (to find the police waiting for them), they discovered that the owner of the car they were driving was a Mr. Thomas Baker, no relation to Richard Baker. Thus, both Mr. Bakers were at the same shopping center at the same time, with identical cars and with matching keys. The police estimated the odds as "a million to one." ◆

EXAMPLE 7.23
Winning the Lottery Twice

Moore (1997, p. 330) reported on a *New York Times* story of February 14, 1986, about Evelyn Marie Adams who won the New Jersey lottery twice in a short time period. Her winnings were $3.9 million the first time and $1.5 million the second time. When Ms. Adams won for the second time, the *New York Times* claimed that the odds of one person winning the top prize twice were about 1 in 17 trillion. Then, in May 1988, Robert Humphries won a second Pennsylvania lottery, bringing his total winnings to $6.8 million. ◆

Most people think that the events just described are exceedingly improbable, and they are. *What is not improbable is that someone, somewhere, someday will experience those events or something similar.*

When we examine the probability of what appears to be a startling coincidence, we ask the wrong question. For example, the figure quoted by the *New York Times* of 1 in 17 trillion is the probability that a *specific* individual who plays the New Jersey State Lottery exactly twice will win both times (Diaconis and Mosteller, 1989, p. 859.) However, millions of people play the lottery every day, and it is not surprising that someone, somewhere, someday would win twice.

In fact, Purdue professors Stephen Samuels and George McCabe (cited in Diaconis and Mosteller, 1989, p. 859) calculated those odds to be practically a sure thing. They calculated that there was at least a 1 in 30 chance of a double winner in a four-month period and better than even odds that there would be a double winner in a seven-year period somewhere in the United States. And they used conservative assumptions about how many tickets past winners had purchased.

When you experience a coincidence, remember that there are over 6 billion people in the world and over 280 million in the United States. If something has a 1 in a million probability of occurring to each individual on a given day, it will occur to an average of over 280 people in the United States *each day* and over 6000 people in the world *each day.* Of course probabilities of specific events depend on individual circumstances, but we hope you can see that it is not unlikely that something surprising will happen quite often.

EXAMPLE 7.24
Sharing the Same Birthday

Here is a famous example that you can use to test your intuition about surprising events. How many people would need to be gathered together to be at least 50% sure that two of them share the same birthday (month and day, not necessarily year)? Most people provide answers that are much higher than the correct one, which is only 23 people.

There are several reasons why people have trouble with this problem. If your answer was somewhere close to 183, or half the number of birthdays, then you may have confused the question with another one, such as the probability that someone in the group has *your* birthday or that two people have a specific date as their birthday.

It is not difficult to see how to calculate the appropriate probability, using our probability rules. Notice that the only way to avoid two people having the same birthday is if all 23 people have different birthdays. To find that probability, we simply use the rule that applies to the word *and* (Rule 3), thus multiplying probabilities. The probability that the first three people have different birthdays is the probability that the second person does not share a birthday with the first, which is 364/365 (ignoring February 29), and the third person does not share a birthday with either of the first two, which is 363/365. (Two dates were already taken.)

Continuing this line of reasoning, the probability that none of the 23 people share a birthday is

$$\frac{(364)(363)}{(365)(365)} \cdots \frac{(343)}{(365)} = .493$$

The probability that at least two people share a birthday is the probability of the complement, or $1 - .493 = .507$.

If you find it difficult to imagine this could be correct, picture it this way. Imagine each of the 23 people shaking hands with the other 22 people and asking them about their birthday. There would be 253 handshakes and birthday conversations. Surely there is a relatively high probability that at least one of those pairs would discover a common birthday.

By the way, the probability of a shared birthday in a group of ten people is already better than one in nine, at .117. (There would be 45 handshakes.) With only 50 people it is almost certain, with a probability of .97. (There would be 1225 handshakes.) ◆

The technique used in Example 7.24 can be used to illustrate why some coincidences are not at all unlikely. Consider the situation described in Example 7.21 in which two George D. Brysons held the same hotel room in succession. It is not at all unlikely that occasionally two successive occupants of a hotel room somewhere, sometime will have the same name. To see that this is so, consider the probability of the complement—that no matter who occupies a hotel room, the next occupant will have a different name. Even ignoring common names, adding these probabilities across many thousands of hotel rooms and many days, weeks, and years, it would be extremely unlikely that successive occupants would always have different names.

EXAMPLE 7.25
*Unusual Hands
in Card Games*

As a final example of unlikely coincidences, consider a card game such as bridge, in which a standard 52-card deck is dealt to four players, so they each receive 13 cards. Any specific set of 13 cards is equally likely, each with a probability of about 1 in 635 billion. You would probably not be surprised to get a mixed hand, say the 4, 7, and 10 of hearts; 3, 8, 9, and jack of spades; 2 and queen of diamonds; and 6, 10, jack, and ace of clubs. Yet, that specific hand is just as unlikely as getting all 13 hearts! The point is that any very specific event, surprising or not, has extremely low probability, but there are many, many surprising events and their combined probability is quite high.

Magicians sometimes exploit the fact that many small probabilities add up to one large probability by doing a trick in which they don't tell you what to expect in advance. They set it up so that *something* surprising is almost sure to happen. When it does, you are likely to focus on the probability of *that particular outcome*, rather than realizing that a multitude of other outcomes would have also been surprising and that one of them was likely to happen.

To summarize, most coincidences only seem improbable if we ask for the probability of that specific event occurring at that time, to us. If, instead, we ask the probability of it occurring some time, to someone, the probability can become quite large. Further, because of the multitude of experiences we each have every day, it is not surprising that some of them may appear to be improbable. That specific event is undoubtedly improbable. What is not improbable is that something "unusual" will happen to each of us once in awhile. ◆

The Gambler's Fallacy

Another common misperception about random events is that they should be self-correcting. Another way to state this is that people think the long-run frequency of an event should apply even in the short run. This misperception has classically been called the **gambler's fallacy.** Researchers William Gehring and Adrian Willoughby have discovered that this fallacy and related decision making while gambling are reflected in activity in the brain, in "a medial-frontal region in or near the anterior cingulate cortex" (p. 2279).

The gambler's fallacy can lead to poor decision making, especially if applied to gambling. For example, people tend to believe that a string of good luck will follow a string of bad luck in a casino. Unfortunately, independent chance events have no such memory. Making ten bad gambles in a row doesn't change the probability that the next gamble will also be bad.

Notice that the gambler's fallacy primarily applies to independent events. The gambler's fallacy may not apply to situations where knowledge of one outcome affects probabilities of the next. For instance, in card games using a single deck, knowledge of what cards have already been played provides information about what cards are likely to be played next, and gamblers routinely make use of that information. If you normally receive lots of mail but have received none for two days, you would probably (correctly) assess that you are likely to receive more than usual the next day.

A somewhat different but related misconception is what Tversky and Kahneman (1982) call the belief in the **law of small numbers,** "according to which [people believe that] even small samples are highly representative of the populations from which they are drawn" (p. 7). They report that "in considering tosses of a coin for heads and tails, for example, people regard the sequence HTHTTH to be more likely than the sequence HHHTTT, which does not appear random, and also more likely than the sequence HHHHTH, which does not represent the fairness of the coin" (p. 7). Remember that any specific sequence of heads and tails is just as likely as any other sequence if the coin is fair, so the idea that the first sequence is more likely is a misperception.

7.8

turn on your mind

If you wanted to pretend to be psychic you could do a "cold reading" on someone you do not know. Suppose you are doing this for a 25-year-old woman. You make statements such as the following:

◆ I see that you are thinking of two men, one with dark hair, and the other one with slightly lighter hair or complexion. Do you know who I mean?

◆ I see a friend who is important to you but who has disappointed you recently.

◆ I see that there is some distance between you and your mother that bothers you.

Using the material in this section, explain why this would often work to convince people you are psychic.*

KEY TERMS

EXERCISES   Blue = Basics   **Bold, Bold** = Answer in back

Sections 7.1 and 7.2

7.1   According to a U.S. Department of Transportation website (http://www.dot.gov/airconsumer), 76.1% of domestic flights flown by the top ten U.S. airlines from June 1998 to May 1999 arrived on time. Represent this in terms of a random circumstance and an associated probability.

7.2   Suppose you live in a city that has 125,000 households with telephones and a polling organization randomly selects 1000 of them to phone for a survey. What is the probability that your household will be selected?

7.3   Jan is a member of a class with 20 students. Each day for a week (Monday to Friday) a student in Jan's class is randomly selected to explain how to solve a homework prob-

lem. Once a student has been selected, he or she is not selected again that week. If Jan was not one of the four students selected earlier in the week, what is the probability that she will be picked on Friday? Explain how you found your answer.

7.4   Is each of the following values a legitimate probability value? Explain any "no" answers.

a. .50
b. .00
c. 1.00
d. 1.25
e. −.25

7.5   Which interpretation of probability applies to each of the following situations? If it's the relative frequency interpretation, explain which of the three methods listed in the "In Summary" box at the end of Section 7.2 applies.

a. If a spoon is tossed 10,000 times and lands with the rounded head face up 3,000 of those times, we would say that the probability of the rounded head landing face up for that spoon is about .30.

b. In a debate with you, a friend says that she thinks there is a 50–50 chance that God exists.

c. Based on data from the 1991 to 1993 General Social Survey, the probability in those years was about 612/1669 = .367 that a randomly selected adult who had ever been married had divorced.

7.6 A car dealer has noticed that one out of 25 new-car buyers returns the car for warranty work within the first month.

a. Write a sentence expressing this fact as a proportion.

b. Write a sentence expressing this fact as a percent.

c. Write a sentence expressing this fact as a probability.

7.7 Explain which interpretation of probability (relative frequency or personal) applies to each of these statements and how you think the probability was determined.

a. According to Krantz (1992, p. 161), the probability that a randomly selected American will be injured by lightning in a given year is 1/685,000.

b. According to my neighbor, the probability that the tomato plants she planted last month will actually survive to produce fruit is only 1/2.

c. According to the nursery where my neighbor purchased her tomato plants, if a plant is properly cared for, the probability it will produce tomatoes is .99.

d. The probability that a husband will outlive his wife (for U.S. couples) is 3/10 (Krantz, 1992, p. 163).

7.8 Identify three "random circumstances" in the following story and give the possible outcomes for each of them:

> It was Robin's birthday and she knew she was going to have a good day. She was driving to work and when she turned on the radio her favorite song was playing. Besides, the traffic light at the main intersection she crossed to get to work was green when she arrived, something that seemed to happen less than once a week. When she arrived at work, rather than having to search as she usually did, she found an empty parking space right in front of the building.

7.9 Refer to the previous exercise. Suppose Robin wants to find the probability associated with the outcomes in the random circumstances contained in the story. Identify one of the circumstances and explain how she could determine the probabilities associated with its outcomes.

7.10 Casino games often use a "fair die" that has six sides with 1 to 6 dots on them. When the die is tossed or rolled, each of the six sides is equally likely to come out on top. Using the physical assumption that the die is fair, determine the probability of each of the following outcomes for the number of dots showing on top after a single roll of a die:

a. Six dots.

b. One or two dots.

c. An even number of dots.

7.11 A computer solitaire game uses a standard 52-card deck and randomly shuffles the cards for play. Theoretically, it should be possible to find optimal strategies for playing and then to compute the probability of winning based on the best strategy. Not only would this be an extremely complicated problem but also the probability of winning for any particular person will depend on that person's

skill. Explain how an individual could determine his or her probability of winning this game. (*Hint:* It might take a while to determine the probability!)

7.12 Find information on a random circumstance in the news. Identify the circumstance and possible outcomes, and assign probabilities to the outcomes. Explain how you determined the probabilities.

7.13 Give an example of a situation for which a probability statement makes sense, but for which the relative frequency interpretation could not apply, such as the probability given by Carl Sagan for an asteroid hitting the Earth.

7.14 Alicia's statistics class meets 50 times during the semester, and each time it meets the probability that she will be called on to answer the first question is 1/50. Does this mean that Alicia will be called on to answer the first question exactly once during the semester? Explain.

7.15 Every day, John buys a lottery ticket with the number 777 for the simple lottery described in Example 7.2. He has now played 999 times and has not won a single time. He reasons that since tomorrow will be his 1000th time, and since the probability of winning is 1/1000, he will have to win tomorrow. Explain whether or not John's reasoning is correct.

7.16 Refer to Example 7.5. What is the probability that a randomly selected child who slept in darkness would develop some degree of myopia?

7.17 When 190 students were asked to pick a number from 1 to 10, the number of students selecting each number were as follows:

Number	1	2	3	4	5	6	7	8	9	10	Total
Frequency	2	9	22	21	18	23	56	19	14	6	190

a. What is the approximate probability that someone asked to pick a number from 1 to 10 will pick the number 3?

b. What is the approximate probability that someone asked to pick a number from 1 to 10 will pick one of the two extremes, 1 or 10?

c. What is the approximate probability that someone asked to pick a number from 1 to 10 will pick an odd number?

Section 7.3

7.18 A student wants to send a bouquet of roses to her mother for Mother's Day. She can afford to buy only two types of roses, and decides to randomly pick two from the following four varieties: Blue Bell, Yellow Success, Sahara, and Aphrodite. Label the varieties B, Y, S, A.

a. Make a list of the six simple events in the sample space.

b. Assuming all outcomes are equally likely, what is the probability that she will pick Sahara and Aphrodite?

7.19 Remember that the event A^C is the complement of the event A.

a. Are A and A^C mutually exclusive? Explain.

b. Are A and A^C independent? Explain.

7.20 A penny and a nickel are tossed. Explain whether the outcomes for the two coins are:

a. Independent events.

b. Complementary events.

c. Mutually exclusive events.

7.21 Suppose events A and B are mutually exclusive with $P(A) = 1/2$ and $P(B) = 1/3$.
  a. Are A and B independent events? Explain how you know.
  b. Are A and B complementary events? Explain how you know.

7.22 Suppose A, B, and C are all disjoint possible outcomes for the same random circumstance. Explain whether each of the following sets of probabilities is possible.
  a. $P(A) = 1/3$, $P(B) = 1/3$, $P(C) = 1/3$.
  b. $P(A) = 1/2$, $P(B) = 1/2$, $P(C) = 1/4$.
  c. $P(A) = 1/4$, $P(B) = 1/4$, $P(C) = 1/4$.

7.23 Jill and Laura have lunch together. They flip a coin to decide who pays for lunch, and then flip a coin again to decide who pays the tip. Define a "possible outcome" to be who pays for lunch and who pays the tip, in order, for example "Jill,Jill."
  a. List the simple events in the sample space.
  b. Are the simple events equally likely? If not, why not?
  c. What is the probability that Laura will have to pay for lunch and leave the tip?

7.24 Refer to Example 7.7 in which you and your friend Vanessa each enter a drawing for a free lunch in week 1 and again in week 2. Events defined were: A = you win in week 1, B = Vanessa wins in week 1, C = Vanessa wins in week 2.
  a. Are events B and C independent? Explain.
  b. Suppose that after week 1, the cards not drawn as the winning card are retained in the bowl for the drawing in week 2. Are events B and C independent? Explain.

7.25 When a fair die is tossed, each of the six sides (numbers 1 to 6) is equally likely to land face up. Two fair dice, one red and one green, are tossed. Explain whether the following pairs of events are disjoint:
  a. A = red die is a 3; B = red die is a 6.
  b. A = red die is a 3; B = green die is a 6.
  c. A = red die and green die sum to 4; B = red die is a 3.
  d. A = red die and green die sum to 4; B = red die is a 4.

7.26 Refer to the previous exercise. For each part, explain whether the two events are independent.

7.27 According to Krantz (1992, p. 102), "Women between the ages of 20 and 24 have a 90 percent chance of being fertile while women between 40 and 44 have only a 37 percent chance of bearing children [i.e., being fertile]." Define appropriate events, and write these statements as conditional probabilities, using appropriate notation.

7.28 Refer to the previous exercise. Which method of finding probabilities do you think was used to find the "90 percent chance" and "37 percent chance"? Explain.

7.29 Refer to the previous two exercises. Suppose an American woman is randomly selected. Are her age and her fertility status independent? Explain.

7.30 Refer to Case Study 7.1. Define C_1, C_2, and C_3 to be the events that Alicia is called upon to answer questions 1, 2, and 3, respectively.
  a. Based on the physical situation used to select students, what is the (unconditional) probability of each of these events? Explain.
  b. What is the *conditional* probability of C_3, *given* that C_1 occurred?
  c. Are C_1 and C_3 independent events? Explain.

7.31 Use the information given in Case Study 7.1 and the "physical assumption" method of assigning probabilities to argue that on any given day, the probability that Alicia has to answer one of the three questions is 3/50.

Section 7.4

7.32 A fair coin is tossed three times. The event A = getting all heads, has probability = 1/8.
  a. Describe in words what the event A^C is.
  b. What is the probability of A^C?

7.33 Two fair dice are rolled. The event A = "getting the same number on both dice" has probability = 1/6.
  a. Describe in words what the event A^C is.
  b. What is the probability of A^C?

7.34 Two fair coins are tossed. Define:

A = Getting a head on the first toss.
B = Getting a head on the second toss.
A and B = Getting a head on both the first and second tosses.
A or B = Getting a head on the first toss, or the second toss, or both tosses.

  a. Find $P(A)$ = the probability of A.
  b. Find $P(B)$ = the probability of B.
  c. Using the multiplication rule (Rule 3b), find $P(A$ and $B)$.
  d. Using the addition rule (Rule 2a), find $P(A$ or $B)$.

7.35 Julie is taking English and history. Suppose at the outset of the term, her probabilities for getting A's are:

P(grade of A in English class) = .70.
P(grade of A in history class) = .60.
P(grade of A in both English and history classes) = .50.

  a. Are the events "grade of A in English class" and "grade of A in history class" independent? Explain how you know.
  b. Use the addition rule for two events (Rule 2) to find the probability that Julie will get at least one A between her English and history classes.

7.36 In a recent election, 55% of the voters were Republicans and 45% were not. Of the Republicans, 80% voted for Candidate X and of the non-Republicans, 10% voted for Candidate X. Consider a randomly selected voter. Define events:

A = Voter is Republican.
B = Voted for Candidate X.

  a. Write values for $P(A)$, $P(A^C)$, $P(B|A)$, and $P(B|A^C)$.
  b. Find $P(A$ and $B)$ and write in words what outcome it represents.
  c. Find $P(A^C$ and $B)$ and write in words what outcome it represents.
  d. Using the results in parts (b) and (c), find $P(B)$. (*Hint:* The events in parts (b) and (c) cover all of the ways B can happen.)
  e. Use the result in part (d) to state what percent of the vote Candidate X received.

7.37 In each of the following situations, explain whether the selection is made with replacement or without replacement.
  a. The three digits in the simple lottery in Example 7.2.
  b. The three students selected to answer questions in Case Study 7.1.
  c. The five people selected for extra security screening while boarding a particular flight.
  d. The two football teams selected to play in the Rose Bowl in a given year.
  e. The cars stopped by the police for speeding in five consecutive mornings on the same stretch of highway.

7.38 In Example 7.12 we found the probability that both of two unrelated strangers share your birth month. In this exercise, we find the probability that at least one of the two strangers shares your birth month. Assume all 12 months are equally likely.

a. What is the probability that the first stranger does *not* share your birth month?

b. What is the probability that the second stranger does *not* share your birth month?

c. What is the probability that *neither* of them shares your birth month?

d. Use the result from part (c) to find the probability that at least one of them shares your birth month.

7.39 Refer to the previous exercise. In this exercise another method is used for finding the probability that at least one of two unrelated strangers shares your birth month.

a. What is the probability that the first stranger shares your birth month?

b. What is the probability that the second stranger shares your birth month?

c. What is the probability that both of them share your birth month?

d. Use Rule 2a (for "either A or B") to find the probability that at least one of the strangers shares your birth month.

7.40 In Example 7.11 we found the probability that a woman with two children (not twins) has two girls or two boys is .5002. What is the probability that she has one child of each sex?

7.41 Harold and Maude plan to take a cruise together, but they live in separate cities. The cruise departs from Miami, and they each book a flight to arrive in Miami an hour before they need to be on the ship. Their travel planner explains that Harold's flight has an 80% chance of making it on time for him to get to the ship, and Maude's flight has a 90% chance of making it on time.

a. How do you think the travel planner determined these probabilities?

b. Assuming the probabilities quoted are long-run relative frequencies, do you think whether Harold's plane is on time is independent of whether Maude's plane is on time on the particular day they travel? Explain. (*Hint:* Consider reasons why planes are delayed.)

c. Whether realistic or not, assuming the probabilities are independent, what is the probability that Harold and Maude will both arrive on time?

d. What is the probability that one of the two will be cruising alone?

7.42 A robbery has been committed in an isolated town. Witnesses all agree that the criminal was driving a red pickup truck and had blond hair. From evidence at the scene, the criminal also smoked cigarettes. Police determine that 1/50 of the vehicles in town are red pickup trucks, 30% of the residents smoke, and 20% of the residents have blond hair. The next day they notice a red pickup truck whose driver has blond hair and is smoking. They arrest the driver for the robbery.

a. Discuss whether or not you think it's reasonable to assume that whether someone drives a red pickup truck, smokes cigarettes, and has blond hair are all independent traits.

b. Assuming the traits listed are all independent, what proportion of the vehicle owners in town are red pickup truck owners who smoke and have blond hair?

c. Continuing to assume the traits listed are independent, if there are 10,000 vehicle owners in town, how many of them fit the description of the criminal?

d. Assuming there is no other evidence, what is the probability that the driver arrested by the police is innocent of the robbery?

e. The prosecuting attorney argues that the probability that someone would own a red pickup truck and smoke cigarettes and have blond hair is very small, so the person arrested by the police must be guilty. Do you agree with this reasoning? Explain.

7.43 A raffle is held in a club in which 10 of the 40 members are good friends with the president. The president draws two winners.

a. If the two winners are drawn *with replacement,* what is the probability that a friend of the president wins each time?

b. If the two winners are drawn *without replacement,* what is the probability that a friend of the president wins each time?

c. If the two winners are drawn *with replacement,* what is the probability that neither winner is a friend of the president?

d. If the two winners are drawn *without replacement,* what is the probability that neither winner is a friend of the president?

Section 7.5

7.44 A public library carries 50 magazines that focus on either news or sports. Thirty of them focus on news and the remaining 20 focus on sports. Among the 30 news magazines, 20 include international news and 10 include national, state, or local news only. Among the 20 sports magazines, 5 focus on international sports and the remaining 15 focus on national, state, or local sports.

a. Create a table illustrating these numbers, with type of magazine (news, sports) as the row variable.

b. A customer randomly picks a magazine from the shelf and notices that it is a news magazine. Given that it is a news magazine, what is the probability that it includes international news?

c. What proportion of the magazines include international news or sports?

7.45 In a large general education class, 60% (.6) are science majors and 40% (.4) are liberal arts majors. Twenty percent (.2) of the science majors are seniors, while 30% (.3) of the liberal arts majors are seniors.

a. If there are 100 students in the class, how many of them are science majors?

b. If there are 100 students in the class, how many of them are science majors and seniors?

c. Create a hypothetical table of 100 students with major (science, liberal arts) as the row variable and class (senior, nonsenior) as the column variable, illustrating the proportions given in the exercise.

d. Use the table created in part (c) to determine what percent of the class are seniors.

7.46 Refer to the previous exercise.

a. Create a tree diagram for this situation.

b. Use the tree diagram in part (a) to determine what percent of the class are seniors.

7.47 In a computer store, 30% (.3) of the computers in stock are laptops and 70% (.7) are desktops. Five percent (.05) of the laptops are on sale, while 10% (.1) of the desktops are on sale. Use a tree diagram to determine what percent of the computers in the store are on sale.

7.48 In an Italian restaurant, a waitress has observed that 80% of her customers order coffee, and 25% of her customers order both biscotti and coffee. Define events:

A = a randomly selected customer orders coffee.
B = a randomly selected customer orders biscotti.

a. Express the waitress' observations as probability statements involving events A and B.
b. What is the conditional probability that a randomly selected customer would order a biscotti, given that he or she orders coffee?
c. What is the conditional probability that a customer would not order a biscotti, given that he or she orders coffee?

7.49 Two students each use a random number generator to pick a number between 1 and 7. What is the probability that they pick the same number?

7.50 A standard poker deck of cards contains 52 cards, of which four are aces. Suppose two cards are drawn sequentially, so that one random circumstance is the result of the first card drawn and the second random circumstance is the result of the second card drawn. Go through the five steps listed under "Specific Set of Steps for Finding Probabilities" to find the probability that the first card is an ace and the second card is not an ace.

7.51 Refer to the example toward the end of Section 7.4, of drawing two students without replacement from a class of 30 students in which 3 are left-handed. Draw a tree diagram to illustrate that the probability of selecting two left-handed students is 1/145.

7.52 Suppose that a magnet high school includes grades 11 and 12, with half of the students in each grade. Half of the senior class and 30% of the junior class are taking calculus. Create a hypothetical table of 100 students for this situation. Use grade (junior, senior) as the row variable.

7.53 Refer to the previous exercise. Suppose a calculus student is randomly selected to accompany the math teachers to a conference. What is the probability that the student is a junior?

7.54 An airline has noticed that 40% of its customers who buy tickets don't take advantage of "advance-purchase" fares, and the remaining 60% do. The "no-show" rate for those who don't have advance-purchase fares is 30%, while for those who do have them it is only 5%.

a. Create a tree diagram for this situation.
b. Create a "hypothetical hundred thousand" table for this situation.
c. Using the tree diagram from part (a) or the table from part (b), find the percent of customers who are "no-shows."
d. Given that a customer is a no-show, what is the probability that he or she had an advance-purchase fare?
e. Refer to the answer you found in part (d). Write a sentence presenting this result that someone with no training in statistics would understand.

7.55 In a test for ESP, a picture is randomly selected from four possible choices and hidden away. Participants are asked to describe the hidden picture, which is unknown to anyone in the environment. They are later shown the four possible choices and asked to identify the one they thought was the hidden target picture. Because the correct answer had been randomly selected from the four choices before the experiment began, the probability of guessing correctly by chance alone is 1/4 or .25. Each time the experiment is repeated, four new pictures are used.

a. Researchers are screening people for potentially gifted ESP participants for a later experiment. They will only accept people who get three correct answers in three repetitions of the screening experiment. What is the probability that someone who is just guessing will be accepted for the later experiment?
b. Refer to part (a). Suppose that an individual has some ESP ability and can correctly guess with probability .40 each time. What is the probability that such a person will be accepted for the later experiment?
c. Refer to parts (a) and (b). Suppose that half of the people in the population being tested are just guessing and have no ESP ability, while the other half can actually guess correctly with probability .40 each time. Given that someone is accepted for the upcoming experiment, what is the probability that they actually have ESP ability?

Section 7.6

7.56 Five fair dice were tossed and the sum of the resulting tosses was recorded. This process was repeated 10,000 times using a computer simulation. The number of times the sum of the five tosses equaled 27 was 45. What is the estimated probability that the sum of the five dice will be 27?

7.57 The observed risk of an accident per month at a busy intersection without any stoplights was 1%. The potential benefit of adding a stoplight was studied using a computer simulation modeling the typical traffic flow for a month at that intersection. Based on 10,000 repetitions, a total of 50 simulated accidents occurred.

a. What is the estimated probability of an accident in a month at the intersection with a stoplight added?
b. Would adding the stoplight be a good idea? Explain.

7.58 Refer to Example 7.19 and use the results given in Table 7.3 to estimate probabilities of the following outcomes:
a. Prize 4 is received at least three times.
b. Prize 4 is received at least three times *given* that the full collection of all four prizes was not received.
c. Prize 4 is received at least three times *and* the full collection of all four prizes was received.

7.59 Refer to the simulation given for Example 7.20. What is the estimated probability that a participant would guess four or more correctly?

7.60 Refer to Example 7.20. Explain how you would change the simulation procedure if the assumption was that everyone was randomly guessing, so that the probability of a correct guess was .20 instead of .30 each time.

7.61 Refer to Example 7.20. Suppose the probability of a correct guess each time is .40.

a. Explain how you would simulate this situation.
b. Carry out the simulation and estimate the probability that a participant will be identified as gifted.

7.62 Suppose that in a lottery game players choose three digits, each from the set 0 to 9. A winning sum is then selected from the possibilities 0 (0 + 0 + 0) to 27 (9 + 9 + 9) by randomly choosing three digits and using their sum. For instance, if the three digits 483 are selected, then a winning ticket is any ticket in which the 3 digits sum to 4 + 8 + 3 = 15. Suppose the winning sum is 15.

   a. Using the physical assumption that all 1000 choices (000, 001, . . . , 999) are equally likely, find the probability that three digits chosen at random will sum to 15.

   b. Simulate playing this game 1000 times, randomly selecting the three digits each time. Based on the simulation, find the approximate probability of winning when the winning sum is 15.

   c. Based on information about how people respond when asked to pick random digits, do you think the proportion of people who would actually pick three digits summing to 15 is close to the probabilities you found in parts (a) and (b)? Explain.

7.63 Janice has noticed that on her drive to work there are several things that can slow her down. First, she hits a red light with probability .3. If she hits the red light, she also has to stop for the commuter train with probability .4, but if she doesn't hit the red light she only has to stop with probability .2.

   a. Find the probability that Janice has to stop for both the red light and the train.

   b. Find the probability that Janice has to stop for the red light *given* that she has to stop for the commuter train.

   c. Explain how you would conduct a simulation to estimate the probabilities in parts (a) and (b).

   d. Conduct the simulation described in part (c). Use at least 50 repetitions.

   e. Compare the answers you computed in parts (a) and (b) to the estimated probabilities from your simulation in part (d).

Section 7.7

7.64 The PAP smear is a screening test to detect cervical cancer. Estimate the sensitivity and specificity of the test if a study of 200 women with cervical cancer resulted in 160 testing positive, and in another 200 women without cervical cancer, 4 tested positive.

7.65 In tossing a fair coin ten times, if the first nine tosses resulted in all tails, will the chance be greater than .5 that the tenth toss will turn up heads? Explain.

7.66 Which of the following sequences resulting from tossing a fair coin five times is most likely: HHHHH, HTHHT, or HHHTT? Explain your answer.

7.67 Using material from Section 7.7, explain what is wrong with the following statement: "The probability that you will win the million dollar lottery is about the same as the probability that you will give birth to quintuplets."

7.68 The *U.C. Berkeley Wellness Encyclopedia* contains the following statement in its discussion of HIV testing (1991, p. 360): "In a high-risk population, virtually all people who test positive will truly be infected, but among people at low risk the false positives will outnumber the true positives. Thus, for every infected person correctly identified in a low-risk population, an estimated ten noncarriers [of HIV] will test positive." Suppose you have a friend who is part of this low-risk population, but who has just tested positive.

   a. Using the numbers in the statement above, what is the probability that your friend actually carries the virus?

   b. Understandably, your friend is upset and doesn't believe that the probability of being infected with HIV isn't really near 1. After all, the test is accurate and it came out positive! Explain to your friend how the quoted statement can be true, even though the test is very accurate both for people with HIV and for people who don't carry it. If it's easier, you can make up numbers to put in a table to support your argument.

7.69 A rare disease occurs in about 1 out of 1000 people who are similar to you. A test for the disease has sensitivity of 95% and specificity of 90%.

   a. Create a "hypothetical one hundred thousand" table illustrating this situation, where the row categories are disease (yes, no) and the column categories are test results (positive, negative).

   b. Draw a tree diagram for this situation.

   c. Using the table from part (a) or the tree diagram from part (b), find the proportion of people who will test positive for the disease.

   d. Find the probability that you actually have the disease given that your test results are positive.

7.70 Suppose there are 30 people in your statistics class and you are divided into 15 teams of 2 students each. You happen to mention that your birthday was last week, upon which you discover that your teammate's mother has the same birthday you have (month and day, not necessarily year). Assume the probability is 1/365 for any given day.

   a. What is the probability that your teammate's mother would have the same birthday as yours?

   b. Suppose your teammate has two siblings and two parents, for a family of size 5. What is the probability that at least one of your teammate's family has the same birthday as yours, assuming their birth dates are all independent?

   c. Is the fact that your teammate's mother has the same birthday as yours a surprising coincidence? Explain.

7.71 Give an example of a situation where the gambler's fallacy would not apply because the events are not independent.

7.72 A friend has three boys and would like to have a girl. She explains to you that the probability that her next baby will be a girl is very high, because the law of averages says she should have half of each and she already has three boys. Is she correct? Explain.

7.73 A friend, quite upset, calls you because she had a dream that a building had been bombed and she was helping to search for survivors. The next day, a terrorist bombs an embassy building in another country. Your friend is convinced that her dream was a warning and that she should have told someone in authority. Comment on this situation.

7.74 Tomorrow morning when you first arise, pick a three-digit number (anything from 000 to 999). You can choose randomly or simply decide what number you want to use. As you go through the day, notice whether or not you encounter that number. It could be in a book, in a newspaper or magazine, on a digital clock when you happen to glance at it, part of the serial number on a bill, and so on. Write down all of the instances in which you encounter your chosen three-digit number. Are you surprised at how many or how few times you encountered the number? Explain.

7.75 Give an example of a coincidence that has occurred in your life. Using the material from this chapter, try to approximate the probability of exactly that event happening. Discuss whether or not the answer convinces you that something very odd happened to you.

7.76 Suppose you are seated next to a stranger on an airplane and you start discussing various topics like where you were born (what state or country), what your favorite movie of all time is, your spouse's occupation, and so on. For simplicity, assume the probability that your details "match" for any given topic is 1/50 and is independent from one topic to the next. If you discuss ten topics, how surprising would it be to find that you "match" on at least one of them?

7.77 Do you think that all coincidences can be explained by random events? Explain why or why not, using probability as the focus of your explanation. (There is no correct answer; your reasoning is what counts.)

Chapter Exercises

7.78 New spark plugs have just been installed in a small airplane with a four-cylinder engine. For each spark plug, the probability that it is defective and will fail during its first 20 minutes of flight is 1/10,000, independent of the other spark plugs.
   a. For any given spark plug, what is the probability that it will *not* fail during the first 20 minutes of flight?
   b. What is the probability that none of the four spark plugs will fail during the first 20 minutes of flight?
   c. What is the probability that at least one of the spark plugs will fail?

7.79 A psychological test identifies people as being one of eight types. For instance, Type 1 is "Rationalist" and applies to 15% of men and 8% of women. Type 2 is "Teacher" and applies to 12% of men and 14% of women. Each person fits one and only one type.
   a. What is the probability that a randomly selected male is either "Rationalist" or "Teacher"?
   b. What is the probability that a randomly selected female is not a "Teacher"?
   c. Suppose college roommates have a particularly hard time getting along with each other if they are both "Rationalists." A college randomly assigns roommates of the same sex. What proportion of male roommate pairs will have this problem?
   d. Refer to part (c). What proportion of female roommate pairs will have this problem?
   e. Using your answers to parts (c) and (d) and assuming that half of college roommate pairs are male and half are female, what proportion of all roommate pairs will both be "Rationalists"?

7.80 Refer to the previous exercise. A psychologist has noticed that "Teachers" and "Rationalists" get along particularly well with each other, and she thinks they tend to marry each other. One of her colleagues disagrees and thinks that the "types" of spouses are independent of each other.
   a. If the "types" are independent, what is the probability that a randomly selected married couple would consist of one "Rationalist" and one "Teacher"?
   b. In surveys of thousands of randomly selected married couples, she has found that about 5% of them have one "Rationalist" and one "Teacher." Does this contradict her colleague's theory that the types of spouses are independent of each other? Explain.

7.81 In Chapter 6 we learned that if there is no relationship be-

tween two categorical variables in a population, a "statistically significant" relationship will appear in samples from that population 5% of the time. Suppose two researchers independently conduct studies to see if there is a relationship between drinking coffee (regularly, sometimes, never) and having migraine headaches (frequently, occasionally, never).
   a. If there really is no relationship in the population, what is the probability that the first researcher finds a statistically significant relationship?
   b. If there really is no relationship in the population, what is the probability that both researchers find a statistically significant relationship?

7.82 A professor has noticed that, even though attendance is not a component of the grade for his class, students who attend regularly obtain better grades. In fact, 40% of those who attend regularly receive A's in the class, while only 10% of those who do not attend regularly receive A's. About 70% of students attend class regularly. Find the following percents:
   a. The percent who receive A's *given* that they attend class regularly.
   b. The percent who receive A's *given* that they do not attend class regularly.
   c. The overall percent who receive A's.

7.83 Refer to the previous exercise. Draw a tree diagram and use it to find the overall percent who receive As.

7.84 Refer to the previous two exercises. Construct a "hypothetical hundred thousand" table for this situation.

7.85 Refer to the previous three exercises. Given that a randomly chosen student receives an A grade, what is the probability that he or she attended class regularly?

7.86 Recall from Chapter 2 that the median of a dataset is the value with half of the observations at or above it and half of the observations at or below it. Suppose four individuals are randomly selected *with replacement* from a large class and asked how many hours they studied last week. Assume that there are an even number of students in the class and that nobody has a response exactly equal to the median.
   a. What is the probability that a particular individual will give a response that is above the median for the class?
   b. Use the Extension of Rule 3b to find the probability that all four individuals will give a response that is above the median for the class.
   c. If the individuals had been selected without replacement, would the Extension of Rule 3b still be applicable? Explain.

7.87 About 1/3 of all adults in the United States have Type O+ blood. If three randomly selected adults donate blood, find the probability of each of these events:
   a. All three are Type O+.
   b. None of them is Type O+.
   c. Two out of the three are Type O+.

7.88 In October 1999, experts at the U.S. Geological Survey's San Francisco Bay Area Earthquake Hazards Project announced that "the likelihood of a powerful earthquake occurring in the next 30 years in the Bay Area is 70 percent" (*Sacramento Bee*, Eddie Lau, Oct. 15, 1999, p. A1). Do you think this figure is based on personal probability, long-run relative frequency, physical assumptions about the world, or some combination? Explain.

7.89 According to the U.S. Census Bureau "only 35 percent of the foreign-born people in the United States in 1997 were naturalized citizens, compared with 64 percent in 1970" (*Sacramento Bee,* Oct. 15, 1999, p. A1).

  a. What is the probability that two randomly selected foreign-born people in the United States in 1997 were both naturalized citizens?

  b. Refer to part (a) of this exercise. Suppose a married couple was randomly selected instead of two separate individuals. Do you think the probability that they were both naturalized citizens would be the same as the probability in part (a)? Explain.

  c. Do you think the probabilities reported by the Census Bureau are relative frequency probabilities or personal probabilities? Explain.

  d. A student writing a report about these statistics wrote, "If you had lived in the United States in 1970 and were foreign-born, the probability that you would be a naturalized citizen would have been .64. But by 1997 if you still lived in the United States, the probability that you would be a naturalized citizen would be only .35." Rewrite this sentence in a way that conveys the information correctly.

7.90 Recall that the Empirical Rule in Chapter 2 stated that for bell-shaped distributions about 68% of the values fall within 1 standard deviation of the mean. The heights of women at a large university are approximately bell-shaped, with a mean of 65 inches and standard deviation of 2.5 inches. Use this information to answer the following questions:

  a. What is the probability that a randomly selected woman from this university is 67.5 inches or taller?

  b. What is the probability that two randomly selected women from this university are both 62.5 inches or shorter?

  c. What is the probability that of two randomly selected women, one is 62.5 inches or shorter and the other is 62.5 inches or taller?

  d. What is the probability that two randomly selected women are both 65 inches or taller?

The following scenario applies to the remaining exercises. In Chapter 6 we discussed a random sample of people who had ever *been married and demonstrated the proportions who smoked and who had ever been divorced. The numbers are shown again here.*

Smoking and divorce, GSS surveys 1991–1993

Smoke?	Ever Divorced?		
	Yes	No	Total
Yes	238	247	485
No	374	810	1184
Total	612	1057	1669

Data Source: SDA archive at UC Berkeley website (http://csa.berkeley.edu:7502/).

Because this survey was based on a random sample in the United States in the early 1990s, the data should be representative of the adult population who had ever been married at that time. Answer these questions for a randomly selected member of that population.

7.91 Draw a tree diagram illustrating this situation, where the first set of branches represents smoking status and the second set represents "ever divorced."

7.92 What is the approximate probability that the person smoked?

7.93 What is the approximate probability that the person had ever been divorced?

7.94 Given that the person smoked, what is the probability that he or she had been divorced?

7.95 Given that the person had been divorced, what is the probability that he or she smoked?

7.96 Suppose two people were randomly selected from that population, without replacement. What is the probability that they had both been divorced?

7.97 Suppose two people were randomly selected from that population, without replacement. What is the probability that one of them smoked but the other one did not (in either order)?

7.98 Suppose two people were randomly selected from that population. Given that one of them had been divorced, what is the probability that the other one had also been divorced?

REFERENCES

Diaconis, P., and F. Mosteller (1989). "Methods for studying coincidences," *Journal of the American Statistical Association,* Vol. 84, pp. 853–861.

Eddy, D. M. (1982). "Probabilistic reasoning in clinical medicine: Problems and opportunities," Chapter 18 in D. Kahneman, P. Slovic, and A. Tversky (eds.), *Judgment under Uncertainty: Heuristics and Biases,* Cambridge, U.K.: Cambridge University Press.

Gehring, W. J., and A. R. Willoughby (2000). "The medial frontal cortex and the rapid processing of monetary gains and losses," *Science,* Vol. 295, pp. 2279–2284.

Information Please Almanac (1991). Otto Johnson (ed.), Boston: Houghton Mifflin.

Krantz, Les (1992). *What the Odds Are,* New York: Harper Perennial.

Moore, D. S. (1997). *Statistics: Concepts and Controversies,* 4th ed., New York: W. H. Freeman.

Paulos, John Allen (1995). *A Mathematician Reads the Newspaper,* New York: Basic Books.

Plous, S. (1993). *The Psychology of Judgment and Decision Making,* New York: McGraw-Hill.

Stinchfield, R. (2001). "A comparison of gambling by Minnesota public school students in 1992, 1995 and 1998," *Journal of Gambling Studies,* Vol. 17, No. 4, pp. 273–296.

Tversky, A., and D. Kahneman (1982). "Judgment under uncertainty—Heuristics and biases," Chapter 1 in D. Kahneman, P. Slovic, and A. Tversky (eds.), *Judgment under Uncertainty: Heuristics and Biases,* Cambridge, U.K.: Cambridge University Press.

University of California, Berkeley (1991). *The Wellness Encyclopedia,* Boston: Houghton Mifflin.

Weaver, W. (1963). *Lady Luck: The Theory of Probability,* Garden City, NY: Doubleday.

Random Variables

What's random about this event? See Example 8.1.

If a veterinarian had to learn a different pattern for treating every different breed, it might be impossible for any individual to learn enough to be able to treat dogs in general. Similarly, situations involving uncertainty and probability fall into certain broad classes, and we can use the same set of rules and principles for all situations within a class.

The numerical outcome of a random circumstance is called a *random variable*. In this chapter, we'll learn how to characterize the pattern of the distribution of the values that a random variable may have, and we'll learn how to use the pattern to find probabilities.

Patterns make life easier to understand and decisions easier to make. For instance, dogs come in a variety of breeds, sizes, and temperaments, but all dogs fit certain patterns that veterinarians can rely upon when treating nearly any type of dog. If a veterinarian had to learn a different pattern for treating every different breed, it might be nearly impossible for any individual to learn enough to be able to treat dogs in general.

Similarly, situations involving uncertainty and probability fall into certain broad classes, and we can use the same set of rules and principles for all situations within a class. We encountered this idea in Chapter 2 when we learned the Empirical Rule for bell-shaped distributions. All variables that follow a bell-shaped distribution have the same pattern, which is that about 68% of the values fall within 1 standard deviation of the mean, about 95% of the values fall within 2 standard deviations of the mean, and so on. This pattern holds whether the variable is heights of adult males, handspans of college-age females, or SAT scores of high school seniors. ◆

8.1 | WHAT IS A RANDOM VARIABLE?

definition A **random variable** assigns a number to each outcome of a random circumstance, or, equivalently, a random variable assigns a number to each unit in a population.

It is easier to create rules for broad classes of situations and then identify how a specific example fits into a class than it is to create rules for each specific example. We can employ this strategy quite effectively for working with a wide variety of situations involving probability and random outcomes. We categorize these situations by defining a generic numerical outcome, or "random variable," for similar random circumstances. Identifying the type of random variable appropriate in a given situation makes it easy to find probabilities and other information that would be difficult to derive from first principles.

There are two different broad classes of random variables:

1. A **continuous random variable** can take any value in an interval or collection of intervals.
2. A **discrete random variable** can take one of a countable list of distinct values.

Discrete or Continuous?

> *tech note*   Sometimes a random variable fits the technical definition of a discrete random variable but it is more convenient to treat it as a continuous random variable. Examples include incomes, prices, and exam scores. Sometimes continuous random variables are rounded off to whole units, giving the appearance of a discrete random variable, such as age in years or pulse rate to the nearest beat. In most of these situations, the number of possible values is large and we are more interested in probabilities concerning intervals than specific values, so the methods for continuous random variables will be used.

EXAMPLE 8.1
Random Variables at an Outdoor Graduation or Wedding

Suppose you are participating in a major outdoor event, like a graduation or wedding ceremony. There are a number of random factors that will determine how enjoyable the event will be, such as the temperature and the number of airplanes that fly overhead during the important speeches. If you are responsible for setting the date for the event, you might try to get some information on likely values for these random outcomes on different dates, so you can optimize the likelihood of an enjoyable event. In this context, *temperature* is a *continuous random variable* because it can take on any value in an interval. We often round off continuous random variables to the nearest whole number, like temperature in degrees, but conceptually the value can be anything in an interval. In contrast, the *number of airplanes* that fly overhead during the event is a *discrete random variable*. The value can be 0, 1, 2, 3, and so on but cannot be anything in between the integers, like 2.5 airplanes. ◆

EXAMPLE 8.2
Probability an Event Occurs Three Times in Three Tries

As an example of a class of random variables, think about what the following three questions have in common:

♦ What is the probability that three tosses of a fair coin will result in three heads?

♦ Assuming boys and girls are equally likely each time (which we learned in Chapter 7 is not quite true), what is the probability that three births will result in three girls?

♦ Assuming the probability is 1/2 that a randomly selected individual will be taller than the median height of a population, what is the probability that three randomly selected individuals will all be taller than the median?

These three questions all have the same answer, which is 1/8, found using the multiplication rule in Chapter 7. Furthermore, if each question had asked about the probability of getting one outcome of one type and two of the other type, such as one head and two tails or one boy and two girls, the answers to all three questions would also have been the same. It would have been 3/8.

Probabilities for the number of heads in three tosses, girls in three births, and individuals falling above the median in three random selections are all found using the exact same process. In each case, a random variable can be defined as X = number of times the "outcome of interest" occurs in three independent tries. It doesn't matter if the "outcome of interest" is a head on a coin toss, a girl in a birth, or someone taller than the median in a randomly selected male. The pattern for finding probabilities will be the same. ◆

8.1

turn on your mind

If you know that the number of possible values a random variable can have is finite, do you know whether the random variable is discrete or continuous? Answer the same question for a random variable that can have an infinite number of possible values.*

8.2 | DISCRETE RANDOM VARIABLES

We consider discrete and continuous random variables separately because probabilities are computed and used differently for them. For discrete random variables, we are interested in probabilities of exact outcomes or a series of them. For continuous random variables, we are interested in the probability of the outcome falling into a specific interval. For instance, suppose you are waiting to fly on standby and you have first priority. You would want to know the probability that the number of standby passengers who will be able to board the plane (a discrete random variable) is one or more. You might also want to know the probability that the flying time (a continuous random variable) will be no more than the time specified in the flight schedule. The probability that the flying time is *exactly* that amount would be essentially zero, and it doesn't make sense to talk about probabilities of exact values for continuous random variables.

Probability Notation for Discrete Random Variables

formula X = the random variable.

k = a number the discrete random variable could assume.

$P(X = k)$ is the probability that X equals k.

Remember that a *discrete random variable* is one that can only result in a countable set of possibilities. Although a discrete random variable often has a finite number of outcomes, that is not always the case. Example 8.3 illustrates a discrete random variable with an infinite number of possible values.

EXAMPLE 8.3
It's Possible to Toss Forever

Consider repeatedly tossing a fair coin, and define the random variable:

X = number of tosses until the first head occurs

Notice that, theoretically, X could equal any value from 1 to infinity because the coin could continue to come up tails indefinitely. The number of tosses required to get the first head is not likely to be large, but any number of flips is a possible outcome.

To find the probability that k tosses are needed to get the first head, we can use the multiplication rule in Chapter 7 (extension of Rule 3b):

$$P(X = k) = (1/2)^k$$

For instance, $P(X = 1) = 1/2, P(X = 2) = (1/2)(1/2) = 1/4$, and so on. The same pattern of probabilities applies to the number of births until the first girl occurs (assuming boys and girls are equally likely), the number of people randomly selected until the first person taller than the population median is found, and so on. ◆

The Probability Distribution of a Discrete Random Variable

The purpose of defining a random variable usually is to find probabilities associated with its possible values. In Chapter 7 we learned that the sample space for a random circumstance consists of a list of the unique possible outcomes, called simple events. When a random variable X is defined, a value for X is given to each simple event in the sample space. The probability for any particular value of X can then be found by adding the probabilities for all of the simple events that have that value of X.

Using the Sample Space to Find Probabilities for Discrete Random Variables

Step 1: List all simple events in the sample space.

Step 2: Find the probability for each simple event (often they are equally likely).

Step 3: List the possible values for the random variable X and identify the value for each simple event.

Step 4: Find all simple events for which $X = k$, for each possible value k.

Step 5: $P(X = k)$ is the sum of the probabilities for all simple events for which $X = k$.

EXAMPLE 8.4
How Many Girls Are Likely?

If a family has three children and the probability of a girl is 1/2 for each birth,[1] what are the probabilities of having 0, 1, 2, or 3 girls? We could use the rules in Chapter 7 to solve this problem, but to organize the solution we list the sample space, assign probabilities to each simple event, and then, for each simple event, determine a value of the random variable "number of girls":

Sample Space   For each birth, write either B for boy or G for girl. There are eight possible arrangements of B and G for three births. These are the *simple events.*

Sample Space and Probabilities   The eight simple events are equally likely.

---

[1] In Chapter 7 we learned that P(girl) is about .488, but for simplicity here we use .5.

Random Variable X = number of girls in three births. For each simple event, the value of the random variable X is the number of Gs listed. The following table displays the value of X for each simple event.

Simple Event	BBB	BBG	BGB	GBB	BGG	GBG	GGB	GGG
Probability	1/8	1/8	1/8	1/8	1/8	1/8	1/8	1/8
X = # of Girls	0	1	1	1	2	2	2	3

We can find the probability for each value of X by adding the probabilities of the simple events that have that value. The probabilities for the possible values of X are

$P(X = 0) = 1/8$

$P(X = 1) = 3/8$ (added probabilities for the simple events with $X = 1$)

$P(X = 2) = 3/8$ (added probabilities for the simple events with $X = 2$)

$P(X = 3) = 1/8$

Notice that these probabilities sum to 1 over all possible values of X. ◆

> **definition** The **probability distribution function (pdf)** for a discrete random variable X is a table or rule that assigns probabilities to the possible values of the random variable X.

It is often useful to represent a probability distribution function wih a picture similar to a histogram or bar graph. The possible values are placed on the horizontal axis and their probabilities on the vertical axis. A bar is drawn centered on each possible value, with the height of the bar equal to the probability for that value. Sometimes the bars are scaled so that their total area is 1. Then the probability for any combination of values can be found as the area of the bars (rectangles) for those values. This method will be displayed in the next example.

EXAMPLE 8.4—CONTINUED
The Probability Distribution for Number of Girls

The probabilities for all possible values of X = number of girls in three births make up the probability distribution of X. These probabilities can be written in the table:

k	0	1	2	3
$P(X = k)$	1/8	3/8	3/8	1/8

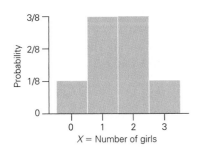

FIGURE 8.1   **The pdf for X = Number of Girls in Three Births**

Figure 8.1 displays the pdf. Notice that the bar over each value forms a rectangle that has a width of 1 and a height equal to the probability for that value. Therefore, the area of each bar is equivalent to the probability for that value. For instance, $P(X = 2) = 3/8$ coincides with the area of the rectangle centered on $X = 2$, a rectangle that has height = 3/8 and width = 1. Later in this chapter, you will learn that equating probability to an area is a crucial and necessary idea when working with continuous variables. For discrete variables, however, we generally can use more direct ways to find the probability that X takes a particular value, so, for discrete variables, we usually don't have to find the area of a rectangle to find a probability. ◆

Conditions for Probabilities for Discrete Random Variables

Two conditions must always apply to the probabilities for discrete random variables:

Condition 1   The sum of the probabilities over all possible values of a discrete random variable must equal 1. Stated mathematically

$$\sum_k P(X = k) = 1$$

Condition 2   The probability of any specific outcome for a discrete random variable must be between 0 and 1. Stated mathematically

$$0 \le P(X = k) \le 1 \qquad \text{for any value } k$$

The Cumulative Distribution Function of a Discrete Random Variable

Sometimes the question of interest involves the probability that a random variable is less than or equal to a specific value. For instance, imagine that you take a quiz that has ten multiple-choice questions. You are not prepared so you have to guess on every question. Suppose that if you get six or fewer correct, you fail the test. Define the random variable X = number correct. The probability of interest to you is $P(X \le 6)$.

> **definition**   The **cumulative distribution function (cdf)** for a random variable X is a rule or table that provides the probabilities $P(X \le k)$ for any real number k. Generally, the term **cumulative probability** refers to the probability that X is less than or equal to a particular value.

EXAMPLE 8.4—CONTINUED
Cumulative Distribution for the Number of Girls

The cumulative distribution function for the number of girls in a family with three children is

k	0	1	2	3
$P(X \le k)$	1/8	4/8	7/8	1

For example, the probability of two or fewer girls among three children is $P(X \le 2) = 7/8$. Notice that this is simply $P(X = 0) + P(X = 1) + P(X = 2) = 1/8 + 3/8 + 3/8$. ◆

Finding Probabilities for Complex Events Based on Random Variables

The probability rules in Chapter 7 all apply to events defined for random variables and can be used to find probabilities of complicated events.

EXAMPLE 8.4—CONTINUED
A Mixture of Children

What is the probability that a family with three children will have at least one child of each sex? In Example 8.4 we defined the random variable X = number of girls in three children. If there is at least one child of each sex, then either the family has one girl and two boys (X = 1) or two girls and one boy (X = 2). The probability can be found as

$$P(X = 1 \text{ or } X = 2) = P(X = 1) + P(X = 2) = 6/8 = 3/4$$

Notice that we can simply add these probabilities because the events X = 1 and X = 2 are mutually exclusive events. A family with three children cannot have both exactly one girl (X = 1) and exactly two girls (X = 2). ◆

8.2

turn on your mind

In the preceding example, we added the probabilities of X = 1 and X = 2 because they were mutually exclusive events. For any discrete random variable X, is it always true that X = k and X = m are mutually exclusive events, where k and m represent two values that X can have? Explain.*

EXAMPLE 8.5
Two Dice

Many gambling games use dice in which the number of dots rolled is equally likely to be 1, 2, 3, 4, 5, or 6. For instance, craps is a game in which two dice are rolled and the sum of the dots on the two dice determines whether the gambler wins, loses, or continues rolling the dice. Let X = sum of two fair dice. Here is the sample space for the two dots and the corresponding values of the random variable X:

Dots	X	Dots	X	Dots	X	Dots	X	Dots	X	Dots	X
1,1	2	2,1	3	3,1	4	4,1	5	5,1	6	6,1	7
1,2	3	2,2	4	3,2	5	4,2	6	5,2	7	6,2	8
1,3	4	2,3	5	3,3	6	4,3	7	5,3	8	6,3	9
1,4	5	2,4	6	3,4	7	4,4	8	5,4	9	6,4	10
1,5	6	2,5	7	3,5	8	4,5	9	5,5	10	6,5	11
1,6	7	2,6	8	3,6	9	4,6	10	5,6	11	6,6	12

There are 36 equally likely simple events in the sample space, so each simple event has probability 1/36. To construct the probability distribution (pdf) for X, count the number of simple events resulting in each value of X and divide by 36.

The probability distribution for the sum of two dice is

k	2	3	4	5	6	7	8	9	10	11	12
$P(X = k)$	1/36	2/36	3/36	4/36	5/36	6/36	5/36	4/36	3/36	2/36	1/36

Figure 8.2 displays the pdf with the rectangles for X = 4, 5, and 6 shaded. We can find $P(a \leq X \leq b)$ by adding the areas of the rectangles over those values, or by

HINT: See step 4 on page 252. Are there simple events for which $X = k$ and $x = m$ at the same time?

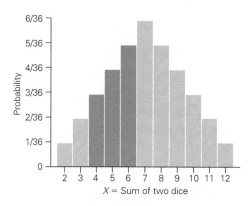

FIGURE 8.2   **Probability Distribution Function for Sum of Two Dice Showing $P(4 \leq X \leq 6)$**

adding the probabilities for all individual values in that range. For instance, $P(4 \leq X \leq 6) = 3/36 + 4/36 + 5/36 = 12/36 = 1/3$. ◆

8.3

turn on your mind

Refer to the probability distribution for the sum of two dice. What is the value of $P(X \leq 4)$? What does this probability measure? Explain what is measured by the value of $1 - P(X \leq 4)$.*

8.3 | EXPECTATIONS FOR RANDOM VARIABLES

Generally, for any random variable in which the probabilities of the outcomes are known, the average value over the long run can be predicted. Suppose you play a lottery every week. Although the specific outcome for a given week cannot be predicted in advance, the average amount you can expect to win or lose per play over the long run can be predicted accurately. This long-run prediction is provided by the *expected value* or, synonymously, the **mean value of the random variable** that describes the possible outcomes on each play.

> *definition*   The **expected value** of a random variable is the mean value of the variable X in the sample space, or population, of possible outcomes. *Expected value* can also be interpreted as the mean value that would be obtained from an infinite number of observations of the random variable.

For a discrete random variable, calculating the expected value, or mean value, is simple and the logic of the calculation is somewhat intuitive. Imagine, for instance, a gambling game in which on any play, the probabilities are .3 that

HINT: What values of k are included if $X \leq 4$?

a player wins $2 and .7 that a player loses $1. In ten plays of the game, the relative frequencies of wins and losses will not necessarily correspond exactly with the theoretical probabilities, but to develop an intuitive feel for expected value let's suppose that ten games go exactly according to theory.

Because the probabilities for winning and losing are .3 and .7, respectively, theory suggests that ten games would result in three wins and seven losses. With three wins of $2 and seven losses of $1, the total money won and lost is $2 \times 3 + (-\$1) \times 7$, and the average result per play is

$$\frac{\$2 \times 3 + (-\$1) \times 7}{10} = \frac{-\$1}{10} = -\$0.10$$

This is the *expected value* of X = amount won or lost per play, and in this instance, the outlook isn't good for the player. If the game goes according to theory, which it will in the long run, a player can expect to lose an average of 10 cents per play.

To do our calculation, we assumed ten plays would follow theory exactly, but in fact, the calculation of the expected value of a random variable is not tied to any particular number of plays. We could use the strategy described in the previous paragraph for any arbitrary number of plays, and the answer would still be $-\$0.10$ per play. The probability distribution of a discrete random variable determines the expected value of the variable. In our imagined gambling game, the expected value can be computed as $\$2 \times .3 + (-\$1) \times .7 = -\$0.10$, which is the result of summing up "value $\times$ probability" over all possible values of the random variable.

Calculating Expected Value for a Discrete Random Variable

formula If X is a random variable with possible values $x_1, x_2, x_3, \ldots$, occurring with probabilities $p_1, p_2, p_3, \ldots$, then the **expected value** of X is calculated as

$$E(X) = \sum x_i p_i$$

♦ The formula says to calculate "value times probability" separately for each possible value of X, and then calculate the sum of these "value times probability" quantities.

♦ The Greek letter "mu" (μ) can be used to represent the mean or expected value of X. In other words, $\mu = E(X)$.

EXAMPLE 8.6
California Decco Lottery Game

The California lottery has offered a number of games over the years. One such game is Decco, in which a player chooses one card from each of the four suits in a regular deck of playing cards. For example, the player might choose "4 of hearts," "3 of clubs," "10 of diamonds," and "jack of spades." A winning card is then drawn from each suit. If one or more of the choices matches the winning cards drawn, a prize is awarded. It costs $1.00 for each play, so the net gain for any prize is $1.00 less than the prize. Define the random variable to be X = net gain for any single ticket. Table 8.1 shows the prizes, net gain, and probability of winning each prize, taken from the back of a Decco game card. Notice that we count the free ticket as an even trade because it is worth $1.00, the same amount it cost to play the game, but see the technical note following this example for further explanation.

TABLE 8.1 ■ Probabilities for the Decco Game

Number of Matches	Prize	X = Net Gain	Probability
4	$5,000	$4,999	.000035
3	$50	$49	.00168
2	$5	$4	.0303
1	Free ticket	0	.242
0	None	−$1	.726

How much would you win or lose per ticket in this game, over the long run? The expected value of X, denoted as $E(X)$, is the answer, and the calculation is

$$E(X) = (\$4,999 \times .000035) + (\$49 \times .00168) + (\$4 \times .0303)$$
$$+ (\$0 \times .242) + (-\$1 \times .726)$$
$$= -\$0.35$$

This tells us that over many repetitions of the game, players will *lose* an *average* of 35 cents per play. From the perspective of the Lottery Commission, this means that they pay out about 65 cents in prizes for each $1 ticket they sell for this game. ◆

Free Tickets Are Not Worth the Price

tech note   The situation is actually worse than presented in Example 8.6. Many lottery games give a free ticket as a prize, and you may think the value of that ticket is equal to its cost, usually $1.00. It's not, unless you can sell the ticket to someone else for that price. The real value of the ticket is the expected win for one play of the game. In the computation in Example 8.6, for simplicity we used a "net gain" of 0 when the prize was a free ticket, but because it is actually worth less than that, the average loss per play is even more than $.35. We will continue to use an expected loss of $.35 for simplicity in discussions of the Decco game.

Notice that the expected value in Example 8.6 is not one of the possible outcomes, so the phrase "expected value" is a bit misleading. In other words, the expected value may not be a value that is ever expected on a single random outcome. Instead, it is the average over the long run.

8.4

turn on your mind

Suppose the probability of winning in a gambling game is .001, and when a player wins, his or her net gain is $999. When a player loses, the net amount lost is $1 (the cost to play). Is this game fair? Why or why not? How would you define a fair game? Does the number of times the game is played affect your view of whether the game is fair? Explain.*

*HINT: A game is fair if the expected value of the gain is the same as the cost to play.

Standard Deviation for a Discrete Random Variable

We first encountered the idea of standard deviation in Chapter 2, where we learned how to compute the standard deviation as a measure of spread for a quantitative variable and then used it in the Empirical Rule. Similarly, the **standard deviation of a discrete random variable** can be useful to quantify how spread out the possible values of a discrete random variable might be, weighted by how likely each value is to occur. As with the standard deviation of a set of measurements, the standard deviation of a random variable is essentially the average distance the random variable falls from its mean, or expected value, over the long run.

Variance and Standard Deviation of a Discrete Random Variable

formula   If X is a random variable with possible values of $x_1, x_2, x_3, \ldots$, occurring with probabilities $p_1, p_2, p_3, \ldots$, and with expected value $E(X) = \mu$, then,

Variance of X $= V(X) = \sigma^2 = \Sigma(x_i - \mu)^2 p_i$

Standard deviation of X $=$ square root of $V(X) = \sigma = \sqrt{\Sigma(x_i - \mu)^2 p_i}$

The sum is taken over all possible values of the random variable X.

EXAMPLE 8.7
Stability or Excitement—Same Mean, Different Standard Deviations

Suppose you decide to invest $100 in a scheme you hope will make some money. You have two choices of investment plans, and you must decide which one to choose. For each $100 invested under the two plans, the possible net gains one year later and their probabilities are as shown:

Plan 1		Plan 2	
$X =$ Net Gain	Probability	$Y =$ Net Gain	Probability
$5,000	.001	$20	.3
$1,000	.005	$10	.2
$0	.994	$4	.5

Examine the possible gains and associated probabilities. Which plan would you choose? Let's calculate the expected value for each plan. The expected value will tell us what the average long-run gain (loss?) per investment is for a particular plan.

For Plan 1,

$$E(X) = \$5,000 \times (.001) + \$1,000 \times (.005) + \$0 \times (.994) = \$10.00$$

For Plan 2,

$$E(Y) = \$20 \times (.3) + \$10 \times (.2) + \$4 \times (.5) = \$10.00$$

In other words, the expected net gain is the same for the two plans.

What's different about the two plans is the variability in the possible net gains. Under the first plan, you could make a lot of money, but with a low probability. Most likely, you will make nothing at all. Under the second plan, you will be sure to make a small amount, but there is no possibility of a big gain. This difference in the variability in possible amounts under the two plans can be quantified by finding the standard deviations.

TABLE 8.2 ■ **Standard Deviation Calculations for Example 8.7**

Plan 1			Plan 2		
$(X - \mu)^2$	p	$(X - \mu)^2 p$	$(Y - \mu)^2$	p	$(Y - \mu)^2 p$
$(\$5,000 - \$10)^2 = \$24,900,100$	.001	\$24,900.1	$(\$20 - \$10)^2 = \$100$	.3	\$30
$(\$1,000 - \$10)^2 = \$980,100$	.005	\$4,900.5	$(\$10 - \$10)^2 = 0$	.2	0
$(\$0 - \$10)^2 = 100$	.994	\$99.4	$(\$4 - \$10)^2 = \$36$	.5	\$18

The calculations of the standard deviations are displayed in Table 8.2. Summing the third column under each plan provides the variances. Taking the square root of a variance provides the standard deviation of the net gain for a plan.

For Plan 1,

$$V(X) = \$29,900.00 \quad \text{and} \quad \sigma = \sqrt{29,900.00} = \$172.92$$

For Plan 2,

$$V(Y) = \$48.00 \quad \text{and} \quad \sigma = \sqrt{48} = \$6.93$$

These values demonstrate that the possible outcomes for Plan 1 are much more variable than the possible outcomes for Plan 2. If you wanted to invest cautiously, you would choose Plan 2, but if you wanted to have the chance to gain a large amount of money, you would choose Plan 1. ◆

Expected Value (Mean) and Standard Deviation for a Population

When we have a population of measurements, we can think of each individual measurement as the value of a random variable, and we can calculate the mean and standard deviation in either of two ways. We can create a probability distribution for the measurements and use the definitions of expected value and standard deviation in this section. Or, we can find the mean and standard deviation by using the individual measurements directly in the formulas of Chapter 2. The two methods will give the same answers.

TABLE 8.3 ■ **Hours of Study Yesterday for a Population of College Students**

X = Hours of Study	Number of Students	Probability
0	16	16/200 = .08
1	28	28/200 = .14
2	50	50/200 = .25
3	36	36/200 = .18
4	26	26/200 = .13
5	22	22/200 = .11
6	14	14/200 = .07
7	6	6/200 = .03
8	2	2/200 = .01
Total	200	1.00

EXAMPLE 8.8
Mean Hours of Study for the Class Yesterday

A class of $N = 200$ students is asked, "To the nearest hour, how many hours did you study yesterday?" The instructor is interested only in the responses of the students in his class, so the 200 students in the class constitute a population. The probability distribution of the responses is shown in Table 8.3.

What is the mean number of hours studied the previous day in this population? The answer can be found using the formula $E(X) = \Sigma x_i p_i$, and the calculation is

$$E(X) = (0 \times .08) + (1 \times .14) + (2 \times .25) + (3 \times .18) + (4 \times .13)$$
$$+ (5 \times .11) + (6 \times .07) + (7 \times .03) + (8 \times .01)$$
$$= 2.96 \text{ hours}$$

This mean can also be calculated in the usual way that we average 200 individual values, which is that we can total the 200 individual values and divide that total by $N = 200$. ◆

Mean and Standard Deviation for a Population

> *formula*   Suppose a population has N individuals and a measurement X is of interest. Define:
>
> k_i = value of X for individual i.
>
> $x_1, x_2, x_3, \ldots$ as the distinct possible values for the measurement X.
>
> $p_1, p_2, p_3, \ldots$ as the proportions of the population with the values $x_1, x_2, x_3, \ldots$.
>
> Then, the population mean and standard deviation are
>
> $$E(X) = \mu = \frac{1}{N}\sum k_i = \sum x_i p_i$$
>
> $$\text{Standard deviation of } X = \sigma = \sqrt{\frac{\Sigma(k_i - \mu)^2}{N}} = \sqrt{\Sigma(x_i - \mu)^2 p_i}$$

8.4 | BINOMIAL RANDOM VARIABLES

We learned in Section 8.2 that a random variable is either a *discrete* random variable or a *continuous* random variable. Within each of these two broad types, certain classes of random variables are so common that they also have a name. Formulas for the probability distribution functions of these common classes of variables have been developed, and many computer software programs and calculators are programmed to provide probabilities for them.

In this section, we consider an important class of *discrete* random variables. A variable in this class is called a *binomial random variable*. Certain conditions must be met for a variable to fall into this class, but the basic idea is that a binomial random variable is a count of how many times an event occurs (or does not occur) in a particular number of observations or trials that make up a random circumstance.

Binomial Experiments and Binomial Random Variables

The number of heads in three tosses of a fair coin, the number of girls in six independent births, and the number of men who are six feet tall or taller in a random sample of ten adult men from a large population are all examples of binomial random variables. A binomial random variable is the result of a binomial experiment.

> *definition*   A **binomial experiment** is defined by the following conditions:
>
> 1. There are n "trials" where n is determined in advance and is not a random value.
> 2. There are two possible outcomes on each trial, called "success" and "failure" and denoted S and F.
> 3. The outcomes are independent from one trial to the next.
> 4. The probability of a "success" remains the same from one trial to the next, and this probability is denoted by p. The probability of a "failure" is $1 - p$ for every trial.

A **binomial random variable** is defined as X = number of successes in the n trials of a binomial experiment. Each row in Table 8.4 contains an example of a

TABLE 8.4 ■ Examples of Binomial Experiments and Binomial Random Variables

Random Circumstance	Random Variable	Success	Failure	*n*	*p*
(1) Toss three fair coins	X = number of heads	Head	Tail	3	1/2
(2) Roll a die eight times	X = number of 4s and 6s	4, 6	1, 2, 3, 5	8	2/6 = 1/3
(3) Randomly sample 1000 U.S. adults	X = number who have seen a UFO	Seen UFO	Have not seen UFO	1000	Proportion of all adults who have seen a UFO
(4) Roll two dice once	X = number of times sum is 7	Sum is 7	Sum not 7	1	6/36 = 1/6

binomial experiment and a binomial random variable. For each example, go through the conditions for a binomial experiment and make sure you understand why those conditions apply to that example.

The following four examples illustrate a few subtle features of binomial random variables that could initially be confusing. Keep these points in mind when trying to determine whether a random variable fits the binomial description:

♦ *There may be more than two possible outcomes for each trial,* but the random variable counts how many times a particular subset of the possibilities occurs. Anything in that subset is a "success" and anything not in the subset is a "failure." For example, a single die can display either 1, 2, 3, 4, 5, or 6 dots, but a success can be defined by a particular set of them, while a failure is anything else. Look at the second example in Table 8.4.

♦ *Sample surveys can produce a binomial random variable* when we count how many individuals in the sample have a particular opinion or trait (see the third example in Table 8.4). A "trial" is one sampled individual. A "success" is that the individual has the opinion or trait. The probability of "success" is the proportion in the population who have the opinion or trait. If a random sample is taken without replacement from a large population, the conditions of a binomial experiment are considered to be met, although the probability of a "success" actually changes very slightly from one trial to the next as each sampled individual is removed from eligibility.

♦ *Sampling without replacement from a small population does not produce a binomial random variable.* Suppose a class consists of ten boys and ten girls. Five children are randomly selected to be in a play. X = the number of girls selected. Notice that X is *not* a binomial random variable because the probability that a girl is selected each time depends on who is already in the sample and who is left, violating the condition that the probability of "success" must remain the same on each trial. X is an example of a *hypergeometric random variable,* discussed on the CD accompanying this book.

♦ *Any individual random circumstance can be treated as a binomial experiment* with n = 1 and p = probability of a particular outcome. In this case, the random variable X is either 0 or 1, and the random variable may also be called a **Bernoulli random variable.** The fourth example in Table 8.4 illustrates such a variable.

The word *binomial* is from the Latin *bi* = "two," and *nomen* = "name." Explain why the word *binomial* is appropriate for a binomial random variable.*

Finding Probabilities for Binomial Random Variables

For a binomial random variable, the probabilities for the possible values of X are given by the formula

$$P(X = k) = \frac{n!}{k!(n - k)!} p^k(1 - p)^{n-k} \qquad \text{for } k = 0, 1, 2, \ldots, n$$

The formula for $P(X = k)$ is made up of two parts.

1. The first part, $n!/k!(n - k)!$, gives the number of simple events in the sample space (consisting of all possible listings of successes and failures in n trials) that have exactly k successes. The notation $n!$ is read "n-factorial," and it is the product of the integers from 1 to n. For instance, $3! = 1 \times 2 \times 3 = 6$. By convention, $0! = 1$.

2. The second part, $p^k(1 - p)^{n-k}$, gives the probability for each of the simple events for which $X = k$. It follows from the extension of Rule 3b in Chapter 7. If $X = k$, there are k successes and $(n - k)$ failures. Multiply p for each success and $(1 - p)$ for each failure to get $p^k(1 - p)^{n-k}$.

Remember that a *probability distribution function* for a discrete random variable is a table or rule that assigns probabilities to the possible values of the random variable X. It is synonymous to say that a random variable X is a *binomial random variable* and to say that X has a **binomial distribution.** In both cases, the *probability distribution function* for X is the formula just given for $P(X = k)$.

EXAMPLE 8.9
Probability of Two Wins in Three Plays

Suppose that the probability that you win a game is .2 for each play and plays of the game are independent of one another. Let X = number of wins in three plays. What is $P(X = 2)$, the probability that you win exactly twice in three plays? For this problem, X is a binomial random variable with $n = 3$ and success probability $p = .2$. Also, $1 - p = .8$ and $k = 2$ in the formula for $P(X = k)$.

◆ There are

$$\frac{3!}{2!(3 - 2)!} = \frac{6}{2(1)} = 3$$

simple events that produce $X = 2$. The three sequences with two wins are WWL, WLW, and LWW.

◆ For each of these simple events, the probability is $p^k(1 - p)^{n-k} = (.2)^2(.8)^1 = .032$.

◆ So the probability of exactly two wins is $P(X = 2) = 3(.032) = .096$.

The complete probability distribution function (pdf) for X = number of wins in three plays is graphed in Figure 8.3. See if you can verify that $P(X = 1) = .384$. ◆

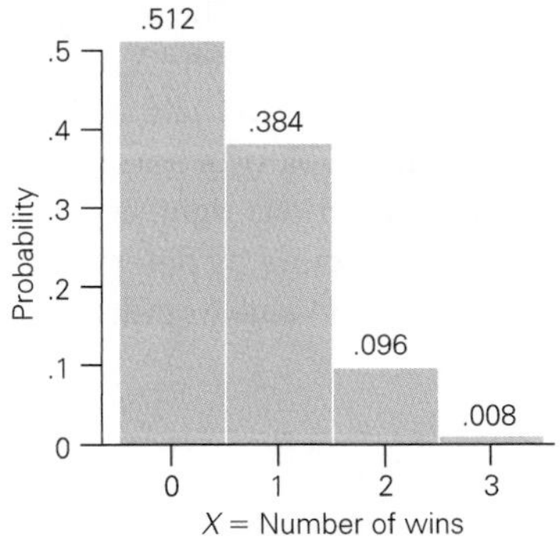

FIGURE 8.3 **Probability distribution function for binomial random variable with $n = 3$ and $p = .2$**

HINT: See the second criterion in the definition of a binomial experiment.

Using Excel to Find Binomial Probabilities

 tech note   Fortunately, binomial probabilities are available in many computer software programs and calculators. To find binomial probabilities using Excel,

♦ $P(X = k)$, is calculated with the command BINOMDIST(k,n,p,false). The "false" indicates that we want the probability for exactly k successes.

♦ $P(X \leq k)$ is calculated with the command BINOMDIST(k,n,p,true). The "true" indicates that the desired probability is "cumulative" and that we want the probability of k or fewer successes.

EXAMPLE 8.10
Excel Calculations for Number of Girls in Ten Births

Let X = number of girls in ten births, and assume that $p = .488$ is the probability that any birth is a girl. As noted in Chapter 7, this value of p is based on birth records in the United States. We can use Excel to find that the probability of exactly seven girls in ten births is = BINOMDIST(7,10,.488,false) = .106. The probability of seven or fewer girls is = BINOMDIST(7,10,.488,true) = .953. ♦

Using Minitab to Find Binomial Probabilities

tech note   ♦ Use **Calc>Probability Distributions>Binomial**

♦ In the dialog box, select "Probability" or "Cumulative Probability" depending on whether you want $P(X = k)$ or $P(X \leq k)$. Specify the number of trials and the probability of success.

♦ Click on "Input constant" and fill in the corresponding box with the value of k.

Note: To find probabilities for several values of k at once, first store the values in a column of the worksheet, and then specify that column as "Input Column."

EXAMPLE 8.11
Guessing Your Way to a Passing Score

You've been busy lately, so busy you're surprised to learn when you arrive at today's statistics class that a 15-question True-False quiz is on the agenda. The quiz is about readings that haven't been discussed during class and you haven't done the readings, so you're forced to guess at every question. You'll pass the quiz if you get ten or more correct answers, so you wonder about $P(X \geq 10)$, where X = number of correct answers. X is a binomial random variable with $n = 15$ trials, and $p = .5$ is the success probability for any question. To find the probability of ten or more correct answers, note that you'll either get ten or more questions right, or you'll get nine or fewer right. So, the answer for $P(X \geq 10)$ can be found by determining the cumulative probability $P(X \leq 9)$, and then subtracting that value from 1. Here's Minitab output with the value of $P(X \leq 9)$:

```
Cumulative Distribution Function
Binomial with n = 15 and p = 0.500000
        x        P(X <= x)
       9.0        0.8491
```

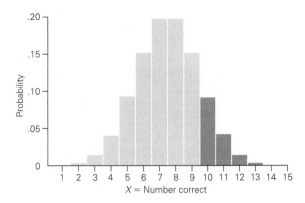

FIGURE 8.4 **Probabilities for guessing on a 15-question true-false quiz**

The probability of a passing score is $1 - .8491 = .1509$. You've got a chance to pass, although the probability you don't pass is .8491! Figure 8.4 illustrates this probability. ◆

Expected Value (Mean) and Standard Deviation for a Binomial Random Variable

To find the mean value of a binomial random variable, we don't have to use the formula from Section 8.3 for expected value. There is a much simpler formula that applies to all binomial random variables, and this formula is easy to understand. If you flip a fair coin 100 times, for instance, how many heads would you expect to result, on average? The answer is $100 \times 1/2 = 50$ heads, which is the number of flips times the probability of heads for any single flip. Or, if you guess the answer for every question on a multiple-choice test with 25 questions, each with 5 choices, you could expect to get about $25 \times 1/5 = 5$ right answers. For both of these examples, we determined the mean, μ, by calculating np, the product of the number of trials and the probability of success.

There also is a simplified formula for the standard deviation of a binomial random variable. The formulas for the mean (expected value) and standard deviation of a binomial random variable were derived using algebra and the formulas introduced earlier in this chapter for expected value, standard deviation, and $P(X = k)$ when X is a binomial random variable. You won't have to know how to do these derivations, but the results are useful for later applications in this textbook, so remember where to find them.

Mean, Standard Deviation, and Variance of a Binomial Random Variable

formula   For a *binomial random variable X* based on n trials with success probability p,

The **mean** is $\mu = E(X) = np$.

The **standard deviation** is $\sigma = \sqrt{np(1 - p)}$.

Note: For any random variable, the standard deviation is the square root of the **variance**. For a binomial random variable, the variance is $V(X) = np(1 - p)$, which leads to the formula for standard deviation.

EXAMPLE 8.12
Is There Extraterrestrial Life?

Suppose that 50% of a large population would say "yes" if they were asked, "Do you believe there is extraterrestrial life?" A sample of $n = 100$ is taken from this population, and each person in the sample is asked the question about belief in extraterrestrial life. The random variable X = number in the sample who say "yes" is approximately a binomial random variable. For this variable, $n = 100$ and $p = .5$, so the mean of X is $\mu = (100)(.5) = 50$, and the standard deviation is $\sigma = \sqrt{100(.5)(1 - .5)} = 5$. In other words, in repeated samples of size 100 from this population, on average 50 people would say "yes" to the question. The amount by which that number would differ from sample to sample is represented by the standard deviation of 5. We will discuss this kind of "sample variability" in much more detail in Chapter 9. ◆

8.6

turn on your mind

In Example 8.11, we determined the probability that you could guess your way to a passing score on a quiz with 15 True-False questions. If you did guess at each of 15 True-False questions, what is the expected value of X = number of correct answers? Is the expected value a possible score on the quiz? What exactly does the expected value tell us?*

8.5 | CONTINUOUS RANDOM VARIABLES

> *definition* A **continuous random variable** is one for which the outcome can be any value in an interval or collection of intervals.

In practice, all measurements are rounded to a specified number of decimal places, so we may not be able to accurately observe all possible outcomes of a continuous variable. For example, the limitations of weighing scales keep us from observing that a weight may actually be 128.3671345993 pounds. With most scales, we would be forced to round such a weight to 128 pounds, or, with a digital scale, perhaps to 128.4 pounds. Generally, however, we call a random variable a continuous random variable if there are a large number of observable outcomes covering an interval or set of intervals. For instance, measurements of height, time, weight, and monetary values are all treated as continuous random variables.

The way that we determine probabilities for continuous random variables differs in one important respect from how we determine probabilities for discrete random variables. For a discrete random variable, we can find the probability that the variable X exactly equals a specified value. We can't do this for a continuous random variable. For a continuous random variable, we are only able to find the probability that X falls between two values. We do this by determining the area between the two values under a curve called the **probability density function** of the random variable. In other words, unlike discrete random variables, continuous random variables do not have probability distribution functions specifying the exact probabilities of specified values. Instead, they have probability density functions, which are used to find probabilities that the random variable falls into a specified interval of values.

*HINT: Use the formula for $E(X)$ for a binomial random variable.

> **definition** The **probability density function** for a continuous random variable X is a curve such that the area under the curve over an interval equals the probability that X is in that interval. In other words, the probability $P(a \leq X \leq b)$ is the area under the density curve over the interval between the values a and b.

8.7

turn on your mind

The total area under the probability density function over the entire range of values the random variable X can possibly have is the same for all continuous random variables. What is that total area? What probability does it represent?

Suppose the random variable is the amount of rainfall in Davis, California, for a randomly selected year and can range from 0 inches to 50 inches. What is the area under the appropriate density curve over the range from 0 to 50 inches? What probability does it represent?*

EXAMPLE 8.13
Time Spent
Waiting for the Bus

A bus arrives at a bus stop every 10 minutes. If a person arrives at the bus stop at a random time, how long will he or she have to wait for the next bus? Define the random variable X = waiting time until the next bus arrives. The value of X could be any value between 0 and 10 minutes, and X is a continuous random variable. (In practice, the limitations of watches would force us to round off the exact time.) Figure 8.5 shows the probability density function for the waiting time. Possible waiting times are along the horizontal axis, and the vertical axis is a density scale. The height of the "curve" is .1 for all X between 0 and 1, so the total area between 0 and 10 minutes is $(10)(.1) = 1$. ◆

The density function shown in Figure 8.5 is a flat line that covers the interval of possible values for X. There is a "uniformity" to this density curve in that every interval with the same width has the same probability. A random variable with this property is called a **uniform random variable** and is the simplest example of a continuous random variable.

EXAMPLE 8.13—*CONTINUED*

Suppose we want to find the probability that the waiting time X was in the interval from 5 to 7 minutes. The general principle for any continuous random vari-

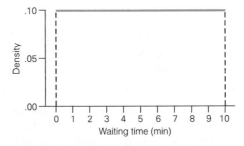

FIGURE 8.5 **A uniform probability density function for Example 8.13**

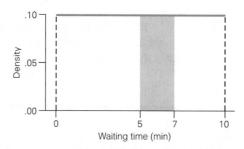

FIGURE 8.6   **The probability that waiting time is between 5 and 7 minutes**

able is that the probability $P(a \le X \le b)$ is the "area under the curve" over the interval from a to b. In this example, the "area under the curve" is the area of a rectangle that has width $= 7 - 5 = 2$ minutes and height $= .1$. This area is $(2)(.1) = .2$, which is the probability that the waiting time is between 5 and 7 minutes. In Figure 8.6, the shaded area represents the desired probability. ◆

Theoretically, the use of calculus is needed to find an area under a density curve (unless it's a simple rectangle or other simple shape, as in Example 8.13). In practice, however, tables of appropriate probabilities usually are available. Computer software and graphing calculators also can be used to "automate" the calculations for the most commonly encountered models.

8.6 | NORMAL RANDOM VARIABLES

We first encountered normal random variables in Chapter 2, as a special case of bell-shaped distributions. If a population of measurements follows a normal curve, and if X is the measurement for a randomly selected individual from that population, then X is said to be a **normal random variable.** X is also said to have a **normal distribution.** Any normal random variable can be completely characterized by specifying its mean, μ, and standard deviation, σ.

Normal random variables are the most common type of *continuous random variables.* As with any continuous random variable, the probability that X falls into some specified interval is equivalent to the area under a probability density curve, which in this case is the bell-shaped **normal curve.** Nature provides numerous examples of measurements that follow a normal curve. The fact that so many different kinds of measurements follow a normal curve is not surprising. On many attributes, the majority of people are somewhat close to average, and as you move further from the average, either above or below, there are fewer people with such values.

Here are some features shared by all normal curves and normal random variables (X):

1. As with any continuous random variable, $P(X = k) = 0$ for any value k.
2. The curve is symmetric on either side of the mean, μ, so $P(X \le \mu) = P(X \ge \mu) = .5$. For instance, half of all women's heights are above the mean and half are below the mean.
3. $P(X \le \mu - d) = P(X \ge \mu + d)$ for any number d. For instance, the probability that a randomly selected woman is at least two inches shorter than

the mean is the same as the probability that she is at least two inches taller than the mean. In this case, X = woman's height and $d = 2$.

4. The Empirical Rule holds:

- $P(\mu - \sigma \le X \le \mu + \sigma) \approx .68$
- $P(\mu - 2\sigma \le X \le \mu + 2\sigma) \approx .95$
- $P(\mu - 3\sigma \le X \le \mu + 3\sigma) \approx .997$

EXAMPLE 8.14
College Women's Heights

Data collected in several classes by the authors of this text and some of their colleagues suggest that the distribution of the heights of college women can be described reasonably well by a normal curve with mean $\mu = 65$ inches (5 foot 5 inches) and standard deviation $\sigma = 2.7$ inches. A normal curve with these characteristics is shown in Figure 8.7. Heights are shown along the horizontal axis, with tick marks given at the mean and at 1, 2, and 3 standard deviations above and below the mean. Notice that half (.5) of the area is above the mean of 65.0 and half is below it.

Most of the normal curve is over the interval of height from 56.9 inches to 73.1 inches. This is consistent with the Empirical Rule that we encountered in Chapter 2. One part of the Empirical Rule is that for a bell-shaped curve, about 99.7% of the values fall within 3 standard deviations of the mean in either direction. Here, the interval of heights within 3 standard deviations of the mean is $65 \pm 3 \times 2.7$, which is 65 ± 8.1 inches, or 56.9 and 73.1 inches. The Empirical Rule is generally used as an approximate rule for describing sample data with a bell-shaped curve, but the features of that rule are exact characteristics of a normal curve model. ◆

Standardized Scores

Once the mean, μ, and the standard deviation, σ, have been specified, finding probabilities is a simple process for a normal random variable. We simply have to convert the endpoints of an interval of interest to **standardized scores** and then use a table, calculator, or computer software to find probabilities associated with these standardized scores. A standardized score is also called a **z-score.** We first encountered z-scores in Chapter 2; the definition is repeated here, using notation for random variables.

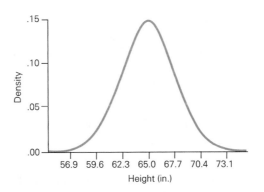

FIGURE 8.7   Normal curve for heights of college women

Calculating a *z*-Score

formula   The formula for converting any value x to a **z-score** is

$$z = \frac{\text{Value} - \text{Mean}}{\text{Standard deviation}} = \frac{x - \mu}{\sigma}$$

A *z*-score measures the number of standard deviations that a value falls from the mean.

EXAMPLE 8.14—*CONTINUED*
The z-Score for a Height of 62 Inches

For a population of college women, the *z*-score corresponding to a height of 62 inches is

$$z = \frac{\text{Value} - \text{Mean}}{\text{Standard deviation}} = \frac{62 - 65}{2.7} = \frac{-3}{2.7} = -1.11$$

This *z*-score tells us that 62 inches is 1.11 standard deviations below the mean height for this population. If you are a college woman who is 62 inches tall, your height is 1.11 standard deviations below the mean height for other college women. ◆

Finding Probabilities for *z*-Scores

Converting any normal random variable to *z*-scores is equivalent to converting the random variable of interest to a normal random variable that has mean $\mu = 0$ and standard deviation $\sigma = 1$. A normal random variable with these characteristics is said to be a **standard normal random variable** and to have a **standard normal distribution.** Tables and software packages are designed to give probabilities for the standard normal distribution. The Appendix of this book contains a table of standard normal probabilities. To read Table A.1, Standard Normal Probabilities,

♦ The body of the table contains $P(Z \leq z^*)$, which is the probability that the value of a standard normal variable Z takes a value that is less than the specific value z^*.

♦ The left-most column of the table shows the algebraic sign, the digit before the decimal place, and the first decimal place for z^*.

♦ The second decimal place of z^* is in the column heading across the top of the table.

Technical Detail: $P(Z = z^*) = 0$, so it is equivalent to write $P(Z \leq z^*)$ or $P(Z < z^*)$.

As an example, Table A.1 shows that $P(Z \leq 1.82) = .9656$. To see this, look in the portion of the table of positive values of z. In the first column (labeled z), locate the row for 1.8. In that row, move over to the ".02" column to find the cumulative probability for z = 1.82. The general idea is

z	.00	.01	.02	.03	.04	.05	.06	.07	.08	.09
1.8	$\longrightarrow$		.9656							

Here are some other examples that you should verify to be sure you understand how to read the table:

$$P(Z \leq - 2.59) = .0048$$
$$P(Z \leq 1.31) \quad = .9049$$
$$P(Z \leq 2.00) \quad = .9772$$

Notice at the bottom of both pages of the table, there is a section titled "In the Extreme" where cumulative probabilities are given for selected "extreme" z-scores. For instance, from that section of the table you can learn that $P(Z \leq -4.75) = .000001$ (one in a million!).

To find probabilities for other types of intervals, simply add and subtract appropriate probabilities of the form $P(Z \leq z^*)$. When using a table like ours, it is usually best to draw a picture of the problem, highlight the desired area, and then figure out how the area relates to probabilities of the form $P(Z \leq z^*)$.

There are some simple probability relationships that are useful for solving normal curve problems. We state them for a standard normal random variable Z here, and for any normal random variable X later. In the Exercises, you will be asked to show how they follow from the probability rules in Chapter 7.

1. $P(Z > a) = 1 - P(Z \leq a)$
2. $P(Z > a) = P(Z < -a)$
3. $P(a \leq Z \leq b) = P(Z \leq b) - P(Z \leq a)$

Examples 8.15 and 8.16 demonstrate these relationships.

EXAMPLE 8.15
Probability That Z Is Greater Than 1.31

There are two equivalent ways to find the probability that Z is greater than 1.31:

$$P(Z > 1.31) = 1 - P(Z \leq 1.31)$$
$$= 1 - .9049 = .0951$$

This is an application of the general relationship $P(Z > a) = 1 - P(Z \leq a)$. Figure 8.8 illustrates the area of interest and the solution. Notice that the desired probability equals the area to the right of 1.31. We could also use the symmetry relationship,

$$P(Z > a) = P(Z < -a),$$

so

$$P(Z > 1.31) = P(Z < -1.31) = .0951 \quad \blacklozenge$$

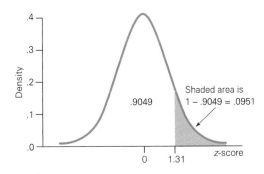

FIGURE 8.8   **Area to the right of** $Z = 1.31$

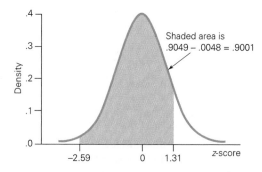

FIGURE 8.9   **Area between $Z = -2.59$ and $Z = 1.31$**

EXAMPLE 8.16
Probability That Z Is
Between −2.59 and 1.31

The probability that a standard normal variable Z is between -2.59 and 1.31 is found by taking the difference between the probabilities to the left of these two values.

$$P(-2.59 \leq Z \leq 1.31) = P(Z \leq 1.31) - P(Z \leq -2.59)$$
$$= .9049 - .0048 = .9001$$

Figure 8.9 shows the area under the normal curve for this example. This is an example of using the relationship:

$$P(a \leq Z \leq b) = P(Z \leq b) - P(Z \leq a) \; \blacklozenge$$

How to Solve General Normal Curve Problems

Every probability problem about a normal curve can be solved using z-scores. The following example illustrates the process.

EXAMPLE 8.14—CONTINUED
Probability That Height Is
Less Than 62 Inches

If we assume that college women's heights follow a normal curve with $\mu = 65$ inches and $\sigma = 2.7$ inches, we can find probabilities associated with any possible range of heights. For example, what is the probability that a randomly selected college woman is 62 inches or shorter? Equivalently, what proportion of college women are 62 inches or shorter?

$$P(X \leq 62) = P\left(Z \leq \frac{62 - 65}{2.7}\right)$$
$$= P(Z \leq -1.11) = .1335$$

In other words, about 13% of college women are 62 inches or shorter. Figure 8.10 illustrates the area of interest under the normal curve for college women's heights. $\blacklozenge$

The area displayed in Figure 8.10, the probability that a randomly selected college woman has a height less than 62 inches, is called the cumulative probability for 62 inches. A cumulative probability is a "less than" type of probability. We encountered this idea for discrete random variables when we defined the *cumulative distribution function* as $P(X \leq k)$. The same definition holds for continuous random variables, and the probability is simply the area under the density curve to the left of the value k.

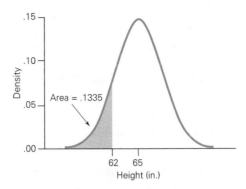

FIGURE 8.10   College women's heights and
P(height $\leq$ 62 inches)

To find a cumulative probability for any random variable with a normal distribution, we simply need to know its mean and standard deviation, find the z-score corresponding to k, and find the area under the standard normal curve to the left of that z-score.

Finding a Cumulative Probability $P(X \leq k)$ for any Normal Random Variable

If X is a normal random variable with known mean μ and standard deviation σ, to find $P(X \leq k)$, the probability that X is less than or equal to k:

Step 1: Calculate a z-score for the value k; call it z^*.

Step 2: Use a table, calculator, or computer to find $P(Z \leq z^*)$.

EXAMPLE 8.14—CONTINUED
Proportion of Women Who Are Taller Than 68 Inches

Suppose we want to find the proportion of college women who are taller than 68 inches. The simplest solution is to first find the probability that a woman is shorter than 68 inches and then subtract that answer from 1. The relationship is $P(X > 68) = 1 - P(X \leq 68)$. To find $P(X \leq 68)$, we convert it to an equivalent question about the z-score for 68 inches. The z-score for 68 inches is $(68 - 65)/2.7 = 1.11$, and

$$P(Z > 1.11) = 1 - P(Z \leq 1.11)$$
$$= 1 - .8665 = .1335$$

About 13% of the women in this population are at least 68 inches tall. Figure 8.11 illustrates the problem and the solution. ◆

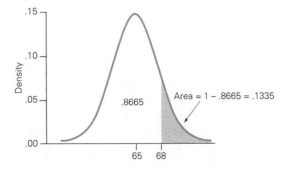

FIGURE 8.11   Probability that college woman is taller than
68 inches

You may have noticed that the proportion taller than 68 inches equals the proportion shorter than 62 inches. The equivalence is not a coincidence. Both problems have to do with being more than 3 inches from the mean. By the symmetry of the normal curve, the probability that a woman is at least 3 inches shorter than the mean equals the probability that a woman is at least 3 inches taller than the mean.

Useful Probability Relationships for Normal Random Variables

The following relationships are useful for working with probabilities for a normal random variable X.

- To find the probability that X **is greater than b,** subtract the probability that X is less than b from 1. In mathematical terms, $P(X > b) = 1 - P(X \le b)$.

- The probability that X is *more* **than d units *above* the mean** is the same as the probability that X is *less* **than d units *below* the mean**. In mathematical terms, $P(X > \mu + d) = P(X < \mu - d)$.

- To find the probability that X **is between a and b,** take the difference between the probability that X is less than b and the probability that X is less than a. In mathematical terms, $P(a \le X \le b) = P(X \le b) - P(X \le a)$.

EXAMPLE 8.14—*CONTINUED*
The Proportion of Women Between 62 and 68 Inches Tall

To find the probability that a college woman's height is between 62 and 68 inches, use the relationship $P(62 \le X \le 68) = P(X \le 68) - P(X \le 62)$. In other words, take the difference between the cumulative probabilities for 62 inches and 68 inches. The probabilities that we need were determined in previous parts of this example, and the answer is $.8665 - .1335 = .733$. About 73% of college women are between 62 and 68 inches tall. ◆

Finding Percentiles

There probably have been several instances in your life where information about your percentile ranking on a particular variable has been provided to you. For example, you may have been told that your Verbal SAT score was at the 80th percentile of all Verbal SAT scores, or that your height was at the 50th percentile for individuals of your sex and age. Remember from Chapter 2 that the kth percentile for a dataset is a number that has k% of the data values at or below it. The same definition holds for random variables. If your Verbal SAT score was at the 80th percentile, then your score was higher than the scores of 80% of the other test takers (and lower than 20%).

In some problems, we may want to know what value of a variable defines a specified percentile ranking. We may, for example, want to know what IQ score is the 98th percentile, or what pulse rate is the 25th percentile of pulse rates for your gender. You should notice that the word **percentile** refers to the *value* of a variable, while **percentile ranking** refers to the *proportion* below that value. For instance, if the 25th percentile of pulse rates is 64 beats per minute, then 25% of pulse rates are below 64 and 75% are above 64. The *percentile* is 64 beats per minute, and the *percentile ranking* is 25% or .25.

In probability terms, the percentile rank for the value of a variable corresponds to the *cumulative probability* for that value. For example, the 25th percentile of pulse rates is the pulse rate for which .25 is the cumulative probability (area to the left under the density curve). Figure 8.12 illustrates this concept.

To determine a percentile for a specified percentile ranking (or cumulative probability) for a normal random variable, there are two steps:

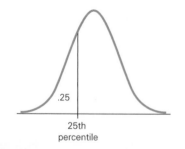

FIGURE 8.12   The 25th percentile for a random variable with a normal distribution

Step 1: Find the z-score that has the specified cumulative probability. This step does not involve calculation; it involves a table search (or a computerized version of a table search). For instance, using Table A.1 in the Appendix, find the percentile rank in the body of the table and read the z-score from the row and column headings.

Step 2: Calculate the value of the variable that has the z-score found in step 1. This can be done using the relationship $x = z\sigma + \mu$.

EXAMPLE 8.17
The 75th Percentile of Systolic Blood Pressures

Suppose that the blood pressures of men aged 18 to 29 years old can be described with a normal curve having mean $\mu = 120$ and standard deviation $\sigma = 10$. What is the 75th percentile? In other words, what is the blood pressure value x such that $P(\text{Blood pressure} \leq x) = .75$?

Using the table of standard normal probabilities, we learn that $z = .67$ is approximately the z-score for which the cumulative probability is the desired .75. (Search for .75 within the table, then look at the row and column labels to read the value of z.) The blood pressure with this z-score is determined from $x = z\sigma + \mu$, and the answer is $.67(10) + 120 = 6.7 + 120 \approx 127$. ◆

Finding a Percentile or a Value with Specified Cumulative Probability
If X is a normal random variable with mean μ and standard deviation σ, and p is a specified probability, then to find the value x for which $P(X \leq x) = p$:

Step 1: Find the value z^* for which $P(Z \leq z^*) = p$ using a table, computer, or calculator.

Step 2: Compute $x = z^*\sigma + \mu$.

8.8

turn on your mind

Which of the following measurements do you think are likely to have a normal distribution: heights of college men, incomes of 40-year-old women, pulse rates of college athletes? Explain your reasoning for each variable. For those variables that are likely to be normally distributed, give approximate values for the mean and standard deviation.*

Minitab Tip

 tech note   **Calculating Normal Curve Probabilities and Percentiles**

- ◆ Use **Calc>Probability Distributions>Normal.**
- ◆ Specify the mean and standard deviation.
- ◆ To find $P(X \leq k)$, select "Cumulative Probability" and also specify the value of k in the box labeled "Input Constant."
- ◆ To find a percentile, select "Inverse Cumulative" and also specify the cumulative probability for the percentile in the box labeled "Input Constant."

Note: It's not necessary to compute z-scores when using Minitab for determining normal curve probabilities.

8.7 | APPROXIMATING BINOMIAL DISTRIBUTION PROBABILITIES

One useful application of the normal distribution is that it can be used to approximate probabilities for some other types of random variables. In this section, we learn how to use the normal distribution to approximate cumulative probabilities for binomial random variables. When X has a binomial distribution with a large number of trials, the binomial probability formula is difficult to use because the factorial expressions in the formula become very large. The work required to find binomial probabilities when n is large is enormous, and even computer programs and calculators may not be able to do the task. Fortunately, the normal distribution can be used to approximate probabilities for a binomial random variable when this situation occurs.

The **normal approximation to the binomial distribution** is based on the following result, derived from mathematics. If X is a binomial random variable based on n trials with success probability p, and n is large, then the random variable X is also approximately a normal random variable. For this normal random variable,

$$\text{Mean} = \mu = np$$
$$\text{Standard deviation} = \sigma = \sqrt{np(1-p)}$$

Conditions: The approximation works well when both np and $n(1-p)$ are at least 10.

EXAMPLE 8.18
The Number of Heads in 30 Flips of a Coin

Figure 8.13 displays the probability distribution function of a binomial random variable based on $n = 30$ trials and a success probability $p = .5$. This distribution could, for example, describe X = number of heads when a coin is flipped $n = 30$ times, or the number correct if you are just guessing on a 30-question True-False quiz. The bell-shaped pattern of the distribution is clear, and a normal curve could be used to approximate this distribution because both np and $n(1-p)$ are greater than 10. Recall that 99.7%, or nearly all, of a normal curve falls within 3 standard deviations of the mean. For the binomial random variable displayed in Figure 8.13, $\mu = 15$, the standard deviation is $\sigma = \sqrt{30 \times .5 \times (1 - .5)}$ = 2.74, and the interval $\mu \pm 3\sigma$ is approximately 15 ± 8, or 7 to 23. The probability is small that X would take a value outside this interval. ◆

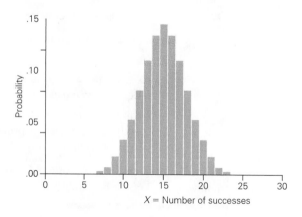

FIGURE 8.13   **Binomial distribution for $n = 30$ and $p = .5$**

Approximating Cumulative Probabilities for a Binomial Random Variable

The normal curve approximation can be used to find cumulative probabilities for binomial random variables, as follows:

$$P(X \leq k) \approx P(Z \leq z^*)$$

where

$$z^* = \frac{k - np}{\sqrt{np(1 - p)}}$$

In other words, to find a cumulative probability, first calculate a z-score for the value of interest, k, using the formulas for the mean and the standard deviation of a binomial variable. Then, use the standard normal curve to determine the cumulative probability for this z-score.

More complex probabilities can be found as well, using the same relationships as for any normal random variable X. For example, find the probability that X is between two numbers a and b as follows:

$$P(a \leq X \leq b) = P(X \leq b) - P(X \leq a) \approx P\left(Z \leq \frac{b - np}{\sqrt{np(1 - p)}}\right)$$
$$- P\left(Z \leq \frac{a - np}{\sqrt{np(1 - p)}}\right)$$

It is important to note that you should not use the normal curve approximation if your statistical software or calculator is able to determine a binomial probability exactly. In this regard, the capabilities of different software programs and calculators vary greatly. For the next example, for instance, version 13 of Minitab is able to provide an exact answer, but version 12 of Minitab is not.

EXAMPLE 8.19
Political Woes

A politician is convinced that at least 50% of her constituents favor a woman's right to choose abortion but is concerned because the latest poll of 500 adults in her district found that slightly less than half, only 240, or 48% of the sample, supported this position. If indeed 50% of adults in the district support abortion, what is the probability that a random sample of 500 adults would find 240 or fewer of them holding this position?

To solve this problem, notice that if X = number in sample who support abortion, and if 50% of all adults in the district actually support it, then X is a binomial random variable with $n = 500$ and $p = .5$. The desired probability is $P(X \leq 240)$. It would be quite tedious to find this probability by adding the individual probabilities from 0 to 240! It is much easier to use the normal approximation, with

$$\mu = np = 250$$
$$\sigma = \sqrt{np(1 - p)} = 11.2$$

The solution is $P(X \leq 240) \approx \left(P(Z \leq \frac{240 - 250}{11.2}\right) = P(Z \leq -.89) = .1867$.

This means that it is not unlikely that she could observe a minority of 48% or less of the sample favoring abortion, even if 50% of the district favors it. ◆

EXAMPLE 8.18—*CONTINUED*
Guessing and Passing
a True-False Test

In Example 8.18 and Figure 8.13 we displayed probabilities for a binomial random variable with $n = 30$ and $p = .5$. Suppose you need 70%, or 21 questions, correct to pass a True-False test on which you are just guessing. Find $P(X \geq 21)$. Notice that the complement of this event is *not* $P(X \leq 21)$; it's $P(X \leq 20)$. Using the normal approximation to the binomial with $n = 30$ and $p = .5$:

$$P(X \geq 21) = 1 - P(X \leq 20) \approx 1 - P\left(Z \leq \frac{20 - np}{\sqrt{np(1 - p)}}\right) = 1 - P(Z \leq 1.83)$$
$$= 1 - .9664 = .0336.$$

Using Minitab, the exact probability that $X \geq 21$ is $1 - .9786 = .0214$.

Figure 8.13 illustrates the exact binomial pdf for this situation. Notice that $P(X \geq 21)$ corresponds to the areas of the rectangles above 21, 22, . . . , 30, of which only the ones above 21, 22, and 23 are visible. After that, the probabilities, and thus heights of the rectangles, are essentially 0. For instance, $P(X = 24) = .0006$. ◆

Continuity Correction

tech note   Notice in Figure 8.13 that the rectangle centered on $X = 21$ actually begins at 20.5, not at 21.0. But in the normal approximation to the binomial calculation we found the area under a normal curve starting at 21, not 20.5. In doing so, we omitted half of the rectangle centered at 21. To make the approximation more accurate, sometimes a **continuity correction** is used by adding or subtracting .5, based on which rectangles are desired. For Example 8.18,

$$P(X \geq 21) \approx P\left(Z \leq \frac{20.5 - (30)(.5)}{\sqrt{(30)(.5)(1 - .5)}}\right) = P(Z \geq 2.01) = P(Z \leq -2.01)$$
$$= .0222$$

which is much closer to the exact probability of .0214 than was the approximation of .0336 found without the continuity correction.

8.8 | SUMS, DIFFERENCES, AND COMBINATIONS OF RANDOM VARIABLES

There are many instances where we want information about combinations of random variables. Suppose, for example, that your final score in a class is found by adding together 25% of each of two midterm exam scores (Exam1 and Exam2) and 50% of your final exam score (Exam3). Expressed as an equation, the final score is calculated as

Final score = $.25 \times$ Exam1 + $.25 \times$ Exam2 + $.50 \times$ Exam3

If you know the mean for each exam, it is easy to calculate the mean final score. It probably makes sense to you that the mean final score can be found by combining the mean exam scores in the same way that an individual's scores are combined. If the means on the three exams are μ_1, μ_2, and μ_3, the formula for the mean final score is

Mean of final scores = $.25 \times \mu_1$ + $.25 \times \mu_2$ + $.50 \times \mu_3$

For instance, if the exam means are 72, 76, and 80, respectively, then the mean of the final scores is

$$\text{Mean of final scores} = (.25 \times 72) + (.25 \times 76) + (.50 \times 80)$$
$$= 18 + 19 + 40 = 77$$

We are assuming the class constitutes the entire population of interest so the means are represented as population means (μ) instead of sample means ($\bar{x}$). The formula for calculating the mean final score, however, would hold for sample means as well.

The combination of exam scores that we just considered is an example of a "linear combination" of random variables. In a linear combination, we add (or subtract) variables, but some of the combined variables may be multiplied by a numerical value, as occurred in calculating the final score. For two random variables X and Y, the most commonly encountered linear combinations are the sum $X + Y$ and the difference $X - Y$.

> *definition* A **linear combination** of random variables, X, Y, . . . is a combination of the form
>
> $$L = aX + bY + \cdots$$
>
> where a, b, etc. are numbers, which could be positive or negative. The most commonly encountered linear combinations of two variables are
>
> Sum $= X + Y$
>
> Difference $= X - Y$

A number of rules tell us about the statistical properties of a linear combination of random variables. The most basic rule is for the mean. This rule applies to any set of random variables, whether they are discrete or continuous, independent of each other or not, and regardless of their distributions. The only assumption is that the variables combined all have finite means.

Mean of a Linear Combination of Random Variables (Including Sums and Differences)

> *formula* If X, Y, . . . are random variables, a, b, . . . are numbers, either positive or negative, and
>
> $$L = aX + bY + \cdots$$
>
> The mean of L is
>
> $$\text{Mean}(L) = a\,\text{Mean}(X) + b\,\text{Mean}(Y) + \cdots$$
>
> In particular,
>
> $$\text{Mean}(X + Y) = \text{Mean}(X) + \text{Mean}(Y)$$
> $$\text{Mean}(X - Y) = \text{Mean}(X) - \text{Mean}(Y)$$

Rules for the variance and standard deviation of a linear combination are complicated, and we will only consider a specific situation, which is that the random variables are independent. Two random variables are statistically **independent** if the probability for any event associated with one random variable is not altered by whether or not any event for the other random variable has happened. In a more practical sense, it is usually safe to say that *two random variables are independent if there is no physical connection between the two variables, or if there is no apparent reason why the value of one variable should influence the value of the other.*

Variance and Standard Deviation of a Linear Combination of Independent Random Variables

formula If X, Y, etc. are independent random variables, a, b, etc. are numbers, and

$$L = aX + bY + \cdots$$

then, the *variance* and *standard deviation* of L are

$$\text{Variance}(L) = a^2\,\text{Variance}(X) + b^2\,\text{Variance}(Y) + \cdots$$
$$\text{Standard Deviation of } L = \sqrt{\text{Variance}(L)}$$

In particular,

$$\text{Variance}(X + Y) = \text{Variance}(X) + \text{Variance}(Y)$$
$$\text{Variance}(X - Y) = \text{Variance}(X) + \text{Variance}(Y)$$

Keep in mind that the standard deviation is the square root of the variance. Notice also that the variance of the *difference* is the *sum* of the variances because $b = -1$ and $b^2 = +1$.

Simply knowing the mean and standard deviation of a combination of random variables is of little practical use in most cases. To find probabilities associated with various outcomes, we also need to know the distribution.

Combining Independent Normal or Binomial Random Variables

Some classes of random variables keep the same shape when linear combinations of variables within the class are formed. This occurs for normal curve distributions. Any linear combination of normally distributed variables also has a normal distribution, but we only consider independent variables and focus on rules for the **sum** and for the **difference** of two such variables.

Linear Combinations of Independent Normal Random Variables

formula If X, Y, etc. are independent, normally distributed random variables, and a, b, etc. are numbers, either positive or negative, then the random variable $L = aX + bY + \cdots$ is normally distributed. In particular,

$X + Y$ is normally distributed with mean $\mu_X + \mu_Y$ and standard deviation $\sqrt{\sigma_X^2 + \sigma_Y^2}$.

$X - Y$ is normally distributed with mean $\mu_X - \mu_Y$ and standard deviation $\sqrt{\sigma_X^2 + \sigma_Y^2}$.

EXAMPLE 8.20
Will Meg Miss Her Flight?

Meg travels often and lately has become lax about giving herself enough time to get to the airport. She leaves home 45 minutes before the last call for her flight will occur. Her travel time from her front door to the airport parking lot is normally distributed with mean of 25 minutes and standard deviation of 3 minutes. From the parking lot, she must then take a shuttle bus to the terminal and go through security screening. The mean time for doing this is 15 minutes and the standard deviation is 2 minutes, and this time also is normally distributed. The driving time and the airport time are independent of each other. What is the probability that Meg will miss her flight because her total time for getting to the plane is more than 45 minutes?

Let's define some random variables:

X = driving time; normally distributed with μ_X = 25 min. and σ_X = 3 min.
Y = airport time; normally distributed with μ_Y = 15 min. and σ_Y = 2 min.
$T = X + Y$ = total time.

The random variable T has a normal distribution because it is a sum of two independent, normally distributed random variables. For T, the mean is the sum of the means for X and Y, which is μ = 25 + 15 = 40 min., and the standard deviation is $\sigma = \sqrt{\sigma_X^2 + \sigma_Y^2} = \sqrt{3^2 + 2^2} = \sqrt{9 + 4} = \sqrt{13} = 3.6$. Using Table A.1 in the Appendix (or statistical software or the right calculator), we find that the probability the total time T exceeds 45 minutes is

$$P(T > 45) = P\left(Z > \frac{45 - 40}{3.6}\right)$$
$$= P(Z > 1.39) = 1 - P(Z < 1.39)$$
$$= 1 - .9177 = .0823$$

Meg should leave sooner. If she continues this behavior, she will miss her flight about 8% of the time. ◆

EXAMPLE 8.21
Can Alison Ever Win?

Alison and her sister Julie each swim a mile every day. Alison's times are normally distributed with mean = 37 minutes and standard deviation = 1 minute. Julie is faster but less consistent than Alison, and her times are normally distributed with mean = 33 minutes and standard deviation = 2 minutes. On any day, their times are independent of each other. Can Alison ever beat Julie?

Let's define three random variables for a given day:

X = Alison's time; normally distributed with μ_X = 37 min. and σ_X = 1 min.
Y = Julie's time; normally distributed with μ_Y = 33 min. and σ_Y = 2 min.
$D = X - Y$ = Difference in their times.

The random variable D is normally distributed because it is the difference of two normally distributed variables. For D, the difference between the sisters' times, the mean is μ = 37 − 33 = 4 minutes and the standard deviation is $\sigma = \sqrt{\sigma_X^2 + \sigma_Y^2}$ $= \sqrt{1^2 + 2^2} = \sqrt{5} = 2.236$. Alison beats Julie when $X < Y$ or, equivalently, when $D = X - Y < 0$. The probability that $D < 0$ is

$$P(D < 0) = P\left(Z < \frac{0 - 4}{2.236}\right) = P(Z < -1.79) = .0367$$

Alison swims a faster time about 3.7% of the time, which is about one day per month. ◆

8.9

turn on your mind

In Example 8.21, the time it takes Alison to swim a mile on any given day was assumed to be *independent* of the time it takes Julie to swim a mile on that same day. Refer to the explanation of when two random variables are independent, given earlier in this section. Explain whether it is reasonable to assume Alison's and Julie's times on the same day are independent in each of the following scenarios:

1. They swim at different times, and the one who swims first does not report her time to the other until after they are both done.
2. They swim side-by-side in two lanes of a pool.
3. They swim at different times, but the one who swims second knows the time it took the other to swim the mile that day.*

Combining Independent Binomial Random Variables

A linear combination of binomial random variables is generally not a binomial variable, but there is one situation where it is. The sum of independent binomial variables, each with the same success probability, has a binomial distribution. Put another way, independent binomial experiments with the same success probability can be combined and analyzed as a single binomial experiment. Imagine that you flip a coin five times while one of your friends flips a coin ten times. Probability questions about the total number of heads flipped by you and your friend can be answered using the binomial distribution for $n = 5 + 10 = 15$ trials and $p = .5$ (assuming you both flipped fairly!).

Adding Binomial Random Variables with the Same Success Probability

If X, Y, etc. are independent binomial random variables with n_X, n_Y, etc. trials and all have the same success probability p, then the sum $X + Y + \cdots$ is a binomial random variable with $n = n_X + n_Y + \cdots$, and success probability p.

Note: If the success probabilities differ, the sum is not a binomial random variable.

EXAMPLE 8.22
Donations Add Up

A volunteer organization is having a fund drive. Three volunteers agree to call potential donors. In past drives, about 20% of those called agreed to make a donation, independent of who called them. If the three volunteers make 10, 12, and 18 calls, respectively, what is the probability that they get at least ten donors?

Let's define a random variable for each volunteer:

X = number of donors secured by volunteer 1; binomial $n = 10$, $p = .2$.
Y = number of donors secured by volunteer 2; binomial $n = 12$, $p = .2$.
W = number of donors secured by volunteer 3; binomial $n = 18$, $p = .2$.

The total number of donors, $T = X + Y + W$, is a binomial random variable with $n = 10 + 12 + 18 = 40$ trials and $p = .2$. Notice that either there will be ten or more donors or there will be nine or fewer, so $P(T \geq 10) = 1 - P(T \leq 9) = 1 -$

*HINT: In each case, is there any apparent reason why the value of one should influence the value of the other?

.7318 (from Minitab) = .2682. So, in about 27% of the cases in this type of fund drive, there will be at least ten donors when 40 people are called. ◆

EXAMPLE 8.23
Strategies for Studying When You Are Out of Time

You have a two-part multiple-choice test tomorrow, with 10 questions on one part and 10 on the other; all questions have four choices. You don't have time to study all the material well. From past experience you know that if you study all of the material in the time you have, you can narrow all 20 questions down to two choices and get them correct with probability .5, so your grade would be a binomial random variable with $n = 20$ and $p = .5$. If you study only the first set of material, you will get the questions right for that set with probability .8 but have to guess completely on the other set, which means $p = .25$ for those 10 questions. You need to get 13 or more questions right to pass the test. What should you do?

Strategy 1: Study all material. The score for the test has a binomial distribution with $n = 20$ and $p = .5$. The probability you pass is $P(\text{Score} \geq 13) = 1 - P(\text{Score} \leq 12)$, which is $1 - .8684$ (from Minitab) = .1316. The mean and standard deviation of the score will be useful for comparing the two strategies:

$$\text{Mean(Score)} = np = (20)(.5) = 10 \text{ questions}$$
$$\text{Variance(Score)} = np(1 - p) = (20)(.5)(1 - .5) = 5$$
$$\text{Standard deviation} = 2.24 \text{ questions}$$

Strategy 2: Study only set one. Score $= X + Y$, where $X =$ number correct on first part and $Y =$ number correct on second part. First, determine the mean and variance for each of X and Y:

X is binomial with $n = 10$, $p = .8$	Y is a binomial with $n = 10$, $p = .25$
$\text{Mean}(X) = np = 10(.8) = 8$	$\text{Mean}(Y) = np = 10(.25) = 2.5$
$\text{Variance}(X) = np(1 - p)$ $= 10(.8)(.2) = 1.6$	$\text{Variance}(Y) = np(1 - p)$ $= 10(.25)(.75) = 1.875$

With these values, we can determine the mean and standard deviation of Score $= X + Y$.

$$\text{Mean(Score)} = \text{Mean}(X) + \text{Mean}(Y) = 8 + 2.5 = 10.5 \text{ questions}$$
$$\text{Variance(Score)} = \text{Variance}(X) + \text{Variance}(Y) = 1.6 + 1.875 = 3.475$$
$$\text{Standard deviation} = \sqrt{3.47} = 1.86 \text{ questions}$$

Strategy 1 has a lower mean (10) than strategy 2 (10.5), so in the long run, strategy 2 will be slightly better. But, you are only taking a single exam, so an effective long-run strategy is not your concern. Strategy 1 has a higher standard deviation (2.24) than strategy 2 (1.86), so perhaps the chance of a score well above the mean is greater for strategy 1. This turns out not to be the case. For strategy 1, the passing score of 13 is $(13 - 10)/2.24 = 1.34$ standard deviations above the mean. For strategy 2, a score of 13 is $(13 - 10.5)/1.86 = 1.34$ standard deviations above the mean. It does not appear to matter which strategy you use.

Unfortunately, when the success probabilities are unequal (as in strategy 2), it can be tedious to find probabilities for a sum of binomial random variables with a small number of trials. For strategy 2, calculating the probability of passing involves finding probabilities for every possible combination of X and Y for which the sum is at least 13. This is a case where simulation may be an effective way to determine the probability. Using the Minitab package, strategy 2 was simulated by randomly generating values for X and Y and adding them together. This was done 1000 times, and a passing grade of 13 or more was achieved in 130 of the 1000 repetitions. The estimated probability that you pass the test using strategy 2 is about $130/1000 = .130$, almost identical to the probability of .1316 for strategy 1. Neither strategy offers you much hope! ◆

CASE STUDY 8.1
Does Caffeine Enhance the Taste of Cola?

Soft drink manufacturers claim that caffeine enhances the flavor of cola drinks, but in a study reported in the *Archives of Family Medicine* (Griffiths, 2000) researchers from Johns Hopkins University dispute this claim. In a taste test done by the researchers, 25 participants each tried 20 times to identify which of two cola drinks was "sample A" and which was "sample B." Unknown to the participants, one of the cola samples (A or B) contained caffeine, while the other cola sample did not. The particular sample (A or B) containing caffeine was the same for all 20 trials done by an individual. On a single trial, an individual tasted drinks from two unlabeled cups, and then guessed which cup contained sample A and which contained sample B. After each trial, the participant was told whether he or she was correct. Prior to the 20 trials that counted, each participant performed 5 practice trials.

If a participant could make 15 or more correct identifications during the 20 trials that counted, his or her flavor detection performance was called "significant" by the researchers. Only 2 of the 25 participants achieved this "significant" level. Further, over the 500 total trials done by the 25 participants, correct identifications were made only 53% of the time, a performance level that, according to the investigators, was not significantly better than chance performance (50%).

The research team used the binomial distribution to develop the criterion for individual "significance," which was 15 or more correct identifications in 20 tries. Recall that after each trial a participant learned whether he or she was correct. If this feedback were effective, the probability of success would increase during the 20 trials, so this study would not be a binomial experiment. For a binomial experiment, we need the same probability of success for each trial. If we as-

sume, however, that a participant cannot detect the difference and makes a random guess every trial, $X =$ the number of correct guesses for an individual is a binomial random variable with $n = 20$ and $p = .5$. For this binomial distribution, $P(X \leq 14) \cong .98$, and $P(X \geq 15) = 1 - .98 = .02$. The probability is only .02 that somebody who randomly guesses every time could get 15 or more correct, so doing this well would be "significant."

If all 25 participants randomly guessed for all trials, the "expected" number of "significant" participants would be $25 \times .02 = .5$, a value that could loosely be interpreted as about 0 or 1 participants. Only 2 participants achieved "significance," which is just slightly above the number we would expect if all participants randomly guess every time. A final piece of evidence is that correct identifications occurred only in 265 (53%) of all 500 trials performed by the 25 participants. This result would not be unusual if a random guess were made on every trial. For a binomial distribution with $n = 500$ and $p = .5$, $P(X \geq 265) \cong .10$.

Soft drink manufacturers were critical of this study. Some of the criticisms had to do with the sample sizes, both for participants and trials. The most pointed criticism, though, concerned the preparation of the two drink samples. The investigators created the two drink samples by either adding or not adding caffeine to caffeine-free Coca Cola. According to soft drink manufacturers, other ingredients must also be added along with caffeine in order to gain the flavor enhancement effects of caffeine. In their report, the investigators admitted that this was a weakness of the study, and suggested that additional studies might be needed to determine if caffeine does affect flavor.

KEY TERMS

EXERCISES Blue = Basics Bold, **Bold** = Answer in back

Sections 8.1 and 8.2

8.1 A book is randomly chosen from a library shelf. For each of the following characteristics of the book, decide whether the characteristic is a continuous or a discrete random variable:
a. Weight of the book (e.g., 2.3 pounds).
b. Number of chapters in the book (e.g., 10 chapters).
c. Width of the book (e.g., 8 inches).
d. Type of book (0 = hardback or 1 = paperback).
e. Number of typographical errors in the book (e.g., 4 errors).

8.2 Decide whether each of the following characteristics of a television news broadcast is a continuous or a discrete random variable:
a. Number of commercials shown (e.g., five commercials).
b. Length of the first commercial shown (e.g., 15 seconds).
c. Whether there were any fatal car accidents reported (0 = there were no fatal accidents reported, 1 = there was at least one reported).
d. Whether or not rain was forecast for the next day (0 = no rain forecast, 1 = rain forecast).

8.3 What is the missing value, represented by "?" in each of the following probability distribution functions?
a.

k	1	4	5	7
P(X = k)	1/6	1/6	1/6	?

b.

k	100	200	300	400	500
P(X = k)	.1	.2	.3	.3	?

8.4 A professor gives a weekly quiz with varying numbers of questions and uses a randomization device to decide how many questions to include. Let the random variable X = the number of questions on an upcoming quiz. The probability distribution for X is given in the following table, but one probability is missing. What is the probability that X = 30?

No. of Questions, X	10	15	20	25	30
Probability	.05	.20	.50	.15	?

8.5 Let the random variable X = number of phone calls you will get in the next 24 hours. Suppose the possible values for X are 0, 1, 2, or 3 and their probabilities are .1, .1, .3, and .5, respectively. For instance, the probability that you will receive no calls is .1.
a. Verify that the "Conditions for Probabilities for Discrete Random Variables" given in Section 8.2 are met.
b. Draw a picture of the probability distribution function.
c. Find the cumulative distribution function.

8.6 For a fair coin tossed three times, the eight possible simple events are: HHH, HHT, HTH, THH, HTT, THT, TTH, TTT. Let X = number of heads. Find the probability distribution for X by writing a table showing each possible value of X along with the probability that value occurs.

8.7 Suppose the probability distribution for X = number of jobs held during the past year for students at a school is as follows:

No. of Jobs, X	0	1	2	3	4
Probability	.14	.37	.29	.15	.05

a. Find $P(X \leq 2)$, the probability that a randomly selected student held two or fewer jobs during the past year.
b. Find the probability that a randomly selected student held either one or two jobs during the past year.
c. Find $P(X > 0)$, the probability that a randomly selected student held at least one job during the past year.

8.8 A kindergarten class has three left-handed children and seven right-handed children. Two children are selected without replacement for a shoe-tying lesson. Let X = the number who are left-handed.
a. Write the simple events in the sample space. For instance, one simple event is RL, indicating that the first child is right-handed and the second one is left-handed.
b. Find the probability for each of the simple events in the sample space. (*Hint:* A tree diagram may help you solve this.)

c. Find the probability distribution function for X.

d. Draw a picture of the probability distribution function for X.

8.9   Refer to Example 8.5, in which the probability distribution is given for the sum of two fair dice. Use the distribution to find the probability that the sum is even.

8.10   Consider three tosses of a fair coin. Write the sample space, and then find the probability distribution function for each of the following random variables:

   a. X = number of tails.

   b. Y = the difference between the number of heads and the number of tails.

   c. Z = the sum of the number of heads and the number of tails.

8.11   A woman decides to have children until she has her first girl, or until she has four children, whichever comes first. Let X = number of children she has. For simplicity, assume that the probability of a girl is .5 for each birth.

   a. Write the simple events in the sample space. Use B for boy and G for girl. For instance, one simple event is BG, because the woman quits once she has a girl.

   b. Find the probability for each of the simple events in the sample space.

   c. Find the probability distribution function for X.

   d. Draw a picture of the probability distribution function for X.

8.12   Refer to Example 8.1, the scheduling of an outdoor event. Give an example of another continuous random variable (in addition to temperature) and another discrete random variable (in addition to number of planes flying overhead) that would influence the enjoyment of the event. Give the sample space for those random variables.

8.13   Refer to Example 8.5. Find the cumulative distribution function (cdf) for the sum of two fair dice.

8.14   Explain which would be of more interest in each of the following situations, the pdf or the cdf for X. If you think both would be of interest, explain why.

   a. A politician wants to know how her constituents feel about a proposed new law. She hires a survey firm to take a random sample of voters in her district, and X = number in the sample who oppose the new law.

   b. Each time someone is exposed to a virus he or she could become infected with it. Let X = number of exposures a person can sustain before becoming infected. For instance, if $X = 0$, they become infected on the first exposure; if $X = 1$, they become infected on the second exposure, and so on.

   c. A pharmaceutical company wants to show that its new drug is effective for lowering blood pressure. The drug is administered to a sample of 800 patients with high blood pressure, and X = the number for whom the drug reduces blood pressure.

   d. A caterer who serves dinner at wedding receptions is told in advance the number of people who have said they will attend; X is the number of people who actually attend the dinner.

Section 8.3

8.15   Burt pays $30 a year for "towing" insurance. He thinks that the probability that he will need to have his car towed once in the next year is 1/10 (.1) and the probability that he will have to have it towed more than once is zero. It will cost $100 if his car is towed if he doesn't have insurance, but will cost nothing if he does have insurance. Let X = Burt's cost next year for towing and/or insurance.

   a. If Burt buys the insurance, X has only one possible value. What is it?

   b. If Burt doesn't buy the insurance, X has two possible values. List the two values and their probabilities.

   c. Refer to parts (a) and (b). In each case, find $E(X)$. Using these two values for $E(X)$, explain whether Burt should buy the insurance.

8.16   The Brann family wants to have children. They are working with a financial advisor who informs them that based on families with similar characteristics, the probability distribution for the random variable X = number of children they might have is

No. of Children	0	1	2	3
Probability	.05	.60	.30	.05

   a. What is the expected value of X?

   b. Explain what "expected value" means in this example.

   c. Is $E(X)$ a possible outcome for the number of children the Brann family will have?

8.17   The probability that Mary will win a game is .01, so the probability she will not win is .99. If Mary wins, she will be given $100, while if she loses, she must pay $5. If X = amount of money Mary wins (or loses), what is the expected value of X?

8.18   A random variable X has the following probability distribution:

Values of X	−1	0	1
Probability	.25	.50	.25

   a. Calculate the mean of X.

   b. Calculate the variance of X.

   c. Calculate the standard deviation of X.

8.19   A random variable X has the following probability distribution:

Values of X	−2	0	2
Probability	.25	.50	.25

   a. Calculate the mean of X.

   b. Calculate the variance of X.

   c. Calculate the standard deviation of X.

8.20   Find the expected value for the number of girls in a family with three children, assuming boys and girls are equally likely. (*Hint:* The probability distribution function was found in Example 8.4.)

8.21   Find the expected value for the sum of two fair dice. (*Hint:* The probability distribution function was found in Example 8.5.)

8.22   Find the standard deviation for the sum of two fair dice.

8.23   Find the standard deviation for the net gain in the California Decco lottery game in Example 8.6.

8.24   An insurance company expects 10% of its policyholders to collect claims of $500 this year, and the remaining 90%

to collect no claims. What is the expected value for the amount they will pay out in claims per person?

8.25 Refer to the previous exercise. If the insurance company wants to make a net profit of $10 per policyholder for the year, how much should they charge each person for insurance? Ignore administrative and other costs.

8.26 In 1991, 72% of children in the United States were living with both parents, 22% were living with mother only, 3% were living with father only, and 3% were not living with either parent (*World Almanac,* 1993, p. 945). What is the expected value for the *number* of parents a randomly selected child was living with in 1991? Does the concept of expected value have a meaningful interpretation for this example? Explain.

8.27 Suppose the probability that you get an A in any class you take is .3 and the probability that you get a B is .7. To construct a grade point average, an A is worth 4.0 and a B is worth 3.0. What is the expected value for your grade point average? Would you expect to have this grade point average for each quarter or semester of your school career? Explain.

8.28 Suppose you have to cross a train track on your commute. The probability that you will have to wait for a train is 1/5, or .20. If you don't have to wait, the commute takes 15 minutes, but if you have to wait it takes 20 minutes.
   a. What is the expected value of the time it takes you to commute?
   b. Is the expected value ever equal to the actual commute time? Explain.

Section 8.4

8.29 A fair coin is flipped 200 times. The random variable X = number of heads out of the 200 tosses.
   a. Is X a binomial random variable? If so, specify n and p. If not, explain why not.
   b. What is the expected value of X?

8.30 For each of the examples below, decide if X is a binomial random variable. If so, specify n and p. If not, explain why not.
   a. X = number of heads from flipping the same coin ten times, where the probability of a head = 1/2.
   b. X = number of heads from flipping two coins five times each, where the probability of a head for one coin = 1/2 and the probability of a head for the other coin = 1/4.
   c. X = number of cities in which it will rain tomorrow among five neighboring cities located within ten miles of each other.
   d. X = number of children who will get the flu this winter in a kindergarten class with 20 children.

8.31 For each of the following binomial random variables, specify n and p:
   a. A fair die is rolled 30 times. X = number of times a 6 is rolled.
   b. A company puts a game card in each box of cereal and 1/100 of them are winners. You buy ten boxes of cereal and X = number of times you win.
   c. Jack likes to play computer solitaire and wins about 30% of the time. X = number of games he wins out of his next 20 games.

8.32 Refer to the previous exercise. Find μ in each case.

8.33 Assuming X is a binomial random variable with $n = 10$ and $p = .20$, find the probability for each of the following values of X:
   a. $X = 5$.
   b. $X = 2$.
   c. $X = 1$.
   d. $X = 9$.

8.34 Find the mean and standard deviation for a binomial random variable X with:
   a. $n = 10, p = .50$.
   b. $n = 1, p = .40$.
   c. $n = 100, p = .90$.
   d. $n = 30, p = .01$.

8.35 Explain which of the conditions for a binomial experiment is *not* met for each of the following random variables:
   a. A football team plays 12 games in its regular season. X = number of games the team wins.
   b. A woman buys a lottery ticket every week for which the probability of winning anything at all is 1/10. She continues to buy them until she has won three times. X = the number of tickets she buys.
   c. A poker hand consists of 5 cards drawn from a standard deck of 52 cards. X = the number of aces in the hand.

8.36 A computer chess game and a human chess champion are evenly matched. They play ten games. Find probabilities for the following events.
   a. They each win five games.
   b. The computer wins seven games.
   c. The human chess champion wins at least seven games.

8.37 In an ESP test, a "participant" tries to draw a hidden "target" photograph that is unknown to anyone in the room. After the drawing attempt, the participant is shown four choices and asked to determine which one had been the real target. The real target is randomly selected from the four choices in advance, so the probability of a correct match by chance is 1/4. The test is repeated ten times using four new photographs each time.
   a. Go through the conditions for a binomial experiment, and explain how this situation fits each one of them, assuming the participant is just guessing each time.
   b. Let X = number of correct choices in the ten tests. If the participant is just guessing, is X a binomial random variable? If not, explain why not. If so, specify n and p.
   c. If the participant is just guessing, find $P(X \geq 6)$.
   d. Suppose the participant actually has some psychic ability and can get each answer correct with probability .5 instead of .25. Find $P(X \geq 6)$.
   e. Compare the answers in parts (c) and (d). If the participant actually selects six of the ten answers correctly, would you believe he or she was just guessing, or that he or she was using some psychic ability? Explain your answer. (Note that there is no correct answer here; your reasoning is what counts.)

8.38 For each of the following situations, assume X is a binomial random variable with the specified n and p, and find the requested probability.
   a. $n = 10, p = .5, P(X = 4)$.
   b. $n = 10, p = .3, P(X \geq 4)$.
   c. $n = 10, p = .3, P(X \leq 3)$.
   d. $n = 5, p = .1, P(X = 0)$.
   e. $n = 5, p = .1, P(X \geq 1)$.

8.39 For each of the following scenarios, write the desired probability in a format such as $P(X \leq 10)$ and specify n and p. Do not actually compute the desired probability. If you cannot specify a numerical value for p, write in words what it represents.

a. A random sample of 1000 adults is drawn from the United States. $X =$ the number in the sample who are living with a partner but are not married. The desired probability is the probability that at least 1/4 of the sample fits this description.

b. A pharmaceutical company claims that 20% of those taking its new allergy medication will experience drowsiness. To test this claim, it randomly assigns 500 people to take the new medication and measures $X =$ the number who experience drowsiness. The desired probability is the probability that 110 or more people in the sample experience drowsiness if the claim is true.

c. A student has not studied the material for a 20-question True-False test and simply guesses on each question. A passing grade is 70%; the desired probability is the probability that the student passes the test.

8.40 Find the expected value and standard deviation for a binomial random variable with each of the following values of n and p:

a. $n = 10, p = 1/2$.
b. $n = 100, p = 1/4$.
c. $n = 2500, p = 1/5$.
d. $n = 1, p = 1/10$.
e. $n = 30, p = .4$.

8.41 Use the direct formulas for expected value and standard deviation to verify that the mean and standard deviation for a binomial random variable with $n = 2$ and $p = .5$ are $\mu = 1$ and $\sigma = 0.7071$, respectively. (*Hint:* The only possible values of X are 0, 1, 2. Find their probabilities and use the formulas at the end of Section 8.3.)

Sections 8.5 and 8.6

8.42 Suppose that the time students wait for a bus can be described by a uniform random variable X, where X is between 0 minutes and 60 minutes.

a. What is the probability that a student will wait between 0 and 30 minutes for the next bus?

b. What is the probability that a student will have to wait at least 30 minutes for the next bus?

8.43 In each situation below, calculate the standardized score (or z-score) for the value x:

a. Mean $\mu = 0$, standard deviation $\sigma = 1$, value $x = 1.5$.
b. Mean $\mu = 10$, standard deviation $\sigma = 6$, value $x = 4$.
c. Mean $\mu = 10$, standard deviation $\sigma = 5$, value $x = 0$.
d. Mean $\mu = -10$, standard deviation $\sigma = 15$, value $x = -25$.

8.44 For each value of z^*, find the cumulative probability $P(Z \leq z^*)$:

a. $z^* = 0$.
b. $z^* = -0.35$.
c. $z^* = 0.35$.
d. $z^* = 1.96$.
e. $z^* = -2.33$.
f. $z^* = 2.58$.
g. $z^* = 1.65$.

8.45 Weights (X) of men in a certain age group have a normal distribution with mean $\mu = 180$ pounds and standard deviation $\sigma = 20$ pounds. Find each of the following probabilities:

a. $P(X \leq 200) =$ probability the weight of a randomly selected man is less than or equal to 200 pounds.

b. $P(X \leq 165) =$ probability the weight of a randomly selected man is less than or equal to 165 pounds.

c. $P(X > 165) =$ probability the weight of a randomly selected man is more than 165 pounds.

8.46 A game is played with a spinner on a circle, like the minute hand on a clock. The circle is marked evenly from 0 to 100, so, for example, the 3:00 position corresponds to 25, the 6:00 position to 50, and so on. The player spins the spinner and the resulting number is the number of seconds he or she is given to solve a word puzzle. Let $X =$ amount of time the player is given to solve the puzzle.

a. Is X a uniform random variable, a binomial random variable, a normal random variable, or none of these? Explain how you know.

b. Write down the density function for X. Be sure to specify the range of values for which it holds.

c. Find $P(X \leq 15$ seconds).

d. Find $P(X \geq 40$ seconds).

e. Draw a picture of the density function of X, and use it to illustrate the probabilities you found in parts (c) and (d).

f. What is the expected value of X? This was not covered in the text, so explain your reasoning.

8.47 Give an example of a uniform random variable that might occur in your daily life.

8.48 Draw the "curve" corresponding to each of the following random variables, then shade the area corresponding to the desired probability. You *do not* need to compute the probability.

a. X is a uniform random variable from 10 to 20, $P(10 \leq X \leq 13)$.

b. X is a normal random variable with $\mu = 75$ and $\sigma = 5$, $P(70 \leq X \leq 85)$.

c. X is a normal random variable with $\mu = 15$ and $\sigma = 10$, $P(-5 \leq X \leq 20)$.

8.49 Find the following probabilities for a standard normal random variable Z:

a. $P(Z \leq -1.4)$.
b. $P(Z \leq 1.4)$.
c. $P(-1.4 \leq Z \leq 1.4)$.
d. $P(Z \geq 1.4)$.

8.50 Find the following probabilities for a standard normal random variable Z:

a. $P(Z \leq -3.72)$.
b. $P(-3.72 \leq Z \leq 3.72)$.
c. $P(Z \geq 15)$.

8.51 Find the value z^* that satisfies each of the following probabilities for a standard normal random variable Z:

a. $P(Z \leq z^*) = .025$.
b. $P(Z \leq z^*) = .975$.
c. $P(-z^* \leq Z \leq z^*) = .95$.

8.52 For each of the following formulas given in this chapter, use the rule referenced from Chapter 7 to verify that the relationship is correct for a standard normal random variable Z:

a. Use Rule 1 to verify that $P(Z > a) = 1 - P(Z \leq a)$.

b. Use Rule 2b to verify that $P(Z \leq b) = P(Z \leq a) + P(a \leq Z \leq b)$. Use that result to show that $P(a \leq Z \leq b) = P(Z \leq b) - P(Z \leq a)$.

8.53 Find the following probabilities for Verbal SAT test scores X, for which the mean is 500 and the standard deviation is 100. Assume that SAT scores are described by a normal curve.
a. $P(X \leq 500)$.
b. $P(X \leq 650)$.
c. $P(X \geq 700)$.
d. $P(500 \leq X \leq 700)$.

8.54 Refer to Example 8.14. Find the proportion of college women whose heights fall into the following ranges:
a. Between 62 inches and 65 inches.
b. Between 60 inches and 70 inches.
c. Less than 70 inches.
d. Greater than 60 inches.
e. Either less than 60 inches *or* greater than 70 inches.

8.55 Refer to Example 8.14. Find the height such that about 25% of college women are shorter than that height. What is the percentile ranking for that height?

8.56 Refer to Example 8.14. Find the height such that about 10% of college women are taller than that height. What is the percentile ranking for that height?

8.57 Based on data from Penn State students, assume that right handspan measurements for college women are approximately normally distributed, with mean 20 cm and standard deviation 1.8 cm, and for men they are normally distributed, with mean 22.5 cm and standard deviation 1.5 cm. Measure your own right handspan.
a. Assuming you fit with the population of college students of your sex, what is the *z*-score corresponding to your right handspan measurement? (Be sure to give your sex and right handspan measurement with your answer.)
b. What proportion of students of your sex have right handspan measurements smaller than yours?

8.58 Suppose the yearly rainfall totals for a city in northern California follow a normal distribution, with mean of 18 inches and standard deviation of 6 inches. For a randomly selected year, what is the probability that total rainfall will be in each of the following intervals?
a. Less than 10 inches.
b. Greater than 30 inches.
c. Between 15 and 21 inches.
d. Greater than 35 inches.

8.59 Refer to the previous exercise. Suppose that in a given year the total rainfall is only 6 inches. You work for the local newspaper, and your editor has asked you to write a story about the terrible drought the town is suffering and how abnormal the situation is. Write a few sentences that you could use to explain the statistical facts to your readers (and your editor). Be sure to comment on whether or not you agree that the situation is terribly abnormal.

Section 8.7

8.60 Suppose that a fair coin is flipped $n = 100$ times.
a. Calculate the mean and standard deviation of $X =$ number of heads. (*Hint:* The variable X has a binomial distribution.)
b. Use the normal approximation to the binomial distri-

bution to estimate the probability that the number of heads is greater than or equal to 60.
c. Repeat part (a) using the continuity correction.

8.61 Suppose $p = .512$ is the proportion of one-child families in which the child is a boy.
a. For a random sample of $n = 50$ one-child families, estimate the probability that there will be 20 or fewer boys. Use the normal approximation to the binomial distribution.
b. Repeat part (a) using the continuity correction.

8.62 Use the normal approximation to the binominal distribution to approximate the stated probability in each of the following scenarios:
a. A random sample of 1000 eligible voters is drawn and $X =$ number who actually voted in the last election. It is known that 60% of all eligible voters did vote. Find (approximately) $P(X \leq 620)$.
b. To be eligible for a certain job, women must be at least 62 inches tall, and 87% of women meet this criterion. In a random sample of 2000 women, $X =$ number who qualify for the job (based on height). Find (approximately) $P(X \leq 1700)$.

8.63 In a test for extrasensory perception, the "participant" repeatedly guesses the suit of a card randomly sampled with replacement from an ordinary deck of cards. There are four suits, all equally likely. The participant guesses 100 times, and $X =$ number of correct guesses.
a. Explain why X is a binomial random variable, and specify n and p, assuming the participant is just guessing.
b. Find the mean and standard deviation for X if the participant is just guessing.
c. Suppose the participant guesses correctly 33 times. Find the approximate probability of guessing this well or better by chance.
d. Suppose the participant guesses correctly 50 times. Find the approximate probability of guessing this well or better by chance. In that circumstance, would you be convinced that the participant was doing something other than just guessing? Explain.

Section 8.8

8.64 Suppose the heights of adult males in a population have a normal distribution with mean $\mu = 70$ inches and standard deviation $\sigma = 2.8$ inches. Two unrelated men will be randomly sampled. Let $X =$ height of the first man and $Y =$ height of the second man.
a. Consider $D = X - Y$, the difference between the heights of the two men. What type of distribution will the variable D have?
b. What is the mean value for the distribution of D?
c. Assuming independence between the two men, find the standard deviation of D.
d. Determine the probability that the first man is more than 3 inches taller than the second man. That is, find $P(D > 3)$.
e. Find the probability that one of the men is at least 3 inches taller than the other. That is, find the probability that either $(D > 3)$ or $(D < -3)$.

8.65 Suppose the length of time a person takes to use an ATM machine is normally distributed with mean $\mu = 100$ seconds and standard deviation $\sigma = 10$ seconds. There are

$n = 4$ people ahead of Jackson in a line of people waiting to use the machine. He is concerned about T = total time the four people will take to use the machine.

a. What is the mean value of T = total time for the four people ahead of Jackson?

b. Assuming the times for the four people are independent of each other, determine the standard deviation of T.

c. Jackson hopes the total time T is less than or equal to 360 seconds (6 minutes). Find $P(T < 360)$, the probability that the total waiting time is less than 360 seconds.

8.66 Ed and Taylor work together on a group quiz that has 15 multiple-choice questions, each with four choices for the possible answer. Unfortunately, neither had time to study so they decide to randomly guess at all answers. Ed guesses answers for the first 7 questions, while Taylor guesses for the other 8 questions.

a. For any single question on the quiz, what is p = chance of a correct guess?

b. Let X = number of correct guesses that Ed makes. What are the values of n and p for the binomial distribution that describes X?

c. Let Y = number of correct guesses that Taylor makes. What are the values of n and p for the binomial distribution that describes Y?

d. Consider $X + Y$ = total correct guesses that Ed and Taylor make. What are the values of n and p for the binomial distribution that describes $X + Y$?

8.67 The variable X has a normal distribution with mean $\mu = 75$ and standard deviation $\sigma = 6$. The variable Y has a normal distribution with mean $\mu = 70$ and standard deviation $\sigma = 8$. Variables X and Y are independent variables.

a. Find the mean and standard deviation of the sum $X + Y$.

b. Find the mean and standard deviation of the difference $X - Y$.

8.68 Give the mean, variance, and standard deviation of the sum $X + Y$ in each of the following cases. If possible, name what distribution the sum has as well.

a. X is a binomial random variable with $n = 10, p = .5$. Y is a binomial random variable with $n = 20, p = .4$. X and Y are independent.

b. X is a normal random variable with $\mu = 100$ and $\sigma = 15$. Y is a normal random variable with $\mu = 50$ and $\sigma = 10$. X and Y are independent.

c. X is a normal random variable with $\mu = 100$ and $\sigma = 15$. Y is a binomial random variable with $n = 200, p = .25$. X and Y are independent.

8.69 Ethan has a midterm in his statistics class, which starts 10 minutes after the scheduled end of his biology class. The biology teacher rarely ends class on time though, and the amount of time he is overtime is approximately normally distributed, with mean of 2 minutes and standard deviation of 1/2 minute. The time it takes Ethan to get from one class to another is also normal, with mean 6 minutes and standard deviation 1 minute.

a. Is it reasonable to assume that the two times are independent? Explain.

b. Assuming the two times are independent, what is the probability that Ethan will be late for his exam?

8.70 Joe performs remarkably well on "remote viewing" ESP tests, which require the "viewer" to draw a picture, then determine which of four possible photos was the intended "target." Because the target is randomly selected from

among the four choices, the probability of a correct match by chance is 1/4, or .25. Joe participates in three experiments with $n = 10, 20$, and 50 trials, respectively. In the three experiments, his numbers correct are 4, 8, and 20, respectively, for a total of 32 correct out of 80 trials.

a. For each experiment, what is the expected number correct if Joe is just guessing?

b. Over all 80 trials, what is the expected number correct? Explain how you found your answer.

c. For each experiment separately, find the approximate probability that someone would get as many correct as Joe did, or more, if they were just guessing.

d. Out of the 80 trials overall, find the approximate probability that someone would get as many correct as Joe did (32), or more, if they were just guessing.

e. Compare your answers in parts (c) and (d). If Joe were trying to convince someone of his ability, would it be better to show the three experiments separately, or would it be better to show the combined data? Explain.

8.71 Annmarie is trying to decide whether to take the train or the bus into the city. The train takes longer but is more predictable than the bus because there are no traffic delays. Train times are approximately normally distributed, with mean 60 minutes and standard deviation 2 minutes, while bus times are approximately normally distributed, with mean 50 minutes and standard deviation 8 minutes. The bus and train times are independent of each other. Find the probability that the train is faster on any given day.

8.72 Charles, Julia, and Alex are in grades 4, 3, and 2, respectively, and are representing their school at a spelling bee. The school's team score is the sum of the number of words the individual students spell correctly out of 50 words each. Different words are given for each grade level. From practicing at school, it is known that the probability of spelling each word correctly is .9 for Charles and .8 for the younger two, Julia and Alex.

a. Find the mean and standard deviation for the number of correct words for each child.

b. Find the mean and standard deviation for the team score.

c. Assume the individual scores are independent. Does the team score have a binomial distribution? Explain.

d. Although not obvious from the material in this chapter, the team score would be approximately normal with the mean and standard deviation you were asked to find in part (b). If last year's team score was 131, what is the approximate probability that this year's team scores as well or better?

Chapter Exercises

8.73 Find the following probabilities for X = pulse rates of women, for which the mean is 75 and the standard deviation is 8. Assume a normal distribution.

a. $P(X \le 71)$.

b. $P(X \ge 85)$.

c. $P(59 \le X \le 95)$.

8.74 Refer to the previous exercise about the pulse rates of women. What is the 10th percentile of women's pulse rates?

8.75 The vehicle speeds at a particular interstate location can be described by a normal curve. The mean speed is 67 mph and the standard deviation is 6 mph. What proportion of vehicle speeds at this location are faster than 75 mph?

8.76 Do you think that a normal curve would be a good approximation to the distribution of the ages of all individuals in the world? Briefly explain your answer.

8.77 A histogram is drawn of the weights of all students in a class of 100 men and 100 women. Would this histogram have a bell shape? Briefly explain your answer.

8.78 Suppose that 10% of a population is left-handed. What is the probability that in a sample of $n = 10$ individuals, 3 or more individuals are left-handed?

8.79 New spark plugs have just been installed in a small airplane with a four-cylinder engine. There is one spark plug per cylinder, so four spark plugs have been installed. For each spark plug, the probability that it is defective and will fail during its first 20 minutes of flight is 1/10,000, independent of the other spark plugs.
   a. For each spark plug, what is the probability that it will not fail?
   b. If one spark plug fails, the plane will shake and not climb higher, but it can be landed safely. What is the probability that this happens?
   c. If two or more spark plugs fail, the plane will crash. What is the probability that this happens?

8.80 In the casino game of roulette, a gambler can bet on which of 38 numbers will be the result when the roulette wheel is spun. On a $2 bet, a gambler gains $70 if he or she picks the right number, but loses the $2 otherwise.
   a. Let X = amount gained or lost on a $2 bet on a roulette number. Write out the probability distribution of X.
   b. Calculate $E(X)$, the mean value of X. What does this value indicate about the advantage that a casino has over roulette players?

8.81 Suppose that a college determines the following distribution for X = number of courses taken by full-time students this semester:

k	3	4	5	6	7
$P(X = k)$	.07	.14	.52	.25	.02

   a. Write out the cumulative distribution function of X.
   b. What is the probability that a randomly selected full-time student is taking five or fewer courses this semester?
   c. What is the probability that a randomly selected full-time student is taking more than five courses?

8.82 Refer to exercise 8.81. What is the mean number of courses taken by full-time students?

8.83 Explain which of the conditions for a binomial experiment is *not* met for each of the following random variables:
   a. A ten-question quiz has five True-False questions and five multiple-choice questions, each with four possible choices for the answer. A student randomly picks an answer for every question. X = number of answers that are correct.
   b. Four students are randomly picked without replacement from a class of ten women and ten men. X = number of women among the four selected students.

8.84 The standard medical treatment for a certain disease is successful in 60% of all cases.
   a. The treatment is given to $n = 200$ patients. What is the probability that the treatment is successful for 70% or more of these 200 patients? (*Tip:* 70% of $n = 200$ is 140 patients.)
   b. The treatment is given to only $n = 20$ patients. What is the probability that the treatment is successful for 70% or more of these 20 patients?

8.85 Kim and her sister Karen each plan to have four children. Assume the probability of a girl is .50, independent across births.
   a. If X = number of girls Kim will have, what is the distribution of X?
   b. If Y = number of girls Karen will have, what is the distribution of Y?
   c. What is the distribution for T, the total number of girls Kim and Karen have?

8.86 Shaun (3 years old) and Patrick (4 years old) are each allowed to pick one book for bedtime stories, and the parent on duty reads the two books sequentially. The lengths of time it takes to read the books from which they select are approximately normally distributed, with mean 5 minutes and standard deviation 2 minutes.
   a. Does it make sense to assume the times for the two books are independent? Explain.
   b. On about what proportion of nights will storytime exceed 15 minutes, assuming the times for the two books are independent?

8.87 You will need a computer program that simulates a large number of binomial random variables at once for this exercise. Refer to Example 8.23, "Strategies for Studying When You Are Out of Time." Simulate what would happen if you used strategy 2, in which the total score was the sum of two binomial random variables, one with $n = 10$ and $p = .8$, the other with $n = 10$ and $p = .2$. Run 1000 simulations, and determine the proportion of them for which you would have received a passing grade (13 or more). Explain what you did.

REFERENCES

Griffiths, R. R., and E. M. Vernotica (2000). "Is caffeine a flavoring agent in cola soft drinks?" *Arch. Fam. Med.,* Vol. 9, pp. 727–734.

World Almanac and Book of Facts (1993). Mark S. Hoffman (ed.), New York: Pharos Books.

CHAPTER 9

Means and Proportions As Random Variables

Video games again? Has their favorite TV show been cancelled?
See Example 9.7.

Network Productions/Index Stock Imagery

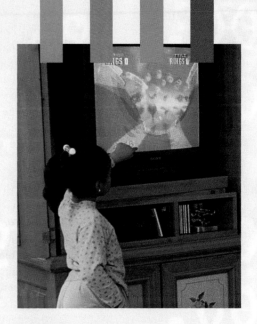

This chapter introduces the reasoning that allows researchers to make conclusions about entire populations using relatively small samples of individuals. The secret to understanding how things work is to understand what kind of dissimilarity we should expect to see among different samples from the same population.

I n Chapter 8 we learned how to work with random variables, including how to make probability statements about ranges of possible values, what to expect as the long-run average, and how to identify special classes of random variables. This chapter considers what happens if we regard a summary statistic for an entire random sample as a random variable. For instance, if we take a random sample of adults and find the proportion who have a certain trait or opinion, that proportion is the numerical outcome of a random circumstance. In other words, the sample proportion is itself a random variable.

This chapter serves as an introduction to the reasoning that allows researchers to make conclusions about entire populations on the basis of a relatively small sample of individuals. By understanding how a sample mean or proportion behaves as a random variable, we can begin to understand the population from which it was found.

The basic idea is that we must work backwards, from a sample to a population. We start with a question about a population like: How many teenagers are infected with HIV? At what average age do left-handed people die? What is the average income of all students at a large university? We collect a sample from the population about which we have the question and measure the variable of interest. We can then answer the question of interest for the sample. Finally, based on statistical theory, we will be able to determine how close our sample answer is to what we really want to know, the true answer for the population. ◆

9.1 | UNDERSTANDING DISSIMILARITY AMONG SAMPLES

The secret to understanding how things work is to understand what kind of dissimilarity we should expect to see in various samples from the same population. For example, suppose we knew that most samples were likely to provide an answer that is within 10% of the population answer. Then we would also know the population answer should be within 10% of whatever our specific sample gave. Armed only with our sample value, we could make a good guess about the population value. You have already seen this idea at work in Chapter 4, when we used the margin of error for a sample survey to estimate results for the entire population. Statisticians have worked out similar techniques for a variety of sample measurements.

Statistics and Parameters

We have already encountered the idea of a single random variable derived from an entire sample in Chapter 8. Remember that if we take a random sample from a population and define X = number in the sample with a certain opinion, then X is a binomial random variable. If we repeated the entire sampling procedure over and over again, we would get different values for X each time.

A **statistic** is a numerical value computed from a sample. Examples of statistics when the sample consists of a quantitative variable are the mean, the median, and the standard deviation. For example, for the sample of 103 Penn State women whose right handspan measurements were discussed in Chapter 2, the mean was about 20 cm and the standard deviation was about 1.8 cm. These values are examples of *statistics* associated with that sample of measurements. In contrast, a **parameter** is a number associated with a population, and it is generally assumed that the values of parameters are fixed, unchanging numbers. The average right handspan for the population of all college women is an example of a parameter.

For categorical variables, statistics associated with a sample include the number or the proportion of the sample who fall into various categories. For example, when Penn State students were asked to choose a number from 1 to 10, 19 out of 190, or exactly 10%, chose the number 8. Both the frequency of 19 and the percentage of 10% are statistics associated with that sample.

The distinction between a sample statistic and a population parameter is crucial. To be clear which is being referred to in formulas, different symbols are used to represent a statistic and the corresponding population parameter. You might recall that in Chapter 2 we used the symbols $\bar{x}$ and s to represent the mean and standard deviation of a sample. In Chapter 8, however, we used the symbols μ and σ for the mean and standard deviation of a population. For instance, if the mean pulse rate is 75.3 for a sample of 16 women, we should express this mean as $\bar{x} = 75.3$. If we used this sample mean to estimate the mean pulse rate of all women, we would write that $\bar{x} = 75.3$ estimates the unknown value of the population mean μ.

For a categorical variable, the symbol p is used to represent the proportion of a population that has a particular characteristic or trait. The symbol $\hat{p}$ (read as "p hat") is used to represent the proportion of a sample that has the characteristic or trait of interest. For example, if we sample 100 students at our school and there are 53 females in the sample, we would write that $\hat{p} = .53$ is the proportion of females in the sample. On the other hand, if we learn from the school registrar that 51.2% of all enrolled students are female, we would write that $p = .512$ is the proportion of all students who are female.

Sampling Distributions

Every time a new sample is taken, the sample statistics will change. For instance, if we were to sample a different collection of 103 Penn State women, we would get a different mean right handspan value. *The distribution of possible values of a*

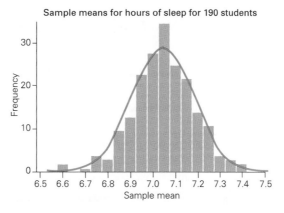

Sample means for hours of sleep for 190 students

FIGURE 9.1   **The sampling distribution for mean hours of sleep for 200 different samples, each with $n = 190$ students**

statistic for repeated samples of the same size from a population is called the **sampling distribution** *of the statistic. Think of the statistic as a random variable, and the sampling distribution as the distribution for that random variable. As we will see in this and subsequent chapters, many statistics of interest have sampling distributions that are approximately normal distributions.*

EXAMPLE 9.1
Mean Hours of Sleep for College Students

The sample of Penn State students first discussed in Chapter 2 included the question "How many hours of sleep did you get last night?" The mean of the 190 responses was 7.1 hours. Suppose we were to ask another 190 students that same question. It is unlikely that the mean response would be exactly 7.1 hours again.

Figure 9.1 shows a histogram of possible sample means we might get, found from simulating this experiment 200 times. A normal curve is superimposed on top of the histogram to demonstrate that the sampling distribution of possible sample means is approximately a normal distribution. We will return to this idea later in this chapter.

To understand how this picture was developed, think about a university that has 50,000 students. You and 199 friends (you are very popular) each go out and take a random sample of 190 of those students. You ask the students in your sample how many hours they slept last night and then calculate the mean of the 190 answers. Finally, you and your friends (200 of you) get together and draw a histogram of your 200 different sample means. You would get a picture similar to Figure 9.1. ◆

9.1

turn on your mind

Suppose you and your friends each asked 1900 people how many hours they slept last night, instead of asking 190 people each, so that you each compute a sample mean based on 1900 answers. When the 200 of you created the histogram of your results, how do you think it would compare to Figure 9.1? Would it be less spread out? More spread out? In other words, would possible sample means based on 1900 people be more variable or less variable than possible sample means based on 190 people, with the samples taken from the same population?*

*****HINT:** Trust your intuition on which sample size may generally provide more accuracy. Think about how that might relate to how means from different samples vary.

Statistic, Parameter, and Sampling Distribution

◆ A **statistic** is a numerical summary of a sample. Its value may differ for different samples.

◆ A **parameter** is a numerical summary of a population. It is considered to be fixed and unchanging.

◆ The **sampling distribution** for a statistic is the distribution of possible values of the statistic for repeated random samples of the same size taken from a population.

9.2 | SAMPLING DISTRIBUTIONS FOR SAMPLE PROPORTIONS

Suppose we conduct a binomial experiment with n trials and get successes on x of the trials. Or, suppose we measure a categorical variable for a representative sample of n individuals, and x of them have responses in a certain category. In each case, we can compute the statistic $\hat{p}$ = the **sample proportion** = x/n, the proportion of trials resulting in success, or the proportion in the sample with responses in the specified category. If we repeated the binomial experiment or collected a new sample, we would probably get a different value for the sample proportion.

For instance, suppose we would like to know what proportion of a large population carries the gene for a certain disease. We sample 25 people and use the sample proportion from that sample to estimate the true answer. Suppose that in truth 40% of the population carries the gene, although this fact is unknown to us.

What will happen if we randomly sample 25 people from this population? Will we always find 10 people (40%) with the gene and 15 people (60%) without? Or, will the number and proportion with the gene differ for different samples of $n = 25$? You may recognize that this situation is a binomial experiment and that if X = number (out of 25) who carry the gene, then X is a *binomial random variable* with $n = 25$ and $p = .4$.

Many Possible Samples

Consider four different random samples of 25 people taken from this population. Remember that we are trying to estimate the proportion of the population with the gene, based on the sample *statistic,* which is the *sample proportion.* We do not know that in truth the population proportion (the parameter) is actually 40%. Here is what we would have concluded about the proportion of people who carry the gene, given four possible samples with X as specified:

Sample 1: $X = 12$, proportion with gene = 12/25 = .48 = 48%.
Sample 2: $X = 9$, proportion with gene = 9/25 = .36 = 36%.
Sample 3: $X = 10$, proportion with gene = 10/25 = .40 = 40%.
Sample 4: $X = 7$, proportion with gene = 7/25 = .28 = 28%.

Notice that each one of these samples would have given a different answer, and the sample answer may or may not have matched the truth about the population, which is that 40% carry the gene.

In practice, when a researcher conducts a study similar to this one or a polling organization randomly samples a group of people to measure public opinion, only one sample is collected. There is no way to determine whether or not the sample is an accurate reflection of the population. However, statisticians have calculated what to expect for the vast majority of possible samples.

The Normal Curve Approximation Rule for Sample Proportions

In Chapter 8 we learned if X is a binomial random variable with large n, then X is also approximately a normal random variable. This result can also be applied to the proportion X/n, since dividing every value by n does not change the shape of the distribution of possible values. In other words, the *sampling distribution for a sample proportion is approximately normal.*

Let's give this result a name. We will call it the **Normal Curve Approximation Rule for Sample Proportions.** Sometimes we will refer to it simply as the **Rule for Sample Proportions.** This rule can be applied in two different situations:

Situation 1: A random sample is taken from an actual population.
Situation 2: A binomial experiment is repeated numerous times.

Conditions for Which the Normal Curve Approximation Rule for Sample Proportions Applies

In each situation, three conditions must all be met for the Normal Curve Approximation Rule for Sample Proportions to apply:

Condition 1: The Physical Situation   Situation 1: There is an actual population with a fixed proportion who have a certain trait, opinion, disease and so on.

or

Situation 2: There is a repeatable situation for which a certain outcome is likely to occur with a fixed relative frequency probability.

Condition 2: Data Collection   In Situation 1, a random sample is selected from the population, thus ensuring that the probability of observing the characteristic is the same for each sample unit.

or

In Situation 2, the situation is repeated numerous times, with the outcome each time independent of all other times.

Condition 3: The Size of the Sample or Number of Trials   The size of the sample or the number of repetitions is relatively large. The necessary size depends on the proportion or probability under investigation. It must be large enough so that we are likely to see at least five of each of the two possible responses or outcomes, in other words, np and $n(1 - p)$ must be at least 5, and it is preferable if they are each at least 10.

Examples of Scenarios for Which the Rule for Sample Proportions Applies

From your study of binomial random variables in Chapter 8, you should recognize that these are simply the conditions for a binomial random variable with large n. Here are some examples of scenarios that meet these conditions.

Scenario 1: Election Polls   A pollster wants to estimate the proportion of voters who favor a certain candidate. The voters are the population units and favoring the candidate is the opinion of interest. A large sample is taken.

Scenario 2: Television Ratings A television rating firm wants to estimate the proportion of households with television sets that are tuned to a certain television program. The collection of all households with television sets makes up the population and being tuned to that particular program is the trait of interest.

Scenario 3: Consumer Preferences A manufacturer of soft drinks wants to know what proportion of consumers prefer a new mixture of ingredients compared with the old recipe. The population consists of all consumers and the response of interest is preference for the new formula over the old.

Scenario 4: Testing ESP A researcher studying extrasensory perception wants to know the probability that people can successfully guess which of five symbols is on a hidden card. Each card is equally likely to contain each of the five symbols. There is no physical population. The repeatable situation of interest is a guess and the response of interest is a successful guess. The researcher wants to see if the probability of a correct guess is higher than .20, the chance for a successful guess if there were no such thing as extrasensory perception. The number of guesses made by each person should be at least 25 for Condition 3 (number of trials) to hold. With random guessing, $p = 1/5 = .2$, so $n = 25$ trials would lead to $np = 5$ and $n(1 - p) = 20$.

9.2

turn on your mind

Each of scenarios 1 to 4 can be thought of as a binomial experiment. Specify what constitutes a "success" in each case. Then construct your own example of a scenario for which the Rule for Sample Proportions would hold, and specify what constitutes a "success" for your example.*

---

definition The **Normal Curve Approximation Rule for Sample Proportions** can be defined as follows:

Let p = population proportion of interest or binomial probability of success.

Let $\hat{p}$ = corresponding sample proportion or proportion of successes.

If numerous samples or repetitions of the same size n are taken, the distribution of possible values of $\hat{p}$ is approximately a normal curve distribution with

Mean = p

Standard deviation = s.d.$(\hat{p}) = \sqrt{\dfrac{p(1 - p)}{n}}$

This approximate normal distribution is called the **sampling distribution of $\hat{p}$.**

Technical Note: The n individuals in the sample or the repetitions must be independent, equivalent to Condition 3 in a binomial experiment.

EXAMPLE 9.2
Possible Sample Proportions
Favoring a Candidate

Suppose that of all voters in the United States, 40% are in favor of Candidate X for president. Pollsters take a sample of 2400 voters. What proportion of the sample would be expected to favor Candidate X? The rule tells us that the pro-

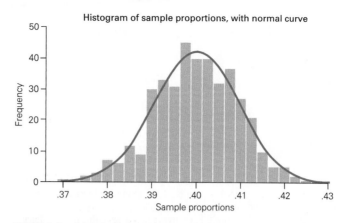

Histogram of sample proportions, with normal curve

FIGURE 9.2 **Histogram of 400 sample proportions based on $n = 2400$, $p = .4$**

portion of the sample who favor Candidate X is a random variable that has a normal distribution. The mean and standard deviation for the distribution are

Mean $= p = .40$ (40%)

$$\text{s.d.}(\hat{p}) = \sqrt{\frac{p(1 - p)}{n}} = \sqrt{\frac{(.4)(1 - .4)}{2400}} = \sqrt{\frac{.24}{2400}} = \sqrt{.0001} = .01$$

Figure 9.2 shows a histogram of the sample proportions resulting from simulating this situation 400 times, with the appropriate normal curve superimposed on the histogram. Notice that as expected from the Empirical Rule in Chapter 2, the possible values cover the range $\mu \pm 3(\text{s.d.})$, in this case, $0.40 \pm 3(.01)$. ◆

9.3

turn on your mind

For Example 9.2, into what range of possible values should the sample proportion fall 95% of the time, based on the Empirical Rule? If the polling organization used a sample of only 600 voters instead, would this range of possible sample proportions be wider, more narrow, or the same? Explain your answer, and explain why it makes intuitive sense.*

EXAMPLE 9.3
Caffeinated or Not?

Case Study 8.1 described a study in which 25 people each tried 20 times to guess whether a cola they taste is caffeinated or not caffeinated. For some of the 20 trials, the cola being tasted contained caffeine while in the others it did not. Suppose we take the view that people cannot judge merely by taste whether caffeine is present. If this were so, then participants would actually be randomly guessing on each trial, so $p = .5$, where p is the probability of correctly guessing whether caffeine is present or not on any trial. If this is the case for all individuals, then the overall experiment can be seen as a binomial experiment with $n = 500$ trials (25 people $\times$ 20 trials each) and $p = .5$.

We can use the Rule for Sample Proportions to approximate the sampling distribution of potential values of $\hat{p}$, the proportion of correct guesses in the sample of 500 trials. The sampling distribution will be approximately a normal curve with the following mean and standard deviation:

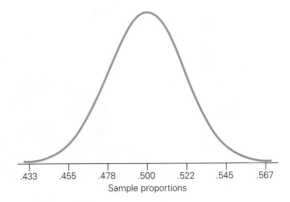

.433   .455   .478   .500   .522   .545   .567
Sample proportions

FIGURE 9.3   **Approximate sampling distribution of possible sample proportions when $n = 500$, $p = .5$**

Mean $= p = .5$

Standard deviation $=$ s.d. $(\hat{p}) = \sqrt{\dfrac{.5\,(1 - .5)}{500}} = .0224$

Figure 9.3 shows this normal curve. Based on the Empirical Rule, we know values fall in the interval $\mu \pm (2 \times$ s.d.) about 95% of the time. So, in this situation there's about a 95% chance that the proportion of correct guesses in a sample of 500 trials will be in the interval $.5 \pm (2 \times .0224)$, or between about .455 and .545. In the actual experiment, there were 265 correct guesses made, so the sample proportion was $\hat{p} = 265/500 = .53$. This is well within the interval of values that would occur for about 95% of samples of $n = 500$ trials where a random guess is made on every trial. In other words, $\hat{p} = .53$ is not strong evidence against the hypothesis that in general people cannot taste whether a cola contains caffeine or not.

Estimating the Population Proportion from a Single Sample Proportion

In practice, when we actually take a random sample of 2400 voters in a political poll, we have only one sample proportion and we don't know the true population proportion. However, we do know how far apart the sample proportion and the true population proportion are likely to be. That information is contained in the **standard deviation of $\hat{p}$,**

$$\text{s.d.}(\hat{p}) = \sqrt{\dfrac{p(1 - p)}{n}}$$

which can be estimated using the sample proportion $\hat{p}$ in the formula. The estimated version is called the **standard error of $\hat{p}$,**

$$\text{s.e.}(\hat{p}) = \sqrt{\dfrac{\hat{p}(1 - \hat{p})}{n}}$$

For instance, if $\hat{p} = .39$ and $n = 2400$, the standard error is $\sqrt{.39\,(1 - .39)/2400} = .01$. This value estimates the theoretical standard deviation of the sampling distribution for sample proportions, based on a single sample. Because we know that the mean, which is the true proportion p, is almost surely within 3 standard deviations of the observed value $\hat{p}$, we know that p is almost surely within the range $\hat{p} \pm 3(\text{s.e.}) = .39 \pm 3(.01) = .39 \pm .03$. So we know the true proportion who support the candidate is almost surely between .36 and .42. Notice that the only numerical value we needed to determine this was the sample proportion $\hat{p}$, and of course the sample size n. We will explore this idea in much more detail in Chapter 10, "Estimating Proportions with Confidence."

9.3 | WHAT TO EXPECT OF SAMPLE MEANS

In the previous section, the value of interest was the proportion falling into one category of a categorical variable or the probability of success in a binomial experiment. We saw that if we knew the size of the sample and the magnitude of the true proportion, we could determine an interval of values that was likely to cover the sample proportion.

We now turn to the case where the information of interest involves the mean or means of quantitative variables. For example, researchers might want to find the mean difference in age at death for left- and right-handed siblings. A company that sells oat products might want to know the mean cholesterol level people would have if everyone had a certain amount of oat bran in their diet. To help determine financial aid levels, a large university might want to know the mean income of all students on campus who work.

Many Possible Samples

Suppose a population consists of thousands or millions of individuals, and we are interested in estimating the mean of a quantitative variable. If we sample 25 people and compute the mean of the variable for that sample, how close will that *sample mean* be to the *population mean* we are trying to estimate? Each time we take a sample we will get a different sample mean. Can we say anything about what we expect those means to be?

For example, suppose we are interested in estimating the average weight loss for everyone who attends a national weight-loss clinic for ten weeks. Suppose, unknown to us, the distribution of weight losses for everyone in this population is approximately normal with a mean of 8 pounds and a standard deviation of 5 pounds. Figure 9.4 shows a normal curve with these characteristics. If the weight losses are approximately normal, we know from the Empirical Rule in Chapter 2 that 95% of the individuals will fall within 2 standard deviations, or 10 pounds, of the mean of 8. In other words, 95% of the individual weight losses will fall between -2 (a gain of two pounds) and 18 pounds lost.

Table 9.1 lists some possible samples that could result from randomly sampling 25 people from this population; these were indeed the first four samples produced by a computer simulation of this situation. The weight losses have been put into increasing order for ease of reading. A negative value indicates a weight gain. (As an aside, notice that, as expected, there are $5/100 = 5\%$ of the values outside of the range -2 and 18.) We are interested in the behavior of the possible sample means for samples such as these.

Here are the sample means and standard deviations for each of these four samples. You can see that the sample means, although all different, are relatively

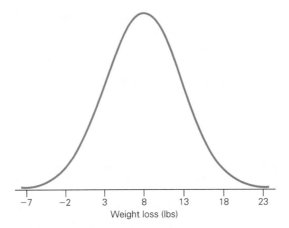

FIGURE 9.4   Normal curve for individual weight losses with mean $\mu = 8$ pounds and standard deviation $\sigma = 5$ pounds

TABLE 9.1 ■ Four Potential Samples from a Population with $\mu = 8$, $\sigma = 5$

Sample 1:	1, 1, 2, 3, 4, 4, 5, 6, 7, 7, 7, 8, 8, 9, 9, 11, 11, 13, 13, 14, 14, 15, 16, 16
Sample 2:	−2, −2, 0, 0, 3, 4, 4, 4, 5, 5, 6, 6, 8, 8, 9, 9, 9, 9, 10, 11, 12, 13, 13, 16
Sample 3:	−4, −4, 2, 3, 4, 5, 7, 8, 8, 9, 9, 9, 9, 10, 10, 11, 11, 11, 12, 12, 13, 14, 16, 18
Sample 4:	−3, −3, −2, 0, 1, 2, 2, 4, 4, 5, 7, 7, 9, 9, 10, 10, 10, 11, 11, 12, 12, 14, 14, 14, 19

close to the population mean of 8. You can also see that the sample standard deviations are relatively close to the population standard deviation of 5. This latter fact is important, because although we are interested in using the sample mean to estimate the population mean, we will need to use the sample standard deviation to help find a margin of error for this estimate.

Sample 1: Mean = 8.32 pounds, standard deviation = 4.74 pounds.
Sample 2: Mean = 6.76 pounds, standard deviation = 4.73 pounds.
Sample 3: Mean = 8.48 pounds, standard deviation = 5.27 pounds.
Sample 4: Mean = 7.16 pounds, standard deviation = 5.93 pounds.

Conditions for Which the Normal Curve Approximation Rule for Sample Means Applies

The mean of a sample is another example of a statistic. Because it is a numerical outcome of a random circumstance, it is also a random variable. As with sample proportions, statisticians have developed a rule to tell us what to expect for the possible distribution of sample means in repeated sampling from the same population. We call this rule the **Normal Curve Approximation Rule for Sample Means,** or simply the **Rule for Sample Means.** The Rule for Sample Means applies in both of the following types of situations:

Situation 1   The population of the measurements of interest is bell-shaped and a random sample of any size is measured.
Situation 2   The population of measurements of interest is not bell-shaped, but a *large* random sample is measured. Thirty is usually used as an arbi-

trary demarcation of "large," but if there are extreme outliers it is better to have a larger sample.

There are actually only a limited number of situations for which the Rule for Sample Means does *not* apply. It does not apply at all if the sample is not random, and it does not apply for small random samples unless the original population is bell-shaped. In practice, it is often difficult to get a random sample. Researchers are usually willing to use the Rule for Sample Means as long as they can get a representative sample with no obvious sources of confounding or bias.

Examples of Scenarios for Which the Rule for Sample Means Applies

Here are some examples of scenarios that meet the conditions.

> *Scenario 1: Average Weight Loss* A weight-loss clinic is interested in measuring the average weight loss for participants in its program. It makes the assumption that the weight losses will be bell-shaped, so the Rule for Sample Means will apply for any sample size. The population of interest is all current and potential clients and the measurement of interest is weight loss.

> *Scenario 2: Average Age At Death* A researcher is interested in estimating the average age at which left-handed adults die, assuming they have lived to be at least 50. Because ages at death are not bell-shaped, the researcher should measure at least 30 such ages at death. The population of interest is all left-handed people who live to be at least 50 years old. The measurement of interest is age at death.

> *Scenario 3: Average Student Income* A large university wants to know the mean monthly income of students who work. The population consists of all students at the university who work. The measurement of interest is monthly income. Because incomes are not bell-shaped and there are likely to be outliers (a few people with high incomes), the university should use a large random sample of students. They should take particular care to reach the people who are actually selected to be in the sample. There could be a large bias if, for example, they were willing to replace the desired respondent with a roommate who happened to be home when the researcher called. The students working the longest hours, and thus making the most money, would probably be hardest to reach by phone and the least likely to respond to a mail questionnaire.

9.4

turn on your mind

Construct an example of interest to you personally for which the Rule for Sample Means applies and for which a study could be done to estimate a population mean.*

> *definition* The **Normal Curve Approximation Rule for Sample Means** can be defined as follows:
>
> Let μ = mean for the population of interest.
> Let σ = standard deviation for the population of interest.
> Let $\bar{x}$ = mean for the sample = sample mean.
>
> If numerous random samples of the same size n are taken, the distribution of possible values of $\bar{x}$ is approximately normal, with
>
> Mean = μ
>
> Standard deviation = s.d.$(\bar{x})$ = $\dfrac{\sigma}{\sqrt{n}}$
>
> This approximate normal distribution is called the **sampling distribution of $\bar{x}$** or the **sampling distribution of the mean.**
>
> *Technical Note:* The n observations in each sample must all be independent, which they will be if random samples are used.

Be careful that you do not confuse the standard deviation for the original population of measurements, σ, with the **standard deviation of the sample means,** $\sigma/\sqrt{n}$. The parameter σ is a measure of the variability among individual measurements within the population. The parameter $\sigma/\sqrt{n}$ is a measure of the variability among sample means for the many different random samples of size n that can be taken from the population.

EXAMPLE 9.4
Hypothetical Mean Weight Loss
For our hypothetical weight-loss example, the population mean and standard deviation were μ = 8 pounds and σ = 5 pounds, respectively, and we were taking random samples of size 25. The rule tells us that potential sample means $\bar{x}$ could be anything from a normal curve with a mean μ of 8 pounds and standard deviation s.d. $(\bar{x})$ of $\sigma/\sqrt{n}$ = 5/5 = 1.0. (We divide the population standard deviation of 5 by the square root of n = 25, which also happens to be 5, to find the standard deviation of potential sample means.)

From the Empirical Rule in Chapter 2, we know the following facts about possible sample means in this situation, based on intervals extending 1, 2, and 3 standard deviations from the mean of 8:

♦ There is a *68%* chance that the sample mean will be between *7 and 9.*

♦ There is a *95%* chance that the sample mean will be between *6 and 10.*

♦ It is *almost certain* that the sample mean will be between *5 and 11.*

If you look at the four hypothetical samples we chose (Table 9.1), you will see that the sample means range from 6.76 to 8.48, well within the range we expect to see using these criteria. Figure 9.5 displays a histogram and superimposed normal curve for 400 simulated sample means, each based on a sample of 25 weight losses from a population with a mean of 8 pounds and a standard deviation of 5 pounds. ♦

This discussion presumes that we know the population mean and the standard deviation. Obviously, that's not much use to us in real situations when the population mean is what we are trying to determine. In Chapter 12 we will see

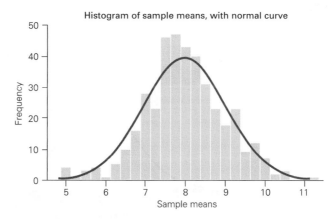

FIGURE 9.5   **Histogram of 400 sample means for samples of $n = 25$,**
$\mu = 8$, $\sigma = 5$

how to modify the Rule for Sample Means to accurately estimate the population
mean when all we have available is a single sample for which we can compute
the sample mean and the sample standard deviation.

Standard Error of the Mean

In practice, the population standard deviation σ is rarely known, so the sample
standard deviation s is used in its place when determining the standard deviation for the sampling distribution of sample means. Consistent with what we did
for sample proportions in the previous section, when making this substitution
we call the result the **standard error of the mean.** The terminology makes sense
because the standard error measures roughly how much, on average, the sample
mean $\bar{x}$ is in error as an estimate of the population mean μ.

We denote the standard error of the mean as s.e.$(\bar{x})$, and the formula is

$$\text{s.e.}(\bar{x}) = \frac{s}{\sqrt{n}}$$

For the $n = 25$ weight losses in Sample 1 shown in Table 9.1, the sample standard
deviation is $s = 4.74$ pounds. Based on this sample, the standard error of the
mean is $s/\sqrt{n} = 4.74/\sqrt{25} = 0.948$. This value estimates $\sigma/\sqrt{n}$, the theoretical
standard deviation of the sampling distribution for sample means. If we were to
use a different sample of $n = 25$ observations from Table 9.1, the standard error
of the mean would have a different value.

Increasing the Size of the Sample

Suppose we had considered samples of 100 people in the weight-loss example
rather than samples of 25. Notice that the mean of the possible sample means
would still be 8 pounds, but the standard deviation, s.d.$(\bar{x})$, would decrease. It
would now be $\sigma/\sqrt{n} = 5/\sqrt{100} = 0.5$, instead of $5/\sqrt{25} = 1.0$. Therefore, for
samples of size $n = 100$, the standard deviation of potential sample means is only
half of what it is for samples of size $n = 25$. In Example 9.4 we applied the Empirical Rule to see that for samples of $n = 25$, the sample means are likely to range
between 8 ± 3 pounds, or between about 5 pounds and 11 pounds. In contrast, for
samples of $n = 100$, the sample means are likely to range only between about $8 \pm$
1.5 pounds, or between 6.5 pounds and 9.5 pounds. Figure 9.6 compares the sam-

FIGURE 9.6   **Sampling distributions of potential sample means for samples of $n = 25$ and $n = 100$ taken from population that has mean $\mu = 8$ and standard deviation $\sigma = 5$**

pling distributions for samples of $n = 25$ and $n = 100$ and shows clearly that there is less variability among potential sample means for the larger sample size.

In general, a fourfold increase in sample size cuts the standard deviation of the distribution of possible means, and thus the range of likely means, in half. A ninefold increase in sample size cuts the standard deviation of possible means to a third of what it was, and so on. It's obvious that the Rule for Sample Means tells us the same thing our common sense tells us: Larger samples tend to result in more accurate estimates of population values than smaller samples.

9.5

turn on your mind

From the weight-loss example discussed in this section, we learned that increasing the sample size fourfold would about halve the range of possible sample means. Would the range of *individual* weight losses in the sample be likely to increase, decrease, or remain about the same if the sample size were increased fourfold? Explain.*

Sampling for a Long, Long Time: The Law of Large Numbers

The Rule for Sample Means tells us how much variability in possible sample means to expect for different sample sizes. There is a much simpler technical result in statistics called the **Law of Large Numbers,** which guarantees that the sample mean $\bar{x}$ will eventually get "close" to the population mean μ *no matter how small a difference* you use to define "close." The result requires that the population mean be finite (not infinite) and that the observations in the sample be independent of each other. "Eventually" could be a very long time, depending on how much variability there is in the population of measurements. In practice, the Law of Large Numbers says that for any specific population, the larger the sample size, the more you can count on $\bar{x}$ to be an accurate representation of μ.

The Law of Large Numbers is also used by insurance companies, casinos, and so on to give them peace of mind about what will happen to their average

*HINT: Which sample size might be more likely to include some of the more extreme weight losses for individuals in the population, leading to a wider range?

profit (or loss) "in the long run." They know that eventually, after enough gamblers have bet or customers have bought insurance and claims have been paid, they can count on the mean net profit to be close to the theoretical expected value or mean. This peace of mind comes at a price; they must make sure they have enough cash on hand to pay the claimant or gambler through the natural fluctuations in the process.

EXAMPLE 9.5
The Long Run for the Decco Lottery Game

In Chapter 8 we computed the expected value of the California Decco lottery game and found that the state gains an average of $0.35 for every dollar played. In other words, over all tickets sold, it pays out an average of $0.65 and keeps $0.35. Obviously, this average is not achieved in the short run. The state knows that to achieve this average it must sell hundreds of thousands of tickets. For instance, the first ten tickets sold might all be losers, or there might be a $5000 prize winner. The state must be prepared to pay winnings in the short run. States and casinos that operate gambling games have large funds they can use to pay winning players. For this reason, even when a game is an even bet, a gambler with limited funds will still eventually lose while the "house" weathers the lows (and highs). ◆

turn on your computer

Finding the Pattern in Sample Means

The main idea for any sampling distribution is that it gives the pattern for how the potential value of a statistic may vary from sample to sample. The Rule for Sample Means tells us that in two common situations, a normal curve approximates the sampling distribution of the sample mean. The **SampleMeans** applet lets us see the pattern that emerges when we look at the means of many different random samples from the same population. Figure 9.7 illustrates the appearance of the applet when it is started. The histogram shown is a population

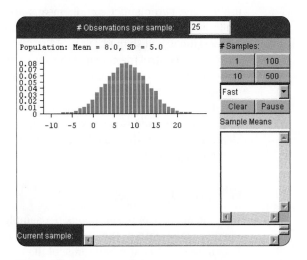

FIGURE 9.7   **The SampleMeans applet starting point**

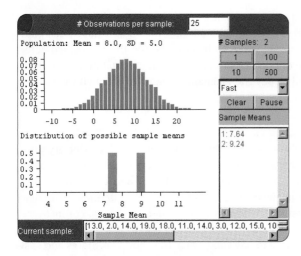

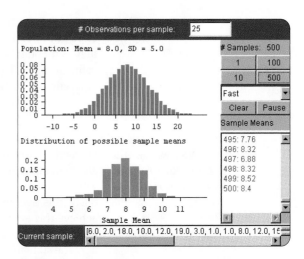

FIGURE 9.8   Example of the SampleMeans applet after two samples of *n* = 25 have been selected

FIGURE 9.9   Example of the SampleMeans applet after 500 samples of *n* = 25 have been selected

of individual measurements with $\mu = 8$ and $\sigma = 5$, as for the weight-loss example in this section. Notice that the distribution of individual measurements is bell-shaped, so the Rule for Sample Means should hold for any sample size. At the start, the number of observations per sample is set at $n = 25$.

What Happens

The applet simulates choosing simple random samples from the population. For each sample selected, the mean is calculated, displayed in the box under "Sample Means," and graphed in a histogram. The individual measurements in the most recently selected sample are shown at the bottom of the display. The buttons under "# Samples" can be used to select either 1, 10, 100, or 500 different samples at a time. Figure 9.8 illustrates an example in which two different samples of $n = 25$ per sample have been selected, while Figure 9.9 shows an example in which 500 different samples of $n = 25$ were selected. Notice that in Figure 9.8, the two distinct sample means are evident in the bottom histogram, while in Figure 9.9 the histogram of the 500 sample means (the bottom histogram) looks bell-shaped.

You can control the speed of the applet with the menu under the "# Samples" button. With slow and fast sampling you see the histogram change as samples are added. With "batch" sampling, the histogram of sample means is not updated until all requested samples have been selected. The "# Observations per sample" box is used to change the sample size per sample. The "Clear" button clears all results and should be used whenever changing the sample size ("# Observations per sample").

What to Do

With the number of observations per sample set at 25, generate many different samples. Take note of the resulting shape of the histogram of sample means. Take note of the center and range of the distribution of sample means. Use the

Clear button to clear the histogram, and then enter 100 as "# Observations per sample." Generate many different samples for samples of this size. Again, take note of the shape, center, and spread of the histogram of sample means. Verify that the range of the histogram of sample means is approximately $\mu \pm 3 \times (\sigma/\sqrt{n})$. Do the same things for "# Observations per sample" = 200. Experiment with the applet to formulate answers to the following questions. What feature of the distribution of sample means is affected by changing the sample size? What features are not affected by changing the sample size? How does changing the sample size affect the chance that a sample mean will fall in the interval 7.5 to 8.5 (within 0.5 pound of the true mean)?

Lessons Learned

This applet lets you see that a normal curve approximates the distribution of sample means for different random samples of the same size from a population. This is evident from the shape of the histogram for sample means, assuming you select many different samples of the same size. You can also see that increasing the number of observations in a sample decreases the variability among sample means. Notice that regardless of sample size, the histogram of sample means is approximately a normal curve centered at 8 pounds, the population mean. But, increasing the sample size increases the likelihood that a sample mean will be close to 8 pounds, the population mean.

9.4 | WHAT TO EXPECT IN OTHER SITUATIONS: CENTRAL LIMIT THEOREM

We have discussed two common situations that arise in assessing public opinion, conducting medical research, and many other applications. The first situation arises when we want to know what proportion of a population fall into one category of a categorical variable or want to estimate the probability of success in a binomial experiment. The second situation occurs when we want to know the mean of a population for a measurement variable.

There are numerous other situations for which researchers would like to use results from a sample to say something about a population or to compare two or more populations. Statisticians have determined rules similar to those in this chapter for most of the situations researchers are likely to encounter. Most of these rules are derived from the same basic statistical result, called the **Central Limit Theorem.**

definition The **Central Limit Theorem** states that if *n* is sufficiently large, the sample means of random samples from a population with mean μ and finite standard deviation σ are approximately normally distributed with mean μ and standard deviation $\sigma/\sqrt{n}$.

Technical Note: The mean and standard deviation given in the Central Limit Theorem hold for any sample size; it is only the "approximately normal" shape that requires *n* to be sufficiently large.

You may notice that the Central Limit Theorem is nothing more than a re-statement of the Rule for Sample Means, except that in the latter we specified the conditions needed to satisfy "if n is sufficiently large." The Central Limit Theorem is often used in situations where it isn't obvious that the statistic of interest is actually a sample mean. In fact, both of the rules in this chapter are special cases of the Central Limit Theorem.

The Rule for Sample Proportions follows from the Central Limit Theorem by defining each observation in the sample to be either 1 or 0. The observation is 1 if the individual sampled has the desired trait or opinion, and the observation is 0 otherwise. The sample mean is simply the average of the 1s and 0s in the sample, which is the sample proportion $\hat{p}$. The population mean $= p$, the proportion of 1s in the population. The population standard deviation is the standard deviation of the 1s and 0s in the population, which can be shown to be $\sigma = \sqrt{p(1 - p)}$, so $\sigma/\sqrt{n} = \sqrt{p(1 - p)/n}$.

9.6

turn on your mind

Verify that if the raw data for each individual in a sample is 1 when the individual has a certain trait, and 0 otherwise, then the sample mean is equivalent to sample proportion with the trait. You can do this by using a formula, explaining it in words, or constructing a numerical example.*

EXAMPLE 9.5—CONTINUED
California Decco Winnings

In Chapter 8 and in Example 9.5 of this chapter we discussed the California Decco lottery game, for which the mean amount lost per ticket over millions of tickets sold is $\mu = \$0.35$. The standard deviation is $\sigma = \$29.67$, reflecting the large variability in possible amounts won or lost, ranging from a net win of \$4999 to a net loss of \$1. Suppose a store sells 100,000 tickets in a year. What are the possible values for the average loss per ticket? The Central Limit Theorem tells us the answer: Assuming $n = 100,000$ is sufficiently large, the distribution of possible sample means is approximately normal, with a mean (loss) of \$0.35 and a standard deviation of $\sigma/\sqrt{n} = \$29.67/\sqrt{100,000} = \$0.09$. Using the Empirical Rule, the mean loss is almost surely in the range $\$0.35 \pm 3(\$0.09)$, or between 8 cents and 62 cents. Remember that this is the average loss per ticket for a collection of 100,000 tickets. Notice that the *total* loss for the 100,000 is therefore likely to be between ($\$0.08 \times 100,000$) and ($\$0.62 \times 100,000$), or between \$8000 and \$62,000! Certainly you can think of better ways to invest \$100,000. ◆

Mean or Median as "Central"?

The Central Limit Theorem provides information about what to expect of the mean in large samples, but the median remains the statistic of choice for representing the "central" value in an extremely skewed set of numbers. For instance, consider two random samples of net winnings for ten Decco tickets:

Net Amount Won ($n = 10$)	Mean	Median
$-1,-1,-1,-1,-1,-1,-1, 0, 0$	$-\$0.80$ (80 cent loss)	$-\$1.0$ (\$1.00 loss)
$-1,-1,-1,-1,-1,-1,-1, 0, 0, 4999$	\$499.20 (won)	$-\$1.0$ (\$1.00 loss)

*HINT: Write out a short list of 0s and 1s; then find the mean for the list and compare that to the proportion of 1s in the list.

Clearly, the median is a better measure of the "typical" net win in ten plays of this game. The problem is that for the occasional sample with a large outlier, the mean will be inflated, but this is not representative of the entire population. Remember that in this case, the population mean is 35 cents lost, and the population median is −$1.00. In fact, 72.6% of all tickets (as shown in Chapter 8) result in $1.00 lost or a −$1.00 net win.

9.7

turn on your mind

The Central Limit Theorem does not specify what is meant by "a sufficiently large sample." What factor(s) about the population of values do you think determine how large is large enough for the approximate normal shape to hold? Consider the California Decco example. Do you think $n = 30$ would be large enough for the distribution of possible values for the average loss to be approximately normal? Why or why not?

Now consider the handspan measurements of females. Do you think $n = 30$ would be large enough for the approximate normal shape to hold? What is different about these two examples?*

9.5 | SAMPLING DISTRIBUTION FOR ANY STATISTIC

In Section 9.1 we defined the sampling distribution of a statistic as the distribution of possible values of a statistic for repeated samples of the same size from a population. Two special cases discussed in this chapter were the sampling distribution of a sample proportion $\hat{p}$ and the sampling distribution of the sample mean. In both cases, under specified conditions the sampling distribution was approximately normal.

Every statistic has a sampling distribution, but the appropriate distribution may not always be normal, or even be approximately bell-shaped. Statisticians have developed a theory that helps determine the appropriate sampling distribution for many common statistics. It is also possible to construct an approximate sampling distribution for a statistic by actually taking repeated samples of the same size from a population and constructing a relative frequency histogram or table for the values of the statistic over the many samples. The next example illustrates this method.

EXAMPLE 9.6
Winning the Lottery by Betting on Birthdays

In the Pennsylvania Cash 5 lottery game, players select five numbers from the integers 1 to 39, and the grand prize is won by anyone who selects the same five numbers as the ones randomly drawn by the lottery officials. Suppose that in such a game someone bets numbers corresponding to the days of the month on which five family members were born, which is anecdotally a common strategy. Obviously, the highest integer someone using that strategy could select is 31, so there is no chance of winning the grand prize at all if the highest of the winning draws is bigger than 31—that is, if it is 32 to 39. What is the probability of that happening?

The statistic in question is the *highest* of five integers randomly drawn without replacement from the integers 1 to 39; let's call it *H*. For instance, if the num-

*HINT: See Table 8.1 for the Decco game probability distribution. See Figure 2.4 in Section 2.5 for a histogram of female handspans.

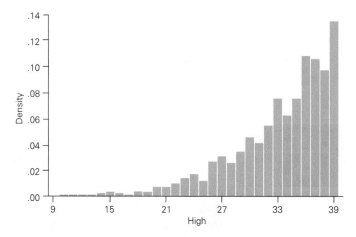

FIGURE 9.10   **Approximate sampling distribution for highest Cash 5 number**

bers selected are 3, 12, 22, 36, and 37, then $H = 37$. Determining the actual sampling distribution of H is a complicated exercise in probability. However, we can approximate the sampling distribution of H using lottery data supplied by the Pennsylvania Lottery Commission for repeated plays of the Cash 5 game.

The relative frequency histogram in Figure 9.10 shows the values of H for the 1560 games between April 23, 1992 and May 18, 2000, obtained from the website www.palottery.com. (The game was played weekly at first, then daily.) Table 9.2 displays some of the possible values of H and the frequency with which they occurred in the 1560 games. For instance, for one game, the highest of the five numbers was only 10, while for 70 out of the 1560 games (about 4.5% of the time) the high was 30. (Examples noted in this paragraph are in boldface in the table to

TABLE 9.2 ■ **Partial Sampling Distribution for Highest Cash 5 Number (examples from text are in bold)**

H = high	Count	Cumulative	Percent	Cum. Percent
10	**1**	1	0.06	0.06
11	1	2	0.06	0.13
12	1	3	0.06	0.19
13	1	4	0.06	0.26
14	2	6	0.13	0.38
15	3	9	0.19	0.58
16	2	11	0.13	0.71
⋮	⋮	⋮	⋮	⋮
29	55	309	3.53	19.81
30	**70**	379	**4.49**	24.29
31	65	**444**	4.17	**28.46**
32	85	529	5.45	33.91
33	118	647	7.56	41.47
34	98	745	6.28	47.76
35	118	863	7.56	55.32
36	169	1032	10.83	66.15
37	165	1197	10.58	76.73
38	152	1349	9.74	86.47
39	**211**	1560	**13.53**	100.00

help you find them.) Notice that the high was 31 or less for 444 of the games, which represents 28.46% of the games. In other words, all of the winning numbers are contained in the integers 1 to 31 in just over 28% of the games. For the remaining 72% of the games, the highest number is over 31. In fact, the most common outcome is $H = 39$, the highest possible number, which occurred in 211/1560, or about 13.5% of all games played.

Notice that the shape of the probability distribution for H is not symmetric and is skewed to the left. This example illustrates that not all sample statistics have bell-shaped sampling distributions. ◆

9.8

turn on your mind

Example 9.6 described a sample statistic, H = highest number drawn, for the Cash 5 lottery game. Give another example of a sample statistic for the Cash 5 game, and describe what you think the shape of its sampling distribution would be.*

9.6 | STANDARDIZED STATISTICS

In Chapter 2 we learned that sometimes it is useful to transform a raw score into a standardized score, or z-score, measuring how many standard deviations the raw score falls above or below the mean. The z-scores for raw scores from a normal population with mean μ and standard deviation σ are determined by the following formula:

$$z = \frac{x - \mu}{\sigma}$$

The resulting z-scores form a *standard normal population,* with $\mu = 0, \sigma = 1$.

Similarly, sometimes it is useful to transform a raw sample statistic into its standardized version. Doing this transformation requires knowledge of the mean and standard deviation of the sampling distribution for the sample statistic. If the sampling distribution is approximately normal, then the standardized statistic has, approximately, a standard normal distribution.

As we learned earlier in this chapter, many sample statistics have approximately normal sampling distributions. Researchers often conduct studies in which they observe one value of such a statistic (such as a sample proportion or a sample mean), and they want to know how far that value falls from a hypothetical center of the sampling distribution. Sometimes it is useful to obtain that information in standardized form. In other words, it is useful to find the standardized version of the observed sample value. Let's look at how to find the standardized version of sample means and proportions.

Standardized z-Statistics for Sample Means and Proportions

Assuming appropriate conditions are met for the Rule for Sample Proportions and the Rule for Sample Means to hold, as given in Sections 9.2 and 9.3, the following **standardized statistics** have, approximately, a standard normal distribution:

HINT: Some possibilities are lowest value, median value, and the mean value.

$$\text{For sample means: } z = \frac{\bar{x} - \mu}{\text{s.d.}(\bar{x})} = \frac{\bar{x} - \mu}{\sigma/\sqrt{n}} = \frac{\sqrt{n}(\bar{x} - \mu)}{\sigma}$$

$$\text{For sample proportions: } z = \frac{\hat{p} - p}{\text{s.d.}(\hat{p})} = \frac{\hat{p} - p}{\sqrt{\dfrac{p(1 - p)}{n}}}$$

EXAMPLE 9.7
Unpopular TV Shows

It is common for television networks to cancel shows with consistently low ratings. Ratings are based on a random sample of households, and the sample proportion of households tuned to the show ($\hat{p}$) is an estimate of p, the population proportion watching the show. Suppose a network wants p to be at least .20 or the show will be cancelled. In a random sample of 1600 households, 288, or a proportion of .18, are watching. Is this close enough to the desired population proportion of .20 to be attributable to random fluctuations in possible sample proportions, even if p really is .20 or higher?

The sampling distribution of $\hat{p}$ is approximately normal, with p = actual population proportion watching the show. If p = .20, then the mean and standard deviation of the sampling distribution are p = .20 and s.d. ($\hat{p}$)= .01. Therefore, the standardized version of $\hat{p}$ = .18 is

$$z = \frac{\hat{p} - p}{\text{s.d.}(\hat{p})} = \frac{\hat{p} - p}{\sqrt{\dfrac{p(1 - p)}{n}}} = \frac{.18 - .20}{\sqrt{\dfrac{(.2)(.8)}{1600}}} = \frac{.18 - .20}{.01} = -2.00$$

The sample proportion of .18 is about 2 standard deviations below the mean of .20. That probably isn't far enough below .20 to rule out sampling variability as the reason for such a low proportion, but it probably would be if the ratings were consistently that low. ◆

9.7 | STUDENT'S *t*-DISTRIBUTION: REPLACING σ WITH *s*

We have a dilemma. Computing a standardized score for $\bar{x}$ requires knowledge of the *population* standard deviation σ, which is rarely available. The best we can do is to approximate σ with the *sample* standard deviation *s,* and thus approximate s.d.$(\bar{x}) = \sigma/\sqrt{n}$ with s.e.$(\bar{x}) = s/\sqrt{n}$. Unfortunately, for small sample sizes this approximation is often off the mark, so the standardized statistic doesn't exactly conform to the standard normal distribution. Instead, under certain conditions (see In Summary box on the next page), it has a probability distribution called **Student's *t*-distribution,** or just ***t*-distribution** for short.

Theoretically, the *t*-distribution arises when a standardized score or statistic is calculated for a normally distributed score or statistic using the *sample* standard deviation in place of the *population* standard deviation. The Student's *t*-distribution was named for William Gosset, who published a paper about it in 1908 using the pseudonym "A Student" so as not to reveal that his place of employment, the Guinness Brewery, was using statistical methods. A *t*-distribution has a bell shape, it's centered at 0, and it is more spread out than the standard normal curve in that there's more probability in the extreme areas than there is for the standard normal curve.

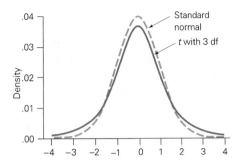

FIGURE 9.11   **A *t*-distribution with df = 3 and a standard normal distribution**

A parameter called **degrees of freedom,** abbreviated as **df,** is associated with any *t*-distribution. In most applications, this parameter is a function of the sample size for the problem, but the specific formula for the degrees of freedom depends on the type of problem. For the standardized version of a sample mean $\bar{x}$, df $= n - 1$, where n is the sample size. A property of the *t*-distribution is that as the degrees of freedom value increases, the distribution gets closer to the standard normal curve. The *t*-distribution with df $= \infty$ (infinity) is identical to the standard normal curve. In practice, if degrees of freedom are very large, the *t*-distribution is so close to the standard normal distribution that they are used interchangeably.

Figure 9.11 shows a *t*-distribution with df $= 3$ along with the standard normal curve. As can be seen in this figure, the *t*-curve is more spread out than the standard normal. For the *t*-distribution, there's slightly more probability in the extreme tails of the distribution than there is for the standard normal. This difference diminishes as the degrees of freedom increase.

in summary   Standardized *z*- and *t*-Statistics

If a small random sample is taken from a normal population or a large random sample is taken from any population (in which case these results are approximate), then the standardized statistic

$$z = \frac{\bar{x} - \mu}{\text{s.d.}(\bar{x})} = \frac{\bar{x} - \mu}{\sigma/\sqrt{n}} = \frac{\sqrt{n}(\bar{x} - \mu)}{\sigma}$$ has a standard normal distribution, and

$$t = \frac{\bar{x} - \mu}{\text{s.e.}(\bar{x})} = \frac{\bar{x} - \mu}{s/\sqrt{n}} = \frac{\sqrt{n}(\bar{x} - \mu)}{s}$$ has a *t*-distribution with df $= n - 1$.

EXAMPLE 9.8
Standardized Mean Weights

In Section 9.3 we considered four hypothetical samples of $n = 25$ people who were trying to lose weight at a clinic. We played the role of the all-knowing sage and assumed we knew that $\mu = 8$ and $\sigma = 5$. If the value for μ is correct, then the standardized statistic

$$t = \frac{\bar{x} - \mu}{s/\sqrt{n}} = \frac{\bar{x} - 8}{s/\sqrt{25}}$$

has a t-distribution with df $= 25 - 1 = 24$. If we were to generate thousands of random samples of size 25 and draw a histogram of the resulting standardized t-statistics, they would adhere to this t-distribution.

In practice, we do not draw thousands of samples and we do not know μ. Suppose we speculated that $\mu = 8$ pounds and drew one random sample, the first one given in Table 9.1, for which $\bar{x} = 8.32$ pounds and $s = 4.74$ pounds. Are the sample results consistent with the speculation that $\mu = 8$ pounds? In other words, is a sample mean of 8.32 pounds reasonable to expect if $\mu = 8$ pounds? The standardized statistic is

$$t = \frac{\bar{x} - \mu}{s/\sqrt{n}} = \frac{\bar{x} - 8}{s/\sqrt{25}} = \frac{8.32 - 8}{4.74/5} = 0.34$$

This statistic tells us that the sample mean of 8.32 is only about one-third of a standard error above 8, which is certainly consistent with a population mean weight loss of 8 pounds. ◆

Areas and Probabilities for Student's t-Distribution

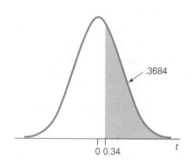

FIGURE 9.12 **A t-distribution with df $= 24$, illustrating location of $t = 0.34$**

Because Student's t-distribution differs for each possible df value, we can't summarize the probability areas in one table like we could for the standard normal distribution. We would need a separate table for each possible df value. Instead, tables for the t-distribution are tailored to specific uses, and we will explore two types of t-distribution tables in Chapters 12 and 13.

Many calculators and computer software programs provide probabilities (areas) for specified t-values and t-values for specified areas. For example, the Excel command TDIST(k,d,1) provides the area above the value k for a t-distribution with degrees of freedom d. (The reason for including the third value, 1, will become clear in Chapter 13.) In other words, it provides $P(t > k)$. For the situation in Example 9.8, TDIST(0.34,24,1) = 0.3684. Figure 9.12 illustrates this area.

Excel Tip

tech note   To find a t-value corresponding to a specified area, the Excel command is a bit tricky. The command TINV(p,d) provides the value k from the t-distribution with df $= d$ for which p is the *combined* area in the region above k and below $-k$. For instance, TINV(0.05,24) = 2.06. This indicates that the area below -2.06 plus the area above 2.06 is 0.05, for a t-distribution with df $= 24$. Notice that this also implies that 95% of the area is between -2.06 and $+2.06$, in contrast to the standard normal curve for which 95% of the area is between about -2 and $+2$.

9.8 | STATISTICAL INFERENCE

The results in this chapter will be used for the remainder of the book to make conclusions about populations on the basis of samples. The procedures we will use for making these conclusions are a subset of **statistical inference** procedures. The two most common procedures are to find *confidence intervals* and conduct *hypothesis tests*. Here, we give just a brief introduction to these procedures, which will be developed throughout the rest of the book.

Confidence Intervals

In the next several chapters, we will explore the two basic techniques researchers use to summarize their statistical results. The first technique is to create a **confidence interval,** which is an interval of values that the researcher is fairly sure covers the true value for the population parameter.

We encountered confidence intervals in Chapter 4 when we learned about the margin of error. Adding and subtracting the margin of error to the reported sample proportion creates an interval that we are 95% "confident" covers the truth. That interval is the confidence interval. We will explore confidence intervals further in Chapter 10 and again in Chapters 12 and 14.

Hypothesis Testing

The second statistical technique is called **hypothesis testing** or **significance testing.** Hypothesis testing uses sample data to attempt to reject the hypothesis that nothing interesting is happening—that is, to reject the notion that chance alone can explain the sample results.

We encountered this idea in Chapter 6 when we learned how to determine whether or not the relationship between two categorical variables is "statistically significant." The hypothesis researchers set about to reject in that setting is that two categorical variables are unrelated to each other. In most research settings, the *desired* conclusion is that the variables under scrutiny are related. Achieving **statistical significance** is equivalent to rejecting the idea that chance alone can explain the observed results. For instance, in Example 9.8, in which we obtained a random sample of weight-loss values for a clinic, we might want to see if we can reject the idea that there is *no* weight loss on average—that is, that $\mu = 0$ pounds. For our sample mean and standard deviation of 8.32 and 4.74 pounds, if $\mu = 0$ the standardized sample mean would be $t = \sqrt{25}(8.32 - 0)/4.74 = 8.78$. Clearly, a sample mean that is 8.78 standard errors above the population mean is virtually impossible, so we would *reject* the notion that $\mu = 0$. We will explore hypothesis testing further in Chapters 11 and 13.

CASE STUDY 9.1
Do Americans Really Vote When They Say They Do?

On November 8, 1994, a historic election took place, in which the Republican Party won control of both houses of Congress for the first time since 1952. But how many people actually voted? On November 28, 1994, *Time Magazine* (p. 20) reported that in a telephone poll of 800 adults taken during the two days following the election, 56% reported that they had voted. Considering that only about 68% of adults are registered to vote, that isn't a bad turnout.

But *Time* reported another disturbing fact along with the 56% reported vote. *Time* reported that, in fact, only 39% of American adults had voted, based on information from the Committee for the Study of the American Electorate.

Could it be the case that the results of the poll simply reflected a sample that, by chance, voted with greater frequency than the general population? The Rule for Sample Proportions can answer that question. Let's suppose that the truth about the population is, as reported by *Time*, that only 39% of American adults voted. Then the Rule for Sample Proportions tells us what kind of sample proportions we can expect in samples of 800 adults, the size used by the *Time Magazine* poll. The mean of the possibilities is .39, or 39%. The standard deviation is the square root of (.39)(.61)/800 = .017, or 1.7%.

Therefore, we are almost certain that the sample percent based on a sample of 800 adults should fall within $3 \times 1.7\% =$ 5.1% of the truth of 39%. In other words, if respondents were telling the truth, the sample percent should be no higher than 44.1%—nowhere near the reported percent of 56%.

In fact, if we combine the Rule for Sample Proportions with what we learned about normal curves in Chapter 8, we can say even more about how unlikely this sample result would be. If in truth only 39% (0.39) of the population voted, the standardized score for the reported value of 56% (0.56) is $z =$ (.56 − .39)/.017 = 10.0. We know from Chapter 8 that it is virtually impossible to obtain a standardized score of 10.

Another example of the fact that *reported* voting tends to exceed *actual* voting occurred in the 1992 U.S. presidential election. According to the *World Almanac* (1995, p. 631), 61.3% of American adults reported voting in the 1992 election. In a footnote, the Almanac explains:

Total reporting voting compares with 55.9 percent of population actually voting for president, as reported by Voter News Service. Differences between data may be the result of a variety of factors, including sample size, differences in the respondents' interpretation of the questions, and the respondents' inability or unwillingness to provide correct information or recall correct information.

Unfortunately, because figures are not provided for the size of the sample, we cannot assess whether or not the difference between the actual percent of 55.9 and the reported percent of 61.3 can be explained by the natural variability among possible sample proportions.

KEY TERMS

Section 9.1
statistic, 294, 296
parameter, 294, 296
sampling distribution, 294–295, 296

Section 9.2
sample proportion, 296
normal curve approximation rule for
    sample proportions, 297, 298
sampling distribution of $\hat{p}$, 298
standard deviation of $\hat{p}$, 300
standard error of $\hat{p}$, 300

Section 9.3
normal curve approximation rule for
    sample means, 302–303, 304

sampling distribution of $\bar{x}$, 304
sampling distribution of the mean,
    304
standard deviation of the sample
    mean, 304
standard error of the mean, 305
law of large numbers, 306

Section 9.4
central limit theorem, 309

Section 9.6
standardized statistic, 313–314
standardized z-statistic, 313–314, 315

Section 9.7
Student's t-distribution, 314
t-distribution, 314
degrees of freedom, (df), 315
standardized t-statistic, 315

Section 9.8
statistical inference, 316
confidence interval, 317
hypothesis testing, 317
significance testing, 317
statistical significance, 317

EXERCISES   Blue = Basics   **Bold, Bold** = Answer in back

Section 9.1

9.1 In each situation, explain whether the value given in bold print is a statistic or a parameter:
   a. A polling organization samples 1000 adults nationwide and finds that **72%** of those sampled favor tougher penalties for persons convicted of drunk driving.
   b. In their year 2000 census, the United States Census Bureau found that the median age of all American citizens was about **35** years.

   c. For a sample of 20 men and 25 women, there is a **14** centimeter difference in the mean heights of the men and women
   d. A writer wants to know how many typing mistakes there are in his manuscript, so he hires a proofreader who reads the entire manuscript and finds **15** errors.

9.2 A polling organization plans to sample 1000 adult Americans to estimate the proportion of Americans who think crime is a serious problem in this country. In the context of this poll, explain the difference between a statistic and a parameter. What is the parameter of interest to the polling organization? What will be the statistic?

9.3 Explain whether $\hat{p}$ or p is the correct statistical notation for each proportion described:

a. The proportion that smokes in a randomly selected sample of $n = 300$ students in the 11th and 12th grades.

b. The proportion that smokes among all students in the 11th or 12th grade in the United States.

c. The proportion that is left-handed in a sample of $n = 250$ individuals.

9.4 Suppose that a simple random sample of $n = 2$ numbers will be selected from the list of values 1, 3, 5, 7, 9.

a. There are ten possible equally likely samples of $n = 2$ numbers that could be selected (1 and 3, 1 and 5, etc.). List the ten possible samples, and calculate the sample mean $\bar{x}$ for each sample.

b. Summarize the results of part (a) into a table showing the sampling distribution of possible sample means. To do this, list each possible value for the sample mean along with the probability the value would occur.

9.5 Explain whether $\bar{x}$ or μ is the correct statistical notation for each mean described.

a. The mean hours of study per week was 15 hours for a sample of $n = 30$ students at a college.

b. A university administrator determines that the mean age of all students at a college is 20.2 years.

9.6 Some stockholders want to know if the mean salary for male employees in a large company is higher than the mean salary for female employees. The company allows them access to salary information for a random sample of 100 male and 100 female employees, and the mean salaries are $41,000 for the males and $39,500 for the females.

a. Are the mean salaries in this example statistics or parameters? Explain.

b. Based on these means, can the shareholders determine that the mean salary for males in the company is higher than the mean salary for females? Explain.

c. If they selected new random samples of 100 males and 100 females, would the average salaries of those samples be $41,000 and $39,500? Explain, using the concept of sampling distribution in your explanation.

9.7 Refer to the previous exercise. Suppose the 100 men and 100 women in the sample were all of the company's employees. Now answer questions a and b, repeated here:

a. Are the mean salaries in this example statistics or parameters? Explain.

b. Based on these means, can the shareholders determine that the mean salary for males in the company is higher than the mean salary for females? Explain.

9.8 A soft drink called Crash is so popular that vending machines allocate the top two selection buttons to it. Over the long run, of those who buy Crash 60% push the top button and 40% push the lower button, and this behavior seems to be independent from one purchase to the next. Suppose a sample of $n = 10$ people buy Crash at a vending machine one morning and $X =$ the number who push the top button.

a. Is X a statistic? Explain.

b. Describe the sampling distribution of X.

9.9 In a large retirement community, 60% of households have no dogs, 30% have one dog, and 10% have two dogs. Following a news story about how the elderly have trouble walking their dogs in the winter weather, a magnanimous group of teenagers decides that it will randomly select two households each and call and offer to walk their dog(s). For each teen who participates, T is the *total* number of dogs in the two households called.

a. List all possible values for T.

b. Find the sampling distribution for T. (*Hint:* This is simply a list of possible values for T and their probabilities.)

c. If there are no dogs in the two households ($T = 0$), the teen starts over with a new sample of two households. If 1000 teens participate, for about how many of them will $T = 0$ for their first sample?

9.10 The *I Ching* is an ancient Chinese system of asking for advice. In one version, three pennies are flipped and if the number of heads is odd (1 or 3), a "broken line" is recorded, while if it is even (0 or 2), a "solid line" is recorded. This process is repeated six times, then the results are used to identify one of the $2^6 = 64$ possible patterns of solid and broken lines and corresponding advice. Assume the coins are fair and the flips are independent. Define B to be the number of broken lines out of the six.

a. For each of the six lines, what is the probability that it is a "broken line"?

b. What are the possible values for B?

c. What is the probability that $B = 0$, so that all of the lines are solid?

d. Find the sampling distribution for B.

9.11 Are there situations for which the sampling distribution of a statistic consists of a single possible value, which has probability 1 of occurring each time? If not, explain why not. If so, explain how that could happen and give an example.

Section 9.2

9.12 Assuming the Rule for Sample Proportions applies, calculate the mean and the standard deviation of the sampling distribution of possible sample proportions for each combination of sample size (n) and population proportion (p).

a. $n = 400, p = .5$.

b. $n = 1600, p = .5$.

c. $n = 64, p = .8$.

d. $n = 256, p = .8$.

9.13 Refer to the previous exercise, and notice that for parts (a) and (b), the values of n are different while p is the same. This pattern also occurs in parts (c) and (d). Use the answers to the previous exercise to describe how changing the sample size affects the mean and standard deviation of the distribution of possible sample proportions.

9.14 A polling organization polls $n = 100$ randomly selected registered voters in order to estimate the proportion of a large population that intends to vote for Candidate Y in an upcoming election. Although it is not known by the polling organization, $p = .55$ is the actual proportion of the population that prefers Candidate Y.

a. Give the numerical value of the mean of the sampling distribution of $\hat{p}$.

b. Calculate the standard deviation of the sampling distribution of $\hat{p}$.

c. Use the Empirical Rule to find values that fill in the blanks in the following sentence. In about 99.7% of all randomly selected samples of $n = 100$ from this population, the sample proportion preferring Candidate Y will be between _____ and _____.

9.15 In a random sample of $n = 200$ drivers, 50 individuals say they never wear a seatbelt when driving.

a. Give a numerical value of $\hat{p}$ = sample proportion that never wears a seatbelt when driving.

b. Calculate the standard error of $\hat{p}$.

c. In a different survey of $n = 400$ drivers, 100 people say they never wear a seatbelt when driving. Give numerical values for $\hat{p}$ and the standard error of $\hat{p}$.

9.16 In a random sample of $n = 500$ adults, 300 individuals say they believe in love at first sight.

a. Calculate the value of $\hat{p}$ = sample proportion that believes in love at first sight.

b. Calculate the standard error of $\hat{p}$.

9.17 Suppose the probability is $p = .2$ that a person purchasing an instant lottery ticket wins money, and this probability holds for every ticket purchased. Consider different random samples of $n = 64$ purchased tickets. Let $\hat{p}$ = sample proportion of winning tickets in a sample of 64 tickets.

a. Give the numerical value of the mean of the sampling distribution of $\hat{p}$.

b. Calculate the standard deviation of the sampling distribution of $\hat{p}$.

c. Use the Empirical Rule to find values that fill in the blanks in the following sentence. In about 68% of all randomly selected samples of $n = 64$ instant lottery tickets, the proportion of tickets that will be money winners will be between _____ and _____.

d. Use the Empirical Rule to find values that fill in the blanks in the following sentence. In about 95% of all randomly selected samples of $n = 64$ instant lottery tickets, the proportion of tickets that will be money winners will be between _____ and _____.

9.18 Suppose medical researchers think that $p = .70$ is the proportion of all teenagers with high blood pressure whose blood pressure would decrease if they took calcium supplements. To test this theory, the researchers plan a clinical trial (experiment) in which $n = 200$ teenagers with high blood pressure will take regular calcium supplements.

a. Assume $p = .70$ actually is the population proportion that would experience a decrease in blood pressure. What are the numerical values of the mean and standard deviation of the sampling distribution of $\hat{p}$, the sample proportion, for samples of $n = 200$ teenagers?

b. Use the results of part (a) to calculate an interval that will contain the sample proportion $\hat{p}$ for about 99.7% of all samples of $n = 200$ teenagers.

c. In the clinical trial, 120 of the 200 teenagers taking calcium supplements experienced a decrease in blood pressure. What is the value of $\hat{p}$ for this sample? Is this value a parameter or a statistic?

d. Given the answers for parts (b) and (c), explain why

the observed value of $\hat{p}$ could be used as evidence that the researchers might be wrong to think that $p = .70$.

9.19 An automobile club comes to the aid of stranded motorists who are members. Over the long run, about 5% of the members utilize this service in any 12-month period. A small town has 400 members of the club. Consider the 400 members to be representative of the larger club membership. Let $\hat{p}$ be the proportion of them who will utilize the service in the coming 12-month period.

a. Explain why conditions 1 to 3 for the Normal Curve Approximation Rule for Sample Proportions are met in this scenario. State any assumptions you need to make to do so.

b. What are the values of n and p in this situation?

c. Use the Rule for Sample Proportions to describe the sampling distribution of $\hat{p}$, including values for the mean and standard deviation.

d. The towing service in town contracts with the club to come to the aid of up to 28 members in the next 12-month period. What proportion is that of the 400 members in town? What is the approximate probability that the actual proportion requiring aid will exceed that value?

9.20 Refer to the previous exercise where $\hat{p}$ is the sample proportion of 400 randomly selected club members who require aid in a 12-month period. Based on the Empirical Rule, into what interval should $\hat{p}$ fall about 95% of the time?

9.21 Explain the difference between the *standard error of $\hat{p}$*, and the *standard deviation of the sampling distribution of $\hat{p}$*. Write down the formula for each one. Which one is more likely to be used in practice? Why?

9.22 For each of the following, *if* the scenario fits the Rule for Sample Proportions, describe the sampling distribution of $\hat{p}$ and draw a picture of it. If the scenario doesn't fit, explain why not (in which case you do not have the tools to describe the sampling distribution of $\hat{p}$).

a. An auto insurance company has 1500 customers in a city, and over the long run 6% of them will file a claim in any given year. Define $\hat{p}$ to be the proportion who file a claim in the next year.

b. A dean has found that over the years, about 15% of students who begin their college work in her program do not finish. This year, 90 students will begin her program; define $\hat{p}$ to be the proportion who will finish.

c. An essay contest has three winners, but the number of entrants varies each time it is offered, so the proportion of entrants who are winners also varies. Define $\hat{p}$ to be the proportion of entrants who will be winners the next time the contest is offered.

9.23 Recent studies have shown that about 20% of American adults fit the medical definition of being obese. A large medical clinic would like to estimate what percent of their patients are obese, so they take a random sample of 100 patients and find that 18 are obese. Suppose in truth, the same percent holds for the patients of the medical clinic as for the general population, 20%. Give a numerical value for each of the following:

a. The population proportion of obese patients in the medical clinic.

b. The proportion of obese patients for the sample of 100 patients.

c. The standard error of $\hat{p}$.

d. The mean of the sampling distribution of $\hat{p}$.

e. The standard deviation of the sampling distribution of $\hat{p}$.

9.24 Refer to the previous exercise, in which 20% of the patients in a medical clinic are obese. If the clinic took repeated random samples of 100 observations and found the sample proportion who were obese, into what interval should those sample proportions fall about 95% of the time?

9.25 A student commented, "Once a poll has been taken, $\hat{p}$ (the sample proportion with a certain opinion) is a known value, so it cannot have a distribution of possible values. Therefore, I don't understand what you mean by the sampling distribution of $\hat{p}$." Write an explanation for this student.

Sections 9.3 and 9.4

9.26 Explain whether the Rule for Sample Means can be used to describe the possible values of the sample mean in each scenario.

a. Mean normal body temperature will be determined for a randomly selected sample of 18 individuals. In the population of all humans, normal body temperature has approximately a normal distribution with mean $\mu = 98.2$ degrees Fahrenheit and standard deviation $\sigma = 0.5$.

b. Mean number of music CDs owned will be determined for a randomly selected sample of 4 college students. In the population of all college students, the distribution of number of CDs owned is skewed to the right.

c. Refer to the previous part. The mean number of music CDs owned will be determined for a randomly selected sample of 900 college students.

9.27 The weights of men in a particular age group have mean $\mu = 170$ pounds and standard deviation $\sigma = 24$ pounds.

a. For randomly selected samples of $n = 16$ men, what is the standard deviation of the sampling distribution of possible sample means?

b. For randomly selected sample of $n = 64$ men, what is the standard deviation of the sampling distribution of possible sample means?

c. In general, how does increasing the sample size affect the standard deviation of the sampling distribution of possible sample means? The previous two parts provide a hint.

9.28 Example 9.1 concerned selecting random samples of $n = 190$ from a population of student responses to the question "How many hours of sleep did you get last night?" Suppose that in a large population of students the mean amount of sleep the previous night was $\mu = 7.05$ hours and the standard deviation $\sigma = 1.75$ hours. Consider randomly selected samples of $n = 190$ students.

a. What is the value of the mean of the sampling distribution of possible sample means?

b. Calculate the standard deviation of the sampling distribution of possible sample means.

c. Use the Empirical Rule to find values that fill in the blanks at the end of the following sentence. For 68% of all randomly selected samples of $n = 190$ students, the mean amount of sleep the previous night will be between ___ and ___ hours.

d. Use the Empirical Rule to fill in the blanks at the end of the following sentence. For 95% of all randomly selected samples of $n = 190$ students, the mean amount of sleep will be between ___ and ___ hours.

9.29 The **cholest** dataset on the CD accompanying this book includes cholesterol levels measured for 28 heart attack patients two days after their attacks. The sample mean for this sample is 253.9 and the standard deviation is 47.7.

a. Assuming this was a sample from a larger population of heart attack patients, what symbols should be used to represent the values given for the mean and standard deviation?

b. Calculate the standard error of the sample mean.

9.30 A randomly selected sample of $n = 60$ individuals over 65 years old takes a test of memorization skills. The sample mean is $\bar{x} = 53$ and the standard deviation is $s = 7.2$. Give the numerical value of the standard error of the mean.

9.31 Vehicle speeds at a certain highway location are believed to have approximately a normal distribution with mean $\mu = 60$ mph and standard deviation $\sigma = 6$ mph. The speeds for a randomly selected sample of $n = 36$ vehicles will be recorded.

a. Give numerical values for the mean and standard deviation of the sampling distribution of possible sample means for randomly selected samples of $n = 36$ from the population of vehicle speeds.

b. Use the Empirical Rule to find values that fill in the blanks in the following sentence. For a random sample of $n = 36$ vehicles, there is about a 95% chance that mean vehicle speed in the sample will be between ___ and ___ mph.

c. Sample speeds for a random sample of 36 vehicles are measured at this location, and the sample mean is 66 mph. Given the answer to part (b), explain whether this result is consistent with the belief that the mean speed at this location is $n = 60$ mph.

9.32 Small planes cannot fly well if the cargo (people and luggage) weigh too much. Suppose an airline runs a commuter flight that holds 40 people. They know that the weights of passenger + luggage for typical customers on this flight is approximately normal with a mean of 210 pounds and a standard deviation of 25 pounds.

a. Draw a picture of this distribution.

b. Using the Rule for Sample Means, describe the sampling distribution of the mean weight of passenger + luggage for a random sample of 40 customers.

c. Draw a picture superimposing the distributions from parts (a) and (b). (Label it clearly, and remember that the total area under each curve must equal 1.)

d. Assume customers on any particular flight are similar to a random sample. If the *total* weight of passengers and their luggage should not exceed 8800 pounds, what is the probability that a sold-out flight (40 passengers and their luggage) will exceed the weight limit? (*Hint:* Rewrite the desired limit as an average per passenger.)

9.33 Explain the difference between the standard deviation of the sampling distribution of the mean and the standard error of the mean. Explain which one is more likely to be used in practice and why.

9.34 Describe the sampling distribution for the statistic of interest in each of the following stories, including numerical values for the mean and standard deviation of the sampling distribution.

   a. A fisherman takes tourists out fishing and has noticed that over the long run the weights of a certain type of fish typically caught is approximately normal with a mean of 10 pounds and a standard deviation of 2 pounds. During a good day, the boatload of eight people catches the limit of 2 fish each, or a total of 16 fish. The statistic of interest is the mean weight of the 16 fish caught on a good day.

   b. A fisherman hangs out at the local bar in the evening and hears tourists talking about the weights of the fish they caught that day. He notices that the weights mentioned seem to have a mean of about 20 pounds and a standard deviation of about 4 pounds. He records what he hears as the weights for the next 50 "fish stories" at the bar. The statistic of interest is the mean weight for the 50 stories. Assume they represent a random sample of all such stories.

9.35 Consider the population of net gains for tickets in the California Decco lottery game described in Example 9.5. The possible values are $4999, $49, $4, 0 and −$1; the mean is −$0.35 and the standard deviation is $29.67. Suppose someone buys ten tickets each week.

   a. Explain why the Rule for Sample Means (or the Central Limit Theorem) would *not* hold for the distribution of possible mean net gains for the weekly purchases of ten tickets.

   b. Although the possible means for samples of ten tickets are *not* approximately normal, you can still specify numerical values for the mean and standard deviation of the sampling distribution of the mean in this situation. What are they?

9.36 A rental car company has noticed that the distribution of the number of miles customers put on rental cars per day is somewhat skewed to the right, with an occasional high outlier. The distribution has a mean of 80 miles and a standard deviation of 50 miles.

   a. Draw a picture of a normal curve with this mean and standard deviation (80 miles and 50 miles), and use the information in the picture to verify that the distribution of number of miles must be skewed to the right and/or have occasional high outliers rather than be normally distributed.

   b. What is the approximate distribution for the *mean* number of miles per day put on a typical one of the company's rental cars in a year (365 days)?

   c. What is the approximate distribution for the *total* number of miles put on a typical one of the rental cars in a year (365 days)?

   d. Do you think the necessary conditions for using the Rule of Sample Means to find the answer in part (b) are met in this situation? Explain.

Section 9.5

9.37 Suppose that a simple random sample of $n = 2$ numbers will be selected from the list of values 1, 2, 3, 4, 5.

   a. There are ten possible equally likely samples of $n = 2$ numbers that could be selected (1 and 2, 1 and 3, etc.).

List the ten possible samples, and give H = highest number for each sample.

   b. Summarize the results of part (a) into a table showing the sampling distribution of H. To do this, list each possible value for H along with the probability the value would occur.

   c. Which value is most likely to be the highest number in the sample?

9.38 Refer to the previous exercise.

   a. For each of the ten possible samples listed in part (a) of the previous exercise, give the value of the range $R = H − L$, where H is the highest number and L is the lowest number.

   b. Use the results of part (a) to find the probability that $R = 4$.

   c. Summarize the results of part (a) into a table showing the sampling distribution of R. To do this, list each possible value for R along with the probability the value would occur.

   d. Which value of R is most likely to occur? Which value is least likely to occur?

9.39 Refer to the discussion of the Cash 5 lottery game in Example 9.6 and the accompanying Table 9.2.

   a. In what proportion of the games is the highest number 35 or more?

   b. What is the median value of H for the 1560 Cash 5 games represented in Example 9.6?

   c. In what proportion of the games is the highest number 15 or less?

9.40 Define L to be the *lowest* of the five numbers drawn in the Cash 5 lottery game. Describe the shape of the sampling distribution of L, and explain how you know.

9.41 Use a computer to simulate the numbers drawn for the Cash 5 lottery game 1000 times, and draw a histogram for the values of H = highest number drawn. Compare your histogram to the one shown in Figure 9.10.

9.42 Suppose two fair dice are rolled and H = higher of the two faces. If both dice show the same value, H is that value. Construct the sampling distribution of H, listing all possible values and their probabilities.

9.43 Suppose someone who takes a ten-question True-False test doesn't know any of the answers and randomly selects True or False for each question. Define the statistic X = number correct.

   a. Describe the sampling distribution of X. (*Hint:* This distribution was introduced in Chapter 8.)

   b. What is the mean of this sampling distribution?

   c. What is the standard deviation of this sampling distribution?

9.44 Refer to the previous exercise. Now define the statistic of interest to be the *proportion* correct, $X/10$. What is the *mean* of the sampling distribution of this statistic? Explain how you found your answer.

Section 9.6

9.45 In each part, give the value of the standardized statistic (*z*-score) for the sample proportion.

   a. $\hat{p} = .60, p = .50$, $n = 100$.

b. $\hat{p} = .60, p = .50, n = 200$.

c. $\hat{p} = .78, p = .80, n = 400$.

d. $\hat{p} = .82, p = .80, n = 400$.

e. $\hat{p} = .25, p = .40, n = 900$.

9.46 Based on past history, a car manufacturer knows that 10% ($p = .10$) of all newly made cars have an initial defect. In a random sample of $n = 100$ recently made cars, 13% ($\hat{p} = .13$) have defects. Find the value of the standardized statistic (z-score) for this sample proportion.

9.47 In each part, give the value of the standardized statistic (z-score) for the sample mean:

a. $\bar{x} = 74, \mu = 72, \sigma = 10, n = 25$.

b. $\bar{x} = 70, \mu = 72, \sigma = 10, n = 25$.

c. $\bar{x} = 92, \mu = 100, \sigma = 16, n = 4$.

d. $\bar{x} = 92, \mu = 100, \sigma = 16, n = 64$.

e. $\bar{x} = 10.15, \mu = 10.0, \sigma = 5, n = 10,000$.

9.48 Home prices in a city have mean $\mu = \$200,000$ and standard deviation $\sigma = \$25,000$. For $n = 25$ randomly selected homes, the mean price is $\bar{x} = \$208,000$. Find the value of the standardized statistic (z-score) for this sample mean.

9.49 In addition to the sample size n, what population value(s) must be known in order to find a standardized score for a sample proportion $\hat{p}$?

9.50 In addition to the sample size n, what population value(s) must be known in order to find a standardized score for a sample mean $\bar{x}$?

9.51 A blind taste test is done to compare Cola 1 and Cola 2. Among $n = 75$ participants, $\hat{p} = .64$ is the proportion preferring Cola 1. If, actually, the two colas are equally preferred in a larger population of tasters, $p = .5$ is the corresponding population proportion. Assuming $p = .5$, find the value of the standardized statistic (z-score) for the sample proportion observed in the taste test.

9.52 Suppose a random sample of 36 IQ scores is drawn from a population of IQ scores with mean $= 100$ and standard deviation $= 15$.

a. Find the standardized statistic for $\bar{x} = 97$.

b. Find the standardized statistic for $\bar{x} = 105$.

c. Give numerical values for the mean and standard deviation of the sampling distribution of $\bar{x}$.

d. Draw a picture of the sampling distribution of $\bar{x}$, and identify where $\bar{x} = 97$ and $\bar{x} = 105$ fall on the picture.

e. Draw a picture of the standard normal curve, and identify where the standardized statistics found in parts (a) and (b) fall on the picture.

f. What is the relationship between the pictures in parts (d) and (e)?

9.53 Suppose an ESP test consists of $n = 75$ independent tries, for which there are four possible choices on each try. Suppose someone is just guessing, so the probability of a correct guess on each try is $p = .25$. Consider two possible sample proportions, $\hat{p} = .20$ (15 correct) and $\hat{p} = .33$ (25 correct).

a. Find the standardized z-statistics for $\hat{p} = .20$ and $\hat{p} = .33$.

b. Draw a picture of the sampling distribution of $\hat{p}$, and identify where $\hat{p} = .20$ and $\hat{p} = .33$ fall on the picture.

c. Draw a picture of the standard normal curve, and identify where the standardized statistics found in part (a) fall on the picture.

d. What is the relationship between the pictures in parts (b) and (c)?

Sections 9.7 and 9.8

9.54 Explain whether or not each of the following would ever differ for two random samples of the same size from the same population.

a. The sample mean $\bar{x}$.

b. The standard deviation of the sampling distribution of $\bar{x}$.

c. The standard error of $\bar{x}$.

d. The standardized z-score for $\bar{x}$.

e. The population mean μ.

9.55 In each situation, find the value of the t-statistic for the sample mean $\bar{x}$ and give the value of degrees of freedom (df).

a. $\bar{x} = 5, \mu = 10, s = 20, n = 16$.

b. $\bar{x} = 15, \mu = 10, s = 20, n = 16$.

c. $\bar{x} = 56, \mu = 50, s = 15, n = 25$.

d. $\bar{x} = 50, \mu = 50, s = 20, n = 9$.

9.56 Explain the difference between what is represented by s and σ, the two different symbols for standard deviation.

9.57 In each situation, find the value of the standardized statistic for the sample mean, and indicate whether the standardized statistic is a t-statistic or a z-statistic.

a. $\bar{x} = 175, \mu = 170, s = 24, n = 4$.

b. $\bar{x} = 175, \mu = 170, \sigma = 20, n = 4$.

c. $\bar{x} = 161, \mu = 170, s = 18, n = 36$.

9.58 Draw a picture of each of the following distributions. Shade the area above the value given, and label the proportion of the distribution that falls in that region, as in Figure 9.12. You do not have to label the vertical axis. *Note:* For parts (b) and (c), the use of either statistical software or Excel is necessary.

a. Standard normal distribution; $z = .70$.

b. t-distribution with df $= 10, t = .70$.

c. t-distribution with df $= 10, t = -.70$.

9.59 Are there any (finite) values for which the area above that value is the same for all t-distributions? If so, specify the value(s) and the area(s). If not, explain why not.

9.60 In each of the following situations, which of the two distributions would be more spread out?

a. Standard normal distribution or t-distribution with df $= 10$.

b. t-distribution with df $= 5$ or t-distribution with df $= 25$.

c. t-distribution with df $= 100$ or normal distribution with standard deviation $= 100$.

9.61 Compute the standardized statistic for the sample mean in each of these situations.

a. A random sample of 25 IQ scores from a population with mean $100; \bar{x} = 105, s = 10$.

b. A random sample of 100 salaries of women who work in a traditional male job for which the population mean salary is $\$80,000; \bar{x} = \$78,000, s = \$4000$.

9.62 Refer to the previous exercise. Draw a picture of the appropriate distribution for the standardized statistic in each case, and find the area below the value of the standardized statistic. (*Note:* The use of either statistical software or Excel is necessary.)

9.63 Refer to the parts of the previous two exercises that concern the 100 salaries of women. Suppose allegations were made that the population mean salary of women who work in that job is lower than the known population mean salary of $80,000 for men.
  a. Does the sample information provided for the women seem to support that allegation? Explain.
  b. The question in part (a) is an example of hypothesis testing, the goal of which was described in Section 9.8 as "to reject the notion that chance alone can explain the sample results." Explain how the question in part (a) fits that description of hypothesis testing.

9.64 Draw a picture illustrating each of the following distributions, showing the *t*-values marking the specified areas and the proportion of the *t*-distribution that falls in that area. *Note:* The use of either statistical software or Excel is necessary.
  a. *t*-distribution with df = 10, middle 95%.
  b. *t*-distribution with df = 20, area above 1.725.
  c. *t*-distribution with df = 20, area between 1.725 and −1.725.
  d. *t*-distribution with df = 10, upper 5%.
  e. *t*-distribution with df = 10, area below −*t* and above +*t* (same *t*) totals 5%.

Chapter Exercises

9.65 Suppose you want to estimate the proportion of students at your college who are left-handed. You decide to collect a random sample of 200 students and ask them which hand is dominant. Go through the Conditions for Which the Rule for Sample Proportions Applies and explain why the rule would apply to this situation.

9.66 Refer to the previous exercise. Suppose the truth is that .12 or 12% of the students are left-handed and you take a random sample of 200 students. Use the Rule for Sample Proportions to draw a picture similar to Figure 9.3, showing the possible sample proportions for this situation.

9.67 According to the *Sacramento Bee* (2 April 1998, p. F5), "A 1997–98 survey of 1027 Americans conducted by the National Sleep Foundation found that 23% of adults say they have fallen asleep at the wheel in the last year."
  a. Conditions 2 and 3 needed to apply the Rule for Sample Proportions are met because this result is based on a large random sample of adults. Explain how condition 1 is also met.
  b. The article also said that (based on the same survey) "37 percent of adults report being so sleepy during the day that it interferes with their daytime activities." If in truth 40% of all adults have this problem, find the interval in which about 95% of all sample proportions should fall, based on samples of size 1027. Does the result of this survey fall into that interval?
  c. Suppose a survey based on a random sample of 1027 college students was conducted and 25% reported being so sleepy during the day that it interferes with their daytime activities. Would it be reasonable to conclude that the population proportion of college students who have this problem differs from the proportion of all adults who have the problem? Explain.

9.68 A recent Gallup Poll found that of 800 randomly selected drivers surveyed, 70% thought that they were better-than-average drivers. In truth, in the population, at most only 50% of all drivers can be "better than average."
  a. Draw a picture of the possible sample proportions that would result from samples of 800 people from a population with a true proportion of .50.
  b. Would you be unlikely to see a sample proportion of .70, based on a sample of 800 people, from a population with a proportion of .50? Explain, using your picture from part (a).

9.69 Suppose you are interested in estimating the average number of miles per gallon of gasoline your car can get. You calculate the miles per gallon for each of the next nine times you fill the tank. Suppose in truth, the values for your car are bell-shaped, with a mean of 25 miles per gallon and a standard deviation of 1. Draw a picture of the possible sample means you are likely to get based on your sample of nine observations. Include the intervals into which 68%, 95%, and almost all of the potential sample means will fall, using the Empirical Rule from Chapter 2.

9.70 Refer to the previous exercise. Redraw the picture under the assumption that you will collect 100 measurements instead of only 9. Discuss how the picture differs from the one in the previous exercise.

9.71 Give an example of a scenario of interest to you for which the Rule for Sample Proportions would apply. Explain why the conditions allowing the rule to be applied are satisfied for your example.

9.72 Suppose the population of IQ scores in the town or city where you live is bell-shaped, with a mean of 105 and a standard deviation of 15. Describe the distribution of possible sample means that would result from random samples of 100 IQ scores.

9.73 Suppose that 35% of the students at a university favor the semester system, 60% favor the quarter system, and 5% have no preference. Would a random sample of 100 students be large enough to provide convincing evidence that the quarter system is favored? Explain.

9.74 According to *USA Today* (20 April 1998 Snapshot), a poll of 8709 adults taken in 1976 found that 9% believed in reincarnation, while a poll of 1000 adults taken in 1997 found that 25% held that belief.
  a. Assuming a proper random sample was used, verify that the sample proportion for the 1976 poll represents the population proportion to within about 1%.
  b. Based on these results, would you conclude that the proportion of all adults who believe in reincarnation was higher in 1997 than it was in 1976? Explain.

9.75 Suppose 20% of all television viewers in the country watch a particular program.
  a. For a random sample of 2500 households measured by a rating agency, describe the distribution of the possible sample proportions who watch the program.
  b. The program will be cancelled if the ratings show less than 17% watching in a random sample of households. Given that 2500 households are used for the ratings, is the program in danger of getting cancelled? Explain.

9.76 Use the Rule for Sample Means to explain why it is desirable to take as large a sample as possible when trying to estimate a population value.

9.77 According to the *Sacramento Bee* (2 April 1998, p. F5), Americans get an average of 6 hours and 57 minutes of sleep per night. A survey of a class of 190 statistics students at a large university found that they averaged 7.1 hours of sleep the previous night, with a standard deviation of 1.95 hours.

a. Assume that the population average for adults is 6 hours and 57 minutes, or 6.95 hours of sleep per night, with a standard deviation of 2 hours. Draw a picture illustrating how the Rule for Sample Means would apply to sample means for random samples of 190 adults.

b. Would the mean of 7.1 hours of sleep obtained from the statistics students be a reasonable value to expect for the sample mean of a random sample of 190 adults? Explain.

c. Can the sample taken in the statistics class be considered a representative sample of all adults? Explain.

9.78 Explain whether or not each of the following scenarios meets the conditions for which the Rule for Sample Proportions applies. If not, explain which condition is violated.

a. Unknown to the government, 10% of all cars in a certain city do not meet appropriate emissions standards. The government wants to estimate that percentage, so they take a random sample of 30 cars and compute the sample proportion that do not meet the standards.

b. The Census Bureau would like to estimate what proportion of households have someone at home between 7 P.M. and 7:30 P.M. on weeknights to determine whether or not that would be an efficient time to collect census data. They survey a random sample of 2000 households and visit them during that time to see whether or not someone is at home.

c. You want to know what proportion of days in typical years have rain or snow in the area where you live. For the months of January and February, you record whether or not there is rain or snow each day, and then you calculate the proportion.

d. A large company wants to determine what proportion of its employees are interested in on-site day care. For a random sample of 100 employees, the company calculates the sample proportion who are interested.

9.79 Explain whether or not you think the Rule for Sample Means applies to each of the following scenarios. If it does apply, specify the population of interest and the measurement of interest. If it does not apply, explain why not.

a. A researcher wants to know what the average cholesterol level would be if people restricted their fat intake to 30% of calories. He gets a group of patients who have had heart attacks to volunteer to participate, puts them on a restricted diet for a few months, then measures their cholesterol and calculates the mean value.

b. A large corporation would like to know the average income of the spouses of its workers. Rather than go to the trouble to collect a random sample, they post someone at the exit of the building at 5 P.M. Everyone who leaves between 5 P.M. and 5:30 P.M. is asked to complete a short questionnaire on the issue; there are 70 responses.

c. A university wants to know the average income of its alumni. They select a random sample of 200 alumni and mail them a questionnaire. They follow up with a phone call to those who do not respond within 30 days.

d. An automobile manufacturer wants to know the average price for which used cars of a particular model and year are selling in a certain state. It is able to obtain a list of buyers from the state motor vehicle division, from which a random sample of 20 buyers is selected. The manufacturer makes every effort to find out what those people paid for the cars and is successful in doing so.

9.80 In Case Study 9.1, we learned that about 56% of American adults actually voted in the presidential election of 1992, whereas about 61% of a random sample claimed that they had voted. The size of the sample was not specified, but suppose it was based on 1600 American adults, a common size for such studies.

a. Into what interval of values should the sample proportion fall 68%, 95%, and almost all of the time?

b. Do you think the observed value of 61% is reasonable, based on your answer to part (a)?

c. Now suppose the sample had been of only 400 people. Compute a standardized score to correspond to the reported percentage of 61%. Comment on whether or not you believe people in the sample could all have been telling the truth, based on your result.

9.81 Suppose the population of grade point averages (GPAs) for students at the end of their first year at a large university has a mean of 3.1 and a standard deviation of 0.5.

a. Draw a picture of the distribution of the sample mean GPA for a random sample of 100 students.

b. Find the probability that the sample mean will be 3.15 or greater.

9.82 The administration of a large university wants to take a random sample to measure student opinion of a new food service on campus. It plans to use a continuous scale from 1 to 100, where 1 is complete dissatisfaction and 100 is complete satisfaction. The administration knows from past experience with such questions that the standard deviation for the responses is going to be about 5, but it does not know what to expect for the mean. It wants to be almost sure that the sample mean is within plus or minus 1 point of the true population mean value. How large will the random sample have to be?

Dataset Exercises

9.83 The data for this exercise are in the **GSS-93** dataset. The variable ***gunlaw*** is whether a respondent favors or opposes stronger gun control laws. Of the 1055 respondents, 870 are in favor. *For this exercise, assume these respondents represent a population.*

a. What is the population proportion p who favor stronger gun control laws?

b. Suppose random samples of $n = 60$ are drawn from this population. Describe and draw the approximate sampling distribution for the proportion $\hat{p}$ who would favor stronger gun control laws.

c. Simulate 200 samples of size 60 from this population, and draw a histogram of the sample proportions who favor stronger gun control laws.

d. Compare your simulated distribution in part (c) with the sampling distribution you described in part (b).

9.84 Use the **pennstate1** dataset for this exercise. The data for the variable *HrsSleep* are responses by $n = 190$ students to the question, "How many hours did you sleep last night?" For this exercise, suppose they represent a population.
  a. Simulate 200 samples of $n = 10$ responses to *HrsSleep.* Show the commands you used or explain how you did the simulation.
  b. Draw a histogram of the 200 sample means.
  c. Describe the simulated sampling distribution you found in part (b).
  d. Draw a histogram of the 200 sample medians for the samples you found in part (a).
  e. Compare the sampling distributions for the sample mean and the sample median.

9.85 Use the data in the **GSS-93** dataset for this exercise. One of the questions asked was age in years. A five-number summary for age is 18, 32, 43, 58, and 89.
  a. Draw a boxplot of the ages for the entire dataset.
  b. Let H = highest age in the sample for samples of size $n = 10$. Do any of the rules given in this chapter provide information about the sampling distribution of H? If so, explain.
  c. Simulate 200 samples of size 10 and find H for each one. Create a histogram for the 200 values of H.
  d. Using the histogram in part (c) and any other numerical or graphical information you wish to provide, describe the sampling distribution of H.

9.86 Use the **Fantasy5** dataset for this exercise, with data from 2318 games of California's version of the same scheme as the Pennsylvania Cash 5 game.
  a. Draw a picture of the sampling distribution of H, the highest number each day, and compare it to the equivalent picture for the Cash 5 game, shown in Figure 9.10. Do you expect them to be similar? Are they?
  b. Consider each game to be a random sample of size 5, drawn without replacement from the integers 1 to 39. Which column in the dataset represents the median for each of these random samples?
  c. Draw a picture of the sampling distribution of the median.
  d. Find the mean of each of the 2318 samples of size 5. Draw a picture of the sampling distribution of the mean.
  e. Compare the sampling distributions of the median and the mean. Which one is more spread out? Why do you think that is the case?

9.87 Use the **Cash5** dataset for this exercise, with data from 1560 games of Pennsylvania's Cash 5 lottery game described in Section 9.5. The variables *High* and *Low* give the highest and lowest numbers picked in each game.
  a. For each game, find $R = High - Low$, the range between the highest and lowest numbers. Draw a histogram of R, and describe the shape of this histogram.
  b. Find the mean for each of the variables R, *High*, and *Low.* Verify that the mean for R equals the difference between the means for *High* and *Low.*
  c. What is the maximum possible value of the range R in the Cash 5 game? What values of *High* and *Low* would lead to this value?
  d. Tally how often each value of R occurred in the 1560 games given in the dataset. How often did the maximum possible value of R occur?

Turn On Your Computer

*For Exercises 9.88 to 9.90, use the **SampleMeans** applet described in Section 9.3. It is on the CD for this text. The applet selects random samples from a bell-shaped population in which the mean $\mu = 8$ and the standard deviation $\sigma = 5$.*

9.88 This exercise concerns possible sample means for random samples of $n = 36$.
  a. Use the applet to generate 500 different random samples of $n = 36$ observations. What is the approximate shape of the resulting histogram of sample means?
  b. Approximately, what were the smallest and largest values of the sample mean among the 500 samples you generated?
  c. For random samples of $n = 36$, use the Empirical Rule to find the interval of values in which about 99.7% of all sample means will fall. Compare that interval to your answer for part (b).

9.89 This exercise concerns possible sample means for random samples of $n = 75$.
  a. Use the applet to generate 500 different random samples of $n = 75$ observations. What is the approximate shape of the resulting histogram of sample means?
  b. Approximately, what were the smallest and largest values among the sample mean in the 500 samples you generated?
  c. For random samples of $n = 75$, use the Empirical Rule to find the interval of values into which the sample mean will fall about 99.7% of the time. Compare the interval to your answer for part (b).
  d. Describe any difference between the histograms created for part (a) of this exercise and part (a) of the previous exercise. (If you have not already generated the histogram for part (a) of the previous exercise, do so now.)

9.90 This exercise compares sample means for random samples of $n = 10$ and random samples of $n = 100$.
  a. Use the applet to generate ten different random samples of $n = 10$. List the ten sample means, and identify the lowest and highest values in the list.
  b. Use the applet to generate ten different random samples of $n = 100$. List the ten sample means, and identify the lowest and highest values in the list.
  c. Compare the results of parts (a) and (b). What is indicated about the effect of sample size on the variation among sample means for different samples?

9.91 Use the **TVMeans** applet, which selects random samples from a population modeled using responses given by college students to a question asking how many hours they watch television in a typical week. The mean for the population is $\mu = 8.352$ hours and the standard deviation is $\sigma = 7.723$ hours.
  a. Generate 500 different random samples of $n = 5$ observations. Draw a sketch showing the shape of the histogram of sample means for random samples of $n = 5$.
  b. Generate 500 different random samples of $n = 49$ observations. Draw a sketch showing the shape of the histogram of sample means for random samples of $n = 49$.
  c. Refer to the two situations, given in Section 9.3, for which the Normal Curve Approximation Rule for Sample Means holds. Explain which situation is pres-

ent in the **TVMeans** applet. Also, explain how parts (a) and (b) illustrate that situation.

9.92 Refer to the previous exercise about the **TVMeans** applet. Assume the Normal Curve Approximation Rule for Sample Means holds for random samples of $n = 49$ observations.

a. Use the Empirical Rule to find the interval of values into which the sample mean will fall about 95% of the time for random samples of $n = 49$.

b. Use the Empirical Rule to find the interval of values into which the sample mean will fall about 68% of the time for random samples of $n = 49$.

REFERENCE

World Almanac and Book of Facts (1995). Robert Famighetti. Mahwah, NJ: Funk and Wagnalls.

CHAPTER 10

Estimating Proportions With Confidence

How many teens have dated someone of another race or ethnic group?
See Example 10.1.

One of the most common types of inference procedures is to construct a *confidence interval* estimate of the unknown value of a population parameter. Here is a typical confidence interval statement: Based on this sample, we have 95% confidence that somewhere between 33% and 39% of all Americans suffer from allergies.

In this chapter, we will learn how to use a sample of data to estimate the proportion of a population that falls into a particular category of a categorical variable. Suppose, for instance, that we have been asked to estimate the proportion of students at your school who think that marijuana should be legalized. How can we go about developing our estimate? One possibility that may occur to you is that we could use information from a random sample of students to estimate the proportion for the whole population.

Let's imagine that we survey 150 randomly selected students and that about 41% of these students think that marijuana should be legalized. Figure 10.1 illustrates the situation.

Because we only have information from a sample of 150 students, we should be concerned about whether the sample result (41%) is an accurate estimate of the population value. Some questions about accuracy that typify those that we will examine in this chapter are

Population of all students	What percent thinks marijuana should be legalized?
↓	
Random sample of 150 students	41% think marijuana should be legalized.

FIGURE 10.1 **Population and sample results**

◆ How much difference might there be between the sample estimate, 41%, and the true population value?

◆ How does the sample size affect the accuracy of our sample estimate?

◆ If we report that between 33% and 49% of all students at the college think that marijuana should be legalized, how confident can we be that we are correct?

The last of these questions is connected to the idea of a **confidence interval**, an interval of estimates that is likely to capture the population value. The primary objective of this chapter is to describe how to calculate and interpret a confidence interval estimate of a population proportion. The general concepts that we learn here will also apply to many other estimation problems that we will encounter later in the text.

Remember from Chapters 3 and 9 that the term *statistical inference* is used to describe the use of sample data to make judgments or decisions about populations. The method of using a confidence interval for estimating a population value is one of the two principal techniques of statistical inference. In this chapter, we introduce confidence intervals by illustrating their use for proportions. In Chapter 12, we broaden the discussion and show how to find confidence intervals for a variety of other situations.

The second method of statistical inference is hypothesis testing, which is a method for using sample data to determine whether a specific statement about a population may be true. In Chapter 6, we used a chi-square test to determine if there was a statistically significant relationship between two categorical variables. That procedure was an example of a hypothesis test. We will illustrate the concepts of hypothesis testing by demonstrating their use for proportions in the next chapter (11), then elaborate on the use of hypothesis tests for some other situations in Chapter 13. ◆

10.1 | THE LANGUAGE AND NOTATION OF ESTIMATION

To make our discussion of estimation clear, let's summarize and review some of the language and notation associated with the estimation problem.

- ◆ A **unit** is an individual person or object to be measured.
- ◆ The **population** (or **universe**) is the entire collection of units about which we would like information or the entire collection of measurements we would have if we could measure the whole population. The population might be imagined rather than actual, such as the population of outcomes if 100,000 coin flips were to be conducted.
- ◆ The **sample** is the collection of units we will actually measure or the collection of measurements we will actually obtain.
- ◆ The **sample size,** denoted by the letter n, is the number of units or measurements in the sample.
- ◆ The symbol p denotes the **population proportion,** the fraction of the population that has a certain trait or characteristic or the probability of success in a binomial experiment. The value of the *parameter p* is not known; the sample proportion estimates it.
- ◆ The symbol $\hat{p}$ denotes the **sample proportion,** the fraction of the sample that has a certain trait or characteristic. The *statistic $\hat{p}$* is an estimate of p.

Finally, remember that we would ideally like to have a *randomly selected sample* from the population, but in Chapters 3 and 4 we learned that is not always possible and that sometimes we can settle for less. Let's review the crucial criterion for statistical inference to be valid.

> *definition* The **Fundamental Rule for Using Data for Inference** is that available data can be used to make inferences about a much larger group *if the data can be considered to be representative with regard to the question(s) of interest.*

10.1

turn on your mind

Each day, Maria gets dozens of e-mail messages. She keeps track of what proportion of the messages are "junk" and what proportion are interesting each day. If the collection of messages on a single day is considered to be a sample of all e-mail messages she ever receives, explain the meaning of each of the definitions in this section in the context of this example. Discuss whether you think the Fundamental Rule for Using Data for Inference would allow Maria to draw conclusions about the population proportion based on a sample proportion.*

10.2 | MARGIN OF ERROR

In our imaginary survey of student opinion about the legalization of marijuana, we raised questions about the accuracy of a sample estimate. One commonly reported measure of accuracy is the margin of error, a number that provides a likely upper limit for the difference between $\hat{p}$, the sample proportion, and p, the unknown population proportion that we're trying to estimate.

The Meaning of the Margin of Error Given with Survey Results

The **margin of error** provided in media descriptions of survey results has these characteristics:

◆ The difference between the sample proportion and the population proportion is *less* than the margin of error *about 95% of the time,* or for about 19 of every 20 sample estimates.

◆ The difference between the sample proportion and the population proportion is *more* than the margin of error *about 5% of the time,* or for about 1 of every 20 sample estimates.

In other words, for most sample estimates, about 95% of them, the actual error is quite likely to be smaller than the margin of error. Occasionally, about 5% of the time, the error might be larger than the margin of error. Unfortunately, we never know the actual amount of error in a particular estimate. We only know that most of the time the actual error is less than the reported margin of error.

Some polling organizations use the phrase "95% confidence" in conjunction with the margin of error. As we'll see later, researchers occasionally determine a value for the margin of error associated with a "confidence level" other than 95%. For instance, a margin of error associated with 90% confidence has the characteristic that the actual sampling error will be less than this number for about 90% of all sample estimates.

EXAMPLE 10.1
Teens and Interracial Dating:
Case Study 1.3 Revisited

In Case Study 1.3, we described a 1997 *USA Today*/Gallup Poll of teenagers in which one finding was that 57% of the 496 teens in the sample who date said they had been out on a date with someone of another race or ethnic group. The margin of error for this estimate was about 4.5%.

What does the margin of error indicate about the difference between *the sample estimate* of 57% and *the true percent* of all dating American teens who have been out on a date with someone of another race or ethnic group? The answer is that in surveys of this size, the difference between the sample and population percents is likely to be less than 4.5% one way or the other. There is, however, a small chance that the sample estimate might be off by more than 4.5%. ◆

EXAMPLE 10.2
If I Won the Lottery I'd Consider Quitting

What would you do for the rest of your life if you won a lot of money in a lottery? In a 1997 poll conducted by the Gallup Organization, one of the questions was "If you won 10 million dollars in the lottery would you continue to work, or would you stop working?" The results were reported at the Gallup Organization's website (www.gallup.com).

Surprisingly, 59% of the 616 employed respondents answered that they would continue working, 40% said they would stop working, and 1% had no opinion. The website article also gave this information about the poll:

> The current results are based on telephone interviews with a randomly selected sample of 1,014 adults, conducted August 22–25, 1997. Among this group, 616 are employed full-time or part-time. For results based on this sample of "workers," one can say with 95% confidence that the error attributable to sampling could be plus or minus 4 percentage points.

Gallup describes the margin of error with the phrase "could be plus or minus 4 percentage points," but the phrase "could be *as large as* plus or minus 4 percentage points" would have been more informative. The margin of error is a likely upper limit on the sampling error. Here, there is a 95% chance that the sampling error is actually smaller than 4 percentage points. ◆

10.3 | CONFIDENCE INTERVALS

One of the most common types of inference procedures is to construct a *confidence interval* estimate of the unknown value of a population parameter.

> *definition* A **confidence interval** is an interval of values computed from sample data that is likely to include the true population value.

Here is a typical confidence interval statement: "Based on this sample, we have 95% confidence that somewhere between 33% and 39% of all Americans suffer from allergies." Notice that this statement conveys a range of estimates of a population value as well as the likelihood that the interval does indeed capture the population value.

The phrase **confidence level** is used to describe the chance that an interval actually contains the true population value in the following sense. Most of the time (quantified by the confidence level) intervals computed in this way will capture the truth about the population, but occasionally they will not. In any given instance, the interval either captures the truth or it does not, but we will never know which is the case. Therefore, our confidence is in the *procedure*—it works most of the time—and the "confidence level" or "level of confidence" is the percent of the time we expect it to work. For instance, a 95% confidence level means that confidence intervals computed using the same procedure will include the true population value for 95% of all possible random samples from the population. In practice, we can't know for sure whether our confidence interval actually does capture the population value. We can feel fairly certain that it does because the procedure that we use will be successful most of the time.

---

in summary | Interpreting the Confidence Level

♦ For a confidence interval, the **confidence level** is the probability that the procedure used to determine the interval will provide an interval that includes the population parameter.

♦ The confidence level has a relative frequency probability interpretation: If we consider all possible randomly selected samples of the same size from a population, the *confidence level* is the fraction or percent of those samples for which the confidence interval includes the population parameter.

Note: It is commonplace to express the confidence level as a percent.

The most common confidence level that researchers use is 95%. In other words, researchers define "likely to include the true population value " to mean that they are 95% certain the procedure will work. So, they are willing to take a 5% risk that the interval does not actually include the true value. Sometimes researchers employ only 90% confidence, and occasionally they use higher confidence levels like 98% or 99%.

It would be wonderful to be 100% confident that a confidence interval contains the population value. Unfortunately, 100% confidence is impossible unless either we sample the entire population or we provide an absurdly wide interval of estimates. For instance, if we said that the percent of American college students who think marijuana should be legalized is somewhere between 0% and 100%, we would have 100% confidence that we're right. The cost of a high confidence level might be that the interval is so wide that it's not informative.

Constructing a 95% Confidence Interval for a Population Proportion

formula   An approximate 95% confidence interval for a population proportion is easy to calculate once the appropriate margin of error is known. The interval is

Sample estimate ± Margin of error

In the long run, about 95% of all confidence intervals computed in this way will capture the population value of the proportion, and about 5% of them will miss the population value.

Be careful when giving information about a specific confidence interval computed from an observed sample. The confidence level only expresses how often the confidence interval procedure works in the long run. It does not tell us the probability that a specific interval includes the population value. For example, suppose that a 95% confidence interval estimate of the percent of all Americans suffering from allergies is 33% to 39%. This interval either does or does not include the true unknown value of the population percent, but we can never know which is the case because we can't know the population value.

EXAMPLE 10.1—*CONTINUED*
Teens and Interracial Dating

The *USA Today*/Gallup Poll finding was that 57% of the dating teens in the sample had been out with somebody of another race or ethnic group. The margin of error for this estimate was reported as 4.5%. Consequently, a 95% confidence interval is 57% ± 4.5%, which is 52.5% to 61.5%. We have 95% confidence that somewhere between 52.5% and 61.5% of all American teens who date have gone out with somebody of another race or ethnic group. ◆

EXAMPLE 10.2—*CONTINUED*
Winning the
Lottery and Work

What percent of the entire American employed adult population would say they would quit working if they won the lottery? In the Gallup Poll described in Example 10.2, the sample estimate of this percent was 40% and the margin of error was 4%. A 95% confidence interval estimate is

$$\text{Sample percentage} \pm \text{Margin of error}$$
$$40\% \pm 4\%$$
$$36\% \text{ to } 44\%$$

With 95% confidence, we can say that somewhere between 36% and 44% of working Americans would say they would quit working if they won $10 million in the lottery.

Notice that the interval does not cover 50%; it resides completely below 50%. Therefore, it would be fair to conclude, with high confidence, that fewer than half of all working Americans think they would quit if they won the lottery (and more than half think they would continue working). ◆

10.2

turn on your mind

Explain in your own words what it means to say that we have 95% confidence in the interval estimate. Then give an example of something you do in your life that illustrates the same concept—you follow the same procedure each time, and it either works (most of the time) or does not work to produce the desired result. What confidence level would you assign to the procedure in your example; i.e., what percent of the time do you think it produces your desired result?*

10.4 CALCULATING A MARGIN OF ERROR FOR 95% CONFIDENCE

The margin of error of $1/\sqrt{n}$ given in Chapter 4 is actually a conservative approximation that works best when p is close to .5. The formula given next describes a more accurate margin of error for the *proportion* of the sample that has a particular trait. A proportion is a fraction or decimal fraction that has a value between 0 and 1. To determine the margin of error for a percent, first calculate the margin of error for the proportion and then multiply by 100.

*HINT: What is a task you frequently perform that you can't always do successfully?

Calculating the 95% Margin of Error for a Proportion

formula For a 95% confidence level, a formula for the approximate **margin of error for a sample proportion** is

$$\text{Margin of error} \approx 2\sqrt{\frac{\hat{p}(1 - \hat{p})}{n}}$$

Recall that in Section 9.2, we learned that the **standard error of a sample proportion** is

$$\text{s.e.}(\hat{p}) = \sqrt{\frac{\hat{p}(1 - \hat{p})}{n}}$$

Thus, the "95% margin of error" is simply two standard errors, or 2 s.e.($\hat{p}$).

Notice from the formula that three factors determine the margin of error.

1. *The sample size, n.* When the sample size is increased, the margin of error decreases. The effect of sample size on margin of error is intuitive. It makes sense that the accuracy of an estimate will improve when the sample size is increased.
2. *The sample proportion, $\hat{p}$.* Within this context, $\hat{p}$ is a measure of the natural variability among the units. If the proportion is close to either 1 or 0 most individuals have the same trait or opinion, so there is little natural variability and the margin of error is smaller than if the proportion is near .5.
3. *The "multiplier" 2.* This multiplier is connected to the "95% of the time" aspect of the margin of error. Later in the chapter, you'll learn how to change the multiplier in order to change the confidence level. The general theory for the multiplier comes from the normal curve approximation rule for sample proportions described in Section 9.2.

Technical Detail: For reasons explained in Section 10.5, the precise multiplier is 1.96, so the 95% margin of error would be more precisely computed as 1.96 s.e.($\hat{p}$). Using the value 2 as the multiplier provides a 95.44% confidence level, which is of course approximately 95%. Using the value 2 rather than 1.96 gives a more direct connection to the Empirical Rule, and we generally will compute the 95% margin of error as 2 s.e.($\hat{p}$).

10.3

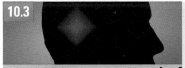

turn on your mind

As noted toward the end of Section 9.2, s.e.($\hat{p}$) is an estimate of s.d.($\hat{p}$), and it is generally very close. Use the Empirical Rule from Chapters 2 and 8, and the Normal Curve Approximation Rule for Sample Proportions from Section 9.2 to draw a picture of possible sample proportions, using s.e.($\hat{p}$) in place of s.d.($\hat{p}$). Show what percent of sample proportions you expect to fall into the ranges:

Population proportion $\pm$ s.e.($\hat{p}$)
Population proportion $\pm$ 2 s.e.($\hat{p}$)
Population proportion $\pm$ 3 s.e.($\hat{p}$)

Then identify what connection margin of error has with the value "95%" in this picture.*

EXAMPLE 10.3
The Pollen Count
Must Be High Today

In April of 1998, the Marist College Institute for Public Opinion surveyed a random sample of 883 American adults about allergies. According to a report posted at the Institute's website (www.mipo.marist.edu), 36% of the sample answered "yes" to the question "Are you allergic to anything?" The sample proportion is $\hat{p} = .36$ and $n = 883$, so the margin of error is

$$95\% \text{ margin or error} \approx 2 \times \sqrt{\frac{\hat{p}(1 - \hat{p})}{n}}$$

$$= 2 \times \sqrt{\frac{.36(1 - .36)}{883}} = .032$$

A 95% confidence interval is $.36 \pm .032$, which is roughly .33 to .39. We can be 95% confident that somewhere between 33% and 39% of all adult Americans have allergies. Remember that the confidence level describes our confidence in the procedure used to determine the interval. In the long run, the procedure will be correct about 95% of the time. ◆

EXAMPLE 10.4
College Men and Ear Pierces

During the 1990s, it became more common for American men, particularly young men, to wear an earring. In class surveys done between 1996 and 1998 in statistics classes at Penn State, 141 of 565 college men indicated that they had at least one ear pierce. The sample proportion with an ear pierce was $\hat{p} = 141/565 = .25$. The approximate margin of error for a 95% confidence level is

$$2\sqrt{\frac{.25(1 - .25)}{565}} = .036$$

A 95% confidence interval for the population proportion is $.25 \pm .036$. This is .214 to .286 which, in percentage terms, is 21.4% to 28.6%.

There is an important question that should be asked about this sample, which is: What population does it represent? Because all 565 men were from the same school, the sample may not represent all college men in the United States. It may not even represent all Penn State men because the surveyed classes were taken only by students in the liberal arts and social sciences. Perhaps the population represented is Penn State men in the liberal arts and social sciences.

Another difficulty here is that the sample was a convenience sample that simply included the men who happened to be in certain classes. In the theoretical development of a 95% confidence interval, the assumption is that we have a random sample. Rather than attempting to use the sample to estimate a population proportion, maybe we only should report that 25% of these 565 men had at least one ear pierce. It can be argued, however, that even though the sample was not randomly selected, it is likely to be representative of a larger group and therefore can be used to make inferences about that group. ◆

The Conservative Estimate of Margin of Error

The formula $1/\sqrt{n}$ provides a **conservative estimate of the margin of error** in that it usually overestimates the actual size of the margin of error. This conservative number is used by polling organizations so they can report a single margin of error for all questions on a survey. The more precise formula involves the sample proportion, so the exact margin of error might change from one question to the next within the same survey. The formula $1/\sqrt{n}$ provides a margin of error that works (conservatively) for all questions based on the same sample size, even if the sample proportions differ from one question to the next.

How do we reconcile the two different formulas for the margin of error? The two formulas for the margin of error are equivalent when the proportion used in the more complicated formula is .5. When we use .5 for $\hat{p}$, the margin of error is

$$2 \times \sqrt{\frac{.5(1 - .5)}{n}} = \frac{1}{\sqrt{n}}$$

An important part of this story is that when you use any proportion other than .5 in the more exact formula, the answer is smaller than what you get when you use .5. This means that the conservative formula will almost always overestimate the size of the margin of error.

EXAMPLE 10.5
The Gallup Poll Margin of Error for n = 1000

The Gallup Organization often uses random samples of about 1000 randomly selected Americans. For $n = 1000$ the conservative estimate of margin of error is $1/\sqrt{1000} = .032$, or about 3.2%. ◆

EXAMPLE 10.3—CONTINUED
Allergies and Really Bad Allergies

In the Marist Institute allergy survey, about 3% said they experienced "severe" allergy symptoms. The sample size is $n = 883$, so the conservative margin of error is $1/\sqrt{883} = .034$, or 3.4%. Using this conservative margin of error, a 95% confidence interval estimate of the percent of all Americans who have severe allergies is 3% ± 3.4%, or −0.4% to 6.4%. Notice that the lower end of this interval is negative, an impossible value for a population percentage.

Generally, when the sample proportion $\hat{p}$ is far from .5, as it is for the severe allergy symptoms group, the conservative margin of error is too conservative. Using $\hat{p} = .03$ in the more complicated exact formula produces .011 or 1.1% as the margin of error value. The corresponding 95% confidence interval estimate of the population percent with severe allergy symptoms is 3% ± 1.1%, which is 1.9% to 4.1%. ◆

10.4

turn on your mind

Suppose the legislature in a particular state wanted to know what proportion of students graduating from the state university last year were permanent residents of the state. The university had information for all students, and it showed that 3900 of the 5000 graduates were state residents. Is a confidence interval appropriate for this situation? If so, compute the appropriate interval. If not, explain why not.*

10.5 | GENERAL THEORY OF CONFIDENCE INTERVALS FOR A PROPORTION

First, we'll consider the theory behind the development of a 95% confidence interval and then we'll learn how to compute intervals with other confidence levels.

***HINT:** Do the 5000 graduates constitute a sample or a population?

Developing the 95% Confidence Interval

The key to developing a 95% confidence interval for a proportion is the Normal Curve Approximation Rule for Sample Proportions described in Chapter 9. That rule describes the distribution of the sample proportions that would occur if we took many different random samples of the same size from a population. By this rule, if the sample size is sufficiently large, the distribution of possible values of $\hat{p}$ is approximately a normal curve. For this normal distribution,

◆ The mean is p, the population proportion.

◆ The standard deviation is

$$\sqrt{\frac{p(1-p)}{n}}$$

Because the distribution of possible sample proportions has a normal curve, we can use the Empirical Rule to make the following statement: *In about 95% of all samples, the sample proportion $\hat{p}$ will fall within 2 standard deviations of p, the true population proportion, so for about 95% of all samples,*

$$-2 \text{ standard deviations} < \hat{p} - p < 2 \text{ standard deviations}$$

This means that in about 95% of all samples, the difference between the sample proportion and the true population proportion is less than 2 standard deviations. The previous sentence basically defines the 95% margin of error.

We have one difficulty. The standard deviation formula involves p, the true population proportion, a value that we don't know. The obvious solution is to put $\hat{p}$, the sample proportion, in the place of p, the standard deviation formula. As discussed in Chapter 9, when this is done, many researchers use the phrase **standard error** to describe the result. Let's review that terminology.

> *definition* The **standard error of a sample proportion,** denoted by s.e.$(\hat{p})$, is
>
> $$\text{s.e.}(\hat{p}) = \sqrt{\frac{\hat{p}(1-\hat{p})}{n}}$$

If we assume that the standard error of $\hat{p}$ is a reasonably close approximation to the standard deviation of $\hat{p}$, we can use the standard error in place of the standard deviation. So, for approximately 95% of all random samples from a population, the difference between the sample proportion and the population proportion is described by the mathematical inequality

$$-2 \text{ standard errors} < \hat{p} - p < 2 \text{ standard errors}$$

This mathematical inequality says that in about 95% of all samples, the difference between the sample proportion and the population proportion is less than 2 standard errors. With two steps of algebra, this inequality can be changed to

$$\hat{p} - 2 \text{ standard errors} < p < \hat{p} + 2 \text{ standard errors}$$

This holds for about 95% of all samples and thus provides the formula for the 95% confidence interval.

in summary   General Description of the Approximate 95% Confidence Interval for a Proportion

An approximate 95% confidence interval for a population proportion is

$\hat{p} \pm 2$ standard errors

The standard error is

$$\text{s.e.}(\hat{p}) = \sqrt{\frac{\hat{p}(1 - \hat{p})}{n}}$$

Interpretation: For about 95% of all randomly selected samples from the population, the confidence interval computed in this manner captures the population proportion.

Necessary Conditions: The confidence interval derived from the normal curve can safely be used when $n\hat{p}$ and $n(1 - \hat{p})$ are both greater than 10. It is also assumed that the sample is randomly selected.

Reminders

1. The confidence level describes the chance that the procedure we use to determine the interval will work. For a specific sample, we won't know whether or not the confidence interval actually contains the population proportion. With a 95% confidence level, we know there's a good chance that the interval contains the population value, because it will for approximately 95% of all possible random samples from the population.
2. The exact multiplier for a 95% confidence interval is 1.96, but it is common practice to round this multiplier to 2.

Other Levels of Confidence and Other Types of Confidence Intervals

Researchers don't always use the 95% confidence level. Occasionally, they use a lower level like 90%, and sometimes they use a higher level like 98%. Additionally, researchers estimate many different types of parameters. In Chapter 12, we will learn procedures for finding confidence intervals for means, differences in two means, and differences in two proportions. All of these situations can be accommodated by one general formula. The details for the formula change based on the situation, but the format of the calculation remains the same.

General Format for Confidence Intervals for Proportions and Means

formula   For any confidence level, whether it's 95% or some other value, a confidence interval for either a population proportion or a population mean can be expressed as

Sample estimate $\pm$ Multiplier $\times$ Standard error

The multiplier is affected by the choice of confidence level.

TABLE 10.1 ■ Confidence Intervals for a Population Proportion

Confidence Level	Multiplier	Confidence Interval
90	1.645 or 1.65	$\hat{p} \pm 1.65$ standard errors
95	1.96, often rounded to 2	$\hat{p} \pm 2$ standard errors
98	2.33	$\hat{p} \pm 2.33$ standard errors
99	2.58	$\hat{p} \pm 2.58$ standard errors

For a 95% confidence level, the appropriate **multiplier** is close to 2 and is often rounded off to 2. To change the *confidence level,* we simply change the *multiplier.* The larger the multiplier, the greater the confidence. A multiplier larger than 2 provides a confidence level higher than 95% because the interval will be wider than the 95% confidence interval. If the multiplier is smaller than 2, the confidence level will be lower than 95%.

For confidence intervals for proportions, the normal curve is used to determine the multiplier for a specific confidence level. For example, for any normal curve, about 98% of the values are within plus or minus 2.33 standard deviations of the mean. Using the Normal Curve Approximation Rule for Sample Proportions in the same way we did for a 95% confidence interval, we can determine that the correct multiplier for a 98% confidence interval is 2.33 and the associated confidence interval is $\hat{p} \pm 2.33$ standard errors.

Table 10.1 shows the multipliers and the corresponding confidence intervals for four frequently used confidence levels. Notice that when the confidence level increases, the value of the multiplier also increases. With a greater multiplier, the width of the interval will increase. With a wider interval, we'll be more confident that we've captured the population proportion.

EXAMPLE 10.6
Is There Intelligent Life on Other Planets?

In a 1997 Marist Institute survey of 935 randomly selected Americans, 60% of the sample answered "yes" to the question "Do you think there is intelligent life on other planets?" (*Source:* www.mipo.marist.edu). Let's use this sample estimate to calculate a 90% confidence interval for the proportion of all Americans who believe there is intelligent life on other planets. The sample proportion is $\hat{p} = .60$ and $n = 935$. The standard error of the sample proportion is

$$\text{s.e.}(\hat{p}) = \sqrt{\frac{.6(1-.6)}{935}} = .016$$

For a 90% confidence level, the multiplier in Table 10.1 is 1.65, and a 90% confidence interval for the population proportion is

$$.60 \pm 1.65 \times .016$$
$$.60 \pm .026$$

With 90% confidence, we can say that in 1997 the proportion of Americans who believed there is intelligent life on other planets was in the range $.60 \pm .026$ (or, $60\% \pm 2.6\%$).

For 98% confidence, the interval is *sample proportion $\pm$ 2.33 standard errors.* The calculation is $.60 \pm 2.33 \times .016$, which is $.60 \pm .037$. When converted to percents, the 98% confidence interval is $60\% \pm 3.7\%$. We can be fairly sure that in

1997 roughly between 56% and 64% of Americans believed there is life on other planets. Because the entire interval is above 50%, we can also state with high confidence that in 1997 a majority of Americans believed there is intelligent life on other planets. ◆

---

in summary   Formula for a Confidence Interval for a Population Proportion p

A formula for the confidence interval for a population proportion is

$$\hat{p} \pm z^* \sqrt{\frac{\hat{p}(1 - \hat{p})}{n}}$$

where

- ◆ $\hat{p}$ is the sample proportion.
- ◆ z^* denotes the multiplier.
- ◆ $\sqrt{\dfrac{\hat{p}(1 - \hat{p})}{n}}$ is the standard error of the sample proportion.

Table 10.1 has z^* multipliers for the most commonly used confidence levels. The multiplier z^* is such that the area under the standard normal curve between $-z^*$ and z^* corresponds to the confidence level.

Conditions for Using the Formula

Whenever we use a sample to infer something about a population, we have to be sure that the sample satisfies certain conditions. In order to use the procedure described here, we should verify that data meet two conditions:

1. The sample is a randomly selected sample from the population.
2. The normal curve approximation to the distribution of possible sample proportions assumes a "large" sample size. Both $n\hat{p}$ and $n(1 - \hat{p})$ should be at least 10 (although some authors say these quantities need only to be at least 5).

The first condition is an idealistic one that is sometimes difficult to achieve. A more lenient condition is given by the Fundamental Rule for Using Data for Inference, which we repeat here: Available data can be used to make inferences about a much larger group *if the data can be considered to be representative with regard to the question(s) of interest.* In the context of this chapter, a confidence interval based on a sample proportion can be used to estimate the population proportion if the individuals in the sample can be considered to be representative of the individuals in the population for the trait, opinion, etc. of interest.

More About the Multiplier z^*

In the formula for a confidence interval for a proportion, the multiplier z^* is the standardized score such that the area between $-z^*$ and $+z^*$ under the standard normal curve corresponds to the desired confidence level. Figure 10.2 illustrates this relationship. In practice, it would be unusual for anybody to use a confidence

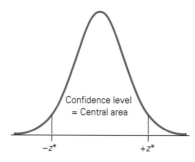

FIGURE 10.2 **The relationship between the confidence level and the multiplier z*. The confidence level is the probability between −z* and z* in the standard normal curve.**

FIGURE 10.3 **Finding z* for the 50% confidence level**

level other than the four shown in Table 10.1. Theoretically, however, any confidence level could be specified, and the standard normal curve would be used to determine the associated z^* multiplier.

EXAMPLE 10.6—CONTINUED
50% Confidence Interval for Proportion Believing Intelligent Life Exists Elsewhere

Suppose we want a 50% confidence interval for the 1997 proportion that believed intelligent life exists elsewhere. Figure 10.3 illustrates the problem that we have to solve in order to find the z^* value for a 50% confidence level. To use the Standard Normal Curve table in Appendix A.1, we observe from Figure 10.3 that if the area between $-z^*$ and $+z^*$ is .50, the area to the right of z^* is .25 and so the area to the left of z^* is .75. From Appendix A.1, we learn that the z-value for which the cumulative probability is .75 is about $z^* = .67$. This means that a 50% confidence interval for a population proportion is *sample proportion* $\pm$ *.67 standard errors,* which in this example is $.60 \pm .67 \times .016$, or $.60 \pm .011$. Notice that this interval is more narrow than the 90% and 98% confidence intervals computed previously. Using a lower confidence level produces a more narrow interval. ◆

10.5

turn on your mind

Suppose that we collect data on "hours of sleep last night" from 64 students who are present at an 11:00 A.M. statistics class. The sample mean is 6.8 hours, the standard deviation of the data is 1.6 hours, and the standard error of the mean is 0.2 hours. What population, if any, is represented by this sample? Assuming there is a population represented by this sample, explain why we can not use the formula

$$\hat{p} \pm z^* \sqrt{\frac{\hat{p}(1 - \hat{p})}{n}}$$

to compute a 95% confidence interval for the population mean. What general formula in this section could be used to calculate the interval? Calculate the confidence interval.*

Minitab Tab

> **tech note** **Calculating a Confidence Interval for a Proportion**
>
> ♦ To compute a confidence interval for a proportion, use **Stat>Basic Statistics>1 Proportion.** (This procedure is not in versions earlier than Version 12.)
>
> ♦ If the raw data are in a column of the worksheet, specify that column. If the data have already been summarized, click on "Summarized Data," and then specify the sample size and the count of how many observations have the characteristic of interest.
>
> *Note:* To calculate intervals in the manner described in this chapter, use the *Options* button, and click on "Use test and interval based on normal distribution." Note also that the confidence level can be changed by using the *Options* button.

10.6 | CHOOSING A SAMPLE SIZE FOR A SURVEY

TABLE 10.2 ■ Relationship Between Sample Size and Margin of Error for 95% Confidence

Sample Size n	Margin of Error = $1/\sqrt{n}$
100	.10 (10%)
400	.05 (5%)
625	.04 (4%)
1000	.032 (3.2%)
1600	.025 (2.5%)
2500	.02 (2%)
10,000	.01 (1%)

When surveys are planned, the choice of a sample size is an important issue. One commonly used strategy is to use a **sample size** that provides a **desired margin of error** for a 95% confidence interval. Table 10.2 displays the margin of error for several different sample sizes. The margin of error calculations were done using the "conservative" formula $1/\sqrt{n}$. This is commonly done by polling organizations because, before the sample is observed, there is no way to know what sample proportion to use in the more exact margin of error formula. With a table like Table 10.2, researchers can pick a sample size that provides suitable accuracy for any sample proportion, within the constraints of the time and money available for the survey.

Two important features of Table 10.2 are

1. When the sample size is *increased,* the margin of error *decreases.*
2. When a large sample size is made even larger, the improvement in accuracy is relatively small. For example, when the sample size is increased from 2500 to 10,000, the margin of error only decreases from 2% to 1%. In general, cutting the margin of error in half requires a fourfold increase in sample size.

Polling organizations determine a sample size that is accurate enough for their purposes and is also economical. Many national surveys use a sample size of about 1000 which, as you can see from Table 10.2, makes the margin of error roughly 3%. This is a reasonable degree of accuracy for most questions asked in these surveys.

Some federal government surveys utilize much larger sample sizes, sometimes as large as $n = 120,000$, to make accurate estimates of quantities like the unemployment rate. Also, when researchers want to make accurate estimates for subgroups within the population, they have to use a very large overall sample size. For instance, to get information from approximately 1000 African-American women in the 18- to 29-year-old age group, a random sample of 120,000 Americans might be necessary.

The Effect of Population Size

You might wonder how the number of people in the population affects the accuracy of a survey. The surprising answer is that for most sample surveys, the number of people in the population has almost no influence on the accuracy of sample estimates. The margin of error for a sample size of 1000 is about 3% whether the number of people in the population is 30,000 or 200 million.

The formulas for margin of error in this chapter were derived assuming that the number of units in the population is essentially infinite. In practice, as long as the population is at least 10 times as large as the sample, we consider only how sample size affects accuracy and we ignore the specific size of the population. For small populations a "finite population correction" is used. We will not discuss it in this book, but you can consult any book on survey sampling for details.

10.6

turn on your mind

Suppose that a survey of 400 students at your school is conducted to assess student opinion about a new academic honesty policy. Based on Table 10.2, about what will be the margin of error for the poll? How many students attend your school? Given this figure, do you think the values in Table 10.2 should be used to estimate the margin of error for a survey of students at your school? Explain.*

10.7 | USING CONFIDENCE INTERVALS TO GUIDE DECISIONS

Two research questions that investigators often consider about population proportions are

♦ Is it reasonable to reject a specific hypothesized value of a population proportion?

♦ Is it reasonable to conclude that two proportions are different from each other?

In later chapters, we will learn more efficient and powerful procedures that we can use to study these questions. Confidence intervals, however, can be used as a somewhat informal method for evaluating these issues.

Principles for Using Confidence Intervals to Guide Decision Making

Two important principles are useful for examining these questions. Both principles can be applied to any situation in which confidence intervals are calculated. We state the principles only in the context of proportions, but they can be used to answer questions about population means or any other population parameter.

Principle 1. A value not in a confidence interval can be rejected as a possible value of the population proportion. A value in a confidence interval is an "acceptable" possibility for the value of a population proportion.

*HINT: The sample size is $n = 400$. Is the number of students at your school more than 10 times this sample size?

Principle 2. When the confidence intervals for proportions in two different populations do not overlap, it is reasonable to conclude that the two population proportions are different.

In Chapter 12 we will learn how to find a confidence interval directly for the difference between two population proportions, and we will also learn how to find a confidence interval estimate for the difference between two means. A direct confidence interval for the difference is more efficient than the use of Principle 2 for comparing two population proportions (or means), but if a difference is found using Principle 2, it provides clear evidence of a real difference in the population proportions.

To better understand Principles 1 and 2, let's look at some examples.

EXAMPLE 10.7
Which Drink Tastes Better?

Imagine a taste test done to compare two different soft drinks. In the test, 60 people taste both drinks and 55% of these 60 participants say they like the taste of drink A better than the taste of drink B. The makers of drink A will be excited that their drink was picked by more than half of the sample and might even create commercials to brag about the results. The makers of drink B, however, can use a 95% confidence interval to show that there is not enough evidence to claim that drink A would be preferred by a majority of the population represented by the sample.

An approximate 95% confidence interval for *p*, the population proportion that prefers drink A, is .42 to .68. The calculation is sample proportion ± margin of error:

$$.55 \pm 2 \sqrt{\frac{.55(1 - .55)}{60}}$$
$$.55 \pm .13$$

Here, the confidence interval leaves the issue unsettled. Most of the interval is above .50 so the makers of drink A may argue that it's reasonable to claim that more than half of the population prefers their drink. On the other hand, the makers of drink B can point out that it is possible that a majority of the population actually prefers their drink because the confidence interval also includes some estimates that are less than .50 (50%)—in fact as low as only 42%.

The difficulty with this hypothetical experiment is that it's too small to be definitive. In actual practice, a much larger sample size should be used to generate a more precise estimate of the proportion that prefers drink A. ◆

CASE STUDY 10.1
Extrasensory Perception Works with Movies

Extrasensory perception (ESP) is the apparent ability to obtain information in ways that exclude ordinary sensory channels. Early ESP research focused on having people try to guess at simple targets, like symbols on cards, to see if they could guess at a better rate than would be expected by chance. In recent years, experimenters have used more interesting targets, like photographs, outdoor scenes, or short movie segments.

In a study of ESP reported by Bem and Honorton (1994), subjects called "receivers" described what another person, the "sender," was seeing on a television screen in another room. The receivers were shown four pictures and asked to pick which one they thought the sender had actually seen. The actual image shown to the sender had been randomly picked by the investigators from among these four choices.

Sometimes the sender was looking at a single, "static" image on the television screen and sometimes at a "dynamic" short video clip, played repeatedly. The additional three choices shown to the receiver for judging were always of the same type (static or dynamic) as the actual target to eliminate biases due to a preference for one type of picture.

Results from the experiment are shown in Table 10.3. Because the right answer is one of four possibilities, receivers who are randomly guessing will be right about 25% of the time. For the static pictures, the 27% success rate is about what would be expected from random guessing. The 41% success rate for the dynamic pictures, however, is noticeably higher than the 25% that would result from random guessing.

A skeptic might raise the possibility that the results for the dynamic pictures were the product of good luck. Is there enough evidence to safely say that the percent of correct guesses for the dynamic pictures is significantly above 25%, the percent expected by chance? A confidence interval helps us answer this question.

For the dynamic pictures, the 95% margin of error is

TABLE 10.3 ■ Results of the Bem and Honorton ESP Study

	Successful Guess?			
	Yes	No	Total	Percent Success
Static Picture	45	119	164	27.4%
Dynamic Picture	77	113	190	40.5%

Source: Bem and Honorton, 1994.

$$\text{Margin of error} = 2 \times \sqrt{\frac{.405 \times (1 - .405)}{190}} = .072$$

So, an approximate 95% confidence interval for the proportion is .405 ± .072, which is .333 to .477. In percentage terms, the interval ranges from 33.3% to 47.7%, an interval that does not include 25%. This means that it's reasonable to reject the possibility that the true percent of correct guesses is 25%. The researchers can claim that the true percent of correct guesses is, in fact, significantly better than what would occur from random guessing.

CASE STUDY 10.2
Nicotine Patches Versus Zyban®

Some of you may know from personal experience that quitting smoking is difficult. Many people trying to quit use nicotine replacement methods like nicotine patches or nicotine gum to ease nicotine withdrawal symptoms. Recently, medical researchers have begun investigating whether the use of an antidepressant medication might be a more effective aid to those attempting to give up cigarettes. In a study reported in the March 4, 1999 New England Journal of Medicine, Dr. Douglas Jorenby and colleagues compared the effectiveness of nicotine patches to the effectiveness of the antidepressant buproprion, which is marketed with the brand name Zyban.

The 893 participants were randomly allocated to four treatment groups: placebo, nicotine patch only, Zyban only, and Zyban plus nicotine patch. To keep participants blind as to their treatments, they all used a patch (nicotine or placebo) and took a pill (Zyban or placebo). For instance, in the placebo-only group, participants used both a placebo patch and took placebo pills. The Zyban group also used placebo patches, and so on. The treatments were used for nine weeks.

TABLE 10.4 ■ 95% Confidence Intervals for Proportion Not Smoking after Six Months

Treatment	Subjects	Proportion Not Smoking	Approx. 95% CI
Placebo only	160	.188	.13 to .25
Nicotine patch	244	.213	.16 to .26
Zyban	244	.348	.29 to .41
Zyban and nicotine patch	245	.388	.33 to .44

Table 10.4 displays, for each treatment group, an approximate 95% confidence interval for the proportion not smoking six months after the start of the experiment. Each interval is a range of estimates of the proportion that would not be smoking after six months in a population of individuals using that particular method. A more direct way to compare the four success rates and determine if there are differences will be given in Chapter 15. At this point, we can use the intervals shown in the table to gauge how the four treatments might differ.

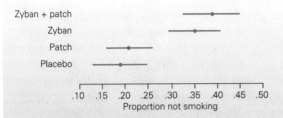

FIGURE 10.4   **95% Confidence intervals for proportion not smoking after six months**

The display in Figure 10.4 compares the 95% confidence intervals graphically, clearly showing an appropriate conclusion for this experiment.

Based on the graph, we can make the following generalizations:

♦ Zyban is effective. The Zyban groups had higher success rates and the confidence intervals for the two groups that used Zyban do not overlap the intervals for the two groups not using Zyban.

♦ The nicotine patch is not particularly effective. There is substantial overlap in the range of estimates in the intervals for the nicotine patch and placebo groups, so we can't conclude that the patch is better than the placebo. Similarly, there is substantial overlap between the intervals for the Zyban-only group and the Zyban-plus-patch group, so these two treatments do not significantly differ.

CASE STUDY 10.3
What a Great Personality

Students in a statistics class at Penn State were asked, "Would you date someone with a great personality even though you did not find them attractive?" By gender, the results were

♦ 61.1% of 131 women answered "yes."

♦ 42.6% of 61 men answered "yes."

There clearly is a difference between the men and the women in these samples. Can this difference be generalized to the populations represented by the samples? This question brings up another question. What are the populations that we're comparing? These men and women weren't randomly picked from any particular population, but for this example we'll assume they are like a random sample from the populations of all American college men and women.

A comparison of the 95% confidence intervals for the population percent will help us make a generalization.

♦ For men, the approximate 95% confidence interval is 30.2% to 55%.

♦ For women, the approximate 95% confidence interval is 52.7% to 69.4%.

The two intervals are compared graphically in Figure 10.5. There's a slight overlap in the range of estimates contained in the two intervals. For the most part, however, the interval

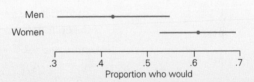

FIGURE 10.5   **95% Confidence intervals for proportions that would date someone with a great personality who wasn't attractive**

for the men is below the interval for the women. It's probably safe to generalize that, compared to college men, a higher proportion of college women would say, "Yes, I would date someone with a great personality even if that someone wasn't attractive." In Chapter 12, we will learn how to find a confidence interval for the *difference* in the proportions of men and women who would answer yes to the question.

We can also see the effect of sample size on interval width in Figure 10.5. The confidence interval for women is not as wide as the interval for men. There were more than twice as many women as there were men in the class, and the larger sample size for women leads to a more precise estimate of the population proportion.

10.7

turn on your mind

A randomly selected sample of 400 students is surveyed about whether additional coed dorms should be created at their school. Of those surveyed, 57% say there should be more coed dorms. The 95% margin of error for the survey is 5%. Compute a 95% confidence interval for the population percent in favor of more coed dorms. Based on this confidence interval, can we conclude that more than 50% of all students favor more coed dorms? Explain. Can we reject the possibility that the population proportion is .60?*

in summary **Finding a Confidence Interval for a Population Proportion**

In this chapter, each method covered for finding a confidence interval estimate of a population proportion (p) is an instance of the same general format, which is

Sample p ± Multiplier × Standard error

The methods covered were:

Confidence interval for p with exact multiplier for any confidence level:

$$\hat{p} \pm z^* \sqrt{\frac{\hat{p}(1 - \hat{p})}{n}}$$

where the symbol $\hat{p}$ represents the sample proportion, and the multiplier z^* is such that the area under the standard normal curve between $-z^*$ and z^* is the confidence level. For 95% confidence, the exact multiplier is $z^* = 1.96$.

Approximate 95% confidence interval for p:

$$\hat{p} \pm 2 \sqrt{\frac{\hat{p}(1 - \hat{p})}{n}}$$

This formula results from rounding the multiplier $z^* = 1.96$ to the value 2. The corresponding confidence level is 95.44%, or approximately 95%.

Conservative 95% confidence interval for p:

$$\hat{p} \pm \frac{1}{\sqrt{n}}$$

This method, which is the simplest, was covered in Chapter 4 as well. It is used by many polling organizations and results from substituting $\hat{p} = .5$ in the formula for the standard error when determining the approximate 95% confidence interval. The confidence level for this procedure generally is greater than 95%.

KEY TERMS

*HINT: See Example 10.7 in Section 10.7 and Example 10.2—*CONTINUED* at the end of Section 10.3.

EXERCISES   Blue = Basics   **Bold, Bold** = Answer in back

Sections 10.1, 10.2, and 10.3

10.1 In each part of this question, explain whether the proportion described is a sample proportion or a population proportion. Also in each part, indicate which of the two notations for a proportion, *p* or $\hat{p}$, should be used to denote the given value.

a. In the 1990 United States Census, it was found that about 1 in 9 Americans were at least 65 years old at that time.

b. A randomly selected group of 500 registered voters in your state is asked whom they intend to vote for in an upcoming election for governor. Based on the proportion choosing each candidate, the polling organization predicts the election winner.

c. In a clinical trial done to assess the effectiveness of a new medication for asthma, a satisfactory relief from symptoms was experienced by 55% of *n* = 80 participants.

10.2 In a 1997 survey done by the Marist College Institute for Public Opinion, 36% of a randomly selected sample of *n* = 935 American adults said they do not get enough sleep each night (*source:* www.mipo.marist.edu). The margin of error was reported to be 3.5%.

a. Use the survey information to create a 95% confidence interval for the percent that feels they don't get enough sleep each night. Write a sentence that interprets this interval. Specify the population.

b. Do you think this sample could be used to estimate the percent of college students who think they don't get enough sleep each night? Why or why not?

10.3 Suppose that a polling organization reports that the margin of error is 4% for a sample survey. Explain what this indicates about the possible difference between a percent determined from the survey data and the population value of the percent.

10.4 A CNN/Time Poll conducted in the United States October 23–24, 2002 asked, "Do you favor or oppose the legalization of marijuana?" In the nationwide poll of *n* = 1007 adults, 34% said they favored legalization. The margin of error was given as 3.1% (*Source:* www.pollingreport.com).

a. Find a 95% confidence interval estimate of the percent of American adults who favored the legalization of marijuana at the time of the poll.

b. Write a sentence that interprets the interval computed in part (a).

10.5. A Gallup Organization poll of *n* = 1004 randomly selected American adults in July 2002 found that 55% of those surveyed felt their weight was about right. The margin of error for the survey was given as 3% (*Source:* www.gallup.com).

a. Find a 95% confidence interval estimate of the percent of American adults who think their weight is about right.

b. Based on the interval computed in part (a), explain whether it is reasonable to say that more than 50% of American adults think their weight is about right.

10.6 In each situation, explain why you think the sample proportion should or should not be used to estimate the population proportion.

a. An Internet news organization asks visitors to its website to respond to the question "Are you satisfied with the president's job performance?" Of *n* = 3500 respondents, 61% say they are not satisfied with the president's performance. Based on this survey, the organization writes an article in which they say that a majority of Americans are not satisfied with the president.

b. A convenience sample of *n* = 400 college students in two classes at the same university is used to estimate the proportion that is left-handed in the nationwide population of college students.

10.7 A federal law that lowered the limit for a legal blood alcohol level for automobile drivers was signed by President Clinton in October 2000. At their website, the Gallup Organization reported the following survey results in an article dated October 26, 2000:

> 72% of Americans support lowering the drunk driving limit to 0.08% BAC. . . . A total 1,002 telephone interviews were conducted between July 20–Aug. 3, 2000, with a representative sample of the U.S. public age 16 and older. The findings are based on 930 respondents who identified themselves as licensed drivers. The margin of error equals plus or minus three percentage points.

a. The first sentence of the information from the Gallup Organization states, "72% of Americans support lowering the drunk driving limit to 0.08% BAC." Considering the difference between a sample and a population, explain why this sentence is not necessarily correct. Rewrite the sentence so that it is correct.

b. The article provides the information that "the margin of error equals plus or minus three percentage points." Write one or two sentences interpreting this value that could be understood by someone who does not know anything about statistics.

c. Using the information provided by the Gallup Organization, calculate a 95% confidence interval for the proportion that supports the lower legal blood alcohol limit. Write a sentence that interprets this interval. Be sure to specify the appropriate population.

d. Based on the interval computed in part (c), is it reasonable to conclude that more than half of American licensed drivers support the lower blood alcohol limit?

10.8 Suppose 200 different researchers all randomly select samples of $n = 400$ individuals from a population. Each researcher uses his or her sample to compute a 95% confidence interval for the proportion that has blue eyes in the population. About how many of the confidence intervals will capture the population proportion? About how many of the intervals will not capture the population proportion? Briefly explain how you determined your answers.

10.9 Suppose that a margin of error for a sample percent is reported to be 3%. What is the probability that the difference between the sample percent and the population percent will be more than 3%? Interpret the meaning of this probability.

10.10 Taking into account the purpose of a confidence interval described in Section 10.3, explain what is wrong with the following statement: "Based on the survey data, a 95% confidence interval estimate of the sample proportion is .095 to .117."

Section 10.4

10.11 For each combination of sample size and sample proportion, find the approximate margin of error for the 95% confidence level.
  a. $n = 100, \hat{p} = .56$.
  b. $n = 400, \hat{p} = .56$.
  c. $n = 400, \hat{p} = .20$.
  d. $n = 400, \hat{p} = .80$.
  e. $n = 1000, \hat{p} = .50$.

10.12 Suppose a new treatment for a certain disease is given to a sample of $n = 200$ patients. The treatment was successful for 166 of the patients. Assume that these patients are representative of the population of individuals who have this disease.
  a. Calculate the sample proportion successfully treated.
  b. Determine a 95% confidence interval for the proportion successfully treated. Write a sentence that interprets this interval.

10.13 In a survey of 190 college students, 134 students said they believe there is extraterrestrial life (*Data source:* **pennstate3** dataset on the CD for this book).
  a. Find $\hat{p}$ = sample proportion that believes there is extraterrestrial life.
  b. Calculate the approximate margin of error for the 95% confidence level.
  c. Using the margin of error found in part (b), find a 95% confidence interval estimate of the proportion of all college students who believe there is extraterrestrial life.

10.14 Suppose a polling organization is conducting a survey to estimate the proportion of Americans who regularly attend religious services. They plan to gather data from a randomly selected sample of 550 individuals. Based on the "conservative" formula, what will be the margin of error for the survey?

10.15 In a poll done by Princeton Survey Research Associates in October of 1998 for *Newsweek Magazine,* 56% of 753 randomly sampled American adults answered "yes" to the question "Do you personally believe that abortion is wrong?" (*Source:* www.pollingreport.com/abortion.htm.)
  a. Calculate the margin of error necessary for a 95% confidence interval.
  b. Calculate a 95% confidence interval for the percent of all Americans who believe that abortion is wrong.
  c. Based on this confidence interval, is it reasonable to conclude that more than half of all Americans think abortion is wrong? Explain.

10.16 In a Gallup Youth Survey done in 2000, $n = 501$ randomly selected American teenagers were asked about how well they get along with their parents.
  a. According to the Gallup Organization, the margin of error for the poll was 5%. Verify that this figure is approximately correct.
  b. A survey result was that 54% of the sample said they get along "very well" with their parents. Using the reported margin of error, calculate a 95% confidence interval for the population proportion that gets along "very well" with their parents. Write a sentence that interprets this interval.
  c. Using the more exact formula for margin of error in Section 10.4, calculate a 95% confidence interval. Compare the answer to the answer in part (b).
  d. Another result in the same survey was that only 5% said that cheating on exams was "not at all serious." Using the reported margin of error, compute a 95% confidence interval for the population proportion that would say this. Also, compute the 95% confidence interval using the more exact formula for margin of error. Which interval is narrower?
  e. You should have found that the intervals in parts (b) and (c) were quite similar to each other, but the two intervals computed in part (d) were not. Explain why the two intervals agreed more closely in parts (b) and (c) than they did in part (d).

10.17 In Example 10.3—*CONTINUED* the information given was that 3% of a nationwide randomly selected sample of $n = 883$ suffered from severe allergies.
  a. Determine the standard error of the sample proportion in this problem.
  b. Verify that the margin of error is about 1.1% for a 95% confidence interval for the percent that suffers from severe allergies in the population represented by this sample.

Section 10.5

10.18 For each confidence interval procedure, provide the confidence level.
  a. Sample proportion $\pm 1.645 \times$ standard error.
  b. Sample proportion $\pm 2 \times$ standard error.
  c. Sample proportion $\pm 2.33 \times$ standard error.
  d. Sample proportion $\pm 2.58 \times$ standard error.

10.19 Explain whether the width of a confidence interval would increase, decrease, or remain the same as a result of each of the following changes:
  a. Increase the confidence level from 95% to 99%.

b. Decrease the confidence level from 95% to 90%.

10.20 In a randomly selected sample of $n = 400$ registered voters in a community, 220 individuals say they plan to vote for Candidate Y in the upcoming election.

    a. Find $\hat{p}$ = sample proportion planning to vote for candidate Y.

    b. Calculate the standard error of the sample proportion.

    c. Find a 95% confidence interval for the proportion of the registered voter population who plan to vote for Candidate Y.

    d. Find a 98% confidence interval for the proportion of the registered voter population who plan to vote for Candidate Y.

10.21 In an ABC News.com nationwide poll done in 2001, the proportion of respondents who thought it should be illegal to use a handheld cellular telephone while driving a car was $\hat{p} = .69$ (69%). The poll's sample size was $n = 1027$.

    a. Find the value of the standard error of the sample proportion.

    b. Find a 95% confidence interval estimate of the population proportion that thinks it should be illegal to use a cellular telephone while driving.

    c. Find a 90% confidence interval estimate of the population proportion that thinks it should be illegal to use a cellular telephone while driving.

10.22 Refer to Example 10.6 of this chapter where for a sample of $n = 935$ American adults, $\hat{p} = .60$ was the proportion that thinks intelligent life exists elsewhere. Compute a 99% confidence interval for the population proportion.

10.23 Refer to exercise 10.12. Calculate a 98% confidence interval for the proportion successfully treated. Is this interval wider or narrower than the interval computed in part (b) of exercise 10.12?

10.24 A randomly selected sample of $n = 15$ individuals is asked whether they are right-handed or left-handed. In the sample, only one person is left-handed. Explain why a confidence interval for the population proportion should not be computed using the methods described in this chapter.

10.25 Determine the value of the z^* multiplier that would be used to compute an 80% confidence interval for a population proportion.

Sections 10.6 and 10.7

10.26 Suppose that a researcher is designing a survey to estimate the proportion of adults in your state who oppose a proposed law that requires all automobile passengers to wear a seat belt.

    a. What would be the approximate margin of error if the researcher randomly sampled 400 adults?

    b. What sample size would be needed to provide a margin of error of about 2%?

10.27 Explain whether the width of a confidence interval would increase, decrease, or remain the same as a result of each of the following changes.

    a. Increase the sample size from 1000 to 2000.

    b. Decrease the sample size from 1000 to 500.

    c. Increase the population size from 10 million to 20 million.

10.28 Suppose a health expert has claimed that 28% of college students smoke cigarettes. To investigate this claim, researchers survey a random sample of college students. Using this sample, a 95% confidence interval for the percent of college students who smoke is found to be 19% to 24%. Based on this interval, explain whether the claim that 28% of all college students smoke is reasonable or not.

10.29 A university is contemplating switching from the quarter system to a semester system. The administration conducts a survey of a random sample of 400 students and finds that 240 of them prefer to remain on the quarter system.

    a. Construct a 95% confidence interval for the true proportion of all students who would prefer to remain on the quarter system.

    b. Does the interval you computed in part (a) provide convincing evidence that more than half of all students prefer to remain on the quarter system? Explain.

10.30 In which of the following three samples will the margin of error be the smallest? Explain. Assume that each sample is a random sample.

    Sample A: sample of $n = 1000$ from a population of 10 million.

    Sample B: sample of $n = 2500$ from a population of 200 million.

    Sample C: sample of $n = 400$ from a population of 50,000.

10.31 Suppose that a 95% confidence interval for the proportion of men who experience sleep apnea (irregular breathing during sleep) is .11 to .17 and a 95% confidence interval for the proportion of women who experience sleep apnea is .04 to .08. Based on these intervals, is it reasonable to conclude that the population proportions experiencing sleep apnea differ for men and women? Explain.

10.32 A college dean plans a student survey to estimate the percent of presently enrolled students who plan to take classes during the next summer session. She wants the 95% margin of error for the estimate to be at most 5%. What is the necessary sample size?

10.33 An epidemiologist plans a survey to estimate the prevalence of Alzheimer's disease in the population of adults aged 65 years or older. It's desired that the 95% margin of error for the sample estimate be no more than 3%. What sample size is needed?

10.34 Exercise 10.5 describes a 2002 Gallup Organization poll in which the finding was that 55% of adult Americans surveyed said their weight was about right. The margin of error for the survey was 3%. The website article about this survey also contained the information that in a 1990 survey done by Gallup, 46% of the respondents thought their weight was about right. Assuming the margin of error for the 1990 survey was also 3%, discuss whether it is reasonable to conclude that the population percent thinking their weight is about right is higher in 2002 than in 1990.

Chapter Exercises

10.35 In Case Study 10.1, we saw the results of an ESP experiment in which there was a 1/4 chance of correct response if the "receiver" was merely guessing at what image a "sender" in another room was viewing. For static images, the "receivers" responded correctly in 45 of 164 trials.

a. Calculate the sample proportion of correct guesses at the static images.

b. Calculate the standard error for this sample proportion.

c. Calculate a 95% confidence interval for the true proportion of correct guesses at static images.

d. Based on the confidence interval in part (c), do you think that these data provide evidence that there is extrasensory perception? Explain.

10.36 Suppose that in a random sample $n = 300$ of employed Americans, there are 57 individuals who say they would fire their boss if they could. Calculate a 95% confidence interval for the population proportion. Write a sentence or two that interprets this interval.

10.37 Refer to the previous exercise. Calculate a 90% confidence interval for the population proportion.

10.38 *U.S. News and World Report* (Dec. 19, 1994, pp. 62–71) reported on a survey of 1000 American adults, conducted by telephone on December 2–4, 1994, designed to measure beliefs about apocalyptic predictions. One of the results reported was that 59% of the sample said they believe the world will come to an end.

a. Calculate the standard error of the sample proportion who believe the world will come to an end.

b. Calculate a 95% confidence interval for the population proportion. Interpret the interval in a way that could be understood by a statistically naïve reader.

10.39 In Chapter 2, we saw data from a statistics class activity in which 190 students were asked to randomly pick one of the numbers 1, 2, 3, 4, 5, 6, 7, 8, 9, 10. The number 7 was picked by 56 students.

a. For the sample, calculate the proportion of students who picked 7.

b. Calculate the standard error for this sample proportion.

c. Calculate a 90% confidence interval for the population proportion.

d. Calculate a 95% confidence interval for the population proportion.

e. Calculate a 98% confidence interval for the population proportion.

f. What do the results of parts (c–e) indicate about the effect of confidence level on the width of a confidence interval?

g. Based on these confidence intervals, do you think that students choose numbers "randomly"? Explain.

10.40 A study reported in the *Journal of Occupational and Environmental Medicine* (Franke et al., 1998, 40:441– 444) found that retired male Iowa policemen are more likely to have heart disease compared to other men with similar ages but different occupations. Data from the study were that about 32% of a sample of 232 retired policemen had heart disease, but only 18% of a sample of 817 men with other occupations had heart disease.

a. In Chapter 3, we learned about the various types of studies. Is this an observational study or a randomized experiment? Explain.

b. Do you think that we can attribute the observed difference in heart disease percentages to job-related factors? Explain.

c. Graphically compare the policemen and the other men using a bar chart.

d. Calculate a 95% confidence interval for the proportion of retired Iowa policemen.

e. Calculate a 95% confidence interval for the proportion of other retired men who have heart disease.

f. Based on these two confidence intervals, do you think it is safe to conclude that police officers are more likely to experience heart disease than other men? Explain.

g. Why are the widths of the two confidence intervals different from each other?

10.41 Use an example from this chapter to explain the difference between a sample proportion and a population proportion.

10.42 A professor wants to know if her class of 60 students would prefer the final exam to be given as a take-home exam or an in-class exam. She surveys the class and learns that 45 of the 60 students would prefer a take-home. Explain why she should not use these data to compute a 95% confidence interval for the proportion preferring a take-home exam.

10.43 Suppose that a margin of error for a survey is reported to be 4%. Write a brief explanation of what this margin of error tells us about the accuracy of sample percentages from this survey.

10.44 The Gallup Organization used two different wordings of a question in a February 1999 poll about the death penalty. The two different questions were asked of two different random samples of Americans. Results reported at the Gallup website were

Question 1: Are you in favor of the death penalty for a person convicted of murder? (Based on 543 adults: margin of error plus or minus 5 percentage points)

	For	Against	No Opinion
99 Feb 8–9	71%	22%	7%

Question 2: What do you think should be the penalty for murder—the death penalty or life imprisonment with absolutely no possibility of parole?

(Based on 511 adults: margin of error plus or minus 5 percentage points)

	Death Penalty	Life Imprisonment	No Opinion
99 Feb 8–9	56%	38%	6%

a. Compare the two questions using a bar chart.

b. The margin of error for each question was reported as 5%. Verify that this is approximately true.

c. For the first question, calculate a 95% confidence interval for the percent of all Americans who are "For" the death penalty. Use the margin of error reported by the Gallup Organization. Write a sentence that interprets this confidence interval.

d. For the second question, calculate a 95% confidence interval for the percent of all Americans who would answer "Death Penalty" when asked whether the penalty for murder should be the death penalty or life imprisonment. Use the margin of error reported by the Gallup Organization. Write a sentence that interprets this interval.

10.45 In a survey reported in a special edition of *Newsweek* (Spring/Summer 1999, *Health for Life*), only 3% of a sample of 757 American women responded "Not at all satisfied" to the question "How satisfied are you with your overall physical appearance?"

  a. The margin of error for the poll was reported as 3.5%. Use the conservative formula for margin of error to verify that this is approximately correct.

  b. Based on the reported margin of error, calculate a 95% confidence interval for the percent of all American women who are "not at all satisfied" with their physical appearance. Are all values in this interval valid estimates of the population percent? Explain.

  c. Use the "exact" formula to calculate the margin of error.

  d. Based on the margin of error in part (c), calculate a 95% confidence interval for the population percent. Write a sentence that interprets this confidence interval for somebody who doesn't know very much about statistics.

10.46 What is the probability that a 95% confidence interval will not cover the true population value? Explain.

10.47 In 1998, two statistics classes for students in the liberal arts at a large northeastern university were asked, "Do you have a tattoo?" The responses were

	Yes	No
Women	46	227
Men	32	175

  a. What proportion of the women in this sample has a tattoo?

  b. What proportion of the men in this sample has a tattoo?

  c. Compare the men and women using a bar graph.

  d. What population do you think is represented by this sample? In other words, to whom do you think the results can be generalized?

  e. For the college women, calculate a 95% confidence interval for the proportion of the population that has a tattoo. Write a sentence that interprets this interval.

  f. For the college men, calculate a 95% confidence interval for the proportion of the population that has a tattoo. Write a sentence that interprets this interval.

  g. Use the results of parts (e) and (f) to compare college men and women with regard to the proportion that has a tattoo.

10.48 Find the reported results of a poll in which a margin of error is also reported. Look in a weekly news magazine such as *Newsweek* or *Time,* in a newspaper such as the *New York Times,* or on the Internet.

  a. Explain what question was asked in the poll and what margin of error was reported. Verify the margin of error with a calculation.

  b. Present a 95% confidence interval for the results.

Explain in words what the interval means for your example.

10.49 For Case Study 10.2 (nicotine patches and Zyban), verify the confidence intervals reported in Table 10.4.

10.50 *Parade Magazine* reported that "nearly 3200 readers dialed a 900 number to respond to a survey in our Jan. 8 cover story on America's young people and violence" (Feb. 19, 1995, p. 20). Of those responding, "63.3% say they have been victims or personally know a victim of violent crime." Can the methods in this chapter legitimately be used to compute a 95% confidence interval for the proportion of Americans who fit that description? Explain why or why not.

Dataset Exercises

10.51 Use the **GSS-93** dataset for this exercise. The dataset contains data from the 1993 General Social Survey, and the variable *polparty* indicates the political party preference of the respondent. Calculate a 95% confidence interval for the proportion of Americans who indicated that they prefer the Democratic party.

10.52 Use the **GSS-93** dataset for this exercise. The dataset contains data from the 1993 General Social Survey, and the variable *marijuan* indicates the respondent's opinion about the legalization of marijuana. Calculate a 95% confidence interval for the proportion of Americans who are opposed to the legalization of marijuana.

10.53 Use the **pennstate3** dataset for this exercise. The data are from a student survey in a statistics class at Penn State. The variable *atfirst* gives data for whether or not a student believes in love at first sight.

  a. What is the sample proportion that believes in love at first sight?

  b. Find a 95% confidence interval for the population proportion that believes in love at first sight.

  c. Write a sentence that interprets the interval found in part (b).

10.54 Refer to the previous exercise about the variable *atfirst* in the **pennstate3** dataset.

  a. Create a two-way table that shows the relationship between the variables *atfirst* and *Sex.* (See Sections 2.3 and 6.1 to review two-way tables.)

  b. What proportion of the females in the sample believes in love at first sight? What proportion of the males believes in love at first sight?

  c. For each sex separately, find a 95% confidence interval for the population proportion that believes in love at first sight.

  d. Compare the two confidence intervals found in part (c). What does the comparison indicate about the difference between the proportions of males and females who believe in love at first sight?

| REFERENCE

Bem, D., and C. Honorton (1994). "Does psi exist? Replicable evidence for an anomalous process of information transfer," *Psychological Bulletin,* Vol. 115, No. 1, pp. 4–18.

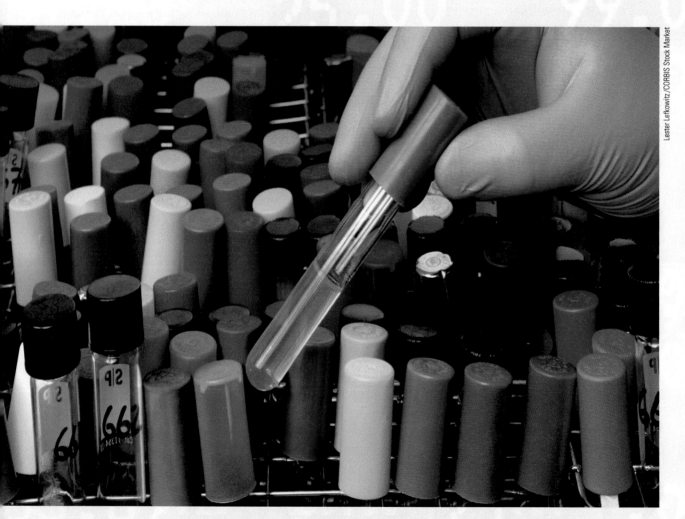

CHAPTER 11

Testing Hypotheses About Proportions

Lester Lefkowitz/CORBIS Stock Market

How do pharmaceutical companies test medication side effects?
See Examples 11.1 and 11.1—CONTINUED.

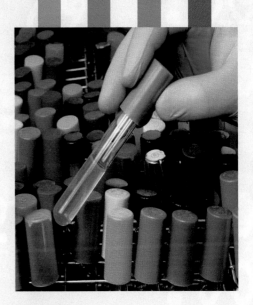

The logic of statistical hypothesis testing is similar to the "presumed innocent until proven guilty" logic of the American judicial system. In hypothesis testing, we assume that the null hypothesis is a possible truth until the sample data conclusively demonstrate otherwise.

Suppose that your state legislature is considering a proposal to lower the legal limit for the blood alcohol level that constitutes drunk driving. A legislator wants to determine if a majority of adults in her district favor this proposal. To gather information, she surveys 200 randomly selected individuals from her district and learns that 59% of these people favor the proposal.

Can the legislator conclude that a majority of all adults in her district favor this proposal? Because the result is based on a sample, there is the possibility that the observed majority might have occurred just by the "luck of the draw." If a majority of the whole population actually opposes the proposal, how likely is it that 59% of a random sample would favor the proposal?

In this chapter, we will learn how to use the method of *statistical hypothesis testing* to analyze this type of issue. The hypothesis testing method uses data from a sample to judge whether or not a statement about a population may be true. For example, is it true that a majority of all adults in the legislator's district favor the proposal for the tougher blood alcohol standard?

Hypothesis testing and confidence interval estimation are related methods, and often both methods can be used to analyze the same situation. As we learned in Chapter 10, a confidence interval is a numerical answer to the question "What is the population value?" A hypothesis test is used to answer questions about particular values for a population parameter, or particular relationships in a population, based on information in the sample data.

In this chapter, we focus on testing hypotheses about a population proportion, but the basic steps are the same for any hypothesis test. Additional situations will be considered in Chapters 13 to 16. The five steps for any hypothesis test, first introduced in Chapter 6, are as follows.

Steps in Any Hypothesis Test

Step 1: *Determine the* null *and* alternative *hypotheses.*

Step 2: *Verify necessary data conditions, and if met, summarize the data into an appropriate* test statistic.

Step 3: *Assuming the null hypothesis is true, find the p-value.*

Step 4: *Decide whether or not the result is* statistically significant *based on the p-value.*

Step 5: *Report the conclusion in the context of the situation.* ◆

11.1 | FORMULATING HYPOTHESIS STATEMENTS

Many of the questions that researchers ask can also be expressed as questions about which of two statements might be true for a population. Consider, for instance, the nature of these research questions:

◆ Does a majority of the population favor a new legal standard for the blood alcohol level that constitutes drunk driving?

◆ Do female students study, on average, more than male students do?

◆ Will side effects be experienced by fewer than 20% of people who take this new medication?

All of these questions can be answered either with a "no" or a "yes," and each possible answer makes a specific statement about the situation. For instance, we can view the research question about the proportion favoring a new legal standard for drunk driving as a choice between two competing *hypothesis* statements:

Hypothesis 1: The proportion favoring the new standard *is not a majority.*
Hypothesis 2: The proportion favoring the new standard *is a majority.*

Or, for the question about the comparative study habits of women and men, we can view the research question in terms of a choice between these two statements:

Hypothesis 1: On average, women *do not* study more than men do.
Hypothesis 2: On average, women *do* study more than men do.

Terminology for the Two Choices

In the language of statistics, the two possible answers to questions like the ones we just encountered are called the **null hypothesis** and the **alternative hypothesis.**

definition The **null hypothesis,** represented by the symbol H_0, is a statement that there is nothing happening. The specific null hypothesis varies from problem to problem, but generally it can be thought of as the status quo, or no relationship, or no difference. In most situations, the researcher hopes to disprove or reject the null hypothesis.

> The **alternative hypothesis,** represented by the symbol H_a, is a statement that something is happening. In most situations, this hypothesis is what the researcher hopes to prove. It may be a statement that the assumed status quo is false, or that there is a relationship, or that there is a difference.

Each of the following statements is an example of a null hypothesis:

- There is no extrasensory perception.
- There is no difference between the mean pulse rates of men and women.
- There is no relationship between exercise intensity and the resulting aerobic benefit.

Some examples of alternative hypotheses are

- There is extrasensory perception.
- Men have lower mean pulse rates than women do.
- Increasing exercise intensity increases the resulting aerobic benefit.

EXAMPLE 11.1
Are Side Effects Experienced by Fewer Than 20% of Patients?

Suppose that a pharmaceutical company wants to be able to claim that for its newest medication the proportion of patients who experience side effects is less than 20%. The issue can be addressed with these null and alternative hypotheses:

Null: 20% (or more) of users will experience side effects.
Alternative: Fewer than 20% of users will experience side effects.

Notice that the claim that the company hopes to prove is used as the alternative hypothesis. ◆

EXAMPLE 11.2
Does a Majority Favor the Proposed Blood Alcohol Limit?

For the blood alcohol question, suppose that the legislator's plan is to vote for the proposal if there is conclusive evidence that a majority of her constituents favor the proposal. In statistical terms, the null and alternative hypotheses for the legislator are

$H_0: p \leq .5$ (not a majority)
$H_a: p > .5$ (a majority)

As in Chapters 9 and 10, p represents a population proportion. In this case, p is the proportion of her constituents that favors the proposal. The alternative hypothesis is a "something happening" statement in the sense that its truth will cause the legislator to vote for the new limit. ◆

In Example 11.1, the alternative hypothesis is that the percent experiencing side effects is *less than* 20%. In Example 11.2, the alternative hypothesis is that the proportion of the population in favor of the legislator's plan is *more than* .5. Both of these alternative hypotheses describe values that differ from the null hypothesis in a particular numerical direction. When the alternative hypothesis specifies a single direction, the test is called a **one-sided** or **one-tailed hypothesis test.** In practice, most hypothesis tests are one-sided tests because investigators usually have a particular direction in mind when they consider a question.

When the alternative hypothesis includes values in either direction from a specific standard, the test is called a **two-sided** or **two-tailed hypothesis test.** Suppose, for example, that an alternative hypothesis is that men and women have different verbal abilities. This statement does not specify a particular direction for the difference, so the hypothesis test is a two-sided test.

11.1

turn on your mind

Confidence intervals and hypothesis testing are the two major categories of "statistical inference." Based on this information, do you think null and alternative hypotheses are generally statements about populations, samples, or both? Explain.*

11.2 | THE LOGIC OF HYPOTHESIS TESTING: WHAT IF THE NULL IS TRUE?

The logic of statistical hypothesis testing is similar to the "presumed innocent until proven guilty" logic of the American judicial system. In hypothesis testing, we assume that the null hypothesis is a possible truth until the sample data conclusively demonstrate otherwise. The "something is happening" hypothesis is chosen only when the data show us that we can reject the "nothing is happening" hypothesis.

Unfortunately, the hypothesis test method is a somewhat indirect strategy for making a decision. We will not be able to determine the chance that a hypothesis statement is either true or false. We can only assess whether or not the observed data are consistent with an assumption that the null hypothesis is true about the population, within the reasonable bounds of sampling variability discussed in Chapter 9. If the data would be unlikely when the null hypothesis is true, we *reject* the statement made in the null hypothesis.

The Probability Question on Which Hypothesis Testing Is Based

If the null hypothesis is true about the population, what is the probability of observing sample data like that observed? Let's look at two examples that illustrate how the answer to this question is useful for deciding whether or not to reject the null hypothesis.

EXAMPLE 11.3
Psychic Powers

A popular cartoon once featured two characters playing a coin-flipping game. After one had correctly guessed the outcome 100 times, supposedly using psychic abilities, the other still insisted that it must have been a coincidence. When the first character successfully guessed that the next flip would result in seven rotations followed by hovering in the air, the skeptic resorted to chanting the word "luck" repeatedly, still refusing to believe in psychic abilities.

*HINT: See the discussion of statistical inference at the beginning of Section 9.8.

This cartoon nicely captures the thought process of hypothesis testing. We all realize that correctly guessing 100 times in a row is unlikely to be a coincidence. It seems nearly impossible that anybody could be this lucky. Suppose, however, that we accept the skeptic's explanation and assume that the cartoon character is indeed only guessing. If this is true, how likely is it that he could correctly guess 100 consecutive times in a fair coin toss?

We can use the methods of Chapter 7 to calculate that the probability of 100 correct guesses in a row is $(1/2)^{100}$. As you might expect, the answer is extraordinarily small. After the decimal point, there are 30 zeroes before the first nonzero digit appears. Basically, there is no chance that anybody could be this lucky. It is reasonable to conclude that the character must have been using psychic powers, or some method other than just guessing. We would reject the null hypothesis that he was just guessing because the sample results are extremely inconsistent with that hypothesis. ◆

EXAMPLE 11.4
Stop the Pain Before It Starts

A headline at the CNN website on October 21, 1996 read, "Study: Painkillers More Effective Before Surgery Than Afterward." The article described a University of Pennsylvania research study done to test the theory that the most effective pain relief strategy is to stop the pain before it starts. In the study, men undergoing surgery for prostate cancer were randomly assigned either to an "experimental" group that began taking painkillers before the operation or to a "control" group that followed the standard practice of waiting until after the operation to begin taking painkillers. The author of the website article presented the key result in terms of the likelihood that the observed data could have occurred just by chance:

> But 9 1/2 weeks later . . . only 12 members of the 60 men in the experimental group were still feeling pain. Among the 30 control group members, 18 were still feeling pain. Gottschalk said the likelihood of this difference being due to chance was only 1 in 500.

The null hypothesis, the statement that nothing is happening, is that the effectiveness of the painkillers would be the same whether they were started before or after the operation. According to the investigator, if we assume that this null hypothesis is true, the probability is only 1 in 500 that the observed difference could have been as large as it was or larger. Based on this evidence, it seems reasonable to reject the null hypothesis that the two timings are equally effective. ◆

11.2

turn on your mind

For each of the two examples in this section, explain what the null hypothesis and the alternative hypothesis would be. Then write a sentence answering "the probability question at the center of a hypothesis test" for each example. The sentence should be of the form: "If [fill in null hypothesis] is true, then the likelihood that [fill in event] would have happened is [fill in likelihood]."*

11.3 | REACHING A CONCLUSION ABOUT THE TWO HYPOTHESES

When we do a hypothesis test, the objective is to decide between the null and alternative hypotheses.

- ◆ The data summary that we use to evaluate the two hypotheses is called the **test statistic.**

- ◆ The likelihood that we would have observed a *test statistic* as extreme as what we did, or something even more extreme, if the null hypothesis is true is called the **p-value.**

- ◆ The decision is made to accept the alternative hypothesis if the *p*-value is smaller than a designated **level of significance,** denoted by the Greek letter α (alpha), and usually set by researchers at 0.05, less commonly at 0.10 or 0.01.

Computing the *p*-Value of a Hypothesis Test

definition The **p-value** is computed by assuming the null hypothesis is true and then determining the probability of a result as extreme (or more extreme) as the observed test statistic in the direction of the alternative hypothesis.

In the language of Chapter 7, the *p*-value is the *conditional probability of observing a test statistic as extreme as that observed or more so, given that the null hypothesis is true.* "Extreme" is understood to mean in the direction supporting the alternative hypothesis. We will learn details of how to compute a "test statistic" for specific situations in this and subsequent chapters. In general, a test statistic is simply a summary that compares the sample data to the null hypothesis. The chi-square statistic introduced in Chapter 6 is an example of a test statistic.

Notice that because the *p*-value is a probability, it must be between 0 and 1. It indicates the strength of the evidence against the null hypothesis. The smaller the *p*-value is, the more conclusive the evidence is against the null hypothesis. For example, the evidence against the null hypothesis is more conclusive when the *p*-value is 0.001 than when it is 0.25. As we learned earlier in this chapter, the logic of hypothesis testing is indirect. A *p*-value *does not* tell us the probability that the null hypothesis is true. Instead, it only tells us the probability that our test statistic could have been as extreme as it is, if we assume the null hypothesis is true.

An Advanced Technical Note—Bayesian Statistics

tech note The *p*-value represents the *conditional probability* $P(A|B)$, where

A = observing a test statistic value as extreme as that observed or more so, and

B = the null hypothesis is true.

We would really prefer to know $P(B|A)$, the probability that the null hypothesis is actually true, *given* the observed data. Suppose we try using Rule 3 or 4 from Chapter 7 to find this conditional probability. We would need to find $P(A \text{ and } B)$, and to find that, we would need to know $P(B)$. But that's the probability that the null hypothesis is true. If we knew that, we wouldn't have to conduct the hypothesis test! That's why we must rely on the indirect information provided by the p-value to make our conclusion. In fact, the null hypothesis is either true or not, so even considering $P(B)$ only makes sense if we think of it as a personal probability representing our belief that the null hypothesis is true. There is a branch of statistics, called **Bayesian statistics,** that utilizes the approach of assessing $P(B)$ and then combining it with the data to find an updated $P(B)$.

Rejecting the Null Hypothesis

The phrase **statistically significant** is used to describe the results when the researcher has decided that the p-value is small enough to decide in favor of the alternative hypothesis. The **level of significance,** also called the α **level** ("alpha" level), is the borderline for deciding that the p-value is small enough to justify choosing the alternative hypothesis. A result is statistically significant when the p-value is less than the chosen level of significance.

Most researchers use the convention that we can reject the null hypothesis when the p-value is less than 0.05 (or 5%). In other words, the *level of significance* is usually set at $\alpha = 0.05$, and the result is *statistically significant* when the p-value is less than 0.05. In some research disciplines, the phrase *highly significant* is used to describe the result when the p-value is less than 0.01 (1%), and *marginally significant* is used when the p-value is between 0.05 and 0.10. p-Values greater than 0.10 are rarely considered sufficient evidence to reject the null hypothesis. Researchers frequently criticize these somewhat arbitrary borderlines, but they are used by many scientific journals.

in summary   Interpreting a *p*-Value

In any statistical hypothesis test, the smaller the p-value is, the stronger the evidence is against the null hypothesis. It is common research practice to call a result *statistically significant* when the p-value is less than 0.05.

Stating the Two Possible Conclusions

The two possible conclusions of a hypothesis test are

- When the p-value is small, we *reject the null hypothesis* or, equivalently, we *accept the alternative hypothesis.* "Small" is defined as a p-value $\leq \alpha$, where α = level of significance (usually 0.05).

- When the p-value is not small, we conclude that we *cannot reject the null hypothesis* or, equivalently, *there is not enough evidence to reject the null hypothesis.* "Not small" is defined as a p-value $> \alpha$, where α = level of significance (usually 0.05).

The conclusion that we "cannot reject the null hypothesis" may seem wordy to you, and you may be tempted to say that you accept the null hypothesis. Resist that temptation because *it is almost never correct to say,* "I accept the null hypothesis." The problem with "accepting the null" is that this wording makes it seem that we are convinced that the null hypothesis is true. The strategy of hypothesis testing is to reject the null hypothesis when the evidence is convincingly against it. If we only collect a small sample amount of data, we may not see convincing evidence for the alternative hypothesis because the sampling error is so large. That is certainly *not* equivalent to accepting that the null hypothesis is true. For instance, if we observe three births and two are boys, we would certainly not be willing to *accept* the hypothesis "2/3 of all births are boys" even though the observed data don't provide evidence that it is false.

11.3

turn on your mind

Suppose an ESP test is conducted by having someone guess whether each of n coin flips will result in heads or tails. The null hypothesis is that $p = .5$, and the alternative is that $p > .5$, where p = probability of guessing correctly. Suppose one participant guesses $n = 10$ times and gets 6 right, while another guesses $n = 100$ times and gets 60 right. In each case, the percent correct was 60%. Do you think the p-value would be lower in one case than in the other, or would it be the same? Explain.*

EXAMPLE 11.5
A Jury Trial

If you are on a jury in the American judicial system, you must presume that the defendant is innocent unless there is enough evidence to conclude that he or she is guilty. Therefore the two hypotheses are

Null hypothesis: The defendant is innocent.
Alternative hypothesis: The defendant is guilty.

The prosecution collects evidence, much like researchers collect data, in the hope that the jurors will be convinced that such evidence would be extremely unlikely if the assumption of innocence were true. Consistent with our thinking in hypothesis testing, in many cases we would not *accept* the hypothesis that the defendant is innocent. We would simply conclude that the evidence was not strong enough to rule out the possibility of innocence. In fact, in the United States the two conclusions juries are instructed to choose from are "guilty" and "not guilty." A jury would never conclude, "the defendant is innocent." ◆

There are two different errors that can be made in hypothesis testing, just as in the jury system. The first type of error is equivalent to a "guilty" verdict when in fact the defendant is innocent. This might be called a false positive. In hypothesis testing, this is equivalent to rejecting the null hypothesis when it is true. The second type of error is equivalent to a "not guilty" verdict when the defendant actually committed the crime. This might be called a false negative. In hypothesis testing, this is equivalent to not rejecting the null hypothesis when in fact the alternative hypothesis is true.

*HINT: The *p*-value is the conditional probability of observing 60% or more correct, given that the participant is just guessing. Would it be harder to guess at least 6 correct in 10 tries, or at least 60 correct in 100 tries?

In the judicial system in the United States, the first type of error is seen as more serious. This is what leads to the reasoning that a defendant should be considered "innocent until proven guilty." In any hypothesis testing situation, the two types of errors should be considered to determine which is more serious, and the level of significance should be adjusted accordingly. These errors and how they affect the decision will be covered in more detail in Section 11.7 and in Chapter 13, Section 13.6.

11.4 | TESTING HYPOTHESES ABOUT A PROPORTION

In this section, we illustrate the five steps to hypothesis testing in the context of testing a specified value for a population proportion.

Steps in any Hypothesis Test

Step 1: *Determine the* null *and* alternative *hypotheses.*

Step 2: *Verify necessary data conditions, and if met, summarize the data into an appropriate* test statistic.

Step 3: *Assuming the null hypothesis is true, find the p-value.*

Step 4: *Decide whether or not the result is* statistically significant *based on the p-value.*

Step 5: *Report the conclusion in the context of the situation.*

Examples 11.1 and 11.2 were illustrations of how to write the null and alternative hypotheses in words and in formulas when the parameter of interest is a population proportion. For instance, in Example 11.2 about the proportion favoring a lower legal blood alcohol limit, the null hypothesis was $H_0: p \leq .5$ and the alternative was $H_a: p > .5$. The specific value specified in the hypotheses for the population proportion of interest is called the **null value** and is denoted by the symbol p_0. In Example 11.2 just described, the value of p_0 is .5.

The possible null and alternative hypotheses are one of these three choices, depending on the research question:

1. $H_0: p = p_0$ versus $H_a: p \neq p_0$ (two-sided)
2. $H_0: p \geq p_0$ versus $H_a: p < p_0$ (one-sided)
3. $H_0: p \leq p_0$ versus $H_a: p > p_0$ (one-sided)

Often the null hypothesis for a one-sided test is written as $H_0: p = p_0$ instead. We will write it both ways in this chapter, to give you practice with the two ways you may encounter the null hypothesis in journal articles. Remember that a *p*-value is computed by assuming the null hypothesis is true, and the specific null value p_0 is what is assumed to be the truth about the population for that computation.

The *z*-Test for a Proportion

When we have a sufficiently large random sample, we can use a **z-test** to examine hypotheses about a population proportion. The test is called a "*z*-test" because the **test statistic** is a standardized score (*z*-score) for measuring the difference between the sample proportion and the null hypothesis value of the population proportion. The logic of the test is as follows:

♦ Determine the sampling distribution of possible sample proportions when the true population proportion is p_0 (called the *null value*), the value specified in H_0.

- Using properties of this sampling distribution, calculate a standardized score (z-score) for the observed sample proportion $\hat{p}$.
- If the standardized score has a large magnitude, conclude that the sample proportion $\hat{p}$ would be unlikely if the null value p_0 is true, and reject the null hypothesis.

The principal idea is that we determine how likely it would have been for the sample proportion to have occurred if the null hypothesis is true. For example, if the null value is $p_0 = .5$ and the observed sample proportion is $\hat{p} = .65$, we would determine how likely it is that we could observe a sample proportion as large as .65 (or larger) if the population proportion was .5.

Conditions for Conducting the z-Test

Whenever we conduct a hypothesis test, we must make sure the data meet certain conditions. These conditions are the assumptions that were made when the theory was derived for the test statistic that we are using to test our hypotheses. For testing proportions with the procedure described in this section, there are two conditions that should be true for the sample:

1. The sample should be a random sample from the population.
2. The quantities np_0 and $n(1 - p_0)$ should both be at least 10.

The first condition is not always practical, and most researchers are willing to use the test procedure as long as the sample is considered to be representative of the population for the question of interest. For instance, a college statistics class may be representative of all college students on questions like which of two soft drinks is preferred or whether their right foot is longer than their left foot.

The second condition is a sample size requirement. To test the null hypothesis that $p = .5$, for example, we would need a sample of at least $n = 20$ to meet this condition. If the null hypothesis is that $p = .1$, the sample size would have to be at least $n = 100$. Our standard may be somewhat conservative; some authors suggest that np_0 and $n(1 - p_0)$ only need to be larger than 5 (e.g., Ott, 4th ed., p. 370).

Let's go through the five steps of hypothesis testing for an example, and then formalize the details.

EXAMPLE 11.6
The Importance of Order

This example was first introduced in Chapter 2. In a student survey, a statistics teacher asked his students to "randomly pick a letter from these two choices — S or Q." For about half of the students, the order of the letters S and Q was reversed so that the end of the instruction read "Q or S." The purpose of the activity was to determine if there might be a preference for choosing the first letter. A tendency to pick the first choice offered has been noted in several settings, including in elections.

Step 1: *Determine the null and alternative hypotheses.*
Use the letter p to represent the proportion of the population that would pick the first letter. The null hypothesis is a statement of "nothing happening." If there is no general preference for either the first or second letter, $p = .5$ (because there are two choices). So the "null value" for p is $p_0 = .5$.

The alternative hypothesis usually states the researcher's belief or speculation. The purpose of the activity was to see if there is a general preference for picking the first choice, and a preference for the first letter would mean that p is greater than .5. The null and alternative hypotheses can be summarized as

$H_0: p = .5$

$H_a: p > .5$

◆ These hypotheses are statements about the larger population that this sample represents. Hypothesis tests are always used to say something about the population from which the sample has been taken.

◆ A more literal statement of the null hypothesis would be $H_0: p \le .5$ because it is possible that less than half of the population would choose the first letter. Even if the null hypothesis is modified in this way, the value .5 is used as the assumed null value in the calculations.

Step 2: *Verify necessary data conditions, and if met, summarize the data into an appropriate test statistic.*

Before computing the test statistic, we verify that our sample meets the necessary conditions for using the z-statistic. With $n = 190$ and $p_0 = .5$, both np_0 and $n(1 - p_0)$ equal 95, a quantity larger than 10, so the sample size condition is met. The sample, however, is not really a random sample—it's a convenience sample of students who were enrolled in this class. It does not seem that this will bias the results for this question, so we will behave as though the sample was a random sample.

Among 92 students who saw the order "S or Q," 61 picked S, the first choice. Among the 98 students who saw the order "Q or S," 53 picked Q, the first choice. In all, 114 of 190 students picked the first choice of letter. Expressed as a proportion, this is $114/190 = .60$.

Data analysts nearly always use statistical software to do the calculations for a hypothesis test. Figure 11.1 displays output for this problem from the Minitab statistical program. We first work through the remainder of the hypothesis test utilizing this output. Following that, we will show the detailed calculations for a hypothesis test for a population proportion.

Test of p = 0.5 vs p > 0.5

X	N	Sample p	95.0 % CI	Z-Value	P-Value
114	190	0.60	(0.53, 0.67)	2.76	0.003

FIGURE 11.1   **Minitab (Version 12) output for the *S* or *Q* choice**

The output items labeled "X," "N," and "Sample p" summarize the calculation of the sample proportion. The sample proportion, $\hat{p} = .60$, is the primary information for the test statistic, but we need to determine the corresponding z-statistic to find the p-value. From the output, we see under the label "Z-Value" that the value of the z-statistic is 2.76. The z-value is a standardized score for measuring the difference between the sample proportion, $\hat{p} = .60$, and the null hypothesis value, $p_0 = .50$.

Step 3: *Assuming the null hypothesis is true, find the p-value.*

The *p*-value for this hypothesis test is the answer to this question: *If the true p is .5, what is the probability that, for a sample of 190 people, the sample proportion could be as large as .60 (or larger)?*

The answer to this question is also the answer to a corresponding question about the *z*-statistic: *If the null hypothesis is true, what is the probability that the z-statistic could be as large as 2.76 (or larger)?*

We can either use computer output to find this value, or we can find it from Table A.1, the Standard Normal Table in the Appendix. Details of using the table will be given later in this chapter. In the Minitab output, we can locate the answer, "0.003," at the far right under the heading "P-Value." If the population proportion is really .5, the probability is only 0.003, about 3 in 1000, that we could observe a sample proportion as large as .60 or larger.

> **Note:** In the specific context of hypothesis tests for proportions, it is unfortunate that the letter "*p*" could have two different meanings. Do not confuse the population proportion "*p*" with the *p*-value for the test, which is sometimes abbreviated to just "*p*" in research articles and computer output. You should be able to sort out which is which based on the context.

Step 4: *Decide whether or not the result is statistically significant based on the p-value.*

The convention used by most researchers is to declare statistical significance when the *p*-value is smaller than 0.05. The *p*-value in this example is 0.003, so we can reject the null hypothesis.

Step 5: *Report the conclusion in the context of the situation.*

The statistical conclusion was to reject the null hypothesis that $p = .50$. In this situation, the conclusion is that *there is statistically significant evidence that the first letter presented is preferred.* This conclusion is a generalization that applies to the population represented by this sample. In other words, we conclude that for the entire population of individuals represented by these students, there would be a preference for choosing the first letter presented.

You may have noticed that the output in Figure 11.1 also provided a 95% confidence interval for the population proportion. With 95% confidence we can say that the population proportion who would choose the first letter presented is somewhere between .53 and .67. With only 190 responses, the margin of error is somewhat large (.07 or 7%) so the confidence interval is not particularly precise. The true proportion that picks the first letter may be only a slight majority (.53) or it could be as much as a two-thirds majority (.67).

Conclusions are strengthened when another study replicates the results. The instructor repeated this activity in another class of 327 students. In that class, 58% of the students picked the first letter, which is very close to the 60% found in the original study. ◆

Details for Calculating the z-Statistic

Our fundamental concern is the difference between the sample proportion and the null hypothesis value for the population proportion. If the sample proportion is sufficiently far from the null value, we can reject the null hypothesis. For example, if the null hypothesis is that $p = .5$, a sample proportion of .9 based on a relatively large random sample would be strong evidence against the null hypothesis. A sample proportion equal to .52 would be far less convincing evidence against the statement that the true $p = .5$.

We can measure the difference between the sample proportion and the null hypothesis value with a standardized score. From the Rule for Sample Proportions in Chapter 9, we know that the possible values of the sample proportion $\hat{p}$, based on a sample of size n, are approximately normal with

- mean $= p =$ true population proportion
- standard deviation $= \sqrt{\dfrac{p(1 - p)}{n}}$

When we assume the null hypothesis is true, so that $p = p_0$, we assign special names to the mean and standard deviation. In particular, the term *null value* is used for p_0, and the term *null standard error* is used for the standard deviation when p_0 is substituted for p. Under the null hypothesis, the sampling distribution of $\hat{p}$ is approximately normal with

- mean $=$ null value $= p_0$
- standard deviation $=$ null standard error $= \sqrt{\dfrac{p_0(1 - p_0)}{n}}$

The z-statistic for the significance test is

$$z = \frac{\text{Sample estimate} - \text{Null value}}{\text{Null standard error}} = \frac{\hat{p} - p_0}{\text{Null standard error}} = \frac{\hat{p} - p_0}{\sqrt{\dfrac{p_0(1 - p_0)}{n}}}$$

- $\hat{p}$ represents the sample estimate of the proportion
- p_0 represents the specific value in the null hypothesis
- n is the sample size

EXAMPLE 11.6—*CONTINUED*
Calculating
the z-Statistic for
the S or Q Problem

For the "random" choice between S and Q, the null hypothesis was $p = .5$, and the proportion of the sample of $n = 190$ students that picked the first letter was $\hat{p} = .6$. In Figure 11.1, we saw that the z-statistic for the hypothesis test is 2.76. The calculation is

$$z = \frac{\text{Sample estimate} - \text{Null value}}{\text{Null standard error}} = \frac{.6 - .5}{\sqrt{\dfrac{.5(1 - .5)}{190}}} = \frac{.10}{.0362} = 2.76 \; \blacklozenge$$

EXAMPLE 11.1—*CONTINUED*
Do Fewer Than
20% Experience
Medication Side Effects?

Suppose that a pharmaceutical company wants to claim that side effects will be experienced by fewer than 20% of the patients who use a particular medication. In a clinical trial with $n = 400$ patients, they find that 68 patients experienced side effects.

Step 1: *The null and alternative hypotheses are*

H_0: $p \geq .20$ (company's claim is not true)

H_a: $p < .20$ (company's claim is true)

Notice that the pharmaceutical company's claim is used as the alternative hypothesis. Also notice that the null hypothesis is a region of values. To calculate the z-statistic, it is standard practice to use the value that separates the null and alternative hypothesis regions, in this case $p_0 = .20$.

Step 2: *Verify necessary data conditions, and if met, summarize the data into an appropriate test statistic.*

There were 400 patients, so both np_0 and $n(1 - p_0)$ are large enough to proceed with a test based on the z-statistic. Although most clinical trials use volunteer patients, presumably the company would choose volunteers who are representative of the larger population of potential users of the medication, so for practical purposes we will accept that the necessary conditions are met. Out of 400 patients, 68 experienced side effects. The sample proportion that experienced side effects is $\hat{p} = 68/400 = .17$. The z-statistic for the hypothesis test is

$$z = \frac{\text{Sample estimate} - \text{Null value}}{\text{Null standard error}} = \frac{.17 - .20}{\sqrt{\dfrac{.20(1 - .20)}{400}}} = \frac{-.03}{.02} = -1.5$$

Notice that the z-statistic is negative. This occurs because the sample proportion is less than the null value, the result that the pharmaceutical company wanted. We will complete the remaining three steps for this example after we present the general format for finding a p-value. ◆

Computing the p-Value for the z-Test

Recall that a p-value is computed by assuming the null hypothesis is true and then determining the probability of a result as extreme, or more extreme, as the observed test statistic in the direction of the alternative hypothesis. For the z-test of hypotheses about a population proportion, the p-value probability is found using the normal curve. This is a consequence of the Normal Curve Approximation Rule for Sample Proportions introduced in Chapter 9. The details of "determining the probability of a result as extreme (or more extreme) as the observed test statistic" are consistent with the direction specified in the alternative hypothesis:

- For a *greater than* alternative hypothesis, find the probability that the test statistic z could have been *equal to or greater than* what it is.
- For a *less than* alternative, find the probability that the test statistic z could have been *equal to or less than* what it is.
- For a *two-sided alternative hypothesis,* the p-value includes the probability areas in both extremes of the distribution of the test statistic z.

The correspondence between the type of alternative hypothesis and the p-value area is summarized in Table 11.1.

TABLE 11.1 ■ Alternative Hypothesis Regions and p-Value Areas

Statement of H_a		p-Value Area	Normal Curve Region
$p < p_0$	(less than)	Area to the left of z (even if $z > 0$)	
$p > p_0$	(greater than)	Area to the right of z (even if $z < 0$)	
$p \neq p_0$	(not equal)	$2 \times$ area to the right of $|z|$	

The reasoning behind including both extremes for the two-sided alternative hypothesis is as follows. Suppose we want to test whether the true percentage of heads is 50% when we spin a coin on its edge and watch how it lands. We spin the coin on its edge 100 times, and it lands "heads-up" 60 times. Remember that "*the p-value is computed by assuming the null hypothesis is true and then determining the probability of a result as extreme (or more extreme) as the observed test statistic in the direction of the alternative hypothesis.*" In this case, "in the direction of the alternative hypothesis" includes both above and below 50%. So 40% heads is as extremely far into the alternative hypothesis region (as far from the null value of 50%) as is 60% heads. Both extremes provide equivalent support for the alternative hypothesis.

If we use Minitab to do the hypothesis test, the program will automatically compute and report the *p*-value. To calculate the *p*-value "by hand," we can use Table A.1, the Standard Normal Table, or we could use a spreadsheet program like Excel (the command NORMSDIST(z) finds the area to *left* of z).

EXAMPLE 11.1—*CONTINUED*
The Medication
Side Effects Problem

We already have done steps 1 and 2 for this example. The null and alternative hypotheses are H_0: $p \geq .20$ and H_a: $p < .20$, and the *z*-statistic is $z = -1.5$. We now complete the final three steps.

Step 3: *Assuming the null hypothesis is true, find the p-value.*

The alternative hypothesis is that the *proportion is less than* a specified value, so the *p*-value is the *area to the left* of the observed *z*-statistic. We can use Table A.1, the Standard Normal Table, to determine this probability, or we can use the Excel instruction NORMSDIST(-1.5). For $z = -1.5$, the area to the left is about 0.067, and this is the *p*-value. It is the answer to this question: *If the true p is .2, what is the probability that, for a sample of 400 people, the sample proportion could be as small as .17 (or smaller)?*

The relationship between the *p*-value and the *z*-statistic for this problem is illustrated in Figure 11.2.

Step 4: *Decide whether or not the result is statistically significant based on the p-value.*

If the usual 0.05 standard for statistical significance is used, the *p*-value of 0.067 is not quite small enough to reject the null hypothesis.

Step 5: *Report the conclusion in the context of the situation.*

The sample evidence was in the desired direction for the pharmaceutical company, but it was not strong enough to conclusively reject the null hypothe-

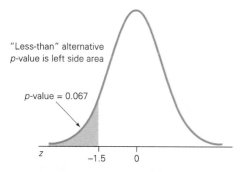

"Less-than" alternative
p-value is left side area

p-value = 0.067

z −1.5   0

FIGURE 11.2   *p*-Value for medication side effects example

sis. The company cannot reject the idea that the proportion of the population who would experience side effects is .20 (or more). If this is an important issue for the company, they should consider gathering additional data. As we will learn in the next section, sample size affects statistical significance. This example also illustrates why it is not a good idea to "accept the null hypothesis." We would not be convinced that 20% or more of the population would experience side effects when only 17% of the sample did so. ◆

EXAMPLE 11.6—CONTINUED
The p-Value for the
"Greater Than"
Alternative in
the S or Q Example

For the "choose S or Q" problem, the alternative hypothesis is $H_a: p > .5$. When an alternative hypothesis is that a *proportion is greater than* a specified value, the p-value is the *area to the right* of the observed z-statistic. We determined before that $z = 2.76$ and the corresponding p-value is 0.003. The p-value, which is the area to the right of 2.76, is illustrated in Figure 11.3.

To determine this p-value "by hand," we can use Table A.1 in the Appendix to learn that for $z = 2.76$, the area to the left is roughly 0.997. This is the probability that we could get a z-score smaller than 2.76, so the probability we could get a z-score greater than 2.76 is $1 - 0.997 = 0.003$. To calculate this p-value with Excel, enter $=1-@NORMSDIST(2.76)$ into a cell of the spreadsheet. (The @ symbol tells Excel to invoke that function.) ◆

EXAMPLE 11.7
A Two-Sided Test:
Are Left and Right
Foot Lengths Equal?

Students in a statistics class measured the lengths of their right and left feet to the nearest millimeter. The right and left foot measurements were equal for 103 of the 215 students, but the two foot lengths were different for 112 students.

Let's consider the 112 individuals with unequal measurements, and use them to represent the population of adults with unequal foot lengths. Among those with unequal lengths, we can use the letter p to represent the proportion that has a longer right foot. If we have no advance belief that either foot will tend to be longer, the null and alternative hypotheses for p are

$H_0: p = .5$
$H_a: p \neq .5$

These two hypotheses are statements about the population represented by this sample of students. The null hypothesis states that among the population of people who have different foot lengths, exactly half will have a longer right foot

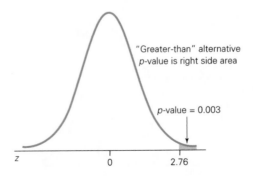

FIGURE 11.3   *p*-Value for the "*S* or *Q*" example

Test of p = 0.5 vs p not = 0.5					
X	N	Sample p	95.0 % CI	Z-Value	P-Value
63	112	0.5625	(0.471, 0.654)	1.32	0.186

FIGURE 11.4 **Minitab output for foot length example**

and exactly half will have a longer left foot. The alternative states that this is not the case, but does not specify a direction.

Both np_0 and $n(1 - p_0)$ are greater than 10, so we can proceed with the test, assuming that we think the students in the sample are representative of the larger population. In the sample, a longer right foot was reported by 63 of the 112 students who reported different foot lengths. The corresponding proportion with a longer right foot is $\hat{p} = 63/112 = .56$. Minitab output for the hypothesis test is shown in Figure 11.4. We see that the p-value is 0.186, so we cannot reject the null hypothesis. Although there was a tendency toward a longer right foot in the sample, there is insufficient evidence to conclude that the proportion in the population with a longer right foot is different from the proportion with a longer left foot.

The calculation of the z-value (the answer is shown in the output as Z-value = 1.32) is

$$z = \frac{\text{Sample estimate} - \text{Null value}}{\text{Null standard error}}$$

$$= \frac{.5625 - .5}{\sqrt{\dfrac{.5(1 - .5)}{112}}} = \frac{0.0625}{0.0472} = 1.32$$

The two-tailed p-value is the total of the area to the right of $z = 1.32$ and the area to the left of $z = -1.32$, an area illustrated in Figure 11.5. ◆

The Rejection Region Approach to Hypothesis Testing

Before computers and calculators capable of finding p-values were widely available, hypothesis testing was routinely conducted by using what is called the

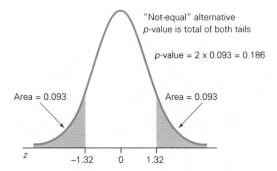

FIGURE 11.5 **Two-tailed p-value for foot length example**

"rejection region" approach. In this approach, instead of finding a p-value and comparing it to the desired level of significance, the computed test statistic is compared to a "rejection region." If the test statistic falls in the rejection region, the null hypothesis is rejected. If not, the null hypothesis cannot be rejected.

The **rejection region** in a hypothesis test is the region of possible values for the test statistic that would lead to rejection of the null hypothesis. *If* the null hypothesis is true, the probability that the computed test statistic will fall in the rejection region is α, the desired level of significance.

Like p-values, rejection regions depend on whether the alternative hypothesis is one-sided or two-sided. Here are the rejection regions and rules for a z-test with levels of significance $\alpha = 0.05$ and 0.01:

	Rejection Region Rule	
Alternative Hypothesis	$\alpha = 0.05$	$\alpha = 0.01$
$H_a: p < p_0$	Reject H_0 if $z < -1.645$	Reject H_0 if $z < -2.33$
$H_a: p > p_0$	Reject H_0 if $z > +1.645$	Reject H_0 if $z > +2.33$
$H_a: p \neq p_0$	Reject H_0 if $|z| > 1.96$	Reject H_0 if $|z| > 2.58$

Notice that the form of the rejection region (upper tail, lower tail, or both tails) is the same as the form of the p-value areas given in Table 11.1. In both cases, the decision to reject the null hypothesis is only made if the test statistic falls into a tail that supports the alternative hypothesis. To understand how the rejection region boundaries are found, examine the table of Standard Normal Probabilities in the Appendix. In each case, the rejection region is the part of the standard normal curve that

- includes values of the test statistic z that support the alternative hypothesis
- has total area of α in that region

In other words, the probability that a standard normal z-score falls into the rejection region is the specified α. When H_0 is true, the z-statistic is simply a standard normal z-score, so using this method ensures that the probability that the null hypothesis will be rejected if it is actually true is α. To find rejection regions for other values of α, find the region of the standard normal curve that supports the alternative hypothesis and has total area of α.

EXAMPLE 11.6—*CONTINUED*
Rejecting the
Hypothesis of Equal Choices

For the "choose S or Q" problem, the test statistic is $z = 2.76$ and the alternative hypothesis is that $p > .5$. Based on the rejection region rule for $\alpha = 0.05$, which is to reject H_0 if $z > +1.645$, we conclude that the null hypothesis can be rejected at $\alpha = 0.05$. Using a more stringent $\alpha = 0.01$, we can also reject the null hypothesis because the test statistic $z = 2.76$ is greater than 2.33. The conclusion would be stated, "The null hypothesis can be rejected at $\alpha = 0.01$." In the context of the example, the result might be stated, "There is statistically significant evidence that the first letter presented is preferred using $\alpha = 0.01$." ◆

11.4

turn on your mind

Here are two questions about *p*-values and one-sided versus two-sided tests:

1. Under what conditions would the *p*-value for a one-sided *z*-test be greater than 0.5?
2. When the data are consistent with the direction of the alternative hypothesis for a one-sided test, the *p*-value for the corresponding two-sided test is double what it would be for the one-sided test. Use this information to explain why it would be "cheating" to look at the data before deciding whether to do a one- or two-sided test.*

Minitab Tip

 tech note   **Testing Hypotheses about a Proportion**

◆ To test hypotheses about a proportion, use **Stat**>**Basic Statistics**>**1 Proportion.** (This procedure is not in versions earlier than Version 12.)

◆ If the raw data are in a column of the worksheet, specify that column. If the data have already been summarized, click on "Summarized Data," then specify the sample size and the count of how many observations have the characteristic of interest.

◆ Use the ***Options*** button, specify the value of p_0, select the type of alternative hypothesis, and click on "Use test and interval based on normal distribution."

◆ If the "Use . . . normal distribution" option is not selected, then the reported *p*-value will be exact, based on adding the relevant binomial probabilities. The confidence interval will also be exact. See the Minitab Help feature for details on how it is computed.

◆ In Version 13, if the alternative hypothesis selected is one-sided, the reported confidence interval will also be one-sided. For instance, if the alternative hypothesis is "greater than p_0" a lower bound will be given for the confidence interval. The interval extends from the lower bound to 1.0. To produce a two-sided confidence interval, go back to the default option of "not equal" as the alternative hypothesis.

11.5 | THE ROLE OF SAMPLE SIZE IN STATISTICAL SIGNIFICANCE

There is a big difference between the following two beginnings to an advertisement for a toothpaste:

◆ 2 out of 3 dentists recommend . . .

◆ 2/3 of the 500 dentists surveyed recommend . . .

*HINT: Q1: Study Table 11.1. Q2: The *p*-value is supposed to reflect how unlikely such extreme data would be by chance. Would all possibilities be covered if the alternative hypothesis was altered based on looking at the data?

We should be suspicious that the first claim may be based literally on the recommendations of only three dentists. If this is the case, we know that the claim is meaningless. A sample of just three individuals is not large enough to be conclusive. On the other hand, the second claim seems stronger. A sample of 500 dentists seems like a pretty big sample, although we should ask how the 500 dentists were selected for whatever survey was done.

The size of the sample affects our ability to make firm conclusions based on that sample. With a small sample, we may not be able to conclude anything. With larger samples, there is more chance that we can make firm conclusions in hypothesis testing situations, and in fact, with large samples we may find statistical significance even though the effect is minor and unimportant. The results of hypothesis testing should always be interpreted with the size of the sample in mind. We will learn more about this idea in the next section and in Chapter 13.

Cautions About Sample Size and Statistical Significance

- ◆ When there is a small to moderate effect in the population, a small sample has little chance of providing statistically significant support for the alternative hypothesis.
- ◆ With a large sample, even a small and unimportant effect in the population may lead to a conclusion of statistical significance.

EXAMPLE 11.8
How the Same Sample Proportion Can Produce Different Conclusions

In Example 10.7 of Chapter 10, we used a confidence interval to analyze a taste test in which 55% of the 60 participants liked the taste of drink A better than the taste of drink B. Based on the 95% confidence interval for the "true" proportion that prefers drink A, we were unable to conclude whether a majority of the population prefers the taste of drink A.

We can also examine these data with a hypothesis test in which the null hypothesis is that there is no general preference for either drink. The null and alternative hypotheses are

H_0: $p = .5$ (no preference)
H_a: $p \neq .5$ (preference for one or the other)

where the letter p represents the proportion in the population that would prefer drink A.

Now, suppose that a much larger sample size of 960 was used and that the result was still that 55% of the sample prefers drink A. What effect will the larger sample size have on the statistical significance of the data?

Figure 11.6 displays hypothesis test and confidence interval results (from using Minitab) for both sample sizes, assuming the sample proportion remains at 55%. When the sample size is 60, the p-value is 0.439, so we cannot reject the null hypothesis as a possible truth. When the sample size is 960, the p-value is 0.002, so the result is *statistically significant*. In that case, we can reject the null hypothesis and conclude that a majority of the population would prefer drink A.

The sample size also influences the width of the 95% confidence intervals for the true p. When the sample size is only 60, the 95% confidence interval for the true p is .42 to .68, an imprecise, wide range of estimates. When the sample size is 960, the 95% confidence interval is .52 to .58, a relatively precise range of estimates and an interval range that is entirely in the region defined by the alternative hypothesis. ◆

Test of p = 0.5 vs p ≠ 0.5

Results when n = 60 and sample p = 0.55

X	N	Sample p	95.0 % CI	Z-Value	P-Value
33	60	0.55	(0.42, 0.68)	0.77	0.439

Results when n = 960 and sample p = 0.55

X	N	Sample p	95.0 % CI	Z-Value	P-Value
528	960	0.55	(0.52, 0.58)	3.10	0.002

FIGURE 11.6   **Taste test results for $n = 60$ and $n = 960$**

This example shows us again why it's not advisable to use the phrase "accept the null hypothesis." The sample of only 60 participants was too small to be conclusive about whether or not we should reject the statement that the true p is .5. The larger sample resulted in a sample proportion that would be very unlikely if in fact the true population proportion is .5 and thus allowed a stronger conclusion.

Why is the same sample proportion more significant for a relatively larger sample size? The conceptual, or intuitive, answer to this question is that, with more data, we have more accurate sample estimates and we reduce our uncertainty about what population values are likely. The technical answer is that increasing the sample size decreases the standard error of the sample proportion.

The z-value for the hypothesis test is

$$z = \frac{\text{Sample estimate} - \text{Null value}}{\text{Null standard error}}$$

For both of our hypothesis tests, the sample proportion is .55 and the null hypothesis value is .5, so the top portion of the calculation is the same for both cases. The z-value changes because the sample size affects the standard error.

- When the sample size is $n = 60$, the null standard error $= \sqrt{\dfrac{.5(1 - .5)}{60}} \approx$ .065.

- When the sample size is $n = 960$, the null standard error $= \sqrt{\dfrac{.5(1 - .5)}{960}} \approx$ .016.

Notice that increasing the sample size decreases the null standard error. Generally, a standard error roughly measures the "typical difference" between a statistic and a population parameter. If the null hypothesis that $p = .5$ were actually true, the consequence of taking a larger sample is that the sample proportion would be likely to fall closer to the null value (.5) than it would for a smaller sample. As a result, the difference between the sample proportion of .55 and the null value of .5 is relatively greater when the sample size is large than when it is small.

One more comment is in order about the example just presented. If in fact the null hypothesis were true, and $p = .50$, then a sample proportion as large as .55 would probably not have occurred in the larger sample. It is quite feasible for a sample of $n = 60$ to produce a sample proportion that differs from the truth by as much as .55 differs from .50. But it is quite unlikely for a sample of $n = 960$ to produce a sample proportion this far from the true proportion.

In summary, it is the size of the standard error that changes based on the size of the sample, and increasing the sample size gives a smaller standard error. As a result, a particular absolute difference between the sample proportion and null value is more significant with a large sample than with a small sample. No matter how large the sample, the sample proportion is likely to fall within two or so standard errors of the true population proportion. If the difference between the sample proportion and the null value is more than this, it is significant.

11.5

turn on your mind

If the null hypothesis is true, the correct conclusion is "cannot reject the null hypothesis." If the alternative hypothesis is true, the correct conclusion is "reject the null hypothesis." Increasing the sample size increases the probability of making the correct conclusion in one of these cases, but not in the other. Your job is to figure out which is which. Here is a hint: The conclusion "cannot reject the null hypothesis" is made as long as the sample proportion falls within a reasonable number of standard errors of the null value. When the null hypothesis is true, does the likelihood of this happening change as the sample size increases? Explain, and use this explanation to determine which conclusion has increased probability of being made correctly with increasing sample size.*

11.6 | REAL IMPORTANCE VERSUS STATISTICAL SIGNIFICANCE

The phrase *statistically significant* only means that the data are strong enough to reject a null hypothesis. A result that is significant in the statistical meaning of the word is not necessarily significant in the more common meaning of the word. One reason for this, of course, is that the research study might not address an important real-world issue. Even when the research issue is important, however, statistical significance does not guarantee practical significance.

A *p*-value provides information about the conclusiveness of the evidence against the null hypothesis, but it does *not* provide information about the *magnitude* of the effect. In some instances, the magnitude of a statistically significant effect can be so small that the practical effect is not important. If the sample size is large enough, almost any null hypothesis can be rejected be-

*__HINT:__ Think about the probability that the sample proportion falls within 2 standard errors of the null value p_0 when it is the truth. Does that probability depend on the sample size?

cause there is almost always at least a slight relationship between two variables, or a slight difference between two groups, or a slight deviation from the status quo.

<table>
<tr><td>EXAMPLE 11.9
Birth Month and Height</td><td>The headline of a Reuters news article posted at the Yahoo Health News website February 18, 1998 was "Spring Birthday Confers Height Advantage." The article describes an Austrian study of the heights of 507,125 military recruits. In an article in the journal Nature, the researchers reported their finding that men born in the spring were, on average, about 0.6 centimeters taller than men born in the fall (Weber et al., Nature, 1998, 391:754–755). This is a small difference; 0.6 centimeters is only about 1/4 of an inch. The sample size for the study is so large that even a very small difference will earn the title statistically significant. Do you think the practical import of this difference warranted the headline? ◆</td></tr>
</table>

CASE STUDY 11.1
The Internet and Loneliness: Case Study 1.7 Revisited

We encountered the concept that a statistically significant result may not have practical importance when we read Case Study 1.7. That case study examined research done at Carnegie Mellon University in which the principal finding was that Internet usage may lead to feelings of loneliness and depression. This finding received a lot of media attention, but a close look at the study shows that the actual effects were quite small. For example, according to the *New York Times,* "one hour a week on the Internet was associated, on average, with an increase of 0.03, or 1 percent on the depression scale" (Harman, 30 August 1998, p. A3).

11.6

turn on your mind

In this section, we noted that a research finding of "statistical significance" does not necessarily indicate that the finding is of practical importance. In situations where the hypothesis test is about a specified value for a population parameter, explain why it would be helpful to present a confidence interval for the parameter along with the finding of statistical significance.*

11.7 | WHAT CAN GO WRONG: THE TWO TYPES OF ERRORS

Whenever we use a sample of data to make a decision about a larger population, we may make a mistake. In testing statistical hypotheses, there are two potential decisions and each decision brings the possibility of an error. Decision makers and researchers should consider the consequences of these possible errors when they create and apply their decision-making rules.

*HINT: Think about what information a confidence interval for a proportion provides.

EXAMPLE 11.5—_CONTINUED_
**The Courtroom Analogy**

Let's use the courtroom analogy as an illustration. Viewed from within the hypothesis testing framework, the two hypothesis are

> _Null hypothesis:_ The accused is _innocent._
> _Alternative hypothesis:_ The accused is _guilty._

and the two possible decisions for a judge or jury are

> _Do not reject the null hypothesis:_ The accused is _not guilty._
> _Reject the null hypothesis:_ The accused is _guilty._

For trials in general, here are the possible errors and the consequences that accompany those errors:

- _Possible error 1:_ A "guilty" verdict for a person who is really innocent.
  Consequence: An innocent person is falsely convicted. The guilty party remains free.

- _Possible error 2:_ A "not guilty" verdict for a person who committed the crime.
  Consequence: A criminal is not punished.

In the American court system, a false conviction (possible error 1) is generally viewed as the more serious error. Not only is an innocent person punished but also a guilty one remains free. Courtroom rules and rules affecting pretrial investigations tend to reflect society's concern about incorrectly punishing an innocent person. ◆

EXAMPLE 11.10
**A Medical Analogy**

Imagine that you are tested to determine if you have a disease. The lab technician or physician who evaluates your results must make a choice between two hypotheses:

> _Null hypothesis:_ You do not have the disease.
> _Alternative hypothesis:_ You have the disease.

Unfortunately, many laboratory tests for diseases are not 100% accurate. There is a chance the result is wrong. Consider the two possible errors and their consequences:

- _Possible error 1:_ You are told you have the disease, but you actually don't. The test result was a **false positive.**
  Consequence: You will be unnecessarily concerned about your health and you may receive unnecessary treatment.

- _Possible error 2:_ You are told that you do not have the disease, but you actually do. The test result was a **false negative.**
  Consequence: You do not receive treatment for a disease that you have. If this is a contagious disease, you may infect others.

Which error is more serious? In most medical situations, the second possible error, a false negative, is more serious but this could depend on the disease and the follow-up actions that are taken. For instance, in a screening test for cancer, a false negative could lead to a fatal delay in treatment. Initial test results that are "positive" for cancer are usually followed up with a retest so a false positive may be discovered quickly. ◆

Type 1 and Type 2 Errors
in Statistical Hypothesis Testing

The situation encountered in statistical hypothesis testing is about the same as in the courtroom and medical analogies. One notable difference is that in statistical hypothesis testing, random sampling error causes the errors defined in this section. When a sample is used, the "luck of the draw" could be such that the sample statistic does not properly represent the population value. This is particularly likely when the sample size is small and the corresponding margin of error is large.

In the terminology of statistical hypothesis testing, the two possible errors are called the **type 1** and **type 2** errors.

> *definition* A **type 1 error** can only occur when the null hypothesis is actually true. The error occurs by concluding that the alternative hypothesis is true.
>
> A **type 2 error** can only occur when the alternative hypothesis is actually true. The error occurs by concluding that the null hypothesis cannot be rejected.

The numbering of the error types indicates which of the two hypotheses, (1) null or (2) alternative, is actually true. For example, a type 1 error is the error that occurs when the first hypothesis, the null, is really true but we decide in favor of the alternative.

EXAMPLE 11.11
Calcium and the Relief of Premenstrual Symptoms

Suppose researchers are planning a randomized "blind" trial in which 400 women who suffer from premenstrual symptoms are randomly assigned either to take calcium supplements or a placebo. The research group believes that the use of calcium supplements will reduce the severity of the symptoms. For three months, the researchers will track the participants' premenstrual symptoms and will use the sample data to evaluate these hypotheses:

H_0: For reducing symptoms, calcium is not better than placebo.
H_a: For reducing symptoms, calcium is better than placebo.

A type 1 error would occur if the researchers decide that calcium is better than placebo when, in fact, it is not (the null hypothesis is true). A type 2 error would occur if the researchers decide that calcium is not better than placebo when, in fact, it is (the alternative hypothesis is true).

In 1998, a research article describing a study like our hypothetical example was published in the *American Journal of Obstetrics and Gynecology* (Thys-Jacobs et al., 1998). The authors concluded that there was a statistically significant difference between the effectiveness of calcium supplements and placebo. Ideally, this conclusion is correct and no error was made. If future research and experience proves that calcium supplements are actually not effective, these researchers will have made a type 1 error by choosing the alternative when the null hypothesis is true. If a type 1 error was made in this situation, women may be taking calcium to reduce their symptoms when it does not actually work. On the other hand, if the researchers had not found a difference but calcium really is effective (a type 2 error) then women would not know about a treatment that is actually effective. ◆

EXAMPLE 11.10—CONTINUED
The Medical Analogy

In Example 11.10, we saw the two possible errors that might occur when you are tested for the presence of disease. Let's rephrase the possible errors in statistical terminology.

- ◆ A type 1 error occurs when the diagnosis is that you have the disease when actually you do not. In other words, *a type 1 error is a false positive.*

- ◆ A type 2 error occurs when the diagnosis is that you do not have the disease when actually you do. In other words, *a type 2 error is a false negative.* ◆

The Trade-Off Between the Risks of the Two Possible Errors

There always is a trade-off between the chances of making the two types of errors. For instance, in the American court system, the procedures designed to minimize the probability of a false conviction carry with them an increased risk of erroneous not guilty verdicts. But, if court rules were made more lenient to decrease the risk of incorrect acquittals, the probability of false convictions would increase.

Determining the safer direction in which to err depends upon the situation as well as the consequences of each type of potential error. HIV screening tests tend to err on the side of false positives because the consequence of failing to detect HIV could be disastrous. Because HIV screening does produce many false positives, people who test positive with an inexpensive screening test for HIV generally are tested again with an extremely accurate but more expensive test before they are given the results.

In cases when the null hypothesis is true, *the probability of making a type 1 error is the level of significance α.* Therefore, the researcher actually determines the probability that a type 1 error will occur by deciding what to use as the significance level, α. A type 1 error occurs when the *p*-value $< \alpha$, leading to the conclusion that the null hypothesis is false. But when the null hypothesis is true, the probability of choosing a sample that results in a *p*-value less than α is simply α. For instance, with a *z*-statistic and a two-sided test, the *p*-value is less than 0.05 if $|z| > 1.96$, which happens with probability 0.05.

Determining the probability of a type 2 error is much more difficult. That probability depends on the sample size, the form of the test statistic, the true parameter value, and the level of significance. We will discuss probabilities associated with the two types of errors in more detail in Chapter 13.

11.7

turn on your mind

Draw a tree diagram (see Chapter 7) where "H_0 true" and "H_a true" are the two choices for the first set of branches, and the two possible decisions are the choices for the second set of branches. For each of the four resulting pathways, identify whether the pathway results in a correct decision, a type 1 error, or a type 2 error.*

CASE STUDY 11.2
An Interpretation of a p-Value Not Fit to Print

One of the most common mistakes that researchers and journalists make has to do with the interpretation of the *p*-value. We learned that a *p*-value does not tell us the probability that a hypothesis is true. When a *p*-value is erroneously interpreted in this manner, the resulting statements can be completely misleading.

In an article entitled, "Probability Experts May Decide Pennsylvania Vote," the *New York Times* (April 11, 1994, p. A15) reported on the use of statistics to try to decide whether there was fraud in a special election held in Philadelphia. When a state senator from Pennsylvania's Second Senate District died in 1993, a special election was held to fill the seat. The Democratic candidate, William Stinson, defeated the Republican candidate, Bruce Marks, by the narrow margin of 20,518 votes to 20,057 votes, a difference of only 461 votes.

The Republicans were disturbed when they saw the comparison of voting booth results and absentee ballot results, shown in Table 11.2. The Republican Marks beat Stinson in the voting booths, but Stinson, the election winner, had a huge advantage in the absentee ballots. The Republicans charged that the election was fraudulent and asked the courts to disallow the absentee ballot votes on the basis of suspicion of fraud. In February 1994, three months after the election, Philadelphia Federal District Court Judge Clarence Newcomer disqualified all absentee ballots and ruled that the Republican, Marks, should be seated. The Democrats appealed this ruling, and both sides hired statisticians to help sort out what might have happened.

One statistical expert, Orley Ashenfelter, examined 22 previous senatorial elections in Philadelphia to determine the relationship between votes cast in the voting booth and those cast by absentee ballot. Using the previous data, he calculated a regression equation to predict the difference in absentee ballot votes for the two parties based on a given amount of difference between the parties in the voting booth.

In the voting booth, there was a difference of 564 votes in favor of the Republicans. Using his equation, Ashenfelter estimated that when there was this much difference in favor of the Republicans in the voting booths, there would be a difference of 133 votes in favor of the Republicans in the absentee ballots. Instead, the difference for absentee ballots in the disputed election was 1025 votes in favor of the *Democrats*.

Of course, everyone knows that chance events play a role in determining what happens in any given election. A hypothesis test can be used to evaluate the possible effects of randomness. Ashenfelter considered the null hypothesis that there was no fraud and calculated that the *p*-value was 6%. In other words, he determined that *if there was no fraud,* the probability was 6% that the Democratic advantage in absentee votes would be as large as 1025 votes when the Republican advantage in the voting booths was 565 votes.

Unfortunately, the author of the *New York Times* article misinterpreted this probability in a way that leads readers to believe that the election was probably fraudulent. When you read the following quote from the article, see if you can detect the mistake in interpretation:

> More to the point, there is some larger probability that chance alone would lead to a sufficiently large Democratic edge on the absentee ballots to overcome the Republican margin on the machine balloting. And the probability of such a swing . . . Professor Ashenfelter calculates, was about 6 percent. Putting it another way, if past elections are a reliable guide to current voting behavior, *there is a 94 percent*

TABLE 11.2 ■ **Election Results by Type of Vote**

	Stinson	Marks	Difference
Voting Booth	19,127	19,691	−564
Absentee	1391	366	+1025
Total	20,518	20,057	+461

chance that irregularities in the absentee ballots, not chance alone, swung the election to the Democrat, Professor Ashenfelter concludes (Passell, 1994, p. A15, italics added).

The author's statement that there is a 94% chance that irregularities swung the election is wrong. He mistakenly interpreted the *p*-value to be the probability that the null hypothesis is true so he reported what he thought to be the probability that the election was fraudulent. In this case, the *p*-value only tells us that, if we assume there was no fraud, there is a 6% chance that we would see results like these. The *p*-value cannot be used to find the probability that the election was fraudulent.

The case went through two appeals, but the original decision made by Judge Newcomer to disallow the absentee ballots was upheld each time. The statistical evidence was not a major factor in these decisions. The appeal judges found that there was enough evidence of irregular absentee voting procedures to justify Judge Newcomer's decision.

KEY TERMS

Section 11.1
null hypothesis, 356
alternative hypothesis, 357
one-sided hypothesis test, 357
one-tailed hypothesis test, 357
two-sided hypothesis test, 358
two-tailed hypothesis test, 358

Sections 11.2 and 11.3
test statistic, 360
p-value, 360
level of significance, 360, 361
Bayesian statistics, 360–361

statistically significant, 361
α level, 361

Section 11.4
null value, 363
z-test for a proportion, 363
z-test statistic for proportion, 363, 367
p-value, test for proportion, 368
rejection region, 372

Section 11.5
sample size and statistical significance, 374

Section 11.6
statistical significance vs. importance, 376

Section 11.7
false positive, 378
false negative, 378
type 1 error, 379
type 2 error, 379

EXERCISES   Blue = Basics   **Bold, Bold** = Answer in back

Section 11.1

11.1 Determine whether each of these statements is an example of a null hypothesis or an alternative hypothesis.
  a. The average weight of Canadian geese is the same as the average weight of Canadian warblers.
  b. The proportion of books in the local public library that are novels is higher than the proportion of books in the university library that are novels.
  c. The average price of wool jackets in New York City is lower in the summer than in the winter.
  d. The proportion of students who receive A grades from Professor Harrington is the same as or higher than the proportion of students who receive A grades from Professor Cantor.

11.2 For each of the following situations, write the alternative hypothesis.
  a. The null hypothesis is H$_0$: $p = .30$ and it's a two-sided hypothesis test.
  b. The null hypothesis is H$_0$: $p \leq .45$.
  c. The null hypothesis is H$_0$: $p \geq .60$.

11.3 Is each of the following statements a valid null hypothesis? If not, explain why not.
  a. In a sample of students, the mean pulse rate for the men is equal to the mean pulse rate for the women.
  b. The average weight of newborn boys is the same as the average weight of newborn girls.
  c. The proportion of cars in California that are white is higher than the proportion of cars in Maine that are white.

11.4 State the null and alternative hypotheses for each of the following potential research questions. In each situation, also indicate whether the hypothesis test will be one-sided or two-sided.
   a. Do female college students study more, on average, than male college students do?
   b. Compared to men who are not bald, are bald men more likely to have heart disease?
   c. Is there a correlation between height and head circumference?
   d. Will an increase in the speed limits on interstate highways lead to an increase in the highway fatality rate?
   e. When a coin is spun on its edge, is the probability that it will land "heads-up" equal to .5?

11.5 Suppose that a statistics teacher asks his students to each randomly pick one of the numbers 0, 1, 2, 3, 4. His general theory is that the proportion who pick the number 0 will be less than what would be expected from random selection. Use p to represent the population proportion that would pick the number 0.
   a. What is the specific value of p that corresponds to true random selection?
   b. In terms of p, write null and alternative hypotheses for this situation.

11.6 Suppose the present success rate in the treatment of a particular psychiatric disorder is .65 (65%). A research group hopes to demonstrate that the success rate of a new treatment will be better than this standard. Use the letter p to represent the success rate of the new treatment. Write null and alternative hypotheses for p.

11.7 Do you think researchers should determine whether to use a one-sided or two-sided hypothesis test before they look at the sample data or after they look at it? Explain.

11.8 For each of the following situations, write the null and alternative hypotheses in words (as in Example 11.1) and in symbols (as in Example 11.2).
   a. In the last census, taken five years ago, it was determined that 6% of school-aged children in a certain state lived with their grandparent(s). To support a bill on tax breaks for seniors, a congressional member plans to take a random sample of school-aged children to determine if that percent has increased.
   b. An anthropologist is trying to determine if the people in a certain region descend from the same ancestors as another region she has studied. She knows that in the region she has studied, 15% of the people have a certain unique genetic trait. She plans to take a random sample of people in the new region and test them for that trait.
   c. Paul likes a certain candy that comes in a bag with mixed colors, each with their own flavor. The candy company's website claims that 30% of these candies are red, which is Paul's favorite. He doubts their claim and thinks less than 30% are red. He is willing to assume that the candy is randomly placed into bags, and he plans to buy several bags of candy and count the proportion of red pieces.

11.9 Refer to the previous exercise. In each situation, the hypotheses are about a population proportion p. Explain what the population is and what the proportion of interest is in each case.

Sections 11.2 and 11.3

11.10 Consider this quote: "In a recent survey, 61 out of 100 consumers reported that they preferred plastic bags instead of paper bags for their groceries. If there is no difference in preference in the population, the chance of such extreme results in a sample of this size is about 0.03. Because 0.03 is less than 0.05, we can conclude that there is a statistically significant difference in preference." Give a numerical value for each of the following.
   a. The p-value.
   b. The level of significance, α.
   c. The sample proportion.
   d. The sample size.

11.11 State the conclusion that would be made in each of the following situations.
   a. Level of significance = 0.05, p-value = 0.10.
   b. Level of significance = 0.05, p-value = 0.01.
   c. Level of significance = 0.01, p-value = 0.99.
   d. Level of significance = 0.01, p-value = 0.002.

11.12 Suppose that a woman thinks she might be pregnant so she takes a pregnancy test. Considering this situation to be analogous to hypothesis testing, write each of the following in words.
   a. The null hypothesis. (*Hint:* Remember that the null hypothesis generally states that there is nothing going on.)
   b. The alternative hypothesis.
   c. The conclusion if there is not enough evidence to reject the null hypothesis.
   d. The conclusion if the null hypothesis is rejected.

11.13 Consider testing the null hypothesis that there is no relationship between smoking and getting a certain disease versus the alternative hypothesis that smokers are more likely than nonsmokers to get the disease. Explain in words what would be concluded about the relationship in the population if
   a. The p-value is 0.33 and the level of significance is 0.05.
   b. The p-value is 0.03 and the level of significance is 0.05.

11.14 Refer to part (a) of the previous exercise. Use the scenario to explain why it is not appropriate to *accept* the null hypothesis.

11.15 About 10% of the human population is left-handed. Suppose that a researcher speculates that artists are more likely to be left-handed than are other people in the general population. The researcher surveys 150 artists and finds that 18 of them are left-handed.
   a. State the researcher's null and alternative hypotheses.
   b. What proportion of the sample of artists is left-handed?
   c. To calculate a p-value for the hypothesis test, what probability should the researcher calculate? Make your answer specific to this situation.

11.16 An article in *USA Today* (Elias, June 3, 1999, p. D1) describes a study done by Georgia State University psychologist James Dabbs in which he found that women who are trial lawyers (litigators) are more likely to have male children than women lawyers who are not trial lawyers. According to the article, "58% of litigators' kids were boys vs. 44% [boys] for the others. The odds of this happening by chance are less than 5%, he says."

a. Consider the second sentence in the quote. What statistical term describes this result?

b. The quote from the article tells us that a *p*-value is less than 5%. Write one sentence that describes exactly what the *p*-value measures in this setting.

c. Dabbs believes the result can be attributed to the women's testosterone levels because, in a previous study, he found that, on average, women litigators have higher testosterone levels than women lawyers who aren't litigators. Do you think this conclusion is justified? Explain why or why not.

11.17 Given the convention of declaring that a result is "statistically significant" if the *p*-value is 0.05 or less, what decision would be made concerning the null and alternative hypotheses in each of the following cases? Be explicit about the wording of the decision.

a. *p*-value = 0.35.
b. *p*-value = 0.001.
c. *p*-value = 0.04.

11.18 Two researchers are testing the null hypothesis that a population proportion *p* is .25 and the alternative hypothesis that *p* > .25. Both take a sample of 100 observations. Researcher A finds a sample proportion of .29 and Researcher B finds a sample proportion of .33. For which researcher will the *p*-value of the test be smaller? Explain without actually doing any computations.

11.19 A physician claims that as soon as his patients have a positive pregnancy test he is generally able to predict the sex of the baby and that his probability of being right is greater than the one-half that would be expected if he was just guessing. A skeptic challenges his claim, and the physician decides to collect data for the next ten pregnancies to try to support his claim.

a. From the perspective of the physician, what are the null and alternative hypotheses for this situation?

b. Out of the ten pregnancies, he is correct six times. Write in words what probability needs to be computed to find the *p*-value.

c. The *p*-value for this test is 0.377. Does that prove that the skeptic is correct? Explain.

d. State the appropriate conclusion, using $\alpha = 0.05$.

e. Assuming the physician really does have some ability to make these predictions, what would you recommend that he do to increase the chance of proving his claim?

Section 11.4

11.20 Find the *p*-value for each of these situations, taking into account whether the test is one-sided or two-sided.

a. *z*-statistic = 2.10, $H_0: p = .10$, $H_a: p \neq .10$.
b. *z*-statistic = −2.00, $H_0: p = .6$, $H_a: p < .6$.

c. *z*-statistic = −1.09, $H_0: p = .5$, $H_a: p < .5$.
d. *z*-statistic = 4.25, $H_0: p = .25$, $H_a: p > .25$.

11.21 Refer to the previous exercise. For each of parts (a) to (d), specify the rejection region for $\alpha = 0.05$, then make a conclusion for the test using the rejection region rule.

11.22 In each of the following, determine whether the conditions for conducting a *z*-test for a proportion are met. If not, explain why not.

a. Twenty students are randomly selected from the list of all sorority and fraternity members at a university, to determine if a majority of sorority and fraternity students favor a new policy on alcohol on campus. The hypotheses are
$H_0: p = .50$.
$H_a: p > .50$.

b. Twenty employees of a large company are randomly selected to determine if the proportion of company employees who are left-handed exceeds the national proportion of 10% who are left-handed. The hypotheses are
$H_0: p = .10$.
$H_a: p > .10$.

c. A company employs 500 stockbrokers. They are all surveyed to find out if a majority believes the market will go up in the next year.
$H_0: p = .50$.
$H_a: p > .50$.

d. A market research firm wants to know if more than 30% of the people who visit a mall actually buy something. A researcher stands by the exit door starting at noon and asks 50 people as they are leaving whether they bought anything.
$H_0: p = .30$.
$H_a: p > .30$.

11.23 Refer to the previous exercise. In each of the parts define in words the population parameter *p*.

11.24 For each of the following calculate the *z*-statistic:

a. Sample size $n = 30$; sample proportion $\hat{p} = .60$.
$H_0: p = .50$.
$H_a: p \neq .50$.

b. Sample size $n = 60$; sample proportion $\hat{p} = .10$.
$H_0: p = .25$.
$H_a: p < .25$.

c. Sample size $n = 500$; sample proportion $\hat{p} = .30$.
$H_0: p = .20$.
$H_a: p > .20$.

d. Sample size $n = 200$; sample proportion $\hat{p} = .50$.
$H_0: p = .80$.
$H_a: p < .80$.

11.25 Refer to the previous exercise. In each case, calculate the *p*-value for the test.

11.26 Explain the difference between the *null standard error* used in the denominator of a *z*-statistic for a test for a proportion and the *standard error* used in finding a confidence interval for a proportion.

11.27 *Time Magazine* reported that in a 1994 survey of 507 randomly selected adult American Catholics, 59% answered yes to the question "Do you favor allowing women to be priests?" (*Time*, 26 December–2 January 1995, pp. 74–76).

a. Set up the null and alternative hypotheses for deciding whether more than half of American Catholics favor allowing women to be priests.

b. What conditions are necessary for using a z-statistic to test the hypotheses in part (a)? Are those conditions met here? Explain.

c. Compute the test statistic for this situation.

d. Calculate the p-value for the test.

e. Based on the p-value, make a conclusion for this situation. Write it in both statistical language and in words that someone with no training in statistics would understand.

f. Calculate a 95% confidence interval for the proportion of American Catholics who favor allowing women to be priests. Does this confidence interval confirm the conclusion that a majority of American Catholics favor allowing women priests? Explain.

11.28 In Exercise 11.15, we described a survey done to determine whether artists are more likely to be left-handed than others in the general population. If we use p to represent the proportion of all artists who are left-handed, the hypotheses are H_0: $p = .10$ and H_a: $p > .10$. The sample result was that 18 artists of 150 surveyed (or 12%) are left-handed.

a. From the given information, do we know if the conditions necessary to use a z-statistic for this test are met? Explain.

b. Conduct a hypothesis test. Clearly give the details of the five steps. Be sure to write a conclusion.

11.29 Suppose a one-sided test for a proportion resulted in a p-value of 0.04. What would the p-value be if the test was two-sided instead?

11.30 Suppose a two-sided test for a proportion resulted in a p-value of 0.07.

a. Using the usual criterion for hypothesis testing, would we conclude that the population proportion was different from the null hypothesis value? Explain.

b. Suppose the test had been constructed as a one-sided test instead and that the sample proportion was in the direction to support the alternative hypothesis. Using the usual criterion for hypothesis testing, would we be able to decide in favor of the alternative hypothesis? Explain.

11.31 In Example 11.7, results were given for a survey of students in a statistics class who measured the lengths of their right and left feet to the nearest millimeter. The right and left foot measurements were equal for 103 of the 215 students. Assuming this class is representative of all college students, is there evidence that the proportion of college students whose feet are the *same* length differs from one-half? Go through the five steps of hypothesis testing for this situation.

11.32 A Gallup Poll released on October 13, 2000 (Chambers, 2000) found that 47% of the 1052 U.S. adults surveyed classified themselves as "very happy" when given the choices of "very happy," "fairly happy," or "not too happy." Suppose that a journalist who is a pessimist took advantage of this poll to write a headline titled "Poll finds that U.S. adults who are very happy are in the minority." If p = proportion of all U.S. adults who are very

happy, go through the five steps of hypothesis testing and determine whether the headline is justified. Be sure to comment on the headline in your conclusion in step 5.

Sections 11.5 and 11.6

11.33 Suppose the null and alternative hypotheses in a test are
H_0: $p = .70$.
H_a: $p \neq .70$.
For each of the following sample sizes calculate the null standard error.

a. $n = 40$.
b. $n = 100$.
c. $n = 500$.
d. $n = 1000$.

11.34 Refer to the previous exercise. In each case, suppose the sample proportion is $\hat{p} = .75$ and compute the test statistic z and the p-value. Then make a conclusion using a level of significance of 0.05. Comment on the relationship between the sample size and the conclusions.

11.35 Sometimes a result that is statistically significant does not have practical significance. Is this more likely to happen when the sample size is very large or when it is very small? Explain.

11.36 One possible problem in hypothesis testing is that researchers fail to find a statistically significant result even though the null hypothesis is false. Is this problem more likely to occur with a very small sample or with a very large sample? Explain.

11.37 Researchers know that 20% of a certain ethnic group has a distinctive trait. They want to know if the proportion with the trait is higher in a second ethnic group. They take a random sample of n members of the second group and find the sample proportion $\hat{p}$ with the trait. The parameter of interest is p, the population proportion with the trait for the second group. In each of the following scenarios, determine which situation is more likely to lead to a statistically significant finding, assuming all other conditions remain the same. Explain your answer.

a. $n = 100$ or $n = 1000$.
b. $p = .25$ or $p = .45$.
c. $\hat{p} = .25$ or $\hat{p} = .45$.

11.38 When reporting the results of a study, explain why a distinction should be made between "statistical" significance and significance as the term is used in ordinary language.

11.39 Which do you think is more informative when you are given the results of a hypothesis test, the p-value or the decision about whether or not to reject the null hypothesis? Explain.

11.40 Which do you think is more informative when you are given the results of a study, a confidence interval or a p-value? Explain.

11.41 Suppose you were to read in your local newspaper that a new study based on 100 men had found that there was *no difference* in heart attack rates for men who exercised regularly and men who did not. Do you think the study found *exactly* the same rate of heart attacks for the two groups of men? In the context of the material in this chapter, what would you suspect was the reason for that reported finding?

11.42 Suppose that a study is designed to choose between the hypotheses

Null hypothesis: Population proportion is .20.
Alternative hypothesis: Population proportion is higher than .20.

On the basis of a random sample of size 400, the sample proportion is .25.
   a. Compute the *z*-score corresponding to the sample proportion of .25, assuming the null hypothesis is true.
   b. What is the *p*-value for the standardized score computed in part (a)?
   c. Based on the result from part (b), make a conclusion. Be explicit about the wording of your conclusion and justify your answer.
   d. Suppose that the sample size had only been 100, rather than 400, but the sample proportion was again .25. Using this smaller sample size, repeat parts (a) to (c).
   e. Explain what this problem illustrates about the effect of sample size on statistical significance.

11.43 An advertisement for Claritin, a drug for seasonal nasal allergies, made this claim: "Clear relief without drowsiness. In studies, the incidence of drowsiness was similar to placebo" (*Time,* Feb. 6, 1995, p. 43). The advertisement also reported that 8% of the 1926 Claritin takers and 6% of the 2545 placebo takers reported drowsiness as a side effect. A one-sided test of whether or not a higher proportion of Claritin takers than placebo takers would experience drowsiness in the population results in a *p*-value of about 0.005.
   a. From this information, would you conclude that the incidence of drowsiness for the Claritin takers is statistically significantly higher than for the placebo takers?
   b. Does the answer to part (a) contradict the statement in the advertisement that the "incidence of drowsiness was similar to placebo"? Explain.
   c. Use this example to discuss the importance of making the distinction between the common use and the statistical use of the word *significant.*

Section 11.7

11.44 Explain whether each of the following statements is true or false.
   a. The *p*-value is the probability that the null hypothesis is true.
   b. If the null hypothesis is true, then the level of significance is the probability of making a type 1 error.
   c. A type 2 error can only occur when the null hypothesis is true.
   d. The probability of making a type 1 error plus the probability of making a type 2 error is 1.

11.45 Can the two types of error both be made in the same hypothesis test? Explain.

11.46 Define events as follows: A = Null hypothesis is true. A^C = Alternative hypothesis is true. B = Null hypothesis

is not rejected. B^C = Null hypothesis is rejected. For each of the following outcomes explain whether a type 1 error, a type 2 error, or a correct decision has been made.
   a. A and B.
   b. A^C and B.
   c. A and B^C.
   d. A^C and B^C.

11.47 A medical insurance company wants to know if the proportion of its customers requiring a hospital stay during a year will decrease if it provides coverage for certain types of alternative medicine. The company conducts a one-year study in which it gives insurance coverage for alternative medicine to 5000 randomly selected customers. Based on this study, the company tests the following hypotheses about the effect of offering the alternative medicine coverage to its customers:

   H_0: proportion requiring a hospital stay
     will not decrease
   H_a: proportion requiring a hospital stay
     will decrease

If the null hypothesis is rejected, the company will offer this coverage to all of its customers in the future.
   a. Explain what a type 1 error would be in this situation.
   b. Explain what a type 2 error would be in this situation.
   c. Explain which type of error would be more serious for the insurance company.
   d. Explain which type of error would be more serious for the customers.

11.48 Medical researchers now believe there may be a link between baldness and heart attacks in men.
   a. State the null hypothesis and the alternative hypothesis for a study used to investigate whether or not there is such a relationship.
   b. Discuss what would constitute a type 1 error in this study.
   c. Discuss what would constitute a type 2 error in this study.

11.49 Consider medical tests, in which the null hypothesis is that the patient does not have the disease and the alternative hypothesis is that they do.
   a. Give an example of a medical situation in which a type 1 error would be more serious.
   b. Give an example of a medical situation in which a type 2 error would be more serious.

11.50 Explain which type of error, type 1 or type 2, could be made in each of the following cases.
   a. The null hypothesis is true.
   b. The alternative hypothesis is true.
   c. The null hypothesis is not rejected.
   d. The null hypothesis is rejected.

11.51 Refer to Example 11.6 in which convincing evidence was found for the importance of order in a "random" selection between two letters. Suppose a student in your class ran for president of the campus student association and lost. After reading Example 11.6, she realized that because her name is at the end of the alphabet, she was listed after all of her opponents on the ballot and the election was unfair to her. She demands a reelection with names listed in random order.

a. Which type of error, type 1 or type 2, could have been made in Example 11.6? Explain.

b. If the type of error you specified in part (a) was made, is the reelection justified? Explain.

c. Now suppose the other type of error had been made, and the student read the results of the study in that case instead. Explain what the consequences would be for the student and the student government.

d. Which type of error do you think is more serious for the student who ran for president? Explain.

11.52 A politician is trying to decide whether to vote for a new tax bill that calls for substantial reforms. A random sample of voters in his district led him to believe the alternative hypothesis, H_a: $p > .5$, where p is the proportion of all voters in his district who support the bill. As a consequence, he decides to vote for the bill.

a. What would a type 1 error be in this situation, and what would be the consequences for the politician?

b. What would a type 2 error be in this situation, and what would be the consequences for the politician?

c. Explain which error would be more serious, if either, for the politician in this example.

d. Given the situation described, could the politician have made a type 1 error or a type 2 error?

Chapter Exercises

11.53 Consider the two conditions necessary for conducting a z-test for a proportion. One is a sample size condition, and the other is a condition about how the sample was collected. For each of the two conditions, explain why it is required in order for the test and the results to be valid.

11.54 Refer to the five steps of any hypothesis test, given in the introduction to this chapter and again in Section 11.4. Which step(s) can be completed before collecting any data?

11.55 A student has been accused of cheating on an examination by copying another student's paper, and you have been asked to serve on the panel that must decide the student's fate. If the student is found guilty, he will fail the course and will have to write an essay on honesty for the school paper.

a. What are the null and alternative hypotheses for this situation?

b. What is a type 1 error in this situation, and what are the consequences?

c. What is a type 2 error in this situation, and what are the consequences?

d. As a member of the panel making the decision, you must evaluate the seriousness of the two types of error. Explain which type you think is more serious.

11.56 In a survey of 240 students in an elementary statistics class at the University of California, Davis (UCD), 20 said they were left-handed and 220 said they were right-handed. Assume the students are representative of all students at the school. Does this provide evidence that the proportion of UCD students who are left-handed differs from the national proportion of .10? Carry out the five steps of the hypothesis test for this situation.

11.57 Max likes to keep track of birthdays of people he meets. He has 170 birthdays listed on his birthday calendar. One cold January night, he comes up with the theory that people are more likely to be born in October than they would be if all 365 days were equally likely. He consults his birthday calendar and finds that 22 of the 170 birthdays are in October.

a. Write down the null and alternative hypotheses for Max's test. Be sure to carefully specify what p represents.

b. Carry out the remaining four steps of the hypothesis test for this situation.

11.58 Specify the null and alternative hypotheses in words for each of the following research questions.

a. Does listening to Mozart increase performance on an intelligence test?

b. Does talking to plants result in better growth for the plants?

c. Does drinking fluoridated water lead to increased bone fractures in elderly people?

11.59 For the following two situations, define the population parameter in words. Then specify the null and alternative hypotheses in symbols.

a. For people suffering from a certain type of chronic pain, 70% experience temporary relief when they take a standard medication. If a new medication appears to be more effective, it will replace the standard. Does the new medication provide pain relief to a larger proportion than the standard medication?

b. A student at a large university is thinking about starting a new service in which students can order their textbooks from his website and he will buy them at the bookstore and deliver them for a small service charge. He plans to survey a random sample of students and ask them if they would be willing to pay for such a service. If he is convinced that at least 5% of students would use his service, he will go forward with it.

11.60 Refer to the previous exercise. For each of the two situations described, explain the consequences of a type 1 error and the consequences of a type 2 error. For part (a), explain which type would be more serious for the patients, and for part (b) explain which type would be more serious for the student who is planning the new service.

11.61 Find the p-value for each of these situations, taking into account whether the test is one-sided or two-sided.

a. z-statistic = 1.45, H_0: $p = .50$, H_a: $p \neq .50$.

b. z-statistic = -1.78, H_0: $p = .3$, H_a: $p < .3$.

c. z-statistic = 1.78, H_0: $p = .3$, H_a: $p < .3$.

d. z-statistic = 2.25, H_0: $p = .75$, H_a: $p > .75$.

11.62 Refer to the previous exercise. For each of parts (a) to (d), specify the rejection region for $\alpha = 0.05$, then make a conclusion for the test using the rejection region rule.

11.63 For a test of H_0: $p = .25$ versus H_a: $p > .25$, for what range of values of the sample proportion $\hat{p}$ will the p-value for the test be *greater* than 0.5? Explain your answer.

11.64 For a one-sided hypothesis test for a proportion in which the alternative hypothesis is H_a: $p < p_0$, for what values of the test statistic z will the p-value be *greater* than 0.5? Explain your answer.

11.65 In Chapter 2, we saw data from a statistics class activity in which students were asked to "randomly" pick a number (integer) from 1 to 10. Of the 190 students, 56 picked the number 7. Carry out the five steps of hypothesis testing to determine if people similar to these students are more likely to pick the number 7 than would be expected by chance if all numbers were equally likely.

11.66 A professor planned to give an examination in a large class on the Monday before Thanksgiving vacation. Some students asked if he could change the date because so many of their classmates had at least one other exam on that date. They speculated that at least 40% of the class had this problem. The professor agreed to poll the class, and if there was convincing evidence that the proportion with at least one other exam on that date was greater than .40, he would change the date. Of the 250 students in the class, 109 reported that they had another exam on that date.
   a. What proportion of the class reported that they had another exam on that date?
   b. Is the proportion you found in part (a) a sample proportion or a population proportion?
   c. The professor conducted a z-test of $H_0: p = .40$ versus $H_a: p > .40$ and found $z = 1.16$ and p-value = 0.125. He said he would not move the exam because the null hypothesis cannot be rejected, and there is not convincing evidence that the population proportion is greater than .40. What is wrong with his reasoning? [*Hint:* Refer to part (b).]

11.67 According to *USA Today* (Snapshot, April 20, 1998, also referenced in exercise 9.74), a random sample of 8709 adults taken in 1976 found that 9% believed in reincarnation. A poll of 1000 adults in 1997 found that 25% believed in reincarnation. Because the margin of error for the 1976 poll is so small, we will treat the sample proportion of .09 as if it were the population proportion with this belief in 1976. Test the hypothesis that the proportion of adults believing in reincarnation in 1997 was higher than the proportion in 1976.

11.68 In a survey of students at the University of California, Davis, students were asked which of two popular soft drinks they preferred—let's call them brand C and brand P. Of the 159 respondents, 80 preferred brand P

and 79 preferred brand C. Assuming these students represent all students at UCD, test whether there is a preference for one drink over the other for students at UCD.

11.69 Refer to the previous exercise. Some students were asked if they preferred C or P, while other students were asked if they preferred P or C. Of the 159 respondents, 86 responded with the first drink presented. Test the hypothesis that the first drink presented is more likely to be selected than the second drink presented.

Dataset Exercises

11.70 Use the dataset **UCDavis2.** The variable *Friends* is a response to the question "Who do you find it easiest to make friends with? People of the (circle one) Same Sex or Opposite Sex?" The responses are S = same or O = opposite.
   a. Is there sufficient evidence that students find it easier to make friends with the opposite sex than with the same sex? What assumption(s) did you have to make about the sample in order for the testing procedure to be valid?
   b. Conduct the analysis separately for men and for women, using the variable "Sex" to identify males (M) and females (F).
   c. Refer to part (b). Compare the results for males and females by writing a summary of the results in words that would be understood by someone who has not studied statistics.
   d. Compare your results in parts (a) and (b). Explain how they are similar and how they are different, if at all. Explain any discrepancies you found.

11.71 Use the dataset **UCDavis2.** The variable *Seat* is a response to the question "Where do you typically sit in a classroom?" Possible responses were F = Front, M = Middle, B = Back.
   a. Test the hypothesis that a majority of students prefer to sit in the middle of the room.
   b. Specify the population of interest, and comment on whether this sample is an appropriate representation of it.

REFERENCES

Chambers, Chris (2000). "Americans are overwhelmingly happy and optimistic about the future of the United States," Gallup Poll Press Release, October 13, 2000, www.gallup.com/poll/releases/pr001013.asp.

Ott, R. L. (1998). *An Introduction to Statistical Methods and Data Analysis,* 4th ed., Belmont, CA: Duxbury Press.

Passell, Peter (1994). "Probability experts may decide Pennsylvania vote," *New York Times,* April 11, 1994, p. A15.

Thys-Jacobs, S., P. Starkey, D. Bernstein, J. Tian, and the Premenstrual Syndrome Study Group (1998). "Calcium carbonate and the premenstrual syndrome: Effects on premenstrual and menstrual symptoms," *American Journal of Obstetrics and Gynecology,* 179, 2, pp. 444–452.

CHAPTER 12

More About Confidence Intervals

Ron Sherman /Stock, Boston /PictureQuest

Do men lose more weight from dieting or from exercising? See Example 12.4 on pages 398 and 402.

When complicated procedures are needed to compute confidence intervals, journal articles provide completed intervals. Your job as a reader is to interpret those intervals. Principles in this chapter for understanding confidence intervals for means and proportions can be used to understand any confidence interval.

I n Chapter 10 we learned how to form and interpret a confidence interval for a population proportion. Remember that a *confidence interval* is an interval of values computed from sample data that is likely to include the true population value. For example, based on a sample survey of 1000 Americans, we may be able to say with 95% confidence that the interval from .23 to .29 (or 23% to 29%) will cover the true proportion of all Americans who favor the legalization of marijuana. The *confidence level* for an interval describes our confidence in the procedure we used to determine the interval. We are confident that most of the confidence intervals we compute using the procedure will contain the true population value.

In this chapter, we expand the use of confidence intervals to other characteristics of populations, like the mean of a quantitative variable, or the difference in means for two populations, or the difference between proportions in two populations. We may, for example, wish to know what is the mean number of hours per day that college students watch television. Or, we may want to know how much difference there is between the mean pulse rates of women and men. A psychiatric researcher may want to know how much difference there is between the proportions of successful outcomes for two different treatments of clinical depression. In each of these types of situations, the objective is the same. We use sample information to form a confidence interval estimate of a population value. ◆

12.1 | EXAMPLES OF DIFFERENT ESTIMATION SITUATIONS

To begin, let's review the following two definitions, which are relevant to our discussion of the estimation of population values:

◆ A **parameter** is a population characteristic. The numerical value of a parameter usually cannot be determined because we cannot measure all units in the population. We have to estimate the parameter using sample information.

♦ A **statistic,** or **estimate,** is a characteristic of a sample. A statistic estimates a parameter.

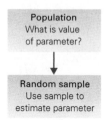

Population
What is value
of parameter?

Random sample
Use sample to
estimate parameter

FIGURE 12.1 **Sample information is
used to estimate a population parameter**

Figure 12.1 illustrates the statistical estimation problem. We wish to estimate a characteristic of a population. In more technical terms, we want to estimate a *parameter.* To do this, we take a random sample from the population and use the sample to calculate a sample *statistic* that estimates the parameter.

Following are descriptions of four common research situations that can be analyzed using a confidence interval estimate of the value of a population parameter. The parameters in these four different situations are

1. p = a population proportion
2. μ = a population mean
3. $p_1 - p_2$ = the difference between two population proportions
4. $\mu_1 - \mu_2$ = the difference between two population means

We've already covered the estimation of a proportion in Chapter 10, but we include that situation here to emphasize that the confidence intervals presented in this chapter all have the same general structure that a confidence interval for a proportion does. For each situation, we provide two examples, as well as the notation and description for the parameter and the sample estimate.

Situation 1. Estimating the Proportion Falling into a Category of a Categorical Variable

♦ *Example research questions:*

What proportion of American adults believe there is extraterrestrial life? In what proportion of British marriages is the wife taller than her husband?

♦ *Population parameter:* p = proportion in the population falling into that category

♦ *Sample estimate:* $\hat{p}$ = proportion in the sample falling into that category

Situation 2. Estimating the Mean of a Quantitative Variable

♦ *Example research questions:*

What is the mean time that college students watch TV per day? What is the mean pulse rate of women?

♦ *Population parameter:* μ (spelled "mu" and pronounced "mew") = population mean for the variable

♦ *Sample estimate:* $\bar{x}$ = the sample mean for the variable

Situation 3. Estimating the Difference Between Two Populations with Regard to the Proportion Falling into a Category of a Categorical Variable

♦ *Example research questions:*

How much difference is there between the proportions that would quit smoking if taking the antidepressant buproprion (Zyban) versus if wearing a nicotine patch?

How much difference is there between men who snore and men who don't snore with regard to the proportion who have heart disease?

♦ *Population parameter:* $p_1 - p_2$, where p_1 and p_2 represent the proportions in populations 1 and 2, respectively

♦ *Sample estimate:* $\hat{p}_1 - \hat{p}_2$, the difference between the two sample proportions

Situation 4. Estimating the Difference Between Two Populations with Regard to the Mean of a Quantitative Variable

♦ *Example research questions:*

How much difference is there in average weight loss for those who diet compared to those who exercise to lose weight?

How much difference is there between the mean foot lengths of men and women?

♦ *Population parameter:* $\mu_1 - \mu_2$, where μ_1 and μ_2 represent the means in populations 1 and 2, respectively

♦ *Sample estimate:* $\bar{x}_1 - \bar{x}_2$, the difference between the two sample means

12.1

turn on your mind

Pick one of the example research questions provided in one of the four situations just described. Explain an appropriate sampling procedure, and then describe what the population parameter and the sample estimate would be for your example.*

Independent Samples

Situations 3 and 4 both involve finding the difference in parameters (means or proportions) for two independent samples. Two samples are called **independent samples** when the measurements in one sample are not related to the measurements in the other sample. For example, a comparison of the mean pulse rates of men and women is a comparison of two *independent samples* as long as the individuals sampled are not related pairs, like siblings or spouses.

Independent samples are generated in a variety of ways. Here are the most common methods:

♦ Random samples are taken separately from two populations and the same response variable is recorded for each individual.

♦ One random sample is taken and a variable recorded for each individual, but then units are categorized as belonging to one population or another, such as male and female.

♦ Participants are randomly assigned to one of two treatment conditions, such as diet or exercise, and the same response variable, such as weight loss, is recorded for each individual unit.

♦ Two random samples are taken from a population and a separate variable is measured in each sample. For example, one sample may be asked about hours of Internet use, whereas a separate sample is asked about hours of television viewing. Then the results are compared. This method for collecting data is not used very often.

*HINT: Sampling methods are covered in Chapter 4, Sections 4.2 and 4.3.

Depending upon whether the response variable is quantitative or categorical, a researcher might compare two independent groups by looking at the difference between two means or by looking at the difference between two proportions.

Paired Data: A Special Case of One Mean

An important special case of a single mean of a population occurs when two quantitative variables are collected in pairs and we desire information about the difference between the two variables. For example, we might measure the IQ score of each person in a sample after he or she listens to a relaxation tape and again after he or she listens to a Mozart tape. The difference between the two IQ measurements can be computed for each person, and we could use the sample differences to estimate the mean population difference. This would provide information about whether listening to Mozart produces higher IQ scores, on average, than listening to a relaxation tape does.

The term *paired data* (or *paired samples*) is used when pairs of variables are collected and used in this way. Generally, in such situations we only are interested in the population (and sample) of *differences,* and not in the original data. Therefore, for paired quantitative variables, it is appropriate to use methods designed for inferences about a single population mean. The mean in these situations is the mean for the population of differences that would result if we measured both variables on all units in the population.

---

definition   The term **paired data** means that the data have been observed in natural pairs. Some ways paired data can occur are

- Each person is measured twice. The two measurements of the same characteristic or trait are made under different conditions.

- Similar individuals are paired prior to an experiment. During the experiment, each member of a pair receives a different treatment. The same response variable is measured for all individuals.

- Two different variables are measured for each individual. There is interest in the amount of difference between the two variables.

12.2 | STANDARD ERRORS

Whenever we use a sample to estimate a population parameter, there is the possibility of an "error" due to the act of sampling. It is unlikely, for example, that the mean pulse rate of a sample of 25 women would exactly equal the mean pulse rate in the population of women represented by the sample. For any particular observed sample estimate, we can't know the exact amount of difference between the sample estimate and the population parameter because we don't know the value of the parameter. However, we are able to determine approximately the "average" sampling error that would occur over all possible random samples that can be taken from a population.

We encountered the phrase *standard error* when we calculated confidence intervals for the population proportion in Chapter 10. Recall from Section 10.5 that the *margin of error* for an approximate 95% confidence interval for a proportion was expressed as $2 \times$ standard error. From this connection between margin of error and standard error, you should realize that a standard error somehow measures the accuracy of a sample statistic. The phrase *standard error* can be used in conjunction with any type of statistic, such as a mean or a difference between two means. In nontechnical terms, the standard error is a rough guide to the potential size of sampling error.

We learned in Chapter 9 that a sample statistic is a random variable because the value of a statistic varies over the different samples that could be taken from the same population. The mean pulse rate of a sample of 25 women, for instance, may be different for each possible random sample that could be taken from the population of all women. The **sampling distribution** of a statistic like a sample mean or a sample proportion is the distribution of possible values of the statistic for all possible random samples of a specified size from the population. In technical terms, the **standard error** of a statistic is the estimated standard deviation of the sampling distribution of the statistic.

definition Rough Definition: The **standard error** of a sample statistic measures, roughly, the average difference between the statistic and the population parameter. This "average difference" is over all possible random samples of a given size that can be taken from the population.

Technical Definition: The **standard error** of a sample statistic is the estimated standard deviation of the sampling distribution for the statistic.

Calculating the Standard Error

The concept of standard error is always the same, but the formula for determining the standard error depends upon the type of sample statistic. For instance, the formula for the standard error of a sample mean is different from the formula for the standard error of a sample proportion. The formula for the standard error of a sample proportion and the formula for the standard error of a sample mean are shown again here. These two formulas were first introduced in Chapter 9, and the formula for the standard error of a sample proportion was emphasized in Chapter 10. The notation s.e.(statistic) represents a standard error. As it has throughout, n represents the sample size.

Standard Errors for Sample Proportion and Sample Mean

formula **Standard Error of a Sample Proportion**

$$\text{s.e.}(\hat{p}) = \sqrt{\frac{\hat{p}(1 - \hat{p})}{n}}, \qquad \hat{p} = \text{sample proportion}$$

Standard Error of a Sample Mean

$$\text{s.e.}(\bar{x}) = \frac{s}{\sqrt{n}}, \qquad s = \text{sample standard deviation}$$

EXAMPLE 12.1
Revisiting Intelligent
Life on Other Planets

In Chapter 10 we used data from a 1997 Marist Institute survey of 935 randomly selected Americans to estimate the proportion of Americans who would answer "yes" to the question, "Do you think there is intelligent life on other planets?" The sample proportion of "yes" answers was $\hat{p} = .60$. Based on the sample size of $n = 935$, the standard error is

$$\text{s.e.}(\hat{p}) = \sqrt{\frac{\hat{p}(1 - \hat{p})}{n}} = \sqrt{\frac{(.6)(.4)}{935}} = .016$$

The $\hat{p}$ observed in this sample was one of many possibilities for the sample proportion in the sense that a different sample of $n = 935$ might provide a different value of $\hat{p}$. The standard error of .016 is roughly the average difference between the statistic, $\hat{p}$, and the population parameter, p, for all possible random samples of $n = 935$ from this population. Theoretically, the standard error is the estimated standard deviation for the sampling distribution of possible sample proportions that would result from asking this question of different random samples of 935 individuals. The distribution of these sample proportions is centered on the unknown value of the parameter p, and the standard error, .016, estimates the standard deviation of this distribution. ◆

EXAMPLE 12.2
Mean Hours per
Day That Penn
State Students Watch TV

In a class survey at Penn State, a question was "In a typical day, about how much time do you spend watching television?" Here is a numerical summary, generated by Minitab, of the responses (in hours):

Variable	N	Mean	Median	TrMean	StDev	SE Mean
TV	175	2.09	2.000	1.950	1.644	0.124

Based on this information, what is our estimate of the mean hours of television per day in the *population* represented by this sample? The sample mean, $\bar{x} = 2.09$ hours per day, is the statistic that estimates μ, the population mean. From the Minitab output, we see that the standard error of the sample mean is $\text{s.e.}(\bar{x}) = 0.124$ (look under "SE Mean"). The calculation of this value is

$$\text{s.e.}(\bar{x}) = \frac{s}{\sqrt{n}} = \frac{1.644}{\sqrt{175}} = 0.124 \ \blacklozenge$$

The standard error in Example 12.2 measures, roughly, the average difference between the unknown value of the population mean μ and the sample mean for samples of $n = 175$ from this population. Technically, the standard error estimates the standard deviation of the sampling distribution of possible sample means. The sample mean $\bar{x} = 2.09$ hours observed in this sample is just one of a plethora of possibilities for the sample mean. The distribution of these possibilities for $\bar{x}$ is centered on the unknown value μ hours, and the estimated standard deviation of the distribution of sample means is 0.124 hours.

The Standard Error of a Difference for Independent Samples

Remember that two samples are called *independent samples* when the measurements in one are not related to the measurements in the other; situations in which such samples arise were discussed in Section 12.1. Depending upon whether the response variable is quantitative or categorical, a researcher might compare two independent groups either by looking at the difference between two means or by looking at the difference between two proportions. In either case, the **standard error of the difference** between statistics from independent samples is determined as

$$\text{s.e.(difference)} = \sqrt{[\text{s.e.(statistic 1)}]^2 + [\text{s.e.(statistic 2)}]^2}$$

This formula leads to the following formulas for the standard error of a difference between two sample proportions and the difference between two sample means. In these formulas, a subscript of 1 or 2 indicates that the measure is for the sample from population 1 or 2, respectively.

Standard Errors for Difference Between Two Proportions and Difference Between Two Means

> *formula* **Standard Error of the Difference Between Two Sample Proportions**
>
> $$\text{s.e.}(\hat{p}_1 - \hat{p}_2) = \sqrt{\frac{\hat{p}_1(1 - \hat{p}_1)}{n_1} + \frac{\hat{p}_2(1 - \hat{p}_2)}{n_2}}$$
>
> **Standard Error of the Difference Between Two Sample Means**
>
> $$\text{s.e.}(\bar{x}_1 - \bar{x}_2) = \sqrt{\frac{s_1^2}{n_1} + \frac{s_2^2}{n_2}}$$

EXAMPLE 12.3
Nicotine Patches or Antidepressants If You Want to Quit Smoking?

Case Study 10.2 presented the results of a study done to determine whether the antidepressant buproprion (also called Zyban) is more effective than the nicotine patch in helping people to quit smoking (Jorenby et al., 1999). Volunteers were randomly allocated to four possible treatments. For this example, we compare two of the treatments, nicotine patch (administered along with a placebo pill) and Zyban (administered along with a placebo patch). There were $n = 244$ participants randomly assigned to each of these two treatments.

After six months, 85 of the 244 Zyban users had quit smoking, while only 52 of the 244 nicotine patch users had quit. The corresponding sample proportions who quit and the difference between these proportions are

$$\hat{p}_1 = \frac{85}{244} = .348, \text{ for Zyban}$$

$$\hat{p}_2 = \frac{52}{244} = .213, \text{ for nicotine patch}$$

$$\hat{p}_1 - \hat{p}_2 = .348 - .213 = .135$$

We see that with Zyban the success rate is .135 (or 13.5%) higher than the success rate is with the nicotine patch. The sample difference $\hat{p}_1 - \hat{p}_2 = .135$ estimates the population parameter $p_1 - p_2$, the difference in the proportions who would quit under each method for the population of all smokers like those in this experiment. The standard error of the statistic $\hat{p}_1 - \hat{p}_2$ is

$$\text{s.e.}(\hat{p}_1 - \hat{p}_2) = \sqrt{\frac{\hat{p}_1(1 - \hat{p}_1)}{n_1} + \frac{\hat{p}_2(1 - \hat{p}_2)}{n_2}}$$

$$= \sqrt{\frac{.348(1 - .348)}{244} + \frac{.213(1 - .213)}{244}} = .040$$

In this example, the standard error roughly measures the average difference between the statistic $\hat{p}_1 - \hat{p}_2$ and the population parameter $p_1 - p_2$. Theoretically, the standard error estimates the standard deviation of the sampling distribution of possible sample differences in proportions, $\hat{p}_1 - \hat{p}_2$. Other samples of 244 in each treatment condition could produce other estimates of the difference, so the observed difference is just one of a plethora of possibilities for the sample difference. The distribution of all possibilities for the sample difference is centered on the unknown value of the parameter $p_1 - p_2$ and has an estimated standard deviation of .040. ◆

EXAMPLE 12.4
Do Men Lose More
Weight by Diet or by Exercise?

In a study done by Wood et al. (1988), 42 sedentary men were placed on a diet while 47 previously sedentary men were put on an exercise routine (study also reported by Iman, 1994, p. 258). The group on a diet lost an average of 7.2 kg, with a standard deviation of 3.7 kg. The men who exercised lost an average of 4.0 kg, with a standard deviation of 3.9 kg.

The difference between the sample means is an estimate of $\mu_1 - \mu_2$, the difference in the means of two hypothetical populations defined by the two weight-loss strategies in the study. The first hypothetical population is the population of weight losses for all sedentary men like the ones in this study if they were to be placed on this diet for a year. The second hypothetical population is the population of weight losses for those same men if they were to follow the exercise routine for a year.

The difference between the two means is $\bar{x}_1 - \bar{x}_2 = 7.2 - 4.0 = 3.2$ kg (about 7 pounds), with the dieters losing more weight than the exercisers. The standard error of the statistic $\bar{x}_1 - \bar{x}_2$ is

$$\text{s.e.}(\bar{x}_1 - \bar{x}_2) = \sqrt{\frac{s_1^2}{n_1} + \frac{s_2^2}{n_2}}$$

$$= \sqrt{\frac{3.7^2}{42} + \frac{3.9^2}{47}} = 0.81$$

In this example, the standard error measures, roughly, the average difference between the statistic $\bar{x}_1 - \bar{x}_2$ and the population parameter $\mu_1 - \mu_2$. Technically, the standard error estimates the standard deviation of the sampling distribution of possible sample differences in means, $\bar{x}_1 - \bar{x}_2$, for samples of sizes 42 and 47 from the populations. The observed sample difference of 3.2 kg is just one of many possibilities for the sample difference. For the distribution of the many possible values of the difference in sample means, the estimated standard deviation is s.e.$(\bar{x}_1 - \bar{x}_2) = 0.81$ kg. ◆

12.2

turn on your mind

Notice that all of the standard error formulas in this section have the sample size(s) in the denominator. This tells us that if the sample size is increased, the standard error will decrease (assuming the sample statistics remain about the same). Refer to the "rough definition" of standard error and explain why this relationship between sample size and standard error makes sense, based on that definition.*

*HINT: Roughly, a standard error measures the average difference between a sample estimate and a parameter, so it measures how closely the sample estimate approximates the parameter.

12.3 | APPROXIMATE 95% CONFIDENCE INTERVALS

The general format for determining a confidence interval is the same for each situation that we consider in this chapter. This format, which we first encountered in Chapter 10, can be written as

Sample estimate ± Multiplier × Standard error

In other words, we form a confidence interval by adding and subtracting an appropriate number of standard errors to (and from) the sample estimate. The **multiplier** depends upon the confidence level, the sample size, and the type of parameter under study.

In Chapter 10, we illustrated how to find approximate 95% confidence intervals for a population proportion. For an approximate 95% confidence interval for a proportion, the appropriate number of standard errors is 1.96, which is often rounded to 2. This same technique can be used to determine approximate 95% confidence intervals for the three new situations that we've introduced in this chapter. The Normal Curve Approximation Rules for means and proportions in Chapter 9 provide the theoretical foundation. With a sufficient sample size, for about 95% of all random samples from a population, the difference between the sample statistic and the population parameter is less than 2 standard errors. This leads to a simple and conceptually convenient way to determine an **approximate 95% confidence interval** for a parameter.

> ***definition*** For sufficiently large samples, the interval
>
> **Sample estimate ± 2 × Standard error**
>
> is an **approximate 95% confidence interval** for a population parameter. This is so for a proportion, a mean, the difference between two proportions, and the difference between two means.
>
> ***Note:*** The 95% confidence level describes how often the procedure provides an interval that includes the population value. For about 95% of all random samples of a specific size from a population, the confidence interval captures the population parameter.

Necessary Conditions for Computing Approximate 95% Confidence Intervals

The approximate 95% confidence intervals described in this section are only valid if the sample sizes are large enough for the Normal Approximation Rules in Chapter 9 to hold. Conditions for which confidence intervals for one mean or a difference in two means can be computed with small sample sizes are presented in Sections 12.4 and 12.5. As guidelines for the situations we consider, the following sample size requirements should be met to use the method for approximate 95% confidence intervals in this section:

For one proportion: Both $n\hat{p}$ and $n(1 - \hat{p})$ are at least 5, preferably at least 10. These quantities are the number of observations in the category of interest and not in that category, respectively.

For one mean: n is greater than 30.

For two proportions: $n\hat{p}$ and *$n(1 - \hat{p})$* are at least 5 (preferably 10) for each sample.

For two means: n_1 and *n_2* are each greater than 30.

In addition to the sample size requirements, another requirement is that the samples are randomly selected. In practice, it is sufficient to assume that samples are representative of the population for the question of interest. For problems that concern the difference between two means or two proportions, there is one more condition:

Independence of samples: For the confidence intervals for the difference between two proportions or two means, the two samples must be *independent* of each other.

EXAMPLE 12.1—*CONTINUED*
Confidence Interval
for Proportion of
Americans Who Believe
There Is Intelligent
Life on Other Planets

The sample proportion that answered "yes" to the question about extraterrestrial life was $\hat{p} = .60$. The sample size was $n = 935$. We determined that the standard error is s.e.$(\hat{p}) = .016$. An approximate 95% confidence interval for the proportion of Americans who think there is intelligent life on other planets is

Sample estimate $\pm\ 2 \times$ Standard error

$.60 \pm 2 \times .016$

$.60 \pm .032$

$.568$ to $.632$

In percent terms, the interval ranges from 56.8% to 63.2%. We are approximately 95% confident that this interval is correct, meaning that it captures the population percent that believes there is intelligent life on other planets. The confidence level is a confidence in the procedure used to determine the interval. For about 95% of all random samples from the population, the corresponding confidence interval captures the population parameter. We don't know if this particular interval does or does not capture the population value. ◆

EXAMPLE 12.2—*CONTINUED*
Confidence Interval
for Mean Hours
per Day That Penn
State Students Watch TV

The sample mean, based on a sample $n = 175$ students, was $\bar{x} = 2.09$ hours per day. The standard error is s.e.$(\bar{x}) = 0.124$, and an approximate 95% confidence interval estimate of μ, the population mean, is

Sample estimate $\pm\ 2 \times$ Standard error

$\bar{x} \pm 2 \times$ s.e.$(\bar{x})$

$2.09 \pm 2 \times 0.124$

2.09 ± 0.248

1.842 to 2.338 hours

In a research article, this confidence interval might be described as follows: *We are 95% confident that the mean time that Penn State students spend watching television per day is somewhere between 1.842 and 2.338 hours.* Actually the report would probably round off the numbers and declare that, with 95% confidence, the mean is between 1.8 and 2.3 hours. Remember what is meant technically by that statement: We are 95% confident that the interval from 1.842 to 2.338 hours is correct, in that it captures the mean television viewing hours for Penn State students. ◆

12.3

turn on your mind

◆ What population do you think is represented by the sample of 175 students in Example 12.2? Do you think the Fundamental Rule for Using Data for Inference holds in this case?

◆ Does the confidence interval in Example 12.2 tell us that *95% of the students* watch television between 1.842 and 2.338 hours per day? If not, what exactly does the interval tell us?*

The first of the next two examples involves finding an approximate 95% confidence interval for the difference between two population proportions, while the second involves finding an approximate 95% confidence interval for the difference between two population means. When considering a confidence interval for a difference between two parameters, it is informative to see whether the interval covers the value 0 or not. If a confidence interval for a difference between two parameters covers (includes 0), it is possible the two population values are equal because 0 is a plausible value for the difference between them. When a confidence interval for a difference between two parameters does not cover 0, we have evidence of a difference between the population parameters because 0 (no difference) is an implausible estimate of the difference between them.

EXAMPLE 12.3—*CONTINUED*
Estimating the Difference Between Nicotine Patches and Antidepressants

The sample difference $\hat{p}_1 - \hat{p}_2 = .135$ estimates the population parameter $p_1 - p_2$, the difference in the proportions who would quit smoking under each method for the population of all smokers like those in this experiment. The standard error of the statistic $\hat{p}_1 - \hat{p}_2$ is s.e.$(\hat{p}_1 - \hat{p}_2) = .040$. An approximate 95% confidence interval for the difference between population proportions $p_1 - p_2$ is

$$\text{Sample difference} \pm 2 \times \text{Standard error}$$

$$.135 \pm 2 \times .040$$

$$.135 \pm .080$$

$$.055 \text{ to } .215$$

With 95% confidence, we can say that this interval covers the difference between the proportions who would quit smoking in a population taking Zyban and a population using the nicotine patch. Expressed as percents, this represents a difference of somewhere between about 5.5% and 21.5%, with Zyban having a higher success rate. We also note that the interval does not include the value 0, so it is reasonable to rule out the possibility that there actually may be no difference between the success rates of the two methods. ◆

*HINT: Refer to the statement in Example 12.2—*CONTINUED* that shows how the interval might be described in a research article.

Group 1 is the "diet" group and group 2 is the "exercise" group. The sample difference between the mean weight losses for the two methods is $\bar{x}_1 - \bar{x}_2 = 7.2 - 4.0 = 3.2$ kg (about 7 pounds). We found that the standard error of the statistic $\bar{x}_1 - \bar{x}_2$ is s.e.$(\bar{x}_1 - \bar{x}_2) = 0.81$. An approximate 95% confidence interval for the difference between population means is

$$\text{Sample difference} \pm 2 \times \text{Standard error}$$
$$3.2 \pm 2 \times 0.81$$
$$3.2 \pm 1.62$$
$$1.58 \text{ to } 4.82 \text{ kg}$$

We are 95% confident that the interval from 1.58 to 4.82 kg covers the increased mean weight loss for dieters compared to those who exercised. Because the interval does not cover 0, we can be fairly certain that this difference was not just for this particular sample of men but also holds for the population as well. ◆

The Confidence Level in Action

In Chapter 10, we learned that a confidence level has a relative frequency probability interpretation. If we consider all possible randomly selected samples of the same size from a population, the confidence level is the fraction or percent of these samples for which the confidence interval includes the population parameter. The **ConfidenceLevel** applet on the CD for the text lets you see this concept in action.

What Happens

The applet simulates choosing random samples of $n = 16$ from a normally distributed population of measurements with mean $\mu = 170$ and standard deviation $\sigma = 20$, roughly the characteristics of weights of men aged 18 to 24 years old. For each sample, a confidence interval for the population mean is found and graphed. Figure 12.2 is an example of how the display looks when the applet is

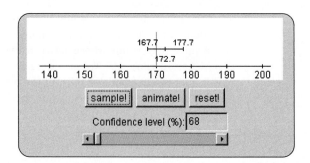

FIGURE 12.2   **Example of the initial ConfidenceLevel applet display**

first started. Notice that the initial confidence level is 68% for the procedure being used to estimate the population mean. The red vertical line in the display is at the value of the population mean, $\mu = 170$. In Figure 12.2, the confidence interval shown, 167.7 to 177.7, covers the population mean.

Use the ***sample!*** button to generate a new sample. Figure 12.3 is an example of how the display might appear after this button is clicked. Notice that the confidence interval found from this new sample also covers the population mean (located at the red line), and at the top of the display the information "1 out of 1 (100%) captures" is given. For the first new sample generated, the confidence interval captured the population mean, so the procedure has been successful 100% of the time thus far in the simulation.

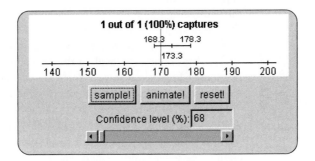

FIGURE 12.3   **The ConfidenceLevel applet display after one new sample has been generated**

The applet continues to tally how often the confidence interval captures the population value (170) as new samples are generated. The ***sample!*** button is used to generate one new sample, whereas using the ***animate!*** button causes the applet to repeatedly generate samples until ***stop!*** is clicked. (The ***stop!*** button appears after ***animate!*** is clicked.)

Figure 12.4 shows how the display looked after 103 different random samples had been generated. At the top of the display, we see that 70.87% of the 103 samples gave confidence intervals that captured the population parameter. This is close to what we would expect for the 68% confidence level. Over many different samples, the confidence interval procedure captures the population mean

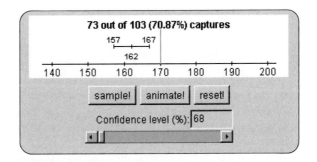

FIGURE 12.4   **The ConfidenceLevel applet display after 103 new samples have been generated**

about 68% of the time. Notice, by the way, that the interval shown in Figure 12.4 did not cover the red line at 170, so that interval does not capture the population mean.

What to Do

Carry out the process just described. Keep the confidence level set at 68% and generate several new samples. Take note of how often the confidence intervals determined from these samples cover the population mean. Eventually, after you generate many new samples, you will see that about 68% of the samples you generate will capture the population mean (the red line). Change the confidence level by using the scrollbar at the bottom of the display. When this is done, the applet will automatically reset the tally of how often the procedure has captured the parameter. Using this new confidence level, generate many samples and take note of how often the samples give intervals that capture 170, the population mean. Over many samples, the percent shown at the top of the display will be close to the confidence level for the procedure. Examine what happens when the confidence level is set at 99%. You'll see that the confidence interval will capture the population mean (170) for nearly every sample generated.

It's informative to watch what happens to the displayed confidence intervals when the scrollbar is used to change the confidence level. You'll see an interval become wider as the confidence level is increased, and become narrower as the confidence level is decreased. Figure 12.5 shows the 68% and the 99% confidence intervals for the same random sample. The interval for the 99% level is much wider than the interval for the 68% level. Notice that the 99% confidence interval has captured the parameter, but the 68% confidence interval has not. Generally, the wider interval is more likely to capture the parameter value.

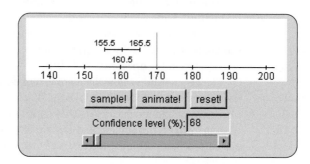

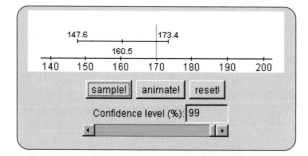

FIGURE 12.5   **The 68% and 99% confidence intervals for the population mean found using the same random sample**

Lessons Learned

The applet illustrates the idea that if we consider many different randomly selected samples of the same size from a population, the confidence level is approximately the fraction or percent of these samples for which the confidence interval includes the population parameter. In other words, the confidence level expresses our confidence that the procedure works in the long run. Also, you will see that for the same random sample, the higher the confidence level, the wider the interval. These principles apply to all confidence interval procedures, regardless of the parameter being estimated.

12.4 | GENERAL CONFIDENCE INTERVALS FOR ONE MEAN OR PAIRED DATA

In this section, we describe how to determine a confidence interval for a population mean using a sample of any size, large or small, and with any confidence level. We may, for instance, want to use a small sample of only $n = 9$ forearm lengths to create a 95% confidence interval for the mean forearm length in a population. Or, we may want to use a 98% confidence level rather than a 95% level.

A **confidence interval estimate of the mean of a population** is sometimes called a *t*-**interval** because the calculations involve the probability distribution called the *Student's t*-**distribution,** which was covered in Chapter 9. As a starting point for developing the *t*-interval, we can use the general format of a confidence interval:

$$\text{Sample estimate} \pm \text{Multiplier} \times \text{Standard error}$$

When the parameter is the mean of a population, the *sample estimate* is $\bar{x}$ = the sample mean for the variable and the *standard error* is $\text{s.e.}(\bar{x}) = s/\sqrt{n}$. The **multiplier** is denoted as t^***,** and it is determined using the Student's *t*-distribution. After introducing an example, we describe how to find the value of t^*.

EXAMPLE 12.5
The Mean Forearm Length of Men

Suppose that the forearm lengths (cm) for a randomly selected sample of $n = 9$ men are

25.5, 24.0, 26.5, 25.5, 28.0, 27.0, 23.0, 25.0, 25.0

The sample mean is $\bar{x} = 25.5$ cm and the sample standard deviation is $s = 1.52$ cm. The standard error of the mean is $\text{s.e.}(\bar{x}) = s/\sqrt{n} = 1.52/\sqrt{9} = 0.507$. A 95% confidence interval for the mean in the population is sample mean $\pm$ multiplier $\times$ standard error, which is $25.5 \pm t^* \times 0.507$. ◆

Determining the t^* Multiplier

Remember that theoretically the *t*-distribution arises when a standardized statistic is calculated using the sample standard deviation in place of the population standard deviation. This almost always is what happens when estimating means, because the population standard deviation σ is rarely known.

A *t*-distribution has a bell shape, it's centered at 0, and it is more spread out than the standard normal curve in that there's more probability in the extreme areas than there is for the standard normal curve. This additional variability results from using *s,* which differs for each sample from the same population, instead of *σ,* which is a fixed constant for a given population of measurements.

A parameter called **degrees of freedom,** abbreviated as **df,** is associated with any *t*-distribution. For problems involving a *single mean,* df = $n - 1$, where *n* is the sample size. As df gets large, the *t*-distribution gets closer to the standard normal curve because the sample standard deviation *s* becomes a more accurate estimate of the population standard deviation *σ.* The *t*-distribution with df = infinity is identical to the standard normal curve.

> **definition** For a confidence interval for a population mean, the **t^* multiplier** is the value in a *t*-distribution with df = $n - 1$ such that the area between $-t^*$ and $+t^*$ equals the desired confidence level.

Most statistical software packages have a facility for determining a confidence interval for a mean. If you are forced to do confidence interval calculations "by hand," it's relatively simple to complete the calculations. To find the multiplier for the desired confidence level, all you need is a table of the *t*-distribution (or the right calculator). Table A.2 in the Appendix shows t^* multipliers for four different confidence levels and varying degrees of freedom. To use this table, compute the degrees of freedom, choose a confidence level, and then look in the row and column for these values in the table.

EXAMPLE 12.5—*CONTINUED*
Calculating the 95%
Confidence Interval
for Forearm Length

We determined that a confidence interval for mean forearm length (cm) is $25.5 \pm t^* \times 0.507$. For the multiplier t^*, the degrees of freedom are df = $n - 1 = 9 - 1 = 8$. In Table A.2, we find that the appropriate multiplier is $t^* = 2.31$, so the 95% confidence interval is $25.5 \pm 2.31 \times 0.507$, which is 25.5 ± 1.17, or 24.33 cm to 26.67 cm. We can say with 95% confidence that in the population represented by the sample, the mean forearm length is between 24.33 and 26.67 cm. ◆

Conditions Required for Using the *t* Confidence Interval

The methods presented in this section are derived mathematically by assuming that the sample has been randomly selected from a population in which the response variable has a normal distribution. The *t*-interval procedure, however, is a *robust* procedure because it works well over a wide range of situations. Put another way, the stated confidence level for a *t*-interval is approximately correct in many situations where the assumption about a normally distributed response variable is not correct.

For large sample sizes, a *t*-interval is a valid estimate of the population mean, even in the presence of skewness. For small sample sizes, a *t*-interval can be used if the data are not skewed and contain no outliers.

Two Situations for Which a
t Confidence Interval for One Mean Is Valid

Situation 1: The population of the measurements is bell-shaped and a random sample of any size is measured. In practice, for small samples, the

FIGURE 12.6   **Dotplot of the forearm lengths for Example 12.5**

data should show no extreme skewness and should not contain any outliers.

Situation 2: The population of measurements is not bell-shaped, but a *large* random sample is measured. A somewhat arbitrary definition of a "large" sample is $n \geq 30$, but if there are extreme outliers, it is better to have a larger sample.

Before calculating a confidence interval for a mean, first check that one of the situations just described holds. To look for outliers or skewness, plot the data using either a histogram, boxplot, dotplot, or stemplot. The sample mean and median can also be compared to each other. Differences between the mean and the median usually occur if the data are skewed—that is, contain outliers in one direction. If $n \geq 30$, the procedure in this section usually produces a valid confidence interval estimate of the population mean, but if the data are obviously skewed, you should question whether the median might be a better measure of location than the mean.

EXAMPLE 12.5—CONTINUED
Checking the Necessary Conditions for the Forearm Length Confidence Interval

Figure 12.6 is a dotplot of the nine forearm lengths used to compute the confidence interval for the population mean. There is no obvious skewness and there are no outliers. Assuming the sample can be thought of as a random sample, Situation 1 holds and the necessary conditions for computing a confidence interval for the mean are present. ◆

in summary   Calculating a Confidence Interval for a Population Mean

A confidence interval for a population mean μ is

$$\bar{x} \pm t^* \times \text{s.e.}(\bar{x}), \quad \text{which is } \bar{x} \pm t^* \frac{s}{\sqrt{n}}$$

To determine this interval (also called a *t-interval*),

1. Make sure the appropriate conditions apply.
2. Choose a confidence level.
3. Determine the sample mean and standard deviation ($\bar{x}$ and s).
4. Calculate the standard error of the mean. s.e.$(\bar{x}) = \frac{s}{\sqrt{n}}$.
5. Calculate df $= n - 1$.
6. Use Table A.2 (or statistical software) to find the multiplier t^*.

EXAMPLE 12.6
What Type of
Students Sleep More?

On the second day of classes in Spring 2000, a Monday, students in two statistics classes at the University of California at Davis were given a survey. One of the questions asked was, "How many hours of sleep did you get last night, to the nearest half hour?" One class was Statistics 10, a statistical literacy course for liberal arts majors ($n = 25$), while the other was Statistics 13, a large introductory class in statistical methods for more technical majors ($n = 148$). Here is Minitab output that summarizes the information on this question for the two classes:

class	N	Mean	StDev	SE Mean
Stat 10	25	7.66	1.34	0.27
Stat 13	148	6.81	1.73	0.14

Notice that Minitab has computed the standard errors. For instance, for the Statistics 10 class, s.e.$(\bar{x}) = s/\sqrt{n} = 1.34/\sqrt{25} = 0.27$. The standard deviation for the Statistics 13 class is actually larger than for the Statistics 10 class, but the standard error is much smaller because the sample size n is so much larger. The larger the sample, the more accurate the sample mean is as an estimate of the population mean.

Let's find 95% confidence intervals for the mean hours of sleep for the *populations* represented by these two classes. Notice that there are some differences between the hypothetical populations. For the Statistics 10 class, students are liberal arts majors and the course is a general education elective. The Statistics 13 students represent a wide variety of majors, and the course is required for most of them. For both classes, the night in question was a Sunday and many of the students had just returned from spring break that day (skipping the first day of classes, a Friday).

Checking the Conditions

For each group, we must make the assumption that these students are equivalent to a random sample from the population of interest. Although not strictly true, the students in these two classes are probably representative of all students who take these and similar classes over the years. Second, for the Statistics 10 class the sample size is only 25, so we must assume that the population of sleep times is approximately bell-shaped. A histogram of the sample values (not shown) indicated that this assumption is reasonable.

Calculating the Confidence Intervals

Class	n	df $= n - 1$	Mean	t^*	s.e.(Mean)	95% Confidence Interval
Stat 10	25	24	7.66	2.06	0.27	7.10 to 8.22 hours
Stat 13	148	147	6.81	1.98	0.14	6.53 to 7.09 hours

Interpreting the Confidence Intervals

Each interval indicates the range of values that we think covers the true *average* number of hours students in each population sleep. For instance, we can say with 95% confidence that the average hours of sleep for all students similar to those in Statistics 10 is covered by the interval from 7.10 to 8.22 hours. Notice that the interval is much wider for the Statistics 10 situation, because the sample size was much smaller. Notice also that the two intervals do not overlap.

Therefore, it appears that the liberal arts students' average hours of sleep really is higher than the general students' average hours of sleep. ◆

Paired Data: Confidence Interval for the Mean Difference in Paired Variables

Remember that an important special case of a single mean of a population occurs when two quantitative variables are collected in pairs and we desire information about the *difference* between the two variables. For example, we might want to know the average difference between Verbal SAT scores for individuals before and after taking a training course. Or we may want to know the average difference in manual dexterity for the dominant and nondominant hands. In both of these examples, we would collect two measurements from each individual in the sample.

To analyze paired data, we begin by calculating the difference in the two measurements for each pair in the sample. As notation for an analysis of the differences, we could simply use the notation already developed for a single mean, but it is preferable to use notation emphasizing that the data consist of differences. Here is notation that can be used for paired data:

Notation for Paired Differences

Data: two variables for each of n individuals or pairs; use the difference $d = x_1 - x_2$.

Population parameter: μ_d = mean of differences for the population = $\mu_1 - \mu_2$.

Sample estimate: $\bar{d}$ = sample mean of the differences = $\bar{x}_1 - \bar{x}_2$.

Standard deviation and standard error: s_d = standard deviation of the sample of differences; s.e.$(\bar{d})$ = $s_d/\sqrt{n}$.

Confidence interval for μ_d: $\bar{d} \pm t^* \times$ s.e.$(\bar{d})$, where df = $n - 1$ for the multiplier t^*.

EXAMPLE 12.7
Screen Time—
Computer versus TV

The 25 students in a liberal arts course in statistical literacy were given a survey that included questions on how many hours per week they watched television and how many hours a week they used a computer. The responses are shown in Table 12.1, along with the difference d for each student. From these data, let's

TABLE 12.1 ■ **Data on Weekly Hours of Computer Use and TV Viewing**

Student	Computer	TV	Difference	Student	Computer	TV	Difference
1	30	2.0	28.0	14	5	6.0	−1.0
2	20	1.5	18.5	15	8	20.0	−12.0
3	10	14.0	−4.0	16	30	20.0	10.0
4	10	2.0	8.0	17	40	35.0	5.0
5	10	6.0	4.0	18	15	15.0	0.0
6	0	20.0	−20.0	19	40	5.0	35.0
7	35	14.0	21.0	20	3	13.5	−10.5
8	20	1.0	19.0	21	21	35.0	−14.0
9	2	14.0	−12.0	22	2	1.0	1.0
10	5	10.0	−5.0	23	9	4.0	5.0
11	10	15.0	−5.0	24	14	0.0	14.0
12	4	2.0	2.0	25	21	14.0	7.0
13	50	10.0	40.0				

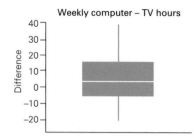

FIGURE 12.7 **Boxplot for difference between computer and TV hours per week,** $n = 25$

construct a 90% confidence interval for μ_d, the average *difference* in hours spent using the computer versus watching television (Computer use − TV) for the population of students represented by this sample.

First, check that the conditions for a confidence interval for one mean hold for the differences. The sample size is under 30, so it is important to make sure there are no major outliers or extreme skewness. The sample mean and median are 5.36 and 4.0 hours, respectively. In data ranging from −20 to +40, these statistics are close enough to rule out extreme skewness. The boxplot of the differences in Figure 12.7 provides further evidence that the appropriate conditions are satisfied.

The standard deviation of the differences is 15.24 hours, and with $n = 25$, the standard error is $15.24/\sqrt{25} = 3.05$. The df $= 25 − 1 = 24$, so, from Table A.2, for a 90% confidence interval $t^* = 1.71$. The computation for a 90% confidence interval is

$$\bar{d} \pm t^* \times s.e.(\bar{d})$$
$$5.36 \pm (1.71)(3.05)$$
$$5.36 \pm 5.22 \text{ or } 0.14 \text{ to } 10.58 \text{ hours}$$

Interpretation: We are 90% confident that the average difference between computer usage and television viewing for students represented by this sample is covered by the interval from 0.14 to 10.58 hours per week, with more hours spent on computer usage than on television viewing. ◆

12.4

turn on your mind

For a fixed sample, explain why it is logical that a 95% confidence interval covers a wider range of values than a 90% confidence interval. Explain this in terms of our confidence that the procedure works in any given case.*

Minitab Tip

tech note **Computing a Confidence Interval for a Mean**

- ◆ To compute a confidence interval for a mean, use **Stat**>**Basic Statistics**>**1-sample t.** Specify the column that contains the raw data. To change the confidence level, use the ***Options*** button. The default confidence level is 95%.

- ◆ For *paired data,* first calculate a column of differences using **Calc**>**Calculator,** then use the *1-sample t* procedure.

- ◆ Alternatively, for *paired data,* use **Stat**>**Basic Stats**>**Paired t.** Specify the two columns that contain the raw data for the pair of measurements.

Note: Use the ***Graphs*** button to create visual displays of the data.

12.5 | GENERAL CONFIDENCE INTERVAL FOR THE DIFFERENCE BETWEEN TWO MEANS (INDEPENDENT SAMPLES)

As is the case in confidence intervals for a single mean, the t-distribution is used to determine the multiplier in the confidence interval for the difference in means for independent samples. The general format of a confidence interval for the difference in two means is

$$\text{Difference in sample means} \pm t^* \times \text{Standard error}$$

The *standard error* of the difference in sample means is

$$\text{s.e.}(\bar{x}_1 - \bar{x}_2) = \sqrt{\frac{s_1^2}{n_1} + \frac{s_2^2}{n_2}}$$

Unfortunately, there's a muddy mathematical story underneath the calculation of a confidence interval for the difference between two population means. On the surface, however, the story appears to be easy and can be summarized as follows.

Confidence Interval for the Difference Between Two Means (Independent Samples)

> *formula*   An approximate **confidence interval for $\mu_1 - \mu_2$** is
>
> $$\bar{x}_1 - \bar{x}_2 \pm t^* \sqrt{\frac{s_1^2}{n_1} + \frac{s_2^2}{n_2}}$$
>
> The multiplier t^* is a t-value such that the area between $-t^*$ and $+t^*$ in the appropriate t-distribution equals the desired confidence level. Appropriate degrees of freedom depend on whether we assume the two population variances are similar.

The difficulty is that for this confidence interval procedure, it's not exactly mathematically correct to use a t-distribution to determine the multiplier. It is approximately correct to do so, but the approximation involves a complicated formula for the degrees of freedom. That approximation formula (often called **Welch's approximation**) is

$$\text{df} \approx \frac{\left(\dfrac{s_1^2}{n_1} + \dfrac{s_2^2}{n_2}\right)^2}{\dfrac{1}{n_1 - 1}\left(\dfrac{s_1^2}{n_1}\right)^2 + \dfrac{1}{n_2 - 1}\left(\dfrac{s_2^2}{n_2}\right)^2}$$

Statistical software, such as Minitab, will determine this quantity and will also automate the process of finding the multiplier t^*. If software is not available, a conservative "by-hand" approach is to use the lesser of $n_1 - 1$ and $n_2 - 1$ for the degrees of freedom.

Equal Variances and Pooled Standard Error

> *tech note*   If we are willing to make the assumption that the two populations have the same (or similar) variance, then there is a procedure for which the t^* multiplier *is* mathematically correct. It involves "pooling" both samples to estimate the common variance. The procedure is discussed at the end of this section.

Two Situations for Which a t Confidence Interval for Two Means Is Valid

An important condition required for the formulas in this section to be valid is that the samples must be *independent* of each other. In addition, one of two different situations must hold:

> *Situation 1:* The populations of measurements are both bell-shaped, and random samples of any size are measured. In practice, for small samples the observed data should not show extreme skewness and there should not be any outliers.
>
> *Situation 2: Large* random samples are measured. A somewhat arbitrary definition of a "large" sample is $n \geq 30$, but if there are extreme outliers or extreme skewness in the measurements, it is better to have an even larger sample.

Note: For a confidence interval for the difference in two means, one of these situations must hold for both groups.

EXAMPLE 12.8
The Effect of a Stare on Driving Behavior

Social psychologists at the University of California at Berkeley wanted to study the effect that staring at drivers would have on driver behavior (Ellsworth, Carlsmith, and Henson, 1972). In a randomized experiment, the researchers either stared or did not stare at the drivers of automobiles stopped at a campus stop sign. The researchers timed how long it took each driver to proceed from the stop sign to a mark on the other side of the intersection. Suppose that the crossing times, in seconds, were

> No Stare Group ($n = 14$): 8.3, 5.5, 6.0, 8.1, 8.8, 7.5, 7.8, 7.1, 5.7, 6.5, 4.7, 6.9, 5.2, 4.7
>
> Stare Group ($n = 13$): 5.6, 5.0, 5.7, 6.3, 6.5, 5.8, 4.5, 6.1, 4.8, 4.9, 4.5, 7.2, 5.8

Based on these data, let's determine a 95% confidence interval for $\mu_1 - \mu_2$, the difference between the mean crossing times in the populations represented by these two independent samples.

Checking the Conditions and Preliminary Graphical Analysis

The two samples are *independent* because different drivers were measured in the two different experimental conditions and measurements are not paired in any way. Boxplots of the data (see Figure 12.8) indicate that there are no outliers

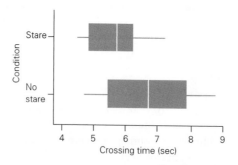

FIGURE 12.8   Boxplots of the intersection crossing time data for Example 12.8

```
Two-sample T for CrossTime

Group      N     Mean     StDev    SE Mean
NoStare    14     6.63     1.36      0.36
Stare      13     5.59     0.822     0.23

95% CI for mu (NoStare) − mu (Stare ): (0.14, 1.93)
T-Test mu (NoStare) = mu (Stare) (vs not =): T = 2.41   P = 0.025   DF = 21
```

FIGURE 12.9   **Minitab output for Example 12.8**

and that the shape of the data is more or less symmetric within each group. The boxplots also illustrate that the crossing times in the stare sample were generally faster than crossing times in the no stare sample. It also looks like the data within the stare group are less variable than the data within the no stare group, so it is probably not reasonable to assume that the populations have equal variances.

Calculating the Confidence Interval

Figure 12.9 displays Minitab output that includes a 95% confidence interval for the difference between population means. This output was produced by the "two-sample t" procedure, and it includes descriptive statistics for each group, a 95% confidence interval for the difference between means, and a significance test concerning the population means. We'll examine this significance test in Chapter 13.

For the no stare data, the sample mean is $\bar{x}_1 = 6.63$ seconds; for the stare data, $\bar{x}_2 = 5.59$ seconds; and the difference between the sample means is $6.63 - 5.59 = 1.04$ seconds. The 95% confidence interval for the difference between population means, $\mu_1 - \mu_2$, is 0.14 to 1.93 seconds.

We see from the output that df = 21 for this problem. Minitab calculated this quantity using the approximation formula for degrees of freedom. Table A.2 can be used to determine that when df = 21, $t^* = 2.08$ at the 95% level. Minitab calculated the confidence interval reported on the output as

Sample estimate $\pm$ Multiplier $\times$ Standard error

$$\bar{x}_1 - \bar{x}_2 \pm 2.08 \times \sqrt{\frac{s_1^2}{n_1} + \frac{s_2^2}{n_2}}$$

$$(6.63 - 5.59) \pm 2.08 \times \sqrt{\frac{1.36^2}{14} + \frac{0.822^2}{13}}$$

0.14 to 1.93 seconds

(Actually, the numbers given produce a lower endpoint of 0.15 instead of 0.14. Minitab obtained 0.14 by using more decimal places in its calculations.) If the approximate df provided by Minitab had not been available, we could have used the "conservative" degrees of freedom, the minimum of the two values $n_1 - 1$ and $n_2 - 1$, which is $13 - 1 = 12$. With df = 12, $t^* = 2.18$ (see Table A.2) and the resulting interval is 0.11 to 1.97 seconds, an interval only slightly wider than the interval provided by Minitab. ◆

12.5

turn on your mind

In Section 12.4 we learned how to find a confidence interval for the mean of paired differences, which we used in Example 12.7 to estimate the mean difference in weekly computer and TV hours for a population of liberal arts students.

◆ Explain why it would not have been appropriate to use the methods in this section, for two independent samples, to estimate that mean difference, even though in either case the sample estimate is the difference in sample means, 5.36 hours.

◆ If the methods in this section had been erroneously used, by treating computer usage and TV viewing hours as independent samples, do you think the standard error of the sample estimate would have been larger or smaller than it was in Example 12.7? Explain your answer using common sense, not formulas. Think about how much natural variability there would be in the data for two independent samples, compared with measuring both sets of hours on the same individuals.*

The Equal Variance Assumption and the Pooled Standard Error

When estimating the difference between two population means, it may sometimes be reasonable to assume that the populations have equal standard deviations. The term *variance* describes the squared standard deviation, so the assumption of equal standard deviations for the two populations is the same as assuming the variances are equal. Using statistical notation, we can express the assumption of equal population variances as $\sigma_1^2 = \sigma_2^2 = \sigma^2$, where σ^2 represents the common value of the variance. With this assumption, information from both groups is combined in order to estimate the value of σ^2. The estimate of variance based on the combined or "pooled" data is called the **pooled variance**. The square root of the pooled variance is called the **pooled standard deviation,** and it is computed as

$$\text{Pooled standard deviation} = s_p = \sqrt{\frac{(n_1 - 1)s_1^2 + (n_2 - 1)s_2^2}{n_1 + n_2 - 2}}$$

tech note   Notice that the pooled variance is a "weighted" average of the individual sample variances. The weights are $(n_1 - 1)/(n_1 + n_2 - 2)$ and $(n_2 - 1)/(n_1 + n_2 - 2)$, giving the variance of the larger sample more weight. If $n_1 = n_2$, then the weights are equal, and $s_p^2 = (s_1^2 + s_2^2)/2$.

*HINT: Remember that the standard error measures how much the sample estimate is likely to vary from sample to sample. Do you think the paired sample estimate $\bar{d}$ would be likely to vary more than or less than the difference in the two separate means?

Replacing the individual standard deviations s_1 and s_2 with the pooled version s_p in the formula for standard error leads to the **pooled standard error for the difference between two means:**

$$\text{Pooled s.e.}(\bar{x}_1 - \bar{x}_2) = \sqrt{\frac{s_p^2}{n_1} + \frac{s_p^2}{n_2}} = \sqrt{s_p^2\left(\frac{1}{n_1} + \frac{1}{n_2}\right)} = s_p\sqrt{\frac{1}{n_1} + \frac{1}{n_2}}$$

This all may seem quite complicated, but if the assumption of equal population variances is correct, this complication actually provides a cleaner mathematical solution for the determination of the multiplier t^*. In this case, the degrees of freedom are simply df $= n_1 + n_2 - 2$.

Pooled Confidence Interval for the Difference Between Two Independent Means

formula If we assume the population variances are the same, then the confidence interval for $\mu_1 - \mu_2$, the difference between the population means, is

$$\bar{x}_1 - \bar{x}_2 \pm t^* \sqrt{s_p^2\left(\frac{1}{n_1} + \frac{1}{n_2}\right)}$$

t^* is found using a t-distribution with df $= n_1 + n_2 - 2$, and s_p is the pooled standard deviation.

Minitab Tip

tech note In Minitab, the default option for the two-sample t procedure is the "unpooled" version in which the population variances are not assumed to be equal. To get the pooled version, check the dialog box item that says "Assume Equal Variances."

EXAMPLE 12.9
Pooled t-Interval for Difference Between Mean Female and Male Sleep Times

The introductory statistical methods class (Statistics 13) discussed in Example 12.6 consisted of 83 females and 65 males. Let's assume these students are equivalent to a random sample of all students who take introductory statistics. How much difference is there between how long female and male students represented by this sample slept the previous night? To answer that question, we'll find a 95% confidence interval for $\mu_1 - \mu_2$ = difference in mean sleep hours for females versus males. Here is the Minitab output for the pooled procedure in which we assume equal population variances for males and females

---

Two-sample T for sleep [with "Assume Equal Variance" option]

Sex	N	Mean	StDev	SE Mean
Female	83	7.02	1.75	0.19
Male	65	6.55	1.68	0.21

Difference = mu (Female) − mu (Male   )
Estimate for difference: 0.461
95% CI for difference: (−0.103, 1.025)
T-Test of difference = 0 (vs not =): T-Value = 1.62 P-Value = 0.108 DF = 146
Both use Pooled StDev = 1.72

Notice that the sample standard deviations are very similar (1.75 for females and 1.68 for males), so it may be reasonable to assume that the population variances are similar as well. The sample mean given for females is $\bar{x}_1 = 7.02$ hours, the sample mean given for males is 6.55 hours, and the difference between these two sample means is reported on the output as "Estimate for difference: 0.461 hours." Notice that the sample means were rounded to two decimal places in the output, and that causes an inconsistency because the difference between 7.02 and 6.55 is 0.47. The value 0.461 is, however, the correct difference between the sample means.

The 95% confidence interval for the difference in mean hours of sleep for the populations of female and male students is −0.103 to 1.025 hours (in bold and underlined in the output display). Because the interval covers 0, we can't rule out the possibility that the population means are equal for men and women, although for this sample, women slept an average of about half an hour more than the men did.

The pooled standard deviation given at the bottom of the output is $s_p = 1.72$. Although not given in the output, the pooled standard error is 0.284. These two values can be found as follows:

$$s_p = \sqrt{\frac{(83-1)(1.75)^2 + (65-1)(1.68)^2}{83+65-2}} = \sqrt{2.957} = 1.72$$

$$\text{Pooled s.e.}(\bar{x}_1 - \bar{x}_2) = \sqrt{\frac{(1.72)^2}{84} + \frac{(1.72)^2}{65}} = 1.72\sqrt{\frac{1}{84} + \frac{1}{65}} = 0.284$$

In the pooled procedure, the degrees of freedom are found as df $= n_1 + n_2 - 2$, which in this example equals $83 + 65 - 2 = 146$. If Table A.2 is used, a conservative estimate of the multiplier t^* is 1.98 (for df = 100 and 0.95 confidence). The confidence limits found by Minitab can be verified by calculating 0.461 ± (1.98)(0.284). ◆

Pooled or Unpooled?

In Example 12.9, the sample standard deviations for females and males had about the same values, so it was reasonable to use the assumption that the population standard deviations were equal. The confidence interval for the difference in means, however, would have been about the same even if the assumption of equal standard deviations had not been made. With the unpooled procedure, the 95% confidence interval for the difference in population means is −0.10 to 1.03 hours, quite close to the pooled version. One advantage for the pooled version is that finding the value of the degrees of freedom is simpler.

Sample standard deviations in two independent samples will almost never be identical in practice. So, how do we know when it might be reasonable to use the pooled version of a confidence interval for a difference between two population means? And, what is the risk of using the pooled procedure when, in truth, the population standard deviations differ? We will explore that question in detail when we consider hypothesis testing for the difference between two means in Chapter 13, but here we give some preliminary guidance.

If the larger value of the two sample standard deviations is from the group with the larger sample size, the pooled procedure will tend to give a wider confidence interval than the unpooled version and so would be a conservative estimate of the true difference, as the next example illustrates. Similar to when we used the conservative margin of error in a confidence interval for one proportion, it is acceptable to use the more conservative pooled procedure. But, it is not good practice to knowingly create an interval that is wider than necessary. On the other hand, if the smaller of the two sample standard deviations is from the group with the larger sample size, the pooled version of the procedure may produce a misleading narrow interval. Generally, it's best to use the unpooled procedure unless the sample standard deviations are quite similar.

EXAMPLE 12.6—CONTINUED
Sleep Time with and without the Equal Variance Assumption

In Example 12.6 we compared confidence intervals for a single mean for the average amount of sleep for two types of statistics students. We can also find a confidence interval for the difference in mean hours of sleep for the two types of students. Here is the Minitab output for doing so, with and without the "Assume Equal Variance" option:

Two-Sample T-Test and Confidence Interval

Two-sample T for sleep [without "Assume Equal Variance" option]

class	N	Mean	StDev	SE Mean
10	25	7.66	1.34	0.27
13	148	6.81	1.73	0.14

95% CI for mu (10) − mu (13): (0.23, 1.46)
T-Test mu (10) = mu (13) (vs not =): T = 2.79   P = 0.0083   DF = 38

Two-sample T for sleep [with "Assume Equal Variance" option]

class	N	Mean	StDev	SE Mean
10	25	7.66	1.34	0.27
13	148	6.81	1.73	0.14

95% CI for mu (10) − mu (13): (0.13, 1.57)
T-Test mu (10) = mu (13) (vs not =): T = 2.33   P = 0.021   DF = 171
Both used Pooled StDev = 1.68

For this example, it is not reasonable to assume equal variances. Notice that doing so increases the width of the confidence interval. Without the assumption the interval is from 0.23 to 1.46, but with the assumption it is 0.13 to 1.57. A comparison of the standard error of the difference for the two situations illustrates why the width increased. Using the pooled estimate increases the standard error of the mean for the sample with $n = 25$.

$$\text{Unpooled s.e.}(\bar{x}_1 - \bar{x}_2) = \sqrt{\frac{(1.34)^2}{25} + \frac{(1.73)^2}{148}} = \sqrt{0.07 + 0.02} = 0.30$$

$$\text{Pooled s.e.}(\bar{x}_1 - \bar{x}_2) = \sqrt{\frac{(1.68)^2}{25} + \frac{(1.68)^2}{148}} = \sqrt{0.11 + 0.02} = 0.36$$

This example illustrates that it is conservative to use the pooled procedure if the two sample sizes are decidedly different and the larger sample standard deviation accompanies the larger sample size. ◆

Minitab Tip

 tech note   **Computing a Confidence Interval for the Difference Between Two Independent Means**

- To compute a confidence interval for the difference in two means, use **Stat>Basic Statistics>2-sample t.** Specify the location of the data. The raw data for the response may be in one column (*Samples*), and the raw data for group categories (*Subscripts*) may be in a second column. Or, the raw data for the two independent groups may be in two separate columns.
- To change the confidence level, use the **Options** button.
- To use the *pooled* standard error, click on **Assume Equal Variances.**

Note: Use the **Graphs** button to create a comparative dotplot or a comparative boxplot.

12.6 | THE DIFFERENCE BETWEEN TWO PROPORTIONS (INDEPENDENT SAMPLES)

The objective in this section is to form a confidence interval for the difference between two population proportions. Again, we start with the same general format that we've used throughout this chapter, which is

Sample estimate ± Multiplier × Standard error

The *sample estimate* is $\hat{p}_1 - \hat{p}_2$, the difference between the two sample proportions. The *standard error* is

$$\text{s.e.}(\hat{p}_1 - \hat{p}_2) = \sqrt{\frac{\hat{p}_1(1 - \hat{p}_1)}{n_1} + \frac{\hat{p}_2(1 - \hat{p}_2)}{n_2}}$$

The multiplier is denoted as z^*, and it is determined using the standard normal distribution.

Confidence Interval for
the Difference Between
Two Population Proportions

formula   A **confidence interval for $p_1 - p_2$** is

$$\hat{p}_1 - \hat{p}_2 \pm z^* \sqrt{\frac{\hat{p}_1(1 - \hat{p}_1)}{n_1} + \frac{\hat{p}_2(1 - \hat{p}_2)}{n_2}}$$

z^* is the value of the standard normal variable with the desired confidence level as the area between $-z^*$ and z^*.

Note: Values of z^* for common confidence levels can be found in the last row of Table A.2, because the *t*-distribution with infinite degrees of freedom is equivalent to the standard normal distribution. These simply are more precise versions of the z^* multipliers provided in Table 10.1, page 340.

Conditions for a Confidence Interval for the Difference in Two Proportions

As is the case for all statistical inference procedures, there are conditions that should be present in order to use the confidence interval just described. For a confidence interval for the difference between two proportions, the principal conditions have to do with the sample sizes for the observed samples. Both conditions must hold.

Condition 1: Sample proportions are available based on independent, randomly selected samples from the two populations.

Condition 2: All of the quantities $n_1\hat{p}_1$, $n_1(1 - \hat{p}_1)$, $n_2\hat{p}_2$, and $n_2(1 - \hat{p}_2)$ are at least 5 and preferably at least 10. These quantities represent the counts observed in the category of interest and not in that category, respectively, for the two samples.

EXAMPLE 12.10
Snoring and Heart Attacks

P. G. Norton and E. V. Dunn conducted a study to determine whether there is a relationship between snoring and risk of heart disease (Norton and Dunn, 1985). They found that of the 1105 snorers they sampled, 86 had heart disease, while only 24 of the 1379 nonsnorers had heart disease. We will define population 1 to be snorers and population 2 to be nonsnorers. In each case, p is the (unknown) population proportion with heart disease.

How much difference is there between the proportions with heart disease for the two populations? We can answer this question with a confidence interval. First recognize that the conditions for calculating this confidence interval are satisfied. Condition 1 is satisfied because the researchers collected independent samples from each population, and Condition 2 is satisfied because the relevant observed counts all are greater than 5. In the group that snores, the numbers with and without heart disease, respectively, are 86 and 1019, while in the group that doesn't snore, the numbers with and without heart disease are 24 and 1355, respectively.

The sample proportions with heart disease in the two groups and the standard error of the difference between the two sample proportions are

$$\hat{p}_1 = \frac{86}{1105} = .0778, \quad \hat{p}_2 = \frac{24}{1379} = .0174, \quad \text{and} \quad \hat{p}_1 - \hat{p}_2 = .0604$$

$$\text{s.e.}(\hat{p}_1 - \hat{p}_2) = \sqrt{\frac{\hat{p}_1(1 - \hat{p}_1)}{n_1} + \frac{\hat{p}_2(1 - \hat{p}_2)}{n_2}}$$

$$= \sqrt{\frac{.0778(.9222)}{1105} + \frac{.0174(.9826)}{1379}} = .0088$$

In general, the confidence interval estimate of the difference $p_1 - p_2$ is

$$\hat{p}_1 - \hat{p}_2 \pm z^* \, \text{s.e.}(\hat{p}_1 - \hat{p}_2)$$

$$.0604 \pm z^*(.0088)$$

Based on this general statement, the following table includes confidence intervals for three different confidence levels. For each level, we show the appropriate z^* multiplier and the completed answer to $.0604 \pm z^*(.0088)$. The df = ∞ row of Table A.2 was used to determine the multipliers.

Confidence Level	z^*	Confidence Interval
90%	1.645	.046 to .075
95%	1.960	.043 to .078
99%	2.576	.038 to .083

As is always the case, the higher the level of confidence, the wider the interval. From these intervals, it appears that the proportion of snorers with heart disease in the population is about 4% to 8% higher than the proportion of non-snorers with heart disease.

As a final note about this example, we point out that it is also informative to compute the relative risk of heart disease for snorers compared to nonsnorers. This relative risk is the ratio of the sample proportions, which is $\hat{p}_1/\hat{p}_2 = .078/.0174 = 4.5$. In other words, we estimate that the risk of heart disease for snorers is about 4.5 times what the risk is for nonsnorers. Unfortunately, it is not straightforward to compute a confidence interval for relative risk in the population. Also, remember that on the basis of an observational study such as this, we can only conclude that there is a relationship between snoring and heart attacks, not a cause-and-effect influence. ◆

EXAMPLE 12.11
Do You Always Buckle Up When Driving?

How often do you wear a seatbelt when driving a car? This was asked in the 2001 Youth Risk Behavior Surveillance System, a nationwide biennial survey of 9th through 12th graders in the United States. Possible responses to the question about seatbelt use were as follows: never, rarely, sometimes, most times, and always. Exercise 2.15 presented data on the connection between seatbelt use and course grades usually attained in school for 12th graders who said they drive. In this example, we compare female and male 12th-grade drivers. To do so, we find a 95% confidence interval for $p_1 - p_2 =$ difference between the population proportions of 12th-grade female and male drivers who would say they always wear a seatbelt when driving. Following is the Minitab output for this confidence interval. (The data are in the **YouthRisk** dataset on the text CD.)

Test and CI for Two Proportions

Success = always

Sex	X	N	Sample p
Female	747	1443	0.517672
Male	677	1572	0.430662

Estimate for p(Female) − p(Male): 0.0870099
95% CI for p(Female) − p(Male): (0.0514590, 0.122561)
Test for p(Female) − p(Male) = 0 (vs not = 0): Z = 4.78 P-Value = 0.000

The sample proportions of females and males who said they always wear a seatbelt are given toward the top of the output under "Sample p." The values under "X" and "N" are, respectively, the number who said they always wear a seatbelt and the sample size for each sex. Rounded to three decimal places, the sample proportion for females is $\hat{p}_1 = 747/1443 = .518$ and the sample proportion for males is $\hat{p}_2 = 677/1572 = .431$. We see that females are more likely to say they always wear a seatbelt, and the difference between the sample proportions is $\hat{p}_1 - \hat{p}_2 = .518 - .431 = .087$ (8.7%). This value is given in the line of output that begins "Estimate for . . ."

The 95% confidence interval for $p_1 - p_2$ rounded to three decimal places is .051 to .123. This information is given in the next-to-last line of output. The confidence interval estimates the difference in population proportions of female and male 12th-grade drivers who would say they always wear a seatbelt when driving. As always, the 95% confidence level expresses our confidence in the procedure used to find the interval. Because the interval does not include 0, it's reasonable to conclude that there is a difference between the population proportions. Apparently, 12th-grade female drivers are more likely than 12th-grade male drivers to say they always buckle up when driving.

The last line of output gives results for a hypothesis test in which the null hypothesis is that there is no difference between the female and male population proportions. The details for that type of hypothesis test will be covered in Chapter 13. Based on your knowledge of the principles of hypothesis testing covered in Chapter 11, however, you may know how to use the results in the last line of output to make a conclusion in this situation. The *p*-value for the test, given as 0.000 at the end of the output, is small, so the null hypothesis of no difference can be rejected. This is consistent with the finding that the 95% confidence interval did not include 0, the value that would indicate no difference. ◆

Minitab Tip

> **tech note** **Determining the Interval for the Difference in Proportions**
>
> ◆ To compute a confidence interval for the difference in two proportions, use **Stat>Basic Statistics>2 Proportions.** See the following note for information about inputting data.
>
> ◆ To change the confidence level, use the ***Options*** button. The default confidence level is 95%.
>
> ***Note:*** The raw data for the response may be in one column, and the raw data for group categories (Subscripts) may be in a second column. Or the raw data for the two independent groups may be in two separate columns. Or the data may already be summarized. If so, click ***Summarized Data,*** then specify the sample size and the *number* of successes for each group.

12.6

turn on your mind

An environmental group is suing a manufacturer because chemicals dumped into a nearby river may be harming fish. A sample of fish from upstream (no chemicals) is compared with a sample from downstream (chemicals), and a 95% confidence interval for the difference in proportions of healthy fish is .01 to .11 (with a higher proportion of healthy fish upstream). First, interpret this interval. The statistician for the manufacturer produces a 99% confidence interval ranging from $-.01$ to $+.13$, and tells the judge that because it includes 0, and because it has higher accompanying confidence than the other interval, we can't conclude that there is a problem. Comment.*

*You could also turn the argument around by noting the upper end of the 99% interval.
HINT: Does knowing the 99% interval change the interpretation of the 95% interval?*

12.7 | UNDERSTANDING ANY CONFIDENCE INTERVAL

The statistics and parameters that researchers examine are not limited to proportions, means, differences in means, or differences in proportions. Throughout this book, we've seen several other statistics, such as the median, the lower and upper quartiles, the correlation coefficient, and relative risk. For each of these statistics, there are formulas and procedures that allow us to compute confidence intervals for the corresponding population parameter. Some of those formulas and procedures, however, are quite complex.

In cases where a complicated procedure is needed to compute a confidence interval, authors of journal articles usually provide the completed intervals. Your job as a reader is to be able to interpret those intervals. The principles you have learned for understanding confidence intervals for means and proportions are directly applicable to understanding any confidence interval. As an example, let's consider the confidence intervals reported in one of our earlier case studies.

CASE STUDY 12.1
Confidence Interval for Relative Risk: Case Study 3.4 Revisited

In Case Study 3.4, we discussed a study relating heart disease to baldness in men. A parameter of interest in that study was the relative risk of heart disease based on the degree of baldness. The investigators focused on the relative risk (RR) of myocardial infarction (a heart attack) for men with baldness compared to men without any baldness. Here is how they reported some of the results:

> For mild or moderate vertex baldness, the age-adjusted RR estimates were approximately 1.3, while for extreme baldness the estimate was 3.4 (95% CI, 1.7 to 7.0). . . . For any vertex baldness (i.e., mild, moderate, and severe combined), the age-adjusted RR was 1.4 (95% CI, 1.2 to 1.9). (Lesko et al., 1993, p. 1000)

The 95% confidence intervals for age-adjusted relative risk are not simple to compute, and they don't take the form "sample estimate $\pm 2 \times$ standard error." This is evidenced by the fact that the intervals are not symmetric about the sample relative risks given. However, these intervals have the same interpretation as any other confidence interval. For instance, with 95% confidence, we can say that the ratio of risks of a heart attack in the populations of men with extreme baldness and men with no baldness is somewhere between 1.7 and 7.0. In other words, men with extreme baldness are probably somewhere between 1.7 to 7 times as likely to experience a heart attack as men of the same age who have no baldness. Of course, these results assume that the men in the study are representative of the larger population.

12.7

turn on your mind

Part of the quote in Case Study 12.1 said: "For any vertex baldness (i.e., mild, moderate, and severe combined), the age-adjusted RR was 1.4 (95% CI, 1.2 to 1.9)." Explain what is wrong with the following interpretation of this result, and write a correct interpretation:

Incorrect Interpretation: There is a .95 probability that the age-adjusted relative risk of a heart attack (for men with any vertex baldness compared to men without any) is between 1.2 and 1.9.*

CASE STUDY 12.2
Premenstrual Syndrome? Try Calcium

The front-page headline in the *Sacramento Bee* was "Study says calcium can help ease PMS" (Maugh, 1998). The article described a randomized, double-blind experiment in which women who suffered from premenstrual syndrome (PMS) were randomly assigned to take daily either a placebo or 1200 mg of calcium in the form of four Tums E-X tablets (Thys-Jacobs et al., 1998). The participants were 466 women with a history of PMS. In the experiment, 231 of these women were randomly assigned to the calcium treatment group and 235 women were in the placebo group.

The primary measure of interest was a composite score based on 17 PMS symptoms (insomnia, six mood-related symptoms, five water-retention symptoms, two involving food cravings, and three related to pain). Participants were asked to rate each of the 17 symptoms daily on a scale from 0 (absent) to 3 (severe). The actual "symptom complex score" was the mean rating for the 17 symptoms. Thus, a score of 0 would imply that all symptoms were absent, and a score of 3 would indicate that all symptoms were severe. The original article (Thys-Jacobs et al., 1998) presents results individually for each of the 17 symptoms in addition to the composite score.

The treatments were continued for three menstrual cycles. We report the symptom scores for the baseline premenstrual time (7 days) before treatments began and for the premenstrual time before the third cycle. Table 12.2 shows some results given in the journal article, including the mean symptom complex scores ± 1 standard deviation and the sample sizes. We see that the mean symptom scores for the two treatment groups were about equal at the baseline time but differed more noticeably before the third cycle. Notice also that the sample sizes for the third cycle are slightly reduced because patients dropped out of the study.

One interesting outcome is that the mean symptom score was substantially reduced for both the placebo and the calcium-treated groups. For the placebo group, the mean symptom score dropped by about a third; and for the calcium-treated group, the mean was more than cut in half. The purpose of the experiment is to see if taking calcium diminishes symptom severity. But we see that placebo alone can be responsible for reducing symptoms, so the appropriate comparison is between the placebo and calcium-treated groups. We should compare those two groups to each other rather than simply examine the reduction in scores for only the calcium-treated group.

We can use the results in Table 12.2 to compute a confidence interval for $\mu_1 - \mu_2$, the difference between the placebo and calcium mean symptom scores before the third cycle for the entire population of PMS sufferers. The difference in sample means (placebo $-$ calcium) is $\bar{x}_1 - \bar{x}_2 = 0.60 - 0.43 = 0.17$. The standard error is

$$\text{s.e.}(\bar{x}_1 - \bar{x}_2) = \sqrt{\frac{0.52^2}{228} + \frac{0.40^2}{212}} = 0.044$$

An approximate 95% confidence interval for the difference in population means is

$$\bar{x}_1 - \bar{x}_2 \pm 2 \times \text{s.e.}(\bar{x}_1 - \bar{x}_2)$$

$$0.17 \pm 2(0.044)$$

$$0.08 \text{ to } 0.26$$

To put this in perspective, remember that the scores are averages over the 17 symptoms. Therefore, a reduction from a mean of 0.60 to a mean of 0.43 would, for instance, correspond to a reduction from (0.6)(17) = 10.2 or about 10 mild symptoms (rating of 1) to (0.43)(17) = 7.31, or just over 7 mild symptoms. In fact, examination of the full results of the study shows that for each one of the 17 symptoms, the reduction in mean severity score was greater in the calcium-treated group than in the placebo group. Because this is a randomized experiment and not an observational study, we can conclude that the calcium treatment actually *caused* the greater reduction in PMS symptoms.

TABLE 12.2 ■ Results for Case Study 12.2

| | Symptom Complex Score: Mean ± s.d. | |
	Placebo Group	*Calcium-Treated Group*
Baseline	0.92 ± 0.55 (*n* = 235)	0.90 ± 0.52 (*n* = 231)
Third Cycle	0.60 ± 0.52 (*n* = 228)	0.43 ± 0.40 (*n* = 212)

SUMMARY OF CONFIDENCE INTERVAL PROCEDURES

The basic structure of intervals for the parameters in the following table is

Sample statistic $\pm$ Multiplier $\times$ Standard error

The table describes the specific details for each type of parameter.

	Parameter	Statistic	Standard Error	Multiplier	Example
One Mean	μ	$\bar{x}$	$\dfrac{s}{\sqrt{n}}$	t^* (see note 1)	12.5
Mean Difference in Paired Variables	μ_d	$\bar{d}$	$\dfrac{s_d}{\sqrt{n}}$	t^* (see note 1)	12.7
Difference Between Means (unpooled)	$\mu_1 - \mu_2$	$\bar{x}_1 - \bar{x}_2$	$\sqrt{\dfrac{s_1^2}{n_1} + \dfrac{s_2^2}{n_2}}$	t^* (see note 2)	12.8
Difference Between Means (pooled)	$\mu_1 - \mu_2$	$\bar{x}_1 - \bar{x}_2$	$s_p\sqrt{\dfrac{1}{n_1} + \dfrac{1}{n_2}}$	t^* (see note 3)	12.9
One Proportion	p	$\hat{p}$	$\sqrt{\dfrac{\hat{p}(1-\hat{p})}{n}}$	z^* (see note 4)	10.6
Difference Between Proportions	$p_1 - p_2$	$\hat{p}_1 - \hat{p}_2$	$\sqrt{\dfrac{\hat{p}_1(1-\hat{p}_1)}{n_1} + \dfrac{\hat{p}_2(1-\hat{p}_2)}{n_2}}$	z^* (see note 4)	12.10

[1] Use Table A.2, df $= n - 1$.
[2] Use Table A.2,

$$df \approx \frac{\left(\dfrac{s_1^2}{n_1} + \dfrac{s_2^2}{n_2}\right)^2}{\dfrac{1}{n_1 - 1}\left(\dfrac{s_1^2}{n_1}\right)^2 + \dfrac{1}{n_2 - 1}\left(\dfrac{s_2^2}{n_2}\right)^2}$$

or use df $= \min(n_1 - 1, n_2 - 1)$.
[3] Use Table A.2, df $= n_1 + n_2 - 2$; see Section 12.5 for the formula for s_p.
[4] Use last row of Table A.2, or the z^* multipliers:

Conf. Level	z^*
0.90	1.645 or 1.65
0.95	1.960 or 2.00
0.98	2.326 or 2.33
0.99	2.576 or 2.58

KEY TERMS

Section 12.1
parameter, 391–392
statistic, 392
estimate, 392
independent samples, 393

paired data, 394

Section 12.2
sampling distribution, 395
standard error, general definition, 395

standard error, one proportion, 395
standard error, one mean, 395
standard error for a difference, 397
standard error, difference in means, 397

EXERCISES Blue = Basics **Bold, Bold** = Answer in back

Section 12.1

12.1 In a random sample of 300 parents in a school district, 104 supported a controversial new education program. The purpose of the survey was to estimate the proportion of all parents in the school district who support the new program.
   a. What is the research question of interest for this survey?
   b. What is the population parameter in this study? What is the appropriate statistical notation (symbol) for this parameter?
   c. What is the value of the sample estimate (statistic) in this study? What is the appropriate statistical notation (symbol) for this estimate?

12.2 A large Internet provider conducted a survey of its customers. One question it asked was how many e-mail messages the respondent had received the previous day. The mean number was 13.2.
   a. What is the research question of interest for this survey?
   b. What is the population parameter in this study? What is the appropriate statistical notation (symbol) for this parameter?
   c. What is the value of the sample estimate (statistic) in this study? What is the appropriate statistical notation (symbol) for this estimate?

12.3 A medical researcher wants to estimate the difference in the proportions of women with high blood pressure for women who use oral contraceptives versus women who do not use oral contraceptives. In an observational study involving a sample of 900 women, the researcher finds that .15 (15%) of the 500 women who used oral contraceptives had high blood pressure, whereas only .10 (10%) of the 400 women who did not use oral contraceptives had high blood pressure.
   a. What is the research question of interest for this study?
   b. What is the population parameter in this study? What is the appropriate statistical notation for this parameter?

   c. What is the value of the sample estimate (statistic) in this study? What is the appropriate statistical notation for this estimate?

12.4 A student doing a project for a statistics class wants to estimate the difference between the mean number of music CDs owned by male and female students. He surveys 50 male students and 45 female students about the number of music CDs they own. The mean number for the males is 110 and the mean number for females is 90.
   a. What is the research question of interest for this survey?
   b. What is the population parameter in this study? What is the appropriate statistical notation for this parameter?
   c. What is the value of the sample estimate (statistic) in this study? What is the appropriate statistical notation for this estimate?

12.5 In each of the following situations, explain whether the comparison involves paired data or data from two independent samples:
   a. Twenty sophomores are randomly selected from campus dormitories at a college, and twenty other sophomores are randomly selected from students who live off-campus. The mean grade point averages of the two groups are compared.
   b. Thirteen individuals each take a strength test both before and again after they participate in a six-week weight-training program. The investigator wants to estimate the average gain in strength due to the training program.
   c. A polling organization compares the proportions of men and women who favor a particular candidate in an upcoming election.

12.6 Refer to exercise 12.2. The study was a retrospective study because the Internet customers were asked how many e-mail messages they received the previous day. Give one disadvantage for that method and one advantage compared to asking the customers in the sample to keep track for the next day.

12.7 A study was done by randomly assigning 200 volunteers with sore throats to either drink a cup of herbal tea or use a throat lozenge to ease their pain. The percents reporting relief for the two methods were compared. What are the research question, the population parameter, and the sample estimate for this study?

12.8   A sample of 100 students at a university was asked how many hours a week they spent studying and how many they spent socializing. The difference was computed for each student. What are the research question, the population parameter, and the sample estimate for this study?

12.9   Refer to the previous exercise. Does the situation described represent independent samples or paired data? Explain.

12.10   For each of the following research questions, would it make more sense to collect independent samples or paired data? Explain.
   a. In the United States, on average what is the age difference between husbands and wives?
   b. What is the difference in average ages at which teachers and plumbers retire?
   c. What is the difference in average salaries for high school graduates and college graduates?

12.11   Give an example of a research question for which the population parameter of interest would be $p_1 - p_2$.

12.12   Give an example of a research question for which the population parameter of interest would be $\mu_1 - \mu_2$.

Sections 12.2 and 12.3

12.13   In each part, use the information given to calculate the standard error of the mean, and find an approximate 95% confidence interval for the population mean.
   a. Mean height for a sample of $n = 81$ women is $\bar{x} = 64.2$ inches, and the standard deviation is $s = 2.7$ inches.
   b. Mean systolic blood pressure for a sample of $n = 100$ men is $\bar{x} = 123.5$, and the standard deviation is $s = 9$.
   c. Mean systolic blood pressure for a sample of $n = 324$ men is $\bar{x} = 123.5$, and the standard deviation is $s = 9$.

12.14   For a sample of 36 men, the mean head circumference is 57.5 cm with a standard deviation equal to 2.4 cm. For a sample of 36 women, the mean head circumference is 55.3 cm with a standard deviation equal to 1.8 cm.
   a. Find the value of the difference between the sample means for men and women.
   b. Find the standard error of the difference between the sample means in this context.
   c. Find an approximate 95% confidence interval for the difference between population mean head circumferences for men versus women.

12.15   Suppose a randomly selected sample of $n = 64$ men has a mean foot length of $\bar{x} = 27.5$ cm, and the standard deviation of the sample is 2 cm.
   a. Calculate the standard error of the sample mean. Write one or two sentences that interpret this value.
   b. Calculate an approximate 95% confidence interval for the mean foot length of men. Write a sentence that interprets this interval.

12.16   Refer to the previous exercise about the foot lengths of men. A randomly selected sample of $n = 100$ women has a mean foot length of $\bar{x} = 24.0$ cm, and the standard deviation of the sample is 2 cm.
   a. Calculate the standard error of the mean. Explain why the value is smaller than the standard error for the men in the previous exercise.
   b. Now consider the difference between the mean foot lengths of men and women. Compute the standard error for the difference between sample means for the men and women.
   c. Compute an approximate 95% confidence interval for the difference between the mean foot lengths of men and women. Write a sentence that interprets this interval.

12.17   In a survey of college students, 70% (.70) of the 100 women surveyed said they believe in love at first sight, whereas only 40% (.40) of the 80 men surveyed said they believe in love at first sight.
   a. Find the value of the difference between the sample proportions for men and women.
   b. Find the standard error of the difference between the sample proportions.
   c. Find an approximate 95% confidence interval for the difference between population proportions believing in love at first sight for men versus women.

12.18   The pulse rates of $n = 50$ people are measured. These people then march in place for one minute, and the pulse rates are measured again. We are interested in estimating the mean difference between the two pulse rates for the population represented by this sample. Explain how you would compute the standard error for the sample mean difference. Be specific about what formula you would use.

12.19   Example 12.4 of Sections 12.2 and 12.3 described a study that compared mean weight loss for a diet plan to the mean weight loss for an exercise plan. In the study, $n = 42$ men were put on a diet. The men who dieted lost an average of 7.2 kg, with a standard deviation of 3.7 kg.
   a. Compute the standard error of the mean for the men who dieted. Write a sentence or two to explain what is measured by this value.
   b. Compute an approximate 95% confidence interval for the mean weight loss for the men who dieted. Write a sentence that interprets this interval.

12.20   Suppose that a teacher asks her class how many hours they studied for the midterm exam. For the 40 students enrolled in the class, the mean was 5.5 hours and the standard deviation was 2 hours. Explain why the teacher should not calculate a standard error for the mean and should not calculate a confidence interval for the mean.

12.21   Example 12.2 in Sections 12.2 and 12.3 used a sample of $n = 175$ students to estimate the mean daily hours that Penn State students watch television. The following summary shows results for daily hours of television by gender:

Sex	N	Mean	St Dev	SE Mean
Female	116	1.95	1.51	0.14
Male	59	2.37	1.87	0.24

   a. Calculate the difference between the mean values for the females and males. Is this a statistic or a parameter? Explain.

b. For each gender, verify the standard error of the mean by substituting appropriate values into the correct formula.

c. An approximate 95% confidence interval for the difference between means is -0.14 to $+0.97$ hours. Based on this interval, what can we conclude, if anything, about the difference in the mean daily television watching times of men and women? Justify your answer.

d. What formula was used to compute the interval given in part (c)? Substitute appropriate values into this formula.

12.22 On January 30, 1995, *Time* magazine reported the results of a poll of adult Americans in which it asked, "Have you ever driven a car when you probably had too much alcohol to drive safely?" The exact results were not given, but from the information given we can guess at what they were. Of the 300 men who answered, 189 (63%) said yes and 108 (36%) said no. The remaining 3 men weren't sure. Of the 300 women, 87 (29%) said yes and 210 (70%) said no; the remaining 3 women weren't sure.

a. Compute an approximate 95% confidence interval for the difference in proportions of men and women who would say yes to this question.

b. Write a sentence or two interpreting this interval.

12.23 Refer to the previous exercise. Calculate an approximate 95% confidence interval for the proportion of men who would say they have ever driven a car when they probably have had too much to drink, and write a sentence or two that interprets the interval. Be specific about the population that the interval describes.

Section 12.4

12.24 In each case, use the information given to compute a confidence interval for the population mean μ. Assume all necessary conditions are present for using the method described in Section 12.4.

a. $\bar{x} = 76$, $s = 6$, $n = 9$, 95% confidence level.
b. $\bar{x} = 76$, $s = 6$, $n = 9$, 90% confidence level.
c. $\bar{x} = 76$, $s = 6$, $n = 16$, 90% confidence level.
d. $\bar{x} = 76$, $s = 8$, $n = 16$, 95% confidence level.
e. $\bar{x} = 100$, $s = 8$, $n = 16$, 95% confidence level.

12.25 What three factors affect the width of a confidence interval for a population mean? For each factor, indicate how an increase in the numerical value of the factor affects the interval width.

12.26 Use Table A.2 to find the multiplier t^* for calculating a confidence interval for a single population mean in each of the following situations:

a. $n = 22$; confidence level = 0.98.
b. $n = 5$; confidence level = 0.90.
c. $n = 5$; confidence level = 0.99.
d. $n = 25$; confidence level = 0.95.
e. $n = 81$; confidence level = 0.95.

12.27 A sample of $n = 9$ men between 30 and 39 years old is asked to do as many situps as they can in one minute. The mean number is $\bar{x} = 26.2$ and the standard deviation is $s = 6$.

a. Find the value of the standard error of the sample mean. Write a sentence that interprets this value (refer back to Section 12.2 for guidance).

b. Find a 95% confidence interval for the population mean.

c. Write a sentence that interprets the confidence interval in the context of this situation.

12.28 Volunteers who had developed a cold within the previous 24 hours were randomized to take either zinc or placebo lozenges every 2 to 3 hours until their cold symptoms were gone (Prasad et al., 2000). Twenty-five participants took zinc lozenges, and 23 participants took placebo lozenges. The mean overall duration of symptoms for the zinc lozenge group was 4.5 days, and the standard deviation of overall duration of symptoms was 1.6 days. For the placebo group, the mean overall duration of symptoms was 8.1 days, and the standard deviation was 1.8 days.

a. Calculate a 95% confidence interval for the mean overall duration of symptoms in a population of individuals like those who used the zinc lozenges.

b. Calculate a 95% confidence interval for the mean overall duration of symptoms in a population of individuals like those who used the placebo lozenges.

c. Based on the intervals computed in parts (a) and (b), is it reasonable to conclude generally that taking zinc lozenges reduces the overall duration of cold symptoms? Explain why you think this is or is not an appropriate conclusion.

d. In their paper, the researchers say they tested the null hypothesis that the data were sampled from a normal curve population and this hypothesis was not rejected. How is this relevant to the calculations done in parts (a) and (b)?

12.29 Refer to the previous exercise. Compute a 99% confidence interval for the mean duration of symptoms for individuals using the placebo lozenges. Write one or two sentences that interpret this interval.

12.30 A randomly selected sample of $n = 12$ students at a university is asked, "How much did you spend for textbooks this semester?" The responses, in dollars, are

200 175 450 300 350 250 150 200 320 370 404 250

Computer output with a 95% confidence interval for the population mean is

```
Variable    N    Mean    StDev   SE Mean       95.0% CI
spent      12   284.9    96.1      27.7   (223.9, 346.0)
```

a. Draw either a dotplot or a boxplot of the data. Briefly discuss whether the necessary conditions for doing a confidence interval for the population mean are present or not.

b. The standard error of the mean given in the output is 27.7 (under "SE Mean"). Verify this value by giving the correct formula and substituting appropriate values into this formula.

c. What are the degrees of freedom for the t^* multiplier? What is the value of the t^* multiplier for the given confidence interval?

d. Write a sentence that interprets the confidence interval. Be specific about the population that is being described.

e. Calculate a 90% confidence interval for the population mean.

12.31 Refer to the previous exercise. Use the Empirical Rule to create an interval that estimates the textbook expenses of 95% of the individual students at the university.

12.32 Suppose that a highway safety researcher is studying the design of a highway sign and is interested in the mean maximum distance at which drivers are able to read the sign. The maximum distances (in feet) at which $n = 16$ drivers can read the sign are

$$
\begin{array}{cccccccc}
440 & 490 & 600 & 540 & 540 & 600 & 240 & 440 \\
360 & 600 & 490 & 400 & 490 & 540 & 440 & 490 \\
\end{array}
$$

a. Verify the necessary conditions for computing a confidence interval for the population mean distance. Assume the sample can be considered to be a random sample from the population of interest.

b. Estimate the mean maximum distance at which drivers can read the sign. Use a 95% confidence interval, and write a sentence that interprets this interval.

12.33 For a sample of $n = 20$ women aged 18 to 29, responses to the question, "How tall would you like to be?" are recorded along with actual heights. In the sample, the mean desired height is 66.7 inches, the mean actual height is 64.9 inches, and the mean difference is $\bar{d} = 1.8$ inches. The standard deviation of the differences is $s_d = 2.1$ inches.

a. Compute a 95% confidence interval for the mean difference between desired and actual height, and write a sentence that interprets this interval. Be specific about what population is described by the interval.

b. What are the necessary conditions for the validity of the confidence interval computed in part (a)?

c. Explain why the following statement is not correct: "Based on the confidence interval computed in part (a), we can conclude that all women aged 18 to 29 would like to be taller."

Section 12.5

12.34 For each of the following situations identify whether it would be appropriate to use a paired procedure (described in Section 12.4) or a two-sample procedure (described in Section 12.5) to estimate the difference of interest:

a. A researcher wants to estimate the difference between the mean scores on a memorization test for people older than 60 compared to people under 40.

b. Women give their actual and desired weights in a survey. An estimate of the mean difference is desired.

c. Two treatments for reducing cholesterol are compared. Forty people with high cholesterol use the first treatment and 40 other people with high cholesterol use the second treatment. An estimate of the difference between the mean decrease in cholesterol for treatment 1 and the mean decrease in cholesterol for treatment 2 is desired.

12.35 Suppose you were given a 95% confidence interval for the difference in two population means. What could you conclude about the population means if

a. The confidence interval did *not* cover zero?

b. The confidence interval *did* cover zero?

12.36 Data on the testosterone levels (ng/dl in saliva) of men in different professions were given in a paper published in the *Journal of Personality and Social Psychology* (Dabbs et al., 1990). The researchers suggest that there are occupational differences in mean testosterone level. Medical doctors and university professors were two of the occupational groups for which means and standard deviations were given along with a dotplot of the raw data. Computer output for a 95% confidence interval for the difference in mean testosterone levels of medical doctors and university professors is

```
Two-sample T for MD vs Profs

           N      Mean     StDev    SE Mean
MD    16      11.60     3.39      0.85
Prof  10      10.70     2.59      0.82

Difference = mu MD − mu Profs
Estimate for difference: 0.90
95% CI for difference: (−1.54, 3.34)
DF = 22
```

a. The 95% confidence interval is given as -1.54 to 3.34. The unpooled procedure was used to compute this interval. Show how the interval was computed by giving the formula and identifying numerical values for all elements of the formula. Note the degrees of freedom are given as "DF = 22."

b. Interpret the confidence interval for the difference in means. Be specific about the populations that are described. What assumptions are you making in this interpretation?

c. Based on the 95% confidence interval given, what can be concluded generally about the difference in mean testosterone levels of medical doctors and professors?

12.37 What assumption is necessary in order to use the pooled procedure for finding a confidence interval for the difference between two population means?

12.38 Each of 63 students in a statistics class used their nondominant hand to print as many letters of the alphabet,

```
Two-sample T for Exercise 12.38

Sex       N      Mean     StDev    SE Mean
Female  29     12.55     4.01      0.74
Male    34     13.65     4.46      0.77

Difference = mu (Female) − mu (Male )
Estimate for difference: −1.10
95% CI for difference: (−3.23, 1.04)
T-Test of difference = 0 (vs not =):
T-Value = −1.03  P-Value = 0.309  DF = 60
```

in order, as they could in 15 seconds. The output for this exercise gives results for a 95% confidence interval for the difference in population means for females and males. The "unpooled" procedure was used (*Data source:* **letters** dataset on the CD for the text).

a. What was the mean number of letters printed by females in the sample? What was the mean number printed by males? What is the difference between the sample means for men and women?

b. What is the 95% confidence interval given in the output for the difference between population means? Write a sentence that interprets this interval.

c. Refer to the previous part. Based on the 95% confidence interval, what conclusion can be made about whether the population means for men and women differ or not? Explain.

d. Find the value of the (unpooled) standard error of the difference between sample means.

e. Note that the value for degrees of freedom for this problem are given at the end of the output as "DF=60." Use Table A.2 to find the value of t^* that was used in finding the interval.

12.39 Refer to the output for the previous exercise about letters printed with the nondominant hand.

a. Find the value of s_p = pooled standard deviation for these data.

b. For the pooled two-sample procedure, find the (pooled) standard error of the difference in sample means.

c. What would be the degrees of freedom for the pooled procedure?

12.40 Refer to exercise 12.28 about the effect of zinc lozenges on the duration of cold symptoms. For $n = 25$ in the zinc lozenge group, the mean overall duration of symptoms was 4.5 days and the standard deviation was 1.6 days. For $n = 23$ in the placebo group, the mean overall duration of symptoms was 8.1 days and the standard deviation was 1.8 days.

a. Calculate $\bar{x}_1 - \bar{x}_2$ = difference in sample means and also compute the unpooled s.e.$(\bar{x}_1 - \bar{x}_2)$ = standard error of the difference in means.

b. Compute a 95% confidence interval for the difference in mean days of overall symptoms for the placebo and zinc lozenge treatments, and write a sentence interpreting the interval. Use the unpooled standard error and use the smaller of $n_1 - 1$ and $n_2 - 1$ as a conservative estimate of degrees of freedom.

c. Is the interval computed in part (b) evidence that the population means are different? Explain.

12.41 Refer to the previous exercise. Use the pooled procedure to compute a 95% confidence interval for the difference in mean days of symptoms for the zinc and placebo treatments.

12.42 Following are data for $n = 20$ individuals on resting pulse rate and whether the individual regularly exercises or not. Calculate a 95% confidence interval for the difference in means for the two groups defined by whether the individual regularly exercises or not. Be sure to verify necessary conditions and state any assumptions.

Person	Pulse	Regularly Exercises
1	72	No
2	62	Yes
3	72	Yes
4	84	No
5	60	Yes
6	63	Yes
7	66	No
8	72	No
9	75	Yes
10	64	Yes
11	62	No
12	84	No
13	76	No
14	60	Yes
15	52	Yes
16	60	No
17	64	Yes
18	80	Yes
19	68	Yes
20	64	Yes

Section 12.6

12.43 In each situation explain whether the method covered in Section 12.6 for finding a confidence interval for the difference in two proportions should be used or not:

a. A survey is done to estimate the difference between the proportions of college students and high school students who smoke cigarettes. Data on cigarette smoking habits are gathered from randomly selected samples of 500 college and 500 high school students.

b. Two new treatments for a serious disease are compared. Each treatment is used for five patients. The first treatment is successful for three patients of the five patients who used it. The second treatment is successful for only one of the five patients who used that treatment.

c. An economist wants to estimate the difference between the mean annual income of college graduates and the mean annual income of high school graduates who did not go to college. Income data are collected from samples of 200 individuals in each educational degree group.

12.44 In the General Social Survey, an ongoing nationwide survey done by the National Opinion Research Center at the University of Chicago, a question asked is whether a respondent favors or opposes capital punishment (the death penalty) for persons convicted of murder. The output for this exercise compares the proportions who said they were opposed to the death penalty in the year 2000 and the year 1993 (*Sources:* **GSS-93** dataset for this text and http://csa.berkeley.edu:7502/archive.htm).

Sample	X	N	Sample p
2000	801	2565	0.312
1993	337	1488	0.226

Estimate for p(1) − p(2): 0.086
95% CI for p(1) − p(2): (0.058, 0.114)

a. What proportion of the year 2000 sample was opposed to the death penalty? What proportion of the year 1993 sample was opposed?

b. What is the estimated difference between the proportions opposed to the death penalty in the two years?

c. Write the 95% confidence interval given in the output. Then, interpret this interval in the context of this situation.

d. Provide the formula used to calculate the interval, and substitute appropriate numerical values into the formula.

12.45 Refer to the output given for the previous exercise.

a. Find the value of s.e.$(\hat{p}_1 - \hat{p}_2)$ = standard error of the difference between the two sample proportions.

b. Find a 90% confidence interval for the difference between the population proportions opposed to the death penalty in the years 2000 and 1993. Use Example 12.10 for guidance.

12.46 In a study done in Maryland, investigators surveyed individuals by telephone about how often they get tension headaches (Schwartz et al., 1998). One response variable measured was whether or not the respondent had experienced an episodic tension-type headache (ETTH) in the prior year. A headache pattern was called "episodic" if the headaches occurred less often than 15 times a month; otherwise, the headaches were called "chronic." Of the 1600 women in the survey aged 18 to 29, 653 said they had experienced episodic tension-type headaches in the last year. Of the 2122 women in the 30–39-year-old age group, the number having experienced episodic headaches was 995.

a. Estimate the proportion in each group that experienced an episodic headache in the prior year, and compute the difference in these two proportions.

b. Compute a 95% confidence interval for the difference between the proportions for these age groups in the population. Write a sentence that interprets this confidence interval.

12.47 Refer to the previous exercise. In the sample, there were 4594 individuals with at least a college degree and $n = 7076$ individuals with at least a high school diploma (but not a college degree). Following is Minitab output with a 95% confidence interval for the difference in proportions experiencing episodic tension-type headaches in the two educational groups:

Sample	X	N	Sample p
1	2140	4594	0.466
2	2690	7076	0.380

Estimate for p(1) − p(2): 0.086
95% CI for p(1) − p(2): (0.068, 0.104)

a. Write two or three sentences that interpret the results.

b. Provide the formula used to calculate the interval, and substitute appropriate numerical values into the formula.

12.48 Suppose a randomly selected sample of $n = 900$ registered voters is surveyed in order to estimate the proportions that will vote for the two candidates in an upcoming election. Fifty-five percent of those sampled say they will vote for one candidate, while 45% indicate a preference for the other candidate. Explain why the method in Section 12.6 for computing a confidence interval for a difference in proportions should not be used to estimate the difference in the proportions planning to vote for the two candidates.

12.49 In Case Study 10.3, students in a statistics class at Penn State were asked, "Would you date someone with a great personality even though you did not find them attractive?" By gender, the results were that 61.1% of 131 women answered "yes" while 42.6% of 61 men answered "yes" (*Source:* **pennstate** dataset).

a. Calculate a 95% confidence interval for the difference in proportions of men and women who would say "yes" to the question if asked. Write a sentence that interprets the interval.

b. What populations do you think are represented by these samples of men and women?

c. Does the interval computed in part (a) include the value 0? What does this tell us about whether there is a difference between college men and women for this question?

12.50 Refer to the previous exercise.

a. Compute a 99% confidence interval for the difference in proportions.

b. How does the width of the 99% confidence interval computed in part (a) of this problem compare to the width of the 95% confidence interval computed in part (a) of the previous exercise?

c. Would a 90% confidence interval for the difference in proportions be wider or narrower than the 99% confidence interval computed in part (a)? Explain.

Section 12.7 and Case Study 12.2

12.51 Responses from $n = 204$ college students to the question "About how many CDs do you own?" are used to determine 95% confidence intervals for the median and the mean. (*Note:* The data are in the dataset **pennstate2**.)

a. A 95% confidence interval for the population median is 50 to 60. Write two or three sentences interpreting this result. Be specific about the population that the interval describes, and also describe any implied assumptions about the sample.

b. A 95% confidence interval for the mean μ is 62.7 to 82.9. Compare this result to the result in part (a), and explain why this comparison suggests that the data for music CDs owned may be skewed.

c. Sample statistics summarizing the data are $\bar{x} = 72.8$, $s = 72.2, n = 204$. Use this information to verify the 95% confidence interval for the mean given in part (b).

12.52 Suppose you were given a 95% confidence interval for the relative risk of disease under two different conditions. What could you conclude about the risk of disease under the two conditions if

a. The confidence interval did not cover 1.0?

b. The confidence interval did cover 1.0?

12.53 In a twelve-year study done at ten medical centers, Cole et al. (2000) investigated whether the decrease in heart rate over the first two minutes after stopping treadmill exercise was a useful predictor of subsequent death during the study period. Based on observations of $n = 5234$ participants, the investigators concluded: "Abnormal heart rate recovery predicted death (relative risk 2.58 [CI, 2.06 to 3.20]). After adjustment for standard risk factors, fitness, and resting and exercise heart rates, abnormal heart rate recovery remained predictive (adjusted relative risk, 1.55 [CI, 1.22 to 1.98])." Explain why the given confidence intervals are evidence that abnormal heart rate recovery after treadmill exercise is a predictor of subsequent death during the study period.

12.54 Refer to Case Study 12.2. Use the baseline data for the placebo group to find an approximate 95% confidence interval for the mean PMS complex score for the population of all women like the ones in this study. Write a sentence interpreting the interval.

12.55 Refer to Case Study 12.2.
a. Use the baseline data to find an approximate 95% confidence interval for the difference in means for the populations represented by the placebo and calcium groups at the start of the study.
b. Explain why the researchers would want the interval computed in part (a) to cover zero.

Chapter Exercises

Be sure to include a check of the appropriate conditions as part of your work when you compute a confidence interval.

12.56 Would it be appropriate to use the ages of death of First Ladies given in Chapter 2 (Table 2.5) to find a 95% confidence interval for the mean? If your answer is yes, what is the parameter of interest? If your answer is no, explain why not.

12.57 A sample of college students was asked if they would return the money if they found a wallet on the street. Of the 93 women, 84 said "yes," and of the 75 men, 53 said "yes." Assume these students represent all college students (*Source:* **UCDavis2** dataset).
a. Find separate approximate 95% confidence intervals for the proportions of college women and college men who would say "yes" to this question.
b. Find an approximate 95% confidence interval for the difference in the proportions of college men and women who would say "yes" to this question.
c. Write a few sentences interpreting the intervals in parts (a) and (b).

12.58 Find an exact 95% confidence interval (use t^*) for the mean weight loss after a year of exercise for the population of men represented by those in the study in Example 12.4. There were 47 men in the exercise group in the sample, with mean weight loss of 4.0 kg and standard deviation of 3.9 kg.

12.59 In computing a confidence interval for a population mean μ, explain whether the interval would be wider, more narrow, or neither as a result of each of the following changes. Assume features not mentioned (confidence level, mean, standard deviation, sample size) remain the same.

a. The level of confidence is changed from 90% to 95%.
b. The sample size is doubled.
c. A new sample of the same size is taken, and $\bar{x}$ increases by 10.

12.60 Example 2.11 reported that a random sample of 199 married British women had a mean height of 1602 mm, with standard deviation of 62.4 mm.
a. Find a 99% confidence interval for the mean height of all women represented by this sample. Write a sentence interpreting the interval.
b. Give a 99% confidence interval for the mean height *in inches* of all women represented by those in this sample (1 mm = 0.03937 in.).

12.61 Refer to the previous exercise. The sample included the heights of the women's husbands as well. For these men, the mean height was 1732.5 mm, with standard deviation 68.8 mm.
a. Find a 90% confidence interval for the mean height of the population of men represented by this sample.
b. Given the information provided in this and the previous exercise, is it possible to compute an approximate 95% confidence interval for the average difference in height between the husband and wife in British couples? If so, compute the interval. If not, explain what additional numerical information you would need.

12.62 Example 2.7 gave the weights in pounds of the 18 men on the crew teams at Oxford and Cambridge universities in 1991–92. The data were

Cambridge: 188.5, 183.0, 194.5, 185.0, 214.0, 203.5, 186.0, 178.5, 109.0
Oxford: 186.0, 184.5, 204.0, 184.5, 195.5, 202.5, 174.0, 183.0, 109.5

a. Explain why it is not appropriate to use the methods in this chapter to compute a confidence interval for the mean weight of college crew team members, even if we assume these 18 men represent a random sample of all college crew team members.
b. The first 8 values listed for Cambridge represent the weights of the 8 rowers on the team. Assuming these 8 men represent a random sample of all Cambridge crew team rowers over the years, compute a 90% confidence interval for the mean of that population.
c. Make the same assumption as in part (b) about the weights of the first 8 men in the Oxford sample. Compute a 90% confidence interval for the difference in mean weights of Cambridge and Oxford rowers. Explain whether you used the pooled or unpooled standard error, and why.
d. Write a sentence interpreting the interval in part (c).

12.63 In Stroop's Word Color Test, 100 words that are color names are shown in colors different from the word. For example, the word *red* might be displayed in blue. The task is to correctly identify the display color of each word; in the example just given the correct response would be blue. Gustafson and Kallmen (1990) recorded the time needed to complete this test for $n = 16$ individuals after they had consumed alcohol and for $n = 16$ other individuals after they had consumed a placebo drink flavored to taste as if it contained alcohol. Each group included 8 men and 8 women. In the alcohol group, the mean completion time was 113.75 seconds and the standard deviation was 22.64 seconds. In the placebo group, the mean completion time was 99.87 seconds and the standard deviation was 12.04 seconds.

a. Calculate the unpooled standard error for the difference in the two sample means.

b. Calculate a 95% confidence interval for the difference in population means. For the unpooled procedure, the approximate degrees of freedom are df = 22.

c. Based on the confidence interval computed in part (b), can we conclude that the population means for the two groups are different? Why or why not?

d. Can we verify the necessary conditions for computing the confidence interval in part (b)? If so, verify the conditions. If not, explain why it is not possible.

12.64 Example 6.2 presented data collected between 1996 and 1998 on ear pierces and tattoos for male Penn State students. Assume these men represent a random sample of male Penn State students. The results were

	Tattoo?		
Ear Pierce?	*No*	*Yes*	*Total*
No	381	43	424
Yes	99	42	141
Total	480	85	565

a. For the population of men with no ear pierce, find a 90% confidence interval for the proportion with a tattoo.

b. For the population of men with an ear pierce, find a 90% confidence interval for the proportion with a tattoo.

c. Find a 99% confidence interval for the difference in proportions of men with a tattoo for the populations with and without an ear pierce. Write a sentence interpreting the interval.

12.65 An experiment was done by 15 students in a statistics class at the University of California at Davis to see if manual dexterity was better for the dominant hand compared to the nondominant hand (left or right). Each student measured the number of beans they could place into a cup in 15 seconds, once with the dominant hand and once with the nondominant hand. The order in which the two hands were measured was randomized for each student.

a. Explain whether a comparison of beans placed using the dominant and nondominant hands is a comparison of paired data or two independnt samples.

b. Referring to material earlier in the book, explain why the order of the two hands was randomized rather than, for instance, having each student test the dominant hand first.

c. The data are presented in the table below and are given also in the **beans** dataset on the CD for this text. Assuming these students represent a random sample from the population, compute a 90% confidence interval for the mean difference in the number of beans that can be placed into a cup in 15 seconds by the dominant and nondominant hands.

Student	1	2	3	4	5	6	7	8	9	10	11	12	13	14	15
Dominant	22	19	18	17	15	16	16	20	17	15	17	17	14	20	26
Nondom.	18	15	13	16	17	16	14	16	20	15	17	17	16	18	25
Difference	4	4	5	1	−2	0	2	4	−3	0	0	0	−2	2	1

d. Write a sentence or two using the interval in part (c) to address the question of whether manual dexterity is better, on average, for the dominant hand.

12.66 In a random sample of 199 married British couples (described in Chapter 2), there were 170 for which both ages were reported. The average difference in husband's age and wife's age was 2.24 years, with standard deviation of 4.1 years.

a. Find an approximate 95% confidence interval for the average age difference for all married British couples. Write a sentence interpreting the interval.

b. Were the samples of husband ages and wife ages collected as paired data or as two independent samples? Briefly explain.

12.67 A study was conducted on pregnant women and subsequent development of their children (Olds et al., 1994). One of the questions of interest was whether the IQ of children would differ for mothers who smoked at least 10 cigarettes a day during pregnancy and those who did not smoke at all. The mean IQ at age 4 for the children of the 66 nonsmokers was 113.28 points, while for the children of the 47 smokers it was 103.12 points. The standard deviations were not reported, but from other information provided, the pooled standard deviation was about 13.5 points.

a. Assuming these women and children are a representative sample, find a 95% confidence interval (use t^*) for the difference in mean IQ scores at age 4 for children of mothers who do not smoke during pregnancy and those whose mothers smoke at least 10 cigarettes a day during pregnancy. Write a sentence interpreting the interval.

b. One of the statements in the article was "after control for confounding background variables . . . the average difference observed at 36 and 48 months was reduced to 4.35 points (95% CI: 0.02, 8.68) [Olds et al., p. 224]." Explain the purpose of this statement and interpret the result given.

12.68 In Example 12.8 we compared the time in seconds to cross an intersection when someone was or was not staring at the driver. We did not assume equal population variances. Here's the Minitab (Version 12) output that resulted from clicking "Assume Equal Variance":

```
Two-sample T for CrossTime

Group      N      Mean     StDev    SE Mean
NoStare    14     6.63     1.36     0.36
Stare      13     5.592    0.822    0.23

95% CI for mu (NoStare) − mu (Stare) : (0.14, 1.94)
T-Test mu (NoStare) = mu (Stare) (vs >): T = 2.37
P = 0.013   DF = 25
Both use Pooled StDev = 1.14
```

a. What is the value of s_p?

b. Compare the 95% confidence interval with the one in Example 12.8, and discuss whether it is reasonable to use the "equal variance" assumption for this study.

12.69 Suppose 100 researchers each plan to independently gather data and construct a 90% confidence interval for a population mean. If X = the number of those intervals that actually cover the population means, then X is a binomial random variable.

a. What is a "success" for this binomial random variable?

b. What is the numerical value of p, the probability of a success?

c. What is the expected number of intervals that will cover their population means?

d. Will each researcher know whether he or she has a "successful" interval? Explain.

e. What is the probability that all 100 researchers actually get intervals that cover their population means of interest?

12.70 Fatty acids present in fish oil may be useful for treating some psychiatric disorders. An article reported September 3, 1998 at the Yahoo Health website described a randomized experiment done by a Harvard Medical School researcher in which 14 bipolar patients received fish oil daily, while 16 other patients received a placebo daily. After four months, 9 of the 14 patients who received fish oil had responded favorably, but only 3 of the 16 placebo patients had done so.

a. Calculate the difference between the proportions showing favorable response in the two groups, and also calculate a standard error for this difference.

b. Discuss whether the method described in Section 12.6 should be used to calculate a confidence interval for the difference. If you believe it should, calculate the confidence interval.

c. In Chapter 3, blind and double-blind procedures were discussed. Explain how those concepts would be applied to this experiment.

Dataset Exercises

12.71 Use the dataset **pennstate1** for this exercise. Case Study 1.1 presented data given by college students in response to the question, "What is the fastest you have ever driven a car? _____ mph" The variable **fastest** contains the responses to this question. Determine a 95% confidence interval for the difference in the mean response of college men and college women. Interpret the interval, state any assumptions about the sample, and verify necessary conditions.

12.72 Use the dataset **pennstate1** for this exercise. The variable **RtSpan** has the raw data for measurements of the stretched right handspans of $n = 190$ Penn State students.

a. Calculate a 95% confidence interval for the mean stretched handspan in the population of men represented by this sample. Write a sentence that interprets the interval.

b. Calculate a 95% confidence interval for the mean stretched handspan in the population of women represented by this sample. Write a sentence that interprets the interval.

c. Compute a 95% confidence interval to estimate the difference in the mean handspans of college men and women. Write a sentence that interprets the interval.

12.73 Use the dataset **UCDavis2** for this exercise. In the survey, students reported ideal height (***IdealHt***) and actual height (***height***).

a. For the men in the sample, calculate a 90% confidence interval to estimate the mean difference between ideal and actual height. Be certain to graphically analyze the data in order to verify necessary conditions.

b. Repeat part (a) for the women in the sample.

c. Based on the intervals computed in parts (a) and (b), is there a difference between men and women with regard to mean difference between ideal and actual height? Explain.

12.74 Use the dataset **GSS-93**. The variable ***owngun*** indicates whether the respondent owns a gun or not, and the variable ***polparty*** contains the respondent's political party preference. Determine a 95% confidence interval for the difference in proportions of Republicans and Democrats who owned a gun that year.

12.75 Use the dataset **cholest**. The variable ***control*** contains cholesterol levels for individuals who have not had a heart attack, while the variable ***2-day*** contains cholesterol levels for heart attack patients two days after the attack.

a. Calculate a 98% confidence interval for the mean cholesterol level of individuals who have not had a heart attack. Interpret the interval, state any assumptions, and verify necessary conditions.

b. Calculate a 98% confidence interval for the mean cholesterol level of heart attack patients two days after the attack. Interpret the interval, state any assumptions, and verify necessary conditions.

c. Calculate a 98% confidence interval for the mean difference in the cholesterol levels of the populations represented by the two samples described in this problem. Interpret the interval, state any assumptions, and verify necessary conditions.

12.76 Use the **deprived** dataset for this exercise. Students in a statistics class were asked whether they generally felt sleep deprived (variable name = ***Deprived***) and also were asked how many hours they usually slept per night (variable name = ***SleepHrs***).

a. For the sample, find the mean hours of sleep per night for students who said they are sleep deprived and for students who said they are not sleep deprived. What is the difference in the two sample means?

b. Find a 95% confidence interval for the difference in population mean of hours of sleep for students who would say they are not sleep deprived versus students who would say they are sleep deprived. Interpret the interval in the context of this situation.

Turn On Your Computer

For these exercises, use the **ConfidenceLevel** *applet described in Section 12.3. It is on the CD for this text.*

12.77 Set the confidence level at 68%.

   a. Use the ***start!*** button to generate a new random sample. Write the confidence interval displayed, and indicate whether it captures the population mean (170) or not.

   b. Generate 150 different samples. How many times did the confidence interval capture the population mean? What percent of the samples gave a confidence interval that captured the population mean?

   c. Refer to the previous part. Compare the number and percent of times that the confidence interval cap-

tured the population mean to what might be expected for the 68% confidence level.

12.78 Change the confidence level to 95%. Repeat the parts of exercise 12.77 using the 95% confidence level.

12.79 Change the confidence level to 99%. Repeat the parts of exercise 12.77 using the 99% confidence level.

12.80 For the same random sample, give the 90%, 95%, and 99% confidence intervals for the population mean. (This can be done by observing what occurs when the scrollbar is used to change the confidence level.) What is indicated about the relationship between the width of the confidence interval and the confidence level?

12.81 Write a definition of the confidence level for a confidence interval procedure.

REFERENCES

Cole, C. R., J. M. Foody, E. H. Blackstone, and M. S. Lauer (2000). "Heart rate recovery after submaximal exercise as a predictor of mortality in a cardiovascularly healthy cohort," *Annals of Internal Medicine,* Vol. 132, pp. 552–555.

Dabbs, J. M., D. de La Rue, and P. Williams (1990). "Testosterone and occupational choice: Actors, ministers, and other men," *Journal of Personality and Social Psychology.* Vol. 59, pp. 1261–1265.

Ellsworth, P. C., J. M. Carlsmith, and A. Henson, (1972). "The stare as a stimulus to flight in human subjects: A series of field experiments," *Journal of Personality and Social Psychology,* Vol. 21, pp. 302–311.

Gustafson, R., and H. Kallmen (1990). "Alcohol and Color Word Test," *Perceptual and Motor Skills,* Vol. 71, pp. 99–105.

Iman, R. L. (1994). *A Data-Based Approach to Statistics,* Belmont, CA: Wadsworth.

Jorenby, D. E., S. J. Leischow, M. A. Nides, S. I. Rennard, J. A. Johnston, A. R. Hughes, S. S. Smith, M. L. Muramoto, D. M. Daughton, K. Doan, M. C. Fiore, and T. B. Baker (1999). "A controlled trial of sustained-release bupropion, a nicotine patch, or both for smoking cessation," *New England Journal of Medicine,* Vol. 340, No. 9, pp. 685–691.

Lesko, S. M., L. Rosenberg, and S. Shapiro (1993). "A case-control study of baldness in relation to myocardial infarction in men," *Journal of the American Medical Association,* Vol. 269, No. 8, pp. 998–1003.

Maugh, Thomas H., II. "Study says calcium can help ease PMS," *Sacramento Bee,* 26 August 1998, pp. A1 and A9.

Norton, P. G., and E. V. Dunn (1985). "Snoring as a risk factor for disease," *British Medical Journal,* Vol. 291, pp. 630–632.

Olds, D. L., C. R. Henderson, Jr., and R. Tatelbaum (1994). "Intellectual impairment in children of women who smoke cigarettes during pregnancy," *Pediatrics,* Vol. 93(2), Feb. 1994, pp. 221–227.

Prasad, A. S., J. T. Fitzgerald, B. Bao, F. W. J. Beck, and P. H. Chandrasekar (2000). "Duration of symptoms and plasma cykotine levels in patients with the common cold treated with zinc acetate," *Annals of Internal Medicine,* Vol. 133, pp. 245–252.

Schwartz, B. S., W. F. Stewart, D. Simon, and R. B. Lipton (1998). "Epidemiology of tension-type headache," *Journal of the American Medical Association,* Vol. 279, pp. 381–383.

Thys-Jacobs, S., P. Starkey, D. Bernstein, J. Tian, and the Premenstrual Syndrome Study Group (1998). "Calcium carbonate and the premenstrual syndrome: Effects on premenstrual and menstrual symptoms," *American Journal of Obstetrics and Gynecology,* Vol. 179, No. 2, pp. 444–452.

Wood, R. D., M. L. Stefanick, D. M. Dreon, B. Frey-Hewitt, S. C. Garay, P. T. Williams, H. R. Superko, S. P. Fortmann, J. J. Albers, K. M. Vranizan, N. M. Ellsworth, R. B. Terry, and W. L. Haskell (1988). "Changes in plasma lipids and lipoproteins in overweight men during weight loss through dieting as compared with exercise," *New England Journal of Medicine,* Vol. 319, No. 18, pp. 1173–1179.

CHAPTER 13

More About Significance Tests

Would your behavior change if she were staring at you? See Example 13.3.

To evaluate the quality of a research study, consider such features as sampling procedure, methods used to measure individuals, wordings of questions, and possible lurking variables. When conclusions are based on hypothesis tests, additional issues and cautions discussed in this chapter should be considered.

I n Chapter 11, we learned the logic and basic steps of hypothesis testing and applied them to z-tests for one proportion. In this chapter, we'll look at the details of hypothesis tests for the same situations for which we developed confidence intervals in Chapter 12:

- ◆ Hypotheses about a population mean or the mean difference for paired data. For example, we might wish to determine whether or not the mean body temperature for humans is 98.6 degrees Fahrenheit.

- ◆ Hypotheses about the difference between the means of two populations. For example, we might ask whether or not the mean time of television watching per week is the same for men and women.

- ◆ Hypotheses about the difference between two population proportions. For example, we might question whether or not the proportion favoring the death penalty is the same for teenagers as it is for adults.

Before we delve into the details, it is worth reviewing three cautions we have already encountered concerning the use of data to make inferences beyond the sample:

1. Inference is only valid if the sample is representative of the population for the question of interest.
2. Hypotheses and conclusions apply to the larger population(s) represented by the sample(s).
3. If the distribution of a quantitative variable is highly skewed, we should consider analyzing the median rather than the mean. Methods for testing hypotheses about medians are a special case of **nonparametric methods,** covered as Supplemental Topic 2 on the CD and briefly in Section 16.3. ◆

13.1 | THE GENERAL IDEAS OF SIGNIFICANCE TESTING

The terms **hypothesis testing** and **significance testing** are synonymous. The term *significance testing* arises because the conclusion about whether to reject a null hypothesis is based on whether a sample statistic is "significantly" far from what would be expected if the null hypothesis were true in the population. Equivalently, we declare **statistical significance** and reject the null hypothesis if there is a relatively small probability that an observed difference or relationship in the sample would have occurred if the null hypothesis holds in the population. One major principle for all significance tests is that we declare "statistical significance" when the *p*-value of the test is "small."

The significance tests for the three situations that we examine in this chapter all have the same general format because the test statistic is a standardized score that measures the difference between an observed statistic and the null value of a parameter. This was also the case in Chapter 11 where we used a *z*-statistic to test hypotheses about a population proportion. The basic format that we followed in Chapter 11 and will also follow in this chapter is as follows:

◆ *The null hypothesis defines a specific value of a population parameter, called the null value.* In Example 13.1 below, for instance, the null hypothesis is that the mean normal body temperature of humans is $\mu = 98.6$ degrees Fahrenheit. Sometimes the null value is defined for the difference between two population parameters. In Example 13.4, the null hypothesis is that the difference between the mean amounts of time college men and women watch television in a typical day is $\mu_1 - \mu_2 = 0$.

◆ *A relevant statistic is calculated from sample information and summarized into a "test statistic."* In each case, we begin by determining the sample equivalent of the parameter of interest. For instance, we use $\bar{x}$ = mean of a sample of temperature measurements to estimate μ = population mean temperature. We then measure the difference between the sample statistic and the null value using the **standardized statistic:**

$$\frac{\text{Sample statistic } - \text{ Null value}}{\text{Null standard error}}$$

The Distribution of the Standardized Statistic

For hypotheses about means, the *standardized statistic* is called a *t*-statistic and the *t*-distribution is used to find the *p*-value.

For hypotheses about proportions, the *standardized statistic* is called a *z*-statistic and the standard normal distribution is used to find the *p*-value.

◆ *A p-value is computed based on the standardized "test statistic."* The *p*-value is calculated by temporarily assuming the null hypothesis to be true and then calculating the probability that the test statistic could be as large in magnitude as it is (or larger) in the direction(s) specified by the alternative hypothesis.

◆ *Based on the p-value, we either reject or fail to reject the null hypothesis.* The most commonly used criterion (level of significance) is that we reject the null hypothesis when the *p*-value is less than 0.05. In many research articles, *p*-values are simply reported and readers are left to draw their own conclusions. Remember that a *p*-value measures the strength of the evidence against the null hypothesis, and the smaller the *p*-value, the stronger the evidence against the null (and for the alternative).

These general ideas are consistent with the five steps outlined in Chapters 6 and 11 that are used for *any* hypothesis test. Let's review those five steps:

Step 1: Determine the *null* and *alternative* hypotheses.

Step 2: Verify necessary data conditions, and if met, summarize the data into an appropriate *test statistic*.

Step 3: Assuming the null hypothesis is true, find the *p-value*.

Step 4: Decide whether or not the result is *statistically significant* based on the *p-value*.

Step 5: Report the conclusion in the context of the situation.

13.2 | TESTING HYPOTHESES ABOUT ONE MEAN OR PAIRED DATA

For questions about **the mean** of a quantitative variable **for one population,** the null hypothesis typically has the form

$$H_0: \mu = \mu_0 \quad \text{(mean is a specified value)}$$

The alternative may either be one-sided ($H_a: \mu < \mu_0$ or $H_a: \mu > \mu_0$) or two-sided ($H_a: \mu \neq \mu_0$), depending on the research question of interest. The usual procedure for testing these hypotheses is called a **one-sample *t*-test** because the *t*-distribution is used to determine the *p*-value. Let's look at an example of a situation where a one-sample *t*-test would be used.

EXAMPLE 13.1
Normal Human Body Temperature

What is normal body temperature? A paper published in the *Journal of the American Medical Association* presented evidence that normal body temperature may be less than 98.6 degrees Fahrenheit, the long-held standard (Mackowiak et al., 1992). The value 98.6 degrees seems to have come from determining the mean in degrees Celsius, rounding up to the nearest whole degree (37 degrees), and then converting that number to Fahrenheit using $32 + (1.8)(37) = 98.6$. Rounding up may have produced a result higher than the actual average, which may therefore be lower than 98.6 degrees. To test this, the null hypothesis is $\mu = 98.6$, and we are only interested in rejecting in favor of lower values, so the alternative is $\mu < 98.6$. We can write these hypotheses as

$$H_0: \mu = 98.6$$
$$H_a: \mu < 98.6$$

Suppose that a random sample of $n = 18$ normal body temperatures is

98.2 97.8 99.0 98.6 98.2 97.8 98.4 99.7 98.2
97.4 97.6 98.4 98.0 99.2 98.6 97.1 97.2 98.5

For these data, the sample mean is $\bar{x} = 98.217$. This is lower than 98.6, but to determine whether this is a statistically significant difference from 98.6, the question we must answer is: What is the probability that the sample mean could be 98.217 or less if the population mean is actually 98.6 (the null value)?

The answer is the *p*-value that we will use to decide between the two hypotheses. We will return to this example after we provide some details for the five steps of a one-sample *t*-test, but we won't keep you in suspense. The *p*-value for this example is 0.015, so the data support the alternative hypothesis. ◆

For a one-sample *t*-test, details of the five steps in the hypothesis test are

Step 1: Determine the Null and Alternative Hypotheses

Remember that in general the null hypothesis states the status quo and the alternative hypothesis states the research question of interest. For a one-sample *t*-test, the possible null and alternative hypotheses are one of these three choices, depending on the research question:

(1) $H_0: \mu = \mu_0$ versus $H_a: \mu \neq \mu_0$ (two-sided)

(2) $H_0: \mu = \mu_0$ versus $H_a: \mu < \mu_0$ (one-sided)

(3) $H_0: \mu = \mu_0$ versus $H_a: \mu > \mu_0$ (one-sided)

Sometimes, when the alternative hypothesis is one-sided, the null hypothesis is written to include values in the other direction from the alternative hypotheses as well as equality, for instance $H_0: \mu \leq \mu_0$, but the "null value" used when computing the test statistic is always μ_0.

Step 2: Verify Necessary Data Conditions, and If Met, Summarize the Data into an Appropriate Test Statistic

Recall from the previous two chapters that whenever we carry out a statistical inference procedure, we must check to see if certain data conditions are met. These conditions are connected to the assumptions that were made when the theory was derived for the particular situation. Carrying out a *t*-test for one population mean requires that one of the same two situations holds as for constructing a confidence interval for a mean, given in Chapter 12. Here are those situations, slightly modified from the way they were stated in Chapter 12:

Situations for Which a One-Sample t-Test Is Valid

Situation 1: The population of the measurements of interest is approximately normal, and a random sample of any size is measured. In practice, the method is used as long as there is no evidence that the shape is notably skewed or that there are extreme outliers.

Situation 2: The population of measurements of interest is not approximately normal, but a *large* random sample is measured. Thirty is usually used as an arbitrary demarcation of "large," but if there are extreme outliers or extreme skewness, it is better to have a larger sample.

For small or moderate sample sizes, use a boxplot, histogram, dotplot, or stem-and-leaf plot to check for notable skewness or extreme outliers. Checking the relative sizes of the sample mean and sample median might also be useful. Skewness and outliers both cause these two statistics to differ from each other. If either skewness or outliers are present, a one-sample *t*-test should not be used. In this event, a statistical test called the *sign test* can be used to analyze hypotheses about the *median*. We provide the details of the sign test in Supplemental Topic 2 on the CD. The procedure is available in most statistical software, including Minitab.

For a large sample size, the *t*-test will work well for testing hypotheses about the mean even if there is some skewness. However, when the data are obviously skewed, you should question whether the mean is the appropriate parameter to analyze. For skewed data, the median may be a better measure of location, and test procedures for analyzing the median might be more appropriate than the *t*-test.

Continuing Step 2: The Test Statistic for a One-Sample t-Test

The next part of step 2 is to compute a test statistic. The statistic $\bar{x}$, the sample mean, estimates the population mean μ. The "null standard error" for the denominator is the usual standard error of $\bar{x}$, s.e.$(\bar{x}) = s/\sqrt{n}$. Because this standard error does not depend on the null value μ_0, the word *null* can be omitted from the description of the denominator standard error. The test statistic, called the *t*-statistic, is a standardized score for measuring the difference between the sample mean and the null hypothesis value of the population mean and is written as

$$t = \frac{\text{Sample mean} - \text{Null value}}{\text{Standard error}} = \frac{\bar{x} - \mu_0}{s/\sqrt{n}}$$

This particular *t*-statistic has approximately a *t*-distribution with df $= n - 1$.

Step 3: Assuming the Null Hypothesis Is True, Find the p-Value

Using the *t*-distribution with df $= n - 1$, the *p*-value is the area in the tail(s) beyond the test statistic *t*, as follows:

- For H_a: $\mu < \mu_0$ (a one-sided test), the *p*-value is the area below *t*, even if *t* is positive.

- For H_a: $\mu > \mu_0$ (a one-sided test), the *p*-value is the area above *t*, even if *t* is negative.

- For H_a: $\mu \neq \mu_0$ (a two-sided test), the *p*-value is $2 \times$ area above $|t|$.

Table 13.1 summarizes and illustrates this information. While some specifics will differ for the other hypothesis-testing situations considered in this chapter, the

TABLE 13.1 ■ **Alternative Hypothesis Regions and p-Value Areas**

Statement of H_a		p-Value Area	t-Curve Region
$\mu < \mu_0$	(less than)	Area to the left of *t* (even if $t > 0$)	
$\mu > \mu_0$	(greater than)	Area to the right of *t* (even if $t < 0$)	
$\mu \neq \mu_0$	(not equal)	$2 \times$ area to the right of $|t|$	

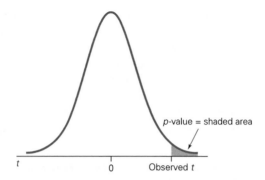

FIGURE 13.1 **The *p*-value for a one-tailed *t*-test with H$_a$: $\mu > \mu_0$**

general connection between the *p*-value and the computed area under the appropriate distribution holds in all cases that we consider.

Most software programs, including Minitab and Excel will do the work of finding the *p*-value for you. You can also find a range for the *p*-value using tables of the Student *t*-distribution. Table A.3 in the Appendix gives the areas to the right of eight different values of *t* for various values of degrees of freedom. The type of area given in Table A.3 is shown in Figure 13.1, which shows the area comprising the *p*-value for a one-tailed *t*-test with H$_a$: $\mu > \mu_0$. For instance, in Example 13.2 (p. 446), the *p*-value is the area to the right of $t = 2.68$ and the degrees of freedom are df $= 9$. In Table A.3, the *t*-value $t = 2.68$ is between the column headings 2.5 and 3.0, so the *p*-value is somewhere between 0.015 and 0.007. A *t*-distribution is symmetric, so Table A.3 can also be used to estimate *p*-values for a "less than" alternative hypothesis. This will be demonstrated when we complete Example 13.1.

Steps 4 and 5: Decide Whether or Not the Result Is Statistically Significant Based on the p-Value and Report the Conclusion in the Context of the Situation

These two steps remain the same for all of the hypothesis tests considered in this book. Choose a level of significance α, and reject the null hypothesis if the *p*-value is less than α. Otherwise, conclude that there is not enough evidence to support the alternative hypothesis.

EXAMPLE 13.1—*CONTINUED*
The Five Steps for Testing
the Hypotheses About
Normal Body Temperature

Step 1: The appropriate null and alternative hypotheses for this situation are

H$_0$: $\mu = 98.6$ degrees

H$_a$: $\mu < 98.6$ degrees

The parameter μ is the mean body temperature in the human population. The research question is whether μ is smaller than the long-held standard, so the alternative hypothesis displays a one-sided test.

Step 2: Verify necessary data conditions, and if met, summarize the data into an appropriate test statistic. The boxplot in Figure 13.2 illustrates that there are no outliers and the shape does not appear to be notably skewed. Although not shown on the boxplot, the sample mean $= \bar{x} = 98.217$ is almost identical to the median of 98.2. This comparison pro-

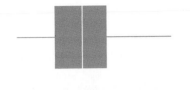

97.0 97.4 97.8 98.2 98.6 99.0 99.4 99.8
Temperature

FIGURE 13.2   Boxplot of the sample for Example 13.1

vides additional evidence that skewness and outliers are not a problem, so the one-sample *t*-test can be used.

We used Minitab to carry out the test, and we can identify the elements necessary for constructing the *t*-statistic using the following Minitab output:

```
Test of mu = 98.600 vs mu < 98.600
Variable      N      Mean    StDev    SE Mean        T       P
Temperature  18    98.217    0.684      0.161    −2.38   0.015
```

The key elements are

- The sample statistic is $\bar{x} = 98.217$ (under "Mean").
- The standard error is $\text{s.e.}(\bar{x}) = \dfrac{s}{\sqrt{n}} = \dfrac{0.684}{\sqrt{18}} = 0.161$ (under "SE Mean").
- $t = \dfrac{\text{Sample statistic} - \text{Null value}}{\text{Standard error}} = \dfrac{98.217 - 98.6}{0.161} = \dfrac{-0.383}{0.161}$
  $$= -2.38 \text{ (under "T").}$$

Step 3: The *p*-value is given as 0.015 in the last column of output. It was calculated as the area to the left of $t = -2.38$ in a *t*-distribution with $n - 1 = 18 - 1 = 17$ degrees of freedom, and Figure 13.3 illustrates this area. If we use Table A.3, we can determine that the *p*-value is between 0.016 and 0.010. Because the *t*-distribution is symmetric, the area to the left of $t = -2.38$ equals the area to the right of $t = +2.38$. The value $t = 2.38$ is between the column headings 2.33 and 2.58 in the table, and for 17 degrees of freedom, the corresponding one-sided *p*-values shown in the table are 0.016 and 0.010.

Step 4: Using $\alpha = 0.05$ as the level of significance criterion, the results are statistically significant because 0.015, the *p*-value of the test, is less than 0.05. In other words, we can reject the null hypothesis.

Step 5: We can conclude, based on these data, that the mean temperature in the human population is actually less than 98.6 degrees. ◆

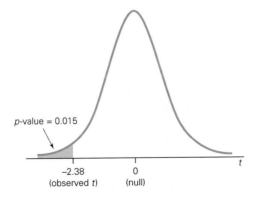

p-value = 0.015

−2.38
(observed *t*)

0
(null)

t

FIGURE 13.3   *p*-Value region for Example 13.1

**Using Excel
to Find the *p*-Value**

tech note   In Example 13.1, the *p*-value can also be found in Excel by typing @TDIST(2.38,17,1) in any cell. Notice that Excel requires you to give the absolute value of the test statistic. The "1" indicates that you want the area in one tail only, since this is a one-tailed test.

Caution about using Excel for one-sided alternative hypotheses: If the sample mean happens to be in the direction opposite to that specified by the alternative hypothesis, then *p*-value > 0.5 and Excel gives 1 − *p*-value. For instance, in Example 13.1, if the sample mean had been above 98.6 and had resulted in $t = +2.38$, then the appropriate *p*-value would *still* be the area to the *left* of *t*, or to the *left* of 2.38, which is 1 − 0.015 = 0.985. Excel only gives areas to the *right* of the specified value of *t* for one-tailed tests, and only allows positive values of *t* to be specified.

in summary   The Steps for Testing a Single Mean with a "One-Sample *t*-Test"

Step 1: Determine the *null* and *alternative* hypotheses.

Null hypothesis: $H_0: \mu = \mu_0$

Alternative hypothesis: $H_a: \mu \neq \mu_0$ or $H_a: \mu > \mu_0$ or $H_a: \mu < \mu_0$

where the format of the alternative hypothesis depends on the research question of interest.

Step 2: Verify necessary data conditions, and if met, summarize the data into an appropriate *test statistic*.

If *n* is large, or if there are no extreme outliers or skewness, compute

$$t = \frac{\text{Sample mean} - \text{Null value}}{\text{Standard error}} = \frac{\bar{x} - \mu_0}{s/\sqrt{n}}$$

Step 3: Assuming the null hypothesis is true, find the *p-value*.

Using the *t*-distribution with df = $n - 1$, the *p*-value is the area in the tail(s) beyond the test statistic *t*, as follows:

For $H_a: \mu \neq \mu_0$, the *p*-value is $2 \times$ area above $|t|$ (a two-tailed test).

For $H_a: \mu > \mu_0$, the *p*-value is the area above *t* (a one-tailed test) even if *t* is negative.

For $H_a: \mu < \mu_0$, the *p*-value is the area below *t* (a one-tailed test) even if *t* is positive.

Step 4: Decide whether or not the result is *statistically significant* based on the *p-value*.

Choose a significance level ("alpha"); the standard is $\alpha = 0.05$. The result is statistically significant if the *p*-value $\leq \alpha$.

Step 5: Report the conclusion in the context of the situation.

Consider the two possible one-sided alternative hypotheses in a one-sample t-test:

$$H_a: \mu > \mu_0 \quad \text{and} \quad H_a: \mu < \mu_0$$

In each case, what range of values of the t-statistic would result in a p-value > 0.5? What range of values of the sample mean would result in a p-value > 0.5? Write a general rule for one-sided tests explaining conditions under which the p-value > 0.5.*

Paired Data and the Paired t-Test

Remember from Chapter 12 that the term **paired data** is used to describe data collected in natural pairs. In Chapter 3 we learned about *matched-pair* designs in which units are paired and one in each pair receives each treatment. Data are collected in pairs in other types of studies as well, such as when cases and controls are matched in case-control studies. Often, paired data occur when the researcher collects two measurements from each observational unit. For instance, if we record weights both before and after a diet program for each person in a sample, we have paired data. Or, we might record performance on a college entrance exam for each individual before and after a training program designed to boost performance on that type of exam.

In most cases paired data are collected because the researchers want to know about the differences, and not about the original observations. In particular, it is often of interest to know if the mean difference in the population is different from 0. A one-sample t-test can be used on the sample of differences to examine whether the sample mean difference is significantly different from 0. When this is done, the test is called a **paired t-test**. It is nothing more than a one-sample t-test conducted on the n differences. To emphasize that the data used in the test are differences, it is commonplace to use d_i instead of x_i to denote the original data values, $\overline{d}$ instead of $\overline{x}$ for the sample mean of the differences, s_d instead of s for the sample standard deviation of the differences, and μ_d instead of μ for the population mean of the differences. Other than those notational differences, once the difference value has been computed for each pair, the test proceeds exactly like a one-sample t-test.

in summary The Steps for a Paired t-Test

Step 1: Determine the *null* and *alternative* hypotheses.

Null hypothesis: $H_0: \mu_d = 0$

Alternative hypothesis: $H_a: \mu_d \neq 0 \quad or \quad H_a: \mu_d > 0 \quad or \quad H_a: \mu_d < 0$

*HINT: Remember that for $H_a: \mu < \mu_0$, the p-value is the area below the test statistic t. What values of t have more than half of the area below them? What relationship between the sample mean and μ_0 would result in those values of t?

where the format of the alternative hypothesis depends on the research question of interest and the order in which the differences are taken.

Step 2: Verify necessary data conditions, and if met, summarize the data into an appropriate *test statistic.*

Before proceeding with the details of this step, calculate the difference d between the two observations for each pair. Then verify that n is large or that there are no extreme outliers or skewness in the *differences.* Compute the sample mean and standard deviation of the differences, $\bar{d}$ and s_d, and then compute the test statistic:

$$t = \frac{\text{Sample mean} - \text{Null value}}{\text{Standard error}} = \frac{\bar{d} - 0}{s_d/\sqrt{n}}$$

Steps 3, 4, and 5: Proceed exactly as instructed in the In Summary "The Steps for Testing a Single Mean with a One-Sample *t*-Test" on page 444, except in the instructions for Step 3, replace μ with μ_d and μ_0 with 0.

EXAMPLE 13.2
The Effect of Alcohol on Useful Consciousness

Ten pilots performed tasks at a simulated altitude of 25,000 feet. Each pilot performed the tasks in a completely sober condition and, three days later, after drinking alcohol. The response variable is the time (in seconds) of useful performance of the tasks for each condition. The longer a pilot spends on useful performance, the better. The research hypothesis is that useful performance time decreases with alcohol use, so the data of interest is the decrease (or increase) in performance with alcohol compared to when sober. The data (Devore and Peck, 1993, p. 575) are as follows:

Pilot	No Alcohol	Alcohol	Difference = No Alcohol − Alcohol
1	261	185	76
2	565	375	190
3	900	310	590
4	630	240	390
5	280	215	65
6	365	420	−55
7	400	405	−5
8	735	205	530
9	430	255	175
10	900	900	0

Step 1: This is a paired-data design. Let μ_d = population mean difference between no alcohol and alcohol measurements, if all pilots were to take these tests. Null and alternative hypotheses about μ_d are

H_0: $\mu_d = 0$ seconds

H_a: $\mu_d > 0$ seconds   (i.e., no alcohol > alcohol)

The alternative hypothesis is one-sided because we hope to show that if performance does change, there is longer useful performance in the "No Alcohol" condition.

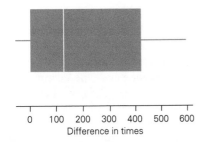

0   100   200   300   400   500   600
Difference in times

FIGURE 13.4 **Boxplot of differences for Example 13.2**

Step 2: Figure 13.4 displays a boxplot of the differences for the ten participants. A check of the necessary conditions for doing a *t*-test reveals that while the sample size is small and the dataset of differences for the sample does have some skewness, outliers and extreme skewness do not appear to be serious problems. So, a paired *t*-test will be used to examine this question.

Minitab output for analyzing the mean difference follows. Notice that the analysis involves only the sample of *n* = 10 differences and does not otherwise utilize the original performance scores.

Test of mu = 0.0 vs mu > 0.0						
Variable	N	Mean	StDev	SE Mean	T	P
Diff	10	195.6	230.5	72.9	2.68	0.013

The *t*-statistic shown in the output is *t* = 2.68 (under "T" in the output). The calculation of the test statistic is

- The sample statistic is the observed mean difference, $\bar{d} = 195.6$.
- The standard error is s.e.$(\bar{d}) = \dfrac{s_d}{\sqrt{n}} = \dfrac{230.5}{\sqrt{10}} = 72.9$.

$$t = \frac{\text{Sample statistic} - \text{Null value}}{\text{Standard error}} = \frac{195.6 - 0}{72.9} = 2.68.$$

Step 3: At the right side of the output, we see that the *p*-value is 0.013. Because the alternative hypothesis was "greater than," this *p*-value was computed as the area to the right of 2.68 in a *t*-distribution with df = 10 − 1 = 9, an area illustrated in Figure 13.5. If we had used Table A.3, we would have found that 0.007 < *p*-value < 0.015. Finding the exact *p*-value of 0.013 requires a computer or calculator that gives areas for the *t*-distribution. For instance, in Excel if you type @TDIST(2.68,9,1) into any cell, the result will be 0.013 (rounded to three decimal places).

Steps 4 and 5: The *p*-value is 0.013, so we can reject the null hypothesis using the standard significance level of 0.05. Even with such a small experiment, we can declare that alcohol has a statistically significant effect and decreases useful performance time. ◆

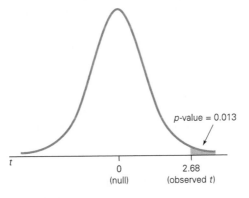

p-value = 0.013

t

0
(null)

2.68
(observed *t*)

FIGURE 13.5 **p-Value region for Example 13.2**

13.2

turn on your mind

Suppose in Example 13.2 the purpose of the study was to determine whether pilots should be allowed to consume alcohol the evening prior to their flights and the alcohol consumption occurred 12 hours before the measurement of time of useful performance. Refer to the discussion of type 1 and type 2 errors in Chapter 11. Explain what the consequences of each type of error would be in this example. Which would be more serious? Given the data and results of the study, which type of error could have been made?*

The Rejection Region Approach for *t*-Tests

In Chapter 11, Section 11.4, we learned that the decision in hypothesis testing can be made by finding a **rejection region,** which is the region of possible values for the test statistic that would lead to rejection of the null hypothesis. The method is based on finding the **critical value,** which is a value such that if the test statistic is beyond it in one or both tails (depending on H_a), the result is statistically significant. Using this approach, the null hypothesis is rejected if the test statistic falls into the rejection region.

This method consists of replacing Steps 3 and 4 with:

Substitute Step 3: Find the critical value and rejection region for the test.

Substitute Step 4: If the test statistic is in the rejection region, conclude that the result is *statistically significant* and reject the null hypothesis. Otherwise, do not reject the null hypothesis.

In Chapter 11 we learned what values are in the rejection region for *z*-tests with a level of significance of 0.05 or 0.01. This approach can be used for *t*-tests as well, but the rejection region changes depending on the degrees of freedom accompanying the test. Table A.2 can be used to find the critical value and rejection region.

Steps for Finding the Critical Value and Rejection Region for a t-Test

1. Determine the degrees of freedom for the test.
2. Decide on α, the level of significance for the test; 0.05 is the most common but sometimes 0.10, 0.01, or some other value is used.
3. In Table A.2, read the critical value from the row with appropriate degrees of freedom for the test. Use the critical value to construct the rejection region, as follows:

   ◆ For H_a: *Parameter > null value,* read the critical value from the column with confidence level $1 - 2\alpha$. For instance, for $\alpha = 0.05$, use the 0.90 column, because $1 - 2\alpha = 1 - 2(0.05) = 1 - 0.10 = 0.90$. Reject the null hypothesis if $t \geq$ critical value. For example, to test $H_a: \mu > 0$ with df = 10 and $\alpha = 0.05$, the critical value is 1.81. The rejection region is $t \geq 1.81$. If the test statistic *t* falls in that region, reject the null hypothesis.

◆ For H_a: *Parameter < null value,* also read the critical value from the column with confidence level $1 - 2\alpha$, but add a negative sign. Reject the null hypothesis if $t \leq$ critical value. For example, to test H_a: $\mu < 0$ with df = 10 and $\alpha = 0.05$, the critical value is -1.81. The rejection region is $t \leq -1.81$. If the test statistic t falls in that region, reject the null hypothesis.

◆ If the test is two-sided (H_a: *Parameter ≠ null value*), use the column with confidence level $1 - \alpha$. For instance, for $\alpha = 0.05$, use the column headed 0.95. Reject the null hypothesis if $|t| \geq$ critical value. For example, to test H_a: $\mu \neq 0$ with df = 10 and $\alpha = 0.05$, the critical value is 2.23. The rejection region is $t \leq -2.23$ and $t \geq 2.23$. If the test statistic falls in that region, reject the null hypothesis.

Here is a summary and examples of the procedure for finding the critical value and rejection region for any t-test. Always use the row of Table A.2 corresponding to the degrees of freedom for the test.

Alternative Hypothesis	Column Heading in Table A.2	Column in Table A.2 for $\alpha = 0.05$	Example: Rejection Region for df = 10, $\alpha = 0.05$
H_a: Parameter ≠ null value	$1 - \alpha$	0.95	$t \leq -2.23$ and $t \geq 2.23$
H_a: Parameter > null value	$1 - 2\alpha$	0.90	$t \geq 1.81$
H_a: Parameter < null value	$1 - 2\alpha$	0.90	$t \leq -1.81$

EXAMPLE 13.1—CONTINUED
The Critical Value and Rejection Region for Testing Normal Body Temperature

In Example 13.1, the alternative hypothesis was H_a: $\mu < 98.6$ degrees, the degrees of freedom = 17, and $\alpha = 0.05$. From Table A.2, the critical value is found to be -1.74, using the df = 17 row and confidence level = 0.90 column. The rejection region is $t \leq -1.74$. The test statistic $t = -2.38$ is in the rejection region, so the null hypothesis is rejected. This is the same conclusion reached by finding the p-value and comparing it to 0.05. ◆

EXAMPLE 13.2—CONTINUED
The Critical Value and Rejection Region for Alcohol and Useful Consciousness

To find the critical value for Example 13.2, use Table A.2 with df = 9. Because the alternative hypothesis is H_a: $\mu_d > 0$, for $\alpha = 0.05$ use the 0.90 column. The critical value is 1.83 and the rejection region is $t \geq 1.83$. Because the test statistic $t = 2.68$ is in the rejection region, we reject the null hypothesis. This is the same conclusion we reached in step 4 of the example, based on the p-value. ◆

Comparing the p-Value Approach to the Rejection Region Approach

Once the level of significance α has been decided, the rejection region method and the p-value method will always arrive at the same conclusion about statistical significance. It is always true that if the p-value $\leq \alpha$ then the test statistic falls into the rejection region, and vice versa. However, the p-value method provides additional information because it allows us to determine what decision would be made for every possible value of α. The rejection region method only provides a decision for the specified α. For that reason, and because statistical software programs and research journals generally report p-values, we will continue to emphasize the p-value approach.

Minitab Tip

tech note   **Computing a One-Sample *t*-Test or a Paired *t*-Test**

◆ To carry out a one-sample *t*-test, use **Stat>Basic Statistics> 1-Sample t.** Specify the column that contains the raw data, and specify the *null value* of the mean in the "Test mean:" box. To specify the *alternative hypothesis,* use the **Options** button.

◆ For *paired data,* first calculate a column of differences using **Calc>Calculator,** then use the *1-sample t* procedure to test that the mean difference is 0 (the null value).

◆ Alternatively, for *paired data,* use **Stat>Basic Stats>Paired t.** Specify the two columns that contain the raw data for the pair of measurements.

◆ In Version 12 a confidence interval is not automatically provided. Beginning with Version 13, a confidence interval is provided, and if the alternative hypothesis selected is one-sided, the reported confidence interval will also be one-sided.

Note: For both the *1-sample* and *Paired t,* the **Graphs** button can be used to create visual displays of the data.

13.3 | TESTING THE DIFFERENCE BETWEEN TWO MEANS (INDEPENDENT SAMPLES)

It is often of interest to determine whether the means of populations represented by two independent samples of a quantitative variable differ. The two populations may be represented by two categories of a categorical variable, such as males and females, or they may be two hypothetical populations represented by different treatment groups in an experiment. In most cases, when comparing two means, the null hypothesis is that they are equal:

$$H_0: \mu_1 - \mu_2 = 0 \qquad (\text{or } \mu_1 = \mu_2)$$

The procedure for testing this null hypothesis is called the **two-sample *t*-test.** Let's look at an example of a situation where a two-sample *t*-test would be used.

EXAMPLE 13.3
The Effect of a Stare on Driving Behavior

In Example 12.8, we discussed an experiment done by social psychologists at the University of California at Berkeley. The researchers either did not stare or did stare at automobile drivers stopped at a campus stop sign. In the experiment, the response variable was the time (in seconds) it took the drivers to drive from the stop sign to a mark on the other side of the intersection. The two populations represented by the observed times are the hypothetical ones that would consist of the times drivers like these would take to move through a similar intersection, either under normal conditions (no stare) or the experimental condition (stare). An hypothesis the researchers wished to test was that the stare would speed up the crossing times, so the mean crossing time would be greater (slower) for those who did not experience the stare than it would be for those who did. So, the null and alternative hypotheses are

$$H_0: \mu_1 - \mu_2 = 0 \quad (\text{or } \mu_1 = \mu_2)$$
$$H_a: \mu_1 - \mu_2 > 0 \quad (\text{or } \mu_1 > \mu_2)$$

In these hypotheses, the subscript 1 is used to denote the No Stare population and the subscript 2 is used to denote the Stare population. For the data given in Chapter 12, the mean crossing time was $\bar{x}_1 = 6.63$ seconds for $n = 14$ drivers who crossed under normal conditions (No Stare) and $\bar{x}_2 = 5.59$ seconds for $n = 13$ who crossed in the experimental condition (Stare). The difference between the sample means is 1.04 seconds. Is this difference large enough to be statistically significant evidence against the null hypothesis? We will answer this question after describing the details of the five hypothesis-testing steps for a two-sample *t*-test. ◆

Step 1: Determine the Null and Alternative Hypotheses

The *null* hypothesis is usually that the difference in means is 0:

$$H_0: \mu_1 - \mu_2 = 0 \quad (\text{or } \mu_1 = \mu_2)$$

The *alternative* hypothesis may either be one-sided or two-sided:

$$H_a: \mu_1 - \mu_2 > 0 \quad or \quad H_a: \mu_1 - \mu_2 < 0 \quad or \quad H_a: \mu_1 - \mu_2 \neq 0$$

In one-sided tests, the null hypothesis may be written to include an inequality in the opposite direction from the alternative hypothesis.

Step 2: Verify Necessary Data Conditions, and If Met, Summarize the Data into an Appropriate Test Statistic

The situations in which the *t*-test for the difference in two means is valid are similar to those given in Chapter 12 for constructing a confidence interval for the difference in two means.

Situations for Which a t-Test for the Difference in Two Population Means Is Valid

Situation 1: Both populations represented by the measurements of interest are approximately normal, and random samples of any size are measured. In practice, the method is used as long as there is no evidence that the shapes are notably skewed or that there are extreme outliers.

Situation 2: The populations of measurements of interest are not approximately normal, but a *large* random sample is measured from each one. Thirty is usually used as an arbitrary demarcation of "large," but if there are extreme outliers or extreme skewness, it is better to have larger samples.

Independence: The samples must be independent. In other words, they must not have been measured as paired or blocked data.

To verify the necessary conditions, examine histograms, stem-and-leaf plots, boxplots, or dotplots for each sample. Within each sample, a comparison of the mean and median can also provide information about possible skewness and outliers. If both of the two independent samples are large, we are in "Situation 2" and the two-sample *t*-test generally is valid for comparing the means unless there are remarkably extreme outliers. Keep in mind, however, that for skewed data the median may be the better measure of location.

Continuing Step 2: The Test Statistic for a Two-Sample t-Test

The relevant sample statistic is $\bar{x}_1 - \bar{x}_2$ = the difference between sample means. As with a one-sample t-test, the standard error of $\bar{x}_1 - \bar{x}_2$ does not depend on whether the null hypothesis is true, so the term *null* is dropped from the denominator standard error. The "standardized" test statistic is

$$t = \frac{\text{Sample statistic} - \text{Null value}}{\text{Standard error}} = \frac{\bar{x}_1 - \bar{x}_2 - 0}{\sqrt{\dfrac{s_1^2}{n_1} + \dfrac{s_2^2}{n_2}}}$$

Step 3: Assuming the Null Hypothesis Is True, Find the p-Value

To find the p-value, use the t-distribution with appropriate degrees of freedom:

- For H_a: $\mu_1 - \mu_2 < 0$, the p-value is the area below t, even if t is positive.
- For H_a: $\mu_1 - \mu_2 > 0$, the p-value is the area above t, even if t is negative.
- For H_a: $\mu_1 - \mu_2 \neq 0$, the p-value is $2 \times$ area above $|t|$.

As discussed in Chapter 12, the t-distribution is only an approximation for the distribution of the t-statistic, and appropriate degrees of freedom are found by a complicated formula called "Welch's approximation." The formula is given in Section 12.5 and will not be repeated here. In practice, if computer software such as Minitab is used, it will provide the numerical value of degrees of freedom found from the approximation. If software is not available, a conservative approach is to use the smaller of $n_1 - 1$ and $n_2 - 1$ as the degrees of freedom.

Equal Variances and Pooled Standard Error

tech note If we are willing to make the assumption that the two populations we are comparing have the same (or similar) variance, then there is a procedure for which the t-distribution *is* the correct distribution of the t-statistic when the null hypothesis is true. It involves "pooling" both samples to estimate the common variance. The procedure is called a *pooled two-sample t-test*, and is discussed at the end of this section.

***Steps 4 and 5: Decide Whether or Not the Result
Is Statistically Significant Based on the p-Value
and Report the Conclusion in the Context of the Situation***

These steps proceed as with any hypothesis test. Choose a significance level ("alpha"), usually $\alpha = 0.05$, and declare the difference in means to be statistically significant if the p-value $\leq \alpha$. Report a conclusion appropriate for the situation. When drawing a conclusion about differences between two populations, it also is important to consider the way in which the data were gathered. Remember from Chapter 3 that data collected in an experiment can provide stronger evidence of causation than data from an observational study.

EXAMPLE 13.3—*CONTINUED*
***The Effect of a Stare
on Driving Behavior***

Step 1: *State the hypotheses.* The subscript 1 is used to represent the No Stare population and the subscript 2 to represent the Stare population. As stated above, the appropriate null and alternative hypotheses are

$$H_0: \mu_1 - \mu_2 = 0 \qquad (\text{or } \mu_1 = \mu_2)$$
$$H_a: \mu_1 - \mu_2 > 0 \qquad (\text{or } \mu_1 > \mu_2)$$

The alternative hypothesis reflects the fact that the researchers thought staring would cause drivers to speed up, so the mean time should be slower (larger values) for the No Stare group and faster (smaller values) for the Stare group.

Step 2: *Verify necessary data conditions, and if met, determine the test statistic.* The data conditions were checked in Example 12.8. We saw that the conditions for conducting the *t*-test appeared to be valid, as there were no extreme outliers and no extreme skewness in the data. There were $n_1 = 14$ observations in the No Stare group and $n_2 = 13$ observations in the Stare group. The following Minitab (Release 12) output provides a confidence interval for the difference between the population means and results for a one-tailed test:

Two-sample T for CrossTime

Group	N	Mean	StDev	SE Mean
NoStare	14	6.63	1.36	0.36
Stare	13	5.59	0.822	0.23

95% CI for mu (NoStare) − mu (Stare): (0.14, 1.93)
T-Test mu (NoStare) = mu (Stare) (vs >): T = 2.41   P = 0.013   DF = 21

The last line of output shows us that the *t*-statistic is T = 2.41. The elements of the calculation are

- The sample statistic is $\bar{x}_1 - \bar{x}_2 = 6.63 - 5.59 = 1.04$ seconds.

- $\text{s.e.}(\bar{x}_1 - \bar{x}_2) = \sqrt{\dfrac{s_1^2}{n_1} + \dfrac{s_2^2}{n_2}} = \sqrt{\dfrac{1.36^2}{14} + \dfrac{0.822^2}{13}} = 0.43.$

- $t = \dfrac{\text{Sample statistic} - \text{Null value}}{\text{Standard error}} = \dfrac{\bar{x}_1 - \bar{x}_2 - 0}{\text{s.e.}(\bar{x}_1 - \bar{x}_2)} = \dfrac{1.04 - 0}{0.43} = 2.41.$

Steps 3, 4, and 5: *Determine the p-value and make a conclusion in context.* Note from the output that the *p*-value of the test is 0.013, so we can reject the null hypothesis and attach the label "statistically significant" to the results. The *p*-value is the probability that a sample difference could be as far or further from 0 as 1.04 seconds is *in the positive direction,* if the population difference is actually 0. This probability is determined using a *t*-distribution with df = 21 (the approximate degrees of freedom computed by Minitab using the Welch approximation formula described in Chapter 12) and finding the area to the right of the test statistic value, $t = 2.41$. From Table A.3, we would learn that the *p*-value is between 0.009 and 0.015. We can conclude that if all drivers were stared at, the mean crossing times at an intersection would be faster than under normal conditions. It can also be noted that these data were collected in a randomized experiment, so it's reasonable to conclude that the staring or not staring caused the difference between the mean crossing times.

Substitute Steps 3 and 4: As is always the case, the same conclusion is reached using the *rejection region* approach. To find the *critical value* for this example, use Table A.2 with df = 21. (If Minitab had not provided the degrees of freedom, we would use the conservative value of smaller sample size -1, which is $13 - 1 = 12$, but we will assume we know df $=$ 21.) Because the alternative hypothesis is one-sided, H_a: $\mu_1 - \mu_2 > 0$, for $\alpha = 0.05$ use the 0.90 column. The critical value is 1.72 and the rejection region is $t \geq 1.72$. Because the test statistic $t = 2.41$ is in the rejection region, we reject the null hypothesis. This is the same conclusion we reached based on the p-value of 0.013, and because the p-value is more informative than the rejection region approach, it is always better to report it if it is known. ◆

EXAMPLE 13.4
A Two-Tailed Test of Television Watching for Men and Women

In Example 12.2 we used information from $n = 175$ Penn State students to estimate the mean amount of time that college students watch television in a typical day. Do you think that the mean time watching television is *different* for the population of college men than it is for the population of college women?

Step 1: A two-sided alternative hypothesis is appropriate because there is no prior knowledge that one specific sex might have a higher mean. Therefore, if μ_1 and μ_2 are the mean population daily television viewing hours for men and women, respectively, for the populations represented by these students, then the appropriate hypotheses are

$$H_0: \mu_1 - \mu_2 = 0$$
$$H_a: \mu_1 - \mu_2 \neq 0$$

Step 2: The conditions are met for a two-sample t-test to be valid because television viewing hours are available for large independent samples of men and women. Minitab provides the test statistic and furnishes the information necessary to show how to compute it by hand:

```
Sex          N       Mean      StDev     SE Mean
Male         59      2.37      1.87      0.24
Female       116     1.95      1.51      0.14

95% CI for mu (Male) − mu (Female): (−0.14, 0.98)
T-Test of mu (Male) − mu (Female) (vs not =): T = 1.49   P = 0.140   DF = 97
```

In the last line of output, we see that the test statistic is T $= 1.49$. The calculation is

- $\bar{x}_1 - \bar{x}_2 = 2.37 - 1.95 = 0.42$ hours

- s.e.$(\bar{x}_1 - \bar{x}_2) = \sqrt{\dfrac{s_1^2}{n_1} + \dfrac{s_2^2}{n_2}} = \sqrt{\dfrac{1.87^2}{59} + \dfrac{1.51^2}{116}} = 0.281$

- $t = \dfrac{\text{Sample statistic} - \text{Null value}}{\text{Standard error}} = \dfrac{0.42 - 0}{0.281} = 1.49$

Steps 3, 4, and 5: *p-value and conclusion.* The p-value is the probability that a sample mean difference could be as far or further from 0 as 0.42 hours is, *in either direction,* if the population mean difference is actually 0. This is determined by finding the probability that the value of a Student's t-distribution is above 1.49 or below -1.49. For this test, use approximate df $= 97$ (see Minitab output above) or if necessary, use df $= 59 - 1 = 58$ (minimum sample size $- 1$). In either case, the *p-value* is 2 times

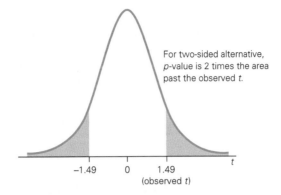

FIGURE 13.6   *p*-Value region for Example 13.4

the area to the right of 1.49 in a *t*-distribution with the stated degrees of freedom (97 or 58), which is 0.14 for either degrees of freedom. Figure 13.6 illustrates this area and demonstrates that it is actually the area to the left of -1.49 plus the area to the right of 1.49. It is simpler computationally to find $2 \times$ the area to the right of 1.49.

Notice that although the sample mean of the daily viewing hours is higher for the men, the *p*-value of 0.14 is greater than 0.05, so we cannot reject the null hypothesis that $\mu_1 - \mu_2 = 0$. On the basis of these *samples,* there is insufficient evidence to conclude that the mean *population* television viewing hours for college men and women are different.

Substitute Steps 3 and 4: As is always the case, the same conclusion is reached using the *rejection region* approach. The conclusion in this case is that we cannot reject the null hypothesis. To find the critical value for this example, use Table A.2 with df = 58. (If Minitab had not provided the degrees of freedom, we would have to use the conservative value of smaller sample size $- 1$, which is $59 - 1 = 58$, so we will use it here.) Because the alternative hypothesis is two-sided, H_a: $\mu_1 - \mu_2 \neq 0$, for $\alpha = 0.05$ use the 0.95 column. The critical value falls between 2.01 and 2.00; we will use the more conservative 2.01 as the critical value. The rejection region is $t \leq -2.01$ and $t \geq 2.01$. Because the test statistic $t = 1.49$ is *not* in the rejection region, we *cannot* reject the null hypothesis. This is the same conclusion we reached based on the *p*-value of 0.14. ◆

---

in summary   **The Steps for a Two-Sample**
t-Test (Unpooled)

Step 1: Determine the *null* and *alternative* hypotheses.

Null hypothesis: H_0: $\mu_1 - \mu_2 = 0$

Alternative hypothesis: H_a: $\mu_1 - \mu_2 \neq 0$ *or* H_a: $\mu_1 - \mu_2 > 0$ *or*
                              H_a: $\mu_1 - \mu_2 < 0$

where the format of the alternative hypothesis depends on the research question of interest and the order in which population 1 and population 2 are defined.

Step 2: Verify necessary data conditions, and if met, summarize the data into an appropriate *test statistic*.

Verify that both n's are large *or* that there are no extreme outliers or skewness in either sample. The samples must also be independent. Compute the test statistic:

$$t = \frac{\text{Sample statistic} - \text{Null value}}{\text{Standard error}} = \frac{\bar{x}_1 - \bar{x}_2 - 0}{\sqrt{\dfrac{s_1^2}{n_1} + \dfrac{s_2^2}{n_2}}}$$

Steps 3, 4, and 5: Proceed exactly as instructed in the In Summary "The Steps for Testing a Single Mean with a One-Sample *t*-Test" on page 444, except in the instructions for step 3, use df = (smaller of $n_1 - 1$, $n_2 - 1$) and replace μ with $(\mu_1 - \mu_2)$ and μ_0 with 0.

Pooled Two-Sample *t*-Test

The use of the *t*-distribution for finding *p*-values for the two-sample *t*-test is an approximation. However, if the population standard deviations are the same, then there is a more precise method available. The **pooled two-sample *t*-test** is based on the assumption that $\sigma_1 = \sigma_2 = \sigma$, the common standard deviation for both populations. The sample variances are combined to provide a **pooled sample variance, s_p^2**, and **pooled standard deviation, s_p**. The formula for the pooled sample variance is

$$\text{Pooled sample variance} = s_p^2 = \frac{(n_1 - 1)s_1^2 + (n_2 - 1)s_2^2}{n_1 + n_2 - 2}$$

The computations for the *t*-statistic and *p*-value remain the same as with the regular two-sample *t*-test except for two small changes. First, the pooled sample variance is used in place of the individual sample variances when computing the standard error. Second, the degrees of freedom are df = $n_1 + n_2 - 2$.

in summary   Pooled Two-Sample *t*-Test

The test statistic is

$$\text{Pooled } t = \frac{\text{Sample statistic} - \text{Null value}}{\text{Pooled standard error}}$$

where

$$\text{Pooled standard error} = \text{Pooled s.e.}(\bar{x}_1 - \bar{x}_2) = \sqrt{\frac{s_p^2}{n_1} + \frac{s_p^2}{n_2}} = s_p\sqrt{\frac{1}{n_1} + \frac{1}{n_2}}$$

Under the null hypothesis, the pooled *t*-statistic has a *t*-distribution with df = $n_1 + n_2 - 2$. All other steps are the same as for the unpooled two-sample *t*-test.

Although the pooled t-test provides an exact solution and the "unpooled" version provides only an approximate solution, we do not recommend that the pooled t-test be used except in very specific circumstances. It is better to have an approximate solution that is known to work well than to use an exact solution based on an assumption that cannot be verified.

Guidelines for Using the Pooled Two-Sample t-Test

- When $n_1 = n_2$, the pooled and unpooled standard errors are equal and so the t-statistic also is the same for both the unpooled and pooled procedures. The pooled procedure, however, is not exact unless the population standard deviations are equal, so generally it is preferable to use Welch's approximate df. If this value is not available, when the two sample sizes are equal it is an acceptable substitute to use df $= n_1 + n_2 - 2$. This recommendation can be extended to include situations where the sample sizes are close.

- When n_1 and n_2 are very different, the pooled test can be quite misleading unless the sample standard deviations are similar. Some books recommend using the pooled test as long as the ratio of sample standard deviations (larger s/smaller s) is ≤ 2, but this cutoff is completely arbitrary and we do not recommend it.

- It can be shown using algebra that

$$\text{Pooled s.e.}(\bar{x}_1 - \bar{x}_2) \approx \sqrt{\frac{s_1^2}{n_2} + \frac{s_2^2}{n_1}}$$

where the symbol "$\approx$" means "is approximately equal to." Therefore, using the pooled standard error is essentially equivalent to reversing the roles of n_1 and n_2 in the standard error. If the larger sample produces the smaller sample standard deviation, the standard error will tend to be underestimated, the t-statistic will tend to be too large, and the null hypothesis will be rejected too easily. Therefore, if the sample sizes are very different and the smaller standard deviation accompanies the larger sample size, we do not recommend using the pooled procedure.

- If the sample sizes are very different, the standard deviations are similar, and the larger sample size produced the larger standard deviation, the pooled t-test is acceptable because it will be conservative.

EXAMPLE 13.4 — *CONTINUED*
Misleading
Pooled t-Test for
Television Watching
for Men and Women

In Example 13.4, we compared television viewing hours for male and female college students and could not reject the hypothesis that they had the same population means. The sample size for males was only about half of what it was for females, but the standard deviation was larger for males. Here are the summary statistics:

	Sample Size	Mean	Standard Deviation	Variance
Male	$n_1 = 59$	2.37	1.87	3.50
Female	$n_2 = 116$	1.95	1.51	2.28

The difference in means is 0.42 hour, the unpooled standard error is 0.281, the test statistic is 1.49, and the resulting p-value is 0.14. Here are the computations for the *pooled t-test:*

$$s_p^2 = \frac{(n_1 - 1)s_1^2 + (n_2 - 1)s_2^2}{n_1 + n_2 - 2} = 2.69, \qquad s_p = 1.64$$

$$\text{Pooled s.e.}(\bar{x}_1 - \bar{x}_2) = \sqrt{\frac{s_p^2}{n_1} + \frac{s_p^2}{n_2}} = s_p\sqrt{\frac{1}{n_1} + \frac{1}{n_2}} = 1.64\sqrt{\frac{1}{59} + \frac{1}{116}} = 0.262$$

$$t = \frac{\text{Sample statistic} - \text{Null value}}{\text{Pooled standard error}} = 0.42/0.262 = 1.60$$

$$\text{df} = 59 + 116 - 2 = 173; \qquad p\text{-value} = 0.11$$

Although the p-value for the pooled test still would not lead to rejection of the null hypothesis, it is noticeably smaller than the p-value for the unpooled test. In similar situations, in which sample sizes are very different and the larger sample has the smaller variance, the pooled *t*-test and inflated test statistic could provide a misleading conclusion to reject the null hypothesis. ◆

EXAMPLE 13.5
Legitimate Pooled t-Test for Comparing Male and Female Sleep Time

In Example 12.9, we compared the mean sleep time for male and female college students by finding a confidence interval for the difference. The data were collected in statistics classes at the University of California, Davis, at the beginning of the Spring 2000 quarter. Here is a summary of the results from Minitab, displaying both the unpooled and pooled versions:

Two Sample T-Test and Confidence Interval

Two sample T for sleep [without "Assume Equal Variance" option]

sex	N	Mean	StDev	SE Mean
f	83	7.02	1.75	0.19
m	65	6.55	1.68	0.21

95% CI for mu (f) − mu (m): (−0.10, 1.02)
T-Test mu (f) = mu (m) (vs not =): T = 1.62   P = 0.11   DF = 140

Two sample T for sleep [with "Assume Equal Variance" option]

sex	N	Mean	StDev	SE Mean
f	83	7.02	1.75	0.19
m	65	6.55	1.68	0.21

95% CI for mu (f) − mu (m): (−0.10, 1.03)
T-Test mu (f) = mu (m) (vs not =): T = 1.62   P = 0.11   DF = 146
Both use Pooled StDev = 1.72

Notice that in this case, the sample sizes are similar, as are the sample standard deviations. Consequently, the pooled standard deviation of 1.72 is similar to the separate standard deviations of 1.75 and 1.68. The test statistic of 1.62 is identical under both procedures, and the p-value of 0.11 is the same. The use of the pooled procedure was warranted in this case. ◆

Minitab Tip

tech note **Computing a Two-Sample *t*-Test to Compare Means**

♦ To carry out a two-sample *t*-test, use **Stat>Basic Statistics> 2-sample t.** Specify the location of the data. There are two ways the data can be organized. The raw data for the response may be in one column (*Samples*) and the raw data for group categories (*Subscripts*) in a second column, or the raw data for the two independent groups may be in two separate columns.

♦ To compute a *pooled* two-sample *t*-test, click on **Assume Equal Variances.**

♦ To specify the alternative hypothesis, use the **Options** button.

Note: Use the **Graphs** button to create a comparative dotplot or a comparative boxplot.

13.3

turn on your mind

The paired *t*-test introduced in Section 13.2 and the two-sample *t*-test introduced in this section are both used to compare two sets of measurements, and the null hypothesis in both cases is usually that the mean population difference is 0. Explain the difference in the situations for which they are used. Suppose researchers wanted to know if college students spend more time watching TV or exercising. Explain how they could collect data appropriate for a paired *t*-test and how they could collect data appropriate for a two-sample *t*-test.*

13.4 | TESTING THE DIFFERENCE BETWEEN TWO POPULATION PROPORTIONS

Researchers often wish to examine the difference between two populations with regard to the proportions falling into a particular category of a response variable. It is almost always of interest to test whether the two population proportions are equal, and that is the only case we will consider. The two populations may be represented by two categories of a categorical variable, such as when we want to compare the proportions of Republicans and Democrats who support a certain political issue. Or, the two populations may be hypothetical, represented by different treatments in an experiment. For instance, we may want to compare the proportions of smokers who would quit smoking if wearing a nicotine patch versus if wearing a placebo patch.

When two proportions are equal, the standard errors of the sample statistics (the sample proportions) are equal as well. This fact will be used to estimate the

***HINT:** If you were in the study and they asked you (and other participants) about both time watching TV and time exercising, would the data be paired or independent samples?

null standard error for the test statistic. So, unlike in tests for means, the null standard error formula used for the test differs from the standard error formula used in Chapter 12 to find confidence intervals for the difference in two proportions. Also, it is appropriate to use the phrase "null standard error" rather than simply "standard error" because the calculation is connected to assuming the null hypothesis to be true.

EXAMPLE 13.6 ***The Prevention*** ***of Ear Infections***	Based on its biochemical properties, Finnish researchers hypothesized that regular use of the sweetener xylitol might be useful for preventing ear infections in preschool children and carried out a study to test this hypothesis (Uhari, 1998). In a randomized experiment, $n_1 = 165$ children took five daily doses of placebo syrup, and 68 of these children got an ear infection during the three months of the study. Another $n_2 = 159$ children took five daily doses of xylitol, and 46 of these children got an ear infection during the study. The sample proportions getting an ear infection are $\hat{p}_1 = 68/165 = .412$ for the placebo group and $\hat{p}_2 = 46/159 = .289$ for the xylitol group, and the difference between these two proportions is .123 (12.3%). Is this observed difference in proportions large enough to conclude in general that using xylitol reduces the risk of ear infection? We will return to this example after summarizing the steps for the **hypothesis test for comparing two population proportions.** ◆

Step 1: Determine the Null and Alternative Hypotheses

The *null* hypothesis is that there is no difference in population proportions:

$$H_0: p_1 - p_2 = 0 \quad (\text{or } p_1 = p_2)$$

The *alternative* hypothesis may be either two-sided or one-sided, depending on the research question of interest:

$$H_a: p_1 - p_2 \neq 0 \quad or \quad H_a: p_1 - p_2 > 0 \quad or \quad H_a: p_1 - p_2 < 0$$

The alternative hypothesis may also be written as

$$H_a: p_1 \neq p_2 \quad or \quad H_a: p_1 > p_2 \quad or \quad H_a: p_1 < p_2$$

The direction of the alternative hypothesis for a one-sided test depends on which group is defined as population 1 and which is defined as population 2. It is often easier to clarify the correct direction by writing the alternative hypothesis in the second format.

Step 2: Verify Necessary Data Conditions, and If Met, Summarize the Data into an Appropriate Test Statistic

Conditions Necessary for a z-Test of the Difference in Two Proportions to Be Valid

- ◆ Independent samples are available from the two populations.
- ◆ The number with the trait or response of interest and the number without the trait or response of interest is at least 5 in each sample, and preferably at least 10.

Make sure the data collection was done so as to ensure independent samples, then simply make sure there are at least 5 (or 10) with and without the trait or response of interest in each of the two samples.

Continuing Step 2: Computing the Test
Statistic for a z-Test for Two Proportions

The sample statistic $\hat{p}_1 - \hat{p}_2$ (difference between sample proportions) estimates the parameter $p_1 - p_2$ (difference between population proportions). To find the null standard error, assume the null hypothesis is true, so that $p_1 = p_2 = p$. Estimate the common population proportion p using all of the data:

$$\hat{p} = \frac{n_1\hat{p}_1 + n_2\hat{p}_2}{n_1 + n_2}$$

Despite the complicated formula, this combined estimate is simply the sample proportion for both samples combined. It is used instead of separate estimates of p_1 and p_2 to find the null standard error. The rationale for this substitution is that the test is based on the distribution of the test statistic *assuming the null hypothesis is true.* If $p_1 = p_2$, then $\hat{p}$ is the best estimate for each of the population proportions because it makes use of all available sample data. The standardized test statistic is

$$z = \frac{\text{Sample statistic} - \text{Null value}}{\text{Null standard error}} = \frac{\hat{p}_1 - \hat{p}_2 - 0}{\sqrt{\dfrac{\hat{p}(1 - \hat{p})}{n_1} + \dfrac{\hat{p}(1 - \hat{p})}{n_2}}}$$

$$= \frac{\hat{p}_1 - \hat{p}_2 - 0}{\sqrt{\hat{p}(1 - \hat{p})\left(\dfrac{1}{n_1} + \dfrac{1}{n_2}\right)}}$$

If the null hypothesis is true, the sampling distribution of this z-statistic is approximately the standard normal curve.

Step 3: Assuming the Null Hypothesis is True, Find the p-Value

The standard normal curve is used to find the *p*-value:

- For H_a: $p_1 - p_2 > 0$, the *p*-value is the area above z (a one-tailed test), even if z is negative.

- For H_a: $p_1 - p_2 < 0$, the *p*-value is the area below z (a one-tailed test), even if z is positive.

- For H_a: $p_1 - p_2 \neq 0$, the *p*-value is $2 \times$ area above $|z|$ (a two-tailed test).

Do not confuse the *p-value* with the population or sample *proportions,* which also use the letter *p.*

Steps 4 and 5: Decide Whether or Not the Result
Is Statistically Significant Based on the p-Value
and Make a Conclusion in the Context of the Situation

Choose a significance level ("alpha"); standard practice is $\alpha = 0.05$. The result is statistically significant if the *p*-value $\leq \alpha$. Interpret the conclusion in the context of the situation. Whenever two populations are compared, the manner in which the data were collected should also be considered. Remember from Chapter 3 that an experiment is generally a stronger proof of causation than an observational study.

EXAMPLE 13.6—*CONTINUED*
The Prevention
of Ear Infections

Step 1: *Determine the null and alternative hypotheses.* The researchers hoped to show that xylitol reduces ear infections. The parameter p_1 is the proportion who would get an ear infection in the population of children similar to those in the study if taking the placebo. The parameter p_2 is the proportion who would get an ear infection in that population if taking the xylitol. Therefore, the null and alternative hypotheses of interest are

$$H_0: p_1 - p_2 = 0 \quad \text{(or } p_1 = p_2\text{)}$$
$$H_a: p_1 - p_2 > 0 \quad \text{(or } p_1 > p_2\text{)}$$

A one-sided alternative is used because the researchers want to show that the proportion getting an ear infection is significantly lower in the xylitol group than in the placebo group.

Step 2: *Verify necessary data conditions, and if met, summarize the data into an appropriate test statistic.* There are at least 10 children in each sample who did and did not get ear infections, so the conditions are met.

♦ $\hat{p}_1 = \dfrac{68}{165} = .412$ and $\hat{p}_2 = \dfrac{46}{159} = .289$.

♦ The sample statistic is $\hat{p}_1 - \hat{p}_2 = .412 - .289 = .123$.

♦ The combined proportion is $\hat{p} = \dfrac{68 + 46}{165 + 159} = \dfrac{114}{324} = .35$.

♦ null s.e.$(\hat{p}_1 - \hat{p}_2) = \sqrt{\hat{p}(1 - \hat{p})\left(\dfrac{1}{n_1} + \dfrac{1}{n_2}\right)} = \sqrt{(.35)(.65)\left(\dfrac{1}{165} + \dfrac{1}{159}\right)} = .053.$

♦ $z = \dfrac{\text{Sample statistic} - \text{Null value}}{\text{Null standard error}} = \dfrac{.123}{.053} = 2.32.$

Steps 3, 4, and 5: Because the alternative is $H_a: p_1 - p_2 > 0$, the p-value is the area above $z = 2.32$. Figure 13.7 illustrates this probability. From the normal probability table (Appendix Table A.1), we learn that the probability is 0.9898 that z is less than 2.32, so p-value $= 1 - 0.9898 = 0.0102$. We can reject the null hypothesis and attach the label "statistically significant" to the result because the p-value is small. Based on this experiment, we can conclude that taking xylitol would reduce the proportion of ear infections in the population of similar preschool children in comparison to taking a placebo. ♦

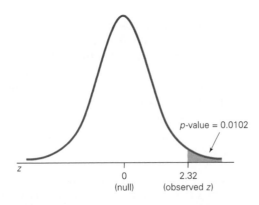

p-value = 0.0102

z

0
(null)

2.32
(observed z)

FIGURE 13.7   *p-Value region for Example 13.6*

in summary The Steps for a z-Test for the Difference in Two Proportions

Step 1: Determine the *null* and *alternative* hypotheses.

Null hypothesis: $\qquad$ $H_0: p_1 - p_2 = 0$

Alternative hypothesis: $\quad$ $H_a: p_1 - p_2 \neq 0$ $\quad$ or $\quad$ $H_a: p_1 - p_2 > 0$ $\quad$ or $\quad$ $H_a: p_1 - p_2 < 0$

where the format of the alternative hypothesis depends on the research question of interest and the order in which population 1 and population 2 are defined.

Step 2: Verify necessary data conditions, and if met, summarize the data into an appropriate *test statistic*.

Verify that samples are large enough so that for each sample, $n\hat{p}$ and $n(1 - \hat{p})$ are at least 5, preferably 10. The samples also must be independent. Compute the test statistic:

$$z = \frac{\text{Sample statistic} - \text{Null value}}{\text{Null standard error}} = \frac{(\hat{p}_1 - \hat{p}_2) - 0}{\sqrt{\hat{p}(1 - \hat{p})\left(\dfrac{1}{n_1} + \dfrac{1}{n_2}\right)}}$$

Step 3: Assuming the null hypothesis is true, find the *p-value*.

Using the *z* (standard normal) distribution, the *p*-value is the area in the tail(s) beyond the test statistic *z* as follows:

For $H_a: p_1 - p_2 \neq 0$ the *p*-value is $2 \times$ area above $|z|$ (a two-tailed test).
For $H_a: p_1 - p_2 > 0$ the *p*-value is the area above *z* even if *z* is negative.
For $H_a: p_1 - p_2 < 0$ the *p*-value is the area below *z* even if *z* is positive.

Steps 4 and 5: Proceed exactly as instructed in the In Summary "The Steps for Testing a Single Mean with a One-Sample *t*-Test" on page 444.

Using Minitab for a Test of Two Proportions

Output from the Minitab (Release 12) procedure for examining two proportions for Example 13.6 is shown below:

```
Sample        X          N        Sample p
Placebo       68         165        0.412
Xylitol       46         159        0.289

Estimate for p(1) − p(2): 0.123
95% CI for p(1) − p(2): (0.020, 0.226)
Test for p(1) − p(2) = 0 (vs > 0): Z = 2.34   P-Value = 0.010
```

The default in Minitab is *not* to use the combined sample proportion in the formula for the standard error, because the Minitab procedure for two proportions is used to compute a confidence interval as well as to carry out a test of hypotheses. In other words, Minitab is using the standard error formula in Chapter 12 in the denominator of the test statistic, rather than the null standard error formula given in this chapter. However, the results are just slightly different and the conclusion is the same. This will generally, but not always, be the case.

Minitab Tip

tech note **Computing a Two-Sample z-Test for the Difference in Proportions**

◆ To test hypotheses about the difference in two proportions, use **Stat>Basic Statistics>2 Proportions.** See note below for information about inputting data.

◆ To specify the alternative hypothesis, use the **Options** button.

◆ To compute the z-statistic described in this section, use **Options,** and then click **Use pooled estimate of p for test.**

Note: There are three possibilities for inputting data. The raw data for the response may be in one column and the raw data for group categories (*Subscripts*) may be in a second column. Or, the raw data for the two independent groups may be in two separate columns. Or, the data may already be summarized. If so, click **Summarized Data,** then specify the sample size and the *number* of successes for each group.

turn on your mind

The raw data for Example 13.6 can be thought of as two categorical variables (with two possible categories each) for each participant in the experiment. What are the two variables and their categories? Construct a contingency table in the format learned in Chapter 6, with the explanatory variable as rows. In Chapter 6, you learned how to look for relationships by finding a chi-square statistic and associated *p*-value. In the context of this example, how do you think the null and alternative hypotheses would be stated if the problem is viewed from that perspective? (You will learn how to do this in Chapter 15.)*

13.5 | THE RELATIONSHIP BETWEEN SIGNIFICANCE TESTS AND CONFIDENCE INTERVALS

In the situations covered in Chapters 10–13, you may have noticed a direct correspondence between the values covered by a confidence interval and the results of two-sided hypothesis tests. The correspondence is precise for tests involving one or two population means and a two-sided alternative.

*****HINT:** One variable is treatment (xylitol or placebo). What else did the researchers measure for each child?

Confidence Intervals and Tests with Two-Sided Alternatives

When testing one population mean or the difference in two population means with the hypotheses

H_0: parameter = null value   *and* H_a: parameter $\neq$ null value

- If the null value is covered by a $(1 - \alpha)100\%$ confidence interval, the null hypothesis is not rejected and the test is not statistically significant at level α.

- If the null value is not covered by a $(1 - \alpha)100\%$ confidence interval, the null hypothesis is rejected and the test is statistically significant at level α.

Don't be confused by the cumbersome notation $(1 - \alpha)100\%$. The correspondence is between a 95% confidence interval and a significance level of 0.05, a 99% confidence interval and a significance level of 0.01, and so on.

EXAMPLE 13.4—*CONTINUED*
Mean Daily Television Hours of Men and Women

In Example 13.4, we tested whether the population mean daily television viewing hours differed for male and female college students. The Minitab output is reprinted here:

```
Sex          N       Mean      StDev     SE Mean
Male        59       2.37      1.87       0.24
Female     116       1.95      1.51       0.14

95% CI for mu (Male) − mu (Female): (−0.14, 0.98)
T-Test of mu (Male) − mu (Female) (vs not =): T = 1.49   P = 0.140   DF = 97
```

Notice that a 95% confidence interval for the difference in population means is −0.14 to +0.98 hours. In other words, with 95% confidence we can say that $-0.14 \leq \mu_1 - \mu_2 \leq 0.98$ hours. The null value for the test was 0 hours, which is covered by this interval. Therefore, the difference in sample means, which is 0.42 hours, is not significantly different from the population null value of 0.

The correspondence also holds for one or two proportions, with one caveat. In those situations, the standard error used for the confidence interval is slightly different from the null standard error used for the hypothesis tests. Therefore, the correspondence may not hold if the null value is close to one of the boundaries of the confidence interval. In most cases, however, this minor technical detail will not interfere with the correspondence.

This correspondence means that a confidence interval can be used as an alternative way to conduct a two-sided significance test. Some researchers think that whenever possible, a confidence interval should be used to test hypotheses because an interval provides information about the value of a parameter as well. ◆

Confidence Intervals and One-Sided Tests

It is possible to construct one-sided confidence intervals by allowing one end of the interval to extend to the minimum or maximum possible value of the parameter, then adjusting the confidence level appropriately. In that case, the same correspondence would hold between one-sided confidence intervals and one-sided tests. It is also possible to use a standard two-sided confidence interval to test a one-sided alternative by appropriately adjusting the significance level of the test or the confidence level for the interval. We present the general result, but the caveat just given in the two-sided case for one or two proportions holds in this case as well.

When testing the hypotheses H_0: parameter = null value versus a one-sided alternative, compare the null value to a $(1 - 2\alpha)100\%$ confidence interval:

- If the null value is covered by the interval, the test is not statistically significant at level α.

- For the alternative H_a: parameter > null value, the test is statistically significant at level α if the entire interval falls *above* the null value.

- For the alternative H_a: parameter < null value, the test is statistically significant at level α if the entire interval falls *below* the null value.

For instance, if a 90% confidence interval falls completely above the null value for a test and the alternative hypothesis is H_a: parameter > null value, then the null hypothesis can be rejected at a significance level of $\alpha = 0.05$. As an illustration, a 90% confidence interval for $\mu_1 - \mu_2$ that contained only positive values would allow researchers to accept the alternative hypothesis H_a: $\mu_1 - \mu_2 > 0$ using $\alpha = 0.05$.

EXAMPLE 13.6—CONTINUED
Ear Infections and Xylitol

Consider Example 13.6 in which a 95% confidence interval for $p_1 - p_2$, the difference in proportions of children who would get ear infections with placebo and xylitol, is .020 to .226. This interval tells us that we can reject H_0: $p_1 - p_2 = 0$ and accept H_a: $p_1 - p_2 > 0$ with $\alpha = 0.025$, because the entire 95% confidence interval falls above the null value of 0. The *p*-value for the test was 0.01, and since $0.01 < 0.025$, this conclusion is confirmed using the standard approach as well. Notice that if the alternative hypothesis had been in the opposite direction, that $p_1 - p_2 < 0$, the null hypothesis would *not* be rejected even though the null value of 0 is not contained in the interval. This conclusion fits with our common sense. The interval indicates that the possible values for the difference are all *above* 0 (.02 to .226), so the alternative hypothesis that the true difference is *less* than 0 is certainly not supported by the interval. ◆

13.5

turn on your mind

Refer to the continuation of Example 13.6. A 95% confidence interval for the difference in proportions who would get ear infections with placebo compared to with xylitol was .02 to .226. Based on this information, specify a one-sided 97.5% confidence interval and explain how you would use it to test H_0: $p_1 - p_2 = 0$ versus H_a: $p_1 - p_2 > 0$ with $\alpha = 0.025$.*

*HINT: The maximum possible value for $p_1 - p_2$ is 1.0, so that's the upper end of the interval.

13.6 | CHOOSING AN APPROPRIATE INFERENCE PROCEDURE

In this chapter and the previous three, we have learned how to construct confidence intervals and conduct hypothesis tests to make inferences for several different population parameters. The focus has been on how to carry out and interpret these inference procedures after the procedure and population parameter of interest have already been identified. In this section, we provide guidance on how to identify the appropriate procedure based on the research question(s) of interest. Necessary decisions include what parameter to investigate and whether to construct a confidence interval, conduct a hypothesis test, or do both.

Confidence Interval or Hypothesis Test?

When using sample data to answer a question about a larger population, how can you decide whether to construct a confidence interval, conduct a hypothesis test, or do both? The key point to consider is whether the main purpose is to estimate the numerical value of a parameter or to make a "maybe not" or "maybe yes" type of conclusion about a specific hypothesized value. If the purpose is to estimate a numerical value, a confidence interval is appropriate. If the purpose is to make a conclusion about a specific value, hypothesis testing is appropriate. Because these procedures provide different types of information about the population, it may be appropriate to use both in many situations.

As an example, think about the difference between the types of information asked for by the following two questions:

Question 1: What is the mean number of hours that students study each week?

Question 2: Is there a difference between mean hours of study per week for females versus males?

Notice that question 1 asks for a numerical value. The answer might be something like "about 18 hours per week." A confidence interval can be used to give an estimate that reflects the uncertainty due to using a sample to estimate the population parameter. For example, we might answer the question about mean number of hours studying with a statement like "With 95% confidence, we estimate that the mean hours of study per week for all students at our school is between 17.2 and 18.8 hours." In general, a confidence interval is used if the main purpose is to estimate the value of a parameter.

How would you answer question 2? It doesn't ask us to estimate numerical values of mean hours of study for men and women, but instead simply asks if there is a difference. Given the question wording, we only have to answer with something like "Yes, there appears to be a difference" or "We cannot say there is a difference." We can create an answer by conducting a hypothesis test (also called a significance test) of the null hypothesis that the difference in means for men and women is 0 versus the alternative hypothesis that the difference in means is not 0. In general, a hypothesis test is used if the main purpose is to provide a "maybe not" or "maybe yes" type of answer for a research question.

In many situations, it may be informative to conduct a significance test and construct a confidence interval as well. For question 2 above, for instance, it would not only be useful to know whether there was a difference, it would also be informative to know the magnitude of a possible difference. A confidence interval for the difference in means for the populations of men and women would give us that information. It is not always the case that both procedures should be used. When the primary purpose is to estimate the numerical value of a single parameter, it usually doesn't make sense to conduct a hypothesis test because there's no specific value of interest. As an example, there's no specific or hypothesized value for the parameter of interest for question 1 above.

Let's summarize what can be learned from constructing a confidence interval or conducting a hypothesis test.

- A confidence interval estimate provides a range of values that is likely to contain the truth about the population parameter, so it gives information about the *magnitude* of the parameter. The confidence level, typically 95%, gives information about how often the procedure will result in an interval that successfully captures its prey (the parameter) in the long run.

- The *p*-value and conclusion from hypothesis testing provide a "maybe not" or "maybe yes" answer to the question, "Is the parameter equal to (or different from) a certain value?" They do not give information about the magnitude of a parameter.

- In many cases where hypothesis testing is the primary goal, it makes sense to construct a confidence interval to accompany the results of the hypothesis test.

- In most cases where a confidence interval estimate is the primary goal, it does not make sense to conduct a hypothesis test to accompany the interval because there is no specific parameter value to be tested.

Determining the Appropriate Parameter

In Chapters 10–13 we learned inference procedures for five specific population parameters:

p: One proportion = population proportion in a category of a categorical variable, or long-run probability of a particular outcome.

μ: One mean = mean for a quantitative variable in a population, or a quantitative outcome in a random circumstance.

μ_d: Paired difference mean = population mean for the difference in two paired variables or quantitative outcomes; use when paired samples are available.

$p_1 - p_2$: Difference in two population proportions or long-run probabilities; use when independent samples are available.

$\mu_1 - \mu_2$: Difference in two means = difference in population means for two populations, use when independent samples are available.

Determining which of these is the parameter of interest depends on the answers to these questions:

- Is there one sample or two? If there are two, are they independent samples or are they paired?
- For one sample, is the variable measured on each unit quantitative or categorical?
- For two independent samples, one variable identifies the two samples and is categorical. Is the other variable also categorical?

TABLE 13.2 ■ **The Parameters and Types of Data Used for Inferences About Them**

Variable Type (Parameter Type)	One Sample (No Pairing)	Paired Data	Two Independent Samples
Categorical (Proportions)	p	none	$p_1 - p_2$
Quantitative (Means)	μ	μ_d	$\mu_1 - \mu_2$

Based on the answers to these questions, you can identify which of the five parameters is appropriate. Table 13.2 illustrates the process.

When you are first learning to distinguish among the situations, it helps to have some clues. Here are tips for helping you determine which parameter to use, assuming the choices are from the five covered in Chapters 10–13.

◆ *Are two different sample sizes given, or is it clear that two independent samples were taken?* If so, the parameter of interest must be either $p_1 - p_2$ or $\mu_1 - \mu_2$.

◆ *Are one or more sample means given?* If so, the parameter is probably a mean or difference in two means.

◆ *Are sample counts or proportions given?* If so, the parameter is probably a proportion or a difference in two proportions.

After you determine the parameter of interest and whether to conduct a hypothesis test and/or construct a confidence interval, you can use the summary tables at the end of this chapter and at the end of Chapter 12 to review the computational details of the analysis.

Examples of Choosing an Inference Procedure

The following examples are quotes about studies from other chapters in this textbook. In each case, think about what type of inference is appropriate.

EXAMPLE 13.7
Kids and Weight Lifting

In Case Study 3.2, a randomized experiment was presented in which children were randomly assigned to one of two weight-lifting conditions or a control condition. Muscular strength and endurance were measured after eight weeks. One of the results reported in Case Study 3.2 was "leg extension strength significantly increased in both exercise groups compared with that in the control subjects."

Notice that the researchers are comparing each of the two weight-lifting conditions to the control condition. Let's focus on comparing the heavy-lifting group to the control group for the reported response variable, leg extension strength.

Decision 1: Confidence interval, hypothesis test or both? Based on the statement about the results, the researchers were clearly interested in knowing *if* there is a significant difference in leg extension strength after heavy lifting compared with no weight lifting. They were also most likely interested in the *magnitude* of the difference. Therefore, both inference procedures would be appropriate.

Decision 2: What is the appropriate parameter to investigate? Let's investigate the three questions used to determine which parameter is appropriate.

◆ *Is there one sample or two? If there are two, are they independent samples or are they paired?* It is clear that there are two samples and that they are independent. One group of children did heavy lifting and the other group did no weight training.

◆ *For one sample, is the variable measured on each unit quantitative or categorical?* This question is not relevant because there are two samples.

◆ *For two independent samples, one variable identifies the two samples and is categorical. Is the other variable also categorical?* The training (heavy or none) identifies the two samples. The other variable measured is the leg extension strength, which is not categorical. Presumably, a quantitative measurement was made for each child.

Based on the answers to these questions, the appropriate column of Table 13.2 is "Two Independent Samples" and the appropriate row is "Quantitative (Means)." Therefore, the parameter of interest is $\mu_1 - \mu_2$, the difference in population means for leg extension strength if all similar children were to participate in the heavy-lifting or control conditions. ◆

EXAMPLE 13.8
Loss of Cognitive Functioning

Example 3.5 reported on an observational study of 6000 older people, which found that 70% of the participants did not lose functioning over time. What inference procedure can be used for this result?

Decision 1: Confidence interval, hypothesis test, or both? There is no information provided about the study that would lead to a natural hypothesis-testing question. The reported result, that 70% of the *sample* lost cognitive functioning over time, leads to a consideration of the margin of error and confidence interval estimate for the proportion of the *population* in this age group that loses cognitive functioning over time. Therefore, hypothesis testing is not appropriate, but a confidence interval is.

Decision 2: What is the appropriate parameter to investigate? The sample statistic reported is a sample proportion for a single sample. People in the study were categorized by whether or not they lost cognitive functioning. Therefore, the parameter of interest is p = proportion that loses cognitive functioning over time for the population of older people represented by this sample. ◆

13.7 | THE TWO TYPES OF ERRORS AND THEIR PROBABILITIES

In Chapter 11, we learned that if the null hypothesis is true but it is rejected, a type 1 error has been made, while if the null hypothesis is false but we fail to reject it, a type 2 error has been made. In most situations, a type 1 error is more serious because it means that the status quo is overturned, and some consequential action is likely. There are situations where it is more serious to make a type 2 error because failure to reject the null hypothesis when it is false could result in the end of a promising line of research.

Determining which type of error is more serious in a given situation is important, especially since researchers have some control over the associated probabilities. In this section, we will learn how decisions can be made to minimize the more serious type of error.

When we describe the probability of making an error, we can only talk in conditional terms. For instance, by definition a type 1 error can only occur when the null hypothesis is true. This means that any description of type 1 error has to include the condition "if the null hypothesis is true." The difficulty is that in practice we never know what is actually true. If we did, we wouldn't need statistical methods. Therefore, it is necessary to consider both possible types of error in any situation.

Probability of a Type 1 Error and the Level of Significance

Recall that a type 1 error occurs when the decision is for the alternative hypothesis but the null hypothesis is actually true. Also, remember that the *level of significance,* or α-level, is the borderline used to decide if a p-value is small enough to justify a decision in favor of the alternative. The level of significance that we use for a hypothesis test also provides the (conditional) **probability of a type 1 error.**

> *definition* When the null hypothesis is true, the **probability of a type 1 error,** the level of significance, and the α-level are all equivalent. When the null hypothesis is not true, a type 1 error cannot be made.

To see the correspondence between the level of significance and the probability of a type 1 error, suppose the null value is the correct population parameter value. In that case, the distribution of the test statistic (z or t) is known and is either the standard normal or the Student's t-distribution. The p-value is the tail area at and beyond the observed test statistic in the tail(s) specified by the alternative hypothesis. Suppose the 0.05 level of significance is being used. By chance alone, the test statistic will fall into the most extreme 5% of the distribution just 5% of the time. When that happens, the p-value will be <0.05, the null hypothesis will be rejected, and a type 1 error will have been made. The same holds for any specified value for α.

This correspondence means that with the standard level of significance of 0.05 or 5%, about 5% of all hypothesis tests done *when the null hypothesis is really true* will result in a false claim of statistical significance. Notice that this is not the same thing as saying that 5% of all rejected null hypotheses should not have been rejected. In fact, some statisticians and researchers argue that in the "real world," the null hypothesis is rarely true. If this argument is correct, the overall number of type 1 errors in practice may be quite small.

One caution to keep in mind is that most research projects involve many hypothesis tests, each done using a significance level of 0.05 or 0.01. We should be cautious when we read that a statistical analysis involved many different hypothesis tests but only a small number of the results were found to be statistically significant. A possible explanation is that all of the various null hypotheses are actually true, but with the 0.05 standard for the level of significance, about 5% of the tests resulted in a conclusion for the alternative hypothesis by chance.

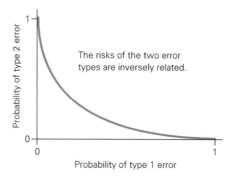

FIGURE 13.8   **The general relationship between the probabilities of the two errors**

The media often fails to report this **multiple-testing** phenomenon, focusing instead on the one or two tests that were statistically significant out of many that were conducted in a study.

The Trade-Off in Probability for the Two Types of Error

If we wanted to be sure that we rarely made a type 1 error, we could simply set the level of significance at a ridiculously low value, making it almost impossible to reject the null hypothesis when it was true. However, if we did this, we would obviously be at great risk of making a type 2 error, because our stringent criterion would make it difficult to reject the null hypothesis even when it was not true.

There is an inverse relationship between the probabilities of the two types of error, illustrated in Figure 13.8. As you can see, an increase in the probability of a type 1 error leads to a decrease in the probability of a type 2 error (and vice versa). The figure is only intended to illustrate the general pattern of the trade-off between the two risks. The exact probabilities will depend on the sample size and the type of test statistic used in a particular situation. Notice that it is *not* the case that the probabilities of the two types of errors sum to 1.0, or to any other specified value.

Type 2 Errors and Power

The probability of making a type 1 error is easy to specify because it involves the assumption that the population parameter is equal to a specific null value. With that assumption, we know precisely what distribution the test statistic has and can thus find probabilities associated with possible outcomes.

It is not so simple to find the **probability of a type 2 error.** Remember that a type 2 error is made when the alternative hypothesis is true. But the alternative hypothesis covers a wide range of possibilities. If the truth is close to the null value, it may be difficult for sample data to provide adequate evidence to reject the null hypothesis, and the probability of making a type 2 error will be high. If the truth is far from the null value, then the sample data will likely provide enough evidence to reject the null value, and the probability of a type 2 error will be low.

There are three factors that affect the probability of making a type 2 error:

1. The sample size; larger *n* reduces the probability of a type 2 error without affecting the probability of a type 1 error.

2. The level of significance used for the test; larger α reduces the probability of a type 2 error by increasing the probability of a type 1 error.
3. The actual value of the population parameter, which is not in the researcher's control. The farther the truth falls from the null value (as long as it is in the alternative hypothesis), the lower the probability of a type 2 error.

Rather than focusing on the risk of making a mistake, many investigators prefer to focus on the chance that their sample will provide the evidence necessary to make the right choice. A common question when a study is planned is "If something is really going on in the population, what is the probability that we'll be able to detect it?" This question leads to the statistical meaning of the word *power:*

> **definition** When the alternative hypothesis is true, the probability of making the correct decision is called the **power** of a test.

Power is simply the flip side of the risk of a type 2 error, and the same factors that influence the risk of a type 2 error also affect the power.

The concept of power is the same for all statistical hypothesis tests, but the technical formulas and details differ depending on the situation. The "by hand" calculations can be difficult, but fortunately some statistical software programs (including Minitab) can be used to easily determine the power of a test under specified conditions.

EXAMPLE 13.9
Planning a Student Survey

A university is considering a plan to offer regular classes year-round by making the summer session a regular term but will only do so if there is sufficient student interest. A university administrator is planning a student survey to determine if a majority of all students at the school would attend summer session under that structure. The plan will only be implemented if a majority would attend, so the status quo is to assume that the proportion who would attend is not a majority. With p representing the proportion of all students who would attend in the summer, a hypothesis testing structure is

$H_0: p \le .50$ (the proportion who would attend is not a majority)
$H_a: p > .50$ (a majority would attend)

Notice that the alternative hypothesis includes a broad range of possibilities and does not specify an exact value. If the true population proportion who would attend is any value greater than .50, the correct decision is to pick the alternative hypothesis.

Table 13.3 shows the *power* for three different "true" proportions and for three different sample sizes. As you look at the table, keep in mind that the power is the probability that the sample evidence leads us to conclude that a majority of the student population would attend a regular summer term. For example, suppose that in truth 60% of students think they would attend a regular summer term and $n = 100$ students are surveyed. The probability that the sample proportion would be large enough to conclude that $p > .50$ is given in Table 13.3 as .64. That means the probability is .36 that a type 2 error would be

TABLE 13.3 ■ **Power for Selected Sample Sizes and True Proportions**

| Sample Size | True Population Proportion | | |
	.52	.60	.65
$n = 50$	.09	.41	.69
$n = 100$	.11	.64	.92
$n = 400$	.20	.99	nearly 1

made, and the null hypothesis would not be rejected. Similarly, if the truth is that 52% think they would attend, and a sample of 400 is chosen, the power is only .20 and the probability of a type 2 error is .80.

These power values were determined for tests done with a 0.05 level of significance. Don't worry about how to do the calculations (Minitab was used to get these numbers). ◆

Example 13.9 illustrates that power is a function of multiple factors. What patterns can we see in Table 13.3? You should be able to detect two important relationships that apply to power for all hypothesis tests:

◆ *The **power** increases when the **sample size** is increased.* We can see this by looking down any column of the table. This makes sense because when the sample size is increased, the standard error is decreased, leading to larger values of the test statistic. Also, the sample statistic is a more accurate estimate of the population value, making it easier to detect a difference between the true population value and the null value.

◆ *The power increases when the difference between the true population value and the null hypothesis value increases.* We can see this looking across any row of the table. This makes sense because the probability of detecting a large difference is higher than the probability of detecting a small difference. However, remember that the truth about the population is not something the researcher can control or change.

Researchers should evaluate power before they collect data that will be used to do hypothesis tests to make sure they have sufficient power to make the study worthwhile. In Example 13.9, we see that a sample of 50 students would have low power even if the true proportion who would attend in the summer were as high as .60 or even .65, a definite majority. If this hypothesis test is important to the administrator for making a decision, he or she should sample more than 50 students. We also see that if the true population proportion is .52, only a slight majority, there is little chance that the administrator will be able to decide in favor of the alternative, even if 400 students are surveyed.

Occasionally, news reports, especially in science magazines, will insightfully note that a study may have failed to find a relationship between two variables because the test had low power. This is a common consequence of conducting research with samples that are too small, but it is one that is often overlooked in media reports.

13.6

turn on your mind

Draw a tree diagram (Chapter 7) illustrating the possible errors in hypothesis testing by making the first set of branches "the truth" (null or alternative) and the second set of branches the decision (do not reject the null, reject the null). Show where the α-level, the probability of a type 2 error, and the power fit on the tree, and how they relate to each other. For any branches on which you cannot assign probabilities, explain why you can't assign them.*

*HINT: Remember that conditional probabilities go on the second set of branches—in this case, the probability of a specific decision, given that the null (or alternative) hypothesis is true.

13.8 | EFFECT SIZE

In most of the hypothesis-testing situations in Chapters 11 and 13, we are interested in comparing a population mean or proportion to a specific null value, or to another population mean or proportion. In many research situations, we would like to know something about the magnitude of the comparison. The test statistic and p-value for a test are not useful for this purpose because they depend on the size of the sample. A confidence interval may not be useful because it depends on the units of measurement, and we want a measure that is independent of the units of measurement. This is particularly true if we want to compare research results across studies, where different measurement units may have been used or slightly different treatments may have been assigned.

In general, the **effect size** for a research question is a measure of how much the truth differs from chance or from a control condition. The most common effect-size measure used for a single mean is

$$d = \frac{\mu_1 - \mu_0}{\sigma}$$

where μ_1 is the true population mean, μ_0 is the null value, and σ is the population standard deviation. Notice that d measures the distance between the true mean and the null mean value in terms of number of standard deviations.

As an example, suppose it is known that the mean IQ in a certain population under usual conditions is 110, with a standard deviation of 15. Researchers speculate that listening to classical music temporarily boosts IQ. If indeed the mean IQ after listening to classical music is 115, then the effect size is $(115 - 110)/15 = 1/3$. In other words, listening to classical music boosts the mean IQ by one-third of a standard deviation.

The most common effect-size measure for comparing two means is

$$d = \frac{\mu_1 - \mu_2}{\sigma}$$

where μ_1 and μ_2 are the two population means and σ is the population standard deviation, assumed to be the same for both populations. If this assumption is not reasonable, and if one population corresponds to a control group condition, then the standard deviation for the control condition is used. If that is not possible either, then a pooled standard deviation is used. Notice that d measures the distance between μ_1 and μ_2 in terms of number of standard deviations, using the standard deviation for the individual populations as the yardstick. In most situations, the order of the difference is not important to the magnitude of the effect, so the absolute value of d is reported.

As an example, suppose pulse rates for those who don't exercise have a mean of 72 and standard deviation of 4 beats per minute, while pulse rates for those who do exercise have a mean of 68 with the same standard deviation. Then the effect size for the difference is $(72 - 68)/4 = 1$. In other words, average pulse rates for those who exercise and those who don't exercise differ by 1 standard deviation.

There are many uses for effect sizes, some of which require d to be estimated from data. There are various suggestions for estimating d based on complicated statistical principles (see, e.g., Hedges and Olkin, 1985), but the simplest method is to substitute sample values for the population parameters in d.

Estimating Effect Sizes for One and Two Samples

> **formula**   For a single sample, the estimated effect size is $\hat{d} = \dfrac{\bar{x} - \mu_0}{s}$, where $\bar{x}$ and s are the sample mean and standard deviation, respectively.
>
> For two samples, the estimated effect size is $\hat{d} = \dfrac{\bar{x}_1 - \bar{x}_2}{s}$, where $\bar{x}_1$ and $\bar{x}_2$ are the two sample means and s is either the standard deviation of the control condition measurements (if there is one) or the pooled sample standard deviation.

Notice that there is a relationship between the test statistic t and the estimated effect size. The formula for the estimated effect size includes everything in the formula for the t statistic *except* the influence of the sample size(s).

Relationship Between Test Statistic t and Effect Size

> **formula**
>
> For one sample: $t = \dfrac{\bar{x} - \mu_0}{\dfrac{s}{\sqrt{n}}} = \dfrac{\sqrt{n}(\bar{x} - \mu_0)}{s} = \sqrt{n}\,\hat{d}$, so $\hat{d} = \dfrac{t}{\sqrt{n}}$
>
> For two samples: $Pooled\ t = \dfrac{\bar{x}_1 - \bar{x}_2}{s\sqrt{\dfrac{1}{n_1} + \dfrac{1}{n_2}}} = \dfrac{\hat{d}}{\sqrt{\dfrac{1}{n_1} + \dfrac{1}{n_2}}}$

Although we won't cover other effect-size measures, the relationship for t-tests holds in most hypothesis-testing situations for which effect sizes are used. Rosenthal (1991) provides a summary of many of these procedures, and notes that in most cases,

Test statistic = Size of effect × Size of study

as we have seen in the tests for means.

Interpreting an Effect Size

Effect sizes provide information about how strong a difference or effect is in the population, relative to another population or a hypothesized value. The interpretation is similar to the interpretation of a standardized score for a specific individual value. In fact, you should notice that the effect size d for a single mean of a normal population is simply the standardized score for μ_1 relative to the normal distribution with mean μ_0 and standard deviation σ.

Cohen (1988) defined small, medium, and large effect sizes for $|d|$ somewhat arbitrarily to be 0.2, 0.5, and 0.8, respectively. In other words, if the true mean μ_1 is half of a standard deviation away from the null mean value ($|d| = 0.5$), Cohen called this a medium effect. If the true mean μ_1 is only 1/5 of a standard deviation away from the null mean ($|d| = 0.2$), Cohen called it a small effect; similarly for 0.8 as a large effect. These are arbitrary, but he said that a small effect should be detectable only through statistics, a medium effect should be obvious to a careful observer, and a large effect should be obvious to any observer.

EXAMPLE 13.10
Could Aliens Tell
That Women Are Shorter?

Suppose an alien were to visit Earth and observe humans. Would it be obvious that men are taller, on average, than women? The mean heights of adult men and women are about 70 inches and 65 inches, respectively, with standard deviations of about 2.5 inches within each population. Therefore, the effect size for the difference in heights is approximately $d = (70 - 65)/2.5 = 2.0$. Such a large difference should be immediately obvious to anyone.

However, suppose the difference in men's and women's heights was smaller. The following table shows what differences correspond to small, medium, and large effect sizes. Think about whether you would notice the difference in mean heights for two groups whose means differed by these amounts. ◆

Effect Size Magnitude	Difference in Heights when $\sigma = 2.5$	Interpretation
Small ($d = 0.2$)	$2.5 \times .2 = 0.50$ inch	Not obvious without statistics
Medium ($d = 0.5$)	$2.5 \times .5 = 1.25$ inches	Obvious to careful observer
Large ($d = 0.8$)	$2.5 \times .8 = 2.00$ inches	Obvious to most observers

EXAMPLE 13.1—*CONTINUED*
Normal Body Temperature

Have you noticed that many people comment on how their normal body temperature seems to be lower than the previously held standard of 98.6? If so, then you have detected a medium effect size. In Example 13.1, data were presented for normal body temperature for 18 people. The sample mean and standard deviation were 98.217 and .684, respectively. The estimated effect size for comparing normal body temperature to the previously held standard of 98.6 is

$$\hat{d} = \frac{\bar{x} - \mu_0}{s} = \frac{98.217 - 98.6}{.684} = -0.56.$$

This is a medium effect size, which should be evident to a careful observer such as a health care worker who routinely measures the temperature of healthy individuals. ◆

Comparing Effect Sizes Across Studies

Effect sizes have become increasingly important in the past few decades with the increase in the use of **meta-analysis,** which is the statistical combination of results on the same topic across studies. Studies are all somewhat different, and may use different units of measurement, different sample sizes and so on. It is useful to have a method of comparison across studies that isn't influenced by sample size or units of measurement, and effect sizes serve that purpose.

In early attempts to review many studies on the same topic, researchers made the mistake of using *p*-values. In fact, they often used a **vote count,** in which they simply counted the proportion of studies that achieved statistical significance. As we have learned, the problem with this method is that statistical significance is heavily dependent on sample size. To illustrate the problem, consider the scenario in the following example.

EXAMPLE 13.11
The Hypothesis-
Testing Paradox

Suppose a researcher conducts a one-sample *t*-test in a study with $n = 100$ and finds that the test statistic $t = 2.5$, so with a two-tailed test the *p*-value is 0.012. The results of the study are clearly statistically significant. Just to be sure, the researcher decides to repeat the study, but this is just for confirmation, so a smaller sample size of $n = 25$ is used. The researcher is disappointed to find that in the replication study, $t = 1.25$, so the *p*-value is only 0.21, and the result is not statistically significant. Perplexed about why the effect disappeared, the researcher decides to combine the data. For the combined data, the researcher is very surprised to find that $t = 2.795$ and the p-value is 0.0052! The paradox is that when the researcher considered the second study alone, it seemed to detract from the evidence for an effect because it was not statistically significant. When the researcher considered the second study in conjunction with the first study, it seemed to strengthen the evidence for an effect.

Now let's look at the effect size for each study and for the combined studies. Here is a summary of the results:

	Sample Size	Test Statistic t	p-Value	Effect Size $\hat{d} = t / \sqrt{n}$
Study #1	100	2.50	0.012	0.25
Study #2	25	1.25	0.21	0.25
Combined	125	2.795	0.0052	0.25

Notice that the effect size is exactly the same for all three studies! The problem is that the researcher was using statistical significance as the basis for the conclusion about whether the first study replicated the second one. The different sample sizes rendered that comparison meaningless. ◆

Thus, effect sizes are quite useful for comparing the results of studies on the same topic. Replication of results requires that similar effect sizes be obtained across studies, and not that statistical significance or the lack of it be obtained. Comparing p-values or statistical significance across studies is valid only if the sample sizes are similar.

Effect Size and Power

It is obvious from Table 13.3 that the *power* for a test depends on the difference between the null value and the true value of the parameter. However, the difference alone is not sufficient. For means, the relevant difference is the effect size, d.

Suppose a researcher wants to find a statistically significant result as long as the truth is a certain size effect, say D. All that he or she needs to do in addition to specifying D is to choose a significance level, usually 0.05 or 0.01. There is then a trade-off between sample size(s) and power that can be quantified. Many researchers aim for power of 0.80, meaning that there is an 80% chance of achieving statistical significance if the true effect size is D. Many software packages will compute the sample size(s) needed to achieve the specified power, or the power that will result from a specified sample size.

EXAMPLE 13.12
Planning a Weight-Loss Study

Suppose you were convinced that your new weight-loss plan worked, and you wanted to conduct a study to verify that. How would you decide how many participants to include? You need to specify four things: (1) the effect size you hope to detect, (2) the planned level of significance α, (3) whether the test is one- or two-tailed, and (4) the desired power. Let's suppose you hope to detect a medium effect size of 0.5, using $\alpha = 0.05$ for a one-tailed test, and want power =

0.80. Using Minitab, we find that a sample of $n = 27$ participants is required. To detect a small effect size of 0.2 with power of 0.80, a sample of $n = 156$ is required.

The interpretation of an effect size of 0.2 or 0.5 in terms of weight lost depends on the standard deviation of the weight losses. If the standard deviation is 10 pounds, then effect sizes of 0.2 and 0.5 correspond to average weight losses of 2 pounds and 5 pounds, respectively.

Table 13.4 shows some additional power and sample size results for this situation. Notice that if indeed the effect is very small ($d = 0.1$), it will be very difficult to achieve statistical significance. Even with $n = 100$ participants, the probability of detecting a statistically significant effect is only .26. On the other hand, if the true effect is a medium effect size, then even with only 20 participants there is a fairly high probability (.695) of achieving a statistically significant effect. ◆

TABLE 13.4 ■ **Power Based on True Effect Size Values for One-Sided, One-Sample *t*-Test, $\alpha = 0.05$**

	True Effect Size			
Sample Size	0.1	0.2	0.5	0.8
$n = 20$	.11	.22	.695	.964
$n = 50$	.17	.40	.967	nearly 1
$n = 100$	.26	.63	.9996	nearly 1

Minitab Tip

tech note **Computing Sample Size for Specified Power or Power for Specified Sample Size**

◆ To compute power for a one-sample *t*-test, use **Stat>Power and Sample Size>1-Sample t.** Use the default sigma = 1.0, and for the differences specify the effect sizes for which you want power information.

There are three choices for what to compute:

◆ **Calculate power for each sample size.** If you want to use this option, fill in the sample sizes for which you want to find power, and for "difference" specify the effect size you hope to detect.

◆ **Calculate power for each difference.** If you want to use this option, fill in a list of effect sizes you hope to detect as the "differences." Then specify the sample size.

◆ **Calculate sample size for each power value.** If you want to use this option, fill in a list of power values and the effect size you hope to detect as the "difference."

◆ Use ***Options*** to specify the form of the alternative hypothesis (not equal to, greater than, less than), the level of significance, and optional storage locations.

13.9 | EVALUATING SIGNIFICANCE IN RESEARCH REPORTS

To evaluate the quality of a research study, you should always consider features like the sampling procedure, the methods used to measure individuals, the wording of questions, and the possibility of lurking variables. When the conclusions are based on hypothesis tests, several additional items should be considered:

1. Is the *p-value* reported? If you know the *p*-value, you can make your own decision, based on the severity of a type 1 error and the size of the *p*-value.

2. If the word *significant* is used to describe a result, determine if the word is being used in the everyday sense or in the statistical sense only. The phrase *statistically significant* just means that a null hypothesis has been rejected, which is no guarantee that the result has "real-world" importance.

3. If you read that "no difference" or "no relationship" has been found in a study, try to determine if the sample size was small. The hypothesis test may have had very low power because not enough data were collected to be able to make a firm conclusion.

4. Think carefully about conclusions based on extremely large samples. If a study is based on a very large sample size, even a weak relationship or a small difference can be statistically significant.

5. If possible, determine what confidence interval should accompany the hypothesis test. This interval will provide better information about the magnitude of the effect as well as information about the margin of error in the sample estimate.

6. Determine how many hypothesis tests were conducted in the study. Sometimes researchers perform a multitude of tests, but only a few of the tests achieved statistical significance. If all of the null hypotheses tested are actually true, then about 1 in 20 tests will achieve statistical significance just by chance at the 0.05 level of significance.

SUMMARY OF PROCEDURES FOR HYPOTHESIS TESTS

The basic structure of hypothesis testing for the parameters in the table below is

Null hypothesis: H_0: parameter = null value

Alternative hypothesis: $\left\{\begin{array}{l} H_a\text{: parameter} \neq \text{null value} \\ H_a\text{: parameter} > \text{null value} \\ H_a\text{: parameter} < \text{null value} \end{array}\right\}$ Choose one.

Test statistic: $t \text{ or } z = \dfrac{\text{Sample statistic} - \text{Null value}}{\text{Null standard error}}$

p-value   For H_a: parameter $\neq$ null value, *p*-value is $2 \times$ area above $|t|$ or $|z|$.
For H_a: parameter $>$ null value, *p*-value is the area *above t* or *z*, even if negative.
For H_a: parameter $<$ null value, *p*-value is the area *below t* or *z*, even if positive.

If *p*-value $>$ significance level, do not reject H_0.
If *p*-value $\leq$ significance level, reject H_0:, accept H_a, and conclude result is statistically significant.

	Parameter	Statistic	Null Value	Null Standard Error	t or z; df for t	Example
One Mean	μ	$\bar{x}$	μ_0	$\dfrac{s}{\sqrt{n}}$	t df $= n - 1$	13.1
Mean Difference in Paired Variables	μ_d	$\bar{d}$	Usually 0	$\dfrac{s_d}{\sqrt{n}}$	t df $= n - 1$	13.2
Difference Between Means (unpooled)	$\mu_1 - \mu_2$	$\bar{x}_1 - \bar{x}_2$	Usually 0	$\sqrt{\dfrac{s_1^2}{n_1} + \dfrac{s_2^2}{n_2}}$	t df = Welch's approximation or smaller of $n_1 - 1, n_2 - 1$	13.3
Difference Between Means (pooled)	$\mu_1 - \mu_2$	$\bar{x}_1 - \bar{x}_2$	Usually 0	$s_p\sqrt{\dfrac{1}{n_1} + \dfrac{1}{n_2}}$	t df $= n_1 + n_2 - 2$	13.5
One Proportion	p	$\hat{p}$	p_0	$\sqrt{\dfrac{p_0(1 - p_0)}{n}}$	z	11.7
Difference Between Proportions	$p_1 - p_2$	$\hat{p}_1 - \hat{p}_2$	Usually 0	$\sqrt{\hat{p}(1 - \hat{p})\left(\dfrac{1}{n_1} + \dfrac{1}{n_2}\right)}$	z	13.6

KEY TERMS

Section 13.1
nonparametric methods, 437
hypothesis testing, 438
significance testing, 438
statistical significance, 438
standardized statistic, 438

Section 13.2
t-test for one mean, 439–442, 444
one-sample t-test, 439
conditions for one sample t-test, 440
paired data, 445
paired t-test, 445
rejection region, 448
critical value, 448

Section 13.3
t-test for difference in two means, 450–452
two-sample t-test, 450
conditions for two-sample t-test, 451
pooled two-sample t-test, 456
unpooled two-sample t-test, 455–456
pooled sample variance, s_p^2, 456
pooled standard deviation, s_p, 456

Section 13.4
z-test (hypothesis test) for difference in two proportions, 460–461
conditions for z-test for difference in two proportions, 460

Section 13.7
type 1 error probability, 471
multiple testing, 472
type 2 error probability, 472
power, 473
power and sample size, 474

Section 13.8
effect size, 475
meta-analysis, 477
vote count, 477

EXERCISES   Blue = Basics   **Bold, Bold** = Answer in back

For all exercises requiring hypothesis tests, make sure you check conditions, define all parameters, and state your conclusion in words in the context of the problem.

Sections 13.1 and 13.2

13.1 For each of the following research questions specify the "parameter" and the "specific value" that constitute the null hypothesis of "parameter = specific value." In other words, define the population parameter of interest and specify the null value that is being tested.
 a. Do a majority of Americans between the ages of 18 and 30 think the use of marijuana should be legalized?
 b. Is the mean of the Math SAT scores in California in a given year different from the target mean of 500 set by the test developers?
 c. Is the mean age of death for left-handed people lower than it is for right-handed people?

d. Is there a difference in the proportions of male and female college students who smoke cigarettes?

13.2 Refer to the previous exercise. In each case, specify whether the alternative hypothesis would be one-sided or two-sided.

13.3 Explain whether or not each of the following statements is true.
   a. Hypotheses and conclusions from hypothesis testing apply only to the samples on which they are based.
   b. The p-value is calculated assuming that the null hypothesis is true.
   c. One of the two possible conclusions in hypothesis testing is to accept the null hypothesis.
   d. The statements "reject the null hypothesis" and "accept the alternative hypothesis" are equivalent.

13.4 Give the value of the test statistic t in each of the following situations.
   a. H_0: $\mu = 50$, $\bar{x} = 60$, $s = 90$, $n = 100$.
   b. H_0: $\mu_d = 0$, $\bar{d} = -4$, $s_d = 15$, $n = 50$.
   c. Null value = 100, sample mean = 98, $s = 15$, sample size = 40.
   d. H_0: $\mu = 250$, $\bar{x} = 270$, standard error = 5, $n = 100$.

13.5 Find the p-value and draw a sketch showing the p-value area for each of the following situations in which the value of t is the test statistic for the hypotheses given:
   a. H_0: $\mu = \mu_0$, H_a: $\mu > \mu_0$, $n = 28$, $t = 2.00$.
   b. H_0: $\mu = \mu_0$, H_a: $\mu > \mu_0$, $n = 28$, $t = -2.00$.
   c. H_0: $\mu = \mu_0$, H_a: $\mu \neq \mu_0$, $n = 81$, $t = 2.00$.
   d. H_0: $\mu = \mu_0$, H_a: $\mu \neq \mu_0$, $n = 81$, $t = -2.00$.

13.6 Use Table A.2 to find the critical value and rejection region in each of the following situations. Then determine whether the null hypothesis would be rejected. In each case the null hypothesis is H_0: $\mu = 100$.
   a. H_a: $\mu > 100$, $n = 21$, $\alpha = 0.05$, test statistic $t = 2.30$.
   b. H_a: $\mu > 100$, $n = 21$, $\alpha = 0.01$, test statistic $t = 2.30$.
   c. H_a: $\mu \neq 100$, $n = 21$, $\alpha = 0.05$, test statistic $t = 2.30$.
   d. H_a: $\mu \neq 100$, $n = 21$, $\alpha = 0.01$, test statistic $t = 2.30$.
   e. H_a: $\mu > 100$, $n = 10$, $\alpha = 0.05$, test statistic $t = 1.95$.
   f. H_a: $\mu < 100$, $n = 10$, $\alpha = 0.05$, test statistic $t = -1.95$.
   g. H_a: $\mu < 100$, $n = 10$, $\alpha = 0.05$, test statistic $t = 1.95$.
   h. H_a: $\mu \neq 100$, $n = 10$, $\alpha = 0.05$, test statistic $t = 1.95$.

13.7 The dataset **cholest** on the CD accompanying this book includes cholesterol levels for heart attack patients and for a group of control patients. It is recommended that people try to keep their cholesterol level below 200. The following Minitab output is for the control patients.

```
Test of mu = 200.00 vs mu < 200.00

Variable    N    Mean    StDev   SE Mean      T       P
control    30   193.13   22.30     4.07    -1.69   0.051
```

a. What are the null and alternative hypotheses being tested? Write them in symbols.
b. What is the mean cholesterol level for the sample of control patients?
c. How many patients were in the sample?
d. Use the formula for the standard error of the mean to show how to compute the value of 4.07 reported by Minitab.

e. What values does Minitab report for the test statistic and the p-value?
f. Identify the numbers that were used to compute the t-statistic, and verify that the reported value is correct.
g. What conclusion would be made in this situation, using a 0.05 level of significance?

13.8 Suppose a study is done to test the null hypothesis H_0: $\mu = 100$. A random sample of $n = 50$ observations results in $\bar{x} = 102$ and $s = 15$.
   a. What is the null standard error in this case?
   b. Plug numbers into the formula

$$\frac{\text{Sample statistic} - \text{Null value}}{\text{Null standard error}}$$

   c. Based on the information given, can the p-value for this test be found? If so, find it. If not, explain what additional information would be needed.

13.9 It has been hypothesized that the mean pulse rate for college students is about 72 beats per minute. A sample of Penn State students recorded their sexes and pulse rates. Assume the samples are representative of all Penn State men and women for pulse rate measurements. The summary statistics were as follows:

Sex	n	Mean	StDev
Female	35	76.9	11.6
Male	57	70.42	9.95

   a. Test whether the pulse rates of all Penn State men have a mean of 72.
   b. Test whether the pulse rates of all Penn State women have a mean of 72.
   c. Write a sentence or two summarizing the results of parts (a) and (b) in words that would be understood by someone with no training in statistics.

13.10 Most people complain that they gain weight during the December holidays, and Yanovski et al. (2000) wanted to determine if that was the case. They sampled the weights of 195 adults in mid-November and again in early to mid-January. The mean weight change for the sample was a gain of 0.37 kg, with a standard deviation of 1.52 kg. State and test the appropriate hypotheses. Be sure to carefully define the population parameter(s) you are testing.

13.11 In Exercise 12.65 a study was reported in which students were asked to place as many dried beans into a cup as possible in 15 seconds with their dominant hand, and again with their nondominant hand (in randomized order). The differences in number of beans (dominant hand–nondominant hand) for 15 students were as follows:

4, 4, 5, 1, −2, 0, 2, 4, −3, 0, 0, 0, −2, 2, 1

The data also are given in the CD dataset **beans**.
   a. The research question was whether students have better manual dexterity with their dominant hand than with their nondominant hand. Write the null and alternative hypotheses.

b. Check the necessary conditions for doing a one sample t-test.

c. Carry out the test using $\alpha = 0.05$.

d. Carry out the test using $\alpha = 0.10$.

e. Write a conclusion about this situation that would be understood by other students of statistics.

13.12 Data from the CD dataset **UCDavis1** included information on height (*height*) and mother's height (*momheight*) for 93 female students. Here is the output from the Minitab paired t procedure comparing these heights:

```
Paired T for height − momheight

             N     Mean    StDev   SE Mean
height      93    64.342   2.862    0.297
momheigh    93    63.057   2.945    0.305
Difference  93     1.285   3.136    0.325

95% CI for mean difference: (0.639, 1.931)
T-Test of mean difference = 0 (vs > 0): T-Value = 3.95
P-Value = 0.000
```

a. It has been hypothesized that college students are taller than they were a generation ago, and therefore that college women should be significantly taller than their mothers. State the null and alternative hypotheses to test this claim. Be sure to define any parameters you use.

b. Using the information in the Minitab output, the test statistic is $t = 3.95$. Identify the numbers that were used to compute the t-statistic, and verify that the stated value is correct.

c. What are the degrees of freedom for the test statistic?

d. Carry out the remaining steps of the hypothesis test.

e. Draw a sketch that illustrates the connection between the t-statistic and the p-value in this problem.

Section 13.3

13.13 In each of the following situations, determine whether the alternative hypothesis was Ha: $\mu_1 - \mu_2 > 0$, or Ha: $\mu_1 - \mu_2 < 0$, or Ha: $\mu_1 - \mu_2 \neq 0$.

a. H_0: $\mu_1 - \mu_2 = 0$, $t = 2.33$, df = 8, p-value = 0.048.

b. H_0: $\mu_1 - \mu_2 = 0$, $t = -2.33$, df = 8, p-value = 0.024.

c. H_0: $\mu_1 - \mu_2 = 0$, $t = 2.33$, df = 8, p-value = 0.976.

d. H_0: $\mu_1 - \mu_2 = 0$, $t = -2.33$, df = 8, p-value = 0.976.

13.14 For each of the following situations, identify whether a paired t-test or a two-sample t-test is appropriate:

a. The weights of a sample of 15 marathon runners were taken before and after a training run to test if marathon runners lose dangerous levels of fluids during a run.

b. Random samples of 200 new freshmen and 200 new transfer students at a university were given a 50-question test on current events to test if the level of knowledge of current events differs for new freshmen and transfer students.

c. Sixty students were matched by initial pulse rate, with the two with the highest pulse forming a pair,

and so on. Within each pair, one student was randomly chosen to drink a caffeinated beverage, while the other one drank an equivalent amount of water. Their pulse rates were measured 10 minutes later, to test if caffeine consumption elevates pulse rates.

13.15 Calculate the value of the test statistic t in each of the following situations. In each case, assume the null hypothesis is H_0: $\mu_1 - \mu_2 = 0$.

a. $\bar{x}_1 = 35$, $s_1 = 10$, $n_1 = 100$; $\bar{x}_2 = 33$, $s_2 = 9$, $n_2 = 81$.

b. The difference in sample means is 48, s.e. $(\bar{x}_1 - \bar{x}_1) = 22$.

c. Minitab output:

```
              N     Mean    StDev   SE Mean
Sample 1     68    80.58    4.22     0.51
Sample 2     68    78.55    3.31     0.40
```

13.16 Do hard- and softcover books likely to be found on a professor's shelf have the same average number of pages? Data on the number of pages for eight hardcover and seven softcover books from a professor's shelf were presented in Example 3.4 and are in the file **ProfBooks** on the CD accompanying this book. Here is the Minitab output from the "2-sample t" procedure. Assume the books are equivalent to a random sample.

```
Cover    N     Mean    StDev   SE Mean
Hard     8     307     134      47
Soft     7    429.4    80.9     31

95% CI for mu (Hard) − mu (Soft) : ( −246,  2)
T-Test mu (Hard) = mu (Soft)(vs not =) : T = −2.16
P = 0.054 DF = 11
```

a. Give the null and alternative hypotheses using symbols.

b. What is the value of the test statistic t?

c. Identify the numbers that were used to compute the t-statistic, and verify that the reported value is correct.

d. What conclusion would be made using a 0.05 level of significance? Write the conclusion in statistical terms and in the context of the problem.

13.17 Example 2.7 gave the weights of eight rowers on each of the Cambridge and Oxford crew teams. The weights are shown again here. Assuming these men represent appropriate random samples, test the hypothesis that the mean weight of rowers on the Cambridge and Oxford crew teams are equal versus the alternative that they are not equal.

Cambridge: 188.5, 183.0, 194.5, 185.0, 214.0, 203.5, 186.0, 178.5

Oxford: 186.0, 184.5, 204.0, 184.5, 195.5, 202.5, 174.0, 183.0

13.18 Case Study 1.1 presented data given in response to the question "What is the fastest you have ever driven a car? _____ mph." The summary statistics are:

Females: $n = 102$, mean = 88.4, standard deviation = 14.4

Males: $n = 87$, mean $= 107.4$, standard deviation $= 17.4$

Assuming these students represent a random sample of college students, test whether the mean fastest speed driven by college men and college women is equal versus the alternative that it is higher for men.

13.19 Example 12.6 presented results for the number of hours slept the previous night from a survey given in two statistics classes. One class was a liberal arts class, while the other class was a general introductory class. The survey was given following a Sunday night after classes had started. For simplicity, let's assume these classes represent a random sample of sleep hours for college students in liberal arts and non-liberal arts majors. The data are given next.

	n	Mean	St. Dev.
Lib. arts	25	7.66	1.34
Non-Lib. arts	148	6.81	1.73

a. Test the hypothesis that the mean number of hours of sleep for the two populations of students are equal versus the alternative that they are not equal. Use the unpooled t-test. (*Note:* The approximate df $= 38$ for the unpooled test.)

b. The figure below displays a dotplot of the data. Briefly explain what is indicated about the necessary conditions for doing a two-sample t-test.

c. Repeat the hypothesis test using the pooled procedure. Compare the results to those in part (a), and discuss which procedure you think is more appropriate in this situation.

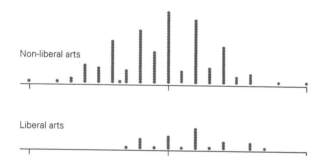

EXERCISE 13.19(b) **Dotplot of sleep values for exercise 13.19**

13.20 Example 12.4 presented data from a study in which sedentary men were randomly assigned to be placed on a diet or exercise for a year to lose weight. Forty-two men were placed on a diet, while the remaining 47 were put on an exercise routine. The group on a diet lost an average of 7.2 kg, with a standard deviation of 3.7 kg. The men who exercised lost an average of 4.0 kg, with a standard deviation of 3.9 kg.

a. State and test appropriate null and alternative hypotheses to determine if the mean weight loss would

be different under the two routines for the population of men similar to those in this study.

b. Explain how you decided whether to do a pooled or unpooled test in part (a).

13.21 Do students sleep more in Pennsylvania or in California? Data from surveys in elementary statistics classes at Penn State University and the University of California at Davis resulted in the following summary statistics for the number of hours students sleep:

	n	Mean	St. Dev.	S.E. Mean
UC Davis	173	6.93	1.71	0.13
Penn State	190	7.11	1.95	0.14

Assume these students are representative of all students at those two schools. Is there sufficient evidence to conclude that the mean hours of sleep are different at the two schools? Carry out all steps of the hypothesis test, and define all parameters.

13.22 Students in a statistics class at Penn State were asked: About how many minutes do you typically exercise in a week? Responses from the *women* in the class were:

60, 240, 0, 360, 450, 200, 100, 70, 240, 0, 60, 360, 180, 300, 0, 270

Responses from the *men* in the class were:

180, 300, 60, 480, 0, 90, 300, 14, 600, 360, 120, 0, 240

a. Draw appropriate graphs to check if the conditions for conducting a two-sample t-test are met. Discuss the results of your graphs.

b. What additional assumption or condition is required if conclusions are to be made about amount of exercise for the population of all Penn State students based on these sample results?

c. Assume that the conditions are met, and conduct a test to determine if the mean amount of exercise differs for men and women.

Section 13.4

13.23 Find the p-value and draw a sketch of the p-value area for each of the following situations in which the value of z is the test statistic for the hypotheses given:
a. $H_0: p_1 - p_2 = 0$, $H_a: p_1 - p_2 > 0$; $z = 1.75$.
b. $H_0: p_1 - p_2 = 0$, $H_a: p_1 - p_2 > 0$; $z = -1.75$.
c. $H_0: p_1 - p_2 = 0$, $H_a: p_1 - p_2 \neq 0$; $z = 1.75$.
d. $H_0: p_1 - p_2 = 0$, $H_a: p_1 - p_2 \neq 0$; $z = -1.75$.

13.24 State a conclusion for each of the following situations, using $\alpha = 0.05$:
a. $H_0: p_1 - p_2 = 0$, $H_a: p_1 - p_2 < 0$; $z = -1.99$.
b. $H_0: p_1 - p_2 = 0$, $H_a: p_1 - p_2 > 0$; $z = 1.78$.
c. $H_0: p_1 - p_2 = 0$, $H_a: p_1 - p_2 < 0$; $z = 0.33$.
d. $H_0: p_1 - p_2 = 0$, $H_a: p_1 - p_2 > 0$; $z = 0.33$.

13.25 Refer to the previous exercise and to the discussion of the rejection region approach to hypothesis testing (for z-tests) in Section 11.4. In each part (a to d), find the rejection region that would be used for $\alpha = 0.05$, then state a conclusion for the z-statistic given.

13.26 Is the proportion of men who write a shopping list before going shopping less than the proportion of women who do so? Let p_1 and p_2 represent the population proportions of men and women, respectively, who use shopping lists. Suppose a random sample of 50 men and 50 women was asked if they use a shopping list when they have more than ten items to buy. Of the 50 men, 20 said yes and of the 50 women 30 said yes.
   a. Write the null and alternative hypotheses in terms of p_1 and p_2, taking into account the initial question asked at the beginning of this exercise.
   b. Provide numerical values for $\hat{p}_1$ and $\hat{p}_2$.
   c To find the null standard error, the combined sample proportion $\hat{p}$ is required. Compute $\hat{p}$ for this situation.
   d. Find the test statistic for this situation.
   e. Make a conclusion using the 0.05 level of significance.

13.27 Exercises 6.6 and 6.56 presented data on grumpy old men and heart disease. In Chapter 6, the goal was to determine if there was a relationship between the two variables. A one-tailed test may also make sense. We might hypothesize that if there is a difference in the probability of developing heart disease for men with no anger and men with lots of anger, the latter group would have a higher probability. Minitab output for testing this claim follows. Note that p_1 is the probability of developing heart disease for men with no anger and p_2 is the probability of developing heart disease for men with the most anger.

```
Sample    X      N      Sample p
1         8      199    0.040201
2         59     559    0.105546

Estimate for p(1) − p(2): 0.0653446
95% CI for p(1) − p(2): (−0.102675, −0.0280137)
Test for p(1) − p(2) = 0 (vs < 0): Z = −2.79 P-Value
= 0.003
```

   a. Write the null and alternative hypotheses in terms of p_1 and p_2, taking into account the claim being tested.
   b. What is the value of the test statistic?
   c. What conclusion would you make? Write your conclusion in statistical terms and in the context of the problem.

13.28 Exercise 12.57 presented results of a survey asking college students if they would return the money if they found a wallet on the street. Of the 93 women, 84 said they would, and of the 75 men, 53 said they would. Assume these students represent all college students. Test the hypothesis that equal proportions of college men and women would say they would return the money versus the alternative hypothesis that a higher proportion of women would do so.

13.29 Refer to exercise 12.64, in which men were classified according to whether they had a pierced ear and a tattoo. Of the 424 men with no ear pierce, 43 had a tattoo. Of the 141 men with at least one ear pierce, 42 had a tattoo. Assuming these men are a random sample of college men,

test the hypothesis that college men with at least one ear pierce are more likely to have a tattoo than college men with no ear pierces.

13.30 A Gallup Poll taken in May 2000 asked the question "In general, do you feel that the laws covering the sale of firearms should be made: more strict, less strict, or kept as they are now?" Of the $n = 493$ men who responded, 52% said "more strict," while of the $n = 538$ women who responded, 72% said "more strict." Assuming these respondents constitute random samples of U.S. men and women, is there sufficient evidence to conclude that a higher proportion of women than men in the population think these laws should be made more strict? Justify your answer.

13.31 Refer to the previous question. The same poll asked the question, "Which of the following do you think is the primary cause of gun violence in America—the availability of guns, the way parents raise their children, or the influences of popular culture such as movies, television, and the Internet?" 51% of the $n = 493$ men and 38% of the $n = 538$ women responded, "Way parents raise kids."
   a. Is there sufficient evidence to conclude that a higher proportion of men than women in the population think the "way parents raise kids" is the primary cause? Justify your answer.
   b. Refer to the data in this exercise as well as the previous one. Notice that 52% of the men thought laws for firearm sales should be more strict, and 51% of men thought the way parents raise kids is the primary cause of gun violence. Can the two-sample test for proportions covered in Section 13.4 be used with these data to test whether the corresponding population proportions differ? If so, carry out the test. If not, explain why not.

13.32 Case Study 10.3 reported on a survey of Penn State students asking the question, "Would you date someone with a great personality even though you did not find them attractive?" Of the $n = 131$ women, 61.1% said yes, and of the $n = 61$ men, 42.6% said yes. Is there sufficient evidence to conclude that for the populations represented by these students, a higher proportion of women than men would answer yes to this question?

Sections 13.5 and 13.6

13.33 In each of the following cases, explain whether the null hypothesis H_0: $\mu = 25$ can be rejected. Use $\alpha = 0.05$.
   a. 95% confidence interval for μ is (10 to 30), H_a: $\mu \neq 25$.
   b. 95% confidence interval for μ is (26 to 50), H_a: $\mu \neq 25$.
   c. 90% confidence interval for μ is (10 to 30), H_a: $\mu > 25$.
   d. 90% confidence interval for μ is (10 to 30), H_a: $\mu < 25$.
   e. 90% confidence interval for μ is (26 to 50), H_a: $\mu > 25$.
   f. 90% confidence interval for μ is (26 to 50), H_a: $\mu < 25$.

13.34 Refer to the rules for the relationship between confidence intervals and two-sided alternatives, given in the two bullets on page 465.
   a. Rewrite the rules specifically for $\alpha = 0.05$.
   b. Rewrite the rules specifically for $\alpha = 0.01$.

13.35 Refer to the rules for the relationship between confidence intervals and one-sided tests, given in the three bullets and sentence preceding them on page 466.
a. Rewrite the rules specifically for $\alpha = 0.05$.
b. Rewrite the rules specifically for $\alpha = 0.01$.

13.36 Refer to the five parameters given in Table 13.2. For each of the following situations identify which of the five is or are appropriate. Give the parameter(s) in symbols, and define what the symbols represent in the context of the situation.
a. Researchers want to compare the mean running times for the 50-yard dash for first grade boys and girls. They select a random sample of 35 boys and 32 girls in first grade and time them running the 50-yard dash.
b. Researchers want to know what proportion of a certain type of tree growing in a national forest suffers from a disease. They test a representative sample of 200 of the trees from around the forest and find that 15 of them have the disease.
c. Researchers want to know what percent of adults have a fear of going to the dentist. They also want to know the average number of visits made to a dentist in the past 10 years for adults who have that fear. They ask a random sample of adults whether or not they fear going to the dentist and also how many times they have gone in the past 10 years.
d. Refer to part (c). Researchers also want to compare the average number of visits made by adults who fear going to the dentist with the average number of visits for those who don't have the fear.

13.37 Refer to the previous exercise. In each case, explain whether a confidence interval, a hypothesis test, or both would be more appropriate.

13.38 Each of the following presents a two-sided 95% confidence interval and the alternative hypothesis of a corresponding hypothesis test. In each case, state a conclusion for the test, including the level of significance you are using.
a. C.I. for μ is (101 to 105), H_a: $\mu \neq 100$.
b. C.I. for p is (.12 to .28), H_a: $p < .10$.
c. C.I. for $\mu_1 - \mu_2$ is (3 to 15), H_a: $\mu_1 - \mu_2 > 0$.
d. C.I. for $p_1 - p_2$ is $(-.15$ to $.07)$, H_a: $p_1 - p_2 \neq 0$.

13.39 As stated in Section 13.5, "a confidence interval can be used as an alternative way to conduct a two-sided significance test." If a test were conducted using this method, would the p-value for the test be available? Explain.

13.40 For each of the following situations, can you conclude whether a 90% confidence interval for μ would include the value 10? If so, make the conclusion. If not, explain why you can't tell.
a. H_0: $\mu = 10$, H_a: $\mu < 10$, do not reject the null hypothesis for $\alpha = 0.05$.
b. H_0: $\mu = 10$, H_a: $\mu < 10$, reject the null hypothesis for $\alpha = 0.05$.
c. H_0: $\mu = 10$, H_a: $\mu \neq 10$, do not reject the null hypothesis for $\alpha = 0.10$.
d. H_0: $\mu = 10$, H_a: $\mu \neq 10$, reject the null hypothesis for $\alpha = 0.10$.

13.41 Give an example of a situation for which the appropriate inference procedure would be each of the following:

a. A hypothesis test for one proportion.
b. A hypothesis test and confidence interval for a paired difference mean.
c. A confidence interval for one mean.
d. A confidence interval for the difference in two means for independent samples.

13.42 Refer to each of the following scenarios from exercises in various chapters of this book. In each case, determine the most appropriate inference procedure(s), including the appropriate parameter. If you think inference about more than one parameter may be of interest, answer the question for all parameters of interest. Explain your choices.
a. A sample of college students was asked if they would return the money if they found a wallet on the street. Of the 93 women, 84 said "yes," and of the 75 men, 53 said "yes." Assume these students represent all college students.
b. A study was conducted on pregnant women and subsequent development of their children (Olds et al., 1994). One of the questions of interest was whether the IQ of children would differ for mothers who smoked at least 10 cigarettes a day during pregnancy and those who did not smoke at all.
c. Max likes to keep track of birthdays of people he meets. He has 170 birthdays on his birthday calendar. One cold January night, he comes up with the theory that people are more likely to be born in October than they would be if all 365 days were equally likely. He consults his birthday calendar and finds that 22 of the 170 birthdays are in October.
d. The dataset **cholest** reports cholesterol levels of heart attack patients 2, 4, and 14 days after the heart attack. Data for days 2 and 4 were available for 28 patients. The mean difference (2 day–4 day) was 23.29, and the standard deviation of the differences was 38.28.

Sections 13.7, 13.8, and 13.9

13.43 A researcher is deciding whether to use a sample size of 100 or whether to increase the sample size to 200. Explain how this choice will affect the power of any hypothesis tests done using data from the resulting sample.

13.44 A researcher is deciding whether to use a level of significance equal to 0.05 or a level of significance equal to 0.01. Explain how this choice will affect the power of the hypothesis test.

13.45 Explain which type of error (1 or 2) could be made in each of the following situations. If both are possible, state that as well.
a. The null hypothesis is true.
b. The alternative hypothesis is true.
c. The null hypothesis is rejected
d. The null hypothesis is not rejected.

13.46 Compute the effect size for each of the following situations, and state whether it would be considered closer to a small, medium, or large effect:
a. In a one-sample test with $n = 100$, the test statistic is $t = 2.24$.

b. In a one-sample test with $n = 50$, the test statistic is $t = -2.83$.

c. In a paired-difference test with $n = 30$ pairs, the test statistic is $t = 1.48$.

d. In a test for the difference in two means with independent samples, with $n_1 = 40$ and $n_2 = 50$, the test statistic is $t = -2.33$.

13.47 Refer to Table 13.4, which presents power for a one-sided, one-sample t-test. In a test of H_0: $\mu_d = 0$ versus H_a: $\mu_d > 0$, suppose the truth is that the population of differences is a normal distribution with mean $\mu_d = 2$ and standard deviation $\sigma = 4$.

a. Recalling the Empirical Rule from Chapter 2, draw a picture of this distribution, showing the ranges into which 68% and 95% of the differences fall.

b. On your picture, indicate where the null value of 0 falls.

c. If a sample of size 20 is taken, what is the power for the test, assuming a 0.05 level of significance will be used?

d. Explain in words what probability the power of the test represents.

13.48 In Table 13.4, it is shown that the power is 0.40 for a one-sided, one-sample t-test with 0.05 level of significance, $n = 50$, and true effect size of 0.2. Would the power be higher or lower for each of the following changes?

a. The true effect size is 0.4.

b. The sample size used is $n = 75$.

c. The level of significance used is 0.01.

13.49 Refer to the list of items in Section 13.9. Explain which ones should be of concern if the sample size(s) for a test are large.

13.50 Refer to the list of items in Section 13.9. Explain which ones should be of concern if the sample size(s) for a test are small.

13.51 Suppose a one-sample t-test of H_0: $\mu = 0$ versus H_a: $\mu \neq 0$ results in a test statistic of $t = 0.65$ with df = 14. Suppose a new study is done with $n = 150$, and the sample mean and standard deviation turn out to be exactly the same as in the first study.

a. What conclusion would you make in the original study, using $\alpha = 0.05$?

b. What conclusion would you make in the new study, using $\alpha = 0.05$?

c. Compare your results in parts (a) and (b) and comment.

13.52 Minitab can provide power for a variety of situations. Suppose a test for ESP has four choices, and the probability of a correct guess by chance on each trial is .25. A researcher believes the true probability of a correct guess is .33. The following output shows the power of the one-sided test for this situation for three possible sample sizes:

```
Test for One Proportion
Testing proportion = 0.25 (versus > 0.25)
Calculating power for proportion = 0.33
Alpha = 0.05   Difference = 0.08
Sample
Size      Power
  50      0.3776
 100      0.5740
 400      0.9705
```

a. What is the power of the test if $n = 50$ trials are used?

b. Write a sentence providing the power of the test for $n = 100$ and explaining its meaning.

c. If the researcher wants to have at least a .95 probability of detecting ESP in the study and is correct that the true probability of a success is .33, would a sample of size 400 be sufficient? Explain.

d. If the true probability of success is actually .40 on each trial, would the power for each sample size be higher or lower than that shown in the output? Explain.

13.53 Refer to Case Study 1.6, comparing heart attack rates for men who had taken aspirin or placebo. Suppose the observed proportions of .017 and .0094 are actually the correct population proportions who would have heart attacks with placebo and with aspirin. The following Minitab output shows the power of a one-sided test for two proportions for this situation, for three sample sizes. The samples are the number of participants in *each* group (aspirin and placebo). Suppose you are the statistician advising a research team about conducting a new study to confirm the results of the old study. The researchers comment that samples of size 500 in each condition should be sufficient, since the effect is obviously so strong, based on the small p-value for the previous study. What would you advise? Explain.

```
Testing proportion 1 = proportion 2 (versus >)
Calculating power for proportion 1 = 0.017 and
proportion 2 = 0.0094
Alpha = 0.05   Difference = 0.0076

Sample
Size      Power
  500     0.3677
 1000     0.5392
 3000     0.8828
```

13.54 A study is conducted to see if results of an IQ test are significantly higher after listening to Mozart than after sitting in silence. Explain what has happened in each of the following scenarios:

a. A type 1 error was committed.

b. A type 2 error was committed.

c. The power of the test was too low to detect the difference that actually exists.

d. The power of the test was so high that a very small difference resulted in a statistically significant finding.

13.55 (Computer software required.) Find the power for the following one-sample t-test situations. In each case, assume a 0.05 level of significance will be used.

a. Effect size = 0.3, sample size = 45, H_a: $\mu > \mu_0$.

b. Sample size = 30, H_a: $\mu \neq 10$, true mean = 13, $\sigma = 4$.

c. Effect size = -1.0, sample size = 15, H_a: $\mu < \mu_0$.

13.56 (Computer software required.) In parts (a) to (d), find the sample size necessary to achieve 80% power for a one-sample t-test with H_a: $\mu > \mu_0$ and level of significance of 0.05 for each of the following effect sizes:

a. 0.2

b. 0.4

c. 0.6

d. 0.8

e. Make a scatterplot of the sample size (vertical axis) versus the effect size for the effect sizes in parts (a) to (d). Does the relationship between the effect size and the sample size required to achieve 80% power appear to be linear? If not, what is the nature of the relationship?

13.57 For a z-test for one proportion, a possible effect size measure is $(p_1-p_0)/\sqrt{p_0(1-p_0)}$ where p_0 is the null value and p_1 is the true population proportion.

a. What is the relationship between this effect size and the z-test statistic for this situation?

b. Does the effect size fit the relationship "Test statistic = Size of effect × Size of study?" If not, explain why not. If so, show how it fits.

c. What would be a reasonable way to estimate this effect size?

13.58 Refer to the effect-size measure in the previous exercise. For parts (a) to (c), compute the effect size.

a. $p_1 = .35, p_0 = .25$.

b. $p_1 = .15, p_0 = .05$.

c. $p_1 = .95, p_0 = .85$.

d. Based on the results in parts (a) to (c), does this effect size stay the same when $p_1 - p_0$ stays the same? Explain.

e. In statistical software for computing power for a test for a single proportion, unlike for a single mean, both p_1 and p_0 must be specified, rather than just the difference between them. Explain why it is not enough to specify the difference, using the results of the previous parts of this exercise.

13.59 Explain why it is more useful to compare effect sizes than p-values when trying to determine if many studies about the same topic have found similar results.

13.60 Refer to item 6 in the list of concerns in Section 13.9. Is that statement the same thing as saying that the null hypothesis is likely to be true in about 1 out of 20 tests that have achieved statistical significance? Explain.

13.61 Refer to the list of items in Section 13.9.

a. For which of the concerns would the p-value for a test be useful to have? Explain why in each case.

b. For which of the concerns would a confidence interval estimate for the parameter be useful to have? Explain why in each case.

c. For which of the concerns would the sample size(s) be useful to know? Explain why in each case.

Chapter Exercises

13.62 In a random sample of 170 married British couples, the difference between the husband's and wife's ages had a mean of 2.24 years and a standard deviation of 4.1 years.

a. Test the hypothesis that British men are significantly older than their wives, on average.

b. Explain what is meant by the use of "significant" in part (a), and discuss how it compares with the everyday use of the word.

13.63 A Gallup Poll taken on a random sample of Canadian adults in February 2000 asked the question, "Do you favour or oppose marriages between people of the same sex?" A similar poll was taken in April 1999 (Edwards and Mazzuca, 2000). The Minitab output for the "two proportions" procedure (with the "pooled estimate for the test") is as follows, where Sample 1 is the February 2000 poll and Sample 2 is the April 1999 poll, and X is the number who answered "favour":

Sample	X	N	Sample p
1	431	1003	0.429711
2	360	1000	0.360000

Estimate for p(1) − p(2): 0.0697109
95% CI for p(1) − p(2): (0.0270067, 0.112415)
Test for p(1) − p(2) = 0 (vs not = 0): Z = 3.19
P-Value = 0.001

a. Define appropriate notation and write the null and alternative hypotheses to test whether the proportion of adult Canadians who favor marriages between people of the same sex was different in April 1999 and February 2000.

b. Using the Minitab output, go through the remaining four steps of hypothesis testing to test the hypotheses you defined in part (a).

c. Use the confidence interval given in the Minitab output to test the hypotheses in part (a).

13.64 Refer to Example 13.6, comparing the proportion of children with ear infections while taking xylitol or a placebo. Read the discussion of type 1 and type 2 errors, and explain the consequences of each type of error if it were to have been made in this study.

13.65 Suppose a highway safety researcher makes modifications to the design of a highway sign. The researcher believes that the modifications will make the mean maximum distance at which drivers are able to read the sign greater than 450 feet. The maximum distances (in feet) at which $n = 16$ drivers can read the sign are

440　490　600　540　540　600　240　440
360　600　490　400　490　540　440　490

Use this sample to determine whether the mean maximum sign-reading distance at which drivers can read the sign is greater than 450. Show all five steps of a hypothesis test, and be sure to state a conclusion. Also, describe any assumptions that you make.

13.66 Case Study 1.6 presented data on 22,071 physicians who were randomly assigned to take aspirin or a placebo every other day for five years. Of the 11,037 taking aspirin, 104 had a heart attack, while of the 11,034 taking placebo, 189 had a heart attack.

a. Test whether the proportion having heart attacks in the population of men similar to the ones in this study would be smaller if taking aspirin than if taking a placebo.

b. What would the consequences of type 1 and type 2 errors be for this study? Which do you think would be more serious?

13.67 Refer to the previous exercise. The test showed that the difference in proportions that had heart attacks after taking aspirin and after taking a placebo was highly statistically significant. Suppose the study had 2,200 participants instead of over 22,000, but that the proportions having heart attacks in the two groups were about the same as they were in the original study. In other words, suppose 10 out of 1100 in the aspirin group had a heart attack and 19 out of 1100 in the placebo group had a heart attack. For a two-sided test of the hypothesis that the proportions likely to have a heart attack are equal after taking aspirin and taking placebo, the test statistic is $z = 1.68$.

a. Using $\alpha = 0.05$, what would you conclude?

b. Discuss this example in the context of the material presented in Section 13.9.

13.68 In exercise 12.67 a study is described in which the mean IQs at age 4 for children of smokers and nonsmokers were compared. The mean for the children of the 66 nonsmokers was 113.28 points, while for the 47 smokers it was 103.12 points. Assume the pooled standard deviation for the two samples is 13.5 points and that a pooled t-test is appropriate. Test the hypothesis that the population mean IQ at age 4 is the same for children of smokers and nonsmokers versus the alternative that it is higher for children of nonsmokers.

13.69 Refer to the previous exercise. One of the statements made in the research article and reported in exercise 12.67 was: "After control for confounding background variables . . . the average difference observed at 36 and 48 months was reduced to 4.35 points (95% CI: 0.02, 8.68)." Use this statement to test the null hypothesis that the difference in the mean IQ scores for the two populations is 0 versus the alternative that it is greater than 0. (Notice that the results have now been adjusted for confounding variables such as parents' IQ, whereas the data given in the previous exercise had not.)

13.70 It is believed that regular physical exercise leads to a lower resting pulse rate. Following are data for $n = 20$ individuals on resting pulse rate and whether the individual regularly exercises or not. Assuming this is a random sample from a larger population, use this sample to determine whether the mean pulse is lower for those who exercise. Clearly show all five steps of the hypothesis test.

Person	Pulse	Regularly Exercises
1	72	No
2	62	Yes
3	72	Yes
4	84	No
5	60	Yes
6	63	Yes
7	66	No
8	72	No
9	75	Yes
10	64	Yes
11	62	No
12	84	No
13	76	No
14	60	Yes
15	52	Yes
16	60	No
17	64	Yes
18	80	Yes
19	68	Yes
20	64	Yes

13.71 In Case Study 5.1, results were presented for a sample of 63 men who were asked to report their actual weight and their ideal weight. The mean difference between actual and ideal weight was 2.48 pounds, and the standard deviation of the differences was 13.77 pounds. Is there sufficient evidence to conclude that for the population of men represented by this sample the actual and ideal weights differ, on average? Justify your answer by showing all steps of a hypothesis test.

13.72 Perry et al. (1999) wanted to test the folklore that women who have not been given information about the sex of their unborn child can guess it at better than chance levels. They asked a sample of 104 pregnant women to guess the sex of their babies, and 57 guessed correctly. Assuming chance guessing would result in 50% correct guesses, test the hypothesis that women can guess at a better than chance level. Carry out the test using $\alpha = 0.05$, and make sure to state a conclusion. Note that the hypothesis involves only one proportion, so you may need to refer to an earlier chapter for guidance.

13.73 Refer to the previous exercise. The authors also wanted to test whether women with different levels of education would differ in their ability to guess the sex of their babies correctly. Of the $n = 45$ women with more than 12 years of education, 32 guessed correctly. Of the $n = 57$ women with 12 or fewer years of education, 24 guessed correctly. (Two women did not report their level of education.) Is there sufficient evidence to conclude that women in the populations with these two different levels of education differ in their ability to guess the sex of their baby? Carry out the test using $\alpha = 0.05$, and make sure to state a conclusion.

13.74 Exercise 6.9 described a case control study comparing short to not-short English secondary school students. Of $n = 92$ short students, 42 said they had been bullied in school. Of $n = 117$ not-short students, 30 said they had been bullied in school. Here is Minitab output for comparing two proportions:

Sample	Bullied	N	Sample p
Short	42	92	0.456522
Not Short	30	117	0.256410

Estimate for p(1) − p(2): 0.200111
95% lower bound for p(1) − p(2): 0.0919200
Test for p(1) − p(2) = 0 (vs > 0): Z = 3.02
P-Value = 0.001

a. The researchers wanted to know if short students are bullied more often. Write the null and alternative hypotheses for this question, defining and using appropriate notation.

b. Use the Minitab output to carry out the remaining steps of the hypothesis test.

c. The Minitab procedure found a one-sided 95% confidence interval for the difference in the two proportions, and the lower end of the interval is given in the output. What is the upper end of the interval? Write the complete interval.

d. Use the one-sided 95% confidence interval to test the hypotheses stated in part (a).

13.75 A Gallup Poll taken in August 2000 (Chambers, 2000) asked U.S. adults in a random sample of $n = 1019$ about their satisfaction with K–12 education. One question was: "Overall, how satisfied are you with the quality of education students receive in grades kindergarten through grade twelve in the U.S. today—would you say: completely satisfied, somewhat satisfied, somewhat dissatisfied or completely dissatisfied?" There were 622 respondents who said that they were somewhat or completely dissatisfied. Is this sufficient evidence to conclude that a majority of U.S. adults were dissatisfied in August 2000? Carry out the test using $\alpha = 0.05$, and make sure to state a conclusion.

13.76 Refer to the previous exercise. A Gallup Poll the previous August (1999) asked $n = 1028$ U.S. adults the same question, and 524 responded that they were somewhat or completely dissatisfied.

a. Repeat the test in the previous exercise and make a conclusion for August 1999.

b. Referring to the data presented in the previous exercise and in this one, and assuming the samples were taken independently, is there sufficient evidence to conclude that the proportion of U.S. adults who were dissatisfied changed from August 1999 to August 2000? Justify your answer.

13.77 In an experiment conducted by one of the authors, ten students in a graduate-level statistics course were given this question about the population of Canada: "The population of the U.S. is about 270 million. To the nearest million, what do you think is the population of Canada?" (The population of Canada at the time was slightly over 30 million.) The responses were

20, 90, 1.5, 100, 132, 150, 130, 40, 200, 20

Eleven other students in the same class were given the same question with different introductory information: "The population of Australia is about 18 million. To the nearest million, what do you think is the population of Canada?" The responses were

12, 20, 10, 81, 15, 20, 30, 20, 9, 10, 20

The experiment was done to demonstrate the *anchoring effect*, which is that responses to a survey question may be "anchored" to information provided to introduce the question. In this experiment, the research hypothesis was that the individuals who saw the U.S. population figure would generally give higher estimates of Canada's population than the individuals who saw the Australia population figure.

a. Write null and alternative hypotheses for this experiment. Use proper notation.

b. Test the hypotheses stated in part (a). Be sure to state a conclusion in the context of the experiment.

c. As a step in part (b), you should have created a graphical summary to verify necessary conditions. Do you think any possible violations of the necessary conditions have affected the results of part (b) in a way that produced a misleading conclusion? Explain why or why not.

13.78 The dataset **cholest** reports cholesterol levels of heart attack patients 2, 4, and 14 days after the heart attack. Data for days 2 and 4 were available for 28 patients. The mean difference (2 day − 4 day) was 23.29, and the standard deviation of the differences was 38.28. A histogram of the differences was approximately bell-shaped. Is there sufficient evidence to indicate that the mean cholesterol level of heart attack patients decreases from the 2nd to the 4th day after the heart attack?

13.79 Refer to the previous exercise. Suppose physicians will use the answer to that question to decide whether to retest patients' cholesterol levels on day 4. If there is no conclusive evidence that cholesterol goes down, they will use the day 2 level to decide whether to prescribe drugs for high cholesterol. If there is evidence that cholesterol goes down between days 2 and 4, patients will all be retested on day 4 and the prescription drug decision will be made then.

a. What are the consequences of type 1 and type 2 errors for this setting?

b. Which type of error do you think is more serious?

Dataset Exercises

13.80 Refer to the previous two exercises. Using the dataset **cholest,** determine whether there is sufficient evidence to conclude that the cholesterol level drops, on average, from day 2 to day 14 after a heart attack.

13.81 The dataset **UCDavis2** includes information on *Sex, Height,* and *Dadheight.* Use the data to test the hypothesis that college men are taller, on average, than their fathers. Assume the male students in the survey represent a random sample of college men.

13.82 The dataset **GSS-93** includes information on *sex* and on whether respondents think marijuana should be legal (*marijuan*). Use the dataset to test the hypothesis that the proportions of males and females who thought marijuana should be legal differed for the 1993 population.

13.83 The dataset **UCDavis2** includes grade point average *GPA* and answers to the question: "Where do you typically sit in a classroom (circle one): Front, Middle, Back." The answer to this question is coded as F, M, B for the variable *Seat.* Assuming these students represent all college students, test whether there is a difference in mean GPA for students who sit in the front versus the back of the classroom.

REFERENCES

Chambers, Chris (2000). "Americans dissatisfied with U.S. education in general, but parents satisfied with their kids' schools," Gallup Poll Release, Sept. 5, 2000 (www.gallup.com).

Cohen, J. (1988). *Statistical Power Analysis for the Behavioral Sciences*, 2nd ed., Hillsdale, NJ: Lawrence Erlbaum Associates.

Devore, J., and R. Peck (1993). *Statistics: The Exploration and Analysis of Data,* 2nd ed., Belmont, CA: Duxbury Press.

Edwards, Gary, and Josephine Mazzuca (2000). "About four-in-ten Canadians accepting of same sex marriages, adoption," Gallup Poll Release, March 7, 2000 (www.gallup.com).

Faigenbaum, Avery D., Wayne L. Westcott, Rita LaRosa Loud, and Cindy Long (1999). "The effects of different resistance training protocols on muscular strength and endurance development in children," *Pediatrics Electronic Article*, Vol. 104, No. 1, p. e5.

Hedges, L. V., and I. Olkin (1985). *Statistical Methods for Meta-Analysis*, New York: Academic Press.

Mackowiak, P. A., S. S. Wasserman, and M. M. Levine (1992). "A critical appraisal of 98.6 degrees F, the upper limit of the normal body temperature, and other legacies of Carl Reinhold August Wunderlich," *Journal of the American Medical Association,* Vol. 268, No. 12 (Sep. 23), pp. 1578–1580.

Olds, D. L., C. R. Henderson, Jr., and R. Tatelbaum (1994). "Intellectual impairment in children of women who smoke cigarettes during pregnancy," *Pediatrics*, Vol. 93, No. 2, pp. 221–227.

Perry, D. F., J. DiPetro, and K. Costigan (1999). "Are women carrying 'basketballs' really having boys? Testing pregnancy folklore," *Birth,* Vol. 26, pp. 172–177.

Rosenthal, R. (1991). *Meta-Analytic Procedures for Social Research*, revised ed., Newbury Park, CA: Sage Publications.

Uhari, M., T. Kenteerkar, and M. Niemala (1998). "A novel use of Xylitol sugar in preventing acute Otitis Media," *Pediatrics*, Vol. 102, pp. 879–884.

Yanovski, J. A., S. Z. Yanovski, K. N. Sovik, T. T. Nguyen, P. M. O'Neil, and N. G. Sebring (2000). "A prospective study of holiday weight gain," *The New England Journal of Medicine,* March 23, 2000, Vol. 342, No. 12, pp. 861–867.

CHAPTER 14

More About Regression

Bob Daemmrich/Stock Boston/PictureQuest

When you get older, how much closer will you have to get to read highway signs? See Example 14.3.

In Chapter 5 we used regression to describe a relationship in a sample. Now we make inferences about the population represented by the sample. What is the relationship between handspan and height in the population? What is the mean handspan for people 65 inches tall? What interval covers the handspans of most individuals of that height?

We learned in Chapter 5 that often a straight line describes the pattern of a relationship between two quantitative variables. For instance, in Example 5.1 we explored the relationship between the handspans (cm) and heights (in.) of 167 college students and found that the pattern of the relationship in this sample could be described by the equation

Average handspan = −3 + 0.35 Height

An equation like the one relating handspan to height is called a *regression equation,* and the term **simple regression** is sometimes used to describe the analysis of a straight-line relationship (*linear relationship*) between a response variable (*y* variable) and an explanatory variable (*x* variable).

In Chapter 5, we only used regression methods to describe a sample and did not make statistical inferences about the larger population. Now, we consider how to make inferences about a relationship in the population represented by the sample. Some questions involving the population that we might ask when analyzing a relationship are

1. Does the observed relationship also occur in the population? For example, is the observed relationship between handspan and height strong enough to conclude that the relationship also holds in the population?
2. For a linear relationship, what is the slope of the regression line in the population? For example, in the larger population, what is the slope of the regression line that connects handspans to heights?
3. What is the mean value of the response variable (*y*) for individuals with a specific value of the explanatory variable (*x*)? For example, what is the mean handspan in a population of people 65 inches tall?

4. What interval of values predicts the value of the response variable (*y*) for an individual with a specific value of the explanatory variable (*x*)? For example, what interval predicts the handspan of an individual 65 inches tall? ◆

14.1 | SAMPLE AND POPULATION REGRESSION MODELS

A **regression model** describes the relationship between a quantitative response variable (the *y* variable) and one or more explanatory variables (*x* variables). The *y* variable is sometimes called the *dependent variable,* and because regression models may be used to make predictions, the *x* variables may be called the *predictor variables.* The labels *response variable* and *explanatory variable* may be used for the variables on the *y* axis and *x* axis, respectively, even if there is not an obvious way to assign these labels in the usual sense.

Any regression model has two important components. The most obvious component is the equation that describes how the mean value of the *y* variable is connected to specific values of the *x* variable. The equation for the connection between handspan and height, Average handspan = −3 + 0.35 (Height), is an example. In this chapter, we focus on *linear relationships,* so a straight-line equation will be used, but it is important to note that some relationships are *curvilinear.*

The second component of a regression model describes how individuals vary from the regression line. Figure 14.1, which is identical to Figure 5.6, displays the raw data for the sample of *n* = 167 handspans and heights along with the regression line that estimates how the mean handspan is connected to specific heights. Notice that most individuals vary from the line. When we examine sample data, we will find it useful to estimate the general size of the deviations from the line. When we consider a model for the relationship within the population represented by a sample, we will state assumptions about the distribution of deviations from the line.

If the sample represents a larger population, we need to distinguish between the **regression line for the sample** and the **regression line for the population.** The observed data can be used to determine the regression line for the sample, but the regression line for the population can only be imagined. Because we do not observe the whole population, we will not know numerical values for the intercept and slope of the regression line in the population. As in nearly every sta-

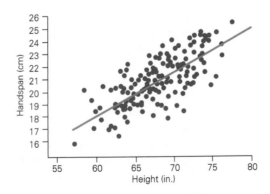

FIGURE 14.1   **Regression line linking handspan and height for a sample of college students**

tistical problem, the statistics from a sample are used to estimate the unknown population parameters, which in this case are the slope and intercept of the regression line.

The Regression Line for the Sample

In Chapter 5, we introduced this notation for the regression line that describes sample data:

$$\hat{y} = b_0 + b_1 x$$

In any given situation, the sample is used to determine values for b_0 and b_1.

- $\hat{y}$ is spoken as "y-hat" and it is also referred to either as *predicted y* or *estimated y*.
- b_0 is the **intercept** of the straight line. The *intercept* is the value of $\hat{y}$ when $x = 0$.
- b_1 is the **slope** of the straight line. The *slope* tells us how much of an increase (or decrease) there is for $\hat{y}$ when the x variable increases by one unit. The sign of the slope tells us whether $\hat{y}$ increases or decreases when x increases. If the slope is 0, there is no linear relationship between x and y because $\hat{y}$ is the same for all values of x.

The equation describing the relationship between handspan and height for the sample of college students can be written as

$$\hat{y} = -3 + 0.35x$$

In this equation,

- $\hat{y}$ estimates the average handspan for any specific height x. If height = 70 in., for instance, $\hat{y} = -3 + 0.35(70) = 21.5$ cm.
- The *intercept* is $b_0 = -3$. While necessary for the line, this value does not have a useful statistical interpretation in this example. It estimates the average handspan for individuals who have height = 0 in., an impossible height far from the range of the observed heights. It also is an impossible handspan.
- The *slope* is $b_1 = 0.35$. This value tells us that the *average increase* in handspan is 0.35 cm for every 1-inch increase in height.

Reminder: The Least-Squares Criterion

In Chapter 5, we described the least-squares criterion. This mathematical criterion is used to determine numerical values of the intercept and slope of a sample regression line. The least-squares line is the line, among all possible lines, that has the smallest sum of squared differences between the sample values of y and the corresponding values of $\hat{y}$.

Deviations from the Regression Line in the Sample

The terms *random error, residual variation,* and *residual error* all are used as synonyms for the term **deviation.** Most commonly, the word **residual** is used to describe the deviation of an observed y value from the sample regression line. A *residual* is easy to compute. It simply is the difference between the observed y value for an individual and the value of $\hat{y}$ determined from the x value for that individual.

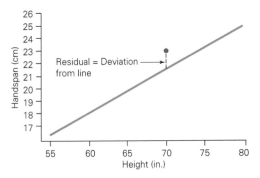

FIGURE 14.2   **Residual for a person 70 inches tall with a handspan = 23 cm.**
The residual is the difference between observed $y = 23$ and $\hat{y} = 21.5$, the predicted
value for a person 70 inches tall.

EXAMPLE 14.1
Residuals in
the Handspan
and Height Regression

Consider a person 70 inches tall whose handspan is 23 centimeters. The sample regression line is $\hat{y} = -3 + 0.35x$, so $\hat{y} = -3 + 0.35(70) = 21.5$ cm for this person. The *residual* = observed y − predicted $y = y - \hat{y} = 23 - 21.5 = 1.5$ cm. Figure 14.2 illustrates this residual. ◆

> **definition** For an observation y_i in the sample, the **residual** is
>
> $$e_i = y_i - \hat{y}_i$$
>
> y_i = the value of the response variable for the observation.
>
> $\hat{y}_i = b_0 + b_1 x_i$, where x_i is the value of the explanatory variable for the observation

> **tech note** The sum of the residuals is 0 for any least-squares regression line. The "least-squares" formulas for determining the equation always result in $\sum y_i = \sum \hat{y}_i$, so $\sum e_i = 0$.

The Regression Line for the Population

The regression equation for a simple linear relationship in a population can be written as

$$E(Y) = \beta_0 + \beta_1 x$$

- ◆ $E(Y)$ represents the mean or expected value of y for individuals in the population who all have the same particular value of x. Note that $\hat{y}$ is an estimate of $E(Y)$.
- ◆ β_0 is the **intercept** of the straight line in the **population.**
- ◆ β_1 is the **slope** of the line in the **population.** Note that if the slope $\beta_1 = 0$, there is no linear relationship in the population.

Unless we measure the entire population, we cannot know the numerical values of β_0 and β_1. These are population parameters that we estimate using the corresponding sample statistics. In the handspan and height example, $b_1 = 0.35$ is a sample statistic that estimates the population parameter β_1, and $b_0 = -3$ is a sample statistic that estimates the population parameter β_0.

Multiple Regression

tech note　　In **multiple regression,** the mean of the response variable is a function of two or more explanatory variables. Put another way, in multiple regression we use the values of more than one explanatory (predictor) variable to predict the value of a response variable. For example, a college admissions committee might predict college GPA for an applicant based on Verbal SAT, Math SAT, high school GPA, and class rank. The general structure of an equation for doing this might be

$$\text{College GPA} = \beta_0 + \beta_1 \text{ Verbal SAT} + \beta_2 \text{ Math SAT} + \beta_3 \text{ HS GPA} + \beta_4 \text{ Class Rank}$$

As in simple regression, numerical estimates of the parameters $\beta_0, \beta_1, \beta_2, \beta_3$, and β_4 would be determined from a sample. On the CD for this text, multiple regression is covered in Supplemental Topic 4.

Assumptions About Deviations from the Regression Line in the Population

To make statistical inferences about the population, two assumptions about how the *y* values vary from the population regression line are necessary. First, we assume that the general size of the deviation of *y* values from the line is the same for all values of the explanatory variable (*x*), an assumption called the **constant variance** assumption. This assumption may or may not be correct in any particular situation, and a scatterplot should be examined to see if it is reasonable or not. In Figure 14.1, the constant variance assumption looks reasonable because the magnitude of the deviation from the line appears to be about the same across the range of observed heights.

The second assumption about the population is that for any specific value of *x*, the distribution of *y* values is a normal distribution. Equivalently, this assumption is that deviations from the population regression line have a normal curve distribution. Figure 14.3 illustrates this assumption along with the other

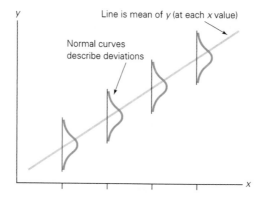

FIGURE 14.3　**Regression model for population**

elements of the population regression model for a linear relationship. The line $E(Y) = \beta_0 + \beta_1 x$ describes the mean of y, and the normal curves describe deviations from the mean.

The Simple Regression Model for a Population

A useful format for expressing the components of the population regression model is

$$y = \text{Mean} + \text{Deviation}$$

This conceptual equation states that for any individual, the value of the response variable (y) can be constructed by combining two components:

1. The **mean,** which in the population is the line $E(Y) = \beta_0 + \beta_1 x$ if the relationship is linear. There are other possible relationships, such as curvilinear, a special case of which is a quadratic relationship, $E(Y) = \beta_0 + \beta_1 x + \beta_2 x^2$. Relationships that are not linear will not be discussed in this book.
2. The individual's **deviation = y – mean,** which is what is left unexplained after accounting for the mean y value at that individual's x value.

This format also applies to the sample, although technically we should use the term *estimated mean* when referring to the sample regression line.

EXAMPLE 14.1—CONTINUED
Mean and Deviation
for Height and
Handspan Regression

Recall that the sample regression line for handspans and heights is $\hat{y} = -3 + 0.35x$. Although it is not likely to be true, let's assume for convenience that this equation also holds in the population. If your height is $x = 70$ in. and your handspan is $y = 23$ cm, then

$$\text{Mean} = -3 + 0.35(70) = 21.5,$$
$$\text{Deviation} = y - \text{Mean} = 23 - 21.5 = 1.5, \text{ and}$$
$$y = 23 = \text{Mean} + \text{Deviation} = 21.5 + 1.5$$

In other words, your handspan is 1.5 cm above the mean for people with your height. ◆

In the theoretical development of procedures for making statistical inferences for a regression model, the collection of all *deviations* in the population is assumed to have a normal distribution with mean 0 and standard deviation σ (so the variance is σ^2). The value of the standard deviation σ is an unknown population parameter that is estimated using the sample. This standard deviation can be interpreted in the usual way that we interpret a standard deviation. It is, roughly, the average distance between individual values of y and the mean of y as described by the regression line. In other words, it is roughly the size of the average deviation across all individuals in the range of x values.

Keeping the regression notation straight for populations and samples can be confusing. Although we have not yet introduced all relevant notation, a summary at this stage will help you keep it straight.

in summary **Simple Linear Regression Model: Population and Sample Versions**

For (x_1, y_1), (x_2, y_2), . . . , (x_n, y_n), a sample of n observations of the explanatory variable x and the response variable y from a large population, the simple linear regression model describing the relationship between y and x follows.

Population Version

$$\text{Mean:} \quad E(Y) = \beta_0 + \beta_1 x$$

$$\text{Individual:} \quad y_i = \beta_0 + \beta_1 x_i + \varepsilon_i = E(Y_i) + \varepsilon_i$$

The deviations ε_i are assumed to follow a normal distribution with mean 0 and standard deviation σ.

Sample Version

$$\text{Mean:} \quad \hat{y} = b_0 + b_1 x$$

$$\text{Individual:} \quad y_i = b_0 + b_1 x_i + e_i = \hat{y}_i + e_i$$

where e_i is the *residual* for individual i. The sample statistics b_0 and b_1 *estimate* the population parameters β_0 and β_1. The mean of the residuals is 0, and the residuals can be used to estimate the population standard deviation σ.

14.2 | ESTIMATING THE STANDARD DEVIATION FOR REGRESSION

Recall that the standard deviation in the regression model measures, roughly, the average deviation of y values from the mean (the regression line). Expressed another way, the **standard deviation for regression** measures the general size of the residuals. This is an important and useful statistic for describing individual variation in a regression problem, and it also provides information about how accurately the regression equation might predict y values for individuals. A relatively small standard deviation from the regression line indicates that individual data points generally fall close to the line, so predictions based on the line will be close to the actual values.

The calculation of the estimate of standard deviation is based on the sum of the squared residuals for the sample. This quantity is called the **sum of squared errors** and is denoted by **SSE**. Synonyms for "sum of squared errors" are **residual sum of squares** or **sum of squared residuals.** To find the SSE, residuals are calculated for all observations, then the residuals are squared and summed. The *standard deviation from the regression line* is

$$s = \sqrt{\frac{\text{Sum of Squared Residuals}}{n - 2}} = \sqrt{\frac{\text{SSE}}{n - 2}}$$

and this sample statistic estimates the population standard deviation σ.

Estimating the Standard Deviation for a Simple Regression Model

formula The formula for estimating the standard deviation for a simple regression model is

$$SSE = \sum(y_i - \hat{y}_i)^2 = \sum e_i^2$$

$$s = \sqrt{\frac{SSE}{n-2}} = \sqrt{\frac{\sum(y_i - \hat{y}_i)^2}{n-2}}$$

The statistic s is an estimate of the population standard deviation σ.

Technical Note: Notice the difference between the estimate of σ in the regression situation compared to if we simply had a random sample of the y_i's without information about the x_i's:

$$\text{Sample of } y\text{'s only:} \quad s = \sqrt{\frac{\sum(y_i - \bar{y})^2}{n-1}}$$

$$\text{Sample of } (x,y) \text{ pairs, linear regression:} \quad s = \sqrt{\frac{\sum(y_i - \hat{y}_i)^2}{n-2}}$$

Remember that in the regression context, σ is the standard deviation of the y values at *each* x, not the standard deviation of the whole population of y values.

EXAMPLE 14.2
Relationship Between Height and Weight for College Men

Figure 14.4 displays regression results from the Minitab program and a scatterplot for the relationship between y = weight (pounds) and x = height (inches) in a sample of n = 43 men in a Penn State statistics class. The regression line for the sample is $\hat{y} = -318 + 7x$, and this line is drawn onto the plot. We see from

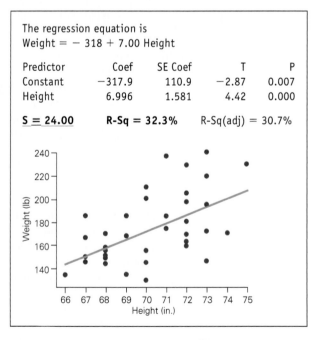

FIGURE 14.4   **The relationship between weight and height for n = 43 college men**

the plot that there is considerable variation from the line at any given height. The standard deviation, shown in the row of computer output immediately above the plot, is "S = 24.00." This value roughly measures, for any given height, the general size of the deviations of individual weights from the mean weight for the height.

The standard deviation from the regression line can be interpreted in conjunction with the Empirical Rule for bell-shaped data stated in Section 2.7. Recall, for instance, that about 95% of individuals will fall within 2 standard deviations of the mean. As an example, consider men who are 72 inches tall. For men with this height, the estimated average weight determined from the regression equation is $-318 + 7.00(72) = 186$ pounds. The estimated standard deviation from the regression line is $s = 24$ pounds, so we can estimate that about 95% of men 72 inches tall have weights within $2 \times 24 = 48$ pounds of 186 pounds, which is 186 ± 48, or 138 to 234 pounds. Think about whether this makes sense for all the men you know who are 72 inches (6 feet) tall. ◆

14.1

turn on your mind

Regression equations can be used to predict the value of a response variable for an individual. What is the connection between the accuracy of predictions based on a particular regression line and the value of the standard deviation from the line? If you were deciding between two different regression models for predicting the same response variable, how would your decision be affected by the relative values of the standard deviations for the two models?*

The Proportion of Variation Explained by x

In Chapter 5, we learned that a statistic denoted as r^2 is used to measure how well the explanatory variable actually does explain the variation in the response variable. This statistic is also denoted as R^2 (rather than r^2), and the value is commonly expressed as a percent. Researchers typically use the phrase "**proportion of variation explained by x**" in conjunction with the value of r^2. For example, if $r^2 = 0.60$ (or 60%), the researcher may write that the explanatory variable explains 60% of the variation in the response variable.

The formula for r^2 presented in Chapter 5 was

$$r^2 = \frac{\text{SSTO} - \text{SSE}}{\text{SSTO}}$$

The quantity SSTO is the sum of squared differences between observed y values and the sample mean $\bar{y}$. It measures the size of the deviations of the y values from the overall mean of y, whereas SSE measures the deviations of the y values from the predicted values y.

EXAMPLE 14.2—CONTINUED
R^2 for Heights and
Weights of College Men

In Figure 14.4, we can find the information "R-sq = 32.3%" for the relationship between weight and height. A researcher might write "the variable height explains 32.3% of the variation in the weights of college men." This isn't a particularly impressive statistic. As we noted before, there is substantial deviation of individual weights from the regression line, so a prediction of a college man's weight based on height may not be particularly accurate. ◆

14.2

turn on your mind

Look at the formula for SSE and explain in words under what condition SSE = 0. Now explain what happens to r^2 when SSE = 0, and explain whether that makes sense according to the definition of r^2 as "proportion of variation in y explained by x."*

EXAMPLE 14.3
*Driver Age
and Highway
Sign-Reading Distance*

In Example 5.2, we examined data for the relationship between y = maximum distance (feet) at which a driver can read a highway sign and x = the age of the driver. There were n = 30 observations in the dataset. Figure 14.5 displays Minitab regression output for these data. The equation describing the linear relationship in the sample is

$$\text{Average distance} = 577 - 3.01 \times \text{Age}$$

From the output, we learn that the standard deviation from the regression line is s = 49.76 and R-sq = 64.2%. Roughly, the average deviation from the regres-

```
The regression equation is
Distance = 577 − 3.01 Age

Predictor          Coef      SE Coef         T         P
Constant         576.68        23.47     24.57     0.000
Age             −3.0068       0.4243     −7.09     0.000

S = 49.76      R-Sq = 64.2%      R-Sq (adj) = 62.9%

Analysis of Variance

Source            DF         SS         MS         F         P
Regression         1     124333     124333     50.21     0.000
Residual Error     28      69334       2476
Total              29     193667

Unusual Observations
Obs     Age    Distance        Fit     SE Fit     Residual     St Resid
 27    75.0      460.00     351.17      13.65       108.83        2.27R

R denotes an observation with a large standardized residual
```

FIGURE 14.5   Minitab output: Sign reading distance and driver age

sion line is about 50 feet, and the proportion of variation in sign reading distances explained by age is .642, or 64.2%.

The "Analysis of Variance" table provides the pieces needed to compute r^2 and s:

$$\text{SSE} = 69{,}334$$

$$s = \sqrt{\frac{\text{SSE}}{n-2}} = \sqrt{\frac{69{,}334}{28}} = 49.76$$

$$\text{SSTO} = 193{,}667$$

$$\text{SSTO} - \text{SSE} = 193{,}667 - 69{,}334 = 124{,}333$$

$$r^2 = \frac{124{,}333}{193{,}667} = .642, \text{ or } 64.2\% \; \blacklozenge$$

14.3 | INFERENCE ABOUT THE LINEAR REGRESSION RELATIONSHIP

When researchers do a regression analysis, they occasionally know based on past research or common sense that the variables are indeed related. In some instances, however, it may be necessary to do a hypothesis test in order to make the generalization that two variables are related in the population represented by the sample. The **statistical significance of a linear relationship** can be evaluated by testing whether or not the slope is 0. Recall that if the slope is 0 in a simple regression model, the two variables are not related because changes in the x variable will not lead to changes in the y variable. The usual null hypothesis and alternative hypothesis about β_1, the slope of the population regression line $E(Y) = \beta_0 + \beta_1 x$, are

$H_0: \beta_1 = 0$ (the population slope is 0, so y and x are *not linearly related*)
$H_a: \beta_1 \neq 0$ (the population slope is not 0, so y and x *are linearly related*)

The alternative hypothesis may be one-sided or two-sided, although most statistical software uses the two-sided alternative.

The test statistic used to do the hypothesis test is a t-statistic with the same general format that we saw in Chapter 13. That format, and its application to this situation, is

$$t = \frac{\text{Sample statistic} - \text{Null value}}{\text{Standard error}} = \frac{b_1 - 0}{\text{s.e.}(b_1)}$$

This is a standardized statistic for the difference between the sample slope and 0, the null value. Notice that a large value of the sample slope (either positive or negative) relative to its standard error will give a large value of t. If the mathematical assumptions about the population model described in Section 14.1 are correct, the statistic has a t-distribution with $n - 2$ degrees of freedom. The p-value for the test is determined using that distribution.

"By hand" calculations of the sample slope and its standard error are cumbersome. Fortunately, the regression analysis of most statistical software includes a t-statistic and a p-value for this significance test.

Formula for the Sample Slope and Its Standard Error

formula   In case you ever need to compute the values by hand, here are the formulas for the sample slope and its standard error:

$$b_1 = r\frac{s_y}{s_x}$$

$$\text{s.e.}(b_1) = \frac{s}{\sqrt{\Sigma(x_i - \overline{x})^2}} \qquad \text{where } s = \sqrt{\frac{\text{SSE}}{n-2}}$$

In the formula for the sample slope, s_x and s_y are the sample standard deviations of the x and y values, respectively, and r is the correlation between x and y.

EXAMPLE 14.3 — *CONTINUED*
Driver Age
and Highway
Sign-Reading Distance

Figure 14.5 (p. 502) presents the Minitab output for the regression of sign-reading distance and driver age. The sample estimate of the slope is $b_1 = -3.01$. This sample slope is different from 0, but is it different enough to enable us to generalize that a linear relationship exists in the population represented by this sample?

The part of the Minitab output that can be used to test the statistical significance of the relationship is shown in bold in Figure 14.5, and the relevant *p*-value is underlined (by the authors of this text, not by Minitab). This line of the output provides information about the sample slope, the standard error of the sample slope, the *t*-statistic for testing statistical significance and the *p*-value for the test of

$H_0: \beta_1 = 0$ (the population slope is 0, so y and x are *not linearly related*)
$H_a: \beta_1 \neq 0$ (the population slope is not 0, so y and x *are linearly related*)

The test statistic is

$$t = \frac{\text{Sample statistic} - \text{Null value}}{\text{Standard error}} = \frac{b_1 - 0}{\text{s.e.}(b_1)} = \frac{-3.0068 - 0}{0.4243} = -7.09$$

The *p*-value is, to three decimal places, 0.000. This means the probability is virtually 0 that the observed slope could be as far from 0 or farther than it is if there is no linear relationship in the population. So, as we might expect for these variables, we can conclude that the relationship between the two variables in the sample represents a real relationship in the population. ◆

tech note   Most statistical software reports a *p*-value for a two-sided alternative hypothesis when doing a test for whether the slope in the population is 0. It may sometimes make sense to use a one-sided alternative hypothesis instead. In that case, the *p*-value for the one-sided alternative is (reported *p*/2) if the sign of b_1 is consistent with H_a, but is 1 − (reported *p*/2) if it is not.

Confidence Interval for the Population Slope

The significance test of whether or not the population slope is 0 only tells us if we can declare the relationship to be statistically significant. If we decide that the true slope is not 0, we might ask, "What is the value of the slope?" We can answer this question with a confidence interval for β_1, the population slope.

The format for this confidence interval is the same as the general format used in Chapters 10 and 12, which is

$$\text{Sample estimate} \pm \text{Multiplier} \times \text{Standard error}$$

The estimate of the population slope β_1 is b_1, the slope of the least-squares regression line for the sample. As shown already, the standard error formula is complicated and we'll usually rely on statistical software to determine this value. The "multiplier" will be labeled t^* and is determined using a t-distribution with df = $n - 2$. Table A.2 can be used to find the multiplier for the desired confidence level.

Formula for
Confidence Interval for
β_1, the Population Slope

> **formula**   A confidence interval for β_1 is
>
> $$b_1 \pm t^* \text{ s.e.}(b_1)$$
>
> The multiplier t^* is found using a t-distribution with $n - 2$ degrees of freedom and is such that the probability between $-t^*$ and $+t^*$ equals the confidence level for the interval.

EXAMPLE 14.3—*CONTINUED*
95% Confidence Interval
for Slope Between Age
and Sign-Reading Distance

In Figure 14.5, we see that the estimated slope is $b_1 = -3.01$ and s.e.$(b_1) = 0.4243$. There are $n = 30$ observations so df = 28 for finding t^*. For a 95% confidence level, $t^* = 2.05$ (see Table A.2). The 95% confidence interval for the population slope is

$$-3.01 \pm 2.05 \times 0.4243$$
$$-3.01 \pm 0.87$$
$$-3.88 \text{ to } -2.14$$

With 95% confidence, we can estimate that in the population of drivers represented by this sample, the *mean* sign-reading distance decreases somewhere between 3.88 and 2.14 feet for each one-year increase in age. ◆

14.3

turn on your mind

In previous chapters, we learned that a confidence interval can be used to determine whether a hypothesized value for a parameter can be rejected. How would you use a confidence interval for the population slope to determine if there was a statistically significant relationship between x and y? For example, why is the interval just computed for the sign-reading example evidence that sign-reading distance and age are related?*

Testing Hypotheses About the Correlation Coefficient

In Chapter 5, we learned that the correlation coefficient is 0 when the regression line is horizontal. In other words, if the slope of the regression line is 0, the correlation is 0. This means that the results of a hypothesis test for the population slope can also be interpreted as applying to equivalent hypotheses about the correlation between x and y in the population.

As we did for the regression model, we use different notation to distinguish between a correlation computed for a sample and a correlation within a population. It is commonplace to use the symbol ρ (pronounced "rho") to represent the correlation between two variables within a population. Using this notation, null and alternative hypotheses of interest are

H_0: $\rho = 0$ (x and y are not correlated)
H_a: $\rho \neq 0$ (x and y are correlated)

The results of the hypothesis test described before for the population slope β_1 can be used for these hypotheses as well. If we reject H_0: $\beta_1 = 0$, we also reject H_0: $\rho = 0$. If we decide in favor of H_a: $\beta_1 \neq 0$, we also decide in favor of H_a: $\rho \neq 0$.

Many statistical software programs, including Minitab, will give a p-value for testing whether the population correlation is 0 or not. This p-value will be the same as the p-value given for testing whether the population slope is 0 or not.

In the following Minitab output for the relationship between pulse rate and weight in a sample of 35 college women, notice that 0.292 is given as the p-value for testing that the slope is 0 (look under P in the regression results) and for testing that the correlation is 0. Because this is not a small p-value, we cannot reject the null hypotheses for the slope and the correlation.

Regression Analysis: Pulse Versus Weight

The regression equation is
Pulse = 57.2 + 0.159 Weight

Predictor	Coef	SE Coef	T	P
Constant	57.17	18.51	3.09	0.004
Weight	0.1591	0.1487	1.07	0.292

Correlations: Pulse, Weight

Pearson correlation of Pulse and Weight = 0.183
P-Value = 0.292

The Effect of Sample Size on Significance

The size of a sample always affects whether a specific observed result achieves statistical significance. For example, $r = 0.183$ is not a statistically significant correlation for a sample size of $n = 35$, as in the pulse and weight example, but it would be statistically significant if $n = 1000$. With very large sample sizes, weak relationships with low correlation values can be statistically significant. The "moral of the story" here is that with a large sample size, it may not be saying much to say that two variables are significantly related. This only means that we think the correlation is not precisely 0. To assess the practical significance of the result, we should carefully examine the observed strength of the relationship.

tech note   The usual *t*-statistic for testing whether the population slope is 0 in a linear regression could also be found using a formula that involves only n = sample size and r = correlation between x and y. The algebraic equivalence is

$$t = \frac{b_1}{\text{s.e.}(b_1)} = \sqrt{n-2} \, \frac{r}{\sqrt{1-r^2}}$$

In the output for the pulse rate and body weight example just given, notice that the *t*-statistic for testing whether the slope $\beta_1 = 0$ is $t = 1.07$. This was calculated as

$$t = \frac{b_1}{\text{s.e.}(b_1)} = \frac{0.1591}{0.1487} = 1.07$$

The sample size is $n = 35$ and the correlation is $r = 0.183$, so an equivalent calculation of the *t*-statistic is

$$t = \sqrt{n-2} \, \frac{r}{\sqrt{1-r^2}} = \sqrt{35-2} \, \frac{0.183}{\sqrt{1-0.183^2}} = 1.07$$

This second method for calculating the *t*-statistic illustrates two ideas. First, there is a direct link between the correlation value and the *t*-statistic used to test whether the slope is 0. Second, notice that for any fixed value of r, increasing the sample size n will increase the size of the *t*-statistic. And, the larger the value of the *t*-statistic, the stronger the evidence against the null hypothesis.

14.4 | PREDICTING THE VALUE OF *y* FOR AN INDIVIDUAL

An important use of a regression equation is to estimate or predict the unknown value of a response variable for an *individual* with a known specific value of the explanatory variable. Using the data described in Example 14.3, for instance, we can predict the maximum distance at which an individual can read a highway sign by substituting his or her age for x in the sample regression equation. Consider a person 21 years old. The predicted distance for such a person is approximately $\hat{y} = 577 - 3(21) = 514$ feet.

There will be variation among 21-year-olds with regard to the sign-reading distance, so the predicted distance of 514 feet is not likely to be the exact distance for the next 21-year-old who views the sign. Rather than predicting that the distance will be exactly 514 feet, we should instead predict that the distance will be within a particular interval of values. A **95% prediction interval** for the value of the response variable (y) accounts for the variation among individuals with a particular value of x. This interval can be interpreted in two equivalent ways:

1. The 95% prediction interval estimates the central 95% of the values of y for members of the population with a specified value of x.
2. The probability is .95 that a randomly selected individual from the population with a specified value of x falls into the corresponding 95% prediction interval.

Notice that a prediction interval differs conceptually from a confidence interval. A confidence interval estimates an unknown population parameter, which is a numerical characteristic or summary of the population. An example in this chapter is a confidence interval for the slope of the population line. A prediction interval, however, does not estimate a parameter; instead, it estimates the potential data value for an individual. Equivalently, it describes an interval into which a specified percentage of the population may fall.

14.4

turn on your mind

If we knew the population parameters β_0, β_1, and σ, under the usual regression assumptions, we would know that the population of y values at a specific x value was normal with mean $\beta_0 + \beta_1 x$ and standard deviation σ. In that case, what interval would cover the central 95% of the y values for that x value? Use your answer to explain why a prediction interval would not have zero width even with complete population details.*

As with most regression calculations, the "by hand" formulas for prediction intervals are formidable. Statistical software can be used to create the interval. Figure 14.6 shows Minitab output that includes the 95% prediction intervals for three different ages (21, 30, and 45). The intervals are toward the bottom-right side of the display in a column labeled "95% PI" and are highlighted with bold type. (***Note:*** The term "Fit" is a synonym for $\hat{y}$, the estimate of the average response at the specific x value.) Here is what we can conclude:

♦ The probability is .95 that a randomly selected 21-year-old will read the sign at somewhere between roughly 407 and 620 feet.

♦ The probability is .95 that a randomly selected 30-year-old will read the sign at somewhere between roughly 381 and 592 feet.

♦ The probability is .95 that a randomly selected 45-year-old will read the sign at somewhere between roughly 338 and 545 feet.

We can also interpret each interval as an estimate of the sign-reading distances for the central 95% of a population of drivers with a specified age. For instance, about 95% of all drivers 21 years old will be able to read the sign at a distance somewhere between 407 and 620 feet.

We're not limited to using only 95% prediction intervals. With Minitab, we can describe any central percentage of the population that we wish. For example, here are 50% prediction intervals for the sign-reading distance at the three specific ages we considered above.

Age	Fit	50.0% PI
21	513.54	(477.89, 549.18)
30	486.48	(451.38, 521.58)
45	441.37	(406.76, 475.98)

*HINT: Generally, standard deviation measures how individuals vary from the mean. The regression equation gives mean y for a specific x.

```
The regression equation is
Distance = 577 − 3.01 Age

Predictor          Coef      SE Coef         T         P
Constant         576.68        23.47     24.57     0.000
Age             −3.0068       0.4243     −7.09     0.000

S = 49.76      R-Sq = 64.2%      R-Sq(adj) = 62.9%

Analysis of Variance

Source               DF         SS        MS         F         P
Regression            1     124333    124333     50.21     0.000
Residual Error       28      69334      2476
Total                29     193667

Unusual Observations
Obs     Age    Distance         Fit    SE Fit    Residual    St Resid
 27    75.0      460.00      351.17     13.65      108.83        2.27R

R denotes an observation with a large standardized residual

Predicted Values for New Observations

New Obs        Fit    SE Fit         95.0% CI             95.0% PI
1           513.54     15.64    ( 481.50, 545.57)    ( 406.69, 620.39)
2           486.48     12.73    ( 460.41, 512.54)    ( 381.26, 591.69)
3           441.37      9.44    ( 422.05, 460.70)    ( 337.63, 545.12)

Values of Predictors for New Observations
New Obs        Age
1             21.0
2             30.0
3             45.0
```

FIGURE 14.6   Minitab output showing prediction intervals of distance

For each specific age, the 50% prediction interval estimates the central 50% of the maximum sign-reading distances in a population of drivers with that age. For example, we can estimate that 50% of drivers 21 years old would have a maximum sign-reading distance somewhere between about 478 feet and 549 feet. The distances for the other 50% of 21-year-old drivers would be predicted to be outside this range, with 25% above 549 feet and 25% below 478 feet.

> *definition* A **prediction interval** estimates the value of y for an individual with a particular value of x, or equivalently, the range of values of the response variable for a specified central percentage of a population with a particular value of x.

tech note   The formula for the prediction interval for y at a specific x is

$$\hat{y} \pm t^*\sqrt{s^2 + [\text{s.e.(fit)}]^2}$$

where

$$\text{s.e.(fit)} = s\sqrt{\frac{1}{n} + \frac{(x - \bar{x})^2}{\Sigma(x_i - \bar{x})^2}}$$

The multiplier t^* is found using a t-distribution with $n - 2$ degrees of freedom and is such that the probability between $-t^*$ and $+t^*$ equals the desired level for the interval.

Note:

- The s.e.(fit), and thus the width of the interval, depends upon how far the specified x value is from $\bar{x}$. The further the specific x is from the mean, the wider the interval.

- When n is large, s.e.(fit) will be small, and the prediction interval will be approximately $\hat{y} \pm t^*s$.

14.5 | ESTIMATING THE MEAN y AT A SPECIFIED x

In the previous section, we focused on the estimation of the values of the response variable for individuals. A researcher may instead want to estimate the *mean* value of the response variable for individuals with a particular value of the explanatory variable. We might ask, "What is the mean weight for college men who are 6 feet tall?" This question only asks about the mean weight in a group with a common height, and it is not concerned with the deviations of individuals from that mean.

In technical terms, we wish to estimate the population mean $E(Y)$ for a specific value of x that is of interest to us. To make this estimate, we use a confidence interval. The format for this confidence interval is again:

Sample estimate $\pm$ Multiplier $\times$ Standard error

The *sample estimate* of $E(Y)$ is the value of $\hat{y}$ determined by substituting the x value of interest into $\hat{y} = b_0 + b_1x$, the least-squares regression line for the sample. The *standard error* of $\hat{y}$ is the s.e.(fit) shown in the Tech Note box in the previous section, and its value is usually provided by statistical software. The *multiplier* is found using a t-distribution with df $= n - 2$, and Appendix A.2 can be used to determine its value.

EXAMPLE 14.2—*CONTINUED*
Estimating Mean
Weight of College
Men at Various Heights

Based on the sample of $n = 43$ college men in Example 14.2, let's estimate the mean weight in the population of college men for each of three different heights: 68 inches, 70 inches, and 72 inches. Figure 14.7 shows Minitab output that includes the three different confidence intervals for these three different heights. These intervals are toward the bottom of the display in a column labeled "**95% CI**." The first entry in that column is the estimate of the population mean weight for men who are 68 inches tall. With 95% confidence, we can estimate that the mean weight of college men 68 inches tall is somewhere between 147.78 and

```
The regression equation is
Weight = − 318 + 7.00 Height

Predictor        Coef      SE Coef        T         P
Constant       −317.9        110.9     −2.87     0.007
Height           6.996        1.581      4.42     0.000

S = 24.00        R-Sq = 32.3%      R-Sq(adj) = 30.7%

--- Some Output Omitted ---

Predicted Values for New Observations

New Obs       Fit     SE Fit       95.0% CI            95.0% PI
1          157.80       4.96   ( 147.78, 167.81)   ( 108.31, 207.29)
2          171.79       3.66   ( 164.39, 179.19)   ( 122.76, 220.82)
3          185.78       4.72   ( 176.25, 195.31)   ( 136.38, 235.18)

Values of Predictors for New Observations

New Obs     Height
1             68.0
2             70.0
3             72.0
```

FIGURE 14.7   **Minitab output with confidence intervals for mean weight**

167.81 pounds. The second row under "**95% CI**" contains the information that the 95% confidence interval for the mean weight of college men 70 inches tall is 164.39 to 179.19 pounds. The 95% confidence interval for the mean weight for men 72 inches tall is 176.25 to 195.31 pounds.

Again, it is important to realize that the confidence intervals for $E(Y)$ do not describe the variation among *individuals*. They only are estimates of the *mean* weights for specific heights. The prediction intervals for individual responses describe the variation among individuals. You may have noticed that 95% prediction intervals, labeled "95% PI," are next to the confidence intervals in the output. Among men 70 inches tall, for instance, we would estimate that 95% of the individual weights would be in the interval from about 123 to about 221 pounds. ◆

Minitab Tip

 tech note   **Creating Prediction Intervals for *y* and Confidence Intervals for *E(Y)***

◆ Use **Stat**>**Regression**>**Regression,** then use the ***Options*** button of the dialog box.

◆ In the box labeled "Prediction intervals for new observations," either specify the numerical value of a single *x* value of interest or specify a worksheet column that contains two or more different *x* values of interest. The confidence level can be specified in the box labeled "Confidence Level."

Note: Minitab computes both a prediction interval for *y* and a confidence interval for $E(Y)$ for each specified value of *x*.

14.5

turn on your mind

Draw a picture similar to the one in Figure 14.3, illustrating the regression line and the normal curves for the *y* values at several values of *x*. Use it to illustrate the difference between a prediction interval for *y* and a confidence interval for the mean of the *y*'s, at a specific value of *x*. *

14.6 | CHECKING CONDITIONS FOR USING REGRESSION MODELS FOR INFERENCE

There are a few conditions that should be at least approximately true when we use a regression model to make an inference about a population. Of the five conditions that follow, the first two are particularly crucial.

Conditions for Linear Regression

1. The form of the equation that links the mean value of *y* to *x* must be correct. For instance, we won't make proper inferences if we use a straight line to describe a curved relationship.
2. There should not be any extreme outliers that influence the results unduly.
3. The standard deviation of the values of *y* from the mean *y* is the same regardless of the value of the *x* variable. In other words, *y* values are similarly spread out at all values of *x*.
4. For individuals in the population with the same particular value of *x*, the distribution of the values of *y* is a normal distribution. Equivalently, the distribution of deviations from the mean value of *y* is a normal distribution. This condition can be relaxed if the sample size is large.
5. Observations in the sample are independent of each other.

Checking the Conditions with Plots

A scatterplot of the raw data and **plots of the residuals** provide information about the validity of the assumptions. Remember that a residual is the difference between an observed value and the predicted value for that observation and that some assumptions made for a linear regression model have to do with how *y* values deviate from the regression line. If the properties of the residuals for the sample appear to be consistent with the mathematical assumptions made about deviations within the population, we can use the model to make statistical inferences.

Conditions 1, 2, and 3 can be checked using two useful plots:

♦ A scatterplot of *y* versus *x* for the sample
♦ A scatterplot of the residuals versus *x* for the sample

If Condition 1 holds for a linear relationship, then:

♦ The plot of *y* versus *x* should show points randomly scattered around an imaginary straight line.
♦ The plot of residuals versus *x* should show points randomly scattered around a horizontal line at residual = 0.

*HINT: Each bell curve in Figure 14.3 describes individual variation at a specific *x* value. How does this relate to the purpose of a prediction interval?

If Condition 2 holds, extreme outliers should not be evident in either plot. If Condition 3 holds, neither plot should show increasing or decreasing spread in the points as *x* increases.

14.6

turn on your mind

A residual is the difference between an observed value of *y* and the predicted value of *y* for that observation. Based on the size of a residual for an observation, how would you decide whether an observation was an outlier? Is it enough to know the value of the residual, or do you need to know other information to make this judgment? How could you apply the methods for detecting outliers described in Chapter 2?*

EXAMPLE 14.2—CONTINUED
Checking the
Conditions for the
Weight and Height Problem

Figure 14.4 (p. 500) displayed a scatterplot of the weights and heights of *n* = 43 college men. In that plot, it appears that a straight line is a suitable model for how mean weight is linked to height. In Figure 14.8 there is a plot of the residuals (e_i) versus the corresponding values of height for these 43 men. This plot is further evidence that the right model has been used. If the right model has been used, the way in which individuals deviate from the line (residuals) will not be affected by the value of the explanatory variable. The somewhat random-looking blob of points in Figure 14.8 is the way a plot of residuals versus *x* should look if the right equation for the mean has been used. Both plots (Figures 14.4 and 14.8) also show that there are no extreme outliers and that the heights have approximately the same variance across the range of heights in the sample. Therefore, Conditions 2 and 3 appear to be met. ◆

Condition 4, which is that deviations from the regression line are normally distributed, is difficult to verify but it is also the least important of the conditions because the inference procedures for regression are *robust*. This means that if there are no major outliers or extreme skewness, the inference procedures work well even if the distribution of *y* values is not a normal distribution. In Chapters 12 and 13, we saw that confidence intervals and hypothesis tests for a mean or a difference between two means also were robust.

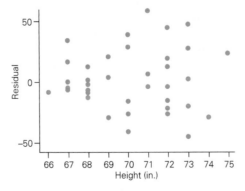

FIGURE 14.8 **Plot of residuals versus *x* for Example 14.2; the absence of a pattern indicates the right model has been used**

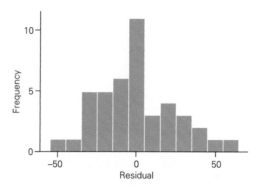

FIGURE 14.9   **Histogram of residuals for Example 14.2**

To examine the distribution of the deviations from the line, a *histogram of the residuals* is useful, although for small samples a histogram may not be informative. A more advanced plot called a *normal probability plot* can also be used to check whether the residuals are normally distributed, but we do not provide the details in this text. Figure 14.9 displays a histogram of the residuals for Example 14.2. It appears that the residuals are approximately normally distributed, so Condition 4 is met.

Condition 5 follows from the data collection process. It is met as long as the units are measured independently. It would not be met if the same individuals were measured across the range of x values, such as if x = average speed and y = gas mileage were to be measured for multiple tanks of gas on the same cars. More complicated models are needed for *dependent* observations, and those models will not be discussed in this book.

Corrections When Conditions Are Not Met

There are some steps that can be taken if Conditions 1, 2, or 3 are not met. If Condition 1 is not met, more complicated models can be used. For instance, Figure 14.10 shows a typical plot of residuals that occurs when a straight-line model is used to describe data that are curvilinear. It may help to think of the residuals as prediction errors that would occur if we use the regression line to predict the value of y for the individuals in the sample. In the plot shown in Figure 14.10, the "prediction errors" are all negative in the central region of x and nearly all positive for outer values of x. This occurs because the wrong model is being used to make the predictions. A curvilinear model, such as the quadratic model discussed earlier, may be more appropriate.

Condition 2, that there are no influential outliers, can be checked graphically with the scatterplot of y versus x and the plot of residuals versus x. The appropriate correction if there are outliers depends on the reason for the outliers. The same considerations and corrective action discussed in Chapter 2 would be taken, depending on the cause of the outlier. For instance, Figure 14.11 shows a scatterplot and a residual plot for the data of exercise 5.55. A potential outlier is seen in both plots.

In this example, the x variable is weight and the y variable is time to chug a beverage. The outlier probably represents a legitimate data value. The relationship appears to be linear for weights ranging up to about 210 pounds, but then it appears to change. It could either become quadratic, or it could level off. We do not have enough data to determine what happens for higher weights. The so-

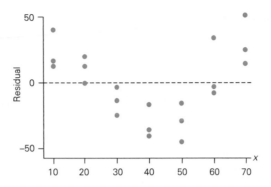

FIGURE 14.10   **A residual plot indicating the wrong model has been used**

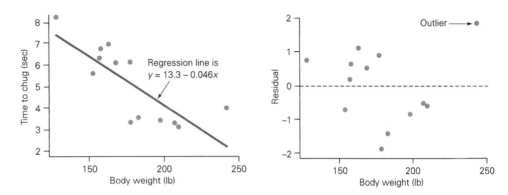

FIGURE 14.11   **Scatterplot and corresponding residual plot with an outlier**

lution in this case would be to remove the outlier and use the linear regression relationship only for body weights under about 210 pounds. Determining the relationship for higher body weights would require a larger sample of individuals in that range.

If either Condition 1 or Condition 3 is not met, a **transformation** may be required. This is equivalent to using a different model. Fortunately, often the same transformation will correct problems with Conditions 1, 3, and 4. For instance, when the response variable is monetary, such as salaries, it is often more appropriate to use the relationship

$$\ln(y) = b_0 + b_1x + e$$

In other words, to assume that there is a linear relationship between the natural log of *y* and the *x* values. This is called a *log transformation on the y's*. We will not pursue transformations further in this book.

Minitab Tip

tech note   **Plotting and Storing Residuals**

◆ Use **Stat>Regression>Regression.** The *Graphs* button of the dialog box offers options for several possible residual plots for the regression.

◆ To store residuals in a column of the worksheet, use the *Storage* button of the dialog box for regression.

CASE STUDY 14.1
A Contested Election

Case Study 11.1 discussed allegations of fraud in a 1993 Philadelphia special election for state senator. The Democratic candidate, William Stinson, beat the Republican candidate, Bruce Marks, by a difference of 461 votes, but Judge Clarence Newcomer overturned the results in a decision issued April 24, 1994. Judge Newcomer wrote, "The court will order the certification of Bruce Marks as the winner of the 1993 Special Election in the Second Senatorial District, because this court finds that the record of evidence overwhelmingly supports the finding that Bruce Marks would have won the election but for wrongdoing" (Newcomer, 1994).

Judge Newcomer partially based his decision on statistical evidence presented by expert witnesses. Other evidence suggested that a number of absentee ballots had been filed illegally, and a statistical analysis indicated that the absentee count was indeed unusual when compared to the machine vote count.

The data used for the statistical analysis consisted of two variables for each of the 21 senatorial elections held in the previous 11 years (1982–1992) in the Philadelphia area. The variables were:

$y = Diff\ absentee = $ (Democrat candidate − Republican candidate) votes by absentee ballot

$x = Diff\ machine = $ (Democrat candidate − Republican candidate) votes by machine ballot

The data for the 21 prior elections were given by economist and expert witness Orley Ashenfelter in a report to Judge Newcomer (Ashenfelter, 1994), and they are presented in Table 14.1 along with the contested 1993 results.

Figure 14.12 shows a plot of the data, with the contested election marked in red. In the contested election, the observed difference (Democrat − Republican) appears well above what might be expected based on the overall connection between absentee and machine votes. Notice also that there is an additional outlier, for the election held in District 1 in 1992. No explanation or discussion of that outlier occurred in the court records.

Is the combination of absentee and machine differences in the contested election at all reasonable, if all other factors remain similar to circumstances of the other elections? The output shown on the next page are for a simple linear regression computed using data from the 21 prior elections. Included in the results are 95% confidence and prediction intervals for the difference in absentee ballots when the

TABLE 14.1 ■ **Differences in Democratic and Republican Votes in Philadelphia Elections**

Year	District	Diff Absentee	Diff Machine
82	2	346	26427
82	4	282	15904
82	8	223	42448
84	1	593	19444
84	3	572	71797
84	5	−229	−1017
84	7	671	63406
86	2	293	15671
86	4	360	36276
86	8	306	36710
88	1	401	21848
88	3	378	65862
88	5	−829	−13194
88	7	394	56100
90	2	151	700
90	4	−349	11529
90	8	160	26047
92	1	1329	44425
92	3	368	45512
92	5	−434	−5700
92	7	391	51206
93 (Contested)	2	1025	−564

machine ballot difference is −564, the value observed in the contested election. In particular, notice that the 95% prediction interval for the absentee ballot difference for this machine ballot difference is −854.7 to 588.6. The actual ab-

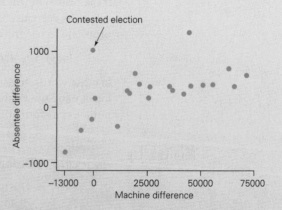

FIGURE 14.12 **Plot of absentee difference versus voting machine difference**

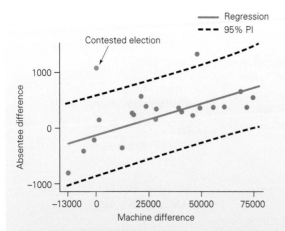

FIGURE 14.13 **Prediction limits for Diff Absentee, given machine difference**

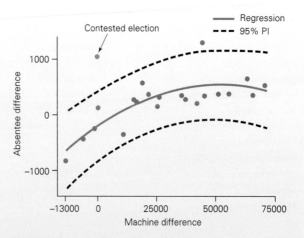

FIGURE 14.14 **Prediction limits for quadratic model**

sentee difference in the contested election was +1025, a difference far outside this range. Figure 14.13 displays this result graphically, giving "prediction limits" for the entire range of possible values of machine differences covered by the data.

```
The regression equation is
Diff Absentee = − 126 + 0.0127 Diff Machine
Predictor        Coef      StDev        T        P
Constant       −125.9      114.3    −1.10    0.284
Diff Mac     0.012703    0.002980     4.26    0.000

S = 324.8      R-Sq = 48.9%      R-Sq(adj) = 46.2%

Predicted Values

   Fit    StDev Fit       95.0% CI           95.0% PI
−133.1       115.6   ( −375.0, 108.8)   ( −854.7, 588.6)
```

The analysis reported in the *New York Times,* and quoted in Case Study 11.1, used the linear relationship we have just used. However, an examination of the plot of the data in Figure 14.12 indicates that the relationship may actually be curvilinear. A plot of the residuals versus *x* (not shown) confirms this effect. Therefore, another analysis was done by including a "quadratic" term, (Diff Machine)^2, in the regression equation. Results are shown in the output in the next column, including 95% confidence and prediction intervals for the contested election. Notice that the prediction interval is even more disparate with the observed result of +1025 than it was with the simple linear regression equation.

```
The regression equation is
Diff Absentee = − 219 + 0.0297 Diff Machine −0.000000
Quadratic

Predictor         Coef         StDev        T       P
Constant        −219.0         105.4    −2.08   0.052
Diff Mac      0.029709      0.006887     4.31   0.000
Quadrati   − 0.00000028    0.00000011   −2.67   0.016

S = 282.6       R-Sq = 63.3%      R-Sq(adj) = 59.3%

Predicted Values

   Fit    StDev Fit       95.0% CI           95.0% PI
−235.9       107.7   ( −462.1, −9.6)   ( −871.2, 399.5)
```

The *p*-value reported for the "quadratic term" is 0.016 and it is for a test of the null hypothesis that the quadratic term is not needed. Therefore, it is clear that the new model, including the quadratic term, is better than the simple linear model. Figure 14.14 shows the "prediction limits" based on the quadratic model over the range of machine differences for the model including the quadratic term.

The regression analysis and accompanying figures cast doubt on the results of the contested election, *assuming* all other factors were the same as in the past. There may have been other factors that led more people who cast votes for the Democratic candidate to do so by absentee ballot in this election. That issue cannot be addressed using the statistical evidence available, but Judge Newcomer was convinced that other potential differences could not account for the statistical anomaly displayed by the regression analysis.

KEY TERMS

EXERCISES   Blue = Basics   **Bold, Bold** = Answer in back

Sections 14.1, 14.2, and 14.3

14.1 The **temperature** dataset on this book's CD gives $y =$ mean April temperature (Fahrenheit) and $x =$ geographic latitude for 20 U.S. cities. The simple linear regression equation for the sample is $\hat{y} = 119 - 1.64\,x$.
  a. The value of latitude for Pittsburgh is 40. What is the predicted April temperature for Pittsburgh?
  b. The mean April temperature for Pittsburgh is 50. What is the residual for Pittsburgh?

14.2 Refer to the previous exercise. Minitab output for the linear regression is

```
The regression equation is
AprTemp = 119 - 1.64 latitude

Predictor    Coef     SE Coef      T       P
Constant     118.776    4.467    26.59   0.000
latitude     -1.6436    0.1165  -14.11   0.000

S = 2.837      R-Sq = 91.7%
```

  a. Write null and alternative hypotheses for testing whether there is a linear relationship between mean April temperature and latitude. Use proper statistical notation.
  b. Use information given in the output to test the hypotheses written in part (a). State a conclusion and give a reason for the conclusion.
  c. Using values given in the output, show how to calculate the t-statistic for testing the hypotheses stated in part (a).

14.3 Refer to the previous two exercises.
  a. In the output, what value is given for the standard deviation from the regression line? Write a sentence that interprets this value.
  b. In the output, the value of R^2 is given as 91.7%. Write a sentence that interprets this value.

14.4 The **UCDavis1** dataset on the text CD includes grade point averages and self-reported hours per week of watching television for students in a statistics class. In a simple linear regression for the relationship between $y =$ grade point average and $x =$ hours per week of television watching, the p-value is 0.552 for testing H_0: $\beta_1 = 0$ versus H_a: $\beta_1 \neq 0$.
  a. Is the observed relationship statistically significant or not? Explain.
  b. What would be the p-value for testing the null hypothesis that correlation between the variables is 0 in the population represented by the sample? Assume a two-sided alternative hypothesis.

14.5 For men over the age of 40, a linear regression is done to examine the relationship between $y =$ systolic blood pressure and $x =$ age. A 95% confidence interval for the population slope β_1 is 0.3 to 0.7. In the context of this situation, write a sentence that interprets this confidence interval.

14.6 The population model for simple linear regression can be defined as
$$y_i = \beta_0 + \beta_1 x_i + \varepsilon_i$$
  a. Explain what the parameters β_0 and β_1 represent.
  b. Write the equation that represents how the mean of the y variable relates to the x variable.

14.7 Find r^2 in each of the following situations:
  a. SSTO = 500, SSE = 300.
  b. SSTO = 200, SSE = 40.
  c. SSTO = 80, SSE = 0.
  d. SSTO = 100, SSE = 95.

14.8 Example 14.3 in Section 14.2 gave the regression equation $y = 577 - 3.01x$ for the relationship between $y =$ maximum distance at which a driver can read a highway sign and $x =$ driver age.
  a. What is the predicted value of the maximum sign-reading distance for a driver 21 years old?
  b. Compute the residual for a 21-year-old driver who can read the sign at a maximum distance of 525 feet.

c. The standard deviation from the regression line in this example is approximately $s = 50$ feet. Use the Empirical Rule to give an interval that describes the maximum sign-reading distances for about 95% of all drivers who are 21 years old.

d. Would it be unusual for a 21-year-old driver to be able to read the sign from 650 feet? Justify your answer.

14.9 In the simple linear regression model for a population, the relationship between the x variable and the mean of the y variable is $E(Y) = \beta_0 + \beta_1 x$.

   a. Suppose $\beta_1 = 0$. What would be the appearance of this line? Draw a sketch illustrating your answer.

   b. Explain how the answer to part (a) illustrates the lack of a linear relationship between x and y.

14.10 Data for y = hours of sleep the previous day and x = hours of studying the previous day for $n = 116$ college students were shown in Figure 5.12 and described in Example 5.9. Some regression results for those data are

---

The regression equation is
Sleep = 7.56 − 0.269 Study

Predictor	Coef	SE Coef	T	P
Constant	7.5555	0.2239	33.74	0.000
Study	−0.26917	0.06616		0.000

S = 1.509   R-Sq = 12.7%   R-Sq(adj) = 11.9%

---

   a. What is the estimated mean decrease in hours of sleep per 1-hour increase in hours of studying? What notation is used for this value?

   b. Calculate an approximate 95% confidence interval for β_1. Write a sentence that interprets this interval.

   c. Using proper statistical notation, write null and alternative hypotheses for assessing the statistical significance of the relationship.

   d. We omitted from the output the t-statistic for testing the hypotheses of part (c). Compute the value of this t-statistic using other information shown in the output. What are the degrees of freedom for this t-statistic?

   e. Is there a statistically significant relationship between hours of sleep and hours of studying? Justify your answer based on information shown in the output.

14.11 Refer to the previous problem about hours of sleep and hours of study.

   a. What is the value of the standard deviation from the regression line? Write a sentence that interprets this value.

   b. Calculate the predicted value of hours of sleep the previous day for a student who studied 4 hours the previous day.

   c. Using the Empirical Rule, determine an interval that describes hours of sleep for approximately 95% of students who studied 4 hours the previous day.

   d. The value of R^2 is given as 12.7%. Write a sentence that interprets this value.

14.12 Refer to the previous two exercises about hours of sleep and hours spent studying. What is the intercept of the

regression line? Does this value have a useful interpretation in the context of this problem? If so, what is the interpretation? If not, why not?

14.13 The relationship between y = hours of watching television in a typical day and x = age was examined in Example 5.8. The data were gathered in the 1996 General Social Survey done by the National Opinion Research Center at the University of Chicago, and there were $n = 1913$ observations. The correlation between the variables is $r = .12$, a value indicative of a weak connection between hours of watching television and age.

The regression equation is
tvhours = 2.19 + 0.0173 age

Predictor	Coef	SE Coef	T	P
Constant	2.1899	0.1577	13.89	0.000
age	0.017255	0.003348	5.15	0.000

S = 2.371   R-Sq = 1.4%   R-Sq(adj) = 1.3%

---

   a. What is the estimated increase in average daily hours of television watching for each 1-year increase in age?

   b. Using proper statistical notation, write null and alternative hypotheses for testing the statistical significance of the relationship between the two variables.

   c. Use information in the output to determine if there is a statistically significant relationship between age and daily hours of watching television. Include relevant information in your answer.

   d. Explain whether or not you think the observed relationship has practical significance.

14.14 The least-squares regression line is $\hat{y} = 9 + 2x$ for these six observations of x and y:

x	1	1	3	3	5	5
y	10	12	13	17	17	21

   a. For each observation, calculate the residual. Verify that the sum of the residuals is 0.

   b. Compute SSE, the sum of squared errors (residuals).

   c. For the sample, calculate the standard deviation from the regression line.

14.15 In Example 14.2, a sample of $n = 43$ college men was used to determine the regression equation, Weight = $-318 + 7$ (Height). Weights were measured in pounds and heights were measured in inches.

   a. The slope of the line is 7. Explain whether the proper notation for this slope is b_1 or β_1.

   b. The standard error for the slope was given as 1.581 in Figure 14.4. Calculate an approximate 95% confidence interval for the slope in the population. Write a sentence that interprets this interval.

   c. It has been stated that for each 1-inch increase in height, average weight increases by 5 pounds. Explain whether the interval computed in part (b) supports this statement or not.

   d. Explain why it would not be useful to compute a confidence interval for the population intercept in this example.

14.16 Refer to the previous exercise in which a regression equation is given for the relationship between weight and height for college men. What is the value of the residual for a college man 72 inches tall who weighs 160 pounds?

Sections 14.4 and 14.5

14.17 For each part of this question, explain whether a confidence interval for the mean or a prediction interval for a value of y should be used.
a. Estimate the first-year college GPA for a student whose high school GPA was 3.5.
b. Estimate the mean first-year college GPA for students whose high school GPA was 3.5.
c. Estimate the average income for individuals who have 20 years of experience within a particular occupation.
d. Estimate the adult height of a daughter of a woman who is 64 inches tall.

14.18 Suppose a regression model is used to analyze the relationship between y = grade point average and x = number of classes missed in a typical week for college students.
a. In the context of this situation, explain what would be predicted by a prediction interval for y when $x = 2$ classes missed per week.
b. In the context of this situation, explain what would be estimated by a confidence interval for $E(Y)$ when $x = 2$ classes missed per week.

14.19 A college finds that among students who had a total SAT score of approximately 1200, about 90% have a first-year GPA in the range 2.7 to 3.7. Explain whether this interval is a prediction interval or a confidence interval for the mean.

14.20 Forty students measure their resting pulse rates, then march in place for one minute and measure their pulse rates after the marching. The regression line for the sample is $\hat{y} = 17.79 + 0.894x$, where y = pulse after marching and x = pulse before marching. The following Minitab output gives a confidence interval and a prediction interval for pulse after marching when pulse before marching is 70 (*Data source:* **pulsemarch** dataset on the text CD).

Fit	SE Fit	95.0% CI	95.0% PI
80.35	1.15	(78.02, 82.67)	(65.50, 95.19)

a. Write the 95% confidence interval for $E(Y)$. In the context of this situation, write a sentence that interprets this interval.
b. Write the 95% prediction interval for y. In the context of this situation, write a sentence that interprets this interval.

14.21 Example 2.11 described the heights of a sample of married British women. The ages of the women and their husbands were available in the same dataset for $n = 170$

couples. For the sample, the linear regression line relating y = husband's age and x = wife's age is $\hat{y} = 3.59 + 0.967x$. The following results computed with Minitab give a confidence interval and prediction interval for husband's age when wife's age is 40:

Fit	SE Fit	95.0% CI	95.0% PI
42.258	0.313	(41.641, 42.875)	(34.200, 50.316)

a. Verify that the "Fit" is consistent with the predicted value that would be given by the regression equation.
b. Interpret the "95% CI" given by Minitab. Be specific about what the interval estimates.
c. Interpret the "95% PI" given by Minitab. Be specific about what the interval estimates.
d. Explain why the "95% PI" is much wider than the "95% CI."

14.22 Refer to the previous exercise. Using the general format for a 95% confidence interval, verify the confidence interval for the mean given by Minitab. Notice that the standard error of the "Fit" is given.

14.23 Exercise 14.10 gave linear regression results for the relationship between y = hours of sleep the previous day and x = hours spent studying the previous day. Following is Minitab output showing a confidence interval and a prediction interval for hours of sleep when hours of studying = 3 hours:

Fit	SE Fit	95.0% CI	95.0% PI
6.748	0.142	(6.466, 7.029)	(3.746, 9.750)

Write down the interval given for predicting the hours of sleep when hours of studying is 3 hours. Give two different interpretations of this interval.

14.24 Suppose a linear regression analysis of the relationship between y = systolic blood pressure and x = age is done for women between 40 and 60 years old. For women who are 45 years old, a 90% confidence interval for $E(Y)$ is determined to be 128.2 to 131.3. Explain why it is incorrect to conclude that about 90% of women who are 45 years old have a systolic blood pressure in this range. Write a sentence that correctly interprets the interval.

Section 14.6

14.25 There are five conditions listed at the beginning of Section 14.6 that should be at least approximately true for linear regression. Which of the conditions can be checked using each of the following methods? In each case, list all of them that can be checked.
a. Drawing a histogram of the residuals.
b. Drawing a scatterplot of the residuals versus the x values.

c. Learning how the data were collected.

d. Drawing a scatterplot of the raw data, y versus x.

14.26 Refer to exercise 14.20 about a linear regression for $y =$ pulse after marching in place and $x =$ pulse before marching in place. The figure for this exercise is a plot of residuals versus the pulse before marching for a sample of 40 students. Discuss what the plot indicates about Conditions 1, 2, and 3 for linear regression listed at the beginning of Section 14.6.

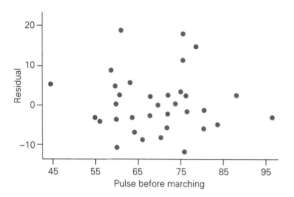

EXERCISE 14.26 **Residuals versus pulse before marching**

14.27 The figure for this exercise is a histogram of the residuals for a linear regression relating $y =$ height (inches) and $x =$ foot length (cm) for a sample of college men. Discuss what the histogram indicates about Conditions 2 and 4 for linear regression listed at the beginning of Section 14.6 (*Data source:* **heightfoot** dataset on the text CD).

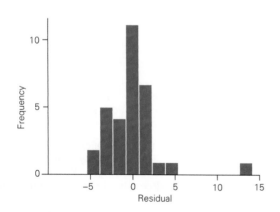

EXERCISE 14.27 **Histograms of residuals**

14.28 Regression results for the relationship between $y =$ hours of sleep the previous day and $x =$ hours spent studying the previous day were given in exercise 14.10.

The figure accompanying this exercise is a plot of residuals versus hours spent studying. What does the plot indicate about the necessary conditions for doing a linear regression? Be specific about which of the five conditions given in Section 14.6 are verified by this plot.

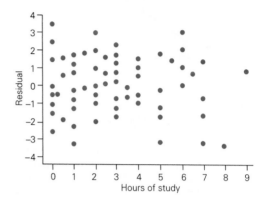

EXERCISE 14.28 **Residuals versus hours spent studying**

14.29 Refer to the previous exercise. The figure accompanying this exercise is a histogram of the residuals for the regression relating hours of sleep and hours spent studying. What does this plot indicate about the necessary conditions for doing a linear regression? Be specific about which of the five necessary conditions are verified in this figure.

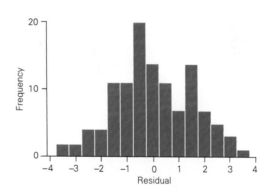

EXERCISE 14.29 **Histogram of residuals**

14.30 Plot residuals versus x for the data given in exercise 14.14.

14.31 Observed data along with the sample regression line for the relationship between body weight (lbs) and neck girth (in.) in 19 female bears of various ages are shown in the figure on the next page. (*Note:* The data are in the dataset **bears-female** on the data CD.)

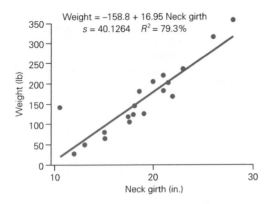

EXERCISE 14.31 **Data and regression line for the body weight and neck girth of $n = 19$ female bears**

a. Which of the necessary conditions for linear regression appears to be violated in this dataset?
b. What corrective actions would you consider in order to properly estimate the relationship between body weight and neck girth?
c. Sketch a histogram that illustrates the pattern of the distribution of the residuals for this problem. Your sketch does not have to be accurate in the numerical details, but should correctly show the pattern.

14.32 The accompanying figure shows data for the relationship between the average stopping distance (ft) of a car when the brakes are applied and vehicle speed (mph). The regression line for these data is also shown on the plot. (*Note:* The raw data were given in exercise 5.7.)

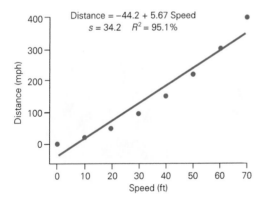

EXERCISE 14.32 **Stopping distance and vehicle speed for automobiles**

a. Which of the five necessary conditions for linear regression appears to be violated in this situation?
b. What corrective action would you take in order to correctly estimate the connection between stopping distance and vehicle speed?
c. Make a sketch that illustrates the pattern of a plot of residuals versus speed for the data shown in the

figure in this exercise. Your sketch does not need to be numerically accurate, but should correctly show the pattern of the plot.

Chapter Exercises

14.33 Sketch sample data for which the standard deviation from the regression line is $s = 0$.

14.34 An example in Sections 14.1 and 14.2 described the relationship between y = handspan (cm) and x = height (in.). The sample consisted of measurements of both variables for $n = 167$ college students. Computer output for this example is

```
The regression equation is
HandSpan = − 3.00 + 0.351 Height

Predictor      Coef     SE Coef       T       P
Constant     −3.002       1.694   −1.77   0.078
Height       0.35057     0.02484   14.11   0.000

S = 1.301              R-Sq = 54.7%
```

a. What is the value of the standard deviation from the regression line? Write a sentence that interprets this value.
b. What is the value of R^2 given in the output? Write a sentence that interprets this value.

14.35 Refer to the previous exercise. Compute a 90% confidence interval for the population slope. Write a sentence that interprets this interval.

14.36 This output is for a linear regression relating y = GPA and x = hours per week spent using the computer for $n = 162$ college students (*Note:* The data are in the **UCDavis1** dataset).

```
The regression equation is
GPA = 3.01 − 0.00555 computer

162 cases used 11 cases contain missing values

Predictor       Coef     SE Coef       T       P
Constant     3.00588     0.07335   40.98   0.000
computer    −0.005548    0.003979   −1.39   0.165
```

a. Is there a statistically significant relationship between the two variables? Justify your answer using information from the output. Be specific about the null and alternative hypotheses that you're evaluating.
b. Suppose that ρ denotes the correlation between the two variables in the population represented by the sample. What is the p-value for testing $H_0: \rho = 0$ versus $H_a: \rho \neq 0$?

14.37 These data are x = average on five quizzes prior to midterm exam and y = score on midterm exam for $n = 11$ students randomly selected from a statistics class of about 950 students:

x = Quizzes	80	68	94	72	74	83	56	68	65	75	88
y = Exam	72	71	96	77	82	72	58	83	78	80	92

a. Plot the data, and describe the important features of this plot.

b. Using statistical software, calculate the regression line for this sample.

c. What is the predicted midterm exam score for a student with a quiz average equal to 75?

d. With statistical software, determine a 50% prediction interval for the midterm exam score of a student whose quiz average was 75.

14.38 This exercise refers to the following Minitab output, relating y = son's height to x = father's height for a sample of $n = 76$ college males. (*Note:* The data are in the dataset **UCDavis1** on the data CD.)

```
The regression equation is
Height = 30.0 + 0.576 dadheight

76 cases used 3 cases contain missing values

Predictor      Coef      SE Coef      T       P
Constant     29.981       5.129     5.85   0.000
dadheigh     0.57568     0.07445    7.73   0.000

S = 2.657       R-Sq = 44.7%

Predicted Values [for dad's heights of 65, 70 and 74]

Fit     SE Fit      95.0% CI            95.0% PI
67.400   0.415   ( 66.574, 68.226)   ( 62.041, 72.759)
70.279   0.318   ( 69.645, 70.913)   ( 64.946, 75.612)
75.581   0.494   ( 71.596, 73.566)   ( 67.195, 77.967)
```

a. What is the equation for the regression line?

b. Identify the value of the *t*-statistic for testing whether or not the slope is 0. Verify that the value is correct, using the formula for the *t*-statistic and the information provided by Minitab for the parts that go into the formula.

c. State and test the hypotheses about whether or not the population slope is 0. Use relevant information provided in the output.

d. Compute a 95% confidence interval for β_1, the slope of the relationship in the population. Write a sentence that interprets this interval.

14.39 Refer to the previous exercise.

a. What is the value of R^2 for the observed linear relationship between height and father's height? Write a sentence that interprets this value.

b. What is the value of the correlation coefficient r?

14.40 Refer to the previous two exercises. Notice that Minitab provided prediction intervals and confidence intervals for father's heights of 65, 70, and 74 inches.

a. Verify that the "Fit" given by Minitab for dad's height of 65 inches is consistent with the predicted height that would be given by the regression equation.

b. Write down the interval Minitab provided for predicting an individual son's height if his dad's height is 70

inches. Provide two different interpretations for the interval.

c. Write a sentence that interprets the "95% CI" given for son's height when father's height is 74 inches.

d. Explain why the prediction interval is much wider than the corresponding confidence interval for each father's height provided.

e. The accompanying figure is a plot of the residuals versus father's height. Which of the five necessary conditions for regression listed in Section 14.6 appears to be violated? What corrective actions should you consider?

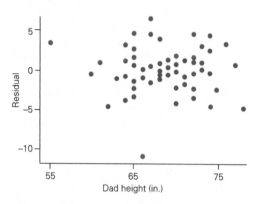

EXERCISE 14.40(e)   Residuals versus father's height

14.41 The five steps for hypothesis testing were given in Chapters 11 and 13. Describe those steps as they apply to testing whether there is a relationship between two variables in the simple regression model.

14.42 A sample of 837 ninth-grade girls was asked how much time they spent watching music videos each week. The girls also were asked to rate how concerned they were about their weight on a scale of 0–100 (100 = extremely concerned) as well as to rate their perception of how important appearance is on a scale of 1–6 (6 = very important). The researchers (Borzekowski et al., 2000) wrote the following about the results: "When media use was separated into distinct media genres, only hours of watching music videos was related to perceived importance of appearance and weight concerns ($r = .12$, $p < 0.001$, and $r = .08$, $p < 0.05$, respectively)."

a. What are the null and alternative hypotheses for which *p*-values are given in the researchers' statement? What conclusions have the researchers made about these hypotheses?

b. Do the correlation values given by the researchers indicate weak or strong relationships between the variables? Support your answer with a sketch illustrating the appearance of a scatterplot for the given correlation values.

14.43 Explain why rejecting H_0: $\beta_1 = 0$ in a simple linear regression model does not prove that the relationship is linear. To answer this question, you might find it helpful to consider the figure in exercise 14.32, which shows stopping distance and vehicle speed for automobiles.

Dataset Exercises

14.44 Use the dataset **letters** for this exercise. A sample of 63 students wrote as many letters of the alphabet, in order as capital letters, as they could in 15 seconds using their dominant hand, and then repeated this task using their nondominant hand. The variables **dom** and **nondom** contain the raw data for the results.

a. Plot $y = $ **dom** versus $x = $ **nondom.** Describe the important features of the plot.

b. Compute the simple regression equation for the relationship. What is the equation?

c. What are the values of the standard deviation from the regression line and R^2? Interpret these values in the context of this problem.

d. Determine a 95% confidence interval for the population slope. Write a sentence that interprets this interval.

e. Consider the statement, "On average, a student can write about 23 more letters in 15 seconds with the dominant hand than with the nondominant hand." What regression equation would accompany this statement? Based on your answers to parts (b) and (d), explain why this statement is reasonable.

14.45 Refer to the previous exercise about letters written with the dominant (y) and nondominant (x) hands.

a. Plot residuals versus $x = $ **nondom.** What does this plot indicate about conditions for using the linear regression model?

b. Create a histogram of the residuals. What does this plot indicate about the conditions for using the linear regression model?

14.46 Use the **bears-female** dataset for this exercise. Weights (lbs) and chest girths (in.) are given for $n = 19$ female wild bears. The corresponding variable names are **Weight** and **Chest.**

a. Plot $y = $ **Weight** versus $x = $ **Chest.** Describe the important features of the plot.

b. Compute a simple linear regression equation for $y = $ **Weight** and $x = $ **Chest.**

c. What is the value of R^2 for this relationship? Write a sentence interpreting this value.

d. What is the predicted weight for a bear with a chest girth of 40 inches?

e. Compute a 95% prediction interval for the weight of a bear with a chest girth of 40 inches. Write a sentence interpreting this interval.

f. Compute a 95% confidence interval for the mean weight of bears with a chest girth of 40 inches. Write a sentence interpreting this interval.

14.47 Use the dataset **heightfoot.** Heights (in.) and foot lengths (cm) are given for 33 men.

a. Plot $y = $ height versus $x = $ foot length. What important features are evident in the plot?

b. Omit any outliers evident in the plot in part (a), and compute the linear regression line for predicting $y = $ height from $x = $ foot length.

c. Determine a 90% prediction interval for the height of a man whose foot length is 28 centimeters.

d. Discuss whether height can be accurately predicted from foot length. Use regression results to justify your answer.

e. For the data used for part (b), plot residuals versus $x = $ foot length. What does this plot indicate about the necessary conditions for doing a linear regression?

14.48 Refer to the previous exercise about the relationship between height and foot length.

a. Do not omit any outliers. Use the complete dataset to determine a 90% prediction interval for the height of a man whose foot length is 28 centimeters.

b. Explain why the interval computed in part (a) is wider than the interval computed for part (c) of the previous exercise.

c. For the regression based on all data points, plot residuals versus $x = $ foot length. What does this plot indicate about the necessary conditions for doing a linear regression?

REFERENCES

Ashenfelter, Orley (1994). "Report on expected absentee ballot," revised March 29, 1994. Unpublished report submitted to Judge Clarence Newcomer, U.S. District Court, Eastern District of Pennsylvania, March 30, 1994.

Borzekowski, D. L. G, T. N. Robinson, and J. D. Killen (2000). "Does the camera add 10 pounds? Media use, perceived importance of appearance, and weight concerns among teenage girls," *Journal of Adolescent Health,* Vol. 26, pp. 36–41.

Newcomer, Clarence (1994). Judgment in the Civil Action No. 93–6157, Bruce S. Marks et al. v. William Stinson et al., United States District Court for the Eastern District Court of Pennsylvania, entered April 26, 1994.

CHAPTER 15

More About Categorical Variables

With whom is it easiest to make friends? See Example 15.2.

Are the digits drawn in lotteries actually equally likely, as claimed? Are belief and performance on ESP tests related? Do males and females have the same opinions about whether it's easier to make friends with the same sex or the opposite sex? Chi-square tests can be used to answer these kinds of questions about categorical variables.

n Chapter 6, we learned techniques for analyzing a fundamental question that researchers often ask about two categorical variables, which is

Is there a relationship between the variables so that the chance that an individual falls into a particular category for one variable depends upon the particular category they fall into for the other variable?

For instance, in Example 6.1 we saw that the likelihood of divorce is greater for smokers than it is for nonsmokers. A procedure for assessing the statistical significance of a relationship between categorical variables is the chi-square test. We introduced the basic ideas of this statistical method in Chapter 6, and in this chapter we examine the chi-square test more fully. We will use the chi-square procedure to test hypotheses about two-way tables, and also we will learn how the chi-square procedure is used to test hypotheses about a single categorical variable. ◆

15.1 | THE CHI-SQUARE TEST FOR TWO-WAY TABLES

In Chapter 6, we learned these terms:

- ◆ The raw data from a **categorical variable** consist of group or category names that don't necessarily have any logical ordering. Your sex (male or female) and your handedness (left or right), for instance, are both categorical variables.

- ◆ A **two-way table** displays the counts of how many individuals fall into each possible combination of categories of two categorical variables. A two-way table may also be called a **contingency table.**

◆ Each combination of a row and a column is referred to as a **cell** of the contingency table.

◆ **Row percents** are the percents across a row of a contingency table. They are based on the total number of observations in the row.

◆ **Column percents** are the percents down a column of a contingency table. They are based on the total number of observations in the column.

As usual, there are five steps required to assess statistical significance. In this case, the question of interest is whether a relationship observed in a sample can be used to infer that there is a relationship in the population(s) from which the sample(s) was drawn.

Step 1: The Null and Alternative Hypotheses

The **null** and **alternative hypotheses** about the categorical variables that form a two-way table are

H_0: The two variables are not related.
H_a: The two variables are related.

It is commonplace to use the word *associated* in place of the word *related*. Within a specific context, we may be able to write more informative versions of the general statements about the relationship.

EXAMPLE 15.1
Ear Infections and Xylitol Sweetener

Xylitol is a food sweetener that may also have antibacterial properties. In an experiment conducted in Finland (and discussed in Example 13.6), researchers investigated whether the regular use of chewing gum containing Xylitol could reduce the risk of a middle ear infection for children in daycare centers (Uhari et al., 1998). The investigators randomly divided 533 children in daycare centers into three groups. One group regularly chewed gum that contained Xylitol, another group regularly took Xylitol lozenges, and the third group regularly chewed gum that did not contain Xylitol. The experiment lasted for three months and, for each child, the researchers recorded whether the child had an ear infection during that period. (In Example 13.6, the data concerned Xylitol administered in a syrup form rather than in gum.)

Table 15.1 displays the data along with row percents. As usual, the explanatory variable, which is the type of gum or lozenge each child took, is displayed as rows. The response variable, which is whether the child had an ear infection, is displayed as columns. The results of the test would be the same if the vari-

TABLE 15.1 ■ **Ear Infections and the Use of Xylitol**

	Ear Infection in Three Months?		
Group	No	Yes	Total
Placebo Gum	129 (72.5%)	49 (27.5%)	178
Xylitol Gum	150 (83.8%)	29 (16.2%)	179
Xylitol Lozenge	137 (77.8%)	39 (22.2%)	176
Total	416 (78%)	117 (22%)	533

ables in the rows and columns were reversed, with the explanatory variable as columns. However, displaying the categories of the explanatory variable as rows makes it easier to find and interpret the conditional percents that are usually of interest, the row percents. The display in Table 15.1 readily allows us to see that only 16.2% of the children in the Xylitol gum group got an ear infection during the experiment, compared to 22.2% of the Xylitol lozenge group and 27.5% of the placebo gum group.

The purpose of the experiment is to compare the three groups with regard to the proportion of children who experienced an ear infection. The goal is to see if the sample results allow us to infer that differences would exist in the population of all children if they were to be administered these treatments. For this purpose, there are three relevant parameters.

p_1 = proportion who would get an ear infection in a population given placebo gum

p_2 = proportion who would get an ear infection in a population given Xylitol gum

p_3 = proportion who would get an ear infection in a population given Xylitol lozenges

If the chance of falling into the ear infection category is not related to treatment method, the risk of an ear infection would be the same for the three treatments. So, null and alternative hypotheses about the parameters are

H_0: $p_1 = p_2 = p_3$. (No relationship between treatment and outcome.)
H_a: p_1, p_2, and p_3 are not all the same. (There is a relationship.)

Notice that the alternative hypothesis simply states that the three proportions are not all the same. A limitation of chi-square tests is that no particular direction for the relationship can be stated in the alternative hypothesis. In contrast, if we were comparing only two proportions, as in Chapter 13, we would be able to specify a one-sided alternative hypothesis if it were appropriate. ◆

EXAMPLE 15.2
With Whom Do You Find It Easiest to Make Friends?

Students in a Penn State statistics class were asked, "With whom do you find it easiest to make friends?" Possible responses were "opposite sex," "same sex," and "no difference." Students were also categorized as male or female. We would like to determine whether there is a statistically significant relationship between the sex of the respondent and response. To emphasize the comparison of men and women, we might express the null and alternative hypotheses as

H_0: There would be no difference in the distribution of responses of men and women if the populations of them were asked this question. (No relationship between gender and response.)

H_a: There would be a difference in the distribution of responses of men and women if the populations of them were asked this question. (There is a relationship between gender and response.)

As is always the case in hypothesis testing, these hypotheses are statements about the larger populations represented by the samples of men and women. Again, notice that the alternative hypothesis does not specify any particular way in which the men and women might differ.

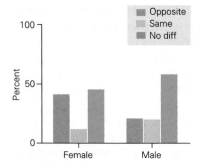

TABLE 15.2 ■ Data For Example 15.2

| | With Whom Is It Easiest to Make Friends? | | | |
	Opposite Sex	Same Sex	No Difference	Total
Females	58 (42%)	16 (12%)	63 (46%)	137
Males	15 (22%)	13 (19%)	40 (59%)	68
Total	73 (36%)	29 (14%)	103 (50%)	205

Table 15.2 compares the responses of males and females, and Figure 15.1 displays the relevant conditional percentage distributions. We see that there appears to be a relationship. For instance, a decidedly higher percentage of females than males responded "opposite sex." ◆

Homogeneity and Independence

tech note It is generally sufficient to state the null and alternative hypotheses as H_0: No relationship and H_a: There is a relationship. At the theoretical level, however, there are two specific variations of these general statements, and the method of sampling dictates which variation is appropriate in a particular situation. If samples have been taken from separate populations, the null hypothesis statement is a statement of **homogeneity** (sameness) among the populations. Example 15.1 is such an instance. If a sample has been taken from a single population, and two categorical variables measured for each individual, the statement of no relationship is a statement of **independence** between the two variables. Example 15.2 is such an instance. (*Note:* Independence was discussed in Chapter 7.) Fortunately, for sufficiently large samples, the same chi-square test is appropriate for both situations, so generally we will not be concerned about whether the null hypothesis is about homogeneity or about independence.

Step 2: The Chi-square Statistic for Two-Way Tables and Necessary Conditions

The chi-square test described in Section 6.5 can be used to assess statistical significance for tables with any numbers of rows and columns. This procedure is an approximate method that requires a "large" sample. The larger the sample, the better the approximation. Commonly used guidelines for the term *large sample* are

1. All expected counts should be greater than 1.
2. At least 80% of the cells should have an expected count greater than 5.

We will provide more details about the chi-square test shortly, but first let's review the basic ideas from Section 6.5.

- ◆ The counts in the cells of a two-way table of the sample data are called the **observed counts.**
- ◆ The chi-square statistic measures the difference between the observed counts and corresponding **expected counts.** The *expected counts* are hy-

pothetical counts that would occur if the null hypothesis were true. The expected counts can be calculated as

$$\text{Expected} = \frac{\text{Row total} \times \text{Column total}}{\text{Total } n}$$

◆ The **chi-square statistic** is

$$\chi^2 = \sum_{\text{all cells}} \frac{(\text{Observed} - \text{Expected})^2}{\text{Expected}}$$

The symbol Σ stands for "sum," and the sum is over all cells of the two-way table. A large chi-square value occurs when there is a large difference between the observed and expected counts.

◆ The **p-value** of the chi-square test is the probability that the chi-square statistic, χ^2, could be as large as or larger than it is if the null hypothesis is true. A chi-square probability distribution is used to determine this probability. The degrees of freedom for the chi-square distribution are given by df = (Rows − 1)(Columns − 1), where "Rows" indicates the number of rows in the table (excluding the row of totals), and "Columns" indicates the number of columns in the table (excluding the column of totals).

Notation for Chi-square Statistic for Two-Way Tables

tech note   The following mathematical notation can be used for the elements of the chi-square test:

O_{ij} = observed count for the cell in the ith row and jth column of the table

E_{ij} = expected count for the cell in the ith row and jth column of the table

R_i = total count of observations in the ith row

C_j = total count of observations in the jth column

n = total count

$E_{ij} = \dfrac{R_i C_j}{n}$ = expected count for the cell in the ith row and jth column

$$\chi^2 = \sum_{i,j} \frac{(O_{ij} - E_{ij})^2}{E_{ij}}$$

r = number of rows; c = number of columns

EXAMPLE 15.1—*CONTINUED*
Chi-square Results for the Xylitol and Ear Infection Data

Minitab output for testing the significance of the Xylitol and ear infection relationship is displayed in Figure 15.2 (see next page). Toward the bottom of the output, we see that the p-value is 0.035, which is below the usual significance level standard of 0.05. As a result, we can conclude that there is a statistically significant relationship between the risk of an ear infection and the preventative treatment used. Notice that expected counts are shown below observed counts in the results and that values for the chi-square statistic and the degrees of freedom are also given. There are three rows and two columns, so the degrees of freedom are df = (3 − 1)(2 − 1) = 2. ◆

```
Rows:        Treatment    Columns:     Infectn

             No           Yes          All
Placebo      129          49           178
             138.93       39.07        178.00

Xyl Gum      150          29           179
             139.71       39.29        179.00

Xyl Loz      137          39           176
             137.37       38.63        176.00

All          416          117          533
             416.00       117.00       533.00

Chi-Square = 6.690,   DF = 2,   P-Value = 0.035

Cell Contents:   Observed
                 Expected
```

FIGURE 15.2   **Minitab output for Example 15.1**

Interpreting and Calculating Expected Counts

The expected counts in a chi-square analysis are the counts that would be expected to occur if the null hypotheses were true. Three important properties of the expected counts for a two-way table are

- The expected counts have the same row and column totals as the observed counts.
- The pattern of row percents is identical for all rows of expected counts.
- The pattern of column percents is identical for all columns of expected counts.

Calculating Expected Counts

formula   For each cell in a two-way table,

$$\text{Expected count} = \frac{\text{Row total} \times \text{Column total}}{\text{Total } n}$$

"Row total" is the total sample size in the row, "Column total" is the total sample size in the column, and "Total n" is the total sample size over the entire table.

There are several equivalent ways to derive the formula for calculating the expected counts. For instance, we could utilize the property that the row percents would be identical for all rows if the null hypothesis were true. In Table 15.1 for the Xylitol and ear infection example, the proportion that experienced an ear infection in the total sample was 117/533. Note that this is the sample size in the second column divided by the total sample size. Under the null hypothesis, the proportion experiencing an ear infection is the same for all treatments, so the quantity 117/533 estimates the *proportion* with an ear infection for any treatment. For any treatment, the expected *count* of those who would get an ear infection can be determined by multiplying the sample size for the treatment (a row total) by the overall proportion with an ear infection (column total/total n). The same argument could be made for the expected counts of those who do not get an ear infection.

EXAMPLE 15.1—*CONTINUED*
*Calculation of
Expected Counts
and Chi-square for
the Xylitol and
Ear Infection Data*

Consider the "Placebo Gum, Yes Ear Infection" cell. There are 178 observations in the "Placebo Gum" row, and 117 observations in the "Yes Ear Infection" column. For the cell in question, the expected count is

$$\frac{\text{Row total} \times \text{Column total}}{\text{Total } n} = \frac{178 \times 117}{533} = 39.07$$

The calculation of all expected counts for this example is shown in Table 15.3. The calculation of the chi-square statistic is

$$\chi^2 = \sum_{\text{all cells}} \frac{(\text{Observed} - \text{Expected})^2}{\text{Expected}}$$

$$= \frac{(129 - 138.93)^2}{138.93} + \frac{(49 - 39.07)^2}{39.07} + \frac{(150 - 139.71)^2}{139.71} + \frac{(29 - 39.29)^2}{39.29}$$

$$+ \frac{(137 - 137.37)^2}{137.37} + \frac{(39 - 38.63)^2}{38.63} = 6.69 \; \blacklozenge$$

Step 3: The p-Value for the Chi-square Test

The p-value for a chi-square test is the probability that the chi-square statistic could have been as large or larger if the null hypotheses were true. This probability is determined using a chi-square distribution with degrees of freedom = (Rows − 1)(Columns − 1) = $(r - 1)(c - 1)$, where r = Rows is the number of rows in the contingency table and c = Columns is the number of columns. This number is equivalent to the minimum number of cells for which expected counts need to be computed by the formula. The remaining expected counts are then determined by the fact that the row and column totals are fixed in advance. For instance, in the 3×2 table in Example 15.1, once you compute $(3 - 1) \times (2 - 1) = 2$ expected counts, the rest are determined by the row and column totals. So you are only "free" to fill in two cells before the others are determined. In Table 15.3, notice that after the counts of 138.93 and 139.71 had been computed, the rest of the counts could be found by subtraction from knowing what the row and column totals must be.

TABLE 15.3 ■ Calculation of Expected Counts for Example 15.1

	No Ear Infection	Yes Ear Infection	Row Total
Placebo Gum	$\frac{178 \times 416}{533} = 138.93$	$\frac{178 \times 117}{533} = 39.07$	178
Xylitol Gum	$\frac{179 \times 416}{533} = 139.71$	$\frac{179 \times 117}{533} = 39.29$	179
Xylitol Lozenge	$\frac{176 \times 416}{533} = 137.37$	$\frac{176 \times 117}{533} = 38.63$	176
Column Total	416	117	533

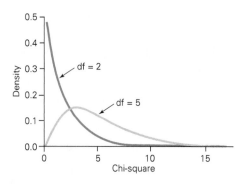

FIGURE 15.3   Two different chi-square distributions

> **formula**   For the chi-square statistic for a two-way table,
>
> $$\text{Degrees of freedom} = (r - 1)(c - 1)$$
>
> r = number of rows in the table, and c = number of columns in the table.

The Chi-square Family of Distributions

A **chi-square distribution** is a skewed probability distribution that stretches to the right. The minimum value is 0 for a variable with a chi-square distribution. A single parameter, called *degrees of freedom,* completely determines the precise characteristics of a specific chi-square distribution. Figure 15.3 shows a chi-square distribution with 2 degrees of freedom and also shows a chi-square distribution with 5 degrees of freedom.

EXAMPLE 15.1—*CONTINUED*
p-Value for the
Xylitol Example

Figure 15.4 illustrates the *p*-value area for the Xylitol and ear infection problem. The chi-square statistic was 6.69, degrees of freedom = $(3 - 1)(2 - 1) = 2$, and the *p*-value is the probability that a chi-square statistic with df = 2 would be 6.69 or larger. This is the area to the right of 6.69 under a chi-square probability density curve (df = 2). ◆

Three Ways to Determine the *p*-Value

The chi-square test for two-way tables is used so frequently that any statistical software program will include this procedure and provide the *p*-value necessary

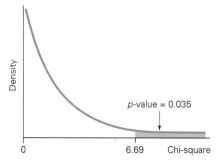

FIGURE 15.4   *p*-Value for Example 15.1

for deciding between the null and alternative hypotheses about the table. Some of you might not be using statistical software, however, so we consider three different ways to determine the p-value:

- Use statistical software to do the chi-square test. The p-value will be part of the output (as in Figure 15.1 of this chapter).

- Use the Excel command CHIDIST(chi-square value, df). This command will return the area to the right of the value you specify. For instance, CHIDIST (6.69,2) returns 0.035, the p-value for Example 15.1.

- Use Table A.5 in the Appendix to give a range for the p-value.

Using Table A.5 to Approximate the p-Value

First, determine the degrees of freedom for your two-way table. Then, look in the corresponding "df" row of Table A.5. Scan across that row until you locate approximately where the calculated chi-square statistic falls.

- If the value of the chi-square statistic falls between two table entries, the p-value is between the values of p (column headings) for these two entries.

- If the value of the chi-square statistic is larger than the entry in the rightmost column (labeled $p = 0.001$), the p-value is less than 0.001 (written as $p < 0.001$).

- If the value of the chi-square statistic is smaller than the entry in the leftmost column (labeled $p = 0.50$), the p-value is greater than 0.50 ($p > 0.50$).

EXAMPLE 15.3
A Moderate p-Value

Suppose that a two-way table has three rows and three columns and the chi-square statistic is $\chi^2 = 8.12$. The degrees of freedom are df $= (3 - 1)(3 - 1) = 4$. To find the p-value, we scan the df $= 4$ row in Table A.5 and learn that 8.12 is between the entries 7.78 ($p = 0.10$) and 8.50 ($p = 0.075$). Thus, the p-value is between 0.075 and 0.10. We would write this as $0.075 < p\text{-value} < 0.10$. Or, often it is written simply as $0.075 < p < 0.10$. In Excel, the command CHIDIST (8.12,4) tells us that the p-value is 0.087. ◆

EXAMPLE 15.4
A Tiny p-Value

Suppose that a two-way table has four rows and two columns and the chi-square statistic is $\chi^2 = 17.67$. The degrees of freedom are $(4 - 1)(2 - 1) = 3$. In Table A.5, we see that 17.67 is larger than the rightmost entry in the df $= 3$ row, so the p-value is less than 0.001 ($p < 0.001$). In Excel, the command CHIDIST (17.67,3) tells us that the p-value is 0.00051. ◆

15.1

turn on your mind

Consider Example 15.2 about gender and the question about with whom it's easiest to make friends. What are the degrees of freedom for the chi-square statistic for these data? To be statistically significant at the 0.05 level, how large would the calculated chi-square have to be?*

Steps 4 and 5: Making a Decision and Reporting a Conclusion

An approximate *p*-value, or even a range for the *p*-value, is enough information to make a decision about the null hypothesis. If we use the 0.05 significance level, we simply have to determine whether the *p*-value is less than 0.05. In Example 15.3, for instance, we learned from Table A.5 that the *p*-value is between 0.075 and 0.10. Thus, we know that it is not less than 0.05 and we would fail to reject the null hypothesis.

The value in the 0.05 column of Table A.5 is referred to as the **critical value** for the 0.05 significance level. The region of chi-square values greater than the critical value is called the **rejection region.** The *p*-value will be less than 0.05 when the chi-square statistic is greater than this critical value, in other words, if the chi-square statistic is in the rejection region. Consequently, if the level of significance is $\alpha = 0.05$, two equivalent rules for declaring statistical significance based on a chi-square statistic are

- ◆ Reject the null hypothesis when the *p*-value is less than 0.05.
- ◆ Reject the null hypothesis when the chi-square statistic is greater than the entry in the 0.05 column of Table A.5 (the critical value), in other words, when the chi-square statistic is in the rejection region.

Reporting a Conclusion in Context

Remember that the two possible conclusions for hypothesis tests are "Do not reject the null hypothesis" or "Reject the null hypothesis." The latter conclusion is equivalent to "accept the alternative hypothesis" or "conclude that the results are statistically significant."

In chi-square tests for two-way tables, it is important to write these conclusions in context. Suppose we were testing whether there is a relationship between smoking (yes or no) and drinking alcohol (never, occasionally, often). Here are various ways to write the possible conclusions.

Ways to write the conclusion "do not reject the null hypothesis"

- ◆ The relationship between smoking and drinking alcohol is not statistically significant.
- ◆ The proportions of smokers who never drink, drink occasionally, and drink often are not significantly different from the proportions of nonsmokers who do so.
- ◆ There is insufficient evidence to conclude that there is a relationship in the population between smoking and drinking alcohol.

Ways to write the conclusion "reject the null hypothesis"

- ◆ There is a statistically significant relationship between smoking and drinking alcohol.
- ◆ The proportions of smokers in the population who never drink, drink occasionally, and drink often are not the same as the proportions of nonsmokers who do so.
- ◆ Smokers have significantly different drinking behavior than nonsmokers.

EXAMPLE 15.2—*CONTINUED*
Making Friends

Figure 15.5 shows partial Minitab output for a chi-square test of the relationship between sex and response to the question "With whom is it easiest to make

```
Expected counts are printed below observed counts

            Opposite    Same    No Diff    Total
Female         58         16        63        137
             48.79      19.38     68.83

Male           15         13        40         68
             24.21       9.62     34.17

Total          73         29       103        205

Chi-Sq =    1.740 + 0.590 + 0.494 +
            3.507 + 1.188 + 0.996 = 8.515
```

FIGURE 15.5   **Minitab output for Example 15.2**

friends?" Recall that the possible responses concerned the sex of the friends. In the last line of output, we see that the chi-square statistic is 8.515. Although Minitab provides the p-value, this value has been omitted to provide practice using Table A.5, the chi-square distribution table. The contingency table has two rows and three columns, so df $= (2 - 1)(3 - 1) = 2$. In the df $= 2$ row of Table A.5, the computed chi-square falls between the entries in the 0.025 column (7.38) and the 0.01 column (9.21). The p-value is between 0.01 and 0.025, so the result is statistically significant if we use the standard 0.05 significance level.

Equivalently, find the critical value in Table A.5. Using the df $= 2$ row and the 0.05 column, the critical value is 5.99. Reject the null hypothesis because the computed chi-square statistic of 8.515 is greater than the critical value of 5.99.

In the context of the situation, the conclusion is that there is a statistically significant relationship between sex and response to the question asked. Equivalently, conclude that there would be a difference in the distribution of responses of men and women if the populations of them were asked this question. Using the bar chart of row percents shown in Figure 15.1 (p. 530), we can describe the nature of the difference between the females and males. Compared to men, women are more likely to say "opposite sex" and less likely to say "same sex." ◆

Supporting Analyses

We don't learn anything about the specific nature of a relationship from a chi-square test. The results of a statistically significant chi-square test should be accompanied by some other descriptive or inferential statistics that elaborate on the connection between the variables. Some or all of the following procedures may be useful for this purpose:

- ◆ Description of row (or column) percents.

- ◆ Bar chart of counts or percents.

- ◆ Examination of $\dfrac{(\text{Observed} - \text{Expected})^2}{\text{Expected}}$ within each cell. These values are called "contributions to chi-square." The cells with the largest values have contributed the most to the statistical significance of the relationship, so they deserve attention in any description of the relationship.

- ◆ Confidence intervals for important proportions or for differences between proportions. In Example 15.1, for instance, confidence intervals for the proportions getting an ear infection in the three treatment groups would be informative.

---

in summary | **The Five Steps in a Chi-square Test of a Relationship Between Two Variables**

Step 1: *Determine the null and alternative hypotheses.*

Null hypothesis: H_0: The two variables are not related.

Alternative hypothesis: H_a: The two variables are related.

Step 2: *Verify necessary data conditions, and if met, summarize the data into an appropriate test statistic.* If at least 80% of the expected counts are greater than 5 and none are less than 1, compute

$$\chi^2 = \sum_{\text{all cells}} \frac{(\text{Observed} - \text{Expected})^2}{\text{Expected}}$$

The *expected count* for a cell is computed as $\dfrac{\text{Row total} \times \text{Column total}}{\text{Total } n}$.

Step 3: *Assuming the null hypothesis is true, find the p-value.* Using the χ^2 distribution with df $= (r - 1)(c - 1)$, where $r =$ number of rows and $c =$ number of columns in the two-way table, the *p*-value is the area in the tail to the right of the calculated test statistic χ^2.

Step 4: *Decide whether or not the result is statistically significant based on the p-value.* Choose a significance level ("alpha"); the standard is $\alpha = 0.05$. The result is statistically significant if the *p*-value $\leq \alpha$.

Step 5: *Report the conclusion in the context of the situation.*

Minitab Tip

tech note   **Computing a Chi-square Test for a Two-Way Table**

◆ If the raw data are stored in columns of the worksheet, use **Stat>Tables>Cross Tabulation.** In the dialog box, specify the two columns of interest and also click on ***Chi-square analysis.***

◆ If the data are already summarized into counts, enter the table of counts into columns of the worksheet and then use **Stat>Tables>Chi-Square Test.** In the dialog box, specify the columns containing the counts.

15.2 | ANALYZING 2 × 2 TABLES

There are a number of special circumstances that apply to analyzing 2 × 2 tables. First, there is a handy computational shortcut for computing the chi-square statistic for a 2 × 2 table that does not require computing expected counts. It can be accomplished with a calculator, without needing to write down any intermediate results.

Shortcut Formula for a 2 × 2 Table

Suppose we label a 2 × 2 table as follows:

	Column 1	Column 2	Total
Row 1	A	B	R_1
Row 2	C	D	R_2
Total	C_1	C_2	N

Then the test statistic is

$$\chi^2 = \frac{N(AD - BC)^2}{R_1 R_2 C_1 C_2}$$

with df = 1.

EXAMPLE 6.10—*CONTINUED* *Order and Choice of S or Q*   In Example 6.10 of Chapter 6, we examined the results of a survey in which students were asked to "Randomly choose one of the letters S or Q" or "Randomly choose one of the letters Q or S." The Minitab output for examining the relationship between the form of the question and the letter picked is shown in Example 6.10 and again here.

Minitab Output for the *S* or *Q* Experiment (Example 6.10)

Expected counts are printed below observed counts

	Letter Picked		
Form	S	Q	Total
S first	61	31	92
	51.33	40.67	
Q first	45	53	98
	54.67	43.33	
Total	106	84	190

Chi-Sq = 1.823 + 2.301 +
         1.712 + 2.160 = 7.995
DF = 1,   P-Value = 0.005

The value of the chi-square statistic is 7.995. The shortcut formula results in precisely the same value and is found as follows:

$$\chi^2 = \frac{N(AD - BC)^2}{R_1 R_2 C_1 C_2} = \frac{190(61 \times 53 - 31 \times 45)^2}{92 \times 98 \times 106 \times 84} = 7.995$$

The remaining steps of the test are the same as always. ◆

Chi-square Test or *z*-Test for Difference in Two Proportions?

In Section 13.4, we learned that a *z*-test can be used to compare two proportions. In such situations, we also can create a 2 × 2 table of the observed counts. The two groups would constitute the two rows, and whether or not the trait of interest is present would constitute the two columns. When the data are presented as a contingency table, we may naturally consider using a chi-square test. Does it make a difference whether we choose to use the z-test of Section 13.4 or the chi-square test to compare two proportions? The answer depends upon the nature of the alternative hypothesis. If the desired alternative hypothesis has no specific direction (is two-sided), the two tests give exactly the same p-value. If the desired alternative hypothesis has a direction (is one-sided), the z-test should be used because in a chi-square test a specific direction cannot be specified in the alternative hypothesis.

The only essential difference between the two tests is the ability to specify a one-sided alternative hypothesis. In fact, there is an algebraic connection between the values of the test statistics for the two procedures. For any 2×2 table, the squared value of the z-statistic equals the chi-square statistic ($z^2 = \chi^2$). Or, put another way, $|z| = \sqrt{\chi^2}$. This connection between the test statistics is also the connection between the theoretical standard normal distribution and the theoretical chi-square distribution with df = 1.

15.2

turn on your mind

Suppose that you read that men are more likely to be left-handed than women are. To investigate this claim, you survey your class and find that 11 of 84 men and 7 of 78 women are left-handed. Should you compare the men and women using a z-test or a chi-square test? Or does it matter?*

EXAMPLE 15.5
Age and Tension Headaches

Exercise 12.46 was about a study for which the response variable was whether or not the respondent had experienced an episodic tension-type headache during the previous year (Schwartz et al., 1998). Table 15.4 is a contingency table that compares the incidence of tension headaches for women 18 to 29 years old and women 30 to 39 years old.

Let p_1 and p_2 represent the proportions experiencing tension headaches in the populations of women aged 18 to 29 and women aged 30 to 39, respectively. Because the researchers did not speculate about the possible relative sizes of p_1 and p_2, the alternative hypothesis is two-sided. Null and alternative hypotheses are

$H_0: p_1 = p_2$
$H_a: p_1 \neq p_2$

TABLE 15.4 ■ **Age Group and the Incidence of Tension Headaches**

| Age | Episodic Tension Headaches | | Total |
	Yes	No	
18 to 29	653 (40.8%)	947 (59.2%)	1600
30 to 39	995 (46.9%)	1127 (53.1%)	2122
Total	1648 (44.3%)	2074 (57.7%)	3722

The null hypothesis is equivalent to stating that there isn't a relationship between age group and the risk of episodic tension headaches. In this example, we can use either a chi-square test or a two-sample z-test because no specific direction is specified in the alternative hypothesis. Using statistical software (Minitab) to do a chi-square test, we found that $\chi^2 = 13.66$ and the p-value was reported to be 0.000 (only three decimal places were given). The observed relationship between age group and the incidence of tension headaches is statistically significant, and the row percents show us that the older women are more likely to experience tension headaches. If we had done a z-test for comparing two proportions, the value of z would have been $z = \sqrt{13.66} \approx 3.70$, and the p-value would have been identical to the p-value for the chi-square test. ◆

EXAMPLE 15.6
Sheep, Goats, and ESP

In parapsychology, the sheep–goat effect is that people who believe in extrasensory perception (sheep) tend to be more successful in ESP experiments than people who do not (goats). The effect is slight, but it has been observed in many forced-choice ESP experiments (Lawrence, 1993; Schmeidler, 1988, pp. 56–58). In a forced-choice experiment, the participant "guesses" which of several known possibilities has been (or will be) selected by the experimenter.

Students in a statistics class at the University of California at Davis classified themselves as sheep (believers) or goats (nonbelievers). Among 192 students, there were 112 sheep and 80 goats. Each student was paired with another student in the same belief group. One member of each pair flipped a coin ten times while the other member guessed the outcome of each flip. Students then reversed their roles and repeated the flipping, so each person was able to make ten guesses. The guessing process was uncontrolled, as each student could decide whether he or she would guess in advance of the flip, during the flip, or after the flip. Table 15.5 displays data for the numbers of successful and unsuccessful guesses in each group. The sheep did slightly better than the goats, guessing correctly about 52% of the time compared to 49% for the goats.

The activity was done to determine whether sheep would do better, so a one-sided alternative hypothesis is appropriate. Define p_1 and p_2 to be the population proportions of successful guesses for sheep and goats. The null and alternative hypotheses of interest are

$$H_0: p_1 \leq p_2$$
$$H_a: p_1 > p_2$$

A z-test for comparing two proportions should be done rather than a chi-square test because the alternative hypothesis describes a relationship in a specific direction. Figure 15.6 displays Minitab output for this test. From the bottom line of output, we learn that the p-value is 0.075. The null hypothesis cannot be rejected at the 0.05 significance level. ◆

TABLE 15.5 ■ ESP Belief and Success at Guessing Coin Flips

Group	Successful Guess		Total
	Yes	*No*	*Total*
Sheep (Believers)	582 (52%)	538 (48%)	1120
Goats (Nonbelievers)	389 (49%)	411 (51%)	800
Total	971 (51%)	949 (49%)	1920

```
Sample       X        N       Sample p
1           582      1120     0.519643
2           389       800     0.486250

Estimate for p(1) − p(2): 0.0333929
Test for p(1) − p(2) = 0 (vs > 0): Z = 1.44   P-Value = 0.075
```

FIGURE 15.6   **Minitab output for Example 15.6**

Fisher's Exact Test for 2 × 2 Tables

For 2 × 2 tables, **Fisher's Exact Test** is another test that can be used to analyze the statistical significance of the relationship. In theory, this test can be used for any 2 × 2 table, but most commonly it is used when necessary sample size conditions for using the z-test or the chi-square test are violated. In large part, this has to do with computational difficulties that occur for large sample sizes.

Although the computations are cumbersome, the idea behind Fisher's Exact Test is easy. Suppose, for example, that a randomized experiment is done to see if taking the herb echinacea reduces the risk of getting a cold, and the observed data are 1 of 10 people taking echinacea get a cold during the study while 4 of 10 taking a placebo get a cold. In all, 5 of the 20 participants got a cold, but only 1 was in the echinacea group. The p-value for a one-sided Fisher's Exact Test is the answer to this question:

> *Given that 5 of 20 participants get a cold regardless of treatment method, what is the probability that just 1 or fewer would be in the echinacea group?*

Notice that the test statistic is simply the count of how many got a cold in the echinacea group. As always, the p-value question addresses how likely it is that the test statistic would be as extreme or more extreme as it is in the direction of the alternative hypothesis if the null hypothesis is true. The answer (it's 0.152) is determined using a probability distribution called the *hypergeometric distribution,* which is discussed further in Supplemental Topic 1 on the CD accompanying this book.

Some, but not all, statistical software programs include the Fisher's Exact Test. The Statistical Package for the Social Sciences (SPSS) does, but Minitab does not (as of Version 13). Several websites provide a calculator designed to give the p-value for Fisher's Exact Test.

EXAMPLE 15.7
Butterfly Ballots   The winner of the 2000 United States presidential election (George W. Bush) was not determined until about a month after election day. There were several court hearings in Florida about the legality of vote counting and voting procedures in that state. One of the Florida controversies concerned a ballot format called the butterfly ballot used in Palm Beach County. Candidates were listed in two columns, and to indicate a choice, a voter punched a hole in the appropriate place in an area between the two columns of names. The first three presidential candidates were listed as follows:

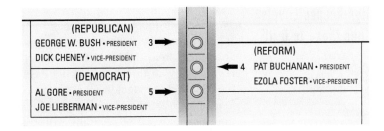

After the election, several Palm Beach County voters said they meant to vote for Al Gore, but mistakenly voted for Pat Buchanan, the Reform Party candidate. These voters said they punched a hole in the second punch location because they saw Al Gore's name listed second in the left column. That location, however, was for Pat Buchanan who was listed in the right column. Perhaps not coincidentally, Buchanan's vote total in Palm Beach County was decidedly higher than expected.

A brief communication published in *Nature* (Sinclair et al., 2000) gave results from an experiment done in Canada to study whether the butterfly ballot increases the likelihood of voter mistakes. Shortly after the United States election, the researchers recruited people in an Edmonton, Alberta, shopping mall to vote in a mock election for the prime minister of Canada. Participants were randomly assigned to use either the double-column butterfly format or the more conventional single-column format. After they voted, the participants were asked for whom they voted. Of 55 voters using the butterfly format, four voted for a different candidate than they intended. Of 52 voters using the single-column format, none made a mistake.

Is the observed result statistically significant? Define p_1 = population proportion that makes a mistake with the butterfly ballot and p_2 = population proportion that makes a mistake with the single-column ballot. The null and alternative hypotheses of interest are

$H_0: p_1 \leq p_2$
$H_a: p_1 > p_2$

The observed counts don't satisfy the necessary conditions for doing a z-test, which are that at least five observations with and without the trait of interest should be observed in each group (see Section 13.4). Fisher's Exact Test is more appropriate for these data, and the *p*-value can be determined by answering this question:

Given that 4 of 107 participants will make a mistake, what is the probability that all 4 are among the 55 voters randomly selected to use the butterfly ballot?

The answer is 0.0661, a *p*-value not quite below the usual 0.05 standard for statistical significance. It is important to note, however, that given that 4 participants will make a mistake, the evidence for the alternative is as strong as possible since all 4 were using the butterfly format, so it may be reasonable to use a higher level of significance and reject the null hypothesis. Also, the researchers asked all participants to rate the confusion level of the ballot they used on a 7-point scale, with 7 representing the most confusing. The mean confusion score for the butterfly ballot was significantly higher than for the single-column format. ◆

**Significance Levels
and *p*-Values Close to 0.05**

tech note   Although we have used the common standard of rejecting the
null hypothesis when the *p*-value ≤ 0.05, there is nothing magic
about 0.05. In Examples 15.6 and 15.7, the *p*-values were 0.075 and 0.0661,
respectively. In these and similar cases it is up to you as the reader of
the research to decide whether or not to reject the null hypothesis.
Remember that the level of significance used corresponds to the conditional probability of rejecting a true null hypothesis. Sometimes there
may be reasons to set that at a higher (or lower) level than 0.05. Where
to set the cutoff is something that you as a reader should always decide,
which is why it is important for researchers to report *p*-values rather
than to simply report a decision about whether or not to reject the null
hypothesis.

15.3 | TESTING HYPOTHESES ABOUT ONE CATEGORICAL VARIABLE: GOODNESS OF FIT

15.3

turn on your mind

Imagine tossing a six-sided die 60 times. How many times would you expect each side to occur? What did you assume when you calculated these
expected counts? How would you measure the difference between the
observed and expected counts of how often each side occurs in the 60
tosses?*

We sometimes wish to test whether the probabilities of falling into the possible
categories of a single categorical variable are given by a specified set of values.
For example, if a lottery drawing involves randomly drawing digits between 0
and 9, we may wish to analyze observed data to confirm that the probability
over the long run is 1/10 for drawing each of the ten digits from 0 to 9. With two
modifications from how it is applied to two-way tables, the chi-square statistic
can be used to test hypotheses about the probability distribution of a single categorical variable. In such instances, the significance test is called the **chi-square
goodness of fit test.**

The first modification of the chi-square procedure necessary for the goodness of fit situation involves the calculation of the expected counts. This calculation is straightforward and intuitively obvious. Suppose we hypothesize,
for example, that 45% of a population has brown eyes, 35% has blue eyes, and
20% has an eye color other than brown or blue. If we randomly select $n = 200$
persons from this population, it probably makes sense to you that we would
expect about 45% of 200 $= .45 \times 200 = 90$ persons to have brown eyes if our
hypothesis is correct. We also would expect about $.35 \times 200 = 70$ persons to
have blue eyes, and $.20 \times 200 = 40$ persons to have an eye color other than
brown or blue.

The other modification of the chi-square procedure concerns the degrees of freedom. For a goodness of fit test, the degrees of freedom are computed as $df = k - 1$, where k is the number of categories for the variable of interest. In the eye color example of the previous paragraph, there were three eye color categories. Consequently, the degrees of freedom for a chi-square goodness of fit test would be $df = 3 - 1 = 2$.

15.4

turn on your mind

Remember that the "degrees of freedom" for the chi-square test for a two-way table represents the largest number of cells for which you were "free" to find expected counts. The remaining expected counts were determined because the row and column totals had to be the same as they were for the observed counts. Explain how the same principle applies in specifying the degrees of freedom for a chi-square goodness of fit test, which are $k - 1$ when there are k categories.*

in summary The Five Steps in a Chi-square Goodness of Fit Test

Step 1: *Determine the null and alternative hypotheses.*

Null hypothesis: H_0: The probabilities for the k categories of a categorical variable are given by $p_1, p_2, \ldots, p_k$.

Alternative hypothesis: H_a: Not all probabilities specified in H_0 are correct.

Note: The probabilities specified in the null hypothesis must sum to 1.

Step 2: *Verify necessary data conditions, and if met, summarize the data into an appropriate test statistic.* If at least 80% of the expected counts are greater than 5 and none are less than 1, compute

$$\chi^2 = \sum_{\text{all categories}} \frac{(\text{Observed} - \text{Expected})^2}{\text{Expected}}$$

where the expected count for the ith category is computed as np_i.

Step 3: *Assuming the null hypothesis is true, find the p-value.* Using the χ^2 distribution with $df = k - 1$, the p-value is the area in the tail beyond the test statistic χ^2.

Step 4: *Decide whether or not the result is statistically significant based on the p-value.* Choose a significance level ("alpha"); the standard is $\alpha = 0.05$. The result is statistically significant if the p-value $\leq \alpha$. Equivalently, the result is statistically significant if the test statistic χ^2 is at least as large as the value in the α column and $df = k - 1$ row of Table A.5.

Step 5: *Report the conclusion in the context of the situation.*

*HINT: The total expected count must equal the total observed count. If you know $k - 1$ expected counts, what must the remaining one be?

EXAMPLE 15.8
The Pennsylvania
Daily Number

The Pennsylvania Daily Number is a state lottery game in which the state constructs a three-digit number by drawing a digit between 0 and 9 from each of three different containers. If the digits drawn, in order, were 3, 6, and 3, for example, then the daily number would be 363. In this example, we focus only on draws from the first container. If numbers are randomly selected, each value between 0 and 9 would be equally likely to occur. This leads to the following null hypothesis:

$$H_0: p = \frac{1}{10} \text{ for each of the 10 possible digits in first container}$$

Simply stated, the alternative hypothesis is that the null hypothesis is false. In this setting, that would mean that the probability of selection for some digits is different from 1/10.

Figure 15.7 shows the frequency distribution of draws from the first container for the $n = 500$ days between July 19, 1999 and November 29, 2000. The observed data were downloaded from the Pennsylvania lottery website. The expected count for each of the 10 possible outcomes is $1/10 \times 500 = 50$, and the red dashed line in the figure marks this value. The greatest difference between observed and expected occurs for the number 5, which was drawn from the first container only 39 times over these 500 days.

The chi-square goodness of fit statistic for these data is

$$\chi^2 = \sum_{\text{categories}} \frac{(\text{Observed} - \text{Expected})^2}{\text{Expected}}$$

$$= \frac{(47-50)^2}{50} + \frac{(50-50)^2}{50} + \frac{(55-50)^2}{50} + \frac{(46-50)^2}{50} + \frac{(53-50)^2}{50}$$

$$+ \frac{(39-50)^2}{50} + \frac{(55-50)^2}{50} + \frac{(55-50)^2}{50} + \frac{(44-50)^2}{50} + \frac{(56-50)^2}{50} = 6.04$$

There are ten possible outcomes for the number drawn, so df = 10 − 1 = 9. To find the *p*-value, we find the probability that a chi-square statistic would be as large as or larger than 6.04 using a chi-square distribution with df = 9. From Table A.5, the chi-square distribution table, we learn that the *p*-value is greater than 0.50 because 6.04 is smaller than (to the left of) the entry of 8.34 under 0.50 in the row for df = 9. The Excel command CHIDIST(6.04,9)

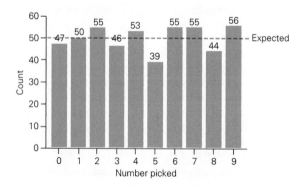

FIGURE 15.7 **Observed and expected counts for first digit drawn in the Pennsylvania Daily Number Game, July 19, 1999 through November 29, 2000**

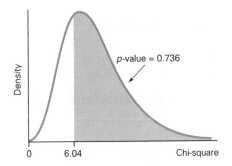

FIGURE 15.8   *p*-Value for Example 15.8 is area to right of 6.04 in chi-square distribution with df = 9

provides the information that the *p*-value is 0.736. This *p*-value is illustrated in Figure 15.8. The result is not statistically significant; the null hypothesis is not rejected. ◆

Mathematical Notation for Chi-square Goodness of Fit Statistic

tech note   The following mathematical notation can be used for the chi-square goodness of fit test:

O_i = observed count in the *i*th category

p_i = hypothesized probability for the *i*th category

$E_i = np_i$ = expected count in *i*th category

$$\chi^2 = \sum_i \frac{(O_i - E_i)^2}{E_i}$$

k = number of categories; df = $k - 1$

Sample Size and the Goodness of Fit Test

The null hypothesis often is the desired hypothesis for the investigators when they do a goodness of fit test. In Example 15.8 about the Pennsylvania Daily Number, lottery officials would hope to "prove" that all numbers have an equal chance to be selected. This creates a technical and logical difficulty because with a small sample, a null hypothesis might be retained simply because there is not enough data to reject it. This was the basis for the advice given in Chapter 11 to use the phrase "cannot reject the null" rather than "accept the null." If the goal is to not reject the null hypothesis, the most scientifically valid approach is to use as large a sample as possible. This prevents the possible criticism that the null hypothesis was retained only because the sample was not large enough to provide conclusive evidence. On the other hand, the risk of a large sample size is that small, relatively unimportant departures from the null hypothesis can achieve statistical significance. It is often useful to include confidence intervals for the parameters if possible, to determine the magnitude of departures from the null hypothesis.

Minitab Tip

> **tech note** **Calculating the Chi-square Statistic for Goodness of Fit**
>
> Minitab does not have a chi-square goodness of fit procedure, but it is not difficult to compute the chi-square statistic using the Minitab calculator. The basic steps are
>
> ◆ Enter the observed counts into a column. Suppose it is C1.
>
> ◆ Enter the null hypothesis proportions into a second column. Suppose it is C2.
>
> ◆ Use **Calc>Calculator.** Create a column of expected counts by multiplying C2 by the total sample size. Suppose it is C3.
>
> ◆ Again use **Calc>Calculator.** Create (by computation) a column (say, C4) that contains a chi-square value. Given the column designations of the previous steps, the expression is SUM((C1−C3)**2/C3). Look carefully at the parenthesis locations. You can also compute (C1−C3)**2/C3 and store the results in C4, then sum C4. That will allow you to determine which categories are contributing the most to the value of the test statistic.

CASE STUDY 15.1
Do You Mind If I Eat the Blue Ones?

You'll find six different colors of M&Ms in a bag of plain M&Ms: brown, red, yellow, blue, orange, and green. If you're like some people, you may have a color preference (or dislike) when it comes to eating M&Ms and might have fleeting thoughts about what the color distribution is or should be. At the M&Ms website (http://www.m-ms.com/factory/history/faq1.html), the distribution of colors for plain M&Ms is given as: brown 30%, red 20%, yellow 20%, blue 10%, orange 10%, and green 10%.

Students in a University of California at Davis statistics class (Fall 2000 term) counted the frequency of each color among 6918 plain M&Ms from about 130 small (1.69 ounces) bags. All bags were purchased at the same store in California. The observed distribution of colors in this sample was

	Color					
	Brown	Red	Yellow	Blue	Orange	Green
Count	1911	1072	1308	804	821	1002
Percent	27.6%	15.5%	18.9%	11.6%	11.9%	14.5%
Expected %	30%	20%	20%	10%	10%	10%

Generally, the observed percents in the UC Davis data are not far from the percents advertised by the manufacturer, but some differences are evident. Most notably (especially for those who like red M&Ms), there were fewer red and more green candies than expected.

We can use a chi-square goodness of fit test to determine if the difference between the expected and observed distributions is statistically significant. If we assign numbers to colors using the order in which the colors are listed above (1 = brown, 2 = red, and so on), the null hypothesis of interest is

$$H_0: p_1 = .3, p_2 = .2, p_3 = .2, p_4 = .1, p_5 = .1, p_6 = .1$$

The first step in computing the chi-square statistic is to calculate the expected counts for each color. To do so, multiply the null hypothesis proportion for a color by the total sample size, $n = 6918$. For example, the expected count for brown is $.3 \times 6918 = 2075.4$. Figure 15.9 displays expected counts and observed counts for each color. As noted before, the largest differences between observed and expected counts occur for red and green.

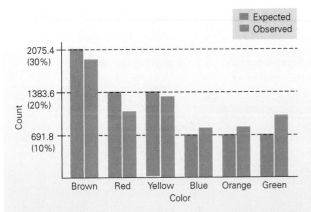

FIGURE 15.9   **Observed and expected counts for a sample of 6918 plain M&Ms**

The chi-square goodness of fit statistic for these data is $\chi^2 = 268.75$, with degrees of freedom = number of categories $- 1 = 6 - 1 = 5$. In Table A.5, the entry under 0.001 for df = 5 is 20.51. The computed chi-square statistic, 268.75, is so much larger than 20.51 that it's reasonable to say that the p-value is essentially 0. The result is highly significant in that it would be nearly impossible for a random sample of 6918 M&Ms to have a color distribution that differed from the null hypothesis distribution by as much (or more) as the observed sample does.

This experiment provided an opportunity to examine the data in another interesting way. Twenty-five student teams sorted and counted the M&Ms; for most teams, the sample size was approximately 275 (five bags). A separate chi-square statistic was computed for each team's sample, and statistical significance was achieved for most, but not all, samples. For 16 of the 25 samples, the p-value was less than 0.05, and in most of these cases, the p-value was much less than 0.05.

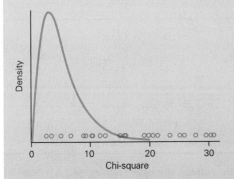

FIGURE 15.10   **Chi-square values for 25 samples of M&Ms and the chi-square distribution for df = 5**

Figure 15.10 shows the chi-square distribution for 5 degrees of freedom along with the 25 calculated chi-square values, indicated by the blue circles along the horizontal axis. If many, many chi-square tests are performed and the null hypothesis is always true, Figure 15.10 illustrates that when df = 5, the test statistic should generally fall between 0 and about 10. In fact, when df = 5, the *critical value* for the 0.05 significance level is 11.07 (look under 0.05 in Table A.5). Computed chi-square values of 11.07 or more are statistically significant. We see that the majority of the computed chi-square values were greater than 11.07, and several were much greater than 11.07. Such large chi-square values offer strong evidence against the null hypothesis. The results summarized in Figure 15.10 also show us why it's useful to replicate studies. Although the results were not significant for a few teams, the consistency of the significance over most teams helps us believe that there is a real difference.

After obtaining these results, one of the authors posted a message about them to an internet "listserv" for teachers of Advanced Placement statistics courses. She received several replies from other instructors who had done this activity. Nearly all described statistically significant departures from the color distribution given at the M&Ms website, but the nature of the difference varied considerably. In some cases, for example, the number of red candies was much more than expected, while in other cases the number of red candies was much less than expected.

To further investigate sample-to-sample variation, one of the authors counted the frequency of the six colors in four one-pound bags of plain M&Ms purchased at four different stores in Pennsylvania. The color distribution in the total sample was reasonably close to the expected distribution, but there were substantial differences among the bags. For instance, the observed percent of brown M&Ms ranged from 23% in one bag to 40% in another. And the null hypothesis was rejected for three of the four bags. See exercise 15.36 for details.

Why do so many different samples provide statistically significant evidence against the distribution given by the manufacturer? The answer probably has to do with the manufacturing and distribution process. A bag of M&Ms, or a group of bags purchased at the same store, may not be a *random sample* from a larger population. The color composition of the bags produced in a manufacturing plant on a given day could be affected by the available quantities of the various colors. Also, the process used to put candies into the bags may not produce a well-mixed random sampling of the colors. In other words, students counting M&M colors most likely are not using random or representative samples of the larger population.

KEY TERMS

Section 15.1
categorical variable, 527
two-way table, 527
contingency table, 527
cell, 528
row percent, 528
column percent, 528
null hypothesis for two-way tables, 528
alternative hypothesis for two-way
  tables, 528

chi-square test for homogeneity, 530
chi-square test for independence, 530
observed counts for chi-square test,
  530
expected counts for chi-square test,
  530–531, 532
chi-square test statistic, 531
p-value, 531, 533
degrees of freedom, 534
chi-square distribution, 534

critical value, 536
rejection region, 536

Section 15.2
Fisher's Exact Test, 542

Section 15.3
chi-square goodness of fit test, 544

EXERCISES   Blue = Basics   **Bold, Bold** = Answer in back

Sections 15.1 and 15.2

15.1 For each pair of variables, indicate whether or not a two-way table would be appropriate for summarizing the relationship. In each case, briefly explain why or why not.
   a. Satisfaction with quality of local K–12 schools (satisfied or not satisfied) and political party (Republican, Democrat, etc.).
   b. Height (centimeters) and foot length (centimeters).
   c. Gender and amount willing to spend on a home theater system.
   d. Age group (under 20, 21–29, etc.) and handedness (right-handed, left-handed, or ambidextrous).

15.2 In each of the following situations, give the p-value for the given chi-square statistic. Either use the information in Table A.5 to estimate a range for the p-value or use software to determine an exact value.
   a. $\chi^2 = 3.84$, df = 1.
   b. $\chi^2 = 6.7$ for a table with 3 rows and 3 columns.
   c. $\chi^2 = 26.23$ for a table with 2 rows and 3 columns.
   d. $\chi^2 = 2.28$, df = 9.

15.3 Recall that the critical value for a chi-square test is the chi-square value for which the area to its right equals the level of significance. An observed relationship is statistically significant if the calculated chi-square statistic is greater than or equal to the critical value. Use Table A.5 to determine the critical value in each of the following situations.
   a. Level of significance is $\alpha = 0.05$; df = 1.
   b. Level of significance is $\alpha = 0.01$; table has 3 rows and 4 columns.
   c. Level of significance is $\alpha = 0.05$; df = 6.

15.4 For each of the following situations determine whether the result is statistically significant at the 0.05 level of significance.
   a. $\chi^2 = 2.89$, df = 1.
   b. $\chi^2 = 5.00$, df = 1.
   c. $\chi^2 = 23.60$, df = 4.
   d. $\chi^2 = 23.60$, df = 15.

15.5 Refer to the previous exercise. For each part determine whether the result is statistically significant at the 0.01 level of significance.

15.6 Suppose investigators conduct a study on the relationship between birth order (first or only child, not first or only child) and activity preference (indoor or outdoor).
   a. Suppose the p-value of the study is not small enough to reject the null hypothesis. Write this conclusion in the context of the situation.
   b. Now suppose the p-value of the study is small enough to reject the null hypothesis. In the context of the situation, express the conclusion in two different ways.

15.7 Students from two different statistics classes at UC Davis reported their gender (male or female) and recorded which class they were taking. One class is for liberal arts students and the other is for non-liberal-arts students. (These data are in the file **UCDavis1** on the CD accompanying the text.) The results for the 173 students are given below. In each cell the observed counts are printed first, with the expected counts below them. Assume these students are a representative sample of all UC Davis students who would take either class.

	NonLib	LibArt	All
Female	83	11	94
	80.42	13.58	94.00
Male	65	14	79
	67.58	11.42	79.00
All	148	25	173
	148.00	25.00	173.00

   a. State the null and alternative hypotheses that could be tested from these data.
   b. What are the degrees of freedom for the chi-square test statistic?

c. Compute the value of the chi-square test statistic.

d. Find the *p*-value or *p*-value range for the chi-square statistic found in part (c).

e. Make a conclusion and write it in the context of the situation. Be sure to state the level of significance you are using.

15.8 The data for this exercise are from a sample of 12th graders, collected as part of the 2001 Youth Risk Behavior Surveillance System, in the dataset **YouthRisk** on the CD accompanying this book. The students were asked how often they wear a seat belt while driving, and for this exercise we combine the responses for "never" and "rarely" and for "most times" and "always" and ignore the "sometimes" responses. Here is a contingency table of the results for males and females.

	Seat Belt Use		
	Most Times or Always	*Rarely or Never*	*Total*
Female	964	97	1061
Male	924	254	1178
Total	1888	351	2239

Data source: http://www.cdc.gov/nccdphp/dash/yrbs/

a. Calculate the row percents for females and the row percents for males. Compare them.

b. Specify the null and alternative hypotheses that could be tested using a chi-square statistic in this situation.

c. Calculate the expected count for the cell "Male, Most times or Always."

d. Use the expected count you calculated in part (c) and obtain the expected counts for the remaining cells by subtraction.

e. Compute the chi-square statistic.

f. Use the chi-square statistic computed in part (e) to find a *p*-value or *p*-value range.

g. Make a conclusion and write it in the context of the situation. Be sure to state the level of significance you are using.

15.9 Refer to the previous exercise, in which the relationship between sex and seat belt use was examined.

a. Compute the chi-square statistic using the shortcut formula given in Section 15.2. Show your work.

b. What are the degrees of freedom for this situation?

c. Find the *p*-value or *p*-value range for the chi-square statistic found in part (a).

d. Make a conclusion and write it in the context of the situation. Be sure to state the level of significance you are using.

15.10 In the 1993 General Social Survey conducted by the National Opinion Research Center at the University of Chicago, participants were asked:

> Do you favor or oppose the death penalty for persons convicted of murder?
>
> Do you think the use of marijuana should be made legal or not?

A two-way table of counts for the responses to these two questions is

		Marijuana?		
		Legal	*Not Legal*	*Total*
Death Penalty?	**Favor**	152	561	713
	Oppose	61	159	220
	Total	213	720	933

Data source: http://csa.berkeley.edu:7502/archive.htm

a. Is there an obvious choice for which variable should be the explanatory variable in this situation? Explain.

b. Calculate row and/or column percents for the table. Use these percents to describe the relationship (or absence of a relationship).

c. State null and alternative hypotheses about the two variables that have been used to create the contingency table.

d. Do a chi-square test of the hypotheses stated in part (c). State a conclusion and support your conclusion with a *p*-value.

e. If you did not already do so in part (d), use the "shortcut" computational formula to find the value of the test statistic. Show how the numbers fit into the formula.

15.11 The following two contingency tables separate the data of exercise 15.10 by sex of the respondent. The first table shows the responses of males while the second table displays the responses of females.

Males Only

		Marijuana?		
		Legal	*Not Legal*	*Total*
Death Penalty?	**Favor**	80	238	318
	Oppose	30	41	71
	Total	110	279	389

Females Only

		Marijuana?		
		Legal	*Not Legal*	*Total*
Death Penalty?	**Favor**	72	323	395
	Oppose	31	118	149
	Total	103	441	544

a. For each table, compute relevant conditional percents. Based on these percents, briefly discuss, for each gender, the nature of the relationship between the variables.

b. For males, do a chi-square test to assess the statistical significance of the relationship between opinions about marijuana and the death penalty. State a conclusion within the context of the problem.

c. For females, do a chi-square test to assess the statistical significance of the relationship between opinions about marijuana and the death penalty. State a conclusion within the context of the problem.

15.12 Refer to the previous two exercises. Based on the results from exercise 15.10, a reporter wrote, "There is a significant relationship between opinions on the death penalty and legalization of marijuana. While about 28% of those who oppose the death penalty think marijuana should be legal, only about 21% of those who favor the death penalty think marijuana should be legal."

   a. Referring to the data in exercise 15.11, make appropriate changes and rewrite the reporter's statement based on men only.

   b. Make appropriate changes and rewrite the reporter's statement based on women only.

   c. Discuss the validity of the reporter's statement based on your results from parts (a) and (b). Write a paragraph explaining the results taking the sex of the respondents into account.

15.13 For the expected counts shown in Table 15.3 for Xylitol and ear infection data, verify that the null hypothesis "expected" proportion getting an ear infection is the same for the three treatment groups.

15.14 An article at the Gallup Poll website entitled "SOCIAL AUDIT, Gambling in America" included the following comparison of the responses of teenagers and adults to the question, "Generally speaking, do you approve or disapprove of legal gambling or betting?" The survey was conducted in April 1999.

	Opinion of Legal Gambling			
	Approve	*Disapprove*	*No Opinion*	*Total*
Adults	959 (63%)	488 (32%)	76 (5%)	1523
Teens	261 (52%)	235 (47%)	5 (1%)	501
Total	1220	723	81	2024

Source: http://www.gallup.com/poll/socialaudits/gambling2.asp

   a. State null and alternative hypotheses for this contingency table.

   b. Here's Minitab output for a chi-square test. What conclusion can we make about the hypotheses stated in part (a)? Justify this conclusion using information from the output.

```
Expected Counts are shown below observed counts

Rows: Age Group    Columns: Opinion

          Approve   Disappro   No Opini      All

Adults        959        488         76     1523
           918.01     544.04      60.95  1523.00

Teens         261        235          5      501
           301.99     178.96      20.05   501.00

All          1220        723         81     2024
          1220.00     723.00      81.00  2024.00

Chi-Square = 45.723,   DF = 2,   P-Value = 0.000
```

   c. What is the expected count for the "Teens, Approve" cell? Show how to calculate this value.

15.15 Refer to the previous exercise. Would a *z*-test for the difference in two proportions have been appropriate instead of a chi-square test? If your answer is yes, explain

whether the results would have been identical to the results of the chi-square test. If your answer is no, explain why not.

15.16 In each of the following situations, explain which test would be most appropriate: a chi-square test, a one-sided *z*-test for the difference in two proportions, or a Fisher's Exact Test.

   a. The manufacturer of a safety seal used in cars wants to know if the safety seals perform as well in extreme cold temperatures as they do in normal temperatures. Testing the seals is expensive, so the manufacturer tests only six seals at an extreme cold temperature and six other seals at a normal temperature. Two of the six seals tested at the extreme cold fail and none of the six seals tested at a normal temperature fails.

   b. In June, before an upcoming November presidential election, a random sample of 1000 voters was asked which candidate they would vote for if the election were held then. In September, a new random sample of 1000 voters is asked the same question. The polling agency wants to know if the population proportions planning to vote for each candidate are different in September than they were in June.

   c. Frequent computer use may be a cause of carpal tunnel syndrome, a painful condition that affects peoples' hands and wrists. Researchers hypothesized that people who took typing classes in school would be less likely to suffer from carpal tunnel syndrome than those who did not take typing classes. To examine this hypothesis, the researchers asked a random sample of 3000 people who frequently used computers in their jobs if they had ever taken typing classes and if they had ever suffered from carpal tunnel syndrome.

15.17 Refer to the previous exercise. In each case, specify the null and alternative hypotheses.

15.18 The use of magnets has been proposed as a cure for various illnesses. Suppose researchers conduct a study with ten participants to determine whether using magnets as therapy reduces pain from migraine headaches. Five participants are randomly assigned to receive the magnet treatment and of those, two report that their pain is reduced. The remaining five participants are given an indistinguishable sham treatment and of those, none report that their pain is reduced. Fisher's Exact Test would be appropriate in this situation.

   a. Write in words the question that the *p*-value would answer in this situation.

   b. (Appropriate software required.) Carry out Fisher's Exact Test.

15.19 In exercise 2.15, data were presented on seat belt use and grades for a sample of 2530 12th graders, collected as part of the 2001 Youth Risk Behavior Surveillance System. Students were asked how often they wear a seat belt while driving, and possible choices were never, rarely, sometimes, most times, and always. For this exercise, we combine the responses for "never" and "rarely" and for "most times" and "always" and ignore the "sometimes" responses. The contingency table on the next page summarizes the results.

Seat Belt Use			
Typical Grades	*Most Times or Always*	*Rarely or Never*	*Total*
A or B	1354	180	1534
C	428	125	553
D or F	65	40	105
Total	1847	345	2192

Data source: http://www.cdc.gov/nccdphp/dash/yrbs/

Carry out a chi-square test for the relationship between seat belt use and typical grades for 12th graders. Be sure to cover all five steps.

15.20 The following drawing illustrates the water-level task. Several developmental psychologists have investigated performance on this task. The figure to the left shows the water level in a glass of water that's half full (or is it half empty?). The figure on the right shows the same glass tipped to the right, but the water level is not shown. The task is to correctly draw the water line in this glass.

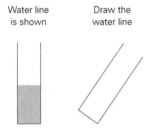

Water line is shown   Draw the water line

A University of South Carolina psychologist examined the water-level task success rate of 50 students from each of five different colleges within the university (Kalichman, 1986). Within each college, the sample included 25 men and 25 women. The investigators showed each participant eight different drawings of tipped glasses. If the participant correctly drew the water line on four or more of the drawings, he or she was given a "passing" result. Here's a contingency table of the results.

Result on Task			
College	*Pass*	*Fail*	*Total*
Business	33	17	50
Language Arts	32	18	50
Social Sciences	25	25	50
Natural Sciences	38	12	50
Engineering	43	7	50
Total	171	79	250

a. Compare the colleges using row percents. What differences are apparent from these percents?
b. Write null and alternative hypotheses for this table.
c. What are the degrees of freedom for a chi-square test?
d. The chi-square statistic for this table is 16.915. Determine a *p*-value, and state a conclusion about the null and alternative hypotheses.
e. For each college, what are the expected counts for "Pass" and "Fail" outcomes?

f. (Obviously, optional) What is the correct water line in the glass at the right above?

15.21 The data in the table below first appeared in exercise 6.9. The variables are height (short or not) and whether or not the student had ever been bullied in school for 209 secondary school students in England. The researchers gathered the data to test their hypothesis that short students are more likely to be bullied in school than other students are.

Height and Bullying in School

	Ever Bullied		
Height	*Yes*	*No*	*Total*
Short	42	50	92
Not Short	30	87	117
Total	72	137	209

a. Should these data be analyzed using a chi-square test or a *z*-test for comparing two proportions? Explain.
b. Explain why it makes sense to designate height as the explanatory variable.
c. Carry out an appropriate hypothesis test. Be sure to state null and alternative hypotheses, and clearly indicate your conclusion about these hypotheses.
d. Calculate separate 95% confidence intervals for the proportion ever bullied for short students and for students who are not short. Compare these two intervals. What does this comparison indicate about the relationship between height and the risk of being bullied?

Section 15.3

15.22 In the following situations, give the expected count for each of the *k* categories.
a. $k = 3$, H_0: $p_1 = p_2 = p_3 = 1/3$, and $n = 300$.
b. $k = 3$, H_0: $p_1 = 1/4$, $p_2 = 1/4$, $p_3 = 1/2$, and $n = 1000$.
c. $k = 4$, H_0: $p_1 = .2$, $p_2 = .4$, $p_3 = .1$, $p_4 = .3$, and $n = 2000$.
d. $k = 5$, H_0: all p_i are the same, and $n = 2500$.

15.23 In a chi-square goodness of fit test, is it possible for all of the expected counts to be larger than the corresponding observed counts? Explain.

15.24 Explain whether each of these is possible in a chi-square goodness of fit test.
a. The chi-square statistic is negative.
b. The chi-square statistic is 0.
c. The expected counts are not whole numbers.
d. The observed counts are not whole numbers.
e. The probabilities specified in the null hypothesis sum to less than 1.
f. The degrees of freedom are larger than the number of categories.

15.25 The following table below shows the results from 190 students at Penn State (dataset **pennstate1** on the CD) "randomly" choosing among the numbers from 1 to 10. For example, there were 2 students who chose the digit 1, and 9 students who chose the digit 2.

Digit	1	2	3	4	5	6	7	8	9	10
Frequency	2	9	22	21	18	23	56	19	14	6

Assuming that the students were actually choosing digits at random, the expected number of students choosing any digit is 19 (19 = 190/10), so all expected counts are 19.

a. State the null and alternative hypotheses. (*Hint:* Refer to Example 15.8.)
b. Calculate the chi-square goodness of fit test statistic.
c. What are the degrees of freedom for this test statistic?
d. Find the *p*-value or *p*-value range.
e. Make a conclusion and write it in the context of the situation. Be sure to state the level of significance you are using.

15.26 Suppose that on a typical day the proportion of students who drive to campus is .3 (30%), the proportion who bike is .6 (60%), and the remaining .1 (10%) come to campus in some other way (for example, walk, take the bus, get a ride). The campus sponsors a "spare the air" day to encourage people not to drive to campus on that day. They want to know if the proportions using each mode of transportation on that day differ from the norm. To test this hypothesis, a random sample of 300 students that day was asked how they got to campus, with the following results:

Method of Transportation	Drive	Bike	Other	Total
Frequency	80	200	20	300

a. State the null and alternative hypotheses.
b. Find the expected counts for the three modes of transportation.
c. Calculate the chi-square goodness of fit statistic.
d. Find the *p*-value or *p*-value range.
e. Make a conclusion and write it in the context of the situation. Be sure to state the level of significance you are using.

15.27 In a class survey done in a statistics class at Penn State, students were asked, "Suppose you are buying a new car and the model you are buying is available in three colors: silver, blue, or green. Which color would you pick?" Of the *n* = 111 students who responded, 59 picked silver, 27 picked green, and 25 picked blue. Is there sufficient evidence to conclude that the colors are not equally preferred? Carry out a significance test. Be sure to state the null hypothesis and specify the population to which your conclusion applies.

15.28 Refer to the previous exercise. Suppose a car manufacturer had hypothesized that 50% would prefer silver, 30% would prefer blue, and 20% would prefer green. Test the manufacturer's hypothesis.

15.29 The following table contains the observed distribution of the last digit of the forecasted high temperature on December 10, 2000 for *n* = 150 United States and international cities on December 10, 2000 (*Source: New York Times,* Dec. 10, 2000, p. 47).

Last Digit	0	1	2	3	4	5	6	7	8	9
Count	11	21	11	23	10	17	11	15	13	18

a. Compute expected counts for the null hypothesis that all digits 0, 1, . . . , 9 are equally likely to be the last digit of the forecasted high temperature.
b. Calculate the chi-square goodness of fit statistic for these data. What are the degrees of freedom for this statistic?
c. State a conclusion about the null hypothesis that all digits are equally likely to be the last digit selected. Explain.

15.30 Suppose a statistics teacher assigns her class of 60 students the homework task of flipping a coin two times, counting the number of heads, and submitting that number to her during the next class period.

a. List the possible sequences of results (in order) for two flips of a coin. Using this list, determine the probability distribution for *X* = number of heads in two flips if the coin is fair.
b. Using proper notation, express the probabilities determined in part (a) as a null hypothesis about the number of heads that may occur in two flips of a fair coin.
c. The distribution of the number of heads reported by the 60 students in the class was

Number of Heads	0	1	2
Number of Students	8	40	12

Using these data, do a chi-square goodness of fit test to test the null hypothesis stated in part (b). Clearly show all steps, and state a conclusion about the null hypothesis.
d. If you were the teacher, what would you conclude about how the class may have done this assignment? Briefly justify your answer.

15.31 The California Daily 3 lottery game is identical to the Pennsylvania Daily Number game described in Example 15.8. The following table contains the observed distribution of all digits drawn in the California Daily 3 on the 200 days between May 14, 2000 and November 29, 2000. Three digits are drawn each day, so the sample size is *n* = 600 for this table.

Last Digit	0	1	2	3	4	5	6	7	8	9
Count	49	61	64	62	50	64	59	65	63	63

Carry out a significance test of the null hypothesis that all digits 0, 1, . . . , 9 are equally likely to be drawn.

Chapter Exercises

15.32 In a survey reported in a special issue of *Newsweek* magazine (Special Edition: Health for Life, Spring/Summer 1999), *n* = 747 randomly selected women were asked, "How satisfied are you with your overall appearance?" There were four possible responses to this question, and the following table shows the distribution of counts for the possible responses for each of three age groups. (*Note:* The counts were estimated from percents given in *Newsweek.*)

How Satisfied Are You with Your Overall Appearance?					
Age	Very	Somewhat	Not Too	Not at All	Total
Under 30	45	82	10	4	141
30–49	73	168	47	6	294
Over 50	106	153	41	12	312
Total	224	403	98	22	747

a. Determine conditional percents within each age group. Summarize these data using a bar chart, and describe what is shown about the relationship between age and satisfaction with appearance.
b. Minitab output for a chi-square test of association between age group and satisfaction with appearance follows. Verify that the degrees of freedom shown are correct.
c. Is there a statistically significant association between the two variables for this problem? Justify your answer with information from the output.
d. Refer to the output for part (b). Draw a sketch that illustrates the p-value for this problem, and write a sentence interpreting the p-value.
e. Refer to the output for part (b). What is the expected count for the "50+, Not Too Satisfied" cell? Show how to calculate this expected count.

```
Expected counts are printed below observed counts

          Very    Somewhat   Not Too   Not at All   Total
18-29      45        82         10          4         141
         42.28     76.07      18.50       4.15

30-49      73       168         47          6         294
         88.16    158.61      38.57       8.66

50+       106       153         41         12         312
         93.56    168.32      40.93       9.19

Total     224       403         98         22         747

Chi-Sq = 0.175 + 0.463 + 3.904 + 0.006 +
         2.607 + 0.556 + 1.842 + 0.816 +
         1.655 + 1.395 + 0.000 + 0.860 = 14.278
DF = 6, P-Value = 0.027
1 cells with expected counts less than 5.0
```

15.33 Refer to the previous exercise. Notice that the "contributions to chi-square" are given in the output for all cells. For instance, the "contribution to chi-square" for the row "18–29" and the column "Very" is 0.175, and for the row "18–29" and the column "Not at All" it is 0.006.
   a. Identify the two cells with the highest "contributions to chi-square." Specify the numerical value of the "contribution" and the row and column categories for each of the two cells.
   b. For each of the two cells identified in part (a), determine whether the expected count is higher or lower than the observed count.
   c. Using the information in parts (a) and (b), explain how the women in those category combinations contribute to the overall conclusion for this study.

15.34 Exercise 6.45 gave data on ear pierces and tattoos for a sample of 678 college women. The data are presented again in the following table. The ear pierce response is

the total number of ear pierces for a woman, and this has been categorized.

Ear Pierces and Tattoos, 678 College Women

Pierces	No Tattoo	Have Tattoo
2 or less	245	19
3 or 4	210	26
5 or 6	91	32
7 or more	25	30

Data source: One of the authors.

a. Describe the relationship with relevant percents and an appropriate graph.
b. Write null and alternative hypotheses for the relationship between ear pierces and tattoos.
c. Test the null and alternative hypotheses written for part (b). Use $\alpha = 0.05$ for the level of significance. State a conclusion.

15.35 In a study reported in the *Annals of Internal Medicine* (Lotufo et al., 2000), the investigators examined the possible relationship in men between baldness and the risk of coronary heart disease. Other researchers have reported a possible link between these two variables (see Case Study 3.4, for example). In this study, 19,112 men aged 40 to 84 years old were followed for 11 years. All men were free of coronary heart disease at the beginning of the study. During the study, the men were asked about any baldness pattern they may have had at the age of 45. The following table shows counts for the cross-classification of hair loss pattern at age 45 and whether a participant developed coronary heart disease during the study period or not. (*Note:* Vertex baldness occurs on top in the area of the crown or peak of the head.)

Hair Loss Pattern and Coronary Heart Disease

	Coronary Heart Disease		
Hair Pattern	Yes	No	Total
No Baldness	548	7611	8159
Baldness			
Frontal	333	4075	4408
Mild Vertex	275	3148	3423
Moderate Vertex	163	1608	1771
Severe Vertex	127	1224	1351
Total	1446	17666	19112

a. Analyze the relationship between hair loss pattern and the risk of coronary heart disease. Write a short report in which you provide relevant descriptive statistics as well the results of a test for statistical significance. If there is an association, describe the nature of the association.
b. Is this an observational study or an experiment? Briefly explain how the answer affects the interpretation of any observed link between hair loss pattern and coronary heart disease in men.

15.36 One of the authors of this book purchased four 1-pound bags of plain M&Ms at different stores in Pennsylvania to compare the color distribution to the one stated at the manufacturer's website. The observed results for the combined bags, and the proportions alleged by the manufacturer, are given in the following table. State and test the appropriate hypotheses to determine if it is reasonable to assume that the observed colors are a random sample from a population with the manufacturer's alleged proportions.

	Brown	Red	Yellow	Blue	Orange	Green	Total
Observed	602	396	379	227	242	235	2081
	(.289)	(.190)	(.182)	(.109)	(.116)	(.113)	
Alleged Proportions	.30	.20	.20	.10	.10	.10	

15.37 Refer to Example 15.6, describing an experiment in which students at the University of California at Davis were classified as "sheep" who believe in ESP or as "goats" who do not. Each student then guessed the results of 10 coin tosses. Classify students as "Stars" if they guessed 5 or more correctly, and as "Duds" if they did not. The results are shown in the following table.

	Stars	Duds	Total
Sheep	79	33	112
Goats	48	32	80
Total	127	65	192

a. Describe the relationship between belief and performance with relevant percents and an appropriate graph.
b. Write null and alternative hypotheses for the relationship between belief and performance. Be sure to state the population to which your hypotheses apply.
c. Test the null and alternative hypotheses written for part (b). Use $\alpha = 0.05$ for the level of significance. State a conclusion.

15.38 Refer to the previous exercise in which each student guessed the results of 10 coin flips. If all students are just guessing, and if the coins are fair, then the number of correct guesses for each student should follow a binomial distribution.
a. What are the parameters n and p for the binomial distribution, assuming the coins are fair and students were just guessing?
b. Specify the probabilities of getting 0 correct, 1 correct, . . . , 10 correct for this experiment if students were just guessing. (*Hint:* These are the probabilities in the pdf for a binomial distribution with parameters specified in part (a).)
c. The following table shows how many students got ≤2 right, 3 right, 4 right, and so on, separately, for students classified as sheep (believe in ESP) and classified as goats (don't believe in ESP). Using your results from part (b), fill in the "null probabilities" that correspond to the hypothesis that students are just guessing.

Number Correct	Sheep	Goats	Null Probabilities
≤ 2	6	5	
3	11	12	
4	16	15	
5	29	19	
6	28	16	
7	14	10	
≥ 8	8	3	
Total	112	80	

d. Test the hypothesis that the population of sheep represented by these students guess according to the null probabilities specified in part (c). Give a p-value, and state a conclusion.
e. Repeat part (d) for the population of goats represented by these students.

15.39 Household sizes for the households participating in the 1996 General Social Survey conducted by the National Opinion Research Center at the University of Chicago are shown in the following table. The table also shows the proportion of households of each size in the survey and the corresponding proportions of all U.S. households of each size.

Household Size	Number of Cases	Sample Proportion	U.S. Proportion
1	744	0.256	0.257
2	988	0.340	0.322
3	454	0.156	0.169
4	453	0.156	0.149
5 or more	265	0.091	0.103
Total	2904		

Sources: *Sample data:* SDA data archive, http://csa.berkeley.edu:7502; *Population data:* www.census.gov/populatio/socdemo/hh-fam/98ppla.txt (Table A. Households by Type and Selected Characteristics, 1998).

a. Carefully state the null and alternative hypotheses for testing whether the sizes of households in the General Social Survey reflect the size of households for the United States as a whole.
b. Carry out the appropriate test for your hypotheses in part (a). State your conclusion in the context of the situation.

15.40 The data in this exercise were first presented in exercise 6.48. In the 1996 General Social Survey, religious preference and opinion about when premarital sex might be wrong were among the measured variables. The contingency table of counts for these variables is shown in exercise 6.48 and again here.

Religious Preference and Opinion About Premarital Sex

Religion	When Is Premarital Sex Wrong?				
	Always	Almost Always	Sometimes	Never	Total
Protestant	355	117	227	384	1083
Catholic	62	37	120	226	445
Jewish	0	3	14	34	51
None	20	13	45	147	225
Other	15	13	23	40	91
Total	452	183	429	831	1895

Source: SDA archive at http://csa.berkeley.edu:7502.

a. Are the conditions necessary for carrying out a chi-square test met? Explain.
b. Test whether or not there is a statistically significant relationship between these two variables. Show all five steps for the hypothesis test.

15.41 Case Study 10.3 described a survey in which students in a statistics class at Penn State were asked, "Would you date someone with a great personality even though you did not find them attractive?" The results were that 80 of

131 women answered "yes" while 26 of 61 men answered "yes."

a. Construct a contingency table for this situation, being careful to identify the explanatory and response variables.

b. State the appropriate hypotheses for this situation.

c. Given the hypotheses you specified in part (b), would it be more appropriate to conduct a chi-square test, a z-test, or does it not matter?

d. Conduct the appropriate test of the hypotheses you specified in part (b). Carry out all five steps.

15.42 Refer to the previous exercise. Use the shortcut formula for 2×2 tables to compute the chi-square statistic. Show the formula with all numbers entered.

15.43 Weindling et al. (1986; also in Hand et al., 1994, p. 15) were interested in the health of juvenile delinquents. They classified 16 boys who failed a vision test by whether or not they wore glasses and whether or not they were a juvenile delinquent. They were interested in knowing if the likelihood of wearing glasses differed for juvenile delinquents compared to nondelinquents. The results are shown in the following table.

Data for Exercise 15.43

	Wears Glasses	Does Not Wear Glasses	Total
Delinquent	1	8	9
Nondelinquent	5	2	7
Total	6	10	16

a. Specify the appropriate null and alternative hypotheses.

b. Explain why a chi-square test is not appropriate in this situation.

c. Find statistical software or a website that will conduct a Fisher Exact Test, and carry out the test.

d. Explain in words what the p-value for this test represents.

15.44 Wilding and Cook (2000) asked 352 males and 376 females to listen to a male voice and a female voice. One week later they attempted to identify the voices they had heard in lineups of six male and six female voices. The results are shown in the following table. Using appropriate subsets of the data, conduct a test of the null hypotheses in parts (a) to (d).

	Identified Male Voice?		Identified Female Voice?	
Listener's Sex	*Yes*	*No*	*Yes*	*No*
Male (n = 352)	145	207	132	220
Female (n = 376)	162	214	191	185
Total (n = 728)	307	421	323	405

a. H_0: Sex of listener and ability to identify a male voice are not related.

b. H_0: Sex of listener and ability to identify a female voice are not related.

c. H_0: Sex of listener and ability to identify a voice of the same sex are not related.

d. H_0: Sex of listener and ability to identify a voice of the opposite sex are not related.

e. Using the results from parts (a) to (d), write a short paragraph about the relationship between listener's sex, speaker's sex, and ability to subsequently identify a voice.

15.45 In a class survey, Penn State statistics students were asked, "Which one of these choices describes your perception of your weight: about right, overweight, underweight?" The table in exercise 6.7 displayed the results by sex. Displayed below are these results along with the Minitab output for a chi-square test. (*Source:* The authors.)

```
Expected counts are printed below observed counts

              About right    Overwt    Underwt    Total
F                    87          39          3      129
                  91.88       25.56      11.56

M                    64           3         16       83
                  59.12       16.44       7.44

Total               151          42         19      212

Chi-Sq = 0.259 +   7.072 + 6.340 +
             0.403 + 10.991 + 9.853 = 34.918
DF = 2,    P-Value = 0.000
```

a. State the null and alternative hypotheses being tested in this situation.

b. Make a conclusion for the test using $\alpha = 0.05$.

c. Using the results shown in the Minitab output, identify the cells with large "contributions to chi-square." Explain in words that would be understood by someone with no training in statistics why the contributions are so large for those cells.

15.46 In the 1996 General Social Survey, participants were asked, "Should divorce in this country be easier or more difficult to obtain than it is now?" The results are shown in the following table and Minitab output.

Data for Exercise 15.46

Sex	Easier	More Difficult	Stay Same	Total
Male	247	413	151	811
Female	280	547	206	1033
Total	527	960	357	1844

Data source: 1996 SDA archive at http://csa.berkeley.edu:7502/.

```
Minitab Results for Exercise 15.46

            Easier    More Diff.    Same     Total
M              247          413      151       811
            231.78       422.21   157.01

F              280          547      206      1033
            295.22       537.79   199.99

Total          527          960      357      1844

Chi-Sq = 1.000 + 0.201 + 0.230 +
             0.785 + 0.158 + 0.181 = 2.554
DF = 2,    P-Value = 0.279
```

a. Carry out the five steps for a chi-square test for this situation.

b. Draw a picture of the appropriate chi-square distribution and shade the region for the *p*-value for this test.

15.47 Refer to the previous exercise. Suppose the same question were to be asked in many independent surveys. Assuming the null hypothesis is true, into what range should the test statistic fall about 95% of the time, where 0 is at the lower end of the range?

15.48 Explain why a chi-square test statistic cannot be negative.

15.49 Students (*n* = 183) were asked to identify their own eye color as well as the eye color to which they are most attracted. The results are shown here.

Eye Color and Attraction

Own Eyes	Eyes Attracted To				
	Brown	Blue	Hazel	Green	Total
Brown	30	22	6	13	71
Blue	15	37	3	11	66
Hazel	4	12	7	7	30
Green	4	8	1	3	16
Total	53	79	17	34	183

a. The Minitab results of a chi-square analysis follow. Based on these results, explain why a chi-square analysis is not appropriate.

	Brown	Blue	Hazel	Green	Total
Brown	30	22	6	13	71
	20.56	30.65	6.60	13.19	
Blue	15	37	3	11	66
	19.11	28.49	6.13	12.26	
Hazel	4	12	7	7	30
	8.69	12.95	2.79	5.57	
Green	4	8	1	3	16
	4.63	6.91	1.49	2.97	
Total	53	79	17	34	183

Chi-Sq = 4.331 + 2.441 + 0.054 + 0.003 +
2.530 + 0.070 + 6.369 + 0.365 +
0.886 + 2.541 + 1.599 + 0.130 +
0.087 + 0.173 + 0.159 + 0.000 = 21.738
DF = 9, P-Value = 0.010
4 cells with expected counts less than 5.0

b. Combine the categories for "hazel" and "green" and rerun the analysis. Carry out all five steps of the hypothesis test.

c. Refer to the results from part (b). Identify the cells that have the largest "contributions to chi-square," and explain why the results in those cells support the alternative hypothesis.

15.50 Refer to the previous exercise. Using the original data (not combining green and hazel) construct a contingency table for the two variables:

Explanatory variable: Eye color.
Response variable: Finds own eye color most attractive, yes or no.

a. Conduct a chi-square test to determine if these two variables are related. Specify all five steps of the test.

b. Determine which eye color(s) contributes the most to the chi-square statistic. Explain whether that eye color(s) is more attractive to people who have it as their own color than would be expected, or less so.

15.51 Gillespie (1999) and Chambers (2000) reported on two Gallup polls, taken in August 1999 and August 2000 using independent samples, which asked parents the question, "How satisfied are you with the quality of education your oldest child is receiving? Would you say completely satisfied, somewhat satisfied, somewhat dissatisfied or completely dissatisfied?" The results of the two polls are shown in the following table.

Results of Gallup Polls Taken in 1999 and 2000

	August 24–26, 1999	August 24–27, 2000
Completely Satisfied	125	87
Somewhat Satisfied	155	133
Somewhat Dissatisfied	41	34
Completely Dissatisfied	7	17
Just Starting School (Volunteered Answer)	7	11
No Opinion	3	0
Total	338	282

a. Refer to the discussion of the technical difference between tests for homogeneity and tests for independence. Which is more appropriate for this situation, for comparing the results of the survey for the two years? Specify the appropriate null and alternative hypotheses.

b. Ignore the last two categories (Just starting school; no opinion). Carry out the five steps for a chi-square test to determine if opinions differed in 1999 and 2000. Be sure to identify the appropriate populations represented by these data.

Dataset Exercises

15.52 Use the dataset **GSS-93** for this exercise. The variable *owngun* indicates whether the respondent owns a gun or not, and the variable *polparty* contains the respondent's political party preference. Is there a significant relationship between *owngun* and *polparty?*

15.53 Use the dataset **UCDavis2.** Respondents were categorized as male or female (*Sex*) and were asked if they typically sit in the front, middle, or back of the classroom (*Seat*).

a. Carry out the five steps to determine whether there is a significant relationship between these two variables.

b. The *p*-value for your test in part (a) should be about 0.02. Explain in words which cells contribute the most to the chi-square statistic and how those cells support the alternative hypothesis.

15.54 Use the dataset **UCDavis2.** Two variables measured were whether the respondent was left- or right-handed

(**Hand**) and whether they find it easier to make friends with people of the same or opposite sex (**Friends**). Carry out the five steps to determine if there is a significant relationship between those variables.

15.55 Use the dataset **UCDavis2.** Identify two variables for which it would be of interest to you to test whether or not there is a relationship. Carry out the five steps of the chi-square test. If one or both of the variables are quantitative, create reasonable categories. For instance, you could classify students as nondrinkers, moderate drinkers, or heavy drinkers using the variable **Alcohol.** Make sure you explain what variables you used and any recoding you did.

REFERENCES

Chambers, Chris (2000). "Americans dissatisfied with U.S. education in general, but parents satisfied with their kids' schools," Gallup Poll Release, Sept. 5, 2000.

Gillespie, Mark (1999). "Local schools get passing grades: Americans support higher pay for teachers," Gallup Poll Release, Sept. 8, 1999.

Hand, D. J., E. Daly, A. D. Lunn, K. J. McConway and E. Ostrowski (1994). *A Handbook of Small Data Sets,* London: Chapman & Hall.

Kalichman, S. C. (1986). "Horizontality as a function of sex and academic major," *Perceptual and Motor Skills,* Vol. 63, pp. 903–908.

Lawrence, T. R. (1993). "Gathering in the sheep and goats. A Meta-analysis of forced choice sheep–goat ESP studies, 1947–1993," *Proceedings of Presented Papers: The 36th Annual Convention of the Parapsychological Association,* pp. 75–86.

Lotufo, P. A., C. U. Chae, U. A. Ajani, C. H. Henneken, and J. E. Manson (2000). "Male pattern baldness and coronary heart disease: The physicians' health study," *Arch. Intern. Med.,* Vol. 160, pp. 165–171.

Schmeidler, Gertrude R. (1988). *Parapsychology and Psychology: Matches and Mismatches,* Jefferson, NC: McFarland.

Schwartz, B. S., W. F., Stewart, D. Simon, and R. B. Lipton (1998). "Epidemiology of tension-type headache," *Journal of the American Medical Association,* Vol. 279, pp. 381–383.

Sinclair, R. C., M. M. Mark, S. E. Moore, L. A. Lavis, and A. S. Soldat (2000). "An electoral butterfly effect," *Nature,* Vol. 408, pp. 665–666.

Uhari, M., T. Kenteerkar, and M. Niemala (1998). "A novel use of Xylitol sugar in preventing acute Otitis Media," *Pediatrics,* Vol. 102, pp. 879–884.

Weindling, A. M., F. N. Bamford, and R. A. Whittall (1986). "Health of juvenile delinquents," *British Medical Journal,* Vol. 292, p. 447.

Wilding, J., and S. Cook (2000). "Sex differences and individual consistency in voice identification," *Perceptual and Motor Skills,* Vol. 91, pp. 535–538.

Analysis of Variance

CHAPTER 16

Mark Reinstein/Index Stock Imagery

Do actors have higher testosterone levels than other men? See Example 16.2.

Analysis of variance is a versatile tool for analyzing how the mean value of a quantitative response variable is affected by one or more categorical explanatory factors. For instance, it can be used to compare the mean weight loss for three different weight-loss programs, or the mean testosterone levels of men in seven different occupations.

Suppose that a researcher wants to compare the mean weight loss for three different weight-loss programs. Or, that another researcher wants to compare the mean testosterone levels of men in seven different occupations. What statistical methods can be used to make the desired comparisons? In the data analysis, the researchers might, at some point, use confidence intervals and significance tests to compare two means at a time (for example, compare mean testosterone levels of occupations 1 and 2, occupations 1 and 3, and so on). Usually, however, an important first step in the analysis of more than two means is to do a significance test to determine if there are any differences at all among the population means being compared. The significance test for doing this is part of a procedure called the **analysis of variance,** which is also sometimes referred to as **ANOVA.**

In this chapter, we focus on the comparison of the means of more than two populations. When different values or levels of a single categorical explanatory variable (weight-loss programs, for instance) define the populations being compared, the ANOVA procedure is called **one-way analysis of variance.** In general, *analysis of variance* is a versatile tool for analyzing how the mean value of a quantitative response variable is related to one or more categorical explanatory factors. While most of the chapter is about one-way analysis of variance, the final section gives an overview of the concepts of *two-way analysis of variance,* which is used to examine the effects of two categorical explanatory variables on the mean value of a quantitative response variable. ◆

16.1 | COMPARING MEANS WITH AN ANOVA *F*-TEST

When we compare the means of populations represented by independent samples of a quantitative variable, a null hypothesis of interest is that all means have the same value. An alternative hypothesis is that the means are not all equal.

Notice that this alternative hypothesis does not require that all means must differ from each other. The alternative would be true, for example, if only one of the means were different from the others. If k = the number of populations, the null and alternative hypotheses for comparing population means can be written as

$H_0: \mu_1 = \mu_2 = \ldots = \mu_k$
H_a: The means are not all equal.

An **F-statistic** that arises from a *one-way analysis of variance* of the sample data is used to test the hypotheses about the population means, and the significance test is called an **F-test.** The F-statistic is sensitive to differences among a set of sample means. The greater the variation among the sample means, the larger the value of the test statistic. The smaller the variation among the observed means, the smaller the value of the test statistic. In this section, we are concerned with the general ideas of the F-test. The specific details and formulas are given in the next section.

Conceptually, the F-statistic can be viewed as follows:

$$F = \frac{\text{Variation among sample means}}{\text{Natural variation within groups}}$$

The "variation among sample means" is 0 if all k of the sample means are exactly equal and gets larger the more spread out they are. If that variation is large enough, it provides evidence that at least one of the k population means is different from the others, so the null hypothesis would be rejected. The denominator of the F-statistic, the "natural variation within groups," provides a yardstick for determining whether the numerator is large enough to reject the null hypothesis. Much like the standard error in a z-statistic, it "standardizes" the numerator so that the p-value can be found from common tables. In fact, the denominator of the F-statistic is simply a pooled estimate of the variance within each group, a fact that will be discussed in more detail in the next section.

To find the p-value, which is the probability the computed F-statistic would be as large as it is (or larger) if the null hypothesis is true, a probability distribution called the **F-distribution** is used. As with all other significance tests, the null hypothesis is rejected if the p-value is as small or smaller than the desired level of significance (usually $\alpha = 0.05$). When the null hypothesis is rejected, the conclusion is that the population means do not all have the same value.

EXAMPLE 16.1
Classroom Seat Location and Grade Point Average

Is it true that the best students sit in the front of a classroom, or is that a false stereotype? In surveys done in two statistics classes at the University of California at Davis, students reported their grade point averages and also answered the question, "Where do you typically sit in a classroom (front, middle, back)?" In all, 384 students gave valid responses to both questions, and among these students, 88 said they typically sit in the front, 218 said they typically sit in the middle, and 78 typically sit in the back. Figure 16.1 shows a boxplot comparing the GPAs of the students for the three seat locations and the analysis of variance results from Minitab with an F-test for comparing the mean grade point averages. In the boxplot, we see that students sitting in the front generally have slightly higher GPAs than the others; toward the bottom of the computer output the sample means are given as: Front = 3.2029,

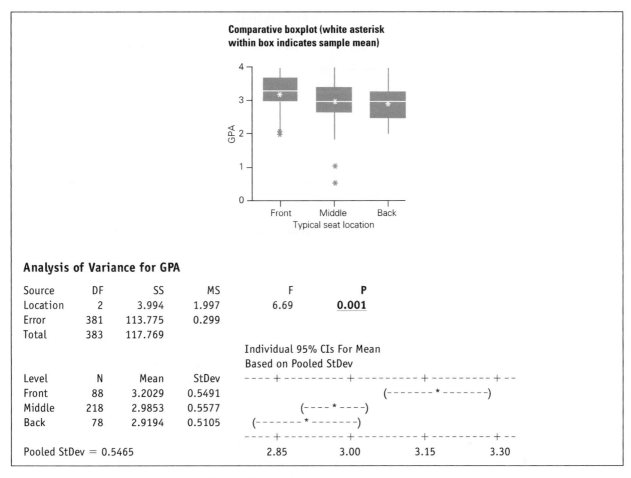

Analysis of Variance for GPA

Source	DF	SS	MS	F	P
Location	2	3.994	1.997	6.69	**0.001**
Error	381	113.775	0.299		
Total	383	117.769			

Individual 95% CIs For Mean
Based on Pooled StDev

Level	N	Mean	StDev
Front	88	3.2029	0.5491
Middle	218	2.9853	0.5577
Back	78	2.9194	0.5105

```
                                    ---- + --------- + --------- + --------- + --
Front                                                  (------- * ------)
Middle                                   (---- * ----)
Back                           (------- * -------)
                                    ---- + --------- + --------- + --------- + --
                                    2.85        3.00        3.15        3.30
```

Pooled StDev = 0.5465

FIGURE 16.1 **Comparison of GPA for three classroom seat locations**

Middle = 2.9853, Back = 2.9194. The analysis of variance results can be used to test

H_0: $\mu_1 = \mu_2 = \mu_3$
H_a: The three means are not all equal.

where μ_1, μ_2, and μ_3 are the *population* mean GPAs for the populations of students who would typically sit in the front, middle, and back of the classroom, respectively.

The details of the analysis of variance will be shown later, but it is relatively easy to interpret the result. The *p*-value for the *F*-test is under "P" in the rightmost column of the table entitled "Analysis of Variance for GPA," and its value is 0.001 (bold, underlined). With a *p*-value this small, we can reject the null hypothesis and thus conclude that there are differences among the means in the populations represented by the samples. Notice that the output in Figure 16.1 also shows 95% confidence intervals for the three population means. The location of the interval for the "Front" mean does not overlap with the other two intervals, which indicates a significant difference between the mean GPA for the front-row sitters and the mean GPA for the other students. It is not clear whether there is a significant difference between the "Middle" and "Back" groups since their confidence intervals overlap. ◆

Notation for Summary Statistics

Useful notation for summarizing statistics from the observed samples is

k = number of groups

$\bar{x}_i$, s_i, and n_i are the mean, standard deviation, and sample size for the ith sample group

N = total sample size ($N = n_1 + n_2 + \cdots + n_k$)

EXAMPLE 16.1—*CONTINUED*
Application of
Notation to the GPA
and Classroom Seat Sample

Three seat locations (1 = front, 2 = middle, 3 = back) are compared, so $k = 3$. The group sample sizes are $n_1 = 88$, $n_2 = 218$, $n_3 = 78$. The total sample size is $N = 88 + 218 + 78 = 384$. Toward the bottom of the output shown in Figure 16.1, the sample means given are $\bar{x}_1 = 3.2029$, $\bar{x}_2 = 2.9853$, $\bar{x}_3 = 2.9194$. The sample standard deviations given in Figure 16.1 are $s_1 = 0.5491$, $s_2 = 0.5577$, $s_3 = 0.5105$. ◆

Assumptions and Necessary Conditions for the *F*-Test

In the derivation of the *F*-statistic, the assumptions are similar to those for the pooled two-sample *t*-procedures described in Chapters 12 and 13. The assumptions about the populations and samples representing them are

♦ The samples are independent random samples.

♦ The distribution of the response variable is a normal curve within each population.

♦ The different populations may have different means.

♦ All populations have the same standard deviation, σ.

These assumptions make up a model for the probability distributions in the populations being compared. Figure 16.2 illustrates, for three populations, how this model might look if the alternative hypothesis were true, and how it would look if the null hypothesis were true. Notice that in the alternative hypothesis case, the only difference among the populations is the difference among their means, μ_1, μ_2, and μ_3. The spread of the normal curve is assumed to be the same for each population.

When we compare two means, it is not imperative to assume equal population standard deviations because an "unpooled" procedure is available that does not require this assumption. Unfortunately, when we do a one-way analysis of variance, the equal standard deviations assumption is necessary. In practice, equality of the observed standard deviations does not have to hold exactly for the *F*-test to provide a valid significance test of differences among population means. One commonly used criterion is that the *F*-test can be used if the largest of the sample standard deviations is not more than twice as large as the smallest of the sample standard deviations. There are significance tests for the equality of several standard deviations, but those tests tend not to work well when the data are not normally distributed. They can also have low power for small or moderate sample sizes, leading to false acceptance of equal variances when they are actually quite different. Therefore, we do not recommend using those tests.

The assumption of normally distributed data is not strictly necessary in practice either. Unless there are extreme outliers, or extreme skewness in the data, the *F*-test works well even for relatively small sample sizes. When the raw

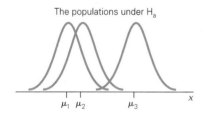

The populations under H_a

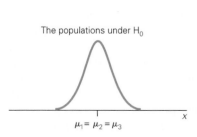

The populations under H_0

FIGURE 16.2 **The model for one-way analysis of variance under the two different hypotheses**

data are available, a visual display should be created and examined in order to evaluate whether skewness or outliers are present.

in summary **Necessary Conditions for Using the *F*-Statistic to Compare Means**

- ◆ The *F*-statistic can be used if the data are not extremely skewed, there are no extreme outliers, and the group standard deviations are not markedly different.

- ◆ As with the *t*-tests and confidence intervals in Chapters 12 and 13, tests based on the *F*-statistic are valid for data with skewness or outliers if the sample sizes are large.

- ◆ A rough criterion for standard deviations is that the largest of the sample standard deviations should not be more than twice as large as the smallest of the sample standard deviations.

EXAMPLE 16.1—*CONTINUED*
Assessing the Necessary Conditions for the GPA and Seat Location Data

The boxplot in Figure 16.1 (p. 563) shows two outliers in the group of students who typically sit in the middle of a classroom, but there are 218 students in that group so these outliers don't have much influence on the results. The standard deviations for the three groups are nearly the same, and the data do not appear to be skewed. The necessary conditions for doing an *F*-test are satisfied in this example. ◆

16.1

turn on your mind

To what populations do the conclusions of Example 16.1 apply? Do you think it matters that the data were collected at a single university? Does it matter that the surveys were done only in statistics classes?*

EXAMPLE 16.2
Occupational Choice and Testosterone Level

Many research studies have been done to examine how testosterone affects human behavior, and, conversely, some studies have considered how behavior affects testosterone level. In a study done at Georgia State University, psychologists compared the salivary testosterone concentrations of men who were ministers, salesmen, firemen, professors, physicians, professional football players, and actors. There were 66 men in the overall sample, and the sample sizes in the seven occupational groups ranged from 6 (actors) to 16 (physicians).

The researchers reported in the *Journal of Personality and Social Psychology* (Dabbs et al., 1990, p. 1262) that "analysis of variance showed an overall difference among the groups, $F(6,59) = 2.50$, $p < 0.05$, and a Newman-Keuls test indicated that actors and football players were significantly higher than ministers."

*HINT: How universal do you think are the characteristics of students selecting the three different classroom seat locations?

In this quote, the information given is that the p-value for an F-test was less than 0.05, so the null hypothesis that all population means are the same was rejected. Additional information is given about the pattern of the difference, which is that actors and football players had higher testosterone levels than ministers. Presumably, all other differences involving the other occupational groups were not statistically significant. The researchers focused on the difference between actors and ministers and reported on two additional studies they did that replicated the finding. In their discussion, they related the observed testosterone differences to the social, competitive, and dominance behaviors of ministers and actors. ◆

The Family of F-Distributions

An F-distribution is used to find the p-value for an ANOVA F-test of the null hypothesis that several population means are equal. The family of F-distributions is a family of skewed distributions, each with a minimum value of 0. A specific F-distribution is indicated by two parameters called *degrees of freedom*. The first of the two parameters is called the **numerator degrees of freedom;** the second is called the **denominator degrees of freedom.** The values of the two degrees of freedom parameters always are given in the order *numerator df, denominator df.* In one-way ANOVA, the numerator df $= k - 1$ (number of groups $- 1$), and the denominator df $= N - k$ (total sample size $-$ number of groups).

Figure 16.3 shows an F-distribution with 2 and 30 degrees of freedom along with an F-distribution with 6 and 30 degrees of freedom. Notice that both curves are skewed and the minimum possible value is 0. These are properties of all F-distributions, regardless of the values for the numerator and denominator degrees of freedom.

Determining the p-Value

All statistical software programs incorporate analysis of variance procedures, and the p-value will be reported as part of the output. In situations where an F-statistic has been computed without statistical software, the Excel command FDIST(*value, numerator df, denominator df*) can be used to find the p-value. When software is not available a range for the p-value can be found using tabled values for the appropriate F-distribution. Table A.4 in the Appendix gives **critical values** for two different levels of significance, $\alpha = 0.05$ and $\alpha = 0.01$. If the observed

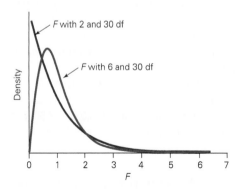

FIGURE 16.3   **An F-distribution with 2 and 30 df and an F-distribution with 6 and 30 df**

F-statistic is greater than the critical value for a particular level of significance, the result is statistically significant at that level. The region of *F*-statistic values greater than the critical value is called the **rejection region** for the test.

Using Table A.4 to Judge Statistical Significance
First, determine values for the numerator degrees of freedom and the denominator degrees of freedom. Possible values for the numerator degrees of freedom are given as column headings across the top of Table A.4. Possible values for the denominator degrees of freedom are given as row labels in the leftmost column.

♦ If the value of the *F*-statistic is greater than the critical value in the $\alpha = 0.05$ portion of the table, the result is statistically significant at the 0.05 significance level. In this case, the *p*-value is less than 0.05, which may be written $p < 0.05$.

♦ If the value of the *F*-statistic is greater than the critical value in the $\alpha = 0.01$ portion of the table, the result is statistically significant at the 0.01 significance level. In this case, the *p*-value is less than 0.01, which may be written $p < 0.01$.

♦ If the value of the *F*-statistic is between the critical values given for $\alpha = 0.05$ and $\alpha = 0.01$, the *p*-value is between 0.05 and 0.01 ($0.01 < p < 0.05$). In this case, the result is statistically significant for $\alpha = 0.05$ but not for $\alpha = 0.01$.

As an example, suppose the *F*-statistic for comparing four means is $F = 4.26$ and numerator df = 3 and denominator df = 20. In Table A.4, for $\alpha = 0.05$, the critical value is given as 3.10 (in the column labeled "3" and row labeled "20"). Because the observed $F = 4.26$ is greater than the critical value = 3.10, the result is statistically significant at the $\alpha = 0.05$ level. The critical value for the $\alpha = 0.01$ is given as 4.94 in Table A.4. Because 4.26 is not greater than this critical value, the result is not significant at the 0.01 level. Thus, the *p*-value is between 0.01 and 0.05.

EXAMPLE 16.2—*CONTINUED*
The p-Value for the
Testosterone and
Occupational
Choice Example

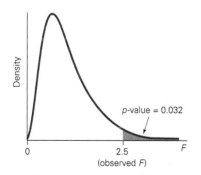

FIGURE 16.4   The *p*-value for Example 16.2 is the area to the right of *F* = 2.5 under an *F*-distribution with 6 and 59 degrees of freedom

The authors reported that the value of the *F*-statistic for comparing the seven occupations was $F = 2.5$ and the *p*-value was less than 0.05. With $k = 7$ occupational groups and $N = 66$ observations in the total sample, the degrees of freedom are $7 - 1 = 6$ and $66 - 7 = 59$. Figure 16.4 illustrates the *p*-value, which is the area to the right of 2.5 under an *F*-distribution with 6 and 59 df. In Excel, FDIST(*value, numerator df, denominator df*) can be used to find the probability of an *F*-statistic as large as or larger than the specified value. In this case, FDIST(2.5,6,59) provides the information that the *p*-value is 0.032. Using Table A.4, we learn that the approximate critical value is 2.25 for $\alpha = 0.05$. This is the value given for numerator df = 6 and denominator df = 60. Because 2.5 is larger than this critical value, the result is statistically significant for the 0.05 significance level, and the *p*-value is smaller than 0.05.♦

Multiple Comparisons

The term **multiple comparisons** is used when two or more comparisons are made to examine the specific pattern of differences among means. The most commonly analyzed set of multiple comparisons is the set of all pairwise comparisons among population means. In Example 16.1 about GPA and classroom seat location, the possible pairwise comparisons are Front versus Middle,

Middle versus Back, and Front versus Back. In Example 16.2 about occupation and testosterone level, the mean testosterone levels for 21 different pairs of occupations can be compared (actor versus minister, football player versus professor, and so on).

Either of two equivalent approaches can be used to make inferences about pairs of means. For each pair, a significance test could be done to determine if the two means significantly differ. Or, a confidence interval for the difference in each pair of means could be computed, and interpreted in terms of statistical significance. If a confidence interval for a difference does not include the value 0, there is a statistically significant difference. In its one-way analysis of variance procedure, Minitab uses the confidence interval approach.

When many comparisons are made within the same study, some statistically significant results may occur just by chance. Remember that when the $\alpha = 0.05$ significance level is used, about 1 in 20 independent statistical tests will achieve statistical significance even if all null hypotheses are true. In other words, when many statistical tests are done there is an increased risk of making at least one type I error (erroneously rejecting a null hypothesis). Consequently, several procedures have been developed to control the overall **family type I error rate** or the overall **family confidence level** when inferences for a set (family) of multiple comparisons are done. **Tukey's procedure** is one such procedure for the family of pairwise comparisons. If the family error rate is not a concern, **Fisher's procedure** is used.

---

definition ◆ A **family error rate** for a set of significance tests is the probability of making one or more type I errors (erroneously rejecting a null hypothesis) when more than one significance test is done.

◆ A **family confidence level** for a procedure used to create a set of confidence intervals is the proportion of times that all intervals in the set capture their true parameter values.

EXAMPLE 16.1—*CONTINUED*
Pairwise Comparisons
of GPAs Based
on Seat Locations

Figure 16.5 shows Minitab output for pairwise comparisons of the mean GPA by seat location. The family confidence level used for the Tukey procedure was 0.95 (95%), while for Fisher's procedure a 0.95 (95%) confidence level was used for each individual interval. For both methods, the output gives confidence intervals for the difference in mean GPAs for each of the three possible comparisons of seat locations (Front versus Middle, Front versus Back, and Middle versus Back). The two numbers given for each combination of two seat locations are the lower and upper limits of a confidence interval for the difference in mean GPAs for the corresponding populations. In the results for the Tukey procedure, for instance, the values given for the "Front" (column label) versus "Back" (row label) combination are 0.0846 and 0.4824. Thus, a confidence interval for the difference in means ($\mu_{\text{Front}} - \mu_{\text{Back}}$) is 0.0846 to 0.4824. In the results given for the Fisher procedure, the confidence interval for ($\mu_{\text{Front}} - \mu_{\text{Back}}$) is 0.1164 to 0.4506.

Tukey's pairwise comparisons
Intervals for (column level mean) − (row level mean)

	Front	Middle
Middle	0.0561	
	0.3791	
Back	0.0846	−0.1028
	0.4824	0.2347

Fisher's pairwise comparisons
Intervals for (column level mean) − (row level mean)

	Front	Middle
Middle	0.0819	
	0.3533	
Back	0.1164	−0.0758
	0.4506	0.2077

FIGURE 16.5 Confidence intervals for pairwise differences in the GPA and seat location example

In general, two means are significantly different if the confidence interval for the difference does not cover 0. Notice that the two procedures lead to the same conclusions about statistical significance in this example, but that will not always be the case. In both procedures, the only confidence interval that covers 0 is the one for $(\mu_{\text{Middle}} - \mu_{\text{Back}})$. So, we can conclude that the population mean GPAs differ for students who sit in the front and middle of the room and for those who sit in the front and back of the room, but not for those who sit in the middle and back.

Figure 16.6 is a graph of the confidence intervals found using the Tukey method. Each interval estimates the difference between the population mean GPAs for two different seat locations. A vertical line is drawn at 0, the value that would indicate no difference between two means. Notice that the confidence interval for $(\mu_{\text{Middle}} - \mu_{\text{Back}})$ covers the line drawn at 0, whereas confidence intervals for $(\mu_{\text{Front}} - \mu_{\text{Back}})$ and $(\mu_{\text{Front}} - \mu_{\text{Middle}})$ do not. ◆

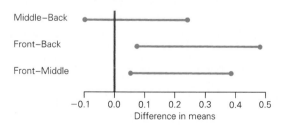

FIGURE 16.6 Confidence intervals for differences between pairs of means in the GPA and seat location example (Tukey procedure)

Minitab Tip

tech note   **One-Way Analysis of Variance**

- Use **Stat**>**ANOVA**>**One-way** if values of the response variable are in one column (Response) and values or names for groups are in a second column (Factor). In the dialog box, the ***Comparisons*** button is used for pairwise comparisons.

- Use **Stat**>**ANOVA**>**One-way (unstacked)** if the data for different groups are stored in separate columns. Specify the separate columns for the groups in the dialog box. There is not a pairwise comparisons capability in this procedure (Version 13 or before).

16.2 | DETAILS OF ONE-WAY ANALYSIS OF VARIANCE

In this section, we provide some computational details for the F-statistic and give the necessary conditions for using the statistic. In practice, statistical software is nearly always used to do a one-way analysis of variance, so it is not necessary to learn formulas in order to do the computations "by hand." The formulas, however, provide useful insights into the concepts of analysis of variance and how the F-test is constructed.

The Analysis of Variance Table

A fundamental concept in one-way analysis of variance is that the variation among the data values in the overall sample can be separated into (1) differences between group means, and (2) natural variation among observations within a group. The calculations and theory for analysis of variance stem from the fact that for a particular way of measuring variation, the sum of the variation between group means and the variation among observations within groups equals the total variation. Expressed as an equation, the relationship is

Total variation = Variation between groups + Variation within groups

An **analysis of variance table,** like the one shown in Figure 16.1 for Example 16.1 (p. 563), is used to display information about the sources of variation in the response variable. The F-statistic used to compare population means measures the relative size of the variation between group means and the natural variation within groups.

EXAMPLE 16.3
Comparison of Weight-Loss Programs
Suppose that a researcher does a randomized experiment to compare the mean weight loss for three different programs for losing weight, and the observed weight losses after three months are as follows:

Program 1	Program 2	Program 3
7	9	15
9	11	12
5	7	18
7		

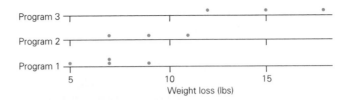

FIGURE 16.7   Dotplot for Example 16.3

A look at the dotplot of the data shown in Figure 16.7 shows that over the total dataset, the weight losses ranged from 5 to 18 pounds. The sample means for the three programs are $\bar{x}_1 = 7$, $\bar{x}_2 = 9$, $\bar{x}_3 = 15$. While there is some variation among individuals within each program, generally it appears that differences *between* weight-loss programs account for much of the variation in the total dataset. The weight losses for program 3 in particular are noticeably greater than the weight losses for the other two programs. ◆

Measuring Variation Between Groups

The variation between group means is measured with a weighted sum of squared differences between the sample means (the $\bar{x}_i$) and $\bar{x}$, the overall mean of all data. Each squared difference is multiplied by the appropriate group sample size, n_i, in this sum. This quantity is called **sum of squares for groups** or **SS Groups.** A formula is

$$\text{SS Groups} = n_1(\bar{x}_1 - \bar{x})^2 + n_2(\bar{x}_2 - \bar{x})^2 + \cdots + n_k(\bar{x}_k - \bar{x})^2 = \sum_{\text{groups}} n_i(\bar{x}_i - \bar{x})^2$$

The numerator of the *F*-statistic for comparing means is called the **mean square for groups** or **MS Groups,** and it is calculated as

$$\text{MS Groups} = \frac{\text{SS Groups}}{k - 1}$$

Measuring Variation Within Groups

To measure the variation among individuals within groups, find the sum of squared deviations between data values and the sample mean in each group, and then add these quantities. This is called the **sum of squared errors** or **SSE.** A formula in terms of sample standard deviations is

$$\text{SS Error} = (n_1 - 1)s_1^2 + (n_2 - 1)s_2^2 + \cdots + (n_k - 1)s_k^2 = \sum_{\text{groups}} (n_i - 1)s_i^2$$

The denominator of the *F*-statistic is called the **mean square error** or **MSE,** and it is calculated as

$$\text{MSE} = \frac{\text{SSE}}{N - k} = \frac{(n_1 - 1)s_1^2 + (n_2 - 1)s_2^2 + \cdots + (n_k - 1)s_k^2}{n_1 + n_2 + \cdots + n_k - k}$$

Notice that MSE is just a weighted average of the sample variances for the k groups. In fact, if all n_i are equal, MSE is simply the average of the k sample variances. The square root of MSE, denoted by s_p and called the **pooled standard deviation,** estimates the population standard deviation of the response variable.

Recall that the populations being compared are assumed to have equal standard deviations.

> ***definition*** The **pooled standard deviation** $s_p = \sqrt{\text{MSE}}$ estimates the population standard deviation, σ. This assumes that each population has the same value of σ.

Measuring Total Variation

The total variation in all samples combined is measured by computing the sum of squared deviations between data values and the mean of all the data. This quantity is referred to as the **total sum of squares** or **SS Total**. The total sum of squares may also be referred to as SSTO. A formula for the sum of squared differences from the overall mean is

$$\text{SS Total} = \sum_{\text{values}} (x_{ij} - \bar{x})^2$$

where x_{ij} represents the jth observation within the ith group, and $\bar{x}$ is the mean of all observed data values. Notice that SS Total would be the numerator of the sample variance (with denominator $N - 1$) if all the data were combined and treated as a single sample.

The relationship between SS Total, SS Groups, and SS Error is

$$\text{SS Total} = \text{SS Groups} + \text{SS Error}$$

This additive relationship is useful computationally. For example, if the values of SS Total and SS Groups are known, then SS Error can be calculated as

$$\text{SS Error} = \text{SS Total} - \text{SS Groups}$$

EXAMPLE 16.3—CONTINUED
Analysis of Variation Among Weight Losses

For Example 16.3, the $k = 3$ sample means are $\bar{x}_1 = 7$, $\bar{x}_2 = 9$, $\bar{x}_3 = 15$, and the mean of all $N = 10$ observations is $\bar{x} = 10$.

$$\text{SS Groups} = n_1(\bar{x}_1 - \bar{x})^2 + n_2(\bar{x}_2 - \bar{x})^2 + n_3(\bar{x}_3 - \bar{x})^2$$

$$= 4(7 - 10)^2 + 3(9 - 10)^2 + 3(15 - 10)^2 = 114$$

$$\text{MS Groups} = \frac{114}{3 - 1} = 57$$

$$\text{SS Total} = (7 - 10)^2 + (9 - 10)^2 + (5 - 10)^2 + (7 - 10)^2 + (9 - 10)^2$$
$$+ (11 - 10)^2 + (7 - 10)^2 + (15 - 10)^2 + (12 - 10)^2$$
$$+ (18 - 10)^2 = 148$$

$$\text{SS Error} = \text{SS Total} - \text{SS Groups} = 148 - 114 = 34$$

$$\text{MSE} = \frac{34}{10 - 3} = 4.857$$

$$F = \frac{57}{4.857} = 11.74 \qquad \text{with 2 and 7 df}$$

Figure 16.8 shows Minitab output for Example 16.3. The analysis of variance table format used is standard for most software. The line labeled "Programs" gives information about SS Groups and MS Groups, and also includes the

Analysis of Variance

```
Source      DF      SS      MS       F      P
Programs     2   114.00   57.00   11.74   0.006
Error        7    34.00    4.86
Total        9   148.00
```

                                Individual 95% CIs For Mean
                                Based on Pooled StDev

```
Level       N     Mean    StDev   ----------+---------+---------+-----
Program1    4    7.000    1.633   (------*-----)
Program2    3    9.000    2.000      (-------*------)
Program3    3   15.000    3.000                      (------*-------)
                                    ----------+---------+---------+-----
Pooled StDev =   2.204                      8.0      12.0      16.0
```

FIGURE 16.8   **Minitab output for Example 16.3**

F-statistic and the *p*-value. The label for this line is the name the user gives the explanatory variable when the dataset is created. In some instances, "Factor" may be used as a generic label for the explanatory variable. The line labeled "Error" gives information about SS Error and MSE. At the bottom of the output, the pooled standard deviation is given as 2.204. This can be computed as $\sqrt{MSE} = \sqrt{4.86}$. ◆

General Format of a One-Way ANOVA Table

In summary, the general format of the one-way analysis of variance table is

Source	df	SS	MS	F
Between groups (due to factor)	$k-1$	$SS\ Groups = \sum_{groups} n_i(\bar{x}_i - \bar{x})^2$	$\dfrac{SS\ Groups}{k-1}$	$F = \dfrac{MS\ Groups}{MSE}$
Error (within groups)	$N-k$	$SSE = \sum_{groups} (n_i-1)s_i^2$	$\dfrac{SSE}{N-k}$	
Total	$N-1$	$SSTO = \sum_{values} (x_{ij} - \bar{x})^2$		

EXAMPLE 16.4
Top Speeds of Supercars

Kitchens (1998, p. 783) gives data gathered by *Car and Driver* magazine on the top speeds of five supercars from five different countries—Acura NSX-T from Japan, Ferrari F355 from Italy, Lotus Esprit S4S from Great Britain, Porsche 911 Turbo from Germany, and Dodge Viper RT/10 from the United States. The data represent the top speeds for six runs on each car, using as much distance as necessary without exceeding the engine's redline. There were three runs in each direction on the test facility, to cancel grade or wind effects. Figure 16.9 on the next page includes a dotplot of the data, as well as output for a one-way analysis of variance that compares the five cars. Some important features of the results shown in the figure are

◆ The *p*-value is 0.000, so we can reject the null hypothesis that the population mean speeds are the same for all five cars.

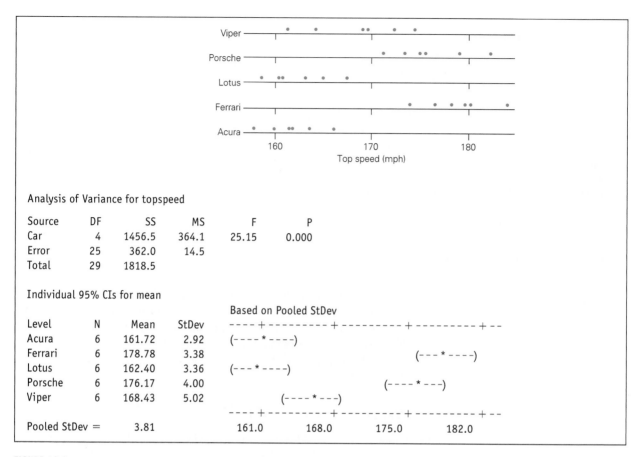

FIGURE 16.9   Dotplot and analysis of variance output for Example 16.4

♦ $F = 25.15$. The calculation was $F = $ MS Cars/MS Error $= 364.1/14.5$. An F-distribution with 4 and 25 df was used to determine the p-value.

♦ The necessary conditions for doing an ANOVA F-test are present. The data are not skewed and there are no extreme outliers. The largest sample standard deviation (5.02 for Viper) is not more than twice as large as the smallest standard deviation (2.92 for Acura).

♦ MS Error $= 14.5$ is an estimate of the variance of the top speed for the hypothetical distribution of all possible runs with one car. The estimated standard deviation for each car is $\sqrt{\text{MS Error}} = \sqrt{14.5} = 3.81$. This value is given as the pooled standard deviation at the bottom of the output.

♦ Based on the sample means and corresponding confidence intervals for population means, the Porsche and Ferrari seem to be significantly faster than the other three cars. ♦

Computation of 95% Confidence Intervals for the Population Means

It is informative to examine and compare confidence intervals for the population means. In Examples 16.1 and 16.4, we saw that the Minitab output for one-way analysis of variance includes a graph showing a 95% confidence interval for each population mean. These intervals are computed using the same general format we used in Chapter 12 for a confidence interval for a mean:

$$\text{Sample mean} \pm \text{Multiplier} \times \text{Standard error}$$

Because it is assumed that all populations have the same standard deviation, $s_p = \sqrt{\text{MSE}}$ is used to estimate the standard deviation within each group. This affects the standard error and the degrees of freedom. For the ith sample mean, $\text{s.e.}(\overline{x}_i) = s_p/\sqrt{n_i}$. Notice that the pooled standard deviation is used regardless of group, but the sample size is specific to the group. The "multiplier" is determined using a t-distribution as it was for a single mean in Section 12.4, but in this situation, $\text{df} = N - k$. These degrees of freedom are used because they are associated with the *mean squared error*, which is used to estimate the standard deviation.

Confidence Interval for a Population Mean

formula In one-way analysis of variance, a **confidence interval for a population mean** μ_i is

$$\overline{x}_i \pm t^* \frac{s_p}{\sqrt{n_i}}$$

where $s_p = \sqrt{\text{MSE}}$ and t^* is such that the confidence level is the probability between $-t^*$ and t^* in a t-distribution with $N - k$ degrees of freedom.

EXAMPLE 16.4—CONTINUED
95% Confidence Intervals for Mean Car Speeds

The pooled standard deviation for Example 16.4 is $s_p = 3.81$ mph, a value displayed at the bottom of Figure 16.9. For each car, $n_i = 6$, so the standard error for any car is $\text{s.e.}(\overline{x}_i) = 3.81/\sqrt{6}$. The df for the t^* multiplier are $N - k = 30 - 5 = 25$. From the table of t^* multipliers (Table A.2), we learn that for a 0.95 confidence level and $\text{df} = 25$, the multiplier is $t^* = 2.06$. A 95% confidence interval for any mean is $\overline{x}_i \pm 2.06(3.81/\sqrt{6})$, or $\overline{x}_i \pm 3.02$. For example, the 95% confidence interval for the Acura is 161.72 ± 3.02 mph, for the Ferrari it is 178.78 ± 3.02 mph, and so on. ◆

16.2

turn on your mind

In Example 16.4, each 95% confidence interval had the same width. Why did this happen? When would the 95% confidence intervals have different widths?*

in summary Steps for the *F*-Test for Comparing Several Means

Step 1: *Determine the* null *and* alternative *hypotheses.*

Null hypothesis: $H_0: \mu_1 = \mu_2 = \ldots = \mu_k$

Alternative hypothesis: H_a: The μ's are not all equal.

Step 2: *Verify necessary data conditions, and if met, summarize the data into an appropriate* test statistic. The *F*-statistic can be used if the data are not extremely skewed, there are no extreme outliers, and the group standard deviations are not markedly different. A criterion for standard deviations is that the largest of the sample deviations should not be more than twice as large as the smallest of the sample standard deviations. The test statistic is

$$F = \frac{\text{MS Groups}}{\text{MS Error}} = \frac{\dfrac{\Sigma n_i(\bar{x}_i - \bar{x})^2}{k - 1}}{\dfrac{\Sigma(n_i - 1)s_i^2}{N - k}}$$

Step 3: *Assuming the null hypothesis is true, find the p-value.* Using the *F*-distribution with numerator df $= k - 1$ and denominator df $= N - k$, the *p*-value is the area in the tail to the right of the test statistic *F*.

Step 4: *Decide whether or not the result is* statistically significant *based on the p-value.* Choose a significance level ("alpha"); standard is $\alpha = 0.05$. The result is statistically significant if the *p*-value $\leq \alpha$.

Step 5: *Report the conclusion in the context of the situation.* In analysis of variance, when the null hypothesis is rejected these steps are usually followed by a multiple comparison procedure to determine which group means are significantly different from each other.

16.3 | OTHER METHODS FOR COMPARING POPULATIONS

You probably won't be surprised to learn that the necessary conditions for using an analysis of variance *F*-test don't hold for all datasets. In this section, we discuss methods that can be used when one or both of the assumptions about equal population standard deviations and normal distributions are violated. It is important to remember that no inference method is appropriate if the observed data do not represent the population for the question of interest.

EXAMPLE 16.5
Drinks per Week and Seat Location

In the two surveys described for Example 16.1, students were asked, "How many alcoholic beverages do you consume each week?" Let's compare responses for the same three groups compared in Example 16.1: students who typically sit in the front, middle, or back of a classroom. Figure 16.10 displays a boxplot of the data and Table 16.1 contains summary statistics for the three seat locations. The sample sizes are a bit different here than in Example 16.1 because some students did not give a response to every question.

The information in Figure 16.10 and Table 16.1 reveals that the students who typically sit in the back report drinking more alcohol than the other students do. The information in the figure and table also shows that the group standard deviations differ, and the data appear to be skewed. The boxplot shows much more variation in the responses of the back of the classroom group than in the other two groups. In Table 16.1, we see that the standard deviation in the "back" group (10.5) is more than twice as large as the standard deviation in the "front" group

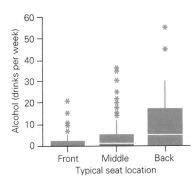

FIGURE 16.10   Boxplot by seat location for number of alcoholic beverages per week

TABLE 16.1 ■ Summary Statistics by Seat Location for Number of Alcoholic Beverages per Week

Location	n	Mean	Median	s.d.
Front	87	1.6	0	3.4
Middle	207	3.9	1	6.5
Back	79	8.5	5	10.5

(3.4). Also, the mean is greater than the median in each group, which is evidence of skewness in the data. The necessary conditions for doing an analysis of variance are violated in this dataset. ◆

Hypotheses About Medians

When the observed data are skewed, or when extreme outliers are present, it usually is better to analyze the median rather than the mean. This is also what should usually be done if the response variable is an ordinal variable. When several population medians are compared, null and alternative hypotheses of interest are

H_0: Population medians are equal.
H_a: Population medians are not all equal.

The notation used for a population median varies from author to author. The most commonly used symbol is η (pronounced "eta"). With this notation, the null hypothesis about the medians of k populations is $H_0: \eta_1 = \eta_2 = \ldots = \eta_k$. The letter M is generally used to denote a sample median. When considering several samples, the median of the ith sample would be written M_i.

Kruskal–Wallis Test for Comparing Medians

One test for comparing medians is the **Kruskal–Wallis Test.** It is based on a comparison of the relative rankings (sizes) of the data in the observed samples, and for this reason is called a **rank test.** The term **nonparametric test** also is used to describe this test because there are no assumptions made about a specific distribution for the population of measurements.

The general idea is that values in the total data set of N observations are ranked from lowest to highest (lowest = 1, highest = N). The ranks of the values are averaged for each group, and the test statistic measures the variation among the average ranks of the groups. If most of the small data values were in one particular group, for example, that group would have a lower average rank than the other groups. A p-value can be determined by finding the probability that the variation among the set of rank averages for the groups would be as large (or larger) as it is if the null hypothesis is true. More information about the Kruskal–Wallis Test as well as other nonparametric methods is given in Supplemental Topic 2 on the CD for this book.

EXAMPLE 16.5—*CONTINUED*
Kruskal–Wallis Test for
Alcoholic Beverages
per Week by Seat Location

Figure 16.11 contains output from Minitab for a Kruskal–Wallis Test of the null hypothesis that the *median* number of alcoholic beverages consumed per week is the same for the three classroom seat locations. The p-value shown at the bottom of the output is P = 0.000, which indicates strong evidence against the null hypothesis. You'll see that two p-values are shown; the second is followed by the phrase "adjusted for ties." There is a "tie" in the rankings when two or more observations have the same value. For example, all students who reported 0 drinks per week are tied with each other. It is possible to determine an adjustment to the p-value based on the number of ties that occur. In practice, the adjusted and unadjusted values rarely differ by much.

The output in Figure 16.11 on the next page includes the sample median and the average rank within each group. Oddly, the medians are given by Minitab in

> **Kruskal–Wallis Test on alcohol**
>
> | Seat | N | Median | Ave Rank | Z |
> |------|-----|----------|----------|-------|
> | Front | 87 | 0.00E+00 | 143.7 | −4.27 |
> | Middle | 207 | 1.00E+00 | 183.6 | −0.68 |
> | Back | 79 | 5.00E+00 | 243.6 | 5.25 |
> | | | | | |
> | Overall | 373 | | 187.0 | |
>
> $H = 35.98$ DF = 2   P = 0.000
> $H = 40.18$ DF = 2   P = 0.000 (adjusted for ties)

FIGURE 16.11   **Kruskal–Wallis Test for comparing median number of alcoholic beverages per week in three classroom locations**

scientific notation. Notice that the median number of alcoholic beverages per week for the "back" group is 5, which is clearly higher than the medians for the other two groups. Because the reported data values tended to be higher in the back group, the average rank is highest for this group. The data values tended to be lowest for the front group (median = 0), so the average rank is lowest for that group. The Kruskal–Wallis statistic measures the variation among the average ranks shown for the three groups much like the F-statistic measures the variation among the sample means in analysis of variance. ◆

Mood's Median Test for Comparing Medians

TABLE 16.2 ■ **Format of the Two-Way Table for Mood's Median Test. M = Median of All Data in Overall Dataset**

Group	Number ≤ M	Number > M
1		
2		
⋮		
k		

Another *nonparametric* test used to compare population medians is **Mood's Median Test.** The idea is easy to grasp. First, the median (M) of the total data set with all groups combined is determined. Then, within each group, the number of observations less than or equal to M and the number of observations greater than M are counted. These counts can be displayed in the two-way table shown in Table 16.2. A chi-square statistic for two-way tables (Chapter 15) is used to test the null hypothesis that the population medians are the same. The test is equivalent to testing that the two variables creating the rows and columns in Table 16.2 are not related. A statistically significant result indicates that the medians are not all the same.

16.3

turn on your mind

Show why the null hypothesis of equal population medians is equivalent to the null hypothesis that the two variables in Table 16.2 are not related as follows. Assume for simplicity that no values are tied with the sample median M. In that case, fill in the marginal totals for Table 16.2 using the notation for group sizes of $n_1, n_2, \ldots, n_k$; $N = n_1 + n_2 + \cdots + n_k$. What would be the expected cell counts for the test of the null hypothesis that the two variables are unrelated? Explain why those are the same cell counts that would be expected under the null hypothesis that all population medians are equal.*

*<small>**HINT:** If the null were true, what fraction of each group would be on either side of the overall median? See Section 15.1 to review expected counts for a two-way table.</small>

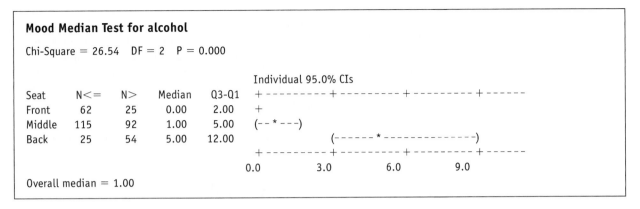

Mood Median Test for alcohol

Chi-Square = 26.54   DF = 2   P = 0.000

```
                                      Individual 95.0% CIs
Seat    N<=   N>   Median   Q3-Q1    + --------- + --------- + --------- + ------
Front    62   25    0.00    2.00     +
Middle  115   92    1.00    5.00     (-- * ---)
Back     25   54    5.00   12.00                 (------ * -------------)
                                     + --------- + --------- + --------- + ------
                                     0.0        3.0         6.0         9.0

Overall median = 1.00
```

FIGURE 16.12   **Mood's Median Test for the alcoholic beverages per week by seat location example**

EXAMPLE 16.5—CONTINUED
Mood's Median Test for the Alcoholic Beverages and Seat Location Example

Output from Minitab for Mood's Median Test in the alcoholic beverages consumed per week by classroom seat location example is shown in Figure 16.12. The first line shows that the *p*-value for the chi-square test is 0.000, indicating that the null hypothesis of equal population medians can be rejected. The overall median of all responses is shown at the bottom of the output as "Overall median = 1.00." In the central portion of the output, information is given about how many responses in each seat location group were less than or equal to this value and how many were greater than this value. In the "front" group, for instance, 62 students reported consuming one or fewer alcoholic beverages per week and 25 reported drinking more than this. A much different pattern is evident in the "back" group. In that group, 25 reported consuming one or fewer drinks per week compared to 54 who reported drinking more than one drink per week. Notice also that sample medians and interquartile ranges are given for each group along with a 95% confidence interval for the median of the population represented by each group. ◆

Minitab Tip

tech note   **Nonparametric Procedures for Comparing Several Medians**
The Kruskal–Wallis and Mood's Median tests are listed in the menu that results from using **Stat>Nonparametrics.**

Advanced Technical Note

tech note   **Transforming the Response Variable for Analysis of Variance**
When the group standard deviations and the group means are related, it may be possible to transform the values of the response variable so that the necessary conditions for ANOVA are satisfied on the transformed scale. An analysis of variance is then done on the transformed data. Three transformations that frequently work for this purpose are square root, logarithm, and reciprocal. For instance, if the ratio $s_i/\bar{x}_i$ is about the same for all groups, then the values of log(response) tend to have equal standard deviations for all groups. Using this "log transformation" frequently works for financial data, such as salaries, for which the variability increases as the mean increases.

The type of pattern for which a transformation might work is present in Example 16.5. Notice that sample means and sample standard deviations are ordered in the same way over the three groups. In this example, if $x =$ alcoholic beverages per week, the group standard deviations are nearly equal for the transformed response $1/(0.5 + x)$. (Adding 0.5 to x avoids dividing by 0.) It is difficult, however, to interpret the transformed responses, so a comparison of medians may be preferable.

16.4 | TWO-WAY ANALYSIS OF VARIANCE

A **two-way analysis of variance** is used to examine how two categorical explanatory variables affect the mean of a quantitative response variable. For example, an industrial psychologist may want to see how type of background music and loudness of background music affect productivity in a workplace. Or an economist may be interested to learn the effects of gender and race on mean income. In problems like these, there is interest in the effect of each separate explanatory factor, and there is interest in the combined effect of the two explanatory factors.

The **interaction** between two variables is usually the most interesting feature of a two-way analysis of variance problem. When two variables interact, the effect on the response variable of one explanatory variable depends upon the specific value or level present for the other explanatory variable. A statement like "being overweight caused greater increases in blood pressure for men than for women" is a statement describing an interaction. The effect on blood pressure of weight (overweight or not) depends upon gender (male or female).

The term **main effect** is used to describe the overall effect of a single explanatory variable. In the type of background music and loudness of music example just described, the main effect of the explanatory variable "music loudness" is the effect on productivity of loudness averaged over all music types. A main effect may not be meaningful if an interaction is present. For instance, it may not be sensible or useful to report the effect on blood pressure of being overweight without reporting that the effect is different for men than it is for women.

EXAMPLE 16.6
Happy Faces and Restaurant Tips

When a restaurant server writes a friendly note or draws a "happy face" on your restaurant check, is this just a friendly act or is there a financial incentive? Temple University psychologists conducted a randomized experiment to investigate whether drawing a happy face on the back of a restaurant bill increased the average tip given to the server (Rind and Bordia, 1996). One female server and one male server in a Philadelphia restaurant either did or did not draw a happy face on checks during the experiment. In all, they drew happy faces on 45 checks (22 for the female, 23 for the male) and did not draw happy faces on 44 other checks (23 for the female and 21 for the male). The sequence of drawing the happy face or not was randomized in advance.

Figure 16.13 is a graph of the mean tip percent for each of the four combinations of server gender (female or male) and check message (none or happy face drawing). The type of graph shown is called an **interaction plot.** The mean

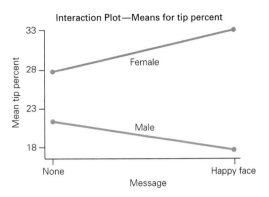

FIGURE 16.13   Mean tip percent related to sex of server and message on check (none or happy face)

response (tip percent) is graphed on the vertical axis and message type (none or happy face) is graphed on the horizontal axis. The higher line in the figure is for the female server (she got better tips than the male). We see that her mean tip percent was about 5% higher for the "happy face" checks. The lower line in the figure shows the results for the male server, and for him, drawing a happy face decreased the mean tip percent by about 4%. The effect of drawing a happy face depended upon gender, so there is an interaction between sex of server and message type. The researchers speculated that customers might have felt that drawing a happy face was not gender appropriate for males. ◆

16.4

turn on your mind

In Example 16.6, there was only one server of each sex. What problem does this cause in the interpretation and generalization of the results? How would you have designed the experiment to better examine the interaction between sex of the server and drawing a happy face (or not)?*

EXAMPLE 16.7
You've Got to Have Heart

Psychologist Lee Salk (*Scientific American,* May 1973) observed 287 mothers within four days after giving birth and found that 83% of the right-handed mothers and 78% of the left-handed mothers held their babies on the left side. When asked why they chose the left side, the right-handed mothers said it was so their right hand would be free. The left-handed mothers said it was because they could hold the baby better with their dominant hand. Salk speculated that "it is not in the nature of nature to provide living organisms with biological tendencies unless such tendencies have survival value." He surmised that there must be survival value to placing a newborn infant close to the sound of the mother's heart.

To test his conjecture, Salk arranged for a baby nursery at a New York City hospital to have the continuous sound of a human heartbeat played over a loudspeaker. At the end of four days, he measured how much weight $n = 102$ babies

*HINT: Do the results reflect a general gender difference or simply the difference between two servers?

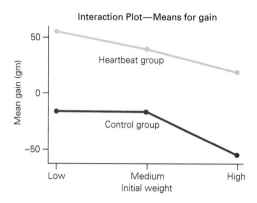

FIGURE 16.14   Mean weight gain (or loss) by initial weight and experimental conditions (heartbeat or not)

in the nursery had gained or lost. Later, with a new group of $n = 112$ babies in the nursery, no sound was played and weight gains (or losses) were again measured after four days. Because initial birth weight affects weight gain or loss in the early stages of life, Salk also categorized the babies into three birth-weight categories.

In all, there are six possible combinations of experimental group (heartbeat or not) and birth weight (low, medium, high). Figure 16.14 is an interaction plot of the sample mean weight gain or loss (grams) for these combinations. (Salk did not give means; we have estimated them from the data shown in a dotplot in his *Scientific American* report.) Considering the purpose of the investigation, the most important finding revealed by Figure 16.14 is that the weight gain was generally greater for the heartbeat group. This confirmed what Salk had suspected. Although they did not eat more than the control group, the infants treated to the sound of the heartbeat gained more weight (or lost less). Further, they spent much less time crying. Salk's conclusion was that "newborn infants are soothed by the sound of the normal adult heartbeat." Somehow, mothers intuitively know that it is important to hold their babies on the left side.

The difference in weight gain evident in Figure 16.14 for all three birth-weight groups indicates that there is a *main effect* for the explanatory variable of "heartbeat or control group." The difference between the mean weight gain or loss in the heartbeat and control groups is roughly the same in each of the birth-weight groups. This is evident from the approximately equal distance between the two lines (heartbeat and control) shown in Figure 16.14 regardless of initial weight. This similarity across groups indicates that there may not be an *interaction* between the experimental condition variable and initial birth-weight group. In this example, it's sensible to report the main effect of heartbeat versus control averaged over birth-weight groups. ◆

Two-Way Analysis of Variance and *F*-Tests

In a two-way analysis of variance, three *F*-statistics are constructed. One is used to test the statistical significance of the interaction, while the other two are used to test the significance of the two separate main effects. The computational details and a more extensive discussion of two-way ANOVA are in Supplemental Topic 4 on the CD for this text.

Source	DF	Adj SS	Adj MS	F	P
Message	1	14.7	14.7	0.13	0.715
Sex	1	2602.0	2602.0	23.69	0.000
Interaction	1	438.7	438.7	3.99	0.049
Error	85	9335.5	109.8		
Total	88	12407.9			

FIGURE 16.15   Two-way analysis of variance of restaurant tipping data

EXAMPLE 16.6—CONTINUED
Two-Way Analysis of Variance for Happy Face Example

The Minitab output in Figure 16.15 is for a two-way analysis of variance of the data for the happy face and restaurant tip example. (Professor Bruce Rind of Temple University provided the raw data). Only consider the p-values shown in the last column of the table, and don't worry about the other details.

The significance test of the effect of "Message" (happy face or none) has a p-value of 0.715, indicating a nonsignificant result. That result, however, is nearly meaningless because, as we saw before, there is an interaction between message type and sex of server. The interaction, which is significant with a p-value of 0.049, was that drawing a happy face increased the tip percent for the woman, but decreased it for the man. For the main effect of sex of server, the p-value is 0.000, indicating a statistically significant difference in average tips for the female and male.

In the last Turn On Your Mind, you were asked to think about the problem caused by having only one server of each sex. The answer is that we can't be certain whether the observed effects have to do with a gender difference or with the difference between these particular individuals. Multiple servers of each sex should be included in the study in order to determine whether there really is a gender difference. ◆

KEY TERMS

Section 16.1
analysis of variance (ANOVA), 561
one-way analysis of variance, 561
F-statistic for comparing means, 562
F-test for comparing means, 562, 575–576
F-distribution, 562, 566
assumptions and conditions for F-test, 564–565
numerator degrees of freedom, 566
denominator degrees of freedom, 566
critical values, 566–567
rejection region, 567
multiple comparisons, 567
family type I error rate, 568

family confidence level, 568
Tukey's multiple comparison procedure, 568
Fisher's multiple comparison procedure, 568

Section 16.2
analysis of variance table, 570, 573
sum of squares (SS) for groups, 571
mean square (MS) for groups, 571
sum of squared errors (SSE), 571
mean squared error (MSE), 571
pooled standard deviation in ANOVA, 571–572
total sum of squares (SS Total, SSTO), 572

confidence interval for a population mean in ANOVA, 575

Section 16.3
Kruskal–Wallis test, 577
rank test, 577
nonparametric test, 577
Mood's median test, 578

Section 16.4
two-way analysis of variance, 580
interaction, 580
main effect, 580
interaction plot, 580–581

EXERCISES   Blue = Basics   **Bold, Bold** = Answer in back

Section 16.1

16.1 In each situation, determine whether one-way analysis of variance is an appropriate method for analyzing the data described. Briefly explain why or why not for each part.

a. A researcher compares the mean blood pressures of men over 50 years old for three different ethnic groups. He samples 100 men in each ethnic group, and measures their blood pressures.

b. A psychiatrist compares four treatment programs for clinical depression. The response variable is whether a patient shows improvement after two months of treatment or not. A randomized experiment is done in which 20 patients are randomly allocated to each treatment.

c. Three methods for memorizing information are compared. Forty-five participants are randomly divided into three groups, and each group memorizes information with a different method. All participants then take a test on the memorized information, and the scores are used to compare the methods.

d. Fifty individuals all listen to five songs, and rate each song on a scale of 0 to 100. The mean scores for the five songs are compared.

16.2 Researchers studying the connection between body weight and age report the following finding: "The p-value was 0.003 for a one-way analysis of variance done to compare body mass index values for the three age groups."

a. What null hypothesis did the researchers test? Write the null hypothesis in words, and also write it using proper statistical notation.

b. Explain what conclusion can be made about the comparison of body mass index values for the three age groups.

16.3 The output for this exercise is an analysis of variance comparing hours spent watching television in a typical day for five categories of highest educational degree attained for $n = 1591$ respondents in the 1993 General Social Survey. Educational degree groups are: graduate, bachelor's, junior college, high school, and less than high school (*Data source:* **GSS-93** dataset on the CD for this book).

a. Write null and alternative hypotheses for this situation. Write the hypotheses in words, and also write the null hypothesis using proper notation.

b. What are the values of the F-statistic and the p-value for testing the hypotheses written in part (a)? What conclusion can be made about the hypotheses?

c. Compare the sample means given in the output below the analysis of variance table. Describe how mean hours of watching television per day relates to highest degree attained.

16.4 For $n = 153$ female students in the **UCDavis2** dataset on the CD accompanying this book, mean height (inches) by student's preferred seat location in a classroom is as follows:

Location	Mean
Front ($n = 38$)	63.9
Middle ($n = 93$)	64.8
Back ($n = 22$)	66.5

a. The p-value is 0.001 for an F-test that compares the mean heights of female students in the three seating locations. In the context of this situation, what conclusion can be made?

b. Describe how mean height of female students in the dataset relates to preferred seating location.

16.5 Refer to the previous exercise about female height and preferred classroom seating location. The following output from Minitab gives confidence intervals for all pairwise comparisons of seating locations. A Tukey procedure with 95% family confidence interval was used.

Intervals for (column level mean) − (row level mean)		
	Back	Front
Front	1.018	
	4.362	
Middle	0.270	−2.142
	3.230	0.261

```
Analysis of Variance for tvhours
Source          DF          SS          MS          F          P
degree          4          639.70      159.92      35.98      0.000
Error           1586        7050.14     4.45
Total           1590        7689.84

Level           N           Mean
Bachelor        252         2.060
Graduate        118         1.797
HighScho        834         2.969
JunColl         96          2.635
NotHS           291         3.928
```

a. What confidence interval is given for the difference between the mean heights of female students who prefer to sit in the back versus those who prefer to sit in the front? Explain whether the interval gives evidence that the population means differ for these two locations.

b. What confidence interval is given for the difference between the mean heights of female students who prefer to sit in the back versus those who prefer to sit in the middle? Explain whether the interval gives evidence that the population means differ for these two locations.

c. What confidence interval is given for the difference between the mean heights of female students who prefer to sit in the front versus those who prefer to sit in the middle? Explain whether the interval gives evidence that the population means differ for these two locations.

16.6 In each situation use Table A.4 to find a critical value and then state a conclusion for an F-test of the null hypothesis of equal population means:

a. F-statistic $= 6.27$ with 2 and 12 degrees of freedom; $\alpha = 0.05$.

b. F-statistic $= 1.63$ with 5 and 70 degrees of freedom; $\alpha = 0.05$.

c. F-statistic $= 3.27$ with 3 and 20 degrees of freedom; $\alpha = 0.05$.

d. F-statistic $= 3.27$ with 3 and 20 degrees of freedom; $\alpha = 0.01$.

16.7 In the 1993 General Social Survey, a randomly selected sample of U.S. adults was asked what they think is the ideal number of children for a couple to have. The accompanying output is for a one-way analysis of variance that compares the mean response in four age groups: 18–29, 30–44, 45–59, and 60+ (*Source:* SDA archive at csa.berkeley.edu:7502/).

a. Write null and alternative hypotheses for this problem. State the hypotheses in words and also state them using mathematical notation. To what populations do these hypotheses apply?

b. What values are given in the output for the F-statistic and the p-value? What conclusion can be made about the hypotheses?

c. Based on the 95% confidence intervals given for the population means, describe the differences among the age groups.

d. Is the assumption of equal population standard deviations reasonable for these data? Briefly explain.

16.8 Refer to the previous exercise about the ideal number of children for a couple to have. The following output is for a Tukey procedure done to examine all pairwise comparisons of the four age groups. A 95% family confidence level was used.

Intervals for (column level mean) − (row level mean)			
	18−29	30−39	40−59
30−39	−0.0854		
	0.3023		
40−59	−0.1650	−0.2507	
	0.2675	0.1363	
60+	−0.5099	−0.5952	−0.5608
	−0.0854	−0.2170	−0.1369

a. Which pairs of age groups exhibit statistically significant differences? In one or two sentences, summarize the differences in mean response for the four age groups.

b. Briefly explain what it means to say that a 95% family confidence level was used for the six confidence intervals shown in the output for this problem.

16.9 To evaluate a standard test of the flammability of fabric for children's sleepwear, the American Society for Testing Materials had five laboratories each test 11 pieces of the same type of fabric. The response variable is the length of the char mark made when the fabric sample is held over a flame for a specified time period. Ideally, all labs using the standardized test to test the same fabric should observe about the same value for this response variable. Ryan and Joiner (2001, p. 269) give the following data for the observed char lengths (the measurement unit was not specified by Ryan and Joiner).

```
Analysis of Variance for chldidel
Source    DF       SS       MS      F        P
agegrp     3    23.519    7.840   10.91   0.000
Error    955   686.128    0.718
Total    958   709.648

                          Individual 95% CIs For Mean
                          Based on Pooled StDev
Level    N     Mean     StDev    + ---------- + --------- + --------- + ------
1       202   2.4010   0.8654              (----- * -----)
2       335   2.2925   0.7409    (---- * ---)
3       203   2.3498   0.8150      (---- * -----)
4       219   2.6986   1.0003                           (----- * -----)
                                  + ---------- + --------- + --------- + ------
Pooled StDev =   0.8476                  2.40       2.60       2.80
```

EXERCISE 16.7

Lab 1: 2.9 3.1 3.1 3.7 3.1 4.2 3.7 3.9 3.1 3.0 2.9
Lab 2: 2.7 3.4 3.6 3.2 4.0 4.1 3.8 3.8 4.3 3.4 3.3
Lab 3: 3.3 3.3 3.5 3.5 2.8 2.8 3.2 2.8 3.8 3.5 3.8
Lab 4: 3.3 3.2 3.4 2.7 2.7 3.3 2.9 3.2 2.9 2.6 2.8
Lab 5: 4.1 4.1 3.7 4.2 3.1 3.5 2.8 3.5 3.7 3.5 3.9

a. Graph the data in a way that is useful for comparing the laboratories. Describe any differences among laboratories that can be identified in your graph.

b. Use the graph drawn for part (a) to assess whether the necessary conditions are present for using one-way analysis of variance to compare the five laboratories.

16.10 Refer to the previous exercise about testing the flammability of children's sleepwear. Minitab output for a one-way analysis of variance of the data is shown below.

a. Write null and alternative hypotheses for comparing the mean char lengths for the five labs. State the hypotheses in words, and also state them using mathematical notation. To what populations do these hypotheses apply?

b. Are there statistically significant differences among the labs? Justify your answer using the *F*-statistic and *p*-value found in the output.

c. Draw a sketch illustrating how the *p*-value was determined for this problem. See Figure 16.4 (p. 567) for guidance.

d. Based on sample means and the 95% confidence intervals given for the population means, describe the differences among the five laboratories. Be specific about which laboratories appear to have different mean values from the others.

16.11 Koopmans (1987, p. 93) gave data on the testosterone levels (measured as milligrams per 100 milliliters of blood samples) of 46 women classified into three occupational groups: (1) not employed, (2) employed in job not requiring an advanced degree, and (3) employed in job requiring advanced degree. The data are displayed in the accompanying dotplot.

a. Write null and alternative hypotheses for comparing the mean testosterone levels in the three groups. Use proper notation.

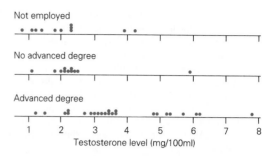

EXERCISE 16.11 **Dotplot of testosterone levels of women by degree required for profession**

b. What does the dotplot indicate about the necessary conditions for doing a one-way analysis of variance of the data? Do any conditions appear to be violated? If so, which conditions?

Section 16.2

16.12 Give a value for each of the missing elements in the following analysis of variance table:

Source	df	SS	MS	F
Between Groups	5	40	—	—
Error	10	60	—	
Total	—		—	

16.13 Give a value for each of the missing elements in the following analysis of variance table:

Source	df	SS	MS	F
Between Groups	2	10	—	—
Error	—	—	—	
Total	30	300		

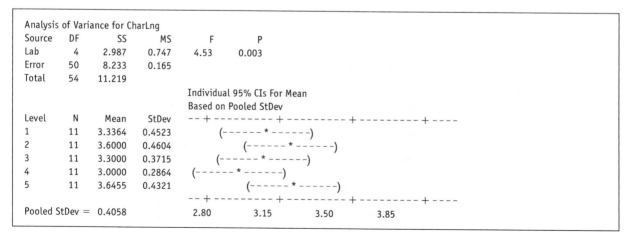

```
Analysis of Variance for CharLng
Source    DF       SS      MS       F       P
Lab        4    2.987   0.747    4.53    0.003
Error     50    8.233   0.165
Total     54   11.219

                       Individual 95% CIs For Mean
                       Based on Pooled StDev
Level    N     Mean    StDev   -- + --------- + --------- + --------- + ----
1       11   3.3364   0.4523        (------ * ------)
2       11   3.6000   0.4604              (------ * ------)
3       11   3.3000   0.3715       (------ * ------)
4       11   3.0000   0.2864   (------ * ------)
5       11   3.6455   0.4321              (------ * ------)
                               -- + --------- + --------- + --------- + ----
Pooled StDev =  0.4058         2.80      3.15      3.50      3.85
```

EXERCISE 16.10

16.14 Refer to exercises 16.4 and 16.5 about female student height and preferred classroom seating location. Sample sizes, means, and standard deviations by seating location are as follows:

Location	N	Mean	Std. Dev.
Front	38	63.9	2.09
Middle	93	64.8	2.80
Back	22	66.6	2.76
All	153	64.8	

a. Show calculations verifying that SS Groups is approximately 102.

b. Use the formula $\text{SS Error} = \sum_{\text{groups}} (n_i - 1)s_i^2$ to verify that SS Error is approximately 1043.

c. The value of df for error is 150. Find the value of MSE, and find the value of the pooled standard deviation s_p.

16.15 Suppose that SS Groups = 0 in an analysis of variance. What would this indicate about the sample means?

16.16 Thirty male college students were randomly divided into three groups of 10, and the groups received different doses of caffeine (0, 100, and 200 mg). Two hours after consuming the caffeine, each participant tapped a finger as rapidly as possible, and the number of taps per minute was recorded. The data are displayed in a comparative boxplot in the following figure (*Data source:* Hand et. al., 1994, dataset 50).

a. Write null and alternative hypotheses for comparing the mean taps per minute in the three caffeine amount groups. Use proper notation.

b. Using the figure, evaluate the necessary conditions for doing a one-way analysis of variance to compare the mean taps per minute for the three caffeine amount groups.

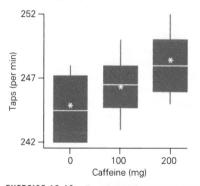

EXERCISE 16.16   Boxplot of finger taps per minute by caffeine amount

16.17 Refer to the previous exercise about finger tapping and caffeine amount. Here is a partial analysis of variance table for the problem with some elements intentionally omitted:

Source	df	SS	MS	F	p
Caffeine	—	61.40	—	—	0.006
Error	=	—	—		
Total	29	195.50			

a. Write out the completed analysis of variance table. Indicate how you determined a value for each element not shown in the table.

b. Calculate the pooled standard deviation, s_p. Describe what parameter is estimated by this statistic.

c. Based on the p-value given in the ANOVA table, what conclusion can be made about the mean taps per minute in the population for the three caffeine amounts?

16.18 Refer to exercises 16.9 and 16.10 about testing the flammability of children's sleepwear. Assuming that the equal standard deviations assumption is valid, calculate 95% confidence intervals for each of μ_1, μ_2, μ_3, μ_4, and μ_5. The output for exercise 16.10 shows the sample means and the pooled standard deviation.

16.19 Suppose that four soil treatments that might be useful for improving the yield of alfalfa grown in fields are compared in an experiment. Each treatment is used in six fields, and the response variable is the crop yield per acre. Suppose further that SS Groups = 150 and SS Error = 200.

a. Write null and alternative hypotheses for comparing the mean crop yields in the four groups. Use proper notation.

b. Calculate the F-statistic for comparing the mean yield of the four treatments.

c. What are the degrees of freedom for the F-statistic?

d. The correct p-value is about 0.01. Draw a sketch illustrating how the p-value is found.

e. Based on the p-value given in part (d), what conclusion can be made about the mean yields for the four soil treatments?

16.20 Refer to the previous exercise. Use the information given or determined in that exercise to write out a completed analysis of variance table.

16.21 Suppose that three drugs used to reduce cholesterol are compared in a randomized experiment in which three people use each drug for a month. The data for the reductions in cholesterol level for the $N = 9$ participants are

Drug 1	Drug 2	Drug 3
6	10	9
4	14	12
2	9	6

a. Calculate the overall mean, $\bar{x}$, and the group means, $\bar{x}_1$, $\bar{x}_2$, and $\bar{x}_3$.

b. Calculate SS Groups, the sum of squares for groups.

c. Calculate SS Total, the total sum of squares.

d. Determine SS Error, the sum of squared errors.

e. Calculate the F-statistic for comparing the mean cholesterol reductions for the three drugs. What are the degrees of freedom for this statistic?

Section 16.3

16.22 Refer to exercise 16.3 about hours of watching television in a typical day and the highest educational degree attained for respondents in the 1993 General Social Survey. Minitab output for a Mood's Median Test of the same data is as follows:

```
Mood median test for tvhours

Chi-Square = 138.16    DF = 4    P = 0.000

degree      N<=     N>    Median
Bachelor    182     70    2.00
Graduate    94      24    2.00
HighScho    409     425   3.00
JunCol      62      34    2.00
NotHS       90      201   4.00

Overall median = 2.00
```

a. In the context of this situation, write the null and alternative hypotheses that are tested by the Mood's Median Test.
b. What is the p-value for testing the hypotheses written in part (a)? Explain what conclusion can be made about the hypotheses.
c. Which group had the highest median hours of television watched in a typical day? What was the median value for that group?
d. The overall median for the sample is 2 hours of watching television in a typical day. What percent of respondents with a bachelor's degree said they watch television more than 2 hours in a typical day? What percent of those who did not get a high school degree watch more than 2 hours of television in a typical day?

16.23 A sample of $n = 729$ college students is asked to rate how much they like various types of music on a scale of 1 to 6, where 1 = don't like at all and 6 = like a lot. The students also were asked whether their hometown was a big city, rural, a small town, or suburban. Results for a Kruskal–Wallis test comparing ratings of reggae music for the four types of hometown are given in the output for this exercise.
a. Write null and alternative hypotheses for comparing the four hometowns with regard to the rating of reggae music.
b. What p-value is given in the output? Explain what conclusion can be made based on this p-value.
c. For which type of hometown was the median rating of reggae the highest? What was the median rating in that type?

16.24 In the same survey described in the previous exercise, students were asked how many times they pray per week and what they felt was the importance of religion in their life (very important, fairly important, or not very). Descriptive statistics comparing number of times praying per week for the three religious importance groups are

Importance	N	Mean	Median	StDev
Very	169	9.57	7	8.64
Fairly	312	4.76	3	2.15
Not very	252	0.77	0	1.83

Why would it be preferable to compare the prayer frequency for three religious importance groups using a nonparametric technique rather than analysis of variance? (*Hint:* Which of the necessary conditions for using an *F*-statistic to compare means are violated by these data?)

16.25 A sample of $n = 235$ college students was asked, "Consider how important a person's personality and looks (attractiveness) are to you. Rate this importance on a scale of 1 (personality is most important) to 25 (looks are most important)."
a. Explain whether the response is a quantitative variable, a categorical variable, or an ordinal variable.
b. Results for a Mood's Median Test that compares the responses of men and women are shown in the Minitab output given on the next page. What are the null and alternative hypotheses of the Mood's Median Test in this instance? Make your answer specific to this situation.
c. What is the overall median for all responses? What percent of the women gave an answer that was less than or equal to the overall median? What percent of the men gave an answer that was less than or equal to the overall median?
d. What conclusion can be made about the difference between men and women with regard to the relative importance of looks versus personality? Explain how you made this decision, and be specific about the populations to which you think the conclusion applies.

16.26 Refer to the previous exercise. The p-value is given as $P = 0.000$, and the value of the chi-square statistic is given as Chi-Square = 15.05. Explain the connection between the p-value and the chi-square statistic.

16.27 Refer to exercise 16.11 about women's testosterone levels. Results are shown in the accompanying output for a Kruskal–Wallis test done to compare the testosterone levels of the three groups of women.

```
Kruskal–Wallis Test on Reggae

Hometown     N     Median   Ave Rank     Z
Big city     89    5.000    476.2      5.32
Rural        96    3.000    335.2     -1.49
Small town   176   3.000    360.3     -0.34
Suburban     368   3.000    348.2     -2.18
Overall      729            365.0

H = 29.17    DF = 3    P = 0.000
```

```
group      N     Median   Ave Rank     Z
Adv Degr   24    3.400    30.1       3.46
No Adv D   11    2.200    17.6      -1.67
Not Empl   11    2.000    15.1      -2.38
Overall    46             23.5

H = 12.19   DF = 2   P = 0.002
H = 12.21   DF = 2   P = 0.002 (adjusted for ties)
```

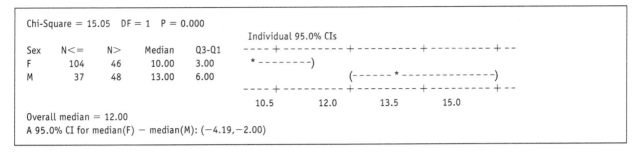

```
Chi-Square = 15.05   DF = 1   P = 0.000

                                         Individual 95.0% CIs
Sex    N<=    N>    Median    Q3-Q1    ---- + --------- + --------- + --------- + --
F      104    46    10.00     3.00      * --------)
M       37    48    13.00     6.00                      (------ * -------------- -)
                                       ---- + --------- + --------- + --------- + --
                                          10.5        12.0        13.5        15.0

Overall median = 12.00
A 95.0% CI for median(F) − median(M): (−4.19,−2.00)
```

EXERCISE 16.25

a. Write null and alternative hypotheses for the Kruskal–Wallis test. Make your answer specific to this situation.
b. Based on the output, what conclusion can be made about testosterone levels in the three groups? Justify your answer using information given in the output.
c. What are the sample medians for the three groups? Based on these medians, and the appearance of the dotplot in the figure for Exercise 16.11, describe the difference among the three groups.

Section 16.4

16.28 For each scenario explain whether an interaction is described or not. If there is an interaction, what are the two variables that interact?
  a. For women, there was no difference between the mean hours spent studying per week for members and nonmembers of Greek organizations. For men, there was a five-hour difference between mean hours spent studying per week for members of Greek organizations versus nonmembers.
  b. The difference between the mean survival times for the two treatments was about six months in each patient age group.

16.29 Explain whether the following statement is an example of a main effect or an interaction: The mean number of classes missed per week was significantly lower for students who think religion is very important than it was for students who think religion is either fairly or not very important.

16.30 Exercise 16.23 described a survey in which college students were asked to rate various types of music on a 1 to 6 scale where 1 = don't like and 6 = like a lot. The figure for this exercise is an interaction plot showing how the mean rating of rock music relates to hometown and gender.
  a. Which gender liked rock music better?
  b. What is the evidence of a possible main effect of hometown?
  c. Discuss whether you think there is evidence of a possible interaction between gender and hometown.

16.31 The figure for this exercise shows how mean hours slept the previous night is related to gender and preferred classroom seat location for a sample of $n = 173$ college students (*Data source:* **UCDavis** dataset).
  a. For males, describe how mean hours slept the previous night is related to preferred classroom seat location.
  b. For females, describe how mean hours slept the previous night is related to preferred classroom seat location.
  c. Explain why the plot is evidence of a possible two-way interaction between gender and seat location.

16.32 Give an example not given in this chapter in which two-way analysis of variance would be used to make a comparison of means. Be specific about what the response variable of interest is, what the explanatory variables are, and what specific levels or categories of the explanatory variables are used.

16.33 In Example 16.1 about mean GPA and typical classroom seat location, the finding was that there were differences among the mean grade point averages for the three lo-

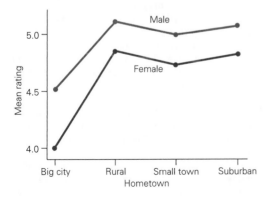

EXERCISE 16.30

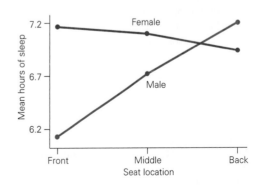

EXERCISE 16.31

cations. Suppose that the sex of the students is also considered along with the seat location.

a. What would be indicated about the difference in the mean GPA of men and women if there were an interaction between student gender and seat location?

b. What would be indicated about the difference in the mean GPA of men and women if there were not an interaction between student gender and seat location?

16.34 Students in a statistics class gave information on their height and weight and also reported their perception of their weight (about right, underweight, overweight). The mean body mass index, BMI, is shown in the following table, along with sample size, for each combination of student gender and perception of weight category. (BMI is calculated as Weight in kilograms/(Height in meters)^2.)

Mean Body Mass Index by Gender and Perception of Weight

	Perception of Weight		
	Underweight	About Right	Overweight
Females	19.3 ($n = 7$)	21.1 ($n = 107$)	24.4 ($n = 31$)
Males	20.1 ($n = 14$)	23.9 ($n = 56$)	27.8 ($n = 13$)

a. Draw an interaction plot of the means. Figures 16.13 (p. 581) and 16.14 (p. 582) may provide guidance for how to do this.

b. Based on the given data, do you think gender and perception of weight are interacting variables? Briefly explain why you think this.

16.35 Ryan and Joiner (2001) give data collected in an experiment done to examine the effects of storage temperature on the rot that occurs in stored potatoes. Potatoes were injected with bacteria known to cause potato rot, and three different bacteria amounts (low, medium, and high) were used. For each bacteria amount, half of the injected potatoes were stored at 10°C, while the others were stored at 16°C. The response variable was the diameter (mm) of the rot in a potato after being stored. The mean rot diameters for all combinations of bacteria amount and temperature are shown in the following table. For each combination, the sample size is 9.

Mean Diameter of Potato Rot by Storage Temperature and Bacteria Amount

Bacteria	Temperature	
	10°C	16°C
Low	3.6	7.0
Medium	4.8	13.6
High	8.0	19.6

a. Draw an interaction plot of the means. Figures 16.13 (p. 581) and 16.14 (p. 582) may provide guidance for how to do this.

b. What is the evidence that there may be an interaction between bacteria amount and storage tempera-

ture? Briefly describe the pattern of this possible interaction.

Chapter Exercises

16.36 Give an example not already given anywhere in this chapter in which one-way analysis of variance could be used to make a comparison of means. Be specific about what the response variable of interest is, and what groups are compared.

16.37 Refer to Figure 16.1 for Example 16.1 about GPA by classroom seat location. Explain why the 95% confidence intervals for the mean GPA in the three seat locations have unequal widths.

16.38 Students in grades 3 to 8 in 11 public schools in Ohio were asked how often they engage in violent behaviors and how often they watch television (Singer et al., 1998). A violent behaviors score was calculated by adding frequency scores (0 = never, 3 = almost every day) for five different violent acts: threatening, hitting before being hit, hitting after being hit, beating up, and attacking with knife. For five groups determined by self-reported hours of television, the sample size, sample mean, and sample standard deviation are

Daily Hours of Television	n_i	$\bar{x}_i$	s_i
<1	227	2.94	2.73
1–2	526	2.59	2.44
3–4	666	2.87	2.36
5–6	310	3.10	2.45
>6	488	4.03	2.81

a. Write null and alternative hypotheses for comparing the mean violent behaviors score for the five television-watching groups. State the hypotheses in words, and also state them using mathematical notation.

b. What do you think are the populations to which the results of an analysis of variance F-test would apply?

c. The researchers did a one-way analysis of variance and reported the results as $F = 22.95$, $p < 0.001$. What does this result indicate about the null and alternative hypotheses for this problem?

d. Notice that the highest mean violent behaviors score is in the group that watches the most television. Explain why this cannot necessarily be interpreted to mean that watching a lot of television causes violent behavior in children. What is another explanation for the observed result?

16.39 Refer to the previous exercise.

a. Based on the information given, which of the necessary conditions for doing a one-way analysis of variance appear to be satisfied? What is the evidence of this?

b. For children who watch television less than 1 hour per day, use the Empirical Rule (see Section 2.7) to estimate the interval in which the middle 95% of scores would fall if the data were bell-shaped. Considering that 0 is the lowest possible violent behaviors score, explain why the result of your calculation is evidence that the data either are skewed or contain outliers.

c. Is the difficulty noted in part (b) also present in the other television-watching groups? Show calculations that support your answer.

16.40 Refer to the previous two exercises. The investigators reported results separately for boys and girls in the five television-watching groups. In this two-way classification, the approximate observed mean violent behaviors scores were

	Hours of Daily Television Watching				
	<1	1–2	3–4	5–6	6+
Boys	3.7	3.0	3.4	3.4	4.1
Girls	2.3	2.3	2.4	2.8	3.9

Explain whether there is an interaction between sex and amount of television watching or not. If there is an interaction, describe the pattern of the interaction.

16.41 Refer to Example 16.4 about the top speeds of supercars. The accompanying output shows Fisher's procedure for pairwise comparisons, with a 95% confidence level for each individual confidence interval. Interpret the output. Specifically, use the output to describe the statistically significant differences among the mean top speeds of the cars. Look back at Example 16.4 to see which were the fastest and slowest cars.

```
Intervals for (column level mean) − (row level mean)

            Acura     Ferrari    Lotus     Porsche

Ferrari    −21.593
           −12.541

Lotus       −5.209    11.857
            3.843     20.909

Porsche    −18.976    −1.909   −18.293
           −9.924     7.143    −9.241

Viper      −11.243    5.824    −10.559    3.207
           −2.191     14.876   −1.507     12.259
```

REFERENCES

16.42 At a private university in southern California, 334 freshman (197 males and 137 females) reported their frequency of drinking alcoholic beverages and also completed a test of personality and psychological characteristics (Ichimaya and Kruse, 1998). One response variable was the score on a 12-item test of conscientiousness for which a high score indicates dependability. Summary statistics for three groups defined by frequency of binge drinking (five or more drinks in one session) are

Drinking Group	n_i	$\bar{x}_i$	s_i
Nonbinge	162	32.59	7.15
Occasional Binge	67	29.93	6.43
Frequent Binge	105	30.10	6.45

a. Write null and alternative hypotheses for comparing the mean conscientiousness score for the three groups. Write the hypotheses in words, and also write the null hypothesis using proper statistical notation.

b. What do you think are the populations to which the results of an analysis of variance F-test would apply?

c. The researchers did a one-way analysis of variance and reported the results as $F = 5.95$, $p < 0.0005$. What does this result indicate about the null and alternative hypotheses for this problem? (*Note:* The p-value reported by the researchers is incorrect. The correct p-value is $p = 0.003$).

d. Using the reported sample means, describe the differences among the mean conscientiousness scores for the three groups. Explain whether you think any observed differences have practical significance or not.

e. Is it reasonable to assume that population standard deviations are equal? Why or why not?

16.43 Refer to the previous exercise. Use formulas in Section 16.2 to compute SS Error, MSE, and the pooled standard deviation, s_p.

16.44 Refer to exercise 16.16 about finger tapping and amount of caffeine consumed. Notice that caffeine amount is a quantity, so it could be analyzed as a quantitative variable. What statistical technique other than one-way analysis of variance could be used to analyze the relationship between taps per minute and caffeine amount? What would be an advantage of using that technique to analyze this relationship? (*Tip:* It might help to look again at the boxplot for exercise 16.16.)

Dabbs, J. M., D. de LaRue, and P. Williams (1990). "Testosterone and occupational choice," *Journal of Personality and Social Psychology*, Vol. 59, No. 6, pp. 1261–1265.

Hand, D. J., F. Daly, A. D. Lunn, K. J. McConway, and E. Ostrowski (1994). *A Handbook of Small Data Sets*, London: Chapman and Hall.

Ichimaya, M. A., and M. I. Kruse (1998). "The social contexts of binge drinking among university freshmen," *Journal of Alcohol and Drug Education*, Vol. 44, pp. 18–33.

Kitchens, L. J. (1998). *Exploring Statistics: A Modern Introduction to Data Analysis and Inference*, 2nd ed., Boston: Duxbury Press.

Koopmans, L. H. (1987). *An Introduction to Contemporary Statistical Methods*, 2nd ed., Boston: Duxbury Press.

Rind, B., and P. Bordia (1996). "Effect on restaurant tipping of male and female servers drawing a happy face on the backs of customers' checks," *Journal of Social Psychology*, Vol. 26 (3), pp. 215–225.

Ryan, B., and B. L. Joiner (2001). *MINITAB Handbook*, Fourth Edition., Belmont: Duxbury Press.

Salk, L. (1973). "The role of the heartbeat in the relations between mother and infant," *Scientific American*, May, pp. 262–264.

Singer, M. J., K. Slovak, T. Frierson, and P. York (1998). "Viewing preferences, symptoms of psychological trauma, and violent behaviors among children who watch television," *J. Am. Acad. Child Adolesc. Psychiatry*, Vol. 37, No. 10, pp. 1041–1049.

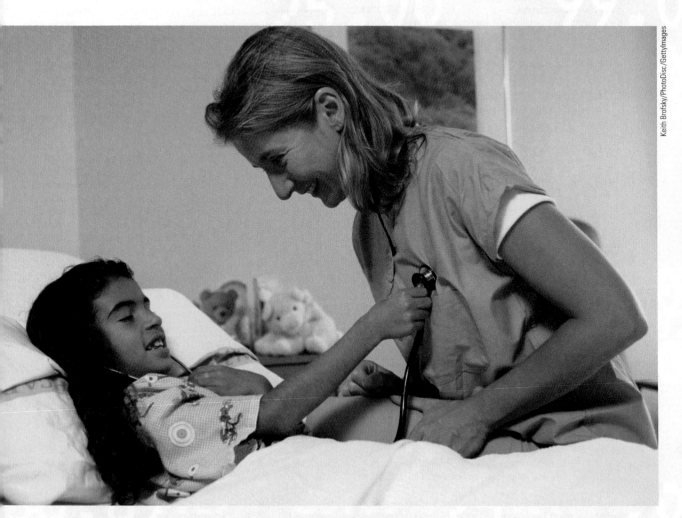

Turning Information Into Wisdom

Would you trust her less if she were selling cars? See Example 17.9.

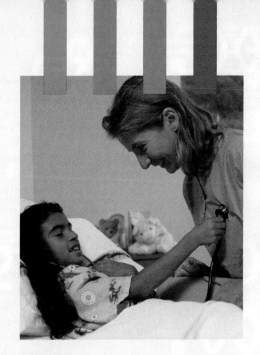

Information developed through the use of statistics has enhanced our understanding of how life works, helped us learn about each other, allowed control over some societal issues, and helped individuals make informed decisions. Nearly every area of knowledge has been advanced by statistical studies.

I n the opening paragraph of Chapter 1, we said, "we hope to convince you that learning about this subject [statistics] will be interesting and useful." By the time you have read this far in the book, we hope you have seen some interesting examples and information. But are the methods in this book useful? Why would anyone care about what can be done with statistics?

In this chapter, we speculate on the wisdom to be gained from statistical studies and why people are interested in such studies. Certainly you can live without them. But information developed through the use of statistics has enhanced our understanding of how life works, helped us learn about each other, allowed control over some societal issues, and helped individuals make informed decisions. There is almost no area of knowledge that has not been advanced by statistical studies. As individuals, we learn from our own and others' experiences. But as a society, we learn through scientific studies—many of them based on statistical methods.

This chapter contains a number of examples that illustrate the wisdom to be gained from statistical studies. Before delving into examples, let's review the basic situations that allow us to turn data into information and information into wisdom. ◆

17.1 | BEYOND THE DATA

Much of the appeal of statistical methods is that they allow us to describe, predict, and sometimes control the world around us. This is possible because with the methods of statistical inference we can use relatively small amounts of data to provide information and sometimes make conclusions about immense populations. This process is one of the truly remarkable features of modern statistics.

However, it is important to remember that the extent to which data descriptions can be generalized to something more rests on two issues. These issues are *what group of individuals was measured,* and, if relevant, *whether or not randomization was used to assign conditions.* These are two different aspects of study design and lead to two different possible extensions of simple descriptive measures.

Random, Representative, or Restrictive Sample?

If pressed to be completely intellectually honest, most statisticians would have to agree with the statement made in *The Statistical Sleuth* (Ramsey and Schafer, 1997, p. 7): "Inferences to **populations** can be drawn from random sampling studies, but not otherwise." The mathematics supporting the material on statistical inference in this book demands simple random samples. However, most researchers, including statisticians, realize that true random samples are almost impossible to obtain. Methods of statistical inference would be of little use if they were restricted to situations in which true random samples were available. Instead, in practice most researchers follow the Fundamental Rule for Using Data for Inference we introduced in Chapter 3.

> *definition* The **Fundamental Rule for Using Data for Inference** is that available data can be used to make inferences about a much larger group *if the data can be considered to be representative with regard to the question(s) of interest.*

One of the key steps in interpreting a statistical study is the capacity to determine whether this rule holds for the questions of interest in the study. We will look at some examples in this chapter.

Randomized Experiments, Observational Studies, and Causal Conclusions

One of the most common errors made by the media in interpreting statistical studies is to conclude that a causal relationship has been established when that conclusion is not warranted by the way the study was conducted. If a statistically significant relationship between the explanatory and response variables is demonstrated, it is tempting to assume that the differences in the explanatory variable *caused* the differences in the response variable. But it is important to remember that even if a cause-and-effect conclusion is sensible, it is not justified by the results of an observational study.

> *definition* The **Rule for Concluding Cause and Effect** is that cause-and-effect relationships can be inferred from randomized experiments, but not from observational studies.

The reasoning is simple. When individuals are randomized into different treatment conditions, the effect of confounding variables should be similar in all treatment groups. Therefore, differences in the response variable(s) can be attributed to the one thing that is known to differ across groups—the explanatory variable, which is the set of treatment conditions. In observational studies, the groups defining the explanatory variable occur naturally and they may have other natural differences between them in addition to the explanatory variable. These other possible differences produce confounding variables, the effect of which cannot be separated from the effect of the explanatory variable. Therefore, differences in the response variable cannot be attributed to differences in the explanatory variable.

Here are some examples of headlines from various news services on the Internet, all based on observational studies. In each instance, the headline implies a cause-and-effect relationship. We're sure you can think of confounding variables that may have led to the observed relationship:

- *Emotional Support Helps Breast Cancer Survival* (Reuters News Service, http://dailynews.yahoo.com/headlines/hl/, Dec. 2, 2000)
- *Study: Even a Little* [of the drug] *Ecstasy can Lower IQ* (USA Today Health News, http://www.usatoday.com/life/health/archive.htm, May 16, 2000)
- *Study: Junk Food Raises Teens' Risk of Heart Disease* (CNN Health News, http://www.cnn.com/2000/HEALTH/03/14/teen.arteries/index.html, Mar. 14, 2000)
- *Lack of Folic Acid Causes Defects* (Associated Press, http://dailynews. yahoo.com/htx/ap/20001129/hl/folic_acid_1.html, Nov. 29, 2000)
- *City Living Increases Men's Death Risk* (ABC News, http://www.abcnews. go.com/sections/living/DailyNews/cityrisk001130.html, Nov. 30, 2000)

In most cases, neither the original researchers nor the authors of the news articles made the mistake made in the headline. The reporters who write the articles usually do not write the headlines, and the reporters may be better trained in how to interpret studies than are headline writers. Unfortunately, the public may not read the fine print beyond the headline.

Using Nonstatistical Considerations to Assess Cause and Effect

You might wonder why researchers conduct observational studies at all, given that the goal is probably to make a causal conclusion. There are some nonstatistical considerations that can be used to help assess whether a causal link is reasonable based on observational studies. Here are some features that lend evidence to a causal connection.

1. *There is a reasonable explanation of cause and effect.*

A potential causal connection will be more believable if an explanation exists for how the cause and effect occurs. For instance, in Example 3.4, we established that for hardcover books the number of pages is correlated with the price. We would probably not contend that higher prices cause more pages, but could reasonably argue that more pages cause higher prices. We can imagine that publishers set the price of a book based on the cost of producing it and that the more pages there are, the higher the cost of production. Thus, we have a reasonable explanation for how an increase in the length of a book could cause an increase in the price.

2. *The connection happens under varying conditions.*

If many observational studies conducted under different conditions all find the same link between two variables, that strengthens the evidence for a causal connection. This is especially true if the studies are not likely to have the same confounding variables. The evidence is also strengthened if the same type of relationship holds when the explanatory variable falls into different ranges.

For example, numerous observational studies have related cigarette smoking and lung cancer. Further, the studies have shown that the higher the number of cigarettes smoked, the greater the chances of developing lung cancer; similarly, a connection has been established with the age at which smoking began. These facts make it more plausible that smoking actually causes lung cancer.

3. *Potential confounding variables are ruled out.*

When a relationship appears in an observational study, potential confounding variables may immediately come to mind. For example, the researchers in Case Study 3.1, which showed a relationship between lead exposure and tooth decay in children, did consider that income level, carbohydrates, calcium, and lack of dental care may have been confounding variables. However, they were able to measure those variables and examine them in the analysis, and the relationship between lead exposure and tooth decay persisted. The greater the number of confounding factors that can be ruled out, the more convincing the evidence for a causal connection.

---

in summary   **Guidelines About Cause and Effect and Using Data for Inference**

◆ If the sample *does not* represent a larger population for the question of interest and *randomization* to treatments *was not used,* no inferences can be drawn.

◆ If the sample *does* represent a larger population for the question of interest but *randomization* to treatments *was not used,* statistically significant results *can* be extended to the larger population but generally not with a cause-and-effect explanation.

◆ If the sample *does not* represent a larger population for the question of interest but *randomization* to treatments *was used,* the relationship observed in the sample can be inferred to be causal, but cannot be extended to a larger population.

◆ If the sample *does* represent a larger population for the question of interest and *randomization* to treatments *was used,* causal inferences can be drawn about the larger population.

17.2 | TRANSFORMING UNCERTAINTY INTO WISDOM

We live in a world filled with uncertainty and variability. The field of statistics exists because this is so. Statistical methods allow us to gain information and control because we can use them to measure variability and find predictable patterns in the presence of uncertainty. Here are some reasons that statistical methods are popular and useful:

◆ As individuals, we need to *make personal decisions* about things like:

What to eat to remain healthy.
How to enhance our children's well-being.
Which treatment to undergo in a medical situation.
How to invest our time to enhance our enjoyment of life.

◆ As a society, we want to *have some control* over things like:

Reducing rates of cancer, heart attacks, and other diseases.
Growing better plants (pest-resistant, high-yield, and so on).
Determining what public education strategies help reduce risky behavior
    for HIV infection.
Deciding what new laws to enact to enhance driver safety.

◆ As intelligent and curious beings, we want *to understand* things like:

Are psychic abilities real and if so, under what conditions?
Do left-handed people die at a younger average age?
Does listening to classical music really improve scores on intelligence
    tests?
Are there differences in how men's and women's brains work?

◆ As social and curious beings, we want to *know about other people:*

Who are they planning to vote for in the next election?
What television programs are they watching?
How much alcohol do they drink?
How healthy are they?

17.3 | MAKING PERSONAL DECISIONS

Results of statistical studies and other statistical information can sometimes help when you are required to make a decision involving uncertainty. Such a decision usually involves both factual and emotional reasoning, so statistical information alone is often not sufficient. It is sometimes helpful to think about the decision in the framework of hypothesis testing and to consider the consequences of the two types of error we discussed. In many cases, the decision can be formulated as follows:

H_0: I will be better off if I take no action.
H_a: I will be better off if I do take action.

A type 1 error would correspond to taking action when you would have been better off not doing so. A type 2 error would correspond to taking no action when you would have been better off taking action.

EXAMPLE 17.1
Playing the Lottery

Suppose there is a lottery in your area and the prize money is many millions of dollars (or the equivalent in your currency). You have picked the numbers you would like to play but can't decide whether to buy a ticket. For simplicity, let's forget about the smaller possible prizes and consider only the decision about whether or not to spend money for a ticket based on the big prize. Here are your hypotheses:

H_0: The numbers I have chosen will not win the big prize.
H_a: The numbers I have chosen will win the big prize.

Let's consider the possible consequences of choosing each of these hypotheses and then analyze the choices.

	Likelihood	H₀ Is Chosen (Don't Buy)	Hₐ Is Chosen (Buy Ticket)
H_0 Is True (Won't Win)	Very high	No loss	Lose cost of ticket
H_a Is True (Would Win)	Very low	Lose millions, agony of seeing your numbers win	Win the big prize

The likelihood that the null hypothesis is true is very high, yet many people behave as if the alternative hypothesis is true. The reason becomes obvious by examining the consequences of each choice in the last two columns of the table. Although there is no loss for correctly choosing H_0, the possible error associated with that choice is devastating. The possible error associated with choosing H_a is minor for many people (lose cost of ticket) and the possible payoff is very high.

To summarize, if you choose H_a, the likelihood that you are making a type 1 error is very high but the consequences of it are minor. If you choose H_0, the likelihood that you are making a type 2 error is extremely small, but the consequences of it are not minor. By the way, the long-run average loss of 30 to 60 cents per ticket in most lotteries is apparently insignificant to most individual ticket buyers, who make their decision (consciously or not) based on the consequences shown in the table. ◆

EXAMPLE 17.2
Surgery or Uncertainty?

Sometimes life-or-death decisions must be made on the basis of little information. A somewhat common situation is as follows. Suppose your doctor discovers a lump and cannot tell whether it is a malignant or benign growth. You have two choices. You can have the affected organ removed with surgery, or you can wait and see if the lump continues to grow or to spread. What would you do? The hypotheses you must choose between are

H_0: The lump is benign.
H_a: The lump is malignant.

Let's examine the choices and their consequences:

	Likelihood	H₀ Is Chosen (No Surgery)	Hₐ Is Chosen (Surgery)
H_0 Is True (Benign)	??	No loss	Lose organ needlessly
H_a Is True (Malignant)	??	Possibly life-threatening	Stop possible spread

Statistical information may be available to assess the likelihood of each hypothesis, and presumably the medical practitioner could provide reasonable probabilities. You must then weigh the possible consequences of each choice based on nonstatistical issues. For instance, depending on which organ is involved, its loss may be minor or it may be extremely serious and require lifelong medical intervention. ◆

EXAMPLE 17.3
Fish Oil and
Psychiatric Disorders

A friend's child was recently diagnosed with a possible psychiatric disorder, and the child's physician recommended that the parents give the child fish oil. In an Internet search for more information, the parents found the following news story.

Thursday September 3, 1998

Fish Oil May Fight Psychiatric Disorders

NEW YORK, Sep 03 (Reuters) — The consumption of omega-3 polyunsaturated fatty acids found in fish and fish oil may reduce the symptoms of a variety of psychiatric illnesses, including schizophrenia, bipolar disorder, and depression, researchers report.

"Research suggests that (fatty acids) may have a role in psychiatric disorders," said Dr. Joseph Hibbeln of the National Institute on Alcohol Abuse and Alcoholism, part of the National Institutes of Health (NIH) in Bethesda, Maryland.

Hibbeln is one of a number of researchers attending an NIH-sponsored workshop on the issue in Bethesda this week.

The workshop was prompted in part by the results of three recent studies.

Findings from one study, conducted by Dr. Andrew Stoll of the Harvard Medical School in Boston, Massachusetts, suggest that fish oil supplementation could help alleviate the symptoms of bipolar (manic-depressive) disorder.

For a 4-month period, Stoll gave 14 bipolar patients daily supplements of either fish oil or a "dummy pill," or placebo. He found that "overall, 9 of 14 patients responded favorably to the addition of omega-3 fatty acids (to their diet), compared to only 3 of 16 patients receiving placebo."

Another study focused on the effects of one fish-oil fatty acid, eicosapentaenoic (EPA), in the treatment of schizophrenia. A 3-month trial conducted by Dr. Malcolm Peet of Northern General Hospital in Sheffield, England, concluded that [there was] "a 25% improvement (in schizophrenic symptoms) in the EPA treated group," compared with patients receiving either docosahexaenoic acid (DHA, another omega-3 fatty acid) or placebo.

A third study, conducted by Hibbeln, focused on levels of omega-3 fatty acids in the blood of 50 patients hospitalized after attempting suicide.

Hibbeln found that, among nondepressive (but not depressive) patients, high blood concentrations of EPA "predicted strikingly lower (better) scores in 6 different psychological rating scales which are related to suicidal risk." The NIH researcher says these findings suggest that "some subgroups of suicidal patients may reduce their suicidal risk with the consumption of EPA."

Hibbeln also noted that another study showed that dietary intake of EPA and DHA may influence serotonin function in the brain. "Such an alteration in serotinergic function may possibly reduce depressive, suicidal and violent behavior, but these changes have not yet been demonstrated in . . . clinical trials," he said in a statement.

Hibbeln explained that the brain's synaptic membranes, where much of the brain's neurological signaling takes place, "have a large proportion of essential fatty acids in them—fatty acids which are derived entirely from the diet."

He points out that "in the last century, (Western) diets have radically changed and we eat grossly fewer omega-3 fatty acids now. We also know that rates of depression have radically increased by perhaps a hundred-fold" over the same period of time.

Links between fish consumption and neurological health may be supported by the results of global studies. According to Hibbeln, those findings suggest that "rates of major depression are markedly different across countries, depending upon how much fish is consumed in those countries."

Source: Mundell, E. J. (1998). "Fish oil may fight psychiatric disorders," Reuters News press release, Sept. 3, 1998.

What would you do if you were the parents of this child? Would you start giving fish oil to your child? The two hypotheses are

H_0: Fish oil will not help my child.
H_a: Fish oil will help my child.

The possible decisions and consequences are

	Likelihood	H_0 Is Chosen (No Fish Oil)	H_a Is Chosen (Fish Oil)
H_0 Is True (Fish Oil Won't Help)	??	No loss or gain	Child takes fish oil needlessly; presumably no harm
H_a Is True (Fish Oil Will Help)	??	Child does not receive a treatment that would help	Child is helped by fish oil

In this case, the parents must assess the likelihood that fish oil will help their child, and the consequences of making each decision. Some of the research discussed in the article is based on randomized experiments, so in those studies there appears to be a causal benefit from fish oil. The participants in those studies may or may not be representative of the same group as this particular child, and the parents need to assess that issue. Finally, the consequences of choosing H_a erroneously are minor, so with a moderate probability that it is true, the parents would be wise to decide in favor of giving fish oil to the child. ◆

17.4 | CONTROL OF SOCIETAL RISKS

Sometimes statistical studies can be used to guide policy decisions. In these cases, lawmakers, government regulatory agencies, and other decision makers must weigh decisions and their consequences.

EXAMPLE 17.4
Go, Granny, Go or Stop, Granny, Stop?

Efforts to improve driving safety are often based on results of statistical studies. For instance, studies have shown that wearing a seat belt is likely to reduce the chances of death or serious injury in an accident, that driving after consuming alcohol increases the risk of an accident, and so on. Laws have been passed to help protect drivers and passengers based on these findings. But there is clearly a trade-off between protection and personal freedom. If you were a lawmaker concerned about driver safety, would the following article convince you to take action?

Tuesday April 7, 1998 6:46 PM EDT   Yahoo 1998

Visual Field Loss Ups Elderly Car Crashes

NEW YORK (Reuters) — A 40% loss in range of vision among older drivers more than doubles their risk for a car accident, experts say. They believe around one third of all seniors suffer from such vision impairment.

"Visual dysfunction and eye disease deserve further examination as causes of motor vehicle crashes and injury," say ophthalmology researchers at the University of Alabama at Birmingham, and the Western Kentucky University in Bowling Green, Kentucky.

Their study, published in the April 8th issue of The Journal of the American Medical Association (JAMA), focused on the 3-year motor vehicle accident rates of 294 Alabama drivers between 55 and 87 years of age. Each of the individuals received various vision tests, including field of vision examinations.

The researchers discovered that, of all the vision-related factors they studied, "impaired useful field of view was the only one that demonstrated a marked elevation (in risk). Older drivers with a 40% or greater reduction in the useful field of view were 2.1 times more likely to have incurred a crash . . . compared with those with less than 40% reduction."

They found that an older driver's crash risk increased by 16% with every 10-point drop in their field of vision.

Since previous research has found that one in three older adults has a greater than 40% reduction in their field of vision, the study authors speculate that field of vision tests might "be a good candidate for inclusion in a functional test battery" aimed at determining driver safety. At the present time, most of the nation's drivers are only obligated to pass visual acuity tests that assess their sharpness of vision in order to obtain license renewals.

However, JAMA contributing editor Dr. Thomas Cole believes field of view tests are "probably too time-consuming and expensive to be used as a screening test in driver licensing offices, and should instead be considered a diagnostic test for drivers with suspected subtle (vision) impairment."

Source: The Journal of the American Medical Association (1998), 279(14):1083–1088.

Should additional vision screening be required for older drivers? There are statistical and nonstatistical issues involved in that decision. First, the research was based on an observational study; drivers cannot be randomly assigned to have vision impairment or not. There are obviously potential confounding factors that may affect accident rates. Also, the researchers mentioned that they studied many aspects of vision but that "impaired useful field of view" was the only one that was related to accident rates. It is possible that they made a type 1 error, which can easily happen for one or more hypotheses when a large number are tested. Finally, it is not clear how representative the participants in this study are of all older drivers, and the results may not apply to all older drivers.

Even if the relationship is real and causal, it may not be appropriate to restrict driving privileges based on visual field impairment. In addition to the statistical issues, there are issues of personal freedom and of the cost of vision testing. Policy makers must weigh all of these factors when making decisions based on statistical studies. ◆

EXAMPLE 17.5
When Smokers Butt Out Does Society Benefit?

The debate over the health risks of breathing smoke from other peoples' cigarettes has been largely statistical in nature, and new information released at the end of 2000 added fuel to the fire. After more than ten years of active antismoking measures, the lung cancer rate in California was down substantially compared to the rest of the United States. The situation was summarized in this news article:

Thursday November 30, 2000 8:13 PM ET

Anti-Tobacco Measures Lessen Cancer

By JENNIFER COLEMAN, Associated Press Writer

SACRAMENTO, Calif. (AP) — California's tough anti-smoking measures and public health campaigns have resulted in a 14 percent decrease in lung cancer over the past 10 years, the government reported Thursday.

Other regions of the country reported only a 2.7 percent decrease over the same period, the Centers for Disease Control and Prevention said.

"Based on the California experience, we would hope to see similar effects in other states using similar programs," said Dr. Terry Pechacek, CDC associate director for science and public health.

Lung cancer develops slowly and the full benefits of quitting can take up to 15 years to be realized. However, Pechacek said, researchers can start seeing some results within five years.

Smoking rates in California began dropping in the late 1980s, helped in part by Proposition 99 in 1988. The voter-approved measure added a 25-cent-per-pack tax on tobacco products that paid for anti-smoking and education programs. Local governments also began restricting smoking in public buildings and workplaces.

Two years ago, voters bumped the price of cigarettes an additional 50 cents per pack, money also earmarked for education. And this year alone, the state will spend $136 million on smoking prevention, cessation and research—some $45 million of it on anti-tobacco advertising.

"California has the most comprehensive program for protecting nonsmokers from secondhand smoke," said Ken August, spokesman for the state health department. "Restaurants, bars and almost all indoor workplaces are smoke-free."

The effect of the anti-tobacco efforts has been fewer smokers and fewer deadly cases of cancer related to smoking, health officials said. August and Pechacek both said they expect the trend to continue.

August said that means there will be up to 4,000 fewer lung cancer cases in California this year and about 2,000 fewer deaths.

In its report, the CDC compared cancer registries in California, Connecticut, Hawaii, Iowa, New Mexico and Utah, as well as Seattle, Atlanta and Detroit.

In 1988, the lung cancer rate in California was 72 cases per 100,000 people, slightly higher than that of the other regions studied. By 1997, California's rate had dropped to about 60 per 100,000.

The CDC averages the statistics for the first two years and the last two years studied to arrive at an accurate representation, health officials said. The numbers the CDC used were 71.9 for 1988 and 70.3 for 1989, averaging to 71.1; and 62.2 for 1996 and 60.1 for 1997, averaging to 61.15. That computes to a 14 percent drop in lung cancer cases.

While lung cancer rates for women in the other regions rose 13 percent, the rate for California women dropped 4.8 percent. Among California men, lung cancer rates dropped 23 percent, compared with a 13 percent drop among men elsewhere.

Dr. David Burns, a volunteer with the American Lung Association in California, said: "This is an accomplishment of Proposition 99 money being invested wisely by the state to help people change their smoking behavior."

Source: http://dailynews.yahoo.com/htx/ap/20001130/hl/cancer_study_2.html.

Suppose you were a lawmaker in another jurisdiction and read these results. Would you attempt to enact legislation similar to that in California? The evidence is certainly tempting, but there are some statistical issues that need to be considered. First, these results are based on observational data. California was not randomly chosen to apply tough antismoking laws. People in California may be more health conscious than people in other states. California has other strict air pollution legislation that was enacted in the same time period, such as tough maintenance and inspection laws for vehicle emissions. California industry has changed over the years, favoring high-tech industry likely to employ younger, healthier workers.

If you were a lawmaker, you would need to weigh consequences of possible decisions. For instance, as mentioned, California has had an active antismoking education program. The consequences of launching such a program would presumably not be harmful, so a decision to do so would have positive or neutral consequences. On the other hand, a decision to ban smoking in bars and restaurants would involve more controversial consequences. ◆

17.5 | UNDERSTANDING OUR WORLD

Sometimes statistical studies are done to help us understand ourselves and our world, without involving any decisions. There are thousands of academic journals containing the results of statistical studies, most of which will never be used to change personal or societal decisions or behavior. Scan any major news source for a few weeks and you will find reports of many interesting studies that are done to help us understand the world. Many of these studies are exploratory in nature and have results that are controversial. That's part of why they make interesting news.

EXAMPLE 17.6
Is It Wining or Dining That Helps French Hearts?

French citizens have lower rates of heart disease than people in neighboring countries, and some recent speculation has focused on red wine as a partial cause. The following article discusses some other possible explanations. Notice that no one is likely to change laws or behavior as a result of this research, it is simply interesting information.

Friday May 28 1:24 PM ET (1999)

Wine May Not Explain France's Lower Heart Disease Rate

NEW YORK, May 28 (Reuters Health) — Previous research has suggested that red wine consumption may explain why the French have a much lower rate of heart disease than other nations. But in a report published this week in the British Medical Journal, two UK experts dispute this theory, suggesting instead that the reduced risk lies in the fact that the French diet traditionally contains less animal fat.

And because the levels of animal fat and cholesterol in the French diet have risen in the last 15 years, their explanation suggests that it is only a matter of time before the heart disease rate in France catches up with the rate in Britain, where heart disease mortality is about four times higher.

Dr. Malcolm Law and Professor Nicholas Wald from the Wolfson Institute of Preventive Medicine in London, UK, suggest that the tendency of French doctors to attribute heart disease deaths to other causes "could account for about 20% of the difference," according to the report.

Law and Wald do give red wine some credit as a preventive factor, but say that this effect is small. The high consumption of red wine in France, they write, "explains (less than 5%) of the difference."

On the other hand, they provide considerable statistical evidence to support their "time lag" theory. "Mortality from . . . heart disease," the authors write, "was strongly associated with past animal fat consumption . . . and past (serum cholesterol) values, but not with recent values."

"Animal fat consumption and serum cholesterol concentration have been similar in France and Britain for a relatively short time—about 15 years," write Law and Wald. "Serum cholesterol concentration in 1970 was . . . lower in France than in Britain . . . and this explains most of its lower mortality from heart disease," they suggest.

Several related editorials question Law and Wald's hypothesis. Meir Stampfer and Eric Rimm from Harvard University, Boston, Massachusetts, write, "Obviously, other factors must play a role. . . . We think it more likely that the difference in coronary mortality rests on behavioral (especially dietary) differences that have not received adequate attention."

In another commentary, D.J.P. Barker from the University of Southampton in Southampton, UK, writes that "recent trends in coronary heart disease are only weakly related to trends in serum cholesterol" and argues that "coronary heart disease originates in utero, through adaptations that the fetus makes to undernutrition."

Finally, Johan Mackenbach and Anton Kunst from Erasmus University in Rotterdam, the Netherlands, contend that "heterogeneity of populations should be taken into account."

But Law and Wald dismiss these arguments. "We believe," they write in response, "that the time lag explanation is the major reason and that the alternative explanations offered in the commentaries are quantitatively unimportant."

Source: British Medical Journal (1999), 318:1471–1480. ◆

EXAMPLE 17.7
Give Her the Car Keys

Memory is a fascinating ability, and most of us wish we had more of that ability. Studies about memory may eventually help us understand ways to improve it. In the meantime, the following study is simply interesting. If it leads to any decision at all, it would be related to who thinks they should get the car keys and who actually should. We'll let you figure it out.

Thursday March 26, 1998 1:30 PM EST   YAHOO Health News

Women Remember Item Location Better

NEW YORK (Reuters) — Women are better at remembering where objects are than men, but show less confidence in their memory, according to a study.

"When it comes to memory, women have more skill than confidence, and men have more confidence than skill," concludes Dr. Robin West, a University of Florida (UF) psychology professor and researcher.

West, along with UF psychology graduate student Duana Welch, compared the spatial memories of over 300 healthy men and women of various ages in a study funded by the National Institutes of Mental Health.

They used specially-designed computer tests that had each participant place 20 common household "objects" into one of 12 "rooms" (e.g., kitchen, bedroom, bathroom) depicted on the screen. After a 40-minute interval, each participant was asked to remember the location of each object.

According to Welch, the test focused on "something that has very important day-to-day meaning for people; that is, the ability to find where you put something."

The results? West and Welch say they found "younger adults performing better than older adults, and women performing better than men." In fact, women scored an average of 14.4 points on the test, compared with the men's average score of 13.5.

Those scores didn't meet male expectations of their own memory skills, the researchers say. In a statement issued by the university, West and Welch say that when questioned, "men tended to overestimate their ability to remember object locations," while women tended to underestimate their powers of recall. The study authors note these findings "are in keeping with other literature suggesting that women are not as confident about their cognitive (intellectual) abilities as they should be."

Those types of gender-based insecurities may be ending, however. In a previous study involving married couples, West discovered that gender-specific differences in memory-confidence disappeared among younger (ages 35 to 45) couples. West credits those results on "historical changes in the beliefs and attitudes of our culture. The older women grew up in a time when men were thought to have more mental ability than women. Such beliefs—learned in childhood and reinforced over time—are hard to change." ◆

17.6 | GETTING TO KNOW YOU

As social beings, we are curious about how others think and behave. What do they do with their time? Are we in the majority with our opinions on controversial issues? At what age do people typically get married? What proportion of the population is left-handed? What proportion is gay or lesbian? Are people basically honest? Many of these questions can be answered by surveying random or representative samples.

Most national governments have agencies that collect samples to answer some of these questions on a routine basis. The United States government collects diverse and numerous statistics on the behavior and opinions of its people. The website http://www.fedstats.gov is headlined "The gateway to statistics from over 100 U.S. Federal agencies" and provides links to all kinds of information about the U.S. population.

EXAMPLE 17.8
Lifestyle Statistics
from the Census Bureau

The United States Census Bureau collects voluminous data on many aspects of American life. The ongoing "Current Population Survey" polls a random sample of U.S. households on a wide variety of topics. From this survey, trends in lifestyle decisions can be tracked. Here are a few examples of trends reported in 1995 ("Marital Status and Living Arrangements," Arlene F. Saluter, http://www.census.gov/population/www/pop-profile/msla.html):

♦ "The estimated median age at first marriage is higher than ever before. In 1994, the median age at first marriage was 26.7 years for men and 24.5 years for women, approximately $3\frac{1}{2}$ years higher than the median age in 1970 (23.2 years for men and 20.8 years for women).

♦ An unmarried-couple household is composed of two unrelated adults of the opposite sex (one of whom is the householder) who share a housing unit with or without the presence of children under 15 years old. There were 7 unmarried couples for every 100 married couples in 1994, compared with only 1 for every 100 in 1970. About one-third had children under 15 years old present in the home.

♦ Children living with one parent (18.6 million) represented 27 percent of all children under 18 years old in 1994, up from 12 percent in 1970. The majority lived with their mother, but an increasing proportion lived with their father. In 1994, 12 percent of the children in a one-parent situation lived with their father, up from 9 percent in 1970."

Notice that these statistics are presented as if they were known for the population, but in fact, they are based on random samples of various sizes. Consequently, they have a margin of error that could be computed from knowing the sample size. ♦

EXAMPLE 17.9
In Whom Do We Trust?

If you want to know about the opinions of Americans on almost any topic, visit the website for the Gallup Organization (http://www.gallup.com) and type in the key word of your choice. (Unfortunately, Gallup now charges for this service.) For instance, a news release on November 27, 2000 was headlined "Nurses Remain at Top of Honesty and Ethics Poll, Car Salesmen Still Seen as Least Honest and Ethical." The accompanying story (Darren K. Carlson, http://

www.gallup.com/poll/releases/pr001127.asp) reported on a poll that has been taken yearly since 1977. Respondents were asked, "Please tell me how you would rate the honesty and ethical standards of people in these different fields—very high, high, average, low, or very low" and were then given a list of several dozen occupations, in random order. Some of the results highlighted in the news release were

- "For the second year in a row, Gallup's survey on honesty and ethics in professions finds that the American public rates nursing as the field with the highest standards of honesty and ethics. Almost eight in 10 Americans—79%—say nurses have 'very high' or 'high' ethical standards. Pharmacists finish second with 67%. Pharmacists had consistently finished first in the survey, until nurses were added to the list in 1999.

- Only one profession is rated as having 'low' or 'very low' standards by a majority of Americans: car sales.

- Americans remain skeptical of the honesty and ethics of their elected officials. As with every previous year, less than half the public said any elected official on Gallup's list had 'very high' or 'high' honesty and ethics.

- The long-term trends of Gallup's honesty and ethics survey reveal a growing skepticism among the American public regarding the ethics of news professionals and lawyers. The three news professions surveyed all remain significantly lower than when they were first placed on the list. Twenty-one percent of the public says journalists are honest and ethical, a percentage that has declined steadily from its debut of 33% in 1977.

- Lawyers are often the punch line to jokes regarding professional ethics and honesty. They debuted on Gallup's survey list in 1977 with 26%. Lawyers have not been rated as having high ethical standards by more than 20% of the public since 1991, and the latest poll shows a rating of 17%."

College teachers were rated highly by 59% and grade school and high school teachers by 62%. And, of course, to interpret the results correctly, you need to know that "the results reported here are based on telephone interviews with a randomly selected national sample of 1,028 adults, 18 years and older, conducted November 13–15, 2000. For results based on the whole sample, one can say with 95 percent confidence that the maximum error attributable to sampling and other random effects is plus or minus 3 percentage points." ◆

17.7 | WORDS TO THE WISE

We hope that by now you realize that you are likely to encounter statistical studies in your personal and professional life and that they can provide useful information. We also hope you realize that results from such studies can be misleading if you don't interpret them wisely.

Throughout this book we have presented warnings and examples of how statistical studies are often misinterpreted. The ten guiding principles presented here are a synthesis of those warnings. Keeping these principles in mind when you read statistical studies will help you gain wisdom about the world around you while maintaining a healthy dose of skepticism about legitimate conclusions.

in summary   Ten Guiding Principles

1. A representative sample can be used to make inferences about a larger population, but descriptive statistics are the only useful results for an unrepresentative sample.

2. Cause and effect can be inferred from randomized experiments, but generally not from observational studies, where confounding variables are likely to cloud the interpretation.

3. A conservative estimate of *sampling* error in a survey is the margin of error, $1/\sqrt{n}$. This provides a bound on the difference between the true proportion and the sample proportion that holds for at least 95% of properly conducted surveys.

4. The margin of error does *not* include nonsampling error, such as errors due to biased wording, nonresponse, and so on.

5. When the individuals measured constitute the whole population, there is no need for statistical inference because the truth is known.

6. A significance test based on a very large sample is likely to produce a statistically significant result even if the true value is close to the null value. In such cases, it is wise to examine the magnitude of the parameter with a confidence interval to determine if the result has practical importance.

7. A significance test based on a small sample may not produce a statistically significant result even if the true value differs substantially from the null value. It is important that the null hypothesis not be "accepted" on this basis.

8. When deciding how readily to reject the null hypothesis (what significance level to use), it is important to consider the consequences of type 1 and type 2 errors. If a type 1 error has serious consequences, the level of significance should be small. If a type 2 error is more serious, a higher level of significance should be used.

9. A study that examines many hypotheses could find one or more statistically significant results just by chance, so you should try to find out how many tests were conducted when you read about a significant result. For instance, with a level of significance of 0.05, about 1 test in 20 should result in statistical significance when all of the null hypotheses are correct and the tests are independent. It is common in large studies to find that one test attracts media attention, so it is important to know if that test was the only one out of many conducted that achieved statistical significance.

10. You will sometimes read that researchers were surprised to find "no effect" and that a study "failed to replicate" an earlier finding of statistical significance. In that case, consider two possible explanations. One is that the sample size was too small and the test had low power. The other possibility is that the result in the first study was based on a type 1 error. This is particularly likely if the effect was moderate and was part of a larger study that covered multiple hypotheses.

If you still think statistics is a boring and useless subject, check to make sure you are still breathing, your heart is beating, and your mind has not turned off!

EXERCISES   Blue = Basics   **Bold, Bold** = Answer in back

Chapter Exercises

Exercises 1 to 15 are based on the following reports of three studies taken from news organization websites. In each case, the headline and a few sentences from the news story are provided.

Study #1: "*Calcium Lowers Blood Pressure in Black Teens:* In the new study, researchers followed 116 African-American teens who were enrolled in grades 10 through 12 at three high schools in Los Angeles. Over the course of eight weeks, the study participants were given either a placebo or a calcium supplement. They were also asked to fill out food questionnaires. Researchers measured the teens' blood pressure at the outset of the study and two, four and eight weeks later." (Linda Carroll, Medical Tribune News Service, Sept. 7, 1998; study published in the *American Journal of Clinical Nutrition* (1998), Vol. 68, 648–655.)

Study #2: "*Daily Two-Mile Walk Halves Death Risk:* Between 1980 and 1982, multicenter researchers in the Honolulu Heart Program studied 707 nonsmoking, retired men, aged 61 to 81 years, and collected mortality data on these men over the following 12 years. During the study, 208 of the men died. The study results show that while 43.1% of men who walked less than one mile per day died, only half this figure—21.5%—of the men who walked more than two miles per day died." (Reuters News, Jan. 8, 1998; study published in *The New England Journal of Medicine* (1998), Vol. 338, 94–99.)

Study #3: "*Tea Doubles Chance Of Conception:* Tea for two might make three, according to a new study. The investigators asked 187 women, each of whom said they were trying to conceive, to record information concerning their daily dietary intake over a one-year period. According to the researchers, an analysis of the data suggests drinking one-half cup or more of tea daily approximately doubled the odds of conception per cycle, compared with non-tea drinkers. The mechanism behind tea's apparent influence on fertility remains unclear. But the investigators point out that, on average, tea drinking is associated with a 'preventive or healthier' lifestyle, which might encourage conception." (Reuters News, Feb. 27, 1998; study published in the *American Journal of Public Health* (1998), Vol. 88, No. 2: 270–274.)

17.1 Each of the three headlines implies a causal relationship between an explanatory and response variable. For each of the three studies, describe the explanatory and response variables.

17.2 Do you think Study #1 was a randomized experiment or an observational study? Explain. Based on your answer, explain whether or not the headline is justified.

17.3 Do you think Study #2 was a randomized experiment or an observational study? Explain. Based on your answer, explain whether or not the headline is justified.

17.4 Do you think Study #3 was a randomized experiment or an observational study? Explain. Based on your answer, explain whether or not the headline is justified.

17.5 Give an example of a possible confounding variable for Study #2. Explain why you think it fits the definition of a confounding variable.

17.6 Give an example of a possible confounding variable for Study #3. Explain why you think it fits the definition of a confounding variable.

17.7 Can the results of Study #1 be applied to a larger population? If so, to what population? If not, why not?

17.8 Can the results of Study #2 be applied to a larger population? If so, to what population? If not, why not?

17.9 Can the results of Study #3 be applied to a larger population? If so, to what population? If not, why not?

17.10 In Study #1, participants were also asked to fill out a food questionnaire. Another quote from the news article was: "Overall, diastolic blood pressure—the second of the two numbers given when blood pressure is measured—dropped about two points in the group given calcium supplements. But the drop was almost five points in teens with a particularly low intake of calcium-containing foods."
   a. Why do you think the researchers wanted the information provided by the food questionnaire?
   b. Is "intake of calcium-containing foods" a confounding variable or an interacting variable in this study? Explain.

17.11 Here are some additional quotes from the article for Study #2. Comment on each quote using issues covered in this chapter.
   a. "The investigators also report that '. . . when the distance walked is increased by one mile per day . . . the risk of death can be reduced by 19%.'"
   b. "Cancer was the most common cause of death in the men studied. The research team found that 13.4% of the men who walked less than one mile per day died of cancer, but only 5.3% of those who walked more than two miles per day died of cancer. Even when age was included in the analysis, this result held."
   c. "Walking also appeared to protect against dying from heart disease and stroke, but the findings were not statistically significant, meaning that they could have occurred by chance."

17.12 The article for Study #3 also noted: "The study results also show that the women who consumed the most tea '. . . had significantly higher energy and fat intakes' than women who drank less tea."
   a. Do you think the word "significantly" in this quote refers to statistical significance? If not, why not? If so, describe in words the null and alternative hypotheses you think the researchers tested to reach that conclusion.
   b. Are "energy and fat intake" confounding variables or interacting variables in this study? Explain.

17.13 The article for Study #3 also said: "The California researchers say they found no significant association between coffee intake and fertility, but '. . . in later cycles . . . there was a suggestion that both total caffeine and coffee were associated with a nonsignificant reduction in fertility,' a finding in keeping with previous research which pointed to the possibility that coffee or caffeine might lower conception rates."
   a. The phrase "*no* significant association between coffee intake and fertility" seems to contradict the "suggestion that both total caffeine and coffee were associated with a nonsignificant reduction in fertility." Explain this apparent contradiction.

b. Refer to item 10 in Section 17.7 and discuss it in the context of this quote.

17.14 The two main variables measured in Study #1 were the treatment given to the participant and the participant's blood pressure.

a. For each of the two variables, determine if it was recorded as a categorical variable or a quantitative variable. If it was a categorical variable, specify the categories.

b. Researchers measured the participants' blood pressure at the beginning of the study and two, four, and eight weeks later. If they wanted to determine whether blood pressure had dropped significantly from the beginning of the study to eight weeks later for the participants in the calcium group, would they use a paired t-test or a test for the difference in means for independent samples? Explain.

c. Refer to part (b). Write the null and alternative hypotheses the researchers would use.

d. If the researchers wanted to compare the change in blood pressure after eight weeks of taking calcium compared to eight weeks of taking a placebo, what hypothesis-testing method would they use?

e. Refer to part (d). Write the null and alternative hypotheses the researchers would use.

17.15 Refer to the headline in Study #2 and to the statement "While 43.1% of the men who walked less than one mile per day died, only half this figure—21.5%—of the men who walked more than two miles per day died."

a. What two categorical variables measured on each participant are used in making that statement? What are the categories for each one?

b. If the researchers wanted to determine if the result was statistically significant, what inference procedure would be appropriate? Be specific.

17.16 Find an example of an observational study in the news and answer these questions about it:

a. Explain why it fits the definition of an observational study rather than a randomized experiment.

b. Describe an explanatory and response variable considered in the study.

c. Using the variables in part (b), give an example of a possible confounding variable and explain why it fits the definition of a confounding variable.

d. Write two headlines to accompany the study—one that is correct and the other that implies a conclusion that is not justified. Explain which is which, and why. (You may use the actual headline accompanying the story as one of these.)

e. Can the results of the study be extended to a larger population? Explain.

17.17 Find an example of a randomized experiment in the news and answer these questions about it:

a. Explain why it fits the definition of a randomized experiment rather than an observational study.

b. Describe an explanatory and response variable considered in the study.

c. Using the variables in part (b), give an example of a possible interacting variable and explain why it fits the definition of an interacting variable. You may use one that is actually measured in the study and discussed in the news report.

d. Give the headline that was provided with the news article and discuss whether it is justified based on the study.

e. Can the results of the study be extended to a larger population? Explain.

17.18 In each of the following cases, explain whether the results can be extended to a larger population. If so, explain what the population is. If not, explain why not.

a. A company measured the salaries of all of its employees and found that the average salary for men was 10% higher than the average salary for women.

b. A geologist at Yellowstone National Park measured the length of time for each eruption and the waiting time until the next eruption for the Old Faithful geyser from Aug. 1–8 and 16–23, 1978 (data from Weisberg, 1985, p. 231). The correlation between the two measurements was 0.877, indicating that waiting time until the next eruption is strongly correlated with the duration of the previous eruption.

c. A poll following the presidential debates of 2000 was conducted by using random-digit dialing. When someone answered the phone, they were asked if they had watched the debates. If the answer was yes, they were asked who won. If the answer was no, the call was terminated. The question of interest was the proportion of U.S. adults who thought each of the two candidates had won the debate.

17.19 Refer to Example 17.5 describing California's antismoking measures and reduction in lung cancer. An article in *The New England Journal of Medicine* (Fichtenberg and Glantz, 2000) studied mortality from heart disease in California during the same period. The conclusion the authors reached was: "A large and aggressive tobacco-control program is associated with a reduction in deaths from heart disease in the short run."

a. The conclusion is based on results obtained through methods similar to those in Example 17.5. Is the wording of the conclusion justified? Explain.

b. Write two headlines to accompany a news report on this study, one that presents the conclusion accurately and one that implies a conclusion that is not justified. Explain your reasoning.

17.20 Example 17.5 describes California's antismoking measures and subsequent reduction in lung cancer rates. Read the example and the material that follows it. Using the "nonstatistical considerations to assess cause and effect" given in Section 17.1, discuss the extent to which you think a cause-and-effect conclusion can be made about the relationship between the antismoking measures and reduction in lung cancer rates.

REFERENCES

Fichtenberg, C. M., and S. A. Glantz (2000). "Association of the California Tobacco Control program with declines in cigarette consumption and mortality from heart disease," *New England Journal of Medicine,* Vol. 343, No. 24, 1772–1777.

Ramsey, F., and D. Schafer (1997). *The Statistical Sleuth: A Course in Methods of Data Analysis,* Belmont, CA: Duxbury Press.

Weisberg, S. (1985). *Applied Linear Regression,* 2nd ed. New York: Wiley and Sons.

Appendix of Tables

TABLE A.1 ■ Standard Normal Probabilities (for $z < 0$)

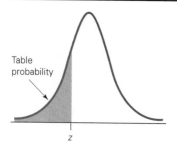

z	.00	.01	.02	.03	.04	.05	.06	.07	.08	.09
−3.4	.0003	.0003	.0003	.0003	.0003	.0003	.0003	.0003	.0003	.0002
−3.3	.0005	.0005	.0005	.0004	.0004	.0004	.0004	.0004	.0004	.0003
−3.2	.0007	.0007	.0006	.0006	.0006	.0006	.0006	.0005	.0005	.0005
−3.1	.0010	.0009	.0009	.0009	.0008	.0008	.0008	.0008	.0007	.0007
−3.0	.0013	.0013	.0013	.0012	.0012	.0011	.0011	.0011	.0010	.0010
−2.9	.0019	.0018	.0018	.0017	.0016	.0016	.0015	.0015	.0014	.0014
−2.8	.0026	.0025	.0024	.0023	.0023	.0022	.0021	.0021	.0020	.0019
−2.7	.0035	.0034	.0033	.0032	.0031	.0030	.0029	.0028	.0027	.0026
−2.6	.0047	.0045	.0044	.0043	.0041	.0040	.0039	.0038	.0037	.0036
−2.5	.0062	.0060	.0059	.0057	.0055	.0054	.0052	.0051	.0049	.0048
−2.4	.0082	.0080	.0078	.0075	.0073	.0071	.0069	.0068	.0066	.0064
−2.3	.0107	.0104	.0102	.0099	.0096	.0094	.0091	.0089	.0087	.0084
−2.2	.0139	.0136	.0132	.0129	.0125	.0122	.0119	.0116	.0113	.0110
−2.1	.0179	.0174	.0170	.0166	.0162	.0158	.0154	.0150	.0146	.0143
−2.0	.0228	.0222	.0217	.0212	.0207	.0202	.0197	.0192	.0188	.0183
−1.9	.0287	.0281	.0274	.0268	.0262	.0256	.0250	.0244	.0239	.0233
−1.8	.0359	.0351	.0344	.0336	.0329	.0322	.0314	.0307	.0301	.0294
−1.7	.0446	.0436	.0427	.0418	.0409	.0401	.0392	.0384	.0375	.0367
−1.6	.0548	.0537	.0526	.0516	.0505	.0495	.0485	.0475	.0465	.0455
−1.5	.0668	.0655	.0643	.0630	.0618	.0606	.0594	.0582	.0571	.0559
−1.4	.0808	.0793	.0778	.0764	.0749	.0735	.0721	.0708	.0694	.0681
−1.3	.0968	.0951	.0934	.0918	.0901	.0885	.0869	.0853	.0838	.0823
−1.2	.1151	.1131	.1112	.1093	.1075	.1056	.1038	.1020	.1003	.0985
−1.1	.1357	.1335	.1314	.1292	.1271	.1251	.1230	.1210	.1190	.1170
−1.0	.1587	.1562	.1539	.1515	.1492	.1469	.1446	.1423	.1401	.1379
−0.9	.1841	.1814	.1788	.1762	.1736	.1711	.1685	.1660	.1635	.1611
−0.8	.2119	.2090	.2061	.2033	.2005	.1977	.1949	.1922	.1894	.1867
−0.7	.2420	.2389	.2358	.2327	.2296	.2266	.2236	.2206	.2177	.2148
−0.6	.2743	.2709	.2676	.2643	.2611	.2578	.2546	.2514	.2483	.2451
−0.5	.3085	.3050	.3015	.2981	.2946	.2912	.2877	.2843	.2810	.2776
−0.4	.3446	.3409	.3372	.3336	.3300	.3264	.3228	.3192	.3156	.3121
−0.3	.3821	.3783	.3745	.3707	.3669	.3632	.3594	.3557	.3520	.3483
−0.2	.4207	.4168	.4129	.4090	.4052	.4013	.3974	.3936	.3897	.3859
−0.1	.4602	.4562	.4522	.4483	.4443	.4404	.4364	.4325	.4286	.4247
−0.0	.5000	.4960	.4920	.4880	.4840	.4801	.4761	.4721	.4681	.4641

In the Extreme (for $z < 0$)

z	−3.09	−3.72	−4.26	−4.75	−5.20	−5.61	−6.00
Probability	.001	.0001	.00001	.000001	.0000001	.00000001	.000000001

S-PLUS was used to determine information for the "In the Extreme" portion of the table.

TABLE A.1 ■ Standard Normal Probabilities (for z > 0)

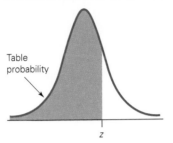

Table probability

z

z	.00	.01	.02	.03	.04	.05	.06	.07	.08	.09
0.0	.5000	.5040	.5080	.5120	.5160	.5199	.5239	.5279	.5319	.5359
0.1	.5398	.5438	.5478	.5517	.5557	.5596	.5636	.5675	.5714	.5753
0.2	.5793	.5832	.5871	.5910	.5948	.5987	.6026	.6064	.6103	.6141
0.3	.6179	.6217	.6255	.6293	.6331	.6368	.6406	.6443	.6480	.6517
0.4	.6554	.6591	.6628	.6664	.6700	.6736	.6772	.6808	.6844	.6879
0.5	.6915	.6950	.6985	.7019	.7054	.7088	.7123	.7157	.7190	.7224
0.6	.7257	.7291	.7324	.7357	.7389	.7422	.7454	.7486	.7517	.7549
0.7	.7580	.7611	.7642	.7673	.7704	.7734	.7764	.7794	.7823	.7852
0.8	.7881	.7910	.7939	.7967	.7995	.8023	.8051	.8078	.8106	.8133
0.9	.8159	.8186	.8212	.8238	.8264	.8289	.8315	.8340	.8365	.8389
1.0	.8413	.8438	.8461	.8485	.8508	.8531	.8554	.8577	.8599	.8621
1.1	.8643	.8665	.8686	.8708	.8729	.8749	.8770	.8790	.8810	.8830
1.2	.8849	.8869	.8888	.8907	.8925	.8944	.8962	.8980	.8997	.9015
1.3	.9032	.9049	.9066	.9082	.9099	.9115	.9131	.9147	.9162	.9177
1.4	.9192	.9207	.9222	.9236	.9251	.9265	.9279	.9292	.9306	.9319
1.5	.9332	.9345	.9357	.9370	.9382	.9394	.9406	.9418	.9429	.9441
1.6	.9452	.9463	.9474	.9484	.9495	.9505	.9515	.9525	.9535	.9545
1.7	.9554	.9564	.9573	.9582	.9591	.9599	.9608	.9616	.9625	.9633
1.8	.9641	.9649	.9656	.9664	.9671	.9678	.9686	.9693	.9699	.9706
1.9	.9713	.9719	.9726	.9732	.9738	.9744	.9750	.9756	.9761	.9767
2.0	.9772	.9778	.9783	.9788	.9793	.9798	.9803	.9808	.9812	.9817
2.1	.9821	.9826	.9830	.9834	.9838	.9842	.9846	.9850	.9854	.9857
2.2	.9861	.9864	.9868	.9871	.9875	.9878	.9881	.9884	.9887	.9890
2.3	.9893	.9896	.9898	.9901	.9904	.9906	.9909	.9911	.9913	.9916
2.4	.9918	.9920	.9922	.9925	.9927	.9929	.9931	.9932	.9934	.9936
2.5	.9938	.9940	.9941	.9943	.9945	.9946	.9948	.9949	.9951	.9952
2.6	.9953	.9955	.9956	.9957	.9959	.9960	.9961	.9962	.9963	.9964
2.7	.9965	.9966	.9967	.9968	.9969	.9970	.9971	.9972	.9973	.9974
2.8	.9974	.9975	.9976	.9977	.9977	.9978	.9979	.9979	.9980	.9981
2.9	.9981	.9982	.9982	.9983	.9984	.9984	.9985	.9985	.9986	.9986
3.0	.9987	.9987	.9987	.9988	.9988	.9989	.9989	.9989	.9990	.9990
3.1	.9990	.9991	.9991	.9991	.9992	.9992	.9992	.9992	.9993	.9993
3.2	.9993	.9993	.9994	.9994	.9994	.9994	.9994	.9995	.9995	.9995
3.3	.9995	.9995	.9995	.9996	.9996	.9996	.9996	.9996	.9996	.9997
3.4	.9997	.9997	.9997	.9997	.9997	.9997	.9997	.9997	.9997	.9998

In the Extreme (for z > 0)

z	3.09	3.72	4.26	4.75	5.20	5.61	6.00
Probability	.999	.9999	.99999	.999999	.9999999	.99999999	.999999999

S-PLUS was used to determine information for the "In the Extreme" portion of the table.

TABLE A.2 ■ **The t^* Multipliers for Confidence Intervals for Means or Difference Between Means**

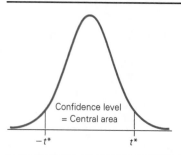

Confidence level
= Central area

$-t^*$ t^*

df	Confidence Level			
	0.90	0.95	0.98	0.99
1	6.31	12.71	31.82	63.66
2	2.92	4.30	6.96	9.92
3	2.35	3.18	4.54	5.84
4	2.13	2.78	3.75	4.60
5	2.02	2.57	3.36	4.03
6	1.94	2.45	3.14	3.71
7	1.89	2.36	3.00	3.50
8	1.86	2.31	2.90	3.36
9	1.83	2.26	2.82	3.25
10	1.81	2.23	2.76	3.17
11	1.80	2.20	2.72	3.11
12	1.78	2.18	2.68	3.05
13	1.77	2.16	2.65	3.01
14	1.76	2.14	2.62	2.98
15	1.75	2.13	2.60	2.95
16	1.75	2.12	2.58	2.92
17	1.74	2.11	2.57	2.90
18	1.73	2.10	2.55	2.88
19	1.73	2.09	2.54	2.86
20	1.72	2.09	2.53	2.85
21	1.72	2.08	2.52	2.83
22	1.72	2.07	2.51	2.82
23	1.71	2.07	2.50	2.81
24	1.71	2.06	2.49	2.80
25	1.71	2.06	2.49	2.79
26	1.71	2.06	2.48	2.78
27	1.70	2.05	2.47	2.77
28	1.70	2.05	2.47	2.76
29	1.70	2.05	2.46	2.76
30	1.70	2.04	2.46	2.75
40	1.68	2.02	2.42	2.70
50	1.68	2.01	2.40	2.68
60	1.67	2.00	2.39	2.66
70	1.67	1.99	2.38	2.65
80	1.66	1.99	2.37	2.64
90	1.66	1.99	2.37	2.63
100	1.66	1.98	2.36	2.63
1000	1.65	1.96	2.33	2.58
Infinite	1.645	1.960	2.326	2.576

Note that the t-distribution with infinite df is the standard normal distribution.

TABLE A.3 ■ One-Sided *p*-Values for Significance Tests Based on a *t*-Statistic

◆ A *p*-value in the table is the area to the right of *t*.
◆ Double the value if the alternative hypothesis is two-sided (not equal).

	Absolute Value of *t*-Statistic							
df	*1.28*	*1.50*	*1.65*	*1.80*	*2.00*	*2.33*	*2.58*	*3.00*
1	0.211	0.187	0.173	0.161	0.148	0.129	0.118	0.102
2	0.164	0.136	0.120	0.107	0.092	0.073	0.062	0.048
3	0.145	0.115	0.099	0.085	0.070	0.051	0.041	0.029
4	0.135	0.104	0.087	0.073	0.058	0.040	0.031	0.020
5	0.128	0.097	0.080	0.066	0.051	0.034	0.025	0.015
6	0.124	0.092	0.075	0.061	0.046	0.029	0.021	0.012
7	0.121	0.089	0.071	0.057	0.043	0.026	0.018	0.010
8	0.118	0.086	0.069	0.055	0.040	0.024	0.016	0.009
9	0.116	0.084	0.067	0.053	0.038	0.022	0.015	0.007
10	0.115	0.082	0.065	0.051	0.037	0.021	0.014	0.007
11	0.113	0.081	0.064	0.050	0.035	0.020	0.013	0.006
12	0.112	0.080	0.062	0.049	0.034	0.019	0.012	0.006
13	0.111	0.079	0.061	0.048	0.033	0.018	0.011	0.005
14	0.111	0.078	0.061	0.047	0.033	0.018	0.011	0.005
15	0.110	0.077	0.060	0.046	0.032	0.017	0.010	0.004
16	0.109	0.077	0.059	0.045	0.031	0.017	0.010	0.004
17	0.109	0.076	0.059	0.045	0.031	0.016	0.010	0.004
18	0.108	0.075	0.058	0.044	0.030	0.016	0.009	0.004
19	0.108	0.075	0.058	0.044	0.030	0.015	0.009	0.004
20	0.108	0.075	0.057	0.043	0.030	0.015	0.009	0.004
21	0.107	0.074	0.057	0.043	0.029	0.015	0.009	0.003
22	0.107	0.074	0.057	0.043	0.029	0.015	0.009	0.003
23	0.107	0.074	0.056	0.042	0.029	0.014	0.008	0.003
24	0.106	0.073	0.056	0.042	0.028	0.014	0.008	0.003
25	0.106	0.073	0.056	0.042	0.028	0.014	0.008	0.003
26	0.106	0.073	0.055	0.042	0.028	0.014	0.008	0.003
27	0.106	0.073	0.055	0.042	0.028	0.014	0.008	0.003
28	0.106	0.072	0.055	0.041	0.028	0.014	0.008	0.003
29	0.105	0.072	0.055	0.041	0.027	0.013	0.008	0.003
30	0.105	0.072	0.055	0.041	0.027	0.013	0.008	0.003
40	0.104	0.071	0.053	0.040	0.026	0.012	0.007	0.002
50	0.103	0.070	0.053	0.039	0.025	0.012	0.006	0.002
60	0.103	0.069	0.052	0.038	0.025	0.012	0.006	0.002
70	0.102	0.069	0.052	0.038	0.025	0.011	0.006	0.002
80	0.102	0.069	0.051	0.038	0.024	0.011	0.006	0.002
90	0.102	0.069	0.051	0.038	0.024	0.011	0.006	0.002
100	0.102	0.068	0.051	0.037	0.024	0.011	0.006	0.002
1000	0.100	0.067	0.050	0.036	0.023	0.010	0.005	0.001
Infinite	0.1003	0.0668	0.0495	0.0359	0.0228	0.0099	0.0049	0.0013

Note that the *t*-distribution with infinite df is the standard normal distribution.

TABLE A.4 ■ Critical Values for *F*-test ($\alpha = 0.05$)

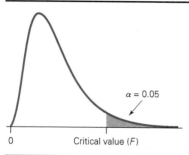

$\alpha = 0.05$

0   Critical value (*F*)

Denom df	\multicolumn{10}{c}{Numerator df}									
	1	2	3	4	5	6	7	8	9	10
1	161.45	199.50	215.71	224.58	230.16	233.99	236.77	238.88	240.54	241.88
2	18.51	19.00	19.16	19.25	19.30	19.33	19.35	19.37	19.38	19.40
3	10.13	9.55	9.28	9.12	9.01	8.94	8.89	8.85	8.81	8.79
4	7.71	6.94	6.59	6.39	6.26	6.16	6.09	6.04	6.00	5.96
5	6.61	5.79	5.41	5.19	5.05	4.95	4.88	4.82	4.77	4.74
6	5.99	5.14	4.76	4.53	4.39	4.28	4.21	4.15	4.10	4.06
7	5.59	4.74	4.35	4.12	3.97	3.87	3.79	3.73	3.68	3.64
8	5.32	4.46	4.07	3.84	3.69	3.58	3.50	3.44	3.39	3.35
9	5.12	4.26	3.86	3.63	3.48	3.37	3.29	3.23	3.18	3.14
10	4.96	4.10	3.71	3.48	3.33	3.22	3.14	3.07	3.02	2.98
11	4.84	3.98	3.59	3.36	3.20	3.09	3.01	2.95	2.90	2.85
12	4.75	3.89	3.49	3.26	3.11	3.00	2.91	2.85	2.80	2.75
13	4.67	3.81	3.41	3.18	3.03	2.92	2.83	2.77	2.71	2.67
14	4.60	3.74	3.34	3.11	2.96	2.85	2.76	2.70	2.65	2.60
15	4.54	3.68	3.29	3.06	2.90	2.79	2.71	2.64	2.59	2.54
16	4.49	3.63	3.24	3.01	2.85	2.74	2.66	2.59	2.54	2.49
17	4.45	3.59	3.20	2.96	2.81	2.70	2.61	2.55	2.49	2.45
18	4.41	3.55	3.16	2.93	2.77	2.66	2.58	2.51	2.46	2.41
19	4.38	3.52	3.13	2.90	2.74	2.63	2.54	2.48	2.42	2.38
20	4.35	3.49	3.10	2.87	2.71	2.60	2.51	2.45	2.39	2.35
21	4.32	3.47	3.07	2.84	2.68	2.57	2.49	2.42	2.37	2.32
22	4.30	3.44	3.05	2.82	2.66	2.55	2.46	2.40	2.34	2.30
23	4.28	3.42	3.03	2.80	2.64	2.53	2.44	2.37	2.32	2.27
24	4.26	3.40	3.01	2.78	2.62	2.51	2.42	2.36	2.30	2.25
25	4.24	3.39	2.99	2.76	2.60	2.49	2.40	2.34	2.28	2.24
26	4.23	3.37	2.98	2.74	2.59	2.47	2.39	2.32	2.27	2.22
27	4.21	3.35	2.96	2.73	2.57	2.46	2.37	2.31	2.25	2.20
28	4.20	3.34	2.95	2.71	2.56	2.45	2.36	2.29	2.24	2.19
29	4.18	3.33	2.93	2.70	2.55	2.43	2.35	2.28	2.22	2.18
30	4.17	3.32	2.92	2.69	2.53	2.42	2.33	2.27	2.21	2.16
40	4.08	3.23	2.84	2.61	2.45	2.34	2.25	2.18	2.12	2.08
50	4.03	3.18	2.79	2.56	2.40	2.29	2.20	2.13	2.07	2.03
60	4.00	3.15	2.76	2.53	2.37	2.25	2.17	2.10	2.04	1.99
70	3.98	3.13	2.74	2.50	2.35	2.23	2.14	2.07	2.02	1.97
80	3.96	3.11	2.72	2.49	2.33	2.21	2.13	2.06	2.00	1.95
90	3.95	3.10	2.71	2.47	2.32	2.20	2.11	2.04	1.99	1.94
100	3.94	3.09	2.70	2.46	2.31	2.19	2.10	2.03	1.97	1.93
200	3.89	3.04	2.65	2.42	2.26	2.14	2.06	1.98	1.93	1.88
500	3.86	3.01	2.62	2.39	2.23	2.12	2.03	1.96	1.90	1.85
1000	3.85	3.00	2.61	2.38	2.22	2.11	2.02	1.95	1.89	1.84

TABLE A.4 ■ Critical Values for *F*-test ($\alpha = 0.01$)

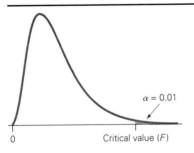

$\alpha = 0.01$

Critical value (*F*)

0

					Numerator df					
Denom df	1	2	3	4	5	6	7	8	9	10
1	4052	4999	5404	5624	5764	5859	5928	5981	6022	6056
2	98.50	99.00	99.16	99.25	99.30	99.33	99.36	99.38	99.39	99.40
3	34.12	30.82	29.46	28.71	28.24	27.91	27.67	27.49	27.34	27.23
4	21.20	18.00	16.69	15.98	15.52	15.21	14.98	14.80	14.66	14.55
5	16.26	13.27	12.06	11.39	10.97	10.67	10.46	10.29	10.16	10.05
6	13.75	10.92	9.78	9.15	8.75	8.47	8.26	8.10	7.98	7.87
7	12.25	9.55	8.45	7.85	7.46	7.19	6.99	6.84	6.72	6.62
8	11.26	8.65	7.59	7.01	6.63	6.37	6.18	6.03	5.91	5.81
9	10.56	8.02	6.99	6.42	6.06	5.80	5.61	5.47	5.35	5.26
10	10.04	7.56	6.55	5.99	5.64	5.39	5.20	5.06	4.94	4.85
11	9.65	7.21	6.22	5.67	5.32	5.07	4.89	4.74	4.63	4.54
12	9.33	6.93	5.95	5.41	5.06	4.82	4.64	4.50	4.39	4.30
13	9.07	6.70	5.74	5.21	4.86	4.62	4.44	4.30	4.19	4.10
14	8.86	6.51	5.56	5.04	4.69	4.46	4.28	4.14	4.03	3.94
15	8.68	6.36	5.42	4.89	4.56	4.32	4.14	4.00	3.89	3.80
16	8.53	6.23	5.29	4.77	4.44	4.20	4.03	3.89	3.78	3.69
17	8.40	6.11	5.19	4.67	4.34	4.10	3.93	3.79	3.68	3.59
18	8.29	6.01	5.09	4.58	4.25	4.01	3.84	3.71	3.60	3.51
19	8.18	5.93	5.01	4.50	4.17	3.94	3.77	3.63	3.52	3.43
20	8.10	5.85	4.94	4.43	4.10	3.87	3.70	3.56	3.46	3.37
21	8.02	5.78	4.87	4.37	4.04	3.81	3.64	3.51	3.40	3.31
22	7.95	5.72	4.82	4.31	3.99	3.76	3.59	3.45	3.35	3.26
23	7.88	5.66	4.76	4.26	3.94	3.71	3.54	3.41	3.30	3.21
24	7.82	5.61	4.72	4.22	3.90	3.67	3.50	3.36	3.26	3.17
25	7.77	5.57	4.68	4.18	3.85	3.63	3.46	3.32	3.22	3.13
26	7.72	5.53	4.64	4.14	3.82	3.59	3.42	3.29	3.18	3.09
27	7.68	5.49	4.60	4.11	3.78	3.56	3.39	3.26	3.15	3.06
28	7.64	5.45	4.57	4.07	3.75	3.53	3.36	3.23	3.12	3.03
29	7.60	5.42	4.54	4.04	3.73	3.50	3.33	3.20	3.09	3.00
30	7.56	5.39	4.51	4.02	3.70	3.47	3.30	3.17	3.07	2.98
40	7.31	5.18	4.31	3.83	3.51	3.29	3.12	2.99	2.89	2.80
50	7.17	5.06	4.20	3.72	3.41	3.19	3.02	2.89	2.78	2.70
60	7.08	4.98	4.13	3.65	3.34	3.12	2.95	2.82	2.72	2.63
70	7.01	4.92	4.07	3.60	3.29	3.07	2.91	2.78	2.67	2.59
80	6.96	4.88	4.04	3.56	3.26	3.04	2.87	2.74	2.64	2.55
90	6.93	4.85	4.01	3.53	3.23	3.01	2.84	2.72	2.61	2.52
100	6.90	4.82	3.98	3.51	3.21	2.99	2.82	2.69	2.59	2.50
200	6.76	4.71	3.88	3.41	3.11	2.89	2.73	2.60	2.50	2.41
500	6.69	4.65	3.82	3.36	3.05	2.84	2.68	2.55	2.44	2.36
1000	6.66	4.63	3.80	3.34	3.04	2.82	2.66	2.53	2.43	2.34

TABLE A.5 ■ Chi-square Distribution

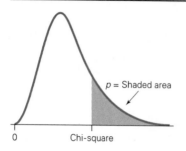

p = Shaded area

0   Chi-square

				p = Area to Right of Chi-square Value					
df	0.50	0.25	0.10	0.075	0.05	0.025	0.01	0.005	0.001
1	0.45	1.32	2.71	3.17	3.84	5.02	6.63	7.88	10.83
2	1.39	2.77	4.61	5.18	5.99	7.38	9.21	10.60	13.82
3	2.37	4.11	6.25	6.90	7.81	9.35	11.34	12.84	16.27
4	3.36	5.39	7.78	8.50	9.49	11.14	13.28	14.86	18.47
5	4.35	6.63	9.24	10.01	11.07	12.83	15.09	16.75	20.51
6	5.35	7.84	10.64	11.47	12.59	14.45	16.81	18.55	22.46
7	6.35	9.04	12.02	12.88	14.07	16.01	18.48	20.28	24.32
8	7.34	10.22	13.36	14.27	15.51	17.53	20.09	21.95	26.12
9	8.34	11.39	14.68	15.63	16.92	19.02	21.67	23.59	27.88
10	9.34	12.55	15.99	16.97	18.31	20.48	23.21	25.19	29.59
11	10.34	13.70	17.28	18.29	19.68	21.92	24.73	26.76	31.26
12	11.34	14.85	18.55	19.60	21.03	23.34	26.22	28.30	32.91
13	12.34	15.98	19.81	20.90	22.36	24.74	27.69	29.82	34.53
14	13.34	17.12	21.06	22.18	23.68	26.12	29.14	31.32	36.12
15	14.34	18.25	22.31	23.45	25.00	27.49	30.58	32.80	37.70
16	15.34	19.37	23.54	24.72	26.30	28.85	32.00	34.27	39.25
17	16.34	20.49	24.77	25.97	27.59	30.19	33.41	35.72	40.79
18	17.34	21.60	25.99	27.22	28.87	31.53	34.81	37.16	42.31
19	18.34	22.72	27.20	28.46	30.14	32.85	36.19	38.58	43.82
20	19.34	23.83	28.41	29.69	31.41	34.17	37.57	40.00	45.31
21	20.34	24.93	29.62	30.92	32.67	35.48	38.93	41.40	46.80
22	21.34	26.04	30.81	32.14	33.92	36.78	40.29	42.80	48.27
23	22.34	27.14	32.01	33.36	35.17	38.08	41.64	44.18	49.73
24	23.34	28.24	33.20	34.57	36.42	39.36	42.98	45.56	51.18
25	24.34	29.34	34.38	35.78	37.65	40.65	44.31	46.93	52.62
26	25.34	30.43	35.56	36.98	38.89	41.92	45.64	48.29	54.05
27	26.34	31.53	36.74	38.18	40.11	43.19	46.96	49.65	55.48
28	27.34	32.62	37.92	39.38	41.34	44.46	48.28	50.99	56.89
29	28.34	33.71	39.09	40.57	42.56	45.72	49.59	52.34	58.30
30	29.34	34.80	40.26	41.76	43.77	46.98	50.89	53.67	59.70

Answers to Selected Exercises

*The following are partial or complete answers to the exercises numbered in **bold** in the text.*

Chapter 1

1.2 a. .00043
1.5 a. 400
1.7 c. Randomized experiment.
   d. Observational study.
1.11 189/11,034, or about 17/1000, based on placebo group.
1.15 a. 150 mph.
   b. 55 mph.
   c. 80 mph.
   d. 1/2
   e. 51
1.19 No.
1.22 The base rate for that type of cancer.
1.26 a. 212/1525 = .139.
   b. $1/\sqrt{1525}$ = .026.
   c. .113 to .165.
1.28 a. Self-selected or volunteer.
   b. No. Readers with strong opinions will respond.

Chapter 2

2.1 a. Categorical.
   b. Quantitative.
   c. Quantitative.
   d. Categorical.
2.2 a. Categorical.
   b. Ordinal.
2.4 a. Not continuous.
2.5 a. Explanatory is amount of walking or running; response is lung function.
2.6 a. Population.
   b. Sample.
2.8 a. Support ban or not; categorical.
   b. Gain on verbal and math SATs after program; quantitative.

c. Smoker or not and Alzheimer sufferer or not; both categorical.
2.9 a. Question 1a.
2.11 Example: Letter grades (A, B, etc.) converted to GPA.
2.14 a. 1427/2530 = .564, or 56.4%.
   b. 100% − 56.4% = 43.6%.
2.15 a. 1700/2470 = .688, or 68.8%.
   b. 1056/1700 = .621, or 62.1%.
2.16 c. Overweight = 26.57%; about right = 69.23%; underweight = 4.20%.
2.18 a. Explanatory is smoked or not; response is developed Alzheimer's disease or not.
2.21 Either could be justified as being more informative.
2.23 a. Skewed to the right.
   b. 13 ear pierces may be an outlier.
   c. 2 ear pierces; about 45 women had this number.
   d. About 32 or so.
2.25 a. Roughly symmetric.
   b. Highest = 92.
   c. Lowest = 64.
   d. 5/20 = .25, or 25%
2.29 Example: The age of a person who is 80 years old would be an outlier at a traditional college, but not at a retirement home.
2.31 Whether it's the male author (then not an outlier) or the female author (then an outlier).
2.34 Yes. Values inconsistent with the bulk of the data will be obvious.
2.36 a. This is personal preference; some may prefer a very large family.
   b. An outlier (in the high direction).
2.37 a. Median = (72 + 76)/2 = 74; mean = 74.33.
   b. Median = 7; mean = 25.
2.39 a. Range = 225 − 123 = 102.
   b. IQR = 35.
   c. 50%

2.40 a Median $= 12$.

2.41 d. There are no outliers.

2.44 The median is 16.72 inches. The data values vary from 6.14 to 37.42 inches. The middle 1/2 of the data is between 12.05 and 25.37 inches, so "typical" annual rainfall covers quite a wide range.

2.48 0, 20, 55, 175, 450; data values are skewed to the right and there is an extreme outlier of 450 CDs. (Quartile values may differ slightly if using the computer.)

2.51 32, 45.5, 50, 57, 74.

2.54 a. Between 5.3 and 8.7 hours.
b. Between 3.6 and 10.4 hours.

2.56 a. $z = (200 - 170)/20 = 1.5$.

2.57 a. $\bar{x} = 20$; $s = 1.581$.

2.58 a. Range $= 98 - 41 = 57$.
b. $s \approx 57/6 = 9.5$.

2.60 The Empirical Rule predicts about 68%, 95%, 99.7% within 1, 2, and 3 standard deviations of the mean; data show 72%, 97%, 98%, so the set of measurements fits well.

2.62 a. Population.
b. Population, 14.77.

2.66 a. Would hold without the two outliers; should still be close.
b. Yes, range is 10.75 cm, close to 6 standard deviations. Expect between 4 and 6 standard deviations.

2.68 Example: Male height of 73, $z = 1.00$.

2.70 a. $z = -0.5$; 0.3085.
b. $z = 2.5$; 0.9938.

2.72 50, 50, 50, 50, 50, 50, 50; no.

2.75 a. Mean $= 51.47$ years; standard deviation $= 8.92$ years (population standard deviation $= 8.85$).
b. Range is 42 years, 4.7 standard deviations, so it holds.
c. z for youngest CEO is -2.18, z for oldest CEO is 2.53; about as expected from the Empirical Rule.

2.78 a. Categorical.
b. Quantitative.

2.80 a. Yes; night light use, for example.
b. No.

2.84 a. Set 2—it covers a much wider range of heights.

2.86 a. Amount of beer consumed per unit of time (week, etc.) and systolic blood pressure.
b. Calories of protein consumed per day on average and whether or not they had colon cancer.

2.89 Question 5a: Do the students who studied the most last week tend to be the students with the highest grade point averages?

Chapter 3

3.4 c. Observational study.

3.6 a. Response variable is daughter's height.

3.8 a. Doesn't hold; professional basketball players do not represent any larger population.
b. Probably holds, students taking statistics most likely have representative pulse rates.

3.9 a. Probably not, because long-term meditation is a matter of choice, not easily randomly assigned.
b. Yes, volunteers could be randomly assigned to attend the program or not.

3.10 a. The explanatory variable is long-term practice of meditation; the response is blood pressure.

3.11 a. Amount of salt and sodium in the diet or other diet-related factors.

3.16 No. Although all songs have the same probability of being sampled, all *sets* of four songs do not. For instance, a sample consisting of the first four songs on the first CD is impossible.

3.19 a. No.
c. Yes.
e. No.

3.22 Completely randomized design.

3.24 a. Yes.
b. No.
c. No.

3.27 a. Single-blind; customers knew what plan they had but the technician did not.

3.28 a. Matched pairs.

3.29 a. The explanatory variable is the rate plan; the response is usage during peak hours.

3.30 a. A control group was used (matched with the treatment group); a placebo was not.

3.31 a. A random sample was used, so results can be extended to all customers.

3.37 a. Observational study.
b. The explanatory variable was whether or not the couple owned a pet, and the response variables were marriage satisfaction and stress levels.
c. An example is the amount of business travel they do. Couples who travel frequently may be less likely to own pets and also have more stress.

3.38 a. Interacting variable.

3.41 Explanatory variable is taking the new medication or not, response variable is weight gain or loss, interacting variable is gender.

3.45 a. Yes.
b. Yes.
c. No.

3.49 c. Confounding variables and the implication of causation (e.g., current diet). Relying on memory; it would be hard for people to remember how high in fat their childhood diet was.

3.52 Observational study.

3.56 Postmenopausal women who did not use hormone therapy at all.

3.60 Extending results inappropriately. If women today take lower levels of hormones than the women in the study, these results may not apply to women currently on hormone therapy.

3.63 Question 4a: Are the measurements similar across categories? Is self-esteem and self-judgment the same for the three groups, on average?

3.66 This is an example of an interacting variable, since the effect on self-esteem of thinking about their bad hair is different for men than for women.

3.67 a. Descriptive statistics.
b. Inferential statistics.

3.72 a. Individual unit is a tomato plant. Two variables were the number of tomatoes produced and whether the tomato plant was raised in full sunlight or partial shade.

3.74 a. Yes
   b. Yes.
   c. No.

Chapter 4

4.3 .014 or 1.4%.
4.6 c. Nonresponse bias.
4.9 b. 40% ± 3.15% or 36.85% to 43.15%.
4.12 For example, testing manufactured parts where the test damages the product.
4.15 a. .49 ± .03 = .46 to .52.
   b. .47 ± .03 = .44 to .50.
   c. No, the two intervals both cover 50% and overlap with each other.
4.17 a. Selection bias.
   b. Nonresponse bias.
4.22 a. Use 01 to 49 as is and subtract 50 from 51 to 99 to get 15, 23, 20, 21, 29, 5.
   b. It doesn't matter.
4.26 Any list that contains the two-digit strings in any order: 00, 07, 15, 19, 24, 33, 44, 51, 65, 99. For instance, 24190 03351 99076 54415.
4.30 Simple random sample.
4.34 a. Stratified sample: Use the three types of schools as strata. Create a list of all students for each of the three strata; draw a simple random sample from each of the three lists.
   b. Cluster sample: Use individual schools or individual classes as clusters. Take a random sample of clusters; measure all students in those clusters.
   c. Simple random sample: Obtain a list of all students in the classes at all schools; take a simple random sample from that combined list.
4.37 Cluster sample because a sample of exchanges is found and then only numbers within those exchanges are sampled.
4.39 a. All taxpayers.
   b. Parents of all the school children.
4.45 Anonymous testing.
4.48 a. Dentists who subscribe to one of two dental magazines. Yes, because not all dentists subscribe to those two magazines.
   b. Nonresponse.
   c. Send a reminder or call those who didn't respond.
4.51 a. Put an ad in the local paper asking people to fill out the survey.
   b. Ask "Don't you agree that there is too much trash in our streets and that more public trash containers are needed?"
4.53 Any two questions in which one changes the way respondents would think about the other. An example: "Are you aware that over 30% of homeless people in this city are mothers with children?" and "Do you think more public money should be used to help homeless people?"
4.56 Desire to please; confidentiality and anonymity.
4.59 a. Open-form question.
   b. Yes, because of all the publicity he had just received.
   c. Probably lower.
4.65 a. All students at the university.

b. All students enrolled in statistics classes.
   c. The 500 students to whom the survey was mailed.
4.67 The sample sizes or margin of error. The 20% versus 25% may be within the margin of error for the surveys.
4.70 The quickie poll would probably be most representative.
4.72 Nonresponse.
4.73 b. Send the survey to a legitimate random sample but make the questions so outrageous that only those who support the position would respond; others would not take it seriously.
4.77 No, only those likely to vote should be used.
4.80 Larger; the sample size for Republicans only would be smaller.
4.82 a. .078; .66 ± .078 or 58.2% to 73.8%.
   b. .066; .38 ± .066 or 31.4% to 44.6%.
   c. Yes, intervals do not overlap.

Chapter 5

5.1 a. Negative association.
   b. No association.
5.2 a. Negative association.
   b. Roughly linear.
   c. Highest average math SAT is about 600; less than 5% took the test.
   d. Lowest average math SAT is about 475; about 85% took the test.
5.3 a. Yes, both variables are quantitative.
5.7 a. The speed of the car is the explanatory variable and the stopping distance is the response variable.
   b. Positive association, somewhat linear but possibly curvilinear.
5.9 a. Average weight = − 250 + 6 (70) = 170 lb.
   b. On average, weight increases 6 pounds per each 1-inch increase in height.
5.11 b. Predicted average = 575 − 1.11 (8) = 566.12.
   c. Residual = 573 − 566.12 = 6.88.
5.12 Deterministic relationship.
5.14 a. Height increases an average of 0.7 inches for each centimeter increase in handspan.
   b. 65.1 in.
   c. Residual = 66.5 − 65.1 = 1.4 in.
5.20 The two variables do not have a linear association.
5.21 a. Chest girth increases as length increases.
   b. The value of r is high, so the relationship apparently is strong.
   c. $r = +0.82$.
5.24 It would still be 0.95. Changing the units of measurement does not change the correlation.
5.27 a. Graph 2 is the strongest; Graph 3 is the weakest.
5.31 Both variables will have relatively high values in the winter and relatively low values in the summer.
5.34 Gender differences create the observed negative correlation. Females tend to be shorter, and have more ear pierces.
5.36 a. Estimated stopping distance when speed is 80 mph is −45 + 5.7(80) = 411 ft. No, this is probably not an accurate estimate. The relationship is probably not linear.

b. From the plot the relationship looks curvilinear. Estimated stopping distance is about 500 ft.

5.38 Men and women should not be combined. Women probably have higher scores but lower heights.

5.42 b. Positive, because larger cities have more of both.
c. Negative, because strength decreases with age.

5.44 $r^2 = 0.64$.

5.47 a. For a man, $53 + 0.7(140) = 151$ pounds. For a woman, $44 + 0.6(140) = 128$ pounds. The man wants to weigh 11 pounds more; the woman wants to weigh 12 pounds less.
b. No, there are no actual weights close to 0.
c. Yes. For each increase of 1 pound in actual weight, the slope provides the estimated average increase in ideal weight, which is 0.6 pounds for women and 0.7 pounds for men.

5.50 b. -0.312
c. The correlation for hardcover books only is 0.348. The correlation for softcover books only is 0.637.

5.54 a. Perhouse $= 44.9 - (0.0212)$(Year). The estimated number of persons per household in 2010 is $44.9 - (0.0212)(2010) = 2.288$ persons.
b. Slope $= -0.0212$, indicating that the average number of people per household decreases by about 0.02 per year, or about 0.2 every 10 years.

5.56 a. For line 1, SSE $= 10$; for line 2, SSE $= 4$.
b. Line 2 is better because SSE is smaller.

5.61 b. Diff $= -52.5 + 0.312$ (Actual). For men who weigh 150 pounds the estimated average difference is $-52.5 + 0.312(150) = -5.7$ pounds. This is actual − ideal, so they want to weigh more.
d. $r^2 = 0.353$ or 35.3%.

Chapter 6

6.3 a. Yes, both variables are categorical.
c. No, both variables are quantitative.

6.4 No. Totals are given for categories of each variable but counts for combinations are not provided.

6.6 a.

Anger?	Heart Disease	No Heart Disease	Total
No Anger	8	191	199
Most Anger	59	500	559
Total	67	691	758

b. $8/199 = 4.0\%$.
c. $59/559 = 10.6\%$.

6.10 a. 1.0

6.11 a. $10/100 = .1$.

6.12 a. $.1/.05 = 2$.

6.13 a. 2.11

6.17 1.4

6.20 a. Relative risk is $.106/.04 = 2.65$.
b. Percent increase in risk is $100\% \times (10.6 - 4.0)/4.0 = 165\%$.

6.23 a. Aged 18 to 29, 13.9%; aged 30 or over, 10.6%.
b. Relative risk is $.139/.106 = 1.3$. Adults under 30 are 1.3 times as likely to report seeing a ghost as adults 30 years old or older.

6.26 Probably not. The relationship between blood pressure and religious activity would need to be reversed when separate categories of a third variable are considered.

6.28 Occupation; men may be more likely to have jobs that require long-distance driving.

6.31 a. Response variable is outcome (successful or not).
c. Compare treatments separately within the two initial severity groups.

6.34 b. Do not reject the null hypothesis because the p-value is greater than .05.
f. Reject the null hypothesis because the chi-square statistic is greater than 3.84.

6.37 a. Yes
b. Yes.
c. No.

6.40 a. Null hypothesis is that there is no relationship between gender and opinions about capital punishment. Alternative hypothesis is that there is a relationship.
b. The relationship is not statistically significant because $0.19 > 0.05$.

6.41 a. Chi-square statistic $= 1.714$.

6.45 a. Yes, there appears to be a relationship based on the following percents:

Pierces	% with Tattoo
2 or less	7.2%
3 or 4	11.0%
5 or 6	26.0%
7 or more	54.5%

c. $(32 + 30)/107 = 57.9\%$ of women with a tattoo have five or more ear pierces. $(91 + 25)/571 = 20.3\%$ of women with no tattoo have five or more ear pierces.
d. $107/678 = 15.8\%$.
e. $245/678 = 36.1\%$.

6.49 a.

	Cancer	Control	Total
Bird	98	101	199
No Bird	141	328	469
Total	239	429	668

b. Bird owners: $98/199 = .4925$, or 49.25%. Nonowners: $141/469 = .301$, or 30.1%.
c. No. This was a case control study in which the researchers purposely sampled more lung cancer patients than would naturally occur in a group of 668 people. The sample percents falling into the cancer category are much higher than you would see in a random sample.
d. The relative risk for bird owners is $.4925/.301 = 1.64$.
e. The "baseline" risk of lung cancer for people like yourself.
f. No. This is an observational study and there may be confounding factors that explain the results.
g. Compare the smoking habits of the bird owners and nonowners and see whether or not the bird owners generally smoke more.

6.54 Chi-square $= 4.817$, p-value $= 0.028$; relationship is statistically significant.

6.58 Using the approximate odds given in Exercise 6.57, the odds ratio is $24/8.5 = 2.82$. The precise odds ratio is found by taking $(59 \times 191)/(8 \times 500) = 2.817$. The odds of remaining free of heart disease versus getting heart disease for men with no anger are about 2.8 times the odds of those events for men with the most anger.

6.61 a. For men, the odds for Program A are 400 to 250, or about 1.6 to 1. For women, the odds are 50 to 25, or 2 to 1. The odds ratio for women compared to men is therefore 2/1.6, or 1.25. The odds of being admitted versus being denied admittance for women are about 1.25 times what they are for men, so women have better odds.

b. For men, the odds for the combined programs are 450 to 550, or about .8 to 1. For women, the odds are 175 to 325, or about .54 to 1. The odds ratio (women to men) is therefore about $.54/.8 = .675$. The odds of being admitted versus being denied admittance for women are about 2/3 of what they are for men, so women have worse odds.

c. The last sentence in the solutions for parts (a) and (b) can be used for this purpose.

Chapter 7

7.2 1/125

7.4 c. Yes.
d. No.

7.7 a. Relative frequency; probably determined by observing the number injured by lightning for many years, divided by the average population in those years.
b. Personal; based on her assessment of the health of the plants and growing conditions.

7.9 Random circumstance: traffic light is green or not. Determine probability by observing the proportion of time it's green over many months of driving to work.

7.11 Play over and over again and record how many games he or she won out of the total number of games played.

7.13 Example: the probability that the United States President will be assassinated this year.

7.16 17/172.

7.19 a. Yes.
b. No.

7.22 a. Yes.
b. No.
c. Yes.

7.25 a. Yes, red die cannot be both 3 and 6.
b. No, red die can be 3 in the same toss that green die is 6.

7.26 a. No, knowing A occurred changes $P(B)$ to 0.
b. Yes, knowing the red die is a 3 does not change $P(B)$.

7.29 No, knowing the woman's age changes the probability that she is fertile.

7.32 a. Getting at least one tail.
b. 7/8

7.35 a. No.
b. .8

7.38 a. 11/12
b. 11/12
c. 121/144
d. 23/144

7.41 a. Long-run relative frequency of these flights arriving on time to get to the ship.
b. No, in Miami bad weather would increase the chances of being late for both.
c. .72
d. .26

7.43 a. .0625
b. .0577
c. .5625
d. .5577

7.44 b. 2/3
c. 1/2

7.47 .085

7.50 (1/13)(48/51)

7.53 $P(\text{calculus student}) = .4$; $P(\text{Junior}|\text{calculus student}) = .15/.4 = 0.375$.

7.56 45/10000

7.58 a. 8/50
b. 7/31
c. 1/50

7.60 Use only two digits, such as 8 and 9, to represent correct guesses.

7.63 a. .12
b. .4615

7.66 They are equally likely.

7.70 a. 1/365
b. .0136
c. No, that specific event has low probability but it is not unlikely that someone in the class would have a birthday matching a teammate's family member's birthday.

7.72 No, birth outcomes are independent.

7.76 Not surprising; $1 - P(\text{no match}) = .1829$.

7.79 a. .27
b. .86
c. .0225
d. .0064
e. .0145

7.82 a. 40%
b. 10%
c. 31%

7.86 a. .5 (problem stated that no responses equal median).
b. .0625
c. No, they would not be independent.

7.89 a. .1225
b. No, their statuses are not independent.
c. Relative frequency.
d. Statement must be about a separate randomly selected foreign-born person in each of the two years.

7.92 485/1669

7.95 238/612

7.97 .4125

Chapter 8

8.2 a. Discrete.
b. Continuous.
c. Discrete.
d. Discrete.

8.7 a. .80

8.8   c.

k	0	1	2
$P(X = k)$	42/90	42/90	6/90

8.12 Continuous example: amount of rainfall during the event; S includes the range from 0 to the maximum possible rain in one day. Discrete example: number of emergency vehicles with sirens driving by during event; $S = \{0,1,2, \ldots , k\}$, where k is the logical maximum for the situation.

8.15 a. $30
       b. $0 and $100 with probabilities .9 and .1.

8.17 −$3.95

8.20 $E(X) = 1.5$.

8.23 Standard deviation = $29.67.

8.26 $E(X) = 1.69$; not a possible value, so meaningful only as a long-run average.

8.29 a. Yes, 200, .5
       b. 100

8.31 a. $n = 30, p = 1/6$.

8.32 a. 5

8.35 a. The probability of success does not remain the same from one trial to the next.
       b. There are not a prespecified number of trials.
       c. Outcomes are not independent from one trial to the next; probability of success changes.

8.38 a. .2051
       b. .3504

8.39 b. The desired probability is $P(X \geq 110)$, n is 500, and p is .20.

8.43 b. $z = -1.0$.

8.44 b. .3632
       c. .6368

8.46 a. X is a uniform random variable.
       b. $f(x) = 1/100$ for any x between 0 and 100; $f(x) = 0$ for any x not between 0 and 100.
       c. $P(X \leq 15 \text{ seconds}) = (15 - 0)/100 = .15$.

8.49 a. .0808

8.51 a. −1.96

8.54 a. .3665

8.55 $P(Z \leq -.675)$ is about .25, so about 25% of the women are shorter than $-.675 \times 2.7 + 65 = 63.2$ inches.

8.58 a. .0918 (for $z = -1.33$)
       b. .0228
       c. .3830
       d. .0023

8.61 a. .0571
       b. .0749

8.65 a. 400 seconds.
       b. 20 seconds.
       c. .0228

8.68 b. $X + Y$ is normal with mean = 150, variance = 325, standard deviation = 18.03.

8.71 $P(Z < -1.21) = .1131$.

8.73 a. $P(Z \leq -0.5) = .3085$.

8.75 .0918 (for $z = -1.33$)

8.77 Probably not. It's a mixture of two bell-shaped distributions with different means.

8.80 a. X is −$2, or $70; $P(X = -\$2) = 37/38$, $P(X = \$70) = 1/38$.

b. $E(X) = -\$4/38 = -\$.1053$, players lose about ten cents per $2 bet over the long run.

8.83 a. Probability of success is not the same for all trials.
       b. Outcomes are not independent from one trial to the next.

8.86 a. It makes sense to assume independence unless the children influence each others' choices, or some other common factor leads them both to pick a long or short story.
       b. $P(Z > 1.77) = .0384$.

Chapter 9

9.1   a. Statistic.
       b. Parameter.
       c. Statistic.
       d. Parameter.

9.3   a. $\hat{p}$
       b. p
       c. $\hat{p}$

9.5   a. $\bar{x}$
       b. μ

9.7   a. Parameters; they represent the population values.
       b. Yes, they know the means exactly, and the mean for males is $1500 higher.

9.10 a. 1/2
       b. Integers from 0 to 6.
       c. $(1/2)^6 = 1/64$.
       d. B is binomial with $n = 6$ and $p = 1/2$; probabilities for $B = 0, 1, 2, 3, 4, 5, 6$ are 1/64, 6/64, 15/64, 20/64, 15/64, 6/64, and 1/64, respectively.

9.12 a. Mean = .5; s.d. = s.d. = $\sqrt{\dfrac{(.5)(.5)}{400}} = .025$.
       b. Mean = .5; s.d. = .0125.

9.14 a. .55
       b. $\sqrt{\dfrac{(.55)(.45)}{100}} = .0497$, or about .05.
       c. $.55 \pm 3(.05)$, or between about .40 and .70.

9.16 a. $\hat{p} = 300/500 = .60$.
       b. s.e.$(\hat{p}) = .022$.

9.20 $.05 \pm 2\sqrt{\dfrac{(.05)(.95)}{400}}$, or .03 to .07.

9.23 a. .20
       b. .18
       c. .0384
       d. .20
       e. .04

9.26 a. Yes, this falls into Situation 1 described in Section 9.3.
       b. No. For skewed population, sample size is too small.
       c. Yes, this falls into Situation 2.

9.27 a. 6
       b. 3
       c. s.d.$(\bar{x})$ decreases when sample size is increased.

9.29 a. $\bar{x}$ and s.
       b. s.e.$(\bar{x}) = 47.7/\sqrt{28} = 9.014$.

9.32 b. Approximately normal with a mean of 210 pounds and a standard deviation of 3.95.
       d. $P(z > 2.53) = .0057$.

9.33 Standard deviation of the sampling distribution is $\sigma/\sqrt{n}$.

Standard error of the mean replaces population σ with the sample version s and is more commonly used because σ is rarely known.

9.35   a. The population of possible net gains is highly skewed (not bell-shaped) and the sample size is small.
      b. $-\$0.35$; $\$9.38$

9.40   Because of the symmetry of the situation, it should be a mirror image of the sampling distribution of H, the highest number, given in Figure 9.4, so it should be highly skewed to the right.

9.43   a. Binomial; $n = 10$, $p = .5$.
      b. 5
      c. 1.58

9.45   a. $z = 2$.
      b. $z = 2.828$.

9.47   a. $z = 1$.
      b. $z = -1$.

9.50   Mean μ and standard deviation σ.

9.53   a. -1.0 and $+1.6$.

9.55   a. $t = -1$; df $= 16-1 = 15$.

9.57   a. $t = 0.417$.
      b. $z = 0.5$.
      c. $t = -3$.

9.60   a. t-distribution.
      b. df $= 5$.
      c. Normal distribution.

9.61   a. $t = 2.5$.

9.65   Actual population exists (students at your college); fixed proportion are left-handed; $n = 200$ is large enough for number of left-handers to be sufficient.

9.68   b. Yes; the sample proportion is almost surely in the range .447 to .553, so .70 is unlikely.

9.72   Approximately normal with a mean of 105 and a standard deviation of 1.5.

9.75   a. Approximately normal, mean $= .20$, standard deviation $= \sqrt{.2 \times .8/2500} = .008$.
      b. Not likely. We expect virtually all samples to have between 17.6% and 22.4% of viewers.

9.78   a. No, sample size is too small.
      b. Yes.
      c. No, days in January and February only do not constitute a random sample.
      d. Yes.

9.82   225

Chapter 10

10.1   c. Sample proportion. $\hat{p} = .55$.

10.2   a. $36\% \pm 3.5\%$, or 32.5% to 39.5%. With 95% confidence, we can say that the percent of American adults who feel they don't get enough sleep is between 32.5% and 39.5%.
      b. If college students generally differ from others on this question, then this sample won't correctly estimate the percent for students.

10.5   a. $55\% \pm 3\%$, or 52% to 58%.
      b. Confidence interval is entirely above 50%, so it's reasonable to say more than 50% of population thinks their weight is about right.

10.8   About $0.95 \times 200 = 190$ intervals will capture the population proportion, so about 10 intervals will not.

10.9   The probability is .95 that the difference between sample and population proportions (or percents) is less than the margin of error, so the probability that the difference is greater than the margin of error (3% here) is $1 - .95 = .05$.

10.10   A confidence interval estimates a population value (not a sample value).

10.11   a. $2\sqrt{\dfrac{.56(1 - .56)}{100}} = .0993$.
      b. .0496

10.12   a. $\hat{p} = \dfrac{166}{200} = .83$.
      b. $.83 \pm 2\sqrt{\dfrac{(.83)(1 - .83)}{200}}$, or $.83 \pm .053$. With 95% confidence, we can say that in the population of patients with this disease, the proportion who would be cured with this treatment is in this interval.

10.16   a. $\dfrac{1}{\sqrt{501}} = .045$, or 4.5%. They apparently rounded up to 5%.

10.17   a. This can be calculated as $\sqrt{\dfrac{(.03)(.97)}{883}} = .006$.
      b. $2\sqrt{\dfrac{(.03)(.97)}{883}} = .011$.

10.18   a. .90.
      b. .95.
      c. .98.
      d. .99.

10.20   a. $\hat{p} = \dfrac{220}{400} = .55$.
      b. s.e.$(\hat{p}) = \sqrt{\dfrac{.55(1 - .55)}{400}} = .025$.
      c. $.55 \pm (1.96)(.025)$, or .501 to .599.
      d. $.55 \pm (2.33)(.025)$, or .492 to .608.

10.23 $.83 \pm 2.33\sqrt{\dfrac{(.83)(.17)}{200}}$, or $.83 \pm .062$. The 98% confidence interval is wider than the 95% interval.

10.25 $z^* = 1.28$. In a standard normal curve, the area under the curve between -1.28 and $+1.28$ is about .80.

10.26   a. 5% (or, .05).
      b. About $n = 2500$.

10.28   The 28% claim is not reasonable because it is not within the confidence interval.

10.32   At least $n = 400$.

10.34   95% confidence intervals for population percents in the two years do not overlap. It's reasonable to conclude that the population percent is higher in 2002.

10.35   a. $\hat{p} = \dfrac{45}{164} = .274$.
      b. $\sqrt{\dfrac{(.274)(1 - .274)}{164}} = .035$.
      c. $.274 \pm (2 \times .035)$, or $.274 \pm .07$.

d. The interval contains 1/4 = .25, which is the proportion that would result from guessing. Based on this interval, we cannot rule out the possibility that the participants are merely guessing.

10.37 $.19 \pm 1.645 \sqrt{\dfrac{.19(1 - .19)}{300}}$.

10.40 a. Observational study. The researchers did not assign individuals to these groups.

b. There may be other differences between the two groups that could account for the difference. For instance, policeman may have worse diets or may smoke more.

f. The confidence intervals do not overlap so it is reasonable to conclude the two groups differ.

10.46 5%.

10.50 A confidence interval should not be computed because this is not a randomly selected sample, nor is it likely to be a representative sample. It is a self-selected sample, and this type of sample often is biased toward a particular trait or opinion.

Chapter 11

11.3 a. No.
b. Yes.
c. No.

11.5 a. There are five choices, so $p = 1/5$ or .2.
b. $H_0: p = .2$, $H_a: p < .2$.

11.7 Before they look at the data.

11.9 a. Population is all school-aged children in the state; p is the proportion of them living with one or more grandparents.

11.11 a. Do not reject the null hypothesis.
b. Reject the null hypothesis.

11.13 a. There is not sufficient evidence to conclude that smokers are more likely to get the disease.

11.17 a. Cannot reject the null hypothesis.
b. Reject the null hypothesis (or accept the alternative hypothesis).
c. Reject the null hypothesis (or accept the alternative hypothesis).

11.20 a. 0.0358
b. 0.0228
c. 0.1379
d. 0.00001

11.22 a. Yes.
b. No.
c. No.
d. No.

11.24 b. -2.68

11.25 b. 0.0037

11.26 Null standard error uses the null value p_0, and standard error uses the sample proportion.

11.28 a. No, don't know if it was a random sample.
b. Step 1: $H_0: p = 0.1$, $H_a: p > 0.1$.
Step 2: Sample size condition is met; see part (a) for other. Sample proportion is .12,

$$z = \frac{.12 - .1}{\sqrt{\dfrac{.1(.9)}{150}}} = 0.82$$

Step 3: Exact p-value = 0.242; p-value for z is 0.206 (or 0.207).
Step 4: Cannot reject the null hypothesis; result is not statistically significant.
Step 5: Cannot conclude that artists are more likely to be left-handed than the general population.

11.30 a. No, $0.07 > 0.05$.
b. Yes.

11.33 a. .0725
d. .0145

11.35 Very large.

11.37 a. 1000
b. .45
c. .45

11.41 Probably the finding was that there was no *significant* difference, in the statistical meaning, not the ordinary-language meaning. It could be because there really is no difference, or because the sample was too small to detect it and a type 2 error was made.

11.44 a. False.
b. True.
c. False.
d. False.

11.46 a. Correct decision.
b. Type 2 error.

11.49 a. Example: a diagnosis that leads to major surgery.
b. Example: an infection that could be cured by antibiotics but gets very serious if untreated.

11.52 c. Type 1 is probably more serious—voting for the bill that implements substantial change when actually a majority do not support it.
d. Type 1.

11.56 Step 1: $H_0: p = .1$, $H_a: p \neq .1$.
Step 2: Sample conditions are met. Sample proportion is $20/240 = .0833$,

$$z = \frac{.0833 - .1}{\sqrt{\dfrac{.1(.9)}{240}}} = -.86$$

Step 3: Exact p-value = 0.395; p-value for z is 0.3898.
Step 4: Cannot reject the null hypothesis; result is not statistically significant.
Step 5: Cannot conclude that UCD students' proportion who are left-handed differs from national proportion.

11.59 a. Population parameter = proportion of all people who suffer from this chronic pain that would experience temporary relief if taking the new medication. Hypotheses are $H_0: p = .7$, $H_a: p > .7$.

11.61 a. 0.1470
b. 0.0375

11.64 $z > 0$.

11.66 b. Population—only this class is of interest.

11.69 Assume students represent a random sample of a population of interest on this question and p = proportion of population who would choose first drink. $H_0: p = .5$, $H_a: p > .5$. Both 86 and 73 are large enough to meet conditions. $z = 1.03$, p-value = 0.1515, not statistically significant. Cannot conclude that the first drink presented is more likely to be selected.

Chapter 12

12.1 a. What proportion of parents in the school district support the new program?

b. Parameter is p = proportion of parents in school district who support the new program.

c. Sample estimate is $\hat{p} = 104/300 = .347$.

12.4 a. Is the mean number of CDs owned different for the populations of males and females?

b. Parameter $= \mu_1 - \mu_2$, where μ_1 = population mean for one gender (e.g., males) and μ_2 = population mean for the other (e.g., females).

c. $\bar{x}_1 - \bar{x}_1 = 110 - 90 = 20$.

12.5 a. Two independent samples.

12.8 One research question of interest would be, "What is the mean difference between hours spent studying and hours spent socializing?" The parameter is μ_d = mean difference for all students at the university. The sample estimate is $\bar{d}$ = mean difference for the 100 students in the sample.

12.9 Paired data. Two variables are measured on each individual.

12.13 a. s.e.$(\bar{x}) = \dfrac{2.7}{\sqrt{81}}$ 0.3; approximate 95% CI is 64.2 ± 0.6.

12.14 a. 2.2 cm.

b. $\sqrt{\dfrac{2.4^2}{36} + \dfrac{1.8^2}{36}} = 0.5$.

c. $2.2 \pm (2 \times 0.5)$, or 1.2 to 3.2 cm.

12.15 a. s.e. $(\bar{x}) = \dfrac{2}{\sqrt{64}} = 0.25$ cm. Roughly, for samples of this size, the average difference between the sample and population means is 0.25 cm.

12.18 Calculate the difference for each person. The standard error of the sample mean difference is calculated using the formula $s/\sqrt{n}$, where s = standard deviation of the sample of differences and $n = 50$.

12.21 d. The formula for a confidence interval for the difference between two independent means was used. The calculation is $(2.37 - 1.95) \pm 2\sqrt{\dfrac{1.87^2}{59} + \dfrac{1.51^2}{116}}$.

12.22 a. $(.63 - .29) \pm 2\sqrt{\dfrac{(.63)(1 - .63)}{300} + \dfrac{(.29)(1 - .29)}{300}}$.

12.24 a. $76 \pm 2.31\dfrac{6}{\sqrt{9}}$.

e. $100 \pm 2.13\dfrac{8}{\sqrt{16}}$.

12.26 a. $t^* = 2.52$ (df = 21).

b. $t^* = 2.13$ (df = 4).

12.31 a. Mean $\pm 2s$, which is $284.9 \pm 2 \times 96.1$, which is 284.9 ± 192.2. This interval describes expenditures for individuals and is not a confidence interval for a parameter.

12.34 a. Two-sample.

b. One–sample (for paired difference).

c. Two-sample.

12.35 a. The population means differ.

b. We cannot say the population means differ.

12.36 a. $(11.6 - 10.7) \pm 2.07\sqrt{\dfrac{3.39^2}{16} + \dfrac{2.59^2}{10}}$.

12.37 The variances (or, standard deviations) in the two populations are equal.

12.41 $s_p = 1.7$. The 95% confidence interval is $(8.1 - 4.5) \pm 2.01\sqrt{\dfrac{1.7^2}{23} + \dfrac{1.7^2}{25}}$.

12.43 a. Yes, there are two independent samples with sufficiently large sample sizes.

b. No, the sample sizes are too small.

c. No, methods of Section 12.5 should be used because the question is about mean values.

12.47 b. $(.466 - .380) \pm 2\sqrt{\dfrac{.466(1 - .466)}{4594} + \dfrac{.380(1 - .380)}{7076}}$.

12.48 This is a difference between the proportions in two different categories of a variable in the same sample. The method in Section 12.6 is for a difference between proportions with the same trait in two independent samples.

12.51 c. The interval is approximately $72.8 \pm 2\dfrac{72.2}{\sqrt{204}}$, or 72.8 ± 10.1.

12.53 Both intervals are entirely above 1, so it is reasonable to conclude that risk of death is greater in the abnormal heart rate recovery group than in the normal heart rate group.

12.59 a. The interval will be wider for 95% confidence.

b. The interval will become more narrow because the standard error will decrease.

c. Assuming the standard deviation stays the same, the interval width stays the same.

12.62 a. On each team, the ninth weight is the weight of the coxswain, who gives instructions about the rowing cadence but does not row. A coxswain's weight is much less than the weights of the rowers, so the distribution of weights is not symmetric.

12.66 b. This is paired data. The difference between the ages of a husband and wife can be determined for each married couple.

12.69 a. A "success" is an interval that captures the population mean.

b. .90.

e. $.90^{100}$.

Chapter 13

13.1 a. Parameter = proportion of adult Americans between the ages of 18 and 30 who think the use of marijuana should be legalized; null value = .5.

c. Parameter = difference in mean ages of death for left- and right-handed people; null value = 0.

13.4 a. 1.11

d. 4.00

13.6 a. Rejection region is $t \geq 1.72$; reject H_0.

c. Rejection region is $|t| \geq 2.09$; reject H_0.

g. Rejection region is $t \leq -1.83$; do not reject H_0.

13.9 a. H_0: $\mu = 72$ beats per minute, H_a: $\mu \neq 72$. Since $n = 57$ is large, the test can proceed. Test statistic is $t = -1.20$, df = 56, exact p-value $= 2(0.1176) = 0.2352$. Cannot reject the null hypothesis; mean male pulse rate is not significantly different from 72.

13.10 $t = 3.4$; reject the null hypothesis.

13.13   b. H_a: $\mu_1 - \mu_2 < 0$.
c. H_a: $\mu_1 - \mu_2 < 0$.

13.15   a. 1.414

13.17   Plots show necessary conditions are satisfied, $t = .43$; don't reject the null hypothesis.

13.20   a. Unpooled $t = 3.97$, pooled $t = 3.96$; reject the null hypothesis.
b. Can use pooled because sample sizes and standard deviations are close.

13.23   a. 0.0401
b. 0.9599

13.24   a. Reject the null hypothesis or accept the alternative hypothesis.
b. Reject the null hypothesis or accept the alternative hypothesis.

13.25   c. $z < -1.645$; do not reject the null hypothesis.
d. $z > 1.645$; do not reject the null hypothesis.

13.28 $z = 3.26$, $p = .001$; reject the null hypothesis and conclude a higher proportion of women would claim that they would return the money.

13.33   a. No.
c. No.
e. Yes.

13.36   a. $\mu_1 - \mu_2$ where μ_1 and μ_2 are the mean running times for the 50-yard dash for the populations of first-grade boys and girls, respectively.

13.38   a. Reject H_0 for $\alpha = 0.05$.
b. Do not reject H_0 for $\alpha = 0.025$.

13.40   a. Can't tell. The entire interval could be greater than 10 or it could include 10.

13.42   a. Estimate the difference in proportions of college men and women who would answer yes, $p_1 - p_2$, and test whether $p_1 - p_2 = 0$. May also want to estimate p_1 and p_2 separately.

13.45   a. Type 1.
c. Type 1.

13.47   a. 68% of the differences fall in the range -2 to $+6$.
c. .695

13.49   Items 2, 4, and 5.

13.53   Larger samples should be used. Power for samples of 500 is only .3677.

13.55   a. .632

13.58   a. .23
d. No.

13.61   a. All except item 5 rely on knowing the p-value.
b. Items 2, 3, and 4.

13.63   b. $z = 3.19$; samples are large enough and independent, p-value $= 0.001$, conclude the population proportions were significantly different.

13.66   b. Type 1, people would take aspirin although it doesn't help; type 2, people would not take aspirin and heart attacks that could be prevented would not be; type 2 is more serious.

13.69   Reject the null hypothesis using $\alpha = 0.025$.

13.72 $z = 0.98$, p-value $= 0.163$ (exact p-value $= 0.189$); do not reject H_0; cannot guess at significantly better than chance level.

13.76   a. $z = 0.62$, p-value $= 0.266$; do not reject H_0 for $\alpha = 0.05$.
b. $z = 4.59$; yes.

13.79   a. Type 1, patients are retested perhaps without cause; type 2, patients need to be retested but are not, so the cholesterol readings may be too high.

b. Type 2 seems more serious because a medical decision is not made using the most accurate data.

13.82 $z = 3.30$, p-value $= 0.001$; conclude proportions were significantly different.

Chapter 14

14.1   a. $\hat{y} = 119 - 1.64(40) = 53.4$.
b. $y - \hat{y} = 50 - 53.4 = -3.4$.

14.3   a. $s = 2.837$ is roughly the average deviation of y-values from the sample regression line.
b. Geographic latitude explains 91.7% of the variation in mean April temperatures.

14.4   a. The p-value is not less than 0.05 so result is not statistically significant.
b. 0.552

14.7   a. $r^2 = \dfrac{\text{SSTO} - \text{SSE}}{\text{SSTO}} = \dfrac{500 - 300}{500} = 0.40$.

14.8   a. $\hat{y}_i = 513.79$, or about 514 ft.
b. $e_i = 11.21$, or about 11 ft.
c. Approximately 514 ± 100 ft.
d. 650 ft is more than two standard deviations from the mean distance for drivers 21 years old, so it would be unusual.

14.10   a. $b_1 = -0.269$.
b. $-0.26917 \pm (2 \times 0.06616)$, or about -0.401 to -0.137.
c. H_0: $\beta_1 = 0$ versus H_a: $\beta_1 \neq 0$.
d. $t = -4.07$, df $= 114$.
e. The relationship is statistically significant (p-value $= 0.000$).

14.11   a. $s = 1.509$. This is roughly the average deviation of individual y-values from the regression line.

14.12 $b_0 = 7.56$. This is the mean hours of sleep for students who studied 0 hours.

14.13   d. The result may not have practical significance. The slope indicates only a small increase in television watching per one-year increase in age, and R^2 is small so the relationship is weak.

14.14   b. SSE $= 18$.
c. $s = \sqrt{\dfrac{18}{6 - 2}} = 2.12$.

14.17   a. Prediction interval for a value of y.
b. Confidence interval for the mean.

14.18   a. Grade point average of an individual who misses two classes per week.
b. Mean grade point average of all who miss two classes per week.

14.21   a. $\hat{y}_i = 3.59 + (.967)(40)$.
d. The width of the prediction interval reflects the variation among the individual ages of husbands married to women 40 years old. The confidence interval is narrow because, with $n = 170$, the mean age can be estimated with good precision.

14.22 $42.258 \pm (2 \times 0.313)$, which gives approximately the interval provided by Minitab.

14.23 $(3.746, 9.750)$. Of students in the population who studied 3 hours, about 95% slept between 3.746 and 9.75 hours. Or, the probability is .95 that the hours of sleep will be in the given interval for a student randomly selected from the population of students who studied 3 hours.

14.25 a. Conditions 2 and 4.
 b. Conditions 1, 2, and 3.
 c. Condition 5.
 d. Conditions 1, 2, and 3.

14.27 There is an outlier; aside from the outlier the distribution might be normal.

14.28 Conditions 1, 2, and 3 hold. The form of the equation is probably correct, there are no outliers, and the standard deviation is about the same for all values of x.

14.29 Condition 4 seems to hold. It's not unreasonable to assume that the residuals have a normal distribution.

14.31 a. There appears to be an outlier so Condition 2 is violated.

14.32 c. The plot will have a U shape.

14.36 b. 0.165

14.37 b. $\hat{y} = 25.38 + 0.7069x$.
 c. $\hat{y} = 78.4$.
 d. 72.97 to 83.83.

14.39 a. $R^2 = 44.7\%$. Father's height explains about 44.7% of the variation in son's height.
 b. $r = \sqrt{0.447} = 0.67$.

14.42 a. $H_0: \rho = 0$ versus Ha: $\rho \neq 0$. It may be that in reality the researchers' alternative hypothesis was $\rho > 0$, but computer software routinely provides a p-value for the two-sided alternative. The researchers have decided to reject the null hypotheses.

14.46 a. The two observations with the greatest chest girths could be outliers, or there might be a gently curving pattern.
 b. $\hat{y} = -206.9 + 10.76x$.
 c. $R^2 = 95.1\%$.
 d. $\hat{y}_i = 223.5$.
 e. 95% prediction interval is (180.47, 266.49).
 f. 95% confidence interval is (211.41, 235.55).

Chapter 15

15.1 a. Appropriate. Both variables are categorical.
 b. Not appropriate. Both variables are quantitative.

15.2 a. p-value = 0.05.
 b. $0.10 < p$-value < 0.25 (0.153).

15.3 b. 16.81 (df = 6).

15.5 a. No, $\chi^2 < 6.63$.
 b. No, $\chi^2 < 6.63$.
 c Yes, $\chi^2 > 13.28$.
 d. No, $\chi^2 < 30.58$.

15.7 a. H_0: Gender and type of class taken are not related for the population of students. H_a: Gender and type of class taken are related for the population of students.
 b. df = 1.
 c. 1.258
 d. p-value = 0.262.
 e. Do not reject the null hypothesis for $\alpha = 0.05$. The relationship between gender and type of class taken is not statistically significant.

15.10 c. H_0: Opinion about death penalty and opinion about marijuana legalization are not related; H_a: Opinion about death penalty and opinion about marijuana legalization are related.

---

 d. $\chi^2 = 3.92$, df = 1, p-value < 0.05 (about 0.048).
 e. $\chi^2 = 933(152 \times 159 - 561 \times 61)^2/(713 \times 220 \times 213 \times 720) = 3.92$.

15.13 For expected counts, the proportion with an ear infection is .22 within each treatment.

15.15 No. The response variable has 3 categories.

15.18 a. Given that 2 out of 10 participants have reduced pain, what is the probability that both of them would be in the magnet-treated group?

15.20 f. We're not telling; ask an engineer.

15.21 a. The researcher probably thought that short students would be more likely to be bullied. That is a one-sided hypothesis, so a z-test is appropriate.
 c. $z = 3.02$, p-value = 0.001.

15.22 a. 100 for each of the 3 categories.

15.24 a. No.
 b. Yes.
 c. Yes.
 d. No.
 e. No.
 f. No.

15.26 a. $H_0: p_1 = .3, p_2 = .6, p_3 = .1$ where p_1, p_2, and p_3 are the population proportions who drove, biked, and used another way that day, respectively.
 c. 6.67

15.28 $\chi^2 = 1.766$, df = 2, $0.25 < p$-value < 0.50 (0.413).

15.30 a. HH, TH, HT, TT. $X = 0$, $p = 1/4$; $X = 1$, $p = 1/2$; $X = 2$, $p = 1/4$.
 b. $H_0: p_0 = .25, p_1 = .50, p_2 = .25$.
 c. $\chi^2 = 7.2$, df = 2, $0.025 < p$-value < 0.05 (0.027).

15.34 b. H_0: Number of ear pierces and likelihood of having a tattoo are not related, H_a: Number of ear pierces and likelihood of having a tattoo are related.
 c. $\chi^2 = 90.544$, df = 3, p-value < 0.001. Decide H_a.

15.36 $\chi^2 = 15.8$, df = 5, $0.005 < p$-value < 0.01. Reject H_0: proportions are as stated at M&M website, conclude at least two proportions are not as stated.

15.38 a. $n = 10$, $p = .5$.
 c.

Number Correct	Null Probabilities
≤2	.0547
3	.1172
4	.2051
5	.2461
6	.2051
7	.1172
≥8	.0547

15.40 a. The conditions are met.
 b. $\chi^2 = 157$, df = 12.

15.44 a. $\chi^2 = 0.267$, df = 1, not significant.
 b. $\chi^2 = 13.025$, df = 1, significant.
 c. $\chi^2 = 6.748$, df = 1, significant.
 d. $\chi^2 = 2.356$, df = 1, not significant.

15.47 Between 0 and 5.99.

15.49 b. $\chi^2 = 15.5$, df = 4, $0.001 < p$-value < 0.005. There is a statistically significant relationship.
 c. The largest contributions occur in cells where student eye color and eye color student finds attractive are both blue or both brown.

15.51. a. Homogeneity.

Chapter 16

16.1 a. Appropriate.
d. Not appropriate. Not a comparison of independent groups.

16.2 a. Mean body weight is equal for the populations in the three age groups; H_0: $\mu_1 = \mu_2 = \mu_3$.
b. Mean body weight is not equal for the populations in the three age groups.

16.5. a. 1.018 to 4.362; interval does not cover 0 so it's reasonable to say means differ.

16.6 a. Reject the null; F-statistic is greater than 3.89, the critical value.

16.8 a. 60+ age group is significantly different from all other age groups.
b. 95% confident that all six intervals capture the corresponding population parameters.

16.9 b. Variation is about the same for each lab and there are no outliers.

16.10 a. H_0: $\mu_1 = \mu_2 = \mu_3 = \mu_4 = \mu_5$ versus H_a: Not all μ_i the same.
b. Yes. $F = 4.53$, p-value $= 0.003$.
c. p-value is area to the right of 4.53 under a skewed curve.
d. The mean for lab 4 is lower than the means for labs 2 and 5. Other comparisons are more difficult to judge.

16.12 Completed table is:

Source	df	SS	MS	F
Between groups	5	40	8	1.333
Error	10	60	6	
Total	15	100		

16.14 c. MSE $= 1043/150 = 6.953$; $s_p = \sqrt{6.953} = 2.637$.

16.17 a.

Source	df	SS	MS	F	p
Caffeine	2	61.40	30.70	6.18	0.006
Error	27	134.10	4.97		
Total	29	195.50			

b. $s_p = \sqrt{4.97} = 2.23$.

16.18 Each interval has the form $\bar{x}_i \pm 2.01\dfrac{0.4058}{\sqrt{11}}$, or $\bar{x}_i \pm 0.246$.

16.19 b. $F = 50/10 = 5$.
c. df $= 3$ and 20.

16.21 a. $\bar{x} = 8$, $\bar{x}_1 = 4$, $\bar{x}_2 = 11$, $\bar{x}_3 = 9$.
b. SS Groups $= 78$.
c. SS Total $= 118$.
d. SSE $= 118 - 78 = 40$.

16.23 a. Null is that median ratings would be equal for populations of students from the four types of hometowns; alternative is that median ratings would not be equal for the four types of hometowns.
b. p-value $= 0.000$; conclude that median ratings would not be equal.
c. Big city, median $= 5$.

16.25 a. Ordinal.

16.27 a. H_0: Medians are the same for the three populations of occupational groups; H_a: Population medians are not all the same.
b. Decide in favor of H_a (p-value $= 0.002$).

16.28 a. Interaction; amount of difference between members and nonmembers of Greek organizations depends upon gender.

16.30 a. Males.
b. Students from big cities rate rock music lower than students from other types of hometowns.
c. Pattern of relationship between rating and hometown is about the same for males and females so the interaction is weak or nonexistent.

16.33 a. The amount of difference between mean GPA of men and women would depend upon seat location.
b. The amount of difference between men's and women's mean GPAs would be the same in each seat location.

16.35 b. As the bacteria amount increases, the difference in mean rot for 10°C and 16°C increases.

16.38 a. H_0: $\mu_1 = \mu_2 = \mu_3 = \mu_4 = \mu_5$ versus H_a: Not all μ_i the same.
b. Population might be all public school children of this age in the United States.
c. Decide in favor of H_a. Not all the means are the same.
d. Perhaps children who engage in more violent behaviors also like to watch more television.

16.40 There may be interaction. The difference between boys and girls is smaller in the 6+ hours of television group than it is in other television watching groups.

16.43 SSE $= 15,286$, $s_p = \sqrt{46.18} = 6.796$.

16.44 Regression methods could be used. Both variables are quantitative.

Chapter 17

17.1 Study #1; explanatory variable is taking calcium or placebo and response variable is blood pressure.

17.4 Observational study; headline is not justified.

17.6 Drinking coffee or not. People who don't drink coffee may be more likely to drink tea and may also be more likely to conceive for other reasons.

17.9 Probably. We are not told who was in the sample, but there is no indication that it was an unrepresentative group with regard to diet and conception.

17.12 a. Statistical significance; the null hypothesis is that energy and fat intake are not related to tea consumption.
b. Confounding variables.

17.13 a. There was an association but it was not strong enough to be *statistically* significant for the sample size used.

17.15 a. Amount walked per day (less than 1 mile, between 1 and 2 miles, more than 2 miles) and whether the man died during the study (yes, no).

17.18 a. No, the entire population was already measured.
b. Yes, assuming the mechanism causing geyser eruptions stays the same.

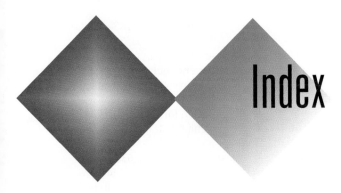

Index

Credits

This page constitutes an extension of the copyright page. We have made every effort to trace the ownership of all copyrighted material and to secure permission from copyright holders. In the event of any question arising as to the use of any material, we will be pleased to make the necessary corrections in future printings. Thanks are due to the following authors, publishers, and agents for permission to use the material indicated.

Photos

xxii © Tom Carroll/Phototake/PictureQuest; **12** © Bob Daemmrich/Stock Boston/PictureQuest; **58** © Tom Stewart/The Stock Market; **88** © Mark Scott/FPG International/PictureQuest; **130** © David Hurrell, Rex Interstock/Stock Connection/PictureQuest; **170** © Joel Gordon; **202** © Will Hart/PhotoEdit/PictureQuest; **248** © Joseph Sohm, ChromoSohm Inc./CORBIS; **292** © Network Productions/Index Stock Imagery; **328** © Ron Chapple/FPG International/PictureQuest; **354** © Lester Lefkowitz/CORBIS Stock Market; **390** ©Ron Sherman/Stock Boston/PictureQuest; **436** © Stockbyte/PictureQuest; **492** © Bob Daemmrich/Stock Boston/PictureQuest; **526** © Chuck Savage/CORBIS Stock Market; **560** © Mark Reinstein/Index Stock Imagery; **592** © Keith Brofsky/PhotoDisc/GettyImages

Text

Chapter 1 **6** Case Study 1.7: From "Sad, Lonely World Discovered in Cyberspace," by A. Harmon, *New York Times*, August 30, 1998, p. A3. Copyright © 1998 by the New York Times Co. Reprinted by permission.

Chapter 2 **33** Example 2.9 excerpt: Reprinted by permission of *The Davis Enterprise*.

Chapter 3 **66** Case Study 3.1: Copyright 1999, USA TODAY. Reprinted with permission. **68** excerpt: Reprinted by permission of the *Sacramento Bee*. **78** Example 3.5 excerpt: Reprinted by permission of the *Sacramento Bee*.

Chapter 4 **107** Example 4.8 excerpt: From "The Year of Believing in Prophecies," by T. Watanabe, *The Los Angeles Times,* March 31, 1999. Copyright © 1999 The Los Angeles Times Syndicate. Reprinted by permission. **117** Example 4.18 quote: Reprinted by permission of *The Davis Enterprise*. **122** questions in Exercises 4.14 and 4.15: Copyright © 1999 The Gallup Organization.

Chapter 5 **162** table: Reprinted with permission from *The World Almanac and Book of Facts 1999.* Copyright © 1999 World Almanac Education Group. All rights reserved.

Chapter 10 **322** Example 10.2 excerpt: Copyright © 1997 The Gallup Organization.

Chapter 11 **377** quote: From "Sad, Lonely World Discovered in Cyberspace," by A. Harmon, *New York Times*, August 30, 1998, p. A3. Copyright © 1998 by the New York Times Co. Reprinted by permission. **381** excerpt: From "Probability Experts May Decide Pennsylvania Vote," by P. Passell, *New York Times,* April 11, 1994, A15. Copyright © 1994 by the New York Times Co. Reprinted by permission.

Chapter 13 **485** Exercises 13.30, 13.31: Copyright © 2000 The Gallup Organization. **488** Exercise 13.63: Copyright © 2000 The Gallup Organization. **490** Exercises 13.75, 13.76: Copyright © 2000 The Gallup Organization.

TO THE OWNER OF THIS BOOK:

We hope that you found *Mind on Statistics* useful. So that this book can be improved in a future edition, would you take the time to complete this sheet and return it? Thank you.

School and address: _____

Department: _____

Instructor's name: _____

1. What I like most about this book is: _____

_____

_____

2. What I like least about this book is: _____

_____

_____

3. My general reaction to this book is: _____

_____

4. My reaction to the book CD is: _____

_____

5. The name of the course in which I used this book is: _____

_____

6. Were all of the chapters of the book assigned for you to read? _____

   If not, which ones weren't? _____

7. In the space below, or on a separate sheet of paper, please write specific suggestions for improving this book and anything else you'd care to share about your experience in using the book.

_____

_____

_____

_____

OPTIONAL:

Your name: _____ Date: _____

May Duxbury quote you, either in promotion for *Mind on Statistics*, or in future publishing ventures?

Yes: _____ No: _____

Sincerely,

Carolyn J. Crockett

ATTN: Carolyn J. Crockett, Statistics
BROOKS/COLE—THOMSON LEARNING
10 DAVIS DRIVE
BELMONT, CA   94002-9801

CD Datasets and Text Examples

There are 46 datasets on the CD for this text; all are provided in MINITAB, Microsoft Excel, SPSS, JMP, and text formats. Full descriptions are in the files readme.html and printme.html within the dataset directory of the CD. When a dataset is either necessary or helpful for doing an exercise, the name of the relevant dataset is given within the exercise.

The connection between text Examples/Case Studies and the datasets is shown below. As an example, in Chapter 1, the dataset called **pennstate1** includes the data used for Case Study 1.1.

Chapter	Dataset	Where Used
1	**pennstate1**	Case Study 1.1
2	**pennstate1**	Examples 2.1, 2.3, 2.5
	MusicCDs	Example 2.8
	rainfall	Example 2.9
	pennstate1M	Example 2.10
	UCDavis1,pennstate1	Selected variables from each are used in the **Empirical** applet of Section 2.7
3	**ProfBooks**	Example 3.4
4	**chap4-heights**	Data used in **Sampling** applet of Section 4.2
5	**handheight**	Example 5.1
	signdist	Example 5.2
	pennstate1	Example 5.6
	sleepstudy	Example 5.9
	idealwt or **idealwtmen, idealwtwomen**	Case Study 5.1
6	**pennstate1**	Example 6.10
9	**Cash5**	Example 9.6
10	**pennstate3**	Case Study 10.3
11	**pennstate1**	Example 11.6
12	**pennstate5**	Example 12.2
	UCDavis1	Examples 12.6, 12.7, 12.9
	YouthRisk	Example 12.11
13	**UCDavis1**	Examples 13.4, 13.5
14	**handheight**	Example 14.1
	wthghtM	Example 14.2, Figures 14.8 and 14.9
	signdist	Example 14.3
	chugtime	Figure 14.11
15	**pennstate2**	Example 15.2
16	**UCDavis1,UCDavis2** (combined)	Examples 16.1 and 16.4 (GPAs > 4.0 deleted for Example 16.1 as was 78th observation of **UCDavis1**. They actually gave seat location as front/middle.)
	happyface	Example 16.6
Supp. 2	**UCDavis2**	Examples S2.2, S2.4
Supp. 3	**temperature**	Example S3.1
Supp. 4	**UCDavis1**	Example S4.1
	happyface	Example S4.4

Insert the Student's Suite CD-ROM from the opposite page to access:

◆ Datasets formatted for MINITAB, Microsoft Excel, SPSS, SAS, JMP, and ASCII

◆ Java applets from Section 2.7, Section 4.2, Section 5.3, Section 9.3, and Section 12.3. These applets will help you complete the recommendations in those sections and the "Turn On Your Computer" exercises at the end of Chapters 2, 4, 5, 9, and 12.

◆ Microsoft PowerPoint presentation slides to help you follow along in class

◆ Links to both the Book Companion Web Site and *Internet Companion for Statistics* by Michael Larsen

◆ Links to Web resources, including exercises and tutorial quizzes for each chapter

◆ Technology manuals to help you work through text examples using MINITAB, SPSS, Excel, or TI-83

◆ Supplemental topics for further study

Supplemental Topic 1: Additional Discrete Random Variables
S1.1 Hypergeometric Distribution / S1.2 Poisson Distribution / S1.3 Multinomial Distribution

Supplemental Topic 2: Nonparametric Tests of Hypotheses
S2.1 The Sign Test / S2.2 The Two-Sample Rank-Sum Test / S2.3 The Wilcoxon Signed-Rank Test / S2.4 The Kruskal–Wallis Test

Supplemental Topic 3: Multiple Regression
S3.1 The Multiple Linear Regression Model / S3.2 Inference About Multiple Regression Models / S3.3 Checking Conditions for Multiple Linear Regression

Supplemental Topic 4: Two-Way Analysis of Variance
S4.1 Assumptions and Models for Two-Way ANOVA / S4.2 Testing for Main Effects and Interactions

Supplemental Topic 5: Ethics
S5.1 Ethical Treatment of Human and Animal Participants / S5.2 Assurance of Data Quality / S5.3 Appropriate Statistical Analysis / S5.4 Fair Reporting of Results

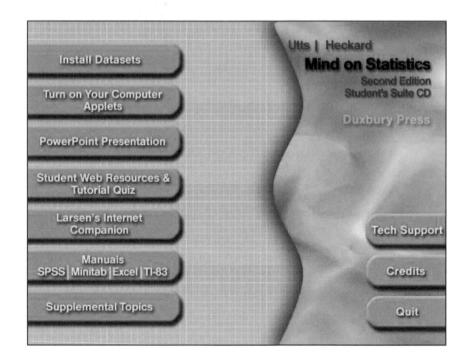